HANDBOOK OF
CHILD PSYCHOLOGY

HANDBOOK OF CHILD PSYCHOLOGY

SIXTH EDITION

Volume Three: Social, Emotional, and Personality Development

Volume Editor

NANCY EISENBERG

Editors-in-Chief

WILLIAM DAMON and RICHARD M. LERNER

WILEY

John Wiley & Sons, Inc.

Library of Congress Cataloging-in-Publication Data:

Handbook of child psychology / editors-in-chief, William Damon & Richard M. Lerner.—
  6th ed.
     p.   cm.
  Includes bibliographical references and indexes.
  Contents: v. 1. Theoretical models of human development / volume editor,
Richard M. Lerner — v. 2. Cognition, perception, and language / volume editors,
Deanna Kuhn, Robert Siegler — v. 3. Social, emotional, and personality development /
volume editor, Nancy Eisenberg — v 4. Child psychology in practice / volume editors, K.
Ann Renninger, Irving E. Sigel.
  ISBN 0-471-27287-6 (set : cloth)
  — ISBN 0-471-27288-4 (v. 1 : cloth) — ISBN 0-471-27289-2 (v. 2 : cloth)
  — ISBN 0-471-27290-6 (v. 3 : cloth) — ISBN 0-471-27291-4 (v. 4 : cloth)
  1. Child psychology.   I. Damon, William, 1944–   II. Lerner, Richard M.
  BF721.H242   2006
  155.4—dc22
                                                            2005043951

Printed in the United States of America.
  10 9 8 7 6 5 4 3 2 1

In memory of Paul Mussen, whose generosity of spirit touched our lives and helped build a field.

Contributors

John E. Bates
Department of Psychology
Indiana University
Bloomington, Indiana

Sheri A. Berenbaum
Department of Psychology
The Pennsylvania State University
University Park, Pennsylvania

Daphne Blunt Bugental
Department of Psychology
University of California
Santa Barbara, California

William M. Bukowski
Department of Psychology
Concordia University
Montreal, QC, Canada

Raymond Buriel
Department of Psychology
Pomona College
Claremont, California

Joseph J. Campos
Department of Psychology
University of Califorina
Berkeley, California

Linda A. Camras
Department of Psychology
DePaul University
Chicago, Illinois

Avshalom Caspi
Department of Psychology
University of Wisconsin
Madison, Wisconsin

John D. Coie
Department of Psychology
Duke University
Durham, North Carolina

W. Andrew Collins
Institute of Child Development
University of Minnesota
Minneapolis, Minnesota

Pamela Davis-Kean
Institute for Social Research
University of Michigan
Ann Arbor, Michigan

Kenneth A. Dodge
Department of Psychology
Duke University
Durham, North Carolina

Jacquelynne S. Eccles
Department of Psychology
University of Michigan
Ann Arbor, Michigan

Nancy Eisenberg
Department of Psychology
Arizona State University
Tempe, Arizona

Richard A. Fabes
Department of Family and Human Development
Arizona State University
Tempe, Arizona

Nathan A. Fox
Department of Human Development
University of Maryland
College Park, Maryland

Joan E. Grusec
Department of Psychology
University of Toronto
Toronto, Ontario, Canada

Susan Harter
Department of Psychology
University of Denver
Denver, Colorado

Jerome Kagan
Department of Psychology
Harvard University
Cambridge, Massachusetts

Donald Lynam
Department of Psychology
University of Kentucky
Lexington, Kentucky

Carol Lynn Martin
Department of Family and Human Development
Arizona State University
Tempe, Arizona

Ross D. Parke
Department of Psychology
University of California
Riverside, California

Jeffrey G. Parker
Department of Psychology
Pennsylvania State University
University Park, Pennsylvania

Robert W. Roeser
The Eliot-Pearson
Department of Child Development
Tufts University
Medford, Massachusetts

Mary K. Rothbart
Department of Psychology
University of Oregon
Eugene, Oregon

Kenneth H. Rubin
Center for Children, Relationships, and Culture
Department of Human Development
University of Maryland
College Park, Maryland

Diane N. Ruble
Department of Psychology
New York University
New York, New York

Carolyn Saarni
Department of Counseling
Sonoma State University
Rohnert Park, California

Ulrich Schiefele
Department of Psychology
Universität Bielefeld
Bielefeld, Germany

Rebecca L. Shiner
Department of Psychology
Colgate University
Hamilton, New York

Tracy L. Spinrad
Department of Family and Human Development
Arizona State University
Tempe, Arizona

Laurence Steinberg
Department of Psychology
Temple University
Philadelphia, Pennsylvania

Ross A. Thompson
Department of Psychology
University of California
Davis, California

Elliot Turiel
Graduate School of Education
University of California
Berkeley, California

Allan Wigfield
Department of Human Development
University of Maryland
College Park, Maryland

David Witherington
Department of Psychology
University of New Mexico
Albuquerque, New Mexic

Reviewers

Daphne Blunt Bugental
Department of Psychology
University of California
Santa Barbara, California

W. Andrew Collins
Institute of Child Development
University of Minnesota
Minneapolis, Minnesota

Keith Crnic
Department of Psychology
Arizona State University
Tempe, Arizona

Nathan A. Fox
Department of Human Development
University of Maryland
College Park, Maryland

Doran C. French
Department of Psychology
Professor and Chair
Illinois Wesleyan University
Bloomington, Illinois

William G. Graziano
Department of Psychology
Purdue University
West Lafayette, Indiana

Leon Kuczynski
Department of Family Relations and
    Applied Nutrition
University of Guelph
Guelph, Ontario, Canada

Brett Laursen
Professor of Psychology
Florida Atlantic University
Fort Lauderdale, Florida

Kathryn Lemery
Department of Psychology
Arizona State University
Tempe, Arizona

Terrie Moffitt
Institute of Psychiatry
London, United Kingdom

Ross D. Parke
Department of Psychology
University of California
Riverside, California

Concetta Pastorelli
Department of Psychology
University of Rome
Rome, Italy

Mary Rothbart
Department of Psychology
University of Oregon
Eugene, Oregon

Ellen Skinner
Department of Psychology
Portland State
Portand, Oregon

Judi Smetana
Department of Clinical and Social Sciences
    in Psychology
University of Rochester
Rochester, New York

Carolyn Zahn-Waxler
National Institute of Mental Health and
Departments of Psychology and Psychiatry
University of Wisconsin
Madison, Wisconsin

Preface to Handbook of Child Psychology, *Sixth Edition*

WILLIAM DAMON

Scholarly handbooks play several key roles in their disciplines. First and foremost, they reflect recent changes in the field as well as classic works that have survived those changes. In this sense, all handbooks present their editors' and authors' best judgments about what is most important to know in the field at the time of publication. But many handbooks also influence the fields that they report on. Scholars—especially younger ones—look to them for sources of information and inspiration to guide their own work. While taking stock of the shape of its field, a handbook also shapes the stock of ideas that will define the field's future. It serves both as an indicator and as a generator, a pool of received knowledge and a pool for spawning new insight.

THE *HANDBOOK*'S LIVING TRADITION

Within the field of human development, the *Handbook of Child Psychology* has served these key roles to a degree that has been exceptional even among the impressive panoply of the world's many distinguished scholarly handbooks. The *Handbook of Child Psychology* has had a widely heralded tradition as a beacon, organizer, and encyclopedia of developmental study for almost 75 years— a period that covers the vast majority of scientific work in this field.

It is impossible to imagine what the field would look like if it had not occurred to Carl Murchison in 1931 to assemble an eclectic assortment of contributions into the first *Handbook of Child Psychology*. Whether or not Murchison realized this potential (an interesting speculation in itself, given his visionary and ambitious nature), he gave birth to a seminal publishing project that

not only has endured over time but has evolved into a thriving tradition across a number of related academic disciplines.

All through its history, the *Handbook* has drawn on, and played a formative role in, the worldwide study of human development. What does the *Handbook*'s history tell us about where we, as developmentalists, have been, what we have learned, and where we are going? What does it tell us about what has changed and what has remained the same in the questions that we ask, in the methods that we use, and in the theoretical ideas that we draw on in our quest to understand human development? By asking these questions, we follow the spirit of the science itself, for developmental questions may be asked about any endeavor, including the enterprise of studying human development. To best understand what this field has to tell us about human development, we must ask how the field itself has developed. In a field that examines continuities and changes, we must ask, for the field itself, what are the continuities and what are the changes?

The history of the *Handbook* is by no means the whole story of why the field is where it is today, but it is a fundamental part of the story. It has defined the choices that have determined the field's direction and has influenced the making of those choices. In this regard, the *Handbook*'s history reveals much about the judgments and other human factors that shape a science.

THE CAST OF CHARACTERS

Carl Murchison was a scholar/impresario who edited *The Psychological Register;* founded and edited key psychological journals; wrote books on social psychology, politics, and the criminal mind; and compiled an assortment of handbooks, psychology texts, autobiographies of renowned psychologists, and even a book on psychic beliefs (Sir Arthur Conan Doyle and Harry Houdini were among the contributors). Murchison's initial *Handbook of Child Psychology* was published by a small university press (Clark University) in 1931, when the field itself was still in its infancy. Murchison wrote:

> Experimental psychology has had a much older scientific and academic status [than child psychology], but at the present time it is probable that much less money is being spent for pure research in the field of experimental psychology than is being spent in the field of child psychology. In spite of this obvious fact, many experimental psychologists continue to look upon the field of child psychology as a proper field of research for women and for men whose experimental masculinity is not of the maximum. This attitude of patronage is based almost entirely upon a blissful ignorance of what is going on in the tremendously virile field of child behavior. (Murchison, 1931, p. ix)

Murchison's masculine allusion, of course, is from another era; it could furnish some good material for a social history of gender stereotyping. That aside, Murchison was prescient in the task that he undertook and the way that he went about it. At the time Murchison wrote the preface to his *Handbook,* developmental psychology was known only in Europe and in a few forward-looking American labs and universities. Nevertheless, Murchison predicted the field's impending ascent: "The time is not far distant, if it is not already here, when nearly all competent psychologists will recognize that one-half of the whole field of psychology is involved in the problem of how the infant becomes an adult psychologically" (Murchison, 1931, p. x).

For his original 1931 *Handbook,* Murchison looked to Europe and to a handful of American centers (or "field stations") for child research (Iowa, Minnesota, the University of California at Berkeley, Columbia, Stanford, Yale, Clark). Murchison's Europeans included a young "genetic epistemologist" named Jean Piaget, who, in an essay on "Children's Philosophies," quoted extensively from interviews with 60 Genevan children between the ages of 4 and 12 years. Piaget's chapter would provide American readers with an introduction to his seminal research program on children's conceptions of the world. Another European, Charlotte Bühler, wrote a chapter on children's social behavior. In this chapter,

which still is fresh today, Bühler described intricate play and communication patterns among toddlers, patterns that developmental psychology would not rediscover until the late 1970s. Bühler also anticipated the critiques of Piaget that would appear during the sociolinguistics heyday of the 1970s:

> Piaget, in his studies on children's talk and reasoning, emphasizes that their talk is much more egocentric than social . . . that children from 3 to 7 years accompany all their manipulations with talk which actually is not so much intercourse as monologue . . . [but] the special relationship of the child to each of the different members of the household is distinctly reflected in the respective conversations. (Buhler, 1931, p. 138)

Other Europeans included Anna Freud, who wrote on "The Psychoanalysis of the Child," and Kurt Lewin, who wrote on "Environmental Forces in Child Behavior and Development."

The Americans whom Murchison chose were equally notable. Arnold Gesell wrote a nativistic account of his twin studies, an enterprise that remains familiar to us today, and Stanford's Louis Terman wrote a comprehensive account of everything known about the "gifted child." Harold Jones described the developmental effects of birth order, Mary Cover Jones wrote about children's emotions, Florence Goodenough wrote about children's drawings, and Dorothea McCarthy wrote about language development. Vernon Jones's chapter on "children's morals" focused on the growth of *character,* a notion that was to become lost to the field during the cognitive-developmental revolution, but that reemerged in the 1990s as the primary concern in the study of moral development.

Murchison's vision of child psychology included an examination of cultural differences as well. His *Handbook* presented to the scholarly world a young anthropologist named Margaret Mead, just back from her tours of Samoa and New Guinea. In this early essay, Mead wrote that her motivation in traveling to the South Seas was to discredit the views that Piaget, Levy-Bruhl, and other nascent "structuralists" had put forth concerning "animism" in young children's thinking. (Interestingly, about a third of Piaget's chapter in the same volume was dedicated to showing how Genevan children took years to outgrow animism.) Mead reported some data that she called "amazing": "In not one of the 32,000 drawings (by young 'primitive' children) was there a single case of personalization of animals, material phenomena, or inanimate objects" (Mead, 1931, p. 400). Mead parlayed these data into a tough-minded critique of Western psychology's ethnocentrism, making the point that animism and other beliefs are more likely to be culturally induced than intrinsic to early cognitive development. This is hardly an unfamiliar theme in contemporary psychology. Mead also offered a research guide for developmental fieldworkers in strange cultures, complete with methodological and practical advice, such as the following: Translate questions into native linguistic categories; don't do controlled experiments; don't do studies that require knowing ages of subjects, which are usually unknowable; and live next door to the children whom you are studying.

Despite the imposing roster of authors that Murchison assembled for the 1931 *Handbook of Child Psychology*, his achievement did not satisfy him for long. Barely 2 years later, Murchison put out a second edition, of which he wrote: "Within a period of slightly more than 2 years, this first revision bears scarcely any resemblance to the original *Handbook of Child Psychology*. This is due chiefly to the great expansion in the field during the past 3 years and partly to the improved insight of the editor" (Murchison, 1933, p. vii). The tradition that Murchison had brought to life was already evolving.

Murchison saw fit to provide the following warning in his second edition: "There has been no attempt to simplify, condense, or to appeal to the immature mind. This volume is prepared specifically for the scholar, and its form is for his maximum convenience" (Murchison, 1933, p. vii). It is likely that sales of Murchison's first volume did not approach textbook levels; perhaps he received negative comments regarding its accessibility.

Murchison exaggerated when he wrote that his second edition bore little resemblance to the first. Almost half of the chapters were virtually the same, with minor additions and updating. (For the record, though, despite Murchison's continued use of masculine phraseology, 10 of the 24 authors in the second edition were women.) Some of the authors whose original chapters were dropped were asked to write about new topics. So, for example, Goodenough wrote about mental testing rather than about children's drawings, and Gesell wrote a general statement of his maturational theory that went well beyond the twin studies.

But Murchison also made some abrupt changes. He dropped Anna Freud entirely, auguring the marginalization of psychoanalysis within academic psychology. Leonard Carmichael, who was later to play a pivotal role

in the *Handbook* tradition, made an appearance as author of a major chapter (by far the longest in the book) on prenatal and perinatal growth. Three other physiologically oriented chapters were added as well: one on neonatal motor behavior, one on visual-manual functions during the first 2 years of life, and one on physiological "appetites" such as hunger, rest, and sex. Combined with the Goodenough and Gesell shifts in focus, these additions gave the 1933 *Handbook* more of a biological thrust, in keeping with Murchison's long-standing desire to display the hard science backbone of the emerging field.

Leonard Carmichael was president of Tufts University when he organized Wiley's first edition of the *Handbook*. The switch from a university press to the long-established commercial firm of John Wiley & Sons was commensurate with Carmichael's well-known ambition; indeed, Carmichael's effort was to become influential beyond anything that Murchison might have anticipated. The book (one volume at that time) was called the *Manual of Child Psychology*, in keeping with Carmichael's intention of producing an "advanced scientific manual to bridge the gap between the excellent and varied elementary textbooks in this field and the scientific periodical literature" (Carmichael, 1946, p. viii).

The publication date was 1946, and Carmichael complained that "this book has been a difficult and expensive one to produce, especially under wartime conditions" (Carmichael, 1946, p. viii). Nevertheless, the project was worth the effort. The *Manual* quickly became the bible of graduate training and scholarly work in the field, available virtually everywhere that human development was studied. Eight years later, now head of the Smithsonian Institution, Carmichael wrote, in the preface to the 1954 second edition, "The favorable reception that the first edition received not only in America but all over the world is indicative of the growing importance of the study of the phenomena of the growth and development of the child" (Carmichael, 1954, p. vii).

Carmichael's second edition had a long life: Not until 1970 did Wiley bring out a third edition. Carmichael was retired by then, but he still had a keen interest in the book. At his insistence, his own name became part of the title of the third edition; it was called, improbably, *Carmichael's Manual of Child Psychology*, even though it had a new editor and an entirely different cast of authors and advisors. Paul Mussen took over as the editor, and once again the project flourished. Now a two-volume set, the third edition swept across the social sciences, generating widespread interest in developmental psychology and its related disciplines. Rarely had a scholarly compendium become both so dominant in its own field and so familiar in related disciplines. The set became an essential source for graduate students and advanced scholars alike. Publishers referred to *Carmichael's Manual* as the standard against which other scientific handbooks were compared.

The fourth edition, published in 1983, was now redesignated by John Wiley & Sons to become once again the *Handbook of Child Psychology.* By then, Carmichael had passed away. The set of books, now expanded to four volumes, became widely referred to in the field as "the Mussen handbook."

WHAT CARMICHAEL CHOSE FOR THE NOW EMERGENT FIELD

Leonard Carmichael, who became Wiley's editor for the project in its now commercially funded and expanded versions (the 1946 and 1954 *Manuals*), made the following comments about where he looked for his all-important choices of content:

> Both as editor of the *Manual* and as the author of a special chapter, the writer is indebted . . . [for] extensive excerpts and the use of other materials previously published in the *Handbook of Child Psychology, Revised Edition.* (1946, p. viii)

> Both the *Handbook of Child Psychology* and the *Handbook of Child Psychology, Revised Edition,* were edited by Dr. Carl Murchison. I wish to express here my profound appreciation for the pioneer work done by Dr. Murchison in producing these handbooks and other advanced books in psychology. The *Manual* owes much in spirit and content to the foresight and editorial skill of Dr. Murchison. (1954, p. viii)

The first quote comes from Carmichael's preface to the 1946 edition, the second from his preface to the 1954 edition. We shall never know why Carmichael waited until the 1954 edition to add the personal tribute to Carl Murchison. Perhaps a careless typist dropped the laudatory passage from a handwritten version of the 1946 preface and its omission escaped Carmichael's notice. Or perhaps 8 years of further adult development increased Carmichael's generosity of spirit. (It also may be possible that Murchison or his family com-

plained.) In any case, Carmichael acknowledged the roots of his *Manuals,* if not always their original editor. His choice to start with those roots is a revealing part of the *Handbook*'s history, and it established a strong intellectual legacy for our present-day descendants of the early pioneers who wrote for the Murchison and Carmichael editions.

Although Leonard Carmichael took the 1946 *Manual* in much the same direction established by Murchison back in 1931 and 1933, he did bring it several steps further in that direction, added a few twists of his own, and dropped a couple of Murchison's bolder selections. Carmichael first appropriated five Murchison chapters on biological or experimental topics, such as physiological growth, scientific methods, and mental testing. He added three new biologically oriented chapters on animal infancy, physical growth, and motor and behavioral maturation (a tour de force by Myrtal McGraw that instantly made Gesell's chapter in the same volume obsolete). Then he commissioned Wayne Dennis to write an adolescence chapter that focused exclusively on physiological changes associated with puberty.

On the subject of social and cultural influences in development, Carmichael retained five of the Murchison chapters: two chapters on environmental forces on the child by Kurt Lewin and by Harold Jones, Dorothea McCarthy's chapter on children's language, Vernon Jones's chapter on children's morality (now entitled "Character Development—An Objective Approach"), and Margaret Mead's chapter on "primitive" children (now enhanced by several spectacular photos of mothers and children from exotic cultures around the world). Carmichael also stayed with three other Murchison topics (emotional development, gifted children, and sex differences), but he selected new authors to cover them. But Carmichael dropped Piaget and Bühler.

Carmichael's 1954 revision, his second and final edition, was very close in structure and content to the 1946 *Manual.* Carmichael again retained the heart of Murchison's original vision, many of Murchison's original authors and chapter topics, and some of the same material that dated all the way back to the 1931 *Handbook.* Not surprisingly, the chapters that were closest to Carmichael's own interests got the most significant updating. Carmichael leaned toward the biological and physiological whenever possible. He clearly favored experimental treatments of psychological processes. Yet he still kept the social, cultural, and psychological analyses by Lewin, Mead, McCarthy, Terman, Harold Jones, and

Vernon Jones, and he even went so far as to add one new chapter on social development by Harold and Gladys Anderson and one new chapter on emotional development by Arthur Jersild.

The Murchison and Carmichael volumes make for fascinating reading, even today. The perennial themes of the field were there from the start: the nature-nurture debate; the generalizations of universalists opposed by the particularizations of contextualists; the alternating emphases on continuities and discontinuities during ontogenesis; and the standard categories of maturation, learning, locomotor activity, perception, cognition, language, emotion, conduct, morality, and culture—all separated for the sake of analysis, yet, as authors throughout each of the volumes acknowledged, all somehow inextricably joined in the dynamic mix of human development.

These things have not changed. Yet, much in the early editions is now irrevocably dated. Long lists of children's dietary preferences, sleeping patterns, elimination habits, toys, and somatic types look quaint and pointless through today's lenses. The chapters on children's thought and language were written prior to the great contemporary breakthroughs in neurology and brain/behavior research, and they show it. The chapters on social and emotional development were ignorant of the processes of social influence and self-regulation that soon would be revealed through attribution research and other studies in social psychology. Terms such as *cognitive neuroscience, neuronal networks, behavior genetics, social cognition, dynamic systems,* and *positive youth development* were of course unknown. Even Mead's rendition of the "primitive child" stands as a weak straw in comparison to the wealth of cross-cultural knowledge available in today's *cultural psychology.*

Most telling, the assortments of odd facts and normative trends were tied together by very little theory throughout the Carmichael chapters. It was as if, in the exhilaration of discovery at the frontiers of a new field, all the facts looked interesting in and of themselves. That, of course, is what makes so much of the material seem odd and arbitrary. It is hard to know what to make of the lists of facts, where to place them, which ones were worth keeping track of and which ones are expendable. Not surprisingly, the bulk of the data presented in the Carmichael manuals seems not only outdated by today's standards but, worse, irrelevant.

By 1970, the importance of theory for understanding human development had become apparent. Looking back

on Carmichael's last *Manual,* Paul Mussen wrote, "The 1954 edition of this *Manual* had only one theoretical chapter, and that was concerned with Lewinian theory which, so far as we can see, has not had a significant lasting impact on developmental psychology" (Mussen, 1970, p. x). The intervening years had seen a turning away from the norm of psychological research once fondly referred to as "dust-bowl empiricism."

The Mussen 1970 edition—or *Carmichael's Manual,* as it was still called—had a new look and an almost entirely new set of contents. The two-volume edition carried only one chapter from the earlier books, Carmichael's updated version of his own long chapter on the "Onset and Early Development of Behavior," which had made its appearance under a different title in Murchison's 1933 edition. Otherwise, as Mussen wrote in his preface, "It should be clear from the outset . . . that the present volumes are not, in any sense, a *revision* of the earlier editions; this is a completely new *Manual*" (Mussen, 1970, p. x).

And it was. In comparison to Carmichael's last edition 16 years earlier, the scope, variety, and theoretical depth of the Mussen volumes were astonishing. The field had blossomed, and the new *Manual* showcased many of the new bouquets that were being produced. The biological perspective was still strong, grounded by chapters on physical growth (by J. M. Tanner) and physiological development (by Dorothy Eichorn) and by Carmichael's revised chapter (now made more elegant by some excerpts from Greek philosophy and modern poetry). But two other cousins of biology also were represented, in an ethological chapter by Eckhard Hess and a behavior genetics chapter by Gerald McClearn. These chapters were to define the major directions of biological research in the field for at least the next 3 decades.

As for theory, Mussen's *Handbook* was thoroughly permeated with it. Much of the theorizing was organized around the approaches that, in 1970, were known as the "three grand systems": (1) Piaget's cognitive-developmentalism, (2) psychoanalysis, and (3) learning theory. Piaget was given the most extensive treatment. He reappeared in the *Manual,* this time authoring a comprehensive (and, some say, definitive) statement of his entire theory, which now bore little resemblance to his 1931/1933 sortings of children's intriguing verbal expressions. In addition, chapters by John Flavell, by David Berlyne, by Martin Hoffman, and by William Kessen, Marshall Haith, and Philip Salapatek all gave major treatments to one or another aspect of Piaget's body of work. Other approaches were represented as well. Herbert and Ann Pick explicated Gibsonian theory in a chapter on sensation and perception, Jonas Langer wrote a chapter on Werner's organismic theory, David McNeill wrote a Chomskian account of language development, and Robert LeVine wrote an early version of what was soon to become "culture theory."

With its increased emphasis on theory, the 1970 *Manual* explored in depth a matter that had been all but neglected in the book's previous versions: the mechanisms of change that could account for, to use Murchison's old phrase, "the problem of how the infant becomes an adult psychologically." In the process, old questions such as the relative importance of nature versus nurture were revisited, but with far more sophisticated conceptual and methodological tools.

Beyond theory building, the 1970 *Manual* addressed an array of new topics and featured new contributors: peer interaction (Willard Hartup), attachment (Eleanor Maccoby and John Masters), aggression (Seymour Feshbach), individual differences (Jerome Kagan and Nathan Kogan), and creativity (Michael Wallach). All of these areas of interest are still very much with us in the new millennium.

If the 1970 *Manual* reflected a blossoming of the field's plantings, the 1983 *Handbook* reflected a field whose ground cover had spread beyond any boundaries that could have been previously anticipated. New growth had sprouted in literally dozens of separate locations. A French garden, with its overarching designs and tidy compartments, had turned into an English garden, a bit unruly but glorious in its profusion. Mussen's two-volume *Carmichael's Manual* had now become the four-volume Mussen *Handbook,* with a page-count increase that came close to tripling the 1970 edition.

The grand old theories were breaking down. Piaget was still represented by his 1970 piece, but his influence was on the wane throughout the other chapters. Learning theory and psychoanalysis were scarcely mentioned. Yet the early theorizing had left its mark, in vestiges that were apparent in new approaches, and in the evident conceptual sophistication with which authors treated their material. No return to dust bowl empiricism could be found anywhere in the set. Instead, a variety of classical and innovative ideas were coexisting: Ethology, neurobiology, information processing, attribution theory, cultural approaches, communications theory, behavioral genetics, sensory-perception models, psycholinguistics, sociolinguistics, discontinuous stage theories, and continuous memory theories all took their places, with none

quite on center stage. Research topics now ranged from children's play to brain lateralization, from children's family life to the influences of school, day care, and disadvantageous risk factors. There also was coverage of the burgeoning attempts to use developmental theory as a basis for clinical and educational interventions. The interventions usually were described at the end of chapters that had discussed the research relevant to the particular intervention efforts, rather than in whole chapters dedicated specifically to issues of practice.

This brings us to the efforts under the present editorial team: the *Handbook*'s fifth and sixth editions (but really the seventh and eighth editions, if the germinal two pre-Wiley Murchison editions are counted). I must leave it to future commentators to provide a critical summation of what we have done. The volume editors have offered introductory and/or concluding renditions of their own volumes. I will add to their efforts here only by stating the overall intent of our design and by commenting on some directions that our field has taken in the years from 1931 to 2006.

We approached our editions with the same purpose that Murchison, Carmichael, and Mussen before us had shared: "to provide," as Mussen wrote, "a comprehensive and accurate picture of the current state of knowledge—the major systematic thinking and research—in the most important research areas of the psychology of human development" (Mussen, 1983, p. vii). We assumed that the *Handbook* should be aimed "specifically for the scholar," as Murchison declared, and that it should have the character of an "advanced text," as Carmichael defined it. We expected, though, that our audiences may be more interdisciplinary than the readerships of previous editions, given the greater tendency of today's scholars to cross back and forth among fields such as psychology, cognitive science, neurobiology, history, linguistics, sociology, anthropology, education, and psychiatry. We also believed that research-oriented practitioners should be included under the rubric of the "scholars" for whom this *Handbook* was intended. To that end, for the first time in 1998 and again in the present edition, we devoted an entire volume to child psychology in practice.

Beyond these very general intentions, we have let chapters in the *Handbook*'s fifth and sixth editions take their own shape. We solicited the chapters from authors who were widely acknowledged to be among the leading experts in their areas of the field, although we know that, given an entirely open-ended selection process and no limits of budget, we would have invited a large number of other leading researchers whom we did not have the space—and thus the privilege—to include. With very few exceptions, every author whom we invited agreed to accept the challenge. Our only real, and great, sadness was to hear of the passing of several authors from the 1998 edition prior to our assembly of the present edition. Where possible, we arranged to have their collaborators revise and update their chapters.

Our directive to authors was simple: Convey your area of the field as you see it. From then on, the authors took center stage—with, of course, much constructive feedback from reviewers and volume editors. No one tried to impose a perspective, a preferred method of inquiry, or domain boundaries on any of the chapters. The authors expressed their views on what researchers in their areas attempt to accomplish, why they do so, how they go about it, what intellectual sources they draw on, what progress they have made, and what conclusions they have reached.

The result, in my opinion, is still more glorious profusion of the English garden genre, but perhaps contained a bit by some broad patterns that have emerged over the past decade. Powerful theoretical models and approaches—not quite unified theories, such as the three grand systems—have begun once again to organize much of the field's research and practice. There is great variety in these models and approaches, and each is drawing together significant clusters of work. Some have been only recently formulated, and some are combinations or modifications of classic theories that still have staying power.

Among the formidable models and approaches that the reader will find in this *Handbook* are the dynamic system theories, the life span and life course approaches, cognitive science and neuronal models, the behavior genetics approach, person-context interaction theories, action theories, cultural psychology, and a wide assortment of neo-Piagetian and neo-Vygotskian models. Although some of these models and approaches have been in the making for some time, they have now come into their own. Researchers are drawing on them directly, taking their implied assumptions and hypotheses seriously, using them with specificity and control, and exploiting their implications for practice.

Another pattern that emerges is a rediscovery and exploration of core processes in human development that had been underexamined by the generation of researchers just prior to the present one. Scientific interest has a way of moving in alternating cycles (or spirals, for those who wish to capture the progressive nature of scientific development). In our time, developmental study has cycled away from classic topics such as motivation and learning—not in the sense that they were entirely forgotten, or that good work ceased to be done in such areas, but in the sense that they no longer were the most prominent subjects of theoretical reflection and debate. Some of the relative neglect was intentional, as scholars got caught up in controversies about whether psychological motivation was a "real" phenomenon worthy of study or whether learning could or should be distinguished from development in the first place. All this has changed. As the contents of our current edition attest, developmental science always returns, sooner or later, to concepts that are necessary for explaining the heart of its concerns, progressive change in individuals and social groups over time, and concepts such as learning and motivation are indispensable for this task. Among the exciting features of this *Handbook* edition are the advances it presents in theoretical and empirical work on these classic concepts.

The other concept that has met some resistance in recent years is the notion of development itself. For some social critics, the idea of progress, implicit in the notion of development, has seemed out of step with principles such as equality and cultural diversity. Some genuine benefits have accrued from that critique; for example, the field has worked to better appreciate diverse developmental pathways. But, like many critique positions, it led to excesses. For some, it became questionable to explore issues that lie at the heart of human development. Growth, advancement, positive change, achievement, and standards for improved performance and conduct, all were questioned as legitimate subjects of investigation.

Just as in the cases of learning and motivation, no doubt it was inevitable that the field's center of gravity sooner or later would return to broad concerns of development. The story of growth from infancy to adulthood is a developmental story of multifaceted learning, acquisitions of skills and knowledge, waxing powers of attention and memory, growing neuronal and other biological capacities, formations and transformations of character and personality, increases and reorganizations in the understanding of self and others, advances in emotional and behavioral regulation, progress in communicating and collaborating with others, and a host of other achievements documented in this edition. Parents, teachers, and other adults in all parts of the world recognize and value such developmental achievements in children, although they do not always know how to understand them, let alone how to foster them.

The sorts of scientific findings that the *Handbook*'s authors explicate in their chapters are needed to provide such understanding. The importance of sound scientific understanding has become especially clear in recent years, when news media broadcast story after story based on simplistic and biased popular speculations about the causes of human development. The careful and responsible discourse found in these chapters contrasts sharply with the typical news story about the role of parents, genes, or schools in children's growth and behavior. There is not much contest as to which source the public looks to for its information and stimulation. But the good news is that scientific truth usually works its way into the public mind over the long run. The way this works would make a good subject for developmental study some day, especially if such a study could find a way to speed up the process. In the meantime, readers of this edition of the *Handbook of Child Psychology* will find the most solid, insightful

and current set of scientific theories and findings available in the field today.

February 2006
Palo Alto, California

REFERENCES

Bühler, C. (1931). The social participation of infants and toddlers. In C. Murchison (Ed.), *A handbook of child psychology.* Worcester, MA: Clark University Press.

Carmichael, L. (Ed.). (1946). *Manual of child psychology.* New York: Wiley.

Carmichael, L. (Ed.). (1954). *Manual of child psychology* (2nd ed.). New York: Wiley.

Mead, M. (1931). The primitive child. In C. Murchison (Ed.), *A handbook of child psychology.* Worcester, MA: Clark University Press.

Murchison, C. (Ed.). (1931). *A handbook of child psychology.* Worcester, MA: Clark University Press.

Murchison, C. (Ed.). (1933). *A handbook of child psychology* (2nd ed.). Worcester, MA: Clark University Press.

Mussen, P. (Ed.). (1970). *Carmichael's manual of child psychology.* New York: Wiley.

Mussen, P. (Ed.). (1983). *Handbook of child psychology.* New York: Wiley.

Acknowledgments

A work as significant as the *Handbook of Child Psychology* is always produced by the contributions of numerous people, individuals whose names do not necessarily appear on the covers or spines of the volumes. Most important, we are grateful to the more than 150 colleagues whose scholarship gave life to the Sixth Edition. Their enormous knowledge, expertise, and hard work make this edition of the *Handbook* the most important reference work in developmental science.

In addition to the authors of the chapters of the four volumes of this edition, we were fortunate to have been able to work with two incredibly skilled and dedicated editors within the Institute for Applied Research in Youth Development at Tufts University, Jennifer Davison and Katherine Connery. Their "can-do" spirit and their impressive ability to attend to every detail of every volume were invaluable resources enabling this project to be completed in a timely and high quality manner.

It may be obvious, but we want to stress also that without the talent, commitment to quality, and professionalism of our editors at John Wiley & Sons, this edition of the *Handbook* would not be a reality and would not be the cutting-edge work we believe it to be. The breadth of the contributions of the Wiley staff to the *Handbook* is truly enormous. Although we thank all these colleagues for their wonderful contributions, we wish to make special note of four people in particular: Patricia Rossi, Senior Editor, Psychology, Linda Witzling, Senior Production Editor, Isabel Pratt, Associate Editor, and Peggy Alexander, Vice President and Publisher. Their creativity, professionalism, sense of balance and perspective, and unflagging commitment to the tradition of quality of the *Handbook* were vital ingredients for any success we may have with this edition. We are also deeply grateful to Pam Blackmon and her colleagues at Publications Development Company for undertaking the enormous task of copy editing and producing the thousands of pages of the Sixth Edition. Their professionalism and commitment to excellence were invaluable resources and provided a foundation upon which the editors' work was able to move forward productively.

Child development typically happens in families. So too, the work of editors on the *Handbook* moved along productively because of the support and forbearance of spouses, partners, and children. We thank all of our loved ones for being there for us throughout the several years on which we have worked on the Sixth Edition.

Numerous colleagues critiqued the chapters in manuscript form and provided valuable insights and suggestions that enhanced the quality of the final products. We thank all of these scholars for their enormous contributions.

William Damon and Richard M. Lerner thank the John Templeton Foundation for its support of their respective scholarly endeavors. In addition, Richard M. Lerner thanks the National 4-H Council for its support of his work. Nancy Eisenberg thanks the National Institute of Mental Health, the Fetzer Institute, and The Institute for Research on Unlimited Love—Altruism, Compassion, Service (located at the School of Medicine, Case Western Reserve University) for their support. K. Ann Renninger and Irving E. Sigel thank Vanessa Ann Gorman for her editorial support for Volume 4. Support from the Swarthmore College Provost's Office to K. Ann Renninger for editorial assistance on this project is also gratefully acknowledged.

Finally, in an earlier form, with Barbara Rogoff's encouragement, sections of the preface were published in *Human Development* (April 1997). We thank Barbara for her editorial help in arranging this publication.

Preface to Volume Three
Social, Emotional, and Personality Development

NANCY EISENBERG

As for the fifth edition, this volume has been a labor of love. When I was a graduate student, we read many of the chapters from the 1970 edition of the *Mussen Handbook of Child Psychology* is our classes. Even then, in my mind it was the "bible" of the field. Moreover, my mentor was Paul Mussen, so I frequently borrowed one of his extra copies of the *Handbook,* and he gave me that copy as a gift when I graduated. When the 1983 edition of the *Handbook* was being prepared, I was fortunate as a young scholar to get to review a couple of chapters; in addition, I heard the occasional grumblings of Paul Mussen about the chapters that were late. At that time in my career it was my dream that I would someday get to contribute a chapter to the *Handbook.*

Thus, I was pleased and honored (as well as a little apprehensive) when I was asked to edit a volume of this very important set of books for the fifth edition, and now the sixth edition. Editing the volume has been an exceptional learning experience. I have had the privilege to work with some of the best people in the field and to read (and reread) a year or two before other people the very exciting work that is in this volume. I have learned much from my fellow contributors to the volume.

The contributors to this volume deserve much thanks. All of the people who were requested to contribute agreed to do so, and all of the chapters were completed. The authors spent tremendous energy and time constructing their very thoughtful and integrative chapters,

and then editing them to fit within the stringent space limitations and page restrictions. The contributors to this volume poured their souls into their chapters; I was fortunate to work with such a talented, cooperative, and personable group of people.

I also thank the many other people who made this volume possible. First and foremost, I thank my husband, Jerry Harris, for his continuing support throughout this and my other time-consuming projects. I also thank Richard Lerner for his assistance in dealing with administrative issues related to the volume. The senior editors, Richard Lerner and William Damon, allowed the volume editors to shape their own volumes, which I greatly appreciated. Numerous colleagues who critiqued the chapters in manuscript form also provided valuable insights and suggestions that enhanced the quality of the final product.

In addition, I thank my colleagues and students who shared their ideas with me in the course of this task. I also appreciate the financial support that I received over the last few years from the National Institutes of Mental Health and the National Institute of Drug Abuse. Finally, I thank Paul Mussen, my friend and mentor, who has provided me with intellectual and emotional support for approximately three decades. His death has left a hole in my life and that of many others. It has been a privilege and joy to carry on the tradition of the *Handbook* that he edited twice in his career, and I dedicate this book to him.

Contents

CHAPTER 1

Introduction

NANCY EISENBERG

The sixth edition of the *Handbook of Child Psychology* was written approximately 8 years after the 1998 fifth edition. As was true for the last edition, the goal of the authors in this volume of the *Handbook* was to present state-of-the-art reviews of conceptual and empirical work on social, emotional, and personality development. Each author or set of authors has provided the reader with an integrative summary of the current status of an important topic within the domain of social and personality development and, to some degree, with a vision for the future. Although research on social, emotional, and personality development is a cumulative endeavor with few abrupt, dramatic changes in knowledge, the field does have a somewhat different look from 8 years ago, and differs greatly from that depicted in the fourth edition of the *Handbook* in 1983. In this chapter, I note some of the themes in this volume, with an eye to changes in themes in the past 20 or so years.

AN EMPHASIS ON PROCESS (MEDIATION) AND MODERATION

As developmental psychologists have produced and accumulated more knowledge about the occurrence and frequency of variables of interest (e.g., descriptive data) as well as about relations among constructs (i.e., correlational data), they have begun to ask more complex questions than in the past. This trend is very evident in this volume of the *Handbook,* even more so than in the fifth edition (1998). For example, in addition to routinely questioning assumptions of directionality of causality, there is evidence in the chapters of an increased concern with *process,* as reflected in questions about mediation. Mediating processes are the processes underlying the relation between two variables (a predictor and a criterion). Mediators help clarify how or why a given relation occurs (Baron & Kenny, 1986; MacKinnon, Lockwood, Hoffman, West, & Sheets, 2002).

Work on this chapter was supported by a grant from the National Institute of Mental Health. Thanks to Mary Rothbart for her comments on a draft of this chapter and to Joseph Campos for his discussion with me of some of the ideas therein.

In addition, based in part on the contemporary concern with context, diversity, biological substrates and predispositions, and indices of individual differences (see later discussion), there is considerable interest in moderating variables, that is, in variables such as sex, socioeconomic class, race/ethnicity, personality, prior socialization experiences, and type of situation that affect the direction or strength of the relation between an independent or predictor variable and a dependent or criterion variable (Baron & Kenny, 1986). To study moderation, investigators generally examine the interaction of the independent variable with the potential moderator (e.g., age, high or low level of regulation) when predicting an outcome or criterion variable or comparing the equivalence of structural models for different groups.

Mediating or moderating processes are discussed directly or indirectly by all chapter authors, but are a more central focus in some chapters. For example, in their discussion of relations of temperament to children's adjustment, Rothbart and Bates (Chapter 3, this *Handbook,* this volume) explicitly discuss two types of indirect relations: mediated linkage, as when temperament influences transactions with the environment, which, in turn, shape the child's developing adjustment, and moderated relations, as when temperament and some facet of the environment affect children's adjustment. Bugental and Grusec (Chapter 7, this *Handbook,* this volume) also explicitly emphasize moderation in the socialization process, and Dodge, Coie, and Lynam (Chapter 12, this *Handbook,* this volume) review studies of moderating effects, concluding that such research is essential for delineating the combinations of factors that predict antisocial behavior.

A few more specific examples of how authors discuss mediation and moderation illustrate the types of issues that are the focus of contemporary work in developmental psychology and related disciplines. First, consider mediation. Collins and Steinberg (Chapter 16, this *Handbook,* this volume) conclude that the impact of pubertal maturation on adolescent psychosocial development is more likely to be interpersonally mediated than due to the direct action of hormonal changes on mood or emotional functioning. Similarly, multiple authors note that the quality of relationships or social interactions likely mediates between distal environmental factors (e.g., economic resources, quality of the neighborhood), family structure, or social institutions and youths' adjustment and other socioemotional developmental outcomes (e.g., Dodge et al., Chapter 12; Parke & Buriel, Chapter 8; Thompson, Chapter 2, this *Handbook,* this volume). Harter (Chapter 9, this *Handbook,* this volume) argues for mediation by

others' approval of the relation between genes (as expressed, for example, in temperament or attractiveness) and self-esteem. Kagan and Fox (Chapter 4, this *Handbook,* this volume) discuss a number of biological systems that mediate between heredity or biological structures and psychological or behavioral responses, whereas Ruble, Martin, and Berenbaum (Chapter 14, this *Handbook,* this volume) note that genes and hormones are often viewed as proximal mediators of the effect of evolutionary forces on gender differences. Eisenberg, Fabes, and Spinrad (Chapter 11, this *Handbook,* this volume) present data indicating that sympathy at least partly mediates the relations between moral judgment or perspective taking and children's prosocial behavior, whereas children's regulation mediates the relation between parental expression of negative emotion in the family and children's sympathy. They also present a model in which a number of more proximal factors mediate the relations of more distal factors (e.g., biological factors, socialization, and antecedent sociocognitive and dispositional characteristics of the child) to prosocial behavior.

Mediation is invoked repeatedly in discussions of parenting, parent-child attachment, family variables, and developmental outcomes. After a review of the literature on attachment, Thompson calls for additional exploration of the mediators of the relations of attachment security to outcome variables. Rubin, Bukowski, and Parker (Chapter 10, this *Handbook,* this volume) present data indicating that lower levels of parental skill have been associated with higher levels of antisocial behavior and lower levels of academic performance, which in turn have been associated with higher levels of peer rejection. Dodge et al. (Chapter 12, this *Handbook,* this volume) discuss social-cognitive processes as mediators of the relations between parenting (e.g., abuse) and offsprings' externalizing behavior. They also argue that parenting is a mediator of the relation between the macrolevel variable of family poverty and children's aggression. Wigfield, Eccles, Schiefele, Roeser, and Davis-Kean (Chapter 15, this *Handbook,* this volume) suggest that a range of parental beliefs and practices mediate between family demographics and achievement-related outcomes. In their model, specific parental behaviors (e.g., time spent with the child, teaching strategies) at least partially mediate relations between parental general beliefs and behaviors (e.g., locus of control, gender-role stereotypes, parenting style) and children's outcomes (e.g., goals, persistence, performance). Bugental and Grusec (Chapter 7, this *Handbook,* this volume) examine a range of potential mediators in regard to the relation of socialization to developmental outcomes, including children's acquired ways of cognitively representing their social worlds, hormones (and neurotransmitters) involved in children's responses to socialization experiences, and gene expression in the continuous reorganization of the brain in response to experience. Finally, Caspi and Shiner (Chapter 6, this *Handbook,* this volume) discuss a variety of mediating processes related to personality and note the need for further investigation of both the proximal relationship-specific processes that mediate personality effects on relationship outcomes and mediators (e.g., parental attributions) of the association between parental personality and parenting behavior. The list could go on and on; what is impressive is how mediating processes have become such a central focus in work on socioemotional development.

Moderational processes are also repeatedly emphasized in this volume. For example, Bugental and Grusec discuss the ways that parental goals serve to moderate parental behavior (including their affective responses) on different occasions, as well as the role of culture as a moderator of the relation between socialization experiences and children's development. Collins and Steinberg (Chapter 16, this *Handbook,* this volume) cite evidence indicating that the impact of puberty on psychological functioning is moderated by the social context in which adolescents mature. They also cite research indicating that aspects of parenting—for example, parenting style and parenting practices—may interact with one another in the prediction of outcome variables such as youths' adjustment. Numerous other authors in this volume review empirical interactions between children's temperament (e.g., emotionality or regulation) or personality and their parenting experiences in predicting children's behavior or socioemotional development (e.g., Kagan & Fox, Chapter 4; Rothbart & Bates, Chapter 3; Thompson, Chapter 2, this *Handbook,* this volume). Components of temperament or personality may also interact with one another: For example, Eisenberg et al. (Chapter 11, this *Handbook,* this volume) summarize data indicating that the interaction of individual differences in emotionality and regulation predicts children's prosocial behavior and sympathy better than the consideration of only the main effects of these predictors.

Demographic characteristics that reflect diversity are other common moderators of predictors of developmental outcomes. Wigfield et al. (Chapter 15, this *Handbook,* this volume) suggest that competence-related beliefs and school performance may predict school performance for White but not African American children and that academic self-concept of ability is less predictive of general self-esteem for at least some African American children

than for White American children. Dodge et al. (Chapter 12, this *Handbook,* this volume) note that harsh discipline (but not abuse) is a predictor of later aggressive behavior for White but not African American children. Further, Ruble et al., Chapter 14, and Turiel and others, Chapter 13, this *Handbook,* this volume, discuss ways in which the sex of the child may moderate the effects of social experience on various social behaviors (although authors did not always use the term *moderation*). Thus, moderators that have received substantial attention include temperament/personality, children's sex, race, culture, and parenting style or support.

One moderator of the effects of the socializing environment that has received relatively little attention in the past is genetic differences between children. Recently, Caspi et al. (2002) reported such moderation for the long-term effects of maltreatment. Those children whose genotype resulted in high levels of MAOA (monoamine oxidase A, an enzyme that metabolizes neurotransmitters such as serotonin, and thus renders them inactive) were more likely than children without this genetic tendency to exhibit antisocial problems if they were maltreated (see Caspi & Shiner, Chapter 6, this *Handbook,* this volume). With the new wave of research on genes, neurotransmitters, and other biological factors, investigators are likely to obtain much more evidence of interactions between biological indices and environmental factors or experiences in the next decade (see Cadoret, Yates, Troughton, Woodworth, & Stewart, 1995). Such research, as well as research on interactions involving the kinds of variables already discussed, is producing a more differentiated understanding of "when" relations and processes occur—an issue that is an essential complement to the more basic mediational question of "why" relations occur (Parke, 2004). Moreover, as dynamical systems approaches become more popular, evidence of indirect, nonlinear relations among multiple variables is likely to be more common than at the present (e.g., Lewis, 2002).

A FOCUS ON EMOTION

The fifth edition of the *Handbook* (1998) was the first to include a chapter dedicated solely to the topic of emotion (rather than the more general topic of socioemotional development in infancy). The neglect of emotion in prior editions is not surprising given the history of the study of emotion in psychology in the past 50 years. Due to the influence of behaviorism and then cognitive approaches in psychology, emotion was considered a nuisance variable (and something of no relevance) for many years. In the past 10 to 15 years, however, emotion has become central to the study of social development, as well as to many other topics in psychology.

The current emphasis on emotion is a dramatic departure from the previous view of emotions as intrapsychic events "which do not play a causal role in behavior and which are secondary by-products of more significant processes" (Campos, 1984, p. 148). Today emotions are viewed as motivational forces that play a role in much of our social behavior. As noted by Parke (1994), in contemporary psychology, emotions are viewed as "both products and processes of social interactions, relationships, and contexts" (p. 158).

The central role of emotion in contemporary developmental psychology is reflected in most of the chapters in this volume. This focus is, of course, most evident in Saarni, Campos, Camras, and Witherington's chapter on emotional development (Chapter 5, this Handbook, this volume). Saarni et al. take a functionalist perspective in which emotion is closely linked to the context and what a person is trying to do. Emotion is viewed as synonymous with the significance of a person-event transaction for the individual.

Due to the immense body of work relevant to emotion, Saarni et al. (Chapter 5, this Handbook, this volume) limit their coverage, focusing primarily on the conceptualization of emotion, developmental changes in emotion and emotion communication, the role of culture in emotion in emotional development, and the components of emotional competence, their development, and their relations to adjustment and social competence. Saarni et al.'s review of this portion of the emotion literature demonstrates that children's understanding of emotion and its expression, as well as children's communication of, and coping with, emotion, change considerably with age. Moreover, emotional understanding and communication seem to have a profound influence on social interaction, although the relation between social interaction and these aspects of functioning is doubtlessly reciprocal. Saarni et al.'s review reflects major domains of interest in recent work on emotion and provides a contemporary, contextually oriented perspective on emotional development.

Temperament, Personality, and Emotion

Emotion can be viewed in both situationally specific and dispositional terms. In theory and research on temperament and personality, enduring individual differ-

ences in reactivity are fundamental constructs; thus, dispositional emotional tendencies are salient topics in the two chapters that deal with temperament (Kagan & Fox, Chapter 4; Rothbart & Bates, Chapter 3, this Handbook, this volume) and the chapter on personality (i.e., Caspi & Shiner, Chapter 6, this Handbook, this volume).

Temperament is defined by Rothbart and Bates as constitutionally based individual differences in reactivity and self-regulation. Reactivity includes emotional responding, both in regard to specific emotions (e.g., fear) and more general constructs of emotion (e.g., negative emotionality or emotional intensity; see Larsen & Diener, 1987; Rothbart & Bates, Chapter 2, this Handbook, this volume). Regulation pertains to the modulation of temperamental reactivity (Ahadi & Rothbart, 1994; Eisenberg, 2002; Rothbart & Derryberry, 1981). Research on temperament/personality, and hence on emotional reactivity and self-regulation, has increased greatly in volume in the past 1 to 2 decades.

Kagan and Fox (Chapter 4, this Handbook, this volume) view temperament as a "biologically based bias for correlated clusters of feelings, thoughts, and actions that appear during childhood, but not always in the opening months, and are sculpted by varied rearing environments into a large but still limited number of traits that comprise an individual's personality profile." Thus, like Rothbart and Bates (Chapter 3, this Handbook, this volume), they include emotion in their definition of temperament. However, they do not emphasize regulatory components of temperament to the same degree as Rothbart and Bates, and they tie dispositional biases to thought patterns (Rothbart & Bates view the content of thought as personality rather than temperament), as well as to actions.

Dispositional emotionality also plays an important role in concepts of personality. In fact, Caspi (1998) defined personality as "individual differences in the tendency to behave, think, and feel in certain consistent ways" (p. 312). Personality theorists often include in personality not only traits, but also personal concerns (i.e., a wide array of motivational, developmental, or strategic constructs that are contextualized in time, place, or role) and life stories (McAdams, 1995). As noted by Caspi and Shiner (Chapter 6, this Handbook, this volume), "personality is typically seen as including a wider range of individual differences in feeling, thinking, and behaving than is temperament." Similarly, Kagan and Fox (Chapter 4, this Handbook, this volume) assert that, "the stable variation in behaviors and emotions observed in older children, adolescents and adults are personality traits, not temperamental biases, although the latter make a contribution to the profile that emerges later in development." Analogously, Rothbart and Bates (Chapter 3, this *Handbook,* this volume) note that, "Temperament represents the affective, activational, and attentional core of personality, whereas personality includes much more than temperament, particularly the content of thought, skills, habits, values, defenses, morals, beliefs, and social cognition. Social cognition includes the perception of the self, others, and the relation of self to objects, events, and others."

Despite these definitional distinctions, as noted by Caspi and Shiner, there is a striking similarity between the constructs of temperament and personality. Both can be observed in animals (at least to some degree) as well as humans; both involve moderate genetic influence but are also affected by experience; and, importantly, "many traits from both domains are characterized by specific habitual positive and negative emotions" (Caspi & Shiner, Chapter 6, this *Handbook,* this volume). If we view temperament as representing the building blocks from which personality develops (Rothbart & Bates, Chapter 3, this *Handbook,* this volume), these similarities are not surprising.

Caspi and Shiner (Chapter 6, this *Handbook,* this volume; Caspi, 1998), as well as Rothbart and Bates (Chapter 3, this *Handbook,* this volume), speculate on how aspects of temperament in childhood are linked to the structure of adult personality (i.e., aspects of the "big five" components of personality). For example, temperamental negative emotionality is believed to contribute to the personality construct of neuroticism and agreeableness (inversely related) whereas temperamental positive affect or surgency (and sociability) are associated with agreeableness and extraversion in adults. In addition, aspects of temperament believed to be involved in the regulation or control of emotionality and emotionally driven behavior have been linked to personality. For example, temperamental behavioral inhibition (see Kagan & Fox, Chapter 4, this *Handbook,* this volume) is viewed as related to adult neuroticism and low levels of extraversion (Caspi & Shiner, Chapter 6, this *Handbook,* this volume). Moreover, temperamental attentional regulation and inhibitory control likely contribute to the adult personality characteristic of constraint, and perhaps also agreeableness (although the latter may also have a more proximal temperamental correlate in childhood; see Rothbart & Bates, Chapter 3, this *Handbook,* this volume).

Emotion and Social Behavior

In addition to playing a role in later personality, and consistent with much of the review in the Saarni et al.'s Chapter 5 (this *Handbook,* this volume) on emotion, individual differences in temperamental emotionality, including directly experienced negative emotions such as anger and vicariously induced emotion (e.g., sympathy or empathy), frequently have been found to predict variation among children in socioemotional development (see Dodge et al., Chapter 12; Eisenberg et al., Chapter 11; Turiel, Chapter 13, this *Handbook,* this volume). For example, to a much greater degree than 8 years ago, there is empirical support for relations between dispositional emotionality—irritability/anger, fearfulness, and positive emotionality—and social competence or adjustment, including internalizing and externalizing problem behavior (see Caspi & Shiner, Chapter 6; Kagan & Fox, Chapter 4; Rothbart & Bates, Chapter 3, this *Handbook,* this volume). Moreover, much more often than a decade ago, investigators are identifying distinct relations between different types of negative emotions (e.g., anger versus anxiety or sadness, fear of novelty versus fear of strangers) and the prediction of specific internalizing and externalizing problems or related psychological problems (e.g., Eisenberg et al., 2001, 2005; Rothbart & Bates, Chapter 3, this *Handbook,* this volume).

Ruble et al. (Chapter 10, this *Handbook,* this volume) noted an increased focus on emotion in the peer literature since the fifth edition of the *Handbook.* They list among topics recently introduced to the discipline the relation of jealousy and other emotional processes to the maintenance and dissolution of peer relationships. Dispositional emotionality clearly plays a role in the quality of social functioning in peer interactions and relationships; for example, emotional reactivity has been linked to social withdrawal (Rubin et al., Chapter 10, this *Handbook,* this volume; Spinrad et al., 2004), as well as information processing in social encounters, although there is relatively little research on the latter issue (see Arsenio & Lemerise, 2004; Crick & Dodge, 1994). Researchers have found that cheerful children appear to be relatively popular, whereas children prone to intense negative emotions are lower in social status (see Rubin et al., Chapter 10, this *Handbook,* this volume). Relations between peer interactions/relationships and emotion no doubt are reciprocal; as noted by Rubin et al. (Chapter 10, this *Handbook,* this volume), experiences with peers affect social, emotional, and cognitive functioning beyond the influences of family, school, and neighborhood.

Contextually specific emotional reactions, in addition to dispositional emotionality, are seen as playing a major role in peer and other types of relationships. Rubin et al. (Chapter 10, this *Handbook,* this volume) define *relationships* as referring to the meanings, expectations, and emotions that derive from a succession of interactions between two individuals known to each other. As noted by Thompson (Chapter 2, this *Handbook,* this volume), "Emotion is a more salient feature of social interaction compared to most encounters with objects—including the emotions that precede social interaction and the changes in emotions that arise from interactive activity." Thompson also notes that differences in attachment security are believed to affect early emotional development and the style of young children's emotion regulation, and that these emerging aspects of the individual influence children's social, emotional, and personality development in subsequent years. Thus, social relationships are affected by dispositional differences in emotionality as well as by emotions experienced when interacting with others, and the quality of social relationships with parents, peers, and others contribute to emerging individual differences in situational and dispositional emotionality.

Emotion, the Self, and Goals

Emotion is also an integral aspect of conceptions of the self. For example, low self-esteem seems to be highly related to feelings of depression and hopelessness (Harter, Chapter 9, this *Handbook,* this volume). Moreover, emotions tied to attachment status (e.g., Kochanska, 2001) may affect children's self-esteem and working model of the self in relation to others. In addition, young children's understanding of emotion (e.g., identification of emotions, knowing when various emotions are likely to occur) is viewed by both Harter and Thompson (Chapter 2, this *Handbook,* this volume) as affecting the child's construction of the self.

In the 1998 edition of this volume, Eccles, Wigfield, and Schiefele concluded that the highest priority in the research on achievement was closer consideration of the influence of emotion on motivation. Although there is more work on this issue than a decade ago, there is not as much as one might expect. Nonetheless, as noted by Wigfield et al. (Chapter 15, this *Handbook,* this volume), emotional development plays a role in some theories regarding individual differences (and likely developmental change) in achievement-related beliefs, values, and goals. Success and failure are associated with emotional reactions; level of anxiety can affect performance; and emotion-related self-evaluations play a role in achievement-related behavior and vice versa. For example, high levels of trait-like intrinsic motivation appear to foster positive emotional experience and well-being (Ryan & Deci, 2000), as well as self-esteem (Ryan, Connell, & Deci, 1985). Wigfield et al. (Chapter 15, this *Handbook,* this volume) note that there has been increasing interest recently in the research on relations between motivation and affect, and they expect the volume of work on this topic to increase.

Emotion and Morality

The role of emotion in the study of morality has varied greatly as a function of the conception of morality. In Kohlbergian work on moral reasoning, emotion traditionally plays a minor role in comparison to cognition (see Kohlberg, 1984; Rest, 1983). In contrast, emotions such as empathy-related reactions or guilt have been highlighted in some work on moral *behavior,* including theory and research on prosocial tendencies (e.g., Eisenberg & Fabes, 1990; Eisenberg et al., Chapter 11, this *Handbook,* this volume; Hoffman, 2000), feelings of guilt (Saarni et al., Chapter 5; Thompson, Chapter 2, this *Handbook,* this volume; Zahn-Waxler & Kochanska, 1990), and conscience (Thompson, Chapter 2, this *Handbook,* this volume). For example, in work on prosocial behavior, both enduring tendencies toward experiencing moral emotions (i.e., dispositional sympathy) and situational emotional reactions (e.g., situational sympathy or guilt) are viewed as motivating altruistic action (see Eisenberg et al., Chapter 11, this *Handbook,* this volume). And in recent work, emotional reactions such as guilt and empathy are one of two components of conscience (Aksan & Kochanska, 2005).

Some contemporary theorists, including Wilson (1993), assume that there is a biologically based emotional basis to morality (see Turiel, Chapter 13, this *Handbook,* this volume). According to Kagan (1984), moral principles are determined by the intensity of the community's affective reactions to the specific content of the principle. Turiel recognizes the importance of emotion in morality, but also emphasizes cognition more than theorists such as Hoffman, Kagan, and Shweder, concluding, as he did in 1998, "As important as are emotions—especially sympathy, empathy, and respect—for moral functioning, emotions occur in and among persons who can think about them with regard to other people and in relation to complicated social agendas, goals, and arrangements. The relationships among emotions, moral judgments, reflections, and deliberations require a great deal of attention in research and in theoretical formulations." Thus, the magnitude of the role of emotion in morality is still an issue of discussion.

Sex and Emotion

In the past decade, investigators have not examined sex differences in measures of emotional functioning as much as might be expected. As one might expect, there are sex differences in the emotions that boys and girls tend to display—for example, girls tend to display more sadness, fear, shame, and guilt (Eisenberg, Martin, & Fabes, 1996; Ruble et al., Chapter 14, this *Handbook,* this volume)—although little is known about the degree to which boys and girls differ in internally experienced emotion (albeit adolescent girls report more anxiety and depression than do boys). Nonetheless, gender differences in the degree or type of expression of anger and frustration may be a factor in the gender difference in children's externalizing behavior and aggression (see Dodge et al., Chapter 12, this *Handbook,* this volume). Findings regarding gender differences in empathy or sympathy are weaker, although some measures favor females (Eisenberg et al., Chapter 11, this *Handbook,* this volume). Guilt is another emotion that girls likely experience more than boys; if this is true, there are implications for both the development of conscience and for children's adjustment (see Zahn-Waxler & Robinson, 1995). In addition, there is evidence that females are better at expressing and decoding emotions than are males (Ruble et al., Chapter 14, this *Handbook,* this volume), which has implications for gender differences in social communication and skills. Because of the centrality of emotion in recent research and theory on the quality of children's social functioning, it is likely that investigators will attend more to gender differences in the experience and expression of emotion in the near future.

Emotion in Socialization and the Socialization of Emotion

Socialization is an area of study in which emotion has received increased attention in recent years (Parke & Buriel, Chapter 8, this *Handbook,* this volume). As noted by Parke and Buriel (1998), affect played a relatively minor role in socialization theories until the recent past.

Until the 1980s, affect was discussed primarily in regard to the degree of warmth, support, and harmony versus conflict or hostility in the parent-child relationship or expressed in parents' "parenting style" (see Collins & Steinberg, Chapter 16, this *Handbook,* this volume). In contrast, the topic of affect/emotion permeates contemporary work on socialization, far beyond the emotional tone of parents' interactions with their children.

Before highlighting some of the recently emerging topics in regard to emotion and socialization, it is noteworthy that nearly every chapter in this volume contains some discussion of the relation of the emotional climate in the home and/or school—that is, between parents and children, teachers and children, and/or between parents—to children's social, emotional, or achievement-related development. Most authors of the chapters have noted that the emotional tone of the relationship between the socializing adult and a child is associated with the quality of children's social behavior (e.g., social competence, prosocial and aggressive behavior, peer interactions), their conceptions of self and emotional autonomy, the quality of their interpersonal relationships, their academic-related outcomes, or their adjustment (e.g., chapters by Bugental & Grusec; Collins & Steinberg; Dodge et al.; Eisenberg et al.; Parke & Buriel; Rubin et al.; and Thompson, this *Handbook,* this volume). Indeed, one of the more consistent findings across domains of socioemotional development is the importance of supportive, positive (versus hostile) relationships with socializing adults for children's healthy development. Although this is an old topic of study, investigators are still delineating the many ways in which the emotional tone of relationships with other people may affect the course of children's development.

According to Bugental and Grusec (Chapter 7, this *Handbook,* this volume), emotion is one outcome of socialization: "it [socialization] includes their [children's] ability and motivation to acquire individual and culturally shared competencies at a social, emotional, and cognitive level." Thus, in addition to providing an emotional context for socialization, socialization-related interactions are believed to affect the valence and degree of emotionality, in part through influencing children's felt security and attachment, conceptions of the self, and the associations, interpretations, and attributions they make regarding people, contexts, and events in their lives.

In addition, Bugental and Grusec (Chapter 7, this *Handbook,* this volume) suggest that emotion affects a variety of cognitive processes fundamental to the socialization process, including attentional focus, memory retrieval, appraisal and response selection, and the capacity for rational or reflective processing. These processes affect, for example, children's responses to socialization attempts and parents' reactions to their children's negative behaviors. Bugental and Grusec's conception of the role of emotion in socialization is more complex, multilayered, and encompassing than in most existing theory.

It is no surprise that emotion plays a central role in both biologically oriented and culturally oriented socialization theories. In biologically-based theories, affect and emotion are conceptualized as basic processes to be regulated, as regulators of relationships (e.g., attachment relationships), or as consequences of socializing relationships. One relatively recent focus has been the long-term influences of socialization practices on the regulation (or dysregulation) of the child's neurohormonal responses, which often co-occur with emotional experience and are part of emotional responses. Emotional processes are also viewed as functional regulators of other processes central to socialization (see Bugental & Grusec, Chapter 7, this *Handbook*, this volume).

In recent sociocultural perspectives, the expression, experience, interpretation, and naming of emotions are derived, at least in part, from the culture (see Bugental & Grusec, Chapter 7, this *Handbook*, this volume; Kitayama & Markus, 1994; Saarni et al., Chapter 5, this *Handbook*, this volume). Thus, socialization by the culture influences emotional reactions, as well as a range of social behaviors. Saarni et al. illustrate this point in their discussion of "how emotion communication accompanies and helps to inculcate cultural values, affects pre- and perinatal emotionality, determines the types of events to which an infant or child is exposed, and creates the 'emotional climate' within which a person is immersed." As a consequence of the recent increased awareness of cultural contributions to emotional experience and expression, a number of our current conceptions of emotional development are likely to be challenged (see the discussion of culture that follows).

In summary, in the past 2 decades, the topic of emotion has moved to center stage in the study of social and personality development. This surge of interest in emotion has been accompanied by, and perhaps is related causally to, elevated interest in biological inputs to development and temperament. In addition, contemporary concern with culture and context has had a powerful influence on thinking about emotional development.

A FOCUS ON REGULATION

Because emotional experience and expression often involve regulation (or the lack thereof), contemporary discussion and research on emotion regulation also have been revitalized. Until the early 1990s, popular approaches to the topic of regulation included emphases on parental control and discipline; children's compliance, delay of gratification, and resistance to temptation; children's internalization of societal values regarding behaviors such as aggression and prosocial behavior; and the role of fear, anxiety, and guilt in fostering internalization or at least compliance (e.g., Hoffman, 1970, 1983; Maccoby & Martin, 1983; see Dodge et al., Chapter 12; Eisenberg et al., Chapter 11; Turiel, Chapter 13, this *Handbook*, this volume). Although there is still considerable interest in these topics, in recent years investigators concerned with regulatory processes also have focused on mechanisms by which children regulate their emotion and emotion-driven behavior, and the relation of individual differences in regulation to social competence and adjustment. Even though children's regulation was clearly an important emerging topic in the fifth edition of the *Handbook* (1998), more authors discuss this topic in this edition of the *Handbook*, and in considerably greater depth. Perhaps this is because many view the regulation of emotion, as much as the emotion itself, as related to quality of social behavior and relationships (Rubin et al., Chapter 10; Saarni et al., Chapter 5, this *Handbook*, this volume).

Contemporary Work on Regulation

Contemporary thinking on the aforementioned topics has diverse origins in the discipline. The work of the Blocks (Block & Block, 1980) on ego control has had an important impact on this topic of study. Also important is work by temperament theorists on constructs such as attentional control (e.g., the ability to shift and focus attention), impulsivity, and effortful control (i.e., superordinate self-regulatory systems that can assert control over the reactive and self-regulatory processes of other temperament systems; Rothbart, Ahadi, Hershey, & Fisher, 2001; Rothbart & Rueda, 2005). Similarly, mechanisms for adaptation discussed by coping theorists (e.g., Carver, Scheier, & Weintraub, 1989; Lazarus & Folkman, 1984) for decades can be viewed as modes of dealing with, or regulating, emotion and behavior in stressful contexts. In addition, some of the adult personality work on constructs such as constraint or conscientiousness (Caspi & Shiner, Chapter 6, this *Handbook,* this volume) is relevant to developmental scientists interested in regulatory processes.

Self-regulation is discussed, in one form or another, in most of the chapters in this volume. For example, Kagan and Fox (Chapter 4, this *Handbook,* this volume), as well as Rothbart and Bates (Chapter 3, this *Handbook,* this volume), discuss the temperamental (including physiological) basis of regulation of reactivity; in addition, Rothbart and Bates emphasize the attentional basis of some forms of self-regulation and review parts of the growing literature pertaining to the relations of temperamental regulation to adjustment. Caspi and Shiner (Chapter 5, *Handbook,* this volume) note that constraint is a component of all contemporary systems of personality, and highlighted the role of temperamental regulation in the emergence of personality traits such as constraint (or conscientiousness) and neuroticism. Saarni et al. focus on social communicative mechanisms used by infants to regulate their behavior (e.g., social referencing), as well as on the relation of emotion regulation to adjustment, coping, and emotional competence. They also discuss emotion and language as regulators of behavior.

Thompson (Chapter 2, *Handbook,* this volume) reviews the early development of self-regulation, whereas Rubin et al. (Chapter 10, this *Handbook,* this volume) summarized literature on the role of self-regulation in peer competence. The latter also note that peer interactions, especially friendships, provide opportunities to develop and use emotion regulation capacities. In addition, Dodge et al. (Chapter 12, this *Handbook,* this volume) discuss the role of children's emerging regulatory abilities in age-related changes in aggression; they also note the association of individual differences in children's aggression with problems in emotion regulation, attentional deficits, and impulsivity. Similarly, Eisenberg et al. (Chapter 11, this *Handbook,* this volume) report findings consistent with the view that regulatory processes are intimately involved in the vicariously induced emotions of sympathy and personal distress, as well as in the performance of prosocial behavior. Further, Wigfield et al. (Chapter 15, this *Handbook,* this volume) consider links between motivation and self-regulation and how motivation is translated into regulated behavior. They also discuss the importance of internally (versus externally) regulated motivation and behavior in the

achievement of goals and learning, as well as academic performance.

Bugental and Grusec (Chapter 7, this *Handbook,* this volume), Parke and Buriel (Chapter 8, this *Handbook,* this volume), Dodge and Coie (Chapter 12, this *Handbook,* this volume), and Collins and Steinberg (Chapter 16, this *Handbook,* this volume) focus, to varying degrees, on the socialization correlates of the development of children's self-regulation—a topic that has flourished in the past decade. For example, Bugental and Grusec note the increasing interest in the long-term effects of socialization practices on the regulation (or dysregulation) of the child's neurohormonal responses. They, as well other authors (e.g., Collins & Steinberg, Chapter 16; Thompson, Chapter 2, this *Handbook,* this volume; also see "A Focus on Relationships" that follows), discuss the co-regulation of the protective care (attachment) system by parent and offspring. This protective care relationship (especially parental warmth), in turn, is viewed as facilitating the acquisition of self-regulation skills. Moreover, Bugental and Grusec briefly discuss socialization practices and behaviors most associated with children's autonomous regulation. In addition, Parke and Buriel review literature on the potential role of emotional and attentional regulation as mediators between parenting and child outcomes and the likely mutual causal relations between socialization experiences and individual differences in children's regulation.

The Development of Emotion-Related Regulation

Based on the literature reviewed in various chapters (e.g., Saarni et al., Chapter 5; and Thompson, Chapter 2, this *Handbook,* this volume), several developmental trends in emotion-related regulation are evident (also see Eisenberg & Morris, 2002; Thompson, 1994; Walden & Smith, 1997). First, with increasing age in early infancy and childhood, regulation of emotion and behavior is shifted gradually from external sources in the social world (e.g., socializers) to self-initiated, internal (i.e., child-based) resources. Caregivers soothe young children, manage young children's emotion by selecting the situations they are in, and provide children with information (e.g., facial cues, narratives) to help the child interpret events (Thompson, Chapter 2, this *Handbook,* this volume). With age and cognitive development, children are better able to manage emotion themselves. Second, mentalistic strategies for emotion regulation, such as thinking about situations in a positive light, cognitive avoidance, and shifting and focusing attention, increase with use in age. The use of such strategies is probably facilitated by the development of children's understanding of emotion, including the factors that elicit, maintain, and modulate emotion, as well as by other cognitive advances and physical changes. Third, with greater maturity, children develop greater capacity to modulate the course of their physiological and emotional arousal, for example, the intensity and duration of arousal, an ability that would be expected to have dramatic effects on behavior (e.g., aggression, venting of emotion, emotional expression). Fourth, with age, individuals likely become more adept at selecting, managing, and construing situations and relationships in a manner that minimizes the need to deal with negative emotions and stress (Carstensen, 1991; see Saarni et al., Chapter 5, this *Handbook,* this volume). Fifth, the ability to match strategies with the nature of stressors appears to improve with development. Thus, children improve in the ability to select appropriate coping solutions for everyday problems. Moreover, children appear to become better at distinguishing between stressors that can be controlled and those that cannot, and at choosing the most effective strategies for these stressors (e.g., emotion-management strategies such as blunting or cognitive distraction in uncontrollable contexts; see Saarni et al., Chapter 5, this *Handbook,* this volume). These developmental changes are likely to impact development in many aspects of social, emotional, and academic functioning.

Neurological changes, especially in the prefrontal cortex and cingulate gyrus, likely account for some of the age-related changes in self-regulation and executive attention (see Rothbart & Bates, Chapter 3; Thompson, Chapter 2, this *Handbook,* this volume). A topic of recent interest has been the continued growth and change in multiple regions of the prefrontal cortex throughout the course of adolescence, especially with respect to processes of myelination and synaptic pruning (both of which increase the efficiency of information processing; see Collins & Steinberg, Chapter 14, this *Handbook,* this volume). These changes are believed to underlie improvements in executive functioning (long-term planning, metacognition, self-evaluation, and the coordination of affect and cognition; Keating, 2004), which plays a central role in self-regulation. Research on the neurological bases of self-regulation is clearly an important emerging area of work.

Modes of Regulation

Conceptual issues or empirical data related to different types of regulation or control were not discussed much in the 1998 *Handbook* (except in this introduction), and Rothbart and Bates note that this state of affairs has changed. Numerous authors at least address implicitly or explicitly, several types of children's regulatory/control capacities, including the regulation of attention, physiology, or behavior, as well as the social context. For example, in the discussion of temperament and/or personality (e.g., Caspi & Shiner, Chapter 6; Kagan & Fox, Chapter 4; Rothbart & Bates, Chapter 3, this *Handbook,* this volume), authors review findings related to the abilities to effortfully manage attention and to effortfully activate or inhibit behavior as needed when necessary, especially when one is not inclined to do so. Developmental theorists frequently have highlighted constructs such as inhibitory control, self-regulation, constraint, and ego control, which involve the ability to modulate the behavioral expression of impulses and feelings (e.g., Block & Block, 1980; Kopp, 1982; Pulkkinen, 1982; Rothbart et al., 2001), and such abilities are addressed in numerous chapters in discussion of their relations to adjustment and social competence (e.g., Caspi & Shiner, Chapter 6; Dodge et al., Chapter 12; Rothbart & Bates, Chapter 3; Saarni et al., Chapter 5, this *Handbook,* this volume).

Another type of regulation—managing or regulating the stressful situation that elicited the emotional arousal—has been discussed primarily by coping theorists, who view problem-focused coping (efforts to modify the source of the problem) as an important type of coping (Lazarus & Folkman, 1984). This type of regulation generally includes planning and direct problem solving or instrumental coping in response to the experience of emotion. In addition, people often proactively manage situations to reduce exposure to stress and negative emotion in the future (Aspinwall & Taylor, 1997; Carstensen, 1991). An example is when socially anxious individuals choose not to attend social events that elicit discomfort. Unfortunately, few investigators have examined children's efforts to proactively shape or select their experiences; this remains an important gap in our knowledge.

Appropriate regulation depends, in part, on the particular context. Effective emotion-related regulation is viewed as flexible and relevant to one's goals (Cole, Michel, & Teti, 1994; Eisenberg & Morris, 2002). For example, appropriate expression of emotion depends on the situation, and a person skilled in regulation adjusts his or her behavior accordingly. Moreover, it is important to differentiate between regulation and how it is measured. If regulation is operationalized as control or inhibition of behavior, particularly high levels are likely to be maladaptive (Block & Block, 1980). For example, some children appear to be highly inhibited temperamentally; these children are prone to fears, negative affect, avoidant behavior, and social withdrawal (see Kagan & Fox, Chapter 4; Rothbart & Bates, Chapter 3, this *Handbook,* this volume), and are more likely than other children to develop anxiety disorders in adulthood (Rosenbaum et al., 1993). We (and, to some degree, Rothbart & Bates, 1998, Chapter 3, this *Handbook,* this volume) have argued that it is important to differentiate between control (i.e., inhibition) that is more effortfully managed and that which is somewhat involuntary and, hence, often rigid and extreme so that only the former should be labeled as *self-regulation* (e.g., Eisenberg & Spinrad, 2004; Eisenberg et al., 2004). In reality, the degree to which various control processes are effortful or not may usually vary on a continuum rather than categorically. Moreover, this distinction may not be as useful in regard to physiological regulation, although physiological processes related to emotion sometimes can be modulated by effortful processes (e.g., focusing attention away from a distressing event, thought, or person) and vagal processes may be involved in effortful regulation (see Rothbart & Bates, Chapter 3, this *Handbook,* this volume).

One important reason for differentiating between more effortful and less voluntary aspects of control or regulation is that they may be combined in various ways that seem to be associated with different types of behavior in children (Eisenberg & Morris, 2002). For example, early in elementary school, externalizing problems have been linked to low levels of effortful attentional control and inhibitory control, as well as with reactive undercontrol (impulsivity). In contrast, younger children with internalizing behavior problems (not comorbid with externalizing) tend to be low in effortful attentional but not inhibitory control, and high on less voluntary overcontrol (e.g., very low in impulsivity; Eisenberg et al., 2001; also see Caspi, 2000; Caspi & Shiner, Chapter 6, this *Handbook,* this volume). As children move through elementary school, however, internalizing problems may no longer be linked to deficits in attentional control (Eisenberg et al., 2005). In contrast, children who are

well adjusted tend to be high in attentional and inhibitory effortful control and moderate in impulsivity (Eisenberg et al., 2001, 2005).

In summary, a recent theme in the developmental literature has been on multidimensional, emotion-related conceptions of regulation. This work is a natural accompaniment to the current emphasis on emotion and temperament, as well as the concern with adjustment, stress, and coping in the larger domain of psychology. However, as is noted by Collins and Steinberg (Chapter 16, this *Handbook,* this volume), the issues of both emotional development and self-regulation have attracted only tangential attention from adolescence researchers. Thus, the role of various aspects of regulation and control in healthy and maladaptive adolescent development is a natural area for future investigation.

A FOCUS ON COGNITION

Another trend in developmental psychology in recent years has been increased links between work on cognition with theory and empirical research on emotion and social behavior (Parke, 2004). Cognition plays an obvious and fundamental role in most aspects of emotional and social functioning. Saarni et al. (Chapter 5, this *Handbook,* this volume) review the early emergence of a cognitive understanding of facial expressions and others' emotions (e.g., social referencing). They also provide many examples of how cognitive advances in infancy and early childhood are reflected in emotion-related capabilities. For example, they note a number of competencies the child needs to be emotionally competent, including the following that involve social-cognitive skills: (a) awareness of one's own emotional state; (b) the ability to discern and understand others' emotions; (c) skill in using the vocabulary of emotion and expression terms commonly available in one's subculture and at more mature levels skill in acquiring cultural scripts that link emotion with social roles; (d) the capacity for empathy and sympathy (which involves some understanding of others' emotional states); (e) understanding that inner emotional state need not correspond to outer expression and that one's emotional-expressive behavior may impact on another; and (f) awareness that the structure or nature of relationships is in large part defined by how emotions are communicated within the relationship. Related skills discussed by authors in this volume include the abilities to comprehend and take into account unique information about others' internal states (intentions, emotions, motivations, cognitions), to analyze elements of a social context and the consequences of various modes of action, and to devise appropriate cognitive strategies for sensitive social interaction in relationships, management of aggressive impulses, and altruistic behavior (Dodge et al., Chapter 12; Eisenberg et al., Chapter 11; and Rubin et al., Chapter 10, this *Handbook,* this volume).

In addition, conceptions of the self are in large part cognitive constructions, although they also are imbued with emotion (Harter, Chapter 9, this *Handbook,* this volume). In fact, Harter argued that developmental achievements in understanding others' behaviors and cognitions (e.g., how others view the self), as well as emotional processes, underlie age-related changes in self-conceptions. Similarly Thompson (Chapter 2, this *Handbook,* this volume) argues that a host of cognitive skills underlie the early emergence of the self and the understanding of self in relation to others.

In his chapter on moral development, Turiel (Chapter 13, this *Handbook,* this volume) discusses a range of ways in which cognitions are integral to moral thinking. For example, cognition obviously is critical for differentiating moral from nonmoral (e.g., conventional and personal) concerns, in constructing conceptions about morality, in analyzing information about elements in a specific morally relevant situation, and in making morally relevant decisions based on situational information and values, beliefs, and goals. As is evident from the passage from Turiel's chapter quoted earlier, he argues that cognition is central to moral development.

In his discussion of early socioemotional development, Thompson (Chapter 2, this *Handbook,* this volume) reviews some of the ways in which young children's working models of attachment figures and relationships are modified with the growth of understanding of psychological processes (e.g., work on the theory of mind). Individuals' working models of relationships, which have a cognitive as well as an affective component, are expected to influence relationships not only in childhood (also see Rubin et al., Chapter 10, this *Handbook,* this volume), but later in life (Main, Kaplan, & Cassidy, 1985; see Collins & Steinberg, Chapter 16, this *Handbook,* this volume). In addition, Collins and Steinberg discuss cognitive and sociocognitive changes in adolescence—for example, in executive attention, decision-making processes, problem solving, abstract reasoning, and perspective taking—that are relevant to psychosocial changes during that period of life.

The role of cognition in the motivation to succeed has been a topic of considerable discussion. Wigfield et al. (Chapter 15, this *Handbook,* this volume) organized their review of theory and research on the motivation to succeed around three broad questions: Can I do this task? Do I want to do this task and why? and What do I need to do to succeed on this task? It is obvious that cognition is central to assessing and dealing with all of these questions, although, of course, emotion also plays a critical role in achievement motivation. As an example of how cognitions affect the motivation to succeed, Wigfield et al. reviewed literature concerning the ways in which children's understanding of competence-related constructs (e.g., ability, effort, task difficulty) affect motivation.

Interest in cognitive processes as explanatory mechanisms in socialization has changed markedly in recent years. In the past 2 decades, social learning theory accounts of socialization have become much more cognitive in orientation; in addition, cognitive constructs from the cognitive sciences and social psychology have been assimilated into developmental conceptions of socialization. In their chapter, Bugental and Grusec (Chapter 7, this *Handbook,* this volume) argue that socialization interactions are organized by the ways experiences are represented at a cognitive level. Cognitions often mediate or moderate socialization processes, and cognitive processes involved in socialization may be deliberate and reflective or relatively automatic. They also discuss the role of children's acquired ways of cognitively representing their social worlds (including conceptions of the self, family members, and peers) in mediating the effects of socialization on developmental outcomes, as well as how parental cognitions—for example, biases, attributions—affect the quality of parenting. In brief, socialization is achieved partly through caregivers' influence on the development of children's conceptions of relationships, and parents' beliefs about children likely are influenced by their own working models of relationships (also see Rubin et al., Chapter 10, this *Handbook,* this volume).

Like Bugental and Grusec (Chapter 7, this *Handbook,* this volume), Parke and Buriel (Chapter 8, this *Handbook,* this volume) suggest that the role of cognition in socialization is varied and multilevel: "the role of cognition comes in many guises, including the child's own cognitive capacities as a determinant of socialization strategies, as well as parents' cognitions, beliefs, values and goals concerning their parental role as constraints on their socialization practices. . . . Equally important is the recognition of the importance of the ways in which parents perceive, organize and understand their children's behaviors and beliefs for appreciating how parent-child relationships are regulated and change." Moreover, like Bugental and Grusec, Parke and Buriel view cognitions as mediators of the relation between socialization or family experiences (parenting, marital conflict) and children's developmental outcomes. Parental cognitions, ideas, beliefs, values—also are viewed as mediating the relation of family socioeconomic status to children's development.

Finally, cognitive perspectives such as cognitive developmental theory and schema-based models are important in contemporary work on gender issues. Among the most fundamental issues in the study of gender are the role of cognition in gender-typed behavior, the development of an understanding of gender-relevant constructs early in life, and the role of social factors in children's gender-relevant cognitions. The current focus on cognition has contributed a conception of gender development in which the child's conceptions play a significant role in his or her own development (see Ruble et al., Chapter 14, this *Handbook,* this volume).

In brief, cognitive processes of many sorts (including those studied in neuropsychology) are being integrated into theory and research on diverse aspects of social and emotional development. This trend, which has likely increased in the past decade, has resulted in richer conceptualizations of children and their social and emotional development, as well as of the socialization process.

A FOCUS ON CONTEXTUAL AND ENVIRONMENTAL INPUTS TO DEVELOPMENT

Investigation of social and emotional development is becoming more differentiated and sophisticated in its conception of the social context. This change in the field is based, in part, on Bronfenbrenner's (1979) early efforts to increase the field's awareness of the multiple levels of the child's social ecology and the need to consider the interaction between the larger social world (e.g., the neighborhood and culture) and the family and individual. The social environment provides affordances for the expression of individual characteristics—it is the niche for biologically based characteristics to operate (or not). And, as mentioned previously, the field is increasingly recognizing the importance of gene-environment interactions (i.e., when the effect on a person of exposure to a particular environment varies depending on their genotype or, conversely, when environmental experiences moderate gene expression).

Similarly, life-span psychologists also have heightened our awareness of the interplay of historical, cultural, biological, and psychological influences on behavior (Baltes, Lindenberger, & Staudinger, 1998; Baltes, Reese, & Lipsitt, 1980). From a life-span perspective, changes in the individual's social context across the life span interact with the individual's unique history of experiences, roles, and biology to produce an individualized developmental pathway. Further, increased interest in individual differences in temperament, personality, and social functioning sometimes has contributed to a focus on context as a possible explanation for these differences (e.g., Rothbart & Bates, Chapter 3, this *Handbook,* this volume).

Diversity

One manifestation of current interest in the context of development is the recent emphasis in the discipline on recognizing and examining diversity (Parke, 2004). This trend is consistent with the life-span emphasis on individual variation in developmental trajectories. An emphasis on diversity can refer to a host of differences among people that are correlated with different life experiences, including differences in sex, sexual orientation, and masculinity/femininity; in culture and subcultural background/experiences; in socioeconomic status and associated living conditions; and in the composition and structure of families.

For years, many developmentalists have acknowledged that research on differences among various groups (e.g., cultures or subcultures) is valuable in delineating factors that influence diverse courses of development. However, in the past decade or two, we have moved beyond solely identifying differences *between* groups on particular variables.

Of particular importance, developmental scientists are acknowledging the value of studying differences in *processes* of development in different groups. Often in the past, the implicit assumption has been that the causes of development were similar or identical across groups but that various groups differed in degree of exposure to various causal agents or in biological predispositions. Thus, gender, ethnicity, and other group-level variables were considered unwanted error variance and were often treated as control variables—nonpsychological and nonbehavioral variables of little interest. Investigators are finding that contributors to development, and the configuration and operation of influential factors, sometimes vary in different contexts and for different groups. Examples were provided in the prior discussion of moderation effects.

Types and Examples of Contextual Influence

The importance of the various types of contextual influences on social and emotional development is evident in many of the chapters in this volume. Consistent with the past *Handbook* chapters on socialization, Parke and Buriel (Chapter 8, this *Handbook,* this volume) review in some detail the relations of aspects of the proximal family context (e.g., parental socialization-related practices and cognitions) to social, personality, and emotional development. This ongoing interest in the role of the proximal family environment is also reflected in a number of other chapters, such as those focused on early social, self-related and moral development (Thompson, Chapter 2, this *Handbook,* this volume), aggression (Dodge et al., Chapter 12, this *Handbook,* this volume), prosocial development (Eisenberg et al., Chapter 11, this *Handbook,* this volume), peer relationships (Rubin et al., Chapter 10, this *Handbook,* this volume), achievement (Wigfield et al., Chapter 15, this *Handbook,* this volume), and socioemotional development in adolescence (Collins & Steinberg, Chapter 16, this *Handbook,* this volume).

Parke and Buriel's Chapter 8, Bugental and Grusec's Chapter 7 (this *Handbook,* this volume) on socialization processes, and, to some degree, a number of other chapters include content pertaining to other aspects of context. These include family structure and organization (e.g., as assessed by parental employment status, marital status, and number of parents in the home) and subcultural and cultural factors. Although research on socialization in minority families and communities is still quite limited in quantity, such work has been assigned new importance in the past 2 decades (see Parke & Buriel, Chapter 8, this *Handbook,* this volume). Developmental scientists are increasingly acknowledging that the values, socialization goals, and strategies in ethnic minority families may differ in important ways from those in the majority culture. Moreover, there are unique issues and challenges with regard to socialization and development in contexts where children must interact effectively in two cultures (e.g., the cultures of the minority and major-

ity groups), cultures that often conflict in particular values and expectations. Similarly, the context of poverty—a situation in which increasing numbers of families are finding themselves—is a topic of growing interest in the developmental community (see Parke, 2004; Parke & Buriel, Chapter 8, this *Handbook,* this volume).

Although developmental psychology has been influenced by cultural anthropology for a long time (e.g., Whiting & Whiting, 1975), interest in the role of culture in psychological development has increased in the past 15 years, particularly with regard to the study of emotion, the self, and moral development (e.g., Kitayama & Markus, 1994; Oyserman, Coon, & Kemmelmeir, 2002; Turiel, Chapter 13, this *Handbook,* this volume). As one example, Saarni et al. (Chapter 5, this *Handbook,* this volume) proposed that culture plays a role in the construction of the meaning of events that can elicit emotion (e.g., in emotion-relevant appraisals of events and others' behaviors and reactions) and in rendering some emotional responses more probable than others. Culture also influences how members of a society regulate and express emotion through a transactional process. Specifically, culture determines what one notices in the feedback from the body; influences communication patterns and, hence, socially induced affect; determines one's role in society and, consequently, emotional experiences that are associated with roles; and influences the selection and expression of emotional responses. This view of emotion differs somewhat from the common perspective that emotional expression and feeling are strongly rooted primarily in biology and that many emotion-related processes are universal.

Given the links among emotion, perceptions of the self, and relationships (Harter, Chapter 9, this *Handbook,* this volume; Thompson, Chapter 2, this *Handbook,* this volume), it is not surprising that contemporary theorists expect culture to play a role in the development of the self. Harter (Chapter 9, this *Handbook,* this volume) noted that the self is likely culturally saturated. Thus, the Western view of self may differ in important ways from that in cultures in which self-definition is deeply embedded in social relationships and obligations. This proposition is consistent with the contemporary argument that people in different cultures have different construals of the self due to cultural differences in concepts of individuality (Markus & Kitayama, 1991). In some cultures (e.g., many Asian cultures), the self is viewed as interdependent and there likely is more emphasis on attending to others, fitting in, and harmony with others. In contrast, some have argued that in many Western cultures, independence from others rather than overt connectedness is valued. Although there may be more diversity within groups in regard to an emphasis on individualism than sometimes is acknowledged (Turiel, Chapter 13, this *Handbook,* this volume) so that distinctions between individualistic and collectivistic cultures do not hold (Oyserman et al., 2002), it appears that there is some variation across cultures in normative self-conceptions. This variation probably is reflected in processes underlying the development of self-perceptions early in life. For this reason and others (e.g., the content of certain items may not be relevant or meaningful; see Harter, Chapter 9, this *Handbook,* this volume), measures of self-perceptions developed in the United States may not be appropriate for use in non-Western or nonindustrialized cultures.

Culture is an especially salient theme in Turiel's Chapter 13 (this *Handbook,* this volume) on moral development. Although coming from a predominantly cognitive perspective, Turiel notes the dynamic interplay among various personal and social (including cultural) goals in moral development. He also acknowledges that social reasoning is flexible and takes into account different and varied aspects of the social world. In discussing contrasting perspectives on cross-cultural findings, Turiel makes the point that differences in assumptions about reality (e.g., assumptions about practices that are harmful to the dead) and in informational assumptions (e.g., regarding the expected effects of physical punishment on children) are important to consider when interpreting cultural differences in moral and social conventional reasoning. As is evident in Turiel's chapter, there is disagreement in the field in regard to the interpretation of some cross-cultural differences in reasoning about moral and social conventional issues, with Turiel viewing moral development as being more similar across cultures than do most cultural psychologists (e.g., Shweder, Mahapatra, & Miller, 1987). However, Turiel emphasizes another aspect of context more than do most cultural psychologists; he argues that a focus on contextual variations between cultures has led to little consideration of variations in moral reasoning associated with contextual differences *within* cultures. Turiel and his colleagues' work (e.g., Wainryb & Turiel, 1995) on the diversity of perspectives within cultures stemming from factors such as gender roles

and status hierarchies is an important direction for research on moral development.

The emphasis on different groups within a society serving as different socialization contexts is echoed in recent work on the separate cultures of girls and boys (Maccoby, 1990). Segregation by sex in childhood seems to be a universal phenomenon, although it varies to some degree with variables such as the availability of same-sex peers and opportunities to choose one's associates (Ruble et al., Chapter 14, this *Handbook,* this volume). Within sex-segregated groups, girls and boys appear to develop different styles of interaction, goals, and values, as well as different perceptions of the self (Harter, Chapter 9; Ruble et al., Chapter 14, this *Handbook,* this volume). These subcultural differences likely have substantial and long-term implications for social, emotional, and personality development.

Also evident in this volume of the *Handbook* is the increased recognition in recent decades of connections among contexts within a society, for example, among family, school, and peer cultures (e.g., Collins & Steinberg, Chapter 16; Dodge et al., Chapter 13; Wigfield et al., Chapter 15; Parke & Buriel, Chapter 8; Rubin et al., Chapter 14, this *Handbook,* this volume). However, these connections are seldom examined in empirical study of development and in theory, or acknowledged in the real world (e.g., there often is little communication between schools and parents). Culture doubtlessly has important effects on the nature of the connections across settings within a culture; for example, the links between parents and schools may be stronger in majority culture families than in some minority groups (especially in some neighborhoods) who feel little connection to the majority culture. However, research on the role of culture in the forging (or inhibiting) of connections across settings within cultures would enrich an ecological perspective of development.

A FOCUS ON BIOLOGICAL PERSPECTIVES

There can be little doubt that there has been a resurgence of interest in individual differences, and especially the biological and constitutional bases of individual differences. Plomin (1994) noted that 78% of the text pages in the 1983 *Handbook of Child Psychology* were devoted predominantly (more than half the page) to normative or group difference approaches. In contrast, individual differences were a major focus of attention in the 1998 edition of the *Handbook* and in this edition. Indeed, in three of the chapters in Volume 3, constitutionally based individual differences are the primary focus (i.e., Caspi & Shiner, Chapter 6; Kagan & Fox, Chaper 4; Rothbart & Bates, Chapter 3, this *Handbook,* this volume).

The current focus on constitutionally based individual differences is not unprecedented. After a period of heavy reliance on biological explanations of social behavior earlier in this century, biological perspectives appeared to go out of fashion in developmental and social psychology. Behaviorism and then social learning perspectives became more popular during the middle half of the century, whereas biologically based explanations of social behavior and personality were de-emphasized. In the past 25 years, the pendulum has swung back once more.

Noticeable differences in the field between now and when the 1998 edition of the *Handbook* was published are in regard to the degree of acceptance of genetics and biological factors as major contributors to socioemotional development and, of equal importance, in the greater understanding that genetic contributions to development do not preclude environmental contributions. The field is more cognizant that genetic factors usually are moderated or mediated by the environment, including the social environment, and are not independent of environmental inputs to development. Thus, as was noted by Caspi and Shiner (Chapter 6, this *Handbook,* this volume), in the past decade the pitting of nature versus nurture has increasingly come to a halt.

For the most part, developmental scientists now accept that both genetic and other biological factors affect development, and that even behaviors with a strong hereditary basis can be strongly affected by the environment in which the organism develops. Most also are aware of the relevant caveats in interpreting the results of behavioral genetics studies, two of which are aptly spelled out by Dodge et al. (Chapter 12, this *Handbook,* this volume): "it is understood that genetic effects may be mediated environmentally through gene-environment transactions in which genes influence surrounding environments, which, in turn, influence phenotypic expression. . . . In behavior genetics studies, the effects of such transactions are included in the heritability estimates and not counted as environmental effects. Second, all estimates are context specific. That is, the influence of genes on behavior varies across social contexts, and a change in the social context may change the relative im-

portance of genes and environment." Increased understanding of these issues has led to a more balanced and complex view of the role of nature and nurture in socioemotional development.

Caspi and Shiner (Chapter 6, this *Handbook,* this volume) suggest that the use of molecular genetic techniques is contributing to the trend to replace the nature-nurture conjunction "versus" with the more appropriate conjunction "and." Other factors that have likely contributed to movement in this regard include sophisticated discussions of interpretational and statistical issues (e.g., Bronfenbrenner & Ceci, 1994; Collins, Maccoby, Steinberg, Hetherington, & Bornstein, 2000; Rutter & Silberg, 2002; Turkheimer & Gottesman, 1996) in premier publication outlets, as well as studies demonstrating the complexity of relations between environmental and genetic or biological factors (see Caspi & Shiner, Chapter 6, this *Handbook,* this volume, and the discussion of moderated relations later).

Biology, Temperament, and Personality

As noted previously, Rothbart and Bates (Chapter 3), as well as Kagan and Fox (Chapter 4, this *Handbook,* this volume), focus primarily on issues related to temperament. It is often assumed that behaviors with a temperamental basis are inherited, but current definitions of temperament are more complex. Rothbart and Bates (Chapter 3) define temperament as "constitutionally based individual difference in reactivity and self-regulation, in the domains of affect, activity, and attention. . . . By the term *constitutional,* we refer to the biological bases of temperament, influenced over time by heredity, maturation, and experience." Thus, temperament is influenced not only by heredity, but by environmental factors that affect an individual's biological being (e.g., trauma or drugs) and by the social context.

Similarly, for Kagan and Fox (Chapter 4, this *Handbook,* this volume), temperament "refers to a biologically based bias for correlated clusters of feelings, thoughts, and actions that appear during childhood, but not always in the opening months, and are sculpted by varied rearing environments into a large but still limited number of traits that comprise an individual's personality profile." Thus, they emphasize the role of both biological and environmental factors in children's early dispositional characteristics. Similarly, Caspi and Shiner (Chapter 6, this *Handbook,* this volume) argue that personality, viewed as social and cognitive elaborations on temperament, is moderately influenced by both heredity and environment (especially unshared environmental factors that are not shared by twins or siblings). Thus, there is consensus among these authors on the importance of both hereditary and the environmental influences on temperament and personality.

Developmental scientists increasingly are using physiological/neurological measures of dispositional characteristics, situational reactivity, regulation, approach/ avoidance tendencies, and various types of cognitive, attentional, or emotional processing related to temperament. For example, Kagan and Fox (Chapter 4, this *Handbook,* this volume) summarize research on cerebral asymmetry and its association with behavioral inhibition, other physiological correlates of inhibited and uninhibited behavior, and the relation of neurochemical systems in the brain to mood and action. They further note that people with different temperaments will not react in the same way, behaviorally or biologically, to a given experience. Accordingly, they suggest that we invent constructs that capture this fact—that we "replace the current constructs, which describe children and their environments (parents, sibling, school settings) separately, with single synthetic constructs that represent a particular temperamental type growing up in a particular set of contexts. . . . As environments shape children of varied temperaments into different phenotypes, it will be useful to invent new concepts, rather than rely on the language of ANOVA that describes interactions between the temperamental type of child and a rearing environment."

Rothbart and Bates (Chapter 3, this *Handbook,* this volume) discuss associations of the major dimensions of temperamental reactivity (approach, fear, anger, etc.) and self-regulation (e.g., attention) with the neural systems identified as underlying these dimensions. They discuss neurological processes involved in effortful control, defined as "the efficiency of executive attention, including the ability to inhibit a dominant response and/or to activate a subdominant response, to plan, and to detect errors." Rothbart and Bates also review research on the behavioral and emotional correlates of autonomic reactivity (e.g., heart rate, vagal tone, skin conductance) and cortisol responding, as well as hemispheric asymmetry, as a way of further examining the biological bases of temperament and their expression in behavior. These measures, which tend to be related to some indices of temperament, are sometimes used as proxies for temperament, and sometimes as separate

constructs that inform us about aspects of temperament that relate to them.

After concisely summarizing the behavioral genetics literature, Caspi and Shiner (Chapter 6, this *Handbook,* this volume) highlight recent work on molecular genetics and personality. They note that individual genes have not consistently mapped onto personality, but that this may be due (among other reasons) to personality being predicted by a combination of genes and gene X environment interactions. Caspi and Shiner believe that developmental psychologists can contribute to this line of work by helping to refine the measurement of psychological phenotypes for inclusion in genetic research and helping to measure developmental contexts and environmental risks that may interact with genetic factors to shape personality (or temperament) and its development.

Biology and Socioemotional Development

As is reflected in the chapters in this volume, much contemporary work on the biological bases of socioemotional development is based on complex frameworks that posit interconnected causal roles of biological/constitutional and environmental factors in human functioning. For example, Bugental and Grusec (Chapter 7, this *Handbook,* this volume) depict development as the result of a dynamic co-regulation of aspects of the individual (from neural to behavioral) and the environment (from physical to social). The emergence of structure in both people and their environments results from a process of mutual influence and regulation. They present literature consistent with the view that children are biologically prepared for socialization, and argue that biologically based differences in children (e.g., in temperament, physical attractiveness) elicit different socialization experiences from the environment. Similarly, biological factors that affect parenting are discussed, with a recognition that biologically influenced parental characteristics are played out in a social context. They further argue, using an evolutionary perspective, that humans may be designed for preferential receptivity to proximity-maintenance with specific others in the presence of distress (e.g., attachments), for the use and recognition of signals denoting power or dominance, for differentiating between in-groups and out-groups in social life, and for the reciprocal obligations associated with communal life. These biological predispositions are viewed as emerging in a social context in which cultural factors, as well as situational cognitive and emotional factors, act as mediators and moderators of their effects on the socialization process and its outcomes. Thus, Bugental and Grusec view socialization in a complex process-oriented manner, influenced by the ongoing interaction of biological and environmental factors.

As is evident in Ruble et al.'s chapter (Chapter 14, this *Handbook,* this volume), biological approaches play an increasingly visible role in the study of gender-related development. They discuss possible evolutionary contributions to sex differences, as well as more proximal biological correlates or contributors—such as hormones and brain structure—to gender-related development and behavior. They conclude that prenatal androgens and hormones during early development appear to affect gender-related self-perceptions, preferences, or behaviors, and that the effects of sex hormones in adolescence are evident, but probably more modest. They further note that hormones have different effects on different characteristics; for example, prenatal androgen seems to have a large effect on some aspects of functioning (activities and interests), a modest effect on others (e.g., sexual orientation), and a small effect on others (gender identity). In addition, they conclude that gender socialization processes at home, at school, in interaction with peers, and through the media all contribute to gender differentiation in concepts, preferences, behaviors, and/or values, although relations often are found under some conditions. They conclude that biological and environmental factors interact in complex ways: "There is increasingly sophisticated understanding of biological effects, and recognition that they are not immutable. Genes are activated or suppressed by environmental factors. Hormones and brain functioning are almost certainly influenced by the different environments in which girls and boys are raised, by their different toy and activity choices, and by joint effects of biology and the social environment."

In their chapter on aggression, Dodge et al. (Chapter 12, this *Handbook,* this volume) conclude that there is indisputable evidence of the role of heredity in aggression (also see Rhee & Waldman, 2002), especially for those who develop aggressive tendencies early and are stable in their aggression into adulthood (also see Caspi & Shiner, Chapter 6, this *Handbook,* this volume). They further conclude that the contribution of shared or common environment is small whereas that of children's nonshared environment is moderate. Thus, "person-specific" experiences of individuals in families appear to be an important environmental factor contributing to aggression and other antisocial behavior. Dodge et al.

also review a large body of work linking environment factors such as family and peer factors to aggression and, more importantly in regard to causal conclusions, research indicating that prevention/intervention programs can reduce the incidence of antisocial behavior. Experimental interventions that involve random assignment are perhaps the best way to demonstrate that environmental factors contribute to antisocial tendencies in youth, despite the strong role of heredity. An issue that merits attention is how partly hereditary factors such as temperament influence the effectiveness of interventions in deterring antisocial behavior.

Dodge et al. (Chapter 12, this *Handbook,* this volume) also discuss evidence for gene by environment interactions. For example, they highlight research demonstrating that children who are genetically predisposed to antisocial tendencies are especially likely to manifest them if they grow up in a risky social environment, such as one in which they are victims of maltreatment. Dodge et al. conclude that some of the most important discoveries in the next decade will come from studies of gene-environment interactions, as well as from experimental prevention/intervention studies.

Eisenberg et al. (Chapter 11, this *Handbook,* this volume) view heredity as contributing to both the development of prosocial and empathy-related responding in the species and to individual differences in aspects of emotionality and regulation (e.g., attentional regulation) that contribute to prosocial behavior and empathy in childhood. Similar to Dodge et al. (Chapter 12, this *Handbook,* this volume), they review studies demonstrating links between environmental factors and prosocial development, as well as experimental prevention studies demonstrating that children's prosocial tendencies can be modified by environmental interventions. However, it is likely that the effects of heredity are not as strong for prosocial as for antisocial behavior (e.g., Krueger, Hicks, & McGue, 2001), although heredity does contribute to empathy/sympathy (see Eisenberg et al., Chapter 11, this *Handbook,* this volume). For example, in a study of stepfamilies, Deater-Deckard et al. (2001) found that most of the variance in adults' reports of children's prosocial behavior was due to environmental rather than hereditary factors, especially aspects of the environment that were not shared by the children (although there was significant variance for shared environmental effects). Unfortunately, there has been little research conducted as yet on the prediction of prosocial tendencies from the interaction between heredity and the environment.

A FOCUS ON RELATIONSHIPS

As noted by Rubin et al. (Chapter 10, this *Handbook,* this volume), interest in relationships other than the parent-child relationship has grown tremendously in recent decades. In addition, researchers studying the family increasingly have examined not just the parent-child dyad, but also the larger family unit, associations between the quality of parent-parent and parent-child relationships, and links between the quality of familial interactions and quality of sibling and peer relationships (Parke & Buriel, Chapter 8, this *Handbook,* this volume). For example, there is now evidence that marital discord is related to problems with children's adjustment, social withdrawal, and low social competence, all of which compromise the quality of peer relationships. Moreover, investigators have begun to study the role of social relationships outside the family (e.g., as reflected in social support) for quality of interaction within the family (see Parke & Buriel; Rubin et al., this *Handbook,* this volume) and for the provision of social opportunities for children (e.g., adult social networks as a source of potential peer contacts for children). In addition, a relatively new emphasis in the literature in recent years has been the impact of settings such as schools, workplaces, volunteer activities, leisure pursuits, and neighborhoods on developmentally significant interpersonal experiences, especially in adolescence (Collins & Steinberg, Chapter 16, this *Handbook,* this volume).

As is discussed in some of the chapters, it has been suggested that the oft-cited causal relation of emotion-related capacities with quality of relationships can be reversed (or more likely, can be bi-directional)—for example, that early attachment relationships play a role in the development of emotion regulation and reflect strategies for regulating emotion in interpersonal contexts (Saarni et al., Chapter 5; Thompson, Chapter 2, this *Handbook,* this volume). The securely attached infant whose parent is consistently and appropriately responsive to the infant's distress signals is believed to learn that it is acceptable to express distress and to actively seek the assistance of others for comfort when upset. In contrast, avoidant infants, due in part to their parents' nonresponsiveness to their distress signals, may learn to inhibit emotional expressiveness as well as other-directed self-regulatory strategies (e.g., contact-seeking and maintaining behaviors; Cassidy, 1994).

The internal working model developed in the context of early attachment relationships is believed to affect the quality of children's subsequent relationships because of the assumptions and expectations about relationships that are inherent in internal working models (Bretherton & Waters, 1985; Parke & Buriel, Chapter 8; Rubin et al., Chapter 10; Thompson, Chapter 2, this *Handbook,* this volume). One way early attachment relationships may affect other relationships is through their influence on the developing sense of self in the infant as lovable or unworthy of love (Bretherton, 1991; Harter, Chapter 9, this *Handbook,* this volume).

Clearly, the topic of attachment and early parent-child relationships is still a central issue in the study of relationships in developmental psychology. Attachments are hypothesized to affect the development of the self, a range of cognitions relevant to quality of relationships, emotion regulation and emotions attached to various relationships, sympathetic and prosocial behavior with others, social competence with peers, and personality development (see Collins & Steinberg, Chapter 16; Eisenberg et al., Chapter 3; Harter, Chapter 9; Rubin et al., Chapter 10; Thompson, Chapter 2, this *Handbook,* this volume). However, most researchers no longer believe that working models consolidate in early childhood with little or no further modification. This broader conception of working models is reflected in Thompson's discussion of some of the questions that require attention in the future, including the following: (a) to what extent is security of attachment definitive of the parent-child relationship? Are there important features of this relationship that are outside the scope of attachment? (b) How is it that attachment security becomes increasingly an attribute of the person, rather than of a specific relationship with maturity? Is it possible that both relationship-specific and person-specific features of attachment security coexist within the attachment-related representational systems that exist in adulthood? (c) How are multiple attachment relationships developmentally influential? How do the expectations arising from multiple attachments become integrated into coherent ways of relating to others, representing relationships, and self-understanding? and (d) why should attachment security be related to other features of psychological development? Some of these questions are related to issues raised by Harter (1998, Chapter 9, this *Handbook,* this volume) and merit additional attention in the next decade.

Close peer relationships such as friendships have been increasingly examined by developmental scientists in the past 2 decades and have been viewed as a source of support; a factor affecting self-perceptions; a context for learning about emotions, conflict, social negotiation, and caring behavior; an impetus for cognitive, social, and emotional development; and an influence on the development of antisocial behavior and substance abuse (Collins & Steinberg, Chapter 16; Dodge et al., Chapter 12; Harter, Chapter 9; Rubin et al., Chapter 10, this *Handbook*, this volume). However, a type of close peer relationship that has received relatively little attention until the last decade is romantic relationships. Collins and Steinberg conclude that relationships with peers are a primary context for the transmission and realization of expectations about romantic relationships. According to the research they review, the quality of romantic relationships, including aggression within them and feelings of rejection, is correlated with the quality of other relationships with peers and family members: Youth with healthy familial and peer (e.g., friendship or peer group) relationships tend to have more positive romantic relationships. They also note that the developmental outcomes of romantic relationships can be positive or negative, depending partly on the quality of these relationships. Consequently, the effects of early family and peer relationships on subsequent adjustment and well-being in adulthood (and in adult relationships) likely are partly mediated through experiences in adolescent romantic relationships. Moreover, partner relationships in late adolescence and early adulthood seem to play an important role in determining an individual's trajectory in antisocial behavior (i.e., its cessation or continuation) in early adulthood (Caspi & Shiner, Chapter 6, this *Handbook*, this volume). Thus, the topic of romantic relationships would seem to be an important one for further study, especially as it relates to success in adult development.

A FOCUS ON APPLICATION

Another trend in the developmental research in the past 2 decades has been renewed interest in application and real-world problems. This emphasis in the discipline is reflected in the fact that for the first time, one volume of the 1998 *Handbook* (Volume 4) was devoted to applied issues, and that volume is also part of this edition of the *Handbook*. Although much of the applied work on socioemotional development is discussed in that volume, the contemporary concern with application is also reflected to some degree in this volume.

This concern can be seen in both the topics of study and the ways in which people are conducting research on certain topics. Work on aggression, regulation, coping, and social competence is burgeoning, for example, no doubt in part because of concern in society about children's psychological health, violence, and related social issues (e.g., see Caspi et al., Chapter 6; Collins & Steinberg, Chapter 16; Dodge et al., Chapter 12; Eisenberg et al., Chapter 11; Rubin et al., Chapter 10; Saarni et al., Chapter 5, this *Handbook*, this volume). In the past decade or two, the focus on developmental psychopathology, in particular, has increased in the writings of developmental scientists. Moreover, investigators increasingly have been turning their attention to development in stressful contexts such as families in poverty, one-parent families, and families of divorce (Parke & Buriel, Chapter 8, this *Handbook*, this volume). Concern with clinical issues and prevention is not without precedent, of course; much of the early work in child development grew out of a desire to understand the origins of typical childhood problems.

In addition, work on topics that have been a focus of interest for a long time is increasingly being conducted outside the laboratory in real-world contexts so that findings have direct applicability to prevention, clinical, and policy issues. For example, developmental scientists are becoming involved in the process of obtaining knowledge that can be used to design programs that lessen the probability of negative effects from exposure to stressors (e.g., divorce, poverty) or that promote prosocial behavior or inhibit aggressive tendencies in school settings (Dodge et al., Chapter 12; Eisenberg et al., Chapter 11, this *Handbook*, this volume). Moreover, developmental scientists are deeply involved in evaluating programs such as day care that have implications for both families and policy (see Volume 4). It is likely that the increasing trend for developmental scientists to apply their theory and methods to real-life issues in real-world contexts will continue into the next decade and well into the 21st century.

SUMMARY

In general, the chapters in this volume highlight the emerging themes, constructs, and methods in the field, and a recent permeability in the intellectual boundaries of the field. Many of the changes in the study of social and emotional development in the past 2 decades can be characterized by increasing integration and differentiation. In this context, I am using the term *integration* to mean the assimilation (usually with some accommodation) into the study of socioemotional functioning of ideas and methods from diverse approaches and topics in developmental psychology, other subdisciplines of psychology, and even other disciplines such as sociology, genetics, and anthropology. The integration of novel methods, constructs, and theoretical perspectives has broadened not only our understanding of social and emotional development, but also the entire framework on which we design and interpret research findings.

Differentiation within the field of socioemotional development may be viewed in terms of contexts, constructs, and causal inferences. As noted previously, the burgeoning interest in context in developmental psychology is reflected in the study of many levels of influence, including diversity in culture and subculture, race and ethnicity, biological sex and gender, types of families and groups, and genetic and constitutional influences. In regard to constructs, our thinking is becoming less global and more conditional, multifaceted, and complex. Similarly, proposed causal influences of various social processes are becoming more multifaceted. Mediated and moderated relations, as well as those based on dynamic systems perspectives, are more central in theory and research.

Moreover (and related), researchers are increasingly acknowledging and examining the multiplicative and covarying contributions of various types of environmental and biologically based influences on socioemotional functioning. Increasingly children are being viewed as producers of their environment as well as the products of socialization; parents and children are viewed as coregulators of each other's behaviors and affective states; and development is characterized as a consequence of social interactions that are shaped by contextual factors and characteristics of all participants in the interaction. Although interactional and reciprocal causal models are not new, they are becoming a part of our everyday thinking about psychological phenomena. As one might expect, implementation of complex interactive models into research designs lags behind conceptual models. However, analytic methods for exploring reciprocal, additive, and interactive causal influences, as well as analyses for examining nonlinear relations and growth curves, are becoming more common, so developmental scientists are increasingly able to test complex conceptions of development empirically. The next decade, like the past one, will undoubtedly be an exciting time for the study of social, emotional, and personality development.

REFERENCES

Ahadi, S. A., & Rothbart, M. K. (1994). Temperament, development, and the big five. In C. F. Halverson Jr., G. A. Kohnstamm, & R. P. Martin (Eds.), *The developing structure of temperament and personality from infancy to adulthood* (pp. 189–207). Hillsdale, NJ: Erlbaum.

Aksan, N., & Kochanska, G. (2005). Conscience in childhood: Old questions, new answers. *Developmental Psychology, 41,* 506–516.

Arsenio, W. F., & Lemerise, E. A. (2004). Aggression and moral development: Integrating social information processing and moral domain models. *Child Development, 75,* 985–1002.

Aspinwall, L. G., & Taylor, S. E. (1997). A stitch in time: Self-regulation and proactive coping. *Psychological Bulletin, 121,* 417–436.

Baltes, P. B., Lindenberger, U., & Staudinger, U. M. (1998). Life-span theory in developmental psychology. In W. Damon (Editor-in-Chief) & R. M. Lerner (Vol. Ed), *Handbook of child psychology* (5th ed., Vol. 1, pp. 1029–1143). New York: Wiley.

Baltes, P. B., Reese, H. W., & Lipsitt, L. P. (1980). Life-span developmental psychology. *Annual Review of Psychology, 31,* 65–110.

Baron, R. M., & Kenny, D. A. (1986). The moderator-mediator variable distinction in social psychological research: Conceptual, strategic, and statistical considerations. *Journal of Personality and Social Psychology, 51,* 1173–1182.

Block, J. H., & Block, J. (1980). The role of ego-control and ego-resiliency in the organization of behavior. In W. A. Collins (Ed.), *Minnesota Symposia on Child Psychology: Vol. 13. Development of cognition, affect, and social relations* (pp. 39–101). Hillsdale, NJ: Erlbaum.

Brenner, E. M., & Salovey, P. (1997). Emotion regulation during childhood: Developmental, interpersonal, and individual considerations. In P. Salovey & D. Sluyter (Eds.), *Teaching in the heart of the classroom: Emotional development, emotional literacy, and emotional intelligence* (pp. 168–192). New York: Basic Books.

Bretherton, I. (1991). Pouring new wine into old bottles: The social self as internal working model. In M. R. Gunnar & L. A. Sroufe (Eds.), *Minnesota Symposia on Child Development: Vol. 23. Self-processes and development* (pp. 1–41). Hillsdale, NJ: Erlbaum.

Bretherton, I., & Waters, E. (1985). Growing points of attachment theory and research. *Monographs of the Society for Research in Child Development, 50*(Serial No. 209).

Bronfenbrenner, U. (1979). *The ecology of human development.* Cambridge, MA: Harvard University Press.

Bronfenbrenner, U., & Ceci, S. J. (1994). Nature-nurture reconceptualized in developmental perspective: A bioecological model. *Psychological Review, 101,* 568–586.

Cadoret, R. J., Yates, W. R., Troughton, E., Woodworth, G., & Stewart, M. A. (1995). Genetic-environmental interaction in the genesis of aggressivity and conduct disorders. *Archives of General Psychiatry, 52,* 916–924.

Campos, J. (1984). A new perspective on emotions. *Child Abuse and Neglect, 8,* 147–156.

Carstensen, L. L. (1991). Selectivity theory: Social activity in life-span context. In K. W. Schaie (Ed.), *Annual review of gerontology and geriatrics* (Vol. 11, pp. 195–217). New York: Springer.

Carver, C. S., Scheier, M. F., & Weintraub, J. K. (1989). Assessing coping strategies: A theoretically based approach. *Journal of Personality and Social Psychology, 56,* 267–283.

Caspi, A. (1998). Personality development across the life course. In W. Damon (Editor-in-Chief) & N. Eisenberg (Vol. Ed.), *Handbook of child psychology: Vol. 3. Social, emotional and personality development* (pp. 311–388). New York: Wiley.

Caspi, A. (2000). The child is father of the man: Personality continuities from childhood to adulthood. *Journal of Personality and Social Psychology, 78,* 158–172.

Caspi, A., McClay, J., Moffitt, T., Mill, J., Martin, J., & Craig, I. W. (2002). Role of genotype in the cycle of violence in maltreated children. *Science, 297,* 851–854.

Cassidy, J. (1994). Emotion regulation: Influences of attachment relationships [Special issue]. *Monographs of the Society for Research in Child Development, 59*(Serial No. 240), 228–249.

Cole, P. M., Michel, M. K., & Teti, L. O. (1994). The development of emotion regulation and dysregulation: A clinical perspective. *Monographs of the Society for Research in Child Development, 59*(2/3, Serial No. 240), 73–100.

Collins, W. A., Maccoby, E. E., Steinberg, L., Hetherington, E. M., & Bornstein, M. H. (2000). Contemporary research on parenting: The case nature and nurture. *American Psychologist, 55,* 218–232.

Crick, N. R., & Dodge, K. A. (1994). A review and reformulation of social information-processing mechanisms in children's social adjustment. *Psychological Bulletin, 115,* 74–101.

Deater-Deckard, K., Dunn, J., O'Connor, T. G., Davies, L. Golding, J., & the ALSPAC Study Team. (2001). Using the stepfamily genetic design to examine gene-environmental processes in child and family functioning. *Marriage and Family Review, 33,* 131–156.

Eccles, J. S., Wigfield, A., & Schiefele, U. (1998). Motivation to succeed. In W. Damon (Editor-in-Chief) and N. Eisenberg (Vol. ed.), *Handbook of child psychology* (5th ed. Vol. 3, pp. 1017–1095). New York: Wiley.

Eisenberg, N. (2002). Emotion-related regulation and its relation to quality of social functioning. In W. W. Hartup & R. A. Weinberg (Eds.), *Minnesota Symposia of Child Psychology: Vol. 32. Child psychology in retrospect and prospect* (pp. 133–171). Hillsdale, NJ: Erlbaum.

Eisenberg, N., Cumberland, A., Spinrad, T. L., Fabes, R. A., Shepard, S. A., Reiser, M., et al. (2001). The relations of regulation and emotionality to children's externalizing and internalizing problem behavior. *Child Development, 72,* 1112–1134.

Eisenberg, N., & Fabes, R. A. (1990). Empathy: Conceptualization, assessment, and relation to prosocial behavior. *Motivation and Emotion, 14,* 131–149.

Eisenberg, N., Fabes, R. A., Guthrie, I. K., & Reiser, M. (2000). Dispositional emotionality and regulation: Their role in predicting quality of social functioning. *Journal of Personality and Social Psychology, 78,* 136–157.

Eisenberg, N., Martin, C. L., & Fabes, R. A. (1996). Gender development and gender differences. In D. C. Berliner & R. C. Calfee (Eds.), *The handbook of educational psychology* (pp. 358–396). New York: Macmillan.

Eisenberg, N., & Morris, A. S. (2002). Children's emotion-related regulation. In R. Kail (Ed.), *Advances in child development and behavior* (Vol. 30, pp. 190–229). Amsterdam: Academic Press.

Eisenberg, N., Sadovsky, A., Spinrad, T. L., Fabes, R. A., Losoya, S. H., Valiente, C., et al. (2005). The relations of problem behavior status to children's negative emotionality, effortful control, and impulsivity: Concurrent relations and prediction of change. *Developmental Psychology, 41,* 193–211.

Eisenberg, N., & Spinrad, T. L. (2004). Emotion-related regulation: Sharpening the definition. *Child Development, 75,* 334–339.

Eisenberg, N., Spinrad, T. L., Fabes, R. A., Reiser, M., Cumberland, A., Shepard, S. A., et al. (2004). The relations of effortful control and impulsivity to children's resiliency and adjustment. *Child Development, 75,* 25–46.

Harter, S. (1998). The development of self-representations. In W. Damon (Editor-in-Chief) & N. Eisenberg (Vol. Ed.), *Handbook of child psychology: Vol. 3. Social, emotional, and personality development* (5th ed., pp. 553–617). New York: Wiley.

Hoffman, M. L. (1970). Moral development. In P. H. Mussen (Ed.), *Carmichael's manual of child development* (Vol. 2, pp. 261–359). New York: Wiley.

Hoffman, M. L. (1982). Development of prosocial motivation: Empathy and guilt. In N. Eisenberg (Ed.), *The development of prosocial behavior* (pp. 281–313). New York: Academic Press.

Hoffman, M. L. (1983). Affective and cognitive processes in moral internalization. In E. T. Higgins, D. N. Ruble, & W. W. Hartup (Eds.), *Social cognition and social development: A sociocultural perspective* (pp. 236–274). Cambridge, England: Cambridge University Press.

Hoffman, M. L. (2000). *Empathy and moral development: Implications for caring and justice.* Cambridge, England: Cambridge University Press.

Kagan, J. (1984). *The nature of the child.* New York: Basic Books.

Keating, D. (2004). Cognitive and brain development. In R. Lerner & L. Steinberg (Eds.), *Handbook of adolescent psychology* (2nd ed., pp. 45–84). Hoboken, NJ: Wiley.

Kitayama, S., & Markus, H. R. (Eds.). (1994). *Emotion and culture: Empirical studies of mutual influence.* Washington, DC: American Psychological Association.

Kochanska, G. (2001). Emotional development in children with different attachment histories: The first three years. *Child Development, 72,* 474–490.

Kochanska, G., Aksan, N., Knaack, A., & Rhines, H. (2004). Maternal parenting and children's conscience: Early security as a moderator. *Child Development, 75,* 1229–1242.

Kochanska, G., Coy, K. C., Tjebkes, T. L., & Husarek, S. J. (1998). Individual differences in emotionality in infancy. *Child Development, 64,* 375–390.

Kohlberg, L. (1984). *Essays on moral development: Vol. 2. The psychology of moral development.* San Francisco: Harper & Row.

Kopp, C. B. (1982). Antecedents of self-regulation: A developmental perspective. *Developmental Psychology, 18,* 199–214.

Krueger, R. F., Hicks, B. M., & McGue, M. (2001). Altruism and antisocial behavior: Independent tendencies, unique personality correlates, distinct etiologies. *Psychological Science, 12,* 397–402.

Larsen, R. J., & Diener, E. (1987). Affect intensity as an individual difference characteristic: A review. *Journal of Research in Personality, 21,* 1–39.

Lazarus, R. S., & Folkman, S. (1984). *Stress, appraisal, and coping.* New York: Springer.

Lewis, M. D. (2002). Interacting time scales in personality (and cognitive) development: Intentions, emotions, and emergent forms. In J. Parziale & N. Granott (Eds.), *Microdevelopment: Transition processes in development and learning* (pp. 183–212). New York: Cambridge University Press.

Maccoby, E. E. (1990). Gender and relationships: A developmental account. *American Psychologist, 45,* 513–520.

Maccoby, E. E., & Martin, J. A. (1983). Socialization in the context of the family: Parent-child interaction. In P. H. Mussen (Series Ed.) & E. M. Hetherington (Vol. Eds.), *Handbook of child psychology: Vol. 4. Socialization, personality, and social development* (4th ed., pp. 1–101). New York: Wiley.

MacKinnon, D. P., Lockwood, C. M., Hoffman, J. M., West, S. G., & Sheets, V. (2002). A comparison of methods to test mediation and other intervening variables. *Psychological Methods, 7,* 83–104.

Main, M., Kaplan, N., & Cassidy, J. (1985). Security in infancy, childhood, and adulthood: A move to the level of representation. In I. Bretherton & E. Waters (Eds.), *Monographs of the Society for Research in Child Development, 50*(Serial No. 209), 66–104.

Markus, H. Z., & Kitayama, S. (1991). Culture and the self: Implications for cognition, emotion, and motivation. *Psychological Review, 98,* 224–253.

McAdams, D. P. (1995). What do we know when we know a person? *Journal of Personality, 63,* 365–396.

Oyserman, D., Coon, H. M., & Kemmelmeier, M. (2002). Rethinking individualism and collectivism: Evaluation of theoretical assumptions and meta-analyses. *Psychological Bulletin, 128,* 3–72.

Parke, R. D. (1994). Progress, paradigms, and unresolved problems: Recent advances in our understanding of children's emotions. *Merrill-Palmer Quarterly, 40,* 157–169.

Parke, R. D. (2004). The society for research in child development at 70: Progress and promise. *Child Development, 75,* 1–24.

Parke, R. D., & Buriel, R. (1998). Socialization in the family: Ethnic and ecological perspectives. In W. Damon (Editor-in-Chief) & N. Eisenberg (Vol. Ed.), *Handbook of child psychology: Vol. 3. Social, emotional, and personality development* (5th ed., pp. 463–552). New York: Wiley.

Plomin, R. (1994). Nature, nurture, and social development. *Social Development, 3,* 37–53.

Pulkkinen, L. (1982). Self-control and continuity from childhood to late adolescence. In P. B. Baltes & O. G. Brim Jr. (Eds.), *Life-span development and behavior* (Vol. 4, pp. 63–105). New York: Academic Press.

Rest, J. R. (1983). Morality. In P. H. Mussen (Series Ed.) & J. H. Flavell & E. M. Markman (Vol. Eds.), *Handbook of child psychology: Vol. 3. Cognitive development* (4th ed., pp. 556–629). New York: Wiley.

Rhee, S. H., & Waldman, I. D. (2002). Genetic and environmental influences on antisocial behavior: A meta-analysis of twin and adoption studies. *Psychological Bulletin, 128,* 490–529.

Rosenbaum, J. F., Biederman, J., Bolduc-Murphy, E. A., Faraone, S. V., Chaloff, J., Hirshfeld, D. R., et al. (1993). Behavioral inhibition in childhood: A risk factor for anxiety disorders. *Harvard Review of Psychiatry, 1,* 2–16.

Rothbart, M. K., Ahadi, S. A., Hershey, K., & Fisher, P. (2001). Investigations of temperament at 3 to 7 years: The children's behavior questionnaire. *Child Development, 72,* 1394–1408.

Rothbart, M. K., Ahadi, S. A., & Hershey, K. L. (1994). Temperament and social behavior in childhood. *Merrill-Palmer Quarterly, 40,* 21–39.

Rothbart, M. K., & Bates, J. E. (1998). Temperament. In W. Damon (Editor-in-Chief) & N. Eisenberg (Vol. Ed.), *Handbook of child psychology: Vol. 3. Social, emotional, personality development* (pp. 105–176). New York: Wiley.

Rothbart, M. K., & Derryberry, D. (1981). Development of individual differences in temperament. In M. E. Lamb & A. L. Brown (Eds.), *Advances in developmental psychology* (Vol. 1, pp. 37–86). Hillsdale, NJ: Erlbaum.

Rothbart, M. K., & Rueda, M. R. (2005). The development of effortful control. In U. Mayr, E. Awh, & S. Keele (Eds.), *Developing individuality in the human brain: A tribute to Michael Posner* (pp. 167–188). Washington, DC: American Psychological Association.

Rutter, M., & Silberg, J. (2002). Gene-environment interplay in relation to emotional and behavioral disturbance. *Annual Review of Psychology, 53,* 463–490.

Ryan, R. M., Connell, J. P., & Deci, E. L. (1985). A motivational analysis of self-determination and self-regulation in education. In C. Ames & R. Ames (Eds.), *Research on motivation in education* (Vol. 2, pp. 13–51). Orlando, FL: Academic Press.

Ryan, R. M., & Deci, E. L. (2000). Self-determination theory and the facilitation of intrinsic motivation, social development, and well-being. *American Psychologist, 55,* 68–78.

Shweder, R. A., Mahapatra, M., & Miller, J. G. (1987). Culture and moral development. In J. Kagan & S. Lamb (Eds.), *The emergence of morality in young children* (pp. 1–83). Chicago: University of Chicago Press.

Spinrad, T. L., Eisenberg, N., Harris, E., Hanish, L., Fabes, R. A., Kupanoff, K., et al. (2004). The relation of children's everyday nonsocial peer play to their emotion, regulation, and social functioning. *Developmental Psychology, 40,* 67–80.

Thompson, R. A. (1994). Emotional regulation: A theme in search of definition. *Monographs of the Society for Research in Child Development, 59*(Serial No. 240), 25–52.

Turiel, E. (1998). The development of morality. In W. Damon (Editor-in-Chief) & N. Eisenberg (Vol. Ed.), *Handbook of child psychology: Vol. 3. Social, emotional, and personality development* (pp. 863–932). New York: Wiley.

Turkheimer, E., & Gottesman, I. I. (1996). Simulating the dynamics of genes and environment in development. *Development and Psychopathology, 8,* 667–677.

Wainryb, C., & Turiel, E. (1995). Diversity in social development: Between or within cultures. In M. Killen & D. Hart (Eds.), *Morality in everyday life: Developmental perspectives* (pp. 283–313). Cambridge, England: Cambridge University Press.

Walden, T. A., & Smith, M. C. (1997). Emotion regulation. *Motivation and Emotion, 21,* 7–25.

Whiting, B. B., & Whiting, J. W. M. (1975). *Children of six cultures: A psychocultural analysis.* Cambridge, MA: Harvard University Press.

Wilson, J. Q. (1993). *The moral sense.* New York: Free Press.

Zahn-Waxler, C., & Kochanska, G. (1990). The origins of guilt. In R. Thompson (Ed.), *Nebraska Symposium on Motivation: Vol. 37. Socioemotional development* (pp. 183–258). Lincoln: University of Nebraska Press.

Zahn-Waxler, C., & Robinson, J. (1995). Empathy and guilt: Early origins of feelings of responsibility. In J. Tangney & K. Fischer (Eds.), *Self-conscious emotions* (pp. 143–173). New York: Guilford Press.

CHAPTER 2

The Development of the Person: Social Understanding, Relationships, Conscience, Self

ROSS A. THOMPSON

What constitutes the development of a person? In moral philosophy, "personhood" is not inherent in human existence but rather is contingent on the achievement of self-awareness, moral autonomy, and other constituents of distinctly human capability. Developmental scientists offer a more nuanced answer to this question, describing how the development of personhood emerges in a continuous relational context in which infants and young children develop their earliest understandings of who they are, who others are, and how to relate to other people.

This chapter is concerned with early sociopersonality development. Because other chapters of this *Handbook* are devoted to temperamental individuality, the development of emotion, peer relationships, and other processes related to personality, the goal is not to comprehensively describe the emergence of early personality or to identify individual characteristics that foreshadow adult personality traits. Instead, and consistent with a developmental perspective, the goal is to describe how central facets of social and personality

Every author of a *Handbook* chapter should have such an opportunity to write a revision—to try to portray the field more accurately, to correct mistakes and misinterpretations, and to see how far the field can advance in a few years. In the previous edition, I gratefully thanked many colleagues who were willing to contribute to my "meandering ponderings" about the issues of this chapter. I remain grateful to them because they have continued to stimulate my thinking. I am also grateful to a remarkable group of student colleagues: Rebecca Goodvin, Debbie Laible, Sara Meyer, Lenna Ontai, and Abbie Raikes.

They have contributed to the ideas considered here, and the chapter is dedicated to them. My deepest appreciation also to Nancy Eisenberg, whose patience and good heart made it easier to complete this project during a period of personal challenge. Although I have sought to identify major contributors to each of the topics reviewed here, the length limitations prohibited appreciative citations to all relevant and important papers. Consequently, I offer an apology to respected colleagues whose work is not explicitly noted as frequently as they merit, but whose thinking and research have been influential.

development emerge through the growth of social understanding, self-awareness, early conscience and cooperation, and the relationships that infuse these early achievements. These are some of the most important ways that make a 6-year-old a fundamentally different person from a newborn and form the foundation for individuality and social relatedness in the years to come. The development of social understanding, relationships, self, and conscience constitute the most important ways that developing individuality intersects with the social world. These topics have also provoked the most concerted research attention in the study of sociopersonality development during the past decade.

The research literatures surveyed in this chapter identify several themes about early sociopersonality development and developing persons. First, relationships are central. Indeed, this chapter is a study of relationships and their developmental influence, whether considering face-to-face interaction and the growth of social expectations, parent-child discourse and autobiographical self-awareness, the growth of a mutually cooperative orientation between parent and child, security of attachment, or children's representations of self and relational processes. This chapter reflects an emerging view that relational experience is generative of new understanding, whether of emotions, self, morality, or people's beliefs, and highlights the need for a developmental relational science of the future that focuses on relational influences across diverse developmental domains. Such a developmental relational science could integrate the most valuable perspectives offered by attachment theory, neo-Vygotskian thinking, sociolinguistic approaches to cognitive growth, and other perspectives into a thoughtful understanding of how early relational experience contributes to fundamental competencies and the emergence of individual differences in thinking, sociability, and personality development.

Second, because relational experience is important, early sociopersonality development is best understood not as socialization or constructivism but rather as the appropriation of understanding from shared activity (Rogoff, 1990). The literatures reviewed in this chapter describe how psychological development arises from the powerfully inductive capacities of the young mind interacting with the conceptual catalysts of social exchange, whether in the conflict of wills between parents and a locomoting toddler, interactions about broken toys and mishaps, or conversations about the day's events that reflect cultural values. Integrating understanding of the constructivist mind with the influence of relationships in early sociopersonality development requires comprehending the nature of the shared activity of young children and those who care for them. This is an important research challenge because a model of appropriated understanding through shared activity can potentially further understanding of many features of early sociopersonality growth. In attachment theory, research on the shared activities and conversations of young children and their caregivers can help to clarify how specific representations of experience and self (or internal working models) develop from relational security or insecurity. In theory of mind, studies of shared experiences and discourse can elucidate some of the conceptual catalysts fostering preschoolers' understanding of people's desires, feelings, beliefs, and thoughts (Thompson, 2006a). A model of appropriated understanding from shared activity offers, more than traditional socialization or constructivist views, the opportunity to integrate social and cognitive aspects of early sociopersonality development.

Third, thinking and understanding in early childhood is a conceptual foundation for what develops afterward. Although this seems a truism, it was not long ago that characterizations of young children as egocentric, concrete, preconventional, and preconceptual made this developmental period seem discontinuous with the conceptual achievements of middle childhood and later. If early childhood establishes the foundations for the development of social cognition, moral judgment, and self-understanding of the years that follow, then relationships and other influences experienced in the early years set the context for the growth of an empathic, humanistic orientation toward others, balanced self-concept, capacities for relational intimacy, social sensitivity, and other capacities conventionally viewed as achievements of middle childhood and adolescence. Understanding how this occurs is a current and future research opportunity.

In the contemporary climate of developmental science, relational influences in the family are understood in concert with heritable influences shared by family members. Although students of early sociopersonality development have been slow to enlist genetically sensitive research designs into studies of family influences (see Collins, Maccoby, Steinberg, Hetherington, & Bornstein, 2000), research on genetic and shared and nonshared environmental influences on the security of attachment and other relational variables has advanced understanding of the interaction of heredity and environment. Contemporary scholarship also benefits from a far less polarized view of the influences of nature and nurture than what was true only a few years ago. Heritability estimates, while important, are now recognized as being both sample- and context sensitive and having little implication for the potency of environmental influences (Committee on Integrating the Science of Early Childhood Development, 2000; Rutter, 1997). Equally important have been the contributions of developmental behavioral genetics for conceptualizing the differentiating experiences of siblings in the family (nonshared environment) and for understanding how children's characteristics are evocative of parenting practices (gene-environment correlation), both long integrated into developmental theory but now receiving renewed attention. At the same time, an expanding body of research is underscoring the importance of studying long-neglected gene-environment interactions—by which children with different heritable characteristics are affected differently by the environment—for informing developmental theory concerning family relationships (see, e.g., Ge et al., 1996, and O'Connor, Caspi, DeFries, & Plomin, 2003, for illustrations). Such studies highlight that the interaction term in the quantitative model for partitioning heritable and environmental influences on behavior may be the most important one. Molecular genetics research has the power to elucidate gene-environment interactions and the probabilistic nature of genetic effects (Rutter, Silberg, O'Connor, & Simonoff, 1999), and comparative studies highlight the influence of the environment in gene expression in studies of rats and primates (see Gunnar & Vasquez, in press, for a review). Taken together, contemporary research is affirming the wisdom of the lesson repeatedly learned by prior generations of developmental scientists: the inseparability of nature and nurture. What has advanced significantly is the technology for elucidating their interaction.

This is an exciting time for studying the development of the person because of a new appreciation of the generative influence of relational experience and respect for what young individuals bring to these relationships.

SOCIAL UNDERSTANDING

Understanding the world of people—the psychological processes that guide behavior and relationships, the na-

ture of social roles and institutions, group processes, and other social phenomena—is essential to psychological growth. At each age, social cognitive understanding contributes to social competence, interpersonal sensitivity, and an awareness of how the self relates to other individuals and groups in a complex social world. Social cognition is also central to the development of emotion understanding, moral awareness, and self understanding. Early social cognitive development creates a foundation to these achievements as young children begin to comprehend how human behavior is related to mental goals, intentions, feelings, desires, thoughts, and beliefs, and how social interaction is affected by the juxtaposition of these mental states in two or more individuals. Moreover, attachment theory and other theories of social development view early childhood as the period when individual differences in social beliefs and dispositions emerge from children's social experiences, especially in close relationships. Taken together, the study of early social cognitive development offers the opportunity to understand how young children derive their initial insights into the psychological world of people, and why children begin to create markedly different expectations for this social world. These early developmental processes color social understanding throughout life.

Developmental study of social cognition has traditionally been the stepchild of research on cognitive development, based on the assumption that the same conceptual processes organize children's thinking about the social and nonsocial worlds. Beginning with the Piagetian era, when the study of social-cognitive development began in earnest, this meant that relatively little attention was devoted to social cognition in infancy and early childhood because this period was theoretically characterized as one of egocentrism, concrete thinking, and a focus on appearances rather than underlying, invisible realities. Students of social cognitive development also inherited from Piagetian theory the constructivist model, with its emphasis on the autonomous child's induction of understanding from individual experience.

The current post-Piagetian era of cognitive developmental research has offered new opportunities to explore early social cognitive development because of a new view of the developing mind. The assumption of early childhood egocentrism has been replaced by the realization that understanding the mental world of other people, and the differences between people's mental states, is one of the early and consuming interests of infants and young children. In their investigations of the growth of joint attention; inferences of intentionality, desires, and beliefs; theory of mind; and other conceptual processes, researchers have highlighted how remarkably early and apparently easily young children acquire insight into the psychological world and the relevance of these achievements to later social understanding.

Contemporary study of early social cognition also contributes to a more sophisticated understanding of the processes by which social understanding develops in early childhood. At a time when cognitive developmental scholars are questioning the adequacy of explanations of conceptual growth that focus solely on the inductive, constructivist mind and are exploring the social origins of psychological understanding (e.g., Carpendale & Lewis, 2004; Hobson, 2002), research into early face-to-face interaction, the impact of locomotor experience on parent-infant relations, social referencing, parental socialization of social domain understanding, and parent-child conversation contribute new insight into the developmental catalysts to early psychological understanding. By exploring these social catalysts, the ideas of social and cognitive developmentalists are usefully integrated in contemporary social cognitive research. This is especially so because inquiry into early social cognitive development can help to clarify central constructs in social developmental theories (such as the "internal working models" of attachment theory) while also providing insight into the consequences of differences in early social experiences for children's understanding of mental states. Therefore, contemporary research on early social cognitive development is not only an instantiation of the traditional view that conceptual achievements are applied to the social and nonsocial worlds alike but also a new opportunity to explore how the scaffolding of everyday social experience provides uniquely social catalysts to the development of psychological understanding.

The study of early social cognition encompasses developments in social skills, general knowledge of the social world (including the psychological functioning of people), and person-specific social expectations. In each of these areas, infancy and early childhood is a period of significant advance.

Early Social Discriminations and Expectations

In traditional developmental theory, a fundamental conceptual challenge for the newborn is to distinguish the internal world from the surround. From this perspective, early social cognition requires the emergence from initial symbiosis or egocentrism. But an alternative view is offered by contemporary perceptual theory (e.g., Gibson, 1995), which argues that the integrated perceptual experiences yielded by movement and activity contribute to a fundamental distinction between internal experience and surrounding stimulation from shortly after birth. According to this view, the tight synchrony of multimodal experience (e.g., integrated visual, tactile, kinesthetic, and auditory experiences) that arises from self-initiated movement is perceptually different from incoming stimulation arising from objects that are acted on or that move of themselves. Gibson and others (e.g., Neisser, 1995) have argued that, in this way, perception distinguishes self-initiated action from surrounding activity and gradually contributes to self-awareness. Indeed, Gibson goes on to argue that the development of new behavioral capabilities coincides with the perception of new affordances of objects in the surrounding world, such as how flat surfaces begin to be perceived as traversible when infants can locomote, and how people begin to be perceived as arousing and responsive when infants can interact socially. In this sense, social cognition and self-awareness each arise from the new perceptual experiences yielded by action, including social activity.

The social and inanimate worlds are potentially distinguishable early in life in several ways. People are spontaneous agents and act in a self-initiated manner, but this is not true of inanimate objects. People interact in a reciprocal, contingent, coordinated, and communicative fashion with the infant, predictably responding to the baby's signals but responding with considerable variability. Emotion is a more salient feature of social interaction compared to most encounters with objects—including the emotions that precede social interaction and the changes in emotions that arise from interactive activity. Most important, the locus of causality for people's behavior is intentional goal-directed mentality for which no comparable sources of causality exist for objects.

During the 1st year, infants begin to discriminate between the social and animate worlds in many of these ways (see Raikson & Poulin-Dubois, 2001). These discriminations are founded on early perceptual preferences that orient young infants toward social events. Newborns visually track facelike stimuli, reflecting the influence of dedicated subcortical neural circuits that affect the development of, and are later supplanted by, cortically mediated facial preferences at 2 to 3 months of age (Johnson & Morton, 1991; Mondloch et al., 1999). Newborns exhibit a visual preference for their mothers' faces based on global perceptual discriminations that will later become more refined when infants begin scanning interior facial features at 2 to 3 months of age (Pascalis, de Schonen, Morton, Deruelle, & Fabre-Grenet, 1995; Walton, Bower, & Bower, 1992). By 3 months, when infants' facial scanning has moved to the interior of faces, infants also begin to discriminate the pictures of familiar persons (Barrera & Maurer, 1981; but see Bartrip, Morton, & de Shonen, 2001, for evidence of earlier recognition ability). Newborns are also capable of recognizing the sound of the mother's voice based on prenatal auditory experience (DeCasper & Fifer, 1980; DeCasper & Spence, 1986). This may be related to newborns' preference for the sounds of human speech and, in particular, for "infant-directed speech" that is characterized by exaggerated prosody, repetition, and simple syntax (Cooper & Aslin, 1990). Infants' preference for infant-directed speech endures throughout the early months and adult vocalizations can evoke emotional responses in the infant that are consistent with the positive or negative tone of the adult voice. Infants respond positively to vocalizations signaling affirmation or warmth (with exaggerated melodic contour) and negatively to vocalizations signaling anger or prohibition (with sharp, staccato intonations; Fernald, 1985, 1996). People are, in short, uniquely compelling elements of the newborn's world: The constellation of stimulus properties they possess captivate the young infant's attention and arouse emotion, perhaps owing to the developing brain's preparedness to respond to human stimulation.

People are captivating to infants not only because of their stimulus properties but also because of their behavioral propensities. Young infants discover that people respond to their initiatives in ways that create excitement and generate positive arousal. This becomes especially apparent after 2 to 3 months of age when, with the behavioral state fluctuations of the neonatal period subsiding and longer periods of awake alertness emerging, infants and their caregivers begin to engage in episodes of face-to-face play. These episodes are typically characterized by focused social interaction without competing caregiving goals or other demands on either partner, with infant and adult facing each other in close proximity and interacting facially, vocally, tactilely, and with behavioral gestures. Developmental scientists have been interested in episodes of face-to-face play not because of their ubiquity or universality, but rather because they constitute some of the earliest experiences of focused social interaction that contribute to the growth of social skills and the development of social expectations for familiar caregivers.

Detailed microanalyses of the course of infant and adult behavior during social interaction reveal several characteristics of face-to-face play that underscore the complexity and richness of this social experience for young infants. First, in responding contingently to the baby's socioemotional expressions, adults do not merely mimic or mirror the infant's actions. In addition, they express emotion in ways that are comparable to the baby's own but using different expressions, such as responding with a smile and a lilting voice when the baby coos. Moreover, adults also model positive expressions and differentially reinforce the baby's emotional responses. Malatesta's elegant microanalyses of maternal and infant emotional expressions during face-to-face play revealed that mothers maintained a generally positive demeanor and, while they matched the emotion of most infant emotional expressions (including joy, interest, surprise, and even sadness and anger), the baby's negative expressions (such as pain or "knit brow") were likely to be ignored or, in the case of anger, evoke the mother's surprised response (Malatesta, Culver, Tesman, & Shepard, 1989; Malatesta, Grigoryev, Lamb, Albin, & Culver, 1986). Mothers seemed committed to maintaining the baby in a positive emotional state and, over a period of weeks, maternal modeling and contingent responding to infant emotional expressions helped to account for increased rates of infant joy and interest expressions in face-to-face play. Adult contingent responsiveness is complex and often involves responses that do not match the infant's own but instead are intended to alter or guide the baby's emotional responding.

Second, although face-to-face play is commonly characterized as the establishment and maintenance of well-coordinated synchrony, with adults sensitively scaffolding their initiatives to accord with the baby's signals, it is mistaken to portray this social activity so simply. Tronick and his colleagues, based on their own microanalytic studies, have concluded that well-coordinated interactions occur only about 30% or less of the time that mothers and infants engage in face-to-face interactions, with nonsynchronous or uncoordinated exchanges occurring when infants become fussy, mothers are distracted, or for other reasons (Gianino & Tronick, 1988; Tronick, 1989). They argue that other interactive goals—such as interactive reparation and self-regulation—accompany the goal of maintaining interactive coordination. Therefore, infants are faced with a more complex interactive activity than merely responding to a sensitively scaffolded social situation. In their earliest experiences of social play, infants are also learning that social interaction is dynamic and changing, and are acquiring the social skills of managing its dyadic course and its emotional effects. They are discovering that their social and emotional responses have effects on the adult's behavior—sometimes highly predictable effects—and that their emotions are central to the dynamics of interaction with a human partner. They are also discovering that their own emotional experience is affected not only by the initiatives of the caregiver but also by the interaction that arises from mutual responsiveness.

These experiences may help to explain why, by 2 to 3 months of age, infants respond differently to people compared to objects, directing more positive facial expressions and vocalizations to responsive people than toward interactive objects (e.g., puppets), and showing distress to nonresponsive people but rarely toward noninteractive objects (Ellsworth, Muir, & Hains, 1993; Legerstee, 1997; Legerstee, Pomerleau, Malcuit, & Feider, 1987). By 2 to 3 months of age, infants appear to expect that people will respond to them and interact with them. This conclusion is supported by studies of the "still-face" effect in infants in which mothers alternate episodes of face-to-face interaction with an episode in which they look at the infant but are impassive and unresponsive. Studies of infants age 2 to 6 months show that babies reliably respond with diminished positive affect, withdrawal, self-directed behavior, and sometimes with social elicitations (e.g., brief smiles, momentarily increased vocalizing and reaching) and negative affect during the still-face episode. When mothers subsequently respond normally, infants become more sociable but also remain subdued (see Adamson & Frick, 2003, for a review of this literature). The still-face effect is robust: It has been observed in response to strangers as well as to parents (Ellsworth et al., 1993; Kisilevsky et al., 1998), in comparisons of infants from Western and non-Western cultures (Kisilevsky et al., 1998), and in conditions when the adult's reasons for ceasing social interaction were systematically varied such as turning away to look at another person (Striano, 2004). This suggests that the expectation that people will be responsive is not person specific and seems to be generalized to a range of interactive experiences in the early months.

The still-face procedure was originally designed to simulate the infant's interactive experience when mothers are depressed. Individual differences in maternal behavior and affect are significant influences on how infants respond socially (Adamson & Frick, 2003). Several studies have found that depressed mothers are less responsive and emotionally more negative and subdued in face-to-face play with their infants, for example, and the offspring of depressed mothers are also less responsive and emotionally less animated as early as 2 to 3 months (e.g., Cohn, Campbell, Matias, & Hopkins, 1990; Field, Healy, Goldstein, & Guthertz, 1990; Field et al., 1988). Field and her colleagues (1988) found that 3- to 6-month-old infants of depressed mothers remained more subdued and less animated when subsequently interacting with a nondepressed stranger. Dawson and colleagues did not replicate this finding with 13- to 15-month-old infants, but reported that the atypical patterns of frontal brain activity characteristic of the infants of depressed mothers during social interaction with their mothers were also apparent when these infants subsequently interacted with a nondepressed familiar adult (Dawson et al., 1999). Differences in early social experience seem to be important, therefore, for how infants interact with other partners, which may reflect the early emergence of generalized and specific social expectations. This may help to explain why early differences in infant affective and self-regulatory behavior in the still-face paradigm predict later attachment security (Braungart-Rieker, Garwood, Powers, & Wang, 2001; Cohn, Campbell, & Ross, 1992) and other psychosocial sequelae. Much more research on the origins and outcomes of individual differences in infant behavior in the still-face procedure is needed to clarify the specific social expectations it reflects. However, by 2 to 3 months of age, infants have begun to expect that people will respond positively to their initiatives, and marked differences in adult responsiveness have significant effects on the infant's social and emotional reactions that generalize to other partners.

As these studies suggest, adult responding that is contingent on the infant's initiatives contributes to the socially and emotionally engaging quality of early social interaction. By 2 to 3 months of age, infants respond with positive emotion to contingent responding but become affectively negative if the contingency is interrupted (Lewis, Alessandri, & Sullivan, 1990; Rovee-Collier,

1989; J. Watson, 1985). Contingency in an environmental response is positively arousing perhaps because it contributes to the infant's sense of agency. Initiating actions that have a predictable effect is a salient indication that one can exert control over important outcomes, whether social or nonsocial. J. S. Watson (1995) has argued that young infants are especially sensitive to perfectly response-contingent events because these indicate self-generated outcomes (e.g., movement of a mobile contingent on the baby's leg kicking) and that such experiences contribute to self-awareness. Later, at about 2 to 3 months, he argues, infants become sensitized to imperfect response-contingent events that are more likely to be social in nature (see also Gergely & Watson, 1999). In each case, contingency is salient because of the sense of control and effectance it creates. Murray and Trevarthen (1985) showed that a small sample of 2- to 3-month-olds responded animatedly when viewing live images of their mothers talking to them through closed-circuit television but later, when the same images of their mothers were replayed (and were thus noncontingent), infants turned away in apparent disinterest or distress (see Bigelow, MacLean, & MacDonald, 1996; Hains & Muir, 1996; and Legerstee & Varghese, 2001, for partial replications and extensions; but note also Rochat, Neisser, & Marian, 1998, for a failure to replicate this effect). The contingency of face-to-face interaction thus seems important to the social and emotional potency of early social play.

There are other advances in social cognition and social skills emerging from early face-to-face play and related experiences of social interaction. First, because social play is so richly affective, infants learn about the emotional expressions of people. By 3.5 months, infants can discriminate the dynamic, multimodal expressions of different emotions enacted by their mothers and they prefer congruence between facial and vocal expressions (Kahana-Kalman & Walker-Andrews, 2001; Montegue & Walker-Andrews, 2002; Walker-Andrews, 1997). This is not observed, however, in response to the emotional expressions of unfamiliar women until 5 to 7 months of age. This suggests that partner familiarity may be important to the earliest comprehension of emotional expressions and their meaning, with some evidence that infants respond in an emotionally resonant manner to the dynamic emotional expressions of their mothers by 3 months (Haviland & Lelwica, 1987). Infants as young as 5 months also react in an emotionally differential manner to positive and negative emotions conveyed through speech alone (Fernald, 1996). Regular experiences of face-to-face play in which these emotional expressions are salient features of social communication would contribute to these forms of nascent emotion understanding. Second, social play also provides opportunities for infants to learn about the distinctive behavioral characteristics of familiar partners. Fathers play differently than mothers in face-to-face encounters with young infants, for example, and infants later show differentiated expectations for the social behavior of each parent (see M. Lamb, 1997, for a review). Finally, to the extent that in the early months, infants begin to represent others' actions as "like me" when they can also be performed by the self (Meltzoff & Gopnik, 1993), the coordination of the socioemotional initiatives of the self and a sensitive partner during early episodes of social play is likely to consolidate this nascent representational capability by 3 months of age.

Social play is not the only interactive context for the development of early social discriminations and expectations. In light of the salience of distress, the association between parental soothing and subsequent relief is likely to be meaningful and easily learned by an infant, contributing to expectations that an adult's arrival will bring distress relief (M. Lamb, 1981). In this context, differences in adult responsiveness are again likely to be important, at least to the extent that they affect developing expectations for the caregiver's arrival and soothing when infants are upset. Several research groups have found that by 6 months, distressed infants began quieting in apparent anticipation of the arrival of their mothers when they could hear the adult's approaching footsteps; infants also protested loudly if the adult approached but did not pick them up (Gekoski, Rovee-Collier, & Carulli-Rabinowitz, 1983; M. Lamb & Malkin, 1986). These studies suggest that during the initial months of the 1st year, infants are learning the association between their distress, a caregiver's approach, soothing ministrations, and subsequent comfort. Much more research is needed to understand the effects of reliable differences in the caregiver responsiveness (such as differences in the adult's efficacy in soothing the infant) on these emergent social expectations related to distress relief, especially as they are mediated by the infant's emotional tendencies.

Intentions and Inferring Intentionality

Interest in face-to-face play wanes after 7 months as infants become more mobile and interested in more active forms of interaction. The growth of self-produced loco-motion not only changes infant-parent interaction but also is, according to Campos and his colleagues, a setting event for a variety of socioemotional and conceptual advances in the child (Campos, et al., 2000; Campos, Kermoian, & Zumbahlen, 1992). These advances occur because locomotor experience dramatically changes the relation of the infant to the environment. Rather than merely reaching toward objects or responding to events that appear before them, infants are now capable of approaching objects and people of interest and initiating independent exploration. As a consequence, self-produced locomotion is associated with a cascade of conceptual changes related to person-environment relations (such as postural compensation to changes in peripheral optic flow perception, advances in distance perception and increased wariness of heights, and more sophisticated spatial search strategies), which include advances in referential communication, means-ends understanding, and social interaction across a distance.

The onset of locomotor experience is also associated with socioemotional changes in the infant and challenges for the family system. The infant's independent locomotion means that the child is becoming capable of wandering away from the parent, acting in a dangerous or disapproved manner, and pursuing independent goals, together with the feelings of self-efficacy of doing so. Parents respond to these changes by more vigilantly monitoring the infant's activity (and childproofing the house), using distal communicative modes (such as calling across a distance), and intervening more often with distractions, prohibitions, and sanctions and thus, at times, frustrating the infant's goal-directed efforts. The stage is set, therefore, for a significant conflict of intention between the infant and parent. Indeed, at the same time that attachment security is emerging, infant-parent relationships are being shaped by how each partner is negotiating the challenges associated with the onset of infant locomotor activity. Parental reactions to this developmental transition are likely to vary significantly. The evolution of offspring from immobile to self-propelled excites most parents, but many also find that the monitoring, intervening, and proaction required to supervise a mobile child is a significant new challenge for them, along with the conflict of wills and testing of limits that accompanies infants' responses to their efforts. A parent's capacity to re-main sensitive to and supportive of the infant's emergent competencies during this period contributes to maintaining parent-infant harmony just as parental coercion and frustration are likely to undermine it.

There are thus many reasons to perceive the locomotor transition as a catalyst for early socioemotional and conceptual development and for parent-infant relationships. But the social consequences of this transition have been little studied thus far. In an exploratory study, Campos and colleagues (1992) interviewed the mothers of locomotor and prelocomotor 8-month-olds and found that mothers' perceptions of the child and reports of their own activities varied significantly based on the child's locomotor status. The parents of locomotor infants indicated that they used more verbal prohibitions, had higher expectations for the child's compliance, and engaged in greater disciplinary activity than did the parents of prelocomotor infants. Parents also reported that their offspring showed greater sensitivity to the parents' location and emotional signals, and exhibited increased expressions of anger and frustration, but also showed more intense affectionate behavior.

Observational studies provide some support for these interview results. Biringen, Emde, Campos, and Appelbaum (1995) reported—in an age-held-constant observational study—that the onset of walking was accompanied by greater "testing of wills" between mothers and infants in prohibition contexts, and by diminished maternal praise of the child, although there were no differences in infant emotionality. Zumbahlen and Crawley (1996) observed a greater number of parental prohibitions directed to crawling than nonlocomotor infants, and that crawling infants showed greater anger and also more often visually checked back with the parent across a distance. In another age-held-constant observational study, Hendrix (2004) reported that the mothers of locomotor infants used "no" more often in a prohibitive context compared to mothers of prelocomotor infants, but there were no group differences in proactive discipline (such as using distractors), child compliance, or infant emotional reactions. The parents of locomotor infants also reported using a greater number of discipline practices at home. Some of these studies have also reported changes in parental behavior over time *regardless* of the child's locomotor status, such as greater childproofing of the home (Hendrix, 2004). This suggests that the anticipation of the baby's self-produced locomotion is important to parents, helping them to prepare for the physical maturation and behavioral competence of their young offspring and the new requirements of their parenting.

That the growth of independent locomotion during the second half of the 1st year is associated with significant changes in parent-child interaction derives, in part, from how locomotion contributes to a more agentic and goal-directed infant. The emergence of intentional, goal-oriented behavior has been a familiar characterization of the 8- to 12-month-old infant from Piaget's (1952) description of the fourth sensorimotor substage. As Campos and his colleagues (2004) have noted, locomotion spurs more sophisticated means-ends behavior because infants must maintain a specific goal in mind (such as moving toward an interesting object) while assembling the specific movements and secondary strategies necessary for achieving it. Not only are infants becoming more volitional during this transition but also, as a consequence, they are being exposed to a range of social responses that underscore the discordant intentions of others, whether they consist of parental prohibitions, verbal admonitions (conveyed in the tone of voice), cautionary facial expressions in response to social referencing, or other forms of referential communication. Self-produced locomotion enhances the expression of infant volition, and also contributes to an awareness of others' intentions (Campos et al., 2000). Indeed, these may be developmentally allied achievements because of how parental interventions over conflicting goals enhance the salience of the volition of another as it contrasts with the infant's own, and motivates efforts to comprehend the difference (see also Tomasello, Carpenter, Call, Behne, & Moll, in press; Tomasello & Rakoczy, 2003).

There are many indications that by 9 to 12 months, infants begin to perceive peoples' actions as intentional and goal directed as infants interpret actions in relation to the objects to which they are directed. In a study by Woodward (1998), for example, infants were habituated to a scene of a hand reaching across a stage to grasp one of two toys. After habituation, the positions of the toys were reversed and the hand either reached to grasp the original toy in its new location (requiring a different trajectory) or a new toy in the original location (using the same reaching motion as before). Six-month-olds and 9-month-olds each looked longer to the latter trials, suggesting that infants had encoded the original action as directed to a particular toy. In this study, infants did not respond comparably when a mechanical arm rather than a human hand reached to grasp the objects, consistent

with infants' differential encoding of human and nonhuman activity. At least by 7 months of age, for example, infants distinguish the movement of people as being self-initiated whereas objects move by external force (Spelke, Phillips, & Woodward, 1995), and this may occur even earlier (Legerstee, 1994). Using a similar habituation procedure, Woodward has also shown that by 12 months, infants understand the object directedness of a person's gazing (Woodward, 2003) and pointing (Woodward & Guajardo, 2002) and have also begun to comprehend the distinction between goals and the actions enacted to achieve them (Woodward & Sommerville, 2000). Baldwin, Baird, Saylor, and Clark (2001) have likewise shown that 10- to 11-month-olds organize their perceptions of people's actions by the completion of goal-directed activity (see Baird & Baldwin, 2001).

Inferences of the intentions underlying actions like reaching, gazing, and pointing are easy for infants to comprehend because they are the same actions that often express their own intentions. By 6 months of age, infants are familiar with the sight of their own hand reaching toward an object and may be more likely, as a consequence, to interpret other object-directed reaches they observe as similarly goal oriented. Understanding the object directedness of gazing and pointing emerges later with growing comprehension of referential communication and joint attention. Moreover, when caregivers respond to the intentionality they infer in the behavior of their infant offspring, they also scaffold emergent comprehension of the intentional structure of behavior (Meins, Fernyhough, Fradley, & Tuckey, 2001; Meins et al., 2003). When mothers punctuate their verbal responses to the infant's goal-directed activity with affirmative utterances when the goal is achieved, for example, they help to parse the sequence of behavioral acts in terms that organize the perception of behavior in goal-oriented units. Caregivers who are attuned to the intentional orientation of infant behavior (or "mind-minded," according to Meins and her colleagues; see Meins et al., 2001, 2003) are especially likely to interactively scaffold early comprehension of the goal orientation of behavior in these ways.

The perception of people as subjective, intentional agents is a signal accomplishment for early social cognitive development. By the first birthday or shortly thereafter, there are further indications that infants are responding in a more sophisticated manner to the actions of people as subjective, intentional agents (see

Carpenter, Nagell, & Tomasello, 1998, Tomasello, 1995a, 1999, and Tomasello & Rakoczy, 2003 for reviews). Infants create joint attentional states with adults by looking in the direction of the adult's gaze or looking from a toy to the adult's face and back to the toy again. They not only follow an adult's gaze but also look in the direction of the adult's pointing or gesturing. They produce protodeclarative gestures (such as pointing to or holding up an object while alternating gaze between the object and the adult's face) and protoimperative gestures (such as reaching for an object while alternating gaze between the object and the adult's face), each apparently intended to alter the adult's subjective orientation and elicit a desired response. They also exhibit social referencing behavior (discussed later). To be sure, there has been some debate over whether these behaviors reflect true perceptions of intentionality rather than conditioned learning of social behavior (Moore & Corkum, 1994) or affective sharing (Baldwin & Moses, 1996). However, the intercoordinated developmental emergence of these achievements suggests that a more fundamental transition has occurred in the infant's person perception. By the first birthday, infants have begun regarding people as intentional agents with subjective viewpoints that can be altered. Later in the 2nd year, further evidence of this transition emerges with the ability of 14- to 18-month-olds to imitate adults' intended rather than accidental actions (Carpenter, Akhtar, & Tomasello, 1998; Meltzoff, 1995), their enlistment of inferences concerning the intentions of adult speakers in learning new words (Baldwin, Markman, Bill, Desjardins, & Irwin, 1996; Tomasello & Barton, 1994), and their use of intention inferences in new social learning (Carpenter, Call, & Tomasello, 2002). There are many further advances in intentionality understanding after age 2. Young children have much to learn about how intentions connect to other mental states, the influences that mediate the transition from intention to action, and the nature of nonintentional action, as well as other psychological processes.

Understanding people's behavior as goal directed and intentional takes the infant a long way toward a mentalistic comprehension of human behavior, but observing rather prosaic behaviors like reaching and pointing does not provide much insight into how infants begin to understand the salient experiences of social interaction. Little is known of how a dawning appreciation of other people as subjective, intentional agents alters other features of developing social cognition and the growth of infant-parent relationships. How much does the emergent "testing of limits" of the toddler period, for example, arise from the young child's perception of the adult's intentionality when blocking, deterring, or otherwise frustrating the child's goal-directed activity? How does a 1-year-old interpret an adult's emotional behavior in relation to objects in the framework of intentionality inferences? How does this infant regard the intentionality of the adult's emotional behavior toward herself? Are a caregiver's nurturant actions perceived by a 1-year-old as intentional and goal directed, and how is this related to emergent social expectations and the developing security of their relationship? Twelve- to fourteen-month-old infants enlist emotional demeanor and gaze direction in their inferences of the intentions of an adult actor toward toy kittens (Phillips, Wellman, & Spelke, 2002). Do toddlers derive similar intentionality judgments in their observations of everyday social behavior?

Social Referencing

Limited answers to such questions can be gleaned from the research on social referencing (Campos & Stenberg, 1981; Klinnert, Campos, Sorce, Emde, & Svejda, 1983). Social referencing describes the use of another's emotional cues to clarify the interpretation of an ambiguous or uncertain event. The enlistment of this emotional information may derive from active information seeking (such as when one adult looks to another's face to clarify the meaning of an ambiguous statement) or may capitalize on the availability of another's emotional cues in the course of affective sharing or seeking reassurance (Baldwin & Moses, 1996). In either case, the importance of social referencing is twofold. First, it indicates that by the first birthday, infants are fairly good consumers of the emotional cues of others and can enlist this information in their own responses to events. Second, social referencing inaugurates the processes by which young children vicariously acquire an understanding of events through the signals provided by others and thus appropriate socially constructed meaning systems. Both are lifelong features of social development.

The research on social referencing indicates that it has important but modest effects on infant behavior (Feinman, Roberts, Hsieh, Sawyer, & Swanson, 1992). The influence of social referencing is especially apparent when infants are uncertain how to respond, but another's emotional cues can be influential even when they are not unsure (Feinman et al., 1992; Zarbatany &

Lamb, 1985). Hertenstein and Campos (2004) have demonstrated the retention of social referencing influences for up to 1 hour in 14-month-olds, but much more research into the longer-term effects of social referencing is needed. Infant responses to uncertain situations can be influenced by facial expressions alone (e.g., Klinnert, Emde, Butterfield, & Campos, 1986; Sorce, Emde, Campos, & Klinnert, 1985; Zarbatany & Lamb, 1985), vocal cues alone (Mumme, Fernald, & Herrera, 1996), multimodal emotional cues (sometimes including gestures; e.g., Hirshberg & Svejda, 1990; Hornik, Risenhoover, & Gunnar, 1987; Walden & Ogan, 1988), and even televised images (Mumme & Fernald, 2003). In everyday situations, infants commonly have access to the unsolicited multimodal emotional cues of their caregivers as they traverse, experiment, and explore the limits of their known universe.

Consistent with the research on infants' understanding of the subjectivity of others' actions, social referencing studies have also shown that as young as 12 to 14 months of age, infants understand the object specificity of another's emotional message (Hornik et al., 1987; Repacholi, 1998; Walden & Ogan, 1988), and can use that person's referential cues, such as gaze direction, to guide the interpretation of the person's emotional expressions (Moses, Baldwin, Rosicky, & Tidball, 2001). This suggests that another's emotional message has considerable informational value for 1-year-olds because they can comprehend its referential intent. But the emotional cues of an adult also have emotional impact, and studies have shown that the adult's signals influence the infant's general emotional demeanor, especially toward the object of referential focus (Hirshberg & Svejda, 1990; Klinnert et al., 1986; Moses et al., 2001; Mumme et al., 1996; Sorce et al., 1985). These dual influences of social referencing are not inconsistent. When reading another's emotional expressions in the presence of an ambiguous event, infants are emotionally alerted by the adult's affective demeanor at the same time that they are interpreting the meaning of this demeanor for the event of shared referential focus.

Social referencing illustrates, therefore, the sensitivity of 1-year-olds to the meaning underlying an adult's emotional orientation. By the beginning of the 2nd year, 1-year-olds comprehend that another's emotional expressions can be evoked with reference to a specific object or event, and this knowledge influences their interpretation of that event. This awareness is enlisted not only in situations when infants are uncertain about ambiguous events but also in circumstances when caregivers' emotional expressions serve to alert, caution, interest, reassure, or otherwise motivate their young offspring in relation to events of shared attention. In these circumstances, the same understanding of object specificity and referential intent enables infants to comprehend that the adult's sharp, imperative voice is with reference to the potted plant that the child is reaching toward, or that the caregiver's smiling expression provides reassurance with respect to the kitten they are stroking.

In light of these early achievements in referential understanding and emotional communication, it is somewhat surprising that there has not been exploration of further development in these processes during the 2nd and 3rd years, when a young child's interpretation of the psychological meaning of an adult's emotional expressions becomes more insightful. Studies of early language acquisition show that as early as 18 months, for example, toddlers' inferences of the intentions of adult speakers—usually gleaned from their emotional displays—provide a basis for initial word learning (e.g., Baldwin, 2000; Baldwin et al., 1996), and future research might be devoted to examining other conceptual achievements that are facilitated by early emotional communication. For example, what does it mean for a young child's perception of other people, especially other family members or peers, when they are the targets of a caregiver's emotionally referential focus? When do young children begin to comprehend that they can themselves be objects of an adult's emotional responding, and what is the impact of this awareness for early self-concept and the development of security in close relationships? Variations in emotional communication appear to be relevant to the earliest feelings of self-confidence and pride when the adult's referential focus on the child or the child's accomplishments is accompanied by emotionally affirmative cues (Stipek, 1995). Conversely, emotional communication can be enlisted by parents in conveying behavioral standards (such as looking sternly at the child who is initiating disapproved activity) and in inducing shame or guilt when these standards are violated (Emde & Buchsbaum, 1990).

The impact of social referencing experiences on the adult also merits further research attention. Informal observations of spontaneous referencing behavior in my laboratory indicate that parents are acutely aware of the social referencing of their young offspring and often deliberately pose salient emotional expressions to reassure, instill caution, and provide other socioemotional messages. If this is true, it suggests that social referencing should be viewed as a dyadic process of referential communication through which infants and young children appropriate an understanding of events of significance to them, and caregivers facilitate that understanding through deliberate emotional cuing.

Understanding Social Events

After 18 months, a transition occurs in psychological development when young children strive to comprehend normative standards for the social world. Developmental scientists have observed this in many behavioral domains. With respect to early conscience, for example, this is the period when toddlers respond with heightened interest and concern to objects that are damaged or flawed, applying normative standards for the wholeness, appearance, and integrity of objects (Kagan, 1981, in press; S. Lamb, 1993). As discussed later, this subsequently becomes manifested in an intuitive morality that causes young children to regard rules as obligatory, even though children commonly violate them (Wellman & Miller, 2003). With respect to the development of self-awareness, the responses of 18-month-olds to the familiar rouge task not only reveal self-recognition before a mirror but also their evident embarrassment when detecting a spot of red on their noses (Lewis, 2000; Lewis & Brooks-Gunn, 1979). Toddlers have internalized a normative standard for their physical appearance that does not include a rouge-marked nose. One of the most important manifestations of the young child's search for normative standards at this age is in language development, where they strive to comprehend the appropriate nominal reference of the words they are acquiring at such a rapid pace (Tomasello & Rakoczy, 2003).

With respect to event representation, young children reveal further their search for normative standards. By the end of the 2nd year, they begin to create generalized scripts for familiar social experiences such as bedtime rituals, mealtimes and other regular family routines, arrivals and departures from child care, and other common events (Hudson, 1993; Nelson, 1978, 1989; Nelson & Gruendel, 1981). These scripts provide a conceptual scaffold for knowledge of general routines and for memory of specific experiences that incorporate routine events, and they constitute the young child's normative expectations for how those routines should occur in the future. Indeed, young children can be inflexible in their fidelity to scripted expectations (Hudson, 1990, de-

scribes one 2-year-old who became distressed when she was given her bath before—rather than after—dinner because she thought this meant that she would not be fed that evening). These scripts increase in complexity and scope throughout the preschool years as they become integrated into broader knowledge systems.

Studies by Nelson and her colleagues indicate that the content, organization, and structure of early event representation is shaped not only by the child's prelinguistic representation of experiences but also by the verbal structure applied to them in parent-child discourse. In the context of shared conversations, beginning as soon as children can talk about events, parents help to review, reconstruct, and consolidate young children's memory of generalized routines and specific experiences (Fivush, 1993; Hudson, 1990; Nelson, 1989, 1993a). Furthermore, parents often help children to anticipate future events, and the verbal structure they provide may help to organize the child's representation of that experience as it subsequently occurs (Nelson, 1989, 1993a). There is also evidence that the style of parental discourse is important. Parents who are more elaborative in their conversational style provide considerable background and contextual information in their shared discussion of events in the child's life. Several studies have found that the offspring of more elaborative mothers have a more complete and sophisticated representation of their past experiences (including representations of routine events) not only owing to the direct impact of parental discourse style but also because of the child's appropriation of the adult's narrative approach (Hudson, 1990; Nelson, 1993a; Reese & Fivush, 1993).

Generalized event representations, or scripts, provide a foundation for young children's understanding of social events. However, with researchers' focus on rather prosaic routines (such as restaurant visits), little is known about how young children represent everyday experiences that involve greater emotional and relational depth such as separations and reunions, bedtime routines, and distress relief. Such events are important in how young children comprehend emotion and relationships, the quality of parental nurturance, and the reliability of care. The child's direct experience of these events, as well as the verbal structure of parental discourse in subsequent conversation, are each important to how children comprehend these experiences. Further study of children's representations of these experiences may also contribute to understanding the origins of the differences in relational security and trust that underlie parent-child attachment.

Feelings and Desires

Social referencing research is important because it illustrates the significance of emotion to the infant's behavioral regulation and to social understanding. Social referencing is important also because processes of emotional communication are ubiquitous in child-parent interaction, including the routine events that are the foundation for generalized event representations. Not surprisingly, among the most important subsequent advances in early social cognition is developing understanding of people's desires, beliefs, and feelings (Thompson & Lagattuta, 2005).

Toddlers display a remarkable comprehension of the differences between people in what they desire, contrary to the traditional portrayal of early egocentrism. In an important study, Repacholi and Gopnik (1997) presented 14- and 18-month-olds with two snacks: goldfish crackers (which the children liked) and broccoli (which the children disliked). Then the adult tasted each snack, smiling and exhibiting pleasure ("mmmm!") with one, and frowning and saying "ewww!" with the other. In the "match" condition, the adult's preferences were the same as the child's; in the "mismatch" condition, the adult preferred the broccoli and disliked the crackers. Then the adult extended her hand and said, "I want some more, can you give me more?" The 18-month-olds (but not the younger toddlers) reliably gave the adult the food she desired in both the match and mismatch conditions. By contrast, the 14-month-olds overwhelmingly gave the adult more goldfish crackers. The sensitivity to differences in desire among 18-month-olds is consistent with evidence that spontaneous verbal references to desire emerge by 18 months, and somewhat later children use contrastive statements about desire (e.g., comparing what one person wants with what another desires; Bartsch & Wellman, 1995).

By age 2, toddlers can be overheard making spontaneous verbal references to emotions, the causes of emotion, and even emotion regulatory efforts (e.g., "I scared of the shark. Close my eyes" at 28 months; Bartsch & Wellman, 1995; Bretherton, Fritz, Zahn-Waxler, & Ridgeway, 1986; Brown & Dunn, 1991; Dunn, Bretherton, & Munn, 1987; Wellman, Harris, Banerjee, & Sinclair, 1995). The emergence of expressive emotion-related utterances is preceded by months of receptive comprehension of emotion-related discourse (Ridgeway, Waters, & Kuczaj, 1985). Careful analysis of the content of young children's emotion references has shown that even in their initial utterances, children regard emotions not just as behavioral events but as subjective, psychological conditions, distinct from the situations and behaviors with which they are associated. By contrast with their descriptions of pain, for example, children as young as 2 describe emotion as referential (e.g., sad *about* something) and involving volition, consistent with their developing understanding of intentionality and referentiality. Moreover, even in these initial utterances, toddlers explicitly differentiate people's feelings, often contrasting another's emotions with their own in a nonegocentric manner (Bartsch & Wellman, 1995; Wellman et al., 1995). By age 2.5, young children comprehend better the connections between desire and emotion: People are happy when they get or see what they want and unhappy when their desires are denied (Repacholi & Gopnik, 1997; Wellman & Woolley, 1990).

It appears that early childhood witnesses the growth of young children's intuitive theories of emotion that incorporate not only the belief-desire reasoning described by theory of mind researchers but also their dawning understanding of the internal (including visceral) and external determinants of emotion, the subjectivity and referentiality of emotional experience, the outcomes of emotional arousal, and emotional regulatory processes. These intuitive theories of emotion expand markedly during the preschool years (Denham, 1998; Fabes, Eisenberg, Nyman, & Michaelieu, 1991). In their efforts to comprehend the causes of emotion, preschoolers begin to conceptually map the typical situations and goal states that are associated with different feelings, such as that blocked goals elicit anger and loss is associated with sadness (Harris, 1989; Stein & Levine, 1989). This reflects their awareness that both situational and internal factors are relevant to eliciting emotion (Dunn & Hughes, 1998; Fabes et al., 1991). For example, 3-year-olds know that feelings are associated with beliefs and expectations about events such as the surprise a visitor feels after seeing giraffes on a farm (Wellman & Banerjee, 1991). Young children's understanding of the connection between emotion and thought is also revealed in their appreciation that feelings can be evoked by mental reminders of past emotionally evocative experiences. By age 5, for example, children understand that someone can feel sad when seeing a cat who reminds her of a pet who ran away (Lagattuta, Wellman, & Flavell, 1997; see also Lagattuta & Wellman, 2001). Young children are thus beginning to comprehend the personal and idiosyncratic influences on emotional responding (Dunn & Hughes, 1998).

As a consequence of these causal understandings, and perhaps also because they are more motivated to do so, young children better understand the causes of negative than positive emotions they observe in others (Dunn & Hughes, 1998; Fabes et al., 1991). Their understanding is limited, however. Young children have considerably greater difficulty understanding how emotions can be based on *false* belief, for example, and it is not until about age 6 that they appreciate that someone will feel delighted before opening a box of candy because she thinks it contains chocolates rather than the pebbles her older brother has substituted (de Rosnay & Harris, 2002; de Rosnay, Pons, Harris, & Morrell, 2004; Harris, Johnson, Hutton, Andrews, & Cooke, 1989). Moreover, consistent with the younger child's straightforward association of emotions with specific mental states, it is not until middle childhood that children begin to grasp that multiple emotions of different valence can be experienced simultaneously, and that ambivalence and emotional equivocation can occur (Harter & Buddin, 1987; Wintre & Vallance, 1994).

Young children's developing understanding of how to manage or regulate their emotions reflects these conceptions of the origins of emotional experience (see reviews by Thompson, 1990, 1994). In early childhood, preschoolers believe that emotion can be managed by fleeing, removing, restricting perception of, or ignoring emotionally arousing events, revealing an awareness of the connections between emotion, perception, and thought. Children also recognize that emotion can be managed through reassuring self-talk, seeking nurturance, ceasing to think about emotionally arousing events, distraction, or other strategies that change the mental states that contribute to emotional arousal (Harris, Guz, Lipian, & Man-Shu, 1985; Lagattuta et al., 1997). Consistent with their developing comprehension of the distinction between appearance and reality, older preschoolers also begin to understand the value of managing emotional expressions to dissemble one's feelings or protect the feelings of others, and they begin to use display rules in everyday circumstances (Banerjee, 1997; Cole, 1986). The intuitive theories of emotion that guide young children's understanding of the origins of emotions are also enlisted in their efforts to regulate emotional arousal.

Young children are highly motivated to understand emotions because their desires and feelings are compelling experiences and others' emotions are salient and significant influences on them. Although desires and emotions may seem conceptually simple (especially by comparison with other mental states), they are actually quite challenging for young children to understand because they are invisible, multidetermined motivators of behavior. Emotions have complex internal causes and can be manifested in diverse facial, vocal, and behavioral expressions that are not always intercoordinated, which makes understanding the associations between desires, feelings, perceptions, beliefs, and behavior a conceptually daunting task.

Young children are assisted in developing coherent intuitive theories of emotion, however, by their conversations with adults who label, describe, and explain the causes and consequences of the emotion to them (Thompson, Laible, & Ontai, 2003). The influence of these verbal references to emotion begins early: In one study, references to feelings by mothers and older siblings when toddlers were 18 months were positively correlated with the child's emotion-related utterances at 24 months (Dunn et al., 1987). With increasing age, emotion-related discussions are integrated into conversations of recent events or current experiences, story reading, talking about upcoming events, personal storytelling, or other conversational forums. The influence of these conversations on emotion understanding derives from (a) the growth of language competence that provides a lexical foundation to shared understanding of psychological experiences that are otherwise difficult to define, comprehend, or convey to another; and (b) adult mind-mindedness that causes them to induct young children into the psychological world they inhabit whenever they talk with the child about people. Thus, whenever young children ask "why" about the feelings and behavior they observe in others, they are tutored about the mental world by adults who cannot help but do so because psychological understandings of people have become intuitive to mature thinkers. Moreover, language also enables thought about emotional experience outside of its immediate context, when young children (and often their parents) are more capable of thoughtful reflection and discussion. Indeed, language content and structure has many potentially important influences on the growth of psychological understanding in children (see Budwig, 2002, for a review of these), but the essential feature of these linguistic contributions is that they are also social.

Parent-child conversation about desires, feelings, behavior, and thought thus helps to organize psychological understanding through the lexicalization of mental and emotional life: Words categorize psychological experience in ways that provide coherence and a basis for shared reference and understanding. They help to make explicit the implicit knowledge that young children have intuited. When preschoolers discuss desires and feelings with an adult, they also begin to comprehend that the same event can be experienced differently by people who may feel differently about it (Levine, Stein, & Liwag, 1999). Conversational discourse enables young children to compare their own representation of an experience with that of the adult, and by comparing primary and secondary representations (the latter conveyed in shared conversation) young children are likely to derive new ways of understanding and thinking about personal experiences. More broadly, conversations about emotions provide a forum for the transmission of cultural values, causal attributions, moral evaluations, and other belief systems of the caregiver that are also part of the adult's intuitive understanding of the psychological motivators of people's behavior. As a consequence, young children learn about emotion in conversations that can link emotion to standards of conduct and social awareness. This may explain why parental conversational references to feelings are a more significant predictor of early conscience development than are parents' explicit references to rules (Laible & Thompson, 2000).

Parents who discuss emotions more frequently and with greater elaboration, therefore, have children with more accurate and richer conceptualizations of emotion (Brown & Dunn, 1996; Denham, Zoller, & Couchard, 1994; Dunn, Brown, & Beardsall, 1991; Dunn, Brown, Slomkowski, Tesla, & Youngblade, 1991; Fivush, 1993; Jenkins, Turrell, Kogushi, Lollis, & Ross, 2003; Laible, 2004a, 2004b; Ontai & Thompson, 2002). There are many elements of elaborated, emotion-related discourse that are likely to provoke young children's emotion understanding, including the adult's descriptive statements, explanations of the causes of emotion or its consequences, linking emotion in another person to the child's experience, asking questions of children that further their understanding of emotion, and coaching children in strategies of emotion management (Ontai & Thompson, 2002). The frequency of mothers' and children's emotion references and, in particular, their talk about the causes of emotion are especially influential for the development of emotion understanding (Brown & Dunn, 1996; Dunn & Brown, 1993; Dunn, Brown, & Beardsall, 1991; see also Dunn, Brown, Slomkowski, et al., 1991), although more research on this issue is necessary. Parents and young children tend to discuss negative emotions more frequently than positive feelings

because the former are conceptually more complex and are also more troubling to the child, and thus there is a stronger inherent need to understand, regulate, and/or prevent intense negative feelings (Lagattuta & Wellman, 2002). Parents also talk about emotions differently with daughters than with sons, using more elaboration, reassurance, and a greater relational focus in their emotion-related conversations with daughters (Fivush, 1998).

Research on the influence of parent-child conversation on the early development of emotion understanding also highlights two other conclusions. First, conversations with adults are not the only important conversational catalysts to emotion understanding. Young children talk about feelings and thoughts more frequently with friends and siblings than they do with their mothers (Brown, Donelan-McCall, & Dunn, 1996), and these conversations also contribute significantly to children's developing understanding of emotion (Hughes & Dunn, 1998). Sibling interactions (especially interaction with an older sibling) offer unique contexts for the growth of emotion understanding, such as in pretend play that permits animated role taking of feelings and coping strategies (Dunn et al., 1991; Youngblade & Dunn, 1995), and sibling conflict that involves negotiating desires and needs with other family members (Dunn & Herrera, 1997; N. Howe, Patrakos, & Rinaldi, 1998). These contexts for emotion conversation among coequals may be even more provocative of developing emotion understanding because young children can be more direct in conveying their own desires and emotions and their reasons for feeling these ways.

Second, by contrast with simple constructivist or socialization models of the development of knowledge, the growth of emotion understanding derives from an interaction of a child's comprehension of psychological realities with the catalysts of the adult's psychological references in shared conversation. Both the child's constructivist effort and the adult's provocation are important, and probably necessary. Young children clearly have powerful inductive capacities for comprehending psychological states in themselves and others, but to assume that children build theories about mental states independently of the scaffolding of child-parent discourse and other relational incentives may overstate either the insightfulness of the child's inductive inferences or the clarity of the observational material on which the young child relies. Considerably more research is needed, however, to understand how these discourse elements interact with the child's conceptual capabilities and other social influences in helping children to develop more sophisticated understanding of the psychological world.

Because of this, an essential future research task is to understand the broader network of relational influences that are associated with differences in parent-child conversational discourse about emotion. It seems likely that individual differences in the richness of adult speech about psychological states would be complemented by other affective dimensions of the parent-child relationships. Securely attached children are more advanced in emotion understanding (Laible & Thompson, 1998; Ontai & Thompson, 2002; Raikes & Thompson, 2005a), for example, and the broader family emotional climate, the adult's emotional expressiveness, and other features of early emotion socialization have important influences on young children's developing emotion understanding (Denham, 1998; Raikes & Thompson, 2005a). The few studies that have assessed the importance of emotional influences in the family in relation to conversational discourse find that each are important to emotion understanding (e.g., Denham et al., 1994). Further study of this question is necessary, however, for understanding how developments in young children's conceptual comprehension of emotion are facilitated by language, elements of the family emotional climate, and their interaction.

Understanding Psychological Characteristics and Social Roles

After age 3, other significant advances occur in young children's understanding of the psychological world. Most notably, children develop a more fully representational view of the mind that incorporates an awareness that beliefs can be inconsistent with reality (Wellman, 2002; Wellman, Cross, & Watson, 2001). Young children's dawning understanding of false belief is significant not only because it reflects an awareness of the potential independence of mental events from objective reality but also because it is a gateway to the comprehension of other psychological realities such as the privacy of personal mental experience, the induction of mistaken beliefs in others, and the mind's activity independent of experience (e.g., interpretations, expectations). For these reasons, there has been a significant research literature exploring the origins of this developmental achievement that is more extensively reviewed in another chapter of this *Handbook*.

Individual differences in children's understanding of false belief are strongly correlated with differences in emotion understanding (Cutting & Dunn, 1999; de Rosnay et al., 2004; Hughes & Dunn, 1998). Both capacities rely on an awareness of the subjectivity of psychological states: People can share the same experience but be psychologically affected in different ways, thus the potential privacy of psychological experience. However, the association between emotion understanding and false belief awareness may also derive from their common association with differences in language ability, family background, or children's experiences in family relationships (Cutting & Dunn, 1999; Ruffman, Slade, Rowlandson, Rumsey, & Garnham, 2003). As with the research on conversational discourse and emotion understanding, for example, many studies have found that children's conversations with parents and peers about mental and emotional themes predict later differences in false belief understanding (Bartsch & Wellman, 1995; Brown et al., 1996; Dunn, Brown, & Beardsall, 1991; Dunn, Brown, Slomkowski, et al., 1991; Hughes & Dunn, 1998; Ruffman, Slade, & Crowe, 2002; Ruffman et al., 2003; Sabbagh & Callanan, 1998; Welch-Ross, 1995; see generally Astington & Baird, 2005). Sabbagh and Callanan (1998) found that when 3- to 5-year-old offspring initiated conversational references to the mind by implicitly contrasting different mental states or saying "I don't know," their parents often responded by highlighting the representational aspects of mental states, which commonly elicited further explicit mental state talk from their children. Other researchers have also found that parents' mental state causal language (Dunn, Brown, Slomkowski, et al., 1991) and explicit mental state discourse are especially important to the development of false belief understanding in children (e.g., Ruffman et al., 2002). A recent training study with 3-year-olds showed that only training conditions involving language improved children's subsequent performance on false belief tasks, and that language conditions involving both perspective-shifting discourse (i.e., discussing mental deception using deceptive objects, such as a pen that looks like a flower) and syntactic prompts (e.g., sentential complements such as "*Peter knows* that Mommy's home") were each independently effective (Lohmann & Tomasello, 2003).

These findings are consistent with the general view that adult discourse about phenomena that interest young children is influential in conceptual growth, especially when the phenomena are otherwise elusive or difficult for children to comprehend. Harris (in press; Harris & Koenig, 2005) has argued that children accept the testimony, or claims, of adults on a wide range of issues of importance to them, from understanding the shape of the earth and other natural phenomena, to the association between mind and brain and other psychological phenomena, to the nature of God, the afterlife, and other metaphysical phenomena. Children early develop understanding of these phenomena based on their acceptance of the truthfulness of what they are told but cannot independently confirm, he argues, and this knowledge is readily integrated into knowledge systems based on personal experience. Young children are not passive recipients of this knowledge, of course, because their inquiries about animals, people's beliefs, or God provoke the conversations that inform them, and as they attempt to juxtapose their current conceptions with what they learn, children's comments, queries, and objections further guide the discussion. Research on the early growth of social and emotional understanding, and of mental states, is consistent with this view.

Recent studies indicate that individual differences in mental state understanding have surprisingly early origins. Wellman, Phillips, Dunphy-Lelii, and LaLonde (2004) reported that 14-month-olds who showed greater sensitivity to intentional human activity in a habituation procedure (see Phillips et al., 2002, and described earlier) were more proficient on a battery of theory of mind tasks at age 4. The source of the continuity over several years was unexplained, but relational influences may be pertinent. Meins and her colleagues (2002) found that 6-month-olds whose mothers commented on their actions in ways that reflected awareness of the baby's intentions, goals, or other psychological states (i.e., "mind-mindedness") were more advanced on false belief assessments at age 4. Ruffman, Perner, and Parkin (1999) noted that preschoolers' false belief understanding was even predicted by mothers' use of disciplinary procedures that involved asking the child to reflect on the victim's feelings. These findings suggest that individual differences in social cognitive development across the early years are related to the quality of early relational experience in ways that merit further study. Thus, the preschooler's inductive reasoning about psychological experiences in others has developmental antecedents from early in life.

The developmental outcomes of these differences in social cognitive competence are potentially important. Dunn, Denham, and their colleagues have found that individual differences in false belief understanding and emotion understanding each predict young children's social competence in friendship with peers in contemporaneous and longitudinal assessments (Brown et al., 1996; Denham et al., 2003; Denham, Caverly, et al., 2002; Dunn, 1995; Dunn, Cutting, & Demetriou, 2000; see also Cutting & Dunn, 2002; Schultz, Izard, & Ackerman, 2000). Understanding the features of parent-child interaction and later conversation that contribute to these differences in psychological understanding—especially in the broader context of the emotional climate of the family—can contribute to a better grasp of the influences that contribute to the growth of interpersonal sensitivity in early childhood.

As with the research on conversation and emotion understanding, the contexts and partners with whom young children share their understandings of the mind are also important. Children commonly discuss their own feelings and mental states in conversations with their mothers, but when talking with peers or siblings *both* children share their views about mutual interests or concerns in positive, cooperative contexts (Brown et al., 1996; Dunn, 1999) or in negotiation or dispute resolution (Howe et al., 1998). False belief understanding was predicted, in one study, by mental state discourse between siblings and friends involving contrastives (i.e., differentiating one person's preferences from another's), activity suggestions involving mental terms (e.g., "*I think* I'm gonna . . ."), and assertions involving mental referents (Brown et al., 1996). In their encounters with peers and siblings, therefore, young children are likely to encounter discrepancies between their own mental states and those of another, and differences between another's descriptions of reality and the reality that the child knows.

Understanding false belief is complemented by other advances in psychological understanding in the late preschool years. By ages 5 and 6, for example, young children begin to perceive others in terms of psychological motives and traits and can predict future behavior on the basis of the traits they infer, including differences in ability (Heyman, Gee, & Giles, 2003; Heyman & Gelman, 1999, 2000; Yuill & Pearson, 1998). They have much to learn about traits as psychological entities, however, and this is revealed in their optimism concerning the controllability and changeability of traits in others that is also reflected in self-perception, as discussed later in this chapter (see Lockhart, Chang, & Story, 2002). By age 3 or 4, as discussed later, young children distinguish behavioral violations that are moral from those that are social conventional, regarding moral violations as more serious due, in part, to their harm to others (Smetana, 1981, 1997; Smetana & Braeges, 1990). In making this distinction, they are tutored by their mothers who justify moral rules because of their interpersonal consequences (Smetana, Kochanska, & Chuang, 2000). Mother-child conversations also contribute to young children's essentialist thinking about gender differences (Gelman, Taylor, & Nguyen, 2004). Finally, older preschoolers also begin to consider fairness issues in relation to ingroup-outgroup relations, particularly associated with gender exclusion, although major advances in their comprehension of social roles and group processes awaits middle childhood (Killen, Pisacane, Lee-Kim, & Ardile-Rey, 2001; Theimer, Killen, & Stanger, 2001).

Summary

At least three conclusions emerge from these literatures that point to future directions in research on early social cognition.

First, social experiences are uniquely generative of new understanding of people and the psychological world. Early infant-caregiver interactions contribute fundamentally to the development of generalized social expectations and specific expectations for the behavior of familiar partners. Emotional exchanges in infant-parent interaction contribute to the multimodal discrimination of emotional signals and later, in the context of social referencing, understanding of the referentiality of emotional cues. Changes in parent-child interaction associated with the growth of self-produced locomotion may help to foster developing perceptions of the intentionality and subjectivity of other people. Comprehension of everyday social events is aided by the organization and structure provided by adult discourse about these events. Emotion understanding is fostered not only by everyday emotional interactions between young children and their caregivers but also by parent-child and peer conversations that embed insight into the psychological world—people's desires, feelings, intentions, and thoughts—into discussions of everyday experiences. The semantics and structure of such conversations also usher young children into a broader appreciation of how mental events can be shared or divergent, beliefs can be accurate or inaccurate, and psychological experience can be hidden or disclosed. As parents naturally treat their offspring as psychological beings from infancy, commenting on their intentions and

feelings, punctuating their activity with nonverbal affirmations of goal achievement, and talking with them about the psychological world they inhabit, they induct the child into the world of the mind through their testimony. Contrary to a long tradition of social cognitive research, social cognition is not only the generalization of intellectual skills that children have independently constructed but also the unique developmental catalysts embedded into the everyday experience of social interaction from early in life.

Second, individual differences in social experience are important for differences in early social understanding. Differences in infants' experience in face-to-face interaction (such as when mothers are depressed) affect how they respond to the social overtures of other partners and may have more generalized influences on social expectations. Differences in early parental sensitivity and "mind-mindedness" during the 1st year may be important for how young children begin to comprehend the nature of others' intentions as they are gradually constructing a theory of mind. Differences in the content, richness, and structure of parent-child conversations are important for individual differences in the growth of emotion understanding, comprehension of false belief, and other elements of psychological understanding that are predictive of important dimensions of socioemotional competence in the preschool years and beyond. Although the tenor of research on developing social cognition (particularly theory of mind) has little attended to individual differences in these developmental processes and their implications, recent research shows how important early social influences are for the emergence of differences in social expectations, dispositions, and beliefs in the early years. Further study along these lines is warranted.

Third, integrating understanding of early social cognitive development from cognitivist perspectives and social viewpoints is important to theories of sociopersonality development, especially those that emphasize the representational dimensions of early relational experience. The developmental account of early psychological understanding is the account on which a theory of the development of "internal working models" derived from early attachments, for example, should be based. More generally, such an integrative approach to further research on early social cognition is likely to contribute added insight to the growth of sociability and the understanding of mind by highlighting how the powerful inductive capacities of the young child's thinking juxtapose with the incentives of social experience to yield conceptions of the psychological world that are rich, informed, and individualized (Dunn, 1996; Harris, 1997, 1999).

RELATIONSHIPS

Young children develop in an environment of relationships.[1] Their experiences over time with people who know them well, and whose characteristics and tendencies children begin to comprehend, are core influences on early conceptual and sociopersonality development (Committee on Integrating the Science of Early Childhood Development, 2000). This theme runs across the literatures surveyed in this chapter and in many other developmental formulations. These include the viewpoints of neo-Vygotskian theorists and other students of cognitive growth, discussed in the previous section, who emphasize relational influences on the construction of early thinking and understanding (e.g., Nelson, 1996; Rogoff, 1990). They include research on parent-infant interaction, parent-child relationships, and inquiry into the influence of sibling relationships, peers, and other social partners discussed elsewhere in this *Handbook* (e.g., Dunn, 1993, 2004). They include the work on social networks and social support that highlights how relationships are developmental catalysts and avenues for enhanced knowledge and information, skill acquisition, and emotional support through their stress buffering, scaffolding of new competencies, social exchange, and other influences from an early age (e.g., Cochran, Larner, Riley, Gunnarsson, & Henderson, 1990; Thompson, 1995; Thompson, Flood, & Goodvin, 2005). Current work in developmental psychopathology also emphasizes the centrality of close relationships to the constellation of risk and protective factors that predict the emergence of child pathology or psychological well-being (Cicchetti & Cohen, 1995; Cicchetti, Toth, & Lynch, 1995). Indeed, it is time for developmental scientists to begin integrating these multifaceted perspectives into a coherent developmental relational science.

Relational processes have been extensively studied in early development. In parent-child interaction, these processes include the caregiver's warmth, sensitivity, and contingent responding, the scaffolding of shared ac-

tivity, the emotional climate of the home, the verbal richness of family interaction, incentives for exploratory competence, expectations for mature behavior, imitative learning, conceptual catalysts in parent-child conversational discourse, parent's flexibility and adaptability, the use of proactive discipline, processes of negotiation and bargaining between parent and child, family routines and rituals, the effects of physical punishment, the child's construals of the adult's behavior, and the dyad's attachment security, shared positive affect, emotional synchrony, and mutual responsiveness (Baumrind, 1973, 1996; Grusec & Goodnow, 1994; Grusec, Goodnow, & Kuczynski, 2000; for general reviews, consult Laible & Thompson, in press; Maccoby & Martin, 1983; see also Parke & Buriel, Chapter 8; Saarni et al., Chapter 5, this *Handbook,* this volume).

The outcomes of these multifaceted relational influences on social and personality development are equally diverse and include the development of social skills, social expectations, emotion regulation, behavioral self-control, relational schemas, self-confidence, trust in others, social and emotional understanding, conscience development, and the enhancement or deterioration of emotional well-being and psychological competence. The relational influences of parents, siblings, child-care providers, peers, teachers, extended kin, and others contribute to these important developmental outcomes.

At the center of this relational network is the parent-child relationship, which is important because its influences are unique, comprehensive, ubiquitous, and potentially enduring. Ever since Freud's (1940) famous dictum that the infant-mother relationship is "unique, without parallel, established unalterably for a whole lifetime as the first and strongest love-object and as the prototype of all later love-relations" (p. 45), developmental theorists have in concert emphasized this relationship as the foundation of personality growth. In now-classic formulations, developmentalists like Baumrind (1978, 1989) and Hoffman (1983, 2000) integrated multiple dimensions of warmth, authority, responsiveness, and demand into parenting patterns that were significantly predictive of the competence and adjustment of offspring. More recent perspectives have emphasized the direct and indirect effects of family members on each other (Belsky, 1981), transactional models of family influences extended over time (Sameroff & Chandler, 1975), the embeddedness of family processes in larger social, cultural, and economic systems (Bronfenbrenner, 1979), and the significance of children's constructions of experience in their interactions with

---

[1] I am indebted to my colleagues on the National Scientific Council on the Developing Child for helping me to develop this concept for the Council's working paper, which can be found at www.developingchild.net.

family members (Grusec & Goodnow, 1994; Rogoff, 1990). Each of these perspectives provides significant continuing catalysts to new thinking about early sociopersonality development in family relationships.

For more than 3 decades, developmental thinking about parent-child relationships has also been guided by attachment theory (Ainsworth, 1973; Bowlby, 1969/1982, 1973, 1980). It is not difficult to account for its influence. Attachment theory explores some of the most compelling questions about early sociopersonality development and its later consequences. How significant are early experiences (especially in intimate relationships) for psychosocial growth? What processes guide continuity and change in personality characteristics throughout life? How are childhood experiences of care linked to later social relatedness? In what ways do early experiences in relationships contribute to psychological vulnerability and strength? Such questions are central to developmental theory, and the creation and validation of the Strange Situation and other assessment procedures has enabled developmental scientists to investigate these questions with growing sophistication and scope. Several decades of research on child-parent attachment have yielded provisional answers to these central questions of developmental theory, and have yielded more questions to ponder.

This section is concerned with theory and research on early parent-child attachment, not because attachment theory is the only important theoretical approach to understanding early relational influences, but because the breadth of its theoretical scope and the body of empirical literature it has produced are uniquely generative of new ideas concerning the impact of early parent-child relationships on sociopersonality development. The continuing vitality of attachment theory will derive, however, from its inclusion of other conceptual and empirical approaches to early relational influences. A number of recent, authoritative reviews of research in attachment (Cassidy & Shaver, 1999; Colin, 1996) reflect the breadth of developmental, personality, and clinical research directions inspired by attachment formulations. The following review focuses on the early development of child-parent attachment and its enduring influence.

Attachment and Its Development

Attachment can be defined as an enduring affectional tie that unites one person to another over time and across space (Ainsworth, 1973). Attachment figures are a source of security that permit confident exploration and

mastery, a safe haven in stress or danger, and who contribute to self-regulation in difficult or anxious circumstances. Sustained separation from the attachment figure is a source of stress and disruption. Parents are typically the first and primary attachment figures for infants, but other reliable, enduring caregivers can also become attachment figures such as grandparents, stepparents, or sometimes child-care providers. In light of typical conditions of infant care in the United States and elsewhere, multiple attachment relationships are normative, although the development of such relationships is based not on the adult's role or responsibilities but rather on the nature of the child's expectations for that person's behavior from past experience. Given the functions of attachment figures in early childhood development, occasional babysitters, older peers, and teachers are unlikely to be attachment figures and, at later ages, close friends and romantic partners may assume attachment-like functions but are not attachment figures in the same sense (compare Ainsworth, 1989 with Hazen & Shaver, 1994).

Attachment theory offers multilevel explanations for why attachments develop in infancy. On a developmental level, attachment emerges from the variety of social cognitive advances that enable infants to develop individualized expectations for the partner's behavior that help to define the affective quality of their relationship. These advances, discussed in the preceding section, include:

- The recognition of the partner's face, voice, and other features
- The growth of expectations for the partner's behavior (especially related to distress relief and pleasure in sociability) that contribute to an affective preference for that person
- A developing awareness of the partner as a person (with subjective, mental states, and an intentional stance toward the infant) with whom a relationship gradually develops

These and other conceptual achievements contribute to the consolidation of initial attachment relationships by the first birthday.

Attachment relationships continue to develop after the first birthday as the child becomes psychologically more sophisticated and can regard the partner and the relationship in more complex ways (Ainsworth, 1990; Crittenden, 2000). In early childhood, for example, young children increasingly rely on mental representations of the partner's characteristics, especially his or her physical and psychological accessibility when children are stressed. Children also acquire, as earlier noted, enhanced capacities for understanding the mental and emotional perspectives of the partner, comprehending and accommodating to the partner's goals and interests, and communicating more effectively their own needs and concerns (Harris, 1997). This development of attachment was described by Bowlby (1969/1982, 1973) as the "goal-corrected partnership." In later years, this partnership becomes more complex, mutual, and dynamic as the children mature psychologically. In middle childhood, children understand relationships to be based on psychological sharing between partners, enduring despite conflict, and children begin to explicitly conceptualize relational processes for the first time while seeking psychological support as well as physical proximity to their attachment figures (Raikes & Thompson, 2005b). They may also begin deriving security from the broader network of family relationships they share as well as specific parent-child relationships (Davies & Cummings, 1994; Davies & Forman, 2002). In adolescence, attachment relationships are transformed by a young person's efforts to clarify and differentiate self from others, reflect on complex abstract realities (such as the nature of human relationships), and develop capacities for emotional reflection and self-regulation (Allen & Land, 1999). Attachment relationships develop, in short, with the child's developing psychological sophistication.

On an ethological or evolutionary level, attachments are believed to have evolved to promote infant survival (and inclusive fitness) by maintaining the protective proximity of adults, especially in conditions of alarm or danger. Seeking physical closeness to a caregiver helped to ensure (in the environment of evolutionary adaptedness) that infants were protected and were not lost or abandoned, and that they would also be nurtured and could learn from the adult behavior they observed until they reached maturity.

Complementary biologically based motivational systems fostering nurturance in adults are also believed to have arisen from this evolutionary legacy (Thompson et al., 2005). But the inclusive fitness considerations of the mother are more complicated than those of the infant because maternal energy, time, and other resources must be divided between the needs of several offspring and the mother herself, including her survival and future reproductive potential. From a biological perspective, maternal solicitude is contingent on many factors, including the number of siblings, environmental resources (e.g., food, social support), the adult's health and age, and the age, health, and other characteristics of the child (Blurton-Jones, 1993; Clutton-Brock, 1991; Hrdy, 1999). In some circumstances, maternal withdrawal or psychological abandonment may be associated with an inability to invest adequate nurturance in offspring. This is consistent with the report of Valenzuela (1990, 1997) that 93% of a sample of chronically undernourished, low-income toddlers were insecurely attached (compared with 50% of a comparison sample of adequately nourished, low-income toddlers) and that their mothers were significantly less sensitive than the mothers of adequately nourished toddlers during observations with the child. It is also consistent, unfortunately, with high rates of infanticide in circumstances and cultures characterized by resource deprivation and other obstacles to adequate early care (Hrdy, 1999). In more typical conditions, there is likely to be greater maternal investment but also significant differences between the mother's willingness to invest in a child (through nurturance and attention) and the child's demands for further investment, such as when weaning conflicts occur (Bateson, 1994; Trivers, 1985). In these circumstances, the mother's insensitivity and rejection are as biologically adaptive for her as are the child's efforts to entice greater nurturance adaptive for the child. Parental solicitude is, in short, a biologically contingent phenomenon, with maternal insensitivity and child-parent conflict not only normative but also biologically adaptive at times in light of the different fitness considerations of each partner.

In addition to developmental and ethological perspectives, Bowlby's (1969/1982, 1973, 1980) theory included two other levels of explanation for the development of attachment relationships that contribute to the conceptual richness of attachment theory. First, he borrowed concepts from cybernetic control systems theory to explain the flexible organization of specific attachment behaviors into a behavioral system characterized by continuous goal-correctedness, hierarchical organization, and the functional interrelations among specific behaviors. Thus, attachment develops as a behavioral system when the child has psychologically matured sufficiently that the functional goals underlying the system (e.g., protective proximity to a caregiver) can organize specific attachment behaviors (e.g., reaching, locomotion to the adult, or crying). This functionalist approach to behavioral organization has been an important contribution to assessing attachment in the Strange Situation and other procedures. Second, Bowlby's developmental theory was also significantly influenced by his psychoanalytic orientation. His concept of the "internal working model" of self and attachment figure, arising from early relational experience and coloring later relationships, is similar to central features of object relations theory. In addition, his formulations concerning unconscious defensive processes in children, the influence of inconsistent mental representations arising from different experiences of care, and the importance of the therapist as an attachment figure all derive from his orientation as a psychoanalytic therapist. These influences contribute to the depth of attachment formulations although, like many concepts deriving from the psychoanalytic tradition, their heuristic power is accompanied by some conceptual ambiguity and difficulty in assessment.

Differences in Attachment Security

Attachment theory is important as a normative theory of the development of early relationships, but the majority of research attention has been devoted to individual differences in the security of attachment and their broader influence. The characterization of these differences in terms of security is consistent with Bowlby's ethological view of the protective functions of attachment relationships, and with Ainsworth's observations of the importance of maternal sensitivity to the infant's emotional well-being. Moreover, the concept of security is also consistent with other well-known characterizations of early psychosocial growth (especially the Eriksonian concept of "basic trust versus mistrust" in infancy) and recasts the meaning of infant behaviors earlier described as "dependent" in a more positive, psychologically constructive light. Although attachment as a species-typical phenomenon has biological origins, individual differences in the security of attachment do not appear to have strong genetic foundations. Three recent studies—two large twin studies of infants (Bokhorst et al., 2003) and preschool children (O'Connor & Croft, 2001) and the third a study of the concordance of foster infants' attachment security with the foster mothers' attachment states of mind (Dozier, Stovall, Albus, & Bates, 2001)—together suggest that nongenetic processes are predominant in the development of secure or insecure attachments. Evidence for the influence of both shared environment (environmental influences that make siblings similar) and nonshared environment (influences that make siblings different) was stronger than evidence for genetic influences in explaining differences in attachment security.

Attachment theory portrays individual differences in the security of attachment as the outcome of variations in maternal sensitivity to the infant during the 1st year. Moreover, differences in attachment security are believed to influence emergent features of social, emotional, and personality development in the years that follow. But in this general formulation there are a number of specific issues related to the interpretation of differences in the security of attachment and their broader significance. The following four receive particular attention here: (1) the concept of security as definitional of the child-parent relationship, (2) the developmental transition from security as relationship specific to security as a personal attribute, (3) the integration of multiple relational experiences into attachment security, and (4) the association between the security of attachment and psychological development.

First, to what extent is the security of attachment definitive of the parent-child relationship? Are there important features of this relationship that are outside the scope of attachment? Bowlby believed that even in infancy attachment is only one of several dimensions of the parent-child relationship and is supplemented by their complementary roles in feeding, play, instruction, and other activities that are guided by other behavioral systems. The parent's skill as a playmate or teacher does not necessarily have consequences for the attachment system. Moreover, there exists a rich literature describing other features of parent-infant relationships that underscore the importance of parental teaching and guidance, the intellectual richness of the home environment, and the adult's sensitivity and responsiveness in fostering the child's conceptual and language development (see Dunn, 1993, and Bornstein, 2002, for reviews). Despite this, few researchers have sought to study the development of parent-child relationships more inclusively, such as by exploring how the emergence of attachment security intersects with other relational influences. This would be a valuable goal in light of recent evidence that the security of attachment moderates the influence on the child of parenting practices such as discipline approach (Kochanska, Aksan, Knaack, & Rhines, 2004) and maternal conversational discourse (Thompson et al., 2003). In addition, understanding the developing dynamics of parent-infant relationships may provide added insight into the origins of attachment security. As earlier described, at the same time that the security of attachment is emerging during the 1st year, the quality of the parent-child relationship is also being influenced by the growth of self-produced locomotion and the conflict of wills that occurs as infants become more agentic and goal directed. How parents manage conflict with the child may be important, along with sensitive responsiveness in other contexts, to the development of security in offspring.

Second, attachment theorists agree that with growing maturity, attachment security becomes increasingly an attribute of the person, rather than of a specific relationship. In infancy and early childhood, we typically think of children as secure or insecure with respect to a specific caregiver; in adolescence and adulthood, we commonly think of secure or insecure persons. But how and why does this developmental transition occur? Investigating this theoretically crucial question is impaired, to some extent, by assessment procedures: Measures of attachment security for older persons have predominantly incorporated the assumption that attachment styles or states of mind are characteristic of the person, and researchers have rarely considered whether adolescents or adults also maintain relationship-specific forms of security or insecurity with particular partners. Yet, when the findings of studies using different procedures for assessing attachment security are compared, there is evidence for *both* security as a relationship-specific quality and security as a personal attribute in studies of children in middle childhood and adolescence (see Raikes & Thompson, 2005b, and contributors to Kerns & Richardson, 2005). This suggests that security as a personal attribute may develop over an extended period as personality development becomes influenced by the representational systems inspired by multiple attachment relationships throughout childhood and youth. But these findings also raise another question. Is it possible that both relationship-specific and person-specific features of attachment security coexist in the attachment-related representational systems that exist in adulthood?

Third, how are multiple attachment relationships developmentally influential (Thompson, 2005)? Attachment theorists agree that in infancy and at later ages, attachments commonly develop with more than one caregiver, and the security of these relationships is independent of the others. How do the expectations arising from multiple attachments become integrated into coherent ways of relating to others, representing relationships, and self-understanding? Do children acquire

multiple, perhaps somewhat inconsistent, representations of self and relationships if their security varies with different attachment partners? Or are these representations integrated or harmonized in some way? Over the years, there have been different ways of responding to this issue. Attachment relationships are believed by some to be hierarchical in influence (with mother-child attachments primary), while others believe that attachment security affects psychosocial growth in a domain-specific fashion (such that maternal attachments influence different aspects of sociopersonality development than do relationships with fathers or child-care providers; see, e.g., Main & Weston, 1981; Oppenheim, Sagi, & Lamb, 1988). At present, however, neither empirical evidence nor theory offers a clarified picture.

Fourth, why should attachment security be related to other features of psychological development? Thoughtful theoretical attention to this question should guide research into the sequelae of early attachment security and enable researchers to interpret expected and unexpected associations between attachment and later behavior. Attachment researchers have been guided, however, by a broad expectation that secure attachment predicts more positive social and personality functioning. Empirically, this has resulted in a large research literature in which attachment has been studied in relation to a dizzying variety of later outcomes, including cognitive and language development; frustration tolerance; self-recognition; behavior problems; relations with peers, friends, and siblings; interactions with unfamiliar adults; exploration and play; competence in preschool and kindergarten classrooms; curiosity; ego resiliency; and math achievement (see Thompson, 1999, and following). As Belsky and Cassidy (1994) asked, one might wonder if there is anything to which attachment security is *not* related.

Why has there been a search for so many diverse sequelae of attachment security? One reason is that attachment theory provides a conceptual umbrella for broad and narrow constructions of the developmental impact of attachment relationships. The most narrow view, and the one that is best supported by empirical evidence, is that security of attachment should predict the child's later trust and confidence in the attachment figure and other close relational partners. Waters, Kondo-Ikemura, Posada, and Richters (1991) have broadened this view with their argument that because attachment security indexes the continuing harmony of the parent-child relationship, a variety of socialization outcomes should result from attachment security related to identification, imitation, learning, cooperation and compliance, and prosocial motivation. A yet broader perspective is that attachment security should foreshadow cognitive competence, exploratory skill, and communication style through its effects on the child's self-confidence, initiative, and other broader personality processes, together with the support afforded by continuing sensitive parenting. Weinfield, Sroufe, Egeland, and Carlson (1999) have further proposed that attachment influences later development as it affects (a) neurodevelopment, (b) affect regulation, (c) behavioral regulation and relational synchrony, and (d) early representations (e.g., the internal working models proposed by Bowlby and discussed later). Although they argue that attachment relationships should be most strongly predictive of sequelaelike psychological adjustment, interpersonal competence, and self-understanding, it is easy to see how a much wider variety of outcomes can be encompassed in the four sources of influence they describe. Adding further complexity is the view (now current in evolutionary biology and behavioral ecology) that different attachment patterns are each evolved behavioral strategies that are adapted to different conditions of environmental resources and parental solicitude (see Chisholm, 1999). Whether attachment patterns predict adaptive or maladaptive later behavior depends, in part, on whether the environmental conditions characterizing early development endure or change over the child's life.

Whether conceptualized in a developmental or evolutionary framework, theoretical clarity concerning the association between attachment security and psychological development is essential. When attachment researchers are unclear or disagree over the hypotheses that can be reasonably derived from the theory, it is difficult to determine whether empirical findings confirm, disconfirm, or do not directly address theoretical claims at all. As a consequence, both convergent and discriminate validities are obscured. Moreover, theoretical precision is necessary to guide expectations for whether the association of attachment with other psychological developments will be strong or weak, direct or mediated, moderated by other variables, or nonexistent. Once expectations are clear, then unexpected relations between attachment security and other variables can be examined more incisively (e.g., by exploring for mediating variables). The need for theoretical clarity is perhaps the most important challenge facing attachment theory and research in the next decade of its development (Thompson & Raikes, 2003). Attempting to bootstrap theory development on the findings of empirical research conceived under the umbrella of many different conceptions of attachment outcomes risks both theoretical obscurantism and holding attachment theory accountable for formulations it should not and perhaps cannot embrace (Sroufe, 1988).

Security of Attachment in the Strange Situation

The Strange Situation has been an empirical and a conceptual anchor for attachment research because of the careful validational work of Ainsworth and her followers (see Ainsworth, Blehar, Waters, & Wall, 1978, for procedural and coding details). By linking detailed longitudinal observations of the secure-base behavior of infants at home with patterns of attachment in the Strange Situation, Ainsworth demonstrated that a straightforward 20-minute laboratory procedure could capture important and reliable dimensions of relational security in infancy. As evidence accumulated for the moderate stability and predictive validity of attachment classifications derived from the Strange Situation, a large body of research was generated to explore the origins, correlates, and sequelae of individual differences in attachment using this procedure. To be sure, the reliance on a single attachment assessment had disadvantages: The identity of the security of attachment construct with Strange Situation behavior made it impossible to examine how prior experiences might affect Strange Situation behavior independently of attachment security (Lamb, Thompson, Gardner, & Charnov, 1985). But the reliance on a single procedure also enabled researchers to integrate a wide variety of research findings because each used the same assessment. The Strange Situation has also had broader significance for attachment research. Attachment assessments for older children and adults are often validated by showing that they yield classifications that are longitudinally consistent with earlier Strange Situation classifications, and attachment researchers still rely on adaptations of the threefold (later fourfold) Strange Situation classification categories when they are studying attachment in older children, adolescents, or adults.

The strategy of the Strange Situation is to create conditions of moderately escalating stress to activate the attachment behavioral system of 1-year-olds. Based on the infant's behavior throughout the procedure, but especially during reunions with the partner after brief separation episodes, an attachment classification is assigned. Infants who are considered securely attached (Group B) organize their behavior around the caregiver as a secure base throughout the procedure and show fairly unequivocal pleasure at the adult's return. Infants who are insecure-avoidant (Group A) show relatively little secure-base behavior and exhibit avoidance of the partner during reunions either by failing to greet or delaying in greeting the adult. Infants who are insecure-resistant (Group C) also show little secure-base behavior during preseparation episodes (during which they remain preoccupied with the adult) and mingle their efforts to achieve proximity to the caregiver during reunions with angry resistance. Although these dual insecure groups are different in their behavioral characteristics, understanding the distinctive origins and sequelae of these groups has been hindered by the long-standing tendency of researchers to combine avoidant and resistant classifications in their analysis, together with the enlistment of sample sizes that are too small to permit reliable comparisons between these groups.

Although these three groups constituted the extent of the classification options for Strange Situation research for many years, a new insecure classification category emerged in the late 1980s as the result of difficulties in appropriately characterizing the attachment behavior of certain infants, especially those in at-risk conditions. Main and Solomon (1986, 1990) created the classification of disorganized/disoriented (Group D) to describe infants who, for a time, appear to *lack* an organized, coherent strategy for interacting with the caregiver in the Strange Situation. This can be manifested in many ways, most notably in contradictory behavior (e.g., strong avoidance combined with strong contact-seeking), but also in undirected, incomplete, or interrupted movements, inexplicable freezing or stilling, stereotyped or other anomalous postures, apparent fear of the adult, and other indications of disorganization or disorientation. These behaviors can be fleeting and initially difficult to detect, although with training and experience reliable assignment of the D classification can be accomplished. In a sense, infants in the D classification are distinct from those in both the secure classification (group B)—because infants are distinctly insecure—and from the two insecure (groups A and C) classifications, because infants are disorganized rather than exhibiting an organized (albeit insecure) behavioral strategy. Even so, classification as D is often accompanied by a secondary assignment to one of the three organized attachment groups reflecting a "best fitting" alternative classification. Although the D classification originated in efforts to describe the attachment behavior

of infants who had been maltreated, were growing up in difficult family conditions, or were otherwise at risk for later problems, infants in the disorganized/disoriented group are often found in nonclinical middle-class samples, although in widely varying rates, with one meta-analytic estimate that 15% of the infants from middle-class samples are classified in the D group (van Ijzendoorn, Schuengel, & Bakermans-Kranenberg, 1999). By contrast, roughly 25% of the infants in lower-income samples are in the D group, with much higher proportions in some clinical samples. In low-risk, middle-class samples the secondary classification for D-group infants is predominantly secure, while in higher-risk samples the secondary classification is more commonly insecure (Lyons-Ruth & Jacobvitz, 1999; Lyons-Ruth, Repacholi, McLeod, & Silva, 1991).

Why do infants become disorganized or disoriented in the Strange Situation? In a return to Bowlby's clinical interests in the enduring effects of early trauma, Main and her colleagues (Main & Hesse, 1990; Main & Solomon, 1990) have argued that infant disorganization develops in response to the frightening or frightened behavior of the caregiver, which can occur when the adult has an unresolved personal history of traumatic or frightening experiences, especially when memories of these experiences are evoked by current circumstances (e.g., domestic violence). When caregivers act this way, it puts the infant in the terrible paradox of fearing the person from whom they must also find comfort in stress, and disorganized behavior can be the result. In support of this view, the incidence of infant disorganized attachment is much higher in samples characterized by sociodemographic risk, especially child maltreatment (in which the parent necessarily acts in a frightening manner). However, parental depression or marital discord is not necessarily associated with increased frequency of infant disorganization, suggesting that the conditions of family risk that are most generative of the D classification are those that most directly imperil infant-parent relationships and the child's emotional well-being (e.g., Barnett, Ganiban, & Cicchetti, 1999; Carlson, 1998; see Lyons-Ruth & Jacobvitz, 1999, and van Ijzendoorn et al., 1999 for reviews). There is also a significant association between parental classification as "unresolved/disorganized" in the Adult Attachment Interview and infant disorganized/disoriented attachment, which is important because of the belief that this adult state of mind reflects continued difficulty over past experiences of trauma or loss

(Hesse, 1999; van Ijzendoorn, 1995).[2] The more important question, however, is whether the parent's stresses and attachment state of mind are manifested in frightening or frightened conduct in the presence of the infant. The few studies that have directly addressed this question have revealed a modest but inconsistent association between maternal frightening behavior and attachment disorganization in infants, often depending on the form of disorganization the infant exhibits (Lyons-Ruth, Bronfman, & Parsons, 1999; Schuengel, Bakermans-Kranenburg, & van Ijzendoorn, 1999). This suggests that further research is necessary to fully elucidate the origins of infant disorganized/disoriented attachment in the infant-caregiver relationship.

The D classification in infancy is distinguished from the other attachment classifications because it is not an organized strategy. But surprisingly, when attachment security is assessed in separation-reunion procedures in preschoolers, the manifestations of disorganization for most children appear to be highly organized in the form of controlling strategies for managing and regulating mother-child interaction (Moss, Bureau, Cyr, Mongeau, & St.-Laurent, 2004; Teti, 1999). A variety of controlling (group D) subgroups in preschoolers, including controlling-caregiving and controlling-punitive strategies, reflect different behavioral and affective approaches to the caregiver. Because these categories for classifying disorganization in preschoolers were derived

inductively from two small longitudinal follow-up studies of infants earlier deemed disorganized/disoriented (Main & Cassidy, 1988, $N = 12$; Wartner, Grossmann, Fremmer-Bombik, & Suess, 1994, $N = 13$), there is no clear theoretical explanation for why children who are so distinctly *dis*organized in infancy should become preschoolers who are so organized that they seek to control the caregiver's behavior. The extent to which this reflects sequelae of disorganized attachment, changes in parent-child interaction, psychological development in the child, or the influence of other variables is still being explored. This developmental transition remains an empirical and conceptual challenge for attachment theory and research and, together with the need for a better understanding of the origins of infant disorganization, suggests the urgent need for further prospective longitudinal research on these issues.

Taken together, in typical, nonclinical middle-class samples, approximately 62% of infants are deemed secure, 15% avoidant, 9 to 10% resistant, and the remaining 15% disorganized. The proportion of insecure and disorganized groups is larger in lower-income samples, clinical groups, and families at sociodemographic risk (van Ijzendoorn et al., 1999). Multiple classification subgroups associated with each category reflect considerable variation on each classification theme, but little research has been devoted to understanding these differences. There have also been challenges to the suitability of the Strange Situation as an attachment assessment for infants with distinct experiential backgrounds, such as those with substantial experience in child care, which highlight the importance of understanding the backgrounds of infants in the Strange Situation when interpreting their responses to the separation episodes and encounters with a stranger (Clarke-Stewart, Goossens, & Alhusen, 2001).

Attachment researchers have long recognized the analytic limitations of a categorical outcome measure like attachment classification and, over the years, have proposed modifications or adaptations of the classification system to permit continuous scores (e.g., Gardner, Lamb, Thompson, & Sagi, 1986; M. Lamb et al., 1985; Richters, Waters, & Vaughn, 1988) or dimensional approaches to assessing attachment security (e.g., Waters & Deane, 1985). More recently, Fraley and Spiker (2003) have proposed that attachments are fundamentally ordered along two continua (proximity-seeking versus avoidance and high versus low anger/resistance) and have urged attachment researchers to use

---

[2] Although findings such as these are commonly interpreted as supporting the predictive validity of the Adult Attachment Interview (AAI), they should be interpreted cautiously because the AAI was developed explicitly to predict infant attachment classifications. The AAI was developed from a sample of interview responses of parents for whom the attachment classifications of their infant offspring from Strange Situation assessments conducted several years earlier were known (Hesse, 1999). The AAI coding and classification system were developed by searching for commonalities in the interview responses of parents whose infants shared the same attachment classification. This helps to explain why AAI classifications so closely parallel infant Strange Situation classifications and why many researchers have reported a correspondence between parental AAI groups and their infants' Strange Situation classifications. Predicting infant attachment status was what the AAI was originally created to accomplish. But documentation of the predictive validity of the AAI in this manner is not the same thing as if the adult attachment assessment had been developed completely independently of knowledge of the attachment security of offspring.

a dimensional rather than a taxonomic approach to studying differences in attachment security. Although the use of multiple continua can have important advantages in attachment research, the Fraley and Spieker analysis is limited because they excluded infants in the D classification, rendering their conclusions of limited applicability in light of growing interest in infant disorganization. More generally, a dimensional strategy would require far more than two continua to capture the richness of the organizational approach to attachment assessment and its sequelae, and it requires further research to determine whether a dimensional approach can do so without undermining many of the other advantages of this approach.

Other Behavioral Assessments of Attachment Security

As children mature, attachment assessments must also change to accommodate the child's developing behavioral sophistication. Two other behavioral assessments of attachment security have been developed for preschoolers (representational assessments are discussed later in the section on internal working models). Each has presented attachment researchers with the challenge of mapping heterotypic continuity in attachment security: How can age-appropriate manifestations of a secure attachment be identified that capture the same attachment construct as is assessed in the infant Strange Situation (see Solomon & George, 1999)?

One approach is the Cassidy and Marvin (1992) procedure for preschoolers (i.e., 3- to 5-year-olds), based on an earlier approach by Main and Cassidy (1988) for 6-year-olds, which focuses on reunions with the parent after one or more separations. Preschool attachment classification categories closely parallel those of the Strange Situation. A similar separation-reunion procedure by Crittenden (1992, 1994; see also Crittenden, 2000) uses somewhat different classification categories for older children, including secure, insecure-defended, insecure-coercive, and other insecure groups. Each approach borrows the strategy of the Strange Situation that preschoolers' attachment organization is activated by the stress of separations from the caregiver, and sometimes separation episodes are lengthened to better ensure that this occurs for older children. Although they are similar, the two approaches differ from each other, and from the Strange Situation coding procedures, in how secure behavior is

indexed. The Cassidy-Marvin procedure focuses on body position, affect, speech, gaze, and physical proximity and contact, whereas Crittenden's classification procedure also encompasses affect regulation and open communication with the parent. The Cassidy-Marvin procedure is widely used, and individual differences in security assessed in this procedure are modestly but reliably associated with prior measures of maternal sensitivity and responsiveness and are also modestly associated with infant Strange Situation classifications[3] (Barnett, Kidwell, & Leung, 1998; Moss, Bureau, Cyr, Mongeau, & St.-Laurent, 2004; Moss, Cyr, Bureau, Tarabuley, & Dubois-Comtois, 2004; National Institute of Child Health and Human Development Early Child Care Research Network, 2001; Stevenson-Hinde & Shouldice, 1995). But by contrast with their careful attention to the standardized use of the Strange Situation with infants, attachment researchers have tended to modify the procedure and scoring conventions of the Cassidy-Marvin procedure in different studies, sometimes using the Strange Situation, sometimes extending the separation episodes and eliminating episodes with the stranger, and sometimes including other assessments in the midst of the procedure (e.g., Moss, Bureau, Cyr, Mongeau, & St.-Laurent, 2004; National Institute of Child Health and Human Development Early Child Care Research Network, 2001; Stevenson-Hinde & Shouldice, 1995). This

---

[3] It is important to note that the classification of preschool attachment behavior in the Cassidy and Marvin (1992) and Main and Cassidy (1988) assessments is based on procedures created explicitly to identify early childhood correlates of infant attachment classifications. In a procedure resembling the development of the Adult Attachment Interview, Main and Cassidy (1988) created the preschool attachment categories in an iterative process involving samples of young children for whom their attachment classifications in infancy were known throughout measurement development. By searching for commonalities in the preschool separation-reunion behavior of children who, as infants, shared the same attachment classification, the close parallel between infant Strange Situation and preschool attachment classifications was ensured. However, this approach makes the consistency between infant and preschool classifications less impressive than if preschool classifications had been derived independently, and because it is based on inductive rather than deductive procedures, this approach to measurement development also creates theoretical challenges (e.g., explaining why infants who are deemed disorganized become highly strategic, controlling preschoolers).

makes it difficult to know how comparable the findings are from the different variations of the procedure and how far the validity evidence can extend to significant alterations of the Strange Situation.

A different strategy for assessing attachment security in preschoolers is the Attachment Q-Sort (AQS; Waters & Deane, 1985). Based on extensive home observations, a well-trained observer or the mother sorts 90 descriptive statements into nine groups based on how accurately each statement describes the child. This distribution is then correlated with a criterion sort to yield a correlation coefficient that is the child's security score. The AQS seeks to describe secure base behavior at home rather than provoking attachment behavior in the laboratory, based on an effort to directly assess the secure base behavior that is, to some attachment theorists, the gold standard of any attachment assessment (Waters & Cummings, 2000). Consequently, children are observed under a variety of conditions, but inevitably less often in circumstances that deliberately heighten the activation of attachment behavior. The criteria for secure attachment are thus broader than for Strange Situation-based procedures. In addition to secure base behavior, for example, items that are high in the security criterion sort include:

- "Child follows mother's suggestions readily, even when they are clearly suggestions rather than orders."
- "Child uses mother's facial expressions as a good source of information when something looks risky or threatening."
- "Child recognizes when mother is upset. Becomes quiet or upset himself. Tries to comfort her."
- "Child is strongly attracted to new activities and new toys."

By incorporating into the security criterion sort many of the hypothesized correlates of attachment security (such as the child's obedience, social referencing, empathy, and exploratory interest) the AQS enlists a much broader operationalization of attachment security that is perhaps better suited to a home observational measure, in contrast with the more narrow focus on secure base behavior of the laboratory separation-reunion procedures. The AQS is also an assessment of security alone; there are no consistent procedures for distinguishing secure from insecure attachments on the continuous security score, nor does the procedure yield differentiated forms of insecurity such as those provided by assessments based on the Strange Situation.

The AQS is suitable for use with children from 1 to 5 years of age.

A meta-analysis of research using the AQS by van Ijzendoorn, Vereijken, Bakermans-Kranenburg, and Riksen-Walraven (2004) showed that the average security score for nonclinical samples was .32, with an average score of .21 in clinical samples. With a theoretical range of security scores (like correlation coefficients) from −1.00 to +1.00, this is consistent with Strange Situation evidence that most infants are secure, but that there is variability in security. They also reported that AQS security scores were moderately associated with security assessed in the Strange Situation (combined effect size .23) and with measures of maternal sensitivity (effect size .31), but were also negatively associated with assessments of temperamental reactivity (effect size .27), conclusions that are consistent with narrative reviews of this literature (e.g., Thompson, 1998). These findings were consistent for security scores derived from observers and from maternal report, although van Ijzendoorn and his colleagues (2004) concluded that research findings better support the validity of observer sorts. Their conclusion is consistent with the greater likelihood of report bias from mothers, but Teti and Mc-Gourty (1996) have delineated procedures designed to minimize this influence, and maternal sorts may be more valid with the training and supervision they suggest (the meta-analysis did not distinguish maternal-report studies employing the Teti and McGourty procedures from those that did not).

Do these behavioral assessments capture the same attachment construct that is assessed in the infant Strange Situation procedure? The careful design of these measures, their predicted associations with differences in maternal sensitivity, and their modest associations with infant Strange Situation classifications each suggest that their shared variance indexes a consistent attachment construct. However, differences in external correlates (such as temperament), operationalizations of security, and measurement strategy each indicate that these assessments capture significant sources of independent variance as well. This is perhaps inevitable in light of the challenges of mapping heterotypic continuity in behavior during a period of rapid developmental change. But this means that attachment theorists are wise to be cautious in generalizing findings across research studies using different measures of the security of attachment. As one illustration, a recent report from the National Institute of Child Health and Human Development (NICHD) Study of Early Child Care found different associations between mother- and caregiver-reported child behavior problems at age 3 and attachment assessments at 15 months (using the Strange Situation), 24 months (using the AQS), and 36 months (using the Cassidy-Marvin procedure), and there was very modest consistency in security and disorganization scores derived from these attachment assessments at each age (McCartney, Owen, Booth, Clarke-Stewart, & Vandell, 2004). As we shall see, the interpretive cautions of generalizing across attachment assessments are also required when generalizing to representational measures of attachment in early childhood and later years.

Origins of Attachment Security

To attachment theorists, the caregiver's sensitivity to the infant is the adult's core contribution to the development of a secure attachment. Sensitivity is a broad conceptual rubric for the quality of adult caregiving that has diverse consequences for offspring, and it can have different meanings in different theoretical traditions. In Vygotskian theory, for example, sensitivity entails the careful scaffolding of shared activity to foster conceptual growth within the child's readiness for new challenges (Rogoff, 1990), while a learning theorist would emphasize the construction of environmental contingencies that foster adaptive behavior. To attachment theorists, sensitivity consists of a constellation of response attributes that includes attention to the infant's signals, accurate interpretation of their meaning, and appropriate and prompt responsiveness to promote the infant's trust in the caregiver (Ainsworth, 1973; Ainsworth et al., 1978). Empirically, sensitivity tends to be operationalized in ways that also include caregiver warmth, cooperation, interactional synchrony, and other related processes (Belsky, 1999; De Wolff & van Ijzendoorn, 1997; Thompson, 1998). Bowlby himself characterized sensitivity as "respect for the child."

A 1997 meta-analysis by De Wolff and van Ijzendoorn on the association between maternal sensitivity and infant attachment security concluded that there is a modest but reliable association (combined effect size .22) between sensitivity and security (De Wolff & van Ijzendoorn, 1997), which is consistent with the results of several other reviews of this literature (Belsky, 1999; Thompson, 1998) and with findings from the large, longitudinal NICHD Study of Early Child Care (NICHD Early Child Care Research Network, 1997, 2001). This is true whether the infant Strange Situation, the AQS,

or the Cassidy-Marvin procedure is used to assess attachment. Paternal sensitivity is also reliably associated with security of attachment, but more weakly than for mothers (van Ijzendoorn & De Wolff, 1997), and sensitivity is also a predictor of security with nonparental caregivers (Howes, 1999). A meta-analytic review of the results of intervention studies designed to improve maternal sensitivity concluded that carefully designed interventions could be effective in increasing sensitive responsiveness, especially when they were relatively short, behaviorally focused programs. Moreover, these interventions also had a small but significant effect in enhancing the security of attachment, supporting the causal role of maternal sensitivity in fostering attachment security (Bakermans-Kranenburg, van Ijzendoorn, & Juffer, 2003). Parental sensitivity is an important and reliable but modest predictor of the security of attachment.

De Wolff and van Ijzendoorn (1997) concluded that other dimensions of parenting are also important in fostering security, and suggested that researchers look to the contexts of parent-child interaction for clues about these influences. Attachment researchers have responded to their suggestion. Not surprisingly, they have found that the caregiver's psychological attributes are predictive of attachment security. In the NICHD Study of Early Child Care, for example, the mothers of securely attached infants were higher than mothers of insecure infants on a composite of measures of psychological adjustment that indexed depression, neuroticism, and anxiety (each reverse scored), sociability, extraversion, and other variables (NICHD Early Child Care Research Network, 1997). Attachment researchers have also explored other psychological resources of the mother that might foster secure attachment. Meins has reported that maternal "mind-mindedness," which describes mothers' tendencies to impute mental and psychological states to their infant offspring, is associated with sensitive responding and predicts attachment security in 1-year-olds (Meins et al., 2001, 2003). In a similar vein, Oppenheim and his colleagues explored differences in maternal "insightfulness" into the infant's internal experiences and motives and found that mothers deemed positively insightful were rated as more sensitive during mother-infant play sessions, and their offspring were more likely to be securely attached in the Strange Situation (Koren-Karie, Oppenheim, Dolev, Sher, & Etzion-Carasso, 2002; Oppenheim & Koren-Karie, 2002). Both mind-mindedness and insightfulness assessments explained variance in infant security beyond the effects of maternal sensitivity.

Such studies are helpful in bridging the "transmission gap" highlighted by van Ijzendoorn (1995) in his meta-analytic review of studies associating adult attachment representations, parental responsiveness, and infant attachment security. His review focused on the adult representations of early childhood care, including recollections of feeling loved and secure and perceptions of the feelings and motives of caregivers, which are characterized as attachment "states of mind" and are assessed in the Adult Attachment Interview (see Hesse, 1999, for a review of this literature). Reviewing an extensive body of research, van Ijzendoorn (1995) concluded that these adult attachment representations are significantly associated with independent measures of parental responsiveness (combined effect size .34), with adults in the autonomous (secure) group responding more sensitively to their offspring than adults in the insecure, preoccupied, and dismissing groups. Furthermore, adult attachment representations are also strongly associated with the attachment classifications of infant offspring in the Strange Situation, even when adult attachment was assessed prenatally (combined effect sizes .31 to .48). Autonomous adults tend to have children who are securely attached, and adults in the preoccupied and dismissing groups have offspring who are more likely to be insecure.[4] Thus, one important contribution to the security of attachment are caregivers' personal representations of the care they received as young children and its influence on the sensitivity of care they provide to their own offspring. As van Ijzendoorn (1995) pointed out, however, a substantial proportion of the association between adult attachment representations and infant attachment security is *not* explained by differences in parental sensitivity, and he suggested that this "transmission gap" warranted further exploration by attachment researchers. What other influences do adult attachment representations have on the development of security in offspring that are not mediated by sensitive care? Studies of maternal mind-mindedness and insightfulness may provide one response to this question (see Meins, 1999).

Beyond the mother-infant dyad, the amount and quality of child care has not been found to be a significant influence on the security of infant-mother attachment, according to the NICHD Study of Early Child Care, al-

though there was some evidence that when maternal sensitivity was low, greater amounts of child care and/or poorer quality care increased the risk of insecure attachment (NICHD Early Child Care Research Network, 1997, 2001). In other cultural settings where the quality of child care is very poor, there is evidence that child care can have a directly adverse impact on infant-mother attachment as well as interacting with maternal insensitivity (Sagi, Koren-Karie, Gini, Ziv, & Joels, 2002).

The quality of the marital relationship has also been found to predict attachment security in several studies, with mothers who report greater marital satisfaction and harmony having infants with more secure attachments, although this association is not found consistently across the research literature (e.g., Belsky & Isabella, 1988; Howes & Markman, 1989; Owen & Cox, 1997; see Belsky, 1999). Marital conflict is likely to have direct and indirect implications for the security of attachment. Maritally conflicted couples may have greater difficulty maintaining sensitivity to infant signals and needs in the midst of their own emotional turmoil. Owen and Cox (1997) also found that marital conflict and sensitive responding each made independent contributions to attachment security, such that conflict was negatively related to attachment security even among young children whose mothers or fathers remained sensitive when interacting with them. The negative emotional climate of the home may be one influence that can account for the impact of marital conflict independently of parental sensitivity: Young children may be made anxious by parental arguing and conflict even when each parent is a sensitive caregiver.

This conclusion is consistent with Cummings and Davies' (1994; Davies & Cummings, 1994) portrayal of how young children's security is affected not just by their relationships with each parent but also by their emotional experience in the family system as a whole. Their "emotional security hypothesis" argues that marital conflict can threaten young children's security in the family and can provoke distress, motivate children's efforts to regulate conflict, and instill hostile representations of family life—qualities that resemble insecure attachment (see Davies & Forman, 2002; Davies, Harold, Goeke-Morey, & Cummings, 2002). Security may, in short, be a function not just of the child-parent relationship but of children's experience of the broader family emotional climate. Understanding the direct and indirect influences of the family environment, especially as it is affected by marital conflict, domestic violence, and

---

[4] See note 2, p. 49.

other negative family experiences, is particularly significant in light of the relatively weak association between measures of parental sensitivity and infant disorganized attachment (van Ijzendoorn et al., 1999). Family influences that are related to angry and frightening parental conduct may, independently of sensitivity, be important to the genesis of infant disorganization and possibly also other forms of attachment insecurity.

Insecure attachment is more frequent in lower-income and socioeconomically stressed samples owing, in part, to the greater incidence of stresses within and around the family that can affect parental sensitivity and the security of attachment (Barnett et al., 1999; van Ijzendoorn et al., 1999; Vondra, Shaw, Swearingen, Cohen, & Owens, 2001). Furthermore, De Wolff and van Ijzendoorn (1997) noted in their meta-analysis that the socioeconomic status of the family is also a significant moderator of the influence of sensitivity on attachment. Thus, there is a weaker association between maternal sensitivity and attachment security in lower-income than middle-income families. A study by Raikes and Thompson (2004c) explored this further by showing, in a sample of low-income Early Head Start families, that while the impact of economic risks (associated with poverty) on attachment security was mediated by its effects on maternal responsiveness, the effects of emotional risks (such as domestic violence, alcohol or drug abuse) had direct effects on the security of attachment that were unmediated by maternal behavior. These risk factors, which altered the broader emotional climate of the family, were associated with lower attachment security independently of variations in maternal sensitivity. Emotional risk factors also moderated the association between maternal behavior and child security such that material responsiveness was less strongly associated with attachment security in families with many emotional risks. In short, in homes with many stresses and risk factors, sensitive responsiveness is less likely to shape the security of attachment and the difficulties of family life are likely to have a greater direct impact on the child's sense of security. Further research of this kind, especially research that distinguishes different kinds of risk, is essential to understand better the effects of family stresses and buffers on the security of attachment in socioeconomically stressed and middle-income families as a way of better comprehending the influences on attachment beyond parental sensitivity.

Taken together, the literature on the origins of attachment security not only highlights new directions for

further research but also compels a reconceptualization of the nature of parental sensitivity in a manner that is consistent with De Wolff and van Ijzendoorn's (1997) call for attention to context. Attachment researchers have tended to portray differences in sensitivity as characterological and traitlike, deriving from the enduring legacy of childhood experiences captured in the Adult Attachment Interview. But contemporary approaches to parenting also emphasize the situationally adaptive, flexible nature of caregiving (Grusec & Goodnow, 1994; Grusec et al., 2000; Kuczynski, Marshall, & Schell, 1997). Parents approach their children with consistent values and goals, but their parenting is also affected by the child's immediate behavior, situational and long-term goals, the constraints of the circumstances, and the behavior of other people (such as a spouse or sibling). Their parenting is adapted to characteristics of the child but also of the family, marital relationship, and circumstances as well as the parent's relational history. Such a view is consistent with the conclusions of a meta-analysis by Holden and Miller (1999) on the stability of parenting across time, children, and situations. They found that although child-rearing practices are fairly consistent across different children and over time, parents are much less consistent in their behavior across situations, and they suggested that developmentalists must increasingly view parenting practices as both enduring (rooted in adult values, goals, and beliefs concerning child care) and different (adapting to situational demands and children's immediate needs). The same is likely to be true of the variations in parental sensitivity that contribute to attachment security.

Viewed in this light, variations in parental sensitivity may not be uniformly influential on attachment security, but rather in particular contexts and circumstances relevant to developing security. For example, sensitivity may be an important influence when it is exhibited in the contexts most relevant to attachment—when the child is distressed or alarmed—than during nonstressful episodes of play, teaching, or feeding (Thompson, 1997). The sensitivity with which caregivers manage conflicts of will with their offspring may also be important in light of the growth of parent-child limit testing when children become locomotor, as earlier noted. Sensitivity may be influential in relationships when the parent can be a reliable, protective haven of support, in contrast to conditions in which marital conflict, neighborhood violence, or poor child care impose emotional threats that a sensitive parent cannot buffer. Moreover, sensitivity may be especially influential when sensitive care is maintained over time as a continuing source of emotional support for adaptive functioning (Belsky & Pasco Fearon, 2002a, 2002b). In these situations, sensitivity is developmentally important because the conditions of care make sensitivity more salient to the infant.

This suggests that the baby's construal of the adult's responsiveness is also an important part of the context influencing the impact of sensitive care on developing attachment security. As Watson (1979) noted, the contingency perception that forms the basis for an awareness of sensitive responding is affected by the base rates of both the child's behavior and the adult's response: Infants who are temperamentally fussy may, for example, have a more difficult time detecting a caregiver's responsiveness to their cries than infants who are temperamentally more pacific (Thompson, 1986). But research on the association between infant temperament and attachment security has yielded a fairly consistent conclusion in studies using the Strange Situation procedure: There is not a reliable, direct association between temperament and attachment security (see Thompson, 1998, and Vaughn & Bost, 1999 for reviews). There is also no reliable association between temperament and the infant disorganized/disoriented classification (van Ijzendoorn et al., 1999). However, research using the Attachment Q-Sort has shown that infants who are temperamentally more negatively reactive and difficult are likely have low security scores (van Ijzendoorn et al., 2004; Vaughn & Bost, 1999), which probably arises from the manner in which attachment security is operationalized in the AQS. Taken together, the research literature does not support the view that attachment security derives from antecedent differences in infant temperament.

This desirably straightforward conclusion is, in some senses, unfortunate because it has caused researchers to fail to explore further a number of indirect associations between temperament and attachment (see Thompson, Connell, & Bridges, 1988). Mangelsdorf, Gunnar, Kestenbaum, Lang, and Andreas (1990) reported that patterns of maternal care had different consequences for the development of security when infants who were high or low in temperamental proneness-to-distress were distinguished. Nachmias, Gunnar, Mangelsdorf, Parritz, and Buss (1996) reported that toddlers who are behaviorally inhibited may especially benefit from a secure attachment relationship when coping with stressful challenges. Taken together, these findings suggest that temperament may interact with maternal caregiving in the

development of attachment security and in the sequelae of attachment in ways that merit further exploration.

Finally, an important influence on the development of attachment security is culture. Cultural practices influence normative conditions of early childhood care, and cultural beliefs and values shape the characteristics that parents value and seek to foster in offspring. Theory and research on attachment has, from the beginning, grown within the conceptual tension of recognizing the importance of culture to the development of attachment while also appreciating the evolutionarily adaptive, species-typical process shaping attachment in humans and other animals. Understanding attachment as a universal developmental phenomenon shaped by cultural influences continues to be one way that research on attachment remains sensitive to context.

This conceptual tension was initially manifested in efforts by researchers in several Western and non-Western nations to use the Strange Situation to determine whether infants in their societies exhibited the same patterns of security and insecurity that were initially identified in the United States. The findings of this research literature, including studies in Israel, Japan, China, Africa, Chile, Sweden, Great Britain, and the Netherlands, yielded several conclusions (see Thompson, 1998, and van Ijzendoorn & Sagi, 1999, for reviews). First, when the Strange Situation is used inappropriately (e.g., allowing separation episodes to endure despite heightened infant distress) or inconsistently with normative child-rearing practices, infant behavior in the procedure does not necessarily reflect attachment security. Infants living on Israeli kibbutzim who rarely encountered strangers and children in Japanese homes who had rarely been separated from their mothers responded with unusual distress in the Strange Situation because the procedure entailed experiences with strangers and separation that were more atypical for their background than for infants living in the United States. This is important because the Strange Situation was designed to be a *moderately* stressful assessment based on the experiences of typically developing children in the United States, and when the procedure is highly stressful it is unlikely to yield a valid assessment of attachment security. These findings underscore the significance of ensuring that assessments of attachment are based on a thoughtful appreciation of the typical conditions of early childhood care for the samples under study.

Second, especially when these considerations are taken into account, studies from a wide variety of nationalities indicate that infants develop attachments to their parents and other caregivers. Moreover, with a few exceptions (e.g., Grossmann, Grossmann, Huber, & Wartner, 1981), the most common attachment classification in nonstressed, nonclinical samples is secure. Attachment is indeed a universal phenomenon and, although infants may manifest security through distal, proximal, or contact-seeking behaviors, most infants appear to be securely attached. Furthermore, researchers who examined parental perceptions of desirable child behavior found that in most countries, parents endorse a profile of behavior that is consistent with that of securely attached children, although parents from different countries often differ in their reasons for this preference, their preferred manifestations of security, and their evaluations of various patterns of insecurity (Harwood, Miller, & Irizarry, 1995; Posada et al., 1995). It appears that secure attachment is both broadly desirable and normative. Third, when multiple studies were conducted within a single national group (such as in Japan, Israel, Germany, and the United States), they indicated that there is often considerable variability in patterns of attachment *within* nationalities. This within-national variability suggests that cultures are not homogeneous in how they influence the development of attachment security, and the values and practices shared within any nationality are significantly adapted to local conditions (e.g., rural versus urban, kibbutz versus city, or middle-income versus lower-income).

Finally, cultural research on the security of attachment indicates that there is somewhat less consistency across national samples in how the quality of care contributes to attachment security, and in the outcomes of a secure or insecure attachment (Thompson, 1998; van Ijzendoorn & Sagi, 1999). These are the ways in which cultural differences in child care and values concerning children are most likely to be influential. None of a battery of measures of parental attitudes and behavior and parent-child interaction obtained throughout the 1st year succeeded, for example, in discriminating infants who were securely attached from insecure in Sweden (M. Lamb et al., 1985). Likewise, in a study of Israeli infants raised in the kibbutz, Oppenheim et al. (1988) found that attachment security to mother or father had no association with measures of later sociopersonality development. To be sure, the association between parental sensitivity and security of attachment is only of moderate strength in U.S. samples, as noted earlier, and research concerning the sequelae of attachment security

in the United States has yielded a mixed pattern of findings as well. But there is also considerably greater diversity in cross-national findings concerning the origins of attachment security and its outcomes.

Based on these considerations related to attachment research in Japan, Rothbaum, Weisz, Pott, Miyake, and Morelli (2000) have questioned the universal applicability of three core claims of attachment theory: (1) caregiver sensitivity leads to secure attachment, (2) secure attachment leads to later social competence, and (3) children who are securely attached use the caregiver as a secure base for exploration. They argue that these conclusions reflect Western beliefs about the nature of the child and of infant-parent relationships and thus cannot properly be generalized to non-Western cultures (see also Rothbaum, Pott, Azuma, Miyake, & Weisz, 2000). The answer, according to Rothbaum and his colleagues (2000), is to develop unique, indigenous theories and methods of studying parent-child attachment relationships. Indeed, given the amount of variability in attachment observed within nationalities, their recommendation might be extended to the creation of context-specific attachment research for different subgroups within cultural settings.

By contrast, the conclusions yielded by research on attachment and culture suggest a less extreme solution. Hypotheses concerning the origins and outcomes of attachment security derived from attachment theory should be evaluated with attention to the cultural contexts of child care and the values guiding parent-child interaction in specific groups. This includes constant attention to the validation of measures derived from studies of children in the United States for use with non-Western groups and, when necessary, the creation of new assessments. To evaluate whether parental sensitivity predicts attachment security in non-Western contexts, for example, it is important to develop culturally appropriate assessments of sensitivity. Theoretical predictions concerning attachment outcomes must also be evaluated with regard to the contexts and values of early care. Indeed, even the documentation that secure attachment is normative in different nationalities is not necessarily evidence that the Strange Situation procedure is valid until convergent evidence (such as confirming an association between the child's attachment behavior at home with secure behavior in the Strange Situation) is obtained. However, the existing research literature suggests that rather than abandoning the theory and methods of contemporary attachment research, these tools may continue to be useful as they are adapted to work in specific cultures and settings in which child-parent relationships develop. If such inquiry can be conducted in a culturally sensitive manner, it might be a preferable alternative to the generation of a collection of indigenous attachment methods and theories and would also inform the development of attachment theory.

Indeed, further studies on attachment and culture can usefully enable research into the origins of attachment security to become more context sensitive whether or not it is used to evaluate the generality of attachment theory. Sagi, van Ijzendoorn, Aviezer, Donnell, and Mayseless (1994), for example, compared the attachment security of Israeli infants in two kibbutz arrangements: (1) a "familist" arrangement in which infants returned home for the night after spending the day in group care, and (2) a "traditional" arrangement entailing communal sleeping conditions involving supervision by professional caretakers. From attachment theory they predicted and subsequently confirmed that infants in the latter group would be more insecurely attached to their mothers because of the inconsistent responsiveness of the professional caretakers and their mothers' inaccessibility to them at night. In another kibbutz study, Oppenheim and colleagues (1988) found that the security of attachment of young children to their *metaplot* (communal caretakers) predicted which children were later more empathic, purposive, dominant, achievement oriented, and independent, even though mother-child attachment security did not predict these dimensions of later psychosocial competence. The importance of the child-*metaplot* attachment relationship to these outcome measures (which were assessed in the context of communal care) may have heightened the influence of these attachments to context-relevant psychosocial skills. In each case, research on attachment in a different cultural setting permitted researchers to test hypotheses that could not be readily evaluated in the United States. These are examples of how further studies of attachment and culture can contribute to a greater understanding of the ways that context influences the early development of security in close relationships.

Consistency and Change in the Security of Attachment

The current era of attachment research emerged out of a desolate period in which researchers had difficulty devising reliable measures of infant-parent interaction and,

as a result, could not identify stable, meaningful individual differences in interactive quality (Masters & Wellman, 1974). One of the first studies of the stability of attachment classifications contributed to the validation of the Strange Situation by showing that when evaluated within the organizational perspective of Ainsworth's coding system, individual differences in infant-parent attachment could be highly stable over a 6-month period (Waters, 1978). This finding was consistent with the theoretical tradition shaping attachment theory (derived from psychoanalytic theory) that early parent-child relationships would be a consistent, formative influence on sociopersonality development. Thus, the development of a reliable methodology and the discovery that individual differences in relationship quality could be stable over time contributed to the enthusiasm initially generated for attachment theory and research.

Since that time, however, there have been many studies of the stability of attachment security, none of them confirming the initial expectation that attachments are highly consistent over time. Table 2.1 summarizes studies examining the stability of early attachment classifications. Studies were included in this table when the Strange Situation was used on each occasion because these studies provide the most valid window into the consistency of attachment relationships over time (studies using different attachment measures on each occasion, by contrast, confound change in attachment with measurement differences, and the Strange Situation is the best-validated attachment assessment). The table shows that the proportion of infants who retain the same attachment classification on each occasion varies widely, from under 50% to nearly 100%, over periods of only 6 to 8 months.

Similar conclusions are yielded from studies using other behavioral measures of attachment over longer intervals. Symons, Clark, Isaksen, and Marshall (1998) reported a correlation of .44 between observer-sorted AQS assessments of 44 children at ages 2 and 5; and Moss, Cyr, Bureau, Tarabulsy, and Dubois-Comtois (2004) reported that 67% of their sample of 120 children retained consistent classifications when assessed in the Cassidy-Marvin procedure at age 3 to 4 and the closely related Main and Cassidy (1988) procedure at age 5 to 6. The first longitudinal studies comparing infant Strange Situation classifications with mid- to late-adolescent Adult Attachment Interview states of mind have yielded mixed results: Two studies (Hamilton, 2000; Waters, Merrick, Treboux, Crowell,

TABLE 2.1 Stability of Attachment Classifications in the Strange Situation

Study	N	Age at Time 1	Age at Time 2	Stability
Middle-class samples				
Belsky et al. (1996)[a]				
–Pennsylvania State mothers	124	12	18	52
–Pennsylvania State fathers	120	13	20	46
–Pittsburgh mothers	90	12	18	46
Easterbrooks (1989)[b]		13	20	
–mothers	60			58
–fathers	60			56
Frodi, Grolnick, and Bridges (1985)	38	12	20	66
Jacobsen et al. (1997)	32	12	18	50
Main and Weston (1981)		12	20	
–mothers	15			73
–fathers	15			87
Owen et al. (1984)		12	20	
–mothers	59			78
–fathers	53			62
Takahashi (1986, 1990)	48	12	23	60
Thompson et al. (1982)	43	12.5	19.5	53
Waters (1978)	50	12	18	96
Lower-income samples				
Barnett et al. (1999)		12	18	
–maltreated subsample	18			66
–nonmaltreated subsample	21			62
Lyons-Ruth et al. (1991)	46	12	18	30
Minnesota Study of Risk and Adaptation[c]		12	18	
Vaughn et al. (1979)	100			62
Egeland and Sroufe (1981)				
–maltreated subsample	25			48
–excellent care subsample	32			81
Egeland and Farber (1984)	189			60
Schneider-Rosen et al. (1985)		12	18	
–maltreated subsample	12			42
–nonmaltreated subsample	17			76
Vondra et al. (2001)	195	12	18	45

Notes: Age is in months. Overall stability of attachment classification is expressed as the proportion of the sample maintaining the same classification at each age.

[a] Pennsylvania State samples included exclusively firstborn sons. Pittsburgh sample was recruited for a study of postpartum depression; depression was unrelated to attachment classification or its stability over time.

[b] Sample was equally divided between full-term and low-birthweight preterm infants. Term status was unrelated to attachment classification or to its stability. Strange Situation assessments with mothers and fathers were separated by approximately 1 month.

[c] Stability estimates from these studies are based on overlapping subsamples.

& Albersheim, 2000) found that nearly two-thirds of the sample obtained the same attachment classification in infancy and adolescence, whereas three studies (Lewis, Feiring, & Rosenthal, 2000; Weinfield, Sroufe, & Egeland, 2000; Zimmermann & Grossmann, 1997) found no continuity. Other evidence also indicates that consistency in attachment classification over time should not necessarily be anticipated. Dozier and colleagues (2001) found that by only a few months after their foster care placements, infants' attachment security had already begun to be predictable by knowledge of the foster mothers' attachment states of mind at a level comparable to that found in biological mother-child dyads. There is, in short, no normative stability to attachment relationships from the early years.[5] Attachment relationships sometimes stay the same, but sometimes they change (Thompson, 2000).

This conclusion does not threaten the validity of the Strange Situation because of the extensive external validity for the procedure. However, because it conflicts with certain theoretical expectations, it requires explanation. Are the changes that occur in attachment security random or systematic, perhaps even lawful? Serious attention to this issue is important not just for theoretical reasons. Understanding the causes of continuity and change in attachment security could be relevant to identifying protective factors for the maintenance of security in the lives of some children and catalysts to security in the lives of others whose early experiences have been relationally insecure.

One suggestion offered by these studies is that secure attachments tend to be more stable than insecure ones (see Thompson, 1998). Bowlby (1969/1982) explained this in terms of the self-perpetuating mutual satisfactions that the caregiver and infant derive from a secure relationship. However, the handful of stability studies enlisting the D classification suggest that infant disorganization/disorientation may also be more stable than the organized, insecure classifications, perhaps because of the extremity and consistency of the antecedent caregiving conditions giving rise to disorganized attachment (van Ijzendoorn et al., 1979). Therefore, there can be catalysts to relational consistency of both positive and negative kinds, although this clearly merits greater research attention.

Attachment researchers have hypothesized that attachment relationships are more likely to change when stresses alter familiar patterns of parent-child interaction, and there is some evidence in support of this view. Vaughn, Egeland, Sroufe, and Waters (1979) found that the mothers of infants who shifted from securely attached at 12 months to insecurely attached at 18 months reported significantly higher amounts of life stress compared with the mothers of infants who maintained secure attachment at each age. These findings are consistent with the association between stressful events and height-

ened attachment insecurity in the socioeconomically stressed samples earlier described. In longer-term studies, the frequency of negative life events between attachment assessments is associated with changes in the security of attachment from infancy to adulthood, especially shifts toward insecure adult attachment representations (Hamilton, 2000; Lewis et al., 2000; Waters, Weinfield, & Hamilton, 2000; Weinfield et al., 2000; see also Beckwith, Cohen, & Hamilton, 1999). These events include parental divorce or serious illness, parental loss, child maltreatment, and other intervening events of significance and severity, although some of them (particularly divorce) are experienced by a high proportion of children in countries like the United States.

Stresses may not be the only influences provoking changes in attachment. Thompson, Lamb, and Estes (1982) found with a middle-class sample that comparatively nonstressful changes in parent-infant interaction, such as those resulting from the mother's return to work and the onset of nonmaternal care, were associated with changes in attachment security. These life events were associated with changes from insecurity to security and the reverse. Thus, change and stress can alter familiar patterns of parent-child interaction and, as a consequence, the security of attachment, with stress promoting a change toward insecurity. This may help to explain why the proportion of stable attachment relationships in middle-class samples is not strikingly higher than those for lower-income samples (Table 2.1), and why studies with samples that were specifically selected to exclude such influences reported higher consistency in attachment relationships over time (e.g., Main & Weston, 1981). Owen, Easterbrooks, Chase-Lansdale, and Goldberg (1984) did not find an association between changes in attachment and shifts in maternal employment, however, although the latter were associated with changes in the security of infant-*father* attachments.

A somewhat more refined hypothesis is that changes in the quality or sensitivity of caregiving—which may result from changing or stressful life conditions—are associated with change in attachment security. Frodi, Grolnick, and Bridges (1985) found no associations between the stability of attachment and intervening life events or child care patterns, but reported associations with the sensitivity of maternal care. Infants who were either consistently secure or became secure from 12 to 20 months had mothers who were more sensitive and less controlling at 12 months. A similar conclusion derives from the NICHD Study of Early Child Care, which found that changes in

---

[5] Although Fraley (2002) concluded from a meta-analysis review of many of these studies that there is moderate stability of attachment security across the first 19 years of life, his analysis focused exclusively on the secure-insecure distinction and thus ignored important changes that occur between the insecure classifications, which tend to be more unstable over time than the secure group.

maternal sensitivity were significantly associated with changes in attachment security from 15 months (assessed via the Strange Situation) to 36 months (assessed via the Cassidy-Marvin procedure; NICHD Early Child Care Research Network, 2001). Only 46% of the sample maintained the same attachment classification over time, with low or decreasing maternal sensitivity in home observations from 24 to 36 months predicting which infants would change from secure to insecure, and higher sensitivity over this period predicting which infants would change from insecure to secure (but see Belsky, Campbell, Cohn, and Moore, 1996, for a failure to find similar differences). Thus, changes in the security of attachment may be associated with changes in the sensitivity of parental care, which is consistent with attachment theory.

Changes in the sensitivity of care can derive from many influences. In a study using the AQS, Teti, Sakin, Kucera, Corns, and Das Eiden (1996) found that the attachment security of firstborn preschoolers decreased following the birth of a new sibling. The children whose security scores dropped most dramatically had mothers with significantly higher scores on depression, anxiety, and/or hostility compared with the mothers of children who maintained high security scores. In this study, furthermore, firstborns' security scores were also predicted by measures of the mothers' marital harmony and affective involvement with the firstborn. Thus, the impact of the secondborn's birth on the security of mother-firstborn attachment was moderated by the mother's capacities to cope successfully with the new birth, which was itself predicted not only by her personality style but also by the support she received from her partner. It seems likely that similar processes of coping and adjustment would mediate the impact of family events on the sensitivity of parental care and the consistency of child-parent attachments over time. When caregivers can cope adaptively with changing life circumstances and negative events, sometimes with the assistance of others, they are more likely to maintain familiar patterns of interaction and consistent attachment relationships over time.

Taken together, these studies collectively portray the continuity of attachment security as a relational process that is influenced both by the quality of care in infancy and the subsequent quality of care after infancy. Such a view is consistent with Bowlby's claim that attachment patterns are a product both of personal history and current circumstances. It suggests that rather than early experience launching children on highly predictable developmental pathways, or psychological growth deriving

from current experience alone (Fraley, 2002), relational history and current experience each exert important influences on a child's psychosocial functioning.

But further exploration of the determinants of stability and change in attachment security is essential for several reasons. First, far greater understanding of the conditions that are associated with relational changes, and why they are influential, is needed. The pattern of findings thus far suggests that different kinds of influences are associated with changes from security to insecurity compared to the reverse, but these are confounded with the broader socioeconomic circumstances of the family and thus require further study. Second, the association between negative life events and change in attachment is moderate but not strong, suggesting that other influences are also relevant and perhaps preeminent in altering prior relational patterns (Thompson, 2000; Waters, Weinfield, & Hamilton, 2000). These could include the coping capacities of the parent (as noted earlier) or the child, as suggested by the emotional security hypothesis of Davies and Cummings (1994). Other potential influences include the availability of other attachment partners who provide greater relational stability to the child, the child's personal construals of the caregiver's behavior that could moderate the impact of stressful events on the child's expectations for care, and temperamental qualities that may alter a child's vulnerability or resiliency to the personal impact of negative life events. Each of these hypotheses merits further empirical exploration, and few have yet been studied. Third, our understanding is especially impoverished with respect to the influences that can cause formerly insecure children to become secure, despite the relevance of this to preventive and interventive efforts. Although parent-child therapeutic interventions informed by attachment theory have been shown to benefit young children growing up in at-risk circumstances (e.g., Cicchetti, Toth, & Rogosch, 1999), little is known about the ordinary conditions that can provoke transitions to secure attachment in nontherapeutic contexts. Further study of this issue can have potential importance for fostering more positive early parent-child relationships and to the study of early childhood mental health.

Early Attachment and Subsequent Psychological Development

If the consistency of attachment relationships is due to an interaction of early sensitive care and subsequent experience, then this should also be true of the sequelae of attachment security: The extent to which attachment predicts later sociability, behavior problems, or other outcomes should depend on both early security and the child's subsequent experiences, particularly of sensitive care. Belsky and Pasco Fearon (2002a) confirmed this expectation from attachment theory using data from the NICHD Study of Early Child Care. Analyzing Strange Situation classifications at 15 months and subsequent measures of maternal sensitivity at 24 months, they reported that the children who obtained the highest scores on a broad range of social and cognitive measures at 36 months were those who were securely attached and who subsequently experienced sensitive care. Those performing most poorly at 36 months were insecurely attached in infancy and experienced later insensitive care. Interestingly, of the two intermediate groups, children who were initially insecurely attached but subsequently experienced sensitive care scored higher on all outcome measures than children who were initially secure but later experienced insensitive care. Similar findings have been reported by other attachment researchers (e.g., Easterbrooks & Goldberg, 1990; Egeland, Kalkoske, Gottesman, & Erickson, 1990; Erikson, Sroufe, & Egeland, 1985; Sroufe, Egeland, & Kreutzer, 1990). Belsky and Pasco Fearon (2002a) also found that maternal-report measures of life stress, depression, social support, and family resources at 24 months helped to explain why some securely attached infants subsequently experienced insensitive care, and why some initially insecure infants later experienced sensitive maternal care. In each case, maternal insensitivity was positively associated with the number of negative life events and lack of support that mothers experienced when children were age 2. In a corollary report from the same NICHD study, Belsky and Pasco Fearon (2002b) reported that a cumulative measure of contextual risk during the child's first 3 years moderated some of the associations between early attachment and later behavior.

In another reanalysis of the NICHD Study of Early Child Care, Raikes and Thompson (2005d) expanded on these findings. They examined the association between multiple early assessments of attachment security (at 15, 24, and 36 months) and later measures of parent-child relationship quality with children's social-cognitive functioning at 54 months and first grade. They found that *both* concurrent parenting quality and early attachment security were associated with social-cognitive outcomes, and that children with insecure attachment histories

were more sensitive to the effects of parenting quality later in life than children with secure attachment histories. Moreover, attachment security at 24 and 36 months (when children's mental representations are maturing) but not at 15 months was predictive of later social cognition, and security at multiple ages was more predictive than a secure attachment at only one assessment. It was, in short, cumulative relational experience that predicted children's social-cognitive functioning at school entry, which included assessments of children's attributions for peer behavior, their ability to generate appropriate responses to social problems, and self-perceived loneliness.

These findings, taken together, indicate that early security interacts with the quality of subsequent experience (particularly maternal care and broader life stresses) in predicting developmental outcomes. Indeed, these findings suggest that later caregiving may be at least as important as early security in predicting later behavior. Unfortunately, most of the research on the outcomes of early attachment is insensitive to these developmentally interactive influences. Although virtually all attachment theorists agree that the consequences of a secure or insecure attachment arise from an interaction between early security and the continuing quality of parental care, most studies are designed in a simple pre-post manner in which security in an antecedent assessment is associated with a later behavioral outcome. This makes it impossible to determine whether early security is linked to later behavior because caregivers have remained consistently supportive (or unsupportive) over time, or even whether the child's attachment has remained consistently secure or insecure. If either is true, then predictive relations between attachment and later behavior may be better attributed to the continuing influences of parental sensitivity or attachment security. Moreover, few studies are designed to enable an assessment of possible moderators of the association between early security and its hypothesized outcomes, which include not only the sensitivity of parental care and family stress but also other features of parental behavior that can facilitate or impede later developmental outcomes. Thus, research on the predictive relations between attachment and later behavior is often agnostic concerning its causes (Thompson, 1999).

This is unfortunate because attachment theory is ready to move beyond simple pre-post research to a more incisive exploration of the conditions underlying continuity and change in psychological growth. It is as important today to understand *why* early security is (or is not) related to later psychological functioning as it is to establish a predictive relation. In this regard, theory development must proceed in tandem with more sophisticated research designs to enable the examination of more complex, interactive predictive models than the simple expectation that early security predicts later psychosocial functioning.

Guided by a general expectation that a secure attachment predicts better later functioning, as noted earlier, researchers have studied a wide range of hypothesized outcomes. It is important, however, to distinguish different outcome domains in assessing the importance of attachment security for psychological development. This is because a secure attachment might be expected to have stronger, more enduring, and more direct associations with sequelae that are more specifically related to issues of relational trust and security than to outcomes that are not.

The most direct result of a secure attachment would be for the *parent-child relationship:* An early secure attachment should predict more positive subsequent parent-child interaction. This expectation is confirmed in short-term follow-up studies during the 2nd year in which securely attached children showed greater enthusiasm, compliance, and positive affect (and less frustration and aggression) during shared tasks with their mothers (e.g., Frankel & Bates, 1990; Matas, Arend, & Sroufe, 1978; Slade, 1987). Secure infants tend to maintain more harmonious relations with their mothers in the 2nd year. However, in each of these studies, the mothers of securely attached infants were themselves more sensitive and helpful toward offspring in follow-up assessments, and thus supported the positive behavior of their children. It is more appropriate, therefore, to conclude that securely attached *dyads* tend to maintain interactive harmony in the 2nd year. This continuity in parent-child harmony provides significant benefits for child socialization and personality development for securely attached children (Waters et al., 1991). However, the beneficial effects of a secure attachment in infancy may wane over time. Researchers have not found longer-term associations between security in infancy and parent-child interaction at ages 3 (Youngblade & Belsky, 1992) and 5 (van Ijzendoorn, van der Veer, & van Vliet-Visser, 1987), even though long-term associations have sometimes been demonstrated, as noted earlier, between attachment measures at different ages. This is consistent with the findings of studies concerning the stability of attachment classifications, which indicate, as noted ear-

lier, that relationships may remain consistent or change after infancy. Consequently, although attachment security in infancy may inaugurate short-term consistency in the harmony of parent-child relations, the evidence concerning long-term continuity is mixed, with continuity likely depending on important mediating conditions in the ecology of family life.

What about the benefits of attachment security for children's experience of *other close relationships?* A meta-analysis by Schneider, Atkinson, and Tardif (2001) found a modest association between parent-child attachment and children's peer relationships (combined effect size .20) and confirmed that this association is stronger for studies of children's close friendships (effect size .24) than for relationships with other peers (effect size .14), which is consistent with other reviews of this literature (Thompson, 1998, 1999). Strange Situation, AQS, and representational attachment assessments for older children were used in the studies reviewed in this meta-analysis, and findings for each were consistent with these conclusions. Schneider and colleagues also concluded that this association is stronger for peer relations in middle childhood and adolescence than in early childhood and suggested that this derives from the consolidation and sophistication of representational processes related to friendship in older children. However, this conclusion integrates studies involving long-term prediction from infant attachment with studies in which attachment and peer relations were each assessed in childhood or adolescence, and thus the meaning of this association is not entirely clear from this meta-analysis.

Other studies support the conclusion that attachment security is more strongly associated with children's functioning in close relationships. In the Minnesota Study of Risk and Adaptation (see Sroufe, Egeland, Carlson, & Collins, 2005), for example, infants who were securely attached were later less dependent on their preschool teachers and functioned better in the preschool setting (Sroufe, 1983). Bost, Vaughn, Washington, Cielinski, and Bradbard (1998) found that secure preschoolers (assessed via observer AQS scores) had more extensive and supportive social networks and were also higher on sociometric assessments of peer competence (see Booth, Rubin, & Rose-Krasnor, 1998, and DeMulder, Denham, Schmidt, & Mitchell, 2000, for similiar results). Anan and Barnett (1999) also found (in a sample of lower-income African American 6.5-year-olds) that secure attachment (assessed 2 years earlier) was associated with children's perceptions of greater social support, and social support mediated the association between secure attachment and lower scores on externalizing and internalizing problems. To be sure, there is evidence that securely attached infants are also more sociable with unfamiliar adults during the 2nd or 3rd year (e.g., Main & Weston, 1981; Thompson & Lamb, 1983), which may derive from the generalization of the social skills that secure infants acquire with their mothers. However, mothers were present during stranger sociability assessments in these studies, and each study in which concurrent maternal behavior was evaluated yielded differences indicating that the mothers of secure children were more supportive and child centered with their offspring. Thus, differences in stranger sociability may be a dyadic phenomenon. Differences in more intimate relationships appear, by contrast, to be a function of the capacity of securely attached children to create more positive relationships.

Attachment researchers have also studied the associations between relational security and *personality development*. The Minnesota Study of Risk and Adaptation, a uniquely comprehensive, prospective longitudinal study of children and families in poverty, has focused extensively on the association between attachment and personality within the organizational perspective of attachment theory and Sroufe's portrayal of the "continuity of adaptation" of age-related developmental challenges. In this study, children were recruited with their families in infancy and followed through age 28, with personality characteristics assessed regularly through behavioral observations, interviews, observer ratings, semiprojective instruments, and self-reports. Sroufe and his colleagues found significant continuities between early attachment security (assessed in the Strange Situation at 12 and 18 months) and personality dimensions throughout childhood and adolescence, including associations between secure attachment and measures of emotional health, self-esteem, agency and self-confidence, positive affect, ego resiliency, and social competence in interactions with peers, teachers, camp counselors, romantic partners, and others (see Sroufe et al., 2005, for a comprehensive report, which also includes a list of citations to specific research reports and a comprehensive list of measures). Moreover, consistent with the emphasis on both developmental history and current experience, Sroufe and his colleagues found that the prediction of these and other personality features was enhanced when (a) early attachment measures were supplemented by other indicators of the quality of early care, (b) there was consideration of continuity in the quality of care between infancy and later ages, and (c)

early measures were supplemented by more contemporaneous assessments of relational functioning and/or personality, especially when long-term prediction was involved (e.g., Carlson, Sroufe, & Egeland, 2004). Taken together, this study yielded impressive evidence of the predictable organization of personality and behavioral functioning from childhood to early adulthood as a function of the interactive effects of early caregiving, subsequent experiences, and relational influences. Although some of the findings of this project have not been replicated by others (e.g., Easterbrooks & Goldberg, 1990; Frankel & Bates, 1990), the study offers an important portrayal of the place of attachment security in the multifactorial construction of personality development (Thompson, in press).

Security of attachment as a protective or risk factor to the development of *psychopathology* has also been the focus of research inquiry. In the Minnesota study, insecure-resistant attachment in infancy predicted anxiety disorders in adolescence, but there were few other associations between the organized insecure classifications and later psychopathology (Sroufe et al., 2005). In another at-risk sample, Lyons-Ruth, Easterbrooks, and Cibelli (1997) reported that avoidant attachment in the Strange Situation was associated with teacher-report internalizing symptomatology indexed by the Child Behavior Checklist (CBCL) at age 7, although there was no association with teacher-reported anxiety or behavior problems at age 5 (Lyons-Ruth, Alpern, & Repacholi, 1993). A number of studies have failed to discern a reliable association between early organized insecurity in the Strange Situation and the development of behavioral problems, especially in middle-class samples (e.g., Bates & Bayles, 1988; Erickson et al., 1985; Fagot & Kavanagh, 1990). However, analyses from the NICHD Study of Early Child Care found that insecurity at 24 months (on the AQS) predicted maternal and caregiver CBCL ratings at age 3 of internalizing and externalizing behavior problems, and insecurity at 36 months (using the Cassidy-Marvin procedure) predicted internalizing problems on the same assessments (McCartney et al., 2004). Thus, research evidence concerning the association between organized insecure attachment and the development of behavior problems in childhood is quite mixed. There is some evidence that this association is stronger in lower-income families, which are subject to other risk factors for child problems, than in middleclass homes, but the research evidence is inconclusive.

Further attention to the clinical implications of attachment security has accompanied the creation of the disorganized/disoriented (group D) classification. Children in this group may be at risk for the development of later clinical problems, especially when they are in stressed or lower-income families. In the Minnesota study, infants who were classified D in the Strange Situation later obtained significantly higher scores on a global index of psychopathology and, in particular, of dissociative symptomatology in adolescence (Sroufe et al., 2005; see also Carlson, 1998). Lyons-Ruth and her colleagues (1995, 1997) reported that disorganized attachment in the Strange Situation was associated with teacher-reported externalizing symptoms on the CBCL at age 7, and with teacher-reported hostility at age 5 (see also Shaw, Owens, Vondra, Keenan, & Winslow, 1996, for similar findings using the Strange Situation with a low-income sample, and Moss, Parent, et al., 1996, and Moss, Bureau, et al., 2004, for comparable findings using the Cassidy-Marvin procedure with older children from middle-class families).[6] Shaw, Keenan, Vondra, Delliquadri, and Giovanelli (1997) and Moss, Bureau, and colleagues (2004) also reported higher scores for D children on internalizing symptomatology, and Moss, Cyr, and Dubois-Comtois (2004) have found contemporaneous associations between disorganized attachment and behavior problems in school-age children, with the different D subgroups predicting externalizing and internalizing problems. However, in a somewhat discordant report, McCartney and colleagues (2004), analyzing data from the NICHD Study of Early Child Care, found no reliable associations between disorganized attachment in the Strange Situation (at 15 months) or the Cassidy-Marvin procedure (at 36 months) and mother- or caregiver-reported behavior problems at age 3.

These mixed findings suggest that further examination of the association between insecure attachment and the development of behavior problems is warranted. In doing so, two interpretive cautions should be noted. First, since the origins of infant attachment disorganization are based in the same risk factors that also contribute to later psychopathology (such as maternal psychosocial problems and depression, family stress, and other factors), it

is unsurprising that in studies that have included these additional risks in predictive models, both disorganized attachment and other family risks combine to predict later child psychopathology (e.g., Carlson, 1998; Lyons-Ruth et al., 1993; Shaw et al., 1997). This is one of the reasons that the association between attachment insecurity and later behavior problems tends to be stronger in socioeconomically distressed families, but it also suggests that the sequelae of insecurity derive, in part, from continuity in the risk factors that initially contributed to attachment insecurity earlier in the child's life. Second, it should be clear that insecure attachment—even disorganized attachment—is not an index of psychopathology but only a risk factor. These findings show that although insecurity increases the chances of later behavior problems, the prediction of child psychopathology should be viewed in the context of multifactorial models involving early caregiving influences, continuing family adversity, ineffective parenting, and atypical child characteristics (Greenberg, 1999).

Indeed, the same conclusion is true of the other sequelae of the security of attachment. Because each of these hypothesized outcomes is multidetermined, attachment security is likely to explain a significant but small proportion of variance in each, with the amount of variance declining over time as other developmental influences emerge. This is one reason why future studies that include multiple predictors of later outcomes will be more informative in situating the security of attachment in the constellation of other influences that predict later parent-child relationships, social competence, personality, and risk for psychopathology. Furthermore, the large majority of research studies on the outcomes of attachment security focus on child-mother attachment relationships, even though attachment theorists recognize that children develop meaningful relationships with fathers and other attachment partners. It seems likely that studies incorporating the influence of multiple attachment relationships will have greater predictive power than those focusing on the child-mother relationships alone, but few studies have considered the roles of fathers and other caregivers.

What can we conclude, therefore, about the association between early attachment and later psychological development? Early security clearly makes a difference for the child's future in concert with other family influences. It inaugurates a more harmonious mother-child relationship that provides continuing benefits for the young child's receptivity to mothers' socialization incentives. It is associated with more positive personality

---

[6] These findings are consistent with a meta-analytic review by van Ijzendoorn and De Wolff (1997) who reported that there is a moderately strong association between disorganized/disoriented attachment and externalizing behavior (combined effect size .29), but the extraordinary heterogeneity of the samples and the assessments of disorganization for the 12 studies they summarized makes the meaning of this conclusion uncertain.

characteristics and greater social competence, especially in other close relationships with peers and adults. Attachment security is also a protective factor in the development of psychological well-being, with insecure attachment—especially disorganized insecurity—a risk factor for the development of behavioral problems. A secure attachment alone is not necessarily a strong predictor of long-term outcomes but, in concert with continuing supportive care, it meaningfully improves the odds for positive psychological growth. What is less clear is why these outcomes emerge. Attachment security is likely to be associated with more positive social skills, self-regulatory capacities, modes of social and emotional understanding, motivational processes, social expectations, causal attributions, and self-referential beliefs that contribute to the benefits of a secure attachment and the challenges of an insecure one. Attachment security is also likely to be associated with continuing parental sensitivity that provides ongoing support for healthy psychological growth. But thus far, researchers have yet to incisively explore the psychological processes underlying the association between early attachment security and its later psychological outcomes. This constitutes a central agenda for future attachment research.

A recent study by Denham, Blair, Schmidt, and DeMulder (2002) provides an example of the kind of research that would advance this understanding. In this study, multiple measures of attachment security (including observer AQS) were assessed when children were age 3, along with multiple measures of emotional (in)competence, including assessments of emotion understanding, regulation, and anger expression. Children were later studied in their kindergarten classrooms to assess peer competence through sociometric ratings and teacher-rated social competence measures. Latent variable path-analytic procedures were used to confirm two avenues from preschool attachment security to kindergarten social competence: (1) a direct pathway and (2) an indirect path through emotional competence (see also Denham et al., 2001). As we shall see, there is considerable research elucidating how securely attached children develop skills of emotion understanding through the more open conversation shared with their mothers, and this research suggests that skills in emotional competence may be one means by which the social skills of secure children are enhanced. To Denham and colleagues, the mediating influence of emotional competence illustrates one of several facets of the internal working models generated by the security of attachment.

Internal Working Models

One of Bowlby's most heuristically powerful formulations is the view that attachment security influences psychological growth through children's developing mental representations, or *internal working models* (IWMs), of the social world. Internal working models are based on young children's expectations for the behavior of their attachment figures that develop into broader representations of themselves, their attachment figures, interpretations of their relational experiences, and decision rules about how to interact with others. These working models also become interpretive filters through which children (and adults) reconstruct their understanding of new experiences and relationships in ways that are consistent with past experiences and expectations, sometimes enlisting unconscious defensive processes in doing so. As a consequence, children choose new partners and behave with them in ways that are consistent with, and thus help to confirm, the expectations created from earlier attachment relationships. In this manner, IWMs constitute the bridge between the infant's experience of sensitive or insensitive care and the development of beliefs and expectations that affect subsequent experience in close relationships (Bretherton & Munholland, 1999). Furthermore, young children are believed to internalize conceptions of themselves from early relational experience that are incorporated into developing IWMs and that also constitute a perceptual lens for experiences that affect self-concept and other developing self-referential beliefs. In this manner, secure or insecure attachments shape the organization of personality through the influence of mental working models arising from attachment security.

This is a valuable way of thinking about socioemotional development that is representational, integrative, affectively oriented, and relationally based. Its breadth, however, poses some conceptual challenges for attachment theory. Grossmann (1999) has pointed out that at least two formulations of IWMs can be found in Bowlby's theory. One conceptualizes IWMs in a manner resembling the dynamic unconscious by which relational experience is interpreted through the perceptual-affective schemas of infancy; these prelinguistic models have enduring influence but remain largely inaccessible to conscious reflection. The other conceptualizes IWMs as resembling other, conscious representational models like scripts and schemas that evolve developmentally and can be consciously accessed. These are different formulations and have different implications for theory and assessment. Perhaps as a consequence, basic questions concerning how

IWMs develop, how their development is affected by other facets of conceptual growth, and changes in IWMs over time remain unclear in attachment theory (Thompson & Raikes, 2003). Another problem is the explanatory breadth that IWMs can assume. As Hinde (1988) noted, "in the very power of such a model lies a trap: it can too easily explain anything" (p. 378), a concern shared by other developmental scientists (Belsky & Cassidy, 1994; Rutter & O'Connor, 1999). Over the years, as attachment security has been studied in relation to a widening array of developmental outcomes, the concept of internal working models has been enlisted to account for unexpected as well as hypothesized associations, giving credence to Belsky and Cassidy's (1994) concern that IWMs would constitute a "catch-all, post hoc explanation" for such research findings. The inclusiveness of the IWM construct has expanded with every new empirical finding that is "explained" with reference to it.

This has also presented a considerable challenge for efforts to assess children's mental working models derived from attachment relationships. Attachment researchers have created a variety of assessments of children's mental representations of relational experience, many of them based on semiprojective narrative approaches that involve children's responses to doll-play materials, story-completion probes, evocative pictures, and other materials (see Solomon & George, 1999, and Stevenson-Hinde & Verschueren, 2002, for reviews of these methods). These procedures rely on the assumption that in responding to materials that are designed to evoke attachment-related issues, children will project onto the materials their own feelings and beliefs associated with their attachment experiences. Surprisingly, no procedures have been developed to directly assess children's expectations for the behavior of their attachment figures in familiar situations or their scripts for social interaction with their attachment figures.

Considerable thoughtful creativity has been devoted to semiprojective measurement development, but Solomon and George (1999) have chastised the "frontier mentality" of researchers who have produced these representational assessments with inadequate attention to their validation, especially by comparison to the careful validation of behavioral measures of attachment security. This may be due to the challenges inherent in such validational efforts. The coherence, emotional themes, and resolution of young children's narrative responses to semiprojective assessments are likely affected not only by the representations of relationships that researchers

hope to assess but also by other influences on narrative content and quality that derive from children's linguistic skills and verbal fluency, parent-child discourse, social desirability influences, culture, and ethnicity. There are also developmental considerations related to validation because the coherence of young children's story-completion discourse probably means something different compared to coherence in an adolescent's or adult's response to Adult Attachment Interview (AAI) probes. Attachment researchers have generally sought to validate representational measures of attachment security by establishing predictive or contemporaneous associations with behavioral attachment measures, even though security assessed by narrative coherence and emotional openness is not the same thing as security assessed by secure base behavior. But the important task of elucidating the meaning of differences in narrative responses to semiprojective probes and their association with parent-child interaction at home remains to be accomplished (Raikes & Thompson, 2005b; Waters & Cummings, 2000).

There have been at least two recent efforts to contribute greater theoretical clarity to the IWM construct in ways that have implications for assessment. Bretherton (1990, 1991; Bretherton & Munholland, 1999) has described mental working models in terms of the formulations of script theory and constructive memory and emphasized the openness of communication between parent and child as a significant developmental influence on the construction of working models in early childhood. More generally, she describes IWMs as a system of hierarchically organized representational systems that involve different levels of generalizability and are relevant to various broader belief systems, suggesting that elements of IWMs can be studied in the context of other conceptual achievements of the childhood years.

Building on this view, Thompson (1998, 2000) has proposed a developmental account that associates the growth of IWMs with other developing mental processes that encode, represent, interpret, and remember social experiences.[7] Drawing on literatures concerning the de-

---

[7] In a related view, Spangler and Delius (2003) have proposed that IWMs should be portrayed as a "theory of attachment" (or, perhaps, a "theory of relationships") involving coherently integrated knowledge of relational processes and causal influences that generate specific predictions and expectations for relational experience. Such a view, drawn from theory-theory of young children's intuitive beliefs about mind, physics, and biological kinds (Wellman, 2002), also offers considerable potential utility in clarifying the IWM construct.

velopment of implicit memory, event representation, autobiographical memory, theory of mind, and other features of social understanding, he portrays the growth of IWMs as building on and integrating these allied conceptual achievements that concern, like IWMs do, understanding of people and social events, self-understanding, and interpretations of relational experience. In this developmental view, IWMs change considerably with age, especially during periods of significant representational advance (such as the transition to symbolic representational capacities in early childhood, and the emergence of abstract thought in adolescence) when earlier representational systems become reorganized (see also Ainsworth, 1989; Crittenden, 2000). Thompson also argues that IWMs may have greatest influence on other aspects of sociopersonality growth during the developmental periods when these capabilities are maturing most significantly. The working models associated with a secure attachment may influence emotion understanding most strongly in early childhood, for example, when children's conceptions of others' feelings begin to become consolidated. Finally, in this view, IWMs are shaped not only by the child's direct experience of close relationships but also by the secondary representations of experience mediated by language through parent-child conversation. Consistent with literatures reviewed elsewhere in this chapter, he argues, language provides young children with considerable insight into others' feelings, thoughts, knowledge, and motives and are likely to significantly influence developing IWMs as they shape children's emergent conceptions of emotion, intention, and mind (see Thompson et al., 2003).

These newer portrayals of the development of mental working models emphasize the associations between IWMs and other conceptual systems and suggest that rather than trying to study working models directly through semiprojective procedures and other avenues, attachment researchers might equally fruitfully glean an understanding of their developmental influence by studying the representational correlates of differences in attachment security. By understanding how secure and insecure attachments are associated with differences in emotion understanding, self-awareness, and other characteristics, it might be possible to identify the influence of working models. There is now emerging an empirical literature documenting how the security of attachment is associated with representations of self, others, and relationships.

Belsky, Spritz, and Crnic (1996) hypothesized that differential processing of schema-consistent information, owing to the influence of IWMs, would cause securely attached children to remember positive events more accurately than insecure children. In a study in which 3-year-olds' delayed recognition memory for positive and negative events during a previously viewed puppet show was assessed, this expectation was confirmed. A recent study using data from the NICHD Study of Early Child Care also showed attachment-related differences in attentional processes, with disorganized children showing especially poor attentional performance (Pasco Fearon & Belsky, 2004). The conclusion that children with different attachment histories differentially attend to and remember emotionally related events merits further investigation because of its relevance to understanding the influence of the mental representations associated with attachment history and its broader implications for understanding attachment functioning.

Attachment security should be associated with children's conceptions of relationships, and one study has confirmed this to be true of peer relationships. Cassidy, Kirsh, Scolton, and Parke (1996) examined the associations between attachment security and children's sensitivity to the feelings of peers and attributions concerning peer motivations in response to hypothetical stories involving negative actions with ambiguous intent. Although attachment security from infant Strange Situation assessments did not confirm the expectation that securely attached 4-year-olds would be more likely to attribute benign motives to story characters, this expectation was confirmed when attachment security and peer measures were obtained contemporaneously in kindergarteners and first graders. Moreover, these representations of peer relationships in the older children were found to mediate the association between attachment security and peer sociometric status. Consistent with the findings of Denham, Blair, and colleagues (2002) described earlier, representations of the feelings and intentions of other children helped to account for the greater social competence of secure children. As noted earlier, furthermore, Raikes and Thompson (2005d) found that attachment history (especially in concert with subsequent supportive parenting) predicted children's attributions for peer behavior and social problem solving at 54 months and first grade, especially when children were securely attached on multiple early assessments.

Several studies have found that securely attached children are more competent in emotion understanding in contemporaneous associations using the AQS (Laible & Thompson, 1998; Ontai & Thompson, 2002) and in predictive associations from infant Strange Situation classifications (Steele, Steele, Croft, & Fonagy, 1999) or early childhood AQS (Raikes & Thompson, 2005a; see also de Rosnay & Harris, 2002). These studies also indicate that securely attached children are especially proficient at understanding negative emotions and mixed feelings, which are each conceptually complex. Why do secure children better understand emotions? There is some indication that secure children acquire this understanding because of how they talk about emotion with their mothers. Ontai and Thompson (2002) found that attachment security interacted with elaborative maternal discourse in predicting emotion understanding: More secure 5-year-olds whose mothers had earlier used a more descriptively rich, elaborative style of conversation about emotion with them (in storybook reading and discussions of past events) were more advanced in positive emotion understanding (see also Laible, 2004b, for similar findings). Because the mothers of securely attached children have been found to be generally more elaborative in their style of conversation with offspring (Farrant & Reese, 2000; Laible, 2004b; Laible & Thompson, 2000; see Reese, 2002, for a review), these findings offer support for the view from attachment theory that secure dyads share a more "open, fluid communication" style that enables discussion of feelings (particularly mixed or negative emotions) and the child's greater comprehension of them (Bretherton, 1990). One of the benefits of more open shared communication between mother and child—in which mothers provide more detailed information concerning emotions and other psychological experiences—is that young children can share troubled or confusing feelings with their caregivers and obtain an understanding response. This research thus suggests important associations between mother-child discourse style, the development of IWMs and of emotion understanding, and attachment security, consistent with the earlier review of research concerning the growth of emotion understanding in preschoolers. Indeed, Raikes and Thompson (2005a) found that the quality of mother-child conversations about emotion mediated the association between attachment security and emotion understanding in 3-year-olds. The influence of maternal discourse also suggests one way that the intergenerational transmission of attachment security and related representations might occur.

Similar influences may also account for the association between attachment and conscience development. A secure attachment is associated with conscience development (Laible & Thompson, 2000) but, as discussed later, attachment security is especially influential for children who are temperamentally relatively fearless, for whom the emotional incentives of the mother-child relationship motivate moral compliance (Kochanska, 1991, 1995). Attachment security is accompanied by mother-child discourse style in shaping early conscience development, with mothers who more richly and elaboratively discuss the feelings of other people contributing most to young children's internalization of moral values (Laible & Thompson, 2000). As noted in a later section, this conclusion is consistent with Hoffman's (1983, 2000) classic formulations concerning the nature of parental communication contributing to moral internalization. Further evidence of how attachment interacts with other parental influences derives from the findings of Kochanska and colleagues (2004) of how attachment security interacts with parental discipline practices on the growth of conscience. In their longitudinal analysis, they found that for securely attached children, the parent's use of responsiveness and gentle discipline predicted later conscience, but for insecure children there was no such association. These findings suggest that the security of attachment moderates the influence of other relational influences on early socialization. With respect to conscience, for example, the adult's disciplinary practices may have differential emotional impact depending on the broader relationship shared by parent and child.

Attachment theory argues that the IWMs deriving from a secure or insecure attachment influence self-concept, particularly conceptions of the self as loved and loveable. In a study of contemporaneous associations between attachment and multiple measures of self-understanding, Cassidy (1988) found that securely attached 6-year-olds described themselves in generally positive terms but were capable of admitting that they were imperfect. Insecurely attached children either revealed a more negative self-image or resisted admitting flaws. Clark and Symons (2000) found stronger contemporaneous associations between attachment security and two assessments of self-concept at age 5 than predictive associations with attachment at age 2, but the associations depended on the measure of self-concept. Goodvin, Meyer, Thompson, and Hayes (2005) also found that securely attached preschoolers viewed themselves more positively and self-concept was more stable over time than for insecure children, while maternal emotional difficulties (depression and parenting stress) predicted children's negative self-perceptions. In problem-solving tasks, insecurely attached preschoolers expressed greater frustration and inability and asked for help sooner and in unnecessary circumstances (Colman & Thompson, 2002). These findings suggest that attachment security and developing self-concept are associated, and warrant further exploration of the mediating processes by which this occurs.

Finally, attachment theory does not make strong predictions concerning the benefits of a secure attachment for understanding others' thoughts and beliefs and, perhaps as a consequence, there is mixed evidence for the association between attachment security and theory of mind. Meins et al. (2002) found no association between early attachment and children's later performance on theory of mind tasks, but Symons and Clark (2000) found a contemporaneous association between attachment and theory of mind in 5-year-olds. In light of the variety of assessments of theory of mind in preschoolers and the direct and indirect avenues by which attachment relationships might be influential in its development, further reflection is warranted on whether and why an association between these constructs might exist.

Taken together, the research on the representational correlates of attachment security contributes to an appreciation of why the mental models associated with secure or insecure attachments are so conceptually exciting for developmental analysis. The conclusions of these studies suggest:

- Mental representations of peer intentions, emotional inferences, and other psychological processes mediate between attachment security and its behavioral outcomes, such as social competence.

- Differences in processes of parent-child discourse may interact with the broader security of the parent-child relationship to shape young children's developing emotion understanding and, quite likely, conscience development, and possibly contribute to the intergenerational transmission of expectations and beliefs associated with the security of attachment.

- Attachment security and its allied representations may moderate the influence of other parental practices, such as discipline approaches, on children's conscience development and possibly other behavioral outcomes.

- A child's relational history may also sensitize or blunt attention to other features of social experience in ways suggested by the findings of Belsky and his colleagues.

- For many domains of psychological development, such as theory of mind, greater reflection on the role of attachment security is needed.

Further research on the representational correlates of the security of attachment may contribute to understanding how multiple attachment relationships become enfolded into the development of secure or insecure persons by adolescence or early adulthood. It is noteworthy that most of the research reviewed here has not sought to directly assess internal working models, but rather has sought to comprehend their functioning through more specific analyses of the associations between attachment and conceptions of peer relationships, emotion understanding, self-concept, and other psychological processes associated with the mental models derived from attachment relationships. In so doing, we derive a portrayal of working models as rapidly developing processes that mediate between attachment security and its behavioral outcomes, interacting with other relational influences between parents and offspring, and sensitizing awareness of social processes.

Summary

Despite its controversial status in developmental psychology (Thompson, 2005), attachment theory remains uniquely generative because of how it integrates ideas concerning the effects of early relational experience on socioemotional and personality development, constructivist views on the growth of social relatedness, the development of representations concerning relationships and self, and the relevance of these for the growth of psychological well-being and psychopathology. Its future potential for remaining a central view of early personality development depends on the capacities of attachment theorists and researchers to update Bowlby's provocative formulations with the thinking of contemporary developmental science and the yield of their own empirical studies. The findings of the studies reviewed in this section suggest that there remains considerable potential for the generation of new ideas within the attachment framework.

CONSCIENCE

Conscience development is concerned with how children construct and act consistently with generalizable, internal standards of conduct. It is closely tied to moral judgment, but the growth of conscience also encompasses the affective, temperamental, and relational influences that, together with moral judgment, shape moral conduct. The study of conscience thus provides a window into how emotional, cognitive, and relational influences intersect to guide young children's developing views of themselves in relation to others and the broader values of the social world (Kochanska & Thompson, 1997; Thompson, Meyer, & McGinley, 2006).

Not surprisingly, contemporary research on conscience has emerged in the shadow of moral development theory. Traditional approaches to moral development, such as learning theory and the cognitive-developmental views of Piaget and Kohlberg, have portrayed morality in early childhood as distinct from that of older children and adolescents because of the younger child's egocentric, preconventional moral orientation. By contrast with older children who are concerned with maintaining harmonious social relations, and adolescents who are viewed as ethical, humanistic moralists, young children are portrayed as authoritarian, utilitarian moralists who are guided by rewards, punishment, and obedience. But new research, together with new understandings of young children's conceptual skills and relational experiences, have contributed to a new view of early conscience and of the importance of early childhood to the development of mature morality. It is now becoming clear that conscience in early childhood shares much in common with the morality of later years because of preschoolers' sensitivity to the feelings of others and the relational incentives for cooperation. Parental influences encompass far more than sanctions and reinforcements and include maintaining a relationship of mutual responsiveness and trust, enlisting conversational catalysts for moral understanding, and proactive efforts that foster cooperation and compliance in young children. Early childhood is increasingly viewed as providing a foundation for the morality of values, humanistic regard, and relationships of later years.

Intuitive Morality of Early Childhood

In early childhood, the conceptual foundations of moral development become established. Young children are not egocentric but rather, as earlier noted, are intensely interested in the desires, intentions, feelings, and thoughts of other people. Their sensitivity to others' reactions contributes to their anticipation of and responsiveness to disapproval and, later, to a dawning understanding of normative standards of appearance and behavior late in the 2nd year. As noted earlier, by 18 to 19 months of age, young children begin to respond with heightened interest and concern to objects that are damaged or flawed (Kagan, 1981, in press; S. Lamb, 1993). Kagan (1981) has interpreted this phenomenon as an emergent moral sense, based on caregivers' reactions to damaged objects and the young child's emergent sensitivity to standards. Consistent with this view, Kochanska, Casey, and Fukumoto (1995) found that older children (26- to 41-month-olds) who responded with greater concern to flawed objects also showed greater distress to rigged mishaps for which they believed they were responsible. These studies suggest that young children internalize normative standards for appearance and integrity based, in part, on their observations of how adults respond to violations of these standards in everyday experience (such as cleaning or discarding soiled toys). This is at the same time that toddlers begin to respond with embarrassment and concern to a spot of rouge on their noses, reflecting their awareness of normative standards for personal appearance (Lewis, 2000; Lewis & Brooks-Gunn, 1979).

Young children also appropriate behavioral standards and distinguish between different domains of behavioral obligation (see Turiel, Chapter 13, this *Handbook*, this volume). Much as adults do, 3- and 4-year-olds distinguish between moral and social-conventional standards, viewing moral violations as more serious and less revocable owing, in part, to their harm to others (Smetana, 1981, 1997; Smetana & Braeges, 1990). In complex social situations, such as gender exclusion in peer play, preschoolers prioritize equal treatment over convention in their consideration for fairness by age 5 (Killen et al., 2001; Theimer et al., 2001). By age 4, furthermore, individual differences in emotion understanding and knowledge of mental states (i.e., theory of mind) predict differences in children's moral judgments in friendship relations (Dunn, Cutting, & Demetriou, 2000; see also Dunn, Brown, & Maguire, 1995). Thus, young children develop an intuitive morality that arises from the socialization efforts of caregivers in tandem with their own sensitivity to the feelings and thoughts of others and their developing grasp of normative standards of appearance and behavior.

Young children's focus on normative standards is unsurprising in light of their search for other constancies in everyday experience. This is one reason why they acquire such an early grasp of obligation in moral, conventional, and prudential concerns. As Harris and Nunez (1996) have shown, even 3-year-olds are highly skilled in understanding how a prescriptive rule applies to different circumstances (e.g., "Mom says if Cathy rides her bike she should put her helmet on"), even though they are not as skilled at applying a similar descriptive, but not prescriptive, maxim (e.g., "When Cathy rides her bike, she always wears her helmet"). In a provocative analysis, Wellman and Miller (2003) have proposed that just as 3-year-olds have difficulty conceptualizing beliefs that are discordant with reality, so also they have difficulty understanding obligation that is discordant with behavior, so they are prone to assert that rules cannot be broken and obligations must necessarily be fulfilled. Behavioral obligations describe normative reality in the eyes of young children, according to Wellman and Miller, and violations are special sources of concern. This concern with what is obligatory and normative, which is similar to the moral absolutism observed in young children long ago by Piaget (1965), is consistent with young children's interest in objects that are flawed and mirror appearances that are rouge marked, and suggests that an important conceptual foundation for early conscience development is young children's attunement to the normative standards and behavioral expectations that are part of their developing representations of what they might typically expect in everyday experience.

Young children's developing representations of normative and behavioral standards are conceptually salient because they are likely to be embedded in broader prototypical knowledge structures by which children represent everyday experiences (Hudson, 1993; Nelson, 1978). Many of the moral, conventional, and prudential standards conveyed to young children are related to routine events and are repeatedly confirmed in these contexts, whether consisting of prohibitions about making "messes" and breaking things, self-control with respect to waiting, sharing, aggression, and eating, withdrawing from touching dangerous objects, self-care, or participation in family routines (Gralinski & Kopp,

1993; Smetana et al., 2000). Caregivers distinguish between different obligatory domains in their discussion of expectations with young children, justifying moral rules for their interpersonal consequences, for example, and prudential rules by safety concerns (Smetana, 1997; Smetana et al., 2000). Thus, preschoolers' understanding of *how things are done* includes standards for *how one should act* in these and other everyday situations, and this may help to explain young children's inflexibility with the application of behavioral expectations just as they are rigid in their beliefs about how common routines are conducted. Expectations for how a person acts may become regarded as normative and obligatory just as are expectations for how others will act in these prototypical situations.

Ironically, the normative absolutism of the young child's thinking about obligation does not necessarily translate into behavioral compliance, as every parent knows. This arises, in part, because many moral situations involve frustrating present desires in favor of broader (often future) goals, which is a conceptual challenge for young children (Lagattuta, 2005). It is also challenging to comprehend the feelings and interests of multiple participants in interpersonal conflict, especially when self-interest is involved. As Arsenio and his colleagues have shown, for example, young children perceive victimizers as feeling positively about their misconduct, partly because children focus on the satisfaction of the victimizer's desires rather than the victim's distress (Arsenio & Lover, 1999). These studies highlight that even with their sensitivity to others' feelings, comprehending simultaneously the emotional perspectives of multiple people is still difficult for young children. Thus, the young intuitive moralist's deontic understanding does not readily translate into moral compliance. The result is everyday experience with the disapproval of caregivers and the feelings of guilt that may result.

Moral Emotion

Moral emotion also emerges early, and contributes to the incentives for moral compliance because of its relevance to the self and relationships. As noted elsewhere, the development of self-understanding occurs in concert with the emergence of self-referent emotions that are elicited in everyday situations in which adults make salient attributions of responsibility for achievement or wrongdoing. With respect to guilt and shame, parental responses to a young child's misbehavior typically make explicit the behavioral values the child has violated, and it is remarkable how early children begin to respond with these emotions (Barrett, 1998; Lewis, 2000; Thompson et al., 2005). Kochanska, Gross, Lin, and Nichols (2002) observed children's affective and behavioral responses at 22, 33, and 45 months to experimental situations involving rigged mishaps for which children believed they were responsible. Young children exhibited concern and distress at each age, and individual differences in these responses were stable over time and were modestly predictive of a battery of conscience assessments at 56 months. Moreover, children who displayed more of these behaviors at each age were found to be temperamentally more fearful, and their mothers used less power assertion in discipline encounters. These developmental findings are consistent with maternal reports concerning the development of guilt in offspring, which also report significant growth in the affective and behavioral manifestations of guilt over this period (Kochanska, DeVet, Goldman, Murray, & Putnam, 1994; Stipek, Gralinski, & Kopp, 1990; Zahn-Waxler & Robinson, 1995; see Eisenberg, Fabes, & Spinrad, Chapter 11, this *Handbook,* this volume). At the same time that young children are becoming aware of normative and behavioral expectations, they are also becoming prone to self-referent moral emotions that can significantly motivate compliance.

Temperamental individuality is an important mediator of children's experience of the affective discomfort and anxiety associated with wrongdoing. In a theoretical analysis, Kochanska (1993) proposed that conscience development may assume two developmental pathways: (1) through the motivation to avoid the emotional discomfort associated with wrongdoing, and (2) through the motivation to maintain good relations with caregivers by exercising behavioral self-control. She proposed that a child's temperamental profile is influential in determining which developmental pathway predominantly contributes to the growth of conscience. This view was subsequently elaborated in two studies showing that for temperamentally fearful young children, conscience was predicted by maternal control strategies that deemphasized power and instead enlisted nonassertive guidance and "gentle discipline." These children are naturally prone to fear and anxiety after wrongdoing, Kochanska reasoned, and thus nonpunitive discipline that enlists the child's preexisting worry without creating overwhelming distress is likely to contribute best to moral internalization. By contrast, for children who were temperamentally relatively fearless, conscience was instead best predicted by the security of attachment and maternal warm responsiveness. For these children, the relational incentives of the mother-child relationship better motivated moral internalization and helped to consolidate a positive, mutually responsive parent-child relationship (Kochanska, 1991, 1995; see Kochanska, 1997a, and Kochanska et al., 2002, however, for somewhat different findings). These findings suggest that temperament may influence conscience development because it mediates children's emotional experience of parenting practices in response to wrongdoing.

Temperament may be related to conscience development in other ways. Young children who are high on effortful (or inhibitory) control are more capable of exercising self-restraint to comply or desist, and research by Kochanska and her colleagues suggests that these children are also higher on measures of conscience in both contemporaneous and longitudinal assessments (e.g., Kochanska, 1993; Kochanska, Murray, & Coy, 1997). Kochanska and her colleagues (1994) also reported that preschool girls who were higher on temperamental reactivity obtained higher scores on a maternal report measure of the child's guilt, consistent with the view that reactive children would be more sensitive to disapproval and criticism.

The temperament research underscores that there are alternative avenues to conscience development because young children are not morally cooperative for the same reasons. For some, cooperation springs from broader capacities for self-control; for others, maintaining good relations with caregivers (and the threats to relational harmony arising from misbehavior) is central; for still others, moral cooperation derives from efforts to avoid the fear and anxiety that arises from disapproval. This suggests that the moral socialization efforts of parents must be adapted to the child's temperamental profile and other characteristics. Furthermore, this literature suggests that not only moral resources but also moral vulnerabilities inhere in these temperamental profiles. Temperamentally fearful children may be vulnerable to becoming guilt-prone and morally inflexible as a result; temperamentally fearless children may misbehave when they can escape detection or avoid worry about the caregiver's loss of love. Because moral emotions are such powerful motivators of moral compliance, the influences of temperament on the emotional tendencies and self-regulatory capacities that underlie moral conduct are potentially important for healthy and unhealthy forms of moral motivation.

There is yet another emotional resource for conscience development that emphasizes the prosocial over the prohibitive side of morality. Empathy begins to emerge during the 2nd year and continues to unfold with growth in emotion understanding in early childhood (Zahn-Waxler, 2000; Zahn-Waxler & Radke-Yarrow, 1990; Zahn-Waxler & Robinson, 1995). To be sure, the sight and sound of another person's distress, fear, or anger is a motivationally complex and stressful event for young children. It may lead to sympathetic feelings and prosocial initiatives, but young children may also ignore, laugh at, or aggress toward another in distress, or seek comfort for themselves because of threats to their own emotional security and limited social understanding. This is one reason why it is important to index empathy in young children as an affective response rather than as an instrumental (i.e., prosocial) behavior. However, when adults can assist the child in understanding the emotions they are witnessing in another, especially by clarifying causality and responsibility, raw empathic arousal can become enlisted into prosocial initiatives toward another person, and into guilt when the child is the perpetrator of another's distress (Zahn-Waxler & Radke-Yarrow, 1990; Zahn-Waxler & Robinson, 1995). Moreover, as children mature throughout the preschool years, their vicarious emotional responding becomes increasingly predictive of prosocial behavior (Eisenberg & Fabes, 1998; see also Eisenberg & Fabes 1995; Miller, Eisenberg, Fabes, & Shell, 1996). Viewed in this light, empathy alone may not reliably elicit moral responding in young children, but instead is a setting condition from which prosocial initiatives may arise. Equally important, empathy is one of the emotional catalysts for young children developing a moral awareness in which the feelings and needs of other people are central.

Relational Influences

Fortunately, young children are not alone in their efforts to comply and cooperate. Parents and other caregivers contribute in many ways to the development of conscience. Beginning in infancy, when animated facial and vocal expressions of emotion are used by parents to warn or deter a locomoting child from a dangerous or disapproved activity, social referencing is enlisted to instill certain behaviors with emotional meaning and an-ticipated disapproval (Campos et al., 1999; Emde & Buchsbaum, 1990). Later, as the distal warning becomes remembered, behavioral compliance arises from the toddler "referencing the absent parent" in memory (Emde, Biringen, Clyman, & Oppenheim, 1991; Emde & Buchsbaum, 1990). Parents intervene to remove the child from disapproved conduct and sanction disobedience, but they also proactively avoid discipline encounters by distracting attention, providing anticipatory guidance or alternative activities, or other diversionary tactics (Holden & West, 1989). There is also considerable direct instruction of young children about moral, conventional, and prudential rules of conduct by parents who strive to enlist children's cooperation (Smetana et al., 2000). Beyond these, at least three other facets of the parent-child relationship contribute significantly to conscience development in the preschool years: (1) the overall warmth and cooperativeness of the parent-child relationship, (2) child management strategies used by parents in discipline encounters, and (3) broader conversational discourse between parents and offspring that incorporates morally relevant themes.

The warmth and cooperativeness of the parent-child relationship is important, especially early in life, because conscience development is part of a child's broader induction into a relational system of reciprocity characterized by mutual obligations (Kochanska, 1997b; Waters et al., 1991). The human consequences of personal conduct become experienced directly for the first time in a parent-child relationship, and thus the quality of that relationship, especially its mutual responsiveness, helps to orient a young child's moral sensitivity to humanistic concerns and heighten the child's receptiveness to the parent's socialization initiatives. In several studies in which the mutual responsiveness of parents with young children was assessed during extended home observations, Kochanska and her colleagues found that dyadic differences in this relational quality predicted measures of the child's conscience development both contemporaneously and longitudinally (e.g., Kochanska, 1997b; Kochanska, Forman, & Coy, 1999; Kochanska & Murray, 2000; see also Laible & Thompson, 2000). Related research has helped to explain why. Mothers in mutually responsive relationships use less power assertion with offspring and they are more empathic, as are their children in response to maternal simulations of distress (Kochanska, 1997b; Kochanska et al., 1999). In a behavior genetic study, Deater-Deckard and O'Connor (2000) concluded that dyadic mutually responsive orientation exemplifies an evocative gene-environment correlation in the parent-child relationship, which is consistent with the temperament research reviewed earlier.

Another index of relational quality is the security of attachment, and, as earlier noted, there is research evidence that a secure attachment is positively associated with cooperation and conscience development (e.g., Kochanska, 1995; Laible & Thompson, 2000). Interestingly, neither research group has reported a significant association between measures of attachment security and mutually responsive orientation between parent and child, despite their apparent conceptual overlap. Taken together, these studies underscore the importance of a harmonious relationship of positive mutuality between parent and child as a foundation for the growth of conscience and for cooperative conduct in young children.

A second feature of the parent-child relationship that contributes to conscience development is how the parent responds when young children misbehave. The discipline encounter has been the focus of extensive study for many years, and research findings with toddlers and preschoolers are consistent with those of older children in concluding that interventions that are coercive and power assertive elicit not only children's situational compliance but also young children's frustration and occasionally defiance. However, discipline that emphasizes reasoning and provides justification for compliance is more likely to foster internalized values in young children, even though children may also assert their autonomy through bargaining and negotiation (Crockenberg & Litman, 1990; Kuczynski, Kochanska, Radke-Yarrow, & Girnius-Brown, 1987; Laible & Thompson, 2002). This is likely to be one reason why, over the course of the preschool years, parents increasingly rely on verbal strategies over physical interventions for enlisting children's compliance (Dunn & Munn, 1987; Kuczynski et al., 1987).

Parental explanations, justifications, and reasoning may be especially important for young children who, in the context of heated emotions over misbehavior, may not immediately comprehend what is wrong or who is culpable. In their intervention, most parents provide a cognitive structure that explicitly links their response to the standards the parent has previously conveyed ("You know better than to hit your sister!"), invokes salient attributions of responsibility ("Why did you hit her?"), identifies consequences for another ("Look, she's crying!"), and often directly induces the self-referent evaluation and affect ("Bad boy! You should be ashamed of yourself!"). In doing so, the parent not only explicitly denotes causal associations between the child's behavior, consequences for another, the parent's response, and the experience of moral affect but also may provide an interpretation of the event that is different from the child's own. To the extent to which this is clearly communicated and understood by young children, this experience can be conceptually provocative to young children who are otherwise striving to understand others' beliefs, feelings, motives, and their associations with the child's own. Furthermore, parental explanations and reasoning in the discipline encounter also introduce young offspring to cultural and moral interpretations of the child's behavior. As Miller and her colleagues have shown, for example, mothers in the United States tend to attribute child misconduct to spunk or mischievousness, but Chinese and Chinese-American mothers emphasize much more the shame inherent in misbehavior, each consistent with their cultural values (Miller, Fung, & Mintz, 1996; Miller, Wiley, Fung, & Liang, 1997).

This straightforward and rationalist account of the effects of discipline in early conscience is complicated, however, in several ways (Grusec & Goodnow, 1994; Grusec, Goodnow, & Kuczynski, 2000). First, multiple parental goals are likely to compete in how parents respond to any discipline encounter. In many circumstances, a priority on moral tutelage must vie with other goals, including effecting immediate child compliance, enabling children to responsibly choose among behavioral alternatives, enhancing parent-child communication and understanding, allowing children to assert themselves, and other worthwhile aims (Hastings & Grusec, 1998; Holden & Miller, 1999). The reasons for the child's misbehavior, the child's characteristics (such as temperament), and situational constraints (e.g., public versus private setting) are among the important influences on the goals that parents choose to pursue during conflict with the child, and this helps to explain why parents are not necessarily consistent in their parenting practices across different situations (Holden & Miller, 1999). The clarity of the parent's moral message is thus likely to be obscured by the alternative socialization goals that are also being pursued, or by the parent's effort to integrate inconsistent goals (e.g., values transmission while enabling child autonomy).

Second, not only what the parent says but the broader relational context influences conscience development. A clear explanation warranting compliance is likely to have different meaning to a child who shares a warm and supportive relationship with the caregiver compared to a child who has experienced considerable prior conflict or distrust in that person. The view that children in warm, secure relationships may be more responsive to parental discipline practices than children in insecure relationships was recently tested by Kochanska et al. (2004), who assessed attachment security at 14 months, parental disciplinary practices at 14 to 45 months, and conscience at 56 months. For securely attached children, there was a significant positive longitudinal association between parental gentle discipline/responsiveness and later conscience; for insecure children, there was no such association. The expectation that specific parental practices have differential consequences based on the broader tenor of the parent-child relationship is consistent with other studies of the effects of parent-child conversational discourse on conscience development (Thompson et al., 2003; see following), and suggests that adult explanations may "sound differently" to children who share different kinds of relationships with them.

Third, young children are participants in the process of values appropriation. They interpret what they are told in the discipline encounter in light of their own perceptions of fairness, the emotional effects of the parent's behavior (e.g., threats to security or a sense of autonomy), and the relevance and consistency of the parental message with what else they know (Grusec & Goodnow, 1994; Kuczynski et al., 1997). The importance of children's constructions of parental values is consistent with the literature on temperament and conscience discussed earlier and with the studies highlighting the mediating influence of the parent-child relationship on discipline effects. Furthermore, parental attitudes and discipline practices vary in relation to the outcome expectancies of parents—parents intervene based, in part, on how they anticipate the child will react to their intended intervention (Holden, Miller, & Harris, 1999; Holden, Thompson, Zambarano, & Marshall, 1997). Thus, a child's construal of the discipline encounter is important not only for its effects on conscience development but also for how it influences the child's behavioral response which, in turn, affects future parental conduct. Studies such as these are important for reaffirming the importance of bidirectional and transactional models of early moral socialization, by contrast with traditional portrayals of values internalization.

Fourth, although conflict is conceptually provocative and contributes to values clarification, conflict between a young child and a parent is also threatening to young children, and the emotion generated by the discipline encounter may undermine the child's comprehension and processing of the parent's moral message. This is consistent with Hoffman's (1983, 2000) classic formulation of the discipline encounter, but it emphasizes how much the difference in power between participants in conflict can make a full and accurate comprehension of the message from an authority difficult. As noted by Thompson (1998), from a depth of processing memory model it is likely that a young child's coherent processing and understanding of the parent's message will be undermined by the heightened arousal created by the discipline encounter, even when parents are careful to use discipline approaches that do not unduly heighten the child's discomfort. This is especially likely if the young child's cognitive resources are also being mobilized for negotiation or bargaining (Crockenberg & Litman, 1990; Kuczynski et al., 1987).

This is one reason that students of conscience development have focused on a third feature of the parent-child relationship that is associated with conscience development: conversations that occur outside the discipline encounter. These conversations may be planned or spontaneous and their topics may concern (a) events in the past, such as the child's prior misbehavior or admirable conduct; (b) a shared experience in the future, such as going to a public setting where good behavior is necessary; (c) immediate events, such as a sibling's temper tantrum; (d) storybook reading; (e) pretend play; or (f) other shared experiences. In these contexts, even when parents are not explicitly intending these conversations to be a means of transmitting moral lessons, the judgments, values, inferences, assumptions, and other interpretations that parents naturally incorporate into these conversations make them potentially potent forums for early moral understanding and conscience development. Equally important, the young child's cognitive resources are more likely to be focused on understanding and responding to the parent's message with less competing emotional arousal than in the discipline encounter.

Variations in the content and style of parental discourse in conversation influence early conscience development. Laible and Thompson (2000) recorded conversations between parents and their 4-year-olds about past incidents in which the child had either misbehaved or behaved appropriately. Mothers who more frequently referred to the feelings of other people had children who were more advanced on measures of conscience, but maternal references to rules and the consequences of breaking them from the same conversations were unrelated to conscience. These findings were replicated in a prospective longitudinal study in which maternal references to feelings (but not references to rules and moral evaluations) during conflict with the child at 30 months predicted the child's conscience development 6 months later (Laible & Thompson, 2002). In another study, 2- to 3-year-old children whose mothers used reasoning and humanistic concerns in resolving conflict with them were more advanced in measures of moral understanding in follow-up assessments in kindergarten and first grade (Dunn et al., 1995). These findings suggest that one of the most important features of parent-child conversations on morally relevant themes is how they sensitize young children to the human dimensions of misbehavior and good conduct, helping children to comprehend the effects of their actions on how people feel. In a sense, these conversations put a human face on morality.

Just as in the discipline encounter, the warmth, emotional tone, and constructiveness of the parent's demeanor can be as important as what is said to the child. When they were in conflict with their young offspring, mothers who took the initiative to resolve conflict, using justifications to explain and clarify their expectations, and who managed to avoid aggravating and exacerbating tension (such as through threats or teasing) had young children who were more advanced on measures of conscience development at age 3 (Laible, 2004a; Laible & Thompson, 2002; see also Dunn et al., 1995 described earlier). By contrast, mothers who were conversationally "power assertive" when recounting the child's misbehavior in the recent past—conveying a critical or negative attitude, feelings of disappointment or anger, or involving reproach or punishment—had preschool children who obtained lower scores on measures of "moral cognition" assessed via children's story-completion responses to moral dilemmas (Kochanska, Aksan, & Nichols, 2003). As Hoffman (1983, 2000) has long argued, power assertion in the discipline encounter heightens children's anxiety and defensiveness and undermines retention of the parent's moral message, and it is likely that the same occurs in conversations about moral issues outside of discipline. Conversely, just as the well-documented effects of in-

ductive discipline on moral internalization occur when the adult combines warmth with a rational explanation that reduces threat to the child, similar influences occur in conversations outside of the discipline encounter as well. These conclusions also suggest that conscience development in young children is influenced by parent-child discourse in a manner similar to how older children are affected (Thompson et al., 2003).

Finally, just as the broader affective quality of the parent-child relationship is an important mediator of the effects of discipline in young children (Kochanska et al., 2004), the same is true of the effects of parent-child conversational discourse. Mothers' references to people's feelings interacts with the shared warmth of the parent-child relationship in its association with conscience development (Laible & Thompson, 2000; Thompson et al., 2003). Thus, broader relational quality combines with specific features of parent-child discourse to shape young children's conscience development.

Summary

The dissonance between the portrayal of conscience development emerging from these studies and traditional portrayals of the self-interested, preconventional, egocentric young child is an incentive to expanding understanding of the intuitive morality of early childhood and its developmental influences. These studies make it apparent that young children are acquiring moral orientations that are simpler, but fundamentally similar to, those of older children and adolescents, and therefore the experiences and influences of early childhood may provide an essential foundation for moral development at later ages. Viewed in this light, young children's conceptual growth, developing emotional understanding, and relational experiences may provide essential cornerstones for the later emergence of the internal, humanistic, self-committed morality of older children. Young children clearly are not "premoral" in any serious sense.

The study of conscience development has also offered developmentalists new questions and interesting methodologies with which to explore them. Beyond longitudinal studies that integrate the morality of early childhood with the better-studied moral reasoning of middle childhood, greater exploration of how young children conceptualize moral obligations would contribute to understanding how they perceive themselves as moral actors and (in Kochanska's evocative phrase) "moral selves." The relational catalysts to conscience development also merit further exploration, especially in efforts to integrate understanding of parental practices in conversation, discipline, and other interactive situations that contribute to the development of moral awareness in young children. Given the growing evidence that conscience emerges not primarily from the prohibitive morality of parental discipline but from the incentives provided by a harmonious, mutually cooperative parent-child relationship, a portrayal of early moral growth that underscores children's appropriation of values from shared activity in the family may be more appropriate than the traditional internalization formulation. By underscoring the multifaceted shared contexts in which early conscience develops, such an approach highlights how parents and children mutually create the moral environment they share as a family.

SELF

The development of self-awareness provides a window into the psychological growth of the child. Over the course of a few years, young children acquire capacities to engage with others intersubjectively, visually recognize their mirror images, attribute behavioral and psychological qualities to themselves, create autobiographical accounts, and situate themselves temporally as individuals with continuity into the past and future. With each developmental advance the child becomes a more complex, multidimensional *self* while also becoming more insightfully self-aware. Advances in self-awareness also transform young children's social interactions. They make children more psychologically self-conscious social actors who also possess greater insight into others. Like emotional development, the growth of self in early childhood involves the progressive elaboration of biologically basic capacities in ways that integrate the influences of conceptual growth, relational processes, and the child's own constructions of experience. These features of the development of self have stimulated considerable recent research into this topic, although important questions remain to be addressed.

Developmentally Emergent Dimensions of Self

It is common to describe the 2nd year as when *the self* emerges, but enduring aspects of self-awareness have developmentally earlier origins. Both Gibson (1995) and Neisser (1995) argue that the earliest forms of prerepre-

sentational self-awareness arise from the integrated perceptual experiences deriving from movement and activity beginning soon after birth. The synchronous multimodal perceptual experience arising from self-produced activity fundamentally distinguishes the perceiver from objects (and people) acted on or that move around the infant. Neisser's portrayal of this "ecological self" addresses the traditional assumption that infants are born adualistic (i.e., incapable of differentiating the external from the internal world) by noting that perceptual experience itself distinguishes subjective from surround—in Gibson's (1995) evocative words, "to perceive the world is to coperceive oneself" (p. 6). Indeed, in this Gibsonian view, subsequent developmental changes in the perception of affordances in the environment also entail developmental changes in self-awareness (e.g., awareness of emergent capabilities) such as in how flat, extended surfaces afford walking to a 15-month-old toddler but not a 6-month-old. Moreover, these integrated perceptual experiences provide avenues for other, more complex forms of self-awareness to develop. By 5 months, the integration of kinesthetic and visual experience during movement enables a primitive kind of featural self-recognition: Infants can distinguish videos of their own leg movements from those of another infant (Bahrick & Watson, 1985; Rochat & Morgan, 1995). The initial organization and integration of experience around an implicit frame of reference thus constitutes one of the earliest forms of self-awareness.

Another is the experience of agency. As earlier noted, very young infants respond to contingency and by 2 to 3 months they respond with positive affect to contingent responding but become affectively negative if the contingency is interrupted (Lewis et al., 1990; Rovee-Collier, 1989; Watson, 1985). Initiating actions that have a predictable impact on objects and people, and the positive affect that results from the awareness of control, are together likely to be highly salient experiences contributing to self-awareness early in infancy. Early social interaction taps into the young infant's contingency awareness, which contributes to the delight of face-to-face play, and variability in caregiver responsiveness, such as the subdued responding of depressed mothers, consequently has a significant impact on infant affect and sociability. Taken together, therefore, the earliest forms of prerepresentational self-awareness are perceptual, affective, and agentic in quality, contributing to the emergence of initial *existential self-awareness,* and the foundation of James's (1890) "I-self."

By the final months of the 1st year, infants are not only agentic but also volitional. In their goal-directed efforts, as Piaget noted, infants can substitute an alternative means for one that has been frustrated and act strategically to accomplish their intentions. This inaugurates, according to Tomasello (1995b, 1999; Tomasello & Rakoczy, 2003), a conceptual advance in which infants begin to perceive others also as intentional actors. As earlier discussed, this is manifested in a variety of behaviors that reflect the infant's awareness that other people have subjectivity that can be understood and intentions that can be influenced, including joint attention, social referencing, imitative learning, and the emergence of intentional communicative efforts (Carpenter, Nagell, & Tomasello, 1998). Moreover, by the end of the 1st year, the infant's experience of goal directedness often conflicts with others' goals and intentions (of which every parent of a locomotor infant is aware), contributing to the self-awareness that derives from conflicts between his or her own goals and those of another. As a result, social interaction involves the infant's goal directedness combined with a dawning awareness that subjective, intentional states are at the root of others' behavior. According to Tomasello (1995b), it is not only the development of a new intersubjective capacity that inaugurates an advance in self-awareness but also the infant's growing realization that the self can be the object of another's attention, intention, and emotional response. Just as infants enlist another's emotional evaluation of objects and events in social referencing, they also become sensitive to the adult's emotional demeanor when attention is focused on themselves, and variability in the caregiver's warmth, emotional tone, and sensitivity become increasingly important at this time. This awareness sets the stage for the growth of self-referent emotions, like embarrassment, and self-referential evaluative emotions, like pride, guilt, and shame, later in the 2nd year. The end of the 1st year witnesses, therefore, the emergence of *the intersubjective self.*

When do infants begin to exhibit *featural self-recognition*—the ability to recognize their physical features? This is commonly taken as the central index of self-awareness, but as noted earlier, recognition that one's features and actions are familiar can mean different things at different ages. Legerstee, Anderson, and Schaffer (1998) found that 8-month-old infants could discriminate static and dynamic video images of their faces from those of peers (5-month-olds could discrimi-

nate only dynamic images), and infants of both ages could also discriminate the sound of their nondistressed vocalizations from those of other infants. Prior experience with vocal play and mirror images could contribute to these discriminations, with the strong integration of visual-kinesthetic and auditory-kinesthetic perceptual experience during these activities marking them as self-initiated (see Bahrick, Moss, & Fadil, 1996, for findings with younger infants). But these results do not necessarily imply that infants are recognizing themselves in these facial and vocal displays. By 18 months, however, after their noses have been surreptitiously marked with a spot of rouge, toddlers reliably show mark-directed behavior when placed before a mirror (Lewis & Brooks-Gunn, 1979). Featural self-recognition is based on the contingency between movement and motion in the mirror, but this behavior also reflects additional psychological achievements: Young children exhibit self-referent emotions like embarrassment at this age (Lewis, 2000), becoming aware of standards for appearance and behavior that also evoke special attention to soiled toys or faces (Kagan, 1981; S. Lamb, 1993). Consequently, toddlers' responses to the classic rouge task entails more complex influences than mere featural self-recognition, and its psychological meaning incorporates greater self-awareness and the application of standards for normative appearance (i.e., my nose is not ordinarily red). Mirror self-recognition at 18 months builds on the achievements of intersubjective self-awareness at age 1 to consolidate the beginning of objective self-awareness in young children, or James's (1890) "me-self."

In light of the development of the "me-self," it is unsurprising that late in the 2nd year and early in the third, toddlers exhibit emerging indications of other representational forms of self-awareness. These include increased verbal self-referential behavior (e.g., "me big!"; Bates, 1990) and verbal labeling of internal experiences (such as emotions; Bretherton et al., 1986), assertions of competence and responsibility as autonomous agents (such as in self-monitoring, refusing assistance, and insisting on "do it myself"; Bullock & Lutkenhaus, 1988, 1990; Stipek, Gralinski, & Kopp, 1990), growing sensitivity to evaluative standards and the emergence of conscience (Thompson, Meyer, & McGinley, 2006), assertions of ownership (Fasig, 2000), the emergence of self-control (Kopp & Wyer, 1994), categorizing the self by gender and in other ways, and young children's growing interest in how their behavior is regarded by others (Emde & Buchsbaum, 1990; Stipek, Recchia, & Mc-

Clintic, 1992). The more complex self-representations of early childhood are reflected also in the emergence of self-referential emotions during the 2nd and 3rd years. By the end of the 2nd year and increasingly in the third, the simple joy of success becomes accompanied by looking and smiling to an adult and calling attention to the feat; the simple sadness of failure becomes accompanied either by avoidance of eye contact with the adult and turning away or by reparative activity and confession; and in response to conspicuous attention toddlers increasingly respond with smiling, gaze aversion, and self-touching (Barrett, 1998; Barrett, Zahn-Waxler, & Cole, 1993; Kochanska et al., 2002; Lewis, 2000; Stipek, 1995; Stipek et al., 1992).

Taken together, young children are beginning to regard themselves in more multidimensional and evaluative ways early in the 3rd year as they increasingly perceive themselves as objects of the attention and thought of others. This is part of the legacy of the intersubjectivity that emerges by the first birthday, and the greater sensitivity to the evaluations of others arising from developing psychological understanding and intersubjective awareness as featural self-recognition is attained. Moreover, during the 2nd year, developing capacities for receptive language clarify not only the child's status as the object of others' evaluations but also lexicalizes these evaluations as they are conveyed through language. Young children not only appropriate others' evaluations of themselves but also the evaluative standards they use as part of children's effort to comprehend constancies and expectations for everyday experience. These processes contribute to the emergence of the *conceptual self* (the "cognitive self" of Howe & Courage, 1993, 1997) that will continue to evolve in sophistication and scope in the years that follow.

Somewhat later, in the 4th and 5th years, young children begin to perceive themselves in more explicitly characterological terms at about the same time that they begin to perceive others in terms of psychological traits (Marsh, Ellis, & Craven, 2002; Measelle, Ablow, Cowan, & Cowan, 1998). To be sure, young children often rely on concrete, observable features and action tendencies in their spontaneous self-descriptions but they can also use psychological trait terms provided by other people appropriately as personality self-descriptions (e.g., "I am naughty sometimes, but good with adults"; Eder, 1989, 1990). Although young children's use of trait terms like *good* and *naughty* lacks the rich meaning inherent in how older people use these con-

cepts, these self-descriptions are like personality traits in that they show stability over time, are similar to how others (such as their mothers and teachers) describe them, and show convergent validity when correlated with external measures of the same characteristics (Eder & Mangelsdorf, 1997; Goodvin et al., 2005; Marsh et al., 2002; Measelle et al., 1998). Even a preschooler's use of a concrete feature, such as describing his- or herself as a girl or boy, is accompanied by a basic understanding of the psychological attributes and stereotypes associated with being male or female (Ruble & Martin, Chapter 14, this *Handbook,* this volume). To be sure, young children's personality self-descriptions show greater stability and convergent validity with increasing age, consistent with growth in children's understanding of personality characteristics more generally (Marsh, Craven, & Debus, 1998). Moreover, young children tend to be unduly optimistic about the modifiability of individual traits, particularly the stability of positive qualities and the changeability of negative ones. Current research confirms, however, the emergence of the conceptual self in early childhood and of psychological self-descriptors in the child's self-concept.

Another important advance in self-awareness occurs when young children can perceive themselves in a temporal context. Comprehending how past experiences can influence the present self, and the ability to anticipate the self in future contexts, are significant advances in self-awareness because of their relevance to strategic planning, delay of gratification, moral compliance, performance evaluation, autobiographical memory, and self-understanding. These advances depend on a capacity to perceive an identity between the present self and the self that existed in the past and that will exist in the future. The realization that it is the same "I" in each temporal context distinguishes this kind of self-awareness from earlier-developing capacities to evoke expectations from past events, recall specific past experiences, or anticipate future events (Moore & Lemmon, 2001). Povinelli (1995, 2001) has shown that temporal self-awareness begins to emerge at about 4 years of age. In experimental procedures that are analogous to the mirror self-recognition tasks, young children were videotaped playing with an experimenter who surreptitiously (but on film) placed a large sticker on the child's head. When they later watched themselves on the videotapes, most 4-year-olds located and removed the sticker that was still on their heads. By contrast, younger 3-year-olds recognized themselves in the videos but most did not touch the stickers on their heads, apparently unable to associate the event on film with their current condition (Povinelli, Landau, & Perilloux, 1996; Povinelli & Simon, 1998; see also Povinelli, Landry, Theall, Clark, & Castille, 1999 for similar results using different procedures).

The growth of the *temporal self* by age 4, as indexed by the delayed self-recognition task, is believed to be associated with at least two interrelated conceptual achievements: (1) a dawning awareness of the representational nature of knowledge (also relevant to theory of mind development) and (2) the ability to reason in a causal temporal-spatial manner (Povinelli, 2001; Welch-Ross, 2001). Together they contribute to the child's realization that knowledge is subjective and personal, knowledge will vary even though the self remains constant, and current experience and knowledge are affected by past influences on the self. There has not, however, been definitive empirical examination of these ideas. Performance on the delayed self-recognition task is positively correlated with delay of gratification in preschoolers (Lemmon & Moore, 2001) and with some aspects of autobiographical memory, although not with performance on theory of mind tasks (Welch-Ross, 2001; Zelazo, Sommerville, & Nichols, 1999). Much more research clearly is needed.

Self-Regulation

Accompanying these multifaceted changes in self-awareness is growth in the young child's capacities for self-management. According to Kopp's (1982; Kopp & Wyer, 1994) well-known formulation, the preschool years witness significant advances in behavioral self-control because of growth in children's capacities for remembering, representing, and generalizing behavioral standards, conceiving the self as an autonomous and responsible agent, altering behavior in response to remembered standards, and (somewhat later) engaging in a more continuous and self-generated monitoring of compliance with these standards. Kopp regards the 2nd and 3rd years as central to the development of self-control. The more mature and autonomous skills of self-regulation are an achievement of the 4th year.

This formulation has been expanded in recent years with new appreciation of the temperamental, neurobiological, and caregiving contributions to the growth of self-regulation (see Eisenberg, 2002, for a review related to emotion regulation). Temperament theorists, most notably Rothbart (1989), have long recognized that temperamental qualities index the self-regulatory and reactive qualities of behavioral style (see Rothbart & Bates, Chapter 3, this *Handbook,* this volume). Differences in temperamental effortful control best reflect this feature of individuality, which have been found to emerge early in childhood and to be associated with better emotion regulation, conscience development, and other adaptive qualities (Kochanska, 1993; Kochanska, Murray, & Coy, 1997; Kochanska, Murray, & Harlan, 2000). Although neurobiological studies of the development of self-regulation are still limited with children, it is apparent that the growth of self-control is associated with maturation of multiple regions of the prefrontal cortex that are associated with emotional, attentional, cognitive, and behavioral self-control (Johnson, 1997). Finally, an extensive body of empirical literature documents the association between self-regulatory competence in early childhood and sensitive, supportive maternal care and the association between parental overcontrol, punitiveness, and negative affect and children's behavioral dysregulation (see Eisenberg, 2002; Fox & Calkins, 2003).

These advances help to account for expanding research interest in the development of self-regulation, but this remains an extraordinarily difficult area of study. Research into emotion regulation illustrates why (see Cole, Martin, & Dennis, 2004, and commentaries that follow; also Eisenberg & Spinrad, 2004). Emotional regulatory processes can be automatic or effortful, but distinguishing these is important to understanding their developmental course. The processes of and influences on emotion regulation are often indistinguishable from those affecting emotional arousal, leading to uncertainty over whether regulatory processes can be independently identified and studied. Moreover, emotion regulation can arise from external sources (such as the efforts of caregivers) as well as self-initiated efforts, and, although each manages emotion, extrinsic and intrinsic regulatory efforts entail different influences and developmental course (Thompson & Meyer, in press). This means that a child can display moderate levels of emotional arousal appropriate to the situation, but this can arise because of (a) the child's temperamental effortful control; (b) the coaching, support, and incentives of caregivers; (c) the fact that this child was not highly aroused in the circumstances (owing to temperament, prior experience, or other factors); and/or (d) the child's enlistment of emotional self-regulatory strategies. Distinguishing these influences on emotionality is a conceptual and empirical challenge. Finally, individual differences in emotion regulation must be studied functionally to comprehend their relevance to broader differences in emotional or social competence (Thompson, 1994). Young children may develop strategies of emotion regulation that are adaptive in some social contexts but maladaptive in others, and individual differences in attentional, behavioral, cognitive, and emotional self-regulation may have common bases but also different developmental pathways.

Taken together, these challenges do not mitigate the value of studying the development of self-regulation and the origins and consequences of individual differences in self-control. But they do indicate that considerably greater conceptual and empirical clarification of the nature of self-regulation—and its attentional, emotional, cognitive, and behavioral components—is needed to guide future inquiry.

Development of Autobiographical Memory

Autobiographical memory can be defined as explicit memory of past events that is organized around the significance of these events for the self. The growth of autobiographical memory during the preschool years reflects advances in self-awareness but also other developing capacities, including the developing representation of events in memory, social influences on the reconstruction and recall of past experiences, conceptual skills related to the representation of knowledge, and the influence of language in the construction of memory and its reporting (Reese, 2002). Because of its complexity, there has been considerable debate among developmental scientists concerning the nature of autobiographical memory and its developmental influences, accompanied by significantly expanded research attention to this phenomenon.

One influential view has been offered by Howe and Courage (1993, 1997), who have proposed that autobiographical memory emerges late in the 2nd year after the development of the "cognitive self," a knowledge structure that organizes memories of personal experiences. The development of the cognitive self is, according to these theorists, revealed at 18 months by the visual self-recognition of toddlers in the mirror-rouge task and by other indicators of self-awareness at this time. Howe and Courage argue that evidence for autobiographical memory during this period can be found in research showing that personal events can be recalled by infants and young children several weeks or months after their occurrence, and the recall of these children, although reliant on carefully designed nonverbal responses or the interrogatory assistance of questioners, is generally coherent and accurate (Howe & Courage, 1997; see generally Bauer 2002a, 2002b). In their view, once toddlers have become capable of representing themselves physically and conceptually by the end of the 2nd year, personal memories become mnemonically tagged as autobiographical.

Most other developmentalists portray the emergence of autobiographical memory at a later age, however, owing in part to a stronger distinction between episodic and autobiographical memory (see Fivush, 2001). In their view, autobiographical memory is distinctive because it incorporates an awareness of the personal, present significance of the past event. To Welch-Ross (1995, 2001), the social metacognitive skills essential to the development of autobiographical memory concern knowledge representation—understanding how knowledge is connected to unique experiences in the personal past—together with a personal, subjective stance to remembered events, and the ability to reason about causal connections between events across time. Perner (2001; Perner & Ruffman, 1995) likewise implicates metacognitive skills, especially the capacity to comprehend autobiographical memories as personal "reexperiences" of, and thus deriving from, past events directly experienced. Nelson and Fivush (2004; see also Nelson, 1993b, 1996; Fivush, 2001) portray autobiographical memory as a distinct memory system that builds on the development of a sense of self, theory of mind, knowledge representations, and an awareness of the temporal connections between past and present events. They also emphasize the influence of narrative discourse between the child and a caregiver during reminiscence as the means by which many of these conceptual foundations of autobiographical memory are fostered in early childhood.

The conclusion of these theorists that autobiographical memory emerges at age 3.5 or 4 is easy to reconcile with research findings that most adults do not remember personal events from earlier than about age 3.5 (the end of "childhood amnesia") and to integrate with other developing conceptual achievements of early childhood, including theory of mind, self-understanding, and comprehension of psychological causality. In one empirical test of alternative theoretical views, Harley and Reese (1999) assessed 19-month-olds' self-recognition in the mirror-rouge task along with maternal reminiscing style in conversation with the child. They found that each variable uniquely predicted children's later memory skill: children who developed featural self-recognition earlier and the offspring of mothers with an elaborative reminiscing style were each more proficient in recalling personal experiences. However, subsequent analyses revealed that by age 2, the effects of early self-recognition ability on subsequent autobiographical recall were mediated by maternal reminiscing style (Reese, 2002). Thus, it seems that the emergence of the cognitive self in early childhood is an important contributor to the development of autobiographical memory, but especially in juxtaposition with social influences on the construction of memory.

Regardless of their theoretical bent concerning age of onset, many developmental theorists agree that the growth of autobiographical memory entails social influences as well as conceptual achievements. Nelson and Fivush (2004) argue, in particular, that the content and structure of narrative discourse with an adult about shared experiences provides essential catalysts to the representation of autobiographical events and the development of self. These conceptual catalysts through narrative include: (a) helping young children understand the personal significance of remembered events, sometimes with reference to prior experiences; (b) enabling young children to conceptualize their experience in a temporal-causal framework in which past events relate to present experience; (c) contributing to children's comprehension of the distinctiveness of their subjective remembrance, partly as it compares (and conflicts) with the adult's own recollection; and (d) helping to structure and reorganize the child's direct representation of the experience into a form that is more memorable and can be shared. By scaffolding a young child's memory through narrative, adults foster the temporal understanding, sense of self, subjective orientation, and other metacognitive skills relevant to autobiographical memory (Nelson & Fivush, 2004). Similar views have been offered by Miller (1994, Miller et al., 1997; Wiley, Rose, Burger, & Miller, 1998), who has emphasized how cultural and subcultural beliefs about the self become appropriated by young children through the content of narrative discourse—or "personal storytelling"—with family members.

Autobiographical memory is thus not an individual recollection but rather a shared construction. This is especially true early in childhood when direct representations of experience are likely to be somewhat disorganized and incomplete, and when the adult narrative can provide the structure and interpretive framework that establishes the significance of personal events to the child and makes them more memorable. Consider,

for example, the following brief conversation between a 21-month-old and his mother about conflict over breakfast cereal earlier in the morning (from Dunn & Brown, 1991, p. 97):

Child: Eat my Weetabix. Eat my Weetabix. Crying.
Mother: Crying, weren't you? We had quite a battle. "One more mouthful, Michael." And what did you do? You spat it out!
Child: (pretends to cry)

In the mother's elaborated representation of their shared experience, she provides her son with a temporal sequence of events leading to his emotional reaction (which was the source of his conversational prompt), emphasizing the significance of the event for him, and at the same time conveying a representation of the event that was likely to be quite different from his own. In doing so, she not only enlisted his direct representation into a narrative structure for verbal sharing but also sequenced essential features of their shared experience in a manner that made the episode more memorable. She also contributed to his developing self-awareness by clarifying that although they shared this experience, their viewpoints were different and thus the understanding they derived from it was different (and thus that knowledge is subjective). The mother provided, in short, a memorable narrative structure and lessons in understanding and self. Although it is uncertain how much this shared retelling would, at 21 months, contribute to the development of an autobiographical memory, the mother's scaffolding of her son's representations of events over time would be likely to contribute to memories that are autobiographical in nature.

Consistent with this view, longitudinal research shows that mothers with a more elaborative narrative style (i.e., richly descriptive and evaluative, providing background and contextual information and eliciting information from the child) have children who themselves are later found to engage in more detailed, richer reminiscing and provide more extensive autobiographical accounts compared to the offspring of mothers with a less elaborative narrative style (Farrant & Reese, 2000; Haden, Haine, & Fivush, 1997; Harley & Reese, 1999; Reese, Haden, & Fivush, 1993; see Reese, 2002 for a review). Individual differences in maternal narrative style are consistent across the preschool years (Farrant & Reese, 2000; Reese et al., 1993) and across siblings (Haden, 1998), although child characteristics (such as age and gender) also influence maternal elaborativeness

(Reese, 2002). One study found that in a socioeconomically disadvantaged sample, mothers who were trained to use an elaborative style in conversation with their 3.5-year-olds were found to use more contextual questions and open-ended prompts a year later. By age 5.5, their children themselves were more elaborative in their narrative style (Peterson, Jesso, & McCabe, 1999). Taken together, these findings suggest that the detail and richness of young children's autobiographical memories are significantly influenced by the quality of reminiscing they share with their caregivers, and that conceptions of self may also be conceptually elaborated in these conversational contexts. This conclusion is consistent with those of earlier discussions in this chapter concerning the influence of conversational catalysts on the development of emotion understanding, theory of mind, and other aspects of psychological understanding.

In the context of shared reminiscing, young children are likely to appropriate not only organized personal memories and a narrative style but also much more. Reconsider the earlier conversation between Michael and his mother over Weetabix and notice the other lessons provided by the adult in her representation of the morning's confrontation. The mother instructed her son about emotion and morality: In her portrayal, crying is associated with misbehavior and defiance (not with having to eat horrible breakfast cereal, which may have been her son's initial representation). She provided lessons about the self: Good boys cooperate, but Michael was uncooperative and that is why he cried. There were also lessons about relationships, which, according to his mother, are harmonious when sons are cooperative with their mothers' requests but are disrupted by filial defiance (rather than by maternal insistence). In short, the mother interpreted the morning's events in her framework of assumptions, causal attributions, beliefs, and values. These beliefs constitute part of the context of mother-child reminiscing and, although it is unclear how many of these lessons are likely to be internalized at age 2, they are likely to have a significant influence on young children's developing conceptions of emotion, morality, self, and relationships as such conversations become part of the landscape of parent-child interaction during the preschool years (Thompson et al., 2003).

Adults incorporate certain values into their shared conversations with young children because they are cultural members who nonconsciously embrace cultural beliefs about the self, relationships, and morality. In an observational study, Miller and her colleagues showed, for example, how the "personal storytelling" of Chinese and American mothers portrayed the child's experience consistently with the broader values of their cultures. Chinese and Chinese-American mothers used storytelling with their children to convey moralistic themes, with an emphasis on the shame inherent in misconduct, while American mothers used storytelling for its entertainment value, emphasizing instead the child's spunk or mischievousness over misconduct (Miller, Potts, Fung, Hoogstra, & Mintz, 1990; Miller et al., 1996, 1997). Wang, Leichtman, and Davies (2000) noted that American mothers co-constructed reminiscences with their preschool offspring that emphasized the child's personal predilections and opinions, while Chinese mothers focused on moral rules and behavioral standards (see also Mullen & Yi, 1995). The influence of these conversational foci is reflected in the self-descriptions and autobiographical accounts of Asian and American young children. American children have been found to be more self-focused, use more internal state language and evaluations, and provide more detail about specific past events, by contrast with the greater emphasis on social roles and relationships and daily routines of Asian children (Han, Leichtman, & Wang, 1998; Wang, 2004). These findings suggest that the shared construction of autobiographical narrative, and the self-understanding that relates to it, is one way that cultural values concerning the self, relationships, and morality are conveyed intergenerationally (Fivush, 2004).

Young children do not merely appropriate the representations of personal experience interpreted by their caregivers: They are active construers of their own direct experiences. Although the language and the narrative structure offered by the adult are extremely important influences in shaping children's personal representations through conversation (partly owing to how language articulates and clarifies internal psychological realities), as children develop competencies in representing, interpreting, and remembering personal experience they are likely to object to parental constructions of their experience that are dissonant with their own. Levine, Stein, and Liwag (1999) showed that parents and young children commonly disagree about the child's feelings and experiences during shared events, often when adults make assumptions about the child's goals that are incorrect, and that disagreements occur most frequently for negative emotions. Disagreements between parents and offspring also commonly arise when adults omit from their narrative crucial aspects of the experience that figure prominently in children's own recollections. Little is known, however, about how children respond to such discrepancies in parent-child conversation, and this is a topic meriting further inquiry because of its relevance to children's comprehension of the personal, subjective nature of knowledge as well as to attachment theorists' views about the origins of the relational origins of defensive exclusion.

Summary

The conclusion that the early development of self derives from an interaction of the child's construals of personal experience and the adult's scaffolding of personal understanding confers on this topic unique research opportunities and challenges. Contrary to other forms of psychological understanding, children have special expertise concerning their characteristics, experiences, and self-knowledge that will increasingly vie with the adult's interpretations as children mature and acquire more robust, internally consistent self-referent beliefs. Yet, because of their psychological sophistication, caregivers are also uniquely insightful about the feelings, motivations, and individuality of the children they care for. Moreover, they begin to shape young children's self-awareness from an early age, beginning with the emotional signals they convey concerning the child's activities, to their appraisals of the child's successes and failures, to the construction of autobiographical memory in conversations about everyday events. Yet, there are elements of the child's experiences—and construals of that experience—that are always private and inaccessible to the adult, in part because they cannot easily be conveyed. Somehow, in the context of the shared activity of a young child, who is both expert and novice in self-understanding, and an adult, who has limited but sophisticated insight into the child's characteristics, self-understanding is jointly constructed. Understanding this developmental process is an important and valuable challenge for future research.

CONCLUSION

Often the most innovative thinking in developmental science is integrative. A field that commonly parcels the developmental process into separable domains or periods benefits from efforts to integrate insight from studies of cognitive and social functioning, or across stages of growth, or between typically and atypically developing populations. This is certainly true of the study of early sociopersonality development. The most notable reflection of this integrative potential is in the study of early social cognition, where the developmentally downward extension of theory of mind research touches on the long-standing interests of social developmentalists in the expectations and self-awareness deriving from social interaction in infancy. Research on conscience development likewise integrates understanding of emotion, temperament, cognition, and parenting in new ways of conceptualizing the interaction of child and adult in the appropriation of moral standards. Attachment theory and research benefits from the integration of research on event representation, autobiographical memory, and parent-child narrative in theoretical conceptions of the internal working models associated with security. The broader science of developing relationships is also increasingly integrating biological perspectives into understanding of the nature and consequences of early family relationships.

In these and other domains of early sociopersonality growth, development arises from the interaction of a young child, equipped with a powerfully inductive mind, and people with whom the child is in continuous relationship. Relational partners are conceptual catalysts because of the ubiquity of their shared experiences with the young child; their intimate knowledge of the child's characteristics, individuality, and developmental needs; and the opportunities they enlist to stimulate behavioral and conceptual growth (often without awareness of doing so) in interactive activities. Throughout this review of research on early social understanding, conscience, and development of self, the importance of parents, peers, siblings, and other relational partners is continuously apparent.

For this reason, the developmental model that seems most useful in comprehending early sociopersonality development is not socialization (which emphasizes the child as the recipient of understanding) or constructivism (which emphasizes the independently inductive mind), but rather a model of the appropriation of understanding through shared activity (Rogoff, 1990). This neo-Vygotskian formulation emphasizes the shared creation of knowledge through the interaction of the child with a partner in the everyday activities highlighted in this review, such as social interaction, relief of distress, conflict of wills, and shared conversation. Such a theoretical orientation enables an integration of the profound insights into the developing mind provided by cognitive-developmental scholars with the exquisite studies of early social interaction offered by students of sociopersonality development and has the potential of generating new insights into early development. The value of such an orientation has been highlighted throughout this review, from research describing the association of maternal "mind-mindedness" with the development of psychological understanding, to research on attachment security as a mediator of the influence of parental discipline practices on moral internalization, to studies of the influence of parent-child conversation on the development of autobiographical memory. In each case, conceptual growth arises from the generative influence of social experience on a young mind that is powerfully prepared to glean new understanding from that experience.

Bridging the conceptual perspectives of cognitive and sociopersonality research is a significant advance for future research, just as are efforts to bridge biological and social perspectives to relationships, and to bridge understanding of typical and atypical developmental processes. Each is important because in the end, the continuing vitality of research in this area derives from our success in reassembling the developing child: one who thinks, feels, and relates, who is both biological and social, who maintains continuity across time while dramatic developmental changes occur, and who is in relationship with multiple partners in diverse social ecologies. Our capacities as research scientists to see the developing child as a coherent, integrated being underlies our capacities to imagine the developmental process for all of its complexity, scope, and vitality.

REFERENCES

Adamson, L., & Frick, J. (2003). The still face: A history of a shared experimental paradigm. *Infancy, 4,* 451–473.

Ainsworth, M. D. S. (1973). The development of infant-mother attachment. In B. Caldwell & H. Ricciuti (Eds.), *Review of child development research* (Vol. 3, pp. 1–94). Chicago: University of Chicago Press.

Ainsworth, M. D. S. (1989). Attachments beyond infancy. *American Psychologist, 44,* 709–716.

Ainsworth, M. D. S. (1990). Some considerations regarding theory and assessment relevant to attachments beyond infancy. In M. Greenberg, D. Cicchetti, & E. Cummings (Eds.), *Attachment in the preschool years* (pp. 463–488). Chicago: University of Chicago Press.

Ainsworth, M. D. S., Blehar, M., Waters, E., & Wall, S. (1978). *Patterns of attachment.* Hillsdale, NJ: Erlbaum.

Allen, J., & Land, D. (1999). Attachment in adolescence. In J. Cassidy & P. Shaver (Eds.), *Handbook of attachment* (pp. 319–335). New York: Guilford Press.

Anan, R., & Barnett, D. (1999). Perceived social support mediates between prior attachment and subsequent adjustment: A study of urban African American children. *Developmental Psychology, 35,* 1210–1222.

Arsenio, W., & Lover, A. (1999). Children's conceptions of sociomoral affect: Happy victimizers, mixed emotions, and other expectancies. In M. Killen & D. Hart (Eds.), *Morality in everyday life: Developmental perspectives* (pp. 87–128). New York: Cambridge University Press.

Astington, J., & Baird, J. (Eds.). (2005). *Why language matters for theory of mind.* New York: Oxford University Press.

Bahrick, L., Moss, L., & Fadil, C. (1996). Development of visual self-recognition in infancy. *Ecological Psychology, 8,* 189–208.

Bahrick, L., & Watson, J. (1985). Detection of intermodal proprioceptive-visual contingency as a potential basis of self-perception in infancy. *Developmental Psychology, 21,* 963–973.

Baird, J., & Baldwin, D. (2001). Making sense of human behavior. In B. Malle, L. Moses, & D. Baldwin (Eds.), *Intentions and intentionality* (pp. 193–206). Cambridge, MA: MIT Press.

Bakermans-Kranenburg, M., van Ijzendoorn, M., & Juffer, F. (2003). Less is more: Meta-analyses of sensitivity and attachment interventions in early childhood. *Psychological Bulletin, 129,* 195–215.

Baldwin, D. (2000). Interpersonal understanding fuels knowledge acquisition. *Current Directions in Psychological Science, 9,* 40–45.

Baldwin, D., Baird, J., Saylor, M., & Clark, M. (2001). Infants parse dynamic action. *Child Development, 72,* 708–717.

Baldwin, D., Markman, E., Bill, B., Desjardins, R., & Irwin, J. (1996). Infants' reliance on a social criterion for establishing word-object relations. *Child Development, 67,* 3135–3153.

Baldwin, D., & Moses, L. (1996). The ontogeny of social information-processing. *Child Development, 67,* 1915–1939.

Banerjee, M. (1997). Hidden emotions: Preschoolers' knowledge of appearance-reality and emotion display rules. *Social Cognition, 15,* 107–132.

Barnett, D., Ganiban, J., & Cicchetti, D. (1999). Maltreatment, negative expressivity, and the development of type D attachments from 12 to 24 months of age. *Monographs of the Society for Research in Child Development, 64*(Serial No. 258) 97–118.

Barnett, D., Kidwell, S., & Leung, K. (1998). Parenting and preschooler attachment among low-income urban African American families. *Child Development, 69,* 1657–1671.

Barrera, M., & Maurer, D. (1981). Discrimination of strangers by the 3-month-old. *Child Development, 52,* 558–563.

Barrett, K. (1998). The origins of guilt in early childhood. In J. Bybee (Ed.), *Guilt and children* (pp. 75–90). San Diego, CA: Academic Press.

Barrett, K., Zahn-Waxler, C., & Cole, P. (1993). Avoiders versus amenders: Implications for the investigation of guilt and shame during toddlerhood? *Cognition and Emotion, 7,* 481–505.

Bartrip, I., Morton, I., & de Schonen, S. (2001). Responses to mother's face in 3-week to 5-month-old infants. *British Journal of Developmental Psychology, 19,* 219–232.

Bartsch, K., & Wellman, H. (1995). *Children talk about the mind.* London: Oxford University Press.

Bates, E. (1990). Language about me and you: Pronominal reference and the emerging concept of self. In D. Cicchetti & M. Beeghly

(Eds.), *The self in transition: Infancy to childhood* (pp. 165–182). Chicago: University of Chicago Press.

Bates, J., & Bayles, K. (1988). Attachment and the development of behavior problems. In J. Belsky & T. Nezworski (Eds.), *Clinical implications of attachment* (pp. 253–299). Hillsdale, NJ: Erlbaum.

Bateson, P. (1994). The dynamics of parent-offspring relationships in mammals. *Trends in Ecology and Evolution, 9*, 399–403.

Bauer, P. (2002a). Developments in early recall memory: Normative trends and individual differences. In R. Kail (Ed.), *Advances in child development and behavior* (Vol. 20, pp. 103–152). San Diego, CA: Academic Press.

Bauer, P. (2002b). Early memory development. In U. Goswami (Ed.), *Handbook of cognitive development* (pp. 127–146). Oxford, England: Blackwell.

Baumrind, D. (1973). The development of instrumental competence through socialization. In A. Pick (Ed.), *Minnesota Symposia on Child Psychology* (Vol. 7, pp. 3–46). Minneapolis: University of Minnesota Press.

Baumrind, D. (1978). Parental disciplinary patterns and social competence in children. *Youth and Society, 9*, 239–276.

Baumrind, D. (1989). Rearing competent children. In W. Damon (Ed.), *Child development today and tomorrow* (pp. 349–387). San Francisco: Jossey-Bass.

Baumrind, D. (1996). A blanket injunction against disciplinary use of spanking is not warranted by the data. *Pediatrics, 98*, 828–831.

Beckwith, L., Cohen, S., & Hamilton, C. (1999). Maternal sensitivity during infancy and subsequent life events relate to attachment representation at early adulthood. *Developmental Psychology, 35*, 693–700.

Belsky, J. (1981). Early human experience: A family perspective. *Developmental Psychology, 17*, 3–23.

Belsky, J. (1999). Interactional and contextual determinants of attachment security. In J. Cassidy & P. Shaver (Eds.), *Handbook of attachment* (pp. 249–264). New York: Guilford Press.

Belsky, J., Campbell, S., Cohn, J., & Moore, G. (1996). Instability of infant-parent attachment security. *Developmental Psychology, 32*, 921–924.

Belsky, J., & Cassidy, J. (1994). Attachment: Theory and evidence. In M. Rutter & D. Hay (Eds.), *Development through life* (pp. 373–402). Oxford, England: Blackwell.

Belsky, J., & Isabella, R. (1988). Maternal, infant, and social-contextual determinants of attachment security. In J. Belsky & T. Nezworski (Eds.), *Clinical implications of attachment* (pp. 41–94). Hillsdale, NJ: Erlbaum.

Belsky, J., & Pasco Fearon, R. (2002a). Early attachment security, subsequent maternal sensitivity, and later child development: Does continuity in development depend upon continuity of caregiving? *Attachment and Human Development, 4*, 361–387.

Belsky, J., & Pasco Fearon, R. (2002b). Infant-mother attachment security, contextual risk, and early development: A moderational analysis. *Development and Psychopathology, 14*, 293–310.

Belsky, J., Spritz, B., & Crnic, K. (1996). Infant attachment security and affective-cognitive information processing at age 3. *Psychological Science, 7*, 111–114.

Bigelow, A., MacLean, B., & MacDonald, D. (1996). Infants' response to live and replay interactions with self and mother. *Merrill-Palmer Quarterly, 42*, 596–611.

Biringen, Z., Emde, R., Campos, J., & Appelbaum, M. (1995). Affective reorganization in the infant, the mother, and the dyad: The role of upright locomotion and its timing. *Child Development, 66*, 499–514.

Blurton-Jones, N. (1993). The lives of hunter-gatherer children: Effects of parental behavior and parental reproductive strategy. In M. Pereira & L. Fairbanks (Eds.), *Juvenile primates* (pp. 309–326). New York: Oxford University Press.

Bokhorst, C., Bakermans-Kranenburg, M., Pasco Fearon, R., van Ijzendoorn, M., Fonagy, P., & Schuengel, C. (2003). The importance of shared environment in mother-infant attachment security: A behavioral genetic study. *Child Development, 74*, 1769–1782.

Booth, C., Rubin, K., & Rose-Krasnor, L. (1998). Perceptions of emotional support from mother and friend in middle childhood: Links with social-emotional adaptation and preschool attachment security. *Child Development, 69*, 427–442.

Bornstein, M. (2002). Parenting infants. In M. Bornstein (Ed.), *Handbook of parenting: Vol. 1. Children and parenting* (2nd ed., pp. 3–43). Mahwah, NJ: Erlbaum.

Bost, K., Vaughn, B., Washington, W., Cielinski, K., & Bradbard, M. (1998). Social competence, social support, and attachment: Demarcation of construct domains, measurement, and paths of influence for preschool children attending Head Start. *Child Development, 69*, 192–218.

Bowlby, J. (1973). *Attachment and loss: Vol. 2. Separation—Anxiety and anger.* New York: Basic Books.

Bowlby, J. (1980). *Attachment and loss: Vol. 3. Loss—Sadness and depression.* New York: Basic Books.

Bowlby, J. (1982). *Attachment and loss: Vol. 1. Attachment* (2nd ed.). New York: Basic Books. (Original work published 1969)

Braungart-Rieker, J., Garwood, M., Powers, B., & Wang, X. (2001). Parental sensitivity, infant affect, and affect regulation: Predictors of later attachment. *Child Development, 72*, 252–270.

Bretherton, I. (1990). Open communication and internal working models: Their role in the development of attachment relationships. In R. A. Thompson (Ed.), *Nebraska Symposium on Motivation: Vol. 36. Socioemotional development* (pp. 57–113). Lincoln: University of Nebraska Press.

Bretherton, I. (1991). Pouring new wine into old bottles: The social self as internal working model. In M. Gunnar & L. Sroufe (Eds.), *Minnesota Symposia on Child Psychology: Vol. 23. Self processes and development* (pp. 1–41). Hillsdale, NJ: Erlbaum.

Bretherton, I., Fritz, J., Zahn-Waxler, C., & Ridgeway, D. (1986). Learning to talk about emotions: A functionalist perspective. *Child Development, 57*, 529–548.

Bretherton, I., & Munholland, K. (1999). Internal working models in attachment relationships: A construct revisited. In J. Cassidy & P. Shaver (Eds.), *Handbook of attachment* (pp. 89–111). New York: Guilford Press.

Bronfenbrenner, U. (1979). *The ecology of human development.* Cambridge, MA: Harvard University Press.

Brown, J., Donelan-McCall, N., & Dunn, J. (1996). Why talk about mental states? The significance of children's conversations with friends, siblings, and mothers. *Child Development, 67*, 836–849.

Brown, J., & Dunn, J. (1991). "You can cry, mum": The social and developmental implications of talk about internal states. *British Journal of Developmental Psychology, 9*, 237–256.

Brown, J., & Dunn, J. (1996). Continuities in emotion understanding from 3 to 6 years. *Child Development, 67*, 789–802.

Budwig, N. (2002). A developmental-functionalist approach to mental state talk. In E. Amsel & J. Byrnes (Eds.), *Language, literacy, and cognitive development* (pp. 59–86). Mahwah, NJ: Erlbaum.

Bullock, M., & Lutkenhaus, P. (1988). The development of volitional behavior in the toddler years. *Child Development, 59,* 664–674.

Bullock, M., & Lutkenhaus, P. (1990). Who am I? Self-understanding in toddlers. *Merrill-Palmer Quarterly, 36,* 217–238.

Campos, J., Anderson, D., Barbu-Roth, M., Hubbard, E., Hertenstein, M., & Witherington, D. (2000). Travel broadens the mind. *Infancy, 1,* 149–219.

Campos, J., Kermoian, R., & Zumbahlen, M. (1992). Socioemotional transformations in the family system following infant crawling onset. In N. Eisenberg & R. Fabes (Eds.), *Emotion and its regulation in early development* (pp. 25–40). San Francisco: Jossey-Bass.

Campos, J., & Stenberg, C. (1981). Perception, appraisal, and emotion: The onset of social referencing. In M. Lamb & L. Sherrod (Eds.), *Infant social cognition* (pp. 273–314). Hillsdale, NJ: Erlbaum.

Carlson, E. (1998). A prospective longitudinal study of attachment disorganization/disorientation. *Child Development, 69,* 1107–1128.

Carlson, E., Sroufe, L., & Egeland, B. (2004). The construction of experience: A longitudinal study of representation and behavior. *Child Development, 75,* 66–83.

Carpendale, J. I. M., & Lewis, C. (2004). Constructing an understanding of mind: The development of children's social understanding within social interaction. *Behavioral and Brain Sciences, 27,* 79–96.

Carpenter, M., Akhtar, N., & Tomasello, M. (1998). Fourteen- to 18-month-old infants differentially imitate intentional and accidental actions. *Infant Behavior and Development, 21,* 315–330.

Carpenter, M., Call, J., & Tomasello, M. (2002). Understanding "prior intentions" enables two-year-olds to imitatively learn a complex task. *Child Development, 73,* 1431–1441.

Carpenter, M., Nagell, K., & Tomasello, M. (1998). Social cognition, joint attention, and communicative competence from 9 to 15 months of age. *Monographs of the Society for Research in Child Development, 63*(4, Serial No. 255).

Cassidy, J. (1988). Child-mother attachment and the self in 6-year-olds. *Child Development, 59,* 121–134.

Cassidy, J., Kirsh, S., Scolton, K., & Parke, R. (1996). Attachment and representations of peer relationships. *Developmental Psychology, 32,* 892–904.

Cassidy, J., & Marvin, R. (1992). *Attachment organization in 3- and 4-year-olds: Procedures and coding manual.* Unpublished manuscript, Attachment Working Group, Department of Psychology, University of Virginia, Charlottesville.

Cassidy, J., & Shaver, P. (Eds.). (1999). *Handbook of attachment: Theory, research, and clinical applications.* New York: Guilford Press.

Chisholm, J. (1999). *Death, hope and sex: Steps to an evolutionary ecology of mind and morality.* New York: Cambridge University Press.

Cicchetti, D., & Cohen, D. (1995). Perspectives on developmental psychopathology. In D. Cicchetti & D. Cohen (Eds.), *Developmental psychopathology: Vol. 1. Theory and methods* (pp. 3–20). New York: Wiley.

Cicchetti, D., Toth, S., & Lynch, M. (1995). Bowlby's dream comes full circle: The application of attachment theory to risk and psychopathology. In T. Ollendick & R. Prinz (Eds.), *Advances in clinical child psychology* (Vol. 17, pp. 1–75). New York: Plenum Press.

Cicchetti, D., Toth, S., & Rogosch, F. (1999). The efficacy of toddler-parent psychotherapy to increase attachment security in offspring of depressed mothers. *Attachment and Human Development, 1,* 34–66.

Clark, S., & Symons, D. (2000). A longitudinal study of Q-sort attachment security and self-processes at age 5. *Infant and Child Development, 9,* 91–104.

Clarke-Stewart, K. A., Goossens, F., & Alhusen, V. (2001). Measuring infant-mother attachment: Is the strange situation enough? *Social Development, 10,* 143–169.

Clutton-Brock, T. (1991). *The evolution of parental care.* Princeton, NJ: Princeton University Press.

Cochran, M., Larner, M., Riley, D., Gunnarsson, L., & Henderson, C. (1990). *Extending families: The social networks of parents and their children.* New York: Cambridge University Press.

Cohn, J., Campbell, S., Matias, R., & Hopkins, J. (1990). Face-to-face interactions of postpartum depressed and nondepressed mother-infant pairs at 2 months. *Developmental Psychology, 26,* 15–23.

Cohn, J., Campbell, S., & Ross, S. (1992). Infant response in the still-face paradigm at 6 months predicts avoidant and secure attachment at 12 months. *Development and Psychopathology, 3,* 367–376.

Cole, P. (1986). Children's spontaneous control of facial expressions. *Child Development, 57,* 1309–1321.

Cole, P., Martin, S., & Dennis, T. (2004). Emotion regulation as a scientific construct: Methodological challenges and directions for child development research. *Child Development, 75,* 317–333.

Colin, V. (1996). *Human attachment.* New York: McGraw-Hill.

Collins, W., Maccoby, E., Steinberg, L., Hetherington, E., & Bornstein, M. (2000). Contemporary research on parenting: The case for nature *and* nurture. *American Psychologist, 55,* 218–232.

Colman, R. A., & Thompson, R. A. (2002). Attachment security and the problem-solving behaviors of mothers and children. *Merrill-Palmer Quarterly, 48,* 337–359.

Committee on Integrating the Science of Early Childhood Development. (2000). *From neurons to neighborhoods: The science of early childhood development* (J. Shonkoff & D. Phillips, Eds.). Washington, DC: National Academy Press.

Cooper, R., & Aslin, R. (1990). Preference for infant-directed speech in the first month after birth. *Child Development, 61,* 1584–1595.

Crittenden, P. (1992). Quality of attachment in the preschool years. *Development and Psychopathology, 4,* 209–241.

Crittenden, P. (1994). *Preschool assessment of attachment.* Unpublished manuscript, Family Relations Institute, Miami, FL.

Crittenden, P. (2000). A dynamic-maturational approach to continuity and change in patterns of attachment. In P. Crittenden & A. Claussen (Eds.), *The organization of attachment relationships* (pp. 343–358). New York: Cambridge University Press.

Crockenberg, S., & Litman, C. (1990). Autonomy as competence in 2-year-olds; Maternal correlates of child defiance, compliance, and self-assertion. *Developmental Psychology, 26,* 961–971.

Cummings, E., & Davies, P. (1994). *Children and marital conflict.* New York: Guilford Press.

Cutting, A., & Dunn, J. (1999). Theory of mind, emotion understanding, language, and family background: Individual differences and interrelations. *Child Development, 70,* 853–865.

Cutting, A., & Dunn, J. (2002). The cost of understanding other people: Social cognition predicts young children's sensitivity to criticism. *Journal of Child Psychology and Psychiatry, 43,* 849–860.

Davies, P., & Cummings, E. (1994). Marital conflict and child adjustment: An emotional security hypothesis. *Psychological Bulletin, 116,* 387–411.

Davies, P., & Forman, E. (2002). Children's patterns of preserving emotional security in the interparental subsystem. *Child Development, 73,* 1880–1903.

Davies, P., Harold, G., Goeke-Morey, M., & Cummings, E. (2002). Child emotional security and interparental conflict. *Monographs of the Society for Research in Child Development, 67*(Serial No. 270).

Dawson, G., Frey, K., Panagiotides, H., Yamada, E., Hessl, D., & Osterling, J. (1999). Infants of depressed mothers exhibit atypical frontal electrical brain activity during interactions with mother and with a familiar, nondepressed adult. *Child Development, 70,* 1058–1066.

Deater-Decker, K., & O'Connor, T. (2000). Parent-child mutuality in early childhood: Two behavioral genetic studies. *Developmental Psychology, 36,* 561–570.

DeCasper, A., & Fifer, W. (1980). Of human bonding: Newborns prefer their mother's voice. *Science, 208,* 1174–1176.

DeCasper, A., & Spence, M. (1986). Prenatal maternal speech influences newborn's perception of speech sounds. *Infant Behavior and Development, 9,* 133–150.

DeMulder, E., Denham, S., Schmidt, M., & Mitchell, J. (2000). Q-sort assessment of attachment security during the preschool years: Links from home to school. *Developmental Psychology, 36,* 274–282.

Denham, S. (1998). *Emotional development in young children.* New York: Guilford Press.

Denham, S., Blair, K., DeMulder, E., Levitas, J., Sawyer, K., Auerbach-Major, S., et al. (2003). Preschool emotional competence: Pathway to social competence. *Child Development, 74,* 238–256.

Denham, S., Blair, K., Schmidt, M., & DeMulder, E. (2002). Compromised emotional competence: Seeds of violence sown early? *American Journal of Orthopsychiatry, 72,* 70–82.

Denham, S., Caverly, S., Schmidt, M., Blair, K., DeMulder, E., Caal, S., et al. (2002). Preschool understanding of emotions: Contributions to classroom anger and aggression. *Journal of Child Psychology and Psychiatry, 43,* 901–916.

Denham, S., Mason, T., Caverly, S., Schmidt, M., Hackney, R., Caswell, C., et al. (2001). Preschoolers at play: Co-socializers of emotional and social competence. *International Journal of Behavioral Development, 25,* 290–301.

Denham, S., Zoller, D., & Couchoud, E. A. (1994). Socialization of preschoolers' emotion understanding. *Developmental Psychology, 30,* 928–936.

de Rosnay, M., & Harris, P. (2002). Individual differences in children's understanding of emotion: The roles of attachment and language. *Attachment and Human Development, 4,* 39–54.

de Rosnay, M., Pons, F., Harris, P., & Morrell., J. (2004). A lag between understanding false belief and emotion attribution in young children: Relationships with linguistic ability and mothers' mental-state language. *British Journal of Developmental Psychology, 22,* 197–218.

De Wolff, M., & van Ijzendoorn, M. (1997). Sensitivity and attachment: A meta-analysis on parental antecedents of infant attachment. *Child Development, 68,* 571–591.

Dozier, M., Stovall, K., Albus, K., & Bates, B. (2001). Attachment for infants in foster care: The role of caregiver state of mind. *Child Development, 72,* 1467–1477.

Dunn, J. (1993). *Young children's close relationships.* Newbury Park, CA: Sage.

Dunn, J. (1995). Children as psychologists: The later correlates of individual differences in understanding of emotions and other minds. *Cognition and Emotion, 9,* 187–201.

Dunn, J. (1996). Children's relationships: Bridging the divide between cognitive and social development. *Journal of Child Psychology and Psychiatry, 37,* 507–518.

Dunn, J. (1999). Mindreading, emotion, and relationships. In P. Zelazo, J. Astington, & D. Olson (Eds.), *Developing theories of intention* (pp. 229–242). Mahwah, NJ: Erlbaum.

Dunn, J. (2004). *Children's friendships.* Oxford, England: Blackwell.

Dunn, J., Bretherton, I., & Munn, P. (1987). Conversations about feeling states between mothers and their young children. *Developmental Psychology, 23,* 132–139.

Dunn, J., & Brown, J. (1991). Relationships, talk about feelings, and the development of affect regulation in early childhood. In J. Garber & K. A. Dodge (Eds.), *The development of emotion regulation and dysregulation* (pp. 89–108). Cambridge: Cambridge University Press.

Dunn, J., & Brown, J. (1993). Early conversations about causality: Content, pragmatics, and developmental change. *British Journal of Developmental Psychology, 11,* 107–123.

Dunn, J., Brown, J., & Beardsall, L. (1991). Family talk about feeling states and children's later understanding of others' emotions. *Child Development, 27,* 448–455.

Dunn, J., Brown, J., & Maguire, M. (1995). The development of children's moral sensibility: Individual differences and emotion understanding. *Developmental Psychology, 31,* 649–659.

Dunn, J., Brown, J., Slomkowski, C., Tesla, C., & Youngblade, L. (1991). Young children's understanding of other people's feelings and beliefs: Individual differences and their antecedents. *Child Development, 62,* 1352–1366.

Dunn, J., Cutting, A., & Demetriou, H. (2000). Moral sensibility, understanding others, and children's friendship interactions in the preschool period. *British Journal of Developmental Psychology, 18,* 159–177.

Dunn, J., & Herrera, C. (1997). Conflict resolution with friends, siblings, and mothers: A developmental perspective. *Aggressive Behavior, 23,* 343–357.

Dunn, J., & Hughes, C. (1998). Young children's understanding of emotions within close relationships. *Cognition and Emotion, 12,* 171–190.

Dunn, J., & Munn, P. (1987). The development of justifications in disputes. *Developmental Psychology, 23,* 781–798.

Easterbrooks, M. (1989). Quality of attachment to mother and to father: Effects of perinatal risk status. *Child Development, 60,* 825–830.

Easterbrooks, M., & Goldberg, W. (1990). Security of toddler-parent attachment: Relation to children's sociopersonality functioning during kindergarten. In M. Greenberg, D. Cicchetti, & E. Cummings (Eds.), *Attachment in the preschool years* (pp. 221–244). Chicago: University of Chicago Press.

Eder, R. (1989). The emergent personologist: The structure and content of $3^{1}/_{2}$-, $5^{1}/_{2}$-, and $7^{1}/_{2}$-year-olds' concepts of themselves and other persons. *Child Development, 60,* 1218–1228.

Eder, R. (1990). Uncovering children's psychological selves: Individual and developmental differences. *Child Development, 61,* 849–863.

Eder, R., & Mangelsdorf, S. (1997). The emotional basis of early personality development: Implications for the emergent self-concept. In R. Hogan & S. Briggs (Eds.), *Handbook of personality psychology* (pp. 209–240). Orlando, FL: Academic Press.

Egeland, B., & Farber, E. (1984). Infant-mother attachment: Factors related to its development and changes over time. *Child Development, 55,* 753–771.

Egeland, B., Kalkoske, M., Gottesman, N., & Erickson, M. (1990). Preschool behavior problems: Stability and factors accounting for change. *Journal of Child Psychology and Psychiatry, 31,* 891–909.

Egeland, B., & Sroufe, L. (1981). Attachment and early maltreatment. *Child Development, 52,* 44–52.

Eisenberg, N. (2002). Emotion-related regulation and its relation to quality of social functioning. In W. Hartup & R. Weinberg (Eds.), *Minnesota Symposia on Child Psychology: Vol. 32. Child psychology in retrospect and prospect* (pp. 133–171). Mahwah, NJ: Erlbaum.

Eisenberg, N., & Fabes, R. (1995). The relation of young children's vicarious emotional responding to social competence, regulation, and emotionality. *Cognition and Emotion, 9,* 203–228.

Eisenberg, N., & Fabes, R. (1998). Prosocial development. In W. Damon (Editor-in-Chief) & N. Eisenberg (Vol. Ed.), *Handbook of child psychology: Vol. 3. Social, emotional, and personality development* (5th ed., pp. 701–778). New York: Wiley.

Eisenberg, N., & Spinrad, T. (2004). Emotion-related regulation: Sharpening the definition. *Child Development, 75,* 334–339.

Ellsworth, C., Muir, D., & Hains, S. (1993). Social competence and person-object differentiation: An analysis of the still-face effect. *Developmental Psychology, 29,* 63–73.

Emde, R., Biringen, Z., Clyman, R., & Oppenheim, D. (1991). The moral self of infancy: Affective core and procedural knowledge. *Developmental Review, 11,* 251–270.

Emde, R., & Buchsbaum, H. (1990). "Didn't you hear my Mommy?" Autonomy with connectedness in moral self-emergence. In D. Cicchetti & M. Beeghly (Eds.), *The self in transition: Infancy to childhood* (pp. 35–60). Chicago: University of Chicago Press.

Erickson, M., Sroufe, L., & Egeland, B. (1985). The relationship between quality of attachment and behavior problems in preschool in a high-risk sample. *Monographs of the Society for Research in Child Development, 50*(Serial No. 209), 147–166.

Fabes, R., Eisenberg, N., Nyman, M., & Michaelieu, Q. (1991). Young children's appraisals of others' spontaneous emotional reactions. *Developmental Psychology, 27,* 858–866.

Fagot, B., & Kavanagh, K. (1990). The prediction of antisocial behavior from avoidant attachment classifications. *Child Development, 61,* 864–873.

Farrant, K., & Reese, E. (2000). Maternal style and children's participation in reminiscing: Stepping stones in children's autobiographical memory development. *Journal of Cognition and Development, 1,* 193–225.

Fasig, L. (2000). Toddlers' understanding of ownership: Implications for self-concept development. *Social Development, 9,* 370–382.

Feinman, S., Roberts, D., Hsieh, K.-F., Sawyer, D., & Swanson, D. (1992). A critical review of social referencing in infancy. In S. Feinman (Ed.), *Social referencing and the social construction of reality in infancy* (pp. 15–54). New York: Plenum Press.

Fernald, A. (1985). Four-month-old infants prefer to listen to "motherese." *Infant Behavior and Development, 8,* 181–195.

Fernald, A. (1996). Approval and disapproval: Infant responsiveness to vocal affect in familiar and unfamiliar languages. *Child Development, 64,* 657–674.

Field, T., Healy, B., Goldstein, S., & Guthertz, M. (1990). Behavior-state matching and synchrony in mother-infant interactions of nondepressed versus depressed dyads. *Developmental Psychology, 26,* 7–14.

Field, T., Healy, B., Goldstein, S., Perry, S., Bendell, D., Schanberg, S., et al. (1988). Infants of depressed mothers show "depressed" behavior even with nondepressed adults. *Child Development, 59,* 1569–1579.

Fivush, R. (1993). Emotional content of parent-child conversations about the past. In C. Nelson (Ed.), *Minnesota Symposia on Child Psychology: Vol. 23. Memory and affect in development* (pp. 39–77). Hillsdale, NJ: Erlbaum.

Fivush, R. (1998). Gendered narratives: Elaboration, structure, and emotion in parent-child reminiscing across the preschool years. In C. Thompson & D. Herrmann (Eds.), *Autobiographical memory: Theoretical and applied perspectives* (pp. 79–103). Mahwah, NJ: Erlbaum.

Fivush, R. (2001). Owning experience: Developing subjective perspective in autobiographical narratives. In C. Moore & K. Lemmon (Eds.), *The self in time* (pp. 35–52). Mahwah, NJ: Erlbaum.

Fivush, R. (2004). Voice and silence: A feminist model of autobiographical memory. In J. Lucariello, J. Hudson, R. Fivush, & P. Bauer (Eds.), *The development of the mediated mind* (pp. 79–99). Mahwah, NJ: Erlbaum.

Fox, N., & Calkins, S. (2003). The development of self-control of emotion: Intrinsic and extrinsic influences. *Motivation and Emotion, 27,* 7–26.

Fraley, R. (2002). Attachment stability from infancy to adulthood: Meta-analysis and dynamic modeling of developmental mechanisms. *Personality and Social Psychology Review, 6,* 123–151.

Fraley, R., & Spieker, S. (2003). Are infant attachment patterns continuously or categorically distributed? A taxometric analysis of strange situation behavior. *Developmental Psychology, 39,* 387–404.

Frankel, K., & Bates, J. (1990). Mother-toddler problem solving: Antecedents in attachment, home behavior, and temperament. *Child Development, 61,* 810–819.

Freud, S. (1940). *An outline of psychoanalysis.* New York: Norton.

Frodi, A., Grolnick, W., & Bridges, L. (1985). Maternal correlates of stability and change in infant-mother attachment. *Infant Mental Health Journal, 6,* 60–67.

Gardner, W., Lamb, M., Thompson, R., & Sagi, A. (1986). On individual differences in strange situation behavior: Categorical and continuous measurement systems in a cross-cultural data set. *Infant Behavior and Development, 9,* 355–375.

Ge, X., Conger, R., Cadoret, R., Neiderhiser, J., Yates, W., Troughton, E., et al. (1996). The developmental interface between nature and nurture: A mutual influence model of child antisocial behavior and parent behaviors. *Developmental Psychology, 32,* 574–589.

Gekoski, M., Rovee-Collier, C., & Carulli-Rabinowitz, V. (1983). A longutudinal analysis of inhibition of infant distress: The origins of social expectations? *Infant Behavior and Development, 6,* 339–351.

Gelman, S., Taylor, M., & Nguyen, S. (2004). Mother-child conversations about gender: Understanding the acquisition of essentialist beliefs. *Monographs of the Society for Research in Child Development, 69*(Serial No. 275).

Gergely, G., & Watson, J. (1999). Early socio-emotional development: Contingency perception and the social-biofeedback model. In P. Rochat (Ed.), *Early social cognition* (pp. 101–136). Mahwah, NJ: Erlbaum.

Gianino, A., & Tronick, E. (1988). The mutual regulation model: The infant's self and interactive regulation and coping and defensive capacities. In T. Field, P. McCabe, & N. Schneiderman (Eds.), *Stress and coping* (Vol. 2, pp. 47–68). Hillsdale, NJ: Erlbaum.

Gibson, E. (1995). Are we automata. In P. Rochat (Ed.), *The self in infancy* (pp. 3–15). Amsterdam: North Holland-Elsevier.

Goodvin, R., Meyer, S., Thompson, R. A., & Hayes, R. (2005). *Self-understanding in early childhood: Associations with attachment security, maternal perceptions of the child, and maternal emotional risk.* Unpublished manuscript, University of Nebraska, Lincoln.

Gralinski, J., & Kopp, C. (1993). Everyday rules for behavior: Mothers' requests to young children. *Developmental Psychology, 29,* 573–584.

Greenberg, M. (1999). Attachment and psychopathology in childhood. In J. Cassidy & P. Shaver (Eds.), *Handbook of attachment* (pp. 469–496). New York: Guilford Press.

Grossmann, K. E. (1999). Old and new internal working models of attachment: The organization of feelings and language. *Attachment and Human Development, 1,* 253–269.

Grossmann, K. E., Grossmann, K., Huber, F., & Wartner, U. (1981). German children's behavior towards their mothers at 12 months and their fathers at 18 months in Ainsworth's strange situation. *International Journal of Behavioral Development, 4,* 157–181.

Grusec, J., & Goodnow, J. (1994). Impact of parental discipline methods on the child's internalization of values: A reconceptualization of current points of view. *Developmental Psychology, 30,* 4–19.

Grusec, J., Goodnow, J., & Kuczynski, L. (2000). New directions in analyses of parenting contributions to children's internalization of values. *Child Development, 71,* 205–211.

Gunnar, M., & Vazquez, D. (in press). Stress neurobiology and developmental psychopathology. In D. Cicchetti & D. Cohen (Eds.), *Developmental psychopathology: Vol. 3. Risk, disorder, and adaptation* (2nd ed.). New York: Wiley.

Haden, C. (1998). Reminscing with different children: Relating maternal stylistic consistency and sibling similarity in talk about the past. *Developmental Psychology, 34,* 99–114.

Haden, C., Haine, R., & Fivush, R. (1997). Developing narrative structure in parent-child reminiscing across the preschool years. *Developmental Psychology, 33,* 295–307.

Hains, S., & Muir, D. (1996). Effects of stimulus contingency in infant-adult interactions. *Infant Behavior and Development, 19,* 49–61.

Hamilton, C. (2000). Continuity and discontinuity of attachment from infancy through adolescence. *Child Development, 71,* 690–694.

Han, J., Leichtman, M., & Wang, Q. (1998). Autobiographical memory in Korean, Chinese, and American children. *Developmental Psychology, 34,* 701–713.

Harley, K., & Reese, E. (1999). Origins of autobiographical memory. *Developmental Psychology, 35,* 1338–1348.

Harris, P. (1989). *Children and emotion.* Oxford, England: Blackwell.

Harris, P. (1997). Between strange situations and false beliefs: Working models and theories of mind. In W. Koops, J. Hoeksma, & D. C. van den Boom (Eds.), *Development of interaction and attachment* (pp. 187–199). Amsterdam: Elsevier.

Harris, P. (1999). Individual differences in understanding emotion: The role of attachment status and psychological discourse. *Attachment and Human Development, 1,* 307–324.

Harris, P., Guz, G., Lipian, M., & Man-Shu, Z. (1985). Insight into the time course of emotion among Western and Chinese children. *Child Development, 56,* 972–988.

Harris, P., Johnson, C., Hutton, D., Andrews, G., & Cooke, T. (1989). Young children's theory of mind and emotion. *Cognition and Emotion, 3,* 379–400.

Harris, P., & Nunez, M. (1996). Understanding of permission rules by preschool children. *Child Development, 67,* 1572–1591.

Harris, P. L. (in press). What do children learn from testimony? In P. Carruthers, M. Siegel, & S. Stich (Eds.), *Cognitive bases of science.* Cambridge: Cambridge University Press.

Harris, P. L., & Koenig, M. A. (2005). *Trust in testimony: How children learn about science and religion.* Unpublished manuscript, Harvard University.

Harter, S., & Buddin, B. (1987). Children's understanding of the simultaneity of two emotions: A five-stage developmental acquisition sequence. *Developmental Psychology, 23,* 388–399.

Harwood, R., Miller, J., & Irizarry, N. (1995). *Culture and attachment.* New York: Guilford Press.

Hastings, P., & Grusec, J. (1998). Parenting goals as organizers of responses to parent-child disagreement. *Developmental Psychology, 34,* 465–479.

Haviland, J., & Lelwica, M. (1987). The induced affect response: 10-week-old infants' responses to three emotion expressions. *Developmental Psychology, 23,* 97–104.

Hazen, C., & Shaver, P. (1994). Attachment as an organizational framework for research on close relationships. *Psychological Inquiry, 5,* 1–22.

Hendrix, R. (2004). *Emergence of parental prohibition in response to self-produced locomotion and its accompanying emotional changes.* Unpublished doctoral dissertation, University of Nebraska, Lincoln.

Hertenstein, M., & Campos, J. (2004). The retention effects of an adult's emotional displays on infant behavior. *Child Development, 75,* 595–613.

Hesse, E. (1999). The adult attachment interview: Historical and current perspectives. In J. Cassidy & P. Shaver (Eds.), *Handbook of attachment* (pp. 395–433). New York: Guilford Press.

Heyman, G., Gee, C., & Giles, J. (2003). Preschool children's reasoning about ability. *Child Development, 74,* 516–534.

Heyman, G., & Gelman, S. (1999). The use of trait labels in making psychological inferences. *Child Development, 70,* 604–619.

Heyman, G., & Gelman, S. (2000). Preschool children's use of trait labels to make inductive inferences. *Journal of Experimental Child Psychology, 77,* 1–19.

Hinde, R. (1988). Continuities and discontinuities: Conceptual issues and methodological considerations. In M. Rutter (Ed.), *Studies of psychosocial risk* (pp. 367–383). Cambridge: Cambridge University Press.

Hirshberg, L., & Svejda, M. (1990). When infants look to their parents: Pt. 1. Infants' social referencing of mothers compared to fathers. *Child Development, 61,* 1175–1186.

Hobson, P. (2002). *The cradle of thought.* New York: Macmillan.

Hoffman, M. (1983). Affective and cognitive processes in moral internalization. In E. Higgins, D. Ruble, & W. Hartup (Eds.), *Social cognition and social development* (pp. 236–274). New York: Cambridge University Press.

Hoffman, M. (2000). *Empathy and moral development: Implications for caring and justice.* New York: Cambridge University Press.

Holden, G., Miller, P., & Harris, S. (1999). The instrumental side of corporal punishment: Parents' reported practices and outcome expectancies. *Journal of Marriage and the Family, 61,* 908–919.

Holden, G., & Miller, P. C. (1999). Enduring and different: A meta-analysis of the similarity in parents' child rearing. *Psychological Bulletin, 125,* 233–254.

Holden, G., Thompson, E., Zambarano, R., & Marshall, L. (1997). Child effects as a source of change in maternal attitudes toward corporal punishment. *Journal of Social and Personal Relationships, 14,* 481–490.

Holden, G., & West, M. (1989). Proximate regulation by mothers: A demonstration of how differing styles affect young children's behavior. *Child Development, 60,* 64–69.

Hornik, R., Risenhoover, N., & Gunnar, M. (1987). The effects of maternal positive, neutral, and negative affect communications on infant responses to new toys. *Child Development, 58,* 937–944.

Howe, M., & Courage, M. (1993). On resolving the enigma of infantile amnesia. *Psychological Bulletin, 113,* 305–326.

Howe, M., & Courage, M. (1997). The emergence and early development of autobiographical memory. *Psychological Review, 104,* 499–523.

Howe, N., Petrakos, H., & Rinaldi, C. (1998). "All the sheeps are dead—He murdered them": Sibling pretense, negotiation, internal state language, and relationship quality. *Child Development, 69,* 182–191.

Howes, C. (1999). Attachment relationships in the context of multiple caregivers. In J. Cassidy & P. Shaver (Eds.), *Handbook of attachment* (pp. 671–687). New York: Guilford Press.

Howes, P., & Markman, H. (1989). Marital quality and child functioning: A longitudinal investigation. *Child Development, 60,* 1044–1051.

Hrdy, S. (1999). *Mother nature.* New York: Ballantine Books.

Hudson, J. (1990). The emergence of autobiographical memory in mother-child conversation. In R. Fivush & J. Hudson (Eds.), *Knowing and remembering in young children* (pp. 166–196). Cambridge: Cambridge University Press.

Hudson, J. (1993). Understanding events: The development of script knowledge. In M. Bennett (Ed.), *The child as psychologist: An introduction to the development of social cognition* (pp. 142–167). New York: Harvester Wheatsheaf.

Hughes, C., & Dunn, J. (1998). Understanding mind and emotion: Longitudinal associations with mental-state talk between young friends. *Developmental Psychology, 34,* 1026–1037.

Jacobsen, T., Huss, M., Fendrich, M., Kruesi, M., & Ziegenhain, U. (1997). Children's ability to delay gratification: Longitudinal relations to mother-child attachment. *Journal of Genetic Psychology, 158,* 411–426.

James, W. (1890). *The principles of psychology.* New York: Henry Holt.

Jenkins, J., Turrell, S., Kogushi, Y., Lollis, S., & Ross, H. (2003). A longitudinal investigation of the dynamics of mental state talk in families. *Child Development, 74,* 905–920.

Johnson, M. (1997). *Developmental cognitive neuroscience.* Oxford, England: Blackwell.

Johnson, M., & Morton, J. (1991). *Biology and cognitive development: The case of face recognition.* Oxford, England: Blackwell.

Kagan, J. (1981). *The second year: The emergence of self-awareness.* Cambridge, MA: Harvard University Press.

Kagan, J. (in press). Human morality and temperament. In G. Carlo & C. Pope-Edwards (Eds.), *Nebraska Symposium on Motivation: Vol. 51. Moral motivation through the lifespan.* Lincoln: University of Nebraska Press.

Kahana-Kalman, R., & Walker-Andrews, A. (2001). The role of person familiarity in young infants' perception of emotional expressions. *Child Development, 72,* 352–369.

Kerns, K., & Richardson, R. (Eds.). (2005). *Attachment in middle childhood.* New York: Guilford Press.

Killen, M., Pisacane, K., Lee-Kim, J., & Ardila-Rey, A. (2001). Fairness or stereotypes? Young children's priorities when evalu-

ating group exclusion or inclusion. *Developmental Psychology, 37,* 587–596.

Kisilevsky, B., Hains, S., Lee, K., Muir, D., Xu, F., Fu, G., et al. (1998). The still-face effect in Chinese and Canadian 3- to 6-month-old infants. *Developmental Psychology, 34,* 629–639.

Klinnert, M., Campos, J., Sorce, J., Emde, R., & Svejda, M. (1983). Emotions as behavior regulators: Social referencing in infancy. In R. Plutchik & H. Kellerman (Eds.), *Emotion—Theory, research, and experience: Vol. 2. Emotions in early development* (pp. 57–86). New York: Academic Press.

Klinnert, M., Emde, R., Butterfield, P., & Campos, J. (1986). Social referencing: The infant's use of emotional signals from a friendly adult with mother present. *Developmental Psychology, 22,* 427–432.

Kochanska, G. (1991). Socialization and temperament in the development of guilt and conscience. *Child Development, 62,* 1379–1392.

Kochanska, G. (1993). Toward a synthesis of parental socialization and child temperament in early development of conscience. *Child Development, 64,* 325–347.

Kochanska, G. (1995). Children's temperament, mother's discipline, and security of attachment: Multiple pathways to emerging internalization. *Child Development, 66,* 597–615.

Kochanska, G. (1997a). Multiple pathways to conscience for children with different temperaments: From toddlerhood to age 5. *Developmental Psychology, 33,* 228–240.

Kochanska, G. (1997b). Mutually responsive orientation between mothers and their young children: Implications for early socialization. *Child Development, 68,* 94–112.

Kochanska, G., Aksan, N., Knaack, A., & Rhines, H. (2004). Maternal parenting and children's conscience: Early security as a moderator. *Child Development, 75,* 1229–1242.

Kochanska, G., Aksan, N., & Nichols, K. (2003). Maternal power assertion in discipline and moral discourse contexts: Commonalities, differences, and implications for children's moral conduct and cognition. *Developmental Psychology, 39,* 949–963.

Kochanska, G., Casey, R., & Fukumoto, A. (1995). Toddlers' sensitivity to standard violations. *Child Development, 66,* 643–656.

Kochanska, G., DeVet, K., Goldman, M., Murray, K., & Putnam, S. (1994). Maternal reports of conscience development and temperament in young children. *Child Development, 65,* 852–868.

Kochanska, G., Forman, D., & Coy, K. (1999). Implications of the mother-child relationship in infancy for socialization in the second year of life. *Infant Behavior and Development, 22,* 249–265.

Kochanska, G., Gross, J., Lin, M.-H., & Nichols, K. (2002). Guilt in young children: Development, determinants, and relations with a broader system of standards. *Child Development, 73,* 461–482.

Kochanska, G., & Murray, K. (2000). Mother-child mutually responsive orientation and conscience development: From toddler to early school age. *Child Development, 71,* 417–431.

Kochanska, G., Murray, K., & Coy, K. (1997). Inhibitory control as a contributor to conscience in childhood: From toddler to early school age. *Child Development, 68,* 263–277.

Kochanska, G., Murray, K., & Harlan, E. (2000). Effortful control in early childhood: Continuity and change, antecedents, and implications for social development. *Developmental Psychology, 36,* 220–232.

Kochanska, G., & Thompson, R. A. (1997). The emergence and development of conscience in toddlerhood and early childhood. In J. Grusec & L. Kuczynski (Eds.), *Parenting and children's internalization of values* (pp. 53–77). New York: Wiley.

Kopp, C. (1982). Antecedents of self-regulation: A developmental view. *Developmental Psychology, 18,* 199–214.

Kopp, C., & Wyer, N. (1994). Self-regulation in normal and atypical development. In D. Cicchetti & S. L. Toth (Eds.), *Rochester Symposium on Developmental Psychopathology: Vol. 5. Disorders and dysfunctions of the self* (pp. 31–56). Rochester, NY: University of Rochester Press.

Koren-Karie, N., Oppenheim, D., Dolev, S., Sher, E., & Etzion-Carasso, A. (2002). Mothers' insightfulness regarding their infants' internal experience: Relations with maternal sensitivity and infant attachment. *Developmental Psychology, 38,* 534–542.

Kuczynski, L., Kochanska, G., Radke-Yarrow, M., & Girnius-Brown, O. (1987). A developmental interpretation of young children's noncompliance. *Developmental Psychology, 23,* 799–806.

Kuczynski, L., Marshall, S., & Schell, K. (1997). Value socialization in a bidirectional context. In J. Grusec & L. Kuczynski (Eds.), *Parenting and children's internalization of values* (pp. 23–50). New York: Wiley.

Lagattuta, K. (2005). When you shouldn't do what you want to do: Young children's understanding of desires, rules, and emotions. *Child Development, 76,* 713–733.

Lagattuta, K., & Wellman, H. (2001). Thinking about the past: Young children's knowledge about links between past events, thinking, and emotion. *Child Development, 72,* 82–102.

Lagattuta, K., & Wellman, H. (2002). Differences in early parent-child conversations about negative versus positive emotions: Implications for the development of emotion understanding. *Developmental Psychology, 38,* 564–580.

Lagattuta, K., Wellman, H., & Flavell, J. (1997). Preschoolers' understanding of the link between thinking and feeling: Cognitive cuing and emotional change. *Child Development, 68,* 1081–1104.

Laible, D. (2004a). Mother-child discourse surrounding a child's past behavior at 30 months: Links to emotional understanding and early conscience development at 36 months. *Merrill-Palmer Quarterly, 50,* 159–180.

Laible, D. (2004b). Mother-child discourse in two contexts: Links with child temperament, attachment security, and socioemotional competence. *Developmental Psychology, 40,* 979–992.

Laible, D., & Thompson, R. A. (1998). Attachment and emotional understanding in preschool children. *Developmental Psychology, 34,* 1038–1045.

Laible, D., & Thompson, R. A. (2000). Mother-child discourse, attachment security, shared positive affect, and early conscience development. *Child Development, 71,* 1424–1440.

Laible, D., & Thompson, R. A. (2002). Mother-child conflict in the toddler years: Lessons in emotion, morality, and relationships. *Child Development, 73,* 1187–1203.

Laible, D., & Thompson, R. A. (in press). Foundations of socialization. In J. Grusec & P. Hastings (Eds.), *Handbook of socialization* (2nd ed.). New York: Guilford Press.

Lamb, M. (1981). Developing trust and perceived effectance in infancy. In L. Lipsitt (Ed.), *Advances in infancy research* (Vol. 1, pp. 101–127). New York: Ablex.

Lamb, M. (1997). The development of father-infant relationships. In M. Lamb (Ed.), *The role of the father in child development* (3rd ed., pp. 104–120). New York: Wiley.

Lamb, M., & Malkin, C. (1986). The development of social expectations in distress-relief sequences: A longitudinal study. *International Journal of Behavioral Development, 9,* 235–249.

Lamb, M., Thompson, R. A., Gardner, W., & Charnov, E. (1985). *Infant-mother attachment: The origins and developmental significance of individual differences in strange situation behavior.* Hillsdale, NJ: Erlbaum.

Lamb, S. (1993). First moral sense: An examination of the appearance of morally related behaviors in the second year of life. *Journal of Moral Education, 22,* 97–109.

Legerstee, M. (1994). Patterns of 4-month-old infant responses to hidden silent and sounding people and objects. *Early Development and Parenting, 3,* 71–80.

Legerstee, M. (1997). Contingency effects of people and objects on subsequent cognitive functioning in 3-month-old infants. *Social Development, 6,* 307–321.

Legerstee, M., Anderson, D., & Schaffer, A. (1998). Five- and eight-month-old infants recognize their faces and voices as familiar and social stimuli. *Child Development, 69,* 37–50.

Legerstee, M., Pomerleau, A., Malcuit, G., & Feider, H. (1987). The development of infants' responses to people and a doll: Implications for research in communication. *Infant Behavior and Development, 10,* 81–95.

Legerstee, M., & Varghese, J. (2001). The role of maternal affect mirroring on social expectancies in 3-month-old infants. *Child Development, 72,* 1301–1313.

Lemmon, K., & Moore, C. (2001). Binding the self in time. In C. Moore & K. Lemmon (Eds.), *The self in time* (pp. 163–179). Mahwah, NJ: Erlbaum.

Levine, L., Stein, N., & Liwag, M. (1999). Remembering children's emotions: Sources of concordant and discordant accounts between parents and children. *Developmental Psychology, 35,* 790–801.

Lewis, M. (2000). Self-conscious emotions: Embarrassment, pride, shame, and guilt. In M. Lewis & J. Haviland-Jones (Eds.), *Handbook of emotions* (pp. 563–573). New York: Guilford Press.

Lewis, M., Alessandri, S., & Sullivan, M. (1990). Violation of expectancy, loss of control, and anger expressions in young infants. *Developmental Psychology, 26,* 745–751.

Lewis, M., & Brooks-Gunn, J. (1979). *Social cognition and the acquisition of self.* New York: Plenum Press.

Lewis, M., Feiring, C., & Rosenthal, S. (2000). Attachment over time. *Child Development, 71,* 707–720.

Lockhart, K., Chang, B., & Story, T. (2002). Young children's beliefs about the stability of traits: Protective optimism? *Child Development, 73,* 1408–1430.

Lohmann, H., & Tomasello, M. (2003). The role of language in the development of false belief understanding: A training study. *Child Development, 74,* 1130–1144.

Lyons-Ruth, K., Alpern, L., & Repacholi, B. (1993). Disorganized infant attachment classification and maternal psychosocial problems as predictors of hostile-aggressive behavior in the preschool classroom. *Child Development, 64,* 572–585.

Lyons-Ruth, K., Bronfman, E., & Parsons, E. (1999). Maternal frightened, frightening, or atypical behavior and disorganized infant patterns. *Monographs of the Society for Research in Child Development, 64*(Serial No. 258), 67–96.

Lyons-Ruth, K., Easterbrooks, M., & Cibelli, C. (1997). Infant attachment strategies, infant mental lag, and maternal depressive symptoms: Predictors of internalizing and externalizing problems at age 7. *Developmental Psychology, 33,* 681–692.

Lyons-Ruth, K., & Jacobvitz, D. (1999). Attachment disorganization: Unresolved loss, relational violence, and lapses in behavioral and attentional strategies. In J. Cassidy & P. Shaver (Eds.), *Handbook of attachment* (pp. 520–554). Chicago: University of Chicago Press.

Lyons-Ruth, K., Repacholi, B., McLeod, S., & Silva, E. (1991). Disorganized attachment behavior in infancy: Short-term stability, maternal and infant correlates, and risk-related subtypes. *Development and Psychopathology, 3,* 377–396.

Maccoby, E., & Martin, J. (1983). Socialization in the context of the family: Parent-child interaction. In P. Mussen (Series Ed.) & E. Hetherington (Vol. Ed.), *Handbook of child psychology: Vol. 4. Socialization, personality, and social development* (4th ed., pp. 1–101). New York: Wiley.

Main, M., & Cassidy, J. (1988). Categories of response to reunion with the parent at age 6: Predictable from infant attachment classifications and stable over a 1-month period. *Developmental Psychology, 24,* 415–426.

Main, M., & Hesse, E. (1990). Parents' unresolved traumatic experiences are related to infant disorganized attachment status: Is frightened and/or frightening parental behavior the linking mechanism. In M. Greenberg, D. Cicchetti, & E. Cummings (Eds.), *Attachment in the preschool years* (pp. 161–182). Chicago: University of Chicago Press.

Main, M., & Solomon, J. (1986). Discovery of an insecure-disorganized/disoriented attachment pattern. In T. Brazelton & M. Yogman (Eds.), *Affective development in infancy* (pp. 95–124). Norwood, NJ: Ablex.

Main, M., & Solomon, J. (1990). Procedures for identifying infants as disorganized/disoriented during the Ainsworth strange situation. In M. Greenberg, D. Cicchetti, & E. Cummings (Eds.), *Attachment in the preschool years* (pp. 121–160). Chicago: University of Chicago Press.

Main, M., & Weston, D. (1981). The quality of the toddler's relationship to mother and to father: Related to conflict behavior and the readiness to establish new relationships. *Child Development, 52,* 932–940.

Malatesta, C., Culver, C., Tesman, J., & Shepard, B. (1989). The development of emotion expression during the first 2 years of life. *Monographs of the Society for Research in Child Development, 54*(1/2, Serial No. 219).

Malatesta, C., Grigoryev, P., Lamb, C., Albin, M., & Culver, C. (1986). Emotion socialization and expressive development in preterm and full-term infants. *Child Development, 57,* 316–330.

Mangelsdorf, S., Gunnar, M., Kestenbaum, R., Lang, S., & Andreas, D. (1990). Infant proneness-to-distress temperament, maternal personality, and mother-infant attachment: Associations and goodness of fit. *Child Development, 61,* 820–831.

Marsh, H., Craven, R., & Debus, R. (1998). Structure, stability, and development of young children's self-concepts: A multicohort-multioccasion study. *Child Development, 69,* 1030–1053.

Marsh, H., Ellis, L., & Craven, R. (2002). How do preschool children feel about themselves? Unraveling measurement and multidimensional self-concept structure. *Developmental Psychology, 38,* 376–393.

Masters, J., & Wellman, H. (1974). The study of human infant attachment: A procedural critique. *Psychological Bulletin, 81,* 218–237.

Matas, L., Arend, R., & Sroufe, L. (1978). Continuity of adaptation in the second year: The relationship between quality of attachment and later competence. *Child Development, 49,* 547–556.

McCartney, K., Owen, M., Booth, C., Clarke-Stewart, A., & Vandell, D. (2004). Testing a maternal attachment model of behavior problems in early childhood. *Journal of Child Psychology and Psychiatry, 45,* 765–778.

Measelle, J., Ablow, J., Cowan, P., & Cowan, C. (1998). Assessing young children's views of their academic, social, and emotional lives: An evaluation of the self-perception scales of the Berkeley Puppet Interview. *Child Development, 69,* 1556–1576.

Meins, E. (1999). Sensitivity, security and internal working models: Bridging the transmission gap. *Attachment and Human Development, 1,* 325–342.

Meins, E., Fernyhough, C., Fradley, E., & Tuckey, M. (2001). Rethinking maternal sensitivity: Mothers' comments on infants' mental processes predict security of attachment at 12 months. *Journal of Child Psychology and Psychiatry, 42,* 637–648.

Meins, E., Fernyhough, C., Wainwright, R., Clark-Carter, D., Gupta, M., Fradley, E., et al. (2003). Pathways to understanding mind: Construct validity and predictive validity of maternal mind-mindedness. *Child Development, 74,* 1194–1211.

Meins, E., Fernyhough, C., Wainwright, R., Gupta, M., Fradley, E., & Tuckey, M. (2002). Maternal mind-mindedness and attachment security as predictors of theory of mind understanding. *Child Development, 73,* 1715–1726.

Meltzoff, A. (1995). Understanding the intentions of others: Re-enactment of intended acts by 18-month-old children. *Developmental Psychology, 31,* 838–850.

Meltzoff, A., & Gopnik, A. (1993). The role of imitation in understanding persons and developing a theory of mind. In S. Baron-Cohen, H. Tager-Flusberg, & D. Cohen (Eds.), *Understanding other minds* (pp. 335–366). London: Oxford.

Miller, P. (1994). Narrative practices: Their role in socialization and self-construction. In U. Neisser & R. Fivush (Eds.), *The remembering self* (pp. 158–179). Cambridge: Cambridge University Press.

Miller, P., Eisenberg, N., Fabes, R., & Shell, R. (1996). Relations of moral reasoning and vicarious emotion to young children's prosocial behavior toward peers and adults. *Developmental Psychology, 32,* 210–219.

Miller, P., Fung, H., & Mintz, J. (1996). Self-construction through narrative practices: A Chinese and American comparison of early socialization. *Ethos, 24,* 237–280.

Miller, P., Potts, R., Fung, H., Hoogstra, L., & Mintz, J. (1990). Narrative practices and the social construction of self in childhood. *American Ethologist, 17,* 292–311.

Miller, P., Wiley, A. R., Fung, H., & Liang, C.-H. (1997). Personal storytelling as a medium of socialization in Chinese and American families. *Child Development, 68,* 557–568.

Mondloch, C., Lewis, T., Budreau, D., Maurer, D., Dannemiller, J., Stephens, B., et al. (1999). Face perception during early infancy. *Psychological Science, 10,* 419–422.

Montague, D., & Walker-Andrews, A. (2002). Mothers, fathers, and infants: The role of person familiarity and parental involvement in infants' perception of emotional expressions. *Child Development, 73,* 1339–1352.

Moore, C., & Corkum, V. (1994). Social understanding at the end of the first year of life. *Developmental Review, 14,* 349–372.

Moore, C., & Lemmon, K. (2001). The nature and utility of the temporally extended self. In C. Moore & K. Lemmon (Eds.), *The self in time* (pp. 1–13). Mahwah, NJ: Erlbaum.

Moses, L., Baldwin, D., Rosicky, J., & Tidball, G. (2001). Evidence for referential understanding in the emotions domain at 12 and 18 months. *Child Development, 72,* 718–735.

Moss, E., Bureau, J.-F., Cyr, C., Mongeau, C., & St.-Laurent, D. (2004). Correlates of attachment at age 3: Construct validity of the preschool attachment classification system. *Developmental Psychology, 40,* 323–334.

Moss, E., Cyr, C., Bureau, J.-F., Tarabulsy, G., & Dubois-Comtois, K. (2004). *Correlates and stability of attachment between preschool and early school-age.* Unpublished manuscript, University of Quebec at Montreal.

Moss, E., Cyr, C., & Dubois-Comtois, K. (2004). Attachment at early school age and developmental risk: Examining family contexts and behavior problems of controlling-caregiving, controlling-punitive, and behaviorally disorganized children. *Developmental Psychology, 40,* 519–532.

Moss, E., Parent, S., Gosselin, C., Rousseau, D., & St.-Laurent, D. (1996). Attachment and teacher reported behavior problems during the preschool and early school age period. *Development and Psychopathology, 8,* 511–525.

Mullen, M. K., & Yi, S. (1995). The cultural context of talk about the past: Implications for the development of autobiographical memory. *Cognitive Development, 10,* 407–419.

Mumme, D., & Fernald, A. (2003). The infant as onlooker: Learning from emotional reactions observed in a television scenario. *Child Development, 74,* 221–237.

Mumme, D., Fernald, A., & Herrera, C. (1996). Infants' responses to facial and vocal emotional signals in a social referencing paradigm. *Child Development, 67,* 3219–3237.

Murray, L., & Trevarthen, C. (1985). Emotional regulation of interactions between 2-month-olds and their mothers. In T. M. Field & N. A. Fox (Eds.), *Social perception in infants* (pp. 177–197). Norwood, NJ: Ablex.

Nachmias, M., Gunnar, M., Mangelsdorf, S., Parritz, R., & Buss, K. (1996). Behavioral inhibition and stress reactivity: The moderating role of attachment security. *Child Development, 67,* 508–522.

National Institute of Child Health and Human Development Early Child Care Research Network. (1997). The effects of infant child care on infant-mother attachment security: Results of the NICHD Study of Early Child Care. *Child Development, 68,* 860–879.

National Institute of Child Health and Human Development Early Child Care Research Network. (2001). Child-care and family predictors of preschool attachment and stability from infancy. *Developmental Psychology, 37,* 847–862.

Neisser, U. (1995). Criteria for an ecological self. In P. Rochat (Ed.), *The self in infancy* (pp. 17–34). Amsterdam: North Holland-Elsevier.

Nelson, K. (Ed.). (1978). *Event knowledge: Structure and function in development.* Hillsdale, NJ: Erlbaum.

Nelson, K. (Ed.). (1989). *Narratives from the crib.* Cambridge, MA: Harvard University Press.

Nelson, K. (1993a). Events, narratives, memory: What develops. In C. Nelson (Ed.), *Minnesota Symposia on Child Psychology: Vol. 26. Memory and affect in development* (pp. 1–24). Hillsdale, NJ: Erlbaum.

Nelson, K. (1993b). The psychological and social origins of autobiographical memory. *Psychological Science, 4,* 7–14.

Nelson, K. (1996). *Language in cognitive development: The emergence of the mediated mind.* New York: Cambridge.

Nelson, K., & Fivush, R. (2004). The emergence of autobiographical memory: A social-cultural developmental theory. *Psychological Review, 111,* 486–511.

Nelson, K., & Gruendel, J. (1981). Generalized event representations: Basic building blocks of cognitive development. In M. Lamb & A. Brown (Eds.), *Advances in developmental psychology* (pp. 131–158). Hillsdale, NJ: Erlbaum.

O'Connor, T., Caspi, A., DeFries, J., & Plomin, R. (2003). Genotype-environment interaction in children's adjustment to parent separation. *Journal of Child Psychology and Psychiatry, 44,* 849–856.

O'Connor, T., & Croft, C. (2001). A twin study of attachment in preschool children. *Child Development, 72,* 1501–1511.

Ontai, L., & Thompson, R. A. (2002). Patterns of attachment and maternal discourse effects on children's emotion understanding from 3- to 5-years of age. *Social Development, 11,* 433–450.

Oppenheim, D., & Koren-Karie, N. (2002). Mothers' insightfulness regarding their children's internal worlds: The capacity underlying secure child-mother relationships. *Infant Mental Health Journal, 23,* 593–605.

Oppenheim, D., Sagi, A., & Lamb, M. (1988). Infant-adult attachments on the kibbutz and their relation to socioemotional development 4 years later. *Developmental Psychology, 24,* 427–433.

Owen, M., & Cox, M. (1997). Marital conflict and the development of infant-parent attachment relationships. *Journal of Family Psychology, 11,* 152–164.

Owen, M., Easterbrooks, M., Chase-Lansdale, L., & Goldberg, W. (1984). The relation between maternal employment status and the stability of attachments to mother and to father. *Child Development, 55,* 1894–1901.

Pascalis, O., de Schonen, S., Morton, J., Deruelle, C., & Fabre-Grenet, M. (1995). Mother's face recognition by neonates: A replication and an extension. *Infant Behavior and Development, 18,* 79–85.

Pasco Fearon, R., & Belsky, J. (2004). Attachment and attention: Protection in relation to gender and cumulative social-contextual adversity. *Child Development, 75,* 1677–1693.

Perner, J. (2001). Episodic memory: Essential distinctions and developmental implications. In C. Moore & K. Lemmon (Eds.), *The self in time* (pp. 181–202). Mahwah, NJ: Erlbaum.

Perner, J., & Ruffman, T. (1995). Episodic memory an autonoetic consciousness: Developmental evidence and a theory of childhood amnesia. *Journal of Experimental Child Psychology, 59,* 516–548.

Peterson, C., Jesso, B., & McCabe, A. (1999). Encouraging narratives in preschoolers: An intervention study. *Journal of Child Language, 26,* 49–67.

Phillips, A., Wellman, H., & Spelke, E. (2002). Infants' ability to connect gaze and emotional expression to intentional action. *Cognition, 85,* 53–78.

Piaget, J. (1952). *The origins of intelligence in children.* New York: International Universities Press.

Piaget, J. (1965). *The moral judgment of the child.* New York: Harcourt, Brace.

Posada, G., Gao, Y., Posada, R., Tascon, M., Schoelmerich, A., Sagi, A., et al. (1995). The secure-base phenomenon across cultures: Children's behavior, mothers' preferences, and experts' concepts. *Monographs of the Society for Research in Child Development, 60*(Serial No. 244), 27–48.

Povinelli, D. (1995). The unduplicated self. In P. Rochat (Ed.), *The self in early infancy* (pp. 161–192). Amsterdam: North Holland-Elsevier.

Povinelli, D. (2001). The self: Elevated in consciousness and extended in time. In C. Moore & K. Lemmon (Eds.), *The self in time* (pp. 75–95). Mahwah, NJ: Erlbaum.

Povinelli, D., Landau, K., & Perilloux, H. (1996). Self-recognition in young children using delayed versus live feedback: Evidence of a developmental asynchrony. *Child Development, 67,* 1540–1554.

Povinelli, D., Landry, A., Theall, L., Clark, B., & Castille, C. (1999). Development of young children's understanding that the recent past is causally bound to the present. *Developmental Psychology, 35*, 1426–1439.

Povinelli, D., & Simon, B. (1998). Young children's understanding of briefly versus extremely delayed images of the self: Emergence of the autobiographical stance. *Developmental Psychology, 34*, 188–194.

Raikes, H. A., & Thompson, R. A. (2005a). Family emotional climate, attachment security, and young children's emotion understanding in a high-risk sample. *British Journal of Developmental Psychology, 23*, 1–17.

Raikes, H. A., & Thompson, R. A. (2005b). Relationships past, present, and future: Reflections on attachment in middle childhood. In K. Kerns & R. Richardson (Eds.), *Attachment in middle childhood* (pp. 255–282). New York: Guilford Press.

Raikes, H. A., & Thompson, R. A. (2005c). Links between risk and attachment security: Models of influence. *Applied Developmental Psychology, 26*, 440–455.

Raikes, H. A., & Thompson, R. A. (2005d). *Early attachment and subsequent parenting quality as predictors of early social cognitive development.* Unpublished manuscript, University of California, Davis.

Rakison, D., & Poulin-Dubois, D. (2001). Developmental origin of the animate-inanimate distinction. *Psychological Bulletin, 127*, 209–228.

Reese, E. (2002). Social factors in the development of autobiographical memory: The state of the art. *Social Development, 11*, 124–142.

Reese, E., & Fivush, R. (1993). Parental styles of talking about the past. *Developmental Psychology, 29*, 596–606.

Reese, E., Haden, C., & Fivush, R. (1993). Mother-child conversations about the past: Relationships of style and memory over time. *Cognitive Development, 8*, 403–430.

Repacholi, B. (1998). Infants' use of attentional cues to identify the referent of another person's emotional expression. *Developmental Psychology, 34*, 1017–1025.

Repacholi, B., & Gopnik, A. (1997). Early reasoning about desires: Evidence from 14- and 18-month-olds. *Developmental Psychology, 33*, 12–21.

Richters, J., Waters, E., & Vaughn, B. (1988). Empirical classification of infant-mother relationships from interactive behavior and crying during reunion. *Child Development, 59*, 512–522.

Ridgeway, D., Waters, E., & Kuczaj, S. (1985). Acquisition of emotion-descriptive language: Receptive and productive vocabulary norms for ages 18 months to 6 years. *Developmental Psychology, 21*, 901–908.

Rochat, P., & Morgan, R. (1995). Spatial determinants in the perception of self-produced leg movements by 3- to 5-month-old infants. *Developmental Psychology, 31*, 626–636.

Rochat, P., Neisser, U., & Marian, V. (1998). Are young infants sensitive to interpersonal contingency? *Infant Behavior and Development, 21*, 355–366.

Rogoff, B. (1990). *Apprenticeship in thinking.* New York: Oxford University Press.

Rothbart, M. (1989). Temperament in childhood: A framework. In G. Kohnstamm, J. Bates, & M. Rothbart (Eds.), *Temperament in childhood* (pp. 59–73). New York: Wiley.

Rothbaum, F., Pott, M., Azuma, H., Miyake, K., & Weisz, J. (2000). The development of close relationships in Japan and the United States: Paths of symbiotic harmony and generative tension. *Child Development, 71*, 1121–1142.

Rothbaum, F., Weisz, J., Pott, M., Miyake, K., & Morelli, G. (2000). Attachment and culture: Security in the United States and Japan. *American Psychologist, 55*, 1093–1104.

Rovee-Collier, C. (1989). The joy of kicking: Memories, motives, and mobiles. In P. R. Solomon, G. Goethals, C. Kelley, & B. Stephens (Eds.), *Memory: Interdisciplinary approaches* (pp. 151–180). New York: Springer-Verlag.

Ruffman, T., Perner, J., & Parkin, L. (1999). How parenting style affects false belief understanding. *Social Development, 8*, 395–411.

Ruffman, T., Slade, L., & Crowe, E. (2002). The relation between children's and mothers' mental state language and theory-of-mind understanding. *Child Development, 73*, 734–751.

Ruffman, T., Slade, L., Rowlandson, K., Rumsey, C., & Garnham, A. (2003). How language relates to belief, desire, and emotion understanding. *Cognitive Development, 18*, 139–158.

Rutter, M. (1997). Nature-nurture integration: The example of antisocial behavior. *American Psychologist, 52*, 390–398.

Rutter, M., & O'Connor, T. (1999). Implications of attachment theory for child care policies. In J. Cassidy & P. Shaver (Eds.), *Handbook of attachment* (pp. 823–844). New York: Guilford Press.

Rutter, M., Silberg, J., O'Connor, T., & Simonoff, E. (1999). Genetics and child psychiatry: Pt. 1. Advances in quantitative and molecular genetics. *Journal of Child Psychology and Psychiatry, 40*, 3–18.

Sabbagh, M., & Callanan, M. (1998). Metarepresentation in action: 3-, 4-, and 5-year-olds' developing theories of mind in parent-child conversations. *Developmental Psychology, 34*, 491–502.

Sagi, A., Koren-Karie, N., Gini, M., Ziv, Y., & Joels, T. (2002). Shedding further light on the effects of various types and quality of early child care on infant-mother attachment relationship: The Haifa Study of Early Child Care. *Child Development, 73*, 1166–1186.

Sagi, A., van Ijzendoorn, M., Aviezer, O., Donnell, F., & Mayseless, O. (1994). Sleeping out of home in a kibbutz communal arrangement: It makes a difference for infant-mother attachment. *Child Development, 65*, 992–1004.

Sameroff, A., & Chandler, M. (1975). Reproductive risk and the continuum of caretaking casualty. In F. Horowitz, E. Hetherington, S. Scarr-Salapatek, & G. Siegel (Eds.), *Review of child development research* (Vol. 4, pp. 187–244). Chicago: University of Chicago Press.

Schneider, B., Atkinson, L., & Tardif, C. (2001). Child-parent attachment and children's peer relations: A quantitative review. *Developmental Psychology, 37*, 86–100.

Schuengel, C., Bakermans-Kranenburg, M., & van Ijzendoorn, M. (1999). Frightening maternal behavior linking unresolved loss and disorganized infant attachment. *Journal of Consulting and Clinical Psychology, 67*, 54–63.

Schultz, D., Izard, C., & Ackerman, B. (2000). Children's anger attribution bias: Relations to family environment and social adjustment. *Social Development, 9*, 284–301.

Shaw, D., Keenan, K., Vondra, J., Delliquadri, E., & Giovanelli, J. (1997). Antecedents of preschool children's internalizing problems: A longitudinal study of low-income families. *Journal of the American Academy of Child and Adolescent Psychiatry, 36*, 1760–1767.

Shaw, D., Owens, E., Vondra, J., Keenan, K., & Winslow, E. (1996). Early risk factors and pathways in the development of early disruptive behavior problems. *Development and Psychopathology, 8*, 679–699.

Slade, A. (1987). Quality of attachment and early symbolic play. *Developmental Psychology, 23,* 78–85.

Smetana, J., & Braeges, J. (1990). The development of toddler's moral and conventional judgments. *Merrill-Palmer Quarterly, 36,* 329–346.

Smetana, J., Kochanska, G., & Chuang, S. (2000). Mothers' conceptions of everyday rules for young toddlers: A longitudinal investigation. *Merrill-Palmer Quarterly, 46,* 391–416.

Smetana, J. G. (1981). Preschool children's conceptions of moral and social rules. *Child Development, 52,* 1333–1336.

Smetana, J. G. (1997). Parenting and the development of social knowledge reconceptualized: A social domain analysis. In J. Grusec & L. Kuczynski (Eds.), *Parenting and children's internalization of values* (pp. 162–192). New York: Wiley.

Solomon, J., & George, C. (1999). The measurement of attachment security in infancy and childhood. In J. Cassidy & P. Shaver (Eds.), *Handbook of attachment* (pp. 287–316). New York: Guilford Press.

Sorce, J., Emde, R., Campos, J., & Klinnert, M. (1985). Maternal emotional signaling: Its effect on the visual cliff behavior of 1-year-olds. *Developmental Psychology, 21,* 195–200.

Spangler, G., & Delius, A. (2003, August). *The inner working model as a "theory of attachment."* Paper presented at the 11th European Conference on Developmental Psychology in Milano, Italy.

Spelke, E., Phillips, A., & Woodward, A. (1995). Infants' knowledge about object motion and human action. In D. Sperber, D. Premack, & A. Premack (Eds.), *Causal cognition* (pp. 44–78). Oxford, England: Clarendon.

Sroufe, L. A. (1983). Infant-caregiver attachment and patterns of adaptation in preschool: The roots of maladaptation and competence. In M. Perlmutter (Ed.), *Minnesota Symposia on Child Psychology: Vol. 16. Development and policy concerning children with special needs* (pp. 41–83). Hillsdale, NJ: Erlbaum.

Sroufe, L. A. (1988). The role of infant-caregiver attachment in development. In J. Belsky & T. Nezworski (Eds.), *Clinical implications of attachment* (pp. 18–38). Hillsdale, NJ: Erlbaum.

Sroufe, L. A., Egeland, B., Carlson, E., & Collins, W. (2005). *Minnesota Study of Risk and Adaptation from birth to maturity: The development of the person.* New York: Guilford Press.

Sroufe, L. A., Egeland, B., & Kreutzer, T. (1990). The fate of early experience following developmental change: Longitudinal approaches to individual adaptation in childhood. *Child Development, 61,* 1363–1373.

Steele, H., Steele, M., Croft, C., & Fonagy, P. (1999). Infant-mother attachment at 1 year predicts children's understanding of mixed emotions at 6 years. *Social Development, 8,* 161–178.

Stein, N., & Levine, L. (1989). The causal organization of emotional knowledge: A developmental study. *Cognition and Emotion, 3,* 343–378.

Stevenson-Hinde, J., & Shouldice, A. (1995). Maternal interactions and self-reports related to attachment classifications at 4.5 years. *Child Development, 66,* 583–596.

Stevenson-Hinde, J., & Verschueren, K. (2002). Attachment in childhood. In P. Smith & C. Hart (Eds.), *Blackwell handbook of childhood social development* (pp. 182–204). Oxford, England: Blackwell.

Stipek, D. (1995). The development of pride and shame in toddlers. In J. P. Tangney & K. W. Fischer (Eds.), *Self-conscious emotions* (pp. 237–252). New York: Guilford Press.

Stipek, D., Gralinski, J., & Kopp, C. (1990). Self-concept development in the toddler years. *Developmental Psychology, 26,* 972–977.

Stipek, D., Recchia, S., & McClintic, S. (1992). Self-evaluation in young children. *Monographs of the Society for Research in Child Development, 57*(Serial No. 226).

Striano, T. (2004). Direction of regard and the still-face effect in the first year: Does intention matter? *Child Development, 75,* 468–479.

Symons, D., & Clark, S. (2000). A longitudinal study of mother-child relationships and theory of mind in the preschool period. *Social Development, 9,* 3–23.

Symons, D., Clark, S., Isaksen, G., & Marshall, J. (1998). Stability of q-sort attachment security from age 2 to 5. *Infant Behavior and Development, 21,* 785–791.

Takahashi, K. (1986). Examining the strange-situation procedure with Japanese mothers and 12-month-old infants. *Developmental Psychology, 22,* 265–270.

Takahashi, K. (1990). Are the key assumptions of the "strange situation" procedure universal? A view from Japanese research. *Human Development, 33,* 23–30.

Teti, D. (1999). Conceptualizations of disorganization in the preschool years. In J. Solomon & C. George (Eds.), *Attachment disorganization* (pp. 213–242). New York: Guilford Press.

Teti, D., & McGourty, S. (1996). Using mothers versus observers of children's secure base behavior: Theoretical and methodological considerations. *Child Development, 67,* 597–596.

Teti, D., Sakin, J., Kucera, E., Corns, K., & Das Eiden, R. (1996). And baby makes four: Predictors of attachment security among preschool-aged firstborns during the transition to siblinghood. *Child Development, 67,* 579–596.

Theimer, C., Killen, M., & Stangor, C. (2001). Preschool children's evaluations of exclusion in gender-stereotypic contexts. *Developmental Psychology, 37,* 18–27.

Thompson, R. A. (1986). Temperament, emotionality, and infant social cognition. In J. Lerner & R. Lerner (Eds.), *Temperament and social interaction during infancy and childhood* (pp. 35–52). San Francisco: Jossey-Bass.

Thompson, R. A. (1990). Emotion and self-regulation. In R. A. Thompson (Ed.), *Nebraska Symposium on Motivation: Vol. 36. Socioemotional development* (pp. 383–483). Lincoln: University of Nebraska Press.

Thompson, R. A. (1994). Emotion regulation: A theme in search of definition. In N. Fox (Ed.), *Monographs of the Society for Research in Child Development, 59*(Serial No. 240), 25–52.

Thompson, R. A. (1995). *Preventing child maltreatment through social support.* Thousand Oaks, CA: Sage.

Thompson, R. A. (1997). Sensitivity and security: New questions to ponder. *Child Development, 68,* 595–597.

Thompson, R. A. (1998). Early sociopersonality development. In W. Damon (Editor-in-Chief) & N. Eisenberg (Vol. Ed.), *Handbook of child psychology: Vol. 3. Social, emotional, and personality development* (5th ed., pp. 25–104). New York: Wiley.

Thompson, R. A. (1999). Early attachment and later development. In J. Cassidy & P. Shaver (Eds.), *Handbook of attachment* (pp. 265–286). New York: Guilford Press.

Thompson, R. A. (2000). The legacy of early attachments. *Child Development, 71*(1), 145–152.

Thompson, R. A. (2005). Multiple relationships multiply considered. *Human Development, 48,* 102–107.

Thompson, R. A. (2006). Conversation and developing understanding: Introduction to the special issue. *Merrill-Palmer Quarterly, 52,* 1–16.

Thompson, R. A. (in press). Developing persons, relationships, and science. *Human Development.*

Thompson, R. A., Braun, K., Grossmann, K. E., Gunnar, M., Heinrichs, M., Keller, H., et al. (2005). Early social attachment and its consequences: The dynamics of a developing relationship. In C. Carter, L. Ahnert, K. E. Grossmann, M. Lamb, S. Porges, & N. Sachser (Eds.), *Attachment and bonding: A new synthesis* (Dahlem Workshop report 92, pp. 349–383). Cambridge, MA: MIT Press.

Thompson, R. A., Connell, J., & Bridges, L. (1988). Temperament, emotion, and social interactive behavior in the strange situation: A component process analysis of attachment system functioning. *Child Development, 59,* 1102–1110.

Thompson, R. A., Flood, M., & Goodvin, R. (2005). Social support and developmental psychopathology. In D. Cicchetti & D. Cohen (Eds.), *Developmental psychopathology: Vol. 3. Risk, disorder, and adaptation* (2nd ed.). New York: Wiley.

Thompson, R. A., & Lagattuta, K. (2005). Feeling and understanding: Early emotional development. In K. McCartney & D. Phillips (Ed.), *The Blackwell handbook of early childhood development.* Oxford, England: Blackwell.

Thompson, R. A., Laible, D., & Ontai, L. (2003). Early understanding of emotion, morality, and the self: Developing a working model. In R. Kail (Ed.), *Advances in child development and behavior* (Vol. 31, pp. 137–171). San Diego, CA: Academic Press.

Thompson, R. A., & Lamb, M. (1983). Security of attachment and stranger sociability in infancy. *Developmental Psychology, 19,* 184–191.

Thompson, R. A., Lamb, M., & Estes, D. (1982). Stability of infant-mother attachment and its relationship to changing life circumstances in an unselected middle-class sample. *Child Development, 53,* 144–148.

Thompson, R. A., & Meyer, S. (in press). The socialization of emotion regulation in the family. In J. Gross (Ed.), *Handbook of emotion regulation.* New York: Guilford Press.

Thompson, R. A., Meyer, S., & McGinley, M. (2006). Understanding values in relationship: The development of conscience. In M. Killen & J. Smetana (Eds.), *Handbook of moral development* (pp. 267–297). Mahwah, NJ: Erlbaum.

Thompson, R. A., & Raikes, H. A. (2003). Toward the next quarter-century: Conceptual and methodological challenges for attachment theory. *Development and Psychopathology, 15,* 691–718.

Tomasello, M. (1995a). Joint attention as social cognition. In C. Moore & P. Dunham (Eds.), *Joint attention* (pp. 105–130). Hillsdale, NJ: Erlbaum.

Tomasello, M. (1995b). Understanding the self as social agent. In P. Rochat (Ed.), *The self in infancy* (pp. 449–460). Amsterdam: North Holland-Elsevier.

Tomasello, M. (1999). *The cultural origins of human cognition.* Cambridge, MA: Harvard University Press.

Tomasello, M., & Barton, M. (1994). Learning words in nonostensive contexts. *Developmental Psychology, 30,* 639–650.

Tomasello, M., Carpenter, M., Call, J., Behne, T., & Moll, H. (in press). Understanding and sharing intentions: The origins of cultural cognition. *Behavioral and Brain Sciences,* in press.

Tomasello, M., & Rakoczy, H. (2003). What makes human cognition unique? From individual to shared to collective intentionality. *Mind and Language, 18,* 121–147.

Trivers, R. (1985). *Social evolution.* Menlo Park, CA: Benjamin/Cummings.

Tronick, E. (1989). Emotions and emotional communication in infants. *American Psychologist, 44,* 112–119.

Valenzuela, M. (1990). Attachment in chronically underweight young children. *Child Development, 61,* 1984–1996.

Valenzuela, M. (1997). Maternal sensitivity in a developing society: The context of urban poverty and infant chronic under nutrition. *Developmental Psychology, 33,* 845–855.

van Ijzendoorn, M. (1995). Adult attachment representations, parental responsiveness, and infant attachment: A meta-analysis on the predictive validity of the adult attachment interview. *Psychological Bulletin, 117,* 387–403.

van Ijzendoorn, M., & De Wolff, M. (1997). In search of the absent father: Meta-analyses of infant-father attachment: A rejoinder to our discussants. *Child Development, 68,* 604–609.

van Ijzendoorn, M., & Sagi, A. (1999). Cross-cultural patterns of attachment: Universal and contextual dimensions. In J. Cassidy & P. Shaver (Eds.), *Handbook of attachment* (pp. 713–734). New York: Guilford Press.

van Ijzendoorn, M., Schuengel, C., & Bakermans-Kranenburg, M. (1999). Disorganized attachment in early childhood: Meta-analysis of precursors, concomitants, and sequelae. *Development and Psychopathology, 11,* 225–249.

van Ijzendoorn, M., van der Veer, R., & van Vliet-Visser, S. (1987). Attachment 3 years later: Relationships between quality of mother-infant attachment and emotional/cognitive development in kindergarten. In L. Tavecchio & M. van Ijzendoorn (Eds.), *Attachment in social networks* (pp. 185–224). Amsterdam: Elsevier.

van Ijzendoorn, M., Vereijken, C., Bakermans-Kranenburg, M., & Riksen-Walraven, J. (2004). Assessing attachment security with the attachment q sort: Meta-analytic evidence for the validity of the observer AQS. *Child Development, 75,* 1188–1213.

Vaughn, B., & Bost, K. (1999). Attachment and temperament: Redundant, independent, or interacting influences on interpersonal adaptation and personality development. In J. Cassidy & P. Shaver (Eds.), *Handbook of attachment* (pp. 198–225). New York: Guilford Press.

Vaughn, B., Egeland, B., Sroufe, L., & Waters, E. (1979). Individual differences in infant-mother attachment at 12 and 18 months: Stability and change in families under stress. *Child Development, 50,* 971–975.

Vondra, J., Shaw, D., Swearingen, L., Cohen, M., & Owens, E. (2001). Attachment stability and emotional and behavioral regulation from infancy to preschool age. *Development and Psychopathology, 13,* 13–33.

Walden, T., & Ogan, T. (1988). The development of social referencing. *Child Development, 59,* 1230–1240.

Walker-Andrews, A. (1997). Infants' perception of expressive behaviors: Differentiation of multimodal information. *Psychological Bulletin, 121,* 437–456.

Walton, G., Bower, N., & Bower, T. (1992). Recognition of familiar faces by newborns. *Infant Behavior and Development, 15,* 265–269.

Wang, Q. (2004). The emergence of cultural self-constructs: Autobiographical memory and self-description in European American and Chinese children. *Developmental Psychology, 40,* 3–15.

Wang, Q., Leichtman, M., & Davies, K. (2000). Sharing memories and telling stories: American and Chinese mothers and their 3-year-olds. *Memory, 8,* 159–178.

Wartner, U., Grossmann, K., Fremmer-Bombik, E., & Suess, G. (1994). Attachment patterns at age 6 in South Germany:

Predictability from infancy and implications for preschool behavior. *Child Development, 65,* 1014–1027.

Waters, E. (1978). The reliability and stability of individual differences in infant-mother attachment. *Child Development, 49,* 483–494.

Waters, E., & Cummings, E. (2000). A secure base from which to explore close relationships. *Child Development, 71,* 164–172.

Waters, E., & Deane, K. (1985). Defining and assessing individual differences in attachment relationships: Q-methodology and the organization of behavior in infancy and early childhood. In I. Bretherton & E. Waters (Eds.), *Monographs of the Society for Research in Child Development, 50*(Serial No. 209), 41–65.

Waters, E., Kondo-Ikemura, K., Posada, G., & Richters, J. (1991). Learning to love: Mechanisms and milestones. In M. Gunnar & L. Sroufe (Eds.), *Minnesota Symposia on Child Psychology: Vol. 23. Self processes and development* (pp. 217–255). Hillsdale, NJ: Erlbaum.

Waters, E., Merrick, S., Treboux, D., Crowell, J., & Albersheim, L. (2000). Attachment security in infancy and early adulthood: A 20-year longitudinal study. *Child Development, 71,* 684–689.

Waters, E., Weinfield, N., & Hamilton, C. (2000). The stability of attachment security from infancy to adolescence and early adulthood: General discussion. *Child Development, 71,* 703–706.

Watson, J. (1979). Perception of contingency as a determinant of social responsiveness. In E. Thoman (Ed.), *Origins of the infant's social responsiveness* (pp. 33–64). Hillsdale, NJ: Erlbaum.

Watson, J. (1985). Contingency perception in early social development. In T. Field & N. Fox (Eds.), *Social perception in infants* (pp. 157–176). Norwood, NJ: Ablex.

Watson, J. S. (1995). Mother-infant interaction: Dispositional properties and mutual designs. In N. Thompson (Ed.), *Perspectives in ethology* (pp. 189–210). New York: Plenum Press.

Weinfield, N., Sroufe, L., & Egeland, B. (2000). Attachment from infancy to early adulthood in a high-risk sample: Continuity, discontinuity, and their correlates. *Child Development, 71,* 695–702.

Weinfield, N., Sroufe, L. A., Egeland, B., & Carlson, E. (1999). The nature of individual differences in infant-caregiver attachment. In J. Cassidy & P. Shaver (Eds.), *Handbook of attachment* (pp. 68–88). New York: Guilford Press.

Welch-Ross, M. (1995). An integrative model of the development of autobiographical memory. *Developmental Review, 15,* 338–365.

Welch-Ross, M. (2001). Personalizing the temporally extended self: Evaluative self-awareness and the development of autobiographical memory. In C. Moore & K. Lemmon (Eds.), *The self in time* (pp. 97–120). Mahwah, NJ: Erlbaum.

Wellman, H. (2002). Understanding the psychological world: Developing a theory of mind. In U. Goswami (Ed.), *Handbook of childhood cognitive development* (pp. 167–187). Oxford, England: Blackwell.

Wellman, H., & Banerjee, M. (1991). Mind and emotion: Children's understanding of the emotional consequences of beliefs and desires. *British Journal of Developmental Psychology, 9,* 191–214.

Wellman, H., Cross, D., & Watson, J. (2001). Meta-analysis of theory-of-mind development: The truth about false belief. *Child Development, 72,* 655–684.

Wellman, H., Harris, P., Banerjee, M., & Sinclair, A. (1995). Early understanding of emotion: Evidence from natural language. *Cognition and Emotion, 9,* 117–149.

Wellman, H., & Miller, J. (2003). *Integrating deontic reasoning and theory of mind.* Manuscript submitted for publication.

Wellman, H., Phillips, A., Dunphy-Lelii, S., & LaLonde, N. (2004). Infant social attention predicts preschool social cognition. *Developmental Science, 7,* 283–288.

Wellman, H., & Woolley, J. (1990). From simple desires to ordinary beliefs: The early development of everyday psychology. *Cognition, 35,* 245–275.

Wiley, A., Rose, A., Burger, L., & Miller, P. (1998). Constructing autonomous selves through narrative practices: A comparative study of working-class and middle-class families. *Child Development, 69,* 833–847.

Wintre, M., & Vallance, D. (1994). A developmental sequence in the comprehension of emotions: Intensity, multiple emotions, and valence. *Developmental Psychology, 30,* 509–514.

Woodward, A. (1998). Infants selectively encode the goal object of an actor's reach. *Cognition, 69,* 1–34.

Woodward, A. (2003). Infants' developing understanding of the link between looker and object. *Developmental Science, 6,* 297–311.

Woodward, A., & Guajardo, J. (2002). Infants' understanding of the point gesture as an object-directed action. *Cognitive Development, 17,* 1061–1084.

Woodward, A., & Sommerville, J. (2000). Twelve-month-old infants interpret action in context. *Psychological Science, 11,* 73–77.

Youngblade, L., & Belsky, J. (1992). Parent-child antecedents of 5-year-olds' close friendships: A longitudinal analysis. *Developmental Psychology, 28,* 700–713.

Youngblade, L., & Dunn, J. (1995). Individual differences in young children's pretend play with mother and sibling: Links to relationships and understanding of other people's feelings and beliefs. *Child Development, 66,* 1472–1492.

Yuill, N., & Pearson, A. (1998). The development of bases for trait attribution: Children's understanding of traits as causal mechanisms based on desire. *Developmental Psychology, 34,* 574–586.

Zahn-Waxler, C. (2000). The development of empathy, guilt, and internalization of distress: Implications for gender differences in internalizing and externalizing problems. In R. J. Davidson (Ed.), *Anxiety, depression, and emotion* (pp. 222–265). New York: Oxford University Press.

Zahn-Waxler, C., & Radke-Yarrow, M. (1990). The origins of empathic concern. *Motivation and Emotion, 14,* 107–130.

Zahn-Waxler, C., & Robinson, J. (1995). Empathy and guilt: Early origins of feelings of responsibility. In J. Tangney & K. Fischer (Eds.), *Self-conscious emotions* (pp. 143–173). New York: Guilford Press.

Zarbatany, L., & Lamb, M. (1985). Social referencing as a function of information source: Mothers versus strangers. *Infant Behavior and Development, 8,* 25–33.

Zelazo, P., Sommerville, J., & Nichols, S. (1999). Age-related changes in children's use of external representations. *Developmental Psychology, 35,* 1059–1071.

Zimmermann, P., & Grossmann, K. E. (1997). Attachment and adaptation in adolescence. In W. Koops, J. Hoeksma, & D. van den Boom (Eds.), *Development of interaction and attachment* (pp. 281–292). Amsterdam: North-Holland.

Zumbahlen, M., & Crawley, A. (1996, April). Infants' early referential behavior in prohibition contexts: The emergence of social referencing. In R. A. Thompson (Chair), *Taking perspective on social referencing: New viewpoints.* Invited symposium conducted at the biennial meeting of the International Society for Infant Studies, Providence, RI.

CHAPTER 3

Temperament

MARY K. ROTHBART and JOHN E. BATES

Recent years have witnessed major advances in our understanding of temperament in childhood. Early views on temperament as unchanging and stable have been replaced by more dynamic views of developmental change in temperament. An early emphasis on temperament in infancy has been extended to the study of childhood and adolescence, and research on temperament has burgeoned (Rothbart & Derryberry, 2002). In addition, rapid advances have been made in our understanding of temperament-environment interactions. In this chapter, we explore both historical influences and more recent advances in our understanding of individual differences

in temperament, differences observed by parents and physicians long before their systematic study by students of human development.

A DEFINITION OF TEMPERAMENT

Gordon Allport (1961) defined temperament as "the characteristic phenomena of an individual's emotional nature, including his susceptibility to emotional stimulation, his customary strength and speed of response, the quality of his prevailing mood, these phenomena being regarded as dependent upon constitutional make-up and, therefore, largely hereditary in origin" (p. 34). Allport's definition focused on individual differences in emotional reactivity. Thomas and Chess (1977), however, took a broader approach to temperament, including individual differences in attention and activity level.

Taking into account both of these approaches, we have defined temperament as constitutionally based individual differences in reactivity and self-regulation, in the domains of affect, activity, and attention (Rothbart & Bates, 1998; Rothbart & Derryberry, 1981). By the term *constitutional,* we refer to the biological bases of temperament, influenced over time by heredity, maturation, and experience. *Reactivity* and *self-regulation* are umbrella terms that broadly organize the temperament domain. By *reactivity,* we refer to responsiveness to change in the external and internal environment. Reactivity includes a broad range of reactions (e.g., the emotions of fear, cardiac reactivity) and more general tendencies (e.g., negative emotionality), thus it is not limited to general reactivity. Parameters of reactivity are measured by the latency, duration, and intensity parameters of motor, affective, and attentional reactions (e.g., fear, anger, positive affect, or orienting; Rothbart & Derryberry, 1981). Emotional reactivity also includes action tendencies. Thus, fear predisposes freezing, attack, and/or inhibition, and positive affectivity predisposes approach. The expression or inhibition of these behavioral tendencies can feed back to influence the ongoing emotional reaction. By *self-regulation,* we refer to processes such as effortful control and orienting that function to modulate reactivity. We believe (as does Kagan, 1998) that other important dimensions of temperament are likely to be identified in the future.

Temperament describes tendencies or dispositions that are not continually expressed but require appropriate eliciting conditions. Fearful children, for example, are not continually distressed and inhibited, but under conditions of novelty, sudden change in stimulation, or signals of punishment, they may be particularly prone to a fearful reaction. Easily frustrated children are not continually irritable or angry, but when their goals are blocked or there is a failure of their expectations, they will be particularly prone to frustration.

Temperament and Personality

Temperament represents the affective, activational, and attentional core of personality, whereas personality includes much more than temperament, particularly the content of thought, skills, habits, values, defenses, morals, beliefs, and social cognition. Social cognition includes the perception of the self, others, and the relation of self to objects, events, and others. Over time, social cognition becomes increasingly important in eliciting and moderating temperamental processes. This happens, for example, when anger comes to be elicited by judgments that others have broken the rules when we have been following them. These perceptions can be influenced by temperament (Derryberry & Reed, 1994), but they involve separable thought processes as well. Personality traits have been defined as patterns of thoughts, emotion, and behavior that show consistency across situations and stability over time, and that "affect the individual's getting along with other people and with himself" (Hilgard, 1962, p. 447). Temperament traits similarly show consistency across situations and stability over time, but they are limited to basic processes of reactivity and self-regulation, and do not include the specific content of thought or the use of conceptually based defenses (e.g., paranoia).

In our view, *temperament* is the appropriate term for describing individual differences in reactivity and self-regulation in nonhuman animals and young infants. Although some researchers refer to individual differences in animals as their "personality" (e.g., Gosling & John, 1999), we find it helpful to consider the aspects of individuality we share with other animals separately from those involving the content of thought that are more distinctly human. Animal models of temperament allow investigations of affective and cognitive neuroscience that are not possible in humans, and aid in the study of the neural underpinnings of temperament. Strelau (1983) takes a similar position to ours, arguing that temperament results from biological evolution, and is "peculiar to both humans and animals, which cannot be said of personality" (p. 258). In addition, "The individual has a temperament from the moment of birth, since it is determined by inborn physiological mechanisms which, in turn, may be modified under environmental influences" (p. 258).

We begin this chapter with a brief history of temperament research, considering its recent history, its ancient roots, and its study in adulthood. In the second section, we examine the structure of temperament as it has emerged from research on child development and from some of the major theoretical models of the neurosciences. We also consider results of the search for a taxonomic structure of adult personality traits, and relate temperament structure to the resulting Big Three and Big Five factors of personality.

In the third section, we discuss methods and measures for the study of temperament, considering both the benefits and liabilities of some of the major empirical approaches. Because the use of parent-report in temperament research has been questioned (Kagan, 1994, 1998; Kagan & Fox, Chapter 4, this *Handbook,* this volume), we critically consider contributions of parent-report. In the fourth section, we focus on temperament and development, considering issues of continuity and change. In the fifth section, we discuss relations between temperament and behavioral adjustment. The final section presents our conclusions and indicates future directions for the study of temperament and development. Overall, we organize research findings on temperament in a developmental framework. The literature review is not comprehensive, but we hope it captures some of the major issues and approaches to the study of temperament in childhood. We now begin with a historical review of temperament in childhood and adulthood.

HISTORY OF TEMPERAMENT: RESEARCH ON CHILDHOOD

Several lines of inquiry have contributed to contemporary temperament research on children. One is the research of the normative child psychologists in the 1920s and 1930s, who observed large numbers of children to establish the normal sequences of motor and mental development and studied small samples of children intensively over time. In doing so, they noted striking temperamental variability among the children they observed (Gesell, 1928, as cited in Kessen, 1965; Shirley, 1933). Shirley's intensive study of the motor development of a group of infants during the first 2 years led to her observation of the infant's "core of personality." Shirley (1933) noted that developmentally, "Both constancy and change characterize the personality of the baby. Traits are constant enough to make it plausible that a nucleus of personality exists at birth and that this nucleus persists and grows and determines to a certain degree the relative importance of (other) traits" (p. 56). She devoted a full volume to these traits, even though her original intention had been to study only motor and intellectual development. Fifteen years later, Neilon (1948) located 15 of Shirley's 25 babies, asking judges to match Shirley's infant personality sketches to descriptions of the children as adolescents, based on as-

sessments by clinicians blind to their identity. These matches were more successful than would have been expected by chance.

Gesell (1928, as cited in Kessen, 1965) identified the critical importance of the child's temperament in what he called the developmental "web of life." His views of alternative developmental pathways, so important to recent thinking, are illustrated in the case of C. D.:

> This girl exhibited a striking degree of amenability, sociality, and good nature as early as the age of 9 months. . . . She is now 5 years of age, and in spite of a varied experience in boarding homes and institutions she has not lost these engaging characteristics. They are part and parcel of her make-up quite as much as the lowered tempo and the lowered trend of her general development. It can be predicted with much certainty that she will retain her present emotional equipment when she is an adolescent and an adult. But more than this cannot be predicted in the field of personality. For whether she becomes a delinquent, and she is potentially one, will depend upon her subsequent training, conditioning, and supervision. She is potentially also a willing, helpful, productive worker. Environment retains a critical role even though heredity sets metes and bounds. (Gesell, 1928, pp. 372–373)

Three important concepts from Gesell and Shirley are further elaborated in this chapter. First, temperament traits are constitutionally based characteristics that provide the core of personality and influence directions for development. Second, although some stability of temperament is expected across age, developmental outcomes will also depend on the child's experience in the social context. Finally, as in the case of C. D., a given set of temperamental characteristics allows for multiple possible outcomes. Different trajectories and outcomes may occur for children with similar temperamental traits, and children differing in temperament may come to similar developmental outcomes via different pathways (Kochanska, 1995).

Clinical Research

A second major line of research on temperament in childhood came from biologically oriented clinicians. Bergman and Escalona (1949) identified children who were particularly reactive to low intensities of stimulation in one or more sensory modalities. In Escalona's (1968) groundbreaking book, *The Roots of Individuality,* she proposed the concept of "effective experience," the idea that events in children's lives are experienced only as they are filtered through the individual child's nervous system. A given event will thus differ in its effects for children who differ in temperament. An adult's vigorous play, for example, may lead to pleasure in one child and distress in another. Escalona noted that objective coding of environmental events alone will not capture essential information about the individual child's reaction to them. Infants observed by Escalona (1968) were followed in developmental studies of vulnerability, resiliency and coping by Murphy and Moriarty (1976). In other studies, Fries and Woolf (1954) identified and studied congenital activity type, Korner (1964) studied neonatal individuality and developed an extensive assessment schedule for the newborn, and Birns (1965) and her associates developed and implemented some of the earliest standardized assessments of temperament.

Among clinical investigators, Thomas, Chess, Birch, Hertzig, and Korn (1963) published the first of their volumes on the extremely influential New York Longitudinal Study (NYLS). Inspired by differences among their own children, Chess and Thomas studied individual differences in what they called the "primary reaction patterns," collecting interviews from parents of infants on repeated occasions. Beginning when their initial sample of 22 infants was 3 to 6 months of age, parents were extensively interviewed about their infants' behavior in varying contexts. Each infant reaction and its context was then typed on a separate sheet of paper, and Birch inductively sorted the descriptions into categories that came to represent the nine NYLS temperament dimensions (Chess & Thomas, personal communication, October, 1992; Thomas et al., 1963): (1) Activity Level, (2) Approach/Withdrawal, (3) Adaptability, (4) Mood, (5) Threshold, (6) Intensity, (7) Distractibility, (8) Rhythmicity, and (9) Attention Span/Persistence. Later, Michael Rutter suggested the term *temperament* to describe their area of study, and this term was adopted by the NYLS group (Chess & Thomas, personal communication, October, 1992).

Acceptance of Temperament Research

Reports from the NYLS arrived at an opportune time, when researchers in social development were becoming increasingly aware of the contributions of individual children to their own development. One influence was the burgeoning of infancy research, with researchers studying the initial state of the individual and its subsequent adaptations (Osofsky, 1979). Because the initial state

varied from child to child (Korner, 1964), early differences could be seen as providing the raw material for later development. Ideas originally put forward by Robert Sears and associates (e.g., Sears, Maccoby, & Levin, 1957) were also reemerging regarding bidirectionality in the effects of socialization, from child to caregiver and caregiver to child (Bell, 1968). Finally, cognitive approaches stressed children's influences on their own development via their perceptual and cognitive mental representations of events (Kohlberg, 1969). Research on temperament would now introduce the idea that, in addition to individual differences in thought patterns, individual differences in children's *emotional* processing could bias their affective representations of experience, with important implications for their development.

HISTORY OF TEMPERAMENT IN ADULTHOOD

Adult studies of temperament have a much longer history than developmental work, much of it focused on biological aspects of personality. Temperament ideas go back to Greco-Roman physicians over 2,000 years ago, and to even earlier traditions in China and India (Diamond, 1974; Needham, 1973). In this thinking, psychological characteristics were consistently linked to the physiology of the individual as it was understood at the time. Thus, ancient Greco-Roman physicians identified the well-known fourfold typology and linked it to the bodily humors: the sanguine individual, positive and outgoing (with a predominance of blood); the melancholic person, prone to fear and sadness (with a predominance of black bile); the choleric person, irritable and prone to aggression (with a predominance of yellow bile); and the phlegmatic person, slow to excitation (with a predominance of phlegm; Diamond, 1974). The fourfold typology was used throughout the Middle Ages and in the writings of Kant. By the time of Wundt (1903), however, a shift was made away from positing temperamental "types" to studying dimensions of variability in temperament, a shift that has only recently been reversed in Kagan's (1994, 1998) and others' (Caspi, Sugden, et al., 2003) use of temperament typologies.

Jung's Theory

Psychological types were put forward by Jung (1923), but they differed in important ways from current typologies. In Jung's view, introverted and extraverted tendencies were universal and reflected in thinking, feeling, sensation, and intuition. Jung argued that introverted *and* extraverted tendencies are present in all persons, but that, for a given person, one attitude becomes more elaborated and conscious, while the other is less elaborated, more primitive, and, for the most part, unconscious. Differences among children in extraversion and introversion, he wrote, can be seen early in life:

> The earliest mark of extraversion in a child is his quick adaptation to the environment, and the extraordinary attention he gives to objects, especially to his effect upon them. Shyness in regard to objects is very slight; the child moves and lives among them with trust. He makes quick perceptions, but in a haphazard way. Apparently he develops more quickly than an introverted child, since he is less cautious, and as a rule, has no fear. Apparently, too, he feels no barrier between himself and objects, and hence he can play with them freely and learn though them. He gladly pushes his undertakings to an extreme, and risks himself in the attempt. Everything unknown seems alluring. (Jung, 1928, as cited in Fordham, 1953, p. 303)

Objects as described by psychoanalysts include both physical and social entities, so the more introverted child would be expected to dislike new social situations and to approach strangers with caution and fear. Jung suggests that the introvert would also be inclined toward pessimism about the future, and the extravert would show more ready approach and action on objects (impulsivity), greater sociability, and more optimism about the future (Jung, 1923).

Eastern and Western Schools of Temperament and Personality

In addition to Jung's theoretical model of introversion-extraversion, similar dimensions emerged from early factor-analytic studies of temperament in adults. In Great Britain, Webb (1915) analyzed self-report items referring to emotionality, activity, qualities of the self, and intelligence and thus identified two broad factors. One, labeled "w," was defined as "consistency of action resulting from deliberate volition or will" (Webb, 1915, p. 34). This factor bears similarities to temperamental Effortful Control in childhood (Kochanska, Murray, & Harlan, 2000; Rothbart, Ahadi, Hershey, & Fisher, 2001), and to the higher-order personality factors more recently labeled Control, Constraint, or Conscientiousness (Digman & Inouye, 1986). A second factor assessed distress proneness or negative emotionality, sometimes

labeled emotional stability-instability; Eysenck (1967) would later call it Neuroticism. By 1937, Burt had also identified the factor of Extraversion-Introversion, and later factor-analytic research on questionnaire assessed personality has repeatedly identified three factors: Extraversion, Neuroticism, and Conscientiousness. These three factors, sometimes called the Big Three, along with factors of Agreeableness and Openness to experience, have been extracted from factor analyses of trait descriptive words and personality items, and constitute what have been called the Big Five personality factors (Costa & McCrae, 1988; Goldberg, 1990).

Soviet and Eastern European research on temperament began with Pavlov's (1955/1935) observations of individual differences among dogs in conditioning experiments, and led to an active research tradition described by Strelau (1983). Pavlov linked temperamental differences among the animals, which he also generalized to humans, to qualities of the central nervous system, including strength of neural activation. Strength of activation was related to the "law of strength" in classical conditioning, whereby increasing the intensity of a conditioned stimulus led to the increased intensity of the animal's response. For some animals, however, increasing stimulus intensity led to failure to respond. Pavlov described these animals as having a weak nervous system; animals with a strong nervous system maintained the law of strength even at high levels of stimulus intensity. Additional Pavlovian temperament constructs included strength of inhibition, balance between activation and inhibition, and mobility—flexibility of nervous system adjustment to changing conditions. Soviet researchers began their work in the laboratory, but a lack of generality of their measures across stimulus and response modalities, a phenomenon they called partiality, led to a general shift in their focus from the laboratory to the use of questionnaire methods (Strelau, 1983).

Although British and Soviet schools took different historical directions in the study of temperament, with British researchers moving from questionnaires to the laboratory, and Eastern European researchers from the laboratory to questionnaires, both schools remain actively involved in the study of temperament, and both link individual differences in temperament to hypothetical nervous system function. We now review studies of the structure of temperament as it has emerged from research on infancy and childhood and describe neural models conceptually related to this structure.

THE STRUCTURE OF TEMPERAMENT

In this section, we consider research on temperament that has led to revision of the original list of nine NYLS dimensions (Tables 3.1 and 3.2). Much of this research employed factor analysis of large sets of items within the temperament domain. Factor analysis allows researchers to see simultaneously the relations and nonrelations among large sets of behavior descriptions. A major limitation of the factor analytic method is that the dimensions yielded by the analysis depend on the descriptors included in the initial data matrix. Several broad dimensions of temperament have consistently emerged from different sets of data.

Infant Studies

In a review of the structure of temperament as indicated by infant studies (Rothbart & Bates, 1998; Rothbart & Mauro, 1990), six dimensions were identified that provided a shorter list of temperament variables for future researchers (Table 3.1). Individual differences in positive emotionality were differentiated from negative emotionality, and two kinds of negative emotion were identified: fear and anger/irritable distress.

Infant scales with different names often measure similar constructs. Goldsmith and Rieser-Danner (1986) had both mothers and day-care teachers of 4- to 8-month-old infants fill out the Revised Infant Temperament Questionnaire (RITQ; W. Carey & McDevitt, 1978), the Infant Characteristics Questionnaire (ICQ; Bates, Freeland, & Lounsbury, 1979), and the Infant Behavior Questionnaire (IBQ; Rothbart, 1981). Distress to novelty was assessed by all three of these instruments: IBQ Fear, ICQ Unadaptable, and RITQ Approach-Withdrawal scales. Intercorrelations across these scales were high. For mothers, they ranged from .60 to .69, with the

average $r = .64$; for day-care teachers, the intercorrelations ranged from .51 to .73, with the average $r = .63$ (Goldsmith & Rieser-Danner, 1986).

The second shared dimension was Irritable Distress, assessed by IBQ Distress to Limitations, RITQ Negative Mood (which includes positive affect at one pole), and ICQ Fussy/Difficult scales. Intercorrelations among these scales for mothers ranged from .44 to .63, with an average of .54; for day-care teachers, the correlations ranged from .66 to .74, with an average of .71. The third shared temperament dimension was Activity Level, assessed only on the RITQ and IBQ scales, where the correlation for both mothers and day-care teachers was .65.

Gartstein and Rothbart (2003) have recently studied the factor structure of expanded scales measuring parent-reported infant temperament, as adapted from dimensions identified in research on temperament in childhood (Table 3.2). Factor analysis of a large data set describing 3- to 12-month-old children yielded three broad dimensions: *Surgency/Extraversion,* defined primarily from scales of Approach, Vocal Reactivity, High Intensity Pleasure (stimulation seeking), Smiling and Laughter, Activity Level and Perceptual Sensitivity; *Negative Affectivity,* with loadings from Sadness, Frustration, Fear, and loading negatively, Falling Reactivity; and *Orienting/Regulation,* with loadings from Low Intensity Pleasure, Cuddliness, Duration of Orienting, and Soothability and a secondary loading for Smiling and Laughter. As early as infancy, there is thus evidence for three broad temperament dimensions.

A number of important conclusions have emerged from factor analytic studies on the structure of infant temperament as reviewed by Rothbart and Mauro (1990) and Rothbart and Bates (1998). First, the structure appears to correspond more to dimensions of reactivity in the basic emotions and attention/regulation than to a general style. Second, bipolar constructs such as ap-

TABLE 3.1   Dimensions of Temperament in Infancy

Broad Factors	Narrow Dimensions	
Negative emotionality	Fear	Sadness
	Frustration/irritability	Falling reactivity
Surgency/extraversion	Approach	Smiling and laughter
	Vocal reactivity	Activity level
	High intensity pleasure	Perceptual sensitivity
Orienting/regulation	Low intensity pleasure	Cuddliness
	Duration of orienting	Soothability
Rhythmicity		

TABLE 3.2   Dimensions of Temperament in Childhood

Broad Factors	Narrow Dimensions	
Negative emotionality	Fear	Resistance to control
	Shyness	Sadness
	Frustration/irritability	Soothability
		Discomfort
Surgency/extraversion	Activity level	Positive anticipation
High intensity pleasure	Sociability	
Effortful control/self-regulation	Inhibitory control	Low intensity pleasure
	Attentional focusing	Perceptual sensitivity
	Persistence	
Agreeableness/adaptability	Manageability	Affiliation

proach versus withdrawal and good versus bad mood have not emerged from these analyses; instead, unipolar constructs of infant temperament have gained support. Third, these dimensions also correspond to individual differences emerging from studies of nonhuman animals (Gosling & John, 1999), allowing links between temperament constructs in humans and the psychobiology of individual differences.

Childhood Studies

Factor analyses of questionnaire items based on the NYLS for older children have similarly revealed a shorter list of broad temperament factors (Table 3.2). Analysis of mother reports for 3- to 8-year-olds on the Thomas and Chess (1977) Childhood Temperament Questionnaire in the Australian Temperament Project (ATP) yielded factors of *Inflexibility* (irritability and uncooperativeness), *Persistence, Sociability,* and *Rhythmicity* (Sanson, Smart, Prior, Oberklaid, & Pedlow, 1994); second-order factors extracted from the ATP data were labeled *Negative Emotionality, Self-Regulation,* and *Sociability.*

The Children's Behavior Questionnaire (CBQ; Rothbart et al., 2001) has also consistently yielded three broad factors, found in U.S. replications and in research performed in the People's Republic of China and Japan (Ahadi, Rothbart, & Ye, 1993; Kochanska, DeVet, Goldman, Murray, & Putnam, 1993; Rothbart et al., 2001). The first, called *Surgency/Extraversion,* is defined primarily by the scales of Approach, High Intensity Pleasure (sensation-seeking), Activity Level, and a negative contribution from Shyness. The second, called *Negative Affectivity,* is defined by the scales of Discomfort, Fear, Anger/Frustration, Sadness, and loading negatively, Soothability. The third factor, labeled *Effortful Control,* is defined by the scales of Inhibitory Control, Atten-

tional Focusing, Low Intensity Pleasure, and Perceptual Sensitivity. These three factors map well on the second-order factors identified by Sanson et al. (1994): Surgency/Extraversion on Sociability; Negative Affectivity on Negative Emotionality, and Effortful Control on Self-Regulation.

The first three factors emerging from a recent factor analysis of NYLS-inspired Middle Childhood Temperament Questionnaire items (Hegvik, McDevitt, & Carey, 1982) for 8- to 12-year-olds (McClowry, Hegvik, & Teglasi, 1993) also show similarity to these factors: *Approach/Withdrawal, Negative Reactivity,* and *Task Persistence.* McClowry et al.'s (1993) two smaller factors, *Activity* and *Responsiveness,* also parallel smaller factors in the ATP (Sanson et al., 1994).

Presley and Martin's (1994) analysis of teacher reports of 3- to 7-year-olds on the Temperament Assessment Battery for Children yielded five factors demonstrating some overlap with those described above. These include *Social Inhibition, Negative Emotionality, Agreeableness/Adaptability, Activity Level,* and *Task Persistence.* In their review of factor analytic studies on infant and child temperament, Martin, Wisenbaker, and Huttunen (1994) note the robustness of the general temperament factors of Negative Emotionality, Task persistence, Adaptability, and Social Inhibition. They see Activity Level as more problematic because it is related to both negative and positive affect early in life.

The factors emerging from research on temperament in childhood show strong conceptual similarities with the Big Three factors and three of the Big Five or FFM factors that have been extracted from analyses of self- and peer descriptions of personality in adults (Goldberg, 1993) and children (Ahadi & Rothbart, 1994; Caspi, Chapter 6, this *Handbook,* this volume; Digman & Inouye, 1986). The *Negative Affectivity* factor from childhood measures is conceptually similar to the broad adult dimension of *Neuroticism* or *Negative Emotionality.* The *Surgency and Sociability* factors are similar to the broad adult dimension of *Extraversion* or *Positive Emotionality.* The *Persistence, Self-Regulation,* or *Effortful Control* factors map upon the adult dimension of *Control/Constraint* (see Ahadi & Rothbart, 1994), and Martin et al.'s (1994) *Agreeableness/Adaptability* factor onto the adult dimension of *Agreeableness.*

In our research on adults, we have found strong one-to-one correlations between factor scores derived from factor analysis of temperament scales and Big Five measures (Rothbart, Ahadi, & Evans, 2000), between Negative Emotionality and Neuroticism, Positive Emotionality and Extraversion, and Effortful Control and Conscientiousness. In addition, Perceptual Sensitivity was related to Openness, and temperamental Affiliation to Agreeableness. Neuroticism, however, often contains negative judgments about the self that may be strongly related to an individual's experiences with others; these may or may not have a strong temperamental base, and research on temperament and personality in childhood becomes very important.

In research with the Combined Temperament and Personality Scales (CTPQ) describing 565 children between the ages of 3 and 12, we have extracted factors that included Positive Emotion, Gregariousness, Warmth, and Soothability (*Sociable Extraversion*); Anxiety, Self-consciousness, Dependency, and Depression/Sadness (*Internalizing Negative Emotionality*); Inhibitory Control, Order, Diligence, Self-discipline, Attentional focusing, and low Distractibility (*Conscientiousness*); Aesthetics/Creative Ideas, Intellect, and Perceptual Sensitivity (*Openness*); and Excitement seeking, Assertiveness, Self-centered, Noncompliance/Aggression, Manipulative, Activity, and Anger/Hostility and Impulsivity (*Unsocialized Stimulation Seeking*; Rothbart & Victor, 2004). This research differentiates fearful and angry negative affect, and links aspects of extraversion with both unsocialized stimulation seeking and sociable extraversion. Longitudinal research will be important in identifying the experiential and self-regulatory temperament influences on these two outcomes.

Shiner (1998) has also recently contributed an important review of the structure of personality in middle childhood. Her preliminary taxonomy includes these dimensions: sociability, social inhibition, prosocial disposition, dominance, aggressiveness, negative emotionality, mastery motivation, inhibitory control, per-

sistence/attention, and activity level. Shiner indicates the importance of placing these dimensions in a developmental context. We can, for example, study irritability in infants, but aggression cannot be observed until later in the development. The hierarchical structure of Shiner's (1998) additional dimensions will also be of interest. Does dominance, for example, relate more to extraversion/surgency, or to agreeableness/affiliation? Does anger proneness relate more to negative emotionality or agreeableness/affiliation (Shiner, 1998)? In Rothbart and Victor's (2004) research, it loads on the Unsocialized Stimulation Seeking factor.

Summary

As noted earlier, work to date on temperament structure in infancy and in childhood suggests revisions of the original NYLS nine dimensions to include (with broad, aggregated constructs in parentheses): Positive Affect and Activity Level (Surgency/Extraversion), Fearful Distress, Irritable Distress (General Negative Emotionality), Effortful Control/Task Persistence, and Agreeableness/Adaptability. In our next section, we make tentative links between these constructs and models developed in the neurosciences.

NEURAL MODELS OF TEMPERAMENT

We now describe neural models developed to enhance our understanding of temperament. Cloninger (1986), Gray (1991), LeDoux (1989), Panksepp (1998), and Zuckerman (1984) have all made contributions to the development of neural models for temperament (see review by Rothbart, Derryberry, & Posner, 1994). We begin by describing models for positive emotionality and approach (Surgency/Extraversion), and fear. Irritability/anger is also discussed, and it is seen, along with fear, discomfort, and sadness, to represent part of a general construct of susceptibility to negative affect or negative emotionality. The emotion-based dimensions are related to differences observed in nonhuman animals (Gosling & John, 1999; Panksepp, 1998), and to factor structures extracted from studies of personality in adults and temperament in childhood. The fourth dimension, Effortful Control, will be further discussed in connection with neural models for individual differences in executive attention (Posner & Fan, in press).

Emotion as an Information-Processing System

Emotions can be seen as broadly integrative systems that order feeling, thought, and action (LeDoux, 1989). They also represent the output of information processing networks assessing the meaning or affective significance of events for the individual (LeDoux, 1989). Whereas object recognition systems and spatial processing systems address the questions, "What is it?" and "Where is it?" neural emotion processing networks address the questions, "Is it good for me?" "Is it bad for me?" and "What shall I do about it?" When there are individual differences in temperamental emotionality, there are thus differences in object perception as well.

In neural processing of emotion, thalamic connections route information about object qualities of a stimulus through sensory pathways (LeDoux, 1989). Simultaneously, information is routed to the limbic system and the amygdala, where memories of the affective meaning of the stimulus further influence the process. Later object processing can update the emotional analysis, but in the meantime, back projections from the amygdala can influence subsequent sensory processing. Output of the amygdala to organized autonomic reactions via the hypothalamus and to motor activation via the corpus striatum reflects the motivational aspect of the emotions (LeDoux, 1989).

Attention as a Control System

Neuroimaging studies demonstrate connections between emotional processing networks and the executive attention system that allow the selection of emotional information for conscious processing so that we may or may not be aware of our emotional evaluations (Bush, Luu, & Posner, 2000; Posner & Rothbart, 1991). Attentional systems can select for conscious processing aspects of emotional analyses, and emotion can also influence the focusing and shifting of attention (Derryberry & Reed, 1996, 2002; Gray, 1991). An important aspect of social adaptation involves the appropriateness of a child's social interaction and the related acceptance of the child by others (Parker & Asher, 1987). Information about the state of others will thus be an important contributor to appropriate social action, and failure of this information to access action and consciousness can be a critical element in the development of disordered functioning. When attention is focused on threatening stimuli or on

the self, access to information about others is likely to be less accessible. These are important examples of information-processing aspects of temperament that have major implications for social development, and we discuss them again in the section on temperament and the development of personality.

Positive Emotionality/Approach and Extraversion

We now briefly review neural models developed to describe a physical substrate for approach and fearful inhibition. Based on animal research, Gray (1991) described the behavioral activation system (BAS), involving sensitivity to rewards, and the behavioral inhibition system (BIS), involving sensitivity to punishment, nonreward, novelty, and innate fear stimuli (see applications to children by Blair, 2003). These two systems are seen as mutually inhibitory, with their balance determining degrees of extraversion-introversion. Gray also posited a fight-flight system that moderates unconditioned punishment (Gray, 1991). According to Gray's BAS model, reward-related projections from the amygdala to the nucleus accumbens activate a motor program that increases proximity to the desired stimulus and facilitates goal-oriented behavior (Gray & McNaughton, 1996).

In a broader behavioral facilitation system (BFS), Depue and Collins (1999) proposed a circuit involving the nucleus accumbens, ventral pallidum, and dopaminergic neurons that codes the intensity of the rewarding stimuli, with related circuits involving the medial orbital cortex, amygdala, and hippocampus integrating the "salient incentive context." Individual differences in the functioning of this network are thought to arise from variation in the dopaminergic projections that encode the intensity of incentive motivation. With development, dopaminergic facilitation can enhance responsivity to positive incentive stimuli (Depue & Collins, 1999) and provide a neural basis for a positive feedback system. This system can lead initially approaching children to become even more approaching, and temperamental differences in extraversion to become greater with time.

Depue and Iacono (1989) used the BFS to account for initiation of locomotor activity, incentive-reward motivation, exploration of environmental novelty (if stronger than opposing fear reactions), and irritable aggression. Panksepp (1982, 1986b, 1998) concluded that "the general function of DA [dopamine] activity in appetitive behavior is to promote the expression of motivational excitement and anticipatory eagerness—the heightened energization of animals searching for and expecting rewards" (1986a, p. 91). Cloninger (1986, 1987) also specified a novelty-seeking dimension related to DA functioning, as did Zuckerman (1984) in his dimension of sensation seeking (see review by Rothbart, 1989a).

A broad approach dimension has also been linked to positive affect. Tellegen's (1985) research on personality yielded a broad factor of Positive Emotionality, including pleasure and positive anticipation, and Watson and Clark (1997) have argued that positive affect is the core of individual differences in Extraversion. The children's temperament factor of Surgency/Extraversion (Rothbart et al., 2001) fits well with these models. In research on infants (Rothbart, 1988; Rothbart, Derryberry, & Hershey, 2000), expressions of smiling and laughter were related to their rapid latency to approach objects, and predicted their anticipatory eagerness about upcoming positive events at the age of 7 years.

In recent functional Magnetic Resonance Imagery (fMRI) research with adults, Canli et al. (2001) found that persons higher in extraversion showed greater brain response to positive than negative stimuli in widespread frontal, temporal, and limbic activation of both hemispheres. Those higher in neuroticism reacted more to negative than to positive stimuli, showing more circumscribed activation (fronto-temporal on the left side) and deactivation in a right frontal area. In a follow-up study focusing on the amygdala, extraversion was correlated with left amygdala activation to happy, but not to fearful, faces (Canli, Sivers, Whitfield, Gotlib, & Gabrieli, 2002). Neuroticism was not correlated with activation to any of the emotional faces, except for significant amygdala activation for the fearful expression.

Fear and Behavioral Inhibition

Fear is an emotional response activated in the presence of threat or signals of upcoming danger, and its function appears to be a defensive one. Fear activation is accompanied by inhibition of ongoing motor programs and preparation of response systems controlling coping options such as fleeing, fighting, or hiding (see review by Rothbart, Derryberry et al., 1994). In Gray's (1991) behavioral inhibition system model (BIS), the fear-related BIS is based on circuits including the orbital frontal cortex, medial septal area, and the hippocam-

pus. However, the amygdala has been more often identified as the critical structure in the processing of conditioned fear (LeDoux, 1989). Emotional networks involving the amygdala also appear to respond more strongly to novel than to familiar stimuli (Nishijo, Ono, & Nishino, 1988). Amygdala lesions in rodents disrupt autonomic and cortisol reactions, behavioral freezing, and fear vocalizations; similar findings have been reported in primates (Lawrence & Calder, 2004). In humans, functional neuroimaging studies by Calder, Lawrence, and Young (2001) and others support involvement of the amygdala in both acquiring and expressing fear, although not in the voluntary production of facial expressions of fear (Anderson & Phelps, 2002). The amygdala also is involved in the recognition of fear in the human face (Calder et al., 2001), and there is evidence in humans that amygdala damage is related to reduced fear experience (Adolphs et al., 1999; Sprengelmeyer et al., 1999).

Projections from the amygdala implement autonomic and behavioral components of fear, including startle, motor inhibition, facial expression, and cardiovascular and respiratory changes (Davis, Hitchcock, & Rosen, 1987). Individual variability in the structure and functioning of any of these subsystems may be related to variations in behavioral expressions of fear, and multiple components of other affective motivational systems, such as approach/positive affect and anger/irritable distress, would also be expected.

The amygdala also appears to affect information processing in the cortex. For example, the basolateral nucleus of the amygdala projects to frontal and cingulate regions involved in the executive attention system (Posner & Petersen, 1990), as well as to ventral occipital and temporal pathways involved in processing object information. These connections are consistent with findings that anxious individuals show enhanced attention to threatening sources of information (e.g., Derryberry & Reed, 1994). A more detailed analysis of structures related to behavioral inhibition can be found in Kagan and Fox's chapter, Chapter 4, this *Handbook,* this volume.

A psychobiological analysis of fear suggests there may be less disagreement about temperament variables than had been previously thought. Fear as we have described it includes arousal, felt emotion, motor response preparation for flight and/or attack (with responses often inhibited), and attention toward the fear-inducing stimulus and/or possible escape routes (Davis et al., 1987). When temperament researchers study aspects of this construct, they sometimes stress (a) the motivational aspects of the individual's response (e.g., Thomas & Chess's, 1977, Approach/Withdrawal; Kagan's, 1994, behavioral inhibition), (b) the distress proneness aspects (Buss & Plomin's, 1975, Emotionality; Goldsmith & Campos', 1982, Fear), (c) its duration and susceptibility to interventions (Rothbart's, 1981, Soothability), (d) its relation to arousal (Strelau's, 1983, reactivity), or (e) multiple components of response (Rothbart & Derryberry's, 1981, Fear). If we take the broader view of fear suggested by neuroscience work, agreement is more evident, and intercorrelations among scales measuring the differently named constructs as discussed earlier further support this contention (Goldsmith, Rieser-Danner, & Briggs, 1991).

We have now touched on possible neural substrates for approach/positive affect systems related to reward seeking, and for fear, linked to the inhibition of approach and of sensation seeking that might lead to punishment ("harm avoidance"). An important aspect of these constructs for students of social development is that they describe individual differences in susceptibility to reward and punishment, suggesting that some children will be more activated by reward and some children will find stopping an activity easier when there is a high likelihood of punishment (Rothbart, Ahadi, & Hershey, 1994). When a situation involves both potential rewards and punishments, such as interactions with a stranger, the balance between approach and fear tendencies based on temperament and previous experience will be critical to behavioral outcomes.

This model has direct applications to child socialization. If we consider a toddler performing an enjoyable act, such as shredding the pages of a book, the child's initial activities will be influenced by the approach or extraversion system. Now the parent gives a sharp, punishing command for the child to stop. Will the child's activity be inhibited? Patterson (1980) found that parents of nonproblem children were effective in stopping their children's aversive behavior on three out of four occasions when they punished. When parents of problem children used punishment, however, children were likely to actually continue the punished behavior (Patterson, 1980; Snyder, 1977). Although parenting skills are also involved, children's temperament is likely to make a basic contribution to this situation.

Individual differences in risky behaviors and accident-proneness (Matheny, 1991; Schwebel, 2004),

mastery motivation (Rothbart & Hwang, 2005), and affective representations of the environment (Derryberry & Reed, 1994) are all likely to be influenced by temperamental approach and inhibition tendencies in interaction with past experience. The coping strategies children use will also be influenced by their tendencies to approach or inhibit action. Quay (1993) has employed Gray's constructs of the BAS and BIS to analyze the development of undersocialized aggressive conduct disorder. In the next section, we describe temperament systems related to distress, overstimulation, irritability and anger, and possible controls offered by affiliative tendencies.

Optimal Levels of Stimulation and Distress to Overstimulation

We have now described individual differences in systems of fear and approach/extraversion. However, processes related to arousability have also been proposed to underlie approach and withdrawal. One model incorporates the idea of "optimal level" of stimulation. This approach derives temperament from general arousability or "strength of nervous system," put forward in the Soviet and Eastern European schools—Eysenck's (1967) model—and ideas developed by Bell (1974). In the theory of Berlyne (1971), arousal potential (created by stimulus intensity, novelty, and surprise) activates two motivational systems: one related to pleasure and approach (elicited at lower levels of arousal potential), the other to distress and withdrawal (elicited at higher levels of arousal potential). The two systems oppose each other. Individual differences in the strength of each of these two systems support a level of optimal arousal—the point where approach and pleasure are at their highest, but withdrawal processes do not yet dominate.

Schneirla (1959) put forward similar ideas, describing Approach and Withdrawal systems across species related to the intensity of stimuli. Eysenck (1967) argued that introverts are more arousable and sensitive to stimulation at low intensity levels than extraverts, linking this arousal to the Ascending Reticular Activation System. Introverts were seen to experience both pleasure and discomfort at lower levels of stimulus intensity; this lower optimal level of arousal would lead them to seek lower stimulus levels. In Strelau's (1983) model, more strongly reactive individuals engage in self-regulatory activities to maintain their optimal levels of stimulation. Soviet researchers' concept of nervous system strength of activation or endurance under high-intensity stimulation, and Strelau's reactivity construct are dimensions involving both sensitivity and susceptibility to distress that might be present in early life. More recently, Aron and Aron (1997) have also linked sensory sensitivity and reactivity to distress.

Developmental research on temperament shows mixed support for a positive relation between sensitivity and susceptibility to distress. Miller and Bates (1986) found significant positive correlations between temperature sensitivity and susceptibility to the negative emotions. In Keogh's (Keogh, Pullis, & Caldwell, 1982) Teacher Temperament Questionnaire, the third factor, labeled Reactivity, included both negative affect and sensitivity items. In research with the CBQ, positive correlations between perceptual sensitivity and discomfort are regularly obtained (Goldsmith, Buss, & Lemery, 1997; King & Wachs, 1995; Rothbart, Posner, & Hershey, 1995), but in the CTPQ, perceptual sensitivity was moderately related to openness and social extraversion (including *positive* affect), and slightly negatively related to the internalizing negative affects. Andersson, Bohlin, and Hagekull (1999) found that parent reported reactivity to sensory stimulation at 10 months was related to greater stranger wariness at 10 months and social inhibition at 25 months. Martin et al. (1994) have also reviewed three factor analytic studies finding sensitivity items to load with items assessing negative emotionality. Laboratory research assessing children's sensory thresholds along with their thresholds for pleasure and discomfort would be helpful in further testing this theoretical relationship.

Anger/Irritability

In Gray's (1991) model, the fight-flight system is constituted by circuits connecting the amygdala, ventromedial nucleus of the hypothalamus, central gray region of the midbrain, and somatic and motor effector nuclei of the lower brain stem processing information involving unconditioned punishment and nonreward. When there is detection of painful or frustrating input, the brain stem effectors produce aggressive or defensive behavior. Individual differences in reactivity of this fight-flight system are also thought to underlie aggressive aspects of Eysenck's general Psychoticism dimension,

and Panksepp (1982) describes similar neural circuitry in connection with a "rage" system (see review by Rothbart, Derryberry, et al., 1994).

Important distinctions have more recently been made, however, among varieties of aggression and anger, and their underlying neural systems. Aggression as a self-defense reaction seems to be based on the functioning of the same amygdala circuits as involved in the production of fear (Blanchard & Takahashi, 1988). Aggression linked to protection of resources, competition, and offensive aggression, however, involves a different system based on the monoamine dopamine (DA; Lawrence & Calder, 2004). The DA system has been linked to both the production of offensive aggression (Smeets & González, 2000), and to the recognition of anger in the human face (Lawrence, Calder, McGowan, & Grasby, 2002). In Lawrence et al.'s study, DA blockade impaired the recognition of anger, while sparing recognition of other emotions and of facial identity.

We have noted earlier that Depue and Iacono (1989) suggest the dopaminergic system may facilitate irritable aggression aimed at removing a frustrating obstacle, consistent with findings that DA agonists (e.g., amphetamine) can enhance aggressive behaviors. Their view suggests links between approach and frustration/anger, and children's activity level and anger have been consistently positively related in parent-reported temperament (Rothbart & Derryberry, 2002). In addition, infant activity level predicts not only positive emotionality at age 7, but also higher anger/frustration and low soothability-falling reactivity (Rothbart, Derryberry, & Hershey, 2000). Together with findings relating 7-year surgency to aggression (Rothbart et al., 2000), this suggests that strong approach tendencies may be linked to negative and positive emotions (Derryberry & Reed, 1994; Rothbart et al., 2000). Children who showed a short latency to grasp objects at 6.5, 10, and 13.5 months showed high levels of positive anticipation and impulsivity at age 7, as well as high anger-frustration and aggression, again suggesting that strong approach tendencies can contribute to both later anger-related negative emotions and to positive emotions.

Negative Emotionality or General Distress Proneness

Negative Emotionality or distress proneness is often viewed as a general dimension subsuming emotions of fear, anticipatory anxiety, sadness, frustration/anger, guilt, and discomfort. For example, the Five-Factor model of adult personality includes negative emotions as components of the Neuroticism superfactor. Neuroticism/Negative Emotionality has been found to be orthogonal to Extraversion/Positive Emotionality (Eysenck & Eysenck, 1985; Tellegen, 1985; Watson & Clark, 1992). As evident in our previous discussion, however, the positive relationship between anger/frustration and strong approach tendencies suggests that a more differentiated model is needed.

As noted earlier, separable neural systems have been found to be related to different forms of negative affect. There are nevertheless several possibilities for identifying higher order negative emotion reactions. One is the link between systems supporting fear and defensive aggression (Blanchard & Takahashi, 1988). Defensive aggression in animal models seems to be based on the same amygdalar circuits as fear, and in humans, anger in response to threat may also be linked to fear.

Negative affect systems are also regulated by more general neurochemical systems including dopaminergic and serotonergic projections arising from the midbrain, and by circulating gonadal and corticosteroid hormones (Rothbart, Derryberry, et al., 1994; Zuckerman, 1995). Neurochemical influences may thus also provide coherence of emotional states in an individual, and support more general factors of temperament such as negative emotionality. For example, serotonergic projections from the midbrain raphe nuclei appear to moderate limbic circuits related to anxiety and aggression (Spoont, 1992). Low serotonergic activity may thus increase an individual's vulnerability to both fear and frustration, contributing to a general factor of negative affectivity, including depression. Gonadal hormones are related to both positive affect and aggressiveness (Zuckerman, 1991), possibly influencing individual differences in positive and angry states. Neural structures can thus support variability at broad and specific levels, although more research in the area is definitely needed.

Affiliativeness/Agreeableness

We share with other animals, including mammals, birds, and fish, systems of affiliation that support pair bonds and the care of the young (Insel, 2003). Panksepp (1986c) indicates that affiliative and prosocial behav-

iors may depend in part on opiate projections from higher limbic regions (e.g., amygdala, cingulate cortex) to the ventromedial hypothalamus, with brain opiates promoting social comfort and bonding, and opiate withdrawal promoting irritability and aggressiveness. Because ventromedial hypothalamic lesions dramatically increase aggression, Panksepp (1986a) also suggests that this brain region normally inhibits aggressive behaviors controlled by the midbrain's central gray area. Hypothalamic projections can allow for friendly, trusting, and helpful behaviors between members of a species by suppressing aggressive tendencies. Mechanisms underlying prosocial and aggressive behaviors would in this way be reciprocally related, in keeping with the bipolar Agreeableness-Hostility dimension found in Five Factor Models of personality. Panksepp (1993) has also reviewed research suggesting links between social bonding and the hypothalamic neuropeptide oxytocin (OXY), involved in maternal behavior, feelings of social acceptance and social bonding, and reduction of separation distress. OXY is also released during sexual activity by both females and males.

Agreeableness, including at the high end, the prosocial emotions and behaviors and affiliative tendencies, and at the low end, aggression and manipulativeness, has been increasingly studied in childhood (Graziano, 1994; Graziano & Eisenberg, 1997; Graziano & Tobin, 2002). Like other originally bipolar dimensions, prosocial and antagonistic dispositions have also been studied separately (Bohart & Stipek, 2001), and Graziano and Eisenberg (1997) suggest that the two dispositions may be separable, even though negatively related. On a related issue, Shiner and Caspi (2003) point out that antisocial and prosocial behavior have different etiologies (Krueger, Hicks, & McGue, 2001). Any temperamental predisposition to prosocial behavior needs to be seen as an open system, interacting with social experience for its outcomes. In research described earlier linking temperament to personality in early and middle childhood, two forms of extraversion/surgency have been identified; one linked to prosocial behavior and the other to antisocial behavior and aggression (Victor, Rothbart, & Baker, 2006), again suggesting the importance of socialization to pro- or antisocial behavior, and reminiscent of Gesell's (1928, as cited in Kessen, 1965) comment earlier in our chapter that C.D. could become either a delinquent or a willing and responsible worker, depending on her training.

Attentional Networks

Functional neuroimaging has allowed many cognitive tasks to be analyzed by the brain areas they activate, and studies of attention have been among the most often examined (Corbetta, Kincade, & Shulman, 2002; Driver, Eimer, & Macaluso, in press; Posner & Fan, in press). Imaging data support the presence of three networks related to different aspects of attention, carrying out the functions of alerting, orienting, and executive attention (Posner & Fan, in press). We discuss orienting and executive attention in this section, although alerting is also likely to prove of interest to future temperament studies.

Orienting involves aligning attention to a source of signals. It may be overt (as in eye movements) or covert (occurring without any movement; Posner, 1980). Orienting can be manipulated by presenting a cue indicating where in space an event will occur, thereby directing attention to the cued location (Posner, 1980). Orienting to visual events has been associated with posterior brain areas, including the superior parietal lobe and temporal parietal junction and the frontal eye fields (Corbetta et al., 2002). Lesions of the parietal lobe and superior temporal lobe have been consistently related to difficulties in orienting (Karnath, Ferber, & Himmelbach, 2001).

Orienting early in life is a reactive aspect of attention, and children differ both in their latency to orient and their duration of orienting (see review by Ruff & Rothbart, 1996). In the IBQ, individual differences in duration of orienting in infancy are positively related to smiling and laughter and vocal activity, suggesting that orienting may be part of an early positive reactivity or interest system (Rothbart, 1988; Rothbart, Derryberry, et al., 2000).

The second major control system over reactive approach and action (the first is fearful inhibition as discussed earlier) is that of effortful control, supported by development of the executive attention network (Posner & Rothbart, 2000). Executive attention and effortful control are related to volition and awareness of input (Posner & Rothbart, 1991). There are limits on how much we can simultaneously attend to in directed thought or action. Areas of the midfrontal lobe, including the anterior cingulate gyrus, appear to underlie a general executive attentional network (Vogt, Finch, & Olson, 1992), in combination with lateral prefrontal areas. The anterior cingulate represents the outflow of the limbic system, and is thus closely tied to emotion. It also has close connections to adjacent motor systems. Activity of the anterior cingulate is modified by dopamine input from the underlying basal ganglia. The anterior cingulate structure consists of alternating bands of cells with close connections to the dorsolateral frontal cortex and to the posterior parietal lobe (Goldman-Rakic, 1988), suggesting a highly integrative role. The anterior cingulate thus appears to provide an important connection between widely different aspects of attention (e.g., attention to semantic or emotional content, or visual location).

Persistence, a dimension of personality conceptually related to effortful control in temperament, has been related to brain activation (Gusnard et al., 2003). The effects of persistence act strongly on midline and lateral prefrontal areas that are quite different than those found active for positive and negative affect, suggesting regulatory aspects of persistence. An increasingly accepted view (Posner & Rothbart, 2000) is that effortful control, represented in midline frontal areas, acts to regulate brain areas like the amygdala that are more clearly related to reactive aspects of negative affect.

In additional research, children who showed rapid approach as infants tended to be low in attentional control and inhibitory control at age 7, consistent with findings of a negative relation between Surgency/Extraversion and Effortful Control (Rothbart, Derryberry, et al., 1994), and suggesting that strong approach tendencies may constrain the development of voluntary self-control. If approach tendencies are viewed as the "accelerator" toward action, and inhibitory tendencies as the "brakes," stronger accelerative tendencies may weaken the braking influence of inhibitory control (Rothbart & Derryberry, 2002).

Executive control of attention is often studied by tasks that involve conflict, such as varieties of the Stroop task, where subjects are asked to respond with the color of ink (e.g., red) while ignoring the color word name (e.g., blue; Bush et al., 2000). Resolving conflict in the Stroop task activates midline frontal areas (anterior cingulate) and lateral prefrontal cortex (Botvinick, Braver, Barch, Carter, & Cohen, 2001; Fan, Flombaum, McCandliss, Thomas, & Posner, 2003). There is also evidence for activation of this network in tasks involving conflict between a central target and surrounding flankers that may be congruent or incongruent with the target (Botvinick et al., 2001; Fan, McCandliss, Sommer, Raz, & Posner, 2002).

Regulatory Functions of Executive Attention

The anterior cingulate gyrus, one of the main nodes of the executive attention network has been linked to a variety of specific functions (Posner & Fan, in press), including working memory (Duncan & Owen, 2000), emotion (Bush et al., 2000), pain (Rainville, Duncan, Price, Carrier, & Bushnell, 1997), monitoring for conflict (Botvinick et al., 2001), and monitoring for error (Holroyd & Coles, 2002). In emotion studies, the cingulate is often seen as part of a network involving orbital frontal and limbic (amygdala) structures. The frontal areas seem to have the ability to interact with the limbic system (Davidson, Putnam, & Larson, 2000), fitting well with the idea of their supporting self-regulation.

A self-regulatory role for the cingulate has been identified in imaging studies with adults. Cingulate activity was greater when subjects were instructed to control the amount of negative affect felt in viewing a picture (Ochsner, Bunge, Gross, & Gabrieli, 2002). When hypnotism was used to control the perception of pain due to heat, cingulate activity also reflected the perceived degree of pain rather than the physical intensity of the heat stimulus (Rainville et al., 1997). Finally, large lesions of the anterior cingulate either in adults or children result in great difficulty in regulating behavior, particularly in social situations (Anderson, Damasio, Tranel, & Damasio, 2001). Smaller lesions may produce only a temporary inability to deal with conflict in cognitive tasks (Ochsner et al., 2002; Turken & Swick, 1999). These results link the anterior cingulate to regulation of neural activity related to emotion and behavior, and provide evidence for a role of the cingulate as a part of a network involved in regulation, cognition, and affect (Bush et al., 2000; Rueda, Posner, & Rothbart, 2004).

Development of executive attention between 2 and 7 years is indexed by marked changes in the ability to deal with conflict and to detect errors and slow subsequent responses (Mezzacappa, 2004: Rueda, Fan, et al., 2004; see reviews by Rothbart, Posner, & Kieras, in press; Rothbart & Rueda, 2005). Between 30 to 36 months, children are able to perform a variant of the Stroop task, the Spatial Conflict key press task, which in adults is related to activation of the anterior cingulate. In this task, conflict occurs when a stimulus is presented on the side of the screen opposite its corresponding key. The dominant response is to press the key consistent with the object's spatial location; the subdominant response is to press the key that matches the stimulus. At 24 months, children are unable to properly perform this task, but by 30 months, most children can perform it but are slowed by the conflict, as are adults (Gerardi-Caulton, 2000; Rothbart, Ellis, Rueda, & Posner, 2003). Children performing more efficiently on spatial conflict were rated by their parents as having relatively higher levels of effortful control and lower levels of negative affectivity.

Summary

Models from neuroscience have been developed related to general dimensions of Approach, Fear/Inhibition or Harm Avoidance, Irritability (Fight-Flight or Rage), and Affiliativeness or Social Reward Dependence, Orienting, and executive attention as a basis of Effortful Control. Optimal level models proposing a link between sensitivity and affect have also found some support in the developmental literature. These dimensions offer a beginning for future work that will more finely differentiate the temperament domain, its development, and relation to the development of personality. In our review, we now move to considering measurement issues in the study of temperament in childhood, providing extensive evaluation of parent reports. It will be helpful for the reader to consider this material in addition to that put forward by Kagan and Fox in Chapter 4, this *Handbook,* this volume. We then discuss recent genetics research and other psychobiological approaches to the study of temperament.

MEASUREMENT APPROACHES

Approaches to measuring temperament in children have included caregiver reports, self-reports for older children, naturalistic observations, and structured laboratory observations (see Table 3.3). Each of these approaches offers relative advantages for temperament study. Caregiver-report questionnaires, for example, can tap the extensive knowledge base of caregivers, who have seen the child in many different situations over a long period of time. Questionnaires are also convenient—they are relatively inexpensive to develop, administer, and analyze, and allow the study of multiple variables (Bates, 1989b, 1994). Alternatively, naturalistic observations can possess high degrees of objectivity and ecological validity, whereas laboratory observations allow the researcher to precisely control the context and specific elicitors of the child's behavior, as well as the time course and intensity of the child's reaction.

TABLE 3.3   Potential Sources of Measurement Error in Three Child Temperament Assessment Methods

	A. Rater Characteristics Relatively independent of child behavior	B. Bias in Assessment As a function of child behavior or rater-child interaction	C. Method Factors Relatively independent of both child and rater characteristics
I. Parent questionnaires	1. Comprehension of instructions, questions, and rating scales 2. Knowledge of child's behavior (and general impression rater has of the child) 3. Inaccurate memory: recency effects, selective recall 4. State when completing rating task (e.g., anxiety) 5. Response sets (e.g., social desirability and acquiescence) 6. For ratings, knowledge of implicit reference groups 7. Accuracy in detecting and coding rare but important events 8. Kind of impression (if any) raters wants child/self to make on researcher	1. Observed child behavior occurring in response to parental behavior 2. Parents' interpretations of observed behavior a function of parental characteristics	1. Need to inquire about rarely observed situations 2. Adequacy of item selection, wording, and response options
II. Home observation measures (in vivo coding)	1. Limited capacity of coder to process all relevant behavior 2. Coding of low-intensity ambiguous behaviors 3. State of coder during observation 4. Limits of precision of coding 5. For ratings, knowledge of implicit reference groups	1. Caregiver-child interaction moderating behavior coded (including I.8) 2. For ratings, halo effects	1. Change in child and caregiver behavior due to presence of coder (e.g., decreased conflict) 2. Difficulties of sensitively coding the context of behavior 3. Limitations to number of instances of behavior (especially rated ones) that can be observed 4. Lack of normative data 5. Lack of stability in observational time windows; limited sample of behavior
III. Laboratory measures (Objective measures scored from videotape in episodes designed to elicit temperament-related reactions)	1. Scoring of low-intensity ambiguous reactions 2. For ratings, knowledge of implicit reference groups 3. Limited capacity of coder to process all relevant behavior 4. State of coder during observation 5. Limits of precision of coding 6. Accuracy in detecting and coding of rare but important events	1. Effects of uncontrolled caregiver behavior or other experience prior to or during testing 2. Selection of sample, including completion of testing on the basis of child reactions (e.g., distress-prone infants not completing procedures) 3. Subtle variations in experimenter reactions to different children (e.g., more soothing behavior toward distress-prone infants)	1. Lack of adequate normative data 2. Limitations of number of instances of behavior that can be recorded 3. Carryover effects in repeated testing 4. Constraints on range of behavioral options 5. Novelty of laboratory setting 6. Adequate identification of episodes appropriate to evoking temperamental reactions

Adapted from Bates (1989) as adapted from Rothbart & Goldsmith (1985).

In addition to their respective advantages, each technique also is subject to error. In caregiver report measures, there may be perceptual or response biases in the informant. Naturalistic observations are expensive, and often show relatively low day-to-day reliability so that it becomes difficult for researchers to collect an adequate sample of relevant behaviors. Laboratory procedures often limit the kinds of behavior that can be elicited, and the repeated testing necessary to measure a complex trait in the laboratory may be unfeasible or involve carryover effects. More detail on measurement issues can be found in Bates (1987, 1989b, 1994), Goldsmith and Rothbart (1991), Rothbart and Goldsmith (1985), and Slabach, Morrow, and Wachs (1991). In the present chapter, we focus on the issue of the scientific acceptability of caregiver reports. Although the literature often provides admonitions about parent reports, it frequently does not analyze the strengths and limitations of each approach. We have recognized limitations of caregiver report (e.g., Bates, 1980), but nevertheless have found that caregiver reports have broadly established validity (Rothbart & Bates, 1998).

Meanings of Parent Reports

Parent reports have been extensively used in personality, clinical, and developmental research, including the study of temperament. At the same time, the validity of parent reports about children's temperament has been particularly questioned, especially by Kagan (1998; Kagan & Fox, Chapter 4, this *Handbook,* this volume). We provide an alternative view to the one he has presented.

Digital versus Analog Validity

Determining the validity of parent reports has often been framed in an absolute or "digital" way, leading to a simple judgment of whether parent reports are valid. Thomas et al. (1963) asked whether a significant correlation existed between parent reports and independent ratings, and finding significant correlations, concluded that parent reports were valid measures of temperament. More typically, when statistically significant correlations between parent ratings and independent ratings have been fairly small in size, the conclusion has been that parent reports are not valid. Any low correlation could be due to problems with observer ratings as well as parent ratings, but this issue is seldom addressed.

Early in the discussion of the meaning of parent reports of temperament, Kagan (1982) advocated a digital view of validity, and has continued to elaborate this view. In his earlier writings, Kagan (1994, 1998) argues that parent reports are not worthy of use in scientific studies of temperament. Kagan and Fox (Chapter 4, this *Handbook,* this volume), concluded that parent-report data should be supplemented by observation. Our own position, reached more or less independently (Bates, 1994; Rothbart, 1995; Rothbart & Hwang, 2002), is also that temperament research benefits from the use of multiple measures. We would agree with the statement of Vaughn et al. (1992), discussing measures of attachment security, that "it would be most unfortunate if pretensions to methodological rigor forced investigators to ignore sources of relevant developmental information" (p. 470).

Caregivers' Vantage Point versus Bias and Inaccuracy

One argument for the continued use of parent reports of temperament is that they provide a useful vantage point for observations. Temperament dimensions are by definition general patterns of responses by the child, and parents are in a good position to observe the child's behavior on multiple occasions, including infrequently occurring behavior that nevertheless may be critical to defining a particular temperament dimension. Most families minimize noxious stimulation for their babies, for example, so that it is difficult to observe such situations naturalistically. Parents, in contrast, can describe an infant's response to a variety of naturally occurring stimuli, like being given a shampoo, or hearing the vacuum cleaner start up. Parent observations also meet both concerns about ecological validity and ethical constraints about creating aversive situations to assess temperament in the laboratory.

Kagan (1994, 1998), on the other hand, has argued that parent reports have problems with bias and inaccuracy. Bias and inaccuracy are real concerns, but, in our view, they are not as great a problem as Kagan suggests. Similar concerns have been extensively dealt with in personality research, and the dominant conclusion has been that traits can be reliably assessed by ratings of knowledgeable informants, including the self, friends, and parents (Kenrick & Funder, 1988; Moskowitz & Schwarz, 1982). In addition, validity is a problem for structured and naturalistic observational measures of temperament as well as for parent reports, and we have summarized potential sources of measurement error in three temperament assessment methods in Table 3.3.

Behaviors reliability coded in precisely defined situations have a high degree of objectivity. But this does not mean that the observations also have high validity. Observational research needs to demonstrate the same kinds of validity (content, construct, convergent, discriminant) required of a parent-report measure (Bates, 1989b; Rothbart & Goldsmith, 1985). There are some very promising laboratory assessments of temperament (e.g., Garcia-Coll, Halpern, Vohr, Seifer, & Oh, 1992; Goldsmith & Rothbart, 1991; Kagan, Reznick, & Snidman, 1988; Matheny, Wilson, & Thoben, 1987), but none has become so established that it can be seen as the gold standard for temperament measurement.

Kagan (1994) has also argued that the language of an individual item on a temperament questionnaire is subject to multiple interpretations. This ambiguity, however, is the main reason why researchers use *scales* of items rather than individual items to measure temperament. Attempts are made to write the best possible items, but the researcher does not expect that by doing this, all sources of error will be eliminated. Basic psychometric theory holds that the reason a set of convergent, but imperfectly correlated items tends to have better test-retest reliability, better stability over time, and better validity is that the error components of individual items tend to cancel each other out when the item scores are added to each other, yielding a closer approximation to a "true" score. This principle is true of aggregation across multiple observations as well as multiple items. Fortunately, one need not be limited to simply adding items and hoping that error is thereby reduced. With analytical tools such as LISREL and EQS, one can also explicitly model linkages between items' and scales' error components, creating latent constructs that more precisely control for measurement error. Other approaches to reducing concerns about validity are to use validity scale filters as in the Minnesota Multiphasic Personality Inventory (MMPI), and to study the ways parents construe child behavior and the items researchers present to them (Bates, 1994).

A Components-of-Variance Approach to Validity

We prefer to frame the question of validity of parent reports in terms of components of variance, judging a measure's validity on a continuum rather than an absolute judgment. Bates and Bayles (1984) asked how much variance in parent reports could be explained by reports of independent observers in a series of second-order empirical analyses on data from their longitudinal study. They found that: (a) mother ratings of their children on an array of temperament and nontemperament traits showed appropriate convergent and discriminant relations on similar sets of scales from 6 months to 3 years of age; (b) fathers and mothers agreed at generally moderate levels; (c) mothers and observers (in both naturalistic and structured contexts) agreed at generally modest but significant levels; and (d) factors such as anxiety or the tendency to describe oneself in socially desirable ways, which could reflect subjective biases, accounted for only modest portions of the variance.

Measured subjective factors thus did not overshadow measured objective factors as explanations of differences in parents' perceptions of their children. In addition to these components of parents' perceptions, there remained other error components.

Matheny et al. (1987) provided independent support for this model, using an array of laboratory measures. Their aggregated maternal report scores correlated moderately to strongly with laboratory scores of temperament: $r = .52$ at 12 months, .38 at 18 months, and .52 at 24 months. Their conclusion was that "the objective component of maternal ratings was clearly demonstrable and prominent" (Matheny et al., 1987, p. 324). They also showed that maternal personality characteristics were not only correlated with mothers' perceptions of the child but also correlated with their children's behavior as independently observed in laboratory situations, a finding congruent with genetically based similarities between mother and child.

A pattern of moderate to strong validity correlations for parent report can now be found in a number of places in the literature. One important requirement for ascertaining construct validity is that both measures demonstrate adequate reliability, and often the observational or mechanical measures, not the parent-report measures, are deficient in this regard. To produce adequate reliability, aggregation across multiple measures is often necessary (Rushton, Brainerd, & Pressley, 1983). Eaton (1983) recorded activity level from actometers worn by preschoolers over repeated nursery school free play sessions. Reliability of the actometers was .13 in a single session, but rose to .75 when multiple sessions were aggregated (Eaton, 1994). Aggregated scores also correlated .75 with parent report temperament ratings using the Colorado Childhood Temperament Inventory (CCTI) activity level scale and .73 with composite staff ratings of child activity level.

Asendorpf (1990) used multiple measures on multiple occasions to assess children's behavioral inhibition to strangers (shyness) across a 4-year period beginning at age 3. Measures included a parent-report assessment as well as observations of children's behavior with strange adults and children. Of all the measures taken by Asendorpf, parent report consistently showed the strongest relations with the other measures; for example, parent reported shyness predicted latency to talk to a stranger at 3 years with $r = .67$; the overall average r between parent-report and other shyness measures across the 4 years ranged from .43 to .53. Bishop, Spence, and

McDonald (2003) also reported convergence between parent ratings on a new behavioral inhibition questionnaire and both teacher questionnaires and structured observation measures.

Laboratory measures have also been found to be positively related to the Infant Behavior Questionnaire (IBQ) and Toddler Behavior Assessment Questionnaire (TBAQ) (see Goldsmith & Rothbart, 1991) and between temperament measures and model tasks designed to reflect underlying brain function; for example, a positive relation was found between a laboratory spatial conflict task designed to assay executive attention and the CBQ measure of inhibitory control ($r = .66$) for 36-month-old children (Gerardi-Caulton, 2000). Rothbart, Ellis, and Posner (2004) also reported relations between effortful control scales and spatial conflict scores. These findings provide further validational support for parent reports of temperament, but agreement is not always found (see Kagan & Fox, Chapter 4, this *Handbook,* this volume). A comprehensive review of validity studies in the measurement of temperament is needed.

Goldsmith et al. (1991) correlated mother reports with those of day-care teachers in samples of preschoolers, toddlers, and infants. Using a variety of standard temperament scales, they found strong convergence between scales from different questionnaires measuring the same construct, and generally acceptable divergence between scales expected to differ. Correlations between mother and day-care teacher for two older groups were in the typical range for correlations between parents and other observers (.11 to .50 for preschoolers, with the highest correlation on activity level, and .00 to .35 for toddlers, with the highest correlation also for activity), and perhaps a little above this range for infants (.21 to .60, with the highest correlation on one of the measures of approach-sociability). Day-care teachers would presumably be well acquainted with the children, although Goldsmith et al. did not report the degree of acquaintance. However, Goldsmith et al. (1991) emphasize the difference in contexts between mother and teacher observations.

As evidence for potential impact of failure to control context, they cite the Hagekull, Bohlin, and Lindhagen (1984) study. Hagekull et al. (1984) asked parents to directly record infant behavior, such as infants' reactions to loud sounds, over extended periods in specific situations. Parent data converged strongly with independent observers' data: Correlations between parents' and observers' direct observation data for two, 4-hour visits

ranged from .60 (for attentiveness) to .83 (for sensory sensitivity). Contrary to the argument of Seifer, Sameroff, Barrett, and Krafchuk (1994), this suggests that parents are not necessarily deficient or strongly biased in their powers of observation, especially since their training for the task was minimal. Hagekull et al. (1984) also found that for an open time frame, general questionnaire scales completed by the parents converged to a modest to moderately strong degree with scales based on independent direct observation, with correlations ranging from .21 to .63. We attribute the apparent improvements in observer-parent agreement coefficients more to the study's careful effort to observe sufficiently large numbers of key events than to any conceptual or psychometric advantages in the questionnaire they used (the Baby Behavior Questionnaire; BBQ). Although BBQ scales were developed through factor analysis, some of the scales in this instrument have some difficulties in interpretation, related to apparently heterogeneous content.

Prenatal Perception Studies

Researchers have also studied parent expectations of temperament before the child is born, which are often significant predictors of postnatal ratings of temperament (Diener, Goldstein, & Mangelsdorf, 1995; Mebert, 1991), and we discussed these in detail in our 1998 *Handbook* chapter. Diener et al. (1995), for example, looked at mother and father agreement over time. Prenatally, mothers' and fathers' temperament expectations were only modestly to moderately correlated, and the correlation pattern was generally nondifferentiated. Mothers' expectations of unadaptability to novelty, for example, were more highly related to fathers' fussy/difficult expectations than to the father's unadaptability expectations. Postnatally, however, mother-father convergence was considerably stronger, and there was also a strong pattern of discriminant validity. For example, mothers' ratings of unadaptability were correlated with fathers' ratings of unadaptability .67, and with fathers' ratings of difficultness only .28.

Mebert (1991) and Diener et al. (1995) speculated that prenatal expectations reflected a vague internal working model of the infant before birth, which might influence temperament through expectancy confirmation processes (Darley & Fazio, 1980). However, the fact that mother and father perceptions of the infant become so much closer in both a convergent and a discriminant sense from before to after their actual experience with the baby can be interpreted as evidence for an objective component in the ratings.

Recent Attempts to Make Parent and Observer Perspectives More Similar

Although some writers have argued that modest parent-observer agreement is simply a product of low validity in the parents' reports, this is not a necessary conclusion. Modest correlations could, for example, reflect observers simply not seeing the behavior parents based their reports on. Naturalistic and structured observation measures are often based on between 30 minutes and 4 hours of observation, and only a few are based on as much as 6 hours total. There is also little evidence that these measures show high test-retest reliability.

Two extensive home observation studies attempted to address such problems (Bornstein, Gaughran, & Segui, 1991; Seifer et al., 1994). In our 1998 handbook chapter, we described these studies in detail, indicating limitation in the designs, and concluding that the ideal large scale study for the limits of the objective component of parent reports of temperament has not yet appeared (Rothbart & Bates, 1998). Studies approaching the ideal would require conceptually well-developed measures with careful attention to both parent-report and observer-report forms. Extra attention would be devoted to validating observer- and parent-report measures, testing for convergence and divergence among measures, as well as studying relations between the measures and alternate ways of observing (e.g., summary ratings versus independently recorded molecular behavior frequencies or naturalistic versus structured observations). One recent example of such a study is that of Forman et al. (2003), who showed that aggregating laboratory measures of temperament across multiple tasks enhanced convergence with mother-report questionnaire measures.

The design would also pay greater attention to assessing contexts of temperament-relevant behavior. Although the concept of temperament implies some degree of cross-situational consistency, there is no reason to suppose that any given trait should be equally well revealed in all contexts, given variability in instigation of the response. The issue of context is crucial to all forms of temperament assessment, and will prove important as early temperament characteristics are linked to developing coping strategies across varying situations.

Shall We Use Parent Reports?

As we concluded in 1998, evidence to date supports the careful use of parent-report measures of temperament. Two basic reasons to use parent-report measures are (1) that they provide a useful perspective on the temperament of children because parents can see a wide range of child behaviors, and (2) that they have established a fair degree of objective validity. In addition, parent-report measures have contributed to substantial empirical advances, including our understanding of the structure of temperament in relation to the Big Five or Big Three models, as described earlier, and their parallels in psychophysiological systems (Bates, Wachs, & Emde, 1994; Rothbart, Derryberry, et al., 1994). A further reason for using parent reports is that the social relationship aspects of temperament elicited from parents may in themselves be important to understanding development.

Although we draw the conclusion that caregiver reports are useful in research, we share the concerns expressed in the literature about their measurement issues. Caregiver reports must be carefully interpreted as reflecting a combination of subjective and objective factors (Seifer, 2003). Improvements in caregiver-report measures should recognize possible sources of bias, such as parents' tendency to contrast one child with another in rating temperament (Saudino, 2003) on some, but not all, parent report questionnaires (Hwang & Rothbart, 2003). We should also develop subscales to detect specific biases in reporters and improve the generalizibility of the observational measures we use to validate caregiver reports (Goldsmith & Hewitt, 2003).

Observational and laboratory measures are appealing and should also be employed in temperament studies; however, they should not at this time be the sole measure of temperament. The primary arguments for this position are that (a) the validity of a number of such measures of temperament is not strongly established, and (b) even if the measures were well validated, they would often be awkward and highly expensive to use. Improvements in *both* parent-report and observational measures are needed. Parent reports can likely be made more objective, and the subjective components can be modeled more accurately and even controlled for (see Bates, 1994). The construct validity of observational measures can also be improved. We now turn to a review of research on additional temperament-related measures assessing the neural substrates of temperament-related behavior.

PSYCHOBIOLOGICAL RESEARCH APPROACHES

Gunnar (1990) describes five assumptions guiding psychobiological research on temperament: (1) "the assumption that temperament variation is regulated by the central nervous system"; (2) "the assumption that measures of peripheral systems inform us about the physiological bases of temperament because peripheral activity is regulated centrally," allowing the use of nonintrusive measures such as heart rate or electrodermal response; (3) "the assumption that fundamental temperament and emotional processes reflect a common mammalian heritage (Panksepp, 1982)," allowing research on animal models; (4) "the assumption that the aspects of central functioning related to temperament variation are those linked to broad or general behavioral tendencies"; and (5) "Finally, as reflected in Rothbart and Derryberry's theory (1981), concepts such as reactivity or arousal and self-regulation or inhibition are central to most physiological theories of temperament" (all quotations from p. 393). We have already adopted a number of these assumptions in the course of this review, and they are further illustrated in this section.

Behavioral Genetics

One reason for adopting a psychobiological approach to temperament is the considerable body of research indicating genetic contributions to the development of temperament and personality. Results of this work are reported extensively by Caspi and Shiner (Chapter 6, this *Handbook,* this volume), Goldsmith (1989; Goldsmith, Losoya, Bradshaw, & Campos, 1994), Plomin (Plomin, Chipuer, & Loehlin, 1990), Bouchard and Loehlin (2001), and for animal studies, Wimer and Wimer (1985). Because these reviews are available elsewhere, we briefly review findings that appear promising for an understanding of temperament and social development. Heritability estimates from behavioral genetics studies calculate the proportion of phenotypic (observable) variance in a characteristic attributable to genetic variation in a population, and heritability has proven to be substantial for most broad temperament and personality traits. In the area of personality, broad traits tend to show heritability estimates in the vicinity of .50 (Bouchard & Loehlin, 2001).

Tellegen et al. (1988) reported studies of adult monoygotic (MZ) and dizygotic (DZ) twins who had been reared either together or apart. Overall correlations of traits for MZ twins reared apart were surprisingly of a magnitude usually found for identical twins raised together (average *r* = .49), with heritability estimates of about .50. Correlations for MZ twins raised apart were .61 for stress reaction, .48 for sense of well-being, .50 for control, .49 for low risk taking, and .46 for aggression. For the three superfactors of Positive Emotionality (extraversion), Negative Emotionality (neuroticism) and Constraint (effortful and fearful control), only Positive Emotionality showed evidence of higher correlations for MZ and DZ twins raised together in comparison with twins raised apart (MZ apart *r* = .34, together = .63; DZ apart *r* = −.07, together = .18).

Goldsmith et al. (1997) have reviewed developmental behavioral genetics research and presented their own findings. Reviewing major twin studies, Goldsmith et al. (1997) reported that parent-report measures yield MZ twin correlations ranging from .50 to .80, with DZ correlations ranging from zero to .50. For scales based on Buss and Plomin's (1984) Emotionality, Activity, Sociability (EAS) measure, DZ correlations are typically less than half MZ correlations and often near zero, creating problems for heritability estimates. Although this pattern could also be due to the interactive effects of multiple genes, it seems more likely to be due to perceptual tendencies to contrast fraternal twins (Saudino, 2003). Despite the tendency for contrast effects to spuriously inflate heritability estimates, there is substantial evidence of heritability. For example, Silberg et al. (2004) showed heritability for ICQ traits in infants, even controlling for contrast effects.

Evidence for larger DZ correlations that are more in line with expected values has been found using observational methods (see Kagan and Fox's discussion of the genetics of behavioral inhibition, Chapter 4, this *Handbook,* this volume), and for parent-report studies employing the IBQ (Goldsmith, 1993) and the TBAQ, but not the CBQ (Goldsmith et al., 1997). Research employing these last three measures also suggests shared family influence, as did the MacArthur Longitudinal Twin Study (Plomin et al., 1993) for parent-reported positive affect and approach (Goldsmith et al., 1997). Goldsmith and Gottesman (1977) have also found evidence for genetic and shared family influences on CBQ effortful control scales.

In a study involving 3- to 16-month-old infants using the IBQ and a laboratory supplement at 9 months, genetic and shared environmental effects depended on the particular dimensions of temperament studied (Goldsmith, Lemery, Buss, & Campos, 1999). Additive genetic effects accounted fully for Distress to Limitations, Fear, and Activity Level measures, shared family effects accounted for Soothability, and genetic, shared, and nonshared environmental effects accounted for Smiling and Laughter and Duration of Orienting. The covariation of mother and father report and lab measures of stranger distress reflected chiefly genetic influences. Arseneault et al. (2003) similarly combined data across multiple reporters and settings, finding stronger genetic effects for antisocial behavior across than within situations in 5-year-old children. Saudino and Cherny (2001) found that covariation between mother and father reports on the CCTI shyness scale in infants from 14 to 36 months was mediated by genetic factors, but to a lesser extent than it was mediated by nonshared environment factors.

Goldsmith's positive affect/approach findings are congruent with Tellegen et al.'s (1988) study of MZ and DZ twins raised together and apart, in that shared family effects are found for positive emotionality. The shared environmental effect on effortful control reported by Goldsmith et al. (1997) requires replication, but shared family experience may also prove to be important in the development of attentional control. These findings may stimulate research into conditions that promote approach, orienting, positive affect, and self-control in the child's early social environment. Silberg et al. (2004) support the finding of a shared environment effect in addition to genetic influence on an aggregated sociability and positive affect scale on the ICQ. They also found evidence for a shared environment effect in unadaptability (novelty distress), as well as genetic heritability.

Although behavior genetics research indicates strong heritability of individual differences in temperament in the populations studied to date, these findings are based on the usual environmental circumstances experienced by developing children, and any heritability estimates reflect genes and environment operating together. The results do not tell us what *might* be accomplished via environmental intervention. They also do not reveal the specific developmental processes involved in temperament and personality outcomes. To learn more about the latter questions, studies furthering our understanding of temperament and development are essential. Zuckerman

(1995) addressed the question of "What is inherited?" and proposed this answer:

> We do not inherit personality traits or even behavior mechanisms as such. What is inherited are chemical templates that produce and regulate proteins involved in building the structure of nervous systems and the neurotransmitters, enzymes, and hormones that regulate them.... How do these differences in biological traits shape our choices in life from the manifold possibilities provided by environments?... Only cross-disciplinary, developmental, and comparative psychological research can provide the answers. (pp. 331–332)

We now recognize that experiential and environmental processes themselves build changes in brain structure and functioning (Posner & Raichle, 1994), both before and after birth (Black & Greenough, 1991). This situation is a far cry from the view that genetics gives us hardwiring that determines our future temperament and personality, and it demands developmental research. An exciting recent approach takes advantage of new methods of molecular genetics, and we review briefly some of the research in this area.

MOLECULAR GENETICS AND TEMPERAMENT

The mapping of the human genome has provided a promising new direction for studying genes and environment in development (G. Carey, 2003; Plomin & Caspi, 1999). Genetic alleles identified in previous adult research, for example, have been examined in children. An association between the 7-repeat allele of the dopamine D4 receptor (DRD4) and novelty seeking in adults was reported in 1996 (Benjamin, Ebstein, & Belmaker, 1996; Ebstein et al., 1996), although replication of these results has been inconsistent. In addition, variation in the 5-HTTLPR, a serotonin transporter gene, had been associated with Five Factor Model Neuroticism scores and with measures of fear and harm avoidance (see review by Lesch, Greenberg, Higley, Bennett, & Murphy, 2002). In a recent imaging study, presentation of fear stimuli also resulted in increased activation of the right amygdala in adults with the l/s or s/s form of the 5-HTTLPR gene (Hariri et al., 2002).

Ebstein and his colleagues used a longitudinal sample to investigate these two genetic polymorphisms in relation to neonatal and later infant behavior (Auerbach et al., 1999; Ebstein et al., 1998). Ebstein and Auerbach used the Neonatal Behavioral Assessment Scale (NBAS) to measure temperament during the neonatal period, and the IBQ to measure temperament at 2 months (Auerbach et al., 1999; Ebstein et al., 1998). In the newborn examination, the DRD4 long variant that has been linked to sensation seeking in adults was associated with orientation, range of state, regulation of state, and motor organization. In addition, an interaction was found between DRD4 and the 5-HTTLPR polymorphisms. The serotonin transporter gene s/s polymorphism that has been linked to fear and distress in adults was related to lower orientation scores, but only for neonates who did not have the long repeat variant of DRD4. For those who did, presence of the 5-HTTLPR s/s genotype had no effect.

Newborns who demonstrated high orientation and motor organization showed lower negative emotionality at 2 months. In addition, 2-month-old infants with long repeat DRD4 alleles had lower scores on IBQ negative emotionality and distress to limitations. Infants with the s/s 5-HTTLPR genotype previously related to fear and distress in adults had higher scores on negative emotionality and distress, and infants who shared both short repeat DRD4 alleles and short repeat 5-HTTLPR alleles showed the highest levels of negative emotionality and distress. Thus, the balance between orientation and distress found at the behavioral level (Harman, Rothbart, & Posner, 1997) may also be reflected at the genetic level. Finally, at 1 year of age, infants with the long DRD4 allele had lower negative emotionality scores, and showed less fear and less social inhibition (Auerbach et al., 1999).

Suomi and his colleagues have recently reported interactions between genes and environment in rhesus monkey studies of the 5-HTTLR gene and development (Barr et al., in press; Bennett et al., 2002). A standardized temperament assessment was carried out at 7, 14, 21, and 30 days of age, and monkeys with the 5-HTTLR short repeat allele showed higher levels of distress, as in human studies (Bennett et al., 2002). In human infants, the short allele was also linked to lower orientation scores (Auerbach et al., 1999; Ebstein et al., 1998), but analysis of monkey data revealed an environment by gene interaction. The short repeat allele was related to lower orientation scores, but only for monkeys who had been nursery-reared with peers, not for mother-reared monkeys. The authors note that a number of factors may account for the interaction. One is that a general tendency

to distress related to being reared in the nursery may be related to their distractibility; another is that mothers may buffer their infants' experience so as to moderate the expression of the genetic characteristic. Bennett et al. (2002) further reported an interaction between the short repeat form of the 5-HTTLR genotype and rearing condition in relation to CSF concentrations of 5-HIAA, a marker for a disposition to aggressive behavior.

Barr et al. (in press) found that nursery-reared young monkeys engaged in more social play than mother-reared monkeys, but if they had the short form of the distress-related 5-HTTLR allele, nursery-reared monkeys showed lower levels of social play, similar to the amount of play of mother-reared monkeys. Nursery-reared animals with the l/s genotype were more aggressive than either the mother-reared or l/l nursery-reared animals, suggesting the involvement of serotonin in development of aggression, but only in animals exposed to early life stress and maternal deprivation. The authors note that human research also supports both genetic and environmental contributions to the etiology of aggressive disorders (e.g., G. Carey, 1996; Dodge & Pettit, 2003).

In a study of 4-year-olds, Schmidt and Fox (2002) found a relation between the long repeat form of DRD4 and high scores on observed disruptive behavior and parent-reported aggressive and delinquent behavior. Schmidt, Fox, Perez-Edgar, Hu, and Hamer (2001) also found a link between the long repeat form and mothers' reports of attention problems. No links were found between serotonin transporter alleles and shyness, although they had been predicted. Children with the long 7-repeat allele of DRD4 related to sensation seeking in adults show behavioral aspects of ADHD, but do not demonstrate deficits in conflict performance as measured by the color-word Stroop task (Swanson et al., 2000). Sensation seeking might well be a prominent characteristic in at least some children diagnosed with ADHD. Evidence from evolutionary studies suggests that the 7-repeat allele is under positive selective pressure (Ding et al., 2002), which might be related to its association with sensation seeking, a possible advantage during human evolution (Ding et al., 2002).

In research on individual differences in attention (Posner & Fan, in press), the anterior cingulate, associated with executive attention, is only one synapse away from the ventral tegmental area, a major source of DA, and the five types of DA receptors are all expressed in the cingulate. The Attention Network Task (ANT), which assesses efficiency of alerting, orienting, and executive attention, was used in a small-scale twin study (Fan, Wu, Fossella, & Posner, 2001). In this study, the executive attention network score showed high enough heritability (.89) to justify the search for specific genes. At least two candidate genes were found to be related to executive attention (Fossella, Posner, Fan, Swanson, & Pfaff, 2002): the DRD4 gene and the monoamine oxidase A (MAOA) gene, related to the synthesis of DA and norepinepherine. In a neuroimaging study, these genes also were related to differences in brain activation in the anterior cingulate gyrus (Fan, Fossella, Sommer, Wu, & Posner, 2003). The presence of the more common 4 repeat allele, rather than the long repeat allele of DRD4 that has been related to sensation seeking, was associated with greater difficulty in resolving conflict (Fossella et al., 2002).

These findings are all recent and require further confirmation and extension, but they indicate the possible utility of relating genetic differences to specific brain networks and temperamental characteristics. It will be particularly interesting to look at relationships at different ages and in connection with different life experiences. Human studies have also identified significant interactions between gene and environment in maladaptive outcomes, and we discuss these in the Temperament and Adjustment section.

Approach/Withdrawal and Hemispheric Asymmetry

We now consider developmental research taking a psychobiological perspective and employing psychophysiological indicators. In the first of these, differences in cerebral hemispheric activation have been related to temperamental tendencies toward approach versus inhibition-withdrawal. Evidence from electrophysiological (EEG) and lesion studies has related higher anterior left hemisphere activation in response to stimulation to increased positive affect and/or decreased negative affect (see reviews by Davidson et al., 2003; Davidson & Tomarken, 1989). The reverse relationships—higher anterior right hemisphere activation related to higher negative affect and/or decreased positive affect—have also been reported. Resting EEG asymmetries have also been related to positive and negative emotional reactivity (e.g., Davidson & Fox, 1989; Tomarken, Davidson, Wheeler, & Doss, 1992). Harmon-Jones and Allen (1997), for example, reported greater left than right-frontal cortical activity in women subjects with higher scores on Carver and

White's (1994) BAS questionnaire. The BIS measure was not related to asymmetry. Buss et al. (2003) found relations between extreme right EEG asymmetry and high basal and reactive cortisol, replicating previous primate findings from Kalin and his colleagues (Kalin, Larson, Shelton, & Davidson, 1998).

Fox, Calkins, and Bell (1994) reported that infants with stable right frontal EEG asymmetry between 9 and 24 months of age displayed more fearfulness and inhibition in the laboratory than other children. At 4 years, children who showed more reticence and social withdrawal were also more likely to show right frontal asymmetry. Calkins, Fox, and Marshall (1996) also found that children selected for high motor activity and negative affect to laboratory stimulation at 4 months showed greater right frontal asymmetry at 9 months, greater mother reports of fear at 9 months, and more inhibited behavior at 14 months. However, no concurrent relation was found between behavior and frontal asymmetry at 9 and 14 months, and greater activation of both right and left frontal areas was related to higher inhibition scores at 14 months. The authors (Calkins et al., 1996) suggest a need to differentiate between fearful and angry distress, as discussed earlier in the Structure of Temperament section. They also hypothesize that high motor/high negative affect and high motor/high positive affect may be associated with later different kinds of problems. For high motor/high positive affect, the problems would be associated with difficulties in self-control.

Autonomic Reactivity and Self-Regulation

By assuming central controls on peripheral reactivity, psychobiological researchers have developed models of centrally regulated systems that can be studied early in life. In this section, we consider briefly some of the research on electrodermal responding, heart rate, and vagal tone.

Electrodermal Reactivity

Several early studies reported a relationship between electrodermal response and introversion (see review by Buck, 1979). Jones (1960), for example, compared the 10 highest and 10 lowest electrodermal responders age 11 to 18 in the Berkeley Adolescent Growth Study. High electrodermal responders were described as showing high emotional control, quiet, reserve and deliberation, and as being calm and responsible. Low electrodermal responders were rated as more impulsive, active and talkative, more attention seeking, assertive and bossy. Adult studies have also found stable individual difference in electrodermal reactivity to be negatively related to measures of extraversion (e.g., Crider & Lunn, 1971). Fowles (1982) reported that electrodermal responding, but not heart rate reactivity, was related to measures of Gray's Behavioral Inhibition System. Indeed, Fowles and Kochanska (2000) found that electrodermal reactivity served as a substitute for laboratory and mother report fear, moderating relations between socialization and conscience development at age 4.

Fabes et al. (1994) studied kindergarten and second-grade children's facial expressions of distress and skin conductance (SC) reactivity to a film about children being hurt in an accident. For both ages, SC reactivity, used as a marker of personal distress, was positively related to facial distress and negatively related to helping. Results were seen to reflect an interference of personal negative affect with children's prosocial behavior. In a study of older children (third and sixth graders), SC was positively related to facial expressions of distress to a film and negatively related to mothers' report of dispositional helpfulness, but for girls only (Fabes, Eisenberg, & Eisenbud, 1993). Evidence has thus been found for electrodermal response as both a sign of distress and behavioral inhibition. Lang and his associates (Lang, Bradley, & Cuthbert, 1997), however, have found that adults' SC to viewing pictures increased for *both* aversive and pleasant stimuli, so that the sympathetic response measured in SC may be more general than previously thought.

Heart Rate and Vagal Tone

A good deal of recent research has focused on heart rate and on vagal tone as a measure of parasympathetic cardiac control. In her review of heart rate (HR) research, Von Bargen (1983) reported HR reactivity to stimulation to be the most stable and reliable of HR measures. As noted by Kagan (1998), HR variability has been linked to low behavioral inhibition in some, but not all, studies. Fabes, Eisenberg, Karbon, and Troyer (1994) found HR variability to be positively related to kindergarten and second-grade children's instrumental coping to a baby's crying. Fabes et al. (1993) also found positive relationships between HR variability and measures of sympathy (dispositional sympathy for girls, concerned attention to others' distress for boys) in third and sixth grade children.

Cardiac vagal tone has also been related to temperament (Bornstein & Suess, 2000; El-Sheikh, 2001). Respiratory Sinus Arrhythmia (RSA), the fluctuation in heart rate occurring at the frequency of respiration, has been used to assess parasympathetic control via the vagal nerve (Porges, 1986). There is an increase in HR during inspiration and a decrease during expiration that is extracted from HR variation, and Porges argued that variability in RSA reflects individual differences in tonic parasympathetic vagal tone. Higher baseline vagal tone is also related to greater vagal suppression to stimulation, although some infants with regulatory disorders show high RSA but do not demonstrate suppression of RSA with attention (DeGangi, DiPietro, Greenspan, & Porges, 1991). Vagal suppression is often seen as reflecting attentional strategies to cope with the environment or respond to stress (Huffman et al., 1998). Berntson, Cacioppo, and Quigley (1993) note RSA is not a direct equivalent to tonic vagal control of the heart because it is determined by multiple peripheral and central processes. They nevertheless conclude that RSA is an important noninvasive measure that "shows a high degree of sensitivity to psychological and behavioral variables" (p. 193).

Keeping these concerns in mind, we can consider some of the findings relating vagal tone or RSA measures to temperament variables. Porges, Doussard-Roosevelt, and Maiti (1994) reviewed studies relating newborn vagal tone to irritability and found that young infants with high baseline levels of vagal tone were also highly reactive and irritable. Later in development, however, vagal tone has been found to be related positively to interest and positive expressiveness and negatively to internalizing distress (for a more extensive review of these findings, see Beauchaine, 2001; Porges, 1991). Thus, RSA after 5 to 6 months tends to be associated with positive emotionality and approach as well as irritability. Richards and Cameron (1987) found that baseline RSA was positively correlated with parent-reported approach at 6- and 12-months, and Fox and Stifter (1989) reported more rapid approach to strangers in infants with higher RSA at 14 months. Stifter, Fox, and Porges (1989) found that 5-month-olds with higher RSA looked away from the stranger more during a strangers' approach and showed higher levels of interest and positive affect, although this pattern was not found at 10 months. Evidence of stability of vagal tone is only found after about 9 months of age (Porges & Doussard-Roosevelt, 1997).

Stifter and Corey (2001) found that greater suppression of vagal tone to cognitive challenge in 12-month-olds was associated with experimenter ratings of approach, and Fox and Field (1989) reported more rapid adjustment to preschool in 3-year-olds with higher vagal tone; these children also showed higher positive affect and greater adaptability. Katz and Gottman (1995) found that children with low vagal tone at age 5 showed a stronger correlation between marital hostility at age 5 and problem behaviors at age 8 than children with high vagal tone ($rs = .65$ and $.25$), although the interaction was not significant. Katz and Gottman saw their finding as congruent with a buffering effect of higher vagal tone that might operate through attentional self-regulation. El-Sheikh, Harger, and Whitson (2001) also found an interaction: 8- to 12-year-olds with higher vagal tone appeared to be buffered against anxiety related to high verbal marital conflict. Finally, El-Sheikh (2001) found that higher vagal suppression to a taped argument in 6- to 12-year-olds was related as a protective factor to internalizing, externalizing, and other social problems related to parental problem drinking, whereas negative affectivity was a vulnerability factor in the effects of parental drinking.

Beauchaine's (2001) interpretation of developmental findings is that higher vagal tone is associated with more adaptive functioning at any given age: in the neonate, it is linked to irritability; in the older infant and child, it is linked to approach and positive affect as well as to irritability. Later higher vagal tone is associated with more appropriate social behaviors and adaptation to stressors, along with lower depressive and anxious psychopathology (see review by Beauchaine, 2001). However, the links between attentional regulation and vagal tone or suppression suggest more specific interpretations of these findings. In infancy, irritability and anger are positively related to approach, positive affect, and duration of orienting (Rothbart & Derryberry, 2002), and infants high in vagal tone may be showing a stronger approach system linked to parasympathetic function in these responses. Later, infants high in vagal tone and vagal suppression may be showing stronger attentional regulation. At 9 months, Porges, Doussard-Roosevelt, Portales, and Suess (1995) found vagal tone to be positively correlated with ICQ fussy/difficultness. For a small longitudinal sample, however, even after partialling out 9-month ICQ difficulty, 9-month vagal tone predicted lower difficulty at 3 years, possibly re-

lated to attention regulation and even to the development of the executive attention system across this period. Research with adults has recently linked high heart-rate variability to performance on tasks involving executive attention (Hansen, Johnsen, & Thayer, 2003), and children with higher vagal tone have been found to show greater ability to sustain attention (Suess, Porges, & Plude, 1994). In sum, relations between vagal tone and temperament vary depending on the age of the child and include both reactive and self-regulative processes.

Cortisol Reactivity

Another approach that takes into account both reactivity and self-regulatory control is the work of Gunnar and others on cortisol reactivity. During stress reactions, the adrenal cortex secretes steroid hormones, including the glucocorticoids, cortisol and corticosterone (Carter, 1986). These hormones increase blood glucose and work with catecholamines to produce glucose from free fatty acids, also serving an anti-inflammatory function for injury and disease. Gunnar and her associates have investigated cortisol reactivity in relation to individual differences in temperamentally based self-regulation, and have reviewed links between stress hormone activity and development (Gunnar & Cheatham, 2003). Decreases in cortisol reactivity are found between 2 and 4 months, and further decreases between 6 and 18 months (Gunnar, Brodersen, Krueger, & Rigatuso, 1996; Lewis & Ramsay, 1995).

Both temperament and child care are related to cortisol levels. Dettling, Parker, Lane, Sebanc, and Gunnar (2000) found that children high in temperamental negative emotionality and low in self-regulation showed the greatest increase in cortisol levels when they were in less than optimal child-care situations. Donzella, Gunnar, Krueger, and Alwin (2000) investigated stress responses to competition in 3- to 5-year-olds. Children played against a familiar adult experimenter and initially won 3 games, but then lost 3. Temperamental surgency assessed via teacher report was related to both positive affect during winning and to tense and angry affect during losing. Although most children did not show increases in cortisol to competition, the 15% who did were higher in temperamental surgency and lower in effortful control. The authors concluded that more extraverted, surgent children are most vulnerable to stress during competition. This is an important finding, because it indicates links between stress hormones and positive affect as well as negative affect systems.

Gunnar (1994) also found an initially surprising relation between cortisol levels and preschool children's adjustment to a group setting. Rather than finding higher levels of cortisol for 3- to 5-year-old inhibited (and presumably more stress-prone) children early in the school year, Gunnar found that measures of cortisol reactivity to the school experience were related to mother-report CBQ (Rothbart et al., 2001) surgency measures of high activity, stimulation seeking, and impulsivity, with a trend toward less shyness. Teachers also reported fewer internalizing problems, greater popularity, and independence for children with higher cortisol levels. Later in the school year, however, higher cortisol reactivity was associated with teacher reports of greater internalizing behavior and CBQ reports of sensitivity to discomfort.

Gunnar (1994) suggests that temperamentally linked coping activities of children may mediate their cortisol reactions so that more shy children will be less likely to experience stressful interactions initially because of avoidant or inhibitory coping strategies. More outgoing children will be more likely to seek out stress and show its effects in early, but not later, group experience when they may have mastered the social challenge (Gunnar, 1994). Gunnar's work indicates the importance of studying reactive measures in the context of regulatory coping. In more recent research, peer reactions to a child's behavior have also been found to be related to cortisol function. Gunnar, Sebanc, Tout, Donzella, and Van Dulmen (2003) reported that children with higher cortisol levels in the nursery school classroom were those whose temperamentally based behavior (high surgency; low effortful control) led other children to reject them. These findings reflect recent increases in complexity of temperament-environment relationships that we discuss later in the chapter.

Summary

Behavior genetics research supports the idea that the chemical templates we inherit are reflected in our temperament, social, and personality characteristics, and recent research suggests that gene-environment interaction may be particularly important in relation to personality and social development. More developmental research is needed, however, to specify how developing brain mechanisms interact with environmental events to support these outcomes. In research linking temperament to psychophysiology, recent investigations have related tendencies toward approach and withdrawal to left and right hemisphere brain activity, respectively. In addition, electrodermal responding has been linked to reserve and negative emotionality. HR variability and vagal tone have also been studied, with the latter taken as a measure of parasympathetic function. HR variability has been linked to prosocial responding and inversely, in some studies, to behavioral inhibition. Vagal tone has been linked to behavioral irritability, approach, positive affect, and attention, with the direction of the linkage varying depending on the age of the child. Both vagal tone and cortisol research stress the importance of both reactive and self-regulative variables in the understanding of psychophysiology and development, and all of these approaches are promising for tracing links between genetic inheritance, experience, and behavioral outcomes.

TEMPERAMENT AND DEVELOPMENT

Early theorists of temperament stressed the importance of finding stability of temperament over time. Thus, for Buss and Plomin (1975), to qualify as a "temperament," a characteristic must demonstrate stability from its early appearance to late in life. More recent approaches to the field, however, have noted that temperament itself develops, and the study of this development allows us a greater understanding of both normative and individual differences (Goldsmith et al., 1997; Rothbart, 1989b; Rothbart & Derryberry, 1981). Temperamental measures can fail to show normative stability, for example, but genetically related individuals may show strong similarities in their patterns of change. These results have been found in behavioral genetics work on both activity level (Eaton, 1994) and behavioral inhibition (Matheny, 1989).

Even for dimensions showing normative stability, expressions of temperament are likely to change over time. In measuring negative emotionality, for example, 6-year-olds spend much less time crying than do 6-month-olds, but worry a good deal more. To appropriately assess stability of temperamental characteristics, it is necessary to establish continuity in the temperament constructs studied across time. Pedlow, Sanson, Prior, and Oberklaid (1993) assessed the ATP sample at intervals from infancy to 7 to 8 years of age. By using structural equation modeling, they identified factors that applied across the entire age range (Approach/Sociability, Rhythmicity), or across several of the time intervals studied (Irritability, Persistence, Cooperation-Manageability, and Inflexibility). A model correcting for error of measurement was then used to assess individual stability on these factors from year to year, and estimates were considerably higher than those previously reported, mostly in the range of 0.7 to 0.8. Even with these levels of stability, however, there is considerable room for individual change in their children's relative position on these characteristics.

Since our last review, an important meta-analysis of studies on the stability of personality traits, including temperament, has been carried out by Roberts and DelVecchio (2000). This review was organized according to the Five-Factor model, and began with studies of temperament and personality in infancy. Considerable stability was found in measures of these variables after about the age of 3 years, with estimated cross-time correlations for 0 to 2.9 years = .35; 3 to 5.9 years = .52; 6 to 11.9 years = .45; and 12 to 17.9 years = .47. The increase at 3 to 6 years is of interest, given evidence for the rapid development of executive attention and effortful control during the first 3 years of life, possibly related to early instability. As attention systems stabilize, controls over earlier more reactive tendencies may increase prospects for stability of temperament and personality. Beyond childhood, levels of stability continue to increase through adolescence and young adulthood, not peaking until after the age of 50 (Roberts & DelVecchio, 2000).

In the next section, we consider issues of temperament stability and change in relation to social-emotional development and the development of personality. We review research examining the development of temperament in the areas of positive affect/approach and inhibition, distress proneness, activity level, and effortful control. Individual differences in emotional and motor reactivity can be seen early in life, and they will be influenced over time by the development of more regulatory systems, one of their emotionally based (fear or behavioral inhibition), the other more directly self-regulative (effortful control). The first system develops earlier than the second, and both are developing during the period when Roberts and DelVecchio (2000) reported the lowest levels of normative stability.

Contributions of Temperament to Development

Temperament constructs are fundamental to thinking about trajectories of social-emotional and personality development (Rothbart, Ahadi, et al., 1994). As noted earlier, temperament is implicated in social learning, with some children more responsive to reward, others to punishment. Some children will be highly responsive to both. Temperament is also closely linked to the development of coping strategies. If one child tends to experience high distress to strangers, for example, and another child little distress, coping strategies involving avoidance of strangers may be elicited and reinforced for the first child, but not for the second. If the second child also experiences delight in the interaction with a stranger, more rapid and confident approach to interactions with strangers is likely in the future. Thus, the practice and reinforcement of children's temperamentally based responses may serve to magnify initial differences through a positive feedback process. Individual differences in temperament also promote the child's active seeking or avoiding of environments. Scarr and McCartney (1983) describe these genotype/environment interactions as "niche picking." The child who stays at the edge of a nursery school class or a party is selecting a different experience than the child who goes directly to the center of social excitement.

In Gray's (1991) theory, extraverts, high in positive affect and approach (the BAS), are seen as more susceptible to reward, and introverts, high in fear and shyness, to punishment (the BIS). This model suggests that caregiver treatment may have differing developmental outcomes, depending on differences among children. In other models, optimal level theories (e.g., Bell, 1974; Strelau, 1983) stress individual preferences for high or low levels of stimulation. A child easily overwhelmed by stimulation will try to keep things quiet, whereas a child who requires high levels of stimulation for pleasure will attempt to keep things exciting. Mismatches in optimal levels between a parent and child, or among siblings, may require major adaptations from one or more of the children or parents. Situational challenges, such as an intense day-care experience for an easily overstimulated infant, or demands for extended quiet time for a stimulus-seeking older child, may lead to problems for both child and caregiver.

Scarr and McCartney (1983) also describe evocative interactions where the child's temperamental characteristics elicit reactions from others that may influence the child's development. Thus, a positive and outgoing disposition may serve as a protective factor eliciting the support of others in a high-risk environment (Werner, 1985). Radke-Yarrow and Sherman (1990) noted that in a high-risk situation, a buffering effect can occur when the child's characteristics meet the needs of the parent (these needs may be quite idiosyncratic). Acceptance by adults can then lead children to feel there is something special or important about them personally. This notion is very similar to Thomas and Chess's (1977) "goodness-of-fit" argument.

Because temperament itself develops (Rothbart, 1989b), new systems of behavioral organization (e.g., smiling and laughter, frustration, executive attention) will also come "online" over time. Any new systems that serve to regulate action and emotion will also come to modulate characteristics that were previously present, yielding potential instability of temperament across the developmental transition. In addition to the direct effects of developing control systems of fear and effortful control, children who develop a given control system early in life may have quite different experiences than children who develop the system later (Rothbart & Derryberry, 1981). For example, the child who develops fear-related inhibition late is likely to experience a greater number of interactions with potentially threatening objects or situations than the child who develops fearful inhibition early. The child who is fearful and inhibited to potential dangers early in development may spend more time watching and making sense of events in the environment than the less inhibited child. We now consider some of the major dimensions of temperament in a developmental context.

Extraversion/Surgency versus Shyness and Behavioral Inhibition

By 2 to 3 months, infants show a pattern of smiling, vocalization, and motor cycling of the limbs described by Kistiakovskaia (1965) and termed the "animation complex, including smiling, quick and animated generalized movements with repeated straightening and bending of hands and feet, rapid breathing, vocal reactions, eye blink, and so on" (p. 39). These reactions appeared to increase in duration and decrease in latency into the second and third months of life (Kistiakovskaia, 1965). Werner (1985) reviewed cross-cultural evidence for both an increase in smiling between 2 and 4 months and in vocalization at 3 to 4 months. This cluster of intercorre-

lated behaviors (smiling and laughter; vocal and motor activity) is also found in parents' reports of temperament and in home observations (Rothbart, 1986). It is displayed toward exciting and novel objects as well as toward people (Bradley, 1985). However, Aksan and Kochanska (2004a) used confirmatory factor analysis to determine that observed social and non-social positive affect at 7 months formed two separate factors.

Beyond 3 to 4 months, positive affect shows normative increases in probability and duration across the first year of life, both in home observation and parent-report data (Rothbart, 1981, 1986). Stability has also been found for individual differences on a composite positive emotionality measure including smiling and laughter, motor and vocal activity, as assessed by parent-report and home observation between 3 to 9 months, and stability of a laboratory measure of smiling and laughter between 3 and 13.5 months of age (Rothbart, 1986). Smiling and laughter in infancy as observed in the laboratory also predicted both concurrent (Rothbart, 1988) and 6- to 7-year-old approach tendencies (Rothbart et al., 2001). Pedlow et al. (1993) also found stability from infancy to 7 to 8 years on their dimension of Approach/Sociability.

Later in the first year, an important form of inhibition and control over approach develops: some infants who were highly approaching at 5 or 6 months now come to inhibit their approach responses when the stimuli are unfamiliar and/or intense (Rothbart, 1988; Schaffer, 1974). In our laboratory, we found increases in infants' latency to grasp novel and intense toys from 6.5 to 10 months of age (Rothbart, 1988). Infants' approach latency to low-intensity stimuli showed stability from 6.5 months to later ages (10 and 13.5 months), but to high-intensity stimuli, it did not. This finding is congruent with the idea that behavioral inhibition is developing late in the first year, with the inhibitory reactions particularly evident in response to high-intensity stimuli. Once inhibition of approach is established, longitudinal research suggests that individual differences in approach versus inhibition to novelty or challenge will be a relatively enduring aspect of temperament. In familiar or low-intensity situations, however, chiefly positive activation will be evident. The inhibiting aspect of fear qualifies it as a control system that modulates other response tendencies, and we elaborate this argument in discussing Kochanska's (1993) research later in the chapter.

By early childhood, social inhibition with strangers shows moderate stability (Asendorpf, 1993; Gest,

1997). Honzik (1965) also noted that longitudinal Fels subjects' scores on "spontaneity" versus "social interaction anxiety" were stable and predictive over long periods for both males (the first 3 years to adulthood) and females (6 to 10 years to adulthood; Kagan & Moss, 1962). Bayley and Schafer (1963) found their most stable and persistent category between infancy to 18 years to be "active, extraverted" versus "inactive, introverted" behavior. Tuddenham (1959) reported stability on scales indexing "spontaneity" versus "inhibition" for subjects from 14 to 33 years in the Oakland Growth Study. Finally, Honzik (1965) found that for the period between 21 months and 18 years of age, the two most stable dimensions were "introversion" versus "extraversion" and "excessive reserve" versus "spontaneity."

These results can be added to evidence from Kagan (1998; Kagan & Fox, Chapter 4, this *Handbook,* this volume) on stability of behavioral inhibition, and to Caspi and Silva's (1995) and Pfeifer, Goldsmith, Davidson, and Rickman's (2002) recent work on stability of outgoingness and inhibition. In Pfeifer et al.'s (2002) research, children were examined at 4 and 7 years with laboratory, TBAQ, and CBQ assessments of behavioral inhibition and uninhibited behavior. At the younger age, children were classified as extremely inhibited, extremely uninhibited, or intermediate. Close to half the children remained in their original subgroup over the 3-year period. More than half changed subgroup, but the change tended to be to the intermediate group rather than to the other extreme. Caspi and Silva (1995) identified a group of children high on approach or confidence at age 3 to 4, who were outgoing and eager to undertake tasks, and adjusted easily to challenging situations. At age 18, these children were relatively low on self-reported control (i.e., more impulsive) and high on social potency (leadership and low shyness). Children identified in the preschool period as inhibited (fearful, with problems in sustaining attention) were, at age 18, high on harm avoidance, notably low on aggression, and low on social potency. Caspi and Silva's (1995) finding that inhibition or fearfulness served as a protective factor against the later development of aggression is also congruent with the positive correlations found between temperamental fearfulness and the development of conscience described later.

In summary, evidence for approach tendencies related to positive affect can be seen early in development. Later in infancy, behavioral inhibition related to fear develops. Once established, tendencies toward approach versus inhibition demonstrate significant stability over

relatively long developmental periods, with important implications for social development and for the measurement of temperament (Rothbart & Sheese, in press).

Activity Level

Another major temperamental characteristic that can be measured early in development is activity level. Using both ultrasound imaging and mothers' reports, activity level can also be measured prenatally, and evidence for temperamental stability has been found over the short periods that have been measured (Eaton & Saudino, 1992). In early research, Fries (Fries & Woolf, 1954) and Escalona (1968) identified activity level as a major dimension of individual differences among infants. Birns, Barten, and Bridger (1969) found no stability of activity level from the newborn period to ages 3 and 4 months, but some stability was found from 4 weeks to later assessments.

A possible explanation for instability of early activity level is the tendency for activity to be linked to both negative and positive emotional reactivity. When high levels of activity occur in the newborn, they are often linked to the expression of negative affect (e.g., Korner, Hutchinson, Koperski, Kraemer, & Schneider, 1981). Escalona (1968) observed that newborns engage in their highest motor activity during distress; positive states were associated with quiescence. Later in development, however, the infant often becomes motorically aroused while in an alert and nondistressed state, as noted by Kistiakovskaia (1965), and activity frequently occurs when the infant is orienting toward novel objects or receiving caregiver stimulation (Wolff, 1965). Links between activity and newborn expression of negative affect may account for its failure to predict later activity. Indeed, when Korner et al. (1985) measured nondistress motor activity in the newborn, vigor of activity predicted high daytime activity and high approach scores on the BSQ at ages 4 to 8 years. Another finding is that activity at 4 months, coupled with negative affect, predicted later behavioral inhibition (Fox, Henderson, Rubin, Calkins, & Schmidt, 2001; Kagan, 1998); activity coupled with positive affect predicted later uninhibited behavior (Calkins & Fox, 1994; Fox et al., 2001).

Saudino and Eaton (1995), using actometer measures in a twin study, did not find normative stability in activity level from 7 to 36 months. Nevertheless, in Saudino and Eaton's (1995) study, MZ twins were more similar than DZ twins at both ages, and MZ twins were also more concordant in their changes in activity from 7 to

36 months than were DZ twins. Lower levels of stability of activity level from the first year to later periods have also been reported. Roberts and DelVecchio (2000) found the lowest mean levels of stability for activity level among other temperament/personality dimensions studied ($r = .28$); other dimensions ranged from .35 to .47 in consistency over time.

At least two explanations are possible for early instability. One, presented earlier, is that activity can be related to both positive and negative affect, so that the two kinds of activity should be differentiated. Second, the onset of inhibition as an aspect of fearfulness late in the first year may lead to lower activity for a number of children under conditions of novelty or high intensity. A second form of control over impulsive activity will also be developing beginning late in the first year and during the preschool years. This is the effortful control system, related to the development of executive attention, to be discussed later in this section. Its development coincides with normative decreases in activity level, which in a meta-analysis of activity level studies showed a peak between 7 and 9 years (Eaton, McKeen, & Campbell, 2001).

Attentional Orienting and Effortful Control

Attention has both reactive and self-regulative aspects. In reactive attention—orienting to exogenous stimulation—consistency of rates of infant looking have been found across three quite different measures in 3-month-olds: (1) a visual discrimination paradigm, (2) an auditory discrimination paradigm, and (3) rate of looking toward the mother in social interaction (Coldren, Colombo, O'Brien, Martinez, & Horowitz, 1987). Byrne, Clark-Touesnard, Hondas, and Smith (1985) also reported stability from 4 to 7 months in average looking time and duration of first look in visual habituation tasks.

A developmental shift in visual orienting appears to occur late in the first year of life. Kagan, Kearsley, and Zelazo (1978) noted a U-shaped developmental pattern of fixation times to clay faces with scrambled and unscrambled features in both North American and Guatemalan children. From 4 to 8 months, there is a steep decline in the amount of time children spend looking at both kinds of faces. Between 13 and 36 months, however, there is an increase in looking time that is stronger for scrambled than for unscrambled faces. Kagan et al. (1978) argue that "stability of duration of orienting from 8 to 13 and 13 to 27 months, without comparable 8 to 27 month continuity, suggests

that determinants of fixation time change between 8 and 27 months" (p. 81). No stability was found between 4 months and later measures. These changes are in keeping with findings that signs of executive attention begin to emerge toward the end of the first year (Kochanska, Murray, & Harlin, 2000), allowing increased attentional control and planning, and presumably changing the meaning of individual differences in looking at objects (see also discussion in Ruff & Rothbart, 1996).

The development of effortful control—the efficiency of executive attention—including the ability to inhibit a dominant response and/or to activate a subdominant response, to plan, and to detect errors, also appears to be linked to the child's developing ability to maintain a sustained focus of attention. Krakow, Kopp, and Vaughn (1981) studied sustained attention to a set of toys in 12- to 30-month-old infants. Duration increased across this period, with stability of individual differences between 12 and 18 months, and between 24 and 30 months. Sustained attention was also positively related to self-control measures, independent of developmental quotient, at 24 months. In a major longitudinal study, Kochanska (Kochanska & Knaack, 2003; Kochanska, et al., 2000) used multiple methods to assess effortful control and emotionality. Mother report of effortful control was aggregated with laboratory measures, which included delay, slowing motor activity, lowering the voice, suppressing and initiating activity to a signal, and effortful attention at 22, 33 and 45 months of age. Focused attention at 9 months predicted children's later effortful control, and effortful control was related to regulation of anger at 22 and 33 months and joy at 33 months (Kochanska, et al., 2000). Measures of effortful control showed increasing coherence and stability across 22 to 45 months, so that between 33 and 45 months, stability was equivalent to that of IQ. Children who had shown more regulated anger and joy and more fear-related inhibition at 22 months demonstrated later higher levels of effortful control (Kochanska & Knaack, 2003). The link between inhibition and later effortful control was further supported by Aksan and Kochanska (2004b). These are exciting findings, worthy of future replication.

Krakow and Johnson (1981), using measures of self-control under verbal instructions with children age 18 to 30 months, found large age effects in inhibitory control. They also found moderate levels of stability of inhibitory self-control across the 12-month period. Vaughn, Kopp, and Krakow (1984) reported on two aspects of self-control: delay and compliance. Cross-task consistency and coherence across the two broader measures increased across age, and the authors concluded "that individual differences in self-control emerge and are consolidated during the 2nd and 3rd years of life" (p. 990). Reed, Pien, and Rothbart (1984) found strong age effects in two measures of self-control (a pinball game and Simon-Says game) in a cross-sectional study of children aged 40 to 49 months. These studies together indicate increases in self-regulation across 18 to 49 months of age. In our research using the Stroop-like spatial conflict tasks described earlier, children began to demonstrate effective management of conflict at 30 months, and 36-month-old children who showed greater interference in reaction time for conflicting responses were reported by their mothers as exhibiting lower levels of inhibitory control (Rothbart et al., 2004). Less accurate children were also reported as showing higher levels of anger/frustration in the IBQ (Gerardi-Caulton, 2000), suggesting attentional control over emotion as well as action. Additional research with conflict tasks indicates development of conflict performance between the ages of 2 and 7 (see review by Rothbart & Rueda, 2005).

Murphy, Eisenberg, Fabes, Shepard, and Guthrie (1999) studied children longitudinally at 4 to 6, 6 to 8, 8 to 10, and 10 to 12 years of age, using parent and teacher report. Children were reported as increasing control over attentional shifting and inhibitory control across age, and girls also decreased in impulsivity. With the exception of attention shifting, the measures of self-regulation showed considerable stability across this period of development.

Attention and Distress

A consistent theme of the relation between attention and distress is that the two mutually influence each other. In a study of attentional orienting and soothing in 3- to 6-month-old infants (Harman et al., 1997), infants were first shown a sound and light display; about 50% of the infants became distressed to the stimulation. They then strongly oriented to interesting visual and auditory soothing events when these were presented. While the infants oriented, facial and vocal signs of distress disappeared. However, as soon as the orienting stopped, for example, when the object was removed, the infants' distress returned to almost exactly the levels shown prior to its presentation. Apparently, the loss of overt signs of distress is not always accompanied by a genuine loss of distress. Instead, some internal system, which we termed the *distress keeper,* appears to hold a computation of the initial level of distress. Repeating the soothing

stimulus also appeared to reduce its soothing effectiveness (habituation) at 6 months, but not at 3 to 4 months.

Regulatory behaviors were studied in a longitudinal study of 66 children seen at 3, 6, 10, and 13 months of age (Rothbart, Ziaie, & O'Boyle, 1992). The infants were presented with stimuli that varied in intensity and predictability, and children showed considerable active coping with their own distress and excitement. At 6 months, children's disengagement of attention could be reliably coded. Overall disengagement of attention was not stable from 6 to 10 months, but from 10 to 13 months, children demonstrated stability in their tendency to disengage from distress-producing visual stimuli such as masks and mechanical toys. Infant disengagement was also related to lower levels of negative affect at 13 months. Stability from 10 to 13 months was also found in infants' use of mouthing, hand to mouth (e.g., thumb sucking), approach, and withdrawing the hand, suggesting that some of the infants' self-regulation strategies were becoming habitual by this time.

Direct links have also been found between children's disengagement of attention and decreases in negative affect (Stifter & Braungart, 1995). Correlations also have been found between infants' use of self-regulation in anger inducing situations and their early childhood ability to delay responses (Calkins & Williford, 2003), suggesting that mechanisms used to cope with negative emotion may later be transferred to control of cognition and behavior, as suggested by Posner and Rothbart (1998). Further support of this idea was found by Mischel and his colleagues (Sethi, Mischel, Aber, Shoda, & Rodriguez, 2000). Toddlers were briefly separated from their mothers and children's coping strategies coded. Later, at age 5, their behavior was observed in a situation where they could delay gratification for a more valued reward. Children who used more distraction strategies during the maternal separation at the younger age were later able to delay longer.

Long-term stability in the ability to delay gratification and later attentional and emotional control has been reported (Mischel, 1983). In Mischel's work, the number of seconds delayed by preschool children while waiting for rewards that were physically present (a conflict situation) significantly predicted parent-reported attentiveness and ability to concentrate when the children were adolescents (Shoda, Mischel, & Peake, 1990). Children less able to delay in preschool were also reported as more likely to "go to pieces" under stress as teenagers, and to show lower academic competence in SAT scores, even when controlling for intelligence (Shoda et al., 1990). In follow-up studies, preschool delay predicted goal setting and self-regulatory abilities when the participants reached their early 30s (Ayduk et al., 2000), suggesting remarkable continuity in self-regulation.

In Caspi and Silva's (1995) study, preschool children characterized as "well adjusted" were described as flexible in orientation, and "capable of reserve and control when it was demanded of them" (p. 492). These children's flexibility of responsiveness may have been linked to greater executive attention and effortful control, as well as to higher ego resiliency (Block & Block, 1980) as described later. At age 18, children earlier identified as "well adjusted" by Caspi and Silva had high scores on Social Potency, including leadership and low social shyness. Interesting positive links have been found between activity level as assessed through actometers and children's performance on motor conflict tasks (Campbell, Eaton, & McKeen, 2002). Active 4- to 6-year-old children, especially the younger children, showed better performance on tasks that required them to inhibit a habitual response to perform a nonhabitual response. Their "paper highlights . . . the potentially functional, yet much neglected role that physical movement may play in young children's development" (p. 295).

Attention thus shows major developments over the first years of life, with a more self-regulative system added to a more reactive one (Rothbart, Posner, & Rosicky, 1994). As noted earlier, Caspi and Silva's (1995) Factor 1 (Lack of Control), including a combination of irritability and lack of self-regulation at age 3 to 4 years, was strongly related to negative emotionality at 18. Studies are now underway exploring contributions of both temperament and parent treatment to the development of self-control, as in Silverman and Ragusa's (1992) study predicting 4-year-old self-control from 24-month child temperament and maternal variables. Olson, Bates, and Bayles (1990) have also found relationships between parent-child interaction at 13 months and 2 years (but not at 6 months) and children's self-control at age 6.

Two Control Systems

Early individual differences in motor and emotional reactivity thus appear to be influenced by development of at least two temperament-related control systems: One is part of an emotional reaction (fear and behavioral inhibition), the other is more completely self-regulatory (attentional control), with the first system developing earlier than the second. This view is related to the theory of ego-control and ego-resiliency developed by Jean and Jack Block (Block & Block, 1980). The Blocks posited two control systems: (1) ego-control, involving fearful or inhibitory control over impulsive approach; and (2) ego-resiliency, defined by flexible adaptation to changing circumstances. The latter system is related to the temperamental characteristic of attentional effortful control, and research by Eisenberg et al. (1996) supports the predicted relationship between ego-resiliency and CBQ attentional control in kindergarten to third grade children. Resiliency was also related to social status and to teacher-reported socially appropriate behavior. Effects of self regulation were also significantly stronger for children who were high in negative emotionality (Eisenberg et al., 1996).

Eisenberg et al. (2004) have studied parent- and teacher-reported effortful control and impulsivity in relation to ego resiliency in children 4.5 to 8 years, with a 2-year follow-up. At both ages, effortful control and impulsivity predicted unique direct variance in resiliency and externalizing, and they also predicted internalizing problems indirectly, through resiliency. A moderating effect was also found on teacher-reported anger and the relation between effortful control, impulsivity, and externalizing. All relations held in predictions from Time 1 to Time 2, except the path from impulsivity to externalizing.

In the Blocks' theory, resiliency or flexibility contributes to the development of adaptation and mental health. As Block and Kremen (1996) put it:

> Adaptability in the long-term requires more than the replacement of unbridled impulsivity or *under-control,* with categorical, pervasive, rigid impulse control. This would be *over-control* of impulse, restriction of the spontaneity that provides the basis for creativity and interpersonal connection. Instead and ideally, *dynamic and resourceful regulation and equilibrium of impulses and inhibitions* must be achieved. It is this *modulation of ego-control* that we more formally mean by *the construct of ego-resiliency.* It can be said that the human goal is to be as under-controlled as possible and as over-controlled as necessary. (p. 351)

In the ego-control construct, when fear and its correlates develop into a relatively constricted life, approach tendencies are strongly opposed, and rigid functioning may result. Ego-resiliency, alternatively, is strengthened by a set of life experiences that build on capacities for both expression and control of impulses. Effortful control appears to provide an important underlying system for the development of ego resiliency, with impulsivity also related. The Blocks' theory stresses the importance of experience in the development of adaptation, with endogenous control systems allowing cultural influence on the behaviors, thoughts, and emotions that are controlled, as well as on the particular self-regulatory capacities and strategies used by the child.

Summary

Because temperament systems themselves develop, in this section we have presented a brief account of the early development of aspects of positive affect and approach, activity level, and distress in relation to attentional control. (For further information on the development of temperamental distress, see Rothbart & Bates, 1998.) Some of these developmental changes lead us to expect temperamental stability in only limited time windows. Early reactive systems of emotionality and approach become overlain by the development of at least two temperamentally linked control systems. The first, fearful inhibition, is linked to developments in fearfulness late in the 1st year of life. The second, effortful attentional control, develops across the preschool period and shows considerable stability. Another likely control mechanism for the support of socialization is the development of a social reward system, connected with children's desires to please and to refrain from hurting their parents and other persons, likely linked to temperamental affiliativeness. Any failure of these controls may be linked to the development of behavior problems. Because these temperamental systems are open to experience, appropriate socialization will be necessary for positive outcomes.

TEMPERAMENT AND THE DEVELOPMENT OF PERSONALITY

Life experiences influence connections between children's emotional reactions, their conceptual understanding of events, and their use of coping strategies to deal with these events. These mental habits are influenced by the child's temperament, expectancies, beliefs, values, goals, self-evaluations, appraisals, as well as understandings of the situation, the self, and/or others (Mischel & Ayduk, 2004; Teglasi & Epstein, 1998). In Mischel and Ayduk's (2004) model, individuals differ in the "ease of accessibility" of cognitive-affective units and in the organization among them.

Coping strategies, which may have been originally based on temperamental predispositions, become part of these units, and may be consolidated or inhibited depending in part on their consequences. Mischel and Ayduk (2004) give the example of individual differences in rejection sensitivity (RS):

> RS is a chronic processing disposition characterized by anxious expectations of rejection and a readiness to encode even ambiguous events in interpersonal situations [e.g., partner momentarily seems inattentive] as indicators of rejection that rapidly trigger automatic hot reactions [e.g., hostility-anger, withdrawal-depression, self-silencing]. Probably rooted in prior rejection experiences, these dynamics are readily activated when high RS people encounter interpersonal situations in which rejection is a possibility, triggering in them a sense of threat and foreboding. (Mischel & Ayduk, 2004, p. 118)

As RS becomes habitual, the person's attention may become quite narrowly focused on the likelihood of rejection, and defensive behaviors (e.g., anger or preventative rejection of the other) may develop to fend off the expected rejection. Different levels of generality of such a disposition are also possible. RS, for example, might extend to a wide range of human relationships, but the sensitivity may also be more specific so that only rejection by the child's peers, but not by adults, has been sensitized. RS may be so specific that it is limited to a single person in a single kind of situation. Mental habits are particularly likely to develop in connection with intimate relationships, as in the family, but they may be carried over to new relationships when more positive expectations and coping methods are lacking. Thus, the experience of early criticism and rejection, which may have its strongest impact on children prone to distress, can have long-term consequences for problems in development.

Mischel and Ayduk's (2004) analysis of RS describes an anxious or defensive set, but alternatively, children's experiences with others may be generally of acceptance. If so, the child will be less likely to be on guard about rejection or to show a defensive perceptual set. Instead, the child's attention can be directed more broadly, allowing greater conscious awareness of the state and needs of others. More distress prone, fearful, and irritable children may be more likely to develop such habits as RS, but after experiencing high levels of rejection, even a low distress-prone child would be likely to develop RS. Surgent and approaching children may also be more likely to expect acceptance, but even the more distress prone child may lack the conditions for becoming sensitive to rejection when others are not critical and rejecting. This model stresses temperament-environment interactions for a number of social-emotional processes that are likely to be differentiated by context, and we review some of these important interactions in the next section.

When repeatedly exercised, habitual activations of clusters of thoughts, emotions, and action tendencies to a particular stimulus or situation become very likely to occur and difficult to change. When mental habits involve distress, how might they be weakened or disconnections achieved in the habit? In Eastern traditions, this is done partly through diminishing the role of the ego so that situations can become less threatening to the self. Mental discipline and meditation also allow weakening of links between thoughts and emotions or thoughts and action tendencies. Western therapy similarly works through the clients' patterns of reaction, attempting to reconstruct previously consolidated patterns and provide new frameworks for meaning. Taking a developmental view, however, one would wish to give the child the kinds of experiences that will form favorable and noninjurious mental habits in the first place.

Socialization in the United States and other Western cultures often strongly emphasizes habits related to the individual or ego, promoting the pursuit of individual security, satisfaction of individual desires, and achievement of a positive self-concept. In other cultures, the shaping of the child's mental habits can be quite different. Mascolo, Fischer, and Li (2003) suggest, for example, that the biological mechanisms on which pride and shame are based are similar across cultures, while the responses can be shaped in quite different directions:

> For example, in American dyads, pride experiences develop as socialization agents praise children's accomplishments; shame experiences develop in social contexts in which children are made aware of their flawed identities. In contrast, in China, modest self-harmonization develops as parents efface their children's accomplishments while relatives and other significant others praise them; shame is a normative emotion that develops as parents use explicit shaming techniques to socialize filial piety in children. (pp. 401–402)

In this view, the biological equipment or temperament is similar across cultures, but the mental habits and representations of self, the world and other, will vary from culture to culture, and, we would add, context to context. By the time a child is a well-socialized member of the society, more biologically based temperament will have been shaped into a set of values, goals, and representations of the self and others that specify what is good and bad for the person. Even for children who are not well-socialized, values stressed by the culture may nevertheless have an effect. Children in the United States, for example, may still attempt to promote a positive self-concept, and pursue it though a delinquent peer group, even when the goals and values followed to achieve the positive concept may not be socially acceptable ones.

Shiner and her colleagues have recently been studying the continuity of personality from the period 8 to 12 to 20 years (Shiner, Masten, & Tellegen, 2002) and 30 years (Shiner, Masten, & Roberts, 2003). The 8 to 12 year variables, taken from parent and child interviews and teacher questionnaires, included measures of mastery motivation, academic conscientiousness, surgent engagement, agreeableness, and self-assurance versus anxious insecurity. Adaptation in childhood and adulthood was assessed by academic achievement, rule abiding conduct versus antisocial behavior, and social competence. Adult measures employed self- and parent-report questionnaires, including the Multidimensional Personality Questionnaire (MPQ; Tellegen, 1985), as well as data on academic achievement, rule compliance, social competence, job competence, and romantic competence.

Tellegen's self-report MPQ contains three broad personality factors: (1) Positive Emotionality (PEM) includes scales for well-being, achievement, social potency, and social closeness; (2) Negative Emotionality (NEM) includes scales for stress reaction, alienation, and aggression; and (3) Constraint (CON) includes scales for control, harm avoidance, and traditionalism. PEM was moderately predicted at age 20 by mastery motivation, surgent engagement, and self-assurance in middle childhood (Shiner et al., 2002). PEM was also related to concurrent social and romantic competencies at 20 years, but adult PEM was not linked to any of the childhood measures of adaptation. NEM at 20, however, was related to low adaptation in all areas in childhood, and to all concurrent adaptation measures except romantic competence. Even controlling for childhood personality, lower academic achievement and greater conduct problems in childhood continued to predict adult NEM.

Childhood mastery motivation and surgent engagement were also inversely related to NEM in adulthood. At age 20, CON was predicted by earlier lower self-assurance and higher academic competence, but when childhood personality was controlled, it was not related to childhood adaptation.

Shiner et al. (2002) suggest that positive emotionality may be more closely linked to current adaptation, whereas negative emotionality shows more continuity with earlier adaptation. In our section on adjustment, we note strong links between negative emotionality and psychopathology, both in childhood and adulthood. Negative emotionality is also particularly linked to behavior problems when effortful control is low (Caspi, 2000; Eisenberg, Fabes, Guthrie, & Reiser, 2000). Shiner et al. (2002) note that adults high on negative emotionality tend to be particularly upset by daily problems (Suls, Martin, & David, 1998). How might the development of mental habits contribute to these findings? First, habits related to distress may have involved attempts to decrease distress through mental processing, which in turn may have included repeatedly thinking about problematic events. Positive experiences would be less of a challenge and tend to be less intense, so they are likely to have been less rehearsed. When mental habits have been tied to difficult and painful situations in the past, one faces not only current problems, but also representations in memory that bring forward the mental habits linked to similar situations. Well-practiced associations may make negative affect, cognition, and action links stronger. Thus, early failure, for example, poor achievement in school, may create the possibility of long-term negative affect or neuroticism that extends to achievement situations later in life.

Caspi, Harrington et al. (2003) linked observations of 1000 children at age 3 to their self-reported personality at age 26 (96% of the original sample). Undercontrolled children (10% of the sample) had been temperamentally impulsive, restless, distractible, and negativistic at age 3; Confident children (28%) were friendly, eager, and somewhat impulsive; Inhibited children (8%) were fearful, reticent, and easily upset; Reserved children (15%) were timid but not extreme in shyness; Well-adjusted children (40%) appeared to be capable of self-control, adequately self-confident, and did not become upset during testing. At age 26, previously Undercontrolled children were higher in negative emotionality, more alienated, and subject to stress reactions. They also tended to follow a traditional morality. Formerly Inhibited and Reserved children were high in harm avoid-

ance, low in social potency (less vigorous, dynamic, forceful), and low in achievement. Both previously Undercontrolled and Confident children were low in harm avoidance. Confident children were high on social potency as adults; Inhibited children were high in Constraint and low in Positive Emotionality.

Caspi, Harrington, et al.'s (2003) findings provide evidence that the temperament of the child truly provides the core of aspects of the developing personality. Undercontrolled children, who combined extraversion/surgency, negative affect, and low attentional control at age 3, showed neurotic and alienated tendencies as adults. Confident extraverted children were confident and unfearful as adults. More shy and fearful Inhibited and Reserved children maintained their caution and harm avoidance into adulthood and were low in social potency, whereas the more extreme Inhibited children were also high in Constraint (a mixture of fearfulness and self-control) and low in Positive Emotionality and social support. The most interesting aspect of the results, however, goes beyond temperament to touch on alienation, traditional values, and social support.

Kubzansky, Martin, and Buka (2004) related children's personality/temperament at age 7 as derived from observer ratings to self ratings at age 35. Children's behavioral inhibition did not predict adult functioning, but their anger proneness (Distress) predicted adult Hostility/Anger, and inappropriate interpersonal self-regulation in childhood predicted adult Interpersonal Sensitivity. Strong relations were found between child Distress Proneness and adult somatization, another very intriguing finding. Overall, we expect that these studies will inspire more contributions to the longitudinal literature related to these variables in the future.

TEMPERAMENT AND ADJUSTMENT

In the preceding section, devoted to temperament and personality, we have begun to consider temperament and some aspects of adjustment. In this section, we consider in more detail theoretical models and research findings relating temperament to individual differences in adjustment. By *adjustment* we mean not only psychopathology but also positive behaviors including the development of conscience. We are more interested in dimensions of adjustment than in categorical diagnostic systems, and think of adjustment as adaptation to particular contexts. A child may carry temperament traits from one context to another, but their implications for adjustment will depend on the specific context and expectations of the parent, peer, or teacher (Chess & Thomas, 1984; Lerner & Lerner, 1994), in connection with experiences and adaptations to specific situations as suggested in the mental habits model described previously.

Does Temperament Predict Adjustment?

Meaningful patterns of relationship exist between constructs of temperament and constructs of adjustment in the development of children. This was clear by the late 1980s (Bates, 1989a) and has become more firmly established since then, with many studies showing temperament links with psychopathology (e.g., see reviews by Eisenberg et al., 2000; Lonigan, Vasey, Phillips, & Hazen, 2004; Rothbart & Bates, 1998; Rothbart & Posner, in press; Sanson, Hemphill, & Smart, 2004; Wachs & Bates, 2001). In these studies, temperament and adjustment have been measured in a variety of ways, including parent reports, teacher reports, and direct observation, with adjustment assessed at home and at school, using both cross-sectional and longitudinal designs. In this review, we focus primarily on patterns of relations that indicate a differentiated view of how temperament might contribute to the child's adjustment. We mention two methodological and conceptual issues before describing findings.

The issue of measurement "contamination" (Sanson, Prior, and Kyrios, 1990) has been of continuing interest to researchers. Sanson et al. argued that relations observed between a temperament measure and an adjustment measure might be an artifact of content overlap between the two supposedly distinct measures. Item content in a temperament scale, for example, might concern behaviors that are the same as those in the measure of psychopathology or vice versa. Bates (1990) argued that adjustment and temperament should actually have some conceptual overlap. The child's adjustment could reflect a component of temperament, and psychopathology could be, at least in part, an extreme point on a temperament dimension. For theoretical reasons, however, we tend to regard temperament and adjustment as separate concepts.

Temperament characteristics may also be contributors to adjustment rather than equivalent to adjustment. This possibility can be supported, if studies show that temperament-adjustment links exist even after correcting for content overlap, or if studies show links between temperament and adjustment that transcend the simple content overlap model. Studies where expert raters and psychometric principles are used to remove items with overlapping content do demonstrate links between tem-

perament and psychopathology even after "decontamination" (Lemery, Essex, & Smider, 2002; Lengua, West, & Sandler, 1998; Oldehinkel, Hartman, de Winter, Veenstra, & Ormel, 2004). The second way of supporting a distinction between temperament and adjustment is shown by a variety of studies. One study, for example, found that therapy led to changes in parents' descriptions of their children's psychopathology but not their temperament (Sheeber, 1995). Other studies address the question of the developmental processes through which temperament and adjustment are related, and these are discussed after considering the second methodological issue.

The second methodological issue is source bias. As we have argued, caregivers' reports do show validity. However, when a conceptual relation is inferred between two constructs measured via the same source, for example, parents, the possibility exists that relations are due to preconceptions in the minds of the informant rather than the behavior of the subject. Bates and Bayles (1984) have nevertheless argued (on the basis of many different tests of subjective and objective components in parents' perceptions of their children) that measures of subjective bias do not account for more of the variance than measures of objective phenomena. In addition, as is detailed later, the different measures are related to one another within and across time in a differentiated pattern, for example, with early novelty distress predicting later novelty distress or internalizing problems more than externalizing problems. Recent studies have also shown credible levels of objectivity in caregivers' descriptions of children's temperament, even when subjective factors, such as depression, play some role (e.g., Bishop et al., 2003; Forman et al., 2003). Thus, source biases are not as powerful as one might have feared, and caregivers perceive children's behavioral traits in relatively differentiated rather than global or unitary ways. This brings us to the central question: How does temperament predict adjustment?

Temperament might be involved in the development of behavior problems in a number of ways. Clark, Watson, and Mineka (1994) listed four ways in which mood and anxiety disorders might be related to personality characteristics (also see Shiner & Caspi, 2003):

1. A *vulnerability model,* where there is a predisposition to the development of disorders (e.g., in response to stressors)
2. The *pathoplasty model,* a variant of vulnerability in which personality shapes the course of a disorder

(e.g., by producing an environment that maintains the disorder)

3. The *scar hypothesis,* in which a disorder produces enduring changes in personality (e.g., increased levels of insecurity)

4. The *spectrum or continuity hypothesis,* where the psychopathological condition is an extreme manifestation of the underlying personality trait

Clark et al. (1994) point out that the four models need not be mutually exclusive. These models may also extend to behavioral disorders, and to positive outcomes as in:

1. A *protective model,* where the person is predisposed to deal adequately with challenging situations

2. The *boost from positive adaptation model,* in which the experience of overcoming challenge strengthens feelings of optimism and well-being

3. The *spectrum or continuity model,* in which the positive outcome is itself the manifestation of an underlying set of characteristics, such as a positive outlook on experience

These and other possible processes linking temperament, risk conditions, and psychopathology are listed in Table 3.4. Generally, available evidence does not allow for a choice among the models, but, in recent years, behavioral and molecular genetics research is offering the promise of choices (e.g., Eaves, Silberg, & Erkanli, 2003).

Direct Linkage

Most studies of the relations between temperament and adjustment have considered direct, linear effects, where a particular temperament trait contributes to the development of an adjustment pattern. Additive effects of multiple temperament traits are also possible, as when two or more temperament traits linearly increase the risk of some disorder, such as negative affectivity and lack of impulse control predicting behavior problems (Eisenberg et al., 1996), both negative emotionality and fearfulness predicting levels of young boys' internalizing problems (Gilliom & Shaw, 2004), or both impulsivity and negative emotionality associated with adolescents' antisocial behavior (Stice & Gonzales, 1998).

In evaluating direct linkage models, studies considering multiple temperament traits in relation to multiple dimensions of adjustment are critical. According to current theories of psychopathology, individual differences

in specific temperament-related brain circuits are linked to specific forms of motivation or functioning (Bates et al., 1994; Clark et al., 1994; Fowles, 1994; Gray, 1991; MacDonald, 1988; Rothbart, Derryberry, et al., 1994; Rothbart & Posner, in press), as discussed earlier. There is some, but not complete, agreement on the specific systems and how they map onto behavioral traits. In previous sections, we discussed systems controlling inhibition to novelty and conditioned signals of punishment and nonreward, as well as unconditioned fear, positive affectivity and reward seeking, sensitivity to social rewards, and attentional control. We now use these systems as general constructs to organize the evidence on temperament and adjustment. At this time, only a limited number of studies permit a differentiated view of temperament-adjustment linkages, and none of the studies are methodologically strong enough to stand alone in support or rejection of a psychobiological systems model. However, enough convergence exists that we are confident about the broad outlines of direct linkage models.

Theoretical Expectations

Direct linkage models will become more detailed as neurobehavioral systems are better understood and as measures of adjustment are meaningfully differentiated. For now, a researcher would expect early irritability, or general tendencies toward negative affect, to predict a wide variety of adaptive difficulties, including internalizing, or anxiety problems, and externalizing, or conduct problems, as well as deficits in positive social competencies. As measures of irritability are more finely differentiated, however, more clearly defined pathways to later adjustment may be identified. For example, sensitivity to minor aversive stimuli might predispose a child to both internalizing (e.g., whining and withdrawal) and externalizing (e.g., reactive aggression) behavior problems, whereas irritability to frustration of reward or of stimulation-seeking behavior (Rothbart, Derryberry, et al., 1994) would likely pertain more to externalizing tendencies than to internalizing ones.

Temperamental tendencies toward fearfulness in novel or potentially punishing situations should predict internalizing-type adjustments most directly, although they may also serve to predict externalizing problems in inverse or interactive ways, as discussed later. A finer differentiation of fearfulness will ultimately be important for predicting different kinds of internalizing adjustment. For example, separation distress may differ in some ways from novelty fear (see Fowles's, 1994, dis-

TABLE 3.4   Processes That May Link Temperament and Adjustment

Processes	Examples
A. Direct, Linear Effects	
1. Temperament extreme constitutes psychopathology or positive adaptation.	Extreme shyness, Attention-Deficit/Hyperactivity Disorder
	High attentional control
2. Temperament extreme predisposes to a closely related condition.	Fearfulness → Anxiety Disorder, Agoraphobia/Panic Disorder
	High attentional control → good social adjustment
3. Temperament characteristics affect particular symptomatology of a disorder.	Anxiety versus hopelessness in depression
B. Indirect, Linear Effects	
1. Temperament structures the immediate environment, which then influences development of positive adjustment or psychopathology.	High stimulation seeking → leaving home early, marrying poorly
	High attentional control → planning → good school adjustment
2. Temperament biases others to behave in ways that provide experiences leading to risk factors, pathology, or more positive outcome.	High positive affect → attention from caregivers in institutional situations
	Infant irritability → coercive cycles in parent-child interactions
3. Temperament biases processing of information about self and others, predisposing to cognitively based psychopathology or positive adjustment.	Negative affectivity → negatively biased social information processing → aggression
	Positive affectivity → positively biased social information processing → optimism about others
C. Temperament × Environment Interactions	
1. Temperament buffers against risk factors or stressors.	Fear protecting against aggression or criminal socialization
	Positive affect protecting against peer or parent rejection
2. Temperament heightens response to event.	Negative affectivity augmenting response to stress, increasing risk of depression or likelihood of post-traumatic stress disorder
	Attentional orienting augmenting response to teachers' instructions.
D. Temperament × Temperament Interactions	
1. Self-regulation of a temperament extreme qualitatively changes its expression.	High surgency with nonregulation → Attention-Deficit/Hyperactivity Disorder, whereas same trait with good regulation → high competence
	High negative emotionality with low attentional control → sensitization and increasing anxiety, whereas negative emotionality plus high attentional control → no maladjustment
2. One temperament trait protects against risk consequences of another temperament-based trait.	Fearfulness or higher attentional control protecting against impulsivity
E. Miscellaneous	
1. Different temperament characteristics may predispose to similar outcomes.	Shyness, impulsivity, lack of affiliativeness, and negativity may each predispose to development of social isolation
2. Temperament or personality may be shaped by psychopathological disorder.	Anxiety Disorder → increased dependency

Source: Adapted from "Temperament, Attention, and Developmental Psychopathology" (pp. 315–340), by M. K. Rothbart, M. I. Posner, and K. Hershey, in *Manual of Developmental Psychopathology*, Vol. 1, D. Cicchetti and J. D. Cohen (Eds.), 1995, New York: Wiley. Some of the wording and examples have been changed. Note that many of the examples are theoretically plausible, but not based on empirical evidence.

cussion of theories placing separation fear in a panic or fight/flight brain system and novelty fear in a behavioral inhibition system, and see our sections on Panksepp's, 1998, psychobiological theory).

Positive affectivity or surgency, involving activity, stimulation seeking, assertiveness, and possibly some

aspects of manageability, should be involved more closely in externalizing than in internalizing problems, except that depression has a strong component of low positive affectivity (Tellegen, 1985). However, a trait of prosocial tendency, affiliation and agreeableness, perhaps involving sensitivity to social rewards (MacDonald, 1992), might prove separable from the more general extraversion or surgency (positive affectivity) system, as Rothbart and Victor's (2004) findings suggest. Low levels of prosocial interest and concern would be expected to be associated with the development of externalizing and not internalizing problems, and perhaps with the failure to acquire positive social competencies independent of behavioral problems.

Finally, systems controlling attention, especially the executive attention system described earlier, would be expected to be related to both externalizing and internalizing, but to have more to do with externalizing problems than with internalizing ones. As with fear systems, attentional control should also play an additive or interactive role with other temperament characteristics. In addition, a well-functioning set of attentional controls is likely to be linked to more positive developmental outcomes.

Empirical Findings of Direct Linkage

A number of studies provide support for the models just described. In general, predictive relations between temperament and adjustment are of modest to moderate size. Correlations between infancy measures and adjustment in late preschool and middle childhood tend to be smaller, and those between preschool or middle childhood and later periods larger. Even though the correlations may be modest to moderate in size, they have been well replicated, and they are clearly not chance findings. Moreover, the size of the relations is usually not less than and sometimes greater than predictions from other theoretically linked variables, such as parenting quality. Lytton (1995), for example, performed a meta-analysis of studies predicting conduct disorder (a diagnosis of extreme externalizing problems) and criminality, finding child temperament variables to be the single most powerful predictor of the outcomes, even in comparison with qualities of parenting.

In the Bloomington Longitudinal Study (BLS), infancy and toddlerhood ICQ temperamental difficultness (frequent and intense negative affect and attention demanding) predicted later externalizing and internalizing problems as seen in the mother-child relationship, from the preschool to the middle-childhood periods (Bates & Bayles, 1988; Bates, Bayles, Bennett, Ridge, & Brown, 1991; Bates, Maslin, & Frankel, 1985; Lee & Bates, 1985). Early negative reactivity to novel situations (unadaptability) predicted less consistently, but when it did, it predicted internalizing problems more than external-

izing problems. Early resistance to control (perhaps akin to the manageability dimension of Hagekull, 1989, and perhaps at least partly related to the construct of effortful control) predicted externalizing problems more than internalizing problems. This was also found in predicting externalizing problems at school in both the BLS and a separate longitudinal study, the Child Development Project (CDP; Bates, Pettit, Dodge, & Ridge, 1998).

In a structural modeling analysis of CDP data, dealing with the overlap in externalizing and internalizing symptoms, Keiley, Lofthouse, Bates, Dodge, and Pettit (2003) separated mother and teacher reports of behavior problems across 5 to 14 years into pure externalizing, pure internalizing, and covarying factors, and then considered early childhood predictors of each of these factors. Resistant temperament (unmanageability) predicted the pure factors of mother- and teacher-rated externalizing problems, but not the pure internalizing factors. Unadaptable temperament (novelty distress) predicted positively both mother and teacher pure internalizing factors, and to a lesser degree, and *negatively,* the pure mother and teacher externalizing factors. That is, unadaptable temperament predicted higher levels of internalizing problems and, less strongly, lower levels of externalizing problems. Although a disposition to fearfulness would not necessarily constrain dispositions to aggressive and uncooperative behaviors, it is intuitively reasonable that children who are fearful and sensitive to potential punishment would be likely to inhibit externalizing behavior (Bates, Pettit, & Dodge, 1995). And finally, difficult temperament (negative emotionality and demandingness) predicted, in this multivariate context, none of the pure factors, but only the covarying externalizing plus internalizing factor in mothers' reports.

These predictions are all consistent with models where temperament extremes either constitute pathology dimensions or predispose to risk for these conditions. The linkages are of modest size, but they obtain from early in life, and are not eliminated by the inclusion of family and parenting characteristics in prediction, so they are not simply artifacts of family functioning. Also supporting the general pattern, Gilliom and Shaw (2004) found that, in a sample of preschool-age boys from low-income families, high levels of negative emotionality were associated with initial levels of both externalizing and internalizing problems, whereas high levels of fearfulness were associated with decreases in externalizing problems over time. High initial levels of internalizing problems were associated with increases in internalizing problems over time. In partial contrast, Russell, Hart, Robinson, and Olsen (2003) found that negative emotionality as measured by parent report on the EAS did not predict preschoolers' adjustment as rated by teachers. However, EAS shyness was related to both lower prosocial behavior and lower aggressive behavior at preschool.

Lemery et al. (2002) also provide support for a differential linkage model. Composited mother CBQ ratings of child temperament at 3 and 4 years predicted both mother and father reports of behavior problem symptoms at age 5, in a differentiated pattern. Whether or not the temperament scales were "purified" by removing items overlapping with preschool-age behavior problems, early anger predicted later externalizing problems more strongly than it predicted later internalizing problems, early fear and sadness predicted later internalizing problems more strongly than they predicted later externalizing problems, and early inhibitory control inversely predicted later externalizing or Attention-Deficit/Hyperactivity Disorder (ADHD) problems more strongly than it predicted later internalizing problems.

The Dunedin Longitudinal Study (Caspi & Silva, 1995), mentioned previously in the context of personality development, provides further support and extends measures of temperament from parent to experimenter ratings. Ratings based on the child's behavior during testing sessions, aggregated from 3 and 5 years, predicted aggregated ratings of parents and teachers in late childhood (over ages 9 and 11) and early adolescence (over ages 13 and 15). Early approach (outgoing responses to strangers and test materials—the inverse of inhibition) predicted, inversely, internalizing problems better than externalizing problems for boys. It did not predict either kind of problem for girls. Early sluggishness (a factor combining lack of positive affect, passivity, and wariness/withdrawal from novelty) predicted later internalizing and externalizing problems for girls, but not boys, as well as the relative absence of positive competencies for both girls and boys. It is not clear how approach and sluggishness emerged separately from a factor analysis describing similar dimensions, but whatever the underlying distinction between the two dimensions, they predicted outcomes differently for the two genders. A third temperament dimension, combining lack of control, irritability, and distractibility (corresponding approximately to the resistance to control or manageability factors from parent-report questionnaires), predicted, for both genders, externalizing prob-

lems more strongly than internalizing problems or positive competencies. The discovery of differentiated patterns in studies such as the BLS, CDP, and Dunedin study has occurred despite the tendency for externalizing and internalizing adjustment scores to be somewhat correlated with each other, making the pattern all the more remarkable.

In other recent studies, Morris et al. (2002) found that irritable temperament was positively associated with first and second graders' externalizing and internalizing problems equally, whereas effortful control was negatively associated with externalizing more strongly than internalizing problems. Patterson and Sanson (1999) found that 5-year-olds' low persistence (attentive and on-task) was associated with externalizing, whereas low approach to people and novel objects was associated with internalizing problems. Lengua, Wolchik, Sandler, and West (2000) found 9- to 12-year-old impulsivity (CBQ) to be associated with conduct problems and not with depression and positive emotionality Dimensions of Temperament Survey (DOTS) to be negatively associated with depression, an association stronger than with conduct problems. In partial contrast to the general pattern, however, Lengua et al. also reported that negative emotionality (DOTS) was associated with depressive symptoms more strongly than with conduct problem symptoms.

Mun, Fitzgerald, von Eye, Puttler, and Zucker (2001), also using the DOTS, reported that withdrawal tendencies at 3 to 5 years were more strongly predictive of internalizing than externalizing problems 3 years later. Their negative emotional reactivity scale also failed to confirm the general pattern of roughly equal associations with both externalizing and internalizing problems, instead predicting externalizing more strongly than internalizing problems. Murphy, Shepard, Eisenberg, and Fabes (2004) found that both negative emotionality and self-regulation (whether assessed by teacher or parent questionnaires) in middle childhood predicted social competence and behavior problems in early adolescence as rated by teacher or parent reports. And Eisenberg et al. (2001) found that anger, impulsivity, and low self-regulation (observed and parent/teacher-rated) were more strongly associated with externalizing problems (parent/teacher-rated), whereas sadness and low impulsivity were more strongly related to internalizing problems.

Also notable is the study by Rothbart, Ahadi, et al. (1994). Temperamental negative affectivity (CBQ) was concurrently associated with a full range of social traits in 6- to 7-year-olds, including aggressiveness, guilt, help seeking, and negativity (e.g., in response to suggestion of a new activity). However, subcomponents of the general negative affect factor were associated with the social traits in a more differentiated way: Fear and sadness were more related to traits such as empathy and anger, whereas discomfort was more related to aggression and help seeking. A small subsample in the Rothbart, Ahadi, et al. (1994) sample had been tested in the laboratory as infants. Temperament as assessed in the laboratory 5 to 6 years earlier showed a somewhat similar pattern of linkage with the social behavior outcomes: Infant laboratory activity (again, usually regarded as part of surgency or positive affectivity) predicted aggressiveness and negativity, as did early smiling (another component of surgency); infant anger/frustration predicted both higher aggressiveness and help seeking; fear predicted lower levels of aggressiveness and higher levels of empathy and guilt/shame. A number of other studies also deserve mention for addressing the question of differentiated linkages between temperament and adjustment, including Biederman et al. (1990); Guerin, Gottfried, Oliver, and Thomas (1994); Hagekull (1994); Hegvik et al. (1982); McClowry et al. (1993); Rende (1993); Teglasi and MacMahon (1990); and Wertlieb, Weigel, Springer, and Feldstein (1987). These studies considered clinical as well as community samples of children at different ages and in different countries. In broad overview, their findings converge with the general, differential linkage pattern.

Several additional studies whose designs do not permit a full test of the differential linkage model because they lack a full range of temperament or adjustment variables can be interpreted as roughly conforming to the pattern described here. Among a number of examples, Prior, Smart, Sanson, and Oberklaid (2000) found that children who were stable in shyness had a higher likelihood of being diagnosed with an anxiety disorder in adolescence. Eisenberg et al. (1996) found correlations between teacher and parent ratings of emotional and behavioral low self-regulation, lower baseline heart rate, and acting-out behavior problems. Keane and Calkins (2004) measured self-regulation differences in toddlers by suppression of heart-rate variability associated with respiration, which theoretically reflects vagal regulation and indexes sustained attention and active coping. Low vagal regulation in challenging tasks at age 2 years predicted high levels of mother-rated externalizing behavior and emotional negativity and lability at age

4. In another longitudinal study with a low-income Pittsburgh sample, Keenan and Shaw (1994) found that an ICQ composite of difficultness and resistance to control predicted laboratory measures of aggression in 18-month-old boys, but not girls. Also, in a low-income Pittsburgh sample restricted to only boys, Shaw, Gilliom, Ingoldsby, and Nagin (2003) showed that a persistently high trajectory of conduct problems across ages 2 to 8 years was predicted by fearlessness in the laboratory at age 2.

In the Quebec longitudinal study, Vitaro, Brendgen, and Tremblay (2002) studied the antecedents of extreme groups of reactively aggressive, proactively aggressive, combined reactive and proactive, or nonaggressive children at age 11 and 12. Reactive aggression involves response to provocations and anger, whereas proactive aggression involves less negative emotion and more concern with material and social gain. Vitaro et al. (2002) found that temperament at age 6 (parent report on the DOTS) predicted in ways at least partly consistent with the differential linkage model. Reactively aggressive children were lower on attention span, higher on distractability, and more motorically active and intense in responses than both nonaggressive and proactively aggressive children. However, both reactively and proactively aggressive children were more approaching and adaptable to novelty than the nonaggressive group: Note that our interpretation here, based on the DOTS scoring instructions (by R. Lerner, dated May 7, 1982), is opposite to Vitaro et al.'s (2002), who assumed that the scale signified withdrawal rather than approach. Thus, both forms of aggression can be seen as reflecting consistency with temperamental roots. Proactively aggressive children were temperamentally similar to nonaggressive children, except for being more outgoing, whereas reactively aggressive children, consonant with the dysregulated, emotional nature of their aggression, had been, in addition to highly outgoing, also more active, intense, and less attentive or well-regulated.

The focus of this section has been primarily on psychopathology or negative adjustment, consistent with the emphasis of the literature. However, positive adjustment (including empathy, conscience, intelligence, self-regulation, resiliency, and cooperation) is an area of at least equal importance in development. In our sections on Psychobiological Approaches and Temperament and Development, we have presented additional evidence on such constructs (also see the Temperament and Attachment section in Rothbart & Bates, 1998). Conceptually, there are two ways in which positive and negative adjustment can be distinguished. The first one is by the positive or negative valence of the trait or behaviors (e.g., cooperative versus defiant). More interesting, the second is whether a given prosocial construct reflects chiefly the inverse of a negative adjustment trait (e.g., in the relation between cooperation and aggressive-disruptive behavior problems), or whether the construct is substantially independent of standard negative adjustment items. This question has only occasionally been addressed (e.g., Bates et al., 1991). Future research may discover how temperament antecedents of positive and negative adjustment components vary, in ways paralleling the differentiation between internalizing and externalizing (see also discussion by Rothbart, 1989b, and Rothbart and Hwang, 2005, on the development of mastery motivation). Nevertheless, there is evidence that measures of positive adjustment are related to temperament in understandable ways. One key example is the work on moral development by Kochanska (1997). For example, Kochanska and Knaack (2003) found that effortful control, assessed in laboratory tasks at ages 2 and 3, predicted more advanced conscience development at age 4, indexed by both laboratory tasks and child self-report, and fewer mother-reported externalizing behaviors at age 6.

Summary

In summary, the literature on temperament and adjustment supports a direct linkage model. With a few exceptions, specific temperament dimensions also relate in a differentiated way to internalizing and externalizing adjustments, with early inhibition relating more to later internalizing, and early unmanageability relating more to later externalizing, and with early negative affect relating to both outcomes. Positive adjustment dimensions are not as clearly articulated, nor measured often enough to demonstrate differential linkages at this point.

Evidence at this point also does not yet answer the question of which of the direct linkage models listed in Table 3.4 applies best to the observed relations between temperament and adjustment. Given generally modest predictive relations, we would favor a vulnerability or predisposition model; a spectrum/continuity model might also apply. However, early individual differences likely become transformed, via developmental processes that include experience, into the more complex forms of adjustment in later years, and these processes must shape adjustment outcomes. Many child temperament researchers seem to agree with Thomas, Chess, and Birth (1968) that temperament in itself does not constitute a negative versus positive adjustment, but that it

conditions developmental processes that determine adjustment. This concept fits a vulnerability model better than a simpler continuity (or spectrum) model.

Empirical and Theoretical Limits on Continuity

As noted, predictive correlations tend to be modest to moderate in size, especially when temperament is assessed in early life. This is likely due to several factors. Measurement error is almost always a problem, but when power is sufficient, it can be controlled in structural models. However, even with such a statistical control for measurement error, there will be limited predictive power (e.g., see Keiley et al., 2003). Limited predictiveness can also occur because of conceptual limitations in the measure of either temperament or adjustment. For example, the sample of situations used in a set of items may not be sufficient to capture the relevant construct. One particular problem is accounting for the lower levels of prediction from temperament at home to adjustment at school. This is sometimes ascribed to parental rating biases, but many differences in incentive conditions are present at home and school, and even if a child's temperament is measured accurately, the child's expression of that temperament could differ in the two settings. For example, the same child could be resistant and angry with the mother and yet inhibited and adequately compliant at school, a pattern seen empirically by Dumas and LaFreniere (1993) and clinically in our treatment program for young children with oppositional behavior problems. It is not that such a child is inconsistent in temperament, but rather that a child with a disposition toward anxiety can be quite uncooperative and disruptive in familiar situations and more reserved in the highly stimulating and more novel school setting. Alternatively, a child with an anxiety-prone temperament could be angry as a way to reduce anxiety aroused in a chaotically stressful home, by gaining a sense of control, and be calm in the well-ordered, supportive school environment. The habit model described earlier (linking thoughts, emotions, and actions) allows for different experiences across situations that differ in the constraints they offer for temperament expression and for different histories of experience that may be relatively idiosyncratic.

Another factor in limiting prediction is that temperament itself can change in the course of development, as a result of either experience or later-emerging traits such as attentional control. It remains an interesting possibility that we may discover laws to account for changes in temperament. Asendorpf (1994) found that the adaptive behavior of shy children who were highly intelligent improved more over development than that of shy children who were less intelligent. Fox et al. (2001) found that negatively reactive infants, at high risk for behavioral inhibition, were more likely to show continuous behavioral inhibition across age 14 months to 4 years if they also showed right frontal EEG asymmetry (indicating in another way a strong disposition to negative affect), and they were also more likely to be continuously inhibited if they were exclusively in the care of their parents rather than receiving some nonparental care.

It is also possible that the limited size of prediction from temperament to adjustment is due to the action of other major factors in development such as parenting, family stress, or school environment. In other words, temperament might be linked to adjustment through one of the indirect processes listed in Table 3.4. These include mediator models, as when a child's negative temperament influences negative parenting, which, in turn, plays the dominant role in producing the child's aggressive behavior problems, or moderator models, as when a child's negative temperament has one implication for development of adjustment in the context of negative parenting and another in the context of positive parenting. We next consider such processes, most sharply focusing on temperament × environment moderator models.

Moderated Linkage

Rothbart and Bates (1998) discussed two possible indirect processes by which temperament and adjustment could be related. The first was mediated linkage in which temperament influences transactions with the environment, which, in turn, shape the child's developing adjustment. For example, a child's negative emotional reactivity might evoke hostile responses from caregivers, which build habitual frustration and hostility in the child. Research showing such temperament-parenting-adjustment processes was generally lacking at the time the 1998 chapter was prepared, especially longitudinal research, and relatively few studies have explored this kind of process in the intervening years. There have been some careful evaluations of mediation between one temperament trait and another temperament trait in accounting for adjustment, such as the structural modeling work of Eisenberg and her colleagues (Eisenberg et al., 2000; Eisenberg, Guthrie, et al., 2000). However, space does not permit review of this work.

The second indirect process we considered was moderated linkage in which we are primarily interested in how temperament and a feature of the environment might interact in the development of adjustment. For example, a child with high temperamental negative emotionality exposed to stress might be more likely to develop behavior problems than a less reactive child. In 1998, there were more relevant studies on moderated than mediated linkage, and, subsequently, there has been a striking growth in studies of moderated linkage. This direction in research is especially exciting because developmental theory discussed in the early sections of this chapter has emphasized the likelihood of temperament-environment interaction. Although these connections have been posited for decades, they are just now beginning to take empirical shape.

Rothbart and Bates (1998) identified three subtopics of moderated linkage: temperament × environment interactions, temperament × temperament interactions, and temperament × gender interactions. In recent years, the greatest empirical growth has occurred in the first of these, temperament × environment interaction. Temperament × temperament interaction findings are more slowly growing, and would be worth review if space were available. Most notably, Eisenberg's research team and others have shown that relations between effortful control and externalizing and prosocial behavior are stronger for children high in negative emotionality than for children low in negative emotionality (Belsky, Friedman, & Hsieh, 2001; Diener & Kim, 2004; Eisenberg, Fabes, et al., 2000; Eisenberg, Guthrie et al., 2000; Stifter, Spinrad, & Braungart-Rieker, 1999).

Temperament × gender interactions were somewhat numerous as of the time of the Rothbart and Bates (1998) chapter and have continued to accumulate at a moderate pace. However, our previous impression of a nonsystematic pattern of temperament × gender findings appears to still hold. So, to allow more space for discussing the more dynamic temperament × environment interaction literature, we leave the temperament × gender findings for another review. In the following, we review recent temperament × environment interaction findings extensively. In addition to Rothbart and Bates (1998), consider other reviews by Bates and McFadyen-Ketchum (2001); Gallagher (2002); Putnam, Sanson, and Rothbart (2002); and Sanson et al. (2004). Wills, Sandy, Yaeger, and Shinar (2001) have also reviewed a substantial portion of the literature in connection with an empirical report.

Researchers sometimes focus on how a temperament trait's association with adjustment is moderated by an environmental characteristic, as in parental hostility moderating the relation between child negative emotionality and adjustment. They also focus on how an environmental feature is moderated by the child's temperament, as in self-regulation tendencies moderating the adjustment implications of family stress. Choice between perspectives reflects the basic interests of the researchers, but an interaction from one perspective could often have also been described from the other perspective, although the results may not always be identical.

A bigger methodological challenge, however, is simply to find the interaction effect. Nonexperimental studies typically have to deal with correlated predictor and moderator variables, problems in the joint distributions of the variables, and insufficient statistical power for detecting effects (McClelland & Judd, 1993; Stoolmiller, 2001; Wachs & Plomin, 1991). Sometimes, interaction effects may be present but not found by statistical tests or statistically significant effects may be sample-specific or spurious. For these reasons, we focus especially on effects that have been replicated in some fashion. Because research in our area so seldom exactly repeats the methods of even the most fundamental studies, it is too much to require full replication. However, the literature is beginning to show some interesting patterns.

We also describe a few failures to find interaction effects, especially when they might constitute nonreplications of a previously found pattern. Given the assumed statistical bias against finding possible interaction effects, we focus mostly on positive findings. Many, but not all, consider the interaction of temperament and environment in the context of the main effects, and not all control for these effects by entering an interaction term in a multiple regression equation following entry of the main effects terms. We concentrate more on the substantive patterns of results than on methodological features (see Bates & McFadyen-Ketchum, 2001, for more discussion of methods).

Most of the emerging literature concerns three kinds of temperament trait: Those related to (a) lack of self-regulation, including low effortful control, unmanageability, and resistance to control, and probably related to the Big Five personality dimensions of agreeableness and conscientiousness; (b) negative emotional reactivity, sometimes called difficult temperament; and (c) novelty distress, fear, or unadaptability. Depending on how they are assessed, these constructs often partially overlap with one another, but for conceptual purposes, they are separated here. As developmental scientists, we are especially drawn to studies showing temperament × environment interaction effects in longitudinal studies of development of adjustment, but some useful cross-sectional findings have also emerged.

Self-Regulation × Environment

Temperamental tendencies toward dysregulation, such as impulsivity or resistance to control, may be rooted not only in underdeveloped effortful control systems, but also in the behavioral approach system, or surgency, as we have previously discussed. Such tendencies have shown direct associations with adjustment, especially with externalizing problems, as also discussed. At least twenty recent studies show traits in this broad domain interacting with characteristics of the rearing environment in the development of adjustment, and most of these consider the effects of temperament and parenting.

One theme emerging across studies is that dysregulation traits are more highly associated with problem behavior when parenting is negative or harsh rather than gentle. Calkins (2002) found that 18-month-old children high on distress and resistance in frustrating situations were likely to be high on angry and aggressive behavior in similar situations at 24 months when their mothers were low in positive parenting, but not when their mothers were highly positive. Rubin, Burgess, Dwyer, and Hastings (2003) measured children's self-regulation in laboratory tasks at age 2 and mother reports on the TBAQ at age 2. They also measured intrusive and hostile mothering in a snack situation and by mother report. Poor child self-regulation predicted mother-reported externalizing behavior problems at age 4 to a greater extent for children who at age 2 received higher levels of intrusive and hostile mothering. This pattern was found cross-sectionally at age 2 in the same study, but only for boys (Rubin, Hastings, Chen, Stewart, & McNichol, 1998).

Other cross-sectional examples of the pattern include the finding that positive parenting as measured by interview and incidental observations mattered more for temperamentally unmanageable children's preschool adjustment than for less resistant children (Bates, Viken, & Williams, 2003). Morris et al. (2002) found that children rated by their mothers as low in effortful control (CBQ) showed an especially strong relationship between mother hostility (child report) and teacher-reported externalizing behavior, whereas Patterson and Sanson (1999) reported that mother-rated temperamental inflexibility (negative emotionality and resistance to demands) was more strongly associated with mother-reported externalizing problems when the mothers described themselves as relatively high in harsh punishment.

The general pattern also extends to a prosocial behavior—expression of sympathy. Valiente et al. (2004) found that parents' expressivity of negative emotion (self-rated and observed) was associated with children's self-reported sympathetic responses, but only when the child was high in effortful control (parent and teacher ratings on the CBQ and observation). This was true for self-rated general dispositions and personal distress responses to an empathy-inducing film, but not for sympathy responses to the film. In a sample of children who had experienced divorce, inconsistent maternal discipline (mother and child report) was more strongly associated with both depression and conduct problems in children who had impulsive temperaments (mother and child report on the CBQ) than for those who were not impulsive (Lengua et al., 2000). Finally, elementary school children's self-described externalizing behavior problems were more strongly associated with angry discipline by both mothers and fathers, when the children described themselves as low rather than high in agreeableness (Prinzie et al., 2003). This pattern was essentially replicated by Van Leeuwen, Mervielde, Braet, and Bosmans (2004) using parent ratings of child personality and adjustment and both parent and child descriptions of parenting.

A second theme that has emerged in the literature is supported by fewer studies, but it raises an important possibility—that disciplinary responses by parents can have positive rather than adverse implications for children with temperamental or personality tendencies toward dysregulation. Stice and Gonzales (1998) found that adolescents' ratings of parental control and support were positively correlated and that, for highly impulsive youths, high levels of parental control and support were more associated with low levels of adolescent antisocial behavior than for nonimpulsive youths. Even more clearly showing that control can be especially effective for dysregulated children, Stoolmiller (2001) found that boys who were highly unmanageable (disposed to have tantrums) in their early years showed a stronger relationship between maternal unskilled discipline and increasing externalizing problems (as rated by teachers

from elementary school to middle school) than boys who were low or medium in their unmanageability.

Bates et al. (1998) found, in two separate studies with community samples, that early childhood temperamental resistance to control (mother report on the ICQ) better predicted externalizing behavior problems in middle childhood (mother and teacher reports) for children who received low levels of parental control (observed in the home) than for children receiving high levels of control. Parental control was measured as reactions to misbehavior, and these reactions were sometimes but not always negative, for example, scolding. The researchers almost never saw harsh discipline such as spanking. Although hostile parenting and lack of warmth might well make it more likely that children's dysregulated temperament traits will become acting-out behavior problems, the findings of Stice and Gonzales (1998) and Bates et al. (1998) suggest that parental control might also serve to lessen the likelihood that dysregulated temperament will lead to problem behavior if unmanageability is overcome by high levels of parental management effort. However, high levels of parental control may not be ideal for all children: Bates et al. (1998) also noted that high levels of maternal control with highly manageable children sometimes resulted in higher levels of externalizing behavior than would have been predicted by temperament alone, with the possibility that the mothers' control somehow prevented the development of truly internalized self-control.

A third theme concerns a somewhat different trait, not discussed in the main temperament literature, the core psychopathy trait, *callous-unemotional,* which involves tendencies to be nonempathic, manipulative, and lacking anxiety and guilt. This pattern seems likely to be a form of temperamental dysregulation, even though its regulatory core appears to concern low prosocial orientation more than reward-sensitive impulsivity or low effortful control. It may also be related to very low levels of fear, but this does not seem likely to be the dominant component. Wooten, Frick, Shelton, and Silverthorn (1997) found in a combined clinical and normal sample that when children were described by parents and teachers as low on the callous-unemotional scale, less positive parenting, as described by parent and child, was associated with greater conduct problems as measured by parent and teacher report. When high on the callous-unemotional scale, however, children were high on conduct problems whether the parenting was positive or not. This pattern was replicated, in essence, by B. O'Connor and Dvorak (2001) in a community sample, and by Oxford, Cavell, and Hughes (2003) in a sample more similar to that of Wooten et al. (1997).

The findings of regulatory temperament × parenting interactions are interesting, and it is encouraging that some common patterns of findings have been found that can be interpreted as reflecting differential effects of parenting on children with different temperaments. However, especially when interaction effects are not found, the studies cannot provide sufficient evidence on developmental process. The parent and child are also genetically related, and interaction effects might be confounded or obscured by gene-environment correlation. This makes it valuable to have relevant findings from studies considering variables other than standard temperament/personality, behavioral adjustment, and parenting. One example is the Hart, Atkins, and Fegley (2003) study, which shows, among other things, that Head Start experience was especially beneficial in developing academic skills for children with resilient (well-regulated) personalities living in highly stressful family environments. Bates et al. (2003) found that disrupted sleep schedules (mother daily report) and lack of positive parenting (mother interview) had stronger paths to children's maladjustment in preschool (teacher reports) for children who were high in resistance to control (mother report on the ICQ).

Lengua and Long (2002) reported that children in a community sample showed a stronger association between family stress and internalizing behavior problems when the children were low in self-regulation (on the CBQ and Early Adolescent Temperament Questionnaire [EATQ]), all measures based on child and mother reports. Fabes et al. (1999) found that preschool children whose teachers rated them high in effortful control (CBQ) had an adaptive advantage compared to less self-regulated children, with lower levels of negative emotion and higher competence in peer interactions, but only in high intensity interactions (vigorous, highly emotional games). Effortful control did not make much difference when the peer interaction events were of lower intensity. Finally, Goodnight, Bates, Newman, Dodge, and Pettit (2004) found that teens, especially boys, with impulsive tendencies in a laboratory card-playing task, showed a stronger linkage between having antisocial friends (teen and parent report) and increases in their own externaliz-

ing behavior problems (teen and parent report) than did teens with nonimpulsive tendencies.

Considering studies with nonstandard measures of temperament-related traits, El-Sheikh et al. (2001) found that high vagal tone (a measure of self-regulation via the parasympathetic nervous system, described earlier) reduced the risks of externalizing and internalizing behavior and health problems for children exposed to frequent marital quarrels. Although not showing an interaction as such, Donzella et al. (2000) put preschool children in a competitive game and found that those who showed a cortisol increase, as opposed to those who did not, were described by teachers on the CBQ as high in surgency and low in effortful control. Booth, Johnson, Granger, Crouter, and McHale (2003) measured testosterone, which could indicate temperament-like dispositions toward surgency, in children and adolescents. Testosterone levels were not directly related to adjustment, but when quality of mother-child and father-child relationship (parent- and child-rated) was low, higher levels of testosterone were associated with higher levels of conduct problems and lower levels of depression. These relationships were lower and opposite in direction when relationship quality was high.

Finally, we consider a study that measured particular genes with relevance to individual differences. The Dunedin study of a birth cohort in New Zealand (Caspi et al., 2002) showed that boys (and in supplemental analyses, girls) who had a less active allele for MAOA (a gene on the X chromosome coding for an enzyme that metabolizes neurotransmitters such as dopamine and influences aggressive behavior) showed a stronger relationship between the experience of adverse experiences in the family (harsh and indifferent parenting, loss of primary caregiver, and retrospectively reported abuse) and later antisocial behavior. The study (Caspi, Sugden, et al., 2003) also showed that those with two copies of the short allele of the 5-HTT gene (a gene that influences the efficiency of serotonin functioning in response to stress and consequently anxiety responses) had a stronger relationship between the number of stressful life events they had experienced from age 21 to 26 years and their level of depression than those with a short and a long or two copies of the long allele of the gene. Both of these genes can be seen as affecting emotional and behavioral self-regulation traits of individuals, and both showed interactions with stressful experience in predicting adjustment outcomes.

Summary

In summary, research has begun to demonstrate that child characteristics related to the temperament domain of dysregulation interact with a range of environmental qualities in the development of competencies and problems. In general, negative experiences and the absence of positive experiences appear to have less adverse effects on the development of children with stronger self-regulatory tendencies, and greater effects on the development of children with weaker self-regulation. Ten years ago, this pattern was essentially undiscovered. Now, after an inspiring flurry of scientific activity, we can begin to envision research on the actual developmental processes by which temperament and environment moderate one another's effects on child adjustment. What are the limits of the phenomena? More precisely, which environmental factors interact with which particular child characteristics? What are the developmental processes by which these effects are found? What are the psychological products of the temperament and environment? In the next subsections, we review comparable literatures on interactions involving negative emotional reactivity and novelty distress traits, and features of the environment.

Negative Emotionality × Environment

Negative emotionality traits, which tend to predict both internalizing and externalizing adjustment outcomes, also interact with environment characteristics in shaping the development of children's adjustment. To an even greater extent than the preceding section, this section is not conceptually pure: Temperament measures classified as negative emotionality often include other temperament constructs that might better be treated separately. For example, sometimes a negative emotionality measure may reflect not only the general negative reactivity but also the correlated, yet conceptually separable, discomfort in a novel situation. Or a measure might combine negative emotionality and poor self-regulation. Nevertheless, for the sake of simpler organization, studies with such measures are placed here.

The majority of studies in this section concern negative emotionality in interaction with measures of parenting, consistent with the strong emphasis on parenting in the social development literature. Belsky, Hsieh, and Crnic (1998) found that intrusive and negatively affective parenting during toddlerhood was more predictive of externalizing behavior at age 3 for boys who as infants were high rather than low in negative emotionality (parent IBQ ratings and lab observation of both frustration and fear). The Belsky et al. (1998) study also provides an important illustration of the fact that although externalizing problems are often found to be substantially correlated with internalizing problems in children, the two kinds of problems may have different antecedents (Bates, 1989a). Belsky et al. (1998) found that temperamentally negative infants who received more negative and less positive fathering were *less* inhibited in the laboratory at 3 years, whereas the relation between fathering and inhibition was nonsignificant for infants low in negative emotionality.

The Belsky et al. (1998) finding resembles a finding of Arcus (2001) in which infants observed in the laboratory to be high in negative reactivity were less likely to show behavioral inhibition in the laboratory at 14 months if their mothers were observed to be high in limit setting. Arcus also found that negatively reactive infants with boisterous and annoying siblings were less likely to show behavioral inhibition than those experiencing less intrusive behavior from siblings, even beyond the effect of maternal limit setting. Arcus suggests that mild frustrations and challenges, such as those from firm mothers and intrusive siblings, may promote reactive infants' self-regulatory abilities better than a highly accommodating environment.

In contrast, a study by Pauli-Pott, Mertesacker, and Beckman (2004) appears to find, at least partially, the opposite of the Arcus pattern: Maternal insensitivity at 4 months predicted infant stranger distress at 12 months more strongly for infants who had been high rather than low in negative emotionality in the lab at 4 months. The discrepancy could be due to many different aspects of sample and procedure, but the difference may be related to: (a) slight but potentially important developments taking place between 12 and 14 months, (b) differences in the meaning of an assessment battery confronting the child with a wide variety of novel objects versus one centered on only a strange person, or less likely (c) subtle cultural differences between the United States and Germany. Paralleling the Pauli-Pott et al. (2004) findings, although with more of an externalizing outcome, Feldman, Greenbaum, and Yirmiya (1999) found that mother-infant affect synchrony in play during the first year, likely related to maternal sensitivity, was more predictive of toddlers' self-control (compliance with do and don't commands) observed at age 2 years when the infants had been high rather than low on negative emotionality (mother ICQ and lab observations).

Related patterns have also been found with older children. Morris et al. (2002) reported that mothers' overt hostility (child-rated) showed stronger associations with teacher reports of externalizing behavior problems for children temperamentally high in anger to frustration (mother CBQ) than for less irritable children. More irritable children also showed a stronger relation between child-rated maternal covert hostility and intrusive control of the child's feelings and teacher reports of children's internalizing. In a similar effect, high levels of mother-reported family conflict were associated with high levels of teacher-reported externalizing and internalizing problems, but only for children rated by teachers on the Keogh Teacher Temperament Questionnaire as high on a composite of negative emotionality and dysregulation (Tschann, Kaiser, Chesney, Alkon, & Boyce, 1996). Also showing how difficult temperament might change the implications of stressful environments are findings of Kilmer, Cowan, and Wyman (2001).

Further supporting the general trend of negativity × family environment effects, Gilliom, Shaw, Beck, Schonberg, and Lukon (2002) reported that toddlers' negative emotionality (ICQ difficultness) was more predictive of relatively ineffective self-regulation in a gift-delay task 2 years later when their mothers had been observed to be high in negative control and low in warmth than when the mothers had been low in negative control and high in warmth. Hemphill and Sanson (2001), in a preliminary report, described a related effect. Lengua et al. (2000) did not find an interaction between negative emotionality (mother and child reports on the EAS) and parenting. They did, however, find that low positive emotionality (mother and child reports on the DOTS) was associated with stronger relations between maternal rejection (ratings by mother and child) and child externalizing behavior and depression (mother and child ratings). The latter finding is described here because it is one of very few interactions reported between positive emotionality and environment in relation to child adjustment.

Returning to interactions involving negative emotionality, if one assumes that a mother's negative emotionality is genetically transmitted to her child, the findings of T. O'Connor, Caspi, DeFries, and Plomin (2003) confirm the general finding that negative emotionality predisposes a child to be more susceptible to negative rearing conditions. O'Connor et al. found that

adopted children's biological mothers' negative emotionality (EAS) predicted the children's behavior problems at age 12, but only if the children's adoptive parents had separated. This effect was statistically significant for parent reports of externalizing and internalizing problems, in the same direction but not significant for teacher reported problems, and significant for observer ratings of low social responsibility. In a different adoption study, Stams, Juffer, and van Ijzendoorn (2002) found that adopted children with the combination of disorganized attachment and challenging temperament (composite of all ICQ factors) in the early years showed lower levels of cognitive development and less optimal ego control at age 7 than those with none or only one of these risk factors. Stams et al. (2002) interpreted the disorganized attachment as reflecting a less optimal relationship with the mother, and this is plausible. However, the meaning of the disorganized attachment construct is not well developed (Thompson, 1998). In addition to stressful or abusive rearing conditions (Thompson, 1998), it has sometimes also been interpreted as due to infants' neural development having been compromised (Green & Goldwyn, 2002). Therefore, the temperament × environment interpretation in this instance needs to be provisional.

Adjustment is typically measured at a point in time, but increasingly as trajectories across time. Owens and Shaw (2003) provide a rare example of an interaction between child temperament and rearing environment in forecasting change in adjustment. They showed that the expected decline in externalizing behavior across age 2 to age 6 (e.g., Keiley, Bates, Dodge, & Pettit, 2000) was slower for children who had been observed at 18 months to be high on negative emotionality and who had mothers with high levels of depression, than for children with depressed mothers but lower levels of negative emotionality. This is consistent with the general trend emerging in the literature for negative emotionality to amplify environmental risk factors for behavior problem development. However, to enrich the picture, Owens and Shaw (2003) also found that with mothers who had been low in depression across early childhood, children observed to be highly negative at 18 months showed a slightly steeper decline in externalizing behavior problems than low negative children. At age 2, the high negative children with nondepressed mothers had about 20% more symptoms than low negative emotionality children with nondepressed mothers, but by age 6, they were practically as low in symptoms as the low negative children.

Wills et al. (2001) provide another example of temperament-environment interaction forecasting growth in problem behavior. Because of the nature of the temperament composites, this study could also have been reviewed in the self-regulation × environment section. In a large sample of youths followed from age 11 to 13, Wills et al. (2001) found a pattern in which negative temperament (negative emotionality plus high activity level) amplified relations between parenting risk factors, such as parent-child conflict and parent tobacco and alcohol use, and both intercept level and slope of youths' substance use. The reverse applied to positive temperament (positive emotionality with task orientation): High positive temperament reduced the relations between parenting risk factors and the intercept and slope of youths' substance use. These findings obtained for both self- and teacher-report measures of temperament. The findings are comparable to those of Mun et al. (2001), who found stronger links between some preschool-age temperament variables (parent report on the DOTS) and parent reports of middle childhood behavior problems when the parents were high in alcohol and antisocial behavior problems than when they reported low levels of these problems. Although activity level and distractibility showed this moderator effect, emotional reactivity and unadaptability did not.

Finally, we consider two studies using biological measures and interactions between temperament-like characteristics and nonfamily environmental factors. Dettling et al. (2000) asked how diurnal patterns of cortisol in response to the stresses of day care were affected by temperament. When at home, children's cortisol levels peak in the early morning and decline over the day, but children in day care often show increases from morning to afternoon. Dettling et al. (2000) found that day-care children higher on a composite parent- and day-care teacher-report (CBQ) measure of negative affectivity and low effortful control showed a greater increase in afternoon cortisol than those lower on this temperament composite, even after controlling for quality of day care the children received. Finally, a study by Quas, Bauer, and Boyce (2004) concerned psychophysiological reactivity measured in the laboratory in 4- to 6-year-olds, which we interpret as a temperament index. The environmental variable was whether an interviewer took a supportive or nonsupportive approach to the child, and the "adjustment" variable was the child's performance in recalling episodes that occurred in the lab. Quas et al. (2004) found that children high on autonomic reactivity gave more correct answers in the memory task when the interviewer was supportive than when she was unsupportive. For low-reactive children, however, interviewer supportiveness did not make a difference in recall, although the low-reactive children did offer more "don't know" answers to a supportive than to an unsupportive interviewer.

Summary

In summary, although explicit replications are largely lacking and even approximate replications are sometimes not found, there appear to be some general patterns in the findings reviewed. First, negative emotionality traits tend to foreshadow externalizing behavior problems, but to be more strongly linked to externalizing behavior problems in the presence of adverse rearing environments. Conversely, environmental adversities tend to predict child behavior problems more strongly in the presence of negative child temperament. Perhaps we can adapt coercion training theory (Patterson, Reid, & Dishion, 1992) to envision a "Velcro" process by which this interaction effect operates so that negatively emotional children tend to acquire coercive tendencies more easily than less irritable children because they have the relevant "hooks." These coercive tendencies are especially established when there are environmental triggers and responses to this irritability, such as a hostile parent. And these behavioral and emotional habits become dysfunctionally habitual and generalized.

This complements an older, fairly well-established pattern of findings (Bates, 1989a), showing that more difficult infants develop less well cognitively in noisy homes than do easy infants (e.g., Wachs, 1987). However, in the latter findings, strong emotional responses may impair the child's ability to extract meaningful information in a confusing environment rather than to selectively respond to and elicit negativity from the social environment. Second, negative emotionality often foreshadows internalizing problems, but environmental adversities may play a different role here, with moderately challenging, directive and unsupportive behavior reducing the chances of development of anxious behavior patterns. Arcus's (2001) suggested process makes sense here, with moderate challenge forcing an otherwise withdrawing child to develop more adaptive regulatory abilities.

As in the self-regulation × environment area, empirical progress in describing negative emotionality × environment moderator effects has been striking. However, much work remains to be done. More consistent and precise operational definitions of negative emotionality will be important in clarifying which aspects of temperament are interacting with the environment. As always, definition of the crucial aspects of the environment would help as well (Wachs, 2000). As patterns of interaction become more firmly established, it will also be important to identify the developmental processes by which an interaction effect is mediated. Finally, although not all articles mentioning the search for interactions found them, and not all of those reported follow the same pattern, consistent-enough patterns of moderator effects have been reported in recent years that it seems unlikely that "file drawer" nonreplications will swamp the published effects. Nevertheless, it might also be helpful if researchers were to reserve a portion of their work for explicit attempts to replicate intriguing interaction effects, and if journals reserved space for notes on the success or failure of these attempts. It will be theoretically valuable to identify not only consistently found moderator effects, but also those that are consistently *not* found, despite methodologically plausible attempts.

Fearfulness × Environment

Our final section on temperament × environment interaction concerns temperamental fearfulness. Temperament constructs in this domain describe distress and withdrawal or slow adaptation to novel or potentially harmful situations. Theoretically, as discussed earlier, they are rooted in individual variations in brain circuits, especially those comprising the fear system. Empirically, there is evidence that highly inhibited, fearful, unadaptable young children are sometimes at greater risk of developing anxiety problems, and that unusually fearless young children are at greater risk of developing conduct problems, as discussed. In studies of the interaction of fearful temperament and environment, the temperament measures have been more typically pure representatives of the focal concept than in the other kinds of temperament-environment interaction we have reviewed. However, even here there remain some methodological uncertainties. For example, measures of low levels of behavioral inhibition could reflect not only the primary construct, lack of fear, but also high approach or low levels of self-regulation. Fearful temperament was the topic for which there was the most compelling evidence for a temperament-parenting interaction in the development of children's adjustment at the time of Rothbart and Bates (1998) original review. In sheer numbers of relevant studies, this literature has not grown as fast in the intervening

years as the other two topics we have reviewed. However, there has been progress.

Kochanska (1991) showed that highly fearful 8- to 10-year-old children showed more signs of conscience when their mothers used gentle rather than harsh control, whereas the gentleness of maternal control did not make a difference for the relatively fearless children. This finding was consistent with a theoretically based assumption that highly anxious children are susceptible to overarousal, impeding their cognitive processing and internalizing of rules in harsh discipline encounters, whereas fearless children are not as susceptible to overarousal. More recently, this finding has been supported with a slightly older sample of boys, by Colder, Lochman, and Wells (1997). Temperamentally fearful children whose parents used harsh discipline showed more teacher-rated aggression than either low-fear children with harsh parents or high-fear children with gentle parents.

Kochanska (1995) replicated and extended this finding in a study of younger children. She reported that gentle discipline mattered more in the self-control of children above the median on novelty fear than for the children below the median on fear. Moreover, and very importantly, she also reported that a positive mother-child relationship, indexed by the attachment Q-sort, mattered more in the self-control of relatively fearless children than for the relatively fearful ones. The latter finding was predicted by a model assuming that fearless children could be more easily motivated to acquire social rules by positive and enjoyable aspects of the parent-child relationship. Kochanska (1997) also extended the pattern of findings by following the toddlers in her 1995 study at two further time points. Temperamental fearfulness was still measured at Time 1 (average age 33 months) by a composite of mother reports on the CBQ and observations in standard laboratory challenge situations, and maternal discipline was measured by observations in toy clean-up situations at home and in the lab. At Time 2 (average age 46 months), Kochanska (1997) found that relatively fearful children's conscience (resistance to temptation to cheat in a game and responses to hypothetical moral dilemmas) was more advanced if their mothers had been gentle in their control rather than harsh.

Relatively fearless children's conscience was not dependent on gentle versus harsh discipline, but instead was predicted by how securely attached they had been. At Time 3 (age 60 months), however, Time 1 gentle control did not matter for the conscience of fearful children, and Time 1 attachment security did not matter for the fearless children, although Time 1 maternal responsiveness, which is conceptually and empirically related to attachment security, did predict conscience at Time 3 for fearless children. Interestingly, Fowles and Kochanska (2000) found, in the same sample, that when fearfulness was defined by electrodermal reactivity, the pattern of findings was fairly similar to those based on the behavioral definition of temperament, even though there was little convergence between the two measures.

Independent replications of the Kochanska temperament × parenting interaction effects in predicting indexes of moral development were attempted by van der Mark, Bakermans-Kranenburg, and van Ijzendoorn (2002) and van der Mark, van Ijzendoorn, and Bakermans-Kranenburg (2002) in a study of girls at 16 and 22 months. Fearfulness was assessed in the laboratory and committed compliance and empathy responses were the measures of moral development. However, van der Mark et al. did not find temperament-parenting interaction effects. These nonreplications may have been due to the very young age of the children in the study, to the fact that the sample was restricted to girls and relatively high in socioeconomic status, or to a variety of other method differences. Although not explicitly attempting to replicate the Kochanska (1997) pattern, findings in a preliminary report by Hemphill and Sanson (2001) could be interpreted as showing that highly punitive parenting appeared to amplify a small group of uninhibited children's risk for externalizing problems, in potential contrast with Kochanska's (1997) finding that harsh control was not predictive of conscience development for uninhibited children. Maternal punitiveness at age 2 was not different for the groups of children moderate or high on inhibition and with or without behavior problems.

The accumulating literature provides both replications and nonreplications of the rich fear × parenting pattern. The meaning of the nonreplications is not established, because key methodological issues are not resolved. On balance, the fear × parenting effect is well replicated for such a complex pattern, and it is potentially of considerable theoretical importance. However, further replications, using a variety of methods, will be needed for the pattern to become a solidly established developmental phenomenon. And, despite the exceptionally well-developed theoretical background for the pattern, studies will also be needed to identify the processes mediating the observed interaction effect.

Next, we ask how fearful temperament interacts with rearing environment in the prediction of more standard behavior problem symptoms. First, considering possible moderator processes in development of internalizing behavior, Tschann et al. (1996) found that preschool children relatively low on approach, as rated by their teachers on Keogh's questionnaire, were more likely to be observed as socially withdrawn when their mothers described low levels of family conflict than when their mothers described high levels of family conflict. High-approach children, alternatively, showed the lowest levels of social withdrawal when their families were low in conflict. This is conceptually similar to the effect previously discussed, where negative emotionality predicted behavioral inhibition less when parents were more rather than less directive or challenging, although the effect is concurrent rather than longitudinal, as in the Arcus (2001) and Park, Belsky, Putnam, and Crnic (1997) studies. Bates (2003) presented preliminary analyses from two longitudinal studies that partly converge with this effect: Mother-rated temperamental unadaptability (ICQ) in early childhood predicted mother-rated internalizing problems across middle childhood more strongly in families where the mothers had been observed to be low in control than where they had been observed to be more highly directive and restrictive.

In partial contrast, however, a rather different kind of temperament × parenting interaction was found by Rubin, Burgess, and Hastings (2002). Rubin et al. found that inhibited tendencies with a peer observed at age 2 predicted social reticence with unfamiliar peers at age 4, but only for children whose mothers were observed at age 2 to be high in psychological control—derisive or intrusive with affection or help on a task. Inhibition at age 2 was not predictive of social inhibition at age 4 for children who received less psychological control from their mothers. A possible key to reconciling the earlier studies is to note that Rubin et al. (2002) may have captured dimensions of parenting that either underchallenged or overchallenged children with fearful temperament, whereas the Arcus (2001) and Park et al. (1997; or Belsky et al., 1998) and Bates (2003) studies may have measured parenting dimensions more consistent with Arcus's (2001) model of optimal challenge accelerating self-regulation of anxiety responses. This interpretation is consistent with the more clinical insights of Chess and Thomas (1984), who observed in their longitudinal study that withdrawing children developed best when parents provided repeated and firm, but not overwhelming, challenges to their children to deal with novel situations, with overprotectiveness not as beneficial.

Finally, Eaves et al. (2003) offer an interesting perspective on the question of how gene-environment interaction and gene-environment correlation can be simultaneously modeled in a twin study. This is of importance to the study of temperament × environment interactions because we assume that some portion of temperament is based on the genome. One important window on processes where genes and temperament-relevant expressions of genes influence psychological outcomes is gene-environment interaction. These interactions have become of great interest in developmental psychopathology recently, as evidenced by the frequent mention of the findings by Caspi et al. (2002; Caspi, Sugden, et al., 2003) described previously. Children of contrasting genotype might be differently affected by a similar environment.

However, equally important for understanding developmental process is the phenomenon of gene-environment correlation. A child with a given genotype might be exposed to a particular environment associated with the development of behavior problems because close relatives share the same genotype, or a child's genotype might lead to temperament traits that elicit environmental responses that, in turn, promote the development of behavior problems. Interpreting gene-environment interaction effects in human studies is often difficult because it is difficult to assume that the environment dimension is not at the same time also a function of the genotype. In the past, this issue was dealt with by only evaluating gene-environment interaction effects where it could be demonstrated that there was no correlation between environment and gene (e.g., Caspi et al., 2002). Eaves et al. (2003), however, developed a Bayesian approach to simultaneously model gene main effects, gene-environment interaction effects, and gene-environment correlation effects.

Using this approach in a longitudinal study of adolescent twin girls, Eaves et al. (2003) found that genes explained the development of depression in several paths. Some genes influenced depression specifically. Other genes affected anxiety early on, and then depression later, through three pathways: (1) a genetic main effect in which girls' early anxiety increased their risk of later anxiety, (2) a gene-environment correlation in which girls at high risk for anxiety were especially likely to be exposed to depressogenic life events, and (3) a gene-environment interaction in which girls with this higher

genetic risk of anxiety and exposure to stressful events are more sensitive to the depressogenic life events. This study is only indirectly relevant to temperament per se, but it is exciting to consider how studies with early measures of temperament and environment in a genetically informative sample might help advance our understanding of the processes involved in the development of children's adjustment.

Summary and Future Directions

To conclude this section, it is greatly encouraging to have seen such a rapid accumulation of temperament-environment interaction findings. The field has gone from mostly thinking about complex processes in theoretical writings to vigorously instantiating such effects in empirical work. As we have shown, there are several patterns with some broadly converging support. As usual in our complex field, these replications are far from exact or widespread, but some patterns are beginning to stand out, and they are not always patterns that would have been intuitively expected. As mentioned previously, methodological and definitional issues are important in replication studies, and more attention needs to be allocated to such studies. In addition, much work remains in detailing the mediating processes by which temperament-environment interactions have their role in development.

It also may be valuable to more extensively explore interactions between multiple temperament variables and environmental variables simultaneously. As of about 10 years ago, the typical limit of complexity was to consider temperament and environment variables' main effects as linear, additive contributors to a developmental outcome. Currently, the typical limit considers main effects plus the interaction of one temperament variable and one environment variable as predictors of an outcome, or main effects plus the interaction of two temperament variables (e.g., negative emotionality × effortful control) as predictors. However, for reasons suggested earlier, where the meaning of a given temperament variable in isolation is not always clear, it might be helpful to consider the effect of a profile of temperament variables as moderating or moderated by an environmental variable (see also Rothbart & Sheese, in press).

For example, fearful temperament might have different implications depending on both its temperament context, such as the tendency toward dysregulation, and its environmental context such as family stress. Not coincidentally, this example is a direction we have been exploring (Bates, Sandy, Pettit, & Dodge, 2000), and we hope to have useful findings to offer in the next edition of this handbook. Similarly, profiles of environments, such as parental harsh discipline in the context of warm involvement versus minimal involvement, might also be important in understanding the interactions with temperament. However, in a chapter on temperament, we should not go further in thinking about this direction. Future progress on understanding the role of temperament will require both relatively mundane replications and new, more exciting, highly complex studies.

CHAPTER CONCLUSIONS AND FUTURE DIRECTIONS

Over the past 2 decades, there has been considerable progress in identifying the broad outlines and the more specific dimensions of temperament in childhood. The general framework for temperament now constitutes a revision of the NYLS dimensions, and includes broad dimensions of Positive Affect and Approach, Negative Affectivity, including subconstructs of Irritability and Fear, Effortful Control, and possibly Affiliativeness or Social Orientation. These broad dimensions share similarities with four of the Big Five Factors of Personality (Extraversion, Neuroticism, Conscientiousness, and Agreeableness), and with all of the Big Three broad factors of personality (Extraversion, Neuroticism, and Conscientiousness), but they are by no means identical. Research establishing linkages between measures of these dimensions of early temperament and later personality has now begun to accumulate, and will continue to be one of the major continuing tasks for our area, as will further differentiating our temperament and personality measures.

Differentiating Temperament Dimensions

In our previous review, we suggested the importance of differentiating between fearful and irritable distress, and in this review we note that both biological and clinical studies have benefited from this distinction. Findings on the psychobiology of temperament showing overlap between networks subserving defensive fear and defensive aggression may help to account for findings of general neurotic tendencies, and they may also suggest further means of differentiating reactive and instrumental aggression in relation to temperament.

Further evidence links anger and early surgency/extraversion to the development of externalizing problems and indicates that fear may be a protective factor against aggression and other externalizing problems as well as a contributor to the early development of conscience. A great deal of recent research has established connections between effortful control and the regulation of both affect and behavior. Future research will consider the limits of fearful and effortful control on adaptation, in connection with the Blocks' (1980) construct of overcontrol, and allow us to study the way in which effortful control may become part of a resilient approach to life's challenges.

Probably the most striking new findings in this review involve temperament × environment interactions. In interaction studies, the child's effortful control, manageability, and agreeableness have been found to moderate the effects of adverse environments, and negative emotionality has been found to amplify the effects of adverse experience. Unexpectedly, we have found that more fearful or inhibited children appear to benefit from early challenge, at least in measures of the later strength of this system. However, fearful or inhibited preschoolers' conscience appears to develop better in the context of gentle socialization methods.

Measures

Good measures of temperament are crucial to our theoretical understanding. Further advances in defining the structure of temperament and understanding the neural and developmental substrates of temperament will continue to rely on advances in measurement. As an additional goal of research, we advocate the further development of sound measures, using parent-report, naturalistic observation, and structured or laboratory observation measures to be used in converging and complementary ways. We have advocated an analog approach to questions of validation rather than a digital, yes-no approach to ascertaining the value of methods and measures. Aside from the important future work of comparing results of alternative methods, another important focus in research should be identification of *non*-relationships among constructs—tests for discriminant as well as convergent validity. Partly on the basis of differential, discriminating patterns of correlations between parent-reports of temperament and other measures, we are able to argue for the validity of parent-reports. The use of brain marker tasks in the study of development of executive attention and effortful control has made significant strides in the past 5 years. We encourage the continued use of marker tasks to link performance to the development of brain functioning.

Development

As the dimensions of temperament have been further delineated and measures improved, real advances have occurred in our understanding of temperament-environment interactions. Future research is needed to examine the processes supporting these effects. There may be times when emotionality or effortful control systems are more sensitive to environmental conditions than others, or times when the child's irritable and frustrative distress might be most easily directed toward or away from coercive responses and tendencies to aggressive action. These are basic developmental questions with profound implications for our understanding of the nature of temperament and the development of personality.

Establishing closer links with our understanding of the developing neurophysiological substrate of temperament is a related task for our area. In this work, findings from each domain of study will illuminate the other. Thus, behavioral research on the developing structure of temperament helps to specify the operations necessary to link the psychology of temperament to its neurophysiology. Reviewers who relate parallel research carried out in these two domains will help in this work. The use of physiological assays, behavioral measures in research designs and the use of marker tasks will lead to further advances.

Finally, we have identified possible trajectories in the development of social and personality traits from early temperamental characteristics, most strongly in Kochanska's (1995) work on multiple routes to conscience. The task of identifying routes to other significant outcomes requires progress in all of the tasks described earlier, and it is of critical importance to our enterprise. The study of developmental trajectories requires establishing stronger links between our work and more environmentally oriented areas of our field such as social learning and social cognition research. As we have indicated, temperament constructs do not conflict with these areas of research: The temperament dimensions we have described are open to experience, although some systems are likely more open than others. In addition, the functioning of control systems will be highly dependent on what the culture indicates should be controlled. Prospects for effective longitudinal research will be much improved by an integration of the study of individual differences, cross-cultural, social learning, and social cognition.

Developmental research in our area may also eventually answer questions like the following: To what degree is temperament plastic and susceptible to change? To what degree does experience alter only the *expression* of temperamental characteristics? If distress and maladaptive social cognitions can result from a painful life history, how much of early temperament may have been overlain by these negative experiences? Could the original core of temperament be uncovered by imaginative assays, intervention, further social experience, or even by further changes in social or physical development? We know someone who, through the aging process, lost many of her memories, including information that had troubled her over many years and led to major conflicts in herself and with others. What remained after her memory loss was a positive and expressive person, loved by all who met her. Was this the child she once was? If so, could other less serious interventions have uncovered it? Better yet, could developmental research inform both child rearing and children's prospects in society so that the accumulating pain might never have occurred? We have made much progress in our field in the past decades, but a number of questions remain. Many of these questions are hopeful about a future for us, our parents, and our children.

REFERENCES

Adolphs, R., Tranel, D., Hamann, S., Young, A. W., Calder, A. J., Phelps, E. A., et al. (1999). Recognition of facial emotion in nine individuals with bilateral amygdala damage. *Neuropsychologia, 37*, 1111–1117.

Ahadi, S. A., & Rothbart, M. K. (1994). Temperament, development and the Big Five. In C. F. Halverson, G. A. Kohnstamm, & R. P. Martin (Eds.), *The developing structure of temperament and personality from infancy to adulthood* (pp. 189–207). Hillsdale, NJ: Erlbaum.

Ahadi, S. A., Rothbart, M. K., & Ye, R. (1993). Children's temperament in the United States and China: Similarities and differences. *European Journal of Personality, 7*, 359–378.

Aksan, N., & Kochanska, G. (2004a). Heterogeneity of joy in infancy. *Infancy 6*(1), 79–94.

Aksan, N., & Kochanska, G. (2004b). Links between systems of inhibition from infancy to preschool years. *Child Development 75*(5), 1477–1490.

Allport, G. W. (1961). *Pattern and growth in personality.* New York: Holt, Rinehart and Winston.

Anderson, A. K., & Phelps, E. A. (2002). Is the human amygdala critical for the subjective experience of emotion?: Evidence of intact dispositional affect in patients with amygdala lesions. *Journal of Cognitive Neuroscience, 14*(5), 709–720.

Anderson, S. W., Damasio, H., Tranel, D., & Damasio, A. R. (2001). Long-term sequelae of prefrontal cortex damage acquired in early childhood. *Developmental Neuropsychology, 18,* 281–296.

Anderson, K., Bohlin, G., & Hagekull, B. (1999). Early temperament and stranger wariness as predictors of social inhibition in 2-year-olds. *British Journal of Developmental Psychology, 17,* 421–434.

Arcus, D. (2001). Inhibited and uninhibited children: Biology in the social context. In T. D. Wachs & G. A. Kohnstamm (Eds.), *Temperament in context* (pp. 43–60). Mahwah, NJ: Erlbaum.

Aron, E. N., & Aron A. (1997). Sensory-processing sensitivity and its relation to introversion and emotionality. *Journal of Personality and Social Psychology, 73*(2), 345–368.

Arseneault, L., Moffitt, T. E., Caspi, A., Taylor, A., Rijsdijk, F. V., Jaffee, S. R., et al. (2003). Strong genetic effects on cross-situational antisocial behaviour among 5-year-old children according to mothers, teachers, examiner-observers, and twins' self-reports. *Journal of Child Psychology and Psychiatry, 44,* 832–848.

Asendorpf, J. B. (1990). Development of inhibition during childhood: Evidence for situational specificity and a two-factor model. *Developmental Psychology, 26,* 721–730.

Asendorpf, J. B. (1993). Social inhibition: A general-developmental perspective. In H. C. Traue & J. W. Pennebaker (Eds.), *Emotion inhibition and health* (pp. 80–99). Ashland, OH: Hogrefe & Huber.

Asendorpf, J. B. (1994). The malleability of behavioral inhibition: A study of individual developmental functions. *Developmental Psychology, 30,* 912–919.

Auerbach, J., Geller, V., Letzer, S., Shinwell, E., Levine, J., Belmaker, R. H., et al. (1999). Dopamine D4 receptor (D4DR) and serotonin transporter promoter (5-HTTLPR) polymorphisms in the determination of temperament in 2-month-old infants. *Molecular Psychiatry, 4,* 369–374.

Ayduk, O., Mendoza-Denton, R., Mischel, W., Downey, G., Peake, P. K., & Rodriguez, M. (2000). Regulating the interpersonal self: Strategic self-regulation for coping with rejection sensitivity. *Journal of Personality and Social Psychology, 79,* 776–792.

Barr, C. S., Newman, T. K., Becker, M. L., Parker, C. C., Champoux, M., Lesch, K. P., et al. (in press). Early experience and rh5-HTTLPR genotype interact to influence social behavior and aggression in nonhuman primates. *Genes, brain, and behavior.*

Bates, J. E. (1980). The concept of temperament. *Merrill-Palmer Quarterly, 26,* 299–319.

Bates, J. E. (1987). Temperament in infancy. In J. D. Osofsky (Ed.), *Handbook of infant development* (2nd ed., pp. 1101–1149). New York: Wiley.

Bates, J. E. (1989a). Applications of temperament concepts. In G. A. Kohnstamm, J. E. Bates, & M. K. Rothbart (Eds.), *Temperament in childhood* (pp. 321–355). Chichester, England: Wiley.

Bates, J. E. (1989b). Concepts and measure of temperament. In G. A. Kohnstamm, J. E. Bates, & M. K. Rothbart (Eds.), *Temperament in childhood* (pp. 3–26). Chichester, England: Wiley.

Bates, J. E. (1990). Conceptual and empirical linkages between temperament and behavior problems: A commentary on the Sanson, Prior, and Kyrios study. *Merrill-Palmer Quarterly, 36,* 193–199.

Bates, J. E. (1994). Parents as scientific observers of their children's development. In S. L. Friedman & H. C. Haywood (Eds.), *Developmental follow-up: Concepts, domains, and methods* (pp. 197–216). New York: Academic Press.

Bates, J. E. (2003, April). *Temperamental unadaptability and later internalizing problems as moderated by mothers' restrictive control.* Presented at meeting of the Society for Research in Child Development, Tampa, FL.

Bates, J. E., & Bayles, K. (1984). Objective and subjective components in mothers' perceptions of their children from age 6 months to 3 years. *Merrill-Palmer Quarterly, 30,* 111–130.

Bates, J. E., & Bayles, K. (1988). The role of attachment in the development of behavior problems. In J. Belsky & T. Nezworski (Eds.), *Clinical implications of attachment* (pp. 253–299). Hillsdale, NJ: Erlbaum.

Bates, J. E., Bayles, K., Bennett, D. S., Ridge, B., & Brown, M. M. (1991). Origins of externalizing behavior problems at eight years of age. In D. Pepler & K. Rubin (Eds.), *Development and treatment of childhood aggression* (pp. 93–120). Hillsdale, NJ: Erlbaum.

Bates, J. E., Freeland, C. A. B., & Lounsbury, M. L. (1979). Measurement of infant difficultness. *Child Development, 50,* 794–803.

Bates, J. E., Maslin, C. A., & Frankel, K. A. (1985). Attachment security, mother-child interaction, and temperament as predictors of behavior-problem ratings at age three years. *Monographs of the Society for Child Development, 50*(1/2, Serial No. 209), 167–193.

Bates, J. E., & McFadyen-Ketchum, S. (2001). Temperament and parent-child relations as interacting factors in children's behavioral adjustment. In V. J. Molfese & D. L. Molfese (Eds.), *Temperament and personality across the life span* (pp. 141–176). Mahwah, NJ: Erlbaum.

Bates, J. E., Pettit, G. S., & Dodge, K. A. (1995). Family and child factors in stability and change in children's aggressiveness in elementary school. In J. McCord (Ed.), *Coercion and punishment in long-term perspectives* (pp. 124–138). New York: Cambridge University Press.

Bates, J. E., Pettit, G. S., Dodge, K. A., & Ridge, B. (1998). The interaction of temperamental resistance to control and restrictive parenting in the development of externalizing behavior. *Developmental Psychology, 34,* 982–995.

Bates, J. E., Sandy, J. M., Pettit, G. S., & Dodge, K. A. (2000, October). *Child and adolescent adjustment as a function of child temperament and family stress.* Paper presented at the First Expert Workshop on Personality Psychology, Ghent, Belgium.

Bates, J. E., Viken, R. J., & Williams, N. (2003, April). *Temperament as a moderator of the linkage between sleep and preschool adjustment.* Paper presented at meeting of Society for Research in Child Development, Tampa, FL.

Bates, J. E., Wachs, T. D., & Emde, R. N. (1994). Toward practical uses for biological concepts of temperament. In J. E. Bates & T. D. Wachs (Eds.), *Temperament: Individual differences at the interface of biology and behavior* (pp. 275–306). Washington, DC: American Psychological Association.

Bayley, N., & Schafer, E. S. (1963). Maternal behavior, child behavior, and their intercorrelations from infancy through adolescence. *Monographs of the Society for Research in Child Development, 28,* 127.

Beauchaine, T. (2001). Vagal tone, development, and Gray's motivational theory: Toward an integrated model of autonomic nervous system functioning in psychopathology. *Development and Psychopathology, 13,* 183–214.

Bell, R. Q. (1968). A reinterpretation of the direction of effects in studies of socialization. *Psychological Review, 75,* 81–95.

Bell, R. Q. (1974). Contributions of human infants to caregiving and social interaction. In M. Lewis & L. A. Rosenblum (Eds.), *The effect of the infant on its caregiver* (pp. 1–19). New York: Wiley.

Belsky, J., Friedman, S., & Hsieh, K. (2001). Testing a core emotion-regulation prediction: Does early attentional persistence moderate the effect of infant negative emotionality on later development? *Child Development, 72,* 123–133.

Belsky, J., Hsieh, K., & Crnic, K. (1998). Mothering, fathering, and infant negativity as antecedents of boys' externalizing problems and inhibition at age 3 years: Differential susceptibility to rearing experience? *Development and Psychopathology, 10,* 301–319.

Benjamin, J., Ebstein, R. P., & Belmaker, R. H. (Eds.). (1996). *Molecular genetics and the human personality.* Washington, DC: American Psychiatric Publishing.

Bennett, A. J., Lesch, K. P., Heils, A., Long, J. C., Lorenz, J. G., Shoaf, S. E., et al. (2002). Early experience and serotonin transporter gene variation interact to influence primate CNS function. *Molecular Psychiatry, 7,* 118–122.

Bergman, P., & Escalona, S. K. (1949). Unusual sensitivities in very young children. *Psychoanalytic Study of the Child, 3,* 333–352.

Berlyne, D. E. (1971). *Aesthetics and psychobiology.* New York: Appleton-Century-Crofts.

Berntson, G. G., Cacioppo, J. T., & Quigley, K. S. (1993). Respiratory sinus arrhythmia: Autonomic origins, physiological mechanisms, and psychophysiological implications. *Psychophysiology, 30,* 183–196.

Biederman, J., Rosenbaum, J. F., Hirshfeld, D. R., Faraone, S. V., Bolduc, E. A., Gersten, M., et al. (1990). Psychiatric correlates of behavioral inhibition in young children of parents with and without psychiatric disorders. *Archives of General Psychiatry, 47,* 21–26.

Birns, B. (1965). Individual differences in human neonates' responses to stimulation. *Child Development, 36,* 249–256.

Birns, B., Barten, S., & Bridger, W. (1969). Individual differences in temperamental characteristics of infants. *Transactions of the New York Academy of Sciences, 31,* 1071–1082.

Bishop, G., Spence, S. H., & McDonald, C. (2003). Can parents and teachers provide a reliable and valid report of behavioral inhibition? *Child Development, 74,* 1899–1917.

Black, J. E., & Greenough, W. T. (1991). Developmental approaches to the memory processes. In J. L. Martinez Jr., & R. P. Kesner (Eds.), *Learning and memory: A biological view* (2nd ed., pp. 61–91). San Diego, CA: Academic Press.

Blair, C. (2003). Behavioral inhibition and behavioral activation in young children: Relations with self-regulation and adaptation to preschool in children attending Head Start. *Developmental Psychobiology, 42,* 301–311.

Blanchard, D. C., & Takahashi, S. N. (1988). No change in intermale aggression after amygdala lesions which reduce freezing. *Physiology and Behavior, 42,* 613–616.

Block, J., & Kremen, A. (1996). IQ and ego-resiliency: Their conceptual and empirical connections and separateness. *Journal of Personality and Social Psychology, 70,* 349–361.

Block, J. H., & Block, J. (1980). The role of ego-control and ego-resiliency in the organization of behavior. In W. A. Collins (Ed.), *Minnesota Symposia on Child Psychology* (Vol. 13, pp. 39–101). Hillsdale, NJ: Erlbaum.

Bohart, A. C., & Stipek, D. J. (2001). What have we learned. In A. C. Bohart & D. J. Stipek (Eds.), *Constructive and destructive behavior: Implications for family, school, and society* (pp. 367–397). Washington, DC: American Psychological Association.

Booth, A., Johnson, D. R., Granger, D. A., Crouter, A. C., & McHale, S. (2003). Testosterone and child and adolescent adjustment: The moderating role of parent-child relationships. *Developmental Psychology, 39,* 85–98.

Bornstein, M., & Suess, P. E. (2000). Child and mother cardiac vagal tone: Continuity, stability, and concordance across the first 5 years. *Developmental Psychology, 36,* 54–65.

Bornstein, M. H., Gaughran, J. M., & Segui, I. (1991). Multi-method assessments of infant temperament: Mother questionnaire and mother and observer reports evaluated and compared at five months using the infant temperament measure. *International Journal of Behavioral Development, 14,* 131–151.

Botvinick, M. M., Braver, T. S., Barch, D. M., Carter, C. S., & Cohen, J. D. (2001). Conflict monitoring and cognitive control. *Psychological Review, 108,* 624–652.

Bouchard, T. J., Jr., & Loehlin, J. C. (2001). Genes, evolution, and personality. *Behavior Genetics, 31*(3), 243–273.

Bradley, B. S. (1985). Failure to distinguish between people and things in early infancy. *British Journal of Developmental Psychology, 3,* 281–291.

Buck, R. W. (1979). Individual differences in nonverbal sending accuracy and electrodermal responding: The externalizing-internalizing dimension. In R. Rosenthal (Ed.), *Skill in non-verbal communication: Individual differences.* Cambridge, MA: Oelgeschlager, Gunn, & Hain.

Burt, C. (1937). The analysis of temperament. *British Journal of Medical Psychology, 17,* 158–188.

Bush, G., Luu, P., & Posner, M. I. (2000). Cognitive and emotional influences in anterior cingulate cortex. *Trends in Cognitive Sciences, 4,* 215–222.

Buss, A. H., & Plomin, R. (1975). *A temperament theory of personality development.* New York: Wiley.

Buss, A. H., & Plomin, R. (1984). *Temperament: Early developing personality traits.* Hillsdale, NJ: Erlbaum.

Buss, K. A., Schumacher, J. R. M., Dolski, I., Kalin, N. H., Goldsmith, H. H., & Davidson, R. J. (2003). Right frontal brain activity, cortisol, and withdrawal behavior in 6-month-old infants. *Behavioral Neuroscience, 117*(1), 11–20.

Byrne, J. M., Clark-Touesnard, M. E., Hondas, B. J., & Smith, I. M. (1985, April). *Stability of individual differences in infant visual attention.* Paper presented at the meeting for the Society for Research in Child Development, Toronto, Canada.

Calder, A. J., Lawrence, A. D., & Young, A. W. (2001). Neuropsychology of fear and loathing. *Nature Reviews Neuroscience, 2,* 352–363.

Calkins, S. D. (2002). Does aversive behavior during toddlerhood matter? The effects of difficult temperament on maternal perceptions and behavior. *Infant Mental Health Journal, 23,* 381–402.

Calkins, S. D., & Fox, N. A. (1994). Individual differences in the biological aspects of temperament. In J. E. Bates & T. D. Wachs (Eds.), *Temperament: Individual differences at the interface of biology and behavior* (pp. 199–217). Washington, DC: American Psychological Association.

Calkins, S. D., Fox, N. A., & Marshall, T. R. (1996). Behavioral and psychological antecedents of inhibition in infancy. *Child Development, 67,* 523–540.

Calkins, S. D., & Williford, A. P. (2003, April). *Anger regulation in infancy: Consequences and correlates.* Paper presented at the meeting of the Society for Research in Child Development, Tampa, FL.

Campbell, D. W., Eaton, W. O., & McKeen, N. A. (2002). Motor activity level and behavioural control in young children. *International Journal of Behavioral Development, 26,* 289–296.

Canli, T., Sivers, H., Whitfield, S. L., Gotlib, I. H., & Gabrieli, J. D. E. (2002). Amygdala response to happy faces as a function of extraversion. *Science, 296,* 2191.

Canli, T., Zhao, Z., Desmond, J. E., Kang, E., Gross, J., & Gabrieli, J. D. E. (2001). An fMRI study of personality influences on brain reactivity to emotional stimuli. *Behavioral Neuroscience, 115,* 33–42.

Carey, G. (1996). Family and genetic epidemiology of aggressive and antisocial behavior. In D. M. Stoff & R. B. Cairns (Eds.),

Aggression and violence: Genetic, neurobiological, and biosocial perspectives (pp. 3–21). Mahwah, NJ: Erlbaum.

Carey, G. (2003). *Human genetics for the social sciences.* London: Sage.

Carey, W. B., & McDevitt, S. C. (1978). Revision of the infant temperament questionnaire. *Pediatrics, 61,* 735–739.

Carter, C. S. (1986). The reproductive and adrenal systems. In M. G. H. Coles, E. Donchin, & S. E. Porges (Eds.), *Psychophysiology: Systems, processes, and applications* (pp. 172–182). New York: Guilford Press.

Carver, C. S., & White, T. L. (1994). Behavioral inhibition, behavioral activation, and affective responses to impending reward and punishment: The BIS/BAS Scales. *Journal of Personality and Social Psychology, 67,* 319–333.

Caspi, A. (2000). The child is father of the man: Personality continuities from childhood to adulthood. *Journal of Personality and Social Psychology, 78,* 158–172.

Caspi, A., Harrington, H., Milne, B., Amell, J. W., Theodore, R. F., & Moffitt, T. E. (2003). Children's behavioral styles at age 3 are linked to their adult personality traits at age 26. *Journal of Personality, 71,* 495–513.

Caspi, A., McClay, J., Moffitt, T., Mill, J., Martin, J., Craig, I. W., et al. (2002). Role of genotype in the cycle of violence in maltreated children. *Science, 297,* 851–854.

Caspi, A., & Silva, P. A. (1995). Temperament qualities at age three predict personality traits in young adulthood: Longitudinal evidence from a birth cohort. *Child Development, 66,* 486–498.

Caspi, A., Sugden, K., Moffitt, T. E., Taylor, A., Craig, I. W., Harrington, H., et al. (2003). Influence of life stress on depression: Moderation by a polymorphism in the 5-HTT gene. *Science, 301,* 386–389.

Chess, S., & Thomas, A. (1984). *Origins and evolution of behavior disorders.* New York: Brunner/Mazel.

Clark, L. A., Watson, D., & Mineka, S. (1994). Temperament, personality, and the mood and anxiety disorders. *Journal of Abnormal Psychology, 103,* 103–116.

Cloninger, C. R. (1986). A unified biosocial theory of personality and its role in the development of anxiety states. *Psychiatric Developments, 3,* 167–226.

Cloninger, C. R. (1987). A systematic method for clinical description and classification of personality variants. *Archives of General Psychiatry, 44,* 573–588.

Colder, C. R., Lochman, J. E., & Wells, K. C. (1997). The moderating effects of children's fear and activity level on relations between parenting practices and childhood symptomatology. *Journal of Abnormal Child Psychology, 25*(3), 251–263.

Coldren, J. T., Colombo, J., O'Brien, M., Martinez, R., & Horowitz, F. D. (1987, April). *The relationship of infant visual attention across social interaction and information processing tasks.* Paper presented at the meeting for the Society for Research in Child Development, Baltimore, MD.

Corbetta, M., Kincade, J. M., & Shulman, G. L. (2002). Neural systems for visual orienting and their relationships to spatial working memory. *Journal of Cognitive Neuroscience, 14,* 508–523.

Costa, P. T., Jr., & McCrae, R. R. (1988). From catalog to classification: Murray's needs and the five-factor model. *Journal of Personality and Social Psychology, 55,* 258–265.

Crider, A., & Lunn, R. (1971). Electrodermal lability as a personality dimension. *Journal of Experimental Research in Personality, 5,* 145–150.

Darley, J., & Fazio, R. (1980). Expectancy confirmation processes arising in the social interaction sequence. *American Psychologist, 35,* 867–881.

Davidson, R. J., & Fox, N. A. (1989). Frontal brain asymmetry predicts infants' response to maternal separation. *Journal of Abnormal Psychology, 98,* 127–131.

Davidson, R. J., Putnam, K. M., & Larson, C. L. (2000). Dysfunction in the neural circuitry of emotion regulation: A possible prelude to violence. *Science, 289,* 591–594.

Davidson, R. J., Scherer, K. R., Goldsmith, H. H., Pizzagalli, D., Nitschke, J. B., Kalin, N. H., et al. (2003). Neuroscience. In R. J. Davidson, K. R. Scherer, H. H. Goldsmith, D. Pizzagalli, J. B. Nitschke, N. H. Kalin, et al. (Eds.), *Handbook of affective sciences: Part I. Series in affective science* (pp. 3–128). London: Oxford University Press.

Davidson, R. J., & Tomarken, A. J. (1989). Laterality and emotion: An electrophysiological approach. In F. Boller & J. Grafman (Eds.), *Handbook of neuropsychology* (pp. 419–441). Amsterdam: Elsevier.

Davis, M., Hitchcock, J. M., & Rosen, J. B. (1987). Anxiety and the amygdala: Pharmacological and anatomical analysis of the fear-potentiated startle paradigm. In G. Bower (Ed.), *The psychology of learning and motivation: Vol. 21. Advances in research and theory* (pp. 263–305). San Diego, CA: Academic Press.

DeGangi, G. A., DiPietro, J. A., Greenspan, S. I., & Porges, S. W. (1991). Psychophysiological characteristics of the regulatory disordered infant. *Infant Behavior and Development, 14,* 37–50.

Depue, R. A., & Collins, P. F. (1999). Neurobiology of the structure of personality: Dopamine, facilitation of incentive motivation, and extraversion. *Behavioral and Brain Sciences, 22,* 491–569.

Depue, R. A., & Iacono, W. G. (1989). Neurobehavioral aspects of affective disorders. In M. R. Rosenzweig & L. Y. Porter (Eds.), *Annual review of psychology* (Vol. 40, pp. 457–492). Palo Alto, CA: Annual Reviews.

Derryberry, D., & Reed, M. (1994). Temperament and attention: Orienting toward and away from positive and negative signals. *Journal of Personality and Social Psychology, 66,* 1128–1139.

Derryberry, D., & Reed, M. A. (1996). Regulatory processes and the development of cognitive representations. *Development and Psychopathology, 8,* 215–234.

Derryberry, D., & Reed, M. A. (2002). Anxiety-related attentional biases and their regulation by attentional control. *Journal of Abnormal Psychology, 111,* 225–236.

Dettling, A. C., Parker, S., Lane, S. K., Sebanc, A. M., & Gunnar, M. R. (2000). Quality of care and temperament determine whether cortisol levels rise over the day for children in full-day childcare. *Psychoneuroendocrinology, 25,* 819–836.

Diamond, S. (1974). *The roots of psychology: A sourcebook in the history of ideas.* New York: Basic Books.

Diener, M. L., Goldstein, L. H., & Mangelsdorf, S. C. (1995). The role of prenatal expectations in parents' reports of infant temperament. *Merrill-Palmer Quarterly, 41,* 172–190.

Diener, M. L., & Kim, D.-Y. (2004). Maternal and child predictors of preschool children's social competence. *Applied Developmental Psychology, 25,* 3–24.

Digman, J. M., & Inouye, J. (1986). Further specification of the five robust factors of personality. *Journal of Personality and Social Psychology, 50,* 116–123.

Ding, Y. C., Chi, H. C., Grady, D. L., Morishima, A., Kidd, J. R., Kidd, K. K., et al. (2002). Evidence of positive selection acting at the human dopamine receptor D4 gene locus. *Proceedings of the National Academy of Sciences, USA, 99*, 309–314.

Dodge, K. A., & Pettit, G. S. (2003). A biopsychosocial model of the development of chronic conduct problems in adolescence. *Developmental Psychology, 39*, 349–371.

Donzella, B., Gunnar, M. R., Krueger, W. K., & Alwin, J. (2000). Cortisol and vagal tone response to competitive challenge in preschoolers: Associations with temperament. *Developmental Psychobiology, 37*, 209–220.

Driver, J., Eimer, M., & Macaluso, E. (in press). Neurobiology of human spatial attention: Modulation, generation, and integration. In N. Kanwisher & J. Duncan (Eds.), *Attention and performance XX: Functional brain imaging of visual cognition.*

Dumas, J. E., & LaFreniere, P. J. (1993). Mother-child relationships as sources of support or stress: A comparison of competent, average, aggressive, and anxious dyads. *Child Development, 64*, 1732–1754.

Duncan, J., & Owen, A. M. (2000). Dissociative methods in the study of frontal lobe function. In S. Monsell & J. Driver (Eds.), *Control of cognitive processes: Attention and performance XVII* (pp. 567–576). Cambridge, MA: MIT Press.

Eaton, W. O. (1983). Measuring activity level with actometers: Reliability, validity, and arm length. *Child Development, 54*, 720–726.

Eaton, W. O. (1994). Temperament, development, and the Five-Factor Model: Lessons from activity level. In C. F. Halverson Jr., G. A. Kohnstamm, & R. P. Martin (Eds.), *The developing structure of temperament and personality from infancy to adulthood* (pp. 173–187). Hillsdale, NJ: Erlbaum.

Eaton, W. O., McKeen, N. A., & Campbell, D. W. (2001). The waxing and waning of movement: Implications for psychological development. *Developmental Review, 21*, 205–223.

Eaton, W. O., & Saudino, K. J. (1992). Prenatal activity level as a temperament dimension? *Infant Behavior and Development, 15*, 57–70.

Eaves, L., Silberg, J., & Erkanli, A. (2003). Resolving multiple epigenetic pathways to adolescent depression. *Journal of Child Psychology and Psychiatry, 44*, 1006–1014.

Ebstein, R. P., Levine, J., Geller, V., Auerbach, J., Gritsenko, I., & Belmaker, R. H. (1998). Dopamine D4 receptor and serotonin transporter promoter in the determination of neonatal temperament. *Molecular Psychiatry, 3*, 238–246.

Ebstein, R. P., Novick, O., Umansky, R., Priel, B., Osher, Y., Blaine, D., et al. (1996). Dopamine D4 receptor (D4DR) exon III polymorphism associated with the human personality trait of novelty seeking. *Nature Genetics, 12*(1), 78–80.

Eisenberg, N., Cumberland, A., Spinrad, T. L., Fabes, R. A., Shepard, S. A., Reider, M., et al. (2001). The relations of regulation and emotionality to children's externalizing and internalizing problem behavior. *Child Development, 72*, 1112–1134.

Eisenberg, N., Fabes, R. A., Guthrie, I. K., Murphy, B. C., Poulin, R., & Shepard, S. (1996). The relations of regulation and emotionality to problem behavior in elementary school children. *Development and Psychopathology, 8*, 141–162.

Eisenberg, N., Fabes, R. A., Guthrie, I. K., & Reiser, M. (2000). Dispositional emotionality and regulation: Their role in predicting quality of social functioning. *Journal of Personality and Social Psychology, 78*, 136–157.

Eisenberg, N., Guthrie, I. K., Fabes, R. A., Shepard, S., Losoya, S., Murphy, B. C., et al. (2000). Prediction of elementary school children's externalizing problem behaviors from attentional and be-

havioral regulation and negative emotionality. *Child Development, 71*(5), 1367–1382.

Eisenberg, N., Spinrad, T. L., Fabes, R. A., Reiser, M., Cumberland, A., Shepard, S. A., et al. (2004). The relations of effortful control and impulsivity to children's resiliency and adjustment. *Child Development, 75*(1), 25–46.

El-Sheikh, M. (2001). Parental drinking problems and children's adjustment: Vagal regulation and emotional reactivity as pathways and moderators of risk. *Journal of Abnormal Psychology, 110*, 499–515.

El-Sheikh, M., Harger, J., & Whitson, S. M. (2001). Exposure to interparental conflict and children's adjustment and physical health: The moderating role of vagal tone. *Child Development, 72*, 1617–1636.

Escalona, S. K. (1968). *The roots of individuality: Normal patterns of development in infancy.* Chicago: Aldine.

Eysenck, H. J. (1967). *The biological basis of personality.* Springfield, IL: Charles C Thomas.

Eysenck, H. J., & Eysenck, M. W. (1985). *Personality and individual differences: A natural science approach.* New York: Plenum Press.

Fabes, R. A., Eisenberg, N., & Eisenbud, L. (1993). Behavioral and physiological correlates of children's reactions to others in distress. *Developmental Psychology, 29*, 655–663.

Fabes, R. A., Eisenberg, N., Jones, S., Smith, M., Guthrie, I., Poulin, R., et al. (1999). Regulation, emotionality, and preschoolers' socially competent peer interactions. *Child Development, 70*, 432–442.

Fabes, R. A., Eisenberg, N., Karbon, M., Bernzweig, J., Speer, A. L., & Carlo, G. (1994). Socialization of children's vicarious emotional responding and prosocial behavior: Relations with mothers' perceptions of children's emotional reactivity. *Developmental Psychology, 30*, 44–55.

Fabes, R. A., Eisenberg, N., Karbon, M., & Troyer, D. (1994). The relations of children's emotion regulation to their vicarious emotional responses and comforting behaviors. *Child Development, 65*, 1678–1693.

Fan, J., Flombaum, J. I., McCandliss, B. D., Thomas, K. M., & Posner, M. I. (2003). Cognitive and brain consequences of conflict. *NeuroImage, 18*, 42–57.

Fan, J., Fossella, J. A., Sommer, T., Wu, Y., & Posner, M. I. (2003). Mapping the genetic variation of executive attention onto brain activity. *Proceedings of the National Academy of Sciences, USA, 100*, 7406–7411.

Fan, J., McCandliss, B. D., Sommer, T., Raz, A., & Posner, M. I. (2002). Testing the efficiency and independence of attentional networks. *Journal of Cognitive Neuroscience, 14*, 340–347.

Fan, J., Wu, Y., Fossella, J., & Posner, M. I. (2001). Assessing the heritability of attentional networks. *BMC Neuroscience, 2*, 14.

Feldman, R., Greenbaum, C. W., & Yirmiya, N. (1999). Mother-infant affect synchrony as an antecedent of the emergence of self-control. *Developmental Psychology, 35*, 223–231.

Fordham, F. (1953). *An introduction to Jung's psychology.* New York: Plenum Press.

Forman, D. R., O'Hara, M. W., Larsen, K., Coy, K. C., Gorman, L. L., & Stuart, S. (2003). Infant emotionality: Observational methods and the validity of maternal reports. *Infancy, 4*, 541–565.

Fossella, J., Posner, M. I., Fan, J., Swanson, J. M., & Pfaff, D. W. (2002). Attentional phenotypes for the analysis of higher mental function. *Scientific World Journal, 2*, 217–223.

Fowles, D. C. (1982). Heart rate as an index of anxiety: Failure of a hypothesis. In J. T. Cacioppo & R. E. Petty (Eds.), *Perspectives in cardiovascular psychophysiology* (pp. 93–126). New York: Guilford Press.

Fowles, D. C. (1994). A motivational theory of psychopathology. In W. Spaulding (Ed.), *Nebraska Symposium on Motivation: Vol. 41. Integrated views of motivation and emotion* (pp. 181–238). Lincoln: University of Nebraska Press.

Fowles, D. C., & Kochanska, G. (2000). Temperament as a moderator of pathways to conscience in children: The contribution of electrodermal activity. *Psychophysiology, 37,* 788–795.

Fox, N. A., Calkins, S. D., & Bell, M. A. (1994). Neural plasticity and development in the first two years of life: Evidence from cognitive and socioemotional domains of research. *Development and Psychopathology, 6,* 677–696.

Fox, N. A., & Field, T. (1989). Individual differences in preschool entry behavior. *Journal of Applied Developmental Psychology, 10,* 527–540.

Fox, N. A., Henderson, H. A., Rubin, K. H., Calkins, S. D., & Schmidt, L. A. (2001). Continuity and discontinuity of behavioral inhibition and exuberance: Psychophysiological and behavioral influences across the first four years of life. *Child Development, 72,* 1–21.

Fox, N. A., & Stifter, C. A. (1989). Biological and behavioral differences in infant reactivity and regulation. In G. Kohnstamm, J. Bates, & M. K. Rothbart (Eds.), *Temperament in childhood* (pp. 169–183). Chichester, England: Wiley.

Fries, M. E., & Woolf, P. (1954). Some hypotheses on the role of congenital activity type in personality development. *Psychoanalytic Study of the Child, 8,* 48–64.

Gallagher, K. C. (2002). Does child temperament moderate the influence of parenting on adjustment? *Developmental Review, 22,* 623–643.

Garcia Coll, C. T., Halpern, L. F., Vohr, B. R., Seifer, R., & Oh, W. (1992). Stability and correlates of change of early temperament in preterm and full-term infants. *Infant Behavior and Development, 15,* 137–153.

Gartstein, M. A., & Rothbart, M. K. (2003). Studying infant temperament via the revised infant behavior questionnaire. *Infant Behavior and Development, 26,* 64–86.

Gerardi-Caulton, G. (2000). Sensitivity to spatial conflict and the development of self-regulation in children 24 to 36 months of age. *Developmental Science, 3,* 397–404.

Gesell, A. (1928) *Infancy and human growth.* New York: MacMillan.

Gest, S. D. (1997). Behavioral inhibition: Stability and associations with adaptation from childhood to early adulthood. *Journal of Personality and Social Psychology, 72*(2), 467–475.

Gilliom, M., & Shaw, D. (2004). Codevelopment of externalizing and internalizing problems in early childhood. *Development and Psychopathology, 16,* 313–333.

Gilliom, M., Shaw, D. S., Beck, J. E., Schonberg, M. A., & Lukon, J. L. (2002). Anger regulation in disadvantaged preschool boys: Strategies, antecedents, and the development of self-control. *Developmental Psychology, 38,* 222–235.

Goldberg, L. R. (1990). An alternative "description of personality": The Big-Five factor structure. *Journal of Personality and Social Psychology, 59,* 1216–1229.

Goldberg, L. R. (1993). The structure of phenotypic personality traits. *American Psychologist, 48,* 26–34.

Goldman-Rakic, P. S. (1988). Topography of cognition: Parallel distributed networks in primate association cortex. *Annual Review of Neuroscience, 11,* 137–156.

Goldsmith, H. H. (1989). Behavior-genetic approaches to temperament. In G. A. Kohnstamm, J. E. Bates, & M. K. Rothbart (Eds.), *Temperament in childhood* (pp. 111–132). Chichester, England: Wiley.

Goldsmith, H. H. (1993). Temperament: Variability in developing emotion systems. In M. Lewis & J. M. Haviland (Eds.), *Handbook of emotion* (pp. 353–364). New York: Guilford Press.

Goldsmith, H. H., Buss, K. A., & Lemery, K. S. (1997). Toddler and childhood temperament: Expanded content, stronger genetic evidence, new evidence for the importance of environment. *Developmental Psychology, 33,* 891–905.

Goldsmith, H. H., & Campos, J. J. (1982). Toward a theory of infant temperament. In R. Emde & R. Harmon (Eds.), *Attachment and affiliative systems* (pp. 161–193). New York: Plenum Press.

Goldsmith, H. H., & Gottesman, I. I. (1977). An extension of construct validity for personality scales using twin-based criteria. *Journal of Research in Personality, 11,* 381–397.

Goldsmith, H. H., & Hewitt, E. C. (2003). Validity of parental report of temperament: Distinctions and needed research. *Infant Behavior and Development, 26,* 108–111.

Goldsmith, H. H., Lemery, K. S., Buss, K. A., & Campos, J. J. (1999). Genetic analyses of focal aspects of infant temperament. *Developmental Psychology, 35,* 972–985.

Goldsmith, H. H., Losoya, S. H., Bradshaw, D. L., & Campos, J. J. (1994). Genetics of personality: A twin study of the five-factor model and parental-offspring analyses. In C. Halverson, R. Martin, & G. Kohnstamm (Eds.), *The developing structure of temperament and personality from infancy to adulthood* (pp. 241–265). Hillsdale, NJ: Erlbaum.

Goldsmith, H. H., & Rieser-Danner, L. (1986). Variation among temperament theories and validation studies of temperament assessment. In G. A. Kohnstamm (Ed.), *Temperament discussed: Temperament and development in infancy and childhood* (pp. 1–9). Lisse: Swets & Zeitlinger.

Goldsmith, H. H., Rieser-Danner, L. A., & Briggs, S. (1991). Evaluating convergent and discriminant validity of temperament questionnaires for preschoolers, toddlers, and infants. *Developmental Psychology, 27,* 566–579.

Goldsmith, H. H., & Rothbart, M. K. (1991). Contemporary instruments for assessing early temperament by questionnaire and in the laboratory. In A. Angleitner & J. Strelau (Eds.), *Explorations in temperament: International perspectives on theory and measurement* (pp. 249–272). New York: Plenum Press.

Goodnight, J. A., Bates, J. E., Newman, J. P., Dodge, K. A., & Pettit, G. S. (2004). *The interactive influence of friend deviance, disinhibitory tendencies, and gender on the development of externalizing behavior during early and middle adolescence.* Manuscript submitted for publication.

Gosling, S. D., & John, O. P. (1999). Personality dimensions in nonhuman animals: A cross-species review. *Current Directions in Psychological Science, 8,* 69–75.

Gray, J. A. (1991). The neuropsychology of temperament. In J. Strelau & A. Angleitner (Eds.), *Explorations in temperament: International perspectives on theory and measurement* (pp. 105–128). New York: Plenum Press.

Gray, J. A., & McNaughton, N. (1996). The neuropsychology of anxiety: Reprise. In D. A. Hope (Ed.), *Nebraska Symposium on Motivation: Vol. 43. Perspectives on anxiety, panic, and fear—Current theory and research in motivation* (pp. 61–134). Lincoln: University of Nebraska Press.

Graziano, W. G. (1994). The development of agreeableness as a dimension of personality. In C. F. Halverson, G. A. Kohnstamm, &

R. P. Martin (Eds.), *The developing structure of temperament and personality from infancy to adulthood* (pp. 339–354). Hillsdale, NJ: Erlbaum.

Graziano, W. G., & Eisenberg, N. (1997). Agreeableness: A dimension of personality. In R. Hogan, J. A. Johnson, & S. Briggs (Eds.), *Handbook of personality psychology* (pp. 795–824). San Diego, CA: Academic Press.

Graziano, W. G., & Tobin, R. M. (2002). Agreeableness: Dimension of personality or social desirability artifact? *Journal of Personality, 70*, 695–727.

Green, J., & Goldwyn, R. (2002). Annotation: Attachment disorganisation and psychopathology—New findings in attachment research and their potential implications for developmental psychopathology in childhood. *Journal of Child Psychology and Psychiatry, 43*, 835–846.

Guerin, D. W., Gottfried, A. W., Oliver, P. H., & Thomas, C. W. (1994). Temperament and school functioning during early adolescence. *Journal of Early Adolescence, 14*, 200–225.

Gunnar, M. R. (1990). The psychobiology of infant temperament. In J. Colombo & J. Fagen (Eds.), *Individual differences in infancy: Reliability, stability, prediction* (pp. 387–409). Hillsdale, NJ: Erlbaum.

Gunnar, M. R. (1994). Psychoendocrine studies of temperament and stress in early childhood: Expanding current models. In J. E. Bates & T. D. Wachs (Eds.), *Temperament: Individual differences at the interface of biology and behavior* (pp. 175–198). Washington, DC: American Psychological Association.

Gunnar, M. R., Brodersen, L., Krueger, K., & Rigatuso, J. (1996). Dampening of adrenocortical responses during infancy: Normative changes and individual differences. *Child Development, 67*, 877–889.

Gunnar, M. R., & Cheatham, C. L. (2003). Brain and behavior interface: Stress and the developing brain. *Infant Mental Health Journal, 24*, 195–211.

Gunnar, M. R., Sebanc, A. M., Tout, K., Donzella, B., & Van Dulmen, M. M. H. (2003). Peer rejection, temperament, and cortisol activity in preschoolers. *Developmental Psychobiology, 43*, 346–358.

Gusnard, D. A., Ollinger, J. M., Shulman, G. L., Cloninger, C. R., Price, J. L., Van Essen, D. C., et al. (2003). Persistence and brain circuitry. *Proceedings of the National Academy of Sciences, USA, 100*, 3479–3484.

Hagekull, B. (1989). Longitudinal stability of temperament within a behavioral style framework. In G. A. Kohnstamm, J. E. Bates, & M. K. Rothbart (Eds.), *Temperament in childhood* (pp. 283–297). Chichester, England: Wiley.

Hagekull, B. (1994). Infant temperament and early childhood functioning: Possible relations to the five-factor model. In J. C. J. Halverson, G. A. Kohnstamm, & R. P. Martin (Eds.), *The developing structure of temperament and personality* (pp. 227–240). Hillsdale, NJ: Erlbaum.

Hagekull, B., Bohlin, G., & Lindhagen, K. (1984). Validity of parental reports. *Infant Behavior and Development, 7*, 77–92.

Hansen, A. L., Johnsen, B. H., & Thayer, J. F. (2003). Vagal influence on working memory and attention. *International Journal of Psychophysiology, 48*, 263–274.

Hariri, A. R., Mattay, V. S., Tessitore, A., Kolachana, B., Fera, F., Goldman, D., et al. (2002). Serotonin transporter genetic variation and the response of the human amygdala. *Science, 297*, 400–403.

Harman, C., Rothbart, M. K., & Posner, M. I. (1997). Distress and attention interactions in early infancy. *Motivation and Emotion, 21*, 27–43.

Harmon-Jones, E., & Allen, J. J. B. (1997). Behavioral activation sensitivity and resting frontal EEG asymmetry: Covariation of putative indicators related to risk for mood disorders. *Journal of Abnormal Psychology, 106*, 159–163.

Hart, D., Atkins, R., & Fegley, S. (2003). Personality and development in childhood: A person-centered approach. *Monographs of the Society for Research in Child Development, 68*, 74–85.

Hegvik, R. L., McDevitt, S. C., & Carey, W. B. (1982). The middle childhood temperament questionnaire. *Developmental and Behavioral Pediatrics, 3*, 197–200.

Hemphill, S., & Sanson, A. (2001). Matching parenting to child. *Family Matters, 59*, 42–47.

Hilgard, E. R. (1962). *Introduction to psychology: Under the general editorship of Claude E. Buxton* (3rd ed.). New York: Harcourt, Brace, & World.

Holroyd, C. B., & Coles, M. G. H. (2002). The neural basis of human error processing: Reinforcement learning, dopamine, and the error-related negativity. *Psychological Review, 109*, 679–709.

Honzik, M. P. (1965). Prediction of behavior from birth to maturity [Review of the book *Birth to maturity*]. *Merrill-Palmer Quarterly, 11*, 77–88.

Huffman, L. C., Bryan, Y. E., del Carmen, R., Pedersen, F. A., Doussard-Roosevelt, J. A., & Porges, S. W. (1998). Infant temperament and cardiac vagal tone: Assessments at twelve weeks of age. *Child Development, 69*, 624–635.

Hwang, J., & Rothbart, M. K. (2003). Behavior genetics studies of infant temperament: Findings vary across parent-report instruments. *Infant Behavior and Development, 26*, 112–114.

Insel, T. R. (2003). Is social attachment an addictive disorder? *Physiology and Behavior, 79*, 351–357.

Jones, H. E. (1960). The longitudinal method in the study of personality. In I. Iscoe & H. W. Stevenson (Eds.), *Personality development in children* (pp. 3–27). Chicago: University of Chicago Press.

Jung, C. G. (1923). *Psychological types or the psychology of individuation.* New York: Harcourt Brace.

Kagan, J. (1982). The construct of difficult temperament: A reply to Thomas, Chess, and Korn. *Merrill-Palmer Quarterly, 28*, 21–24.

Kagan, J. (1994). *Galen's prophecy: Temperament in human nature.* Cambridge, MA: Harvard University Press.

Kagan, J. (1998). Biology and the child. In W. Damon (Editor-In-Chief) & N. Eisenberg (Vol Ed.), *Handbook of child psychology: Vol. 3. Social, emotional and personality development* (5th ed., pp. 177–235). New York: Wiley.

Kagan, J., Kearsley, R. B., & Zelazo, P. R. (1978). *Infancy: Its place in human development.* New York: Wiley.

Kagan, J., & Moss, H. A. (1962). *Birth to maturity.* New York: Wiley.

Kagan, J., Reznick, J. S., & Snidman, N. (1988). Biological bases of childhood shyness. *Science, 240*(4849), 167–171.

Kalin, N. H., Larson, C., Shelton, S. E., & Davidson, R. J. (1998). Asymmetric frontal brain activity, cortisol, and behavior associated with fearful temperament in rhesus monkeys. *Behavioral Neuroscience, 112*, 286–292.

Karnath, H.-O., Ferber, S., & Himmelbach, M. (2001). Spatial awareness is a function of the temporal not the posterior parietal lobe. *Nature, 411*, 951–953.

Katz, L. F., & Gottman, J. M. (1995). Vagal tone protects children from marital conflict. *Development and Psychopathology, 7*, 83–92.

Keane, S. P., & Calkins, S. D. (2004). Predicting kindergarten peer social status from toddler and preschool problem behavior. *Journal of Abnormal Child Psychology, 32*(4), 409–423.

Keenan, K., & Shaw, D. S. (1994). The development of aggression in toddlers: A study of low-income families. *Journal of Abnormal Child Psychology, 22*, 53–77.

Keiley, M. K., Bates, J. E., Dodge, K. A., & Pettit, G. S. (2000). A cross-domain growth analysis: Externalizing and internalizing behaviors during 8 years of childhood. *Journal of Abnormal Child Psychology, 28*, 161–179.

Keiley, M. K., Lofthouse, N., Bates, J. E., Dodge, K. A., & Pettit, G. S. (2003). Differential risks of covarying and pure components in mother and teacher reports of externalizing and internalizing behavior across ages 5 to 14. *Journal of Abnormal Child Psychology, 31*, 267–283.

Kenrick, D. T., & Funder, D. C. (1988). Profiting from controversy: Lessons from the person-situation debate. *American Psychologist, 43*, 23–34.

Keogh, B., Pullis, M. E., & Caldwell, J. (1982). A short form of the teacher temperament questionnaire. *Journal of Educational Measurement, 19*, 323–329.

Kessen, W. (1965). *The child.* New York: Wiley.

Kilmer, R. P., Cowen, E. L., & Wyman, P. A. (2001). A micro-level analysis of developmental, parenting, and family milieu variables that differentiate stress-resilient and stress-affected children. *Journal of Community Psychology, 29*, 391–416.

King, B. R., & Wachs, T. D. (1995, March). *Multimethod measurement of stimulus sensitivity in infants, preschoolers, and parents.* Paper presented at the meeting of the Society for Research in Child Development, Indianapolis, IN.

Kistiakovskaia, M. I. (1965). Stimuli evoking positive emotions in infants in the first months of life. *Soviet Psychology and Psychiatry, 3*, 39–48.

Kochanska, G. (1991). Socialization and temperament in the development of guilt and conscience. *Child Development, 62*, 1379–1392.

Kochanska, G. (1993). Toward a synthesis of parental socialization and child temperament in early development of conscience. *Child Development, 64*, 325–347.

Kochanska, G. (1995). Children's temperament, mothers' discipline, and security of attachment: Multiple pathways to emerging internalization. *Child Development, 66*, 597–615.

Kochanska, G. (1997). Multiple pathways to conscience for children with different temperaments: From toddlerhood to age 5. *Developmental Psychology, 33*, 228–240.

Kochanska, G., DeVet, K., Goldman, M., Murray, K. T., & Putnam, S. P. (1993). Maternal reports of conscience development and temperament in young children. *Child Development, 65*, 852–868.

Kochanska, G., & Knaack, A. (2003). Effortful control as a personality characteristic of young children: Antecedents, correlates, and consequences. *Journal of Personality, 71*, 1087–1112.

Kochanska, G., Murray, K. T., & Harlan, E. T. (2000). Effortful control in early childhood: Continuity and change, antecedents, and implications for social development. *Developmental Psychology, 36*, 220–232.

Kohlberg, L. (1969). Stage and sequence: The cognitive developmental approach to socialization. In D. A. Goslin (Ed.), *Handbook of socialization theory and research* (pp. 347–480). Chicago: Rand McNally.

Korner, A. F. (1964). Some hypotheses regarding the significance of individual differences at birth for later development. *Psychoanalytic Study of the Child, 19*, 58–72.

Korner, A. F., Hutchinson, C. A., Koperski, J., Kraemer, H. C., & Schneider, P. A. (1981). Stability of individual differences of neonatal motor and crying patterns. *Child Development, 52*, 83–90.

Korner, A. F., Zeanah, C. H., Linden, J., Kraemer, H. C., Kerkowitz, R. I., & Agras, W. S. (1985). Relation between neonatal and later activity and temperament. *Child Development, 56*, 38–42.

Krakow, J. B., & Johnson, K. L. (1981, April). *The emergence and consolidation of self-control processes from 18 to 30 months of age.* Paper presented at the meeting of the Society for Research in Child Development, Boston, MA.

Krakow, J. B., Kopp, C. B., & Vaughn, B. E. (1981, April). *Sustained attention during the second year: Age trends, individual differences, and implications for development.* Paper presented at the meeting of the Society for Research in Child Development, Boston.

Krueger, R. F., Hicks, B. M., & McGue, M. (2001). Altruism and antisocial behavior: Independent tendencies, unique personality correlates, distinct etiologies. *Psychological Science, 12*, 397–402.

Kubzansky, L. D., Martin, L. T., & Buka, S. L. (2004). Early manifestations of personality and adult emotional functioning. *Emotion, 4*, 364–377.

Lang, P. J., Bradley, M. M., & Cuthbert, B. N. (1997). Motivated attention: Affect, activation, and action. In P. J. Lang, R. F. Simmons, & M. T. Balaban (Eds.), *Attention and orienting: Sensory and motivational processes* (pp. 97–135). Mahwah, NJ: Erlbaum.

Lawrence, A. D., & Calder, A. J. (2004). Homologizing human emotions. In D. Evans & P. Cruse (Eds.), *Emotions, evolution, and rationality* (pp. 15–47). Oxford, England: Oxford University Press.

Lawrence, A. D., Calder, A. J., McGowan, S. M., & Grasby, P. M. (2002). Selective disruption of the recognition of facial expressions of anger. *NeuroReport, 13*, 881–884.

LeDoux, J. E. (1989). Cognitive-emotional interactions in the brain. *Cognition and Emotion, 3*, 267–289.

Lee, C. L., & Bates, J. E. (1985). Mother-child interaction at two years and perceived difficult temperament. *Child Development, 56*, 1314–1325.

Lemery, K. S., Essex, M. J., & Smider, N. A. (2002). Revealing the relation between temperament and behavior problem symptoms by eliminating measurement confounding: Expert ratings and factor analyses. *Child Development, 73*, 867–882.

Lengua, L. J., & Long, A. C. (2002). The role of emotionality and self-regulation in the appraisal-coping process: Tests of direct and moderating effects. *Applied Developmental Psychology, 23*, 471–493.

Lengua, L. J., West, S. G., & Sandler, I. N. (1998). Temperament as a predictor of symptomatology in children: Addressing contamination of measures. *Child Development, 69*, 164–181.

Lengua, L. J., Wolchik, S. A., Sandler, I. N., & West, S. G. (2000). The additive and interactive effects of parenting and temperament in predicting adjustment problems of children of divorce. *Journal of Clinical Child Psychology, 29*, 232–244.

Lerner, J. V., & Lerner, R. M. (1994). Explorations of the goodness-of-fit model in early adolescence. In W. B. Carey & S. C. McDevitt (Eds.), *Prevention and early intervention: Individual differences as risk factors for the mental health of children—A festschrift for Stella Chess and Alexander Thomas* (pp. 161–169). New York: Brunner/Mazel.

Lesch, K. P., Greenberg, B. D., Higley, J. D., Bennett, A., & Murphy, D. L. (2002). Serotonin transporter, personality, and behavior:

Toward a dissection of gene-gene and gene-environment interaction. In J. Benjamin, R. P. Ebstein, & R. H. Belmaker (Eds.), *Molecular genetics and the human personality* (pp. 109–136). Washington, DC: American Psychiatric Publishing.

Lewis, M., & Ramsay, D. S. (1995). Stability and change in cortisol and behavioral response to stress during the first 18 months of life. *Developmental Psychobiology, 28,* 419–428.

Lonigan, C. J., Vasey, M. W., Phillips, B. M., & Hazen, R. A. (2004). Temperament, anxiety, and the processing of threat-relevant stimuli. *Journal of Clinical Child and Adolescent Psychology, 33,* 8–20.

Lytton, H. (1995, March). *Child and family factors as predictors of conduct disorder and criminality.* Paper presented at the meeting of the Society for Research in Child Development, Indianapolis, IN.

MacDonald, K. (1988). *Social and personality development: An evolutionary synthesis.* New York: Plenum Press.

MacDonald, K. (1992). Warmth as a developmental construct: An evolutionary analysis. *Child Development, 63,* 753–773.

Martin, R. P., Wisenbaker, J., & Huttunen, M. (1994). The factor structure of instruments based on the Chess-Thomas model of temperament: Implications for the big five model. In C. F. Halverson, G. A. Kohnstamm, & R. P. Martin (Eds.), *The developing structure of temperament and personality from infancy to adulthood* (pp. 339–347). Hillsdale, NJ: Erlbaum.

Mascolo, M. F., Fischer, K. W., & Li, J. (2003). Dynamic development of component systems of emotions: Pride, shame, and guilt in China and the United States. In R. J. Davidson, K. R. Scherer, & H. H. Goldsmith (Eds.), *Handbook of affective sciences* (pp. 375–410). New York: Oxford University Press.

Matheny, A. P., Jr. (1989). Children's behavioral inhibition over age and across situations: Genetic similarity for a trait during change. *Journal of Personality, 57,* 215–235.

Matheny, A. P., Jr. (1991). Children's unintentional injuries and gender: Differentiation by environmental and psychosocial aspects. *Children's Environment Quarterly, 8,* 51–61.

Matheny, A. P., Wilson, R. S., & Thoben, A. S. (1987). Home and mother: Relations with infant temperament. *Developmental Psychology, 23,* 323–331.

McClelland, G. H., & Judd, C. M. (1993). Statistical difficulties of detecting interactions and moderator effects. *Psychological Bulletin, 114*(2), 376–390.

McClowry, S. G., Hegvik, R., & Teglasi, H. (1993). An examination of the construct validity of the middle childhood temperament questionnaire. *Merrill-Palmer Quarterly, 39,* 279–293.

Mebert, C. J. (1991). Dimensions of subjectivity in parents' ratings of infant temperament. *Child Development, 62,* 352–361.

Mezzacappa, E. (2004). Alerting, orienting, and executive attention: Developmental properties and sociodemographic correlates in an epidemiological sample of young, urban children. *Child Development, 75,* 1373–1386.

Miller, E. M., & Bates, J. E. (1986, April). *Relationships between mother perceptions and observed episodes of infant distress: Components of perceived difficult temperament.* Paper presented at the meeting of the International Conference on Infant Studies, Los Angeles, CA.

Mischel, W. (1983). Delay of gratification as process and as person variable in development. In D. Magnusson & V. P. Allen (Eds.), *Human development: An interactional perspective* (pp. 149–165). New York: Academic Press.

Mischel, W., & Ayduk, O. (2004). Willpower in a cognitive-affective processing system: The dynamics of delay of gratification. In R. F. Baumeister & K. D. Vohs (Eds.), *Handbook of self-regulation: Research, theory, and applications* (pp. 99–129). New York: Guilford Press.

Morris, A. S., Silk, J. S., Steinberg, L., Sessa, F. M., Avenevoli, S., & Essex, M. J. (2002). Temperamental vulnerability and negative parenting as interacting predictors of child adjustment. *Journal of Marriage and Family, 64,* 461–471.

Moskowitz, D. S., & Schwarz, J. C. (1982). Validity comparison of behavior counts and ratings by knowledgeable informants. *Journal of Personality and Social Psychology, 42,* 518–528.

Mun, E. Y., Fitzgerald, H. E., von Eye, A., Puttler, L. I., & Zucker, R. A. (2001). Temperamental characteristics as predictors of externalizing and internalizing child behavior problems in the contexts of high and low parental psychopathology. *Infant Mental Health Journal, 22,* 393–415.

Murphy, B. C., Eisenberg, N., Fabes, R. A., Shepard, S., & Guthrie, I. K. (1999). Consistency and change in children's emotionality and regulation: A longitudinal study. *Merrill-Palmer Quarterly, 45,* 413–444.

Murphy, B. C., Shepard, S. A., Eisenberg, N., & Fabes, R. A. (2004). Concurrent and across time prediction of young adolescents' social functioning: The role of emotionality and regulation. *Social Development, 13*(1), 56–86.

Murphy, L. B., & Moriarty, A. E. (1976). *Vulnerability, coping, and growth: From infancy to adolescence.* New Haven, CT: Yale University Press.

Needham, J. (1973). *Chinese science.* Cambridge, MA: MIT Press.

Neilon, P. (1948). Shirley's babies after 15 years. *Journal of Genetic Psychology, 73,* 175–186.

Nishijo, H., Ono, T., & Nishino, H. (1988). Single neuron responses in amygdala of alert monkey during complex sensory stimulation with affective significance. *Journal of Neuroscience, 8,* 3570–3583.

Ochsner, K. N., Bunge, S. A., Gross, J. J., & Gabrieli, J. D. E. (2002). Rethinking feelings: An fMRI study of the cognitive regulation of emotion. *Journal of Cognitive Neuroscience, 14,* 1215–1229.

O'Connor, B. P., & Dvorak, T. (2001). Conditional associations between parental behavior and adolescent problems: A search for personality-environment interactions. *Journal of Research in Personality, 35,* 1–26.

O'Connor, T. G., Caspi, A., DeFries, J. C., & Plomin, R. (2003). Genotype-environment interaction in children's adjustment to parental separation. *Journal of Child Psychology and Psychiatry and Allied Disciplines, 44*(6), 849–856.

Oldehinkel, A. J., Hartman, C. A., de Winter, A. F., Veenstra, R., & Ormel, J. (2004). Temperamental profiles associated with internalizing and externalizing problems in preadolescence. *Development and Psychopathology, 16,* 421–440.

Olson, S. L., Bates, J. E., & Bayles, K. (1990). Early antecedents of childhood impulsivity: The role of parent-child interaction, cognitive competence, and temperament. *Journal of Abnormal Child Psychology, 18,* 317–334.

Osofsky, J. D. (1979). *Handbook of infant development.* New York: Wiley.

Owens, E. B., & Shaw, D. S. (2003). Predicting growth curves of externalizing behavior across the preschool years. *Journal of Abnormal Child Psychology, 31,* 575–590.

Oxford, M., Cavell, T. A., & Hughes, J. N. (2003). Callous/unemotional traits moderate the relation between ineffective parenting and child externalizing problems: A partial replication and extension. *Journal of Clinical Child and Adolescent Psychology, 32,* 577–585.

Panksepp, J. (1982). Toward a general psychobiological theory of emotions. *Behavioral and Brain Sciences, 5,* 407–467.

Panksepp, J. (1986a). The anatomy of emotions. In R. Plutchik & H. Kellerman (Eds.), *Emotion—Theory, research and experience: Vol. 3. Biological foundations of emotions* (pp. 91–124). San Diego, CA: Academic Press.

Panksepp, J. (1986b). The neurochemistry of behavior. *Annual Review of Psychology, 37,* 77–107.

Panksepp, J. (1986c). The psychobiology of prosocial behaviors: Separation distress, play, and altruism. In C. Zahn-Waxler, E. M. Cummings, & R. Iannotti (Eds.), *Altruism and aggression: Biological and social origins* (pp. 19–57). Cambridge, England: Cambridge University Press.

Panksepp, J. (1993). Neurochemical control of moods and emotions: Amino acids to neuropeptides. In M. Lewis & J. M. Haviland (Eds.), *Handbook of emotions* (pp. 87–107). New York: Guilford Press.

Panksepp, J. (1998). *Affective neuroscience: The foundations of human and animal emotions.* New York: Oxford University Press.

Park, S. Y., Belsky, J., Putnam, S., & Crnic, K. (1997). Infant emotionality, parenting, and 3-year inhibition: Exploring stability and lawful discontinuity in a male sample. *Developmental Psychology, 33,* 218–227.

Parker, J. G., & Asher, S. R. (1987). Peer relations and later personal adjustment: Are low-accepted children at risk? *Psychological Bulletin, 102,* 357–389.

Patterson, G., & Sanson, A. (1999). The association of behavioural adjustment to temperament, parenting and family characteristics among 5-year-old children. *Social Development, 8,* 293–309.

Patterson, G. R. (1980). Mothers: The unacknowledged victims. *Monographs of the Society for Research in Child Development, 45*(5, Serial No. 186).

Patterson, G. R., Reid, J. B., & Dishion, T. J. (1992). *Antisocial boys.* Eugene, OR: Castalia.

Pauli-Pott, U., Mertesacker, B., & Beckman, D. (2004). Predicting the development of infant emotionality from maternal characteristics. *Development and Psychopathology, 16,* 19–42.

Pavlov, I. P. (1955). General types of animal and human higher nervous activity. In J. Gibbons (Ed.), *Selected works.* Moscow: Foreign Language Publishing House. (Original work published 1935)

Pedlow, R., Sanson, A. V., Prior, M., & Oberklaid, F. (1993). The stability of temperament from infancy to eight years. *Developmental Psychology, 29,* 998–1007.

Pfeifer, M., Goldsmith, H. H., Davidson, R. J., & Rickman, M. (2002). Continuity and change in inhibited and uninhibited children. *Child Development, 73,* 1474–1485.

Plomin, R., & Caspi, A. (1999). Behavioral genetics and personality. In L. A. Pervin & O. P. John (Eds.), *Handbook of personality: Theory and research* (2nd ed., pp. 251–276). New York: Guilford Press.

Plomin, R., Chipuer, H. M., & Loehlin, J. C. (1990). Behavioral genetics and personality. In A. L. Pervin (Ed.), *Handbook of personality theory and research* (pp. 225–243). New York: Guilford Press.

Plomin, R., Emde, R. N., Braungart, J. M., Campos, J., Corley, R., Fulker, D. W., et al. (1993). Genetic change and continuity from 14 to 20 months: The MacArthur Longitudinal Twin Study. *Child Development, 64,* 1354–1376.

Porges, S. W. (1986). Respiratory sinus arrhythmia: Physioslogical basis, quantitative methods, and clinical implications. In P. Grossman, K. Janssen, & D. Vaitl (Eds.), *Cardiorespiratory and cardiosomatic psychophysiology* (pp. 101–115). New York: Plenum Press.

Porges, S. W. (1991). Autonomic regulation and attention. In B. A. Campbell, H. Hayne, & R. Richardson (Eds.), *Attention and information processing in infants and adults* (pp. 201–223). Hillsdale, NJ: Erlbaum.

Porges, S. W., & Doussard-Roosevelt, J. A. (1997). The psychophysiology of temperament. In J. D. Noshpitz, S. Greenspan, S. Wieder, & J. Osofsky (Eds.), *Handbook of child and adolescent psychiatry* (pp. 163–179). New York: Wiley.

Porges, S. W., Doussard-Roosevelt, J. A., & Maiti, A. K. (1994). Vagal tone and the physiological regulation of emotion. *Monographs of the Society for Research in Child Development, 59*(2/3), 167–186, 250–283.

Porges, S. W., Doussard-Roosevelt, J. A., Portales, A. L., & Suess, P. E. (1995). Cardiac vagal tone: Stability and relation to difficultness in infants and 3-year-olds. *Developmental Psychobiology, 27,* 289–300.

Posner, M. I. (1980). Orienting of attention. *Quarterly Journal of Experimental Psychology, A, 32,* 3–25.

Posner, M. I., & Fan, J. (in press). Attention as an organ system. In J. Pomerantz (Ed.), *Neurobiology of perception and communication: From synapse to society* (The 4th De Lange Conference). Cambridge, England: Cambridge University Press.

Posner, M. I., & Petersen, S. E. (1990). The attention system of the human brain. *Annual Review of Neuroscience, 13,* 25–42.

Posner, M. I., & Raichle, M. E. (1994). *Images of the mind.* New York: Scientific American Library.

Posner, M. I., & Rothbart, M. K. (1991). Attentional mechanisms and conscious experience. In M. Rugg & A. D. Milner (Eds.), *The neuropsychology of consciousness* (pp. 91–112). London: Academic Press.

Posner, M. I., & Rothbart, M. K. (1998). Attention, self-regulation, and consciousness. *Philosophical Transactions of the Royal Society of London, B, 353,* 1915–1927.

Posner, M. I., & Rothbart, M. K. (2000). Developing mechanisms of self-regulation. *Development and Psychopathology, 12,* 427–441.

Presley, R., & Martin, R. P. (1994). Toward a structure of preschool temperament: Factor structure of the temperament assessment battery for children. *Journal of Personality, 62,* 415–448.

Prinzie, P., Onghena, P., Hellinckx, W., Grietens, H., Ghesquiere, P., & Colpin, H. (2003). The additive and interactive effects of parenting and children's personality on externalizing behaviour. *European Journal of Personality, 17,* 95–117.

Prior, M., Smart, D., Sanson, A., & Oberklaid, F. (2000). Does shy-inhibited temperament in childhood lead to anxiety problems in adolescence? *Journal of the American Academy of Child and Adolescent Psychiatry, 39,* 461–468.

Putnam, S. P., Sanson, A. V., & Rothbart, M. K. (2002). Child temperament and parenting. In M. Bornstein (Ed.), *Handbook of parenting* (2nd ed., 255–278). Mahwah, NJ: Erlbaum.

Quas, J. A., Bauer, A., & Boyce, W. T. (2004). Physiological reactivity, social support, and memory in early childhood. *Child Development, 75,* 797–814.

Quay, H. C. (1993). The psychobiology of undersocialized aggressive conduct disorder: A theoretical perspective—Toward a developmental perspective on conduct disorder. *Development and Psychopathology, 5,* 165–180.

Radke-Yarrow, M., & Sherman, T. (1990). Hard growing: Children who survive. In J. Rolf, A. S. Masten, D. Cicchetti, K. H. Neuchterlin, & S. Weintraub (Eds.), *Risk and protective factors in the development of psychopathology* (pp. 97–119). New York: Cambridge University Press.

Rainville, P., Duncan, G. H., Price, D. D., Carrier, B., & Bushnell, M. C. (1997). Pain affect encoded in human anterior cingulate but not somatosensory cortex. *Science, 277*, 968–971.

Reed, M., Pien, D., & Rothbart, M. K. (1984). Inhibitory self-control in preschool children. *Merrill-Palmer Quarterly, 30*, 131–148.

Rende, R. D. (1993). Longitudinal relations between temperament traits and behavioral syndromes in middle childhood. *Journal of the American Academy of Child and Adolescent Psychiatry, 32*, 287–290.

Richards, J. E., & Cameron, D. (1987, April). *Infant heart rate variability and behavioral developmental status.* Paper presented at the meeting of the Society for Research in Child Development, Baltimore, MD.

Roberts, B. W., & DelVecchio, W. F. (2000). The rank-order consistency of personality traits from childhood to old age: A quantitative review of longitudinal studies. *Psychological Bulletin, 126*, 3–25.

Rothbart, M. K. (1981). Measurement of temperament in infancy. *Child Development, 52*, 569–578.

Rothbart, M. K. (1986). Longitudinal observation of infant temperament. *Developmental Psychology, 22*, 356–365.

Rothbart, M. K. (1988). Temperament and the development of inhibited approach. *Child Development, 59*, 1241–1250.

Rothbart, M. K. (1989a). Biological processes of temperament. In G. Kohnstamm, J. Bates, & M. K. Rothbart (Eds.), *Temperament in childhood* (pp. 77–110). Chichester, England: Wiley.

Rothbart, M. K. (1989b). Temperament and development. In G. Kohnstamm, J. Bates, & M. K. Rothbart (Eds.), *Temperament in childhood* (pp. 187–248). Chichester, England: Wiley.

Rothbart, M. K. (1995). Concept and method in contemporary temperament research [Review of the book *Galen's prophecy*]. *Psychological Inquiry, 6*, 334–348.

Rothbart, M. K., Ahadi, S. A., & Evans, D. E. (2000). Temperament and personality: Origins and outcomes. *Journal of Personality and Social Psychology, 78*, 122–135.

Rothbart, M. K., Ahadi, S. A., & Hershey, K. L. (1994). Temperament and social behavior in childhood. *Merrill-Palmer Quarterly, 40*, 21–39.

Rothbart, M. K., Ahadi, S. A., Hershey, K., & Fisher, P. (2001). Investigations of temperament at 3 to 7 years: The children's behavior questionnaire. *Child Development, 72*, 1394–1408.

Rothbart, M. K., & Bates, J. E. (1998). Temperament. In W. Damon (Editor-In-Chief) & N. Eisenberg (Vol. Ed.), *Handbook of child psychology: Vol. 3. Social, emotional, and personality development* (5th ed., pp. 105–176). New York: Wiley.

Rothbart, M. K., & Derryberry, D. (1981). Development of individual differences in temperament. In M. E. Lamb & A. L. Brown (Eds.), *Advances in developmental psychology* (Vol. 1, pp. 37–86). Hillsdale, NJ: Erlbaum.

Rothbart, M. K., & Derryberry, D. (2002). Temperament in children. In C. von Hofsten & L. Bäckman (Eds.), *Psychology at the turn of the millennium: Vol. 2. Social, developmental, and clinical perspectives* (pp. 17–35). East Sussex, England: Psychology Press.

Rothbart, M. K., Derryberry, D., & Hershey, K. (2000). Stability of temperament in childhood: Laboratory infant assessment to parent report at seven years. In V. J. Molfese & D. L. Molfese (Eds.), *Temperament and personality development across the life span* (pp. 85–119). Hillsdale, NJ: Erlbaum.

Rothbart, M. K., Derryberry, D., & Posner, M. I. (1994). A psychobiological approach to the development of temperament. In J. E.

Bates & T. D. Wachs (Eds.), *Temperament: Individual differences at the interface of biology and behavior* (pp. 83–116). Washington, DC: American Psychological Association.

Rothbart, M. K., Ellis, L. K., & Posner, M. I. (2004). Temperament and self-regulation. In R. F. Baumeister & K. D. Vohs (Eds.), *Handbook of self-regulation: Research, theory, and applications* (pp. 357–370). New York: Guilford Press.

Rothbart, M. K., Ellis, L. K., Rueda, M. R., & Posner, M. I. (2003). Developing mechanisms of temperamental effortful control. *Journal of Personality, 71*, 1113–1143.

Rothbart, M. K., & Goldsmith, H. H. (1985). Three approaches to the study of infant temperament. *Developmental Review, 5*, 237–260.

Rothbart, M. K., & Hwang, J. (2002). Measuring infant temperament. *Infant Behavior and Development, 25*(1), 113–116.

Rothbart, M. K., & Hwang, J. (2005). Temperament and the development of competence and motivation. In A. J. Elliot & C. S. Dweck (Eds.), *Handbook of competence and motivation* (pp. 167–184). New York: Guilford Press.

Rothbart, M. K., & Mauro, J. A. (1990). Questionnaire approaches to the study of infant temperament. In J. W. Fagen & J. Colombo (Eds.), *Individual differences in infancy: Reliability, stability and prediction* (pp. 411–429). Hillsdale, NJ: Erlbaum.

Rothbart, M. K., & Posner, M. I. (in press). Temperament, attention, and developmental psychopathology. In D. Cicchetti (Ed.), *Handbook of developmental psychopathology*. Hoboken, NJ: Wiley.

Rothbart, M. K., Posner, M. I., & Hershey, K. (1995). Temperament, attention, and developmental psychopathology. In D. Cicchetti & J. D. Cohen (Eds.), *Manual of developmental psychopathology* (Vol. 1, pp. 315–340). New York: Wiley.

Rothbart, M. K., Posner, M. I., & Kieras, J. (in press). Temperament, attention, and the development of self-regulation. In K. McCartney & D. Phillips (Eds.), *Blackwell handbook of early child development*. Malden, MA: Blackwell.

Rothbart, M. K., Posner, M. I., & Rosicky, J. (1994). Orienting in normal and pathological development. *Development and Psychopathology, 6*, 635–652.

Rothbart, M. K., & Rueda, M. R. (2005). The development of effortful control. In U. Mayr, E. Awh, & S. Keele (Eds.), *Developing individuality in the human brain: A festschrift honoring Michael I. Posner—May, 2003* (pp. 167–188). Washington, DC: American Psychological Association.

Rothbart, M. K., & Sheese, B. (in press). Temperament and emotion regulation, In J. J. Gross (Ed.) *Handbook of emotion regulation*. New York: Guilford.

Rothbart, M. K., & Victor, J. (2004, October). *Temperament and the development of personality.* Paper presented at the Occasional Temperament Conference, Athens, GA.

Rothbart, M. K., Ziaie, H., & O'Boyle, C. G. (1992). Self-regulation and emotion in infancy. In N. Eisenberg & R. A. Fabes (Eds.), *Emotion and its regulation in early development: Vol. 55. New directions for child development—The Jossey-Bass education series* (pp. 7–23). San Francisco: Jossey-Bass.

Rubin, K. H., Burgess, K. B., Dwyer, K. M., & Hastings, P. D. (2003). Predicting preschoolers' externalizing behaviors from toddler temperament, conflict, and maternal negativity. *Developmental Psychology, 39*, 164–176.

Rubin, K. H., Burgess, K. B., & Hastings, P. D. (2002). Stability and social-behavioral consequences of toddlers' inhibited temperament and parenting behaviors. *Child Development, 73*, 483–495.

Rubin, K. H., Hastings, P., Chen, X., Stewart, S., & McNichol, K. (1998). Intrapersonal and maternal correlates of aggression, conflict, and externalizing problems in toddlers. *Child Development, 69,* 1614–1629.

Rueda, M. R., Fan, J., Halparin, J., Gruber, D., Lercari, L. P., McCandliss, B., et al. (2004). Development of attention during childhood. *Neuropsychologia, 42,* 1029–1040.

Rueda, M. R., Posner, M. I., & Rothbart, M. K. (2004). Attentional control and self-regulation. In R. F. Baumeister & K. D. Vohs (Eds.), *Handbook of self-regulation: Research, theory, and applications* (pp. 283–300). New York: Guilford Press.

Ruff, H. A., & Rothbart, M. K. (1996). *Attention in early development: Themes and variations.* New York: Oxford University Press.

Rushton, J. P., Brainerd, C. J., & Pressley, M. (1983). Behavioral development and construct validity: The principle of aggregation. *Psychological Bulletin, 94,* 18–38.

Russell, A., Hart, C. H., Robinson, C. C., & Olsen, S. F. (2003). Children's sociable and aggressive behavior with peers: A comparison of the U.S. and Australia, and contributions of temperament and parenting styles. *International Journal of Behavioral Development, 27,* 74–86.

Sanson, A., Hemphill, S. A., & Smart, D. (2004). Connections between temperament and social development: A review. *Social Development, 13,* 142–170.

Sanson, A., Prior, M., & Kyrios, M. (1990). Contamination of measures in temperament research. *Merrill-Palmer Quarterly, 36,* 179–192.

Sanson, A. V., Smart, D. F., Prior, M., Oberklaid, F., & Pedlow, R. (1994). The structure of temperament from 3 to 7 years: Age, sex, and sociodemographic influences. *Merrill-Palmer Quarterly, 40,* 233–252.

Saudino, K. J. (2003). Parent ratings of infant temperament lessons from twin studies. *Infant Behavior and Development, 26,* 100–107.

Saudino, K. J., & Cherny, S. S. (2001). Sources of continuity and change in observed temperament. In R. N. Emde & J. K. Hewitt (Eds.), *Infancy to early childhood: Genetic and environmental influences on developmental change* (pp. 89–110). New York: Oxford University Press.

Saudino, K. J., & Eaton, W. O. (1995). Continuity and change in objectively assessed temperament: A longitudinal twin study of activity level. *British Journal of Developmental Psychology, 13,* 81–95.

Scarr, S., & McCartney, K. (1983). How people make their own environments: A theory of genotype-environment effects. *Child Development, 54,* 242–435.

Schaffer, H. R. (1974). Cognitive components of the infant's response to strangeness. In M. Lewis & L. A. Rosenblum (Eds.), *The origins of fear* (pp. 11–24). New York: Wiley.

Schmidt, L. A., & Fox, N. A. (2002). Molecular genetics of temperamental differences in children. In J. Benjamin, R. P. Ebstein, & R. H. Belmaker (Eds.), *Molecular genetics and the human personality* (pp. 245–255). Washington, DC: American Psychiatric Publishing.

Schmidt, L. A., Fox, N. A., Perez-Edgar, K., Hu, S., & Hamer, D. H. (2001). Association of DRD4 with attention problems in normal childhood development. *Psychiatric Genetics, 11,* 25–29.

Schneirla, T. C. (1959). An evolutionary and developmental theory of biphasic processes underlying approach and withdrawal. In M. R. Jones (Ed.), *Nebraska Symposium on Motivation* (Vol. 7, pp. 297–339). Lincoln: University of Nebraska Press.

Schwebel, D. C. (2004). Temperamental risk factors for children's unintentional injury: The role of impulsivity and inhibitory control. *Personality and Individual Differences, 37,* 567–578.

Sears, R. R., Maccoby, E. E., & Levin, H. (1957). *Patterns of child rearing.* Evanston, IL: Row, Peterson.

Seifer, R. (2003). Twin studies, biases of parents, and biases of researchers. *Infant Behavior and Development, 26,* 115–117.

Seifer, R., Sameroff, A. J., Barrett, L. C., & Krafchuk, E. (1994). Infant temperament measured by multiple observations and mother report. *Child Development, 65,* 1478–1490.

Sethi, A., Mischel, W., Aber, J. L., Shoda, Y., & Rodriguez, M. L. (2000). The role of strategic attention deployment in development of self-regulation: Predicting preschoolers' delay of gratification from mother-toddler interactions. *Developmental Psychology, 6,* 767–777.

Shaw, D. S., Gilliom, M., Ingoldsby, E. M., & Nagin, D. S. (2003). Trajectories leading to school-age conduct problems. *Developmental Psychology, 39*(2), 189–200.

Sheeber, L. B. (1995). Empirical dissociations between temperament and behavior problems: A response to the Sanson, Prior, and Kyrios study. *Merrill-Palmer Quarterly, 41,* 554–561.

Shiner, R. L. (1998). How shall we speak of children's personalities in middle childhood? A preliminary taxonomy. *Psychological Bulletin, 124*(3), 308–332.

Shiner, R. L., & Caspi, A. (2003). Personality differences in childhood and adolescence: Measurement, development, and consequences. *Journal of Child Psychology and Psychiatry, 44,* 2–32.

Shiner, R. L., Masten, A. S., & Roberts, J. M. (2003). Childhood personality foreshadows adult personality and life outcomes 2 decades later. *Journal of Personality, 71,* 1145–1170.

Shiner, R. L., Masten, A. S., & Tellegen, A. (2002). A developmental perspective on personality in emerging adulthood: Childhood antecedents and concurrent adaptation. *Journal of Personality and Social Psychology, 83,* 1165–1177.

Shirley, M. M. (1933). *The first two years: A study of 25 babies.* Minneapolis: University of Minnesota Press.

Shoda, Y., Mischel, W., & Peake, P. K. (1990). Predicting adolescent cognitive and self-regulatory competencies from preschool delay of gratification: Identifying diagnostic conditions. *Developmental Psychology, 26,* 978–986.

Silberg, J. L., Febo San Miguel, V., Murrelle, E. L., Prom, E., Bates, J. E., Canino, G., et al. (2004). *Genetic and environmental influences on temperament in the first year of life: The Puerto Rico Infant Twin Study.* Unpublished manuscript.

Silverman, I. W., & Ragusa, D. M. (1992). A short-term longitudinal study of the early development of self-regulation. *Journal of Abnormal Child Psychology, 20,* 415–435.

Slabach, E. H., Morrow, J., & Wachs, T. D. (1991). Questionnaire measurement of infant and child temperament: Current status and future directions. In J. Strelau & A. Angleitner (Eds.), *Explorations in temperament: International perspectives on theory and measurement* (pp. 205–234). New York: Plenum Press.

Smeets, W. J. A. J., & González, A. (2000). Catecholamine systems in the brain of vertebrates: New perspectives through a comparative approach. *Brain Research Reviews, 33,* 308–379.

Snyder, J. A. (1977). A reinforcement analysis of interaction in problem and nonproblem children. *Journal of Abnormal Psychology, 86,* 528–535.

Spoont, M. R. (1992). Modulatory role of serotonin in neural information processing: Implications for human psychopathology. *Psychological Bulletin, 112,* 330–350.

Sprengelmeyer, R., Young, A. W., Schroeder, U., Grossenbacher, P. G., Federlein, J., Buettner, T., et al. (1999). Knowing no fear. *Proceedings of the Royal Society of London. Series B, Biological Sciences, 266,* 2451–2456.

Stams, G. J. M., Juffer, F., & van Ijzendoorn, M. H. (2002). Maternal sensitivity, infant attachment, and temperament in early childhood predict adjustment in middle childhood: The case of adopted children and their biologically unrelated parents. *Developmental Psychology, 38,* 806–821.

Stice, E., & Gonzales, N. (1998). Adolescent temperament moderates the relation of parenting to antisocial behavior and substance use. *Journal of Adolescent Research, 13,* 5–31.

Stifter, C. A., & Braungart, J. M. (1995). The regulation of negative reactivity in infancy: Function and development. *Developmental Psychology, 31,* 448–455.

Stifter, C. A., & Corey, J. M. (2001). Vagal regulation and observed social behavior in infancy. *Social Development, 10,* 189–201.

Stifter, C. A., Fox, N. A., & Porges, S. W. (1989). Facial expressivity and vagal tone in 5- and 10-month-old infants. *Infant Behavior and Development, 12,* 127–137.

Stifter, C. A., Spinrad, T. L., & Braungart-Rieker, J. M. (1999). Toward a developmental model of child compliance: The role of emotion regulation in infancy. *Child Development, 70,* 21–32.

Stoolmiller, M. (2001). Synergistic interaction of child manageability problems and parent-discipline tactics in predicting future growth in externalizing behavior for boys. *Developmental Psychology, 37,* 814–825.

Strelau, J. (1983). *Temperament personality activity.* New York: Academic Press.

Suess, P. E., Porges, S. W., & Plude, D. J. (1994). Cardiac vagal tone and sustained attention in school-age children. *Psychophysiology, 31,* 17–22.

Suls, J., Martin, R., & David, J. P. (1998). Person-environment fit and its limits: Agreeableness, neuroticism, and emotional reactivity to interpersonal conflict. *Personality and Social Psychology Bulletin, 24,* 88–98.

Swanson, J. M., Flodman, P., Kennedy, J., Spence, M. A., Moyzis, R., Schuck, S., et al. (2000). Dopamine genes and ADHD. *Neuroscience and Biobehavioral Reviews, 24,* 21–25.

Teglasi, H., & Epstein, S. (1998). Temperament and personality theory: The perspective of cognitive-experiential self-theory. *School Psychology Review, 27,* 534–550.

Teglasi, H., & MacMahon, B. V. (1990). Temperament and common problem behaviors of children. *Journal of Applied Developmental Psychology, 11,* 331–349.

Tellegen, A. (1985). Structures of mood and personality and their relevance to assessing anxiety, with an emphasis on self-report. In A. H. Tuma & J. D. Maser (Eds.), *Anxiety and the anxiety disorders* (pp. 681–706). Hillsdale, NJ: Erlbaum.

Tellegen, A., Lykken, D. T., Bouchard, T. J., Jr., Wilcox, K. J., Segal, N. L., & Rich, S. (1988). Personality similarity in twins reared apart and together. *Journal of Personality and Social Psychology, 54,* 1031–1039.

Thomas, A., & Chess, S. (1977). *Temperament and development.* New York: New York University Press.

Thomas, A., Chess, S., & Birch, H. G. (1968). *Temperament and behavior disorders in children.* New York: New York University Press.

Thomas, A., Chess, S., Birch, H. G., Hertzig, M. E., & Korn, S. (1963). *Behavioral individuality in early childhood.* New York: New York University Press.

Thompson, R. A. (1998). Early sociopersonality development. In W. Damon (Editor-In-Chief) & N. Eisenberg (Vol. Ed.), *Handbook of child psychology: Vol. 3. Social, emotional, and personality development* (5th ed., pp. 25–104). New York: Wiley.

Tomarken, A. J., Davidson, R. J., Wheeler, R. E., & Doss, R. C. (1992). Individual differences in anterior brain asymmetry and fundamental dimensions of emotion. *Journal of Personality and Social Psychology, 62,* 676–687.

Tschann, J. M., Kaiser, P., Chesney, M. A., Alkon, A. & Boyce, W. T. (1996). Resilience and vulnerability among preschool children: Family functioning, temperament, and behavior problems. *Journal of the American Academy of Child and Adolescent Psychiatry, 35,* 184–192.

Tuddenham, R. D. (1959). The constancy of personality ratings over 2 decades. *Genetic Psychology Monographs, 60,* 3–29.

Turken, A. U., & Swick, D. (1999). Response selection in the human anterior cingulate cortex. *Nature Neuroscience, 2,* 920–924.

Valiente, C., Eisenberg, N., Fabes, R. A., Shepard, S. A., Cumberland, A., & Losoya, S. (2004). Prediction of children's empathy-related responding from their effortful control and parents' expressivity. *Developmental Psychology, 40,* 911–926.

van der Mark, I. L., Bakermans-Kranenburg, M. J., & van Ijzendoorn, M. H. (2002). The role of parenting, attachment, and temperamental fearfulness in the prediction of compliance in toddler girls. *British Journal of Developmental Psychology, 20,* 361–378.

van der Mark, I. L., van Ijzendoorn, M. H., & Bakermans-Kranenburg, M. J. (2002). Development of empathy in girls during the second year of life: Associations with parenting, attachment, and temperament. *Social Development, 11,* 451–468.

Van Leeuwen, K. G., Mervielde, I., Braet, C., & Bosmans, G. (2004). Child personality and parental behavior as moderators of problem behavior: Variable and person-centered approaches. *Developmental Psychology, 40,* 1028–1046.

Vaughn, B. E., Kopp, C. B., & Krakow, J. B. (1984). The emergence and consolidation of self-control from 18 to 30 months of age: Normative trends and individual differences. *Child Development, 55,* 990–1004.

Vaughn, B. E., Stevenson-Hinde, J., Waters, E., Kotsaftis, A., Lefever, G. B., Shouldice, A., et al. (1992). Attachment security and temperament in infancy and early childhood: Some conceptual clarifications. *Developmental Psychology, 28,* 463–473.

Victor, J. B., Rothbart, M. K., & Baker, S. R. (2006). Manuscript in preparation.

Vitaro, F., Brendgen, M., & Tremblay, R. E. (2002). Reactively and proactively aggressive children: Antecedent and subsequent characteristics. *Journal of Child Psychology and Psychiatry and Allied Disciplines, 43*(4), 495–506.

Vogt, B. A., Finch, D. M., & Olson, C. R. (1992). Functional heterogeneity in cingulate cortex: The anterior executive and posterior evaluative regions. *Cerebral Cortex, 2,* 435–443.

Von Bargen, D. M. (1983). Infant heart rate: A review of research and methodology. *Merrill-Palmer Quarterly, 29,* 115–149.

Wachs, T. D. (1987). Specificity of environmental action as manifest in environmental correlates of infants' mastery motivation. *Developmental Psychology, 23,* 782–790.

Wachs, T. D. (2000). *Necessary but not sufficient: The respective roles of single and multiple influences on individual development.* Washington, DC: American Psychological Association.

Wachs, T. D., & Bates, J. E. (2001). Temperament. In G. Bremner & A. Fogel (Eds.), *Blackwell handbook of infant development: Handbooks of developmental psychology* (pp. 465–501). Malden, MA: Blackwell.

Wachs, T. D., & Plomin, R. (1991). Overview of current models and research. In T. D. Wachs & R. Plomin (Eds.), *Conceptualization and measurement of organism-environment interaction* (pp. 1–8). Washington, DC: American Psychological Association.

Watson, D., & Clark, L. A. (1992). On traits and temperament: General and specific factors of emotional experience and their relation to the five-factor model. *Journal of Personality, 60,* 441–476.

Watson, D., & Clark, L. A. (1997). The measurement and mismeasurement of mood: Recurrent and emergent issues. *Journal of Personality Assessment, 68,* 267–296.

Webb, E. (1915). Character and intelligence. *British Journal of Psychology, 1,* 3.

Werner, E. E. (1985). Resilient offspring of alcoholics: A longitudinal study from birth to age 18. *Journal of Studies on Alcohol, 47,* 34–40.

Wertlieb, D., Weigel, C., Springer, T., & Feldstein, M. (1987). Temperament as a moderator of children's stressful experiences. *American Journal of Orthopsychiatry, 57,* 234–245.

Wills, T. A., Sandy, J. M., Yaeger, A., & Shinar, O. (2001). Family risk factors and adolescent substance use: Moderation effects for temperament dimensions. *Developmental Psychology, 37,* 283–297.

Wimer, R. E., & Wimer, C. C. (1985). Animal behavior genetics: A search for the biological foundations of behavior. *Annual Review of Psychology, 36,* 171–218.

Wolff, P. H. (1965). The development of attention in young infants. *Annals of the New York Academy of Sciences, 118,* 8–30.

Wooton, J. M., Frick, P. J., Shelton, K. K., & Silverthorn, P. (1997). Ineffective parenting and childhood conduct problems: The moderating role of callous-unemotional traits. *Journal of Consulting and Clinical Psychology, 65,* 301–308.

Wundt, W. (1903). *Grundzuge der physiologischen psychologie* [Lectures on human and animal psychology] (5th ed., Vol. 3). Leipzig, Germany: W. Engelmann.

Zuckerman, M. (1984). Sensation seeking: A comparative approach to a human trait. *Behavioral and Brain Sciences, 7,* 413–471.

Zuckerman, M. (1991). *Psychobiology of personality.* New York: Cambridge University Press.

Zuckerman, M. (1995). Good and bad humors: Biochemical bases of personality and its disorders. *Psychological Science, 6,* 325–332.

CHAPTER 4

Biology, Culture, and Temperamental Biases

JEROME KAGAN and NATHAN A. FOX

An unreserved acceptance of the idea that biological processes contribute to psychological phenomena has waxed and waned over time. Although attributing a feeling of fatigue to a bacterial infection is currently noncontroversial, the suggestion that a dysphoric mood could be due, in part, to an inherited physiology encountered more resistance during the last century. One historical source of the skepticism was the decision by Greek philosophers two millennia ago to separate soul and body rather than to follow the classic Chinese philosophers and assume that mental and bodily events are joined in as seamless a unity as color, shape, and motion in the conscious perception of a cloud at sunset.

The basis for denying biology a significant role in mood and behavior during the middle third of the twentieth century was the understandable desire, especially among Americans, to minimize biological variation among varied immigrant or ethnic groups. This ideology was in the service of defending the optimistic hope that proper family experience and education could create a

Jerome Kagan is indebted to his recent colleagues, Nancy Snidman, Mark McManis, Sue Woodward, and Vali Kahn, and, earlier colleagues, Doreen Arcus and J. Steven Reznick, for their wisdom in the research on high and low reactive infants. Kagan also acknowledges current research support from the Bial Foundation, Metanexus Institute, the COUQ Foundation, and past support from the William T. Grant and John D. and Catherine T. MacArthur Foundations. Nathan Fox thanks Peter Marshall, Louis Schmidt, and Heather Henderson, and acknowledges research support from NICHD in the form of Grant HD 17895.

community of citizens that possessed roughly equivalent ability, motivation, civility, and capacity for happiness (May, 1959).

Second, a broad conceptual moat must be jumped when the vocabularies of biology and psychology occur in the same sentence. No one has difficulty understanding "The boy ran away because he felt afraid" because everyone's experience validates the association between a feeling of fear and the act of fleeing. But many find it more difficult to understand "The boy ran away because of a limbic discharge" because they have not consciously experienced that brain event, and, further, such a sentence occurs rarely in social discourse. Hence, both the sense and referential meanings of the second sentence are less clear and a causal association between flight and a limbic discharge seems less valid. Ease of assimilation is always easier when the statement contains ideas to which a listener is accustomed. Fifteenth-century Europeans would have experienced far less difficulty than modern ones in understanding, and accepting as true, the declaration: "The woman died because she was bewitched."

A third obstacle to combining biological and psychological terms, which is related to the issue of different vocabularies, is inherent in all emergent phenomena; the tides offer an example. Most people who have had the relevant education believe that the changing height of the oceans during each day is due to changes in the gravitational relation between the moon and the earth, even though there is a bit of mystery surrounding the idea that the gravitational attraction between moon and earth affects the waterline at the beach. No feeling of mystery— or certainly much less—is engendered when the linked phenomena are at the same level of description, as in "The child cried after she fell," because our phenomenology supplies the mediating feeling of pain or surprise that we know produces a cry. The contemporary public is ready to believe the recent, and surprising, declaration that a bacterium (*Heliobacter pylori*) can cause ulcers because it is easy to imagine how swarms of bacteria could devour the stomach's delicate mucosal lining. An earlier generation was considerably more resistant to the psychosomatic hypothesis that conflict over dependency could produce ulcers because it was harder to imagine how an unconscious psychological state could be responsible for this materialistic condition.

When the mind must leap from gravitational force to tides or from psychological states to ulcers, and the intermediate events are not completely clear, people must rely on faith in authority to accept both statements as true. When knowledge of the mediating event is incomplete, as it is for most propositions that relate brain physiology to psychology, considerable faith is required. The resulting feeling of disquiet mars the aesthetic feeling that is a distinguishing feature of a completely satisfying explanation.

That is why psychologists continue to disagree on the relative contributions of genetic programs and the epigenetic events following conception to the observed phenotype, even though both influences are always formative. A gardener who plants tomato seeds in the spring cannot know the exact size, coloring, or taste of the plant picked months later because of the unpredictability of temperature, rainfall, and pests. But she knows with certainty that the fruit picked in the fall will be a tomato and not an apple.

All psychological phenotypes are the products of cascades of events, many unpredictable, but the genome of the child constrains seriously the envelope of possible profiles that a particular child might display. It seems wise, therefore, to acknowledge, as the ancients did, that genes and experience act coordinately and cease quarreling over which force is stronger.

The emergent nature of psychological events from biology is analogous to the temperature and pressure of a closed container of gas. Pressure and temperature describe the emergent consequences of large numbers of molecular collisions and are inappropriate terms for a single molecule. The assumption that every psychological phenomenon can be explained by or derived from the activity of particular neuronal ensembles, as the temperature and pressure of a vessel of gas are explained by equations describing the collisions of large numbers of atoms, is flawed because the motion of each atom is assumed to be independent of the motion of every other atom. This assumption does not apply to brains for each neuron is influenced by the activity of others. Anxiety is a property of a person and not of the neurons that participate in that emotional state. Thus, the scholar who acknowledges that thought, feeling, and action depend on and emerge from brain events but who insists that these events must be described in a language different from the one that describes underlying brain processes is not a metaphysical dualist. All of nature cannot be described with one vocabulary because brains have qualitatively different structures than schemata and semantic networks.

This argument is not a rejection of attempts to understand the biological contributions to psychological processes. Even though complete translation of the latter events into the language of the former is probably impossible, research that looks for the biological correlates has advantages. First, the products of this work deepen our understanding of the molar events. The discovery that connections between temporal and frontal structures mature during the last half of the 1st year implies that there should be major improvements in working memory at this time, and that inference leads to a new conceptualization of the phenomenon Piaget called object permanence (Diamond, 1990).

A failure to find expected correspondences between brain and behavior often provides fruitful seeds for new ideas. The fact that lesions of the dorsolateral prefrontal cortex impair working memory, but do not impair the retrieval of motor habits invites a distinction among different kinds of memories. The fact that an intact amygdala is necessary for a rat to display a potentiated startle reflex to a loud sound presented after a conditioned stimulus, but is not necessary for the startle reflex invites a distinction between two types of startles. Thus, learning more about the relation of brain activity to psychological events contributes to theory, even though a complete translation of mind to brain is probably not possible.

One reason why the description of a profile of neuronal activation cannot be a substitute for psychological structure is that the context and the agent's past experience determine which particular neural patterns, and therefore which psychological structures will be activated. No sample of adults of the same age, sex, social class, and health, tested at the same time of day produces identical profiles of brain activity to a particular stimulus because each person brings a different history to the context of evaluation. Two groups of adults subject to similar torture provide a more complex example of this principle. One group comprised well-educated political activists, the second consisted of less well-educated, apolitical men. Although all prisoners experienced similar acts of torture, more of the apolitical men developed anxiety, depression, or posttraumatic stress disorder (Basoglu et al., 1997). The fact that fewer political activists developed these symptoms has to be due in part to their intellectual commitment to the causes that led to their incarceration. But the psychological state we call intellectual commitment to a cause cannot be translated into sentences whose words only describe brain processes.

A psychological representation of a class of events is a hypothetical network consisting of many interrelated features that can include representations from several sensory modalities, motor programs, and language. The particular subset of features activated in a person at a particular time and place is not knowable until the incentive is specified. Further, different incentives will activate different parts of the large network. The features of the network for thunderstorms evoked in a person caught outside in a summer storm are different from those activated when the same person is in an office building or flying in an airplane as lightning is scarring the night sky. Thus, a summer storm can activate a large number of representations and no member of this family is knowable until the scientist intervenes with a probe to measure it. No member is more essential than any other, and none is active when the person is sipping coffee on a sunny June morning. This means that the neural pattern of activation in a person lying in a positron-emission tomography (PET) or functional magnetic resonance imaging (fMRI) scanner looking at pictures of snakes is not to be regarded as the true or only neural configuration that these stimuli would provoke. The same pictures would create a different brain state if the person were looking at them on a television screen in his living room. There is no master clock for the universe and there is no God's eye view of the brain's response to an incentive because each person has a particular frame of mind and brain state in each class of situation, and that frame affects which neuronal ensembles and representations will be activated. Put differently, a number of possible brain states are possible the moment a new event occurs. The context, the immediately prior state, and the person's temperament and past history combine to select one outcome from the set of candidates: That is the phenomenon scientists measure. Thus, probabilistic quantum principles operate the moment an event occurs; classical principles take over milliseconds later when one outcome has been chosen.

BIOLOGY AND BRAIN MATURATION

Biological processes affect psychological growth in two obvious but very different ways. Initially, the lawful maturation of the nervous system is accompanied by universal changes in emotion, cognition, and behavior. For example, the 1st year consists of two important transitions. One occurs at 2 to 3 months, and the second at 7 to 12 months of age. The first transition is accompanied by disappearance of newborn reflexes, endogenous smiling, a decrease in crying, the appearance of circadian rhythm, and the enhancement of recognition memory.

The disappearance of the reflexes is believed to be due to cortical inhibition of brain stem neurons (Volpe, 1995). Although descending axons from the supplementary motor area reach the brain stem and spinal cord targets before birth, actual synaptic contacts do not appear until 2 to 3 months after birth (Kostovic, 1990).

The transition between 7 and 12 months is marked by the ability to activate a representation for a past event that is no longer present, hold that representation online, and relate it to features in the current situation in a hypothetical process that is called working memory. The enhancement in working memory is accompanied by a spurt of growth and differentiation in both pyramidal and inhibitory interneurons in the prefrontal cortex (Kostovic, 1990). Not surprisingly, this anatomical growth is accompanied by increased glucose uptake in the lateral frontal cortex and the dorsolateral prefrontal cortex (Chugani, 1994; Huttenlocher, 1979).

The 2nd year is characterized by the initial comprehension and expression of speech, the capacity to infer selected mental and feeling states in others, representations of actions that are prohibited, and the conscious awareness of some of the self's feelings and intentions. One basis for these changes is the growth that occurs in the neurons in layer three of the prefrontal cortex, which elongate and grow spines. Layer three represents the neurons that participate in the corpus callosum, which unites the hemispheres. When the neurons of one hemisphere make contact with those of the opposite hemisphere through the corpus callosum, the speed of integrating information from both hemispheres is accelerated (Mrzljak & Uylings, 1990).

Finally, after the 2nd year of life, over the next 3 or 4 years, there is maturation of at least five cognitive abilities: (1) the reliable integration of past with present, (2) anticipation of the future, (3) appreciation of causality, (4) enhanced reliance on semantic categories, and (5) detection of shared relations between events and categories. These changes are accompanied by a dramatic increase in the total cortical surface so that the human brain attains 90% of its adult weight by the time the child is 8 years old (Giedd et al., 1996). Further, the balance between the number of new synapses formed and the number eliminated shifts after the sixth birthday to a ratio that favors the latter process. There is a parallel increase in myelination and an increase in the interconnectedness that involves both hemispheres, anterior and posterior cortical sites, as well as cortical and subcortical structures. This story is being told in several chapters in this *Handbook*.

BIOLOGY AND TEMPERAMENT

Some of the stable psychological variation found among children in all cultures represents a second domain in which biology influences growth. This idea, which is the sense meaning of the concept *temperament,* comprises the primary focus of this chapter. However, the biological processes and psychological experiences that mediate the maturation of a particular class of behavior are usually different from those that are responsible for the variation in that behavior. Fear of unfamiliar adults in infancy provides a nice example of this claim. It is believed that the display of distress to and avoidance of strangers appears in most children by 7 to 9 months as a result of maturation of circuits from limbic sites to the frontal lobe (Diamond, 1990; Kagan, 1994). The variation in the intensity and chronicity of fearful behavior to strangers is believed to be due to differences in the chemistry of the amygdala and experiences with strangers rather than completion of the circuits that link the limbic structures with the frontal lobe (Kagan, 1994). Although inquiry into human temperaments is becoming more popular, there is no consensus on basic terms, measurement procedures, or robust generalizations. Hence, it is not possible in one chapter to summarize, in an integrative style, all that has been published. The interested reader is referred to several books that present the diverse views on this theme; they include Kohnstamm, Bates, and Rothbart (1989), Strelau and Angleitner (1991), Bates and Wachs (1994), and Plomin and McClearn (1993). The first task in every science is to categorize the phenomena that define its domain with concepts that capture nature's plan. Four cognitive biases interfere with this assignment. These include (a) the tendency to award priority to easily observed features, (b) the desire to honor parsimony by inventing categories with the fewest number of features, (c) a preference for concepts that imply temporal stability rather than change, and (d) the urge to believe that the inferred category refers to a real entity in nature and not simply a clever invention.

The sense meaning of temperament held by many, but not all, scientists refers to a biologically based bias for correlated clusters of feelings, thoughts, and actions that appear during childhood, but not always in the opening months, and are sculpted by varied rearing environments into a large but still limited number of traits that comprise an individual's personality profile. Hence, the stable variation in behaviors and emotions observed in older children, adolescents, and adults are personality traits, not temperamental biases, although the latter make a contribution to the profile that emerges later in development. In addition, students of human temperaments exclude stable variation in cognitive functions from this category because of the typical failure to find consistent correlations between a temperamental bias and quality of perceptual, memorial, or inferential abilities. There is no good evidence to suggest that irritability, activity, or reactivity in infants predicts differences in IQ score or other cognitive abilities in later childhood. The independence of these two domains is reasonable because the presumed physiological bases for differences in perception, memory, and reasoning are different from those that mediate the temperamental biases. The biological biases that are the foundations of temperaments can be due to heritable variation in anatomy or neurochemistry or the result of prenatal events that are not strictly genetic in origin. Each of the many temperamental profiles that has been or will be discovered in the future is a concept. The more knowledge that accumulates around the concept, the more complete the cognitive appreciation of the concept and the events to which it refers. However, the biological features that enrich a temperamental concept, and are necessary for the emergent psychological profile, cannot replace it. A small number of neurobiologists believe that one day the idea of consciousness will be reduced to a particular set of neural activities, implying that consciousness is no more than a network of circuits. The reason for rejecting that premise is the same as the rationale for rejecting the idea that a chemical description of the toxins produced by the malarial parasites is equivalent to a description of the patient's malaise. A tornado has a shape, speed, direction of motion, and color, and these features are not derivable from lengthy descriptions of groups of air molecules in the tornado. Similarly, the transparent quality of a pane of glass is not explained by a description of the chemical structure of silica. Genes select or stabilize a form, but unless we know the exact conditions under which the organism is developing it is not possible to predict or understand the final form (Goodwin, 1994). "We inherit dispositions, not destinies . . . lives are not simple consequences of genetic consignments. Genetic determinism is improbable for simple acts of the fruit fly, implausible for complex human behavior" (Rose, 1995, p. 648).

The remarkable advances in neuroscience have tempted some to hope that many psychological concepts will eventually be replaced with a specification of a neural circuit. Such optimism is not warranted. A tem-

porally delimited pattern of brain activation, produced by an incentive, does not necessarily reflect a person's conscious feelings. Nor can the circuit represent the sequences of thoughts, preparation for action, and autonomic reactions that will occur subsequently. All of these events are referents for the psychological state.

The psychological meaning of *fear* is not a momentary brain state, even though a brain state accompanies the psychological state and, therefore, cannot be ignored. The neurophysiological phenomena should be given their own conceptual label. Three different sources of evidence are often used to infer a fear state: (1) a behavioral profile, (2) a pattern of physiological reactions, and (3) a self-report. At the moment, the correlations among these three referents are not high enough to treat them as redundant. There are two complementary, but different, frames for descriptions of human emotional states. One originates in phenomenology, the other in physiology. The concepts, their interrelations, and their time courses are sufficiently different in the two frames that it is wise to distinguish clearly between the words that are presumed to refer to the same state.

This position is neither a defense of traditional mind-brain duality nor an attack on biological reduction. It merely states that all psychological phenomena, including temperament, are emergent with respect to underlying biological events. A particular PET scan showing high metabolic activity in areas of the visual cortex does not explain completely why a person perceives a small, red sphere moving slowly to the right rather than a large, gray background moving slowly to the left. Each perception, behavior, emotion, and thought represents more than the brain circuits that are necessary for its actualization, a position Sperry (1977) maintained during the final years of his productive career. Thus, the description of a temperamental category is not equivalent to a description of the biological features that comprise part of its foundation. A wave is more than the moving particles of water that comprise it (Einstein & Infeld, 1938).

This chapter first presents a brief historical perspective on the concept of temperament and the reasons for its appeal, and then a description of the nodes of agreement and disagreement among investigators. The two most important controversies involve the validity of parental reports of children's behavior and whether temperamental qualities should be conceived of as continua or categories. The heart of the chapter is a summary of the most robust generalizations regarding the temperamental characteristics of irritability in infants and sociability and shyness in older children. The final sections consider, more briefly, the relevance of temperament to attachment, psychopathology, ethnicity, and morality. The chapter focuses on infancy and early childhood and does not consider in detail the interesting research on the temperamental contributions to the behaviors of adolescents and adults.

HISTORICAL BACKGROUND

The Greeks and Romans believed that a balance among the four humors of yellow and black bile, blood, and phlegm created an opposition in each of two complementary universal qualities: warm versus cool and dry versus moist (Siegel, 1968). These qualities were related to the four fundamental substances in the world: fire, air, earth, and water. The Greeks assumed—without a detailed appreciation of genetics or physiology—that the balance among these qualities created an inner state responsible for the observed variation in rationality, emotionality, and behavior. Children were impulsive and irrational because they were born with an excess of the moist quality.

Galen, an extraordinarily perceptive second-century physician born in Asia Minor, elaborated these Hippocratic ideas by positing nine temperamental types derived from the four humors (Roccatagliatta, 1986). The ideal personality was exquisitely balanced on the complementary characteristics of warm-cool and dry-moist. In the remaining four less ideal types one pair of qualities dominated the complementary pair; for example, warm and moist dominated cool and dry. These four were the temperamental categories Galen called melancholic, sanguine, choleric, and phlegmatic. Each was the result of an excess of one of the bodily humors that produced, in turn, the imbalance in qualities: The melancholic was cool and dry because of an excess of black bile, the sanguine was warm and moist because of an excess of blood, the choleric was warm and dry because of an excess of yellow bile, and the phlegmatic was cool and moist because of an excess of phlegm.

Although the concentrations of the four humors and the relative dominance of the derived qualities were inherent in each person's physiology, they were, nonetheless, susceptible to the influence of external events, especially climate and diet. The body, naturally, became warmer and more moist in the spring; hence, people became more sanguine. When the body became cooler and

drier in the fall, a melancholic mood became more prevalent. Because humans lived in different climates and ate different foods, they differed in these temperamental qualities.

Although the Chinese view of human nature articulated two millennia earlier shared some features with Galen's ideas, it differed from it in several important ways (Yosida, 1973). First, the critical balance was among sources of energy rather than the bodily humors. The energy of the universe—called ch'i—is regulated by a complementary relation between the active initiating force of yang and the more passive, completing force of yin. The two forces must be in balance for optimal physiological and psychological functioning. Like the Greeks, the Chinese linked the emotion of sadness with autumn, joy with early summer, and fear with winter. But the Greeks would have been surprised that the Chinese linked anger with spring—April and May are the months of Galen's sanguine temperament. However, the more important fact is that the Chinese were not interested in temperamental types. Because the energy of ch'i is always changing, a person's moods and behavioral style cannot be too permanent. The notion of a person inheriting a stable emotional bias was inconsistent with the Chinese premise of continual transformation. A person might be sad temporarily, but not because he or she was a melancholic type.

Galen's inferences, which remained popular in Europe until the end of the nineteenth century, were not seriously different from contemporary speculations that the brains of schizophrenics might possess an excess of dopamine while those of depressives may have insufficient norepinephrine (Healy, 1997). Kant (1785/1959) accepted Galen's four types with only minor changes but distinguished between affect and action because he recognized the imperfect relation between invisible, internal processes and overt behavior. Kant believed that humans possessed a will that could control the behavioral consequences of strong desires.

This contrast was captured in the nineteenth century in the comparison between temperament and character. The former referred to inherited emotional biases, the latter to the expression of these biases in actions that were a function of both life experiences and inborn temperament. The pragmatist, for example, was a character type who could possess either a sanguine or a melancholic temperament.

Two centuries later, Roback (1931) modernized Kant's views by suggesting that individuals inherited, to different degrees, dispositions for certain desires and emotions. But, unlike animals, humans could control behaviors that violated their ethical standards; this is Roback's version of Freud's belief that ego tames id. The sanguine type must inhibit, occasionally, the tendency to act impulsively because of strong feelings; the melancholic must suppress the urge to become anxious and withdrawn. Thus, a temperamentally sanguine person who has made too many ill-advised decisions can become overly cautious; a melancholic who has learned to inhibit fear may appear to others to be spontaneously sociable. The idea that the character type does not always provide a reliable insight into temperament is the essence of Jung's distinction between each person's hidden anima and public persona.

Nineteenth-century essays on temperament focused on the biology of the brain and searched for visible signs of that biology on the surface of the body. Franz Gall (1835) incurred the enmity of a segment of his community by suggesting that variation in human intentions and emotions, derived from differences in brain tissue, could actually be detected with measurements of the skull. Gall's crass materialism angered many colleagues who did not believe that a person's character was determined by brain tissue and, therefore, was not controllable by each agent's will. A second reason for the hostility toward Gall is that many nineteenth-century scholars did not believe that the anatomy of the brain had any implications for human behavior because psychology was not part of natural science.

Spurzheim (1834) consolidated Gall's ideas by retaining the essential premise of a location for each primary human characteristic and, reflecting nineteenth-century prejudice, assigning more space in the cranial cavity to emotional than to intellectual processes. Love was in the cerebellum, aggression in the temporal lobe, and timidity in the upper lateral and posterior part of the head near the parietal area. The vigorous positivism in Spurzheim's arguments was motivated by the need to expunge metaphysical and religious ideas from scientific explanations of human nature; it was time to place human behavior in its proper place as a part of natural law.

Thus, by the end of the nineteenth century most scholars had accepted the fact that psychiatry rested on biology. Listen to Adolph Meyer in 1897: "We cannot conceive a disorder of the mind without a disorder of function of those cell mechanisms which embody that part of the mind" (1897/1994, p. 44).

The first transformation of these ideas was an expansion of the number of revealing physical features and, more important, an appreciation that these features were only indirect signs of the real, but still unknown, causes. In a book that enjoyed eight editions, Joseph Simms (1887) awarded the face more diagnostic power than Paul Ekman or Carroll Izard would have dared. Even American schoolteachers were indoctrinated with these ideas: Jessica Fowler (1897) wrote a manual to help teachers diagnose their young pupils' psychological qualities. A "veneration for elders" was predictable from excessively drooping eyes.

Cesare Lombroso (1911) and Ernst Kretschmer (1925), in classic treatises, suggested an association between body type, on the one hand, and crime or mental disease, on the other. Lombroso acknowledged that crime had social and climatic correlates, but claimed that adults who fell at one of the extremes of a normal body type were more often represented among criminals, and dark-haired men were more likely to be criminals than those who were blonde. Kretschmer invented new names—asthenic, pyknic, and athletic—for the three classical body physiques and awarded differential vulnerability to major mental illness to the first two body types. Schizophrenics were more often tall, thin, narrow-faced asthenics; manic depressives were more often chubby, broad-faced, pyknic types.

These speculations formed the basis for Sheldon's (1940) famous book on personality and physique. Sheldon measured a large number of morphological dimensions from the photographs of 4,000 college men and collapsed the resulting 76 categories into three basic body types, each rated on a 7-point scale and each having a corresponding set of psychological qualities. The tall, thin ectomorph was an introvert; the chubby endomorph was an extrovert; and the broad, athletically built mesomorph was energetically assertive.

Sheldon's work began as the eugenics movement in America had reached a crest and was published the year that the Nazis were threatening Europe. The idea that inherited physical qualities, associated with different ethnic groups, were associated with human behavior was too close to Hitler's version of Aryan types, and this research, as well as a growing eugenics movement, stopped suddenly. Promotion of the formerly popular idea that the obvious physical differences among Scandinavians, Italians, Jews, and Blacks were linked to intelligence and morality had become a sign of both irrationality and amoral prejudice. The abrupt end to public discussion of these hypotheses is not surprising; tucked away in Sheldon's book is the provocative suggestion that Blacks are more often aggressive mesomorphs, whereas Jews are more often intellectual ectomorphs. Ernest Hooton's (1939) book, which suggested that some bodily constitutions were naturally inferior and linked to criminal behavior, had a defensive tone because he was aware of how unpopular this view had become to many Americans. Temperamental ideas, which had enjoyed the support of professors, presidents, and corporation heads during the 1st decade of the century, were forced underground for almost 50 years.

Freud's Influence

Freud (1933/1965) was a critical figure in this story because he made important changes in the remnants of Galen's views. First, he substituted one bodily substance, the energy of the libido, for the four humors. This idea of psychological energy, the sense meaning of libido, was not a completely novel notion. Nineteenth-century physicians had elaborated the ancient belief that the amount of energy was an inherited personal quality. The *vis nervosa,* an idea related to the eighteenth-century notion that inanimate objects varied in their ability to retain and give off heat, was less abundant in those unfortunate persons who developed fears, depression, and neurasthenia.

Pavlov (1928) also exploited this idea to explain why some dogs became conditioned easily while others, who resisted the laboratory procedures, were difficult to condition. Pavlov thought that the former group of animals had a stronger nervous system, permitting them to be more resilient to the unfamiliarity of the laboratory conditioning procedures. Pavlov intended that description to be flattering, because functional and adaptive evaluations, which were absent in Galen, colored temperamental concepts after Darwin's seminal work. Galen had written as if each psychological type sought an adaptation to fit his or her bodily humor. Pavlov inserted the evaluative ethic of adaptation and implied that some temperaments functioned better than others. The sanguine was the best type; the melancholic, who had a weaker brain, was the least desirable.

The idea that individuals vary in psychological energy and, therefore, in strength of brain activity may seem odd to modern readers. However, norepinephrine, the primary neurotransmitter of the sympathetic nervous system, maintains body temperature by producing bodily energy (Paxinos, 1990). Current psychiatric the-

ory holds that depressives have low levels of central norepinephrine. The mechanism of one of the therapeutic drugs acts to increase the concentration of norepinephrine in the synaptic cleft. Moreover, infants differ in the vigor of motor activity and loudness of vocalizations. Some 4-month-olds thrash their limbs and squeal with delight; others lie passive and quiet. A high energy level leaps to mind as the best description of the former infants. In the classic monograph on hysteria, Breuer and Freud (1956) wrote, "Differences which make up a man's natural temperament are based on profound differences in his nervous system—on the degree to which the functionally quiescent cerebral elements liberate energy" (p. 198). The creative element in Freud's thinking was to award the free-floating energy of libido an origin and a target in sexuality, while accepting the popular view that heredity influenced the total amount of libido possessed. Although Freud's early writings awarded influence both to temperamental differences in amount of libido and excitability of the nervous system, as well as childhood experiences, the latter ascended in importance in his later writings and, accordingly, the temperamental contribution faded.

The current popularity of the premise that childhood experiences are part of the causal web in adult anxiety and depression prevents a proper appreciation of the revolutionary character of Freud's ideas. Although the ancients were open to the suggestion that psychological variation in the normal range could be influenced by childhood experience—even Plato accepted that argument—the serious mental afflictions of depression, mania, and schizophrenia were regarded as solely physiological in origin. Although the ancients believed that some environmental factors were potent, including air, diet, exercise, rest, and excretion and retention of fluid, none of these causes was social in nature.

By softening the division between serious mental disorder and normal variation in worry and sadness, Freud persuaded many that both a terror of leaving home and worry about one's debts could be derivatives of the same conflict. The assumption of an experiential basis for fears and anxieties that was appropriate for all—everyone felt guilt over sexual and hostile motives—implied that every person could develop a phobia. Freud (1909/1950) let his readers believe that "little Hans" was no different temperamentally from any other child; his extreme fear of horses was the result of very unusual experiences in his family. It is of interest that contemporary reports on children's phobias have returned to the notions prevalent decades before Freud. Clinical cases in psychiatric journals are now described as if they were physiological diseases to be treated with drugs; there is little or no discussion of conflict, trauma, or early family experience.

Psychoanalytic theory slowly turned minds away from a category of person who was especially vulnerable to acquiring a phobia to the idea of environmental encounters that produce fear. The adjective *fearful* now became a continuous dimension on which any person could be placed. Because all individuals experienced conflict, anyone could become phobic. The idea of a vulnerable temperamental type was replaced with the notion of unusually stressful experiences.

A metaphor that captures this contrast is a bridge that collapses under a load. The traditional assumption was that all bridges must carry loads of varying weight; hence, a bridge that collapsed under a load that was in the normal range must have been structurally weak. This is the temperamental premise. Freud, and especially his followers, argued that, most of the time, the collapse was caused by an unusually heavy load. The psychological loads included childhood seduction, harsh socialization of hostility and sexuality, loss of a love object, and fear of the anger of an authoritarian parent. Even though there are many more children who are socialized harshly by autocratic parents or rejected by indifferent ones than there are hysterical patients, this theoretical stance won admirers quickly because of political factors.

Many Americans were threatened when, after World War I, a number of prominent scientists joined by influential journalists suggested that some immigrants were less fit genetically than indigenous Americans (May, 1959). An opposing group of politically more liberal scientists and journalists quieted this provocative claim by suggesting that Pavlov's discoveries of conditioning meant that all children were essentially similar at birth and conditioned experiences supplied the only shaping hand. McDougall's (1908) acerbic critique of this position in his text *Social Psychology* was drowned out by the rising voice of Watsonian behaviorism. America celebrates the individual, who, through wit and perseverance, makes or invents a reliable product that has pragmatic value. Thomas Edison and Henry Ford are prototypic American heroes. The most celebrated American scientists of this same era performed laboratory experiments yielding hard facts presumed to have implications for human life. Many American psychologists studied the phenomenon of learning in rats because this animal permitted experimental manipulations that could produce more certain facts, and therefore, a deeper understanding of the mechanisms behind the child's learning of new habits. This knowledge would serve the needs of an egalitarian society.

The European mind at the end of the nineteenth and the beginning of the twentieth century was more friendly to temperament because it held a different ethic. The European city enjoyed greater loyalty than the same size community in geographically mobile America. The residents of Paris, London, and Florence took more pride from their cities' long history than did citizens in New York, Philadelphia, or Washington. The vitality and stability of the community had precedence over the upwardly mobile achieving individual in American society. That preference was correlated with a desire to maintain social harmony through citizen acceptance of and conformity to local mores and Europeans were receptive to the idea that variation in stability could be due to biology. Americans wanted to deny biology any force. Every person with an intact brain and body could actualize her goals if she worked hard and exploited her inherent cleverness. No person's acceptability to others or future success should be shackled by their inheritance.

The appeal and acceptability of scientific ideas are always influenced by the societal context in which they appear. Darwin's inference of natural selection, influenced by Malthus's suggestion that the increasing fecundity of populations would outstrip food supplies, overcame initial resistance quickly because many overcrowded European cities contain large numbers of very poor families producing large numbers of children. A half century later, when many east coast American cities contained crowded ghettoes of European immigrants, our society had to choose between scientific declarations claiming that the foreigners were genetically compromised and the arguments of egalitarian scholars who argued that the habits and values of the immigrants were experientially based. The latter explanation became ascendant for almost 50 years until a new wave of immigrants with color arrived. But this time the American economy had less need for their labor and the biological sciences had made important discoveries.

Thus, the current receptivity to temperamental ideas cannot be understood without acknowledging history and recent theory and research in neuroscience, psychology, and psychiatry. The period from 1910 to 1970 was characterized by the conviction that, excepting the small number of brain-damaged children, most were fundamentally similar, and the development of different skills and personalities was due, in the main, to experience, especially conditioned habits. This popular and dominant premise was shaken by several historical events.

First, the conceptual gap between the principles of classical and operant conditioning and the novel forms observed in children's speech and behavior became difficult to repress. The resulting dissonance led, over time, to a broad dissatisfaction with the traditional view, but still no replacement. At the same time, Piaget's (1950) ideas of stages of psychological development became popular. Although Piaget insisted on the importance of the child's actions in the world, his arguments imposed some constraint on the effectiveness of experience. No 2-month-old could possess an object concept no matter what his experiences. Although Piaget did not favor the biological determinism implied by the concept of maturation, his writings created a renewed enthusiasm for maturational processes. Chomsky's ascerbic critique of Skinner's explanation of language acquisition abetted the maturational argument. Thus, the community became receptive to the influences of biology and the older ideas on temperament.

When the dissemination of PET and fMRI data promised an eager audience objective quantification of the brain's biology, the dam that was repressing an enthusiasm for biology burst. Only 2 decades ago, the probability was high that a paper on behavioral genetics submitted to *Child Development* or *Developmental Psychology* would be rejected. Today, similar reports are usually accepted by referees because of a change in the community's premises. The essential data have not changed very much; what has changed is the credibility of the importance of biological processes.

There is, however, a danger in an excessive enthusiasm for biological determinism. A nativistic view of the infant, which is gaining popularity, resembles the preformationist assumption that a tiny child was hidden in each sperm. Infants are being awarded cognitive talents that psychologists would have satirized 25 years ago. The permissive attitude toward these claims could not have occurred without the prior perceived failures of behaviorism and psychoanalytic theory, just as the popularity of Picasso and other modernists required the prior idealism of Courbet and Monet. Picasso's *Nude in a Red Chair* would not have been regarded as a great work of art had not Western artists, during prior centuries, painted serene, beautiful, unclothed women.

A quarter-century ago, psychologists loyal to stimulus response learning theory invented possible explanations of almost every stable behavior. Readers will recall, for example, that Skinner (1981) suggested that operant conditioning principles could explain the child's acquisition of speech. Contemporary neuroscientists are being equally creative when they propose neurophysiological bases for many diverse and complex behaviors. We do not criticize this inventive energy, but only note that, as with the earlier behavioristic accounts, most of these explanations will turn out to be either too simple or simply incorrect (Hu & Fox, 1988).

RENAISSANCE OF TEMPERAMENTAL IDEAS

An important reason for the return of temperamental ideas was the bold, influential work of Thomas and Chess (1977). Although Solomon Diamond (1957) anticipated the current interest in temperament at about the same time that Alexander Thomas and Stella Chess published their first papers, historical forces awarded priority to the two psychiatrists because their categories were more closely related to parental experiences with infants and to later childhood pathology. It is useful to recall their strategy of discovery. Thomas and Chess (1977) conducted, at regular intervals, lengthy interviews with well-educated parents of infants and inferred nine temperamental dimensions together with three more abstract categories from those interviews. The nine temperamental dimensions were: (1) activity level; (2) rhythmicity or regularity of bodily functions like hunger, sleep, and elimination; (3) initial reaction to unfamiliarity, especially approach or withdrawal; (4) ease of adaptation to new situations; (5) responsiveness to subtle stimulus events; (6) amount of energy; (7) dominant mood, primarily whether happy or irritable; (8) distractibility; and (9) attention span and persistence.

The three temperamental categories represented a profile on two or more of the nine dimensions. The most frequent category, about 40% of the sample, was the easy child, who was regular in bodily activity and approached unfamiliar objects with a happy, engaging mood. The second, comprising about 15% of the sample, was slow to warm up and, like the children Kagan, Reznick, and Snidman (1988) called inhibited, they react to unfamiliarity with withdrawal and occasionally mild distress. The third category, comprising about 10% of the sample, was called difficult and was characterized by minimal regularity, frequent irritability, withdrawal from unfamiliarity, and poor adaptation. This category of child was most likely to develop psychiatric symptoms—two-thirds had developed such symptoms by age 10. These three categories comprised about two-thirds of the Chess and Thomas sample; the remaining third were difficult to classify.

Continuous evaluation of the children through the 5th year revealed minimal preservation of most of the dimensions. The largest correlations, about .3, reflected stability across the preschool years. But there was not much predictability from early infancy to age 4. As a result, Thomas and Chess concluded that the nine temperamental dimensions, as phenotypes, were not very stable. They revisited these subjects when they were between 18 and 22 years of age, using clinical interviews and questionnaires to evaluate degree of adjustment. Although there was no relation between the possession of an easy or a difficult temperament in the first 2 years and later adult adjustment, the children who had been classed as difficult in the 3rd and 4th years were judged to be less able to cope with life stresses than those children who had an easy temperament. However, Chess and Thomas (1990) noted, wisely, that the outcomes of a difficult temperament depended on the goodness-of-fit— the match—between the child's temperament and the family's ideals for the child. Both must be assessed if one is to predict future pathology.

Animal Research

The discovery that closely related strains of animals raised under identical laboratory conditions behaved differently to the same intrusions provided another set of persuasive facts. Over 35 years ago, John Paul Scott and John Fuller (1965) observed over 250 puppies from five different breeds—basenji, beagle, cocker spaniel, Shetland sheepdog, and fox terrier—at the secluded Jackson laboratories in Bar Harbor, Maine. In one assessment of an animal's timidity, a handler took a puppy from its cage to a common room, placed the puppy one or two feet away, stood still, and observed the animal's behavior. The handler then slowly turned and walked toward the puppy, squatted down, held out his hand, stroked the puppy, and finally picked it up. The puppies that ran to the corner of the room, crouched, and issued a high-pitched yelp early in the sequence were classified as timid. The five breeds of dogs differed dramatically in degree of timidity, for the basenjis, terriers, and shelties were more timid than the beagles and cocker spaniels. But the rearing environment was important: All

the dogs were less timid if they had been raised at home rather than in the laboratory. Twenty years later, Goddard and Beilharz (1985) discovered that Labradors, Australian kelpies, boxers, and German shepherds differed in the avoidance of unfamiliar objects: The German shepherds were the most timid, and the Labradors were the least fearful.

Pavlov noted over 75 years ago that some dogs in his laboratory were unusually tame with humans while others cowered when an adult made an unexpected movement. Pavlov called the former dogs excitable and the latter inhibited (Pavlov, 1928). Factor analyses of behavioral observations on over 15,000 dogs from 164 different breeds revealed a broad factor best interpreted as a shy-bold continuum (Svartberg & Forkman, 2002).

House cats, too, differ in timidity. The small proportion of cats who consistently withdraw to novelty and fail to attack rats have a lower threshold of excitability in specific areas of the amygdala than the majority of cats who do not withdraw and generally attack rats (Adamec, 1991). Similar stories can be told for a great many species. Mice, rats, wolves, cows, monkeys, birds, and even paradise fish differ, within species or among closely related strains, in the tendency to approach or to avoid novelty. A review of this variation by a team of evolutionary biologists concluded, "There can be little doubt that the shy-bold continuum is an important source of behavioral variation in many species that deserves the attention of behavioral ecologists" (Wilson, Clark, Coleman, & Dearstyne, 1994, p. 7).

It is not surprising that fearful behavior can be bred in animals, but it is surprising that it requires such a small number of generations. Some quail chicks become chronically immobile when placed on their back in a cradle and restricted by a human hand; remaining immobile is one measure of fear in birds. If chicks who display the fearful trait are bred with other fearful animals, it takes only eight generations to produce a relatively uniform line of birds that shows immobility for as long as 2 minutes (Williamson et al., 2003). It is equally easy to establish a pedigree of birds that shows very brief periods of immobility, implying minimal fear, and possible to select quail who secrete high or low levels of corticosterone. The strain with higher levels is more fearful of novelty than the strain with low levels of this steroid (Jones, Satterlee, & Ryder, 1994).

The Maudsley Reactive strain of rats was bred over generations to be emotionally reactive to unfamiliarity, where the amount of defecation in a brightly lit open field, aversive for a rat, was the index of reactivity. A second strain of rats was bred to be minimally reactive. The differences between the reactive and nonreactive strains emerge early, by 30 days, and are not due to postnatal experiences. The reactive, compared with the nonreactive, animals have lower levels of catecholamines in body tissue and lower levels of norepinephrine in the blood, but compensate by having an increased density of beta adrenergic receptors on the heart (Blizard, Liang, & Emmel, 1980). However, later research revealed that the low reactive rats failed to defecate because they possessed higher levels of norepinephrine in the colon due to greater sympathetic activation. That condition led to constriction of the smooth muscle of the colon, and therefore, less defecation (Blizard & Adams, 2002). This fact illustrates the danger of conceptual inferences from incomplete evidence for the low reactive animals are, in fact, high reactive sympathetically.

Strain differences in the reaction to unfamiliarity exist in primate groups. South American squirrel monkeys of two different strains, reproductively isolated by only a thousand miles of jungle, vary in their morphology, physiology, and behavior (Snowdon, Coe, & Hodun, 1985). About 20% of rhesus monkeys are extremely timid in unfamiliar environments, have a tense muscle tone as infants, and show physiological reactivity in bodily targets that are linked to fearfulness (Suomi, 1987). There are even sanguine, melancholic, and choleric monkeys. When the behaviors of three closely related species of macaques were compared with respect to their tendency to approach or to withdraw from an unfamiliar human, bonnets were most likely to approach, whereas crabeaters, the smallest of the three species, were the most fearful. The largest animals—rhesus—were the most aggressive (Clarke, Mason, & Moberg, 1988). When these three species were observed under different conditions of novelty and restraint, the aggressive rhesus were least disturbed and showed the smallest increases in heart rate. The fearful crabeaters were the most disturbed and showed the largest increases in both heart rate and glucocorticoids. The bonnets, who are passive and avoidant, showed modest increases in both heart rate and glucocorticoids. However, when crabeater, rhesus, and pigtail monkey infants were reared in isolation for 6 months, the rhesus displayed the most disturbed social behavior, whereas crabeater monkeys showed almost normal social behavior (Sackett, Ruppenthall, Farenbuch, Holm, & Greenough, 1981). Thus, the influence of temperament on development

varies with the nature of the imposed stressor (Magnusson, 1988).

Temperamental factors are even linked to immune function in monkeys. One group of crabeater males was assigned to a stable group of four or five other monkeys for the 26 months of the experiment. A second, stressed group of animals also lived with four or five other monkeys, but the composition of the group changed each month. These frequent changes generated uncertainty in the crabeater monkey. The scientists also observed the animals twice a week for about a half hour to determine which were social and affiliative—they groomed and stayed close to other monkeys—and which were social isolates. After the 2 years of either stressful or minimally stressful social experience, the integrity of each animal's immune system was measured by drawing blood from each monkey for 3 weeks and evaluating the ability of the T lymphocytes to respond appropriately to an antigen. Lower levels of cell proliferation to the antigen index are assumed to reflect a compromised immune system. Only the animals that lived under stress and, in addition, were temperamentally prone to be social isolates showed a severely compromised immune system. The affiliative animals that had experienced the same level of stress showed a healthier immune response. This finding illustrates the principle that a disease state requires both a stress and a vulnerable organism (Cohen, Kaplan, Cunnick, Manuck, & Rabin, 1992).

The fact that very small variations in the genetic composition of closely related animals are associated with distinct profiles of behavior and physiology requires accommodation. If an animal's temperament influences its reaction to total isolation and immune competence, it is likely that similar factors are operative in human psychological functions. Thus, diverse, independent forces combined to render temperamental ideas as attractive candidates in interpretations of human behavior.

NEUROCHEMISTRY AND TEMPERAMENT

It is likely that the biological bases for many, but certainly not all, temperamental categories are heritable neurochemical profiles, a hypothesis anticipated earlier in the twentieth century (McDougall, 1929; Rich, 1928). Research on voles, a small rodent, is illustrative. Prairie and Montane voles, two closely related strains, differ in a psychologically significant behavior. Males and females from the former strain pair bond following several hours of mating, while members of the latter strain do not. Variation in the promoter regions of the genes that influence the distribution of receptors for vasopressin in males and oxytocin in females contributes to this behavioral difference (Insel, Wang, & Ferris, 1994). The DNA of the promoter region determines whether the gene will be activated in a particular site. Both strains secrete vasopressin and oxytocin and both strains have receptors for these molecules, but the strains differ in the locations of the relevant receptors. Only the prairie vole has receptors in limbic sites believed to mediate states of pleasure.

There is heritable variation in the concentration of and density and location of receptors for more than a 150 different molecules that affect brain function. This fact implies a very large number of neurochemical profiles. Even if the majority have little function or relevance for mood or behavior, given the extraordinarily large number of profiles it is likely that human populations contain many temperaments, each defined by a neurochemistry that influences the usual psychological reaction to classes of events.

Two important factors determine brain neurochemistry and, therefore, temperamental biases. First, some brain molecules are excitatory and some are inhibitory and a balance between these processes determines the brain state. For example, the balance between opioids and corticotropin-releasing hormone (CRH) in the locus ceruleus determines the organism's reaction to a stressor (Van Bockstaele, Bajic, Proudfit, & Valentino, 2001). Second, the variation in the density of receptors for a molecule can be independent of the concentration of that molecule. Some mice strains show high levels of tyrosine hydroxylase in the cortex (an enzyme involved in the synthesis of dopamine and norepinephrine) but a low density of receptors for norepinephrine. Other strains are high or low on both properties (Dyaglo & Shishkina, 2000). If we assume that the concentration of a particular neurotransmitter or modulator, and the density of its receptors, can be low, moderate, or high, there can be nine possible profiles for each molecule and, assuming 150 different molecules, at least 1400 neurochemical profiles that could reciprocally influence each other. This state of affairs implies a very large number of possible temperamental biases.

There are at least four different ways brain chemistry can affect the excitability of a particular neuronal ensemble with consequences for behavior. The ensemble can (a) secrete a greater amount of neurotransmitter or

modulator, (b) have more receptors for a particular molecule, (c) project to neurons that secrete a particular molecule, or (d) can be inhibited or disinhibited by another ensemble. Given the brain's massive interconnectedness, it is reasonable to assume a very large number of ways in which neurochemistry can influence emotion and behavior. Only some of these influences are inherited (Placidi et al., 2001).

Some molecules that appear to be significant include norepinephrine, CRH, glutamate, GABA (γ-aminobutyric acid), dopamine, serotonin, opioids, vasopressin, prolactin, and oxytocin. For example GABA-ergic and serotonergic circuits usually inhibit neuronal excitement. Infants born with a compromise in either transmitter system should be less effective in modulating extreme states of distress. This speculation has some support for very irritable 2-year-olds, compared with relaxed toddlers, possessing the shorter form of an allele in the promoter region for the serotonin transporter gene (Auerbach et al., 1999). It is relevant that samples of Japanese adults are more likely than samples of Europeans to possess the long version of this allele and Japanese infants are less irritable than European-Caucasian infants (Kumakiri et al., 1999). Further, adults who inherit the shorter allele show greater amygdala activity to fear-provoking stimuli, compared with adults who possess the longer form (Hariri et al., 2002); although, very shy Israeli children inherit the longer form of this allele (Arbelle et al., 2003).

The lateral nucleus of the amygdala secretes a molecule called gastrin-releasing peptide that acts on the receptors of interneurons to release GABA, which in turn inhibits neural activity. Mice without the gene for this class of receptor fail to release GABA in amygdala neurons and, as a consequence, these animals preserve traces of the association between a conditioned stimulus and electric shock for a longer period of time (Shumyatsky, 2002). It is possible that children who possess this allele will have compromised GABA activity in the amygdala and a tendency to preserve a fearful posture (Maren, Yep, & Goosens, 2001; Sanders, 2001).

Variation in dopamine release and in the density of its varied receptors are related to cortical excitability, intensity of sensory pleasure, and reaction to novelty. There is an immediate release of dopamine in the nucleus accumbens the moment a rat places his forepaws in a novel environment, which can last for as long as 8 seconds (Rebec, Christianson, Guevra, & Bardo, 1997). Further, high dopamine levels in the cortex suppress neuronal activity in the corpus striatum. As a result, there are fewer volleys from striatum to cortex, and, therefore, a lower level of cortical excitability. In addition, higher dopamine activity in the cortex implies a smaller proportional rise in dopamine following exposure to novelty. A person sated on chocolate experiences less pleasure from a chocolate bar than one who has not tasted chocolate for several days. These facts suggest that children with higher dopaminergic activity in the cortex might have a lower preference for novel experiences than those with greater dopaminergic activity. It is of interest that females have more dopamine receptors in the cortex than males and fewer females than males seek novel experiences.

Variation in norepinephrine and its receptors modulates the preferred reaction to novelty, level of alertness, sustained attention in the face of distraction, and thresholds for detecting subtle changes in sensory signals. This variation should have consequences for psychological qualities. Rats from the Wistar strain who explore unfamiliar areas have greater norepinephrine activity in the nucleus accumbens; hence, volleys from the amygdala are enhanced when they arrive at the nucleus accumbens (Roozendaal & Cools, 1994). The amygdalar release of norepinephrine is potentiated by epinephrine acting on norepinephrine receptors in the basolateral nucleus (McGaugh & Cahill, 2003). Hence, variation in the density of receptors for norepinephrine in the amygdala and the sensitivity of the basolateral receptors to epinephrine could affect behaviors that are classified as temperamental (Cecchi, Khoshbouei, Javors, & Morilak., 2002).

Opioids modulate the intensity of visceral afferent feedback from the body to the nucleus tractus solitarius in the medulla. Hence, less opioid activity implies that the medulla's projection to the amygdala will be more intense, and, as a consequence, the orbitofrontal prefrontal cortex, a target of the amygdala, will be vulnerable to greater activation. One possible consequence of this cascade is a greater state of worry, tension, or dysphoria and/or greater difficulty extinguishing a conditioned fear (McNally & Westbrook, 2003). Individuals with greater opioid activity in the medulla should experience more frequent moments of serenity and imperturbability (Miyawaki, Goodchild, & Pilowsky, 2002; Wang & Wessendorf, 2002). It is important to appreciate that not all variation in opioid activity is genetic in origin for some can originate in prenatal events. For example, female mice embryos lying between two males, or next to a male, compared with those lying between two

females, are affected by the surge in testosterone secreted by the male embryos. One consequence of this prenatal position is increased density of mu-opioid receptors in the midbrain, which, postnatally, is accompanied by a higher pain threshold (Morley-Fletcher, Palanza, Parolaro, Vigano, & Laviola, 2003).

CRH secreted by the hypothalamus, influences many systems, but especially the hypothalamic pituitary adrenal axis (HPA). One product of activity in this axis is secretion of the hormone cortisol by the adrenal cortex. Capuchin monkeys with high cortisol levels are more avoidant than animals with lower cortisol levels (Byrne & Suomi, 2002). Further, there is evidence for a relation between an allele at a CRH locus and behavioral inhibition in children, especially among those with one or more parents with panic disorder (Smoller et al., in press). Infusion of high doses of glucocorticoids, especially to the central nucleus, potentiates the release of CRH, startles (Lee, Schulkin, & Davis, 1994), and freezing in rats (Takahashi & Rubin, 1994). It is also relevant that monkeys who exhibited high fear to novelty and had high cortisol levels showed greater relative right, rather than left, frontal activation in the electroencephalogram (EEG; Kalin, Larson, Shelton, & Davidson, 1998), and monkeys who showed extreme right frontal activation had higher levels of CRH across the interval from 4 to 52 months of age (Kalin, Shelton, & Davidson, 2000).

However, there is no simple relation between cortisol levels, on the one hand, and either the reaction to an aversive event or self-reported mood, on the other. Adults administered either 20 or 40mg of cortisol, or a placebo, were asked to rate unpleasant and neutral words and pictures and in addition to describe their mood. Although the subjects given cortisol showed a rise in circulating hormone, there was no relation between their self-reported feelings, or their ratings of the words and pictures, and cortisol level (Abercrombie, Kalin, Thurow, Rosenkranz, & Davidson, 2003).

Gunnar (1994), who has explored the ability of salivary cortisol to detect different types of children, has also concluded that biological variables are ambiguous in meaning. Salivary cortisol levels are too subject to varied temporary states to be relied on alone as a sensitive sign of a stable temperamental type. Bold, outgoing preschool children are much more active than shy, timid ones early in the school year and have occasional days with very high cortisol levels. But several months later, when the originally less active, shy children have become acclimated to the school setting and venture forth to socialize with others, they begin to show occasional days with very high salivary cortisol levels. Thus, the variation in cortisol spikes is closely related to the child's temporary psychological state and level of activity. Our laboratory found no significant relation between early morning salivary cortisol levels in 87 infants 5 and 7 months old and reactivity, smiling, or fear (Kagan, 1994). Further, infants between 12 and 18 months of age vary in the class of event most likely to provoke the secretion of cortisol, and in the time to attain a peak cortisol level (Goldberg et al., 2003). A particular average cortisol value has no univocal meaning across samples of infants or children.

Although we have emphasized the influence of neurochemistry, some temperamental categories could be derivatives of special anatomical features. Adults with a larger than average volume of the right anterior cingulate reported more frequent bouts of worry and shyness with strangers (Pujol et al., 2002). Also relevant, the volume of the right medial ventral prefrontal cortex in monkeys, an area that is active in anxious adults, is a heritable feature (Lyons, Afarion, Schatzberg, Sawyer-Glover, & Moseley, 2002).

Unfortunately, the immaturity of current knowledge relating brain neurochemistry to human psychological states frustrates any attempt to posit a specific relation between a chemical profile and a temperament. Because genetic variation accounts for less than 10% of the variation in most complex behaviors, it is unlikely that a single allele responsible for a particular neurotransmitter level or receptor distribution will determine a temperamental type. In light of these problems, it is impossible to define any temperament at the present time by a specific neurobiological profile. Further, the number of possible neurochemical profiles that can affect behavior is much larger than the number of behavioral profiles. There is a limited number of ways a child can display shyness with a group of children on a playground. The child can stand apart from the group, remain quiet, play alone at a task, or stare vigilantly at the other children. A much larger number of neurochemical patterns could accompany each of those behaviors, just as a large number of bodily states can create a stomach cramp.

THE COMPLEXITY OF BRAIN-BEHAVIOR RELATIONS

Scientists appreciate that the influence of a biological profile on behavior is more complex than earlier scholars expected. The earlier assumptions were based on facts like the relation between a trisomy on chromosome 21 and the mental retardation of Down syndrome. This fact, and related discoveries, seduced many scientists into minimizing the indeterminacy, complexity, and counterintuitive quality of the intermediate processes between genes and a psychological profile (Hu & Fox, 1988). Consider the counterintuitive nature of the following fact: The activity of the sweat glands in the skin of an adult is sympathetic in origin but is mediated by cholinergic neurons. The puzzle is that the embryo's sweat gland is noradrenergic and it requires sympathetic innervation to induce a molecule that, in turn, changes the neurotransmitter from noradrenergic to cholinergic (Habecker & Landis, 1994). Very few biologists sitting quietly in their study 50 years ago would have imagined this mechanism.

Behavioral data are equally complex and it will be necessary to view variation in behaviors like aggression, affiliation, sociability, fear, and depression historically, for each phenotype can result from a different life history. Consider two rats, one unfamiliar and one familiar with mice. If the septum of the former is lesioned, the animal is likely to attack a mouse placed in its visual field. But if the rat had been first familiarized with mice, the attack is less likely following the septal surgery. Similarly, stimulation of the periaqueductal gray of a rat that formerly would not attack mice is likely to produce an attack. But the same level of stimulation applied to an experienced rat that has attacked mice in the past causes the animal to interrupt its attack when stimulation begins (Karli, 1956, 1981, 1991).

Equivalent behavioral outcomes do not always imply similar prior conditions. The concept of equivalence in physics holds that if the same mathematical description applies to an event that was produced by different conditions, the phenomena are to be considered equivalent theoretically. A classic example is the concave surface of the water in a bucket that is rotating on a table. However, if one imagines the universe rotating and the bucket remaining still, the surface of the water will appear concave. Because the mathematics that describe the concave surface is the same for a rotating bucket or a rotating universe, the two events are considered equivalent. The increased reliance on complex machines that purport to measure brain states has led some scientists to a tacit acceptance of a form of equivalence. They assume that the PET or fMRI profile reflects a particular psychological state, regardless of the conditions or the context of assessment. This assumption is probably incorrect. The unconditioned nictitating membrane reflex to a puff of air involves a brain state different from the one activated by the conditioned form of the reflex, even though the reflex appears identical under the two conditions (the cerebellar nuclei are required for the conditioned reflex but not for the unconditioned one; R. Thompson et al., 1987).

One reason for the lack of a determinant relation in humans between an underlying biology and a psychological profile is that the person's historical and cultural context typically influences the profile. The journals of the writer John Cheever (1993), who died in the second half of this century, and the biography of William James's sister Alice James (Strouse, 1980), who died 100 years earlier, imply that both writers inherited a very similar, if not identical, diathesis that favored a chronically dysphoric, melancholic mood. But Cheever, whose premises about human nature were formed when Freudian theories were ascendant, assumed that his angst was due to childhood experiences, and he tried to overcome the conflicts that he imagined his family had created with the help of drugs and psychotherapy. By contrast, Alice James believed, with a majority of her contemporaries, that she had inherited her dour mood. Hence, she concluded, after trying baths and galvanic stimulation, that because she could not change her heredity she wished to die. The historical era of these creative writers exerted a profound influence on the coping strategies each selected and, by inference, on the quality of their emotional lives.

No single peripheral physiological measure is likely to be an especially valid index of a temperamental type because each is subject to local influences that are unrelated to central brain mechanisms that are the primary features of the temperament. However, an aggregate of different measures might do better. When the standard scores for eight peripheral physiological variables that are related to limbic excitability were averaged, the correlation between this aggregate index and behavioral inhibition was much higher than the relation between any one variable and the index of inhibited behavior (Kagan et al., 1988).

The traditional view that the relation between brain and behavior is unidirectional is being replaced with a more dynamic perspective that expects that psychological states influence brain physiology and the activity of particular genes and their products. Glucocorticoids and other chemicals produced by psychological states can turn on or off genes that control the density of receptors on neurons and, as a consequence, alter the reactivity of the central nervous system. Each afternoon as the light fades, a gene is activated that initiates the sequence of protein synthesis (Takahashi & Hoffman, 1995). A child who inherited a physiology that biased her to be fearful (or impulsive) might, through experience, gain control of that behavior. The new profile could change both the child's psychological state and the genome that contributed to her initial behavior. An extremely inhibited 2-year-old boy in a longitudinal sample was not very fearful as an adolescent, and the reactive sympathetic nervous system he displayed as a toddler was much less apparent when he was 13 years old (Kagan, 1994). Further, the neural structures necessary for the acquisition of a conditioned avoidance or a freezing response may not be necessary for long-term maintenance of the same behavior. For example, the central nucleus of the amygdala is required if an animal is to learn to avoid a place associated with pain. But once the association has been established, the avoidant behavior can occur without involvement of the amygdala (Parent, West, & McGaugh, 1994). Thus, the physiology that is the basis for learning a habit need not be similar to the physiology that maintains it.

Specificity

A principle of specificity is as important as a belief in dynamic reciprocity in probing the relation of brain to behavior. The area of the cortex that is essential for the retrieval of words that represent actions may be different from the area that is important in the retrieval of nouns (Damasio, 1994). The areas of the brain that cause a rat to avoid an electric probe that delivered shock are not the same as those that cause the rat to bury wood chips following the same experience of shock: The amygdala is necessary for display of the former, the septum for the latter (Treit, Pesold, & Rotzinger, 1993a, 1993b). The circuit that mediates defensive aggression to a noxious stimulus does not require the amygdala; the freezing response to an intruder does require the amygdala but not the hypothalamus. However, the rise in heart rate to an intruder is likely to involve the lateral hypothalamus (Fanselow, 1994).

It is a truism that the history of every scientific discipline is marked by new theoretical conceptions. It is less well recognized that changes in the evidential bases for a concept, which are the product of new methods, are equally characteristic of the history of disciplines. The microscope, for example, changed the meaning of life to include forms that could not be seen. The radio telescope, which permitted the measurement of microwave radiation, led to the idea of dark matter and a new conception of the mass of the cosmos.

Psychology continues to be concerned with a small number of fundamental ideas that include consciousness, emotion, memory, thought, and pathology. Prior to the invention of machines that could measure brain activity, it was understood that the definitions of each of these concepts rested either on a person's phenomenological statements or observations of behavior. But after scientists gained access to the EEG, and later to the PET and fMRI, the primary referents for the psychological terms changed. It is possible that, in time, psychological information will come to be regarded as less objective, less accurate, or both. That trend is dangerous because psychological data are inherent in the meanings of words like *consciousness* and *emotion.*

Consciousness is a psychological state, not a pattern of brain activity, even though the latter is the basis for the former. An enabling condition should never be confused with its emerging products. A child's perception of a gull swooping down on the sea is not synonymous with the description of the circuits that make that perception possible. No one would confuse the tides with the gravitational attraction between earth and moon, a burning tree with the lightning that struck it, obesity with levels of lipids and carbohydrates, nor a protein with the DNA and RNA that were responsible for its manufacture. Yet, some scientists are committing the error of confusing ideas like fear, consciousness, and depression with specific neurochemistries and brain circuits. It is correct to state that a child's immobility to a spider requires a circuit that includes the thalamus, amygdala, and central gray. However, that statement is not equivalent to saying that the conscious feeling of fear is nothing more than, or identical with, discharge of that circuit. This philosophical error is chasing psychological investigations of emotion and cognition to the periphery in a legitimate excitement over the powerful advances in our understanding of the brain conditions that form the bases for a psychological state.

It is unlikely that the concepts that originate in observations of behavior will map neatly on the concepts of neurophysiology. The structure of psychological processes is different from the structure of brain processes, just as the structure of the brain is different from the molecular structure of the genes that influenced its formation. It will be necessary, as noted ear-

lier, to invent new concepts to name the neural circuits activated when certain psychological states occur rather than simply adopt the older, popular, psychological terms. For example, LeDoux, Iwata, Cicchetti, and Reis (1988) have described elegantly the brain structures necessary for a rat's acquisition of a conditioned freezing response or increase in blood pressure to a light that had been associated with electric shock. They call these brain structures a fear circuit. But this meaning of fear must be distinguished from the meaning of "fear" to describe a child who says he is afraid of failing a school examination.

Agreements and Disagreements

Most investigators of temperamental biases agree on several issues. One is that the major structures of the limbic system—hippocampus, cingulate, septum, hypothalamus, and amygdala—and their projections to motor and autonomic targets are important participants in the variation that defines the major constructs. Second, the variation in the excitability of these brain structures is likely to be influenced by many genes rather than by a single allele. Third, the peripheral biological measurements often used to define the temperamental categories—for example, cortisol, blood pressure, heart rate, vagal tone, EEG—have only very modest associations with the behavioral components of the category (Bates & Wachs, 1994; Gunnar, 1994; Kagan, 1994). Schwartz, Snidman, and Kagan (1999) failed to find a robust relation between any one of a large number of peripheral physiological variables and temperament in a group of adolescents who had been classified as inhibited or uninhibited in the 2nd year of life.

This trio of agreements is set against four nodes of controversy. One source of tension is captured by the contrast between scientists who begin their work with a priori theoretical concepts and those who are comfortable with a host of tiny facts when an area of inquiry is young. The former scholars, who outnumber the latter at the present time, often begin with a theoretical view of the human temperaments and devise measures for them. The smaller group, following Francis Bacon, allows the data to guide the invention of temperamental concepts.

A second subtle issue involves the idea of essences. Some investigators conceive of a temperamental type as an essence with a fixed behavioral and physiological profile—the way many diseases are classified. One strategy treats the initial temperamental profile in the

1st year as an original, enduring structure that is preserved for life.

A less popular view holds that the child begins life with a particular temperamental profile that undergoes change as a result of experience with parents, initially, and later with teachers and peers. As each of these categories of experiences is encountered and accommodated, psychological changes occur. Thus, the category psychologists assign to a garrulous 10-year-old who was a very irritable infant should incorporate the traits of the former child. Because many behavioral changes occur in the first dozen years, the temperamental categories assigned to infants will differ from the personality constructs used to describe adolescents. Imagine two containers of glycerine, but only one contains a small drop of black ink that, having been stirred in the container, is invisible. Despite the fact that the drop of ink cannot be seen, it has altered the composition of the glycerine. An infant temperamental bias, like the drop of ink, may not be observable in adolescents, even though it can influence the mood and reactions of youth to particular events. This conception of temperament is similar to the biologists' view of evolution. Even though the evolutionary origin of all dog breeds was the gray wolf, the features of dogs are distinctly different from those of the gray wolf, and biologists differentiate the features of beagles from those of pit bulls.

There is no essential dog: Some are aggressive, some are not; some are spotted, some not; some bark, some do not. Nonetheless, all dogs share an evolutionary history and a set of anatomical structures, physiologies, and behaviors that distinguish them from cats and cows, which have also been domesticated. One day scientists will discover the critical features that define each of the many temperamental types. But because the study of temperaments is at an early stage of inquiry, most investigators rely on behavioral characteristics, each mediated by different biologies, as the critical defining features of a temperament.

SOURCES OF EVIDENCE

Perhaps the most important controversy refers to the source of evidence used to define a temperamental type or bias (see Rothbart & Bates, Chapter 3, this *Handbook,* this volume). The validity of every empirically based inference is always influenced by the nature of the observations. This principle is true for all of the sciences. Estimates of the age of an animal species, or the phylogenetic relation between two species, can vary considerably if fossils rather than proteins are the basis for the judgment. Hence, the validity of a theoretical position can change when the source of information changes, even though investigators may use the same construct.

Statements about the origins and consequences of a temperamental bias can be based on three very different sources of data. The first and most common, at present, are verbal reports provided by an informant, usually a parent, but, occasionally, by an older child, teachers, or peers. A second, less frequent source is derived from behavioral observations in a laboratory or, less often, at home or in a school setting. The third, least frequent source involves biological measures, like vagal tone, heart rate, or cortisol level. Each of these sources has a unique structure and a unique set of advantages and limitations. Extensive behavioral observations are not a good proxy for parental descriptions or biology. Biological measures are not a valid proxy for behavior or parent perceptions, and parental reports are not always a good proxy for behavioral observations gathered across diverse situations.

Behavioral Observations

The major advantages of gathering behavioral observations, especially when they are recorded on film, is that the information is, presumably, closer to the referent that the investigators wish to know—most theorists want to know how a child usually behaves in a particular class of settings. However, there are serious limitations on most observational data. First, the usual setting is an unfamiliar laboratory room where the child interacts with an unfamiliar adult while occasionally a parent sits nearby. Children can behave in special ways in this uncommon context. A child who is aggressive with peers might show no aggression in this setting. Second, most behavioral corpora are based on less than 1 hour of observation. It is unlikely that a majority of children will reveal signs of their important temperamental biases in such a short period. Finally, proper ethical restrictions limit seriously the incentives psychologists can present, even though these incentives might occur in the child's environment.

In general, behavioral observations are more valid when the constructs refer to cognitive competences, usual reactions to novel social and nonsocial events, and degree of sociability with unfamiliar adults or children. Behavioral observations are far less valid if the constructs refer to beliefs, motives, conflicts, or usual emotional reactions to frustration, danger, ethical violations, or gaining a desired goal.

ADULT VERBAL DESCRIPTIONS

Verbal descriptions provided by a parent or teacher have the obvious advantage of sampling behaviors across a variety of settings over a long period. Investigators can ask parents about their child's reaction to events that could not be simulated in the laboratory (e.g., reaction to punishment, to injury, to illness, or to attack).

The most popular questionnaires are the ICQ (Bates, 1989); the IBQ (Rothbart, 1981); the CBQ (Rothbart, Ahadi, & Hershey, 1994); the RITQ (Carey & McDevitt, 1978); and the EAS (Buss & Plomin, 1984). The questionnaires designed for infants and children usually ask about characteristics that parents are interested in and can observe easily, especially irritability, smiling, activity, shyness, and fear.

Most questionnaires do not ask about qualities that are subtle or of minimal interest to parents but nonetheless might be theoretically important; for example, how long a child takes to eat, preferred use of the right or left hand, or the fullness of each smile. Obviously, investigators cannot ask parents about qualities that are not observable, like asymmetry of cerebral activation or sympathetic reactivity. Because scientists can only ask parents about psychological qualities they understand with words that are part of a consensual vocabulary, most psychologists restrict their temperamental categories to a small number of easily understood ideas; for example, activity level, smiling, fear of strangers, crying to limitations, soothability, and duration of attention to events. However, there is a small group of infants who, in addition to being minimally irritable, smile frequently, have a low heart rate, low muscle tension, and greater activation of the EEG in the left frontal area. A psychologist who invented a novel temperamental name for this combination of qualities could not ask a mother to rate her child on this quality for the parent does not have access to the child's biology.

If a majority of parents (or teachers) consistently provided accurate descriptions of children's behaviors,

questionnaires would be a preferred and valuable source of data. But, as with behavioral observations, this class of evidence has its special set of limitations.

First, parents vary considerably in the accuracy of their descriptions, where accuracy is defined by an objective record of the child's usual reactions. This variability among parents is due to differential comprehension of the questions, an understandable desire, often unconscious, to emphasize traits parents view as desirable and to deny features that do not fit the parents' ego ideal, and variation in the extensiveness of parental retrieval of the child's past behaviors. For example, parents of 9-month-olds did not agree in their attribution of fearfulness, smiling, or sociability to their infant because the fathers interpreted high activity levels in the young child as reflecting a positive emotional mood, whereas the mothers regarded the same behavior as reflecting anger (Goldsmith & Campos, 1990).

One reason for the discrepancies between two informants, or between a verbal description and behavioral observations, is that a person's verbal products, whether answers to interview questions or checkmarks on questionnaires, have special features that are not characteristic of the phenomena the sentences are intended to describe. Sentences demand logical consistency, possess a structure different from that of the events they intend to describe, and pass through a psychological filter that evaluates their social desirability. Over 35 years ago, Charles Osgood and his colleagues (Osgood, Suci, & Tannenbaum, 1957) demonstrated that people from many different cultures use the evaluative contrast good versus bad as a first dividing principle when they categorize people, objects, and events. Most parents, too, impose a construction on their child's behavior that represents their conception of the ideal child. The parent who wants an outgoing child and is threatened by a quiet one may deny extreme shyness and exaggerate sociability. This evaluative frame colors informants' answers to all questions.

Individuals are sensitive to the logical consistency in a series of related sentences. If a mother says (or checks on a form) that her child is happy, there will be resistance to acknowledging that her child occasionally feels sad, tense, or anxious. There is no such demand for consistency in a person's behavior or physiology.

Each verbal description of a child competes with a nonverbal representation composed of prior experiences with the child. The verbal categories invite a consistency to which the perceptual schemata are indifferent.

Verbal descriptions pass through a psychological filter that removes inconsistency and exaggerates small differences to create a clearer, more consistent, and more desirable picture of the child. An infant who both smiles frequently to playful bouts but also cries to frustration presents an inconsistent profile with respect to the complementary notions of a happy or unhappy infant. As a result, many parents exaggerate one of these profiles and mute the other to avoid the inconsistency. Hence, they are likely to tell the interviewer that their baby is usually happy or usually irritable but not both (Goldsmith & Campos, 1990).

Most words refer to discrete categories of events, making it difficult to describe blends. There is no English word that describes the feeling generated when one hopes for good news about a hospitalized loved one but fears the worst, or the feeling that combines the satisfaction experienced when a misfortune befalls an enemy with the guilt over the malevolent wish. Languages are not rich enough to describe all the important feelings and behaviors that are part of the human competence. Hence, questionnaires must use the best words available, even though they may be inadequate.

Further, every sentence assumes, often tacitly, a comparison. When a parent reads the sentence "Does your child like to go to parties?" she unconsciously compares that preference with others. If one parent compares "going to parties" with an activity the child dislikes, while a second parent compares it with one that is also preferred, the former parent is more likely to endorse the item, even though both children may like parties equally well.

When the question asks about an emotion, like cheerfulness or fear, the opportunity to emphasize different features of a concept is enhanced. If the investigator and the parent have different features of the concept in mind, each will impose a different meaning on the question. Wittgenstein (1953) suggested in *Philosophical Investigations* that every sentence, written or spoken, assumes a comparison context. When a mother answers a query about her child's fear of strangers, she is unconsciously comparing her idea of fear with related concepts that might refer, for example, to anger, sensitivity, or developmental maturity. Psychologists cannot expect uniformity among parents in the outcome of those comparisons and, as a result, similar parental replies can have different meanings (see Forman et al., 2003).

Variation in the parents' experience with children can also be important. A young mother with her first infant has a less accurate base for judging her child than a parent who has had three children. The level of agreement between descriptions of infants by primiparous mothers and laboratory observations of the same child are poorer than the agreement between the laboratory observations and the reports of mothers who have had more than one child (Forman et al., 2003). Mothers with their first infants are prone to describe them as more irritable and more demanding than more experienced mothers. But if the first child of the experienced parent were extremely irritable and the second only a little less irritable, but still more irritable than most children, the mother is likely to rate the second child as less irritable than observations would reveal because the mother contrasts the second with the first child. This phenomenon occurs with mothers of fraternal twins who usually rate the two siblings as much less similar than observers do because the mother exaggerates the differences between them (Kagan & Saudino, 2001).

Every mother watching her child retreat from an unfamiliar adult does not conclude that her child is afraid of strangers. A mother might (a) generate no categorization, (b) regard the child as tired, (c) categorize the stranger as ominous, or (d) conclude that the child is behaving adaptively with a stranger. This example, and many others like it, is stored in the parent's long-term memory until the day the psychologist asks, "Is your child afraid of strangers?" The consequences of reading a question are difficult to predict because the psychologist does not know the categories a parent used to store and to retrieve the relevant past observations of their child or the parents' state at the moment they were being questioned. This suggestion is supported by the fact that the social class and personality of the parents influence their descriptions of their children. Mothers who never attended college describe their infants as less adaptive and less sociable than college-educated parents (Spiker, Klebanov, & Brooks-Gunn, 1992). Mothers experiencing stress, for whatever reason, have a lower frustration tolerance and, therefore, are prone to exaggerate their infant's irritability. Depressed mothers with their first child described their 6-week-old infants as more irritable than did experienced mothers or mothers free of depression (Green, 1991). The ratings made by depressed mothers of the irritability of their 6-month-olds were poorly correlated with laboratory observations, while the ratings made by healthy mothers were somewhat more accurate (Forman et al., 2003).

Mothers who described their children on the Carey Temperament Questionnaire as difficult were more anxious, suspicious, and impulsive than mothers who described their children as easy (Vaughn, Bradley, Joffe, Seifer, & Barglow, 1987; see also Matheny, Wilson, & Thoben, 1987; Mebert, 1991 for similar results). On some occasions, questionnaire evidence leads to conclusions that violate both biology and common sense. One team of investigators interviewed 794 pairs of adult female twins about their physical health and emotional states. The replies to these questions posed by a stranger, revealed the surprising fact that self-esteem was as heritable as physical health (Kendler, Myers, & Neale, 2000). We suspect that had the evidence consisted of a physical examination with laboratory tests and direct observations of behavior, the results might have been different.

An exhaustive review of the degree of agreement among parents, teachers, and peers with respect to the occurrence of children's behavioral and emotional problems, in over 269 samples, revealed poor concordance among different informants as to whether a child was fearful, aggressive, or impulsive. The average correlation between two informants was less than .3 (Achenbach, 1985; see also, Klein, 1991; Spiker, Klebanov, & Brooks-Gunn, 1992).

These limitations, inherent in questionnaire data, are the major reason why the relations between parental reports and behavioral observations for apparently similar traits, are usually low to modest. For example, the stability of behavioral observations of shyness and fearfulness from 14 to 36 months in a large study of same-sex monozygotic and dizygotic twins was significantly smaller than the stability of parental ratings of the same qualities (.3 versus .6; Kagan & Saudino, 2001; see also Guerin & Gottfried, 1994; Fagot & O'Brien, 1994; Plomin & Foch, 1980). Moreover, the heritability of the behaviorally based indexes of inhibition to unfamiliarity decreased with age, while the heritability of the parental descriptions of a similar quality increased with age (Emde & Hewitt, 2001). The heritability of behavioral observations of inhibition from 14 to 36 months decreased from .51 at 14 months to .24 at 36 months, while the heritability of parental descriptions of similar behaviors increased from .21 at 14 months to .37 at 36 months. At some ages, the heritability of parental rat-

ings of avoidant behavior in the child was close to 1.0—a value so high it is likely that the parents' ratings were a serious distortion of the children's actual behavior (Kagan & Saudino, 2001; see also, Saudino, McGuire, Reiss, Hetherington, & Plomin, 1993; Rose, 1995).

A well-designed study assessing the accuracy of parental descriptions of children's behavior with strangers in an unfamiliar situation revealed that the mothers' descriptions were only accurate for preschool children who were extremely shy or extremely sociable with a stranger in a laboratory setting. The parental ratings were not correlated with the child's behavior for over 80% of the sample because many mothers who described their child as sociable had children who were very shy with a stranger in the laboratory (Bishop, Spence, & McDonald, 2003). Rosicky (1993) compared the laboratory behavior of 135 1-year-olds to four events that often elicit a fear reaction—for example, a toy spider or masks—with the mothers' ratings of their children's fearfulness to these same events. The mothers were remarkably inaccurate in predicting how their child would behave.

In one investigation, 50 firstborn infants were observed at home weekly from 4 to 6 months of age. The parents and the observers were consistent over time in their independent evaluations of the baby's dominant mood, approach to unfamiliarity, activity, and intensity of response. But the correlations between the parents' ratings and the observers' evaluations of the same qualities were low (about .2). The authors wrote, "The most important implication of our findings is . . . a cautionary message about the large published literature based on parent report of their infant's behavioral style . . . mothers are a poor source of information about their infants' behavioral style" (Seifer, Sameroff, Barrett, & Krafchuk, 1994, pp. 1488–1489).

In a similar study, observers visited the homes of 5-month-old infants on two occasions and noted the frequency of smiling, vocalizing, fretting, crying, banging, and kicking. The observers also asked the mothers to make ratings of these same behaviors in their infants. Once again, the two sources of data were in poor accord; the correlations averaged only about .2 (Bornstein, Gaughran, & Segui, 1991). There is not even a positive correlation between the degree of intentionality actually displayed by 9-month-old infants in a laboratory and the degree to which their mothers attributed intentionality to their infants on a questionnaire (Reznick, 1999).

Thus, both theoretical analyses and empirical data imply that generalizations about behavior and emotion that are based only on questionnaires (or interviews) have a special meaning. Norbert Schwarz (1999) notes that "retrospective behavioral reports are highly fallible and strongly affected by the research instrument used" (p. 100). "We view our questionnaires as measurement devices—what we overlook is that our questionnaires are also a source of information that respondents draw on in order to determine their task and arrive at a useful and informative answer" (p. 103).

The writer Julia Blackburn (2002) captures the slipperiness of words:

> I suppose I have often mistrusted the spoken word. You give a quick tug on the line, and out they come from the dark continent of the mind. Those little raps of sound that jostle together, shoulder to shoulder and supposed to be able to give shape to what you really think or feel or know. But words can so easily miss the point. They drift off in the wrong direction, or they insist on providing a clear shape for something that by its very nature is lost when it is pinned down.

SUMMARY

Even though parents have opportunities to observe their children in a variety of natural situations over long periods, and laboratory contexts are often artificial and the observations of short duration, there are unique influences on parental, teacher, or peer descriptions that are absent when behaviors requiring minimal inference are recorded on film and coded by disinterested observers.

We are not the first to question the validity of parental reports when they are intended to describe how the child behaves rather than the parents' conceptions of their children's behaviors. Over 65 years ago, a team of child psychologists noted the poor relation between what actually happened during the 1st year of an infant's life and the maternal descriptions of those events less than a year later (Pyles, Stolz, & MacFarlane, 1935; see also Yarrow, Campbell, & Burton, 1970).

It is possible that the verbal categories parents use to describe their children's behavior, compared with the categories derived from frame-by-frame analyses of children's behavior, are incommensurable (Goldsmith, Lemery, Buss, & Campos, 1999) because the concepts used to describe the analyses of the films do not exist in the vocabulary of the parents. For example, the language used by Ekman (1992) and Izard (1991) to describe brief changes in facial muscles award meanings to words like *anger* or *fear* that are different from those understood by parents or observers watching one child strike another or flee from a large animal.

If asking parents about their children's behavior and moods were an accurate source of information, the field of personality development would be one of the most advanced domains in the social sciences. Many investigators have asked parents to describe their children and have used the data to construct theories. We interpret the limited progress to mean that verbal statements by parents, teachers, or friends, have some, but limited, value. Over 20 years ago, Bates (1983) noted, "Empirical and theoretical considerations call into question the assumption that parent reports of a difficult temperament are essentially measures of characteristics residing within the child" (p. 95). Stifter and Wiggins (2004) affirmed that conclusion 21 years later, "parental reports of infant temperament and difficultness may be influenced by factors that have little association with infant emotionality and behaviors" (p. 88).

Thus, the review of empirical research that follows will not, with some exceptions, cover the very large number of reports that have relied on parental questionnaires as the only source of evidence. The preceding discussion was detailed because it is a defense of that decision.

If, as we believe, future discoveries of theoretical significance are likely to come from behavioral observations combined with parental or teacher reports, rather than from either source of data alone, we should not treat conclusions based on any one of these sources of information as having equivalent meaning to the other. Georg von Bekesy, recipient of a Nobel Prize for research on hearing, once advised a young instructor worried about his research career: "The method is everything." The older scientist explained that he always measured a phenomenon with at least five different methods on the assumption that the features shared across them might reveal the critical properties of the phenomenon of interest (Evans, 2003). Our constructive conclusion is that each method—questionnaire, behavioral observation, or biology—provides different information and requires distinct concepts. We do not suggest that questionnaire evidence be ignored, only that investigators who rely only on this procedure recognize that the validity of their inferences is restricted to this class of information and is not a proxy for direct observation. The same caveat applies to those who rely only on behavioral data.

The authors believe, although they remain ready to be proven wrong, that future research will reveal that substantial theoretical progress will follow greater reliance on a combination of informant report and behavioral observations gathered across diverse settings.

CONTINUOUS TRAITS OR CATEGORIES

A final source of disagreement is whether a temperamental category should be conceived of as a continuum or as a qualitative category (Meehl, 1973, 1995).

A central tension in empirical studies of individual differences is whether people differ quantitatively on the same set of dimensions—therefore, each individual is described best as a set of values on factor scores—or whether some individuals belong to qualitative groups. A strong bias for simplicity favors continuous functions over categories. The theoretical power and popular success of relativity theory in physics supports this bias. Einstein suggested that, in the frame of an observer, objects shorten as their velocity approaches the speed of light. To universalize this law in the service of parsimony, he suggested that this shortening occurs even when a person swings her tennis racket, although the velocity is so small the shortening of the object is not detectable with any instrument. However, water does not begin to form very tiny ice crystals as it cools from 30° to 28° centigrade. The function relating temperature to the formation of ice is nonlinear.

Nonlinear functions are common in the life sciences and, at transition points, novel qualities, which can be viewed as categories, emerge. For example, the behavior of a single ant, or a small number, appears random and without coherence, but, "When the density of a colony reaches a critical value . . . chaos begins to turn into order and rhythmic patterns emerge over the colony as a whole" (Goodwin, 1994, p. 189). A large colony of ants has distinct qualities that cannot be predicted from or explained by an additive model that sums the behavior of a large number of ants considered one at a time.

Nonlinear functions are common in many domains of psychology; for example, the magnitude of potentiated startle in a rat has an inverted-U function with intensity of shock during training (Davis, 1984). Thus, current statistical procedures like regression can distort relations in nature (see Hinde, Tamplin, & Barrett, 1993, for a similar position). These analytic procedures assume that the forces producing the values for the variables under study are the same at all ranges; the force varies only in magnitude. This persistent preference for continua, although tacit, has been inimical to progress in psychology. A biologist phrased the case well for qualitative categories: "The study of biological form begins to take us in the direction of a science of qualities that is not an alternative to, but complements and extends, the science of quantities" (Goodwin, 1994, p. 198).

Thomas and Chess (1977) regarded the three major types of children—easy, difficult, and slow to warm up—as categories, but treated the variation in each of their nine dimensions as continuous. They wrote about the approach-withdrawal dimension as if all infants could be placed on a continuum with respect to the tendency to withdraw or to approach unfamiliar events. By failing to say otherwise, they seemed to reject the possibility that infants who rarely approach unfamiliar people might be qualitatively, not just quantitatively, different from those who occasionally avoid strangers. It is likely, however, that extremely shy children are qualitatively different from those who are moderately shy. One reason is that extreme shyness, which is characteristic of a very small proportion of children, is linked with other characteristics that seem unrelated to shy behavior, including eye color, asymmetry of EEG activation, and sympathetic reactivity. Support for this claim is presented later in this chapter.

One reason psychologists have preferred continua over categories is a derivative of the contagion of ideas among disciplines. Before relativity theory, physicists assumed that object and energy were qualitatively different things. A burning log was distinct from the heat or energy the log emitted. Einstein suggested, however, that there was only the field and, therefore, only energy: "The difference between matter and field is a quantitative rather than a qualitative one" (Einstein & Infeld, 1938, p. 242). Surely, if a log and the heat it can emit can be placed on an abstract continuum of energy, psychologists could defend the notion that no individual is qualitatively different from anyone else on any psychological dimension.

A more obvious, and perhaps less controversial, reason is the training in statistics given to young psychologists. By World War II, the use of inferential statistics became the mark of the sophisticated social scientist. The correlation coefficient, t-test, and analysis of variance should be computed on continuous variables. Hence, psychologists found it useful to assume that there were no qualitative types of people; all humans could be treated as substantially similar in their sensations, perceptions, memories, and emotions. Statistical analyses were performed on continuous scores produced by different experimental conditions, not by different kinds of people.

The domination of research in both personality and development by analysis of variance and regression has frustrated a small group of investigators who have had the intuition that some subjects are qualitatively different from the majority in their sample. However, when the group of subjects is small in number, the usual inferential statistics often do not reach the popular .05 level required for referee approval. Further, there is no consensus on an algorithm that permits an investigator to conclude that some subjects belong to a distinct group. Consider, as an example, an investigator who did not know about Down syndrome studying the relation of maternal age to children's intelligence in a sample of 600 families. The correlation between the two variables would reveal no statistically significant relation. However, examination of a scatter plot might reveal that two children with very low IQ scores had the two oldest mothers in the sample. Reflection on that fact might tempt the investigator to consider the possibility that these two children were qualitatively different from the other 598 and, perhaps, that these two families provided a clue to a relation between age of mother and intelligence of the child for a very small proportion of the population. Hence, there is an initial enthusiasm for considering individual cases and small subgroups with extreme scores.

CURRENT VIEWS OF THE INFANT

Current ideas on temperament vary with the developmental stage of the subject and the sources of evidence; hence, this discussion accommodates to these factors. It is also necessary to impose a conservative attitude toward evidence. Infants and children differ on a large number of characteristics and it is unlikely that most of this variation is temperamental in origin, even though an investigator conducting a cross-sectional study may claim otherwise. Thus, we restrict this discussion to a small number of characteristics for which the evidence implies a temperamental contribution to avoid the error psychologists made a half-century earlier when they assumed that all variation was due to social experience.

Aesthetic considerations influence the selection of scientific strategies. Western standards of beauty in science celebrate two forms of discovery. In the natural sciences, especially biology and chemistry, experimental control of a phenomenon through techniques that rely on machines generates an aesthetic feeling. A second route to beauty is through elegant formal theory that presumably explains diverse phenomena. Einstein's theory of relativity is a classic example. Because no student of temperament can gain experimental control of a child's behavior, most psychologists in this domain drift toward the invention of theoretical ideas that might provide an aesthetic structure to the phenomena of interest.

It is natural to ask ontological questions when a domain of inquiry is young. The Greeks asked, "What is matter?" Twentieth-century physicists have answered that question with a set of mathematical functions that predict and, therefore, presumably explain the events that follow the bombardment of a hydrogen atom with high energy. Eighteenth-century naturalists asked, "What is a species?" Biologists answered with a set of relations among the evolutionary histories, anatomical and physiological features, and profiles of interbreeding among different animals. In most natural sciences, except psychology, a set of functions replaced abstract Platonic conceptions of an event—a set of empirical relations became the answer to the earlier ontological query.

Replacement of Platonic definitions with robust functions is moving at a slower pace in developmental psychology. Many journal reports still begin with an ontological definition of a concept, like coping, secure attachment, empathy, or reactivity rather than with a concept that was invented a posteriori to explain observations. Thomas and Chess (1977), for example, define temperament as the style of a person's behavior; Goldsmith and Campos (1990) regard temperaments as processes that modulate an emotional profile. These a priori declarations are useful early in the investigation of a domain, but they limit the scope of empirical work and should be abandoned when new evidence erodes their usefulness.

All observers recognize that variation in irritability is a moderately stable characteristic in the 1st year and psychologists could declare that irritability is a temperamental trait. However, after the second birthday, many infants who had been highly irritable lose this quality and become timid. Thus, either a new term is needed to describe this class of 2-year-old or the investigator can move up the ladder of abstraction and suggest that "ease of arousal" is the temperamental quality that explains the relation between infant irritability and subdued behavior in a 2-year-old. One problem with this solution is that some infants display "ease of arousal" by babbling, rather than crying, and these children develop behavioral profiles different from those who are irritable.

We do not suggest that psychologists abandon ontological questions, only that they remain receptive to evidence and move toward concepts defined by a set of related functions. For example, 20% of healthy 4-month-old infants become very active and fretful to auditory, visual, and olfactory stimuli; two-thirds of these easily aroused infants become fearful in the 2nd year. This relation begins to define a temperamental type that future investigators will refine. One can emphasize the 4-month behavior and call these infants easily aroused, or focus on the timid behavior at 2 years and call these children fearful. This choice is less important than appreciating that the primary meaning of either term is a set of developmental functions. New temperamental concepts will be needed once we have learned more about development. We should not treat a temperamental bias as an essence. The psychological outcomes of each temperament will be informed by the historical era and culture in which children grow and the specific experiences they encountered. The biological conditions that are the foundation of a temperament do not produce any single or fixed profile later in life; they only set a bias for a particular envelope of outcomes.

Rothbart's Dimensions

Mary Rothbart's bold, synthetic ideas dominate discussions of infant temperament. Rothbart (1989) posits two primary dimensions on which infants vary—ease of arousal and self-regulation—and both are controlled continually by the social environment:

> Temperament [is defined as] constitutionally based individual differences in reactivity and self-regulation, with constitutional referring to the person's relatively enduring biological makeup inferred over time by heredity, maturation, and experience. Reactivity refers to the arousability of motor activity, affect, autonomic and endocrine responses. Self-regulation refers to processes that can modulate (facilitate or inhibit) reactivity and those processes include attention, approach, withdrawal, attack, behavioral inhibition, and self-soothing. (p. 59)

Reactivity

Reactivity can reflect pleasant or distressed states. The referents for the former category are vocalization, smiling, and nondistressed motor activity; the referents for the latter are thrashing, fretting, and crying. A low-intensity stimulus usually produces vocalization and smiling; a moderately intense stimulus leads to vocalization or fretting; an intense stimulus more often provokes cries of distress. Rothbart (1989) suggests that either a pleasant or unpleasant state can be expressed through somatic, cognitive, or neuroendocrine responses and experienced as a feeling of pleasure or distress. The valence linked to the state of the reactivity—whether pleasant or unpleasant—will influence the specific self-regulatory reactions displayed. Thumb sucking, clutching a part of the body, or moving toward or away a novel incentive are three obvious self-regulatory reactions.

The idea of reactivity has obvious face validity. Fetuses and newborns differ in their reactivity to stimulation, and the variation is related to a modest degree to early postnatal behavior (Madison, Madison, & Adubato, 1986; Strauss & Rourke, 1978). In addition, maternal reports of fetal movements are moderately stable from gestational weeks 28 to 35 (Eaton & Saudino, 1992). DiPietro and colleagues (DiPietro, Hodgson, Costigan, & Johnson, 1996; DiPietro et al., 2000, 2002) examined the relation between fetal activity and heart rate (beginning at 20 weeks of gestation), on the one hand, and infant temperament at 3 and 6 months, using the ICQ, on the other (Bates, Freeland, & Lounsbury, 1979). High levels of fetal activity predicted irritability and a less adaptive profile (a factor on the ICQ) when the infants were 3 and 6 months old (DiPietro et al., 1996). In a separate study, individual differences in heart rate were preserved from 24 weeks of gestation through 1 year postnatal (DiPietro et al., 2000). However, the evidence on fetal activity from this second sample led to conclusions slightly different from those implied by the earlier investigation. More active fetuses showed less distress to limitations when they were 1 year old and were less behaviorally inhibited at 2 years of age (DiPietro et al., 2002).

The specific source of the arousing stimulation, whether visual, tactile, olfactory, or auditory, cannot be ignored when classifying an infant as high or low in reactivity to stimulation. Four-month-old infants who cry to the recorded voice of a woman speaking short sentences are not psychologically similar to those who cry to a moving visual stimulus. Goldsmith and Campos (1990) found no correlation between an infant's tendency to cry when placed on the visual cliff and the following encounter with a stranger.

The nature of the response is also important in judging the infant's reactivity. Infants can cry, fret, smile, move, or vocalize to auditory stimuli; and do or do not struggle to restraint of their arms. An infant's preferred reaction to a particular incentive is due, partly, to temperamental and maturational factors that are not yet understood. For example, in a longitudinal sample of 23 infants observed at 7, 10, 13, and 16 weeks, an index of motor arousal to varied stimuli based on limb movement increased with age, while the frequency of tongue protrusions, vocalization, and crying decreased with age. Only individual variation in tongue protrusions was stable from 7 to 16 weeks (Rezendes, 1993).

Thus, a potential problem with the concept of reactivity or "ease of arousal" is an indifference to the exact nature of the incentive. The brain circuits that mediate smiling are likely to be different from those that mediate babbling or thrashing (Gainotti, Caltagirone, & Zoccolotti, 1993).

Self-Regulation

The concept of self-regulation is a derivative of two older ideas: The first originates in the learning theories of the 1950s; the second in Freud's writings. Dollard and Miller (1950) suggested that a reinforcement was any event that reduced stimulation and level of internal arousal. This hypothesis is derived from Freud's suggestion that humans seek quiescence and a reduction in the vis nervosa. This hypothesis assumes, as a deep premise, that organisms naturally seek a low—or optimal—level of internal arousal. This idea remains popular despite the fact that children prefer to run rather than to sit and to explore rather than to sit quietly with a new toy.

Freud changed the internal state that caused symptoms from the popular vis nervosa to anxiety, which was attractive to many readers. Freud added that cognitive, affective, and behavioral reactions to anxiety were directed at reducing the intensity of this unpleasant state. Because anxiety is an obvious enemy, the responses to it could reasonably be called defenses. This idea, which remains popular among psychiatrists and psychologists, renders the concept of self-regulation appealing.

The idea of self-regulation, however, shares some of the same problems that burden reactivity. A 1-year-old infant who shows a wary face to a stranger and then retreats to the mother may be different temperamentally from one who also displays a wary face but does not retreat and, subsequently, vocalizes to the intruder. Even though both infants may appear to be regulating the un-

certainty generated by the unfamiliar adult, the former infant becomes more timid and shy in the 2nd year than the latter. Because all infants do something when aroused by events, most regulate to some degree. It is important to attend to both the specific source of the arousal and the specific self-regulatory behaviors that follow, because different temperamental types may be hidden in these categories.

Although self-regulation seems an apt way to describe some infant behaviors, it may be less appropriate for older children because the incentive is not an intense stimulus that produces a level of arousal, but is often an unfamiliar event. When an adult dressed as a clown enters a room where a 2-year-old child has been playing quietly, most children stop playing and stare at the intruder. This stereotyped reaction occurs because the clown is a discrepant event, not because it is an intense stimulus, and children usually react to discrepancies with cessation of activity. But it is not obvious that the immobility, even if accompanied by retreat to the mother, is self-regulating for it may not reduce the child's arousal. Indeed, staring at an unfamiliar intruder while clutching the parent may increase the child's level of uncertainty and physiological arousal.

Two eminent students of animal behavior have noted "careful attention to specific patterns of behavior . . . is prerequisite to an understanding of the relation between biological and behavioral systems . . . an adequate description of behavior must include reference to the stimuli and situations that normally produce that behavior and to its normal consequences in the environment" (Blanchard & Blanchard, 1988, p. 63).

This suggestion is not intended to replace Rothbart's creative ideas. Rather, we urge psychologists to use her fruitful hypotheses while acknowledging Whitehead's (1928) admonition that we should not reason about predicates severed from their noun and object partners. The action verb *kiss* has very different meanings in the following three sentences: (1) The woman kissed her lover, (2) The baby kissed his grandmother, and (3) The winning jockey kissed his horse.

Biologists share a consensual meaning when they use a theoretical predicate. *Bleach* describes what rods in the retina do to light. *Phagocytosis* refers to what natural killer cells do to bacteria. *Digest* is what the intestinal villi do to proteins, fats, and carbohydrates. Social scientists are looser in their use of predicates. The predicate *learn* is often applied to diverse organisms, from worms to chimps, on the assumption that the process of learning is the same in all animals. The indifference to agents and targets is due, in part, to the fact that psychologists are primarily interested in process rather than in the agents in whom the processes occur.

Because psychology is one of the least mature of the natural sciences, its practitioners are tempted to take as a model the highly respected discipline of physics. The Newtonian declaration that force equals mass times acceleration holds for all objects—cars, stones, and snowflakes—in all earthly situations. Einstein even declared that the laws of the theory of general relativity apply to all parts of the cosmos. If psychologists were friendlier to biology than to physics, they would realize that specificity, not generality, is the more useful rule in the life sciences.

IRRITABILITY IN INFANCY

Studies of variation in irritability dominate all other infant qualities while studies of shy-timid versus sociable-bold behavior dominate investigations of children. These facts imply that scientists who quantified other behaviors found less stable, or less coherent, results and did not publish their data. It is hard to believe that most developmental psychologists have restricted their observations to these few characteristics and more likely that irritability in infancy and a timid or sociable posture in childhood are popular targets because they are obvious, relatively easy to code, and of concern to parents.

Extreme irritability in young infants is preserved to a modest degree through part or all of the 1st year. Crying and fretting are stable over the first 4 months, and newborn irritability predicts less frequent smiling and babbling to adults at 4 months of age (Birns, Barten, & Bridger, 1969). Newborns whose cries were of high pitch and of shorter duration—and unpleasant to the ear—were rated by mothers at 3 months as more irritable and difficult (Huffman et al., 1994). Extreme distress to a heel stick during the newborn period predicted degree of distress to an inoculation 2 months later (correlation of .4; Worobey & Lewis, 1989) and was related to maternal descriptions of the 6-month-old as minimally distressed by limitations, but not to maternal descriptions of soothability or frequency of smiling at 6 months (Gunnar, Porter, Wolf, Rigatuso, & Larson, 1995). Facial expressions, coded in the Ekman-Izard scheme as either anger or sadness, to an inoculation were

moderately stable from 2 to 19 months ($r = .5$; Izard, Hembree, & Huebner, 1987). However, the frequency of spontaneous irritability should not be equated with ease of being soothed by a pacifier. Newborns who took a long time to be soothed by a pacifier were rated by their mothers at 9 months as more active and less likely to avoid unfamiliar events (Riese, 1995).

Some, but not all, irritable infants develop a reserved, timid, and fearful style in the preschool years. Four-month-old infants who showed frequent irritability together with vigorous limb activity to varied classes of stimuli were more fearful to unfamiliar events in the 2nd and 3rd years than those who showed only irritability without motor activity, or only vigorous motor arousal without irritability. Newborn twins who were unusually irritable, hard to soothe, and minimally attentive to stimulation were less sociable and more labile when they were 9 to 24 months old (Matheny et al., 1987). Similarly, newborns who became extremely irritable to a chilled metal disk placed against their thigh, compared with those who were far less irritable, became children with a more serious emotional demeanor ($r = .36$) and less sociability ($r = .38$; Riese, 1987). However, variation in crying is not always predictive of later behavior (see M. Fish, Stifter, & Belsky, 1991, for an example).

Although the evidence implies that extreme irritability to stimulation in the opening weeks predicts a less sociable, more dour child 6 to 24 months later, the crying behavior in most of these studies was either spontaneous or a reaction to varied stimuli. In a few studies, however, the crying was produced by the frustration of restraint, typically holding the infant's hands or arms. Infants who cry to this incentive, or any other frustrating event, may not have the same temperament as those who cry spontaneously to visual or auditory stimulation. Infants who cry to restraint have high vagal tone; infants who cry to visual or auditory stimulation have lower vagal tone (Fox, 1989).

The modest stability of variation in irritability over the first 2 years could be due to the fact that the incentives for crying change with age. Irritability in a 2-month-old is due, in large measure, to a low threshold of responsivity to the discomfort of cold, hunger, loud noises, and bright lights. Irritability in a 9-month-old is influenced in a more important way by threshold of reaction to unfamiliarity (Hebb, 1946). Irritability in a 1-year-old is influenced by a vulnerability to separation distress and prior conditioning experiences in which certain events have become acquired cues for distress.

By 3 years of age, the reasons for crying are more varied and include frustrations and prior reinforcements for crying. Thus, we should not be surprised that the correlation between irritability at 1 month and crying at 3 years is relatively low. Each of the small number of responses that children can display when distressed—crying, withdrawal, thrashing, or freezing—is preferentially elicited by different incentives and involves different brain circuits.

As might be expected, extremely irritable and nonirritable infants elicit different reactions from their mothers. A group of 89 lower-class infants were observed in the first 2 weeks of life on the Brazelton Neonatal Behavioral Assessment Scale. One group of 15 infants were extremely irritable and another group of 15 were minimally irritable; these groups represented the top and bottom 17% of the sample. These infants and their mothers were observed at home monthly over the first 6 months. The mothers of the highly irritable, compared with the minimally irritable, infants had less physical contact with their children but soothed them more frequently during the first few months. The mothers of nonirritable infants were more constant in their soothing overtures over time. However, the two groups of mothers became increasingly similar in their responsiveness as time passed. By 6 months, the two groups experienced similar maternal behaviors, and there were few differences between the infant groups in their behavior (Van den Boom & Hoeksma, 1994).

Smiling in Infancy

Crying during the opening months is more salient and more frequent than smiling and, in addition, has an analogue in the distress calls of primates. Smiling has no obvious analogue in most animals; perhaps that is why fewer investigators have probed individual differences in infant smiling, even though variation in this response appears to be heritable (Freedman & Keller, 1963; Reppucci, 1968). Frequent smiling to adults does not appear until about 3 months of age and may be impaired by damage to posterior sites in the right hemisphere (Reilly, Stiles, Larsen, & Trauner, 1995). Differences in smiling appear to be stable from 3 months to the end of the 1st year. In one study, variation in smiles to moderately discrepant events at 4 months predicted smiling following success on a cognitive test at 27 months of age, and variation in smiling is more stable over this period than variation in attentiveness, crying, or vocalization (Kagan, 1971).

Over half of a large sample of 4-month-olds never smiled to visual, auditory, and olfactory stimuli, while 10% smiled three or more times to the same incentives. Although three smiles may seem to be a small number in an absolute sense, it represented the 90th percentile of the distribution. When these high smiling infants were matched with infants of the same sex and level of motor arousal and irritability who did not smile at all, the former group had significantly lower sitting diastolic blood pressure when they were 21 months old. This result suggests that frequent smiling at 4 months is associated with low sympathetic tone in the cardiovascular system, an idea supported by the fact that 2-week-olds who showed high levels of heart rate variability to stimulation were frequent smilers at 4 months (S. Fish & Fish, 1995). Four-month-old infants who showed low levels of motor activity and crying to stimulation—called low reactive infants—smiled more frequently at 4, 14, and 21 months as well as at 11 years of age, compared with infants who showed high levels of motor activity and crying—called high reactive. The low reactive-high smiling children had low baseline heart rates when they were 11 years old (Kagan & Snidman, 2004). Thus, frequent smiling to nonsocial stimuli may reflect a special temperamental quality.

Activity in Infancy

The popular temperamental trait called activity level changes its referential meaning between infancy and 3 years of age. Hence, it is not surprising that there is not much preservation of variation in activity level from infancy to the toddler years (Dunn & Kendrick, 1981; Feiring & Lewis, 1980; Matheny, 1983). One study assessed activity in 112 healthy, middle-class newborns using a pressure transducer mattress that distinguished activity during crying from activity during nondistress periods. Fifty of the 112 infants were assessed again when they were between 4 and 8 years of age. Activity in the older children was monitored for 24 hours using an ambulatory microcomputer along with a parental questionnaire. There was only a modest correlation between the vigor of activity during the newborn period and vigorous activity during the day in the older children ($r = .29$). Further, there was no correlation between day and night activity in older children and no relation between newborn activity and parental ratings of activity in older children (Korner et al., 1985). The independence of day and night activity implies that a concept of general activity is not useful.

Activity level in monozygotic (MZ) and dizygotic (DZ) twins, assessed at 14, 20, and 24 months, was moderately stable and heritable (Saudino & Cherny, 2001). The stability coefficient from 14 to 24 months was only .23 and the heritability value .20 (see Saudino & Eaton, 1991, for a similar result with a smaller sample of twins, and Goldsmith & Gottesman, 1981). Matheny (1983) also reported very modest stability of activity in a laboratory from 6 to 24 months but a more robust heritability coefficient. Apparently, a general activity construct that does not stipulate age, context of assessment, or time of day is probably not theoretically useful.

Attentional Processes

The discoveries of cognitive neuroscience have penetrated the study of temperament and led investigators to examine variation in the distribution of attention. Rothbart, Derryberry, and Posner (1994) describe three aspects of attention that might turn out to have a temperamental contribution.

Infants differ in the rapidity and consistency with which they orient to a moving object or a sound in the periphery. The posterior attention network is especially involved in directing an infant's attention to sensory stimuli. It is believed that the posterior attentional network involves portions of the parietal cortex, thalamus, and superior colliculus and activity in these sites is modulated by noradrenergic axons from the locus ceruleus.

The anterior attentional network involves parts of the prefrontal cortex, anterior cingulate cortex, and the supplementary motor area. This network participates more in effortful control of behavior and the inhibition of activity to distracting or irrelevant stimuli, as well as in the effortful search for specific targets. It is believed that dopaminergic inputs from the ventral tegmental area and the basal ganglia modulate this network.

Finally, Posner and Petersen (1990) posit a vigilance system that mediates maintenance of an alert state over a prolonged duration. Preliminary evidence implicates the role of the right lateral midfrontal cortex as important, which, like the posterior system, is influenced by noradrenergic axons from the locus ceruleus.

Observations of children at 1, 2, and 3.5 years of age revealed stability of inattentiveness from 2 to 3.5 years of age (Ruff, Lawson, Parinello, & Weissberg, 1990). Distractability in a laboratory playroom—flitting from one toy to another—in a sample of 3.5-year-old children showed a modest association with teacher ratings of hyperactivity at 6 to 8 years of age (Carlson, Jacobvitz, &

Sroufe, 1995; Riese, 1988). A longitudinal study of variation in attentiveness, indexed by duration of fixation time to human faces or forms, revealed no stability from 4 months to 13 or 27 months, and only modest stability from 13 to 27 months ($r = .2$), and parental education predicted attentiveness for girls but not boys in the 2nd year (Kagan, 1971). Further, variation in infant attentiveness was not related to the child's IQ or reading ability at 10 years of age (Kagan, Lapidus, & Moore, 1978). Because the psychological bases for attentiveness to an event change from attention to discrepancy at 4 months to the activation of cognitive structures in the 2nd year, we should not expect much preservation of long or short periods of attentiveness to new events.

In sum, irritability, smiling, activity, and attention are probably influenced by temperamental biases and each is usually assessed in parental questionnaires for temperament (see Goldsmith & Rothbart, 1991).

TEMPERAMENTS IN OLDER CHILDREN

The most popular temperamental qualities in children older than age 2 bear some resemblance to those studied in infants, even though new characteristics emerge after the first birthday. Bates (1989) summarizes some of these qualities. The concept of *negative emotionality* refers to the display of distress, fear, and anger and is similar in sense meaning to one of the three major adult temperaments proposed by Buss and Plomin (1984). A second factor is *difficultness,* a derivative of the Thomas and Chess category that refers to irritability, a vulnerability to stress, and a demanding posture with adults. Bates (1980) acknowledges that this quality is, in part, a construction on the part of the parent. A third, *adaptability to novelty,* describes a child's tendency to approach unfamiliar events and situations. *Reactivity,* a fourth category, is close in meaning to Rothbart's (1989) definition, and *activity* is a fifth temperamental factor. *Attention regulation,* which refers to the tendency to shift attention when distracted by external stimulation, resembles Rothbart's (1989) infant quality of soothability. And Bates (1989) suggests that *sociability and positive reactivity* comprise important temperaments. Finally, Eisenberg et al. (2003) argue that the variation among school-age children in the ability to regulate emotion and relevant behaviors represents important traits that might have a temperamental origin. This regulation can be voluntary or involuntary, and can be influenced by the quality of parental emotional reactions toward the child (Eisenberg & Spinrad, 2004). These categories may turn out to be stable, but at the present time the evidence is most extensive for the reaction to unfamiliar events and situations. We now summarize this evidence.

Reaction to Unfamiliarity

Two temperamental categories studied extensively refer to a child's reaction to an unfamiliar person, object, event, or context, whether affective restraint, caution, or avoidance, on the one hand, or a spontaneous approach, on the other. The reaction to an unfamiliar event depends on whether it is perceived as a threat, the ease with which it is assimilated, and the availability of an appropriate response. All 1-year-olds reach toward a new toy after playing with a different one because the new object poses no threat, is assimilated at once, and a relevant action is available. However, not all 1-year-olds reach toward a stranger who has extended a hand because this event is not assimilated quickly, and the child is uncertain as to what response to display. Thus, children, like adults, live in a corridor bordered on one side by the appeal of new experiences and, on the other side, by fear of the unfamiliar.

There are three good reasons for an interest in the reaction to unfamiliarity. The relevant behaviors are moderately stable, easily quantified, and the intraspecific variation in these behaviors is present in almost every species studied, including mice, rats, wolves, dogs, cows, monkeys, birds, and fish. For example, the reactions to novel objects among infant monkeys reared either with a female dog or a fur-covered plastic toy were assessed regularly in the laboratory. The behavioral variation in the reaction to novelty during the 3rd year was more clearly a function of the animal's early temperamental bias to remain close to or distant from its surrogate object (the dog or the toy) than to the different conditions of rearing (Mason & Capitanio, 1988).

There is preservation of a timid compared with a nontimid reaction to unfamiliarity when behavior or questionnaire data comprise the evidence (Stevenson-Hinde & Shouldice, 1996). A group of over 1800 Canadian children were rated for fearfulness, prosocial behavior, and restlessness by different teachers from kindergarten through grade six. Most children rated as very high or low in fearfulness when they were in kindergarten were given a similar rating when they were

in the sixth grade (Cote, Tremblay, Nagin, Zoccolillo, & Vitaro, 2002; see also Rimm-Kaufman et al., 2002). A longitudinal study of non-European infants adopted by Dutch parents confirms the preservation of a bias for shy and/or anxious behavior. Young children who had been described by their adopted mothers as shy and prone to a dysphoric mood in the 2nd year were most likely to show internalizing traits when they were 7 years old. Neither the family's social class, nor the mother's early sensitivity with the infant predicted these qualities at age 7 (Stams, Juffer, & van Ijzendoorn, 2002).

The heritability of inhibited or uninhibited behavior to unfamiliarity, based on behavioral observations of a large sample of monozygotic and dizygotic twins observed at 14, 20, 24, and 36 months approached .5 (Kagan & Saudino, 2001). Inhibited children remained close to their mother and avoided playing with both toys and peers, while uninhibited children showed the complementary behaviors. Heritability estimates were over .90 when the sample was restricted to children who were extremely inhibited or uninhibited in a play session consisting of four children (DiLalla, Kagan, & Reznick, 1994). However, only 10% of the children were consistently shy and inhibited at all four ages from 14 to 36 months (Kagan & Saudino, 2001).

Longitudinal data from the Berkeley Guidance Study reveals that boys described by their mothers as very shy in late childhood had distinct traits when they were over 40 years old. The adults who had been shy married, became parents, and established a career later than their less shy peers. Very shy girls, on the other hand, married at normative times but, unlike their less shy peers, did not develop a career, terminated a job when they married or had a child, and conformed to the traditional sex-role norms for that era in American history (Caspi, Elder, & Bem, 1988).

Longitudinal observations of a large group of New Zealand children affirm the preservation of a shy profile. Over 1,000 3-year-olds were rated on a variety of characteristics following a 1-hour interaction in a laboratory setting. About 15% were rated as shy and subdued, and 30% as sociable and spontaneous. When these same subjects were 18 years old, they filled out a personality questionnaire. The adolescents who had been shy at 3 years of age described themselves as cautious, minimally aggressive, and likely to avoid dangerous situations (Caspi & Silva, 1995).

Not all shy, timid, 2- or 3-year-olds become excessively shy adolescents because parents, teachers, and peers have encouraged bolder behavior, and because the shy, inhibited children try to develop a more relaxed, sociable profile. Those who are unsuccessful may have had a different set of experiences. Rubin and colleagues (2002) found that 2-year-olds who were inhibited in the laboratory setting were only likely to preserve that style if they had intrusive, hypercritical mothers. The shy 2-year-olds were less likely to remain reticent if their mothers discouraged shyness (Rubin, Burgess, & Hastings, 2002). The change from shy to sociable behavior is of course more likely in cultures, like our own, that favor the latter as an ideal. This is less likely in Asian cultures which favor a quiet, less bold child (Kerr, Lambert, & Bem, 1996; Rickman & Davidson, 1994).

There is an intriguing relation between season of conception and observer ratings of shyness in both American and New Zealand samples. The preschool children in a large American longitudinal cohort, the National Longitudinal Sample of Youth (NLSY), were rated on shyness by trained home visitors on two different occasions. The 15% of the sample who were rated as very shy on both occasions, separated by 2 years, were most likely to be conceived during the period from late July to late September. Thus, the brain would be completing its basic organization during the period of September to November when the amount of daylight is decreasing most rapidly. The New Zealand children who were rated as shy were most likely to be conceived in January and February. Because New Zealand is in the Southern Hemisphere, daylight begins to decrease during these 2 months. Thus, both groups of fetuses who became shy children spent the first 4 months of their gestation at a time of decreasing daylight (Gortmaker, Kagan, Caspi, & Silva, 1997). The decrease in daylight is accompanied by increases in level of melatonin but decreases in serotonin in the pregnant mother. It is possible that these biochemical changes affect the brains of those embryos who are genetically disposed to develop shyness and increases the probability of that behavioral outcome. Nature can act in surprising ways.

We noted a modest positive relation between infant irritability and a shy profile in the older child. However, as with irritability, a shy posture with children or adults can have different antecedents and, therefore, different meanings. A 4-year-old in a social setting can play alone because (a) uncertainty is generated over the unfamil-iarity of the setting, (b) the child feels concern over being evaluated by others, (c) the child prefers to play alone, or (d) the child has experienced traumatic, fear-arousing encounters with other children and has developed a conditioned avoidance to peers. An investigator who codes only "time playing apart from other children" could have etiologically heterogeneous groups with similar scores. On the other hand, if the investigator codes several variables—time playing alone, time staring at peers, talking, smiling, and reaction to overtures from others—it will be easier to parse the isolated children into separate groups, only some of whom possess a temperamental bias to be shy. Every class of behavior is ambiguous as to its antecedent conditions.

The research of Rubin and his colleagues, which relies on behavioral observations, is exemplary. Rubin (1993) makes a distinction between the child who plays alone but who shows signs of anxiety (called reticent) and the equally solitary child who is actively engaged in activities but who does not show signs of uncertainty (called solitary-passive). Both types are stable over time, but the former more often stares at peers and resembles the behaviorally inhibited child (Coplan, Rubin, Fox, Calkins, & Stewart, 1994). *Social reticence* is characterized by an absence of social interaction with others, especially staring at peers while being unoccupied. Other children who also play alone explore objects or engage in constructive behaviors and these children are called *solitary-passive* (Rubin, 1982). Preschool children who are solitary-passive show neither signs of anxiety nor do they display internalizing or externalizing symptoms (Rubin, Coplan, Fox, & Calkins, 1995). Further, 2-year-olds who were able—or motivated—to tolerate a two-minute delay before engaging in an interesting activity (because the examiner made that request) and, in addition, were behaviorally inhibited were most likely to be reticent with peers when they were 4 years old (Henderson, Marshall, Fox, & Rubin, 2004).

Asendorpf (1991) also finds shy behavior to be stable over time, although more intelligent children show a greater decrease in shyness over time compared with their less intelligent peers (Asendorpf, 1994). Shy, reticent behavior with strangers was stable in a group of 99 German children observed in varied settings from the preschool years through the third grade ($r = .6$; Asendorpf, 1990). Asendorpf agrees with Rubin that a child can be shy because of the unfamiliarity of the situation, a concern over evaluation of task competence by another, or anxiety over peer rejection (Asendorpf, 1989, 1991, 1993). Buss (1986) argues that some shy school-age children display fearful behaviors to the unfamiliar during the first 2 years of life, while others do not display this trait until they are 3 or 4 years of age.

A similar conclusion emerged from a study of 212 Swedish children followed over a 6-year interval. Psychologists rated the children's behavior in the 1st and 2nd years and annually until 6 years of age. (In addition, mothers rated their infants four times during the 1st year, twice during the 2nd year, and annually until they were 6 years old.) The children who were exceptionally shy or sociable (15% at each end of the distribution) preserved their style from the second to the 6th year of life. The stability was greater for girls than for boys and smaller in magnitude when the whole sample was treated as if sociability were a continuum (Kerr, Lambert, Stattin, & Klackenberg-Larsson, 1994).

A second group of Swedish investigators followed 144 firstborn children from 16 months through the 4th year of life, a 2-year interval. Some children were attending day care and some were raised only at home. Shy behavior with an unfamiliar adult, based on observations at home, was stable from 28 to 40 months ($r = .4$) but not from 16 to 40 months, and there was no effect of day care attendance on shyness (Broberg, Lamb, & Hwang, 1990). "The increased contact with strange adults that followed from enrollment in out of home care did not affect children's inhibition at 28 and 40 months of age, which suggests that inhibition in the 1st year of life is best viewed as a fairly stable dimension that is not systematically affected by ordinary life changes like those implicit in the initiation of out of home care" (p. 1161). The fact that the children attending day care were not more sociable than those at home with their mothers surprised the authors and will surprise some developmental psychologists.

Alternatively, placement in day care before the age of 2 years apparently influences behavioral inhibition in a middle-class sample. Infants who displayed a combination of high motor activity and distress to unfamiliar auditory and visual stimuli, a profile that predicts behavioral inhibition at age 2, were less reticent with unfamiliar peers at age 4 if they had been placed in out-of-home day care than if they had remained at home with their mothers (Fox, Henderson, Rubin, Calkins, & Schmidt, 2001). An infant's temperament interacts with rearing conditions. In addition, children placed in different types of surrogate care outside the home who

were rated by observers as low in self-control showed larger increases in cortisol secretion from morning to afternoon than most other children (Dettling, Gunnar, & Donzella, 1999; Dettling, Parker, Lane, Sebanc, & Gunnar, 2000; Watamura, Sebanc, & Gunnar, 2002). A similar result was found for infant boys in surrogate care who were rated as shy or anxious (Tout, de Haan, Campbell, & Gunnar, 1998).

INHIBITED VERSUS UNINHIBITED CHILDREN

Kagan and Snidman (2004) regard shyness with strangers, whether peers or adults, as only one feature of a broader temperamental category called inhibition to the unfamiliar (Arcus, 1991; Kagan, 1994). Inhibited children react to different types of unfamiliarity with an initial avoidance, distress, or subdued affect when they reach the maturational stage when discrepancies elicit uncertainty, usually 7 to 9 months in humans. The comparable ages in other species are 2 to 3 months in monkeys, 30 to 35 days in cats, and 5 to 7 days in ducklings (Kagan, 1994). The source of the unfamiliarity can be people, animals, situations, objects, or dynamic events. An inhibited child might, with experience, learn to control an initial avoidance of strangers and, therefore, not appear shy, but still retain an avoidant style to unfamiliar challenges or places or be prone to a serious, dour mood. An inhibited temperament assumes that a child can display an avoidant style in any one of a number of contexts. Membership in this temperamental category is not defined by only one class of behavior, like shyness with an unfamiliar peer. Hence, children who are not particularly shy might have an inhibited temperament.

The complementary category, called uninhibited to the unfamiliar, is characterized by a sociable, affectively spontaneous reaction to unfamiliar people, situations, and events. As with the inhibited child, the category refers to an envelope of profiles whose form changes with development.

Shy or sociable behavior in a specific class of situation can be the product of different biologies and past histories. The independence of an entity (in this case a child) from its functions (behavior in a particular situation) was a major node of disagreement between Whitehead and Russell. Russell (1940) believed that the two ideas were independent, whereas Whitehead insisted that they were a unity. In the statement "Lions stalk gazelles" Russell would have argued that the predicate *stalk* was applicable to a variety of animals and could be treated as an independent function. Whitehead (1928) would have claimed that lions stalk in a particular way that is different from that of hyenas; therefore, no scholar should posit separate classes of agents and functions that can be combined in any way. We side with Whitehead, as do all who believe that the motives, emotional moods, and postures of an agent who "gives an order to another" are different if the agent is a 3-year-old talking to a peer, a burglar with a victim, an army officer with a private, or a parent with an adolescent. The behavior of temperamentally inhibited children in unfamiliar social situations is not exactly like the profile of those who acquired their shy, timid demeanor through experience alone. The former group displays fewer spontaneous smiles and greater muscle tension. Thus, we should not treat the predicate "is shy" as a quality separable from the child's life history, physiology, and the context of observation. This suggestion applies to all predicates referring to psychological dispositions.

Inhibited and uninhibited profiles appear to be heritable. Identical twins are more similar in the display of shy, timid behavior during childhood than are fraternal twins (Emde et al., 1992; Matheny, 1983, 1990), thus matching data on adults (Davis, Luce, & Kraus, 1994). The Institute of Behavioral Genetics at the University of Colorado has studied a large number of same-sex twin pairs at 14 and 21 months. The heritability coefficients for inhibited and uninhibited behavior, based on direct observations were between .5 and .6 (Kagan & Saudino, 2001). But readers should be aware of the fact that the heritability equations that produce the estimates are vulnerable to the critique of assuming additivity of genes and environment, ignoring epistasis, and failing to measure the environmental factors directly to compute the interaction between genes and experience.

The Biological Bases for Reaction to Unfamiliarity

The brain states created by unfamiliarity, classical conditioning, evolutionarily significant stimuli, and anticipation of the future involve different neural circuits. This claim rests, in part, on evidence from animal studies (Treit et al., 1993a, 1993b) and the fact that the most probable profile of responses is different for these four incentives. An unfamiliar event, for example, a person with a mask, typically produces cessation of activity in a 2-year-old child. This response is mediated by a circuit involving the amygdala and the ventral peri-aqueductal gray. However, acquiring a classically conditioned rise in heart rate does not require the central gray, but the amygdala and its projections to the hypothalamus and the sympathetic chain. A startle reaction to a looming object or loud sound need not involve the amygdala. Classically conditioned avoidance of specific tastes, but not odors, can be acquired in anaesthetized rats, suggesting that the conditioned avoidance of tastes may be biologically different from learned avoidance to novel sights (Rattoni, Forthman, Sanchez, Perez, & Garcia, 1988). Unfortunately, scientists do not know the circuits that mediate the conscious reports of anxiety over a future threat or challenge. We do know that children and adults can report feeling anxious without any accompanying peripheral physiological changes. In light of this evidence, it seems reasonable to reject the idea of a single fear state and to assume, until data prove otherwise, that discrepancy, classical conditioning, biologically significant events, anticipation of future unpleasantness, as well as separation from a target of attachment create different physiological and psychological states. It is reassuring that physiologists also reject the idea of a unitary state of physiological stress: Hemorrhage, hypotension, and hypoglycemia produce different profiles of secratog release (Sapolsky, 1992).

Each brain, or peripheral, site that participates in a circuit that produces a behavioral or biological reaction has a different responsibility. For example, a child's bodily freezing to the sudden entrance of a stranger wearing a mask requires a sensory cortex to register the features of the person, a parahippocampal region to detect the stranger's discrepant features, and an amygdala to provoke the neurons of the central gray to produce the immobility. Scientists emphasize the contribution of the amygdala because it is the most immediate origin of projections to the structures that produce the immobility. But a child with no sensory cortex could not perceive the person and therefore would not freeze. If the variable of interest had been the perception of the unfamiliar person, rather than the immobility, scientists would emphasize the significance of the sensory cortex.

Scientists are biased to attribute causal status to the structure or process that is the immediate origin of a set of observations. The ancients believed that the emotions of love and anger originated in the heart because a perception of a racing heart always preceded the emotional experience. Suppose that available technology permitted psychologists to quantify moment-to-moment changes in a number of neurotransmitters and modulators during the presentation of visual and auditory stimuli to young infants and they discovered that variation in norepinephrine secretion from the locus ceruleus predicted variation in inhibited behavior in the 2nd year of life. Under these conditions, the scientists might have argued that the responsivity of the locus ceruleus was the basis for the temperamental biases. The dependent variable selected influences, in a serious way, the brain sites or physiologies awarded causal status. A painful event evokes activity in the amygdala and the HPA. Scientists who measure fMRI activity in the amygdala will emphasize the significance of this structure while those who quantified increases in cortisol would award more importance to the HPA axis. No temperamental bias is located in a particular brain structure. All a scientist can say is that a particular structure is relevant.

One obstacle to progress in understanding temperamental vulnerabilities to variation in avoidance of the unfamiliar is the assumption that there is only one basic fear state with variation in intensity. An infant monkey's distress calls to separation from the mother, a quail chick's immobility to restriction of movement, an increase in heart rate or blood pressure to a conditioned stimulus that had been paired with shock, and flight from a novel object are sometimes regarded as indexes of the same basic fear state. These theoretical discussions of fear ignore the variation in species, incentive event, and specific response quantified and assume that the same emotional state is generated in each of the above instances. This assumption is likely to be incorrect.

Other psychologists (Panksepp, 1990) claim that separation of a mammalian infant from its mother elicits a fear state. Separation, unlike unfamiliarity or a conditioned stimulus that signals pain, produces distress vocalizations, not freezing, defensive aggression, or flight. A kitten faced with an unfamiliar event often shows arching of the back mediated by the central gray. A kitten separated from its mother displays different behaviors. Thus, it is probably an error to use the distress that accompanies separation as a model for fear. This is not to say that the state created by separation is not interesting or of theoretical importance, but this state is probably not the best probe for understanding fear to threat, a conditioned cue, or to novelty. It is of interest that posttraumatic stress disorder usually follows events that are dangerous, such as earthquakes, or those that engender a combination of fear and guilt; for example, witnessing an atrocity (Pynoos et al., 1987). That is one reason why there is a low correlation between the occurrence of dis-

tress to separation at home, or in the laboratory, and cries of fear to discrepant events in 1-year-olds and why a temperamental vulnerability to a fear reaction to discrepancy and a child's attachment classification are only modestly related (Kagan, 1994). One implication of these facts is that the generalizations about fear or anxiety based on separation from caretakers, whether in monkeys or children, should not be applied uncritically to the reactions displayed to unfamiliarity, threat, or conditioned cues for aversive events.

The concept of a basic fear circuit is too ambitious. The meaning of "fear state" is different when the defining referent is (a) a self-report, (b) a change in behavior, or (c) an increased activity in a neural circuit. If this suggestion is valid, we will need different theoretical constructs for fear depending upon which referent is used. Even if a particular brain structure were involved in all of the above phenomena, that fact would be insufficient to assume that the states, which were identical for complex events and shared a single feature, were essentially similar. Although all mammals are capable of internal fertilization, there is extraordinary diversity among them in other systems.

Finally, there is the possibility that, as with parental reports and behavioral observations, the description of the brain events that contribute to a psychological state of fear and the verbal descriptions of an agent are incommensurable—one cannot replace one set of sentences with the other without changing the intended meaning.

The Functions of the Amygdala

Observations of 4-month-old infants exposed to visual, auditory, and olfactory stimulation point to the possible physiological bases for the inhibited and uninhibited temperamental profiles that emerge after the first birthday. The early infant behaviors that are predictive of these two categories can be understood if we assume that some infants are born with a low threshold of excitability in the amygdala and its projections to the ventral striatum, hypothalamus, cingulate, frontal cortex, central gray, and medulla.

The amygdala consists of many neuronal collections each with a distinct pattern of connectivity, neurochemistry, and functions. Each collection projects to at least 15 different sites, and receives inputs from about the same number of regions, resulting in about 600 known amygdalar connections (Petrovich, Canteras, & Swanson, 2001; Stefanacci & Amaral, 2002). Although a simplification, most anatomists conceptualize the amygdala as composed of three basic areas: (1) the basolateral, (2) the corticomedial, and (3) the central areas. The basolateral area, which transmits its information to the central nucleus, receives rich thalamic and cortical inputs from many external sensory origins, and some input from the viscera, and is reciprocally connected to cortex, hippocampus, hypothalamus, basal ganglia, brain stem, and the bed nucleus. The behavioral reactions of flight or attack are mediated primarily by projections from the basolateral nucleus to the ventromedial striatum and ventral pallidum (Fudge, Kunishio, Walsh, Richard, & Haber, 2002).

The corticomedial nucleus receives primarily olfactory and taste information and projects to the hippocampus, thalamus, hypothalamus, and central nucleus. The central nucleus, like the basolateral, receives input from taste, vision, audition, and the viscera, but most important, from the basolateral and corticomedial areas.

Further, the central area is the origin of a large number of projections to the bed nucleus, cortex, basal forebrain, hypothalamus, brain stem, and autonomic nervous system. Projections from the central nucleus are more responsible for internal, bodily changes that include secretion of hormones, reactivity to the autonomic nervous system, and subtle alterations in posture and muscle tone. Some investigators have suggested that the central nucleus is activated primarily by acute, punctate events to produce a transient reaction. More continuously stressful conditions activate the bed nucleus of the stria terminalis to create a more chronic state. The level of CRH in the central nucleus is correlated with an animal's reactivity to a phasic event; CRH level in the bed nucleus is more clearly correlated with reactivity to a chronic stressor (Walker, Toufexis, & Davis, 2003). This difference suggests a contrast between an acute state of vigilance produced by seeing a snake or a spider with a chronic state of worry over the future. The central nucleus is needed for the acute state, while the bed nucleus maintains the prolonged state of uncertainty to a longer lasting threat. However, this rule has exceptions (Fendt, Enders, & Apfelbach, 2003).

Fear or Surprise

There is disagreement over the events most likely to activate the amygdala and the psychological states that follow. The central issue is whether the amygdala reacts primarily to imminently threatening events to produce states of fear or to unfamiliar ones to produce states of surprise. Dangerous events should create distinctly different states in brain, and, subsequently, in mind than

unfamiliar ones because not all unfamiliar events pose a threat and some threats are not novel. A female Diana monkey issues a distinct vocalization to the unexpected alarm call of a male leopard. However, she does not vocalize to the same male leopard call if it occurs a second time a few minutes later, even though the leopard remains a threat because the call is no longer a discrepant and therefore not a surprise. This monkey would have vocalized if the second sound had been an eagle's shriek (Seyfarth & Cheney, 2003). The monkey vocalized when the potentially dangerous auditory event was unexpected but not when the same sign of a dangerous event was anticipated. Earlier writers have suggested that mammals show signs of fear to unfamiliar events (Hebb, 1946; Valentine, 1930), and animals with a lesioned amygdala fail to avoid unfamiliar animals or objects. That is why infant monkeys with lesions of the amygdala who had been permanently separated from their mother when they were 6 months of age did not preferentially choose to approach the mother rather than an unfamiliar animal (Bauman, Lavenex, Mason, Capitanio, & Amaral, 2004). The lesioned animals showed no preference because they did not experience the state of uncertainty usually provoked by an unfamiliar adult animal.

Scientists began to focus on the amygdala's contribution to fear rather than surprise after Brown, Kalish, and Farber (1951) reported that the magnitude of an animal's body startle to a loud acoustic probe was enhanced when a light that had been previously paired with electric shock was presented to a rat just before the loud acoustic stimulus. These investigators assumed that rats should be afraid of a light that signaled electric shock, and therefore concluded that the larger startles reflected a state of fear. This assumption was followed by the elegant research of LeDoux (2000), Davis et al. (1994), and others, indicating that the thalamus and the amygdala were necessary for the acquisition of a conditioned reaction of body immobility, potentiated startle, or autonomic reactivity to a neutral stimulus that had signaled an electric shock. Soon a large majority of scientists had concluded that the conditioned stimulus created a state of fear in the animal. This inference was attractive because the concept of fear played an important theoretical role in the middle of the twentieth century when psychoanalytic theory was popular. Fear seemed closely related to anxiety, and Freud had made anxiety the central culprit in neuroses. In addition, the *Diagnostic Statistical Manual* of the American Psychiatric Association had made the anxiety disorders a major mental illness category. This evidence persuaded

Ohman and Mineka (2001, 2003) to suggest that the amygdala reacts primarily to signs of danger rather than to unfamiliarity. They argued that all animals inherit a fear module (located in the amygdala) that reacts, without conscious awareness and free of cognitive control, to events that pose a threat to the integrity of the body. Snakes are presumed to be a classic example of such an event. There are serious problems with this position.

First, the behavioral reactions of most monkeys, chimpanzees, and human infants to a snake are no different from their reaction to discrepant events that are harmless, like a tortoise or seaweed (Marks, 1987). Monkeys born and reared in a laboratory, and therefore protected from contact with live snakes, showed a longer period of motor inhibition to the presentation of a snake, whether alive or an artifact, than to blue masking tape. However that restraint only occurred on the first testing session. During later sessions, the animals showed no more restraint to the snake than to the masking tape. Moreover, a majority of animals failed to show any difference in withdrawal behavior to the snake, compared to the harmless masking tape (Nelson, Shelton, & Kalin, 2003). If snakes were a biologically potent incentive for a fear state, motor restraint should not have habituated so quickly and the majority of monkeys, rather than just 30%, should have shown a withdrawal reaction.

School-age children from a Dakota Indian tribe in Manitoba asked to recall the single most frightening event of their earlier years, most often named either a large domestic animal, like a bull or horse, that had frightened them or a ghost or witch-like figure they believed carried the children away if they disobeyed. Very few children named snakes, even though snakes are common in this area (Wallis, 1954). A critical fact is that select neurons in the amygdala as well as in the bed nucleus, hippocampus, and brain stem respond reliably to discrepant events, whether or not they are harmful (Wilson & Rolls, 1993). Further, the reactivity of these neurons habituates often rapidly as the event loses its unfamiliarity (LaBar, Gatenby, Gore, LeDoux, & Phelps, 1998). Adults in an fMRI scanner looking at faces with neutral expressions showed greater amygdalar activation to new, compared with familiar faces, even though no face had a fearful, or threatening expression (Schwartz, Wright, Shin, Kagan, & Rauch, 2003), as did adults who had shown characteristic avoidance of unfamiliarity during childhood (Schwartz et al., 2003).

Thus, the evidence implies that the amygdala reacts primarily to unfamiliar events, rather than to events that are threatening; unless, the animal knows the event is dangerous. A basic property of the amygdala is a prepared-

ness to receive information from the parahippocampal region indicating that an event that captured attention is deviant from the agent's stored representations. Surprise is a possible name for the psychological state created by such experiences (Whalen, 1998). It is less clear what name(s) is most appropriate for the brain state. But the brain and emergent psychological states that define surprise, following exposure to an unfamiliar event, are different from those that represent a state of fear to the imminent possibility of harm. It is important to differentiate between an unfamiliar event and an unexpected change in the sensory surround (e.g., a sudden loud sound), because the latter need not activate the reciprocal connections between the parahippocampal region and the amygdala.

HIGH AND LOW REACTIVITY TO UNFAMILIARITY

It is assumed, but not yet proven, that 4-month-old infants who show high levels of vigorous motor activity, a great deal of muscle tension, and frequent irritability to a standard laboratory battery composed of visual, auditory, and olfactory stimulation possess low thresholds of excitability in the basolateral and central areas of the amygdala and their projections. These infants, who represent about 20% of an unselected healthy Caucasian sample, are called high reactive. A complementary group who showed low levels of motor arousal and minimal irritability to the same battery, about 40% of the sample, are assumed to have higher amygdalar thresholds to stimulation and are called low reactive. The two patterns of reaction to unfamiliar events are less clear in much younger infants because the connectivity between the amygdala and sites mediating motor activity and distress are not yet mature (Weber, Watts, & Richardson, 2003). However, as noted earlier, the amygdala is part of a circuit that includes the thalamus, sensory and association cortex, and parahippocampal region that are also activated by unfamiliar events. Although the amygdala is the proximal origin of the motor activity in crying, it remains possible that the variation in behavior might be due, in part, to variation in the excitability of another structure in this circuit that primes the amygdala.

Childhood Derivatives of High and Low Reactivity

Kagan and colleagues observed a large number of children at 14 and 21 months who had been high- or low-reactive infants at 4 months. The laboratory batteries at

14 and 21 months consisted of a variety of procedures designed to elicit uncertainty, including intrusion into the child's personal space (placing electrodes on the body or a blood pressure cuff on the arm), exposure to unfamiliar objects (robots, toy animals, or papier-mâché puppets), and encounters with unfamiliar people who behaved in an atypical way or wore a novel costume. A child who cried to any one of these events or did not approach any of the unfamiliar objects when requested to do so was coded as fearful for that episode. High-reactive infants were significantly more fearful at 14 and 21 months than were low-reactive infants. About one-third of the high-reactives were highly fearful at both 14 and 21 months, and only 3% showed minimal fear at the two ages. By contrast, one-third of the low-reactives were minimally fearful at the same two ages and only 4% showed high fear. It is of interest that the remaining children showed intermediate levels of fearfulness (Kagan, 1994).

Support for the claim that these two groups of infants, defined by a combination of motor arousal and crying to stimulation, represent qualitative categories that should not be placed on a continuum of arousal comes from the fact that when the duration of crying to the 4-month battery was either zero (the infant did not cry at all) or longer than 8 seconds, the correlation between degree of motor activity at 4 months and fearfulness at 14 months was close to zero for each of the two cry groups ($r = .13$ for the subjects who did not cry at all, and $r = .10$ for those who cried more than 8 seconds). Conversely, when the infants were divided into groups with motor scores that were low (<40) or high (>50), the correlation between duration of crying at 4 months and fear at 14 months was also low ($r = .25$ for those with low motor behavior; $r = .08$ for those with high motor scores). Thus, once an infant had passed the criteria for motor arousal and crying that defined high reactivity, additional motor activity or crying (in that category) had minimal consequences for how fearful the child would become later.

When the high- and low-reactive infants were evaluated at 4.5 years of age, the former group was much more subdued and talked and smiled less frequently during a 1-hour laboratory assessment with an unfamiliar female examiner. By contrast, the low-reactive children were spontaneous; they asked questions, commented on the procedures, and smiled and laughed more often. The differences between the two groups in smiling were more dramatic than the differences in talking. The three

low-reactive boys who smiled the most (more than 50 times) had been the most relaxed infants when they were 4 months old (Kagan, 1997).

A small proportion of high-reactives talked and smiled frequently during the examination at 4 years. Although their environmental histories probably influenced this profile, it is of interest that during the original assessment at 4 months these children smiled more often than the majority of high-reactive infants who were more subdued at 4.5 years. In addition, the spontaneous high-reactives had a lower and more variable heart rate when they were 14 months old, implying that this small group of high-reactives may have possessed a special temperamental quality.

The fact that spontaneous conversation with a stranger is a sensitive sign of uncertainty after 3 or 4 years of age is supported by a different sample of children classified as inhibited or uninhibited at 21 or 31 months and observed again at 5, 7, and 13 years of age. Infrequent talking to an unfamiliar examiner was the best correlate of the original classification of an inhibited temperament at all three ages. It is possible that the small number of children with elective mutism represent extremely inhibited children (Black, 1992).

Restraint on spontaneous conversation in an unfamiliar social situation seems to be analogous to freezing to a novel event in animals. Both responses are mediated by the fibers of the central gray that are innervated by projections from the amygdala. But restraint on spontaneous speech is not a sensitive measure of uncertainty to the unfamiliar until after the third birthday. There was no significant relation between spontaneous vocalization in the 1st and 2nd year and spontaneous speech with an adult at 4 years of age. Although both variables refer to vocal sounds, the responses are different in meaning. Absence of vocalization in the 1st year reflects low affective arousal; restraint on speech at 4 years reflects anticipatory anxiety. One-year-old children are not old enough to be concerned with the examiner's evaluation of them or to anticipate the laboratory procedures that might be administered.

The high- and low-reactive 4.5-year-old children also differed in their social behavior with two other unfamiliar children of the same age and sex when trios of children were observed in a laboratory playroom for a half hour. Almost 66% of the low-reactive but fewer than 10% of the high-reactive children were outgoing and sociable with the unfamiliar children. By contrast, 40% of the high-reactives were avoidant and quiet compared with only 10% of the low-reactives. Although there was significant preservation of inhibited or uninhibited temperamental styles from 4 months to 4.5 years, these data also imply that environmental factors affect each child's phenotype.

The 4-year-old children who had been high reactive were also more intimidated by the examiner. In one episode, the female examiner asked the older child to perform some actions that would be prohibited by most parents. For example, she opened a photo album containing pictures of herself, took out a large color photograph, and, as she handed it to the child, said, "This is my favorite picture; tear up my favorite picture." More low- than high-reactives either asked her why they should perform that act or, in the case of five children, refused to do so. Moreover, their resistance was not accompanied by any obvious signs of anxiety; they simply appeared to be less afraid of disobeying the requests of an authority figure when that request required them to violate a norm they had acquired. Almost all the high-reactives were reluctant to disobey and, after a 5- to 10-second delay, tore a small corner from the photograph.

Parents of high-reactive infants who became inhibited preschoolers reported that their children were more sensitive to criticism and cried, had a tantrum, or became subdued when chastised. On the face of it, this response does not follow from the hypothesis that high-reactive-inhibited children react to unfamiliarity with uncertainty. Parental criticism is not an unfamiliar event; a person dressed in a clown costume is discrepant. This relation can be understood, however, if we assume that a child older than 3 or 4 years is continually generating representations of the present and immediate future. If an event, like a chastisement, is unexpected, it resembles a discrepant event. Because the amygdala and its circuits are excited by discrepancy, the child might react with crying, withdrawal, or a tantrum. It is possible that adolescents and adults who were high-reactive-inhibited children are more easily threatened by encounters with beliefs, opinions, or philosophical premises that are not in accord with their firm beliefs.

Influence of Experience

Although physiological products of genes make a modest contribution to the inhibited and uninhibited behavioral profiles, they share power with experience. Over one-third of high-reactive infants were not exceptionally fearful or shy in the 2nd year; a small number were fear-

less. Home observations on 50 high- and 50 low-reactive firstborn infants indicated that a mother's actions with the infant affected the probability that a high-reactive child would become inhibited. A nurturing parent who consistently protected her high-reactive infant from all minor stresses made it more, rather than less, difficult for that child to control an initial urge to retreat from strangers and unfamiliar events. Equally accepting mothers who set firm limits for their children, making mundane age-appropriate demands for cleanliness or conformity, helped their high-reactive infants overcome their fearfulness (Arcus, 1991).

The role of experience is illustrated by the variability in each temperamental category. We examined the variability in behavior with the examiner at 4.5 years within two very different groups: high-reactive girls who showed high fear at 14 months ($N = 16$) and low-reactive girls who showed low fear at 14 months ($N = 28$). Although the former, as expected, had significantly fewer spontaneous comments and smiles compared with the latter, the variation within each group was large. For example, although one-third of the high-reactive, fearful girls had fewer than 10 spontaneous comments, one-third had more than 50 comments. One-third displayed fewer than 5 smiles, but one-third had more than 30 smiles. Within the low-reactive, low-fear girls, one-third had fewer than 27 comments and fewer than 21 smiles, but one-third had more than 70 comments and more than 35 smiles. It is fair to suggest that this broad range of outcomes at 4.5 years within these classes of children is due, in part, to differential experience. The envelope of developmental trajectories for each temperamental group is not fixed in a rigid way (Kagan & Snidman, 2004).

Another sample of infants, classified as high reactive or aroused, was observed at 9, 14, 24, and 48 months (Fox et al., 2001). About one-half of the high reactives retained an inhibited persona through 2 years of age, and one-third preserved this profile through the fourth birthday. However, the child's gender and form of rearing influenced the retention or loss of an inhibited persona. High-reactive boys preserved their inhibition more than girls, and those who were placed in day care during the early years were less likely to preserve behavioral inhibition than those raised only at home. Fox et al. (2001) speculated that placement in day care probably influences the preservation of behavioral inhibition because exposure to unfamiliar peers and settings, and freedom from possible overprotection at home, might allow these children to learn coping strategies to unfamiliarity. Rubin, Cheah, and Fox (2001) coded maternal behavior while 4-year-old inhibited children were asked to build a block tower with their mothers. Mothers who were oversolicitous and excessively responsive to their child's crying were most likely to have children who were reticent when playing with peers.

A sample of 164 of the children in Kagan's sample were evaluated when they were 7.5 years old. Data from maternal reports, teacher descriptions and observations revealed that 26% of the total sample had anxious symptoms. This group of 42 anxious children was compared with 107 control children without anxious symptoms. The 7-year-olds who had been high-reactive infants were most likely to possess anxious symptoms; 45% of high-reactives, but only 15% of low-reactives received this classification. Moreover, the high-reactives with anxious symptoms were most likely to have screamed in fear during the 21-month assessment when a person dressed in a clown costume entered a room where they had been playing. About 20% of the sample of high-reactives were consistently inhibited at four ages: 14 and 21 months, as well as 4.5 and 7.5 years. Not one high-reactive infant was consistently uninhibited across all four evaluations (Kagan & Snidman, 2004).

These children were evaluated again when they were between 10 and 12 years of age. About one-third of the high- and low-reactives displayed a style of social behavior with the examiner that was in accord with their earlier infant temperament, while only 16% showed behaviors that were inconsistent with their infant temperament. More high-reactives were quiet, spoke in a soft voice, sat stiffly in the chair, and often looked away from the examiner. By contrast, more low-reactives were relaxed and talked and smiled frequently with the examiner. The number of spontaneous comments with the examiner at age 11 was a particularly sensitive sign of early temperament. High-reactives preserved a serious facial expression from 14 months to 11 years, while the low-reactives smiled and laughed frequently at every assessment. When the children filled out Q-sorts to describe themselves, the low-reactives were more likely than the high-reactives to report that they were "happy most of the time." Forty percent of the high-reactives retained an inhibited profile from 4.5 to 11 years of age, and 70% of the low-reactives retained an uninhibited profile across this same period. Further, 50% of low-reactives, compared with 13% of high-reactives, were described by their mother as extremely

sociable and extraverted, although the childrens' descriptions of their own behavior did not correlate highly with their contemporary behavior with the examiner or with the mothers' descriptions. It is important to note that the 4-month temperamental category was a better predictor of behavior at age 11 than the child's fearfulness at 14 or 21 months.

Biological Assessments

Four biological measures gathered on these subjects at age 11 were regarded as indirect signs of amygdalar activity, even though many brain sites participate in each biological reaction.

EEG Asymmetry

One measure was an asymmetry in EEG activation that favors the left or the right hemisphere, where desynchronization of alpha frequencies is the index of activation. The left frontal area is usually more active than the right when individuals are relaxed and in a happy mood, but the right is more active than the left when the individual is in a state of uncertainty, fear, or anxiety (Davidson, 2003a, 2003b; Fox, 1991, 1994). The results from a number of studies suggest that children and adults who show right frontal activation in the EEG are more likely to react to a discrepant event, unfamiliar situation or new challenge with greater dysphoria and/or an anxious avoidant response. Individuals who show left frontal activation show the complementary pattern of a more relaxed, happy mood and an eagerness to engage new experiences or challenges (Davidson, Ekman, & Saron, 1994; Schmidt & Fox, 1994; Tomarken, Davidson, & Henriques, 1990). A similar relation was observed in infants. Ten-month-old infants showed left frontal activation to a smiling, but not to a crying, adult, but they were more likely to show right frontal activation to the approach of a stranger (Fox & Davidson, 1987) and to a temporary separation from the mother (Davidson & Fox, 1989; Fox & Davidson, 1988). Further, the smiles of infants are usually accompanied by left frontal activation, while behavioral signs of fear are accompanied by right frontal activation (Fox & Davidson, 1987). Moreover, the tendency to show right frontal activation to temporary separation from the mother is a stable trait in the 2nd year (Fox, Bell, & Jones, 1992). Both socially reticent and solitary-passive children—using Rubin's definitions—show right frontal activation. But only the reticent group shows low alpha power across the entire scalp, suggesting a higher level of cortical arousal, and perhaps a hypervigilant mood.

When confronted with a stressful or unexpected incentive, like temporary maternal absence, young children show greater EEG activation on the right, compared with the left, frontal area (Dawson, Panagiotides, Klinger, & Hill, 1992). Thus, it is of interest that inhibited, compared with uninhibited, children showed greater activation in the right frontal area under resting conditions (Davidson, 1994a, 1994b). High-reactive infants showed greater activation of the right frontal area when tested during the 1st and 2nd years; low-reactive infants showed greater activation of the left frontal area (Fox, Calkins, & Bell 1994). Because neural activity in the amygdala is transmitted to the frontal lobe, by the nucleus basalis, it is possible that greater desynchronization of alpha frequencies on the right frontal lobe reflect greater activity in the right amygdala (Kapp, Supple, & Whalen, 1994; Lloyd & Kling, 1991). The distribution of receptors for CRH and/or the level of CRH may contribute to the asymmetry of activation. Monkeys who showed a stable and extreme right frontal activation across a 4-year interval had high CRH levels (Kalin et al., 2000). Further, rhesus monkeys who combined high cortisol levels with high fear to unfamiliarity were most likely to show right frontal activation (Kalin et al., 1998). And 6-month-old infants with high cortisol levels were biased to show right frontal activation (Buss et al., 2003).

The 11-year-old children who had been high-reactive infants had greater activation in the right than in the left hemisphere at parietal sites. The high-reactives who, in addition, had been highly fearful in the 2nd year were more likely than low-reactives to be right hemisphere active at frontal sites as well. Further, the low-reactive, 11-year-old boys who described themselves as "happy most of the time" had greater left frontal activation than low-reactive boys who did not report a chronically happy mood.

The earlier research of Fox, Rubin, and their colleagues, which was an incentive for the work by Kagan's laboratory, along with recent evidence from Fox's laboratory, affirms a relation between direction of asymmetry of activation and a temperamental bias for inhibited or uninhibited behavior. For example, Fox et al. (1995) studied 48 children who were seen at 2 years of age and later at age 4. At age 2, the children were observed in settings designed to elicit behavioral inhibition, including an encounter with an unfamiliar adult and a novel object. The children returned to the laboratory at 4 years of age for a peer play session. Each child was placed in a quartet of four unfamiliar children of the same sex. Each quartet consisted of one behaviorally inhibited child, one uninhibited child, and two children whose inhibition scores were close to the mean based on their behavior at 2 years of age. The children were observed during free play with peers and during a set of standard tasks using Rubin's coding criteria (Rubin, 2000). This scale allows identification of children who are socially reticent (isolated, staring, unoccupied, and displaying long latencies before they speak) and socially competent children who initiate play and often smile and talk.

Measures of EEG were recorded several weeks earlier. Children showing right frontal activation were more likely to be reticent than those who displayed left frontal activation. Maternal ratings of the child's shyness were correlated with both their play behavior and direction of activation. Of great interest is the fact that the very sociable children who showed right frontal activation were described by their mothers as displaying behaviors classified as externalizing (i.e., disobedience and mild aggression). But the reticent 4-year-olds who were also right frontal active were described as displaying internalizing problems (anxious, tense, and extremely shy). Thus, among children who showed right frontal activation, typical behavior at home was a function of their temperament. And inhibited 7-year-olds showed a more obvious increase in the level of right frontal activation to the challenge of preparing a speech than uninhibited children (Schmidt, Fox, Schulkin, & Gold, 1999).

Perhaps, the most relevant work from the Fox laboratory is based on a longitudinal study of a large group of infants who were classified at 4 months (using a battery similar to the one used by the Kagan group) into high-reactive (14% of the group), low-reactive (15% of the group), and infants who displayed high motor activity, vocalization, and smiling, but minimal distress (9%; we might call these children aroused). The high-reactives were most likely to show right frontal activation at 9 months while the aroused children were more likely to show left frontal activation. In addition, the high-reactives had less alpha power at both left and right frontal sites, implying higher cortical arousal.

These children were observed again at 4 and 7 years of age as they played in groups of 4 unfamiliar children of the same sex. Children who had been high-reactive as infants and had shown right frontal activation at 9 months were reticent with peers at 4 years of age; a similar result emerged at 7 years (Polak, Fox, Henderson, & Rubin, 2004). The high-reactives with right frontal activation at 9 months were not only reticent but also were described by their teachers as having internalizing features. The aroused infants who displayed left frontal activation had a complementary set of traits.

Wave 5 in the Brain Stem Auditory Evoked Potential (BAEP)

The biological measure that best separated the high- from the low-reactives at age 11 was the magnitude of the brain stem evoked potential from the inferior colliculus, the fifth structure in the auditory chain. The waveform generated by the colliculus, called wave 5, occurs within 6 ms of the onset of sound. Amygdalar activity enhances the excitability of the inferior colliculus through projections to the locus ceruleus and the central gray, which synapse on the colliculus. This anatomical fact means that children with a more excitable amygdala should have a larger wave 5 to a series of clicks. This expectation was affirmed for high-reactives had larger wave 5 values than low-reactives (Kagan & Snidman, 2004). The high-reactives who had been inhibited with unfamiliar peers at 4.5 years of age had larger wave 5 values than the high-reactives who had been more sociable. Further, the 15% of the sample who smiled infrequently at every assessment had higher wave 5 values than those who smiled frequently.

Event-Related Potential

A third variable that separated high- and low-reactives was the event-related potential (ERP) to unfamiliar scenes. The amygdala sends projections to the locus ceruleus, ventral tegmentum, and basal nucleus of Meynert, which in turn project to cortical pyramidal neurons that mediate the magnitude of the ERP. Children with a more excitable amygdala, therefore, might show larger P300 or N400 to discrepant events. Again, the data affirmed expectation, for high-reactives showed larger N400s to ecologically invalid scenes (e.g., a child's head on an animal's body) than low-reactives. Further, high-reactives with the largest magnitude waveforms to discrepancy at age 11 had more intense symptoms of anxiety or depression 4 years later and showed shallower habituation of the N400 waveform to a different set of discrepant scenes (Kagan & Snidman, 2004).

The P300 and N400 waveforms represent brain activity involving the relation between an incentive event and existing representations. Earlier waveforms in the ERP that occur between 100 and 200 ms reveal different relations to behavior. Fox and colleagues studied a waveform called mismatch negativity (MMN) which occurs to a novel tone inserted in a series of identical ones. The MMN, which occurs with a latency of 200 to 250 ms, is generated by neurons in the primary auditory cortex. Children in two independent samples classified as inhibited showed a smaller MMN to the infrequent auditory stimulus than did controls (Bar-Haim et al., 2003). In addition, 9-month-olds classified as high reactive at 4 months showed a smaller positive waveform to a discrepant auditory stimulus than others (Marshall, Hardin, & Fox, 2004). These two results appear to be inconsistent with the fact that high-reactives at 11 years of age showed larger negative waveforms to discrepant scenes. However, the discrepant scenes shown to the 11-year-olds were meaningful and probably activated the parahippocampal area and its reciprocal connections to the basolateral nucleus of the amygdala. A large negative waveform to an unfamiliar scene (e.g., a chair with one leg) does not have the same significance as the mismatch negativity waveform to a deviant tone because the latter need not involve the amygdala.

Most school-age children show a longer response latency on trials following those on which they made an error—a psychological trait called reflectivity. It is of interest, therefore, that 7-year-olds rated as high on shyness and inhibitory control (based on Rothbart's CBQ) displayed a larger waveform, called error related negativity, on trials in which they made an error, as well as a longer response time on the subsequent trial (Henderson, 2002).

Sympathetic Activity

Activity in the sympathetic nervous system also reflects amygdalar activity because the latter structure projects to the sympathetic nervous system. A spectral analysis of supine heart rate revealed that more high- than low-reactives had more power in the low frequency spectrum, which reflects both sympathetic and parasympathetic activity, and less power in the high frequency band, which reflects vagal or parasympathetic activity. The combination of greater power in the low frequency band and a high resting heart rate was characteristic of one of every three high-reactives (compared with only one of five low-reactives). By contrast, one of every two low-reactives, but only one of sixteen high-reactives, displayed greater power in the higher frequency band and had a low heart rate. Not surprisingly, more children with high vagal tone smiled more often during the 2nd year and described themselves as "chronically happy" at age 11.

Further, more high- than low-reactive infants had higher fetal heart rates (over 140 bpm) a few weeks before birth, and higher 2-week postnatal sleeping heart rates while being held erect, but not when supine. Spectral analysis of the infants' sleeping heart rates revealed that the high-reactive, compared with the low-reactive, infants had greater power in the low-frequency band (between .02 and .10 Hz) when held erect, suggesting greater sympathetic reactivity (Snidman, Kagan, Riordan, & Shannon, 1995). A longitudinal study of 31 pregnant mothers and their fetuses revealed that fetuses with high heart rates had less frequent positive affect at 6 months of age (DiPietro, 1995). A variable heart rate in infancy, reflecting less sympathetic and more vagal tone, is linked to a tendency to approach unfamiliarity (Richards & Cameron, 1989), unfamiliar people (Fox, 1989), and facial expressions of smiling and laughter (Stifter, Fox, & Porges, 1989). Finally, 5- and 7-year-old inhibited, compared with uninhibited, children showed greater pupillary dilation, greater cardiac acceleration, and larger changes in blood pressure to cognitive stressors (Kagan, 1994).

The children Rubin classified as socially reticent displayed less vagal and higher sympathetic tone in the cardiovascular system than the solitary-passive or sociable groups. However, the solitary-passive children who had high baseline heart rates were more inhibited at 2 years than those with low heart rates (Henderson et al., 2004). Further, over the course of the laboratory observation at 4 years of age, the children with higher heart rates began to resemble reticent children as the tasks became more structured. Finally, Schmidt, Fox, and Schulkin (1999) reported that behaviorally inhibited (but not control) 7-year-olds displayed increases in heart rate and decreases in heart rate variability to emotional challenges—signs of less vagal tone.

About one of every four high-reactives and one of every four low-reactives preserved their expected behavioral as well as biological profiles, while only one of twenty children classified as high- or low-reactive at 4 months developed a combination of behavior and biology that was characteristic of the complementary category. Only 10% of high-reactives were fearful in the second year and, in addition, had high values on all four biological variables, but no low-reactive developed these features. These results are remarkably similar to those reported by Fox and his colleagues who followed three temperamental groups first classified at 4 months of age in a battery similar to the one employed in this study.

However, it is important to appreciate that none of the biological variables has the same meaning or significance across individuals with different temperaments. The meaning of left frontal activation in the EEG profiles of the 11-year-olds in the Kagan and Snidman cohort provides an example. The low-reactives who were described by their mother as extremely sociable and outgoing, smiled frequently with the examiner, and had low levels of cortical arousal (as indexed by the beta to alpha ratio) showed extreme left frontal activation. But the high reactives who were described as shy and timid, smiled infrequently with the examiner, and had high cortical arousal were equally likely to show extreme left frontal activation. This fact suggests that left frontal activation does not have the same meaning in youth with different temperaments.

It is likely that this result can be generalized. No measure, whether questionnaire reply, behavior, or biology, has a universal meaning across all individuals. This claim is supported by information on some of the 11-year-olds who were assessed at age 15 years. Six high-reactive boys were extremely subdued and inhibited during a long interview with an examiner conducted in the home. The remaining 17 high-reactive boys were far less restrained. Right frontal activation, high sympathetic tone, and a high ratio of beta to alpha power, along with a large ERP to discrepant scenes at age 11 predicted the extreme inhibition in the six boys who were subdued. But low-reactive 15-year-old girls who showed the opposite traits of garrulousness and sociability during the interview also showed high sympathetic tone and a high ratio of beta to alpha power. Once again, the theoretical significance of a biological variable depended on the type of individual on whom it was measured.

Despite this possibility, most studies of humans—children, college students, or aging adults—treat their samples as if they were relatively homogeneous; gender is the usual exception. This decision is surprising. No behavioral biologist would gather data on a random sample of dogs of different breeds or macaque monkeys from different strains because they know that the strains would react in different ways to an incentive. Hence, psychologists should gather some information on the biology of their subjects. Some candidates include height, weight, body type, eye color, and, if possible, heart rate, blood pressure, cortisol level, EEG asymmetry and ERP waveforms to varied incentives.

Facial Skeleton

High and low reactives differed in physical features, a fact supporting the belief that they belong to different categories. Infants classified as high reactive at 4 months had narrower faces (the ratio of the width of the face at the bizygomatic—high cheekbone—to the length of the face) when they were 14 months old compared with children classified as low reactive (Arcus & Kagan, 1995). The fact that facial skeleton differentiated the two temperamental groups implies the influence of a set of genes that affects features as diverse as the growth of facial bone, ease of arousal in infancy, smiling, and avoidance of unfamiliar events. It is of interest that inbred mouse strains like A/JAX that are susceptible to inhibition of palatal shelf growth following pharmacological doses of glucocorticoids during gestation are more fearful in an open field than strains like C57 BL/6 that are less susceptible to the influence of this steroid on the growth of facial bone (W. Thompson, 1953; B. Walker & Fraser, 1957). This fact implies that the genes that influence the growth of facial bone in response to glucocorticoids are correlated with those that monitor avoidance of novelty.

Second, 11-year-old high-reactives were a little more likely than low-reactives to possess light blue eyes and a small body size (24% of high-reactives, but only 7% of low-reactives had both features). The relation of eye-color and body size to infant temperament in Caucasian children may surprise some readers, but will be less surprising to those who know about the changes in physical characteristics that accompany domestication of wolves, foxes, mink, and cattle. The most extensive work, conducted at a field station in Siberian Russia, was initiated by D. Belyaev and carried on by his colleague, L. N. Trut, after Belyaev's death (Trut, 1999). These investigators selectively bred tame male silver fox with tame females for over 40 years. The wild form, which is not tame, has hairs that are black at the base and silver-white at the outer edge, stiff, erect ears and a tail that turns down. However, the offspring of many generations of breeding tame with tame animals displayed a number of physical features that accompanied the increased tameness and minimal fear of humans. The tame animals developed

white spots on their coat that were free of melanin pigmentation, floppy rather than stiff ears, an upturned tail and a broader face. These physical features are derivatives of neural crest cells. In addition, the offspring of the tame matings had lower levels of cortisol and higher levels of serotonin metabolites and brain dopamine (Trut, 1999). If a minimal fear of unfamiliar adults is associated with distinct physical features in a fox we should not be surprised to find that high- and low-reactive children differ in eye color and body size. It is possible that the genes that mediate the time of migration of the neural crest cells, and perhaps molecular features of these cells, are pleiotropic and contribute to a cluster of physical and behavioral features. Nature works in unexpected ways.

Finally, it is worth noting that extreme values on behavioral or biological variables often separated high- and low-reactives when mean scores did not. There were many occasions when the correlations among variables were low across the whole sample, but the children with values at either extreme were very different. For example, 10% of high-reactives, but not one low-reactive, had a z-score equal to or greater than .5 on the four differentiating biological variables; every one of these seven children showed distinct behaviors at 4 months of age that were indicative of high arousal. Persistent aggression is also characteristic of a small group of children. A longitudinal study of boys from different laboratories revealed that only 4% of a very large sample showed persistent aggression across the childhood years (Brody et al., 2003). Male vervet monkeys who are at either extreme on behavioral measures of impulsivity had a lower social rank than a large number of animals whose scores were in the middle of the distribution (Fairbanks, 2001). Many psychologists place great faith in the informativeness of mean values; any other parameter carries the stain of being less than perfect. This bias is irrational. Because nonlinear functions are common in psychology, current statistical procedures that rely on the mean often fail to reveal important relations. The reluctance to acknowledge the utility of examining extreme groups that might be qualitatively different from the rest of the sample is slowing progress in many domains of psychology.

Temperaments Constrain

Despite the predicted relation between the infant classifications of high and low reactivity and the behavior and biological profiles at age 11, only one-third of the children in the high- and low-reactive groups actualized a behavioral and biological profile that was in accord with expectation. However, very few children showed the profile of the complementary group, a result confirmed by Fox, Rubin, and their colleagues. Most children displayed behavioral and biological patterns characteristic of randomly selected middle-class Caucasian children. Apparently, many high-reactives had learned to cope with their earlier tendency to avoid unfamiliar people and situations and were able to develop a persona that was not obviously shy or timid. Thus, the prediction that a high-reactive infant would not become a sociable, exuberant child with left frontal activation, a small wave 5, and high vagal tone can be made with much greater confidence than the prediction that this child would become a subdued, timid adolescent with high levels of arousal in cortical, brain stem, and autonomic targets. Similarly, the prediction that a low-reactive will not become an extremely shy 11-year-old with high biological arousal is more certain than the prediction that this child will be exuberant and show low biological arousal. Each temperament constrains acquisition of the features of the complementary category. Hidden beneath the common observation that the behaviors and moods of children change from infancy to adolescence is the persistence of temperamental biases that prevent some from attaining a particular psychological profile.

A temperamental bias eliminates many more outcomes than it determines and is like the basic form of the song of a particular species of bird. The animal's genome constrains the basic architecture of the song but does not determine all of its features, for the adult song depends on exposure to songs of conspecifics and the opportunity to hear its own vocal sounds. The constraining power of initial conditions, whether biological or environmental, finds an analogy in a stone rolling down a steep mountain over a 5-minute interval. An observer will be able to eliminate a great many final locations after each 10 seconds of descent, but it is not until the final second that she will be able to predict where the stone will come to rest. When the high promises of the genome project are met and parents can request the complete genomic analysis of their newborn, an expert will be better able to tell parents what the infant will not become than to inform them about the characteristics their infant will possess 2 decades later.

TEMPERAMENT AND ATTACHMENT

There is a lively controversy surrounding the contribution of inhibited or uninhibited temperaments to a child's reactions in the Ainsworth Strange Situation and, therefore, to the classifications of secure or insecure attachment (Connell & Thompson, 1986). The Strange Situation is an unfamiliar setting; therefore, inhibited children should react with greater uncertainty, when either left alone or with a stranger. As a result, more of these children should be difficult to soothe when the mother returns and they are likely to be classified as type C resistant and insecurely attached.

Infants who were classified type C at 14 months were behaviorally inhibited at 2 years, suggesting that the temperamental bias to be inhibited is contributing to their behavior in the Strange Situation (Calkins & Fox, 1992). Ten percent of Dutch infants assessed in the Strange Situation with their hired caregiver, mother, or father showed an insecure attachment to all three adults, implying a temperamental contribution to their behavior in the laboratory (Goossens & van IJzendoorn, 1990). One group of authors, reflecting on these facts, wrote, "Temperament does play a role in Strange Situation behavior through its effects on the quality and intensity of the infant's separation distress. Infants who are high on fearfulness are likely to react more negatively to the separation episodes" (Thompson, Connell, & Bridges, 1988, p. 1109).

A meta-analysis of data from seven different samples ($N = 498$) revealed that the infant's behavior in the laboratory prior to the mother leaving the child predicted better than chance the child's subsequent behavior and the attachment classification. Infants classified as type C showed more crying and resistance to their mother during episode 2, an episode that occurred prior to any separation (Sagi, van IJzendoorn, & Koren-Karie, 1991; but see Fox, 1995).

Fox, Kimmerly, and Schaefer (1991) performed a meta-analysis on studies that examined the concordance of attachment classifications (based on the Strange Situation) to the mother and the father in separate assessments. Infants classified as Type A, B, or C (avoidant, secure, or resistant) to one parent were more likely than chance to be classified in the same way when they were tested with the other parent. This concordance implies a temperamental influence on behavior in the Strange Situation, as well as the possibility that both the mother and the father behave similarly with the infant.

Further support for the role of temperament is found in an independent study of 9- and 13-month-old infants. A temperamental quality called *proneness to distress,* together with the mother's personality, were the best predictors of an insecure attachment in the child. Specifically, infants who were prone to distress and, in addition, had mothers with high scores on a personality trait called *constraint*—these women were rigid, had traditional views, and avoided risks—were more likely to be insecurely attached. There was no effect of the maternal personality trait alone. Distressed infants reared by a mother who was low on constraint were more likely to be securely attached. Among low-distress infants, however, there was no relation between this maternal personality trait and security of child attachment. Variation in maternal behavior seems to be more important for infants who are vulnerable to distress than it is for those who are minimally fretful and irritable (Mangelsdorf, Gunnar, Kestenbaum, Lang, & Andreas, 1990). Thus, as Van den Boom and Hoeksma (1994) argued, both temperament and family experience act together to influence a child's behavior in the Strange Situation.

The investigators who believe that temperament makes a minimal contribution to the attachment classifications have most often relied on maternal questionnaires to measure the child's temperament. A review of many studies suggests that, for most samples, children described by their mothers as irritable at home were more likely to be classified as insecurely attached in the laboratory. One group of authors suggested that although temperament was not the only influence on the attachment classification, "the empirical overlap between these behavioral domains is greater than might have been anticipated" (Vaughn et al., 1992, p. 469).

PSYCHOPATHOLOGY AND TEMPERAMENT

It is likely that temperamental biases contribute to psychopathology. Children and adults differ in their psychological and physiological reactions to an unfamiliar event, even when the event is unusually stressful such as an earthquake, divorce, kidnapping, or witnessing a mass shooting (North, Smith, & Spitznagel, 1994).

The extraordinary variation in the development of symptoms of stress following a trauma is probably influenced by temperament. Usually less than 40% of children react to a traumatic event with anxiety or fear. For example, only 10 of 40 school children who were kidnapped and terrorized for 2 days developed posttraumatic stress disorder (Terr, 1979). During the winter of 1984, a sniper fired at a group of children on the playground of a Los Angeles elementary school. One child was killed, 13 were injured, and a siege followed. Clinicians interviewed the children 1 month later to determine who was experiencing extreme levels of anxiety. Thirty-eight percent were judged anxious, but an equal proportion, 39%, seemed completely free of any unusual level of anxiety. The important fact is that the children who were anxious 1 month after the trauma were those who had shown an inhibited temperament prior to the school violence (Pynoos et al., 1987).

A group of fourth and fifth grade children living in south Florida had been assessed for the presence of an anxious mood over a year before Hurricane Andrew struck the area. The 11% of the children who were still distressed 7 months after the storm were those who had been anxious prior to the hurricane (La Greca, Silverman, & Wassastein, 1998). Similarly, young British children less than 5 years old who became fearful after being taken from their homes during the bombing of London during World War II had been extremely fearful before the bombing raids began (John, 1941). Thus, a temperamental bias favoring a fearful reaction to novelty or threat renders children vulnerable to an extreme reaction to trauma.

The stress associated with entering school for the first time was only associated with an increase in respiratory illness in children who had shown both sympathetic reactivity prior to the beginning of the school year (measured by an increase in heart rate and arterial blood pressure to challenge) and, in addition, had been exposed to stressful experiences at home. Children of the same age and social class who showed low sympathetic reactivity showed no increased rate of respiratory illness, even though they may have lived in a highly stressful home environment (Boyce & Jemerin, 1990).

One team of investigators took advantage of the fact that an earthquake occurred in Northern California (the Loma Prieta earthquake of 1989) in the middle of a study of 20 young children who were entering kindergarten. Six children showed an increase in respiratory illness after the earthquake; five showed a decline. Variation in the change in the helper-suppressor cell ratios and pokeweed mitogen response predicted the children who showed the increase in respiratory illness. The children who showed an up-regulation of the two immune parameters following school entry had a significant increase in respiratory illness after the earthquake. This fact suggests that the children who perceived kindergarten entrance as stressful (indexed by the change in immune reaction) became most vulnerable to respiratory infections following the earthquake (Boyce et al., 1993). Even though the differences between adults who had an easy or difficult temperament at age 3 years were small, Chess and Thomas (1984) suggested that easy children were better-adjusted adults; Werner (1993) reports a similar result.

It is not clear whether the modulatory processes associated with temperament act directly by (a) blunting the limbic system's initial reaction to the stressor, (b) shortening the duration of the stressful reaction, or (c) acting indirectly through inhibitory processes to mute a consciously experienced stress reaction that is no less intense physiologically than it is in the majority of children. All three mechanisms are possible, and each has relevance for the development of psychopathology.

Epidemiological studies in varied Western countries agree that between 1% and 5% of children have simple or social phobias. The range for the looser diagnostic concept of anxiety disorder is larger—5% to 26%—suggesting that the clinical judgment of whether the symptom is disabling enough to be called a disorder is unreliable (Klein & Last, 1989). No more than one-third of preschool children who are very inhibited will be diagnosed with an anxiety disorder 10 years later. This means that most children grow toward health. Although this knowledge represents a major advance compared with the information available 100 years ago, it is, in an absolute sense, only a modest beginning.

There is consensus that some children inherit a physiological vulnerability that renders them especially susceptible to developing one of the many states of anxiety or depression. About 20% to 30% of first-degree relatives of children with an anxiety disorder had a similar symptom, compared with only 10% of controls (Weissman, 1984).

Although the absolute risk is low, children who were high-reactive infants are at a greater risk than most for developing social phobia in adolescence or adulthood. The established lifetime prevalence of social phobia in Americans and Europeans ranges between 5% and 15% (Merikangas, Avenevoli, Acharyva, Zhang, & Angst, 2002). The 3-month prevalence of any anxiety disorder in a large sample of North Carolina youth from 9 to 16

years of age was between 2% and 3% (Costello, Mustillo, Erkanli, Keeler, & Angold, 2003). However, Schwartz, Snidman, and Kagan (1999) reported that 61% of a sample of 13-year-old adolescents who had been inhibited in the 2nd year of life had developed symptoms of social phobia. One half of a sample of 30, 15-year-olds who had been high reactive at 4 months had serious signs of anxiety over social interaction or unfamiliar situations, and three high-reactive girls, but not one low-reactive girl, had been diagnosed with clinical depression (Kagan & Snidman, 2004). However, most high-reactives are likely to find an adaptive adult niche that will protect them from dealing frequently with unfamiliar people on an unpredictable schedule. Fortunately, many vocations and life roles permit this protection while simultaneously awarding dignity, challenge, and financial security to those with this personality trait. Most humans experience uncertainty over one or more of their symbolic features as a result of their life histories. The usual nodes of uncertainty center on acceptability to others, attractiveness, status, wealth, ability, power, and virtue. The high- and-low reactive temperamental biases amplify or mute the intensity of the felt uncertainty. High-reactives experience this emotion more acutely than most; low-reactives experience it less intensely.

The risk categories for low-reactives are failure to conform to community norms because of less uncertainty over criticism or the consequences of risky decisions. This trait is the best predictor of adult psychiatric problems in contemporary North American and European samples because it is correlated with academic failure. Several studies reveal that an extremely uninhibited profile in early childhood is predictive of extreme levels of aggressive behavior during adolescence. For example, 6% of a large sample of lower-class boys were persistently, and seriously, asocial from their second to their 8th year. The best predictor of this small group was a lack of fear to the discrepancy of suddenly hearing the sounds of a gorilla while the child was playing in the laboratory (Shaw, Gilliom, Ingoldsby, & Nagin, 2003). It is of interest that, compared with controls, criminals show less, and social phobics more, amygdalar activity (as measured by fMRI) to neutral faces that function as conditioned stimuli for a painful unconditioned stimulus (Veit et al., 2002). A low-reactive boy raised by a family that did not socialize aggressive behavior effectively who played in a neighborhood containing peer temptations for crime is probably at a slightly higher than average risk for a delinquent career (Farrington, 2000). But far less risk accompanies a low-reactive boy in a well-integrated family without pathology that socialized aggression effectively—this boy is likely to be popular with peers.

Although every child and adult has the capacity for anticipating unpleasant events, the intensity and chronicity of the accompanying bodily feelings are muted in many persons, and therefore the state does not interfere with the performance of everyday tasks. Only, a small proportion experience feelings, which accompany the unwanted anticipations, with great intensity or regularity to a degree that they compromise their ability to deal with daily responsibilities. These are the individuals who are regarded as having an anxiety disorder. Because the majority of these patients have never experienced the events they fear, or if they had, the frequency of encounter was low, theory predicts that their anxious state should have extinguished over time. Because it does not we must ask why. There are several possible reasons.

When psychoanalytic theories were popular a half-century ago, it was assumed that some life histories could create a chronic feeling of guilt over violations of moral standards. One consequent of the guilt was the expectation of harm or loss as a symbolic punishment for the ethical lapse. Because the guilt was chronic, the anxiety persisted. Although this interpretation of chronic anxiety had intuitive appeal earlier, it is less attractive today because of a secular decrease in the frequency and intensity of guilt over sexual and aggressive behavior, yet no decrease in the prevalence of anxiety disorders.

A second mechanism that relies on classical conditioning assumes that the individual had experienced intense distress during an encounter with the feared event; therefore its mental representations persisted. Some anxiety disorders could have been acquired by a Pavlovian mechanism. This might be especially true for some phobias, but it cannot explain all of the anxiety disorders unless we make thought a conditioned stimulus. Americans who avoid public encounters with strangers are afraid of being evaluated in an undesirable way; they are not afraid of strangers qua strangers. They wish to avoid what they imagine to be a critical evaluation by others because of prior experiences in which they felt an unpleasant tension when with strangers. Thus, the thought of entering an unfamiliar social situation provoked the feeling of anxiety.

The hypothesis of inherited physiological profiles acting as a diathesis for an anxiety disorder is an attractive explanatory candidate. These physiological conditions, which are the bases for temperaments, participate in three different explanatory schemes that probably involve the orbitofrontal prefrontal cortex (OBPFC). Activity in the OBPFC is an important origin of an individual's feeling tone. One part of this area receives sensory information from the viscera, as well as external sources related to eating behavior. The OBPFC also receives input from the amygdala and sends its synthesis of information to an area in the OBPFC called the ventromedial prefrontal cortex, which is the origin of projections to the hypothalamus and brain stem (Price, 1999). This arrangement implies that frequent or intense somatic sensations could be due either to an excitable amygdala, an excitable OBPFC, or an active ventromedial prefrontal cortex. If the neural activity pierces consciousness, the person will experience a change in feeling tone and will be motivated to interpret it. The detected change in feeling tone can be interpreted as fear, anxiety, guilt, or excitement, or as a temporary compromise in bodily function. The child or adult who interprets the change in feeling as implying a threatening event can become very anxious. However, the individual could focus on the bodily sensations and fail to impose an interpretation that implied fear or anxiety—a process more common in China than in Europe and North America (Lee & Kleinman, 1997).

The most parsimonious hypothesis is that there is only one diathesis—a neurochemistry that lowers the threshold of excitability of a brain circuit that when activated leads to somatic sensations and a change in feeling tone. The individual's history determines which target will be feared. A much more reasonable hypothesis is that several brain profiles underlie the various anxiety disorders. This view argues that a person with a particular physiological diathesis might develop a blood phobia, while another with a different physiology will develop social phobia.

Moreover, each visceral target—heart, muscle, gut, labyrinth—that sends afferent information to the brain is influenced by a distinct neurochemistry. It is reasonable to assume that genetic features render a particular visceral target more or less reactive and influence the specific events that will be avoided. For example, adolescents with a phobia of blood often report feeling faint when they see large quantities of blood. This fear is most likely in those who possess a brisk vasovagal reaction, which is accompanied by high vagal tone. One adolescent boy in Kagan's longitudinal sample who had a blood phobia but no other fears had been a low-reactive infant, an uninhibited child, and an adolescent with extremely high vagal tone.

ETHNICITY AND TEMPERAMENT

Differences in temperament among varied ethnic groups remain a delicate issue because of the racial and ethnic strife around the world. Many psychologists, understandably, shy away from studies that might reveal genetically based differences in mood or behavior among populations that have been reproductively isolated for a long time. A team of scientists compared the frequencies of over 100 different alleles for physiological markers in the world's geographically separate human populations by averaging the difference in frequencies to create an index of genetic distance between any pair of populations (Cavalli-Sforza, Menozzi, & Piazza, 1994). As expected, the index of genetic distance was largest when Asians, Africans, and European Caucasians were compared with each other. But even in the Caucasoid Europeans, people from Scandinavia, England, and Northern Europe were genetically different from populations living in Spain, Italy, and the Balkans. In general, the greater the geographical and linguistic distance between any two populations, and, therefore, the greater the reproductive isolation, the greater the genetic distance. It is not unreasonable to assume that some of the alleles have implications for emotions and behavior.

The most consistent evidence relating temperament to geographically separated populations compares Asian with Caucasian infants. Over 30 years ago, Freedman and Freedman (1969) reported that newborn Asian American infants, compared with European Americans, were calmer, less labile, less likely to remove a cloth placed on their face, and more easily consoled when distressed. Nine years later, Kagan, Kearsley, and Zelazo (1978) found that Chinese American infants living in Boston were less active, less vocal, less likely to smile to stimulation, and more inhibited during the 1st year compared with European American infants from Boston.

Caudill and Weinstein (1969) observed Japanese infants to be less easily aroused than European American infants, and Lewis, Ramsay, and Kawakami (1993) found Japanese infants to be less reactive than American

infants (during well-baby examinations) and less likely to cry to inoculation. Five-month-old European American infants showed distress following arm restraint more quickly than did Japanese infants, implying a higher threshold of distress to this incentive in Asian infants (Camras, Oster, Campos, Miyake, & Bradshaw, 1992). Kagan and colleagues administered the battery of visual, auditory, and olfactory stimulations described earlier to 4-month-old infants living in Boston, Dublin, and Beijing. The Caucasian infants from Dublin and Boston were more easily aroused and distressed than the Chinese infants from Beijing (Kagan et al., 1994).

These differences in ease of arousal to unfamiliarity during the 1st year have some parallels in older children. Mothers of 6- to 7-year-old children living in Shanghai described them as less active, less impulsive, more controlled, and more shy than did mothers of children living in the Pacific Northwest (Ahadi, Rothbart, & Ye, 1993). Further, the parents of school-age Thai children, compared with those of European American children, were more concerned over low energy, low motivation, somatic problems, and forgetfulness, whereas the parents of European American children reported more concern with disobedience, aggression, and hyperactivity (Weisz et al., 1987, 1988).

It is relevant that Asian American adult psychiatric patients require a lower dose of psychotropic drugs than European American patients (Lin, Poland, & Lesser, 1986), implying that Asian populations may be at a lower level of limbic arousal. There is, in addition, greater genetic diversity in many loci determining blood groups and proteins among Caucasians than among Asians. Europeans and Asians have been reproductively isolated for over 30,000 years—over 1000 generations. It requires only 15 to 20 generations of selective breeding to produce obviously different behavioral profiles in many animal species (Mills & Faure, 1991). Perhaps, scientists should consider the ethnic composition of their samples when the psychological variables they quantify bear some relation to reactivity and ease of arousal.

The influence of culture has been lost in the excitement over the many significant discoveries in biology. A comparison of European and Asian cultures in the seventeenth and eighteenth centuries, before the West's influence on the latter, illustrates the power of culture. The primary entity in European society is the individual; each person must attain salvation, wealth, status, or happiness on their own. By contrast, the imperative for

Asian youth is to seek harmony with, and become part of, a group—first family and later peers and community. Although children and adolescents can develop either an individualistic or a communal attitude, high- and low-reactives may find the two ethics differentially friendly. High-reactive-inhibited children feel more secure in a social network that sets strict rules for behavior, does not regularly pose demands for excessive risk, and rewards loyalty to the community standards with praise. This type of child is vulnerable to uncertainty in an individualistic society where accomplishment requires entrepreneurial risk, competitive posture, dealing with strangers, and confronting unpredictability.

The low-reactive-uninhibited child is less threatened by such an imperative, enjoys the excitement of risk and meeting strangers, and is more likely to bridle when deviance is punished, whether in the form of extreme talent, lack of civility, or domination of others. Both socialization and temperament contribute to the development of a personality type that conforms to the demands of the local culture.

TEMPERAMENT AND MORAL AFFECTS

Variation in the intensity of moral emotions might be influenced by temperament. The experience of anxiety, shame, or guilt as an accompaniment to the contemplation or commission of an act that violates personal or community standards is an important source of restraint on those actions. It is likely (as Kant believed) that individuals vary in the intensity of their shame and guilt, although the biology that accounts for this variation may be different from the physiology that represents the foundation for the appearance of the moral emotions in most children. Even though parental practices and attitudes are most influential, temperamental factors might play a small role. The intensity of the experienced moral affects are due to efferents that originate in limbic sites and excite peripheral organs, as well as the quality of afferent activity in the periphery to the medulla, amygdala, and, eventually, frontal cortex.

Damasio (1994) described the case of an adult male who lost, through surgery, the ventromedial surface of his prefrontal cortex. This neural tissue receives afferent information from the amygdala, which, in turn, receives it from the heart, lung, gut, and muscles via a nucleus in the medulla. Without this neuronal surface the individual cannot have the subtle anticipatory feeling of anxiety over risking money on an investment or changing jobs. This patient, who had been an intelligent and successful man prior to the surgery, began to make impulsive decisions after the surgery despite no change in his measured intelligence.

Consider a hypothetical but common situation. A 5-year-old wants a toy that another is enjoying and thinks about seizing it. One of the factors that will influence the probability of a seizure by the envious child is a feeling of anxiety over the possible consequences of the aggressive act. Although socialization in the home will influence the intensity of that feeling, it is reasonable to suggest that children with equivalent socialization experiences will differ in the intensity of the anxiety state because of temperamental factors. This variation is related to the activation of the sympathetic nervous system and the receipt of information from limbic targets by the frontal cortex. For example, low-reactive 1- and 2-year-old infants show less fear to an examiner's criticism than high-reactives. Kochanska (1991, 1993) has shown that shy, timid children raised by mothers who used reasoning in their socialization had a very strict conscience (using a projective measure of conscience). Neither the form of maternal socialization nor the child's shyness, considered alone, predicted variation in the conscience measure.

It is important to emphasize that most children are capable of the moral emotions of anxiety, shame, and guilt. Further, although some children inherit a temperament that favors an exaggerated guilt reaction, such children need not show any pathology later in life. Nor is it likely that most children with a temperament favoring a less intense affective response will become juvenile delinquents. Most parents of these latter children will impose heavier socialization demands on them. Nonetheless, if the environment is permissive of aggression, stealing, and lying, the child with a temperamental bias for a sluggish anxiety/fear reaction is probably at greater risk for aggressive or delinquent behaviors than other children growing up in the same social context (Kochanska, 1995).

The children who had been high-reactive infants should be more vulnerable than others to bouts of guilt because of greater sympathetic activity, and therefore, greater visceral feedback to the amygdala and the OBPFC. However, a verbal report of guilt can occur with or without an appropriate change in physiology at the time of the ethical violation. Some children might say they feel guilty, but this confession might not be correlated with a physiological reaction. Eleven-year-old children were asked in the home setting to rank 20 Q-sort items descriptive of their personality from most to least characteristic. One item was, "I feel bad if one of my parents says that I did something wrong." There was no difference between high- and low-reactives in the mean rank assigned this item (the mean rank was 10), however, high-reactives who ranked this item as more characteristic of self (a rank less than 10) showed a larger number of biological signs of amygdalar reactivity than the low-reactives who rated this item as equally characteristic of self or the high-reactives who did not admit to feeling guilty. The high-reactives who confessed to feeling guilty had a mean standard score greater than .00 across the biological variables that reflected cortical and autonomic arousal. The low-reactives who admitted to equally frequent feelings of guilt had a mean standard score less than .00 (Kagan & Snidman, 2004). The fact that only high-reactives who admitted feeling bad following parental criticism showed signs of cortical and autonomic reactivity suggests that they may be especially vulnerable to bouts of guilt. Most children can be socialized to feel shame or guilt following violation of a standard, but a small proportion are especially vulnerable to these emotions because of their temperament (Kagan & Snidman, 2004).

The mothers of these children ranked 28 statements describing their child from most to least characteristic of their son or daughter. One item referred to the child's behavior when chastised: "is sensitive to punishment." The high- and low-reactive girls differed in the rank the mothers awarded this item, for many more high- than low-reactive girls were described this way. And the high-reactive girls described by their mothers as sensitive to punishment showed greater right parietal activation in the EEG than the high-reactive girls who were less sensitive to punishment.

Low-reactive boys who had high vagal tone represented a special temperamental category. These boys are likely to become group leaders if they grow up in typical American middle-class homes with loving parents who socialize school achievement and the control of aggression. The same boys raised by indifferent parents in large cities may become delinquents. Antisocial adolescents who showed minimal autonomic reactivity to simple stimulation—a lower heart rate and less frequent skin conductance responses—were more likely to continue a criminal career than equally antisocial adolescents who did not become adult criminals (Raine,

Venables, & Williams, 1990; see also, Katz & Gottman, 1994).

It is possible that the small group of criminals who commit violent crimes (probably fewer than 5% of all delinquents and criminals) possess a special temperament. In a longitudinal study of a large New Zealand cohort, the young adults who were violent had been rated at 3 and 5 years of age as low on control of behavior (Henry, Caspi, & Silva, personal communication). A minority of impulsive, minimally fearful 5-year-old boys became adolescent delinquents; only 28% of high-delinquent boys had been rated by their teachers 8 years earlier as highly asocial (Tremblay, Pihl, Vitaro, & Dubkin, 1994). Thus, only a small proportion of asocial adolescents were born with a temperament that placed them at risk for this profile.

CONCLUSION

The inclusion of biological evidence in studies of temperament and personality is a welcome development. The history of science is rich with examples of the accelerated progress that occurs when two or more previously isolated domains probe common problems with different vocabularies and methods. The fields of biophysics, molecular biology, and radio astronomy are obvious examples. The union of such domains, by providing new information, refines existing terms and eliminates concepts that have outlived their usefulness. This first phase of a collaboration between biology and psychology has led to some new ideas, for example, the realization that the concept of one fear state is not theoretically useful.

As Galen anticipated, children, like animals, inherit different biologies that, in turn, affect the manner in which environmental events influence their psychological growth. Developmental scientists should assume from the beginning that different temperamental types will not react in the same way, behaviorally or biologically, to a given experience and invent constructs that capture that fact.

Psychologists may eventually replace the current constructs, which describe children and their environments (parents, sibling, and school settings) separately, with single synthetic constructs that represent a particular temperamental type growing up in a particular set of contexts. To illustrate, instead of writing about high-reactive infants, on the one hand, and protective, permissive families, on the other, psychologists might invent a new construct that describes the envelope of possible profiles for the category of child developing in this environment. As environments shape children of varied temperaments into different phenotypes, it will be useful to invent new concepts rather than rely on the language of analysis of variance that describes interactions between the temperamental type of child and a rearing environment.

This suggestion is a special instance of the more general rule that the construct chosen depends on the investigator's purpose. Light can be described as a wave, a particle, or as a source of heat or illumination. It can be useful on some occasions to describe a psychological profile with a construct that defines its current features, biological origins, and experiential history, as we do with the concept of bipolar illness and mathematical genius.

Temperament and history act together to create a psychological barrier between a potentially emotionally charged external event and reaction of the limbic system that renders the event less potent. Fifty years ago, these phenomena would have been called a defense. Although all individuals can learn defenses to protect them from distress to threat, a small proportion of children may inherit a temperament that makes it easier for them to establish these defenses. A child's experiential history determines the meaning imposed on an event; a combination of temperament and history determines both the ease with which the interpretation of an event gains access to varied brain circuits as well as the excitability of those structures.

The return of temperamental constructs will, inevitably, increase scientific interest in affective phenomena and, in so doing, alert psychologists to those events that have their primary effect on feeling tone and emotions rather than on behaviors, especially the emotion families called guilt, shame, fear, anger, pride, anxiety, sadness, excitement, surprise, and joy. Individual variation in the frequency and intensity of those affect states is influenced by temperament and the constructions that children create from their encounters. It is reasonable to be optimistic about the future of developmental psychology if scientists search for the coherent profiles that emerge from biological predispositions and life histories and do not insist on reducing each profile either to the actions of genes or the consequences of experiences. We will then attain a synthesis as fruitful as the one that followed the recognition that

evolution required mutation, recombination, geographical isolation, and a natural selection of those features that were adaptive in particular settings.

REFERENCES

Abercrombie, H. C., Kalin, N. H., Thurow, M. E., Rosenkranz, M. A., & Davidson, R. J. (2003). Cortisol variation in humans affects memory for emotionally laden and neutral information. *Behavioral Neuroscience, 117,* 505–516.

Achenbach, T. M. (1985). *Assessment and taxonomy of child and adolescent psychopathology.* Newbury Park, CA: Sage.

Adamec, R. E. (1991). Anxious personality in the cat. In B. J. Carroll & J. E. Barrett (Eds.), *Psychopathology and the brain* (pp. 153–168). New York: Raven Press.

Ahadi, S. A., Rothbart, M. K., & Ye, R. (1993). Children's temperament in the United States and China. *European Journal of Psychiatry, 7,* 359–377.

Arbelle, S., Benjamin, J., Galin, M., Kremer, P., Belmaker, R. H., & Ebstein, R. P. (2003). Relation of shyness in grade school children to the genotype for the long form of the serotonin transporter promoter region polymorphism. *American Journal of Psychiatry, 160,* 671–676.

Arcus, D. M. (1991). *Experiential modification of temperamental bias in inhibited and uninhibited children.* Unpublished doctoral dissertation, Harvard University, Boston, MA.

Arcus, D. M., & Kagan, J. (1995). Temperament and craniofacial skeleton in children. *Child Development, 66,* 1529–1540.

Asendorpf, J. B. (1989). Shyness as a final common pathway for two different kinds of inhibition. *Journal of Personality and Social Psychology, 57,* 481–492.

Asendorpf, J. B. (1990). Development of inhibition during childhood. *Developmental Psychology, 26,* 721–730.

Asendorpf, J. B. (1991). Development of inhibited children's coping with unfamiliarity. *Child Development, 62,* 1460–1474.

Asendorpf, J. B. (1993). Abnormal shyness in children. *Journal of Child Psychiatry, 34,* 1069–1081.

Asendorpf, J. B. (1994). The malleability of behavioral inhibition. *Developmental Psychology, 30,* 912–919.

Auerbach, J., Geller, V., Lezer, S., Shinwell, E., Belmaker, R. H., Levin, J., et al. (1999). Dopamine D4 receptor (D4VR) and seratonin transporter promoter (5-HTTLPR) polymorphisms in the determination of temperament in two-month-old infants. *Molecular Psychiatry, 4,* 369–373.

Bar-Haim, Y., Marshall, P. J., Fox, N. A., Schorr, E. A., & Gordon-Salant, S. (2003). Mismatch negativity in socially withdrawn children. *Biological Psychiatry, 54,* 17–24.

Basoglu, M., Mineka, S., Parker, N., Aker, T., Livanov, M., & Gok, S. (1997). Psychological preparedness for trauma as a protective factor in survivors of torture. *Psychological Medicine, 27,* 1421–1437.

Bates, J. E. (1980). The concept of difficult temperament. *Merrill-Palmer Quarterly, 26,* 299–319.

Bates, J. E. (1983). Issues in the assessment of difficult temperament. *Merrill-Palmer Quarterly, 29,* 89–97.

Bates, J. E. (1989). Concepts and measures of temperament. In G. A. Kohnstamm, J. E. Bates, & M. K. Rothbart (Eds.), *Temperament in childhood* (pp. 3–26). New York: Wiley.

Bates, J. E., Freeland, C. A., & Lounsbury, M. L. (1979). Measurement of infant difficultness. *Child Development, 50,* 950–959.

Bates, J. E., & Wachs, T. D. (1994). *Temperament.* Washington, DC: American Psychological Association.

Bauman, M. D., Lavenex, D., Mason, W. A., Capitanio, J. P., & Amaral, D. G. (2004). The development of mother-infant interactions after neonatal amygdala lesions in rhesus monkeys. *Journal of Neuroscience, 24,* 711–721.

Birns, B., Barten, S., & Bridger, W. (1969). Individual differences in temperamental characteristics of infants. *Transactions of the New York Academy of Sciences, 31,* 1071–1082.

Bishop, G., Spence, S. H., & McDonald, C. (2003). Can parents and teachers provide a reliable and valid report of behavioral inhibition? *Child Development, 74,* 1899–1917.

Black, B. (1992). Elective mutism as a variant of social phobia. *Journal of the American Academy of Child and Adolescent Psychiatry, 31,* 1090–1094.

Blackburn, J. (2002). *Old man Goya.* New York: Random House.

Blanchard, D. C., & Blanchard, R. J. (1988). Ethoexperimental approaches to the biology of emotion. In M. R. Rosenzweig & L. W. Porter (Eds.), *Annual review of psychology* (Vol. 39, pp. 43–68). Palo Alto, CA: Annual Reviews.

Blizard, D. A., & Adams, N. (2002). The Maudsley reactive and nonreactive strains. *Behavior Genetics, 32,* 277–299.

Blizard, D. A., Liang, B., & Emmel, D. K. (1980). Blood pressure, heart rate, and plasma catecholamines under resting conditions in rat strains selectively bred for differences in response to stress. *Behavioral and Neural Biology, 29,* 487–492.

Bornstein, M. H., Gaughran, J. M., & Segui, D. (1991). Multivariate assessment of infant temperament. *International Journal of Behavioral Development, 14,* 131–151.

Boyce, W. T., Chesterman, E. A., Martin, N., Folkman, S., Cohen, F., & Wara, D. (1993). Immunologic changes occurring at kindergarten entry predict respiratory illnesses after the Loma Prieta earthquake. *Developmental and Behavioral Pediatrics, 14,* 296–303.

Boyce, W. T., & Jemerin, J. M. (1990). Psychobiological differences in childhood stress response. *Journal of Developmental and Behavioral Pediatrics, 11,* 86–94.

Breuer, J., & Freud, S. (1956). *Studies in hysteria* [Standard edition]. London: Hogarth. (Original work published 1893–1898)

Broberg, A., Lamb, M. E., & Hwang, P. (1990). Inhibition: Its stability and correlates in 16- to 40-month-old children. *Child Development, 61,* 1153–1163.

Brody, L. M., Tremblay, R. E., Brane, B., Fergusson, D., Horwood, J. L., Laird, et al. (2003). Developmental trajectories of childhood disruptive behaviors and adolescent delinquency. *Developmental Psychology, 39,* 222–245.

Brown, J. S., Kalish, H. I., & Farber, I. E. (1951). Conditioned fear as revealed by magnitude of startle response to an auditory stimulus. *Journal of Experimental Psychology, 41,* 317–328.

Buss, A. H. (1986). A theory of shyness. In W. H. Jones, J. M. Cheek, & S. R. Briggs (Eds.), *Shyness: Perspectives on research and treatment* (pp. 39–46). New York: Plenum Press.

Buss, A. H., & Plomin, R. (1984). *Temperament: Early developing personality traits.* Hillsdale, NJ: Erlbaum.

Buss, K. A., Schumacher, J. R. M., Dolski, I., Kalin, N. H., Goldsmith, H. H., & Davidson, R. J. (2003). Right frontal brain activity, cortisol, and withdrawal behavior in 6-month-old infants. *Behavioral Neuroscience, 117,* 11–20.

Byrne, J., & Suomi, S. J. (2002). Cortisol reactivity and its relation to home cage behavior and personality ratings in tufted capuchin (Cebux apella) juveniles from birth to 6 years of age. *Psychoneuroendocrinology, 27,* 139–154.

Calkins, S., & Fox, N. A. (1992). The relations among infant temperament, security of attachment, and behavioral inhibition at 24 months. *Child Development, 63,* 1456–1472.

Camras, L. A., Oster, H., Campos, J. J., Miyake, K., & Bradshaw, D. (1992). Japanese and American infants' response to arm restraint. *Developmental Psychology, 28,* 578–583.

Carey, W. B., & McDevitt, S. C. (1978). Revision of the infant temperament questionnaire. *Pediatrics, 61,* 735–739.

Carlson, E. A., Jacobvitz, D., & Sroufe, L. A. (1995). A developmental investigation of inattentiveness and hyperactivity. *Child Development, 66,* 37–54.

Caspi, A., Elder, G. H., & Bem, D. J. (1988). Moving away from the world. *Developmental Psychology, 24,* 824–831.

Caspi, A., & Silva, P. A. (1995). Temperamental qualities at age 3 predict personality traits in young adulthood. *Child Development, 66,* 486–498.

Caudill, W., & Weinstein, H. (1969). Maternal care and infant behavior in Japan and America. *Psychiatry, 32,* 12–43.

Cavalli-Sforza, L. L., Menozzi, P., & Piazza, A. (1994). *The history and geography of human genes.* Princeton, NJ: Princeton University Press.

Cecchi, M., Khoshbouei, H., Javors, M., & Morilak, D. A. (2002). Modulatory effects of norepinephrine in the lateral bed nucleus of the stria terminalis on behavioral and neuroendocrine responses to acute stress. *Neuroscience, 112,* 13–21.

Cheever, J. (1993). *The journals of John Cheever.* New York: Ballantine Books.

Chess, S., & Thomas, A. (1984). Genesis and evolution of behavior disorders. *American Journal of Psychiatry, 141,* 1–9.

Chess, S., & Thomas, A. (1990). New York Longitudinal Study: The young adult periods. *Canadian Journal of Psychiatry, 35,* 557–561.

Chugani, H. T. (1994). Development of regional brain glucose metabolism. In G. Dawson & K. Fischer (Eds.), *Human behavior and the developing brain* (pp. 153–175). New York: Guilford Press.

Clarke, A. S., Mason, W. A., & Moberg, G. P. (1988). Differential behavioral and adrenocortical responses to stress among three macaques species. *American Journal of Primatology, 14,* 37–52.

Cohen, S., Kaplan, J. R., Cunnick, J. E., Manuck, S. B., & Rabin, B. S. (1992). Chronic social stress, affiliation, and cellular immune response in nonhuman primates. *Psychological Science, 3,* 301–304.

Connell, J. T., & Thompson, R. (1986). Emotion and social interaction in the strange situation. *Child Development, 57,* 733–745.

Coplan, R. J., Rubin, K. H., Fox, N. A., Calkins, S. D., & Stewart, S. L. (1994). Being alone, playing alone, and acting alone. *Child Development, 65,* 129–137.

Costello, E. J., Mustillo, S., Erkanli, A., Keeler, G., & Angold, A. (2003). Prevalence and development of psychiatric disorders in childhood and adolescence. *Archives of General Psychiatry, 60,* 837–844.

Cote, S., Tremblay, R. E., Nagin, D. S., Zoccolillo, M., & Vitaro, F. (2002). The development of impulsivity, fearfulness, and helpfulness during childhood. *Journal of Child Psychology and Psychiatry, 43,* 609–618.

Damasio, A. (1994). *Descartes' error.* New York: Putnam Press.

Davidson, R. J. (1994a). Asymmetric brain function, affective style, and psychopathology. *Development and Psychopathology, 6,* 741–758.

Davidson, R. J. (1994b). Temperament, affective style, and frontal lobe asymmetry. In G. P. Dawson & K. P. Fischer (Eds.), *Human behavior in the developing brain* (pp. 518–536). New York: Guilford Press.

Davidson, R. J. (2003a). Affective neuroscience and psychophysiology. *Psychophysiology, 40,* 655–665.

Davidson, R. J. (2003b). Right frontal brain activity, cortisol, and withdrawal behavior in 6-month-old infants. *Behavioral Neuroscience, 117,* 11–20.

Davidson, R. J., Ekman, P., & Saron, C. D. (1990). Approach withdrawal and cerebral asymmetry: Emotional expression and brain physiology. *Journal of Personality and Social Psychology, 58,* 330–341.

Davidson, R. J., & Fox, N. A. (1989). Frontal brain asymmetry predicts infants' responses to maternal separation. *Journal of Abnormal Psychology, 98,* 127–131.

Davis, M. (1984). The mammalian startle response. In R. C. Eaton (Ed.), *The neural mechanisms of startle behavior* (pp. 287–351). New York: Plenum Press.

Davis, M. H., Luce, C., & Kraus, S. J. (1994). The heritability of characteristics associated with dispositional empathy. *Journal of Personality, 62,* 369–391.

Dawson, G., Panagiotides, H., Klinger, L. G., & Hill, D. (1992). The role of frontal lobe functioning in the development of infant self-regulatory behavior. *Brain and Cognition, 20,* 152–175.

Dettling, A. C., Gunnar, M. R., & Donzella, B. (1999). Cortisol levels of young children in full-day childcare centers: Relations with age and temperament. *Psychoneuroendocrinology, 24,* 519–536.

Dettling, A. C., Parker, S. W., Lane, S., Sebanc, A., & Gunnar, M. R. (2000). Quality of care and temperament determine changes in cortisol concentrations over the day for young children in childcare. *Psychoneuroendocrinology, 25,* 819–836.

Diamond, A. (1990). Developmental time course in human infants and infant monkeys and the neural bases of inhibitory control and reaching. In A. Diamond (Ed.), *The development and neural bases of higher cognitive functions* (pp. 637–676). New York: New York Academy of Sciences.

Diamond, S. (1957). *Personality and temperament.* New York: Harper.

DiLalla, L. F., Kagan, J., & Reznick, J. S. (1994). Genetic etiology of behavioral inhibition among 2-year-old children. *Infant Behavior and Development, 17,* 401–408.

DiPietro, J. (1995, March). *Fetal origins of neurobehavioral function and individual differences.* Presented at the meeting of the Society for Research in Child Development, Indianapolis, IN.

DiPietro, J. A., Bornstein, M. H., Costigan, K. A., Pressman, E. K., Hahn, C., Painter, K., et al. (2002). What does fetal movement predict about behavior during the first two years of life? *Developmental Psychology, 40,* 358–371.

DiPietro, J. A., Costingan, K. A., Pressman, E. K., & Doussard-Roosevelt, J. A. (2000). Antenatal origins of individual differences in heart rate. *Developmental Psychobiology, 37,* 221–228.

DiPietro, J. A., Hodgson, D. M., Costigan, K. A., & Johnson, T. R. B. (1996). Fetal antecedents of infant temperament. *Child Development, 67,* 2568–2583.

Dollard, J., & Miller, N. E. (1950). *Personality and psychotherapy.* New York: McGraw-Hill.

Dunn, J., & Kendrick, C. (1981). Studying temperament and parent-child interaction. *Annual Progress in Child Psychiatry and Child Development,* 415–430.

Dyaglo, N. N., & Shishkina, G. Q. (2000). Genetic differences in the synthesis and reception of adrenaline in the mouse brain in behavior and novel environments. *Neuroscience and Behavioral Physiology, 30,* 327–330.

Eaton, W. O., & Saudino, K. J. (1992). Prenatal activity level at the temperamental dimension. *Infant Behavior and Development, 15,* 57–70.

Einstein, E., & Infeld, L. (1938). *The evolution of physics.* New York: Simon & Schuster.

Eisenberg, N., Valiente, C., Morris, A. S., Fabes, R. A., Cumberland, A., Reiser, M., et al. (2003). Facial expressions of emotion. *Psychological Science, 3,* 34–38.

Eisenberg, N., & Spinrad, T. L. (2004). Emotion related regulation. *Child Development, 75,* 334–339.

Ekman, P. (1992). Facial expressions of emotion. *Psychological Science, 3,* 34–48.

Emde, R. N., & Hewitt, J. K. (Eds.). (2001). *Infancy to early childhood.* New York: Oxford University Press.

Emde, R. N., Plomin, R., Robinson, J., Corley, R., DeFries, J., Fulker, D. W., et al. (1992). Temperament, emotion, and cognition at 14 months: MacArthur Longitudinal Twin Study. *Child Development, 63,* 1437–1455.

Evans, R. B. (2003). Georg von Bekesy. *American Psychologist, 58,* 742–746.

Fagot, B. I., & O'Brien, M. (1994). Activity level in young children. *Merrill-Palmer Quarterly, 40,* 378–390.

Fairbanks, L. A. (2001). Individual differences in response to a stranger. *Journal of Comparative Psychology, 115,* 22–28.

Fanselow, M. S. (1994). Neural organization of the defensive behavior system responsible for fear. *Psychonomic Bulletin and Review, 1,* 429–438.

Farrington, D. P. (2000). Psychosocial predictors of adult anti-social personality and adult convictions. *Behavioral Science and Law, 18*(5), 605–622.

Feiring, C., & Lewis, M. (1980). Sex differences and stability in vigor, activity, and persistence in the first 3 years of life. *Journal of Genetic Psychology, 136,* 65–75.

Fendt, M., Enders, T., & Apfelbach, R. (2003). Temporary inactivation of the bed nucleus of the stria terminalis but not of the amygdala blocks freezing induced by trimethylthiazoline, a component of fox feces. *Journal of Neuroscience, 23,* 23–28.

Fish, M., Stifter, C. A., & Belsky, J. (1991). Conditions of continuity and discontinuity in infant negative emotionality. *Child Development, 62,* 1525–1537.

Fish, S. E., & Fish, M. (1995, April). *Variability in neonatal heart rate during orientation tasks and its relation to later social and coping behavior.* Poster presented at the meeting of the Society for Research in Child Development, Indianapolis, IN.

Forman, D. R., O'Hara, M. W., Larsen, K., Coy, K. C., Gorman, L. L., & Stuart, S. (2003). Infant emotionality. *Infancy, 4,* 541–565.

Fowler, J. A. (1897). *A manual of mental science for teachers and students.* New York: Fowler & Walls.

Fox, N. A. (1989). Psychophysiological correlates of emotional reactivity during the first year of life. *Developmental Psychology, 25,* 364–372.

Fox, N. A. (1991). If its not left, its right: Electroencephalogram asymmetry and the development of emotion. *American Psychologist, 46,* 863–872.

Fox, N. A. (1994). Dynamic cerebral processes underlying emotion regulation. *Monographs of the Society for Research in Child Development, 59*(2/3, Serial No. 240), 52–166.

Fox, N. A. (1995). Of the way we were: Adult memories about attachment experiences and their role in determining infant-parent relationships—A commentary on van IJzendoorn. *Psychological Bulletin, 117,* 404–410.

Fox, N. A., Bell, M. A., & Jones, N. A. (1992). Individual differences in response to stress and cerebral asymmetry. *Developmental Neuropsychology, 8(2/3),* 161–184.

Fox, N. A., Calkins, S. D., & Bell, M. A. (1994). Neural plasticity and development in the first 2 years of life. *Developmental Psychopathology, 6,* 677–696.

Fox, N. A., & Davidson, R. J. (1987). EEG asymmetry in 10-month-old infants in response to approach of a stranger and maternal separation. *Developmental Psychology, 23,* 233–240.

Fox, N. A., & Davidson, R. J. (1988). Pattern of brain electrical activity during the expression of discrete emotions in 10-month-old infants. *Developmental Psychology, 24,* 230–236.

Fox, N. A., Henderson, H. A., Rubin, K. H., Calkins, S. D., & Schmidt, L. A. (2001). Continuity and discontinuity of behavioral inhibition and exuberance: Psychophysiological and behavioral influences across the first 4 years of life. *Child Development, 72(1),* 1–21.

Fox, N. A., Kimmerly, N. L., & Schaefer, W. D. (1991). Attachment to mother/attachment to father: A meta-analysis. *Child Development, 62,* 210–225.

Fox, N. A., Rubin, K. H., Calkins, S. D., Marshall, T. R., Coplan, R. J., Porges, S. W., et al. (1995). Frontal activation asymmetry and social competence at 4 years of age. *Child Development, 66,* 1770–1784.

Freedman, D. G., & Freedman, N. (1969). Behavioral differences between Chinese-American and American newborns. *Nature, 224,* 12–27.

Freedman, D. G., & Keller, B. (1963). Inheritance of behavior in infants. *Science, 140,* 196.

Freud, S. (1950). Analysis of a phobia in a 5-year-old boy. In A. Strachey & J. Strachey (Trans.), *Collected papers of Sigmund Freud* (Vol. 3, pp. 149–295). London: Hogarth Press. (Original work published 1909)

Freud, S. (1965). *New introductory lectures on psychoanalysis.* New York: Norton. (Original work published 1933)

Fudge, J. L., Kunishio, K., Walsh, P., Richard, C., & Haber, S. N. (2002). Amygdaloid projections to ventromedial striatral subterritories in the primate. *Neuroscience, 110,* 257–275.

Gainotti, G., Caltagirone, L., & Zoccolotti, P. (1993). Left-right and cortical/subcortical dichotomies in neuropsychological study of human emotions. In F. N. Watts (Ed.), *Neuropsychological perspectives on emotion* (pp. 71–93). Hillsdale, NJ: Erlbaum.

Gall, F. J. (1835). *On the organ of the moral qualities and intellectual faculties and the plurality of the cerebral organs* (W. Lewis, Trans.). Boston: Marsh, Copen, & Lyon.

Giedd, J. N., Snell, J. W., Lange, N., Rajapakse, J. C., Casey, B. J., Kuzuch, T. L., et al. (1996). Quantitative magnetic resonance imaging of human brain development. *Cerebral Cortex, 6,* 551–560.

Goddard, M. E., & Beilharz, R. G. (1985). A multivariate analysis of the genetics of fearlessness in potential guide dogs. *Behavioral Genetics, 15,* 69–89.

Goldberg, S., Levitan, R., Levog, E., Masellis, M., Basile, V. S., Nemeroff, C. B., et al. (2003). Cortisol concentrations in 12- to 18-month-old infants. *Biological Psychiatry, 54,* 719–726.

Goldsmith, H. H., & Campos, J. J. (1990). The structure of temperamental fear and pleasure in infants. *Child Development, 61,* 1944–1964.

Goldsmith, H. H., & Gottesman, I. I. (1981). Origins of variations in behavioral style. *Child Development, 52,* 91–103.

Goldsmith, H. H., Lemery, K. S., Buss, K. A., & Campos, J. J. (1999). Genetic analyses of focal aspects of infant temperament. *Developmental Psychology, 35,* 972–985.

Goldsmith, H. H., & Rothbart, M. K. (1991). Contemporary instruments for assessing early temperament by questionnaire and in the laboratory. In J. Strelau & A. Angleitner (Eds.), *Explorations in temperament* (pp. 249–272). New York: Plenum Press.

Goodwin, B. (1994). *How the leopard changed its spots.* New York: Scribners.

Goossens, F. A., & van IJzendoorn, M. H. (1990). Quality of infants' attachment to professional caregivers. *Child Development, 61,* 832–837.

Gortmaker, S. L., Kagan, J., Caspi, A., & Silva, P. A. (1997). Daylight during pregnancy and shyness in children. *Developmental Psychobiology, 31,* 107–114.

Green, J. M. (1991). Mothers' perception of their 6-week-old babies. *Irish Journal of Psychology, 12,* 133–144.

Guerin, D. W., & Gottfried, A. W. (1994). Developmental stability and change in parent reports of temperament. *Merrill-Palmer Quarterly, 40,* 334–350.

Gunnar, M. R. (1994). Psychoendocrine studies of temperament and stress in early childhood. In J. Bates & T. Wachs (Eds.), *Temperament: Individual differences at the interface of biology and behavior.* Washington, DC: American Psychological Association.

Gunnar, M. R., Porter, F. L., Wolf, C. M., Rigatuso, J., & Larson, M. C. (1995). Neonatal stress reactivity. *Child Development, 66,* 1–13.

Habecker, B. A., & Landis, S. C. (1994). Noradrenergic regulation of cholinergic differentiation. *Science, 264,* 1602–1604.

Hariri, A. R., Mattoy, V. S., Tessitore, A., Fera, F., Smith, W. G., & Weinberger, D. R. (2002). Dextroamphetamine modulates the response of the human amygdala. *Neurosystems Pharmacology, 27,* 1036–1040.

Healy, D. (1997). *The antidepressant era.* Cambridge, MA: Harvard University Press.

Hebb, D. O. (1946). On the nature of fear. *Psychological Review, 53,* 259–276.

Henderson, H. A. (2002). *Tempermental contributions to problem solving: Cognitive and affective processes* [Dissertation Abstract].

Henderson, H. A., Marshall, P. J., Fox, N. A., & Rubin, K. H. (2004). Psychophysiological and behavioral evidence for varying forms and functions of nonsocial behavior in preschoolers. *Child Development, 75,* 251–263.

Hinde, R. A., Tamplin, A., & Barrett, J. (1993). Social isolation in 4-year-olds. *British Journal of Developmental Psychology, 11,* 211–236.

Hooton, E. A. (1939). *Crime and the man.* Cambridge, MA: Harvard University Press.

Hu, M. W., & Fox, S. W. (1988). *Evolutionary processes and metaphors.* New York: Wiley.

Huffman, L. C., Bryan, Y. E., Pedersen, F. A., Lester, B. M., Newman, J. D., & del Carmen, R. (1994). Infant cry acoustics and maternal ratings of temperament. *Infant Behavior and Development, 17,* 45–53.

Huttenlocher, P. R. (1979). Synaptic density in human frontal cortex. *Brain Research, 163,* 195–205.

Insel, T. R., Wang, Z., & Ferris, C. (1994). Patterns of vasopressin receptor distribution associated with social organization in monogamous and non-monogamous microtine rodents. *Journal of Neuroscience, 14,* 5381–5392.

Izard, C. E. (1991). *The psychology of emotions.* New York: Plenum Press.

Izard, C. E., Hembree, E. A., & Huebner, R. R. (1987). Infants' emotion expressions to acute pain. *Developmental Psychology, 23,* 105–113.

John, E. M. (1941). A study of the effects of evacuation and air raids on children of pre-school age. *British Journal of Educational Psychology, 11,* 173–182.

Jones, R. B., Satterlee, D. G., & Ryder, F. H. (1994). Fear of humans in Japanese quail selected for low or high adrenocortical response. *Physiology and Behavior, 56,* 379–383.

Kagan, J. (1971). *Change and continuity in infancy.* New York: Wiley.

Kagan, J. (1994). *Galen's prophecy.* New York: Basic Books.

Kagan, J. (1997). Temperament and the reactions to unfamiliarity. *Child Development, 68,* 139–143.

Kagan, J., Arcus, D., Snidman, N., Yufeng, W., Hendler, J., & Greene, S. (1994). Reactivity in infants: A cross-national comparison. *Developmental Psychology, 30,* 342–345.

Kagan, J., Kearsley, R., & Zelazo, P. (1978). *Infancy.* Cambridge, MA: Harvard University Press.

Kagan, J., Lapidus, D. R., & Moore, M. (1978). Infant antecedents of cognitive functioning. *Child Development, 49,* 1005–1023.

Kagan, J., Reznick, J. S., & Snidman, N. (1988). Biological bases of childhood shyness. *Science, 240,* 167–171.

Kagan, J., & Saudino, K. J. (2001). Behavioral inhibition and related temperaments. In R. N. Emde & J. K. Hewitt (Eds.), *Infancy to early childhood* (pp. 111–122). New York: Oxford University Press.

Kagan, J., & Snidman, N. (2004). *The long shadow of temperament.* Cambridge, MA: Harvard University Press.

Kalin, N. H., Larson, C., Shelton, S. E., & Davidson, R. J. (1998). Asymmetric frontal brain activity, cortisol, and behavior associated with fearful temperament in Rhesus monkeys. *Behavioral Neuroscience, 112,* 286–292.

Kalin, N. H., Shelton, S. E., & Davidson, R. J. (2000). Cerebrospinal fluid corticotropin-releasing hormone levels are elevated in monkeys with patterns of brain activity associated with fearful temperament. *Biological Psychiatry, 47,* 579–585.

Kant, I. (1959). *Foundations of the metaphysics of morals* (L. Beck, Trans.). Indianapolis, IN: Bobbs-Merrill. (Original work published 1785)

Kapp, B. S., Supple, W. F., & Whalen, R. (1994). Effects of electrical stimulation of the amygdaloid central nucleus on neocortical arousal in the rabbit. *Behavioral Neuroscience, 108,* 81–93.

Karli, P. (1956). The Norway rat's killing response to the white mouse. *Behavior, 10,* 81–103.

Karli, P. (1981). Conceptual and methodological problems associated with the study of brain mechanisms underlying aggressive behavior. In P. F. Brain & D. Benton (Eds.), *Biology of aggression* (pp. 323–361). Alphenaandenrijn, Holland: Sijt-hoff Noordhoff.

Karli, P. (1991). *Animal and human aggression.* Oxford, England: Oxford University Press.

Katz, L. F., & Gottman, J. M. (1994). Vagal tone buffers children from the effects of marital hostility. *Psychophysiology, 31,* S80.

Kendler, K. S., Myers, J. M., & Neale, M. C. (2000). A multidimensional twin study of mental health in women. *American Journal of Psychiatry, 157,* 506–517.

Kerr, M., Lambert, W. W., & Bem, D. J. (1996). Life course sequellae of childhood shyness in Sweden. *Developmental Psychology, 32,* 1100–1105.

Kerr, M., Lambert, W. W., Stattin, H., & Klackenberg-Larsson, I. (1994). Stability of inhibition in the Swedish longitudinal sample. *Child Development, 65,* 138–146.

Klein, R. G. (1991). Parent-child agreement in clinical assessment of anxiety and other psychopathology. *Journal of Anxiety Disorders, 5,* 182–198.

Klein, R. G., & Last, C. G. (1989). *Anxiety disorders in children.* Newbury Park, CA: Sage.

Kochanska, G. (1991). Socialization and temperament in the development of guilt and conscience. *Child Development, 62,* 1379–1392.

Kochanska, G. (1993). Toward a synthesis of parental socialization and child temperament in early development of conscience. *Child Development, 64,* 325–347.

Kochanska, G. (1995). Children's temperament, mothers' discipline, and security of attachment. *Child Development, 66,* 597–615.

Kohnstamm, G. A., Bates, J. E., & Rothbart, M. K. (1989). *Temperament in childhood.* New York: Wiley.

Korner, A. F., Zeanah, C. H., Linden, J., Berkowitz, R. I., Kraemer, H. C., & Agras, W. S. (1985). The relation between neonatal and later activity and temperament. *Child Development, 56,* 38–42.

Kostovic, I. (1990). Structural and histochemical reorganization of the human prefrontal cortex during prenatal and postnatal life. *Progress in Brain Research, 85,* 223–240.

Kretschmer, E. (1925). *Physique and character* (W. J. H. Sprott, Trans., 2nd ed.). New York: Harcourt Brace.

Kumakiri, C., Kodama, K., Shimizu, E., Yamanouchi, N., Okada, S., Noda, S., et al. (1999). Study of the association between the serotonin transporter gene regulating polymorphism and personality traits in a Japanese population. *Neuroscience Letters, 263,* 205–207.

La Bar, K. S., Gatenby, C., Gore, J. C., Le Doux, J. E., & Phelps, E. A. (1998). Human amygdala activation during conditioned fear acquisition and extinction. *Neuron, 29,* 937–945.

La Greca, A. M., Silverman, W. K., & Wassastein, S. B. (1998). Children's predisaster functioning as a predictor of post-traumatic stress following Hurricane Andrew. *Journal of Consulting and Clinical Psychology, 66,* 883–892.

LeDoux, J. E. (2000). Emotion circuits in the brain. *Annual Review of Neuroscience, 23,* 155–184.

LeDoux, J. E., Iwata, J., Cicchetti, D., & Reis, E. J. (1988). Different projections of the central amygdaloid nucleus mediate autonomic and behavioral correlates of conditioned fear. *Journal of Neuroscience, 8,* 2517–2529.

Lee, S., & Kleinman, A. (1997). Mental illness and social change in China. *Harvard Review of Psychiatry, 5,* 43–46.

Lee, Y., Schulkin, J., & Davis, M. (1994). Effect of corticosterone on enhancement of the acoustic startle reflex by corticotropin releasing factor. *Brain Research, 666,* 93–98.

Lewis, M., Ramsay, D. S., & Kawakami, K. (1993). Differences between Japanese infants and Caucasian-American infants in behavioral and cortisol response to inoculation. *Child Development, 64,* 1722–1731.

Lin, K. M., Poland, R. E., & Lesser, I. N. (1986). Ethnicity and psychopharmacology. *Culture, Medicine, and Psychiatry, 10,* 151–165.

Lloyd, R. L., & Kling, A. S. (1991). Delta activity from amygdala in squirrel monkeys (Saimiri sciureus): Influence of social and environmental contexts. *Behavioral Neuroscience, 105,* 223–229.

Lombroso, C. (1911). *Crime and its causes.* Boston: Little, Brown.

Lyons, P. M., Afarion, H., Schatzberg, A. F., Sawyer-Glover, A., & Moseley, M. E. (2002). Experience dependant asymmetric variation in monkeys (Saimiri sciurencis). *Behavioral Brain Research, 136,* 51–59.

Madison, L. S., Madison, J. K., & Adubato, S. A. (1986). Infant behavior and development in relation to fetal movement and habituation. *Child Development, 57,* 1475–1482.

Magnusson, D. (1988). *Individual development from an interactional perspective.* Hillsdale, NJ: Erlbaum.

Mangelsdorf, S., Gunnar, M., Kestenbaum, R., Lang, S., & Andreas, D. (1990). Infant proneness to distress temperament, maternal personality, and mother-infant attachment. *Child Development, 61,* 820–831.

Maren, S., Yap, S. A., & Goosens, K. A. (2001). The amgydala is essential for the development of neuronal plasticity in the medial geniculate nucleus during auditory fear conditioning in rats. *Journal of Neuroscience, 21,* RC135.

Marks, I. M. (1987). *Fears, phobias, and rituals.* New York: Oxford University Press.

Marshall, P., Hardin, M., & Fox, N. A. (2004). *Temperament and electrophysiological responses to novelty in infancy.* Manuscript in preparation.

Mason, W. A., & Capitanio, J. P. (1988). Formation and expression of filial attachment in rhesus monkeys raised with living and inanimate mother substitutes. *Developmental Psychobiology, 21,* 401–430.

Matheny, A. (1983). A longitudinal twin study of stability of components from Bayley's infant behavior record. *Child Development, 54,* 356–360.

Matheny, A. (1990). Developmental behavior genetics. In M. E. Hahn, J. K. Hewitt, N. D. Henderson, & R. H. Benno (Eds.), *Developmental behavior genetics: Neural, biometrical, and evolutionary approaches* (pp. 25–38). New York: Oxford University Press.

Matheny, A., Wilson, R. S., & Thoben, A. S. (1987). Home and mother: Relations with infant temperament. *Developmental Psychology, 23,* 323–331.

May, H. (1959). *The end of American innocence.* New York: Knopf.

McDougall, W. (1908). *Introduction to social psychology.* London: Methuen.

McDougall, W. (1929). The chemical theory of temperament applied to introversion and extraversion. *Journal of Abnormal and Social Psychology, 24,* 293–309.

McGaugh, J. L., & Cahill, L. (2003). Emotion and memory. In R. J. Davidson, K. R. Scherer, & H. H. Goldsmith (Eds.), *Handbook of affective science* (pp. 93–116). New York: Oxford University Press.

McNally, G. P., & Westbrook, R. F. (2003). Opioid receptors regulate the extinction of Pavlovian fear conditioning. *Behavioral Neuroscience, 117,* 1292–1301.

Mebert, C. J. (1991). Dimensions of subjectivity in parents' ratings of infant temperament. *Child Development, 62,* 352–361.

Meehl, P. E. (1973). Maxcov-Hitmax: A taxonomy search for loose genetic syndromes. In P. E. Meehl (Ed.), *Psychodiagnosis: Selected papers* (pp. 200–224). Minneapolis: University of Minnesota Press.

Meehl, P. E. (1995). Bootstrap taxometrics. *American Psychologist, 50,* 266–275.

Merikangas, K. R., Avenevoli, S., Acharyya, S., Zhang, H., & Angst, J. (2002). The spectrum of social phobia in the Zurich cohort study of young adults. *Biological Psychiatry, 51,* 55–91.

Meyer, A. (1994). A short sketch of the problems of psychiatry. *American Journal of Psychiatry, 151,* 43–47. (Original work published 1897)

Mills, A. D., & Faure, J. M. (1991). Diversion selection for duration of chronic immobility and social reinstatement behavior in Japanese quail (Coturnix Japonica chicks). *Journal of Comparative Psychology, 105,* 25–38.

Miyawaki, T., Goodchild, A. K., & Pilowsky, P. M. (2002). Activation of mu-opioid receptors in rat ventrolateral medulla selectively blocks baroreceptor reflexes while activation of delta opioid receptors blocks somato-sympathetic reflexes. *Neuroscience, 109,* 133–144.

Morley-Fletcher, S., Palanza, P., Parolaro, D., Vigano, D., & Laviola, G. (2003). Intra-uterine position has long term influences on brain u-opiod receptor densities and behavior in mice. *Psychoneuroendocrinology, 28,* 386–400.

Mrzljak, L. H. B., & Uylings, B. H. (1990). Neural development in human prefrontal cortex in prenatal and postnatal stages. *Progress in Brain Research, 85,* 185–222.

Nelson, E. E., Shelton, S. E., & Kalin, N. H. (2003). Individual differences in the responses of naive rhesus monkeys to snakes. *Emotion, 3,* 3–11.

North, C. S., Smith, E. M., & Spitznagel, E. L. (1994). Posttraumatic stress disorder and survivors of a mass shooting. *American Journal of Psychiatry, 151,* 82–88.

Ohman, A., & Mineka, S. (2001). Fears, phobias, and preparedness. *Psychological Review, 108,* 483–522.

Ohman, A., & Mineka, S. (2003). The malicious serpent. *Current Directions in Psychological Science, 12,* 5–9.

Osgood, C. E., Suci, G. J., & Tannenbaum, P. H. (1957). *The measurement of meaning.* Urbana: University of Illinois Press.

Panksepp, J. (1990). The psychoneurology of fear. In G. D. Burrows, M. Roth, & R. Noyes (Eds.), *The neurobiology of anxiety: Vol. 3. Handbook of anxiety* (pp. 3–58). New York: Elsevier.

Parent, M. B., West, M., & McGaugh, J. L. (1994). Memory of rats with amygdala regions induced 30 days after footshock-motivated escape training reflects degree of original training. *Behavioral Neuroscience, 108,* 1080–1087.

Pavlov, I. P. (1928). *Lectures on conditioned reflexes* (W. H. Gantt, Trans., Vol. 1). New York: International Publishers.

Paxinos, G. (1990). *The human nervous system.* New York: Academic Press.

Petrovich, G. D., Canteras, N. S., & Swanson, L. W. (2001). Combinatorial amygdalar inputs to hippocampal and hypothalamic behavioral systems. *Brain Research Reviews, 38,* 247–289.

Piaget, J. (1950). *The psychology of intelligence.* London: Routledge & Kegan Paul.

Placidi, G. P., Oquendo, N. A., Malone, K. M., Huang, Y. Y., Ellis, S. P., & Mann, J. J. (2001). Aggresivity, suicide attempts, and depression. *Biological Psychiatry, 50,* 783–791.

Plomin, R., & Foch, T. T. (1980). A twin study of objectively assessed personality in childhood. *Journal of Personality and Social Psychology, 39,* 680–688.

Plomin, R., & McClearn, G. E. (Eds.). (1993). *Nature, nurture, and psychology.* Washington, DC: American Psychological Association.

Polak, C., Fox, N. A., Henderson, H. A., & Rubin, K. H. (2004). *Behavioral and physiological correlates of socially wary behavior in middle childhood: Does social wary behavior mediate the relation between infant temperament and later child maladjustment.* Manuscript in preparation.

Posner, M. I., & Petersen, S. E. (1990). The attention system of the human brain. *Annual Review of Neuroscience, 13,* 25–42.

Price, J. L. (1999). Prefrontal cortical networks related to visceral function and mood. *Annals of the New York Academy of Sciences, 877,* 383–396.

Pujol, J., Lopez, A., Deus, J., Cardoner, N., Vallejo, J., Capdevila, A., et al. (2002). Anatomical variability of the anterior cingulate gyrus and basic dimensions of human personality. *Neuroimage, 15,* 847–855.

Pyles, M. K., Stolz, H. R., & MacFarlane, J. W. (1935). The accuracy of mothers' reports on birth and developmental data. *Child Development, 6,* 165–176.

Pynoos, R. S., Frederick, C., Nader, K., Arroyo, W., Steinberg, A., Eth, S., et al. (1987). Life threat and post traumatic stress disorder in school-age children. *Archives of General Psychiatry, 44,* 1057–1063.

Raine, A., Venables, P. H., & Williams, M. (1990). Autonomic orienting responses in 15-year-old male subjects and criminal behavior at age 24. *American Journal of Psychiatry, 147,* 933–937.

Rattoni, F. B., Forthman, D. L., Sanchez, M. A., Perez, J. L., & Garcia, J. (1988). Odor and taste aversions conditioned in anesthetized rats. *Behavioral Neuroscience, 102,* 726–732.

Reilly, J. S., Stiles, J., Larsen, J., & Trauner, D. (1995). Affective facial expression in infants with focal brain damage. *Neuropsychologia, 33,* 83–99.

Rebec, G. V., Christianson, J. R., Guevra, C., & Bardo, M. T. (1997). Regional and temporal differences in real time dopamine efflux in the nucleus accumbens during food choice novelty. *Brain Research, 776,* 61–67.

Reppucci, C. (1968). *Hereditary influences upon distribution of attention in infancy.* Unpublished doctoral dissertation, Harvard University, Boston, MA.

Rezendes, M. O. (1993). *Behavioral and autonomic transitions in early infancy.* Unpublished doctoral dissertation, Harvard University, Cambridge, MA.

Reznick, J. S. (1999). Influences on maternal attribution of infant intentionality. In P. D. Zelazo, J. W. Astington, & D. R. Olson (Eds.), *Developing theories of intention* (pp. 243–267). Mahwah, NJ: Erlbaum.

Rich, G. J. (1928). A biochemical approach to the study of personality. *Journal of Abnormal and Social Psychology, 23,* 158–175.

Richards, J. E., & Cameron, D. (1989). Infant heart rate variability and behavioral developmental status. *Infant Behavior and Development, 12,* 45–58.

Rickman, M. D., & Davidson, R. J. (1994). Personality and behavior in parents of temperamentally inhibited and uninhibited children. *Developmental Psychology, 30,* 346–354.

Riese, M. L. (1987). Temperament stability between the neonatal period and 24 months. *Developmental Psychology, 23,* 216–222.

Riese, M. L. (1988). Temperament in full-term and pre-term infants. *Journal of Developmental and Behavioral Pediatrics, 9,* 6–11.

Riese, M. L. (1995). Mothers' ratings of infant temperament. *Journal of Genetic Psychology, 156,* 23–32.

Rimm-Kaufman, S. E., Early, D. M., Cox, M. J., Saluja, G., Pianta, R. C., Bradley, R. H., et al. (2002). Early behavior attributes and teachers' sensitivity as predictors of competent behavior in the kindergarten classroom. *Applied Developmental Psychology, 23,* 451–470.

Roback, A. (1931). *Psychology of character* (2nd ed.). New York: Harcourt Brace.

Roccatagliatta, J. (1986). *A history of ancient psychiatry.* New York: Greenwood Press.

Roozendaal, B., & Cools, A. R. (1994). Influence of the noradrenergic state of the nucleus accumbens in basolateral amygdala mediated changes in neophobia of rats. *Behavioral Neuroscience, 108,* 1107–1118.

Rose, R. J. (1995). Genes and human behavior. In J. T. Spence, J. M. Darley, & D. P. Foss (Eds.), *Annual review of psychology* (pp. 625–654). Palo Alto, CA: Annual Reviews.

Rosicky, J. (1993, March). *The assessment of temperamental fearfulness in infancy.* Poster presented at the Society for Research in Child Development, New Orleans, LA.

Rothbart, M. K. (1981). Measurement of temperament in infancy. *Child Development, 52,* 569–578.

Rothbart, M. K. (1988). Temperament and the development of inhibited approach. *Child Development, 59,* 1241–1250.

Rothbart, M. K. (1989). Temperament in childhood. In G. A. Kohnstamm, J. E. Bates, & M. K. Rothbart (Eds.), *Temperament in childhood* (pp. 59–73). New York: Wiley.

Rothbart, M. K., Ahadi, S. A., & Hershey, K. L. (1994). Temperament and social behavior in childhood. *Merrill-Palmer Quarterly, 40,* 21–39.

Rothbart, M. K., Derryberry, D., & Posner, M. I. (1994). A psychobiological approach to the development of temperament. In J. E. Bates & T. D. Wachs (Eds.), *Temperament* (pp. 83–116). Washington, DC: American Psychological Association.

Rubin, K. H. (1982). Non-social play in preschoolers: Necessarily evil? *Child Development, 53,* 651–657.

Rubin, K. H. (1993). The Waterloo longitudinal project. In K. H. Rubin & J. B. Asendorpf (Eds.), *Social withdrawal, inhibition, and shyness in childhood* (pp. 291–314). Hillsdale, NJ: Erlbaum.

Rubin, K. H. (2000). *The play observation scale* (Rev. ed.). University of Maryland.

Rubin, K. H., Burgess, K. B., & Hastings, D. D. (2002). Stability and social behavioral consequences of toddlers' inhibited temperament and parenting behaviors. *Child Development, 73,* 483–495.

Rubin, K. H., Cheah, C., & Fox, N. A. (2001). Emotion regulation, parenting, and display of social reticence in preschoolers. *Early Education and Development, 12,* 97–115.

Rubin, K. H., Coplan, R. J., Fox, N. A., & Calkins, S. D. (1995). Emotionality, emotion regulation, and preschoolers' social adaptation. *Development and Psychopathology, 7,* 49–62.

Ruff, H. A., Lawson, K. R., Parinello, B., & Weissberg, R. (1990). Long-term stability of individual differences in sustained attention in the early years. *Child Development, 61,* 60–75.

Russell, B. (1940). *An inquiry into meaning and truth.* London: Allen & Unwin.

Sackett, G. P., Ruppenthall, G. C., Fahrenbuch, C. H., Holm, R. A., & Greenough, W. T. (1981). Social isolation rearing effects in monkeys vary with genotype. *Developmental Psychology, 17,* 313–318.

Sagi, A., van IJzendoorn, M. H., & Koren-Karie, N. (1991). Primary appraisal of the strange situation. *Developmental Psychology, 27,* 587–596.

Sanders, S. K. (2001). Cardiovascular and behavioral effects of GABA manipulation in the region of the anterior basolateral amygdala of rats. *Dissertation Abstracts International, Section, B, Sciences and Engineering, 62,* 1060.

Sapolsky, R. M. (1992). *Stress, the aging brain, and the mechanisms of neuron death* (p. 181). Cambridge, MA: MIT Press.

Saudino, K. J., & Cherny, S. S. (2001). Sources of continuity and change in observed temperament. In R. N. Emde & J. K. Hewitt (Eds.), *Infancy to early childhood* (pp. 89–100). New York: Oxford.

Saudino, K. J., & Eaton, W. O. (1991). Infant temperament and genetics. *Child Development, 62,* 1167–1174.

Saudino, K. J., McGuire, S., Reiss, D., Hetherington, E. M., & Plomin, R. (1993). *Clarifying the confusion.* Paper presented at the Center for Developmental and Health Genetics, Pennsylvania State University, Philadelphia, PA.

Schmidt, L., & Fox, N. A. (1994). Patterns of cortical electrophysiology and autonomic activity in adults' shyness and sociability. *Biological Psychology, 38,* 183–198.

Schmidt, L. A., Fox, N. A., & Schulkin, J. (1999). Behavioral and pscyhophysiological correlates of self-presentation in temperamentally shy children. *Developmental Psychobiology, 35,* 119–135.

Schmidt, L. A., Fox, N. A., Schulkin, J., & Gold, P. W. (1999). Behavioral and psychophysiological correlates of self-presentation in temperamentally shy children. *Developmental Psychobiology, 35,* 119–135.

Schwartz, C. E., Snidman, N., & Kagan, J. (1999). Adolescent social anxiety and outcome of inhibited temperament in childhood. *Journal of the American Academy of Child and Adolescent Psychiatry, 38,* 1008–1015.

Schwartz, C. E., Wright, C. E., Shin, L. M., Kagan, J., & Rauch, S. L. (2003). Inhibited and uninhibited children Grown up: Adult amygdalar response to novelty. *Science, 300,* 1952–1953.

Schwartz, C. E., Wright, C. E., Shin, L. M., Kagan, J., Whalen, P. J., McMullin, K. G., et al. (2003). Differential amygdalar response to novel versus newly familiar neutral faces. *Biological Psychiatry, 53,* 854–862.

Schwarz, N. (1999). Self-reports. *American Psychologist, 54,* 93–105.

Scott, J. P., & Fuller, S. (1965). *Genetics and the social behavior of the dog.* Chicago: University of Chicago Press.

Seifer, R., Sameroff, A. J., Barrett, L. C., & Krafchuk, E. (1994). Infant temperament measured by multiple observations and mother report. *Child Development, 65,* 1478–1490.

Seyfarth, R. M., & Cheney, D. L. (2003). Signalers and receivers in animal communication. In S. T. Fiske, D. L. Schacter, & C. Zahn-Waxler (Eds.), *Annual review of psychology* (Vol. 54, pp. 145–173). Palo Alto, CA: Annual Reviews.

Shaw, D. S., Gilliom, M., Ingoldsby, E. M., & Nagin, D. (2003). Trajectories leading to school-age conduct problems. *Developmental Psychology, 39,* 189–200.

Sheldon, W. H. (1940). *The varieties of human physique.* New York: Harper.

Shumyatsky, G. P., Tsvetkov, E., Malleret, G., Vronskaya, S., Hatton, M., Hampton, L., et al. (2002). Identification of a signaling network in lateral nucleus of amygdala important for inhibiting memory specifically related to learned fear. *Cell, 11,* 905–918.

Siegel, R. E. (1968). *Galen's system of physiology and medicine.* Basel, Switzerland: Karger.

Simms, J. (1887). *Physiognomy illustrated* (8th ed.). New York: Murray Hill.

Skinner, B. F. (1981). Selection by consequences. *Science, 213,* 501–504.

Smollar, J. W., Rosenbaum, J. F., Biederman, J., Kennedy, J., Dai, D., Racitte, S., et al. (in press). Association of the genetic marker at the corticotropin releasing hormone locus with behavioral inhibition. *Biological Psychiatry.*

Snidman, N., Kagan, J., Riordan, L., & Shannon, D. (1995). Cardiac function and behavioral reactivity in infancy. *Psychophysiology, 32,* 199–207.

Snowdon, C. T., Coe, C. L., & Hodun, A. (1985). Population recognition of infant isolation peeps in the squirrel monkey. *Animal Behavior, 33,* 1145–1156.

Sperry, R. W. (1977). Bridging science and values. *American Psychologist, 32,* 237–245.

Spiker, D., Klebanov, P. K., & Brooks-Gunn, J. (1992, May). *Environmental and biological correlates of infant temperament.* Poster presented at the meeting of the International Society for Infant Studies, Miami, FL.

Spiker, D., Kraemer, H. C., Constantine, N. A., & Bryant, D. (1992). Reliability and validity of behavior problem checklist as measures of stable traits in low birth weight premature preschoolers. *Child Development, 63,* 1481–1496.

Spurzheim, J. G. (1834). *Phrenology.* Boston: Marsh, Copen, & Lyon.

Stams, G. J. M., Juffer, F., & van IJzendoorn, A. H. (2002). Maternal sensitivity, infant attachment, and temperament in early childhood to predict adjustment in middle childhood. *Developmental Psychology, 38,* 806–821.

Stefanacci, L., & Amaral, D. G. (2002). Some observations on cortical inputs to the macaque amygdala. *Journal of Comparative Neurology, 451,* 301–323.

Stevenson-Hinde, J., & Shouldice, A. (1996). Fearfulness: Developmental consistency. In A. Sameroff & M. Haith (Eds.), *The five to seven year shift: Age of reason and responsibility* (pp. 237–252). Chicago: University of Chicago Press.

Stifter, C. A., Fox, N. A., & Porges, S. W. (1989). Facial expressivity and vagal tone in 5- and 10-month-old infants. *Infant Behavior and Development, 12,* 127–137.

Stifter, C. A., & Wiggins, C. N. (2004). Assessment of disturbances in emotion regulation and temperament. In R. Del Carmen-Wiggins & A. Carter (Eds.), *Handbook of infant, toddler, and preschool mental health assessment* (pp. 79–103). New York: Oxford University Press.

Strauss, M. E., & Rourke, D. C. (1978). A multivariate analysis of the neonatal behavioral assessment scale in several samples. *Monographs of the Society for Research in Child Development, 43*(5/6), 81–91.

Strelau, J., & Angleitner, A. (1991). *Explorations in temperament.* New York: Plenum Press.

Strouse, J. (1980). *Alice James.* Boston: Houghton Mifflin.

Suomi, S. J. (1987). Genetic and maternal contributions to individual differences in rhesus monkey biobehavioral development. In N. A. Krasnegor, E. M. Blass, M. A. Hofer, & W. P. Smotherman (Eds.), *Perinatal development* (pp. 397–420). New York: Academic Press.

Svartberg, K., & Forkman, B. (2002). Personality traits in the domestic dog (Canis familiaris). *Applied Animal Behavior Science, 79,* 133–156.

Takahashi, J. S., & Hoffman, M. (1995). Molecular biological clocks. *American Scientist, 83,* 158–165.

Takahashi, L. K., & Rubin, W. W. (1994). Corticosteriod induction of treat-induced behavioral inhibition in preweanling rats. *Behavioral Neuroscience, 107,* 860–868.

Terr, L. C. (1979). Children of Chowchilla. *Psychoanalytic Study of the Child, 34,* 547–623.

Thomas, A., & Chess, S. (1977). *Temperament and development*. New York: Brunner/Mazel.

Thompson, R. A., Connell, J. P., & Bridges, L. J. (1988). Temperament, emotion, and social interactive behavior in the strange situation. *Child Development, 59*, 1102–1110.

Thompson, R. F., Donegan, N. H., Clark, G. A., Levond, D. G., Lincoln, J. S., Madden, J., et al. (1987). Neural substrates of discrete defensive conditioned reflexes, conditioned fear states, and their interaction in the rabbit. In I. Gormezano, W. F. Prokasy, & R. F. Thompson (Eds.), *Classical conditioning* (3rd ed., pp. 371–399). Hillsdale, NJ: Erlbaum.

Thompson, W. R. (1953). The inheritance of behavior. *Canadian Journal of Psychology, 7*, 145–155.

Tomarken, A. J., Davidson, R. J., & Henriques, J. B. (1990). Resting frontal brain asymmetry predicts affective responses to films. *Journal of Personality and Social Psychology, 59*, 791–801.

Tout, K., de Haan, M., Kipp-Campbell, E., & Gunnar, M. R. (1998). Social behavior correlates of adrenocortical activity in daycare: Gender differences and time of day effects. *Child Development, 69*, 1247–1262.

Treit, D., Pesold, C., & Rotzinger, S. (1993a). Dissociating the antifear effects of septal and amygdaloid lesions using two pharmacologically validated models of rat anxiety. *Behavioral Neuroscience, 107*, 770–785.

Treit, D., Pesold, C., & Rotzinger, S. (1993b). Noninteractive effects of diazepam and amygdaloid lesions in two animal models of anxiety. *Behavioral Neuroscience, 107*, 1099–1105.

Tremblay, R. E., Pihl, R. O., Vitaro, F., & Dubkin, P. L. (1994). Predicting early onset of male antisocial behavior from preschool behavior. *Archives of General Psychiatry, 51*, 732–735.

Trut, L. N. (1999). Early canid domestication. *American Scientist, 87*, 160–169.

Valentine, C. W. (1930). The innate basis of fear. *Journal of Genetic Psychology, 37*, 394–420.

van Bockstaele, E. J., Bajic, D., Proudfit, H., & Valentino, R. J. (2001). Topographic architecture of stress-related pathways targeting the noradrenergic locus ceruleus. *Physiology and Behavior, 73*, 273–283.

Van den Boom, D. C., & Hoeksma, J. B. (1994). The effect of infant irritability on mother-infant interaction. *Developmental Psychology, 30*, 581–590.

Vaughn, B. E., Bradley, C. F., Joffe, L. S., Seifer, R., & Barglow, R. (1987). Maternal characteristics measured prenatally are predictive of ratings of temperamental difficulty on the Carey infant temperament questionnaire. *Developmental Psychology, 23*, 152–161.

Vaughn, B. E., Stevenson-Hinde, J., Waters, E., Kotsaftis, A., Lefaver, G. B., Shouldice, A., et al. (1992). Attachment security and temperament in infancy in early childhood. *Developmental Psychology, 28*, 463–473.

Veit, R., Flor, H., Erb, M., Hermann, C., Lotze, M., Grudd, W., et al. (2002). Brain circuits involved in emotional learning in antisocial behavior and social phobia in humans. *Neuroscience Letters, 328*, 231–233.

Volpe, J. (1995). *Neurology of the newborn*. Philadelphia: Saunders.

Walker, B. E., & Fraser, F. C. (1957). The embryology of cortisone induced cleft palate. *Journal of Embryology and Experimental Morphology, 5*, 201–209.

Walker, D. L., Toufexis, D. J., & Davis, M. (2003). Role of the bed nucleus of the stria terminalis versus the amygdala in fear, stress, and anxiety. *European Journal of Pharmacology, 463*, 199–216.

Wallis, R. S. (1954). The overt fears of Dakota Indian children. *Child Development, 25*, 185–192.

Wang, H., & Wessendorf, M. W. (2002). Mu- and delta-opioid receptor mRNAs are expressed in periaqueductal gray neurons projecting to the rostral ventromedial medulla. *Neuroscience, 109*, 619–634.

Watamura, S. E., Sebanc, A. M., & Gunnar, M. R. (2002). Rising cortisol at childcare: Relations with nap, rest, and temperament. *Developmental Psychobiology, 40*, 33–42.

Weber, M., Watts, N., & Richardson, R. (2003). High illumination levels potentiate the acoustic startle response in prewenaling rats. *Behavioral Neuroscience, 117*, 1458–1462.

Weissman, M. M. (1984). Depression and anxiety disorder in parents and children. *Archives of General Psychiatry, 4*, 847–849.

Weisz, J. R., Suwanlert, S., Chaiyasit, W., Weiss, B., Achenbach, T., & Walter, B. R. (1987). Epidemiology of behavioral and emotional problems among Thai and American children. *Journal of the American Academy of Child and Adolescent Psychiatry, 26*, 890–898.

Weisz, J. R., Suwanlert, S., Chaiyasit, W., Weiss, B., Walter, B. R., & Anderson, W. W. (1988). Thai and American perspectives on over and under control of child behavior problems. *Journal of Consulting and Clinical Psychology, 56*, 601–609.

Werner, E. E. (1993). Risk resilience and recovery. *Development and Psychopathology, 5*, 503–515.

Whalen, P. J. (1998). Fear, vigilance, and ambiguity. *Current Directions in Psychological Science, 7*, 177–187.

Whitehead, A. N. (1928). *Science and the modern world*. New York: Macmillan.

Williamson, D. E., Coleman, K., Bacanu, S., Devlin, B. J., Rogers, J., Ryan, N. D., et al. (2003). Heritability of fearful-anxious endophenotypes in infant rhesus macaques. *Biological Psychiatry, 53*, 284–291.

Wilson, D. S., Clark, A. B., Coleman, K., & Dearstyne, T. (1994). Shyness and boldness in human and other animals. *Trends in Ecology and Evolution, 9*, 442–446.

Wilson, F. A., & Rolls, E. T. (1993). The effect of stimulus novelty and familiarity on neuronal activity in the amygdala of monkeys performing recognition memory tasks. *Experimental Brain Research, 93*, 367–382.

Wittgenstein, L. (1953). *Philosophical investigations*. New York: Macmillin.

Worobey, J., & Lewis, M. (1989). Individual differences in the reactivity of young infants. *Developmental Psychology, 25*, 663–667.

Yarrow, M. R., Campbell, J. D., & Burton, R. V. (1970). Recollections of childhood. *Monograph of the Society for Research in Child Development, 35*(5).

Yosida, M. (1973). The Chinese concept of nature. In S. Nakayama & N. Sivin (Eds.), *Chinese science* (pp. 71–90). Cambridge, MA: MIT Press.

CHAPTER 5

Emotional Development: Action, Communication, and Understanding

CAROLYN SAARNI, JOSEPH J. CAMPOS, LINDA A. CAMRAS, and DAVID WITHERINGTON

Extraordinary changes have been taking place in the study of emotion in the past 30 years. When the chapter dealing with socioemotional development was published in the fourth edition of this *Handbook* (Campos, Barrett, Lamb, Goldsmith, & Stenberg, 1983), the study of emotion and emotional development was just emerging from decades of neglect. As was noted in that chapter, there were two principal reasons for the neglect. The first was the widespread conviction that emotions were epiphenomenal, and the second was that emotions could not be

measured with specificity. The 1983 chapter described the emergence of a functionalist approach to emotions, and showed how, contrary to prior thought, emotions profoundly affected cognitive, perceptual, social, and self-regulatory processes. It also described the close link between emotion and temperamental dispositions, attachment, and parent-child interactions. It also documented major advances in the measurement of emotion in face, voice, and action. The chapter in the fifth edition of this *Handbook* detailed the elaborations in theory

Preparation of this chapter was conducted with the partial support of grant number HD-25066 from the National Institutes of Health, grant number MH-47543 from the National Institute of Mental Health, and a research grant from the John D. and Catherine T. MacArthur Foundation.

We gratefully acknowledge the assistance in the preparation of this chapter of Carl Frankel and Rosemary Campos. The chapter was written with the support of grants HD-399-25 and the National Science Foundation (Grant #BCS-0002001).

and research in emotion and emotional development since 1983, and extended the treatment of emotion to include new concerns about emotion competence.

The remarkable surge of investigation on emotion has continued unabated in the past 10 years, and the results of such investigations are dramatically changing our conceptualization of both the nature of emotions and their function in development. Three major themes in recent research stand out: (1) the close link between emotion and action, (2) the social functions of emotion, and (3) the closing of the gap in knowledge about development between infancy and adolescence.

The present chapter reflects these three emphases. First, we describe a recently revived way of conceptualizing emotion—one that traces its roots to the long-ignored work of John Dewey (1894, 1895). Second, we stress children's understanding of emotion, and how children cope with their emotions and the environmental transactions that evoke them. Third, we are concerned with emotional development in preschool and middle childhood, when the significance of emotion is especially broad in scope. The chapter also contains a number of subordinate themes. For instance, we review some of the intriguing research that has been done with infants and toddlers on how they develop systems of emotional communication. In the process, we show how the emotional expressions of others regulate the behavior of infants and children and result in empathic behavior, emotion regulation, and coping. Furthermore, we discuss why action has become so important in contemporary approaches to emotion, and how cultural approaches to emotion are beginning to draw our attention to the importance of emotion communication in development.

A CONCEPTUAL FRAMEWORK FOR FEELING AND EMOTION

Emotions seem to be most closely linked to what a person is trying to do. One's perception and interpretation of events is never independent of the action that one can perform on them (Adolph, Eppler, & Gibson, 1993; Dewey, 1894, 1895). Indeed, an event can be defined as an opportunity for action. However, not all events generate emotion—only those in which one has a stake in the outcome. Hence, we propose a working definition of emotion that emphasizes action, the preparation for action, and appraisal of the significance or relevance to concerns of

person-environment transactions. This framework includes communication as a central aspect of action.

A Working Definition of Emotion

Emotion is thus the person's attempt or readiness to establish, maintain, or change the relation between the person and her or his changing circumstances, on matters of significance to that person (Campos, Frankel, & Camras, 2004).

The definition may initially appear to be odd because of the absence of any reference to the traditional elements found in the most prevalent definitions of emotion. There is no allusion to feeling, vegetative states, facial indices of internal states, or other intrapersonal criteria. Instead, emotion is determined by the significance of a person-event transaction. Because the definition emphasizes what the person is trying to accomplish, and because it comes from a conception of emotion that stresses the consequences of emotional states, this working definition of emotion is often called a functionalist one (Barrett & Campos, 1987; Campos, Mumme, Kermoian, & Campos, 1994; Frijda, 1986, 1987; Lazarus, 1991).

There are at least four ways by which events become significant. The first is a particularly powerful and pervasive one: goal relevance and its corollaries. Lazarus (1991) specifically links the first step in the generation of emotion to this factor; however, goal relevance ensures the generation only of some kind of affect. To account for whether the affect has a positive or negative hedonic tone and a behavioral valence of approach or withdrawal, Lazarus posits the congruence or incongruence of an event to personal goals: Goal congruent transactions produce positive hedonic tone, and goal incongruent transactions bring about negative tone. To explain how a specific emotion such as fear, anger, or shame comes about, he proposes the factor of ego involvement (this determines the specific nature of the emotion elicited). So, regardless of the specific goal one is working toward, a person who overcomes obstacles to goal attainment is likely to experience happiness or relief. A person who relinquishes a goal experiences sadness, regardless of whether that goal involves physical, social, or psychological loss. A person who encounters obstacles to goal attainment will show frustration or anger. The specific nature of the goal can also affect the experience of a given emotion. Thus, avoidance of threat is linked to fear, wanting to atone is related to guilt, and the wish to escape the scrutiny of others following a transgression is linked to shame. Table 5.1 lists the factors that Barrett and Campos (1987) proposed for the generation and manifestation of a variety of emotional states. Some of these emotions are called "primordial emotions," to denote their likely presence in the neonate and their rudimentary appraisal demands; others are called "concurrent state emotions," to specify their close link to flexible goals and strivings; still others are called "social emotions," to indicate their origin in social rules backed by emotion communication from significant others. For all of these emotions, goal relevance is typically the most fundamental principle of emotion generation

Not all emotions are generated by the relation of events to goals. A second way in which emotion can be generated is through the social signals of others, which have powerful capacities to render a person-environment transaction significant (Klinnert, Campos, Sorce, Emde, & Svejda, 1983; McIntosh, Druckman, & Zajonc, 1994). They do so because social signals can generate a contagious emotional response and tendency for action in the perceiver (Hatfield, Cacioppo, & Rapson, 1994). Social signals can also give meaning to a transaction associated with the signal (such as when an infant catches the mother's fear of dogs and begins to avoid them; e.g., Bowlby, 1972). Finally, social signals play a central, though under-investigated, role in generating emotions such as pride, shame, and guilt through the enduring effects that they can have as accompaniments to the approval and disapproval of others.

A third source of significance comes about through hedonic processes—specifically, when hedonic stimulation is experienced and becomes the object of one's strivings (Frijda, 1986). Hedonic stimulation refers to the sights, sounds, tastes, smells, and tactile stimulations that intrinsically produce irreducible sensations of pleasure or pain. With pleasurable hedonic experience, we are more likely to want to repeat such experience and thus we approach objects and people. It is the opposite with painful experience. Pleasure and pain are affectogenic in the following way, taken from Frijda (1986): If, after one experiences pleasant stimulation and one wants to repeat the experience, the emotion of desire is generated; similarly, if one experiences pain and wants not to repeat the experience, the emotion of aversion is created. Desire and aversion, with further development, can become the core of much more complex emotional transactions, including envy, jealousy, and rage.

The fourth way that events become significant comes from memory of transactions from the past. Although all emotion theories stress the role of memory in generating affect, we would like to emphasize the importance of past experience for the selection of strategies for responding emotionally. Such a link is best represented in the research on working models in attachment (Bretherton, 1985). For example, as Cassidy (1994) has said, avoidantly attached infants typically have a history of interactions in which their attachment figure has ignored the infant's social signals such as bids for comfort. When these bids are consistently rejected by the caregiver, the child is predisposed toward muted affect during reunions with the caregiver. The past history of ignoring social bids makes the risk of present rejection too great. By contrast, infants who are classified as ambivalently attached have a history of interaction with a figure who has responded inconsistently to their social signals. When such children are reunited with the attachment figure following separation, they show exaggerated, rather than muted, emotional reactions. Such exaggeration serves the function, in part, of ensuring the parent's responsiveness and avoiding the parent's insensitivity. Thus, past experiences determine not only the precise nature of the emotion a child undergoes (as in the case of desire and aversion discussed earlier) but also the manner in which the child responds to, or copes with, contemporary interactions with significant others.

Feeling and Emotion

What is the role in the emotion process of what we call feeling—the irreducible quality of consciousness that accompanies evaluations? The layperson's conception places feeling at the core of emotion. That conception goes as follows: Events elicit feeling, feeling organizes expressions (or outward signs) of feeling and autonomic and instrumental behavioral reactions designed both to manifest outwardly and, in addition, to deal with the feeling. In development, many theorists (e.g., Lewis & Michalson, 1983; Sroufe, 1979) have proposed that feeling is absent in the young infant and comes about only after the infant has acquired the capacity to distinguish self from other—an accomplishment that begins to be shown by 9 months of age.

The functionalist approach to emotion gives feeling a major role as a facet of emotion, but not as its core. Feelings are not prior in time to other processes in emotion generation, as orthodox conceptualizations require. We propose that the origins of feeling come from four

TABLE 5.1   Characteristics of Some Emotion Families

Emotion Family	Goal	Appreciation re Self	Appreciation re Other	Action Tendency	Adaptive Functions	Facial Expression[b]	Physiological Reaction	Vocalic Pattern[f]
Disgust	Avoiding contamination or illness	This stimulus may contaminate me, or cause illness	[a]	Active rejection	Avoid contamination and illness; learn about substances/events/attributes to avoid; alert others re contamination	Brows lowered, nose wrinkled, with widened nasal root; raised cheeks and upper lip	Low heart rate and skin temperature; increased skin resistance[c]	Nasal, slightly tense, "very narrow," but fairly full and powerful voice
Fear	Maintaining integrity of the self (physical or psychological integrity)	This stimulus threatens my integrity	[a]	Flight; active withdrawal	Avoid danger (physical and psychological); learn about events/attributes that are dangerous; alert others re danger	Brows raised and often pulled slightly together; eyes very wide and tense, rigidly fixated on stimulus	High, stable heart rate; low skin temperature; "gasping" respiration[c]	"Narrow," extremely tense, very weak, thin, high voice
Anger	Any end state that the organism currently is invested in achieving	There is an obstacle to my obtaining my goal	[a]	Active forward movement, especially to eliminate obstacles	Attain difficult goals; learn to overcome obstacles and achieve goals; communicate power/dominance	Brows lowered and pulled together; mouth open and square or lips pressed tightly together	High heart rate and skin temperature; facial flushing[c]	"Narrow," medium to very tense, medium to extremely full voice
Sadness	Any end state that the organism currently is invested in achieving	My goal is unattainable	[a]	Disengagement; passive withdrawal	Conserve energy; learn which goals are realizable; encourage nurturance by others	Inner corners of brows moved upward; corners of mouth pulled downward, often with middle of chin pulled upward	Low heart rate;[d] low skin temperature and skin resistance	"Narrow," thin, lax, slow, or halting voice
Shame	Maintaining others' respect and affection; preserving self-esteem	I am bad (self-esteem is perceived to be impaired)	Someone/everyone notices how bad I am	Active or passive withdrawal; avoiding others; hiding of self	Behave appropriately; learn/maintain social standards; communicate submission to others and to others' standards	—	Low heart rate; blushing[e]	"Narrow," moderately lax, thin voice
Guilt	Meeting one's own internalized standards	I have done something contrary to my standards	Someone has been injured by my act	Outward movement; inclination to make reparation, to inform others, and to punish oneself	Behave prosocially; learn/maintain moral and prosocial behavior; communicate contrition/good intentions	—	High heart rate and skin conductance; irregular respiration[e]	"Narrow," tense, moderately full voice
Pride	Maintaining the respect of oneself and others	I am good (I have respect for myself)	Someone/everyone thinks (or will think) I am good	Outward/upward movement; inclination to show/inform others about one's accomplishments	Behave appropriately; learn/maintain social standards; communicate ability to meet standards	—	High heart rate[e]	"Wide," medium tense, full voice

[a] No "appreciation re other" is central to primordial or concurrent-goal emotions; however, particular family members might involve such an appreciation.
[b] These facial movements are adapted from Izard (1979).
[c] These are adapted from Ekman, Levenson, and Friesen (1983).
[d] Ekman et al. (1983) found increased heart rate with sadness; however, decreased heart rate is consistent with our theoretical position on sadness. We think it possible that most subjects in Ekman et al.'s study experienced an agitated grief state rather than a sad "giving-up" state.
[e] These are hypothesized physiological reactions.
[f] These vocalic patterns are adapted from Scherer (1986).

sources, some of which are different from the sources that generate emotion and were delineated earlier (Campos et al., 1994). One of these is the conscious accompaniment to the process of *appraisal*—the determination of how an event impinges on one's goals (Lazarus, 1991). The appreciation of the meaning of an event shows that it *matters* to the individual, and feeling is the registration of this significance. In short, feeling accompanies—not precedes—the registration of events.

The second source of feeling is the consciousness of the activation of goal-oriented central motor commands (efference). Efference, unlike return sensory flow to the brain (afference), has rarely been linked to consciousness in psychological theories, yet efference plays a role in the perception of self-motion as well as in the sense of volition—of willing a body movement to take place (Teuber, 1960). This notion of the importance of efference in generating feeling is consistent with the reasoning of Ekman, Levenson, and Friesen (1983), who discussed the importance of motoric commands to create facial patterns and for bringing about both emotion and feeling. It is also consistent with recent theorizing by Damasio (1994) who stated, "the brain learns to connect the fainter image of an 'emotional' body state, without having to reenact it in the body proper" (p. 155). The link between efference and emotion again renders feeling contemporary with emotion generation, not as an antecedent.

The third way feeling can be generated is through the perception of sensations coming from both smooth and striated muscles and from the effects of hormones. Our language is full of references to these internal states such as when we talk of feeling a "cold" fear, being "flushed" in anger, having "butterflies in the stomach," and so forth. In addition, many cultures literally embody emotion by referring to somatic states that occur when one is in distress or euphoria (Shweder, 1993). The role of feedback seems undeniable in creating aspects of feeling (Laird, 1984), but feeling is again not primary. It follows response generation.

The fourth way that feeling can be generated is through the direct perception of emotional expressions in the face, voice, and gesture of another (Hatfield et al., 1994). This is the phenomenon referred to as *socially induced affect* (McIntosh et al., 1994), which is defined as the generation of a like or complementary feeling state in the other as a result of the perception of social displays in another. This phenomenon is quite context specific. At this time, we do not understand the circumstances in which expressions by another most directly generate a similar feeling in the perceiver, those which generate an emotional state that is similar in valence but different in quality, those in which an opposite emotional state is elicited, and those in which no feelings are generated at all. Research on the ontogeny and consequences of affect contagion and socially induced affect is sorely lacking, despite exciting work with socially deprived infant monkeys suggesting that no social experience is necessary for social signals to affect behavior in affectively appropriate ways (Kenney, Mason, & Hill, 1979; Sackett, 1966; see also the subsequent section in this chapter on the related process of empathy). Socially induced affect renders feeling simultaneous with the detection of social signals, not prior to them. Such considerations are what have led us to propose that feeling is a facet of the emotion process, but not its core. In addition, because infants can show facial and instrumental behavior patterns of specific emotions very early in life (e.g., Gaensbauer, 1982; Stenberg & Campos, 1990), appraisal, efference, and afference are available to the young infant, and so may affect emotion contagion (Haviland & Lelwica, 1987). We thus find no reason to deny infants younger than 9 months of age the experience of feeling.

Facial Expressions and Emotion

Facial expressions have been hypothesized to play a particularly important role in the emotion process. One historically influential emotion theorist (Tomkins, 1962) virtually equated emotion with facial responding. For preverbal infants, facial expressions have been proposed to have additional importance because they are presumed by some to be the sole means by which emotions can be communicated before the advent of language. Thus, some scholars have proposed a virtually one-to-one correspondence between emotion and facial expression for postneonatal infants (Izard, 2004; Izard, Ackerman, Schoff, & Fine, 2000) and developed coding systems for infant emotions that rest on the identification of prespecified facial configurations. Such an approach to emotion measurement would have considerable appeal because it provides an easy solution to the problem of identifying emotion in infants. However, we believe it is fundamentally flawed on both an empirical and conceptual level. Recent studies have documented numerous examples of nonconcordance between emotion and these prespecified facial expressions. For example, infants on the visual cliff display clear indications of fear (e.g., refusal to crawl) but do not show prototypic fear expressions. Indeed, they often *smile*! Conversely, infants typically produce the prototypic facial configuration of surprise (involving raised brow and open mouth) as they introduce an object into their mouth for oral exploration (Camras, Lambrecht, & Michel, 1996). Such mismatches do not imply that facial expressions are misleading or irrelevant to infant emotion. As we further argue, we believe that facial expressions serve as critically important components in a larger pattern of information that observers perceive and integrate in making an emotion judgment (see Oster, in press, for a somewhat different but related view of infant emotional facial expressions).

Action Tendencies and the Flexible Manifestation of Emotion

In the course of studying blind infants, Fraiberg (1971) discovered that many parents of such children showed profound disappointment when they encountered low levels of facial responsiveness and eye contact in their children. The parents seemed to withdraw from their children and to lack the incentive to provide them with physical and social stimulation after noting their children's apparent unresponsiveness. Fraiberg (1971) discovered that although blind infants were indeed relatively unresponsive *facially* during social encounters, they seemed extraordinarily articulate in expressing their emotions and social responses through the actions of their *fingers*. When this responsiveness was pointed out to the parents, they dramatically increased their levels of interaction with the infants; the infants, in turn, were able to maintain their digitally mediated level of social responsiveness.

Fraiberg's observations document an important principle about emotions: Many different responses can be in the service of any given emotion—emotional responses exhibit the property of equipotentiality. To expect, as some theories do (e.g., Ekman et al., 1983; Izard, 1977, 1991; Tomkins, 1962, 1963), a close correspondence between a given response or response pattern (e.g., a facial expression) and a given emotional state is likely to lead to errors of inference. The opposite is also true: The same response can be recruited to express many different emotions. Some years ago, Kagan (1971) put it well. He said that the smile serves many masters. Consider that the action of smiling can be in the service of joy, scorn, nurturance, embarrassment, and other emotions, or stereotyped social greeting. Similarly, the action of doing nothing can be in the service of sadness (as in depressive withdrawal), fear (as in keeping still to avoid detection), or anger (as in passive aggressiveness). Emotions are best considered as "syndromes"—alternative patterns of behavior, any of which can under the right circumstances specify the emotion (Lazarus & Averill, 1972). It is not possible to identify a priori an operational definition of a given emotion that can be applied in all circumstances, such that knowing the response or response pattern by itself one can predict the emotional state of a person. A discrete emotion thus lacks a gold standard—an ostensive definition. Neither the face, voice, gesture, specific instrumental behavior nor autonomic signatures are likely to have more than a probabilistic relation to an emotional state; even then, context must be taken into account to interpret the meaning of a response (see Camras et al., 2002).

At present, the concept of *affect families* (Barrett & Campos, 1987; Dewey, 1934; Kagan, 1994) is used to convey the notion that each experience of a given emotion such as anger or fear is likely to differ in important ways from other emotional experiences of the same class. Each instance of an emotion differs from another in social signaling, type of behavior shown in context, and pattern of appraisal, yet, so long as the adaptational intent is the same for two different experiences, it can be said that the different instances bear a "family resemblance" to each other. Through such adaptational intents, emotions can be classified and their differential consequences understood (Shaver, Schwartz, Kirson, & O'Connor, 1987), not by similarity in morphology.

Measuring Emotion via Action Tendencies

The absence of an ostensive criterion for a given emotional state creates serious problems of inference. One attempt to resolve this dilemma has been proposed by Frijda (1986) in his concept of *action tendencies*. Avoidance of threat, for instance, is the action tendency for fear; avoidance of social contact of the scrutinizing other is that for shame; devotion of effort to remove an obstacle is the action tendency for anger, and so on. Table 5.2 lists Frijda's proposed action tendencies and the specific emotions that they denote—a list that he considers incomplete but representative. Note that Frijda's list of action tendencies yields a much larger number of emotions than does reliance on universality of recognition of facial expressions, which usually are limited to fear, sadness, joy, surprise, sadness, disgust, and possibly contempt.

TABLE 5.2   Relational Action Tendencies, Activation Modes, and Inhibitions[a]

Action Tendency	End State	Function	Emotion
Approach	Access	Producing situation permitting consummatory activity	Desire
Avoidance	Own inaccessibility	Protection	Fear
Being with	Contact, interaction	Permitting consummatory activity	Enjoyment, confidence
Attending (opening)	Identification	Orientation	Interest
Rejecting (closing)	Removal of object	Protection	Disgust
Nonattending	No information or contact	Selection	Indifference
Agonistic	Removal of obstruction	Regaining control	Anger
Interrupting	Reorientation	Reorientation	Shock
Dominating	Retained control	Generalized control	Arrogance
Submitting	Deflected pressure	Secondary control	Humility
Deactivation	—	(Recuperation?)	Sorrow
Bound activation	Action tendency's end state	Aim achievement	Effort
Excitement	—	Readiness	Excitement
Free activation	—	Generalized readiness	Joy
Inactivity	—	Recuperation	Contentment
Inhibition	Absence of response	Caution	Anxiety
Surrender	Activation decrease?	Activation decrease or social cohesion?	Laughter, weeping

[a] Adapted from Frijda (1986).

For Frijda, the concept of action tendency in no way refers to a response that can be measured by electromyography or by operational definition of a given response. Rather, action tendency refers to any of a number of flexibly organized phenomena that *serve the function* of, for example, avoiding threat or overcoming an obstacle. In this sense, action tendency is similar to the ethologist's conception of a behavioral system—a conception that replaced notions of fixed action patterns with appreciation of the multiplicity of ways by which an animal can attain an end (Bischof, 1975). The behavioral system for the ethologist, like the concept of a specific emotion, is defined by the function those behaviors serve. How is function measured? The functionalist's answer is: (a) by inference from the organization of behavior, (b) by suppositions about what the person is trying to accomplish, and (c) by noting whether progress toward the inferred goal is proceeding smoothly or with difficulty. The identification of the operation of a discrete emotion is intimately tied in to the context in which the person is found and the types of behavior pattern the person shows in that setting.

Although the task of measuring emotion is much more difficult than initially thought when emotion was re-

stored to its place in scientific study a few years ago, there is a major precedent for measuring the organization of behavior—a precedent that is both intellectually persuasive and highly influential (Sroufe & Waters, 1977). In attachment theory, Bowlby (1969) posited that attachment could be measured by proximity seeking in times of fear or distress. Although proximity seeking can be operationalized by measuring the physical distance of the child from the attachment figure (Coates, Anderson, & Hartup, 1972; L. Cohen & Campos, 1974), such an approach reveals little in the way of stability of individual differences in attachment, nor is it an index that retains its manifestation as the child grows older and shows attachment patterns in a variety of different ways. Attachment theorists (e.g., Ainsworth, Blehar, Waters, & Wall, 1978) have solved this problem of measuring "proximity seeking" by noting first of all whether different behaviors shown by the child in the context of reunion with the caregiver are in the service of proximity-seeking, even though there may be no approach toward the caregiver. There are many alternative ways in which attachment security can be manifested: smiling at the caregiver, making pickup bids, sharing the joy of playing with a toy, and so on. These alternative behavioral strategies are taken as partial evidence for what Sroufe (1979; Sroufe & Waters, 1977) calls "the organization of behavior." The organization stems from the similar ends that morphologically quite different behaviors serve. The crucial factors of avoidance and ambivalence in attachment are similarly inferred by judging the many alternative ways that a child can give the parent the "cold shoulder treatment" specifying avoidance, or the "angry yet relieved" expression of ambivalence. In short, we think investigators of emotion can learn useful lessons from the literature on attachment, especially to the extent that both emotion and attachment exhibit the property of equipotentiality of responses.

This approach to measurement of the action tendencies related to attachment needs to be generalized to the study of other emotional states. It should not be thought that such flexibility of behavior organized around an emotion is limited to the older school-age child and the adult. Fraiberg's (1971) observations of blind infants' social responsiveness described earlier demonstrate this, and so do 8- to 9-month-old infants tested on the visual cliff, a highly reliable fear elicitor (Scarr & Salapatek, 1970). At that age, infants can manifest fear by literal avoidance of descending onto the glass-covered deep side of the cliff, or they can approach the mother, but in a manner indicative of fear. The infants do this by detouring around the deep side, hitching along the sidewalls of the cliff table until they reach the mother (Campos, Hiatt, Ramsay, Henderson, & Svejda, 1978). Behavioral flexibility is the rule, not the exception, in the manifestation of emotion. Restriction of such flexibility in the interests of measuring one or more responses chosen a priori puts at risk the internal validity of a given study, as well as its external or ecological validity.

Component Systems Approaches to Emotion and its Development: Dynamical Systems and Functionalist Perspectives

In the previous section on action tendencies, we emphasized how emotions lack a gold standard because various aspects of emotional action—facial, vocal, and gestural signals, or specific instrumental behavior—are flexibly organized depending on context. Just as any emotion action cannot be fully understood independent of context, so *any* component of emotion, whether it be action or action tendency, goals and concerns, physiological patterning, appraisals, experiential feeling states, or social and physical contexts, cannot explain emotion itself independent of the other components that comprise the system and the relations that exist among

the components. For example, an individual may experience road rage only when he is in a hurry (i.e., the impediment has high significance), when he can find no way around the impeding driver, when he appraises the driver as deliberately obstructive, and when the driver resembles his estranged father. As emphasized by the dynamical systems approach, emotion cannot be reduced to any one of these components; specific components themselves do not engender emotion, only the relations among components. Thus, fully capturing the complexity of emotion and its generation requires a view of emotion as *relational,* deriving from the *interactions* of many components (Fogel & Thelen, 1987; M. D. Lewis, 2000; M. D. Lewis & Granic, 1999; Mascolo & Harkins, 1998).

Such a view has immediate implications for our conceptualization of emotional development. Understanding the difference in emotion between a 12-month-old and an 18-month-old extends beyond a simple acknowledgment of differences in how the two appraise events, and must include consideration of those developmental changes that engender such alterations in appraisal: changes in the infant's goals and concerns as well as the means available to the infant for acting on the world and thus achieving his goals. The source of developmental transformation in emotion thus resides in the *relations* among components that comprise the system (Fogel et al., 1992; Griffin & Mascolo, 1998; Witherington, Campos, & Hertenstein, 2001). As envisioned by dynamical systems approaches, these components influence one another so that the system *self-organizes* into relatively stable patterns that differ across age. By way of contrast, traditional explanations have attributed emotional development to factors that they consider to be external to the emotion system. A classic example of such an approach is evident in Emde, Gaensbauer, and Harmon's (1976) biobehavioral shift model of emotional development. By their account, the emergence of social smiling around 2 months and the emergence of fear in multiple contexts around 8 months *reflect* overarching neuromaturational change. To quote Emde et al.: "The emergent affect behavior is not the organizer, it merely indicates it" (p. 8). From the standpoint of biobehavioral shifts, emotional development is determined by outside factors (Emde, Kligman, Reich, & Wade, 1978). Most cognitive theories of emotional development follow a similar line of approach by arguing that emotional development is attendant on the development of specific cognitive prerequisites that are considered external to emotion, such as new representational and memory abilities, the emergence of objective self-awareness, or the emergence of an ability to evaluate behavior against a standard (e.g., Kagan, 1984; M. Lewis, 1998). From a dynamical systems perspective, these factors are intrinsic components of the emotion system in that they become organized in specific configurations during emotion episodes.

When emotion is viewed as self-organization rather than organization from without, it also becomes clear that development may involve components unique to the emotion system such as appraisal. Appraisal, unlike objective self-awareness or recall memory, is an emotion-specific form of cognition, an evaluation of events by an individual's goals and concerns. As such, appraisal is a cognitive-motivational process rather than a purely cognitive one (Barrett & Campos, 1987; Mascolo & Fischer, 1995). The concept of appraisal again highlights the importance of viewing the components of emotion in relation to one another. *Causality* in the emotion system is multiply determined by the relation of many components. Thus, environmental events do not cause the development of emotion independent of an individual's concerns and goals and vice versa. Similarly, evaluations of events do not cause the development of emotion independent of the individual's action repertoire, their goals and concerns, and so on. All of the components that comprise the emotion system thus assume formative significance in understanding stability and transition in emotional development (Fogel et al., 1992).

As an organizational framework, the functionalist approach also provides a useful heuristic for integrating our understanding of the relations that exist among the components of the emotion system. The functionalist approach adopts as its central level of analysis the goal-mediated relation between person and environment and identifies certain commonalities or themes in significant person-environment transactions (Barrett & Campos, 1987; Campos et al., 1994). What any given person is doing in a particular context can be organized by a set of abstracted functional relations—what Lazarus (1991) has termed *core relational themes*—that hold for all potential person-environment transactions, such as "trying to overcome an obstacle to obtain a goal" or "trying to avoid a threat to one's well-being and safety." We have already discussed these general themes in the context of emotion families and relational action tendencies. To organize the enormous behavioral and contextual variability that characterize the emotion process in real-time person-environment

transactions, the functionalist appeals to those themes involving basic matches/mismatches between an individual's concerns and events in the world (Witherington, 2003). For example, many different concrete events can call forth the emotion of anger: the stubbing of a toe, a traffic jam, or misplacing one's keys. For the functionalist, what unites all of these events is their serving as obstacles to goal attainment. Similarly, many different actions can be in the service of the emotion of anger: striking out at others, stonewalling, or finding an alternate route to work. What unites all of these actions is the function they can serve—the removal of an obstacle.

The functionalist thus adopts an abstract level of explanation for emotion and its development that is grounded in the particularities of a person's real-time encounters with the environment but that extracts from these particulars a set of general functional relations. In this way, the functionalist approach provides an invaluable interpretive framework for understanding the emotion process in all of its complexity (Witherington, 2003). However, the question of how specific emotion actions emerge during specific emotion episodes remains largely unaddressed by the functionalist framework. Dynamic systems approaches to the study of emotional development complement the functionalist approach by attempting to address this question (e.g., Camras, 1992; Fogel et al., 1992; Lewis & Granic, 2000). As earlier described, both the functionalist approach and the dynamic systems approach view emotion as a self-organizing, multicomponential system, the patterning of which is multiply determined such that no one component is any more primary in the emergence of pattern than any other. But whereas the functionalist approach sets its sights on providing a meaningful organizational framework for interpreting person-environment transactions, the dynamic systems approach takes as its charge the explanation of the emotion process at the more specific level of real-time action in context. For example, with respect to smiling, Dickson, Walker, and Fogel (1997) have shown how the fine-grained morphology of infant smiling patterns varies in accordance with the particular form of play in which infants and parents are engaged. When play involved book reading, 12-month-olds predominantly displayed smiles consisting only of lip corner raises, but when parent-infant interactions turned to physical play, infant smiling most characteristically involved opened mouth smiling, and when parents playfully vocalized with their infants, infant smiling typically included both lip corner raises and contraction of the orbicularis oculi muscles surrounding the eyes (termed the *Duchenne* smile after the nineteenth-century French neurologist). Furthermore, Duchenne and non-Duchenne smiles—smiles not involving orbicularis oculi contraction—may grade into one another, reflecting a quantitative dimension of positive engagement. In a longitudinal sample of 1- to 6-month-olds observed during play with their mothers, Messinger, Fogel, and Dickson (1999) found that non-Duchene smiles typically preceded in close temporal proximity Duchenne smiles and that this relational correspondence between the two forms did not vary across the age range studied. These findings reveal how intimately involved contextual factors are in the formation of emotion-related actions during real-time parent-infant interactions. Current applications of dynamic systems principles to emotional development, however, are not specific to emotion; rather, the same principles apply to any action-in-context, emotional or otherwise. In the absence of an organizational framework like that provided by the functionalist approach, dynamic systems approaches have yet to offer specific insight into emotion itself as a content domain. Thus, the contribution of dynamic systems approaches to the study of emotional development *as emotional development* remains largely unexplored.

Change in Person-Environment Relations and Emotional Development

Given the importance of person-environment relations in the generation of emotion, it should come as no surprise that factors that alter the relation of person to environment have important consequences for emotional development (Witherington et al., 2001). In the period of infancy, motor achievements such as visually guided reaching, crawling, and walking fundamentally alter the way infants psychologically engage the world and are widely regarded as important points of transition in cognitive and perceptual development. Treating emotion as a multicomponent system suggests that our investigations of emotional development should target such points of motoric transition as well as pervasive ecological changes, such as entering preschool. Developments in a variety of domains result in changing the relation between the person and the world and thus lead to important changes in emotion.

Considerable evidence supports a link between experience with crawling and emotional development (Berten-thal & Campos, 1990; Saarni, Mumme, & Campos, 1998). For example, experience with self-produced locomotion, either through crawling or through the use of a walker, gives rise to the phenomenon of wariness of heights (Campos, Bertenthal, & Kermoian, 1992; Campos et al., 1978). Parents also report major increases in their infants' displays of anger and temper tantrums following crawling onset (Campos, Kermoian, & Zumbahlen, 1992). Furthermore, the emergence of crawling affects the whole socioemotional climate in which the infant resides. Parents of crawling infants embark on new forms of emotional communication with their infants (Campos et al., 1992; Zumbahlen & Crawley, 1996). Once infants begin to crawl, parents direct much more positive affect toward their infants in the context of exploration and the discovery of new events and situations. At the same time, parents begin to regard their infants as more sophisticated and intentional, assigning them more responsibility for their actions. This change, coupled with the increased chance for a mobile infant to encounter dangerous situations, produces a substantial increase in parental targeting of fear and anger to their infants once crawling begins.

Like crawling, infant walking has long been regarded as functionally related to infant emotional development (Mahler, Pine, & Bergman, 1975; Spitz, 1965). Work by Biringen, Emde, Campos, and Appelbaum (1995) provides preliminary support for such a relation. Infants and their mothers in the study showed increased tendencies to test each other's wills and engage in open confrontations once the infants began to walk independently. Infants acted more willful and defiant, and mothers viewed their infants in much more emotionally negative terms following walking onset. Evidence, therefore, suggests that motor milestones such as walking and crawling fundamentally alter the infant, her social world, and her relation to that world and in the process reorganize her emotional life and the emotional climate in which she lives.

Culture, Emotion, and Emotional Development

Our attempts to understand how culture affects emotion and emotional development have changed considerably in the past 30 years. In the 1970s and 1980s, researchers were mostly concerned with universals in emotion expression. The search for universals generated impressive evidence on the similarity of recognition of facial expressions by preliterate tribes (Ekman, 1973; Ekman,

Sorenson, & Friesen, 1969), and judges in both Western and non-Western countries (Izard, 1972). In turn, this evidence led to the widespread use of facial expressions as the preferred indices of emotional states, and motivated the "emotion revolution" of the 1970s and 1980s. The apparent universality of *recognition* of facial expression also led to studies on the *elicitation* of facial expression patterns of anger and fear in infants of different cultures (Camras, Oster, Campos, & Bakeman, 2003; Camras, Oster, Campos, Miyake, & Bradshaw, 1992; Camras et al. 1998) and the development of methods of facial expression measurement based on anatomical criteria and judgments of emotion by coders (Izard & Dougherty, 1982; Oster, 1995). Although many criticisms have been leveled at research on universality of recognition (Fridlund, 1994; Russell, 1994, 1995), they have on the whole not proven entirely convincing (Ekman, 1995; Izard, 1995). As a result, the search for universals continues in cross-cultural studies of patterns of appraisal (Mesquita & Frijda, 1992), speculations about child-rearing functions (Trevarthen, 1988), and attributional biases (Morris & Peng, 1994).

Recently, the study of culture and emotions has broadened considerably beyond the issue of universality to the role of culture in the generation, manifestation, and regulation of emotion (D'Andrade, 1984; Kitayama & Markus, 1994; Lazarus, 1991). Because a complete review of culture and emotion is beyond the scope of this chapter, we will limit ourselves an illustration of how emotion communication accompanies and helps to inculcate cultural values, affects pre- and perinatal emotionality, determines the types of events to which an infant or child is exposed, and creates the emotional climate in which a person is immersed.

What Is Culture and Does Culture Influence Infants?

The concept of culture is rarely defined. For our purposes, *culture* refers to a set of traditional, explicit and implicit beliefs, values, actions, and material environments that are transmitted by language, symbol, and behavior in an enduring and interacting group of people. Because of the centrality of symbols, language, and values for culture, most studies of culture and emotion deal with adults, and especially the language of adults (Wierzbicka, 1992). Infants and children with minimal language skills are generally assumed to be beyond the pale of symbolic influence (Winn, Tronick, & Morelli, 1989). However, symbols, language, and values can have profound direct and indirect effects on the preverbal child. The direct effects result from diet, housing, and the material and physical implements of the culture that are used in child rearing. The indirect effects are largely mediated by two factors: (1) the physical/social context in which the infant is raised, and (2) the exposure of the child to the characteristic behavior patterns and nonverbal communication strategies of members of that culture (Gordon, 1989). So, subtle yet powerful are these direct and indirect effects that the infant can be said to be acculturated beginning at birth and maybe even before (Tronick & Morelli, 1991).

Parental Practices. Although the demand for provision and protection of infants and meeting their needs must be universal, the way in which those needs are defined and met varies enormously. One way that culture influences the infant is through the mother's selection of interventions for regulating social signaling, including the baby's crying and struggling. For this reason, swaddling methods have received a great deal of attention from anthropologists. They have discussed how in Middle Eastern societies swaddling facilitates sleep and transport (Whiting, 1981), soothes the child, and permits the mother to work nearby in kibbutzim (Bloch, 1966), maximizes proximity between mother and child, facilitates responsiveness to the child's social signals, such as in the Navaho nation (Chisholm, 1983, 1989), and brings about desirable habituation and autonomic regulation in response to stimuli in noisy environments (Landers, 1989). In the United States, by contrast, swaddling has been unpopular largely because it restricts freedom of movement (Lipton, Steinschneider, & Richmond, 1965) and possibly produces undesired yet distinctive effects on the formation of characteristic emotional dispositions (Mead, 1954), some of which, such as passivity, are not valued in the United States (Chisholm, 1989).

Another cultural variation in parenting practice evident even in the neonatal period is that of co-sleeping. Co-sleeping has been proposed as a socialization mechanism that fosters attachment throughout life by creating a powerful motivation to remain close to the parent (Abbott, 1992). Although sleeping in separate beds and separate rooms is the norm in the United States, data collected in eastern Kentucky exemplifies the widespread regional variation that can occur in co-sleeping (Abbott, 1992). Co-sleeping occurred across all social classes in eastern Kentucky, but was less common among the college educated. Interview data suggested that co-sleeping did facilitate greater interdependence in the family and fostered close emotional ties early in life. Findings such as these contradict widespread beliefs that the effects of co-sleeping are uniformly negative (see discussion in Morelli, Rogoff, Oppenheim, & Goldsmith, 1992).

Physical activity and infant positioning are other examples of parenting practices related to emotional development and showing considerable variation across cultures. Compared to Americans, Gusii infants are exposed to more light tossing and vigorous handling. Provision of such vigorous stimulation has been proposed to explain how Gusii infants overcome fear by 3 to 4 months of age (Keefer, Dixon, Tronick, & Brazelton, 1991).

A traumatic influence with potentially long-lasting consequences for the newborn is circumcision. Circumcision is a painful procedure often conducted without anesthesia or analgesia. It may well form the nucleus of disturbing and enduring memories for pain. Moreover, cultural variations exist in the circumcision procedure: What was at one time a religious ceremony conducted in an intimate family gathering has become routine medical practice involving medical personnel with the family excluded. The emotional climate provided to the infant during the circumcision ritual in the home (the bris) is vastly different from that provided on a plastic restraint board in a hospital nursery and may also influence the infant's memories for pain. In addition, in religious ceremonies, the circumcised newborn is often given small amounts of sweetened water to drink. Such oral stimulation may help soothe the infant's pain reactions, in the same manner that Blass and Ciaramitaro (1994) have reported that sucrose does for other painful procedures.

The Significance of Exposure to Events.   Culture determines the types of events to which the child is exposed. Emotional reactions are determined not only by transactions taking place in the present but also by the history of prior encounters with similar events in the past. It is as if an adaptation level of experience is built up, and depending on the discrepancy of an event from that adaptation level, the child will show intense, moderate, or weak emotional reactions.

This principle of *adaptation level* is well exemplified in the literature on culture and attachment patterns. In the attachment literature, there is evidence that infants from northern Germany show a preponderance of apparent avoidant patterns of attachment (Grossmann, Grossmann, Huber, & Wartner, 1981). By contrast, in Japan, there is a preponderance of apparently ambivalent and hard-to-soothe infants (Miyake, Chen, & Campos, 1985). In the kibbutzim in Israel, still another pattern of behavior is shown: Infants are extremely upset by the entry of strangers in the attachment testing situation.

What accounts for such different patterns of behavior (Sagi, Lamb, Lewkowicz, Shoham, Dvir, & Estes, 1985)? Why do children in three different areas of the world react to the same events in such dramatically different ways? One interpretation is that the value system of different cultures affects what events infants are exposed to and thus to what events they become emotionally responsive. In northern Germany, for example, infants are frequently left alone outside of stores or supermarkets or in the home while the mother steps out briefly. The pattern of exposure (the adaptation level) to being alone renders maternal separations in attachment testing not a very great departure from that to which the infant is accustomed. As a result, infants with such a background may show little or no upset on a brief maternal separation and have little reason to give a strong response to the mother on reunion. Not surprisingly, 49% of infants tested in the Ainsworth Strange Situation in Germany show the "A" pattern of not directing much attention to the reentry of the mother.

In Japan, there is a very different value system—one in which the mother desires very close proximity to her child. In Japan, babysitting is rare, and when it occurs, it is usually done by the grandparents. Accordingly, Japanese infants have very few experiences with separation from the mother. As a result, when the mother leaves the infant alone or with a stranger in the attachment test, the separation is extremely discrepant from the infant's past experience. As a result, the infant shows considerable upset, and it is thus no surprise that the infant is hard to console after experiencing intense distress on separation. The difficulty in consoling the child results in classifying the child as a "C" infant.

In the kibbutzim in Israel, security measures and the history of unexpected terrorist attacks make for a strong form of xenophobia. Strangers are looked on askance, and they are typically not allowed to approach infants. Because infants are very sensitive to the emotional communication of significant others by 12 months of age, they have become sensitized to be wary of strangers themselves. As a result, when a stranger enters the room and initiates contact or approach to the child, the infant is set to become intensely fearful. Interestingly, in urban Israel, where the xenophobia is usually much less evident, infants do not show such intense negative reactions to strangers. The adaptation level of the kind of reaction that significant others typically give to the infants determines the intensity level of their negative responses. Much xenophobia in caregivers results in high levels of stranger distress; less xenophobia results in considerably lower levels. In sum, the value system of each culture (expectations of independence in northern Germany, desire for extreme proximity in Japan, and the need to protect the community in Israeli kibbutzim) leads to different levels of experience against which new experiences are compared. The culture thus determines both exposure to events and the context for differential emotional reactions.

Other examples of how exposure and values interact to influence emotional-expressive behavior can be found in patterns of eye contact: It is usually encouraged in Western culture, where looking into a baby's eyes forms "a window into the soul." However, in certain African societies, eye contact is generally discouraged. Certain tribes believe that eye contact allows another person to cast an "evil eye" on the infant. As a result, infants are often kept in dark corners of the living hut, and held in a manner that minimizes the chance of eye contact. The end result for the infant is a cool, subdued demeanor (LeVine et al., 1994).

Still another instance of culture determining what an infant is exposed to stems from the work with the Efe in central Africa on multiple mothering (e.g., Tronick, Morelli, & Ivey, 1992). Because maternal mortality is extremely high among the Efe, the culture attempts to compensate for the negative consequences of maternal loss by fostering multiple caregiving. Infants are thus often passed from one person to another, and the infant becomes accustomed to being handled by more than one caregiver. As a result, the loss of the mother becomes much less traumatic for Efe infants than for infants elsewhere.

Culture and Emotional Climate. Emotional climate refers to the characteristic patterning and intensity of verbal and nonverbal emotional communication that is within earshot and eyeshot of an audience. Cultures often differ in such emotional cli-

mates. In some cultures, loudness and extremes of gesticulation are encouraged or tolerated; in others, quiet and peaceful expression is the expectation. Such emotional climate may influence the emotional reaction of infants, children, and adults quite profoundly (Briggs, 1970).

Consider that vocal expression of affect is very pervasive and quite closely linked to the communication of discrete emotion (Scherer, 1986). It is now well known that the fetus can hear sounds in the womb from the seventh gestational month onward. As a result of the transmission of sounds through the amniotic fluid (DeCasper & Fifer, 1980; DeCasper, Lecanuet, Busnel, Granier-Deferre, & Maugeais, 1994; Fifer & Moon, 1995), the unborn infant can acquire considerable experience about patterns and intensities of vocalic emotional communication. Just as the newborn can identify his or her mother's speech within 3 days of birth, it is possible that the newborn can come into the world with built-in expectations of what the typical emotional climate is in the society in which he or she is born.

In Japan, the emotional climate is one of soft vocalizations, few verbalizations, and much gentle stroking of the infant (Miyake, Campos, Kagan, & Bradshaw, 1986). This pattern of softness and low frequency and volume of speech has been attributed to the rice paper walls of the typical Japanese household, together with the Japanese value for harmony and tranquility in the home. To attain these cultural goals of harmony, mothers are charged with the responsibility of keeping volume of communication low and to keep the infant's crying to a minimum. Thus, Japanese mothers communicate with their infants much more by touch and less by vocalization than do American mothers.

Emotional climate is thus a crucial means by which culture affects emotion. It is known that in cultures differing emotional climates have important effects on children. Thus, parental quarreling and fighting can result in infants and children of that family becoming maladjusted and insecure (Davies & Cummings, 1994).

In concluding this discussion of culture and emotion, the emphasis in this chapter should be clear: Emotions are relational and functional (in that they serve a purpose), they are embedded in social communicative relations, they are flexibly responsive to context, and they link our actions with our goals. Consistent with the preceding material on culture and emotional development and with a functionalist approach, in the remaining sections of the chapter we take a systems approach to emotional communication as *multichannel* (or multibehavioral), which includes facial expression, vocal quality, gesture, touch, eye contact, interpersonal distance, and so forth (Scheflen, 1974). With increased exposure and experience, young children's emotional-expressive behavior begins to resemble the normative emotional communicative patterns, as prescribed by the culture in which they live. Social referencing, which is reviewed in the next section, is a key interactive process for facilitating this learning of emotional meaningfulness.

In addition, a systems approach to communication is very useful for understanding the kinds of emotional-social phenomena that develop in the preschool and elementary school years, which are discussed in later sections. These phenomena include self presentation strategies, empathy-mediated prosocial behavior, emotion management, and coping strategies, among others. Systems communication theorists (e.g., Watzlawick, Beavin, & Jackson, 1967) emphasize further that what may be most important about communication is its involvement in the *regulation* of relationships, and their notion of *metacommunication* describes this regulatory function: A message, conveyed by nonverbal behavior, communicates how the content of what is said should be understood. In short, communication about communication is intended to influence us, and such communications are typically emotion laden. We turn next to a discussion of the early development of emotional communication, emphasizing social referencing, not only because it is a particularly well-investigated emotional communication process, but also because it illustrates this metacommunicative function of relationship regulation.

THE DEVELOPMENT OF EMOTIONAL COMMUNICATION IN EARLY LIFE

In previous sections, we have discussed the evocation of emotions in response to alterations in some significant aspect of the infant's relations in the environment. We now discuss how emotions provide signals indicating such a relational change and how such signals thereby can produce an effect on the infant.

It proves surprisingly difficult to study emotional communication in early life. The difficulty stems from a point made over 30 years ago by John Smith (1977) in

his studies of avian communication. He distinguished between the message and the meaning of a communicative signal. According to Smith, "message" refers to the invariant information encoded in the environmental display that comprises a signal, while the "meaning" of the message refers to the signal's predictive value about the behavior of the communicator within a particular situational context.

Put another way, the message is that which can be physically described in the action of a communicator—what can be put on a photograph or an audiotape. The meaning is what the message forecasts about the future behavior of the communicator—whose smile can predict approach, scornful rejection, manifestations of pity, or a simple farewell. The point in Smith's distinction that is so crucial for the study of communication between parent and infant is that one cannot predict meaning from a message with very much accuracy.

Smith emphasized that messages are interpreted in their context for many reasons. These contextual factors can change the meaning of a message, further weakening the apparent close relation between message and meaning we so often take for granted. Sometimes, features of the context enter into the perception of the message, and cause the impact of messages on recipients to be very different than what one would expect. Take the mother smiling at her infant as an example. That smile (a message), has a different meaning and will have a differential impact on the infant, depending on whether the mother smiles when the infant is distressed (which can imply misattunement by the mother with the infant's state) or if the mother smiles while the infant is playing with the mother, which would be an expectable part of a social transaction. Because our research methods involve manipulating the message, they are often not suited to identifying what the meaning is for the child to the extent that there is a cleavage between message and meaning. To maximize the chances that we are studying meaning in emotional communication, we therefore consider emotion communication to have occurred only when a manipulation is shown to have an emotional impact. Studies that only address discrimination of the display by infants (i.e., habituation studies) will not be emphasized here.

In brief, we consider emotional communication to occur whenever one person exhibits emotional behavior and another person witnesses and is affected by that emotional behavior. We look for three components in a thorough study of emotional communication: (1) on the input side, registration of the emotion signal by the perceiver, and (2) on the output side, a valenced response to that signal manifested in the recipient's own expressive or instrumental activity, and (3) in between, some degree of appraisal of the input such that the appraisal may change both the significance of the input and the nature of the emotional response. Registration refers to the perception of an expression of emotion (or some component of that expression) and includes the ability to distinguish among expressions of different emotions. (Habituation and preferential looking studies focus on the registration of emotion signals.) A valenced response is one that can be reasonably interpreted as reflecting the content of the internal appraisal and motivation processes on the part of the infant such as approach or avoidance, smiling or frowning. Valenced responses, whether expressive or instrumental, can be diffuse (oriented at no particular event in the world) or targeted at some specific object in the world or at one's own actions. We also emphasize that we use the term *appraisal* broadly without implying the necessary involvement of higher-order cognitive processes. As we review empirical findings, one concern that we raise is about the rush that sometimes exists to attribute to the infant understandings of meanings when these three criteria have not been met.

We delineate four phases of increasingly complex emotional communication between an adult and the infant. Phase 1 (prenatal to 6 weeks) describes the infant's initial valenced reactions to emotion signals. Phase 2 (6 weeks to 7 to 9 months) covers the developmental period preceding the advent of referentiality (i.e., understanding that a communicative signal may refer to some external aspect of the environment). Phase 3 (9 months to 18 months/2 years) focuses on the development of referential emotion communication, behavioral regulation (i.e., where the expressive and instrumental behaviors of the child are affected by the other's emotional expressions), and retention of the emotion signal's impact over progressively longer durations. Phase 4 (18 months/2 years and beyond) is marked by the development of what the literature calls self-conscious emotions, but which, following Watson (personal communication, April 1999), we call "other-conscious emotions" because they depend on the child's detecting the expressive and instrumental reactions of others to his or her own behaviors. We also hypothesize that during this period, marked improvements take place in the child's comprehension of the different "meanings" carried out by different negative emotional messages such as fear versus anger.

Phase 1 (Prenatal to 6 Weeks): Initial Reactions to Emotion Signals

In the neonatal period that extends from birth to 4 to 6 weeks, rudimentary valenced responses to emotional messages clearly exist as evidenced by two findings. First, as a consequence of prenatal exposure, newborns respond to the valence of speech prosody produced in their mother's native language but not in nonmaternal languages (Mastropieri & Turkewitz, 1999). Second, newborns appear capable of responding with cries and negative facial expressions to the cries of another neonate (Dondi, Simion, & Caltran, 1999).

Neonates' Responsiveness to Emotion Prosody

Because the newborns' behavioral repertoire is extremely limited, garnering evidence for the infant's responsiveness to emotional expression presents a major challenge to researchers. In an ingenious study, Mastropieri and Turkewitz (1999) examined neonates' eye widening in reaction to speech produced in either the mother's native language or in a novel language using neutral, happy, sad, or angry prosody. Increased eye widening was found in response to happy prosody, but only for speech produced in the maternal language. This pattern of results suggest that early discrimination of vocalic emotion is not an innate capacity, but instead appears to be based on prenatal experience with a specific language. Furthermore, there is as yet no evidence for discrimination beyond the distinction between positive and neutral or negative vocalic emotion.

Neonatal Crying Contagion. Although to date no one has demonstrated discrimination among vocalic expressions of different discrete negative emotions (e.g., anger, sadness, fear), there is strong evidence for a valenced response to crying. The contagious crying phenomenon has been documented repeatedly, and constitutes a remarkable demonstration of the presence of emotional communication in the neonatal period (e.g., Martin & Clark, 1982; Sagi & Hoffman, 1976; Simner, 1971). Newborns tend to cry in response to the cries of another newborn, though not those of an older infant, a chimpanzee, or white noise. In a methodologically rigorous replication of earlier studies, Dondi et al. (1999) found that neonates decreased their rate of sucking and also showed increased facial distress to cries of unfamiliar infants. Because their expressions of distress were demonstrated in a different modality than the distress stimulus itself (viz., the cry of the other neonate), newborns apparently may not have been merely mimicking the vocal stimulus, but rather truly reacting to the meaning of the cry of the other child. Interestingly, Martin and Clark (1982) reported two fascinating phenomena: (1) that recordings of the babies' own cries resulted in some reduction of their own cries, and (2) that the neonatal crying contagion dropped out by 5 months of age. Both phenomena pose challenges for future research because they require replication and, if replicated, careful study of the processes involved in each.

Phase 2 (6 Weeks to 9 Months): Pre-Referential Communication

During this period, the infant can engage in synchronous dyadic interaction with the caregiver. This phenomenon indicates some limited ability to apprehend the caregiver's emotional valence, understand when the caregiver is targeting her or his emotion toward the infant, and then align her or his own emotional valence and behavior to be congruent with that exhibited by the caregiver. Two other phenomena appear to be well established about emotional communication in this time period. First, infants respond differentially to the valence of mothers' vocal contours (Fernald, 1993). Second, infants discriminate facial expressions as stimulus patterns but show no convincing evidence of comprehending their specific emotion meanings. Some investigators have obtained data that they interpret as demonstrating more substantial communication competencies—a relatively full comprehension of the rich emotional messages generated by the caregiver. While these interpretations are plausible, the research paradigms employed are not suitable to yield the unambiguous inferences that have been drawn from them.

Evidence for Rudimentary Emotional Exchange and Its Constituents

As in the previous period, the strongest evidence of infants' responsiveness to emotional signals comes from studies using acoustic stimuli. The responsiveness to vocalic communication markedly exceeds that evidenced in the neonatal period, exhibiting differentially valenced responses to the valence of adults' emotional signals. For example, in a study noteworthy for its methodological rigor and conceptual richness, Fernald (1993) presented 5-month-old infants with acoustic stimuli specifying prohibition or encouragement of ap-

proach. She reported that 5-month-olds smiled more in response to infant-directed messages specifying "approval" than to messages specifying "prohibition" irrespective of whether the message was produced in English or in an unfamiliar language (German or Italian). Negative affect was more likely to occur in response to prohibitions. Fernald's investigation offers a strong demonstration that by 5 months of age, infants are able to discriminate the emotional valence of acoustic messages and to transform differential message content into congruent behavioral reactions that are either appropriately positive or negative. The issue of whether infants can respond at this age to more specific emotional meanings (e.g., fear versus anger) at this age has not been addressed.

A number of other studies investigate infants' differentially valenced responses in dyadic setting. Numerous investigations (e.g., Cohn & Tronick, 1988; Feldman, Greenbaum, & Yirmiya, 1999; Field, Healy, Goldstein, & Guthertz, 1990; Jaffe, Beebe, Feldstein, Crown, & Jasnow, 2001; Moore & Calkins, 2004) have demonstrated what many call "interactional synchrony," but which we conservatively call "expressive coincidence"—contingencies in the timing of positive or negative expressions during face-to-face interactions between mothers and infants even younger than 3 months of age. More specific "matching" (what we prefer to call "co-occurrence") in the level of positive or negative affect has also been shown (Feldman et al., 1999; Tronick & Cohn, 1989; Weinberg, Tronick, Cohn, & Olson, 1999).

Many of these studies claim to have demonstrated a process of direct and unmediated emotion contagion (Haviland & Lelwica, 1987; Stern, 1985; Trevarthen & Hubley, 1978). However, in our own view, what appears to be direct mutual mirroring between mother and child may instead result from the operation of two other powerful and rudimentary determinants of emotion—contingency and agency (or lack thereof). Lewis and his colleagues (e.g., Lewis, Hitchcock, & Sullivan, 2004), following the pioneering work of J. S. Watson (1972), have unequivocally shown that infants as young as 2 months of age smile when their actions produce a contingent effect on the world and evidence distress when a previously operative contingency fails. Studies of affective synchrony may sometimes confound contingency and its failure with direct affective matching. Thus when contingent reciprocal smiling takes place, it might produce similar emotional responses in mother and baby. However, such shared emotion need not depend on either direct contagion or (alternatively) on the infant's in-depth comprehension of the emotional meaning of the smile. A simpler explanation is that the infant smiles contingently at the mother not because the baby sees a smile, but because the baby notices a contingent reaction that happens to be a smile.

In some of the broadest claims in this literature, researchers propose that processes of synchrony and matching may contribute to the development of emotion regulation (Feldman et al., 1999; Moore, Cohn, & Campbell, 2001) and attachment (Jaffe et al., 2001). For example, mothers' positive emotion signals may induce a more positive response in their infants and may also contribute to the development of a secure attachment relationship. This conclusion has obvious intuitive and emotional appeal, in that it reflects the notion that emotional bonds are built on shared evaluations and experiences. However, we think it critically important to also emphasize that not all maternal smiles directed at the infant are positive in their impact: Maternal responses must be context sensitive rather than always synchronous. For example, Stern (1974) reports that if the infant is attempting to terminate an interaction and the mother continues to force her smiling presence into the infant's visual field (effectively making a demand that the infant suppress her or his negative affect and return the smile), then such maternal insensitivity may result in interactional failure. The same may be said if the mother's first response to the infant's crying is to smile, rather than to present the infant first with sympathy, which the mother then transforms into a smile, paced with the infant (Holodinski & Friedlmeier, in press). If such failures are chronic, they may contribute to the etiology of psychopathology (Gergely & Watson, 1996, 1999; Holodinski & Freidlmeier, in press).

The still-face paradigm provides another interesting context in which to appreciate the ambiguities of studying emotion communication in young infants. In the still-face procedure, normal face-to-face infant-adult interaction is disrupted by an episode in which the adult ceases all movement and thus fails to respond to the infant's signals. The still-face effect rests primarily on the cessation of facial rather than vocal signals (Striano & Bertin, 2004). Furthermore, differential effects of positive versus negative or neutral expressions also have been reported. Rochat, Striano, and Blatt (2002) showed that 2-month-old infants maintained their smiling and gazing if the experimenter posed a smile rather than a neutral or sad expression. This finding suggests that infants' affinity/preference for happy expressions can overcome the negative emotional impact of contingency disruption that normally occurs in the still-face procedure, although the effect of the smile is not strong. Alternatively, infants may find the happy still-face to be less discrepant from their normal experience because they are exposed to smiles more often than neutral or sad expressions in the course of their day-to-day social interactions. Interestingly, Rochat et al. (2002) found that 4- and 6-month-old infants responded equivalently to still-face disruptions involving happy, neutral, or sad expressions. However, in a study that manipulated mothers' sequencing of happy or sad expressive behavior during the course of nondisrupted social interaction, D'Entremont and Muir (1999) found that 5-month-old infants smiled more to happy than to sad facial expressions (irrespective of the presence or absence of the voice). Taken together, these findings suggest that older babies perceive differences among emotional expressions but their common response to happy and sad still-face poses may have been determined by the disruption of contingency that was equivalent across the expression conditions. This again illustrates the important point that emotion communication, including the impact of the signal on the recipient, will depend in part on contextual features—in this case, the maintenance and disruption of previously learned contingencies. The flow of contingencies may be as or more important in determining the infant's emotional responses than the flow of emotional contents between persons.

Weaknesses in the Evidence for Discrimination of Discrete Emotional Signals

The evidence reviewed earlier considered infants' discrimination of and responsiveness to the valence of emotional signals. Another substantial body of research has focused on characterizing infants' abilities in this age range to discriminate among discrete emotional signals. Much of this research has employed experimental procedures (i.e., habituation and preferential looking procedures), originally designed to investigate the discrimination of one display from a second, when those two displays differ in only one dimension or feature, for example, in pitch, hue, size, numerosity, and so forth. In our view, the application of these techniques to the problem of differential perception of emotional signals is problematic. The expressive stimuli presented in these studies involve a complex set of features and these studies fail to isolate those aspects of the stimuli to which infants are attending and responding. For example, using a habituation procedure that employed several models showing variations of each emotional expression, Serrano, Iglesias, and Loeches (1992, 1995) claim infants in this age period distinguish between and respond differentially to static facial expressions of happiness, sadness, anger, and fear on the basis of their emotion-defining features. However, the Serrano et al. studies, like many others, make these claims without systematically isolating *which* stimulus features infants attend to and influence their behavior.

Similar problems exist with studies claiming to demonstrate that infants in this age range distinguish among multimodal expressions of emotion. For example, Montague and Walker-Andrews (2002) employed a familiar infant game (peek-a-boo), reporting that 4-month-old infants distinguish between facial and vocal displays of happiness, sadness, anger, and fear. Yet, it is hard to identify in this study the specific determinants of infants' differential responses, whether the stimulus or the violation of some contingent relation that the infant has come to expect, is the basis for their findings.

The problem of attributing to the infant a rich participation in emotional exchange is not restricted to discrimination studies using static displays of emotions but extends as well to studies of dynamic emotion stimuli. Investigations utilizing the intermodal preference method (involving preferential looking toward a facial expression that corresponds to an emotion vocalization) have reported that 14-week-olds can match facial and vocal expressions for happiness, sadness, and anger when they are displayed by their mothers (although not when they are displayed by unfamiliar persons; Kahana-Kalman & Walker-Andrews, 2001; Montague & Walker-Andrews, 2002). Walker-Andrews (1997) has argued that intermodal matching constitutes evidence for some understanding of affective meaning and has labeled this phenomenon emotion *recognition*. However, because intermodal matching may involve simple associative mechanisms, we prefer to interpret these results as evidence for discrimination of one multimodal affective signal pattern from another, but we are skeptical that these studies get at the issue of the infant's recognition of emotion meaning. As with studies involving only facial or only vocal emotion signals, these studies do not tell us what the physical basis for the infant's discriminative responding in multimodal displays, much less the emotional meaning of the displays (in Smith's terms, as discussed previously).

Studies purporting to demonstrate in postneonatal infants contagion not of crying but of quite specific emotions also are subject to overinterpretation. For example, in a study of 10-week-old infants, Haviland and Lelwica (1987) reported that babies mirrored happy and angry facial expressions in response to their mothers' facial and vocal displays, and exhibited nonspecific mouthing movements in response to sad displays. While all these findings are intriguing, we think it an overinterpretation to claim (as do Haviland and Lelwica) that emotion contagion occurred in this study. In our view, to distinguish emotion contagion from the superficial imitation of facial actions, infants must be observed to display clear indicators of the emotion in a form that differs from the observed stimulus. The strong evidence needed to support such broad attributions has not been presented in any study to date.

Phase 3 (9 Months to 18 Months): Behavioral Regulation and Referential Communication

The infant undergoes a major set of cognitive, social, emotional, agentic, and perceptual changes in the age period that we are about to review. These changes have marked impact on the emotional communication of the infant. The most significant change for our purposes is the emergence of the infant's ability to engage in referential gestural communication (i.e., what it is that the mother is emoting about). Prior to 8 to 10 months, infants typically do not show any reliable tendency to follow the gaze or pointing gesture of the parent. By 9 months, infants begin to show such referential understanding, which becomes progressively more specific with the child's advancing age, and culminates in the baby being able to identify the approximate coordinates of where the experimenter or mother is looking or pointing (Bakeman & Adamson, 1984; Campos et al., 2000; Mumme, Bushnell, DiCorcia, & Lariviere, in press). The implications of this new ability is that the infant becomes capable of engaging in what has been called a "two-person communication about a third event," becomes able to link quite precisely the target of the mother's or experimenter's pointing and gaze, and increasingly becomes able to retain the emotional impact of prior emotional messages (i.e., shows affective memory).

During this period, the infant also becomes able to draw another person's attention to events of significance to herself (i.e., the infant shows affective sharing). In addition, the infant becomes increasingly able to retain the affective impact of prior emotional signals (i.e., shows affective memory). The changes shown by the infant during this age period enable her to imbue environmental events with affective meaning as imposed by parents' or others' emotional messages. In some cases, these emotion messages may even alter the valence of infants' reactions to events. However, during this age period, the infant may still show major deficiencies in processing certain aspects of the emotion message (e.g., the specific negative emotion indicated by a negatively valenced signal). As such deficiencies are overcome, the infant is prepared for a fourth stage in development of emotional communication.

Onset of Emotional Communication Involving Environmental Objects

Two studies clearly document how the infant by 8.5 months of age becomes capable of reacting to the social signals of the mother directed at a third event. In one study (Boccia & Campos, 1989), the infant's reaction to strangers was markedly affected by whether the mother posed a stern or cheery greeting and facial expression when a stranger walked into the room. In the second study (Svedja, 1981), the mother's vocalization of the baby's name followed by a nonsense phrase ("tat fobble") resulted in cessation of the infant's approach to a toy that was significantly longer when the vocalization was uttered in a fearful or angry manner than when it was uttered joyfully. These studies demonstrate that referential communication occurs in infants as young as 8.5 months of age for facial and vocal expressions combined and for vocal expressions produced alone. Regarding responses to facial expressions produced alone, while several studies have demonstrated regulatory effects in 12-month-olds (e.g., Camras & Sachs, 1991; Gunnar & Stone, 1984; Klinnert, 1984; Zarbatany & Lamb, 1985), none has investigated infants at younger ages. In addition, no studies to date have examined behavioral regulation in response to emotion signals produced in either modality by babies younger than 8.5 months of age. Thus, the precise age of onset for behavioral regulation with respect to environmental objects or events is not currently known.

Effects of Emotional Communication in Older Infants

In contrast to younger infants, there has been considerable research on older (10- to 14-month-old) infants' behavioral regulation in response to emotion signals. In an early and powerful demonstration of this phenomenon, Sorce, Emde, Campos, and Klinnert (1985) showed that 12-month-old infants referenced their mother (i.e., looked toward her) when they reached a mid-level drop-off on the visual cliff and most proceeded to cross if she displayed a facial expression of happiness or interest but not of sadness, anger, or fear. The mid-level drop-off induced a state of uncertainty in the infants and they therefore sought information from their mother to help them determine whether to proceed across the cliff. Through their actions, infants demonstrated that they did more than merely register their mothers' emotion signals; they displayed a valenced response reflecting an attempt to maintain or change their relation to the environment.

Primacy of Facial versus Vocal Signals

A current controversy among investigators of behavioral regulation centers on the relative effectiveness of emotion signals produced in different modalities (e.g., facial versus vocal). Because it is virtually impossible to ensure that signal intensity is equated across modalities, attempts to make direct comparisons between facial and vocal expressions may be misleading. Furthermore, the fact that vocal signals can be inescapably imposed on the infant more readily than facial signals may create a false impression that vocal expressions are more effective behavioral regulators. In reality, this differential effectiveness may sometimes be attributable to the differential registration of the signal by the infant. Empirical studies of facial versus vocal signaling have produced mixed results. Mumme, Fernald, and Herrera (1996) found that facial but not vocal expressions influenced infants' behavioral reaction toward a toy, and Vaish and Striano (2004) found that infants responded more readily on the visual cliff to maternal positive vocal signals than to smiling. However, as cited earlier, other investigations show that infants do indeed alter their behavior in response to facial expressions produced without accompanying vocalizations. Some inconsistencies across studies may be due to differences in the emotions that are examined and in the nature of the regulatory response observed (e.g., behavior toward the mother versus toward the target object, response to the first delivery of the signal versus later trials). Thus, further research is necessary to identify both the signal and the situational parameters that determine the specific effects of both facial and vocal signals of emotion on infants' behavior. In addition, modalities other than facial expression and vocalization should be examined. For example, in a recent study, Hertenstein and Campos (2001) showed that infants respond to maternal tactile behaviors that might be interpreted as indicating a negative emotional response (i.e., gently squeezing the abdomen as the infant reached toward a toy).

Referential Specificity

Referential specificity constitutes the notion that infants understand that an emotional expression is uniquely directed toward the object of the expresser's attention rather than to other objects in the environment or to no particular object at all. Without referential specificity, infants may misinterpret emotion signals, for example, linking mother's disgust display directed, say, at an insect, to a nontargeted object, or even to the infant herself. Thus, referential specificity requires the infant to identify more precisely the object of an emotion signal and respond in an appropriately selective manner. Several recent studies (e.g., Hertenstein & Campos, 2004; Moses, Baldwin, Rosinsky, & Tidball, 2001; Mumme & Fernald, 2003; Phillips, Wellman, & Spelke, 2002; Rapacholi, 1998) have investigated referential specificity by comparing infants' responses to targeted versus nontargeted objects. Such studies have found evidence for referential specificity in infants as young as 12 months of age. Referentially specific responding implies that the infant's behavior reflects more than merely the general induction of emotion that might affect behavior with respect to all objects and events encountered in the environment. Nonetheless, a generalized emotional reaction and more specific referential responding are not mutually exclusive processes. Indeed, a number of studies have analyzed infants' own emotional expressions in response to the adult's emotion signals and produced evidence for an alteration of the infant's own expressions of emotion as well as the child's instrumental, voluntary behaviors (e.g., Boccia & Campos, 1989; Mumme & Fernald, 2003). However, these effects are inconsistently found (e.g., Hertenstein & Campos, 2004) and the factors that determine whether or not infants' own emotional expressions are altered have yet to be determined.

Affect Specificity

Affect specificity refers to the infant's ability to make qualitative distinctions among emotions of the same valence (e.g., distinguish anger from fear). Most studies of behavioral regulation have compared reactions to positive versus negative emotional expressions (typically happiness versus fear or disgust). The accumulated evidence leaves little doubt that infants respond to the meaning of these signals at the level of their positive or negative emotional valence. However, in contrast to referential specificity, the issue of affect specificity has received relatively little attention.

Regarding distinctions among the negative emotions, Sorce et al. (1985) have attempted to systematically compare fear, anger, and sadness expressions in the same experimental procedure. In their study, almost no infants crossed the modified visual cliff when mothers displayed an expression of fear or anger, while approximately a third of the babies did proceed to cross in response to the sad expression. Although these findings suggest that 12-month-old infants distinguish among different negative emotions, one possible interpretation is that they distinguish on the basis of emotional intensity (i.e., degree of negativity) but do not understand the qualitatively different relational meanings and functional implications of fear versus anger versus sadness.

Another indication that infants in this phase of development may not be differentially responsive to discrete negative emotional signals comes from a study by Bingham, Campos, and Emde (1987). In this study, 13- to 15-month-old infants encountered a doll whose arm appeared to break and fall off when the infant touched it. At the same time, the experimenter uttered the nonsense phrase "Tat fobble" using a facial expression and vocal tone appropriate for one of six basic emotions: fear, sadness, surprise, joy, disgust, or anger. Videotapes of the procedure allowed for manipulation checks of the experimenter's emotion poses and examination of the infant's own expressive and instrumental responses. This study yielded highly significant differentiation of behavior along a hedonic tone dimension, such that negative emotions elicited withdrawal behaviors and positive emotions elicited greater duration of play with the doll than did the negative signals. However, infants did not respond differently in either expression or instrumental behavior to the different negative emotions. This lack of response differentiation took place despite the paradigm affording the opportunity for the infant to respond differently (e.g., showing nurturance to the doll or the experimenter in response to experimenter sadness versus showing avoidance of either the doll or the experimenter in response to anger). The authors concluded that perhaps infants at this age were not yet able to react differentially to emotional signals more specific than positive versus negative. They also cautioned for the need of further research to validate their tentative conclusion about the lack of differential behavioral regulation by discrete emotion signals.

Retention of Valenced Effects of Emotional Communication

Another important issue in the study of behavioral regulation is the duration of a signal's effect on the behavior of the infant. If emotional expressions are to play a significant role in social and emotional development, their impact must extend beyond the immediate context of occurrence.

Relatively few studies have examined the enduring effects of emotion communication. However, not surprisingly, these have found the period of effectiveness to increase with infant age. For example, Svejda's study (1981; summarized in Campos, Thein, & Owen, 2003) of vocal communication provided evidence of carryover effects across trials separated by 1-minute delays for 8.5-month-old infants. Examining older infants, Hertenstein and Campos (2004) found that 11-month-olds showed differential behavioral regulation (i.e., referential specificity) when the delay between exposure to the signal and the infant's opportunity to respond was 3 minutes but not when it was extended to 60 minutes. In contrast, the effectiveness of the emotion signal was retained across a 1-hour delay in 14-month-old babies. One study of behavioral regulation has also provided suggestive data indicating that there may be systematic individual differences in infants' retention of emotion signals. In an investigation of 10- and 15-month-olds, Bradshaw (1986; Campos et al., 2003) found behavioral effects across a 25-minute delay period for only a subset of participants.

The Development of Affective Sharing by the Infant

While studies of behavioral regulation have largely focused on infants' responses to adults' affective expressions, emotion communication is a bidirectional process in which both parties in a dyadic interaction may generate as well as receive emotion signals. Evidence for infants' deliberate targeting of their own emotional expressions can be found for babies as young as 7 months of age. In a study of infants' responses to arm restraint, Stenberg and Campos (1990) found that infants at this age directed their negative expressive responses toward their mothers rather than toward the site of the frustration (i.e., their restrained hands). In a further investigation of the phenomenon, Conrad (1994; Campos et al., 2003) studied the consequences of infants encountering a display of a monkey clashing cym-

bals while the mother was located some distance away. She reported that 11.5-month-old infants (but not 9-month-old infants) directed emotional expression toward their mothers more often when their mothers were facing toward the infant rather than facing away. Likewise, Jones, Collins, and Hong (1991) found that 10-month-old infants produced "anticipatory smiles" (i.e., smiles that were followed by looks toward their mother) more often when mothers were attending to their play rather than reading a magazine. Similar results also were obtained by Striano and Rochat (2000) and Venezia, Messinger, Thorpe, and Mundy (2004) for 10-month-old infants using a different emotion induction procedure. Results of these studies converge to suggest that intentional affect sharing by infants emerges at around the same time as their understanding of referential specificity in the emotion communications of others. Beyond this, infants appear to be attempting to influence the recipient by "bringing affective events to her attention."

Phase 4 (18 Months/2 Years and Beyond): The Rise of Other-Conscious Emotions

In the next phase of the development of emotional communication, we believe that two significant changes take place in the infant's reactions to emotional signals from others. One is the establishment of differential expressive and instrumental behavioral responses to different emotion signals of the same valence (e.g., anger versus fear). The second is a major change in the infant's construal of the two-person communication about a third event leading to what are commonly called the "self-conscious" emotions (e.g., shame, guilt, pride), but which, the reader will recall, we prefer to call "other-conscious" emotions to note the importance of the emotional reactions of others in their generation. In contrast to the previous age periods, we acknowledge that our description of this phase includes considerable—albeit grounded—speculation. Therefore, several of our proposals regarding Phase 4 remain to be confirmed empirically.

Affect Specificity Revisited

To date, strong evidence demonstrating infants' abilities to make qualitative distinctions among emotions of the same valence is lacking. Nonetheless, in an exploratory study involving a small number of participants, E. Anderson (1994) observed a tendency for infants in this age range to respond differentially when an experimenter gazed at an unfamiliar food item while verbalizing "Look at that" using sad, angry, disgusted, fearful, or happy vocalizations and facial expressions. For example, 18-month-old female infants tended to give the item to the experimenter in response to a sad emotion message but tended to pick it up and eat it in response to a happy message.

Beyond such preliminary data, a survey of the infant literature suggests that by 18 months of age infants may indeed understand the specific meanings and implications of some negative emotions. Infants' affect vocabulary develops rapidly around this age (Dunn, Bretherton, & Munn, 1987) and includes words for several negative emotions (e.g., scary, yucky, mad). Furthermore, Zahn-Waxler and Radke-Yarrow (1990) found that by 2 years of age many infants show appropriate empathic/sympathetic responses to other persons' expressions of distress. In a study involving experimenter-produced expressions of disgust, Rapacholi (1998) showed that 18-month-old infants produced an emotionally appropriate response (i.e., avoiding the disgust-targeted food item when choosing a food item for the experimenter). However, data produced in all these studies are subject to possible interpretations that do not involve the necessary imputation of affect specificity in the infant's understanding of the emotion message. Therefore, this issue remains an important challenge in the area of emotion communication.

The Development of Other-Conscious Emotions

The fourth phase in the development of emotional communication also involves the generation of complex emotions that may require, for their generation, the integration of a number of higher-order cognitive, perceptual, and retentive capacities. These emotions include embarrassment, shame, guilt, and pride. According to Michael Lewis (e.g., Lewis, 1993) these emotions begin to develop between 15 and 18 months, and are in part the consequences of the development of self-recognition as indexed by the "rouge" task. In this well-known paradigm, an infant in this developmental phase will detect and respond appropriately to the sight of a dot of rouge surreptitiously placed on her nose and viewed only in a mirror reflection. Successful performance on the rouge/mirror self-recognition task is taken to indicate the origins of a reflective self that in turn permits the emergence of self-conscious emotions (see Lewis & Brooks-Gunn, 1979; Lewis & Ramsay, 2004). Lewis has called these emotions "self-conscious" because of the link between mirror self-recognition and other indices of self-development, on the one hand, and the onset of

these emotions, on the other hand. As indicated earlier, we prefer to designate them as other-conscious emotions because they rest on the child's detecting other persons' reactions to the child or her behavior.

We believe that emotional communication plays a necessary role in the development of these emotions. Indeed, as noted earlier, the emotions of embarrassment, guilt, shame, and pride may come about as a result of the emerging appreciation by the child of the meaning of the communication by others of anger, sadness, fear, contempt, and other emotions. In other words, the child must first perceive these emotions in others, differentiate them one from the other, know to whom these emotions are being targeted, and have a sense of responsibility by the child in the elicitation of these emotions in others. We also believe that some of these emotions, particularly anger and contempt, are likely to be part of the elicitation of some complex emotions (especially shame), but not of others (particularly guilt).

More specifically, we propose that embarrassment and shame come about when the infant conducts an action toward a third event in the world (including toward himself, considered as an object) and that action elicits certain negative emotional signals such as scorn/disgust, anger, sadness, and general disapproval. By way of contrast, we propose that guilt occurs when the infant becomes aware that his or her actions produce emotions in another person that take the form of sadness, pain/suffering, disappointment, fear, and other variants of these emotion families. Thus, the set of emotion signals that produce shame and guilt are overlapping but not identical. For example, if another person shows fear in response to the infant's action, guilt is more likely to be produced than shame because the emotions that produce shame are emotions that typically lower the power and status of the child in the eyes of the other. Fear is not usually relevant to such status reduction. In sum, discrete emotions may be necessary, and the infant may need clearly to distinguish their different meanings, in order for the more complex emotions of shame, guilt, and pride to form.

If this reasoning is supported by empirical data (and we know of none relevant to the point at this writing), the child must begin to differentiate negative emotions from one another as a necessary prerequisite for generating two related but quite different emotions of shame and guilt. Indeed, the general action tendencies linked to shame (attempts to discontinue social intercourse) and guilt (attempts to engage in reparation of damage to another, which damage has been created by one's actions) require that the emotional signaling to which the shamed or guilty person is subjected be different. Another person's fear has no bearing on discontinuance of one's interaction with that person; another person's scorn or anger does. By contrast, when a person reacts with scorn or anger directed at a child who has done something damaging to another, the offending party is not likely to experience or to express guilt. Guilt is a response to the suffering of another presumably caused by one's self; scorn and anger are not indicators of suffering (Campos, Thein, & Owen, 2003).

Furthermore, we believe that the same emotion message (e.g., sadness) may generate different self-conscious emotions depending on the context in which it occurs. For instance, sadness may elicit guilt when it is expressed after a child engages in a disapproved action but may elicit shame when it is directed to the child herself. Anger may not elicit guilt when it is expressed after a child engages in a hurtful action.

In conclusion, our focus has been on early development in illustrating the theoretical perspective taken in this essay. In the next section, we turn to an extended discussion of recent empirical research undertaken with preschoolers, school-age children, and adolescents. Much of the recent research with these older children and youth embeds emotional experience in social interaction, whether the focus is on socialization of emotional expression norms or on emotion knowledge as applied to social effectiveness. There is also a greater emphasis on the development of the self as related to emotional development, and we address this link in our discussion of self-conscious emotions as well as in our discussion of adolescent "true self" development. Finally, we once again examine emotion regulation research in this older age group relative to temperament influence and the development of coping strategies. Throughout the next section, we also suggest topics for further research, which are also highlighted in our conclusion.

EMOTIONAL DEVELOPMENT IN CHILDHOOD AND ADOLESCENCE: SOCIAL EFFECTIVENESS AND POSITIVE ADAPTATION

Noteworthy in recent research has been the greater emphasis given to how children's and youth's emotional development is manifest in their social competence. Although appraisal processes and the regulation of emotion continue to garner much scientific attention, our emphasis on the functional nature of emotional experience is especially relevant to how *social goals* are the fulcrum around which a great deal of emotion is elicited, experienced, and expressed.

Social psychologists have long examined the question of what constitutes well-being or positive adaptation, and a review of that literature is not appropriate here (for a brief review, see Diener & Lucas, 2000); however, what that research does consider is the extent to which social effectiveness and well-being are personality traits or dependent on the situation a person finds her- or himself in, especially if there has been a sudden change. The research on children's emotion regulation suggests that to some extent a proneness to negative emotion, which may function much like a temperamental disposition, may be related to social adjustment (for reviews, see Eisenberg & Morris, 2002; Swanson, Hemphill, & Smart, 2004). As an illustration of such research that attempts to tease apart the influences on children's resilience and adjustment, we consider a recent longitudinal study by Eisenberg and colleagues (Eisenberg et al., 2004).

Social Adjustment and Emotion Regulation

Eisenberg and her colleagues (2004) differentiate between *effortful* control—the ability to voluntarily inhibit or activate behavior—and *reactive* control—the relatively inflexible tendency to be either overly inhibited or impulsive. Although both types of control have their roots in children's temperament, the former construct is considered by Eisenberg and her colleagues as pivotal to their definition of *effortful emotion regulation* (Eisenberg & Spinrad, 2004), whereas the latter construct, reactive control, is less accessible to voluntary control and is linked to temperamental reactivity. Reactive control is also more often linked to problems of adjustment when this characteristic is particularly pronounced in the individual child, in large part due to its involuntary nature. Eisenberg and colleagues cite Block and Kremen's theorizing (Block & Kremen, 1996), which stipulates that most of us would like to operate with as little control as possible and with only as much control as necessary. When these are adaptively functioning and in balance, then the individual is operating in an ego-resilient fashion. However, the individual can be prone to excessive control and thus be maladaptively inhibited or prone to insufficient control and similarly maladaptively impulsive. If these less adaptive tendencies are elicited when faced with taxing stressors, then Block and Kremen suggest that the individual is not responding with resilience.

Eisenberg et al. (2004) examined how effortful control and reactive undercontrol were related to children's internalizing and externalizing problems over a 2-year period. Both parents' and teachers' ratings of the children's behavior were obtained, and the children themselves were observed doing a puzzle that required sustained effort to solve. The sample ranged from 4.5 to 8 years old, and they were reassessed 2 years later. The results were very complex, indicating that there is no simple path between emotion-laden qualities such as effortful control and reactive control to subsequent social adjustment. The clearest outcome was that impulsivity and insufficient effortful control were directly predictive of externalizing problems, and this relationship was even stronger if the children were rated by their teachers as high in dispositional anger. Proneness to sadness did not moderate this relationship, but as the authors point out, such externalizing children often do experience sadness due to peer rejection. The latter is understood to be a situational response of sadness as opposed to a "dispositional" proneness to sadness.

A recent study undertaken with toddlers (Lawson & Ruff, 2004) used constructs similar to the Eisenberg et al. research. The results also indicated that negative emotionality and ability to sustain attention predicted later behavioral outcomes. More specifically, maternal ratings of emotional lability and proneness to irritability at age 2, defined by the authors as their index of "negative emotionality," and trained observers' ratings of attentiveness during frustrating play episodes with the mother combined to predict cognitive function (IQ) and problem behavior ratings (maternal ratings) at age 3.5 years. Their results indicated that when young children have both risk factors, low attentiveness and proneness to negative emotionality, at a young age, they are likely to obtain both lower IQ scores and be rated as significantly demonstrating more problem behavior. The authors refer to this as the "double hazard" of combined risk factors for both concurrent and predicted outcomes. Those children who showed both high levels of negative emotionality and low attentiveness showed a decline in IQ from age 2 to age 3.5, possibly due to the cumulative effects of this double hazard. Children who were prone to negative emotionality but had high attentiveness appeared to be protected against this deleterious outcome (especially for behavior problems). Interestingly, Gumora and Arsenio (2002) found with a considerably older group of children (sixth to eighth graders) that grade point average could be predicted by the young adolescents' emotion regulation and mood-related disposition toward academic activities: Those adolescents who reported more negative affect regarding ordinary academic routines obtained lower grade point averages, even when cognitive ability was controlled for. Lawson and Ruff do caution that both attention and emotionality consist of a variety of components: "Attention includes persistence, intensity, and flexibility; negative emotionality can refer to fear, anger (irritability), or sadness" (p. 164). They note that further research is needed to tease apart these respective components for us to have a complex understanding of how negative emotionality and attention processes work together in children's development.

Other studies undertaken by Eisenberg and her colleagues with preschoolers (e.g., Eisenberg et al., 1997; Fabes, Hanish, Martin, & Eisenberg, 2002) suggest a continuity that may start relatively early in life (e.g., the Lawson and Ruff research), continue through the preschool years, and as the most recent Eisenberg study described earlier and the Gumora and Arsenio study suggest, may continue through the elementary school years and extend into middle school as well. Indeed, in a longitudinal study Valiente et al. (2003) found that when attention shifting and focusing and children's persistence at a puzzle task were aggregated, they predicted a reduced level of externalizing behavior over time: This effect was most pronounced for children prone to negative emotionality. These authors suggested that negative emotionality may be a moderator of the linkages between attentional processes (which they subsumed under the construct of effortful control) and externalizing behavior. Such research, albeit complex, does indicate that developmental psychologists have provided the *preliminary* data needed to inform public policy about early intervention, which may include parent guidance as well as appropriately structured preschool education for addressing the needs of children who are faced with the "double hazard" of low attentiveness and proneness to negative emotionality at a young age.

Emotional Competence

Another way to conceptualize children's emotional development relative to their overall psychological adjustment or well-being is to examine their level of functioning according to the degree to which they access the various skills characteristic of emotional competence. Similar to such constructs as *well-being,*

TABLE 5.3   Skills of Emotional Competence

1. Awareness of one's emotional state, including the possibility that one is experiencing multiple emotions, and at even more mature levels, awareness that one might also not be consciously aware of one's emotions due to unconscious dynamics or selective inattention.

2. Skill in discerning others' emotions, based on situational and expressive cues that have some degree of cultural consensus as to their emotional meaning.

3. Skill in using the vocabulary of emotion and expression terms commonly available in one's subculture and at more mature levels skill in acquiring cultural scripts that link emotion with social roles.

4. Capacity for empathic and sympathetic involvement in others' emotional experiences.

5. Skill in understanding that inner emotional state need not correspond to outer expression, both in oneself and in others, and at more mature levels understanding that one's emotional-expressive behavior may impact on another and to take this into account in one's self-presentation strategies.

6. Skill in adaptive coping with aversive emotions and distressing circumstances by using self-regulatory strategies that ameliorate the intensity or temporal duration of such emotional states (e.g., stress hardiness) and by employing effective problem-solving strategies for dealing with problematic situations.

7. Awareness that the structure or nature of relationships is largely defined by how emotions are communicated in the relationship such as by the degree of emotional immediacy or genuineness of expressive display and by the degree of emotional reciprocity or symmetry in the relationship (e.g., mature intimacy is in part defined by mutual or reciprocal sharing of genuine emotions, but a parent-child relationship may have asymmetric sharing of genuine emotions).

8. Capacity for emotional self-efficacy: The individual views her- or himself as feeling, overall, the way he or she wants to feel. Emotional self-efficacy means that one accepts one's emotional experience, whether unique and eccentric or culturally conventional, and this acceptance is in alignment with the individual's beliefs about what constitutes desirable emotional balance. In essence, one is living in accord with one's personal theory of emotion and moral sense, when one demonstrates emotional self-efficacy.

social adjustment, and *ego-resilience,* the construct *emotional competence* is a superordinate term that subsumes a number of emotion-related skills. The definition of emotional competence is straightforward: It is the demonstration of self-efficacy in emotion-eliciting social transactions. Elsewhere one of us (Saarni, 1999) has extensively reviewed the developmental contributors to emotional competence; briefly, they include the self or ego identity, a moral sense or character, and a person's developmental history. The components of emotional competence are those skills necessary for self-efficacy in emotion-eliciting social transactions. Table 5.3 summarizes the skills of emotional competence.

The derivation of these eight skills was largely based on a survey of empirical investigations in the field of emotional development, although there is relatively less research that directly addresses the last two skills. However, these last two skills reflect implicit assumptions in many studies on emotional development in Western societies: We live in social-emotional systems (reflected in Skill 7 and see especially the work by Gottman and his colleagues on meta-emotion in family functioning, e.g., Gottman, Katz, & Hooven, 1997) and emotional competence should ultimately address personal integrity—we can discern what works best for us, relative to our values (Skill 8). These skills of emotional competence also reflect a Western cultural bias, which is of concern, and thus caution should be exercised when trying to generalize these skills to non-Western societies (e.g., Mesquita, 2001).

Later, we review a variety of studies that illustrate how each of the skills of emotional competence develops or is manifest, and we emphasize research that focuses on how the emotional competence skill facilitates an individual's effectiveness in relationships. In many cases, as children mature, their enhanced developmental functioning reveals itself in more complex manifestations of a given skill with concomitant advances in how interpersonal exchanges are negotiated.

Social Effectiveness and Skill 1: Awareness of Our Emotions

On some very basic level, knowing what we feel clarifies what we want. Theorists who emphasize close links between emotion and motivation readily acknowledge that the intended target or goal is critical for how we understand our subjective experience of emotion (e.g., Lazarus, 1991). Likewise, our emphasis on the functional nature of emotion is consistent with this perspective. By the time children are 2 to 3 years of age, awareness of emotional state is usually empirically examined from the standpoint of how children use emotion labels or descriptive phrases to refer to their subjective feelings. A number of studies have shown that young children spontaneously talk about their own affective states as well as about others' emotions (e.g., Bloom,

1998; Harris, 1997). The conversations between these young children and their family members also imply that they have expectancies for how they *will* feel as well as memories for how they *did* feel. Young children's conceptualization about their own subjective emotional experience encompasses the past, present, and future, and it is most reliably elicited in familiar interpersonal contexts. These everyday sorts of emotion-related communicative exchanges imply to young children that their emotions are part of a whole scenario of events, behaviors, and other people (see also Thompson, Chapter 2, this *Handbook,* this volume). In short, emotional experience is contextualized.

Furthermore, research with young children has shown that they construe their emotions as directed at something or someone as opposed to what elicited or caused the emotional response (Harris, 1995). For example, consistent with an earlier section, when children verbally describe their emotional reactions, they include the target of their feeling in their statements (e.g., mad *at* you, scared *of* snakes, happy *about* the party). They are less likely to talk about the causes of their emotional reactions (e.g., a conflict over a toy that led to one child feeling treated unfairly and thus becoming angry). However, when young children talk about experiencing pain, they do include the cause of pain, saying that they would feel pain on being pricked by a pin, but they would not say that they feel pain *about* pins.

Levine (1995) examined more thoroughly how younger children construed beliefs about the causes of anger and sadness in hypothetical vignettes. Her sample consisted of 5- to 6-year-olds, and she found that for anger they focused both on the aversiveness of the outcome and on the need to have the desired goal reinstated. For sadness, the children more often mentioned the loss felt by the protagonist and the impossibility or futility of having the goal reinstated. Interestingly, Levine used the same event for both anger and sadness stories, but she varied the attributions surrounding goal outcome. Her vignettes featured a child who could not go out to play because of an injury. In one version, the child had to stay inside but did not want to, and in the other version, the child wanted to play outside but helplessly could not. The former elicited attributions of anger and the latter sadness. Her results indicated that children appear to learn (in our culture at least) that their emotions can be explained by the status of their goals—whether the goals are met, violated, endangered, or lost.

Children who know what they feel are more able to negotiate with others when there is a conflict or a need to assert themselves. However, as Gottman, Katz, and Hooven (1997) argue, children are more likely to be effective negotiators when they can "down-regulate" or de-escalate their internal arousal sufficiently that they can attend to the social exchange and respond with useful social compromises to ease the impasse or conflict. Arsenio and Lemerise (2001) take this idea one step further in their model of social information processing, which is integrated with emotion processes such as encoding of affective cues from peers, the affective nature of the relationship a child has with the peer (e.g., hostile versus friendly), and empathic responsiveness. With this model, they suggest that a researcher can examine more effectively how and why children respond to some peer interactions with aggression and to others with social competence.

By early adolescence, well-functioning youth have the confidence to disclose their emotions and opinions to others, thereby revealing a "true self" to others in so far as they choose to express what their genuine emotions are, despite negative interpersonal consequences. Relevant research has been undertaken by Harter and her colleagues on adolescents' perceptions of their true self and under what conditions they present a dissembled self to others (Harter, 1999; Harter & Lee, 1989; Harter, Waters, Whitesell, & Dastelic, 1998). In addition, an early study (Saarni, 1988) found that some preadolescents recognized that although negative social consequences could occur if they revealed their genuine emotions, nonetheless, they contended that they would indeed express their genuine emotions because the emotions *themselves* were deemed important. With this kind of awareness of one's emotions, we can begin to understand how emotions themselves begin to constitute a part of a developing individual's definition of self (see Harter, 1999). This capacity to be aware of one's self and one's emotional responses is also relevant to the development of self-conscious emotions—pride, shame, guilt, hubris, envy, and embarrassment—and we turn next to a discussion of these emotions and their function in children's experience.

Self-Conscious Emotions

Lewis' work (1993, 1995) on the development of pride, hubris, shame, embarrassment, and guilt constitutes a cognitive appraisal view of how such emotions come about (see also Mascolo & Fischer, 1995). According to

Lewis, these self-conscious emotions require that an objective self has developed: Children can refer to themselves and have conscious awareness of themselves as distinct from others. The cognitive appraisals involved include (a) recognition that there are standards to be met, (b) evaluation of the self's performance relative to these standards, and (c) attribution of responsibility to the self on success or failure in meeting the standard. At around the time children acquire objective self-awareness (15 to 24 months, as measured by self-referential behavior; e.g., Lewis & Brooks-Gunn, 1979), they also become aware of parental standards for behavior, rules that they are expected to follow, and desirable goals for comportment. Children learn about these standards through their family's disciplinary practices, and over the next few years their increasing cognitive sophistication also allows them to gauge the degree to which they have met the standards. The sorts of standards young children learn about are rather simple and concrete, for example, "you should say please if you want something," or "how terrible of you to bite your little sister!" As children become older, their beliefs become more differentiated relative to the standards and rules that they believe they should follow and the goals that they think are worthy. Meeting these standards presumably yields positive emotional experience, both from the experience of mastery and in receiving social approval (e.g., Stipek, 1995).

Children also develop an appraisal of self-agency or responsibility: Have they failed or succeeded at reaching the goal or at living up to the standard, or are they performing according to the rule? Although Lewis does not directly address issues of controllability, Weiner's work certainly informs us of how perception of controllability is directly implied in whether people feel responsible for events (e.g., Weiner & Handel, 1985). Dweck and Leggett (1988) have also contended that if individuals view themselves or their world as modifiable and thus controllable, they will have a different appraisal of such a context (and themselves in it), leading to different emotional sequelae, than those who view themselves and their environments as fixed and static.

Young children may believe they do cause things to happen—that they are in control of events, when they are not, due to their cognitive egocentrism that blurs desire and reality (e.g., Harris, 1989). On a simple level, a 2-year-old may believe and act as though "if I want a cookie, then I should have a cookie." But if that same young child believes that "if I want Mommy to love me, then I have to be a good girl for her," she may then egocentrically conclude she must have been a "bad girl," when her mother simply expresses negative feelings that are unrelated to her child's behavior. Research by Zahn-Waxler and her associates (Zahn-Waxler, Cole, & Barrett, 1991; Zahn-Waxler, Kochanska, Krupnick, & McKnew, 1990; Zahn-Waxler & Robinson, 1995) suggests that young children (especially girls) growing up with depressed mothers may be particularly at risk for developing excessive "accountability" for their mothers' feelings and mood state. Such children were very careful in their interaction with others, as though others were quite fragile, and their behavior included higher levels of appeasement, apologizing, and suppression of negative emotion than comparable children of nondepressed mothers. Thus, these 2- to 3-year-old children appeared to believe unrealistically that they had control over events and over their mothers' emotional responses and/or were responsible for them.

The last cognitive appraisal that has to develop before self-conscious emotions are experienced is a focus on one's self from an evaluative standpoint such that either the whole self or a particular aspect of the self is considered the focus of the success or failure at living up to the standard, rule, or reaching a goal. Lewis (2000) contends that the more that the whole self is globally assumed to be responsible for the success or failure, the more that either hubris (arrogance) or shame will be felt, respectively. When specific aspects of the self are seen as leading to the success or failure, then pride or guilt will be felt, respectively. The emotional responses of pride and guilt are specific self-attributions as in "my effort paid off" (pride) or "it was my mistake and I'll deal with this fiasco" (guilt). The prideful feelings of accomplishment and pleasure allow the individual to undertake still further challenges; the guilt felt on one's failure at a particular event or in a particular situation allows for interpersonal repair and future improvement (see also Barrett, Zahn-Waxler, & Cole, 1993, for a discussion of "avoiders versus amenders" in toddlerhood, with the "amenders" apparently experiencing guilt rather than shame or embarrassment).

There is also a critical interpersonal context that needs to be taken into account in distinguishing shame and guilt—whether we are observed or alone. We do not need social *exposure* to feel guilt (although it might help), but it is a significant feature in our feeling ashamed and wanting to hide from others' view (e.g., Barrett et al., 1993). Exposure contributes to another self-conscious emotion, embarrassment, which is not necessarily the same as shame. As an illustration of such research, Lewis and Ramsay (2002) proposed that there are two types of embarrassment, one is simply due to being the object of other's attention (exposure embarrassment) and the other is a more self-evaluative embarrassment that may be linked to shame. They studied 4-year-old children's reactions to a performance task (i.e., yielding success or failure) and a situation designed to emphasize focus on the self (e.g., receiving lavish compliments) and examined the children's cortisol responses after both conditions to see if they differed. The preschoolers who expressed behaviors indicative of shame or of evaluative embarrassment during failure at the task responded with higher cortisol levels, whereas the exposure to attention situation did not result in elevated cortisol responses. They concluded that shame and evaluative embarrassment are more stressful—as evidenced by the higher cortisol secretion—than feeling oneself to be the object of others' focused (and positive) attention.

Differences between shame and guilt have also been extensively studied by Tangney and her colleagues, using self-reported experiences rated according to dimensions devised by the authors (reviewed in Tangney and Fischer, 1995). She found with young adults that personal shame experiences were more often associated with a sense of powerlessness and having less control over the situation as well as feeling exposed to others' judgments. Furthermore, shame-prone individuals were more likely to externalize blame onto some other person or event. Shame experiences were also reliably associated with withdrawal or avoidance of others, whereas guilt was associated with reparation and nonavoidance of others. Fergusson and Stegge (1995) reviewed the attribution literature on the development of guilt and shame, and they argue that not until middle childhood do children more reliably use a causal analysis of events in reporting their emotions.

A somewhat different view of how shame, guilt, and pride develop has been proposed by Barrett (1997). Her emphasis is on *emotion communication* as a necessary component for the development of self-conscious emotions. She attributes the primary significance for the emergence of the self-conscious emotions to the significant relationships in children's lives, most notably, their parents. Her argument is that the standards by which children view their behavior as shameful, guilt-inducing, or prideful would never be internalized if children did not *care* about the emotion-laden responses of their primary caregivers to their behavior. Thus, for self-conscious emotions to develop, young children would also need to be able to recognize and understand their parents' emotion-laden communicative behavior as directed toward them, and that such instances of parental emotion communication have meaning for the desirability or undesirability of their behavior. This may account for why young children do not demonstrate clear instances of shame, pride, or guilt until the 2nd year of life.

Research on children's self-conscious emotions has received considerable attention in the previous decade: Tangney and Fischer's (1995) volume on self-conscious emotions contains a number of chapters that address developmental issues. Reimer (1996) has sought to integrate research with young children's self-conscious emotions with clinical work on adolescents and adults to examine the development of shame in later childhood and adolescence. The development and functioning of self-conscious emotions clearly needs more attention at all age levels. It would appear that the development of self-conscious emotions are especially relevant to clinical practice, whether it be the treatment of depression that occurs with a greater frequency among female adolescents or the development of effective interventions to facilitate a child's coping with the emotional aftermath of sexual abuse (see Tangney, Burggraf, & Wagner, 1995, for a review of shame, guilt, and psychopathology).

Awareness of Multiple Emotions

Also relevant to children's and adolescents' social effectiveness and adaptation is their ability to be aware of experiencing multiple emotions or conflicting emotions (as in ambivalence). This development may appear as early as 5 to 6 years of age (Stein, Trabasso, & Liwag, 2000) or not until late childhood (Harter & Whitesell, 1989), depending on the criteria and methods for eliciting such understanding from children. Stein and Trabasso examined 5- to 6-year-olds and determined that at this age children could readily describe people who make them feel good *and* bad or whom they liked *and* did not like. However, Stein and Trabasso cautioned that this did not mean that children simultaneously felt conflicting emotions: Rather they first focused on one situation to which they attached values and attributions, responded emotionally to its impact on them (e.g., "I don't like her because she took my Halloween candy"), and then focused on another situation with its accompanying values and attributions and respond emotionally to its impact (e.g., "But I like her when she plays with me"). Thus, ambivalence for Stein and Trabasso was viewed as a *sequential* process with different appraisals attached to the different or polarized emotional responses, and they suggested that this process was the same for adults, just much more rapid.

Studies conducted by Harter and Whitesell (1989) and by Donaldson and Westerman (1986) were similarly concerned with children's cognitive construction of their own emotional experience, particularly when multiple emotions are involved. Harter and Whitesell focused on the cognitive developmental prerequisites for understanding the simultaneity of multiple emotions embedded in a situation or relationship. Not until children had the ability to coordinate multiple attributes of a situation with the dimension of emotional valence (at about 10 years of age) could they make sense of opposite valence emotions (happy and sad) about different targets that co-occur in a situation (e.g., "I'm glad I get to live with my dad, but I'm sad about not being able to live with my mom too"). Young adolescents developed further and could integrate simultaneously opposite valence emotions about the same *target* (e.g., "I love my dad, even though I'm mad at him right now"). Harter and Whitesell acknowledged that what may occur as we cognitively integrate contrasting emotions about the same target is a rapid oscillation between the multiple emotion-eliciting aspects of a relationship or situation.

Harter and Buddin (1987) also pointed out that it is not known whether children might experience simultaneously two (or even more) emotions but can only cognitively construct an explanation about the experience that focuses on one emotion. They also noted that children may in some situations experience only one overwhelming emotion, for example, fear, but as they seek to cope with the scary situation or have to communicate about it to some one else, they begin to cognitively construct a more complex system of appraisals about the emotion-eliciting situation or relationship.

Summary

This first skill of emotional competence—the ability to be aware of an emotional experience—facilitates children's problem solving, for knowing how to respond emotionally to a particular eliciting encounter is crucial to deciding on a course of action, especially if a first impulse to action is potentially going to incur some undesirable consequences, and thus be less self-efficacious in the long term. In terms of social effectiveness, knowing how one's self tends to react, whether it is with shame or with a conflicted set of emotions leading to ambivalence, is still a source of important information for the developing child or teen to integrate into his or her self-definition, especially knowing that some emotional experiences render one's self acutely vulnerable in interpersonal situations.

Social Effectiveness and Skill 2: Ability to Discern and Understand Others' Emotions

To understand others' emotions and motives, children need (a) to make sense of others' expressive behavior and action tendencies, (b) to understand common situational elicitors of emotions, and (c) to comprehend that others have minds, intentions, beliefs, and inner states. There is a fairly substantial research literature on these topics and the reader is referred to reviews in Denham (1999); Dunn (2000); Halberstadt, Denham, and Dunsmore (2001); Harris (2000); Underwood (1999); von Salisch (2001); and Thompson, Easterbrooks, and Padilla-Walker (2003). A variety of studies indicate that children who are more accurate in understanding others' emotional experience also tend to be more socially competent (see reviews in Halberstadt et al., 2001). These studies typically establish a given child's social competence either by teachers' ratings or by peers' sociometric choices. Then the children's understanding of emotion terms, of facial expressions, of elicitors of emotion, and so forth are assessed and correlated with the children's social competence ratings (e.g., Hubbard & Coie, 1994). Other investigators have examined children's maladaptive social interaction to see whether deficits in their understanding of others' emotions contribute to their ineffectual social behavior. Specific clinical populations have also been studied for how their understanding of others' emotional experience may differ from nonclinic samples, for example, autistic children, children who have been abused, and children who have witnessed family violence (for brief reviews, see Saarni, 1999, and Southam-Gerow & Kendall, 2002).

Two studies have considerable potential for broadening research on this topic. In the first study, Barth and Bastiani (1997) investigated children's biases in labeling the expressions of their classmates' facial expression photos. Accuracy scores were based on congruence of the judged expression and which expression the classmate was intending to produce expressively for the photo. Bias scores were calculated as the proportionate number of times a child used a particular expression label (e.g., sad, happy, mad, surprised, or afraid) relative to the total number of classmate photos that were judged. The children made these ratings at the beginning of the school year and again 5 months later. The children's peer acceptance, based on sociometric ratings, and their general social adjustment, based on teacher ratings, were also assessed.

Noteworthy among their results was that those children who had a bias for "seeing" angry facial expressions (contrary to what the familiar classmate was trying to produce expressively) were also the ones who had less satisfactory peer relations, and their teachers rated their adjustment more often as hostile dependent. This outcome is consistent with research with older children who used a hostile attribution bias in their peer relationships (e.g., Crick & Dodge, 1994). These results may also be linked to Isley and colleagues' research on parent-child expressed affect and the children's subsequent social competence with peers (Isley, O'Neil, Clatfelter, & Parke, 1999). In that study, negative expressed affect by parents toward their children was associated with their children's impaired social functioning with peers. Similarly, Schultz, Izard, and Ackerman (2000) found that parental depression and family instability predicted preschool children's anger attribution bias, which in turn was associated with peer rejection. These children were also rated as aggressive by their teachers.

The second study we describe in some detail was on how rejected children behave when mildly interpersonally stressed. Hubbard (2001) had 7- and 8-year-olds rate their peers for how liked or not-liked they were as well as who starts the most fights. The former sociometric rating yielded a rejection index and the latter an aggression index. She then observed the children in a rigged game with a confederate whom they did not know and who was 1 year older. The children were under pressure to win the game to obtain a prize. Compared to accepted children, the rejected children were more likely to express both facial and verbal anger during the game. They also expressed more happiness, but only when some game maneuver was to their advantage. Interestingly, aggressive children were not necessarily more likely to express anger (or happiness or sadness) than nonaggressive children. This particular finding is also

consistent with that found by Underwood and Hurley (1999). We would like to see research that combines elements of the Barth and Bastiani approach with Hubbard's approach: For example, would rejected children demonstrate a bias in their perception of emotion in others, or are they simply oblivious and insensitive to emotional cues? Why did this game context not elicit anger in children rated by their peers for being likely to start fights? Is this a context in which a potential bias for perceiving anger in others is not elicited?

Understanding Others' Feelings and Cognitive Development

The ability to understand what others are experiencing emotionally does not develop in isolation from other aspects of emotional development and cognitive development. Emerging insight into others' emotions develops in interaction with increasing awareness of an individual's own emotional experience, with the ability to empathize, and with the ability to conceptualize causes of emotions and their behavioral consequences. The more children learn about how and why people act as they do, the more they can *infer* their emotional state, even if it is not especially obvious or may even be counterintuitive. The studies reviewed show that the growth in emotional development that children show over time is deeply tied to their cognitive development as well. (For a recent review of children's cognitive understanding of emotions, see Harris, 2000.)

Facial Expressions and Emotion-Eliciting Situations. We concur with the view espoused by Lewis and Michalson (1985) that facial expressions can have a dual function; they can be *signs,* in which case they bear a one-to-one correspondence to internal emotional state, or they can function as *symbols,* in which case they refer to something else. When facial expressions are symbolic, they are referring to metacommunicative processes (e.g., Wagner & Lee, 1999; Weber & Laux, 1993), for example, placating someone, deterring someone, or presenting oneself in a more favorable light. The dissociation of facial expression from internal emotional experience is taken up in detail in the discussion of Skill 5.

By mid to late childhood, most children recognize and can verbalize that a person's expression may be both a social and an emotional response (e.g., Underwood & Hurley, 1999). Gross and Ballif (1991) reviewed the early research on children's understanding of emotions in others based on facial expression cues and situational elicitors of emotion. They concluded that as children matured, they became more accurate in their inferences about what others were feeling. The easiest emotions to figure out were positive ones: Smiling faces and situations depicting pleasure and getting what one wants were readily comprehended as associated with happiness. Negative facial expressions depicting sadness, fear, or anger were more difficult for children to decode. However, if paired with a detailed emotion-eliciting situational context, children were much more likely to infer the negative emotion in question.

As children grow older, they combine both facial and situational cues as they attempt to discern and understand the emotional experience of others. Wiggers and van Lieshout (1985) suggested that when there was a contradiction between a facial expression and the emotion-eliciting situation, school-age children were more likely to opt for whichever cue was more clearly presented. An example used by Wiggers and van Lieshout is a scenario depicting a boy with a weak smile about to get a fearsome injection. The situation, in this case, is more definitively portrayed than the boy's facial expression, and as a result, children conclude that the boy is anxious or afraid, despite the attempt at a smile. Children also recognize that others might feel a mixture of feelings about a situation.

The preceding conclusions were largely based on research that was done by having children appraise hypothetical vignettes, photos, and the like. Fabes, Eisenberg, Nyman, and Michealieu (1991) investigated 3- to 6-year-old children's understanding of others' emotions in naturalistic settings. They found that happy reactions were more often correctly identified (according to adult standards) than negative reactions, thus replicating the general outcome of interview-based research. Fabes et al. also examined children's understanding of the causes of emotions and found that children could more readily identify causes for negative emotions. They interpreted this result as based on the greater intensity of negative emotional states and concluded that children more readily evaluate the causes for goal failure (i.e., any undesired outcome). A developmental difference found by Fabes et al. was that their youngest children tended to attribute causes to wants and needs, but the older children in

kindergarten more often made use of others' personality traits in their construal of what gave rise to the emotional response. This use of personalized information in understanding others' emotional experience is further examined in the next section.

Taking into Account Unique Information about the Other. The most relevant studies for more fully describing this feature of understanding others' emotional experience were conducted by Gnepp and Gould (1985) and Gnepp and Chilamkurti (1988) and theoretically elaborated by Gnepp (1989). Gnepp and Gould examined whether children (ages 5 to 10) could use information about a story character's past experience (e.g., being rejected by your best friend) to predict how the character would feel in some new situation (e.g., subsequently meeting the best friend on the playground). Not unexpectedly, the youngest children were more likely to use the current situational information to infer what the character was feeling (e.g., she would be happy at seeing her best friend) and older children were more likely to infer the character's emotional state by taking into account the prior experience (e.g., she would feel sad on seeing her best friend). An interaction also occurred between the hedonic tone (positive/negative) of the emotion and the use of personal information: If the story character experienced a negative *emotion* at Time 1 but encountered a commonly assumed positive *situation* at Time 2, children were more likely to use prior personal history information when inferring how the character would feel at Time 2. Gnepp (1989) suggests that children must first recognize what a person's perspective was at Time 1 and then must apply that inferred perspective from Time 1 to Time 2 to come up with the atypical emotional response.

In an analogous investigation, Gnepp and Chilamkurti (1988) presented stories to elementary school children and adults in which characters' personality traits were systematically described as either desirable or undesirable traits. The story characters then had some experience befall them, and the children were to infer the emotional reaction of the character to this new experience. Older children and adults were more likely to take into account the prior trait information in inferring the emotional response of the character in the new situation. The younger children (6-year-olds) were less consistent in doing so, but a number were able to take personality trait information into account when inferring how someone might emotionally respond to an emotion-eliciting event, even when the emotional reaction might be atypical for the eliciting event. Lagattuta and her colleagues (Lagattuta, Wellman, & Flavell, 1997), determined that even preschoolers could figure out that the same situation could evoke different emotional responses in story characters if the cues were presented very explicitly (e.g., pictorially showing the story protagonists experiencing atypical emotional reactions).

These investigations show us that by school entry, children are well on their way to superimposing multiple frames of reference onto one another across time intervals to predict or infer other people's emotional responses. In Gnepp's research, a distinction was not made between emotional state and emotional-expressive behavior: The assumption was that children would infer emotional state. Whether children could also infer what sort of expressive behavior would be displayed, and whether it would be congruent with an atypical internal emotional state or with the consensually defined "typical" emotion response to the situation, was not part of the focus of these studies. Little research has since been undertaken on this topic, an omission that we would like to see remedied.

Social Competence and Discerning Others' Emotional States. A number of studies indicate that children with emotional problems or who have been abused show deficits in their understanding of links between facial expression and emotion, in producing facial expressions, and in discriminating emotion expressions (e.g., Camras, Grow, & Ribordy, 1983; R. J. Casey, 1996; Pollack, Cicchetti, Hornung, & Reed, 2000; Shipman, Zeman, Penza, & Champion, 2000). The research by Pollack et al. (2000) warrants further description: These investigators found that neglected children had difficulties in discriminating emotions, whereas physically abused children appeared to have a bias to perceive angry facial expressions. Thus, the sorts of early emotion communication experiences that children receive influence how they construct their understanding of others' emotional expressions and emotional states, and as we elaborate under our discussion of Skill 6, this early emotion communication exposure is also linked to their ability to regulate their own emotional arousal with peers and in school (e.g., Gottman et al., 1997).

Do children who are exceptionally socially competent show an enhancement of understanding emotion and expression linkages? Custrini and Feldman (1989) reported that among girls, but not among boys, degree of social competence greatly influenced their overall accuracy score in encoding and decoding others' emotions. Girls who were below average in social competence scored well below boys, regardless of their social competence level, and the highest scoring children were girls who were above average in social competence. Other research undertaken by Walden and Knieps (1996) suggested that preschoolers who obtained high sociometric peer preferences as play partners were also those who tended to be better at discriminating among emotional facial displays and who tended to demonstrate high spontaneous expressivity (but they did not excel in posed expressions). Another study undertaken by Edwards, Manstead, and McDonald (1984) with somewhat older children demonstrated a similar relation: Children's sociometric rating was positively related to their ability to recognize facial expressions of emotion.

Further support for links between social effectiveness and emotion *knowledge* can be found in research undertaken by Denham, McKinley, Couchoud, and Holt (1990) on preschoolers' peer interaction and in a study on family-peer connections by Cassidy, Parke, Butkovsky, and Braungart (1992). The Denham et al. results showed that children who demonstrated greater knowledge of emotion in the puppet task (especially in understanding anger and fear) were perceived by their peers as more likeable. In the Cassidy et al. (1992) study of kindergarten children, emotion understanding was measured by interviewing the children about identification of emotional facial expressions, how particular emotions were situationally elicited, and what were the social consequences to such emotions. They found that children who demonstrated more complex emotion understanding were more accepted by their peers.

More recent research undertaken by Garner and Estep (2001) examined the relations among preschoolers' emotion knowledge and their social skills. Their results indicated that children's understanding of situational clues to infer what emotions would likely be felt was a negative predictor of children's use of nonconstructive anger reactions with their peers. Their assessment of children's ability to provide explanations for the causes and consequences of others' emotions was a significant predictor of the children's initiating social interaction as well as being chosen as recipients of social bids.

Problematic Outcomes and Understanding Others' Emotional States. Discerning and understanding others' emotional experience does not necessarily always contribute to one's skill at emotional communication. Paradoxically, in certain circumstances, some children would be better off tuning out others' emotional behavior. Children who are exposed to and involved in their parents' depressed feelings represent one group who are at risk for an aversive emotion socialization experience, and another group consists of those children exposed to marital conflict accompanied by overt anger. It is unrealistic to assume that children can tune out their parents' negative emotions, but outcomes for children if such experiences are frequent, intense, and started early in life do not bode well. Investigations of how children of chronically depressed parents (for the most part, mothers) develop emotionally has been reviewed by Downey and Coyne (1990) and by Zahn-Waxler and colleagues (Zahn-Waxler et al., 1990). Research on children who witness interadult anger and domestic violence has been reviewed by Osofsky (1999).

Summary

Children's social effectiveness is closely linked to their accurate appraisal of emotional states in others. Even if the expressive cues are ambiguous, they learn to infer what emotions others might be experiencing, based on their expanding knowledge of common elicitors of emotion relevant to their subculture. Preschoolers can anticipate that atypical emotional responses may be experienced, if they are provided with fairly explicit cues. By the early school years, children take into account what they know about another's personality or unique circumstances to infer the target's emotional response. Research on individual differences indicates that maltreatment of children compromises or distorts the development of these social-cognitive skills.

Social Effectiveness and Skill 3: Use of a Vocabulary of Emotion and Expression

With language and symbols, we can traverse time and space to communicate with others about our own and their emotions. Modern technology seems especially designed to promote such communication with "instant messaging," e-mail, and cell phones everywhere. Social psychologists have investigated why it is that we are so compelled to share our emotional experience with oth-

ers, and one hypothesis has been the "stress and affiliation effect" (reviewed in Luminet, Bouts, Delie, Manstead, & Rimé, 2000): When we feel badly, we want the company of others, and, more specifically, we want *to tell* others how we are feeling (with the interesting exception of when we feel shame). This implies that communicating our feelings to another initiates change. Such change may be found in how we experience our subjective feeling state (e.g., internal emotion regulation is affected), or with the support of others, we may devise different ways to cope with a problematic situation.

From a developmental perspective, the "stress and affiliation" pattern is the hallmark of many attachment studies with young children. We also know that young children and their mothers are more likely to use emotion-laden language when there is a dispute or some negative event occurs (Denham, Mitchell-Copeland, Strandberg, Auerbach, & Blair, 1997; Dunn & Brown, 1991; Dunn, Brown, & Beardsall, 1991). Indeed, as Chambers' review indicates (1999), family discourse is critical to young children's learning about emotions, how to speak about feelings, and how to cope with emotion-laden situations. Awaiting further study is how the social psychological research on emotion disclosure undertaken with adults might manifest itself in children's emotion disclosures to peers. On one hand, Gottman et al. (1997) would contend that school-age children should not disclose their feelings to peers if they are to be accepted. On the other hand, with the advent of close friendships in childhood and early adolescence, disclosure of vulnerability-inducing feelings (e.g., anxiety, sadness, or hurt) is more likely to occur (e.g., Asher & Rose, 1997; Saarni, 1988). However, let us return to the beginning: how young children acquire a lexicon of emotion that permits them to represent their own and others' emotional experience.

Ability to Use Concepts, Lexicon, and Scripts Relevant to Emotion and Expression

The ability to represent emotional experience through words, imagery, and symbolism of varied sorts allows children to communicate to others what they want and what problems they are encountering as well as to describe their delight and pleasure. With words, the child can further elaborate these representations of emotional experience, integrate them across contexts, and compare them with others' representations about emotional experiences. Some of the developments in awareness of one's own multiple emotional responses or in understanding others' atypical emotions, described earlier, could not be undertaken if children did not have access to a language or representational system (e.g., sign language) for symbolically encoding and communicating their emotional experiences.

Assuming an intact nervous system and an environment that is not overwhelmingly trauma filled, children do show some commonalities in our culture in learning how to represent emotion. However, individual differences and cultural influence are again strong forces in the development of language-based emotion concepts, which is not surprising, since one of the critical functions of an emotion lexicon is to be able to communicate with others, which obviously entails their reciprocal communication about emotion (e.g., Dunn & Brown, 1991).

Development of Emotion Lexicon. Bretherton, Fritz, Zahn-Waxler, and Ridgeway (1986) reviewed the relevant literature on children's acquisition of emotion words, and they noted that many toddlers could use emotion words toward the end of the 2nd year. However, they cautioned that what was included as an emotion word, for example, crying, may simply be a behavioral action noted by the young child and conceivably was not used by the child to indicate an internal emotional state. By 3 years of age, children could much more readily label the emotions of others in addition to their own feelings. Increasingly, they could also verbally address the consequences of emotional states as well as the situational causes of emotions; for example, "Grandma mad. I wrote on wall."

Researchers have also studied parents' reports of their children's understanding and use of emotion-descriptive words. Using parents' ratings on checklists of words indicating emotion states (e.g., "happy"), emotion traits (e.g., "good"), and physical states (e.g., "sleepy," "clean"), Ridgeway, Waters, and Kuczaj (1985) tabulated the percentages of children at 6-month intervals (starting at 18 months and extending to 6 years of age) comprehending the emotion word and also using it. The most frequently understood words at 18 months were sleepy, hungry, good, happy, clean, tired, and sad (50% to 83% comprehension). By age 6, children comprehended such words as "nervous" (83%), "embarrassed" (77%), "jealous" (60%), and "miserable" (53%). Their corresponding production of these words was one-half to two-thirds of the percentages for comprehension.

Children can also apply emotion terms to pretend play by age 2 to 3, and, indeed, listening to children talk as they enact fantasies with their figurative toys (e.g., dolls, action figures, stuffed animals) is an excellent way to observe a young child's competence with emotion language, for they construct both the causes of the figure's emotional response and the consequences of the emotion, including how the figure copes. Denham and Auerbach (1995) analyzed the emotional content of mothers and preschoolers' dialogues while looking at picture books together (whose contents were emotion laden). They found that such an interaction was rich with adult-child exchanges that included affect labeling and causes and consequences of emotional experience. In addition, both mothers and children used their emotion-descriptive language in ways that suggested social influence of the other; for example, mothers who limited themselves to simple comments about the emotion-laden material in the picture books had children who asked more questions to engage their mothers more. However, those mothers who made use of verbal explanation to a very great degree appeared to stimulate their children further to use more complex and elaborated emotion-descriptive language. These children tended to respond with more guiding and socializing language about the characters' emotional experience.

Conversations about Emotional Responses. The classic research on this topic was undertaken by Dunn et al. (1987) who investigated naturally occurring conversations in the home between young children and their mothers and siblings. They were particularly interested in determining what sorts of functions conversations about emotional reactions had in the social exchange in the home and how children communicated causes of emotional reactions in their exchanges with others. They followed the young children from age 18 months to 24 months and found that conversations about causes of emotional experience increased significantly in the 6 months they tracked the children. They also found that the vast majority of emotion-laden conversations were with the mother as opposed to the older sibling, although such conversations involving all three occurred more often than between just the two children. This finding suggests that access to an adult who is interested in one's emotional reactions may be pivotal to children having opportunities both to talk about emotions and have their understanding of emotions elaborated. Mothers tended to use conversations about emotional responses as a functional way to guide or explain something to their children, whereas the children were more likely to use emotion-descriptive words simply to comment on their own reaction or observation of another. Thus, they were learning to communicate their own self-awareness of emotion states to their mothers, who in turn were likely to communicate meaningfulness to their children by using guiding, persuading, clarifying, or otherwise interpretive emotion-related language.

Dunn et al. (1991) continued their research on naturally occurring conversations about emotions in the home, but this time extended their longitudinal study of children from when they were 3 years old to age 6. They again focused on children's and mothers' exchanges around causes and consequences of emotions and additionally tracked how disputes and conflicts in the home provided occasions for emotional growth by how children were exposed to and had to use emotion-descriptive language to negotiate the conflict. They found a tremendous range in variability among the children in frequency of "emotion talk"—from 0 to 27 occasions per hour of observation. The mothers also showed a similar variability, ranging from 0 to 22 occasions of "emotion talk" per hour of observation. Unfortunately, Dunn et al. did not provide information as to whether the mother-child dyads were matched in their rates of "emotion talk." Given the findings of their earlier study where mothers were pivotal in providing opportunities for children to verbally communicate about their emotional reactions, we can only speculate that if a mother did not talk much about emotions and related inner states, very likely her child did not either.

Another study by Dunn and Brown (1994) sheds further light on the effects of family emotional expression on children's acquisition of emotion-descriptive language. Again, they found that occasions of negative emotional reactions on the part of the child were when most emotion-related discourse occurred between mother and child. This study also documented that families characterized as high in frequency of anger and distress expression had children who were less likely to be engaged in discourse about emotional experience. However, if the families were low in frequency of negative emotional expression, when a negative emotional event did occur for the child, there was a greater likelihood of an emotion-related conversation to ensue between child and parent. This research suggests that children's acquisition of emotion-descriptive language is anchored in relationship contexts: If everyone is angry or distressed a lot of the time, an episode of distress on the part of a child may be viewed as trivial. What may be metacommunicated in such families is that a child's emotional reaction is not very important. We can surmise how differences in the families' emotional milieus provide varying preparatory stages for their children's later emotional experiences in the world beyond the home (e.g., Du Rocher Schudlich, Shamir, & Cummings, 2004).

A recent study by Laible (2004) on mother-child discourse sheds further light on the role that the parent-child relationship plays in children's acquisition of emotion understanding and internalization of behavioral expectations. Attachment classification and proneness to negative emotional reactivity were evaluated in her preschool sample, and then conversations between the mother and her child were examined for elaborative style and discussion of negative emotions. Two discourse situations were sampled where (1) the mother and child reminisced, and (2) they read a story together. It was primarily in the first discourse context in which the mother and her child discussed the child's past experience that Laible found that attachment security was related to maternal elaboration and the dyad's discussion of negative emotions. In turn, such maternal elaboration was associated with children demonstrating higher levels of behavioral internalization and higher levels of emotion understanding. Interestingly, if mothers perceived their children as prone to negative emotional reactivity, they were more likely to elaborate in the reminiscence task and discuss negative emotions more frequently (probably because their children experienced them more often due to their proneness to negative reactivity).

Structural Analysis of Emotion-Descriptive Language. Russell and Ridgeway (1983) examined emotion-descriptive adjectives used by children in elementary school. They found that these words could be statistically analyzed with principal-components analyses and multidimensional scaling. The result was that two bipolar dimensions were found that provided an organizational structure for the many emotion-related terms used by school children. These two dimensions were: (1) degree of pleasure or hedonic tone and (2) degree of arousal.

This dimensional analysis of emotion concepts is of interest for it suggests something about the way emotion is categorized and perhaps even organized as subjective experience. A number of cross-cultural comparisons have been made on emotion concepts used by adults in other languages (reviewed by Russell, 1991), and the pleasure/displeasure dimension has been reliably found in all the cultures studied. Russell suggests that hedonic tone is relevant in all cultures in how feeling states are differentiated, but the English word "emotion" is not necessarily present in all languages, although an equivalent term is more the rule than the exception (exceptions appear to be the Tahitians, the Bimin-Kuskusmin of Papua New Guinea, the Gidjingali aborigines of Australia, the Ifalukians of Micronesia, the Chewong of Malaysia, and the Samoans; cited in Russell, 1991). In these few cultures where no term similar to emotion exists, internal affective states may be referred to as arising in certain body parts or organs; for example, the Chewong view the liver as the source of what for them might be called thoughts and affective responses. The significance of the virtually universal presence of the pleasure/aversion dimension in emotion-descriptive concepts may indicate that what experiencing pleasure/aversion does for us is a basic function: It is embedded in our approach-avoidance actions in relation to the contexts we live in and thus supports the functionalist theoretical perspective espoused in this chapter.

Emotion Script Learning. Acquisition of emotion-descriptive concepts continues throughout childhood and into adolescence, but little research has examined these older age groups. Further development of emotion language in the school-age child and adolescent may be found in their greater ability to add variety, subtlety, nuance, and complexity to their use of emotion-descriptive words with others. What may also develop is that children's scripts for understanding emotional experience are reciprocally influenced by their growing access to increasing complexity of emotion concepts. Russell (1991) defines emotion scripts as "a knowledge structure for a type of event whereby the event is thought of as a sequence of subevents" (p. 442). Russell notes that even in the same culture scripts for the same emotions may differ from person to person because emotion scripts are linked to other belief networks. This is a significant point because, for example, if a script for anger is linked to a network of concepts about sex role, the anger script may well have

additional emphases or omissions if a person's machismo or femininity is implicated in the anger episode. What is important to consider is that scripts for different emotions may merge (or one emotion may cycle into another) under certain circumstances, particularly if individuals appraise a situation as salient for certain beliefs they hold about themselves (see also Lewis, 1992, for a discussion of links between gender and shame scripts).

Emotion scripts may merge with gender role socialization as suggested by some of the sex differences found for how anger and sadness are talked about in families. For example, gender differences in learning to talk about emotional experience were found by Dunn et al. (1987) in their study of young British children and their mothers. Little girls received more comments and inquiries about emotions from their mothers and from their older siblings than did little boys; however, the boys and girls themselves were similar in their initiation of conversations about emotions. In a similar vein, Fivush (1991) undertook an exploratory study with mothers of 3-year-old boys and girls and found that mothers tended to talk in a more elaborated fashion about sadness with their daughters and more about anger with their sons. She found that mothers tended to embed their discussions of emotions in social frameworks more with their daughters than with their sons. Relative to script notions, she also found that when anger was involved, mothers emphasized relationship repair with their daughters and were more accepting of retaliation by their angry sons.

More recently, Widen and Russell (2002) examined young children's attributions of emotion to story characters who varied in gender but who were engaged in identical emotion-eliciting situations. Through computer image manipulation, the faces of two young adolescents, a boy and a girl, were merged into a single androgynous image. The images were then further manipulated by having either a masculine or a feminine stereotyped hairstyle. Boys more often inferred the male protagonist to be feeling disgusted and girls more often inferred the female protagonist to be feeling fearful. Prior research had indicated that preschoolers often attributed anger to boys and sadness to girls when the emotion being felt was ambiguously presented (e.g., Karbon, Fabes, Carlo, & Martin, 1992). But what the authors suggest—that is even more intriguing from a developmental perspective—is that different emotions may be conceptualized by young children by relying on different cues. Their results indicated that clear facial expressions of happiness, sadness, and anger were not "swayed" by gender cues, whereas the emotional displays of disgust and fear appear to be influenced more by gender stereotypes and the verbal label provided.

Last, cultural influence and the acquisition of an emotional lexicon are inseparable, for societies use language to regulate emotion in social interaction. Many societies emphasize some emotional responses over others by attaching special importance to certain emotion-descriptive words. In American culture, the word "love" is such an emotionally loaded word. Much anthropological research has been done that examines emotion-descriptive language. The reader is referred to an edited volume on this topic (Russell, Fernández-Dols, Manstead, & Wellenkamp, 1996). Another useful perspective is that of ethnotheories (or folk theories) of emotion lexicons (e.g., Lutz, 1988). Illustrative of this perspective are Ochs' (1986) review of Samoan children's acquisition of emotion-descriptive language and A. Eisenberg's (1986) ethnographic study of the emotional and social functions of verbal banter (teasing) in recently immigrated Mexican children.

Summary

Young children show a rapid increase in acquiring an emotion lexicon. Having words for their emotional experience allows for seeking support in distressing circumstances, for reciprocal sharing with others about emotional experience, and for being able to conceptualize lexically their emotions and how they came about as well as what the consequences for the self and others might be. Without an emotion lexicon, how could children and youth reflect on themselves as emotion-experiencing individuals? Indeed, we see in cases of severely abused and traumatized children and youth a deficit in the ability to conceptualize what they experience emotionally (e.g., alexithymia; see also Camras, Sachs-Alter, & Ribordy, 1996). This skill of emotional competence functions somewhat like a pivot for the other skills, for it is with access to the language of emotion concepts that children learn to predict how they themselves are likely to emotionally react, to understand others' emotional responses, and to respond empathically and sympathetically to others, as we discuss next.

Social Effectiveness and Skill 4: The Capacity for Empathic and Sympathetic Involvement

Empathy and sympathy are emotional responses that connect us with others. Beginning with early infancy, it is clear that very young babies respond to the crying states of other neonates (Martin & Clark, 1982). This early attentiveness to emotional-expressive cues may pave the way for later vicariously induced emotion, for they cannot be induced to experience another's emotional state unless they notice it and consider it salient. Sympathy differs from empathy in that it can also be experienced when responding to purely symbolic information, such as reading about someone's distress or by hearing about someone's unfortunate circumstances. Empathy tends to be defined as a more immediate emotional response that is experienced by the observer on witnessing someone's emotional state. Empathy may include emotion contagion, but with older children and adults we more often assume that there is some ability to take the perspective of the distressed person, and, consequently, we experience vicariously what we believe the target person to be experiencing. Sympathy is an affective response that contains elements of sorrow or concern for the distressed person. When feeling sympathetic, we do not necessarily vicariously experience the same or similar negative affect of the target (Eisenberg, 2003).

It is hard to imagine that a person could be socially effective and not be empathically involved in their interaction with others. Yet, paradoxically, sometimes too much empathy with another's negative emotional response can disrupt socially effective engagement with the distressed person, resulting in personal distress rather than being able to focus on the other person and respond appropriately. In a number of well-conducted studies, Eisenberg and her colleagues found that children also need to establish psychological boundaries so that they can respond sympathetically and not become overwhelmed by another's distress (e.g., Eisenberg et al., 1996). Such personal distress leads to a preoccupation with their own negative affective response, which then short-circuits their prosocial, sympathetic behavior. Zahn-Waxler and Robinson (1995) have argued that personal distress reactions are most likely to occur when the other's emotional-expressive display is particularly vivid and intense, and if there appears to be little that an individual can do to ameliorate the other's distressing situation. An individual might also experience personal distress when his or her sympathy is undesired by the target of their concern, as might occur when a distressed individual is further distressed by being made to feel self-conscious, helpless, or somehow inadequate through another's sympathetic overtures. We are not aware of any empirical developmental research on this latter topic.

There has been considerable debate among social and developmental psychologists as to whether empathy is a mediator of altruistic and prosocial behavior. Readers are referred to Eisenberg (2003), Eisenberg, Fabes, and Spinrad (Chapter 11, this *Handbook,* this volume; Eisenberg & Fabes, 1998) for a review of the issues. Prosocial behavior can occur simply from wanting to be sociable with others, not necessarily from being empathic to their feelings (Dunn, 1988). However, Roberts and Strayer (1996) present fairly persuasive evidence that empathy, in conjunction with being able to take the perspective of others, does predict prosocial behavior to some degree.

What seems critical to address in empathy research and its influence on children's and youths' relationships is how it combines with a sense of values to predict socially responsible behavior that is accompanied by a sense of compassion. Children who feel a sense of responsibility to help others are among those most likely to behave prosocially (Chapman, Zahn-Waxler, Cooperman, & Iannotti, 1987). There is also research that demonstrates that failures in empathy are implicated in adolescents with conduct disorders (D. Cohen & Strayer, 1996). Arsenio and Lemerise (2001) are particularly vocal in their call for the need to address moral values in research on aggression, and one of the pivotal mediators between values and prosocial behavior may well prove to be empathy.

We need to know more about the sources of individual differences in the capacity for empathic engagement without becoming overwhelmed by one's own personal distress. One possibility is how children develop a tolerance for ambiguity. Would those children and youth who can tolerate ambiguity to greater extent also be those children who turn out to have a higher threshold for tolerating another's intense distress without being overwhelmed by it and becoming personally distressed themselves? Social psychological research indicates that when people are distressed, they are more likely to impulsively indulge themselves in something pleasurable to make themselves feel better, but what they indulge themselves in is not likely to be prosocial (Tice, Brat-

slavsky, & Baumeister, 2001). If a person could tolerate uncertainty about a course of action, such as to how to intercede or not, and thereby gather more information, they might ultimately be more capable of responding not only prosocially but also more effectively in ameliorating the other's distress. This question has not been investigated to our knowledge, or at least not with children and youth; it would appear that tolerance for ambiguity would also be moderated by self-regulatory abilities and cognitive perspective-taking skill. Indeed, Eisenberg and colleagues (e.g., Eisenberg et al., 1996) provide data that show, for children to experience sympathy rather than personal distress in an emotion-evocative situation, they need to be capable of neuro-physiological regulation, use attentional control processes, accurately appraise emotion-eliciting events, infer others' internal emotional states, and cope with situational demands. We turn next to a more in-depth discussion of individual differences in empathy and sympathy, and their relation to socially adaptive behavior in children and youth.

Disposition for Over-Arousal. A significant contributor to experiencing personal distress rather than the more functional sympathetic response is the disposition to experience emotional over-arousal and more intense levels of vicariously induced negative emotion (e.g., Eisenberg et al., 1988). These researchers found that heart rate acceleration was associated with a personal distress response, but sympathy co-occurred with heart rate deceleration. In the latter study, children's heart rate and facial expressions were better predictors of their subsequent helpful overtures than their self-report.

Early Parental Attunement. While there may also be genetic and biological contributions to individual differences in empathic responsiveness and sympathy (reviewed in Eisenberg, 2003), we concur with the position taken by Zahn-Waxler (1991), who argued that the origins of prosocial and altruistic behavior are to be found in the dynamic emotional exchanges of the attachment relationship between parent and infant. She notes that the processes of joint attention, social exchange, and cooperative turn taking between caregiver and infant "create a world of shared meaning, empathic understanding and appropriate linking of one's own emotions with those of others that then generalize beyond the parent-child dyad" (p. 156). In sum, the emotional attunement between parent and baby is essentially the crucible in which empathy and concern for others' well-being are forged.

Related to this early crucible as the foundation for empathy is that for the most part it is mothers whose attunement with their infant is evaluated. Indeed, women undertake the majority of nurturing and caring for others in close relationships. Zahn-Waxler and Robinson (1995) noted that girls are socialized to be attuned more to their relations with others and to feel responsible for others' well-being. When feeling responsible for others is conjoined with discomfort, guilt and empathy may merge together, particularly if family socialization patterns have led children to acquire an overgeneralized sense of responsibility for others' well-being. They argued that young girls are more likely to develop this pattern and consequently may become more "vulnerable to establishing beliefs about their over-responsibility, unworthiness, and blameworthiness for the problems of others" (Zahn-Waxler & Robinson, 1995, p. 165). Such self-attributions are evident in depression, and, by early adolescence, girls exceed boys in incidence of depression. It appears that a healthy dose of self-interest may inoculate young girls against such feelings, and a masculine sex-role orientation (regardless of one's gender) appears to protect against depression as it is associated with assertive self-interest (see also Ruble & Martin, 1998; Zahn-Waxler, 2000).

Influence of Socialization. A recent multi-method, multi-source study on how parents might influence their children's empathy was carried out by Strayer and Roberts (2004a) who found paths between parents' empathy and their children's empathy, but the relationship was mediated by children's anger. More specifically, empathic parents had children who were *less* angry and who also demonstrated more empathy. Parents who were low in empathy were also more controlling, and they subsequently had children who were more angry and less empathic. It was the child's anger and the parents' controlling disciplinary style and associated parenting practices that appeared to mediate the relationship between parent and child empathy.

This relationship between parental insensitivity and negative reactions toward their child and subsequent ineffective social behavior in the child was also substantiated by Snyder, Stoolmiller, Wilson, and Yamamoto (2003). In their observational study, they found that children's anger was associated with frequency of parental behaviors (e.g., displays of anger, contempt, criticism, domineering, threats, stonewalling) shown toward the child. When the parents were unable to provide the child with sensitive and constructive ways to handle anger, their children tended to carry grudges and develop covert antisocial behavior (e.g., retaliation). The authors also found that the children displayed relatively less fear and sadness, and they suggested that a deficit in those more vulnerable feelings might also be associated with a deficit in empathy in these angry, belittled children. Their use of hazard analyses (essentially analyzing the "risk of recurrence" rates of children's anger displays during parent-child interaction as a function of parents' negative emotion) to infer the likelihood of subsequent emotional responses also constituted a methodological innovation in how to examine the mutually influencing effects of parent and child when in an immediate interaction.

Strayer and Roberts (2004b) also investigated more intensively how children's anger and aggression might be related to their empathy. They observed the play behavior of 5-year-olds and found that whereas empathy accounted for 18% of the variance in observed anger and aggression, it only accounted for 8% of the variance in prosocial behavior. Thus, empathic children are less angry, less verbally and physically aggressive, and were involved in fewer object struggles with their peers. In terms of social effectiveness and the ability to be empathically engaged, this study suggests that more harmonious relationships with others are clearly associated with higher levels of empathy.

In terms of sympathy, modeling by the parents appears to be an important factor in children showing more sympathy (see review by Eisenberg, Fabes, Carlo, & Karbon., 1992). Adult women who report empathy after watching distressing films also describe their families of origin in ways that indicate that positive emotions and sympathetic and vulnerable feelings were freely expressed. Along similar lines, in the investigation undertaken by Eisenberg, Fabes, Schaller, Carlo, and Miller (1991), parents' attitudes were assessed using the Parental Attitude toward Children's Expressiveness Scale (PACES; Saarni, 1990), which was modified for use with preschoolers. Parents of children who reported restrictive attitudes toward their children's emotional displays had children who seemed more inclined to experience personal distress rather than sympathetic concern when describing their reaction to another's distress. This effect was more noticeable when the parents espoused controlling beliefs about their children's emotional displays, even when the emotional displays simply expressed the child's own vulnerable feelings (e.g., sadness, anxiety) as opposed to showing one's genuine feelings without regard for whether they could also hurt someone else's feelings (e.g., showing annoyance toward a well-intentioned gift giver). Parents who restricted their children's emotional displays in circumstances where others' feelings might be hurt—but not when their children expressed vulnerable feelings—appeared to have more sympathy-oriented children. The most impacted children appeared to be boys of mothers who endorsed controlling attitudes about their sons' display of emotions in situations where only self-related vulnerable feelings were involved; these boys were the most likely to show personal distress reactions.

Recently, Valiente et al. (2004) examined the relations between parental expressive style, children's ability to access effortful control, and the children's likelihood of responding with empathy. They found that children prone to personal distress were more likely to have low effortful control; in contrast, children who could access greater effortful control were more likely to respond with sympathy rather than with personal distress. Several complex relationships were found with parental expressive style, and the authors concluded that a high level of parental negative expressive style was associated with their children's likelihood of experiencing personal distress, irrespective of their children's attempts at effortful control. We infer from this research that parental derogation (as indexed here by a negative expressive style) undermines children's abilities to regulate their empathic response such that they experience personal distress rather than being able to invoke effortful control and transform their empathy into sympathetic behavior toward a distressed victim. Research by Gottman et al. (1997) yielded similar results: Parental derogation of the child ill prepares the child for harmonious peer relationships or, for that matter, academic achievement. Indeed, Raver (2002) in a Social Policy Report for the Society for Research on Child Development also called for intervention at the levels of family, community, and child-care setting to facilitate young children's emotional development so that their school readiness would be enhanced.

A pair of longitudinal studies that examined empathy and family influence are worth mentioning. Eisen-

berg and McNalley (1993) examined relations between mothers' child-rearing practices over an 8-year period and their adolescents' (age 15 to 16) perspective taking and vicariously induced emotion. They found that mothers who expressed positive emotions and minimal negative affect with their children were more likely to have sympathetic daughters and sons who scored lower in personal distress. Warm maternal communication was also associated with increased perspective taking in youth of both genders. However, mothers' own sympathy was not significantly related to their adolescents' sympathy.

The last study was undertaken by Koestner, Franz, and Weinberger (1990) with adults who had been participants in a longitudinal study since their preschool years. Empathic concern at age 31 was most strongly related to the following variables assessed when the participants were 5 years old: Fathers' involvement in child care, mothers' tolerance of their children's dependency, inhibition of children's aggression, and satisfaction with the role of mother (fathers had not been asked about their satisfaction with their parental role, but their high involvement with their children would seem to show that they were). The authors' conclusion is worth quoting: "children are most likely to grow up to be empathically concerned adults when both of their parents enjoyed being involved with them and when their affiliative and aggressive needs were differentially responded to, with the former being permitted and encouraged and the latter inhibited" (p. 714).

Summary

Empathy and its derivative, sympathy, are critical to emotional communication; indeed, responsiveness to others' emotions is critical to human evolution (e.g., Cosmides & Tooby, 2000). The development of empathy such that it becomes linked with altruistic, prosocial behavior obviously promotes the well-being of those who need support or help, but it also facilitates the well-being of individuals who respond sympathetically. The preceding research suggests that such individuals enjoy more favorable relations with their peers, may themselves be more effective parents, and are able to regulate their emotional arousal such that they can effectively intervene to assist another. The reviewed research also indicates that complex, often indirect, relationships exist between parenting behaviors and children's empathic, sympathetic, and prosocial behavior toward others.

Social Effectiveness and Skill 5: Skill in Differentiating Internal Emotional Experience from External Emotional Expression

Whether a person is trying to protect his or her vulnerability, enhance some advantage to her- or himself, or promote the well-being of another about whom they care, being able to monitor individual emotional-expressive behavior and action tendencies strategically is adaptive, and children learn to do so with increasing finesse as they mature (Saarni, 1989, 1999). In the following discussion, this discrepancy between internal emotional state and external emotional expression is referred to as emotional dissemblance. The term *emotion management* will also be used to refer to children's regulating their experience of emotion by monitoring their expressive behavior. This last topic is also a significant link to the discussion of Skill 6 involving children's coping with aversive emotions in social contexts.

By the preschool years, if not earlier, young children learn how to introduce disparities between their internal emotional state and their external expressive behavior. Such discrepancies indicate that young children have begun to differentiate their inner emotional experience from what they express in their behavior—especially to others. Perhaps the earliest form of this differentiation between internal state and external expression is the exaggeration of emotional-expressive behavior to gain someone's attention (a trivial injury becomes the occasion to howl loudly and solicit comfort and attention). An early observational study by Blurton-Jones (1967) reported that children, ages 3 to 4, in a free-play situation were more likely to cry after injuring themselves if they noticed a caregiver looking at them; they were less likely to cry if they thought they were unattended. Minimization may be the next to appear; it consists of dampening the intensity of emotional-expressive behavior, despite feeling otherwise. Neutralization describes the adoption of a "poker face," but it is probably relatively difficult to carry off, and, indeed, in early research by Ekman and Friesen (1975) it was found that substitution of another expression that differs from what one genuinely feels is probably a more successful strategy (e.g., smiling despite feeling anxious).

Children learn to manage their expressive behavior by taking into account relationship dimensions such as closeness of relationship, power or status similarity/difference, and the degree to which they are exposed (e.g., public versus private situations). Gottman and his colleagues (1997) demonstrated in their longitudinal research that children who were most effective with their peers knew how to regulate their external expressive behavior, but we contend that children believe that it is important to find an adaptive balance between self-presentation, which may require dissemblance as well as genuine display of emotion. An early interview study indicated that school-age children believed that the display of genuine emotion was as regulated as the display of dissembled emotion (Saarni, 1989b). In older age groups, children nominated more reasons or occasions for when it would be appropriate to express one's genuine emotional response. In descending order of frequency, the categories for when it would be appropriate to express one's genuine emotional response were: (a) if the emotion was very intense; (b) if one was sick, injured, or bleeding; (c) if one was with certain people, such as parents or friends (note the close relationship dimension here); (d) if special or unusual misfortunes occurred such as being in a fire; (e) if one was in a special setting that allowed for the display of genuine emotion, such as in an amusement park or while attending a horror movie; (f) if one was a young child; (g) if one was being scolded or had just been caught doing something wrong; and finally (h) if one had been unjustly accused, one should show how one felt about it.

The pattern of responses indicated that with increasing age children demonstrated increased flexibility in the deployment of emotional-expressive behavior, whether it was dissembled or genuine in display. Their expectations also suggest the implicit use of social scripts that take into account age status and relationships (items f and c, respectively), setting (item e), and implied lack of controllability (items a, b, and d). The last two categories (items g and h) suggest interesting relationship contexts that appear to be associated with children's recognition that their expressive behavior can influence the affective and cognitive states of those who are either scolding them or unjustly accusing them. That topic has little empirical research associated with it among older children—with several important exceptions (Fuchs & Thelen, 1988; Saarni, 1992; Shipman, Zeman, Nesin, & Fitzgerald, 2003). Research undertaken by Shipman and Zeman (2001) indicated that children do indeed have expectations that their emotional-expressive displays will be responded to supportively by others, especially parents or adult caregivers. Shipman et al. (2003) also found in their interview study that younger elementary school children

(7 years old) were more likely than older children (10 years old) to believe their expressive behaviors would be acceptable and would elicit support. Interestingly, in this research, which used vignettes as the vehicle for eliciting children's expectations, there was little difference whether the expressive behavior would be directed at mother, father, or best friend (although for the latter, children thought there might be more tolerance of aggressive displays).

Components of Emotional Dissemblance

As summarized some time ago by Shennum and Bugental (1982), children gradually acquire *knowledge* about when, where, with whom, and how to express behaviorally their emotional reactions. They also need to have the *ability to control* the skeletal muscles involved in emotional-expressive behavior. They need to have the *motivation* to manage their emotional-expressive behavior in the appropriate situations. They also need to have reached a certain complexity of *cognitive representation.* We address each of these components in turn as they are reflected in recent research.

Knowledge.   As noted earlier, children can readily nominate reasons for showing their genuine emotions to others, and indeed, across all ages, the most common reason cited for when genuine emotions would be expressed was if they were experienced as very intense (i.e., and thus less controllable; Saarni, 1979). School-age children can also nominate reasons for dissembling their expressive behavior, and that early study found that the majority of their reasons referred to wanting to avoid embarrassment or derision from others for revealing vulnerable emotions such as hurt or fear. Getting attention, making someone feel sorry for you, and getting help were also among the reasons mentioned for dissembling emotional expressive behavior (cf. Shipman et al., 2003). The older children were more likely to make reference to the degree of affiliation with an interactant, status differences, and controllability of both emotion and circumstances as contextual qualities that affected the genuine or dissembled display of emotion.

Other research has elaborated on these contextual influences in children's understanding of emotional-expressive behavioral management. For example, Underwood, Coie, and Herbsman (1992) found that elementary school children reported that they would be more likely to mask angry expressive behavior with their teachers than with their peers, thus recognizing

the salience of authority and possible risk if anger were to be directly expressed. Underwood (1996) also found that age differences in reporting dissemblance of emotion varied according to the emotion felt, with older children reporting greater likelihood of masking disappointment and blunting of very positive affect and younger children (8 years) more likely to mask anger. Across emotion, girls expected more negative reactions from peers to "mismanaged" emotional-expressive behavior than boys did, and children generally expected less positive peer response to "extremely honest" emotional displays (see also Saarni, 1988).

Parker and her colleagues (2001) examined children's knowledge of dissemblance strategies for anger in a hypothetical vignette about unfair treatment of one child by another and then compared their conceptual knowledge with their actual behavior in playing a competitive game with an unfamiliar peer confederate in which they were unfairly made to lose and the confederate overtly cheated. Relative to the vignette, children's strategies for dissembling angry expressive behavior were coded as behavioral (e.g., leave the situation, cover their face) or as cognitive (e.g., focus their mind on a happier event). The investigators also monitored whether children who had been nominated by their peers as aggression prone would behave any differently during the unfair game. Their results were complex, but essentially what they found was that children reported they would feel angrier, be more likely to express their anger, and be less likely to dissemble their anger in the hypothetical story in contrast to what they reported and expressed after having lost to the cheating confederate in the unfair game (similar pattern of results obtained by R. Casey, 1993). The children rated as aggression prone did report feeling angrier and their displays were more intense and lasted longer during the unfair game, but otherwise there was little to distinguish them from the nonaggressive children (i.e., both groups of children had similar understanding of dissemblance strategies).

Another interesting study examined children's ability to conceptualize the difference between internal emotion state and facial expression and how this conceptualization might be related to their *miniaturization* of emotional expression when alone versus when engaged interpersonally (Holodynski, 2004). Children between the ages of 6 and 8 were exposed to a "slot machine" that dispensed a package of candy or an empty package. They coped with the capricious slot machine in two conditions: (1) alone or (2) accompanied by an adult research assistant. They were also extensively interviewed about their understanding of discrimination between expression and feeling, with a summary score denoting the degree of conceptual complexity in making this discrimination. Holodynski argued that the miniaturization of expressive behavior when alone emerges at around 6 years of age as children learn to self-regulate, similar to the earlier transition from private speech to internal speech serving to facilitate self-regulation (Berk, 1992). Indeed, his results revealed that his oldest age group (8 years old) reliably reduced the intensity of their expressions when alone as opposed to being with the research assistant; the 6-year-olds revealed similarly intense expressions across both conditions. Likewise, he found a significant and positive correlation between complexity of conceptualization about emotion state and expression and subsequent miniaturization of expressive behavior when alone and coping with the capricious slot machine. This research is very thought provoking, because Holodynski may have provided the explanation for some of the discrepancies found in research on children's expression of emotion when faced with different emotion-eliciting circumstances. As noted earlier, the degree of exposure, alone or engaged with others, affects emotional-expressive behavior in ways that can evoke expression amplification when with supportive others (Holodynski's study) or expressive dissemblance when faced with disagreeable confederates (the Parker et al. study, 2001; see also Underwood, Hurley, Johanson, & Mosley, 1999).

Ability to Implement Emotional Dissemblance. Control of skeletal muscles, especially in the face, is critical to being able to modify one's emotional-expressive behavior and thus dissemble the outward expression of one's emotional response. Children become capable of this modification voluntarily at a young age (2 to 3 years), and it is readily apparent in their pretend play; for example, they mimic postures, expressions, vocal qualities, and the like of assorted fantasy characters. However, when it comes to deliberately adopting emotional expressions, posing of facial expressions proves to be difficult, especially negatively toned expressions (e.g., M. Lewis, Sullivan, & Vasen, 1987). The difficulty in posing fear, disgust, sadness, and the like may be due to the fairly consistent socialization pressure in our culture to inhibit negative displays of emotion. As Lewis et al. point out, when asked to produce a scared face (i.e., looking afraid), the young children in their

sample produced scary faces instead (as though getting ready for Halloween).

A more recent study examined children's ability to control their facial muscles when asked to suppress expressions of pleasure, which was elicited by a funny routine acted out by a clown (Ceschi & Scherer, 2003). Seven- and 10-year-olds were interviewed about their knowledge of emotional expression control strategies and then divided into two groups: one group saw the clown routines without any instruction to suppress their expression and the second group were asked to try to conceal their amusement during the clown routine. Both groups apparently found the routine fairly intensely amusing, and thus the second group's ability to suppress their mirth was limited. They were able to reduce the duration of their positive expressive behaviors, but not the frequency. They did try to use control behaviors such as pressing their lips together and showed more "false smiles." Noteworthy is that the children were not alone: both the clown and the experimenter were present (cf. Holodynski's research, 2004). There was no noteworthy age difference in expressive behavior in the two groups or in the knowledge of emotion control strategies. The knowledge of emotion control strategies also did not predict either frequency or duration of expressive control strategies in the suppression group. However, Ceschi and Scherer did confirm that those control strategies that were used (false smiling, lip press, lip suck/pucker) were all in the lower part of the face, and muscle contractions in the upper part of the face and around the eyes were not influenced by the suppression condition. They also suggested that evaluating children's knowledge of emotion control strategies might be better done by having them engage in a recognition task rather than having to freely produce or nominate their control strategies.

Motivation. One of us has investigated children's knowledge of how to manage emotional-expressive behavior and their expectations about what motivated story characters to undertake such management strategies (Saarni, 1979). When the children were asked to explain why the story character's emotional reaction had not been genuinely expressed, four broad categories of motivation were apparent in their responses. These four motivation categories are elaborated as follows:

1. Avoidance of negative situational outcomes or enhancement of positive situational outcomes: This common motive is well illustrated in a study by Davis (1995). She had children play a game in which a desirable prize and an undesirable one were placed in two boxes, visible only to the child. The children were told to deceive the experimenter by pretending to like both prizes, and if they succeeded in "tricking" the experimenter to believe they really liked both, they would be able to keep both prizes. If they did not succeed, then the experimenter took both prizes. Thus, for the children to get the attractive prize, they had to persuasively manage their expressive behavior so as to look positive for both attractive and unattractive prizes. The results showed that the girls were more successful at suppressing negative expressive behaviors toward the unattractive prize than the boys. The girls also revealed a greater number of social monitoring behaviors (e.g., rapid glancing at the experimenter) as well as tension behaviors (e.g., touching one's face), and they appeared to monitor the social exchange more closely than the boys, which may have facilitated their expression management. Davis concludes that girls do have more ability in managing the expression of their negative emotions, and she suggests that individual differences (e.g., temperament) may interact with sex-role socialization to yield the gender pattern she observed.

2. Protection of one's self-esteem: Meerum Terwogt and Olthof (1989) found that boys were reluctant to express fear because they worried they would be viewed as cowards by their peers. Fuchs and Thelen (1988) also reported that boys were loathe to reveal their sadness to their fathers but might consider doing so with their mothers. Maintenance of self-image appeared to be the chief motive for these boys and emotion management was sought by adoption of a stoic "emotional front."

DePaulo (1991) reviewed the earlier literature on what is known about the development of self-presentation, emphasizing nonverbal behavior. One point she made was that as children grow older, more of their peers and adult networks hold them accountable for being able to regulate and manage their emotional-expressive behavior. Thus, there is a continual reinforcement of motivation to manage how one presents oneself to others. There is a great need for further research on how children's needs to self-protect or to enhance their self-image in the eyes of others are linked to emotion dissemblance strategies and self-presentation, but this topic, relative to children, has been underresearched in recent years. More common is research on lying and deception (e.g., Talwar & Lee, 2002). Anderson, Ansfield, and DePaulo (1999) have

provided a review of deception and its links to self-presentation in relationships; although their review focuses on adults, it is suggestive for how research could be extended to children and youth and framed in a developmental inquiry.

3. Maintenance or enhancement of relationships and concern for others' well-being: As an illustration of this last motive for emotional dissemblance, von Salisch (1991, 1996) probed how children actually regulated a relationship by monitoring what they expressed. She developed a computer game that was rigged: The computer was cast as the "opponent" and two children were to play as a team. If the airplane "crashed" on the screen, it meant the children had lost; however, its demise was random but appeared to the children to have been caused by one of them. The participating children were 11-years old, and she was able to have the pairs consist of either best friends or of casual acquaintances. In her analyses of the actual conflict episodes, the most frequent expressive behavior was smiling, followed by signs of tension, then contempt, and last by anger (only 3% of the expressions). In many cases, the children also verbalized reproaches about the "crash," but then accompanied the reproach by smiling. With close friends, the incidence of smiling was even greater than with acquaintances, and among girls in close friend pairs, genuine smiles were especially notable in their reciprocity, even through these girls more frequently verbalized their negative feelings about their friend's game-playing skill (or ostensible lack thereof). The boys in close friendship pairs tended to verbalize less, but they showed more signs of tension than any other group. In essence, these preadolescent boys and girls used their smiles to reassure their friend that the relationship was still on firm ground, despite their reproaching their friend for their "incompetence" in making them lose the game against the computer. Expressive behavior has among its functions more than simply the display of emotion; it is also a social message. What von Salisch's research shows us is that children are adept at using this social function of emotional-expressive behavior to manage their relationships, and they do so in a discriminating fashion.

4. Observance of norms and conventions: These are the cultural display rules that provide us with consensually agreed on scripts for how to manage our emotions. A couple of 9- to 10-year-old children's responses illustrate their notions of what are norms for emotional dissemblance: "You should smile when you get a gift, even if you don't like it much," "You shouldn't yell at a grown-up," and "you should apologize, even though you don't feel like it." It is probably noteworthy that cultural display rules often have "shoulds" associated with them (e.g., Gnepp & Hess, 1986). At least a couple of factors might account for why children do not consistently perform cultural display rule scripts, despite knowing them: First, the social stakes may not be sufficiently high for them to feel motivated to do so; second, their distressed, hurt, or angry emotional responses may be experienced as too intense to allow for emotional dissemblance. As mentioned earlier (Saarni, 1989b), intensity of emotional response was cited by school-age children as the chief reason for when emotions would be genuinely expressed. Research by Garner and Power (1996) also indicated that emotional intensity as a temperament factor may influence the likelihood of adopting emotional dissemblance in certain situations.

These four categories for why we may be motivated to dissemble the expression of our emotional responses are not necessarily exhaustive nor are they mutually exclusive, but they all have one significant feature in common: They are concerned with interpersonal consequences, and it is the varying nature of these social consequences that yields the differences among motives. Even the self-esteem motive for dissemblance does not occur in a social vacuum, for the self is embedded in a history of social relationships.

Cognitive Representation. As suggested by Josephs's (1994) research, a pragmatic or implicit knowledge of emotional dissemblance is likely to precede an articulated and verbalized understanding of expressive dissimulation. In the "theory of mind" literature, a large body of research has emerged concerned with children's understanding of real versus apparent phenomena, and this distinction has been applied to inner emotional state as "real" and external expressive behavior as "apparent." By school entry, children generally understand that how one looks on one's face is not necessarily how one feels on the inside (e.g., Harris, 1989; Harris & Gross, 1988). Thus, relatively young children understand that the appearance of one's facial expression can be misleading about the actual emotional state experienced. By age 6, many children can provide justifications for how appearances can conceal reality, in this case, the genuine emotion felt by an individual.

Harris and Gross (1988) examined young children's rationales for why story characters would conceal their emotions by adopting misleading facial expressions. A significant number of the 6-year-olds interviewed gave very complex justifications that included describing the intent to conceal their feelings and to mislead another to believe something other than what was really being emotionally experienced (e.g., "she didn't want her sister to know that she was sad about not going to the party"). Children younger than age 6 can readily adopt pretend facial expressions, but they are not likely to be able to articulate the embedded relationships involved in deliberate emotional dissemblance. Developmental research that illustrates children's understanding of false beliefs and social perspective taking and the relation between these two cognitive markers and coordinated communication with a playmate was undertaken by Slomkowski and Dunn (1996). They suggested that these cognitive aptitudes are indicative of children's abilities "to read each other" as they regulate and coordinate their conversations and behavior with their peers. Harris (1998) also reviewed the relevant literature on emotional appraisal as it relates to young children's pretend play, and one of the features that he emphasized was young children's attributions of *agency* to make-believe others and their appraisal of fictional material in ways that induces emotional experience. In his words, "the creation and consumption of fictional worlds is a pervasive human enterprise" (Harris, p. 353) and is sustained by our engagement with emotional experiences derived by our appraisal of imaginary events. By the 2nd and 3rd year of life, normal children show this capacity for imagination and fantasy play, thus indicating that critical cognitive skills are developing that also become part of their cognitive repertoire for representing what is real and what may be dissembled and being able to attribute agency and emotionally significant meaning to both the genuine emotion and the dissembled expression.

Summary

A person's ability to maneuver emotional-expressive behavior according to interpersonal contexts and emotional responses gives them a rich repertoire of communicative behavior. The intermingling of emotional experience and social interaction is also evident in children's acquisition of emotional dissemblance and emotion management strategies. There are highly adaptive and functional reasons for humans to be able to dissociate their emotional-expressive behavior from their internally felt, subjective emotional experience: One is being able to have reasonably satisfactory relationships with others; another is to be able to get others to provide support and validation for oneself; still another is to exert one's influence on others—as in impression management, persuasive communication, and the like. A reason that children are particularly likely to endorse is that it helps one to avoid getting into trouble, and last, the omnipresent self-appraisal system has its antennae out to try to create experiences that strengthen or protect the self rather than undermine it. Coping effectively with interpersonal conflict and other situational stressors has much to do with how we regulate both our subjective experience of emotion as well as with what we communicate expressively to others.

Social Effectiveness and Skill 6: Skill in Adaptive Coping with Aversive Emotions and Distressing Circumstances

Accumulated research indicates that adaptive coping requires at least three conditions to be met: (1) regulation of one's emotional arousal, (2) adequate appraisal of the problematic situation and what is realistically under one's control, and (3) resolution that yields a sense of mastery and/or resilience (e.g., Aldwin, 1994; Compas, Connor, Saltzman, Thomsen, & Wadsworth, 1999; Wolchik & Sandler, 1997). We address each of these three conditions relative to how they contribute to social effectiveness. In this section, we also briefly comment on research that raises interesting questions about socialization influence and context effects on the development of adaptive coping.

Emotion Regulation

The issues surrounding emotion regulation recur in this chapter for good reason: The topic is theoretically rich with possibilities for understanding emotion processes and for clinical and educational application. We addressed previously some of the contemporary research on emotion regulation and implications for social competence, and we elaborate further some of the current research in this area. The reader is referred to the special issue on emotion regulation that appeared in *Child Development* (vol. 75, 2004) for thoughtful discussions on how to conceptualize emotion regulation, and, in par-

ticular, the distinction should be made between emotion regulating something else (e.g., another's social response to the self) and emotion itself being regulated (e.g., self-soothing). As noted earlier, emotion regulation is dynamically integral to emotion generation itself, and the complexity of feedback in emotion processes will occupy researchers for some time to come. However, for the purposes of linking emotion regulation with social effectiveness, we emphasize that being able to modulate one's degree of emotional arousal facilitates one's coping with an environmental stressor or conflict. This does not mean simple inhibition; amplification of emotional experience and expressive display may also be strategically effective in a particular situation.

Research on children's emotion regulation may take into account:

- Temperamental reactivity (see Rothbart & Bates, 1998)
- Processes that involve deployment of attention (including effortful control as operationally defined by Eisenberg and colleagues; e.g., Valiente et al., 2003)
- Components of emotion (physiological, expressive, and subjective experience)
- Approach/avoidance tendencies, whereby the latter is understood to include individual differences in inhibition and "niche picking" (i.e., seeking out situations in which desired emotional experiences are likely and avoiding those situations in which aversive emotions are likely to be evoked; see Campos et al., 2004)

Brenner and Salovey's (1997) definition of emotion regulation combines these elements: It is the relative capacity to manage one's emotional reactivity (including intensity and duration of arousal) such that alterations in one's physiological-biochemical system, behavioral-expressive system, and experiential-cognitive system are affected. We also add the emphasis of the relational and functionalist perspective used in this chapter such that emotional regulatory processes should be understood as occurring in contexts construed as personally meaningful to the individual. Finally, *optimal* emotion regulation *over time* should also contribute to a sense of well-being or emotional equilibrium, a sense of self-efficacy, and a sense of connectedness to others to the extent that effective emotion regulation facilitates constructive problem-solving strategies and appropriate appraisal of social contexts.

Development of Emotion Regulation and Coping

Thompson et al. (2003) reviewed the maturing emotion regulatory capacities of the infant's nervous system and concluded that during the 1st year, excitatory and inhibitory processes are stabilized so that infants gradually develop a greater ability to inhibit or minimize the intensity and duration of emotional reactions, and at the same time they also acquire a greater diversity of emotional responses. Examples of early regulation of emotional arousal are young infants' soothing themselves through sucking or withdrawal from excessive stimulation, but equally critical is that caregivers assist infants in learning how to regulate their arousal through attending to their infants' distress and providing comfort. Caregivers also regulate the situations that infants are exposed to so that infants' emotional experience is moderated. Thompson has also argued that parents' emotion regulatory interventions may, over time, contribute significantly to their children's style of emotion regulation. His illustration is that of parents who wait until their child's upset has escalated to high levels before they intervene. The effect is that they reinforce their child's rapid rise time of distress and high intensity of responding, which in turn makes it harder for the parents to soothe their infant due to his or her high level of emotional arousal.

By toddlerhood, we can more readily see how emotion regulation plays a *mediating* role between evocative stressors and how young children cope with a particular taxing situation: By regulating their emotional arousal, they can delay their reaction such that they may be able to adopt a different sort of coping behavior than simply fleeing or lashing out at the stressor (e.g., by age 2 children can approach a peer or small animal). However, emotion regulation, viewed from the standpoint of management of emotional-expressive behavior, might in other contexts play a *moderating* role between the interpersonal circumstances one faces and one's motives for a social outcome. For example, sustaining the duration of the expressive display of happiness (a genuine smile) or amplifying one's smile influences the likelihood that one's interactant will respond positively in kind. Managing one's emotional-expressive behavior can be used to increase or decrease the sorts of social interaction one desires with another (e.g., see the discussion of emotion communication in interpersonal negotiation in Saarni & Buckley, 2002; for preschool examples, see Barrett, 1997). Mutually regulating behaviors that involve the exchange of emotional-expressive signals has a long history of research, for the most part with infants and their caregivers (e.g., Gianino & Tronick, 1988; Trevarthen, 1993). Less research has been undertaken with school-age children, but a number of studies suggest that children are well aware that their expressive displays (self-presentation) influence their peers' subsequent responses to them (e.g., Carlson Jones, Abbey, & Cumberland, 1998; Gottman, Guralnick, Wilson, Swanson, & Murray, 1997; Halberstadt et al., 2001; Hubbard, 2001; Parker et al., 2001; Saarni & Weber, 1999; von Salisch, 1996; Zeman & Shipman, 1997).

The Influence of Temperament

The notion of temperament is a multifaceted one and fraught with many definitional and measurement problems (e.g., Rothbart & Bates, 1998, and Chapter 3, this *Handbook,* this volume), but it is a useful construct for thinking about what are some of the influences on how children develop different styles of emotion regulation and coping. Temperament may be viewed as a collection of dispositions that characterize the individual's style in responding to environmental change (or the lack thereof). These dispositions include reactivity, arousability, and temporal dimensions such as latency of response. Some theorists also include as temperamental traits sociability, approach/avoidance tendencies, and degree of attentional control. Most theorists working with temperament regard these dispositions as applicable to both emotional and nonemotional behavior, and many theorists contend that temperamental dispositions have a biophysiological contribution that is influenced by one's genetic makeup.

When we look at temperament as applied to how a person responds emotionally to evocative stimulation, we can examine the intensity of emotional response (both negative and positive valence), the threshold of arousal of emotional response, the duration (and other temporal aspects) of the emotional response, and even the proclivity for what sort of hedonic tone of emotional response is generated (i.e., negative versus positive reactions to change). The construct emotionality has typically been used to refer to temperament's influence on emotional experience; "high" emotionality is often assumed to refer to high intensity of emotional reaction, frequently combined with a negative hedonic tone (but see Strelau, 1987, for a review of six different definitions of emotionality, some of which do not associate a negative hedonic tone with high levels of emotional intensity of response).

Although temperament is a general proclivity in an individual to approach or withdraw from a novel situation and to react strongly or not to a novel situation, temperament is *not* the same as the emotional response elicited in the individual that requires regulation, rather temperament can be thought of as the background on which the emotion plays out. Emotions are also highly contextualized and dependent on the individual's goals and motives of the moment (Campos et al., 1994; M. Lewis, 1997); their nuances and variety are captured by the huge number of emotion-related words in the English language (White, 2000).

Metaphorically, temperament is rather like a season of the year, but emotions are the mercurial weather conditions that shift from day to day, demanding adjustment and accommodation on a frequent basis. In this metaphor, the season provides constraints on the daily weather, just as temperament may provide some degree of limitation on the experience of emotional response. Temperament influences emotion regulation as in figure-ground relationships; it is the ground, but emotions and their regulation are the figure. Thus, the child who is relatively inhibited in temperament (prone to withdrawal from novel situations) and who tends to react strongly to novel situations (less likely to modulate intensity) may be the child who will more often experience emotions of anxiety, fear, and shame. But this same child may also respond to familiar situations with pleasure, sympathy, and caring. Indeed, we find that the more inhibited child is also the one who is more compliant with parents and internalizes a moral conscience more readily than those young children characterized as more bold and active (reviewed in Kochanska & Thompson, 1997).

Using temperament in this fairly global fashion as having to do with how we dispositionally tend to modulate our emotional reactions, we can examine how individual differences in temperament may influence coping efficacy. This approach was taken by Eisenberg and her colleagues in several different research projects on preschoolers' coping efficacy relative to their social functioning. In one investigation, Eisenberg et al. (1993) looked at 4- to 6-year-old children whose temperament-influenced emotional intensity level was rated by both their mothers and their teachers and then examined by the children's social competence (teacher ratings) and sociometric ratings (peer popularity). They also evaluated the children's coping strategies by having the teachers and mothers rate the children's likelihood of using assorted coping strategies in hypo-

thetical situations. Among their very complex results were that greater social competence of boys (but not girls) could be predicted by their displaying constructive coping strategies (e.g., problem solving) and not displaying excessive negative emotion. For girls, social competence could be predicted from their use of avoidant coping strategies rather than by their engaging in acting out or conflict-escalating behaviors. For both boys and girls, high emotional intensity was associated with lower levels of constructive coping and with lower levels of attentional control (shifting and distractable attention versus focused attention, as assessed by teachers). In short, those 4- to 6-year-olds who frequently showed high intensity negative emotions were more likely to be distractable and to demonstrate less constructive coping. They were also regarded by their teachers as less socially mature and by their peers as less attractive as playmates.

In a second study with the same 4- to 6-year-olds, Eisenberg, Fabes, Nyman, Bernzweig, and Pinuelas (1994) investigated relations among temperament (more specifically, emotionality, operationally defined as intensity of reaction and negative tone of emotion, and their ability to control their attention), coping skills, and their management of anger with their peers. The pattern of their findings was complex with some results occurring only for teacher-rated behaviors but not for mother-rated behaviors. Gender of the child was again a variable that affected some of the patterning of results. Overall, children whose temperament was characterized by low levels of emotionality, displayed reactions that were socially desirable—the children used nonhostile verbal strategies to try to deal with the anger provocation. This pattern was stronger for boys than girls, and boys who used socially desirable and constructive responses to anger were also rated as higher in attentional control. Girls who tended to escape the situation when angered were viewed by teachers as socially skilled—the girls' avoidance of anger was apparently seen as not contributing to an escalation of conflict, a desirable outcome from teachers' standpoint. Although the authors were not studying sex-role socialization, it is noteworthy that teachers' approval of sex-typed behaviors (e.g., the girls' avoidance of conflict), even at this relatively young age, may be influencing children's subsequent style of coping with such gender role-laden emotions as anger.

Although the construct of temperament allows us to consider what children might inherently bring with them as they seek to cope with stressful circumstances, it is unlikely that temperament solely affects how constructive one's coping style is. The social environment has also been modulating and giving meaning to the young child's emotional behavior all along, which includes such temperamental dimensions as intensity, hedonic tone, temporal factors, and the like. Cultures that value expressive restraint might ascribe rather different meanings to, for example, intensity of emotional response, than cultures that do not have such an orientation. In the end, adequacy of coping will be best determined by whether individuals experience themselves as efficacious in the sociocultural context in which they find themselves.

Effective and Ineffective Coping and Emotion Regulation with Peers and Family

We find that children who are "good copers" can modulate their emotions such that they can continue to attend to what is going on socially (e.g., Gottman et al., 1997) and that they can avoid negative emotional escalation by circumventing problematic situations (Eisenberg et al., 1993, 2004). Research has also shown that children who enjoy substantial family support and moderate structure have a larger repertoire of coping strategies (Hardy, Power, & Jaedicke, 1993), and it makes sense that a broader repertoire of coping strategies permits adaptation to a wider variety of emotion-provoking circumstances.

One provocative study by Ramsden and Hubbard (2002) described how parental coaching might affect children's emotion regulation (as measured by the Emotion Regulation Checklist; Shields & Cicchetti, 1997), which in turn was hypothesized to predict children's aggression at school. Their coding of parental coaching of emotion included three dimensions: (1) acceptance of child's emotion, (2) awareness of child's emotion, and (3) instruction about emotion to the child. Their results indicated that the most robust link to aggression was the child's own emotion regulation rating, but parental acceptance of child emotion was positively related to higher emotion regulation, and the overall degree of negative expressivity in the family (as measured by the Family Expressiveness Questionnaire; Halberstadt, 1986) influenced the child's emotion regulation rating in a negative way. Thus, family emotion processes, such as acceptance of children's emotion, and the emotional "climate" of the family, in this case, negative emotional expressivity,

may indirectly affect children's relations with peers, but they do so by influencing children's emotion regulation ability.

Another study also examined maternal self-reported acceptance or control of their children's emotional expressiveness as it related to their children's attachment status and their emotion regulation in a frustrating game (Beat the Bell). Berlin and Cassidy (2003) modified the Parent Attitude toward Child Expressiveness Scale (Saarni, 1985, 1990) for use with mothers of preschoolers, who were participants in a longitudinal study. As infants, the children had been classified in the Strange Situation as securely attached, insecure-avoidant, or insecure-anxious. Their results indicated that children with insecure-avoidant attachment classifications were more likely to suppress their anger and not share their sadness in the frustrating game with their mothers, and their mothers reported that they were more controlling of their children's emotional expressivity. Children with an insecure-anxious attachment had mothers who reported significantly less control of their children's emotional expressivity. Mothers of securely attached children were moderate in both their acceptance and control of their children's emotional expressivity. Interestingly, no significant relations were found between attachment classification and children's emotion regulation during the frustrating Beat the Bell game. The authors speculated that this particular game may not have tapped into the emotion regulation abilities of children that are associated with earlier infant-mother attachment.

Peer interaction has also been studied relative to emotion regulation and coping. As an illustration, Wilton, Craig, and Pepler's (2000) research on *victims* of bullies determined that there appeared to be two prototypical coping styles when accosted by a bully in the classroom. The first coping style consisted of a cluster of behaviors that escalated the bullying episode: aggressive reactivity, expressive displays of anger, contempt, interest, and joy, and an emotion regulation disposition to high intensity arousal of negative affect. This cluster was found in 43% of the bullying episodes.

The second coping style was more oriented toward problem solving and tended to de-escalate the bullying episode. Fifty-two percent of the bullying episodes fell in this second group. This cluster was subdivided into two further patterns, which the authors referred to as the passive problem-solving approach (84%) and the active problem-solving approach (only 16%). Both patterns yielded either resolution or de-escalation of the bullying, but with rather different outcomes: For the passive problem solvers, there was essentially capitulation to the bully or avoidance. The authors inferred that such victims were primarily reacting with anxiety and sadness. The authors surmised that this submissive stance would invite further bullying because the bully gets his or her way. As for the active problem solvers, they responded assertively and the bullying episodes were resolved. What is unknown is whether these children effectively reduced their being threatened by the classroom bullies over time. Last, the authors examined same gender and cross-gender bully victim interactions and found no differences in the prevalence of these two general patterns in victim response. Given the recent attention to girls' social and relational aggression (e.g., Underwood, 2003), we would be very interested in seeing observational research that looks at coping styles of the victims who are targeted by girls (and boys) for relational aggression scapegoating.

Research that links coping and emotion regulation with relationships among children and youth needs to address the influence of context, for example, which emotion is elicited under what sort of circumstances and in what sort of relationship. Much of the existing research is also based on hypothetical vignettes or on adult ratings of children's coping. Interestingly, in a recent study that did compare observations of children's anger management strategies with their verbal hypothetical reports, children showed less anger in the live situation compared to what they reported they would express in the hypothetical situation (Parker et al., 2001). Alternatively, Dearing, Hubbard, and Ramsden (2002) found that children nominated by their peers as aggressive were more likely to handle roughly the materials of a rigged game, yet their awareness or knowledge of anger regulation strategies was not directly related to aggressive status.

Coping Strategies

It is not always clear whether coping is different from emotion regulation. Some researchers refer to coping as an aspect of self-regulation because effortful or purposeful responses may be involved when one copes with a challenging situation (e.g., Compas, 1987). Other investigators use the terms *coping* and *emotion regulation* interchangeably (e.g., Brenner & Salovey, 1997), argu-

ing that both are implicated when children use available strategies to manage stressful encounters. Coping research has typically focused on *strategies* used to manage stress-provoking experience or aversive emotions that are evoked by challenging circumstances. From this perspective, coping follows emotion regulation in a temporal sense: first, a person modulates his or her emotional arousal and then seeks to resolve the stressful encounter to his or her benefit. However, given the dynamics of transactional and reciprocal relations in children's and youths' social worlds, it is unlikely that emotion regulation and coping are so simplistically distinguished according to a linear temporal path (e.g., Campos, Frankel, & Camras, 2004; Lazarus, 1999).

Coping researchers often develop new categories to which they assign various coping strategies: (a) Lazarus and Folkman (1984; Lazarus, 1999) proposed a basic dichotomy between emotion-focused coping and problem-focused coping, (b) others simply use approach (active) versus avoidance (passive) to characterize coping efforts, or (c) primary versus secondary control coping strategies (Marriage & Cummins, 2004), or (d) engagement versus disengagement coping (Ebata & Moos, 1991). Ayers and Sandler (1996) used factor analyses to distill a four-factor model of dispositional coping strategies that were also invariant across gender in a preadolescent sample; the factors were active, distraction, avoidant, and support-seeking. Sandstrom (2004) combined various approaches to the assessment of children's coping strategies into a new instrument for evaluating how children cope specifically with peer rejection. Her four coping categories for describing how children cope with this socially aversive context included:

1. Active coping (e.g., problem solving, assertiveness, getting help/support, constructive distraction, humor)
2. Aggressive coping (e.g., retaliation, teasing, arguing, getting angry, getting others to turn against them)
3. Denial coping (e.g., tell oneself it does not matter, do not care, forget about it, ignore)
4. Ruminative coping (e.g., worry about it, withdraw, wish it were not happening)

One of us (Saarni, 1997) examined children's beliefs about "best" and "worst" coping strategies. Five categories of coping strategies were compiled from the research literature, including problem solving, support- seeking (subdivided into solace-seeking and help-seeking), distancing/avoiding, internalizing, and externalizing. The children (ages 6 to 12) read five different vignettes accompanied by schematic drawings and each vignette featured a negative emotion (e.g., fear, hurt, anger, shame, or sadness). All vignettes were ascertained to have moderate controllability of outcome, featured the protagonist as experiencing moderately intense emotions, concerned peer interaction, and were gender neutral. The results indicated that the younger children's justifications were less complex for which coping strategy was nominated as best or worst, but there were no age differences in the choice of what was thought to be the best or worst strategy. Overall, children preferred beneficial coping strategies such as problem solving and support-seeking, except for the vignette featuring "hurt feelings" for which children picked the distancing strategy as the "best." Aggressive externalizing coping responses were most often selected as the worst option across all emotion-category vignettes. For the most part, children's justifications for their best coping choices emphasized the social situational gains, and parallel losses were cited as justifications for the worst coping choice (e.g., externalizing responses).

More research is needed to determine if children know what generally adaptive coping strategies are, and what gets in the way when they do not employ them. One possibility is self-appraisal, attribution of responsibility for the outcome, and controllability (of one's own emotion and the situational aspects) all interact to influence how children and youth cope in taxing circumstances. To add to this complexity is the role that temperament, especially proneness to negative emotionality and attention deficits, plays in children's ability to recruit adaptive and socially effective coping strategies.

Developmental Change in Coping Strategies

In examining what changes about coping strategies as children mature, we find that although use of situation-oriented problem solving is accessible throughout childhood, it becomes more targeted to the specific problem at hand, and children's repertoire of problem-solving strategies broadens with age (e.g., Altshuler & Ruble, 1989). With age, children's ability to consider a stressor from a number of different angles increases, thus older children can more readily consider different problem solutions relative to these different perspectives (Aldwin, 1994). They learn to recruit social support more effectively and subtly, for example, through effective self-

presentation strategies that garner social approval. They expand their capacity to tolerate aversive emotion to the degree that appraisal processes can be redirected and thus reduce distress (e.g., Band & Weisz, 1988). If appraisal indicates that control over the situational stressor or conflict is minimal or extremely risky, effective emotional regulation may also involve distraction, cognitively reframing the meaning of the difficult situation, and use of cognitive blunting or sensitizing (Miller & Green, 1985). Denial and dissociation appear to be less adaptive coping strategies in that emotions are split off from their eliciting context for short-term gain but at long-term expense (e.g., Fischer & Ayoub, 1993).

Last, perceived control over the stressful situation is relevant to how coping efforts are undertaken. As children mature, they become better able to distinguish uncontrollable stressors from controllable ones (Aldwin, 1994). For the uncontrollable situations, older children are more likely to nominate "secondary control" coping strategies, which include reframing, distraction, and avoidance through anticipatory planfulness (e.g., Marriage & Cummins, 2004). Younger children's avoidance is more often of the escape sort such as hiding under the bed to avoid an unpleasant event (Aldwin, 1994). A large literature has developed examining the different coping strategies mentioned earlier, and for further elaboration, the reader is referred to Aldwin's (1994) volume on stress, coping, and development, and reviews by Compas, Connor-Smith, Saltzman, and Thomsen (2001); Skinner and Wellborn (1994); Wolchik and Sandler (1997); and Wyman, Sandler, Wolchik, and Nelson (2000).

Brenner and Salovey (1997) proposed a framework for the analysis of coping that includes several important dimensions that are relevant to developmental change in coping strategy use: (a) the controllability of the stressor, (b) the degree to which the individual invokes solitary strategies as opposed to socially interactive ones, and (c) the use of internal/intrapsychic strategies as opposed to situational-focused strategies. We elaborate on the dimensions of solitary-social strategies and intrapsychic-situational strategies below as they manifest themselves in children at different developmental stages.

The solitary-social dimension in regulatory strategies is readily illustrated by our use of physical exercise to dissipate tension, frustration, and other dysphoric states. Children soothe themselves with physical activities such as thumb sucking; they also make good use of solitary fantasy play as a regulatory strategy (Slade,

1994). Alternatively, throughout our lives we seek social support (e.g., help, comfort) as a way to cope with stressors and regulate our emotional experience. However, the younger the child, the more significant is the need for social support (e.g., Thompson et al., 2003). Young children rely on adults to provide safe environments such that their ability to cope is not overwhelmed, and caregivers provide direct teaching of coping strategies and modeling on how to cope (e.g., Miller, Klieweer, Hepworth, & Sandler, 1994; Valiente, Fabes, Eisenberg, & Spinrad, 2004). Rossman (1992) found that young elementary school-age children (6 to 7 years) were more likely to cite parents as sources of support, whereas older children were more likely to turn to their peers.

The internal-external dimension becomes more salient in older children's coping and emotion regulation due to their ability to introspect and use metacognition in their understanding of themselves. Meerum Terwogt and Olthof (1989) reviewed a number of studies that suggested that the cognitive developmental gains of middle childhood facilitated self-reflection, thus permitting children to use more cognitive strategies to render emotional experience less aversive (by using distraction, thinking optimistically, and being able to shift perspectives to allow for more positive appraisals). However, Harris and Lipian (1989) found what they called "cognitive slippage" in school-age children when dealing with immediate and acute stress (hospitalization). Compared with unstressed children, the hospitalized children seemed to regress to less mature ways of thinking and understanding cognitive and emotional processes. Similarly, in a recent review of depression, temperament, and coping, Compas and his colleagues (Compas, Connor-Smith, & Jaser, 2004) suggested that children and youth who had more control over attentional processes were more likely to make use of more complex cognitive coping strategies, including shifting their attention away from pain (e.g., blunting), reinterpreting the situation in more positive ways, and being able to selectively attend to positive thoughts and circumstances, thereby ameliorating the likelihood of depression.

A methodological concern is that virtually all of these studies used children's and youth's verbal self-report, which may confound the increased ability to use internally focused strategies with the greater verbal skills that also accompany maturation. It is probable that young children (preschoolers) can also access intrapsychic strategies, although they cannot verbalize for us that they are doing so. For example, dissociation is an intrapsychic coping strategy, and it is used by young children as a way of distracting themselves from an intensely stressful situation. It is also useful when children feel powerless and overwhelmed.

Family Influences on Children's Coping

Attachment. A potentially significant influence on children's coping strategies is their early attachment experience with significant caregivers. Cassidy (1994) has theorized how attachment history and emotion regulation may be linked; the reader is referred to her work for further detail and to the *Handbook of Attachment* (Cassidy & Shaver, 1999). We provide only a brief summary of her thinking. She argues that negative emotions, such as anger and fear, for the securely attached infant come to be associated with maternal sympathetic assistance and that these negative feelings are neither associated with any sort of invalidation of the young child nor with denial of the negative feelings. For emotional regulation, this means that the young child comes to be able to tolerate aversive emotion temporarily such that it can begin to make sense of the frustrating or conflictual situation that faces it and figure out an adaptive coping response. The anxious-avoidant attached infant, however, has often experienced its caregiver's rejection when it sought comfort for its distress. Such an infant learns that some emotions are not acceptable and maybe not even safe. The infant develops a wariness and avoidance of his or her caregiver and begins to regulate his or her distress by minimizing their emotional expression when in the presence of the caregiver. The infant's strategy appears to be that when experiencing emotional distress, it suppresses any negative emotional display so as to maintain caregiver involvement—the infant's emotional regulation strategy seems to be, "Mom will stay with me if I don't raise any fuss." The cost, however, to the infant is constant emotional vigilance and suppression of normal distress. In short, development of adaptive problem-solving and support-seeking coping strategies may be short-circuited for insecure infants.

Related research on infants' attachment classification and their propensity to experience different kinds of emotion was examined by Kochanska (2001). She found that over a 26-month period that (a) infants classified as avoidantly attached become progressively more fearful, (b) resistantly attached children appeared to have difficulty responding with joy or pleasure, (c) young children with disorganized attachment classifications became more angry, and (d) the securely attached children showed less fear and anger than children with the other attachment classifications, in spite of being placed in situations designed to elicit those emotions. One study worth mentioning examined adolescents' attachment classification relative to how they coped with distress. Howard and Medway (2004) included measures of attachment, coping style, life stress, and a questionnaire about whom the respondent would turn to in times of stress. Their results indicated that adolescents with secure attachment status were more likely to use family communication as a coping resource and less likely to turn to substance use as a way to avoid coping with distress. Insecure attachment, alternatively, was related to negative avoidant coping strategies. Less report of stress was also associated with secure attachment and more stress was reported by those with insecure attachment scores. Adolescents also tended to prefer their friends over their parents when they did feel distress.

Family Conflict and Dysfunction. Given the relatively few studies that have tracked quality of attachment to children's subsequent coping competence, the ways that families contribute to individual children's coping competence are far from being well understood. There is a larger body of research that has examined the effects of marital conflict and anger on children's functioning—the latter having some links with how well children cope with the aversive feelings that they themselves experience. Cummings and his colleagues (e.g., Cummings, Goeke-Morey, Papp, & Dukewich, 2002) have conducted a number of investigations on this topic, and, not surprisingly, the general conclusion that they reach is that many children do not fare well when faced with frequent and intense marital conflict. If verbal and physical aggression is common between spouses, the boys in particular appear to develop aggressive, externalizing behavior problems. Daughters also demonstrate behavior problems, but more of the girls also show acute distress. Angry exchanges between parents are felt by children as very stressful, even when they play no role in the dispute, and the immediate coping strategies that children bring to bear on such a family crisis probably pivot on the children's perception of controllability of the dispute.

Children growing up with depressed or psychiatrically disturbed parents have also been studied for how such a family environment influences children's emotional and social functioning. Obviously, parental dysfunction co-occurs with higher frequency with other stressful events for children such as divorce, chronic unemployment, and spousal conflict. Goodman, Brogan, Lynch, and Fielding (1993) investigated the socioemotional functioning of children (ages 5 to 10) who had a depressed mother; the children were subdivided further into three groups: (1) some also had a disturbed father in the home, (2) some were in mother-custody homes, and (3) some had a well father in the home. They also had a comparison sample of children whose mothers and fathers were neither depressed nor psychiatrically disturbed.

Their results indicated that it was the combination of a depressed mother and a disturbed father that was associated with the greatest number of problems among older children as opposed to younger children (cf., Zahn-Waxler, 2000). Apparently, as the children matured, living in an emotionally strained household with two psychiatrically ill parents began to take its toll. Younger children did not yet demonstrate such negative effects. Their study also reconfirmed the problematic effect that divorce has on children when living with a depressed parent, particularly on self-regulation variables. Such children tended to be rated as undercontrolled, for example, more often aggressive and impulsive. Children who had a well father and a depressed mother and who were still married and living together did not differ from the children of well parents except for being rated by their teachers as somewhat less popular among their peers.

Parenting Style. Valiente et al. (2004) looked at mothers' and fathers' expressive style (self-reported) and their supportiveness toward their children as the latter coped with ordinary, daily stressors. Their results indicated that mothers who more often used "negative-dominant" expressive style, which included hostile and derogating expressive behavior, had children whose coping was *less* constructive, and who, perhaps as a consequence, reported experiencing more stress in their daily diaries, maintained over a 2-week period. Fathers' expressive style did not correlate with their children's coping ability. Mothers who reported using more supportive strategies had children who, in turn, were more able to access and use constructive coping strategies.

Hardy, Power, and Jaedicke (1993) examined several parenting variables (supportiveness, structure, and control) and children's coping with "daily hassles." Given the homogeneous middle-class sample, they found that only maternal supportiveness and structure were related to children's coping. Specifically, very supportive mothers in moderately low-structured homes had children who generated more coping strategies across situations; mothers who provided more structure had children who used fewer aggressive coping strategies. Supportive mothers also had children who reported more avoidant coping strategies when the children perceived the stressor as uncontrollable. Overall, parental supportiveness was found to be significantly related to the breadth of repertoire of coping strategies. We infer that parental supportiveness is likely to be associated with an ongoing secure attachment between child and parent; thus, supportiveness may be a "proxy" for how attachment may mediate children's development of coping strategies.

Eisenberg and her colleagues (Eisenberg, Gershoff, et al., 2001) found that nonsupportive mothers, in particular mothers who expressed hostile negative emotion, appeared to influence their children's social competence and externalizing behaviors through the children's ability to regulate their emotional arousal. They examined a couple of other alternative models, but found that the earlier pattern best fit their data. Interestingly, they found less relationship between maternal negative expressivity and children's manifesting internalizing problems.

Turning now to an older group of youth, Zimmermann (1999) assessed adolescents' attachment classification, using the Adult Attachment Interview (George, Kaplan, & Main, 1985). He also had the adolescents respond to several questions about five hypothetical social rejection vignettes, about which they were to imagine that the various incidents of social rejection happened to them. He evaluated their open-ended responses by how flexible their appraisal of the distressing social rejection was, how flexible and variable their behavioral strategies were for coping with the social rejection, and how clearly they could articulate how they would feel as well as what sort of rationale they provided for why they would feel that way. The resulting scores were transformed and aggregated to provide a score indicative of "adaptive emotion regulation." The adolescents were also rated by their best friend, their parents, and by two psychologists with the California Adult Q-sort (Block &

Block, 1980) for degree of ego resiliency, which is often used as a personality prototype. The results showed that the securely attached teens obtained a robustly positive correlation between adaptive emotion regulation and ego resiliency ($r = .57$) whereas the correlation coefficient for dismissing (insecure-avoidant) teens was $-.32$ and for preoccupied (insecure-preoccupied) it was $-.41$ (both significant). This study suggests that ego resiliency is likely influenced by style of emotion regulation, which in turn may be influenced by attachment history. The small sample size prohibited this kind of analysis, but Zimmermann's work is very useful for suggesting how personality organization may change as a function of emotion regulation style and attachment status.

Summary

As children mature, their growing cognitive sophistication, exposure to varied social models, and breadth of emotional-social experience contribute to their being able to generate more coping solutions to problematic situations. The older they are when faced with serious distress, the more able they are to see the situation from various perspectives (including those held by other people who may be part of the problematic situation) and figure out a way to resolve it. With maturity, they become more accurate in their appraisals of how much control they really have over the situation and what risks might accompany taking control of a very difficult situation (e.g., intervening in a fight). Effective coping in Western cultures involves acknowledgment of one's emotional responses, awareness of one's self as having some degree of agency, and a functional appraisal of the problematic situation and one's role in it. By late childhood or early adolescence, Western children who have enjoyed secure attachment in their supportive families and escaped severe trauma should generally be capable of emotionally competent coping with concomitant social effectiveness.

Social Effectiveness and Skill 7: Awareness of Emotion Communication in Relationships

This skill requires that the individual minimally recognize that emotions are communicated differently depending on a person's relationship with an interactant, but this particular skill goes beyond that of impression management or self-presentation strategies as defined in

Skill 5. With this skill, we also want to include the awareness and use of emotional experience to differentiate the organization of a person's relations with others. Implied then are the following skills:

- Recognition of the interpersonal consequences of one's emotion communication, not only of how the other is impacted, but also of how the relationship itself is affected.
- The ability to distinguish among different sorts of relationships and thus tailor one's emotion communication accordingly.
- An understanding of how emotion communication is a vehicle for power or control and thus has the potential to shape the "relational space" between the interactants.

The use of the term *emotion communication* entails verbal statements and all channels of nonverbal expression that can convey affective information to an onlooker or interactant.

By middle to late childhood, children recognize and can articulate to some degree that emotion communication varies as a function of the nature of the relationship that they have with someone (e.g., Saarni, 1988). Research also confirms that children distinguish emotion communication between close friends versus ordinary peers (e.g., Asher, Parker, & Walker, 1996). Likewise, children differentiate how they communicate with mothers versus fathers (Fuchs & Thelen, 1988). Not surprisingly, disclosure of emotionally vulnerable information is more often made to close friends and mothers. Observational research also indicates that children use expressive strategies to maintain relationship equilibrium (such as smiling more often) even as they simultaneously express negative feelings (such as contempt or irritation) toward their friends (von Salisch, 1991). In addition, girls (in Western societies) may be more likely to smile than boys as a way of influencing the relational dynamics (e.g., Saarni, 1992).

Secret Keeping and Secret Sharing

Watson and Valtin (1997) investigated children's understanding of interpersonal relations relative to keeping or sharing secrets, and secrets by their very nature are intensely emotion laden. Their results are important here for how they revealed children's use of relationship knowledge in choosing whether to share a secret. The youngest children (5 to 6 years) were more likely to tell mother more secrets than the older children, whereas the older children were more likely to share secrets with their friends—as an expression of, maybe even testimony to, their friendship—than with their mother. The exception was sharing of embarrassing secrets (i.e., wetting one's pants) by the older boys: Very few would confess this to their friend, whereas the older girls were more willing to share "bodily loss of control" with their same-sex friends. Humiliation and fear of loss of reputation were among the reasons cited by the older boys for not telling a friend, but they might tell their mother, because she could be counted on not to embarrass them. As for guilty or dangerous secrets, older children felt a clear sense of tension about whether to maintain their friend's secret as an act of trustworthiness, even as they also worried that perhaps an adult "should" know about the guilt-laden activity (i.e., theft) or dangerous event (i.e., lighting a fire in an empty garage). As one girl put it, "Mother is like half a friend—so sometimes you can share some secrets with her" (p. 448–449, Watson & Valtin, 1997).

From the standpoint of understanding how relationship structure affects our emotional communication, the older children were more consistently concerned with how trust defined a relationship, and by implication, with trust comes a degree of reciprocity and mutuality. Good friends should be able to trust one another. Emotional communication is profoundly affected by the degree of trust one feels toward another with the result that the greater the trust, the more likely one will disclose information about one's experience that is emotionally vulnerable. Emotionally vulnerable information about oneself or about another, such as in secrets, is invariably anxiety provoking, and it takes a mutually respectful relationship for anxiety-laden exchanges to be reassuringly heard.

Interpersonal Closeness

Strayer and Roberts (1997) undertook an ingenious study to examine how emotion processes such as empathy might mediate or moderate children's "felt" closeness toward video-taped characters. They used a felt wall hanging that had a mirror mounted in the center, and the children were asked to place Velcro-attached photos of video characters relatively close or far from the reflected image of themselves, depending on how comfortable they felt with the video-taped character (e.g., a physically punitive parent versus a girl who is excited about an elephant ride at the circus). The results indicated a nearly linear relationship between the degree of empathy (as measured by the Empathy Continuum, which evaluates the degree of affective sharing, perspective taking, and interpersonal understanding) the children felt for the character and how close they placed the character's photo near their own mirror image. This relationship increased with age and was somewhat stronger in girls. Familiarity, status, authority, and intensity of affect might all play a role in how close we allow another into our personal space, yet this study suggested that if empathy were present, then the emotion communication that transpired defined the relationship as different: We can step into the shoes of the other, even if their personal attributes are quite different from our own and they are unfamiliar persons. We would like to encourage the use of this particular methodological technique in other studies of emotion communication with children and youth, especially those that are also concerned with self-representations, boundaries, and relations with others.

Social Roles and Emotion Communication

Relatively uninvestigated is how emotion is differentially communicated and conceptualized relative to different social roles. Social roles refer to age roles, sex roles, occupational roles, authority and/or leadership roles, and so forth. Some research exists on how gender (and by implication, sex role) influences both the pattern and frequency of emotion discourse (e.g., Ruble & Martin, 1998; Shields, 1995). But we do not know how children integrate their knowledge about social roles with beliefs about emotion communication. Research on children's acquisition of social scripts as they are related to different venues of emotion communication is minimal, although children's use of scripts may be implicit in their expectations about emotion expression (e.g., Underwood et al., 1992) and about best versus worst ways to cope with aversive feelings (e.g., Saarni, 1997).

Relative to sex role, young children endorse emotion-specific gender stereotypes that are common in Western societies, such as males are expected to experience more anger and females more sadness (Karbon et al., 1992). Shields (1995) provided a review of how various aspects of emotional experience are gender-coded (e.g., the expressive/emotional female versus the instrumental/rational male), and she was particularly interested in how

children are socialized into expressive styles that are gender-coded (e.g., the conciliatory style of little girls when faced with a conflict compared with the more coercive style of little boys). She also noted the dearth of studies on the developmental processes that link emotional development with gender identity development.

Harter and her colleagues (1998) looked at "level of voice" in adolescents relative to the degree to which they adhered to sex-role stereotypes. Level of voice was assessed by a questionnaire developed by the authors to ascertain whether the adolescent felt confident about being able to disclose his or her feelings and opinions to others (i.e., to reveal a "true self"). Their interesting results showed that stereotypically feminine adolescents had a lower level of voice in public exchange compared to their more androgynous female peers but no difference was obtained in private exchanges. For male adolescents, stereotypically masculine male adolescents had a more assertive level of voice in public exchange but were not as confident or open in "true self" level of voice in private exchanges (e.g., between close friends) as were androgynous male adolescents. Thus, we see in this research a convergence on emotion communication, sex-role beliefs, and the context of relationship (public versus private and close).

Summary

Although we have research that substantiates that socialization is mediated by parental and peer communicated emotion (e.g., derogation is an emotion-laden communication that directly informs the target that the interactant disapproves of both the target and the behavior of the target), we have relatively little research that examines how children and youth recognize and use emotional communication to differentiate the organization of their relations with others. Related issues include how children and youth construe the interpersonal consequences of their emotional communication with the relationship for themselves *and* for their interactants (the focus being on the relational space between the interactants); how they maintain the relationship quality (e.g., equilibrium) or alter it (e.g., by deepening or attenuating it); and how they apply power and control in the relationship. Some research on the meaningfulness of friendship is relevant (e.g., Asher & Rose, 1997), as is Gottman et al.'s (1997) work on parents' coaching their children in ways that facilitate their children's understanding of emotional experience. Infant intersubjectivity and attunement are also examples of emotion communication, but what is missing in our research base is how children and youth acquire an awareness that emotion communication varies as a function of their affectional ties to an interactant, their status (or dominance) relative to the interactant, and the unique emotion-evoking circumstances in which the interaction is embedded (e.g., public or private).

Social Effectiveness and Skill 8: Capacity for Emotional Self-Efficacy

This final skill of emotional competence entails an individual's acceptance of his or her emotional experience, whether eccentric or conventional, negative or positive. With this skill, individuals can tolerate and not feel overwhelmed by intense negative emotion (e.g., despair, melancholy, outrage, or anguish) because they do not view their emotional responses as unjustified. They feel relatively in control of their emotional experience from the standpoint of mastery and positive self-regard. Indeed, a sense of global self-worth may lie at the heart of emotional self-efficacy (Harter, 1999). In our opinion, this sense of emotional self-efficacy is probably not achieved until adolescence, for it is undoubtedly dependent on cognitive development, including the ability to consider the realm of possibility and of reality. We also hypothesize that the emotionally self-efficacious individual has acquired the preceding seven skills of emotional competence to a relatively mature degree.

As for relationships, emotionally self-efficacious adolescents learn that they cannot have it all: Not everyone will adore them or want to spend time with them, and they may feel lonely at times. But rejection does not leave them in a puddle of devastation and self-pity; instead, emotionally self-efficacious individuals seek to resolve the situation relative to their values. They treasure their friendships (Asher & Rose, 1997) and choose a course that is also guided by a moral compass (e.g., Walker & Hennig, 1997). Research on relationship quality in adolescence also suggests that adherence to a true self is more often associated with perception of self-worth and with youth engaged in relationships that were supportive as opposed to contingent on the youth's pleasing either parents or friends (reviewed in Harter, 1999; see also Eisenberg, Spinrad, & Morris, 2002).

Individual differences in emotional self-efficacy may be influenced by personality; for example, agreeableness appears implicated as a significant aspect of emotional intelligence (e.g., Davies, Stankov, & Roberts, 1998), by appraisal style (e.g., a positive appraisal style promotes a general sense of subjective well-being; Lazarus, 1991), which in turn is associated with mood states, and by temperament (e.g., Eisenberg & McNally, 1993; Eisenberg et al., 2004). As diverse as these research inquires are, they may help to guide us in figuring out how to conceptualize the relations among personality traits, mood states, and emotion processing relative to the benefits for emotional self-efficacy for the developing adolescent. We turn next to that debate.

Personality, Mood, and Emotion Processes

How does an individual maintain some degree of emotional balance or even a sense of well-being in the face of adverse events and painful circumstances? Granted, there are buffering or protective factors that facilitate resilience (e.g., secure attachment, supportive relationships), but what does the individual bring to that crucible of adversity that allows him or her to experience appropriate negative affect but then be able to resume her or his life course with equanimity and perhaps even greater insight into her- or himself? Clinicians may have intuitive answers to this question (e.g., Janoff-Bulman & Frantz, 1997), and perhaps the Blocks' research on ego resilience is relevant (e.g., Block & Block, 1980). What we would like to see investigated from a developmental psychology perspective is how emotion-directed information processes such as perception, attention, judgment, and memory recognition and recall (including recall of one's own personal life-history events) are influenced by personality and mood states (both enduring and transient moods). It seems to us that the maintenance of emotional self-efficacy would require the ability to access at least two sorts of emotion-directed information processes: First, the emotion-directed information processes need to provide feedback about our own emotional experience such that we can evaluate it; second, these processes need to provide feedback about the emotion-evoking circumstances such that we can accept our emotional response to the circumstances and then turn our focus to resolving or accepting the adverse circumstances. As an example, an adolescent might experience the divorce of his or her parents as very aversive, but if some degree of emotional self-efficacy has been developed, he or she can accept the feelings of sadness, anger, and anxiety as appropriate to the painful situation, but then redirect his or her focus toward his or her own positive goals and values (e.g., friendships, academic achievement, or community service) rather than ruminating on his or her parents' conflicts and breakup.

Interestingly, a study by Lyubomirsky and Nolen-Hoeksema (1995) provides empirical support for the value of a person redirecting their focus, which they refer to as distraction. They found that rumination by dysphoric participants led to generating less productive solutions to hypothetical interpersonal problems and having a more pessimistic outlook about their future. However, a second group of dysphoric participants were told to distract themselves (i.e., redirect their focus), and this group did not differ from the nondysphoric participants in optimism and effectiveness in problem solving. In sum, a person can feel miserable (dysphoric), and their misery might be very well justified by the circumstances, but being able to redirect their focus rather than to ruminate on the adversity may well facilitate effective problem solving and influence their expectations for an improved future. This outcome is similar to that found by Weyer and Sandler (1998) in a short-term longitudinal study of children whose parents had recently divorced: Efficacy of coping was negatively related to propensity to ruminate. Likewise, O'Brien, Margolin, and John (1995) found that children who could distance themselves from their parents' divorce appeared to fare better.

Rusting (1998) has provided us with a valuable integration of the research on mood states and personality traits as they affect emotion-congruent information processing. She noted that it is the trait theorists, who have posited that an individual's enduring personality traits, for example, proneness to positive or negative affectivity, most strongly influence their mood-congruent information processing. More specifically, if one is predisposed to positive affectivity (trait), one is more likely to report experiencing more positive mood states, and this results in one's retrieval of more positive memory associations, which in turn probably facilitates the continuance of the desirable mood (and the converse being true if one is predisposed to negative affectivity). This "proneness to positive versus negative affectivity" sounds similar to the earlier discussion in this chapter on temperamental disposition to negative emotionality and reflects some personality development theoretical positions that advocate that personality traits are significantly influenced by temperamental dispositions (e.g., Caspi & Silva, 1995).

However, other theorists have emphasized the influence that *temporary* mood states have on emotion infor-

mation processing. This body of research often involves inducing either a positive or negative mood in the research participants and then giving them various cognitive tasks that involve perception, attention, judgment, and recall. An early study by Carlson and Masters (1985) did just that: They induced positive emotional states (self-focused or other-focused) in one group of 5- to 6-year-old children and a control group had a neutral induction. The first group displayed happier facial expressions and did not demonstrate the usual reduced generosity after inequality of rewards as long as they had received the self-focused happy mood induction. The authors interpreted their results as supportive of the position that temporary positive mood states facilitate tolerance of aversive experiences.

What Rusting proposed—and which is relevant to emotional self-efficacy—is that both temporary mood states and more stable personality styles or traits will influence how one processes emotion-laden cues, for these cues evoke memory associations, which in turn are influenced by both personality disposition and temporary mood. Reframing this so that it helps to elucidate emotional self-efficacy is suggested by the following case:

Lily's younger sister, Sharon, age 10, died of cystic fibrosis, and the family was in profound grief, for it had seemed for awhile that Sharon might survive for a number of years more and then she unexpectedly worsened and died. Lily (age 15) had been neither a "difficult" nor an "easy" baby: She had had her share of difficult-to-soothe crying spells in infancy and seemed to have a rather low threshold for pain (e.g., reacting quite intensely to vaccinations and injections). Upon Sharon's death, she felt very bereft and experienced her grief somatically as well (abdominal pain). She stayed home from school for a week, and subsequently, with her parents' help, she created a photo montage to take to Sharon's elementary school classroom. She also collected Sharon's drawings that she had made over the past few years while undergoing therapy in conjunction with her frequent medical interventions and assembled them into a book. She had the book copied in color and gave the copies to various relatives as gifts to remember Sharon's creativity. Lily focused on Sharon's vibrancy rather than her final months of ravaging coughing and breathlessness, and Lily's turning outward to the former school mates and to the extended family drew her into supportive and rewarding social contact. At the time of the first anniversary after Sharon's death, Lily was able to weep easily over the loss of her sister, but she was also able to feel good about herself, appreciated her parents more from an empathic perspective of what they had gone through, was perceived by her peers as a mature and trustworthy person, enjoyed a moderate social life, and had easily maintained her standing on the honor roll. Lily was optimistic about her future plans, and she was looking forward to a community service volunteer position for the summer in the chronically ill children's ward at the local hospital. (author developed, C. Saarni)

Noteworthy in this case is that Lily is not a ruminator, yet she does not minimize or avoid her negative affect. Her personality style appears to be one of moderation; her coping style is a socially engaged one rather than one of withdrawal or avoidance of others, in spite of some initial somatogenic reactions to Sharon's death. Importantly, her parents appear to be able to provide supportive scaffolding, even as they too grieved for Sharon. Lily is future oriented and planful with the expectancy that what lies ahead will be positive and satisfying. She is expressive but neither over- nor undercontrolled. The fact that her peers view her as trustworthy and mature suggests that her emotional communication with them is respectful, genuine, and insightful. She is probably a good listener, and her peers confide in her. Lily demonstrates emotional self-efficacy: She accepts her grief, she accepts the loss of her sister, yet she finds balance and meaningfulness in her life. In spite of deeply felt adversity, she demonstrates well-being and resilience over the long term (see also Wyman et al., 2000).

Summary

Emotional self-efficacy is obviously a superordinate construct, much the way that emotional competence is. It overlaps with resilience in the face of adversity and entails well-developed skills of emotional competence as described in the preceding sections. One of us (Saarni, 1999) has also argued that emotional self-efficacy must entail a moral sense and a willingness to make choices that support one's beliefs that one is doing "the right thing" even if it is uncomfortable or unpopular (Colby & Damon, 1992; Walker & Hennig, 1997; Wilson, 1993). Such moral choices require thoughtfulness and self-reflection and very likely a sense of moral justice tempered with sympathy and compassion. Social effectiveness is also part of emotional self-efficacy: A person's emotion-directed information processing while engaged in a social encounter, especially a challenging or emotionally evocative one, will be influenced by his or her memory associations of similar past encounters and by their current emotional state. Assuming a sup-

portive family history and a personality style that is not burdened by the double hazard of proneness to negative affect and deficits in attention, then a person's memory associations should be benign or resilient and their current emotional state should be moderately regulated. The challenging social encounter should then unfold with minimal defensiveness, appropriate assertiveness, and demonstration of personal integrity (i.e., a person's moral sense).

In conclusion, further theoretical development of the construct of emotional competence is needed; for example, how does it differ from emotional intelligence (Mayer, Salovey, & Caruso, 2000; Saarni, in press) and how might emotional competence skills be structured hierarchically (as has been done with the construct social competence; Rose-Krasnor, 1997). The skills of emotional competence are dynamic and transactional, for these skills are part of an interpersonal exchange that unfolds in a unique context. Indeed, one could design interesting studies simply by pairing together children or teens who differ in the degree to which they can employ the skills of emotional competence and then observe how their interpersonal negotiations unfold.

CONCLUSION

In science, progress is measured not so much by how many questions have been answered, but by how many new ones have been raised. Such is the case in the study of emotion, where there has been a plethora of significant contributions to knowledge in recent years. In conclusion, we review a few of the unresolved issues that we believe represent the frontier of research into emotional development. Given the generally functionalist perspective taken in this chapter, our proposed research questions emphasize goals, the relational rather than the intrapsychic properties of emotions, the flexibility rather than the reflexive nature of emotional behavior, and the embeddedness of emotion in interpersonal transactions.

The functionalist approach liberalizes the study of emotion, but has not yet profoundly influenced how emotions are studied. Consider the following: If one were to do a census of studies on emotions, one would find, even today, an extraordinary overrepresentation of research in which emotions have been treated primarily as responses—as outward signs of internal states. Studies of emotions as antecedents and organizers of personal and social behaviors have been much less prevalent. When emotions are considered purely as responses, the tendency is to stop there, and not consider how those responses can be in the service of changing or maintaining person-environment relations. This imbalance between emotions considered as responses and emotions conceptualized as organizers generates a number of major new areas of research.

One of these areas concerns new aspects of emotional communication. For instance, there is a discrepancy between the wealth of information we have about individual differences in emotional responding (i.e., temperament), and individual differences in emotional perception and subsequent behavior regulation (a phenomenon for which we do not even have a noun, and about which there are consequently few studies). One of the first research questions we raised in several sections about emotional development concerned the little we know about how emotion perception originates, how such perceptions lead to functional consequences for the child, and how infants and children come to react, and subsequently to become dismissive, hyper-vigilant, or appropriately attuned, toward different cues of emotion expressed by others. We also need to investigate which contributing contextual features promote sensitivity to such cues, how such sensitivities eventually become biases to respond, and what are the personal characteristics of infants and children that lead them to be disposed to react appropriately or to make biased attributions of emotion. Volumes await the description and explanation of the answers to these questions.

If emotions are primarily social and relational, the boundary of social psychological research and developmental study becomes very permeable. For instance, the self, it has been said, develops under the watchful eye of the other. This statement captures our point that it is not just cognitive developments linked to the self that lead to so-called self-conscious emotions. The child must notice the presence of such watchful eyes, realize that the eyes reside in significant others, identify what emotion the eyes are communicating, and subsequently behave to have an appropriate effect on those eyes—such as by hiding from them in shame, or showing off to them in pride. The social context and the social signals (expressions) provided by significant others are thus constitutive of new emotions. This phenomenon has not been adequately studied, in comparison to studies of the relation between cognitive and emotional development. Put

another way, rules and standards, and the construct of the self, may not be sufficient to generate later-appearing emotions like pride, shame, and guilt; these emotions may also require the affective sting of the emotional communications of others. If so, we need to study the value added by emotional signals to the imposition of rules and standards.

Another topic at the interface of developmental and social psychology is that of attention in dyadic and group settings. Basic issues such as the targeting of joint attention between two individuals and the quality of the emotional messages exchanged between them may determine the specific emotion generated in such interchanges. The meaning of a joyful reaction by a significant other in the presence of a child has different functional consequences depending on (a) whether the joy is targeted toward an action of the child (laying the basis for the child to experience pride), (b) whether the joy is merely witnessed by the child (leading to an empathic affect sharing but not pride), or (c) whether the joy is oriented toward the child himself or herself (resulting in the child developing affiliative or attachment bonds). Similarly, the quality of the emotion message manifested by the other in such social interactional exchanges (i.e., its fearful nature or its scornful nature) may have dramatically different results on the child. The first permits the child to "catch" the fear of an object expressed by another; the second potentially enters into the generation of shame (as noted before). It seems an inescapable conclusion that emotions are relational processes. If so, the field must develop paradigms that do justice to that relational nature, and permit functional consequences of those emotions to be observed. Few paradigms exist that permit the richness of emotion to be discerned and quantified. Where the paradigms do exist, as in studies involving naturalistic or field observations, the coding schemes often do not do justice to the many different facets and manifestations of emotional behavior.

Emotions, though, do not always seem to be relational. Indeed, they seem to be intrapsychic and private events. For instance, we weep for the loss of a loved one in the privacy of our own room, with no one present, and no apparent social target for the tears. Is it the case that emotions are primarily private and nonrelational? If they *are* relational, as we propose they are, how do they become private, and do such private events themselves have functional *sequelae*? We cannot answer these questions at this time. The process by which emotions considered as external and relational become internal and private has not been the focus of any systematic research to date. We know that in language speech shifts at 5 to 6 years of age from being primarily or exclusively external to potentially internal and private. Such interiorization has great relevance for the growth of self-regulation. Is there a similar process of interiorization that occurs for emotion? Does the interiorization of emotion take place at the same age as the interiorization of speech? And does such possible interiorization have implications for emotion regulation, by analogy to the consequences of the interiorization of speech for self-regulation? The recent work of Holodinski and Friedlmeier (2006) draws our attention to such interiorization processes. We believe that these authors have identified what may be a major yet unsuspected developmental transition in emotional life—one that takes place in the middle of the 1st decade of life. Their theorizing and research proposals can help reconcile two drastically differing views of emotion: (1) emotion as intrapersonal (a relatively late stage in the ontogeny of emotion) and (2) emotion as interpersonal/relational (a process present throughout the life span but not necessarily evident in all manifestations of emotion in older children and adults).

There is another challenge to the view that emotions are relational. Some emotional phenomena such as esthetic emotions do not appear to be in the service of any apparent goal. Music not only soothes the savage beast but also the very young infant. Is the infant's reaction to music an exception to the view that emotions serve a person's strivings? Or is music, as Lazarus argues, a process that draws on reintegration of cues from memory in which some aspects of a musical composition serve as prods bringing to mind previously experienced emotions (in the manner that the sound of drumbeats in music can remind us of our heartbeat in a state of fear)? This type of question is amenable to test, but to date no thorough study has been conducted on music and emotion in early life. Therefore, we cannot provide evidence relevant to Lazarus's functionalist argument or its nativisit counterpart. Systematic study of esthetic emotions thus seems very relevant in evaluating the limits of applicability of a functionalist approach to emotion.

The approach to emotion we have taken is not only relational but also nonmechanistic. It considers emotions not as reflexive but as flexible, even in the very young infant. The functionalist approach stresses that the same event can produce quite different emotions, and the same emotion can result in quite different, indeed equipotential, transactions with the world. The equipotentiality of emotional behaviors renders them flexible rather than reflexive. However, most research on emotion to date has not done justice to the flexibility and equipotentiality characteristics of emotion. Our methods often constrain the possibility of observing flexibly manifested emotional behaviors, or of noting how the same event can be construed differently by different children. Moreover, the research objectives in most studies typically center on the search for the *coherence* of emotional behaviors—the more highly intercorrelated we find behaviors to be, the better we think our findings are. However, emotional behaviors are rarely highly intercorrelated. Such low-to-modest correlations are precisely what one would expect if emotional behaviors are equipotential. Low correlations due to equipotentiality of response would then reflect, not the presence of error variance, but a true state of affairs. How does one statistically and conceptually tease apart situations in which low correlations among behaviors are expectable from those in which there is error variance? This is a vexing problem for researchers to address, and our usual statistical models do not help disentangle the two possibilities. Only research designed to predict what behaviors are shown in what contexts can do so. Attachment researchers address this problem by the use of interpretational methods and judgmental, though reliable, coding systems such as those that quantify maternal sensitivity or classify the meaning of the infant's behaviors into categories such as avoidant, ambivalent, disorganized, or secure. Perhaps we need to quantify emotions using similar approaches but on different emotional phenomena than attachment. To reiterate, we believe that we cannot continue to ignore the problems created (a) by the same event being interpreted differently by different individuals, and (b) by different behaviors being recruited in the service of the same emotion. We stress again: Our paradigms must allow for the manifestation of the flexibility of emotion.

Another important issue in the functionalist approach is the critical role of context. One instantiation of the importance of context is again at the interface of social and developmental psychology. It relates to when and how children's disclosure of differently valenced emotions to different categories of people takes place (e.g., peers versus adults, close relationships versus distant ones, and so forth). Relevant individual differences to consider in such an investigation include personality disposition (e.g., degree of inhibition) and children's cognitive perspective-taking skills. Children's social cognitive expectancies about the reactions of others to emotion-laden disclosures are also relatively underinvestigated.

Also related to context is the process of how individual differences in the capacity for empathic engagement by the child without the child becoming overwhelmed by his or her own personal distress. We raised the possibility of tolerance for ambiguity as related to having a higher threshold for tolerating another's distress as the witnessing person considered avenues of appropriate action for how to help or intervene. Important contextual features of the relationship that exist between target and sufferer are also under investigated; such features can differentially contribute to personal distress reactions. For example, if the target is more dominant or powerful than the actor and now something affects the target to render her or him distressed, at what age will children intervene to assist sympathetically—and in a genuine manner, rather than instrumentally or strategically—as opposed to feeling personally distressed?

A central aspect of context in emotion is that of the role a person is expected to assume. One cannot understand many emotions without understanding the role a person is playing. However, we do not know very much about how children and youth integrate their knowledge about social roles (e.g., age roles, occupational roles, authority/leadership roles), how roles set the stage for different emotional reactions and different beliefs about emotional communication. Some research on gender roles exists, but it appears to be more related to socialization patterns (e.g., girls' conciliatory versus boys' coercive styles when faced with a conflict) or with attributions of propensity about which gender is more likely to experience what sort of emotion. We thus propose more of a focus on how children and youth organize their relationships with regard to social expectations, how those expectations affect the quality, frequency, and intensity of emotions, and how roles have an impact on various dimensions of emotional communication. For example, more smiling appears to occur among friends, even as they may also reproach or express negative affect more frequently with their friends (von Salisch, 1996). Presumably, there is also more emotion-laden disclosure to friends. How do youth differentiate their emotion communication strategies when they first embark on an intimate relationship? What is it that creates awkward-

ness as they begin to learn how to be warmly and genuinely intimate with a partner? How do children and adolescents figure out how emotional communication is different in intimate relationships as compared to their earlier same-sex peer friendships? Daily diary studies may well be a methodology that would prove useful, as would be studies that recruit dyads of adolescents who self-nominate themselves as partnered.

Another frontier of research deals with factors that influence emotion-directed information processes of perception, attention, judgment, and memory. How do individual differences in a child's personality and his or her development affect these psychological processes? How do enduring and transient mood states affect them? We raised the question of how emotional self-efficacy in adolescence may require the ability to access these emotion-directed information processes in ways that allow for feedback to their evaluation of their own emotional experience so that they can accept their emotional response (as opposed to denying their emotional response and having to defend themselves against it). With such emotional self-efficacy, they can then turn their focus to resolving the adverse circumstances.

A final set of questions brings us full circle to the objective of this chapter: Emotional development is the development of what? We need to do research on how some emotions are present in some rudimentary form at birth or shortly thereafter. These nonemergent emotions develop in the sense that new events elicit them, or new motives are served by them, but the relation between the event and the motive stays invariant. However, what is the process by which different events in relation to different goals yield the same emotion? We do not know the answer to the question of how such totally different transactions yield the same or similar emotions. Other emotions are not present from birth but become organized due to the intercoordination of processes such as cognition, exposure to events in the world, the social reactions and attitudes of others, the biological constitution of the child, and the differentiation of the physical and social self. Do these emotions emerge? Or are they evident in some rudimentary, not-readily measurable form early in life? Some recent research suggests that complex emotions such as jealousy, shame, and pride may be evident even in the 1st year of life, contrary to widespread belief (Draghi-Lorenz, Reddy, & Costall, 2001). In cognitive development, we have learned that phenomena once deemed to emerge in late infancy can be shown in some meaningful form in the newborn or young baby. Are similar rudimentary precocities also identifiable in the development of nonbasic emotions? The possibility that emotions may be evident much earlier than the usual indices of emotion leads us to infer that this is an important question. We hope that future editions of this *Handbook* may report answers to the unresolved issues we pose.

REFERENCES

Abbot, S. (1992). Holding on and pushing away: Comparative perspectives on an eastern Kentucky child-rearing practice. *Ethos, 20,* 33–65.

Adolph, K. E., Eppler, M. A., & Gibson, E. J. (1993). Development of perception of affordances. In C. K. Rovee-Collier & L. P. Lipsitt (Eds.), *Advances in infancy research* (Vol. 8, pp. 50–97). Norwood, NJ: Ablex.

Ainsworth, M., Blehar, M., Waters, E., & Wall, S. (1978). *Patterns of attachment.* Hillsdale, NJ: Erlbaum.

Aldwin, C. (1994). *Stress, coping, and development.* New York: Guilford Press.

Altshuler, J., & Ruble, D. (1989). Developmental changes in children's awareness of strategies for coping with uncontrollable stress. *Child development, 60,* 1337–1349.

Anderson, D. E., Ansfield, M., & DePaulo, B. (1999). Love's best habit: Deception in the context of relationships. In P. Philippot, R. S. Feldman, & E. J. Coates (Eds.), *The social context of nonverbal behavior* (pp. 372–409). Cambridge, England: Cambridge University Press.

Anderson, E. (1994). *Young children's understanding of facial and vocal expressions of emotion.* Unpublished doctoral dissertation, DePaul University, Chicago, IL.

Arsenio, W., & Lemerise, E. (2001). Varieties of childhood bullying: Values, emotion processes, and social competence. *Social Development, 10,* 59–73.

Asher, S., Parker, J., & Walker, D. (1996). Distinguishing friendship from acceptance: Implications for intervention and assessment. In W. Bukowski, A. Newcomb, & W. Hartup (Eds.), *The company they keep: Friendship during childhood and adolescence* (pp. 366–405). New York: Cambridge University Press.

Asher, S., & Rose, A. (1997). Promoting children's social-emotional adjustment with peers. In P. Salovey & D. Sluyter (Eds.), *Emotional development and emotional intelligence* (pp. 196–224). New York: Basic Books.

Ayers, T. S., & Sandler, I. (1996). A dispositional and situational assessment of children's coping: Testing alternative models of coping. *Journal of Personality, 64,* 923–958.

Bakeman, R., & Adamson, L. (1984). Coordinating attention to people and objects in mother-infants and peer-infant interaction. *Child Development, 55*(4), 1278–1298.

Band, E., & Weisz, J. (1988). How to feel better when it feels bad: Children's perspectives on coping with everyday stress. *Developmental Psychology, 24,* 247–253.

Barrett, K., & Campos, J. (1987). Perspectives on emotional development: Vol. 2. A functionalist approach to emotions. In J. Osofsky (Ed.), *Handbook of infant development* (2nd ed., pp. 555–578). New York: Wiley.

Barrett, K. C. (1997). Emotion communication and the development of the social emotions. *New Directions for Child Development, 77,* 69–88.

Barrett, K. C., Zahn-Waxler, C., & Cole, P. M. (1993). Avoiders versus amenders: Implications for the investigation of guilt and shame during toddlerhood. *Cognition and Emotion, 7,* 481–505.

Barth, J., & Bastiani, A. (1997). A longitudinal study of emotion regulation and preschool children's social behavior. *Merrill-Palmer Quarterly, 43,* 107–128.

Berk, L. E. (1992). Children's private speech: An overview of theory and the status of research. In R. M. Diaz & L. E. Berk (Eds.), *Private speech: From social interaction to self-regulation* (pp. 17–53). Hillsdale, NJ: Erlbaum.

Berlin, L. J., & Cassidy, J. (2003). Mothers' self-reported control their preschool children's emotional expressiveness: A longitudinal study of associations with infant-mother attachment and children's emotion regulation. *Social Development, 12,* 477–495.

Bertenthal, B., & Campos, J. (1990). A systems approach to the organizing effects of self-produced locomotion during infancy. In C. L. Rovee-Collier (Ed.), *Advances in infancy research* (pp. 2–60). Hillsdale, NJ: Erlbaum.

Bingham, R., Campos, J. J., & Emde, R. N. (1987, April). *Negative emotions in a social relationship context.* Paper presented at the Society for Research on Child Development, Baltimore, MD.

Biringen, Z., Emde, R., Campos, J., & Appelbaum, M. (1995). Affective reorganization in the infant, the mother, and the dyad. *Child Development, 66,* 499–514.

Bischof, N. (1975). A systems approach toward the functional connections of attachment and fear. *Child Development, 46,* 801–817.

Blass, E., & Ciaramitaro, V. (1994). A new look at some old mechanisms in human newborns. *Monographs of the Society for Research in Child Development, 59*(Serial No. 239).

Bloch, A. (1966). The Kurdistani cradle story. *Clinical Pediatrics, 5,* 641–645.

Block, J., & Block, J. (1980). The role of ego-control and ego-resiliency in the organization of behavior. In W. A. Collins (Ed.), *Minnesota Symposia on Child Psychology: Vol. 13. Development of cognition, affect, and social relations* (pp. 39–101). Hillsdale, NJ: Erlbaum.

Block, J., & Kremen, A. (1996). IQ and ego-resiliency: Conceptual and empirical connections and separateness. *Journal of Personality and Social Psychology, 70,* 349–360.

Bloom, L. (1998). Language acquisition in its developmental context. In w& D. Kuhn & R. S. Siegler (Vol. Eds.), *Handbook of child psychology: Vol. 2. Cognition, perception, and language* (5th ed., pp. 309–370). New York: Wiley.

Blurton-Jones, N. (1967). An ethological study of some aspects of social behaviour of children in nursery school. In D. Morris (Ed.), *Primate ethology* (pp. 347–368). London: Weidenfeld and Nicolson.

Boccia, M., & Campos, J. J. (1989). Maternal emotional signals, social referencing, and infants' reactions to strangers. In N. Eisenberg (Ed.), *New directions of child development* (Vol. 44, pp. 25–49). San Francisco: Jossey-Bass.

Bowlby, J. (1969). *Attachment and loss: Vol. 1. Attachment.* New York: Basic Books.

Bowlby, J. (1972). *Attachment and loss: Vol. 2. Separation.* New York: Basic Books.

Bradshaw, D. L. (1986). *Immediate and prolonged effectiveness of negative emotion expressions in inhibiting infants' actions.* Unpublished doctoral dissertation, University of Denver, CO.

Brenner, E., & Salovey, P. (1997). Emotion regulation during childhood: Developmental, interpersonal, and individual considerations. In P. Salovey & D. Sluyter (Eds.), *Emotional literacy and emotional development* (pp. 168–192). New York: Basic Books.

Bretherton, I. (1985). Attachment theory: Retrospect and prospect. *Monographs of the Society for Research in Child Development, 50*(1/2, Serial No. 209), 3–35.

Bretherton, I., Fritz, J., Zahn-Waxler, C., & Ridgeway, D. (1986). Learning to talk about emotions: A functionalist perspective. *Child Development, 57,* 529–548.

Briggs, J. (1970). *Never in anger.* Cambridge, MA: Harvard University Press.

Campos, J., Anderson, D. I., Barbu-Roth, M. A., Hubbard, E. M., Hertenstein, M. J., & Witherington, D. (2000). Travel broadens the mind. *Infancy, 1*(2), 149–219.

Campos, J., Bertenthal, B., & Kermoian, R. (1992). Early experience and emotional development: The emergence of wariness of heights. *Psychological Science, 3,* 61–64.

Campos, J., Frankel, C., & Camras, L. (2004). On the nature of emotion regulation. *Child Development, 75,* 377–394.

Campos, J., Hiatt, S., Ramsay, D., Henderson, C., & Svejda, M. (1978). The emergence of fear on the visual cliff. In M. Lewis & L. Rosenblum (Eds.), *The development of affect* (pp. 149–182). New York: Plenum.

Campos, J., Kermoian, R., & Zumbahlen, M. (1992). Socioemotional transformations in the family system following infant crawling onset. In N. F. Eisenberg & R. A. Fabes (Eds.), *New directions for child development: Vol. 55. Emotion and its regulation in early development* (pp. 25–40). San Francisco: Jossey-Bass.

Campos, J., Thein, S., & Owen, D. (2003). A Darwinian legacy to understanding human infancy: Emotional expressions as behavior regulators. *Annals of the New York Academy of Sciences, 1000,* 110–134.

Campos, J. J., Barrett, K. C., Lamb, M. E., Goldsmith, H. H., & Stenberg, C. (1983). Socioemotional development. In M. Haith & J. Campos (Vol. Eds.), *Handbook of child psychology: Vol. 2. Infancy and developmental psychobiology* (4th ed., pp. 783–915). New York: Wiley.

Campos, J. J., Mumme, D., Kermoian, R., & Campos, R. G. (1994). A functionalist perspective on the nature of emotion. In N. Fox (Ed.), *The development of emotion regulation* (pp. 284–303). Chicago, IL: University of Chicago Press.

Camras, L. A. (1992). Expressive development and basic emotions. *Cognition and Emotion, 6,* 267–283.

Camras, L. A., Grow, G., & Ribordy, S. C. (1983). Recognition of emotional expressions by abused children. *Journal of Clinical and Child Psychology, 12,* 325–328.

Camras, L. A., Lambrecht, L., & Michel, G. (1996). Infant "surprise" expressions as coordinative motor structures. *Journal of Nonverbal Behavior, 20,* 183–195.

Camras, L. A., Meng, Z., Ujiie, T., Dharamsi, S., Miyake, K., Oster, H., et al. (2002). Observing emotion in infants: Facial expression, body behavior, and rater judgments of responses to an expectancy-violating event. *Emotion, 2*(2), 179–193.

Camras, L. A., Oster, H., Campos, J. J., & Bakeman, R. (2003). Emotional facial expressions in European-American, Japanese, and Chinese Infants. In P. Ekman & J. Campos, R. Davidson, & F. de Waal (Eds.), *Annals of the New York Academy of Sciences: Vol.*

1000. Emotions Inside Out. New York: New York Academy of Sciences.

Camras, L. A., Oster, H., Campos, J., Campos, R., Ujiie, T., Miyake, K., et al. (1998). Production of emotional facial expressions in American, Japanese and Chinese infants. *Developmental Psychology, 34,* 616–628.

Camras, L. A., Oster, H., Campos, J., Miyake, K., & Bradshaw, D. (1992). Japanese and American infants' responses to arm restraint. *Developmental Psychology, 28,* 578–583.

Camras, L. A., & Sachs, V. B. (1991). Social referencing and caretaker expressive behavior in a day care setting. *Infant Behavior and Development, 14,* 27–36.

Camras, L., Sachs-Alter, E., & Ribordy, S. (1996). Emotion understanding in maltreated children: Recognition of facial expressions and integration with other emotion cues. In M. Lewis & M. W. Sullivan (Eds.), *Emotional development in atypical children* (pp. 203–225). Mahwah, NJ: Erlbaum.

Carlson, C. R., & Masters, J. C. (1986). Inoculation by emotion: Effects of positive emotional states on children's reaction to social comparison. *Developmental Psychology, 22,* 760–765.

Carlson Jones, D., Abbey, B. B., & Cumberland, A. (1998). The development of display rule knowledge: Linkages with family expressiveness and social competence. *Child Development, 69,* 1209–1222.

Casey, R. (1993). Children's emotional experience: Relations among expression, self-report, and understanding. *Developmental Psychology, 29,* 119–129.

Casey, R. J. (1996). Emotional competence in children with externalizing and internalizing disorders. In M. Lewis & M. W. Sullivan (Eds.), *Emotional development in atypical children* (pp. 161–183). Mahwah, NJ: Erlbaum.

Caspi, A., & Silva, P. A. (1995). Temperamental qualities at age three predict personality traits in young adulthood: Longitudinal evidence from a birth cohort. *Child Development, 66,* 486–498.

Cassidy, J. (1994). Emotion regulation: Influences of attachment relationships. *Monographs of the Society for Research in Child Development, 59*(2/3, Serial No. 240), 228–249.

Cassidy, J., Parke, R., Butkovsky, L., & Braungart, J. (1992). Family-peer connections: The roles of emotional expressiveness within the family and children's understanding of emotions. *Child Development, 63,* 603–618.

Cassidy, J., & Shaver, P. R. (Eds.). (1999). *Handbook of attachment.* New York: Guilford Press.

Ceschi, G., & Scherer, K. (2003). Children's ability to control the facial expression of laughter and smiling: Knowledge and behaviour. *Cognition and Emotion, 17,* 385–411.

Chambers, S. M. (1999). The effect of family talk on young children's development and coping. In E. Frydenberg (Ed.), *Learning to cope: Developing as a person in complex societies* (pp. 130–149). Oxford, England: Oxford University Press.

Chapman, M., Zahn-Waxler, C., Cooperman, G., & Iannotti, R. (1987). Empathy and responsibility in the motivation of children's helping. *Developmental Psychology, 23,* 140–145.

Chisholm, J. S. (1983). *Navajo infancy.* New York: Aldine.

Chisholm, J. S. (1989). Biology, culture and the development of temperament: A Navajo example. In J. K. Nugent, B. Lester, & T. B. Brazelton (Eds.), *The cultural context of infancy: Vol. 1. Biology, culture, and infant development* (pp. 341–364). Norwood, NJ: Ablex.

Coates, B., Anderson, E., & Hartup, W. (1972). Interrelations in the attachment behavior of human infants. *Developmental Psychology, 6,* 218–237.

Cohen, D., & Strayer, J. (1996). Empathy in conduct disordered and comparison youth. *Developmental Psychology, 32,* 988–998.

Cohen, L., & Campos, J. (1974). Father, mother and stranger as elicitors of attachment behaviors in infancy. *Developmental Psychology, 10,* 146–154.

Cohn, J. F., & Tronick, E. Z. (1988). Mother-infant face-to-face interaction: Influence is bidirectional and unrelated to periodic cycles in either partner's behavior. *Developmental Psychology, 24*(3), 386–392.

Colby, A., & Damon, W. (1992). *Some do care: Contemporary lives of moral commitment.* New York: Free Press.

Compas, B. E. (1987). Coping with stress during childhood and adolescence. *Psychological Bulletin, 101,* 393–403.

Compas, B. E., Connor, J. K., Saltzman, H., Thomsen, A. H., & Wadsworth, M. (1999). Getting specific about coping: Effortful and involuntary responses to stress in development. In M. Lewis & D. Ramsey (Eds.), *Soothing and stress* (pp. 229–256). Mahwah, NJ: Erlbaum.

Compas, B. E., Connor-Smith, J., & Jaser, S. (2004). Temperament, stress reactivity, and coping: Implications for depression in childhood and adolescence. *Journal of Clinical Child and Adolescent Psychology, 33,* 21–31.

Compas, B. E., Connor-Smith, J., Saltzman, H., & Thomsen, A. H. (2001). Coping with stress during childhood and adolescence: Problems, progress, and potential in theory and research. *Psychological Bulletin, 127,* 87–127.

Conrad, R. (1994). *Infant affect sharing and it's relation to maternal availability.* Unpublished doctoral dissertation, University of California, Berkeley.

Cosmides, L., & Tooby, J. (2000). Evolutionary psychology and the emotions. In M. Lewis & J. Haviland-Jones (Eds.), *Handbook of emotions* (2nd ed., pp. 91–115). New York: Guilford Press.

Crick, N., & Dodge, K. (1994). A review of social-information processing mechanisms in children's social adjustment. *Psychological Bulletin, 115,* 74–101.

Cummings, E. M., & Davies, P. (1994). *Children and marital conflict.* New York: Guilford.

Cummings, E. M., Goeke-Morey, M. C., Papp, L. M., & Dukewich, T. L. (2002). Children's responses to mothers' and fathers' emotionality and tactics in marital conflict in the home. *Journal of Family Psychology, 16,* 478–492.

Custrini, R., & Feldman, R. S. (1989). Children's social competence and nonverbal encoding and decoding of emotion. *Journal of Child Clinical Psychology, 18,* 336–342.

Damasio, A. (1994). *Descartes' error: Emotion, reason, and the human brain.* New York: Grosset & Dunlap.

D'Andrade, R. (1984). Cultural meaning systems. In R. Shweder & R. LeVine (Eds.), *Culture theory: Essays on mind, self, and emotion* (pp. 88–119). New York: Cambridge University Press.

Davies, M., Stankov, L., & Roberts, R. D. (1998). Emotional intelligence: In search of an elusive construct. *Journal of Personality and Social Psychology, 75,* 989–1015.

Davies, P., & Cummings, M. (1994). Marital conflict and child adjustment: An emotional security hypothesis. *Psychological Bulletin, 116,* 387–411.

Davis, T. (1995). Gender differences in masking negative emotions: Ability or motivation? *Developmental Psychology, 31,* 660–667.

Dearing, K., Hubbard, J., & Ramsden, S. (2002). Children's self-reports about anger regulation: Direct and indirect links to social preference and aggression. *Merrill-Palmer Quarterly, 48,* 308–336.

DeCasper, A. J., Lecanuet, J. P., Busnel, M. C., Granier-Deferre, C., & Maugeais, R. (1994). Fetal reactions to recurrent maternal speech. *Infant Behavior and Development, 17,* 159–164.

DeCasper, W., & Fifer, W. (1980). Of human bonding: Newborns prefer their mother's voices. *Science, 208,* 1174–1176.

Denham, S. (1999). *Emotional development in young children.* New York: Guilford Press.

Denham, S., & Auerbach, S. (1995). Mother-child dialogue about emotions. *Genetic, Social, and General Psychology Monographs, 121,* 301–319.

Denham, S., McKinley, M., Couchoud, E., & Holt, R. (1990). Emotional and behavioral predictors of preschool peer ratings. *Child development, 61,* 1145–1152.

Denham, S., Mitchell-Copeland, J., Strandberg, K., Auerbach, S., & Blair, K. (1997). Parental contributions to preschoolers' emotion competence: Direct and indirect effects. *Motivation and Emotion, 21,* 65–86.

D'Entremont, B., & Muir, D. (1999). Infant responses to adult happy and sad vocal and facial expressions during face-to-face interactions. *Infant Behavior and Development., 22*(4), 527–539.

DePaulo, B. (1991). Nonverbal behavior and self-presentation: A developmental perspective. In R. S. Feldman & B. Rimé (Eds.), *Fundamentals of nonverbal behavior* (pp. 351–397). New York: Cambridge University Press.

Dewey, J. (1894). The theory of emotion: Pt. 1. Emotional attitudes. *Psychological Review, 1,* 553–569.

Dewey, J. (1895). The theory of emotion: Pt. 2. The significance of emotions. *Psychological Review, 2,* 13–32.

Dewey, J. (1934). *Art as experience.* New York: Minton, Balch.

Dickson, K. L., Walker, H., & Fogel, A. (1997). The relationship between smile type and play type during parent-infant play. *Developmental Psychology, 33,* 925–933.

Diener, E., & Lucas, R. E. (2000). Subjective emotional well-being. In M. Lewis & J. Haviland-Jones (Eds.), *Handbook of emotions* (2nd ed., pp. 325–337). New York: Guilford Press.

Donaldson, S. K., & Westerman, M. A. (1986). Development of children's understanding of ambivalence and casual theories of emotion. *Developmental Psychology, 22,* 655–662.

Dondi, M., Simion, F., & Caltran, G. (1999). Can newborns discriminate between their own cry and the cry of another newborn infant? *Developmental Psychology, 35*(2), 418–426.

Downey, G., & Coyne, J. C. (1990). Children of depressed parents: An integrative review. *Psychological Bulletin, 108,* 50–76.

Draghi-Lorenz, R., Reddy, V., & Costall, A. (2001). Rethinking the development of "nonbasic" emotions: A critical review of existing theories. *Developmental Review, 21,* 263–304.

Dunn, J. (1988). *The beginnings of social understanding.* Cambridge, MA: Harvard University Press.

Dunn, J. (2000). Mind-reading, emotion understanding, and relationships. *International Journal of Behavioral Development, 24,* 142–144.

Dunn, J., Bretherton, I., & Munn, P. (1987). Conversations about feeling states between mothers and their young children. *Developmental Psychology, 23,* 132–139.

Dunn, J., & Brown, J. (1991). Relationships, talk about feelings, and the development of affect regulation in early childhood. In J. Garber & K. Dodge (Eds.), *The development of emotion regulation and dysregulation* (pp. 89–108). Cambridge, England: Cambridge University Press.

Dunn, J., & Brown, J. (1994). Affect expression in the family, children's understanding of emotions, and their interactions with others. *Merrill-Palmer Quarterly, 40,* 120–137.

Dunn, J., Brown, J., & Beardsall, L. (1991). Family talk about feeling states and children's later understanding of other's emotions. *Developmental Psychology, 27,* 448–455.

Du Rocher Schudlich, T., Shamir, H., & Cummings, E. M. (2004). Marital conflict, children's representations of family relationships, and children's dispositions towards peer conflict strategies. *Social Development, 13,* 171–192.

Dweck, C., & Leggett, E. (1988). A social-cognitive approach to motivation and personality. *Psychological Review, 95,* 256–273.

Ebata, A., & Moos, R. (1991). Coping and adjustment in distressed and healthy adolescents. *Journal of Applied Developmental Psychology, 12,* 33–54.

Edwards, R., Manstead, A., & MacDonald, C. J. (1984). The relationship between children's sociometric status and ability to recognize facial expressions of emotion. *European Journal of Social Psychology, 14,* 235–238.

Eisenberg, A. R. (1986). Teasing: Verbal play in two Mexicano homes. In B. Schiefflin & E. Ochs (Eds.), *Language socialization across cultures* (pp. 182–198). Cambridge, England: Cambridge University Press.

Eisenberg, N. (2003). Prosocial behavior, empathy, and sympathy. In M. Bornstein & L. Davidson (Eds.), *Well-being: Positive development across the life course* (pp. 253–265). Mahwah, NJ: Erlbaum.

Eisenberg, N., & Fabes, R. (1998). Prosocial development. In N. Eisenberg (Ed.), *Social, emotional, and personality development* (5th ed., Vol. 3, pp. 701–778). New York: Wiley.

Eisenberg, N., Fabes, R. A., Bernzweig, J., Karbon, M., Poulin, R., & Hanish, L. (1993). The relations of emotionality and regulation to preschoolers' social skills and sociometric status. *Child Development, 64,* 1418–1438.

Eisenberg, N., Fabes, R., Bustamante, D., Mathy, R., Miller, P. A., & Lindholm, E. (1988). Differentiation of vicariously induced emotional reactions in children. *Developmental Psychology, 24,* 237–246.

Eisenberg, N., Fabes, R., Carlo, G., & Karbon, M. (1992). Emotional responsivity to others: Behavioral correlates and socialization antecedents. In N. Eisenberg & R. Fabes (Eds.), *New directions in child development: Vol. 5. Emotion and its regulation in early development* (pp. 57–73). San Francisco: Jossey-Bass.

Eisenberg, N., Fabes, R., Murphy, B., Karbon, M., Smith, M., & Maszk, P. (1996). The relations of children's dispositional empathy-related responding to their emotionality, regulation, and social functioning. *Developmental Psychology, 32,* 195–209.

Eisenberg, N., Fabes, R., Nyman, M., Bernzweig, J., & Pinuelas, A. (1994). The relations of emotionality and regulation to young children's anger-related reactions. *Child Development, 65,* 109–128.

Eisenberg, N., Fabes, R., Schaller, M., Carlo, G., & Miller, P. A. (1991). The relations of parental characteristics and practices to children's vicarious emotional responding. *Child Development, 62,* 1393–1408.

Eisenberg, N., Fabes, R., Shepard, S., Murphy, B., Guthrie, I., Jones, S., et al. (1997). Contemporaneous and longitudinal prediction of children's social functioning from regulation and emotionality. *Child Development, 68,* 642–664.

Eisenberg, N., Gershoff, E., Fabes, R., Shepard, S., Cumberland, A., Losoya, S., et al. (2001). Mothers' emotional expressivity and children's behavior problems and social competence: Mediation through children's regulation. *Developmental Psychology, 37,* 475–490.

Eisenberg, N., & McNally, S. (1993). Socialization and mother's and adolescents' empathy-related characteristics. *Psychological Bulletin, 101,* 91–119.

Eisenberg, N., & Morris, A. S. (2002). Children's emotion-related regulation. *Advances in Child Development and Behavior, 30,* 190–229.

Eisenberg, N., & Spinrad, T. (2004). Emotion-related regulation: Sharpening the definition. *Child Development, 75*(2), 334–339.

Eisenberg, N., Spinrad, T., Fabes, R., Reiser, M., Cumberland, A., Shepard, S., et al. (2004). The relations of effortful control and impulsivity to children's resiliency and adjustment. *Child Development, 75,* 25–46.

Eisenberg, N., Spinrad, T., & Morris, A. S. (2002). Regulation, resiliency, and quality of social functioning. *Self and Identity, 1,* 121–128.

Ekman, P. (1973). *Darwin and facial expression.* New York: Academic Press.

Ekman, P. (1995). Strong evidence for universals in facial expressions: A reply to Russell's mistaken critique. *Psychological Bulletin, 115,* 268–287.

Ekman, P., & Friesen, W. V. (1975). *Unmasking the face.* Englewood Cliffs, NJ: Prentice-Hall.

Ekman, P., Levenson, R. W., & Friesen, W. V. (1983). Autonomic nervous activity distinguishes between emotions. *Science* (221), 1208–1210.

Ekman, P., Sorensen, E., & Friesen, W. (1969). Pan-cultural elements in the facial expression of emotions. *Science* (164), 86–88.

Emde, R., Gaensbauer, T., & Harmon, R. (1976). *Emotional expression in infancy: A biobehavioral study—Psychological issues* (Vol. 10, No. 37). New York: International Universities Press.

Emde, R. N., Kligman, D. H., Reich, J. H., & Wade, T. D. (1978). Emotional expression in infancy: Vol. 1. Initial studies of social signaling and an emergent model. In M. Lewis & L. A. Rosenblum (Eds.), *The development of affect* (pp. 125–148). New York: Plenum Press.

Fabes, R., Eisenberg, N., Nyman, M., & Michaelieu, Q. (1991). Young children's appraisals of others' spontaneous emotional reactions. *Developmental Psychology, 27,* 858–866.

Fabes, R., Hanish, L., Martin, C. L., & Eisenberg, N. (2002). Young children's negative emotionality and social isolation: A latent growth curve analysis. *Merrill-Palmer Quarterly, 48,* 284–307.

Feldman, R., Greenbaum, C. W., & Yirmiya, N. (1999). Mother-infant affect synchrony as an antecedent of the emergence of self-control. *Developmental Psychology, 35,* 223–231.

Fergusson, T., & Stegge, H. (1995). Emotional states and traits in children. In K. Fischer & J. Tangney (Eds.), *Self-conscious emotions: The psychology of shame, guilt, embarrassment and pride* (pp. 174–197). New York: Guilford Press.

Fernald, A. (1993). Approval and disapproval: Infant responsiveness to vocal affect in familiar and unfamiliar languages. *Child Development, 64,* 657–674.

Field, T., Healy, B. T., Goldstein, S., & Guthertz, M. (1990). Behavior-state matching and synchrony in mother infant interactions of nondepressed versus depressed dyads. *Developmental Psychology, 26,* 7–14.

Field, T. M., Woodson, R., Greenberg, R., & Cohen, D. (1982). Discrimination and imitation of facial expressions by neonates. *Science, 218,* 179–181.

Fifer, W. P., & Moon, C. M. (1995). The effects of fetal experience with sound. In J.-P. Lecanuet, W. P. Fifer, N. A. Krasnegor, & W. P. Smotherman (Eds.), *Fetal development: A psychobiological perspective* (pp. 351–366). Hillsdale, NJ: Erlbaum.

Fischer, K., & Ayoub, C. (1993). Affective splitting and dissociation in normal and maltreated children: Developmental pathways for self in relationships. In D. Cicchetti & S. Toth (Eds.), *Rochester Symposium on Development and Psychopathology: Vol. 5. Disorders and dysfunctions of the self* (pp. 149–222). Rochester, NY: University of Rochester Press.

Fivush, R. (1991). The social construction of personal narratives. *Merrill-Palmer Quarterly, 37,* 59–82.

Fogel, A., Nwokah, E., Dedo, J., Messinger, D., Dickson, L., Matusov, E., et al. (1992). Social process theory of emotion: A dynamic systems approach. *Social Development, 1,* 122–142.

Fogel, A., & Thelen, E. (1987). Development of early expressive and communicative action: Reinterpreting the evidence from a dynamic systems perspective. *Developmental Psychology, 23,* 747–761.

Fraiberg, S. (1971). *Insights from the blind.* New York: Basic Books.

Fridlund, A. (1994). *Human facial expressions: An evolutionary view.* New York: Academic Press.

Frijda, N. (1986). *The emotions.* Cambridge, England: Cambridge University Press.

Frijda, N. (1987). Emotion, cognitive structure, and action tendency. *Cognition and Emotion, 1,* 115–143.

Fuchs, D., & Thelen, M. (1988). Children's expected interpersonal consequences of communicating their affective states and reported likelihood of expression. *Child development, 59,* 1314–1322.

Gaensbauer, T. (1982). The differentiation of discrete affects: A case report. *Psychoanalytic Study of the Child, 37,* 29–66.

Garner, P. W., & Estep, K. (2001). Emotional competence, emotion socialization, and young children's peer-related social competence. *Early Education and Development, 12,* 29–48.

Garner, P. W., & Power, T. G. (1996). Preschoolers' emotional control in the disappointment paradigm and its relation to temperament, emotional knowledge, and family expressiveness. *Child Development, 67,* 1406–1419.

George, C., Kaplan, N., & Main, M. (1985). *The attachment interview for adults.* Unpublished manuscript, University of California, Berkeley.

Gergely, G., & Watson, J. (1996). The social biofeedback theory of parental affect-mirroring. *International Journal of Psychoanalysis, 77,* 1181–1212.

Gergely, G., & Watson, J. S. (1999). Early socio-emotional development: Contingency perception and the social-biofeedback model. In P. Rochat (Ed.), *Early social cognition: Understanding others in the first months of life* (pp. 101–136). Mahwah, NJ: Erlbaum.

Gianino, A., & Tronick, E. (1988). The mutual regulation model: The infant's self and interactive regulation and coping and defensive capacities. In T. Field, P. McCabe, & N. Schneiderman (Eds.), *Stress and coping across the development* (pp. 47–68). Hillsdale, NJ: Erlbaum.

Gnepp, J. (1989). Children's use of personal information to understand other people's feelings. In C. Saarni & P. Harris (Eds.), *Children's understanding of emotion* (pp. 151–180). New York: Cambridge University Press.

Gnepp, J., & Chilamkurti, C. (1988). Children's use of personality attributions to predict other people's emotional and behavioral reactions. *Child Development, 59,* 743–754.

Gnepp, J., & Gould, M. E. (1985). The development of personalized inferences: Understanding other people's emotional reactions in light of their prior experiences. *Child Development, 56,* 1455–1464.

Gnepp, J., & Hess, D. L. (1986). Children's understanding of verbal and facial display rules. *Developmental Psychology, 22,* 103–108.

Goodman, S., Brogan, D., Lynch, M., & Fielding, B. (1993). Social and emotional competence in children of depressed mothers. *Child Development, 64,* 516–531.

Gordon, S. (1989). The socialization of children's emotions: Emotional culture, competence, and exposure. In C. Saarni & P. Harris (Eds.), *Children's understanding of emotions* (pp. 319–349). New York: Cambridge University Press.

Gottman, J. M., Guralnick, M., Wilson, B., Swanson, C., & Murray, J. (1997). What should be the focus of emotion regulation in children? A nonlinear dynamic mathematical model of children's peer interaction in groups. *Development and Psychopathology, 9,* 421–452.

Gottman, J. M., Katz, L. F., & Hooven, C. (1997). *Meta-emotion.* Hillsdale, NJ: Erlbaum.

Griffin, S., & Mascolo, M. F. (1998). On the nature, development, and functions of emotions. In M. F. Mascolo & S. Griffin (Eds.), *What develops in emotional development?* (pp. 3–27). New York: Plenum Press.

Gross, A. L., & Ballif, B. (1991). Children's understanding of emotion from facial expressions and situations: A review. *Developmental Review, 11,* 368–398.

Grossmann, K. E., Grossmann, K., Huber, F., & Wartner, U. (1981). German children's behavior toward their mothers at 12 months and their fathers at 18 months in Ainsworth's Strange Situation. *International Journal of Behavioral Development, 4,* 157–181.

Gumora, G., & Arsenio, W. (2002). Emotionality, emotion regulation, and school performance in middle school children. *Journal of School Psychology, 40,* 395–413.

Gunnar, M. R., & Stone, C. (1984). The effects of positive maternal affect on infant responses to pleasant, ambiguous, and fear-provoking toys. *Child Development, 55,* 1231–1236.

Halberstadt, A. (1986). Family socialization of emotional expression and nonverbal communication styles and skills. *Journal of Personality and Social Psychology, 51,* 827–836.

Halberstadt, A., Denham, S., & Dunsmore, J. (2001). Affective social competence. *Social Development, 10,* 79–119.

Hardy, D., Power, T., & Jaedicke, S. (1993). Examining the relation of parenting to children's coping with everyday stress. *Child Development, 64,* 1829–1841.

Harris, P. L. (1989). *Children and emotion.* Oxford, England: Blackwell.

Harris, P. L. (1995). Children's awareness and lack of awareness of mind and emotion. In D. Cicchetti & S. Toth (Eds.), *Rochester*

Symposium on Developmental Psychopathology: Vol. 6. Emotion, cognition and representation (pp. 35–37). Rochester, NY: University of Rochester Press.

Harris, P. L. (1997). Between strange situations and false beliefs: Working models and theories of mind. In W. Koops, J. Hoeksma, & D. van den Boom (Eds.), *Early mother-child interaction and attachment: Old and new approaches* (pp. 187–199). Amsterdam: Royal Netherlands Academy of Arts and Sciences.

Harris, P. L. (1998). Fictional absorption: Emotional responses to make-believe. In S. Bråten (Ed.), *Intersubjective communication and emotion in early ontogeny* (pp. 336–353). Paris: Cambridge University Press.

Harris, P. L. (2000). Understanding emotion. In M. Lewis & J. Haviland (Eds.), *Handbook of emotion* (2nd ed., pp. 281–292). New York: Guilford Press.

Harris, P. L., & Gross, D. (1988). Children's understanding of real and apparent emotion. In J. W. Astington, P. L. Harris, & D. R. Olson (Eds.), *Developing theories of mind* (pp. 295–314). Cambridge: Cambridge University Press.

Harris, P., & Lipian, M. S. (1989). Understanding emotion and experiencing emotion. In C. Saarni & P. Harris (Eds.), *Children's understanding of emotion* (pp. 241–258). Cambridge: Cambridge University Press.

Harter, S. (1999). *The construction of the self.* New York: Guilford Press.

Harter, S., & Buddin, B. J. (1987). Children's understanding of the simultaneity of two emotions: A five-stage developmental acquisition sequence. *Developmental Psychology, 23,* 388–399.

Harter, S., & Lee, L. (1989, April). *Manifestations of true and not true selves in adolescents.* Paper presented at the biennial meeting of the Society for Research in Child Development, Kansas City, MO.

Harter, S., Waters, P. L., Whitesell, N., & Dastelic, D. (1998). Level of voice among female and male high school students: Relational context, support, and gender orientation. *Child Development, 34,* 892–901.

Harter, S., & Whitesell, N. R. (1989). Developmental changes in children's understanding of single, multiple, and blended emotion concepts. In C. Saarni & P. Harris (Eds.), *Children's understanding of emotion* (pp. 81–116). Cambridge: Cambridge University Press.

Hatfield, E., Cacioppo, J. T., & Rapson, R. L. (1994). *Emotional contagion.* Cambridge: Cambridge University Press.

Haviland, J., & Lelwica, M. (1987). The induced affect response: Ten-week-old infants' responses to three emotional expressions. *Developmental Psychology, 23,* 97–104.

Hertenstein, M., & Campos, J. (2001). Emotion regulation via maternal touch. *Infancy, 2,* 549–566.

Hertenstein, M. J., & Campos, J. J. (2004). The retention effects of an adult's emotional displays on infant behavior. *Child Development, 75*(2), 595–613.

Holodynski, M. (2004). The miniaturization of expression in the development of emotional self-regulation. *Developmental Psychology, 40,* 16–28.

Holodynski, M., & Freidlmeier, W. (2006). *Development of emotions and their regulation: A socioculturally based internalization model.* Boston: Kluwer Academic.

Howard, M. S., & Medway, F. (2004). Adolescents' attachment and coping with stress. *Psychology in the Schools, 41,* 391–402.

Hubbard, J. (2001). Emotion expression processes in children's peer interaction: The role of peer rejection, aggression, and gender. *Child Development, 72,* 1426–1438.

Hubbard, J., & Coie, J. (1994). Emotional correlates of social competence in children's peer relationships. *Merrill-Palmer Quarterly, 40,* 1–20.

Isley, S. L., O'Neil, R., Clatfelter, D., & Parke, R. D. (1999). Parent and child expressed affect and children's social competence: Modeling direct and indirect pathways. *Developmental Psychology, 35,* 547–560.

Izard, C. E. (1972). *The face of emotion.* New York: Appleton-Century-Crofts.

Izard, C. E. (1977). *Human emotions.* New York: Plenum Press.

Izard, C. E. (1991). *The psychology of emotions.* New York: Plenum Press.

Izard, C. E. (1995). Innate and universal facial expressions: Evidence from developmental and cross-cultural research. *Psychological Bulletin, 115,* 288–299.

Izard, C. E. (2004). The generality-specificity issue in infants' emotion responses: A comment on Bennett, Bendersky, and Lewis, 2002. *Infancy, 6,* 417–423.

Izard, C. E., Ackerman, B., Schoff, K., & Fine, S. (2000). Self-organization of discrete emotions, emotion patterns and emotion-cognition relations. In M. Lewis & I. Granic (Eds.), *Emotion, development, and self-organization: Dynamic systems approaches to emotional development* (pp. 15–36). Cambridge: Cambridge University Press.

Izard, C. E., & Dougherty, L. (1982). Two complementary systems for measuring facial expressions in infants and children. In C. E. Izard (Ed.), *Measuring emotions in infants and children* (pp. 97–126). New York: Cambridge University Press.

Jaffe, J., Beebe, B., Feldstein, S., Crown, C. L., & Jasnow, M. D. (2001). Rhythms of dialogue in infancy: Coordinated timing in development. *Monographs of the Society for Research in Child Development, 66*(Serial No. 265), vi–131.

Janoff-Bulman, R., & Frantz, C. (1997). The impact of trauma on meaning: From meaningless world to meaningful life. In M. Power & C. Brewer (Eds.), *The transformation of meaning in psychological therapies* (pp. 91–106). London: Wiley.

Jones, S. S., Collins, K., & Hong, H. (1991). An audience effect on smile production in 10-month-old infants. *Psychological Science, 2*(1), 45–49.

Josephs, I. E. (1994). Display rule behavior and understanding in preschool children. *Journal of Nonverbal Behavior, 18,* 301–326.

Kagan, J. (1971). *Change and continuity in infancy.* New York: Wiley.

Kagan, J. (1984). The idea of emotion in human development. In C. E. Izard, J. Kagan, & R. B. Zajonc (Eds.), *Emotions, cognition, and behavior* (pp. 38–72). Cambridge, England: Cambridge University Press.

Kagan, J. (1994). On the nature of emotion. *Monographs of the Society for Research in Child Development, 59*(2/3), 7–24, 250–283.

Kahana-Kalman, R., & Walker-Andrews, A. S. (2001). The role of person familiarity in young infants' perception of emotional expressions. *Child Development, 72*(2), 352–369.

Kaitz, M., Meschulach-Sarfaty, O., Auerback, J., & Eidelman, A. (1988). A reexamination of newborn's ability to imitate facial expressions. *Developmental Psychology, 24,* 3–7.

Karbon, M., Fabes, R., Carlo, G., & Martin, C. L. (1992). Preschoolers' beliefs about sex and age differences in emotionality. *Sex Roles, 27,* 377–390.

Keefer, C., Dixon, S., Tronick, E., & Brazelton, T. (1991). Cultural mediation between newborn behavior and later development: Implications for methodology in cross-cultural research. In J. Nugent, B. Lester, & T. Brazelton (Eds.), *The cultural context of infancy: Vol. 2. Multicultural and interdisciplinary approaches to parent-infant relations* (pp. 39–61). Norwood, NJ: Ablex.

Kenney, M., Mason, W., & Hill, S. (1979). Effects of age, objects and visual experience on affective responses of rhesus monkeys to strangers. *Developmental Psychology, 15*(2), 176–184.

Kitayama, S., & Markus, H. (1994). Introduction to cultural psychology and emotion research. In S. Kitayama & H. Markus (Eds.), *Emotion and culture* (pp. 1–19). Washington, DC: American Psychological Association.

Klinnert, M. D. (1984). The regulation of infant behavior by maternal facial expression. *Infant Behavior and Development, 7,* 447–465.

Klinnert, M. D., Campos, J. J., Sorce, J. F., Emde, R. N., & Svejda, M. (1983). Emotions as behavior regulators: Social referencing in infancy. In R. Plutchik & H. Kellerman (Eds.), *Emotion: Theory, research and experience* (pp. 57–86). New York: Academic Press.

Kochanska, G. (2001). Emotional development in children with different attachment histories: The first three years. *Child Development, 72,* 474–490.

Kochanska, G., & Thompson, R. (1997). The emergence and development of conscience in toddlerhood and early childhood. In J. Grusec & L. Kuczynski (Eds.), *Parenting and children's internalization of values: A handbook of contemporary theory* (pp. 53–77). New York: Wiley.

Koestner, R., Franz, C., & Weinberger, J. (1990). The family origins of empathic concern: A 26-year longitudinal study. *Journal of Personality and Social Psychology, 58,* 709–717.

Lagattuta, K., Wellman, H., & Flavell, J. (1997). Preschoolers' understanding of the link between thinking and feeling: Cognitive cuing and emotional change. *Child Development, 68,* 1081–1104.

Laible, D. (2004). Mother-child discourse in two contexts: Links with child temperament, attachment security, and socioemotional competence. *Developmental Psychology, 40,* 979–992.

Laird, J. (1984). The real role of facial response in the experience of emotions: A reply to Tourangeau and Ellsworth and others. *Journal of Personality and Social Psychology, 47,* 909–917.

Landers, C. (1989). A psychobiological study of infant development in South India. In J. K. Nugent & B. M. Lester (Eds.), *The cultural context of infancy: Vol. 1. Biology, culture and infant development* (pp. 169–207). Westport, CT: Ablex.

Lawson, K. R., & Ruff, H. A. (2004). Early attention and negative emotionality predict later cognitive and behavioural function. *International Journal of Behavioral Development, 28*(2), 157–165.

Lazarus, R. S. (1991). *Emotion and adaptation.* New York: Oxford University Press.

Lazarus, R. S. (1999). *Stress and emotion: A new synthesis.* New York: Springer.

Lazarus, R., & Averill, J. (1972). Emotion and cognition with special reference to anxiety. In C. Spielberger (Ed.), *Anxiety: Current directions in theory and research* (pp. 242–283). New York: Academic Press.

Lazarus, R., & Folkman, S. (1984). *Stress, appraisal, and coping.* New York: Springer Verlag.

Levine, L. (1995). Young children's understanding of the causes of anger and stress. *Child Development, 66,* 697–709.

LeVine, R., Dixon, S., LeVine, S., Richman, A., Leiderman, P. H., Keefer, C. H., et al. (1994). *Child care and culture: Lessons from Africa.* New York: Cambridge University Press.

Lewis, M. (1992). *Shame: The exposed self.* New York: Free Press.

Lewis, M. (1993). Self-conscious emotions: Embarrassment, pride, shame, and guilt. In M. Lewis & J. Haviland (Eds.), *The handbook of emotions* (pp. 563–573). New York: Guilford Press.

Lewis, M. (1995). Embarrassment: The emotion of self-exposure and evaluation. In J. Tangney & K. Fischer (Eds.), *Self-conscious emotions: The psychology of shame, guilt, embarrassment and pride* (pp. 198–218). New York: Guilford Press.

Lewis, M. (1997). *Altering fate: Why the past does not predict the future.* New York: Guilford Press.

Lewis, M. (1998). The development and structure of emotions. In M. Mascolo & S. Griffin (Eds.), *What develops in emotional development?* (pp. 29–50). New York: Plenum Press.

Lewis, M. (2000). Self-conscious emotions: Embarrassment, pride, shame, and guilt. In M. Lewis & J. Haviland (Eds.), *Handbook of Emotions* (2nd ed., pp. 623–636). New York: Guilford Press.

Lewis, M., & Brooks-Gunn, J. (1979). *Social cognition and the acquisition of self.* New York: Plenum Press.

Lewis, M., Hitchcock, D. F., & Sullivan, M. W. (2004). Physiological and emotional reactivity to learning and frustration. *Infancy, 6,* 121–143.

Lewis, M., & Michalson, L. (1983). *Children's emotions and moods: Developmental theory and measurement.* New York: Plenum Press.

Lewis, M., & Michalson, L. (1985). Faces as signs and symbols. In G. Zivin (Ed.), *The development of expressive behavior* (pp. 153–178). New York: Academic Press.

Lewis, M., & Ramsay, D. (2002). Cortisol response to embarrassment and shame. *Child Development, 73,* 1034–1045.

Lewis, M., & Ramsay, D. (2004). Development of self-recognition, personal pronoun use, and pretend play during the second year. *Child Development, 75,* 1821–1831.

Lewis, M., Sullivan, M., & Vasen, A. (1987). Making faces: Age and emotion differences in the posing of emotional expressions. *Developmental Psychology, 23,* 690–697.

Lewis, M. D. (2000). Emotional self-organization at three time scales. In M. D. Lewis & I. Granic (Eds.), *Emotion, development, and self-organization: Dynamic systems approaches to emotional development* (pp. 37–69). Cambridge, England: Cambridge University Press.

Lewis, M. D., & Granic, I. (1999). Self-organization of cognition-emotion interactions. In T. Dalgleish & M. Power (Eds.), *Handbook of cognition and emotion* (pp. 683–701). New York: Wiley.

Lewis, M. D., & Granic, I. (Eds.). (2000). *Emotion, development, and self-organization: Dynamic systems approaches to emotional development.* Cambridge, UK: Cambridge University Press.

Lipton, E. L., Steinschneider, A., & Richmond, J. B. (1965). Swaddling, a child care practice: Historical, cultural and experimental observations. *Pediatrics, 34,* 521–567.

Luminet, O., Bouts, P., Delie, F., Manstead, A., & Rimé, B. (2000). Social sharing of emotion following exposure to a negatively valenced situation. *Cognition and Emotion, 14,* 661–688.

Lutz, C. (1988). Ethnographic perspectives on the emotion lexicon. In V. Hamilton, G. H. Bower, & N. Frijda (Eds.), *Cognitive perspectives on emotion and motivation* (pp. 399–419). Norwell, MA: Kluwer Academic.

Lyubomirsky, S., & Nolen-Hoeksema, S. (1995). Effects of self-focused rumination on negative thinking and interpersonal problem solving. *Journal of Personality and Social Psychology, 69,* 176–190.

Mahler, M., Pine, F., & Bergman, A. (1975). *The psychological birth of the human infant.* New York: Basic Books.

Marriage, K., & Cummins, R. (2004). Subjective quality of life and self-esteem in children: The role of primary and secondary control in coping with everyday stress. *Social Indicators Research, 66,* 107–122.

Martin, G. B., & Clark, R. D. (1982). Distress crying in neonates: Species and peer specificity. *Developmental Psychology, 18,* 3–9.

Mascolo, M., & Fischer, K. (1995). Developmental transformations in appraisals for pride, shame, and guilt. In J. Tangney & K. Fischer (Eds.), *Self-conscious emotions: The psychology of shame, guilt, embarrassment and pride* (pp. 64–113). New York: Guilford Press.

Mascolo, M. F., & Harkins, D. (1998). Toward a component systems approach to emotional development. In M. Mascolo & S. Griffin (Eds.), *What develops in emotional development?* (pp. 189–217). New York: Plenum Press.

Mastropieri, D., & Turkewitz, G. (1999). Prenatal experience and neonatal responsiveness to vocal expressions of emotion. *Developmental Psychobiology, 35*(3), 204–214.

Mayer, J. D., Salovey, P., & Caruso, D. (2000). Emotional intelligence as zeitgeist, as personality, and as a mental ability. In R. Bar-On & J. D. Parker (Eds.), *The handbook of emotional intelligence* (pp. 92–117). San Francisco: Jossey-Bass.

McIntosh, D. N., Druckman, D., & Zajonc, R. B. (1994). Socially induced affect. In D. Druckman & R. A. Bjork (Eds.), *Learning, remembering, believing: Enhancing human performance* (pp. 251–276, 364–371). Washington, DC: National Academy Press.

Mead, M. (1954). The swaddling hypothesis: Its reception. *American Anthropologist, 56,* 395–409.

Meerum Terwogt, M., & Olthof, T. (1989). Awareness and self-regulation of emotion in young children. In C. Saarni & P. Harris (Eds.), *Children's understanding of emotion* (pp. 209–237). Cambridge: Cambridge University Press.

Mesquita, B. (2001). Emotions in collectivist and individualist contexts. *Journal of Personality and Social Psychology, 80,* 68–74.

Mesquita, B., & Frijda, N. (1992). Cultural variations in emotion: A review. *Psychological Bulletin, 112,* 179–204.

Messinger, D. S., Fogel, A., & Dickson, K. L. (1999). What's in a smile? *Developmental Psychology, 35,* 701–708.

Miller, P., Kliewer, W., Hepworth, J., & Sandler, I. (1994). Maternal socialization of children's postdivorce coping: Development of a measurement model. *Journal of Applied Developmental Psychology, 15,* 457–487.

Miller, S. M., & Green, M. L. (1985). Coping with stress and frustration: Origins, nature, and development. In M. Lewis & C. Saarni (Eds.), *The socialization of emotions* (pp. 263–314). New York: Plenum Press.

Miyake, K., Campos, J., Kagan, J., & Bradshaw, D. (1986). Issues in socioemotional development in Japan. In H. Azuma, K. Hakuta, & H. Stevenson (Eds.), *Kodomo: Child development and education in Japan* (pp. 238–261). San Francisco: Freeman.

Miyake, K., Chen, S., & Campos, J. (1985). Infant temperament, mother's mode of interaction, and attachment in Japan. *Mono-graphs of the Society for Research in Child Development, 50*(1/2, Serial No. 209) 276–297.

Montague, D., & Walker-Andrews, A. (2002). Mothers, fathers, and infants: The role of person familiarity and parental involvement in infants' perceptions of emotion expressions. *Child Development, 73,* 1339–1352.

Moore, G. A., & Calkins, S. (2004). Infants' vagal regulation in the still-face paradigm is related to dyadic coordination of mother-infant interaction. *Developmental Psychology, 40,* 1068–1080.

Moore, G. A., Cohn, J. F., & Campbell, S. B. (2001). Infant affective responses to mother's still face at 6 months differentially predict externalizing and internalizing behaviors at 18 months. *Developmental Psychology, 37,* 706–714.

Morelli, G., Rogoff, B., Oppenheim, D., & Goldsmith, D. (1992). Cultural variation in infants' sleeping arrangements: Questions of independence. *Developmental Psychology, 28,* 604–613.

Morris, M., & Peng, K. (1994). Culture and cause: American and Chinese attributions for social and physical events. *Journal of Personality and Social Psychology, 67,* 949–971.

Moses, L. J., Baldwin, D. A., Rosicky, J. G., & Tidball, G. (2001). Evidence for referential understanding in the emotions domain at 12 and 18 months. *Child Development, 72,* 718–735.

Mumme, D., Bushnell, E., DiCorcia, J., & Lariviere, L. (in press). Infants' use of gaze cues to interpret others' actions and emotional reactions. In R. Flom, K. Lee, & D. Muir (Eds.), *The ontogeny of gaze following.* Mahwah, NJ: Erlbaum.

Mumme, D., & Fernald, A. (2003). The infant as onlooker: Learning from emotional reactions observed in a television scenario. *Child Development, 74,* 221–237.

Mumme, D., Fernald, A., & Herrera, C. (1996). Infants responses to facial and vocal emotional signals in a social referencing paradigm. *Child Development, 67,* 3219–3237.

O'Brien, M., Margolin, G., & John, R. S. (1995). Relation among marital conflict, child coping, and child adjustment. *Journal of Clinical Child Psychology, 24,* 346–361.

Ochs, E. (1986). From feelings to grammar: A Samoan case study. In B. Schieffelin & E. Ochs (Eds.), *Language socialization across cultures* (pp. 251–272). Cambridge, England: Cambridge University Press.

Osofsky, J. (1999). The impact of violence on children. *Future of Children, 9*(3), 33–49.

Oster, H. (1995). *Baby FACS: Analyzing facial movement in infants.* Unpublished manuscript.

Oster, H. (in press). The repertoire of infant facial expressions: An ontogenetic perspective. In J. Nadel & D. Muir (Eds.), *The future of emotions.* Oxford, England: Oxford University Press.

Parker, E. H., Hubbard, J., Ramsden, S., Relyea, N., Dearing, K., Smithmyer, C., et al. (2001). Children's use and knowledge of display rules for anger following hypothetical vignettes versus following live peer interaction. *Social Development, 10,* 528–557.

Phillips, A., Wellman, H., & Spelke, E. (2002). Infants ability to connect gaze and emotion expressions to intentional actions. *Cognition, 85,* 53–78.

Pollak, S. D., Cicchetti, D., Hornung, K., & Reed, A. (2000). Recognizing emotion in faces: Developmental effects of child abuse and neglect. *Developmental Psychology, 36,* 679–688.

Ramsden, S., & Hubbard, J. (2002). Family expressiveness and parental emotion coaching: Their role in children's emotion regulation and aggression. *Journal of Abnormal Child Psychology, 30,* 657–667.

Rapacholi, B. (1998). Infants' use of attentional cue to identify the referent of another person's emotional expression. *Developmental Psychology, 34,* 1017–1025.

Raver, C. C. (2002). Emotions matter: Making the case for the role of young children's emotional development for early school readiness. *Social Policy Report, 16*(3), 3–18.

Reimer, M. (1996). Sinking into the ground: The development and consequences of shame in adolescence. *Developmental Review, 16,* 321–363.

Ridgeway, D., Waters, E., & Kuczaj, S. A. (1985). Acquisition of emotion-descriptive language: Receptive and productive vocabulary norms for ages 18 month to 6 years. *Developmental Psychology, 21,* 901–908.

Roberts, W. L., & Strayer, J. (1996). Empathy, emotional expressiveness, and prosocial behavior. *Child Development, 67,* 449–470.

Rochat, P., Striano, T., & Blatt, L. (2002). Four 6-month-olds respond to still face irrespective of expression (happy, sad, neutral) while 2-month-olds disrupted less by happy expression more evidence for early "contagion"? *Infant and Child Development, 11,* 289–303.

Rose-Krasnor, L. (1997). The nature of social competence: A theoretical review. *Social Development, 6,* 111–135.

Rossman, B. R. (1992). School-age children's perceptions of coping with distress: Strategies for emotion regulation and the moderation of adjustment. *Journal of Child Psychology and Psychiatry, 33,* 1373–1397.

Rothbart, M., & Bates, J. E. (1998). Temperament. In N. Eisenberg (Ed.), *Social, emotional and personality development* (5th ed., Vol. 3, pp. 105–176). New York: Wiley.

Ruble, D., & Martin, C. L. (1998). Gender development. In N. Eisenberg (Ed.), *Social, emotional and personality development* (Vol. 3, pp. 933–1016). New York: Wiley.

Russell, J., & Ridgeway, D. (1983). Dimensions underlying children's emotion concepts. *Developmental Psychology, 19,* 795–804.

Russell, J. A. (1991). Culture and the categorization of emotion. *Psychological Bulletin, 110,* 426–450.

Russell, J. A. (1994). Is there universal recognition of emotion from facial expression? A review of the cross-cultural studies. *Psychological Bulletin, 115,* 102–141.

Russell, J. A. (1995). Facial expressions of emotion: What lies beyond minimal universality? *Psychological Bulletin, 118*(3), 379–391.

Russell, J. A., Fernandez-Dols, J. M., Manstead, A., & Wellenkamp, J. (Eds.). (1996). *Everyday conceptions of emotion: An introduction to the psychology, anthropology and linguistics of emotion.* Hingham, MA: Kluwer Press.

Rusting, C. L. (1998). Personality, mood, and cognitive processing of emotional information: Three conceptual frameworks. *Psychological Bulletin, 124,* 165–196.

Saarni, C. (1979). Children's understanding of display rules for expressive behavior. *Developmental Psychology, 15,* 424–429.

Saarni, C. (1985). Indirect processes in affect socialization. In M. Lewis & C. Saarni (Eds.), *The socialization of emotions* (pp. 187–209). New York: Plenum Press.

Saarni, C. (1988). Children's understanding of the interpersonal consequences of dissemblance of nonverbal emotional-expressive behavior. *Journal of Nonverbal Behavior, 12,* 275–294.

Saarni, C. (1989a). Children's beliefs about emotion. In M. Luszez & T. Nettelbeck (Eds.), *Psychological development: Perspectives across the life-span* (pp. 69–78). North-Holland: Elsevier Science Publishers.

Saarni, C. (1989b). Children's understanding of strategic control of emotional expression in social transactions. In C. Saarni & P. Harris (Eds.), *Children's understanding of emotion* (pp. 181–208). New York: Cambridge University Press.

Saarni, C. (1990). *Psychometric properties of the Parental Attitude toward Children's Expressiveness Scale (PACES).* Unpublished manuscript. (ERIC Document Reproduction Service No. ED317-301)

Saarni, C. (1992). Children's emotional-expressive behaviors as regulators of others' happy and sad states. *New Directions for Child Development, 55,* 91–106.

Saarni, C. (1997a). Coping with aversive feelings. *Motivation and Emotion, 21,* 45–63.

Saarni, C. (1997b). Emotional competence and self-regulation in childhood. In P. Salovey & D. Sluyter (Eds.), *Emotional development and emotional intelligence* (pp. 35–66). New York: Basic Books.

Saarni, C. (1999). *The development of emotional competence.* New York: Guilford Press.

Saarni, C. (in press). The development of emotional competence: Pathways for helping children become emotionally intelligent. In R. Bar-On, J. Maree, & M. J. Elias (Eds.), *Educating children and adults to be emotionally intelligent: Guidelines for improving performance.* Rondebosch, South Africa: Heinemann Educational Publishers.

Saarni, C., & Buckley, M. (2002). Children's understanding of emotion communication in families. In R. A. Fabes (Ed.), *Emotions and the family: Vol. 34. Marriage and Family Review* (Special issue, pp. 213–242). New York: Guilford Press.

Saarni, C., Mumme, D. L., & Campos, J. J. (1998). Emotional development: Action, communication, and understanding. In W. Damon (Editor-in-Chief) & N. Eisenberg (Ed.), *Handbook of child psychology: Vol. 3. Social, emotional, and personality development* (5th ed., pp. 237–309). New York: Wiley.

Saarni, C., & Weber, H. (1999). Emotional displays and dissemblance in childhood: Implications for self-presentation. In P. Philippot, R. S. Feldman, & E. Coats (Eds.), *The social context of nonverbal behavior* (pp. 71–105). Cambridge, England: Cambridge University Press.

Sackett, G. (1966). Monkeys reared in isolation with pictures as visual input. *Science, 154,* 175–176.

Sagi, A., Lamb, M., Lewkowicz, K., Shoham, R., Dvir, R., & Estes, D. (1985). Security of infant-mother, -father, and -metapelet attachments among kibbutz reared Israeli children. *Monographs of the Society for Research in Child Development. 50*(1-2, Serial No. 209) 257–275.

Sagi, A. H., & Hoffman, M. L. (1976). Empathic distress in the newborn. *Developmental Psychology, 12,* 175–176.

Sandstrom, M. J. (2004). Pitfalls of the peer world: How children cope with common rejection experiences. *Journal of Abnormal Child Psychology, 32,* 67–81.

Scarr, S., & Salapatek, P. (1970). Patterns of fear development during infancy. *Merrill-Palmer Quarterly, 16,* 53–90.

Scheflen, A. (1974). *How behavior means.* Garden City, NY: Anchor Books.

Scherer, K. R. (1986). Vocal affect expression: A review and model for further research. *Psychological Bulletin, 99,* 143–165.

Schultz, D., Izard, C., & Ackerman, B. (2000). Children's anger attribution bias: Relations to family environment and social adjustment. *Social Development, 9,* 284–301.

Serrano, J. M., Iglesias, J., & Loeches, A. (1992). Visual discrimination and recognition of facial expressions of anger, fear, and surprise in 4- to 6-month-old infants. *Developmental Psychobiology, 25,* 411–425.

Serrano, J. M., Iglesias, J., & Loeches, A. (1995). Infants' responses to adult static facial expressions. *Infant Behavior and Development, 18,* 477–482.

Sethi, S., & Nolen-Hoeksema, S. (1997). Gender differences in internal and external focusing among adolescents. *Sex Roles, 37,* 687–700.

Shaver, P., Schwartz, J., Kirson, D., & O'Connor, C. (1987). Emotion knowledge: Further exploration of a prototype approach. *Journal of Personality and Social Psychology, 52,* 1061–1086.

Shennum, W. A., & Bugental, D. B. (1982). The development of control over affective expression in nonverbal behavior. In R. S. Feldman (Ed.), *Development of nonverbal behavior in children* (pp. 101–118). New York: Springer Verlag.

Shields, A., & Cicchetti, D. (1997). Emotion regulation among school-age children: The development and validation of a new criterion q-sort scale. *Developmental Psychology, 33,* 906–916.

Shields, S. (1995). The role of emotion beliefs and values in gender development. In N. Eisenberg (Ed.), *Review of personality and social psychology* (Vol. 15, pp. 212–232). Thousand Oaks, CA: Sage.

Shipman, K., & Zeman, J. (2001). Socialization of children's emotion regulation in mother-child dyads: A development psychopathology perspective. *Development and Psychopathology, 13,* 317–336.

Shipman, K., Zeman, J., Nesin, A., & Fitzgerald, M. (2003). Children's strategies for displaying anger and sadness: What works with whom? *Merrill-Palmer Quarterly, 49,* 100–122.

Shipman, K., Zeman, J., Penza, S., & Champion, K. (2000). Emotion management skills in sexually maltreated and nonmaltreated girls: A developmental psychopathology perspective. *Development and Psychopathology, 12,* 47–62.

Shweder, R. A. (1993). The cultural psychology of the emotions. In M. Lewis & J. M. Haviland (Eds.), *Handbook of emotions* (pp. 417–434). New York: Guilford Press.

Simner, M. L. (1971). Newborn's response to the cry of another infant. *Developmental Psychology, 5,* 136–150.

Skinner, E. A., & Wellborn, J. G. (1994). Coping during childhood and adolescence: A motivational perspective. In R. Lerner (Ed.), *Life-span development and behavior* (pp. 91–133). Hillsdale, NJ: Erlbaum.

Slade, A. (1994). Making meaning and making believe. In A. Slade & D. Wolf (Eds.), *Children at play: Clinical and developmental approaches to meaning representation* (pp. 81–107). New York: Oxford University Press.

Slomkowski, C., & Dunn, J. (1996). Young children's understanding of other people's beliefs and feelings and their connected communication with friends. *Developmental Psychology, 32,* 442–447.

Smith, W. J. (1977). *The behavior of communicating.* Harvard University Press.

Snyder, J., Stoolmiller, M., Wilson, M., & Yamamoto, M. (2003). Child anger regulation, parental responses to children's anger displays, and early child antisocial behavior. *Social Development, 12,* 335–360.

Sorce, J. F., Emde, R. N., Campos, J., & Klinnert, M. D. (1985). Maternal emotional signaling: Its effect on the visual cliff behavior of 1-year-olds. *Developmental Psychology, 21,* 195–200.

Southam-Gerow, M., & Kendall, P. (2002). Emotion regulation and understanding: Implications for child psychopathology and therapy. *Clinical Psychology Review, 22,* 189–222.

Spitz, R. (1965). *The first year of life.* New York: International Universities Press.

Sroufe, L. A. (1979). Socioemotional development. In J. Osofsky (Ed.), *Handbook of infant development* (pp. 462–516). New York: Wiley.

Sroufe, L. A., & Waters, E. (1977). Attachment as an organizational construct. *Child Development, 48,* 1184–1199.

Stein, N., Trabasso, T., & Liwag, M. (2000). A goal appraisal theory of emotional understanding: Implications for development and learning. In M. Lewis & J. Haviland (Eds.), *Handbook of emotions* (2nd ed., pp. 436–457). New York: Guilford Press.

Stenberg, C., & Campos, J. (1990). The development of anger expressions in infancy. In N. L. Stein, B. Leventhal, & T. Trabasso (Eds.), *Psychological and biological approaches to emotion* (pp. 247–282). Hillsdale, NJ: Erlbaum.

Stern, D. (1974). Mothers and infants at play: The dyadic interaction involving facial, vocal, and gaze behavior. In M. Lewis & L. Rosenblum (Eds.), *The effect of the infant upon the caregiver* (pp. 187–214). New York: Wiley.

Stern, D. (1985). *The interpersonal world of the infant.* New York: Basic Books.

Stipek, D. (1995). The development of pride and shame in toddlers. In J. Tangney & K. Fischer (Eds.), *Self-conscious emotions: The psychology of shame, guilt, embarrassment and pride* (pp. 237–252). New York: Guilford Press.

Strayer, J., & Roberts, W. (1997). Children's personal distance and their empathy: Indices of interpersonal closeness. *International Journal of Behavioral Development, 20,* 385–403.

Strayer, J., & Roberts, W. L. (2004a). Children's anger, emotional expressiveness, and empathy: Relations with parents' empathy, emotional expressiveness, and parenting practices. *Social Development, 13,* 229–254.

Strayer, J., & Roberts, W. L. (2004b). Empathy and observed anger and aggression in five-year-olds. *Social Development, 13,* 1–13.

Strelau, J. (1987). Emotion as a key concept in temperament research. *Journal of Research in Personality, 31,* 510–528.

Striano, T., & Bertin, E. (2004). Contribution of facial and vocal cues in the still-face response of 4-month-old infants. *Infant Behavior and Development, 27,* 499–508.

Striano, T., & Rochat, P. (2000). Emergence of selective social referencing in infancy. *Infancy, 1,* 253–264.

Svejda, M. J. (1981). *The development of infant sensitivity to affective messages in the mother's voice.* Unpublished doctoral dissertation, University of Denver, CO.

Swanson, A., Hemphill, S., & Smart, D. (2004). Connections between temperament and social development: A review. *Social Development, 13,* 142–170.

Talwar, V., & Lee, K. (2002). Development of lying to conceal a transgression: Children's control of expressive behaviour during verbal deception. *International Journal of Behavioral Development, 26,* 436–444.

Tangney, J. P., Burggraf, S., & Wagner, P. (1995). Shame-proneness, guilt-proneness, and psychological symptoms. In J. P. Tangney & K. Fischer (Eds.), *Self-conscious emotions: The psychology of shame, guilt, embarrassment, and pride* (pp. 343–367). New York: Guilford Press.

Tangney, J. P., & Fischer, K. (Eds.). (1995). *Self-conscious emotions: The psychology of shame, guilt, embarrassment, and pride.* New York: Guilford Press.

Teuber, H. L. (1960). Perception. In J. Field, H. Magain, & V. Hall (Eds.), *Handbook of physiology: Vol. 3. Neurophysiology* (pp. 1595–1688). Washington, DC: American Physiological Society.

Thompson, R., Easterbrooks, M. A., & Padilla-Walker, L. (2003). Social and emotional development in infancy. In R. Lerner, M. A. Easterbrooks, & J. Mistry (Eds.), *Handbook of psychology: Vol. 6. Developmental psychology* (pp. 91–112). New York: Wiley.

Tice, D., Bratslavsky, E., & Baumeister, R. (2001). Emotional distress regulation takes precedence over impulse control: If you feel bad, do it! *Journal of Personality and Social Psychology, 80,* 53–67.

Tomkins, S. (1962). *Affect, imagery, and consciousness: Vol. 1. The positive affects.* New York: Springer-Verlag.

Tomkins, S. (1963). *Affect, imagery, and consciousness: Vol. 2. The negative affects.* New York: Springer-Verlag.

Trevarthen, C. (1988). Universal cooperative motives: How infants begin to know the language and culture of their parents. In G. Johoda & I. M. Lewis (Eds.), *Acquiring culture: Cross-cultural studies in child development* (pp. 37–90). London: Croom Helm.

Trevarthen, C. (1993). The function of emotions in early infant communication and development. In J. Nadel & L. Cumaioni (Eds.), *New perspectives in early communicative development* (pp. 48–81). London: Routledge.

Trevarthen, C., & Hubley, P. (1978). Secondary intersubjectivity: Confidence, confiders, and acts of meaning in the first year of life. In A. Lock (Ed.), *Action, gesture, and symbol: The emergence of language* (pp. 183–229). New York: Academic Press.

Tronick, E., & Cohn, J. F. (1989). Infant-mother face-to-face interaction: Age and gender differences in coordination and the occurrence of miscoordination. *Child Development, 60,* 85–92.

Tronick, E., & Morellli, G. (1991). Foreword. In B. L. J. Nugent & T. Brazelton (Eds.), *The cultural context of infancy: Vol. 2. Multicultural and interdisciplinary approaches to parent-infant relations* (pp. ix–xiii). Norwood, NJ: Ablex.

Tronick, E., Morellli, G., & Ivey, P. (1992). The Efe forager infant and toddler's pattern of social relationships: Multiple and simultaneous. *Developmental Psychology, 28,* 568–577.

Underwood, M. (2003). *Social Aggression among Girls.* New York: Guilford Press.

Underwood, M., Coie, J., & Herbsman, C. (1992). Display rules for anger and aggression in school-age children. *Child Development, 63,* 366–380.

Underwood, M., & Hurley, J. (1999). Emotion regulation and peer relationships during the middle childhood years. In C. Tamis-LeMonda & L. Balter (Eds.), *Child psychology: A handbook of contemporary issues* (pp. 237–258). Philadelphia: Psychology Press/Taylor & Francis.

Underwood, M., Hurley, J., Johanson, C., & Mosley, J. (1999). An experimental, observational investigation of children's responses to peer provocation: Developmental and gender differences in middle childhood. *Child Development, 70,* 1428–1446.

Underwood, M., Kupersmidt, J. B., & Coie, J. D. (1996). Childhood peer sociometric status and aggression as predictors of adolescent childbearing. *Journal of Research on Adolescence, 6*(2), 201–223.

Vaish, A., & Striano, T. (2004). Is visual reference necessary? Contributions of facial versus vocal cues in 12-month-old's social referencing behavior. *Developmental Science, 7*(3), 261–269.

Valiente, C., Eisenberg, N., Fabes, R., Shepard, S., Cumberland, A., & Losoya, S. (2004). Prediction of children's empathy-related responding from their effortful control and parents' expressivity. *Developmental Psychology, 40,* 911–926.

Valiente, C., Eisenberg, N., Smith, C. L., Reiser, M., Fabes, R., Losoya, S., et al. (2003). The relations of effortful control and reactive control to children's externalizing problems: A longitudinal assessment. *Journal of Personality, 71,* 1171–1196.

Valiente, C., Fabes, R., Eisenberg, N., & Spinrad, T. (2004). The relations of parental expressivity and support to children's coping with daily stress. *Journal of Family Psychology, 18,* 97–106.

Venezia, M., Messinger, D. S., Thorp, D., & Mundy, P. (2004). The development of anticipatory smiling. *Infancy, 6*(3), 397–406.

von Salisch, M. (1991). *Kinderfreundschaften.* Gottingen, Germany: Hogrefe.

von Salisch, M. (1996). Relationships between children: Symmetry and asymmetry among peers, friends, and siblings. In A. E. Auhagen & M. von Salisch (Eds.), *The diversity of human relationships* (pp. 59–77). New York: Cambridge University Press.

von Salisch, M. (2001). Children's emotional development: Challenges in their relationships to parents, peers, and friends. *International Journal of Behavioral Development, 25,* 310–319.

Wagner, H., & Lee, V. (1999). Facial behavior alone and in the presence of others. In P. Philippot, R. S. Feldman, & E. J. Coats (Eds.), *The social context of nonverbal behavior* (pp. 262–286). Cambridge, England: Cambridge University Press.

Walden, T., & Knieps, L. (1996). Reading and responding to social signals. In M. Lewis & M. W. Sullivan (Eds.), *Emotional development in atypical children* (pp. 29–42). Hillsdale, NJ: Erlbaum.

Walker, L. J., & Hennig, K. (1997). Moral development in the broader context of personality. In S. Hala (Ed.), *The development of social cognition* (pp. 297–327). East Sussex, England: Psychology Press.

Walker-Andrews, A. (1997). Infants' perception of expressive behaviors: Differentiation of multimodal information. *Psychological Bulletin, 121,* 437–456.

Watson, A. J., & Valtin, R. (1997). Secrecy in middle childhood. *International Journal of Behavioral Development, 21,* 431–452.

Watson, J. S. (1972). Smiling, cooing and "The Game." *Merrill-Palmer Quarterly, 18,* 341–347.

Watzlawick, P., Beavin, J., & Jackson, D. (1967). *Pragmatics of human communication: A study of interactional patterns, pathologies, and paradoxes.* New York: Norton.

Weber, H., & Laux, L. (1993). Presentation of emotion. In G. V. Heck, P. Bonaiuto, I. Deary, & W. Nowack (Eds.), *Personality psychology in Europe* (Vol. 4). Tilburg, The Netherlands: Tilburg University Press.

Weinberg, K., Tronick, E. Z., Cohn, J. F., & Olson, K. L. (1999). Gender differences in emotional expressivity and self-regulation during early infancy. *Developmental Psychology, 35*(1), 175–188.

Weiner, B., & Handel, S. J. (1985). A cognition-emotion-action sequence: Anticipated emotional consequences of causal attributions and reported communication strategy. *Developmental Psychology, 21,* 102–107.

Weyer, M., & Sandler, I. (1998). Stress and coping as predictors of children's divorce-related ruminations. *Journal of Clinical Child Psychology, 27,* 78–86.

White, G. M. (2000). Representing emotional meaning: Category, metaphor, schema, discourse. In M. Lewis & J. Haviland-Jones (Eds.), *Handbook of emotions* (2nd ed., pp. 30–44). New York: Guilford Press.

Whiting, J. (1981). Environmental constraint on infant care practices. In R. H. Munroe, R. L. Munroe, & B. Whiting (Eds.), *Handbook of cross-cultural human development.* New York: Garland STPM Press.

Widen, S., & Russell, J. A. (2002). Gender and preschoolers' perception of emotion. *Merrill-Palmer Quarterly, 48,* 248–262.

Wierzbicka, A. (1992). Talking about emotions: Semantics, culture, and cognition. *Cognition and Emotion, 6,* 285–319.

Wiggers, M., & van Lieshout, C. (1985). Development of recognition of emotions: Children's reliance on situational and facial expressive cues. *Developmental Psychology, 21,* 338–349.

Wilson, J. Q. (1993). *The moral sense.* New York: Free Press.

Wilton, M., Craig, W., & Pepler, D. (2000). Emotional regulation and display in classroom victims of bullying: Characteristic expressions of affect, coping styles and relevant contextual factors. *Social Development, 9,* 226–245.

Winn, S., Tronick, E. Z., & Morelli, G. A. (1989). The infant and the group: A look at Efe caretaking practices in Zaire. In J. K. Nugent, B. M. Lester, & T. B. Braelton (Eds.), *The cultural context of infancy: Vol. 1. Biology, culture, and infant development* (pp. 87–109). Norwood, NJ: Ablex.

Witherington, D. C. (2003). *Frameworks for understanding emotions and their development: Functionalist and dynamic systems approaches.* Unpublished manuscript.

Witherington, D. C., Campos, J. J., & Hertenstein, M. J. (2001). Principles of emotion and its development in infancy. In G. Bremner & A. Fogel (Eds.), *Blackwell handbook of infant development* (pp. 427–464). Oxford, England: Blackwell.

Wolchik, S. A., & Sandler, I. N. (Eds.). (1997). *Handbook of children's coping: Linking theory and intervention.* New York: Plenum Press.

Wyman, P. A., Sandler, I., Wolchik, S., & Nelson, K. (2000). Resilience as cumulative competence promotion and stress protec-tion: Theory and intervention. In D. Cicchetti, J. Rappaport, I. Sandler, & R. Weissberg (Eds.), *The promotion of wellness in children and adolescents* (pp. 133–184). Washington, DC: Child Welfare League of America Press.

Zahn-Waxler, C. (1991). The case for empathy: A developmental review. *Psychological Inquiry, 2,* 155–158.

Zahn-Waxler, C. (2000). The development of empathy, guilt, and internalization of distress: Implications for gender differences in internalizing and externalizing problems. In R. J. Davidson (Ed.), *Anxiety, depression, and emotion* (pp. 222–265). New York: Oxford University Press.

Zahn-Waxler, C., Cole, P. M., & Barrett, K. C. (1991). Guilt and empathy: Sex differences and implications for the development of depression. In J. Garber & K. Dodge (Eds.), *The development of emotion regulation and dysregulation* (pp. 243–272). New York: Cambridge University Press.

Zahn-Waxler, C., Kochanska, G., Krupnick, J., & McKnew, D. (1990). Patterns of guilt in children of depressed and well mothers. *Developmental Psychology, 26,* 51–59.

Zahn-Waxler, C., & Radke-Yarrow, M. (1990). The origins of empathic concern. *Motivation and Emotion, 14*(2), 107–130.

Zahn-Waxler, C., & Robinson, J. (1995). Empathy and guilt: Early origins of feelings of responsibility. In J. Tangney & K. Fischer (Eds.), *Self-conscious emotions* (pp. 143–173). New York: Guilford Press.

Zarbatany, L., & Lamb, M. E. (1985). Social referencing as a function of information source: Mothers versus strangers. *Infant Behavior and Development, 8,* 25–33.

Zeman, J., & Shipman, K. (1997). Social-contextual influences on expectancies for managing anger and sadness: The transition from middle childhood to adolescence. *Developmental Psychology, 33,* 917–924.

Zimmermann, P. (1999). Structure and functions of internal working models of attachment and their role for emotion regulation. *Attachment and Human Development, 1,* 291–306.

Zumbahlen, M., & Crawley, A. (1996, April). *Infants' early referential behavior in prohibition contexts: The emergence of social referencing?* Paper presented at the meetings of the International Society for Infant Studies, Providence, RI.

CHAPTER 6

Personality Development

AVSHALOM CASPI and REBECCA L. SHINER

This chapter focuses on individual differences in personality, because differences among individuals are the most remarkable feature of human nature. After all, in both genetic and cultural evolution, selection pressures operate on differences among people. Not surprisingly, individual differences pervade all aspects of life, and they demand scientific inquiry: What are the most salient personality differences between people? What gives rise to these differences? Do personality differences shape important life outcomes? How might personality influence the emergence of psychopathology? Answers to these questions are crucial for those who wish to describe, explain, and predict the nature of individual lives across time.

Work on this chapter was supported by grants from the National Institute of Mental Health (MH-45070 and MH-49414), the Medical Research Council, and the William T. Grant Foundation. We thank Terrie E. Moffitt, Brent W. Roberts, William G. Graziano, and Nancy Eisenberg for their helpful comments and ideas. This chapter reviews material available to us through July, 2004.

The fifth edition of the *Handbook of Child Psychology* was the first edition to include a chapter devoted to personality differences (Caspi, 1998; in editions prior to that, coverage of personality development had been scattered about in specialized chapters dealing, for example, with aggression or motivation). We were pleased to be invited to contribute a new chapter, but we had to ask ourselves: Was a new chapter needed? Given the slow progress of soft psychology (Meehl, 1978), it is heartening to recognize that there have been significant advances in research on personality development over the past decade. In this chapter, we have tried to reflect these advances and to anticipate future directions as well.

In reflecting on the past decade of research, we are struck that debates pitting the person versus the situation, nature versus nurture, and continuity versus change are increasingly being brought to a halt. These three tired debates have given way to a more nuanced understanding of personality development.

At the heart of the person-situation debate was the ontological status of personality traits: Are traits real? It is possible to distinguish among descriptive, dispositional, and explanatory conceptions of traits (Zuroff, 1986). According to the first, *descriptive-summary* conception, traits are summary variables that describe observable consistencies in a person's past behavior. As demonstrated by criterion-oriented studies, a descriptive-summary conception serves useful predictive purposes. However, because this conception bypasses the explanatory work of psychology, it is unlikely, by itself, to yield theoretical insights about personality development: "It contributes no more to the science of psychology than rules for boiling an egg contribute to the science of chemistry" (Loevinger, 1957, p. 641).

According to a second *dispositional* conception, traits represent a tendency to behave in certain kinds of ways if in certain kinds of situations. Personality differences are here treated as "if-then" conditional propositions (Mischel, 1990). Dominant individuals dominate when there are subjects for domination but not when they are alone. Likewise, intelligent persons solve problems given the presence of problems: A person does not constantly act smart. Dispositions differ from descriptive summaries in that they indicate nothing about the occurrence of behavior in the absence of eliciting stimuli (Wakefield, 1989; Zuroff, 1986).

According to a third *realist* conception, traits are explanatory concepts. Whereas the descriptive and dispositional conceptions of traits outlined earlier regard

behavioral attributes as "samples of response classes," a realist conception treats them as indicators or "signs of internal [psychological] structures" (Wiggins, 1973, pp. 368–370). Whereas the dispositional, if-then conception of traits is agnostic with regard to explanation, a realist conception attempts to postulate underlying processes that lead traits to cause certain intentional states (Tellegen, 1991):

> Personality is and does something. . . . It is what lies behind specific acts and within the individual. The systems that constitute personality are in every sense determining tendencies, and when aroused by suitable stimuli provoke those adjustive and expressive acts by which personality comes to be known. (Allport, 1937, pp. 48–49)

According to the realist, neo-Allportian conception (Funder, 1991), traits are not observable entities but hypothetical constructs and, like all such constructs, their usefulness needs to be demonstrated and refuted through the procedures of construct validation. The process of "construct validation is nothing more or less than hypothesis testing" in which a construct becomes known by virtue of the interlocking system of laws in which it occurs (Hogan & Nicholson, 1988, p. 622), and the task of empirical research is to keep tightening the nomological net (Meehl, 1986). In this sense, researchers need to embed traits in process theories that lead to new and testable hypotheses about social, psychological, and biological phenomena throughout the life course. Trait explanations are not an end; rather, they are placeholders in an evolving search for fuller explanations of action and motivated behavior (Fletcher, 1993; Wakefield, 1989).

Whereas the 1998 version of this chapter had to justify its neo-Allportian focus on personality traits as real, this is no longer necessary because of advances in understanding the structure of personality. The first two sections of this chapter review this new evidence in detail. We delineate a taxonomy of measurable individual differences in temperament and personality in childhood and introduce a process-focused analysis of personality traits that details what is known about their developmental antecedents and their psychological and biological underpinnings. A personality taxonomy serves at least three research purposes. First, it improves research communication; connecting multiple and different measures of personality to an established and validated personality structure helps to organize and integrate diffuse research findings. Second, it helps researchers to develop new measures of personality; locating new measures in relation to what is already known eliminates redundancy and elucidates psychological constructs. Third, it enables researchers to connect personality measures to more elaborate nomological networks and thereby to interpret research and generate new hypotheses about individual differences in personality. As becomes evident, the personality taxonomy discussed in the second section organizes the remaining sections of our review.

A second, related debate has pitted nature versus nurture. This is the longest-lived controversy in psychology, and there are signs that it too is dissipating. We begin the fourth section with an overview of research showing a genetic contribution to personality. But whereas the 1998 version of this chapter devoted a good deal of space to elaborating the logic of behavioral genetic designs, in this edition we proceed directly to summarizing and updating the empirical evidence and move on to discuss the contributions of molecular genetics to psychological research. The use of molecular genetic techniques is helping to replace the nature-nurture conjunction *versus* with the more appropriate conjunction *and*. Psychological research is being revolutionized by direct measures of specific genotypes for individuals, and this will increasingly allow researchers to investigate how nature and nurture work together to shape behavioral phenotypes.

A third debate has focused on continuity versus change, which also subsumes the question of whether personality traits matter. Trait models are often caricatured as static, nondevelopmental conceptions of personality. This misapprehension arises because personality traits are thought to represent stable and enduring psychological differences between persons; therefore, they are static. Few personality researchers subscribe to this conclusion. Rather, contemporary personality research has sought to formulate the ways in which personality differences, in transaction with environmental circumstances, organize behavior in dynamic ways over time. Personality traits are thus organizational constructs; they influence how individuals organize their behavior to meet environmental demands and new developmental challenges. As Allport (1937) noted, personality traits are "modi vivendi, ultimately deriving their significance from the role they play in advancing adaptation within, and mastery of, the personal environment" (p. 342). The fifth and sixth sections review new and accumulating evidence about continuities in personality development from childhood to adulthood and how personality differences influence various life outcomes. Whereas the 1998 version of this chapter did not include much information about psychopathology, in this edition we devote the seventh section to review how personality differences influence the development of psychiatric disorders. We are able to do this because the unproductive bifurcation of personality and clinical psychology is drawing to an end, and new, developmental research is highlighting etiological and practical considerations linking normal personality variants and clinical syndromes.

THE DEVELOPING STRUCTURE OF PERSONALITY

In this first section, we address three issues that are central to the study of temperament and personality across the life course: (1) How should we conceptualize temperament and personality, and what is similar and distinctive about these two types of individual differences? (2) How are temperament and personality differences structured from infancy through adulthood? and (3) What do we know about personality types, and do these types add something important to our understanding of personality development? It is important that we address these foundational issues from the outset before turning to questions of how individual differences develop and affect the life course.

Temperament and Personality: How Are They Similar? How Are They Distinct?

Humans display a wide range of individual differences during the life span—from birth to old age. Both child psychologists and adult personality researchers study these individual differences, but historically the two groups have done so in different research traditions: Child psychologists have typically studied temperament traits, whereas adult personality researchers have typically studied personality traits.

The contemporary empirical study of early temperament was spurred largely by Thomas and Chess, who initiated the New York Longitudinal Study to examine the significance of biologically based temperament traits in infancy and childhood (Thomas, Chess, Birch, Hertzig, & Korn, 1963). Thomas and Chess challenged the way that social development was studied at the time because they emphasized that children are not merely the products of their rearing environments; rather, infants come into the world with biologically based behavioral tendencies. Like Thomas and Chess, most temperament researchers continue to focus on individual differences that emerge early in life, include differences in emotional processes, and have a presumed biological basis (Goldsmith et al., 1987). However, most contemporary researchers also recognize that temperament is shaped by both hereditary and environmental influences and that temperament includes components of self-regulation and emotion (Rothbart & Derryberry, 2002).

Personality is typically seen as including a wider range of individual differences in feeling, thinking, and behaving than is temperament. Personality differences include personality traits such as Extraversion and Neuroticism, but they also encompass goals, coping styles, defensive styles, motives, attachment styles, life stories, identities, and various other processes (McAdams, 1995). Although much of the research on children's individual differences has focused on traits labeled *temperament,* a great deal of productive research has already been done on childhood traits that could rightly be considered *personality.* Developmentalists have investigated a vast array of children's traits—aggression, delay of gratification, dominance, achievement strivings, empathy, anxiousness, and the list goes on—but sometimes have not explicitly labeled these traits aspects of children's emerging personalities per se (Shiner, 1998).

Recent empirical work has demonstrated a number of striking similarities between temperament traits and personality traits. First, although temperament differences between nonhuman animals have been recognized at least as long as humans have bred animals, important aspects of personality traits can be observed in nonhuman animals as well (Gosling, 2001; Gosling & John, 1999). Observers can rate traits as accurately in nonhuman animals as they can in humans (Gosling, Kwan, & John, 2003). Second, like temperament traits, nearly all self-reported and observed personality traits show moderate genetic influence (Bouchard, 2004; Bouchard & Loehlin, 2001). Third, like personality traits, temperament traits are affected by experience: Behavioral genetic studies have established that temperament in

infancy and early childhood is only partially heritable and is influenced by environmental events (Emde & Hewitt, 2001), including both pre- and postnatal experiences. Occasionally, researchers claim that individual differences measured later in childhood are not temperament because such traits have already been affected by environmental experiences, implying that only individual differences at birth represent genetically influenced temperament. The behavioral genetic findings reviewed later in this chapter reveal the fallacy of such a claim: From infancy through adulthood, to varying degrees and at varying times, genetic and environmental influences are at work shaping both temperament and personality traits. A fourth key similarity between temperament and personality traits is that many traits from both domains are characterized by specific habitual positive and negative emotions (Rothbart, Ahadi, & Evans, 2000; Watson, 2000). Although this point is widely accepted for the so-called temperament traits of Extraversion and Neuroticism, there is evidence that other major traits involve the experience or expression of emotions as well (Tobin, Graziano, Vanman, & Tassinary, 2000; Trierweiler, Eid, & Lischetzke, 2002; Watson & Clark, 1992). A recent study demonstrated that infants' positive and negative emotional expressions predicted their standing on all of the Big Five personality traits at age 3 (Abe & Izard, 1999). Thus, emotional experience and expression are associated with a wide variety of traits across the life span.

Many of the distinctions between temperament and personality traits seem to be breaking down. There may be some advantages to keeping a temperament perspective in view. Temperament traits tend to be defined as more narrow, lower-level traits (Strelau, 2001), a useful complement to the emphasis on higher-level traits in adult personality research. The concept of temperament also reminds researchers to investigate the early expressions, biological underpinnings, and basic processes underlying traits. But temperament and personality increasingly should be studied side by side. A useful approach may be to consider the broadest possible range of individual differences at each point in development rather than to exclude some individual differences from study on the presupposition that some traits are not aspects of temperament. Because temperament and personality traits share so much in common, we discuss temperament and personality systems together throughout this review.

Personality Structure across the Life Span

One of the most striking points of convergence between temperament and personality is their similar structure across most periods of the life span; by structure, we mean the reliable patterns of covariation of traits across individuals. We later describe research findings on the structure of individual differences in infants and toddlers and the structure observed in young children, adolescents, and adults.

The establishment of a personality structure for describing adult personality has been a complicated, contentious enterprise; work on the structure of young children's individual differences is inherently even more complex. As children's motor, cognitive, emotional, and language abilities develop, the range of traits they can express similarly expands. For example, although infants may differ in temperament traits that are likely to be related to later aggression, infants cannot exhibit differences in aggression until they develop the motor and language skills necessary to direct aggressive actions toward others. Similar rapid growth occurs in children's emotional development. Children develop rapidly from manifesting only a small number of emotions during early infancy—interest, contentment, and distress—to manifesting an expanded set of emotions—including joy, sadness, anger, fear, empathy, pride, shame, and guilt—by age 3 (Eisenberg, 2000; Lewis, 2000). Thus, the structure of individual differences is likely to change over the course of childhood because of children's increasing capacities. Like many other aspects of development, children's individual differences are likely to become increasingly differentiated and complex over development. Despite the challenges in mapping the structure of individual differences in infancy and childhood, substantial progress has been made in this area.

As we illustrate in our description of temperament and personality structure, individual differences are organized hierarchically across the life span. Covariation among specific behavioral descriptors (e.g., talkative or friendly) is explained by lower-order traits, and the covariation among these more narrow, lower-order traits (e.g., sociability or social potency) is explained by broad, higher-order traits (e.g., Extraversion). Individual differences exhibit such a hierarchical structure in infancy and early childhood (Putnam, Ellis, & Rothbart, 2001), middle childhood and adolescence (Shiner & Caspi, 2003), and adulthood (Digman, 1990; Markon,

Krueger, & Watson, 2005). We now turn to a discussion of the traits that can be observed (a) during infancy and early childhood and (b) during the preschool through adult years.

Structure of Individual Differences in Infancy and Early Childhood

Lower-Order Traits. During infancy and early childhood, children display a limited range of traits. Much of the early research on temperament in these developmental periods was derived from Thomas and Chess's nine-trait model (Thomas et al., 1963). Thomas and Chess identified a number of traits that have proven to have great clinical significance, particularly children's tendencies toward the intense expression of anger and frustration and toward fearful withdrawal from new situations (Maziade et al., 1990). More recent research has uncovered some limitations of the original Thomas and Chess model, however (for a summary, see Rothbart & Derryberry, 2002, and Shiner & Caspi, 2003), and other models are increasingly used in research instead.

Current models of temperament in infancy and early childhood derive in part from research on caregiver-report questionnaires. A number of different caregiver temperament questionnaires for young children have yielded very similar sets of lower-order traits. Some of the relevant caregiver questionnaires include: the Infant Behavior Questionnaire (Rothbart, 1981); the Infant Characteristics Questionnaire (Bates, Freeland, & Lounsbury, 1979); the Colorado Childhood Temperament Inventory (Rowe & Plomin, 1977); and the Toddler Behavior Assessment Questionnaire (Goldsmith, 1996). Additional evidence for early childhood traits derives from item-level factor analyses of the questionnaires designed to measure Thomas and Chess's original nine-trait model: Although these factor analyses generate fewer than nine factors, they provide consistent support for a smaller set of traits measured across several questionnaires (Martin, Wisenbaker, & Huttunen, 1994). Structured laboratory tasks and home observational systems also provide evidence that a number of traits can be observed and measured reliably in infants and toddlers. For example, the Laboratory Temperament Assessment Battery assesses five traits in young children: (1) Pleasure/Joy, (2) Fearfulness, (3) Anger Proneness, (4) Interest/Persistence, and (5) Activity Level (Goldsmith & Rothbart, 1991). A home-observation coding system developed by Bornstein and colleagues (Bornstein, Gaughran, & Homel, 1986) permits assessment of Positive Affect, Negative Affect, Persistence, Motor Responsivity, and Soothability.

Taken together, the caregiver-questionnaire studies, laboratory-based tasks, and observational models provide the strongest support for the following lower-order temperament traits in the infant and toddler years (Kochanska, Coy, Tjebkes, & Husarek, 1998; Lemery, Goldsmith, Klinnert, & Mrazek, 1999; Martin et al., 1994; Rothbart & Bates, 1998; Rothbart & Mauro, 1990):

- *Positive emotions/pleasure:* This trait measures the child's propensity toward the expression of positive emotions, including smiling and laughter as well as pleasure and excitement in social interaction. Observational and questionnaire measures for infants demonstrate that the disposition toward positive emotions is distinct from the disposition toward negative emotions (Belsky, Hsieh, & Crnic, 1996; Kochanska et al., 1998).

- *Fear/inhibition:* This trait addresses the child's tendency to withdraw and express fear in the face of stressful or novel situations (both social and nonsocial). This trait expresses itself in fearful, withdrawn, and avoidant behavior in situations with strangers and unfamiliar, unpredictable objects (Kagan, 1998; Kochanska et al., 1998).

- *Irritability/anger/frustration:* In early childhood, this trait includes fussing, anger, and poor toleration of frustration and limitations. This trait is an important component of Thomas and Chess's difficult child type. Infants' expressions of distress during the first 3 months of life often do not predict later expressions of distress (Barr & Gunnar, 2000). However, by around 4 months, infants' tendencies toward fearfulness and anger can be distinguished and show some predictive validity for later temperament (Rothbart, Chew, & Gartstein, 2001). Further, fear and irritability each appear to be influenced by unique genetic and environmental sources, further demonstrating the distinct nature of these two traits (Goldsmith, Lemery, Buss, & Campos, 1999).

- *Discomfort:* Infants and toddlers differ in the extent of their negative emotional reactions to irritating or painful sensory stimulation (e.g., loud noises, cold touches, or sour tastes; Kochanska et al., 1998). A similar trait termed *Threshold* is obtained in factor analyses of New York Longitudinal Study questionnaires (Martin et al., 1994); this trait taps children's sensitivity to various sensory experiences.

- *Attention:* Between the 4 and 8 month period, infants vary in their attentiveness to environmental stimuli (Rothbart, Chew, et al., 2001). Questionnaire measures of this trait tap infants' duration of attention to stimuli and their ability to notice environmental variation. In toddlers, this trait also includes the ability to sustain attention over time and persist at a task (Martin et al., 1994).

- *Activity level:* Activity level is an important component of most temperament models; however, the meaning of this trait is likely to change with development. Motor movement in infancy is associated with both anger and positive emotions, whereas motor movement in the toddler years is linked in complex ways with early markers of high Extraversion and low self-control (Eaton, 1994). When activity level is defined as positive activity, it is already highly correlated with markers of Extraversion by the toddler years (Lamb, Chuang, Wessels, Broberg, & Hwang, 2002).

- *Soothability/adaptability:* The evidence for this final trait is not as consistent as that for the preceding six traits. Soothability, as measured by the Infant Behavior Questionnaire (Rothbart, 1981), assesses children's capacity to be soothed when comforted by caregivers. A similar trait indexing early regulation of emotion emerges in factor analyses of questionnaires stemming from Thomas and Chess's model. This trait, labeled Adaptability, taps children's tendencies to exhibit mild emotional responses and to adjust quickly and quietly to various potentially stressful environmental events (Martin et al., 1994). Adaptability is moderately negatively related to measures of Irritability, and further work is needed to determine if these two traits are truly distinct from one another.

Higher-Order Traits.   Most research on early temperament has focused on narrowly defined, lower-order traits. Rothbart and colleagues have more recently explored the structure of higher-order temperament traits in infancy and the toddler years by examining the factor structure of two newly expanded caregiver-report temperament questionnaires (Gartstein & Rothbart, 2003; Putnam et al., 2001; Rothbart & Derryberry, 2002). In samples of American infants and toddlers, three factors emerge. In infancy and the toddler years, a Surgency factor taps children's tendencies toward an eager, positive approach to potentially pleasurable activities; vocal reactivity (in infants) and sociability (in toddlers); expression of positive emotions; enjoyment of high-intensity activities; and high activity level. In infancy and the toddler years, a Negative Affectivity factor taps both children's tendencies toward sadness, irritability and frustration, and fear as well as their abilities to quiet themselves after high arousal (reversed). The third factor differs in the two periods. In infancy the third factor measures soothability, cuddliness, ability to sustain attention, and pleasure in low-intensity situations, whereas in the toddler years this factor (labeled Effortful Control) includes these traits and more sophisticated self-regulatory abilities. The third factor appears to tap young children's emerging behavioral constraint and regulation. As described in the next section, these three higher-order traits are highly similar to three higher-order temperament and personality traits observed among older children and adults.

Structure of Individual Differences from Childhood through Adulthood

We begin by describing studies of personality structure among adults, and then turn to the study of personality structure in younger age groups.

Personality Structure in Adulthood. One of the great achievements in the study of adult personality over the past 2 decades is greater clarity about the higher-order structure of personality. Prior to this emerging consensus, debate raged about which traits are most valid and important. Researchers were prone to the "jingle-jangle" fallacy of studying the same trait under different names (jingle) or using the same name to describe different traits (jangle) (Block, 1996). Research on adult personality has been energized by emerging consensus about personality structure because researchers can now focus their attention on a common set of traits.

The most widespread support has been obtained for a five-trait structure, dubbed the Big Five or the five-factor model (John & Srivastava, 1999; McCrae & Costa, 1999); these traits include Extraversion, Neuroticism, Conscientiousness, Agreeableness, and Openness to Experience/Intellect. Support for this model derives from two main sources of evidence. First, a number of factor analyses of questionnaires designed to measure a broad range of individual differences yield the Big Five traits

(e.g., Costa & McCrae, 1988; McCrae, Costa, & Busch, 1986); in other words, the Big Five traits emerge in measures designed to assess other sets of traits. Second, research stemming from the lexical tradition provides some support for the five-factor model. According to the lexical hypothesis, the most socially relevant and salient personality characteristics have become encoded in everyday language. Accordingly, the personality terms contained in the natural language may provide an extensive, yet finite, set of attributes that people who share that language have found important and useful in their interactions with each other. In most lexical studies, a set of adjectives is drawn from the dictionary to provide a representative sample of personality traits that are important in the natural language. Factor analyses of adjectives drawn from dictionaries in countries, such as the United States, Germany, Poland, and Holland, have resulted in five factors that are at least somewhat congruent across samples (Saucier, Hampson, & Goldberg, 2000); the strongest support has been obtained from lexical analyses of languages deriving from northern European origins.

Several three-factor models of adult personality have also received some support: Eysenck's (1991) three-factor system, Tellegen's (1985) model of personality structure, and Cloninger's model of temperament (Cloninger, Svrakic, & Przybeck, 1993). For example, biologically oriented theorists have often pointed toward three higher-order domains that correspond with postulated neural structures underlying personality: (1) An approach domain manifested in positive emotions, (2) an avoidance domain manifested in negative emotions, and (3) a constraint domain manifested as tendencies to inhibit or express emotion and impulse.

Although there are important differences among these three-factor models and the five-factor model, they overlap to a considerable degree. Extraversion or Positive Emotionality is common to all systems; it describes the extent to which the person actively engages the world or avoids intense social experiences. Neuroticism or Negative Emotionality is also common to all systems; it describes the extent to which the person experiences the world as distressing or threatening. Conscientiousness or Constraint describes the extent and strength of impulse control in task-focused domains; whether the person is able to delay gratification in the service of more distant goals or is unable to modulate impulsive expression. To these three dimensions, the five-factor model adds two more: (1) Agreeableness and (2) Openness to Experience/Intellect. Agreeableness describes a person's interpersonal nature on a continuum from warmth and compassion to antagonism. Agreeable persons are empathic, altruistic, helpful, and trusting, whereas antagonistic persons are abrasive, ruthless, manipulative, and cynical. Openness to Experience (also called Intellect) describes the complexity, depth, and quality of a person's mental and experiential life.

Personality Structure in Childhood and Adolescence. Consensus about the structure of adult personality traits has important implications for developmental research: We now have greater clarity about the adult personality traits that childhood studies should be trying to predict over time. Developmental researchers have explored the possibility that childhood personality structure might map onto the structure observed in adults, and there is now evidence (from the preschool years through adolescence) from a variety of sources that such is the case. First, factor analyses of questionnaires, adjective lists, and the California Child Q-Set have often produced factors similar to the Big Five traits in studies of children from approximately age 3 through late adolescence. A five-factor structure has been obtained in parent reports (Barbaranelli, Caprara, Rabasca, & Pastorelli, 2003; Halverson et al., 2003; John, Caspi, Robins, Moffitt, & Stouthamer-Loeber, 1994; Lamb et al., 2002; Mervielde & De Fruyt, 1999, 2002; van Lieshout & Haselager, 1993, 1994) and in teacher reports (Barbaranelli et al., 2003; Digman, 1994; Digman & Inouye, 1986; Digman & Shmelyov, 1996; Digman & Takemoto-Chock, 1981; Goldberg, 2001; Graziano & Ward, 1992; Mervielde, Buyst, & De Fruyt, 1995; Resing, Bleichrodt, & Dekker, 1999; van Lieshout & Haselager, 1993, 1994; Victor, 1994). Factor analyses of self-report questionnaires have found evidence for five-factor structures in one study of children ages 9 and 10 (Barbaranelli et al., 2003) and in studies of adolescents (De Fruyt, Mervielde, Hoekstra, & Rolland, 2000; McCrae & Costa, 2004). There is also some evidence that many preadolescents, even as young as 5 years of age, can provide coherent, reliable self-reports of the Big Five traits (Graziano, Jensen-Campbell, & Finch, 1997; Markey, Markey, Tinseley, & Ericksen, 2002; Measelle, John, Ablow, Cowan, & Cowan, 2005).

Second, further support for several of the Big Five traits derives from temperament research in older children and adolescents. As noted previously, Rothbart and colleagues have identified three higher-order temperament traits in infants and toddlers—Surgency, Negative Affectivity, and Effortful Control. Rothbart and colleagues have obtained evidence for the same three higher-order traits in children ages 3 to 7 (Ahadi, Rothbart, & Ye, 1993; Putnam et al., 2001; Rothbart, Ahadi, Hershey, & Fisher, 2001) and in young adolescents ages 10 to 15 (Capaldi & Rothbart, 1992; Putnam et al., 2001). An additional fourth factor is obtained in early adolescence; this factor is labeled *Affiliativeness* and includes some components similar to the positive end of the Agreeableness trait. Possibly, a similar Affiliativeness trait could be identified in younger children as well, if such items were included in the relevant questionnaires. This temperament model yields traits highly similar in content to several of the Big Five traits: Surgency (Extraversion), Negative Affectivity (Neuroticism), Effortful Control (Conscientiousness), and Affiliativeness (Agreeableness).

Third, a variety of behavioral-task and observational measures provide support for traits similar to the Big Five (Shiner & Caspi, 2003). We describe specific behavioral-task and observational measures of traits in our detailed discussion of the content of the Big Five traits.

Thus, data from personality and temperament questionnaires, behavioral tasks, and observational measures converge on a Big Five trait structure in children and adolescents. To illustrate the meaning of the factors, Table 6.1 lists items defining the Big Five traits in three types of child measures: (1) teacher reports using a list of trait descriptors (Digman & Shmelyov, 1996), (2) parent reports using the California Child Q-Sort (John et al., 1994; van Lieshout & Haselager, 1993, 1994), and (3) children's self reports using a puppet interview (Measelle et al., 2005).

Some caveats must be noted regarding the appropriateness of the five-factor model for describing the structure of children's and adolescents' individual differences. First, the traits are sometimes measured in a less internally consistent fashion in younger children, especially preschool-age children (e.g., Lamb et al., 2002). Second, studies using the California Child Q-Set have provided evidence for additional traits such as irritability and dependency that are related to but distinct from the Big Five traits (e.g., John et al., 1994); the possibility of factors beyond the Big Five in children warrants further study. Third, the Big Five traits are

TABLE 6.1   Examples of Trait Descriptors, California Child Q-Sort Items, and Self-Report Puppet Interview Items for Five Higher-Order Personality Traits in Children

Higher-Order Personality Trait	Sample Items		
	Trait Descriptors[a]	Child Q-Sort Items[b]	Puppet Interview Items[c]
Extraversion	Gregarious	Emotionally expressive	I'm not shy when I meet new people
	Cheerful	A talkative child	It's easy for me to make new friends
	Energetic	Fast-paced; moves and reacts to things quickly	If kids are playing, I ask if I can play too
	Withdrawn (rev.)	Inhibited or constricted (rev.)	
Neuroticism	Afraid	Fearful and anxious	I'm sad a lot
	Touchy	Tends to go to pieces under stress; becomes rattled and disorganized	I get nervous when my teacher calls on me
	Tearful		I don't like myself
	Steady (rev.)	Appears to feel unworthy	
		Self-reliant, confident (rev.)	
Conscientiousness	Diligent	Attentive and able to concentrate	I think it's important to do well in school
	Planful	Planful; thinks ahead	I try my best in school
	Careful	Persistent in activities; does not give up easily	When I can't figure something out, I don't give up
	Focused	Reflective; thinks and deliberates before speaking or acting	
Agreeableness	Considerate	Warm and kind toward others	I don't get mad at kids at school
	Trusting	Helpful and cooperative	If someone is mean to me, I don't hit them
	Spiteful (rev.)	Tends to give, lend, and share	I don't pick on other kids
	Rude (rev.)	Teases and picks on others (rev.)	
Openness to experience	Original	Curious and exploring	I learn things well
	Perceptive	Appears to have high intellectual capacity (whether expressed in achievement or not)	I have good ideas
	Knowledgeable		I'm a smart kid
	Curious	Creative in perception, thought, work, or play	
		Has an active fantasy life	

Note: Rev. = Item is scored in the reversed direction.

[a] Items defining the factor in a study of 480 Russian children aged 8 to 10 whose teachers rated them. *Source:* From "The Structure of Temperament and Personality in Russian Children," by J. M. Digman and A. G. Shmelyov, 1996, *Journal of Personality and Social Psychology, 71,* pp. 341–351.

[b] Abbreviated California Child Q-sort items defining the factor in two independent studies: (1) a study of 720 Dutch boys and girls who were Q-sorted by parents and teachers and (2) a study of 350 African American and Caucasian boys aged 12 to 13 enrolled in the Pittsburgh Youth Study who were Q-sorted by their mothers. *Source:* From "Personality Development across the Life Course" (pp. 311–388), by A. Caspi, in *Handbook of Child Psychology: Vol. 3. Social, Emotional and Personality Development,* fifth edition, N. Eisenberg (Ed.), 1998, New York: Wiley.

[c] Berkley Puppet Interview items defining the factor in a study of 95 children aged 5 to 7. *Source:* From "Can children provide coherent, stable, and valid self-reports on the Big Five dimensions?" by J. Measelle, O. P. John, J. Ablow, P. A. Cowan, and C. P. Cowan, 2005, *Journal of Personality and Social Psychology, 89,* 90–106.

sometimes defined by somewhat different clusters of items in children than in adults (van Lieshout & Haselager, 1993, 1994). For example, in one study Extraversion was defined by a much broader range of traits than the typical adult trait and included aspects of Agreeableness and Openness to Experience (Halverson et al., 2003). All of these findings highlight the need for continued study of potential developmental differences in the nature of the Big Five traits. More work is particularly needed in the preschool and early elementary school years because children undergo such rapid developmental changes during these periods.

Personality Types

Thus far we have used the term *personality structure* to refer to the pattern of covariation of traits across individuals. Personality structure can also refer to the organization of traits in the individual. Most research on personality development is *variable-centered*; it focuses on the relative standing of persons on dimensional variables. However, the more appropriate unit of analysis may be the person, not the variable. *Person-centered* research focuses on the configuration of multiple personality variables in the person, on how different dimensional variables are organized in the person and how this organization defines different types of persons. Such a model of the person as a system of interacting components is absent from most studies of personality, although investigators have called for approaches in which the person, not the variable, is the focus of analysis (e.g., Bergman & Cairns, 2000).

Just as the study of personality traits has been hampered by the absence of a structural model, the study of personality types has been held back by the absence of empirically derived personality typologies. Typological models of personality need to be held to the same empirical standards as dimensional models of personality: replicability, generalizability, and construct validity. The history of empirical research on these problems is relatively new, dating to Block's (1971) *Lives Through Time.* Block had clinically trained judges complete independent Q-sorts of the study participants. In the Q-sort technique, a sorter describes an individual's personality by sorting a set of cards containing personality attributes into piles ranging from attributes that are least characteristic to those that are most characteristic of the individual. This produces a person-centered description because the sorter explicitly compares each attribute with other attributes in the same individual. The resemblance between two individuals is indexed by the correlation between their respective Q-sorts, which reflects the degree to which the attributes specified by the Q-sort are ordered the same way in the two individuals. The method of inverse factor analysis can then be used to identify clusters of individuals with similar Q-sort profiles.

Over the past decade, several research teams have built on Block's approach and uncovered evidence pointing to the existence of three personality types in childhood and adolescence (Asendorpf, Borkenau, Ostendorf, & van Aken, 2001; Asendorpf & van Aken, 1999; Dubas, Gerris, Janssens, & Vermulst, 2002; Hart, Atkins, & Fegley, 2003; Hart & Hare, 1997; Robins, John, Caspi, Moffitt, & Stouthamer-Loeber, 1996; Weir & Gjerde, 2002). The largest type of persons, labeled *Resilients,* is characterized by being adaptable to change, self-confident, independent, verbally fluent, and able to concentrate on tasks. *Overcontrollers* are without many interpersonal skills, shy, and inward looking. *Undercontrollers* are impulsive, willful, and disagreeable and they show little concern for others. This convergence of three personality types across multiple studies is noteworthy as the studies differ in numerous ways, including age, gender, ethnicity, geographic location in which the study participants grew up, the source of personality information used to derive the types, and even the statistical methods by which the types were derived.

However, the convergence across studies is not perfect, especially in adult samples (Asendorpf, Caspi, & Hofstee, 2002). More typological research needs to be done before anything close to a comprehensive, generalizable personality typology can be said to exist. In this regard, five issues should be kept in mind. First, attention should continue to be given to the replicability of the types across different instruments of trait assessment, the judge or rater providing the personality data, and the method of deriving the types. Second, more information is needed about the generalizability of the types across sex, both in the structure of the types and their developmental correlates. Third, attention must be given to possible age differences in the personality types that are identified. Fourth, the search for replicable subtypes must continue. Although the three types identified thus far are good candidates to become an integral part of any generalizable person-centered typology, this does not mean that there are only three personality types, just as the five factor model does not imply that there are only five personality dimensions. It simply means that, at the broadest level of generalization, psychological theories must account for the development of these types. Fifth, attention needs to be given to the utility of types and their relative benefits, if any, over dimensional, trait models. Some researchers have suggested, on empirical grounds, that knowledge of a person's type membership is useful only because it is a convenient summary of his or her trait standing (Costa, Herbst, McCrae, Samuels, & Ozer, 2002); the evidence for the incremental validity of type membership (over dimensions) is sparse. Other researchers have suggested that fair tests of the incremental validity of types have not yet been carried out. Although types may not win, or fare better, in a head-to-head comparison of the predictive validity of personality types versus dimensions, Robins and Tracy (2003) suggest that for developmental researchers, "adopting a type approach is particularly important because it is unlikely that environmental events and contexts ever influence a single trait in isolation. Parents, teachers, and other socializing agents interact with the whole child, not with one trait at a time" (p. 114). Still others have noted that, even if types do not offer incremental validity, they offer intuitive appeal and clarity. The practical implications of person-centered research are easier than trait-based research to communicate to policymakers and research consumers (Asendorpf, 2003; Hart et al., 2003).

TEMPERAMENT AND PERSONALITY TRAITS: A PROCESS-FOCUSED, DEVELOPMENTAL TAXONOMY FROM CHILDHOOD TO ADULTHOOD

In this section, we elaborate a taxonomy of personality traits in children and adolescents. We draw on three sources of data: (1) recent research on the structure of personality in children and adolescents, (2) developmental research on single traits, and (3) international studies of adult personality structure. Each of these sources of information is important for different reasons. First, the factor-analytic questionnaire studies in youths generate especially useful information about the structure of the higher-order traits. Second, developmental research provides a strong source of information about the nature of the lower-order traits because these traits have been studied using a variety of methods, including naturalistic observation and lab-based studies. Third, the recent work on personality structure in adults is also critically important to the study of individual differences in children. The adult personality research helps to link higher-order traits with their lower-order components and highlights potentially valid and important lower-order traits that may have been overlooked in de-

velopmental research. Further, adult personality research is increasingly international in scope (Church, 2001), particularly the research deriving from the lexical tradition. This international work has the potential to create a personality taxonomy that is more generalizable and replicable (Saucier & Simonds, in press).

It is important to include lower-order traits in our proposed taxonomy. The Big Five are too broad to capture all the interesting variations in human personality, and distinctions at the level of more specific traits are necessary. The advantage of broad categories, such as those described by the five-factor model, is their substantial bandwidth; the disadvantage of broad categories is their low fidelity (John & Robins, 1993). Lower-order traits may provide better prediction of behavioral outcomes than the higher-order traits (Paunonen & Ashton, 2001). Further, behavioral genetic research suggests that personality is "inherited as a large number of genetic dimensions that have relatively specific effects on personality phenotypes and a smaller number of genetic dimensions that have broader effects" (Livesley, Jang, & Vernon, 2003, p. 78). Thus, the lower-order traits are shaped in part by genetic influences that have effects on all of the components of the higher-order traits, but each lower-order trait is also influenced by unique genetic influences. It will not be possible to understand the genetic (and possibly environmental) origins of personality fully without considering the lower-order traits.

In this taxonomy, we integrate what is known about diverse aspects of each trait. First, we present a description of the Big Five traits and the lower-order traits likely to be subsumed by them (see Table 6.2). There is no a priori reason to assume that each higher-order trait will include an equal number of lower-order traits; thus, the number of lower-order components varies for each of the higher-order traits. We also note some of the lower-

TABLE 6.2   **A Proposed Taxonomy of Higher-Order and Lower-Order Personality Traits in Childhood and Adolescence**

Higher-Order Traits	Extraversion (E)	Neuroticism (N)	Conscientiousness (C)	Agreeableness (A)	Openness to Experience (O)
Lower-order traits	Sociability Energy/activity level	Fear Anxiety Sadness	Attention Self-control Achievement motivation Orderliness	Prosocial tendencies Antagonism Willfulness	Intellect Creativity Curiosity
	Low E + N	N + low A	C + A		
	Social inhibition	Anger/irritability Alienation/mistrust	Responsibility		

Note: The lower-order traits shown at the bottom of the table typically load on both of the higher-order traits shown.

order traits that have been identified in adults that have not been studied in children but that may well emerge in childhood or adolescence. Some of the lower-order traits appear to load onto more than one higher-order trait in factor-analytic studies; we note instances where this occurs. We have presented earlier versions of this taxonomy elsewhere (Caspi, Roberts, & Shiner, 2005; Shiner, 1998; Shiner & Caspi, 2003) but have made revisions to it based on more recent research. Second, we review what is known about the early temperamental antecedents of each trait; although there is much more to study, a great deal has already been learned about the early childhood precursors of the personality traits seen in adults and children. Third, we survey theories and evidence about the processes underlying each trait. One of the great benefits of a consensually agreed-upon taxonomy of traits is that it allows researchers to train their lenses on how personality traits express themselves in everyday life and on the fundamental processes underlying variations in these traits. We thus review some of the most interesting current work on the psychological and biological underpinnings of each Big Five trait.

Extraversion

Children vary in their tendencies to be vigorously, actively, and surgently engaged with the world around them. Extraverted children and adolescents are described in Big Five studies as sociable, expressive, high-spirited, lively, socially potent, physically active, and energetic. In contrast, introverted youths are quiet, inhibited, and lethargic. Observations of preschoolers reveal a similar, coherent set of behaviors: high positive affect, energy and zestful engagement, and eager anticipation of enjoyable events (Buckley, Klein, Durbin, Hayden, & Moerk, 2002). The Revised Class Play, a peer nomination measure for elementary school children, also yields a factor resembling Extraversion (Morison & Masten, 1991); children high on this factor are described by peers as outgoing, sociable leaders who wield considerable social influence. Based on observational measures, extraverted children indeed are more talkative, more dominant, and more involved and engaged in interaction than their introverted peers (Markey, Markey, & Tinsley, 2004).

Extraversion: Lower-Order Traits

Extraversion encompasses the lower-order traits of sociability and energy/activity level. Another lower-order trait—social inhibition—is related to both Extraversion and Neuroticism. *Sociability* (or gregariousness) is the most prototypical lower-order component of Extraversion. It includes the preference for being with others rather than alone (A. Buss & Plomin, 1984; D. Buss & Plomin, 1975) and a variety of behaviors that suggest vigorous, active ways of making connections with others: talkativeness, friendliness, vivaciousness, and expressiveness (Peabody & De Raad, 2002).

Sociability can be distinguished conceptually and empirically from *social inhibition,* feelings of discomfort and reluctance to act in novel situations. As noted previously, fear/inhibition is a trait readily identified in infants and toddlers. Shyness appears to be one aspect of a broader inhibition trait in older children. Inhibition consists of a number of related but distinct behaviors: hesitance with new peers and adults, wariness in physically challenging and unfamiliar situations, difficulty with separation from parents, and acute discomfort in performance situations (Bishop, Spence, & McDonald, 2003). This trait has been measured through a variety of observed behaviors in toddlers, preschoolers, and older children, such as a fearful response to novel situations (e.g., a toy robot, a gorilla head mask, an adult dressed as a clown) and reticent, withdrawn behavior with unfamiliar adults or children (Kagan, Snidman, & Arcus, 1998; Pfeifer, Goldsmith, Davidson, & Rickman, 2002; Rubin, Burgess, & Hastings, 2002). Sociability and social inhibition represent distinct traits: Sociability is a pure marker of Extraversion, whereas social inhibition appears to be a more complex blend of low Extraversion and high fear or anxiety in the presence of novel situations (Asendorpf & van Aken, 2003b; Eisenberg, Fabes, & Murphy, 1995; Markon et al., 2005; Nigg, 2000).

Energy and *activity level* are aspects of Extraversion that are easily observed among children. Energetic engagement with pleasurable tasks is a component of Extraversion by around age 2 or 3 (Halverson et al., 2003; Lamb et al., 2002). Because people become less motorically active with age, activity level may no longer be a separate lower-order component of Extraversion by adulthood and instead may be manifest in greater talkativeness, enthusiasm, and energy (Eaton, 1994). As noted previously, activity level can be observed as a reliable individual difference in infants and is sometimes associated with negative emotions. Similarly, older children are also likely to exhibit individual differences in poorly regulated motor output (Goldberg, 2001), as evidenced, for example, in the fidgeting and impulsive motor movements associated with Attention-Deficit/Hyperactivity Disorder (ADHD; American Psychiatric Association, 1994). Such poorly controlled, impulsive activity is not typically focused on the pursuit of productive ends as in high Extraversion and is more likely to be associated with low Conscientiousness and low Agreeableness in children (Goldberg, 2001). The two types of motor activity need to be distinguished in childhood.

Another possible component of Extraversion is *social dominance,* the tendency to be assertive, to exert control over others, and to capture and enjoy others' attention. Such tendencies are related to Extraversion in adults, but also may be associated with low Agreeableness (Markon et al., 2005). Because these traits are likely to be an important contributor to children's emerging capacities for leadership, positive expressions of social dominance are worthy of research attention in children.

Extraversion: Early Childhood Antecedents

A number of early individual differences predict aspects of Extraversion later in childhood. First, questionnaire and observational measures of positive emotions, such as smiling and laughter, predict childhood Extraversion (Fox, Henderson, Rubin, Calkins, & Schmidt, 2001; Rothbart, Derryberry, & Hershey, 2000). In one study, full-face positive emotions in the Strange Situation at 18 months (a presumed marker of high-intensity positive emotions) predicted Extraversion at 3.5 years (Abe & Izard, 1999). Other aspects of childhood Extraversion are also predicted by infant measures of sociability (Hagekull & Bohlin, 2003), positive activity level (Hagekull & Bohlin, 2003; Korner et al., 1985), shorter observed latency to grasp small objects (Rothbart, Derryberry, et al., 2000), and lower observed fear (Rothbart, Derryberry, et al., 2000). Measures of higher infant frustration also predict later aspects of childhood Extraversion (Rothbart, Derryberry, et al., 2000); we return shortly to this interesting link between anger/frustration and Extraversion.

Longitudinal research on social inhibition suggests that infant negative emotional reactivity to overstimulation predicts later inhibition and that inhibition is somewhat stable for a subset of children, particularly those who are extreme on these traits (Kagan et al., 1998; Pfeifer et al., 2002). However, maternal behavior appears to moderate these relations, such that inhibited children receiving intrusive, derisive, or overprotective parenting remain more consistently inhibited across time than inhibited children receiving other parenting

(Arcus, 2001; Park, Belsky, Putnam, & Crnic, 1997; Rubin et al., 2002). Finally, a 23-year longitudinal study found that highly confident, friendly, and zealous 3-year-olds exhibited high Extraversion as adults, whereas socially reticent, fearful 3-year-olds exhibited low scores on this trait in adulthood (Caspi, Harrington, et al., 2003).

Extraversion: Underlying Processes

Three main models have been advanced to explain the basis of the Extraversion trait. Although each model emphasizes different aspects of the trait, the models are clearly related and can be integrated. Moreover, all three models of Extraversion help to make sense of the findings regarding the associations between the emergence of Extraversion and positive emotions, high energy and activity, and active social behavior in the early years of development.

First, Extraversion is often conceptualized as the predisposition to experience positive emotions (Tellegen, 1985; Watson & Clark, 1997). As noted, the expression of positive emotions in infancy is predictive of later markers of Extraversion. These links between Extraversion and the experience of positive emotions are robust in adulthood as well; a meta-analysis obtained an average correlation of .37 between Extraversion and the concurrent experience of positive affect (Lucas & Fujita, 2000). Individuals vary in the extent to which they act extraverted throughout the course of a day; at those times when they act more extraverted, individuals experience greater positive emotions (Fleeson, Malanos, & Achille, 2002). Extraverts also appear to be more motivated and skilled at prolonging the experience of positive emotions than introverts (Hemenover, 2003).

Why are Extraversion and positive affect linked so consistently? One possibility is that more extraverted individuals engage in activities that promote positive affect, such as spending time with friends. Extraverted adults do engage in more social activity, which results in positive affect, but social activity alone does not account for the Extraversion-positive affect link (Watson, Clark, McIntyre, & Hamaker, 1992). An additional explanation is a temperamental view of Extraversion—that there are endogenous links between Extraversion and positive affect. There is good evidence for this contention: Extraversion is robustly associated with both pleasant (e.g., happy, good) and activated (e.g., alert, excited) positive emotions in emotionally neutral conditions (Lucas & Baird, 2004). Extraverts experience more positive emotions than introverts even when alone.

Extraversion is also sometimes associated with increased activated (but not pleasant) positive emotions in pleasant conditions (Lucas & Baird, 2004); thus, there is some more limited evidence that extraverts show greater positive emotional reactivity to positive events. Behavior genetic research provides support for both a genetically and an environmentally mediated link between Extraversion and positive emotions: Sociability and the positive affects covary because of shared genetic and nonshared environmental influences (Eid, Riemann, Angleitner, & Borkenau, 2003).

Second and relatedly, Extraversion has been conceptualized as a biologically based behavioral activation, approach, or appetitive system. The most influential framework for understanding this approach system has been Gray's (1987, 1990) model of the Behavioral Activation System (BAS). According to Gray, the BAS is a neurobiological system that responds to incentives for appetitive behavior, including signals of reward, nonpunishment, and escape from punishment. Individuals with a stronger BAS should be highly attentive to such incentives: When this system is activated, individuals begin to approach or pursue goals. Measures of BAS functioning in children have recently been developed (Blair, 2003; Colder & O'Connor, 2004). Biological evidence for an approach system derives from Davidson and colleagues' work demonstrating that specialized neural substrates for behavioral approach exist in the left anterior cerebral cortex (Davidson, Pizzagalli, Nitschke, & Kalin, 2003). Adults with greater BAS sensitivity do appear to seek out experiences that produce higher levels of positive affect (Gable, Reis, & Elliot, 2000) and derive their sense of well-being from such positive emotional experiences (Updegraff, Gable, & Taylor, 2004). This approach model of Extraversion helps to make sense of the fact that Extraversion can sometimes be associated with experiences of anger and frustration in both adults and children, in addition to its more typical associations with positive affect (Carver, 2004; Donzella, Gunnar, Krueger, & Alwin, 2000); anger may be experienced to a greater degree among extraverted individuals when they fear they may not or actually do not obtain the rewards they pursue with such vigor.

A third, potentially fruitful model of Extraversion is that it represents the tendency to attract, maintain, and enjoy social attention (Ashton, Lee, & Paunonen, 2002). According to this model, Extraversion serves an adaptive, evolutionary function by holding others' attention in ways that provide rewards; thus, this model posits that the reward-seeking tendencies and positive emotions associated with Extraversion are simply correlates of the pursuit of social attention.

Neuroticism

Just as children vary in their predisposition toward positive emotions, they vary in their susceptibility to negative emotions and general distress. In the Big Five studies, children and adolescents who are high on Neuroticism are described as anxious, vulnerable, tense, easily frightened, "falling apart" under stress, guilt-prone, moody, low in frustration tolerance, and insecure in relationships with others. Fewer descriptors define the lower end of this dimension; these include traits such as stability, being "laid back," adaptability in novel situations, and the ability to "bounce back" after a bad experience. As these descriptions of childhood Neuroticism illustrate, the trait appears to include both the child's experience of negative emotions and the child's effectiveness at self-regulating such negative emotions.

Neurotic individuals tend to be self-critical, insecure, and sensitive to criticism and teasing. Neuroticism may actually be part of an underlying personality dimension that includes self-esteem, locus of control, and generalized self-efficacy (Judge, Erez, Bono, & Thoresen, 2002). Neuroticism thus may be one key aspect of a more general tendency to view oneself and the world through a negative lens (Erez & Judge, 2001). Neurotic adults tend to be dissatisfied with major aspects of their lives, including their relationships, work, and health (Heller, Watson, & Ilies, 2004). Behavioral observations confirm the questionnaire descriptions of children high on this trait; childhood Neuroticism is associated with behaviors such as making self-critical statements, expressing a sense of self-pity and guilt, acting irritated, and showing signs of physical tension (Markey et al., 2004). Higher Neuroticism may also be linked with a variety of aversive interpersonal behaviors in childhood. In an observational study of parent-child interaction, higher Neuroticism was correlated with keeping parents at a distance, seeming detached, speaking sarcastically, and exhibiting low levels of upbeat, enthusiastic behavior (Markey et al., 2004).

Neuroticism: Lower-Order Traits

Neuroticism is likely to include a number of lower-order traits, including fear, anxiety, and sadness. Two other lower-order traits appear to be related to both high Neuroticism and low Agreeableness: (1) anger/irritability and (2) alienation/mistrust.

Based on the extensive literature on negative emotions deriving from research on psychopathology, it may be possible to break down the negative emotions included in Neuroticism into at least three distinct but related lower-order traits: (1) fear, (2) anxiety, and (3) sadness (Barlow, 2000; Chorpita, Albano, & Barlow, 1998; Muris, Schmidt, Merckelbach, & Schouten, 2001). *Fear* represents negative affect and bodily symptoms arising from exposure to an actual or an imagined object or situation. The definition of fearfulness in the psychopathology literature is highly similar to the dimensions of fear/social inhibition described previously, in that these individual differences all involve negative emotions arising from actual exposure to a feared situation (e.g., a novel stimulus or exposure to unfamiliar peers); future research will need to determine whether fear and social inhibition should be seen as distinct traits. *Anxiety* taps tendencies toward nervous apprehension, general distress, worry, and physical tension when there is no imminent threat. The symptom-based measures of anxiety are highly comparable to the general measures of Neuroticism used with children and adults. *Sadness* includes behaviors associated with depression, including lowered mood, hopelessness, and dejection arising from experiences of disappointment and loss. Sadness is included as a lower-order trait in some temperament and personality models (e.g., Costa & McCrae, 1992; Rothbart, Ahadi, et al., 2001) but it is usually only a minor component of most Neuroticism measures, which tend to emphasize anxiety. The distinctive aspects of sadness thus may be obscured when only the general Neuroticism trait is assessed (Moon, Hollenbeck, Humphrey, & Maue, 2003). For example, relative to other aspects of Neuroticism, adult sadness is a more robust predictor of life satisfaction (Schimmack, Oishi, Furr, & Funder, 2004) and global self-esteem (Watson, Suls, & Haig, 2002).

In general, much more work is needed to understand the development of individual differences in fear, anxiety, and sadness, especially given their links with a broad spectrum of psychiatric disorders (Watson, 2001). A great deal of productive work has focused on fear/inhibition as a risk factor for the development of anxiety disorders (Kagan & Snidman, 1999). The emergence of individual differences in anxiety and sadness will be equally important to study, especially given evidence that most adolescents with anxiety disorders do not show inhibited temperament as younger children (Prior, Smart, Sanson, & Oberklaid, 2000). A better under-

standing of how early Neuroticism develops could yield crucial information for prevention programs. Such research is important in light of evidence that children's average level of anxiety appears to have increased from the 1950s to the 1990s (Twenge, 2000).

As we noted previously, individual differences in anger and frustration relate to both the higher-order Neuroticism and Agreeableness traits. *Anger/irritability* taps outer-directed, hostile emotions such as anger, jealousy, frustration, and irritation (Halverson et al., 2003); in children, such hostility is often evoked by limits set by adults. In samples of American children and adults, an anger/irritability trait is moderately correlated with both high Neuroticism and low Agreeableness (Halverson et al., 2003; Kochanska, Friesenborg, Lange, & Martel, 2004; Markon et al., 2005). In a number of international lexical studies, anger/irritability is more clearly associated with low Agreeableness than with high Neuroticism (Ashton et al., 2004).

In some studies with both adults and children, anger/irritability has been viewed as part of an overarching Negative Emotionality trait that includes both Neuroticism and anger/irritability (Buckley et al., 2002; Lengua, 2002; Rothbart, Ahadi, et al., 2001; Tellegen, 1985). Questionnaire studies, lab tasks, and naturalistic observations have all demonstrated that children and adults who are prone to experiencing one type of negative emotion are prone to experiencing other types of negative emotions as well. It is important to separate Neuroticism from anger/irritability for several reasons. As noted previously, it is possible to distinguish fear/inhibition from anger/irritability beginning in infancy. These two types of negative emotions appear to require different regulatory strategies; for example, distraction works to reduce anger but not fear in infants (K. Buss & Goldsmith, 1998). Fear and anger have different and sometimes opposite effects on cognitive processing (e.g., fear promotes risk aversion, whereas anger promotes risk-seeking; Lerner & Keltner, 2000). The adaptive profiles associated with each trait differ as well. For example, whereas fearfulness appears to protect against childhood aggression (Raine, Reynolds, Venables, Mednick, & Farrington, 1998), anger and irritability put children at risk for later aggression (Loeber & Hay, 1997).

A final lower-order trait, *alienation/mistrust* has been identified in adults and, like anger/irritability, is related to high Neuroticism and low Agreeableness (Kochanska et al., 2004; Markon et al., 2005; Martin,

Watson, & Wan, 2000). This trait taps an individual's tendency to mistrust others and to feel mistreated (Tellegen & Waller, 1992). Individual differences in interpersonal alienation and mistrust have been identified in research on social information processing in youths (Crick & Dodge, 1994) and in the attachment literature (Sroufe, Carlson, Levy, & Egeland, 1999). In adults, this trait is highly linked with poor life adaptation and may emerge in part from repeated experiences of failure across development (Shiner, Masten, & Tellegen, 2002).

Childhood Neuroticism may include other aspects that are worthy of consideration, including children's tendencies toward *dependence,* low *self-confidence, vulnerability* in the face of stress and *emotional instability.*

Neuroticism: Early Childhood Antecedents

A number of early childhood traits have been identified as predictors of Neuroticism and its components. Emotional expression in the Strange Situation procedure at 18 months predicts Neuroticism at 3.5 years (Abe & Izard, 1999); specifically, high-intensity full-face negative emotions (sadness and anger) predict Neuroticism positively, and milder, more regulated positive emotions (interest and joy) predict Neuroticism negatively (Abe & Izard, 1999). Consistent with this finding, childhood fearfulness and sadness are predicted by infant measures of high fear and low positive emotions (Rothbart, Derryberry, et al., 2000). Childhood sadness is additionally predicted by low infant frustration (Rothbart, Derryberry, et al., 2000). In contrast, childhood anger/frustration is not predicted by infant fear but, instead, is predicted by infant high frustration, high activity level, and short latency to grasp small objects (Rothbart, Derryberry, et al., 2000). Childhood anger/frustration is predicted by early markers of Extraversion, consistent with the previously discussed claim that high Extraversion may generate high frustration when goals are blocked. Thus, childhood fear and anger appear to have relatively distinct and separate antecedents, whereas childhood sadness shares some common infant antecedents with both.

Although fear and anger appear to be separate in childhood, over time greater anger may come to predict higher anxiety and distress. For example, in one longitudinal study, preschool-age children who were irritable, distractible, labile, and uncontrolled grew up to be more Neurotic as adults (Caspi, Harrington, et al., 2003); it may be the case that the greater adult anxiety experienced by previously angry, undercontrolled children

emerges as these children encounter the ill effects of their behavior.

Neuroticism: Underlying Processes

Research with adults has helped to characterize the cognitive style, daily experiences, and interpersonal functioning of individuals high on Neuroticism. Developmental researchers have also studied the links between attention and executive control and children's experiences of negative emotions. In this section, we focus on the processes underlying the anxiety, fear, and sadness aspects of Neuroticism and discuss anger/irritability in our discussion of Agreeableness.

In cognition, adults high on trait anxiety show attentional biases toward information relevant to their personal fears; such biases are consistent with a model of anxiety as helping to prepare individuals for potentially dangerous situations by rapidly focusing attention on threatening material (Mineka, Rafaeli, & Yovel, 2003). In contrast, tendencies toward depression are associated with biases toward remembering and ruminating over past negative experiences (Mineka et al., 2003). Adults high on trait anxiety and adults high on depression are biased toward assuming they will encounter unduly negative experiences in the future. More generally, adult Neuroticism is associated with an emotionally negative tone in individuals' narratives about key experiences in their lives (McAdams et al., 2004) and with greater cognitive processing of unpleasant, negative information (Gomez, Gomez, & Cooper, 2002). Thus, there is good evidence that Neuroticism and its lower-order components are associated, at least in adulthood, with biases toward processing negative information, though the biases may vary somewhat for different lower-order components.

Developmental research provides an interesting perspective on why Neuroticism may be linked with various cognitive biases. Beginning in infancy and continuing throughout childhood, greater attentional control is associated with more effective regulation of negative emotionality (Eisenberg, Smith, Sadovsky, & Spinrad, 2004; Rueda, Posner, & Rothbart, 2004). Initially, parents are an important source of assistance with such emotional regulation, but over time children develop more of their own capacities for self-regulation. Neurotic individuals' bias toward attending to negative information may arise in part from difficulties in executive functioning, particularly with attention. The converse could also be true: Neuroticism may bias individuals toward focusing on negative cues, which could interfere with the allocation of attention (MacCoon, Wallace, & Newman, 2004).

Just as Neuroticism is associated with negative cognitive biases, it is also linked with more negative daily experiences in adults. In lab-based studies, neurotic adults report more negative emotional responses to a variety of negative stimuli than less neurotic adults (Gross, Sutton, & Ketelaar, 1998). Experience-sampling studies have demonstrated that this negative emotional reactivity occurs in daily life as well: Neurotic adults have stronger negative emotional reactions to everyday problems, including both interpersonal conflicts and stress at work and at home (Bolger & Schilling, 1991; Gable et al., 2000; Suls, Martin, & David, 1998). Neurotic individuals may find daily problems to be more stressful, in part, because they tend to use ineffective coping responses, such as escape and avoidance, and high levels of interpersonal confrontation (O'Brien & DeLongis, 1996). Finally, more neurotic individuals tend to show some distinguishing patterns of interpersonal behavior, including more disagreeable and submissive behavior and less agreeable and dominant behavior (Cote & Moskowitz, 1998). Neurotic adults also show more lability across situations in their interpersonal behaviors (Moskowitz & Zuroff, 2004), which may lead others to form the impression that they are unpredictable. The interpersonal behaviors associated with Neuroticism in adults are consistent with the previously described aversive interaction style observed in more neurotic children. In summary, the process-oriented studies with adults have demonstrated that Neuroticism is associated with a variety of difficulties in emotional and behavioral regulation.

All of these findings regarding Neuroticism are consistent with the claim that individual differences in Neuroticism are associated with variation in a biologically based withdrawal, inhibition, or avoidance system. As with Extraversion, one of the most important frameworks for understanding this system has been a model developed by Gray (1987, 1990). According to Gray, individuals differ in the sensitivity of a neurobiological Behavioral Inhibition System (BIS), which serves to inhibit behavior in the face of potential punishment, nonreward, and novelty. Thus, individuals with a strong BIS should be sensitive to signals of threats and should be quick to withdraw or inhibit their behavior when they perceive such signals. Measures of BIS functioning in

children have recently been developed (Blair, 2003; Colder & O'Connor, 2004). As with Extraversion, Davidson and colleagues have shown that there are specialized neural substrates for behavioral withdrawal, in this case in the right anterior cerebral cortex (Davidson et al., 2003). In situations that present both incentives and threats, individuals may experience an approach-avoidance conflict. In such situations, the goal of avoidance is likely to win out over the goal of approach (Gray & McNaughton, 1996), perhaps because negative emotions have more widespread and lasting effects than positive emotions (Larsen & Prizmic, 2004). Although more Neurotic individuals may be motivated to avoid and minimize aversive experiences, they do not appear to be successful at doing so. Rather, they tend to experience more negative life events than less Neurotic individuals (Magnus, Diener, Fujita, & Pavot, 1993) and experience higher levels of negative emotions in response to such experiences (Gable et al., 2000). The findings on the biological and psychological processes associated with Neuroticism should provide impetus to study similar processes associated with the development of Neuroticism in children.

Conscientiousness

An overarching Conscientiousness trait taps children's individual differences in self-control, in large part as control is used in service of completing tasks and striving to meet standards. In Big Five studies, highly Conscientious children and adolescents are described as responsible, attentive, persistent, orderly and neat, planful, possessing high standards, and thinking before acting. Children low on this trait are depicted as irresponsible, unreliable, careless, distractible, and quitting easily. The higher-order Conscientiousness trait is defined by a remarkably similar set of descriptors in lexical studies with adults across a wide variety of languages and countries, thereby providing strong international evidence for the nature of this trait in adulthood (Peabody & De Raad, 2002). Based on parental descriptions of children from a number of countries, parents rarely describe their children by traits linked with Conscientiousness at age 3 years but do use such descriptors more often by age 6 years (Slotboom, Havill, Pavlopoulos, & De Fruyt, 1998); parents may see these descriptors of Conscientiousness as inappropriate until their children are closer to school age. There is evidence from at least one study that some of these more complex manifestations of self-control can be measured with moderate reliability in children as young as ages 3 and 4 years (Halverson et al., 2003). The numerous Big Five questionnaire studies demonstrate that these more complex traits can certainly be measured in children by middle childhood.

Rothbart, Ahadi, and colleagues (2001) have identified in children a similar temperament trait labeled Effortful Control, which includes children's capacities to plan behavior, inhibit inappropriate responses, focus and shift attention, take pleasure in low intensity situations, and perceive subtle external stimuli. In a series of studies, Kochanska and colleagues have developed a battery of tasks to measure children's emerging Effortful Control (Kochanska & Knaack, 2003; Kochanska, Murray, & Coy, 1997; Kochanska, Murray, & Harlan, 2000; Kochanska, Murray, Jacques, Keonig, & Vandegeest, 1996): All of the tasks require a child to exert self-control by suppressing a dominant response in favor of carrying out a subdominant response. The tasks include delay of a pleasant behavior (e.g., waiting to unwrap a toy), slowing down fine or gross motor movements, suppressing a response to one signal and producing a response to another (e.g., producing different responses to red and green signs), whispering, and Stroop-like attention tasks requiring the child to ignore prominent features of a stimulus and to attend to other less salient features. Although children's performance on the tasks is less internally consistent at 22 months, the tasks reveal a more coherent set of behaviors by 33 months and measure a highly coherent, stable trait by 45 months. Thus, questionnaire and observational studies confirm that children differ reliably in their manifest levels of self-control.

Although temperament and personality models both include dimensions related to self-control, the content of these traits differs somewhat. Temperament models tend to emphasize attention and impulse control, which are individual differences that can be identified in a rudimentary form in very young children. In contrast, personality models include not only impulse control but also traits that children do not exhibit until they are older, such as orderliness, dependability, and motivation to meet goals and complete work. There is some preliminary evidence from one questionnaire study that Big Five Conscientiousness is highly related to Effortful Control (Halverson et al., 2003) but much more work

will be needed to clarify the similarities and differences between the personality and temperament conceptions of this higher-order trait. In particular, as we elaborate in our discussion of Agreeableness, temperamental Effortful Control may represent differences in control that can be applied to tasks and achievement (as in the case of Conscientiousness) and to social relationships (as in the case of Agreeableness). There is some evidence that childhood Effortful Control is linked with Agreeableness (Cumberland-Li, Eisenberg, & Reiser, 2004). Questionnaire studies of the Big Five in adults indicate that Conscientiousness and Agreeableness tend to covary and coalesce to form a superordinate trait (Markon et al., 2005); it is certainly possible that a basic tendency toward behavioral constraint versus disinhibition underlies both of these traits.

Conscientiousness: Lower-Order Traits

Conscientiousness in children includes a number of lower-order components: attention, self-control, achievement motivation, orderliness, and responsibility. *Attention* versus distractibility taps children's capacity to focus attention, regulate attention by shifting mental sets, and persist at tasks in the face of distractions. As noted previously, individual differences in attention emerge in infancy. Attention versus distractibility is a lower-order component of Conscientiousness and Effortful Control in questionnaire measures for older children (Halverson et al., 2003; Putnam et al., 2001). Although attention is an important trait in most childhood temperament models (Shiner, 1998), it is not prominent in adult personality models. Descriptors related to attention may have been left out of adult personality questionnaire studies because such terms are often seen as more relevant to the domains of intellect and cognition than to the domain of personality. Further, by adulthood individual differences in attention and executive control may underlie most of the components of Conscientiousness; we return to this point in our discussion of the processes underlying Conscientiousness.

Four other lower-order components of Conscientiousness have been identified in factor-analytic questionnaire studies with children and adults. *Self-control* taps tendencies to be planful, cautious, deliberate, and behaviorally controlled (Peabody & De Raad, 2002; Roberts, Bogg, Walton, Chernyshenko, & Stark, 2004; Rothbart, Ahadi, et al., 2001). *Achievement motivation* (also called work or industriousness) taps the tendency to strive for high standards, to work hard and be productive, and to pursue goals over time in a determined, persistent manner (Halverson et al., 2003; Peabody & De Raad, 2002; Roberts et al., 2004). *Orderliness* (or organization) reflects a propensity to be neat, clean, and organized rather than sloppy, disorganized, and disorderly (Halverson et al., 2003; Mervielde & De Fruyt, 2002; Roberts et al., 2004). These are all behaviors that involve the active structuring of a person's tasks and environment. *Responsibility* ranges from the tendency to be reliable and dependable to the tendency to be irresponsible and unreliable (Goldberg, 2001; Peabody & De Raad, 2002; Roberts et al., 2004); this subcomponent appears to measure Conscientiousness manifested in relation to other people and may be a blend of Conscientiousness and Agreeableness (Goldberg, 2001; Roberts et al., 2004). Achievement motivation, orderliness, and responsibility are traits typically left out of temperament models; these three lower-order traits seem likely to be important for children's development and warrant more thorough study.

Observations of delay of gratification have been used in a number of studies to assess children's self-control; the most well-known work on observed delay of gratification is Mischel's longitudinal research (Mischel & Ayduk, 2004). Delay of gratification is typically assessed in these studies by placing children in a situation in which they have to choose between an immediate but smaller prize and a delayed but larger prize. Although children's ability to delay in this paradigm is related to their attentional capacities, this measure is probably not a pure measure of self-control because children's approach tendencies are also likely to influence their abilities to delay (Eisenberg, Smith, et al., 2004).

Conscientiousness: Early Childhood Antecedents

Childhood markers of self-control are predicted in conceptually coherent ways by several early individual differences, and childhood self-control itself is remarkably stable by the preschool years. Not surprisingly, the ability to focus attention in infancy predicts Effortful Control later in childhood (Kochanska et al., 2000). Individual differences in persistence at tasks (similar to the lower-order attention trait described previously) have been found to be highly stable from the toddler to preschool years and from middle childhood to adolescence (Guerin, Gottfried, Oliver, & Thomas, 2003). As noted previously, observed Effortful Control itself is a moderately stable trait from 22 to 33 months and is a

highly stable trait from 33 to 45 months (Kochanska & Knaack, 2003). Early IQ has also been found to predict persistence at tasks (Guerin et al., 2003) and Effortful Control (Kochanska & Knaack, 2003) later in childhood.

Early differences in emotional reactivity also predict later self-control in several studies. Milder, more regulated positive emotions in the Strange Situation procedure at 18 months have been found to predict Conscientiousness at 3.5 years (Abe & Izard, 1999). In contrast, several early individual differences predict lower levels of self-control in childhood: Earlier anger and intense joy negatively predict preschool Effortful Control (Kochanska & Knaack, 2003), and shorter latency to approach and grasp small objects in infancy negatively predicts attention and self-control in childhood (Rothbart, Derryberry, et al., 2000). These findings regarding the links between early emotional reactivity and later self-control are provocative but difficult to interpret. It seems likely that infants and toddlers with stronger approach tendencies (those with intense positive emotions and a quick approach) and stronger anger may have more difficulty developing self-control because they have stronger emotions to regulate; they must work against their eager or angry tendencies to exhibit self-control. However, it is also possible that children's early expressions of anger and high-intensity positive emotions may partly tap early difficulties with self-control, which could account for why these early emotions predict later self-control. More work will be needed to clarify the transactions between the emotion-based traits and self-control across childhood.

Conscientiousness: Underlying Processes

Conscientiousness indexes a child's or adult's active engagement with various tasks; an individual high on this trait invests greater energy in completing work, upholding commitments, and maintaining order (Ashton & Lee, 2001). Conscientiousness thus should tap a person's capacity to exercise self-control in the service of effective task completion. The adaptive profile associated with Conscientiousness is consistent with such a view of the trait. As we review later in this chapter, childhood Conscientiousness predicts better academic achievement and improvement in academic achievement over time, and adult Conscientiousness is the best personality trait predictor of work success (Judge, Higgins, Thoreson, & Barrick, 1999). One reason that more conscientious adults may excel in school and work is that they tend to use planful problem solving as a way of handling stressors in these domains of their life rather than trying to escape or avoid such problems (O'Brien & DeLongis, 1996). Conscientious adults also tend to set higher goals for themselves, are more committed to meeting those goals, and have greater confidence that they can meet those goals (Barrick, Mount, & Strauss, 1993; Judge & Ilies, 2002). The data on Conscientiousness make clear that this trait is highly relevant to effectiveness in the areas of striving and achieving; however, it is important to recognize that Conscientiousness may be detrimental to performance in certain contexts (see Tett & Burnett, 2003, and Yeo & Neal, 2004, for reviews). An important area of future research will be examining in closer detail the ways that conscientious children and adults approach and accomplish their daily tasks and goals.

The importance of Conscientiousness is not restricted to task-focused endeavors; rather, Conscientiousness is often associated with effective social functioning as well. For example, a study of observed interactions between school-age children and their parents showed that child Conscientiousness was (unsurprisingly) associated with greater exhibited intelligence and ambition and (unexpectedly) with better social skills, warmth, and co-operativeness (Markey et al., 2004). Childhood Conscientiousness also often predicts concurrent and later peer social competence and rule-abiding behavior (Lamb et al., 2002; Shiner, 2000; Shiner, Masten, & Roberts, 2003) and better conflict resolution with peers (Jensen-Campbell & Graziano, 2001). One straightforward reason that Conscientiousness may be linked with effective social functioning is that self-regulation is clearly important for maintaining social relationships in both childhood and adulthood (Eisenberg, Fabes, Guthrie, & Reiser, 2000; Vohs & Ciarocco, 2004).

A second, deeper reason for these links between Conscientiousness and social functioning may involve the underlying nature of the Conscientiousness trait. Based on socioanalytic theory, Hogan and Ones (1997) have argued that individual differences in Conscientiousness reflect variations in the adoption of and compliance with the rules and expectations of the group, as conveyed by various authority figures (e.g., parents and teachers in childhood; work supervisors in adulthood). Indeed, in adulthood some aspects of Conscientiousness are linked with greater valuing of conformity (Roccas, Sagiv, Schwartz, & Knafo, 2002). Consistent with this model, Effortful Control in childhood is associated with toddlers' and preschoolers' "committed compliance" or internalization of parental rules

(Kochanska, Clark, & Goldman, 1997; Kochanska, Coy, & Murray, 2001). Conscientiousness thus may reflect children's and adults' adoption of society's norms for regulated behavior.

Having considered the nature of Conscientiousness from a theoretical point of view, it is important to examine the more basic biological and psychological processes that are likely to underlie individual differences in this trait. Conscientiousness is not the same as self-regulation because self-regulation is relevant to other individual differences as well; however, research on self-regulation may shed some light on Conscientiousness. Researchers studying the biological basis of self-regulation have pointed to the importance of the prefrontal cortex for a variety of self-regulatory skills, including working memory, emotional processing, planning, novelty detection, resolving conflicting information, initiating action, and inhibiting inappropriate responses (Banfield, Wyland, Macrae, Munte, & Heatherton, 2004; Nigg, 2000). Posner, Rothbart, and colleagues (Posner & Rothbart, 2000; Rueda et al., 2004) consider many of these capacities to reflect individual differences in an overarching executive attention capacity, which they likewise link with the development of the frontal cortex, particularly the anterior cingulate cortex. These researchers have examined the development of executive attention across childhood. Infants show differences in alerting and orienting, which are both manifestations of a more reactive attentional system. However, by 9 and 18 months of age, infants also begin to show evidence of more voluntary control of attention. Children show marked growth in executive attention during the 3rd year of life, and this growth continues throughout childhood. Based on this model, children's manifest differences in Effortful Control are driven in large part by differences in executive attention. Some empirical evidence is beginning to substantiate the link between executive attention and Effortful Control (Rothbart, Ellis, Rueda, & Posner, 2003).

The trait of Conscientiousness is typically seen as involving more voluntary control of behavior, as implied by the labels *Effortful Control* (Rothbart, Ahadi, et al., 2001) and *Will* (Digman & Inouye, 1986). This type of executive control is separate from other types of relatively more involuntary tendencies toward inhibited behavior (Eisenberg, Smith, et al., 2004; Nigg, 2000). As we noted in our discussion of Extraversion and Neuroticism, children's behavior may be inhibited because of low approach tendencies (low Extraversion) or because of high fear or anxiety (high Neuroticism); these types of more emotion-based inhibition can be distinguished from the executive control associated with Conscientiousness (Kindlon, Mezzacappa, & Earls, 1995; Nigg, 2000). Children's emerging capacities for executive control may serve, in part, to regulate the approach and avoidance systems in the service of adaptive behavior (Rothbart, Ellis, & Posner, 2004). Active, effortful control in early childhood predicts better self-regulation of anger and joy later in childhood (Kochanska et al., 2000), and, as noted previously, better attentional control is associated throughout childhood with better regulation of negative emotions.

However, much of self-regulation is likely to occur at an automatic, nonvoluntary level. Research with adults suggests that self-regulation of cognition (even working memory) is often automatic, and the same is proving to be true for regulation of emotion and behavior (Fitzsimons & Bargh, 2004). Nonvoluntary self-regulation is important, in part, because the ability to exercise voluntary control of cognition, emotion, and behavior appears to be limited. In a number of studies with adult samples, voluntary self-control appears to operate as a strength that can be depleted temporarily with use rather than as an unlimited resource (Schmeichel & Baumeister, 2004). In short, automatic nonvoluntary regulation may be necessary as a complement to the more effortful forms of self-regulation, given that effortful regulation has limits. It will be important for developmental research to explore the development of both automatic and more voluntary forms of self-regulation in childhood.

Agreeableness

Agreeableness includes a variety of traits seen as very important by developmental psychologists; yet, historically, these traits have been left out of temperament models. The high end of Agreeableness includes descriptors such as warm, considerate, empathic, generous, gentle, protective of others, and kind. The low end of Agreeableness includes tendencies toward being aggressive, rude, spiteful, stubborn, bossy, cynical, and manipulative. In studies with both children and adults, Agreeableness also includes being willing to accommodate others' wishes rather than forcing one's own desires and intentions on others; for children this aspect of the trait also involves how manageable the child is for parents and teachers. Observations of Agreeable chil-

dren interacting with their parents are consistent with questionnaire descriptions of such children (Markey et al., 2004): Children's high Agreeableness is positively associated with expressing agreement and warmth, seeking agreement from parents, and seeming to like parents and is negatively associated with competitiveness, condescending behavior, and criticalness. In short, Agreeableness is linked with a variety of behaviors that are likely to foster congenial relationships with both peers and adults. Given the adaptive significance of this trait, it is not surprising that parents from many countries spontaneously offer a large number of traits from this domain when they are asked to describe their children (Havill, Besevegis, & Mouroussaki, 1998).

Agreeableness: Lower-Order Traits

In our discussion of Neuroticism, we already noted two lower-order traits that are linked with both Neuroticism and Agreeableness: (1) anger/irritability and (2) alienation/mistrust. A number of other lower-order traits appear to be aspects of Agreeableness in childhood: prosocial tendencies, antagonism, and willfulness. *Prosocial tendencies* (also called helpfulness or nurturance) encompasses children's individual differences in traits that demonstrate concern for other people rather than interest only in themselves. Children differ in their tendencies to be empathic, kind, and nurturant (Eisenberg, Fabes, & Spinrad, Chapter 11, this *Handbook,* this volume). Individual differences in prosocial behavior are moderately stable during the preschool- and school-age years (Eisenberg et al., 1987; Graziano & Eisenberg, 1997); there is some preliminary evidence that prosocial behavior may be stable from childhood to early adulthood (Eisenberg et al., 1999) This aspect of Agreeableness may possibly comprise two sets of traits, one tapping warmth and affection and the other tapping altruism and generosity (Saucier & Ostendorf, 1999).

Antagonism ranges from the tendency to be peaceful and gentle to the tendency to be aggressive, spiteful, quarrelsome, and rude (Halverson et al., 2003): Children who are high on this trait express hostility openly toward others. The lower-order trait antagonism includes both physical aggression and relational aggression (e.g., gossiping and social exclusion). There is some evidence from older children, adolescents, and adults that physical aggression and relational aggression tend to covary in individuals (Cillessen & Mayeux, 2004; Rose, Swenson, & Waller, 2004; Tellegen & Waller, 1992), although it is also important to separate the two types of aggression for more fine-grained developmental analyses.

Willfulness refers to the extent to which an individual attempts to assert his or her will over others through domineering behavior (Halverson et al., 2003). Children and adults who are high on this trait are described as bossy, manipulative, overbearing, and defiant rather than accommodating and flexible (Halverson et al., 2003; Peabody & De Raad, 2002). This trait captures some of the most central aspects of Thomas and Chess's difficult child construct (Bates, 1989) and is also similar to a childhood trait labeled by Bates as "resistance to control" (Bates, Pettit, Dodge, & Ridge, 1998). Children high on this trait are likely to pose significant management problems for parents and teachers. Willfulness involves children's tendencies to assert their wills over others; however, it is important to recognize that actual dominance over others is determined by multiple traits, including aspects of extraversion, as noted previously. Specifically, observed dominance is linked with Extraversion, low Neuroticism, and greater physical aggression in both humans and animals (Anderson, John, Keltner, & Kring, 2001; Gosling & John, 1999; Hawley, 2003; Pellegrini & Bartini, 2001).

Other potential aspects of Agreeableness may exist in children. *Modesty* versus conceitedness involves the extent to which an individual is humble rather than arrogant, self-important, or boastful (Goldberg, 2001; Peabody & De Raad, 2002; Saucier & Ostendorf, 1999). *Integrity* refers to the tendency to be honest, principled, sincere, and loyal versus deceptive and disloyal (Peabody & De Raad, 2002). Integrity appears to be close in content to internalized conscience and the moral self as these constructs have been studied by Kochanska and colleagues (Kochanska, Gross, Lin, & Nichols, 2002).

Although Agreeableness is a one-dimensional trait spanning prosocial traits at the high end and antisocial traits at the low end, it may actually turn out to be better thought of as at least two separate dimensions (Graziano, 1994; Graziano & Eisenberg, 1997). Agreeableness forms a single trait in some lexical studies of adults (e.g., English and German), but it splits into two separate factors in a number of languages (Peabody & De Raad, 2002; Saucier, 2003). One of these factors is typically defined by prosocial tendencies, modesty, and integrity, and the other factor is typically defined by antagonism and willfulness. Thus, one trait involves proso-

cial concern and respect for others, whereas the other trait involves irritable, aggressive, and hostile disregard for others. Although prosocial and aggressive tendencies tend to covary negatively later in childhood, they also co-occur in some youths (Haselager, Cillessen, van Lieshout, Riksen-Walraven, & Hartup, 2002) and, when combined, may confer social benefits in some Machiavellian children (Hawley, 2003). The two aspects of Agreeableness are likely to have some overlapping origins, but also some distinct origins (Krueger, Hicks, & McGue, 2001).

Agreeableness: Early Childhood Antecedents

Although Agreeableness has emerged robustly and consistently in questionnaire studies that tap a wide range of children's behaviors, the traits encompassed by this superfactor are not included in most temperament questionnaires. Perhaps these traits have been seen as less basic than other temperament traits: Temperament researchers may have considered prosocial and hostile tendencies as the developmental products of more basic, early-emerging temperaments. There is some support for the idea that Agreeableness arises, in part, from early differences in positive and negative emotions and from early self-regulation, which we discuss later. However, it is also likely that there are unique genetic and environmental contributors to Agreeableness as well. Aspects of Agreeableness emerge fairly early themselves (e.g., aggression; Tremblay, 2002) and seem to develop alongside other temperament traits. Further, many nonhuman animals display Agreeableness-like traits, even though most of these same species do not display behaviors indicating Conscientiousness (Gosling & John, 1999). Thus, it is likely that Agreeableness is not merely a product of other temperament traits. It would be useful for more longitudinal research to measure early individual differences that may be more uniquely associated with later Agreeableness, such as early behaviors indicating affection, closeness to others, and soothability.

Graziano and Eisenberg (1997) have argued that Agreeableness is likely to have its origins in the self-regulation of negative emotions. Recent studies have provided good evidence for this claim. Agreeableness itself and several of its components are predicted negatively by early differences in high-intensity irritability and frustration and positively by early attention and self-control (Abe & Izard, 1999; Eisenberg et al., 2000; Kochanska,

Murray, & Coy, 1997; Kochanska et al., 2000; Laursen, Pulkkinen, & Adams, 2002; Rothbart, Derryberry, et al., 2000; Rubin, Burgess, Dwyer, & Hastings, 2003). Good attentional control may be particularly important for helping children to shift their focus from negative emotions to positive emotions when they are angry, frustrated, or aroused (Wilson, 2003). In contrast to the negative link between early irritability and later Agreeableness, early fearfulness may actually promote higher Agreeableness because fearfulness presages greater compliance and a stronger moral self (Kochanska et al., 2002), higher empathy (Rothbart, Derryberry, et al., 2000), and lower aggression (Raine et al., 1998). However, fear and anxiety may be negatively associated with prosocial behavior toward strangers (reviewed in Eisenberg & Fabes, 1998). The picture that is emerging is that Disagreeableness develops most strongly among children whose high irritability is not constrained by either good self-regulation or by the inhibiting power of fearfulness (see Caspi, Harrington, et al., 2003, for converging longitudinal evidence).

Positive emotions and Extraversion appear to predict childhood Agreeableness in a complex pattern. Mild, regulated positive emotions presage later Agreeableness (Abe & Izard, 1999). Similarly, positive emotionality and sociability are concurrently associated with prosocial behavior and with empathy in children (reviewed in Eisenberg & Fabes, 1998, and Graziano & Eisenberg, 1997) and with prosocial tendencies in adults (Krueger et al., 2001). Agreeableness itself is linked with higher jovial mood in adults (e.g., happy, cheerful, enthusiastic; Watson & Clark, 1992). Conversely, inhibited temperament is linked with less expressed empathy (Young, Fox, & Zahn-Waxler, 1999). Thus, regulated positive emotions and sociability are likely precursors of later prosocial tendencies, though more evidence is needed. In contrast, Extraversion positively predicts later aggression and externalizing behavior problems (X. Chen et al., 2002; Shiner, 2000). High-intensity positive emotions and shorter observed latency to grasp small objects in infancy likewise predict childhood aggression (Rothbart, Derryberry, et al., 2000). Higher approach tendencies may particularly lead to greater externalizing, antisocial behavior when self-regulation is poor (Eisenberg, Spinrad, et al., 2004). As we described previously, children's Extraversion may result in high levels of frustration and anger when goal seeking is thwarted; in turn, this anger and frustration may lead children with poor self-regulation to behave aggressively. Taken together, the data suggest that well-regulated early Extraversion is likely to predict prosocial tendencies, whereas unregulated early Extraversion is likely to predict antisocial tendencies.

Agreeableness: Underlying Processes

There are large psychological literatures associated with the processes underlying the various components of Agreeableness (for reviews, see the chapters by Dodge, Coie, & Lynam on aggression, Chapter 12; Eisenberg et al., Chapter 11, this *Handbook*, this volume, on prosocial behavior): This developmental research is highly relevant for understanding the nature of Agreeableness in childhood. Rather than attempt to describe these literatures, we focus here on research that specifically examines the Big Five trait of Agreeableness in children and adults and describe potential underlying biological systems.

A number of researchers have argued that Agreeableness reflects individual differences in the motivation to maintain harmonious relationships with others; from this point of view, Agreeableness taps differences in the willingness to forgo individual interests out of concern for others (Digman & Takemoto-Chock, 1981; Graziano & Eisenberg, 1997; Graziano, Hair, & Finch, 1997; MacDonald, 1995). A number of recent studies have provided evidence that Agreeableness does reflect individual differences in the motivation to maintain harmonious relationships. One rather straightforward piece of evidence is that, among college students, Agreeableness is moderately correlated with prizing benevolence as a value, meaning concern for people one knows (Roccas et al., 2002). Based on data from experience-sampling studies, high-Agreeable adults react differently to interpersonal situations than do low-Agreeable adults. Specifically, high-Agreeable adults are more distressed than low-Agreeable adults when they face interpersonal conflicts (Suls et al., 1998) and report more negative affect when they themselves behave in a quarrelsome manner (Cote & Moskowitz, 1998). They also report more positive affect when they engage in warm, agreeable behavior than do low-Agreeable adults (Cote & Moskowitz, 1998). When more Agreeable college students anticipate participating in a competitive situation, they expect the situation to be less rewarding and more challenging than do less Agreeable students (Graziano et al., 1997). The data from these diverse studies support the idea that high-Agreeable individuals are concerned with maintaining harmonious relationships and are distressed by potential and real interpersonal conflicts. This fundamental motivation for peaceable, close relationships is reflected in the life stories told by Agreeable individuals; in life narratives provided by college students and adults, higher Agreeableness is associated with themes of love/friendship, caring for others, and unity (McAdams et al., 2004).

Does the motivation to maintain positive relationships translate into distinct approaches to handling conflict among high-Agreeable children and adults? A variety of studies yield an affirmative answer to this question. First, low-Agreeable children, adolescents, and adults are more likely than high-Agreeable individuals to endorse destructive tactics for handling conflict, such as manipulation, coercion, and power assertion, although even low-Agreeable individuals acknowledge that better tactics could be used (D. Buss, 1992; Graziano, Jensen-Campbell, & Hair, 1996; Jensen-Campbell, Gleason, Adams, & Malcolm, 2003; Jensen-Campbell, Graziano, & Hair, 1996). Agreeableness is also positively associated in children and adolescents with stronger endorsement of constructive conflict tactics, such as negotiation and compromise (Jensen-Campbell & Graziano, 2001; Jensen-Campbell et al., 2003). Second, Agreeableness predicts more effective handling of actual conflicts. Teachers and parents describe high-Agreeable children as negotiating conflict better (Jensen-Campbell et al., 2003), whereas peers describe low-Agreeable adolescents as more aggressive (Gleason, Jensen-Campbell, & Richardson, 2004). When children are observed in conflict situations in the lab, low Agreeableness is associated with higher levels of conflict and tension, as well as more destructive conflict tactics such as stand-offs, name-calling, and withdrawals (Jensen-Campbell et al., 2003). In similar lab-based situations with college students, low Agreeableness is likewise predictive of greater conflict (Graziano et al., 1996). Interestingly, greater Agreeableness does not predict more observed submissive behavior in children and adults (Cote & Moskowitz, 1998; Jensen-Campbell et al., 2003); apparently, Agreeable people do not simply solve their interpersonal problems by giving in to other people. In short, more Agreeable youths and adults appear to generate fewer conflicts for themselves and have a greater capacity for handling the interpersonal conflicts that do arise.

There is increasing research interest in understanding the biological systems underlying individual differences in Agreeableness. Differences in empathy, warmth, and nurturance may arise from a biological system designed to promote parental investment in offspring and close family bonds. Some researchers (e.g., MacDonald, 1992, 1995) have argued that evolution yielded a human biological system that typically ensures that an intimate relationship and the care of close others is inherently rewarding and pleasurable and that the loss of such relationships is painful and distressing. Such a system would confer adaptive benefits because it would promote successful care of offspring through the establishment of strong attachment relationships between infants and their caregivers. Some evolutionary theorists have argued that the primary purpose of this evolved system was to promote parent-child attachment and that the system only secondarily began to serve the role of facilitating pair-bonding between reproductive partners (Diamond, 2004). In their tend-and-befriend model, Taylor et al. (2000) have argued that a biological affiliation system is likely to be especially important for understanding the ways that females respond to stress and threat. According to this model, females may be evolutionarily primed to respond to stress by "tending" (caring for others, particularly offspring) and "befriending" (seeking and offering support). Research with animals has pointed to several potential biological substrates of this affectional system, including endogenous opioids and the neuropeptide oxytocin (Carter, 1998; Taylor et al., 2000). Further, there is some preliminary evidence in humans that affectional bonds may activate brain areas that support positive emotions and deactivate brain areas that are linked with aggression, fear, and sadness (Diamond, 2004); this finding is consistent with the emotional profile associated with Agreeableness.

Openness to Experience/Intellect

Openness to Experience/Intellect is perhaps the most debated and least understood of the Big Five traits, yet it includes a number of potentially important characteristics. This trait does not appear in temperament models, despite parents from a number of countries spontaneously using words from this domain of individual differences to describe their children (Mervielde, De Fruyt, & Jarmuz, 1998). In the Big Five studies, children who are high on this trait are described as eager and quick to learn, clever, knowledgeable, perceptive, imaginative, curious, and original. In previous reviews (Shiner, 1998; Shiner & Caspi, 2003), we argued that the evidence for the existence of this trait in children was equivocal. More recently, the accumulating data provide convincing evidence that this trait can be measured reliably by at least age 6 or 7 years. The childhood trait does not appear to be as broad as some adult conceptualizations of the trait, however. For example, in Costa and McCrae's (1992) influential version of Openness to Experience, the trait includes openness to ideas, fantasy, aesthetics, actions, feelings, and values. In most childhood Big Five studies, the Openness trait focuses more narrowly on openness to ideas and actions and tends to emphasize intellectual capacities and creativity. In some studies with children, when the trait is measured with a broader range of items, it does not form an internally coherent trait (Lamb et al., 2002; Markey et al., 2002). By high school, adolescents can reliably describe themselves on most aspects of the broader Openness trait (McCrae & Costa, 2004; McCrae et al., 2002). Thus, it is safe to say that some form of Openness emerges as an individual difference by middle childhood, but the trait is likely to undergo significant developmental elaboration across the years from early childhood through adolescence.

The lower-order components of Openness in childhood are not yet clear, but *intellect* (Halverson et al., 2003; Mervielde & De Fruyt, 1999, 2002) and *curiosity* and *creativity* (Goldberg, 2001; Mervielde & DeFruyt, 1999, 2002) have received some support. In international lexical studies with adults, Openness also appears to include components of unconventionality (Ashton et al., 2004).

Openness to Experience: Early Childhood Antecedents

The developmental precursors of Openness are unknown, but there is suggestive evidence from three lines of research. First, in one study, full-face positive emotions in the Strange Situation at 18 months (a presumed marker of high-intensity positive emotions) predicted Openness at 3.5 years (Abe & Izard, 1999). Second, early signs of Openness may include curiosity and exploration of new situations; these behaviors are markers of an Openness-like trait in a number of animal species (Gosling & John, 1999). Indirect evidence for this possibility comes from longitudinal studies showing that the tendency to seek stimulation and to explore new environments actively in early childhood predicts later academic achievement and IQ (Guerin et al., 2003; Raine, Reynolds, Venables, & Mednick, 2002). High-intensity

positive emotions and active exploration are likely precursors of both Openness and Extraversion. Openness and Extraversion tend to covary across the life span (Digman, 1997; Markon et al., 2005); the two traits may stem from some of the same underlying early processes. Third, orienting sensitivity, which includes the tendency to be sensitive to internal and external sensory stimulation, is concurrently related to Openness in adulthood (Rothbart, Ahadi, et al., 2000). Thus, the extant data on the antecedents of Openness are limited but suggest several potentially interesting early manifestations of the trait.

Openness to Experience: Underlying Processes

McCrae and Costa (1997) suggested that Openness includes two particularly important processes: Openness as a psychic structure and Openness as a motivation to pursue new, complex experiences. First, "open individuals have access to more thoughts, feelings, and impulses in awareness, and can maintain many of these simultaneously" (McCrae and Costa, 1997, p. 838). Openness is associated with numerous indicators of greater access to varied inner experiences in adults: more differentiated self-reports of emotions (Terracciano, McCrae, Hagemann, & Costa, 2003), reduced tendencies to screen out previously irrelevant stimuli (Peterson, Smith, & Carson, 2002), greater dissociation and perceptual aberration (McCrae & Costa, 1997), and heightened experiences of inspiration (Thrash & Elliot, 2003). This greater access to inner experience may be a mixed blessing; for example, in one study of women undergoing a major move, greater Openness predicted both heightened self-esteem and increased depression (Kling, Ryff, Love, & Essex, 2003). More highly open adults are more creative, at least in supportive circumstances (George & Zhou, 2001); it seems likely that a very important source of this creativity is access to a complex world of inner ideas and emotions. Second, open individuals are motivated to seek out interesting new experiences. This view of Openness is consistent with some of the markers of Openness in children, including eagerness to learn new things (both academic and nonacademic).

Among adults, Openness expresses itself in a wide variety of observable behaviors and attitudes. More open adults tend to be more politically liberal, less authoritarian in their attitudes, and less traditional in their beliefs (Jost, Glaser, Kruglanski, & Sulloway, 2003; McCrae, 1996). They produce more structurally complex narratives about their lives (McAdams et al., 2004), have more distinctive offices and bedrooms (Gosling, Ko, Mannarelli, & Morris, 2002), and possess more varied collections of books (Gosling et al., 2002). In contrast, we know strikingly little about the behaviors associated with Openness in children. It will be important to look in the right contexts to find the behavioral signatures of Openness in children. Adult Openness is accurately observed in some contexts and not others; for example, it is more accurately inferred from adults' pantomimes and conversations on hobbies than from their role playing of various social scenarios (Borkenau, Mauer, Riemann, Spinath, & Angleitner, 2004).

Directions for Future Developmental Research on Personality Structure

In this section, we have reviewed a proposed taxonomy of individual differences in personality. A personality taxonomy is an *evolving* classification system whose purpose is to integrate and guide research. This also means that any such system must be open to empirical refutation and requisite modification. There are historical parallels between the use of structural models in personality psychology and the use of a standardized model for describing and diagnosing mental illness in psychiatry. Prior to the advent of the American Psychiatric Association's *Diagnostic and Statistical Manual of Mental Disorders III* (*DSM-III*), clinicians and researchers did not have available explicit criteria to define the boundaries of diagnostic categories. Clinical diagnoses were difficult to compare and cross-sample replications were hard to conduct. The development of *DSM-III* was a big improvement because it provided a common language with which clinicians and researchers could communicate about the disorders they were treating or investigating. *DSM-III* had its share of problems, and subsequent modifications (*DSM-III-R, DSM-IV*) testify to the need for a flexible and evolving system that can accommodate new empirical information, as do recommended modifications in anticipation of *DSM-V* (Kupfer, First, & Regier, 2002). We can similarly hope that the use of a generally accepted trait taxonomy will help to impose structure on unintegrated research findings, reduce the likelihood that old traits will be reinvented under new labels, and advance the study of personality development across the life course.

Toward these goals, we suggest four ways to build on the current success of elucidating the structure of per-

sonality differences across the life course. First, much more work is needed to specify lower-order traits. We have highlighted some potential lower-order traits that warrant consideration in children and adults; other lower-order traits undoubtedly exist as well.

Second, the fields of child development and personality psychology will continue to benefit from creative measurement of individual differences, beyond the sole use of questionnaires. A strength of the temperament field has been its use of multiple measures of temperament traits, including behavior observations and structured laboratory tasks. Additional types of measures can be explored. For example, implicit measures have been used to assess anxiety and shyness in adults (Asendorpf, Banse, & Mucke, 2002; Egloff & Schmukle, 2002); rather than directly inquiring about a person's self-view of personality, these instruments measure indirectly an individual's automatic associations between trait descriptors and the self. Physiological measures can be used to parse groups of individuals into more homogeneous subtypes (Kagan, Snidman, McManis, Woodward, & Hardway, 2002). Puppet interviews have been used to assess self-views of traits in children as young as age 5 years and could be used to measure a wide range of traits early in childhood (Arseneault, Kim-Cohen, Taylor, Caspi, & Moffitt, 2005; Measelle, Ablow, Cowan, & Cowen, 1998; Measelle et al., 2005).

Third, more research is needed about the cross-cultural generalizability of the taxonomic system reviewed here for children and adolescents. Parents from the United States, China, and several European countries consider the Big Five traits to be important in describing their children (Kohnstamm, Halverson, Mervielde, & Havill, 1998). Cross-cultural studies of adult personality structure have been pursued vigorously over the past decade (Church, 2001). There is some research on childhood temperament and personality structure in countries outside the United States and Europe, such as China, Japan, and Russia (Digman & Shmelyov, 1996; Halverson et al., 2003; Rothbart, Ahadi, et al., 2001), but it will be important to explore the structure of childhood personality in other countries. Another crucial task will be to determine when in the life course mean-level cross-cultural differences in personality emerge.

Fourth, it will be important to chart the development of sex differences in mean levels of personality traits. Although there do not appear to be any sex differences in the structure of personality, there are some differences in the mean levels of personality traits (Feingold,

1994). A deeper understanding of the causes of such sex differences will be important for explaining both personality development and the development of psychopathology (Rutter, Caspi, & Moffitt, 2003).

THE DEVELOPMENTAL ELABORATION OF PERSONALITY TRAITS

The process of developmental elaboration refers to the mechanisms by which those temperament attributes that are part of each individual's genetic heritage accumulate response strength through their repeated reinforcement and become elaborated into cognitive and affective representations that are quickly and frequently activated—into personality traits. This elaboration may involve at least six processes (Table 6.3), which we now describe in the order of their hypothesized emergence. For example, learning processes and environmental elicitation are hypothesized to influence the course of personality development in the first few months of life; environmental construal and social comparison processes can influence personality development only following the emergence of necessary cognitive functions in early and middle childhood; and environmental selection and manipulation generally require the emergence of self-regulatory functions in childhood and are likely to become particularly important as youths move into adolescence.

Before describing these six processes, we hasten to remind the reader that examples of these processes appear in nearly all sections of this chapter. The ubiquitous presence of process-focused personality analysis in this chapter is not an accident. As we noted in our chapter introduction, personality research is increasingly based on the recognition that traits are not merely semantic labels but rather reflect organizing and motivating biological and psychological processes (Derryberry, Reed, & Pilkenton-Taylor, 2003; Tellegen, 1991). The purpose of this section is to provide an organizing framework for thinking about and studying the processes by which personality traits develop and increasingly shape behavior.

Learning Processes

Temperament differences may influence several learning mechanisms that are involved in the elaboration process, including positive and negative reinforcement, punishment, discrimination learning, and extinction. In the second section, we described current models positing that Extraversion and Neuroticism reflect individual differences in a BAS and BIS, respectively (Gray, 1987, 1990). In essence, proponents of these models argue that Extraversion and Neuroticism reflect differences in various learning mechanisms (i.e., Extraversion indexes sensitivity to potential rewards and Neuroticism indexes sensitivity to potential threats). If these formulations of Extraversion and Neuroticism are correct, the two traits should correlate with different patterns of learning. There is some evidence for this in adults (Avila, 2001).

TABLE 6.3 Processes through Which Early Temperament/Personality Shapes the Development of Later Personality, Adaptation, and Psychopathology

Process	Definition	Example
Learning processes	Temperament shapes the child's experience of classical and operant conditioning.	Children high on Openness may find complex and novel stimuli to be reinforcing.
Environmental elicitation	Temperament shapes the response of adults and peers to the child.	Children high on Extraversion may attract peers to play with them.
Environmental construal	Temperament shapes the ways that children interpret the environment and their experiences.	Children low on Agreeableness may interpret requests from adults as hostile impositions on their freedom.
Social and temporal comparisons	Temperament shapes the ways children evaluate themselves relative to others and to themselves across time.	Children high on Neuroticism may wrongly view themselves as inadequate relative to their peers.
Environmental selection	Temperament shapes children's choices about their everyday environments.	Children high on Conscientiousness may pursue challenging activities.
Environmental manipulation	Temperament shapes the ways that children alter, modify, and manipulate their environments.	Children high on Extraversion may actively persuade other children to choose them as leaders of school groups.

Differences in sensitivity to rewards and threats should also predict biases in perception, memory, or attention (Canli, 2004). We previously reviewed some evidence that this is indeed the case (e.g., anxiety predicts selective attention to threats). Other traits in addition to Extraversion and Neuroticism should affect learning processes as well. For example, as we have reviewed, children differ strikingly in their persistence and attention, two temperament traits that are likely to influence learning. Agreeableness may be related to sensitivities to anger- or frustration-inducing stimuli, whereas Openness may be associated with attraction to complex or novel stimuli. All of these differences in learning processes should be amenable to investigation through behavioral and neuroscience methods.

More generally, different parental socialization processes are likely to interact with childhood temperament in the development of personality (for recent reviews, see Bates & McFadyen-Ketchum, 2000; Gallagher, 2002; Putnam, Sanson, & Rothbart, 2002). One example may serve to illustrate how children's temperament differences in learning interact with parental socialization. Kochanska (1997) demonstrated that fearful children (i.e., those with greater sensitivity to threats) show more positive conscience development when mothers use subtle, gentle, psychological discipline than when mothers use strongly power-assertive discipline. For such fearful children, their own internal experiences of distress may facilitate the feeling of guilt when they do something wrong, which appears to promote greater compliance (Kochanska et al., 2002). In contrast, gentle maternal discipline does not predict conscience development among fearless children, most likely because gentle discipline does not create enough discomfort; fearless children instead tend to develop stronger internalization when they are securely attached to their mothers and when their mothers are more responsive to them. Identification of other family moderators of temperament outcomes should be a high priority for research on children's individual differences. A better understanding of how temperament influences basic learning processes should help researchers identify which moderators to examine.

Environmental Elicitation

Temperament differences also elicit different reactions from the environment and influence how other people react to children, beginning in the first few months of life (Bell & Chapman, 1986). Research on evocative effects of children's temperament on parents is especially well developed in relation to infants and young children with "difficult" temperaments (i.e., children who are irritable, hostile, prone to cry, and hard to soothe). Many studies have documented that mothers of difficult infants experience lower confidence, greater depression, and lower self-efficacy than do mothers of more temperamentally easy infants (Crockenberg & Leerkes, 2003). Children's intense irritability has rippling negative effects on fathers and the family system more broadly (Crockenberg & Leerkes, 2003), including detrimental immediate and short-term effects on mothers' work outcomes (Hyde, Else-Quest, Goldsmith, & Biesanz, 2004). Children's negative emotions also predict differential negative treatment by parents; more emotionally negative children evoke more negative parental responses than less emotionally negative children in the same family (Jenkins, Rasbash, & O'Connor, 2003).

The evidence for child effects on parents is the most robust in relation to individual differences in negative emotions, but other temperament traits appear to predict parental responses as well (Crouter & Booth, 2003; Parke, 2004; Putnam et al., 2002). In addition, it is important to recognize that the effects of children's temperaments extend beyond the family environment to other caregivers, teachers, and peers. For example, children who express more positive affect are liked by peers and are seen by teachers as friendly and cooperative, whereas children who express high levels of anger are disliked by peers and are viewed as unfriendly, aggressive, and uncooperative by teachers (reviewed in Denham et al., 2001). Thus, children's temperaments play an important role in shaping the interpersonal experiences they encounter in multiple settings. In turn, the responses that children evoke from others are likely to be internalized as part of children's emerging self-concepts.

Research has begun to uncover some of the microprocesses through which children's temperament elicits responses from others. Individual differences in temperament and personality traits are reliably expressed in unique verbal and nonverbal behaviors, and other persons in the immediate environment react to these behaviors and use this information to make inferences and attributions (Borkenau & Liebler, 1995; Gifford, 1994). Perhaps most striking is evidence linking individual differences in adolescent personality and psychopathology to facial expressions of discrete emotions. For example,

Extraversion predicts facial expressions of social approach, Agreeableness is negatively correlated with facial expressions of anger, and Conscientiousness is associated with reduced facial expressions of negative emotion and with embarrassment (Eisenberg et al., 1989; Keltner, 1998; Keltner, Moffitt, & Stouthamer-Loeber, 1995). Such facial expressions of emotions help to coordinate social interactions: These expressions convey information about the motivations and personality of the sender, evoke complementary or similar emotions from others, and provide incentives for particular responses (e.g., positive emotions reinforce desired social behaviors; Keltner, Ekman, Gonzaga, & Beer, 2003). In addition to the facial expression of emotion, children's other individuating characteristics (e.g., vocal properties; Lin, Bugental, Turek, Martorell, & Olster, 2002) are likely to provoke particular interpersonal responses as well.

Temperament characteristics elicit not only behaviors on the part of others but also expectations. Adults have implicit theories about developmental trajectories that they associate with particular temperament attributes. As such, children's temperament-based behaviors may elicit expectancy-based reactions from adult caregivers (Graziano, Jensen-Campbell, & Sullivan-Logan, 1998).

Finally, it is important to recognize that children's effects on others are likely to be moderated by the characteristics of the interaction partner. Even among parents of emotionally negative children, there are some parents in some contexts who respond with heightened attention and sensitivity (Crockenberg & Leerkes, 2003), which suggests the presence of important moderators of parental responses. Parents' beliefs and attitudes moderate how parents respond to children with particular temperaments (Bugental & Johnston, 2000). Parents' own personalities and moods are likely to moderate child effects as well, given the evidence discussed in the sixth section that parental personality predicts parenting styles. Future research on moderators of child effects will help to spell out more clearly how transactions between children's temperaments and their contexts shape their developing personalities.

Environmental Construal

With the emergence of belief systems and expectations, temperament differences may also begin to influence how environmental experiences are construed, thus shaping each person's effective experience of the environment (Hartup & van Lieshout, 1995). Research about the construal process stems from the cognitive tradition in personality psychology, which emphasizes each person's subjective experience and unique perception of the world. This research focuses on what people "do" mentally (Cervone & Mischel, 2002), demonstrating that social information processing—including attention, encoding, retrieval, and interpretation—is a selective process shaped by individual differences in temperament and personality (Derryberry & Reed, 2003; Matthews, Derryberry, & Siegle, 2000).

The role of cognitive factors in personality and psychopathology has been detailed by Crick and Dodge (1994), whose social information-processing model of children's social adjustment includes six steps: (1) to encode information about the event, (2) to interpret the cues and arrive at some decision about their meaning and significance, (3) to clarify goals, (4) to search for possible responses to the situation, (5) to consider the consequences of each potential response and to select a response from the generated alternatives, and (6) to carry out the selected response. Temperament and personality have the potential to shape social information processing at each of these steps.

One of the most important reasons that temperament is likely to influence cognitive processing is that temperament involves emotional processes that are known to shape cognition (Derryberry & Reed, 2003). Lemerise and Arsenio (2000) presented a reformulation of Crick and Dodge's social information-processing model that amplifies the crucial role of emotional processes. These authors argue that children's individual differences in emotionality and emotion regulation affect processes at each of the six stages of social information processing (see also Arsenio & Lemerise, 2004). For example, children's differences in positive and negative emotions will affect the cues they notice in the environment, the goals that are salient to them, and the types of potential responses they generate. Children's differences in self-regulation will help to determine the responses they select and their ability to enact those responses. Although personality influences cognitive processes, cognitive processes likewise influence ongoing emotional experiences (Matthews et al., 2000); thus; there are bidirectional effects between cognitive/perceptual and emotional processing (Derryberry & Reed, 2003).

Throughout our personality taxonomy section, we presented examples of how personality shapes social-cognitive processing. Two other examples illustrate how such processes occur. As noted, Neuroticism in adults is associated with a variety of cognitive biases. Recent research has demonstrated that higher Neuroticism is associated with specific detrimental ways of appraising and coping with difficult situations. Children who are higher on negative emotionality (including both neuroticism and irritability) are more likely to appraise negative life events as threatening and to use avoidant coping as a way of dealing with these life events, which leads to poorer adjustment (Lengua & Long, 2002). Similarly, Neuroticism in adults predicts heightened distress and worry in response to experimentally induced stress in the lab; this link between Neuroticism and distress is, in part, mediated by threat appraisals and by emotion-focused coping (Matthews et al., 2000). These studies demonstrate that one of the reasons that Neuroticism is so robustly associated with poor adjustment is because it is linked with specific social-cognitive biases.

Social-cognitive processes are also implicated in aggression. Children who are high in reactive aggression (aggression aimed at retaliation against someone) are those who show both high frustration/anger and a tendency to assume hostile intentions on the part of others (Dodge, Lochman, Harnish, Bates, & Pettit, 1997). An interesting, similar pattern predicts aggression and hostility in adults. In one study (Meier & Robinson, 2004), adult participants were asked to categorize words as blameworthy (e.g., murder or adultery) or not (e.g., baldness or hurricane). Among participants low on Agreeableness, greater speed at categorizing words as blameworthy predicted greater hostility and arguments in daily life. Thus, for both children and adults, a heightened bias toward assuming and assigning blame predicts greater hostility and aggression among some individuals.

As these examples illustrate, although social-cognitive and trait approaches to personality are often portrayed as antagonistic, they are perfectly complementary and mutually informative. Future work can aim to explore further the ways that children's early temperaments influence the ways that children construe and make sense of their worlds.

Social and Temporal Comparisons

With increased cognitive sophistication (e.g., role-taking skills), two social-psychological processes are hypothesized to influence self-evaluations and identity development: Children learn about themselves by comparing and contrasting themselves to others (social comparisons) as well as to themselves over time (temporal comparisons). The salience and relative importance of social and temporal comparisons may change across the life course (Suls & Mullen, 1982). Age-related changes in social cognition and social roles make it likely that social comparisons may be especially influential from childhood to adolescence and into adulthood and that temporal comparisons may become increasingly important during the adult years.

The microprocesses through which personality may shape social and temporal comparisons also deserve attention. Temperament and personality may shape a range of relevant processes (Cassidy, Ziv, Mehta, & Feeney, 2003; Derryberry & Reed, 2003), including (a) the kinds of feedback that people deliberately seek out about themselves, (b) attentional biases to comparison information, (c) standards used for comparison, and (d) emotional responsivity to comparison information. Extant research offers some hints about the ways in which personality differences may shape comparison processes. For example, greater anxiety and sadness in children predict negative self-views, which predict poorer estimates of competence relative to actual competence over time (Pomerantz & Rudolph, 2003). Other research suggests that subsets of aggressive children have extremely high or extremely low views of their competence relative to others (Brendgen, Vitaro, Turgeon, Poulin, & Wanner, 2004). More systematic research is needed regarding these processes.

Environmental Selection

As self-regulatory competencies increase with age, individuals begin to make choices and display preferences that may reinforce and sustain their characteristics. Children's emerging personalities shape the environments they select, whether consciously or unconsciously. Processes of environmental selection are likely to become increasingly important across the years from childhood to adulthood (Scarr & McCartney, 1983). Even among very young children, temperament is likely to shape the spheres children occupy in the environments chosen for them by adults (e.g., inhibited toddlers may avoid interactions with other children in child care, or children high on intellect may choose more stimulating activities at home). As children move into middle childhood, they are given greater freedom to choose the environments in which they spend their time (Cole & Cole,

1996). During childhood and adolescence, youths' personalities may help determine the activities in which they participate and the ways in which they choose to spend their free time (McHale, Crouter, & Tucker, 2001; Shanahan & Flaherty, 2001). Personality effects on children's peer relationships may be particularly important; particular traits appear to predict the peer groups children join (Denham et al., 2001), children's experiences of peer rejection and acceptance (Hay, Payne, & Chadwick, 2004), and the quality of children's friendships (Pike & Atzaba-Poria, 2003). Children's individual differences also predict the life events they experience; for example, children with externalizing behavior problems experience a greater number of controllable negative life events than children without these problems (Masten, Neeman, & Andenas, 1994).

In adulthood, individuals make personality-based choices regarding education, occupation, and intimate relationships (reviewed in a later section); all of these choices shape individuals' everyday environments. Indeed, by adulthood the most striking personality differences between individuals are to be found not by studying their responses to the same situation but by studying how they choose and construct new situations (Wachtel, 1973). A person's selection and creation of environments is thus one of the most individualizing and pervasive expressions of his or her personality.

The process of environmental selection may also account for the empirical observation that measures typically used to study the environment are subject to substantial genetic influence (Plomin & Bergeman, 1991). A key issue for personality researchers is the extent to which personality contributes to genetic influences on measures of the environment. So far, genetic effects on the Big Five personality traits have been reported to explain genetic influences on some life events (Saudino, Pedersen, Lichtenstein, McClearn, & Plomin, 1997), and personality traits account for about 30% of the genetic influence on divorce risk (Jockin, McGue, & Lykken, 1996). The main implication from these results, as discussed later, is that associations between environmental measures and personality cannot be assumed to be caused environmentally, and, in some instances, the likely direction of effects is the other way around: Individuals differentially select and are differentially exposed to environments (e.g., divorce or stressful life events) as a result of their genetically influenced personality traits.

Environmental Manipulation

Once the self-concept is firmly established, and with the development of more sophisticated self-regulatory capacities, individuals also begin to alter, modify, and manipulate the environments in which they find themselves (D. Buss, 1987). These processes may become particularly important as children become more skilled in regulating their own behavior and more insightful into the causes of others' behaviors. Like adults, children vary in the goals that they pursue in various circumstances (Rose & Asher, 1999), and these goals are likely to influence the ways that children attempt to modify their environments. The ways that individuals select and shape their environments may be especially relevant for self-regulation. Individuals regulate their behavior in the midst of an ongoing emotional experience. But individuals also regulate their behavior and others' behavior proactively by anticipating potential situations and selecting how to handle those situations according to their goals (Eisenberg, 2001; Gross, 1999).

We have described six processes through which an initial disposition is elaborated so that it increasingly organizes emotion, thought, and action. Research is now needed about each of these processes in relation to different temperament and personality traits.

THE ORIGINS OF INDIVIDUAL DIFFERENCES IN PERSONALITY

In this section, we review what is known about genetic influences on personality variation between people, and discuss how measured genes can be incorporated into research on personality development.

Genetic and Environmental Influences on Personality Development across the Life Span

To estimate the relative roles that genes and environments play in personality development, behavioral geneticists employ two basic research designs: (1) twin studies and (2) adoption studies. The logic behind using the twin method to estimate heritable influences is straightforward, and it has three parts. First, a genetic contribution to personality is indicated when the similarity of monozygotic (MZ) twins' personalities is greater than the similarity of dizygotic (DZ) twins' personalities. This inference is based on the fact that MZ twins share all their genes, but DZ twins, like all siblings, share on average only half of their polymorphic genes. Quantitative model fitting usually labels this "A," for additive genetic effects. To use this logic, researchers must test the critical assumption that all of the greater similarity between MZ and DZ twins can safely be ascribed to MZ twins' greater genetic similarity. This is called the "equal environments assumption." In other words, researchers must show that MZ twins have not been treated more alike than DZ twins in ways that are related to their personality outcomes. Research into this question suggests that MZ and DZ twins are not perfectly equal on some environmental experiences. However, some part of the greater MZ than DZ twin similarity in treatment arises because MZ twins' genetically influenced similar behavior evokes similar treatment. Evoked similar treatment does not violate the assumption unless it further exacerbates MZ twin similarity. Moreover, despite the fact that such inequality may have inflated some heritability estimates by a small amount, it has not done so enough to invalidate the inference that genes influence personality differences.

Second, twin studies can show whether environmental experiences influence twin similarity over and above genetic influences. MZ twins' genetic similarity is twice that of DZ twins, and therefore, if nothing more than genes were influencing their personalities, MZ twins' personalities should be at least twice as similar as DZ twins'. If not, this indicates that something more than genes has made the twins similar (i.e., environments that the siblings share in common must have enhanced their similarity). In model fitting, this yields a significant variance component called family wide, shared, or common environmental variance, often labeled "C." It indexes environmental effects on personality that can be detected because they have increased the personality similarity between family members in the study and because the family members shared the experience for reasons completely apart from their genetic similarity.

Third, twin studies also address the perennial question of why family members differ from each other (Plomin & Daniels, 1987), by using the following logic. If MZ twins, despite sharing all their genes, are not perfectly identical in their personality, this indicates that nonshared experience unique to each family member has reduced their similarity. In model fitting, this yields a

significant variance component called child-specific, nonshared, or unique environmental variance, often labeled "E." It indexes environmental effects on personality that can be detected because they have created differences between family members in the study. Phenotype measurement errors can produce such effects, too, because errors in measurement produce scores that look different for twins in a pair.

The fundamental logic behind using the adoption method to estimate heritable influences is also straightforward. The correlation between adoptee and biological parent personality represents genetic transmission, whereas the correlation between adoptee and adoptive parent personality represents social (i.e., environmental) transmission. To use this logic researchers must test the critical assumptions that adoptees share no more than random genes with their adoptive parents (i.e., adoption was extrafamilial and the adoption agency did not try to match the adoptive and birth family's characteristics), and adoptees share not more than random environments with their biological parents (e.g., the quality of prenatal and orphanage care were uncorrelated with adoptees' biological backgrounds). Like twin data, adoption data can be modeled to ascertain A, C, and E components of variance.

With data from large studies throughout the world (Boomsma, Busjahn, & Peltonen, 2002), research has uncovered increasingly reliable and robust evidence that personality traits are substantially influenced by genetic factors. Bouchard and Loehlin (2001; Bouchard, 2004) provide a comprehensive review of this research, pointing to heritability estimates across the Big Five factors in the range of $.50 \pm .10$. There are some fluctuations from study to study, but in general (a) all five superfactors appear to be influenced by genetic factors to the same extent and (b) genetic and environmental factors also affect individual differences in men's and women's personalities to the same extent.

Three clarifications and qualifications deserve special notice. First, twin studies using peer ratings of personality, rather than self-report personality questionnaires, show genetic influences similar to those found in self-report studies (Reimann, Angleiter, & Strelau, 1997). Moreover, multivariate genetic analyses indicate that the same genetic factors are largely involved in self-reports and peer ratings of personality, which provides strong evidence for the genetic validity of self-report ratings. It does not appear to be the case that heritability estimates derived from twin studies are simply an artifact of self-report methodologies in which MZ and DZ twins are asked to rate themselves. Some studies using observational measures of behavior (e.g., empathy; Emde & Hewitt, 2001) yield lower heritability estimates than have been found using questionnaire measures. However, there are still too few such observational studies to know if this is a robust methodological difference.

A second, related methodological challenge has been levied at temperament and personality research with children. Twin studies of younger age groups have relied primarily on ratings by parents, which have yielded an odd result: Correlations for identical (MZ) twins are high, and correlations for fraternal (DZ) twins are very low, sometimes even negative (Saudino & Cherny, 2001). The suggestion is that parents may provide biased ratings of their twins and that behavioral genetic studies that rely on parents for data may not yield valid estimates of genetic and environmental influences on personality functioning. However, the situation is rather less alarming than often claimed. Parents sometimes contrast their twins in ways that generate greater than expected differences between MZ versus DZ twins, but this problem may be restricted to some traits (e.g., symptoms of hyperactivity, temperament ratings of activity level; Simonoff et al., 1998) and may be attenuated by different rating measures (Goldsmith, Buss, & Lemery, 1997).

Third, family and adoption studies of personality yield lower estimates of genetic influences than twin studies (Martin et al., 2000; Plomin, Corley, Caspi, Fulker, & DeFries, 1998). Specifically, parent-child and biological sibling correlations for personality traits average about .1 to .2, with corresponding heritabilities of .3 that are considerably lower than the heritabilities of .5 obtained in twin studies. One possibility is that the discrepant findings result from the fact that parent-offspring and sibling-sibling correlations are derived from different-age pairs and thus (dis)similarity is confounded by age and cohort differences. Another possibility is that nonadditive genetic effects play a larger role in personality than suggested by MZ and DZ correlations. Nonadditive genetic effects refer to effects of genes that interact to influence a trait, in contrast to additive genetic effects in which genes "add up." Nonadditive effects only contribute slightly to the resemblance of DZ twins and other first-degree relatives, whereas MZ twins are identical for all (additive and nonadditive) genetic

effects. Although adoption studies are far fewer and much smaller than twin studies of personality, it is noteworthy that they suggest less genetic influence than twin studies, and the lack of correspondence, at least in relation to personality research, between the results of twin and adoption/family studies merits further scrutiny.

Four novel findings in behavioral genetics research on personality merit mention. First, measures of personality that incorporate multiple viewpoints or perspectives (e.g., by consolidating information from multiple reporters or across multiple situations) yield larger estimates of genetic influences (as well as smaller, but more reliable, estimates of nonshared environmental influences) than measures based on a single viewpoint (e.g., Arseneault et al., 2003; Philips & Matheny, 1997; Scourfield, van den Bree, Martin, & McGuffin, 2004). This finding has been uncovered in studies of young children, adolescents, and adults. It has been suggested that "consensus trait measures," which eliminate specificities or idiosyncracies in different viewpoints about a person, could be used to better identify both specific genes and specific experiences that are correlated with personality (Bouchard & Loehlin, 2001).

Second, as noted earlier, behavioral genetic studies have been used to examine whether there is etiological differentiation in the lower-order traits (or narrow facets) that make up the broader personality superfactors such as the Big Five. The question is whether higher-order dimensions, or superfactors, represent the best level of analysis for research in genetics. Analyses at the lower-order levels of the personality hierarchy offer additional, useful information about the origins of individual differences in personality. For example, analyses at the lower-order trait level suggest that siblings resemble each other in their altruism and prosocial behavior (facets of Agreeableness), in part, because of the rearing environments they share (Jang, McCrae, Angleitner, Riemann, & Livesley, 1998, Sample 1; Krueger et al., 2001), but analyses of the Agreeableness superfactor (which includes many other facets) may conceal this shared environmental influence. Earlier we noted that, for behavioral prediction, it is often a short-sighted strategy to rely exclusively on measures of broad superfactors. Likewise, such exclusive reliance may limit research into the etiology of personality differences.

Third, although it is often said disparagingly that behavioral genetics is adevelopmental and static, recent findings in three different areas of research demonstrate that behavioral genetic methods are ideal for application to questions about age-related changes in etiology, in relation to both normal and abnormal development. First, research on cognitive development shows that the heritability of IQ increases from early childhood through late adolescence (McGue, Bacon, & Lykken, 1993; Plomin, Fulker, Corley, & DeFries, 1997). In this instance, one can think of a heritability estimate as an outcome variable. When it changes with age, this suggests that the balance of genetic versus environmental causal processes differs at successive developmental stages. In the case of IQ, the findings suggest that the effect on IQ of environmental factors shared by siblings dissipates with age, as each child increasingly seeks out environments that are correlated with his or her genetic endowments. Second, research on the development of drug dependence suggests that the causes of initiation and of dependence are not identical so that the factors that lead adolescents to sample drugs are not necessarily the same factors that lead to drug dependence (Kendler et al., 1999). Third, research in developmental psychopathology suggests that the pattern of antisocial behavior that begins early in life, is pervasive across settings, and persists into adulthood is more likely to be influenced by genetic factors than is the pattern of late-onset, situational, transient delinquency (Taylor et al., 2000). In combination, these three sets of findings illustrate how quantitative genetic studies can play an important role in illuminating developmental processes.

Fourth, behavioral genetic methods are also being used to address the processes of continuity and change in personality development. The quantitative methods that behavioral geneticists use to estimate genetic and environmental components of phenotypic variance at a given point in time can be extended to estimate genetic contributions to continuity and change across time by analyzing cross-twin correlations across different times. Longitudinal personality data from twins show that such MZ cross-twin correlations are consistently and significantly larger than DZ cross-twin correlations, providing evidence that a major source of personality continuity in individual differences is attributable to genetic factors (McGue et al., 1993; Pedersen & Reynolds, 1998; Viken, Rose, Kaprio, & Koskenvuo, 1994). This does not mean that genes "fix" personality but rather that genetic factors contribute to the preservation of individual differences over long stretches of the life span, at least from adolescence onwards. A possible interpretation of these findings is the set-point model (Carey, 2003), which argues that environmental fluctuations may produce short-term changes in personality phenotypes but that genetic factors contribute to individual set-points to which individuals will regress (Lykken & Tellegen, 1996). Longitudinal data with multiple, repeated measurements—over both short and long intervals—are needed to fully test the predictions derived from the model.

Molecular Genetic Analysis of Personality

One of the most exciting directions for genetic research on personality involves the use of molecular genetic techniques to identify some of the specific genes responsible for genetic influences on personality. Quantitative genetic studies are widely seen as a necessary preliminary to identifying heritable phenotypes that can be usefully examined at the molecular genetic level (Martin, Boomsma, & Machin, 1997), and finding genes for personality will revolutionize psychological research by providing direct measures of specific genotypes for individuals.

The search for genes for personality is difficult because, unlike classical single-gene disorders in which a single gene is necessary and sufficient to produce the disorder, there is no evidence for such major effects of genes for personality. For quantitative traits like personality, genetic influence is much more likely to involve multiple genes of varying but small effect size, which greatly increases the difficulty of detecting such genes. Genes for complex traits influenced by multiple genes and multiple environmental factors are known as quantitative trait loci (QTLs; Plomin & Crabbe, 2000). The goal is not to find the gene for a personality trait but rather some of the many genes that make contributions of varying effect sizes to the variance of the trait.

Researchers attempting to find QTLs for personality have investigated allelic association using DNA markers that are in or near genes thought to be relevant to the trait. Allelic association refers to a correlation between alleles of a DNA marker and trait scores across unrelated individuals: Allelic association occurs when individuals with a particular allele for the marker have higher scores on the trait. Genes thought to be relevant to a particular trait are often called candidate genes, which is something of a misnomer. For example, for cardiovascular disease, several cholesterol-related genes were good candidate genes because it was known that cholesterol is involved in the process leading to heart disease. However, for personality, much less is known about relevant physiological mechanisms, which means that few specific genes can be suggested as candidates. The phrase *candidate gene* has thus been corrupted to include any genes that might conceivably be related to personality. The problem with this loose use of this phrase is that any gene expressed in the brain could be considered as a candidate gene, so the phrase loses its meaning (Plomin & Caspi, 1999).

A meta-analysis of studies reporting data on associations between candidate genes and personality traits concluded there were few replicable associations (Munafo et al., 2003). Much of the initial excitement about research on molecular genetics and personality has given way to a more sober appreciation of the pitfalls involved in this kind of research (Benjamin, Ebstein, & Belmaker, 2002). The situation is not much better in psychiatric genetics (Plomin & McGuffin, 2003). Several explanations have been invoked to explain some of the failures to find psychiatric genes that withstand replication over time, including but not limited to publication bias, phenotypic heterogeneity, allelic heterogeneity, weak prior probabilities of association, multiple testing, population stratification, and inadequate sample size (Cardon & Palmer, 2003; Colhoun, McKeigue, & Smith, 2003; Lohmueller, Pearce, Pike, Lander, & Hirschhorn, 2003; Merikangas & Risch, 2003; Sullivan, Eaves, Kendler, & Neale, 2001; van den Oord & Sullivan, 2003). These same explanations may account for the slow pace of discovering, and replicating, genes for personality. It may be useful to step back and reflect on the surge of interest in the search for personality genes, which was stimulated by psychiatrists for two reasons. First, it was hoped that the use of quantitative personality traits (rather than categorical psychiatric diagnoses) would offer greater statistical power and thus facilitate the identification of genetic effects of very small effect size. So far, more power has not proven to be a panacea. Second, personality traits were thought to represent endophenotypes for psychiatric disorders—variables that are intermediate on a causal chain from genes to disorder. There was hope that gene associations would be found more successfully with endophenotypes than has been the case with diagnosed disorders because the former are thought to have simpler genetic underpinnings than disorders themselves. Whether personality traits fulfill the criteria for endophenotypes is debatable (Gottesman & Gould, 2003).

It is also likely that genes do not directly encode for personality traits. In fact, it is now recognized that the heritability coefficient indexes not only direct effects of genes but also effects of interactions between genes and environments (Rutter & Silberg, 2002). Gene-environment interactions (GxE) occur when the effect on a person of exposure to a particular environment is conditional upon their genotype (or conversely, when environmental experiences moderate gene expression). Because interactions are independent of main effects, it is possible that even genome-wide scans of very large numbers of people whose personalities are carefully measured will fail to detect genes whose effects are conditional on environmental risk.

In various branches of medicine that deal with complex multifactorial outcomes (e.g., cardiovascular disease), GxE are being discovered and replicated. In the behavioral sciences, several studies also suggest the possibility that some complex traits, instead of resulting from many genes of small effect, result from relatively fewer genes whose effects are conditional on exposure to environmental risk. One study showed that a functional polymorphism in the promoter region of the gene encoding the neurotransmitter-metabolizing enzyme monoamine oxidase A (MAOA) moderated the effect of child maltreatment in the cycle of violence (Caspi et al., 2002). Specifically, maltreated children whose genotype conferred low levels of MAOA expression more often developed conduct disorder than children whose genotype conferred high levels of MAOA. A second study showed that a functional polymorphism in the promoter region of the serotonin transporter gene moderated the influence of stressful life events on depression (Caspi, Sugden, et al., 2003). Specifically, individuals with one or two copies of the short allele exhibited more depression following stressful life events than individuals homozygous for the long allele. Both studies received initial, independent replication (Foley et al., 2004; Kaufman et al., 2004; Kendler, Kuhn, Vittum, Prescott, & Riley, 2005; but this is a fast-moving field, and readers are encouraged to monitor developments that will have no doubt occurred since this writing).

It is possible that bringing together measured genotypes and measured environments to study personality traits and psychiatric disorders more accurately reflects the processes by which personality phenotypes develop than does the study of genetic main effects. However, such GxE research requires careful, deliberate, theory-guided hypothesis testing. Moffitt, Caspi, and Rutter (2005) have outlined several strategic steps for GxE tests in developmental psychopathology, which may be extended to study personality phenotypes. Up to now, developmental psychologists have played a limited role in molecular genetics research. We suggest that they may contribute in two fundamental ways. First, they can help refine the measurement of psychological phenotypes for inclusion in genetic research. Second, they can help to measure developmental contexts and correlated environmental risks that may interact with genetic factors to shape personality development. It may be that ignoring nurture has handicapped the ability of the psychological sciences to better understand nature, and developmental psychologists may be able to rectify the situation.

PERSONALITY CONTINUITY AND CHANGE

The assertion that an individual's personality has changed or remained the same over time is ambiguous. The boy who has daily temper tantrums when he is age 2 but weekly tantrums when he is age 9 has increased his level of emotional control; he has changed in absolute terms. But if he ranks first in temper tantrums among his peers at both ages, he has not changed in relative terms. Further ambiguity arises if the form of the behavior changes. If this boy emerges into adulthood as a man who is irritable and moody, we may grant that the phenotype has changed but claim that the underlying personality has not. A third ambiguity arises when a claim of continuity rests on observations not of an individual but of a sample of individuals. The continuity of an attribute at the group level may be masking large but mutually canceling changes at the individual level. There are several meanings denoted by the term *continuity*. The purpose of this section is to disentangle those meanings. First, we review evidence about three types of continuity and change observed in longitudinal research: differential, mean-level, and ipsative. Second, we review the conceptual challenge of testing and documenting coherence in personality functioning across time and in diverse circumstances.

Types of Continuity Observed in Longitudinal Research

Differential Continuity and Change

Continuity and change are most often indexed by correlations between personality scores across two points in time (i.e., test-retest correlations). These differential, or rank-order stability correlations, reflect the degree to which the relative ordering of individuals on a given trait is maintained over time. Two contradictory predictions have been proposed about the rank-order stability of personality traits. The classical trait perspective argues that personality traits in adulthood are biologically based temperaments that are not susceptible to the influence of the environment and thus do not change over time (McCrae et al., 2000). From this *essentialist* perspective, we would expect the test-retest correlations to be high, even early in life. In contrast, the radical contextual perspective emphasizes the importance of life changes and role transitions in personality development and suggests that personality should be fluid and prone to change and should yield low test-retest correlation coefficients, especially during developmental periods characterized by rapid physical, cognitive, and social changes (Lewis, 2001).

Existing longitudinal studies do not support either of these positions. A meta-analysis of the rank-order stability of personality (organized according to the five-factor model) revealed six major conclusions (Roberts & DelVecchio, 2000):

1. Test-retest correlations over time are moderate in magnitude, even from childhood to early adulthood.

2. Rank-order stability increases with age. Test-retest correlations (unadjusted for measurement error) increased from .41 in childhood to .55 at age 30, and then reached a plateau around .70 between ages 50 and 70.

3. Rank-order stability decreases as the time interval between observations increases.

4. Rank-order stability does not vary markedly across the Big Five traits.

5. Rank-order stability does not vary markedly according to assessment method (i.e., self-reports, observer ratings, and projective tests).

6. Rank-order stability does not vary markedly by gender.

Several implications can be drawn from this meta-analysis. First, the level of continuity in childhood and adolescence is much higher than originally expected (Lewis, 2001), especially after age 3. Even more impressive is the fact that the level of stability increases in a relatively linear fashion through adolescence and young adulthood. Young adulthood has been described as demographically dense, in that it involves more life-changing roles and identity decisions than any other period in the life course (Arnett, 2000). Despite these dramatic contextual changes, personality differences remain remarkably consistent during this time period. Second, personality continuity in adulthood peaks later than expected. According to one prominent perspective, personality traits are essentially fixed and unchanging after age 30 (McCrae & Costa, 1994). However, the meta-analytic findings show that rank-order stability peaks some time after age 50, but at a level well below unity. Thus, individual differences in personality traits continue to change throughout adulthood, but only modestly after age 50. Third, the magnitude of differential stability of personality traits, although not as high as essentialists would claim, is still remarkably high. In this regard, it is interesting to compare personality traits to two overlapping trait domains, which show even higher differential stability: (1) cognitive abilities and (2) interests. Measures of cognitive ability exhibit more longitudinal consistency than measures of personality traits. It is unlikely that this difference is simply a function of the differential reliability of the two kinds of measures because this difference holds up even when the measures are corrected for unreliability. However, a related methodological consideration is that ability measures show greater continuity because ability tests demand maximal performance, whereas personality questionnaires assess representative, typical performance; the former test format may yield evidence of greater continuity (Ackerman & Heggestad, 1997). Measures of interests also exhibit more longitudinal consistency than measures of personality traits, especially during the 20-year period from early adolescence through early adulthood (Low, Yoon, Roberts, & Rounds, 2005). Interests may stabilize at an earlier age because, relative to personality traits, they are more likely to involve motivational processes that lead individuals to select congruent and reinforcing experiences.

Mean-Level Continuity and Change

Mean-level change refers to changes in the average trait level of a population. This type of change is thought to result from maturational processes shared by a population and is typically assessed by mean-level differences in specific traits over time, which indicate whether the sample as a whole is increasing or decreasing on a trait.

Contradictory perspectives—similar to those guiding predictions about differential stability—have also guided expectations about mean-level changes in personality traits. Proponents of the five-factor model of personality argue that personality traits do not demonstrate mean-level changes after adulthood is reached (Costa & McCrae, 1997). In contrast, proponents of a life-span developmental perspective emphasize the importance of life changes and role transitions in personality development and suggest that mean-level changes do occur and often at ages much later than young adulthood (Helson, Kwan, John, & Jones, 2002).

A meta-analysis synthesized and organized (according to the five-factor model) data from 87 longitudinal studies spanning the period from age 10 to 101 years (Roberts, Walton, & Viechtbauer, in press). The pattern of change in the first domain of the Big Five, Extraversion, was complex until this superfactor was divided into constituent elements of social dominance (assertiveness, dominance) and social vitality (talkativeness, sociability). Traits associated with social dominance increased from adolescence through early middle age, whereas traits associated with social vitality increased in adolescence and then showed decreases in young adulthood and old age. Consistent with evidence from cross-sectional comparisons of different age groups (McCrae et al., 2000), traits belonging to the domains of Agreeableness and Conscientiousness increased in young adulthood and middle age. Traits belonging to the domain of Neuroticism decreased mostly in young adulthood. Finally, traits from the Openness to Experience domain showed increases in adolescence and young adulthood and a tendency to decrease in old age.

In general, the longitudinal evidence documents that, at least from adolescence through adult life, most people become more psychologically mature. Two distinct definitions of maturity prevail in developmental theories (Hogan & Roberts, 2004). The first, humanistic definition equates maturity with self-actualization and personal growth and with the process of becoming less defensive and rigid and more creative and open to feelings. According to the longitudinal evidence (Roberts et al., in press), the data do not support this developmental progression; after young adulthood, people do not grow increasingly open to experience and toward old age they actually exhibit declines on traits related to Openness to Experience. The second, functional definition equates maturity with the capacity to become a productive and involved contributor to society, with the process of becoming more planful, deliberate, and decisive, but also more considerate and charitable (traits encompassed by higher levels of Emotional Stability, Conscientiousness, and Agreeableness). According to the longitudinal data, most people do appear to become more functionally mature with age, and those who develop the cardinal traits of psychological maturity earliest are more effective in their love, work, and health (as reviewed later).

Three additional aspects of these longitudinal findings deserve note. First, there are no discernible sex differences in patterns of mean-level continuity and change across the Big Five. Apparently, men and women change in the same ways over the life course, although mean-level differences between the sexes are maintained over time. This suggests that the causes of personality continuity and change across the life course are likely to be the same for the sexes. Second, the majority of mean-level personality change occurs in young adulthood not in adolescence, as we might suspect given traditional theories of psychological development. This pattern of change is not simply a recent historical phenomenon because it was observed in different cohorts across the twentieth century. This finding suggests that the causes of normative personality change are likely to be identified by narrowing research attention to the study of young adulthood. Third, for select trait categories, change occurs well past young adulthood, demonstrating the continued plasticity of personality well beyond typical age markers of maturity.

The evidence base about continuity and change still has several important gaps. First, the best data about personality continuity and change—and hence the most reliable conclusions—continue to be restricted to adult samples. Relatively few studies have used a comprehensive set of personality variables to characterize young children and to track continuities and changes in their personalities over time. Second, most longitudinal studies continue to estimate continuity and change over only two waves of assessment, despite the advent of new methodological approaches that are appropriate for answering more nuanced questions about both short- and long-term temporal dynamics (Biesanz, West, & Kwok, 2003). Finally, and most important, the next generation of studies should move beyond description and attempt to explain patterns of continuity and change (Mroczek & Spiro, 2003).

Ipsative Continuity and Change

Differential and mean-level continuities are indexed by statistics that characterize a sample of individuals. However, continuity at the group level may not mirror continuity at the individual level. For this reason, some researchers examine ipsative continuity, which explic-

itly refers to continuity at the individual level. Ipsative continuity denotes continuity in the configuration of variables in an individual across time. Ipsative continuity could also be called *person-centered continuity*. The latter term derives from Block's (1971) distinction between a variable-centered approach to personality, which is concerned with the relative standing of persons across variables, and a person-centered approach, which is concerned with the salience and configuration of variables in the person (see the first section). An ipsative approach to the study of development seeks to discover continuities in personality functioning across development by identifying each person's salient attributes and their intraindividual organization.

Relatively little longitudinal research has been conducted from an ipsative point of view. An exception is Block's (1971) *Lives Through Time* in which he employed the Q-sort technique of personality description to analyze continuity and change. Continuity and change were indexed by computing correlations across the set of attributes—Q-correlations—between an individual's Q-sort profiles from different measurement occasions; the higher the correlation, the more the configuration of attributes in the individual remained stable across time. Block's analysis showed that aggregate indices of continuity masked large individual differences in personality continuity. For example, the average Q-correlations between early and late adolescence exceeded .70 and those between late adolescence and adulthood exceeded .50, but the intraindividual Q-correlations ranged from moderately negative to the maximum imposed by measurement error. Other studies of personality continuity and change between childhood and adolescence report average Q-correlations ranging from .43 to .71, with considerable variability in the distribution of these scores; intraindividual Q-correlations ranged from −.44 to .92, indicating that from childhood to adolescence people vary widely in how much continuity or change they exhibited (Asendorpf & van Aken, 1991; Ozer & Gjerde, 1989).

An interesting discovery is that there are meaningful individual differences in intraindividual continuity. In a longitudinal American study, Block (1971) originally reported that those persons whose personalities remained stable from adolescence to adulthood (nonchangers) were more intellectually, emotionally, and socially successful as adolescents than the changers, and a measure of adjustment also showed them to be better adjusted. In European samples, Asendorpf and van

Aken (1991) also found that the most resilient children showed the most continuity of personality patterns across time. In a New Zealand sample, Roberts, Caspi, and Moffitt (2001) reported that traits associated with the domains of Agreeableness, Conscientiousness, and Emotional Stability were positively correlated with increased personality consistency: People who were interpersonally effective, planful, decisive, and considerate were less likely to change over time. Although there is no obvious explanation for this replicated finding, one possibility is that Agreeable, Conscientious, and Emotionally Stable people are better equipped to deal with social-developmental challenges across the life course. They have more personal capital in the form of increased resilience, which allows them to master more efficiently the life challenges that they face and to recuperate more quickly from aversive and disappointing life events that they encounter. In contrast, their more brittle counterparts may be more susceptible to the influence of their environment. The robust finding that some people are more prone to change than others calls for research that systematically tests for an explanation.

Personality Coherence

The kinds of continuity discussed so far refer to *homotypic* continuity—continuity of similar behaviors or phenotypic attributes over time. The concept of coherence enlarges the definition of continuity to include *heterotypic* continuity—continuity of an inferred attribute presumed to underlie diverse phenotypic behaviors. Specific behaviors in childhood may not predict phenotypically similar behavior later in adulthood but may still be associated with behaviors that are conceptually consistent with the earlier behavior (Livson & Peskin, 1980). Kagan (1969) noted that heterotypic continuities are most likely to be found from the earlier years of life, when children go through numerous rapid changes. In contrast, homotypic continuities are more likely to be found after puberty, when psychological organization nears completion.

With the coming of age of various longitudinal samples, examples of heterotypic continuities now abound in the psychological literature, as we see in the following section. But it is important to emphasize that coherence and heterotypic continuity refer to conceptual rather than a literal continuity among behaviors: "The notion of coherence refers to a pattern of findings where a construct, measured by several different methods, retains its psychological meaning as revealed in relationships to a variety of other measures" (Ozer, 1986, p. 52) across time and in different contexts. Accordingly, the investigator who claims to have discovered coherence must have a theory—no matter how rudimentary or implicit—that specifies the basis on which the diverse behaviors and attributes can be said to belong to the same equivalence class. The theories behind claims of coherence often amount to appeals to the reader's intuition. In the personality taxonomy that we presented earlier in this chapter, we described current theories about the processes underlying the Big Five traits. As researchers develop richer and more comprehensive theories about the nature of particular individual differences, the task of making theory-based predictions about coherence should become easier. We now review three conceptual approaches to the problem of studying personality coherence across the life course. Each of these social-developmental approaches provides a framework for understanding coherence by focusing on the distinctive ways in which individuals organize their behavior to meet new environmental demands and developmental challenges.

An Organizational-Adaptational Perspective

An organizational-adaptational perspective focuses on tasks and milestones that are encountered during the course of development and on how these are met by different personalities (Masten & Coatsworth, 1995; Masten et al., 1999; van Lieshout, 2000). According to this perspective, personality traits influence problem-solving modalities that individuals use when meeting new developmental challenges at different points in the life course (e.g., developing competent peer relationships in childhood, establishing appropriate cross-sex relationships in adolescence, learning to parent in early adulthood, or providing for dependent parents in middle age). Some of these developmental tasks are universal, whereas others are specific to a sociocultural context and historical period. A useful example of the organizational-adaptational perspective comes from Sroufe and colleagues' work on the links between children's early attachment to mothers and the children's adaptational profiles during later developmental phases. This general approach enabled Sroufe and his colleagues to confer conceptual coherency on their findings that individuals who were securely attached as infants later explored their environments as toddlers (Matas, Arend, & Sroufe, 1978), were less dependent on their teachers in the preschool years (Sroufe, Fox, & Pancake, 1983), attained higher sociometric status and displayed greater competence in peer relations in late childhood (Urban, Carlson, Egeland, & Sroufe, 1991), and appeared to establish appropriate cross-sex relationships in adolescence (Sroufe, Carlson, & Shulman, 1993).

A Sociological Perspective

Beyond childhood the search for coherence becomes more complicated, and it may be that a purely psychological approach is insufficient for the analysis of personality continuity and change as the individual increasingly negotiates social roles defined by the culture (Settersten, 2003). Some researchers have found it useful to adopt a sociocultural perspective and to conceive of the life course as a sequence of culturally defined, age-graded roles (e.g., marriage, work, and parenting) that the individual enacts over time (Caspi, 1987; Helson, Mitchell, & Moane, 1984). In this fashion, the life course can be charted as a sequence of age-linked social roles, and personality coherence can be explored by investigating consistencies in the ways different persons select and perform different sociocultural roles; for example, in whether they opt for conventional or unconventional career paths or in whether they are "off-time" in relation to normative, age-graded tasks such as getting married.

An Evolutionary Psychology Perspective

Bouchard (1995) correctly argued that a purely sociocultural perspective on the life course "ignores the fact that life-histories themselves are complex evolved adaptations" (p. 91). An evolutionary perspective on the life course complements the sociocultural perspective by exploring how personality variation is related to those adaptively important problems with which human beings have had to repeatedly contend: It focuses research on the genetically influenced strategies and tactics that individuals use for survival and reproduction. Evolutionary psychology thus focuses attention on the coherence of behavioral strategies that people use in, for example, mate selection, mate retention, reproduction, parental care, kin investment, status attainment, and coalition building (D. Buss, 1999). Although these ideas have not yet been tested in the context of long-term longitudinal studies, they show the promise of evolutionary psychology for organizing longitudinal-developmental data on personality coherence.

These three approaches, or road maps for studying personality across the life course, share an important assumption: Continuities of personality across the life course are expressed not only through the constancy of behavior across time and in diverse circumstances but also through the consistency over time in the ways that persons characteristically modify their changing contexts as a function of their behavior. We now turn to review evidence of such continuities across the life course.

PERSONALITY AND THE LIFE COURSE: HOW EARLY-EMERGING PERSONALITY DIFFERENCES SHAPE DEVELOPMENTAL PATHWAYS

Two events have served to make research on personality trait development more vibrant over the past 10 years. First, developmental psychologists have begun to measure personality traits rather than ignore them. Second, personality psychologists have become increasingly interested in relating measures of personality traits to something besides other personality measures. The result is robust evidence that early-emerging individual differences in personality shape how individuals experience, interpret, and respond to the developmental tasks they face across the life course. In this section, we review longitudinal evidence about how personality traits shape (a) the cultivation of social relationships, (b) the mastery of educational and work tasks, and (c) the promotion and maintenance of physical health. For each developmental task, we identify the most relevant personality variables and outline the mechanisms by which these personality traits are hypothesized to exert their influence.

Cultivating Relationships: How Personality Shapes Friendships, Intimate Relationships, and Parenting

One of the most important tasks faced by children and adolescents is the establishment of friendships and acceptance among peers (Hartup & Stevens, 1999; Masten & Coatsworth, 1998). Among children, all of the higher-order Big Five traits except Openness are important predictors of social competence. Perhaps so many aspects of personality predict social competence because social functioning requires a wide array of skills, including emotional expression, emotional understanding, and emotional and behavioral regulation (Rubin, Bukowski, & Parker, Chapter 10, this *Handbook,* this volume). Agreeable and Extraverted children show better social competence concurrently and across time and experience growth in perceived social support from early to late adolescence (Asendorpf & van Aken, 2003a; Branje, van Lieshout, & van Aken, 2004; Shiner, 2000; Shiner et al., 2003). Children high on Negative Emotionality or low on aspects of Conscientiousness (e.g., attention and self-control) have a variety of social difficulties concurrently and across time (Eisenberg et al., 2000); the interaction of high Negative Emotionality and low self-regulation may be especially problematic for social functioning (Eisenberg et al., 2000).

Personality continues to be an important predictor of relationships in adulthood. Extraversion predicts positive relationships (Shiner et al., 2002), whereas Neuroticism and Disagreeableness are the strongest and most consistent personality predictors of negative relationship outcomes—including relationship dissatisfaction, conflict, abuse, and, ultimately dissolution (Karney & Bradbury, 1995; Shiner et al., 2002). These effects of Neuroticism and low Agreeableness have been uncovered in long-term studies following samples of children into adulthood and in shorter-term longitudinal studies of adults. The potential contribution of personality differences to shaping abusive relationships has been further underscored by longitudinal studies that find associations between early developing aggressive traits in childhood and subsequent abusive behavior in adult romantic relationships (Andrews, Foster, Capaldi, & Hops, 2000; Ehrensaft, Moffitt, & Caspi, 2004). One study that followed a large sample of adolescents across their multiple relationships in early adulthood discovered that the influence of Neuroticism and low Agreeableness on relationship quality showed cross-relationship generalization: It predicted the same abusive relationship experiences across relationships with different partners (Robins, Caspi, & Moffitt, 2002). Increasingly, sophisticated studies that include dyads (not just individuals) and multiple methods (not just self reports) demonstrate that the link between personality traits and relationship processes is more than simply an artifact of shared method variance in the assessment of these two domains (Donnellan, Conger, & Bryant, 2004; Watson, Hubbard, & Wiese, 2000).

An important research goal is to uncover the proximal relationship-specific processes that mediate these personality effects on relationship outcomes (Reiss, Capobianco, & Tsai, 2002). Personality traits affect relationships by influencing and altering microinteractional processes. First, individuals select their interactional contexts by choosing partners who resemble them. The tendency to form unions with similar others has im-

plications for the course of personality development because similarities between couple members create interpersonal experiences that reinforce initial tendencies (Alwin, Cohen, & Newcomb, 1991; Caspi & Herbener, 1990). Second, personality differences influence people's exposure to relationship events. For example, people high in Neuroticism are more likely to be exposed to daily conflicts in their relationships (Bolger & Zuckerman, 1995). Third, personality differences shape people's reactions to the behavior of their partners. For example, high-Disagreeable individuals may escalate negative affect during conflict (e.g., Gottman, Coan, Carrere, & Swanson, 1998). Similarly, high-Agreeable people are better able to regulate emotions during interpersonal conflicts (Jensen-Campbell & Graziano, 2001). Cognitive processes also come online in creating trait-correlated experiences (Snyder & Stukas, 1999). For example, highly neurotic individuals may overreact to minor criticism from their partner, believe they are no longer loved when their partner does not call, or assume infidelity on the basis of mere flirtation. Fourth, personality differences evoke behaviors from partners that contribute to relationship quality. For example, people high in Neuroticism and low in Agreeableness may be more likely to express four behaviors identified as detrimental to relationships: criticism, contempt, defensiveness, and stonewalling (Gottman, 1994).

Whereas a great deal of research has investigated the influence of personality on friendships and intimate relationships, fewer studies have considered the possibility that parents' personalities shape their parenting styles and relationships with their children (Belsky & Barends, 2002). This is a curious omission. Although researchers interested in psychiatric disorders have documented that maternal psychopathology can compromise effective parenting (Goodman & Gotlib, 2002), developmental researchers have been slower to recognize that parental personality forms a critical part of children's developmental context (Goldsmith, Losaya, Bradshaw, & Campos, 1994). Moreover, behavioral genetic studies suggest that some parenting behaviors may be heritable (Spinath & O'Connor, 2003). This does not mean that there is a gene for parenting styles. Rather, it suggests that individual differences in parenting behaviors may be related to personality characteristics that are influenced by genetic factors.

The handful of studies that have examined personality → parenting associations—using self-reports as well as observations of parenting—suggest that Extraversion and Agreeableness are related to sensitive and responsive parenting, whereas aspects of Neuroticism, such as anxiety and irritability, are related to less competent parenting (e.g., Belsky, Crnic, & Woodsworth, 1995; Clark, Kochanska, & Ready, 2000; Kochanska, Clark, et al., 1997; Kochanska et al., 2004; Losoya, Callor, Rowe, & Goldsmith, 1997; Metsapelto & Pulkkinen, 2003; Prinzie et al., 2004). Much more work needs to be done: First, most of the research to date has focused on parents of very young children to the virtual exclusion of adolescents. Second, most of the research has not tested mediators (e.g., parental attributions) of personality → parenting associations. Third, most of the research has focused on the main effects of personality and has not addressed the conditions under which particular personality attributes are more or less important in explaining parenting behavior (e.g., Are personality main effects moderated by qualities of the martial relationship or by the child's temperament?). For example, there is some evidence that difficult children are particularly likely to be rejected by highly Conscientious mothers during problem-solving tasks (Neitzel & Stright, 2004). Fourth, to our knowledge, no study has examined personality effects on parenting behavior in relation to multiple children in the same family, and this is a design that has the power to test the cross-situational generalizability of personality effects (across offspring) and to estimate the influence of parental personality on family life independently of other family-wide environmental effects.

The study of personality effects on social relationships is exciting territory where hypotheses about personality dynamics can be tested using multiple and creative methodologies. These approaches need not be confined to close relationships. Bugental (2000) proposed a taxonomy of social relationships that offers the promise of helping to coordinate personality research by focusing attention on how personality variables shape behaviors in five domains of social life: (1) attachment relations, (2) mating relations, (3) hierarchical power relations between persons of unequal status, (4) reciprocal relations among persons of equal status, and (5) coalitional-group relations.

Striving and Achieving: How Personality Shapes Performance in School and Work Settings

During the life course, individuals assume multiple performance tasks (e.g., pursuing an education, assuming a job, or managing and allocating resources). Personality

traits from the domain of Conscientiousness are the most important noncognitive predictors of educational achievement and occupational attainment (Judge et al., 1999; Shiner, in press). In fact, childhood Conscientiousness predicts improvements in academic achievement across time into adulthood (Shiner, 2000; Shiner et al., 2003). Similarly, adult Conscientiousness predicts job performance across a wide variety of measures and across nearly all types of jobs (Barrick, Mount, & Judge, 2001). Conscientiousness encompasses many traits that are necessary for completing work effectively: the capacities to sustain attention, to strive toward high standards, and to inhibit impulsive behavior. In contrast, childhood Neuroticism predicts lower adult occupational attainment (Judge et al., 1999). Adult Neuroticism appears to have small negative effects on job performance (Barrick et al., 2001; Hurtz & Donovan, 2000) and is associated with lower academic attainment (Shiner et al., 2002).

Links between the other Big Five traits and academic and work achievement are less consistent and robust but are still found. Openness to Experience/Intellect predicts academic achievement in samples of school-age children, adolescents, and college students (Farsides & Woodfield, 2003; Graziano, Jensen-Campbell, & Finch 1997; John et al., 1994), and child and adult Agreeableness sometimes do as well (Shiner, 2000; Shiner et al., 2002). Meta-analyses reveal that Extraversion, Agreeableness, and Openness predict some more limited aspects of work performance in a subset of occupations (Barrick et al., 2001). Research with children, adolescents, and adults demonstrates that many of the links between personality traits (especially Conscientiousness) and various indices of achievement remain significant after controlling for individual differences in ability (Judge et al., 1999; Shiner, 2000; Shiner et al., 2003), but sometimes the links disappear (Schmidt & Hunter, 2004). The predictive associations between temperament and personality traits and achievement are apparent early in life, at the time that children first enroll in school (Miech, Essex, & Goldsmith, 2001). The finding that personality effects on achievement emerge early in life is important because school adjustment and academic performance have cumulative effects over time (Entwisle & Alexander, 1993).

The personality processes involved may vary across different stages of development, and at least four candidate processes deserve research scrutiny (see Schneider, Smith, Taylor, & Fleenor, 1998). First, the personality

→ achievement associations may reflect "attraction" effects, or "active niche-picking," whereby people actively choose educational and work experiences whose qualities are concordant with their own personalities. For example, people who are more conscientious prefer conventional jobs such as accounting and farming (Gottfredson, Jones, & Holland, 1993). People who are more extraverted prefer jobs that are described as social or enterprising such as teaching or business management (Ackerman & Heggestad, 1997). Moreover, extraverted individuals are more likely to assume leadership roles in multiple settings (Anderson et al., 2001). All of the Big Five have substantial relations with better performance when the personality predictor is appropriately aligned with work criteria (Hogan & Holland, 2003). This indicates that if people find jobs that fit with their dispositions they will experience greater levels of job performance, which should lead to greater success, tenure, and satisfaction across the life course (Judge et al., 1999).

Second, personality → achievement associations reflect "recruitment" effects, whereby people are selected into achievement situations and are given preferential treatment on the basis of their personality characteristics. These recruitment effects begin to appear early in development. For example, children's personalities influence their emerging relationships with teachers at a young age (Birch & Ladd, 1998). In adulthood, job applicants who are more extraverted, conscientious, and less neurotic are liked better by interviewers and are more often recommended for the job (Cook, Vance, & Spector, 2000).

Third, some personality → achievement associations emerge as consequences of "attrition" or "deselection pressures," whereby people leave achievement settings (e.g., schools or jobs) that do not fit with their personality or are released from these settings because of their trait-correlated behaviors (Cairns & Cairns, 1994). For example, longitudinal evidence from different countries shows that children who exhibit a combination of high irritability/antagonism and poor self-control are at heightened risk of unemployment (Caspi, Wright, Moffitt, & Silva, 1998; Kokko, Bergman, & Pulkkinen, 2003; Kokko & Pulkkinen, 2000).

Fourth, personality → achievement associations emerge as a result of direct, proximal effects of personality on performance. Personality traits may promote certain kinds of task effectiveness; there is some evidence that this occurs in part via the processing of information. For example, higher positive emotions facilitate the efficient processing of complex information and are associated with creative problem solving (Ashby, Isen, & Turken, 1999; Fredrickson, 2003). In addition to these effects on task effectiveness, personality may directly affect other aspects of work performance such as interpersonal interactions (Hurtz & Donovan, 2000). Personality traits may also directly influence performance motivation (e.g., Conscientiousness consistently predicts stronger goal setting and self-efficacy, whereas Neuroticism predicts these positive motivations negatively; Erez & Judge, 2001; Judge & Ilies, 2002).

Personality traits not only affect performance in school and at work; they are also influenced by these experiences. The "correspondence principle" summarizes the empirical observation that the most likely effect of achievement-setting experiences on personality development is to deepen the characteristics that lead people to those experiences in the first place (Roberts, Caspi, & Moffitt, 2003). For example, if people assume leadership positions because they are socially dominant, they will become more socially dominant through their experience as leaders. Similarly, some individuals may perform less well in educational settings as a function of their high irritability and aggressiveness. In turn, they are at a heightened risk of becoming increasingly antagonistic and alienated over time through their failure experiences (Shiner et al., 2002). The correspondence principle thus links two mutually supportive life-course dynamics: "social-selection," wherein people select environments that are correlated with their personality traits, and "social-influence," wherein environmental experiences shape personality functioning. According to longitudinal data, the traits that "select" people into specific experiences are the traits that are most "influenced" in response to those experiences. Life experiences do not impinge themselves on people in a random fashion causing widespread personality transformations; rather, the traits that people already possess are changed (i.e., deepened and elaborated) by trait-correlated experiences that they create in achievement settings.

Health Promotion and Maintenance: How Personality Shapes Health Trajectories

The lifelong interplay between psyche and soma is nowhere more apparent than in research documenting that personality traits contribute to the maintenance of physical integrity and health. Especially impressive are life-span studies documenting associations between personality traits related to Conscientiousness with longevity (Friedman et al., 1995). Individuals high in traits related to Disagreeableness (e.g., anger and hostility) appear to be at greatest risk of disease (e.g., cardiovascular illness; Miller, Smith, Turner, Guijarro, & Hallet, 1996). The evidence for the involvement of Neuroticism in ill health is more mixed, with some research pointing to links with increased risk of actual disease and other studies documenting links with illness behavior only (Smith & Spiro, 2002).

The study of health also serves to illustrate the utility of hierarchical structural models of personality in integrating and interpreting research findings. For example, some of the inconsistency that has been observed in studies of hostility and cardiovascular disease may be due to the fact that hostility is a facet or component of both Neuroticism and Agreeableness (versus Antagonism; Smith & Williams, 1992). Measures of hostility that reflect overt interpersonal expressions of anger are facets of Agreeableness that may be the lethal personality risk factor for coronary heart disease, whereas measures of hostility that tap irritation and self-focused negativity are facets of Neuroticism and may be better predictors of health complaints rather than actual health outcomes. A taxonomic model of personality can help researchers to make conceptual and measurement refinements in testing psychosomatic hypotheses.

Personality health associations may reflect at least three distinct processes (Contrada, Cather, & O'Leary, 1999; Rozanski, Blumenthal, & Kaplan, 1999). First, personality differences may be related to pathogenesis—mechanisms that promote disease. This has been evaluated most directly in studies relating various facets of Disagreeableness/hostility to greater reactivity in response to stressful experiences (Smith & Gallo, 2001). However, part of the complexity of testing hypotheses about the role of personality in the physiological processes of a disease involves the need for greater clarity about the disease processes involved and during which disease phases personality effects may be implicated.

Second, personality differences may be related to physical-health outcomes because they are associated with health-promoting or health-damaging behaviors. For example, individuals high in Extraversion may foster social relationships, social support, and social integra-tion, which are positively associated with health outcomes (Berkman, Glass, Brissette, & Seeman, 2000). In contrast, individuals low in Conscientiousness engage in a variety of health-risk behaviors such as smoking, unhealthy eating habits, lack of exercise, unprotected sexual intercourse, and dangerous driving habits (Bogg & Roberts, 2004). The association between Conscientiousness-related traits and health-risk behaviors is especially robust and appears to be stronger among adolescents than adults, suggesting that this risky personality trait merits greater research and public-health attention. Future personality research could be usefully integrated with developmental research from a decision-theory perspective to better understand the decision-making processes that may mediate the links between traits from the Conscientiousness domain and health-risk behaviors (Hampson, Andrews, Barckley, Lichtenstein, & Lee, 2000). Such research has the potential to contribute to a psychology of public health.

Third, personality differences may be related to reactions to illness. This includes a wide class of behaviors, including the possibility that personality differences affect the selection and execution of coping behaviors (e.g., Scheier & Carver, 1993), modulate distress reduction, and shape treatment adherence (Kenford et al., 2002).

The previous processes linking personality traits to physical health are not mutually exclusive. Moreover, different personality traits may affect physical health via different processes. For example, facets of Disagreeableness may be most directly linked to disease processes, facets of low Conscientiousness may be more clearly implicated in health-damaging behaviors, and facets of Neuroticism may contribute to ill-health by shaping reactions to illness.

The study of personality and health has historically been confined to adults. However, this may well change as health psychologists turn their attention to earlier periods in development to understand public-health puzzles. Consider research on social inequalities in health, which has tended to focus on low socioeconomic status in adulthood as the main causal variable and on adults' stress experiences as the main mediating mechanism. However, mounting evidence from life-course research points to the contribution of early life experiences and to the cumulative impact of sustained social disadvantages on adult health, compelling health psychologists to turn their attention to examine the role that personality factors may play in mediating the associations between early social experiences and poor health across the life course (Chen & Mathews, 2002; Gallo & Mathews, 2003).

Predicting All of Behavior All of the Time?

Although personality traits have been shown to shape developmental outcomes in multiple domains and in different age groups, a common refrain is that these predictive associations only account for a fraction of the variance in outcomes of interest. This observation must be balanced by four considerations. First, it seems necessary to periodically reissue the reminder that even small effect sizes are of theoretical and practical significance (McCartney & Rosenthal, 2000). By way of comparison, epidemiological and clinical studies repeatedly uncover associations whose effect sizes range between .1 and .3 (e.g., the association between decreased bone mineral density and risk of hip fracture or between the nicotine patch and smoking abstinence), leading a recent expert panel to recommend rethinking conventional interpretations of psychological research. Given adequate attention to sampling considerations, researchers should be pleased with associations around .2 to .3 (Meyer et al., 2001). Second, debates about the size of personality effects are based on the implicit assumption that every behavior is the product of a single trait. This is implausible, because each individual is characterized by a personal pattern of multiple traits working additively and interactively to influence behavior. This multiple-trait perspective has important implications for effect-size estimates: Simulation studies demonstrate that it is unreasonable and statistically inconceivable in multiply determined systems for any single trait to explain much more than 10% of the variance (Ahadi & Diener, 1989). Further research on the interactions of personality traits may enhance our ability to predict particular outcomes (see, e.g., Witt, Burke, Barrick, & Mount, 2002, on the prediction of work performance from the interaction of Agreeableness and Conscientiousness). Third, social behavior is a product of multiple personalities acting in concert and influencing one another (Asendorpf, 2002). Consider the case of relationship outcomes. If personality effects are additive across partners, the true impact of a personality trait on a relationship should be regarded as the summed effect of two personalities not a single individual's trait (Moffitt, Robins, & Caspi, 2001). Fourth, because the effects of personality differences accumulate over a lifetime, a focus on a single outcome variable measured at a single point in time may underestimate the contribution of personality to the course of developmental trajectories. Abelson (1985) makes this point in noting that differences between baseball players are trivial if considered on the basis of a single at-bat but become meaningful over the course of a game, a season, and a career. These observations are not intended to breed smug self-satisfaction. Rather, they are meant to foster reasonable expectations and aspirations for research on personality development.

PERSONALITY AND THE EMERGENCE OF PSYCHOPATHOLOGY

Just as individual differences in personality shape adaptation over time, childhood personality plays an important role in the development of psychopathology. One of the primary questions that has fueled scholarly and popular interest in temperament research is whether children with particular temperaments are at greater risk of developing psychiatric problems. Much of the early interest in temperament traits was generated by Thomas and Chess's suggestion that children's early individual differences could help set off a chain of transactions between the child and the environment that could lead eventually to the development of clinical disorders (Thomas, Chess, & Birch, 1968). In this section, we address links between temperament/personality and psychopathology. First, we survey several new directions in research about the association between personality and psychopathology. Second, we summarize what is known about the predictive correlations between childhood temperament/personality differences and later psychopathology. Third, we present a conceptual model of possible associations between temperament/personality and psychopathology and provide empirical examples.

New Directions in Research on Personality and Psychopathology

The links between personality and psychopathology are turning out to be complex, and recent research recognizes this complexity. Next we describe three new directions and advances taken in this area of research.

A first advance springs from evidence that clinical disorders often include subgroups of individuals characterized by different temperament or personality profiles. These subgroups may differ from each other in at least four ways: They may (1) have developed the disorder through different pathways, (2) have different profiles of comorbidity and life adaptation, (3) have different prognoses, and (4) respond differently to different treatments. The presence of personality-based subgroups in some clinical disorders is consistent with the principle of equifinality (i.e., children who are following widely different life paths may eventually develop the same set of pathological symptoms). For example, the diagnosis of Anorexia Nervosa appears to contain a subgroup defined by high levels of perfectionism, obsessive-compulsive features, and rigidity as well as excessive inhibition and harm avoidance (Keel et al., 2004; see Westen & Harnden-Fischer, 2001, for a similar subgroup): Relative to other individuals with Anorexia, this subgroup appears to show poorer adaptive functioning and is likely to have a worse outcome.

A second example comes from work on callous-unemotional traits in children with conduct disorder; callous-unemotional traits include lack of empathy, self-serving use of manipulation, restricted emotional expression, and impoverished conscience. Conduct-disordered children with this constellation of traits show higher proactive (unprovoked) aggression, greater delinquency, and greater variety of conduct problems over time than conduct-disordered children without these traits (Frick, Cornell, Barry, Bodin, & Dane, 2003). This subgroup is also characterized by different patterns of social-information processing; for example, greater focus on positive aspects of aggression and lesser hostile attributional biases (Frick, Cornell, et al., 2003; Pardini, Lochman, & Frick, 2003). As these two examples demonstrate, personality research is helping to parse heterogeneous diagnostic groups into more homogeneous subgroups, which may eventually help clinicians in their treatment planning (Harkness & Lilienfeld, 1997).

A second direction followed in this area of research is the recognition that personality differences may help to explain patterns of comorbidity among disorders. Two of the most important patterns of comorbidity in both children and adults involve the co-occurrence of depression and anxiety—the internalizing disorders—and the co-occurrence of conduct problems and hyperactivity—the externalizing disorders. Several researchers have suggested that personality differences may account for patterns of comorbidity: Certain disorders may co-occur because

they spring in part from similar causes, including shared temperament/personality risk factors, whereas each disorder may also be related to other personality traits that are specific to that disorder (Lilienfeld, 2003; Weiss, Susser, & Catron, 1998). Specific models have been proposed to account for the comorbidity of internalizing and externalizing disorders. Watson and Clark (Clark & Watson, 1991; Watson et al., 1995) developed a tripartite model to account for co-occurring internalizing disorders in adults. According to this model, depression and anxiety tend to co-occur because both share high levels of Negative Affect (or Neuroticism); in addition, depression is specifically characterized by low Positive Affect (or Extraversion) and anxiety is specifically characterized by physiological arousal. There is general support for this model in both children and adults (reviewed in Laurent & Ettelson, 2001; also Lonigan, Phillips, & Hooe, 2003), but more recent research has added that social phobia is also specifically characterized by low Positive Affect (Brown, Chorpita, & Barlow, 1998). As for the externalizing disorders, there is evidence that personality traits associated with low Conscientiousness (often called disinhibition) may underlie the co-occurrence of substance dependence and antisocial behavior in adults; further, Conscientiousness appears to be linked with these disorders by virtue of shared genetic origins (Krueger et al., 2002).

A third prominent research question involves the extent to which normal-range personality traits can provide adequate coverage of individual differences relevant to psychopathology. In other words, can prominent trait models like the Big Five capture the relevant variation in abnormal functioning? This question has been particularly important in relation to personality disorders, where some research demonstrates that combinations of the Big Five traits can capture the symptoms of Borderline Personality Disorder (Trull, Widiger, Lynam, & Costa, 2003) and psychopathy (Miller, Lynam, Widiger, & Leukefled, 2001), particularly when combinations of lower-lower traits are used (Reynolds & Clark, 2001). Further, a meta-analysis demonstrated that abnormal personality traits appear to share a hierarchical structure with normal-range personality traits (Markon et al., 2005). However, normal-range personality measures may need to be refined somewhat to cover personality disorder variation more completely. Some normal-range personality measures may do better than others in tapping pathological personality functioning, and scales measuring some Big

Five traits (e.g., Agreeableness and Conscientiousness) include few negative descriptors at their extremes. Future work will need to investigate whether current personality measures could be strengthened by including more extreme depictions of certain traits (Haigler & Widiger, 2001).

The personality traits relevant to some disorders are, quite possibly, not part of typical personality models. Recent work on Obsessive-Compulsive Disorder (OCD) provides a good example. Among preschool-age children, obsessive-compulsive behaviors are highly heritable, but their genetic origins are largely separate from the genetic origins of other anxiety-related behaviors (Eley et al., 2003); OCD may be less related to general distress or Neuroticism than are many of the other anxiety disorders. Instead, OCD may have more specific associations with a particular psychological feature: a disturbance in the emotion-based system that typically enables individuals to feel that closure has been reached and safety has been secured (Szechtman & Woody, 2004). Although this deficit may be related to Big Five traits in some way, it also appears likely to capture an aspect of psychological functioning that is largely separate from the Big Five. The search for other individual differences outside the Big Five is likely to be important in future research linking personality and psychopathology, because such traits may interact with Big Five traits to give rise to specific disorders.

Empirical Evidence for Specific Associations between Personality Traits and Psychological Disorders

Numerous studies have examined associations between temperament and personality differences and psychopathology, both concurrently and longitudinally. Two reviews (Shiner, in press; Tackett & Krueger, 2005; see also Rothbart & Bates, Chapter 3, this *Handbook*, this volume) surveyed the research on the predictive relations between childhood personality and disorders; the conclusions were as follows:

1. Extraversion appears to put children at risk of externalizing behaviors and aggression and protects against internalizing symptoms. In contrast, behavioral inhibition predicts heightened risk for anxiety, depression, and general internalizing symptoms.

2. Neuroticism predicts later internalizing difficulties, whereas early fearfulness appears to protect children

against the development of externalizing symptoms. Neuroticism also appears to be a risk factor for substance use problems. As we noted earlier, early anger and irritability predict externalizing problems such as aggression and conduct problems; later in life, these traits may also lead to greater internalizing symptoms.

3. Children's self-control and attention promote the development of rule-abiding behavior versus externalizing, antisocial behavior; in other words, children who are low on Conscientiousness are at risk of developing externalizing behaviors. Low Conscientiousness also predicts problems with later drug use.

4. Low Agreeableness (as well as low prosocial tendencies and high antagonism) is associated with later antisocial, externalizing behaviors, and boys who are chronically physically aggressive are at a heightened risk of serious delinquency and violence. Children with difficult temperaments (which is most akin to low Agreeableness) likewise develop greater externalizing problems than children with less difficult temperaments.

5. There is no evidence that childhood Openness is predictive of psychopathology, although it should be noted that Openness has been studied less often than the other childhood traits.

Research on personality and psychopathology is in need of significant improvement, as both design and measurement limitations continue to compromise the external and internal validity of many studies: Most samples are small or unrepresentative, reports of personality and psychopathology are often obtained from the same source, and measures of temperament and symptoms often overlap in content. Future research about personality and psychopathology can adopt the more general recommendations outlined by Kraemer and colleagues about how to define and measure risk factors for psychopathology (Jacobi, Hayward, de Zwaan, Kraemer, & Agras, 2004; Kraemer et al., 1997).

Processes Linking Personality Differences and Psychopathology

Much of the current research on personality and psychopathology simply documents correlations between temperament or personality traits and aspects of psychopathology without articulating how the two domains may be connected. We present a conceptual model of possible associations between temperament/personality and psychopathology in childhood and adolescence. In laying out this conceptual model, we draw on models elaborated by others (Clark, Watson, & Mineka, 1994; Rothbart & Bates, 1998; Widiger, Verheul, & van den Brink, 1999). As much as possible, we borrow their terminology to describe the possible associations, to avoid unnecessarily introducing new labels. First, personality may set in motion processes that cause the development of psychopathology (vulnerability association). Second, psychopathology may represent the extreme end of a continuously distributed personality trait or cluster of traits (spectrum association). Third, personality may protect against the development of psychopathology in the face of stress and adversity (resilience association). Fourth, personality may influence the course and prognosis of a disorder, even if the personality trait is not a cause of the disorder (maintenance association). Fifth, psychopathology may influence the course of personality development itself (scarring association). We now elaborate on these five types of association from a developmental perspective.

Vulnerability Association: Personality May Put Children at Risk for the Development of Psychopathology

According to this model, which has garnered the most interest among researchers, personality traits set in motion the processes that lead to psychopathology. However, whereas there are numerous published reports of predictive associations between personality traits and psychiatric disorders, less empirical attention has been given to causal processes. Previously, we outlined six processes through which early temperament differences become elaborated into more broad personality dispositions (see Table 6.3). These same six processes are likely to be the ones through which temperament differences put children at risk for psychopathology as well.

Research on the development of conduct disorder serves to demonstrate how these six processes may operate. Longitudinal research shows that conduct disorder and severe antisocial behavior are predicted by an early history of high negative emotionality, poor self-control, and high unmanageability (Sanson & Prior, 1999). How might these temperament differences contribute to the development of severe antisocial behavior over time?

First, children with conduct disorder are especially sensitive to signals of reward (O'Brien & Frick, 1996) but are relatively insensitive to punishing stimuli (Lytton, 1990). Learning processes may be at work here;

these children may have temperament traits that lead to difficulty learning to inhibit behavior when faced with potential rewards. Second, observational studies show that adopted children who are at genetic risk for antisocial behavior receive more negative control and coercive parenting from their adoptive parents than do adopted children not at genetic risk (O'Connor, Deater-Deckard, Fulker, Rutter, & Plomin, 1998). These findings point to environmental elicitation in which children's genetically influenced temperaments evoke coercive parenting behaviors.

Environmental construal may be seen in the way that aggressive children misinterpret the intentions of others. For example, such children seek less information about social situations and are more likely to assume hostile intent on the part of other persons (Dodge et al., Chapter 12, this *Handbook,* this volume). Related to the process of environmental construal are social comparison processes in which temperament shapes the way that individuals evaluate themselves in relation to others. In some studies, externalizing children overestimate their social competence relative to others (Hughes, Cavell, & Grossman, 1997; Patterson, Kupersmidt, & Griesler, 1990).

Environmental selection may be seen in the ways by which some children "select" situations that can then reinforce particular behaviors. For example, children with poor self-control are more likely to form ties to delinquent peers who, in turn, promote their antisocial behavior (Wright, Caspi, Moffitt, & Silva, 2001). Through environmental manipulation, an individual's personality alters and shapes the environment. For example, disagreeable youth not only perceive more interpersonal conflict in their environment but also attempt to resolve conflict with destructive tactics (Jensen-Campbell & Graziano, 2001).

Spectrum Association: Psychopathology May Be an Extreme Manifestation of Personality

Although psychiatric disorders are typically measured categorically, it is possible that some disorders are not discrete conditions but represent extreme ends of continuously distributed personality dimensions or combinations of dimensions (Sonuga-Barke, 1998; Widiger & Clark, 2000). For example, some researchers have argued that ADHD may be an extreme variant of an underlying temperament or personality trait rather than a discrete condition that is clearly separable from normal functioning (Jensen et al., 1997). Children with ADHD combined type and hyperactive-impulsive type may have a basic deficit in inhibiting a prepotent response when faced with potential reinforcement for that response (i.e., ADHD may represent the extreme low ends of the traits of attention and inhibitory control; Barkley, 1997). ADHD thus appears to be particularly associated with markers of low Conscientiousness (Nigg et al., 2002).

An understudied area where spectrum relationships are likely to be observed is childhood and adolescent personality disorders. Extensive research has linked dimensional personality traits with categorical personality disorders in adults: Some researchers have argued that adult personality disorders should be conceptualized as complex combinations of adaptive and maladaptive personality traits rather than as categorically distinct conditions (Costa & Widiger, 2002; Widiger et al., 1999; Widiger & Simonsen, 2005). Little is known, however, about how child and adolescent personality is related both to concurrent personality disorders and to later-appearing personality disorders in adulthood, although some recent theoretical work has elaborated on potential links (Cohen & Crawford, in press; Geiger & Crick, 2001; Kernberg, Weiner, & Bardenstein, 2000). Children's early personalities are likely to be important predictors of the processes through which personality functioning goes awry and becomes set into maladaptive, rigid patterns (Mervielde, De Clerq, De Fruyt, & van Leeuwen, 2005; Shiner, 2005).

Although we have presented vulnerability and spectrum associations as if they are distinct, the line between the two is blurry. Most of the associations that have been found between personality and psychopathology could be explained equally well by either the vulnerability or the spectrum model. Some disorders may be better described as discrete entities, whereas others may be better described as dimensional conditions. Further, some aspects of the same disorder may be discrete, whereas other aspects may be dimensional (Pickles & Angold, 2003).

Several research strategies can be harnessed to study the distinction between discrete disorders and spectrum associations. First, taxometric methods can be used to distinguish whether differences between groups of individuals (e.g., depressed versus not depressed persons) represent quantitative differences of degree or qualitative differences in kind (Cole, 2004). Taxometric methods are useful in addressing the issues that we raised in an earlier section (i.e., identifying subtypes in disorders; Beauchaine, 2003) and addressing sources of comorbidity (Ruscio & Ruscio, 2004). Such methods also are highly relevant to developmental research because they can be used to identify children who are at risk for disorders and can help pinpoint sensitive periods when discrete disorders may emerge (Beauchaine, 2003).

Second, psychopharmacological studies can also be used to generate evidence about whether personality traits and psychiatric disorders exist on a continuum (e.g., Ekselius & von Knorring, 1999). For example, the antidepressant paroxetine has been shown to reduce negative affect levels in persons without a history of mental disorder (Knutson et al., 1998): Some treatments thought to be targeted at specific syndrome disorders may exert their influence via broader personality variables.

Third, methods in behavioral genetics research can be used to address the question of whether the heritability of a disorder (e.g., ADHD) is the same or different from that of individual differences in a trait (e.g., continuously distributed symptoms of hyperactivity and inattention). For example, with regard to ADHD, genetic analyses suggest that *DSM-III-R* ADHD may be best viewed as an extreme end of a dimension that varies genetically in the population (Levy, Hay, McStephen, Wood, & Waldman, 1997).

Resilience Association: Personality May Avert the Development of Psychopathology in the Face of Stress

Although some personality traits may put children at risk of psychopathology in adverse environments, other traits may promote resilience in the face of adversity: Some personality traits may be protective factors under conditions that, on average, put children at risk for psychiatric disorders (Luthar, Cicchetti, & Becker, 2000; Masten, 2001). For example, Werner and Smith (1992) studied a group of high-risk children who were exposed to perinatal stress, poverty, and multiple family problems. Children who showed positive, resilient adult outcomes were described in infancy as very active: Males were also described as easygoing, and females were also described as affectionate.

It seems obvious that attention must be given to the possibility that some personality factors protect against psychopathology, whereas others predispose to it. However, to the extent that protective and risk factors operate dimensionally—at opposite ends of a continuum—there is little to be gained, either in theory or in practice, from focusing on the beneficial effects of, for example, low Neuroticism more than on the harmful effects of high Neuroticism. But there is a great deal of value in testing two hypotheses: (1) that some personality factors provide protection in the presence of risk, even though they have no effect in the absence of such risk and (2) that higher levels of a trait are necessary for protection under adverse conditions than are necessary for competent functioning in low-risk conditions. Theoretically, the processes through which individual differences in children's temperament and personality traits promote resilience should be the same as those six processes described in reference to personality as a vulnerability factor.

Much remains to be learned about the potential protective role of individual differences in children's personality traits. Researchers have called for increasing focus on the processes underlying resilience (Luthar et al., 2000; Masten, 1999), and personality research should be an important part of future work in this area. Behavior genetic research should also be used to address genetic and environmental sources of resilience. A recent study demonstrated that, for example, children's outgoing temperament promoted resilience in the face of socioeconomic adversity (Kim-Cohen, Moffitt, Caspi, & Taylor, 2004): This link between resilience and sociable temperament was largely accounted for by genetic factors but included environmental processes as well.

Maintenance Association: Personality May Influence the Course and Prognosis of a Disorder

Most risk-factor research on personality has focused on the role of individual differences in causing (or averting) the onset of disorder. In addition, individual differences in personality may influence the manifestation, course, and prognosis of a disorder once it has started. In some cases, such traits may have played a role in the onset of the disorder; in other cases, these traits may not be etiologically related to the disorder. Studies on depression have examined the potential role of personality in maintaining a depressive episode. For example, in one study of depressed adults, those with lower levels of the BAS after the onset of the depressive episode had worse outcomes than those with more initially positive BAS functioning (Kasch, Rottenberg, Arnow, & Gotlib, 2002). Some personality traits appear to predict response to treatment. For example, research on tobacco dependence shows that persons with high Neuroticism are more likely to relapse following participation in smoking cessation treatments (Kenford et al., 2002). Still other personality traits may increase the risk of recurrence of psychiatric conditions (Teasdale & Barnard, 1993). Although these types of associations have been studied in adults (Widiger et al., 1999), they have received very little attention in research with children, despite their potential developmental significance.

Scarring Association: Psychopathology May Alter Personality Functioning

The experience of significant psychopathology has the potential to alter children's personalities in lasting ways. Such a relationship is often referred to as a "scarring" effect of psychopathology on personality (e.g., Rohde, Lewinsohn, & Seeley, 1990). Personality changes that are secondary to physical disorders are well documented, but, at least in adulthood, there is little solid evidence of lasting changes to personality secondary to psychopathology. For example, the possibility of scar effects has been explored in several studies of adult depression; the evidence thus far indicates that, although depression may have negative long-term effects on other aspects of functioning, it does not appear to result in personality change (Ormel, Oldehinkel, & Vollebergh, 2004; Zuroff, Mongrain, & Santor, 2004). The situation may be very different earlier in life. Because identity and a sense of self are under construction throughout childhood and adolescence, children may be particularly vulnerable to the negative effects of psychopathology that emerges early in the life course. This hypothesis has received practically no research attention and warrants further exploration.

CONCLUSION

Throughout this chapter, we have summarized definitive findings, identified promising research leads and hypotheses, and underscored existing methodological limitations. Our concluding comments are thus devoted to sketching the requirements for improved research.

Longitudinal research is the lifeblood of developmental psychology, but simply tracking people over time is not good enough. There is room for improvement on three fronts. First, longitudinal research on personality can be improved through better trait measurement. The availability of a taxonomy of measurable individual differences in temperament and personality is an indispensable aid to developmental research. However, few off-the-shelf measures assess the full range of higher- and lower-order traits described in this chapter: The development of reliable, valid, and comprehensive measures of child and adolescent personality remains an important task. Until these become available, researchers need to consider several issues when selecting methods and instruments for measuring temperament and personality: (a) Ideally, more than one method should be used to provide a more valid assessment of a particular trait; (b) more than one trait should be measured, even in studies focused on single traits in isolation, because this provides critical information about etiological specificity and discriminant validity; (c) researchers need to consider carefully whether a measure truly taps the trait of interest because labels for measures (i.e., scale names on questionnaires) are often misleading; and (d) researchers should consider not just what is included in a particular instrument, but also what is left out, because many measures do not tap the full range of individual differences observed in children. Second, longitudinal research can be improved by relying on theoretically informed data-collection schedules. Rather than dictated by convenience, longitudinal studies should make an effort to organize data collection around well-defined developmental tasks, whether these tasks are defined by evolutionary imperatives, sociological realities, or maturational changes. The organization of data collection across periods of environmental-maturational changes offers an opportunity to test hypotheses about how individuals select and shape their environments (processes of social selection) and how environments influence individuals (processes of social causation). Third, longitudinal research can be improved by integrating epidemiological concepts and methods into studies of personality development to test hypotheses about risk factors and causal processes.

Longitudinal research is not always developmental research and, conversely, many developmental questions require different types of research designs. In particular, little is known about how early-emerging individual differences become elaborated into the consistent ways of behaving, thinking, and feeling that we call personality. Throughout this chapter, we listed some ideas and working hypotheses about these processes. These will need to be examined using traditional observational methods and, increasingly, the tools of neuroscience as well. First, to the extent that the most important sources of influence on the processes of developmental elaboration are to be found in interpersonal settings, the ideal study of individual development ought to be conceived of as a study of social relationships, one in which longitudinal partici-

pants are successively studied alongside their significant others at different points in the life course. These types of studies will include both global ratings of individual differences and minute-to-minute assessments of social interactions to document how behavior patterns are evoked and sustained. Second, just as research in social cognition inspired deeper understanding of personality dynamics in the latter part of the twentieth century, the fusion of differential psychology and neuroscience will lead the way to a fuller understanding of how personality traits are linked to processing emotional stimuli.

Finally, research into personality development will need to embrace genetics. Questions about the extent to which genetic factors influence individual differences in personality are increasingly less interesting, if only because it is by now so well established that genetic factors do have a large influence. But this does not mean that behavioral genetics research has served its purpose and worn out its welcome. To the contrary, discoveries about the human genome open up new research possibilities in which measured genotypes will be used to study the origins of personality differences and the links between personality and psychopathology. To ignore genetics is not only irresponsible but also a missed opportunity.

These concluding observations are intended to stimulate new research into personality development and also to promote discussion about the kind of multidisciplinary (re)training that is increasingly required of new students (and seasoned researchers), spanning psychometric theory, epidemiology, neuroscience, and genetics. It is a daunting and exciting task.

REFERENCES

Abe, J. A., & Izard, C. E. (1999). A longitudinal study of emotion expression and personality relations in early development. *Journal of Personality and Social Psychology, 77,* 566–577.

Abelson, R. (1985). A variance explanation paradox: When a little is a lot. *Psychological Bulletin, 97,* 129–133.

Ackerman, P. L., & Heggestad, E. D. (1997). Intelligence, personality, and interests. *Psychological Bulletin, 121,* 219–245.

Ahadi, S., & Diener, E. (1989). Multiple determinants and effect sizes. *Journal of Personality and Social Psychology, 56,* 398–406.

Ahadi, S. A., Rothbart, M. K., & Ye, R. M. (1993). Children's temperament in the U.S. and China: Similarities and differences. *European Journal of Personality, 7,* 359–377.

Allport, G. W. (1937). *Personality: A psychological interpretation.* New York: Holt.

Alwin, D. F., Cohen, R. L., & Newcomb, T. M. (1991). *Political attitudes over the life-span: The Bennington women after 50 years.* Madison: University of Wisconsin Press.

American Psychiatric Association. (1994). *Diagnostic and statistical manual of mental disorders* (4th ed.). Washington, DC: Author.

Anderson, C., John, O. P., Keltner, D., & Kring, A. M. (2001). Who attains social status? Effects of personality and physical attractiveness in social groups. *Journal of Personality and Social Psychology, 81,* 116–132.

Andrews, J. A., Foster, S. L., Capaldi, D. M., & Hops, H. (2000). Adolescent and family predictors of physical aggression, communication, and satisfaction in young adult couples: A prospective analysis. *Journal of Consulting and Clinical Psychology, 68,* 195–208.

Arcus, D. (2001). Inhibited and uninhibited children: Biology in the social context. In T. D. Wachs & G. A. Kohnstamm (Eds.), *Temperament in context* (pp. 43–60). Mahwah, NJ: Erlbaum.

Arnett, J. J. (2000). Emerging adulthood: A theory of development from the late teens through the twenties. *American Psychologist, 55,* 469–480.

Arseneault, L., Kim-Cohen, J., Taylor, A., Caspi, A., & Moffitt, T. E. (2005). Psychometric evaluation of 5- and 7-year-old children's self-reports of conduct problems. *Journal of Abnormal Child Psychology, 33,* 537–550.

Arseneault, L., Moffitt, T. E., Caspi, A., Taylor, A., Rijsdijk, F., Jaffee, S., et al. (2003). Strong genetic effects on cross-situational antisocial behavior among 5-year-old children according to mothers, teachers, examiner-observers, and twin's self-reports. *Journal of Child Psychology and Psychiatry, 44,* 832–848.

Arsenio, W. F., & Lemerise, E. A. (2004). Aggression and moral development: Integrating social information processing and moral domain models. *Child Development, 75,* 987–1002.

Asendorpf, J. B. (2002). Personality effects on personal relationships over the life span. In A. L. Vangelisti, H. T. Reis, & M. A. Fitzpatrick (Eds.), *Stability and change in relationships* (pp. 36–56). Cambridge: Cambridge University Press.

Asendorpf, J. B. (2003). Head-to-head comparison of the predictive validity of personality types and dimensions. *European Journal of Personality, 17,* 327–346.

Asendorpf, J. B., Banse, R., & Mucke, D. (2002). Double dissociation between implicit and explicit personality self-concept: The case of shy behavior. *Journal of Personality and Social Psychology, 83,* 380–393.

Asendorpf, J. B., Borkenau, P., Ostendorf, F., & van Aken, M. A. G. (2001). Carving personality description at its joints: Confirmation of three replicable personality prototypes for both children and adults. *European Journal of Personality, 15,* 169–198.

Asendorpf, J. B., Caspi, A., & Hofstee, W. K. B. (2002). The puzzle of personality types. *European Journal of Personality, 16,* S1–S5.

Asendorpf, J. B., & van Aken, M. A. G. (1991). Correlates of the temporal consistency of personality patterns in childhood. *Journal of Personality, 59,* 689–703.

Asendorpf, J. B., & van Aken, M. A. G. (1999). Resilient, overcontrolled, and undercontrolled personality prototypes in childhood: Replicability, predictive power, and the trait-type issue. *Journal of Personality and Social Psychology, 77,* 815–832.

Asendorpf, J. B., & van Aken, M. A. G. (2003a). Personality-relationship transaction in adolescence: Core versus surface personality characteristics. *Journal of Personality, 71,* 629–666.

Asendorpf, J. B., & van Aken, M. A. G. (2003b). Validity of big five personality judgments in childhood: A 9-year longitudinal study. *European Journal of Personality, 17,* 1–17.

Ashby, F. G., Isen, A. M., & Turken, U. (1999). A neuropsychological theory on positive affect and its influence on cognition. *Psychological Review, 106,* 529–550.

Ashton, M. C., & Lee, K. (2001). A theoretical basis for the major dimensions of personality. *European Journal of Personality, 15,* 353.

Ashton, M. C., Lee, K., & Paunonen, S. V. (2002). What is the central feature of extraversion? Social attention versus reward sensitivity. *Journal of Personality and Social Psychology, 83,* 245–252.

Ashton, M. C., Lee, K., Perugini, M., Szarota, P., de Vries, R. E., Di Blas, L., et al. (2004). A six-factor structure of personality-descriptive adjectives: Solutions from psycholexical studies in seven languages. *Journal of Personality and Social Psychology, 86,* 356–366.

Avila, C. (2001). Distinguishing BIS-mediated and BAS-mediated disinhibition mechanisms: A comparison of disinhibition models of Gray (1981, 1987), and of Patterson and Newman (1993). *Journal of Personality and Social Psychology, 80,* 311–324.

Banfield, J. F., Wyland, C. L., Macrae, C. N., Munte, T. F., & Heatherton, T. F. (2004). The cognitive resolution of self-regulation. In R. F. Baumeister & K. D. Vohs (Eds.), *Handbook of self regulation: Research, theory, and applications* (pp. 62–83). New York: Guilford Press.

Barbaranelli, C., Caprara, G. V., Rabasca, A., & Pastorelli, C. (2003). A questionnaire for measuring the big five in late childhood. *Personality and Individual Differences, 34,* 645–664.

Barkley, R. A. (1997). *ADHD and the nature of self-control.* New York: Guilford Press.

Barlow, D. (2000). Unraveling the mysteries of anxiety and its disorders from the perspective of emotion theory. *American Psychologist, 55,* 1247–1263.

Barr, R. G., & Gunnar, M. (2000). Colic: The "transient responsivity" hypothesis. In B. Hopkins & J. A. Green (Eds.), *Crying as a sign, a symptom, and a signal: Clinical, emotional and developmental aspects of infant and toddler crying* (pp. 41–66). New York: Cambridge University Press.

Barrick, M. R., Mount, M. K., & Judge, T. A. (2001). Personality and performance at the beginning of the new millennium: What do we know and where do we go next? *International Journal of Selection and Assessment, 9,* 9–30.

Barrick, M. R., Mount, M. K., & Strauss, J. P. (1993). Conscientiousness and performance of sales representatives: Tests of mediating effects of goal setting. *Journal of Applied Psychology, 78,* 715–722.

Bates, J. E. (1989). Concepts and measures of temperament. In G. A. Kohnstamm, J. E. Bates, & M. K. Rothbart (Eds.), *Temperament in childhood* (pp. 3–26). New York: Wiley.

Bates, J. E., Freeland, C. A. B., & Lounsbury, M. L. (1979). Measurement of infant difficultness. *Child Development, 50,* 715–722.

Bates, J. E., & McFadyen-Ketchum, S. (2000). Temperament and parent-child relations as interacting factors in children's behavioral adjustment. In V. J. Molfese & D. L. Molfese (Eds.), *Temperament and personality development across the life span* (pp. 141–176). Mahwah, NJ: Erlbaum.

Bates, J. E., Pettit, G. S., Dodge, K. A., & Ridge, B. (1998). Interaction of temperamental resistance to control and restrictive parenting in the development of externalizing behavior. *Developmental Psychology, 34,* 982–995.

Beauchaine, T. P. (2003). Taxometrics and developmental psychopathology. *Development and Psychopathology, 15,* 501–527.

Bell, R. Q., & Chapman, M. (1986). Child effects in studies using experimental or brief longitudinal approaches to socialization. *Developmental Psychology, 22,* 595–603.

Belsky, J., & Barends, N. (2002). Personality and parenting. In M. Bornstein (Ed.), *Handbook of parenting* (pp. 415–438). Mahwah, NJ: Erlbaum.

Belsky, J., Crnic, K., & Woodsworth, S. (1995). Personality and parenting: Exploring the mediating role of transient mood and daily hassles. *Journal of Personality, 63,* 905–929.

Belsky, J., Hsieh, K., & Crnic, K. (1996). Infant positive and negative emotionality: One dimension or two? *Developmental Psychology, 32,* 289–298.

Benjamin, J., Ebstein, R. P., & Belmaker, H. (Eds.). (2002). *Molecular genetics and the human personality.* Washington, DC: American Psychiatric Association.

Bergman, L. R., & Cairns, R. B. (Eds.). (2000). *Developmental science and the holistic approach.* Mahwah, NJ: Erlbaum.

Berkman, L. F., Glass, T., Brissette, I., & Seeman, T. E. (2000). From social integration to health. *Social Science and Medicine, 51,* 843–857.

Biesanz, J. C., West, S. G., & Kwok, O.-M. (2003). Personality over time: Methodological approaches to the study of short-term and long-term development and change. *Journal of Personality, 71,* 905–941.

Birch, S. H., & Ladd, G. W. (1998). Children's interpersonal behaviors and the teacher-child relationship. *Developmental Psychology, 34,* 934–946.

Bishop, G., Spence, S. H., & McDonald, C. (2003). Can parents and teachers provide a reliable and valid report of behavioral inhibition? *Child Development, 74,* 1899–1917.

Blair, C. (2003). Behavioral inhibition and behavioral activation in young children: Relations with self-regulation and adaptation to preschool children attending Head Start. *Developmental Psychobiology, 42,* 301–311.

Block, J. (1971). *Lives through time.* Berkeley, CA: Bancroft.

Block, J. (1996). Some jangly remarks on Baumeister and Heatherton. *Psychological Inquiry, 7,* 28–32.

Bogg, T., & Roberts, B. W. (2004). Conscientiousness and health behaviors: A meta-analysis of the leading behavioral contributors to mortality. *Psychological Bulletin, 130,* 887–919.

Bolger, N., & Schilling, E. A. (1991). Personality and the problems of everyday life: The role of Neuroticism in exposure and reactivity to daily stressors. *Journal of Personality, 59,* 355–386.

Bolger, N., & Zuckerman, A. (1995). A framework for studying personality in the stress process. *Journal of Personality and Social Psychology, 69,* 890–902.

Boomsma, D., Busjahn, A., & Peltonen, L. (2002). Classical twin studies and beyond. *Nature Reviews Genetics, 3,* 872–882.

Borkenau, P., & Liebler, A. (1995). Observable attributes as manifestations and cues of personality and intelligence. *Journal of Personality, 63,* 1–25.

Borkenau, P., Mauer, N., Riemann, R., Spinath, F. M., & Angleitner, A. (2004). Thin slices of behavior as cues of personality and intelligence. *Journal of Personality and Social Psychology, 86,* 599–614.

Bornstein, M. H., Gaughran, J. M., & Homel, P. (1986). Infant temperament: Theory, tradition, critique, and new assessments. In C. E. Izard & P. B. Read (Eds.), *Measuring emotions in infants and children* (pp. 172–199). New York: Cambridge University Press.

Bouchard, T. J. (1995). Longitudinal studies of personality and intelligence: A behavior genetic and evolutionary psychology perspective. In D. Saklofske & M. Zeidner (Eds.), *International handbook of personality and intelligence* (pp. 81–106). New York: Plenum Press.

Bouchard, T. J. (2004). Genetic influence on human psychological traits: A survey. *Current Directions in Psychological Science, 13,* 148–151.

Bouchard, T. J., & Loehlin, J. C. (2001). Genes, evolution, and personality. *Behavior Genetics, 31,* 243–274.

Branje, S. J. T., van Lieshout, C. F. M., & van Aken, M. A. G. (2004). Relations between big five personality characteristics and perceived support in adolescent families. *Journal of Personality and Social Psychology, 86,* 615–628.

Brendgen, M., Vitaro, F., Turgeon, L., Poulin, F., & Wanner, B. (2004). Is there a dark side of positive illusions? Overestimation of social competence and subsequent adjustment in aggressive and nonaggressive children. *Journal of Abnormal Child Psychology, 32,* 305–320.

Brown, T. A., Chorpita, B. F., & Barlow, D. H. (1998). Structural relations among dimensions of the *DSM-IV* anxiety and mood disorders and dimensions of negative affect, positive affect, and autonomic arousal. *Journal of Abnormal Psychology, 107,* 179–192.

Buckley, M. E., Klein, D. N., Durbin, E., Hayden, E. P., & Moerk, K. C. (2002). Development and validation of a q-sort procedure to assess temperament and behavior in preschool-age children. *Journal of Clinical Child and Adolescent Psychology, 31,* 525–539.

Bugental, D. B. (2000). Acquisition of algorithms of social life: A domain-based approach. *Psychological Bulletin, 126,* 187–219.

Bugental, D. B., & Johnston, C. (2000). Parental and child cognitions in the context of the family. *Annual Review of Psychology, 51,* 315–344.

Buss, A. H., & Plomin, R. (1975). *A temperament theory on personality development.* New York: Wiley.

Buss, A. H., & Plomin, R. (1984). *Temperament: Early developing personality traits.* Hillsdale, NJ: Erlbaum.

Buss, D. M. (1987). Selection, evocation, and manipulation. *Journal of Personality and Social Psychology, 53,* 1214–1221.

Buss, D. M. (1992). Manipulation in close relationships. *Journal of Personality, 60,* 477–499.

Buss, D. M. (1999). *Evolutionary psychology.* Boston: Allyn & Bacon.

Buss, K. A., & Goldsmith, H. H. (1998). Fear and anger regulation in infancy: Effects on the temporal dynamics of affective expression. *Child Development, 69,* 359–374.

Cairns, R. B., & Cairns, B. D. (1994). *Lifelines and risks: Pathways of youth in our time.* New York: Cambridge University Press.

Canli, T. (2004). Functional brain mapping of extraversion and neuroticism: Learning from individual processes in emotion processing. *Journal of Personality, 72,* 1105–1132.

Capaldi, D. M., & Rothbart, M. K. (1992). Development and validation of an early adolescent temperament measure. *Journal of Early Adolescence, 12,* 154–173.

Cardon, L. R., & Palmer, L. J. (2003). Population stratification and spurious allelic association. *Lancet, 361,* 598–604.

Carey, G. (2003). *Human genetics for the social sciences.* Thousand Oaks, CA: Sage.

Carter, C. S. (1998). Neuroendoicrine perspectives on social attachments and love. *Psychoneuroendicrinology, 23,* 779–818.

Carver, C. S. (2004). Negative affects deriving from the behavioral approach system. *Emotion, 4,* 3–22.

Caspi, A. (1987). Personality in the life course. *Journal of Personality and Social Psychology, 53,* 1203–1213.

Caspi, A. (1998). Personality development across the life course. In W. Damon (Editor-in-Chief) & N. Eisenberg (Vol. Ed.), *Handbook of child psychology: Vol. 3. Social, emotional and personality development* (5th ed., pp. 311–388). New York: Wiley.

Caspi, A., Harrington, H., Milne, B., Amell, J. W., Theodore, R. F., & Moffitt, T. E. (2003). Children's behavioral styles at age 3 are linked to their adult personality traits at age 26. *Journal of Personality, 71,* 495–513.

Caspi, A., & Herbener, E. S. (1990). Continuity and change: Assortive marriage and the consistency of personality in adulthood. *Journal of Personality and Social Psychology, 58,* 250–258.

Caspi, A., McClay, J., Moffitt, T. E., Mill, J., Martin, J., Craig, I. W., et al. (2002). Role of genotype in the cycle of violence in maltreated children. *Science, 297,* 851–854.

Caspi, A., Roberts, B. W., & Shiner, R. (2005). Personality development: Stability and change. *Annual Review of Psychology, 56,* 453–484.

Caspi, A., Sugden, K., Moffitt, T. E., Taylor, A., Craig, I. W., Harrington, H., et al. (2003). Influence of life stress on depression: Moderation by a polymorphism in the 5-HTT gene. *Science, 301,* 386–389.

Caspi, A., Wright, B. R., Moffitt, T. E., & Silva, P. A. (1998). Early failure in the job market: Childhood and adolescent predictors of unemployment in the transition to adulthood. *American Sociological Review, 63,* 424–451.

Cassidy, J., Ziv, Y., Mehta, T. G., & Feeney, B. C. (2004). Feedback seeking in children and adolescents: Associations with self-perceptions, attachment representations, and depression. *Child Development, 74,* 6121–6628.

Cervone, D., & Mischel, W. (2002). Personality science. In D. Cervone & W. Mischel (Eds.), *Advances in personality science* (pp. 1–26). New York: Guilford Press.

Chen, E., & Mathews, K. (2002). Socioeconomic differences in children's health: How and why do these relationships change with age? *Psychological Bulletin, 128,* 295–329.

Chen, X., Liu, M., Rubin, K. H., Chen, G., Gao, X., & Li, D. (2002). Sociability and prosocial orientation as predictors of youth adjustment: A 7-year longitudinal study in a Chinese sample. *International Journal of Behavioral Development, 26,* 128–136.

Chorpita, B. F., Albano, A. M., & Barlow, D. H. (1998). The structure of negative emotions in a clinical sample of children and adolescents. *Journal of Abnormal Psychology, 107,* 74–85.

Church, T. A. (Ed.). (2001). Culture and personality. *Journal of Personality, 69,* 6.

Cillesson, A. H. N., & Mayeux, L. (2004). From censure to reinforcement: Developmental changes in the association between aggression and social status. *Child Development, 75,* 157–163.

Clark, L. A., Kochanska, G., & Ready, R. (2000). Mother's personality and its interaction with child temperament as predictors of parenting behavior. *Journal of Personality and Social Psychology, 79,* 274–285.

Clark, L. A., & Watson, D. (1991). Tripartate model of anxiety and depression: Psychometric evidence and taxonomic implications. *Journal of Abnormal Psychology, 100,* 316–336.

Clark, L. A., Watson, D., & Mineka, S. (1994). Temperament, personality and the mood and anxiety disorders. *Journal of Abnormal Psychology, 103,* 103–116.

Cloninger, C. R., Svrakic, D. M., & Przybeck, T. R. (1993). A psychobiological model of temperament and character. *Archives of General Psychiatry, 39,* 1242–1247.

Cohen, P., & Crawford, T. (in press). Development issues: Personality disorder in children and adolescents. In J. M. Oldham, A. E. Skodol, & D. Bender (Eds.), *American Psychiatric Publishing Textbook of Personality Disorders.* Washington, DC: American Psychiatric Publishing.

Colder, C. R., & O'Connor, R. M. (2004). Gray's reinforcement sensitivity model and child psychopathology: Laboratory and questionnaire assessment of the BAS and BIS. *Journal of Abnormal Child Psychology, 32,* 435–451.

Cole, D. A. (2004). Taxometrics in psychpathology research: An introduction to some of the procedures and related methodological issues. *Journal of Abnormal Psychology, 113,* 3–9.

Cole, M., & Cole, S. R. (1996). *The development of children* (3rd ed.). New York: W. H. Freeman.

Colhoun, H. M., McKeigue, P. M., & Smith, G. D. (2003). Problems of reporting genetic associations with complex outcomes. *Lancet, 361,* 865–872.

Contrada, R. J., Cather, C., & O'Leary, A. (1999). Personality and health: Dispositions and processes in disease susceptibility and adaptation to illness. In L. A. Pervin & O. P. John (Eds.), *Handbook of personality* (2nd ed., pp. 576–604). New York: Guilford Press.

Cook, K. W., Vance, C. A., & Spector, P. E. (2000). The relation of candidate personality with selection-interview outcomes. *Journal of Applied Social Psychology, 30,* 867–885.

Costa, P. T., Herbst, J. M., McCrae, R. R., Samuels, J., & Ozer, D. J. (2002). The replicability and utility of three personality types. *European Journal of Personality, 16,* S73–S87.

Costa, P. T., & McCrae, R. R. (1988). Personality in adulthood: A 6-year longitudinal study of self-reports and spouse ratings on the NEO personality inventory. *Journal of Personality and Social Psychology, 54,* 853–863.

Costa, P. T., & McCrae, R. R. (1992). *Revised NEO Personality Inventory (NEO-PI-R) and the NEO Five-Factor Inventory (NEO-FFI) professional manual.* Odessa, FL: Psychological Assessment Resources.

Costa, P. T., & McCrae, R. R. (1997). Longitudinal study of adult personality. In R. Hogan, J. Johnson, & S. Briggs (Eds.), *Handbook of personality psychology* (pp. 269–292). San Diego, CA: Academic Press.

Costa, P. T., & Widiger, T. A. (2002). *Personality disorders and the five factor model of personality* (2nd ed.). Washington, DC: American Psychological Association.

Cote, S., & Moskowitz, D. S. (1998). On the dynamic covariation between interpersonal behavior and affect: Prediction from neuroticism, extraversion, and agreeableness. *Journal of Personality and Social Psychology, 75,* 1032–1046.

Crick, N. R., & Dodge, K. A. (1994). A review and reformulation of social information processing mechanisms in children's social adjustment. *Psychological Bulletin, 115,* 74–101.

Crockenberg, S., & Leerkes, E. (2003). Infant negative emotionality, caregiving, and family. In A. C. Crouter & A. Booth (Eds.), *Children's influence on family dynamics: The neglected side of family relationships* (pp. 57–78). Mahwah, NJ: Erlbaum.

Crouter, A. C., & Booth, A. (2003). *Children's influence on family dynamics: The neglected side of family relationships.* Mahwah, NJ: Erlbaum.

Cumberland-Li, A., Eisenberg, N., & Reiser, M. (2004). Relations of young children's agreeableness and resiliency to effortful control and impulsivity. *Social Development, 13,* 193–212.

Davidson, R. J., Pizzagalli, E., Nitschke, J. B., & Kalin, N. H. (2003). Parsing the subcomponents of emotion and disorders of emotion: Perspectives from affective neuroscience. In R. J. Davidson, K. R. Scherer, & H. H. Goldsmith (Eds.), *Handbook of affective sciences* (pp. 8–24). New York: Oxford University Press.

De Fruyt, F., Mervielde, I., Hoekstra, H. A., & Rolland, J. (2000). Assessing adolescents' personality with the NEO PI-R. *Assessment, 7,* 329–345.

Denham, S., Mason, T., Caverly, S., Hackney, R., Caswell, C., Diener, E., et al. (2001). Preschoolers at play: Co-socializers of emotional and social competence. *International Journal of Behavioral Development, 25,* 290–301.

Derryberry, D., & Reed, M. A. (2003). Information processing approaches to individual differences in emotional reactivity. In R. J. Davidson, K. R. Scherer, & H. H. Goldsmith (Eds.), *Handbook of affective sciences* (pp. 681–697). New York: Oxford University Press.

Derryberry, D., Reed, M. A., & Pilkenton-Taylor, C. (2003). Temperament and coping: Advantages of an individual differences perspective. *Development and Psychopathology, 15,* 1049–1066.

Diamond, L. M. (2004). Emerging perspectives on distinctions between romantic love and sexual desire. *Current Directions in Psychological Science, 13,* 116–119.

Digman, J. M. (1990). Personality structure: Emergence of the five-factor model. *Annual Review of Psychology, 41,* 417–440.

Digman, J. M. (1994). Child personality and temperament: Does the five-factor model embrace both domains. In C. F. Halverson, G. A. Kohnstamm, & R. P. Martin (Eds.), *The developing structure of temperament and personality from infancy to adulthood* (pp. 323–338). Hillsdale, NJ: Erlbaum.

Digman, J. M. (1997). Higher-order factors of the big five. *Journal of Personality and Social Psychology, 73,* 1256.

Digman, J. M., & Inouye, J. (1986). Further specification of the five robust factors of personality. *Journal of Personality and Social Psychology, 50,* 116–123.

Digman, J. M., & Shmelyov, A. G. (1996). The structure of temperament and personality in Russian children. *Journal of Personality and Social Psychology, 71,* 341–351.

Digman, J. M., & Takemoto-Chock, N. K. (1981). Factors in the natural language of personality: Re-analysis, comparison, and interpretation of six major studies. *Multivariate Behavioral Research, 16,* 49–170.

Dodge, K. A., Lochman, J. E., Harnish, J. D., Bates, J. E., & Pettit, G. S. (1997). Reactive and proactive aggression in school children and psychiatrically impaired chronically assaultive youth. *Journal of Abnormal Psychology, 106,* 37–51.

Donnellan, M. B., Conger, R. D., & Bryant, C. M. (2004). The big five and enduring marriages. *Journal of Research in Personality, 38,* 481–504.

Donzella, B., Gunnar, M. R., Krueger, W. K., & Alwin, J. (2000). Cortisol and vagal tone responses to competitive challenge in preschoolers: Associations with temperament. *Developmental Psychobiology, 37,* 209–220.

Dubas, J. S., Gerris, J. R. M., Janssens, J. M., & Vermulst, A. (2002). Personality types in adolescents: Concurrent correlates, antecedents, and type X parenting interactions. *Journal of Adolescence, 25,* 72–92.

Eaton, W. O. (1994). Temperament, development, and the five-factor model: Lessons from activity level. In C. F. Halverson, G. A. Kohnstamm, & R. P. Martin (Eds.), *The developing structure of temperament and personality from infancy to adulthood* (pp. 173–187). Hillsdale, NJ: Erlbaum.

Egloff, B., & Schmuckle, S. C. (2002). Predictive validity of an Implicit Association Test for assessing anxiety. *Journal of Personality and Social Psychology, 83,* 1441–1455.

Ehrensaft, M., Moffitt, T. E., & Caspi, A. (2004). Clinically abusive relationships in an unselected birth cohort: Men's and women's participation and developmental antecedents. *Journal of Abnormal Psychology, 113,* 258–270.

Eid, M., Riemann, R., Angleitner, A., & Borkenau, P. (2003). Sociability and positive emotionality: Genetic and environmental contributions to the covariation between different facets of extraversion. *Journal of Personality, 71,* 319–346.

Eisenberg, N. (2000). Emotion, regulation, and moral development. *Annual Review of Psychology, 51,* 665–697.

Eisenberg, N. (2001). The core and correlates of affective social competence. *Social Development, 10,* 120–124.

Eisenberg, N., & Fabes, R. A. (1998). Prosocial development. In W. Damon (Editor-in-Chief) & N. Eisenberg (Vol. Ed.), *Handbook of child psychology: Vol. 3. Social, emotional and personality development* (5th ed., pp. 701–778). New York: Wiley.

Eisenberg, N., Fabes, R. A., Guthrie, I. K., & Reiser, M. (2000). Dispositional emotionality and regulation: Their role in predicting quality of social functioning. *Journal of Personality and Social Psychology, 78,* 136–157.

Eisenberg, N., Fabes, R. A., Miller, P. A., Fultz, J., Shell, R., Mathy, R. M., et al. (1989). Relation of sympathy and personal distress to prosocial behavior: A multimethod study. *Journal of Personality and Social Psychology, 57,* 55–66.

Eisenberg, N., Fabes, R. A., & Murphy, B. C. (1995). Relations of shyness and low sociability to regulation and emotionality. *Journal of Personality and Social Psychology, 68,* 505–517.

Eisenberg, N., Guthrie, I. K., Murphy, B. C., Shepard, S. A., Cumberland, A., & Carlo, G. (1999). Consistency and development of prosocial dispositions: A longitudinal study. *Child Development, 70,* 1360–1372.

Eisenberg, N., Shell, R., Pasternack, J., Lennon, R., Beller, R., & Mathy, R. M. (1987). Prosocial development during middle childhood: A longitudinal study. *Developmental Psychology, 23,* 712–718.

Eisenberg, N., Smith, C. L., Sadovsky, A., & Spinrad, T. L. (2004). Effortable control: Relations with emotional regulation, adjustment and socialization in childhood. In R. F. Baumeister & K. D. Vohs (Eds.), *Handbook of self-regulation: Research, theory, and applications* (pp. 259–282). New York: Guilford Press.

Eisenberg, N., Spinrad, T. L., Fabes, R. A., Reiser, M., Cumberland, A., Shepard, S. A., et al. (2004). The relations of effortful control and impulsivity to children's resiliency and adjustment. *Child Development, 75,* 25–46.

Ekselius, L., & von Knorring, L. (1999). Changes in personality traits during treatment with sertaline or citalopram. *British Journal of Psychiatry, 174,* 444–448.

Eley, T. C., Bolton, D., O'Connor, T. G., Perrin, S., Smith, P., & Plomin, R. (2003). A twin study of anxiety-related behaviors in preschool children. *Journal of Child Psychology and Psychiatry, 44,* 945–960.

Emde, R. N., & Hewitt, J. (Eds.). (2001). *Infancy to early childhood: Genetic and environmental influences on developmental change.* New York: Oxford University Press.

Entwistle, D. R., & Alexander, K. L. (1993). Entry into school. *Annual Review of Sociology, 19,* 401–423.

Erez, A., & Judge, T. A. (2001). Relationship of core self-evaluation to goal setting, motivation, and performance. *Journal of Applied Psychology, 86,* 1270–1279.

Eysenck, H. J. (1991). Dimensions of personality: 16, 5 or 3? Criteria for a taxonomic paradigm. *Personality and Individual Differences, 12,* 773–790.

Farsides, T., & Woodfield, R. (2003). Individual differences and undergraduate success: The roles of personality, intelligence, and application. *Personality and Individual Differences, 34,* 1225–1243.

Feingold, A. (1994). Gender differences in personality: A meta-analysis. *Psychological Bulletin, 116,* 429–456.

Fitzsimons, G. M., & Bargh, J. A. (2004). Automatic self-regulation. In R. F. Baumeister & K. D. Vohs (Eds.), *Handbook of self-regulation: Research, theory, and applications* (pp. 151–170). New York: Guilford Press.

Fleeson, W., Malanos, A. B., & Achille, N. M. (2002). An intraindividual process approach to the relationship between extraversion and positive affect: Is acting extraverted as "good" as being extraverted? *Journal of Personality and Social Psychology, 83,* 1409–1422.

Fletcher, G. J. O. (1993). The scientific credibility of common-sense psychology. In K. H. Craik, R. Hogan, & R. N. Wolfe (Eds.), *Fifty years of personality psychology* (pp. 251–268). New York: Plenum Press.

Foley, D. L., Eaves, L. J., Wormley, B., Silberg, J. L., Maes, H. H., Kuhn, J., et al. (2004). Childhood adversity, monoamine oxidase A genotype, and risk for conduct disorder. *Archives of General Psychiatry, 61,* 738–744.

Fox, N. A., Henderson, H. A., Rubin, K. H., Calkins, S. D., & Schmidt, L. A. (2001). Continuity and discontinuity of behavioral inhibition and exuberance: Psychophysiological and behavioral influences across the first 4 years of life. *Child Development, 72,* 1–21.

Fredrickson, B. L. (2003). The value of positive emotions. *American Scientist, 91,* 330–335.

Frick, P. J., Cornell, A. H., Barry, C. T., Bodin, S. D., & Dane, H. E. (2003). Callous-unemotional traits and conduct problems in the prediction of conduct problem severity. *Journal of Abnormal Child Psychology, 31,* 457–470.

Frick, P. J., Cornell, A. H., Bodin, S. D., Dane, H. E., Barry, C. T., & Loney, B. R. (2003). Callous-unemotional traits and developmental problems in the prediction of conduct problem severity. *Developmental Psychology, 39,* 246–260.

Friedman, H. S., Tucker, J. S., Schwartz, J. E., Tomlinson-Keasey, C., Martin, L. R., Wingard, D. L., et al. (1995). Psychosocial and behavioral predictors of longevity. *American Psychologist, 50,* 69–78.

Funder, D. C. (1991). Global straits: A neo-Allportian approach. *Psychological Science, 2,* 31–39.

Gable, S. L., Reis, H. T., & Elliot, A. J. (2000). Behavioral activation and inhibition in everyday life. *Journal of Personality and Social Psychology, 78,* 1135–1149.

Gallagher, K. C. (2002). Does child temperament moderate the influence of parenting on adjustment? *Developmental Review, 22,* 623–643.

Gallo, L. C., & Mathews, K. A. (2003). Understanding the association between socioeconomic status and physical health: Do negative emotions play a role? *Psychological Bulletin, 129,* 10–51.

Garstein, M. A., & Rothbart, M. K. (2003). Studying infant temperament via the revised infant behavior questionnaire. *Infant Behavior and Development, 26,* 64–86.

Geiger, T. C., & Crick, N. R. (2001). A developmental psychopathology perspective on vulnerability to personality disorders. In R. E. Ingram & J. M. Price (Eds.), *Vulnerability to psychpathology* (pp. 57–102). New York: Guilford Press.

George, J. M., & Zhou, J. (2001). When openness to experience and conscientiousness are related to creative behavior: An interactional approach. *Journal of Applied Psychology, 86,* 513–524.

Gifford, R. (1994). A lens-mapping framework for understanding the encoding and decoding of interpersonal dispositions in nonverbal behavior. *Journal of Personality and Social Psychology, 66,* 398–412.

Gleason, K. A., Jensen-Campbell, L. A., & Richardson, D. S. (2004). Agreeableness as a predictor of aggression in adolescence. *Aggressive Behavior, 30,* 43–61.

Goldberg, L. R. (2001). Analyses of Digman's child-personality data: Derivation of big five factor scores from each of six samples. *Journal of Personality, 69,* 709–743.

Goldsmith, H. H. (1996). Studying temperament via construction of the toddler temperament behavior assessment questionnaire. *Child Development, 67,* 218–235.

Goldsmith, H. H., Buss, A. H., Plomin, R., Rothbart, M. K., Thomas, A., Chess, S., et al. (1987). Roundtable: What is temperament? *Child Development, 67,* 218–235.

Goldsmith, H. H., Buss, K. A., & Lemery, K. S. (1997). Toddler and childhood temperament: Expanded content, stronger genetic evidence, new evidence for the importance of environment. *Developmental Psychology, 33,* 891–905.

Goldsmith, H. H., Lemery, K. S., Buss, A., & Campos, J. J. (1999). Genetic analyses of focal aspects of infant temperament. *Developmental Psychology, 35,* 972–985.

Goldsmith, H. H., Losoya, S. H., Bradshaw, D. L., & Campos, J. J. (1994). Genetics of personality: A twin study of the five-factor model and parent-offspring analyses. In C. F. Halverson, G. A. Kohnstamm, & R. P. Martin (Eds.), *The developing structure of temperament and personality from infancy to childhood* (pp. 241–266). Hillsdale, NJ: Erlbaum.

Goldsmith, H. H., & Rothbart, M. K. (1991). Contemporary instruments for assessing early temperament by questionnaire and in the laboratory. In J. Strelau & A. Angleitner (Eds.), *Explorations in temperament: International perspectives on theory and measurement* (pp. 249–272). New York: Plenum Press.

Gomez, R., Gomez, A., & Cooper, A. (2002). Neuroticism and extraversion as predictors of negative and positive information processing: Comparing Eysenck's, Gray's, and Newman's theories. *European Journal of Personality, 16,* 333–350.

Goodman, S. H., & Gotlib, I. H. (Eds.). (2002). *Children of depressed parents.* Washington, DC: American Psychological Association.

Gosling, S. D. (2001). From mice to men: What can we learn about personality from animal research? *Psychological Bulletin, 127,* 45–86.

Gosling, S. D., & John, O. P. (1999). Personality dimensions in nonhuman animals: A cross-species review. *Current Directions in Psychological Science, 8,* 69–75.

Gosling, S. D., Ko, S. J., Mannarelli, T., & Morris, M. E. (2002). A room with a cue: Personality judgments based on offices and bedrooms. *Journal of Personality and Social Psychology, 82,* 379–398.

Gosling, S. D., Kwan, V. S. Y., & John, O. P. (2003). A dog's got personality: A cross-species comparative approach to personality judgment in dogs and humans. *Journal of Personality and Social Psychology, 85,* 1161–1169.

Gottesman, I. I., & Gould, T. D. (2003). The endophenotype concept in psychiatry: Etymology and strategic intentions. *American Journal of Psychiatry, 160,* 636–645.

Gottfredson, G. D., Jones, E. M., & Holland, J. L. (1993). Personality and vocational interests: The relation of Holland's six interest dimensions to five robust dimensions of personality. *Journal of Counseling Psychology, 40,* 518–524.

Gottman, J. M. (1994). *What predicts divorce? The relationship between marital processes and marital outcomes.* Hillsdale, NJ: Erlbaum.

Gottman, J. M., Coan, J., Carrere, S., & Swanson, C. (1998). Predicting marital happiness and stability from newlywed interactions. *Journal of Marriage and Family, 60,* 5–22.

Gray, J. A. (1987). *The psychology of fear and stress* (2nd ed.). New York: McGraw-Hill.

Gray, J. A. (1990). Brain systems that mediate both emotion and cognition. *Cognition and Emotion, 4,* 269–288.

Gray, J. A., & McNaughton, N. (1996). The neuropsychology of anxiety: Reprise. In D. A. Hope (Ed.), *Nebraska Symposium on Motivation: Vol. 43. Perspectives on anxiety, panic, and fear* (pp. 61–136). Lincoln: University of Nebraska Press.

Graziano, W. G. (1994). The development of agreeableness as a dimension of personality. In C. F. Halverson, G. A. Kohnstamm, & R. P. Martin (Eds.), *The developing structure of temperament and personality from infancy to adulthood* (pp. 339–354). Hillsdale, NJ: Erlbaum.

Graziano, W. G., & Eisenberg, N. (1997). Agreeableness: A dimension of personality. In R. Hogan, J. Johnson, & S. Briggs (Eds.), *Handbook of personality psychology* (pp. 795–824). San Diego, CA: Academic Press.

Graziano, W. G., Hair, E. C., & Finch, J. F. (1997). Competitiveness mediates the link between personality and group performance. *Journal of Personality and Social Psychology, 73,* 1394–1408.

Graziano, W. G., Jensen-Campbell, L. A., & Hair, E. C. (1996). Perceiving interpersonal conflict and reacting to it: The case for agreeableness. *Journal of Personality and Social Psychology, 70,* 820–835.

Graziano, W. G., Jensen-Campbell, L. A., & Finch, J. F. (1997). The self as mediator between personality and adjustment. *Journal of Personality and Social Psychology, 73,* 392–404.

Graziano, W. G., Jensen-Campbell, L. A., & Sullivan-Logan, G. (1998). Temperament, activity, and expectations for later personality development. *Journal of Personality and Social Psychology, 74,* 1266–1277.

Graziano, W. G., & Ward, D. (1992). Probing the big five in adolescence: Personality and adjustment during a developmental transition. *Journal of Personality, 60,* 425–439.

Gross, J. J. (1999). Emotion and emotion regulation. In L. A. Pervin & O. P. John (Eds.), *Handbook of personality: Theory and research* (2nd ed., pp. 525–552). New York: Guilford Press.

Gross, J. J., Sutton, S. K., & Ketelaar, T. (1998). Relations between affect and personality: Support for the affect-level and affect-reactivity views. *Personality and Social Psychology Bulletin, 24,* 279–288.

Guerin, D. W., Gottfried, A. W., Oliver, P. H., & Thomas, C. W. (2003). *Temperament: Infancy through adolescence.* New York: Kluwer Press.

Hagekull, B., & Bohlin, G. (2003). Early temperament and attachment as predictors of the five factor model of personality. *Attachment and Human Development, 5,* 2–18.

Haigler, E. D., & Widiger, T. A. (2001). Experimental manipulation of NEO-PI-R items. *Journal of Personality Assessment, 77,* 339–358.

Halverson, C. F., Havill, V. L., Deal, J., Baker, S. R., Victor, J. B., Pavlopoulos, V., et al. (2003). Personality structure as derived from parental ratings of free descriptions of children: The inventory of child individual differences. *Journal of Personality, 71,* 995–1026.

Hampson, S. E., Andrews, J. A., Barckley, M., Lichtenstein, E., & Lee, M. E. (2000). Conscientiousness, perceived risk, and risk-reduction behaviors: A preliminary study. *Health Psychology, 19,* 247–252.

Harkness, A. R., & Lilienfeld, S. O. (1997). Individual differences science for treatment planning: Personality traits. *Psychological Assessment, 9,* 349–360.

Hart, D., Atkins, R., & Fegley, S. (2003). Personality and development in childhood: A person-centered approach. *Monographs of the Society for Research in Child Development, 68,* 1–109.

Hart, S. D., & Hare, R. D. (1997). Psychopathy: Assessment and association with criminal conduct. In D. M. Stoff, J. Breiling, & J. D. Maser (Eds.), *Handbook of antisocial behavior* (pp. 22–35). New York: Wiley.

Hartup, W. W., & Stevens, N. (1999). Friendships and adaptation across the life span. *Current Directions in Psychological Science, 8,* 76–79.

Hartup, W. W., & van Lieshout, C. F. M. (1995). Personality development in social context. *Annual Review of Psychology, 46,* 655–687.

Haselager, G. J. T., Cillesson, A. H. N., van Lieshout, C. F. M., Riksen-Walraven, J. M. A., & Hartup, W. W. (2002). Heterogeneity among peer-rejected boys across middle childhood: Developmental pathways of social behavior. *Developmental Psychology, 38,* 446–456.

Havill, V. L., Besevegis, E., & Mouroussaki, S. (1998). Agreeableness as a diachronic human trait. In C. S. Kohnstamm, C. F. Halverson, I. Mervielde, & V. L. Havill (Eds.), *Parental descriptions of child personality: Developmental antecedents of the big five* (pp. 49–64). Mahwah, NJ: Erlbaum.

Hawley, P. H. (2003). Prosocial and coercive configurations of resource control in early adolescence: A case for the well-adapted Machiavellian. *Merrill-Palmer Quarterly, 49,* 279–309.

Hay, D. F., Payne, A., & Chadwick, A. (2004). Peer relations in childhood. *Journal of Child Psychology and Psychiatry, 45,* 84–108.

Heller, D., Watson, D., & Ilies, R. (2004). The role of person versus situation in life satisfaction: A critical examination. *Psychological Bulletin, 130,* 574–600.

Helson, R., Kwan, V. S. Y., John, O. P., & Jones, C. (2002). The growing evidence of personality change in adulthood: Findings from research with personality inventories. *Journal of Research in Personality, 36,* 287–306.

Helson, R., Mitchell, V., & Moane, G. (1984). Personality and patterns of adherence and nonadherence to the social clock. *Journal of Personality and Social Psychology, 46,* 1079–1096.

Hemenover, S. H. (2003). Individual differences in rate of affect change: Studies in affective chronometry. *Journal of Personality and Social Psychology, 85,* 121–131.

Hogan, J., & Holland, B. (2003). Using theory to evaluate personality and job-performance relations: A socioanalytic perspective. *Journal of Applied Psychology, 88,* 100–112.

Hogan, J., & Ones, D. S. (1997). Conscientiousness and integrity at work. In R. Hogan, J. Johnson, & S. Briggs (Eds.), *Handbook of personality psychology* (pp. 849–870). San Diego, CA: Academic Press.

Hogan, J., & Roberts, B. W. (2004). A socioanalytic model of maturity. *Journal of Career Assessment, 12,* 207–217.

Hogan, R., & Nicholson, R. A. (1988). The meaning of personality test scores. *American Psychologist, 43,* 621–626.

Hughes, J., Cavell, T., & Grossman, P. (1997). A positive view of self: Risk or protection for aggressive children? *Development and Psychopathology, 9,* 75–94.

Hurtz, G. M., & Donovan, J. J. (2000). Personality and job performance: The big five revisited. *Journal of Applied Psychology, 85,* 869–879.

Hyde, J. S., Else-Quest, N. M., Goldsmith, H. H., & Biesanz, J. C. (2004). Children's temperament and behavior problems predict their employed mothers' work functioning. *Child Development, 75,* 580–594.

Jacobi, C., Hayward, C., de Zwaan, M., Kraemer, H. C., & Agras, W. S. (2004). Coming to terms with risk factors for eating disorders: Application of risk terminology and suggestions for a general taxonomy. *Psychological Bulletin, 130,* 19–65.

Jang, K. L., McCrae, R. R., Angleitner, A., Riemann, R., & Livesley, W. J. (1998). Heritability of facet-level traits in a cross-cultural twin sample: Support for a hierarchical model of personality. *Journal of Personality and Social Psychology, 74,* 1556–1565.

Jenkins, J. M., Rasbash, J., & O'Connor, T. G. (2003). The role of the shared family context in differential parenting. *Developmental Psychology, 39,* 99–113.

Jensen, P. S., Mrazek, D., Knapp, P. K., Steinberg, L., Pfeffer, C., Schowalter, J., et al. (1997). Evolution and revolution in child psychiatry: ADHD as a disorder of adaptation. *Journal of the American Academy of Child and Adolescent Psychiatry, 36,* 1672–1679.

Jensen-Campbell, L. A., Gleason, K. A., Adams, R., & Malcolm, K. T. (2003). Interpersonal conflict, Agreeableness, and personality development. *Journal of Personality, 71,* 1059–1085.

Jensen-Campbell, L. A., & Graziano, W. G. (2001). Agreeableness as a moderator of interpersonal conflict. *Journal of Personality, 69,* 323–362.

Jensen-Campbell, L. A., Graziano, W. G., & Hair, E. C. (1996). Personality and relationships as moderators of interpersonal conflict in adolescence. *Merrill-Palmer Quarterly, 42,* 148–164.

Jockin, V., McGue, M., & Lykken, D. T. (1996). Personality and divorce: A genetic analysis. *Journal of Personality and Social Psychology, 71,* 288–299.

John, O. P., Caspi, A., Robins, R. W., Moffitt, T. E., & Stouthamer-Loeber, M. (1994). The "little five": Exploring the five-factor model of personality in adolescent boys. *Child Development, 65,* 160–178.

John, O. P., & Robins, R. W. (1993). Gordon Allport: Father and critic of the five-factor model. In K. H. Craik, R. T. Hogan, & R. N. Wolfe (Eds.), *Fifty years of personality research* (pp. 215–236). New York: Plenum Press.

John, O. P., & Srivastava, S. (1999). The big five trait taxonomy: History, measurement, and theoretical perspectives. In L. A. Pervin & O. P. John (Eds.), *Handbook of personality: Theory and research* (2nd ed., pp. 102–138). New York: Guilford Press.

Jost, J. T., Glaser, J., Kruglanski, A. W., & Sulloway, F. J. (2003). Political conservatism as motivated social cognition. *Psychological Bulletin, 129,* 339–375.

Judge, T. A., Erez, A., Bono, J. E., & Thoresen, C. J. (2002). Are measures of self-esteem, neuroticism, locus of control, and generalized self-efficacy indicators of a common core construct? *Journal of Personality and Social Psychology, 83,* 693–710.

Judge, T. A., Higgins, C. A., Thoresen, C. J., & Barrick, M. R. (1999). The big five personality traits, general mental ability, and career success across the life-span. *Personnel Psychology, 52,* 621–652.

Judge, T. A., & Ilies, R. (2002). Relationship of personality to performance motivation: A meta-analytic review. *Journal of Applied Psychology, 87,* 797–807.

Kagan, J. (1969). The three faces of continuity in human development. In D. A. Goslin (Ed.), *Handbook of socialization theory and research* (pp. 983–1002). Chicago: Rand McNally.

Kagan, J. (1998). Biology and the child. In W. Damon (Editor-in-Chief) & N. Eisenberg (Vol. Ed.), *Handbook of child psychology: Vol. 3. Social, emotional and personality development* (5th ed., pp. 177–235). New York: Wiley.

Kagan, J., & Snidman, N. (1999). Early childhood predictors of adult anxiety disorders. *Biological Psychiatry, 46,* 1536–1541.

Kagan, J., Snidman, N., & Arcus, D. (1998). Childhood derivatives of high and low reactivity in infancy. *Child Development, 69,* 1483–1493.

Kagan, J., Snidman, N., McManis, M., Woodward, S., & Hardway, C. (2002). One measure, one meaning: Multiple measures, clearer meaning. *Development and Psychopathology, 14,* 463–475.

Karney, B. R., & Bradbury, T. N. (1995). The longitudinal course of marital quality and stability: A review of theory, method and research. *Psychological Bulletin, 118,* 3–34.

Kasch, K. L., Rottenburg, J., Arnow, B. A., & Gotlib, I. H. (2002). Behavior activation and inhibition systems and the severity of depression. *Journal of Abnormal Psychology, 111,* 589–597.

Kaufman, J., Yang, B.-Z., Douglas-Palumberi, H., Houshyar, S., Lipschitz, D., Krystal, J. H., et al. (2004). Social supports and serotonin transporter gene moderate depression in maltreated children. *Proceedings of the National Academy of Sciences, USA, 101,* 17316–17321.

Keel, P. K., Fichter, M., Quadflieg, N., Bulik, C. M., Baxter, M. G., Thornton, L., et al. (2004). Application of a latent class analysis to empirically define eating disorder phenotypes. *Archives of General Psychiatry, 61,* 192–200.

Keltner, D. (1998). Facial expressions of emotion and personality. In C. Magai & S. H. McFadden (Eds.), *Handbook of emotion, adult development, and ageing* (pp. 385–401). San Diego, CA: Academic Press.

Keltner, D., Ekman, P., Gonzaga, G. C., & Beer, J. (2003). Facial expression of emotion. In R. J. Davidson, K. R. Scherer, & H. H. Goldsmith (Eds.), *Handbook of affective sciences* (pp. 415–432). New York: Oxford University Press.

Keltner, D., Moffitt, T. E., & Stouthamer-Loeber, M. (1995). Facial expressions of emotion and psychopathology in adolescent males. *Journal of Abnormal Psychology, 104,* 644–652.

Kendler, K. S., Kuhn, J. W., Vittum, J., Prescott, C. A., & Riley, B. (2005). The interaction of stressful life events and a serotonin transporter polymorphism in the prediction of episodes of major depression: A replication. *Archives of General Psychiatry, 62,* 529–535.

Kendler, K. S., Neale, M. C., Sullivan, P., Corey, L. A., Gardner, C. O., & Prescott, C. A. (1999). A population-based twin study in women of smoking initiation and dependence. *Psychological Medicine, 29,* 299–308.

Kenford, S. L., Smith, S. S., Wetter, D. W., Jorenby, D. E., Fiore, M. C., & Baker, T. B. (2002). Predicting relapse back to smoking: Contrasting affective and physical models of dependence. *Journal of Consulting and Clinical Psychology, 70,* 216–227.

Kernberg, P. F., Weiner, A. S., & Bardenstein, K. K. (2000). *Personality disorders in children and adolescents.* New York: Basic Books.

Kim-Cohen, J., Moffitt, T. E., Caspi, A., & Taylor, A. (2004). Genetic and environmental processes in young children's resilience and vulnerability to socioeconomic deprivation. *Child Development, 75,* 651–668.

Kindlon, D., Mezzacappa, E., & Earls, F. (1995). Psychometric properties of impulsivity measures: Temporal stability, validity and factor structure. *Journal of Child Psychology and Psychiatry, 36,* 645–661.

Kling, K. C., Ryff, C. D., Love, G., & Essex, M. (2003). Exploring the influence of personality on depressive symptoms and self-esteem across a significant life transition. *Journal of Personality and Social Psychology, 85,* 922–932.

Knutson, B., Wolkowitz, O. M., Cole, S. W., Chan, T., Morre, E. A., Johnson, R. C., et al. (1998). Selective alteration of personality and social behavior by serotonergic intervention. *American Journal of Psychiatry, 155,* 373–379.

Kochanska, G. (1997). Multiple pathways to conscience for children with different temperaments: From toddlerhood to age 5. *Developmental Psychology, 33,* 228–240.

Kochanska, G., Clark, L., & Goldman, M. (1997). Implications of mothers' personality for parenting and their young children's developmental outcomes. *Journal of Personality, 65,* 389–420.

Kochanska, G., Coy, K. C., & Murray, K. T. (2001). The development of self-regulation in the first 4 years of life. *Child Development, 72,* 1091–1111.

Kochanska, G., Coy, K. C., Tjebkes, T. L., & Husarek, S. J. (1998). Individual differences in emotionality in infancy. *Child Development, 64,* 375–390.

Kochanska, G., Friesenborg, A. E., Lange, L. A., & Martel, M. M. (2004). Parents' personality and infants' temperament as contributors to their emerging relationship. *Journal of Personality and Social Psychology, 86,* 744–759.

Kochanska, G., Gross, J. N., Lin, M.-H., & Nichols, K. E. (2002). Guilt in young children: Development, determinants, and relations with a broader system of standards. *Child Development, 73,* 461–482.

Kochanska, G., & Knaack, A. (2003). Effortful control as a personality characteristic of young children: Antecedents, correlates, and consequences. *Journal of Personality, 71,* 1087–1112.

Kochanska, G., Murray, K. T., & Coy, K. C. (1997). Inhibitory control as a contributor to conscience in childhood: From toddler to early school age. *Child Development, 68,* 263–277.

Kochanska, G., Murray, K. T., & Harlan, E. T. (2000). Effortful control in early childhood: Continuity and change, antecedents, and implications for social development. *Developmental Psychology, 36,* 220–232.

Kochanska, G., Murray, K. T., Jacques, T. Y., Koenig, A. L., & Vandegeest, K. (1996). Inhibitory control in young children and its role in emerging internalization. *Child Development, 67,* 490–507.

Kohnstamm, G. A., Halverson, C. F., Mervielde, I., & Havill, V. L. (1998). *Parental descriptions of child personality: Developmental antecedents of the big five?* Mahwah, NJ: Erlbaum.

Kokko, K., Bergman, L. R., & Pulkkinen, L. (2003). Child personality characteristics and selection into long-term unemployment in Finnish and Swedish longitudinal studies. *International Journal of Behavioral Development, 27,* 134–144.

Kokko, K., & Pulkkinen, L. (2000). Aggression in childhood and long-term unemployment in adulthood: A cycle of maladaptation and some protective factors. *Developmental Psychology, 36,* 463–472.

Korner, A. F., Hutchinson, C. A., Koperski, J., Kraemer, H. C., Berkowitz, R. L., & Agras, W. S. (1985). Relation between neonatal and later activity and temperament. *Child Development, 52,* 83–90.

Kraemer, H. C., Kazdin, A. E., Offord, D. R., Kessler, R. C., Jensen, P. S., & Kupfer, D. J. (1997). Coming to terms with the terms of risk. *Archives of General Psychiatry, 54,* 337–343.

Krueger, R. F., Hicks, B. M., & McGue, M. (2001). Altruism and antisocial behavior: Independent tendencies, unique personality correlates, distinct etiologies. *Psychological Science, 12,* 397–402.

Krueger, R. F., Hicks, B. M., Patrick, C. J., Carlson, S. R., Ianoco, W. G., & McGue, M. (2002). Etiologic connections among substance dependence, antisocial behavior and personality: Modeling the external spectrum. *Journal of Abnormal Psychology, 111,* 411–424.

Kupfer, D. J., First, M. B., & Regier, D. A. (2002). *A research agenda for* DSM-V. Arlington, VA: American Psychiatric Publishing.

Lamb, M. E., Chuang, S. S., Wessels, H., Broberg, A. G., & Hwang, C. P. (2002). Emergence and construct validation of the big five factors in early childhood: A longitudinal analysis of their ontogeny in Sweden. *Child Development, 73,* 1517–1524.

Larsen, R. J., & Prizmic, Z. (2004). Affect regulation. In R. F. Baumeister & K. D. Vohs (Eds.), *Handbook of self-regulation: Research, theory, and applications* (pp. 40–61). New York: Guilford Press.

Laurent, J., & Ettelson, R. (2001). An examination of the tripartite model of anxiety and depression and its application to youth. *Clinical Child and Family Psychology Review, 4,* 209–230.

Laursen, B., Pulkkinen, L., & Adams, R. (2002). The antecedents and correlates of agreeableness in adulthood. *Developmental Psychology, 38,* 591–603.

Lemerise, E. A., & Arsenio, W. F. (2000). An integrated model of emotion processes and cognition in social information processing. *Child Development, 71,* 107–118.

Lemery, K. S., Goldsmith, H. H., Klinnert, M. D., & Mrazek, D. A. (1999). Developmental models of infant and childhood temperament. *Developmental Psychology, 35,* 189–204.

Lengua, L. J. (2002). The contribution of emotionality and self-regulation to the understanding of children's responses to multiple risk. *Child Development, 73,* 144–161.

Lengua, L. J., & Long, A. C. (2002). The role of emotionality and self-regulation in the appraisal-coping process: Tests of direct and moderating effects. *Journal of Applied Developmental Psychology, 23,* 471–493.

Lerner, J. S., & Keltner, D. (2000). Beyond valence: Toward a model of emotion-specific influences on judgment and choice. *Cognition and Emotion, 14,* 473–193.

Levy, F., Hay, D. A., McStephen, M., Wood, C., & Waldman, I. (1997). Attention-deficit hyperactivity disorder: A category or continuum? *Journal of the American Academy of Child and Adolescent Psychiatry, 36,* 737–744.

Lewis, M. (2000). The emergence of human emotions. In M. Lewis & J. M. Haviland-Jones (Eds.), *Handbook of emotions* (2nd ed., pp. 265–280). New York: Guilford Press.

Lewis, M. (2001). Issues in the study of personality development. *Psychological Inquiry, 12,* 67–83.

Lilienfeld, S. O. (2003). Comorbidity between and within childhood externalizing and internalizing disorders: Reflections and directions. *Journal of Abnormal Child Psychology, 31,* 285–291.

Lin, E. K., Bugental, D. B., Turek, V., Martorell, G. A., & Olster, D. H. (2002). Children's vocal properties as mobilizers of stress-related physiological responses in adults. *Personality and Social Psychology Bulletin, 28,* 346–357.

Livesley, W. J., Jang, K. L., & Vernon, P. A. (2003). Genetic basis of personality structure. In T. Millon & M. J. Lerner (Eds.), *Handbook of psychology: Personality and social psychology* (pp. 59–83). New York: Wiley.

Livson, N., & Peskin, H. (1980). Perspectives on adolescence from longitudinal research. In J. Adelson (Ed.), *Handbook of adolescent psychology* (pp. 47–98). New York: Wiley.

Loeber, R., & Hay, D. (1997). Key issues in the development of aggression and violence from childhood to early adulthood. *Annual Review of Psychology, 48,* 371–410.

Loevinger, J. (1957). Objective tests as instruments of psychological theory. *Psychological Reports, 3,* 635–694.

Lohmueller, K. E., Pearce, C. L., Pike, M., Lander, E. S., & Hirschhorn, J. N. (2003). Meta-analysis of genetic association studies supports a contribution of common variants to susceptibility to common disease. *Nature Genetics, 33,* 177–182.

Lonigan, C. J., Phillips, B. M., & Hooe, E. S. (2003). Relations of positive and negative affectivity to anxiety and depression in children: Evidence from a latent variable longitudinal study. *Journal of Consulting and Clinical Psychology, 71,* 464–481.

Losoya, S. H., Callor, S., Rowe, D. C., & Goldsmith, H. H. (1977). Origins of familial similarity in parenting: A study of twins and adoptive siblings. *Developmental Psychology, 33,* 1012–1023.

Low, K. S. D., Yoon, M., Roberts, B. W., & Rounds, J. (2005). The stability on interests from early adolescence to middle adulthood: A quantitative review of longitudinal studies. *Psychological Bulletin, 131,* 713–737.

Lucas, R. E., & Baird, B. M. (2004). Extraversion and emotional reactivity. *Journal of Personality and Social Psychology, 86,* 473–485.

Lucas, R. E., & Fujita, F. (2000). Factors influencing the relation between extraversion and pleasant affect. *Journal of Personality and Social Psychology, 79,* 1039–1056.

Luthar, S. S., Cicchetti, D., & Becker, B. (2000). The construct of resilience: A critical evaluation and guidelines for future work. *Child Development, 71,* 562.

Lykken, D. T., & Tellegen, A. (1996). Happiness is a stochastic phenomenon. *Psychological Science, 7,* 186–189.

Lytton, H. (1990). Child and parent effects in boys' conduct disorder: A reinterpretation. *Developmental Psychology, 26,* 683–697.

MacCoon, D. G., Wallace, J. F., & Newman, J. P. (2004). Self-regulation: Context-appropriate balanced attention. In R. F. Baumeister & K. D. Vohs (Eds.), *Handbook of self-regulation: Research, theory, and applications* (pp. 422–444). New York: Guilford Press.

MacDonald, K. (1992). Warmth as a developmental construct: An evolutionary analysis. *Child Development, 63,* 753–773.

MacDonald, K. (1995). Evolution, the five-factor model, and levels of personality. *Journal of Personality, 63,* 525–567.

Magnus, K., Diener, E., Fujita, F., & Pavot, W. (1993). Extraversion and neuroticism as predictors of objective life events: A longitudinal analysis. *Journal of Personality and Social Psychology, 65,* 525–567.

Markey, P. M., Markey, C. N., & Tinsley, B. J. (2004). Children's behavioral manifestations of the five-factor model of personality. *Personality and Social Psychology Bulletin, 30,* 423–432.

Markey, P. M., Markey, C. N., Tinsley, B. J., & Ericksen, A. J. (2002). A preliminary validation of preadolescents' self-reports using the five-factor model of personality. *Journal of Research in Personality, 36,* 173–181.

Markon, K. E., Krueger, R. F., & Watson, D. (2005). Delineating the structure of normal and abnormal personality: An integrative hierarchical approach. *Journal of Personality and Social Psychology, 88,* 139–157.

Martin, M., Boomsma, D., & Machin, G. (1997). A twin-pronged attack on complex traits. *Nature Genetics, 17,* 387–392.

Martin, R., Watson, D., & Wan, C. K. (2000). A three-factor model of trait anger: Dimensions of affect, behavior, and cognition. *Journal of Personality, 68,* 869–897.

Martin, R. P., Wisenbaker, J., & Huttunen, M. (1994). Review of factor analytic studies of temperament measures based on the Thomas-Chess structural model: Implications for the big five. In C. F. Halverson, G. A. Kohnstamm, & R. P. Martin (Eds.), *The de-*

veloping structure of temperament and personality from infancy to adulthood (pp. 157–172). Hillsdale, NJ: Erlbaum.

Masten, A. S. (1999). Resilience comes of age: Reflections on the past and outlook for the next generation of research. In M. D. Glantz & J. L. Johnson (Eds.), *Resilience and development: Positive life outcomes* (pp. 281–296). New York: Kluwer Press.

Masten, A. S. (2001). Ordinary magic: Resilience processes in development. *American Psychologist, 56,* 227–238.

Masten, A. S., & Coatsworth, J. D. (1995). Competence, resilience, and psychopathology. In D. Cicchetti & D. Cohen (Eds.), *Developmental psychopathology: Vol. 2. Risk, disorder, and adaptation* (pp. 715–752). New York: Wiley.

Masten, A. S., & Coatsworth, J. D. (1998). The development of competence in favorable and unfavorable environments: Lessons from research on successful children. *American Psychologist, 53,* 205–220.

Masten, A. S., Hubbard, J. J., Gest, S. D., Tellegen, A., Garmezy, N., & Ramirez, M. L. (1999). Competence in the context of adversity: Pathways to resilience and maladaptation from childhood to late adolescence. *Development and Psychopathology, 11,* 143–169.

Masten, A. S., Neeman, J., & Andenas, S. (1994). Life events and adjustment in adolescents: The significance of event independence, desirability, and chronicity. *Journal of Research on Adolescence, 4,* 71–97.

Matas, L., Arend, R., & Sroufe, L. A. (1978). Continuity of adaptation in the second year: The relationship between quality of attachment and later competence. *Child Development, 49,* 547–556.

Matthews, G., Derryberry, D., & Siegle, G. J. (2000). Personality and emotion: Cognitive science perspectives. In S. E. Hampson (Ed.), *Advances in personality psychology* (pp. 199–237). Philadelphia: Psychology Press.

Maziade, M., Caron, C., Cote, R., Merette, C., Bernier, H., Laplante, B., et al. (1990). Psychiatric status of adolescents who had extreme temperaments at age 7. *American Journal of Psychiatry, 147,* 1531–1536.

McAdams, D. P. (1995). What do we know when we know a person? *Journal of Personality, 63,* 365–376.

McAdams, D. P., Anyidoho, N. A., Brown, C., Huang, Y. T., Kaplan, B., & Machado, M. A. (2004). Traits and stories: Links between dispositional and narrative features of personality. *Journal of Personality, 72,* 761–784.

McCartney, K., & Rosenthal, R. (2000). Effect size, practical importance, and social policy for children. *Child Development, 71,* 173–180.

McCrae, R. R. (1996). Social consequences of experiential openness. *Psychological Bulletin, 120,* 761–784.

McCrae, R. R., & Costa, P. T. J. (1994). The stability of personality: Observation and evaluations. *Current Directions in Psychological Science, 3,* 173–175.

McCrae, R. R., & Costa, P. T. (1997). Conceptions and correlates of openness to experience. In J. Hogan, J. Johnson, & S. Briggs (Eds.), *Handbook of personality: Theory and research* (pp. 825–847). San Diego, CA: Academic.

McCrae, R. R., & Costa, P. T. (1999). A five-factor theory of personality. In L. A. Pervin & O. P. John (Eds.), *Handbook of personality: Theory and research* (pp. 139–153). New York: Guilford Press.

McCrae, R. R., & Costa, P. T. (2004). A contemplated revision of the NEO five-factor inventory. *Personality and Individual Differences, 36,* 587–596.

McCrae, R. R., Costa, P. T., & Busch, C. M. (1986). Evaluating comprehensiveness in personality systems: The California Q-set and the five-factor model. *Journal of Personality and Social Psychology, 54,* 430–446.

McCrae, R. R., Costa, P. T., Ostendorf, F., Angleitner, A., Hrebickova, H., Avia, M. D., et al. (2000). Nature over nurture: Temperament, personality, and life span development. *Journal of Personality and Social Psychology, 78,* 173–186.

McCrae, R. R., Costa, P. T., Terracciano, A., Parker, W. D., Mills, C. J., De Fruyt, F., et al. (2002). Personality trait development from age 12 to age 18: Longitudinal, cross-sectional and cross-cultural analyses. *Journal of Personality and Social Psychology, 83,* 1456–1468.

McGue, M., Bacon, S., & Lykken, D. T. (1993). Personality stability and change in early childhood: A behavioral genetic analysis. *Developmental Psychology, 32,* 604–613.

McHale, S. M., Crouter, A. C., & Tucker, C. J. (2001). Free-time activities in middle childhood: Links with adjustment in early adolescence. *Child Development, 72,* 1764–1778.

Measelle, J., Ablow, J. C., Cowan, P. A., & Cowen, C. P. (1998). Assessing young children's views of their academic, social, and emotional lives: An evaluation of the self-perception scales of the Berkeley puppet interview. *Child Development, 69,* 1556–1576.

Measelle, J., John, O. P., Ablow, J., Cowan, P. A., & Cowan, C. P. (2005). Can children provide coherent, stable, and valid self-reports on the big five dimensions? *Journal of Personality and Social Psychology, 89,* 90–106.

Meehl, P. E. (1978). Theoretical risks and tabular asterisks: Sir Karl, Sir Roland, and the slow progress of soft psychology. *Journal of Consulting and Clinical Psychology, 46,* 806–834.

Meehl, P. E. (1986). What social scientists don't understand. In D. W. Fiske & R. A. Shweder (Eds.), *Metatheory in social science* (pp. 315–338). Chicago: University of Chicago Press.

Meier, G. H., & Robinson, M. D. (2004). Does quick to blame mean quick to anger? The role of agreeableness in dissociating blame and anger. *Personality and Social Psychology Bulletin, 30,* 856–867.

Merikangas, K., & Risch, N. (2003). Will the genomics revolution revolutionize psychiatry? *American Journal of Psychiatry, 160,* 625–635.

Mervielde, I., Buyst, V., & De Fruyt, F. (1995). The validity of the big five as a model for teachers' ratings of individual differences among children aged 4 to 12 years. *Personality and Individual Differences, 18,* 525–534.

Mervielde, I., De Clerq, B., De Fruyt, F., & van Leeuwen, K. (2005). Temperament, personality and developmental psychopathology as childhood antecedents of personality disorders. *Journal of Personality Disorders, 19,* 171–201.

Mervielde, I., & De Fruyt, F. (1999). Construction of the Hierarchical Personality Inventory for Children (HiPIC). In I. Mervielde, I. L. Deary, F. De Fruyt, & F. Ostendorf (Eds.), *Personality psychology in Europe: Proceedings of the eighth European conference on personality psychology* (pp. 107–127). Tilburg, The Netherlands: Tilburg University Press.

Mervielde, I., & De Fruyt, F. (2002). Assessing children's traits with the hierarchical personality inventory for children. In B. De Raad & M. Perugini (Eds.), *Big five assessment* (pp. 129–142). Ashland, OH: Hogrefe & Huber.

Mervielde, I., De Fruyt, F., & Jarmuz, S. (1998). Linking openness and intellect in childhood and adulthood. In C. S. Kohnstamm, C. F. Halverson, I. Mervielde, & V. L. Havill (Eds.), *Parental descriptions of child personality: Developmental antecedents of the big five?* (pp. 105–142). Mahwah, NJ: Erlbaum.

Metsapelto, R. L., & Pulkkinen, L. (2003). Personality traits and parenting: Neuroticism, extraversion, and openness to experience as discriminative factors. *European Journal of Personality, 17,* 59–78.

Meyer, G. J., Finn, S. E., Eyde, L. D., Kay, G. G., Moreland, K. L., Kubiszyn, T. W., et al. (2001). Psychological testing and psychological assessment: A review of evidence and issues. *American Psychologist, 56,* 128–165.

Miech, R., Essex, M. J., & Goldsmith, H. H. (2001). Self-regulation as a mediator of the status-attainment process: Evidence from early childhood. *Sociology of Education, 74,* 102–120.

Miller, J. D., Lynam, D. R., Widiger, T. A., & Leukefeld, C. (2001). Personality disorders as extreme variants of common personality dimensions: Can the five-factor model adequately represent psychopathy? *Journal of Personality, 69,* 253–276.

Miller, T. Q., Smith, T. W., Turner, C. W., Guijarro, M. L., & Hallet, A. J. (1996). A meta-analytic review of research on hostility and physical health. *Psychological Bulletin, 119,* 322–348.

Mineka, S., Rafaeli, E., & Yovel, I. (2003). Cognitive biases in emotional disorders: Information processing and social-cognitive perspectives. In R. J. Davidson, K. R. Scherer, & H. H. Goldsmith (Eds.), *Handbook of affective sciences* (pp. 976–1009). New York: Oxford University Press.

Mischel, W. (1990). Personality dispositions revisited and revised. In L. Pervin (Ed.), *Handbook of personality* (pp. 111–134). New York: Guilford Press.

Mischel, W., & Ayduk, O. (2004). Willpower in a cognitive-effective processing system: The dynamics of delay of gratification. In R. F. Baumeister (Ed.), *Handbook of self-regulation: Research, theory, and applications* (pp. 99–129). New York: Guilford Press.

Moffitt, T. E., Caspi, A., & Rutter, M. (2005). Strategy for investigating interactions between measured genes and measured environments. *Archives of General Psychiatry, 67,* 473–481.

Moffitt, T. E., Robins, R. W., & Caspi, A. (2001). A couples analysis of partner abuse with implications for abuse prevention. *Criminology and Public Policy, 1,* 401–432.

Moon, H., Hollenbeck, J. R., Humphrey, S. E., & Maue, B. (2003). The tripartite model of neuroticism and the suppression of depression and anxiety within an escalation of commitment dilemma. *Journal of Personality, 71,* 345–368.

Morison, P., & Masten, A. S. (1991). Peer reputation in middle childhood as a predictor of adaptation in adolescence: A 7-year follow-up. *Child Development, 62,* 991–1007.

Moskowitz, D. S., & Zuroff, D. C. (2004). Flux, pulse and spin: Dynamic additions to the personality lexicon. *Journal of Personality and Social Psychology, 86,* 880–893.

Mroczek, D. K., & Spiro, A. (2003). Modeling intraindividual change in personality traits: Findings from the Normative Aging Study. *Journal of Gerontology: Psychological Science, 58B,* 153–165.

Munafo, M. R., Clark, T. G., Moore, L. R., Payne, E., Walton, R., & Flint, J. (2003). Genetic polymorphisms and personality in healthy adults: A systematic review and meta-analysis. *Molecular Psychiatry, 8,* 471–484.

Muris, P., Schmidt, H., Merckelbach, H., & Schouten, E. (2001). The structure of negative emotions in adolescents. *Journal of Abnormal Child Psychology, 29,* 331–337.

Neitzel, C., & Stright, A. D. (2004). Parenting behaviors during child problem solving: The roles of child temperament, mother education and personality, and the problem-solving context. *International Journal of Behavioral Development, 28,* 166–179.

Nigg, J. T. (2000). Inhibition/disinhibition in developmental psychopathology: Views from cognitive and personality psychology and a working inhibition taxonomy. *Psychological Bulletin, 126,* 220–246.

Nigg, J. T., John, O. P., Blaskey, L. G., Huang-Pollock, C. L., Willcutt, E. G., Hinshaw, S. P., et al. (2002). Big five dimensions and ADHD symptoms: Links between personality traits and clinical symptoms. *Journal of Personality and Social Psychology, 83,* 451–469.

O'Brien, B. S., & Frick, P. J. (1996). Reward dominance: Associations with anxiety, conduct problems, and psychopathy in children. *Journal of Abnormal Child Psychology, 24,* 223–240.

O'Brien, T. B., & DeLongis, A. (1996). The interactional context of problem-, emotion-, and relationship-focused coping: The role of the big five personality factors. *Journal of Personality, 64,* 775–813.

O'Connor, T. G., Deater-Deckard, K., Fulker, D. W., Rutter, M., & Plomin, R. (1998). Genotype-environment correlations in late childhood and early adolescence: Antisocial behavioral problems in coercive parenting. *Developmental Psychology, 34,* 970–981.

Ormel, J., Oldehinkel, A. J., & Vollebergh, W. (2004). Vulnerability before, during, and after a major depressive episode: A three-wave population-based study. *Archives of General Psychiatry, 61,* 990–996.

Ozer, D. J. (1986). *Consistency in personality: A methodological framework.* New York: Springer.

Ozer, D. J., & Gjerde, P. F. (1989). Patterns of personality consistency and change from childhood through adolescence. *Journal of Personality, 57,* 483–507.

Pardini, D. A., Lochman, J. E., & Frick, P. J. (2003). Callous/unemotional traits and social-cognitive processes in adjucated youths. *Journal of the American Academy of Child and Adolescent Psychiatry, 42,* 364–371.

Park, S. Y., Belsky, J., Putnam, S., & Crnic, K. (1997). Infant emotionality, parenting, and 3-year inhibition: Exploring stability and lawful discontinuity in a male sample. *Developmental Psychology, 33,* 218–227.

Parke, R. D. (2004). Development in the family. *Annual Review of Psychology, 55,* 365–399.

Patterson, C., Kupersmidt, J., & Griesler, P. (1990). Children's perceptions of self and of relationships with others as a function of sociometric status. *Child Development, 61,* 1335–1349.

Paunonen, S. V., & Ashton, M. C. (2001). Big five factors and facets and the prediction of behavior. *Journal of Personality and Social Psychology, 81,* 524–539.

Peabody, D., & De Raad, B. (2002). The substantive nature of psycholexical personality factors: A comparison across languages. *Journal of Personality and Social Psychology, 83,* 983–997.

Pederson, N. L., & Reynolds, C. A. (1998). Stability and change in adult personality: Genetic and environmental components. *European Journal of Personality, 12,* 365–386.

Pellegrini, A. D., & Bartini, M. (2001). Dominance in early adolescent boys: Affiliative and aggressive dimensions and possible functions. *Merrill-Palmer Quarterly, 47,* 142–163.

Peterson, J. B., Smith, K. W., & Carson, S. (2002). Openness and extraversion are associated with reduced latent inhibition: Replication and commentary. *Personality and Individual Differences, 33,* 1137–1147.

Pfeifer, M., Goldsmith, H. H., Davidson, R. J., & Rickman, M. (2002). Continuity and change in inhibited and uninhibited children. *Child Development, 73,* 1474–1485.

Phillips, K., & Matheny, A. P. J. (1997). Evidence for genetic influence on both cross-situation and situation-specific components of behavior. *Journal of Personality and Social Psychology, 73,* 129–138.

Pickles, A., & Angold, A. (2003). Natural categories or fundamental dimensions: On carving nature at the joints and the rearticulation of psychopathology. *Development and Psychopathology, 15,* 529–551.

Pike, A., & Atzaba-Poria, N. (2003). Do sibling and friend relationships share the same temperamental origins? *Journal of Child Psychology and Psychiatry, 44,* 598–611.

Plomin, R., & Bergeman, C. S. (1991). The nature of nurture: Genetic influences on "environmental" measures. *Behavioral and Brain Sciences, 14,* 373–386.

Plomin, R., & Caspi, A. (1999). Behavioral genetics and personality. In L. A. Pervin & O. P. John (Eds.), *Handbook of personality theory and research* (pp. 251–276). New York: Guilford Press.

Plomin, R., Corley, R., Caspi, A., Fulker, D. W., & DeFries, J. C. (1998). Adoption results for self-reported personality: Evidence of non-additive genetic effects? *Journal of Personality and Social Psychology, 75,* 211–218.

Plomin, R., & Crabbe, J. (2000). DNA. *Psychological Bulletin, 126,* 806–828.

Plomin, R., & Daniels, D. (1987). Why are children in the same family so different from one another? *Behavioral and Brain Sciences, 10,* 1–16.

Plomin, R., Fulker, D. W., Corley, R., & DeFries, J. C. (1997). Nature, nurture, and cognitive development from 1 to 16 years: A parent-offspring study. *Psychological Science, 8,* 442–447.

Plomin, R., & McGuffin, P. (2003). Psychopathology in the postgenomic era. *Annual Review of Psychology, 54,* 205–228.

Pomerantz, E. M., & Rudolph, K. D. (2003). What ensues from emotional distress? Implications for competence estimation. *Child Development, 74,* 329–345.

Posner, M. I., & Rothbart, M. K. (2000). Developing mechanisms of self-regulation. *Development and Psychopathology, 12,* 427–441.

Prinzie, P., Onghena, P., Hellinckx, W., Grietens, H., Ghesquiere, P., & Colpin, H. (2004). Parent and child personality characteristics as predictors of negative discipline and externalizing behavioral problems in children. *European Journal of Personality, 18,* 73–102.

Prior, M., Smart, D., Sanson, A., & Oberklaid, F. (2000). Does shy-inhibited temperament in childhood lead to anxiety problems in adolescence? *Journal of the American Academy of Child and Adolescent Psychiatry, 39,* 461–468.

Putnam, S. P., Ellis, L. K., & Rothbart, M. K. (2001). The structure of temperament from infancy through adolescence. In A. Eliasz & A. Angleneiter (Eds.), *Advances in research on temperament* (pp. 165–182). Miami, FL: Pabst Science.

Putnam, S. P., Sanson, A. V., & Rothbart, M. K. (2002). Child temperament and parenting. In M. Bornstein (Ed.), *Handbook of parenting: Vol. 1. Children and parenting* (2nd ed., pp. 255–277). Mahwah, NJ: Erlbaum.

Raine, A., Reynolds, C., Venables, P. H., & Mednick, S. A. (2002). Stimulation seeking and intelligence: A prospective longitudinal study. *Journal of Personality and Social Psychology, 82,* 674.

Raine, A., Reynolds, C., Venables, P. H., Mednick, S. A., & Farrington, D. P. (1998). Fearlessness, stimulation-seeking, and large body size at age 3 years as early predispositions to childhood aggression at age 11 years. *Archives of General Psychiatry, 55,* 745–751.

Reimann, R., Angleitner, A., & Strelau, J. (1997). Genetic and environmental influences on personality: A study of twins reared together using the self- and peer report NEO-FFI scales. *Journal of Personality, 65,* 449–476.

Reiss, H. T., Capobianco, A., & Tsai, F.-T. (2002). Finding the person in personal relationships. *Journal of Personality, 70,* 813–850.

Resing, W. C. M., Bleichrodt, N., & Dekker, P. H. (1999). Measuring personality traits in the classroom. *European Journal of Personality, 13,* 493–509.

Reynolds, S. K., & Clark, L. A. (2001). Predicting dimensions of personality disorder from domains and facets of the five-factor model. *Journal of Personality, 69,* 199–222.

Roberts, B. W., Bogg, T., Walton, K. E., Chernyshenko, O. S., & Stark, S. E. (2004). A lexical investigation of the lower-order structure of conscientiousness. *Journal of Research in Personality, 38,* 164–178.

Roberts, B. W., Caspi, A., & Moffitt, T. E. (2001). The kids are alright: Growth and stability in personality development from adolescence to adulthood. *Journal of Personality and Social Psychology, 81,* 582–583.

Roberts, B. W., Caspi, A., & Moffitt, T. E. (2003). Work experiences and personality development in young adulthood. *Journal of Personality and Social Psychology, 84,* 582–593.

Roberts, B. W., & DelVecchio, W. F. (2000). The rank-order consistency of personality traits from childhood to old age: A quantitative review of longitudinal studies. *Psychological Bulletin, 126,* 25–30.

Roberts, B. W., Walton, K., & Viechtbauer, W. (in press). Patterns in mean-level change in personality traits across the life-course: A meta-analysis of longitudinal studies. *Psychological Bulletin.*

Robins, R. W., Caspi, A., & Moffitt, T. E. (2002). It's not just who you're with, it's who you are: Personality and relationship experiences across multiple relationships. *Journal of Personality, 70,* 925–964.

Robins, R. W., John, O. P., Caspi, A., Moffitt, T. E., & Stouthamer-Loeber, M. (1996). Resilient, overcontrolled, and undercontrolled boys: Three replicable personality types. *Journal of Personality and Social Psychology, 70,* 157–171.

Robins, R. W., & Tracy, J. L. (2003). Setting an agenda for a person-centered approach to personality development. *Monographs of the Society for Research in Child Development, 68*(Serial No. 272), 110–122.

Roccas, S., Sagiv, L., Schwartz, S. H., & Knafo, A. (2002). The big five personality factors and personal values. *Personality and Social Psychology Bulletin, 28,* 789–801.

Rohde, P., Lewinsohn, P. M., & Seeley, J. R. (1990). Are people changed by the experience of having an episode of depression? A further test of the scar hypothesis. *Journal of Abnormal Psychology, 99,* 264–271.

Rose, A. J., & Asher, S. R. (1999). Children's goals and strategies in response to conflicts within a friendship. *Developmental Psychology, 35,* 69–79.

Rose, A. J., Swenson, L. P., & Waller, E. M. (2004). Overt and relational aggression and perceived popularity: Developmental differences in concurrent and prospective relations. *Developmental Psychology, 40,* 378–387.

Rothbart, M. K. (1981). Measurement of temperament in infancy. *Child Development, 52,* 569–578.

Rothbart, M. K., Ahadi, S. A., & Evans, D. E. (2000). Temperament and personality: Origins and outcomes. *Journal of Personality and Social Psychology, 78,* 122–135.

Rothbart, M. K., Ahadi, S. A., Hershey, K. L., & Fisher, P. (2001). Investigation of temperament at 3 to 7 years: The children's behavior questionnaire. *Child Development, 72,* 1394–1408.

Rothbart, M. K., & Bates, J. E. (1998). Temperament. In W. Damon (Editor-in-Chief) & N. Eisenberg (Vol. Ed.), *Handbook of child psychology: Vol. 3. Social, emotional, and personality development* (5th ed., pp. 105–176). New York: Wiley.

Rothbart, M. K., Chew, K. H., & Garstein, M. A. (2001). Assessment of temperament in early development. In L. T. Singer & P. S. Zeskind (Eds.), *Biobehavioral assessment of the infant* (pp. 190–208). New York: Guilford Press.

Rothbart, M. K., & Derryberry, D. (2002). Temperament in children. In C. von Hofsten & L. Backman (Eds.), *Psychology at the turn of the millennium: Vol. 2. Social, developmental, and clinical perspectives* (pp. 17–35). New York: Taylor & Francis.

Rothbart, M. K., Derryberry, D., & Hershey, K. L. (2000). Stability of temperament in childhood: Laboratory infant assessment to parent report at 7 years. In V. J. Molfese & D. L. Molfese (Eds.), *Temperament and personality across the life span* (pp. 85–119). Mahwah, NJ: Erlbaum.

Rothbart, M. K., Ellis, L. K., & Posner, M. I. (2004). Temperament and self-regulation. In R. F. Baumeister & K. D. Vohs (Eds.), *Handbook of self-regulation: Research, theory, and applications* (pp. 357–370). New York: Guilford Press.

Rothbart, M. K., Ellis, L. K., Rueda, M. R., & Posner, M. I. (2003). Developing mechanisms of temperamental effortful control. *Journal of Personality, 71,* 1113–1143.

Rothbart, M. K., & Mauro, J. A. (1990). Questionnaire approaches to the study of infant temperament. In J. W. Fagen & J. Colombo (Eds.), *Individual differences in infancy: Reliability, stability, and prediction* (pp. 411–429). Hillsdale, NJ: Erlbaum.

Rowe, D. E., & Plomin, R. (1977). Temperament in early childhood. *Journal of Personality Assessment, 41,* 150–156.

Rozanski, A., Blumenthal, J. A., & Kaplan, J. (1999). Impact of psychological factors on the pathogenesis of cardiovascular disease and implications for therapy. *Circulation, 99,* 2217.

Rubin, K. H., Burgess, K. B., Dwyer, K. M., & Hastings, P. D. (2003). Predicting preschoolers' externalizing behaviors from toddler temperament, conflict, and maternal negativity. *Developmental Psychology, 39,* 164–176.

Rubin, K. H., Burgess, K. B., & Hastings, P. D. (2002). Stability and social-behavioral consequences of toddlers' inhibited temperament and parenting behaviors. *Child Development, 73,* 483–495.

Rueda, M. R., Posner, M. I., & Rothbart, M. K. (2004). Attentional control and self-regulation. In R. F. Baumeister & K. D. Vohs (Eds.), *Handbook of self-regulation: Research, theory, and applications* (pp. 283–300). New York: Guilford Press.

Rusico, J., & Rusico, A. M. (2004). Clarifying boundary issues in psychopathology: The role of taxometrics in a comprehensive program of structural research. *Journal of Abnormal Psychology, 22,* 24–38.

Rutter, M., Caspi, A., & Moffitt, T. E. (2003). Using sex differences in psychopathology to study causal mechanisms: Unifying issues and research strategies. *Journal of Child Psychology and Psychiatry, 44,* 1092–1115.

Rutter, M., & Silberg, J. (2002). Gene-environment interplay in relation to emotional and behavioral disturbance. *Annual Review of Psychology, 53,* 463–490.

Sanson, A., & Prior, M. (1999). Temperament and behavioral precursors to oppositional defiant disorder and conduct disorder. In H. C. Quay & A. E. Hogan (Eds.), *Handbook of disruptive behavior disorders* (pp. 397–417). New York: Kluwer Academic/Plenum Press.

Saucier, G. (2003). An alternative multi-language structure for personality attributes. *European Journal of Personality, 17,* 179–205.

Saucier, G., Hampson, S. E., & Goldberg, L. R. (2000). Cross-language studies of lexical personality factors. In S. E. Hampson (Ed.), *Advances in personality psychology* (pp. 1–36). Philadelphia: Taylor & Francis.

Saucier, G., & Ostendorf, F. (1999). Hierarchical components of the big five personality factors: A cross-language replication. *Journal of Personality and Social Psychology, 76,* 613–627.

Saucier, G., & Simonds, J. (in press). The structure of personality and temperament. In D. K. Mroczek & T. D. Little (Eds.), *Handbook of personality development.* Mahwah, NJ: Erlbaum.

Saudino, K. J., & Cherney, S. C. (2001). Parental ratings of temperament in twins. In R. N. Emde & J. Hewitt (Eds.), *Infancy to early childhood: Genetic and environmental influences on developmental change* (pp. 73–88). Oxford, England: Oxford University Press.

Saudino, K. J., Pederson, N. L., Lichtenstein, P., McClearn, G. E., & Plomin, R. (1997). Can personality explain genetic influences on life events? *Journal of Personality and Social Psychology, 72,* 196–206.

Scarr, S., & McCartney, K. (1983). How people make their own environments: A theory of genotype-environment effects. *Child Development, 54,* 424–435.

Scheier, M. F., & Carver, C. S. (1993). On the power of positive thinking. *Current Directions in Psychological Science, 2,* 26–30.

Schimmack, U., Oishi, S., Furr, R. M., & Funder, D. C. (2004). Personality and life satisfaction: A facet-level analysis. *Personality and Social Psychology Bulletin, 30,* 1062–1075.

Schmeichel, B. J., & Baumeister, R. F. (2004). Self-regulatory strength. In R. F. Baumeister & K. D. Vohs (Eds.), *Handbook of self-regulation: Research, theory, and applications* (pp. 84–98). New York: Guilford Press.

Schmidt, L. A., & Hunter, J. (2004). General mental ability in the world of work: Occupational attainment and job performance. *Journal of Personality and Social Psychology, 86,* 162–173.

Schneider, B., Smith, D. B., Taylor, S., & Fleenor, J. (1998). Personality and organizations: A test of the homogeneity of personality hypothesis. *Journal of Applied Psychology, 83,* 4.

Scourfield, J., van den Bree, M., Martin, N., & McGuffin, P. (2004). Conduct problems in children and adolescents. *Archives of General Psychiatry, 61,* 489–496.

Settersten, R. A. (2003). Age structuring and the rhythm of the life course. In J. T. Mortimer & M. J. Shanahan (Eds.), *Handbook of the life course* (pp. 81–102). New York: Kluwer Academic.

Shanahan, M. J., & Flaherty, B. P. (2001). Dynamic patterns of time use in adolescence. *Child Development, 72,* 385–401.

Shiner, R. L. (1998). How shall we speak of children's personalities in middle childhood? A preliminary taxonomy. *Psychological Bulletin, 124,* 308–332.

Shiner, R. L. (2000). Linking childhood personality with adaptation: Evidence for continuity and change across time into late adolescence. *Journal of Personality and Social Psychology, 78,* 310–325.

Shiner, R. L. (2005). A developmental perspective on personality disorders: Lessons from research on normal personality development in childhood and adolescence. *Journal of Personality Disorders, 19,* 202–210.

Shiner, R. L. (in press). Temperament and personality and childhood. In D. K. Mroczek & T. D. Little (Eds.), *Handbook of personality development.* Mahwah, NJ: Erlbaum.

Shiner, R. L., & Caspi, A. (2003). Personality differences in childhood and adolescence: Measurement, development, and consequences. *Journal of Child Psychology and Psychiatry, 44,* 2–32.

Shiner, R. L., Masten, A. S., & Roberts, J. M. (2003). Childhood personality foreshadows adult personality and life outcomes 2 decades later. *Journal of Personality, 71,* 1145–1170.

Shiner, R. L., Masten, A. S., & Tellegen, A. (2002). A developmental perspective on personality in emerging adulthood: Childhood antecedents and concurrent adaptation. *Journal of Personality and Social Psychology, 83,* 1165–1177.

Simonoff, E., Pickles, A., Hervas, A., Silberg, J. L., Rutter, M., & Eaves, L. (1998). Genetic influences on childhood hyperactivity: Contrast effects imply parental rating bias, not sibling interaction. *Psychological Medicine, 4,* 825–834.

Slotboom, A.-M., Havill, V. L., Pavlopoulos, V., & De Fruyt, F. (1998). Developmental changes in personality descriptions of children: A cross-national comparison of parental descriptions of children. In G. A. Kohnstamm, C. F. Halverson, I. Mervielde, & V. L. Havill (Eds.), *Parental descriptions of child personality: Developmental antecedents of the big five?* (pp. 127–153). Mahwah, NJ: Erlbaum.

Smith, T. W., & Gallo, L. (2001). Personality traits as risk factors for physical illness. In A. Baum, T. Revenson, & J. Singer (Eds.), *Handbook of health psychology* (pp. 139–174). Hillsdale, NJ: Erlbaum.

Smith, T. W., & Spiro, A. (2002). Personality, health, and aging: Prolegomenon for the next generation. *Journal of Research in Personality, 36,* 363–394.

Smith, T. W., & Williams, P. G. (1992). Personality and health: Advantages and limitations of the five-factor model. *Journal of Personality, 60,* 395–423.

Snyder, M., & Stukas, A. (1999). Interpersonal processes: The interplay of cognitive, motivational, and behavioral activities in social interaction. *Annual Review of Psychology, 50,* 273–303.

Sonuga-Barke, E. J. S. (1998). Categorical models of childhood disorder: A conceptual and empirical analysis. *Journal of Child Psychology and Psychiatry, 39,* 115–133.

Spinath, F. M., & O'Connor, T. G. (2003). A behavioral genetic study of the overlap between personality and parenting. *Journal of Personality, 71,* 785–808.

Sroufe, L. A., Bennet, C., Englund, M., Urban, S., & Shulman, S. (1993). The significance of gender boundaries in preadolescence: Contemporary correlates and antecedents of boundary violation and maintenance. *Child Development, 64,* 455–466.

Sroufe, L. A., Carlson, E. A., Levy, A. K., & Egeland, B. (1999). Implications of attachment theory for developmental psychopathology. *Development and Psychopathology, 11,* 1–13.

Sroufe, L. A., Carlson, E. A., & Shulman, S. (1993). Individuals in relationships: Development from infancy through adolescence. In D. C. Funder, R. D. Parke, C. Tomlinson-Keasey, & K. Widaman (Eds.), *Studying lives through time* (pp. 315–342). Washington, DC: American Psychological Association.

Sroufe, L. A., Fox, N., & Pancake, V. (1983). Attachment and dependency in developmental perspective. *Child Development, 54,* 1615–1627.

Strelau, J. (2001). The concept and status of trait in research on temperament. *European Journal of Personality, 15,* 311–325.

Sullivan, P. F., Eaves, L. J., Kendler, K. S., & Neale, M. C. (2001). Genetic case-control association studies in neuropsychiatry. *Archives of General Psychiatry, 58,* 1015–1024.

Suls, J., Martin, R., & David, D. P. (1998). Person-environment fit and its limits: Agreeableness, Neuroticism, and emotional reactivity to interpersonal conflict. *Personality and Social Psychology Bulletin, 24,* 88–98.

Suls, J., & Mullen, B. (1982). From the cradle to the grave: Comparison and self-evaluation across the life span. In J. Suls (Ed.), *Psychological perspectives on the self* (pp. 97–125). Hillsdale, NJ: Erlbaum.

Szechtman, H., & Woody, E. (2004). Obsessive-compulsive disorder as a disturbance of security motivation. *Psychological Bulletin, 111,* 111–127.

Tackett, J. L., & Krueger, R. F. (2005). Interpreting personality as a vulnerability for psychopathology: A developmental approach to the personality-psychopathology relationship. In B. L. Hankin & J. R. Z. Abela (Eds.), *Development of psychopathology: A vulnerability-stress perspective* (pp. 199–214). Thousand Oaks, CA: Sage.

Taylor, S. E., Klein, L. C., Lews, B. P., Gruenewald, T. L., Gurung, R. A. R., & Updegraff, J. A. (2000). Biobehavioral responses to stress in females: Tend-and-befriend, not fight-or-flight. *Psychological Review, 107,* 411–429.

Teasdale, J. D., & Barnard, P. J. (1993). *Affect, cognition, and change: Re-modeling depressive thought.* Hillsdale, NJ: Erlbaum.

Tellegen, A. (1985). Structure of mood and personality and their relevance to assessing anxiety, with an emphasis on self-report. In A. H. Tuma & J. D. Maser (Eds.), *Anxiety and the anxiety disorders* (pp. 681–706). Hillsdale, NJ: Erlbaum.

Tellegen, A. (1991). Personality traits: Issues of definition, evidence, and assessment. In W. M. Grove & D. Cicchetti (Eds.), *Thinking clearly about psychology: Vol. 2. Personality and psychopathology* (pp. 10–35). Minneapolis: University of Minnesota.

Tellegen, A., & Waller, N. G. (1992). *Exploring personality through test construction: Development of the Multi-Dimensional Personality Questionnaire (MPQ).* Unpublished manuscript.

Terracciano, A., McCrae, R. R., Hagemann, D., & Costa, P. T. (2003). Individual difference variables, affective differentiation, and the structures of affect. *Journal of Personality, 71,* 669–703.

Tett, R. P., & Burnett, D. D. (2003). A personality trait-based interactionist model of job performance. *Journal of Applied Psychology, 88,* 500–517.

Thomas, A., Chess, S., & Birch, H. (1968). *Temperament and behavior disorders in children.* New York: New York University Press.

Thomas, A., Chess, S., Birch, H., Hertzig, M., & Korn, S. (1963). *Behavioral individuality in early childhood.* New York: New York University Press.

Thrash, T. M., & Elliot, A. J. (2003). Inspiration as a psychological construct. *Journal of Personality and Social Psychology, 84,* 871–889.

Tobin, R. M., Graziano, W. G., Vanman, E. J., & Tassinary, L. G. (2000). Personality, emotional experience, and efforts to control emotions. *Journal of Personality and Social Psychology, 79,* 656–669.

Tremblay, R. E. (2002). The origins of youth violence. In C. von Hofsten & L. Backman (Eds.), *Psychology at the turn of the millennium: Vol. 2. Social, developmental, and clinical perspectives* (pp. 77–88). New York: Taylor & Francis.

Trierweiler, L. I., Eid, M., & Lischetzke, T. (2002). The structure of emotional expressivity: Each emotion counts. *Journal of Personality and Social Psychology, 82,* 1023–1040.

Trull, T. J., Widiger, T. A., Lynam, D. R., & Costa, P. T. (2003). Borderline personality disorder from the perspective of general personality functioning. *Journal of Abnormal Psychology, 112,* 193–202.

Twenge, J. M. (2000). The age of anxiety? Birth cohort change in anxiety and neuroticism. *Journal of Personality and Social Psychology, 79,* 1007–1021.

Updegraff, J. A., Gable, S. L., & Taylor, S. E. (2004). What makes experiences satisfying? The interaction of approach-avoidance motivations and emotions in well-being. *Journal of Personality and Social Psychology, 86,* 496–504.

Urban, J., Carlson, E., Egeland, B., & Sroufe, L. A. (1991). Patterns of individual adaptation across childhood. *Development and Psychopathology, 3,* 445–460.

van den Oord, E. J. C. G., & Sullivan, P. F. (2003). False discoveries and models for gene discovery. *Trends in Genetics, 19,* 537–542.

van Lieshout, C. F. M. (2000). Lifespan personality development: Self-organizing goal-oriented agents and developmental outcome. *International Journal of Behavioral Development, 24,* 276–288.

van Lieshout, C. F. M., & Haselager, G. J. T. (1993). *The big five personality factors in the Nijmegen California Child Q-Set (NCCQ).* Nijmegen, The Netherlands: University of Nijmegen.

van Lieshout, C. F. M., & Haselager, G. J. T. (1994). The big five personality factors in Q-sort descriptions of children and adolescents. In C. F. Halverson, G. A. Kohnstamm, & R. P. Martin (Eds.), *The developing structure of temperament and personality from infancy to adulthood* (pp. 293–318). Hillsdale, NJ: Erlbaum.

Victor, J. B. (1994). The five-factor model applied to individual differences in school behavior. In C. F. Halverson, G. A. Kohnstamm, & R. P. Martin (Eds.), *The developing structure of temperament and personality from infancy to childhood* (pp. 355–370). Hillsdale, NJ: Erlbaum.

Viken, R. J., Rose, R. J., Kaprio, J., & Koskenvuo, M. (1994). A developmental genetic analysis of adult personality: Extraversion and neuroticism from 18 to 59 years of age. *Journal of Personality and Social Psychology, 66,* 730.

Vohs, K. D., & Ciarocco, N. J. (2004). Interpersonal functioning requires self-regulation. In R. F. Baumeister & K. D. Vohs (Eds.), *Handbook of self-regulation: Research, theory, and applications* (pp. 392–407). New York: Guilford Press.

Wachtel, P. L. (1973). Psychodynamics, behavior therapy, and the implacable experimenter: An inquiry into the consistency of personality. *Journal of Abnormal Psychology, 82,* 324–334.

Wakefield, J. C. (1989). Levels of explanation in personality theory. In D. M. Buss & N. Cantor (Eds.), *Personality: Recent trends and emerging directions* (pp. 333–346). New York: Springer.

Watson, D. (2000). *Mood and temperament.* New York: Guilford Press.

Watson, D. (2001). Neuroticism. In N. J. Smelser & P. B. Baltes (Eds.), *International encyclopedia of the social and behavioral sciences* (pp. 10609–10612). Oxford, England: Elsevier.

Watson, D., & Clark, L. A. (1992). On traits and temperament: General and specific factors of emotional experience and their relation to the five-factor model. *Journal of Personality, 60,* 441–476.

Watson, D., & Clark, L. A. (1997). Extraversion and its positive emotional core. In J. Hogan, J. Johnson, & S. Briggs (Eds.), *Handbook of personality psychology* (pp. 767–793). San Diego, CA: Academic Press.

Watson, D., Clark, L., McIntyre, C. W., & Hamaker, S. (1992). Affect, personality, and social activity. *Journal of Personality and Social Psychology, 63,* 1011–1025.

Watson, D., Clark, L. A., Weber, K., Assenheimer, J. S., Strauss, M. E., & McCormick, R. A. (1995). Testing a tripartite model: Pt. 2. Exploring the symptom structure of anxiety and depression in student, adult, and patient samples. *Journal of Abnormal Psychology, 104,* 15–25.

Watson, D., Hubbard, B., & Wiese, D. (2000). General traits of personality and affectivity as predictors of satisfaction in intimate relationships. *Journal of Personality, 68,* 413–449.

Watson, D., Suls, J., & Haig, J. (2002). Global self-esteem in relation to structural models of personality and affectivity. *Journal of Personality and Social Psychology, 83,* 185–197.

Weir, R. C., & Gjerde, P. F. (2002). Preschool personality prototypes: Internal coherence, cross-study replicability, and developmental outcomes in adolescence. *Personality and Social Psychology Bulletin, 28,* 1229–1241.

Weiss, B., Susser, K., & Catron, T. (1998). Common and specific features of childhood psychopathology. *Journal of Abnormal Psychology, 107,* 118–127.

Werner, E. E., & Smith, R. S. (1992). *Overcoming the odds: High risk children from birth to adulthood.* Ithaca, NY: Cornell University Press.

Westen, D., & Harnden-Fischer, J. (2001). Personality profiles in eating disorders: Rethinking the distinction between Axis I and Axis II. *American Journal of Psychiatry, 158,* 547–562.

Widiger, T. A., & Clark, L. A. (2000). Toward *DSM-V* and the classification of psychopathology. *Psychological Bulletin, 126,* 946–963.

Widiger, T. A., & Simonsen, E. (2005). Alternative dimensional models of personality disorder. *Journal of Personality Disorders, 19,* 110–130.

Widiger, T. A., Verheul, R., & van den Brink, W. (1999). Personality and psychopathology. In L. A. Pervin & O. P. John (Eds.), *Handbook of personality: Theory and research* (pp. 347–366). New York: Guilford Press.

Wiggins, J. S. (1973). *Personality and prediction: Principles of personality assessment.* Reading, MA: Addison-Wesley.

Wilson, B. J. (2003). The role of attentional processes in children's prosocial behavior with peers: Attention shifting and emotion. *Development and Psychopathology, 15,* 313–329.

Witt, L. A., Burke, L. A., Barrick, M. A., & Mount, M. K. (2002). The interactive effects of conscientiousness and agreeableness on job performance. *Journal of Applied Psychology, 87,* 164–169.

Wright, B. R. E., Caspi, A., Moffitt, T. E., & Silva, P. A. (2001). The effects of social ties on crime vary by criminal propensity: A life-course model of interdependence. *Criminology, 39,* 321–351.

Yeo, G. B., & Neal, A. (2004). A multilevel analysis of effort, practice, and performance: Effects of ability, conscientiousness, and goal orientation. *Journal of Applied Psychology, 89,* 231–247.

Young, S. K., Fox, N. A., & Zahn-Waxler, C. (1999). The relations between temperament and empathy in 2-year-olds. *Developmental Psychology, 35,* 1189–1197.

Zuroff, D. C. (1986). Was Gordon Allport a trait theorist? *Journal of Personality and Social Psychology, 51,* 993–1000.

Zuroff, D. C., Mongrain, M., & Santor, D. A. (2004). Conceptualizing and measuring personality vulnerability to depression: Comment on Coyne and Whiffen, 1995. *Psychological Bulletin, 130,* 489–511.

CHAPTER 7

Socialization Processes

DAPHNE BLUNT BUGENTAL and JOAN E. GRUSEC

Throughout history, parents and communities have been concerned with ways to influence the young. Children are born into many different types of worlds, and caregivers hope to prepare them to cope well in their own particular world. Socialization represents the preparation of the young to manage the tasks of social life and involves the continuous interplay between:

- Biological mechanisms that facilitate receptivity and motivation to acquire competency in the experienced environment
- Social-cultural mechanisms by which the environment serves to shape and strengthen those competencies
- Variations in the child's biological, social, and cognitive outcomes that occur in response to the experienced environment

In this system, biological and social-cultural factors build on each other in a recursive fashion.

Socialization research began with the assumption that the process was based more or less entirely on the tuition of the young by those who were invested in the child's and/or their own welfare, and the child's successful acquisition of relevant knowledge and skills. More recently, developmentalists have come to two new realizations. First, the brain contains the blueprints that determine the routes by which and the ease with which socialization occurs (and thus may be thought of as "experience-expectant"). Socializing experiences act to modify not only the cognitive, socioemotional, and behavioral competencies of the developing individual but also the corrected design of the brain (which thus may be thought of as "experience-dependent"). Second, social context has a significant impact on the effect of socializing experiences. What socialization is and how it works depends on both the immediate social context and the long-term cultural context. Although there are many continuities across time and cultures with respect to socialization, there are also many variations, reflecting the fact that *socialization* is an umbrella term that refers to a suite of processes that serve many different purposes. A related realization is that the domain in which socialization takes place (e.g., protection, tuition in the rules of group life, collaborative work to accomplish a shared task, or the exertion of control over a child whose actions may be dangerous to others) also determines the impact of particular socialization experiences.

Socialization can produce either benefits or costs for both the young and others in their environment. On the one hand, it can function to foster children's individual success in managing their lives and their shared management of life challenges with others in their world. Thus, it includes their ability and motivation to acquire individual and culturally shared competencies at a social, emotional, and cognitive level. On the other hand, socialization may create threats to these ends. Parents, or other agents of socialization, may lack the knowledge, investment, or competency to assist the young in ways that add to the individual and common good. Finally, there are necessary conflicts between the motives of the young and their elders. Such conflicts may occur at points of transition in their individual and shared lives, for example, when the young seek increasing autonomy or when parents have priorities that are discrepant from those of their children. Celebrities receiving awards credit their parents with their successes. Prison inmates curse their parents as causal in their downfall. To some extent, these variations reflect post hoc biases in causal reasoning. At the same time, the reality is such that parents—in collaboration with others—may indeed expand or limit the child's positive possibilities.

Socialization research has been guided by many different theoretical perspectives. It began with psychoanalytic notions about the conflict between the wishes of the individual and the demands of society and moved to a variety of learning theory conceptualizations reflecting approaches dominant across the field of psychology at the time. Increasing attention to cognitive processes (including the developing abilities of individuals to cognitively represent themselves and their social world) and to the role of emotion expression and emotion regulation resulted in work on the part of social and developmental psychologists to determine the way in which social cognitions and emotions were linked. Although attachment theory remained formally apart from traditional theories of socialization, it became increasingly evident that the foundation for socialization provided by the attach-

ment relationship between child and primary caregiver could not be ignored. With the emergence of neuroscience, theorists and researchers began to explore additional pieces of the socialization puzzle, suggesting ways in which socialization processes are routed through and influenced by the central nervous system and associated neurohormonal processes. In addition, cultural psychologists alerted them to the fact that differing societal beliefs and goals affect the practices in which agents of socialization engage in different cultural contexts and the meaning assigned to these practices.

At the same time, researchers began to understand that a complete understanding of the socialization process was not possible without a consideration of the complexity of those who were doing the socializing. Parents, for example, have their own set of expectations and predilections—the ways in which they think about the parenting relationship—that affect the way they approach the tasks of socialization. Initially these expectations and predilections were seen to be deliberate and reflective but increasingly it became clear that at least some of them occurred automatically and with little awareness. Parenting approaches affect the responses of the child, which feed back to affect parental expectations and predilections by confirming and expanding them or, at times, contradicting them. Thus, any discussion of socialization is now seen to require attention not only to the processes involved in children's socialization but also to biological and cultural processes involved in the production of caregiver socialization practices and to the ways in which children and caregivers have a mutual and reciprocal impact on each other.

We begin this chapter with a consideration of the changing nature of the content, theoretical perspectives, and models in the field of socialization. We then move on to give attention to (a) the biological platform on which socialization is built, (b) the sociocultural processes that organize the socialization experiences of the young, and (c) the ways in which biological and sociocultural history combine to influence the child's life outcomes. Finally, we integrate our view of the current status of socialization theory and consider what we believe to be its future directions.

The approach that we follow is not without limitations. The research cited is necessarily representative rather than exhaustive. In addition, attention is focused on socialization processes that involve children and adolescents. Socialization continues during the lifetime, but the present discussion is limited to the age grouping of interest in this *Handbook*. The early years are those in which socialization produces its greatest effects. Finally, central attention is given to socializing relationships between parents and children. Socialization involves a wide spectrum of influences. Beyond parents, for example, there are the powerful influences of peers who come to expand the lens through which children understand and manage their world. But parents, we believe, are primary for a number of reasons, including the fact that they and their children are unique in being part of a biologically intertwined system that strongly supports the socialization process.

In this first section, we review the theoretical approaches that have been taken to socialization and then highlight changing emphases in the field. The latter include shifting models in the exploration of causal processes in socialization and the emerging view of socialization as variable across domain and context.

THEORETICAL APPROACHES AND CHANGING EMPHASES

There have been several classical approaches to socialization and caregiving relationships. These include psychoanalytic theory, attachment theory, and social learning theory.

Psychoanalytic Theory

The first formal approach to understanding socialization emerged from psychoanalytic theory, which viewed the child as hedonistic, with expression of aggressive and sexual impulses needing parental and societal intervention to create a civilized human being (Freud, 1965). The importance of early experience was underlined in the premise that patterns of responding learned when individuals solved conflicts between gratification of bodily desires and the demands of society formed prototypes for later personality functioning (Erickson, 1959), including characteristic ways of dealing with dependency, aggression, gender roles, and conscience. Freud's concept of incorporation or internalization was particularly influential in guiding subsequent thinking about socialization. Thus, children were assumed to resent the imposition of societal values that threatened their autonomy but to repress their hostile feelings because of fear of punishment in the form of abandonment

or loss of love. To maintain the repression, as well as elicit parental approval, they identified with or internalized the values and rules of their parents. Here was the basis for self-punishment and guilt as well as an answer for the puzzling question of how individuals behave in socially acceptable ways without constant surveillance. The concept of internalization also laid the groundwork for a position that values are transmitted in their totality rather than modified or constructed by their recipients.

Attachment Theory

Psychoanalytic theory was adapted and modified in subsequent approaches to understanding socialization. In attachment theory, for example, there was a sharp break in the notion of a conflictual relationship between society and child, which was replaced by a more positive view of the adaptive quality of parent-child relationships. Bowlby drew from ethology and evolutionary biology to argue that, over evolutionary time, relationships between caregivers and their offspring had taken shapes that fostered both the survival and the adaptive skills of the young. The first steps toward that goal took the form of actions, on both sides, which ensured proximity and protection of the young, as well as facilitating compliance with the directives of caregivers (Stayton, Hogan, & Ainsworth, 1971). Retained from the psychoanalytic perspective was a strong concern with the impact of early experiences on later development. That concern is at the core of proposals that the attachment patterns developed in early life are carried forward in the form of working models (mental representations of the caregiving relationship that include both cognitive and emotional components). These working models subsequently influence individuals' close relationships, including the relationship with their own offspring (e.g., Bowlby, 1980; Bretherton, 1980). With attachment theory came, as well, a change in content studied. Of primary interest was the quality of the relationship formed between caregiver and child, a relationship based on the biological need for the provision of protection and comfort as opposed to the linkage between the satisfaction by a caregiver of an oral or hunger drive as posited by psychoanalytic theory (hence the distinction between attachment and dependency). Ultimately, attention turned to the role of attachment in the way in which children learned to regulate their negative emotions (e.g., Cassidy, 1994), which is a further extension of content.

Social Learning Theories

Psychoanalytic theory contributed to the thinking of social learning theorists who combined the rich clinical material of psychoanalysis with the basic principles of learning theory to produce a dynamic but empirically testable view of socialization (e.g., Sears, Maccoby, & Levin, 1957; Sears, Rau, & Alpert, 1964). The approach involved a set of processes that relied heavily on primary and secondary or learned drives that had their origin in maternal reduction of primary drives, such as hunger and thirst, similar to the psychoanalytic focus on hunger but different from the attachment theory focus on protection. These learned drives included dependency—the need to be near the mother and identification—the need to be like the mother (including the reproduction of her values and beliefs). The theory accounted in learning terms for the transmission and internalization of values and promoted research on topics relevant to socialization such as techniques of discipline. Studies of parenting suggested that, for example, reasoning and withdrawal of love worked well, particularly if they occurred in a context of warmth (Sears et al., 1957). The explanation was that they, unlike punishment or assertion of power, took advantage of the reinforcement that came from reproducing the (withdrawn) behavior of a warm and loving agent of socialization.

In a further refinement of social learning theory, Bandura and Walters (1963) presented a "sociobehavioristic" approach that eschewed psychoanalytic notions as well as reliance on the concept of acquired drives. They argued that the social nature of human functioning needed greater emphasis, focusing on the acquisition of novel responses through observational learning, and arguing that this, as opposed to learning through reinforcement, was the central and most important form of learning. Internalization of societal standards comes about through self-regulation, with the suggestion that people maintain their beliefs and values despite changing external circumstances because they judge their own actions—judgments learned through observation and direct learning (Bandura, 1977). Bandura (1977) also moved away from the notion of wholesale incorporation of parental values when he argued that children select from the conflicting information they receive to establish their own standards of behavior, with selection depending on a number of variables including differences in perceived competence between the model and the self and the degree to which behavior is seen to arise from children's efforts rather than being a function of events over which they have no control.

Emerging separately from the social learning approaches of Sears and Bandura was Patterson's social interactional perspective (e.g., Patterson, 1980, 1982, 1997). Patterson maintains that the reinforcement contingencies embedded in social interactions are the important determinants of children's behavior and has shown in a series of finely detailed studies how some mothers have difficulty obtaining compliance from their children because of their negative reinforcement of those children's coercive behavior. Thus, Patterson (1997) suggests that "problem families function as simple short-term maximizing systems that inadvertently contribute to their own long-term misery" (p. 209). Moreover, when positive reinforcement by peers is added to this pattern of parenting, the outcome is high levels of aggressive behavior (Snyder & Patterson, 1995). Missing in Patterson's approach is the concern with internalization that plays such a prominent role in other approaches to socialization, with Patterson (1997) arguing that reinforcement contingencies that control coercive behaviors are embedded in social exchanges and that these events are highly unlikely to be actively processed. Thus, behaviors during conflict are overlearned and shaped without awareness. In a similar vein, Patterson and Fisher (2002) question what is to be gained by developmental models that hypothesize events such as internalized values as mediators between parenting practices and child outcomes.

Parenting Attitudes and Styles

Early theories of socialization emphasized parent actions as predictors of child outcomes. Some researchers, however, came to believe that parenting attitudes might prove to be better predictors of child socialization outcomes. Again, ideas emerged from psychoanalytic approaches. Horney (1933) and Levy (1943), for example, explored socialization through the study of unconscious emotional reactions, such as overprotection or excessive parental control, which determined parenting behavior and therefore children's social, emotional, and cognitive outcomes. Over time, parent attitudes came to be considered as straightforward events that were accessible to conscious awareness rather than as reflections of unconscious processes. Their content was also expanded to include concepts such as warmth versus coldness, acceptance versus rejection, and autonomy versus control (e.g., A. Baldwin, 1955; Schaefer, 1965). Parental attitudes were seen to provide the emotional climate in which parental values and beliefs are transmitted and so they provided a context in which that transmission occurred and presumably affected its success. In addition to dimensions of parenting style, some socialization researchers focused on categories of parenting style, providing a qualitative assessment that captured the complexity and subtlety of combinations of parenting dimensions. The most enduring and influential of these categorical systems is Baumrind's (e.g., 1967), in her division of parents into three groupings: (1) authoritarian, characterized by rigid psychological control; (2) authoritative, marked by firm control, warmth and responsiveness to the child's needs; and (3) permissive.

Cognitive Approaches to Socialization

In the 1960s, there was an emergent interest in experimental psychology in the role of cognitions, an interest that redirected the field of psychology away from a predominant focus on behavior. The new approach focused on the ways in which information is processed in response to relevant stimuli, along with the ways in which such processing serves to guide subsequent responses. However, the guise that cognitive formulations took varied across fields and theorists. Social psychology had a long history of concern with such constructs as social perception, causal reasoning (attribution theory), motivation for cognitive consistency, and so forth. Bandura (1986) formally adopted the title of "social cognitive theory" for a model that had employed cognitive constructs such as attention and imaginal encoding from the very beginning. M. Hoffman (1970) elaborated on the social learning theorists' analysis of discipline techniques in a cognitive developmental approach. The approach emphasized the use of "other-oriented" discipline (providing a rationale that focused on the impact of the child's antisocial actions on others) as particularly effective for moral development. This pattern of discipline was contrasted to power assertion (use of the parent's superior power to exert control), which predicted low levels of moral maturity, and love-withdrawal (withholding approval or affection when the child misbehaves), which was not consistently related to moral maturity.

The inclusion of cognitive constructs in the field of socialization took many different forms. As one varia-

tion, researchers often gave consideration to the role of the child's cognitive development in their responses to socialization experiences. In doing so, they were concerned with the changing abilities of the child as a processor of information. In addition, the child, at all ages, came to be understood as acquiring social knowledge structures. Bowlby, for example, borrowed from the developing interests in cognitive processes to talk about the ways in which the young carry forward their early history with parents as "internal working models." Beginning in the 1980s, Dodge, Coie, and their colleagues (see Coie & Dodge, 1998, for an overview) applied a cognitive approach to children's antisocial responses, with a particular focus on attributional biases that led to the interpretation of the ambiguous actions of others as reflecting hostile intentions. From a social information-processing framework, children were seen as approaching social situations with a history of social experiences represented in memory. Their consequent behavior was determined by the way they encoded, represented, and processed events as a function of interactions between biology, memorial events, and cues in the immediate social situation. In a reconceptualization of parental discipline practices and children's internalization of values, Grusec and Goodnow (1994) emphasized two features of children's cognition that were important in this process. The first was their accurate perception of the parental message and the second was their perception of such features of discipline as its fairness and its noncoerciveness that made acceptance of the message more likely.

Systematic consideration of parental cognitions emerged in the early 1980s (although it was predated by earlier work on parenting attitudes). Parke (1978) pointed out that, up to that point, most analyses of mother-infant interaction had credited the mother with the same degree of cognitive complexity as the infant. Realization that the understanding of socialization processes was seriously limited by failure to consider the important role of parental cognitions led to a reframing of this area of research. The 1980s saw an upsurge of research activity designed to clarify linkages between children's actions, parental thinking, parent actions, and child outcomes (e.g., Bugental & Johnston, 2000; Goodnow & Collins, 1990; S. Miller, 1995; Sigel, McGillicuddy-DeLisi, & Goodnow, 1992). Parental cognitions also appeared in the work of attachment theorists who focused on the way in which caregivers think about their ability to provide protection for their children (e.g., George & Solomon, 1996).

The approach taken to parental cognitions has followed two complementary pathways. The first focuses on parental cognitions as stable knowledge structures or schemas (as described by Bugental, 1992, and Grusec, Hastings, & Mammone, 1994); as such, they represent implicit cognitions that operate automatically, effortlessly, and outside of awareness (Bugental, Lyon, Cortez, & Krantz, 1997; Greenwald & Banaji, 1995). Parental cognitions as stable knowledge structures are learned as summary representations of parents' own past history as a child (e.g., George & Solomon, 1996; Zeanah, Benoit, Hirschberg, Barton, & Regan, 1994) or they may reflect a shared cultural history (e.g., Bornstein et al., 1998). The second approach to parental cognitions focuses on parental cognitions as event-dependent and data driven; as such, they involve reflective appraisal of ongoing events in the caregiving relationship (see Bugental, Johnston, New, & Silvester, 1998, for a review of these two approaches to parental cognitions).

CURRENT DEVELOPMENTS: BIOLOGICAL AND CULTURAL PERSPECTIVES

Two new areas of focus have emerged in recent years, as socialization researchers have responded to increasing interest in biology and culture. No real understanding of any psychological phenomenon is possible without knowledge of how these two interact repeatedly to arrive at the outcome of interest.

Biological Perspectives

In the past decade, the integration of biological and social processes has emerged across a variety of areas, where it has been recognized that these processes act in a complementary fashion. It has been proposed that when these processes are considered together, new insights may be afforded regarding the mechanisms involved in complex interpersonal interactions (Cacioppo, Berntson, Sheridan, & McClintock, 2000). In addition, there has been increased communication and cross-referencing between investigators concerned with parenting relationships among humans and those concerned with nonhuman models. The combined perspectives have provided new insights into many aspects of socialization. These perspectives, discussed in turn, include developmental neuroscience, evolutionary psychology, and behavior genetics.

Developmental neuroscience has moved into a position of central importance as researchers consider me-

diating processes in parent-offspring interactions (Carter, 1998; Fleming, 1990; Fleming, Corter, Stallings, & Steiner, 2002; Liu et al., 1997; Meaney, Aitken, Bodnoff, Iny, & Tatarewicz, 1985). In addition, there has been increasing interest in the long-term influences of socialization practices on the regulation (or dysregulation) of the child's neurohormonal responses (e.g., Bugental, Martorell, & Barraza, 2003; Gunnar, 2000). Behavioral neuroscientists working predominantly with nonhuman models have shown an increased interest in applying their findings to human processes, and social scientists have increasingly discovered that these findings help to inform their understanding of human relationships (e.g., Collins, Maccoby, Steinberg, Hetherington, & Bornstein, 2000).

As a second shift, a bridge has emerged between the traditional interests of socialization or developmental researchers and those of evolutionary psychologists who focus on parental investment theory (Trivers, 1974). These fields have moved together in a shared concern with the experiences of children who are thought of as "costly" from an evolutionary standpoint and "at risk" in developmental psychology (e.g., Bugental & Beaulieu, 2004; Geary, 2000; Geary & Bjorklund, 2000; Hertwig, Davis, & Sulloway, 2002). These theoretical approaches converge to provide predictions with regard to both the negative and positive outcomes for such children as a function of the costs or benefits they provide to parents in the latters' reproductive success. More generally, increasing reference is being made to an emerging field of evolutionary developmental psychology (e.g., Bjorklund & Pellegrini, 2000, 2002; Geary & Bjorklund, 2000). Evolutionary psychology has focused attention on the domain-specific nature of adaptations. Consistent with this perspective, socialization may be conceptualized as involving distinctive algorithms in accomplishing different goals or tasks (Bugental, 2000).

Also seen are continuing shifts in the contribution of developmental behavior genetics to the socialization process. Traditional approaches have focused on the main effects of genes on children's social, emotional, and cognitive responses. More recently, interest has centered on the interplay between genetic and environmental influences (e.g., Collins et al., 2000). Evidence is mounting in support of evocative gene-environment correlations— the ways in which genetically based characteristics of the child come to influence the socializing environment, which feeds back to influence the child's behavior. As a case in point, O'Connor, Deater-Deckard, Fulker, Rutter, and Plomin (1998) found that children who were at genetic risk for antisocial behavior (an assumption based on the prebirth behavior of their biological mothers) were more likely to elicit coercive parenting from their adoptive parents—a pattern that fostered increases in antisocial behavior of children. Evocative gene-environment correlations have also been found for other socializing influences; for example, the mutual responsiveness shown between parents and very young children (Deater-Deckard & O'Connor, 2000), or the negative conflict shown between parents and adolescents (Neiderhiser, Reiss, Hetherington, & Plomin, 1999).

As another causal route, genetic differences between children may serve to moderate the effects of the socializing environment; for example, Caspi et al. (2002) found that the long-term effects of maltreatment are moderated by genetic patterns. Those children whose genotype conferred high levels of monoamine oxidase A (MAOA; an enzyme that metabolizes neurotransmitters, such as serotonin, and thus renders them inactive) were more likely than children without this genetic pattern to respond to maltreatment with antisocial problems. The evidence that genotypes can moderate the child's sensitivity to environmental insults is significant; more generally, Belsky (e.g., Belsky in press; Belsky, Hsieh, & Crnic, 1997) and colleagues have proposed that there are genetic variations in children that lead to differential susceptibility to their parenting experience. This line of research has led to important insights regarding the types of parenting that are more or less effective with children with different temperament patterns (e.g., Bates, Pettit, Dodge, & Ridge, 1998; Kochanska, 1997). In addition, increased consideration is being given to the ways in which environments influence gene expression (e.g., Brown, 1999; Bruer & Greenough, 2001). For example, a very stressful early environment may lead to the expression of genes that control the presence of cortisol receptors in the brain; the resultant changes in children's response reactivity may act back to influence the nature of their social environment. Early experience in the home environment not only may foster problematic gene expression but also hold the possibility for fostering adaptive gene expression in response to environmental challenges. Newer concern with the two-way effects of genetic and experiential influences counter the earlier concerns expressed by many socialization theorists (e.g., Baumrind, 1993; L. Hoffman, 1985) concerning earlier genetic approaches that focused on just one side of the picture.

In summary, developmental neuroscience, evolutionary psychology, and behavior genetics all converge in their focus on the brain. Evolutionary psychology, combined with developmental neuroscience, tells much about the experience-expectant brain. Concerns with gene expression tell about the experience-dependent brain. Developmental neuroscience offers information regarding the couriers and routes through which socializing influences occur. In doing so, these disciplines simultaneously inform understanding of problematic and adaptive socialization of the young.

The Cultural Perspective

Major changes in the orientation of socialization researchers are also evident in a dramatically increasing interest in the impact of context and culture on socialization outcomes. Earlier approaches to the study of culture's impact focused on cross-cultural comparisons as a way of validating the universality of psychological theories or of obtaining a wider variation in variables of interest than would be otherwise possible (e.g., Barry, Child, & Bacon, 1959; Whiting, 1976). More recently, the focus has been on how psychological events can be understood as a reflection of shared cultural meanings and practices, with attempts to find new ways of thinking about psychological functioning that cannot be accounted for in existing theories (J. Miller, 2002). Culture has also been expanded to include not only socialization in different self-contained groups but also socialization in the context of ethnic and minority groups existing in a larger and different cultural context (primarily in North America) and interactions between socioeconomic status and cultural context.

Harkness and Super (2002) note that studies of culture and socialization, regardless of disciplinary paradigm, have in common four assumptions. First, settings, such as types of dwellings and expectable activities for members of the group, are important because they determine the boundaries of children's experience as well embody cultural meanings. Second, the activities and routines that occur in different settings instantiate themes that matter to agents of socialization and thereby communicate cultural messages. Third, there are themes in a culture such that the same ideas or images occur in the meanings that are inherent in settings and activities; as well, the way settings and activities are organized for younger members of the group reflects an integrated system on the part of socialization agents. And, finally, what agents of socialization do to children is affected not only by the cultural experiences of the agents themselves but also by characteristics of children with whom they interact, with these characteristics including temperament differences, skill potentials, and species-specific potentials for growth, transformation, and the organization of experience into meaning (Super & Harkness, 1997). One way in which these ideas have been formalized is in "ecocultural" (Weisner & Garnier, 1992) or "developmental" niches. Super and Harkness (1997), for example, suggest that children are socialized in a developmental niche that includes the physical and social settings of daily life, culturally regulated customs of child rearing, and cultural belief systems or "ethnotheories" of caregivers. These features are coordinated, they are influenced by outside events, and they are affected by the child's individual characteristics to yield particular socialization outcomes.

Cultural psychologists argue that cultures can be understood as created, sustained, and communicated in everyday practices and behavioral routines (Goodnow, Miller, & Kessel, 1995) and that development occurs through participation in activities rather than through the acquisition of knowledge and skills (Rogoff, Pardies, Arauz, Corres-Chavez, & Angelillo, 2003). Fiske, Kitayama, Markus, and Nisbett (1998) write that socialization involves the incorporation of cultural models, meanings, and practices into basic psychological processes, which maintain or transform the cultural system. Moreover, behavioral responses cannot be understood without knowledge of the culturally based meaning they have and the cultural practices to which they are linked (J. Miller, 2002).

These various proposals have affected and will continue to affect the way researchers construe the developmental process. The work of cultural psychologists has underlined the importance of context and meaning for socialization theorists and led to the realization that the central focus on a few specific socialization practices (e.g., reinforcement, discipline, modeling), characterizing much of the history of research in the area, has limited understanding and needs considerable expansion.

CROSS-CUTTING THEMES: DIRECTION OF EFFECT IN SOCIALIZATION RELATIONSHIPS AND SITUATIONAL SPECIFICITY OF SOCIALIZATION

Before moving to a detailed discussion of biology and culture in the remainder of the chapter, we discuss two issues that must be addressed in any conceptualization of the socialization process. They both reflect changes in the way researchers have thought about socialization as a process whereby the agent of socialization transmits standards, rules, and procedures to the child but the nature of the standard, rule, procedure, and so on is irrelevant in the transmission process.

Direction of Effect in Socialization Relationships

A continuing concern in the field of socialization has been with the direction of effects in relationships. Developmentalists have moved away from very simple models that fail to capture the complex nature of causal processes toward the increasing use of models that are concerned with the interplay of causal forces of many types. Models have moved from the depiction of unidirectional causality (socializing agent to child, or child to socializing agent) to bidirectional causality (interdependence in the effects of causal influences in socializing relationships). As a new direction, contingent causality is being explored in socialization processes; in such models, causal influences are seen as contingent on context. Despite the increasing sophistication of socialization models, empirical research has not kept pace with the emerging models. The preponderance of socialization research (in both the questions asked and the methods of analysis) continues to employ unidirectional models (as noted by Collins et al., 2000, and Kuczynski, 2003).

The earliest way of thinking about socialization processes by philosophers, educators, and social scientists was unidirectional—influence flows from parents and society to children. As described by Hirschfeld (2001):

> Socialization has been seen as a causal process in which knowledge is acquired from communal living in a particular social environment. In this view, structure and organization in cultural learning flow from society to child, and consequently from adult to child. . . . Children are treated largely as if they were passive receptacles into whom culture is poured or on whom it is impressed. (p. 109)

The pervasiveness of this view has been documented in comprehensive reviews (e.g., Corsaro, 1997). This view was virtually unchallenged until Bell's highly influential critique (1968). In reviewing what was known about the influence process that occurred between parents and children, Bell made a compelling case that children have just as much (if not more) influence on parents than parents do on children. Children strongly influence their own environments, either by serving to "trigger" parental responses or by selecting some environments more than others (e.g., Scarr & McCartney, 1983).

Ultimately, it came to be accepted that the influence process between socializing agents and children was bidirectional in nature. As well described by Kuczynski (2003), bidirectional models come in many different forms. As a variant of Kuczynski's categorization, we consider ways of conceptualizing socialization that follow from (a) transactional models, (b) circular models, (c) ecological models, (d) systems models, and (e) contingent causality models.

Transactional Models

The earliest break from unilateral models came with the introduction of the notion of socialization transactions by Sameroff (1975). From this perspective, there are continuous reciprocal interchanges between parents and children. Thus, the parent responds to the child's behavior at one point in time, and the parent's response to the child's behavior comes to influence the child's response in the future. Consequently, socializing relationships undergo constant transformation. However, continuous transactional processes are not easily measured. As a result, research following from this approach typically approximates the tenets of the model by measuring a series of unidirectional influences; for example, the influence of the child on the parent at one point in time, followed by the influence of the parent on the child at a later point in time. Causal inference in such models is possible when interventions lead to differences in parental behavior (as a result of an experimental manipulation), which influence child outcomes. LaFreniere and Capuano's (1997) intervention with the mothers of anxious-withdrawn preschool children provides an illustration: This intervention led to reductions in maternal intrusiveness, which was associated with increases in children's social competence.

In biological approaches that focus on the interrelationship of physiological processes and social interactions, transactional models fit well with the evidence. For example, the regulatory systems of mothers and infants are linked, with the internal states of each open to regulation by the presence or responses of the other (e.g., Hofer, 1987). As is noted later, animal models often contribute to understanding such transactional systems in that experimental variations can be produced at various points in the relationships making causal inference possible. Transactional models are also consistent with emerging work in the field of developmental behavior genetics, with demonstrations of the two-way influence processes found between genes and environment, for example.

Circular Models

Circular models represent a variant of transactional models (Kuczynski, 2003). In such models, the parent and child relationship involves a recursive interactional loop that has no beginning or end. As is true for other transactional models, such processes are not easily measured: It is only possible to enter the loop at defined points, and the direction of effects is not easily ascertained. The notion of circularity does, however, have good explanatory value in accounting for observations of socializing interactions. This has been particularly notable in explaining the "vicious circles" described by Patterson and his colleagues (e.g., Patterson, Reid, & Dishion, 1998). These investigators have found repeated evidence for reciprocal influence processes between mothers and aggressive children. In these families, the mother often begins an interchange with an aversive demand, the child counterattacks, the mother backs off, and the child terminates the counterattack. As the mother's influence attempts fail, her confidence declines, and thus her ability to elicit compliance is further eroded. In similar fashion, longitudinal research conducted by Eisenberg and her colleagues (Eisenberg et al., 1999) found bidirectional effects between children's negative emotionality and parents' use of punitive tactics.

Ecological Models

In ecological approaches to socialization, consideration has been given to bidirectionality, not only in the family, but also between the family and the larger social networks in which the family is rooted. The earliest ecological model in the field of socialization emerged with Bronfenbrenner's conceptualizations (1979). The term *ecology* was used to describe the various levels of socializing influence—from the forces operating in the nuclear family to extended family or friends, neighborhoods, and larger community structures. The descriptive adjective "geographical" was applied to this approach (Goodnow et al., 1995) as a way of highlighting the metaphor contained in an ecological model. In models of this kind, the socializing role of parents may follow from their role as guides or managers (e.g., Parke & Bhavnagri, 1989): Rather than serving as direct sources of influence, parents may act to manage or create environments, which, in themselves, serve as socializing influences.

Family Systems Models

A systems model of family processes make uses of principles drawn from general systems theory (as reviewed by Cox & Paley, 1997). In this approach, the focus is on the mutual influences that occur between family members and between subsystems in the family. For example, the parent-child relationship is understood in the context of the relationship between parents. Thus, the term *co-parenting* is used to describe the activity of joint caregivers, with effectively functioning co-parenting units in which the caregivers together convey a context of solidarity and support between them, a consistent set of rules, and a secure home base (McHale et al., 2002). Family processes are conceptualized as organized systems whose properties are not derivable from knowledge about the individuals or family subsystems. For example, it has been suggested that children's emotional security cannot be understood outside the context of the family; in particular, it has been suggested that the child's sense of security will be damaged by destructive conflict between parents (e.g., Cummings & Wilson, 1999). This approach has stressed consideration of the role of fathers (as well as mothers) if a full understanding is to be obtained of children's development (Cox, Paley, & Harter, 2001).

Finally, the approach has stressed the extent to which families can reorganize adaptively in response to challenges and transitions external to the family (e.g., the child's entrance to school). All components in the socializing system (the individuals in it, the social networks in which it is embedded, along with other aspects of the larger environment) are understood to be in constant change, in particular, at points of transition (e.g., Cowan & Cowan, 2000; Fogel & Branco, 1997; Valsiner & Cairns, 1992). Effective parenting is understood to involve collaboration in response to these changes, conflicts, and contradictions (e.g., Holden & Ritchie, 1988). As a constraint posed by this approach, the measurement of reciprocal processes between family subsystems poses a challenge to existing statistical methods—a challenge receiving increased attention (Kenny, Korchmaros, & Bolger, 2003).

Contingent Causality Models

Conditional causality models focus on the "if-then" nature of socialization processes: Socializing forces, rather than being understood primarily as additive or reciprocal effects, are understood to involve contextual contingencies. This type of model has served to influence thought emerging from different theoretical perspectives. Concerns with the fit between socializing style and child temperament represent the earliest use of a conditional causality model (Thomas & Chess, 1977). From this framework, it was proposed that effective socialization was contingent on the match between parental practices and the characteristics of a particular child. More recently, a number of investigators (e.g., Kim, Conger, Lorenz, & Elder, 2001; Kochanska, 1995; Patterson & Sanson, 1999; Stoolmiller, 2001) have expanded this approach, showing how various features of children's temperament, such as fearfulness or irritability, interact with the socialization practices to which they are exposed.

In another line of work, research concerned with the organizing effects of parenting contexts and parental goals has stressed the appropriate variations in parental practices across settings (e.g., Dix, 1992; Grusec & Goodnow, 1994; Grusec, Goodnow, & Kuczynski, 2000; Hastings & Grusec, 1998). From this point of view, parents' understanding of a particular child's characteristics and perspective and the characteristics of the immediate situation, rather than the use of specific strategies or styles, determines their effectiveness (Grusec et al., 2000). Thus, maternal perspective-taking ability has been linked to mother-adolescent conflict intensity (Lundell, Grusec, McShane, & Davidov, 2004; Smetana, 1996) and mothers' knowledge of their children's reactions to different discipline interventions has been linked to their children's compliance (Davidov & Grusec, 2005). Similarly, parents' knowledge of their adolescents' thoughts and feelings during conflicts predicts positive outcomes (Hastings & Grusec, 1997). In addition, socializing practices appropriately vary with shifts in parental goals or aims (e.g., child safety or compliance; Grusec et al., 2000).

From a very different perspective, parental investment theory proposes that the level of parental care provided to the young is contingent on the resources available to the parents (Mann, 1992; Trivers, 1974), combined with the costs imposed by provision of care to a particular child (e.g., the costs of providing care to an at-risk child versus other children). Thus, a high-risk child might be neglected by parents who lack resources (i.e., economic, cognitive, or social) but receive exceptionally high levels of care by parents who have adequate access to resources (Bugental & Beaulieu, 2004).

Finally, biological approaches include many instances of conditional causality in social relationships. For example, reference is often made to "switching mechanisms" (Zupanc & Lamprecht, 2000) in which a pattern of social response (e.g., manifestation of parental behavior) is "turned on" in response to hormonal change. As another example, the hormonal changes that occur during pregnancy are associated with increased interest in care of the young (among both mothers and their partners).

In summary, models of causality in socializing relationships have moved away from simple concern with unidirectional effects (parent to child, child to parent) to models that consider the role of reciprocal influences, along with the role of context. Children are increasingly understood as engaged in continuous transactions in their socializing environment, an environment that includes not only their families but also more extended social networks, the larger community, and the resources available to the family in that community. In addition, interest has emerged in models suggesting a contingent relationship between socialization and context: The outcomes of the same socializing practices are expected to differ (qualitatively as well as quantitatively) as a function of contextual variables.

Situation-Specific Socialization

In the history of socialization theory, different perspectives have been taken on the cross-contextual continuity of socialization. An earlier view focused on general processes that were believed to operate across ages, settings, and cultures. This view was centered in a learning theory approach that focused on domain-general processes. From this perspective, the child is socialized by a set of processes that are equally applicable across context. Although variations might be expected in quantitative processes (e.g., variations in the intensity of rewards and punishments across ages), variations were not predicted for the qualitative nature of socialization across contexts. The perspective was intrinsically appealing in that it offered a guidebook for parents (or those concerned with facilitating or understanding optimal parenting) regarding the socialization processes that worked. The durability of Baumrind's (e.g., 1967, 1971) approach to socialization is a case in point.

Challenges to this view have emerged from different theoretical perspectives. Increased attention has been directed to the possibility that socialization involves processes that are qualitatively distinct across context or domain. Researchers in some areas have suggested that the processes of interest to them are controlled by mechanisms that are specific to a particular response system or a particular type of social relationship. Language acquisition (following the work of Chomsky, 1988) is one such area, with the thesis that children are innately wired to develop language. Attachment processes (following the work of Bowlby, 1973) is another area with its focus on maternal protection as a foundation of personality. Research concerned with empathy and sympathetic distress (following the lead of M. Hoffman, 1981) is a third area in its emphasis on the importance of other-oriented induction—reasoning that addresses the impact of the child's negative actions on others.

In this section, we review the various ways in which single process theories have come to be questioned. We begin with some of the earliest challenges and end with a relatively recent and systematically organized challenge that has been spearheaded by evolutionary psychology.

Privileged Learning

The earliest challenges to general learning theory came from within the field itself. Researchers from this theoretical perspective were faced with limits on the extent to which the postulated learning mechanisms were true for all situations. For example, evidence emerged that some types of learning appeared to be privileged: Learning occurred with exceptional ease and was highly resistant to attempts to override it. Garcia's classic research showing that food aversion can be learned by nonhumans in a single episode provides a case in point (as summarized in Garcia & Koelling, 1996). Seligman (1970) described these predispositions as "prelearning." He proposed that organisms are differentially prepared to associate different kinds of events, with food aversion as an example of those very easily acquired and the establishment and maintenance of responses incompatible with species-specific responses extremely difficult to learn (Breland & Breland, 1966).

Challenges from Attachment Theory

Early challenges to the continuity of socializing processes also arose in the study of attachment relationships where the processes suggested by learning theorists as organizers of socialization did not appear to operate in any simple fashion. Thus, contrary to what would be predicted by learning theory, babies whose mothers responded most quickly and frequently to their crying in the first 3 months of life cried less at the end of their 1st year of life (Ainsworth, Blehar, Waters, & Wall, 1978). Although the provision of food is a benefit of the attachment relationship, it does not serve as a basis for selective attraction to attachment figures or for strengthening of the attachment relationship (Harlow, 1973; Harlow & Harlow, 1965). Instead, such attraction is organized around the species-specific stimulus features that have been associated with mothers across the relevant evolutionary history. In addition, infants show privileged learning in identifying the characteristics of their own mother. In similar fashion, shared play activity serves as a benefit that is often associated with early parent-child relationships but is not associated with attachment: The young seek contact with attachment figures when they are in a state of distress but may seek out a variety of others for social play (e.g., Bretherton, 1985; Higley et al., 1992).

Some investigators have focused specifically on the distinctiveness of the function of attachment. For example, MacDonald (1992), arguing from an evolutionary perspective, suggested that attachment relationships are organized by fear responses (fear of separation), whereas affectional relationship are organized on the basis of emotional warmth. Goldberg, Grusec and Jenkins (1999) pointed out that the key function of attachment is the safety of the young and that the fundamental element in the production of secure attachment revolves around provision by a caregiver of protection and comfort in response to infant distress as opposed to sensitive responding to other forms of affect.

Peers versus Parents as Agents of Socialization

Another challenge to the notion of single-process explanations of socialization came from developmental psychologists who were concerned with peer relationships. From these earliest concerns (Piaget, 1948), it has been suggested that the influence process between peers differs from that between parents and children. In accord with Piagetian views, Youniss, McLellan, and Strouse (1994) suggested that "[p]eer relationship[s] are marked by use of symmetrical reciprocity and guided by the overarching principle of cooperation by equals" (p. 102), an organizational principle that differs from the unilateral authority or power asymmetry that is more characteristic of adult-child relationships.

Domains of Social Knowledge and Judgment

Concern with variations in socialization processes also emerged with respect to the demonstration of distinctions children make in their judgments about social concepts. Specifically, Turiel and his colleagues (see Turiel, 1998) proposed that there are distinctions shown between morality and conventionality across cultures and that these emerge very early in the course of development. Morality involves universal concerns with justice, welfare, and rights whereas conventionality involves consensually agreed-on behavioral routines that are important for the organized functioning of group life. Although both domains are understood as legitimately subject to regulation by those in authority (e.g., parents in the home environment and teachers in the school environment), the moral domain is seen to be obligatory and unalterable, whereas the social conventional domain can be altered by agreement or consensus.

Building on these concepts, Smetana and her colleagues (e.g., Nucci & Smetana, 1996; Smetana, 1997; Smetana & Asquith, 1994) have been concerned with the changing or nonchanging ways that parents and children understand and negotiate moral, conventional, prudential (e.g., safety maintenance and property protection), and personal (e.g., choice of friends) domains across the course of development. Thus, parental regulation and enforcement are always considered legitimate with respect to the moral domain but grow somewhat less so with respect to the social conventional domain. The big difference comes in what is deemed by adolescents to be increasingly under their personal jurisdiction and therefore not subject to parental control. Even sharper disagreement occurs over issues that combine conventional and personal considerations. Keeping one's room clean and neat may be seen as involving the conventional domain by parents, with the room seen as part of the entire house. The same activities may be seen as involving the personal domain by adolescents, with the room seen as their territory (Smetana & Daddis, 2002).

Parenting Goals

A number of socialization theorists have been concerned with the role of parental goals as sources of variability in their socialization practices across contexts. Parental goals serve to moderate the ways in which parents behave (including their affective responses) on different occasions. From this perspective, parents will employ different tactics in different settings depending on what they hope to achieve. Attention has been directed to the specific nature of parental goals (e.g., Dix, 1992; Hastings & Grusec, 1998). So, for example, Dix (1992) suggested that parenting practices vary on the basis of the activation of (a) parents' personal goals (goals that are relevant to efforts to obtain child obedience), (b) parents' empathic goals (goals focused on satisfying children's emotional needs), and (c) parents' socialization goals (goals based on the motivation for children to learn culturally defined values). Hastings and Grusec (1998) focused on shifting parental practices as a function of a similar clustering of goals: (a) parent-centered goals (fostering power assertion), (b) relationship-centered goals (fostering warmth, negotiation, and cooperation), and (c) child-centered goals (fostering reasoning).

Features of the Child as Determinants of Socialization Effectiveness

In addition to observing that agents of socialization may have different outcomes they wish to achieve, socialization theorists have also had to incorporate the differential susceptibility of different kinds of children to socialization experiences in different domains. Thus, the impact of particular socialization practices depends on a number of variables including the social behavior in question (e.g., violations of moral or social conventions), the age and sex of the child, the sex of the parent, and, as noted earlier, the child's temperament and mood (Grusec & Goodnow, 1994).

Domains of Social Life

A number of theoretical approaches have emerged that are specifically concerned with the nature and functioning of the different domains of social life. Domains may be conceptualized as representing bodies of knowledge that act as guides to partitioning the world and that facilitate the solving of recurring problems faced by organisms in that world (Hirschfeld & Gelman, 1994). These approaches, which have typically been in-

fluenced by evolutionary psychology, propose that different social domains are organized by distinctive algorithms, and that they operate in the accomplishment of social tasks that have had adaptive significance across cultures and species. The greatest utility of this approach for socialization theory follows from the implicit need for different types of parental practices in different social domains.

Although different theorists have developed different taxonomies, five domains have regularly been represented (four are directly relevant to the discussion of socialization processes; Bugental, 2000):

1. *Protective care:* Interaction in this domain is organized by mechanisms (e.g., proximity-maintenance) that provide for the safety and feeding of dependent offspring.

2. *Coalitional groups:* Interaction in this domain is organized to facilitate the establishment and maintenance of shared benefits from an in-group and shared defense against threat from outsiders.

3. *Hierarchical power:* Interaction in this domain involves the management of control between individuals who differ in social dominance and resource holding potential.

4. *Reciprocity/mutuality:* Interaction in this domain involves the regulation of matched benefits between functional equals.

5. *Mating:* Interaction in this domain serves to facilitate the selection and protection of access to high-value sexual partners.

BIOLOGICAL PROCESSES THAT CREATE THE PLATFORM FOR SOCIALIZATION

In this section, we review the biological mechanisms that can be thought of as creating the platform for the processes that are involved in socialization. At one level, there are shared genetic influences that reflect the brain's "best guess" as to the kinds of social experiences the young will have. In addition, there are genetic variations in children in the extent to which they are receptive to socialization (considered later in our integration of biological and sociocultural theories). We organize our understanding of the biological platform for socialization in four social domains that appear to have distinctive features (introduced in Bugental & Goodnow, 1998).

Processes in Different Domains

For each domain, we describe (a) the basic tasks of the domain, (b) the ways in which parents and the young are biologically prepared for the domain, and (c) the ways in which interaction in a domain serves to accomplish proximal tasks (e.g., time-limited tasks characteristic of a particular stage of development) as well as providing experiences beneficial for tasks that emerge at later ages.

Protective Care Domain

The protective care domain is the domain that most uniquely involves parents and the young in a relationship. Although there are variations in the extent to which such a relationship may be established with other caregivers, mothers are the most extensively prepared for this relationship as a result of biological processes. Fathers (among those species that involve cooperative care) are also prepared for this relationship, as a result of biological processes, but somewhat differently and more variably than are mothers.

The provision of care to the young must be thought of as conditional in nature: Parents invest more in those offspring who are more likely to serve their reproductive interests; that is, they are more likely to invest in those children who are likely to grow up to have healthy children of their own (Bugental & Beaulieu, 2004; Wilson & Daly, 1994). In addition, parents (without conscious awareness) weigh their investment in one child against their investment in other offspring (or potential offspring in the future). Parents also invest more in the young when they have the resources to do so (e.g., access to food and economic resources or access to supportive others who will facilitate the process of parental care).

To some extent, the processes involved in protective care serve the shared interests of parents and their offspring. For the infant, the relationship is a safety-maintenance system that is essential for survival and normal development. For the parents, the relationship, in promoting the survival and healthy development of the young, enhances the replication of their own genes. At the same time, the protective care system also involves tasks that are not shared between parent and child (Trivers, 1974; Wilson & Daly, 1994). Human offspring have a very long period of dependency and therefore there is a need for an extended period of parental care: The infant's best interests are served by obtaining the largest share possible of the parent's provision of care; in contrast, the parents' best interests are best served by dividing their care provi-

sion across their offspring (and thus optimizing their own reproductive success). Their interests may be thought of as competing. Mothers may have many children, and the level of care provided for one child must be balanced against the level of care provided for other children. Children, however, cannot choose alternative caregivers; as a result, they are prepared to initially maintain contact with the individual (or individuals) who are available to them in a caregiving role.

What Are the Tasks of the Protective Care Domain?   The proximal tasks of the protective care domain are (a) maintenance of safety and nourishment (provisioning) of the young before they are able to do so for themselves and (b) comforting of the young following stress. The long-term tasks of this domain are (a) facilitation of the stress regulation ability of the young and (b) facilitation of the child's understanding of and competence in the caregiving relationship.

How Are the Young Prepared for the Protective Care Domain?   The protective care system (regulated by attachment processes) represents a co-evolved system that involves the distress system of the young and the protective system of the caregiver (Bowlby, 1969; Panksepp, 1996). Under naturally occurring circumstances, the reunion of mother and infant not only allows safety but also, simultaneously, nursing access. However, attachment processes are linked to stimulus features of the mother rather than to provision of nourishment (e.g., Harlow, 1973).

Experience-Expectant Responses of the Young. Because the protective care domain needs to be operational at birth, most of the timing mechanisms that regulate it are online immediately (or in some cases, even prior to birth). Very early in life (beginning on the 1st day), infants show unique sensitivities to the kinds of auditory and visual stimuli that are species-typical (and thus are likely to be characteristic of parents). The ability to quickly recognize their parents is important for survival in that it insures that infants will attempt to maintain contact and proximity with those individuals who are most likely to provide for their care.

As an example, infants are highly receptive to facial cues, and may recognize their mother's face, as early as 2 days of age (Field, Cohen, Garcia, & Greenberg, 1984). Although it was once believed that this process suggested an innate face recognition mechanism, it is now thought of as a privileged learning process in which there is high visual engagement with faces early in life (Johnson, Dziurawiec, Ellis, & Morton, 1991). This process fosters the development of relevant neural structures. In the same way, infants appear to show a privileged learning process in identifying their mother's voice. Indeed, the human fetus shows an ability to recognize the mother's voice. Kisilosevksy et al. (2003) exposed human fetuses to a tape recording of the voice of their own mother or the voice of a female stranger reading the same passage. The fetuses' heart rate was found to increase in response to the voice of their own mother but decrease in response to the voice of a female stranger (differential responses that are consistent with reactions to familiar versus unfamiliar stimuli). At birth, this early preparation is demonstrated by the fact that neonates show a preference for their own mother's voice (DeCasper & Fifer, 1987; Ward & Cooper, 1999). Finally, infants quickly come to recognize their mother's smell—an odor that is associated with breast milk (Bartoshuk & Beauchamp, 1994; Schaal, 1988). This sensitivity allows infants to easily locate the mother's breast.

Activation of Distress Signals. Unlike precocial animals, the human infant is unable to move away from the mother in the first few months of life. It is not until the infant becomes mobile (during the third trimester of the 1st year of life) that distress calls are shown in response to separation or the presence of a stranger. Even though the care of the young shows many different patterns across cultures, the age at which distress calls emerge is quite regular (Konner, 1972). In the same way, the distress call system is also deactivated at a later age. Among nonhumans, such calls are deactivated in response to increasing levels of testosterone in pubescence (Herman & Panksepp, 1981). Changing levels of testosterone among human adolescents may possibly contribute to declines in their dependency on parents at this time (Steinberg & Silverberg, 1986).

How Are Parents Prepared for the Protective Care Domain? Preparation for the protective care domain occurs at different levels. This includes both general preparation and specific preparation at particular time periods.

Generalized Preparation for Protective Care. Because parents are prepared for caregiving relationships with a number of children, their attraction to this domain is broadly based, including attraction to the young (in particular, infants) as a whole. It is important for parents to be attracted to the stimulus features that characterize the young if they are to become invested in their care.

One of the most general stimulus cues to immaturity is appearance. Humans have been found to show a very general attraction to the facial configuration that characterizes immaturity, as in the very general attraction to baby-faces (Zebrowitz, 1997). In addition, the human cry has the capability of eliciting very general attention from others (Ostwald, 1963). Some sex differences are present, however, in the ways in which men versus women respond to the distress calls of the young. Nonparental males typically respond with heart rate deceleration in response to such signals, whereas nonparental females are more likely to respond with heart rate acceleration (Lin, 1999; Power, Hildebrandt, & Fitzgerald, 1982). These differences may be adaptive in that heart rate increases are more consistent with preparation for action (e.g., provision of care), whereas heart rate decreases are more consistent with vigilance (e.g., monitoring the environment for the source of the infant's distress).

Adults share the tendency to interact with the young using prosodic features that are distinctive to this domain. The properties of this style of speech has been referred to as "infant-directed speech" (Fernald et al., 1989), which is a speech style observed very generally across language groups (Kitamura, Thanavisuth, Burnham, & Luksaneeyanawin, 2002). Infant-directed speech (IDS) has been found to be a uniquely effective means of providing comfort to the distressed infant (Papousek & Papousek, 1995). IDS may serve the goals of socialization at younger ages and language acquisition at later ages (Kitamura et al., 2002).

Prenatal and Perinatal Preparation for Parental Care. Preparation for parental care needs to be considered separately for females and males. Biological preparation of females for the mothering experience begins prenatally (among both human and nonhuman mammals). During (and immediately following) pregnancy, there are hormonal changes that prepare the mother for parturition and lactation among both humans and other mammals (e.g., oxytocin, prolactin). In addition, there are hormonal changes that lead to increases in the prospective mother's interest in the young and the provision of care. In this chapter, we are primarily concerned with hormonal influences on the mother's social responses to the young.

Among human mothers, there are increases in the levels of cortisol, estradiol, and prolactin across the course of pregnancy (Bridges, 1996; Coe, 1990; Storey, Walsh, Quinton, & Wynne-Edwards, 2000). Of these hormones, circulating levels of cortisol during pregnancy appear to be most clearly related to subsequent maternal behavior (Storey et al., 2000). Elevated cortisol levels predict higher levels of approach behaviors in response to infants (e.g., patting, cuddling, or kissing the baby; talking, singing, or cooing to the baby; Fleming, 1990). In addition, those women who show higher levels of cortisol are more likely to recognize and be attracted to the odor of their own newborn infant (Fleming, Steiner, & Corter, 1997). Among human mothers, other hormonal changes appear to be more associated with the physiological processes of pregnancy rather than with maternal responses (Storey et al., 2000).

Storey, Walsh, Quinton, and Wynne-Edwards (2000) found that men and women showed equivalent levels of stage-specific changes in hormonal levels; for example, both show higher levels of prolactin and cortisol late in the pregnancy. Men who showed higher levels of reactivity to infant stimuli were found to show the highest levels of prolactin increase. In addition, new fathers with higher prolactin levels were more alert and more positive in response to infant cries than were those with lower prolactin levels (Fleming et al., 2002). Similar benefits (in parental care) were found in both of these studies as a result of declines in males' testosterone (and associated aggressive tendencies) across the pregnancy of their partner. These findings are interpreted as showing that prospective fathers' hormonal changes before and at the time of their child's birth facilitate their demonstration of parental care. At a more general level, married men with children have lower testosterone levels during the day than do unmarried men or married men without children (Gray, Kahlenberg, Barrett, Lipson, & Ellison, 2002).

Shared parental care of the young is typically greater in species that are also monogamous (Yogman, 1990), and shared parental care is maintained by continued contact with mates. Suggesting the effects of this experience on gene expression, males' experience in providing care for the young may also lead to changes at the level of the brain: The medial preoptic area (an area that is important for maternal behavior) becomes similar to that of females (Gubernick, Sengelaub, & Kurz, 1993).

Recognition of the Infant. After birth, it is important that mothers quickly come to recognize their offspring. In doing so, they show privileged learning. For example, human mothers very quickly learn to identify the sound of their own infant's cry (Green & Gustafson, 1983; Wiesenfeld, Malatesta, & De Loach, 1981). Fathers also show some level of privileged learning in the recognition of their infant cries; however, their accuracy is considerably less than that of mothers. In addition, parents' autonomic responses are different in response to the cries of their own versus unrelated infants (Wiesenfeld et al., 1981).

Oxytocin may also play a role in the easy recognition of one's own offspring (among both humans and nonhumans). Oxytocin has been found to facilitate social recognition processes in general; for example, elevations in oxytocin increase the ability of rodents to recognize a conspecific only seen in a brief encounter (Popik & van Ree, 1991), with influences appearing to be at the level of the hippocampus and the amygdala (Ferguson, Aldag, & Insel, 2001; van Wimersma, Greidanus, & Maigret, 1996). Findings are consistent with the general observation that the brain processes social stimuli differently than nonsocial stimuli (Young, 2002).

Coregulation of the Protective Care System. Regulation of the protective care domain involves key time-limited tasks to be accomplished, as well as the socialization of the young for later life experiences. Indeed, attachment relationships, which develop as a result of the infant's need for care and protection, are often not included in discussions of the topic of socialization. Such relationships are included here on the basis that the ways in which the tasks of this domain are carried out will differentially affect the ability of the young to manage stress, as well as their ability to provide parental care themselves, at later times. Therefore, in discussing coregulation processes, we are simultaneously concerned with proximal and distal tasks.

Safety Maintenance. Early protective care involves a dyadic system maintained by the parent (typically the mother) and the child in this relationship. Caregiving relationships, if they are to be adaptive, require the coordinated activity of the neurohormonal systems as well as the behavioral responses of both individuals. As a caveat, it should be noted that the activation of hormones in response to stressful experiences need not act as a continuing regulator of protective care systems. Ultimately such response systems come to operate efficiently with minimal cues. This short cut occurs as a function of the involvement of the amygdala. The initial activation of stress hormones in response to separation has an effect on the amygdala, which plays an important role in memory consolidation, as described by McGaugh (2002): "The basolateral region of the amygdala plays a crucial role in making significant experiences memorable" (p. 456).

The operation of protective care is best observed in response to separation or presence of threat and reunion. When separated from their mothers, nonhuman infants (typically based on observations of rats and nonhuman primates) show hormonal changes consistent with physiological stress responses (e.g., Hofer, 1996; Keverne, Nevison, & Martel, 1997; Laudenslager, Boccia, Berger, & Gennaro-Ruggles, 1995). Their responses include increases in the levels of corticosterones that are produced, combined with declines in their production of beta-endorphins. In response to these changes, their level of distress calls increases. Such calls are well-known triggers to maternal recovery and caregiving responses, as mediated by hormonal responses (e.g., increases in production of oxytocin).

Although such research informs us about processes in nonhuman species, questions may be raised about equivalent processes among humans. It is useful then to consider the supportive evidence (albeit nonexperimental) that may be observed in relationships between mothers and infants. Infants have been found to show cortisol increases in response to 30 minutes of separation from their mother (Gunnar, Larson, Hertsgaard, Harris, & Brodersen, 1992). Spangler and Grossman (1993), assessing infant response to the Strange Situation (with more limited separation times), did not find a general pattern of cortisol increase; instead such increases were limited to infants who were insecurely attached. They did, however, find increases (across attachment groups) in heart rate—another indicator of distress.

Among both humans and nonhumans, reunion is associated with increased affiliative activity. Among humans, this includes the infant's positive greeting and clinging. However, cortisol responses to reunion depend on attachment style. If the attachment relationship is insecure, cortisol levels continue to be high following reunion (Hertsgaard, Gunnar, Erickson, & Nachmias, 1995; Spangler & Grossman, 1993).

Regulatory Systems. The protective care relationship serves both directly and indirectly to foster stress regulation among the young: It serves to both buffer against stress and ultimately facilitate self-regulatory skills. Infants show direct benefits as a result of direct touching contact with their mothers. For example, preterm infants in neonatal intensive care units have been found to demonstrate significant increases in the presence of circulating beta-endorphins in response to skin-to-skin contact with their mothers (Mooncey, Giannakoulopoulos, Glover, Acolet, & Modi, 1997). In addition, preterm infants have been found to show a variety of benefits (e.g., decreases in cortisol levels or weight gain) in response to massage (Field, 1998; Kuhn & Schanberg, 1998).

The protective care relationship also serves to facilitate the acquisition of self-regulation skills. Evidence with respect to the benefits of protective care comes from both human and nonhuman research. The research program of Meaney and his colleagues (e.g., Francis, Caldji, Champagne, Plotsky, & Meaney, 1999; Meaney, Aitken, Bodnoff, Iny, & Tatarewicz, 1985) has demonstrated the long-term regulatory advantages of high levels of early maternal care: Pups who received extra licking and grooming in response to distress demonstrated an enhanced ability to cope with later stress. Specifically, they more quickly habituated to novelty. In addition, the experience of high maternal care predicted the willingness of offspring to move out to explore the environment without fear. As is true with humans, early provision of reliable protection acts to foster later capabilities for autonomy. In the same way, human infants are unable to self-regulate either their behavior or emotional states in the first few months of life and use the mother as an as external organizer of their biobehavioral regulation (e.g., Spangler, Schieche, Ilg, & Maier, 1994).

Preparation of the Young to Become Parents. Finally, the protective care relationship provides a learning experience that produces effects when the young grow up to become parents themselves. Again, we turn to nonhuman research to identify some of the mediating mechanisms that may operate here. Francis, Diorio, Liu, and Meaney (1999) conducted a program of research exploring the cross-generational effects of early maternal care. A comparison was made between a strain of rats in which mothers engaged in high levels of maternal care (e.g., licking and grooming) versus one that engaged in low levels of care. To separate out the effects of genetic influences from experiential ones, the rat pups were cross-fostered by a different strain of rat (i.e., rats from a high lick/groom strain were reared by mothers from a low lick/groom strain, and vice versa). Rat pups were then tracked to observe the parental care they provided to their own young. The parental care provided by the second generation reflected the care they had received from their foster mother (the experience route) rather than the care that was provided by their biological mother to other pups (the genetic route). This suggests the importance of early care as a precursor to effective parenting at a later age.

Among humans, the attachment literature has provided abundant evidence for the cross-generational transmission of attachment styles. A high degree of convergence has been found between the attachment styles of mothers (as reflected by responses to the Adult Attachment Interview) and the attachment styles of their own infants (Benoit & Parker, 1994; Ward & Carlson, 1995).

Summary. More than is true for any other social domain, parents and the young are strongly prepared at a biological level for the tasks of protective care. The tight programming of this domain can be understood by the centrality of its role in the early survival of the young. Among humans, mothers and fathers are both prepared prior to the birth of offspring for parental care. At a general level, they show interest in infant stimuli. More specifically, hormonal changes during pregnancy increase the probability that they will provide appropriate care of the young. The young, in turn, are designed to easily come to recognize their parents and to signal them in response to distress (with separation being a prototypical elicitor of distress). The hormonal responses and signaling systems of mothers and infants are closely coordinated to optimize both retrieval and relief from distress. In addition, protective care in infancy also acts to socialize the child for later experiences: It serves to influence the ability of the young to regulate their own responses to stress and to prepare them for the provision of protective care when they themselves become parents.

Coalitional Group Domain

The young are also prepared for adaptive functioning within coalitional groups. This process involves biological design as well as selective inputs from parents and peers.

What Are the Tasks of the Coalitional Group Domain? The central tasks of the coalitional group domain are (a) the mutual acquisition and sharing of resources within in-groups and (b) mutual defense against external sources of threat (including out-groups). Although this sounds like a coordinated system, there is good evidence in support of the independence of in-group favoritism, provision of group-based benefits, and out-group derogation/aggression (Brewer, 1999b). Therefore, it is useful to consider the biological preparation for these processes separately. Indeed, the developmental course of relevant processes appears to be different for the two aspects of this domain.

For the protective care domain, we focused exclusively on the relationship between parents and the young. For the socialization of the coalitional group domain, we focus on the socialization processes both by parents and by peers. Although some of the same processes may follow in both cases, there may also be differences.

How Are the Young Prepared for the Coalitional Group Domain? There is an emerging body of work that suggests the time course for (a) recognition of and investment in maintaining in-group similarities and adherence to group rules and (b) for the identification of the features of out-groups and the generation of negative responses to those groups.

Preparation for the In-Group. Imitation or mimicry of the actions of others appears to occur automatically in both humans (Chartrand & Bargh, 1999) and group-living nonhumans (Macdonald, 1983). One of the central functions of social groups is mutual defense through the ability of groups to intimidate potential predators (through their appearance as a large cohesive entity as opposed to an aggregation of individuals who can be more safely attacked). Among humans, mindless mimicry occurs soon after birth. At the most basic level, a neural basis has recently been found for the capacity of primates to share their experiences (Gallese, Ferrari, Kohler, & Forgassi, 2002). "Mirror neurons" have been found in which equivalent neural firings occur when an individual carries out an action and when he or she observes that same action being executed by another individual. These neural processes may underlie the operation of imitation—a process that is manifested on the 1st day of life (Meltzoff & Moore, 1999). Late in infancy, categorization processes lead to a perceptual use of group entities: Children begin to show both that they respond to groups of objects and that they expect groups to move together, which is a core feature of social coalitions (Sugarman, 1983).

By 2 years of age, children became receptive to the rules of group life—the "proper" ways of executing eating, dressing, cleanliness, politeness, and other conventional routines (e.g., Dunn & Munn, 1985; Emde, Biringen, Clyman, & Oppenheim, 1991; Smetana, Kochanska, & Chuang, 2000). This is also the point that children show self-aware emotions (e.g., shame, guilt). The possibility now exists for self-regulation to occur in response to violation of group norms.

There are indications that children's increasing awareness of and concern with family conventions is accompanied by a positive valuation of broader in-groups, for example, their own racial group (other ways of defining "us"). During these early years, children show a strong in-group attachment/favoritism (Aboud, 2003; Cameron, Alvarez, Ruble, & Fuligni, 2001) but do not show a negative out-group bias. As noted earlier (Brewer, 1999b), in-group favoritism appears to represent a different process than out-group hostility/derogation. Aboud determined that in-group attachment is particularly apparent during early childhood. Indeed, it has been argued that there is a stronger evolutionary preparation for in-group cohesiveness than for out-group hostility (Hirschfeld, 2001). This may follow from the fact that in-group coalitions were highly adaptive at all ages in our distant evolutionary past, whereas out-group hostility only became adaptive when children moved further away from the family and needed to be aware of potential dangers from neighboring groups.

Preparation for the Out-Group. A full understanding of out-groups does not appear until middle childhood. It is not until children are at least 5 years of age that they first begin to show an association between in-group favoritism and negative bias to out-groups (Aboud, 2003). As observed by Hirschfeld (1996), younger children may know a group label (e.g., a racial label) but do not easily categorize others or respond to others perceptually on the basis of that label. By middle childhood, they demonstrate out-group hostility and active segregation processes based on the arbitrary ways in which children are grouped. As noted by Hirschfeld (1996): "Children do not find races because they are there to be found. They find races because they are following an impulse to categorize the sorts of things there are in the social world" (p. 345). Supporting this notion, children at this age show group biases (favoring their own group over an out-group) when they are arbitrarily distinguished (e.g., by color of shirts worn; Bigler, Spears Brown, & Markell, 2001). Children from minority groups have been identified as at particularly high risk for bullying (Prothrow-Stith & Quaday, 1996).

By middle childhood, there is increasing maturation of the frontal cortex (Stauder, Molenaar, & Van der Molen, 1999), which facilitates the child's ability to integrate information. This change is temporally associated with more complex use of social categories, along with increases in social comparison processes (Rholes, Newman, & Ruble, 1990). Children now respond differently to the implications of different groups. For example, thoughts of death lead to increasing in-group bias (Florian & Mikulincer, 1998), which is a response consistent with the protection offered by their own group.

How Are Humans Generally Prepared for the Coalitional Group Domain? A central prerequisite for the functioning of the coalitional domain is the recognition of social similarities and differences. However, there does not appear to be any biological design for the specific kinds of the classical coalitional group categorizations (e.g., racial or ethnic groupings). Instead, these are groupings that are arbitrary and are not acquired until there is a readiness to do so (at the point that the child becomes involved in group life beyond the family and needs to be sensitive to groupings that have significance for that particular group at that particular time).

Although infants show a very early ability to categorize others based on sex (or age), as measured by the habituation paradigm, they show no equivalent ability to categorize others by such visually distinctive but arbitrary features as color (Fagan & Singer, 1979; Leinbach & Fagot, 1993). Kurzban, Cosmides, and Tooby (2003) found through the use of a memory confusion paradigm (confusing two exemplars from the same social category in memory) that humans are quite rigid in their categorization of others by sex but are much more flexible in their categorization of others by race. It has been persuasively argued that humans are designed by their evolutionary history to make categorizations by sex (and age), which has shared significance across time and setting; however, their categorization of others by other groupings is arbitrary. The arbitrary nature of group categorization is reasonable in light of the ecology that characterized human associations in the distant evolutionary past. Because of mobility constraints, humans typically came in contact with other groups who could not easily be distinguished or categorized on the basis of appearance. Instead, they had to make use of and become sensitive to subtle markers that distinguished a group that might pose an immediate threat to their own group's resources. Thus, it is likely that (as is still true universally) the coalitional group made use of deliberately created markers (variations in appearance) or variations in ways of communicating. As the simplest contemporary example, think of the colors worn and hand signals used by gang members to promote recognition.

Humans are also hormonally sensitive to the relative resource advantage (win-loss) of their own group versus a competing group. Among males in particular, the experience of winning (or watching "their" team win) leads to elevation of testosterone, whereas the experience of losing (or watching their own team lose) leads to declines in testosterone (Dabbs, 2000).

Coregulation of the Coalitional Group Domain. At the point the young demonstrate an awareness of their own "first" group (the family), they are receptive to socialization processes regarding the defining characteristics and routines of that group. Dunn and her colleagues (e.g., Dunn & Brown, 1991; Dunn, Brown, Slomkowski, Tesla, & Youngblade, 1991; Dunn & Munn, 1985) studied mothers as those most likely to be involved in socialization of the rules of social life in the United Kingdom and the United States. In other cultures, it is often the case that peers serve as the primary socializers of group rules (Harris, 1995).

Although the content of the rules is taught by others, the acquisition of those rules does not appear to occur as a result of reinforcement; instead, the rules are easily internalized without the influence of external consequences. Between the ages of 2 and 4 years, children have been observed to display ritualistic and repetitive behavior (Evans et al., 1997). Their focus on the proper display of conventional routines has an almost obsessive quality to it (Emde et al., 1991). Children of younger or older ages do not display the same ritualistic style in the enactment of everyday activities such as eating, going to bed, or getting dressed. Thus, there appears to be a window of opportunity in which mothers (or others who act to socialize the child with respect to group norms) are able to easily and effortlessly exert behavior control over the young.

During this time period, children come to believe that there is a certain way that "we" (the family) do things and there is resistance to efforts to change established routines. This may be thought of as the first indication of sensitivity to the in-group and the ways in which that group is defined by how members act and what they say and what their routines are. What is seen is the combination of a positive valuation of the family's way of doing things and a concern with violation of those rules (which, at a broader level, implies the possibility of group disapproval or exclusion).

Although mothers rarely punish children for their failures in carrying out accepted routines, children appear ashamed or guilty when they don't "get it right." At older ages, these self-aware emotions have been found to have autonomic consequences, which may influence the nature of the child's response to rule violations. Shame is associated with immediate increases in activation of the sympathetic nervous system, consistent with energy-mobilization and perceived threat (e.g., increases in heart rate and blood pressure, Harrald & Tomaka, 2002), followed by a rapid transition to parasympathetic activity, consistent with energy conservation and withdrawal (Schore, 1998). Gilbert and McGuire (1998) have suggested that the parasympathetic-demobilization response (associated with shame in humans) is part of an ancient, basic defense response that signals the individual to "stop."

The strong motivation to comply with group rules may have its origins in the fear of exclusion, which is one of the most intense fears present at later ages (Baumeister & Tice, 1990; Caporael & Brewer, 1991). The group provides an extremely important source of safety and loss of group support provides a threat to safety. Supporting this notion, depletions in the opioid system (which leads to declines in feelings of safety) motivate approach to the group (Panksepp, Siviy, & Normansell, 1985). This feature of groups may provide the primary basis for in-group preference and cohesion. It might be speculated that as the child's dependence on the mother for safety declines, the dependence on the coalitional group for safety emerges.

By middle childhood, when children are able to categorize others into arbitrary groups (as defined by others at that time), they are then subject to the possibility of responding negatively (jointly with members of their own group) to those out-groups. At this age, there is a high level of stereotyping and prejudice against racial/ethnic out-groups (Bigler, 1999). As noted by Bigler, the shift from more virulent forms of racial bias to more subtle forms of bias in society as a whole has not been reflected in a comparable softening of responses shown by children. In addition, no significant relationship has been found between the biases of parents and those of their children; for example, parents who show little bias often have children who hold strong racial stereotypes (Aboud & Doyle, 1996). Without encouragement from adults, children show aggression to arbitrarily created out-groups when those groups offer competition for scarce resources (Sherif, Harvey, White, Hood, & Sherif, 1954).

Summary. Biological preparation for coalitional group processes (including both the preparation for the socialization of the conventional rules that act to maintain similarity with one's own group and a devaluing of and hostility toward those in other groups) occurs in a set of steps. Sensitivity to the conventional rules of group life, along with in-group preference, emerges at an age when children become subject to self-aware emotions, such as shame, an emotion that may be triggered by violation of group rules or standards and that has powerful physiological effects (parasympathetic demobilizing responses). Although parents (as well as peers) are models and advocates of conventional rules, such rules are likely to be acquired through spontaneous internalization. Intergroup hostility, on the other hand, appears to be under the control of peer, rather than parental influence.

The Hierarchical Power Domain

The hierarchical power domain is centrally concerned with the establishment and management of interpersonal relationships that are unequal in the resource holding potential (RHP) of interactants. The basic notion of RHP includes not only the relative dominance or formidability of two individuals but also their relative access to desired objects or events (Parker & Rubenstein, 1981). Unlike protective care or coalitional relationships, processes in this domain are unstable and may involve frequent renegotiation of relationships (whereas protective care or coalitional relationships tend to be relatively stable once a bond is established to an individual or group).

Humans (as is true for other species) are motivated to acquire or maintain their RHP. Some level of dominance and access to resources is necessary for survival. The motivation for dominance is more salient for males than females (because the relative power of males has greater implications for successful mating). However, females are also motivated to maintain a favorable RHP in that higher access to resources provides benefits not only for themselves but also for their young.

What Are the Tasks of the Hierarchical Power Domain?   As is true for other domains, there are both proximal and distal tasks to be accomplished in the hierarchical power domain. At a proximal level, the successful regulation of this domain acts to keep the child safe from harm (and thus simultaneously serves the reproductive interests of parents). In accomplishing this task, the child is prepared for wariness and submission to power cues from others. At a distal level, power-based

relationships in childhood help to prepare the young for the successful negotiation of power-based relationships at later ages. The accomplishment of this task requires preparation for (a) the appropriate use of dominant responses (affording the opportunity for acquiring/and maintaining resources) and (b) the upper-limit control over dominant responses (i.e., a shut-off mechanism that prevents lethal harm to kin). As suggested by Kelley and Thibaut (1978), interdependent relationships, even when they involve unequal resources or power, typically involve benefit to both parties.

Parents, siblings, and unrelated adults or children may all act to socialize hierarchical power relationships. The negotiation of power relationships among the young themselves represents an omnipresent activity across species, in particular among young males.

How Are the Young Prepared for the Hierarchical Power Domain?   The preparation of the young for power-based relationships is shared for some features but sexually dimorphic for others. All children need to be prepared to respond to the warning signals of adults to avoid harm. Even infants show an early preparation for power messages contained in the speaker's vocal properties. Infants are sensitive (and reactive) to the vocal prohibitions of adults. Fernald (1993) has demonstrated the universality with which young infants respond with behavioral inhibition to vocal prohibition signals (vocalizations that involve short, loud, and staccato prosody). This infant response pattern is shown whether adult messages are voiced by their mothers or voiced by unrelated women speaking a different language.

Across many species, there is also a biologically prepared sensitivity to cues to physical power or formidability. Infants, across species, show greater fear in response to unfamiliar adult males than to unfamiliar adult females (Cheney & Seyfarth, 1985; Skarin, 1977). As pointed out by Cheney and Seyfarth, sensitivity to unfamiliar males (among nonhumans) precedes sensitivity to predators, suggesting the high importance of this response. In addition, there is a high level of continuity in response to power signals across ages (Keating & Bai, 1986).

As well as the general preparation for power-based relationships, there is also sexually dimorphic preparation of the young for this domain. First of all, there appears to be some level of prenatal preparation for the power domain among males as a function of the intrauterine hormonal environment. The presence of elevated levels of androgens (male sex hormones) late during gestation or shortly after birth acts to predict later sex differences that are relevant for this domain (Breedlove, 1992; Mazur & Booth, 1996). Although questions have been raised about this process among humans (see Ruble & Martin, 1998), there are indications that, across species, these early hormonal differences organize the architecture of the brain in ways that are manifested in behavioral patterns at later ages. When females are exposed prenatally to androgens (either through the introduction of exogenous androgens or as a result of naturally occurring hormonal anomalies), they show subsequent social responses that are closer to those usually shown by males, including rough and tumble play. Among nonhuman primates, there are also differences in the nature of their social signals in response to threat. Nonhuman primate females are more likely to produce vocalizations that act to recruit attention (and help) from kin. Males (beginning as juveniles), although they are at much greater risk, are less likely to engage in vocal signaling behavior (Bernstein & Ehardt, 1985).

Across the course of postnatal development, sex differences also emerge in the presence of testosterone, a difference that becomes most striking at puberty. At this age, the increasing levels of testosterone among males allows for more serious forms of power assertion, including aggression. There are also some indications that the changing hormonal environment of the young at pubescence may lead to an altered relationship with adults in a position of power. A number of investigators (e.g., Inoff-Germain et al., 1988; Moffitt, 1993; Susman et al., 1987; Udry & Talbert, 1988) have found that that antisocial behavior in the young (e.g., resistance to authority) rises with increases in testosterone, even when the visible signs to the individual's stage of puberty are statistically controlled.

Coregulation of the Hierarchical Power Domain. The coregulation of the hierarchical power domain serves multiple purposes. These include the maintenance of child safety and regulation of rough and tumble play.

Use of the Power Domain in Maintaining Child Safety. The regulation of the hierarchical power domain involves the accomplishment of tasks that serve proximal goals as well as the accomplishment of tasks that serve to prepare the child for later power engagements. As one of the proximal tasks, the safety needs of the young are met by parental regulation at a distance when infants become mobile. The vocal signals of both human and non-

human primates have both informational and motivational properties (Marler, Evans, & Hauser, 1992). As noted earlier, Fernald (1993) has demonstrated that mothers produce a distinctive prohibition vocal signal to preverbal infants as a means of stopping some ongoing action. Such signals are often used by mothers to prohibit touching an object that may pose a hazard to the child, and they have the advantage in that they stop the infant's behavior before the child is old enough to understand speech. This signaling system carries the advantages of effective inhibition of dangerous actions and the preparation of the child for associated prohibitional speech ("No!"). In short, it allows human parents to bootstrap off of a biologically prepared sensitivity to facilitate their tuitional role. Thus, the accomplishment of a proximal task may also extend to the parent's later use of communications that serve in a socializing role.

Regulation of Rough-and-Tumble Play. A distal task of the hierarchical power domain involves the preparation of the young for power engagements at older ages. Juvenile play (in particular, rough-and-tumble play) serves to safely prepare the young for later more serious types of hierarchical power encounters. This play style, much more common among boys than girls, begins in early childhood. Although social play does not constitute aggression, it does prepare the young for later relationships that carry the potential for aggression. The nature of rough-and-tumble play is typically managed (by children themselves) to be 50/50 in wins and losses (Pellis, 2002). In peer relationships, this balance is fairly easily attained.

Adaptive timing features are shown in the deactivation of the playful power struggles of the young. The "clock" for manifestations of rough-and-tumble play is set in such a way as to maintain the utility of this power-relevant social response pattern: Rough-and-tumble play follows a well-defined course during its development across species. The activation pattern represents an inverted U function in which this play style increases and then declines late in middle childhood (Panksepp, 1993). These declines are associated with increases in the presence of testosterone. At this point, young males would be more likely to inflict serious physical harm in the course of such play bouts (thus decreasing their utility). It appears that increases in testosterone at the onset of pubescence mediate the declines in playful types of power struggles. Before this age, rough-and-tumble play involves a dopamine-based reward system in which participants (in particular, males) experience this activity as positive (Panksepp, 1993). In contrast, serious (rather than playful) aggression between the young may be regulated by testosterone (Sanchez-Martin et al., 2000).

Among humans, fathers (as well as juveniles) show an involvement in social play with the young. At one level, social play provides preparation for novel events, an important aspect of socialization (Bekoff & Allen, 2002). More relevant to the current discussion, fathers are differentially involved in play activity (rough-and-tumble play) that may serve to prepare the young for relationships that involve power asymmetry (Jacklin, DiPietro, & Maccoby, 1984). In doing so, they provide experience with different distributions of power. For example, at one time, the father may win disproportionately; at other times, he can shift the balance of power in the play relationship in such a way that the young win disproportionately (Bekoff & Allen, 2002). These experiences train the child for ways of negotiating power-based relationships at later ages: They provide experience with winning and losing, including the submissive or dominance behavior associated with both roles. They also provide experience in escalating the challenge posed to a more dominant individual as a means of testing to see whether they can increase their hierarchical position. Fathers provide realistic (but safe) consequences when a juvenile's play responses become too intense. In this way, the young also learn upper-limit control over fighting with those of their own coalitional group. For example, nonhuman primate fathers make use of play bites that are limited in intensity (Bekoff & Allen, 2002), which is an upper-limit control that is learned by the young. Power contests are used to establish hierarchical position (rather than destruction of another person), and therefore modulation of aggression is adaptive.

As an indication of the significance of fathers for their children's socialization in this domain, Flinn, Quinlan, Decker, Turner, and England (1996) found hormonal effects that followed from father absence. In particular, the endocrine responses of sons (more than daughters) were sensitive to the presence or absence of the father. Sons whose fathers were absent, although showing low cortisol levels during infancy, demonstrated a combination of high cortisol and low testosterone levels in adolescence. This combination is consistent with a subordinate role in power-based relationships with peers.

The long-term occupation of a subordinate role carries high costs; thus, the presence of preparation for the young to optimize their power position is critical. For example, males experiencing social defeat (as opposed to nonsocial stress) show hypercortisolism—strong increases in the activation of the hypothalamic-pituitary-adrenal (HPA) axis (Abbott et al., 2003). As noted earlier, social defeat or subordination also leads to increases in noradrenaline, a change viewed as a "de-escalating response pattern." In contrast, those individuals who achieve higher levels of power show higher levels of serotonin relative to others (i.e., a hormonal advantage). Although most of the evidence for this hormonal correlate of power has come from nonhuman primate research (e.g., Raleigh, McGuire, Bramner, Olkkacjm, & Yuviller, 1991), similar patterns have also been found with humans (e.g., Madsen, 1986).

Summary. The experiences of the young in the hierarchical power domain serve the child's immediate needs (e.g., responsiveness to parents in safety regulation at a distance) and set the stage for later relationships. Their experiences are orchestrated by an integrated system of social signals and hormonal patterns. Preparation for the power domain reveals both uniformities and variations between males and females. Beginning in infancy, both males and females are responsive to the power signals of adults. However, the prenatal hormonal environment of males selectively influences their preparation for physically competitive encounters (e.g., rough-and-tumble play). Rough-and-tumble play at younger ages is hormonally regulated in ways that are consistent with positive play and provides safe experience in power negotiation. In contrast, serious involvements in power contests (more common by puberty) are regulated by testosterone. The engagement of fathers in social play with the young also provides an early training role for the effective management of future relationships involving power asymmetry.

The Mutuality/Reciprocity Domain

As the last social domain to be considered, humans (along with other primates) are prepared by biological processes for interactions based on mutuality or reciprocity. Such relationships are based on the mutual provision of benefits between functional equals. Kin selection theory (Hamilton, 1964) offers an easy account of the reasons why an individual benefits by the provision of aid to kin: The provision of benefits to kin simultaneously serves to benefit a person's own reproductive success. Less easily explained is the provision of benefits to nonkin. However, when the relationship between individuals is based on the possibility of reciprocal benefits, such relationships can be seen as adaptive (Cosmides & Tooby, 1992). Reciprocity in social relationships has been described as the hallmark of primate behavior, although some forms of reciprocity have occasionally been observed in lower species (Wilkinson, 1988). Among primates, reciprocity extends past simple tit-for-tat short-term exchanges, and is reflected in an elaborate cost-benefit accounting that transcends specific behavioral currencies or contexts (Silk, 1992).

Friendships (an important example of mutual/reciprocal relationships) are distinct from other kinds of peer interactions (Newcomb & Bagwell, 1995). Most notably, friendships are characterized by high levels of reciprocity and intimacy (although intimacy is more commonly linked with female than male friendships). In addition, the benefits that follow from peer associations are greater for friends than nonfriends (Newcomb & Bagwell, 1995).

What Are the Tasks of the Mutuality/Reciprocity Domain?   The proximal tasks of the mutuality/reciprocity (MR) domain include (a) the provision of mutual benefits with unrelated others by sharing and reciprocating tangible and/or social-emotional benefits and (b) the collaboration of two individuals to accomplish a goal that neither one can reach alone (e.g., coordinated activity in reaching a goal or defending against an opponent). The long-term tasks of the MR domain include preparation of the young by parents for mutual/reciprocal relationships with their peers.

How Are the Young Prepared for the Mutuality/ Reciprocity Domain?   In early infancy, infants show pleasure in response to contingency; for example, they smile when an object moves in response to their actions (e.g., Watson & Ramey, 1987). Later during the 1st year, they react to contingently responding objects as though they are human. For example, Johnson and her colleagues (Johnson, Dziurawiec, Ellis, & Morton, 1991) found that, by 1 year of age, infants react to an object (even when it is a nondescript blob) as having intentions after it has been observed responding contingently to another person (e.g., making contingent sounds or flashing a light in response to the speech of another person).

Joint Attention as the Basis for Coordination.   By 1 year of age, children show the ability to share attention and to solicit the joint attention of others (Bakeman &

Adamson, 1984). This process involves the infant's active coordination of his or her interest in some object or event with the ongoing attentional engagement and intentions of another person. This new capability involves what may be thought of as coordination or matching of motives. At this point, the young can coordinate their activities with others with a new level of planning and purpose. This capability can be understood as important in the negotiation of reciprocal or shared activities.

Theory of Mind.   By age 4, children have moved one step further in the MR domain by showing that they now understand that others act on the basis of their beliefs, even when those beliefs are false, that is,—they have acquired a theory of mind. This capacity allows the child to understand the thoughts and desires of others in establishing mutually beneficial interactions. Secondary representational capacity (e.g., pretense, means-end reasoning), thought to reflect an early stage in the development of theory of mind, has been observed among the great apes, suggesting some limited level of continuity across species (Suddendorf & Whiten, 2001).

What is the General Preparation for the Mutuality/Reciprocity Domain?   The regulation of the MR domain appears to involve basic computational and neural mechanisms for which there is an evolutionary design. Trevarthen, Kokkinski, and Flamenghi (1999) have suggested that humans are born ready to reciprocate interactions with others. Indeed, Forman and Kochanska (2001) have observed a correlation between young children's willingness to imitate their parent in a teaching context and to comply in a control context, and they suggest that both reflect a responsiveness or receptive stance toward parental socialization. Unlike automatic mimicry or imitation in the coalitional domain, "imitation" in the MR domain appears to involve intentional response matching or turn-taking and may be better thought of as "emulation" (a distinction in concepts that has been proposed by Want and Harris, 2002).

At a higher level, humans (and other primates) appear to have a "cheater detection" mechanism that provides a sensitivity to violation of implicit social contracts (e.g., providing benefits to another but not receiving benefits in return; Cosmides & Tooby, 1992). When other individuals fail to reciprocate benefits, they are subject to penalties in the withholding of future benefits by the individual who has been "cheated." Over a program of research, Cosmides and Tooby have demonstrated the greatly enhanced ability of individuals to solve complex logical problems (the Wason task) when they are framed as social contracts.

Coregulation of the Mutuality/Reciprocity Domain. The ability of young children to engage in successful MR relationships is facilitated by their early interactions with parents (in particular, mothers).

Early Parental Socialization in MR Relationships. Before infants engage in peer interactions, they may be thought of as having a practice period in which their skills in joint regulation processes develop and are honed. Although children may be thought of as experience-expectant for MR interactions, a "guided apprenticeship" with parents, involving jointly coordinated interactions, may be needed before this domain is fully operational. However, this finding may be limited to societies in which mothers (rather than peers) play a predominant role in the early play activities of the young. Thus, there are variations across cultures in the extensiveness of the early role of parents as opposed to peers in the socialization process.

Suggestive support for the experience-expectant nature of MR interactions comes from research conducted in the still face paradigm. The exchange of eye contact and smiles is an important part of the early relationship between mothers and infants, and is associated with positive affect. For example, a high level of contingent responsiveness has been shown by mothers (by their facial expressions) to the facial expression of their infants during nursing (Leveille, Cossette, Blanchette, & Gaudreau, 2001). If the mother violates the infants' expectations by displaying an immobile face, children show heart rate increases, a decrease in vagal tone, and negative affect (Weinberg & Tronick, 1996). The level of distress shown by infants in this setting indicates the significance of mutual interactional engagement with the mother.

Another early manifestation of parental guidance in MR processes is seen in the vocal communication between mothers and infants. At around 3 or 4 months of age, infants are ready for coordinated vocal dialogues with parents that for the first time involve turn-taking (e.g., Papousek & Papousek, 1995), through a dialogue in which parents take the lead. Consistent with the affective consequences of mutuality/reciprocity in relationships, vocal dialogues between infants and mothers are regularly associated with positive affect. The importance of the infant's stage of cortical development for such exchanges is suggested by the deficits shown by premature infants in establishing such dialogues (e.g., Lester, Hoffman, & Brazelton, 1985).

The later initiation by mothers of ritualized MR games (e.g., peekaboo) also serves to further prepare the infant for reciprocal, coordinated activity (Parrott & Gleitman, 1989). Thus, children who were observed to engage in high levels of mutuality in play (play initiations and compliance to initiations) were found to be more socially competent with peers, which was a relationship found to be mediated by increases in children's emotional knowledge (Lindsey, 1998; Lindsey, Mize, & Pettit, 1997). In short, mutuality in interactions with parents provides an opportunity for guided practice in mutual/reciprocal interactions with peers.

Coregulation with Friends. The basic processes that operate to regulate the MR domain are in place when children first form social ties with other children (processes that are shared with nonhuman primates). Some of the mechanisms are fully operational early on, whereas others come online with children's increased cognitive ability. At the most basic level, the interactive system and physiological regulatory systems of friends (beginning when children are only toddlers) appear to be coordinated. Among toddlers, this concordance appears in their baseline heart rate and cortisol levels as well as their play behaviors (Goldstein, Field, & Healy, 1989). This suggests that young children become synchronized with each other not only in their attention and actions but also at a physiological level.

As one outcome of successful MR relationships with peers, the child is buffered against stressful experiences, both at a direct and an indirect level. At the most direct level, friends serve to buffer the child against bullying by other children (Schwartz, Dodge, Pettit, & Bates, 2000; Smith, Shu, & Madsen, 2001). By the alliance with a friend, children are able to accomplish something that they could not do on their own. More indirectly, the presence of a friend serves to buffer against stress: Children show reduced levels of stress (as reflected in cortisol levels) when a preferred friend is present (Field et al., 1992). In addition, children's level of norepinephrine in response to painful medical experiences has been found to be buffered by their level of perceived support from friends (Hockenberry-Eaton, Kemp, & DiTorio, 1994).

A long-term benefit of early involvement in MR ties with peers is the increased ability to engage in affiliative activity of many kinds (e.g., Lindsey, 2002; Vaughn, Colvin, Azria, Caya, & Krzysik, 2001). Early ties may provide an internship in which there is an opportunity to more fully develop both the regulation of mutual benefits and the more complete understanding of the minds and feelings of others. For example, young children who have a stable and mutual friendship were shown to outperform, on a theory of mind task, children who lacked such a relationship (Peterson & Siegal, 2002). Finally, MR relationships also serve to facilitate positive emotional states, as mediated by both the opioid system and the dopamine system, which are involved in social reward (Depue, Luciana, Arbisi, Collins, & Leon, 1994; McClelland, Patel, Stier, & Brown, 1987; Panksepp, 1993; Vanderschuren, Nissick, & Van Ree, 1997).

Summary. The MR domain serves to accomplish mutually beneficial relationships between unrelated individuals who have a peer relationship. Such relationships facilitate the shared provision of social-emotional benefits (e.g., generation of positive affect or reduction in stress), joint collaboration in shared defense (e.g., against bullying), or task accomplishment. In addition, humans (and other primates) have demonstrated the capacity to keep track of the provision of reciprocal benefits with specific others, thus facilitating the likelihood that an equitable, mutually beneficial relationship will be maintained. The capacity for higher-level MR functions (complex coordination or mutual understanding) follows as children develop cognitively. Early in infancy, children may be thought of as expecting the experience of mutuality/and reciprocity. Mothers respond by facilitating the infant's affectively positive engagement with reciprocal and mutual interaction (e.g., coordinated communication activities or games).

Biological Preparation for Different Environments

Some researchers have been concerned with the extent to which children come to demonstrate an adaptive fit with the experienced environment. From a biological standpoint, this is thought of as "facultative polymorphism": The young are designed to respond in adaptive ways to variations in the world to which they are born. For example, Belsky, Steinberg, and Draper (1991) proposed that early social experiences provide the young with information that is diagnostic with respect to the kinds of environments they will face later in their lives. In a facultative fashion, the young may then "select" response strategies best suited to those probable environments. Thus, mothers who are low in sensitivity and high in rejection are more likely to have insecurely at-

tached children (e.g., Ainsworth, Blehar, Waters, & Wall 1978). At the same time, the response strategies characterized by insecurely attached children may be optimal for maintaining contact with a particular type of mother (Cassidy, 1994; Simpson, 1999). At a more general level, such children may develop an opportunistic rather than a stable pattern of close relationships. In mating relationships, this plays out in the form of short-term mating strategies. For example, avoidantly attached adults tend to become involved in unstable short-term sexual relationships that include low parental investment (Brennan & Shaver, 1995; Simpson, 1999). Mating occurs early and in a way that maximizes the number of progeny.

In addition, there are other more direct cues early in life that are diagnostic with respect to future life experiences. For example, a high level of early stress (e.g., parental divorce or marital conflict) or lack of resources may signal a harsh future (Belsky et al., 1991). Such experiences have been found to be associated with faster rates of sexual maturation—a pattern that might influence mating and parental investment strategies in ways that maximize the number of progeny early in life. These formulations are not without their critics (Maccoby, 1991). In addition, there are indications that pubertal timing as a result of early experience follows more from the benefits associated with positive-harmonious family relationships rather than the costs associated with negative-coercive family relationships (Ellis, McFayden-Ketchum, Dodge, Pettit, & Bates, 1999): Girls who experienced a more positive early history (e.g., greater paternal investment or more mother-daughter affection) showed later pubertal onset.

Integration and Segue

In this section, we have considered the ways in which biological processes prepare both the child and the parent for the domains of social life. We have observed that the brain is experience-expectant. As such, there is a prepared sensitivity to social experiences as well as privileged learning in acquiring the social knowledge that is essential to accomplishing the basic tasks of social life.

In reviewing these processes, we have suggested that there are meaningful distinctions in both the tasks and the mechanisms that regulate interactions in different social domains. However, the domains cannot be seen as entirely distinctive in that some tasks are accomplished by one domain at one stage of development (e.g., safety provided by parents in infancy) and by another domain at later stage (e.g., safety provided by coalitional groups at later ages). However, there are meaningful distinctions in the time course, the mechanisms, and the hormonal and emotional processes that serve to regulate the different domains.

We have given considerable attention to the role of hormones in the preparation of the young to function adaptively in different domains. Such processes may be thought of as key mediators in the preparation of the young and their caregivers for the socialization experience.

We have also suggested that evolutionary history (the mechanisms that have evolved to solve recurrent problems in human history) provides some of the basic design features of socialization. We have also pointed out that evolutionary history prepares individuals for the recurrent variations (as well as the regularities) in their experiences. For example, there have been variations in the resources available to parents and in the characteristics of the young. As a result, there are variable strategies available for optimizing the reproductive success of parents and the young in different ecologies.

Socialization is accomplished most effectively when parents are able to read the changing states of their children, as well as the changing motives and capabilities of children across the course of development. In the framework offered here, this process may also be thought of as involving the parent's ability to shift domains in appropriate ways. So, for example, if an infant is distressed, effective parenting involves parental responsiveness to the child's state and the ability to activate responses consistent with the protective care domain. In contrast, if a parent responds to a distressed child with efforts to engage him or her in a reciprocal game (a domain mismatch), parenting is more likely to be unsuccessful—the child will not be calmed and the parent will not succeed in efforts to engage the child.

In short, biology creates a platform on which sociocultural influences are built. Acceptable variations in socialization processes are afforded by virtue of the fact that the evolutionary history of humans has provided alternative designs for the different kinds of environments they have faced.

SOCIOCULTURAL APPROACHES

We move now from a discussion of the biological mechanisms that operate during socialization to a different level of analysis—a consideration of the impact of the so-cial context and of social experiences on development. In so doing, we keep in mind the biological foundation described in the preceding pages of this chapter. The bulk of empirical knowledge about socialization processes and mechanisms, however, comes from decades of research conducted in a different framework. This perspective acknowledged the existence of biological pressures and predispositions but focused on the actions and attitudes of agents of socialization and the impact of these actions and attitudes on children's behavior, cognitions, and emotions. We provide an overview of the research using that framework. What is added in the present discussion, however, is an attempt to see how the findings from a direction that has historically largely characterized the study of socialization can be considered in the domain framework proposed in the previous section. Such a discussion will reveal large gaps in knowledge that need to be filled. At the same time, it may help to organize and to make sense of the existing data.

In this section we consider how agents of socialization operate to produce individuals who fit into their cultural milieu. The focus is on human research. In these points of focus, different kinds of linkages can be drawn with the biological platform discussed in the last section. In cases where there is a high degree of similarity in processes across sociocultural contexts, the linkages are clearer; for example, the central features of the parental care domain show a high level of continuity across cultures, species, and presumably across human history. In other cases, the linkages are less obvious. As humans have accommodated to circumstances that would have been less central in their evolutionary past, socialization processes have arisen culturally to manage contemporary needs. For example, processes relevant to the socialization of independence would have been less relevant in highly interdependent hunter-gatherer societies. Nonetheless, biology places some level of constraints on socialization: Socialization practices that focused too much or too early on autonomy, without sufficient concern for interdependence, would be likely to meet with resistance. Similarly, those who ignored the biologically based need for some form of separation from the group and attempted to inhibit autonomous action would also be likely to meet with resistance.

Much of the focus in this section, as in the previous section, will be on parents as the primary agents of socialization who prepare children for their social roles. The focus on parents is because, as discussed earlier, children and parents comprise a biosocial system that is set up to favor parents as having a heavy investment in child rearing and children as being equipped very early on to respond to parental cues, including such events as recognition of the face, voice, and smell of their primary caregiver. A fundamental need of children is for security and protection, and parents are in a unique position to satisfy this need. Indeed, the need for protection forms a basis for the development of a strong relationship between parent and child and, as will be shown, the quality of relationship between child and agent of socialization is of major significance in ensuring the success of socialization practices. Moreover, the parent-child relationship is fixed and immutable, unable to be altered or terminated except under the most unusual circumstance. In addition to being constrained by legal and kinship definitions, this relationship, because of the long period of dependency of child on parent, also demands long histories of interaction and facilitates the development of routinized patterns of interaction that foster accommodation to family values and expectations (Collins, Gleason, & Sesma, 1997). As well, parents are usually the local representatives of the social mores and therefore society formally assigns them the task of socialization. In this way, society and biology work together to designate the family setting as the primary context in which children are prepared to function in the larger social milieu. From a practical perspective, the prolonged period of dependency and close contact between the parent-child dyad also motivates parents to instill appropriate and desirable behavior in children with whom they have to share a comfortable daily existence. And, finally, close and frequent contact between parent and child affords opportunities for parents to monitor their children and to come to understand and anticipate their beliefs and actions (conditions that are essential for successful socialization).

We begin this section with a discussion of the basic dimensions of interrelatedness and autonomy in the socialization process—traditional concerns of socialization theory. These map well on to the socialization domains already discussed because they involve both different forms of interaction with others and separation from others. It is the latter that is necessitated by the inequality that is inherent in the hierarchical power domain—an inequality that does not exist in the other domains. We then move on to a discussion of different socialization practices and strategies that are employed in the implementation of the different domains of social

life. Finally, we discuss the role of cultural context as an important qualifier of the effects of different socialization practices.

Dimensions of Socialization

Contemporary models of personality and social development frequently converge on two critical aspects of human functioning: (1) the ability to develop and maintain close interpersonal relationships and (2) the growth of self-definition or autonomy (e.g., Blatt, 1995; Deci & Ryan, 1991; Grotevant & Cooper, 1986). This echoes the continuing theme of shared regulatory processes and self-regulatory processes in the last section. Thus, in the context of relatedness to others, infants, children, and adolescents acquire the ability to function as separate and independent individuals who make their own decisions and guide their own behavior. These two processes of interpersonal relatedness and self-definition develop synergistically so that, as one unfolds, changes in the other are enhanced. In attachment, for example, as infants develop a feeling of security with their caregivers they become more ready to explore their environment and their own mental states. This exploration promotes a more detailed sense of self, which promotes the ability to relate to others (Blatt, 1995). Those individuals who are optimally developed maintain relationships without losing their autonomous view of self—striving to achieve individuality without sacrificing links to others. Those who emphasize interdependence with others and sacrifice autonomy are alleged to develop a dependent personality style, whereas those who emphasize self at the expense of relationships are alleged to develop a self-critical personality style (Blatt, 1998). In addition, the two processes assume differential importance in different contexts (Brewer, 1999a).

The concepts of interdependence or interrelatedness and autonomy appear consistently in treatments of socialization practices as researchers have tried to understand how children learn to fit in with the social group but become in some sense independent of or differently dependent on that group. Thus, there is a continuing interest in maintenance of the protective care, coalitional group, hierarchical power, and MR domains—but in changing ways across the course of development and shifting settings.

Socialization involves continued close ties to others, but decreasing power imbalances. The caveat to be signaled here is that the notion of independence from the group is a culturally bound one and that much thinking and research about interrelatedness and autonomy has been conducted in a middle-class and Western European cultural context. The extent to which existing notions about interpersonal relatedness and self-definition and their interactions are universal is an open question that we address later in this section. To anticipate, however, current conceptions seem to be that these are universal aspects of human development and functioning, albeit with different expressions as a function of the ecological niche in which individuals currently find themselves.

Interdependence/Interrelatedness

Already discussed is the importance of the caregiver-child dyadic relationship in the parental care domain: Attachment is a major foundation of social development, promoting safety, comfort in response to distress, emotional self-regulation, and trust in others. Attachment is not the only form of relationship that children develop with socializing agents (Belsky, 1999; Goldberg, Grusec, & Jenkins, 1999; Thompson, 1999). For example, in addition to providing protection to their children in the face of threat and stress, parents can demonstrate warmth and verbal and physical affection in their interactions with them. They can spontaneously hug and praise their offspring, frequently without any obvious eliciting action on the part of the offspring. Warmth has played an important role in early conceptions of socialization and identification (e.g., Sears, Maccoby, & Levin, 1957) and operates in a different way from protection in facilitating the socialization process; for example, making it pleasurable for children to reproduce the actions of nurturant and rewarding agents of socialization. Warmth, however, is governed by a different system from that which operates in the attachment domain (MacDonald, 1992; Goldberg et al., 1999) and provides a different mechanism for assumption of social roles. For example, the provision of protection and responsiveness to the child's distress makes a unique contribution to the prediction of children's negative affect and empathy and prosocial behavior when the effects of warmth are controlled for, whereas warmth does not when the effects of responsiveness to distress are controlled for. Moreover, warmth makes a unique contribution to the prediction of children's regulation of positive affect when the effects of responsiveness to distress are controlled for, whereas responsiveness to distress does not when the effects of warmth are controlled for (Davidov & Grusec, in press).

Protection and warmth expose children to socialization attempts by keeping them near socialization agents and attentive to their actions. But protection may be of particular significance in the socialization of emotion regulation because of the focus on negative affect and distress. Warmth may play a more prominent role in shared actions and shared identity that is part of the coalitional domain. Thus, being a valued and accepted member of the group (as conveyed through social inclusion processes) may motivate conformity to the standards of that group both to confirm a feeling of belongingness and to avoid alienation and separation as well as anxiety about threat from outside.

Autonomy and Control

The basis of successful socialization is the creation of a positive relationship with parents or other agents of socialization that fosters a willingness or desire to be receptive to their directives. Central here is the notion of willingness, with its implication that behavior is self-directed or autonomous. Children are responsive because of positive aspects of the relationship they have with socialization agents. A considerable part of socialization, however, involves control and the imposition of standards of conduct, and it is here that the hierarchical power domain comes into play. Indeed, control has historically been the major focus of attention for socialization researchers. Often, but not always, the desires of the child and the parent are somewhat or distinctly at odds, and one goal of socialization for parents is to make the child's desires more concordant with their own. This has to be done, however, in a way that encourages the child's feelings of autonomously directed action. Parents have the advantage in this particular situation because they control more resources (although children do have many resources in the relationship involving their ability to provide gratification to the parent; see Kuczynski, 2003; Rheingold, 1969). The challenge is to achieve concordance between adult and child desires, or at least some degree of concordance, in a way that minimizes antagonism and maximizes willing compliance and a feeling on the part of the child that behavior is self-directed or autonomously chosen. Indeed, the existence of conflict and its resolution is frequently considered to be an essential ingredient in the development of autonomy and self-regulation (Maccoby & Martin, 1983; Yau & Smetana, 1996) given that it sharpens the distinction between self and other and helps in the achievement of self-direction.

Events in the hierarchical power domain are complicated by the fact that, as described earlier, relationships change in a far more complex way than in the other domains. Although parental care, coalitional, and MR domain relationships all change with children's expanding competencies and interests, relationships in the hierarchical power domain are particularly likely to change as children become less willing to accept control in areas that they now come to see as personal and where they consider intervention by authority figures to be less acceptable (Smetana, 1988, 1997). In the hierarchical power domain, there is constant negotiation and compromise as socializers and objects of their socialization try to find a middle ground between what the two are willing to tolerate (although the extent to which this occurs may be culturally determined; e.g., Trommsdorff & Kornadt, 2003). Driving this particular aspect of development is the latter's changing notion of autonomy and the former's adjustment as to which actions can be tolerated or negotiated (Goodnow, 1994). Always the focus is on autonomy and self-regulation and the child's acceptance of standards of action and conduct as self-regulated and self-imposed. Without such acceptance, socialization is deemed to be unsuccessful, arousing anger, reactance, and hostility (M. Hoffman, 1970). Indeed, support for the emphasis placed by socialization theorists on autonomy and self-regulation emerges from findings by biological researchers who, as noted earlier, have found that the long-term occupation of a subordinate role has high costs with its accompanying detrimental levels of cardiovascular strain and activation of the HPA system (Abbott et al., 2003). Thus, there is a strong biological basis for the traditional position that successful socialization requires an approach that minimizes feelings of subordination and force. And obviously, in this unstable system, there are developmental differences in what is perceived to be subordination. Indeed, there may be sex differences as well, with boys more likely to resist authority as their testosterone levels increase and they become more aggressive (Panksepp, 1993).

Varieties of Control. Control is a complex variable, which can, for example, be used in either an autonomy-supportive or an autonomy-destructive way. This feature of its use has led to considerable confusion in analyses of socialization, as researchers and theoreticians have focused on either the harmful or beneficial consequences of a clearly multifaceted construct. Those who view control as positive, for example, emphasize clarification and consistency of limits in child rearing (Baumrind, 1971; Baumrind & Thompson, 2002). Those who see it as detrimental to the child's development regard it as coercive and synonymous with the use of force to gain compliance, an approach that undermines willing and autonomous action on the part of the recipient (e.g., Deci & Ryan, 1991). The meaning of the term needs further clarification. The most recent way in which this has occurred is through a distinction between psychological and behavioral control (Barber, 1996, 2002; Steinberg, 1990; Steinberg, Dornbusch, & Brown, 1992).

Psychological versus Behavioral Control. A historical description of approaches to control is helpful in understanding the confusion surrounding its meaning. In early analyses of socialization, control carried a substantially negative connotation. Levy (1943), for example, argued that parents whose own emotional needs had been unmet in childhood developed attitudes toward their own children that reflected these unmet needs. These attitudes manifested themselves either in overprotection and intrusiveness in their child-rearing practices or in the behavioral opposite of rejection. Schaefer (1965), in his treatment of control or, more specifically, the dimension of psychological control versus psychological autonomy, treated it as involving intrusiveness, parental direction, and control through guilt. For Baumrind (1971), control was an important feature of both authoritarian and authoritative parenting, but the nature of the control was not distinguished. Disaggregation of authoritarian and authoritative parenting into three parts—acceptance, behavioral control, and psychological control—has helped to make sense of when control is positive and when it is negative in its consequences (e.g., Steinberg, Elmen, & Mounts, 1989).

Behavioral control, the positive aspect of control, refers to the rules, regulations, and restrictions that parents impose on their children as well as their knowledge or awareness of their children's activities that is obtained in an active way through inquiry and observation. It focuses on control over daily actions, and includes parental monitoring of the whereabouts of their children and of the people with whom they associate. *Psychological control,* in contrast, refers to control that undermines the child's autonomous development. It includes parental intrusiveness, guilt induction, and love withdrawal. Psychologically controlling parents are not responsive to the psychological needs and emotions of their children; their actions imply derogation of the child and they interfere with the child's establishment of a sense of identity (Barber, 1996, 2002). Psychological control seems more relevant to the emotional climate in which parenting is conducted.

High levels of psychological control predict both externalizing problems and internalizing problems (e.g., anxiety, depression, and loneliness) and difficulties with academic achievement, low self-esteem, low self-reliance, and self-derogation. In contrast, low levels of behavioral control have been linked with externalizing problems, including drug use, truancy, and antisocial behavior (Barber & Harmon, 2002). Moreover, the evidence seems to indicate that, in accord with a bidirectional analysis, problematic children and adolescents, to some extent, elicit these parenting behaviors but that parental behaviors also promote problem behaviors in children (e.g., Dodge & Pettit, 2003; Laird, Pettit, Bates, & Dodge, 2003). Although the consequences of psychological and behavioral control are opposite in their valence, it appears that the two forms of control are not simply opposite ends of the same continuum: Behavioral control culminates in increased social responsibility and impulse control, whereas psychological control has its outcome in the development of negative self-processes. The motivation behind parental use of psychological control is not the enhancement of social responsibility in children but the domination and manipulation of emotional and psychological boundaries between parent and child in a way that works to satisfy the needs of the parent. In this sense, it has more to do with the nature of the parent-child relationship than it does with the imposition of demands for socially acceptable behavior. Finally, low psychological control and psychological autonomy are not synonymous: Although a parent may not be psychologically controlling, a parent may not engage in the kind of supportive behavior that facilitates autonomy either (Barber, Bean, & Erickson, 2002).

Psychological Control Elaborated. Although the distinction between behavioral and psychological control marks a significant step forward in understanding of socialization processes, the story does not end here, leaving room for still further distinctions. Note, for example, psychological control includes a variety of socialization practices that may have somewhat different impacts on children's social, emotional, and cognitive development. Specifically, psychological control can manifest itself in several different ways—through the suppression of independence of thinking, through

the production of guilt, or in an overprotectiveness of the child. Each of these features of psychological control may have different outcomes that remain to be elucidated (Morris et al., 2002). Consider, for example, suppression of independence of thinking, or what has been labeled by some as "intrusive control" (e.g., Grolnick, 2003; Pomerantz & Eaton, 2001). Adults who are intrusively controlling are overbearing and inhibiting in their interventions with children, allowing them little choice in their actions. They do not, however, engage in emotional manipulation. Intrusively controlling agents of socialization value compliance, pressure children to engage in specified outcomes, and do not engage in discussion and verbal give-and-take. In spite of the fact that they inhibit a child's autonomy and feelings of choice, their intrusiveness can be an indication of caring. Moreover, under certain conditions, intrusive control can be predictive of positive child outcomes (Pomerantz & Eaton, 2001).

Autonomy Support versus Intrusive Control. Intrusive control appears to overlap with the autonomy-threatening style of intervention described by Deci, Ryan, and their colleagues (e.g., Deci & Ryan, 1991; Grolnick, Deci, & Ryan, 1997) in their discussions of self-determination theory. According to self-determination theory, children require structure or the clear setting out of rules and expectations. Structure can be imposed, however, in either an autonomy-supportive or controlling way. Even in high-risk, dangerous environments where parents impose more rules and restrictions (a practice that does not work so well in low-risk environments at least with respect to the development of children's social competence), those who do it in a democratic way and provide explanations have children who are more competent (A. Baldwin, Baldwin, & Cole, 1990). Nor does autonomy support suggest lack of parental involvement. High involvement and high autonomy support together foster the most positive outcomes academically and socioemotionally. High involvement with low autonomy support, however, stifles development, whereas low involvement deprives children of resources and assistance (Grolnick, 2003). Further refinement in an understanding of intrusive control also requires attention to the specific areas in which control is exerted. For example, adolescents who rate parents as restrictive in areas deemed by the adolescents to be personal issues, as opposed to moral or social conventional, rate their parents as higher in psychological control than do those who see those same issues as legitimately subject to parental authority (Smetana & Daddis, 2002).

A significant feature of autonomy support is the provision of choice (Grolnick, 2003). Some caution is in order, however, with the observation that too much choice can be overly challenging. Here, the evidence comes from studies that show adults have difficulty managing large amounts of choice (Dhar, 1997; Shafir, Simonson, & Tversky, 1993; Shafir & Tversky, 1992). When faced with a large number of alternative possibilities, they find the experience enjoyable but feel frustrated and dissatisfied with the alternatives they have chosen (Iyengar & Lepper, 2000). It does not stretch the imagination to suggest that similar outcomes may exist for children. There comes a point when making choices is so demanding that individuals may defer to the more expert opinion of others, including agents of socialization.

Guilt. Possibly more harmful than intrusive control is parental production of guilt. Some time ago, M. Hoffman (1970) suggested that parental withdrawal of love was a practice that promoted "neurotic" guilt. Children who were recipients of love withdrawal felt guilt from awareness of unacceptable impulses rather than from harm done to others. In a similar vein, Grolnick et al. (1997) allude to introjected regulation, a form of internalization of social standards that have been "taken in" by the child but are maintained in their original form. Thus, the regulation that results from this form of internalization is internally, rather than externally, imposed and is not integrated with the self and thereby becomes a source of tension and inner conflict. As an example, introjected regulation is apparent in individuals who pressure themselves to do well on a test rather than to perform well because it is important to be academically proficient or because achievement is an integrated or cohesive part of their self-concept. Withdrawal of love seems to be particularly implicated in the production of neurotic guilt and may also reflect emotional manipulation that threatens feelings of being respected and included as an important member of the social group (Eccles, 2002): In this way, it moves into or takes advantage of events in the coalitional group domain, involving the desire to be an integral and valued member of the group.

Monitoring and Knowledge about Children and Their Activities. Monitoring is a feature of behavioral control that has received considerable attention from socialization theorists as an approach to parenting. It is conceptualized as close surveillance in the form of parents' requests for information about their children's activities (Laird, Pettit, Mize, Brown, & Lindsey, 1994), shared activities with children (Waizenhoffer, Buchanen, & Jackson-Newsom, 2004), and conversations with teachers, peers, and other parents (Crouter, Helms-Erikson, Updegraff, & McHale, 1999). For young children monitoring involves direct supervision by parents themselves or by others, whereas for older children and adolescents more distal forms of monitoring, such as parent-initiated conversation and imposition of rules, are the norm. Many investigators have found significant relations between parental monitoring and positive child outcomes (see Crouter & Head, 2002, for a review), presumably in part at least because monitoring or knowledge of their children's activities enables parents to ensure that their children are not exposed to influences that would have a detrimental effect on their socialization. (Again, the linkage is bidirectional, with high levels of delinquent behavior predicting decreases in parental knowledge, in addition to low levels of parental knowledge predicting increases in delinquent behavior; e.g., Laird et al., 2003). An extension of the concept of monitoring comes with the notion of "collective socialization" (Brody et al., 2001) that alludes to neighborhood monitoring and refers to feelings of trust and cohesiveness in neighbors that promote agreement about what is acceptable behavior. Brody et al. found that collective socialization, or the willingness of adults to monitor and supervise the behavior of both their own children and that of other members of the community, combined with positive parenting, was associated with a reduction in children's associations with deviant peers, particularly as neighborhoods became more disadvantaged. They hypothesize that collective socialization reduces the negative impact of deviant peers by decreasing the amount of antisocial behavior in the community, by determining appropriate standards of conduct, and by providing more opportunities for supervision of children.

Although monitoring, as noted earlier, is seen as attention to and tracking of a child's activities and the setting of limits, Stattin and Kerr (2000) point out that it has been frequently operationalized simply as knowledge of the child's activities and whereabouts. They suggest that knowledge can come from one of three sources: (1) parents' solicitation of information, (2) parents' control over their children's activities, and (3) disclosure by children. Thus, they argue that it is premature to suggest that tracking and limit-setting account for positive links between monitoring and prosocial outcomes when monitoring is measured as knowledge. Indeed, in a study of Swedish adolescents and their families, Stattin and Kerr (2000) found that disclosure was the most important source of parents' knowledge about their children's activities and friends, with the clear implication that children who engage in antisocial behavior probably hide their activities from their parents and that this, at least in part, accounts for the correlation between knowledge and outcomes. Kerr and Stattin (2000) report that low levels of child disclosure were highly predictive of adolescent maladjustment, whereas solicitation of information and control were not.

Kerr and Stattin (2000) and Stattin and Kerr (2000) operationalized parental solicitation and control as parents asking adolescents about their activities and friends and setting limits on their behavior. When monitoring was defined as parents participating in activities with adolescents and questioning knowledgeable adults about their children, Waizenhoffer, Buchanan, and Jackson-Newsom (2004) found that parental monitoring was, contrary to the Swedish results, predictive of their knowledge. Waizenhoffer et al.'s report of mixed results with respect to links between sources of information and adolescent maladjustment underlines the complexity of the issue and suggests that, among other things, monitoring that is too controlling may indeed have a negative impact. In accord with this interpretation, Kerr and Stattin (2000) found that adolescents who reported feeling overly controlled by their parents also reported higher levels of both external (e.g., delinquency or school problems) and internal (e.g., depression or low self-esteem) maladjustment. One conclusion is that surveillance and questioning—done in an autonomy-supportive manner—helps parents head off problems and respond to warning signs. But an additional contributor to the knowledge required for such responding involves the fostering of an atmosphere of warmth and trust—a relationship that makes children and adolescents more likely to disclose information about their activities. Not to be overlooked, children who have few school problems and are low in delinquency are no doubt more willing to disclose.

Summary

Children need to feel interrelated with, as well as separate and autonomous from, others. Interrelatedness and autonomy take place in the context of the domains of socialization we describe in this chapter, with autonomy as a feature of human behavior that has implications for successful handling of events in the hierarchical power domain. Control is the operative concern in the power domain, as the nature of relative power changes over the course of development. Positive relationships foster socialization. But control is also a part of socialization and

for it to be used effectively it must not threaten children's feelings of autonomy. Researchers have distinguished among different forms of control, with some more effective than others at achieving positive socialization outcomes.

Socialization Practices

To this point, we have discussed the manner in which parents influence behavior through their relationship with the child and through the particular way in which they exercise control. Relationships and the manner in which control is exercised have to do with the context in which caregivers socialize children. Ultimately, they convey the generalized motives of socializing agents rather than their motives with respect to a child's specific actions. But socialization also involves specific content as well as goals or outcomes that parents hope to achieve (Darling & Steinberg, 1993). Included in the content are not only discipline practices, such as punishment or various types of reasoning, but also a whole range of other practices. Some of these practices are deliberate and intentional interventions on the part of socializers, designed to achieve desired goals, and others are less intentional and deliberate. Thus, children are deliberately exposed to models deemed worthy of emulation, but at other times they are exposed to the unintended influences of others. Such unintended influences may either be consistent with or counter to the intended goals of socialization. For example, parents (or agents of socialization) may model prosocial actions in their daily lives. Conversely, children may also be inadvertently exposed to less worthy actions modeled by agents of socialization themselves, deviant members of society, or the media. The use of strongly power assertive discipline techniques is another example of a practice that can be deliberate or unintentional as when it sends the message that force and coercion are good ways to achieve wanted outcomes.

The domain approach that forms the core of the present analysis of socialization processes suggests that different types of socialization practices will be appropriate in different social domains, so we organize a discussion of these practices by their relevance to the four domains of protective care, coalitional group, hierarchical power, and mutuality/reciprocity. As noted earlier, such organization may help to make sense of disparate bodies of research as well as clarifying where there are missing gaps in information and underemphases in the focus of empirical investigations of socialization practices. We also remind the reader that, as noted earlier, these strategies are differentially effective as a function of a whole series of variables including child characteristics (e.g., age, sex, or temperament). These are interactions that are revisited in the concluding section of the chapter.

Socialization Practices in the Protective Care Domain: Sensitive and Responsive Caregiving

In the protective care domain, parental sensitivity is the major parenting practice that promotes positive outcomes for children, with these outcomes including mastery, emotion regulation, and interpersonal closeness (Ainsworth, Blehar, Waters, & Wall, 1978; Bowlby, 1969; Sroufe, 1988). Caregivers are positioned along a series of continua involving their sensitivity to the needs of their children, their acceptance or rejection of those needs, the extent to which they cooperate with or are intrusive in their interactions with their offspring, and the degree to which they are accessible (Ainsworth et al., 1978). Those who are sensitively responsive, accepting, and accessible best prepare their offspring to effectively self-regulate negative affect associated with distress. They enable the young to trust their caregivers (and others with whom they form strong attachment relationships) to fulfill their needs for physical and emotional protection and make reasonable demands for compliance to social standards of behavior (Bretherton, Golby, & Cho, 1997). Thus, the human species has evolved to be willingly compliant, given that such compliance markedly increases the chances of individual survival (Stayton, Hogan, & Ainsworth, 1971). Securely attached individuals are also able to explore their physical and psychological worlds because they have a protective base to which they can return. In this way, their developing sense of competence is fostered by the belief that they are supported, and by adjustments they learn to cope with the stress of impending threats of danger. Rejecting and interfering, or rejecting and neglecting, caregivers promote feelings of insecurity, lack of trust, anger, and feelings of helplessness. As a result, they promote lack of willing compliance (Stayton et al., 1971).

Socialization Practices in the Coalitional Group Domain: Cultural Practices, Routines, Rituals, Joint Play, and Observational Learning

The coalitional domain is marked by children's interest in abiding by rules and conventions, doing things in a ritualized way, and conforming to avoid implicit exclusion from the group. This moves us into a discussion of cultural practices and routines, or everyday ways of acting that simply happen, such as assignment of roles and activities to boys and girls, sleeping arrangements, routine work around the house, how people dress, divisions of parenting between mothers and fathers, and distinctions between what is allowed to occur in public and what must be done only in private (Goodnow, 1997). No rationale or explanation is provided for these actions, and they develop a momentum of their own that mitigates against reflection or questioning. They are to be distinguished from special moments that have been the principal focus of socialization theorists for understanding the way in which rules and standards of behavior are most likely to be made explicit (Bugental & Goodnow, 1998). Rituals (e.g., holiday celebrations) also belong in the category of activities that need no explanation but nevertheless impart considerable information about what is proper and expected. They are different from routines by virtue of their symbolism, endurance, associated affect, and meaning that extend across generations (Fiese et al., 2002).

Routines and rituals play their part in socialization by supporting feelings of group belongingness. Families, for example, develop a group identity through their routines and rituals and these events foster a sense of participation in and feeling of group membership (Moore & Myerhoff, 1977). In this way, they foster the transmission of values from one generation to another and strengthen intergenerational relationships that are important for successful transmission. We use the word *transmission* deliberately in this context, struck by the fact that children's input into routine and ritual may be less than it is in other socialization contexts. Routine and ritual denote an unchanging set of conditions where discussions about usefulness or appropriateness are not even contemplated. Indeed, once such discussion ensues, acceptance may well break down.

Other socialization practices can be assigned to the coalitional group domain. One of these is joint play (to be distinguished from rough-and-tumble play associated with the hierarchical power domain). Parents who engage in enjoyable activities with their children, in addition to providing them with the experience of harmonious and rewarding relationships, are also structuring their children's time. Time spent in joint play at age 3 years predicts improvement in conduct problems at age 4, independent of the initial level of those problems (Gardner, Ward, Burton, & Wilson, 2003). In adolescence, joint play transforms itself into time spent together in mutual activities and continues to be an important feature of parent-child functioning that is linked with reduced conflict with fathers although not with mothers for whom time in joint activity and conflict are not correlated. For fathers and sons, there is some suggestion that it is the time spent together that in part accounts for reduction in conflict, in addition to the obvious observation that high conflict makes fathers and adolescents less likely to share activities (Dubas & Gerris, 2002). Although joint play might seem to have some of the features of mutual reciprocity, the evidence suggests that reciprocity is not a major component of joint play in well-functioning families and that parents of children who do not have conduct problems tend to initiate and organize play in contrast to parents of children with conduct problems who are more likely to sit back and let their children take the lead (Gardner, 1994).

Another way in which parents socialize their children that is of relevance to the coalitional group domain is through management of their experiences of and exposure to desirable influences. Parents select children's schools and their after-school activities, and they determine the neighborhoods in which their children live. They monitor their activities and arrange formal and informal play contacts. Through their own social networks, they provide the opportunity for social contacts for their children (Parke et al., 2002). They also cocoon their children or protect them from undesirable events and people (e.g., restricting exposure to certain forms of media or to particular peers) as well as prearm them by warning them of temptation or providing them with ways of avoiding temptation (e.g., P. Miller & Sperry, 1988; Thornton, Chatters, Taylor, & Allen, 1990; Watson-Gegeo, 1992).

Finally, observational learning shares with cultural practices, routines, rituals, joint play, and management a lack of linkage to special moments, a lack of reaction to a child's specific behavior, and, often, a lack of specifically intended transmission of information or intimation about the desirability of particular actions. It is not immediately obvious to observers why they imitate particular actions, and there may be less occasion or need for discussions about the usefulness or appropriateness of modeled actions. Indeed, it is striking how receptive young children become to "proper" ways of acting or conventional routines, many of which are acquired through observation (e.g., Dunn & Munn, 1985; Emde et al., 1991).

Observational learning occurs in different circumstances that may well affect its potency in the socialization process. In some cases, for example, it happens in a setting where instruction is intended as opposed to others where it is not. Rogoff, Pardies, Arauz, Correa-Chavez, and Angelillo (2003) talk about third-party observation that involves keen attention and listening in or eavesdropping in anticipation of engaging in a similar activity at a future time. Although less studied than other forms of teaching, "intent participation" is a particularly powerful form of learning, especially in cultural communities where children have easy access to everyday activities of adults and other children and where they can engage in collaborative actions with other members of the group. H. L. Rheingold's (1982) observations about the early appearance of helping provide a good example of intent participation in American families. She noted that children between 18 and 30 months of age eagerly helped adults engaged in household work, appearing to enjoy themselves and to understand that they were contributing to the management of the household as opposed to playing. Intent participation stands in sharp contrast to the form of tuition in which teachers deliver knowledge (either in the classroom or in the home) and provide incentives for the successful acquisition of that knowledge. In keeping with the horizontal nature of the process, intent participation fosters complementarity of roles and cooperation. Moreover, the intrinsic merit of the activity is self-evident so that, once again, the need for internalization of values and guidelines for behavior is minimized.

Socialization Practices in the Hierarchical Power Domain: Reward and Punishment

Discipline and reward are the parenting practices that have been the primary focus of socialization researchers over many years. Historically, they have been addressed by their ability to facilitate internalization—the taking over by children of societal attitudes and values as their own (Grusec & Goodnow, 1994). Both have a strong element of control, although it may be easier for children to attribute prosocial behavior to their autonomously self-chosen actions after reasoning than after punishment or power assertion (Lepper, 1983).

In addition to disciplining undesirable actions, parents reward desirable ones. Although rewards detract from an inference of freely chosen action and, therefore, internalization, socialization agents still use them (e.g., Warton & Goodnow, 1995) and they play a major part in some socialization theories. Already discussed in the introductory section of this chapter is the important work of Patterson and his colleagues (Dishion, Andrews, & Crosby, 1995; Patterson, 1980), who have demonstrated how coercive cycles of interaction develop in problem families through inadvertent use of negative reinforcement and how this sets the stage for the exposure of children to positive reinforcement for antisocial action from deviant peer groups. Socialization researchers have distinguished between reinforcement of actions and attributions of good behavior to children's prosocial dispositions, with the latter being a more effective form of reinforcement (Grusec & Redler, 1980; Kuczynski, 1984).

The Case of Corporal Punishment. Power assertive strategies of discipline include verbal criticism, social isolation, and corporal punishment. Given space limitations we briefly discuss corporal punishment only, in part because of the considerable debate that exists with respect to its potentially harmful consequences to children. In spite of the controversy, it remains an acceptable intervention for many parents, at least in the United States where most parents report that they have spanked their young children (Straus & Gelles, 1988). This level of usage is in sharp contrast to many countries (specifically, Austria, Croatia, Cyprus, Denmark, Finland, Germany, Israel, Italy, Latvia, Norway, and Sweden) in which corporal punishment has been outlawed. It is also in contrast to Canada, a country where only 48% of mothers of children aged 0 to 17 years reported that they had used it in mild form (smacking, slapping, pinching) in the past year as opposed to 97% of parents responding to the same question in the United States (Oldershaw, 2002; Straus & Gelles, 1988). Although 14 years separates these two reports—the first Canadian and the second American—the relative figures seem unlikely to have changed substantially and point to considerable philosophical differences between two countries in close geographical proximity and seemingly with many shared values. Holden (2002) notes that in the United States legislation banning corporal punishment is highly unlikely to succeed given the importance placed in American history on corporal punishment as an important part of child rearing and beliefs about the privacy of the family and personal freedoms that mitigate against societal and governmental intervention at this level. In Canada, where history and attitudes about personal freedom are somewhat different, the Supreme Court, in January, 2004, upheld a provision of the Criminal Code that allowed teachers, parents, and guardians to use reasonable force to correct children in their charge. It did, however, set guidelines for reasonable force, quoting experts as saying it should not be used

against children younger than two or against teenagers and should never involve use of an object, such as a belt or ruler, and never include a slap or blow to the head.

Opponents of corporal punishment see it as a predictor of later antisocial behavior (e.g., Strassburg, Dodge, Pettit, & Bates, 1994) and as a potential way station to physical abuse (e.g., Straus, 1994). Supporters (e.g., Baumrind, Larzelere, & Cowan, 2002; Baumrind & Thompson, 2002) regard occasional mild corporal punishment (spanking of a child's extremities with an open hand) that is used only between toddlerhood and puberty and occurs in an authoritative context as a helpful tool in parental efforts to socialize their children and one that young children are willing to accept as a reasonable and fair practice on the part of their parents (Siegal & Barclay, 1985). Certainly, at very young ages, children are unable to understand the rationale or justification for corporal punishment and, in such instances, it may serve only as a source of fear or stress. Supporting this notion, Bugental, Martorell and Barraza (2003) found that children who were the recipients of corporal punishment below the age of 1 year were more likely than other children to show high reactivity (production of cortisol) to stress-inducing events (separation from the mother) at older ages. Similarly, high levels of harsh physical punishment are predictive of children's externalizing problems even when previous levels of problem behavior are held constant (e.g., Nix, Pinderhughes, Dodge, Bates, & Pettit, 1999).

Evidence for the argument that corporal punishment can easily shade into physical abuse is seen to come from the observation that the two are correlated (Gershoff, 2002). Moreover, statistics with respect to rates of child homicide support a hypothesis that there are links between favorable attitudes toward corporal punishment and extreme physical abuse: In Sweden, in 1996, three children between the ages of 0 and 4 years were the victims of homicide. In Canada, in 1997, 24 children of that same age were killed. In the United States, in 1998, the comparable homicide figure was 723 (WHO, 2002). Even controlling for differences in population the per capita rate is markedly discrepant among the three countries. These sorts of correlations do not imply causality, and it is plausible that positive attitudes to and the use of corporal punishment and child abuse have different antecedents (Baumrind et al., 2002). Indeed, Jaffee et al. (2004) have found that shared genetic influences account for a very large portion of the correlation between children's antisocial behavior and corporal punishment, whereas child maltreatment does not appear to be genetically mediated. Thus, they argue that corporal punishment and child maltreatment have distinct origins, with the latter lying in the family environment and characteristics of the abuser and the former in characteristics of the child. This does not mean of course that corporal punishment does not contribute to increases in children's antisocial behavior, as well as being elicited by their antisocial behavior.

Holden (2002) suggests that appropriate analyses of the impact of corporal punishment need to consider children's physiological and affective reactions to the intervention and their cognitive appraisals of its meaning. Thus, punishment that arouses fear, anger, or pain in the child is likely to reduce the child's willing compliance and to increase the child's avoidance of the parent, thereby reducing opportunities for socialization or the building of a positive relationship. Alternatively, if punishment is seen as well-intentioned, or as an accepted and expected part of the cultural context in which it occurs, then it may be viewed in a less negative way by the child. Ultimately, the issue may be reduced at least in part to one of impulsivity versus instrumentality in parental use of corporal punishment as well as the meaning its use has for the child.

There is still much to learn about the long-term effects of corporal punishment and the factors (means of implementation, responses of children) that serve to moderate its effects. It is typically associated with negative outcomes for the child, but the associated pathway and the qualifying variables for this relationship are unclear. Corporal punishment in some contexts may be less detrimental in its impact than other forms of punishment such as derogation and humiliation. Socialization researchers have argued for some time that power assertive discipline techniques, including physical punishment, will be effective only if they are moderate and mild in usage, combined with reasoning, and used in the context of a warm and loving relationship (e.g., Hoffman, 1983). Under all circumstances, corporal punishment, even when mild, does convey the message that the use of force is a justifiable way in which to solve conflicts, and this is a criticism that does not seem to have been adequately answered by its proponents and a message that most adults probably do not wish to send.

Socialization in the Mutuality/Reciprocity Domain

Caregivers who are responsive to the reasonable demands of their children have children who, in turn, are responsive to their demands (Parpal & Maccoby, 1985). This mutually responsive orientation facilitates children's willing compliance with caregiver requests, as opposed to situational or forced compliance based on externally imposed threat of punishment or hope of reward. Moreover, it is seen as a precursor to the development of conscience or early internalization (Kochanska & Aksan, 1995). Indeed, Kochanska and Murray (2000) report that parent-child relationships characterized by mutual compliance, harmony, and positivity during the toddler and preschool years predict children's conscience at early school age (guilt after deviation, resistance to temptation in the absence of surveillance, reluctance to violate rules, and maternal reports of moral and prosocial behavior), even after controlling for the developmental continuity of conscience.

Unlike rewards and punishment that function in the hierarchical domain, with parents imposing demands on their children, parent responsiveness moves the socialization process into the MR domain. As well as setting the stage for future willing compliance, it is also one aspect of the guided apprenticeship involving jointly coordinated interactions that is necessary for the MR domain to be fully operative with others. Although parents (as kin with shared interests with the child) will be willing to produce benefits for their related children, other unrelated individuals will be much less likely to do so. When parents create experiences that foster reciprocal relationships (in which there are two-way benefits), the child can be expected to learn the pragmatic rules of exchange that govern much of social life. Such experiences also create a means of negotiating the relationship between parents and children when the young decline in dependence and increase in power—as the relationship becomes more symmetrical. As suggested, there is empirical evidence to support the notion that mutual reciprocity continues to play a significant role in socialization through middle childhood. Labeled as synchrony and referring to interactions that are reciprocal, responsive, interconnected, and engaged, mutual reciprocity is predictive both of low levels of harsh parenting and low levels of antisocial behavior (Criss, Shaw, & Ingoldsby, 2003). In synchronous relationships children engage in mutual exchange with their parents. More than this, they also impart greater amounts of information to their parents (an important feature of effective socialization as noted earlier) and have the opportunity to practice positive social skills (Criss et al., 2003).

Summary

Different social domains require different socialization strategies to achieve the tasks associated with that domain. According to this analysis, parents who use the "wrong" strategy for a particular domain will not be successful in their socialization goals. Children cannot learn the pragmatic rules of exchange that govern much of social life by being punished, nor can they learn to accept rules of behavior through sensitive and accepting parenting. What works when a child is ill is not the same as what works when a child is well, given that different social domains are activated. There are clear interactions between social domain and socialization strategy.

Socialization and the Cultural Context

One of the most powerful moderators of the impact of experience on children's development is the cultural context in which the experience occurs. We turn now to a discussion of its role in socialization. Context gives meaning to a socialization activity; thus, the same action may have a different outcome in a different cultural context because it has a different meaning in each of those contexts. Investigation of culture also increases understanding of mechanisms of socialization and features of human behavior by demonstrating the role of goals and practices that are influenced by the cultural context, as well as identifying those goals and practices that cut across cultures. Context helps address questions, such as why it is that authoritarian parenting leads to negative outcomes in one culture and not in another, or whether autonomy and separation are universal features of psychological functioning independent of the context in which they are exhibited.

A frequently employed distinction in cultural research is that between individualism and collectivism. The distinction has both its advocates and its critics as we note in the following discussion. We use it, however, because it parallels so closely the dimensions of relatedness and autonomy that have been a prominent part of the discussion of socialization presented in this chapter.

Individualism versus Collectivism as Organizers of Culture

Differences between national cultures have been highlighted through the use of dichotomies, such as individualist-collectivist (Hofstede, 1983), agentic-communal (Kashima et al., 1995), and independent-interdependent (Markus & Kitiyama, 1991), all of which emphasize the distinct way that each values the self versus others. Thus, cultures are broadly characterized as focusing on different aspects of the two social-ization dimensions of interrelatedness and autonomy. Some (generally North American and Western European) focus on separation and autonomy of the individual, with the self seen as a distinct entity having unique internal attributes. These individualist cultures emphasize competition, self-actualization, dominance, and open expression of emotion. In contrast, collectivist cultures, more characteristic of most of the rest of the world, highlight interrelatedness and connectedness with the group, social harmony, and the organization of behavior around relationships with others. Cooperation, empathy, accommodation with the needs of others, subtle expressions of emotion, and, sometimes, deference to the authority of others are central in descriptions of collectivist approaches to psychological functioning.

Individualistic and collectivistic orientations arose as a result of adaptation to different environmental conditions and restraints, with specific economic and environmental conditions favoring different developmental pathways (e.g., Berry, 1976). Thus, the interdependent route is linked to small communities and a subsistence economy, where cooperation and interpersonal harmony are necessary features for survival. In contrast, the independent pathway is an adaptive response to large, anonymous, urban centers and a commercial economy, or modes of production that do not require group support. In the small and interdependent community, ideas tend to be transmitted from one generation to the next in a vertical fashion, and so they maximize continuity and facilitate respect for authority. In the more independent context, ideas are negotiated horizontally in generations and subject to influence from outside sources. As a result, there may be less continuity and respect for the traditional ways of doing things (Greenfield, Keller, Fuligni, & Maynard, 2003).

Pure examples of individualism and collectivism are not easy to find in a world that is changing speedily and where technological developments break down cultural distinctions. The dichotomy has been the object of considerable criticism, much of it a result of the tendency of researchers to treat individualism-collectivism as an individual difference variable rather than as a feature of differences between nations as the original proponents of the distinction (e.g., Hofstede, 1983) intended. Individualism and collectivism are orientations that are found in all societies and individuals (Brewer, 1999a; Brewer & Gardner, 1996; Killen & Wainryb, 2000; J. Miller, 2002; Oyserman, Coon, & Kemmelmeier, 2002). Turiel (2002), who maintains that a desire for autonomy from the group is universal rather than just a feature of individualistic cultures, argues that individuals can respond to ideological belief systems in ways that show active acceptance as well as tacit disapproval or rejection. As an example, the Druze in Israel are a hierarchically organized society in which there are differences between men and women in their rights and individual autonomy. Druze women frequently support the rights of men to exercise their power, but they see it as unjust and they see their own endorsement of male rights simply as a way to avoid severe social sanctions (Wainryb & Turiel, 1994). In a similar vein, Helwig, Arnold, Tan, and Boyd (2003) report that Chinese children express concepts of rights, individual autonomy, and democratic norms in their social reasoning as well as use them to critically evaluate existing social practices. Further criticisms emerge in observations that the concepts appear to change as they move across major cultural areas, with collectivism in Asian societies different from that in African or Latin American societies, and individualism in the United States different from that in Europe (Harkness, Super, & van Tijen, 2000).

In spite of these concerns, Oyserman et al. concluded in a meta-analysis that there is good evidence to support the speculation that so-called individualist- and collectivist-focused societies differ in organization, with the latter promoting in-group harmony and group obligation and the former making personal uniqueness salient and requiring separation from others. Oyserman et al. hasten to add that this does not mean that societies uniformly enforce these mandates on all members. But they suggest the dichotomy does signal that some features of human functioning believed to be universal may not be so. For example, not all individuals make sense of the self through high self-esteem or positive self-views to the extent that European Americans do, nor do all individuals have attributional and cognitive styles that lead them to ignore contextual influences on human behavior as much as do European Americans. People, as a function of the cultural context in which they find themselves, are likely to be different in what they consider to be rewarding outcomes and may treat in-group as opposed to out-group members differently. Ultimately, well-being is linked to a considerable degree to the attainment of culturally valued outcomes.

Some have suggested that, given that elements of autonomy and interrelatedness occur in all cultures, a better way of conceptualizing the impact of different goals in so-called collectivist and individualist societies may be to focus on the relative balance of each. This is a point made by Rothbaum, Pott, Azuma, Miyake, and Weisz (2000) in their analysis of close relationships in Japan and the United States, with the analysis shifting from a focus on the importance and strength of relationships to one that concentrates on the meaning and dynamics of relationships. Their argument is that individuation, which characterizes American thinking, and accommodation, which characterizes Japanese thinking, influences the nature of relationships in those cultures rather than individuation diluting relationships. Specifically, the need for affiliation with others involves either a pull toward adaptation of the self to fit the needs of others—the path of symbiotic harmony, or a tug between the desire for proximity and closeness and that for separation and exploration—the path of generative tension. Examples are provided from a variety of domains. In the protective care domain, Japanese infants derive security from the mother's indulgence of their needs and American infants from the use of the mother as a secure base from which to explore the world, a distinction reflected in greater body contact by Japanese mothers and greater eye contact by American mothers (e.g., Barratt, Negayama, & Minami, 1993). In the hierarchical domain, American parents show respect for noncompliance but exercise more direct control. Japanese parents avoid confrontations and often back down when children resist their requests. As well, they are more likely to use guilt and anxiety induction, shaming, and modeling (Lebra, 2000). American parents threaten to ground their disobedient children inside the home, whereas Japanese parents threaten to banish them outside the home (Johnson, 1993). In the MR domain, American adolescents increasingly seek intimacy with peers in sharp contrast to Japanese adolescents who view the parent-child relationship as enduring and mutually supportive across the life span (Lebra, 2000). Indeed, in Japan there are, in contrast to North America, no laws concerning legal and economic independence from parents (Hsu, 1983). In essence, relationships are central in both cultures, but they take a different form as a function of differential emphasis on individuation and accommodation. The Japanese model is only one contrasting possibility, but it offers a means of expanding conceptualizations of how the nature of relationships is affected by cultural goals.

The usefulness of the collectivist-individualist comparison is reflected in the frequency with which it is employed in many studies (a number of which are discussed later) as a source of hypotheses for cultural differences in the socialization of social, emotional, and cognitive development. Moreover, as noted earlier, it maps well onto the basic socialization mechanisms that appear in the social domain analysis presented in this paper. Given these observations, we treat different attitudes toward interdependence and independence as useful organizing and explanatory devices in the following discussion. Ultimately, we conclude that interrelatedness and autonomy/control are important in all cultures, but the way in which they manifest themselves differs as a function of the values and goals that exist in a particular cultural setting (e.g., Greenfield et al., 2003; Rothbaum, Pott, et al., 2000; Rothbaum, Weisz, Pott, Miyake, & Morelli, 2000). Thus, one challenge for investigators is to see how interrelatedness and autonomy are differentially expressed as a function of goals and belief systems that characterize a particular cultural group.

In the following discussion, we first describe how parental goals are affected by different cultural contexts and how those goals are manifested in different socialization practices. We ask what context reveals about mechanisms of socialization in different social domains and discuss developmental pathways and the expansion of meaning of interrelatedness and autonomy that cultural comparisons provide.

What Context Reveals about the Mechanisms of Socialization

In socialization situations, values are transmitted not only in the form of statements about valued behavior ("Family is important," "Learn to think for yourself") but also in modes of intervention. Power assertion, for example, sends the message that obedience is a desirable and important outcome, whereas reasoning indicates that willing acceptance of a particular position is an important social goal. Negotiation and compromise indicate that maintenance of positive relationships should be an aim in social interactions and that what constitutes acceptable behavior can be stretched as a function of discussion and conciliation. The way in which socialization is carried out, as well as the specific content that is conveyed, reflects general values inherent in the culture.

We begin with a general discussion of the impact of culture on goals and socialization practices and then consider, in greater detail, socialization practices in two domains that have received the most attention from cultural researchers—protective care and hierarchical power.

The Impact of Culture on Goals. The collectivist focus on interdependence and group harmony is reflected in different emphases from the individualist focus on autonomy on what are important goals or outcomes for the child. Familial obligation and the duty of children in the maintenance of the household, for example, marks a prime difference between collectivist and individualist orientations. Although family obligations are valued less by adolescents than by their parents regardless of culture (Phinney, Ong, & Madden, 2000) there is greater endorsement of these obligations by collectivist youth than by individualist youth. Thus, Asian American and Mexican American adolescents are more likely than their European American peers to believe they should assist parents and siblings throughout the life span and be willing to make sacrifices for the family (Fuligni, Tseng, & Lam, 1999). In a parallel way, prosocial behavior or a concern with the needs of others is more duty-based and seen as an important achievement of justice among Hindus, whereas concern for the needs and welfare of others involves an element of choice and personal decision in Anglo-Western contexts (J. Miller & Bersoff, 1992). Greenfield et al. (2003) contrast concepts of intelligence as a function of cultural orientation: Individualists value scientific intelligence because it emphasizes the person in relation to the world of objects. The collectivist contrast is valuation of social intelligence and the development of a child who can contribute to the well-being and cohesiveness of the group rather than one who stands out as different and better. Attention is on shared perspectives rather than different perspectives, one possible reason for why collectivists do less well on theory of mind tasks (Vinden, 1999). Finally, with respect to autonomy, American parents value independence, assertiveness, and self-expression, whereas Chinese parents place the emphasis on obedience, reliability, proper behavior, social obligation, and group achievement (Chao, 1995).

The Impact of Goals on Socialization Practices. The attainment of different goals is achieved by the use of different practices. Japanese American families discuss group activities and shared experiences at the dinner table and Caucasian American families focus on children's activities and individual experiences during dining encounters (Martini, 1996). Similarly, American and Israeli comparisons reveal a concern with the individual's daily experience among the former and the telling of stories that include multiple members of the group among the latter (Blum-Kulka, 1997). American children are encouraged to discuss their own feelings and those of others as a way of increasing their understanding of emotion and ability to regulate it, whereas, in Chinese families, attunement to the feelings of others but restraint in the expression of one's own feelings is encouraged as a key to group harmony (Chao, 1995). Chinese children are expected to read or infer the thoughts and feelings of others without being told (Wang & Leichtman, 2000). Chinese parents are also more likely to remind children of their past transgressions, using story-telling, for example, as a way to teach social norms and behavioral standards and to engender a sense of shame over bad behavior: In contrast, American parents avoid stories of transgression so as not to damage their children's self-esteem (P. Miller, Fung, & Mintz, 1996; P. Miller, Wiley, Fung, & Liang, 1997). European American parents are more likely to engage in authoritative parenting, emphasizing the growth of separation and autonomy in a supportive and responsive relationship; Asian American, Latino, and African Americans are more likely to engage in authoritarian parenting with its greater emphasis on obedience and conformity (Steinberg, Mounts, Lamborn, & Dornbusch, 1991). Learning in cultures that foster interdependence involves keen observation, attentiveness, and focused listening (Greenfield et al., 2003; Rogoff et al., 2003) as opposed to direct tuition and formal schooling. Even in school classrooms, however, children in interdependent cultures are more likely than teachers to take responsibility for classroom management and to solve problems together than those in independent cultures (Rogoff et al., 2003).

Maternal behavior in the protective care domain offers a detailed example of how different cultural values are mirrored in the ways that parents handle the tasks of socialization. For example, Keller et al. (2004) have identified two styles of parenting of very young infants: (1) distal with an emphasis on object stimulation and face-to-face exchange (mutual eye contact and frequent use of language) and (2) proximal with an emphasis on body contact and body stimulation. The former, found in individualist settings (German and Greek), links infants to the nonpersonal world of objects and informs them of their ability to influence the world. The latter, characteristic of collectivist settings (Cameroon Nso, Costa Rican, and, partially, Indian Guujarati Rajput), is associated with social cohesion, feelings of belongingness, and the experience of the body as an agent situated in the environment. In an analysis of how sensitivity in mother-infant interactions manifests itself in different cultural settings, Rothbaum, Weiss, et al. (2000) focused on the contrasting emphasis in Japanese and American cultures on independence and interdepend-

ence and how it reveals itself in the way mothers respond to distress and bids for attention in their infants. They suggest that, for example, sensitivity is expressed to American infants in distal forms of contact and encouragement of expression of negative emotion as opposed to its expression to Japanese infants through prolonged skin-to-skin contact and discouraging of emotion expression. Sensitivity occurs in response to children's signals in the American context and in anticipation of children's signals or needs in the Japanese context; sensitivity fosters exploration and autonomy in the former and emotional closeness in the latter. Secure attachment promotes social competence, but competence differs in the two cultures—exploration, autonomy, willingness to express emotion, and a positive self-concept as opposed to dependence, emotional restraint, self-effacement, and indirect expression of feelings. In this cultural approach the universals of attachment—pursuit of proximity and protection and distress at separation—remain unchanged but some of the basic tenets, including the meaning of sensitivity, competence, and the function of the caregiver as a secure base for exploration, assume more culture-specific forms. With this sort of cultural analysis, the understanding of what it means to be securely attached is perceived in more diverse and context-relevant ways. Different goals in different cultures channel caregiving practices, so that close body contact, immediate or anticipatory reactions to infant distress signals, and disapproval of mother-child separation feature in a variety of collectivistic cultural contexts as a way of fostering early close relationships, in contrast to practices more familiar to researchers in individualist cultures (Greenfield et al., 2003).

Turning to practices in the hierarchical power domain, we note that many studies have found Asians to be more restrictive in their parenting (Chao, 2002) and numbers of others have failed to find the usual relations between authoritative and authoritarian parenting and children's cognitive and social outcomes in different cultural groups. For example, the association between authoritative parenting and academic achievement is stronger for European American than for Asian and African American adolescents (Darling & Steinberg, 1993). Authoritarianism is positively related to externalizing problems for European Americans but unrelated for Mexican Americans (Lindahl & Malik, 1999), and authoritarian parenting has positive effects on adolescents' school performance among the Chinese in

Hong Kong (Leung, Lau, & Lam, 1998). Supervision and consistency of discipline are negatively related to delinquency among European Americans but unrelated among Mexican Americans (C. Smith & Krohn, 1995), and corporal punishment is associated with externalizing problems in European American but not African American children (Deater-Deckard, Dodge, Bates, & Pettit, 1996).

A number of factors can plausibly account for the differential impact of authoritarian parenting. First, socialization styles convey values, and values differ in different social contexts. In collectivist contexts, deference to authority would be supported by authoritarian approaches to child socialization to the extent that such deference fosters family coherence and harmony. Second, authoritarian parenting appears to have different meaning in different contexts. Chao (1994, 2001, 2002) notes that authoritarian parenting in China can involve the concept of *guan* or training that emphasizes the importance of hard work, self-discipline, and obedience. When it has this meaning it may well have a more positive outcome, particularly in the area of academic achievement.

The adverse impact of strict and controlling parenting in Western European cultures may stem to a considerable extent from its association with a variety of negative cognitions and emotions experienced by authoritarian parents in interaction with their children. These include rejection and lack of warmth (Baumrind, 1967), negative attributions for children's actions (Dix, Ruble, & Zambarano, 1989), low feelings of control in interactions with difficult children (Bugental, Brown, & Reiss, 1996), and inability to take the perspective of the child (Dekovic, Gerris, & Janssens, 1991). In contrast, control has been found to be unrelated to these negative emotions and cognitions in collectivist cultures (Rudy & Grusec, 2001, in press) and even to have positive associations with warmth and acceptance (Rohner & Pettengill, 1985; Stewart et al., 1998; Trommsdorff & Iwawaki, 1989). Authoritarian parenting in Western European contexts frequently may be pursued to establish authority over children who are felt and thought about in relatively negative terms. In other cultural groups, however, authoritarianism may often be pursued in children's interests. Indeed, it may be the negative cognitions and emotions that ultimately produce the kinds of outcomes that have been attributed to authoritarian parenting across all cultural contexts. In this sense, control is not the issue so much as rejection, hos-

tility and derogation (resulting from negative attributions), and lack of ability and/or willingness to take the perspective of the child. Accordingly, levels of emotional expression but not parent control and directiveness are related to children's social acceptance (Isley, O'Neil, & Parke, 1996), and warmth and involvement are better predictors of academic achievement and socioemotional outcomes among Korean American, Mexican American, and Anglo European adolescents than is control (Kim & Rohner, 2002; Knight, Virdin, & Roosa, 1994). As well, when coercive discipline is operationalized as observed rejection, criticism, and failure to say good-bye or to greet children in a day care setting it is a predictor of conduct problems even among African American children (Kilgore, Snyder, & Lentz, 2000). Similarly, when parental control is defined for Asians not as *guan*, but as domineering or overprotective behavior, it has negative effects (Herz & Gullone, 1999; Stewart et al., 1998) just as it does in a Western European context. Barber and Harmon (2002) also suggest that psychological control has negative correlates in a variety of cultural contexts. These findings all point to the fact that relationships and parenting style are central in socialization and that they moderate the meaning of control for the developing child.

Linkages to Developmental Pathways

The last question to be addressed in this section has to do with differences among cultures in developmental pathways. If the ideal developmental outcome involves a balance between interrelatedness and autonomy (Blatt, 1998), what might one expect with respect to greater emphasis on the one rather than the other in different cultural contexts? Does the emphasis on autonomy and separation in the West serve the needs of the culture but impede optimal development? The general question has been most frequently addressed with respect to the collectivist model with its weight on interdependence and group harmony. Rothbaum, Pott, et al. (2000) suggest that adaptation to group needs over self-assertion may lead to internalizing problems, although Lewis (2000) notes that the suicide rate is lower in Japan than in the United States and that Japanese high school students report fewer feelings of stress, anxiety, and depression. Lebra (2000) describes the difficulty Japanese children have in breaking away from their mothers and the fact that marital relationships are sometimes strained because exclusive intimacy is not legitimized and, as a result, husbands and wives become distanced. The reliance on shame that characterizes some collectivist cultures may be problematic given that it gives rise to more intense levels of physiological arousal than does guilt (Scherer & Wallbott, 1994) and that it is less likely to lead to reparative behaviors than is guilt (Tangney, Wagner, Hill-Barlow, Marschall, & Gramzow, 1997). Alternatively, the psychological well-being of Chinese American adolescents in the United States does not appear to be harmed by the fact that they have more family obligations than their European American counterparts (Fuligni, Yip, & Tseng, 2002).

Autonomy.   Considerable attention has been paid to the issue of autonomy and whether or how interdependence and group harmony undermine it. An extension of this question has to do with whether autonomy is indeed the universal human need suggested by self-determination (Deci & Ryan, 1991) and other theorists (e.g., Killen & Wainryb, 2000). One stance is that the values of autonomy are opposed to those of group cohesion and that autonomy is not important across all cultures. Another suggestion is that yielding to controlling pressure is more satisfying in some cultures than is making decisions in the absence of any external influences (e.g., Iyengar & Lepper, 2000; J. Miller, 1997). In accord with this viewpoint, the adoption of choices made by trusted others has been found to enhance intrinsic motivation for Asian Americans but not for European Americans (Iyengar & Lepper, 2000). Some (e.g., Chirkov & Ryan, 2003; Ryan & Deci, 2000), however, argue that decisions made in conformity with the guidance of others is not an accurate rendering of the concept of autonomy and that autonomy is experienced when individuals perceive their actions to be willingly enacted and when they themselves fully endorse these actions. The autonomous individual is not defined as individualistic or independent (both of which are indicators of low relatedness) nor does the autonomous individual act in independent, detached, or selfish ways. The opposite of autonomy is not dependence or lack of physical separation (Kagitcibasi, 1996) but, rather, heteronomy in which choices are seen as controlled by those who do not share one's own values or interests. In accord with this distinction, Chirkov and Ryan (2003) found that autonomy and well-being were correlated in both individualist and collectivist countries (South Korea, Turkey, Russia, and the United States). They also found that values involving vertical or status-oriented issues were more difficult for people to internalize, possibly because vertical issues frequently require individuals to give up their own freedom of choice as well as restricting the set of people with whom intimacy and connectedness can be established.

The focus on autonomy as willing enactment and endorsement of a position has been labeled "reflective autonomy" (Koestner & Losier, 1996; Koestner et al., 1999) and distinguished from "reactive autonomy," with individuals who are high in reflective autonomy more willing to follow expert advice and those high in reactive autonomy more likely to reject the influence of others even when such action is counterproductive. We note the parallel distinction between willing and situational compliance (Maccoby & Martin, 1983) and the fact that willing or receptive compliance promotes a positive and cooperative stance in relation to agents of socialization that may fit better with collectivist than individualist goals. Indeed, one is reminded of the fact that Asian parents in general will often give in to their children's demands rather than encourage conflict and confrontation (Chao, 2002), either as a way of avoiding confrontation or because they see young children as not responsible for their actions. This is a practice that may not work well when the goal is separation and individuation, but may work well with a goal that actions be seen as freely chosen.

Conflict.   Conflict is a significant contributor to the development of individuation and separation. An important question has to do with the role and extent of conflict in collectivist contexts. Although parent-adolescent conflict may be more discouraged in collectivist settings it does exist and is widespread (Schlegel & Barry, 1991). Thus, even under conditions in which interdependence and family harmony are stressed, there is expressed disagreement between the generations, an indication of growing autonomy. In a study of Chinese (Hong Kong) adolescents Yau and Smetana (1996), for example, report the existence of conflictual interactions, albeit fewer than in American families. Despite the particularly great emphasis on respect for parental authority in Chinese families, Yau and Smetana report that Chinese adolescents reasoned about conflicts as issues of exercising or maintaining personal jurisdiction, similar to the way in which American adolescents express their growing need for individuation and autonomy. These appeals to personal jurisdiction may reflect the fact that parental respect and filial piety seem to have more of the characteristics of family harmony and love and affection than they do of strict obedience (Sung, 1995). Smetana and Yau did find some differences in the content of conflicts, with more disagreement over academic matters and the behavior of parents themselves (e.g., their smoking or their relationship with other family members), with each of these reflecting the greater Chinese emphasis on academic achievement and family functioning. Yau and Smetana conclude that similarities between adolescents in Hong Kong and American adolescents reflect the universal developmental task of separation or de-individuation from parents, with conflict one way of achieving this de-individuation. However, the way in which conflict is expressed, and the extent to which it occurs, is obviously directed by the cultural context in which it occurs.

What do we conclude about the links between relatedness, autonomy, and developmental pathways? An important observation is that interrelatedness and autonomy appear to be important features of all cultures. Analyses of their manifestations in a variety of contexts suggest differences in emphasis and differences in form but an underlying and common concern with feeling related to others and feeling some degree of control over one's own actions. There may be tradeoffs in the ways in which these motives are expressed. Close family ties provide the benefit of a high sense of safety but at the cost of reductions in the individual's ability to achieve personal goals. Rothbaum and Trommsdorff (in press) talk about tradeoffs between forms of relatedness, contrasting trust and assurance. They argue that trust, or faith in the intentions of others that allows people to seek spontaneous relationships with new partners, is associated with autonomy, self-esteem, and self-actualization. However, assurance, or commitment to and guarantee of loyalties and reciprocity from members of a tightly knit group, promotes group cohesion and family security. Thus, culture may be characterized as preference for different social domains or different points of balance but with no one centrality more adaptive than another.

Summary

Culture provides an example of an interactional model of socialization, pointing to the importance of meaning in understanding mechanisms of socialization. The study of socialization in different cultural contexts re-veals how cultures affect goals and, thereby, socialization practices. For example, research suggests that when authoritarian parenting harms children it is because of its association with lack of warmth and respect for the child. Thus, authoritarian parenting, guided by goals of the culture, has a different meaning in those cultures. Cultures have been distinguished by a differential balance of the two basic dimensions of socialization: interrelatedness and autonomy. Nevertheless, interdependence or interconnectedness appears to be important in all cultures, as does autonomy—a willing enactment of a position.

OUTCOMES OF THE YOUNG AS A RESULT OF THEIR LIFE HISTORY

To this point, we have considered the sociocultural processes that operate in socialization as built on a biological platform that is common to all members of the species. We now move to consider individual variation in biological characteristics and how they combine with sociocultural experiences in determining the outcomes of the young. Researchers have proposed different models of contingent causality in conceptualizing the ways in which child characteristics and life history combine to influence the child's ultimate outcomes. As a beginning to our discussion, we briefly review some of these models. The models differ in their starting points. Some investigators begin with a consideration of children's reactivity to novelty and change in their environment as a function of genetic variables (e.g., sex or temperament differences). Others begin by considering the impact of a variety of child characteristics (e.g., learning disorders or negative emotionality) on their receptivity to socialization per se. Still others begin with a focus on the shared (and unshared) characteristics of children that lead them to be able to adapt to changing ecologies. Despite variations in their starting points, there is a high level of overlap in these models.

We then move on to consider the route through which children's long-term outcomes are determined as a function of these interactions. Specifically, we are concerned with the life outcomes of the young as a function of the mediating role of (a) children's acquired ways of cognitively representing their social worlds, (b) hormones in the responses shown to their experiences, and

(c) gene expression in the continuous reorganization of the brain in response to experience.

Child Characteristics as Sources of Influence on and Reactivity to the Environment

Children's early environment necessarily includes both change and stability. The child is increasingly confronted with novel or surprising events that potentially serve as sources of stress. At the same time, children differ in the extent to which and the ways in which they respond to such normative experiences.

Genetic Variations in Children's Reactivity to Stress-Inducing Events

Variations in children's reactivity to the environment have often been found to be due to genetic differences in children. Researchers initially focused on the extent to which children are selectively vulnerable to negative experiences; for example, boys have generally been found to be more reactive to environmental stress than are girls. They show faster rise times and higher levels of physiological arousal to commonly occurring sources of stress (Maccoby, 1988). On a more ongoing basis, boys are more negatively affected than are girls by single parenthood (Hetherington, 1993), poverty (Elder & Rockwell, 1979), and divorce (Needle, Su, Doherty, 1990).

There has also been a continuing line of research focused on children's temperament as an influence on their reactivity to potential stress (e.g., Gunnar, Porter, Wolfe, Rigatuso, & Larson, 1995; Kochanska, 1993; Ramsay & Lewis, 2003; Schmidt, Fox, Rubin, & Steinberg, 1997). Among the ways in which children differ on the basis of temperament, child fearfulness or inhibition has been most strongly associated with vulnerability to potentially stress-inducing events (Goldsmith & Lemery, 2000; Kagan, 2001). An initial focus on temperament differences that led to differential vulnerability to stress was extended to include temperament differences (e.g., positive emotionality) that led to differential resilience in the face of stress or adversity (Wills, Sandy, Yaeger, & Shinar, 2001).

In considering these genetically influenced differences in children, researchers have focused more recently on the interaction between genes and the child's socializing environment in determining their long-term outcomes (Collins et al., 2000). For example, temperamentally fearful children whose mothers use harsh discipline are more likely to exhibit lower levels of con-

science than are those who are low in fearfulness or than do those who are high in fearfulness and have gentle parents (Kochanska, 1997). In addition, fearful boys exposed either to harsh or overinvolved parenting show elevated levels of depression (Colder, Lochman, & Wells, 1997). At the same time, young children who are fearful or display discomfort in strange situations show a greater level of conscience development to the extent their mothers use a gentle disciplinary style. In addition, fearful children may manifest unique regulatory benefits (habituation to repeated stress) when they experience more responsive parenting (Schwartz & Bugental, 2004).

Supporting the notion that temperament and experience interact in a way that allows clear causal inference, Suomi (1997) has demonstrated that rhesus macaques that show a highly fearful temperament, when cross-fostered by average mothers, showed deficits in their exploratory behavior and in their responses to stressful events. In contrast, temperamentally fearful animals that were cross-fostered by very nurturant mothers showed high levels of exploratory behavior and ability to cope with stress.

In the same way, those children who demonstrate irritability (or negative emotionality) early in life, show different outcomes based on the responses shown by their parents. For example, Crockenberg (1987) observed that infant irritability, when combined with angry and punitive mothering, predicted child anger and noncompliance at 2 years of age; no such relationship was found for nonirritable infants. At the same time, children who show early negative emotionality are more likely to show benefits when they experience positive parenting. For example, Blair (2002) found that infants who showed high negative emotionality demonstrated greater cognitive and social benefits (fewer externalizing problems at later ages) than did other children when their parents participated in an early intervention program that afforded enriched rearing experiences.

Children's Responsiveness to Socialization or Tuition

Consistent differences have been found between children in their receptivity or responsiveness to socialization (Belsky, in press). Both at home and school, children differ in the extent to which they are positively responsive or unresponsive to social influence and/or tuitional efforts. In some cases, child unresponsiveness is due to learning disorders such as attention deficit disorder (ADD) or attention-deficit hyperactivity disorder

(ADHD). In other cases, it may involve child characteristics that have sometimes been summarized as involving a "difficult" temperament (Bates, 1980). Finally, some researchers have been concerned with children's physiological response patterns as predictive of their receptivity to socialization.

Ordinarily, children's reduced responsiveness to socialization is maladaptive, and thus might be thought of as having been weeded out by natural selection. In contemporary, stable environments, a child's unresponsiveness to socialization typically poses a potential problem to parents (or teachers). However, Belsky and his colleagues (Belsky, in press; Belsky, Hsieh, & Crnic, 1998) suggest that there are advantages for such unresponsiveness under some circumstances. In unpredictable environments, such children may be less constrained by a socialization history that is not well-suited to the changing demands. For example, it has been suggested (Jensen et al., 1997) that children with ADHD might have fared well in harsh, unstable environments more characteristic of our evolutionary past. These authors suggested that such children show an exceptional readiness to explore their environment (high levels of motor activity) and rapidly changing responses (impulsivity) in reaction to it. During harsh times, they may have had an "edge" in avoiding danger and taking advantage of unstable benefits.

Attention has also been given to variations in children's emotional and physiological reactions as indicators of their receptivity to socialization. For example, Kochanska (1993) has suggested that children are more receptive to socialization to the extent that they are emotionally reactive to punishment and that they engage in effective self-regulation. In infancy, physiological reactivity (e.g., heart rate or cortisol elevations) of children in response to stress acts as a predictor of later responsiveness to socialization (Gunnar et al., 1995; Kagan & Snidman, 1991). Children who show this type of reaction to aversive stimuli may be thought of as showing adaptive neurobehavioral organization (Gunnar et al., 1995).

Context Sensitivity of Children

It has also been proposed that children are quite generally sensitive to context (Boyce & Ellis, in press), with genotypic variations in this sensitivity. Boyce and Ellis conceptualized context-dependent effects as conditional adaptations that have evolved as a basis for calibrating the child's response patterns to match their environment in an adaptive way: Children are seen as designed by their evolutionary history to show a facultative responsiveness to the environment in which they are born. If the environment is harsh, such context sensitivity may lead to increased vigilance for potential threat. If, however, the environment offers positive support, such context sensitivity may lead to increased receptivity to positive aspects of the social environment. In either case, children's context-sensitivity can be expected to increase their reproductive success (in the particular ecology that confronts them). High levels of context sensitivity may set the child in quite different directions on a phenotypic basis. This sensitivity allows children to be able to adapt to the environment they come to experience.

In addition, early experience with stress (or adversity) may also heighten the context-sensitivity of the child. Children who experience early medical problems (and thus experience the stress associated with the neonatal intensive care unit or stress-inducing medical treatments) represent one such example. Research focused on response to early stress or adversity has documented the very different life outcomes such children may experience based on their parenting history. Although early stress may yield negative life outcomes when parents fail to buffer children against the effects of such experiences (the "risk" pathway), early stress may also yield exceptionally positive life outcomes when parents provide a high level of support (an outcome that may be described as "thriving," e.g., Bugental, 2003).

Infant prematurity represents a case in point, in that it is accompanied by the greater likelihood of early stress, combined with limited self-regulation abilities. Although children who were born prematurely are hyper-reactive to environmental stimuli, they often down-regulate their responses in ways that lead to hypo-reactivity (suggested to serve as protective responses against overstimulation; Tronick, Scanlon, & Scanlon, 1990). Mothers often respond to these reactions with excess stimulation efforts, which foster further problems (Brachfield, Goldberg, & Sloman, 1980); in contrast, when mothers show a response style that is better synchronized to infant needs, such children have more positive self-regulatory and interactional outcomes (Feldman, Weller, Sirota, & Eidelman, 2002).

The parenting history of context-sensitive children may ultimately influence their health outcomes. For example, Bugental and Beaulieu (2004) observed that children who were born at medical risk (as assessed by their premature status or elevated Apgar scores) demonstrated either exceptionally positive or negative health outcomes as toddlers as a function of their parenting history. Those born at medical risk (in comparison with low-risk children) demonstrated exceptionally positive health outcomes if their mothers participated in a cognitively based home visitation intervention (which, in turn, fostered reductions in maternal depression). Medically at-risk children whose mothers were in control conditions were more likely to show negative health outcomes. In support of the observation that early stress, under appropriate conditions, can have a beneficial effect on health, young adults whose history included early medical complications have been found to show exceptionally high levels of health (as well as habituation to repeated stress) when they had been the recipients of supportive parenting (Bugental, Beaulieu, Cayan, et al., 2004). In contrast, young adults with a history of early medical complications showed exceptionally low levels of health (and poor ability to habituate to repeated stress) when they had been the recipients of harsh parenting. No equivalent effects were found for young adults who had not experienced medical risk early in life. Such findings are consistent with Boyce and Ellis's (2000) proposal that parental support and protection serve as key moderators of the extent to which context-sensitive children experience negative or positive outcomes.

What Is the Route by Which Children's Experiences Lead to Different Outcomes?

Children's outcomes as a result of early experiences can be mediated by different means. Consideration is given here to both cognitive and biological routes.

The Mediating Role of the Child's Cognitive Representations of the Social World

One route through which children may come to have different life outcomes involves their acquisition of different ways of representing the social world as a function of their early socialization experiences. In family relationships, children's experiences with their own parents form a central influence on their cognitive representations of the caregiving relationship (Grusec, Hastings, & Mammone, 1994). For example, girls who have experienced maltreatment early in life come to have a low perception of their social power in relationship with others (Bugental & Shennum, 2002). Such representations are

predictive of the propensity to become abusive in their relationships with their own children (Bugental & Happaney, 2004). In the same way, socialization history leads some children to acquire a "victim schema," which is predictive of their being more likely to be victimized by other children (Perry, Hodges, & Egan, 2001). Even broader links are found between children's representations of family, peer, and self; negative representations are predictive of dysfunctional social behavior and low peer status (Rudolph, Hammen, & Burge, 1995).

Relationships with significant others early in life serve as the basis for cognitive representations of relational information. M. Baldwin (1992) proposed that individuals, as a result of their relational history, form cognitive structures that include a script for the interaction pattern, a schema for the role of the other person in the relationship, and a schema for the role of self in the relationship. Such relational schemas come to influence the individual's expectations and experiences in subsequent relationships.

The Mediating Role of Hormones

Developmental neuroscience has provided insights into another route through which socialization may influence children's outcomes. In doing so, the field has focused on regulation of stress in early relationships, including parent-child relationships. In the socialization literature, increasing attention has been given to a key stress regulation system—the HPA axis. Across ages (and species), the HPA axis is activated in response to events that might pose a threat; for an infant, this could include as little as an unfamiliar toy or as much as a frightening parent.

Although an activated HPA axis facilitates the effective management of short-term stress, such is not the case if the HPA axis is repeatedly activated without recovery. In this case, there is destructive wear and tear on the system, a process that McEwen (2000) refers to as "allostatic load." As an end product of this process, the individual became decreasingly able to cope with future stress. Over long time periods, the child's dysregulated HPA axis (as indicated either by cortisol hyper-reactivity, hypo-reactivity, or deviant basal levels), following from unrelieved stress early in life, may produce long-term changes in the capacity of the system to respond to stress, and in the effective functioning of other parts of the central nervous system that are affected by the HPA axis.

When the young child is exposed to very high levels of unbuffered stress, the normatively well-functioning

HPA axis is overactivated. As a result, this regulatory system becomes more limited in its ability to manage new sources of stress, and other linked regulatory systems (e.g., the growth system, the immune system) do not function optimally. Ultimately, the continuous activation of the HPA axis (and associated changes in the functioning of other aspects of the central nervous system) may lead to deficits not only in brain development but also in the social-emotional and cognitive functioning of the child and the health and growth of the child (e.g., Bremner & Narayan, 1998).

The immediate effects of an unsupportive environment on children's stress regulation abilities have been demonstrated in a number of different ways. For example, maternal depression has often found to be associated with children's stress regulation problems. Depressed mothers, as well as mothers subject to panic disorder, are less responsive to infant distress than are nondepressed mothers and thus are less likely to buffer the young against stressful experiences (e.g., Donovan, Leavitt, & Walsh, 1998; Warren et al., 2003). Not surprisingly, children of such mothers are dysregulated in their production of cortisol (e.g., Bugental et al., 2003; Dawson & Ashman, 2000; Essex, Klein, Cho, & Kalin, 2002; Field, 1994; Newport, Stowe, & Nemeroff, 2002). In the same way, stress-inducing experiences later on during the life of the child produce problems if those children fail to receive supportive parenting. For example, the loss of a parent, when combined with a hostile or rejecting family environment, predicts long-term dysregulation of the HPA axis (e.g., Luecken, 1998).

McEwen (2001) has suggested that stress (in particular, early stress) may have positive as well as negative long-term outcomes. There may be circumstances under which high levels of stress lead to enhanced functioning of the system—enhanced allostatic efficiency may occur. If stress occurs repeatedly but is regularly followed with recovery, the HPA axis may become more efficient in the management of future stress. In short, we see the adaptive possibilities for the socializing system to foster resilience (and even exceptionally positive outcomes) in response to early stress. Such accommodations may operate when the parent serves in a buffering role.

What is the route by which parental support serves to foster the positive outcomes of infants who experience early stress? Some of the best evidence comes from experimental work with nonhuman animals. Meaney and his colleagues (e.g., Meaney et al., 1985) found that rat pups that were exposed to repeated stress (handling by humans) showed later benefits in their brain develop-

ment, along with their ability to cope with future sources of stress. As described earlier, these benefits were mediated by the response of rat mothers to their distressed pups (Francis et al., 1999). When the pups were returned to the litter, their mothers engaged in vigorous licking and grooming, a response that served to calm the pups and led to changes in the development of the corticotropin-releasing factor (CRF). This developmental change led to changes in the expression of behavioral, endocrine, and autonomic responses to stress (through the activation of forebrain noradrenergic systems), which led to an increased ability to manage stress, and subsequent increases in their health as adults (as a result of their reduced vulnerability to the effects of stress-induced illness). This research provides a concrete example of more general processes that are operating in the area of stress and parental support. Thus, Francis, Champagne, Liu, and Meaney (1999) propose:

> the relationship between early life events and health in adulthood is mediated by parental influences on the development of neural systems that underlie the expression of behavioral and endocrine responses to stress. (p. 64)

Gunnar and her colleagues (Gunnar et al., 2003), in a review of the literature, concluded that mother-infant interactions have effects on the neuroendocrine stress activity of humans as well as nonhumans. For example, maltreatment or unresponsiveness early in life influences stress hormone activity. In addition, children who manifest reactive temperament patterns show increased stress responses as the quality of parental care declines.

The Mediating Role of Gene Expression

Molecular biology provides insights into the "activation mechanisms" by which the effects of the caregiving environment are accomplished. Thus, there has been an emerging focus on gene expression—the ways in which the environment influences the activation of genes (Brown, 1999). This line of inquiry has led to the general study of differential gene expression in response to environmental variables. Specific to our topic, researchers have become increasingly concerned with the ways in which experiences (including socialization experiences) influence gene expression and resultant variations in brain development (e.g., Bruer & Greenough, 2001). For example, stress may lead to changes in the production of hormones, which serve as messengers to relevant brain cells and the subsequent expression (activation) of genes. Although genes are typically located at inactive sites in brain cells, those genes that have most recently been activated are repositioned to locations in the nucleus in which they are easily accessed in response to recurring environmental triggers (Lamond & Earnshaw, 1998).

This altered process of gene expression lies at the heart of the benefits of maternal buffering of pup distress observed by Meaney and his colleagues (2000). It has been suggested that there are two distinct CRF systems—one of which is adaptive and one of which is maladaptive (Schulkin, Gold, & McEwen, 1998). The first system leads to restraint of CRF receptor gene expression in the paraventricular nucleus of the hypothalamus, which then serves to "turn off" the HPA axis when the source of threat has passed. The second system fosters CRF gene expression in the central nucleus of the amygdala, and the resultant perpetuation of chronic elevations in fear and anxiety. Maternal licking and grooming of rat pups leads to restraint of CRF receptor gene expression in the hypothalamus, with the net effect that the HPA axis is more easily turned off. In contrast, the young who are exposed to unbuffered stress are more likely to experience the continuing costs associated with the involvement of the amygdala.

The extent to which processes that follow early stress are reversible is unclear. In addition, it is unclear whether efforts to counteract the effects of early stress produce effects at the level of structural changes or functional changes in the brain. Francis, Diorio, Plotsky, and Meaney (2002) concluded that an enriched environment served to reverse the hormonal and fear responses that resulted from earlier stress but did not alter gluco-corticoid receptor gene expression. Others have argued that altered life experiences may indeed act back to influence gene expression in ways that reverse the effects of earlier stress (e.g., McEwen, 2001). These questions will undoubtedly stimulate considerable research in the coming years.

In summary, behavioral neuroscientists have increasingly asked about the role of molecular biology in the developing child. From this perspective, the human genome does not automatically create a working brain; instead, hormonal processes are influenced by the environment and subsequently act to foster brain development (via the activation of gene expression), which ultimately promotes the child's social development (e.g., Brown, 1999; Schulkin, Gold, & McEwen, 1998). The promise of this field for human development (and socialization) is suggested by Brown (1999):

In child development, gene expression responds to love; security; effective role models; stimulating language and cognitive environments; a positive family environment including support, discipline, values and positive directions; and appropriate management of stress and anxiety. (p. 40)

INTEGRATION

In reviewing the current status of the field of socialization, we have presented an integrated account that spans many aspects of developmental psychology as well as incorporating insights from other disciplines. Countering increasing specialization in the field of psychology, there has been a recent movement toward integration in and across fields. The life outcomes of the developing child have come to be viewed as situated in both the biological and social-cultural networks of the family. As one example, Dodge and Pettit (2003) provided a synthesis of studies looking at the impact of biological predispositions, sociocultural context, parenting, peers, and mental processes on chronic conduct problems in adolescence. Similarly, Repetti, Taylor, and Seeman (2002) offered a model that links risky parenting with mental and physical health disorders, showing linkages between harsh family experiences, deficits in emotional control, emotional expression and social competence, disturbances in physiologic and endocrine system regulation, and health-threatening behavior. Relevant processes begin even before birth and cross-influence each other both in adaptive and maladaptive ways to influence the mental health, social competencies, physical health, and productivity of the young.

In describing the bridges across coordinated biological systems, evolutionary psychology has suggested basic design features; developmental neuroscience has suggested potential mediators operating at the level of the central nervous system; and behavior genetics has suggested the ways in which the brain is receptive to changes in structure and function as a result of the experiences of the child. Thus, biological systems represent recursive processes that involve continuous corrections of the child's capacities in light of changing environments. Although there are biological constraints on such flexibility, there is also considerable openness to modification. Within this flexibility arises the possibility for the benefits (or costs) that may be experienced by children as result of their socialization history. This counters an early (and limited) view of biological forces as dictating fixed outcomes for the young as a function of individual or shared genetic endowment. As developmentalists have come to realize the fallacy of the notion of nature and nurture as competing forces, they have simultaneously come to appreciate the mutual facilitation that occurs between environment and the brain.

Just as developmentalists have come to understand the biosocial processes as recursive and integrated, they have changed in their conceptualization of the social-cultural factors that influence the outcomes of the young. In particular, there has been movement away from the view of effective socialization as involving a fixed design that has general applicability. One of the earliest questionings of this approach followed from consideration of the variations between children in temperament—and thus the socialization methods likely to be effective. Subsequently, there was a questioning of the effectiveness of different patterns of socialization across cultures. It became apparent that there were many variations possible in socialization practices and styles that lead children to live healthy, happy, productive lives in their cultural framework. Finally, increasing consideration has been given to the role of social context (or domain) in determining the differing processes that operate in socialization. In different contexts and settings (acting in the service of different goals or tasks), socialization appears to operate according to different algorithms. Such algorithms have biological, motivational, behavioral, and cognitive components that work together to facilitate the accomplishment of the relevant socialization goals or tasks.

The models used to represent socialization are shifting in ways that reflect the changing processes thought to operate. Unidirectional models (and exclusive reliance on self-report) can be expected to be replaced with bidirectional models that make use of an expanded range of dependent (and mediating) variables. In addition, the increased focus on context can be expected to lead researchers to make greater use of moderator models in which socialization outcomes are measured differentially as a function of contextual variables. In doing so, conditional models can be used to represent the circumstances under which different types of socialization processes may operate or under which different biological "switching mechanisms" may occur.

Along with changes in the ways of conceptualizing socialization, there have been corresponding changes in the variables of interest. In one direction, there has been an increasing interest in physiological processes. Many labs concerned with socialization are exploring changes that occur in neurotransmitters and hormones and the functioning of the sympathetic-adrenal-medullary system. Concern even extends to the level of the brain and its development. New technology (e.g., functional magnetic resonance imaging) and new findings in other fields (e.g., research in molecular biology that has implications for gene expression) can be expected to expand horizons still further.

In another direction, socialization researchers now incorporate knowledge drawn from anthropology and cultural psychology to consider the differing processes and outcomes of socialization in different settings. Such explorations increase understanding not only of the diversity of experiences that foster healthy outcomes for the young but also the ways in which there is continuity across cultures in the socialization of the young. At the same time, consideration is given to the possibility that there are unhealthy societies (e.g., societies that foster extreme discrepancies in the opportunities for the young or that foster continuing stress without recovery) that limit the life experiences of the young.

Finally, the ways in which investigators in the field of socialization operate is changing. With the increasing complexity of knowledge and methodology comes the need for greater collaborative efforts across labs and across disciplines. Behavioral neuroscientists now work either to incorporate the concepts drawn from socialization theory or to collaborate with socialization researchers to bridge understanding of processes that occur across species or that differ in important ways across species. In those projects concerned with human socialization, researchers have capitalized on the opportunities for determining the outcomes of "natural experiments." Researcher teams (as notable illustrations, Rutter and his colleagues, e.g., Rutter & O'Connor, 2004; and Gunnar and her colleagues, e.g., Gunnar, Morison, Chisholm, & Schuder, 2001) have tracked (and continue to track) the changes in life outcomes that follow from the socialization history introduced into the lives of adopted children. In conceptualizing the outcomes of children who experience adversity early in life, there are also changing expectations. The circumstances that foster later risk have expanded to consider not only the circumstances that allow resilience but also the circumstances that foster advantage or thriving.

In these changes are hopeful outlooks for social policy. As developmentalists come to understand the ways the life course of the young changes as a result of their socialization history, doors open for ways to foster the opportunities that are available for them. National funding agencies concerned with facilitating physical and mental health have created opportunities for researchers across many disciplines to come together to consider how shared knowledge can encourage new collaborations, allow new hypotheses, and resolve puzzles that plague researchers who may acquire new insights regarding resolutions available from other fields. Finally, it becomes the obligation of such collaborative teams to inform policymakers of the possibility and feasibility of sustainable socializing environments that can be expected to optimize the life outcomes of the young.

REFERENCES

Abbott, D. H., Keverne, E. B., Bercovitch, F. B., Sjively, C. A., Mendoza, S. P., Saltzman, W., et al. (2003). Are subordinates always stressed? A comparative analysis of rank differences in cortisol levels among primates. *Hormones and Behavior, 43,* 67–82.

Aboud, F. E. (2003). The formation of in-group favoritism and out-group prejudice in young children: Are they distinct attitudes? *Developmental Psychology, 39,* 48–60.

Aboud, F. E., & Doyle, A. B. (1996). Parental and peer influences on children's racial attitudes. *International Journal of Intercultural Relations, 20,* 371–383.

Ainsworth, M. D. S., Blehar, M. C., Waters, E., & Wall, S. (1978). *Patterns of attachment: A psychological study of the strange situation.* Hillsdale, NJ: Erlbaum.

Bakeman, R., & Adamson, L. B. (1984). Coordinating attention to people and objects in mother-infant and peer-infant interaction. *Child Development, 55,* 1278–1289.

Baldwin, A. (1955). *Behavior and development in childhood.* New York: Dryden Press.

Baldwin, A. L., Baldwin, C., & Cole, R. E. (1990). Stress-resistant families and stress-resistant children. In J. E. Rolf, A. S. Masten, D. Cicchetti, K. H. Nuechterlein, & S. Weintraub (Eds.), *Risk and protective factors in the development of psychopathology* (pp. 257–280). New York: Cambridge University Press.

Baldwin, M. W. (1992). Relational schemas and the processing of social information. *Psychological Bulletin, 112,* 461–484.

Bandura, A. (1977). *Social learning theory.* Englewood Cliffs, NJ: Prentice-Hall.

Bandura, A. (1986). *Social foundations of thought and action: A social cognitive theory.* Englewood Cliffs, NJ: Prentice-Hall.

Bandura, A., & Walters, R. H. (1963). *Social learning theory and personality development.* New York: Holt, Rinehart and Winston.

Barber, B. K. (1996). Parental psychological control: Revisiting a neglected construct. *Child Development, 67,* 3296–3319.

Barber, B. K. (Ed.). (2002). *Intrusive parenting: How psychological control affects children and adolescents.* Washington, DC: American Psychological Association.

Barber, B. K., Bean, R. L., & Erickson, L. D. (2002). Expanding the study and understanding of psychological control. In B. K. Barber (Ed.), *Intrusive parenting: How psychological control affects children and adolescents* (pp. 263–289). Washington, DC: American Psychological Association.

Barber, B. K., & Harmon, E. L. (2002). Violating the self: Parental psychological control of children and adolescents. In B. K. Barber (Ed.), *Intrusive parenting: How psychological control affects children and adolescents* (pp. 15–52). Washington, DC: American Psychological Association.

Barratt, M., Negayama, K., & Mirami, T. (1993). The social environments of early infancy in Japan and the United States. *Early Development and Parenting, 2,* 51–64.

Barry, H. I., Child, I. L., & Bacon, M. K. (1959). Relations of child training to subsistence economy. *American Anthropologist, 61,* 51–63.

Bartoshuk, L. M., & Beauchamp, O. K. (1994). Chemical senses. *Annual Review of Psychology, 45,* 419–449.

Bates, J. E. (1980). The concept of difficult temperament. *Merrill-Palmer Quarterly, 26,* 299–319.

Bates, J. E., Pettit, G. S., Dodge, K. A., & Ridge, B. (1998). Interaction of temperamental resistance to control and restrictive parenting in the development of externalizing behavior. *Developmental Psychology, 34,* 982–995.

Baumeister, R. F., & Tice, D. M. (1990). Anxiety and social exclusion. *Journal of Social and Clinical Psychology, 9,* 165–195.

Baumrind, D. (1967). Child care practices anteceding three patterns of preschool behavior. *Genetic Psychology Monographs, 73,* 43–88.

Baumrind, D. (1971). Current patterns of parental authority. *Developmental Psychology, 4,* 1–103.

Baumrind, D. (1993). The average expectable environment is not good enough: A response to Scarr. *Child Development, 64,* 1299–1317.

Baumrind, D., Larzelere, R. E., & Cowan, P. A. (2002). Ordinary physical punishment: Is it harmful? Comment on Gershoff, 2002. *Psychological Bulletin, 128,* 580–589.

Baumrind, D., & Thompson, R. A. (2002). The ethics of parenting. In M. Bornstein (Ed.), *Handbook of parenting* (Vol. 5, pp. 3–34). Mahwah, NJ: Erlbaum.

Bekoff, M., & Allen, C. (2002). The evolution of social play: Interdisciplinary analysis of cognitive processes. In M. Bekoff, C. Allen, & G. M. Burghardt (Eds.), *The cognitive animal* (pp. 429–435). London: MIT Press.

Bell, R. Q. (1968). A reinterpretation of the direction of effects in studies of socialization. *Psychological Review, 75,* 81–95.

Belsky, J. (1999). Interactional and contextual determinants of attachment security. In J. Cassidy & P. R. Shaver (Eds.), *Handbook of attachment: Theory, research, and clinical applications* (pp. 249–264). New York: Guilford Press.

Belsky, J. (in press). Differential susceptibility in rearing influence: An evolutionary hypothesis and some evidence. In B. Ellis & D. Bjorklund (Eds.), *Origins of the social mind: Evolutionary psychology and child development.* New York: Guilford Press.

Belsky, J., Hsieh, K., & Crnic, K. (1998). Mothering, fathering, and infant negativity as antecedents of boys' externalizing problems and inhibition at age 3: Differential susceptibility to rearing influence? *Development and Psychopathology, 10,* 301–319.

Belsky, J., Steinberg, L., & Draper, P. (1991). Childhood experience, interpersonal development, and reproductive strategy: An evolutionary theory of socialization. *Child Development, 62,* 647–670.

Benoit, D., & Parker, K. C. H. (1994). Stability and transmission of attachment across three generations. *Child Development, 65,* 1444–1456.

Bernstein, I. S., & Ehardt, C. L. (1985). Age-sex differences in the expression of agonistic behavior in rhesus monkey (Macca mulatta) groups. *Journal of Comparative Psychology, 99,* 115–132.

Berry, J. W. (1976). *Human ecology and cognitive style: Comparative studies in cultural and psychological adaptation.* New York: Sage.

Bigler, R. S. (1999). The use of multicultural curricula and materials to counter racism in children. *Journal of Social Issues, 55,* 687–705.

Bigler, R. S., Spears Brown, C., & Markell, M. (2001). When groups are not created equal: Effects of group status on the formation of intergroup attitudes in children. *Child Development, 72,* 1151–1162.

Bjorklund, D. F., & Pellegrini, A. D. (2000). Child development and evolutionary psychology. *Child Development, 71,* 1687–1708.

Bjorklund, D. F., & Pellegrini, A. D. (2002). *The origins of human nature: Evolutionary developmental psychology.* Washington, DC: American Psychological Association.

Blair, C. (2002). Early intervention for low birth weight preterm infants: The role of negative emotionality in the specification of effects. *Development and Psychopathology, 14,* 311–332.

Blatt, S. J. (1995). Interpersonal relatedness and self-definition: Two personality configurations and their implications for psychopathology and psychotherapy. In J. L. Singer (Ed.), *Repression and dissociation: Implications for personality theory, psychopathology and health* (pp. 299–335). Chicago: University of Chicago Press.

Blatt, S. J. (1998). Contributions of psychoanalysis to the understanding and treatment of depression. *Journal of the American Psychoanalytic Association, 46,* 723–752.

Blum-Kulka, S. (1997). *Dinner talk: Cultural patterns of sociability and socialization in family discourse.* Mahwah, NJ: Erlbaum.

Bornstein, M. H., Haynes, O. M., Azuma, H., Galerin, C., Maital, S., Ogino, M., et al. (1998). A cross-sectional study of self-evaluations and attributions in parenting: Argentina, Belgium, France, Israel, Italy, Japan, and the United States. *Developmental Psychology, 34,* 662–676.

Bowlby, J. (1969). *Attachment and loss: Vol. 1. Attachment.* New York: Basic Books.

Bowlby, J. (1973). *Attachment and loss: Vol. 2. Separation.* New York: Basic Books.

Bowlby, J. (1980). *Attachment and loss: Vol. 3. Loss.* New York: Basic Books.

Boyce, W. T., & Ellis, B. J. (in press). Biological sensitivity to context: Pt. 1. An evolutionary-developmental theory of the origins and functions of stress reactivity. *Development and Psychopathology.*

Brachfield, S., Goldberg, S., & Sloman, J. (1980). Parent-infant interaction in free play at 8 and 12 months: Effects of prematurity and immaturity. *Infant Behavior and Development, 3,* 289–305.

Breedlove, S. (1992). Sexual differentiation of the brain and behavior. In J. Becker, S. Breedlove, & D. Crews (Eds.), *Behavioral endocrinology* (pp. 39–68). Cambridge, MA: MIT Press.

Breland, K., & Breland, M. (1966). *Animal behavior.* New York: Macmillan.

Bremner, J. D., & Narayan, M. (1998). The effects of stress on memory and the hippocampus throughout the life cycle: Implications for childhood development and aging. *Development and Psychopathology, 10,* 855–871.

Brennan, K. A., & Shaver, P. R. (1995). Dimensions of adult attachment, affect regulation, and romantic functioning. *Personality and Social Psychology Bulletin, 21,* 267–283.

Bretherton, I. (1980). Young children in stressful situations: The supporting role of attachment figures and unfamiliar caregivers. In G. V. Coelho & P. I. Ahmed (Eds.), *Uprooting and development* (pp. 179–210). New York: Plenum Press.

Bretherton, I. (1985). Attachment theory: Pt. 1. Retrospect and prospect. *Monograph of the Society for Research on Child Development* (1/2, Serial No. 209), 3–35.

Bretherton, I., Golby, B., & Cho, E. (1997). Attachment and the transmission of values. In J. E. Grusec & L. Kuczynski (Eds.), *Parenting and children's internalization of values: A handbook of contemporary theory* (pp. 103–134). New York: Wiley.

Brewer, M. B. (1999a). Multiple identities and identity transition: Implications for Hong Kong. *International Journal of Intercultural Relations, 23,* 167–197.

Brewer, M. B. (1999b). The psychology of prejudice: In-group love or out-group hate? *Journal of Social Issues, 55,* 429–444.

Brewer, M. B., & Gardner, W. (1996). Who is this "we"? Levels of collective identity and self-representation. *Journal of Personality and Social Psychology, 71,* 83–93.

Bridges, R. S. (1996). Biochemical basis of parental behavior in the rat. *Advances in the Study of Behavior, 25,* 215–242.

Brody, G., Ge, X., Conger, R., Gibbons, F. X., McBride, M. V., Gerrard, M., et al. (2001). The influence of neighborhood disadvantage, collective socialization, and parenting on African American children's affiliation with deviant peers. *Child Development, 72,* 1231–1246.

Bronfenbrenner, U. (1979). *The ecology of human development.* Cambridge, MA: Harvard University Press.

Brown, B. (1999). Optimizing expression of the common human genome for child development. *Current Directions in Psychological Science, 8,* 37–41.

Bruer, J. T., & Greenough, W. T. (2001). The subtle science of how experience affects the brain. In D. B. Bailey, J. T. Bruer, F. J. Symons, & J. W. Lichtman (Eds.), *Critical thinking about critical periods* (pp. 209–232). Baltimore, MD: Paul H. Brookes.

Bugental, D. B. (1992). Affective and cognitive processes within threat-oriented family systems. In I. E. Sigel, A. McGillicuddy-DeLisi, & J. Goodnow (Eds.), *Parental belief systems: The psychological consequences for children* (pp. 219–248). Mahwah, NJ: Erlbaum.

Bugental, D. B. (2000). Acquisition of the algorithms of social life: A domain-based approach. *Psychological Bulletin, 26,* 187–209.

Bugental, D. B. (2003). *Thriving in the face of childhood adversity.* New York: Psychology Press.

Bugental, D. B., & Beaulieu, D. A. (2004). Maltreatment risk among disabled children: A bio-social-cognitive approach. In R. Kail (Ed.), *Advances in child development and behavior* (Vol. 31, pp. 129–164). New York: Academic Press.

Bugental, D. B., Beaulieu, D., Cayan, L., Fowler, E., O'Brien, E., & Kokotay, S. (2004). *Stress immunization in young adults: The role of early medical adversity and supportive parenting.* Unpublished paper.

Bugental, D. B., Brown, M., & Reiss, C. (1996). Cognitive representations of power in caregiving relationships: Biasing effects on interpersonal interaction and information processing. *Journal of Family Psychology, 10,* 397–407.

Bugental, D. B., & Goodnow, J. G. (1998). Socialization processes. In W. Damon (Editor-in-Chief) & N. Eisenberg (Vol. Ed.), *Handbook of child psychology: Vol. 3. Social, emotional, and personality development* (5th ed., pp. 389–462). New York: Wiley.

Bugental, D. B., & Happaney, K. (2004). Predicting infant maltreatment in low-income families: The interactive effects of maternal attributions and child status at birth. *Developmental Psychology, 40,* 234–243.

Bugental, D. B., & Johnston, C. (2000). Parental and child cognitions in the context of the family. *Annual Review of Psychology, 51,* 315–344.

Bugental, D. B., Johnston, C., New, M., & Silvester, J. (1998). Measuring parental attributions: Conceptual and methodological issues. *Journal of Family Psychology, 12,* 459–480.

Bugental, D. B., Lyon, J. E., Cortez, V., & Krantz, J. (1997). Who's the boss? Accessibility of dominance ideation among individuals with low perceptions of interpersonal power. *Journal of Personality and Social Psychology, 72,* 1297–1309.

Bugental, D. B., Martorell, G. A., & Barraza, V. (2003). The hormonal costs of subtle forms of infant maltreatment. *Hormones and Behavior, 43,* 237–244.

Bugental, D. B., & Shennum, W. A. (2002). Gender, power, and violence in the family [Special issue]. *Child Maltreatment, 7,* 56–64.

Cacioppo, J. T., Berntson, G. G., Sheridan, J. F., & McClintock, M. K. (2000). Multilevel integrative analyses of human behavior: Social neuroscience and the complementing nature of social and biological approaches [Special issue]. *Psychological Bulletin, 12,* 829–843.

Cameron, J. A., Alvarez, J. M., Ruble, D. N., & Fuligni, A. J. (2001). Children's lay theories about ingroups and outgroups. *Personality and Social Psychology Review, 5,* 118–128.

Caporael, L. R., & Brewer, M. B. (1991). Reviving evolutionary psychology: Biology meets society. *Journal of Social Issues, 47,* 187–195.

Carter, C. S. (1998). Neuroendocrine perspectives on social attachment and love [Special issue]. *Psychoneuroendocrinology, 23,* 779–818.

Caspi, A., McClay, J., Moffitt, T., Mill, J., Martin, J., Craig, I. W., et al. (2002). Role of genotype in the cycle of violence in maltreated children. *Science, 297,* 851–854.

Cassidy, J. (1994). Emotion regulation: Influences of attachment relationships. *Monographs of the Society for Research in Child Development, 59,* 228–283.

Chao, R. K. (1994). Beyond parental control and authoritarian parenting style: Understanding Chinese parenting through the cultural notion of training. *Child Development, 65,* 1111–1119.

Chao, R. K. (1995). Chinese and European American cultural models of the self reflected in mothers' childrearing beliefs. *Ethos, 23,* 328–354.

Chao, R. K. (2001). Extending the research on the consequences of parenting style for Chinese Americans and European Americans. *Child Development, 72,* 1832–1843.

Chao, R. K. (2002). Parenting of Asians. In M. H. Bornstein (Ed.), *Handbook of parenting: Vol. 4. Social conditions and applied parenting* (2nd ed., pp. 59–93). Mahwah, NJ: Erlbaum.

Chartrand, T. L., & Bargh, J. A. (1999). The chameleon effect: The perception-behavior link and social interactions. *Journal of Personality and Social Psychology, 76,* 893–910.

Cheney, D. L., & Seyfarth, R. M. (1985). Social and nonsocial knowledge in vervet monkeys. *Philosophical Transactions of the Royal Society of London, 308,* 187–201.

Chirkov, V., & Ryan, R. M. (2003). Parent and teacher autonomy-support in Russian & U.S. adolescents: Common effects on well-being and academic motivation. *Journal of Cross-Cultural Psychology, 32,* 618–635.

Chomsky, N. (1988). *Language and problems of knowledge.* Cambridge, MA: MIT Press.

Coe, C. L. (1990). Psychobiology of maternal behavior in nonhuman primates. In N. A. Krasnegor & R. S. Bridges (Eds.), *Mammalian parenting* (pp. 157–183). Oxford: Oxford University Press.

Coie, J. D., & Dodge, K. A. (1998). Aggression and antisocial behavior. In W. Damon & N. Eisenberg (Eds.), *Handbook of child psychology* (Vol. 3, pp. 779–862). New York: Wiley.

Colder, C. R., Lochman, J. E., & Wells, K. C. (1997). The moderating effects of children's fear and activity level on relations between parenting practices and childhood symptomatology. *Journal of Abnormal Child Psychology, 25,* 251–263.

Collins, W. A., Gleason, T., & Sesma, A. (1997). Internalization, autonomy, and relationships: Development during adolescence. In J. E. Grusec & L. Kuczynski (Eds.), *Parenting and children's internalization of values: A handbook of contemporary theory* (pp. 78–99). New York: Wiley.

Collins, W. A., Maccoby, E. E., Steinberg, L., Hetherington, E. M., & Bornstein, M. H. (2000). Contemporary research on parenting: The case for nature and nurture. *American Psychologist, 55,* 218–232.

Corsaro, W. A. (1997). *The sociology of childhood.* Thousand Oaks, CA: Pine Forge Press.

Cosmides, L., & Tooby, J. (1992). Cognitive adaptations for social exchange. In J. H. Barkow, L. Cosmides, & J. Tooby (Eds.), *The adapted mind: Evolutionary psychology and the generation of culture* (pp. 163–228). London: Oxford University Press.

Cowan, C. P., & Cowan, P. A. (2000). *When partners become parents: The big life change for couples.* Mahwah, NJ: Erlbaum.

Cox, M. J., & Paley, B. (1997). Families as systems. *Annual Review of Psychology, 48,* 243–267.

Cox, M. J., Paley, B., & Harter, K. (2001). Interparental conflict and parent-child relationships. In J. H. Grych & F. D. Fincham (Eds.), *Interparental conflict and child development* (pp. 249–272). Cambridge: Cambridge University Press.

Criss, M. M., Shaw, D. S., & Ingoldsby, E. M. (2003). Mother-son positive synchrony in middle childhood: Relation to antisocial behavior. *Social Development, 12,* 379–400.

Crockenberg, S. (1987). Predictors and correlates of anger toward and punitive control of toddlers by adolescent mothers. *Child Development, 58,* 964–975.

Crouter, A. C., & Head, M. R. (2002). Parental monitoring and knowledge of children. In M. H. Bornstein (Ed.), *Handbook of parenting* (Vol. 3, pp. 461–483). Mahwah, NJ: Erlbaum.

Crouter, A. C., Helms-Erikson, H., Updegraff, K., & McHale, S. M. (1999). Conditions underlying parents' knowledge about children's daily lives in middle childhood: Between- and within-family comparisons. *Child Development, 70,* 246–259.

Cummings, E. M., & Wilson, A. (1999). Contexts of marital conflict and children's emotional security: Exploring the distinction between constructive and destructive conflict from the children's perspective. In M. Cox & J. Brooks-Gunn (Eds.), *Conflict and closeness in families: Causes and consequences* (pp. 105–129). Mahwah, NJ: Erlbaum.

Dabbs, J. M. (2000). *Heroes, rogues, and lovers.* New York: McGraw-Hill.

Daly, M., & Wilson, M. (1984). A sociobiological analysis of human infanticide. In G. Hausfater & S. B. Hrdy (Eds.), *Infanticide: Comparative and evolutionary perspectives* (pp. 487–502). New York: Aldine de Gruyter.

Darling, N., & Steinberg, L. (1993). Parenting style as context: An integrative model. *Psychological Bulletin, 113,* 487–496.

Davidov, M., & Grusec, J. E. (2005). Mothers' knowledge of children's reactions to discipline and its role in compliance and internalized conduct. Unpublished paper.

Davidov, M., & Grusec, J. E. (in press). Untangling the links of parental responsiveness to distress and warmth to child outcomes. *Child Development.*

Dawson, G., & Ashman, S. B. (2000). On the origins of a vulnerability to depression: The influence of the early social environment on the development of psychobiological systems related to risk for affective disorder. In C. A. Nelson (Ed.), *Minnesota Symposia on Child Psychology: Vol. 31. The effects of early adversity on neurobehavioral development* (pp. 245–280). Mahwah, NJ: Erlbaum.

Deater-Deckard, K., Dodge, K. A., Bates, J. E., & Pettit, G. S. (1996). Physical discipline among African American and European American mothers: Links to children's externalizing behaviors. *Developmental Psychology, 32,* 1056–1072.

Deater-Deckard, K., & O'Connor, T. G. (2000). Parent-child mutuality in early childhood: Two behavioral genetic studies. *Developmental Psychology, 16,* 1561–1570.

DeCasper, A. J., & Fifer, W. P. (1987). Of human bonding: Newborns prefer their mothers' voices. In J. Oates & S. Sheldon (Eds.), *Cognitive development in infancy* (pp. 111–118). Hillsdale, NJ: Erlbaum.

Deci, E. L., & Ryan, R. M. (1991). A motivational approach to self: Integration in personality. In R. Dienstbier (Ed.), *Nebraska Symposium on Motivation: Vol. 38. Perspectives on motivation* (pp. 237–288). Lincoln: University of Nebraska Press.

Dekovic, M., Gerris, J. R., & Janssens, J. M. (1991). Parental cognitions, parental behavior, and the child's understanding of the parent-child relationship. *Merrill-Palmer Quarterly, 37,* 523–541.

De Pue, R. A., Luciana, M., Arbisi, P., Collins, P., & Leon, A. (1994). Dopamine and the structure of personality: Relation of agonist-induced dopamine activity to positive emotionality. *Journal of Personality and Social Psychology, 67,* 485–498.

Dhar, R. (1997). Consumer preference for a no-choice option. *Journal of Consumer Research, 24,* 215–231.

Dishion, T. J., Andrews, D. W., & Crosby, L. (1995). Antisocial boys and their friends in early adolescence: Relationship characteristics, quality, and interactional process. *Child Development, 66,* 139–151.

Dix, T. (1992). Parenting on behalf of the child: Empathic goals in the regulation of responsive parenting. In I. E. Sigel, A. V. McGillicuddy-DeLisi, & J. J. Goodnow (Eds.), *Parental belief systems: The psychological consequences for children* (2nd ed., pp. 319–346). Hillsdale, NJ: Erlbaum.

Dix, T., Ruble, D. N., & Zambarano, R. (1989). Mothers' implicit theories of discipline: Child effects, parent effects, and the attribution process. *Child Development, 60,* 1373–1391.

Dodge, K. A., & Pettit, G. S. (2003). A biopsychosocial model of the development of chronic conduct problems in adolescence. *Developmental Psychology, 39,* 349–371.

Donovan, W. L., Leavitt, L. A., & Walsh, R. O. (1998). Conflict and depression predict maternal sensitivity to infant cries. *Infant Behavior and Development, 21,* 505–517.

Dubas, J. S., & Gerris, J. R. M. (2002). Longitudinal changes in the time parents spend in activities with their adolescent children as a function of child age, pubertal status and gender. *Journal of Family Psychology, 16,* 415–462.

Dunn, J., & Brown, J. (1991). Becoming American or English? Talking about the social world in England and the United States. In M. H. Bornstein (Ed.), *Cultural approaches to parenting: Cross-currents in contemporary psychology* (pp. 155–172). Hillsdale, NJ: Erlbaum.

Dunn, J., Brown, J., Slomkowski, C., Tesla, C., & Youngblade, L. (1991). Young children's understanding of other people's feelings and beliefs: Individual differences and their antecedents. *Child Development, 62,* 1352–1366.

Dunn, J., & Munn, P. (1985). Becoming a family member: Family conflict and the development of understanding. *Child Development, 56,* 480–492.

Eccles, J. (2002). Introduction. In B. K. Barber (Ed.), *Intrusive parenting: How psychological control affects children and adolescents* (pp. 1–2). Washington, DC: American Psychological Association.

Eisenberg, N., Fabes, R. A., Shepard, S. A., Guthrie, I. K., Murphy, B. C., & Reiser, M. (1999). Parental reactions to children's negative emotions: Longitudinal relations to quality of children's social functioning. *Child Development, 70,* 513–534.

Elder, G. H., & Rockwell, C. (1979). The life-course and human development: An ecological perspective. *International Journal of Behavioral Development, 21,* 1–21.

Ellis, B. J., McFadyen-Ketchum, S., Dodge, K. A., Pettit, G. S., & Bates, J. E. (1999). Quality of early family relationships and individual differences in the timing of pubertal maturation in girls: A longitudinal test of an evolutionary model. *Journal of Personality and Social Psychology, 77,* 387–401.

Emde, R. N., Biringen, Z., Clyman, R. B., & Oppenheim, D. (1991). The moral self of infancy: Affective core and procedural knowledge. *Developmental Review, 11,* 251–270.

Erikson, E. H. (1959). *Identity and the life cycle.* New York: International Universities Press.

Essex, M. J., Klein, M. H., Cho, E., & Kalin, N. H. (2002). Maternal stress beginning in infancy may sensitize children to later stress exposure: Effects on cortisol and behavior. *Biological Psychiatry, 52,* 776–784.

Evans, D. W., Leckman, J. F., Carter, A., Reznick, J. S., Henshaw, C., King, R. A., et al. (1997). Ritual, habit, and perfectionism: The prevalence and development of compulsive-like behavior in normal young children. *Child Development, 68,* 58–68.

Fagan, J. F., & Singer, L. T. (1979). The role of simple feature differences in infants' recognition of faces. *Infant Behavior and Development, 2,* 39–45.

Feldman, R., Weller, A., Sirota, L., & Eidelman, A. I. (2002). Skin-to-skin contact (Kangaroo Care) promotes self-regulation in premature infants: Sleep-wake cyclicity, arousal modulation, and sustained exploration. *Developmental Psychology, 38,* 194–207.

Ferguson, J. N., Aldag, J. M., & Insel, T. R. (2001). Oxytocin in the medial amygdala is essential for social recognition in the mouse. *Journal of Neuroscience, 21,* 8278–8285.

Fernald, A. (1993). Approval and disapproval: Infant responsiveness to vocal affect in familiar and unfamiliar languages. *Child Development, 64,* 657–674.

Fernald, A., Taescdhner, T., Dunn, J., Papousek, M., DeBoyson-Bardies, B., & Fukui, J. (1989). A cross-language study of prosodic modifications of mothers' and fathers' speech to preverbal infants. *Journal of Child Language, 16,* 477–501.

Field, T. M. (1994). The effects of mother's physical and emotional unavailability on emotion regulation. *Monographs of the Society for Research in Child Development, 59,* 208–227, 250–283.

Field, T. M. (1998). Touch therapy effects on development. *International Journal of Behavioral Development, 22,* 779–797.

Field, T. M., Cohen, D., Garcia, R., & Greenberg, R. (1984). Mother-stranger face discrimination by the newborn. *Infant Behavior and Development, 7,* 19–25.

Field, T., Greenwald, P., Morrow, C. J., Healy, B. T., Foster, T., Guthertz, M., et al. (1992). Behavior state matching during interactions of preadolescent friends versus acquaintances. *Developmental Psychology, 28,* 242–250.

Fiese, B. H., Tomcho, T. J., Douglas, M., Josephs, K., Poltrock, S., & Baker, T. (2002). A review of 50 years of research on naturally occurring family routines and rituals: Cause for celebration? *Journal of Family Psychology, 16,* 381–390.

Fiske, A. P., Kitayama, S., Markus, H. R., & Nisbett, R. E. (1998). The cultural matrix of social psychology. In D. T. Gilbert, S. Fiske, & G. Lindzey (Eds.), Handbook of social psychology (4th ed., Vol. 2, pp. 915–981). Boston: McGraw-Hill.

Fleming, A. S. (1990). Hormonal and experiential correlates of maternal responsiveness in human mothers. In N. A. Krasnegor & R. S. Bridges (Eds.), *Mammalian parenting* (pp. 184–208). Oxford, England: Oxford University Press.

Fleming, A. S., Corter, C., Stallings, J., & Steiner, M. (2002). Testosterone and prolactin are associated with emotional responses to infant cries in new fathers. *Hormones and Behavior, 42,* 399–413.

Fleming, A. S., Steiner, M., & Corter, C. (1997). Cortisol, hedonics, and maternal responsiveness in human mothers. *Hormones and Behavior, 32,* 85–98.

Flinn, M. V., Quinlan, R. J., Decker, S. A., Turner, M. T., & England, B. G. (1996). Male-female differences in effects of parental absence on glucocorticoid stress response. *Human Nature, 7,* 125–162.

Florian, V., & Mikulincer, M. (1998). Terror management in childhood: Does death conceptualization moderate the effects of mortality salience on acceptance of different others? *Personality and Social Psychology Bulletin, 24,* 1104–1112.

Fogel, A., & Branco, A. U. (1997). Meta-communication as a source of indetermination in relationship development. In A. Fogel, M. C. Lyra, & J. Valsiner (Eds.), *Dynamics and indeterminism in developmental and social processes* (pp. 65–92). Hillsdale, NJ: Erlbaum.

Forman, D. R., & Kochanska, G. (2001). Viewing imitation as child responsiveness: A link between teaching and discipline domains of socialization. *Developmental Psychology, 37,* 198–206.

Francis, D. D., Caldji, C., Champagne, F., Plotsky, P. M., & Meaney, M. J. (1999). The role of corticotropin-releasing factor-norepinephrine systems in mediating the effects of early experience on the development of behavioral and endocrine responses to stress. *Biological Psychiatry, 46,* 1153–1166.

Francis, D. D., Champagne, F. A., Liu, D., & Meaney, M. J. (1999). Maternal care, gene expression, and the development of individual differences in stress reactivity. In N. E. Adler & M. Marmot (Eds.), *Annals of the New York Academy of Sciences: Vol. 896. Socioeconomic status and health in industrial nations—Social, psychological, and biological pathways* (pp. 66–84). New York: New York Academy of Sciences.

Francis, D. D., Diorio, J., Liu, D., & Meaney, M. J. (1999). Nongenomic transmission across generations of maternal behavior and stress responses in rats. *Science, 286,* 1155–1158.

Francis, D. D., Diorio, J., Plotsky, P. M., & Meaney, M. J. (2002). Environmental enrichment reverses the effects of maternal separation on stress reactivity. *Journal of Neuroscience, 15,* 7840–7843.

Freud, S. (1965). *Normality and pathology in childhood.* New York: International Universities Press.

Fuligni, A. J., Tseng, V., & Lam, M. (1999). Attitudes toward family obligations among American adolescents with Asian, Latin American, and European backgrounds. *Child Development, 70,* 11030–11044.

Fuligni, A. J., Yip, T., & Tseng, V. (2002). The impact of family obligation on the daily activities and psychological well-being of Chinese American adolescents. *Child Development, 73,* 302–314.

Gallese, V., Ferraari, P., Kohler, E., & Fogassi, L. (2002). The eyes, the hand, and the mind: Behavioral and neurophysiological aspects of social cognition. In M. Bekoff, C. Allen, & G. M. Burghardt (Eds.), *The cognitive animal* (pp. 451–461). London: MIT Press.

Garcia, J., & Koelling, R. A. (1996). Relation of cue to consequence in avoidance learning. In L. D. Houck & L. C. Drickamer (Eds.), *Foundations of animal behavior: Classic papers with commentaries* (pp. 374–375). Chicago: University of Chicago Press.

Gardner, F. (1994). The quality of joint activity between mothers and their children with behaviour problems. *Journal of Child Psychology and Psychiatry and Allied Disciplines, 35,* 935–948.

Gardner, F., Ward, S., Burton, J., & Wilson, C. (2003). The role of mother-child joint play in the early development of children's conduct problems: A longitudinal observational study. *Social Development, 12,* 361–378.

Geary, D. C. (2000). Evolution and proximate expression of human paternal investment. *Psychological Bulletin, 26,* 55–77.

Geary, D. C., & Bjorklund, D. F. (2000). Evolutionary developmental psychology. *Child Development, 71,* 57–65.

George, C., & Solomon, J. (1996). Representational models of relationships: Links between caregiving and attachment. *Infant Mental Health Journal, 17,* 198–216.

Gershoff, E. T. (2002). Corporal punishment by parents and associated child behaviors and experiences: A meta-analytic and theoretical review. *Psychological Bulletin, 128,* 539–579.

Gilbert, P., & McGuire, M. T. (1998). Shame, status, and social roles: Psychobiology and evolution. In P. Gilbert & B. Andrews (Eds.), *Shame: Interpersonal behavior, psychopathology, and culture* (pp. 99–125). New York: Oxford University Press.

Goldberg, S., Grusec, J. E., & Jenkins, J. M. (1999). Confidence in protection: Arguments for a narrow definition of attachment. *Journal of Family Psychology, 13,* 475–483.

Goldsmith, H. H., & Lemery, K. S. (2000). Linking temperamental fearfulness and anxiety symptoms: A behavior-genetic perspective. *Biological Psychiatry, 48,* 1199–1209.

Goldstein, S., Field, T., & Healy, B. T. (1989). Concordance of play behavior and physiology in preschool friends. *Journal of Applied Developmental Psychology, 10,* 337–351.

Goodnow, J. J. (1994). Acceptable disagreement across generations. In J. Smetana (Ed.), *Beliefs about parenting: Origins and developmental implications* (pp. 51–64). San Francisco: Jossey-Bass.

Goodnow, J. J. (1997). Parenting and the transmission and internalization of values: From social-cultural perspectives to within-family analyses. In J. E. Grusec & L. Kuczynski (Eds.), *Handbook of parenting and the transmission of values* (pp. 333–361). New York: Wiley.

Goodnow, J. J., & Collins, A. W. (1990). *Development according to parents: The nature, sources, and consequences of parents' ideas.* Hillsdale, NJ: Erlbaum.

Goodnow, J. J., Miller, P. J., & Kessel, F. (Eds.). (1995). *Cultural practices as contexts for development.* San Francisco: Jossey-Bass.

Gray, P. B., Kahlenberg, S. M., Barrett, E. S., Lipson, S. F., & Ellison, P. T. (2002). Marriage and fatherhood are associated with lower testosterone in males. *Evolution and Human Behavior, 23,* 193–201.

Green, J. A., & Gustafson, G. E. (1983). Individual recognition of human infants on the basis of cries alone. *Developmental Psychobiology, 16,* 485–493.

Greenfield, P. M., Keller, H., Fuligni, A., & Maynard, A. (2003). Cultural pathways through universal development. *Annual Review of Psychology, 54,* 461–490.

Greenwald, A. B., & Banaji, M. R. (1995). Implicit social cognition: Attitudes, self-esteem, and stereotypes. *Psychological Review, 102,* 4–27.

Grolnick W. (2003). *The psychology of parental control: How well-meant parenting backfires.* Mahwah, NJ: Erlbaum.

Grolnick, W. S., Deci, E. L., & Ryan, R. M. (1997). Internalization within the family: The self-determination theory perspective. In J. E. Grusec & L. Kuczynski (Eds.), *Parenting and children's internalization of values: A handbook of contemporary theory* (pp. 135–161). New York: Wiley.

Grotevant, H. D., & Cooper, C. R. (1986). Individuation in family relationships: A perspective on individual differences in the development of identity and role-taking skill in adolescence. *Human Development, 29,* 82–100.

Grusec, J. E., & Goodnow, J. J. (1994). The impact of parental discipline methods on the child's internalization of values: A reconceptualization of current points of view. *Developmental Psychology, 30,* 4–19.

Grusec, J. E., Goodnow, J. J., & Kuczynski, L. (2000). New directions in analyses of parenting contributions to children's acquisition of values. *Child Development, 71,* 205–211.

Grusec, J. E., Hastings, P., & Mammone, N. (1994). Parenting cognitions and relationship schemas. In J. Smetana (Ed.), *Beliefs about parenting: Origins and developmental implications* (pp. 5–20). San Francisco: Jossey-Bass.

Grusec, J. E., & Redler, E. (1980). Attribution, reinforcement, and altruism: A developmental analysis. *Developmental Psychology, 16,* 525–534.

Gubernick, D. J., Sengelaug, D. R., & Kurz, E. M. (1993). A neuroanatomical correlate of paternal and maternal behavior in the biparental California mouse (Peromyscus californicus). *Behavioral Neuroscience, 107,* 194–201.

Gunnar, M. R. (2000). Early adversity and the development of stress reactivity and regulation. In C. A. Nelson (Ed.), *Minnesota Symposia on Child Psychology: Vol. 31. The effects of early adversity on neurobehavioral development* (pp. 163–200). Mahwah, NJ: Erlbaum.

Gunnar, M. R., Larson, M. C., Hertsgaard, L., Harris, M. L., & Brodersen, L. (1992). The stressfulness of separation among 9-month-old infants: Effects of social context variables and infant temperament. *Child Development, 63,* 290–303.

Gunnar, M. R., Morison, S. J., Chisholm, K., & Schuder, M. (2001). Salivary cortisol levels in children adopted from Romanian orphanages [Special issue]. *Development and Psychopathology, 13,* 611–628.

Gunnar, M. R., Porter, F. L., Wolfe, C. M., Rigatuso, J., & Larson, M. C. (1995). Nenonatal stress reactivity: Predictions to later emotional temperament. *Child Development, 66,* 1–13.

Hamilton, W. D. (1964). Genetical evolution of social behavior. *Journal of Theoretical Biology, 7,* 1–52.

Harkness, S., & Super, C. M. (2002). Biology and ecology of parenting. In M. H. Bornstein (Ed.), *Handbook of parenting* (2nd ed., Vol. 2, pp. 253–280). Mahwah, NJ: Erlbaum.

Harkness, S., Super, C. M., & van Tijen, N. (2000). Individualism and the "Western mind" reconsidered: American and Dutch parents' ethnotheories of the child. In S. Harkness, C. Raeff, & C. M. Super (Eds.), *Variability in the social construction of the child: Vol. 87. New directions for child and adolescent development* (pp. 23–39). San Francisco: Jossey-Bass.

Harlow, H., & Harlow, M. (1965). The affectional system. In A. Schrier, H. F. Harlow, & F. Stolnitz (Eds.), *Behavior of nonhuman primates* (Vol. 2, pp. 287–334). New York: Academic Press.

Harlow, H. F. (1973). *Learning to love.* Oxford, England: Ballantine Books.

Harris, J. R. (1995). Where is the child's environment? A group socialization theory of development. *Psychological Review, 102,* 458–489.

Hastings, P. D., & Grusec, J. E. (1997). Conflict outcomes as a function of parental accuracy in perceiving child cognitions and affect. *Social Development, 6,* 76–90.

Hastings, P. D., & Grusec, J. E. (1998). Parenting goals as organizers of responses to parent-child disagreement. *Developmental Psychology, 34,* 465–479.

Helwig, C. C., Arnold, M. L., Tan, D., & Boyd, D. (2003). Chinese adolescents' reasoning about democratic and authority-based decision making in peer, family, and school contexts. *Child Development, 74,* 783–800.

Herman, B. H., & Panksepp, J. (1981). Ascending endorphin inhibition with distress vocalization. *Science, 211,* 1060–1062.

Hertsgaard, L., Gunnar, M., Erickson, M. F., & Nachmias, M. (1995). Adrenocortical responses to the strange situation in infants with disorganized/disoriented attachment relationships. *Child Development, 66,* 1100–1106.

Hertwig, R., Davis, J. N., & Sulloway, F. J. (2002). Parental investment: How an equity motive can produce inequality. *Psychological Bulletin, 128,* 728–745.

Herz, L., & Gullone, E. (1999). The relationship between self-esteem and parenting style: A cross-cultural comparison of Australian and Vietnamese Australian adolescents. *Journal of Cross-Cultural Psychology, 30,* 742–761.

Hetherington, E. M. (1993). An overview of the Virginia Longitudinal Study of Divorce and Remarriage with a focus on early adolescence. *Journal of Family Psychology, 7,* 39–56.

Higley, J. D., Hopkins, W. D., Thompson, W. W., Byrne, E. A., Hirsch, R. M., & Suomi, S. J. (1992). Peers as primary attachment sources in yearling rhesus monkeys (Macaca mulatta). *Developmental Psychology, 28,* 1163–1171.

Hirschfeld, L. A. (1996). *Race in the making: Cognition, culture, and child's construction of human kinds.* Cambridge, MA: MIT Press.

Hirschfeld, L. A. (2001). On a folk theory of society: Children, evolution, and mental representations of social groups. *Personality and Social Psychology Review, 5,* 107–117.

Hirschfeld, L. A., & Gelman, S. A. (1994). Toward a topography of mind: An introduction to domain specificity. In L. A. Hirschfeld & S. A. Gelman (Eds.), *Mapping the mind* (pp. 3–36). Cambridge, England: Cambridge University Press.

Hockenberry-Eaton, M., Kemp, V., & DiLorio, C. (1994). Cancer stressors and protective factors: Predictors of stress experienced during treatment for childhood cancer. *Research in Nursing and Health, 17,* 351–361.

Hofer, M. A. (1987). Early social relationships: A psychobiologist's view. *Child Development, 58,* 633–647.

Hofer, M. A. (1996). Multiple regulation of ultrasonic vocalization. *Psychoneuroendocrinology, 21,* 203–217.

Hoffman, L. W. (1985). The changing genetics/socialization balance. *Journal of Social Issues, 41,* 127–148.

Hoffman, M. L. (1970). Moral development. In P. H. Mussen (Ed.), *Carmichael's manual of child psychology* (Vol. 2, pp. 261–360). New York: Wiley.

Hoffman, M. L. (1981). Is altruism part of human nature? *Journal of Personality and Social Psychology, 40,* 121–137.

Hoffman, M. L. (1983). Affective and cognitive processes in moral internalization. In E. T. Higgins, D. Ruble, & W. Hartup (Eds.), *Social cognition and social development: A sociocultural perspective* (pp. 236–274). Cambridge, England: Cambridge University Press.

Hofstede, G. (1983). National cultures revisited. *Behavior Science Research, 18,* 285–305.

Holden G. (2002). Perspectives on the effects of corporal punishment: Comment on Gershoff, 2002. *Psychological Bulletin, 128,* 590–595.

Holden, G. W., & Ritchie, K. L. (1988). Child rearing and the dialectics of parental intelligence. In J. Valsiner (Ed.), *Child development within culturally structured environments: Parental cognition and adult-child interaction* (pp. 30–59). Norwood, NJ: Ablex.

Horney, K. (1933). Maternal conflicts. *American Journal of Orthopsychiatry, 3,* 445–463.

Hsu, F. L. K. (1983). *Rugged individualism reconsidered: Essays in psychological anthropology.* Knoxville: University of Tennessee Press.

Inoff-Germain, F., Arnold, G. S., Nottelmann, E. D., Susman, E. J., Cutler, G. B., & Chrousos, G. P. (1988). Relations between hormone levels and observational measures of aggressive behavior of young adolescents in family interactions. *Developmental Psychology, 24,* 129–139.

Isley, S., O'Neil, R., & Parke, R. D. (1996). The relation of parental affect and control behaviors to children's classroom acceptance: A concurrent and predictive analysis. *Early Education and Development, 7,* 7–23.

Iyengar, S. S., & Lepper, M. R. (2000). When choice is demotivating: Can one desire too much of a good thing? *Journal of Personality and Social Psychology, 79,* 995–1006.

Jacklin, C. N., DiPietro, J. A., & Maccoby, E. E. (1984). Sex-typing behavior and sex-typing presence in child/parent interaction [Special issue]. *Archives of Sexual Behavior, 13,* 413–425.

Jaffee, S. R., Caspi, A., Moffitt, T. E., Polo-Tomas, M., Price, T. S., & Taylor, A. (2004). The limits of child effects: Evidence for genetically-mediated child effects on corporal punishment, but not on physical maltreatment. *Developmental Psychology, 40,* 1047–1058.

Jensen, P. S., Mrazek, D., Knapp, P. K., Steinberg, L., Pfeffer, C., Schowalter, J., et al. (1997). Evolution and revolution in child psychiatry: ADHD as a disorder of adaptation. *Journal of the American Academy of Child and Adolescent Psychiatry, 36,* 1672–1681.

Johnson, F. A. (1993). *Dependency and Japanese socialization: Psychoanalytic and anthropological investigation into amae.* New York: New York University Press.

Johnson, M. H., Dziurawiec, S., Ellis, H. D., & Morton, S. (1991). Newborns' preferential tracking of face-like stimuli and its subsequent decline. *Cognition, 40,* 1–21.

Kagan, J. (2001). Temperamental contributions to affective and behavioral profiles in childhood. In S. G. Hofman & P. M. DiBartolo (Eds.), *From social anxiety to social phobia: Multiple perspectives* (pp. 216–234). Needham Heights, MA: Allyn & Bacon.

Kagan, J., & Snidman, N. (1991). Temperamental factors in human development. *American Psychologist, 46,* 856–862.

Kagitcibasi, C. (1996). The autonomous-relational self: A new synthesis. *European Psychologist, 1,* 180–186.

Kashima, Y., Yamaguchi, S., Kim, U., Choi, S., Gelfand, M. J., & Yuki, S. (1995). Culture, gender, and self: A perspective from individualism-collectivism research. *Journal of Personality and Social Psychology, 69,* 925–937.

Keating, C. F., & Bai, D. L. (1986). Children's attributions of social dominance from facial cues. *Child Development, 57,* 1269–1276.

Keller, H., Lohaus, A., Kuensemueller, P., Abels, M., Yovsi, R., Voelker, S., et al. (2004). The bio-culture of parenting: Evidence from five cultural communities. *Parenting, 4,* 25–50.

Kelley, H. H., & Thibaut, J. W. (1978). *Interpersonal relations: A theory of interdependence.* New York: Wiley.

Kenny, D. A., Korchmaros, J. D., & Bolger, N. (2003). Lower level mediation in multilevel models. *Psychological Methods, 8,* 115–128.

Kerr, M., & Stattin, H. (2000). What parents know, how they know it, and several forms of adolescent adjustment: Further support for a reinterpretation of monitoring. *Child Development, 36,* 366–380.

Keverne, E. B., Nevison, C. M., & Martel, F. L. (1997). Early learning and the social bond. In C. S. Carter & I. Lederhendler (Eds.), *Annals of the New York Academy of Sciences: Vol. 807. The integrative neurobiology of affiliations* (pp. 329–339). New York: New York Academy of Sciences.

Kilgore, K., Snyder, J., & Lentz, C. (2000). The contribution of parental discipline, parental monitoring, and school risk to early-onset conduct problems in African American boys and girls. *Developmental Psychology, 36,* 835–845.

Killen, J., & Wainryb, C. (2000). Independence and interdependence in diverse cultural contexts. In S. Harkness, C. Raeff, & C. M. Super (Eds.), *New directions for child and adolescent development: Vol. 87. Variability in the social construction of the child* (pp. 5–21). San Francisco: Jossey-Bass.

Kim, K., & Rohner, R. P. (2002). Parental warmth, control, and involvement in schooling: Predicting academic achievement among Korean American adolescents. *Journal of Cross-Cultural Psychology, 33,* 127–140.

Kim, K. J., Conger, R. D., Lorenz, F. O., & Elder, G. (2001). Parent-adolescent reciprocity in negative affect and its relation to early adult social development. *Developmental Psychology, 37,* 775–790.

Kisilevsky, B. S., Hains, S. M. J., Lee, K., Xie, X., Huang, H., Ye, H., et al. (2003). Effects of experience on fetal voice recognition. *Psychological Science, 14,* 220–224.

Kitamura, C., Thanavisuth, C., Burnham, D., & Luksaneeyanawin, S. (2002). Universality and specificity in infant-directed speech: Pitch modifications as a function of infant age and sex in a tonal and non-tonal language. *Infant Behavior and Development, 24,* 372–392.

Knight, G. P., Virdin, L. M., & Roosa, M. (1994). Socialization and family correlates of mental health outcomes among Hispanic and Anglo American children: Consideration of cross-ethnic scalar equivalence. *Child Development, 65,* 212–224.

Kochanska, G. (1993). Toward a synthesis of parental socialization and child temperament in early development of conscience. *Child Development, 64,* 325–347.

Kochanska, G. (1995). Children's temperament, mothers' discipline, and the security of attachment: Multiple pathways to emerging internalization. *Child Development, 66,* 597–615.

Kochanska, G. (1997). Multiple pathways to conscience for children with different temperaments: From toddlerhood to age 5. *Developmental Psychology, 33,* 228–240.

Kochanska, G., & Aksan, N. (1995). Mother-child mutually positive affect, the quality of child compliance to requests and prohibitions, and maternal control as correlates of early internalization. *Child Development, 66,* 236–254.

Kochanska, G., & Murray, K. T. (2000). Mother-child mutually responsive orientation and conscience development: From toddler to early school age. *Child Development, 71,* 417–431.

Koestner, R., Gingras, I., Abutaa, R., Losier, G. F., DiDio, L. G., & Gagne, M. (1999). To follow expert advice when making a decision: An examination of reactive versus reflective autonomy. *Journal of Personality, 67,* 851–872.

Koestner, R., & Losier, G. F. (1996). Distinguishing reactive versus reflective autonomy. *Journal of Personality, 64,* 465–494.

Konner, M. J. (1972). Aspects of the developmental ethology of a foraging people. In N. B. Jones (Ed.), *Ethological studies of child behaviour* (pp. 285–304). Oxford, England: Cambridge University Press.

Kuczynski, L. (1984). Socialization goals and mother-child interaction: Strategies for long-term and short-term compliance. *Developmental Psychology, 20,* 1061–1073.

Kuczynski, L. (2003). Beyond bidirectionality: Bilateral conceptual frameworks for understanding dynamics in parent-child relations. In L. Kuczynski (Ed.), *Handbook of dynamics in parent-child relationships* (pp. 3–24). Thousand Oaks, CA: Sage.

Kuhn, C. M., & Schanberg, S. M. (1998). Responses to maternal separation: Mechanisms and mediators [Special issue]. *International Journal of Developmental Neuroscience, 16,* 261–270.

Kurzban, R., Cosmides, L., & Tooby, J. (2003). Can race be erased? Coalitional computation and social categorization. *Proceedings of the National Academy of Sciences, 98,* 15387–15392.

LaFreniere, P. J., & Capuano, F. (1997). Preventive intervention as means of clarifying directions of effects in socialization: Anxious-withdrawn preschoolers case. *Development and Psychopathology, 9,* 551–564.

Laird, R. D., Pettit, G. S., Bates, J. E., & Dodge, K. A. (2003). Parents' monitoring-relevant knowledge and adolescents' delinquent behavior: Evidence of correlated developmental changes and reciprocal influences. *Child Development, 74,* 752–768.

Laird, R. D., Pettit, G. S., Mize, J., Brown, E. G., & Lindsey, E. (1994). Mother child conversations about peers. *Family Relations: Interdisciplinary Journal of Applied Family Studies, 43,* 425–432.

Lamond, A. I., & Earnshaw, W. C. (1998). Structure and function in the nucleus. *Science, 280,* 547–553.

Laudenslager, M. L., Boccia, M. L., Berger, C. L., & Gennaro-Ruggles, M. M. (1995). Total cortisol, free cortisol, and growth hormones associated with brief social separation experiences in young macaques. *Developmental Psychobiology, 28,* 129–211.

Lebra, T. S. (2000). New insight and old dilemma: A cross-cultural comparison of Japan and the United States. *Child Development, 71,* 1147–1149.

Leinbach, M. D., & Fagot, B. I. (1993). Categorical habituation to male and female faces: Gender schematic processing in infancy. *Infant Behavior and Development, 16,* 317–332.

Lepper, M. (1983). Social control processes, attributions of motivation, and the internalization of social values. In E. T. Higgins, D. N. Ruble, & W. W. Hartup (Eds.), *Social cognition and social development: A sociocultural perspective* (pp. 294–330). New York: Cambridge University Press.

Lester, B. M., Hoffman, J., & Brazelton, T. B. (1985). The rhythmic structure of mother-infant interaction in term and preterm infants. *Child Development, 56,* 15–27.

Leung, K., Lau, S., & Lam, W. L. (1998). Parenting styles and achievement: A cross-cultural study. *Merrill-Palmer Quarterly, 44,* 157–172.

Leveille, E., Cossette, L., Blanchette, I., & Gaudreau, M. (2001). The socialization of emotions during nursing: The role of contingent maternal facial expressions. *International Journal of Psychology, 36,* 260–273.

Levy, D. (1943). *Maternal overprotection.* New York: Columbia University Press.

Lewis, C. S. (2000). Human development in the United States and Japan: New ways to think about continuity across the lifespan. *Child Development, 71,* 1152–1154.

Lin, E. K. (1999). The signal value of children's voices and its effect on adult's physiological and emotional responses. *Dissertation Abstracts International: Section B: Sciences & Engineering, 60,* 855.

Lindahl, K. M., & Malik, N. M. (1999). Marital conflict, family processes, and boys' externalizing behavior in Hispanic American and European American families. *Journal of Clinical and Child Psychology, 28,* 12–24.

Lindsey, E. W. (1998). Parents as play partners: Mechanisms linking parent-child play to children's social competence. *Dissertation Abstracts International: Section B: Sciences and Engineering, 58,* 5700.

Lindsey, E. W. (2002). Preschool children's friendships and peer acceptance: Links to social competence. *Child Study Journal, 32,* 145–156.

Lindsey, E. W., Mize, J., & Pettit, G. S. (1997). Mutuality in parent-child play: Consequences for children's peer competence. *Journal of Social and Personal Relationships, 14,* 523–538.

Liu, D., Diorio, J., Tannenbaum, C., Caldji, C., Francis, D., Freedman, A., et al. (1997). Maternal care, hippocampal glucocorticoid receptors, and hypothalamic-pituitary-adrenal responses to stress. *Science, 277,* 1659–1662.

Luecken, L. J. (1998). Childhood attachment and loss experiences affect adult cardiovascular and cortisol function. *Psychosomatic Medicine, 60,* 765–772.

Lundell, L., Grusec, J. E., McShane, K., & Davidov, M. (2004). *Mother-adolescent conflict: Adolescent goals and maternal management of those goals.* Unpublished manuscript.

Maccoby, E. E. (1988). Gender as a social category. *Developmental Psychology, 24,* 755–765.

Maccoby, E. E. (1991). Different reproductive strategies in males and females. *Child Development, 62,* 676–681.

Maccoby, E. E., & Martin, J. A. (1983). Socialization in the context of the family: Parent-child interaction. In E. M. Hetherington (Ed.), *Handbook of child psychology* (4th ed., Vol. 4, pp. 1–102). New York: Wiley.

Macdonald, D. W. (1983). The ecology of carnivore social behavior. *Nature, 301,* 379–384.

MacDonald, K. (1992). Warmth as a developmental construct: An evolutionary analysis. *Child Development, 63,* 753–773.

Madsen, D. (1986). Power seekers are different: Further biochemical evidence. *American Political Science Review, 80,* 261–269.

Mann, J. (1992). Nurturance or negligence: Maternal psychology and behavioral preference among preterm twins. In J. H. Barkow, L. Cosmides, & J. Tooby (Eds.), *The adapted mind* (pp. 367–390). New York: Oxford University Press.

Markus, H. R., & Kitayama, S. (1991). Culture and the self: Implications for cognition, emotion, and motivation. *Psychological Review, 98,* 224–253.

Marler, P., Evans, C. S., & Hauser, M. D. (1992). Animal signals: Motivational, referential, or both. In H. Papousek, J. Jurgens, & M. Papousek (Eds.), *Nonverbal vocal communication: Comparative and developmental approaches* (pp. 66–86). Cambridge, England: Cambridge University Press.

Martini, M. (1996). "What's new?" at the dinner table: Family dynamics during mealtimes in two cultural groups in Hawaii. *Early Development and Parenting, 5,* 23–34.

Mazur, A., & Booth, A. (1996). Testosterone and dominance in men. *Behavioral and Brain Sciences, 21,* 353–391.

McClelland, D. C., Patel, V., Stier, D., & Brown, D. (1987). The relationship of affiliative arousal to dopamine release. *Motivation and Emotion, 11,* 51–66.

McEwen, B. S. (2000). Allostasis and allostatic load: Implications for neuropsychopharmacology. *Neuropsychopharmacology, 22,* 108–124.

McEwen, B. S. (2001). *The end of stress as we know it.* Washington, DC: Joseph Henry Press.

McGaugh, J. L. (2002). Memory consolidation and the amygdala: A systems perspective. *Trends in Neurosciences, 25,* 456–461.

McHale, J., Khazan, I., Erera, P., Rotman, T., DeCourcey, W., & McConnell, M. (2002). Coparenting in diverse family systems. In M. H. Bornstein (Ed.), *Handbook of parenting* (Vol. 3, pp. 75–107). Mahwah, NJ: Erlbaum.

Meaney, M. J., Aitken, D. H., Bodnoff, S. R., Iny, L. J., & Tatarewicz, J. E. (1985). Early postnatal handling alters glucocorticoid receptor concentrations in selected brain regions. *Behavioral Neuroscience, 99,* 765–770.

Meaney, M. J., Diorio, J., Francis, D., Weaver, S., Yau, J., Chapman, K., et al. (2000). Postnatal handling increases the expression of cAMP-inducible transcription factors in the rat hippocampus: The effects of thyroid hormones and serotonin. *Journal of Neuroscience, 20,* 3926–3935.

Meltzoff, A. N., & Moore, K. (1999). Persons and representation: Why infant imitation is important for theories of human development. In J. Nadel & G. Butterworth (Eds.), *Imitation in infancy: Cambridge studies in cognitive perceptual development* (pp. 9–35). New York: Cambridge University Press.

Miller, J. G. (1997). Cultural conceptions of duty: Implications for motivation and morality. In D. Munro, J. E. Schumaker, & S. C. Carr (Eds.), *Motivation and culture* (pp. 178–192). New York: Routledge.

Miller, J. G. (2002). Bringing culture to basic psychological theory: Beyond individualism and collectivism—Comment on Oyserman et al. (2002). *Psychological Bulletin, 128,* 97–109.

Miller, J. G., & Bersoff, D. M. (1992). Culture and moral judgment: How are conflicts between justice and interpersonal responsibilities resolved. *Journal of Personality and Social Psychology, 62,* 541–554.

Miller, P. J., Fung, H., & Mintz, J. (1996). Self-construction through narrative practices: A Chinese and American comparison of early socialization. *Ethos, 24,* 237–280.

Miller, P. J., & Sperry, L. L. (1988). Early talk about the past: The origins of conversational stories of personal experience. *Journal of Child Language, 15,* 293–315.

Miller, P. J., Wiley, A. R., Fung, H., & Liang, C. H. (1997). Personal storytelling as a medium of socialization in Chinese and American families. *Child Development, 68,* 557–568.

Miller, S. A. (1995). Parents' attributions for their children's behavior. *Child Development, 66,* 1557–1584.

Moffitt, T. E. (1993). Adolescence-limited and life-course-persistent antisocial behavior: A developmental taxonomy. *Psychological Review, 100,* 674–701.

Mooncey, S., Giannakoulopoulos, X., Glover, V., Acolet, D., & Modi, N. (1997). The effect of mother-infant skin-to-skin contact on plasma cortisol and beta-encorphin concentrations in preterm newborns. *Infant Behavior and Development, 20,* 553–557.

Moore, S. F., & Myerhoff, B. G. (1977). *Secular ritual.* Amsterdam: Van Gorcum.

Morris, A. S., Steinberg, L., Sessa, F. M., Avenevoli, S., Silk, J. S., & Essex, M. J. (2002). Measuring children's perceptions of psychological control: Developmental and conceptual considerations. In B. K. Barber (Ed.), *Intrusive parenting: How psychological control affects children and adolescents* (pp. 125–159). Washington, DC: American Psychological Association.

Needle, R. H., Su, S. S., & Doherty, W. J. (1990). Divorce, remarriage, and adolescent substance use: A prospective longitudinal study. *Journal of Marriage and the Family, 52,* 157–169.

Neiderhiser, J. M., Reiss, D., Hetherington, E. M., & Plomin, R. (1999). Relationships between parenting and adolescent adjustment over time: Genetic and environmental contributions. *Developmental Psychology, 35,* 680–692.

Newcomb, A. F., & Bagwell, C. L. (1995). Children's friendship relations: A meta-analytic review. *Psychological Bulletin, 117,* 306–347.

Newport, D. J., Stowe, Z. N., & Nemeroff, C. B. (2002). Parental depression: Animal models of adverse life events. *American Journal of Psychiatry, 159,* 1265–1283.

Nix, R. L., Pinderhughes, E. E., Dodge, K. A., Bates, J. E., & Pettit, G. S. (1999). Do parents' hostile attribution tendencies function as self-fulfilling prophecies? An empirical examination of aggressive transactions. *Child Development, 70,* 896–909.

Nucci, L., & Smetana, J. G. (1996). Mothers' concept of young children's areas of personal freedom. *Child Development, 67,* 1870–1886.

O'Connor, T. G., Deater-Deckard, K., Fulker, D., Rutter, M., & Plomin, R. (1998). Genotype-environment correlations in late childhood and early adolescence: Antisocial behavior problems and coercive parenting. *Developmental Psychology, 34,* 970–981.

Oldershaw, L. (2002). *A national survey of parents of young children.* Toronto, Ontario, Canada: Invest in Kids.

Ostwald, P. F. (1963). *Soundmaking: The acoustic communication of emotion.* Oxford, England: Charles C. Thomas.

Oyserman, D., Coon, H. M., & Kemmelmaier, M. (2002). Rethinking individualism and collectivism: Evaluation of theoretical assumptions and meta-analyses. *Psychological Bulletin, 128,* 3–72.

Panksepp, J. (1993). Rough and tumble play: A fundamental brain process. In K. McDonald (Ed.), *Parent-child play: Descriptions and implications* (pp. 147–184). New York: State University of New York Press.

Panksepp, J. (1996). Affective neuroscience: A paradigm to study the animate circuits for human emotions. In R. D. Kavanaugh & B.

Zimmerberg (Eds.), *Emotion: Interdisciplinary perspectives* (pp. 29–60). Mahwah, NJ: Erlbaum.

Panksepp, J., Siviy, S. M., & Normansell, L. A. (1985). Brain opioids and social emotions. In M. Reite & T. Field (Eds.), *The psychobiology of attachment and separation* (pp. 3–49). Orlando, FL: Academic Press.

Papousek, H., & Papousek, M. (1995). Intuitive parenting. In M. H. Bornstein (Ed.), *Handbook of parenting: Vol. 2. Biology and ecology of parenting* (pp. 117–136). Mahwah, NJ: Erlbaum.

Parke, R. D. (1978). Parent-infant interaction: Progress, paradigms, and problems. In G. P. Sackett (Ed.), *Observing behavior* (Vol. 1, pp. 69–94). Baltimore: University Park Press.

Parke, R. D., & Bhavnagri, N. P. (1989). Parents as managers of children's peer relationships. In D. Belle (Ed.), *Children's social networks and social supports* (pp. 241–259). New York: Wiley.

Parke, R. D., Simpkins, S. D., McDowell, D. J., Kim, M., Killian, C., Dennis, J., et al. (2002). Relative contributions of families and peers to children's social development. In P. K. Smith & C. H. Craig (Eds.), *Blackwell handbook of childhood social development* (pp. 156–177). Malden, MA: Blackwell.

Parker, G. A., & Rubenstein, D. I. (1981). Role assessment, reserve strategy, and acquisition of information in asymmetric animal conflicts. *Animal Behaviour, 29,* 221–240.

Parpal, M., & Maccoby, E. E. (1985). Maternal responsiveness and subsequent child compliance. *Child Development, 56,* 1326–1334.

Parrott, W. G., & Gleitman, H. (1989). Infants' expectations in play: The joy of peek-a-boo [Special issue]. *Cognition and Emotion, 3,* 291–311.

Patterson, G. R. (1980). Mothers: The unacknowledged victims. *Monographs of the Society for Research in Child Development, 45.*

Patterson, G. R. (1982). *Coercive family process.* Eugene, OR: Castalia Press.

Patterson, G. R. (1997). Performance models for parenting: A social interactional perspective. In J. E. Grusec & L. Kuczynski (Eds.), *Parenting and children's internalization of values: A handbook of contemporary theory* (pp. 193–226). New York: Wiley.

Patterson, G. R., & Fisher, P. A. (2002). Recent developments in our understanding of parenting, bidirectional effects, causal models, and the search for parsimony. In M. H. Bornstein (Ed.), *Handbook of parenting* (Vol. 3, pp. 59–88). Mahwah, NJ: Erlbaum.

Patterson, G. R., Reid, J. B., & Dishion, T. J. (1998). Antisocial boys. In J. M. Jenkins & K. Oatley (Eds.), *Human emotions: A reader* (pp. 330–336). Malden, MA: Blackwell.

Patterson, G. R., & Sanson, A. (1999). The association of behavioural adjustment to temperament, parenting and family characteristics among 5-year-old children. *Social Development, 8,* 293–309.

Pellis, S. M. (2002). Keep in touch: Play fighting and social knowledge. In M. Bekoff, C. Allen, & G. M. Burghardt (Eds.), *The cognitive animal* (pp. 421–427). London: MIT Press.

Perry, D. B., Hodges, E. V. E., & Egan, S. K. (2001). Determinants of chronic victimization by peers: A review and new model of family influence. In J. Juvonen & S. Graham (Eds.), *Peer harassment in school: The plight of the vulnerable and victimized* (pp. 73–104). New York: Guilford Press.

Peterson, C. C., & Siegal, M. (2002). Mindreading and moral awareness in popular and rejected preschoolers. *British Journal of Developmental Psychology, 20,* 205–224.

Phinney, J. S., Ong, A., & Madden, T. (2000). Cultural values and intergenerational value discrepancies in immigrant and non-immigrant families. *Child Development, 71,* 528–539.

Piaget, J. (1948). *The moral judgment of the child.* Glencoe, IL: Free Press.

Pomerantz, E. M., & Eaton, M. M. (2001). Maternal intrusive support in the academic context: Transactional socialization processes. *Developmental Psychology, 37,* 174–186.

Popik, P., & van Ree, J. M. (1991). Oxytocin, but not vasopression, facilitates social recognition following injection into the medial preoptic of the rat brain. *European Journal of Pharmacology, 1,* 555–560.

Power, T. G., Hildebrandt, K. A., & Fitzgerald, H. E. (1982). Adults' responses to infants varying in facial expressions and perceived attractiveness. *Infant Behavior and Development, 5,* 33–44.

Prothrow-Stith, D., & Quaday, S. (1996). Communities, schools, and violence. In A. M. Hoffman (Ed.), *Schools, violence, and society* (pp. 153–161). Westport, CT: Praeger.

Raleigh, M. J., McGuire, M. T., Bramner, G. L., Olkkacjm, D. B., & Yuwiler, A. (1991). Serotonergic mechanisms promote dominance acquisition in adult male vervet monkeys. *Brain Research, 559,* 181–190.

Ramsay, D., & Lewis, M. (2003). Reactivity and regulation in cortisol and behavioral responses to stress. *Child Development, 74,* 456–464.

Repetti, R. L., Taylor, S. E., & Seeman, T. E. (2002). Risky families: Family social environments and the mental and physical health of offspring. *Psychological Bulletin, 128,* 330–336.

Rheingold, H. (1969). The social and socializing infant. In D. A. Goslin (Ed.), *Handbook of socialization theory and research* (pp. 779–790). Chicago: Rand McNally.

Rheingold, H. L. (1982). Little children's participation in the work of adults, a nascent prosocial behavior. *Child Development, 53,* 114–125.

Rholes, W. S., Newman, L. S., & Ruble, D. N. (1990). Understanding self and other: Developments and motivational aspects of perceiving persons in terms of invariant dispositions. In E. T. Higgins & R. M. Sorrentino (Eds.), *Handbook of motivation and cognition: Vol. 2. Foundations of social behavior* (pp. 369–407). New York: Guilford Press.

Rogoff, B., Pardies, R., Arauz, R. M., Correa-Chavez, M., & Angelillo, C. (2003). Firsthand learning through intent participation. *Annual Review of Psychology, 54,* 175–203.

Rohner, R. P., & Pettengill, S. M. (1985). Perceived parental acceptance-rejection and parental control among Korean adolescents. *Child Development, 56,* 524–528.

Rothbaum, F., Pott, M., Azuma, H., Miyake, K., & Weisz, J. (2000). The development of close relationships in Japan and the United States: Paths of symbiotic harmony and generative tension. *Child Development, 71,* 1121–1142.

Rothbaum, F., & Trommsdorff, G. (in press). Do roots and wings complement or oppose one another: The socialization of relatedness and autonomy in cultural context. In J. E. Grusec & P. D. Hastings (Eds.), *Handbook of socialization.* New York: Guilford Press.

Rothbaum, F., Weisz, J. R., Pott, M., Miyake, K., & Morelli, G. (2000). Attachment and culture: Security in the United States and Japan. *American Psychologist, 55,* 1093–1104.

Ruble, D. N., & Martin, C. L. (1998). Gender development. In W. Damon (Editor-in-Chief) & N. Eisenberg (Vol. Ed.), *Handbook of child psychology: Vol. 3. Social, emotional, and personality development* (5th ed., pp. 933–1016). New York: Wiley.

Rudolph, K. D., Hammen, C., & Burge, D. (1995). Cognitive representations of self, family, and peers in school-age children: Links with social competence and sociometric status. *Child Development, 66,* 1385–1402.

Rudy, D., & Grusec, J. E. (2001). Correlates of authoritarian parenting in individualist and collectivist cultures and implications for understanding the transmission of values. *Journal of Cross-Cultural Psychology, 32,* 202–212.

Rudy, D., & Grusec, J. E. (in press). The correlates and outcomes of authoritarian parenting in individualist and collectivist groups. *Journal of Family Psychology.*

Rutter, M., & O'Connor, T. G. (2004). Are there biological programming effects for psychological development? Findings from a study of Romanian adoptees. *Developmental Psychology, 40,* 81–94.

Ryan, R. M., & Deci, E. L. (2000). Self-determination theory and the facilitation of intrinsic motivation, social development, and well-being. *American Psychologist, 55,* 68–78.

Sameroff, A. (1975). Transactional models of early social relations. *Human Development, 18,* 65–79.

Sanchez-Martin, J. R., Fano, E., Ahedo, L., Cardas, J., Brain, P. F., & Azpiroz, A. (2000). Relating testosterone levels and free play social behavior in male and female preschool children. *Psychoneuroendocrinology, 25,* 773–783.

Scarr, S., & McCartney, K. (1983). How people make their own environment: A theory of genotype-environment effects. *Child Development, 54,* 424–435.

Schaal, B. (1988). Olfaction in infants and children: Developmental and functional perspectives. *Chemical Senses, 13,* 145–190.

Schaefer, E. S. (1965). Children's reports of parental behavior: An inventory. *Child Development, 36,* 413–424.

Scherer, K. R., & Wallbott, H. G. (1994). Evidence for universality and cultural variation of differential emotion response patterning. *Journal of Personality and Social Psychology, 66,* 310–328.

Schlegel, A., & Barry, H. (1991). *Adolescence: An anthropological inquiry.* New York: Free Press.

Schmidt, L. A., Fox, N. A., Rubin, K. H., & Steinberg, E. M. (1997). Behavioral and neuroendocrine responses in shy children. *Developmental Psychology, 30,* 127–140.

Schore, A. N. (1998). Early shame experiences and infant brain development. In P. Gilbert & B. Andrews (Eds.), *Shame: Interpersonal behavior, psychopathology, and culture* (pp. 57–77). New York: Oxford University Press.

Schulkin, J., Gold, P. W., & McEwen, B. S. (1998). Induction of corticotropin-releasing hormone gene expression by glucocorticoids: Implications for understanding the states of fear and anxiety and allostatic load. *Psychoneuroendocrinology, 23,* 219–243.

Schwartz, A., & Bugental, D. B. (2004). *Infant habituation to repeated stress as an interactive function of child temperament and maternal depression.* Unpublished paper.

Schwartz, D., Dodge, K. A., Pettit, G. S., & Bates, J. E. (2000). Friendship as a moderating factor in the pathway between early harsh home environment and later victimization in the peer group. *Developmental Psychology, 36,* 646–662.

Sears, R. R., Maccoby, E. E., & Levin, H. (1957). *Patterns of child rearing.* Evanston, IL: Row Peterson.

Sears, R. R., Rau, L., & Alpert, R. (1964). *Identification and child rearing.* Stanford, CA: Stanford University Press.

Seligman, M. E. (1970). On the generality of the laws of learning. *Psychological Review, 77,* 406–418.

Shafir, E., Simonson, I., & Tversky, A. (1993). Reason-based choice. *Cognition, 49,* 11–36.

Shafir, E., & Tversky, A. (1992). Thinking through uncertainty: Nonconsequential reasoning and choice. *Cognitive Psychology, 24,* 449–474.

Sherif, M., Harvey, O. J., White, B. J., Hood, W. R., & Sherif, C. (1954). *Experimental study of positive and negative intergroup attitudes between experimentally prejudiced groups: Robbers' Cave experiment.* Norman: University of Oklahoma.

Siegal, M., & Barclay, M. S. (1985). Children's evaluations of fathers' socialization behavior. *Developmental Psychology, 21,* 1090–1096.

Sigel, I. E., McGillicuddy-DeLisi, A. V., & Goodnow, J. J. (Eds.). (1992). *Parental belief systems: The psychological consequences for children.* Hillsdale, NJ: Erlbaum.

Silk, J. B. (1992). The patterning of intervention among male bonnet macaques: Reciprocity, revenge, and loyalty. *Current Anthropology, 33,* 318–324.

Simpson, J. A. (1999). Attachment theory in modern evolutionary perspective. In J. Cassidy & P. R. Shaver (Eds.), *Handbook of attachment: Theory, research, and clinical applications* (pp. 117–141). New York: Guilford Press.

Skarin, K. S. (1977). Cognitive and contextual determinants of stranger fear in 6- and 11-month-old infants. *Child Development, 48,* 537–544.

Smetana, J. (1988). Adolescents' and parents' conceptions of parental authority. *Child Development, 59,* 321–335.

Smetana, J. (1996). Adolescent-parent conflict: Implications for adaptive and maladaptive development. In D. Cicchetti & S. L. Toth (Eds.), *Rochester Symposium on Developmental Psychopathology: Vol. 7. Adolescence—Opportunities and challenges* (pp. 1–46). Rochester, NY: University of Rochester Press.

Smetana, J. (1997). Parenting and the development of social knowledge reconceptualized: A social domain analysis. In J .E. Grusec & L. Kuczynski (Eds.), *Parenting and the internalization of values: A handbook of contemporary theory* (pp. 162–192). New York: Wiley.

Smetana, J. G., & Asquith, P. (1994). Adolescents' and parents' conceptions of parental authority and personal autonomy. *Child Development, 65,* 1147–1162.

Smetana, J. G., & Daddis, C. (2002). Domain-specific antecedents of parental psychological control and monitoring: The role of parenting beliefs and practices. *Child Development, 73,* 563–580.

Smetana, J. G., Kochanska, G., & Chuang, S. (2000). Mothers' conceptions of everyday rules for young toddlers: A longitudinal investigation. *Merrill-Palmer Quarterly, 46,* 391–416.

Smith, C., & Krohn, M. D. (1995). Delinquency and family life among male adolescents: The role of ethnicity. *Journal of Youth and Adolescence, 24,* 69–93.

Smith, P. K., Shu, S., & Madsen, K. (2001). Characteristics of victims of school bullying: Developmental changes in coping strategies and skills. In J. Juvonen & S. Graham (Eds.), *Peer harassment in school: The plight of the vulnerable and victimized* (pp. 332–351). New York: Guilford Press.

Snyder, J. J., & Patterson, G. R. (1995). Individual differences in social aggression: A test of a reinforcement model of socialization in the natural environment. *Behavior Therapy, 26,* 371–391.

Spangler, B., & Grossman, K. E. (1993). Biobehavioral organization in securely and insecurely attached infants. *Child Development, 64,* 1439–1450.

Spangler, G., Schieche, M., Ilg, U., & Maier, U. (1994). Maternal sensitivity as an external organizer for biobehavioral regulation in infancy. *Development and Psychobiology, 27,* 425–437.

Sroufe, L. A. (1988). The role of infant-caregiver attachment in development. In J. Belsky & T. Nezworski (Eds.), *Clinical implications of attachment: Child psychology* (pp. 18–38). Hillsdale, NJ: Erlbaum.

Stattin, H., & Kerr, M. (2000). Parental monitoring: A reinterpretation. *Child Development, 71,* 1072–1085.

Stauder, J. E. A., Molenaar, P. C. M., & Van der Molen, M. W. (1999). Brain activity and cognitive transition during childhood: A longitudinal event-related brain potential study. *Child Neuropsychology, 5,* 41–59.

Stayton, D. J., Hogan, R., & Ainsworth, M. D. (1971). The origins of socialization reconsidered. *Child Development, 42,* 1057–1069.

Steinberg, L. (1990). Autonomy, conflict, and harmony in the family relationship. In S. S. Feldman & G. R. Elliott (Eds.), *At the threshold: The developing adolescent* (pp. 255–276). Cambridge, MA: Harvard University Press.

Steinberg, L., Dornbusch, S. M., & Brown, B. B. (1992). Ethnic differences in adolescent achievement: An ecological perspective. *American Psychologist, 47,* 723–729.

Steinberg, L., Elmen, J., & Mounts, N. (1989). Authoritative parenting, psychosocial maturity, and academic success among adolescents. *Child Development, 60,* 1424–1436.

Steinberg, L., Mounts, N. S., Lamborn, S. D., & Dornbusch, S. M. (1991). Authoritative parenting and adolescent adjustment across varied ecological niches. *Journal of Research in Adolescence, 1,* 9–36.

Steinberg, L., & Silverberg, S. B. (1986). The vicissitudes of autonomy in early adolescence. *Child Development, 57,* 841–851.

Stewart, S. M., Rao, N., Bond, M. H., McBride-Chang, C., Fielding, R., & Kennard, B. D. (1998). Chinese dimensions of parenting: Broadening Western predictors and outcomes. *International Journal of Psychology, 33,* 345–358.

Stoolmiller, M. (2001). Synergistic interaction of child manageability problems and parent-discipline tactics in predicting future externalizing behavior for boys. *Developmental Psychology, 37,* 814–825.

Storey, A. E., Walsh, C. J., Quinton, R. L., & Wynne-Edwards, K. E. (2000). Hormonal correlates of paternal responsiveness in new and expectant fathers. *Evolution and Human Behavior, 21,* 79–95.

Strassburg, L., Dodge, K. A., Pettit, G. S., & Bates, J. E. (1994). Spanking in the home and children's subsequent aggression toward kindergarten peers. *Development and Psychopathology, 6,* 445–461.

Straus, M. A. (1994). *Beating the devil out of them: Corporal punishment and American families.* New York: Lexington Book.

Straus, M. A., & Gelles, R. J. (1988). How violent are American families?: Estimates from the National Family Violence Resurvey and other studies. In G. T. Hotaling, D. Finkelhor, J. T. Kirkpatrick, & M. A. Straus (Eds.). *Family abuse and its consequences: New direction in research* (pp. 14–36). Thousand Oaks, CA: Sage.

Sugarman, D. B. (1983). The development of children's physical and social causal explanations. *Dissertation Abstracts International, 44,* 363.

Sung, K. (1995). Measures and dimensions of filial piety in Korea. *Gerontologist, 35,* 240–247.

Suomi, S. J. (1997). Long-term effects of different early rearing experiences on social, emotional and physiological development in nonhuman primates. In M. S. Keshewen & R. M. Murra (Eds.), *Neurodevelopmental models of adult psychopathology* (pp. 104–116). Cambridge, England: Cambridge University Press.

Super, C. M., & Harkness, S. (1997). Basic processes and human development. In J. W. Berry, P. R. Dassen, & T. S. Saraswathi (Eds.), *Handbook of cross-cultural psychology* (2nd ed., Vol. 2, pp. 1–39). Needham Heights, MA: Allyn & Bacon.

Susman, E. J., Inoff-Germain, G., Nottelman, E. D., Loriaux, D. L., Cutler, G. B., & Chrousos, G. P. (1987). Hormones, emotional dispositions, and aggressive attributes in young adolescents. *Child Development, 58,* 1114–1134.

Tangney, J. P., Wagner, P. E., Hill-Barlow, D., Marschall, D. E., & Gramzow, R. (1997). Relation of shame and guilt to constructive versus destructive responses to anger across the lifespan. *Journal of Personality and Social Psychology, 70,* 797–809.

Thomas, A., & Chess, S. (1977). *Temperament and development.* Oxford, England: Brunner/Mazel.

Thompson, R. (1999). Early attachment and later development. In J. Cassidy & P. R. Shaver (Eds.), *Handbook of attachment: Theory, research, and clinical applications* (pp. 265–286). New York: Guilford Press.

Thornton, M. C., Chatters, L. M., Taylor, R. J., & Allen, W. R. (1990). Sociodemographic and environmental correlates of racial socialization by Black parents. *Child Development, 61,* 401–409.

Trevarthen, C., Kokkinski, T., & Flamenghi, G. A., Jr. (1999). In J. Nadel & G. Butterworth (Eds.), *Imitation in infancy: Cambridge studies in cognitive perceptual development* (pp. 127–185). New York: Cambridge University Press.

Trivers, R. (1974). Parent-offspring conflict. *American Zoologist, 14,* 249–264.

Trommsdorff, G., & Iwawaki, S. (1989). Students' perceptions of socialization and gender role in Japan and Germany. *International Journal of Behavioural Development, 12,* 485–493.

Trommsdorff, G., & Kornadt, H.-J. (2003). Parent-child relations in cross-cultural perspective. In L. Kuczynski (Ed.), *Handbook of dynamics in parent-child relations* (pp. 271–306). Thousand Oaks, CA: Sage.

Tronick, E. Z., Scanlon, R. N., & Scanlon, J. W. (1990). Protective apathy, a hypothesis about behavioral organization and its relation to clinical and physiological status of the preterm infant during the newborn period. *Clinics in Perinatology, 17,* 125–154.

Turiel, E. (1998). The development of morality. (1998). In N. Eisenberg (Ed.), *Handbook of child psychology* (Vol. 3, pp. 863–932). New York: Wiley.

Turiel, E. (2002). *The culture of morality: Social development, context, and conflict.* New York: Cambridge University Press.

Udry, J. R., & Talbert, L. M. (1988). Sex hormone effects on personality at puberty. *Journal of Personality and Social Psychology, 54,* 291–295.

Valsiner, J., & Cairns, R. (1992). Theoretical perspectives on conflict and development. In C. U. Shantz & W. W. Hartup (Eds.), *Conflict in child and adolescent development* (pp. 15–35). New York: Cambridge University Press.

Vanderschuren, L. J., Niesink, R. J., & Van Ree, J. M. (1997). The neurobiology of social play behavior in rats. *Neuroscience and Biobehavioral Reviews, 21,* 309–326.

van Wimersma, Greidanus, T. B., & Maigret, C. (1996). The role of limbic vasopressin and oxytocin in social recognition. *Brain Research, 713,* 153–159.

Vaughn, B. E., Colvin, T. N., Azria, M. R., Caya, L., & Krzysik, L. (2001). Dyadic analyses of friendship in a sample of preschool-age children attending Head Start: Correspondence between measures and implications for social competence. *Child Development, 72,* 862–878.

Vinden, P. (1999). Children's understanding of mind and emotion: A multi-culture study. *Cognition and Emotion, 13,* 19–48.

Wainryb, C., & Turiel, E. (1994). Dominance, subordination, and concepts of personal entitlements in cultural contexts. *Child Development, 65,* 1701–1722.

Waizenhoffer, R. N., Buchanan, C. M., & Jackson-Newson, J. (2004). Mothers' and fathers' knowledge of adolescents' daily activities: Its sources and its links with adolescent adjustment. *Journal of Family Psychology, 18,* 348–360.

Wang, Q., & Leichtman, M. D. (2000). Same beginnings, different stories: A comparison of American and Chinese children's narratives. *Child Development, 71,* 1329–1346.

Want, S. C., & Harris, P. L. (2002). How do children ape? Applying concepts from the study of non-human primates to the developmental study of "imitation" in children. *Developmental Science, 5,* 1–13.

Ward, C. D., & Cooper, R. P. (1999). A lack of evidence in 4-month-old human infants for paternal voice preference. *Developmental Psychobiology, 35,* 40–59.

Ward, M. J., & Carlson, E. A. (1995). Associations among adult attachment representations, maternal sensitivity, and infant-mother attachment in a sample of adolescent mothers. *Child Development, 66,* 69–79.

Warren, S. L., Gunnar, M. R., Kagan, J., Anders, T. F., Simmens, S. J., Rones, M., et al. (2003). Maternal panic disorder: Infant temperament, neurophysiology, and parenting behavior. *Journal of the American Academy of Child and Adolescent Psychiatry, 42,* 814–825.

Warton, J. J., & Goodnow, J. J. (1995). Money and children's household jobs: Parents' views of their interconnections. *International Journal of Behavioral Development, 18,* 235–350.

Watson, J. S., & Ramey, C. T. (1987). Reactions to response-contingent stimulation in early infancy. In J. Oates & S. Sheldon (Eds.), *Cognitive development in infancy* (pp. 77–85). Hillsdale, NJ: Erlbaum.

Watson-Gegeo, K. A. (1992). Thick explanation in the ethnographic study of child socialization: A longitudinal study of the problem of schooling for Kwara'ae (Solomon Islands) children. In W. A. Corsaro & P. J. Miller (Eds.), *New directions for child development: Vol. 58. Interpretive approaches to children's socialization—The Jossey-Bass education series* (pp. 51–66). San Francisco: Jossey-Bass.

Weinberg, K. M., & Tronick, E. Z. (1996). Infant affective reactions to the resumption of maternal interaction after the still-face. *Child Development, 67,* 905–914.

Weisner, T. S., & Garnier, H. (1992). Nonconventional family lifestyles and school achievement: A 12-year longitudinal study. *American Educational Research Journal, 29,* 605–632.

Whiting, J. W. M. (1976). The cross-cultural method. In E. H. Chasdi (Ed.), *Culture and human development: The selected papers of John Whiting* (pp. 76–88). New York: Cambridge University Press.

Wiesenfeld, A. R., Malatesta, C. Z., & DeLoach, L. L. (1981). Differential parental response to familiar and unfamiliar infant distress signals. *Infant Behavior and Development, 4,* 281–295.

Wilkinson, G. (1988). Reciprocal altruism in bats and other mammals. *Ethology and Sociobiology, 9,* 85–100.

Wills, T. A., Sandy, J. M., Yaeger, A., & Shinar, O. (2001). Family risk factors and adolescent substance use: Moderation effects for temperament dimensions. *Developmental Psychology, 37,* 283–297.

Wilson, M., & Daly, M. (1994). The psychology of parenting in evolutionary perspective and the case of human filicide. In S. Parmigiani & F. S. von Saal (Eds.), *Infanticide and parental care* (pp. 73–134). London: Academic Press.

World Health Organization. (2002). *World Report on Violence and Health.* Geneva, Switzerland: Author.

Yau, J., & Smetana, J. G. (1996). Adolescent-parent conflict among Chinese adolescents in Hong Kong. *Child Development, 67,* 1262–1275.

Yogman, M. W. (1990). Male parental behavior in humans and nonhuman primates. In N. A. Krasnegor & R. S. Bridges (Eds.), *Mammalian parenting* (pp. 461–491). London: Oxford University Press.

Young, L. J. (2002). The neurobiology of social recognition: Approach, and avoidance. *Biological Psychiatry, 51,* 18–26.

Youniss, J., McLellan, J. A., & Strouse, D. (1994). "We're popular, but we're not snobs": Adolescents describe their crowds. In R. Montemayor & G. R. Adams (Eds.), *Personal relationships during adolescence: Vol. 6. Advances in adolescent development—An annual book series* (pp. 101–122). Thousand Oaks, CA: Sage.

Zeanah, C. H., Benoit, D., Hirschberg, L., Barton, M. L., & Regan, C. (1994). Mothers' representations of their infants are concordant with infant attachment classification. *Developmental Issues in Psychiatry and Psychology, 1,* 1–14.

Zebrowitz, L. (1997). *Reading faces.* Boulder, CO: Westview Press.

Zupanc, G. K. H., & Lamprecht, J. (2000). Towards a cellular understanding of motivation: Structural reorganization and biochemical switching as key mechanisms of behavioral plasticity. *Ethology, 106,* 467–477.

CHAPTER 8

Socialization in the Family: Ethnic and Ecological Perspectives

ROSS D. PARKE and RAYMOND BURIEL

Socialization is a process in which an individual's standards, skills, motives, attitudes, and behaviors change to conform to those regarded as desirable and appropriate for his or her present and future role in any particular society. Many agents and agencies play a role in the socialization process, including family, peers, schools, and the media. Moreover, it is recognized that these various agents function together rather than independently. Families have been recognized as an early pervasive and highly influential context for socialization. Children are

dependent on families for nurturance and support from an early age, which accounts, in part, for their prominence as a socialization agent.

In this chapter, we have several goals. Our primary goal is to expand our framework for conceptualizing the family's role in socialization. This takes several forms, including treating the family as a social system in which parent-child, marital, and sibling subsystems, among others, are recognized. The diversity of family forms has increased in the past several decades and a second

Preparation of this chapter was facilitated by National Science Foundation grants BNS 8919391 & SBR 9308941 and NICHD grant HD 32391 to Parke. Finally, thanks to Faye Harmer for her preparation of the manuscript.

goal is to explore the implications of various family configurations for the socialization process. Third, cultural and ethnic variations in family traditions, beliefs, and practices are increasingly being recognized, and a further aim of this chapter is to explore how ethnic diversity informs our understanding of family socialization. Fourth, our goal is to locate family socialization in an ecological context to appreciate how family environments shape and constrain their socialization practices. We demonstrate the value of a life-course perspective on socialization that recognizes the importance of both developmental changes in adult lives and the historical circumstances under which socialization unfolds. Finally, we recognize that families are increasingly diverse in their organization, form, and lifestyle. Some issues are beyond the scope of the chapter including the recent work on gay and lesbian families and research on adopted children (see Brodzinsky & Pinderhughes, 2002; C. Patterson, 2002, for reviews).

THEORETICAL APPROACHES TO SOCIALIZATION IN THE FAMILY: HISTORICAL AND CONTEMPORARY PERSPECTIVES

In this section, we examine historical and contemporary theoretical perspectives on the role of socialization in the family.

Historical Perspectives on Family Socialization Theory

To appreciate these goals, an overview of historical changes in socialization theory is necessary. The history of this field over the past century can be traced to two theoretical perspectives: behaviorism and psychoanalysis (Maccoby, 1992). In the 1920s, Watson offered a learning theory approach to socialization, which was based on conditioning as an explanatory mechanism. This legacy continued under Skinner and followers in the behavior modification movement who applied these principles to children's behavior (Bijou & Baer, 1961).

The other legacy was Freudian psychoanalysis. Perhaps no other view has had so wide an influence—even if often unrecognized and unacknowledged—as Freudian theory. Freud's stage theory with its emphasis on the importance of early experience as a determinant of later social and personality was a major force in socialization research for nearly half a century. Although it was difficult to test as originally formulated, the theory provided the outlines for the major socialization products, such as aggression, dependency, moral development, and sex typing, as well as the major sets of formative experiences in the family, especially the mother-child relationship.

In the 1930s, the fusion of Hullian learning theory with psychoanalysis provided the opportunity to empirically evaluate the propositions of psychoanalytic theory by translating them into drive-reduction language. This led to several renowned studies by Whiting and Child (1953) and Sears, Maccoby, and Levin (1957). As Maccoby (1992) noted, "These large scale efforts to merge psychoanalytic and behavior theory and then to predict children's personality attributes from parental socialization methods, were largely unsuccessful" (p. 1009).

The 1960s and 1970s marked the advent of further developments in socialization theory. First, social learning theory (Bandura, 1977; Bandura & Walters, 1963) emerged as an alternative to the Hullian-Freudian legacy (see Grusec, 1992). The distinguishing feature was the emphasis on imitation or observational learning, which emphasized the central role of cognition in social learning and reduced dependence on external reinforcement for the acquisition of new behaviors. In terms of method, social learning theory relied on the experimental analog approach in contrast to the retrospective interview of Sears and colleagues. Moreover, in a break with the Freudian tradition, social learning theorists placed greater emphasis on the plasticity and modifiability of the organism at different points in development and downplayed the psychoanalytically based concept of early experience as a constraining condition on later development. At the same time, the role of social contingencies in shaping parent-child interaction was receiving increased attention (Gewirtz, 1969). Studies of parent-infant interaction (e.g., Stern, 1977) and interactions of parents and children, especially aggressive and/or deviant children, were flourishing (G. Patterson, 1981).

As approaches to socialization, these theories were limited in several ways. First, they were largely nondevelopmental, and it was generally assumed that the principles applied equally to children at all ages. This is surprising in view of the increased interest in the role of cognition in social learning theory (Bandura, 1977).

Second, the role of affect was given a comparatively minor role. Third, genetic factors and biological constraints were given relatively short shrift. Fourth, the agents of socialization were still narrowly defined as primarily mothers. In the late 1960s, John Bowlby's fusion of psychoanalysis and ethology into his theory of attachment and loss foreshadowed changes that materialized in the 1970s and beyond. Concepts of biological preparedness for social interaction combined with emphasis on the importance of early close relationships served to anticipate modern concepts of biological constraints (Schaffer, 1971) and revive early notions of the importance of early experience and critical periods. Finally, Bowlby's focus on the dyad as the unit of analysis led to the recognition of the importance of *relationships* for development.

In the late 1970s to the present, a variety of changes have taken place in our theoretical approaches to socialization that have corrected some of the shortcomings of these earlier analysis and extended our frameworks into new domains as well.

Contemporary Perspectives on Family Socialization Theory

Several themes are evident in current theoretical approaches to socialization. First, systems theory (Sameroff, 1994; Thelen & Smith, 1994) has transformed the study of socialization from a parent-child focus to an emphasis on the family as a social system (Parke, 2004a). To understand fully the nature of family relationships, it is necessary to recognize the interdependence among the roles and functions of all family members. For example, as men's roles in families shift, changes in women's roles in families must also be monitored.

Second, family members—mothers, fathers, and children—influence each other both directly and indirectly (Minuchin, 2002; Parke, Power, & Gottman, 1979). Examples of fathers' indirect impact include various ways in which fathers modify and mediate mother-child relationships. In turn, women affect their children indirectly through their husbands by modifying both the quantity and the quality of father-child interaction. Children may indirectly influence the husband-wife relationship by altering the behavior of either parent that changes the interaction between spouses.

Third, different units of analysis are necessary to understand families. Although the individual—child,

mother, and father—remains a useful level of analysis, recognition of relationships among family members as units of analysis is necessary. The marital relationship, the mother-child relationship, and the father-child relationship require separate analysis (Parke et al., 2001). Finally, the family as a unit that is independent of the individual or dyads in the family requires recognition (Cook, 2001; Sigel & Parke, 1987).

A fourth shift is from unidirectional to transactional models of relationships among family members. There have been various phases in the conceptual thinking in this domain. First, scholars traditionally were guided by unilateral models of parent-child relations (Kuczynski, 2003) in which the direction of causality was unidirectional, from parent to child. The child's role was relatively passive, the focus was on individuals rather than relationships, and power relations were relatively static. In addition, the mother rather than either the father or other family members was the major focus of both theoretical and empirical work.

In the 1960s with Bell's (1968) classic reformulation, the field began to recognize the bidirectional nature of parent-child relationships. This shift occurred in a climate of reevaluation of infant competence; instead of the passive creatures of earlier times, infants and children were viewed as more competent and active in their own development. A bilateral model has emerged as the dominant paradigm in the parent-child relationship domain (Kuczynski, 2003) in which the direction of causality is bidirectional, equal agency on the part of parent and child is recognized, and power relations are characterized as "interdependent asymmetry."

At the same time, views of the pathways through which parents can influence their children expanded. Historically, socialization models directed attention toward the nature of the parent-child relationship and the types of child-rearing practices that parents employ. Research on infant-parent attachment and on parenting styles exemplifies this tradition. More recently, views of parenting have expanded to include parents as active managers of the child's social environment outside the family. In this role, a parent actively regulates the child's access to physical and social resources outside the family (Parke, Killian, et al., 2003) and serves as regulator of opportunities for social contact with extrafamilial social partners. Although peer influence increases as children develop, parents continue to play an important regulatory role as gatekeepers and monitors of children's social contacts, even in adolescence (Mounts, 2000). However, recent thinking has recognized that in the managerial domain, as in other parts of the parent-child relationship, both children and parents play active roles in decisions about children's social opportunities (Kerr & Stattin, 2000).

Fifth, under the influence of Bronfenbrenner's ecological theory (1989), recognition is being given to the embeddedness of families in other social systems as well as the cultures in which they exist (Parke & Kellam, 1994). These include a range of extrafamilial influences, such as extended families, and informal community ties such as friends and neighbors, work sites, and social, educational, and medical institutions (Repetti, 1994).

Sixth, the importance of considering family relationships from a developmental perspective is now recognized. Although developmental changes in infant and child capacities continue to represent the most commonly investigated aspect of development, other aspects of development are viewed as important too. Under the influence of life-course and life-span perspectives (Elder, 1998; Parke, 1988), examination of developmental changes in adults is gaining recognition because parents continue to change and develop during adult years. For example, age at the onset of parenthood has implications for how females and males manage their parental roles. This involves an exploration of the tasks faced by adults such as self-identity, education, and career, and an examination of the relation between these tasks and parenting.

Developmental analysis need not be restricted to the individual level—either child or parent. Relationships (e.g., the marital, the mother-child, or the father-child relationship) may follow separate and partially independent developmental courses over childhood (Parke, 1988). In turn, the mutual impact of different sets of relationships on each other will vary as a function of the nature of the developmental trajectory. Families change their structure (e.g., through the addition of a new child or the loss of a member through death or divorce), norms, rules, and strategies over time. Tracking the family unit itself over development is an important and neglected task (Cook, 2001).

A major shift over the past 2 decades is the challenge to the universality of our socialization theories. This challenge takes several forms. First, as cross-cultural work in development accumulated, it became evident that generalizations from a single culture (e.g., American) may not be valid in other cultural contexts (Rogoff, 2003). Second, social class differences in socialization challenged the generality of findings even in one cultural or national context (Gauvain, 2001; Hoff, Laursen, & Tardif, 2002). Currently, there is an increased awareness of the importance of both recognizing *and* studying variations in families and family socialization strategies in both other cultures (Rogoff, 2003) and across ethnic groups in our own culture (Parke, 2004b). It is important not only to examine the diversity of familial organization, goals, and strategies *across* ethnic groups but it is equally critical to explore variations *within* different ethnic groups (Garcia Coll & Magnuson, 1999; Parke, 2004b). Although there are many similarities across and within groups, appreciation of the variations is of central concern.

Another assumption that guides current theorizing involves the recognition of the impact of secular shifts on families. In recent years, there have been a variety of social changes in American society that have had a profound impact on families including the decline in fertility and family size, changes in the timing of the onset of parenthood, increased participation of women in the workforce, rise in the rates of divorce, and the subsequent increase in the number of single-parent families as well as remarried step families (Elder, 1998; Hetherington & Kelly, 2001). The ways in which these societal changes impact relationships between parents and children merit examination.

A related theme involves the recognition of the importance of the historical time period in which the family interaction is embedded. Historical time periods provide the social conditions for individual and family transitions: Examples include the 1960s (the Vietnam War era), the 1930s (the Great Depression), or the 1980s (Farm Belt Depression; Conger & Elder, 1994; Elder & Conger, 2000). Across these periods, family interaction may be quite different due to the unique conditions of the era. The distinctions among different developmental trajectories, as well as social change and historical period effects, are important because these different forms of change do not always harmonize (Modell & Elder, 2002). For example, a family event such as the birth of a child may have profound effects on a man who has just begun a career in contrast to the effects on one who has advanced to a stable occupational position. Moreover, individual and family developmental trajectories are embedded in both the social conditions and the values of the historical time in which they exist. The role of parents, as is the case with any social role, is responsive to such fluctuations.

To understand the nature of parent-child relationships in families, a multilevel and dynamic approach is required. Multiple levels of analysis are necessary to capture the individual, dyadic, and family unit aspects of operation in the family itself, and to reflect the embeddedness of families in a variety of extrafamilial social systems. The dynamic quality reflects the multiple developmental trajectories that warrant consideration in understanding the nature of families.

The central processes that are involved in accounting for *both* the choice of and regulation of socialization strategies and the effects of socialization on the developing child have undergone a major revision (see Bugental & Grusec, Chapter 7, this *Handbook,* this volume). The renewed interest in the biological bases of behavior has clearly altered our views of socialization. This interest takes several forms including the role of genetics across development, which has produced not only a more sophisticated understanding of the potential role genetics can play in the onset of certain behaviors but also in the unfolding of behavior across development. Moreover, the reformulation of genetic questions has led to studies of the effects of nonshared family environment on children's development (O'Connor, 2003). Finally, this work has suggested that individual differences between children—some of which are genetically based—play a central role in eliciting and shaping parent's socialization strategies (recognition that the child is an active contributor to his or her own socialization). A second focus is found in studies of hormones and behavior, especially during infancy and adolescence (Corter & Fleming, 2002). Third, the increased use of psychophysiological assessments with families represents a further instance of how biological processes are changing socialization studies (Eisenberg, 2000). Fourth, the resurgence of interest in evolutionary approaches to socialization is producing new and provocative hypotheses and research directions (Geary & Bjorklund, 2000).

Affect is increasingly viewed as a central socialization process. The study of affect has assumed a variety of forms, including the development of emotion regulation (Denham, 1998), emotional production, and understanding of the role of emotion in the enactment of the parenting role (Dix, 1991). Cognition is also viewed as central to socialization. Again the role of cognition comes in many guises, including the child's own cognitive capacities as a determinant of socialization strategies and parents' cognitions, beliefs, values, and goals, concerning their parental role as constraints on their socialization practices (Dix & Branca, 2003). Equally important is the recognition of the importance of the ways in which parents perceive, organize, and understand their children's behaviors and beliefs for appreciating how parent-child relationships are regulated and change (Goodnow, 2002). Underlying much of current research is the recognition that these processes are interdependent, mutually influencing each other. Cognition and affect for example, generally operate together in determining parenting practices (e.g., Dix, 1991; Dix & Branca, 2003).

Just as processes are viewed as interdependent, there is an increasing appreciation of the need for perspectives from a variety of disciplines to understand the family socialization process. No longer restricted to developmental psychology, the field of family socialization is increasingly multidisciplinary. History, anthropology, sociology, demography, pediatrics, psychiatry, and economics are all fields that are playing a role in the study of socialization (Parke, 2004b).

Finally, the methodological rigor of the field has increased in recent years. Instead of sole reliance on cross-sectional and/or correlational studies, greater weight is being given to carefully designed longitudinal studies (Gottfried, Gottfried, & Bathurst, 2002) and experimental studies (Cowan & Cowan, 2002) because these approaches allow more confidence in interpreting direction of effects. Second, more recent studies typically avoid the problems of shared method or reporter variance by reliance on either multiple reporters and/or multiple methods. Third, in view of the challenges from other fields, such as behavior genetics (Harris, 1998; Plomin, 1994), there is increasing recognition of rival explanations of apparent socialization effects. Both shared genetic effects and contextual influences are commonly viewed as alternative perspectives that merit consideration in explaining socialization outcomes. Finally, there is a clear trend to move beyond description by the emergence of theories that specify the mediating variables that can account for the relation between parenting and child outcomes (Parke et al., 2004). Closely related is the recognition of moderating influences, such as social context, ethnicity, or family structure on the operation of socialization processes (Mounts, 2002). Throughout our review, we focus on work that meets these new standards of scientific rigor whenever possible.

FAMILY SYSTEMS APPROACH TO SOCIALIZATION

Consistent with a family systems viewpoint, recent research has focused on a variety of subsystems, including parent-child, marital, and sibling-sibling systems. In the next several sections, we focus on each of these subsystems as contexts for socialization. Finally, we examine recent attempts to conceptualize the family as a unit of analysis.

The Parent-Child Subsystem: A Tripartite Approach

In this section, we consider the parent-child subsystem and the relation between this parent-child subsystem and children's social adaptation. Although it has been common in traditional paradigms to focus on the impact of the parent-child relationship or parental child-rearing styles, according to the Parke, Burks, Carson, Neville, and Boyum tripartite model (1994), this represents only one pathway (see Figure 8.1).

In this case, the goal of parent-child interaction is not explicitly to modify or enhance children's relationships with extrafamilial social partners. In addition, this scheme posits that parents may influence their children through a second pathway namely as direct instructor, educator, or consultant. In this role, parents may explic-

itly set out to educate their children concerning appropriate norms, rules, and mores of the culture. This second socialization pathway may take a variety of forms. Parents may serve as coaches, teachers, and supervisors as they provide advice, support, and directions about strategies for managing new social situations or negotiating social challenges. In a third role, parents function as managers of their children's social lives and serve as regulators of opportunities for social contacts and cognitive experiences. Researchers have begun to recognize the managerial function of parents and to appreciate the impact of variations in how this managerial function influences child development (Parke, Killian, et al., 2003). By managerial, we refer to the ways in which parents organize and arrange the child's home environment and the opportunities for social contact with playmates and socializing agents outside the family. Although the model has been largely applied to the issue of family peer relationships, it is useful for explaining a wide range of socialization outcomes such as gender roles and aggression (see S. McHale, Crouter, & Whiteman, 2003, for an application to gender roles).

Parent-Child Relationships: Interaction and Child-Rearing Styles

In this section, we consider descriptive studies of differences in both the quantity of mother versus father involvement with their children and qualitative differences in styles of interaction. Then, we explore the implications of parent-child interactive style and level of involvement for children's socialization outcomes.

Not all forms of parental involvement are conceptually equivalent. Lamb, Pleck, and Levine (1985) have distinguished various types of parental involvement: interaction, availability, and responsibility (see Lamb, 2004). Each is further defined as follows:

> Interaction refers to the parents direct contact with his child through caregiving and shared activities. Availability is a related concept concerning the child's potential availability for interaction, by virtue of being present or accessible to the child whether or not direct interaction is occurring. Responsibility refers to the role the parent takes in ascertaining that the child is taken care of and arranging for resources to be available for the child. (Lamb et al., 1985, p. 125)

Several further distinctions have been offered. Specifically, it is important to distinguish involvement in child-care activities and involvement in play, leisure, or

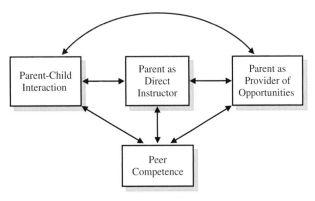

Figure 8.1 A tripartite model of family-peer relationships. (Adapted from "Family-Peer Relationships: A Tripartite Model" (pp. 115–145), in *Exploring Family Relationships with Other Social Contexts: Family Research Consortium— Advances in Family Research,* R. D. Parke, V. M. Burks, J. V. Carson, B. Neville, and L. A. Boyum, 1994, In R. D. Parke & S. Kellam (Eds.), (pp. 115–145). Hillsdale, NJ: Erlbaum.

affiliative activities with the child because there are different determinants of these two types of parental involvement. Absolute and relative involvement need to be distinguished because prior work suggests that these indices are independent and may affect both children's and adults' views of role distributions in different ways (Pleck & Masciadrelli, 2004).

Quantitative Assessments of Mother and Father Involvement in Intact Families

Despite current shifts in cultural attitudes concerning the appropriateness and desirability of shared roles and equal levels of participation in routine caregiving and interaction for mothers and fathers, the shifts toward parity are small but nonetheless real in the majority of intact families. Fathers spend less time with their infants and children than mothers (Pleck & Masciadrelli, 2004) not only in the United States but also in other countries such as Great Britain, Australia, France, Belgium, and Japan (Zuzanek, 2000). Mothers and fathers differ in the amount of time that they spend in actual interaction with their children. Pleck and Masciadrelli (2004) document that fathers' involvement has increased, even if slowly. Compared to the 1970s, proportional engagement (relative to mothers) was about 33%, whereas accessibility was approximately 50%. In contrast, recent estimates for the 1990s suggest that proportional engagement increased to approximately 70%, whereas accessibility was over 70%.

Studies of African American and Hispanic-American families confirm the pattern found for European Americans. Middle-class and lower-class African American and Latino fathers were less involved in caregiving with their infants than mothers (Roopnarine, 2004; Roopnarine, Fouts, Lamb, & Lewis-Elligan, 2005). Comparisons across ethnic groups (African, Hispanic, and European American) revealed few differences in the level of father involvement (Yeung, Sandberg, Davis-Kean, & Hofferth, 2001). These findings are important given past negative characterizations of low-income African American and Hispanic American fathers as uninvolved. The stereotype surrounding fathers of different ethnic backgrounds needs to be discarded as inaccurate and outdated (Roopnarine, 2004). Much of the earlier work was based on single-parent families and failed to recognize differences within cultural groups.

The pattern of contact time between mothers and fathers with their children in infancy continues into middle childhood and adolescence (Collins & Madsen, 2003). In middle childhood (6- to 7-year-olds), Russell and Russell (1987) found that Australian mothers were available to children 54.7 hours/week compared to 34.6 hours/week for fathers. Mothers also spent more time alone with children (22.6 hours/week) than did fathers (2.4 hours/week). However, when both parents and child were together, mothers and fathers initiated interactions with children with equal frequency and children's initiations toward each parent were similar. Adolescents spend less time with their parents than younger children and less time alone with their fathers than their mothers (Larson & Richards, 1994). From infancy through adolescence, mothers and fathers clearly differ in their degree of involvement with their children.

Qualitative Effects: Stylistic Differences in Mother and Father Interaction. Fathers participate less than mothers in caregiving but spend a greater percentage of the time available for interaction in play activities than mothers do. In North American families, fathers regardless of ethnicity (European American, African American, or Hispanic American) spent a greater percentage of their time with their infants in play than mothers, although in absolute terms mothers spent more time than fathers in play with their children (Yeung et al., 2001). The quality of play across mothers and fathers differs, too. For young infants, older infants, and toddlers, fathers play more physically arousing games than mothers. In contrast, mothers played more conventional motor games or toy-mediated activities and were more verbal and didactic (Parke, 1996, 2002).

Nor are these effects evident only in infancy. MacDonald and Parke (1984) found that fathers engaged in more physical play with their 3- and 4-year-old children than mothers, whereas mothers engaged in more object-mediated play than fathers. According to a survey (MacDonald & Parke, 1986), fathers' distinctive role as a physical play partner changes with age. Physical play was highest between fathers and 2-year-olds, and between 2 and 10 years of age, there is a decrease in father-child physical play.

Despite the decline in physical play across age, fathers remain more physical in their play than mothers. In an Australian study of parents and their 6- to 7-year-old children (Russell & Russell, 1987), fathers were more involved in physical/outdoor play interactions and fixing things around the house and garden than mothers. In contrast, mothers were more actively involved in caregiving and household tasks, school work, reading, playing with toys, and helping with arts and crafts. In adolescence, the quality of maternal and paternal involvement continues to differ. Just as in earlier developmental periods, mothers and fathers may complement each other and provide models that reflect the tasks of adolescence—connectedness and separateness. Evidence suggests that fathers may help adolescents develop their own sense of identity and autonomy by being more peer-like and more playful (e.g., joking and teasing), which is likely to promote more equal and egalitarian exchanges. "Fathers, more than mothers conveyed the feeling that they can rely on their adolescents, thus fathers might serve as a 'facilitating environment' for adolescent attainment of differentiation from the family and consolidation of independence" (Shulman & Klein, 1993, p. 53). Although the style of fathers' involvement as a play or recreational partner appears to have reasonable continuity from infancy through adolescence, the meaning and function of this interaction style shifts across development. The positive affect associated with fathers' play in infancy is not as evident in adolescence, although other goals of this age period may be facilitated by this more playful egalitarian style.

A word of caution is in order because fathers in several other cultures do not show this physical play style. In some cultures that are similar to U.S. culture, such as England and Australia, there are similar parental sex differences in play style. In contrast, findings from several other cultures do not find that physical play is a central part of the father-infant relationship (Roopnarine, 2004). Neither Swedish nor Israeli kibbutz fathers were more likely to play with their children or to engage in different types of play (Hwang, 1987). Similarly, Chinese Malaysian, Indian, and Aka pygmy (Central Africa) mothers and fathers rarely engaged in physical play with their children (Hewlett, 2004; Roopnarine, 2004). Instead, both display affection and engage in plenty of close physical contact. In other cultures, such as Italy, neither mothers nor fathers but, instead, other women in the extended family or in the community were likely to play physically with infants (New & Benigni, 1987).

Why do mothers and fathers play differently? Both biological and environment factors probably play a role. Experience with infants, the amount of time spent with infants, the usual kinds of responsibilities that a parent assumes—all of these factors influence the parents' style of play. The fact that fathers spend less time with infants and children than mothers may contribute as well. Fathers may use their distinctive arousing style as a way to increase their salience despite more limited time. Biological factors cannot be ignored given that male monkeys show the same rough-and-tumble physical style of play as American human fathers and tend to respond more positively to bids for rough-and-tumble play than females (Parke & Suomi, 1981). "Perhaps [both monkey and human] males may be more susceptible to being aroused into states of positive excitement and unpredictability than females" (Maccoby, 1988, p. 761)—speculation that is consistent with gender differences in risk taking and sensation seeking. In addition, human males, whether boys or men, tend to behave more boisterously and show more positive emotional expression and reactions than females (Maccoby, 1998). Together these threads of the puzzle suggest that predisposing biological differences between males and females may play a role in the play patterns of mothers and fathers. Yet, the cross-cultural data underscore the ways in which cultural and environmental contexts shape play patterns of parents and remind us of the high degree of plasticity of human social behaviors.

Parent-Child Interaction and Children's Adaptation.   Two approaches to this issue of the impact of parent-child interaction on children's socialization outcomes have been utilized in recent research. Some have adopted a typological approach and examined styles or types of child-rearing practices (Baumrind, 1973). Others have adopted a social interaction approach by focusing on the nature of the interchanges between parent and child (G. Patterson, 2002).

The Typological Approach.   Perhaps the most influential typology has been offered by Baumrind (1973) who distinguished between three types of parental child-rearing typologies. She found that *authoritative* but not *authoritarian* or overly *permissive* behavior by parents led to positive emotional, social, and cognitive development in children. Baumrind has followed her authoritarian, authoritative, and permissive parents and their children from the preschool period through adolescence in a longitudinal study (Baumrind, 1991). She found that authoritative parenting continued to be associated with positive outcomes for adolescents as with younger children and that responsive, firm parent-child relationships were especially important in the development of competence in sons. Moreover, authoritarian child rearing had more negative long-term outcomes for boys than for girls. Sons of authoritarian parents were low in both cognitive and social competence. Their academic and intellectual performance was poor. In addition, they were unfriendly and lacking in initiative, leadership, and self-confidence in their relations with their peers.

Maccoby and Martin (1983) extended the Baumrind typology based on combinations of the warm/responsive, unresponsive/rejecting dimension and the restrictive/demanding, permissive/undemanding dimension and included a fourth type of parenting style, which is characterized by neglect and lack of involvement. These are *disengaged* parents who are "motivated to do whatever is necessary to minimize the costs in time and effort of interaction with child" (Maccoby & Martin, 1983). Such parents are motivated to keep the child at a distance and focus on their own needs rather than the needs of the child. They are parent centered rather than child centered. With older children, this is associated with the parents' failure to monitor the child's activity or to know where the child is, what the child is doing, and who the child's companions are. In infants, such a lack of parental involvement is associated with disruptions in attachment; in older children, it is associated with impulsivity, aggression, noncompliance, moodiness, and low self-esteem (Baumrind, 1991). Older children also show disruptions in peer relations and in cognitive development, achievement, and school performance (Hetherington & Clingempeel, 1992). It is the combined impact of not having the skills to be able to gain gratification in either social or academic pursuits that frequently leads to delinquency in children with neglecting parents (Reid, Patterson, & Snyder, 2002). Parental involvement plays an important role in the development of both social and cognitive competence in children.

The Status of the Typological Approach.   A major concern about the focus on parental *style* is the limited attention to the delineation of the processes that account for the effects of different styles on children's development. Throughout the history of socialization research, there has been a tension between molar and molecular levels of analysis. Over the past 3 decades, the pendulum has swung back and forth between these levels of analysis. Currently, these two strands of research coexist and are seldom united in a single study. On the molecular side, the work of G. Patterson (2002), and Gottman (1994) can be cited. On the molar side, the search for typological answers to parenting style continues (Baumrind, 1991; Steinberg, Dornbusch, & Brown, 1992). Some exceptions can be noted. For example, Hetherington and Clingempeel (1992) have used both parenting style in combination with sequential analyses of children's levels of compliance to parental control, which is a useful bridging of the two levels of analyses.

In an attempt to resolve this issue, Darling and Steinberg (1993) have argued that parental style and parental practices need to be distinguished. Parenting style is "a constellation of attitudes toward the child that are communicated to the child and create an emotional climate in which parents' behaviors are expressed" (p. 493). In contrast to style, "parenting practices are behaviors defined by specific content and socialization goals" (p. 492). These authors cite attending school functions and spanking as examples of parenting practices. Style is assumed to be independent of both the content of parenting behavior and the specific socialization content. Critical to their model is the assumption that parenting style has its impact on child outcomes indirectly. First, style transforms the nature of parent-child interaction and thereby moderates the impact of specific practices. Second, they posit that style modifies the child's openness to parental influence, which, in turn, moderates the association between parenting practices and child outcomes.

A second concern focuses on the issue of direction of effects. It is unclear whether the styles described by Baumrind are, in part, in response to the child's behavior. Placing the typology work in a transactional framework (Sameroff, 1994) would argue that children with certain temperaments and/or behavioral characteristics would determine the nature of the parental style.

A third concern is the universality of the typological scheme. Recent studies have raised serious questions about the generalizability of these styles across either socioeconomic status (SES) or ethnic/cultural groups. Two issues are involved here. First, does the rate of utilization of different styles vary across groups? Second, are the advantages of positive social outcomes associated with a particular style (e.g., authoritative) similar across groups? The answer to both questions seems to be negative. In lower-SES families, parents are more likely to use an authoritarian as opposed to an authoritative style, but this style is often an adaptation to the ecological conditions, such as increased danger and threat, which may characterize the lives of poor families (Furstenberg, Cook, Eccles, Elder, & Sameroff, 1999). Moreover, studies find that the use of authoritarian strategies under these circumstances may be linked with more positive outcomes for children (Baldwin, Baldwin, & Cole, 1990). A second challenge to the presumed universal advantage of authoritative child-rearing styles comes from cross-ethnic studies.

Accumulating evidence underscores the nonuniversality of these stylistic distinctions and suggests the importance of developing concepts that are based on an indigenous appreciation of the culture in question (R. K. Chao, 1994). In summary, it is evident that contextual and cultural considerations need more attention in typological approaches to child rearing.

The Parent-Child Interactional Approach. Research in this tradition is based on the assumption that face-to-face interaction with parents may provide the opportunity to learn, rehearse, and refine social skills that are common to successful social interaction with other social partners. This work has yielded several conclusions. First, the style of the interaction between parent and child is linked to a variety of social outcomes including aggression, achievement, and moral development. To illustrate this approach, studies of children's social competence are considered. Recent studies have found that parents who are responsive, warm, and engaging are more likely to have children who are more socially competent (Grimes, Klein, & Putallaz, 2004). Moreover, high levels of positive synchrony and low levels of nonsynchrony in patterns of mother-child interaction are related to school adjustment rated by teachers, peers, and observers (Harrist, Pettit, Dodge, & Bates, 1994). In contrast, parents who are hostile and controlling have children who experience more difficulty with age-mates in the preschool period (Harrist et al., 1994) and middle childhood.

Evidence suggests that family interaction patterns not only relate to concurrent peer relationships but also predict peer relationships across time. In their study of third grade children, Henggeler, Edwards, Cohen, and Summerville (1992) found that children of fathers who were responsive to their children's requests became more popular over the school year than children of less responsive fathers. Similarly, J. Barth and Parke (1993) found that parents who were better able to sustain their children in play predicted better subsequent adaptation to kindergarten.

Although there is an overlap between mothers and fathers, evidence is emerging that fathers make a unique and independent contribution to their children's social development. Studies (Hart et al., 1998; Isley, O'Neil, & Parke, 1996) have shown that fathers continue to contribute to children's social behavior with peers—after accounting for the mothers' contribution. Although father involvement is quantitatively less than mother involvement, fathers have an important impact on their offspring's development. Quality rather than quantity of parent-child interaction is the important predictor of cognitive and social development.

Differences in interactive style associated with children's social competence and the emotional displays during parent-child interaction are important. The affective quality of the interactions of popular children and their parents differs from the interactions of rejected children and their parents (Parke, Cassidy, Burks, Carson, & Boyum, 1992). Consistently higher levels of positive affect have been found in both parents and children in popular dyads than in the rejected dyads. Negative parental affect is associated with lower levels of peer acceptance (Isley et al., 1996, 1999): Carson and Parke (1996) found that children of fathers who are likely to respond to their children's negative affect displays with negative affect of their own are less socially skilled (e.g., less altruistic, more avoidant, and more aggressive) than their preschool classmates. The results for the reciprocity of negative affect were evident only for fathers, which suggests that men may play a particularly salient role in children's learning how to manage negative emotions in the contexts of social interactions. Boyum and Parke (1995) confirmed the importance of parental negative affect for children's social development but demonstrated that father anger is a particularly salient predictor of children's social acceptance by peers. Less accepted children were likely to receive angry affect from their fathers during observations of family dinner. This finding underscores the importance of distinguishing among specific affective displays rather than reliance on categories of negative or positive emotions.

Together these findings lead to a revision in traditional thinking about the ways that mothers and fathers influence their children's development. This work suggests that fathers may play a larger role in socialization of children's emotion than earlier theories suggested. And it is through the management of their own emotions and their reactions to their children's emotions that fathers may have their greatest impact on their children's social relationships with peers and friends. In summary, both the nature of parent-child interaction and affective quality of the relationship are important correlates of children's social development.

Beyond Description: Processes Mediating the Relations between Parent-Child Interaction and Children's Social Competence. A variety of processes have been hypothesized as mediators between parent-child interaction and peer outcomes. These include emotion-encoding and emotion-decoding skills, emotional regulatory skills, cognitive representations, attributions and beliefs, and problem-solving skills and attention-deployment abilities (Eisenberg, 2000; Ladd, 1992; Parke, McDowell, Kim, & Leidy, 2006; Parke & O'Neil, 1999). These abilities or beliefs are acquired in parent-child interchanges during development and, in turn, guide the nature of children's behavior with their peers. We focus on three sets of processes that seem particularly promising candidates for mediator status: (1) affect-management skills, (2) cognitive representational processes, and (3) attention regulatory processes (see Figure 8.2).

Affect-Management Skills as a Mediating Mechanism. Children learn more than specific affective expressions, such as anger or sadness or joy, in the family. They learn a cluster of processes associated with the understanding and regulation of affective displays, which we term *affect-management skills* (Parke, Cassidy, Burks, Carson, & Boyum, 1992). These skills are acquired during the course of parent-child interaction and are available to the child for use in other relationships. Moreover, it is assumed that these skills play a mediating role between family and children's social competence.

One set of skills that is relevant to successful peer interaction and may, in part, be acquired in the context of parent-child play, especially arousing physical play, is the ability to clearly encode emotional signals and to decode others' emotional states. Through physically playful interaction with their parents, especially fathers, children may be learning how to use emotional signals to regulate the social behavior of others. In addition, they may learn to accurately decode the social and emotional signals of other social partners. Several studies have found positive relations between children's ability to encode emotional expressions and children's social competence with peers (Halberstadt, Denham, & Dunsmore, 2001). Successful peer interaction requires not only the ability to recognize and produce emotions but also a social understanding of emotion-related experiences, of the meaning of emotions, of the cause of emotions, and of the responses appropriate to others' emotions. Cassidy, Parke, Butkovsky, and Braungart (1992), in a study of 5- and 6-year-old children, found that a higher level of peer acceptance was associated with greater (a) ability to identify emotions, (b) acknowledgment of experiencing emotion, (c) ability to describe appropriate causes of emotions, and (d) expectations that they and their parents would respond appropriately to the display of emotions. Family emotional expressiveness—an index of the extent to which family

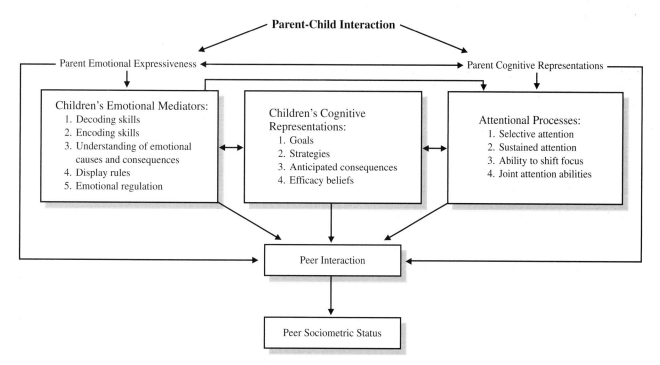

Figure 8.2 Emotional, cognitive, and attentional mediating links between family and peer systems.

members express emotion in the course of everyday interaction—has emerged as a further link between family and peer systems, providing guidelines for the use of emotion in ongoing social interchanges. The expressiveness concept extends emotional learning beyond the acquisition of specific skills, such as encoding or decoding, to the utilization of rules about emotion in multiple contexts (Halberstadt et al., 2001). Several studies have found cross-generational similarities between mother's (Denham, 1998), father's (Boyum & Parke, 1995), and children's levels of expressiveness. Consistent with the assumption that expressiveness is learned in the family and that children transfer their expressive style to their interactions with others outside the family, several studies (Boyum & Parke, 1995; Cassidy et al., 1992) found links between family expressiveness and peer competence. These studies suggest that family emotional expressiveness may be one pathway by which children learn to understand and express their emotions in a socially appropriate manner.

Emotional Regulation.   Research suggests that parental support and acceptance of children's emotions is related to children's ability to manage emotions in a constructive fashion. Several investigators (Eisenberg, 2000; Eisenberg & Fabes, 1992; Parke et al., 2006) have found links between the ability to regulate emotional arousal and social competence. Similarly, children who either have limited knowledge of emotional display rules (Saarni, 1999) or are poor at utilizing display rules are less well accepted by their peers (McDowell, O'Neil, & Parke, 2000; McDowell & Parke, 2000). Parental comforting of children when they experience negative emotion has been linked with constructive anger reactions (Eisenberg & Fabes, 1994). Moreover, children's emotional regulation and their knowledge and affective display rule utilization are linked with high positive parental affect and low levels of parental control (McDowell & Parke, 2000, 2005; McDowell et al., 2000). In addition, parental willingness to discuss emotions with their children is related to children's awareness and understanding of others' emotions (Denham, Cook, & Zoller, 1992; Dunn & Brown, 1994). Eisenberg, Fabes, Schaller, and Miller (1991) found that parental emphasis on direct problem solving was associated with sons' sympathy, whereas restrictiveness in regard to expressing one's own negative emotions was associated with sons' physiological and facial indicators of personal distress. These findings are consistent with work by

Gottman, Katz, and Hooven (1997) on parents' meta-emotion. By *meta-emotion* these researchers refer to parents' emotions about their own and their children's emotions, and *meta-cognitive structure* refers to an organized set of thoughts, a philosophy, and an approach to one's own emotions and to one's children's emotions. Gottman et al. (1997), in a longitudinal analysis, found that fathers' acceptance and assistance with children's sadness and anger at 5 years of age was related to their children's social competence with peers at 8 years of age. Moreover, fathers' assistance with anger predicted academic achievement. The gender of child influenced these relationships: When fathers help daughters with sadness, the daughters are rated as more competent by their teachers. When fathers help their daughters regulate anger, girls are rated as more socially competent by their teachers, show higher academic achievement, and their dyadic interaction with a best friend is less negative. Fathers who are more accepting of their sons' anger and assist them in regulating anger have sons who are less aggressive.

Together, these studies suggest that various aspects of emotional development—encoding, decoding, cognitive understanding, and emotional regulation—play an important role in accounting for variations in peer competence. Our argument is that these aspects of emotion may be learned in the context of family interaction and serve as mediators between the parents and peers. At the same time, the contribution of genetics to individual differences in emotionality and emotional regulation probably plays a role in the emergence of these emotional processes (Eisenberg, 2000; Kochanska, 1993). Finally, the direction of effects remains unclear in these relations; probably both parent and child mutually influence each other in the development of affect-management skills.

Cognitive Representational Models: A Second Mediator between Parents and Peers.   One of the problems facing the area of family peer relationships is how children transfer the strategies they acquire in the family to their peer relationships. Several theories assume that individuals possess internal mental representations that guide their social behavior. Attachment theorists offer working models (Bretherton & Munholland, 1999), whereas social and cognitive psychologists have suggested scripts or cognitive maps that could serve as a guide for social action (Grusec & Ungerer, 2003).

Attachment researchers have found support for Bowlby's argument that representations vary as a function of child-parent attachment history (see Bretherton & Munholland, 1999). For example, children who had been securely attached infants were more likely to represent their family in their drawings in a coherent manner, with a balance between individuality and connection, than were children who had been insecurely attached (Carlson, Sroufe, & Egeland, 2004).

Research in a social interactional tradition reveals links between parent and child cognitive representations of social relationships. Burks and Parke (1996) found some evidence for similarities between children and mothers in their goals, attributions, and anticipated consequences when they responded to a series of hypothetical social dilemmas. This study suggests that children may learn cognitive representational schemes through their family relationships, although the precise mechanism through which these schemas are acquired is not yet specified.

Next, we turn to an examination of the hypothesis that parents of children of different sociometric status differ in their cognitive models of social relationships. Several aspects of cognitive models including attributions, perceptions, values, goals, and strategies have been explored. Pettit, Dodge, and Brown (1988) found that mothers' attributional biases concerning their children's behavior (e.g., the extent to which they view an ambiguous provocation as hostile or benign) and the endorsement of aggression as a solution to interpersonal problems were related to children's interpersonal problem-solving skill that was related to their social competence. Other evidence suggests that parents hold different patterns of beliefs about problematic social behaviors such as aggression and withdrawal and that these patterns are associated with their children's membership in various sociometric status groups (Rubin & Mills, 1990). This work suggests that parents do have a set of beliefs concerning children's social behavior that may, in part, govern their behavior (Goodnow, 2002; Parke, 1978).

MacKinnon-Lewis and her colleagues (1994) found that mothers' and sons' hostile attributions were significantly related to the coerciveness of their interactions. Moreover, mothers' attributions were related to reports of their children's aggression in their classrooms. Similarly, Rubin, Mills, and Rose-Krasnor (1989) found a link between mothers' beliefs and their preschoolers' social problem-solving behavior in the classroom. Mothers who placed higher values on skills, such as making friends, sharing with others, and leading or influencing

other children, had children who were more assertive, prosocial, and competent social problem solvers.

McDowell, Parke, and Spitzer (2002) explored the links between parent and child cognitive representations of social relationships. Parents and their children responded to vignettes reflecting interpersonal dilemmas by indicating how they may react in each situation. Open-ended responses were coded for goals, causes, strategies, and advice. The cognitive representations of social behavior of both fathers and mothers were related to their children's representations. Moreover, fathers' but not mothers' cognitive models of relationships were linked to children's social competence. Fathers' strategies that were related high on confrontation and instrumental qualities were associated with low teacher ratings of children's social competence. Fathers with relational-prosocial goals have children who are rated as more competent by both teachers and peers. Perhaps fathers are more influential in conflict-laden domains, whereas mothers are more influential in social domains involving personal and relationship issues. These data suggest that fathers' cognitive representations of social relationships are important correlates of children's social competence.

Together, these studies suggest that cognitive models of relationships may be transmitted across generations and these models, in turn, may serve as mediators between family contexts and children's relationships with others outside of the family. Finally, this work implies that *both* children and parents actively construct their own dyadic relationships and other social relationships. Moreover, both are influenced in their behavior with each other by these cognitive constructions. One issue that needs more attention is how child and adult constructions change across development and how the pattern of mutual influence between parent and child changes as the child develops (Kuczynski, 2003; Maccoby, 1992). Coordination and coregulation rather than simply a bidirectional pattern of influence probably increasingly characterizes the parent-child relationship in middle childhood and adolescence.

Attention Regulation: A Third Mediating Mechanism. In concert with emotional processes, attentional regulatory processes have come to be viewed as another mechanism through which familial socialization experiences may influence children's social competence. These processes include the ability to attend to relevant cues, to sustain attention, to refocus attention through such processes as cognitive distraction and cognitive restructuring, and other efforts to purposefully reduce the level of emotional arousal in a situation that is appraised as stressful. Attentional processes are thought to organize experience and to play a central role in cognitive and social development, beginning early in infancy. Thus, B. Wilson and Gottman (1994) aptly considered attention regulatory processes as a "shuttle" linking emotional regulation (ER) and sociocognitive processes because attentional processes organize both cognitions and emotional responses and thus influence the socialization of relationship competence. Although studies are only beginning to emerge, evidence suggests that attentional regulation may have direct effects on children's social functioning (Eisenberg, 2000; B. Wilson & Gottman, 1994) and, in some circumstances, attentional control may function in interaction with dimensions of emotionality and social information processing. Other work (Eisenberg & Fabes, 1992) suggests that attentional control and emotional negativity may interact when predicting social competence. Attention regulatory skills appear to be more critical among children who experience higher levels of emotional negativity. Eisenberg, Gutherie, Fabes, Shepard, Losoya, et al. (2000). argued that when children are not prone to experience intense negative emotions, attention regulatory processes may be less essential to positive social functioning. In contrast, the social functioning of children who experience anger and other negative emotions may only be undermined when these children do not have the ability to use attention regulatory processes, such as cognitive restructuring, and other forms of emotion-focused coping (see also, Eisenberg, Cumberland, & Spinrad, 1998).

Attentional processes may work in tandem with emotional regulatory abilities to enhance social functioning (O'Neil & Parke, 2000). Parenting style may be an important antecedent of children's abilities to refocus attention away from emotionally distressing events. Data from fifth graders indicated that when mothers adopted a negative, controlling parenting style in a problem-solving discussion, children were less likely to use cognitive decision making as a coping strategy. Additionally, children were more likely to report greater difficulty in controlling negative affect when distressed. Lower levels of cognitive decision making and higher levels of negative affect were associated with more problem behaviors and higher levels of negative interactions with classmates. Similarly, when fathers adopted a negative, controlling style, children were more likely to use avoidance as a

mechanism for managing negative affect. Additionally, fathers who reported expressing more negative dominant emotions, such as anger and criticism, in everyday intercalations had children who reported greater difficulty controlling negative emotions. Avoidant coping and negative emotionality, in turn, were related to higher levels of parent-reported problem behaviors.

Recent findings from the National Institute of Child Health and Human Development (NICHD) Early Child Care Research Network study of child care and youth development are relevant (NICHD Child Care Research Network, 2003b). The role of attention in a laboratory task as a mediator between parenting and peer outcomes was examined. Parenting was measured by the HOME Observation for Measurement of the Environment (HOME) scale, by maternal sensitivity, and by cognitive stimulation. Attention was indexed by sustained attention and impulsivity. Children viewed a matrix of familiar objects and were required to note when an object appeared and to refrain when a nontarget stimulus was presented. Errors of omission occurred when children responded to a nontarget stimulus. Children who had fewer errors of omission had greater ability to sustain attention; children with errors of commission were more impulsive. Social competence and externalizing behaviors were rated by child-care caregivers at 54 months. There were links between higher-quality family environments and better social competence and lower externalizing. Second, sustained attention and less impulsivity were associated with higher social competence scores. Third, impulsivity served as a mediator between family- and social-outcome measures.

In recent follow-up (NICHD Child Care Network, 2006), attention regulation mediated between mother and father parental sensitivity measures and teacher ratings of children's peer competence and self-reports of loneliness in first grade. In this study, attention was measured by both the Continuous Performance Task (CPT) and by maternal reports of attentional regulatory abilities. Using third grade outcomes of aggression, exclusion by peers, and friendship, and earlier measures (first grade) of mother and father sensitivity predicted these outcomes. Moreover, attentional regulation competence served as a mediator between parenting and later peer outcomes. Together these studies provide evidence for the role of attention as a mediator of the links between family and peer systems.

Parental Instruction, Advice Giving, Consultation, and Rule Provision.   Learning about relationships through interaction with parents can be viewed as an indirect pathway because the goal is often not explicitly to influence children's social relationships with extrafamilial partners such as peers. In contrast, parents may influence children's relationships directly in their role as a direct instructor, educator, or advisor. In this role, parents may explicitly set out to educate their children concerning appropriate ways of initiating and maintaining social relationships and learning social and moral rules.

Several studies have examined these issues. In a study of parental supervision, Bhavnagri and Parke (1991) found that children exhibited more cooperation, turn taking, and had longer play bouts when assisted by an adult than when playing without assistance. Adult assistance enhanced the quality of play for younger (2 to 3.5 years of age) children more than older (3.5 to 6 years of age) children. Although both fathers and mothers were effective facilitators of their children's play with peers, under natural conditions, mothers are more likely to play this supervisory role than fathers (Bhavnagri & Parke, 1991; Ladd & Pettit, 2002).

The quality of advice that mothers provided their children prior to entry into an ongoing play dyad varied as a function of children's sociometric status (Russell & Finnie, 1990). Mothers of well-accepted children were more specific and helpful in the quality of advice that they provided. In contrast, mothers of poorly accepted children provided relatively ineffective kinds of verbal guidance such as "have fun" and "stay out of trouble." The advice was too general to be of value to the children in their subsequent instructions.

As children grow, caregiver forms of management shift from direct involvement or supervision of the ongoing activities of children and their peers to a less public form of management, involving advice or consultation concerning appropriate ways of handling peer problems. This form of direct parental management has been termed *consultation* (Ladd, & Pettit, 2002). Parents report using verbal guidance (e.g., discussion about future consequences, talk of values, and offering their advice) more often than direct interventions (e.g., limiting the adolescent's activities with peers or inviting friends over to the house to shape peer influence; Mounts, 2000). Parental limiting of activities with peers and inviting children's friends over, however, were reported more frequently when parents attempt to influence friend selection (Mounts, 2000). These indirect forms of supervision that emerge as the child reaches adolescence are linked with positive outcomes. Parental supervision

was positively related to adolescents academic competence and psychological adjustment (e.g., low levels of depression; Furstenberg et al., 1999) and negatively related to children's antisocial behavior and association with delinquent peers in late elementary and middle school (Reid et al., 2002) even though parents are not directly involved (e.g., giving instructions) in children's interactions with peers. Perhaps with older children, an adult's presence keeps the children's behavior in line with parental expectations.

Past research on advice giving often has focused on either the content of parent's advice or the manner in which it is given. There is a shift in recent research toward an integrative approach to this topic. As Grusec and Goodnow (1994) suggested, both style and content need to be considered together in determining the impact of parental advice giving on children's peer outcomes. The combined impact of these two aspects of parental advice giving is just beginning to achieve recognition. In their study of children aged 3 to 5 years, Mize and Pettit (1997) found that maternal information giving and guidance (content) predicted, over and above mothers' warmth and responsiveness (style), children's peer acceptance (as rated by teachers) during a play interaction context. These studies did not assess the ways in which children may be contributing to the advice-giving task. McDowell, Parke, and Wang (2003) found similar results showing that the style and content of peer relationships made independent contributions, after controlling for children's behavior during the task.

Most of the research examining parental advice giving assumed that parents advise children; thus, parents hold the key to socialization when giving advice. Many studies neglect the fact that children often raise the subjects that are discussed in the parent-child interaction. In effect, children are actively contributing to their own socialization by selecting issues on which to receive advice. Moreover, whatever the relations are between parental advice giving and children's social competence, the child necessarily holds the power to put into action any advice that is offered. In this sense, children and parents may find themselves as equal partners in facilitating peer relationships. Again, children are active solicitors of parental responses. Either behavioral characteristics during a parent-child interaction or beliefs about the child's behavior in general may affect the relative quality of the parent-child interaction and thus the effectiveness of advice giving. It is also important to note that children may be more or less receptive to parental advice and will shape their own socialization experiences by selectively attending to or ignoring parental offers of advice.

Both parents and children, however, may regard explicit parental advice as less necessary and/or less appropriate as children develop adequate social skills. Instead, by middle childhood, provision of advice would be expected to be used by parents for remediational goals in which the advice giving would be highest for children who functioned poorly socially. McDowell et al. (2003) found that when parents offered more advice and more specific advice about peer dilemmas, children were rated as less positive and more negative by teachers and peers. However, children may act as agents of their own development by eliciting more specific advice to compensate for poor social functioning away from the parent. Other evidence suggests that the type of advice changes further as children enter adolescence and develop a future orientation. In adolescence, parents are likely to try to keep their children from being influenced by peers by talking to them about future consequences of their behavior. Mounts (2000) found that 37% of mothers of adolescents used this direct strategy with their ninth-grade children. This "parental guidance" approach (e.g., "My parents tell me who I have for friends will affect my future") was associated with selection of friends with low levels of antisocial behavior and high levels of academic achievement. Advice giving is a bilateral process in which both parents and children are active participants at all stages of the advice process, from selection of topics to acceptance or rejection of advice.

These studies suggest that direct parental influence in the form of supervision and advice giving can increase the competence of young children and illustrates the utility of examining direct parental strategies as a way of teaching children about social relationships. In these studies, the direction of effects is difficult to determine and parents may be responding to their children's level of social skill. Experimental and longitudinal studies would help place these studies on a clearer interpretative footing.

Another avenue through which parents can regulate their children's peer relationships is the provision of rules or guidelines. Rules concerning children's peer relationships include the guidelines regarding what activities the children can engage in and when, with whom, and where they can play. To date, little attention has been given to the role of rules in the development and maintenance of children's peer relationships. Particularly relevant to the links between rules and peer rela-

tionships is the work of Furstenberg et al. (1999), which explores the relations between parents' restrictions on the activities of their adolescents' social behavior and adolescents' social adjustment. The construct of "restrictions" included, among other aspects, monitoring, rules, teaching good judgment, and restriction of activities. A higher number of restrictions was linked to fewer problem behaviors (e.g., school truancy or substance abuse) and higher social involvement with peers. The operationalization of the restrictions construct combined rules with several parenting skills so that the role of rules alone in the regulation of children's behavior with peers is unclear. Simpkins and Parke (2002) explored the relations between parental play rules and sixth-grade children's loneliness, depression, and friendship quality. Boys whose parents had fewer play rules reported lower levels of depression and more conflict in their best friendship. As in other aspects of parental management, the process by which rules are jointly negotiated by children and their parents is poorly understood. Issues of mutual trust, parental perception of the child's level of responsibility, and self-regulatory ability, and, for the child, the perceived fairness of the rules probably all play a role in both the negotiation process and the extent to which the rules are likely to be followed.

Parents as Managers of Children's Opportunities

Parents influence their children's social relationships not only through their direct interactions with their children but also as managers of their children's social lives (Furstenberg et al., 1999; Parke, Killian, et al., 2003). This parental role is of theoretical importance given the recent claims that parents' impact on children's development is limited and peer group-level processes account for major socialization outcomes (Harris, 1998). In contrast, we conceptualize the parental management of access to peers as a further pathway through which parents influence their children's development (Parke, Killian, et al., 2003). Mothers and fathers differ in their degree of responsibility for management of family tasks; mothers are more likely to assume the managerial role than fathers (Parke, 2002).

Parents make choices about neighborhoods and schools as well as the formal and informal activities in which their children can participate. In these ways, "parents act as designers when they seek to control or influence the settings in which children are likely to meet and interact with peers" (Ladd & Pettit, 2002, p. 286). These design decisions can influence children's social and academic outcomes. Instead of viewing parents as acting alone in their designer roles, we prefer to view parents and children as co-designers in recognition of children's roles as shapers and negotiators across development. Many decisions—even in the designer domain—are influenced by children's and parents' needs, wishes, and decisions. In this section, we consider each of these aspects of the designer role.

Neighborhoods as Determinants of Peer Contact. Although it is assumed that parents choose their neighborhoods, many constraints limit the range of locations from which to choose, especially economic (i.e., cost) and geographic (i.e., distance from work or transportation). Choice of neighborhood is not equally available to parents; lower-SES and minority group parents have a more restricted set of options than higher-SES and non-minority parents. However, there is considerable variability in "neighborhood effects" on children because of the ways in which parents manage their children's access to aspects of their neighborhood setting. Neighborhood choice, therefore, is simply one phase of a multiphase process in which choices made by different parents in similar neighborhoods, as well as the initial choice of neighborhood, are important (Furstenberg et al., 1999). A second conceptual assumption about neighborhoods concerns children's role in neighborhood selection. Although children—especially young children—are not usually direct participants in the choice of neighborhoods, their needs, their safety, and their access to other children and play space usually are considered by parents in their deliberations about choice of neighborhood. Adolescents may be more active participants by articulating their concerns about moving to a new neighborhood that, for example, involves loss of community-based friendships and shifts in school district. Testimony to children's power is evidenced by increases in residential mobility of families after children complete high school.

Neighborhoods vary in their opportunities for peer-peer contact. Especially for young children who have limited mobility, neighborhoods form significant portions of their social world. The most systematic evidence concerning the impact of variations in the quality of neighborhood environments comes from Medrich (1982), who isolated a number of factors—safety, terrain, distance from commercial areas, and child population density—that affect the amount and type of peer social experience.

What is the impact of neighborhood variations on peer competence? Bryant (1985) found that accessibility to neighborhood resources is a correlate of socioemotional functioning. Children who could easily access (by walking or bike) community resources, such as structured and unstructured activities at formally sponsored organizations, were higher both in their acceptance of individual differences and perspective taking. Similarly, using U.S. Census tract data, Coulton and Pandey (1992) found that youngsters in areas with high levels of poverty differed from those in low-poverty areas on several outcomes, including reading scores, birth weight, infant death, and juvenile delinquency. A related Australian study (Homel & Burns, 1989) found that children in the most disadvantaged neighborhoods, reported higher loneliness, feelings of rejection by peers, worry, and lower life satisfaction compared to children in less disadvantaged neighborhoods. Although recent studies find evidence of "neighborhood effects" across a range of developmental outcomes in both adolescents and young children, these effects appear to be modest after taking into account family effects (Leventhal & Brooks-Gunn, 2000). The effects of neighborhoods on children's outcomes are often mediated by parenting practices such as supervision and monitoring. O'Neil, Parke, and McDowell (2001) found that when mothers and fathers perceived their neighborhoods as dangerous and low in social control, they placed more restrictions on their fourth grade children's activities. Parental perceptions were more consistently related to parenting practices than objective ratings of neighborhood quality. Moreover, parental regulatory strategies serve as mediators of the relation between parental perceptions of neighborhood quality and social competence. Mothers and fathers who perceived problems in their neighborhood had children who were more prosocial and less aggressive, but this was mediated by shifts in parental management strategy. Similarly, N. Hill and Herman-Stahl (2002) found that interviewer's ratings of neighborhood safety were associated with mothers' use of hostile socialization strategies. Both mothers and interviewers reports of safety were linked with maternal depression. In turn, mothers' depression mediated the links between neighborhood safety and inconsistent disciplinary practices. Neighborhoods are an important factor in accounting for children's developmental outcomes but much remains to be understood about the mechanisms that account for neighborhood effects and how these mechanisms shift across development.

Parents and Children as Partners in Schooling. Parents choose not only neighborhoods but also, especially for middle-class families, the type and quality of day care and elementary schools that their children will attend. These choices make a difference to children's later development. As studies of child care have shown, the quality of and, to some extent, the amount of time in care are linked to children's cognitive and social development (Clarke-Stewart & Allhusen, 2005). Higher quality child care is associated often with higher cognitive functioning. Social behavior, despite the opportunity to have increased peer contact, is less consistently linked with day-care quality: Some evidence suggests that children who are in day care for more than 40 hours per week may show some increases in aggression (NICHD Early Childcare Research Network, 2003a). As children develop, parents select neighborhoods as a function of quality of the schools that are available (Furstenberg et al., 1999). However, "these choices are constrained by existing economic and social opportunities" (p. 226) and are mainly available to middle-class families. Moreover, the ability to choose is not inconsequential because exercising the ability to choose a school has been linked to adolescent academic outcome (Furstenberg et al., 1999). As a reminder that children can play a role in this process of school choice, there is some evidence that children's behavior in school—their successes and failures in both social and academic domains—influences the nature of the parent-child relationship. Repetti (1996) found that children's positive and negative experiences at school during the day altered the nature of parent-child interaction in the home after school. Although the study did not address the issue of the impact on subsequent decisions to change schools due to this school-based child effect on family dynamics at home, consistent negative school experiences may lead parents to consider shifting schools as an option to reduce negative effects on the child and the family.

School choice is not the only way in which families and schools are linked. The extent to which parents are involved in school-related activities (e.g., parent-teacher associations or school conferences) is positively related to children's academic outcomes (Epstein & Sanders, 2002). Practices of partnerships between parents and schools decline across child development. Parents of children in elementary school are more likely to volunteer, attend parent-teacher conferences, and supervise children's homework. In recognition of adolescent's need for autonomy and independence, parental involvement decreases in high school, but young adolescents still want their families to support their learning and activities at home (Epstein & Sanders, 2002). Even older adolescents endorse

parent involvement at school but in different ways than in earlier school grades. These developmental changes can be interpreted as evidence of the child's role in shaping the form that the parent-school partnership will assume at different points in the child's educational career.

Parents and Children as Active Agents in Involvement in Religious Organizations.   Parental facilitation of children's involvement in religious institutions is another potentially important way in which parents manage their children's lives. It is important to distinguish between the issue of involvement in religious institutions and religious beliefs because these two aspects of religion may have partially independent effects on family functioning and child outcomes (see Mahoney, Pargament, Tarakeshwar, & Swank, 2001, for a review of religious beliefs and parenting practices). Elder and Conger (2000) found that church involvement is a family affair. When both parents attended church on a regular basis, children were more likely to be involved in religious organizations. Similarly, actively involved grandparents tend to have actively involved grandchildren. Church attendance involved more than contact with a broadened network of adults who share similar family and religious values; it also involved exposure to a network of age-mates with common beliefs and values. Involvement in church activities was associated with higher endorsement of not only church but also school, good grades, and—especially for boys—community activities. For those who were less involved in religious activities, athletics and school were given high priority. Religiously involved youth perceived their friends to be less likely to encourage deviant activities, viewed their friends and themselves as less involved in deviance, and were less likely to see friends disapproved of by their parents.

Religious involvement in the 8th grade was predictive of competence by the 12th grade in grades and peer success. Moreover, adolescents who become more religiously involved by the end of high school tend to rank higher on a variety of competence dimensions—from academic and peer success to self confidence and relations with parents. A reciprocal influence model best accounted for those findings. Although the primary flow of influence moved from religious activity and socialization to individual competence in achievement, some adolescents who were successful academically and socially and became more involved in religious activities, further enhanced achievement. Similarly, it is likely that both parents and children are active players in the process of involvement in religious activities. Although parents—through their own involvement and through their introduction of the child to religious beliefs and functions—play an important initial role, children, and especially adolescents, themselves are central agents in choosing to continue their regular participation in religious institutions. These findings are most easily understood through the lens of the bilateral model that guides our chapter. Finally, Brody, Stoneman, and Flor (1996) found that parental religiousness (frequency of church attendance and importance of religion) was associated with better child adjustment as well. Specifically higher maternal and paternal religiousness was associated with less externalizing problems among 9- to 12-year-olds. The effects were mediated by family cohesiveness and lower marital conflict. However, the relative importance of beliefs or involvement in organized religious activities in accounting for these effects remains unclear.

Parental Monitoring.   Another way in which parents can affect their children's social relationships is through monitoring of their children's social activities. This form of management is particularly evident as children move into adolescence and is associated with the relative shift in importance of family and peers as sources of social influence. Moreover, direct monitoring is more common among younger children, whereas distal monitoring is more evident among adolescents. Monitoring refers to a range of activities, including the supervision of children's choice of social settings, activities, and friends. Parents of delinquent and antisocial children engage in less monitoring and supervision of their children's activities, especially concerning children's use of evening time, than parents of nondelinquent children (G. Patterson & Stouthamer-Loeber, 1984). Poorly monitored children have lower academic skills and lower peer acceptance (Sandstrom & Coie, 1999), and they participate in more delinquent and externalizing behavior (Xiaoming, Stanton, & Feigelman, 2000). Nor are the effects of monitoring limited to a reduction in the negative aspects of peer relations. As Krappmann (1986) found, preadolescents of parents who were well informed about their children's peer relationships and activities had closer, more stable, and less problem-ridden peer relationships.

Although monitoring has been viewed as a parent to child effect, Kerr and Stattin (2000) have reconceptualized this issue and argued that monitoring is a process that is jointly co-constructed by the parent and child—a

view consistent with the one guiding our chapter. They suggested that monitoring may be a function of the extent to which children share information about their activities and companion choices with their parents. Given this reconceptualization, prior research could be reinterpreted to suggest that children with poorer social adjustment discussed their activities with parents less than did well-adjusted children. Paternal attempts to learn more about their children's activities must be met with the child's own willingness to discuss such information (Mounts, 2000). Schell (1996), in a qualitative study of high-risk adolescents, found that youth often actively thwart their parents' monitoring attempts. For example, they may mislead the parent concerning their destination or location, which makes it difficult for the parents to accurately track the child's activities. As Kuczynski, Marshall, and Schell (1997) noted: "the proactive and management techniques of parents occur in tandem with proactive management techniques of their children" (p. 43). This reconceptualization is consistent with recent findings with adolescents (Mounts, 2000). Parental guidance (e.g., discussion of future consequences of children's relationships or giving advice) rather than monitoring was consistently correlated with less delinquency, less drug use, and children having more friends with high grade point averages and positive attitudes toward school. The role of parents in the regulation of adolescents' peer relationships in adolescence is not to monitor or to "keep track" of their children's activities; parents' role is to listen to children concerning their relationships, give advice on current dilemmas, and discuss future consequences their children might not think about otherwise. Such willingness may be related to temperamental characteristics of the adolescent. Parental knowledge of child behavior in middle childhood has been linked to characteristics such as expressiveness and sociability (Crouter, Helms-Erikson, Updegraff, & McHale, 1999). In sum, the relations between parental monitoring and adolescent peer activity are more complicated than previously thought. This reconceptualization of monitoring as a shared process between a parent and child is consistent with the theme of both parent and child as active agents in the management of children's social lives.

Recognition of the Interdependence among Components of the Tripartite Socialization Model.   Although we have treated parental style and/or parent-child interaction, advice giving, and parental management as separate influences, these components often operate together to achieve their effects on children's socialization outcomes. A similar argument has been offered by Grusec and Goodnow (1994) who suggested that parental strategies vary in their effectiveness as a function of the quality of the parent-child relationship. As argued elsewhere, these three components can be usefully viewed as a cafeteria model (Parke et al., 1994).

Two issues need to be addressed. First, are there natural occurring combinations of these components? Second, do the different components moderate the relative effectiveness of each component depending on the level of the other components? To illustrate, Mounts (2002) examined the co-occurrence of different types of parenting management practices—prohibiting, guiding, monitoring, supporting—with various parenting styles (authoritarian, authoritative, permissive, and uninvolved). She found that all parents, regardless of their parenting style, use prohibiting and guiding as management strategies. In contrast, monitoring and supporting are more common in authoritative style homes relative to the other parenting style environments. Several other studies illustrate this interdependence across socialization components by demonstration of the joint contributions of parenting style and practices to child outcomes. Steinberg, Lamborn, Dornbusch, and Darling (1992) found that when parents were authoritative, it reduced the effects of parental school involvement in determining school performance, whereas parental involvement in school had a stronger effect in the presence of authoritative parenting style. Similarly, Mize and Pettit (1997) found that when mothers were low in parental responsiveness (parental style) higher levels of constructive coaching (parental practices) aimed at improving peer relationships were linked to lower levels of aggression than when mothers had low levels of responsiveness and low levels of constructive coaching. In contrast, when mothers had moderate or high levels of responsiveness, their level of coaching was unrelated to the level of children's aggression. In this case, coaching compensated for a less adequate parenting style. Finally, Mounts (2001) demonstrated a moderating role of parental style on the effectiveness of parental management of adolescent peer relationships. Parental style was indexed by authoritative, authoritarian, indulgent, and uninvolved approaches, whereas parental management was represented by guiding, prohibiting, monitoring, and supporting their adolescents' friendships. Monitoring operated differently in the context of dif-

ferent parenting styles: with authoritative parents, high levels of monitoring were associated with lower levels of friends and low levels of drug use. For other parenting styles, there were no links between monitoring and friends or drug use. Perhaps adolescents view monitoring differently (i.e., less intrusive) in the context of an authoritative parenting style—a view consistent with monitoring as a dyadic construct. The link between prohibiting and drug use varied as a function of parental style as well; prohibiting was negatively related to drug use for the authoritarian and authoritative style groups but positively linked for the uninvolved parental style group. Because these effects were evident across 1 year, it suggests that a low level of parental involvement may have created a climate in which parent's efforts to prohibit drove adolescents toward higher levels of drug use over time. This underscores the bidirectionality of influence between parents and children in the socialization process as well. In sum, these studies illustrate the interdependence among various components of our tripartite model and suggest that a full understanding of socialization processes requires attention to the moderating effects among the components.

Co-Parenting as a Socialization Strategy

A recent trend is the focus on co-parenting in recognition that mothers and fathers operate as a parenting team and individual parents (J. McHale & Rasmussen, 1998). This work has identified a variety of forms that co-parenting alliances can assume, including "a pattern signifying antagonistic and adult centered or hostile competitive, co-parenting dynamics, a pattern marked by significant imbalance or parenting discrepancy in levels of parental engagement with the child and a pattern reflecting cooperation, warmth, cohesion, and child centeredness or high family harmony" (J. McHale, Lauretti, Talbot, & Pouquette, 2002, p. 142). These patterns have been observed across studies with infants, preschoolers, and school-age children, and in both European and African American families (Brody, Flor, & Neubaum, 1998; Fivaz-Depeursinge & Corboz-Warnery, 1999). Recent work has moved beyond description and revealed links between early co-parenting dynamics and later indices of social adaptation. J. McHale and Rasmussen (1998) found that hostile-competitive co-parenting during infancy was related to aggression, whereas large parenting discrepancies were related to parent-rated anxiety. Others have found links between problematic family alliances in the 1st year and insecure mother-child attachments and clinical symptomatology in the preschool years (Fivaz-Depeursinge & Corboz-Warnery, 1999; J. McHale et al., 2002).

Co-parenting accounts for unique variance in child measures and clearly needs to be distinguished from traditional parent-child and marital level processes (J. McHale et al., 2002). Less is known about the processes that control these various patterns of co-parenting, but recent work on gatekeeping (Allen & Hawkins, 1999; Beitel & Parke, 1998) that focuses on ways in which couples facilitate or hinder the involvement of their partner's interactions with their children is promising. The similarities and differences of the co-parenting relationship for intact and nonintact (divorced or single parent) families are poorly understood (Emery, Kitzmann, & Waldron, 1999). Extensions of theory and empirical work to other family forms (foster parents and birth parents; Erera, 1997), parents and grandparents (Smith & Drew, 2002), and lesbian-parenting partners or these partners and a donor father as co-parent (C. J. Patterson, 2002) would help define the uniqueness of co-parenting forms and process in various family types.

Beyond the Parent-Child Dyad: The Marital Subsystem as a Contributor to Children's Socialization

In the preceding section, parents were conceptualized as active influences, both directly and indirectly, on the development of children's social competence and understanding of relationships. However, children's experiences in families extend beyond their interactions with parents. Children's understanding of relationships is shaped also through their active participation in other family subsystems (e.g., child-sibling) and through exposure to the interactions of other dyadic subsystems (e.g., parent-parent) or participation in triadic relationships (e.g., child-sibling-parent, child-parent-parent).

Influence of Marital Satisfaction and Discord on Child Outcomes

Considerable evidence indicates that marital functioning is related to children's short-term coping and long-term adjustment. Although the size of the associations are not always large, a range of studies link marital discord and conflict to outcomes in children that are likely to impair the quality of interpersonal relationships, including: antisocial behavior; internalizing and externalizing behavior problems; and changes in cognitions, emotions, and physiology in response to exposure to

marital conflict (see Grych & Fincham, 2001, for a recent review). Although less empirical work has been directed specifically toward examination of the "carry-over" of exposure to marital conflict to the quality of children's relationships with significant others (e.g., peers and siblings), exposure to marital discord is associated with poor social competence and adjustment problems (Cummings & Davies, 1994; Davies, Harold, Goeke-Morey, & Cummings, 2002).

Mechanisms Linking Marital Discord to Children's Adjustment

Three alternative, but not mutually exclusive, models have been proposed to account for the impact of marital relations on children's developmental outcomes. Until recently, theoretical frameworks typically conceptualized marital discord as an indirect influence on children's adjustment that operated through its effect on family functioning and the quality of parenting (Fauber & Long, 1991). Factors such as affective changes in the quality of the parent-child relationship, lack of emotional availability, and adoption of less optimal parenting styles have been implicated as potential mechanisms through which marital discord disrupts parenting processes. A second model (Cummings & Davies, 1994; Grych & Fincham, 2001) focuses on the *direct effects* of witnessed marital conflict on children's outcomes rather than on the indirect or mediated effects. Recently, Cummings, Goeke-Morey, and Raymond (2004) have proposed a third model: the interrelations among marital quality, parents' psychological functioning, and children's outcomes. Labeled the "parental mental health hypothesis," this alternative focuses on the role of parental psychological functioning in accounting for the effects of marital conflict either as a risk or protective factor.

Indirect Effects Model. A sizable body of literature supports the view that these two family subsystems are related. Erel and Burman (1995) completed a meta-analytic review of 68 studies that met a variety of criteria, including independent assessment of marital and parent-child relationships. Their review provided support for a positive relation between the quality of the marital relationship and the quality of the parent-child relationship. As Erel and Burman (1995) concluded:

The composite mean weighted effect size representing the association between marital and parent-child quality was

0.46 or approximately one standard deviation in the direction of more positive parent-child relationships in families with more positive relations and more negative parent-child relationships in families with more negative marital relations. (p. 126)

Even when their meta-analysis was restricted to studies of high-quality research or to studies using independent raters and a between-subjects design, the effect sizes were reduced but remained significant. Their review leaves little doubt about the relation between marriage and parent-child relationships.

Theoretically, several models have been offered to account for these effects—the spillover hypothesis and the compensatory hypothesis. According to the spillover perspective, mood or behavior in one subsystem transfers to another subsystem (e.g., from marital subsystem to parent-child subsystem). In contrast, the compensatory hypothesis suggests that positive parent-child relationships can be maintained even in the face of martial conflict and can serve as a buffer on children (Erel & Burman, 1995). The meta-analysis clearly supports the spillover hypothesis and offers no support for the compensatory concept. Their analysis underscores the difficulty of buffering children from marital conflict and discord. Parents may try to buffer their children by limiting their opportunities to witness marital conflicts and disputes; however, as Erel and Burman (1995) suggest, "they cannot shield them from the negative impact that marital discord has on the parent-child relationships" (p. 128). Unfortunately, Erel and Burman's conclusions were largely restricted to Caucasian and intact families.

Several factors have been proposed as moderators of the relation between these two subsystems, including gender of parent, gender of child, age of child, and birth order (Cummings et al., 2004). The quality of the father-child relationship is more consistently associated with the quality of the marital relationship and/or with the amount and quality of marital support than is the mother-child relationship (Parke, 2002). Cummings et al. (2004) labeled this view as the "fathering vulnerability hypothesis." This literature suggests that spousal support is more critical for adequate parenting on the part of fathers than mothers. As marriages deteriorated, men became more negative and intrusive fathers, whereas mothers were less affected by shifts in marital quality (Belsky, Youngblade, Rovine, & Volling, 1991). Moreover, recent meta-analysis (Krishnakumar & Buehler, 2000) of the relation between interparental conflict and parenting supported "the fathering vulnerability hypothesis" including relations with a variety of aspects of parenting, including control, acceptance, harsh discipline, and overall quality of parenting. At the same time, many studies show "parenting vulnerability" (Cummings et al., 2004) in which marital discord affects both mothering and fathering. However, when gender differences do occur, they favor the fathering vulnerability view, with less support for the "mothering vulnerability hypothesis" (Cummings et al., 2004).

A number of factors may aid in explaining the greater vulnerability of fathers. First, father's level of participation is, in part, determined by the extent to which the mother permits participation (Beitel & Parke, 1998). Second, because the paternal role is less well articulated and defined than the maternal role, spousal support may serve to help crystallize the boundaries of appropriate role behavior (Parke, 2002). Third, men have fewer opportunities to acquire and practice skills that are central to caregiving activities during socialization and therefore may benefit more than mothers from informational (i.e., cognitive) support (Parke & Brott, 1999).

Even when research indicates that both mother-child and father-child relationships are both associated with marital relations, mothers and fathers may influence their children's outcomes in different ways. Gottman et al. (1997) found that when parents used a mutually hostile pattern of conflict resolution, fathers were more likely to be intrusive and children were more likely to express anger during a parent-child interaction task. In addition, fathers' intrusiveness predicted more negative peer play and more aggressive play with a best friend. Interestingly, an individual parent's style of handling conflict may be related to the quality of his or her *partner's* relationships with children in the family. When fathers were angry and withdrawn in a conflict resolution task, mothers were more critical and intrusive during interactions with their child. Maternal criticism and intrusiveness, in turn, were associated with unresponsiveness or "tuning out" by the child during mother-child interactions and higher levels of teacher-rated internalizing symptoms (see also Cowan, Cowan, Schulz, & Heming, 1994).

Family systems theory suggests that marital discord not only interferes with the mother-child or father-child relationship but also impairs qualities of the mother-father-child triadic relationship by interfering with the effectiveness of how the mother and father work together with the child (Cox, Paley, & Harter, 2001). Westerman and Schonholtz (1993) found that fathers', but not mothers', reports of marital disharmony and disaffection were significantly related to the effectiveness of joint parental support toward their child's problem-solving efforts. Joint parental support was, in turn, related to fathers' and teachers' reports of children's behavior problems. As Gottman (1994) has shown, women tend to engage and confront, whereas men tend to withdraw in the face of marital disharmony. Men's lack of involvement in the triadic family process may account for these findings.

Although much of the prior work has focused on the transfer of negativity between marital and parent-child subsystems, some evidence suggests that marital satisfaction is a predictor of positive parenting (Russell, 1997). For mothers, but not fathers, greater marital satisfaction was linked to higher levels of warmth, affection, positive involvement, and overall positive parenting.

Direct Effects of Marital Relationships on Children's Outcomes. Despite progress in elucidating specific parenting processes that are impaired by interparental conflict, parental conflict is also associated with behavior problems independent of its influence on the parent-child relationship. Accordingly, attention has turned to elucidating specific processes by which the marital relationship itself *directly* influences children's immediate functioning and long-term adjustment. A parallel research trajectory has been a movement away from a focus on global measures of marital satisfaction to a focus on specific aspects of marital interaction that are most likely to influence children's immediate cognitive, emotional, and physiological functioning. These immediate responses, or "microprocesses," have been hypothesized to be critical links to children's long-term social adjustment when interparental conflict exists (Grych & Fincham, 2001). Recent lab analog studies show that the form of expression of marital conflict plays a critical role in how children react. More frequent interparental conflict and more intense or violent forms of conflict have been found to be particularly disturbing to children and likely to be associated with externalizing and internalizing difficulties (Cummings et al., 2004). McDonald, Jouriles, Norwood, Ware, and Ezell (2000) found that father's interparental aggression was related to children's internalizing problems. Conflict that was child related in content was more likely than conflict involving other content to be associated with behavior problems in children, such as greater shame, re-

sponsibility, self blame, and fear of being drawn into the conflict (Grych, & Cardoza-Fernandez, 2001).

Resolution of conflict, even when it was not viewed by the child, reduces children's negative reactions to exposure to interadult anger and conflict. Exposure to unresolved conflict has been found to be associated with negative affect and poor coping responses in children (Kerig, 1996). In addition, the manner in which conflict is resolved may also influence children's adjustment. Katz and Gottman (1993) found that couples who exhibited a hostile style of resolving conflict had children who tended to be described by teachers as exhibiting antisocial characteristics. When husbands were angry and emotionally distant while resolving marital conflict, children were described by teachers as anxious and socially withdrawn.

Conflict is inevitable in most parental relationships and is not detrimental to family relationships and children's functioning under all circumstances. However, disagreements that are extremely intense and involve threat to the child are likely to be more disturbing to the child. In contrast, when conflict is expressed constructively, is moderate in degree, is expressed in the context of a warm and supportive family environment, and shows evidence of resolution, children may learn valuable lessons regarding how to negotiate conflict and resolve disagreements (Cummings & Davies, 1994).

Parental Mental Health and Marital Quality. Support is beginning to emerge for the view that parental psychological functioning may help account for the effects of marital conflict on children's functions. Consistent with a view of parental psychopathology as a risk factor for children, family discord mediated the effects of maternal depressive symptoms on adolescent girls' social and emotional adjustment (Davies & Windle, 1997). In a later study, marital distress mediated the effects of maternal depression on male and female adolescent externalizing, whereas maternal depression mediated the impact of marital distress on adolescent depressive symptoms (Davies, Dumenci, & Windle, 1999). Other work provides support for the links among poor parental functioning (parental dysphoria), marital conflict, and children's adjustment (DuRocher Schudlich & Cummings, 2003). In this case, depressive conflict style mediated the relations between parental dysphoria and internalizing problems of 8- to 16-year-old children. Consistent with a protective perspective when fathers are supportive of their partners during marital conflict, the impact on the children is reduced (Huffman & Cummings, 2002). Although this mental health perspective is gaining some support, a wider range of mental health problems needs to be examined to determine their links with both marital conflict and children's adjustment. Moreover, the relative importance of this perspective for the direct versus indirect models of influence is not yet established.

Recent Progress in Methodology and Theory. A noteworthy methodological advance is the evaluation of the impact of marital conflict not just through the use of lab analog or questionnaire approaches but the use of parental diary reports of naturally occurring incidents of marital conflict in the home. In support of earlier lab analog studies (Cummings & Davies, 1994), these studies suggested that everyday marital conflict (Goeke-Morey, Cummings, Harold, & Shelton, 2003) and marital physical aggression (O'Hearn, Margolin, & John, 1997) were associated with negative emotional and behavioral reactions. In contrast, parental support and affection were linked with children's positive reactions (Goeke-Morey et al., 2003). These studies increase the ecological validity of the prior findings and the generalizability of the prior work to naturalistic family contexts.

Several competing theoretical frameworks have emerged that focus on cognitive-processing or emotional-regulatory mechanisms. Using a cognitive contextual model, Grych and Fincham (Grych & Cardoza-Fernandes, 2001; Grych & Fincham, 1990) have focused on the cognitive and affective meaning that exposure to conflict has for the child. Davies and Cummings (1994) have offered an emotional security hypothesis that suggests that marital conflict negatively affects children's emotional regulatory abilities, influences children's motivation to regulate their parents' behaviors, and alters their cognitive representations of family relationships. A third position (Crockenberg & Langrock, 2001) focuses on the social learning role of modeling and the role of specific emotions, such as fear and anger, in accounting for the effects of marital conflict on children's adjustment.

In a recent test of competing theoretical positions (i.e., social learning, cognitive appraisal, and emotional security), Davies et al. (2002) found that children responded to interparental conflict with fear and regulation efforts (avoidance or intervention)—reactions that are consistent with emotional security theory. In contrast, the social learning theory prediction (Crocken-

berg & Langrock, 2001) that children would display anger in response to conflict and that they would imitate same-sexed parents was not supported. However, the value of distinguishing among specific types of emotions, such as fear versus anger, rather than on undifferentiated negative affect was clearly supported—a position stressed by Crockenberg's specific emotions perspective on this issue (Crockenberg & Langrock, 2001). In a follow-up study of this sample, Davies et al. found further support for the emotional security position. Child emotional security (assessed by emotional, reactivity, behavioral regulation, and internal representations) mediated the links between interparental conflict and internalizing and externalizing symptoms across a 2-year period. Although the models provided stronger support for the emotional security predictions than cognitive appraisal processes, both sets of processes received some support. In sum, more work is needed before definitive conclusions concerning the theoretical power of these competing, even if overlapping, theoretical perspectives can be drawn. Moreover, as others (Crockenberg & Langrock, 2001) have argued it is critical to examine links among marital conflict, child adjustment, and specific goals (versus a general emotional security goal) that are both directly relevant to emotional security (e.g., worries about family dissolution or fears about being involved in the conflict) and nonsecurity-related concerns (e.g., being a partner in family decision making). It is critical to integrate the recent work on emotional regulation and coping (Eisenberg, 2000; Kerig, 2001) more centrally into these theoretical debates (e.g., Crockenberg & Langrock, 2001). Finally, prior work has been largely adevelopmental and less is known about the impact of exposure to marital conflict on adolescents, especially the effects on their own emerging friendships and close same-sex and opposite-sex relationships.

The Sibling System as a Contributor to Children's Socialization

Descriptions of the normative patterns that characterize sibling relationships over the course of development suggest that, in addition to parents, siblings play a critical role in the socialization of children. Most children are likely to spend more time in direct interaction with siblings than parents and significant others (Dunn, 1993; Larson & Richards, 1994) and that interactions with siblings provide a context for the expression of a range of positive social behaviors as well as numerous conflictual encounters and experiences with conflict resolution (Dunn, 1993). Further, this array of interactions between siblings has been found to be typified by greater emotional intensity than the behavioral exchanges that characterize other relationships. Developmental shifts in sibling relationships suggest that perceptions of warmth and conflict between siblings declined over time, between late middle childhood and early adolescence (Slomkowski & Manke, 2004). A decline in intimacy in sibling relationships is evident from preschool to early adolescence (Dunn, Slomkowski, Beardsall, & Rende, 1994). However, gender influences these developmental patterns: sisters reported more warmth and self-disclosure over this period (Dunn et al., 1994; Slomkowski & Manke, 2004). Despite these shifts, wide individual differences in the quality of sibling relationships and recent evidence suggests change in quality of sibling relationships continues during adolescence (Conger, Bryant, & Brennom, 2004).

Sibling relationships have been hypothesized to contribute to children's socialization in a number of significant ways. A social-learning framework analogous to the one posited to explain parental contributions to the development of children's social competence (Parke & O'Neil, 1999) predicts that through their interactions with siblings children develop specific interaction patterns and social-understanding skills that generalize to relationships with other children. Relationships with siblings also may provide a context in which children can practice the skills and interaction styles that have been learned from parents or others. Older siblings function as tutors, managers, or supervisors of their younger brother's or sister's behavior during social interactions (Edwards & Whiting, 1993) and may function as gatekeepers who extend or limit opportunities to interact with other children outside of the family (Zukow-Goldring, 2002). Also paralleling the indirect influence that the observation of parent-parent interaction has on children, a second avenue of influence on children's development is their observation of parents interacting with siblings. These interactions have been hypothesized to serve as an important context in which children deal with issues of differential treatment and learn about complex social emotions such as rivalry and jealousy.

Influence of Siblings on Child Outcomes

Children's experiences with siblings provide a context in which interaction patterns and social understanding

skills may generalize to relationships with other children. According to Stocker and Dunn (1990), interactions with siblings provide a setting in which children "develop social understanding skills which may enable them to form particularly close relationships with a child of their choice, a close friend."

Studies show only modest evidence of straightforward "carryover" of interaction styles between children's relationships, and when associations emerge they may be complicated by birth order effects and other processes (Dunn, 1993, 2004; Stocker & Dunn, 1990). Adding another complexity to the picture of how sibling and peer relationships are linked are findings from studies, which suggest that sibling relationships may play a role in compensating for other problematic relationships by providing an alternative context for experiencing satisfying social relationships and protecting children from adjustment difficulties. East and Rook (1992), for example, found that children who were socially isolated in their peer relationships were buffered from adjustment problems when they reported positive relationships with a favorite sibling. Similarly, Stocker (1994) reported support for the compensatory role of at least one positive relationship (sibling, friend, or mother) as protection from the development of behavioral conduct difficulties.

The prosocial or deviant interest and activities of siblings are important determinants of the positive or negative influence of siblings on one another. Adolescents who have both close and satisfying relationships and share common deviant interests with their older brothers may be at increased risk for antisocial delinquent behaviors, higher rates of problem behaviors, and problematic interaction patterns with romantic partners (Slomkowski, Rende, Conger, Simmons, & Conger, 2001). Just as for peer-peer relationships, both the type of behavior that they engage in and the quality of the ties between siblings need to be understood before the positive or negative impact of sibling relationships can be predicted.

In view of our focus on bidirectionality of influence, it is important to consider the impact of friendships on sibling relationships. Kramer and Gottman (1992) examined the role that positive relationships with peers play in children's adaptation to the birth of a new sibling. Children who displayed a more positive interaction style with a best friend and who were better able to manage conflict and negative affect, behaved more positively toward their new sibling at both 6 months and 14 months.

They suggest that management of conflict, a valuable skill when interacting with siblings, may be more likely to be learned in interactions with peers than in direct interactions with parents. Recently, Kramer (2004) has developed a social skill training program aimed at improving children's relationships with their siblings. In comparison to a control group of 4- to 6-year-olds, children with a younger sibling who received social skills training showed more positive and less negative sibling relationships and more perspective taking. Although the processes that underlie the success of this program are not yet specified, early evidence suggests that emotional regulatory and attentional factors that are important correlates of peer competence (Eisenberg, 2000; Parke et al., 2006) may play a role in harmonious sibling relationships as well. Brody, Stoneman, Smith, and Gibson (1999) found that 9- to 12-year-old African American children who were higher in self-regulation (e.g., ability to set and attain goals, plan, and persist) experienced more harmonious and less conflictual sibling relationships. Similarly, Volling, McElwain, and Miller (2002) found that preschool-age older siblings who were higher in emotional understanding were less likely to show behavioral dysregulation and negative emotions in a social triangle paradigm in which the mother directed her attention to a younger sibling. Moreover, higher behavioral regulation was associated with more positive sibling-sibling relationships.

The challenge is to discover the contexts under which strong, weak, or compensatory connections may be expected between relationship systems and the processes through which children's experiences with siblings are translated into relationship skills that are used in other relationships. For example, greater generalization of hostile, aggressive interaction styles in both sibling and peer systems may emerge when children lack adequate relationship skills or when children are experiencing stressful, negative family relationships (Dunn, 1993, 2004). In contrast, under other circumstances, the association between sibling relationships and relationships outside the family may be moderated by a number of features that uniquely characterize each relationship. As Dunn (1993) has argued, friendship involves a mutual and reciprocated relationship with another individual, whereas siblings do not necessarily feel this way about one another. In contrast to sibling-sibling relationships, friend and peer relationships represent a more unique combination of backgrounds, experiences, and temperaments that may generate interaction styles that are the result of two unique individuals' approach to re-

lationships. Further, there appear to be different role expectations for sibling versus friend relationships that may differentially influence interaction styles. There is a need to systematically examine the moderating and mediating influences of these factors to uncover normative patterns of associations between sibling and peer relationships.

Siblings as Managers of Children's Social Lives

Just as parents function as managers of children's social lives, siblings in many cultures perform similar management functions in relation to their younger siblings. Cross-cultural work indicates that in African, Polynesian, and Mexican cultures children, especially girls, become involved in sibling caretaking and teaching activities at a relatively early age (Weisner, 1993). Maynard (2002) found that by 4 years of age children took responsibility for initiating teaching situations (e.g., weaving) with their toddler siblings and that by 8 years of age children become highly skilled teachers of culturally relevant skills. Relatively little is known, however, about the caregiving role of siblings in contemporary European American families. Patterns of sibling interaction in New England families suggest that formal caregiving responsibilities may not be as common in American culture as in other cultures (Edwards & Whiting, 1993). However, Bryant (1989) suggests that although parents may not formally assign caretaking duties to children, children frequently voluntarily assume the roles of caretaker, tutor, and teacher of younger siblings and make unique contributions to the socialization of young children. Most work examining these roles has focused on the influence that instruction from older siblings may have on children's cognitive development (Rogoff, 1990, 2003). Relatively little is known about the role that siblings play as supervisors, managers, or advisors of children's social lives. Given the amount of time that most children spend in the company of siblings, this is an area that is ripe for future investigation.

Future Directions for Sibling Research

More fruitful investigation of the links between relationships may come with movement from a socialization framework to a relationships framework. Dunn (1993) notes that one disadvantage of a socialization approach is that it does not adequately take into account that even when a child acquires social competencies through interactions in one relationship, he or she may not be motivated to apply these skills in another relationship. In contrast, a relationships perspective takes into account that each relationship reflects a unique set of demands and rewards as well as different challenges to a child's sociocognitive abilities. This may lead to the generation of questions concerning the unique aspects of child (e.g., temperament, attachment security, or self confidence), the relationship partner, the dynamic of the relationship itself, and the broader social ecology (e.g., family stress or life transitions), which may contribute to a child being motivated or disinclined to behave in a socially competent manner. As Dunn (1993) points out, the goal is to specify "for *which* children, at *which* stages of development, *which* dimensions of particular relationships are likely to show associations with other relationships" (p. 125). A final value of the renewed focus on siblings is the contribution that this work is making to our understanding of the relative roles of genetics and environment in studies of socialization and development (Dunn, 1993; Plomin, 1994).

The Family Unit as a Contributor to Children's Socialization

Parent-child, marital, and sibling influences are clearly the most well-researched aspects of socialization. However, consideration of these units of analysis alone is insufficient because they fail to recognize the family unit itself as a separate and identifiable level of analysis (Minuchin, 2002; Parke, 1988). Consistent with a systems theory perspective (Sameroff, 1994), the properties, functions, and effects of the family unit cannot necessarily be inferred from these smaller units of analysis. Families as units change across development in response to changes in the individual members, life circumstances, and scheduled and unscheduled transitions. Families develop distinct "climates" (Moos & Moos, 1981), "styles" of responding to events (D. Reiss, 1989) and distinct "boundaries" (Boss, 1999), which provide differing socialization contexts for the developing child. Several investigators (Fiese et al., 2002; D. Reiss, 1989) have argued that the family regulates the child's development through a range of processes, including myths, stories, and rituals. Recent evidence suggests the potential importance of these family level processes for understanding socialization in the family.

Family myths: Myths refer to beliefs that influence family process, provide continuity across generations, and are generally not open to discussion or debate (Sameroff,

1994). Wamboldt and Reiss (1989) argue that family myths influence mate selection and marital satisfaction. Individuals can set aside destructive family myths by marrying a person with a different and perhaps healthier history of family myths. To date, there is little direct evidence of the impact of family myths on children's development.

Family stories: Family stories have received more attention as vehicles for socialization of young children (Pratt & Fiese, 2004). Stories are vehicles for the transmission of family values and for teaching family roles. The study of stories as socialization vehicles has taken a variety of forms—in part, depending on the disciplinary perspective of the investigator. Culturally-oriented investigators (e.g., Miller & Sperry, 1987) have established that stories occur in naturalistic contexts in exchange between parents and children or while children are present. In home observations of African American toddlers in south Baltimore, they found that mothers told informal narratives in the presence of their children about events in which someone became angry or responded with verbal or nonverbal aggression. Through these stories, children learn to distinguish between justified and unjustified anger.

Family of origin experiences may be transmitted across generations through stories and shared memories and shape contemporary interaction between family members. Fiese et al. (1999) provided a useful framework for studying family stories by focusing on three narrative dimensions: (1) narrative coherence, (2) narrative styles, and (3) relationship beliefs that characterize the form that the content of family stories assumes. This report provides evidence of the value of this approach for understanding premarital couples (Wamboldt, 1999), family dinner interactions (Fiese & Marjinsky, 1999), couples with an adopted child (Grotevant, Fravel, Gorall, & Piper, 1999), and depressed couples (Dickstein, St. Andre, Sameroff, Seifer, & Schiller, 1999). This approach yielded important insights into child functioning attitudes toward open versus closed adoption, marital satisfaction, and diagnosis of depression (Fiese et al., 1999). Stories are related to family interaction patterns and are linked to children's social competence as well. Putallaz, Costanzo, and Smith (1991) found that mothers with predominantly anxious/lonely recollections of their own childhood experiences with peers took an active role in their children's social development and had the most socially competent children. However, these mothers may be compensating for their own difficult childhoods. Although mothers with positive memories also had socially competent children, mothers with memories of peer rejection had the least socially competent children. Later work (Putallaz, Klein, Costanzo, & Hedges, 1994) involving parent narrations of videotaped interaction of their child with a peer confirmed that mothers and fathers interpretative narrations were shaped, in part, by their recollections of their own childhood peer experiences. Similarly, Prinstein and La Greca (1999) found that mothers of well-liked kindergarteners had positive childhood peer memories, whereas mothers with anxious peer-related memories had less well-liked children. More work is needed to specify when childhood social adversity leads to compensatory reactions and when it leads to intergenerational continuity of social difficulties (see Grimes, Klein, & Putallaz, 2004, for a recent review).

Family rituals and routines: Rituals have been recognized for decades as an important aspect of family life (Bossard & Boll, 1950), but only in the past decade has the socialization function of rituals and routines become apparent (Fiese, 2006a, 2006b; Fiese et al., 2002). Fiese et al. (2002) argue that routines and rituals can be contrasted along the dimensions of communication, commitment, and continuity:

> Routines typically involve instrumental communication in conveying information that is "what needs to be done." The language of routines is direct, implies action, and often includes designation of roles. Routines involve a momentary time commitment and once the act is completed there is little afterthought. Routines are repeated over time, with little alteration, and can be directly observable by outsiders. Rituals, on the other hand, involve symbolic communication and covey this is "who we are as a group." There is an affective commitment that leaves the individual feeling that the activity has a rightness and provides a sense of belonging. When rituals are disrupted there is a threat to group cohesion. (p. 382)

Family routines are associated with better child health and better behavioral regulation in intact families (Fiese et al., 2002). For example, families who observe medication routines are more likely to report higher adherence to medical regimens concerning the management of asthmatic children and, in turn, the children have less asthma-related illness (Fiese, 2006a). Similarly, routines serve a protective function and are linked to better adjustment for both parents and children in single parent, divorced, and remarried households (Fiese et al., 2002).

Wolin, Bennett, and Jacobs (1988) have identified three types of family rituals: (1) family celebrations (e.g., holidays like Christmas), (2) rites of passage (e.g., weddings), (3) family traditions (e.g., birthday customs or family vacations). Failure to attend an important family event, such as a wedding, often indicates a shift in family alliances and definitions of who is in or out of the family (Fiese, 2006a, 2006b). Rituals serve a protective function as well (Fiese et al., 2002), and Wolin, Bennett, and Jacobs (1988) found that children who came from families that were able to preserve family rituals, such as holiday routines, were less likely to become alcoholic as adults. Other studies (Fiese et al., 2002) report that families who attach more meaning to their rituals have adolescents who are higher in self-esteem. In sum, rituals and routines are powerful indices of family functioning and may serve as protective factors for the child.

Questions remain about the uniqueness of rituals relative to other forms of family patterns or child-rearing practices. Are rituals independent vehicles of socialization or merely a reflection of more central causal influences such as the quality of the parent-child relationship (Fiese et al., 2002)? For example, rituals may be less likely in families of alcoholics, which suggest that the degree of alcoholism, either alone or in combination with the lack of rituals, may contribute to future drinking problems. Evidence is needed concerning the contribution of family level variables independently of individual or dyadic levels of analysis. Similarly, the direction of causality in these studies remains unclear. Do harmonious families participate more in family rituals, or does active participation contribute to increased family well-being? Although the answers to these questions are unclear, it is evident that we need to expand our repertoire of avenues through which socialization is enacted in families. Finally, the origin of family level differences is an issue that has received little attention. Given demonstrations (e.g., Plomin, 1994) that genetics may play a role in variations in measures of family home environments, answers are most likely to derive from designs that recognize the contributions of both genetic and environment factors in the emergence of family level differences.

Putting the Pieces Together: Toward a Multiple Sources Model of Socialization in the Family

Our family systems viewpoint argues for the construction of a comprehensive model in which the contribution of parent-child, parent-parent, and sibling relationships are all recognized. Figure 8.3 outlines a comprehensive model of family socialization that includes the influence of all family members. To date, few studies have simultaneously addressed how these subsystems combine to produce their impact on children's relationship learning. Little is known about the relative weighting of parent-child relationships versus other family relationships (Parke & O'Neil, 1999). Nor do we understand how the impact of these different relationships changes as the child develops. The most crucial issue remains the specification of the pathways through which these different relationships exert their influence. In our model, multiple pathways are possible and there is support for both direct and mediated effects. As noted earlier, marital relationships exert both direct (e.g., witnessed effects) and indirect effects (e.g., marital relationships influence parent-child patterns). Similarly, parent-child relationships could influence marital relationships. For example, a disciplinary encounter with a difficult-to-control child could begin a marital conflict due to disagreement about the child's misbehavior or management of the child, the carryover of negative mood, or the alignment of parent and child against a third party. Less is known about the impact of parent-child relationships on marital interactions than the reverse.

Moreover, recent research has begun to identify individual differences across families or family typologies as well as at the level of family subsystems such as marital dyads (Cook, 2001). As a next step, can we characterize families usefully by the relative importance of various subsystems? Some families may invest heavily in directly parenting their children but tend to protect their children from their marital problems. Earlier evidence suggests that exposure to marital conflict is higher for boys than girls (Hetherington & Kelly, 2001). Similarly, some families may encourage close sibling-sibling relationships, whereas others tend to encourage sibs to form separate social spheres. This kind of social arrangement will result in different types of socialization outcomes.

Do all combinations produce equally socially competent children, or are some ingredients in this mix more important than others? Do different combinations produce different, but equally well-adjusted, children in their social relationships? Can children in a family with a poor marriage compensate by investing "relationship energy" into another subsystem such as the sibling-sibling or parent-child system? Studies of divorce (Hetherington & Kelly, 2001) suggest that a close sibling-sibling relationship can help buffer children during a stressful divorce.

DETERMINANTS OF FAMILY SOCIALIZATION STRATEGIES

One of the major advances in the field has been recognition of the importance of understanding the determinants

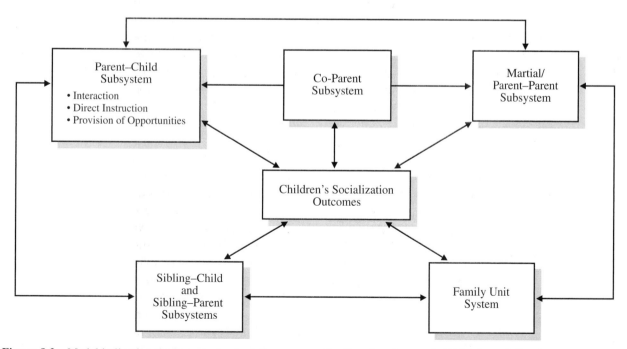

Figure 8.3   Model indicating the hypothesized relations among family subsystems and children's socialization outcomes.

of parenting behavior (Belsky, 1984). For a long time, developmentalists were concerned about the impact of particular styles or practices on children. There was less concern with the conditions that alter parenting behaviors themselves. Several trends have converged to stimulate this interest: First, the recognition of child effects (Bell, 1968) led to a reevaluation of the role of the child in eliciting and shaping parental behaviors. Second, a renewed interest in contextual-ecological issues (Bronfenbrenner, 1989) played a role. Third, closely linked is the increased focus on how cultural, racial, and ethnic background modify parenting behavior (Garcia Coll & Magnuson, 1999). Fourth, interest in the life-course perspective (Elder, 1998) has led to a focus on how timing of entry into parenting roles alters the enactment of parental behaviors. Fifth, recognition of the role of parental cognitions (e.g., goals, values, and attributions) has fueled interest in how cognition shapes parental behavior (Dix & Branca, 2003).

In this section, a variety of factors are considered. Belsky (1984) proposed a three-domain model of the determinants of parenting, which included the personal resources of the parents, the characteristics of the child, and the contextual sources of stress and support. Some of the work relevant to this model is reviewed and recent work on ethnic variations in parenting is reviewed to expand on this earlier theoretical scheme.

Child Characteristics

Child characteristics take two forms: (1) universal predispositions that are shared by all children and (2) individual differences in particular characteristics. An impressive amount of evidence has documented that infants are biologically prepared for social, cognitive, and perceptual challenges and these prepared responses play a significant role in facilitating children's adaptation to their environment. This evolutionary approach has continued to receive support (Geary & Bjorkland, 2000). Under the influence of recent advances in behavior genetics (e.g., Plomin, 1994), there is increasing recognition of the role of individual differences in a wide variety of behavioral characteristics in shaping parental socialization strategies. Perhaps the most well-researched determinant of parenting behavior is child temperament (Putnam, Sanson, & Rothbart, 2002). Although debates about the relative contributions of genetic and experimental factors to the emergence of individual differences in temperament continue (Reid

et al., 2002), temperament plays an important role as a determinant of parental socialization tactics. Infants with difficult temperaments elicit more arousal and distress from caregivers than less difficult infants (Putnam et al., 2002). Children who are more difficult may elicit increasingly coercive strategies from parents (Reid et al., 2002). Alternatively, fearful children may respond optimally to subtle parental socialization strategies (Kochanska, 1997). Other characteristics, in addition to temperament, have been examined, including activity level, social responsiveness, and compliance level. In general, the more active, less responsive, and more noncompliant children elicit more negative parenting and more negative parental arousal and affect (Crouter & Booth, 2003). The impact of these individual differences on parental socialization behavior is not independent of environmental conditions. Crockenberg and Leerkes (2003) showed that the impact of a difficult infant temperament on the parent-infant attachment relationship varied as a function of the degree of social support available to the mother, which underscores the potential modifiability of temperament-based influences.

Personal Resources

Several studies support the prediction that personal resources—conceptualized as knowledge, ability, and motivation to be a responsible caregiver—alter parenting behaviors (Belsky, 1984). Particularly striking are recent studies of how parental psychopathology, such as depression, will alter parenting behavior (Goodman & Gotlib, 2002). From early infancy onward, the patterns of interaction between depressed and nondepressed parents (usually mothers) and their offspring are less positive, less stimulating, and less contingent. In turn, their infants showed less attentiveness, fewer contented expressions, more fussiness, and lower activity levels (Field, 1992). Differences are particularly evident when depression is protracted and not merely transient (Campbell, Cohn, & Meyers, 1995).

These differences in interaction may place the infant at risk for later developmental problems. Infants of depressed mothers are more likely to develop insecure attachments (Goodman & Gotlib, 2002). Recent investigations have found links between severe and chronic depression and disorganized attachment behavior (Lyons-Ruth, Lyubchik, Wolfe, & Bronfman, 2002). This attachment category refers to infants who lack a coherent strategy for accessing their attachment figures and who show confused, conflictful, and fearful behavior in the Strange Situation (see Thompson, Chapter 2, this *Handbook,* this volume). Nor are the effects on child-parent attachment restricted to infancy. Teti, Gelfand, Messinger, and Isabella (1995) found a similar pattern of insecure attachment among preschool-age children of depressed mothers. Although no follow-up studies have revealed the long-term outcomes for these children, other studies of children with poor attachment histories reveal that these children are at risk for later relationship difficulties in adolescence (Carlson et al., 2004). Others' personal problems (e.g., antisocial personality disorder or schizophrenia; limited education and poverty) contribute to poorer parenting (Cummings et al., 2004). At the same time, positive personal characteristics (e.g., high intelligence and self-regulation) and a transpersonal orientation (i.e., a focus on family, work, and child rearing) are linked with better quality parenting (Pulkkinen, Nurmi, & Kokko, 2002). Just as with individual differences in infants and children, recent theorists have argued that some of these individual differences across parents, such as depression and proneness to abuse or coerciveness, may, in part, be genetically based (Caspi et al., 2002). Studies addressing the interplay among genetically based individual differences among infants and parents and environmental factors that enhance or suppress the influence of these characteristics would be valuable.

Parents, Children, and Social Capital

The concept of social capital considers the relations among people, institutions, and organizations of the community outside the immediate family structure. As described by Coleman (1988), social capital is both the flow of information and the sharing of norms and values that serve to facilitate or constrain the actions of people who interact in the community's social structures (e.g., schools, places of worship, or business enterprises). Children benefit from the presence of norm and value consensus among members of their family and the wider community (Coleman, 1988). Monitoring of children is facilitated, as is their socialization, through multiple efforts of network members who hold shared family community norms and values (Elder & Conger, 2000). Moreover, if a child's own family is negligent in fulfilling the socialization role, other adults are available to assume the responsibility.

One important aspect of social capital is the network of social relationships in which families are embedded.

Parents' own social networks of other adults, as well as the child members of parental social networks, provide a source of possible play partners for children. Cochran and Niego (1995) suggested several ways in which these two sets of relationships may be related. First, the child is exposed to a wider or narrower band of possible social interaction partners by exposure to the members of a parent's social network. Second, the extent to which the child has access to the social interactions of his or her parents and members of their social network may determine how well the child acquires a particular style of social interaction. Third, in view of the social support function of social networks, parents in supportive social networks may be more likely to have positive relationships with their children, which may positively affect the child's social adjustment both within and outside the family. Cochran and Niego (1995) reported that there is overlap between parent and child social networks; thirty percent to 40% of 6-year-olds' social networks were also included in the mothers' networks. Children often listed other children as play partners who were children of their mother's friends. Finally, the overlap was higher for relatives than nonrelatives, but both kin and nonkin adult networks provided sources of peer play partners for young children.

Community networking has implications for youth development. Adolescent boys were found to have better school performance and attendance and more positive social behavior when their social networks included large numbers of nonrelated adults (Cochran & Bo, 1989). In a study by Fletcher, Darling, Steinberg, and Dornbusch (1995), when nonrelated adults such as adolescent's friends' parents were perceived as authoritative in their parenting style, adolescents were lower in delinquency and substance abuse, especially when they percieve their own parents to be authoritative. Another way these two networks may be linked was proposed by Coleman (1988), who argued that when both parents and their children are acquainted with other parents and their children, they form network closure. When network closure exists, more shared values and more social control over their offspring are likely, which would be related to better social outcomes. Darling, Steinberg, Gringlas, and Dornbusch (1995) found that social integration (as indexed by network closure) and value consensus were related to adolescent social and academic outcomes. Adolescents who reported high degrees of contact among their parents, their own friends, and their friends' parents were less deviant and higher in academic achievement than their peers who were less socially integrated.

The quality of adult social networks is related to children's social behavior. In an Australian study, Homel, Burns, and Goodnow (1987) found positive relations between the number of "dependable" friends that parents report and 11-year-old children's self-rated happiness, the number of regular playmates and maternal ratings of children's social skills. Recently, Simpkins, O'Neil, Lee, and Parke (2005) found that the more parents enjoyed their own friends, the less the child was disliked and perceived as aggressive by peers. The more contact the parents had with relatives, the less disliked children were by their peers.

Moreover, the quality of the relationship that adults develop with friends in their social network is an important correlate of their children's friendship quality. Doyle and Markiewicz (1996) found that mothers who perceived their own best friends as providing more stimulating ideas and activities but also felt less secure in their friendships had children who experienced more closeness with their best friend. If mothers felt less secure about their best friendship, their own children were more likely to have a best friend. The findings concerning the links between lack of mothers' security about their friendships is consistent with work on maternal recollections of their childhood peer experiences (Putallaz et al., 1991), which supports a compensatory model of parenting. More recently, Simpkins and Parke (2001) found that the quality of both maternal and paternal concurrent friendships was related to children's friendship quality. As these studies illustrate, the quality and scope of adult friendship and social networks are important correlates not only of children's peer competence but also of their friendship qualities.

In sum, the social capital in a community can aid parents' socialization of their children through several pathways. First, when parents and children have community ties, more social support is available. Second, parental awareness of community services and their participation in shaping the institutions of the community promote the maintenance of values and norms that influence their children. Third, parental participation with their children enables closer supervision of children and reduces the time children spend with their own peers. The concept of social capital embodies the notion not only that parenting is a community enterprise (Elder & Conger, 2000) but also that children and adults are active players in the distribution of social capital. More attention needs to be given to children's role as active agents in this process.

Socioeconomic Status as a Determinant of Family Socialization Strategies

There is a long history of research concerning the links between socioeconomic status (SES) and/or social class and parenting beliefs and practices. Although the debate concerning the best strategy for measuring SES continues (Bornstein & Bradley, 2003; Entwisle & Astone, 1994), most scholars agree that SES is multiply determined, and therefore the links with parenting are likely to be multiple as well. Second, in contrast to traditional assumptions that SES is a static state, most (e.g., Featherman, Spenner, & Tsunematsu, 1988; Hoff et al., 2002) argue that SES is a dynamic concept. Over the course of childhood and adolescence, families change social class and change is greatest in the youngest ages. Over 50% of American children change social class prior to entering school (Featherman et al., 1988).

Despite the controversies surrounding the interpretation of this variable, there are SES differences in parental socialization practice and beliefs (Hoff et al., 2002). First, SES differences in parenting style have been found. Lower-SES parents are more authoritarian and more punitive than higher-SES families (Kelley, Sanchez-Hucies, & Walker, 1993; Straus & Stewart, 1999). Second, interaction styles differ across SES levels. Lower-SES mothers are more controlling, restrictive, and disapproving than higher-SES mothers (Hart & Risley, 1995). Additionally, there are more SES differences on language measures than on nonverbal measure with higher-SES mothers being more verbal than lower-SES mothers (Hart & Risley, 1995; Hoff et al., 2002). "Higher SES mothers not only talk more, but provide object labels, sustain conversational topics longer, respond more contingently to their children's speech, and elicit more talk from their children than lower SES mothers" (Hoff-Ginsberg & Tardif, 1995, p. 177). Some SES differences are independent of race and poverty. In China, where there are relatively small differences in income across groups who vary in terms of education, Tardif (1993) found that less educated parents used more imperatives with their toddlers than better educated mothers. Similarly, Hess and Shipman (1965) in their early classic studies of cognitive socialization found clear SES differences in African American lower-class and middle-class families.

Parental cognitions—ideas, beliefs, values—clearly play a major mediating role in accounting for SES differences (Bornstein & Bradley, 2003). Similarly, self-efficacy mediates between SES and parenting goals and practices (Brody, Stoneman, Smith, & Gibson, 1999). Second, ecological factors, such as neighborhood conditions, play a role. One of the challenges is to determine the roles of parental ideas and beliefs and the ecological conditions under which families are operating in determining parental socialization strategies. A more detailed exploration of socioeconomic circumstances is clearly a first step. Perhaps extreme circumstances, such as unsafe and dangerous living conditions, will override parental beliefs and play a more determining role, whereas beliefs may play a role under less extreme conditions. Specification of the types of parenting behavior, which are altered by different factors, is also of interest. Perhaps, differences in verbal stimulation will not vary across contexts in class, but control strategies may be more responsive to environmental circumstances.

THE IMPACT OF SOCIAL CHANGE ON FAMILY SOCIALIZATION

Families are not static but dynamic and are continuously confronted by challenges, changes, and opportunities. A number of society-wide changes have produced a variety of shifts in the nature of family relationships. Fertility rates and family size have decreased, the percentage of women in the workforce has increased, the timing of onset of parenthood has shifted, divorce rates have risen, and the number of single-parent families have increased (Teachman, Tedrow, & Crowder, 2000). These social trends provide an opportunity to explore how families adapt and change in response to these shifting circumstances and represent natural experiments in family adaptation. Moreover, they challenge our traditional assumptions that families can be studied at a single point in historical time because the historical contexts are constantly shifting. Our task is to establish how socialization processes operate similarly or differently under varying historical circumstances. In this section, one issue from this myriad of changes, the effects of recent shifts in family employment and unemployment patterns

are explored to illustrate the impact of social change on family relationships (for reviews of other issues such as timing of parenthood, see Moore & Brooks-Gunn, 2002; for divorce, see Clarke-Stewart & Brentano, 2006; Hetherington & Kelly, 2001). Some of these changes are scheduled or planned such as reentry into the workforce or delaying the onset of parenthood; other changes, such as job loss or divorce, are unscheduled or nonnormative transitions. According to a life-course view both scheduled and unscheduled transitions need to be examined (Elder, 1998) to fully appreciate how these different types of change alter family socialization strategies. These family transitions are adult-focused in contrast to child-focused transitions (e.g., entry to day care or junior high school) and underscore our assumption that adult developmental issues need to be directly addressed to understand how these transitions alter parental socialization beliefs and behaviors. At the same time, child developmental status will play a major role in determining how adults respond to these transitions. We argued earlier it is insufficient to focus on individual levels of analysis—either adult or child. Instead, individual, dyadic, triadic, and family units each follow their own developmental trajectory and the interplay among these separate developmental trajectories can produce a diverse set of effects on the functioning of the units themselves. In addition, the role that these units (i.e., individual, dyad, or family) play in modifying the impact of family transitions will vary as a result of these interlocking developmental curves. Both the timing and nature of family transitions and reactions to these alterations will be determined by the points at which particular individuals, dyads, triads, or families fall along their respective developmental life-course trajectories. Moreover, individual families can vary widely in the particular configuration of life-course trajectories. The central premise is that the particular configuration of these multiple sets of developmental trajectories needs to be considered to understand the impact of societal change on families.

Women's and Men's Employment Patterns and Family Socialization

The relations between employment patterns of both women and men and their family roles are increasingly being recognized (Deutsch, 1999; Hoffman, 2000). In this section, a variety of issues concerning the links between the worlds of work and family are considered to illustrate the impact of recent shifts in work patterns on both men's and women's family roles. We examine the impact of changes in maternal employment on both quantitative and qualitative aspects of mother and father participation and the influence of variations in family work schedules.

Since the 1960s, there has been a dramatic shift in the participation rate of women in the labor force. The rise has been particularly dramatic for married women with children. In the United States in 1998, over 75% of married women with school-age children and over 63% of mothers with children under age 6 were in the paid workforce. In contrast, in 1960 fewer than 19% of mothers with children were employed (Statistical Abstracts, 1999). How have these shifts affected the quantity and quality of the mother's and father's contribution to family tasks such as housework and child care, and what are the implications for children's development?

Maternal Employment and Children's Development

How does maternal employment alter mother-child involvement? There is little difference in the amount of time that mothers spend with their children or in the types of activities engaged in dual or father-only employed families (Gottfried et al., 2002). According to Bianchi (2000), between 1981 and 1997, there was little change in mother's time with children even though there were dramatic increases in maternal employment. Similar findings have been reported for the United States (Galinsky & Swanberg, 2000) and Germany (Ahnert, Rickert, & Lamb, 2000). Moreover, there are few negative outcomes of maternal employment on children, in part, because "there has been reallocation of mothers' time and priorities, delegation of family work to others, increased preschool enrollment of children of employed and nonemployed mothers and redefinition of parenting roles" (Gottfried et al., 2002, p. 214).

Several domains of children's development have been examined including gender roles, achievement, and behavior problems. Maternal employment is associated with more egalitarian views of sex roles by their children, particularly by their daughters (Hoffman & Youngblade, 1999). In middle-class families, maternal employment is related to higher educational and occupational goals in children (Hoffman & Youngblade,

1999). Sons of working mothers, in contrast to sons of unemployed mothers, not only perceive females as more competent, but also view men as warmer and more expressive. Moreover, duration of employment among African American mothers is associated with longer school attendance in their daughters; no link was found for European American mothers (Wolfer & Moen, 1996).

One of the limitations of earlier studies was the lack of long-term follow-up to assess delayed effects of earlier maternal employment on children's development. In a longitudinal study, Gottfried et al. (2002) found that maternal employment was not related to children's development across age (infancy to age 17), developmental domain, and gender. Moreover, prospective analyses indicated that there were no sleeper effects associated with maternal employment. The children of employed and nonemployed mothers were similar in cognitive, socioemotional, academic, motivational, and behavioral domains from infancy through adolescence. This conclusion is not surprising given that the home environment and parenting of employed and nonemployed mothers were very similar in stimulation, nurturing, parent-child interactions, and family climate. The pattern of findings suggests that variations in employed and nonemployed mothers are more significant for child outcomes than differences between groups. In support of this shift away from a "social address" model to a process-oriented approach, Gottfried et al. (2002) found that processes such as parental involvement and the quality of the home environment were clearly linked to children's development—regardless of maternal employment status.

Cohort effects need to be considered in interpreting these findings. As maternal employment becomes more common, the differential effects on select areas of development (e.g., sex roles and independence) may decrease. In part, this may be due to the fact that the shift in maternal employment is part of a changing set of cultural attitudes concerning male and female roles that all children, regardless of their family employment arrangements, are exposed to.

There is some evidence that the child-rearing practices of working mothers may differ from those of nonemployed mothers, particularly in the area of independence training. Except in cases where mothers feel guilty about leaving their children to work, employed mothers encourage their children to become self-sufficient and independent and to assume responsibility for household tasks at an earlier age (Hoffman & Youngblade, 1999). This early independence training may be beneficial in leading to high achievement motivation, achievement behavior, and competence (Hoffman & Youngblade, 1999). Finally, mothers' satisfaction with their employment is related to child outcomes as well in Korean immigrants (K. Kim & Honig, 1998) and European Americans (Gottfried et al., 2002).

In summary, the results of studies of maternal employment suggest it does not usually have detrimental effects on children; positive consequences have usually been obtained, especially for girls. However, the effects of maternal employment can be evaluated only in relation to other factors, such as the reason why the mother is working, the mother's satisfaction with her role, the demands placed on other family members, the attitudes of the other family members toward the mother's employment, and the quality of substitute care and supervision provided for the children.

Quality of Mother and Father Work and Family Socialization

Instead of examining whether one or both parents are employed, researchers have begun to address the impact of the quality and nature of work on both mother and father parenting behavior. This shift in focus is due to the fact that many workers experienced an increase in work hours, a decrease in job stability, a rise in temporary jobs, and, especially among low-wage workers, a decrease in income (Mishel, Bernstein, & Schmitt, 1999). As Crouter (1994) noted, there are two types of linkage between family and work. One type of research focuses on work as an "emotional climate," which may have carryover effects to the enactment of roles in home settings. The focus is generally on short-term effects. A second type of linkage focuses on the type of skills, attitudes, and perspectives that adults acquire in their work-based socialization as adults and how these variations in job experience alter their behavior in family contexts. In contrast to the short-term perspective of the spillover of emotional climate research, this type of endeavor involves more enduring and long-lasting effects of work on family life.

Work in the first tradition has been conducted by Repetti (1994) who studied the impact of working in a high-stress job (air-traffic controller) on subsequent family interaction patterns. She found that the male air traffic controllers were more withdrawn and less angry in marital interactions after high-stress shifts and tended to be behaviorally and emotionally withdrawn during interactions with their children as well. Distressing social experiences at work were associated with higher expressions of anger and greater use of discipline during interaction with the child later in the day. Repetti and Wood (1997) found similar effects for mothers who withdrew from their preschoolers on days when the mothers experienced greater workloads or interpersonal stress on the job. Similarly, Crouter, Bumpus, Maguire, and McHale (1999) found that parents who reported high work pressure and role overload had more conflicts with their adolescents.

Other research suggests that positive work experiences can enhance the quality of fathering. Grossman, Pollock, and Golding (1988) found that high job satisfaction was associated with higher levels of support for their 5-year-olds' autonomy and affiliation, despite the fact that positive feelings about work were negatively related to the quantity of time spent interacting with their child. This finding underscores the importance of distinguishing quantity and quality of involvement.

In contrast to the Repetti studies, the Grossman et al. study focused on general job satisfaction and demandingness rather than daily fluctuations in the level of positivity or negativity experienced in the work setting. Future studies need to assess these two aspects of job-related affect and involvement separately.

Research in the second tradition of family work linkage (the effects of the nature of men's occupational roles on their fathering behavior) dates back to the classic work of Kohn (1995). Several researchers extended this work by focusing on the outcomes of job characteristics for children's development. Cooksey, Menaghan, and Jekielek (1997) found that children had fewer behavior problems when their mother's work involved more autonomy working with people and more problem-solving opportunities. Similarly, fathers with greater job complexity and autonomy were less authoritarian (Grimm-Thomas & Perry-Jenkins, 1994) and responded with greater warmth to their children and with more verbal explanations (Greenberger, O'Neil, & Nagel, 1994). However, the process probably operates in both directions: The home experience of parents affects their job performance as well. Arguments at home with a wife or with a child were negatively related to work performance (Frone, Yardley, & Markel, 1997). These studies underscore the importance of moving beyond employment status per se to a detailed exploration of the nature of work in studies of family work linkages.

Job Loss and Unemployment

Another unscheduled transition that has received attention is the impact of job loss on families (Conger & Elder, 1994; McLoyd, 1998). Several aspects of the parent-child relationship are altered by economic stress including parenting style, parent discipline, parental problem solving, and levels of parent-child conflict and monitoring. Parenting behavior is adversely affected as indexed by increased parental hostility and less consistent, less effective, harsher discipline (Conger & Elder, 1994; Elder, 1974; McLoyd, 1998). Recent extensions of this basic finding to African Americans (Conger et al., 2002) and Mexican Americans (Parke et al., 2004) have been reported. Moreover, under conditions of stress, parental monitoring will be adversely affected with less vigilance on the part of the parent (Crouter, MacDermid, McHale, & Perry-Jenkins, 1990). Although conditions of unemployment or underemployment increase fathers' availability and involvement in child care, unemployed fathers report fewer nurturing behaviors than employed fathers (Harold-Goldsmith, Radin, & Eccles, 1988). Recent research has focused on modifying and mediating variables. Several studies indicate that social support has a positive impact on parent-child relationships under conditions of stress (Conger & Elder, 1994; McLoyd, 1998). Child temperament and physical attractiveness also modify parenting practices. Temperamentally difficult children are treated more harshly by unemployed fathers than temperamentally easy offspring (Elder, Nguyen, & Caspi, 1985). Although physically unattractive daughters are treated more harshly than attractive girls, in some cases they received more support and less harshness (Elder et al., 1985). The quality of the prior father-child relationship is another determinant of how stress impacts changes in the father-child relationship. A positive relationship prior to job loss served as a protective factor in buffering the child from deterioration of the father-child relationship (Elder et al., 1985). Similarly, a positive (warm and affectionate) mother-child relationship reduced harsh treatment of the child by the father (Elder et al., 1985).

A variety of adverse effects on children accompany unemployment and economic stress, including increased depression and loneliness and lowered self-esteem (McLoyd, 1998). Gender differences are evident as well.

Girls respond to stress with internalizing problems, whereas boys tend to show externalizing behaviors (Conger & Elder, 1994). Recent longitudinal studies confirm earlier cross-sectional findings. Conger, Ge, Elder, Lorenz, and Simons (1994) interviewed parents and their adolescents over a 3-year period (seventh to ninth grades). Economic pressure at Wave 1 directly impacted parent-child financial conflict at Wave 2, which was related to adolescent internalizing and externalizing behavior at Wave 3. Moreover, these investigators found support for an indirect path between parental depressed mood and marital conflict, and, in turn, altered parental hostility was linked to adolescent internalizing and externalizing. Even though there were predictable gender differences in levels of symptomatology for boys and girls (i.e., greater externalizing for boys and greater internalizing for girls) the paths were similar for both sexes. Similar support for an indirect pathway model comes from McLoyd's (1998) examination of the impact of unemployment among African American single mothers on parenting and adolescent socioemotional functioning, as well as the Conger et al. (2002) report of the impact of economic pressure on 10- and 11-year-old African American children. Finally, Parke et al. (2004) have found that the economic stress model explains the impact of economic pressure on family processes and child outcomes in Mexican American families as well.

In summary, studies of the impact of unemployment have clearly been fruitful avenues for exploring how families adapt and cope in response to stressful change and underscore the value of a family systems approach to the study of socialization.

Single versus Multiple Transitions

To date, societal changes, such as shifts in the timing of parenting, work participation, or divorce, have been treated relatively independently, but these events co-occur rather than operate in any singular fashion. As earlier work (Simmons & Blyth, 1987) on the impact of multiple transitions, such as the onset of puberty and entry into junior high school, on children's adjustment has found, co-occurrence of several changes can have a cumulative impact on the adolescent's adaptation. Similarly, as the number of environmental risk variables increase, the level of family functioning and child outcomes decrease (Sameroff, 1994). One would expect that the co-occurrence of the arrival of a new infant accompanied by job loss would have different effects than either of these events occurring singly. Moreover, the impact of any historical change may be different as a result of its occurrence in the same period as another change or changes. For example, women's increased presence in the workplace and delay in the onset of parenthood vary, and probably each event has different meaning without the other change. This implies the research need for multivariate designs to capture the simultaneous impact of multiple events on family socialization strategies.

Children and Families of Color in the United States: Issues of Race, Ethnicity, and Culture

Every 10 years, the Census Bureau reaffirms the concept of race, which has a long legacy in this country. Although race has no scientific basis, it is nevertheless a potent social construction that impacts the lives of all people in the United States, especially those considered to be non-White. In the recent past, non-White groups were generally referred to as ethnic minorities. However, because Whites, or European Americans, can also claim ethnic group membership (Waters, 1990), the term *ethnic minority* does not accurately capture the most salient aspects in the lives of non-Whites, which distinguish them from the White population—skin color and physical appearance. For this reason, the term *people of color* has gained greater acceptance as the preferred designation for groups typically considered ethnic minorities—American Indians, African Americans, Latinos, and Asian Americans. The histories of these groups are different but share common experiences of exploitation and subordination by the White majority: (a) the forceful removal of American Indians from their ancestral homelands and relocation on reservations, (b) the enslavement of African Americans and segregation after their emancipation, (c) Latinos' incorporation through military conquest of the Southwest and ambivalent immigration policies, and (d) racist immigration policies toward Asians and their internment during World War II. In addition, mixed race children and families, who now make up 2.4% of the U.S. population (U.S. Bureau of the Census, 2001a), should be included as people of color. Often, these children and families of color experience prejudice and discrimination based on anti-miscegenation attitudes (Root, 1992).

Nationally, people of color today comprise approximately 35% of the U.S. population, and it is estimated that by the year 2020, 40% of all children will be African American or Latino. Child development research, to be relevant in this country, must be more inclusive of children of color and their unique developmental challenges. Parke (2004b) noted the responsibility that the field of child development has to the growing number of children of color:

In view of these demographic shifts there is both an opportunity to evaluate the generalizability of our assumptions about developmental processes and a moral obligation to understand better a larger segment of our population. (p. 10)

Ethnicity refers to an individual's membership in a group sharing a common ancestral heritage based on nationality, language, and culture (Betancourt & Lopez, 1993). Psychological attachment to the group is also a dimension of ethnicity, referred to as ethnic identity (Phinney, 2003). Sometimes ethnicity includes a biological (F. Barth, 1969), or racialized component, that is evident in the phenotype of the group members. Culture is a multidimensional construct referring to the shared values, behaviors, and beliefs of a people that are transmitted from one generation to the next. Unlike ethnicity and race, which are usually self- and other-ascribed attributes, respectfully, culture is learned behavior and can thus vary both across and within ethnic and racial groups. For this reason, it is invalid to equate ethnicity and race with culture. Although in some populations there is an overlap in race, ethnicity, and culture, this convergence should neither be taken for granted nor any of these three attributes considered as a proxy for the other. Consequently, researchers should describe in detail the self-ascribed ethnicity of respondents, their commonly ascribed racial classification, and salient cultural characteristics as determined by appropriate measures of acculturation.

The terminology regarding race, ethnicity, and culture is changing as a result of demographic shifts and more informed awareness of how these factors contribute to development. Nevertheless, *minority group status* in the form of powerlessness and discrimination (Greenfield & Cocking, 1994) is still prevalent among non-White groups in society. Therefore, to maintain consistency between past and present group designations in the literature, the terms *minority group, ethnic minority,* and *people of color* will be used interchangeably, when appropriate, in the remaining section of this chapter.

Conceptual and Methodological Issues for Studying Children and Families of Color

Recent cross-cultural and intracultural theories have emphasized the importance of socialization goals, values, and beliefs as organizing principles for understanding cultural variations (Harkness & Super, 1995). In contrast to the older cultural deficit models of socialization, the recent models emphasize how ecological demands shape socialization goals, values, and practices, and are viewed as adaptive strategies to meet the demands of the ecological settings. Ecological (Bronfenbrenner, 1989) and family systems perspectives (Minuchin, 2002) have been useful in explaining how socialization goals for children derive from their parents' experiences with adaptive strategies that have helped them meet the challenges faced as people of color (Harrison, Wilson, Pine, Chan, & Buriel, 1990). Furthermore, Rogoff (2003) notes that to achieve a valid understanding of development in its cultural context, it is helpful to separate value judgments from observation of events:

> Interpreting the activity of people without regard for *their* meaning system and goals renders observations meaningless. We need to understand the coherence of what people from different communities *do,* rather than simply determining that some other group of people do *not* do what "we" do, or do not do it as well or in the way that we do it, or jumping to conclusions that their practices are barbaric. (p. 17)

Earlier cultural deficit perspectives were reinforced by the popularity of two-group studies that compared samples of European Americans with ethnic/racial minorities and assumed that differences between the groups were cultural in nature. In effect, ethnicity and race were equated with culture as if all members of an ethnic/racial group were equally involved with the culture of their group. An assumption of these studies was that people of color needed to assimilate or become like European Americans to correct deficiencies in their development (Ramirez & Castaneda, 1974; Rogoff, 2003). More recently, the focus on families of color has shifted away from majority-minority comparisons toward within-group studies (Garcia Coll & Magnuson, 1999;

Parke, 2004b). Such studies tell us how within-group cultural variations may account for differences in outcomes among children of the same ethnic/racial group.

One of the problems in cross-cultural or intracultural research about different ethnic groups is the issue of the equivalence of measures across groups. Because most standard measures of family functioning are developed and standardized in White middle-class populations, efforts have been made to develop culturally and linguistically equivalent measures. One innovation is the use of focus groups consisting of members of the ethnic/racial group of interest to generate items and issues that are culturally relevant (De Ment, Buriel, & Villanueva, 2005; Gomel, Tinsley, Clark, & Parke, 1998; Vazquez-Garcia, Garcia Coll, Erkut, Alarcon, & Tropp, 1995). Focus groups are also being used as an integral part of the scale-construction process; they make recommendations for wording changes and identify culturally inappropriate items. Another innovation is the use of translation and back translation to ensure that the meaning is retained in the translation process. In addition, a dual-focus approach (Vazquez-Garcia et al., 1995) is being used in which new concepts and items that arise in the course of the translation process are generated simultaneously in both languages. Work by Knight and colleagues (Knight, Tein, Prost, & Gonzales, 2002; Knight, Virdin, & Roosa, 1994) have provided models for establishing scalar equivalence of commonly used questionnaires for assessment of family functioning. Recent advances in scaling have been applied to this issue as well. Specifically, Reise and his colleagues (Flannery, Reise, & Widaman, 1995; S. Reise, Widaman, & Pugh, 1993) have utilized item response theory (IRT) techniques to address the equivalence of scales across groups. The utility of this approach for establishing gender equivalence (Flannery et al., 1995) and cross-cultural equivalence (e.g., China versus the United States; Reise et al., 1993) suggests that this strategy can be used to establish scalar equivalence across different ethnic groups in our own culture.

The methodological issues involved in doing research with families of color are multifaceted (Bernal, Trimble, Burlew, & Leong, 2003; Betancourt & Lopez, 1993; McLoyd & Steinberg, 1998). In addition to language and scalar equivalence issues, other methodological issues need to be considered. First, families of color are comprised of diverse populations whose presence in the United States has come about through conquest (American Indians), involuntary immigration through slavery (African Americans), and voluntary immigration (Asian Americans and Latino Americans). The nature of these groups' incorporation into the United States has necessitated diverse adaptation strategies, making it useless to combine members of these groups into a single research sample. Even among contemporary immigrant groups, such as Mexican Americans and Chinese Americans, there are communities whose members have lived in this country for several generations. Consequently, researchers need to identify the generation of their samples and their length of U.S. residence (for immigrants) and to avoid overgeneralizations to all members of the group. Researchers must also not overgeneralize cultural characteristics from the country of origin to members of the group who have lived in the United States for generations and who have culturally adapted to new ecological challenges.

Among the dominant ethnic/racial groups in the United States, there is considerable within-group diversity related to national origin and tribal affiliation that could help researchers understand within-group differences in outcomes. For example, combining Korean Americans and Vietnamese Americans together as "Asian Americans," or Mexican Americans and Cuban Americans as "Latinos," can mask historical, language, and social class variables that may contribute to differences in outcomes among members of these groups. Researchers need to identify the national origins of participants in their ethnic/racial sample, and recognize any cultural and sociodemographic variables that may contribute to within-group differences.

The complexity of diversity means that some children of color either belong to two or more ethnic/racial groups or claim an identity that is not consistent with our ethnic/racial categorization system based primarily on color. For example, many biracial children, despite a phenotype of color, claim the ethnic/ racial identity (and cultures) of both their colored and white parents. In other cases, children of color may claim an ethnic identity not typically associated with their phenotype. Thus, some Afro-Latinos from Puerto Rico or the Dominican Republic may self-identify as Latinos, whereas they are identified as African American on the basis their skin color. Researchers need to allow children and families of color to self-identify rather than to assume membership in a racial/ethnic group on the basis of phenotype or surname.

Many children of immigrant families learn English as their second language. Although many speak English at school, they may not be proficient in literacy skills such as reading and writing (Gandara, 1997; Hakuta, Butler, & Witt, 2000). It is imperative to obtain information about children's English language proficiency if they come from homes where parents are immigrants. One in five children in this country comes from homes where at least one parent is an immigrant (U.S. Census Bureau, 2002).

Sample specification should include information on social class, group density, and region of the country, as these variables can impact on within-group differences in outcomes. Social class, based on education and income, can differentiate members of a group sharing a common ethnic/racial identity. Social class can impact cultural orientations in counterintuitive directions, such as higher social class Mexican Americans engaging in more familism (Keefe & Padilla, 1987) and less utilization of professional child-care centers (Buriel & Hurtado-Ortiz, 2000). Due to immigration and mobility, regions of the country are experiencing population booms involving new groups of people of color, such as the influx of Latinos into the South and the Northeast. Because these new groups are acculturating in unfamiliar environments, lacking high densities of same-group members and familiar social supports, their acculturation pathways and outcomes may be different from those of group members in other parts of the country. Geographic location is also important to consider in research with mixed-race populations. As Root (1999) notes, for example, being Asian American and growing up in Honolulu is a different experience than growing up in Los Angeles or Minneapolis. Finally, researchers should take advantage of the natural experiments arising from immigration that produce emic- or group-specific behaviors that have not been considered in traditional developmental theories and models (Buriel, 2003; Parke, 2004b). Examples of research in this vein include children who interpret for their immigrant parents (Buriel, Perez, DeMent, Chavez, & Moran, 1998), Chinese-American reconstruals of the meaning of authoritative parenting as a form of training (Chao, 1994), and a heightened sense of family obligation among children of immigrants (Fuligni, Tseng, & Lam, 1999).

These diverse conceptual and methodological issues represent distal and proximal ecological factors impacting on the lives of children and families of color.

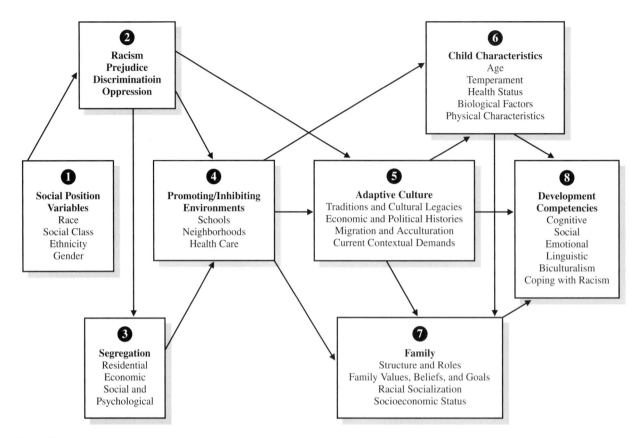

Figure 8.4   Integrative model for the study of developmental competence in minority children. *Source:* "An Integrative Model for the Study of Developmental Competencies in Minority Children," by C. Garcia-Coll et al., 1996, *Child Development, 67,* pp. 1891–1914.

Garcia Coll et al. (1996) have provided a conceptual model for studying developmental competencies in children of color that includes many of the ecological factors presented here (see Figure 8.4). This model outlines relevant sociocultural and demographic variables and their contribution to child outcomes.

Acculturation and Assimilation in U.S. Society

European immigrants to the United States at the turn of the past century underwent acculturation and assimilation in their transformation into European Americans. Acculturation is a process of learning the language, values, and social competencies of the larger society. Assimilation is a possible outcome of acculturation that involves the replacement of the ancestral culture with the culture of the host society (Ramirez, 1983). As European immigrants and their descendants acculturated and replaced their immigrant culture with the mainstream culture, and were accepted as Americans by the larger society, they achieved assimilation. For most European immigrants, the process of

assimilation was completed by the second generation. Assimilation was motivated both by the desire to become part of the mainstream and to eliminate societal discrimination against ethnic immigrants (A. Portes & Rumbaut, 1990). Assimilation was aided by their European phenotype, which they shared with members of the larger society, who were themselves descendants of earlier English and German immigrants. Although ethnicity persists in varying degrees among assimilated European Americans, it is largely a symbolic ethnicity or an optional vestigial attachment to a few ethnic symbols that impose little cost on everyday life (Waters, 1990).

Racial, ethnic, and cultural variation from the European American mainstream remain enduring issues for peoples of non-European descent, including American Indians, Latinos, African Americans, and Asian Americans. Although these groups have been in contact with European Americans for centuries, and have acculturated to varying degrees, they have not assimilated. The non-European phenotype of these groups (and other group markers related to physiognomy, religion, and social class) heightens awareness of their racial and ethnic "otherness," that is associated with beliefs about their behaviors. Often, these beliefs are stereotypes that disparage the lives and cultures of ethnic/racial minorities and limit access to European American society (Padilla & Perez, 2003). According to some theorists, these forms of racism elicit reactionary behaviors that eventually become incorporated as part of the minority group's culture. Ogbu (1991) describes the tendency of some "caste-like" minorities to develop secondary cultural characteristics that include an oppositional identity against the achievement values of European Americans. Jones (2003) theorizes that "Culture can be defined as both an antecedent and consequent of behavior" (p. 282), and as a result, "Reactions to racial biases and stereotypes *produce* the very racial differences that the stereotypes presuppose" (p. 282). As individual members of ethnic minority groups internalize European Americans' stereotypes (Buriel & Vasquez, 1982), they may lead to self-fulfilling prophecies. Steele's (1997) research on stereotype threat describes this situation with African Americans in test-taking situations. Racial stereotyping can also negatively affect young African American children's occupational aspirations (Bigler, Averhart, & Liben, 2003).

Socialization of Children of Color

As with most children, the socialization of children of color usually takes place in a family setting that includes adult caregivers. These adult caregivers are usually biological parents but may include grandparents, relatives, godparents, and other adults who are not biologically related to the children. In some Mexican immigrant families, older children have responsibility for the care and conduct of younger siblings (Valdes, 1996). In addition to ensuring children's physical health and survival, parents attempt to inculcate in children values and behaviors that help them adapt to their environment as it is perceived by the parents. The parents' history of interaction with the larger sociocultural context, including their awareness of their ethnic/racial group's history in the larger society, affects the manner in which they socialize their children. An important dimension of socialization in ethnic minority families is teaching children how to interact effectively in dual cultural contexts; the context of their ethnic/racial group and the context of the larger European American society (Boykin & Toms,

1985). Harrison et al. (1990) have adopted an ecological orientation that views the socialization of ethnic/racial minority children by the interconnectedness between the status of ethnic/racial minority families, adaptive strategies, socialization goals, and child outcomes. Family status involves socioeconomic resources available to group members such as housing, employment, health care, and education. Despite considerable within-group diversity in SES, a growing number of ethnic minority children live in poverty (National Center for Children in Poverty, 2000). Adaptive strategies are the cultural patterns that promote the survival and well-being of group members. Some of these cultural patterns are adaptations of the original ethnic/racial culture to life circumstances in the United States. Other cultural patterns may arise as a result of coping with the conflicting behavioral demands of being an ethnic/racial minority in a predominately European American society. Thus, biculturalism, which is the simultaneous adoption of two cultural orientations, arose originally in response to conflicting cultural demands but is now part of what constitutes the ethnic minority/racial culture. Biculturalism, for example, characterizes the lives of many Mexican American and other ethnic/racial minorities (LaFromboise, Coleman, & Gerton, 1993). In addition to family extendedness and biculturalism, other adaptive strategies include role flexibilities and ancestral worldviews. Emerging out of the adaptive strategies of adults are the socialization goals that they endeavor to inculcate in children to help them meet the ecological challenges they will face as ethnic/racial minorities. Ethnic/racial pride and interdependence are two socialization goals that enable ethnic/racial minority children to function competently as members of both their minority and majority cultures (Harrison et al., 1990). Ethnic/racial pride imparts a sense of personal self-worth in the face of societal prejudice and discrimination (Walker, Taylor, McElroy, Phillip, & Wilson, 1995). Interdependence sustains effective intergroup relations that strengthen ethnic/racial group solidarity (Staples & Johnson, 1993).

Families of Color

Between 1990 and 2000, all groups of people of color increased in size, whereas the number of Whites decreased from 80% to 75% of the U.S. population (U.S. Bureau of the Census, 2000). The percentage of African Americans and American Indians rose slightly from 12.1% to 12.3% and from 0.8% to 0.9%, respectively.

Asian Americans and Latinos had the greatest population increases in the past decade, growing from 2.8% to 3.6% and 9.0% to 12.5%, respectively. Latinos now are the largest minority group in the nation and account for more than half of all new births in California (Richardson & Fields, 2003). Whites have a higher median age and a smaller percentage of children under the age of 18 (37.7 years and 23.5%, respectively) than all groups of people of color: African Americans (30.2 years and 31.4%, respectively); American Indians (28 years and 33.9%, respectively); Asian Americans (32.7 years and 24%, respectively); and Latinos (25.8 years and 35%, respectively; U.S. Census Bureau, 2002). This demographic shift is visible in public schools where nationally approximately 40% of students in kindergarten through 12th grade are children of color (Young, 2002).

The growth of the Asian American and Latino populations was due in large measure to increases in immigration. Overall, foreign-born persons constitute 56 million people with more than half coming from Latin America and a quarter from Asia. In 1997, the majority (61%) of Asian Americans were born in foreign countries (U.S. Bureau of the Census, 1999; 2001b). As immigrant groups, Latinos and Asian Americans share common characteristics, including diverse subpopulations with distinct histories, non-English native languages, and relatively young age. Both groups include economic immigrants who seek a better quality of life and political immigrants who seek refuge from persecution in their countries of origin. Owing to their different motivations for immigration, economic and political immigrants may have different adaptation strategies that influence their socialization goals. For example, compared to economic immigrants, adult political immigrants expecting to return to their countries of origin may be more discouraging of their children's acculturation in areas such as individualism and autonomy (Rumbaut, 1995).

The influx of Latino and Asian immigrants into this country means that these two groups will be constantly characterized by within-group differences in generational status and degree of acculturation. First-generation immigrant parents generally acculturate more slowly than their children (Szapocznik & Kurtines, 1980), particularly after the onset of children's schooling. Yet, despite the more rapid acculturation of children in immigrant families, the socialization of these children is heavily influenced by the socialization goals of their parents' culture and the adaptive strategies developed by immigrants in this country. As the children of immigrants start their own families, their children, the third generation, are socialized in family ecologies that are socioculturally distinct from the ecologies of their parents. The generational status of parents and children contributes to variations in the ecologies of families that have implications for child rearing (Buriel, 1993b). The importance of generational status to diversity in family ecologies is illustrated with an example using Mexican Americans.

Generational Differences in Family Ecologies

The first generation includes those persons born in Mexico who later immigrated to the United States. Some immigrate as single young adults or as married couples, whereas others are brought to this country as young children by their parents. Some parents immigrate with only some of their children, leaving the other children in Mexico under the care of relatives. As the parents' economic condition improves, children are brought to the United States. These children often experience multiple socializing influences in both Mexico and the United States. This transnational socialization experience may also give rise to a dual frame of reference for these parents and children (Perez, 2004; Valenzuela, 1999) that shapes how they perceive opportunities in the United States. At the time of immigration, adults have usually completed the extent of their formal education in Mexico, 7 years on average (Bean, Chapa, Berg, & Sowards, 1994), which is 1 year over compulsory education in Mexico. School-age immigrant children have usually begun their schooling in Mexico and then continue it in this country. Children with prior schooling in Mexico often achieve higher academic levels in U.S. schools relative to native-born Mexican Americans (Padilla & Gonzalez, 2001; Valenzuela, 1999). Preschool immigrant children begin and complete their schooling in the United States. Because these children's formative years are spent in the United States, they are often referred to as the "one and a half" generation. Family income is typically low in the first generation due to parents' lower education and limited knowledge of English. In the first 6 to 8 years after immigration, it is not uncommon for immigrants to live with families of relatives or friends (Blank, 1993; Chavez, 1990) who assist parents with child care. After 8 years, the rate of immigrant families living in single family households is about 75%, which is the same as for U.S. Mexican Americans (Blank, 1993). First-generation children are socialized in home environments influenced by immigrant Mexican culture, which includes elements of Mexican culture, as well as the adaptive strategies of parents associated with the immigrant experience that parents convert into socialization goals (Buriel, 1993b; Delgado-Gaitan, 1994; Valdes, 1996). Elements of Mexican cultural socialization include familism, respect for adults, and interdependence among family and ethnic group members (Delgado-Gaitan, 1994; Rueschenberg & Buriel, 1989). Socialization goals related to the immigrant experience are self-reliance, productive use of time (Buriel, 1993b), and biculturalism (Buriel, 1993a). Immigrant parents and their children both prefer a Mexican ethnic identity (Buriel & Cardoza, 1993), and use Spanish as their primary home language. The parents' and other family members' exposure to English often comes through children's participation in the U.S. schooling system. As a result, many immigrant children serve as interpreters or "cultural brokers" for their parents, which means they are often given adultlike responsibility when acting as the family's representative to the outside English-speaking world. Child cultural brokers play an important role in helping immigrant families adapt and survive in a new environment.

The second generation represents the U.S. born children of immigrant parents. The family environments of these children are in many ways similar to those of their first-generation peers owing to the foreign-born status of their parents. There are some important differences between the two generations that are reflected in the sociocultural characteristics of the family. In some cases, the immigrant parents of second-generation children came to the United States as single young adults who later became partners in generationally endogamous marriages (Murguia, 1982). As a result, they have lived longer in the United States. In those cases where these parents came from Mexico as young children, they may have attended U.S. schools for some or all of their education. Cultural synergisms are most apparent in the families of second-generation children. Thus, although Spanish is usually the native language of second-generation children, English becomes their dominant language after the onset of schooling. However, Spanish continues as the primary language of parents, which creates a strong motivation for the development of bilingualism. Parents strongly encourage the learning of English (Esposito, 2004) but also stress the retention of Spanish as it is the language used to demonstrate respect to adults. Retention of Spanish may help to preserve parental au-

thority during the more rapid acculturation of children. Socialization of first- and second-generation children is similar, particularly in areas such as respect for adults, *personalismo* (Valdes, 1996), and family obligation (Fuligni et al., 1999). The academic achievement of the second generation is often higher than the third generation (Rodriguez, 2002). The second generation's life-long exposure to European American culture impacts on their child-rearing practices as adults. For example, the longer families live in the United States, the more socialization practices and child behavior shift in an individualistic direction, particularly in the area of critical thinking (Delgado-Gaitan, 1994). In the area of ethnic identity, foreign-born parents prefer a Mexican identity, whereas their second-generation children prefer either a Mexican American or Chicano identity (Buriel & Cardoza, 1993). Individuals calling themselves Chicano are more likely to be aware of prejudice against Mexican Americans, and to work through political avenues to improve the status of their group.

The third generation refers collectively to all persons of Mexican descent whose parents were born in the United States. This includes persons in the fourth and subsequent generations whose grandparents and great grandparents were born in this country. Due to immigration and birth rate differences between generations, third-generation children are in the minority in the Mexican American population (Edmonston & Passel, 1994). The third generation is distinguished from previous generations by the absence of any direct parental links to Mexico involving immigration. Consequently, socialization goals derived from immigrant adaptation strategies are not a direct part of the socialization experiences of these children (Buriel, 1993b). Nevertheless, because many members of this generation live in ethnic neighborhoods (barrios) populated by immigrants, socialization practices retain some immigrant influences. For example, familism, or the expectation of support from family members, continues as a socialization goal into later generations (Keefe & Padilla, 1987) even after controlling for SES (Sabogal et al., 1987). Persons in this generation are also socialized in homes where all family members are U.S. citizens, where English is the primary language (Lopez, 1982), where parental schooling has taken place exclusively in the United States, and where children and parents express a Mexican American ethnic identity (Buriel & Cardoza, 1993). Laosa (1982) theorizes that U.S. schooling alters the child-rearing practices of Mexican American parents. Mothers with less education, who are likely to be immigrants, use more modeling to instruct children, whereas mothers with more schooling, who are likely to be native born, use more inquiry and praise to instruct children. This shift in teaching style occurs because more highly schooled mothers adopt the teaching style of school, which emphasizes inquiry and praise. Buriel (1993b) also found that among parents of third-generation children, parental schooling was associated with a child-rearing style involving more support, control, and equality. Divorce is more common among parents of third-generation children, which has implications for child socialization (Buriel, 1993b; Oropesa & Landale, 1995). Teacher ratings of Mexican American children indicate more school maladjustment in boys from single-parent (mothers only) homes than in boys from two-parent homes or in girls of either family type (LeCorgne & Laosa, 1976). Although family incomes are higher in the third generation, schooling outcomes are often lower than in the previous generation. Second-generation children complete more years of schooling and have higher educational aspirations than their third-generation peers (Buriel, 1987, 1994; Valenzuela, 1999).

Acculturation.   Researchers have focused on the construct of acculturation in an effort to unpackage the cultural components of generational status that account for within-group diversity. Acculturation is the process of learning a new culture and is typically measured by increasing English proficiency, English media preferences, and European American friendships (Cuellar, Arnold, & Maldonado, 1995). Recently, the measurement of acculturation has included culturally related values, attitudes, and identity in acknowledgment of the multidimensional nature of this construct (Felix-Ortiz de la Garza, Newcomb, & Meyers, 1995). Multidimensional measures can provide information about the cultural processes associated with behavioral changes in immigrant groups, both within and across generations. The relative predictive power of generation and acculturation varies with the constructs under investigation. For example, acculturation may be a better predictor of ethnic identity than generation (Cuellar, Nyberg, Maldonado, & Roberts, 1997), whereas generation is a better predictor of students' academic achievement (Fuligni, 1997; Padilla & Gonzalez, 2001).

The developmental and socialization outcomes associated with generation and acculturation also have relevance for other U.S. ethnic/racial groups not typically included in the category of immigrants. Landrine and Klonoff (1996) suggested that acculturation is useful for deconstructing race and reviving culture among African Americans, and have developed an African American acculturation scale. In addition, African American families moving from the ghetto into a predominately European American neighborhood may describe their experiences as having to adapt or acculturate to an all-White environment. The same set of experiences may also hold true for American Indian families moving off the reservation to live in a mostly non-Indian environment or for American Indian children attending government boarding schools off their reservation (Garcia Coll, Meyer, & Brillon, 1995).

Acculturation across generations is not a uniform process. In each generation, there is considerable diversity in individuals' involvement with both native and European American culture. In addition, acculturation is not a unidirectional process such that movement toward European American culture is necessarily associated with a corresponding loss of the native culture. Ecological variables such as degree of societal discrimination, educational and employment opportunities, and opportunities to participate in the native culture can all contribute to variations in both the rate and direction of acculturation across generations.

Bicultural Adaptation

For Mexican Americans, the proximity of Mexico and the fact that the southwestern United States was once a part of Mexico create many opportunities for members of this group to participate in their native culture. For Latinos and Asian Americans, a high rate of immigration resulting in densely populated ethnic communities also creates powerful environmental influences for retention of many aspects of the native cultures. Finally, for all ethnic/racial minorities, a non-European phenotype triggers many societal stereotypes and prejudices that limit access to the larger society (Buriel, 1994). Padilla and Perez (2003) argue that a darker phenotype stigmatizes individuals, making it harder and even less desirable for them to acculturate. The combination of these environmental and ethnic/racial group influences differentially operate within and between groups, giving rise to adaptation strategies that do not conform to the assimilationist orientation of European immigrants. Instead, many ethnic/racial minority group members strive for a bicultural orientation that allows for selective acculturation to European American culture while simultaneously retaining aspects of the native culture. This bidirectional adaptation strategy permits individuals to meet the dual cultural expectations that characterize the lives of ethnic/racial minorities as they move in and out of minority and majority cultural environments. The bicultural person learns to function optimally in more than one cultural context and to switch repertoires of behavior appropriately and adaptively as called for by the situation (Harrison et al., 1990). Although all ethnic/racial minority groups have expressed biculturalism in some form as an adaptive strategy (Harrison et al., 1990), most research has focused on immigrant groups, especially Mexican Americans (Chun & Akutsu, 2003; Chun, Balls Organista, & Marin, 2003).

Using Mexican Americans as an example, Figure 8.5 illustrates a bidirectional model of cultural adaptation. This bidirectional model posits four acculturation adaptation styles for Mexican immigrants and their descendants, depending on their involvement with both Mexican immigrant culture and European American culture. The four acculturation styles are: (1) the bicultural orientation, (2) the Mexican orientation, (3) the marginal orientation, and (4) the European American orientation. Ramirez (1983) has defined biculturalism as the simultaneous adoption of the language, values, and social competencies of two cultures. Because culture is multidimensional in nature, involvement in either culture can vary along different dimensions and at different rates. Cultural involvement is represented on a scale of 1 to 5. Thus, persons expressing a bicultural orientation are those above 3 in both Mexican and European American culture. The Mexican orientation is characterized by those individuals who are primarily involved in Mexican culture. This category usually includes many adult recent immigrants, as well as a few later-generation persons living in rural areas.

Also included in this category are the elderly parents of immigrants who are brought to this country to live with the families of their adult children after the children become financially stable. For the elderly, a Mexican orientation seems well suited to their life experiences, which at their stage in life, revolves around family and community rather than schooling and the workplace. The marginal orientation includes a minority of individuals who have become "deculturated" (Berry, 1980) from their ancestral culture and simultaneously alienated from European American society. Deculturation arises from society's denigration of the ethnic/racial group and the internalization of society's stereotypes of the group (Buriel, 1984). Ogbu's (1987) description of Mexican Americans (as well as American Indians and African Americans) as caste-like minorities is probably accurate only for the minority of individuals who adopt a marginal orientation. For example, Vigil (1988) has described hard-core Mexican American gang members in terms characteristic of the marginal orientation. Non-gang members are described as expressing either a traditional or bicultural orientation. Individuals in the European American quadrant of the bidirectional model are those who are primarily involved and identified with European American culture; their preference for friends, language, and social activities are those characteristic of European American culture.

To date, most empirical research on acculturation and biculturalism has been done with adult and adolescent samples. More research is needed with young children to better understand the developmental pathways to bicultural competency (Buriel, 1993a). Some research indicates that ethnic/racial minorities who develop bicultural competencies have better physical and psychological health than those who do not (Buriel & Saenz, 1980; Chun et al., 2003; LaFromboise, Coleman, & Gerton, 1993). Gutierrez and Sameroff (1990) found that mothers' biculturalism is positively associated with the complexity of their concepts about children's development and that more acculturated and more bicultural mothers scored higher in their concepts of development.

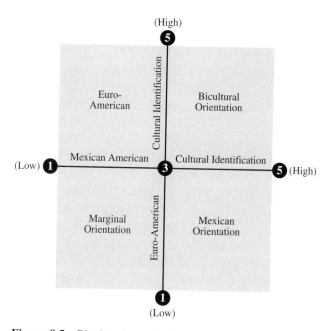

Figure 8.5 Bicultural model of acculturation.

Mothers who were the most bicultural had the highest concept of development scores when compared to the other Mexican American mothers and a sample of highly acculturated European American mothers. They concluded that bicultural mothers have insights into two cultures and realize that child development beliefs associated with each culture are appropriate in different contexts in the same society. LaFromboise et al. (1993) connect biculturalism to self-efficacy theory (Bandura, 1977) by using the term *bicultural efficacy* to describe the belief, or confidence, that one can live effectively, and in a satisfying manner, in two cultural groups without compromising one's sense of identity.

Emic Developmental Research Issues

Immigrants and their children face many sociocultural adaptation challenges that have implications for parenting and child development. Psychology's interest in immigrant groups has generally been threefold. First, to document between-group differences in constructs and measures developed on European American populations (Ramirez, 1983). These studies often erroneously equate race/ethnicity with culture, and conclude that differences are due to culture. A second research line attempts to extend theories, also developed on European Americans, to immigrant groups and their descendents (Parke et al., 2004). The goal is to understand how culture affects the hypothesized pattern of relationships between variables for the different groups and to adjust the theories accordingly. A third area involves identification of emic or unique aspects of a group's behavior arising from the immigrant experience itself. Three experiences common to immigrant families and children include language and cultural brokering, children as family workers, and dual frames of reference.

Language and Cultural Brokers. It is estimated that approximately one in every five children in the United States comes from a home where at least one parent is of foreign birth (Federal Interagency Forum on Child and Family Statistics, 2002). Most of these children are the first members of their families to learn English and attend U.S. schools. As a result, these children are often delegated adultlike responsibilities by their parents, such as interpreting and making decisions with English-speaking agents that affect the whole family (Chao, 2001; DeMent, Buriel, & Villanueva, 2005; Orellana, Dorner, & Pulido, 2003; Tse, 1995, 1996;

Valdes, 2003). "With responsibility as interpreters of the new culture and language, immigrant children are often in a position with no one to translate or interpret for them. Traditional intergenerational authority relationships change and the child also becomes very involved in the worries and concerns of the family, such as hassles with landlords, arranging for medical care, and dealing with the legal system" (Olsen & Chen, 1988, p. 31). Children who serve as interpreters for their non-English speaking parents are referred to as "language brokers." Because these children of immigrants represent the link between their parents' culture and European American society, they can also be considered "cultural brokers."

Child cultural brokers are unique because in addition to the stress related to their own acculturation, they experience additional stressors arising from their role as mediators between their parents and U.S. society. In public, child cultural brokers act with adult authority on behalf of their parents, but at home they are expected to behave as children and show deference and respect to parents. These conflicting expectations and responsibilities represent a form of role strain that may raise children's anxiety to debilitating levels and lower their general well-being. The stress connected to language brokering may be particularly pronounced among young children because their cognitive and social capacities are still in the early stages of development (Weisskirch & Alva-Alatorre, 2002). However, among adolescents, there is little evidence that language brokering is associated with psychological distress (Buriel, Love, & DeMent, in press), particularly among girls. In some groups, such as Mexican Americans, language brokering seems to be associated more with the gender role responsibilities of girls (Buriel et al., in press). In addition, a strong affective parent-child bond buffers adolescents against stress connected to language brokering (Buriel et al., in press).

Language brokers act as adults in interactions with their parents, which often gives rise to role reversals involving the transmission of information. Language brokers must sometimes teach parents things about the new culture while still demonstrating deference and respect consistent with their status as children. Child language brokers must assume a higher-status teaching role without causing parents to lose face in public or in the family. The instructional demands inherent in brokering are thus likely to promote instructional strategies by children that achieve the transmission of information to adults without causing embarrassment to parents. Based on her in-depth study, Valdes (2003) concluded that parent and child act as a team in a language brokering situation "to present the impression of the parent that will be most effective in a given context and that will evoke positive responses from majority individuals" (p. 96). Drawing on Gardner's theory of multiple intelligences, Valdes (2003) argues that competent language brokers exhibit multiple types of cognitive, social, and interpersonal intelligences and should therefore be considered "gifted." Buriel et al. (1998) found that among Latino adolescents, more language brokering was associated with greater biculturalism and more social self-efficacy. Children who broker in diverse settings such as stores, banks, hospitals, and schools have more opportunities to develop accelerated linguistic, cognitive, and interpersonal skills and have higher school grades.

Tse (1995) notes that unlike formal translators, language brokers sometime influence the content and nature of the messages they convey between adult parties. They sometimes favorably paraphrase messages between teachers and their parents. In addition, given their greater knowledge of U.S. culture, language brokers are often assigned responsibility for making decisions with English-speaking agents that affect the entire family (DeMent et al., 2005; Olsen & Chen, 1988). Thus, as a result of the language-brokering role, there is the potential for the modification of traditional intergenerational authority relationships in immigrant families. However, the strong sense of family obligation in immigrant families (Fuligni, Tseng, & Lam, 1999) may mitigate the threat to authority relationships. Rather than threatening parental authority, greater language brokering is associated with a stronger parent-child bond (Buriel et al., in press).

Children as Family Workers.   Family obligation and duty to family are strong values among immigrant children from collectivist cultures (Fuligni et al., 1999). The operationalization of these values often takes the form of young children devoting time assisting parents in their occupations. This assistance, however, is viewed not so much as helping parents as much as contributing to the welfare of the entire family. These work-related situations involve shared parent-child activities that can influence children's perceptions and values about work, family relations, and gender roles.

In addition to household chores, children in immigrant families often assume adultlike responsibilities as workers whose labor is beneficial, and sometimes essential, to the financial well-being of the family (Orellana, 2001). Many immigrants work in manual and service labor occupations where it is not unusual to "bring children along" to help with the work and make extra money. In the past, when Mexican immigrants were involved mostly in agricultural labor, children often worked in the fields with their parents. This situation still exists today, especially during summers, but at a lesser scale due to child labor laws. More typical today, however, is the situation of children working with parents in service and manual labor sectors in jobs such as masonry, gardening and landscaping, painting, construction, cleaning, restaurants, street vending, auto shops, and cottage industries pertaining to garment work and food preparation.

The constructs of parent involvement, family cohesion, and parent-child bonding are typically examined in the context of routine domestic activities and recreation experiences. However, for many immigrant families, economic survival creates roles for children that may promote parental involvement and contribute to family cohesion and parent-child bonding in work-related settings. From a social learning perspective, children in family worker roles may have more opportunities to develop personal responsibility, autonomy, and self-efficacy by observing and modeling their parents in work-related activities. The topic of children as family workers is an area arising from the immigrant experience that deserves further attention.

Dual Frames of Reference.   The immigrant adaptation experience may give rise to a dual frame of reference that allows immigrant children to compare their socioeconomic and cultural status in the United States to their past situation in their country of origin. A dual frame of reference has been discussed in various contexts as an enabling quality that gives foreign-born children higher expectations and feelings of positive self-worth relative to their native-born counterparts (Ogbu, 1991; Suarez-Orozco & Suarez-Orozco, 1995). Although economically poor by U.S. standards, the families of immigrant children experience an immediate increase in their SES on arriving in this country, leading to a relative interpretation of their deprivation. This can bolster the family's sense of optimism and expectations for the future. For example, many immigrant children are frequently exhorted by their parents to take advantage of the opportunities in this country, including education (Perez, 2004; Valenzuela, 1999), and constantly reminded of the hard economic conditions they left behind in their native country. A dual frame of reference may buffer children against the psychologically damaging effects of societal prejudice and discrimination. By having been raised in a culturally supportive environment in their native country, immigrant children have a frame of reference to counter the often negative stereotypes ascribed to many immigrant groups in this country (Buriel & Vasquez, 1982; Perez, 2004). A dual frame of reference represents a useful psychological mechanism for understanding generational differences in school achievement, motivation, and feelings of self-worth.

Socialization Concerns in Ethnic Minority Families

African American Families. Today, approximately 96% of all African Americans are descendants of enslaved people (Reed, 1982) who exhibited extraordinary resiliency to survive in this country without benefit of any human rights. The socially disruptive effects of slavery were felt in all spheres of life, including family formation and functioning. According to M. Wilson (1992), the focus on African American family research has shifted from a pathological/disorganizational model to a strength/resilient model. This shift is characterized by (a) an examination of African Americans in an African American sociocultural context, (b) a consideration of the role of grandmothers and other extended family members in child-rearing activities, and (c) an analysis of the presence of fathers rather than their absence in the family. To this list can be added the role of grandfathers in the transmission of family values and beliefs (McWright, 2002).

"The African American family is a term used to characterize a group of people who are biologically and spiritually bonded or connected and whose members' relations to each other and the outside world are governed by a particular set of cultural beliefs, historical experiences and behavioral practices" (Nobles, Goddard, Cavil, & George, 1987, p. 22). Sudarkasa (1993) notes that to understand African American families, households, and children, it is important to understand that these groupings evolved from an African family structure where coresidential families were the norm. The type and quality of adaptations to enslave-

ment and life in America were perhaps facilitated by the West African heritage of African Americans. From her studies of West African culture, she contends that African extended-family traditions may have proved useful in preserving family ties and for the socialization of children in the face of the disruptive aspects of slavery and its aftermath. Characteristics of African American extended-kin systems include: (a) a high degree of geographical propinquity; (b) a strong sense of family and familial obligations; (c) fluidity of household boundaries, with great willingness to absorb relatives, both real and fictive; (d) frequent interaction with relatives; (e) frequent extended-family get-togethers for special occasions and holidays; and (f) a system of mutual aid (Harrison et al., 1990; Hatchett & Jackson, 1993). Some may surmise that extended-kin behavior among African Americans is a response to poverty rather than an authentic cultural characteristic of the group. However, higher-SES African Americans have greater activity within-kin networks than their lower-SES counterparts (H. McAdoo, 1978). This suggests that higher-SES African Americans continue to derive physical and psychological benefits from these behaviors. Boykin (1983; Boykin & Toms, 1985) has noted similarities between the West African traditions of spirituality, harmony, affect, and communalism and African American culture.

The influence of the extended family among African Americans is important because of the large number of female-headed households that require child-rearing assistance and economic support (M. Wilson, 1992). The proportion of African American households with elderly heads that have young family members is also high, numbering about one in three families (Pearson, Hunter, Ensminger, & Kellam, 1990). When coupled with the fact that many African American grandparents live in close proximity to their married children and families, African American grandparents have many opportunities to influence the development of their grandchildren. Pearson et al. (1990) found that in multigenerational households, mothers were the primary caregivers, followed by grandmothers and then fathers. Grandmothers also showed more supportive behaviors in mother-grandmother families than in mother-father-grandmother families. In mother-absent families, grandmothers were more involved in control and punishment of children. Tolson and Wilson (1990) found that the presence of grandmothers in African American families increases the moral-religious emphasis in the household. Nobles et al. (1987) note that such religious emphasis helps to sustain the African American family and reinforce the sense of family and family solidarity. Although some research suggests that children are better adjusted in grandmother households (Staples & Johnson, 1993), other research suggests that intergenerational conflict may offset the positive effects of grandmother presence. Using systematic observation measures, Wakschlag, Chase-Lansdale, and Brooks-Gunn (1996), found that mothers whose interactions with their *own* mothers were characterized by an open, flexible, and autonomous style, provided their children with more competent parenting. In addition, grandmother directness (e.g., nonconfrontational or assertive maturity demands) was positively related to problem parenting, whereas grandmother emotional closeness was negatively associated with problematic parenting. These results were strongest when the mother and grandmother were not living together, suggesting that intergenerational modeling effects of parenting may occur more readily from a distance. In a compensatory situation where mothers must live with grandmothers, shared child rearing may contribute to tensions between the two adults, which may have negative implications for children. In situations where fathers live with mothers and grandmothers, paternal involvement with caregiving activities is associated with positive relationships with mothers and grandmothers (Krishnakumar & Black, 2003). When grandmothers reported a positive relationship with both mother and father, the mother reported a positive relationship with the father, leading the authors to suggest that grandmothers may play a gatekeeping role in these intergenerational families (Krishnakumar & Black, 2003).

The role of grandfathers has also begun to receive attention. Given that two-parent households were the plurality in the African American community before 1980, many grandfathers are currently involved in the socialization of grandchildren. In a study of the transmission of family values through the use of proverbs, McWright (2002) found that grandfathers' influence was greatest in the area of family connectedness.

Male-present households were the norm in poor African American communities in the period between 1880 and 1925 (Staples & Johnson, 1993). Until the 1980s, most African American families included two parents; today, approximately 35% of all African American children live in two-parent families (U.S. Census Bureau, 1998). According to R. Hill (1988), this decline occurred as the result of economic recessions in the 1970s, which were experienced as depressions in the African American community. Despite the statistical norm of two-parent families until recently, most research on African American fathers focused either on fathers' absence or their maladaptive responses to familial roles (Bowman, 1993). More research is beginning to focus on African American husband/fathers who remain with their families and document their high level of involvement in child rearing, family decision making, as well as the economic provider. J. McAdoo (1993) notes that African American spouses share equally in the major decisions in the family. From an exchange theory perspective, cooperation in decision making has been essential because in most families both spouses have had to work to overcome the lower wages earned by the husband (J. McAdoo, 1993.).

Previous research suggests that persistent economic marginality among African American fathers may lessen their perceptions of the quality of family life and contribute to their separation from their families (Farley & Allen, 1987; W. Wilson, 1987). Bowman (1993) has adopted a role strain model to investigate how African American males perceive economic marginality and how cultural resources facilitate adaptive coping. Subjective cultural strengths, which are transmitted across generations, appear to reduce harmful effects of provider role barriers among husband-fathers and to facilitate coping. African American husband/fathers were much more likely to have jobs (75%) than unmarried fathers (58%); joblessness is a major factor distinguishing unmarried fathers from traditional husband/fathers. Education and employment opportunities are increasing the population of middle-income African American families. However, research with such families is lagging. Due to discrimination, middle-income African American parents face difficulties not encountered by affluent parents of some other racial groups. According to Strom and colleagues (2000), affluent fathers who grew up in low-income areas teach children to distinguish between right and wrong and to expect punishment for breaking rules. As a result, adolescents saw their fathers as overly strict and seldom or never patient. Interestingly, fathers agreed with their children's assessment. Smetana and Chuang (2001) also found that middle-class parents rated limiting adolescents' behavior as more important than encouraging independence, suggesting that parents view firm limits necessary to maintain social order given their particular social ecology.

Working-class African American fathers use more physical than verbal discipline and deliver it in accordance to the transgression's consequences rather than the child's intent (Staples & Johnson, 1993). Although these parents use physical discipline, they rarely couple this with withdrawal of love from children, which may eliminate some of the anxiety and resentment associated with this method. Because African American socialization stresses obedience to adults and physical discipline, parents have often been described as harsh, rigid, and strict (P. Portes, Dunham, & Williams, 1986). The disciplinary style of African American parents is sometimes referred to as being parent centered rather than child centered because it does not focus on the desires of the child (Kelley, Power, & Wimbush, 1992). These descriptions fail to take into account the settings in which parents raise children and the adaptive value of this approach to child rearing. Growing up in dangerous neighborhoods brings with it greater risks for involvement in antisocial behavior. Under these circumstances, strict obedience to parental authority is an adaptive strategy that parents may endeavor to maintain through physical discipline (Dodge, McLoyd, & Lansford, 2005; Kelley et al., 1992). This disciplinary method may also serve to impress on children the importance of following rules in society and the consequences incurred from breaking those rules when one is a member of an ethnic/racial group that is unfairly stereotyped as violent (Willis, 1992). There is considerable diversity in the disciplinary methods used by African American parents. Younger mothers raising their children alone use more physical discipline. Mothers with less education use more restrictive disciplinary practices that include insensitivity, inflexibility, and inconsistent parental behavior. Mothers who are more involved in organized religion also express more child-oriented disciplinary attitudes (Kelley et al., 1992). According to Whaley (2000), African American parents' use of spanking is more a consequence rather than a cause of problem behaviors, unlike European American families where the positive association between spanking and child behavior problems is bidirectional.

An important socialization goal of many ethnic minority parents is fostering a sense of ethnic/racial pride in children (Harrison et al., 1990). Some parents believe that for their children to successfully confront the hostile social environment they will encounter as African Americans, it is necessary to teach them to be comfortable with their Blackness (Harrison, 1985; Peters, 1985). Bowman and Howard's (1985) study of a national sample of African American three-generational families indicated that the manner in which parents oriented their children toward racial barriers was a significant element in children's motivation, achievement, and prospects for upward mobility. Parents of successful children emphasized ethnic pride, self-development, awareness of racial barriers, and egalitarianism in their socialization practices. Using a national sample, Thornton, Chatters, Taylor, and Allen (1990) also report that two out of three African American parents indicate that they either spoke or acted in a manner intended to racially socialize children. African American parents envisioned racial socialization as involving messages regarding their experiences as minority group members, themes emphasizing individual character and goals, and information related to African American cultural heritage. In addition, Thornton et al. (1990), found that (a) older parents were more likely than younger parents to view racial socialization information as a necessary element of socialization; (b) that mothers were more likely than fathers to educate children about race; (c) that never-married parents both women and men, were less likely than their married counterparts to racially socialize their children; (d) that fathers in the Northeast were more likely than those in the South to racially socialize children; and (e) that mothers living in racially integrated neighborhoods were more likely to socialize their children to racial matters than were mothers living in all-African American communities. Murray and Mandara (2002) found that African American youth exposed to race empowerment strategies were higher in racial identity and self-concept than those exposed to a race-defensiveness strategy, which taught dislike of other groups and the usefulness of acting White. They conclude that, "a proactive racial socialization agenda buffers and prepares African American children to face the challenges of racial discrimination" (p. 89).

American Indian Families.   In the recent past, American Indians were known as the "Vanishing Americans." Since 1940, however, the American Indian population has increased at every census count. The Indian population was 345,000 in 1940, but in 2000 numbered over 2,400,000 American Indians and Alaskan Natives (U.S. Census Bureau, 2002). American Indians are a socioculturally diverse group consisting of over 450 distinct tribal units who speak over 100 different languages (Trimble & Medicine, 1993). Typically, American Indians prefer their tribal designation over American Indian (Burgess, 1980). The Navajo of New Mexico and Arizona are the largest tribe, with more than 170,000 members. Other large tribes include the Cherokee, the Sioux, the Chippewa, the Aleuts, and the Eskimos.

Today, approximately 70% of American Indians live off reservations (Banks, 1991), mostly in urban areas, although most research on American Indians focuses on those living on reservations. Due to cultural differences and discrimination, many American Indians have a difficult time adjusting to life in urban areas. For this reason, many reservation American Indians who migrate to urban areas tend to settle in cities and towns near reservations and to maintain contact with their family on the reservation (Banks, 1991). Such living arrangements close to the reservation are more conducive to the development of biculturalism than when Indians live in large urban areas removed from reservations. Contact with European Americans and other cultural groups, such as Latinos, has introduced changes in traditional Indian values and behaviors. Consequently, it is necessary to consider level of acculturation in research involving American Indians even though most studies with American Indians describe the tribe (e.g., Navajo or Sioux) without reference to the study participants' level of acculturation.

American Indian families may be characterized as a collective cooperative social network that extends from the mother and father union to the extended family and, ultimately, the community and tribe (Burgess, 1980). American Indian tribes are resilient in that they have withstood attempts at extermination, removal from their traditional lands, extreme poverty, removal of their children to boarding schools, loss of self-governance, and assimilationist policies aimed at destroying Indian languages, traditions, dress, religions, and occupations (Harjo, 1993). A strong extended-family system and tribal identity characterizes many urban and rural American Indian families (Harrison et al.1990). American Indian patterns of extended family include several households representing significant relatives that give rise to village-like characteristics even in urban areas. In such families, grandparents retain an official symbolic leadership role. Children seek daily contact with grandparents, who monitor children's behavior and have a voice in child rearing (Lum, 1986). Despite the many

social problems faced by these families (e.g., poverty, alcoholism, accidents, and adolescent suicide) the majority are two-parent families. In 1990, nearly 7 out of 10 American Indian families included married couples living together (U.S. Census Bureau, 1995).

Although there are variations among tribes in their value orientations, some common themes can be characterized as traditional American Indian values. These include (a) present-time orientation—a primary concern for the present and acceptance of time as fluid and not segmented; (b) respect for elders—with age comes experience that is transmitted as knowledge that is essential for group survival and harmony in life; (c) identity with group—self-awareness has meaning only in the context of the family and tribe so that the interests of the family and tribe are the same as one's own self-interest; (d) cooperation and partnership—among the Pueblo Indians a common saying is "Help each other so the burden won't be so heavy" (Suina & Smolkin, 1994, p. 121); (e) the concept of partnership is stressed as the desirable way of conducting most activities; and (f) living in harmony with nature—nature, like time, is indivisible, and the person is an integral part of the flow of nature and time.

Traditional American Indian values constitute a worldview that is fundamentally different from Western assumptions about the "proper" relationships among people, the environment, and time. Trimble and Medicine (1993) argue that in its present form, psychology cannot properly describe and explain traditional-oriented American Indian affective and behavioral patterns. A traditional-oriented American Indian worldview represents an "indigenous psychology" (U. Kim & Berry, 1993; Ramirez, 1983) that can only be understood when examined from ecological and sociohistorical perspectives that do not assume the superiority of a Western worldview. For example, in the Iroquoian language, uncles and aunts are called fathers and mothers, respectively. This naming practice implies that parenting is spread across several extended family members. Thus, the parents' primary role in tribal culture is to give children affection and support, whereas supervision and discipline are usually provided by aunts and uncles (Machamer & Gruber, 1998). This may lead to the misperception that parenting is permissive when viewed from a nuclear family perspective. When viewed from an extended family perspective, however, parenting involves both affection and the setting of limits. According to Machamer and Gruber (1998), "the loss of extended family by American Indian adolescents as a result of out-migration (from reservations) signifies the loss of a principal mechanism through which values are transmitted and accountability is learned and enforced" (p. 367). Differences in worldviews represent important theoretical, conceptual, and methodological challenges facing researchers studying American Indian populations (see Table 8.1). Methodological and ethical considerations are beginning to receive attention in the literature (Hudson & Taylor-Henley, 2001; Stubben, 2001).

In traditional-oriented Indian culture, the uses of knowledge and learning are prescribed to help individuals live fulfilling lives as fully integrated members of the family and tribe. For example, among the Navajo, knowledge is organized around three life goals. First, there is knowledge that lasts throughout one's lifetime and concerns language, kinship, religion, customs, values, beliefs, and the purpose of life (Joe, 1994). This kind of knowledge is usually taught informally and using a variety of sources. Among the Pueblo Indians, teaching and learning at this stage is thought to be the responsibility of all Pueblo members (Suina & Smolkin, 1994). The second area of knowledge involves learning an occupation or the means to making a living. This learning often requires an apprenticeship and involves a narrower range of teaching experts such as herders, weavers, and hunters. Learning is through listening, watching, and doing, with a strong emphasis placed on modeling and private practicing of the emerging skill (Suina & Smolkin, 1994). At this stage, children learn the appropriate context for the use of their knowledge. The person learns how knowledge is enmeshed with the history, culture, and survival goals of the tribe. The third category of knowledge is the most restrictive because it is reserved for those interested in becoming healers and religious leaders (Joe, 1994). These are lifetime commitments involving specialized instruction that is usually in addition to learning other means of livelihood.

Differences in the uses and value of knowledge and education have implications for the relative effectiveness of tribal schools versus public schools. Because tribal schools are embedded in a supportive cultural context, they may ameliorate the cultural conflicts in classrooms that can arise when children attend public schools

TABLE 8.1   American Indian Culture versus Dominant Culture Values

American Indian Culture	Dominant Culture
Support of large extended family	Support of, and from, immediate family
Slower, softer speech	Louder, faster speech
Avoids speaker and listener with little or no eye contact	Addressed listener directly, often by name
Interjects less	Interrupts frequently
Deep sense of humor	Light humor
Allows time for thought	Gives instant answers to questions
Nonverbal communication prized	Verbal skills highly prized
Cooperation	Competition
Group needs are most important	Personal goals are most important
Harmony with nature	Power and control of nature
Control of self not others	Control of self and others
Sharing, keep only what one needs	Material things are important
Time is here, be patient	Time is very important, get things done
Noninterference	Need to control all
Patient, allows others to go first	Aggressive and competitive
Talk about good things before criticizing	Criticism is immediate, blunt, to the point
Group-centered society; group emphasis	Individual-centered society, self-emphasis

Source: From "Working with and Conducting Research among American Indian Families," by J. D. Stubben, 2001, *American Behavioral Scientist, 44,* pp. 1466–1481. Reprinted with permission.

where they are exposed to societal values and prejudices. Wall and Madak (1991) found that students attending tribal schools felt that their parents and favorite teacher held higher educational aspirations for them than their peers in public schools. The greater family connectedness found on reservations is also positively associated with more favorable attitudes toward school and less risk-taking behavior among adolescents (Machamer & Gruber, 1998). Public schools may subscribe to academic expectations and practices that are at variance with American Indian learning styles, which can contribute to poorer achievement and lower motivation. Delpit (1995) notes that the American Indian prohibition against speaking for others makes tasks such as writing summaries or book reports difficult for some American Indian children. When given such assignments, American Indian children often prefer to write about their own experiences (Delpit, 1995) and their families' experiences, especially those of their grandparents.

The establishment of boarding schools for American Indian children, far removed from the reservation, was an attempt to destroy traditional child-rearing practices (Harjo, 1993). Between 1890 and 1920, children were forcibly removed from their families for up to 12 years, and parents and relatives were not allowed to visit children during the school year (Harjo, 1993). From 1920 to the 1970s, boarding schools were still a usual part of the childhood and adolescent experience of most American Indian children. Among the many deleterious effects of boarding schools was the deprivation of children from adult parenting models and an undermining of parental authority. Several boarding schools currently exist, although attendance is voluntary. Today, many American Indian grandparents and parents are products of government boarding schools, which impacts on the quality of their parenting. Having been deprived of a parent-child relationship during their childhood, many American Indian parents now experience problems in relations with their own children. Child abuse, particularly in the form of neglect, is cited as a major reason for the removal of Indian children from their families and tribes. American Indian children are placed out of homes at a rate five times higher than other children (Harjo, 1993; Spicer, 1998).

Two major concerns of some tribes are infant health and the child-rearing abilities of adolescents, which are critical for the tribes' survival (Berlin, 1987). American Indian teens are nearly two and a half times more likely to become pregnant before reaching their 18th birthday.

Although infant death at birth is among the lowest of any racial/ethnic group, the rate of sudden infant death syndrome (SIDS) is three times the national average. In addition, due to high rates of alcoholism, American Indian children have a 500% greater chance of being born with Fetal Alcohol Syndrome (Fuller, 2004). Indian Health Services and greater tribal self-determination in the areas of education (the Indian Self-Determination and Education Assistance Act of 1975), family life (The Indian Child Welfare Act of 1978), and culture (The American Indian Religious Freedom Act of 1978) have made it possible for some tribes to sustain healthy families and to recover traditional child-rearing practices. The role of fathers in the socialization of children, especially boys, has special implications for the survival of tribal cultural traditions. An exploratory study with Ojibwa families found a positive association between the amount of time fathers spent as primary caregivers and their sons' academic performance and social development (Williams, Radin, & Coggins, 1996). In addition, fathers with more paternal involvement also had fathers who participated more in their own upbringing. The significance of father involvement for cultural survival may arise from the expectation that as boys grow into adulthood they will assume gender-prescribed leadership roles and therefore need appropriate role models. Leadership expectations for their sons may promote greater father participation in child rearing because fathers are more involved in community leadership activities (Williams et al., 1996).

Zimmerman, Ramirez, Washienko, Walter, and Dyer (1998) have proposed an "enculturation hypothesis" to explain how involvement with American Indian culture buffers children from the negative effects of acculturation, which is associated with alcohol and substance abuse. They developed an empirically derived measure of enculturation that included, (a) cultural affinity, (b) family activities, and (c) Native American identity. In their research with Odawa and Ojibwa tribal members, they found that cultural affinity positively predicted youths' self-esteem. Youth with the highest levels of self-esteem and cultural identity had the lowest levels of alcohol and substance abuse, which was consistent with the enculturation hypothesis. Zimmerman et al. (1998) concluded that enculturation is an important protective factor for American Indian youth. The findings also have implications for preventing depression and reducing suicide, which is three times the national average among American Indian youth (Fuller, 2004).

Asian American Families. The Asian American population includes people from 28 Asian countries or ethnic groups. It is a very diverse group in terms of languages, cultures, number of generations in the United States, and reasons for immigrating to the United States. The first Asian immigrants came from China in the 1840s. However, due to discriminatory immigration policies against Asians, the number of Asian Americans remained low until recently. The growth of the Asian American population in recent years has been accompanied by shifts in ethnicity and national origin. Before 1970, Japanese Americans were the largest Asian ethnic group (41%), followed by Chinese (30%), and Filipinos (24%). Today, the largest groups, in millions, are Chinese Americans (2.7), Filipino Americans (2.4), Asian Indians (1.9), Vietnamese Americans (1.2), Korean Americans (1.2), and Japanese Americans (1.1; U.S. Census Bureau, 2002).

Historically, Japanese, Chinese, and Filipino immigrants came to the United States primarily to improve their economic status. However, Indo-Chinese have arrived primarily as political immigrants or refugees. At the end of the Vietnam War in 1975, 130,000 refugees found asylum in the United States. Beginning in 1978, a massive flow of Indo-Chinese refugees (boat people or second wave) occurred, abruptly ending in 1992 (Rumbaut, 1995). Refugees may suffer more psychological problems and have a more difficult time adjusting to life in the United States than economic immigrants. They tend to experience more undesirable change in the process of acculturation, a greater threat of danger, and a decreasing sense of control over their lives (Rumbaut, 1991).

Little research exists on the structure and process of Asian American families. Most studies have sampled from Chinese and Japanese American populations. Often, examination of Asian American families' socialization processes is for the purpose of identifying the family characteristics that contribute to children's academic performance (Huntsinger & Jose, 1995; Huntsinger, Jose, & Larson, 1998). Of late, research on the adaptive strategies and socialization goals of Asian American parents that bears on the socioemotional development of children has received more attention (see Okagaki & Bojczyk, 2002, for a review). Discussions of Asian American families usually invoke Confucian principles to explain family structure and roles. Confucius developed a hierarchy defining a person's roles, duties, and moral obligations in the state. This hierarchical structure is also applied to the family, and each member's role is dictated by age and gender. Typically, Asian American families are seen as patriarchal, with the father maintaining authority and emotional distance from other members (Ho, 1986; Wong, 1988, 1995). Traditionally, the family exerts control over family members, who are taught to place family needs before individual needs. Children show obedience and loyalty to their parents and, especially for male children, are expected to take care of elderly parents (filial piety). In many Asian countries, subjugation of personal will to elders is an indicator of maturity and persists in intergenerational relationships among Asian American adolescents (Ying, Coombs, & Lee, 1999). Confucian influences on family life are stronger in some Asian American populations (e.g., Chinese and Vietnamese) than others (e.g., Japanese) due to differences in immigration patterns and degree of Westernization of the country of origin. Length of U.S. residence and acculturation also contribute to extensive within-group differences in family structure and roles. Kibria (1993) found that large Vietnamese families varying in age and gender fared better economically than smaller nuclear families. The larger extended family enabled households to connect to a variety of social and economic resources. In Vietnamese families, the kin group is seen as more important than the individual. This perspective has its source in Confucian principles, especially ancestor worship (Kibria, 1993). Ancestor worship for Vietnamese Americans consists of devotion in caring for an altar containing pictures of deceased family members and praying at ritually prescribed times (Chao, 1992). This act affirms the sacredness, unity, and timelessness of the kin group.

Aspects of traditional Asian child-rearing practices appear to be continued by Asian American families (Uba, 1994). Studies tend to be focused primarily on characteristics of parental control. Chiu (1987) compared the child-rearing attitudes of Chinese, Chinese American, and European American mothers. Chinese mothers endorsed restrictive and controlling behavior more than Chinese American and European American mothers, and Chinese American mothers were more restrictive and controlling in their child-rearing attitudes than European American mothers. The intermediate position of Chinese American mothers suggests that their child-rearing attitudes are shifting toward European American norms due to acculturation.

Chao (1994) has argued that the traditional view of Chinese parents as authoritarian, restrictive, and controlling is misleading because these parenting behaviors do not have cross-cultural equivalence for European Americans and Chinese: these child-rearing concepts are rooted in European American culture and are not relevant for describing the socialization styles and goals of Chinese parents. "The 'authoritarian' concept has evolved from American culture and psychology that is rooted in both evangelical and Puritan religious influences" (Chao, 1994, p. 1116). Instead, Chinese parenting should be viewed from the concepts of *chiao shun* and *guan*. *Chiao shun* means "training" or "teaching in appropriate behaviors." Parents and teachers are responsible for training children by exposing them to examples of proper behavior and limiting their view of undesirable behaviors. However, training in the European American sense is conceptualized as strict discipline. This is not the case for Chinese, for whom training is accomplished in the context of a supportive and concerned parent or teacher. The word *guan* means "to govern," "to care for or to love," and parental care and involvement is seen as an aspect of *guan*. Thus, control and governance have positive connotations for the Chinese. Chao (1994) compared European American and immigrant Chinese American mothers on standard measures of control and authoritarian parenting, as well as measures of *chiao shun* and *guan*. Chinese American mothers scored higher on standard measures of parental control and authoritarian parenting. However, they also scored higher on measure reflecting the concepts of *chiao shun* and *guan*. Thus, although Chinese American mothers scored high on the European American concepts of parental control and authoritarian parenting, their parenting style could not be described using European American concepts. Instead, the style of parenting used by the Chinese American mothers is conceptualized as a type of training performed by parents who are deeply concerned and involved in the lives of their children.

The value of this approach is that is helps resolve paradoxes in the literature. In studies on ethnicity achievement, Steinberg, Dornbusch, and Brown (1992) found that Asian American students rated their parents higher on authoritarian parenting than European American and Hispanic groups. Although their parents were lower on the optimal parental style of authoritativeness, Asian students had the highest achievement scores (Steinberg et al., 1992). Chao's (1994) study suggests that confusion between "authoritarian" and "training" child-rearing concepts among Chinese respondents may account for the paradox. Chinese parents may have a different set of

child-rearing values and styles that are distinct from the conventional U.S. child-rearing schemes. The same can be said about the construct of parent-child closeness. Immigrant Chinese American parents express closeness through behaviors emphasizing family harmony, whereas European American families express closeness through romantic themes that include more parent-child physical contact (Rothbaum, Morelli, Pott, & Liu-Constant, 2000).

Future research with Asian American families should take into account within-group difference in child-rearing practices due to generation and acculturation. Studies have found that larger acculturation gaps between Asian immigrant parents and their children are associated with more parental difficulties and communication problems and lower parenting satisfaction (Buki, Ma, Strom, & Strom, 2003; Tseng & Fuligni, 2000).

Latino Families. The term *Latino* is used here to describe those persons often referred to as Hispanics. *Hispanic* is a word coined by the Department of Commerce to enumerate persons in the United States whose ancestry derives from the Spanish-speaking countries and peoples of the Americas. Many people in this group prefer Latino over Hispanic because Latino is the Spanish word for describing this group, whereas Hispanic is an English word imposed on the group. The Latino population consists primarily of Mestizo peoples born of the Spanish conquest of the Americas. They are descendents of Spanish fathers and American Indian women. Although the language of Mestizos is Spanish, much of their culture is a hybrid of Spanish and American Indian influences. Child rearing, in particular, is heavily influenced by American Indian cultures because it was the American Indian women who bore the children of the Spanish conquistadores and raised them in their extended families. As these children grew, they formed unions with other Mestizos and American Indians and extended the predominately American Indian child-rearing practices across generations through their children.

Latinos are now the largest "minority" group in the nation. Mexican Americans make up the vast majority of Latinos (67%), followed by Central and South Americans (14%), Puerto Ricans (9%), and Cuban Americans (4%; U.S. Census Bureau, 2002). It is estimated that if current immigration trends continue, more than half the Latino population for the next 50 years will be made up of immigrants and their children (Edmonston & Passel, 1994). The Latino population will be characterized by sociocultural diversity and change as new immigrants and their children adapt to life in the United States. The direction and nature of this change will be influenced by the sociocultural ecology of the United States, which itself is being gradually transformed by the growing numbers of Latinos and Asians of immigrant families. For many Latinos, especially Mexican Americans, retention of their ethnic and cultural identity is fostered by several factors that include: (a) proximity to the United States-Mexican border, (b) the former historical status of the United States Southwest as a part of Mexico, (c) the continuing growth of the Latino population, (d) mass media and communication between the United States and Latin America, and (e) a non-European phenotype that marks Latinos in this country as *others* (Buriel, 1994).

Ramirez and Castaneda (1974) have described the cultural values of Latinos by four conceptual categories: (1) identification with family, community, and ethnic group; (2) personalization of interpersonal relationships; (3) status and roles based on age and gender; and (4) Latino Catholic ideology. The following discussion of these values recognizes that there are important subgroup variations (e.g., Cuban American, Mexican American, Puerto Rican, and Central and South American) and variations due to acculturation, generation, and social class.

Identification with Family, Community, and Ethnic Group. Latino child-rearing practices encourage the development of a self-identity embedded firmly in the context of the *familia* (family). One's individual identity is therefore part of a larger identity with the familia. For many Latinos, the word family refers to a combination of nuclear and extended family members, including fictive kin such as godparents.

The desire to be close to the familia often results in many members of the same familia living in the same community. The familia network extends further into the community through kinships formed by intermarriage among familias and *el compadrazco,* which is the cultural practice of having special friends become godparents of children in baptisms. Adults united through el compadrazco, called *compadres* and *comadres,* have mutual obligations to each other similar to those of brothers and sisters. Vidal (1988) found that Puerto Rican godparents served as role models and social supports for their godchildren and regarded themselves as potential surrogate parents in the event of the parents' death. Extended familia ties in the community give rise to a sense of identity with one's community.

The worldview of many Latinos includes a sense of identity with *La Raza* (the Race), which is a sense of peoplehood shared by persons of the Americas who are of Mestizo ancestry. The concept of *La Raza* suggests that many Latinos have a more flexible definition of race than the rigid categories typically used in the United States and by the Census Bureau. The Census Bureau and demographers consider Latinos an ethnic group belonging to the White race. However, when responding to the question on race in the 2000 census, 48% of Latinos reported only White, whereas approximately 42% reported only "Some Other Race" (U.S. Census Bureau, 2001a). In contrast, only 0.2% of the total non-Latino population reported "Some Other Race." These data point toward the need for a critical reexamination of how ethnic and racial identity are conceptualized and measured among Latinos.

Personalization of Interpersonal Relationships. Latino culture places a heavy emphasis on sensitivity to the social domain of the human experience. Individuals are socialized to be sensitive to the feelings and needs of others and to personalize interpersonal relationships (*personalismo*). This socialization goal encourages the development of cooperative social motives while discouraging individual competitive behaviors that set apart the individual from the group (Kagan, 1984).

The importance of the social domain for Latinos is reflected in the term *bien educado,* which means "well educated." In Latino culture, however, the term is used to refer not only to someone with a good formal education but also to a person who can function successfully in any interpersonal situation without being disrespectful. Okagaki and Sternberg (1993) found that Mexican immigrant parents emphasized social skills as equal to or as more important than cognitive skills in defining an "intelligent" child. Children in particular are expected to be bien educados in their relations with adults (Valdes, 1996). Addressing adults in Spanish with the formal "you" (*usted*) rather than the informal "you" (*tu*) is an example of being bien educado. Thus, if children lose Spanish and cannot communicate with Spanish monolingual adults, they may be unable to achieve the status of being bien educado in their community.

Status and Roles Based on Age and Gender. Latino culture has clearly defined norms of behavior governing an individual's actions in the familia and the community. Age and gender are important determinants of status and respect. Children are expected to be obedient and respectful toward their parents, even after they are grown and have children of their own. An authoritarian parenting style has been reported among Latinos (Dornbusch, Ritter, Leiderman, Roberts, & Fraleigh, 1987; Schumm et al., 1988). Yet, as Chao (1994) has shown, in the context of non-Western cultures, this parenting style may be experienced as parental support and concern. Grandparents, and older persons in general, receive respect and have considerable status owing to their knowledge of life. Consequently, children are taught to model themselves after adults; as a result, modeling becomes a preferred teaching style (Laosa, 1980).

Gender also influences a person's role in the familia and community. Males are expected to have more knowledge about politics and business, whereas females are expected to know more about child rearing, health care, and education. Because politics and business expose males more to the outside world, they are often perceived as the dominant figures in the familia. However, decision-making studies in the United States reveal that Latino husbands and wives most often share responsibility for major family decisions (Cooney, Rogler, Hurrell, & Ortiz, 1982; Zavella, 1987).

Latino Catholic Ideology. Religion strongly influences the lives of Latinos because Latino Catholicism reinforces and supports cultural values. Latino Catholicism is a synthesis of Spanish European Catholicism and indigenous religious beliefs and practices. Identity with family and community is facilitated through religious practices, such as weddings and el compadrazco, which help extend family networks. Identity with the ethnic group is reinforced by the common Catholic religion shared by more than 80% of La Raza. Religious symbols are often used as markers of ethnic identity. For example, the image of the Virgin of Guadalupe, the Mestizo equivalent of the Virgin Mary, is both a religious symbol and a symbol for La Raza. The cultural emphasis on respect, group harmony, and cooperation in interpersonal relations is in line with the religious themes of peace, community, and self-denial. Many cultural celebrations and developmental milestones are celebrated in religious contexts, such as a *quinceañera,*—a coming-of-age celebration for a young girl on her fifteenth birthday that marks the beginning of adulthood.

The Role of Family in Latino Adaptation

Latino families have 3.71 members on average compared to 2.97 for European American and 3.31 for African American families. Puerto Rican women tend to have their first child before marriage, whereas Mexican American and Cuban American mothers usually have their first child after marriage. Female-headed households are twice as common among Puerto Ricans relative to Mexican Americans and Cuban Americans (see Cauce & Domenech-Rodriguez, 2002, for a summary of family characteristics between Latino subgroups).

The longer immigrants live in the United States, the more their family networks expand. Family networks grow through marriage and birth and from continued immigration of family members. Thus, even as individual family members become acculturated, their local extended family becomes larger (Keefe & Padilla, 1987). Second- and third-generation Mexican Americans have larger and more integrated extended families than immigrants (Keefe & Padilla, 1987). Griffith and Villavicencio (1985) report that for Mexican Americans education and income are the best predictors of increased contact and support from family members.

Buriel (1993b) found that early assumption of responsibility was a dominant socialization goal of Mexican immigrant parents that persists into adolescence. He also found greater similarity in socialization styles among immigrant mothers and fathers than among native-born mothers and fathers. Consensus in socialization styles may reflect an area of domestic interdependence conditioned by the immigrant experience. Because immigrants lack extended kinship networks, parents may depend more on each other for socialization of children, which encourages agreement in parents' socialization styles.

Family research has often focused on how immigration and acculturation affect the adaptation of individual family members. However, the family can be viewed as an adapting entity with its own developmental processes. The family unit undergoes its own development, which transcends the development of its individual members. From a systems perspective (Minuchin, 2002), the Mexican American family can be thought of as an open system with both internal and external aspects of functioning. Internal aspects include the family's patterns of relationships and interactions and also the structure of the family. External aspects include the family's interactions with outside social systems including social institutions and the larger context of U.S. society. Rueschenberg and Buriel (1989) have shown that the Mexican American family is capable of adapting to U.S. social systems while retaining many of its internal characteristics that are cultural in nature.

Research is beginning to examine how traditional theories of parenting and socialization "fit" with family relations and child outcomes in Latino families. N. Hill,

Bush, and Roosa (2003) studied Mexican American and European American mothers and their children to map the relationship between harsh parenting and negative child outcomes. For both groups, families with low levels of conflict and hostile control had children with fewer conduct problems and depressive symptoms. In addition, in the Mexican American sample, lower acculturation, as measured by Spanish/English usage, was associated with a stronger negative relationship between maternal acceptance and child conduct problems. Moreover, among Spanish-speaking parents, hostile control co-occurred with acceptance, which is generally inconsistent with the traditional European American model of parenting. The combination of hostile control and acceptance may represent an adaptive parenting strategy for families living in culturally unfamiliar environments involving high levels of acculturative stress.

Parke et al. (2004), in a longitudinal study examining a family stress model involving economic hardship, family relations, and child outcomes, found that for both Mexican American and European American families, feelings of economic hardship were positively related to depression for both parents. In addition, paternal hostile parenting was related to higher levels of children's internalizing and externalizing behaviors in both European American and Mexican American families. However, among Mexican American families, maternal acculturation was associated with higher levels of marital problems and lower levels of both maternal and paternal hostile parenting. Although higher maternal acculturation may disrupt traditional male-centered authority patterns in the family, it may also serve as the catalyst for altering parenting styles in a less hostile direction.

A widely misunderstood and understudied area in Latino family research involves the role of fathers in parenting and socialization. The stereotype of machismo has led to the belief that Latino fathers are neither caring nor involved with their spouses and children. However, less acculturated Mexican American men supervise and engage their children in conventionally feminine activities more than their more acculturated counterparts (Coltrane, Parke, & Adams, 2004). Paternal participation in family rituals, which are often cultural in nature, is positively associated with monitoring and interacting with children in these families (Coltrane et al., 2004). Father involvement may represent an important dimension of familism, which is the most important value in Latino culture. This is supported by a study with Puerto Rican fathers, which found that fathers' assessments of their commitment to the family and their competence in family matters were positively related to their involvement with their preschool-age children (Roopnarine & Ahmeduzzaman, 1993).

In addition to the role of fathers, research on grandparent involvement, particularly grandmothers, has begun. Owing to the values of familism and status and respect based on age and gender, grandmothers are often the symbolic heads of extended families and are sought after for advise and support in child rearing (Ramos-McKay, Comas-Diaz, & Rivera, 1988). The cultural diversity in the Latino population suggests that the impact of grandmother support may vary as a function of acculturation. Using a Puerto Rican sample, Contreras, Lopez, Rivera-Mosqueda, Raymond-Smith, and Rothstein (1999), examined how acculturation affected relations between grandmother involvement and adolescent mothers' adjustment. Greater grandmother support was related to less symptomatology and parenting stress among less acculturated mothers. When mothers were more unidirectionally acculturated, greater grandmother support was associated with more symptomatology and parenting distress. This research, like the work with fathers, underscores the importance of the moderating role of acculturation in family relationships with Latinos.

Perspectives on Ethnic Influences on Family Socialization

Research on ethnic minority families in the United States has not kept pace with their rapid rate of growth. Until recently, ethnic/racial minority families were lumped together under the category of "minority," which overlooked important differences among ethnic/racial groups and significant diversity in individual groups. Most often, research with ethnic/racial families has compared them against European American families to identify group differences. An implicit assumption in two-group studies is that ethnic/racial minority families are not yet like European American families and that this developmental lag is responsible for the problems besetting ethnic/racial minority families. Recently, some researchers have begun to eschew two-group studies in favor of single-group studies that examine variations in ethnic/racial minority families and their relation to child outcomes. This research is guided by either an ecological or systems perspective that seeks to understand how parents adapt to the challenges they face as ethnic/racial minorities in U.S. society and how these experiences contribute to socialization goals they hold for their children.

The value of the concepts of collectivism and individualism that have been used to distinguish European American families from ethnic minority families (Greenfield & Cocking, 1994; Okagaki & Divecha, 1993) is being questioned as well (Scott-Jones, Lewis, & Shirley, 1996). As our review has indicated, both individualism and collectivism are important elements in the socialization of *both* European American and ethnic minority families and to continue to draw sharp contrasts using these terms serves only to promote stereotypes that are no longer valid. Scott-Jones et al. (1996) have suggested the adoption of Sampson's (1988) notion of ensembled individualism, which "reflects the importance of both individual development and commitment to family as complementary, intertwined elements in the socialization goals of ethnic families" (Scott-Jones et al., 1996, p. 8). Although the precise terminology that is best suited to capture the complexity of ethnic family socialization is still evolving, it is clear that *both* individual and collectivist features will continue to be recognized as important in describing ethnic families.

At present, and for the foreseeable future, the growth of minority families will be due primarily to immigration from Latin America and Asia. Research with families of these groups needs to take into account the acculturation level and generational status of parents and children and the effects these factors have on family processes and child outcomes. Together with acculturation, recognition of biculturalism as both an adaptation strategy and socialization goal should guide future research. The effects of prejudice and discrimination on ethnic minorities, in such areas as social and emotional development, ethnic/racial identity, and achievement motivation, deserve more attention. Language development research should also give greater attention to second-language acquisition (usually English) and bilingualism and their relation to cognitive development and school achievement. More attention must be given to the role of fathers, grandparents, and extended family members in the socialization of children. Finally, observational studies with ethnic/racial minority families have the potential for yielding a contextual richness about the family environments of ethnic/racial minorities that can lead to more culturally relevant insights and theories about their socialization experiences.

REMAINING ISSUES AND FUTURE TRENDS

A number of issues remain to be examined in future research if we are to describe fully the complexities, spec-

ify the determinants and processes, and outline the consequences of family-child relationships. These include the choice of the unit of analysis, the effects of family variation, types of developmental change, the role of historical change, methodological, and contextual issues.

Unit of Analysis

Current work is recognizing the importance of considering parents from a family systems perspective. However, our conceptual analysis of dyadic and triadic units of analysis is still limited (Dickstein, Seifer, et al., 1998; Parke, 1988). Considerable progress has been made in describing the behavior of individual interactants (e.g., mother, father, or child) in dyadic and to a lesser extent triadic settings, but less progress has been achieved in developing a language for describing interaction in dyadic and triadic terms. Even if such terms as *reciprocal* or *synchronous* hold promise, there remains little real advance in this regard. In addition, greater attention needs to be paid to the family as a unit of analysis. A number of researchers have offered differing taxonomies of family types or typologies that move us to this level of analysis (Cook, 2001), but, to date, little effort has been made to apply these notions systematically to family relationships in childhood.

Parenting and Family Variation

One of the clear advances of the past decade is recognition of the importance of individual differences in children; one of the next advances will be the recognition of individual differences among families. Recognition of individual variability across families implies the necessity of expanding sampling procedures. Despite demands for a greater awareness of family diversity, the range of family types that are studied is still relatively narrow. Although progress has been made in describing interaction patterns of parents and children in different cultures (Rogoff, 2003) and in different ethnic groups in the United States (Contreras, Kerns, & Neal-Barnett, 2002; McLoyd, Hill, & Dodge, 2005; McLoyd & Steinberg, 1998), this work represents only a beginning. Particularly critical is an extension of earlier work on parent-child relationships in other ethnic groups to other subsystems such as the marital, sibling, and family systems. Evaluation of family systems notions in families with different ethnic backgrounds, organizations, and structure will provide an opportunity to test the generality of this theoretical perspective. Finally, recent work on gay and lesbian families (Patterson, 2002) and the effects of growing up in these alternative family arrangements on children is raising important questions about the necessity of male-female family arrangements for the rearing of children (Parke, 2002).

Types of Developmental Change

Developmental issues need to be addressed more fully to include children at a wider range of ages. Despite Maccoby's (1984) plea, we still are only beginning to map developmental changes in parental socialization strategies. Moreover, we need to move beyond childhood and examine more closely parental relationships with their adult children—if we are to achieve a life-span view of family socialization. Although development traditionally has marked change in the individual child, it is evident from this review that this perspective is too limited and parents, as well as children, continue to develop across time (Elder, 1998; Parke, 1988). Parents' management of a variety of life-course tasks, such as marriage, work, and personal identity, will clearly determine how they will execute parental tasks; in turn, these differences may find expression in measures of parent-child interaction. Because developmental shifts in children's perceptual, cognitive, and social development may alter parental attitudes and behaviors and/or the nature of the adults' own developmentally relevant choices, such as work or career commitment, this clearly argues for the recognition of two developmental trajectories—a child developmental course and an adult developmental sequence. The description of the interplay between these two types of developmental curves is necessary to capture adequately the nature of developmental changes in a families' role in the socialization process.

Monitoring Secular Trends

There is a continuing need to monitor secular trends and to describe their impact on family relationships (Modell & Elder, 2002). Secular change is complex and clearly does not affect all individuals equally or all behavior patterns to the same extent. It is a serious oversimplification to assume that general societal trends can isomorphically be applied across all individual children, parents, and families. Moreover, better guidelines are necessary to illuminate which particular processes in families are most likely to be altered by historical events

and which processes are less amenable to change (Parke, 2004a). For example, the structural dynamics of early interaction (Stern, 1977) and some qualitative aspects of early parent-infant interactive style may be insulated from the influence of secular shifts. Are fathers biologically prepared to interact in a more physical way, and mothers in a more verbal mode? If this assumption about differences in parental play style is true, rates of interactions would be more likely to change than style when employment opportunities for men and women become more equal. Alternatively, the restraints may be more solely environmental, and as opportunities for adult male and female participation in child care and child rearing equalize, some maternal-paternal stylistic differences may diminish.

Methodological and Design Issues

It is likely that not a single methodological strategy will suffice to understand the development of family socialization. Instead, a wide range of designs and data collection and data analysis strategies is necessary. To date, there is still a paucity of information concerning interrelations across molar and molecular levels of analysis. However, it is becoming increasingly clear that a microanalytic strategy is not always more profitable in describing relationships among interactive partners; in some cases, ratings may be a more useful approach. A set of guidelines concerning the appropriate level of analysis for different questions would be helpful.

Parents' own reports are increasingly being recognized as important sources that can aid in interpretation of observed patterns (Goodnow, 2002; Parke, 1978). Types of self-reports other than structured interviews and questionnaires need to be more frequently employed. Focus groups are commonly used in other disciplines but are used less often by psychologists. A focus group is a type of group interview, which relies on an emergent process of interaction between group members to produce data and insights that would not be found without such interaction. Focus groups are excellent forums in which to explore microlevel experiences of families and examine similarities and differences across different genders, socioeconomic classes, and ethnic groups. These provide a unique opportunity for parents and children to articulate their concerns, values, and goals in a context that is less constrained than the usual interview format. This technique is of particular value in the early stages of research with understudied populations (see Gomel et al., 1998, and Parke et al., 2003, for illustrations of the use of focus groups with African American and Hispanic American groups). As Rutter (2002) has argued, qualitative and quantitative approaches are not incompatible. Quantitative analytic strategies have recently become available for use with the type of qualitative verbal reports generated by focus groups (Richards & Richards, 1991). Recent computer programs (e.g., Nudist, Nonnumerical Unstructured Data Indexing, or Searching and Theory Building) allow the researcher to explore patterns in the data that aid in grounded theory construction, while simultaneously allowing for the application of a coding scheme to the transcript text and then converting the coded text into quantitative information. Recently, Gomel et al. (1998) successfully utilized this program in a focus group study of the impact of economic downturn on ethnic minority families. Ethnographic methodologies can play an important role in family research as well, particularly to gain a better understanding of contextual factors that affect parental functioning (see Burton, & Price-Spratlen, 1999).

Reliance on nonexperimental strategies may be insufficient to address the important issue of direction of effects in work on the impact of parents on children and families. Experimental strategies have been underutilized in studies of families. By experimentally modifying either the type of parental behavior or level of involvement, firmer conclusions concerning the direct causative role that parents play in modifying their children's and their spouse's development will be possible. As Cowan and Cowan (2002) recently argued, intervention studies provide the "gold standard" for testing causal hypotheses. Intervention studies (e.g., Fagan & Hawkins, 2001; Parke, Hymel, Power, & Tinsley, 1980) aimed at modifying fathering behavior provide models for this type of work and, by extending these studies to include measures of child, mother, and father development, they could provide evidence of the impact of changes in parenting behavior on developmental outcomes. Moreover, these experimentally based interventions have clear policy implications by exploring the degree of plasticity of parenting behavior. Similarly, studies in which child behavior is either experimentally modified (Bell & Chapman, 1986) or children with known characteristics (e.g., hyperactivity, conduct disorder) are paired with parental surrogates (Anderson, Lytton, & Romney, 1986) are needed to capture the bidirectionality of family influence effects. By expand-

ing the range of family members or subsystems that are measured, to include nontargeted individuals and subsystems, the impact of modifying the behavior of one family member on other parts of the family system could be evaluated. These interventions can serve as a vehicle for evaluation of alternative theoretical views of parenthood and socialization. In addition to intervention designs, natural experiments continue to be a useful tool for aiding us in sorting out causal issues (Rutter, 2002). For example, recent work on adopted Romanian children has shown that the length of institutionalization is a major predictor of later functioning (Rutter, Pickles, Murray, & Eaves, 2001).

More recognition of the utility of combined sampling strategies is needed. Recently, researchers have begun to use multistage sampling strategies in which survey level information on a national representative sample is secured in combination with the selection of a subsample for purposes of more intensive analyses such as in-depth interviews or observations (Reiss, Neiderhiser, Hetherington, & Plomin, 2000). Together, this strategy ensures greater confidence in the generalizability of the findings and permits access to process-level variables.

For research designs, under the influence of the behavior geneticists (Plomin, 1994), there has been an increased focus on the value of nonshared environmental designs, which allow measurement of the differential impact of families on different children in the same family. Although some have argued for the decreased use of traditional between-family designs that still form the foundation of most of our knowledge of family effects (Plomin, 1994), others (e.g., Hoffman, 1991) have argued for the continued utility of both types of designs with the goal of discovering "what environmental conditions might lead to sibling similarity and dissimilarity" (Hoffman, 1991, p. 199). More conceptual work is needed to provide guidelines concerning the value of within- and between-family designs for different variables and issues.

The field has progressed beyond the simple environment-gene partitioning argument (Harris, 1998) toward a more complex conceptual framework that reframes the debate as gene x environment interactions. According to this view (Reiss, 2003), family processes mediate genetic influence in children's outcomes, and the future challenge is to determine how this gene x environment family model plays out across development. Several designs, including cross-fostering studies with nonhuman primates (Suomi, 2000), modified sibling designs

(Reiss et al., 2000), and prospective adoption designs (Reiss, 2003) are promising new approaches for addressing this issue.

Contextual Issues

Greater attention needs to be paid to the role of context in determining family relationships. How do parent-child interaction patterns shift between home and lab settings and across different types of interaction contexts such as play, teaching, and caregiving? Moreover, it is important to consider the social a well as the physical context. Recognition of the embeddedness of parents in family contexts is critical, and conceptualizing families as embedded in a variety of extrafamilial social settings is important for understanding variation in family functioning. In this regard, it is necessary to recognize that variations in family structure and in ethnicity and social class will modify significantly the ways in which social networks are organized and utilized. For example, the role of the extended family is much more prominent in some groups, such as African American, than in other groups (Gadsen, 1999; McLoyd, Hill, & Dodge, 2005). Similarly, single-parent families may be more directly embedded in a community-based social network than two-parent families. Descriptions of these variations are necessary for an adequate understanding of the role of extrafamilial networks on parent and family functioning.

Locating Families in a Network of Socialization Influences

One of the major challenges is to determine the unique contribution of families to socialization outcomes and the limits of family effects (Harris, 1998). As Maccoby and Martin (1983) argued in their review of the relations between parental functioning and characteristics of children, "in most cases the relationships that have appeared are not large, if one thinks in terms of the amount of variance accounted for" (p. 82). Their conclusion is still valid, if we assume a narrow view of family influence as the direct impact of parents on their children. However, our increased recognition of the family as a *partner* with other institutions, such as peers, schools, media, religious institutions, and government policymakers that together influence children's development, has significantly expanded our view of the family's role in the socialization process and suggests that the family—directly and indirectly—may have a larger impact

on children's outcomes than previously thought. As we have argued, families serve not just as direct influences on children but as indirect influences as well in their roles as managers, modifiers, and negotiators on behalf of children in relation to these social institutions. However, our understanding of the ways in which families influence their children's socialization through their links with other institutions is still poorly understood. Moreover, these agents and institutions (e.g., schools, or peers) play a direct as well as indirect role through the family in the socialization process. Several issues need to be addressed. What are the unique roles that families play in socialization? Are some kinds of outcomes specifically in the family purview such as the development of early social attachments? Are other outcomes influenced largely by other groups (e.g., tastes in music and fashion)? How does the relative role of family and other agents shift across development? Perhaps the most interesting question concerns the ways in which families coordinate their socialization roles with other agents and institutions. Successful socialization requires a gradual sharing of responsibility for socialization with other groups, but we know relatively little about this process of coordination and mutual sharing across socialization agents. It is unhelpful to continue to posit linear models of decreasing family influence across development. Instead, we need models that help us understand the changing nature of family influence relative to other groups and the mechanisms that maintain family values and orientation after direct influence has subsided. Recent work on the intergenerational transmission of working models of relationships (Bretherton & Munholland, 1999) testifies to the prolonged influence of childhood socialization on later adult parenting roles. This work anticipates one of the major themes of future research: the impact of childhood socialization patterns on later adult development—not just in parenting but in other types of adult relationships, including marital, friendship, and work relationships. Closely related is the issue of how families and other institutions are linked. Earlier work has focused on family peer linkages (Parke et al., 2003), family-work ties (Perry-Jenkins, Repetti, & Crouter, 2000), and family-school relationships (Epstein & Sanders, 2002). More recently, there is emerging evidence that the prior neglect of family links with other institutions such as the legal system (Parke & Clarke-Stewart, 2003), religious institutions (Mahoney et al., 2001), social service systems (Olds et al., 1999), and health delivery organizations (Tinsley,

2003) is being corrected. More work on these cross-context relationships is needed. Nor are the processes that promote or constrain family involvement with other institutions well understood. Finally, the bidirectional nature of the linkage needs more attention so that we understand the dynamic and mutual influence of families on other institutions and vice versa.

A Final Word

Families continue to play a central role in the socialization process but their role has undergone dramatic change during the past several decades. To maintain our understanding, it is critical to monitor how changing ecologies of families of different ethnic backgrounds are modifying the socialization of families. Only by a better understanding of these changes will we be able to offer meaningful assistance and support for families. And only by achieving these goals will we be able to fulfill our goal of providing optimal conditions for promoting children's development.

REFERENCES

Ahnert, L., Rickert, H., & Lamb, M. E. (2000). Shared caregiving: Comparisons between home and child care settings. *Developmental Psychology, 36,* 339–351.

Allen, S. M., & Hawkins, A. J. (1999). Maternal gatekeeping: Mothers' beliefs and behavior that inhibit greater father involvement in family work. *Journal of Marriage and the Family, 61,* 199–212.

Anderson, K. E., Lytton, H., & Romney, D. M. (1986). Mothers' interactions with normal and conduct-disordered boys: Who affects whom? *Developmental Psychology, 22,* 604–609.

Baldwin, A. L., Baldwin, C., & Cole, R. E. (1990). Stress resistant families and stress-resistant children. In J. E. Rolf, A. S. Masten, K. Neuchterlein, & S. Weintraub (Eds.), *Risk and protective factors in the development of psychopathology* (pp. 257–280). New York: Cambridge University Press.

Bandura, A. (1977). *Social learning theory.* Englewood Cliffs, NJ: Prentice-Hall.

Bandura, A., & Walters, R. H. (1963). *Social learning and personality development.* New York: Holt, Rinehart and Winston.

Banks, J. A. (1991). *Teaching strategies for ethnic studies* (5th ed.). Boston: Allyn & Bacon.

Barth, F. (1969). *Ethnic groups and boundaries: The social organization of culture difference.* Boston: Little, Brown.

Barth, J. M., & Parke, R. D. (1993). Parent-child relationship influences on children's transition to school. *Merrill-Palmer Quarterly, 39,* 173–195.

Baumrind, D. (1973). The development of instrumental competence through socialization. In A. D. Pick (Ed.), *Minnesota Symposia on Child Psychology* (Vol. 7, pp. 3–46). Minneapolis, MN: University of Minnesota Press.

Baumrind, D. (1991). Parenting styles and adolescent development. In R. Lerner, A. C. Peterson, & J. Brooks-Gunn (Eds.), *The encyclopedia of adolescence* (pp. 746–758). New York: Garland.

Bean, F. D., Chapa, J., Berg, R. R., & Sowards, K. (1994). Educational and sociodemographic incorporation among Hispanic immigrants to the United States. In B. Edmonston & J. S. Passel (Eds.), *Immigration and ethnicity: The integration of America's newest arrivals* (pp. 73–100). Washington, DC: Urban Institute Press.

Beitel, A., & Parke, R. D. (1998). Paternal involvement in infancy: The role of maternal and paternal attitudes. *Journal of Family Psychology, 12,* 268–288.

Bell, R. Q. (1968). A reinterpretation of the direction of effects in studies of socialization. *Psychological Review, 75,* 81–95.

Bell, R. Q., & Chapman, M. (1986). Child effects in studies using experimental or brief longitudinal approaches to socialization. *Developmental Psychology, 22,* 595–603.

Belsky, J. (1984). The determinants of parenting: A process model. *Child Development, 55,* 83–96.

Belsky, J., Youngblade, L., Rovine, M., & Volling, B. (1991). Patterns of marital change and parent-child interaction. *Journal of Marriage and the Family, 53,* 487–498.

Berlin, I. N. (1987). Effects of changing Native American cultures on child development. *Journal of Community Psychology, 15,* 299–306.

Bernal, G., Trimble, J. E., Burlew, A. K., & Leong, F. T. L. (2003). *Handbook of racial and ethnic minority psychology.* Thousand Oaks, CA: Sage.

Berry, J. W. (1980). Acculturation as varieties of adaptation. In A. M. Padilla (Ed.), *Acculturation: Theory, models, and some new findings* (pp. 9–25). Boulder, CO: Westview Press.

Betancourt, H., & Lopez, S. R. (1993). The study of culture, ethnicity, and race in American psychology. *American Psychologist, 48,* 629–637.

Bhavnagri, N. P., & Parke, R. D. (1991). Parents as direct facilitators of children's peer relationships: Effects of age of child and sex of parent. *Journal of Social and Personal Relationships, 8,* 423–440.

Bianchi, S. M. (2000). Maternal employment and time with children: Dramatic change or surprising continuity? *Demography, 37,* 401–414.

Bigler, R. S., Averhart, C. J., & Liben, L. S. (2003). Race and the workforce: Occupational status, aspirations, and stereotyping among African American children. *Developmental Psychology, 39,* 572–580.

Bijou, S. W., & Baer, D. M. (1961). *Child development: Vol. 1. A systematic and empirical theory.* East Norwalk, CT: Appleton-Century-Crofts.

Blank, S. (1993, April). *Household formation and Mexican immigrants: An alternative strategy for meeting the goals of recent migration.* Paper presented at the 20th Annual Center for Studies of the Family Conference, Brigham Young University, Provo, UT.

Bornstein, M. H., & Bradley, R. H. (Eds.). (2003). *Socioeconomic status, parenting, and child development.* Mahwah, NJ: Erlbaum.

Boss, P. (1999). *Ambiguous loss: Learning to live with unresolved grief.* Cambridge, MA: Harvard University Press.

Bossard, J. H. S., & Boll, E. (1950). *Ritual in family living.* Philadelphia: University of Pennsylvania Press.

Bowman, P. J. (1993). The impact of economic marginality among African American husbands and fathers. In H. P. McAdoo (Ed.), *Family ethnicity: Strength in diversity* (pp. 120–137). Thousand Oaks, CA: Sage.

Bowman, P. J., & Howard, C. (1985). Race-related socialization, motivation and academic achievement: A study of Black youths in three-generation families. *Journal of the American Academy of Child Psychiatry, 24,* 134–141.

Boykin, A. W. (1983). The academic performance of Afro-American children. In J. Spence (Ed.), *Achievement and achievement motives: Psychological and sociological approaches* (pp. 321–371). San Francisco: Freeman.

Boykin, A. W., & Toms, F. D. (1985). Black child socialization: A conceptual framework. In H. P. McAdoo & J. L. McAdoo (Eds.), *Black children: Social, educational, and parental environments* (pp. 33–51). Thousand Oaks, CA: Sage.

Boyum, L. A., & Parke, R. D. (1995). The role of family emotional expressiveness in the development of children's social competence. *Journal of Marriage and the Family, 57,* 593–608.

Bretherton, I., & Munholland, K. A. (1999). Internal working models in attachment relationships: A construct revisited. In J. Cassidy & P. R. Shaver (Eds.), *Handbook of attachment: Theory, research, and clinical applications* (pp. 89–111). New York: Guilford Press.

Brody, G. H., Flor, D. L., & Gibson, N. M. (1999). Linking maternal efficacy beliefs, developmental goals, parenting practices and child competence in rural single-parent African American families. *Child Development, 70,* 1197–1208.

Brody, G. H., Flor, D. L., & Neubaum, E. (1998). Coparenting processes and child competence among rural African-American families. In M. Lewis & C. Feiring (Eds.), *Families, risk and competence* (pp. 227–243). Mahwah, NJ: Erlbaum.

Brody, G. H., Stoneman, Z., & Flor, D. (1996). Parental religiosity, family processes and youth competence in rural two-parent African American families. *Developmental Psychology, 32,* 696–706.

Brody, G. H., Stoneman, Z., Smith, T., & Gibson, N. M. (1999, April). *Parent psychological functioning, family processes and sibling relationship quality in rural two parent African American families.* Paper presented at the biennial meeting of the Society for Research and Child Development, Albuquerque, NM.

Brodzinsky, D. M., & Pinderhughes, E. (2002). Parenting and child development in adoptive families. In M. H. Bornstien (Ed.), *Handbook of parenting: Vol. 1. Children and parenting* (2nd ed., pp. 279–311). Mahwah, NJ: Erlbaum.

Bronfenbrenner, U. (1989). Ecological systems theory. In R. Vasta (Ed.), *Six theories of child development: Revised formulations and current issues* (pp. 187–249). Philadelphia: Jessica Kingsley.

Bryant, B. (1985). The neighborhood walk: Sources of support in middle childhood. *Monographs of the Society for Research in Child Development, 50*(3, Serial No. 210).

Bryant, B. K. (1989). The child's perspective of sibling caretaking and its relevance to understanding social-emotional functioning and development. In P. G. Zukow (Ed.), *Sibling interaction across cultures: Theoretical and methodological issues* (pp. 143–164). New York: Springer-Verlag.

Buki, L. P., Ma, T.-C., Strom, R. D., & Strom, S. K. (2003). Chinese immigrant mothers of adolescents: Self-perceptions of acculturation effects on parenting. *Cultural Diversity and Ethnic Minority Psychology, 9,* 127–140.

Burgess, B. J. (1980). Parenting in the Native American community. In M. D. Fantini & R. Cardenas (Eds.), *Parenting in a multicultural society: Practice and policy* (pp. 63–73). New York: Longman.

Buriel, R. (1987). *Academic performance of foreign- and native-born Mexican Americans: A comparison of first-, second-, and third-generation students and parents* (New Directions for Latino Public Policy Research, Working Paper No. 14). A project for the Inter-University Program for Latino Research and the Social Science Research Council, New York.

Buriel, R. (1993a). Acculturation, respect for cultural differences and biculturalism among three generations of Mexican American and Euro-American school children. *Journal of Genetic Psychology, 154,* 531–543.

Buriel, R. (1993b). Childrearing orientations in Mexican American families: The influence of generation and sociocultural factors. *Journal of Marriage and the Family, 55,* 987–1000.

Buriel, R. (1994). Immigration and education of Mexican Americans. In A. Hurtado & E. E. Garcia (Eds.), *The educational achievement of Latinos: Barriers and successes* (pp. 197–226). Santa Cruz: Regents of the University of California.

Buriel, R. (2003, April). *Methodological and conceptual issues for researching Mexican Americans.* Paper presented at the biennial meeting of the Society for Research in Child Development, Tampa, FL.

Buriel, R., & Cardoza, D. (1993). Mexican American ethnic labeling: An intrafamilial and intergenerational analysis. In M. E. Bernal & G. P. Knight (Eds.), *Ethnic identity: Formation and transmission among Hispanics and other minorities* (pp. 197–210). Albany: State University of New York Press.

Buriel, R., & Hurtado-Ortiz, M. T. (2000). Child care practices and preferences among native- and foreign-born Latina mothers and Euro American mothers. *Hispanic Journal of Behavioral Sciences, 22,* 314–331.

Buriel, R., Love, J. A., & DeMent, T. L. (in press). The relationship of language brokering to depression and parent-child bonding among Latino adolescents. In M. H. Bornstein & L. R. Cote (Eds.), *Acculturation and parent-child relationships.* Mahwah, NJ: Lawrence Erlbaum.

Buriel, R., Perez, W., DeMent, T. L., Chavez, D. V., & Moran, V. R. (1998). The relationship of language brokering to academic performance, biculturations, and self-efficacy among Latino adolescents. *Hispanic Journal of Behavioral Sciences, 20,* 283–297.

Buriel, R., & Saenz, E. (1980). Psychocultural characteristics of college-bound and noncollege-bound Chicanas. *Journal of Social Psychology, 110,* 245–251.

Buriel, R., & Vasquez, R. (1982). Stereotypes of Mexican descent persons: Attitudes of three generations of Mexican Americans and Anglo American adolescents. *Journal of Cross-Cultural Psychology, 13,* 59–70.

Burks, V. S., & Parke, R. D. (1996). Parent and child representations of social relationships: Linkages between families and peers. *Merrill-Palmer Quarterly, 42,* 358–378.

Burton, L. M., & Price-Spratlen, T. (1999). Through the eyes of children: An ethnographic perspective on neighborhoods and child development. In A. S. Masten (Ed.), *Minnesota Symposia on Child Psychology: Vol. 29. Cultural processes in child development* (pp. 77–96). Mahwah, NJ: Erlbaum.

Campbell, S. B., Cohn, J. F., & Meyers, T. (1995). Depression in first-time mothers: Mother-infant interaction and depression chronicity. *Developmental Psychology, 31,* 349–357.

Carlson, E. A., Sroufe, L. A., & Egeland, B. (2004). The construction of experience: A longitudinal study of representation and behavior. *Child Development, 75,* 66–83.

Carson, J. L., & Parke, R. D. (1996). Reciprocal negative affect in parent-child interactions and children's peer competency. *Child Development, 67,* 2217–2226.

Caspi, A., McClay, J., Moffitt, T., Mill, J., Martin, J., Craig, I. W., et al. (2002). Role of genotype in the cycle of violence in maltreated children. *Science, 297,* 851–854.

Cassidy, J., Parke, R. D., Butkovsky, L., & Braungart, J. M. (1992). Family-peer connections: The role of emotional expressiveness within the family and children's understanding of emotions. *Child Development, 63,* 603–618.

Cauce, A. M., & Domenech-Rodriguez, M. (2002). Latino families: Myths and realities. In J. M. Contreras, K. A. Kerns, & A. M. Neal-Barnett (Eds.), *Latino children and families in the United States: Current research and future directions* (pp. 3–25). Westport, CT: Praeger.

Chao, C. M. (1992). The inner heart: Therapy with Southeast Asian families. In L. A. Vargas & J. D. Koss-Chioino (Eds.), *Working with culture: Psychotherapeutic intervention with ethnic minority children and adolescents* (pp. 157–181). San Francisco: Jossey-Bass.

Chao, R. (2001, April). *The role of children's linguistic bordering among immigrant Chinese and Mexican families.* Paper presented at the biennial meeting of the Society for Research in Child Development, Minneapolis, MN.

Chao, R. K. (1994). Beyond parental control and authoritarian parenting style: Understanding Chinese parenting through the cultural notion of training. *Child Development, 65,* 1111–1119.

Chavez, L. (1990). Co-residence and resistance: Strategies for survival among undocumented Mexicans and Central Americans in the United States. *Urban Anthropology, 19,* 31–61.

Chiu, L.-H. (1987). Child-rearing attitudes of Chinese, Chinese-American, and Anglo-American mothers. *International Journal of Psychology, 22,* 409–419.

Chun, K. M., & Akutsu, P. D. (2003). Acculturation among ethnic minority families. In K. M. Chun, P. Balls Organista, & G. Marin (Eds.), *Acculturation: Advances in theory, measurement, and applied research* (pp. 95–119). Washington, DC: American Psychological Association.

Chun, K. M., Balls Organista, P., & Marin, G. (Eds.). (2003). *Acculturation: Advances in theory, measurement, and applied research.* Washington, DC: American Psychological Association.

Clarke-Stewart, K. A., & Allhusen, V. (2005). *What we know about childcare.* Cambridge, MA: Harvard University Press.

Clarke-Stewart, K. A., & Brentano, C. (2006). *Divorce: Causes & consequences.* New Haven, CT: Yale University Press.

Cochran, M., & Bo, I. (1989). The social networks, family involvement and pro and anti-social behavior of adolescent males in Norway. *Journal of Youth and Adolescence, 18,* 377–398.

Cochran, M., & Niego, S. (1995). Parenting and social networks. In M. H. Bornstien (Ed.), *Handbook of parenting: Vol. 3. Status and social conditions of parenting* (pp. 393–418). Mahwah, NJ: Erlbaum.

Coleman, J. (1988). Social capital in the creation of human capital. *American Journal of Sociology, 94*(Suppl.), S95–S120.

Collins, W. A., & Madsen, S. D. (2003). Developmental changes in parenting interactions. In L. Kuczynski (Eds.), *Handbook of dynamics in parent-child relations* (pp. 49–66). Thousand Oaks, CA: Sage.

Coltrane, S., Parke, R. D., & Adams, M. (2004). Complexity of father involvement in low-income Mexican American families. *Family Relations: Interdisciplinary Journal of Applied Family Studies, 53,* 179–189.

Conger, K. J., Bryant, C. M., & Brennom, J. M. (2004). The changing nature of adolescent sibling relationships: A theoretical framework for evaluating the role of relationship quality. In R. D. Conger, F. O. Lorenz, & K. A. S. Wickrama (Eds.), *Continuity and change in family relations: Theory, methods and empirical findings* (pp. 319–344). Mahwah, NJ: Erlbaum.

Conger, R., & Elder, G. H., Jr. (Eds.). (1994). *Families in troubled times: Adapting to change in rural America.* Hawthorn, NY: Aldine de Gruyter.

Conger, R. D., Ge, X., Elder, G. H., Lorenz, F. O., & Simons, R. L. (1994). Economic stress, coercive family process and developmental problems of adolescents. *Child Development, 65,* 541–561.

Conger, R. D., Wallace, L. E., Sun, Y., Simons, R. L., McLoyd, V. C., & Brody, G. H. (2002). Economic pressure in African American families: A replication and extension of the family stress model. *Developmental Psychology, 38,* 179–191.

Contreras, J. M., Kerns, K. A., & Neal-Barnett, A. M. (Eds.). (2002). *Latino children and families in the United States.* Westport, CT: Praeger.

Contreras, J. M., Lopez, I. R., Rivera-Mosquera, E. T., Raymond-Smith, L., & Rothstein, K. (1999). Social support and adjustment among Puerto Rican adolescent mothers: The moderating effects of acculturation. *Journal of Family Psychology, 13,* 228–243.

Cook, W. L. (2001). Interpersonal influence in family systems: A social relations model analysis. *Child Development, 72,* 1179–1197.

Cooksey, E. C., Menaghan, E. G., & Jekielek, S. M. (1997). Life course effects of work and family circumstances on children. *Social Forces, 76,* 637–667.

Cooney, R. S., Rogler, L. H., Hurrell, R. M., & Ortiz, V. (1982). Decision making in intergenerational Puerto Rican families. *Journal of Marriage and the Family, 44,* 621–631.

Corter, C. M., & Fleming, A. S. (2002). Psychobiology of maternal behavior in human beings. In M. H. Bornstein (Ed.), *Handbook of parenting: Vol. 2. Biology and ecology of parenting* (2nd ed., pp. 141–82). Mahwah, NJ: Erlbaum.

Coulton, C. V., & Pandey, S. (1992). Geographic concentration of poverty and risk to children in urban neighborhoods. *American Behavioral Scientist, 35,* 238–257.

Cowan, P. A., & Cowan, C. P. (2002). Interventions as tests of family systems theories: Marital family relationships in children's development and psychopathology. *Development and Psychopathology, 14,* 731–759.

Cowan, P. A., Cowan, C. P., Schulz, M. S., & Heming, G. (1994). Prebirth to preschool family factors in children's adaptation to kindergarten. In R. D. Parke & S. G. Kellam (Eds.), *Exploring family relationships with other social contexts* (pp. 75–114). Hillsdale, NJ: Erlbaum.

Cox, M., Paley, B., & Harter, K. (2001). Interparental conflict and parent-child relationships. In J. H. Grych & F. D. Fincham (Eds.), *Interparental conflict and child development: Theory, research, and applications* (pp. 249–272). New York: Cambridge University Press.

Crockenberg, S., & Langrock, A. (2001). The role of emotion and emotional regulation in children's responses to interparental conflict. In J. H. Grych & F. D. Fincham (Eds.), *Interparental conflict and child development: Theory, research, and applications* (pp. 126–156). New York: Cambridge University Press.

Crockenberg, S. C., & Leerkes, E. M. (2003). Parental acceptance, postpartum depression, and maternal sensitivity: Mediating and moderating processes. *Journal of Family Psychology, 17,* 80–93.

Crouter, A. C. (1994). Processes linking families and work: Implications for behavior and development in both settings. In R. D. Parke & S. G. Kellam (Eds.), *Exploring family relationships with other social contexts* (pp. 9–28). Hillsdale, NJ: Erlbaum.

Crouter, A. C., & Booth, A. (Eds.). (2003). *Children's influence on family dynamics: The neglected side of family relationships.* Mahwah, NJ: Erlbaum.

Crouter, A. C., Bumpus, M. F., Maguire, M. C., & McHale, S. M. (1999). Linking parents' work pressure and adolescents' well being: Insights into dynamics in dual-earner families. *Developmental Psychology, 35,* 1453–1461.

Crouter, A. C., Helms-Erikson, H., Updegraff, K., & McHale, S. M. (1999). Conditions underlying parents' knowledge about children's daily lives in middle childhood: Between- and within-family comparisons. *Child Development, 70,* 246–259.

Crouter, A. C., MacDermid, S. M., McHale, S. M., & Perry-Jenkins, M. (1990). Parental monitoring and perceptions of children's school performance and conduct in dual- and single-earner families. *Developmental Psychology, 26,* 649–657.

Cuellar, I., Arnold, B., & Maldonado, R. (1995). Acculturation Rating Scale for Mexican Americans-II: A revision of the original ARSMA Scale. *Hispanic Journal of Behavioral Sciences, 17,* 275–304.

Cuellar, I., Nyberg, B., Maldonado, R. E., & Roberts, R. E. (1997). Ethnic identity and acculturation in a young adult Mexican-origin population. *Journal of Community Psychology, 25,* 535–549.

Cummings, E. M., & Davies, P. (1994). *Children and marital conflict: The impact of family dispute and resolution.* New York: Guilford Press.

Cummings, E. M., Goeke-Morey, M. C., & Raymond, J. A. (2004). Fathers in family context: Effects of marital quality and marital conflict. In M. E. Lamb (Ed.), *The role of the father in child development* (4th ed., pp. 196–221). Hoboken, NJ: Wiley.

Darling, N., & Steinberg, L. (1993). Parenting style as context: An integrative model. *Psychological Bulletin, 113,* 487–496.

Darling, N., Steinberg, L., Gringlas, B., & Dornbusch, S. (1995). *Community influences on adolescent achievement and deviance: A test of the functional community hypothesis.* Unpublished manuscript, Temple University.

Davies, P. T., & Cummings, E. M. (1994). Marital conflict and child adjustment: An emotional security hypothesis. *Psychological Bulletin, 116,* 387–411.

Davies, P. T., Dumenci, L., & Windle, M. (1999). The interplay between maternal depressive symptoms and martial distress in the prediction of adolescent adjustment. *Journal of Marriage and the Family, 61,* 238–254.

Davies, P. T., Harold, G. T., Goeke-Morey, M. C., & Cummings, E. M. (2002). Child emotional security and interparental conflict. *Monographs of the Society of Research in Child Development, 67* (3, Serial No. 270).

Davies, P. T., & Windle, M. (1997). Gender-specific pathways between maternal depressive symptoms, family discord, and adolescent adjustment. *Developmental Psychology, 33,* 657–668.

Delgado-Gaitan, C. (1994). Socializing young children in Mexican-American families: An intergenerational perspective. In P. M. Greenfield & R. R. Cocking (Eds.), *Cross-cultural roots of minority child development* (pp. 55–86). Hillsdale, NJ: Erlbaum.

Delpit, L. (1995). *Other people's children: Cultural conflict in the classroom.* New York: New Press.

DeMent, T., Buriel, R., & Villanueva, C. (2005). Children as language brokers: Recollections of college students. In S. Farideh (Eds.), *Language in multicultural education* (pp. 255–272). Greenwich, CT: Information Age Publishing.

Denham, S. A. (1998). *Emotional development in young children.* New York: Guilford Press.

Denham, S. A., Cook, M., & Zoller, D. (1992). "Baby looks very sad": Implications of conversations about feelings between mother and preschooler. *British Journal of Developmental Psychology, 10,* 301–315.

Deutsch, F. M. (1999). *Halving it all: How equally shared parenting works.* Cambridge, MA: Harvard University Press.

Dickstein, S., Seifer, R., Hayden, L. C., Schiller, M., Sameroff, A. J., Keitner, G., et al. (1998). Levels of family assessment: Pt. 2. Impact of maternal psychopathology on family functioning. *Journal of Family Psychology, 12,* 23–40.

Dickstein, S., St. Andre, M., Sameroff, A., Seifer, R., & Schiller, M. (1999). Maternal depression, family functioning and child outcomes: A narrative assessment. *Monographs of the Society of Research in Child Development, 64*(2, Serial No. 257), 84–103.

Dix, T. (1991). The affective organization of parenting: Adaptive and maladaptive processes. *Psychological Bulletin, 110,* 3–25.

Dix, T., & Branca, S. H. (2003). Parenting as a goal-regulation process. In L. Kuczynski (Eds.), *Handbook of dynamics in parent-child relations* (pp. 167–187). Thousand Oaks, CA: Sage.

Dodge, K. A., McLoyd, V. C., & Lansford, J. E. (2005). The cultural context of physically disciplining children. In V. C. McLoyd, N. E. Hill, & K. A. Dodge (Eds.), *African American family life* (pp. 245–263). New York: Guilford Press.

Dornbusch, S. M., Ritter, P. L., Leiderman, P. H., Roberts, D. E., & Fraleigh, M. J. (1987). The relation of parenting style to adolescent school performance. *Child Development, 58,* 1244–1257.

Doyle, A. B., & Markiewicz, D. (1996). Parents' interpersonal relationships and children's friendships. In W. M. Bukowski, A. F. Newcomb, & W. W. Hartup (Eds.), *The company they keep: Friendship in childhood and adolescence* (pp. 115–136). New York: Cambridge University Press.

Dunn, J. (1993). *Young children's close relationships: Beyond attachment.* Thousand Oaks, CA: Sage.

Dunn, J. (2004). *Children's friendships: The beginnings of intimacy.* London: Blackwell.

Dunn, J., & Brown, J. (1994). Affect expression in the family, children's understanding of emotions and their interactions with others. *Merrill-Palmer Quarterly, 40,* 120–137.

Dunn, J., Slomkowski, C., Beardsall, L., & Rende, R. (1994). Adjustment in middle childhood and early adolescence: Links with earlier and contemporary sibling relationships. *Journal of Child Psychology and Psychiatry, 35,* 491–504.

DuRocher Schudlich, T. D., & Cummings, E. M. (2003). Parental dysphoria and children's internalizing symptoms: Martial conflict styles as mediators of risk. *Child Development, 74,* 1663–1681.

East, P. L., & Rook, K. S. (1992). Compensatory patterns of support among children's peer relationships: A test using school friends, nonschool friends, and siblings. *Developmental Psychology, 28,* 163–172.

Edmonston, B., & Passel, J. S. (1994). The future immigrant population of the United States. In B. Edmonston & J. S. Passel (Eds.), *Immigration and ethnicity: The integration of America's newest arrivals* (pp. 317–353). Washington, DC: Urban Institute Press.

Edwards, C. P., & Whiting, B. B. (1993). "Mother, older sibling and me": The overlapping roles of caregivers and companions in the social world of 2- to 3-year-olds in Ngeca, Kenya. In K. MacDonald (Ed.), *Parent-child play: Descriptions and implications* (pp. 305–329). Albany: State University of New York Press.

Eisenberg, N. (2000). Emotion, regulation, and moral development. *Annual Review of Psychology, 51,* 665–697.

Eisenberg, N., Cumberland, A., & Spinrad, T. (1998). Parental socialization of emotion. *Psychological Inquiry, 9,* 241–273.

Eisenberg, N., & Fabes, R. A. (1992). Emotion, regulation and the development of social competence. In M. S. Clark (Ed.), *Emotion and social behavior: Vol. 14. Review of personality and social psychology* (pp. 119–150). Thousand Oaks, CA: Sage.

Eisenberg, N., & Fabes, R. A. (1994). Mothers' reactions to children's negative emotions: Relations to children's temperament and anger behavior. *Merrill-Palmer Quarterly, 40,* 138–156.

Eisenberg, N., Fabes, R. A., Schaller, M., & Miller, P. (1991). Personality and socialization correlates of vicarious emotional responding. *Journal of Personality and Social Psychology, 61*, 459–470.

Eisenberg, N., Guthrie, I. K., Fabes, R. A., Shepard, S., Losoya, S., Muprhy, B. C., et al. (2000). Prediction of elementary school childrens' externalizing problem behavior from attentional and behavioral regulation and negative emotionality. *Child Development, 71*, 1367–1382.

Elder, G. H., Jr. (1974). *Children of the great depression: Social change in life experience.* Chicago: University of Chicago Press.

Elder, G. H., Jr. (1998). The life course as developmental theory. *Child Development, 69*, 1–12.

Elder, G. H., Jr., & Conger, R. D. (2000). *Children of the land: Adversity and success in rural America.* Chicago: University of Chicago Press.

Elder, G. H., Jr., Nguyen, T. V., & Caspi, A. (1985). Linking family hardship to children's lives. *Child Development, 56*, 361–375.

Emery, R. E., Kitzmann, K. M., & Waldron, M. (1999). Psychological interventions for separated and divorced families. In E. M. Hetherington (Ed.), *Coping with divorce, single parenting, and remarriage: A risk and resiliency perspective* (pp. 323–344). Mahwah, NJ: Erlbaum.

Entwisle, D. R., & Astone, N. M. (1994). Some practical guidelines for measuring youths' race/ethnicity and socioeconomic status. *Child Development, 65*, 1521–1540.

Epstein, J. L., & Sanders, M. G. (2002). Family, school, and community partnerships. In M. H. Bornstein (Ed.), *Handbook of parenting: Vol. 5. Practical issues in parenting* (pp. 407–438). Mahwah, NJ: Erlbaum.

Erel, O., & Burman, B. (1995). Interrelatedness of marital relations and parent-child relations: A meta-analytic review. *Psychological Bulletin, 118*, 108–132.

Erera, P. I. (1997). Step- and foster families: A comparison. *Marriage and Family Review, 26*, 301–315.

Esposito, S. (2004). *Immigrant dreams: A study of Mexican mothers and language choice.* Unpublished doctoral dissertation, Claremont Graduate University, CA.

Fagan, J., & Hawkins, A. J. (Eds.). (2001). *Clinical and educational interventions with fathers.* Binghamton, NY: Haworth Clinical Practice Press.

Farley, R., & Allen, W. R. (1987). *The color line and the course quality of life in America.* New York: Russell-Sage Foundation.

Fauber, R. L., & Long, N. (1991). Children in context: The role of the family in child psychotherapy. *Journal of Consulting and Clinical Psychology, 59*, 813–820.

Featherman, D. L., Spenner, K. I., & Tsunematsu, N. (1988). Class and the socialization of children: Constancy, change, or irrelevance. In E. M. Hetherington, R. M. Lerner, & M. Perlmutter (Eds.), *Child development in life-span perspective* (pp. 67–90). Hillsdale, NJ: Erlbaum.

Federal Interagency Forum on Child and Family Statistics. (2002). *America's children: Key national indicators of well-being.* Washington, DC: Author.

Felix-Ortiz de la Garza, M., Newcomb, M. D., & Meyers, H. F. (1995). A multidimensional measure of cultural identity for Latino and Latina adolescents. In A. M. Padilla (Ed.), *Hispanic psychology: Critical issues in theory and research* (pp. 26–42). Thousand Oaks, CA: Sage.

Field, T. (1992). Infants of depressed mothers. *Development and Psychopathology, 4*, 49–66.

Fiese, B. H. (2006a). Family routines and rituals: Family transactions and individual health. In D. Snyder, J. Simpson, & I. N. Hughes (Eds.), *Emotional regulation in families.* Washington, DC: American Psychological Association.

Fiese, B. H. (2006b). *Family routines and rituals: Promising prospects for the 21st century.* New Haven, CT: Yale University Press.

Fiese, B. H., & Marjinsky, K. A. T. (1999). Dinnertime stories: Connecting family practices with relationship beliefs and child adjustment. *Monographs of the Society for Research in Child Development, 64*(2, Serial No. 257), 52–68.

Fiese, B. H., Sameroff, A. J., Grotevant, H. D., Wamboldt, F. S., Dickstein, S., & Fravel, D. L. (1999). The stories that families tell: Narrative coherence, narrative interaction, and relationship beliefs. *Monographs of the Society of Research in Child Development, 64*(2, Serial No. 257).

Fiese, B. H., Tomcho, T., Douglas, M., Josephs, K., Poltrock, S., & Baker, T. (2002). A review of 50 years of research on naturally occurring family routines and rituals: Cause for celebration? *Journal of Family Psychology, 16*, 381–390.

Fivaz-Depeursinge, E., & Corboz-Warnery, A. (1999). *The primary triangle: A developmental systems view of mothers, fathers, and infants.* New York: Basic Books.

Flannery, W. P., Reise, S. P., & Widaman, K. E. (1995). An item response theory analysis of the general and academic scales of the self-description questionnaire II. *Journal of Research in Personality, 29*, 168–188.

Fletcher, A. C., Darling, N. E., Steinberg, L., & Dornbusch, S. (1995). The company they keep: Relation of adolescents' adjustment behavior to their friends' perceptions of authoritative parenting in the social network. *Developmental Psychology, 31*, 300–310.

Frone, M. R., Yardley, J. K., & Markel, K. S. (1997). Developing and testing an intergrative model of the work-family interface. *Journal of Vocational Behavior, 50*, 145–167.

Fuligni, A. J. (1997). The academic achievement of adolescents from immigrant families: The role of family background, attitudes, and behavior. *Child Development, 68*, 351–363.

Fuligni, A. J., Tseng, V., & Lam, M. (1999). Attitudes toward family obligations among American adolescents with Asian, Latin American, and European backgrounds. *Child Development, 70*, 1030–1044.

Fuller, G. (2004, October 10). *A snapshot report on American Indian youth and families.* Retrieved from http://www.ocbtracker.com/007/snapshot.html.

Furstenburg, F. F., Jr., Cook, T. D., Eccles, J., Elder, G. H., Jr., & Sameroff, A. (1999). *Managing to make it: Urban families and adolescent success.* Chicago: University of Chicago Press.

Gadsen, V. (1999). Black parenting in intergenerational and cultural perspective. In M. E. Lamb (Ed.), *Parenting and child development in "nontraditional" families* (pp. 221–246). Mahwah, NJ: Erlbaum.

Galinsky, E., & Swanberg, J. E. (2000). Employed mothers and fathers in the United States: Understanding how work and family fit together. In L. L. Haas, P. Hwang, & G. Russell (Eds.), *Organizational change and gender equity: International perspectives on fathers and mothers at the workplace* (pp. 15–28). Thousand Oaks, CA: Sage.

Gandara, P. (1997). *Review of research on the instruction of limited English proficient students.* Davis: University of California Linguistic Minority Research Institute, Education Policy Center.

Garcia Coll, C., Crnic, K., Lamberty, G., Wasik, B. H., Jenkins, R., & Garcia, H. V. (1996). An integrative model for the study of developmental competencies in minority children. *Child Development, 67*, 1891–1914.

Garcia Coll, C. T., & Magnuson, K. (1999). Cultural influences on child development: Are we ready for a paradigm shift? In A. S. Masten (Ed.), *Minnesota Symposia on Child Psychology: Vol. 29. Cultural processes in child development* (pp. 1–24). Mahwah, NJ: Erlbaum.

Garcia Coll, C. T., Meyer, E. C., & Brillon, L. (1995). Ethnic and minority parenting. In M. H. Bornstein (Ed.), *Handbook of parenting: Vol. 2. Biology and ecology of parenting* (pp. 189–209). Hillsdale, NJ: Erlbaum.

Gauvain, M. (2001). *The social context of cognitive development.* New York: Guilford Press.

Geary, D. C., & Bjorklund, D. F. (2000). Evolutionary developmental psychology. *Child Development, 71,* 57–65.

Gewirtz, J. (1969). Mechanisms of social learning: Some roles of stimulation and behavior in early human development. In D. Goslin (Ed.), *Handbook of socialization theory and research* (pp. 57–212). Chicago: Rand-McNally.

Goeke-Morey, M. C., Cummings, E. M., Harold, G. T., & Shelton, K. H. (2003). Categories and continua of destructive and constructive marital conflict tactics from the perspective of U.S. and Welsh children. *Journal of Family Psychology, 17,* 327–338.

Gomel, J., Tinsley, B. J., Clark, K., & Parke, R. D. (1998). The effects of economic hardship on family relationships among African Americans, Latino, and Euro-American families. *Journal of Family Issues, 19,* 436–467.

Goodman, S. M., & Gotlib, I. (Eds.). (2002). *Children of depressed parents: Mechanisms of risk and implications for treatment.* Washington, DC: American Psychological Association.

Goodnow, J. J. (2002). Parents' knowledge and expectations: Using what we know. In M. H. Bornstein (Ed.), *Handbook of parenting: Vol. 3. Being and becoming a parent* (2nd ed., pp. 439–460). Mahwah, NJ: Erlbaum.

Gottfried, A. E., Gottfried, A. W., & Bathurst, K. (2002). Maternal and dual-earner employment status and parenting. In M. H. Bornstein (Ed.), *Handbook of parenting: Vol. 2. Biology and ecology of parenting* (2nd ed., pp. 207–230). Mahwah, NJ: Erlbaum.

Gottman, J. M. (1994). *What predicts divorce? The relationship between marital processes and marital outcomes.* Hillsdale, NJ: Erlbaum.

Gottman, J. M., Katz, L. F., & Hooven, C. (1997). *Meta-emotion: How families communicate emotionally.* Hillsdale, NJ: Erlbaum.

Greenberger, E., O'Neil, R., & Nagel, S. K. (1994). Linking workplace and homeplace: Relations between the nature of adults' work and their parenting behaviors. *Developmental Psychology, 30,* 990–1002.

Greenfield, P. M., & Cocking, R. R. (1994). *Cross-cultural roots of minority child development.* Hillsdale, NJ: Erlbaum.

Griffith, J., & Villavicencio, S. (1985). Relationships among acculturation, sociodemographic characteristics, and social supports in Mexican American adults. *Hispanic Journal of Behavioral Sciences, 7,* 75–92.

Grimes, C. L., Klein, T. R., & Putallaz, M. (2004). Parents' relationships with their parents and peers: Influences on children's social development. In J. B. Kupersmidt & K. Dodge (Eds.), *Children's peer relations: From development to intervention* (pp. 141–158). Washington, DC: American Psychological Association.

Grimm-Thomas, K., & Perry-Jenkins, M. (1994). All in a day's work: Job experiences, self-esteem and fathering in working-class families. *Family Relations: Interdisciplinary Journal of Applied Family Studies, 43,* 174–181.

Grossman, F. K., Pollock, W. S., & Golding, E. (1988). Fathers and children: Predicting the quality and quantity of fathering. *Developmental Psychology, 24,* 82–91.

Grotevant, H. D., Fravel, D. L., Gorall, D., & Piper, J. (1999). Narratives of adoptive parents: Perspectives from individual and couple interviews. *Monographs of the Society for Research in Child Development, 64*(2, Serial No. 257), 69–93.

Grusec, J. E. (1992). Social learning theory and developmental psychology: The legacies of Robert Sears and Albert Bandura. *Developmental Psychology, 28,* 776–786.

Grusec, J. E., & Goodnow, J. J. (1994). Impact of parental discipline methods on the child's internalization of values: A reconceptualization of current points of view. *Developmental Psychology, 30,* 4–19.

Grusec, J. E., & Ungerer, J. (2003). Effective socialization as problem solving and the role of parenting cognitions. In L. Kuczynski (Ed.), *Handbook of dynamics in parent-child relations* (pp. 211–228). Thousand Oaks, CA: Sage.

Grych, J. H., & Cardoza-Fernandes, S. (2001). Understanding the impacts of interparental conflict on children: The role of social cognitive processes. In J. H. Grych & F. D. Fincham (Eds.), *Interparental conflict and child development: Theory, research, and applications* (pp. 157–187). New York: Cambridge University Press.

Grych, J. H., & Fincham, F. D. (1990). Marital conflict and children's adjustment: A cognitive-contextual framework. *Psychological Bulletin, 108,* 267–290.

Grych, J. H., & Fincham, F. D. (Eds.). (2001). *Child development and interparental conflict: Theory, research, and applications.* New York: Cambridge University Press.

Gutierrez, J., & Sameroff, A. (1990). Determinants of complexity in Mexican-American and Anglo-American mothers' conceptions of child development. *Child Development, 61,* 384–394.

Hakuta, K., Butler, Y. G., & Witt, D. (2000). *How long does it take English learners to gain proficiency?* (Policy Rep. 2000-1). Stanford University: University of California Language Minority Institute.

Halberstadt, A. G., Denham, S. A., & Dunsmore, J. C. (2001). Affective social competence. *Social Development, 10,* 79–119.

Harjo, S. S. (1993). The American Indian experience. In H. P. McAdoo (Ed.), *Family ethnicity: Strength in diversity* (pp. 199–207). Thousand Oaks, CA: Sage.

Harkness, S., & Super, C. M. (1995). Culture and parenting. In M. H. Bornstein (Ed.), *Handbook of parenting: Vol. 2. Biology and ecology of parenting* (pp. 211–234). Hillsdale, NJ: Erlbaum.

Harold-Goldsmith, R., Radin, N., & Eccles, J. S. (1988). Objective and subjective reality: The effects of job loss and financial stress on fathering behaviors. *Family Perspective, 22,* 309–325.

Harris, J. R. (1998). *The nurture assumption: Why children turn out the way they do.* New York: Free Press.

Harrison, A. O. (1985). The Black family's socializing environment: Self-esteem and ethnic attitude among Black children. In H. P. McAdoo & J. L. McAdoo (Eds.), *Black children: Social, educational, and parental environments* (pp. 174–193). Thousand Oaks, CA: Sage.

Harrison, A. O., Wilson, M. N., Pine, C. J., Chan, S. Q., & Buriel, R. (1990). Family ecologies of ethnic minority children. *Child Development, 61,* 347–362.

Harrist, A. W., Pettit, G. S., Dodge, K. A., & Bates, J. E. (1994). Dyadic synchrony in mother-child interaction: Relation with children's subsequent kindergarten adjustment. *Family Relations: Interdisciplinary Journal of Applied Family Studies, 43,* 417–424.

Hart, B., & Risley, T. R. (1995). *Meaningful differences in the everyday experience of young American children.* Baltimore: Paul H. Brookes.

Hart, C. H., Yang, C., Nelson, D. A., Jin, S., Bazarskava, N., Nelson, L. J., et al. (1998). Peer contact patterns, parenting practices, and preschoolers' social competence in China, Russia, and the United States. In P. Slee & K. Rigby (Eds.), *Peer relation amongst children: Current issues and future directions* (pp. 3–30). London: Routledge.

Hatchett, S. J., & Jackson, J. S. (1993). African American extended kin systems: An assessment. In H. P. McAdoo (Ed.), *Family ethnicity: Strength in diversity* (pp. 90–108). Thousand Oaks, CA: Sage.

Henggeler, S. W., Edwards, J. J., Cohen, R., & Summerville, M. B. (1992). Predicting changes in children's popularity: The role of family relations. *Journal of Applied Developmental Psychology, 12,* 205–218.

Hess, R. D., & Shipman, V. C. (1965). Early experience and the socialization of cognitive modes in children. *Child Development, 36,* 869–886.

Hetherington, E. M., & Clingempeel, W. G. (Eds.). (1992). Coping with marital transitions: A family systems perspective. *Monographs of the Society for Research in Child Development, 57*(2/3, Serial No. 227), 1–242.

Hetherington, E. M., Cox, M., & Cox, R. (1985). Long-term effects of divorce and remarriage on the adjustment of children. *Journal of the American Academy of Child Psychiatry, 24,* 518–530.

Hetherington, E. M., & Kelly, J. (2001). *For better or for worse: Divorce reconsidered.* New York: Norton.

Hewlett, B. (2004). Fathers in nonindustrial cultures. In M. E. Lamb (Ed.), *The role of the father in child development* (4th ed., pp. 182–195). New York: Wiley.

Hill, N. E., Bush, K. R., & Roosa, M. W. (2003). Parenting and family socialization strategies and children's mental health: Low income, Mexican-American and Euro-American mothers and children. *Child Development, 74,* 189–204.

Hill, N. E., & Herman-Stahl, M. A. (2002). Neighborhood safety and social involvement: Associations with parenting behaviors and depressive symptoms among African-American and Euro-American mothers. *Journal of Family Psychology, 16,* 209–219.

Hill, R. B. (1988). Cash and noncash benefits among poor Black families. In H. P. McAdoo (Ed.), *Black families* (2nd ed., pp. 306–318). Thousand Oaks, CA: Sage.

Ho, D. Y. F. (1986). Chinese patterns of socialization: A critical review. In M. H. Bond (Ed.), *The psychology of the Chinese people* (pp. 1–37). London: Oxford University Press.

Hoff, E., Laursen, B., & Tardif, T. (2002). Socioeconomic status and parenting. In M. H. Bornstein (Ed.), *Handbook of parenting: Vol. 2. Biology and ecology of parenting* (2nd ed., pp. 231–252). Mahwah, NJ: Erlbaum.

Hoff-Ginsberg, E., & Tardif, T. (1995). Socioeconomic status and parenting. In M. H. Bornstein (Ed.), *Handbook of parenting: Vol. 2. Biology and ecology of parenting* (pp. 161–188). Hillsdale, NJ: Erlbaum.

Hoffman, L. W. (1991). The influence of the family environment on personality: Accounting for sibling differences. *Psychological Bulletin, 110,* 187–203.

Hoffman, L. W. (2000). Maternal employment: Effects of social context. In R. D. Taylor & M. C. Wang (Eds.), *Resilience across contexts: Family, work, culture, and community* (pp. 147–176). Mahwah, NJ: Erlbaum.

Hoffman, L. W., & Youngblade, L. M. (1999). *Mothers at work: Effects on children's well-being.* New York: Cambridge University Press.

Homel, R., & Burns, A. (1989). Environmental quality and the well-being of children. *Social Indicators Research, 21,* 133–158.

Homel, R., Burns, A., & Goodnow, J. (1987). Parental social networks and child development. *Journal of Social and Personal Relationships, 4,* 159–177.

Hudson, P., & Taylor-Henley, S. (2001). Beyond the rhetoric: Implementing a culturally appropriate research project in first nation communities. *American Indian Culture and Research Journal, 25,* 93–105.

Huffman, D. G., & Cummings, E. M. (2002). *Children's reactions to marital conflict simulations featuring mutual hostility and parental depression.* Unpublished paper, University of Notre Dame.

Huntsinger, C. S., & Jose, P. E. (1995). Chinese American and Caucasian American family interaction patterns in spatial rotation puzzle solutions. *Merrill-Palmer Quarterly, 41,* 471–496.

Huntsinger, C. S., Jose, P. E., & Larson, S. L. (1998). Do parent practices to encourage academic competence influence the social adjustment of young European American and Chinese American children? *Developmental Psychology, 34,* 747–756.

Hwang, P. (1987). The changing role of Swedish fathers. In M. E. Lamb (Ed.), *The father's role: Cross-cultural perspectives* (pp. 115–138). Hillsdale, NJ: Erlbaum.

Isley, S. L., O'Neil, R., Clatfelter, D., & Parke, R. D. (1999). Parent and child expressed affect and children's social competence: Modeling direct and indirect pathways. *Developmental Psychology, 35,* 547–560.

Isley, S., O'Neil, R., & Parke, R. D. (1996). The relation of parental affect and control behaviors to children's classroom acceptance: A concurrent and predictive analysis. *Early Education and Development, 7,* 7–23.

Joe, J. R. (1994). Revaluing Native-American concepts of development and education. In P. M. Greenfield & R. R. Cocking (Eds.), *Cross-cultural roots of minority child development* (pp. 107–113). Hillsdale, NJ: Erlbaum.

Jones, J. M. (2003). Constructing race and deconstructing racism: A cultural psychology approach. In G. Bernal, J. E. Trimble, A. K. Burlew, & F. T. L. Leong (Eds.), *Handbook of racial and ethnic minority psychology* (pp. 276–290). Thousand Oaks, CA: Sage.

Kagan, S. (1984). Interpreting Chicano cooperativeness: Methodological and theoretical considerations. In J. L. Martinez Jr. & R. H. Mendoza (Eds.), *Chicano psychology* (2nd ed., pp. 289–333). Orlando, FL: Academic Press.

Katz, L. F., & Gottman, J. M. (1993). Patterns of marital conflict predict children's internalizing and externalizing behaviors. *Developmental Psychology, 29,* 940–950.

Keefe, S. E., & Padilla, A. M. (1987). *Chicano ethnicity.* Albuquerque: University of New Mexico Press.

Kelley, M. L., Power, T. G., & Wimbush, D. D. (1992). Determinants of disciplinary practices in low-income Black mothers. *Child Development, 63,* 573–582.

Kelley, M. L., Sanchez-Hucies, J., & Walker, R. (1993). Correlates of disciplinary practices in working- to middle-class African-American mothers. *Merrill-Palmer Quarterly, 39,* 252–264.

Kerig, P. K. (1996). Assessing the links between interparental conflict and child adjustment: The conflict and problem-solving scales. *Journal of Family Psychology, 10,* 454–473.

Kerig, P. K. (2001). Children's coping with interparental conflict. In J. H. Grych & F. D. Fincham (Eds.), *Interparental conflict and child development* (pp. 213–248). New York: Cambridge University Press.

Kerr, M., & Stattin, H. (2000). What parents know, how they know it, and several forms of adolescent adjustment: Further support for a reinterpretation of monitoring. *Developmental Psychology, 36,* 366–380.

Kibria, N. (1993). *Family tightrope: The changing lives of Vietnamese Americans.* Princeton, NJ: Princeton University Press.

Kim, K., & Honig, A. S. (1998). Relationship of maternal employment status support for resilience with child resilience among Korean immigrant families in the United States. *Early Child Development and Care, 141,* 41–60.

Kim, U., & Berry, J. W. (1993). *Indigenous psychologies: Research and experience in cultural context.* Thousand Oaks, CA: Sage.

Knight, G. P., Tein, J.-Y., Prost, J. H., & Gonzales, N. A. (2002). Measurement equivalence and research on Latino families: The importance of culturally informed theory. In J. M. Contreras, K. A. Kerns, & A. M. Neal-Barnett (Eds.), *Latino children and families in the United States* (pp. 181–201). Westport, CT: Praeger.

Knight, G. P., Virdin, L. M., & Roosa, M. (1994). Socialization and family correlates of mental health outcomes among Hispanic and Anglo American children: Consideration of cross-ethnic scalar equivalence. *Child Development, 65,* 212–224.

Kochanska, G. (1993). Toward a synthesis of parental socialization and child temperament in early development of conscience. *Child Development, 64,* 325–347.

Kochanska, G. (1997). Multiple pathways to conscience for children with different temperaments: From toddlerhood to age 5. *Developmental Psychology, 33,* 228–240.

Kohn, M. V. (1995). Social structure and personality through time and space. In P. Moen, G. H. Elder Jr., & K. Luscher (Eds.), *Examining lives in context: Perspectives on the ecology of human development* (pp. 141–168). Washington, DC: American Psychological Association.

Kramer, L. (2004). Experimental interventions in sibling relationships. In R. D. Conger, F. O. Lorenz, & K. A. S. Wickrama (Eds.), *Continuity and change in family relations: Theory, methods and empirical findings* (pp. 345–380). Mahwah, NJ: Erlbaum.

Kramer, L., & Gottman, J. M. (1992). Becoming a sibling: "With a little help from my friends." *Developmental Psychology, 28,* 685–699.

Krappmann, L. (1986, December). *Family relationships and peer relationships in middle childhood: An exploratory study of the associations between children's integration into the social network of peers and family development.* Paper presented at the Family Systems and Life-Span Development Conference at the Max Planck Institute, Berlin, Germany.

Krishnakumar, A., & Black, M. M. (2003). Family processes within three-generation households and adolescent mothers' satisfaction with father involvement. *Journal of Family Psychology, 17,* 488–498.

Krishnakumar, A., & Buehler, C. (2000). Interparental conflict and parenting behaviors: A meta-analytic review. *Family Relations: Interdisciplinary Journal of Applied Family Studies, 49,* 25–44.

Kuczynski, L. (Ed.). (2003). *Handbook of dynamics in parent-child relations.* Thousand Oaks, CA: Sage.

Kuczynski L., Marshall, S., & Schell, K. (1997). Value socialization in a bidirectional context. In J. E. Grusec & L. Kuczynski (Eds.), *Parenting and the children's internalization of values: A handbook of contemporary theory* (pp. 23–50). New York: Wiley.

Ladd, G. W. (1992). Themes and theories: Perspective on processes in family-peer relationships. In R. D. Parke & G. W. Ladd (Eds.), *Family-peer relationships: Modes of linkage* (pp. 3–34). Hillsdale, NJ: Erlbaum.

Ladd, G., & Pettit, G. (2002). Parenting and the development of children's peer relationships. In M. H. Bornstein (Ed.), *Handbook of parenting: Vol. 5. Practical issues in parenting* (2nd ed., pp. 269–309). Mahwah, NJ: Erlbaum.

LaFromboise, T., Coleman, H. L., & Gerton, J. (1993). Psychological impact of biculturalism: Evidence and theory. *Psychological Bulletin, 114,* 395–412.

Lamb, M. E. (Ed.). (2004). *The role of the father in child development* (4th ed.). Hoboken, NJ: Wiley.

Lamb, M. E., Pleck, J. H., & Levine, J. A. (1985). The role of the father in child development: The effects of increased paternal involvement. In B. Lahey & E. E. Kazdin (Eds.), *Advances in clinical child psychology* (Vol. 8, pp. 229–266). New York: Plenum Press.

Landrine, J., & Klonoff, E. A. (1996). *African American acculturation: Deconstructing race and reviving culture.* Thousand Oaks, CA: Sage.

Laosa, L. M. (1980). Maternal teaching strategies in Chicano and Anglo-American families: The influence of culture and education on maternal behavior. *Child Development, 51,* 759–765.

Laosa, L. M. (1982). School, occupation, culture, and family: The impact of parental schooling on the parent-child relationship. *Journal of Educational Psychology, 74,* 791–827.

Larson, R., & Richards, M. H. (1994). *Divergent realities: The emotional lives of mothers, fathers, and adolescents.* New York: Basic Books.

LeCorgne, L. L., & Laosa, L. M. (1976). Father absence in low-income Mexican-American families: Children's social adjustment and conceptual differentiation of sex-role attributes. *Developmental Psychology, 12,* 470–471.

Leventhal, T., & Brooks-Gunn, J. (2000). The neighborhoods they live in: The effects of neighborhood residence on child and adolescent outcomes. *Psychological Bulletin, 126,* 309–337.

Lopez, D. E. (1982). *Language maintenance and shift in the United States today—The basic patterns and their social implications: Vol. 1. Overview and summary.* Los Alamitos, CA: National Center for Bilingual Research.

Lum, D. (1986). *Social work practice and people of color: A process-stage approach.* Monterey, CA: Brooks/Cole.

Lyons-Ruth, K., Lyubchik, A., Wolfe, R., & Bronfman, E. (2002). Parental depression and child attachment: Hostile and helpless profiles of parent and child behavior among families at risk. In S. H. Goodman & I. H. Gotlib (Eds.), *Children of depressed parents: Mechanisms of risk and implications for treatment* (pp. 89–120). Washington, DC: American Psychological Association.

Maccoby, E. E. (1984). Socialization and developmental change. *Child Development, 55,* 317–328.

Maccoby, E. E. (1988). Gender as a social category. *Developmental Psychology, 24,* 755–765.

Maccoby, E. E. (1992). The role of parents in the socialization of children: An historical overview. *Developmental Psychology, 28,* 1006–1017.

Maccoby, E. E. (1998). *The two sexes: Growing up apart, coming together.* Cambridge, MA: Belknap Press/Harvard University Press.

Maccoby, E. E., & Martin, J. A. (1983). Socialization in the context of the family: Parent-child interaction. In E. M. Hetherington (Ed.), *Handbook of child psychology: Vol. 4. Socialization, personality, and social development* (4th ed., pp. 1–101). New York: Wiley.

MacDonald, K., & Parke, R. D. (1984). Bridging the gap: Parent-child play interaction and peer interactive competence. *Child Development, 55,* 1265–1277.

MacDonald, K., & Parke, R. D. (1986). Parent-child physical play: The effects of sex and age of children and parents. *Sex Roles, 15(7/8),* 367–378.

Machamer, A. M., & Gruber, E. (1998). Secondary school, family, and educational risk: Comparing American Indian adolescents and their peers. *Journal of Educational Research, 91,* 357–369.

MacKinnon-Lewis, C., Volling, B. L., Lamb, M. E., Dechman, K., Rabiner, D., & Curtner, M. E. (1994). A cross-contextual analysis of boys' social competence: From family to school. *Developmental Psychology, 30,* 325–333.

Mahoney, A., Pargament, K. I., Tarakeshwar, N., & Swank, A. B. (2001). Religion in the home in the 1980s and 1990s: A meta-analytic review and conceptual analysis of links between religion, marriage, and parenting. *Journal of Family Psychology, 15,* 559–596.

Maynard, A. E. (2002). Cultural teaching: The development of teaching skills in Maya sibling interactions. *Child Development, 73,* 969–982.

McAdoo, H. P. (1978). Factors related to stability in upwardly mobile Black families. *Journal of Marriage and the Family, 40,* 761–776.

McAdoo, J. L. (1993). Decision-making and marital satisfaction in African-American families. In H. P. McAdoo (Ed.), *Family ethnicity: Strength in diversity* (pp. 109–119). Thousand Oaks, CA: Sage.

McDonald, R., Jouriles, E. N., Norwood, W., Ware, H. S., & Ezell, E. (2000). Husbands' marital violence and the adjustment problems of clinic-referred children. *Behavior Therapy, 31,* 649–665.

McDowell, D. J., O'Neil, R., & Parke, R. D. (2000). Display rule application in a disappointing situation and children's emotional reactivity: Relations with social competence. *Merrill-Palmer Quarterly, 46,* 306–324.

McDowell, D. J., & Parke, R. D. (2000). Differential knowledge of display rules for positive and negative emotions: Influences from parents, influences on peers. *Social Development, 9,* 415–432.

McDowell, D. J., & Parke, R. D. (2005). Parental control and affect as predictors of children's display rule use and social competence with peers. *Social Development, 14,* 440–457.

McDowell, D. J., Parke, R. D., & Spitzer, S. (2002). Parent and child cognitive representations of social situations and children's social competence. *Social Development, 4,* 486–496.

McDowell, D. J., Parke, R. D., & Wang, S. J. (2003). Differences between mothers' and fathers' advice-giving style and content: Relations with social competence and psychological functioning in middle childhood. *Merrill-Palmer Quarterly, 49,* 55–76.

McHale, J. P., Lauretti, A., Talbot, J., & Pouquette, C. (2002). Retrospect and prospect in the psychological study of coparenting and family group process. In J. P. McHale & W. S. Grolnick (Eds.), *Retrospect and prospect in the psychological study of families* (pp. 127–165). Mahwah, NJ: Erlbaum.

McHale, J. P., & Rasmussen, J. L. (1998). Coparental and family group-level dynamics during infancy: Early family precursors of child and family functioning during preschool. *Development and Psychopathology, 10,* 39–58.

McHale, S. M., Crouter, A. C., & Whiteman, S. D. (2003). The family contexts of gender development in childhood and adolescence. *Social Development, 12,* 125–148.

McLoyd, V. C. (1998). Socioeconomic disadvantage and child development. *American Psychologist, 53,* 185–204.

McLoyd, V. C., Hill, N. E., & Dodge, K. A. (Eds.). (2005). *African American family life.* New York: Guilford Press.

McLoyd, V. C., & Steinberg, L. (Eds.). (1998). *Studying minority adolescents: Conceptual, methodological, and theoretical issues.* Mahwah, NJ: Erlbaum.

McWright, L. (2002). African American grandmothers' and grandfathers' influence in the value socialization of grandchildren. In H. P. McAdoo (Ed.), *Black children: Social, educational, and parental environments* (2nd ed., pp. 27–44). Thousand Oaks, CA: Sage.

Medrich, E. (1982). *The serious business of growing up: A study of children's lives outside school.* Berkeley: University of California Press.

Miller, P., & Sperry, L. L. (1987). The socialization of anger and aggression. *Merrill-Palmer Quarterly, 33,* 1–31.

Minuchin, P. (2002). Looking toward the horizon: Present and future in the study of family systems. In J. P. McHale & W. S. Grolnick. *Retrospect and prospect in the psychological study of families* (pp. 259–278). Mahwah, NJ: Erlbaum.

Mishel, L., Bernstein, J., & Schmitt, J. (1999). *The state of working America.* Ithaca, NY: Cornell University Press.

Mize, J., & Pettit, G. S. (1997). Mothers' social coaching, mother-child relationship style, and children's peer competence: Is the medium the message? *Child Development, 68,* 312–332.

Modell, J., & Elder, G. H. (2002). Children develop in history: So what's new. In W. W. Hartup & R. A. Weinberg (Eds.), *Minnesota Symposia on Child Psychology: Vol. 32. Child psychology in retrospect and prospect* (In celebration of the 75th anniversary of the Institute of Child Development) (pp. 173–206). Mahwah, NJ: Erlbaum.

Moore, M. R., & Brooks-Gunn, J. (2002). Adolescent parenthood. In M. H. Bornstein (Ed.), *Handbook of parenting: Vol. 3. Being and becoming a parent* (2nd ed., pp. 173–214). Mahwah, NJ: Erlbaum.

Moos, R. H., & Moos, B. S. (1981). *Family environment scales manual.* Palo Alto, CA: Consulting Psychologists Press.

Mounts, N. S. (2000). Parental management of adolescent peer relationships: What are its effect on friend selection. In K. A. Kerns, J. M. Contreras, & A. M. Neal-Barnett (Eds.), *Family and peers: Linking two social worlds* (pp. 169–194). Westport, CT: Praeger.

Mounts, N. S. (2001). Young adolescents' perceptions of parental management of peer relationships. *Journal of Early Adolescence, 21,* 92–122.

Mounts, N. S. (2002). Parental management of adolescent peer relationships in context: The role of parenting style. *Journal of Family Psychology, 16,* 58–69.

Murguia, E. (1982). *Chicano intermarriage: A theoretical and empirical study.* San Antonio, TX: Trinity University Press.

Murray, C. B., & Mandara, J. (2002). Racial identity development in African American children: Cognitive and experiential antecedents. In H. P. McAdoo (Ed.), *Black children: Social, educational, and parental environments* (2nd ed., pp. 73–96). Thousand Oaks, CA: Sage.

National Center for Children in Poverty. (2000, Fall). *News and Issues, 10* (NDRI Monograph No. 3). New York: Mailman School of Pubic Health, Columbia University.

National Institute of Child Health and Human Development Early Child Care Research Network. (2003a). Does amount of time spent in child care predict socioemotional adjustment during the transition to kindergarten? *Child Development, 74,* 976–1005.

National Institute of Child Health and Human Development Early Child Care Research Network. (2003b). Do children's attention processes mediate the link between family predictors and school readiness? *Developmental Psychology, 39,* 581–593.

National Institute of Child Health and Human Development Early Child Care Research Network. (2005). *Family-peer linkages: Attributional and attentional processes as mediators.* Unpublished manuscript, National Institute of Child Health and Human Development, Bethesda, MD.

New, R., & Benigni, L. (1987). Italian fathers and infants: Cultural constraints on paternal behavior. In M. E. Lamb (Ed.), *The father's role: Cross-cultural perspectives* (pp. 139–167). Hillsdale, NJ: Erlbaum.

Nobles, W. W., Goddard, L. L., Cavil, W. E., & George, P. Y. (1987). *African-American families: Issues, insight, and directions.* Oakland, CA: Black Family Institute.

O'Connor, T. G. (2003). Behavioral genetic contributions to understanding dynamic processes in parent-child relationships. In L. Kuczynski (Ed.), *Handbook of dynamics in parent-child relations* (pp. 145–163). Thousand Oaks, CA: Sage.

Ogbu, J. U. (1987). Variability in minority responses to schooling: Nonimmigrants versus immigrants. In G. Spindler & L. Spindler (Eds.), *Interpretive ethnography of education: At home and abroad* (pp. 255–280). Hillsdale, NJ: Erlbaum.

Ogbu, J. U. (1991). Immigrant and involuntary minorities in comparative perspective. In M. A. Gibson & J. U. Ogbu (Eds.), *Minority status and schooling: A comparative study of immigrant and involuntary minorities* (pp. 3–36). New York: Garland.

O'Hearn, H. G., Margolin, G., & John, R. S. (1997). Mothers' and fathers' reports of children's reactions to naturalistic martial conflict. *Journal of the American Academy of Child and Adolescent Psychiatry, 36,* 1366–1373.

Okagaki, L., & Bojczyk, K. E. (2002). Perspectives on Asian American development. In G. C. Nagayama Hall & S. Okazaki (Eds.), *Asian American psychology: The science of lives in context* (pp. 67–104). Washington, DC: American Psychological Association.

Okagaki, L., & Divecha, D. J. (1993). Development of parental beliefs. In T. Luster & L. Okagaki (Eds.), *Parenting: An ecological perspective* (pp. 35–67). Hillsdale, NJ: Erlbaum.

Okagaki, L., & Sternberg, R. J. (1993). Parental beliefs and children's school performance. *Child Development, 64,* 36–56.

Olds, D. L., Henderson, C. R., Kitzman, H. J., Eckenrode, J. J., Cole, R. E., & Tatelbaum, R. C. (1999). Parental and infancy home visitation by nurses: Recent findings. *Future of Children, 9,* 44–65.

Olsen, L., & Chen, M. T. (1988). *Crossing the schoolhouse border: Immigrant students and the California public schools.* San Francisco: California Tomorrow Policy Research Report.

O'Neil, R., & Parke, R. D. (2000). Family-peer relationships: The role of emotion regulation, cognitive understanding and attentional processes as mediating processes. In K. A. Kerns, J. M. Contreras, & A. M. Neal-Barnett (Eds.), *Family and peers: Linking two social worlds* (pp. 195–226). Westport, CT: Praeger.

O'Neil, R., Parke, R. D., & McDowell, D. J. (2001). Objective and subjective features of children's neighborhoods: Relations to parental regulatory strategies and children's social competence. *Journal of Applied Developmental Psychology, 22,* 135–155.

Orellana, M. F. (2001). The work kids do: Mexican and Central American children's contributions to households and schools in California. *Harvard Educational Review, 71,* 366–389.

Orellana, M. F., Dorner, L., & Pulido, L. (2003). Accessing assets: Immigrant youth's work as family translators or "para-phrasers." *Social Problems, 50,* 505–524.

Oropesa, R. S., & Landale, N. S. (1995). *Immigrant legacies: The socioeconomic circumstances of children by ethnicity and generation in the United States* (Working Paper 95-01R). Population Research Institute, Pennsylvania State University, University Park, PA.

Padilla, A. M., & Gonzalez, R. (2001). Academic performance of immigrant and U.S. born Mexican heritage students: Effects of schooling in Mexico and bilingual/English language instruction. *American Educational Research Journal, 38,* 727–742.

Padilla, A. M., & Perez, W. (2003). Acculturation, social identity, and social cognition: A new perspective. *Hispanic Journal of Behavioral Sciences, 25,* 35–55.

Parke, R. D. (1978). Parent-infant interaction: Progress, paradigms, and problems. In G. P. Sackett (Ed.), *Observing behavior: Vol. 1.*

Theory and applications in mental retardation (pp. 69–95). Baltimore: University Park Press.

Parke, R. D. (1988). Families in life-span perspective: A multi-level developmental approach. In E. M. Hetherington, R. M. Lerner, & M. Perlmutter (Eds.), *Child development in life-span perspective* (pp. 159–190). Hillsdale, NJ: Erlbaum.

Parke, R. D. (1996). *Fatherhood.* Cambridge, MA: Harvard University Press.

Parke, R. D. (2002). Fathers and families. In M. H. Bornstein (Ed.), *Handbook of parenting: Vol. 3. Being and becoming a parent* (2nd ed., pp. 27–73). Mahwah, NJ: Erlbaum.

Parke, R. D. (2004a). Development in the family. *Annual Review of Psychology, 55,* 365–399.

Parke, R. D. (2004b). The Society for Research in Child Development at 70: Progress and promise. *Child Development, 75,* 1–24.

Parke, R. D., & Brott, A. A. (1999). *Throwaway dads: The myths and barriers that keep men from being the fathers they want to be.* Boston: Houghton-Mifflin.

Parke, R. D., Burks, V. M., Carson, J. V., Neville, B., & Boyum, L. A. (1994). Family-peer relationships: A tripartite model. In R. D. Parke & S. Kellam (Eds.), *Exploring family relationships with other social contexts: Family research consortium—Advances in family research* (pp. 115–145). Hillsdale, NJ: Erlbaum.

Parke, R. D., Cassidy, J., Burks, V. M., Carson, J. L., & Boyum, L. (1992). Family contributions to peer relationships among young children: The role of affective and interactive processes. In R. D. Parke & G. W. Ladd (Eds.), *Family-peer relationships: Modes of linkage* (pp. 107–134). Hillsdale, NJ: Erlbaum.

Parke, R. D., & Clarke-Stewart, K. A. (2003). Effects of parental incarceration on children: Perspectives, promises and policies. In J. Travis & M. Waul (Eds.), *Prisoners once removed: The impact of incarceration and reentry on children, families, and communities* (pp. 189–232). Washington, DC: Urban Institute Press.

Parke, R. D., Coltrane, S., Bothwick-Duffy, S., Powers, J., Adams, M., Fabricius, W., et al. (2003). Measurement of father involvement in Mexican-American families. In R. Day & M. E. Lamb (Eds.), *Reconceptualizing and measuring father involvement* (pp. 17–38). Mahwah, NJ: Erlbaum.

Parke, R. D., Coltrane, S., Duffy, S., Buriel, R., Dennis, J., Powers, J., et al. (2004). Economic stress, parenting and child adjustment in Mexican American and European American families. *Child Development, 75,* 1632–1656.

Parke, R. D., Hymel, S., Power, T. G., & Tinsley, B. R. (1980). Fathers and risk: A hospital based model intervention. In D. B. Sawin, R. C. Hawkins, L. O. Walker, & J. H. Penticuff (Eds.), *Emotional infant: Psychosocial risks in infant-environment transactions* (pp. 174–189). New York: Brunner/Mazel.

Parke, R. D., & Kellam, S. (Eds.). (1994). *Advances in family research: Vol. 4. Family relationships with other social systems.* Hillsdale, NJ: Erlbaum.

Parke, R. D., Killian, C. M., Dennis, J., Flyr, M. V., McDowell, D. J., Simpkins, S., et al. (2003). Managing the external environment: The parent and child as active agents in the system. In L. Kuczynski (Ed.), *Handbook of dynamics in parent-child relations* (pp. 247–270). Thousand Oaks, CA: Sage.

Parke, R. D., Kim, M., Flyr, M., McDowell, D. J., Simpkins, S., Killian, C. M., et al. (2001). Managing marital conflict: Links with children's peer relationships. In J. H. Grych & F. D. Fincham (Eds.), *Interparental conflict and child development: Theory, research, and applications* (pp. 291–314). New York: Cambridge University Press.

Parke, R. D., McDowell, D. J., Kim, M., & Leidy, M. S. (2006). Family-peer relationships: The role of emotional regulatory processes. In D. Snyder, J. A. Simpson, & J. N. Hughes (Eds.), *Emotional regulation in families: Pathways to dysfunction and health.* Washington, DC: American Psychological Association.

Parke, R. D., & O'Neil, R. (1999). Social relationships across contexts: Family-peer linkages. In W. A. Collins & B. Laursen (Eds.), *Minnesota Symposia on Child Psychology: Vol. 30. Relationships as developmental contexts* (pp. 211–239). Hillsdale, NJ: Erlbaum.

Parke, R. D., Power, T. G., & Gottman, J. M. (1979). Conceptualization and quantifying influence patterns in the family triad. In M. E. Lamb, S. J. Suomi, & G. R. Stephenson (Eds.), *Social interaction analysis: Methodological issues* (pp. 231–253). Madison: University of Wisconsin Press.

Parke, R. D., & Suomi, S. (1981). Adult male-infant relationships: Human and nonhuman primate evidence. In K. Immelman, G. W. Barlow, L. Petrinovich, & M. Main (Eds.), *Behavioral development: The Bielefeld interdisciplinary project* (pp. 700–725). New York: Cambridge University Press.

Patterson, C. J. (2002). Lesbian and gay parenthood. In M. H. Bornstein (Ed.), *Handbook of parenting: Vol. 3. Being and becoming a parent* (2nd ed., pp. 317–338). Mahwah, NJ: Erlbaum.

Patterson, G. R. (1981). *Coercive family process.* Eugene, OR: Castalia.

Patterson, G. R. (2002). The early development of coercive family process. In J. B. Reid, G. R. Patterson, & J. Snyder (Eds.), *Antisocial behavior in children and adolescents: A developmental analysis and model for intervention* (pp. 25–44). Washington, DC: American Psychological Association.

Patterson, G. R., & Stouthamer-Loeber, M. (1984). The correlation of family management practices and delinquency. *Child Development, 55,* 1299–1307.

Pearson, J. L., Hunter, A. G., Ensminger, M. E., & Kellam, S. G. (1990). Black grandmothers in multigenerational households: Diversity in family structure and parenting involvement in the Woodlawn community. *Child Development, 61,* 434–442.

Perez, W. (2004). *Is there a dual frame of reference in Mexican immigrant adolescents?* Unpublished doctoral dissertation, Stanford University, CA.

Perry-Jenkins, M., Repetti, R. L., & Crouter, A. C. (2000). Work and family in the 1990s. *Journal of Marriage and the Family, 62,* 981–998.

Peters, M. F. (1985). Racial socialization of young Black children. In H. P. McAdoo & J. L. McAdoo (Eds.), *Black children: Social, educational, and parental environments* (pp. 159–173). Thousand Oaks, CA: Sage.

Petitt, G. S., Dodge, K. A., & Brown, M. M. (1988). Early family experience, social problem solving patterns and children's social competence. *Child Development, 59,* 107–120.

Phinney, J. S. (2003). Ethnic identity and acculturation. In K. M. Chun, P. B. Organista, & G. Marin (Eds.), *Acculturation: Advances in theory, measurement and applied research* (pp. 63–82). Washington, DC: American Psychological Association.

Pleck, J. H., & Masciadrelli, B. P. (2004). Paternal involvement: Levels, sources and consequences. In M. E. Lamb (Ed.), *The role of the father in child development* (pp. 222–271). Hoboken, NJ: Wiley.

Plomin, R. (1994). The Emanuel Miller Memorial Lecture 1993: Genetic research and identification of environmental influences. *Journal of Child Psychology and Psychiatry, 35,* 817–834.

Portes, A., & Rumbaut, R. G. (1990). *Immigrant America: A portrait.* Berkeley: University of California Press.

Portes, P. R., Dunham, R. M., & Williams, S. (1986). Assessing child-rearing style in ecological settings: Its relation to culture, social class, early age intervention, and scholastic achievement. *Adolescence, 21,* 723–735.

Pratt, M. W., & Fiese, B. H. (Eds.). (2004). *Family stories and the life course: Across time and generations.* Mahwah, NJ: Erlbaum.

Prinstein, M. J., & La Greca, A. M. (1999). Links between mothers' and children's social competence and associations with maternal adjustment. *Journal of Clinical Child Psychology, 28,* 197–210.

Pulkkinen, L., Nurmi, J.-E., & Kokko, K. (2002). Individual differences in personal goals in mid-thirties. In L. Pulkkinen & A. Caspi (Ed.), *Paths to successful development: Personality in the life course* (pp. 331–352). New York: Cambridge University Press.

Putallaz, M., Costanzo, P. R., & Smith, R. B. (1991). Maternal recollections of childhood peer relationships: Implications for their children's social competence. *Journal of Social and Personal Relationships, 8,* 403–422.

Putallaz, M., Klein, T. P., Constanzo, P., & Hedges, L. A. (1994). Relating mothers' social framing to their children's entry competence with peers. *Social Development, 3,* 222–237.

Putnam, S. P., Sanson, A. V., & Rothbart, M. K. (2002). Child temperament and parenting. In M. H. Bornstein (Ed.), *Handbook of parenting: Vol. 1. Children and parenting* (pp. 255–278). Mahwah, NJ: Erlbaum.

Ramirez, M., III. (1983). *Psychology of the Americas: Mextizo perspectives on personality and mental health.* New York: Pergamon Press.

Ramirez, M., III, & Castaneda, A. (1974). *Cultural democracy, bicognitive development and education.* New York: Academic Press.

Ramos-McKay, J. M., Comas-Diaz, L., & Rivera, L. A. (1988). Puerto Ricans. In L. Comas-Diaz & E. E. H. Griffith (Eds.), *Clinical guidelines in cross-cultural mental health* (pp. 204–232). New York: Wiley.

Reed, J. (1982). Black Americans in the 1980s. *Population Bulletin, 37,* 1–37.

Reid, J. B., Patterson, G. R., & Snyder, J. (Eds.). (2002). *Antisocial behavior in children and adolescents: A developmental analysis and model for intervention.* Washington, DC: American Psychological Association.

Reise, S. P., Widaman, K. F., & Pugh, R. H. (1993). Confirmatory factor analysis and item response theory: Two approaches for exploring measurement invariance. *Psychological Bulletin, 114,* 552–566.

Reiss, D. (1989). The represented and practicing family: Contrasting visions of family continuity. In A. J. Sameroff & R. N. Emde (Eds.), *Relationship disturbances in early childhood: A developmental approach* (pp. 191–220). New York: Basic Books.

Reiss, D. (2003). Child effects on family systems: Behavioral genetic strategies. In A. C. Crouter & A. Booth (Eds.), *Children's influence on family dynamics: The neglected side of family relationships* (pp. 3–25). Mahwah, NJ: Erlbaum.

Reiss, D., Neiderhiser, J. M., Hetherington, E. M., & Plomin, R. (2000). *The relationship code: Deciphering genetic and social influences on adolescent development.* Cambridge, MA: Harvard University Press.

Repetti, R. V. (1994). Short-term and long-term processes linking job stressors to father-child interactions. *Social Development, 3,* 1–15.

Repetti, R. V. (1996). The effects of perceived daily social and academic failure experiences on school-age children's subsequent interactions with parents. *Child Development, 67,* 1467–1482.

Repetti, R. V., & Wood, J. (1997). Effects of daily stress at work on mothers' interactions with preschoolers. *Journal of Family Psychology, 11,* 90–108.

Richards, L., & Richards, T. (1991). The transformation of qualitative method: Computational paradigm and research processes. In

N. Fielding & R. M. Lee (Eds.), *Using computers in qualitative research* (pp. 38–53). London: Sage.

Richardson, L., & Fields, R. (2003, Feb. 6). Latino majority arrives: Among state's babies. *Los Angeles Times,* pp. A2, A25.

Rodriguez, J. L. (2002). Family environment and achievement among three generations of Mexican American high school students. *Applied Developmental Science, 6,* 88–94.

Rogoff, B. (1990). *Apprenticeship in thinking: Cognitive development in social context.* London: Oxford University Press.

Rogoff, B. (2003). *The cultural nature of human development.* London: Oxford University Press.

Roopnarine, J. (2004). African-American and African Caribbean fathers: Level, quality, and meaning involvement. In M. E. Lamb (Ed.), *The role of the father in child development* (4th ed., pp. 58–97). Hoboken, NJ: Wiley.

Roopnarine, J. L., & Ahmeduzzaman, M. (1993). Puerto Rican fathers' involvement with their preschool-age children. *Hispanic Journal of Behavioral Sciences, 15,* 96–107.

Roopnarine, J. L., Fouts, H. N., Lamb, M. E., & Lewisi-Elligan, T. Y. (2005). Mothers' and fathers' behaviors toward their 3- to 4-month old infants in lower, middle and upper socioeconomic African American families. *Developmental Psychology, 41,* 723–732.

Root, M. P. P. (1992). *Racially mixed people in America.* Thousand Oaks, CA: Sage.

Root, M. P. P. (1999). The biracial baby boom: Understanding ecological constructions of racial identity in the 21st century. In R. Hernandez-Sheets & E. R. Hollins (Eds.), *Racial and ethnic identity in school practices: Aspects of human development* (pp. 67–89). Mahwah, NJ: Erlbaum.

Rothbaum, F., Morelli, G., Pott, M., & Liu-Constant, Y. (2000). Immigrant-Chinese and Euro-American parents' physical closeness with young children: Themes of family relatedness. *Journal of Family Psychology, 14,* 334–348.

Rubin, K. H., & Mills, R. S. (1990). Maternal beliefs about adaptive and maladaptive social behaviors in normal, aggressive and withdrawn preschoolers. *Journal of Abnormal Child Psychology, 18,* 419–435.

Rubin, K. H., Mills, R. S. L., & Rose-Krasnor, L. (1989). Maternal beliefs and children's competence. In B. H. Schneider, G. Attili, J. Nadel, & R. Weissberg (Eds.), *Social competence in developmental perspective* (pp. 313–331). New York: Klewer Academic/Plenum Press.

Rueschenberg, E. J., & Buriel, R. (1989). Mexican American family functioning and acculturation: A family systems perspective. *Hispanic Journal of Behavioral Sciences, 11,* 232–244.

Rumbaut, R. G. (1991). The agony of exile: A study of the migration and adaptation of Indochinese refugee adults and children. In F. L. Ahearn Jr. & J. L. Athey (Eds.), *Refugee children: Theory, research and services* (pp. 53–91). Baltimore: Johns Hopkins University Press.

Rumbaut, R. G. (1995). Vietnamese, Laotian, and Cambodian Americans. In P. G. Min (Ed.), *Asian Americans: Contemporary trends and issues* (pp. 232–270). Thousand Oaks, CA: Sage.

Russell, A. (1997). Individual and family factors contributing to mothers' and fathers' positive parenting. *International Journal of Behavioral Development, 21,* 111–132.

Russell, A., & Finnie, V. (1990). Preschool children's social status and maternal instructions to assist group entry. *Developmental Psychology, 26,* 603–611.

Russell, G., & Russell, A. (1987). Mother-child and father-child relationships in middle childhood. *Child Development, 58,* 1573–1585.

Rutter, M. (2002). Family influences on behavior and development: Challenges for the future. In J. P. McHale & W. S. Grolnick (Eds.), *Retrospect and prospect in the psychological study of families* (pp. 321–351). Mahwah, NJ: Erlbaum.

Rutter, M., Pickles, A., Murray, R., & Eaves, L. (2001). Testing hypotheses on specific environmental causal effects on behavior. *Psychological Bulletin, 127,* 291–324.

Saarni, C. (1999). *The development of emotional competence.* New York: Guilford Press.

Sameroff, A. (1994). Developmental systems and family functioning. In R. D. Parke & S. G. Kellam (Eds.), *Exploring family relationships with other social contexts: Family research consortium—Advances in family research* (pp. 199–214). Hillsdale, NJ: Erlbaum.

Sampson, E. E. (1988). The debate on individualism: Indigenous psychologies of the individual and their role in personal and societal functioning. *American Psychologist, 43,* 15–22.

Sandstrom, M. J., & Coie, J. D. (1999). A developmental perspective on peer ejection: Mechanisms of stability and change. *Child Development, 70,* 955–966.

Schaffer, H. R. (1971). *The growth of sociability.* Harmondsworth, England: Penguin.

Schell Witt, K. (1996). *Family-peer linkages: Adolescents and high risk behavior.* Unpublished doctoral dissertation, University of Guelph, Ontario, Canada.

Schumm, W. R., McCollum, E. E., Bugaighis, M. A., Jurich, A. P., Bollman, S. R., & Reitz, J. (1988). Differences between Anglo and Mexican American family members on satisfaction with family life. *Hispanic Journal of Behavior Sciences, 10,* 39–53.

Scott-Jones, D., Lewis, L. T., & Shirley, K. (1996, March). *Successful pathways through middle childhood: The role of ethnic families of color.* Paper presented at the meeting of the MacArthur Foundation Joint Task Force on Family Processes, Philadelphia, PA.

Sears, R. R., Maccoby, E. E., & Levin, H. (1957). *Patterns of childrearing.* Oxford, England: Row, Peterson.

Shulman, S., & Klein, M. M. (1993). Distinctive role of the father in adolescent separation-individuation. In S. Shulman & A. W. Collins (Eds.), *Father-adolescent relationships: New directions for child development* (pp. 41–57). San Francisco: Jossey-Bass.

Sigel, I. E., & Parke, R. D. (1987). Structural analysis of parent-child research models. *Journal of Applied Developmental Psychology, 8,* 123–137.

Simmons, R. G., & Blyth, D. A. (1987). *Moving into adolescence: The impact of pubertal change and school context.* Hawthorne, NY: Aldine de Gruyter.

Simpkins, S. D., O'Neil, R., Lee, J., & Parke, R. D. (2005). *The relation between parent and children's social networks and children's peer acceptance.* Unpublished manuscript, University of California, Riverside.

Simpkins, S. D., & Parke, R. D. (2001). The relations between parental friendships and children's friendships: Self report and observational analyses. *Child Development, 72,* 569–582.

Simpkins, S. D., & Parke, R. D. (2002). Maternal monitoring and rules as correlates of children's social adjustment. *Merrill-Palmer Quarterly, 48,* 360–377.

Slomkowski, C., & Manke, B. (2004). Sibling relationships during childhood: Multiple perceptions from multiple perspectives. In R. D. Conger, F. O. Lorenz, & K. A. S. Wickrama (Eds.), *Continuity and change in family relations: Theory, methods and empirical findings* (pp. 293–318). Mahwah, NJ: Erlbaum.

Slomkowski, C., Rende, R., Conger, K. J., Simons, R. L., & Conger, R. D. (2001). Sisters, brothers, and delinquency: Evaluating social influence during early and middle adolescence. *Child Development, 72,* 271–283.

Smetana, J., & Chuang, S. (2001). Middle-class African American parents' conceptions of parenting in early adolescence. *Journal of Research on Adolescence, 11,* 177–198.

Smith, P. K., & Drew, L. M. (2002). Grandparenthood. In M. H. Bornstein (Ed.), *Handbook of parenting: Vol. 3. Being and becoming a parent* (2nd ed., pp. 141–172). Mahwah, NJ: Erlbaum.

Spicer, P. (1998). Drinking, foster care, and the intergenerational continuity of parenting in an urban Indian community. *American Indian Culture and Research Journal, 22,* 335–360.

Staples, R., & Johnson, L. B. (1993). *Black families at the crossroads: Challenges and prospects.* San Francisco: Jossey-Bass.

Steele, C. M. (1997). A threat in the air: How stereotypes shape intellectual test performance of African Americans. *American Psychologist, 52,* 613–629.

Steinberg, L., Dornbusch, S. M., & Brown, B. B. (1992). Ethnic differences in adolescent achievement: An ecological perspective. *American Psychologist, 47,* 723–729.

Steinberg, L., Lamborn, S. D., Dornbusch, S. M., & Darling, N. (1992). Impact of parenting practices on adolescent achievement: Authoritative parenting, school involvement, and encouragement to succeed. *Child Development, 63,* 1266–1281.

Stern, D. N. (1977). *The first relationship: Infant and mother.* Cambridge, MA: Harvard University Press.

Stocker, C. M. (1994). Children's perceptions of relationships with siblings, friends, and mothers: Compensatory processes and links with adjustment. *Journal of Child Psychology and Psychiatry, 35,* 1447–1459.

Stocker, C., & Dunn, J. (1990). Sibling relationships in childhood: Links with friendships and peer relationships. *British Journal of Developmental Psychology, 8,* 227–244.

Straus, M. A., & Stewart, J. H. (1999). Corporal punishment by American parents: National data on prevalence, chronicity, severity, and duration, in relation to child and family characteristics. *Clinical Child and Family Psychology Review, 2,* 55–70.

Strom, R. D., Amukamara, H., Strom, S. K., Beckert, T. E., Moore, E. G., Strom, P. S., et al. (2000). African-American fathers: Perceptions of two generations. *Journal of Adolescence, 23,* 513–516.

Stubben, J. D. (2001). Working with and conducting research among American Indian families. *American Behavioral Scientist, 44,* 1466–1481.

Suarez-Orozco, C., & Suarez-Orozco, M. (1995). *Transformations: Migration, family life, and achievement motivation among Latino adolescents.* Stanford: Stanford University Press.

Sudarkasa, N. (1993). Female-headed African American households: Some neglected dimensions. In H. P. McAdoo (Ed.), *Family ethnicity: Strength in diversity* (pp. 81–89). Thousand Oaks, CA: Sage.

Suina, J. H., & Smolkin, L. B. (1994). From natal culture to school culture to dominant society culture: Supporting transitions for Pueblo Indian students. In P. M. Greenfield & R. R. Cocking (Eds.), *Cross-cultural roots of minority child development* (pp. 115–130). Hillsdale, NJ: Erlbaum.

Suomi, S. J. (2000). A biobehavioral perspective on developmental psychopathology: Excessive aggression and serotonergic dysfunction in monkeys. In A. J. Sameroff, M. Lewis, & S. M. Miller (Ed.), *Handbook of developmental psychopathology* (2nd ed., pp. 237–256). Dordrecht, The Netherlands: Kluwer Press.

Szapocznik, J., & Kurtines, W. (1980). Acculturation, biculturalism, and adjustment among Cuban Americans. In A. M. Padilla (Ed.), *Acculturation: Theory, models, and some new findings* (pp. 139–161). Boulder, CO: Westview Press.

Tardif, T. (1993). *Adult-to-child speech and language acquisition in Mandarin Chinese.* Unpublished doctoral dissertation, Yale University, New Haven, CT.

Teachman, J. D., Tedrow, L. M., & Crowder, K. D. (2000). The changing demography of America's families. *Journal of Marriage and the Family, 62,* 1234–1246.

Teti, D. M., Gelfand, D. M., Messinger, D. S., & Isabella, R. (1995). Maternal depression and the quality of early attachment: An examination of infants, preschoolers, and their mothers. *Developmental Psychology, 31,* 364–376.

Thelen E., & Smith, L. B. (1994). *A dynamic systems approach to the development of cognition and action.* Cambridge, MA: MIT Press.

Thornton, M. C., Chatters, L. M., Taylor, R. J., & Allen, W. R. (1990). Sociodemographic and environmental correlates of racial socialization by Black parents. *Child Development, 61,* 401–409.

Tinsley, B. J. (2003). *How children learn to be healthy.* New York: Cambridge University Press.

Tolson, T. F., & Wilson, M. N. (1990). The impact of two- and three-generational Black family structure on perceived family climate. *Child Development, 61,* 416–428.

Trimble, J. E., & Medicine, B. (1993). Diversification of American Indians: Forming an indigenous perspective. In U. Kim & J. W. Berry (Eds.), *Indigenous psychologies: Research and experience in cultural context* (pp. 133–151). Thousand Oaks, CA: Sage.

Tse, L. (1995). Language brokering among Latino adolescents: Prevalence, attitudes, and school performance. *Hispanic Journal of Behavioral Sciences, 17,* 180–193.

Tse, L. (1996). Who decides? The effects of language brokering on home-school communication. *Journal of Educational Issues of Language Minority Students, 16,* 225–234.

Tseng, V., & Fuligni, A. J. (2000). Parent-adolescent language use and relationships among immigrant families with east Asian, Filipino and Latin American backgrounds. *Journal of Marriage and the Family, 62,* 465–477.

Uba, L. (1994). *Asian Americans: Personality patterns, identity, and mental health.* New York: Guilford Press.

U.S. Census Bureau. (1995). *General family and household characteristics of American Indian tribes: 1990.* Retrieved January 19, 2004, from http//www.census.gov/prod/1/pop/profile/95/23_ps.pdf.

U.S. Census Bureau. (1998, March). *Households and family characteristics* (Current population reports, P2-215). Washington, DC: U.S. Department of Commerce.

U.S. Census Bureau. (1999). *Profile of the foreign-born population in the United States: 1997* (Current Population Reports, Series pp. 23–195). Washington, DC: U.S. Government Printing Office.

U.S. Census Bureau. (2000). *USA statistics in brief: Population and vital statistics.* Washington, DC: U.S. Department of Commerce. Retrieved January 15, 2004, from http://www.census.gov./statab/www/poppart.htm.

U.S. Census Bureau. (2001a). *Overview of race and Hispanic origin* (Census 2000 Brief). Washington, DC: U.S. Government Printing Office.

U.S. Census Bureau. (2001b). *Profile of the foreign-born population in the United States* (Current Population Reports Series, pp. 23–206). Washington, DC: U.S. Government Printing Office.

U.S. Census Bureau. (2002, March). *Census 2000, Summary File 1.* Retrieved January 10, 2004, from http://www.census.gov/population/cen2000/Phc-TQ8.

Valdes, G. (1996). *Con respeto: Bridging the distances between culturally diverse families and schools—An ethnographic portrait.* New York: Teachers College Press.

Valdes, G. (2003). *Expanding definitions of giftedness: The case of young interpreters from immigrant communities.* Mahwah, NJ: Erlbaum.

Valenzuela, A. (1999). *Subtractive schooling: U.S.-Mexican youth and the politics of caring.* Albany: State University of New York Press.

Vazquez-Garcia, H. A., Garcia Coll, C., Erkut, S., Alarcon, O., & Tropp, L. (1995, April). *An instrument for the assessment of family values and functioning of Latin parents.* Poster presented at the biennial meeting of the Society for Research in Child Development, Indianapolis, IN.

Vidal, C. (1988). Godparenting among Hispanic Americans. *Child Welfare, 67,* 453–459.

Vigil, J. D. (1988). *Barrio gangs: Street life and identity in Southern California.* Austin: University of Texas Press.

Volling, B. L., McElwain, N. J., & Miller, A. L. (2002). Emotional regulation in context: The jealousy complex between young siblings and its relations with child and family characteristics. *Child Development, 73,* 581–600.

Wakschlag, L. S., Chase-Lansdale, P. L., & Brooks-Gunn, J. (1996). Not just "Ghosts in the nursery": Contemporaneous intergenerational relationships and parenting in young African-American families. *Child Development, 67,* 2131–2147.

Walker, K., Taylor, E., McElroy, A., Phillip, D., & Wilson, M. N. (1995). Familial and ecological correlates of self-esteem in African American children. In M. N. Wilson (Ed.), *New Directions for Child Development: Vol. 68. African American family life—Its structure and ecological aspects* (pp. 23–34). San Francisco: Jossey-Bass.

Wall, C. S., & Madak, P. R. (1991). Indian students academic self concept and their perceptions of teacher and parent aspirations for them in a band-controlled school and a provincial school. *Canadian Journal of Native Education, 18,* 43–51.

Wamboldt, F. (1999). Co-constructing a marriage: Analyses of young couples' relationship narratives. *Monographs of the Society for Research in Child Development, 64*(2, Serial No. 257), 37–51.

Wamboldt, F., & Reiss, D. (1989). Defining a family heritage and a new relationship identity: Two central tasks in the making of a marriage. *Family Process, 28,* 317–335.

Waters, M. C. (1990). *Ethnic options: Choosing identities in America.* Berkeley: University of California Press.

Weisner, T. S. (1993). Overview: Sibling similarity and difference in different cultures. In C. W. Nuckolls (Ed.), *Siblings in south Asia: Brothers and sisters in cultural context* (pp. 1–17). New York: Guilford Press.

Weisskirch, R. S., & Alva-Alatorre, S. (2002). Language brokering and acculturation of Latino children. *Hispanic Journal of Behavioral Sciences, 24,* 369–378.

Westerman, M. A., & Schonholtz, J. (1993). Marital adjustment, joint parental support in a triadic problem-soling task, and child behavior problems. *Journal of Clinical Child Psychology, 22,* 97–106.

Whaley, A. L. (2000). Sociocultural differences in the developmental consequences of the use of physical discipline during childhood for African Americans. *Cultural Diversity and Ethnic Minority Psychology, 6,* 5–12.

Whiting, J. W. M., & Child, I. L. (1953). *Child training and personality: A cross-cultural study.* New Haven, CT: Yale University Press.

Williams, E., Radin, N., & Coggins, K. (1996). Parental involvement in childrearing and the school performance of Ojibwa children: An exploratory study. *Merrill-Palmer Quarterly, 42,* 578–595.

Willis, W. (1992). Families with African American roots. In E. W. Lynch & M. J. Hanson (Eds.), *Developing cross-cultural competence: A guide for working with young children and their families* (pp. 121–150). Baltimore: Paul H. Brookes.

Wilson, B. J., & Gottman, J. M. (1994). Attention: The shuttle between emotion and cognition—Risk, resiliency and physiological bases. In E. M. Hetherington & E. A. Blechman (Eds.), *Stress, coping, and resiliency in children and families: Family research consortium—Advances in family research* (pp. 189–228). Hillsdale, NJ: Erlbaum.

Wilson, M. N. (1992). Perceived parental activity of mothers, fathers, and grandmothers in three-generational Black families. In A. K. H. Burlew, W. C. Banks, H. P. McAdoo, & D. A. Azibo (Eds.), *African American psychology: Theory, research, and practice* (pp. 87–104). Thousand Oaks, CA: Sage.

Wilson, W. J. (1987). *The truly disadvantaged: The inner city, the underclass, and public policy.* Chicago: University of Chicago Press.

Wolfer, L. T., & Moen, P. (1996). Staying in school: Maternal employment and the timing of Black and White daughters' school exit. *Journal of Family Issues, 17,* 540–560.

Wolin, S. L., Bennett, L. A., & Jacobs, J. S. (1988). Assessing family rituals. In E. Imber-Black, J. Roberts, & R. Whiting (Eds.), *Rituals in families and family therapy* (pp. 230–256). New York: Norton.

Wong, M. G. (1988). The Chinese American family. In C. H. Mindel, R. W. Habenstein, & R. Wright Jr. (Eds.), *Ethnic families in America: Patterns and variations* (3rd ed., pp. 230–257). New York: Elsevier.

Wong, M. G. (1995). Chinese Americans. In P. G. Min (Ed.), *Asian Americans: Contemporary trends and issues* (pp. 58–94). Thousand Oaks, CA: Sage.

Xiaoming, L., Stanton, B., & Feigelman, S. (2000). Impact of perceived parental monitoring on adolescent risk behavior over 4 years. *Journal of Adolescent Health, 27,* 49–56.

Yeung, W. J., Sandberg, J. F., Davis-Kean, P. E., & Hofferth, S. L. (2001). Children's time with fathers in intact families. *Journal of Marriage and the Family, 63,* 136–154.

Ying, Y.-W., Coombs, M., & Lee, P. A. (1999). Family intergenerational relationship of Asian American adolescents. *Cultural diversity and Ethnic Minority Psychology, 5,* 350–363.

Young, B. A. (2002, April). *Public school students, staff, and graduate counts by state: School year 2000–2001.* Washington, DC: National Center for Education Statistics.

Zavella, P. (1987). *Women's work and Chicano families: Cannery workers of the Santa Clara Valley.* Ithaca, NY: Cornell University Press.

Zimmerman, M. A., Ramirez, J., Washienko, K. M., Walter, B., & Dyer, S. (1998). Enculturation hypothesis: Exploring direct and protective effects among Native American youth. In H. I. McCubbins, E. A. Thompson, A. I. Thompson, & J. E. Fromer (Eds.), *Resiliency in family series: Vol. 2. Resiliency in Native American and immigrant families* (pp. 199–220). Thousand Oaks, CA: Sage.

Zukow-Goldring, P. (2002). Sibling caregiving. In M. H. Bornstein (Ed.), *Handbook of parenting: Vol. 3. Being and becoming a parent* (pp. 253–286). Mahwah, NJ: Erlbaum.

Zuzanek, J. (2000). *The effects of time use and time pressure on child parent relationships.* Waterloo, Ontario, Canada: Otium.

CHAPTER 9

The Self

SUSAN HARTER

Interest in self-processes has recently burgeoned in many branches of psychology. Cognitive-developmentalists of a neo-Piagetian persuasion have addressed normative changes in the emergence of a sense of self (e.g., Case, 1992; Fischer, 1980; Harter, 1997; Higgins, 1991). Developmentalists interested in memory processes have described how the self is crafted through the construction of narratives that provide the basis for autobiographical memory (see Fivush, 1987; Nelson, 1993; Snow, 1990). Contemporary attachment theorists, building on the earlier efforts of Ainsworth (1979) and Bowlby (1980), have provided new insights into how interactions with caregivers shape the representations of self and others that young children come to construct (see Bretherton, 1991, 1993; Cassidy, 1990; Cicchetti, 1993; Cicchetti & Beeghly, 1990; Cicchetti & Cohen, 1995; Cicchetti & Rogosch, 1996; Pipp, 1990; Rutter & Sroufe, 2000; Sameroff, 2000; Sroufe, 1990). Clinicians in the psychodynamic tradition have also contributed to

our understanding of how early socialization experiences come to shape the structure and content of self-evaluations and contribute to psychopathology (Blatt, 1995; Bleiberg, 1984; Kernberg, 1975; Kohut, 1977; Winnicott, 1965). Moreover, social and personality theorists have devoted considerable attention to those processes that produce individual differences in perceptions of self, particularly among adults (see Baumeister, 1987, 1993; Epstein, 1991; Kihlstrom, 1993; Markus & Wurf, 1987; Steele, 1988).

Although there is a new look to many of these contemporary formulations, the field has also witnessed a return to many of the classic issues that captured the attention of historical scholars of the self. For example, new life has been breathed into James's (1890, 1892) distinction between the I-self as subject, agent, knower and the Me-self as object, as known. In addition, James's analysis of the causes of self-esteem is alive and well. There has also been a resurgence of interest in symbolic interactionists, such as Baldwin (1897), Cooley (1902), and Mead (1934), who placed heavy emphasis on how interactive processes with caregivers shape the developing self.

In this chapter, the emphasis is on self-representations, beginning with toddlers and very early childhood, through late adolescence, where most of recent work on self-development has been conducted. The critical period of the development of the self in infancy was covered in detail in the previous handbook volume (see Harter, 1998; also Thompson, Chapter 2, this *Handbook,* this volume) where there continues to be agreement on the basic processes that govern the period of infancy. More recent treatments (see Fonagy, 2002; Mascolo, Fischer, & Neimeyer, 1999; Rochat & Striano, 2002) echo and refine the role of interactional experiences embedded in the crucible of the primary parent-infant relationship, where sensitive caregiving is critical to healthy self-development. These recent treatments also focus on the importance of the differentiation of the self from caregivers as a foundation for later self-concept development and on intentionality in early social relationships. These acquisitions help motivate the infant to realize that he or she constitutes a self, both independent of, but dependent on, caregivers that supports self-definition.

The first part of this chapter deals with six stages of self-development. Specifically, the focus is on changes in self-understanding and self-evaluation during three periods of childhood, very early, middle, and late childhood, and three periods of adolescence, early, middle, and late adolescence. In each of these six periods, three issues are covered. First, the *normative-developmental features of self-description and self-evaluation* are presented. Features include the salient content of the self, the structure or organization of self-constructs, the valence and accuracy of self-representations, the nature of social comparisons in forming self-judgments, and sensitivity to others as sources of information that may be relevant to self-representations.

Second, the *normative-developmental liabilities* that mark the emergence to each period or stage are described. The very fabric of development involves advances to new stages that may bring with them normative liabilities that should *not* be interpreted as pathological, liabilities that will dissipate as more advanced developments and skills are acquired. Movement to a new stage of cognitive development inevitably leads to liabilities given that the individual lacks "cognitive control" (see Fischer, 1980) over emerging new skills.

Because the self is not only a cognitive construction but also a social construction (Harter, 1999) crafted in the crucible of interactions with significant others, normative-developmental manifestations of the self will necessarily be affected by socialization at the hands of parents and peers, two key influences.

Third, I indicate how at each developmental period there are *individual differences,* against a normative backdrop, the causes of which can lead to healthy forms of self-development. Alternatively, self-development can be seriously derailed due to socialization influences that can result in maladaptive outcomes. These are to be distinguished from normative-developmental liabilities in their severity and the extent to which they compromise the functioning of the child or adolescent.

Before describing each of these three issues at six stages of development during childhood and adolescence, several general themes need to be presented as background: (a) the antecedents of the self as a cognitive and social construction, (b) distinctions between the I-self and the Me-self, (c) recent perspectives on the differentiation of the self and the creation of multiple selves during adolescence, (d) historical formulations and contemporary perspectives, and (e) recent genetic positions on the heritability of self-esteem.

After reviewing the normative-developmental changes in the self, the normative liabilities, and the roots of individual differences leading to healthy versus more maladaptive self-development at each of the six stages, the following issues are explored, drawing on considerable recent research. These themes include (a) the stability of self-esteem, (b) gender differences and the special impact of perceived appearance on self-esteem, (c) cross-cultural differences, and (d) ethnic differences in self-perceptions. For those interested in implications for intervention, the reader is referred to Harter (1999).

ANTECEDENTS OF THE SELF AS A COGNITIVE AND SOCIAL CONSTRUCTION

In examining self-development, this chapter focuses on the antecedents of self-representations as well as on their consequences. With regard to antecedents, the self is a cognitive *and* a social construction—two major themes around which the material to be presented is organized. From a cognitive-developmental perspective, changes in self-representations are inevitable. As neo-Piagetians (e.g., Case, 1992; Fischer, 1980) and self theorists (e.g., Epstein, 1981, 1991; Greenwald, 1980; Kelly, 1955; Markus, 1980; Sarbin, 1962) have forcefully argued, our species has been designed to actively create theories about our world, to make meaning of our experiences, including the construction of a theory of self. Thus, the self is, first and foremost, a cognitive construction.

As a result, the self will develop over time as cognitive processes undergo normative-developmental change. Thus, because the self is a cognitive construction, the particular cognitive abilities and limitations of each developmental period will dictate the features of the self-system or how self-representations are conceptually organized. As such, emphasis is given to the processes responsible for those normative-developmental changes that result in *similarities* in self-representations at a given developmental level.

Previous ontogenetic accounts highlighted major qualitative differences in the nature of self-descriptions associated with broad stages of development. Observers were initially struck by the dramatic differences that defined the stage models of the day (e.g., Piaget, 1960). More recent treatments of self-development fill in the gaps by providing a more detailed account of the progression of the substages of self-understanding. As a result, we have necessarily had to alter our views about whether self-development is best viewed as a discontinuous or continuous process. Employing frameworks of the past, self-development was viewed as largely discontinuous, with an emphasis on the conceptual leaps from one broadly defined stage to another. Thus, theorists highlighted the dramatic differences between the self-descriptions and evaluations of young children, older children, and adolescents. However, there has been a shift in emphasis. The development of self-representations is now viewed as more continuous, in that investigators specify more ministeps or substages that occur, including how such levels build on, and transform, one another.

In focusing on normative-developmental changes, we see how cognitive development impacts two general characteristics of the self-structure, both the *differentiation* and the *integration* that an individual can bring to bear on the postulates in his or her self-theory. With regard to differentiation, emerging cognitive abilities allow the individual to create self-evaluations that differ across various domains of experience. Moreover, they permit the older child to distinguish between real and ideal self-concepts that can then be compared to one another, creating potential discrepancies that have consequences for the self. During adolescence, newfound cognitive capabilities support the creation of multiple selves in different relational contexts.

With regard to integration, cognitive abilities that emerge across development allow the individual to construct higher-order generalizations about the self in the form of trait labels (e.g., demonstrated skills in math, science, and language arts are subsumed under the self-concept of "smart"). Abilities that emerge in middle childhood also permit the individual to construct a concept of his or her worth as a person, an evaluation of his or her global self-esteem. Further cognitive advances in adolescence allow one to successfully intercoordinate seemingly contradictory self-attributes (e.g., "How can I be both cheerful and depressed?") into meaningful abstractions about the self (e.g., "I'm a moody person"). Each of these themes is addressed.

In addition to an exploration of the cognitive-developmental antecedents of the self, emphasis is placed on the self as a social construction. Thus, attention is devoted to how socialization experiences in children's interactions with caregivers, peers, teachers, and in the wider sociocultural context will influence the particular *content* and *valence* of their self-representations. Those building on the symbolic interactionist perspective (Baldwin, 1897; Cooley, 1902; Mead, 1934), as well as those of an attachment theory persuasion (Bretherton & Munholland, 1999), have focused on how socialization experiences with caregivers produce individual differences in the content of self-representations, including whether self-evaluations are favorable or unfavorable. The reactions of significant others determine whether the child comes to view the self as competent versus incapable, as lovable versus undeserving of others' affection and esteem. Although cognitive-developmentalists emphasize the fact that children are active agents in their own development, including the construction of self, the symbolic interactionist and attachment perspectives alert us to the fact that children are also at the mercy of the particular caregiving hand they have been dealt.

To summarize, with regard to antecedents, the self is both a cognitive and a social construction. In examining the self as a cognitive construction, attention focuses on those cognitive-developmental processes that result in changes in the structure of the self-system, namely, how self-representations are organized. This approach provides an account of normative, developmental change, and emphasizes the similarities among individuals at a given stage of development. In treating the self as a social construction, attention turns to those socialization processes that reflect how children are treated by caregivers, interactions that primarily impact the evaluative content of self-representations. Child-rearing practices do impact normative-developmental changes; however, they are also the major causes of individual differences in whether judgments about the self are favorable or unfavorable.

The I-Self and the Me-Self

In addressing these themes, we can draw on a distinction in the literature between the I-self and the Me-self. The majority of scholars who have devoted thoughtful attention to the self have come to a similar conclusion: Two distinct but intimately intertwined aspects of self can be meaningfully identified: (1) self as subject (the I-self) and (2) self as object (the Me-self). William James (1890) introduced this distinction defining the I-self as the actor or knower, whereas the Me-self was the object of one's knowledge, "an empirical aggregate of things objectively known" (p. 197). James also identified particular features or components of both the I-self and the Me-self. Components of the I-self included (a) self-awareness, an appreciation for one's internal states, needs, thoughts, and emotions; (b) self-agency, the sense of the authorship over one's thoughts, and actions; (c) self-continuity, the sense that one remains the same person over time; and (d) self-coherence, a stable sense of the self as a single, coherent, bounded entity. Components of the Me-self included the "material me," the "social me," and the "spiritual me." In contemporary models, this translates into new domains of the self-concept and supports the current multidimensional approaches to the self (see Harter, 1999).

The distinction between the I-self and the Me-self has proved amazingly viable and is a recurrent theme in many theoretical treatments of the self. While more recent scholars have employed somewhat different terminology, the essence of the distinction has been retained. Dickstein (1977), for example, contrasted the "dynamic" self that possesses a sense of personal agency to the self as the object of one's knowledge. Lewis and Brooks-Gunn (1979) initially defined this duality as the existential self and the categorical self. The task of the developing I-self, the self as subject, is to develop the realization that it is "existential" in that it exists as separate from others. The Me-self, the self as object, is referred to as "categorical" in that the developing child must construct categories by which to define the self (e.g., age and gender labels). Wylie (1979, 1989) has summarized the essence of the distinctions that have been drawn by numerous theorists. The I-self is the active observer, whereas the Me-self is the observed, the product of the observing process when attention is focused on the self.

More recently, Lewis (1994) has adopted new terminology. He now refers to the I-self as the "machinery of the self," the basic biological, perceptual, and cognitive processes that allow for the construction of the Me-self as the "idea of me." Such cognitive representations of the self begin to emerge in rudimentary form in the second half of the 2nd year. Both the "machinery of the self" as well as the "idea of me" undergo considerable change during the course of development.

Historically, major attention has been devoted to the Me-self (to the study of the self as an object of one's knowledge and evaluation) as evidenced by the myriad number of studies on self-concept and self-esteem (see Harter, 1983; Wylie, 1979, 1989). More recently, the I-self, which James himself regarded as an elusive if not incorrigible construct, has become more prominent in accounts of self-development. As we come to appreciate, both the structure and content of the Me-self at any given developmental level depend on the particular I-self capabilities (those cognitive processes that define the knower). Thus, cognitive-developmental changes in I-self processes will directly influence the nature of the self-theory that the child is constructing.

Most scholars conceptualize the self as a theory that must be cognitively constructed. Those theorists in the tradition of adult personality and social psychology have suggested that the self-theory should possess the characteristics of any formal theory, defined as a hypothetico-deductive system. Such a personal epistemology should, therefore, meet those criteria by which any good theory is evaluated: that it is parsimonious, empirically valid, internally consistent, coherently organized, testable, and useful. From a developmental perspective, however, the self-theories created by children cannot meet these criteria, given numerous cognitive limitations that have been identified in Piagetian (1960) and neo-Piagetian formulations (e.g., Case, 1992; Fischer, 1980). The I-self in its role as constructor of the Me-self does not, in childhood, possess the capacities to create a hierarchically organized system of postulates that are internally consistent, coherently organized, testable, or empirically valid. It is not until late adolescence or early adulthood that the cognitive abilities to construct a self-portrait meeting the criteria of a good formal theory potentially emerge. Therefore, it is essential to examine how the changing characteristics of the I-self processes that define each developmental stage directly impact the Me-self (the self-theory that is being constructed).

Global versus Domain-Specific Evaluations

The increasing ability with development to differentiate self-domains, as well to integrate self-perceptions into a larger global concept of self, has led contemporary scholars to separate domain-specific perceptions from a global concept of a person's worth or self-esteem. Thus, it has become increasingly important to distinguish between self-evaluations that represent global characteristics of the individual (e.g., "I am a worthwhile person") from those that reflect the individual's sense of adequacy across particular domains such as their cognitive competence (e.g., "I am smart"), social competence (e.g., "I am well liked by peers"), athletic competence (e.g., "I am good at sports"), and so forth (see Bracken, 1996; Epstein, 1991; Harter, 1986b, 1998; Marsh, 1986, 1987; Rosenberg, 1979). Conceptualizations and instruments that aggregate domain-specific self-evaluations into a single score (e.g., Coopersmith, 1967) have been found wanting in that they mask meaningful distinctions between an individual's sense of adequacy across domains. Moreover, the separation of the evaluation of an individual's global worth as a person from more domain-specific attributes has allowed investigators to construct hierarchical models of the relationship among these self-constructs.

With regard to terminology, global self-evaluations have typically been referred to as *self-esteem* (Rosenberg, 1979), *self-worth* (Harter, 1983, 1999) or *general self-concept* (Marsh, 1986, 1987). In each case, the focus is on the overall evaluation of one's worth or value as a person. In this chapter, the terms *self-esteem* and *self-worth* are employed interchangeably. It is important to appreciate that this general evaluation is tapped by a separate set of items that explicitly tap one's perceived worth as a person (e.g., "I feel that I am a worthwhile person"). It is not a summary statement of self-evaluations across specific domains.

In this chapter, the term *self-concept* is primarily reserved for evaluative judgments of attributes in discrete domains, such as cognitive competence, social acceptance, physical appearance, and so forth, or "domain-specific self-evaluations." Such a focus allows the investigator to construct a profile of self-evaluations across domains for individuals or for particular subgroups of interest. Moreover, the separation of global self-esteem or self-worth from domain-specific evaluations allows us to address the issue of whether evaluations in some domains are more predictive of global self-esteem than are others.

Developmental advances allowing older children and adolescent to differentiate self-domains also extend to the development of "multiple selves" that become highly salient in early adolescence (Harter, 1999). Thus, an individual comes to develop a self with each parent, a best friend, a romantic other, and classmates of each gender—selves that often are defined by very different self-descriptors. Although cognitive-developmental processes contribute to the ability to construct multiple selves, social forces, including the pressure to be a particular self in each relational context, also contribute to this differentiation.

Historical Perspectives

These contemporary themes find their roots in the writings of historical scholars of the self. William James clearly contributed with regard to his formulations regarding the origins of our self-esteem, to the differentiation of domains of the self, and to what he labeled the "conflict of the different Me's" across differing relational constructs. The symbolic interactionists, such as Cooley (1902), Baldwin (1895), and Mead (1934), clearly articulated the role of social processes in constructing the self.

The field has witnessed a return to classic issues that captured the attention of historical scholars of the self. Thus, it behooves us to briefly review the scripts of the major actors in this drama as a conceptual backdrop against which more contemporary issues can be examined. The history of interest in the self can be traced back to ancient Greek philosophy, as revealed in the injunction to "know thyself." However, contemporary scholars of the self-concept typically pay major intellectual homage to James (1890, 1892) and to the previously listed symbolic interactionists such as Cooley, Mead, and Baldwin. The reader interested in the history of the self prior to the turn of the twentieth century is referred to excellent treatments by Baumeister (1987), Broughton (1987), and Logan (1987).

The Legacy of William James

The contributions of James (1890, 1892) were legion. Of paramount importance was his distinction between two fundamental aspects of the self, the I-self as subject or knower and the Me-self as object or known. It is the Me-self that took center stage as the major focus of empirical attention. Those interested in individual differences in the self-concept focused primarily on the correlates of favorable versus unfavorable self-evaluations (see Wylie, 1979). In developmental psychology, earlier attempts to identify age-related changes in self-representations concentrated exclusively on the Me-self (see Harter, 1983, 1999). Thus, the data consisted of the differing self-descriptions produced by children at different age levels, with little analysis of what accounted for such shifts (see Montemayor & Eisen, 1977). However, contemporary developmentalists have afforded the I-self a far greater role as the architect of the Me-self. It has become apparent that an appreciation for developmental changes in I-self processes is critical to understand how and why the structure and content of the Me-self changes with age (see Damon & Hart, 1988; Harter, 1983, 1999).

In differentiating various aspects of the self, including the multiplicity of social selves, James (1890) noted that these multiple selves may not all speak with the same voice. For example, James observed that "many a youth who is demure enough before his parents and teachers, swears and swaggers like a pirate among his tough young friends" (p. 169). James further noted that this multiplicity can be harmonious; for example, when an individual is tender to his children but stern to the soldiers under his command. Alternatively, there may be a "discordant splitting" if one's different selves are experienced as contradictory.

The conflict of the different Me's could also be observed in the incompatibility of potential adult roles. James, himself, fantasized about his own desires to be handsome, athletic, rich, and witty, a bon vivant, lady-killer, philosopher, philanthropist, statesman, warrior, African explorer, as well as a tone-poet and a saint. He knowingly concluded that because all of these roles could not possibly coexist, it was necessary to selectively choose, suppressing the alternatives. Thus, "the seeker of his truest, strongest, deepest self must review

the list carefully, and pick out the one on which to stake his salvation" (1890, p. 14).

The repudiation of particular attributes or roles was not, for James (1890), necessarily damaging to the individual's overall sense of worth, the "average tone of self-feeling which each one of us carries about" (p. 171). Thus, his own deficiency at Greek led to no sense of humiliation because he made no pretensions to be proficient at Greek. The role of pretensions became paramount in James's formulation of the causes of self-esteem. Self-esteem could not simply be reduced to the aggregate of perceived successes but rather represented a ratio of successes to one's pretensions. If perceived successes were equal to or greater than one's pretensions or aspirations for success, high self-esteem would result. Conversely, if pretensions exceeded successes (if an individual were unsuccessful in domains deemed important), he or she would experience low self-esteem. Critical to this formulation is the assumption that lack of success in an area in which one does not have pretensions (e.g., Greek for James) will not erode self-esteem because it can be discounted. Thus, both the presence and absence of pretensions figured heavily in James's theorizing. He argued that abandoning certain pretensions can be as much a relief as striving to meet goals: "How pleasant is the day when we give up striving to be young" (p. 201).

For James, therefore, we find many themes that anticipate contemporary issues about the self. First and foremost is the distinction between "I" and "Me" selves. James's multidimensional view of the Me-self has been modernized in recent treatments of the self-structure, where investigators have sought to examine the particular relationships among global and domain-specific self-evaluations. Moreover, the potential conflict between different Me-selves that James observed has served as a springboard to contemporary interest in the construction of multiple selves. As we come to see, differing attributes across role-related selves that appear contradictory (e.g., depressed with parents but cheerful with friends) usher in the potential for conflict. Finally, James's formulation concerning the causes of self-esteem has been revived, leading to empirical investigations of its viability.

The Contribution of the Symbolic Interactionists

In contrast to James, the symbolic interactionists placed primary emphasis on how social interactions with others profoundly shaped the self. For Cooley (1902), Mead (1934), and Baldwin (1897), the self is viewed as a social construction, crafted through linguistic exchanges (symbolic interactions) with others. Several themes have found their way into contemporary theorizing. For example, beginning in childhood, the child (a) engages in the imitation of significant others' behaviors, attitudes, and values or standards; (b) adjusts his or her behavior to garner the approval of salient socializing agents; (c) comes to adopt the opinions that significant others are perceived to hold toward them (these reflected appraisals come to define one's self as a person). The fact that these processes occur in multiple social contexts adds to the complexity of the construction of a self that can be experienced as coherent, as integrated, and as authentic.

Charles Horton Cooley was perhaps the most influential. His formulation was the most metaphorical, given his postulation of the "looking glass self." In his now-famous couplet, he observed that:

> Each to each a looking glass
> Reflects the other that doth pass

For Cooley, significant others constituted a social mirror into which the individual gazes to detect their opinions toward the self. These opinions, in turn, are incorporated into one's sense of self. Cooley contended that what becomes the self is what we imagine that others think of us, including our appearance, motives, deeds, character, and so on: We come to own these reflected appraisals. Such a "self-idea" was comprised of three components: (1) the imagination of our appearance to the other person; (2) the imagination of that person's judgment of that appearance; and (3) some sort of self-feeling—an affective reaction to these reflected appraisals. These components gradually become psychological removed from their initial social sources through an implied internalization process. Cooley writes that the adult is "not immediately dependent on what others think; he has worked over his reflected self in his mind until it is a steadfast portion of his thought, an idea and conviction apart, in some measure, from its external origin. Hence this sentiment requires time for its development and flourishes in mature age rather than in the open and growing period of youth" (1902, p. 199).

Cooley's views on the internalization of others' opinions about the self paved the way for a more developmental perspective on how the opinions of others are incorporated into the self. Moreover, his looking glass self-perspective provides an alternative to James's contentions regarding the determinants of global self-esteem. James focused largely on those cognitive processes in which an individual actively compares particular aspirations to perceived successes in corresponding domains. For Cooley, the antecedents were far more social in nature, and less consciously driven, in that children inevitably internalized the opinions that they believed significant others held toward the self. Cooley also spoke more directly to developmental changes, including the consequences of the internalization process for adults. He contended that the more mature sense of self is not buffeted about by potentially transient or disparate views of significant others. As Cooley (1902) observed, the person with "balanced self-respect has stable ways of thinking about the image of self that cannot be upset by passing phases of praise or blame" (p. 201). His thesis anticipates contemporary interest in whether self-concepts are malleable versus resistant to change.

In George Herbert Mead (1925), we find an elaboration of the themes identified by Cooley, with an even greater insistence on the role of social interaction. For Mead, "We appear as selves in our conduct insofar as we ourselves take the attitude that others take toward us. We take the role of what may be called the 'generalized' other" (p. 270). Mead spoke to the origins of these attitudes in childhood. He postulated a two-stage developmental process through which the child adopted the attitudes of others toward the self, labeling these stages as the play and the game. The *play* involved the imitation of adult roles, which Mead documented in his description of the young child "continually acting as a parent, a teacher, a preacher, a grocery man, a policeman, a pirate, or an Indian" (p. 270). In the subsequent stage of *games,* there are proscribed procedures and rules:

> The child must not only take the role of the other, as he does in the play, but he must assume the various roles of all the participants in the game and govern his actions accordingly. If he plays first base, it is as the one to whom the ball will be thrown from the field or from the catcher. Their organized reaction becomes what I have called the "generalized other" that accompanies and controls his conduct. And it is this generalized other in his experience which provides him with a self. (p. 271)

For Mead, the individual adopts the generalized perspective of a group of significant others that shares a particular perspective on the self. In predicting global judgments of self, Mead's formulation implies a process through which the evaluations of significant others are somehow psychologically weighted to produce an over-all sense of self-worth as a person. However, Mead was not explicit on precisely how other's judgments were combined. Contemporary researchers have begun to address these processes more directly.

For Cooley and Mead, several themes have found their way into contemporary treatments of the self. Paramount is the role of the opinions of others in shaping the self-concept through social interaction. Cooley hinted at a developmental internalization process that has implications for the stability of the self-concept in which the reflected appraisals of specific others become incorporated into relatively enduing attitudes about the self. For Mead, a more generalized sense of self was internalized, although just how the opinions of various others are psychologically homogenized into a collective sense of self remains elusive. Finally, Cooley's observation that self-judgments are accompanied by self-feelings highlighted the role of affective processes in self-concept development, particularly self-conscious emotions such as pride and shame (see Harter, 1999).

Self-Psychology in the Second Half of the Twentieth Century

During the eras of James, Cooley, and later Mead, inquiry into topics concerning the self and psyche flourished. However, with the emergence of radical behaviorism, such constructs were excised from the scientific vocabularies of many theorists and the writings of James and the symbolic interactionists gathered dust on the shelf. It is of interest to ask why the self became an unwelcome guest at the behaviorists' table. Why did constructs such as self, including self-esteem, ego strength, sense of omnipotence, narcissistic injury, and so on, do little to whet the behaviorists' appetite? Several reasons appear responsible.

The very origins of the behaviorist movement rested on the identification of observables. Thus, hypothetical constructs were both conceptually and methodologically unpalatable. Cognitions, in general, and self-representations, in particular, could not be operationalized as observable behaviors. Moreover, self-report measures designed to tap self-constructs were not included on the methodological menu, because people were assumed to be very inaccurate judges of their own behavior. Those more accepting of introspective methodologies found the existing measures of self-concept ungratifying because their content was overly vague. Finally, self-constructs were not satisfying to the behaviorist's palate because their functions were not clearly specified. The very cornerstone of behavioral approaches rested on a functional analysis of behavior. In contrast, approaches to the self did little more than implicate self-representations as correlates of behavior, affording them little explanatory power as causes or mediators of behavior.

Several shifts in emphasis, later in the twentieth century, allowed self-constructs to become more palatable. Hypothetical constructs, in general, gained favor as parsimonious predictors of behavior, often far more economical in theoretical models than a multitude of discrete observables. Moreover, we witnessed a cognitive revolution in both child and adult psychology (Bruner, 1990). For developmentalists, Piagetian and neo-Piagetian models came to the forefront. For experimental and social psychologists, numerous cognitive models found favor. In this revolution, self theorists jumped on the bandwagon, resurrecting the self as a cognitive construction, as a mental representation that constitute a theory of self (e.g., Brim, 1976; Case, 1985; Epstein, 1973, 1981; Fischer, 1980; Greenwald, 1980; Kelly, 1955; Markus, 1980; Sarbin, 1962). Finally, self representations gained increased legitimacy as behaviorally oriented therapists were forced to acknowledge that the spontaneous self-evaluative statements of their clients seemed powerfully implicated in their pathology.

POSSIBLE GENETIC INFLUENCES ON SELF-ESTEEM

The discussion thus far has focused on psychological mechanisms that account for a child's level of self-esteem, describing the contribution of cognitive-developmental and social determinants. For many years, these have been the prevailing approaches. Recently, neurological and genetic models have come to the forefront, the 1990's were declared the decade of the brain, and it became obvious that our splintered subfields needed to be integrated if we are truly to understand development and human behavior. Thus, how might such a genetic perspective be applied to differences in levels of self-esteem in children? Several investigators have recently presented statistical findings (from twin studies) that suggest the heritability of self-esteem. The empirical findings cannot be disputed (see McGuire et al., 1999; Neiss, Sedikides, & Stevenson, 2002).

However, does this mean that there is a self-esteem gene? I think not. Might there be heritability, yes. What might be a thoughtful explanation? We know a great deal about heritability from many compelling studies of intelligence, temperament, athleticism, and creativity to name but a few characteristics. There are also considerable data demonstrating the heritability of conditions such as various learning disabilities, autism, and attention-deficit/hyperactivity disorder (ADHD; see Pennington, 2002). These studies can be linked to the issue of the heritability of self-esteem. If the genetic throw of the dice causes a child to be intellectually competent, athletically competent, or attractive by current societal standards, and if these domains are deemed important, then according to James (and our own findings), this child is on the path to high self-esteem. Conversely, genetically driven negative attributes, where success is viewed as important, will lead to low self-esteem.

A behavioral-genetic twin study by Hur, McGue, and Iacono (1998) comes to a similar conclusion. Findings revealed that 30% of individual differences in the self-concept subscales on the Piers-Harris instrument (Piers, 1976) were associated with genetic factors. The authors suggest two possible mechanisms by which genetic factors could affect self-concept. They first note that the genetic influence could reflect the well-documented genetic influence on actual abilities, personality traits, and physical make-up. Alternatively, they note that genetic factors might affect various dimensions of the self-concept by predisposing identical twins to psychologically evaluate themselves similarly, if they form a close emotional bond. They indicate that sorting out these interpretations will require further research.

Moreover, if children are genetically blessed with a sociable temperament and are rewarded for their sociability by parents, peers, teachers, extended family, and others, from a looking glass self-perspective, this positive feedback will enhance their self-esteem. Thus, it would seem that the constructs identified by James (1892) and Cooley (1902), and documented in our own research (Harter, 1999), are likely to be the mediators of genetic influences, rather than that there exists a direct connection between genes and self-esteem.

DEVELOPMENTAL DIFFERENCES IN SELF-REPRESENTATIONS DURING CHILDHOOD

In the sections to follow, we examine the nature of self-representations and self-evaluations at three periods of childhood: (1) toddlerhood to very early childhood, (2) early to middle childhood, and (3) middle to late childhood. For each period, there is a prototypical

self-descriptive cameo that reflects the cardinal features of the content and structure of the self at that developmental level. Discussion will focus on (a) the normative-developmental changes that are critical as a backdrop and against which we can judge whether a child's self-representations are age-appropriate; (b) the normative-developmental liabilities for the self at this period; and (c) what cognitive and social factors at each period lead to individual differences in self-development, producing positive adjustment outcomes for some versus deviations that can be considered more maladaptive for others.

Toddlerhood to Early Childhood: Verbal Cameo of Normative Self-Representations and Self-Evaluations

> I'm almost 3 years old and I live in a big house with my mother and father and my brother, Jason, and my sister, Lisa. I have blue eyes and a kitty that is orange and a television in my own room. I know all of my ABCs, listen: A, B, C, D, E, F, G, H, J, L, K, O, P, Q, R, X, Y, Z. I can run real fast. I like pizza and I have a nice teacher at preschool. I can count up to 100, want to hear me? I love my dog Skipper. I can climb to the top of the jungle gym, I'm not scared! I'm never scared! I'm always happy. I have brown hair and I go to preschool. I'm really strong. I can lift this chair, watch me! (adapted from Harter, 1999)

Such descriptions will typically be observed in 3- to 4-year-olds. Noteworthy is the nature of the attributes selected to portray the self. Theory and evidence (see Fischer, 1980; Fischer & Canfield, 1986; S. Griffin, 1992; Harter, 1998, 1999; Higgins, 1991; Watson, 1990) indicate that the young child can only construct concrete cognitive representations of observable features of the self (e.g., "I know my ABC's," "I can count," "I live in a big house"). Damon and Hart (1988) label these as categorical identifications; the young child understands the self only as separate, taxonomic attributes that are physical (e.g., "I have blue eyes"), active (e.g., "I can run real fast, climb to the top"), social (e.g., "I have a brother, Jason, and a sister, Lisa"), or psychological (e.g., "I am happy"). Particular skills are touted (running, climbing) rather than generalizations about being athletic or good at sports. Moreover, often these behavioral descriptions will spill over into actual demonstrations of one's abilities ("I'm really strong. I can lift this chair, watch me!"), suggesting that these emerging self-representations are still directly tied to behavior. From a cognitive-developmental perspective, they do not represent higher-order conceptual categories through which the self is defined. In addition to concrete descriptions of behaviors, the young child defines the self by preferences (e.g., "I like pizza; I love my dog Skipper") and possessions ("I have an orange kitty and a television in my own room"). With regard to possessions, Fasig (2000) has specifically studied toddlers' basic understanding of ownership as a facet of the extended self. Those with rudimentary ownership understanding provided richer self-representations than those who did not possess such knowledge. On balance, as Rosenberg (1979) cogently observes, the young child acts as a demographer or radical behaviorist in that his or her self-descriptions are limited to characteristics that are potentially observable by others.

From the standpoint of organization, the self-representations of this period are highly differentiated or isolated from one another. The young child is incapable of integrating these compartmentalized representations of self, and thus self-descriptive accounts appear quite disjointed. This lack of coherence is a general cognitive characteristic that pervades the young child's thinking across a variety of domains (Fischer, 1980; Harter, 1999). As Piaget (1960) observed, young children's thinking is transductive in that they reason from particular to particular in no logical order.

Neo-Piagetians have elaborated on these processes. Case (1992) refers to this level as "Interrelational," in that young children can forge rudimentary links in the form of discrete structures that are defined by physical dimensions, behavioral events, or habitual activities. However, they cannot coordinate two such structures (see also S. Griffin, 1992), in part, because of working memory constraints that prevent young children from holding several features in mind simultaneously. Fischer's (1980) formulation is very similar. He labels these initial structures "Single Representations." Such structures are highly differentiated from one another because the cognitive limitations at this stage render the child incapable of integrating single representations into a coherent self-portrait.

Moreover, self-evaluations during this period are typically unrealistically positive (e.g., "I know all of my ABCs"—which he or she doesn't) because young children have difficulty distinguishing between their desired and their actual competence, which is a confusion initially observed by both S. Freud (1952) and Piaget (1932). Thus, young children cannot yet formulate an ideal self-concept that is differentiated from a real self-

concept. Rather, their descriptions represent a litany of talents that may transcend reality (Harter & Pike, 1984). For contemporary cognitive-developmentalists, such overstated virtuosity stems from another cognitive limitation of this period: The inability of young children to bring social comparison information to bear meaningfully on their perceived competencies (Frey & Ruble, 1990; Ruble & Dweck, 1995). The ability to use social comparison toward the goals of self-evaluation requires that the child be able to relate one concept (e.g., his or her own performance) to another (e.g., someone else's performance), a skill that is not sufficiently developed in the young child. Thus, self-descriptions typically represent an overestimation of personal abilities. It is important to appreciate, however, that these apparent distortions are normative in that they reflect cognitive limitations rather than conscious efforts to deceive the listener.

Another manifestation of the self-structure of very young children is their inability to acknowledge that they can possess attributes of opposing valence, for example, good and bad or nice and mean (Fischer, Hand, Watson, Van Parys, & Tucker, 1984). This all-or-none thinking can be observed in the cameo, in that all of the attributes appear to be positive. Self-representations may also include emotion descriptors (e.g., "I'm always happy"). However, children at this age do not acknowledge that they can experience both positive and negative emotions, particularly at the same time. The majority will deny that they have negative emotions (e.g., "I'm never scared!") as salient features of their descriptive self-portrait. Other procedures reveal that they do have rudimentary concepts of such single negative emotions as mad, sad, and scared (see Bretherton & Beeghly, 1982; Dunn, 1988; Harter & Whitesell, 1989). Evidence now indicates that young children report that they cannot experience seemingly opposing emotional reactions simultaneously (Carroll & Steward, 1984; Donaldson & Westerman, 1986; Gnepp, McKee, & Domanic, 1987; P. Harris, 1983; Harter & Buddin, 1987; Reissland, 1985; Selman, 1980). For Fischer and colleagues (e.g., Fischer & Ayoub, 1994), this dichotomous thinking represents the natural fractionation of the mind. Such "affecting splitting" constitutes a normative form of dissociation that is the hallmark of very young children's thinking about both self and other.

Cognitive limitations of this period extend to the inability of young children to create a concept of their overall worth as a person: a representation of their global self-esteem (Harter, 1990b). This self-representation requires a higher-order integration of domain-specific attributes that have first been differentiated. Young children do describe themselves in terms of concrete cognitive or physical abilities, how they behave, how they look, and the friendships they have formed (Harter, 1990b, 1999). However, these domains are not clearly differentiated from one another, as revealed through factor-analytic procedures (Harter, 1998; Harter & Pike, 1984).

Behaviorally-Presented Self-Esteem in Young Children

The fact that young children cannot cognitively or verbally formulate a general concept of their worth as a person does not dictate that they lack the experience of self-esteem. Rather, our findings (see Harter, 1990a, 1999) indicate that young children manifest self-esteem in their behavior. In examining the construct of "behaviorally presented self-esteem," we first invoked the aid of experienced nursery school and kindergarten teachers. We found that for early childhood educators, self-esteem is a very meaningful concept that distinguishes children from one another. Teachers first provided prototypic descriptors of the high and low self-esteem child, as well as attributes that did not discriminate the two groups. A second group of teachers performed a Q-sort procedure on 84 behavioral descriptors, indicating which described the high self-esteem child, the low self-esteem child, and those that were not relevant to self-esteem.

There were two classes of behaviors that were viewed as characteristic of the high self-esteem child:

1. Active displays of confidence, curiosity, initiative, and independence that included: trusts his or her own ideas, approaches challenge, initiates activities confidently, takes initiative, sets goals independently, is curious, explores and questions, is eager to try doing new things, describes self in positive terms, and shows pride in his or her work.
2. Adaptive reaction to change or stress that included: able to adjust to changes, comfortable with transitions, tolerates frustration and perseveres, and able to handle criticism and teasing.

Similar categories describing the low self-esteem child representing the converse of these two sets of items emerged:

1. Failure to display confidence, curiosity, initiative, and independence that included: doesn't trust his or her own ideas, lacks confidence to initiate, lacks confidence to approach challenge, is not curious, does not explore, hangs back, watches only, withdraws and sits apart, describes self in negative terms, and does not show pride in his or her work.
2. Difficulty in reacting to change or stress that included: gives up easily when frustrated, reacts to stress with immature behavior, and reacts inappropriately to accidents.

Of particular interest are the categories of behaviors that do not seem to discriminate, according to teachers, between high and low self-esteem children. Most noteworthy was the fact that *competence* was not viewed by teachers as indicative of self-esteem in young children. It would appear that confidence, as a behavioral style, is not synonymous with competence, at least at this age level. This is illuminating because it suggests that the origin of a sense of confidence during early childhood does not necessarily reside in the display of skills, more objectively defined. During later childhood, the link between confidence in the self and level of competence apparently becomes stronger. As becomes apparent in describing the antecedents of self-esteem that emerge in middle childhood, competence becomes a much more critical factor. We would argue that, in bridging these two developmental periods, socialization practices that reward displays of confidence will lead the child to engage in behaviors that would allow him or her to develop skills and competencies that will subsequently become a defining predictor of self-esteem.

Additional Functions of the Socializing Environment

Higgins (1991), building on the efforts of Case (1985), Fischer (1980), and Selman (1980), focuses on how self-development during this period involves the interaction between the young child's cognitive capacities and the role of socializing agents. He provides evidence for the contention that at Case's stage of "interrelational development" and Fischer's stage of "single representations," the very young child can place him- or herself in the same category as the parent who shares his or her gender, forming an initial basis for identification with that parent. Thus, the young boy can evaluate his overt behavior with regard to the question: "Am I doing what Daddy is doing?" Similarly, the young girl evaluates her behavior, asking "Am I doing what Mommy is doing?" Attempts to match that behavior impact which attributes become incorporated into the young child's self-definition. Thus, these processes represent one way in which socializing agents impact the self.

Higgins (1991) observes that at the interrelational stage, young children can also form structures allowing them to detect the fact that their behavior evokes a reaction in others, notably parents, which causes psychological reactions in the self (see Thompson, Chapter 2, this *Handbook,* this volume). These experiences shape the self to the extent that the young child chooses to engage in behaviors designed to please the parents. Stipek, Recchia, and McClintic (1992) have provided empirical evidence for this observation, demonstrating that slightly before the age of 2, children begin to anticipate adult reactions, seeking positive responses to their successes and attempting to avoid negative responses to failure. At this age, they also find that young children show a rudimentary appreciation for adult standards, for example, by turning away from adults in seeming distress and hunching their shoulder in the face of failures (see also Kagan, 1984). For Mascolo and Fischer (1995), such reactions constitute rudimentary forms of shame. Shame at this period, like self-esteem, can only be *behaviorally* manifest. Children do not understand the concept at a verbal level (see Harter, 1999). Moreover, although young children are beginning to recognize that their behavior has an impact on others, their perspective-taking skills are extremely limited (see Harter, 1999; Selman, 1980). Thus, they are unable to incorporate others' opinions of the self into a realistic self-evaluation that can be verbalized.

The Role of Narrative in the Co-Construction of the Self

Another arena in which parental figures, in particular, impact children's self-development involves the role of narratives in promoting the young child's autobiographic memory: a rudimentary story of the self. The infantile amnesia that one observes before the age of approximately 2 can only be overcome by learning from adults how to formulate their own memories as *narratives.* Initially, parents recount to the child stories about his or her past and present experiences. With increasing language facility, children come to take on a more active role in that parent and child co-construct the memory of a shared experience (Eisenberg, 1985; Hudson, 1990a, 1990b; Nelson, 1990, 1993; Rogoff, 1990; Snow, 1990).

However, for the young child, such narratives are still highly scaffolded by the parents, who reinforce aspects of experience that they feel are important to codify and remember (Fivush, Gray, & Fromhoff, 1987; Fivush & Hudson, 1990; Nelson, 1989). Through these interactions, an autobiographic account of the self is created. Of further interest are findings demonstrating individual differences in maternal styles of narrative construction (see Bretherton, 1993; Nelson, 1990, 1993). For example, Tessler (1991) has distinguished between an elaborative style (where mothers present an embellished narrative) and a pragmatic style (focusing more on useful information). Elaborative mothers were more effective in establishing and eliciting memories with their young children.

More recently, Nelson (2003) has introduced the concept of a social-cultural-linguistic self that arises from autobiographical memory and a narrative self, between the ages of 2 and 5. The transition to a "cultural self" is dependent on social-linguistic exchanges and exposure to cultural messages that are meaningful to the self. It requires the child's social and cognitive awareness and the capacity for new levels of mental representations that develop during this period. For Nelson, this is a gradual process eventuating in a culturally saturated concept of self, an autobiographical self with both a specific self-history, and an imagined future self that reflects the values and expectations of the culture in which one is embedded. Bem's (1985) gender schema theory is quite consistent with this conceptualization in that she describes how the initial labeling of one's gender leads the young child to look to the culture where they learn that gender distinctions are very important, causing them to attend to the content of gender roles for males and females. Learning that boys are expected to be strong, brave, and assertive but girls are expected to be good, nice, and quiet, boys and girls acquire gender schemas, adopting the characteristics that the culture deems appropriate for their gender.

For most developmental memory researchers, language is the critical acquisition allowing one to establish a personal narrative and to overcome infantile amnesia (Budwig, 2000; Fivush & Hammond, 1990; Hudson, 1990a; Nelson, 1990, 2003; Pillemer & White, 1989). The mastery of language, in general, and of personal pronouns, in particular, enables young children to think and talk about the I-self and to expand their categorical knowledge of the Me-self (Bates, 1990; P. Miller, Potts, Fung, Hoogstra, & Mintz, 1990). Moreover, representations of the self in language are further facilitated by acquisition of the past tense, which occurs toward the latter half of the 3rd year.

Howe (2003) and Howe and Courage (1993) argue, however, that the emergence of language is not sufficient to explain the demise of infantile amnesia and the emergence of an ability to create autobiographical memories. Self-knowledge is also required, in that an appreciation for the self as an independent entity with actions, attributes, affects, and thoughts that are distinct from those of others is necessary for the development of autobiographical memory. Without the recognition of an independent I-self and Me-self, there can be no referent around which personally experienced events can be organized. Thus, for Howe and Courage, the emergence of the toddler's sense of self is the cornerstone in the development of autobiographical memory that further shapes and solidifies one's self definition.

Linguistic interactions with parents also impact the developing child's representation of self in semantic memory (Bowlby, 1969, 1973; Nelson, 1993; Snow, 1990). As Bowlby first noted, early semantic memory is conferred by caregivers. Parents convey considerable descriptive and evaluative information about the child, including labels to distinguish one from others (e.g., "You're a big boy"), evaluative descriptors of the self (e.g., "You are so smart"; "You're a good girl"), as well as rules and standards and the extent to which the child has met parental expectations ("Big boys don't cry"). Consistent with Cooley's (1902) model of the looking glass self, children incorporate these labels and evaluations into their self-definition in the form of general trait knowledge (represented in semantic memory). Thus, the linguistic construction of the self is a highly interpersonal process, with caregivers making a major contribution to its representation in both autobiographical and semantic memory.

More recently, experts on infant memory development have suggested additional processes that may account for childhood amnesia (see Hayne, 2004). Reviewing numerous studies of infant memory, Hayne concludes that there are three developmental processes that may add to our understanding of the infant's failure to retain autobiographical content. The large corpus of research first reveals that the *speed* with which infants encode information increases as a function of age. Secondly, the *retention* interval also dramatically increases as a function of age during infancy. Third, the *flexibility* of memory retrieval also improves during infancy,

meaning that memories are not as bound by specific contextual or proximal cues, whereas changes in such cues can disrupt or preclude memory retrieval in younger infants. Older infants have been found to gradually utilize more or different retrieval cues allowing them to access memories in a wider range of situations. These newer explanations are not incompatible with earlier theories of the function of language and self-development but rather provide additional explanations for the phenomenon of infantile amnesia.

Normative Liabilities for Self-Development during Very Early Childhood

Infantile amnesia precludes a conscious sense of self for the toddler. Even once very young children are able to verbally describe the self, their self-representations are still limited in that they reflect concrete descriptions of behaviors, abilities, emotions, possessions, and preferences that are potentially observable by others. These attributes are also highly differentiated or isolated from one another, leading to rather disjointed accounts, because at this age, young children lack the ability to integrate such characteristics. For some, this lack of a logical self-theory may be cause for concern if not consternation. However, these features are normative in that the I-self processes (i.e., the cognitive structures available at this developmental period) preclude a more logical rendering of the Me-self.

Self-representations are also likely to be unrealistically *positive* for several reasons (see Harter, 1999). First, they lack the cognitive ability to engage in social comparison, for the purpose of self-evaluation. From a cognitive-developmental perspective, this skill, like many of the abilities that are unavailable to the preoperational child as Piaget (1960) revealed, requires that one be able to simultaneously hold two dimensions in mind to compare them (cf. conservation tasks). We apply this analysis to the inability to hold in mind an evaluation of one's own attributes while simultaneously thinking about another's attributes and comparing them.

Second, and for similar reasons, the very young child is unable to distinguish between their *actual* self-attributes and their *ideal* self-attributes. This requires making a discrimination between the two, holding each in mind simultaneously, and comparing the two judgments, a cognitive ability that the very young child lacks. As a result, self-evaluations are unrealistically positive because the fusion of the two favors the ideal or desirable self-concept. When we are dealing with older children, we might interpret such a tendency to reflect socially desirable responding (i.e., the conscious distortion of one's self-evaluation) to be favorable. Cognitive-developmental interpretations lead to a different conclusion: that the very young child's positive evaluations reflect cognitive limitations rather than a conscious attempt to deceive.

Third, young children lack the perspective-taking ability to understand and therefore incorporate the perceived opinions of significant others toward the self (Harter, 1999; Selman, 1980). As becomes evident in the discussion of middle childhood, the ability to appreciate others' evaluations of the self becomes a powerful determinant of a child's sense of worth as he or she emerges in middle childhood.

Cognitive limitations also lead to young children's inability to acknowledge that they can possess both positive and negative self-attributes. The all-or-none, black-and-white thinking that is characteristic of the preoperational child extends to his or her conceptualizations of self: One must be one or the other. To the extent that the majority of socializing agents are relatively benevolent and supportive, the psychological scale will tip toward the imbalance of positive self-attributes. Thus, the young child will bask in the glow of overall virtuosity (even if it is unrealistic).

The inability to possess a verbalizable concept of self-esteem can also be explained by the cognitive limitations of this period. As is documented, the subsequent ability to compare one's actual self-attributes with one's ideal self-attributes will become an important determinant of one's level of self-esteem. Perspective-taking abilities will also become critical given that the internalization of the opinions of significant others becomes a powerful predictor of a child's overall sense of personal worth. It was noted that *behavioral* manifestations of self-esteem do emerge during early childhood, as has been documented. However, it is an interesting empirical question as to whether level of self-esteem as so displayed parallels or predicts the concept of a child's self-esteem that will emerge in middle childhood.

The description of the normative liabilities that impact conceptions and manifestations of the self during early childhood follow from normative cognitive limitations. One may question, however, the extent to which these reflect *psychological* liabilities. Many of the cognitive limitations of this period may serve as *protective* factors, to the extent that the very young child maintains

very positive perceptions of self, even if potentially unrealistic. Positive self-views may serve as motivating factors and emotional buffers, contributing to the young child's development. They may propel the child toward growth-building mastery attempts, they may instill a sense of confidence, and they may lead the child to rebuff perceptions of inadequacy, all of which may foster positive future development. From an evolutionary perspective, such "liabilities" may represent critical strengths, at this developmental level. This issue is revisited as we move up the ontogenetic ladder of representations and evaluations of the self.

Individual Differences: Adaptive and Maladaptive Outcomes during Toddlerhood and Early Childhood

In the previous two sections on the period of toddlerhood to early childhood, the focus was on *normative* self development, including normative liabilities. It is also critical to identify the causes of individual differences in self-development at each period. Individual differences will reflect a combination of the competencies, attributes, and temperament that the child brings into the world. They will also be heavily dependent on the role of socializing agents in the child's life. Thus, we explore what facilitates positive self-evaluations and what compromises the self in terms of negative evaluations. An important goal of this chapter is to distinguish between normative liabilities in the formation of the self and more maladaptive or pathological processes and outcomes at each developmental level.

Findings from the socialization literature in general (see Bugenthal & Goodnow, 1998; Thompson, 1998, and Chapter 2, this *Handbook,* this volume), and attachment theory, in particular (see Bretherton & Munholland, 1999) highlight the critical role of care, sensitivity, and feedback from socializing agents. Theory, going back to Winnicott's (1965) concept of "good enough mothering," suggests that sensitive responding to the infant's and toddler's needs sets the stage for positive self-development (see also Stern, 1985). Soothing, positive affect, interest in the infant's activities, support for mastery attempts, praise, and (nonintrusive) encouragement all lay the groundwork for a healthy sense of self during toddlerhood and early childhood.

Attachment theory (see Bretherton and Munholland, 1999) focuses on the development of working models of self and other, constructed in the crucible of early caregiving experiences. For securely attached infants, a working model of self as valued, loved, and competent will emerge in the context of a working model of parents as emotionally available, loving, sensitive, and supportive of mastery attempts. Conversely, a working model of the self as devalued and incompetent is the counterpart of a working model of parents as rejecting or ignoring of attachment bids and interfering with exploration and mastery attempts.

Moreover, during toddlerhood to very early childhood, other factors could serve to seriously derail normative self-development, leading to outcomes that would seriously compromise a very young child's psychological development. Typically, the causes of severe maladjustment involve an interaction between the child's level of cognitive development and chronic, negative treatment at the hands of caregivers.

The Effects of Abuse.   It is not uncommon for children who experience severe and chronic sexual abuse to have also been subjected to other types of maltreatment, including verbal, physical, and emotional abuse (see Cicchetti, 2004; Harter, 1999; Rossman & Rosenberg, 1998). The normative penchant for very young children to engage in all-or-none thinking (e.g., all good versus all bad) will lead abused children to view the Me-self as *all bad.* As noted earlier, the more typical pattern for children who are socialized by benevolent, supportive parents is to view the self as all good. Abuse, as well as severe neglect (Bowlby, 1980), can lead to early forms of depression in which the very young child eventually becomes listless, unconnected to caregivers, and, eventually numb, emotionally.

Abuse or maltreatment can also affect I-self functions, for example, self-awareness—one of the basic functions of the I-self as originally described by James (1892). Briere (1992) points to a feature of abusive relationships that interfere with the victim's lack of awareness of self. The fact that the child must direct sustained attention to external threats draws energy and focus away from the developmental task of self-awareness. Thus, the hyper-vigilance to others' reactions, what Briere (1989) terms *other directedness,* interferes with the ability to attend to the child's own needs, thoughts, and desires.

Research findings with children support these contentions. Cicchetti (1989) and colleagues (Cicchetti & Rogosch, 2001) found that maltreated children (ages 30 to 36 months) report less internal-state language, particularly negative internal feeling and physiological reactions than do their nonmaltreated, securely attached counterparts (see also Beeghly & Cicchetti, 1994). Similar findings by Beeghly, Carlson, and Cicchetti (1986); Coster, Gersten, Beeghly, and Cicchetti (1989) have also reported that maltreated toddlers use less descriptive speech, particularly about their own feelings and actions. Gralinski, Feshbach, Powell, and Derrington (1993) have also observed that older, maltreated children report fewer descriptions of inner states and feelings than children with no known history of abuse. Thus, there is a growing body of evidence that the defensive processes that are mobilized by maltreated children interfere with one of the primary tasks of the I-self namely awareness of inner thoughts and feelings. Lack of self-awareness should also interfere with the ability to develop autobiographical memory.

Attachment theorists have also contributed to our understanding of how maltreatment in early childhood can adversely influence self-development. There is considerable consensus that the vast majority of maltreated children form insecure attachments with their primary caregivers (Cicchetti & Rogosch, 2001; Crittenden & Ainsworth, 1989; Erickson, Egeland, & Pianta, 1989; Schneider-Rosen, Braunwald, Carlson, & Cicchetti, 1985; Westen, 1993). Findings have documented that maltreated infants are more likely to develop disorganized-disoriented type D attachment relationships (Barnett, Ganiban, & Cicchetti, 1999; Carlson, Cicchetti, & Barnett, 1989). Thus, the effects of early sexual and/or physical abuse, coupled with other forms of parental insensitivity, disrupt the attachment bond, which interferes with the development of positive working models of self and others. The foundation of attachment theory rests on the premise that if the caregiver has fairly consistently responded to the infant's needs and signals, and has respected the infant's need for independent exploration of the environment, the child will develop an internal working model of self as valued, competent, and self-reliant. Conversely, if the parent is insensitive to the infant's needs and signals, inconsistent, and rejecting of the infant's bid for comfort and exploration, the child will develop an internal working model of the self as unworthy, ineffective, and incompetent (Ainsworth, 1979; Bowlby, 1973; Bretherton, 1991, 1993; Crittenden & Ainsworth, 1989; Sroufe & Fleeson, 1986). The parental practices that have been associated with child abuse represent precisely the kind of treatment that would lead children to develop insecure attachments and a concept of self as unlovable and lacking in competence.

As noted earlier, one critical function of parenting is to assist the child in creating a narrative of the self, an autobiographical account that includes the perceptions of self and other (see Hudson, 1990a, 1990b; Nelson, 1986, 2003; Snow, 1990). Initially, these narratives are highly scaffolded by parents, who reinforce aspects of experience that they, the parents, feel are important to codify and to remember or to forget (Fivush & Hudson, 1990; Hudson, 1990a; Nelson, 1986, 1990, 1993; Rogoff, 1990; Snow, 1990). Findings have indicated that the narratives of maltreated children contain more negative self-representations and more negative maternal representations compared to nonmaltreated children (Toth, Cicchetti, Macfie, Maughan, & Vanmeenen, 2000). Moreover, such narratives show less coherence; that is, the self that is represented is less coherent (Crittenden, 1994; Macfie, Cicchetti, & Toth, 2001). These findings document greater signs of dissociative symptoms that reflect disruptions in the integration of memories and perceptions about the self. Thus, maltreatment severely disrupts normative self-development, which leads to associated pathological symptoms, where it has been found that conflictual themes in young children's narratives predict externalizing problems. Moreover, severe, chronic abuse has been associated with disorders, such as borderline personality, where symptoms emerge later in development during adulthood (Putnam, 1993; Westen, 1993).

Language and False-Self Behavior. Language clearly promotes heightened levels of relatedness and allows for the creation of a personal narrative. Stern (1985) also alerts us to the liabilities of language. He argues that language can drive a wedge between two simultaneous forms of interpersonal experience: as it is lived and as it is verbally represented. The very capacity for objectifying the self through verbal representations allows us to transcend, and potentially distort, our immediate experience and to create a fantasized construction of the self. As noted earlier, there is the potential for incorporating the biases of caregivers' perspectives on the self, because initially, adults dictate the content of narratives incorporated in autobiographical memory (Bowlby, 1980; Bretherton, 1987; Crittenden, 1994; Pipp, 1990). Children may receive subtle signals that

certain episodes should not be retold or are best forgotten (Dunn, Brown, & Beardsall, 1991). Bretherton describes another manifestation (defensive exclusion) in which negative information about the self or the other is not incorporated because it is too psychologically threatening (see also Cassidy & Kobak, 1988). Wolf (1990) further describes several mechanisms, such as deceit and fantasy, whereby the young child, as author of the self, can select, edit, or change the facts in the service of personal goals, hopes, or wishes (see also Dunn, 1988).

Such distortions may well contribute to the formation of a self that is perceived as unauthentic if a person accepts the falsified version of experience. Winnicott's (1958) observations alert us to the fact that intrusive or overinvolved mothers, in their desire to comply with maternal demands and expectations, lead infants to present a false outer self that does not represent their own inner experiences. Moreover, such parents may reject the infant's "felt self," approving only of the falsely presented self (Crittenden, 1994). As Stern (1985) notes, the display of false-self, incurs the risk of alienating a person from those inner experiences that represent their true self (see also Main & Solomon, 1990). Thus, linguistic abilities not only allow a person to share his or her experiences with others but also to withhold them as well.

The Impoverished Self. As noted in the discussion of normative-development during early childhood, an important function of parenting is to scaffold the child's construction of autobiographical memory in the form of a narrative of one's nascent life story. However, clinicians observe that maltreatment and neglect sow the seeds for children, beginning in early to middle childhood, to develop what we (Marold & Harter in Harter, 1999) have come to call an "impoverished self," which has its roots in the early socialization practices of caregivers who fail to assist the child in the co-construction of a positive, rich, and coherent self narrative. Research (Tessler, 1991) has revealed individual differences among mothers in that some help to construct an embellished narrative, whereas others focus on a more restricted narrative that focuses on useful information leading to fewer autobiographical memories. Clinical observations reveal that there is another group of parents who, because of their own dysfunction (e.g., depression) and parental inadequacies, do little to nothing in the way of co-constructing with the child a self-narrative. The seeds of an impoverished self, therefore, begin in early childhood and continue into middle childhood and beyond if such children do not receive therapeutic intervention.

When these children come to the attention of family therapists, they lack a vocabulary to define the self, in that there is little in the way of autobiographical memory and descriptive or evaluative concepts about the self. An impoverished self represents a liability in that the individual has few personal referents or self-concepts around which to organize present experiences. As a result, the behavior of such children will often appear to be disorganized. Moreover, to the extent that a richly defined self promotes motivational functions in terms of guides to regulate behavior and to set future goals, such children may appear aimless, with no clear pursuits. A clinical colleague of mine, Donna Marold, has astutely observed that these children do not have dreams for the future, whereas most children do have future aspirations (Marold, personal communication, August 1998). For example, the prototypical child in early to middle childhood indicates that he or she is going to be on a team someday. Marold notes that the families of such children typically do not create or construct the type of narratives that provide a basis for autobiographical memory and a sense of self. Nor do such parents provide the type of personal labels or feedback that would lead to the development of semantic memory for self-attributes. Often, these are parents who do not take photographs of the children or the family, nor do they engage in such activities as posting the child's artwork or school papers on the refrigerator door. Marold has also observed that such parents do not have special rituals such as cooking the child's favorite food or reading (and rereading) cherished bedtime stories.

What type of therapeutic interventions might be applicable, and how can they be guided by developmental theory and research? Therapists (myself included) have learned through trial and error that one cannot, with older children, simply try to instill, teach, or scaffold the self-structures appropriate for their age level; namely, trait labels that represent generalizations that integrate behavioral or taxonomic self-attributes. With such children, there are few attributes to build on. Thus, we must begin at the beginning, utilizing techniques that help the child create the missing narratives, the autobiographical memory, and the self-labels. Marold has successfully employed a number of very basic techniques to achieve this goal, techniques that necessarily enlist the aid of parents. She suggests that the parent and child create a scrapbook in which whatever materials that

might be available (the scant photograph, perhaps from the school picture; a child's drawing; anything that may make a memory more salient) are collected and talked about. Where such materials are not available, Marold suggests cutting pictures out of magazines that represent the child's favorite possessions, activities, preferences, the very features that define the young child's sense of self. If there have been no routines that help to solidify the child's sense of self, Marold recommends that parents be counseled to establish routines, for example, establishing some family rituals (e.g., Friday night pizza) around a child's favorite food. Obviously, these techniques require collaboration with the parents and depend on their ability to recreate their child's past experiences, something that not all parents may be equipped to do. Here, the therapist can serve as an important role model. From the standpoint of our developmental analysis, the prevention of an impoverished self requires this type of support in early childhood. In the absence of such support, such impoverishment will continue into later childhood.

Early to Middle Childhood: Verbal Cameo of Normative Self-Representations and Self-Evaluations

> I have a lot of friends, in my neighborhood, at school, and at my church. I'm good at schoolwork, I know my words, and letters, and my numbers. I can run fast, and I can climb high, a lot higher than I could when I was little and I can run faster, too. I can also throw a ball real far, I'm going to be on some kind of team when I am older. I can do lots of stuff real good. Lots! If you are good at things you can't be bad at things, at least not at the same time. I know some other kids who are bad at things but not me! My parents are real proud of me when I do good at things. It makes me really happy and excited when they watch me! (adapted from Harter, 1999)

Such self-descriptions are typical of children ages 5 to 7. Some of the features of the previous stage persist in that self-representations are still typically very positive, and the child continues to overestimate his or her virtuosity. References to various competencies, for example, social skills, cognitive abilities, and athletic talents are common self-descriptors. With regard to the advances of this age period, children begin to display a rudimentary ability to intercoordinate concepts that were previously compartmentalized (Case, 1985; Fischer, 1980; Harter, 1999). For example, they can form a category or representational set that combines a number of their competencies (e.g., good at running, jumping, schoolwork, having friends in the neighborhood, at school, and at church). However, all-or-none thinking persists. In Case's (1985) model and its application to the self (S. Griffin, 1992), this stage is labeled "unidimentional" thinking. Such black-and-white thinking is supported by another new cognitive process that emerges at this stage. The novel acquisition is the child's ability to link or relate representational sets to one another, to "map" representations onto one another, to use Fischer's (1980) terminology. Of particular interest to self-development is one type of representational mapping that is extremely common in the thinking of young children—a link in the form of opposites. For example, in the domain of physical concepts, young children can oppose up versus down, tall versus short, and thin versus wide or fat.

Opposites can also be observed in the realm of the descriptions of self and others, where the child's ability to oppose "good" to "bad" is especially relevant. As observed earlier, the child develops a rudimentary concept of the self as good at a number of skills. Given that good is defined as the opposite of bad, this cognitive construction typically precludes the young child from being "bad," at least at the same time. Thus, the oppositional mapping takes the necessary form of "I'm good and therefore I can't be bad." However, other people may be perceived as bad at these skills, as the cameo description reveals ("I know other kids who are bad at things but not me!"). Therefore, the structure of such mappings typically leads the child to overdifferentiate favorable and unfavorable attributes, as demonstrated by findings revealing young children's inability to integrate attributes such as nice and mean (Fisher et al., 1984) or smart and dumb (Harter, 1986a). Moreover, the mapping structure leads to the persistence of self-descriptions laden with virtuosity.

These principles also apply to children's understanding of their emotions, in that they cannot integrate emotions of opposing valance such as happy and sad (Harter & Buddin, 1987). There is an advance over the previous period in that children come to appreciate the fact that they can have two emotions of the same valence (e.g., "I'm happy and excited when my parents watch me"). However, the representational set for positive emotions is cognitive separate from negative emotions (e.g., sad, mad, or scared). Thus, children at this stage cannot yet integrate the sets of positive and negative emotions sets that are viewed as conceptually opposites and therefore

incompatible. The inability to acknowledge that a person can possess both favorable and unfavorable attributes, or experience both positive and negative emotions, represents a cognitive liability that is a hallmark of this period of development. Unlike the previous period, the child is now, due to greater cognitive and linguistic abilities, able to verbally express his or her staunch conviction that a person cannot possess both positive and negative characteristics at the same time. As one 5-year-old vehemently put it, "Nope, there is no way you could be smart and dumb at the same time. You only have one mind!"

The Role of the Socializing Environment

Socializing agents also have an impact on self-development, in interaction with cognitive acquisitions. Thus, children acquire an increasing cognitive appreciation for the perspective of others that influences self-development. The child at this level comes to realize that socializing agents have a particular viewpoint (not merely a reaction) toward them and their behavior (Higgins, 1991). As Selman (1980) also observes, the improved perspective-taking skills at this age permit children to realize that others are actively evaluating the self (although children have not yet internalized these evaluations sufficiently to make independent judgments about their attributes.) Higgins observes that the viewpoints of others begin to function as "self-guides" as the child comes to further identify with what he or she perceives socializing agents expect of the self. These self-guides also function to aid the child in the regulation of his or her behavior. However, at this age level, cognitive-developmental limitations preclude the internalization of others' standards and opinions about the self, which will, with later advances, allow the child to personally come to own such standards and opinions.

As Higgins (1991) and Selman (1980) have pointed out, although children at this age do become aware that others are critically evaluating their attributes, they lack the type of self-awareness that would allow them to be critical of their own behavior. In I-self/Me-self terminology, the child's I-self is aware that significant others are making judgments about the Me-self, yet the I-self cannot directly turn the evaluative beacon on the Me-self. These processes will only emerge when the child becomes capable of internalizing the evaluative judgments of others for the purpose of self-evaluation. As a result, children at this age period will show little interest in scrutinizing the self. As Anna Freud (1965) has cogently observed, young children do not naturally take themselves as the object of their own observation. They are much more likely to direct their inquisitiveness toward the outside world of events rather than the inner world of intrapsychic experiences.

There are additional forms of interaction between cognitive-developmental level and the socializing environment that affect the self, including certain advances in the ability to utilize social comparison information. Frey and Ruble (1985, 1990) as well as Suls and Sanders (1982) provide evidence that at this stage children first focus on temporal comparisons (how I am performing now, compared to when I was younger) and age norms rather than individual difference comparisons with age-mates. As our prototypical subject tells us, "I can climb a lot higher than when I was little and I can run faster, too." Suls and Sanders observe that such temporal comparisons are particularly gratifying to young children given the rapid skill development at this age level. As a result, such comparisons contribute to the highly positive self-evaluations that typically persist at this age level.

Evidence (reviewed in Ruble & Frey, 1991) now reveals that younger children do engage in certain rudimentary forms of social comparison; however, it is directed toward different goals than for older children. For example, young children use such information to determine if they have received their fair share of rewards, rather than for purposes of self-evaluation. Findings also indicate that young children show an interest in others' performance to obtain information about the task demands that can facilitate their understanding of mastery goals and improve their learning (Frey & Ruble, 1985; Ruble & Dweck, 1995). However, they cannot yet utilize such information for the purposes of self-evaluation, in large part due to the cognitive limitations of this period; thus, their evaluations continue to be unrealistic.

Normative Liabilities for Self-Development between Early to Middle Childhood

Many of the features of the previous stage persist, in that self-representations are typically very positive, and the child continues to overestimate his or her abilities. Moreover, the child at this period still lacks the ability to develop an overall concept of his or her worth as a person. With regard to advances, children do begin to display a rudimentary ability to intercoordinate self-concepts that were previously compartmentalized; for example, they can construct a representational set that combines a number of their competencies (e.g., good at running, jumping, and schoolwork). However, all-or-none thinking persists due to a new cognitive acquisition in which different valence attributes are verbally conceptualized as opposites (e.g., good versus bad or nice versus mean). Typically this all-or-none structure leads to self-attributes that are all positive, these beliefs are even more intractable than in the previous period given cognitive and linguistic advances that bring such beliefs into consciousness to the extent that the socializing environment supports such positivity.

Rudimentary processes allow the child to appreciate the fact that others are evaluating the self, although cognitive-developmental limitations preclude the child from internalizing these evaluations. Advances include the ability to make temporal comparisons between one's past performance. Given the rapid skill development during these years, such comparisons contribute to the highly positive self-evaluations that typically persist at this age level. The failure to use social comparison information for the purpose of self-evaluation, however, contributes to the persistence of unrealistically favorable self-attributes. As noted in describing the previous period, children at this stage are not consciously distorting their self-perceptions. Rather, they have not yet acquired the cognitive skills to develop more realistic self-perceptions.

Individual Differences: Adaptive and Maladaptive Outcomes during Early to Middle Childhood

A major source of individual differences in self-representations and self-evaluations continues to derive from the caregiving of significant others. During this particular developmental period, rudimentary beginnings of looking glass self-processes emerge (Cooley, 1902), namely, some appreciation for the opinions of significant others that will come to shape opinions of oneself. However, the capacities to engage in looking glass self-processes, as well as to construct working models of self, do not emerge at one particular point in development but evolve gradually over the course of childhood. Children begin, toward middle childhood, to introject parental values and to realize (through rudimentary perspective-taking skills) that not only do parents have standards that they expect will be met, but also that parents form an evaluative opinion about the child (Higgins, 1991; Leahy & Shirk, 1985; Oosterwegel & Oppenheimer, 1993; Selman, 1980). In I-self/Me-self terms, the I-self of the child can realize that others are forming evaluative opinions about one's Me-self. The I-self has not yet *internalized* or come to own the parental evaluations and therefore the I-self cannot yet directly evaluate the Me-self—a process that requires such internalizations. Further advances that allow children to fully engage in Cooley's looking glass self-processes will emerge in the subsequent period of middle to late childhood.

The ability to engage in even the rudimentary processes that emerge during early to middle childhood point to the importance of early socialization in the family as a source of individual differences in children's self-representations. There is considerable evidence from different theoretical perspectives that the quality of caregiving has a tremendous impact on the nature of the child's self-representations; for example, how favorably one evaluates the self (the *content* of one's self image) as well as how features of the self are *organized*. Thus, in general, parents who are nurturant, sensitive, responsive, and approving in the context of demanding realistically high standards will produce children with positive self-evaluations.

Traditional psychodynamic theorists such as Sullivan (1953) and Winnicott (1958) placed heavy emphasis on how the quality of mother-infant interactions impacted self-development, a theme amplified in more contemporary treats of the self (see Stern, 1985). For example, Winnicott described a pattern of "good-enough" mothering that would promote healthy self-development. The good-enough mother responds promptly and appropriately to the infant and toddler's demands, thereby initially promoting feelings of "omnipotence" or power, which certain theorists consider to be a critical precursor of positive feelings about the self (see also Erikson, 1959; Kohut, 1977). The good-enough mother also responds positively to mastery attempts. During periods when the young child's basic needs are met, such a mother retreats, supporting the capacity for her child to play alone, which Winnicott considered essential to the development of a stable and positive sense of self to emerge in early to middle childhood. Small failures in parental responsiveness at this period will lead to some disappointment for the child and less exaggerated feelings of omnipotence. However, according to both Winnicott and Kohut, these experiences play a vital role in self-other differentiation, allowing the children to both separate from the parent and to become more reality-oriented (see also Mahler, 1967).

Similarly, from an attachment theory perspective, a working model of self emerges in the crucible of the caregiver-infant relationship, a process that continues through childhood: Internal working models are believed to reflect experienced interaction patterns between the child and his or her attachment figures, and therefore the developmental working models of self and of the attachment figures are necessarily complementary. Thus, as Bowlby (1969) initially contended, the children who experiences parents as emotionally available, sensitive to his or her needs, loving, and supportive of his or her mastery attempts will construct a working model of the self as lovable and competent—the pattern for securely attached children (see also Bretherton, 1993). Conversely, a working model of self as devalued and incompetent is associated with a working model of parents as rejecting or ignoring of attachment behavior, including interference with exploration.

Although these themes were introduced in describing the earlier period of development, they continue to be relevant during early to middle childhood, from an attachment perspective. Classic models of attachment (e.g., Bowlby, 1969) implied more of a one-time "inoculation" process in which early experiences of maternal sensitivity, emotional availability, love, and support for mastery and exploration would lead, during the critical period of infancy and toddlerhood, to positive self-representations that would carry a person through childhood, adolescence, and beyond. The precursors of a secure attachment relationship leading to positive self-development are necessarily revisited at subsequent stages, given revisions of this earlier model (see Cassidy & Shaver, 1999). These neo-attachment theorists would argue that a person's attachment style and resulting working models or representations of self and others will only remain consistent *to the extent that* the same caregiving pattern continues in subsequent developmental periods. Thus, a more appropriate framework involves a "booster shot model" in which consistency will only be observed if the same pattern of parenting continues, be it contributing to secure or insecure attachment styles and their associated working models (see Thompson, 1998).

Patterns That Are More Maladaptive. In the attachment literature (see Bretherton, 1991; Bretherton & Munholland, 1999; Cassidy & Shaver, 1999; Crittenden, 1990; Main, 1995), there have been further distinctions between less than optimal parenting styles that are associated with three patterns of insecurely attached children, which have implications for the self-development of children described as (1) having an avoidance attachment style, (2) being ambivalently attached, and (3) being disorganized (a more recent style identified by Main).

The (anxious) avoidant style leads the young child to perceive that the mother is unavailable, nonnurturing, and not sharing positive affect. She is viewed as non-soothing in times of need, as turning away when the child is distressed, and sometimes angry. Not feeling loved, the child cuts the self off from emotionally threatening situations. Given this working model of the mother, the working model of the self follows directly. Thus, the child does not feel lovable, nor does he or she feel capable of getting people to meet his or her needs. Sensitivity to being rebuffed leads to occasional periods of anger and hostility. Moreover, the precursors of this style lead the child to eventually feel ineffective in the social domain with peers.

The (anxious) ambivalent child, also labeled as "resistant" by some, perceives the mother to be inconsistently available, sometimes there, sometimes not, leading to the inability to predict and therefore to trust whether she will meet basic and psychological needs. Therefore, distress is expressed in the absence of assurance, leading to a sense that one is not loved and that the mother is not there to support the mastery of new skills. Sometimes, when the mother is present, the child feels good. When she is not available, fussiness and resistance are expressed.

The most recent category describes disorganized-disoriented infants (Main, 1995). This type of child has even more severe doubts about his or her caregiver's ability to adequately provide comfort or reassurance when needed. The caregiver is experienced as highly inconsistent, disorganized, and perhaps neglectful or abusive. Cicchetti's findings (see Cicchetti, Beegley, Carlson, & Toth, 1990) reveal that maltreated, abused infants are more likely to exhibit this D style. Some (see Crittenden, 1990) have suggested that such children manifest a maladaptive combination of child rearing that leads to both avoidant and ambivalent tendencies, including contradictory patterns of behaviors, signs of fear and confusion, crying, depression, freezing, and numbing that reflect more severe disturbances, negativity, and inconsistencies in self-development.

Much of what has been addressed earlier documents negativity in the *content* of self-evaluations. However, of further interest are findings revealing that interactions with caregivers also impact the structure or the *organization* of working models (Bretherton, 1991; Bretherton and Munholland, 1999). Insensitive caregivers who ignore the child's signals will produce insecurely attached children whose working models are less coherently organized from the outset and are less likely to become well integrated. Parental underattunement leads to impoverished working models because it undermines the infant's ability to attend to and subsequently label his or her affective states and thereby incorporate them into a self-portrait (Crittenden, 1994). The child may defensively exclude painful experiments at the hands of insensitive caregivers. At the other extreme, Stern (1985) observes that parental overattunement (or intrusiveness) represents a form of emotional theft in which the parent accentuates how the infant *should* feel rather than how the child actually does feel. Thus, actual feeling states and related perceptions are not shared but become isolated, contributing to fragmentation or a lack of self-coherence.

Crittenden (1994) further distinguishes between securely attached and two types of insecurely attached individuals. Her findings reveal that those with a history of secure attachment can access and integrate the various memory systems, can view themselves from several perspectives, and can accept both their desirable and undesirable features. As a result, they evaluate the self more realistically, including the narrative that they construct of the self. For example, Cassidy (1988) found that securely attached 6-year-olds described themselves in generally positive terms, but they were also able to point out negative attributes, revealing a self-portrait in which they envisage themselves as imperfect.

Those with an *avoidant* attachment history, whom Crittenden labels as "defended" and Bartholomew and Horowitz (1991) identify as "dismissing," have less access to their various memory systems given that some features of the true self have been held out of awareness, whereas others have been defensively "corrected." Those with an ambivalent attachment history, which she (1994) labels as "coercive," also have more fragmented and distorted working models. Their tendency to blame others for their misbehavior robs them of the opportunity to integrate certain behavioral aspects of the self into their working model. Moreover, the inconsistent parenting that they have experienced prevents them from developing an organized or coherent set of internal representations.

The potentials for maladaptive self-development that were identified for very early childhood exist for this subsequent period of development, therefore particularly if the caregiving of socializing agents remains consistently negative. However, the effects may become more evident because the child is more able, given linguistic and cognitive advances, to better verbalize negative self-evaluations.

Abuse at the hands of socializing agents can also continue to derail the self-system. In chronic and severe abuse, the major coping strategy is "dissociation" in which the individual attempts to cognitively split off the traumatic event from consciousness—to detach the self from the traumatic event (Herman, 1992; Putnam, 1993; Terr, 1991). When such abuse occurs at this period of childhood, it conspires with the natural or normative penchant for cognitive dissociation, splitting, or fragmentation (Fischer & Ayoub, 1994). Moreover, the very construction of cognitive structures that consciously lead the child of this age to think in opposites, one must be all good or all bad, lead to a painful awareness that one must be *all bad* or that the self is totally flawed. This can lead to compromising symptoms of depression.

Briere (1992), based on clinical cases, provides a complementary analysis of the sequential "logic" that governs the abused child's attempt to make meaning of his or her experiences. Given maltreatment at the hands of a parent or family member, the child first surmises that either "I am bad or my parents are bad." However, the assumption of young children that parents or adult authority figures are always right leads to the conclusion that parental maltreatment must be due to the fact that they, as children, are bad (that the acts were their fault), and that therefore they deserve to be punished. When children are repeatedly assaulted, they come to conclude that they must be "very bad" contributing to the sense of fundamental badness at their core.

From a cognitive-developmental perspective, the young child who is abused will readily blame the self (Herman, 1992; Piaget, 1932; Watson & Fischer, 1993; Westen, 1993): Given young children's natural egocentrism, they will take responsibility for events they did not cause and cannot control. Moreover, as Piaget demonstrated, young children focus on the deed (e.g., the abusive act) rather than on the intention (e.g., the

motives of the perpetrator). As Herman points out, the child must construct some version of reality that justifies continued abuse and therefore inevitably concludes that his or her innate badness is the cause.

Finally, the preceding section on very early childhood described the rudimentary antecedents of the impoverished self that reside in the fact that caregivers do not adequately support the child's construction of an autobiographical narrative of the child's sense of self. The effects of such lack of scaffolding should become more evident as children move into middle childhood and should be able to verbally express his or her autobiographical sense of self—a narrative of one's past life story, with implications for the future. However, the failure to express dreams for the future, to positively describe one's capabilities, to express pride in one's accomplishments all reflect maladaptive if not pathological distortions of self-development. These symptoms should represent serious red flags that require clinical intervention.

Middle to Late Childhood: Verbal Cameo of Normative Self-Representations and Self-Evaluations

> I'm in fourth grade this year, and I'm pretty popular, at least with my girl friends. That's because I'm nice to people and helpful and can keep secrets. Mostly I am nice to my friends, although if I get in a bad mood I sometimes say something that can be a little mean. I try to control my temper, but when I don't, I'm ashamed of myself. I'm usually happy when I'm with my friends, but I get sad if there is no one to do things with. At school, I'm feeling pretty smart in certain subjects like language arts and social studies. I got As in these subjects on my last report card and was really proud of myself. But I'm feeling pretty dumb in math and science, especially when I see how well a lot of the other kids are doing. Even though I'm not doing well in those subjects, I still like myself as a person, because math and science just aren't that important to me. How I look and how popular I am are more important. I also like myself because I know my parents like me and so do other kids. That helps you like yourself. (adapted from Hartner, 1999)

Such self-descriptions are typically observed in children ages 8 to 11. In contrast to the more concrete self-representations of younger children, older children are much more likely to describe the self in terms such as *popular, nice, helpful, mean, smart,* and *dumb.* Children moving into late childhood continue to describe themselves in terms of their competencies (e.g., "smart," "dumb"). However, self-attributes become increasingly interpersonal as relations with others, particularly peers, become an increasingly salient dimension of the self (see also Damon & Hart, 1988; Rosenberg, 1979).

From the standpoint of emerging cognitive-developmental (I-self) processes, these attributes represent traits in the form of higher-order generalizations, integrating more specific behavioral features of the self (see Fischer, 1980; Siegler, 1991). Thus, in the cameo, the higher-order generalization that she is "smart" is based on the integration of scholastic success in both language arts and social studies. That she also feels "dumb" represents a higher-order construction based on her math and science performance. "Popular" also combines several behaviors: being nice, helpful, and keeping secrets.

This developmental analysis has focused primarily on advances in the ability to conceptualize self-attributes. However, these processes can also be applied to emotion concepts. Thus, the child develops a representational system in which positive emotions (e.g., "I'm usually happy with my friends") are integrated with negative emotional representations (e.g., "I get sad if there is no one to do things with"), as a growing number of empirical studies reveal (Carroll & Steward, 1984; Donaldson & Westerman, 1986; Fischer, Shaver, & Carnochan, 1990; Gnepp et al., 1987; P. Harris, 1983; P. Harris, Olthof, & Meerum-Terwogt, 1981; Harter, 1986b; Harter & Buddin, 1987; Reissland, 1985; Selman, 1980).

This represents a major conceptual advance over the previous two age periods during which young children deny that they can have emotions of opposing valences. Our own developmental findings (see Harter & Buddin, 1987) reveal that at this age, the simultaneous experience of positive and negative emotions can initially only be brought to bear on different targets. As one child subject observed, "I was sitting in school feeling worried about all of the responsibilities of a new pet, but I was happy that I got straight As on my report card." In Fischerian (1980) terms, the child at this level demonstrates a "shift of focus," directing the positive feeling to a positive target or event and then shifting to the experience of a negative feeling that is attached to a negative event. In middle childhood, the concept that the very same target can simultaneously provoke both a positive and a negative emotion is not yet cognitively accessible. However, by late childhood, positive and negative emotions can be brought to bear

on one target given the emergence of representational systems that better allow the child to integrate emotion concepts that were previously differentiated. Sample responses from our empirical documentation of this progression (Harter & Buddin, 1987) were as follows: "I was happy that I got a present but mad that it wasn't what I wanted; If a stranger offered you some candy, you would be eager for the candy but worried about whether it was okay." Elsewhere, we have extended the topic of emotional representations to developmental changes in the understanding of self-affects such as pride and shame. The reader is referred to Harter (1999).

Social Processes

A more balanced view of self in which positive as well as negative attributes of the self are acknowledged is also fostered by new social comparison skills. As our prototypical subject reports, "I'm feeling pretty dumb in math and science, especially when I see how well the other kids are doing." A number of studies conducted in the 1970s and early 1980s presented evidence revealing that it is not until middle childhood that the child can apply comparative assessments with peers in the service of self-evaluation. From a cognitive-developmental perspective, the ability to use social comparison information toward the goal of self-evaluation requires that the child have the ability, which is not sufficiently developed at younger ages, to relate one concept to another simultaneously. In addition to the contribution of advances in cognitive development (see also Moretti & Higgins, 1990), age stratification in school stimulates greater attention to individual differences between age-mates (Higgins & Bargh, 1987; Mack, 1983). More recent findings reveal that the primary motive for children in this age period to utilize social comparison is for personal competence assessment.

The ability to utilize social comparison information for the purpose of self-evaluation is founded on cognitive-developmental advances or the ability to simultaneously compare representations of self and others. However, it is also supported by the socializing environment. For example, evidence reveals that as children move up the academic ladder, teachers make increasing use of social comparison information (Eccles & Midgley, 1989; Eccles, Midgley, & Adler, 1984) and that students are well aware of these educational practices (Harter, 1996). Moreover, parents may contribute to the increasing salience of social comparison, to the extent that they make comparative assessments of how their child is performing relative to siblings, friends, or classmates.

Normative Liabilities for Self-Development during Middle to Late Childhood

A cardinal thesis of this chapter is that cognitive advances bring about, paradoxically, normative liabilities for the self-system. The ability to be able to construct a global perception of one's worth as a person represents a major developmental acquisition—a milestone, as it were—in terms of a shift from mere domain-specific self-perceptions to an integrated sense of one's overall self-esteem. However, other cognitive-developmental acquisitions can serve to lower the valence of this global perception of self, leading to lowered self-esteem. Findings clearly reveal (see Harter, 1999) that beginning in middle childhood self-perceptions become more negative, normatively, compared to the very positive self-perceptions of the majority of young children. The emergence of three cognitive skills is noteworthy in this regard: (1) the ability to use social comparison for the purpose of self-evaluation, (2) the ability to differentiate real from ideal self-perceptions, and (3) increases in social perspective-taking skills.

The ability to employ social comparison for the purpose of self-evaluation (see Maccoby, 1980; Moretti & Higgins, 1990; Ruble & Frey, 1991) leads many, with the exception of the most competent or adequate in any given domain, to fall short in their self-evaluations. If a child therefore judges him- or herself deficient, compared to others, in domains that are deemed important to the self and others, global self-esteem will be eroded. Thus, the very ability and penchant, supported by the culture (e.g., family, peers, schools, and the media) to compare oneself with others makes one vulnerable in valued domains (e.g., appearance, popularity, scholastic competence, athletic performance, and behavioral conduct).

A second newfound cognitive ability to emerge in middle to late childhood involves the capacity to make the distinction between one's real and one's ideal self. From a Jamesian perspective, this skill involves the ability to distinguish between one's actual competencies or adequacies and those to which they aspire and deem important. The cognitive realization that one is not meeting one's expectations (an ability that young children do not possess) will necessarily lower one's overall level of self-esteem, as James's formulation accurately predicts.

Moreover, findings (see Glick & Zigler, 1985; Leahy & Shirk, 1985; Oosterwegel & Oppenheimer, 1993) reveal that the real-ideal discrepancy tends to increase with development. Two causes of such an increase can be identified. First, as noted earlier, social comparison processes lead older children to lower the valence of their self-perceptions, viewing themselves less positively. Second, given increasing perspective-taking skills, children are becoming increasingly cognizant of the standards and ideals that socializing agents hold for their behavior. Moreover, parents, teachers, and peers may normatively raise the bar in terms of their expectations, leading to higher self-ideals.

Increased perspective-taking skills can also *directly* impact self-perceptions, leading them to be more realistic. Protected by limitations in the ability to divine what others truly think of the self, younger children can maintain very positive self-perceptions. The developing ability to more accurately assess the opinions that others hold about one's characteristics, coupled with increasing concern about the importance of the views of others toward the self, normatively leads many older children to realistically lower their self-evaluations.

We can ask whether the processes that lead to more realistic self-evaluations represent liabilities. Many have argued (see review in Harter, 1999) that realistic self-evaluations are more adaptive beginning in middle to late childhood, unlike in early childhood where an overestimation on one's capacities may have a positive motivational function. Yet, in middle to late childhood, despite some potential blows to the ego, the child must seek to realistically readjust his or her self-perceptions and pursue more adaptive paths of development that are consistent with his or her actual attributes.

Individual Differences: Adaptive and Maladaptive Outcomes in Middle to Late Childhood

Several formulations, supported by empirical evidence, speak to the emergence of individual differences in self-representations and associated self-evaluations. From a Jamesian perspective, those who are genetically blessed with talents and/or who are praised for competence in domains deemed important to success will fare the best in terms of positive self-evaluations.

Moreover, child-rearing practices continue to be critical during middle to late childhood. Parental or caregiver approval is particularly critical in the child's domain-specific sense of competence and adequacy as well as global self-worth. Coopersmith (1967), in his seminal efforts to unravel the causes of high and low self-esteem in children, described how the socialization practices of parents impact children's self-esteem. Parents of children with high self-esteem were more likely to (a) be accepting, affectionate, and involved in their child's activities; (b) enforce rules consistently and encourage children to uphold high standards of behavior; (c) prefer noncoercive disciplinary practices, discussing the reasons why the child's behavior was inappropriate; and (d) be democratic in considering the child's opinion around certain family decisions.

More recent evidence also reveals that parental support, particularly in the form of approval and acceptance, is associated with high self-esteem and the sense that one is lovable (see review by Feiring and Taska, 1996). Other studies have built on Baumrind's (1989) typology of parenting styles, linking them to child and adolescent self-evaluations. For example, Lamborn, Mounts, Steinberg, and Dornbusch (1991) reported that those with more authoritative or democratic parents reported significantly higher self-evaluations in the domains of social and academic competence than did those with authoritarian or neglectful parenting.

These findings are consistent with the theorizing of Cooley (1902) and attachment theorists (Bretherton, 1991; Bretherton & Munholland, 1999; Sroufe, 1990; Thompson, Chapter 2, this *Handbook,* this volume). Benevolent socializing agents who readily provide nurturance, approval sensitivity, emotional availability, and support for mastery attempts will produce children who mirror and eventually internalize this support in the form of positive self-evaluations. However, in their search for their image in the social mirror, other children may well gaze through a glass darkly. Caregivers lacking in responsiveness, nurturance, encourage, and approval, as well as socializing agents who are rejecting, punitive, or neglectful, will both cause their children to develop tarnished images of self, feeling unlovable, incompetent, and generally unworthy.

Thus, there is considerable evidence that support from parents as significant others in the child's life will have a powerful influence on self-evaluations (be they domain-specific or global in nature) or overall self-esteem (see Harter, 1999). Our own research documents the fact that parental or caregiver support is a major predictor of global self-worth throughout the childhood years. However, as the child moves up the developmental ladder, other sources of support emerge, where peer support becomes increasingly important. Thus, one can ask

the question "Mirror, mirror on the wall, whose opinion is the most critical of all?" At this particular developmental level, we have documented in numerous studies that of four sources of support: (1) parent, (2) teacher, (3) classmate, and (4) close friend. Parental and classmate support correlate most highly with global self-esteem. Why is close friend support not more predictive? We have argued (Harter, 1999) that, by definition, close friend support must be high. Furthermore, when one examines the various *functions* of support from different significant others, support from close friends typically manifests itself in the form of empathy, caring, and sensitivity to emotions and solutions to personal problems. Classmate support, in contrast, is more consistent with Mead's (1934) model of the "generalized other," more seemingly objective feedback about one's competencies, adequacy, and worth as a person.

As we see in the next sections on adolescence, recent work has begun to address the complexity of the *balance* of support from different significant others. Claims of the past (e.g., Rosenberg, 1979) and the present (J. Harris, 1998) suggest that the impact of parent support declines as a child moves from late childhood to early adolescence when the peer influence becomes paramount. However, current research, including our own (Harter, 1999), demonstrates that nothing is further from the truth.

To return to the theme of the importance of parental child rearing, and more pathological implications in the extreme, children subjected to severe and chronic abuse continue to create images of the self that are despicable, given the difficulty overcoming post-traumatic stress disorder (PTSD), including the psychological pain and symptoms that endure in the form of flashbacks and dissociative symptoms (Briere, 1992; Fischer & Ayoub, 1994; Herman, 1992; McCann & Pearlman, 1992; Terr, 1990; van der Kolk, 1987; Westen, 1993; Wolfe, 1989). More than constructing negative self-perceptions, they view the self as fundamentally flawed. Often excessively high and unrealistic parental standards that are unattainable contribute to these negative views of the self. Thus, the Me-self, both at the level of domain-specific self-perceptions and one's sense of global self-esteem, may be irrevocably damaged.

Finally, to return to the interaction of socializing practices and movement to new stages of cognitive development, such movement can be fostered by socializing agents, or alternatively, can be delayed if such environmental support is not forthcoming. One can imagine scenarios in which there would be little environmental support for the integration of positive and negative attributes or positive and negative emotions. For example, in child-rearing situations where children are chronically and severely abused, family members typically reinforce negative evaluations of the child that are then incorporated into the self-portrait (Briere, 1992; Fischer & Ayoub, 1994; Harter, 1999; Herman, 1992; Terr, 1990; Westen, 1993). As a result, there may be little scaffolding for the kind of self-structure that would allow the child to develop and integrate both positive and negative self-evaluations. Moreover, negative self-evaluations that become automatized (Siegler, 1991) will be even more resistant to change.

Thus, to the extent that there is little or no support for the normative integration of positive and negative attributes, children will not advance cognitively. If the majority of feedback from socializing agents is negative, children in this age range (8 to 12) may remain at the previous level of all-or-none thinking, viewing their behavior as overwhelmingly negative. In addition, at a more affective level, there is a considerable body of research (see review in Harter, 1999) reveals that there is a very robust relationship between negative self-perceptions, including low self-esteem, and depression. Depressive symptoms include lack of energy, profound sadness in the form of depressed affect, and hopelessness. Depression, in turn, is highly predictive of suicidal ideation and suicidal behavior. Thus, caregiving practices resulting in very negative perceptions of the self put children at risk for serious forms of depressive pathology.

In addition to the incorporation of the opinions of significant others, children come to internalize the standards and values of the larger society. Perceptions of one's physical attractiveness, in relation to the importance that is attached to meeting cultural standards of appearance, contribute heavily to one's overall sense of worth as a person (see Harter, 1993, 1999). Those few who feel they have attained the requisite physical attributes will experience relatively high levels of self-esteem. Conversely, those who feel that they fall short of the punishing standards of appearance that represent the cultural ideal will suffer from low self-esteem and depression. Moreover, a related liability can be observed in the eating-disordered behavior of females, in particular, many of whom display symptoms (e.g., associated with anorexia) that are life threatening (Harter, 1999). Our own recent findings (Kiang & Harter, 2004) provide support for a model in which endorsement of the societal standards of appearance leads to low self-esteem that predicts both depression and eating-disordered behavior. Finally, genetic factors leading to physical characteristics that do not meet cultural standards of attractiveness can also contribute to this pattern that may be particularly resistant to change.

Developmental Differences in Self-Representations during Adolescence

The period of adolescence represents a dramatic developmental transition, given pubertal and related physical changes, cognitive-developmental advances, and changing social expectations. With regard to cognitive-developmental acquisitions, adolescents develop the ability to think abstractly (Case, 1985; Fischer, 1980; Flavell, 1985; Harter, 1999; Higgins, 1991). From a Piagetian (1960) perspective, the capacity to form abstractions emerges with the stage of formal operations in early adolescence. These newfound acquisitions, according to Piaget, should equip the adolescent with the hypothetico-deductive skills to create a formal theory. This observation is critical to the topic of self-development, given the claims of many (e.g., Epstein, 1973, 1981, 1991; Greenwald, 1980; Kelly, 1955; Markus, 1980; Sarbin, 1962) that the self is a personal epistemology, a cognitive construction, or a theory that should possess the characteristics of any formal theory. Therefore, a self-theory should meet those criteria by which any good theory is evaluated. Such criteria include the degree to which it is parsimonious, empirically valid, internally consistent, coherently organized, testable, and useful. From a Piagetian perspective, entry into the period of formal operations should make the construction of such a theory possible—be it a theory about elements in the world or a theory about the self.

However, as becomes apparent, the self-representations during early and middle adolescence fall far short of these criteria. The self-structure of these periods is not coherently organized, nor are the postulates of the self-portrait internally consistent. Moreover, many self-attributes fail to be subjected to tests of empirical validity; as a result, they can be extremely unrealistic. Nor are self-representations particularly parsimonious. Thus, the Piagetian framework fails to provide an adequate explanation for the dramatic developmental changes in the self-structure that can be observed across the substages of adolescence. Rather, as in our analysis of how self-representations change during childhood, a neo-Piagetian approach is needed to understand how changes in cognitive-developmental I-self processes result in very different Me-self organizational and content at each three age levels: early adolescence, middle adolescence, and late adolescence. As in our examination of self-development during childhood, for each age level we first provide a cameo self-description. What follows is (a) an analysis of the normative-developmental changes in self-representations and self-evaluations, (b) the exploration of the normative liabilities of each age period, and (c) the discussion of the implications for adaptive and maladaptive self-development at each period of adolescence.

Early Adolescence: Verbal Cameo of Normative Self-Representations and Self-Evaluations

I'm an extrovert with my friends: I'm talkative, pretty rowdy, and funny. I'm fairly good-looking if I do say so. All in all, around people I know pretty well I'm awesome, at least I think my friends think I am. I'm usually cheerful when I'm with my friends, happy and excited to be doing things with them. I like myself a lot when I'm around my friends. With my parents, I'm more likely to be depressed. I feel sad as well as mad and also hopeless about ever pleasing them. They think I spend too much time at the mall with my friends, and that I don't do enough to help out at home. They tell me I'm lazy and not very responsible, and it's hard not to believe them. I get real sarcastic when they get on my case. The fact of the matter is that what they think about is still really important. So when they are on my case, it makes me dislike myself as a person. At school, I'm pretty intelligent. I know that because I'm smart when it comes to how I do in classes, I'm curious about learning new things, and I'm also creative when it comes to solving problems. My teacher says so. I get better grades than most, but I don't brag about it because that's not cool. I can be a real introvert around people I don't know well. I'm shy, uncomfortable, and nervous. Sometimes I'm simply stupid, I mean I act really dumb and say things that are just plain stupid. I worry a lot about what others my age who are not my closest friends must think of me, probably that I'm a total dork. I just hate myself when that happens, because what *they* think is really important. (adapted from Harter, 1999)

With regard to the content of the self-portraits of young adolescents, interpersonal attributes, and social skills that influence interactions with others or one's so-

cial appeal are typically quite salient, as findings by Damon and Hart (1988) indicate. Thus, our prototypical young adolescent admits to being talkative, rowdy, funny, good-looking, and downright awesome, characteristics that may enhance acceptance by peers. In addition to social attributes, self-representations also focus on competencies such as one's scholastic abilities (e.g., "I'm intelligent") and affects (e.g., "I'm cheerful" and "I'm depressed").

From a developmental perspective, there is considerable evidence that the self becomes increasingly differentiated (see Harter, 1998, 1999). During adolescence, there is a proliferation of selves that vary as a function of social context. These include self with father, mother, close friends, romantic partners, peers, as well as the self in the role of student, on the job, and as an athlete (Gecas, 1972; N. Griffin, Chassin, & Young, 1981; Hart, 1988; Harter, Bresnick, Bouchey, & Whitesell, 1997; Harter & Monsour, 1992; Smollar & Youniss, 1985). For example, as the cameo reveals, the adolescent may be cheerful and rowdy with friends, depressed and sarcastic with parents, intelligent, curious, and creative as a student, and shy and uncomfortable around people whom he or she does not know. A critical developmental task, therefore, is the construction of multiple selves that will undoubtedly vary across different roles and relationships, as James (1892) observed over 100 years ago.

In keeping with a major theme of this chapter, both cognitive and social processes contribute to this proliferation of selves. Cognitive-developmental advances, described earlier, promote greater differentiation (see Fischer, 1980; Fischer & Canfield, 1986; Harter, 1990b; Harter & Monsour, 1992; Keating, 1990). Moreover, these advances conspire with socialization pressures to develop different selves in different relational contexts (see Erikson, 1968; Grotevant & Cooper, 1986; Hill & Holmbeck, 1986; Rosenberg, 1986). For example, bids for autonomy from parents make it important to define oneself differently with peers in contrast to parents (see also Steinberg & Silverberg, 1986; White, Speisman, & Costos, 1983). Rosenberg points to another component of the differentiation process in observing that as one moves through adolescence, one is more likely to be treated differently by those in different relational contexts. In studies from our own laboratory (see Harter & Monsour, 1992; Harter et al., 1997), we have found that the percentage of overlap in self-attributes generated for different social contexts ranges from 25% to 30%

among seventh and eighth graders and decreases during adolescence, to a low of approximately 10% among older teenagers.

Many (although not all) of the self-descriptions to emerge in early adolescence represent abstractions about the self, based on the newfound cognitive ability to integrate trait labels into higher-order self-concepts (see Case, 1985; Fischer, 1980; Flavell, 1985; Harter, 1983; Higgins, 1991). For example, as the prototypical cameo reveals, one can construct an abstraction of the self as "intelligent" by combining such traits as smart, curious, and creative. Alternatively, one may create an abstraction that the self is an "airhead" given situations where one feels dumb and "just plain stupid." Similarly, an adolescent could construct abstractions that he or she is an "extrovert" (integrating the traits of rowdy, talkative, and funny) and that he or she is also an "introvert" in certain situations (when one is shy, uncomfortable, and nervous). With regard to emotion concepts, one can be depressed in some contexts (combining sad, mad, and hopeless) as well as cheerful in others (combining happy and excited). Thus, abstractions represent more cognitively complex concepts about the self in which various trait labels can now be appropriately integrated into even higher-order generalizations.

Although the ability to construct such abstractions reflects a cognitive advance, these representations are highly compartmentalized; that is, they are quite distinct from one another (Case, 1985; Fischer, 1980; Higgins, 1991). For Fischer, these "single abstractions" are overdifferentiated, and therefore the young adolescent can only think about each of them as isolated self-attributes. According to Fischer, structures that were observed in childhood reappear at the abstract level. Thus, just as single representations were compartmentalized during early childhood, Fischer argues that when the adolescent first moves to the level of abstract thought, he or she lacks the ability to integrate the many single abstractions that are constructed to define the self in different relational contexts. As a result, adolescents will engage in all-or-none thinking at an abstract level. For Fischer, movement to a qualitatively new level of thought brings with it lack of "cognitive control," and, as a result, adolescents at the level of single abstractions can only think about isolated self-attributes. Thus, contrary to earlier models of mind (Piaget, 1960), in which formal operations usher in newfound cognitive-developmental abilities that should allow one to create an integrated theory of self, fragmentation of

self-representations during early adolescence is more the rule than the exception (Fischer & Ayoub, 1994; Harter & Monsour, 1992).

Another manifestation of the compartmentalization of these abstract attributes can be observed in the tendency for the young adolescent to be unconcerned about the fact that across different roles, certain postulates appear inconsistent, as the prototypical self-description implies (in contrast, at middle adolescence, there is considerable concern). However, during early adolescence, the inability to integrate seemingly contradictory characteristics of the self (e.g., intelligent versus airhead, extrovert versus introvert, or depressed versus cheerful) has the psychological advantage of sparing the adolescent conflict over opposing attributes in his or her self-theory (Harter & Monsour, 1992). Moreover, as Higgins observes, the increased differentiation functions as a cognitive buffer, reducing the possibility that negative attributes in one sphere may spread or generalize to other spheres (see also Linville, 1987; Simmons & Blyth, 1987). Thus, although the construction of multiple selves sets the stage for attributes to be contradictory, most young adolescents do not identify potential contradictions or experience conflict, given the compartmentalized structure of their abstract self-representations.

Evidence comes from our own research (see Harter et al., 1997; Harter & Monsour, 1992), in which we asked adolescents at three developmental levels, early adolescence (seventh grade), middle adolescence (ninth grade), and late adolescence (11th grade) to generate self-attributes across several roles and then indicate whether any of these attributes represented opposites (e.g., cheerful versus depressed, rowdy versus calm, studious versus lazy, at ease versus self-conscious). After identifying any such opposites, they were asked whether any such pairs caused them conflict—were they perceived as clashing in their personality? Across studies, the specific roles have varied. They have included self with a group of friends, with a close friend, with parents (mother versus father), in romantic relationships, in the classroom, and on the job. Across a number of converging indices (e.g., number of opposites, number of conflicts, or percentage of opposites in conflict) the findings revealed that attributes identified as contradictory and experienced as conflicting were infrequent among young adolescents.

An examination of the protocols of young adolescents reveals that there are potential opposites that go undetected. Examples not identified as opposites by young adolescents (but that appeared contradictory to our research team) included being talkative as well as shy in romantic relationships, being uptight with family but carefree with friends, being caring and insensitive with friends, being a good student and a troublemaker in school, being self-conscious in romantic relationships but easygoing with friends, as well as being lazy as a student but hardworking on the job. These observations bolster the interpretation (from Fischer's theory) that young adolescents do not yet have the cognitive ability to simultaneously compare these attributes to one another, and therefore they tend not to detect, or be concerned about, self-representations that are potential opposites. As one young adolescent put it, when confronted with the fact that he had indicated that he was both caring and rude, "Well, you are caring with your friends and rude to people who don't treat you nicely. There's no problem. I guess I just think about one thing about myself at a time and don't think about the other until the next day." When another young adolescent was asked why opposite attributes did not bother her, she succinctly exclaimed, "That's a stupid question. I don't fight with myself!" As becomes apparent, this pattern changes dramatically during middle adolescence.

The differentiation of role-related selves, beginning in early adolescence, can also be observed in the tendency to report differing levels of self-esteem across relational contexts. In the prototypical description, the young adolescent reports that with friends, "I like myself a lot"; however, with parents, I "dislike myself as a person." Around "people I don't know well, I just hate myself." Although the concept of self-esteem has, until now, been reserved for perceptions of global self-esteem, we have introduced the construct of relational self-esteem (Harter, Waters, & Whitesell, 1998).

Beginning in the middle school years, adolescents discriminate their level of perceived self-esteem (i.e., how much they like themselves as a person, across relational contexts). We have examined these perceptions across a number of such contexts including self-worth with parents, with teachers, with male classmates, and with female classmates. Factor-analyses reveal clear factor patterns with high loadings on the designated factors (i.e., each relational context) with negligible cross-loadings. We have also examined the discrepancy between individuals' highest and lowest relational self-esteem scores. Although a minority of adolescents (approximately one-fourth) were found to report little variation in self-esteem across contexts, the vast majority (the remaining three-fourths) report that their self-esteem did vary significantly as a function of the relational context. In the extreme, one female participant reported the lowest possible self-esteem score with parents and the highest possible self-esteem score with female classmates.

In addition to documenting such variability, our goal has been to identify potential causes of these individual differences. In addressing one determinant, we adopted Cooley's (1902) looking glass self-perspective, in which the opinions of significant others are incorporated into one's sense of personal worth. Building on our previous empirical efforts (see Harter, 1990b), we hypothesized that context-specific support, in the form of validation for whom one is as a person, should be highly related to self-esteem in the corresponding context. The findings corroborated the more specific prediction that support in a given relationship was more highly associated with relational self-esteem in that relationship, compared to self-esteem in the other three contexts. Thus, the pattern of results suggests a refinement of the looking glass self-formulation, in that validation from particular significant others will have its strongest impact on how one evaluates one's sense of worth in the context of those particular others.

These findings highlight the fact that with the proliferation of multiple selves across roles, adolescents become very sensitive to the potentially different opinions and standards of the significant others in each context. As the cameo description reveals, the adolescent reports high self-esteem around friends who think he or she is "awesome," lower self-esteem around parents who think he or she is "lazy" and "irresponsible," and the lowest level of self-esteem around strangers who probably think "I'm a total dork." As Rosenberg (1986) observes, adolescents demonstrate a heightened concern with the reflected appraisals of others. He notes that other people's differing views of the self (e.g., the respect of the peer group in contrast to the critical stance of parents) will inevitably lead to variability in the self-concept across contexts.

In addition to their sensitivity to feedback from others, young adolescents continue to make use of social comparison information. However, with increasing age, children shift from more conspicuous to more subtle forms of social comparison as they become more aware of the negative social consequences of overt comparisons; for example, they may be accused of boasting about their superior performance (Pomerantz, Ruble,

Frey, & Greulich, 1995). As the prototypical young adolescent describes in the cameo, "I get better grades than
most, but I don't brag about it because that's not cool."

Normative Liabilities for Self-Development during Early Adolescence

As with the entry into any new developmental level,
there are liabilities associated with these emerging self-
processes. For example, although abstractions are developmentally advanced cognitive structures, they are
removed from concrete, observable behaviors and therefore more susceptible to distortion. The adolescent's
self-concept, therefore, becomes more difficult to verify and is often less realistic. As Rosenberg (1986) observes, when the self comes to be viewed as a collection
of abstractions, uncertainties are introduced because
there are "few objective and unambiguous facts about
one's sensitivity, creativity, morality, dependability,
and so on" (p. 129). Moreover, the necessary skills to
apply hypothetico-deductive thinking to the postulates
of one's self-system are not yet in place. Although the
young adolescent may have multiple hypotheses about
the self, he or she does not yet possess the ability to correctly deduce which are true, leading to distortions in
self-perceptions.

The all-or-none thinking of this period, in the form of
overgeneralizations that the young adolescent cannot
cognitively control (Fischer, 1980), also contributes to
unrealistic self-representations, in that at one point in
time one may feel totally intelligent or awesome, whereas
at another point in time one may feel like a dork. Thus,
the adolescent sense of self will vacillate, given the inability to cognitively control one's self-representations.

In describing this "barometric self" during adolescence, Rosenberg (1986) points to a different set of
more social causes. He cites considerable literature revealing that adolescents experience an increased concern with what their peers think of them, findings that
are relevant to Cooley's looking glass self model. This
heavy dependence on the perceptions of other's opinions tends to set the stage for volatility in one's assessment of the self. However, there is inevitable ambiguity
about others' attitudes toward the self because one can
never have direct access to the mind of another. Thus, attributions about others' thought processes may change
from one time period to another. The second reason for
fluctuating self-evaluations inheres in the fact that different significant others have different opinions of the

self, depending on the situation or moment in time.
Third, adolescents' concern with what others think of
them leads to efforts at impression management, provoking variations in the self across relational contexts.
Finally, at times, adolescents are treated as more adultlike (e.g., on a job) whereas at other times, they are
treated as more childlike (e.g., with parents at home).
Thus, the self fluctuates in tandem.

Our own findings on the emergence of how self-
esteem varies as a function of one's relationships (what
we have termed *relational self-esteem*) is consistent with
Rosenberg's analysis (Harter, 1999). The young adolescent is not yet troubled by what could be viewed as inconsistent self-representations because he or she cannot
simultaneously evaluate them as contradictory. However, there are liabilities associated with this inability.
The compartmentalization of abstractions about the self
precludes the construction of an integrated portrait of
self. The fact that different significant others may hold
differing opinions about the self makes it difficult to develop the sense that the self is coherent. With movement
into middle adolescence, abstract self-descriptors become far less isolated or compartmentalized. However,
the emerging structures that follow bring with them new
liabilities.

Finally, there are domain-specific normative liabilities that are associated with educational transitions.
Young adolescents all shift from an elementary school to
either a middle school or junior high school that typically draws on several elementary feeder schools. Thus,
they must now move into a group of peers, many of
whom they have previously not known (typically two-
thirds to three-fourths of the peer group will be new).
Given the young adolescent's heightened concern with
how others view the self, an important source of global
self-esteem, there may be understandable shifts in
global self-esteem, if individuals perceive that their social acceptance is higher or lower than when they were
in elementary school.

Eccles and Midgley (1989) have also pointed to different emphases in the educational system during the
transition to middle school or elementary school that
have implications for perceptions of a child's scholastic
competence. They note that there is considerably more
emphasis on social comparison (e.g., public posting of
grades, ability grouping, or teachers, in their feedback
to classes, verbally acknowledging the personal results
of competitive activities). These educational practices

represent a mismatch given the adolescent's needs. At a time when young adolescents are painfully self-conscious, the school system heightens the salience of social comparison in conjunction with publicizing each student's performance. In addition to the greater emphasis on social comparison, the standards for performance shift from *effort* to *ability,* according to Eccles and colleagues. They note that in elementary school, there is more emphasis on effort: "Try harder and you can do better." In middle and junior high schools, however, poorer performance is attributed to lack of scholastic ability, leading the young adolescent to feel that he or she does not have the aptitude to succeed or that he or she lacks intelligence. For those not performing well, these practices can lead to declines in self-perceptions of academic ability, shifts that will be exacerbated in contexts of high public feedback and greater social comparison.

Individual Differences: Adaptive and Maladaptive Outcomes during Early Adolescence

The frameworks of James (1892) and Cooley (1902), in conjunction with attachment theory, provide perspectives on the tremendous individual differences that one can observe in self-evaluations beginning in adolescence. From a Jamesian perspective, the congruence or discrepancy between one's perceptions of competence in age-appropriate domains and the *importance of success* attached to each domain have been demonstrated to be a major determinant of one's global self-esteem or self-worth (1990). Thus, those who are able to positively evaluate their successes in domains deemed important to the self will report high self-esteem. A parallel process is the ability to tout the importance of those domains in which one is succeeding. Conversely, those reporting failures in domains of importance will report low self-esteem. Such individuals appear unable to discount the importance of domains in which they are not successful.

Not all researchers in the field endorse the notion that the importance attached to success adds to the prediction of global self-esteem, notably Marsh and his colleagues (Hattie & Marsh, 1996; Marsh, 1993). They base their claims on findings indicating that merely correlating perceived competence or adequacy scores with global self-esteem (ignoring importance) yields values that are comparable to those based on procedures in which perceived importance is also taken into account.

We do not question these statistical findings; they are consistent with our own. We do question the conclusions and suggest that the comparison of these correlations is not the appropriate test (see Harter, 1999).

Why might merely correlating domain-specific competence or adequacy scores with global self-esteem or self-worth result in values comparable to those based on correlating these domain-specific values with global self-worth for just those individuals rating given domains as important? The answer lies in the fact that the vast majority of older children and adolescents (approximately 80%, on average) rate these domains as important, and thus the two correlations will be based on virtually the same set of participants. This is not surprising because as Marsh, himself, acknowledges, those of us that have developed domain-specific measures of self-concept have purposely included those domains important to individuals at various developmental levels.

It is our contention that the more statistically parsimonious empirical models espoused by Marsh and his colleagues in which importance ratings are ignored may obscure the actual psychological processes through which individuals formulate an overall sense of their worth as a person. We would claim, beginning in adolescence, that processes including the ability to think about, to reflect on one's self and the causes of one's overall feelings of self-worth, are not necessarily parsimonious. Considerable literature (see reviews in Harter, 1990a, 1999) reveals the heightened introspectiveness and self-consciousness that emerges in adolescence. Thus, if we truly want to understand the processes underlying adolescents' construction of evaluative judgments about the self (rather than merely predict a value statistically) our own findings indicate that one must take into account the *importance* attached to those self-concept domains that may be relevant to the formulation of an overall view of self.

Elsewhere (Harter, 1999) we have reported on four different empirical approaches that demonstrate the importance of ratings. Additional recent work by MacDonald, Saltzman, and Leary (2003) has demonstrated, with college students, that perceived importance, particularly as it might affect others' judgments of self, directly impacted global self-esteem. In addition, for those interested in clinical or educational interventions, we have also suggested how interventions will be quite different if one takes an approach that only focuses on perceptions of domain-specific competence or adequacy versus an approach in which one also takes into account perceptions of the importance of success in corresponding domains (Harter, 1999).

Cooley's (1902) looking glass formulation and attachment theorists' explorations into working models of the self (see Bretherton & Munholland, 1999), bolster the social framework for viewing individual differences in self-worth, particularly as young adolescents are becoming more cognizant of their own thinking about themselves. However, "more cognizant," as our earlier developmental analysis reveals, does not necessarily translate into more "realistic." The more abstract self-evaluations are further removed from behavioral reality (see Harter, 1999). In early to middle adolescence, teenagers do not have the ability to engage in hypothetico-deductive thinking to arrive at realistic conclusions about the self. It is for this reason that recent findings (reviewed in Harter, 1999) and more classic reviews (see Shrauger & Schoeneman, 1979) have concluded that *self-perceptions* of approval from significant others will be a better predictor of constructs such as self-esteem than actual measures of support from significant others.

In the previous section on late childhood, the issue was raised as to whose opinion—parents or peers—is most critical to the continuing development of a child's overall sense of self-worth or self-esteem. For many years, textbook renditions of the impact of parents and peers have made the assumption that the influence of parents wanes as a child enters adolescence (see Berndt & Burgy, 1996; Harter, 1999). A resurgence of a focus on the impact of peers can also be seen in the work of J. Harris (1998) who makes strong arguments for why parents, with the exception of their genetic contribution, matter little in the psychological development of their children. In contrast, attachment theorists (see Bretherton & Munholland, 1999) continue to assert, as did Bowlby, that the initial attachment with the mother, in particular, is critical to developing a positive working model of self and other that will impact future relationships with peers.

An increasingly sophisticated body of research addresses the more interesting and complex question of the *balance* between parental and peer support because it impacts self-evaluations. Using more advanced statistical techniques, including cluster-analyses and longitudinal predictive designs, recent studies have demonstrated that young adolescents who are able to sustain positive parental support and garner positive peer approval report more positive self-evaluations (Dubois, Reach, Tevendale, & Valentine, 2001; Roberts, Seidman, & Pederson, 2000).

Therefore, beginning in early adolescence, there is a heightened concern with how others view the self, a normative process that has implications for the salience of those determinants of self-esteem that have been articulated in Cooley's (1902) looking glass self-formulation. If significant others provide support for whom the young adolescent is as a person, for those attributes that the young adolescent feels truly define the self, he or she will experience the self as authentic. However, the construction of a self that is too highly dependent on the internalization of the opinions of others can, under some circumstances, lead to the creation of a false self that does not mirror his or her authentic experience. In our own research (Harter, 1999), we have found that it is not until early adolescence that the concept of acting as a false self becomes very salient in the consciousness of young teenagers. The detection of hypocrisy, not only in others but also in the self, emerges as a critical filter in evaluating others as well as the self.

Our own findings (Harter, Marold, Whitesell, & Cobbs, 1996) reveal that unhealthy levels of false-self behavior are particularly likely to emerge if caregivers make their approval contingent on the young adolescent living up to unrealistic standards of behavior, based on unattainable standards dictated by parents. We have labeled this phenomenon "conditional support" although from interviews we have learned that this is a misnomer in that adolescents do not perceive parental responses, in the face of such demands, as "supportive." Rather, conditionality reflects the psychological hoops through which young adolescents must jump to please the parents, given the parental agenda. Those adolescents who experience such a conditional atmosphere are forced to adopt a socially implanted self: They must learn to suppress what they feel are true self-attributes, in an attempt to garner the needed approval from parental caretakers. Here, the terminology purposely switches from *caregiver* to *caretaker* in a metaphorical effort to convey the fact that such socialization practices "take away" from the care of whom one is as a person, one's true self. Our findings indicate that those experiencing high levels of conditionality from parents will express hopelessness about their ability to please the parents that then translates in high levels of false-self behavior in an attempt to garner some level of needed parental support. Of particular relevance is that high levels of false-self behavior are directly related to low levels of self-esteem. As our model has revealed (Harter, 1999), low levels of self-esteem are highly correlated with self-reported depressive symptomatology that can, for some adolescents, lead to suicidal thoughts and actions.

Chronic and severe abuse continues to put an adolescent at even more extreme risk for suppressing his or her true self and displaying various forms of inauthentic or false-self behavior. Such a process has its origins in childhood, given the very forms of parenting that constitute psychological abuse. As described earlier, parenting practices that represent lack of attunement to the child's needs, empathic failure, lack of validation, threats of harm, coercion, and enforced compliance all cause the true self to go underground (Bleiberg, 1984; Stern, 1985; Winnicott, 1958, 1965) and lead to what Sullivan (1953) labeled as "not me" experiences.

Our model of the determinants, correlates, and consequences of self-esteem (see Harter, 1999) becomes increasingly relevant at early adolescence and beyond where there is strong empirical support across numerous studies (see review in Harter, 1999). Findings reveal that lack of both parental and peer support can lead to pathological levels of low self-worth, depressed affect, and hopelessness, which may provoke suicidal ideation if not suicidal behaviors.

Our findings (see Harter, 1999) document that while peer support increases in its predictability of global self-esteem between late childhood and early adolescence, the impact of parental support does *not* decline. Previous textbook portrayals of adolescence imply that parental influences decline as a child moves into adolescence. However, nothing is further from the truth when we examine the impact of parental support, including conditionality, on self-processes including false-self behavior, global self-esteem, and the related correlates of depressed affect, hopelessness, and suicidal ideation.

However, the peer culture does come to loom large in adolescence. Peer support and approval, or its absence, is a powerful predictor of what we have labeled the depression /adjustment composite that includes self-esteem or self-worth, affect/mood (along a continuum of depressed to cheerful), and hope (hopeless to hopeful) that has empirically been demonstrated to predict suicidal thinking. Lack of peer approval appears to be more directly linked to perceived inadequacies in the domains of physical appearance, likability by peers, and athletic competence.

Peer Rejection, Humiliation, and Implications for the High Profile School Shootings.   More recently, we have become focused on the role of peer *rejection,* not merely the lack of peer approval. Our initial interest in this construct came from an analysis of the emerging profiles of the, now, eleven high-profile cases in which White, middle-class older children and adolescents, from small cities or suburbs, have gone on shooting sprees killing peers, and in a few cases, school officials who were random targets rather than specifically identified individuals. What became evident, in the analysis of media reports, is that all of these male youth killers had a history of peer rejection and *humiliation.* As a psychologist who for many years has contributed to (and kept up with) the literature on emotional development in children and adolescents, it was astounding to learn that we have no literature on humiliation. There is ample literature on shame, guilt, embarrassment, but virtually nothing about humiliation. Yet, we can all appreciate the fact (be it from our own experience or the experience of our children) that humiliation is a daily event in schools for many children. For the school shooters, extreme feelings of chronic humiliation by peers, due to excessive teasing, taunting, and physical insults, eventually led them to psychologically "snap," leading to random deaths and in the case of the Columbine teens to suicide.

An examination of the media accounts of the school shooters made it obvious that many of the determinants in our model could be found in the lives of these adolescents (see Harter, Low, & Whitesell, 2003). As a result, we examined a revised model in which we added angry aggression as well as violent ideation. We examined this model in a normative sample of middle school students. Through path-analytic techniques, we demonstrated that the data fit the model exceedingly well: The antecedents in the model, domain-specific perceived inadequacies predicted lack of approval from peers and parents alike. These determinants, in turn, predicted low self-esteem, depressed affect, angry affect, and hopelessness, all of which predicted *both* suicidal ideation and violent ideation. Consistent with the clinical literature on the comorbidity of internalizing and externalizing symptoms, we found a correlation of $r = .55$ between suicidal and violent ideation toward others. Thus, the determinants in our model, if negative, put adolescents at pathological risk for endangering their own and others' lives.

We have also pursued the emotion of humiliation and its role in contributing to violent ideation. In this Harter,

Low, & Whitesell study (2003), we wrote vignettes that simulated some of the types of humiliating events that were experienced by the school shooters. We then asked middle school students what other emotions they might experience (e.g., anger or depression) and what behaviors they might exhibit, along a continuum from doing nothing to acting violently toward the perpetrators or toward anyone (given the randomness of the actual school shooting events). While the majority of students reported that they would be humiliated (given that the vignettes were designed to be humiliating) we identified a group of violent ideators (in the minority) and a group who did not report that they would think about violent revenge. We then sought to determine what distinguished the two groups, finding that those entertaining violent thoughts expressed higher levels of anger and depression. In addition, the violent ideators reported higher levels of negative determinants in the model, such as more peer rejection, less parental support, lower self-concept scores (e.g., appearance or peer likability), lower self-worth, and greater hopelessness. Thus, certain factors in histories of violent ideators propel them to thoughts of seriously harming others and themselves, which are pathological outcomes that may require clinical interventions given that they may be putting themselves and others at serious risk.

In a subsequent study, we sought to more specifically investigate what were some of the factors that lead humiliation to result in violent ideation as well as suicidal ideation, given the paucity of work on the emotion of humiliation. Our findings have documented that teasing and taunting and bullying, particularly in the presence of an *audience who mocks the victim,* lead to humiliation. Humiliation, in turn, serves to provoke prototypical reactions, including revenge, wanting to hide, or attempts to minimize the humiliation (Harter, Kiang, Whitesell, & Anderson, 2003). We are pursuing this prototypical approach to humiliation currently.

Is There a Dark Side to High Self-Esteem?   Our own modeling efforts demonstrate that it is *low* self-esteem that is consistently related to suicidal and violent thinking. These findings are consistent with the broader literature (see Harter, 1999) revealing that high self-esteem is a psychological commodity associated with positive adjustment and mental-health outcomes. Low self-esteem, in contrast, has been viewed as a liability and has been associated with poor adjustment in the literature (e.g., depression, anxiety, conduct problems, or teen pregnancy). However, there is current con-

troversy over whether they may also be a dark side to high self-esteem.

So what is the controversy? One vocal group of theorists (Baumeister, Smart, & Boden, 1996) has argued that there is a subset of individuals with high but fragile self-esteem who are often aggressive in respond to perceived ego threats. Baumeister and colleagues contend that individuals who report high self-esteem in combination with high narcissism, low empathy, and sensitivity to rejection will, in the face of threats to the ego, exhibit violent tendencies.

We (Harter & McCarley, 2004) believe that Baumeister's composite of predictors has some merit, with the exception of the role of self-esteem. Specifically, we predicted that high narcissism, low empathy, sensitivity to rejection coupled with *low* self-esteem (not high self-esteem) would lead young adolescents, in the face of threats to the ego, to violent ideation. To assess violent ideation, participants read humiliating scenarios that represented threats to the ego and were then asked to rate how they would typically response in such a situation, ranging from doing nothing to seriously harming the perpetrator. Self-esteem was measured by our Global Self-Worth Scale (Harter, 1985). Narcissism, empathy, and sensitivity to rejection were assessed by adaptations of previously developed measures, all of which were found to be reliable (alphas ranging from .76 to .87). Regression analyses demonstrated that high narcissism and low empathy significantly predicted violent ideation. However, in contrast to Baumeister's claims, higher self-esteem was associated with lower levels of violent ideation. Further, when self-reported conduct (positive to negative) and the frequency of experiencing humiliating events were included in the model, they both explained a substantial proportion of the variance in violent ideation.

In addition to regression analyses, identification of two extreme groups, those high and low on violent ideation differed significantly with violent ideators reporting higher narcissism, lower empathy, and greater sensitivity to rejection, as Baumeister would predict, but *lower* self-esteem that is not consistent with his formulation. In a subsequent study, we added fluctuating self-esteem, conduct, and the frequency of humiliating, rejection events (Harter & McCarley, 2004). These increased the predictability of violence ideation, both in regression analyses and in comparisons of violent and nonviolent ideators. Violent ideators reported fluctuation self-esteem, greater conduct problems and a greater frequency of having established humiliating events that were ego threatening. Thus, our understanding of thoughts qualifies and broadens the precursors. Not only is self-esteem not predictive of violence but self-esteem and narcissism are uncorrelated ($r = -.01$), indicating that these are different constructs both conceptually, as scales define the two constructs, and empirically. Narcissism entails a sense of entitlement, of superiority, of exhibitionism, whereas high self-esteem is defined as liking and respecting who one is as a person. There is a need to distinguish between these two concepts, conceptually, methodologically, and empirically.

Finally, in this study, we uncovered an interesting finding that is cause for concern. In the high profile cases of the school shooters, the vast majority had not been in any major trouble with the law and had *not* come to the attention of teachers or school personnel as potential troublemakers. Teachers, school officials, and students were astounded that these boys committed such violent acts. Debriefing efforts of the surviving students and families at Columbine, conducted by University of Denver clinicians and some in private practice, revealed that students and their families were realistically fearful that they would not be able to detect who, in the future, might commit such acts because there were few warning signs that they were capable of such behavior. These concerns are real, given findings from Harter and McCarley (2004). In this study, we asked teachers to rate student conduct (e.g., getting in trouble or potential for violent thinking) and among the subgroup of violent ideators who had rated their own conduct as quite negative, teachers incorrectly rated one-third of the group, giving them very positive scores on conduct. This is concerning the difficulty in assessing certain students at risk. Although such violent ideators may not be at risk for violent *action* (given the low percentage of such acts in most schools), violent ideation represents a different kind of pathological risk factor to the extent that it interferes with attention and concentration of scholastic endeavors, with socially appropriate behaviors that would promote positive peer interactions, and so on. The very presence of this subgroup of violent ideators suggests that they represent a type of student with different intrapsychic dynamics compared to those students with histories of conduct problems, delinquency, and acting out patterns, all of whom readily come to the attention of teachers, school officials, and peers. Those not showing these patterns are of concern in terms of their identification. One of our goals is to devise a short-form of our instruments that will allow schools to identify those who may have escaped the attention of school personnel but are nevertheless at pathological risk. Many of these processes begin in early adolescence (and even late childhood) but continue into middle and later adolescence, as the range of ages of the actual school shooters reveals, continuing the presence of risk factors.

Pathological Eating-Disordered Behavior. Our model identifies one self-concept domain that robustly affects global self-esteem across ages and cultures, namely, perceived physical appearance or attractiveness. In reviewing the inextricable link between perceived appearance and self-esteem, between the outer self and the inner self (see Harter, 1999), it became very apparent that this link is profoundly impacted by cultural standards of appearance for each gender. That cultures tout physical attractiveness as the measure of one's worth as a person has been amply demonstrated in contemporary society, as well as historically (Hatfield & Sprecher, 1986). The empirical findings (reviewed in Harter, 1999) indicate that Pearson correlations range from the .40s to the .80s. Moreover, investigators have revealed that these relationships are not merely statistical but are very much embedded in the consciousness of individuals who are aware of this link. In our own work (Kiang & Harter, 2004), we have found strong support for a model in which awareness of current cultural values (e.g., being attractive will lead to higher self-esteem, meeting standards of appearance will make people more popular, and people who are overweight are discriminated against) are highly endorsed. However, there is enough variability in these scores to relate such awareness to perceptions of one's own appearance, which, in turn, predict level of self-esteem and eating-disordered perceptions and behaviors. Specifically, those endorsing these cultural values or links reported more negative views of their appearance, lower self-esteem, more psychological correlates of eating disorders and more eating-disordered behaviors.

This particular study was conducted with college students. However, the seeds of such a model are sown in early adolescence (if not earlier) as teenagers of both genders are well aware of the prevailing norms for desirable appearance. For adult females in the 2000s, one must be tall, very thin, weigh very little (around 110 to 115), have ample breasts, and a pretty face and hair, all of which is an unattainable combination for more than 90% of the female population. Recent statistics (Kilbourne, 1994) indicated that the average American woman is 5'4" and weights 140. Standards have been exceedingly punishing for females for decades. What is new in the past 2 decades is the fact that the bar has been raised for males in our society. No longer is sex appeal to be judged by status, wealth, position, and power but by physical standards of attractiveness as well. Muscular build, abs, biceps, physique, hair (on head as well as face) have all come to define the new ideals for men (see Harter, 1999).

These standards are not lost on our young adolescents. Children succumb to the same discouragement about not being able to emulate the models, singers, and movie stars in the limelight. The importance of meeting these standards becomes particularly salient during early adolescence as teenagers face inevitable pubertal changes that signal their impending adulthood. Thus, they look to the adult standards as the physical markers for what defines attractiveness, appeal, social acceptability, all of which determine one's self-esteem.

The genetic throw of the dice lead some young adolescent males and females to fare better than others in the appearance wars. For example, early maturing girls are at a distinct disadvantage given the current emphasis on thinness and height because on average they are heavier and shorter, compared to later maturing girls who tend to be thinner and taller. The pattern is just the opposite for adolescent males in that earlier maturing teens tend to be taller and more muscular, which gives them a physical edge. Thus, beginning in early adolescent, evaluations of one's appearance take on critical implications for one's global self-esteem. Those not meeting the gold standards are at serious risk for pathological forms of depression and possibly suicide, as well as eating disorders that can be life threatening. Although this preoccupation initially becomes salient in early adolescent, it continues throughout the life span.

Middle Adolescence: Verbal Cameo of Normative Self-Representations and Self-Evaluations

What am I like as a person? You're probably not going to understand. I'm complicated! With my really close friends, I am very tolerant. I mean, I'm understanding and caring. With a group of friends, I'm rowdier. I'm also usually friendly and cheerful but I can get pretty obnoxious and intolerant if I don't like how they're acting. I'd like to be friendly and tolerant all of the time, that's the kind of person I want to be, and I'm disappointed in myself when I'm not. At school, I'm serious, even studious every now and then, but on the other hand, I'm a goof-off too, because if you're too studious, you won't be popular. So I go

back and forth, which means I don't do all that well in terms of my grades. But that causes problems at home, where I'm pretty anxious when I'm around my parents. They expect me to get all As, and get pretty annoyed with me when report cards come out. I care what they think about me, and so then I get down on myself, but it's not fair! I mean I worry about how I probably should get better grades, but I'd be mortified in the eyes of my friends if I did too well. So, I'm usually pretty stressed-out at home, and can even get very sarcastic, especially when my parents get on my case. But I really don't understand how I can switch so fast from being cheerful with my friends, then coming home and feeling anxious, and then getting frustrated and sarcastic with my parents. Which one is the real me? I have the same question when I'm around boys. Sometimes, I feel phony. Say I think some guy might be interested in asking me out. I try to act different, like Britney Spears, I'll be a real extrovert, fun-loving and even flirtatious, and think I am really good-looking. It's important to be good-looking like the models and movie stars. That's what makes you popular. I know in my heart of hearts that I can never look like her, so why do I even try. Its makes me hate myself and feel depressed. Plus, when I try to look and act like her, then everybody, I mean *everybody* else is looking at me like they think I am totally weird! They don't act like they think I'm attractive so I end up thinking I look terrible. I just hate myself when that happens! Because it gets worse! Then I get self-conscious and embarrassed and become radically introverted, and I don't know who I really am! Am I just acting like an extrovert, am I just trying to impress them, when really I'm an introvert! But I don't really care what they think, anyway. I mean I don't want to care, that is. I just want to know what my close friends think. I can be my true self with my close friends. I can't be my real self with my parents. They don't understand me. What do they know about what it's like to be a teenager? They treat me like I'm still a kid. At least at school, people treat you more like you're an adult. That gets confusing, though. I mean, which am I? When you're 15, are you still a kid or an adult? I have a part-time job and the people there treat me like an adult. I want them to approve of me, so I'm very responsible at work, which makes me feel good about myself there. But then I go out with my friends and I get pretty crazy and irresponsible. So, which am I, responsible or irresponsible? How can the same person be both? If my parents knew how immature I act sometimes, they would ground me forever, particularly my father. I'm real distant with him. I'm pretty close to my mother though. But it's hard being distant with one parent and close to the other, especially if we are all together, like talking at dinner. Even though I am close to my mother, I'm still pretty secretive about some things, particularly the things about myself that confuse me. So I think a lot about who is the real me, and sometimes I try to figure it out when I write in my diary, but I can't resolve it. There are days when I wish I could just become immune to myself! (adapted from Harter, 1999)

Self-descriptions are likely to increase in length during this period, as adolescents become increasingly introspective and morbidly preoccupied with what others think of them (Broughton, 1978; Elkind, 1967; Erikson, 1959, 1968; Harter, 1990a; Lapsley & Rice, 1988; Rosenberg, 1979). The unreflective self-acceptance of earlier periods of development vanishes, and, as Rosenberg observes, what were formerly unquestioned self-truths now become problematic self-hypotheses. The tortuous search for the self involves a concern with what or who am I (Broughton, 1978), a task made more difficult given the multiple Me's that crowd the self-landscape. There is typically a further proliferation of selves as adolescents come to make finer differentiations; in the cameo, the adolescent describes a self with really close friends (e.g., tolerant) versus with a group of friends (e.g., intolerant) and a self with mother (e.g., close) versus father (e.g., distant). The acquisition of new roles, for example, self at a job, may also require the construction of new context-specific attributes (e.g., responsible).

Moreover, additional cognitive I-self processes emerge that give the self-portrait a very new look (Case, 1985; Fischer, 1980). Whereas, in the previous stage, single abstractions were isolated from one another, during middle adolescence one acquires the ability to make comparisons between single abstractions, namely, between attributes in the same role-related self or across role-related selves. Fischer labels these new structures "abstract mappings," in that the adolescent can now "map" constructs about the self onto one another or directly compare them. Therefore, mappings force the individual to compare and contrast different attributes. It should be noted that abstract mappings have features in common with the "representational" mappings of childhood, in that the cognitive links that are initially forged often take the form of opposites. During adolescence, these opposites can take the form of seemingly contradictory abstractions about the self (e.g., tolerant versus intolerant, extrovert versus introvert, responsible versus irresponsible, and good-looking versus unattractive as in the cameo).

However, the abstract mapping structure has limitations as a means of relating two concepts to one another in that the individual cannot yet truly integrate such self-representations in a manner that would resolve apparent contradictions. Therefore, at the level of abstract mappings, the awareness of these opposites causes considerable intrapsychic conflict, confusion, and distress (Fischer et al., 1984; Harter & Monsour, 1992; Higgins, 1991), given the inability to coordinate these seemingly contradictory self-attributes. For example, our prototypical adolescent agonizes over whether she is an extrovert or an introvert ("Am I just acting like an extrovert, am I just trying to impress them, when really I'm an introvert?" "So which am I, responsible or irresponsible? How can the same person be both?"). Such cognitive-developmental limitations contribute to the emergence of what James (1892) identified as the "conflict of the different Me's."

In addition to such confusion, these seeming contradictions lead to very unstable self-representations that are also cause for concern (e.g., "I don't really understand how I can switch so fast from being cheerful with my friends, then coming home and feeling anxious, and then getting frustrated and sarcastic with my parents. Which one is the real me?"). The creation of multiple selves, coupled with the emerging ability to detect potential contradictions between self-attributes displayed in different roles, naturally ushers in concern over which attributes define the true self. However, from a normative perspective, the adolescent at this level is not equipped with the cognitive skills to fully solve the dilemma (e.g., "So I think a lot about who is the real me, and sometimes try to figure it out when I write in my diary, but I can't resolve it").

As introduced in the previous section on early adolescence, our own research has been directed toward an examination of the extent to which adolescents at three developmental levels identify opposing self-attributes and report that they are experienced as conflictual (Harter & Monsour, 1992; Harter et al., 1997). We have determined, across several studies, that young adolescents infrequently detect opposites in their self-portrait. However, it was predicted, according to the analysis presented earlier, that there would be a dramatic rise in the detection of opposing self-attributes and an acknowledgment that such apparent contradictions lead to conflict in the self-system at mid-adolescence. Our most recent procedure for examining these issues is described in Harter (1999), as are the findings.

Across three different studies (see Harter et al., 1997), we have found that the number of opposing self-attribute pairs, as well as the number of opposites in conflict, increases between early and middle adolescence. This pattern of findings supports the hypothesis that the abstract mapping structures that emerge in middle adolescence allow one to detect, but not to meaningfully integrate, these apparent contradictions. Thus, they lead to the phenomenological experience of intrapsychic conflict. We have asked teenagers to verbally elaborate on the opposites and conflicts that they reported on our task. As one 14-year-old put it, "I really think I am a happy person and I want to be that way with everyone, not just my friends; but I get depressed with my family, and it really bugs me because that's not what I want to be like." Another 15-year-old, in describing a conflict between self-attributes in the realm of romantic relationships, exclaimed, "I hate the fact that I get so nervous! I wish I wasn't so inhibited. The real me is talkative. I just want to be natural, but I can't." Another 15-year-old girl explained, "I really think of myself as friendly and open to people, but the way the other girls act, they force me to become an introvert, even though I know I'm not." In exasperation, one ninth-grader observed of the self-portrait she had constructed, "It's not right, it should all fit together into one piece!" These comments suggest that at this age level, there is a need for coherence; there is a desire to bring self-attributes into harmony with one another, yet in mid-adolescence, the cognitive abilities to create such a self-portrait are not yet in place.

For across-role opposites, at every age level, females detect more contradictory attributes than do males. These findings replicate two other studies in which similar gender differences were obtained (see Harter et al., 1997). Moreover, in one study in which we asked subjects to indicate how upset they were over conflicting attributes, the pattern revealed that females become more upset over conflicting attributes across early, middle, and late adolescence, whereas males become less upset. Elsewhere, we have offered a general interpretation of this pattern, drawing on those frameworks that emphasize the greater importance of relationships for females than males (Chodorow, 1989; Eichenbaum & Orbach, 1983; Gilligan, 1982; Jordan, 1991; J. Miller, 1986; Rubin, 1985). These theorists posit that the socialization of girls involves far more embeddedness in the family and more concern with connectedness to others. Boys, in contrast, forge a path of independence and autonomy in which the logic of moral and social decisions takes precedence over affective responses to significant others.

In extrapolating from these observations, we have suggested that in an effort to maintain the multiple relationships that girls are developing during adolescence, and to create harmony among these necessarily differentiated roles, opposing attributes in the self become particularly salient as well as problematic. Boys, in contrast, can move more facilely among their different roles and multiple selves to the extent that such roles are logically viewed as more independent of one another. However, these general observations require further refinement, including an empirical examination of precisely which facets of the relational worlds of adolescent females and males are specifically relevant to gender differences in opposing attributes displayed across different contexts.

Closer examination of the gender effects reveals that it is a subset of female adolescents who report more opposites and greater conflict compared to males. We have determined that adolescent females who endorse a feminine gender orientation (eschewing masculine traits) may be particularly vulnerable to the experience of opposing attributes and associated conflict. Feminine adolescent females, compared to females who endorse an androgynous orientation, report more conflict, particularly in roles that involve teachers, classmates, and male friends (in contrast to roles involving parents and female friends). Several hypotheses would be worth pursuing in this regard. Is it that feminine girls report more contradictions in those public contexts where they feel they may be acting inappropriately by violating feminine stereotypes of behavior? Given that femininity as assessed by sex-role inventories is largely defined by caring, sensitivity, and attentiveness to the needs and feelings of others, might female adolescents who adopt this orientation be more preoccupied with relationships, making opposing attributes and accompanying conflict more salient? Moreover, might it be more important for feminine girls to be consistent across relationships, a stance that may be difficult to sustain, to the extent that significant others in different roles are encouraging or reinforcing different characteristics? These are all new directions in which attention to gender issues should proceed.

The challenges posed by the need to create different selves are also exacerbated for ethnic minority youth in this country who must bridge "multiple worlds," as Cooper and her colleagues point out (Cooper, Jackson, Azmitia, Lopez, & Dunbar, 1995). Minority youth must move between multiple contexts, some of which may be with members of their own ethnic group, including family and friends, and some of which may be populated by the majority culture, including teachers, classmates, and other peers who may not share the values of their family of origin. Rather than assume that all ethnic minority youth will react similarly to the need to cope with such multiple worlds, these investigators highlighted several different patterns of adjustment. Some youth are able to move facilely across the borders of their multiple worlds, in large part, because the values of the family, teachers, and peers are relatively similar. Others, for whom there is less congruence in values across contexts, adopt a bicultural stance, adapting to the world of family and to that of the larger community. Others find the transition across these psychological borders more difficult, and some find it totally unmanageable. Particularly interesting is the role that certain parents play in helping adolescents navigate these transitions, leading to more successful adaptations for some than others.

As observed earlier, adolescents during this period become extremely preoccupied with the opinions and expectations of significant others in different roles. As our prototypical respondent indicates, "I care what my parents think about me"; "I want to know what my close friends think"; "I don't care what (everybody else) thinks. I mean I don't want to care, that is"; "I want them (adults at work) to approve of me." Adolescents gaze intently into the social mirror for information about what standards and attributes to internalize. However, as the number of roles proliferates, leading to messages from different significant others that are potentially contradictory, adolescents may become confused or distressed about just which characteristics to adopt. We see this in the cameo self-description with regard to scholastic performance, in that the adolescent feels she "should get better grades" to please her parents but confesses that "I'd be mortified in the eyes of my friends if I did too well." As Higgins (1991) observes, in their attempt to incorporate the standards and opinions of others, adolescents at this level develop conflicting "self-guides" across different relational contexts as they attempt to meet the incompatible expectations of parents and peers. He reports evidence indicating that such discrepancies have been found to produce confusion, uncertainty, and indecision with regard to self-evaluation and self-regulation, which is consistent with our own findings. Moreover, as Rosenberg (1986) notes, the serious efforts at perspective taking that emerge at this

stage make one aware that no human being can have direct access to another's mind, leading to inevitable ambiguity about others' attitudes toward the self, producing yet another source of doubt and confusion.

The potential for displaying differing levels of self-esteem across relational contexts is also exacerbated during this period, to the extent that the significant others are providing different levels of validation for whom one is as a person (see also Rosenberg, 1986). For example, the cameo self-description reveals that the adolescent gets down on herself for not getting the grades her parents expect. She hates herself when she feels peers think she is weird, but she feels good about herself on the job, where supervisors give her more positive feedback. Our own evidence has revealed that not only does self-esteem become differentiated by context beginning in early adolescence but also further differentiated in middle to late adolescence. For example, individuals come to develop different levels of self-esteem with their mothers and their fathers (Harter, 1999); levels that are directly related to their perceptions of approval from each parent.

Normative Liabilities during Middle Adolescence

Mid-adolescence brings a preoccupation with what significant others think of the self, a task that is made more challenging given the proliferation of roles that demand the creation of multiple selves. The addition of new role-related selves can be observed in the fact that adolescents make finer discriminations (e.g., self with a close friend versus self with a group of friends, and self with mother versus self with father). Moreover, there is relatively little overlap in the personal attributes that define the self in each role. The proliferation of multiple selves ushers in the potential for such attributes to be viewed as contradictory. Moreover, the emergence of new cognitive processes, such as abstract mappings, forces the adolescent to compare and contrast different attributes, exacerbating the likelihood that contradictions will be detected. Mappings, in the form of the identification of opposites, are problematic in that the individual cannot yet truly integrate such self-representations in a manner that would resolve the contradictions. Thus, the adolescent is likely to experience conflict, confusion, and distress. Opposites and associated conflict are particularly likely to occur for attributes in different roles rather than in the same role. Females are particularly likely to display these negative outcomes. Opposing self-attributes also lead to unstable self-representations, in addition to concern over which characteristics represent one's true self.

With regard to the impact of the socializing environment, adolescents gaze intently into the social mirror for information about what standards and attributes to internalize. However, contradictory messages from different significant others can lead to confusion about just what characteristics to adopt. Differential support, in the form of approval or validation, will also lead to differing levels of self-worth across relational contexts. The contradictory feedback that adolescents may receive from different sources will, therefore, lead to volatility in self-esteem across interpersonal contexts.

Contradictory standards and feedback can also contribute to a lowering of global self-esteem between early and middle adolescence (see findings reviewed by Harter, 1990a, 1990b), to the extent that one cannot meet the expectations of everyone in each relational context. To the extent that the adolescent does not meet the standards of others, he or she is likely to experience less approval, which will lead to lower global self-esteem. Moreover, the abstract mapping structure, coupled with the penchant for introspection, may also contribute to lowered self-esteem in that it facilitates the comparison of one's ideal and real self-concepts. Such a focus can lead to a heightened awareness of the discrepancy between how one perceives the self to be in reality (e.g., "I can get pretty obnoxious and intolerant") and how one would ideally like to be (e.g., "I'd like to be friendly and tolerant all of the time. That's the kind of person I want to be, and I'm disappointed in myself when I'm not"). The realm of physical appearance is particularly critical. Thus, this adolescent wants to look like Britney Spears, knows she doesn't, and this sets up another painful discrepancy between how she would ideally like to look and how she does. In reality, she does not value her appearance, falling far short of the cultural standards for beauty.

Cognitive-developmental advances during mid-adolescence also represent limitations that can lead to distortions in the interpretation of the opinions of significant others. As observed earlier, with the advent of any new cognitive capacities comes difficulty in controlling and applying them effectively. For example, teenagers have difficulty differentiating their own mental preoccupations from what others are thinking, leading to a form of adolescent egocentrism that Elkind (1967) has labeled the "imaginary audience." Adolescents falsely assume that others are as preoccupied with their behavior and appearance as they themselves are.

As our prototypical respondent exclaims, "Everybody, I mean everybody else is looking at me like they think I am totally weird!" With regard to lack of cognitive control, this phenomenon represents overgeneralization (or failure to differentiate) in that adolescents project their own concerns onto others.

Interestingly, the inability to control and to effectively apply new cognitive structures can result not only in a lack of differentiation between self and other, as in the imaginary audience phenomenon, but also in excessive or unrealistic differentiation. The latter penchant can be observed in another form of egocentrism that Elkind (1967) identified as the "personal fable." In creating narratives that come to define the self, the adolescent asserts that his or her thoughts and feelings are uniquely experienced. No one else can possibly understand or experience the ecstasy of his or her rapture or the intensity of his or her despair. Adults, particularly parents, are likely to be singled out in this regard. As the prototypical adolescent exclaims, "My parents don't understand me. What do they know about what it's like to be a teenager?" Her initial comment to the interviewer when asked to describe what she was like ("You're probably not going to understand") also reflects this type of overdifferentiation between self and other.

The liabilities of this period, therefore, are legion with regard to potential conflict and confusion over contradictory attributes and messages, concern over which characteristics define the true self, distortions in the perception of self versus others, and a preoccupation with discrepancies between the real and ideal self-concepts, all of which can lead to lowered self-worth. Some of these processes would appear to be problematic for particular subgroups of adolescents, for example, females who adopt a feminine gender orientation or ethnic minority youth who are challenged by the need to create selves that bridge "multiple worlds," with one's family, ethnic peers and in the mainstream majority culture.

An appreciation for the ramifications of these normative processes is critical in interpreting the unpredictable behaviors, shifting self-evaluations, and mood swings that are observed in many adolescents during this age period. Such displays are less likely to be viewed as intentional or pathological, and more likely to meet with empathy and understanding to the extent that normative cognitive-development changes can be invoked as in part responsible. For many parents, as well as other adults working closely with teenagers, these seemingly inexplicable reactions often lead to perplexity, exasperation, and anger, provoking power struggles and altercations that strain the adolescent-adult relationship. The realization that this is a normative part of development that should not persist forever may provide temporary comfort to adults who feel beleaguered and ineffectual in dealing with adolescents of this age. Indeed, it gives a more charitable rendering to this period of development.

Individual Differences: Adaptive and Maladaptive Outcomes in Middle Adolescence

With regard to the focus on meeting cultural standards appearance, females are much more likely to suffer from processes that move into the realm of pathology, including depression and eventual eating disorders. From the perspective of our own model of the causes and correlates of self esteem, an intense preoccupation with attempts to meeting the impossible standards of beauty, coupled with very negative perceptions of one's body image, can lead to extremely low self-esteem, depression, and in the extreme, eating-disordered behaviors. We have documented the links between the high importance attached to physical appearance and negative perceptions of one's body image, leading to extremely negative reports of self-esteem and depression among those in mid-adolescence. In the subsequent section on later adolescence and emerging adulthood, we provide further documentation about how these processes can lead to pathological eating-disordered behaviors.

However, numerous findings (reviewed Harter, 1999; see also Nolen-Hoeksema & Girgus, 1994) reveal that dramatic gender differences in depression emerge in middle adolescence. The discrepancy between impossible ideals for appearance and one's perception of one's own body image contributes to very low self-esteem for some, particularly those who are overweight, which leads to profound depression that can require clinical intervention.

While the potential for such internalizing symptoms looms large for girls during middle adolescence, the potential for the escalation of violence and males, as in the case of the high profile cases of school shootings by White, middle-class adolescents is apparent. Intense rejection by peers, at a time when self-consciousness and the need for approval are so salient, sets the stage for violent ideation that can turn to action. The fragile and vacillating self-structures of this particular period can, in the face of humiliation, lead to lack of control, both over cognitions about the self (Harter, 1999) and behaviors that these cognitions may drive. Given the lack of cognitive control (Fischer, 1980), the adolescent during this period may act more impulsively on his thoughts. Recent work on the adolescent brain supports the view that the frontal cortex is not yet completely developed, leading to gaps in executive functions that could serve to curb such impulsive, violent intentions and behaviors.

While the fragmented self is a normative liability of this period of middle adolescence, interactions with a history of severe and chronic physical and sexual abuse may lead to pathological outcomes that can continue as PTSD symptoms even though the abuse occurred in early childhood. The effects of abuse on the self-system are legion (see review in Harter, 1999). From a developmental perspective, a history of abuse can lead to dissociative symptoms that serve to further fragment the fragile multiple selves in the process of psychological construction (see also Putnam, 1993; Westen, 1993) at a time when adolescents have normative challenges to integrating their various selves. As a result, there is no core self at the helm, there is little communication between multiple selves that become "alters," comprising the ability to develop an integrated self. As a result, there is the risk for dissociative identity disorders that represent severe pathological conditions that may require years of treatment.

Late Adolescence: Verbal Cameo of Normative Self-Representations and Self-Evaluations

I'm a pretty conscientious person, particularly when it comes to things like doing my homework. It's important to me because I plan to go to college next year. Eventually I want to go to law school, so developing good study habits and getting top grades are both essential. (My parents don't want me to become a lawyer; they'd rather I go into teaching, but law is what I want to pursue.) Every now and then I get a little lackadaisical and don't complete an assignment as thoroughly or thoughtfully as I could, particularly if our high school has a big football or basketball game that I want to go to with my friends. But that's normal, I mean, you can't just be a total "grind." You'd be pretty boring if you were. You have to be flexible. I've also become more religious as I have gotten older, not that I am a saint or anything. Religion gives me a sense of purpose, in the larger scheme of things, and it provides me with personal guidelines for the kind of adult I'd like to be. For example, I'd like to be an ethical person who treats other people fairly. That's the kind of lawyer I'd like to be, too. I don't always live up to that standard; that is, sometimes I do something that doesn't feel that ethical. When that happens, I get a little depressed because I don't like myself as a person. But I tell myself that it's natural to make mistakes, so I don't really question the fact that deep down inside, the real me is a moral person. Basically, I like who I am, so I don't stay depressed for long. Usually, I am pretty upbeat and optimistic. I guess you could say that I'm a moody person. I'm not as popular as a lot of other kids. You have to look a certain way, have the right body image, wear the right clothes, to be accepted. At our school, it's the jocks who are looked up to. I've never been very athletic, but you can't be good at everything, let's face it. Being athletic isn't that high on my own list of what is important, even though it is for a lot of kids in our school. I try to think that, anyway. But I don't really care what they think anymore, at least I try to convince myself that I don't. I try to believe that what I think is what counts. After all, I have to live with myself as a person and to respect that person, which I do now, more than a few years ago. I'm pretty much being the kind of person I want to be. I'm doing well at things that are important to me like getting good grades. That's what is probably most important to me right now. Having a lot of friends isn't that important to me. I wouldn't say I was unpopular, though. While I am basically an introvert, especially on a date when I get pretty self-conscious, in the right social situation, like watching a ball game with my friends, I can be pretty extroverted. You have to be adaptive around other people. It would be weird to be the same kind of person on a date and with my friends at a football game! For example, when our team has a winning season and goes to the play-offs, everyone in the whole school is proud; what the team does reflects on all of us. On a date, the feelings are much more intimate, just between you and the other person. As much as I enjoy my high school friends and activities, I'm looking forward to leaving home and going to college, where I can be more independent, although I'm a little ambivalent. I love my parents, and really want to stay connected to them, plus, what they think about me is still important to how I feel about myself as a person. So leaving home will be bittersweet. But sometimes it's hard to be mature around them, particularly around my mom. I feel a lot more grown-up around my dad; he treats me more like an adult. I like that part of me because it feels more like my true self. My mom wants me to grow up, but another part of her wants me to remain "her little baby." I'll probably always be somewhat dependent on my parents. How can you escape it? But I'm also looking forward to being on my own. (adapted from Harter, 1999)

With regard to the content of the self-representations that emerge in late adolescence and early adulthood, typically, many of the attributes reflect personal beliefs, values, and moral standards that have become internalized, or alternatively, constructed from their own experiences (see findings by Damon & Hart, 1988). These characteristics are exemplified in the prototypical cameo, in that

the adolescent expresses the personal desire to go to college, which requires good grades and discipline in the form of study habits. Although classmates tout athletics as the route to popularity, there is less concern at this age with what others think ("I used to care but now what I think is important"). In addition, there is a more realistic focus on one's future selves (e.g., not only becoming a lawyer, but also an ethical lawyer, as a personal goal). Noteworthy in this narrative is the absence of an explicit reference to the potential origins of these goals; for example, parental encouragement or expectations that one pursue such a career. Moreover, this adolescent's career choice does not conform to the parents' occupational goals for their child.

The failure to acknowledge the socialization influences that might have led to these choices does not necessarily indicate that significant others, such as peers and parents, had no impact. Findings (see Steinberg, 1990) reveal that the attitudes of adolescents and their parents are quite congruent when it comes to occupational, political, and religious decisions or convictions. That the impact of significant others is not acknowledged suggests that older adolescents and young adults have come to "own" various values as personal choices, rather than attribute them to the sources from which they may have been derived (Damon & Hart, 1988). In Higgins' (1991) terminology, older adolescents have gone through a process in which they have actively selected among alternative "self-guides" and are no longer merely buffeted about by the expectations of significant others; that is, self-guides become increasingly internalized and less tied to their social origins. Moreover, there is a greater sense of direction as the older adolescent comes to envisage future or "possible" selves (Markus & Nurius, 1986) that function as ideals toward which one aspires.

Another feature of the self-portrait of the older adolescent can be contrasted with the period before, in that many potentially contradictory attributes are no longer described as characteristics in opposition to one another. Thus, being conscientious as a student does not appear to conflict with one's lackadaisical attitude toward schoolwork: "That's normal, I mean, you can't just be a total 'grind.' You'd be pretty boring if you were. You have to be flexible." Similarly, one's perception of the self as ethical does not conflict with the acknowledgment that one also has engaged in some unethical behaviors ("It's natural to make mistakes"). Nor does introversion conflict with extroverted behaviors. "You have to be adaptive around other people. It would be weird to be the same kind of person on a date and with my friends at a football game!"

There are cognitive acquisitions that allow the older adolescent to overcome some of the liabilities of the previous period, where potentially opposing attributes were viewed as contradictory and as a cause of internal conflict. The general cognitive advances during this period involve the construction of higher-order abstractions that involve the meaningful intercoordination of single abstractions (see Case, 1985; Fischer, 1980; Fischer & Canfield, 1986). For example, the fact that one is both introverted and extroverted can be integrated through the construction of a higher-order abstraction that defines the self as "adaptive." The observation that one is both depressed and cheerful or optimistic can be integrated under the personal rubric of "moody." Similarly, "flexible" can allow one to coordinate conscientiousness with the tendency to be lackadaisical. The higher-order concept of "ambivalence" integrates the desire to be independent yet still remain connected to parents. Moreover, "bittersweet" reflects a higher-order abstraction combining excitement over going to college with sadness over leaving one's parents. Such higher-order abstractions provide self-labels that bring meaning and therefore legitimacy to what formerly appeared to be troublesome contradictions in the self.

Neo-Piagetians, such as Case (1985), Fischer (1980), and colleagues, observe that developmental acquisitions at these higher levels typically require greater scaffolding by the social environment in the form of support, experiences, instruction, and so on for individuals to function at their optimal level. If these new skills are fostered, they will help the adolescent to integrate opposing attributes in a manner that does not produce conflict or distress. Thus, efforts to assist the adolescent in realizing that it is normal to display seemingly contradictory traits, and perhaps quite appropriate, may alleviate perceptions of conflict. Moreover, helping teenagers to provide higher-order labels that integrate opposing attributes (e.g., flexible, adaptive, moody, and inconsistent) may avert some of the distress that was salient during middle adolescence. These suggestions derive from the observations of Fischer, Case, and others to the effect that these cognitive solutions will not necessarily emerge automatically with development. Nor will the potential benefits derived from movement to late adolescence and early adulthood necessarily accrue; that is, the levels described in this chapter represent a normative sequence of development. However, the age levels are somewhat arbitrary in that certain in-dividuals may not attain a given level at the designated age period. Development may be delayed or even arrested if there is not sufficient support for the transition to a new level of conceptualization, particularly for the higher stages.

The Role of the Socializing Environment

More recent evidence (see Harter et al., 1997) indicates that the ability to resolve potentially contradictory attributes may be more difficult for some role-pair combinations than for others, particularly for females. For example, when all role pairs are combined, there is no decline in the number of opposing attributes identified across roles. For older adolescent females, there is actually a further increase. The fact that six roles were included in the study generating the new data (compared to only four in the original Harter and Monsour study) may have been partly responsible, because the inclusion of additional roles increased the probability that opposing attributes might be detected; there were 15 possible role pairs that might contain contradictions compared to only six role pairs in the original study. In increasing the number of roles, we also separated the reports of self-attributes with mother and with father (whereas in the earlier study, we merely inquired about self with parents).

The separation of self-attributes with each parent potentially enhances the likelihood that characteristics with each may contradict attributes in roles with peers. Examples generated by adolescent respondents in middle to late adolescence included being short-tempered with mother versus a good listener in romantic relationships; respectful with father versus assertive with friends; distant from father but attentive with a romantic interest. Adolescent bids for autonomy from parents (Cooper, Grotevant, & Condon, 1983; Hill & Holmbeck, 1986; Steinberg, 1990), coupled with the increasing importance of the peer group (Brown, 1990; Savin-Williams & Berndt, 1990), would lead to the expectation that attributes expressed with mother and father might well differ from those displayed with peers (i.e., friends and romantic partners), leading to a greater potential for contradictions.

However, the separation of self with mother and self with father also creates the potential for attributes with mother to be in opposition to attributes with father. The potential for attributes with each parent to appear contradictory can be observed in the cameo, where the prototypical older adolescent feels much more mature with father than with mother. Moreover, such conflicts begin to be observed in mid-adolescence, where the prototypical teenager indicated that she was "close" with her mother but "distant" with her father, a difference that became problematic if they were all together such as talking at dinner.

When the findings are broken down by relationship pairs, opposing attributes and associated conflict were most frequent for the combination of self with mother versus self with father, beginning in mid-adolescence, and increasing in late adolescence, a pattern that we have since replicated in a subsequent study. Examples have included being close with mother versus distant with father; stubborn with mother versus respectful with father; open with mother but not with father; at ease with mother but defensive with father; and hostile with mother but cheerful with father. Moreover, such opposites between self with mother versus self with father, as well as associated conflict, increased dramatically for the older girls in particular.

The fact that older female adolescents reported increasing contradiction, whereas male adolescents did not, suggests that cognitive-developmental explanations are incomplete. The separation of attributes with mother and with father, in particular, would appear to make it more difficult for certain adolescents to cognitively resolve or normalize the contradictions (produced by the opposing attributes with mother versus father) that are provoked by these roles, as well as those attributes with each parent that contradict the characteristics that one displays with peers. Contradictions between self with parents and self with peers are more understandable, given developmental bids for autonomy. However, why should adolescents (particularly females) report increasingly different characteristics with mother and father?

Here, we can only speculate. Family therapists observe that children and adolescents typically develop different relationships with each parent, which may cause the salient attributes in each relationship to vary considerably. Contributing to these dynamics is the fact that each parent may have a different set of expectations about those characteristics that he or she values and therefore attempts to foster. First, the adolescent may become caught in a struggle between two parents who are encouraging and reinforcing different facets of his or her personality, provoking opposing attributes and resulting conflict. Second, both of these roles, self with mother and self with father, occur in the same general context (i.e., the family), whereas other multiple roles are not as likely to be called on simultaneously. These particular conditions may exacerbate the contradictions and conflicts that adolescents experience in their respective roles with mother versus father. These family dynamics appear to be relevant to the increase in across-role opposing attributes for female adolescents in particular, who may be more likely to be sensitive to the fact that they are behaving differently with mother versus father. As observed in the previous section on the period of mid-adolescence, females display more concern over relationship issues, which may make opposing attributes more salient. Adolescent females may also feel that, to remain connected to both mother and father, it is important to be consistent across these relationships—a task that can be problematic for the reasons cited earlier.

Although the gender literature suggests that connectedness is more critical to females than to males (Chodorow, 1989; Eichenbaum & Orbach, 1983; Gilligan, 1982; Gilligan, Lyons, & Hanmer, 1989; Jordan, 1991; J. Miller, 1986; Rubin, 1985), the adolescent literature reveals that it is important for teenagers of both genders to remain connected to parents in the process of individuation and the establishment of autonomy (Cooper et al., 1983; Hill & Holmbeck, 1986; Steinberg, 1990). As our prototypical subject reveals, while it is important to go to college where he or she can be more independent, it is also important to stay connected to parents.

Contextual factors, such as the family, therefore will conspire with cognitive development to impact the extent to which opposites and conflicts are experienced. In another example, the role of context can be observed in cross-cultural research by Kennedy (1994). Kennedy has adapted our procedure in comparing the self-understanding of American and Korean youth. He finds that there are different age-related peaks in conflict among adolescents in the two cultures. Korean youth report increased conflict between opposing attributes in 10th and 12th grades, findings that he interprets as the demands of the school context at those particular grade levels. In Korea, 10th grade is the 1st year of high school, and the new students are required to be deferential to the juniors and seniors, a relationship that many 10th graders find oppressive. Kennedy argues that these demands exert a strain on the self-system and destabilize students' sense of self as they struggle to find a niche in the peer hierarchy of high school. During 12th grade, there are different demands, for example, intense preparation for the college entrance exams. This pressure leads to challenges in balancing the demands of academics, peer relationships, and family commitments, resulting in greater conflict.

Future research should attend to such contextual factors and attempt to assess the underlying processes more directly. To return to our own findings in this regard, it would be of interest to determine whether the conflict between self-attributes with mother versus father is more intense if the adolescent is living in a two-parent family where both mother and father are in the same household, or if the parents are divorced and living apart. One hypothesis is that living under the same roof with both parents makes it difficult to avoid conflict if different attributes in each relationship are demanded simultaneously. Alternatively, conflict may be exacerbated in the situation of divorce to the extent that in an acrimonious separation, each parent intensifies his or her differential expectations for the attributes they want the adolescent to display as part of a power struggle in which the adolescent becomes a pawn. Such processes would be intriguing to investigate.

Finally, with regard to developmental changes in the self, evidence from longitudinal studies documents that self-esteem or global self-worth improves in later adolescence (see Engel, 1959; O'Malley & Bachman, 1983; Rosenberg, 1986; Simmons, Rosenberg, & Rosenberg, 1973). Several interpretations of these gains have been suggested (see Harter, 1990b; McCarthy & Hoge, 1982). Reductions in the discrepancy between one's ideal self and one's real self, between one's aspirations and one's successes, according to James's (1892) formulation, may be in part responsible. As the prototypical adolescent indicates, he or she has more self-respect now, compared to a few years ago and observes that "I'm pretty much being the kind of person I want to be. I'm doing well at things that are important to me like getting good grades and being ethical." Gains in personal autonomy and freedom of choice may also play a role, in that the older adolescent may have more opportunity to select performance domains in which he or she is successful. Such freedom may also provide one with more opportunity to select those support groups that will provide the positive regard necessary to promote or enhance self-esteem, consistent with the looking glass self-formulation. Increased role-taking ability may also lead older teenagers to behave in more socially acceptable ways that enhance the evaluation of the self by others, such that the favorable attitudes of others toward the self are internalized as positive self-worth.

These others include parents. Although it has been common in treatments of adolescent development to suggest that the influence of peers increases, whereas the impact of parental opinion declines, findings do not support the latter contention. As our cameo subject indicates, "What my parents think about me is still important to how I feel about myself as a person." Our own findings reveal that the correlation between classmate approval and global self-esteem does increase during childhood and adolescence; however, the correlation between parental approval and global self-esteem, which is high in childhood, does not decline during adolescence (Harter, 1990b). The latter correlation does decline, however, during the college years among students who are away from home.

More specific evaluations of self-esteem continue to vary by relationship context (Harter, Waters, & Whitesell, 1998), throughout the high school years, as adolescents make finer distinctions (e.g., between their self-esteem with mother and with father). However, we did not anticipate the fact that for the vast majority of individuals, self-esteem in one particular relational domain is much more highly related to global self-esteem than is relational self-esteem in all other contexts. The specific domain occupying this position varies from adolescent to adolescent. For example, with our prototypical adolescent, self as student in the academic domain is most important ("Getting good grades is what is most important to me now") and his or her self-esteem in that particular context is higher than in other domains. Thus, focusing on that particular context would appear to be very adaptive in that it should promote more positive feelings of global self-esteem.

Normative Liabilities during Late Adolescence

Many of the limitations of the preceding period of mid-adolescence would appear to be overcome as a result of changes during late adolescence. Attributes reflecting personal beliefs, values, and standards become more internalized, and the older adolescent would appear to have more opportunity to meet these standards, thereby leading to enhanced self-esteem. The focus on future selves also gives the older adolescent a sense of direction. A critical cognitive advance can be observed in the ability to construct higher-order abstractions that involve the meaningful integration of single abstractions that represent potential contradictions in the self-portrait (e.g., depressed and cheerful do not conflict because they are both part of being moody). The older adolescent can also resolve potentially contradictory attributes by asserting that he or she is flexible or adaptive, thereby subsuming apparent inconsistencies under more generalized abstractions about the self. Moreover, older adolescents are more likely to normalize potential contradictions, asserting that it is desirable to be different across relational contexts and that it would be weird or strange to be the same with different people.

Nevertheless, conflict between role-related attributes does not totally abate in later adolescence. Conflict will be more likely to occur if the new skills that allow for an integration of seeming contradictions are not fostered by the socializing environment. Furthermore, opposing attributes across particular role combinations, notably self with mother versus self with father, continue to be problematic in late adolescence, especially for girls. To the extent that one's mother and father elicit or reinforce opposing attributes, cognitive solutions for integrating seeming contradictions would appear to be more difficult to invoke.

Last, although the internalization of standards and opinions that the adolescent comes to own as personal choices and attitudes toward the self represents a developmental advance, there are liabilities as well associated with this process. As Rosenberg (1986) observes, the shift in the locus of self-knowledge from an external to internal source can introduce uncertainty. As long as major truths about the self derive from omniscient and omnipotent adults, then there is little doubt about their veracity. However, when the locus of self-knowledge shifts inward and adolescents must rely on their own autonomous judgment and insight to reach conclusions about the self, the sense of certainty can be compromised.

Individual Differences: Adaptive and Maladaptive Self-Processes and Outcomes in Late Adolescence/Early Adulthood

Many of the pathological processes that have been described in the earlier periods of adolescence can be observed, even if in a somewhat different form, due to developmental advances. Preoccupation with impossible cultural standards of attractiveness looms even larger as the older adolescent anticipates emerging adulthood, making it even more critical to attain these standards to be socially acceptable and successful in the new adult world order (Harter, in press). For females, failure to meet these standards can lead to more pathological processes that may include eating disorders.

For example, in one of our studies conducted by Danis (see Harter, 1999), two eating-disordered groups among women college students were identified, those with symptoms of anorexia and those with symptoms of bulimia. These two groups were compared to a control sample, college women who did not display such symptoms. Both the anorexic and bulimic group reported significantly higher scores on the importance of appearance, toward the very top of the four-point scale, compared to the normative sample. They each reported extremely low scores with regard to their evaluation of their physical appearance, creating a large discrepancy: importance scores vastly higher than perceived appearance scores. This discrepancy, clearly predicted very low self-esteem scores for the two eating-disordered groups compared to the normal sample. These low self-esteem scores, in turn, were highly predictive of extremely high levels of self-reported depression. Of particular interest were the findings that although both eating-disordered groups reported this negative constellation of symptoms, those in the bulimic group were most at risk given the lowest ratings of perceived physical appearance, self-esteem, and depression. Danis interpreted this difference between the two eating-disordered groups in terms of perceptions of control. She argued that those with symptoms of anorexia were objectively thinner, leading them to possibly feel more successful in terms of their weight control. The bulimics, who by definition binge and purge, were interpreted to be less in control; moreover, on average, this group was heavier. That said, those with anorexia are more at risk for malnourishment that can affect bone development, brain development, body development in general, and, in the extreme, they are at risk for death. Those with bulimic symptoms are also at risk for a variety of physical symptoms, including damage to the mouth and esophagus as well as other compromising physical growth symptoms. There are also numerous psychological symptoms including disruptions in the family, compromised academic achievement, and impaired social functioning.

Male adolescents are at continued risk for violence, particularly the type of violence that emanates from peer rejection and humiliation. Chronic rejection and humiliation are likely culprits for violent ideation (Harter, 2004) and for violent action, as in the case of the school shooters. Unlike the impulsive acts of the school shooters in middle adolescents, the acts of those (e.g., Eric Harris and Dylan Kleibold from Columbine) who were older teens were far more *planful*. For over a year, they had developed their strategies, some of which were revealed in Harris's written manifesto. While this is speculative, at this point, in examining the media accounts of the 11 high-profile school shooting cases, it would appear that the dynamics may be different from what we normally consider to be delinquent, conduct-disordered behavior that had come to the attention of teachers, school officials, school psychologists, peers, and parents. In most of these cases, there had been few warning signs with regard to the male shooters having been in trouble with the law, having been identified as troublemakers in the school, having clinical diagnoses, or being placed in special classes for student with a penchant for acting out. As noted earlier (Harter & McCarley, 2004), we found that 33% of those in a normative sample reporting to us that they had serious thoughts of harming others who humiliated them went undetected by their classroom teachers who were given parallel rating forms. Thus, there is a need to discriminate the form of violence that has recently emerged from previous acts that have been committed by known delinquents and conduct-disordered youth who have come to the attention of school and mental health professional, and who commit different types of crimes; for example, drive-by shootings to target one individual versus the random shooting of as many classmates as possible. The dynamics may be different at different developmental stages (e.g., more planful among older adolescents).

The construction of multiple selves, while a normative process, can also have pathological implications. It was pointed out in the section on middle adolescence that the effects of abuse can lead to dissociative symptoms that prevent one's multiple selves from being integrated. In the severest cases, this can lead to dissociative identity disorder (what used to be termed multiple personality disorder). Abuse has also been found to impact the valence (positive or negative) of those attributes judged to be one's core self (versus more peripheral attributes). Normatively, we have found that when asked to rate the attributes across multiple relational context with regard to whether they are central core characteristics or more peripheral, less important attributes that define the self, normative samples of older attributes will define their most important attributes as *positive* and assign their more negative characteristics (less important attributes) to the periphery of the self (Harter & Monsour, 1992). This self-protective strategy has been

defined, normatively, as "beneffectance" by Greenwald (1980); namely, seeing one's positive attributes as central to the self and one's negative attributes as more peripheral.

Our colleagues Fischer and Ayoub (1994) employed our multiple selves procedure with an inpatient sample of seriously abused older adolescent girls, finding just the opposite pattern. Compared to a normative sample, the abused patients identified *negative* attributes as their core self, relegating what few positive characteristics they could identify as peripheral. Herein, we can detect another deleterious effect of abuse on self-processes leading to potential pathological outcomes that require clinical intervention that can hopeful restore a more positive balance of self-perceptions.

STABILITY VERSUS CHANGE IN SELF-REPRESENTATIONS

Initially, it is important to address the question of whether concepts of self, either at a domain-specific or more global level, are immutable or subject to change. If self-representations are relatively stable, then practitioners should be less sanguine about the possibility of promoting positive self-evaluations in individuals with negative self-images. Alternatively, if self-representations are potentially malleable, practitioners can be more optimistic, particularly if there is a cogent analysis of the particular causes of a given individual's negative self-evaluations.

The initial focus in this section is on literature relevant to the actual stability and/or change in the valence of self-representations—how favorably the self is evaluated. A central theme in the literature has been do self-evaluations, notably self-esteem and domain specific self-concepts, change normatively with development? Equally of interest is whether there are individual differences in the extent to which self-evaluations change. Herein is the big debate. Is self-esteem more traitlike or statelike? We return to this controversy after reviewing the normative patterns of self-esteem development (a description of a third issue, do self-evaluations change as function of the situation or short-term intervals, can be found in Harter, 1999).

Normative-Developmental Change

With regard to normative-developmental change, the evidence reveals that self-evaluative judgments become less positive as children move into middle childhood

(Frey & Ruble, 1985, 1990; Harter, 1982; Harter & Pike, 1984; Stipek, 1981). Investigators attribute such a decline to the greater reliance on social comparison information and external feedback, leading to more realistic judgments about one's capabilities (see also Crain, 1996; Marsh, 1989). A growing number of studies suggest that there is another decline at early adolescence (ages 11 to 13), after which global evaluations of worth and domain-specific self-evaluations gradually become more positive over the course of adolescence (Dusek & Flaherty, 1981; Marsh, Parker, & Barnes, 1985; Marsh, Smith, Marsh, & Owens, 1988; O'Malley & Bachman, 1983; Piers & Harris, 1964; Rosenberg, 1986; Savin-Williams & Demo, 1993; Simmons, Rosenberg, & Rosenberg, 1973).

Many of the changes reported coincide with the educational transition to junior high school. Eccles and colleagues (Eccles & Midgley, 1989; Eccles et al., 1984; Wigfield, Eccles, Mac Iver, Reuman, & Midgley, 1991), and Simmons and colleagues (Blyth, Simmons, & Carlton-Ford, 1983; Simmons & Blyth, 1987; Simmons, Blyth, Van Cleave, & Bush, 1979; Simmons & Rosenberg, 1975) have postulated that differences in the school environments of elementary and junior high schools are in part responsible. Junior high school brings more emphasis on social comparison and competition, stricter grading standards, more teacher control, less personal attention from teachers, and disruptions in social networks, all of which lead to a mismatch between the structure of the school environment and the needs of young adolescents. The numerous physical, cognitive, social, and emotional changes further jeopardize the adolescent's sense of continuity, which may, in turn, threaten self-esteem (Leahy & Shirk, 1985). A number of these studies (e.g., Blyth et al., 1983; Nottelmann, 1987; Simmons & Blyth, 1987; Simmons et al., 1979; Wigfield et al., 1991) also report lower self-esteem for girls than for boys (see also Block & Robins, 1993, who find that the gender gap widens from ages 14 to 23).

The magnitude of the decline in perceptions of overall worth is also related to the timing of school shifts and to pubertal change (Brooks-Gunn, 1988; Brooks-Gunn & Peterson, 1983; Simmons & Blyth, 1987). Those making the shift from sixth to seventh grade show greater losses of self-esteem than those who make the school transition a year later, from seventh to eighth grade. Moreover, students making the earlier change, particularly girls, do not recover these losses during the high school years. Early-maturing girls fare the worst.

They are the most dissatisfied with their bodies, in part, because they tend to be somewhat heavier and do not fit the cultural stereotype of female attractiveness emphasizing thinness, as is discussed further in the section on the link between self-esteem and perceived appearance. This, in turn, has a negative effect on their self-worth. Furthermore, according to the developmental readiness hypothesis (Simmons & Blyth, 1987), early maturing girls are not yet emotionally prepared to deal with the social expectations that surround dating or with the greater independence that early maturity often demands (see Lipka, Hurford, & Litten, 1992, for a general discussion of the effects of being "off-time" in one's level of maturational development).

Several interpretations have been offered for the gradual gains in self-esteem that follow from eighth grade through high school (McCarthy & Hoge, 1982). Gains in personal autonomy may provide more opportunity to select performance domains in which one is competent, is consistent with a Jamesian analysis. Increasing freedom may allow more opportunities to select support groups that will provide esteem-enhancing approval, is consistent with the looking glass self-formulation. Increased role-taking ability may also lead teenagers to behave in more socially acceptable ways that garner the acceptance of others. A study by Hart, Fegley, and Brengelman (1993) provides some confirming evidence. In describing their past and present selves, adolescents asserted that with time, they have become more capable, mature, personable, and attractive, describing how they shed undesirable cognitive, emotional, and personality characteristics.

An analysis of changes in mean level of self-worth, however, may mask individual differences in response to educational transitions (see also Block & Robins, 1993). Findings from our own laboratory (see Harter, 1999) on both the transition to junior high school and to college have identified three groups—those whose self-worth increases, decreases, or remains the same. In our own framework, we contend that self-worth leading to an examination of instability or stability as a function of those determinants identified by James (competence in domains of importance) and Cooley (approval from significant others). Results indicate that those whose self-worth increased across educational transitions displayed greater competence in domains of importance and reported more social approval in the new school environment. Students whose self-worth decreased reported both a decline in competence for valued domains and reported less social support after the transition. Students showing no changes in self-worth reported negligible changes in both competence and social support. Demo & Savin-Williams (1992) have also adopted a more idiographic approach, demonstrating that while nearly half of their sample demonstrated stability in their perceptions of overall worth, the remaining subjects manifested varying degrees of instability.

In this literature, there remains controversy, however, among those who claim that self-representations are relatively enduring and those who contend that self-representations are more malleable. One camp of investigators reports evidence that the self-concepts of adults are relatively stable. For example, Swann (1996) provides evidence demonstrating individuals' elaborate and ingenious strategies for self-verification; people go to great lengths to seek information that confirms their self-concept and are highly resistant to information that threatens their view of self (see also Baumeister, 1993; Epstein, 1991; Greenwald, 1980; Rosenberg, 1979). According to Swann, people do not want feedback that may contradict their existing identities. Because such identities provide a psychological blueprint for action, they are the guideposts for how we are to behave. Epstein similarly observes that "people have a vested interest in maintaining the stability of their personal theories of reality, for they are the only systems they have for making sense of their world and guiding their behavior" (p. 97). In Swann's (1996) most recent treatment of this topic, he observes that those with negative self-evaluations are actually ambivalent, in that praise puts them in conflict. Although favorable evaluations would be welcome, they also require unfavorable evaluative feedback, to the extent that such individuals desire verification. He notes that such people are "caught in a crossfire in which the warmth produced by favorable evaluations is chilled by incredulity" (p. 14).

Precisely how this relates to children and adolescents has yet to be determined, given our developmental analysis of normative fluctuations in self-esteem. Just how the adult literature relates to phenomena among younger individuals remains an intriguing issue, all the more so as the field integrates genetic and brain developmental factors. There is a growing consensus that, as James originally suggested, individuals possess both a baseline self-concept and a barometric self-concept (see reviews by Demo & Savin-Williams, 1992; Rosenberg, 1986). Thus, people have a core sense of self that is rel-

atively consistent over time; however, there are also situational variations around this core self-portrait. Others have come to a similar conclusion, postulating that individuals display both trait and state self-esteem (Heatherton & Polivy, 1991; Leary & Downs, 1995). According to some, an individual's baseline sense of self is difficult to alter. Theorists have argued, in the context of hierarchical models of the self, that higher-order schemas, such as global self-worth or esteem, are far more resistant to modification than lower-order, situation-specific constructs (Epstein, 1991; Hattie, 1992). Epstein notes that such higher-order schemas have typically been acquired early in development and are often derived from emotionally significant experiences to which the individual may have little conscious access, making the beliefs difficult to alter.

With regard to the barometric self, adolescence is a time when fluctuations appear to be the more flagrant (Blos, 1962; Demo & Savin-Williams, 1992; Harter, 1990a; Leahy & Shirk, 1985; Rosenberg, 1986). Those of a cognitive-developmental persuasion (e.g., Fischer, 1980; Harter, 1990a; Harter & Monsour, 1992; Higgins, 1991) have attributed these fluctuations to limitation in the ability cognitively to control seemingly contradictory self-attributes (shy versus outgoing), particularly during middle adolescence. Psychoanalytic thinkers (e.g., Blos, 1962; Kohut, 1977) attribute fluctuations to the intense heightened narcissism and self-preoccupation of adolescents whose self-esteem swings from grandiosity to battered self-devaluation. Rosenberg (1986) focuses more on how socialization factors influence the volatility of the self during adolescence. Thus, he observes that the adolescent is preoccupied with what others think of the self but has difficulty divining others' impressions, leading to ambiguity about the self. Moreover, different significant others may have different impressions of the self, creating contradictory feedback. We have recently taken a different perspective, demonstrating that for some adolescents self-esteem remains quite constant across time and context, whereas for others there is considerable variation. We have attempted to investigate the causes, as is discussed in the next section (see also, Harter, 2004).

Individual Differences

Considerable attention has been given to the issue of whether self-esteem is best viewed as a state or trait (see Trzesniewski, Donnellan, & Robins, 2003, for a recent review of this issue). A focus on individual differences in the extent to which self-evaluations are stable or malleable is the primary context in which issues of stability and change in self-evaluations have been examined. Studying adult participants, Kernis and colleagues have examined this issue in its complexity (Greenier, Kernis, & Waschull, 1995; Kernis, 1993; Kernis, Cornell, Sun, Berry, & Harlow, 1993). According to these investigators, there are those whose self-evaluations are more stable and there are those prone to short-term fluctuations in self-esteem. The latter group demonstrate enhanced sensitivity to evaluative events, ego involvement (versus task involvement), preoccupation with self-evaluation, and over reliance on social sources of self-esteem (see also Deci & Ryan, 1987; Rosenberg, 1986). Our own findings indicating greater fluctuations in self-worth for those who consciously endorse a looking glass self-orientation (approval determines self-worth) are consistent with this individual-difference approach (Harter, Stocker, & Robinson, 1996). Moreover, we speculated that the developmental precursors may have involved parenting characterized by inconsistent and/or conditional approval. Greenier et al. (1995) also conjecture that inconsistent as well as controlling feedback will undermine the development of a stable sense of worth (see also Deci & Ryan, 1987, 1995).

Our own position (see Harter, 2004), more consistent with Kernis's, asks whether self-esteem is stable over time for individuals (is it a trait?) or is it subject to fluctuations (more statelike) and therefore the question is false and misguided. We have taken the stance (based on several strands of research) that the construct of self-esteem (or self-worth), in and of itself, is neither a trait nor a state per se (see also DuBois et al., 2002). Rather for *some* individuals self-esteem is stable, whereas for others self-esteem is subject to change. Among adolescents, we have found evidence for this position with regard to self-esteem during the transition to junior high school. As mentioned earlier, some students enhance their self-esteem, others decline in self-esteem, and for a third group self-esteem remains stable. We linked changes versus stability to change or stability in the competence/importance relationship (from James) and to stability or change in social support (from Cooley). Others (see Fenzel, 2002) have related change versus stability in self-worth across transitions to the ability to negotiate the challenges of middle school.

In a second study (Harter, Stocker, & Robinson, 1996) we found that certain adolescents reported virtually no short-term fluctuations in their self esteem over a period of months, whereas others reported great instability, patterns that could be accounted for by their orientation to the approval of others. In a third study (Harter, Waters, & Whitesell, 1998), we found that self-worth varied across relational context (a concept we have labeled "relational self-worth"), with the majority of adolescents reporting different levels of self-worth or esteem depending on whom they were with—father, mother, female peers, or male peers. To summarize, we found that over a relatively long period of time (in the first study) and over short periods of time (in the second study) and across relationship contexts some individuals behaved in a traitlike fashion, whereas others behaved in a statelike fashion. Thus, trait and state attributions lie in individuals, not in the constructs themselves.

Does the conceptualization of self-esteem as neither a trait nor a state cast doubt on the field of personality, which depends on the identification of relatively stable traits? Not necessarily. Many thoughtful investigators are asking just such questions. In a recent study by Hair and Graziano (2003), these investigators examined the stability of self-esteem and the Big Five Personality attributes in a longitudinal study of those moving from middle school to high school. Findings revealed much greater stability over the transition for the personality attributes (Extraversion, Agreeableness, Conscientiousness, Emotional Stability, and Openness to Experience) than for self-esteem, suggesting that the Big Five, as conceptualized, are much more traitlike in nature than is self-esteem, which is amenable to change if its documented causes change, *or* stability if the causes do not change.

GENDER DIFFERENCES IN GLOBAL AND DOMAIN-SPECIFIC SELF-EVALUATIONS

There is now an emerging body of literature that has examined gender differences in subscale scores among older children, adolescents, and college students. For the most part, the findings are quite consistent with regard to a number of gender differences as well as similarities. A major and consistent finding is that females, at every age beginning in middle to late childhood report lower global self-worth than do males. We find this across the life span; however, differences are greatest in middle to late adolescence. An impressive meta-analysis on gender differences in self-esteem by Kling, Hyde, Showers, and Buswell (1999) confirms this finding in that the largest mean effect size favoring boys in the 15- to 18-year-old group. In their meta-analysis these differences are significant, but small and robust across many samples. Interestingly, these differences have not changed in the period between the 1970s and the 1990s despite seeming societal gains for females.

Kling et al. (1999) speculate on several reasons for these gender differences. One potential cause involves the gender role stereotypes that are reinforced in the school setting. Boys are socialized to use dominance, whereas girls are oriented toward shared social activities (see Maccoby, 1990). Girls' influence attempts are more likely to take the form of a polite suggestion, whereas boys are more likely to try to influence others by direct demands (Leaper, 1991). These differing strategies designed to the other present imbalances in mixed-gender interactions in which boys come to ignore the girls' attempt to interact with or influence boys (Maccoby, 1990). Kling et al. conclude that girls' general ability to influence and to gain valuable resources, particularly in unsupervised mixed-gender groups, may make them feel less important and less powerful than boys, which could adversely impact their self-esteem. Maccoby reports that these differences can be observed as early as the preschool years.

Kling et al. (1999) also suggest that different opportunities for athletic participation could also contribute to gender differences in self-esteem. Although Title IX certainly opened more doors for female children and adolescents to participate in sports, more emphasis and status has been given to male athletes and male sports programs. Furthermore, despite greater opportunities for girls, many do not take advantage of the options, fearing it will undermine their femininity. However, studies do show that among males and females who do participate in sports, self-esteem is higher than for those who do not engage in athletics. Our own research still reveals a significant mean difference in perceived athletic ability, favoring males.

J. Crocker and Major's (1989) theoretical model regarding social stigma and self-esteem provides another explanation for the modest gender differences in self-esteem. Stigmatized grounds, in this case females, protect their self-concept by (a) attributing negative feedback they receive to prejudice against members of their group, (b) comparing their own outcomes with members of their own disadvantaged group rather than the advantaged group, and (c) devaluing those domains in which their group does not do well, and, in contrast, valuing those domains in which their group does do well.

Kling et al. (1999) put forth a powerful explanation for gender differences in self-esteem, consistent with our own interpretation on the inextricable link between perceived physical appearance and global self-worth, where correlations range from .66 to .82 across numerous studies. We have argued elsewhere that (Harter, 1999), consistent with Kling's observations, combination of the importance of appearance for females combined with the punishing standards of appearance for females profoundly contributes to their devaluation of their looks. Movies, magazines, and TV all tout the importance of good looks that are impossible to achieve, in part, because many of these looks are due to air-brushing, computer simulation, and the combining of different (the best) body parts from models or movie starts to "achieve the look." Very few ads tout the importance of a physically *fit* female as desirable but rather showcase thinness combined with height and large breasts as the glamour, the ideal of the decade.

Elsewhere, we have depicted gender data across 13 of our own samples from the domains of older children and adolescence where differences are quite marked with girls scoring only at the midpoint of the scale and with boys reporting much higher on both appearance and athletics (Harter, 1999).

Moreover, this pattern has been found to be highly robust across different countries where gender differences for physical appearance and athletic competence are similar in magnitude and highly significant. Thus, in addition to other findings in the United States (see also Hagborg, 1994), the more favorable perceptions of physical appearance and athletic competence by male children and adolescents has been found in other English-speaking countries such as England (Fox, Page, Armstrong, & Kirby, 1994), Australia (Trent, Russell, & Cooney, 1994), and Ireland (Grandlese & Joseph, 1993). The very same pattern has been documented across a range of non-English-speaking countries, including the French-speaking areas of Switzerland (Bolognini, Plancheral, Bettschart, & Halfon, 1996; Pierrehumbert, Plancheral, & Jankech-Caretta, 1987), Italy (Pedrabissi, Santinello, & Scarpazza, 1988), Holland (van Dongen-Melman, Koot, & Verhulst, 1993), China (Meredith, Abbott, & Zheng, 1991; Stigler,

Smith, & Mao, 1985), Japan (Maeda, 1997), and Korea (Rhee, 1993).

The very same gender pattern favoring males on both perceived athletic ability and attractiveness persists at the college level, and the two domains would appear to interact. Our own data reveal that female students feel significantly worse about their appearance ($M - 2.57$) and their athletic competence ($M = 2.67$) than do males (Ms of 2.88 and 3.00, respectively). These same gender differences have been reported in other college samples as well (P. Crocker & Ellsworth, 1990; Klein, O'Bryant, & Hopkins, 1996; McGregor, Mayleben, Buzzanga, Davis, & Becker, 1992).

Interpretations of the gender differences in perceived athletic competence have focused on the fact that, historically, sports have been largely a male domain, with far more opportunities for athletic competition that would allow boys to develop their physical skills. Moreover, male sports figures represent powerful role models that male children and adolescents are eager to emulate. Despite the gains that some females have achieved in entering the world of sports, women athletes have not, for the most part, been viewed as role models for those girls and female adolescents in the mainstream culture.

In the United States, the current female role models are glamorous women who are extremely thin, an image that is not consistent with the muscular, mesomorphic body types of most female athletes. Moreover, images of female attractiveness are very punishing in that they are unattainable by the vast majority of girls and women in the culture. As a result, most females fall far short of these ideals, resulting in the pattern of findings obtained for perceived physical appearance—that females feel particularly inadequate.

The role of adherence to cultural standards of appearance, in consort with pubertal development for adolescent girls extends previous findings (see reviews by Graber, Peterson, & Brooks-Gunn, 1996; Simmons & Blyth, 1987). Early maturing girls, in particular, report lower self-esteem than do those whose pubertal timing is more normative (see Lamb, Jackson, Cassidy, Priest, 1993; William and Currie, 2000). Given the current ideal of thinness for females, early maturing girls must contend with the fact that they are heavier, with larger breasts and wider hips. Because they do not fit the physical mold that the culture dictates, their self-esteem is compromised and they thus acknowledge that they are simply too fat. Their early maturation status also introduces social problems in that they are not psychologically prepared for the sexual advances or taunts that they may received. As Williams and Currie (2000) document, two predictors of self-esteem combine during this period to predict self-esteem: (1) body size ("I'm too fat," whereas many late maturers feel they are too thin) and (2) the perception of how good-looking they are overall.

Moreover, when both genders are considered, evidence indicates that girls and boys experience pubertal changes differently (Graber, Peterson, & Brooks-Gunn, 1996). Boys express greater satisfaction with the changes (e.g., becoming taller, more muscular, and lower voice) changes that signal masculinity (Nolen-Hoeksema & Girus, 1994). In contrast, girls lose their prepubertal body (an image currently valued in our society with regard to thinness) and can be distressed by their new sexual status (Usmiani & Daniluk, 1997; see also Furnham, Badmin, & Sneade, 2002, for links between body dissatisfaction, low self-esteem, and eating-disordered behavior).

Body dissatisfaction becomes critical to the extent that it leads to other mental health concerns such as eating-disordered behavior. There is overwhelming evidence that it is also associated with depression (see reviews by Allgood-Merton, Lewinsohn, & Hops, 1990; Harter, 1999; Marcotte, Fortin, Potvin, & Papillon, 2002; Nolen-Hoeksema & Girgus, 1994; Rosenberg, Schoenback, Schooler, & Rosenberg, 1995; Tobin-Richard, Boxer, Kavrell, & Peterson, 1984). Pollack also reports a strong relationship between body dissatisfaction and depression such that those who perceived themselves to be of normal weight were less depressed than those who thought where were overweight or underweight. In a related study, Furnham and Calnan (1998) presented findings revealing that over two-thirds of adolescent females were dissatisfied with their weight. All females wanted to weigh less. However, males were divided between those (38%) who wanted to gain weight and those (31%) wanted to lose weight. The wish to gain weight was associated with the desire to become more muscular and achieve the masculine ideal of the V-shaped figure.

The playing field has shifted for men in recent years. In former years, males could be judged attractive not only on the basis of their physical features, where they was much more latitude than for females, but by virtue of the fact that they have money, status, or power. (A magazine poll of women just after the Gulf War ended revealed that General Norman Schwartzkopf was judged to be the sexiest man in America.) This observation was made 15 years ago. It is my conjecture, as I look around my world and steep myself in gender literature on appearance and contemporary magazine articles and advertisements that trends are changing rapidly and the bar has been raised for men. Standards of appearance for men have become more important, more salient in our culture as well as more difficult to obtain. Muscles, abs, calves, the V-body shape, and hair (both facial hair and head hair or its absence) all must conform to new and punishing expectations for males, beginning in childhood. Workout centers and plastic surgeons are repeating big benefits but is our culture, when the focus has become so much more on the outer, physical self than on the inner, psychological self?

Returning to the overall pattern of gender differences obtained for both athletic competence and physical appearance, the pattern favoring males is qualified by an examination of particular subgroups of females. For example, in the study of college students by P. Crocker and Ellsworth (1990), the investigators separately examined a subgroup of physical education majors. They found that the females in this group reported significantly higher perceptions of their athletic ability than did the normative sample as a whole. Moreover, among physical education majors, the female students did not differ from the male students. The advantage conferred by the physical education program did not, however, transfer to the domain of physical appearance, where females continued to feel significantly worse about their looks than did males. Marsh and Jackson (1986) report a similar pattern in that female athletes, beginning at the high school level, reported higher physical ability than did nonathletes, although the groups did not differ significantly in their perceptions of their physical appearance.

We have also found across several adolescent samples that gender orientation impacts the perceptions of females in particular. Those females endorsing a feminine orientation (where they identify with feminine sex-role stereotypes but reject masculine attributes) report more negative perceptions of their athletic ability ($M = 2.41$) and their physical appearance ($M = 2.43$) than do androgynous females who endorse both feminine and masculine items ($Ms = 2.92$ and 2.87, respectively). The scores of these androgynous females do not differ significantly from those of either masculine or androgynous males, for whom scores range from 2.92 to 3.18 across the two subscales. Thus, feminine girls are at particular risk for unfavorable evaluations of their physical selves.

To the extent that they view athletics as a male domain, they are likely to avoid sports activities that would allow them to develop physical skills. However, their primarily feminine orientation would appear to lead them to emphasize the importance of physical attractiveness. Attentiveness to this domain may well serve to highlight the difficulty of attaining the impossible standards of beauty that are touted by the culture. As a result, they judge their appearance quite unfavorably relative to the judgments of androgynous females and to both androgynous and masculine males.

Femininity, therefore, will represent a liability in each of these physical domains to the extent that it is not combined with masculine attributes. It should be noted that the feminine girls also reported significantly more negative perceptions of their scholastic competence ($M = 2.80$) compared to their androgynous female peers ($M = 3.14$). Eschewing such masculine attributes as assertiveness and competitiveness, while identifying primarily with such interpersonal attributes as connectedness and concern for others, may divert their attention from academic pursuits. However, such a feminine orientation leads to perceptions of social acceptance and behavioral conduct that are comparable to those of androgynous females, as might be expected given its interpersonal focus.

With regard to gender differences in other domains, at the college level, significant gender differences favoring males have also been found for perceived creativity (Klein et al., 1996; McGregor et al., 1992). In our own data, the gender difference in creativity approaches significance. Thus, while females do not differ from males in their perceptions of either general intellectual ability or scholastic performance, they do judge their creativity to be inferior relative to the ratings of male college students. The gender socialization literature (see Basow, 1992; Beale, 1994; Eagly, Beall, & Sternberg, 2004; Eisenberg, Martin, & Fabes, 1996; Ruble & Martin, 1998) emphasizes that boys receive more encouragement and opportunities for exploration and inventiveness that may, in turn, lead to males' enhanced perceptions of creativity at the college level. (Because the domain of creativity has not been included on the instruments for older children and adolescents, researchers have not yet determined whether there are gender differences at younger ages.)

Across some samples in this country and abroad, gender differences in perceived behavioral conduct favor girls. Two studies at the college level report that females score higher on the morality subscale. However, other studies find no gender differences in conduct or morality. Moreover, when differences are obtained, as in our own samples, they are much smaller in magnitude than the highly consistent gender differences found for athletic competence and physical appearance, favoring males. With regard to global self-worth, studies in this country as well as abroad reveal either no gender differences, or a small but nonsignificant difference, favoring males. Thus, males and females evaluate themselves similarly with regard to their perceptions of overall worth as a person, where scores typically remain around 3.0. In summary, the pattern reveals markedly more favorable self-evaluations for males with regard to perceptions of both athletic prowess and physical attractiveness. At the college level, males also report greater creativity than do females. These differences have been documented across numerous samples and are exacerbated when comparisons are made between feminine girls and males of either androgynous or masculine orientations.

CROSS-CULTURAL COMPARISONS

It has become increasingly common for investigators in other countries to administer self-concept scales, such as our own, to children and adolescents in their own culture. As noted earlier, the finding that males feel better about their athletic competence and physical appearance than do females has been exceedingly consistent across countries. However, there are potential pitfalls in administering measures developed for a given culture to those from other countries. At a minimum, any meaningful interpretation requires that these instruments show comparable psychometric properties. However, attention must also be directed to culturally relevant content, because domains and/or items in a given subscale may need to be tailored to each culture.

Across the studies in non-American countries, the factor pattern itself has been shown to be quite robust. It has been replicated in other English speaking countries, such as Canada (P. Crocker & Ellsworth, 1990) and Australia (Trent, Russell, & Cooney, 1994). It has also been replicated in non-English-speaking samples from Quebec (Boivin, Vitaro, & Gagnon, 1992; Gavin & Herry, 1996), Switzerland (Pierrehumbert et al., 1987), Germany (Asendorpf & van Aken, 1993), Italy (Pedrabissi,

Santinello, & Scarpazza, 1988), Greece (Makris-Botsaris & Robinson, 1991), Japan (Maeda, 1997; Sakurai, 1983), Korea (Rhee, 1993), and China (Stigler et al., 1985). For the most part, the reliabilities have been good to adequate. In certain countries, particular items have attenuated the reliability for a given subscale and have not loaded on their designated factor (although the overall subscale structure has been demonstrated). Some of these item difficulties may reflect translation issues. However, the existence of such items should serve as a red flag that a given instrument may require revisions at the item level to be culturally sensitive to potential differences in how the domains are best defined in a given country.

There are further cautions about the use of our instruments in countries such as China and Japan. For example, Meredith et al. (1991) have reported that only 20 of the 36 items on the Self-Perception Profile for Children factored appropriately. Moreover, in both this Chinese sample as well as the sample studied by Stigler et al. (1985), reliabilities were far from acceptable. The Global Self-Worth subscale was particularly problematic in both studies (alphas of .57 and .54). Lee (C. Lee, personal communication, April 5, 1987) found similar problems with a Chinese American sample and thoughtfully concluded that the concept of global self-worth as defined in the American mainstream culture may not be an appropriate construct to include on an instrument examining meaningful self-perceptions among the Chinese. The Meredith et al. (1991) study reported relatively low reliabilities across all subscales (ranging from .44 to .61) suggesting that there exist items that are inappropriate for each of the domains.

Meredith, Wang, and Zheng (1993) have also argued that there are additional domains of relevance to Chinese children that are not included on our American instruments. As a first step, they added several other possible dimensions and asked Chinese children to rate their importance. Among these additions were items tapping group orientation (e.g., willingness to help others), social conduct (e.g., respect for parental and teacher authority), and social acceptance (e.g., engaging in behaviors such as getting good grades that would meet with peer and adult approval). Such an approach is commendable in that it addresses culturally sensitive issues involving the inclusion of domains that are most relevant for a given culture.

Of further concern is that in Chinese (Stigler et al., 1985), Japanese (Maeda, 1997; Sakurai, 1983), and Korean (Rhee, 1993) samples, the means are considerably lower than are scores in U.S., Canadian, Australian, and European samples. (The domain of social acceptance is perhaps the only exception.) Stigler et al. (1985) offer two possible interpretations for the low scores of his Chinese sample. The first is that the Chinese appear to display a self-effacing style that leads them to be more modest in their report of personal qualities. The second is that our structured alternative format, in which we contrast statements about "Some kids" versus "Other kids," implicitly demands a form of social comparison with others. Stigler and colleagues observe that such social comparison is frowned on in China, where individual differences in competence are downplayed. Thus, Chinese children's unwillingness to report that they may be superior to others leads to a pattern of low scores that may not truly reveal their private perceptions of personal adequacy. These same interpretations may well apply to other Asian countries such as Japan and Korea.

In summary, the use of our instruments would appear to be particularly problematic in Asian cultures where (a) the content of certain items may not be relevant or meaningful, (b) other culturally sensitive content is needed, and (c) response tendencies (e.g., a self-effacing style coupled with an avoidance of social comparison) may require different item content, a different response format, and an instructional set to maximize the report of a true evaluation of one's perceived competencies.

It should be noted that we have never recommended the use of our instruments in other countries, particularly in cultures in which the self may be construed differently, or in which perceptions of self may not be that central to individuals' functioning. Rather, we urge that investigators adopt a more culture-specific perspective, focusing on the very meaning of self-constructs and their potential correlates for a given culture. An emphasis on correlates and consequences of self-perceptions is particularly essential because it is important to address the issue of whether self-judgments do have any predictable impact on other systems (e.g., behavioral or emotional) of interest: Investigators in any country, our own included, need to be clear about the purpose of examining self-perceptions and should attend to their functional role.

The need for such an approach in China is particularly pressing. The intellectual vacuum created by the Cultural Revolution extended to psychology where, for 2 to 3 decades, progress and productivity was effectively halted. This vacuum has exacerbated the current search for methods, measures, and paradigms from Western countries that may be applicable. As I observed at a recent conference in Beijing, many Western psychologists are eager to share their theoretical and methodological wares with their Chinese colleagues. However, in our zeal to be benevolent (or in our less than benevolent quest for fame), we need to guard against imposing frameworks and related instruments that may be inappropriate for a given culture either because they do not adequately tap the construct in question or because the construct may not be that critical to the functioning of individuals in that culture, or both.

ETHNIC DIFFERENCES IN OUR OWN CULTURE

Most of the work on ethnic differences has been comparisons between the self-esteem of African Americans and Europeans in this country. For many years is was merely assumed that Blacks, as they were called at the time, would have lower self-esteem due to their initial status as slaves, their treatment by White society, their status as second-class citizens, and therefore their cultural marginalization. However, with the advent of attention to the Black community by psychologists, using appropriate methodologies, these myths and assumptions were challenged. Two recent, excellent meta-analyses (Gray-Little & Hafdahl, 2000; Twenge & Crocker, 2000) have clearly documented that African Americans in our culture have higher self-esteem than European-Americans, and these and other investigators have developed trenchant analyses of why this might be the case.

The majority of the studies they have reviewed focus on subject populations ranging from late childhood to early adulthood. These analyses indicate few gender differences. However, the studies do suggest an increase in self-esteem as African Americans go through the stages of childhood, adolescence, and young adulthood. The question becomes what are the reasons for what has seemed to be, for some, counterintuitive findings?

Gray-Little and Hafdahl (2000) form two related questions that capture the reader's attention. First, why do Blacks *not* have lower self-esteem? Second, why do they have higher self-esteem compared to Whites? From a Cooley, symbolic-interactionist perspective, which the authors embrace as a social framework on reflected self-appraisals, one needs to ask to whom do Blacks turn as the significant others for feedback about the self? They suggest that Blacks do *not* turn to the larger White society as their reference groups but rather turn to the Black community as their source of support and acceptance; these are the people whose opinions are most important to them. Adhering to these values, accepting them, makes them less vulnerable to their marginalization by the White culture, and allows them to develop a sense of meeting the expectations of their ethnic ingroup, thereby experiencing high self-esteem (as the Jamesian hypothesis would predict).

It is not that the findings indicate that Black self-esteem is equal to that of Whites. Rather, meta-analyses confirm that it is actually higher. Several processes emerge as explanations. For example, social comparison looms large as a factor in impacting an individual's self-esteem. To the extent that Blacks are comparing themselves to other Blacks, rather than White norms for success, this potentially enhances their self-esteem.

A related mechanism suggested by Gray-Little and Hafdahl (2000) is that Blacks engage in a quest for a positive social identity that emphasizes their desirable distinctiveness. To do this means to adopt a Black racial identity, to view your racial heritage as positive, articulated, and meaningful, and that identity is therefore incorporated into your sense of worth as a person.

According to Twenge and Crocker (2002), stigmatization, previously thought to be a potential source of negative self-esteem, has been cast in a new light in these reviews. Developing a positive racial identify may enable racial minorities to attribute negative outcomes to prejudice, to make in-group comparisons, or to use other self-protective mechanisms that membership in a stigmatized group affords. Thus, one devalues the stigmatizing of the majority culture. These authors also point to interesting cohort effects in that the civil rights movement has had an effect. They are quick to point out that there is a time lag in the effects of such movements, approximately 20 years, and they liken this to gains for women given the women's movement. Thus, self-esteem effects in favor of Blacks have increased more recently.

It should be noted that the basic processes underlying self-esteem formation among African Americans appears to be similar to that of White adolescents (see review in Harter, 1990b). Given the notion that an individual incorporates the attitudes of significant others toward the self, the context for self-esteem development in African Americans involves the African American family, peers, and community. Thus, African American children and adolescents internalize the opinions of parents and siblings, as well as African American friends, teachers, and coaches, who serve as their primary social reference groups. Interestingly, the relationship between the attitudes of significant others toward the self and self-esteem has been found to be somewhat stronger among African Americans than among European-Americans (Rosenberg & Simmons, 1972). It has been suggested that the African American community is a source of positive self-concept in African American children and that, under certain conditions, the African American family can filter out destructive racist messages from the White community, supplanting such messages with more positive feedback that will enhance self-esteem (Barnes, 1980).

In keeping with one theme of this chapter, the predictiveness of James's formulation, more recent work (Gray-Little & Hafdahl, 2000) applies such an analysis to the level of self-esteem in African American youth (see also Harter, 1990a). To the extent that African American values differ from those of Whites, different domains will be judged important. For example, there is a stronger correlation between school grades and self-esteem among European Americans than among African Americans, suggesting that the two racial groups may well base their self-esteem on different attributes (Epps, 1975). If we assume that people value those things at which they do well, and try to do well in those domains that they value, we see that African American adolescents may come to value those nonacademic arenas in which they feel they excel and over which they have some control and devalue their negative academic experiences (see Hare, 1985). It has also been suggested (Hunt & Hunt, 1977) that African American male youth, in particular, substitute compensatory values in areas where they can perform more successfully. For example, athletic prowess, musical talent, acting ability, sexuality, and certain antisocial behaviors may become more highly valued than academic performance.

While these theories can be applied to ethnic groups as a whole, it is critical to appreciate the fact that while average levels of self-esteem are somewhat higher among African Americans compared to European Americans there is still tremendous overlap in the distributions, and considerably variability in each group that can also be explained by the theories advanced. We now need to focus on understanding how these processes affect the lives of individual youth, with an eye toward prevention and intervention. Twenge and Crocker (2002) also suggest that we now need to move away from questions about which broad racial groups have higher or lower self-esteem on average and that we need to focus more on questions about individual differences in each culture, including their causes.

More recently, toward this goal, a recent study (Bean, Bush, McKenny, & Wilson, 2003) examined the support offered to African American high school students for academic achievement and global self-esteem. Findings indicated that maternal support and acceptance was significantly related to academic achievement and to adolescent self-esteem (whereas father support was unrelated). They observed that mothers occupy a central role in many African American families including more responsibility for child rearing (see also Collins, 1993). They point out that the mother's role can be seen as especially pivotal because they often take on the instrumental responsibilities and expressive and emotional functions in the family due to the difficulties that African American males have historically encountered in carrying out provider roles (Fine & Schwebel, 1988).

Rowley, Sellers, Chavous, and Smith (1998) provide perhaps a summary statement that can account for many of the more recent findings. They focus on the relationship between *private* racial regard and *personal* self-esteem. Attitudes regarding African Americans were significantly related to the self-esteem of those individuals for whom race plays an important role in defining themselves. Such attitudes were unrelated to self-esteem for those whose race is less central to their definition of self. Thus, African Americans' attitudes about their race are only important to their self-esteem if race is a personally affirmed identity.

CONCLUSIONS

The study of self-development continues to thrive as new theoretical, methodological, and empirical perspectives emerge. There continues to be an interesting marriage between historical formulations about the self, stemming from James (1890), Cooley (1902), Baldwin (1897), and Mead (1934), and more recently Bowlby (1979) and Ainsworth (1979) and many contemporary perspectives that are represented in this chapter. Histor-

ical perspectives have concentrated more heavily on the social construction of the self. More recent treatments have respected this historical perspective, expanding it into how social influences vary depending on the developmental level of the child and the individual differences in the role of caregivers.

Cognitive-developmental differences, at the impetus of neo-Piagetians, have heightened our appreciation for how more subtle and discrete changes in cognitive advances and limitations influence self-development. The I-self has been transmitted into those changing cognitive processes that determine how the Me-self (one's verbalizable sense of self) will necessarily change with age. The field has far more appreciation for how broad stages, previously conceived as childhood and adolescence, must be broken down into the mini-substages in each broad categories of development. With regard to changes in self-development, we have identified three substages in childhood and three substages in adolescence, where self-development makes major leaps in content and organization. Normative cognitive advances and limitations clearly define the self. The contributions of child-rearing practices also make major contributions in terms of the positivity or the negativity of self-evaluations. Genetic advances have also led to speculations about the self.

Two themes have been emphasized: (1) the role of cognitive-development and (2) the role of socializing influences on the self. These clearly lead to normative-developmental trends in self-development. Equally important is how such influences lead to individual differences, particularly in self-evaluations. Thus, major attention has been devoted to theory and empirical findings on such individual differences.

Our explorations need to extend beyond individual differences, to include gender and ethnic differences in our own cultural and cross-cultural considerations. Sensitivity to gender and cultural differences are critical in understanding how the self is constructed. These are the future directions that the study of self-development must take.

REFERENCES

Ainsworth, M. (1979). Infant-mother attachment. *American Psychologist, 34,* 932–937.

Allgood-Merten, B., Lewinsohn, P. M., & Hops, R. (1990). Sex differences and adolescent depression. *Journal of Abnormal Psychology, 99,* 55–63.

Asendorpf, J. B., & van Aken, M. A. G. (1993). Deutsche versionen der Selbstkonzeptskalen von Harter [German versions of Harter's Self-Concept Scales]. *Zeittscrift fur Entwicklungspsychologie und Padagogische Psycholigie, 25,* 64–86.

Baldwin, J. M. (1895). *Social and ethical interpretations in mental development: A study in social psychology.* New York: Macmillan.

Barnes, E. J. (1980). The Black community as a source of positive self-concept for Black children: A theoretical perspective. In R. Jones (Ed.), *Black psychology* (pp. 231–250). New York: Harper & Row.

Barnett, D., Ganiban, J., & Cicchetti, D. (1999). Maltreatment, negative expressivity, and the development of type D attachments from 12 to 24 months of age. *Monographs of the Society for Research in Child Development, 64*(3, Serial No. 258), 97–118.

Bartholomew, K., & Horowitz, L. M. (1991). Attachment styles among young adults: A test of a four-category model. *Journal of Personality and Social Psychology, 61,* 226–244.

Basow, S. A. (1992). *Gender stereotypes and roles* (3rd ed.). Pacific Grove, CA: Brooks/Cole.

Bates, E. (1990). Language about me and you: Pronominal reference and the emerging concept of self. In D. Cicchetti & M. Beeghly (Eds.), *The self in transition: Infancy to childhood* (pp. 1–15). Chicago: University of Chicago Press.

Baumeister, R. F. (1987). How the self became a problem: A psychological review of historical research. *Journal of Personality and Social Psychology, 52,* 90–113.

Baumeister, R. F. (1993). Understanding the inner nature of low self-esteem: Uncertain, fragile, protective, and conflicted. In R. F. Baumeister (Ed.), *Self-esteem, the puzzle of low self-regard* (pp. 201–218). New York: Plenum Press.

Baumeister, R. F., Smart, L., & Boden, J. M. (1996). Relation of threatened egotism to violence and aggression: The dark side of self-esteem. *Psychological Review, 103,* 5–33.

Baumrind, D. (1989). Rearing competent children. In W. Damon (Ed.), *Child development today and tomorrow* (pp. 349–378). San Francisco: Jossey-Bass.

Beale, C. R. (1994). *Boys and girls: The development of gender roles.* New York: McGraw-Hill.

Bean, R. A., Bush, K. R., McKenny, P. C., & Wilson, S. M. (2003). The impact of parental support, behavioral control, and psychological control on the academic achievement and self-esteem of African American and European American Adolescents. *Journal of Adolescent Research, 18,* 523–541.

Beeghly, M., Carlson, V., & Cicchetti, D. (1986, April). *Child maltreatment and the self: The emergence of internal state language in low SES 30-month-olds.* Paper presented at the International Conference on Infant Studies, Beverly Hills, CA.

Beeghly, M., & Cicchetti, D. (1994). Child maltreatment, attachment, and the self-system: Emergence of an internal state lexicon at high social risk. *Development and Psychopathology, 6,* 5–30.

Bem, S. (1985). Androgyny and gender schema theory. In T. B. Sonderegger (Ed.), *Nebraska Symposium on Motivation* (Vol.32, pp. 180–226). Lincoln: University of Nebraska Press.

Berndt, T., & Burgy, L. (1996). The social self-concept. In B. A. Bracken (Ed.), *Handbook of self-concept* (pp. 171–209). New York: Wiley.

Blatt, S. J. (1995). Representational structures in psychopathology. In D. Cicchetti & S. Toth (Eds.), *Rochester Symposium on Developmental Psychology: Vol. 6. Emotion, cognition, and representation* (pp. 1–34). Rochester, NY: University of Rochester Press.

Bleiberg, E. (1984). Narcissistic disorders in children. *Bulletin of the Menninger Clinic, 48,* 501–517.

Block, J. H., & Robins, R. W. (1993). A longitudinal study of consistency and change in self-esteem from early adolescence to early adulthood. *Child Development, 64,* 909–923.

Blos, P. (1962). *On adolescence.* New York: Free Press.

Blyth, D. A., Simmons, R. G., & Carlton-Ford, S. (1983). The adjustment of early adolescents to school transitions. *Journal of Early Adolescence, 3,* 105–120.

Boivin, M., Vitaro, F., & Gagnon, C. (1992). A reassessment of the self-perception profile for children: Factor structure, reliability, and convergent validity of a French version among second through sixth grade children. *International Journal of Behavioral Development, 15,* 275–290.

Bolognini, M., Plancheral, B., Bettschart, W., & Halfon, O. (1996). Self-esteem and mental health in early adolescence: Developmental and gender differences. *Journal of Adolescence, 233–245.*

Bowlby, J. (1969). *Attachment and loss: Vol. 1. Attachment.* New York: Basic Books.

Bowlby, J. (1973). *Attachment and loss: Vol. 2. Separation.* New York: Basic Books.

Bowlby, J. (1980). *Attachment and loss: Vol. 3. Loss, sadness, and depression.* New York: Basic Books.

Bracken, B. (1996). Clinical applications of a context-dependent multi-dimensional model of self-concept. In B. Bracken (Ed.), *Handbook of self-concept* (pp. 463–505). New York: Wiley.

Bretherton, I. (1987). New perspectives on attachment relations: Security, communication, and internal working models. In J. D. Osofsky (Ed.), *Handbook of infant development* (2nd ed., pp. 1061–1101). New York: Wiley.

Bretherton, I. (1991). Pouring new wine into old bottles: The social self as internal working model. In M. R. Gunnar & L. A. Sroufe (Eds.), *Minnesota Symposia on Child Development: Vol. 23. Self processes and development* (pp. 1–41). Hillsdale, NJ: Erlbaum.

Bretherton, I. (1993). From dialogue to internal working models: The co-construction of self in relationships. In C. A. Nelson (Ed.), *Minnesota Symposia on Child Psychology: Vol. 26. Memory and affect* (pp. 237–363). Hillsdale, NJ: Erlbaum.

Bretherton, I., & Beeghly, M. (1982). Talking about internal states: The acquisition of an explicit theory of mind. *Developmental Psychology, 18,* 906–921.

Bretherton, I., & Munholland, K. A. (1999). Internal working models in attachment relationships. In J. Cassidy & P. Shaver (Eds.), *Handbook of attachment* (pp. 89–111). New York: Guilford Press.

Briere, J. (1989). *Therapy for adults molested as children.* New York: Springer.

Briere, J. (1992). *Child abuse trauma: Theory and treatment of the lasting effects.* Newbury Park, CA: Sage.

Brim, O. B. (1976). Life span development of the theory of oneself: Implications for child development. In H. W. Reese (Ed.), *Advances in child development and behavior* (Vol. 11, pp. 82–103). New York: Academic Press.

Brooks-Gunn, J. (1988). Antecedents and consequences of variations in girls' maturational timing. *Journal of Adolescent Health Care, 9,* 365–373.

Brooks-Gunn, J., & Peterson, A. (1983). *Girls at puberty: Biological and psychological perspectives.* New York: Plenum Press.

Broughton, J. (1978). The development of the concepts of self, mind, reality, and knowledge. In W. Damon (Ed.), *Social cognition* (pp. 75–100). San Francisco: Jossey-Bass.

Brown, B. B. (1990). Peer groups and peer cultures. In S. S. Feldman & G. Elliot (Eds.), *At the threshold: The developing adolescent* (pp. 171–196). Cambridge, MA: Harvard University Press.

Bruner, J. (1990). *Acts of meaning.* Cambridge, MA: Harvard University Press.

Budwig, N. (2000). Language and the construction of self. In N. Budwig & I. Uzgiris (Eds.), *Advances in applied developmental psychology* (pp. 83–112). Westport, CT: Ablex.

Bugental, D. B., & Goodnow, J. J. (1998). Socialization Processes. In W. Damon (Editor-in-Chief) & N. Eisenberg (Vol. Ed.), *Handbook of child psychology: Vol. 3. Social, emotional, and personality development* (5th ed., pp. 389–462). New York: Wiley.

Carlson, V., Cicchetti, D., & Barnett, D. (1989). Disorganized/disoriented attachment relationships in maltreated infants. *Developmental Psychology, 25,* 525–531.

Carroll, J. J., & Steward, M. S. (1984). The role of cognitive development in children's understandings of their own feelings. *Child Development, 55,* 1486–1492.

Case, R. (1985). *Intellectual development: Birth to adulthood.* New York: Academic Press.

Case, R. (1992). *The mind's staircase.* Hillsdale, NJ: Erlbaum.

Cassidy, J. (1988). Child-mother attachment and the self in 6-year-olds. *Child Development, 59,* 121–134.

Cassidy, J. (1990). Theoretical and methodological considerations in the study of attachment and the self in young children. In M. T. Greeberg, D. Cicchetti, & E. M. Cummings (Eds.), *Attachment in the preschool years: Theory, research, and intervention* (pp. 87–120). Chicago: University of Chicago Press.

Cassidy, J., & Kobak, R. R. (1988). Avoidance and its relationship to other defensive processes. In J. Belsky & T. Nezworski (Eds.), *Clinical implications of attachment* (pp. 300–326). Hillsdale, NJ: Erlbaum.

Cassidy, J., & Shaver, P. R. (Eds.). (1999). *Handbook of attachment.* New York: Guilford Press.

Chodorow, N. (1989). *Feminism and psychoanalytic theory.* New Haven, CT: Yale University Press.

Cicchetti, D. (1989). How research on child maltreatment has informed the study of child development: Perspectives from developmental psychology. In D. Cicchetti & V. Carlson (Eds.), *Child maltreatment: Theory and research on the causes and consequences of child abuse and neglect* (pp. 309–350). New York: Cambridge University Press.

Cicchetti, D. (1993). Developmental psychopathology: Reactions, reflects, and projections. *Developmental Review, 13,* 471–502.

Cicchetti, D. (2004). An odyssey of discovery: Lessons learned through 3 decades of research on child maltreatment. *American Psychologist, 59,* 728–741.

Cicchetti, D., & Beeghly, M. (1990). *The self in transition: Infancy to childhood.* Chicago: University of Chicago Press.

Cicchetti, D., Beeghly, M., Carlson, V., & Toth, S. (1990). The emergence of the self in atypical populations. In D. Cicchetti & M. Beeghly (Eds.), *The self in transition: Infancy to childhood* (pp. 309–344). Chicago: University of Chicago Press.

Cicchetti, D., & Cohen, D. J. (1995). Perspectives in developmental psychopathology. In D. Cicchetti & D. J. Cohen (Eds.), *Developmental psychopathology: Vol. 1. Theory and methods* (pp. 3–22). New York: Wiley.

Cicchetti, D., & Rogosch, F. A. (1996). Equifinality and multifinality in developmental psychopathology. *Developmental and Psychopathology, 8,* 597–600.

Cicchetti, D., & Rogosch, F. A. (2001). Diverse patterns of neurendocrine activity in maltreated children. *Development and Psychopathology, 13,* 677–694.

Collins, M. (1993). School social context, self-esteem, and locus-of-control among White, Black, and Hispanic youth (Doctoral dissertation, University of Maryland, College Park). *Dissertation Abstracts International, 54,* 692–693.

Cooley, C. H. (1902). *Human nature and the social order.* New York: Charles Scribner & Sons.

Cooper, C. R., Grotevant, H. D., & Condon, S. M. (1983). Individuality and connectedness both foster adolescent identity formation and role taking skills. In H. D. Grotevant & C. R. Cooper (Eds.), *Adolescent development in the family: New directions for child development* (pp. 43–59). San Francisco: Jossey-Bass.

Cooper, C. R., Jackson, J. F., Azmitia, M., Lopez, E., & Dunbar, N. (1995). Bridging students' multiple worlds: African American and Latino youth in academic outreach programs. In R. F. Marcias & R. G. Garcia-Ramos (Eds.), *Changing schools changing students: An anthology of research on language minorities* (pp. 211–234). Santa Barbara: University of California Linguistic Minority Research Institute.

Coopersmith, S. A. (1967). *The antecedents of self-esteem.* San Francisco: Freeman.

Coster, W. J., Gersten, M. S., Beeghly, M., & Cicchetti, D. (1989). Communicative functioning in maltreated toddlers. *Developmental Psychology, 25,* 1020–1029.

Crain, R. M. (1996). The influences of age, race, and gender on child and adolescent multi-dimensional self-concept. In B. A. Bracken (Ed.), *Handbook of self-concept* (pp. 395–420). New York: Wiley.

Crittenden, P. M. (1988). Relationships at risk. In J. Belsky & T. Nezworski (Eds.), *Clinical implications of attachment* (pp. 136–174). Hillsdale, NJ: Erlbaum.

Crittenden, P. M. (1990). Internal representational models of attachment relationships. *Infant Mental Health Journal, 11,* 259–277.

Crittenden, P. M. (1994). Peering into the black box: An exploratory treatise on the development of self in young children. In D. Cicchetti & S. L. Toth (Eds.), *Rochester Symposium on Developmental Psychopathology: Vol. 5. Disorders and dysfunctions of the self* (pp. 79–148). Rochester, NY: University of Rochester Press.

Crittenden, P. M., & Ainsworth, M. D. S. (1989). Child maltreatment and attachment theory. In D. Cicchetti & V. Carlson (Eds.), *Theory and research on the causes and consequences of child abuse and neglect* (pp. 432–463). New York: Cambridge University Press.

Crocker, J., & Major, B. (1989). Social stigma and self-esteem: The self-protective properties of stigma. *Psychological Review, 96,* 608–630.

Crocker, P. R. E., & Ellsworth, J. P. (1990). Perceptions of competence in physical education students. *Canadian Journal of Sports Science, 15,* 262–266.

Damon, W., & Hart, D. (1988). *Self-understanding in childhood and adolescence.* New York: Cambridge University Press.

Deci, E. L., & Ryan, R. M. (1987). The support of autonomy and the control of behavior. *Journal of Personality and Social Psychology, 53,* 1024–1037.

Deci, E. L., & Ryan, R. M. (1995). Human autonomy: The basis for true-self-esteem. In M. Kernis (Ed.), *Efficacy, agency, and self-esteem* (pp. 31–46). New York: Plenum Press.

Demo, D. H., & Savin-Williams, R. C. (1992). Self-concept stability and change during adolescence. In R. P. Lipka & T. M. Brinthaupt

(Eds.), *Self-perspectives across the life span* (pp. 116–150). Albany: State University of New York Press.

Dickstein, E. (1977). Self and self-esteem: Theoretical foundations and their implications for research. *Human Development, 20,* 129–140.

Donaldson, S. K., & Westerman, M. A. (1986). Development of children's understandings of ambivalence and causal theories of emotion. *Developmental Psychology, 22,* 655–662.

DuBois, D. L., Reach, K., Tevendale, H., & Valentine, J. (2001, April). *Self-esteem in early adolescents: Trait, state, or both?* Paper presented at the biennial meeting of the Society for Research in Child Development, New Orleans, LA.

Dunn, J. (1988). *The beginnings of social understanding.* Cambridge, MA: Harvard University Press.

Dunn, J., Brown, J., & Beardsall, L. (1991). Family talk about feeling states and children's later understanding of others' emotions. *Developmental Psychology, 27,* 445–448.

Dusek, J. B., & Flaherty, J. (1981). The development of the self during the adolescent years. *Monograph of the Society for Research in Child Development, 46*(Whole No. 191), 1–61.

Eagley, A. H., Beall, A. E., & Sternberg, R. J. (2004). *The psychology of gender* (2nd ed.). New York: Guilford Press.

Eccles, J. P., & Midgley, C. (1989). State/environment fit: Developmentally appropriate classrooms for early adolescents. In R. Ames & C. Ames (Eds.), *Research on motivation in education* (Vol. 3, pp. 139–181). New York: Academic Press.

Eccles, J. S., Midgley, C., & Adler, T. (1984). Grade-related changes in the school environment: Effects on achievement motivation. In J. G. Nicholls (Ed.), *The development of achievement motivation* (pp. 282–331). Greenwich, CT: JSI Press.

Eichenbaum, L., & Orbach, S. (1993). *Understanding women: A feminist psychoanalytic approach.* New York: Basic Books.

Eisenberg, A. (1985). Learning to describe past experiences in conversations. *Discourse Processes, 8,* 177–204.

Eisenberg, N., Martin, C. L., & Fabes, R. A. (1996). Gender development and gender effects. In D. C. Berliner & R. C. Calfee (Eds.), *Handbook of educational psychology* (pp. 358–396). New York: Simon & Schuster/Macmillan.

Elkind, D. (1967). Egocentrism in adolescence. *Child Development, 38,* 1025–1034.

Engel, M. (1959). The stability of the self-concept in adolescence. *Journal of Abnormal and Social Psychology, 58,* 211–217.

Epps, E. G. (1975). Impact of school desegregation on aspirations, self-concepts, and other aspects of personality. *Law and Contemporary Problems, 39,* 300–313.

Epstein, S. (1973). The self-concept revisited or a theory of a theory. *American Psychologist, 28,* 405–416.

Epstein, S. (1981). The unity principle versus the reality and pleasure principles, or the tale of the scorpion and the frog. In M. D. Lynch, A. A. Norem-Hebeisen, & K. Gergen (Eds.), *Self-concept: Advances in theory and research* (pp. 82–110). Cambridge, MA: Ballinger.

Epstein, S. (1991). Cognitive-experiential self-theory: Implications for developmental psychology. In M. Gunnar & L. A. Sroufe (Eds.), *Minnesota Symposium on Child Development: Vol. 23. Self-processes and development* (pp. 111–137). Hillsdale, NJ: Erlbaum.

Erickson, M. F., Egeland, B., & Pianta, R. (1989). The effects of maltreatment on the development of young children. In D. Cicchetti & V. Carlson (Eds.), *Child maltreatment: Theory and research on the causes and consequences of child abuse and neglect* (pp. 647–684). New York: Cambridge University Press.

Erikson, E. H. (1959). Identity and the life cycle. *Psychological Issues, 1,* 18–164.

Erikson, E. H. (1968). *Identity, youth, and crisis.* New York: Norton.

Fasig, L. G. (2000). Toddler's understanding of ownership: Implications for self-concept development. *Social Development, 9,* 370–382.

Feiring, C., & Taska, L. S. (1996). Family self-concept: Ideas on its meaning. In B. Bracken (Ed.), *Handbook of self-concept* (pp. 317–373). New York: Wiley.

Fenzel, L. M. (2002). Prospective study of changes in global self-worth and strain during the transition to middle school. *Journal of Early Adsolescence, 20,* 93–116.

Fine, M. A., & Schwebel, A. (1988). An emergent explanation of differing racial reactions to single parenthood. *Journal of Divorce, 12,* 175.

Fischer, K. W. (1980). A theory of cognitive development: The control and construction of hierarchies of skills. *Psychological Review, 87,* 477–531.

Fischer, K. W., & Ayoub, C. (1994). Affective splitting and dissociation in normal and maltreated children: Developmental pathways for self in relationships. In D. Cicchetti & S. Toth (Eds.), *Rochester Symposium on Developmental Psychopathology: Vol. 5. Disorders and dysfunctions of the self* (pp. 149–222). Rochester, NY: University of Rochester Press.

Fischer, K. W., & Canfield, R. (1986). The ambiguity of stage and structure in behavior: Person and environment in the development of psychological structure. In I. Levin (Ed.), *Stage and structure: Reopening the debate* (pp. 246–267). New York: Plenum Press.

Fischer, K. W., Hand, H. H., Watson, M. W., Van Parys, M., & Tucker, J. (1984). Putting the child into socialization: The development of social categories in preschool children. In L. Katz (Ed.), *Current topics in early childhood education* (Vol. 5, pp. 27–72). Norwood, NJ: Ablex.

Fischer, K. W., Shaver, P., & Carnochan, P. (1990). How emotions develop and how they organize development. *Cognition and Emotion, 4,* 81–127.

Fivush, R. (1987). Scripts and categories: Inter-relationships in development. In U. Neisser (Ed.), *Concepts and conceptual development: Ecological and intellectual factors in categorization* (pp. 223–248). Cambridge, England: Cambridge University Press.

Fivush, R., Gray, J. T., & Fromhoff, F. A. (1987). Two-year-olds talk about the past. *Cognitive Development, 2,* 393–409.

Fivush, R., & Hamond, N. R. (1990). Autobiographical memory across the preschool years: Toward reconceptualizing childhood amnesia. In R. Fivush & A. Hudson (Eds.), *Knowing and remembering in young children* (pp. 223–248). New York: Cambridge University Press.

Fivush, R., & Hudson, J. A. (Eds.). (1990). *Knowing and remembering in young children.* New York: Cambridge University Press.

Flavell, J. H. (1985). *Cognitive development* (2nd ed.). Englewood Cliffs, NJ: Prentice-Hall.

Fonagy, P. (2002). Understanding of mental states, mother-infant interaction, and the development of the self. In J. Martin Maldonado-Duran (Ed.), *Infant and toddler mental health: Models of clinical intervention with infants and their families* (pp. 58–72). Washington, DC: American Psychiatric Publishing.

Fox, K., Page, A., Armstrong, N., & Kirby, B. (1994). Dietary restraint and self-perceptions in early adolescence. *Personality and Individual Differences, 17,* 87–96.

Freud, A. (1965). *Normality and pathology in childhood.* New York: International Universities Press.

Freud, S. (1952). *A general introduction to psychoanalysis.* New York: Washington Square Press.

Frey, K. S., & Ruble, D. N. (1985). What children say when the teacher is not around: Conflicting goals in social comparison and performance assessment in the classroom. *Journal of Personality and Social Psychology, 48,* 550–562.

Frey, K. S., & Ruble, D. N. (1990). Strategies for comparative evaluation: Maintaining a sense of competence across the life span. In R. J. Sternberg & J. Kolligian Jr. (Eds.), *Competence considered* (pp. 167–189). New Haven, CT: Yale University Press.

Furnham, A., Badmin, N., & Sneade, I. (2002). Body image dissatisfaction: Gender differences in eating attitudes, self-esteem, and reasons for exercise. *Journal of Psychology, 136,* 581–596.

Furnham, A., & Calnan, A. (1998). Eating disturbance, self-esteem, reasons for exercising, and body weight dissatisfaction in adolescent males. *European Eating Disorders Review, 6,* 58–72.

Gavin, D. A., & Herry, Y. (1996). The French self-perception profile for children: Score validity and reliability. *Educational and Psychological Measurement, 56,* 678–700.

Gecas, V. (1972). Parental behavior and contextual variations in adolescent self-esteem. *Sociometry, 36,* 332–345.

Gergen, K. J. (1968). Personal consistency and the presentation of self. In C. Gordon & J. Gergen (Eds.), *The self in social interaction* (pp. 299–308). New York: Wiley.

Gilligan, C. (1982). *In a different voice: Psychological theory and women's development.* Cambridge, MA: Harvard University Press.

Gilligan, C., Lyons, N., & Hanmer, T. J. (1989). *Making connections.* Cambridge, MA: Harvard University Press.

Glick, M., & Zigler, E. (1985). Self-image: A cognitive-developmental approach. In R. Leahy (Ed.), *The development of the self* (pp. 1–54). New York: Academy Press.

Gnepp, J., McKee, E., & Domanic, J. A. (1987). Children's use of situational information to infer emotion: Understanding emotionally equivocal situations. *Developmental Psychology, 23,* 114–123.

Graber, J. A., Peterson, A. C., & Brooks-Gunn, J. (1996). Pubertal processes: Methods, measures, and models. In J. A. Graber (Ed.), *Transitions through adolescence: Interpersonal domains and context* (pp. 23–53). Mahwah, NJ: Erlbaum.

Gralinski, J., Feshbach, N. D., Powell, C., & Derrington, T. (1993, April). *Self-understanding: Meaning and measurement of maltreated children's sense of self.* Paper presented at the meeting of the Society for Research in Child Development, New Orleans, LA.

Grandlese, J., & Joseph, S. (1993). Factor analysis of the self-perception profile for children. *Personality and Individual Differences, 15,* 343–345.

Gray-Little, B., & Hafdahl, A. R. (2000). Factors influencing racial comparisons of self-esteem: A quantitative review. *Psychological Bulletin, 126,* 26–54.

Greenier, K. D., Kernis, M. H., & Waschull, S. B. (1995). Not all high or low self-esteem people are the same: Theory and research on stability of self-esteem. In M. H. Kernis (Ed.), *Efficacy, agency, and self-esteem* (pp. 51–68). New York: Plenum Press.

Greenwald, A. G. (1980). The totalitarian ego: Fabrication and revision of personal history. *American Psychologist, 7,* 603–618.

Griffin, N., Chassin, L., & Young, R. D. (1981). Measurement of global self-concept versus multiple role specific self-concepts in adolescents. *Adolescence, 16,* 49–56.

Griffin, S. (1992). Structural analysis of the development of their inner world: A neo-structured analysis of the development of intrapersonal intelligence. In R. Case (Ed.), *The mind's staircase* (pp. 189–206). Hillsdale, NJ: Erlbaum.

Grotevant, H. D., & Cooper, C. R. (1986). Individuation in family relationships. *Human Development, 29,* 83–100.

Hagborn, W. J. (1994). The Rosenberg Self-Esteem Scale and Harter's self-perception profile for adolescents: A concurrent validity study. *Psychology in the Schools, 30,* 132–136.

Hair, E. C., & Graziano, W. G. (2003). Self-esteem and personality in high school students: A prospective longitudinal study in Texas. *Journal of Personality, 71,* 971–994.

Hare, B. R. (1985). Stability and change in self-perception and achievement among Black adolescents: A longitudinal study. *Journal of Black Psychology, 11,* 29–42.

Harris, J. R. (1998). *The nurture assumption: Why children turn out the way they do—Parents matter less than you think.* New York: Free Press.

Harris, P. L. (1983). What children know about the situations that provoke emotion. In M. Lewis & C. Saarni (Eds.), *The socialization of affect* (pp. 162–185). New York: Plenum Press.

Harris, P. L., Olthof, T., & Meerum-Terwogt, M. (1981). Children's knowledge of emotion. *Journal of Experimental Child Psychology, 36,* 490–509.

Hart, D. (1988). The adolescent self-concept in social context. In D. K. Lapsley & F. C. Power (Eds.), *Self, ego, and identity* (pp. 71–90). New York: Springer-Verlag.

Hart, D., Fegley, S., & Brengelman, D. (1993). Perceptions of past, present and future selves among children and adolescence. *British Journal of Developmental Psychology, 11,* 265–282.

Harter, S. (1982). The perceived competence scale for children. *Child Development, 53,* 87–97.

Harter, S. (1988). Developmental and dynamic changes in the nature of the self-concept: Implications for child psychotherapy. In S. Shirk (Ed.), *Cognitive development and child psychotherapy* (pp. 119–160). New York: Plenum.

Harter, S. (1983). Developmental perspectives on the self-system. In P. Mussen & E. M. Hetherington (Eds.), *Handbook of child psychology: Vol. 4. Socialization, personality, and social development* (4th ed., pp. 275–385). New York: Wiley.

Harter, S. (1985). *The self-perception profile for children.* Unpublished manual, University of Denver, CO.

Harter, S. (1986a). Cognitive-developmental processes in the integration of concepts about emotions and the self. *Social Cognition, 4,* 119–151.

Harter, S. (1986b). Processes underlying the construction, maintenance, and enhancement of the self-concept in children. In J. Suls & A. G. Greenwald (Eds.), *Psychological perspectives on the self* (Vol. 3, pp. 137–181). Hillsdale, NJ: Erlbaum.

Harter, S. (1990a). Adolescent self and identity development. In S. S. Feldman & G. R. Elliot (Eds.), *At the threshold: The developing adolescent* (pp. 352–387). Cambridge, MA: Harvard University Press.

Harter, S. (1990b). Causes, correlates and the functional role of global self-worth: A life-span perspective. In R. Sternberg & J.

Kolligian Jr. (Eds.), *Competence considered* (pp. 67–98). New Haven, CT: Yale University Press.

Harter, S. (1996). Teacher and classmate influences on scholastic motivation, self-esteem, and choice. In K. Wentzel & J. Juvonen (Eds.), *Social motivation: Understanding children's school adjustment* (pp. 11–42). Cambridge, England: Cambridge University Press.

Harter, S. (1997). The personal self in social context: Barriers to authenticity. In R. D. Ashmore & L. Jussim (Eds.), *Self and identity: Fundamental issues* (pp. 81–105). New York: Oxford University Press.

Harter, S. (1998a). The development of self-representations. In W. Damon (Editor-in-Chief) & N. Eisenberg (Vol. Ed.), *Handbook of child psychology: Vol. 3. Social, emotional, and personality development* (5th ed., pp. 553–617). New York: Wiley.

Harter, S. (1998b). The effects of child abuse on the self-system. In B. B. Rossman & M. S. Rosenberg (Eds.), *Multiple victimization of children: Conceptual, developmental, research, and treatment issues* (pp. 147–170). New York: Haworth Press.

Harter, S. (1999). *The construction of the self.* New York: Guilford Press.

Harter, S. (2004). The developmental emergence of self-esteem: Individual differences in change and stability. In D. Mroczek & T. Little (Eds.), *The handbook of personality* (pp. 44–59). New York: Erlbaum.

Harter, S., Bresnick, S., Bouchey, H. A., & Whitesell, N. R. (1997). The development of multiple role-related selves during adolescence. *Development and Psychopathology, 9,* 835–854.

Harter, S., & Buddin, B. J. (1987). Children's understanding of the simultaneity of two emotions: A five-stage developmental acquisition sequence. *Developmental Psychology, 23,* 388–399.

Harter, S., Kiang, L., Whitesell, N. R., & Anderson, A. V. (2003, April). *A prototype approach to the emotion of humiliation in college students.* Poster presented at the biennial meeting of the Society for Research in Child Development, Tampa, FL.

Harter, S., Low, S., & Whitesell, N. R. (2003). What have we learned from Columbine: The impact of the self-system on suicidal and violent ideation among adolescents. *Journal of Youth Violence, 2,* 3–26.

Harter, S., Marold, D. B., Whitesell, N. R., & Cobbs, G. (1996). A model of the effects of parent and peer support on adolescent false self behavior. *Child Development, 55,* 1969–1982.

Harter, S., & McCarley, K. (2004, April). *Is there a dark side to high self-esteem leading to adolescent violence?* Poster presented at the American Psychological Association Convention, Honolulu, HI.

Harter, S., & Monsour, A. (1992). Developmental analysis of conflict caused by opposing attributes in the adolescent self-portrait. *Developmental Psychology, 28,* 251–260.

Harter, S., & Pike, R. (1984). The pictorial scale of perceived competence and social acceptance for young children. *Child Development, 55,* 1969–1982.

Harter, S., Stocker, C., & Robinson, N. S. (1996). The perceived directionality of the link between approval and self-worth: The liabilities of a looking glass self orientation among young adolescents. *Journal of Research on Adolescence, 6,* 285–308.

Harter, S., Waters, P., & Whitesell, N. R. (1998). Relational self-worth: Differences in perceived worth a person across interpersonal contexts. *Child Development, 69,* 756–766.

Harter, S., & Whitesell, N. R. (1989). Developmental changes in children's understanding of single, multiple and blended emotion concepts. In C. Saarni & P. L. Harris (Eds.), *Children's understanding of emotion* (pp. 81–116). Cambridge, England: Cambridge University Press.

Hatfield, E., & Sprecher, S. (1986). *Mirror, mirror. . . . The importance of appearance in everyday life.* New York: State University of New York Press.

Hattie, J. (1992). *Self-concept.* Hillsdale, NJ: Erlbaum.

Hattie, J., & Marsh, H. W. (1996). Theoretical perspectives on the structure of self-concept. In B. A. Bracken (Ed.), *Handbook of self-concept* (pp. 38–90). New York: Wiley.

Hayne, H. (2004). Infant memory development: Implications for childhood amnesia. *Developmental Review, 24,* 33–73.

Heatherton, T. F., & Polivy, J. (1991). Development and validation of a scale for measuring state self-esteem. *Journal of Personality and Social Psychology, 60,* 895–910.

Herman, J. (1992). *Trauma and recovery.* New York: Basic Books.

Higgins, E. T. (1991). Development of self-regulatory and self-evaluative processes: Costs, benefits, and tradeoffs. In M. R. Gunnar & L. A. Sroufe (Eds.), *Minnesota Symposia on Child Development: Vol. 23. Self processes and development* (pp. 125–166). Hillsdale, NJ: Erlbaum.

Higgins, E. T., & Bargh, J. A. (1987). Social cognition and social perception. *Annual Review of Psychology, 38,* 369–425.

Hill, J. P., & Holmbeck, G. N. (1986). Attachment and autonomy during adolescence. In G. J. Whitehurst (Ed.), *Annals of child development* (Vol. 3, pp. 145–189). Greenwhich, CT: JAI Press.

Howe, M. L. (2003). Memories from the cradle. *Current Directions in Psychological Science, 12,* 62–65.

Howe, M. L., & Courage, M. L. (1993). On resolving the enigma of infantile amnesia. *Psychological Bulletin, 113,* 305–326.

Hudson, J. A. (1990a). Constructive processes in children's autobiographical memory. *Developmental Psychology, 26,* 180–187.

Hudson, J. A. (1990b). The emergence of autobiographical memory in mother-child conversation. In R. Fivush & J. A. Hudson (Eds.), *Knowing and remembering in young children* (pp. 166–196). New York: Cambridge University Press.

Hunt, J. G., & Hunt, L. L. (1977). Racial inequality and self-image: Identify maintenance as identity diffusion. *Sociology and Social Research, 61,* 539–559.

Hur, Y., McGue, M., & Iacono, W. G. (1998). The structure of self-concept in female preadolescent twins: A behavior genetic approach. *Journal of Personality and Social Psychology, 74,* 1069–1077.

James, W. (1890). *Principles of psychology.* Chicago: Encyclopedia Britannica.

James, W. (1892). *Psychology: The briefer course.* New York: Henry Holt.

Jordan, J. V. (1991). The relational self: A new perspective for understanding women's development. In J. Strauss & G. Goethals (Eds.), *The self: Interdisciplinary approaches* (pp. 136–149). New York: Springer-Verlag.

Kagan, J. (1984). *The nature of the child.* New York: Basic Books.

Keating, D. P. (1990). Adolescent thinking. In S. S. Feldman & G. Elliot (Eds.), *At the threshold: The developing adolescent* (pp. 54–90). Cambridge, MA: Harvard University Press.

Kelly, G. A. (1955). *The psychology of personal constructs.* New York: Norton.

Kennedy, B. (1994). *The development of self-understanding in adolescence.* Unpublished doctoral dissertation, Harvard University, Cambridge, MA.

Kernberg, O. F. (1975). *Borderline conditions and pathological narcissism.* New York: Aronson.

Kernis, M. H. (1993). The roles of stability and level of self-esteem in psychological functioning. In R. F. Baumeister (Ed.), *Self-esteem: The puzzle of low self-regard* (pp. 167–180). New York: Plenum Press.

Kernis, M. H., Cornell, D. P., Sun, C., Berry, A., & Harlow, T. (1993). There's more to self-esteem than whether it is high or low: The importance of stability of self-esteem. *Journal of Personality and Social Psychology, 65,* 1190–1204.

Kiang, L., & Harter, S. (2004). *Socialcultural values or appearance and attachment processes: An integrated model of eating disorder symptomatology.* Manuscript submitted for publication.

Kihlstrom, J. F. (1993). What does the self look like. In T. K. Srull & R. S. Wyer Jr. (Eds.), *The mental representation of trait and autobiographical knowledge about the self: Vol. 5. Advances in social cognition* (pp. 79–90). New York: Academic Press.

Kilbourne, J. (1994). Still killing us softly: Advertising and the obsession with thinness. In P. Fallon, M. Katzman, & S. Wooley (Eds.), *Feminist perspectives on eating disorders* (pp. 395–418). New York: Guilford Press.

Klein, H. A., O'Bryant, K., & Hopkins, H. R. (1996). Recalled parental authority style and self-perception in college men and women. *Journal of Genetic Psychology, 157,* 5–17.

Kling, K. C., Hyde, J. S., Showers, C. J., & Buswell, B. N. (1999). Gender differences in self-esteem: A meta-analysis. *Psychological Bulletin, 125,* 470–500.

Kohut, H. (1977). *The restoration of the self.* New York: International Universities Press.

Lamb, C. S., Jackson, L., Cassidy, P., & Priest, D. (1993). Body figure preferences of men and women: A comparison of two generations. *Gender Roles, 28,* 345–358.

Lamborn, S. D., Mounts, N. S., Steinberg, L., & Dornbush, S. M. (1991). Patterns of competence and adjustment among adolescents from authoritative, authoritarian, indulgent and neglectful families. *Child Development, 62,* 1049–1065.

Lapsley, D. K., & Rice, K. (1988). The "new look" at the imaginary audience and personal fable: Toward a general model of adolescent ego development. In D. K. Lapsley & F. Power (Eds.), *Self, ego, and identity: Integrative approaches* (pp. 109–129). New York: Springer.

Leahy, R. L., & Shirk, S. R. (1985). Social cognition and the development of the self. In R. L. Leahy (Ed.), *The development of the self* (pp. 123–150). New York: Academic Press.

Leaper, C. (1991). Influence and involvement in children's discourse: Age, gender, and partner effects. *Child Development, 62,* 797–811.

Leary, M. R., & Downs, D. L. (1995). Interpersonal functions of the self-esteem motive: The self-esteem system as a sociometer. In M. H. Kernis (Ed.), *Efficacy, agency, and self-esteem* (pp. 123–140). New York: Plenum Press.

Lewis, M. (1994). Myself and me. In S. T. Parker, R. W. Mitchell, & M L. Boccia (Eds.), *Self-awareness in animals and humans: Developmental perspectives* (pp. 20–34). New York: Cambridge University Press.

Lewis, M., & Brooks-Gunn, J. (1979). *Social cognition and the acquisition of self.* New York: Plenum Press.

Linville, P. W. (1987). Self-complexity as a cognitive buffer against stress-related illness and depression. *Journal of Personality and Social Psychology, 52,* 663–676.

Lipka, R. P., Hurford, D. P., & Litten, M. J. (1992). Self-in school: Age and school experience effects. In R. P. Lipka & T. M. Brinthaupt (Eds.), *Self-perspectives across the life span* (Vol.3, pp. 93–115). Albany: State University of New York Press.

Logan, R. D. (1987). Historical change in prevailing sense of self. In K. Yardley & T. Honess (Eds.), *Self and identity: Psychological perspectives* (pp. 13–26). Chichester, England: Wiley.

Maccoby, E. (1980). *Social development.* New York: Wiley.

Maccoby, E. E. (1990). Gender and relationship: A developmental account. *American Psychologist, 45,* 513–520.

MacDonald, G., Saltzman, J. L., & Leary, M. (2003). Social approval and trait self-esteem. *Journal of Research in Personality, 37,* 23–40.

Macfie, J., Cicchetti, D., & Toth, S. (2001). The development of dissociation in maltreated preschool-aged children. *Development and Psychopathology, 13,* 233–254.

Mack, J. E. (1983). Self-esteem and its development: An overview. In J. E. Mack & S. L. Ablong (Eds.), *The development and sustaining of self-esteem* (pp. 1–44). New York: International Universities Press.

Maeda, K. (1997). [The self-perception profile for children administered to a Japanese sample]. Unpublished raw data, Ibaraki Prefectural University of Health Sciences, Ibaraki, Japan.

Mahler, M. S. (1967). On human symbiosis and the vicissitudes of individuation. *Journal of the American Psychoanalytic Association, 15,* 740–763.

Main, M. (1995). Recent studies in attachment: Overview with selected implications for clinical work. In S. Goldberg, R. Muir, & J. Kerr (Eds.), *Attachment theory: Social, developmental, and clinical implications* (pp. 407–474). Hillsdale, NJ: Analytic Press.

Main, M., & Solomon, J. (1990). Procedures for identifying infants as disorganized/disoriented during the Ainsworth strange situation. In M. Greenberg, D. Cicchetti, & M. Cummings (Eds.), *Attachment during the preschool years: Theory, research, and intervention* (pp. 121–160). Chicago: University of Chicago Press.

Makris-Botsaris, E., & Robinson, W. P. (1991). Harter's self-perception profile for children: A cross-cultural validation in Greece. *Education and Research in Education, 5,* 135–143.

Marcotte, D., Fortin, L., Potvin, P., & Papillon, M. (2002). Gender differences in depressive symptoms during adolescence: Role of gender-typed characteristics, self-esteem, body image, stressful life events, and pubertal status. *Journal of Emotional and Behavioral Disorders, 10,* 1063–4266.

Markus, H. (1980). The self in thought and memory. In D. M. Wegner & R. R. Vallacher (Eds.), *The self in social psychology* (pp. 42–69). New York: Oxford University Press.

Markus, H., & Nurius, P. (1986). Possible selves. *American Psychologist, 41,* 954–969.

Markus, H., & Wurf, E. (1987). The dynamic self-concept: A social psychological perspective. *Annual Review of Psychology, 38,* 299–337.

Marsh, H. W. (1989). Age and sex effects in multiple dimensions of self-concept: Preadolescence to early adulthood. *Journal of Educational Psychology, 81,* 417–430.

Marsh, H. W. (1993). Academic self-concept: Theory, measurement, and research. In J. Suls (Ed.), *Psychological perspectives on the self* (Vol. 4, pp. 59–98). Hillsdale, NJ: Erlbaum.

Marsh, H. W., & Jackson, S. A. (1986). Multidimensional self-concepts, masculinity, and femininity as a function of women's involvement in athletics. *Sex Roles, 15,* 391–415.

Marsh, H. W., Parker, J., & Barnes, J. (1985). Multidimensional adolescent self-concepts: Their relationship to age, sex, and academic measures. *American Educational Research Journal, 22,* 422–444.

Marsh, H. W., Smith, I. D., Marsh, M. R., & Owens, L. (1988). The transition from single-sex to co-educational high schools: Effects on multiple dimensions of self-concept and on academic achievement. *American Educational Research Journal, 25,* 237–269.

Mascolo, M., Fischer, K., & Neimeyer, R. (1999). The dynamic co-development of intentionality, self, and social relations. In R. M. Lerner (Ed.), *Action and self-development: Theory and research through the life span* (pp. 72–98). Thousand Oaks, CA: Sage.

Mascolo, M. F., & Fischer, K. W. (1995). Developmental transformations in appraisals for pride, shame, and guilt. In J. P. Tangney & K. W. Fischer (Eds.), *Self-conscious emotions: The psychology of shame, guilt, embarrassment, and pride* (pp. 64–113). New York: Guilford Press.

McCann, I. L., & Pearlman, L. A. (1992). *Psychological trauma and the adult survivor.* New York: Brunner/Mazel.

McCarthy, J., & Hoge, D. (1982). Analysis of age effects in longitudinal studies of adolescent self-esteem. *Developmental Psychology, 18,* 372–379.

McGregor, K. N., Mayleben, M. A., Buzzanga, V. L., Davis, S. F., & Becker, A. H. (1992). Selected personality characteristics of first-generation college students. *College Student Journal, 18,* 231–234.

McGuire, S., Manke, B., Saudino, K. J., Reiss, D., Hetherington, E. M., & Plomin, R. (1999). Perceived competence and self-worth during adolescence: A longitudinal behavioral genetic study. *Child Development, 70,* 1283–1296.

Mead, G. H. (1925). The genesis of the self and social control. *International Journal of Ethics, 35,* 251–273.

Mead, G. H. (1934). *Mind, self, and society from the standpoint of a social behaviorist.* Chicago: University of Chicago Press.

Meredith, W. H., Abbott, D. A., & Zheng, F. M. (1991). Self-concept and sociometric outcomes: A comparison of only children and sibling children from urban and rural areas in the People's Republic of China. *Journal of Psychology, 126,* 411–412.

Miller, J. B. (1986). *Toward a new psychology of women* (2nd ed.). Boston: Beacon Press.

Miller, P. J., Potts, R., Fung, H., Hoogstra, L., & Mintz, J. (1990). Narrative practices and the social construction of self in childhood. *American Ethnologist, 17,* 292–311.

Montemayor, R., & Eisen, M. (1977). The development of self-conceptions from childhood to adolescence. *Developmental Psychology, 23,* 314–319.

Moretti, M. M., & Higgins, E. T. (1990). The development of self-esteem vulnerabilities: Social and cognitive factors in developmental psychopathology. In R. J. Sternberg & J. Kolligian Jr. (Eds.), *Competence considered* (pp. 286–314). New Haven, CT: Yale University Press.

Neiss, M. B., Sedikides, C., & Stevenson, J. (2002). Self-esteem: A behavioral genetic perspective. *European Journal of Personality, 16,* 351–367.

Nelson, K. (1986). *Event knowledge: Structure and function in development.* Hillsdale, NJ: Erlbaum.

Nelson, K. (Ed.). (1989). *Narratives from the crib.* Cambridge, MA: Harvard University Press.

Nelson, K. (1990). Remembering, forgetting, and childhood amnesia. In R. Fivush & J. A. Hudson (Eds.), *Knowing and remembering in young children* (pp. 301–316). New York: Cambridge University Press.

Nelson, K. (1993). Events, narratives, memory: What develops. In C. A. Nelson (Ed.), *Minnesota Symposia on Child Psychology: Vol. 26. Memory and affect* (pp. 1–24). Hillsdale, NJ: Erlbaum.

Nelson, K. (2003). Narrative and self, myth, and memory: Emergence of a cultural self. In R. Fivush & C. A. Haden (Eds.), *Autobiographical memory and the construction of a narrative self: Developmental and cultural perspectives* (pp. 72–90). Mahwah, NJ: Erlbaum.

Nolen-Hoeksema, S., & Girgus, J. S. (1994). The emergence of gender differences in depression during adolescence. *Psychological Bulletin, 115,* 424–443.

Nottelmann, E. D. (1987). Competence and self-esteem during the transition from childhood to adolescence. *Developmental Psychology, 23,* 441–450.

O'Malley, P., & Bachman, J. (1983). Self-esteem: Change and stability between 13 and 23. *Developmental Psychology, 19,* 257–268.

Oosterwegel, A., & Oppenheimer, L. (1993). *The self-system: Developmental changes between and within self-concepts.* Hillsdale, NJ: Erlbaum.

Pedrabissi, L., & Santinello, M. (1992). Il Self-Perception profile for children di Susan Harter. *Psicologia e Scuola, 61,* 3–14.

Pedrabissi, L., Santinello, M., & Scarpazza, V. (1988). Contributo all'adattamento italiano del "self-perception profile for children" di Susan Harter. *Bollettino di Psicologia Applicata, 185,* 19–26.

Pennington, B. F. (2002). *The development of psychopathology.* New York: Guilford Press.

Piaget, J. (1932). *The moral judgment of the child.* New York: Harcourt, Brace & World.

Piaget, J. (1960). *The psychology of intelligence.* Patterson, NJ: Littlefield-Adams.

Pierrehumbert, B., Plancheral, B., & Jankech-Caretta, C. (1987). Image de soi et perception des compentences propres chez l'enfant. *Revue de Psychlogie Appliquee, 37,* 359–377.

Piers, E. V. (1976). *The Piers-Harris Children's Self-Concept Scale* (Research Monograph No. 1). Nashville, TN: Counselor Recordings and Tests.

Piers, E. V., & Harris, D. B. (1964). Age and other correlates of self-concept in children. *Journal of Educational Psychology, 55,* 91–95.

Pillemer, D. B., & White, S. H. (1989). Childhood events recalled by children and adults. In H. W. Reese (Ed.), *Advances in child development and behavior* (Vol. 21, pp. 297–340). San Diego, CA: Academic Press.

Pipp, S. (1990). Sensorimotor and representational internal working models of self, other, and relationship: Mechanisms of connection and separation. In D. Cicchetti & M. Beeghly (Eds.), *The self in transition: Infancy to childhood* (pp. 243–264). Chicago: University of Chicago Press.

Pomerantz, E. V., Ruble, D. N., Frey, K. S., & Greulich, F. (1995). Meeting goals and confronting conflict: Children's changing perceptions of social comparison. *Child Development, 66,* 723–738.

Putnam, F. W. (1993). Dissociation and disturbances of the self. In D. Cicchetti & S. Toth (Eds.), *Rochester Symposium on Developmental Psychopathology: Vol. 5. Disorders and dysfunctions of the self* (pp. 251–266). Rochester, NY: University of Rochester Press.

Reissland, N. (1985). The development of concepts of simultaneity in children's understanding of emotions. *Journal of Child Psychology and Psychiatry, 26,* 811–824.

Rhee, U. (1993). Self-perceptions of competence and social support in Korean children. *Early Child Development and Care, 85,* 57–66.

Roberts, A., Seidman, E., & Pedersen, S. (2000). Perceived family and peer transactions and self-esteem among urban early adolescents. *Journal of Early Adolescence, 20,* 68–92.

Rochat, P., & Striano, T. (2002). Who's in the mirror? Self—Other discrimination in specular images by 4- and 9-month-old infants. *Child Development, 73,* 35–46.

Rogoff, B. (1990). *Apprenticeship in thinking.* New York: Oxford University Press.

Rosenberg, M. (1979). *Conceiving the self.* New York: Basic Books.

Rosenberg, M. (1986). Self-concept from middle childhood through adolescence. In J. Suls & A. G. Greenwald (Eds.), *Psychological perspective on the self* (Vol. 3, pp. 107–135). Hillsdale, NJ: Erlbaum.

Rosenberg, M., Schoenback, C., Schooler, C., & Rosenberg, F. (1995). Global self-esteem and specific self-esteem: Different concepts, different outcomes. *American Sociological Review, 60,* 141–156.

Rosenberg, M., & Simmons, R. G. (1972). *Black and White self-esteem: The urban school child.* Washington, DC: American Psychological Association.

Rossman, B. B., & Rosenberg, M. S. (Eds.). (1998). *Multiple victimization of children.* New York: Haworth Press.

Rowley, S. J., Sellers, R. M., Chavous, T. M., & Smith, M. A. (1998). The relationship between racial identity and self-esteem in African college and high school students. *Journal of Personality and Social Psychology, 74,* 715–724.

Rubin, L. (1985). *Just friends: The role of friendship in our lives.* New York: Harper.

Ruble, D. N., & Dweck, C. (1995). Self-conceptions, person conception, and development. In N. Eisenberg (Ed.), *Review of personality and social psychology: Vol. 15. The interface* (pp. 109–139). Thousand Oaks, CA: Sage.

Ruble, D. N., & Frey, K. S. (1991). Changing patterns of comparative behavior as skills are acquired: A functional model of self-evaluation. In J. Suls & T. A. Wills (Eds.), *Social comparison: Contemporary theory and research* (pp. 70–112). Hillsdale, NJ: Erlbaum.

Ruble, D. N., & Martin, C. L. (1998). Gender development. In W. Damon (Editor-in-Chief) & N. Eisenberg (Vol. Ed.), *Handbook of child psychology: Vol. 3. Social, emotional, and personality development* (5th ed., pp. 933–1016). New York: Wiley.

Rutter, M., & Sroufe, L. A. (2000). Developmental psychopathology: Concepts and challenges. *Development and Psychopathology, 12,* 265–296.

Sakurai, S. (1983). Development of the Japanese version of Harter's Perceived Competence Scale for Children. *Japanese Journal of Educational Psychology, 31,* 245–249.

Sameroff, A. (2000). Development systems and psychopathology. *Development and Psychopathology, 12,* 297–312.

Sarbin, T. R. (1962). A preface to a psychological analysis of the self. *Psychological Review, 59,* 11–22.

Savin-Williams, R. C., & Berndt, T. J. (1990). Friend and peer relations. In S. S. Feldman & G. Elliot (Eds.), *At the threshold: The developing adolescent* (pp. 277–307). Cambridge, MA: Harvard University Press.

Savin-Williams, R. C., & Demo, P. (1993). Situational and transitional determinants of adolescent self-feelings. *Journal of Personality and Social Psychology, 44,* 820–833.

Schneider-Rosen, K., Braunwald, K. G., Carlson, V., & Cicchetti, D. (1985). Current perspectives in attachment theory: Illustration from the study of maltreated infants. *Monographs of the Society for Research in Child Development, 50,* 104–210.

Selman, R. L. (1980). *The growth of interpersonal understanding.* New York: Academic Press.

Shrauger, J. S., & Schoeneman, T. J. (1979). Symbolic interactionist view of self-concept: Through the looking glass darkly. *Psychological Bulletin, 86,* 549–573.

Siegler, R. S. (1991). *Children's thinking* (2nd ed.). Englewood Cliffs, NJ: Prentice-Hall.

Simmons, R. G., & Blyth, D. A. (1987). *Moving into adolescence: The impact of pubertal change and school context.* New York: Aldine de Gruyter.

Simmons, R. G., Blyth, D. A., Van Cleave, E. F., & Bush, D. (1979). Entry into early adolescence: The impact of school structure, puberty, and early dating on self-esteem. *American Sociological Review, 44,* 553–568.

Simmons, R. G., & Rosenberg, F. (1975). Sex, sex roles, and self-image. *Journal of Youth and Adolescence, 4,* 229–258.

Simmons, R. G., Rosenberg, F., & Rosenberg, M. (1973). Disturbances in the self-images at adolescence. *American Sociological Review, 38,* 553–568.

Smollar, J., & Youniss, J. (1985). Adolescent self-concept development. In R. L. Leahy (Ed.), *The development of self* (pp. 247–266). New York: Academic Press.

Snow, K. (1990). Building memories: The ontogeny of autobiography. In D. Cicchetti & M. Beeghly (Eds.), *The self in transition: Infancy to childhood* (pp. 213–242). Chicago: University of Chicago Press.

Sroufe, L. A. (1990). An organizational perspective on the self. In D. Cicchetti & M. Beeghly (Eds.), *The self in transition: Infancy to childhood* (pp. 281–308). Chicago: University of Chicago Press.

Sroufe, L. A., & Fleeson, J. (1986). Attachment and the construction of relationships. In W. Hartup & Z. Rubin (Eds.), *Relationships and development* (pp. 51–71). New York: Cambridge University Press.

Steele, C. M. (1988). The psychology of affirmation: Sustaining the integrity of the self. In L. Berkowitz (Ed.), *Advances in experimental social psychology* (Vol. 21, pp. 261–302). San Diego, CA: Academic Press.

Steinberg, L. (1990). Interdependence in the family: Autonomy, conflict, autonomy in the parent-adolescent relationship. In S. Feldman & G. Elliot (Eds.), *At the threshold: The developing adolescent* (pp. 255–276). Cambridge, MA: Harvard University Press.

Steinberg, L., & Silverberg, S. B. (1986). The vicissitudes of autonomy in adolescence. *Child Development, 57,* 841–851.

Stern, D. (1985). *The interpersonal world of the infant.* New York: Basic Books.

Stigler, J. W., Smith, S., & Mao, L. (1985). The self-perception of competence by Chinese children. *Child Development, 56,* 1259–1270.

Stipek, D. (1981). Children's perceptions of their own and their classmates' ability. *Journal of Educational Psychology, 73,* 404–410.

Stipek, D. (1995). The development of pride and shame in toddlers. In J. P. Tangney & K. W. Fischer (Eds.), *Self-conscious emotions: The psychology of shame, embarrassment, and pride* (pp. 237–252). New York: Guilford Press.

Stipek, D., Recchia, S., & McClintic, S. (1992). Self-evaluation in young children. *Monographs of the Society for Research in Child Development, 57,* 1–84.

Sullivan, H. S. (1953). *The interpersonal theory of psychiatry.* New York: Norton.

Suls, J., & Sanders, G. (1982). Self-evaluation via social comparison: A developmental analysis. In L. Wheeler (Ed.), *Review of personality and social psychology* (Vol. 3, pp. 67–89). Beverly Hills, CA: Sage.

Swann, W. B., Jr. (1996). *Self-traps.* New York: Freeman.

Terr, L. (1990). *Too scared to cry.* New York: Basic Books.

Terr, L. (1991). Childhood traumas: An outline and overview. *American Journal of Psychiatry, 148,* 10–20.

Tessler, M. (1991). *Making memories together: The influence of mother-child joint encoding on the development of autobiographical memory style.* Unpublished doctoral dissertation, City University of New York Graduate Center, New York.

Thompson, R. (1998). Early sociopersonal development. In W. Damon (Editor-in-Chief) & N. Eisenberg (Vol. Ed.), *Handbook of child psychology: Vol. 3. Social, emotional, and personality development* (5th ed., pp. 25–104). New York: Wiley.

Tobin-Richard, M. H., Boxer, A. M., Kavrell, S. A., & Peterson, A. C. (1984). Puberty and its psychological and social significance. In R. M. Lerner & N. L. Galambos (Eds.), *Experiencing adolescents: A sourcebook for parents, teachers, and teens* (pp. 17–50). New York: Garland.

Toth, S. L., Cicchetti, D., Macfie, J., & Emde, R. N. (1997). Representations of self and others in the narratives of neglected, physically abused, and sexually abused preschoolers. *Development and Psychopathology, 9,* 781–796.

Toth, S. L., Cicchetti, D., Macfie, J., Maughan, & Vanmeenen, K. (2000). Narrative representations of caregivers and self in male pre-schoolers. *Attachment and Human Development, 2,* 271–305.

Toth, S. L., Cicchetti, D., Macfie, J., Rogosch, F. A., & Maughan, A. (2000). Narrative representations of moral-affiliative and conflictual themes and behavioral problems in maltreated preschoolers. *Journal of Clinical Child Psychology, 29,* 307–318.

Trent, L. M., Russell, G., & Cooney, G. (1994). Assessment of self-concept in early adolescence. *Australian Journal of Psychology, 46,* 21–28.

Trzesniewski, K. H., Donnellan, M., & Robins, R. W. (2003). Stability of self-esteem across the life span. *Journal of Personality and Social Psychology, 84,* 205–220.

Twenge, J. M., & Crocker, J. (2002). Race and self-esteem: Meta-analyses comparing Whites, Blacks, Hispanics, Asians, and American Indians and comment on Gray-Little and Hafdahl (2000). *Psychological Bulletin, 128,* 371–408.

Usmiani, S., & Daniluk, J. (1997). Mothers and their adolescent daughters: Relationship between self-esteem, gender role identity, and body image. *Journal of Youth and Adolescence, 26*(1), 45–62.

van der Kolk, B. A. (1987). *Psychological trauma.* Washington, DC: American Psychiatric Press.

van Dongen-Melman, J. E., Koot, H. M., & Verhulst, F. C. (1993). Cross-cultural validation of Harter's self-perception profile in a Dutch sample. *Educational and Psychological Measurement, 53,* 739–753.

Watson, M. (1990). Aspects of self development as reflected in children's role playing. In D. Cicchetti & M. Beeghly (Eds.), *The self in transition: Infancy to childhood* (pp. 281–307). Chicago: University of Chicago Press.

Watson, M. W., & Fischer, K. (1993). Structural change in children's understanding of family roles and divorce. In R. R. Cocking & K. A. Renninger (Eds.), *The development and meaning of psychological distance* (pp. 123–144). Hillsdale, NJ: Erlbaum.

Westen, D. (1993). The impact of sexual abuse on self structure. In D. Cicchetti & S. Toth (Eds.), *Rochester Symposium on Developmental Psychopathology: Vol. 5. Disorders and dysfunctions of the self* (pp. 223–250). Rochester, NY: University of Rochester Press.

White, K., Speisman, J., & Costos, D. (1983). Young adults and their parents: Individuation to mutuality. In H. D. Grotevant & C. R. Cooper (Eds.), *New directions for child development: Adolescent development in the family* (pp. 61–76). San Francisco: Jossey-Bass.

Wigfield, A., Eccles, J. S., Mac Iver, D., Reuman, D. A., & Midgley, C. (1991). Transitions during early adolescence: Changes in children's domain-specific self-perceptions and general self-esteem across the transition to junior high school. *Developmental Psychology, 27,* 552–565.

Williams, J., M., & Currie, C. (2000). Self-esteem and physical development in early adolescence: Pubertal timing and body image. *Journal of Early Adolescence, 20,* 129–149.

Winnicott, D. W. (1958). *From paediatrics to psychoanalysis.* London: Hogarth Press.

Winnicott, D. W. (1965). *The maturational processes and the facilitating environment.* New York: International Universities Press.

Wolf, D. P. (1990). Being of several minds: Voices and version of the self in early childhood. In D. Cicchetti & M. Beeghly (Eds.), *The self in transition: Infancy to childhood* (pp. 183–212). Chicago: University of Chicago Press.

Wolfe, D. (1989). *Child abuse.* Newbury Park, CA: Sage.

Wylie, R. C. (1979). *The self concept: Vol. 2. Theory and research on selected topics.* Lincoln: University of Nebraska Press.

Wylie, R. C. (1989). *Measures of self-concept.* Lincoln: University of Nebraska Press.

CHAPTER 10

Peer Interactions, Relationships, and Groups

KENNETH H. RUBIN, WILLIAM M. BUKOWSKI, and JEFFREY G. PARKER

Experiences with peers constitute an important developmental context for children. In these contexts, children acquire a wide range of behaviors, skills, attitudes, and experiences that influence their adaptation during the life span. Experiences with peers affect social, emotional, and cognitive functioning beyond the influences

of family, school, and neighborhood. In this chapter, we present the current research related to these claims. We begin by commenting briefly on developments in the study of children's peers since the publication of the last *Handbook of Child Psychology* in 1998. Our previous chapter distinguished between processes and effects

The writing of this manuscript was supported, in part, by a grant from the National Institute of Mental Health (# MH58116) to Kenneth H. Rubin and by grants from the

Social Sciences and Humanities Research Council of Canada and the *Fonds Québécois de la recherche sur la société et la culture* to William M. Bukowski.

at the levels of the interactions, relationships, and groups. Our goal is to provide an updated examination of current theory and research on peer relationships and development.

The task of reviewing the literature on peer interactions, relationships, and groups becomes more challenging as the literature becomes more extensive and diverse. The number of relevant papers published in the past 8 years is substantially larger than the number published in any previous 8-year period. Since the publication of our 1998 chapter, several major books have appeared, including:

Children's Peer Relations (Slee & Rigby, 1998)

Sociometry Then and Now: Building on 6 Decades of Measuring Experiences with the Peer Group (Bukowski & Cillessen, 1996)

Family and Peers: Linking Two Social Worlds (Kerns, Contreras, & Neal-Barnett, 2000)

The Role of Friendship in Psychological Adjustment (Nangle & Erdley, 2001)

Peer Harassment in School: The Plight of the Vulnerable and Victimized (Juvonen & Graham, 2001)

How Children and Adolescents Evaluate Gender and Racial Exclusion (Killen, Lee-Kim, McGlothlin, & Stangor, 2002)

Peer Rejection: Developmental Processes and Intervention Strategies (Bierman, 2003)

Enemies and the Darker Side of Peer Relations (Hodges & Card, 2003) *Children's Friendships: The Beginnings of Intimacy* (Dunn, 2004)

Children's Peer Relations: From Development to Intervention (Kupersmidt & Dodge, 2004)

Perhaps even more important, a number of trade books on peer relationships are now available for parents and teachers, including:

Queen Bees and Wannabees: Helping Your Daughter Survive Cliques, Gossip, Boyfriends, and Other Realities of Adolescence (Wiseman, 2002)

The Unwritten Rules of Friendship: Simple Strategies to Help Your Child Make Friends (Elman & Kennedy-Moore, 2003)

The Friendship Factor (Rubin, 2003)

Not only have the topics of children's peer interactions, relationships, and groups experienced increased research and public attention, but the study of the peer system has also become increasingly diverse, more articulated, and more naturalistic. Its diversity is seen not only in the wide range of topics that are studied but also in the participation of children from cultures other than those typically found in Western research. Topics recently introduced to the discipline include the significance of peers and friendships as children mark transitions from one school setting to another; cultural and cross-cultural meanings of acceptable and unacceptable social behaviors and relationships; perceived popularity; jealousy and other emotional processes related to the maintenance and dissolution of peer relationships; the statistical (and conceptual) modeling of growth and change in peer interactions and relationships; peer victimization; mutual antipathies; early romantic relationships; and the relative contribution of peers and friendships to well- and ill-being.

Prior emphases on rejection as necessarily "bad" and friendship as necessarily "good" have been replaced by models that emphasize how sets of variables function together via mediation and moderation to affect outcome. The past decade has seen several changes in peer research, including an increase of interest in victimization, a decrease in interest in *sociometric* rejection, increases in the emphasis on biology and emotion, a concern with the peer *group* per se, and an interest in developing process-oriented explanatory models to account for the factors underlying risk.

In parallel to these changes, research on peer interactions, relationships, and groups has focused on an increasingly articulated set of measures. Although the use of omnibus measures of aggression, withdrawal, sociability, sociometric status, and victimization continues, the use of more specific measures, drawn from more refined thinking about individual characteristics and social interactions, has increased. Now, for example, aggression is measured according to whether it is direct, indirect, relational, physical, reactive, or proactive; withdrawal is measured to the extent that it reflects social reticence, social immaturity, preference for objects rather than people, or social exclusion. Research designs have changed also. The once prevalent preference for one-time-only studies has been coupled with the more frequent use of longitudinal designs that allow an examination of prediction as well as intra-individual change. Thus, the literature on peer interactions, relationships, and groups continues to evolve toward higher levels of complexity and specificity.

In the first section of this chapter, we pay homage to those researchers who established areas of investigation that are still active today. Next, we suggest that the peer system consists of multiple levels of analysis, namely individual characteristics, social interactions, dyadic relationships, and group membership and composition. Our thesis is that interactions, relationships, and groups reflect social participation at different interwoven orders of complexity. Our goal, in introducing these levels of analysis, is to establish a framework for further discussion of the development and significance of children's peer experiences. Moreover, discussion of the interaction, relationships, and group levels of social complexity allows subsequent commentary on conceptual and assessment issues that pertain to individual differences in children's behavioral tendencies and peer relationships. These different levels of analysis receive different amounts of treatment in the theoretical accounts of the significance of peer experiences for normal development. These issues are discussed in the next section where we present theories relevant to the understanding of the peer system.

Next, we describe normative patterns of development from infancy through late childhood and early adolescence. Researchers who study children's peer experiences have long maintained a healthy interest in measurement and measurement issues. In the fifth section, we distinguish between individuals, interactions, relationships, and groups in a discussion of measurement issues. In the final sections, we update the voluminous literature that has emerged concerning the origins and consequences of individual differences in children's experiences with peers. We pay particular attention to the proximal and distal correlates of variables associated with individual differences in popularity and friendship. We consider also the developmental prognosis for children whose peer interaction patterns and relationships are deviant from the norm. The chapter concludes with a discussion of some of the directions that future research might take.

PEER INTERACTIONS AND RELATIONSHIPS—AN HISTORICAL OVERVIEW

The study of children's peer interactions and relationships has had a long and rich history. Charlotte Buhler (1931), in the first *Handbook* chapter on peer interactions and relationships, cited 253 papers, 156 of which

were published in German. Among these early German studies were developmental examinations of social interaction in infants and toddlers; studies of antisocial "tendencies" in children and adolescents; investigations of the evolution of different leadership roles played by children in their peer groups, and observational studies of the development of friendship networks. Thus, prior to World War II, German laboratories were producing research on topics not unknown to contemporaneous peer relationships researchers. Often, the correlates or concomitants of these relationship variables were examined, such as family constellation, institutionalization, and poverty. We continue to grapple with these topics today.

Early North American Research

North American research concerning children's peer interactions and relationships began to blossom in the 1920s when the first Child Welfare Research Stations came into existence. These interdisciplinary research centers produced new observational and statistical procedures to examine developmental and individual differences in children's social behaviors, interactions, and peer relationships. Research reports from these centers emphasized the development of social participation (Parten, 1932); assertiveness (Dawe, 1934); sympathetic and altruistic behaviors (L. Murphy, 1937); conflict and aggression (Maudry & Nekula, 1939); leadership, dominance, and ascendant behavior (Hanfmann, 1935); friendship (Challman, 1932); group dynamics (K. Lewin, Lippitt, & White, 1939); and peer group structure and composition (Moreno, 1934).

By the beginning of World War II, the study of children's social behaviors, interactions, and peer relationships began to wane as many persons who did developmental research had joined the war effort. Nevertheless, during this period, increased attention was directed to topics relevant to group processes and democratic values. Interest in these topics had been heightened by the sociopolitical events associated with the war and led to research on the interface between individual characteristics (e.g., leadership), interactions between group members, and group dynamics. For example, one line of research was concerned with factors that might evoke and maintain intra- and intergroup harmony and conflict. It is not a coincidence that one of the conditions of the K. Lewin et al.'s (1939) classic study of the effect of leadership on peer group processes was labeled "democratic," whereas another was labeled "authoritarian."

A second area of research that flourished during this time of concern with group composition and processes was sociometry. Following the work of Moreno (1934), the war period is noted for the further development of sociometric techniques that provided researchers with a means of studying acceptance and rejection (see Bronfenbrenner, 1944). These techniques were immediately used to study a variety of questions concerning the correlates of children's experiences with peers. Publications by Northway (1944) and Bonney (1944) serve as historical exemplars for current researchers interested in the factors related to children's experiences in groups.

Post–World War II

The arrival of the Cold War fostered limited research concern about children and their extrafamilial social relationships. Instead, attention was directed to children's academic and intellectual prowess. With the launching of the Sputnik satellite by the USSR in 1957, the pressures to train children to become academically oriented and skilled at earlier ages and at faster rates than ever before moved developmental researchers away from the earlier focus on children's social worlds.

In the 1960s, the rediscovery of the Piaget's developmental theory provided an impetus for a structurally oriented research climate that captured the interest of psychologists throughout the Western world. A brief glance at archival child psychology and development journals during the 1960s and 1970s will reveal the domination of the Piagetian Zeitgeist, in conjunction with, or in opposition to, the behaviorist Zeitgeist. This focus on cognition, coupled with continued interest in achievement motivation and behavior, created an environment that was not particularly attuned to the significance of peer interaction and relationships. Nevertheless, researchers in the 1960s and early 1970s appeared to accept the premise that young children were egocentric and were neither willing, nor able, to understand the thoughts, feelings, and spatial perspectives of their peers. Egocentrism also stood in the way of making mature moral judgments and decisions. Given these assumptions, the mind-set seemed to be that studying children's peer relationships would not be productive, at least until the mid-elementary school ages when concrete operations emerged and when egocentric thought vanished.

The coupling of this research and educational climate with the social policy mandate of the mid-1960s regarding the eradication of poverty, led to the development of early education programs for which the primary foci were cognitive and language development and the development of an achievement orientation in young children. Accordingly, nursery schools moved away from emphasizing the development of relationships and social skills and instead aimed to prepare "at-risk" children for elementary school. Additionally, the achievement-oriented middle classes of the 1960s and 1970s increasingly favored cognitively oriented preschool programs.

Despite the emphasis on early cognitive and language development, the preschool and day-care movements of the 1960s and 1970s may have been partly responsible for the reemergence of peer relationships research. In particular, the growth of early education and care centers in North America was dictated, not only by the need to prevent educational failure among the socioeconomically impoverished, but also by the need for out-of-home care for dual income middle-class households. Given that North American children were entering organized peer group settings at earlier ages than ever before and given that children were remaining with peers in age-segregated schools for more years than their cohorts of previous generations, it would have been shortsighted and irresponsible for developmental researchers to ignore the importance of children's peer relationships and social skills.

The current theories about the significance of peer interactions and relationships for normal development are certainly not new. Piaget (1932) himself implicated peer *interaction,* discourse, and negotiation as crucial elements likely to provoke higher levels of operational thinking. Mead (1934) and Sullivan (1953) also wrote persuasively about the importance of friendship and peer *relationships* for adaptive development. Thus, by the end of the 1960s, the time appeared ripe for child developmentalists to be reminded of their early roots. This reminder was issued by Hartup in his 1970 *Manual of Child Psychology* chapter. This chapter, and Hartup's (1983) revision, proved provocative. In 1998, we provided the *Handbook* with an updated look at the literature on peer interactions, relationships, and groups.

The large amount of research attention directed to the study of children's peer interactions, relationships, and groups in the 1980s occurred at the same time that a new approach to understanding the development of psychopathology was proposed. A basic tenet of the approach was that the study of normative development and individual differences and the study of psychopathology were mutually enriching activities (Sroufe & Rutter,

1984). The study of peer interactions and relationships was ideally suited to the field of developmental psychopathology. Researchers recognized that theories, constructs, variables and measures of peer interactions, and relationships were valuable and useful for the study of normal development *and* for the study of maladjustment. The result of this confluence has been that the study of peer interactions, relationships, and groups and the study of the development of psychopathology have become highly complementary activities (e.g., Deater-Deckard, 2001). On the one hand, children's problems with peers, regardless of their source, may contribute to the genesis of behavioral or emotional disorder; on the other hand, children with behavioral and emotional difficulties may be rejected and/or victimized by their peers from the earliest years of life (Hay, Payne, & Chadwick, 2004). A prominent example of the liaison between the study of peers and the study of maladjustment can be seen in current research on bullying and victimization. Following extreme incidents in schools and among youth in groups, investigators became increasingly interested in identifying the complex interactions between individual and group factors that account for the harm that peers can inflict on each other.

In summary, the study of peer interactions, relationships, and groups has a long and rich history. The topics that have attracted the attention of peer researchers have varied in response to intellectual Zeitgeists, advances in theory and research in other domains of developmental psychology, and to social and political events. Currently, peer research balances concerns with the study of individual differences with the study of basic processes. The features of this balance are evident in the sections that follow.

INTERACTIONS, RELATIONSHIPS, AND GROUPS: ORDERS OF COMPLEXITY IN CHILDREN'S PEER EXPERIENCES

Children's experiences with peers can be best understood by referring to several levels of social complexity—in individuals, in interactions, in relationships, and in groups (Hinde, 1987). Moreover, events and processes at each level are constrained and influenced by events and processes at other levels. *Individuals* bring to social exchanges more or less stable social orientations, temperaments that dispose them to be more or less

aroused physiologically to social stimuli, and a repertoire of social skills for social perception, cognition, and social problem solving. Over the short term, their *interactions* with other children vary in form and function in response to fluctuations in the parameters of the social situation, such as the partner's characteristics, overtures, and responses. Further, most interactions are embedded in longer-term *relationships* and thus are influenced by past and anticipated future interactions. Relationships may take many forms and have properties that are not relevant to interactions. At the same time, the nature of a relationship is defined partly by the characteristics of its members, its constituent interactions, and, over the long term, the kinds of relationships individuals form depend on their history of interactions in earlier relationships. Finally, individual relationships are embedded in *groups* or networks of relationships with more or less clearly defined boundaries (e.g., cliques, teams, or school classes). As the highest level of social complexity, groups are defined by their constituent relationships and, in this sense, by the types and diversity of interactions that are characteristic of the participants in those relationships. But groups are more than mere aggregates of relationships; through emergent properties, such as norms or shared cultural conventions, groups help define the type and range of relationships and interactions that are likely or permissible. Further, groups have properties and processes, such as hierarchical organization and cohesiveness, which are not relevant to description of children's experiences at lower levels of social complexity.

To further complicate matters, at any level of social organization the understanding of participants will necessarily differ from that of outsiders. Humorous anecdotes shared between friends, for example, can strike outsiders as unnecessarily cruel (e.g., gossip). Children with many friends can still feel lonely; and seemingly innocuous acts can have great significance to members of a friendship, who understand them differently than do outsiders. Given that neither insiders nor outsiders can claim any specific hegemony on the truth, researchers must be prepared to cross and re-cross perspectives as the problem dictates.

The complexity of the multiple, interrelated levels of social organization that underpin peer experiences can make the prospect of understanding these experiences and their influence on children seem truly dim. Historically, distinctions between the various levels and perspectives of children's peer experiences often have been blurred. For example, investigators have confused phenomena from different levels (e.g., failing to distinguish between group acceptance and friendship) or perspectives (e.g., accepting one child's declaration as evidence of friendship without verifying the reciprocity of this sentiment), and have also sometimes been too facile in making inferences about experiences at one level from measurements at another (e.g., assuming that children who are aggressive in interaction cannot be well-liked or those who are socially removed and withdrawn from interaction cannot have friends). Nevertheless, over the past 25 years, recognition and articulation of the multiple levels of analysis and perspectives that comprise the peer system have greatly increased. Especially significant in this regard has been the contribution of Robert Hinde (e.g., 1987, 1995) who has articulated the features and dialectical relations between successive levels of social complexity.

Borrowing heavily from Hinde, in this section we discuss the nature of three successive levels of complexity in children's experiences with peers—*interactions, relationships,* and *groups.* Our goal is to set the framework for subsequent discussion of the development and significance of children's peer experiences. The interaction, relationship, and group levels of social complexity are also important to the conceptualization and assessment of individual differences in children's behavioral tendencies because individuals can be compared with respect to their functioning at these levels; therefore, the present section serves as an orienting framework for our later discussion of measurement issues. As we indicated, a hierarchy of social complexity should include processes at work at the *individual* (versus interactional, relationship, or group) level of description. These processes would include children's socioemotional/temperamental dispositions, and social knowledge and skills repertoires. In the literature on children's peer experiences, the individual level has been the focus of much interest. However, rather than introduce this well-developed literature here, we embed its discussion into sections on children's interactions and relationships.

Interactions

The simplest order of complexity of peer experience involves interactions. *Interaction* refers to the social exchange of some duration between two individuals. Behaviors that simply (and only) complement one another (like riding on either end of a teeter-totter) would

ordinarily not be considered true interaction unless it was amply clear that they were jointly undertaken. Instead, the term *interaction* is reserved for dyadic behavior in which the participants' actions are interdependent such that each actor's behavior is both a response to, and stimulus for, the other participant's behavior. At its core, an interaction comprises "such incidents as Individual A shows behavior X to Individual B, or A shows X to B and B responds with Y" (Hinde, 1979, p. 15). Conversational turn-taking is a quintessential illustration: Thus, Child A requests information from Child B ("What's your name?"), Child B responds ("My name is Lara. What's yours?"), Child A replies ("Camilla."), and so on.

Such a simple exchange as that of Camilla and Lara belies the richness and complexity of the ways that children of most ages communicate with and influence one another. Thus, besides introducing themselves, children in conversation may argue, gossip, comfort, and support one another, self-disclose, and joke, among other things. And, during interaction, children cooperate, compete, fight, withdraw, respond to provocation, and engage in a host of other behaviors that includes everything from ritualized sexual contact to rough-and-tumble (R&T) play to highly structured sociodramatic fantasy. Typically, researchers have been less interested in cataloguing the myriad of interactional experiences than in understanding the origins and consequences of three broad childhood behavioral tendencies: (1) moving toward others, (2) moving against others, and (3) moving away from others. As a consequence, our understanding of children's experiences at the interactional level is disproportionately organized around the constructs of sociability and helpfulness, aggression, and withdrawal. As much of this literature is oriented toward individual differences among children along these dimensions of interaction, we review this research in later sections. Developmental trends in these behaviors are described in the subsequent section.

Although many social exchanges have their own inherent logic (as in the question-answer sequence of Camilla and Lara), it is also the case that the forms and trajectories of episodes of interaction are shaped by the relationships in which they are embedded. For example, friends are more committed to resolving conflict with each other than nonfriends, are more likely than nonfriends to reach equitable resolutions, and continue to interact following a disagreement (Laursen, 1993; Laursen, Finkelstein, & Betts, 2001; Laursen, Hartup, & Koplas, 1996; Laursen & Koplas, 1995; Newcomb &

Bagwell, 1995). Beyond this, children engaged in interaction vary their behavior as a function of their short-term and long-term personal goals, their understanding of their partner's thoughts and feelings in the situation, the depth of their repertoire of alternative responses, and various "ecological" features of the context of the interactions (such as the presence of bystanders), the physical setting, their own and their partner's relative standing in the group, and the operative local customs or "scripts" for responding. It is precisely the demonstration of such range and flexibility in responding to the challenges of interpersonal interaction, *when considered at the individual level of analysis* that many writers think of as social competence (e.g., Bukowski, Rubin, & Parker, 2001; Rose-Krasnor, 1997).

Relationships

Relationships introduce a second and higher-order level of complexity to children's experiences with peers. *Relationships* refer to the meanings, expectations, and emotions that derive from a succession of interactions between two individuals known to each other. Because the individuals are known to each other, the nature and course of each interaction is influenced by the history of past interactions between the individuals as well as by their expectations for interactions in the future. It has been suggested that the degree of closeness of a relationship is determined by such qualities as the frequency and strength of influence, the diversity of influence across different behaviors, and the length of time the relationship has endured. In a close relationship, influence is frequent, diverse, strong, and enduring. Alternatively, relationships can be defined with reference to the predominant *emotions* that participants typically experience in them (e.g., affection, love, attachment, or enmity). Hinde (1979) further suggests that an essential element of a relationship is *commitment* or the extent to which the partners accept their relationship as "continuing indefinitely or direct their behaviors toward ensuring its continuance or toward optimizing its properties" (p. 29). Finally, it is important to note that, although as social scientists we may speak of abstract categories of relationships (e.g., sibling, best friend, or enemy), children view each instance of these relationships in a particularized way; to children, relationships of even the same general category are not interchangeable.

As a form of social organization, dyadic relationships share features with larger social organizations, such as a family, a class, or a team. In a particularly insightful analysis, McCall (1988) noted that dyads, like larger organizational structures, undergo role differentiation, specialization, and division of labor: "Members' lines of action differ one from the other yet remain interdependent in certain ways" (p. 473). Moreover, participants in a relationship are aware that their relationship, though it may be very much their own local creation, is supported by an objectified, institutionalized social form: "When persons say they are friends, usually they can point to cultural images, rules of conduct, and customary modes of behavior to confirm their claims" (Suttles, 1970, p. 98). In addition, parties to a relationship have a sense of shared membership and belonging: "A sense of shared fate tends to arise as members discover that the surrounding world treats them not so much as separate individuals but rather as a couple, or unit" (McCall, 1988, p. 471). Finally, the creation of a shared culture is a vital part of dyadic relationships. This shared culture includes normative expectations regarding appropriate activities, patterns of communication and revelation, relations to external persons and organizations, and so on. It also includes private terms, or neologisms, for shared concerns or common activities, and rituals, or "dyadic traditions," arising from the routinization of recurrent dyadic activities (such as meeting at the same place after school, flipping a special coin to resolve a dispute, or engaging in an exclusive "buddy shake" to mark a joint promise or planned behavior).

These are all features that relationships have in common with other, larger social organizations. However, McCall indicates that there are certain attitudinal features of the participants in a dyadic relationship that are distinct to this level of social organization and vital to understanding its functioning and impact on interactions and individuals. For example, unlike most social organizations, dyadic relationships do not vary in membership size. Having only two members, the dyad is peculiarly vulnerable, for the loss of a single member terminates the dyad's existence. Because members appreciate this vulnerability, issues of commitment, attachment, and investment loom larger in dyadic relationships than in other forms of social organization. Indeed, an understanding of the surface behavior of members of relationships can be elusive unless note is taken of the deeper meaning of behavior in relation to the relationship's mortality. This same sense of mortality is likely to contribute to a special sense of uniqueness ("there has never been a friendship quite like ours") and to what

McCall calls a "sense of consecration," or a feeling that each member must take responsibility for what happens in the relationship.

Friendship

In the literature on children's peer experiences, one form of dyadic relationship has received attention above all others—*friendship*. The issue of what constitutes friendship is a venerable philosophical debate beyond the scope of this chapter. However, some points from this debate warrant noting here because of their operational significance.

First, there is widespread agreement that friendship is a *reciprocal* relationship that must be affirmed or recognized by both parties. Reciprocity is the factor that distinguishes friendship from the nonreciprocal attraction of only one partner to another. From an assessment perspective, methods that do not verify that the perception of friendship is shared between partners prove difficult because children are sometimes motivated by self-presentational goals to designate as friends other children who do not view them as friends in return. Thus, in the absence of assessing reciprocity, methods of identifying friends may confuse desired relationships with actual ones.

A second point of consensus is that *reciprocity of affection* represents an essential, though not necessarily exclusive, tie that binds friends together (Hays, 1988). The interdependence of the two partners derives primarily from socioemotional rather than instrumental motives. It is customary for children to seek one another out for instrumental reasons. Similarity of talents or interests may bring together children who might not otherwise interact. For example, work and sports teams, musical groups, and even delinquent gangs include members who are not necessarily friends. Similarities or complementarities of talents and interests may lead to friendship and can help sustain them; however, they do not constitute the basis of the friendship itself. The basis is reciprocal affection.

Third, friendships are voluntary, not obligatory or prescribed. In some cultures and in some circumstances, children may be assigned their "friends," sometimes even at birth (Krappmann, 1996). Although these relationships may take on some of the features and serve some of the same interpersonal ends as voluntary relationships, most scholars would agree that their involuntary nature argues against confusing them with friendship.

Until recently, the study of children's dyadic relationships with peers was focused almost exclusively on the study of friendship. Researchers are now turning to the study of mutual antipathies and enmities (e.g., Abecassis, Hartup, Haselager, Scholte, & van Lieshout, 2002; Hodges & Card, 2003). Whereas the topic of disliking is certainly not new (e.g., Hayes, Gershman, & Bolin, 1980), the emphasis of recent research has been on the frequency of mutual antipathies, their correlates, and their developmental significance.

A final point is that relationships must be understood according to their place in the network of other relationships. For example, children's friendships are influenced by the relationships they have at home with parents and siblings. Children's conceptualizations and feelings about their primary relationships are internalized and lead to (a) expectations about what relationships outside of the family might and should be like, and (b) particular interpersonal behaviors and interactions with peers that reflect their internalized models of relationships (Belsky & Cassidy, 1995). Whereas parent-child relationships may influence the early development and maintenance of children's peer relationships, it would make sense to expect that the relations between relationship systems become increasingly reciprocal and mutual with increasing child age: The quality of the child's peer relationships is likely to influence the quality of the parent-child relationship and perhaps even the relationship between the child's parents.

Groups

A *group* is a collection of interacting individuals who have some degree of reciprocal influence over one another. Groups can be formed spontaneously, out of common interests or circumstances, or due to formal external structures (e.g., groups of students organized into classes in school). Hinde (1979) suggests that a *group* is the structure that emerges from the features and patterning of the relationships and interactions present in a population of children. Accordingly, groups possess properties that arise from the manner in which the relationships are patterned but are not present in the individual relationships themselves. Examples of such properties include *cohesiveness,* or the degree of unity and inclusiveness exhibited by the children or manifest by the density of the interpersonal relationships; *hierarchy,* or the extent of intransitivity in the ordering of the individual relationships along interesting dimensions (e.g., If Fred dominates

Brian and Brian dominates Peter, does Fred dominate Peter?); and *homogeneity* or *homophily,* or consistency across members in the ascribed or achieved personal characteristics (e.g., sex, race, age, intelligence, or attitudes toward school). Finally, every group has *norms,* or distinctive patterns of behaviors and attitudes that characterize group members and differentiate them from members of other groups.

Many of our most important means for describing groups speak to these core characteristics or processes. Thus, researchers may address the degree to which the relationships and interactions in a group are segregated along sex or racial lines (e.g., Killen, Crystal, & Watanabe, 2002; Killen, Lee-Kim, McGlothlin, & Strangor, 2002); they may compare the rates of social isolation among groups that differ in composition; or they may investigate the extent to which a group's hierarchies of affiliation, dominance, and influence are linear and interrelated. In addition, group norms can be used as a basis for distinguishing separate "crowds" in the networks of relationships among children in high school (e.g., Brown, 1989). The emergent properties of groups also shape the experiences of individuals in the groups (e.g., Espelage, Holt, & Henkel, 2003). Thus, crowd *labels* constrain, in important ways, adolescents' freedom to explore new identities; *status hierarchies* influence the formation of new friendships; *segregation* influences the diversity of children's experiences with others; and *cohesiveness* influences children's sense of belonging. As such, the group can influence the individual. Indeed, many of the classic developmental studies concerned the peer group per se, including that of K. Lewin et al. (1939) concerning group climate, and Sherif, Harvey, White, Hood, and Sherif's (1961) examination of intragroup loyalty and intergroup conflict. In addition, theorists stressing the importance of children's peer experiences (e.g., Cairns, Xie, & Leung, 1996; Xie, Cairns, & Cairns, 1999, 2001) have generally conceptualized the group as an important developmental context that shapes and supports the behaviors of its constituent members.

In spite of the importance of the group, there has been, until recently, little attention paid to the assessment of group phenomena (see Bukowski & Sippola, 2001). This is surprising because researchers often cite experiences with peers with reference to the "peer group." Cairns et al. (1996) argued that this neglect could be attributed to the complex conceptual and methodological issues related to the study of group structure and organization. However, recently a number of complex statistical procedures have allowed the study of peer groups and peer group effects on children.

Finally, it is worth noting that the construct that has dominated the peer literature during the past 25 years, namely that of *popularity,* is both an individual- and a group-oriented phenomenon. Measures of popularity refer to the group's view of an individual in relation to the dimensions of liking and disliking (Bukowski & Hoza, 1989; Bukowski, Sippola, Hoza, & Newcomb, 2000; Parker, Saxon, Asher, & Kovacs, 1999). In this regard, popularity is a group construct and the processes of rejection and acceptance are group processes. Yet, despite this reality, most peer researchers treat popularity as characteristic of the individual (Asher, Parker, & Walker, 1996; Newcomb, Bukowski, & Pattee, 1993). This confusion exemplifies the significance of recognizing the inextricable links between different levels of analysis. As Bronfenbrenner (1944) wrote over 50 years ago, the study of the peer system requires the "envisagement of the individual and the group as developing organic units" (p. 75).

Culture

It is important to recognize that each of the social levels described earlier falls under the all-reaching umbrella of the cultural macrosystem (e.g., Bronfenbrenner & Crouter, 1983). By culture is meant "the set of attitudes, values, beliefs, and behaviors shared by a group of people, communicated from one generation to the next" (Matsumoto, 1997, p. 5). Cultural beliefs and norms help interpret the acceptability of individual characteristics and the types and ranges of interactions and relationships that are likely or permissible.

As it happens, the cultural and cross-cultural study of children's peer interactions, relationships, and groups has a brief history. A central question asked in this body of work is rather intriguing: Do the "meanings" and significance of given social behaviors or social relationships differ from culture to culture, or are there cultural universals in interpreting given social behaviors and relationships? For example, is social competence defined in a similar fashion across cultures? And what about aggression or socially wariness? Are these behaviors similarly defined and interpreted from culture to culture? Are children's friendships conceptualized in similar ways across culture? Are such relationships viewed as similarly significant from culture to culture? These are but a few questions that are only now being examined by researchers the world over.

Given that the majority of the world's inhabitants do not reside in culturally Westernized countries, the cross-cultural work on peer interactions, relationships, and groups requires careful note: Child development is influenced by many factors. In any culture, children are shaped by the physical and social settings in which they live as well as culturally regulated customs, childrearing practices, and culturally based belief systems (Harkness & Super, 2002). The bottom line is that the psychological "meaning" attributed to any given social behavior is, in large part, a function of the ecological niche in which it is produced. If a given behavior is viewed as acceptable, then parents (and significant others) will attempt to encourage its development; if the behavior is perceived as maladaptive or abnormal, then parents (and significant others) will attempt to discourage its growth and development. And the very means by which people go about encouraging or discouraging the given behavior may be culturally determined and defined. Thus, in some cultures, the response to an aggressive act may be to explain to the child why the behavior is unacceptable; in others, physical discipline may be the accepted norm; in yet others, aggression may be ignored or perhaps even reinforced (for discussions, see Bornstein & Cheah, in press; Harkness & Super, 2002). Another issue is the degree to which cultures allow or encourage peer interactions. For example, in kin-based societies, such as Kenya, peer interactions are discouraged because parents fear the potential for competition and conflict (Edwards, 1992). It would appear most sensible for the international community of child development researchers not to generalize to other cultures their own culture-specific theories of normal and abnormal development. In this regard, we describe relevant extant research pertaining to cross-cultural similarities and differences in children's peer interactions and relationships throughout this chapter.

Summary

To understand children's experiences with peers, researchers have focused on children's interactions with other children and on their involvements in peer relationships and groups. Analyses in each level—interactions, relationships, groups—are scientifically legitimate and raise interesting questions. However, researchers have not always demonstrated a clear understanding of the important ways in which processes at one level are influenced by those at the others. They have sometimes overlooked ways in which conclusions drawn at single levels of analysis can be limited. For example, the observation of two children at play can reveal the rates at which they display different behaviors and the patterning of these behaviors with respect to one another. It can be misleading, however, to attribute these characteristics of interaction solely to individual differences in social competence or temperament; one must also consider relational interdependencies—unique adjustments made by Person A and Person B to one another that define their particular relationship. And events transpiring in a given relationship also reflect realities outside the relationship; for example, tensions produced by individuals' loyalties to other friends in the peer group may affect the quality of social interaction between two specific children.

Until recently, studying individual, dyadic, and group measures was challenging, both conceptually and statistically. Advances in multilevel modeling techniques and in the availability of more-or-less user-friendly software have given researchers the tools to examine the effects of group, dyadic, and individual variables simultaneously. These procedures can be used to assess how the effects of variables describing individual tendencies (e.g., aggressiveness, sociability, or inhibition) on an outcome (e.g., one's subsequent aggressiveness, sociability, or reticence) will vary as a function of dyadic-relationship characteristics (e.g., quality of friendship; quality of the mother-child relationship). In turn, a researcher can assess variations in dyadic effects due to the characteristics of the groups in which they are embedded. The use of these techniques is nearly perfectly suited to some forms of peer relationships research. They have been used with success already (e.g., Kochenderfer-Ladd & Wardrop, 2001).

Yet, despite the remarkable methodological advantages of procedures, such as multilevel modeling, they alone cannot deal with the conceptual ambiguity of many measures currently used in peer research. Specifically, a measure that putatively assesses one level of social analysis may, to some extent, reflect phenomena at another level. For example, having dyadic friendships with aggressive peers, or belonging to an aggressive peer group may reflect individual tendencies such as sociability, risk-taking, and tolerance of aggressiveness and those who are aggressive. At the same time, friendships with aggressive others also carry meaning at the relationship (dyadic friendship) or group levels. Thus, when researchers are examining the effects of group membership, they must also distinguish between the effects of the group per se and the effects of having dyadic relationships in that group. This problem is especially important when one wishes to distinguish between friendship effects and group effects. To the extent that a child's friendships are likely to be embedded in the child's group, researchers need to carefully account for all of these effects and to distinguish between them. Attempts to distinguish between the effects of friendship and the effects of belonging to a peer group are inadequate, or at least limited, when the effects of only one friend are accounted for. In such an instance, some "group effects" may actually be "friendship effects" or the other way around.

Finally, our emphasis on multiple levels of analysis provides us with a basic conceptual model of social competence. Researchers have often treated measures of peer experiences (e.g., sociometric status) as indices of social competence. Our view is that social competence in the peer system refers to a child's capacity to engage effectively and successfully at each level of analysis and in his or her relevant culture. A competent child will be able to (a) become engaged in a peer group structure and participate in group-oriented activities, (b) become involved in satisfying relationships constructed on balanced and reciprocal interactions, and (c) satisfy individual goals and needs and develop accurate and productive means of understanding experiences with peers on both the group and dyadic levels.

THEORIES RELEVANT TO THE STUDY OF CHILDREN'S PEER INTERACTIONS, RELATIONSHIPS, AND GROUPS

Personality Theorists

Psychoanalytic Perspectives

Psychoanalytic or neo-psychoanalytic theorists have rarely ascribed developmental significance to children's peer interactions or relationships. Instead, they regard much of the child's development as resulting from parental behavior and the quality of the parent-child re-

lationship. Perhaps the only psychoanalytically oriented theorist to ascribe developmental significance to children's peer relationships is Peter Blos. For Blos (1967), the major event of adolescence is the process of *individuation* by which adolescents restructure their childhood relationships with their parents and strive to achieve qualitatively different relationships with peers. Individuation involves renegotiating dependency relationships with parents; such renegotiation is precipitated, in part, by adolescent sexual drives. It also involves the introduction of new themes into relationships with peers. Responding to erotic drives, the adolescent turns toward the peer group as a means of finding sexual outlets and venues of emotional closeness; previously, such closeness was available only from parents.

As a function of restructuring their relationships with parents, adolescents come to experience turmoil and anxiety accompanied by feelings of despair, worthlessness, discouragement, and vulnerability. According to Blos, adolescents' capacities to cope with these feelings and experiences rest with their ability to establish qualitatively distinct forms of supportive relationships with peers. In the process of separating from parents and prior to achieving a state of personal autonomy, adolescents turn to peers for "stimulation, belongingness, loyalty, devotion, empathy, and resonance" (Blos, 1967, p. 177).

One potential pitfall of the individuation process for adolescents is that some teenagers become overly dependent on peers, conforming to the norms and standards of the group too readily as part of their search for security outside the family. Blos (1967) argued that, in such cases, dependence on peers is problematic because it precludes the promotion of independence and autonomy. But more generally, it is argued that the peer group is a major determinant of an adolescent's ability to achieve a sense of autonomy and independence from the family.

The effects of the psychoanalytic tradition on peer relationships research can be seen most strongly in two areas of research. The first one takes its inspiration from the argument embedded in *attachment theory* (Bowlby, 1969/1982) that peer relationships are motivated by a human need for relatedness. According to this view, being associated with others increases security because it reduces anxiety and promotes the internalization of positive relational schemas of others. As children develop mechanisms to distinguish between friends and enemies, they are increasingly able to manage their emotions and behavior. A second idea taken from psychoanalytic theory has appeared more recently. Sandstrom and Cramer (2003) applied the concept of *defense mechanisms* to the understanding of girls' responses to rejection. Their findings indicate that the use of denial and projection following rejection vary as a function of sociometric status with their use highest among rejected and neglected girls. They point to the potential adaptive benefits of this use.

Sullivan's Theory of Personality Development

In his developmental model of interpersonal relationships, Sullivan characterized children's peer relationships during the early childhood and the early school-age years as organized largely around play and common activities. During the juvenile period (from approximately age 7 to 9 years), children become increasingly concerned about their place in the peer group as a whole and a sense of belonging to the group becomes increasingly important.

As children entered early adolescence, Sullivan proposed that they begin to develop "chumships" or close, intimate mutual relationships with same-sex peers. As a relationship between "co-equals," chumships were distinct from the hierarchical relationships that children experienced with their parents. Accordingly, Sullivan argued that this close relationship was a child's first true interpersonal experience based on reciprocity and exchange between equals and that the *function* of peer relationships was to promote a sense of well-being. He proposed that it was in chumships that children had their first opportunities to experience a sense of self-validation. This validation would emanate, in large part, from their recognition of the positive regard and care that their chums held for them. Sullivan went so far as to argue that the positive experiences of having a "chum" in adolescence would be so powerful as to enable adolescents to overcome trauma that may have resulted from prior family experiences. Conversely, Sullivan believed that the experience of being isolated from the group, during the juvenile period, would lead a child to have concerns about his or her own competencies and his or her acceptability as a desirable peer. Consequently, Sullivan suggested that children who are unable to establish a position in the peer group would develop feelings of inferiority that could contribute to a sense of psychological ill-being. One posited outcome of the lack of supportive chumships was the development of loneliness, or

"the exceedingly unpleasant and driving experience connected with the inadequate discharge of the need for human intimacy" (Sullivan, 1953, p. 290).

Symbolic Interactionism

Following the lead of William James (1890), who posited that humans have "an innate propensity to get ourselves noticed, and noticed favorably, by our kind" (p. 293), Mead (1934) argued that people defined themselves according to how they believed they were perceived by others. To Mead, for example, the ability to self-reflect, to consider the self in relation to others, and to understand the perspectives of others was largely a function of participation in organized, rule-governed activities with peers. He suggested that exchanges among peers, whether experienced in the arenas of cooperation or competition, conflict or friendly discussion, allowed the child to gain an understanding of the self as both a subject and an object. Understanding that the self could be an object of others' perspectives gradually evolved into the conceptualization of a "generalized other" or an organized and coordinated perspective of the "social" group. In turn, recognition of the "generalized other" led to the emergence of an organized sense of self. Thus, according to symbolic interactionist theory, exchanges between the individual and the peer group are essential to the formation of a "self" concept and a concept of the "other," two constructs thought to be mutually interdependent.

Cognitive Developmental Perspectives

The Piagetian Perspective

Piaget (1932) suggested that children's relationships with peers could be distinguished, in both form and function, from their relationships with adults. The latter relationships were construed as being complementary, asymmetrical, and falling along a vertical plane of dominance and power assertion. As such, children's interactions with adults about cognitions, ideas, and beliefs were thought to be marked by more emotional wariness and less openness and spontaneity than their interactions with age-mates. By contrast, peer exchanges allowed children to actively explore their ideas rather than to risk their devaluation and criticism by adult authority figures. It was also proposed that children come to accept adults' notions, thoughts, beliefs, and rules, not necessarily because they understand them, but rather because obedience is viewed as required. Along the same lines, adults were less likely to follow the dictates of children. Peer relationships, alternatively, were portrayed as being balanced, egalitarian, and as falling along a more-or-less horizontal plane of dominance and power assertion. Thus, it was in the peer context that children could experience opportunities to examine conflicting ideas and explanations, to negotiate and discuss multiple perspectives, to decide to compromise with, or to reject, the notions held by peers. These peer interactive experiences were believed to result in positive and adaptive developmental outcomes for children, such as the ability to understand others' thoughts, emotions, and intentions.

Empirical support for these contentions is drawn from neo-Piagetian research demonstrating that when children work together to solve given problems, they are more likely to advance their knowledge base through discussion than if they work independently and alone. Developmental change occurs because differences of opinion provoke cognitive disequilibria that are sufficiently discomforting so as to elicit attempts at resolution. Each interactor must construct, or reconstruct, a coordinated perspective of the original set of ideas to reinstate a sense of cognitive equilibrium.

From this perspective, it is *intrapersonal* cognitive conflict that evokes a search for homeostasis and resultant developmental change. This intrapersonal conflict may be instigated by disagreements about ideas, thoughts, beliefs; however, it is unlikely that mean-spirited *interpersonal* conflict and hostility brings with it cognitive advancement. Recent views on the role of conflict center on the notion that disagreements between peers about things personal, interpersonal, and impersonal are best resolved through the cooperative exchange of explanations, questions, and reasoned dialogue (e.g., Laursen et al., 2001; Shulman & Laursen, 2002). If the exchange of conflicting ideas is marked by hostility, dysregulated or disabling emotions are not likely to promote cognitive growth and development.

Contemporary perspectives on the role of peer exchange for developmental growth can be seen in the work of co-constructivist thinkers such as Azmitia (Azmitia, Lippman, & Ittel, 1999; Azmitia & Montgomery, 1993) and Rogoff (1997). These writers introduce the notion that the quality of the relationship between the peers who are interacting with each other may contribute to cognitive and social-cognitive growth and development. For example, *friends* can challenge each other with relative impunity. Given that friends are

more sensitive to each others' needs, and more supportive of each others' thoughts and well-being than nonfriends, it may be that children are more likely to talk openly and challenge each others' thoughts and deeds in the company of friends than nonfriends. If this were the case, one would expect exchanges between friends to be more promoting of cognitive and social-cognitive growth than nonfriend peer exchanges. Data supportive of this view are reviewed in later relevant sections.

Vygotsky's Perspective

According to Vygotsky (1978), cognitive growth and development are a function, in large part, of interpersonal exchange. Vygotsky invoked the principle of the "zone of proximal development" (*ZPD*) to explain the significance of social interaction. The *ZPD* represented the distance between what the child could do independently and what he or she could do with the collaboration or assistance of others. Vygotsky indicated that typically assistance was provided by the child's parents. Researchers such as Tudge (1992; Hogan & Tudge, 1999) and Rogoff (1997) have argued that the child's peers can play the role of co-constructivist. Thus, pairing with a more competent, "expert" peer may assist the child's movement through the *ZPD* (e.g., Duran & Gauvain, 1993).

One difference between the Piagetian and Vygotskian perspectives of the links between peer interaction, peer relationships, and growth and development lies in Piaget's belief that it was peer *conflict* that evoked change, whereas Vygotsky contended that it was *cooperation* and the pooling of ideas that promoted change. Contemporary accounts suggest that conflicting ideas and differences in opinion actually elicit cooperation between partners. If partners are positively disposed to one another, it behooves them to discuss their differences, to negotiate, to compromise—in short, to cooperate and to move forward, not only cognitively, but also emotionally in their relationship. Thus, studies of the role that *conflict* plays in cognitive and social-cognitive growth include, in the phenomenon's definition, components of disagreement as well as explanation, questions, agreements, and compromise. A rapprochement between the Piagetian and Vygotskian positions would suggest that *intrapersonal* cognitive conflict triggers the child's attempts to regain some semblance of cognitive homeostasis. If such intrapersonal cognitive conflict is associated with conflictual, negative-spirited interpersonal exchange, cognitive growth is less likely to result than anger, fear, or some other disabling emotion. Alternately, if cognitive conflict is associated with "reasoned dialogue" (Damon & Killen, 1982), cooperative co-construction may occur resulting in a new, more cognitively mature perspective.

In summary, research based on the constructivist theories of Piaget and Vygotsky reveals that:

- Children can, and do, make cognitive advances when they *cooperatively* exchange and discuss conflicting perspectives on various issues (MacDonald, Miell, & Morgan, 2000).

- Children working together can solve problems that neither partner is capable of solving alone (Golbeck, 1998).

- Discussing problems with a peer who has superior knowledge is more likely to evoke intrapersonal conflict and cognitive advancement than discussions with a less competent peer (Duran & Gauvain, 1993; Garton, 2001; Tudge, 1992).

- Transactive exchanges during which children openly criticize each others' ideas and clarify and elaborate their own ideas are more often observed in the company of friends than of nonfriends (e.g., Azmitia & Montgomery, 1993).

Learning and Social Learning Theories, Peer Interaction, and Peer Relationships

Although its influences are less explicit than implied, social learning theory has had a powerful effect on the study of peer interactions, perhaps more so than any other perspective. The traditional learning theory perspective has been that children are behavior control and behavior change agents for each other. Peers punish or ignore nonnormative social behavior and reward or reinforce positively those behaviors considered culturally appropriate and competent. Thus, to the extent that children behave in a socially appropriate manner, they develop positive relationships with their peers; to the extent that children behave in a socially incompetent or nonnormative manner, peer rejection may result.

Perhaps the most relevant and influential social learning was that formulated originally by Bandura and Walters (1963). In their monograph, *Social Learning and Personality Development,* Bandura and Walters noted that children can learn novel social behaviors by observing others. Moreover, children could use observational information about the consequences of specific social behaviors to guide their own exhibition or inhibition of these behaviors. This modeling perspective provides a powerful argument for how the social behaviors of children are quickly and effectively organized, reorganized, and redirected. Observational learning promotes adaptation to new circumstances and new relationships (Cairns, 1979). As Cairns noted, however, once learned, social behaviors are subject to maintenance and change; thus, it is argued that the demonstration of socially learned behaviors will be maintained or inhibited by its actual or expected consequences. Further, the social contexts in which reinforcement and punishment occur (or are expected to occur) matter. The source of the reinforcement or punishment, how, when, and where the consequences are administered, and whether the child believes that he or she can actually produce the desired behavior all affect the production, reproduction, or inhibition of the given behavior. For example, Bandura (1989) speculated that children set standards of achievement for themselves and that they are likely to self-administer reinforcement when the standards are met and punishment when they are not. Self-reinforcement is applied when children see themselves as having exceeded the norms for their relevant comparison group of peers; self-punishment is consequent to having failed to meet perceived group norms.

Also, children's beliefs, cognitions, and ideas about the administrators of rewards/ punishment can influence the strength of the given behaviors. Is the administrator a competent or incompetent peer, an aggressive or nonaggressive age-mate, or a younger or older child? Moreover, the age of the child who is processing this social information must assuredly be of some significance. To the extent that researchers have generally ignored these issues, social learning theory still has some way to go in advancing an understanding of the establishment, maintenance, and dissolution/inhibition of children's peer-directed behaviors.

Human Ethology

Ethology is "the subdiscipline of biology concerned with the biological bases of behavior, including its evolution, causation, function, and development" (Cairns, 1979, p. 358). Although there is no particular ethological theory pertaining specifically to the evolutionary significance of peer interaction or peer relationships, the *methods* and *constructs* used by animal behaviorists have often been adopted by those who study children's social behaviors, peer relationships, and the structural dynamics of the peer group (e.g., Hawley, 2003). To the extent that Bowlby's (1973) ethologically oriented theory of parent-infant attachment relationships has come to influence the study of peer relationships, some consideration of human ethological theory is warranted.

The questions asked by ethologists were outlined by Tinbergen (1951). He suggested that when an organism produces a given behavior, the scientist must ask: (a) Why did the individual demonstrate the particular behavior at the specific time she or he did? (b) How did the individual come to produce such a behavior at such times? and (c) What is the functional significance or survival value of the produced behavior? These questions focus concern on features of motivation, learning and development, and evolutionary adaptation, respectively.

A central tenet of ethological theory is that social behavior, relationships, and organizational structures are limited by biological constraints related to their adaptive, evolutionary function (Hinde & Stevenson-Hinde, 1976). Thus, *aggression,* for example, is viewed as a means by which members of the species survive; protect themselves, their significant others, and their progeny; and ensure reproductive success (Lorenz, 1966). *Altruism* is also seen as a basic facet of human nature, ensuring survival of the species. Likewise, the *attachment relationship* formed during infancy between parent and child not only guarantees the protection of the young from discomfort and threatening predators but also provides the child with an internalized "working model" (Bowlby, 1973) of what human relationships could, should, or might be like. In this latter case, the quality of the primary relationship engenders a set of internalized relationships expectations that affect the initiation and maintenance of extrafamilial (e.g., peer) relationships.

Given the assumption that behavior is best understood when observed in natural settings, ethological theory has influenced contemporary methodologies. Thus, investigators have devoted considerable effort to distinguish *observationally* between different forms and functions of what, on the surface, appear to be the same basic behavioral phenomena. For example, one can distinguish between physical, verbal, and relational aggression (the *forms*) and between hostile and instrumental aggression (the putative *functions*; see Little, Jones, Henrich, & Hawley, 2003). Such distinctions are drawn on the basis

of examining the gestures and facial expressions of the interacting individuals, as well as the ecological (venues) and interpersonal (quality of relationships) contexts in which social interactions occur.

Ethological theory and the questions derived from it evoke analyses of the psychological meanings of different forms of the same behavior (Hawley, 2003). For example, do instrumental and hostile aggressions have different developmental origins and different proximal and distal causes (e.g., Prinstein & Cillessen, 2003)? Similarly, does the frequent expression of behavioral solitude when engaging in constructive activity have different developmental origins and different proximal and distal causes than the frequent expression of behavioral solitude when observing others from afar (Coplan, Rubin, Fox, Calkins, & Stewart, 1994; Henderson, Marshall, Fox, & Rubin, 2004)? Likewise, does a given behavior have the same psychological meaning when produced by a 2-, 4-, and 10-year-old? And finally, does a given behavior have the same psychological meaning when produced by children of the same age, but in different cultures? These are questions pertinent to the study of peer *interaction.* And, given the normalcy/abnormalcy of social behaviors in different contexts and at different ages (Cillessen & Mayeux, 2004), it is also clear how questions derived from ethological theory are relevant to the study of children's peer *relationships.*

Group Socialization Theory

If there was a publication that brought the study of the peer group to the attention of the general reader during the past 10 years it was Judith Rich Harris's essay on group socialization theory (1995) and the book, *The Nurture Assumption,* based on it (1998). Issued just after the writing of our earlier *Handbook* chapter, Harris's essay and book claimed: (a) The effects of parenting on development were, at best, small; (b) the effects of genes on development were strong; and (c) the effect of peer relationships, and especially the peer group, were strong also. At the risk of oversimplification, Harris's ideas can be summarized as follows: First, she criticized research on parenting as being methodologically and substantively flawed. She objected to the claim that parents influence their children because most studies of parenting failed to produce strong effect sizes and were methodologically flawed due to their use of correlational designs rather than of explicitly experimental methods. Second, in support of her arguments regarding the influence of genes, she appropriately called on findings that point to genetic effects on various aspects of development. Third, Harris's claims about the effects of the peer system were, in part, predicated on the view that young people are driven by an atavistic desire to be part of a group. According to Harris, an important repercussion of these tribal motivations is that young people, in an effort to be part of a group, will change their behavior in response to group norms and expectations.

Thus, it was proposed that once children find themselves outside the home, they take on the norms prevalent in the groups in which they spend their time . . . and, for the most part, those groups comprise other children. Drawing from social psychological perspectives on the significance of group norms (a motivation to "fit in"), in-group biases and out-group hostilities, and social cognitive views of group processes, it was argued that children's identities develop primarily from their experiences in the peer group. Although Harris's (1998) views that parent-child and other dyadic relationships (including friendships) are relatively unimportant for individual development has drawn many criticisms (e.g., Collins, Maccoby, Steinberg, Hetherington, & Bornstein, 2000), the elements of her thesis that stressed the significance of peer interactions, relationships, and groups for normal and abnormal development provided some vindication to peer researchers. For decades, these researchers have been challenged by theorists, researchers, and policymakers who have cited the primacy of parenting and the parent-child relationship. With Harris's counterchallenge, a gauntlet was dropped; researchers were called on to address some central questions about the causal roles that genes, biology, family, and peers play in child and adolescent adjustment and maladjustment.

The claims of this book were presented and debated in the review sections of newspapers and magazines and on many "prime time" television programs. The essay managed to win some public praise, typically from people who do not study peer relationships. For good reason, persons who have been advocates of behavioral genetic explanations of a wide variety of social behaviors and personality characteristics (e.g., Pinker, 2002; Rowe, 1995) were supportive of Harris's (1995, 1998) claims of genetic influence. Scholars who study parenting wrote reasoned critiques of Harris's thesis regarding the relative unimportance of parental

socialization (Collins et al., 2000). Perhaps at the writing of the *next* version of this *Handbook* chapter, reliable evidence pertaining to the power of peer group influence will be presented as supporting the provocative thesis proposed by Harris. In the meantime, contemporary research (described later) on the ways in which the composition of peer networks change as a function of children's individual interests and behavioral characteristics may be taken as some evidence of the transactional push-and-pull between individual inclinations and peer group norms.

PEER INTERACTIONS, RELATIONSHIPS, AND GROUPS: A DEVELOPMENTAL PERSPECTIVE

Children's peer experiences become increasingly diverse, complex, and integrated with development. In some cases, the impetus for these developments rests in children (i.e., changes in interpersonal understanding or interpersonal concerns), while others derive from situational or contextual phenomena (Bierman, 2003). In the following sections, we review many developmental mileposts in the *interactional* (changes in the frequency or forms of specific behaviors), *relational* (changes in qualities of friendships or patterns of involvement in friendships), and *group* (changes in configurations of and involvement in cliques and crowds) levels of children's involvement with other children.

Infancy and the Toddler Years

Research on the normative development peer interactions and relationships during infancy and toddlerhood has waned during the past decade. Instead, the focus has appeared to shift from normative development to individual differences to the extent that toddlers initiate social interaction and are capable of regulating social and emotional behavior.

Interaction

Early researchers of children's peer experiences were impressed by what they regarded as the significant social shortcomings in infants. Buhler (1935), for example, reported that prior to the first 6 months of life, babies were oblivious to each other's presence. And it was argued that throughout much of the 1st year infants were interested in each other as objects but not as social partners with whom the development of a relationship was possible (e.g., Maudry & Nekula, 1939). Such a view appears less often in contemporary readings, but it has not disappeared completely; for example, it has been noted that the peer interactions of infants are diffuse and fragmented. These interactions are seen as illustrating the inability of babies to comprehend the social and cognitive needs, capacities, or zones of proximal development of their age-mates (Hay, 1985).

Infants do have obvious social limitations. Yet, careful observation of infants reveals remarkable strides taken during the 1st year of life. These include (a) the seemingly intentional direction of smiles, frowns, and gestures to their play partners (Hay, Nash, & Pederson, 1983); (b) the careful observation of peers representing a clear sign of social interest (Eckerman, 1979); and (c) the response, often in kind, to their play partner's behaviors (Mueller & Brenner, 1977). During the 2nd year of life, toddlers demonstrate monumental gains in their social repertoires. With the emergence of locomotion and the ability to use words to communicate, interactive bouts become lengthier (Eckerman & Stein, 1990), and toddler play becomes organized around particular themes or games. According to Ross (1982), the typical toddler "game" involves extended and patterned interchanges characterized by the mutual exchange of gaze, the direction of social actions to one another, the production of appropriate responses to these social actions, and the demonstration of turn-taking behaviors. Often, these toddler games are marked by reciprocal imitative acts. Reciprocity of imitation suggests not only that a given child is socially interested in the playmate to the point at which she or he is willing to copy that playmate's behavior but also that she or he is also aware of the partner's interest in him or her (i.e., an awareness of being imitated). Mutual imitation, which increases rapidly during the 2nd year, appears to lay the basis for later emerging cooperative interchanges involving pretense (Howes, 1992).

In summary, social skills in toddlerhood comprise (a) the ability to coordinate behavior with that of the play partner; (b) imitation of the peer's activity and an awareness of being imitated; (c) turn-taking that *involves observe peer—respond to peer—observe and wait—respond to peer* interchange sequences; (d) the demonstration of helping and sharing behaviors; and (e) the ability to respond appropriately to the peer partner's characteristics.

These developments promote more effective social commerce between toddlers and contribute a generally positive affective quality to their interaction (Hay, Castle, Davies, Demetriou, & Stimson, 1999). However, toddler social interaction is also marked by conflict (e.g., Hay, Castle, & Davies, 2000; Hay & Ross, 1982; Rubin, Hastings, Chen, Stewart, & McNichol, 1998). Rubin et al. (1998) found that over 70% of 25-month-old children participated in a conflict situation at least once in a 50-minute laboratory setting. In a comparable setting, Hay and Ross (1982) observed 87% of 21-month-old toddlers engaged in at least one conflict. As such, it appears that conflict is neither infrequent nor limited to a small percentage of toddlers.

Indeed, it appears as if many of those toddlers who frequently instigate conflicts with peers are the most socially outgoing and initiating (National Institute of Child Health and Human Development Early Child Care Research Network, 2001; Rubin et al., 1998). It is also the case that (a) toddlers who lose conflicts are more likely than the initial victor to initiate the immediately subsequent conflict (Hay & Ross, 1982); and (b) toddlers are highly attentive to, and are more likely to imitate and initiate interactions with, highly sociable age-mates (Howes, 1983, 1988). Taken together, these data suggest that during the 2nd year of life, toddlers do display social skills of modest complexity.

Relationships

It has been demonstrated that toddlers are more likely to initiate play, direct positive affect to, and engage in complex interactions with familiar than unfamiliar playmates (Howes, 1988, 1996). But can familiarity be equated with the existence of a relationship? According to Ross and Lollis (1989), toddlers do develop positive relationships as they become increasingly familiar with one another. Indeed, these toddler relationships allow the observer to predict the sorts of interchanges that will transpire between dyadic partners (Ross, Conant, Cheyne, & Alevisos, 1992). It is the predictability of the quality of interchange that marks a dyad as constituting a friendship.

Ross and colleagues have carried out an elegant series of studies to demonstrate that toddlers can and do develop relationships and that their relationships can be characterized in several different ways. Ross et al. (1992) begin by noting that a relationship may be inferred when:

Neither the characteristic behavior of Child One, nor the behavior that others typically direct to Child Two, nor the independent, additive influences of both factors taken together are sufficient to predict the behavior of Child One to Child Two. In that sense, relationships cannot be derived from the individual characteristics of the participants; the relationship itself influences the interaction between them. (p. 1)

To this end, Ross and colleagues have demonstrated that toddlers develop *reciprocal* relationships, not only by the mutual exchange of positive overtures, but also by agonistic interactions. Positive interactions are directed specifically to those who have directed positive initiations to the child beforehand; conflict is initiated specifically with those who have initiated conflictual interactions with the child beforehand.

To the extent that reciprocal interchanges of positive overtures may characterize particular dyads, it may be said that toddlers do have friendships. Although the terms of reference vary from those of Ross and colleagues, other researchers have proposed that toddlers have "friends." For example, Howes (1988) defined toddler friendship as encompassing the response to a peer's overture at least *once,* the production of at least *one* complementary or reciprocal dyadic exchange, and the demonstration of positive affect during at least *one* such exchange. Vandell and Mueller (1980) identified toddler friends as those who initiated positive social interaction more often with each other than with other potential partners. During the toddler period, friendships, as defined earlier, do exist; however, it is doubtful that they carry the same strength of psychological meaning as the friendships of older children. Nevertheless, these early relationships may lay the groundwork for the establishment and maintenance of friendships throughout the childhood years.

Groups

Even young toddlers spend much of their time in small groups such as with day-care mates. But there is not much empirical evidence that this level of social organization is salient to, or influential on, these young children. Nevertheless, some authors (e.g., Legault & Strayer, 1991) have observed dominance hierarchies even in small groups of young toddlers, as well as in subsets of children who invest greater attention and interaction to one another than to outside nonmembers. Interestingly, some members of these groups appear

more central to their functioning than others, perhaps illustrating the earliest examples of individual differences in popularity and influence.

New Directions

Major advances in the study of infants' and toddlers' peer interactions and relationships have derived primarily from examinations of *individual differences* in factors such as sociability, behavioral inhibition, conflict, and the regulation of emotional and behavioral tendencies. Much of this research meshes with the current Zeitgeist in which the study of developmental psychopathology dominates in many quarters. Thus, researchers have discovered that those toddlers who frequently initiate conflict with age-mates, especially those who are unable to regulate their emotions and behaviors, evidence difficulties of an externalizing nature in subsequent years (Hay et al., 2000; Rubin, Burgess, Dwyer, & Hastings, 2003). And those toddlers who evidence fearfulness and wariness when faced with unfamiliarity in social settings evidence difficulties associated with social reticence, shyness, and anxiety as preschoolers (e.g., Rubin, Burgess, & Hastings, 2002) and elementary school children (Reznick et al., 1986). Because the focus appears to be turning primarily in the direction of the development of psychopathology, it is important to note that researchers are beginning to find that early individual differences in cooperative, sharing and helping behaviors presage consequent positive aspects of peer interaction. Thus, for example, Howes and Phillipsen (1998) have demonstrated that toddlers' competent play with peers predicts socially competent activity at 4 years and less maladaptive interactive activity at 9 years. Whether individual differences in the peer interactional tendencies of infants and toddlers predict subsequent social relationship and/or group phenomena is, as yet, unknown.

Another new direction derives from the cross-cultural observation of toddlers. Researchers have recently found that Asian toddlers are more compliant than their North American counterparts (Chen, Rubin, et al., 2003); and Chinese and Korean toddlers appear to be more socially inhibited than Italian and Australian toddlers (Chen et al., 1998; Rubin et al., in press). Why these early differences in social behavior exist is only now being explored. Researchers interested in children's peer relationships would do well to examine whether such early cultural differences predict variability in the peer acceptance of children who best "match" their respective cultural norms for compliant and socially outgoing behaviors.

Early Childhood

Interaction

From 24 months to 5 years, the frequency of peer interaction increases and becomes more complex. Parten (1932) described six social participation categories that purportedly unfolded as stages as children matured. In order of presumed maturity, these categories included: unoccupied behavior, solitary play, onlooker behavior (the child observes others but does not participate in the activity), parallel play (the child plays beside but not with other children), associative play (the child plays and shares with others), and cooperative play (the child engages others in interaction that is well coordinated and defined by a division of labor). From her data, Parten concluded that between the ages of 2 and 5 years, children engage in increasing frequencies of associative and cooperative play and in decreasing frequencies of idle, solitary, and onlooker behavior.

A more critical reading of Parten's study and subsequent attempts at replication, however, suggests a more complex set of conclusions (e.g., Rubin, Watson, & Jambor, 1978). To begin with, children at all ages engage in unoccupied, onlooking, solitary, parallel, and group activities. Even at 5 years, children spend *less* of their free play time in classroom settings interacting with others than being alone or near others (Rubin et al., 1978). Indeed, the frequency of "parallel" play appears to remain constant from 3-to-5 years (Rubin et al., 1978). Yet, despite its modest placement in Parten's hierarchy of social participation, parallel play appears to serve as an important bridge to more truly interactive exchanges. More precise, sequential observations of preschool interaction reveal that parallel play often serves as an entrée into more complex, cooperative activity (Robinson, Anderson, Porter, Hart, & Wouden-Miller, 2003). Put another way, competent entry into ongoing peer activity appears to involve the ability to observe what the play participants are doing (onlooking activity), to approach and play beside potential play partners (parallel play), and, finally, to engage the players in conversation about the ongoing activity. A simple consideration of the frequency of particular forms of social participation masks the functional significance of the behavior. Watching and playing near, but not with, others are not necessarily immature. Rather, these behaviors may be sequenced in a competent manner to gain entry into an ongoing play activity.

Further attesting to the limits of Parten's original social participation categories is the fact that the categories of solitary, parallel, and group behavior comprise a variety of play forms that differ in cognitive complexity (see Rubin, Fein, & Vandenberg, 1983, for a review). Thus, whether alone, near, or with others, children may produce simple sensorimotor behaviors (*functional play,* e.g., aimlessly bouncing a ball), construct structures from blocks or draw with crayons (*constructive* play), or engage in some form of pretense (*dramatic* play). These cognitive forms of play, when examined in their social context, reveal interesting developmental trends. For example, solitary-sensorimotor behaviors become increasingly rare over the preschool years, while the relative frequency of solitary-construction or exploration remains the same (Rubin et al., 1978). Furthermore, the only types of social interactive activity to increase over the preschool years are sociodramatic play and games-with-rules (see Goncu, Patt, & Kouba, 2002, for a recent review): Age differences are apparent only for particular forms of social participation. Thus, in contrast to Parten's characterization, it does not appear to be a simple matter of solitary play disappearing over time and being replaced by social interactive activity. Importantly, it is the *form* that solitary or parallel or social activity takes that is of developmental significance.

Perhaps the most complex form of group interactive activity during the preschool years is *sociodramatic play* (Goncu et al., 2002). The ability to engage easily in this form of social activity represents mastery of one of the essential tasks of early childhood—the will and skill to share and coordinate decontextualized and substitutive activities. Researchers have reported that by the 3rd year of life, children are able to share symbolic meanings through social pretense (e.g., Howes, 1988). This is a remarkable accomplishment, as it involves the capacity to take on complementary roles, none of which matches real-world situations, and to agree on the adoption of these imaginary roles in a rule-governed context.

The ability to share meaning during pretense has been referred to as *intersubjectivity* (Goncu, 1993). Goncu (1993) has reported that quantitative differences are present in the extent to which the social interchanges of 3- versus 4.5-year-olds comprise indices of shared meaning or intersubjectivity. For example, the social interactions of older preschoolers involve longer sequences or turns. With increasing age, play partners become better able to agree with each other about the roles, rules, and themes of their pretense. They are also better able to maintain their play interactions by adding new dimensions to their expressed ideas. These developments reflect the preschooler's capacity to take the perspective of the play partner and, even more important, reflect the increasing sophistication of preschooler's naive "theory of mind" (Watson, Nixon, Wilson, & Capage, 1999).

The demonstration of elaborate forms of social pretense during the preschool years is impressive. But is the experience of sociodramatic play developmentally significant? According to Howes (1992), sociodramatic play serves three essential developmental functions. First, it creates a context for mastering the communication of meaning. Second, it provides opportunities for children to learn to control and compromise; these opportunities arise during discussions and negotiations concerning pretend roles and scripts and the rules guiding the pretend episodes (Sawyer, 1997). Third, social pretense allows for a "safe" context in which children can explore and discuss issues of intimacy and trust. Researchers have demonstrated that engaging in sociodramatic play is associated with social perspective-taking skills and the display of skilled interpersonal behavior.

In summary, as pretend play becomes more interactive, it serves increasingly sophisticated psychological functions. At first, social pretense provides opportunities for developing communication skills (Sawyer, 1997). Subsequently, it allows children opportunities to negotiate over roles, rules, and play themes and to practice a variety of roles in particular play scripts (Goncu, 1993). Thus, the addition of understanding pretense and sharing this understanding with others represents a significant milestone in the social lives of young children.

Beyond the developmental differences in how much children interact with one another or engage in cooperative endeavors requiring shared meanings, several other significant advances are made during the preschool period. For one, prosocial caring, sharing, and helping behaviors become more commonplace with increasing age. Researchers have demonstrated that 4-year-olds direct prosocial behavior to their peers more often than 3-year-olds (e.g., Benenson, Markovits, Roy, & Denko, 2003).

And the disposition to behave in a caring, sharing, and helpful manner in early childhood appears rather stable (Eisenberg et al., 1999). Dodge, Coie, & Lynam (Chapter 12, this *Handbook,* this volume) note that aggression increases until age 3 and then declines.

Importantly, the nature of conflict changes from the toddler to the preschool period. During toddlerhood, most conflict appears to center on toys and resources; during the preschool years, conflict becomes increasingly centered on differences of opinion (Chen, Fein, & Tam, 2001; Laursen & Hartup, 1989)—a reflection of the child's growing ability to focus on others' ideas, attitudes, and opinions.

Finally, preschoolers spend a great deal of time simply conversing with their playmates. And their conversations reflect numerous interpersonal goals (e.g., negotiating roles and rules in play; arguing and agreeing; Hay et al., 2004). Older preschool-age children direct more speech to their peers than do their younger counterparts (Levin & Rubin, 1983). And they are more likely to try to make explicit communicative connections with their play partners' ideas (Goncu, 1993; Sawyer, 1997). However, the successful outcome of verbally directed communication is predicted by its technical quality. Preschoolers whose language is comprehensible, who assure that they have obtained listener attention, and who are within arms' length of their social targets are more likely to meet their social goals than those who verbal directives are less skillfully evinced (Mueller, 1972). Relatedly, throughout the preschool years, children demonstrate age-related increases in social-communicative competence. For example, they begin to alter their speech to suit the needs of their listeners (Shatz & Gelman, 1973). Similar adjustments to the characteristics of their social targets have been reported in studies of interpersonal problem solving overtures (Krasnor & Rubin, 1983). These data reflect developmental growth in metacommunicative awareness and "mind-reading" (Dunn, 1999).

Taken together, the data reviewed earlier raise questions concerning Piaget's assumption that the speech of preschoolers is characterized primarily by its socially egocentric quality. Indeed, approximately 60% of preschoolers' utterances are socially directed, comprehensible, and result in appropriate responses (Levin & Rubin, 1983; Mueller, 1972). Furthermore, it has been shown that young children recognize when their verbal repertoires are limited and, in such circumstances, will resort to the use of gestures to communicate meaning (e.g., Sawyer, 1997). Studies of gestural communication actually shed light on Piaget's original ideas concerning egocentric thought and speech. Piaget recognized the significance of gestural communication and wrote that in the explanations of young children, "gestures play as important a part as words." (Piaget, 1959, p. 77). It may well be that Piaget's "take" on communicative competence has been poorly understood, or at best, misjudged. In Piaget's own research, he indicated that only 35% to 40% of young children's utterances were "egocentric." This leads to the conclusion that in almost 60% of the cases, young children demonstrated communicative competence. If one were to add to *verbal* expression the comprehensible use of gestures, preschoolers would clearly be regarded as communicatively skilled.

Relationships

During early childhood, children express preferences for some peers over others as playmates. It appears that one important influence on this process is that preschoolers are attracted to peers who are similar to them in some noticeable regard. For example, similarities in age and sex draw young children together. Furthermore, preschoolers appear to be attracted to, and become friends with peers whose behavioral tendencies are similar to their own, a phenomenon known as *behavioral homophily* (e.g., Kandel, 1978; Ryan, 2001).

Once preschoolers form friendships, their behavior with these individuals is distinctive from their behavior with other children who are familiar but not friends. Among the features that mark the friendships of preschool-age children are supportiveness and exclusivity (Sebanc, 2003). Children as young as 3.5 years direct more social overtures, engage in more social interactions, and play in more complex ways with friends than nonfriends (e.g., Dunn & Cutting, 1999; Dunn, Cutting, & Fisher, 2002). As well, preschool-aged friends tend to cooperate and exhibit more positive social behaviors with each other than with nonfriends (e.g., Dunn et al., 2002). Ladd, Kochenderfer, and Coleman (1996) have shown that not all friendships in early childhood are equally stable. Those friendships that involve higher levels of positive friendship qualities (e.g., validation) and lower levels of negative friendship qualities (e.g., low conflict) are most likely to be stable.

Typically, researchers who study friendship rely on children as informants about with whom they are friends. It has been argued that a "true" friendship is one that relies on friendship nominations from *both* dyadic partners; a unilateral, nonreciprocated friendship has often been taken to mean "wishful thinking" on the part of the single nominator. In keeping with this perspective, Vaughn (2001) recently reported that (a) older preschoolers are more likely to participate in reciprocated friendships than are younger preschoolers; (b) preschoolers who nominate each other as friends interact more frequently with each other than those dyads in which only a unilateral nomination of friendship is evinced.

Importantly, not all young children have a best friend. Approximately 75% of preschoolers have reciprocally nominated best friendships (Dunn, 1993). Friendless preschoolers are less likely than befriended children to initiate and maintain play with peers (e.g., Howes, Matheson, & Wu, 1992). And during this period of early childhood, the ability to make friends, friendship quality, and stability of young children's friendships are associated with, and predicted by, social-cognitive and emotional maturity. For example, the abilities to understand emotional displays and social intent and to perspective-take are associated with friendship formation, maintenance, and friendship quality (Dunn & Cutting, 1999; Dunn et al., 2002; Ladd & Kochenderfer, 1996). Furthermore, the young child's ability to regulate emotions is associated with and predictive of both the number of mutual friends and friendship quality (Walden, Lemerise, & Smith, 1999).

It is not only the positive aspects of behavior that differentiate preschool friendships from nonfriendships—compared to nonfriends, preschool friends also demonstrate more quarreling and more active (assaults and threats) and reactive hostility (refusals and resistance; Dunn & Cutting, 1999; Laursen & Hartup, 1989). Moreover, Hartup and his colleagues (Hartup, Laursen, Stewart, & Eastenson, 1988) demonstrated that preschool children engage in more conflicts with their friends than with neutral associates. These differences are best understood by recognizing that friends spend much more time actually interacting with each other than do nonfriends. Hartup and his colleagues also reported qualitative differences in how preschool friends and nonfriends resolve conflicts and in what the outcomes of these conflicts are likely to be. Friends, as compared with nonfriends, make more use of negotiation and disengagement, relative to standing firm, in their resolution of conflicts. In conflict outcomes, friends are more likely to have equal resolutions, relative to win or lose occurrences. Also, following conflict resolution, friends are more likely than neutral associates to stay in physical proximity and continue to engage in interaction.

In summary, preschoolers behave differently with friends than nonfriends. Preschoolers engage in more prosocial behaviors as well as more conflicts when interacting with friends than with nonfriends. These conflicts are most likely to be resolved through negotiation, and the outcomes are usually equitable. These differences suggest that preschoolers view friendship as a unique context, separate and qualitatively different from their experiences with nonfriends.

Groups

Many researchers have found that the social dominance hierarchy is an important organizational feature of the preschool peer group (e.g., Hawley, 2002; Vaughn, 1999; Vaughn, Vollenweider, Bost, Azria-Evans, & Snider, 2003). And, in keeping with a central tenet of the ethological perspective, researchers have argued that dominance hierarchies develop naturally in groups to serve adaptive functions. In the case of preschool-aged children, dominance hierarchies appear to reduce overt aggression among members of the group. Observations of exchanges between children in which physical attacks, threats, and object conflicts occur reveal a consistent pattern of winners and losers. And children who are losers in object struggles rarely initiate conflict with those who have proven "victorious" over others or who have been victorious over them (Strayer & Strayer, 1976).

Summary

Even in early childhood, one can identify children who are more or less skilled in manipulating their peers or in meeting their interpersonal goals. Dominance hierarchies reflect primarily differences in children's success in struggles over objects. However, achieving the acquisition of desired objects is only one of many interpersonal goals that preschool children may have. Consequently, it remains unknown whether preschool children who have risen to the top of the preschool dominance hierarchy are those who develop and maintain positive relationships with their peers, not only in preschool, but thereafter as well.

As noted earlier, new statistical techniques are now allowing researchers to examine the quantity, composition, and stability of networks in the peer group. In a series of studies, van den Oord and colleagues demonstrated that, as early as the preschool period, children's groups comprise individuals who are behaviorally similar (van den Oord, Rispens, Goudena, & Vermande, 2000; Vermande, van den Oord, Rispens, & Goudena, 2000). Aggression is the most important determinant of social clustering in the preschool classroom: A researcher can best predict the peer group composition for aggressive children—a finding that repeats itself in older groups of children (see following).

Middle Childhood and Early Adolescence

The school-age years represent a dramatic shift in social context for most children in Western cultures. During this time, the proportion of social interaction that involves peers increases. Whereas approximately 10% of the social interaction for 2-year-olds involves peers, the comparable figure for children in middle childhood is more than 30%. Other changes include: the size of the peer group (which becomes considerably larger) and how peer interaction is supervised (it become less closely supervised by adults). Thus, in the years leading up to adolescence, children are brought into contact with a more diverse set of peers, although generally with those who are similar to them in age.

The settings of peer interaction also change. Preschool children's peer contacts are centered in the home and in day-care centers, whereas school-age children come into contact with peers in a wide range of settings. Although the settings for peer interaction in middle childhood have not been well described, there are some key studies. Zarbatany, Hartmann, and Rankin (1990) reported that the most frequent contexts for peer interaction, among middle class young adolescents include, in order of their frequency, conversing, "hanging out," being together at school, talking on the telephone, traveling to and from school, listening to TV and records, and noncontact sports. Boys and girls differed on only one of these activities—more peer interaction took place during phone conversations for girls than for boys. In terms of their perceived *importance,* this sample of early adolescents viewed noncontact sports, watching TV or listening to records, conversing, talking on the telephone, physical games, parties, and "hanging out" as the most important contexts for peer interaction. An important aspect of this research is that these contexts were associated with different types of peer interaction. Noncompetitive activities facilitated socializing and the development of relationships, whereas competitive activities provided opportunities for identifying unique aspects of the self. According to Zarbatany et al. (1990), the full range of activities is necessary for early adolescents to derive broad benefits from peer experiences.

Interaction

During middle childhood, verbal and relational aggression (insults, derogation, threats, gossip) gradually replace direct physical aggression. Further, relative to preschoolers, the aggressive behavior of 6- to 12-year-olds is less frequently directed toward possessing objects or occupying specific territory and more specifically hostile toward others (Dodge, Coie, & Lynam, Chapter 12, this *Handbook,* this volume). With regard to positive social behavior, Eisenberg, Fabes and Spinrad (Chapter 11, this *Handbook,* this volume) report the levels of generosity, helpfulness, or cooperation that children direct to their peers increases somewhat during the primary and middle school years.

The frequency of "pretend" or "nonliteral" aggression, or R&T play fits a U-shaped developmental function (Pellegrini, 2002). Rough-and-tumble play comprises approximately 5% of preschoolers' social activities. In early elementary school, the frequency of R&T ranges from 10% to 17%, thereafter declining in middle childhood and early adolescence to 5% (Humphreys & Smith, 1987). Interestingly, it has been proposed that the primary function of R&T, especially among early adolescent boys, is to establish dominance status and thereby delimit aggression among peers (Pellegrini, 2002). Finally, by middle childhood, increases are found in the frequencies of games with or without formal rules. In these latter activities, children's interactions with peers are highly coordinated, involving both positive (cooperative, prosocial) and negative (competitive, agonistic) forms of behavior.

Children's concerns about acceptance in the peer group rise sharply during middle childhood, and these concerns appear related to an increase in the salience and frequency of *gossip* (Kuttler, Parker, & La Greca, 2002). Gossip, at this age, reaffirms children's membership in important same-sex social groups and reveals, to its constituent members, the core attitudes, beliefs, and behaviors comprising the basis for inclusion in or exclusion from these groups. Thus, gossip may play a role in fostering friendship closeness and in promulgating children's social reputations. Kuttler et al. (2002) recently reported that preadolescents label most talk about a nonpresent other as gossip and consider it to be inappropri-

ate, are more skeptical of gossip than of first-hand information, and are likely to assume that gossipers spread false information out of jealousy.

Two additional forms of interaction have received specific attention in the recent literature. Dishion, McCord, and Poulin (1999) coined the term *deviancy training* to refer the processes of praise, encouragement, imitation, and expectancy by which children increase the level of *aggression* or *antisocial behavior* in their peers. Essentially, deviancy training occurs when children model and reward aggressive behaviors in each other; the process by which these exchanges take place is thought to increase individual tendencies in aggressiveness and to strengthen ties to aggressive and substance-abusing friends and delinquent peer groups. In this regard, deviancy training "hits" at all levels of the social enterprise.

A form of interaction that affects *internalizing* problems has been identified also. Rose (2002) has shown that in the interactions of close friends, especially in the friendships of early adolescent girls, there can be a pattern of interaction described as "co-rumination" in which negative thoughts and feelings are shared and discussed. This joint focus on worries and negative experiences appears more often in the friendships of young adolescent girls than boys and is associated with internalizing problems for 12- to 14-year-olds, but not for 8- to 10-year-olds. Ruminative thoughts in individuals and shared rumination among peers may play a role in sustaining or exacerbating problems of an internalizing nature, thus this topic seems ripe for additional study.

Yet another form of interaction emerging fully blown during middle childhood and early adolescence is *bullying* and *victimization* (Espelage, Bosworth, & Simon, 2000). Bullying refers to acts of verbal and physical aggression on the part of an individual that are chronic and directed toward particular peers (victims). Bullying accounts for a substantial portion of the aggression that occurs in the peer group (Olweus, 1978, 1993). The dimension that distinguishes bullying from other forms of aggressive behavior is its specificity—bullies direct their behavior toward only certain peers, comprising approximately 10% of the school population (National Institute of Child Health and Human Development Early Child Care Research Network, 2001; Olweus, 1984). Research on bullying suggests that bullies are characterized by strong tendencies toward aggressive behavior, relatively weak control over their aggressive impulses, and a tolerance for aggressive behavior (1978, 1993). Further, Perry, Perry, and Kennedy (1992) noted that bullies are most likely to use force unemotionally and outside of an ongoing flow of conflict or interaction. Also, bullies generally do not experience much resistance to their aggressive acts.

Children who are greatest risk for victimization are those who have elevated scores on measures of aggression or social withdrawal. Nearly every study that has assessed the association between aggressiveness and victimization has revealed a positive correlation (e.g., Camodeca, Goossens, Terwogt, & Schuengel, 2002; Hanish & Guerra, 2004; Hodges, Malone, & Perry, 1997; Snyder et al., 2003). These findings appear to be culturally universal; thus victimization and aggression have been found to be positively associated in North American, Southern Asian (Khatri & Kupermidt, 2003) and East Asian (Schwartz, Farver, Chang, & Lee-Shin, 2002) samples. When bullies direct their aggression to other aggressive children, it facilitates a transactional relationship that appears to facilitate the stability of aggression in the bully victim partners (Camodeca et al., 2002; Kochenderfer & Ladd, 1997; Kochenderfer-Ladd 2003). Finally, there is evidence that anxious and socially reticent children are victims of bullying behavior (Hanish & Guerra, 2004; Kochenderfer-Ladd 2003; Olweus, 1993).

As implied by Graham and Juvonen (2001) and Schafer, Werner, and Crick (2002), victimization may occur at multiple levels of social complexity, such as the dyad (Crick & Nelson, 2002) or the group (Bukowski & Sippola, 2001). There are at least two explanations for the observation that aggression and social withdrawal are associated with victimization. One explanation notes that a withdrawn child is likely to be victimized because she or he is an easy and nonthreatening prey who is unlikely to retaliate when provoked (e.g., the construct of "whipping boy"; Olweus, 1978, 1993); alternatively, an aggressive child is victimized because his or her behavior is irritating and likely to provoke victimization from others ("the provocative victim"; Hodges et al., 1997; Olweus, 1993). According to this view different mechanisms underlie victimization for different types of children. Another view uses a single model to explain victimization. It claims that children victimize peers who do not promote the basic group goals of coherence, harmony, and evolution. According to this view, aggressive and withdrawn children do not promote these positive aspects of group functioning and as a result they are victimized.

Relationships

The period of middle childhood and early adolescence brings marked changes in children's understanding of *friendship*. To chart these changes, researchers have asked children questions such as "What is a best friend?" or "What do you expect from a best friend?" (Bigelow, 1977). Although children of all ages indicate that a reciprocal "giving-and-taking" is necessary for friendship (Hartup & Stevens, 1997), researchers have shown that young children's conceptions of a friend are anchored in the here and now, and not easily separated from social activity itself. Early school-age children have friendship concepts that transcend any specific activity, and imply the continuity of relationships over time. Nevertheless, during the early school years, children can still be instrumental and concrete in what they view as a friendship or appropriate friendship behavior. For example, Bigelow's (1977) findings show that children's friendship conceptions at the start of middle childhood (7 to 8 years) involve rewards and costs—friends are individuals who are rewarding to be with, whereas nonfriends are individuals who are difficult or uninteresting to be with. For children of this age, a friend is someone who is convenient (i.e., who lives nearby), has interesting toys or possessions, and shares the child's expectations about play activities. This conception evolves during middle childhood and early adolescence. By about 10 to 11 years, children recognize the value of shared values and shared social understanding. Friends at this age are expected to stick up for and be loyal to one another. Later, at 11 to 13 years, children acquire the view that friends share similar interests, are required to make active attempts to understand each other, and are willing to engage in self-disclosure.

According to Berndt (1996), children do not abandon initial notions about play and mutual association when they eventually recognize the importance of intimacy and loyalty. In support of this view, school-age children's drawings of their friends show clearly that friends are perceived as being similar to each other in many observable ways while at the same time, they show their loyalty and closeness to each other (Pinto, Bombi, & Cordoli, 1997). Moreover, even school-age children appear to recognize that while friends may share objective experiences in their friendships they may be different from each other in their subjective experiences (Little, Brendgen, Wanner, & Krappman, 1999).

Children draw sharper distinctions between the supportiveness of friends and nonfriends with increasing age (Berndt & Perry, 1986). Moreover, children's descriptions of their friendships indicate that loyalty, self-disclosure, and trust increase with age (Berndt, 2002), although these trends are more likely to be observed in girls than in boys (Berndt & Perry, 1986; Strough, Swenson, & Cheng, 2001). Older children of both sexes also possess more intimate knowledge of their friends, describe their friends in a more differentiated and integrated manner, and see their friendships as more exclusive and individualized (Berndt, 2002; Smollar & Youniss, 1982).

Significantly, there is little cross-cultural research on children's *understanding* of friendship. Keller (2004a) has recently questioned whether the notion of emotional intimacy that so characterizes friendship in Western cultures during the later years of childhood and beyond is also typical in non-Western societies. She notes that in some cultures, especially in those that have subsistence economies, a primary function of friendship is instrumental aid and not emotional support (see also Beer, 2001). Moreover, in comparing such Western countries as Germany and the United States with non-Western China, Keller found that children in that latter culture emphasized moral issues and the importance of altruism in their understanding of close friendships. Children in the Western countries were more likely to emphasize relationship intimacy (Keller, 2004b). Given these significant differences in conceptions of friendship, it behooves researchers to examine cultures beyond those investigated by Keller and colleagues. Indeed, it would seem important to study within-cultural/ethnic differences as well (e.g., Way & Chen, 2000).

Changes in the understanding of friendship are accompanied by changes in the patterns and nature of involvement in friendships across middle childhood. Children's friendship choices are more stable and more likely to be reciprocated in middle childhood than at earlier ages, although it is not clear that either the reciprocity or stability of friendship increases during middle childhood (Berndt & Hoyle, 1985). *Stability* of friendships is thought to derive from the positive qualities of, and the positive interactions between, children. Friendships that are high in relationship quality are more likely to persist over time (Berndt, 2004), and this

is also true in early childhood. For example, Ladd, Kochenderfer, and Coleman (1996) found higher levels of positive friendship qualities (e.g., validation) and lower levels of negative friendship qualities (e.g., low conflict) in stable friendships of kindergarteners, relative to unstable friendships. Furthermore, stable friendships in middle childhood and early adolescence are more likely to comprise dyads in which the partners are sociable and altruistic; friendships that dissolve during the course of a school year are more likely to comprise partners who are aggressive and victimized by peers (Hektner, August, & Realmuto, 2000; Wojslawowicz, Rubin, Burgess, Booth-LaForce, & Rose-Krasnor, in press). In addition, children's liking for, and friendship involvement with, *opposite*-sex peers drops off precipitously after 7 years of age (Leaper, 1994).

Friendship dissolution may have a serious impact on children's adjustment. For example, disruptions of close peer relationships have been associated with depression, loneliness, physiological dysregulation, guilt, and anger (e.g., Laursen et al., 1996; Parker & Seal, 1996). In addition, friendship loss in *preadolescence* (typically defined as the late years of middle or junior high school) may be particularly painful, due to the special role of friends' loyalty during this developmental period (Buhrmester & Furman, 1987). Recently, for example, Wojslawowicz et al. (in press) reported that 10- and 11-year-old children who had a best friend at the beginning of the school year but who lost that friendship and failed to replace it by the end of the school year were at increased risk for victimization by peers. Thus, it may be that if a dissolved best friendship is not replaced, the "advantages" of once having a best friend may quickly vanish.

Significantly, researchers have found that the lack of a best friendship, whether at a given point in time or chronically, can be accompanied by numerous risks. Friendless children are more likely to be lonely and victimized by peers (Boulton, Trueman, Chau, Whitehand, & Amatya, 1999; Brendgen, Vitaro, & Bukowski, 2000; Kochenderfer & Ladd, 1997). *Chronic friendlessness* during childhood has been associated contemporaneously with social timidity, sensitivity, and the lack of social skills (Parker & Seal, 1996; Wojslawowicz et al., in press), and predictively with subsequent internalizing problems (Ladd & Troop-Gordon, 2003). Relatedly, investigators have demonstrated that friendship can be an important buffer for children; for example, Hodges and colleagues (Hodges, Boivin, Vitaro, & Bukowksi,

1999) found that peer victimization predicted increases in internalizing and externalizing problems during the school year *only* for those children who lacked a mutual best friendship.

The protective function ascribed to friendship is consistent with the view that close relationships function as security systems (e.g., Sullivan, 1953). Hodges, Malone, and Perry (1997), for example, showed that children who are at risk for victimization because of their own personal characteristics (i.e., being aggressive and/or withdrawn) are less likely to experience victimization in the peer group if they are also befriended rather than friendless. In such studies, it is argued that individual differences in victimization are associated with personal characteristics but that these associations are heightened by the lack of a friendship.

With respect to the *features* of children's friendships in middle childhood and early adolescence, Newcomb and Bagwell (1995) reported that children are more likely to behave in positive ways with friends than nonfriends or to ascribe positive characteristics to their interactions with friends. Although the effect size of this difference may, in some cases be small (Simpkins & Parke, 2002), this pattern of findings is observed across a broad range of studies using a variety of methods, including direct observations (e.g., Simpkins & Parke, 2002), interviews (Berndt, Hawkins, & Hoyle, 1986), and hypothetical dilemmas (Rotenberg & Slitz, 1988). More important, Newcomb and Bagwell's (1995) meta-analysis showed that the expression of affect varied considerably for pairs of friends and nonfriends during middle childhood and early adolescence. In their interactions with friends, relative to interaction with nonfriends, children show more affective reciprocity and emotional intensity, and enhanced levels of emotional understanding. Moreover, young adolescent friends use distraction to keep their friends from potentially harmful rumination about social attributions that may induce guilt or shame (Denton & Zarbatany, 1996). In this regard, friendship is a socially and positive relational context, and it provides opportunities for the expression and regulation of affect (Salisch, 2000). Consistent with the aforementioned views of Sullivan (1953), it has been found that these friend-nonfriend differences are stronger during early adolescence than during either middle childhood or during the preschool years.

One of the few dimensions of interaction in which there are no differences between friends and non-friends is that of *conflict*. Research has shown repeatedly that after early childhood, pairs of friends engage in about the same amount of conflict as pairs of non-friends (Laursen et al., 1996). There is, however, a major difference in the conflict resolution strategies that friends and nonfriends adopt. Friends are more concerned about achieving an equitable resolution to conflicts. More specifically, researchers report that friends are more likely than nonfriends to resolve conflicts in a way that will preserve or promote the continuity of their relationship (see Laursen et al., 2001, for a recent review). Consistent with these findings, friendship motives related to conflict resolution have been observed to be associated with lower levels of anger and more constructive forms of behavior (B. Murphy & Eisenberg, 2002). However, the beneficial effects of friendship are qualified by the characteristics of the best friend: Young adolescents with aggressive friends, compared with those who have nonaggressive friends, adopt increasingly aggressive solutions to social conflicts; young adolescents who are nonaggressive and who have nonaggressive friends use more prosocial solutions to conflicts (Brendgen, Bowen, Rondeau, & Vitaro, 1999). In this respect, experience in a best friendship is linked to the development of social competence; in the best friendship, children and adolescents show a concern for a balance between individual and communal goals.

There appear to be consistent *qualitative* differences in boys' and girls' best friendships in the middle childhood and early adolescent years. For example, the friendships of girls are marked by greater intimacy, self-disclosure, and validation and caring than those of boys (Leaper, 1994; Rubin, Dwyer, et al., 2004; Zarbatany, McDougall, & Hymel, 2000). Ironically, it is because of the intimacy of girls' best friendships that they appear to be less stable and more fragile than those of boys (Benenson & Christakos, 2003; Hardy, Bukowski, & Sippola, 2002). Males' best friendships are characterized by physical activities that do not require the exchange of personal information. According to Benenson and Christakos, intimate disclosure between female friends may become hazardous when best friends have a conflict. In such cases, the conflicting friends can divulge personal information to outsiders (Crick & Grotpeter, 1995). Moreover, girls' close friendships are more likely to occur in isolation, whereas boys' friendships are more likely to occur in a larger social network (Baumeister & Sommer, 1997). Conflict resolution may be aided by third party mediators and allies in the larger group context.

As noted earlier, girls also report more co-rumination (e.g., negative dwelling on emotionally charged and intimate everyday occurrences and feelings), in their friendships than do boys (Rose, 2002). Significantly, when children's peer activities are marked by communal rather than competitive/agentic activities, friendship intimacy is higher. And when boys' best friendships are with girls rather than boys, intimacy is higher, thus suggesting that there may be two different "worlds" of relationships defined by context and activity (Zarbatany et al., 2000).

Thus far we have examined how children think about friendship and how they interact when with their best friends. We have also described the stability of best friendships during the middle childhood/early adolescent period. But who is it that children are attracted to? And with whom do they form best friendships? Just as is the case with young children, older children and young adolescents are drawn to others who are like them. Throughout this age period, children are attracted to and become best friends with those who resemble them in age, sex, ethnicity, and behavioral status (Hartup & Abecassis, 2002). For example, it has been reported that children and young adolescents are attracted to peers whose behavioral tendencies are similar to their own (Rubin, Lynch, Coplan, Rose-Krasnor, & Booth, 1994). Hamm (2000), for example, showed that similarity on a particular dimension varied across children largely due to the importance the child ascribed it. Similarity to their friend on academic performance was highest among children who saw academic performance as important.

Researchers in both Western and Eastern cultures have reported that greater behavioral similarities exist between friends than nonfriends, and children share friendships with other children who resemble themselves in terms of prosocial and antisocial behaviors (e.g., Haselager, Hartup, van Lieshout, & Riksen-Walraven, 1998; Liu & Chen, 2003; Poulin & Boivin, 2000), shyness and internalized distress (e.g., Hogue & Steinberg, 1995; Rubin, Wojslawowicz, Burgess, Booth-LaForce, & Rose-Krasnor, in press), sociability, peer popularity, and academic achievement and motivation (Altermatt & Pomerantz, 2003; Liu & Chen, 2003). Children also dislike those who are different from themselves and terminate relationships with those who are behaviorally unlike themselves (Poulin

& Boivin, 2000). As Hartup and Abecassis (2002) put it: "No evidence exists to suggest that opposites attract" (p. 291).

Finally, as noted earlier, researchers have begun to study enmity and mutual antipathies. Abecassis et al. (2002) have shown that rates vary across classrooms, with the frequencies of dyadic enmity being as high as 58% in some classrooms. Although mutual antipathies are experienced by all children, they are most common among rejected children and they are more common among boys than girls, especially during middle childhood compared with adolescence (Rodkin & Hodges, 2003). But it is important to note that enmity is not simply due to elevated levels of rejection. The specific characteristics of particular pairs of "enemies" appear to be connected to attachment-related experiences (Hodges & Card, 2003). Children whose attachment-related coping styles are incompatible (e.g., one has an avoidant style and the other is preoccupied) are more likely to become enemies than are other children.

The developmental significance of mutual antipathies is unclear. Children in such relationships tend to be more depressed than are other children, and the presence of a mutual antipathy appears to exacerbate the effect of other negative experiences. Nevertheless, participating in the process of mutual disliking may be one means by which young people develop a clearer sense of self as they identify the characteristics that they like and dislike in others.

Many issues related to the study of mutual antipathies require further exploration. Perhaps the most important concerns the issue of how we define and measure the concept of enemy. Just as mutual liking is simply the minimum criterion for friendship, mutual disliking must be considered the minimum criterion for the presence of enmity. To paraphrase the important discussions provided by Hartup and Abecassis (2002), having an enemy implies warfare. Consequently, researchers would do well to examine whether children who nominate each other as "Someone I do not like," actually interact. It may be that mutual antipathies merely capture an affective dimension, not an interactional one. "True" enemies may be proactive about their relationship. They may spread gossip about one another and engage in relational or other forms of aggression. They may be members of different identifiable groups, each of which exclude the other (research on peer exclusion may be particularly relevant, e.g., Horn, 2003; Killen &

Stangor, 2001; Killen, Stangor, Horn, & Sechrist, 2004; Killen et al., 2002). At present, there are virtually no data indicating how and whether those who mutually nominate each other as "Someone I do not like" actually have a clearly defined relationship. As a result, researchers must be careful about how they define and measure the presence of enmity.

Groups

During the upper elementary school and middle school years, the structure of the peer group changes from a relatively unified whole to a more differentiated structure. In this new structure, children organize themselves into social groups, clusters, networks, or cliques (Bagwell, Coie, Terry, & Lochman, 2000; Degirmencioglu, Urberg, Tolson, & Richard, 1998). Peer networks and cliques are voluntary, friendship-based groups, and stand in contrast to the activity or work groups to which children can be assigned by circumstance or by adults. Cliques generally include three to nine same-sex children of the same race (Chen, Chang, & He, 2003; Kindermann, McCollom, & Gibson, 1995). By 11 years of age, children report that most of their peer interaction takes place in the context of the clique, and nearly all children report being a member of one.

With respect to group size, boys, compared with girls, show a preference for larger groups (Benenson, Apostoleris, & Parnass, 1997). It may be that this sex difference has functional significance. Specifically, interaction in smaller groups is less likely than experience in large groups to promote competitiveness and self-criticism (Benenson, Nicholson, Waite, Roy, & Simpson, 2001). Because girls are more likely than boys to have experience in small groups, they may have fewer experiences with competition than boys have. This difference could explain why girls tend to be less competitive than boys (Roy & Benenson, 2002) and why they feel less comfortable with competition (Benenson et al., 2002). This avoidance of competition in favor of more egalitarian strategies may explain why girls experience greater fragility in their same-sex friendships (Benenson & Christakos, 2003).

Peer networks, whether identified observationally (e.g., Gest, Farmer, Cairns, & Xie, 2003) or via peer reports (e.g., Bagwell et al., 2000), or whether identified in or out of school (Kiesner, Poulin, & Nicotra, 2003), are typically organized to maximize within-group homogeneity (Rodkin, Farmer, Pearl, & Van Acker, 2000).

Thus, in recent studies of preadolescents conducted in both Western (e.g., Canada, Finland, United States) and Eastern (e.g., China) cultures, group membership has been found to comprise children similar with regard to the following characteristics: aggression (Espelage et al., 2003; Gest et al., 2003; Kiesner et al., 2003; Xie et al., 1999), bullying (e.g., Salmivalli, Huttunen, & Lagerspetz, 1997), attitudes about bullying (Espelage et al., 2003; Salmivalli & Voeten, 2004), and school motivation and performance (e.g., Chen et al., 2003; Kindermann, 1993; Liu & Chen, 2003; Ryan, 2001; Sage & Kindermann, 1999).

Apart from cliques, the other primary organizational feature of children's groups in middle childhood and early adolescence is the popularity hierarchy. There have been recent attempts to distinguish between *sociometric* popularity and *perceived* popularity. In the case of sociometric popularity or peer acceptance, the questions asked of children are "Who do you most like?" and "Who do you most dislike?" (see following for details about assessment). In the case of perceived popularity, the child is asked who he or she believes is the most popular in the classroom, grade, or school (Parkhurst & Hopmeyer, 1998; LaFontana & Cillessen, 1998, 2002). Unwittingly, these efforts follow Northway's (1946) assertion that being accepted and being popular are different phenomena that have different antecedents and different consequences. Whereas being liked or accepted occurs at the dyadic level (i.e., one person has affection for someone else), the perception of someone as being popular in a classroom or school reflects a group level of analysis (i.e., the person is perceived according to her/his position in the group). Thus, in the study of peer group relationships, the word (and traditional measurement of) *acceptance* is most properly taken as a direct assessment of the extent to which a child is liked by her/his peers, whereas the word *popularity* refers to a child's perceived standing or status in the group.

Recently, researchers have focused on the study of the peer relationship correlates of such negative characteristics such as aggression, bossiness, and untrustworthiness to clarify the distinction between the meanings and measurement of peer acceptance and perceived popularity. Thus, for example, in contradiction to the general finding that aggression impedes a child's *acceptance* among peers, aggression appears to promote a child's perceived *popularity* (Buskirk, Rubin, Burgess, Booth-LaForce, & Rose-Krasnor, 2004; Hawley, Little,

& Pasupathi, 2002; Lease, Kennedy, & Axelrod, 2002). Research regarding the association between aggression and popularity is approached according to basic aspects of group process such as dominance, resource control, and regulation of retaliatory gestures between group members (Hawley, 2003). Findings show that children whose level of aggression is moderately above the mean and who use aggression for instrumental reasons are *perceived* as more popular in their groups than are children who are low in aggression or whose aggression is high and undifferentiated (Hawley, 2003; Little, Jones, Henrich, & Hawley, 2003; Prinstein & Cillessen, 2003; Vaughn at al., 2003).

Although the association between aggression and popularity may be seen even during the preschool period (Vaughn et al., 2003), this association appears to be stronger during early adolescence (Cillessen & Mayeux, 2004; Prinstein & Cillessen, 2003). Whereas aggression is positively associated with measures of popularity during early adolescence (Cillessen & Mayeux, 2004; La-Fontana & Cillessen, 1998, 2002; Parkhurst & Hopmeyer, 1998), it is not related to acceptance (Buskirk et al., 2004). Moderately aggressive children may be given status and power in the peer group; however, this does not mean they are adjusted or that they will receive or benefit from the affection or kindness from their peers.

These findings are consistent with ideas about how groups function and how groups reward persons who promote the group's functioning (see Bukowski & Sippola, 2001). Whereas the main reward that one can provide at the level of the dyad is affection, the main rewards that can be provided at the level of the group are power, attention, and status. And whereas group members victimize peers who impede the group's evolution and coherence, groups give power, attention, and status to group members who promote the group's well-being. Given that group leaders may, at times, have to be forceful, strong, assertive, indeed Machiavellian, their behavior may include a larger coercive or aggressive component than is seen among other children. This tendency to ascribe power and status to moderately aggressive individuals may be more pronounced in adolescence when aggression is seen as a more normative entity than among younger children (Moffitt, 1993). As a result, status, leadership, and aggression may often go together especially for young adolescents (Prinstein & Cillessen, 2003).

Three final points must be made. First, consistent terminology is a prerequisite for learned discussion. As the distinction between how much a child is liked and how popular a child is becomes more frequent, the clarity of the terms used to refer to these constructs becomes increasingly important. The word *acceptance* should be used to refer to a direct assessment of the extent to which a child is liked by her/his peers, whereas the word *popularity* should be used to refer to a person's place in the peer group. The meaning of *acceptance* captures the essence of the construct it refers to (i.e., the extent to which a person is received with favor or approval by others). The word *popularity* is also ideally suited to the construct it is used to represent. Popularity, by definition, refers to someone's position or status among the people. In this respect it is essentially a group-oriented construct.

Second, the "traditional" measures of popularity have been sociometric measures. Sociometry refers to the attractions and repulsions between individuals. To the extent that a measure of perceived popularity is neither a measure of attraction nor repulsion, it is not a sociometric measure. Third, most of the research on acceptance and popularity has been empirically driven. Because researchers have been largely interested in identifying the different correlates of these constructs, little direct attention has been devoted to understanding the conceptual differences between these constructs by their psychological or functional significance. Lease and her colleagues have gone furthest in discussing the link between popularity and power in the peer group (Lease, Kennedy, et al., 2002; Lease, Musgrove, & Axelrod, 2002). Their discussions of how power and status are fused in the construct of popularity provide a strong base for further exploration of how peer groups function and of how their dynamics are controlled by particular peers.

Adolescence

Interaction

The trend of spending increasingly substantial amounts of time with peers that begins in middle childhood continues in adolescence (Larson, Brown, & Mortimer, 2002). For example, during a typical week, even discounting time spent in classroom instruction, high school students spend almost one-third (29%) of their waking hours with peers, an amount more than double that spent with parents and other adults (13%; Csik-szentmihalyi & Larson, 1984). Moreover, adolescent peer interaction takes place with less adult guidance and control than peer interaction in middle childhood, and is more likely to involve individuals of the opposite-sex (Brown & Klute, 2003). These phenomena are largely consistent across cultural groups.

Relationships

As they enter adolescence, both boys and girls already understand a great deal about the reciprocal operations and obligations of friendship, about the continuity of friendships, and about the psychological grounds that evoke behavior. During *early* adolescence, friendship can be seen in overly exclusive terms in the sense that relationships with third parties are inimical to the basic nature of friendship commitment. During adolescence, however, youngsters begin to accept the other's need to establish relationships with others and to grow through such experiences. In particular, perhaps in parallel to their struggles for independence from their parents, adolescents recognize an obligation to grant friends a certain degree of autonomy and independence. Thus, their discussions of friendship and friendship issues show fewer elements of possessiveness and jealousy, and more concern with how the relationship helps the partners enhance their respective self-identities (Berndt & Hoyle, 1985).

During adolescence, friendships are best maintained when the partners have similar attitudes, aspirations, and intellect (e.g., Smollar & Youniss, 1982). Based on this perspective, it appears that children who are different from the other boys and girls in the group are those who are less likely to have a friend. Nonetheless, same-sex friends account for an increasingly larger proportion of adolescents' perceived primary social network, and friends equal or surpass parents as sources of support and advice to adolescents in many significant domains (e.g., Buhrmester, 1998; Furman & Buhrmester, 1992). Moreover, the friendships of adolescents are relatively stable (Berndt, Hawkins, et al., 1986).

One hallmark of friendship in adolescence is its emphasis on intimacy and self-disclosure. Studies consistently indicate that adolescents report greater levels of intimacy in their friendships than do younger children (Buhrmester & Furman, 1986). Furthermore, observations of adolescent friends indicate that intimate self-disclosure is a highly salient feature of friendship interaction. Unlike at earlier ages, self-disclosure during adolescence prompts lengthy and sometimes emotional discussions about the nature of the problem and possible avenues to its resolution.

During adolescence, boys and girls have clear conceptions of the properties that distinguish *romantic* relationships from friendships (Collins, 2003; Connolly, Craig, Goldberg, & Pepler, 2004). Whereas romantic relationships are conceived in terms of passion and commitment, other-sex friendships are largely characterized by affiliation. Although even the youngest of adolescents distinguish between romantic relationships and other-sex friendships, distinctions between these relationships increase with age and with experience in romantic relationships. The study of adolescent romantic relationships by developmental psychologists is a surprisingly new enterprise with nearly all research on this topic stemming from the past 10 years. Relevant research is organized around three questions: (1) When do these relationships first emerge and for whom do they occur? (2) What are the characteristics of these relationships and what accounts for individual differences in their quality? (3) How do romantic relationships affect development?

With regard to developmental timing, romantic relationships are first seen during early adolescence with approximately 25% of 12-year-olds claiming they have had a romantic relationship during the past 18 months (Carver, Joyner, & Udry, 2003). This frequency increases in a largely linear fashion during adolescence with roughly 70% of boys and 75% of girls making this claim at age 18 (Carver et al., 2003; Seiffge-Krenke, 2003). The average duration of a romantic relationship has been observed to be 3.9 months at age 13, and 11.8 months at age 17 months (Seiffge-Krenke, 2003).

Dating and romantic relationships appear to follow a developmental sequence. Connolly et al. (2004) showed that affiliation in mixed-sex groups and dating were qualitatively different phenomena that were sequentially organized. This sequential order followed a path that started with same-sex friendships and moved through an affiliative period of mixed-sex group activities and mixed-sex festive occasions (e.g., parties), followed by dating and being involved in a romantic dyad.

There are large differences between those adolescents who do and do not participate in romantic relationships. These differences vary during the adolescent period and they are often characterized by complex patterns (Collins, 2003). *Early* involvement in romantic relationships has been linked to problem behaviors and emotional difficulties during adolescence (e.g., Davila, Steinberg, Kachadourian, Cobb, & Fincham, 2004), although this difference appears to be strongest among boys and girls who are unpopular among their same-sex peers (Brendgen, Vitaro, Doyle, Markiewicz, & Bukowski, 2002). It has been reported also that early daters show lower levels of scholastic achievement (Seiffge-Krenke, 2003), especially among girls (Brendgen et al., 2002). Among older adolescents, however, participation in romantic relationships is associated with positive experiences among same-sex peers and emotional and behavioral well-being (Seiffge-Krenke, 2003). Connolly, Furman, and Konarski (2000) reported that being part of a small group of close same-sex friends predicted being involved in other-sex peer networks, which, in turn, predicted the emergence of future romantic relationships. The observation that involvement in a romantic relationship is linked to acceptance with same-sex peers resembles prior findings regarding same-sex acceptance and other-sex friendship. These findings, however, have shown that participation in friendship with other-sex peers is linked to same-sex acceptance in a linear and a curvilinear manner in which children who are most liked by same-sex peers, and those who are least liked, have other-sex friends (Bukowski, Sippola, & Hoza, 1999; Kovacs, Parker, & Hoffman, 1996). There is evidence also that the quality of a child's same-sex friendships predicts the quality of their concurrent and subsequent romantic relationships (Connolly et al., 2000). Future research needs to clarify whether this pattern of findings regarding romantic relationships is equally valid for hetero- and homosexual youth.

Although there appears to be some inter-relatedness between romantic relationships and other relationship experiences, this association is often complex. Using an attachment framework, Furman, Simon, Shaffer, and Bouchey (2002) studied adolescents' internal working models for their relationships with parents, friends, and romantic partners. Adolescents' perceived *support* in relationships with their parents tended to be related to their perceived support in romantic relationships and friendships; support in friend and romantic relationships, however, were not related to each other. Nevertheless, self and other *controlling* behaviors in friendships were related to corresponding behaviors in romantic re-

lationships. Perceived *negative interactions* in the three types of relationships were also significantly associated with each other. This pattern of results indicates greater generalizability of negative than positive features across relationship types.

Romantic relationships also appear to have both positive and negative effects on development although the literature on these matters is not yet clear. Whereas there is evidence that participation in romantic relationships can be associated with elevated levels of depressed mood, higher levels of conflict, and emotional lability (Joyner & Udry, 2000), these findings appear to be the result of breakdowns of romance rather than of romance per se. On the positive side, being involved in a romantic relationship indirectly affects the adolescent's sense of well-being via its direct effects on his or her sense of romantic competence (Kuttler, La Greca, & Prinstein, 1999).

Groups

As in middle childhood, cliques are readily observed in adolescence, and membership in cliques is related to adolescents' psychological well-being and ability to cope with stress (Hansell, 1981). Also, as in middle childhood and early adolescence, group membership comprises individuals who are similar with regard to school achievement (Kindermann, 1995), substance use (cigarettes and alcohol; Urberg, Degirmencioglu, & Pilgrim, 1997), and delinquency (Kiesner et al., 2003). Nevertheless, Shrum and Cheek (1987) reported a sharp decline from 11 to 18 years of age in the proportion of students who were clique members and a corresponding increase with age in the proportion of children who had ties to many cliques or children whose primary ties were to other children who existed at the margins of one or more cliques. These authors concluded that there is a general loosening of clique ties across adolescence, a process they label "degrouping." This interpretation meshes well with data suggesting that both the importance of belonging to a group and the extent of intergroup antagonism decline steadily during high school years (Gavin & Furman, 1989). It is consistent also with the observations of ethnographers, who report a dissipation of clique boundaries and a sense of cohesiveness among senior high school class members (Larkin, 1979).

Whereas cliques represent small groups of individuals linked by friendship selections, the concept of peer subcultures, or "crowds" (Brown & Klute, 2003), is a more encompassing organizational framework for segmenting adolescent peer social life. A crowd is a reputation-based collective of similarly stereotyped individuals who may or may not spend much time together. Crowds are defined by the primary attitudes or activities their members share. Thus, crowd affiliation is assigned through the consensus of the peer group and is not selected by the adolescents themselves. Brown (1989) listed the following as common crowd labels among American high school students: jocks, brains, eggheads, loners, burnouts, druggies, populars, nerds, and greasers. Crowds place important restrictions on children's social contacts and relationships with peers (Brown, 1989); for example, cliques are generally formed within (versus across) crowds. Crowd labels may also constrain adolescents' abilities to change their lifestyles or explore new identities by "channeling" them into relationships and dating patterns with those sharing the same crowd nomenclature or classification (Eckert, 1989).

Crowd membership is an especially salient feature of adolescent social life and children's perceptions of crowds change in important ways with age. For example, between the ages of 13 and 16 years, adolescents alter the ways that they identify and describe the crowds in their school (O'Brien & Bierman, 1987). Whereas young adolescents focus on the specific behavioral proclivities of group members, older adolescents center on members' dispositional characteristics and values. This observation reflects broader changes that characterize developmental shifts in person perception between the childhood and adolescent years.

The stigma that is placed on members of a particular crowd channels adolescents into relationships and dating patterns with those sharing a similar crowd label. This may prevent adolescents from the exploration of new identities and discourages a shift to other crowd memberships. There is recent evidence that the stigma associated with some large peer groups or crowds influences the judgments that adolescents form about their peers (Horn, 2003). Consistent with findings from research focused on children's aggressive reputations and social cognitions (e.g., Dodge, 1986), Horn (2003) found that adolescents are biased in their use of reputational or stereotypical information about particular *groups,* particularly when presented with ambiguous situations. It is likely that these crowd-specific evaluations help to perpetuate group stereotypes and the structure of peer groups in a school.

The percentage of students who are able to correctly identify their peer-rated crowd membership increases with age (Brown, Clasen, & Neiss, 1987). An abbreviated list of crowds (populars, jocks, brains, burnouts, nonconformists, and none) used by Prinstein and La Greca (2002) revealed that self-nominations to groups overlapped strongly with findings from peer assignments.

Despite the differences that exist in the structures of peer groups, all of them inevitably disintegrate in the late adolescent years. This is largely due to the integration of the sexes that accompanies this period. To begin with, mixed-sex cliques emerge. Eventually, the larger groups divide into couples, and by late adolescence, girls and boys feel comfortable enough to approach one another directly without the support of the clique. Another contributing factor to the decline in importance of crowds results from adolescents creating their *own* personal values and morals. In this regard, they no longer see it as necessary to broadcast their membership in a particular social group and are therefore content to be separate and apart from particular crowds.

Conclusion

In this section, we have outlined developmental differences that mark the changing nature of social interactions and peer relationships from infancy to adolescence. Hopefully, this review will prove sufficient to provide a normative basis for the discussion that follows concerning the development of individual differences in children's social behaviors and peer relationships.

The nature of children's peer experiences changes with age because of a complex mix of developments with regard to intrapersonal (i.e., changes in interpersonal understanding and concerns), interpersonal (changes in the frequency or forms of specific behaviors), dyadic (changes in qualities of friendships or patterns of involvement in friendships), and group (changes in configurations of and involvement in cliques and crowds) factors. Furthermore, these different factors are not orthogonal; rather, they interlock in complex ways.

SOCIAL BEHAVIORS, INTERACTIONS, RELATIONSHIPS, AND GROUPS: ASSESSMENT ISSUES

The perspective we have adopted for this chapter assumes that children's experiences with peers occur at several orders of social complexity—from interactions to relationships to groups. Implied in such a formulation is that these levels of analyses provide separate windows on the adjustment of individual children with peers: To the extent that individual differences exist in children's adaptation or success with peers, such differences will be reflected in their (a) social interactions, (b) abilities to develop and sustain friendships, and (c) acceptance in peer groups. We examine procedures by which researchers assess peer interactions, relationships, and groups in this section.

Children's Behaviors and Interactions with Peers

Although parents, clinicians, and archival data have all served as sources of information about the valence and nature of children's peer interactions, the most common sources are the reports of other children or teachers or structured observations.

Observations of Behavior

There has been a long tradition of observing children in either naturalistic or laboratory-based play groups and then coding their behavior to reflect particular constructs. For example, *observational procedures* have been used to index the frequency with which individuals engage in particular behavioral styles (e.g., aggression, sociodramatic play, reticence/social wariness, or sharing), adopt particular roles in relation to their partners (e.g., dominant versus submissive roles), or demonstrate social competence (e.g., are successful at entering playgroups). Several well-known coding systems have been developed for these purposes, and discussions of these techniques can be found elsewhere (e.g., Bierman, 2003). These coding schemes have been used profitably to reliably distinguish between children along a variety of behavioral dimensions. For example, Rubin (2001) developed the *Play Observation Scale* (POS), a norm-based time-sampling procedure to assess free play behaviors in early and middle childhood. During free play or unrestricted activity time (in a classroom, on a playground, or in a laboratory playroom), behaviors with and without peers are coded on a checklist that includes the cognitive play categories of functional-sensorimotor, exploratory, constructive, dramatic, and games-with-rules behaviors *nested* in the aforementioned social participation categories of solitary, parallel, and group activities (e.g., Coplan, Gavinski-Molina, Lagace-Seguin, & Wichmann, 2001; Guralnick, Hammond, &

Conner, 2003). In addition, overt and relational aggression, R&T play, unoccupied and onlooker behaviors, and conversations with peers are recorded. Observational procedures such as the POS are useful in targeting children whose behaviors (e.g., different forms of aggression and social withdrawal) deviate from age-group norms. Such procedures can be used to validate peer and teacher assessments of children's social behavior.

Additional observational protocols assess appropriate and inappropriate behavior (e.g., M. L. Lewin, Davis, & Hops, 1999), social competence (e.g., Vaughn et al., 2003), peer group entry (e.g., Putallaz & Gottman, 1981), multiple forms of aggression (e.g., Bierman, Smoot, & Aumiller, 1993), how existing peer dyads respond to newcomers (Zarbatany, Van Brunschot, Meadows, & Pepper, 1996), adolescent conversation and discussion (e.g., Hops, Albert, & Davis, 1997), and group planning (Englund, Levy, Hyson, & Sroufe, 2000).

Although observational methods offer many advantages over the assessments discussed next, they also have specific limitations. First, observations are time-, energy-, and money-consuming. Whereas peer and teacher assessments can be conducted in minutes or hours, observations can require weeks or months of data collection. Second, as children get older, it becomes increasingly difficult to observe them during "free play" (although recent advances in remote audio-visual recording allow observations of children's conversations and interactions from afar; Atlas & Pepler, 1998). Third, situational demands strongly influence the types of behaviors displayed and their frequency. Unless researchers carefully consider or control how subjects' behavior is being influenced by setting demands, observation methods can lead to false conclusions of the willingness of certain individuals to engage in behaviors of interest. Fourth, observations may be reactive; for example, children who are aware that they are being observed may behave in atypical manners, perhaps suppressing negative behaviors or increasing the production of prosocial behaviors. Finally, it should be mentioned that observational strategies have been used rarely to study peer interactions and relationships from a cultural and cross-cultural perspective.

Peer Assessments of Social Behavior

In lieu of direct observations, researchers have often relied on children for information about who it is in the peer group that behaves competently or incompetently, or has qualitatively good or poor relationships. Hymel and Rubin (1985) noted the following advantages of peer informants. First, as "insiders," peers can identify characteristics of children and relationships that are considered relevant from the perspectives of those who ultimately determine a child's social status and integration in the peer group. Second, the judgments of peers are based on many extended and varied experiences with those being evaluated. For example, peers may be able to consider low frequency but psychologically significant events (e.g., a punch in the nose or taking someone's valued possession) that lead to the establishment and maintenance of particular social reputations. These latter events may be unknown to nonpeer "outsiders." Third, peer assessments of children's behaviors and relationships represent the perspectives of many observers with whom the target child has had a variety of personal relationships. The chance that error will be introduced by some idiosyncratic aspect of any single reporter's experience with the child is therefore correspondingly reduced.

In most peer assessment techniques, children are given a set of target behaviors or personality descriptions and asked to nominate peers on the basis of a variety of behavioral roles or character descriptions (e.g., "is a good leader," "gets into fights," or "likes to play alone"). Nominations received from peers are summed in various ways to provide indices of a child's typical social behavior or reputation in the peer group, whether that group comprises a classroom or school grade.

Two commonly used peer assessment techniques are the *Revised Class Play* (Masten, Morrison, & Pellegrini, 1985) and the *Pupil Evaluation Inventory* (PEI; Pekarik, Prinz, Liebert, Weintraub, & Neale, 1976). Factor analysis of children's nominations using these two measures has yielded three similar behavioral factors. For the PEI, the factors obtained were Likeability, Aggression, and Withdrawal. The factors obtained for the Revised Class Play are labeled Sociability-Leadership, Aggressive-Disruptive, and Sensitive-Isolated.

Recent advances in the use of peer assessments have provided a more refined articulation of the dimensions underlying children's social behavior. Thus, Zeller, Vannatta, Schafer, and Noll (2003) computed a confirmatory factor analysis for the Revised Class Play and discovered that the model that best fit the data needed to be substantially more differentiated than a simple three factor model would imply. In a sense, this result is not surprising given previous analyses that have distinguished between different forms of social withdrawal

(e.g., Bowker, Bukowski, Zargarpour, & Hoza, 1998; Rubin & Mills, 1988) and between different forms of aggression (Crick & Bigbee, 1998; Poulin & Boivin, 1999). In the case of aggression, peer assessment procedures to distinguish between physical aggression (fighting, kicking, hitting), verbal aggression (threats, teasing), and relational aggression (spreading rumors, excluding from play) have been developed. Recently, Burgess and colleagues (Burgess, Wojslawowicz, Rubin, Rose-Krasnor, & Booth, 2003) developed a reliable and valid extension of the Revised Class Play to distinguish between forms of social withdrawal, as well as to measure sociability, prosocial/altruistic behavior, and victimization. Embedded items assess peer acceptance, perceived popularity, and rejection.

Like the Revised Class Play, the PEI (Pekarik et al., 1976) has undergone revision. Pope, Bierman, and Mumma (1991) condensed the original scales and added items describing inattentive/immature and disruptive/hyperactive behaviors. By so doing, Pope et al. provided an instrument that could distinguish aggressive children who are rejected from those who are accepted by peers.

Peer behavioral assessment assumes that children's impressions of one another are established over time. Indeed, it has long been assumed that a major advantage of this technique is that it permits researchers to identify children who engage in behaviors that are salient to other children but too infrequent or too subtle for researchers to observe with any reliability. But a disadvantage of peer assessments is that once behavioral reputations consolidate they can be resistant to change (Hymel, 1986). Thus, even though a child's behavior may have changed, their reputation for this behavior persists with peers. As such, the data reaching the researcher may not fully reflect the current state of "reality." In addition, reputations are probably unduly influenced by infrequent but salient events (e.g., embarrassing social gaffs or poignant aggressive outbursts). Although characteristic of the child, the child's reputation for this behavior may overstate the frequency with which it appears in his or her social interchanges. Relatedly, there is evidence that children's recall of their peers' abilities and behavior is affected by their own behavioral reputation, level of peer status, age, and liking for the target; situational factors; and the target's gender, age, and sociometric status (e.g., Hymel, 1986). Finally, a main challenge to the study of peer assessments is the potential variance across cultural contexts in the organization of social constructs (see Bukowski & Sippola, 2001). Because social demands and practices may vary across cultures, children's representations of social constructs may vary also. The cross-cultural research of Chen and colleagues is particularly relevant in this regard and is discussed later (e.g., Chen, Cen, Li, & He, 2005; Chen, Rubin, Li, & Li, 1999; Chen et al., 2004).

Teacher Assessments

Teachers can provide useful data concerning low frequency social exchanges that may contribute toward the quality of a child's peer relationships. One advantage of teacher assessments over peer assessments is that the collection of data is more efficient and less time consuming. A second advantage is that, because they themselves are not members of the peer group, teachers may be more objective in their assessments of social behavior. However, teachers may bring with them an "adultomorphic" perspective that carries with it value judgments about social behaviors that might differ from those of children. Furthermore, teachers may carry with them biases that influence the ways in which they react to their pupils; such teacher reactions may strongly influence children's peer preferences and judgments (White & Kistner, 1992).

Teacher *referrals* are one source of data on children with behavioral difficulties. Many objections might be leveled against this approach, however. In the first place, teachers refer children for academic behaviors (e.g., learning disabilities or motivational problems) that may have only minor implications for social difficulties with peers. Second, even when problematic behavior toward peers is the basis for referral, it is not clear that such referrals will take place when the behavior is not also disruptive of classroom routines and academic progress.

Many standardized measures presently exist and an excellent review of teacher ratings of child behavior may be found in Bierman (2003). Generally, these measures can be broken down into several socioemotional clusters or factors that fall along dimensions of sociability/likeability/leadership, aggression/hostility/conduct disorder, hyperactivity/impulsivity, and anxiety/fearfulness/withdrawal.

Agreement among Sources

Achenbach, McConaughy, and Howell (1987) reported that the correlations between reports of children's behavioral problems average about .60 between similar informants seeing children under generally similar conditions (e.g., pairs of teachers; pairs of parents); .28 between different types of informants seeing the child under different conditions (e.g., parents versus teachers); and .22 between children's self-reports and reports by others, including parents, teachers and mental health workers. Age, sex, and the specific topography of the behavior under consideration have all been shown to be important factors influencing agreement. For example, agreement between teachers and peers concerning social withdrawal appears to increase with age from early to late childhood (Hymel, Rubin, Rowden, & LeMare, 1990), primarily because social withdrawal takes on increased salience to peers (but not teachers) with increasing age. Thus, it would appear as if no single source can substitute for all the others. The goal is not to determine which assessment procedure yields the singular truth about the child but to use what each one reveals about the child's functioning in particular areas or contexts.

Children's Relationships with Friends

Friendship is a subjective relationship and an inherently dyadic construct. Children perceive their friendship partners in particularized rather than role-related ways. They stress the uniqueness of the relationship and reject efforts to treat particular friendship partners as interchangeable with others. Researchers and other observers may note commonalities in personalities or behavioral tendencies across the friendships of a focal child, but the focal child him- or herself is likely to be impressed by the distinctions and diversity among his or her individual partners and relationships.

These subjective and reciprocal properties are challenges to understanding and require special caution in assessment. In early childhood, it is common to ask parents or teachers to identify whether a child is a friend of another child (Howes, 1988). Typically, researchers do not give these informants specific criteria by which the presence of a friendship should be determined. Instead, it is often simply assumed that these informants share the researcher's definition of friendship, which may or may not always be the case. In the assessment of the friendships of older elementary school-age children, the focal child's perceptions of his or her circle of friends must be sought and aligned with independent evidence of reciprocity of affection obtained directly or indirectly from each of these implicated individuals (Asher et al., 1996; Bukowski & Hoza, 1989). Typically, preschoolers and elementary school-age children are presented with a roster or a set of pictures of their same-sex *classmates* (or some other functionally similar group) and asked to circle or otherwise indicate which members are their best or close friends. Researchers who study middle-schoolers may use classroom lists or they may simply ask children to write down the names of their best friends. The pattern of choices is then examined to identify children who nominate one another. Less often, investigators have used reciprocated high ratings as an index of friendship, either alone or in conjunction with friendship nominations (Bukowski, Hoza, & Newcomb, 1994). Both procedures are consistent with the definition of friendship that we presented earlier—friendship requires reciprocity, refers to a free choice on the part of the two children involved, and is predicated on affectional concerns rather than instrumental issues.

Evidence of reciprocity of affection alone may be insufficient to presume or substantiate claims of friendship. Children may enjoy each other's company in school but never spend time together outside of school or in other ways have experiences together that lead them to think of each other as friends. Indeed, sometimes children have only limited direct contact with other children they report liking. For example, children can admire another child from a distance, can be grateful to someone who is only an acquaintance, or have affection for someone whose leadership facilitates group's functioning (Parker, Saxon, et al., 1999). Yet, friendship generally implies that the individuals involved in the relationship not only like or admire one another but also label their relationship a friendship, have some shared history together, are committed to one another, and are comfortable being perceived as a pair of friends by others. Normally, friendship cannot be presumed unless children have been expressly asked whether the relationship in question is a friendship.

One problem that can limit the validity of friendship measures is whether one has adequately assessed the entire domain of a child's peer relationships. Although the peer group at school is typically a child's most salient peer group, it is almost always the case that children have friends outside of school—in their neighborhood or in connection with sports or recreational activities. In this regard, the sole use of school-based data underestimates the extent of children's friendship relations. This problem is further exacerbated if assessments allow only for the nomination of classmates—friendships with children in other classrooms at school are overlooked. This is a particular problem in schools in which children do

not spend their school time in a single class comprising the same group of peers. In North American middle and high schools, for example, it is often the case that students take different courses with different classmates. In this regard, the use of classroom nominations makes little sense. One would fare better by asking all children in a given grade to list their best friends in that particular grade. With increasing age, however, it may also make sense to ask children to nominate their best friends in the given school.

To solve the problem of identifying friendships in a given classroom or school, some researchers have begun to use diary data: They ask children in late middle school (junior high school) or high school to keep a log of who it is they spend time with when they are not at school (e.g., Laursen, Wilder, Noack, & Williams, 2000; Laursen & Williams, 1997). These logs or diaries allow children to indicate the length of time and quality of their interactions with friends.

A second problem occurs when children are permitted only a limited number of friendship nominations (e.g., three choices). This practice may arbitrarily restrict the number friendships a child may have. Furthermore, when the number of choices is specified, children who have one or two classroom friends may feel compelled to add to their list the names of children who are not actually their best friends. This creates the possibility for overestimating the actual number of friendships these children have.

A central benefit of friendship may also be one of its challenges. Whereas friendship may help protect children from inadequacies in their families, the interface between friendship and family may present difficult demands on children. As French (2004) has shown, in cultures that ascribe considerable power or authority to the family system, the significance and meaning of friendship may differ substantially from the meaning of friendship in Western cultures. It is conceivable that friendship may even be seen as a threat to the expected structure and influence of the family. Accordingly, peer research needs to be increasingly sensitive to the cultural variations in the way that friendship is constructed and in the role that friendship is given in children's lives.

Friendship Quality

In addition to determining whether a child has a close dyadic friendship, investigators have shown an increasing concern with the characteristics or qualities of children's relationships with their best friends. Given that children's understanding of friendship changes with age, it is not surprising that there are age differences in the properties of children's friendships. And considering the wide variations in individual characteristics that children bring with them to their friendships, it is reasonable to expect that not all friendships will be alike. The most common approach involves assessing the features of children's friendships through children's own reports (e.g., Berndt & Perry, 1986; Furman & Buhrmester, 1992; Parker & Asher, 1993). Furman (1996) has noted that assessments of this type are usually conducted with questionnaires or interview procedures and are predicated on the belief that a child's impression of a relationship is the best index of this relationship for the child. Drawing from theoretical accounts of friendship (e.g., Sullivan, 1953), the dimensions typically assessed relate to (a) the *functions of friendship* (e.g., provision of companionship, level of intimate disclosure, degree of helpful and advice), (b) *conflict and disagreements,* and (c) the *affective properties* of the friendship (e.g., the affective bonds between friends).

Observational techniques have also sometimes been used to study friends' behavior with one another (e.g., Dunn, Cutting, & Fisher, 2002; Lansford & Parker, 1999), although far less frequently than self-reports. Part of the reluctance of researchers to use observational approaches may stem from the formidable task of isolating the contributions of individual members to the observed patterns of dyadic interaction (Hinde & Stevenson-Hinde, 1987). This is a real concern, but some promising observational methods for describing inter-dyad variation are available (e.g., Howes, 1988; Simpkins & Parke, 2002; Youngblade, Park, & Belsky, 1993). Presumably, any interpersonal behavior between friends may be amenable to observational assessments. Researchers have generally been interested in dimensions of behavior that relate to the putative functions of friendship (e.g., provision of companionship, level of intimate disclosure, degree of helpful and advice) or address the affective properties of the relationship (e.g., the affective bonds between friends). Children's conflict and disagreement with friends have also been of interest.

Children's Peer Acceptance

Much of the dramatic increase in interest in children's peer relationships during the past 25 years can be traced to advances in *sociometry.* Techniques for measuring popularity, especially a procedure developed by Coie, Dodge, and Coppotelli (1982), gave researchers a means by which to represent the extent to which a child is liked and disliked by peers. Much of the activity regarding sociometry is aimed at the challenge of developing valid and efficient measures of the two fundamental sociometric forces, specifically acceptance and rejection, and the measures that derive from them. *Acceptance* refers to how much a child is liked by peers; *rejection* refers to how much a child is disliked. The challenge of creating categorical measures results from the lack of independence between acceptance and rejection. These measures are neither the opposite of each other nor are they unrelated. Accordingly, a child high in acceptance is not necessarily low in rejection and a child high in rejection is not always low in acceptance. Some children could be high on both dimensions or low on both dimensions.

To account for these different patterns of association, derivative scores can be computed to index a child's general likeableness (i.e., sociometric *preference*) and the child's "visibility" in the peer group (i.e., sociometric *impact*). These scores have been used in various ways, most notably to make categorical assignments to the following sociometric groups: (a) *popular*—children who are high in acceptance and low in rejection (i.e., high impact, high preference); (b) *rejected*—children who are low in acceptance and high in rejection (i.e., high impact, low preference); (c) *neglected*—children who are low in both acceptance and rejection (i.e., low impact, mid-range in preference); (d) *average*—children who are average in acceptance and rejection (i.e., mid-range on both variables), and (e) *controversial*—children who are high in acceptance and rejection (i.e., high impact, mid-range on preference). Note well that in the case of sociometric classifications, the term *popular* is used as a synonym for accepted rather than as an index of social prestige or status. Discussions of the stability of sociometric scores and classifications can be found in Cillessen, Bukowski, and Haselager (2000), and in our previous *Handbook* chapter on children's peer interactions, relationships, and groups (Rubin, Bukowski, & Parker, 1998). Discussion of the conceptual, methodological, and potential ethical problems with sociometric techniques classification can be found in Rubin et al. (1998) and Bukowski and Cillessen (1996).

Assessments of the Peer Group

Typically, groups have been studied for three reasons. First, investigators have sought to determine whether and how a child is embedded into a naturally and spontaneously formed group structure. Two techniques, *Social Network Analysis* (SNA; Richards, 1995) and the *Social Cognitive Map* (SCM; Cairns, Gariepy, & Kindermann, 1989) are often used to identify peer networks. Social Network Analysis is based on friendship nominations. Children are asked to list the friends with whom they hang out most often in the school. Group members, liaisons, dyads, and isolates based on patterns of friendship links and the strengths of the links are identified (Richards, 1995). *Group members* are those individuals who belong to a rather exclusive social group that comprises at least three individuals who are linked with other members in the same group and who are connected by paths entirely in the group. *Liaisons* are individuals who have friendships with group members, but are not group members themselves. *Dyads* comprise individuals who have one reciprocated friendship. They do not belong to a group per se, but have mutual friendships. Finally, *Isolates* are children who have no reciprocated friendships. Given that SNA is based on friendship (either reciprocal or nonreciprocal) nominations, groups identified through the program represent *friendship networks.*

Compared with SNA, the SCM technique, developed by Cairns et al. (1989), assesses peer groups more directly. Children are asked, "Are there people in school who hang around together a lot? Who are they?" To ensure that the respondents include themselves, a follow up question is asked "What about you? Do you hang around together a lot with a group? Who are these people you hang around with?" Children are expected to report on groups about which they are most knowledgeable. Based on the reports of all participants, a matrix is constructed from the number of occasions that any two persons co-occurred in the same group. Specifically, each participant's group-membership profile is first generated based on the frequencies of nominations of group-membership with every other child in the class. Then a profile similarity index is derived by correlating pairs of individual group-membership profiles.

Second, following the determination that a child is a member of a group, a researcher can assess the group's structural properties. These properties typically consist of (a) group size, (b) the position of the group in the broader community of peer groups, and (c) the patterns of association in the group. *Size* refers simply to the number of children in the group. The *position of the group* in the broader peer group refers to how many links the group has to other collectives in the general

community of peers. And *group structure* refers to how many links there are between group members. In a *dense* group, most members would be linked to others; in a *loosely organized* group, some members would have no links to others at all.

Finally, a third goal is to assess the psychological characteristics of children's groups. Examples of this approach can be seen in the work of Chen and colleagues (Chen, Chang, & He, 2003), Gest et al. (2003), and Kindermann et al. (1995). In their research, group profiles are schematized, representing the interest and characteristics that its members share. Kindermann and colleagues, for example, have shown that groups vary considerably in their emphasis on academic performance.

Whereas group clustering techniques have been used to account for differences between groups that comprise the larger peer system, they may be an excellent way to capture differences between the structures of the peer group in different cultures. One would expect that, for example, in collectivist cultures, peer groups might be larger in that there might be more links in and between groups than one would see in individualistic cultures. This is an untested empirical question.

THE PROXIMAL CORRELATES OF CHILDREN'S PEER RELATIONSHIPS

The understanding of the origins and correlates of individual differences in children's experiences with peers comprises the largest corpus of peer relationships research in the past 25 years. Much of this research has focused on the processes and variables that either provide the basis for, or are correlated with children's acceptance or rejection by the peer group; a much smaller proportion of the research extant is focused on the correlates and antecedents of individual differences at the level of the dyad (e.g., friendship).

The literature on individual differences in popularity and friendship can be divided into two domains. First, the largest concentration of investigations center on the *individual* characteristics associated with (a) acceptance or rejection in the peer group at large, (b) the ability to make and keep friends, and (c) the quality of friendship. Most of this work focuses on either the display of particular forms of social behavior or the ways that children think about their social environments and relationships.

A second body of research is concerned with the associations between peer acceptance and rejection and friendship and both the child's family relationship experiences and the social environments in which the child functions. This literature deals with the *distal* correlates of peer acceptance and friendship. Although researchers appear to have their own preferences with regard to whether they examine proximal or distal correlates, these factors are truly interdependent; indeed, the study of the links between proximal and distal factors has become the central theme of much contemporary research.

Proximal Correlates—Peer Acceptance

Over 20 years ago, researchers set out to develop a behavioral explanation of peer acceptance and rejection. Studies were conducted using several approaches and designs most notably involving play groups (e.g., Coie & Kupersmidt, 1983) and peer-assessment techniques (Newcomb & Bukowski, 1983). In these investigations, researchers typically examined differences between children who had been classified as sociometrically *popular, rejected, neglected, controversial* and *average*. Literally, hundreds of studies were conducted, making sociometric studies the bread and butter of peer research throughout much of the 1980s.

A thorough review of the literature on the concomitants of popularity was presented in the previous version of this chapter (Rubin et al., 1998). Whereas some reviews of research serve as renaissances that renew the study of a topic, the reviews of the sociometric classification studies served as a requiem. Although many of the basic questions of sociometric classification remain unanswered, research on the differences between children in the five sociometric groups has waned. Here we provide a cursory discussion of what this literature has informed us.

Popular Children

"Popular" children are high in acceptance and low in rejection. Keep in mind that whereas the term *popular* has been traditionally used to refer to these children, this usage varies with the more recent trend to use the word "popular" to refer to children who are high in status and prestige in the group. The children traditionally known as "sociometrically popular" have been shown to have the following characteristics. Relative to other children, those of popular status are skilled at initiating and maintaining qualitatively positive relationships. When entering new peer situations, popular children are more likely than members of other sociometric status groups to consider the frame of reference common to the ongo-

ing playgroup and to establish themselves as sharing in this frame of reference (Putallaz, 1983). Popular children are also less likely to draw unwarranted attention to themselves when entering ongoing playgroups: They do not talk exclusively or overbearingly about themselves and their own social goals or desires, and they are not disruptive of the group's activity (Dodge, McClaskey, & Feldman, 1985). In addition, when entering the ongoing play of both familiar and unfamiliar children, popular children speak clearly, respond contingently to their prospective playmates, and otherwise demonstrate communicative competence that allows the maintenance of connected, coherent interaction (Black & Hazan, 1990). They are seen as cooperative, friendly, sociable, and sensitive by peers, teachers, and observers (e.g., Coie et al., 1982; Newcomb & Bukowski, 1983, 1984; Parkhurst & Hopmeyer, 1998). Specifically, popular children are more likely to be helpful, to interact actively with other children, to show leadership skills, and to engage in constructive play (e.g., Pakaslahti, Karjalainen, & Keltikangas-Jarvinen, 2002). When involved in conflict, sociometrically popular children believe that negotiation and compromise will help them get what they want while simultaneously maintaining positive relationships with peers (e.g., Hart, DeWolf, Wozniak, & Burts, 1992).

Sociometrically popular children do not differ from average children on all aspects of aggression. In a meta-analysis of research on popularity, Newcomb et al. (1993) distinguished between assertive/agonistic behaviors and behaviors that reflected disruptiveness. Popular children did not differ from others on the former category of behavior whereas they did on the latter. Popular children, it appears, can engage in some forms of assertive behavior, but they rarely engage in behaviors that are likely to interfere with the actions and goals of others.

Rejected Children

The most commonly cited behavioral correlate of peer rejection is aggression, regardless of whether aggression is indexed by peer evaluations, teacher ratings, or observations (e.g., Crick, Casas, & Mosher, 1997; Haselager, Cillessen, van Lieshout, Riksen-Walraven, & Hartup, 2002; McNeilly-Choque, Hart, Robinson, Nelson, & Olsen, 1996). The association between rejection and aggression appears to be rather broad; Newcomb et al. (1993) revealed that rejected children, relative to average popular and neglected children, showed elevated levels on three forms of aggression—

specifically, disruptiveness, physical aggression, and negative behavior (e.g., verbal threats). A small number of studies provide evidence of a causal link between aggression and rejection. Two of these are the groundbreaking playgroup studies of Dodge (1983) and Coie and Kupersmidt (1983). In these cleverly designed investigations, the interactions between *unfamiliar* peers in small groups were observed in a laboratory context over several days. Each child's behavior was observationally coded; in addition, each child was assessed in a sociometric interview at the end of each play session. Gradually, some of the children became popular and others became rejected. The behavior that most clearly predicted peer rejection was aggression.

However, aggression is not the only factor linked to rejection. Detailed analyses indicate that aggressive children comprise only between 40% to 50% of the rejected group (Bierman, Smoot, & Aumiller, 1993; Cillessen, van IJzendoorn, van Lieshout, & Hartup, 1992). Indeed, with increasing age, it appears as if aggression becomes decreasingly associated with rejection, especially among boys (e.g., Sandstrom & Coie, 1999). Also, the data extant indicate that aggression may not lead to rejection if it is balanced by a set of positive qualities (e.g., social skill) that facilitate links with other children (Farmer, Estell, Bishop, O'Neal, & Cairns, 2003).

Researchers have found that there is a high level of heterogeneity among the behavioral tendencies of rejected children. For example, children who are highly withdrawn, timid, and wary comprise between 10% to 20% of the rejected group (e.g., Cillessen et al., 1992; Parkhurst & Asher, 1992). Another perspective on this latter statistic is that when extremely withdrawn children are identified, approximately 25% of them fall into the sociometrically rejected group (e.g., Rubin, Chen, & Hymel, 1993).

Finally, victimization has been observed to be associated with peer rejection, either as a correlate (Kochenderfer-Ladd, 2003; Schwartz, 2000), as a mediator that explains the association between withdrawal and victimization, or as a moderator that increases the stability of victimization (e.g., Hanish & Guerra, 2004).

Neglected Children

Few, if any, discrete behaviors have been found to be distinctive of sociometrically neglected children (see Newcomb et al., 1993). Sociometric neglected status is relatively unstable, even over short periods, and in that light, the fact that there are few strong associations between neglected status and specific behaviors is unsurprising.

Controversial Children

Sociometrically, this group is unique in that controversial children are high on both acceptance and rejection. Accordingly, controversial children appear to have many of the characteristics of both popular *and* rejected children. Coie and Dodge (1988), for example, reported that controversial boys, like rejected boys, were aggressive and disruptive, socially withdrawn, prone to anger and rule violations, and highly active. Alternatively, they reported that controversial boys were like popular boys in that they showed high levels of helpfulness, cooperation, leadership, and, in some instances, social sensitivity.

Summary

General conclusions can be drawn as to the features that distinguish sociometrically popular, rejected, neglected, controversial, and average children from one other. These differences generally fall along a positive/negative continuum. Sociometrically rejected children show high levels of negative behaviors and low levels of positive behaviors, whereas the opposite pattern is characteristic of popular children. Average children show moderate amounts of positive and negative behaviors, neglected children demonstrate low levels of each form of social behavior, and controversial children show high levels of both positive and negative behaviors. It should be remembered that the conclusions regarding differences between sociometric groups are based on consistencies across studies. Nevertheless, these general conclusions do not always represent powerful effects. Accordingly one cannot conclude that all aggressive children will be sociometrically rejected and one should not be surprised to discover that some aggressive children are actually liked by their peers. The next wave of research on acceptance, rejection, and children's individual characteristics needs to sort out why some features lead to rejection in one case and acceptance in another.

Recent research has provided some guidance as to what the next set of studies should be like. One direction would be to give further attention to the interactions between variables. Hawley (2003), for example, has shown that aggression is linked with competence when it co-occurs with prosocial tendencies. Alternatively, Prinstein and Cillessen (2003) have pointed to the importance of studying nonlinear effects such as examining whether the association between aggression and competence with peers is best represented as curvilinear. As we noted earlier, several researchers have made the distinction between traditional sociometric dimensions of acceptance and rejection and the conceptualization of *perceived* popularity as an index of a child's status in the group (e.g., Parkhurst & Hopmeyer, 1998).

Variations in the Behavioral Correlates of Popularity: Sex, Group, and Cultural Differences

Groups have norms, or standards, regarding the "goodness" of particular acts. The acceptability of a behavior, and of the child who displays that behavior, is determined by whether the behavior conforms to the group's norms. If a behavior is universally valued, it should correlate with peer acceptance; if the normalcy of a behavior varies across groups, the extent to which the behavior is linked to popularity should vary across these groups also. It is this logic that has provided the basis for much of the research on group variations in the correlates of popularity.

Sex Differences

Given the widespread concern with sex differences in the literature on child development, it seems surprising to discover how little work exists on the topic of sociometric peer acceptance. Typically, researchers have failed to examine whether general findings are equally valid for boys and girls. For that matter, much of the early work focused solely on boys (e.g., Coie & Kupersmidt, 1983; Dodge, 1983) despite published calls for the examination of sex differences in the causes, proximal and distal correlates, and prospective outcomes of peer acceptance and rejection (e.g., Rubin, 1983). Further, sex differences have been neglected despite (a) the long-standing view that the relationships formed and maintained by females are qualitatively distinct from those of males (Leaper, 1994) and (b) the evidence that some aspects of social behavior may be differentially normative for boys and girls (e.g., Humphreys & Smith, 1987).

Sex differences do exist when behavior that is typical for a gender is considered. For example, in an observational study of 8- and 10-year-olds, Moller, Hymel, and Rubin (1992) distinguished styles of play that were engaged in more frequently by females from styles of play that were engaged in more frequently by males. The children were also administered a sociometric rating. The authors found that the relations between the same- or opposite-gender preferred play scores and popularity were nonsignificant for females in either age group. For males, however, the frequent demonstration of female preferred play was significantly, and negatively, associated with acceptance, not only by boys, but also by girls. And this relation held only for the 10-year-old males who frequently produced female sex-stereotyped play.

These latter data are in keeping with a study by Berndt and Heller (1986). Using scenarios in which they described a child who had chosen activities either consistent or inconsistent with gender stereotypes, the participants were asked to make judgments of the actor's popularity among peers. The authors found that 9- and 12-year-old children demonstrated a greater negative reaction to gender inconsistent behavior than did 5-year-olds. Furthermore, they found this intolerance was greater for boys than for girls in that it was more appropriate for girls to behave in a gender inconsistent manner. Taken together, the research on the correlates of popularity for boys versus girls reveals one consistent finding. Males who display female-stereotyped behavior are disliked by both same- and opposite-sex peers; females who display male-stereotyped behavior are generally accepted by both same- and opposite-sex peers. These relations appear to gain strength with increasing age in childhood. Nevertheless, the relevant data base for examining sex differences in the correlates of peer acceptance and rejection is sparse. This gap in the literature is striking and it severely compromises our current understanding of the peer system (see Ruble, Martin, & Berenbaum, Chapter 14, this *Handbook*, this volume, for further discussion).

Variations across Groups

The argument that a child's popularity will be associated with particular peer group norms has been the central focus of a number of investigations. Wright, Giammarino, and Parad (1986) examined the differences in the correlates of popularity in groups at a summer camp for boys with behavioral and emotional problems. For highly aggressive groups of children, the correlation between peer preference and aggression was very low. In nonaggressive groups, this association between preference and aggression was of moderate strength. The opposite pattern was seen in these same groups when social withdrawal was considered. Withdrawal was strongly and negatively correlated to preference in the high aggression groups and uncorrelated to preference in the low aggression groups. Boivin, Dodge, and Coie (1995) reported that reactive aggression, proactive aggression, and solitary play were more negatively linked to a measure of social preference when high levels of these specific behaviors were nonnormative and unrelated to preference when high levels on these behaviors were normative. Stormshak et al. (1999) also found support for the person-group similarity model. These researchers reported that for boys, social withdrawal was associated with peer acceptance in those classrooms in which withdrawal was normative; for boys, aggression was linked to peer preference in those classrooms in which aggression was more normative. Findings for girls were, complex and in some cases not supportive of the person-group similarity model. For example, in classrooms marked by high aggression, aggressive girls were not better liked than nonaggressive girls.

These studies show clearly that the association between a particular form of behavior and popularity depends on whether the behavior is normative for a group. Considering the importance of group norms as moderators of the associations between behaviors and popularity, researchers should be cautious about drawing broad conclusions about the correlates of popularity. Indeed, researchers would do well to assess the *person/group interaction and similarity* as a major determinant of peer acceptance and rejection.

Lastly, the recent study of deviancy training is germane. In this work, researchers find that children who deviate from the norm (typically insofar as their aggressive behavior is concerned) find social support in peer networks of like-behaved counterparts (Bagwell & Coie, 2004; Dishion, Spracklen, Andrews, & Patterson, 1996). It is in such groups that popularity may be determined by behavior that is dysfunctional.

Variations across Culture

Cross-cultural research on the correlates of peer acceptance and rejection has been aimed at asking whether given behaviors known to be associated with acceptance or rejection in North American samples demonstrate similar relations in other cultures. One shortcoming in this work may be that investigators have taken measures originally developed for use in a Western cultural context, and have employed them in other cultural milieus. The general conclusion from this research has been that aggression and helpfulness are associated with rejection and popularity respectively in a wide range of cultures (e.g., Casiglia, Lo Coco & Zappulla, 1998; Chang et al., 2005; Chen, Rubin, & Li, 1995; Cillessen et al., 1992; Tomada & Schneider, 1997). Alternatively, researchers

have found that among young Chinese children, sensitive, cautious, and inhibited behavior are positively associated with competent and positive social behavior and with peer acceptance (Chen et al., 1999; Chen, Rubin, & Sun, 1992). More recently, however, Hart and colleagues (2000) found that social reticence, defined as unoccupied and onlooking behavior (Coplan et al., 1994), was associated with a lack of peer acceptance, not only in young American children, but also among Russian and Chinese youngsters. Furthermore, Chang and colleagues (2005) have recently found that social withdrawal among young Hong Kong Chinese adolescents predicted the lack of peer acceptance 1.5 years hence. Relatedly, Chen et al. (2005) have reported that over the years, since the early 1990s, shy, reserved behavior among Chinese elementary school children has *increasingly* become associated with negative peer reputations. Chen and colleagues have argued that the changing economic and political climate in China is being accompanied by preferences for more assertive, yet competent, social behavior. In short, researchers would do well not to generalize findings drawn from children of one cultural group to children from another context. Moreover, changing socioeconomic climates may prove to have significant influences on that which is deemed acceptable behavior by significant peers and adults in the child's environment (Silbereisen, 2000).

Summary

We have highlighted the notion that acceptance by the peer group (typically defined by classroom composition) is driven by conformity to or deviation from *behavioral* norms. Such a view is admittedly simple conceptually and does not take into account the possibility that correlates of popularity may vary according to whether a child is acquiring or maintaining their status in a group. This latter issue seems ripe for study in the next generation of studies on patterns of liking and disliking among children.

Social Cognitive Correlates of Peer Acceptance and Rejection

Those who study social cognition believe that the child's thoughts about the social universe, especially about specific children, can be evocative or inhibitory because behavioral expression is concerned. Thus, if a child has difficulty understanding the sorts of behaviors required to make proper entry into a group or to obtain desirable objects or to avoid harassment by peers, it may be reflected in their behavior in the peer group. In short, the connection between social cognition and peer acceptance and rejection is best understood by suggesting that thoughts (and emotions for that matter) about things social and relational can evoke particular forms of behavior. In turn, these behaviors lead to acceptance or rejection by peers.

With this in mind, researchers have studied a wide range of social cognitive variables that appear to have some bearing on the child's acceptance by peers. In general, the more social-cognitively astute the child is, the more popular she or he is found to be (e.g., Slaughter, Dennis, & Pritchard, 2002). In this section, we review research in which social cognition has been associated with sociometric status.

Social Information Processing

We begin with a brief description of social information-processing models that are relevant to the study of children's skilled and unskilled social behaviors. In one model, Rubin and Rose-Krasnor (1992) speculated that, when children face an interpersonal dilemma (e.g., making new friends, acquiring a desired object from someone else, or stopping others from acting against them), their thinking follows a particular sequence. First, children select a social goal or a representation of the desired end state of the problem-solving process. Second, they examine the task environment; this involves reading and interpreting relevant social cues. For example, social status, familiarity, and age of the participants in the task environment are likely to influence the child's goal and strategy selection (Krasnor & Rubin, 1983). Third, they access and select strategies; this process involves generating possible plans of action for achieving the perceived social goal, and choosing the most appropriate one for the specific situation. Fourth, they implement the chosen strategy. Finally, it is proposed that children evaluate the outcome of the strategy; this involves assessing the situation to determine the relative success of the chosen course of action in achieving the social goal. If the initial strategy is unsuccessful, the child may repeat it or she/he may select and enact a new strategy or abandon the situation entirely.

Crick and Dodge (1994) proposed a similar social-cognitive model designed specifically to account for aggression in children (see Dodge, Coie, & Lynam, Chapter 14, this *Handbook,* this volume). This model consists of six stages: (1) the encoding of social cues, (2) the interpretation of encoded cues, (3) the clarification of goals, (4) the accessing and generation of potential responses, (5) the evaluation and selection of responses, and (6) the enactment of the chosen response. Recently, Lemerise and Arsenio (2000) integrated *emotional* experiences into the Crick and Dodge's social information-processing model. For example, aggressive children's emotional reactions to problematic social situations might include frustration or anger; anxious/withdrawn children may react with fear. These emotions, in turn, may influence the information that is attended to and the information that is recalled. This mood-congruent information processing might reinforce aggressive children's social schemas or "working models" that the social world is a hostile one or withdrawn children's notions that the social world is fear inducing. These emotional responses may explain, in part, why aggressive and withdrawn children respond in predictable ways to negative events befalling them.

Much research on social cognition and peer relationships has focused on rejected children's deficits or qualitative differences in performance at various stages of these social information-processing models. First, rejected children are distinguished from their nonrejected counterparts on the basis of their spontaneous *motives* for social engagement. Popular children, for example, are more inclined to indicate the reason for interacting with others is to establish new, or enhance ongoing, relationships. Rejected children, however, are more likely to be motivated by goals that would reasonably be expected to undermine their social relationships, such as "getting even with" or "defeating" their peers (e.g., Rabiner & Gordon, 1992).

Second, when considering the motives or intentions of others, *rejected*-aggressive children are more disposed than their popular counterparts to assume that negative events are the product of malicious, malevolent intent on the part of others (e.g., Dodge et al., 2003). This bias is evident when children are asked to make attributions for others' behaviors in situations where something negative has happened but the motives of the instigator are unclear. In these ambiguous situations, rejected-aggressive children appear unwilling to give a provocateur the benefit of the doubt—for example, by assuming that the behavior occurred by accident. This "intention cue bias" is often suggested as an explanation for why it is that aggressive and oppositional-defiant children choose to solve their interpersonal problems in hostile and agonistic ways (e.g., see Orobio de Castro, Veerman, Koops, Bosch, & Monshouwer, 2002, for a recent review).

But why would aggressive children think that when negative, but ambiguously caused events befall them, the protagonist means them harm? In keeping with Lemerise and Arsenio (2000), a transactional perspective would suggest that aggressive children, many of whom are already rejected (and victimized) by their peers, believe that certain others do not like them, those others have a history of rejecting of them or acting mean toward them, and thus the negative act *must* be intentionally caused. This conclusion of intentional malevolence is posited to elicit anger and a rapid fire response of *reactive* aggression. Many researchers have found that when asked how they would react to an ambiguously caused negative event, aggressive children respond with a choice of agonistic strategies (Orobio de Castro et al., 2002). And aggressive children also regard aggression to be an effective and appropriate means to meet their interactive goals (Vernberg, Jacobs, & Hershberger, 1999). The processes leading to the enactment of aggression and the behavioral display itself no doubt reinforces an already negative peer profile.

By the elementary and middle school years, many socially withdrawn children are also rejected by their peers. Thus, one may ask whether these children view their social worlds in ways that vary from those of nonwithdrawn and/or nonrejected children. To begin with, when socially withdrawn 4- and 5-year-olds are asked how they would go about obtaining an attractive object from another child, they produce fewer alternative solutions, display more rigidity in generating alternative responses, and are more likely to suggest adult intervention to aid in the solution of hypothetical social problems when compared to their more sociable agemates (Rubin, Daniels-Beirness, & Bream, 1984).

Observational research has demonstrated that socially reticent and withdrawn children produce fewer overtures to their peers than nonwithdrawn children (Nelson, Rubin, & Fox, 2005; Stewart & Rubin, 1995). Yet, the overtures produced are typically unassertive. Despite this production of unassertive strategies, withdrawn children are more often rebuffed by their peers than are nonwithdrawn children (Nelson et al., 2005; Stewart & Rubin, 1995). This connection between peer rebuff and social withdrawal or reticence may be taken as an in vivo assessment of peer rejection.

Rubin and colleagues (e.g., Rubin, Burgess, Kennedy, & Stewart, 2003) have argued that as a result of frequent interpersonal rejection by peers, withdrawn children may begin to attribute their social failures to internal causes; they may come to believe that there is something wrong with themselves rather than attributing their social failures to other people or situations. Supporting these notions, Rubin and Krasnor (1986) found that extremely withdrawn children tended to blame social failure on personal, dispositional characteristics rather than on external events or circumstances. These results are in keeping with recent findings by Wichmann, Coplan, and Daniels (2004) who reported that when 9- to 13-year-old withdrawn children were presented with hypothetical social situations in which ambiguously caused negative events happened to them, they attributed the events to internal and stable "self-defeating" causes. Moreover, withdrawn children suggested that when faced with such negative situations, they were more familiar with failure experiences and that a preferred strategy would be to withdraw and escape.

Some have suggested that there is a particular group of victimized children who are characterized by a socially withdrawn demeanor. For example, Olweus (1978, 1993) has referred to "whipping boys"—a group of victimized children perceived as easy marks by peers. Hodges and colleagues have referred to some victimized children as "physically weak" and "withdrawn" (Hodges, Boivin, et al., 1999; Hodges, Malone, & Perry, 1997; Rodkin & Hodges, 2003). Not surprisingly, researchers have found that children victimized by peers are also rejected by them (Kochenderfer-Ladd, 2003; Schwartz, 2000). Given the conceptual associations between social withdrawal, victimization, and peer rejection, the earlier noted findings by Wichmann et al. (2004) are reminiscent of work by Graham and Juvonen (1998, 2001). These latter researchers reported that youngsters who identified themselves as victimized by peers tended to blame themselves for their peer relationship problems. And Nolen-Hoeksema, Girgus, and Seligman (1992) have argued that self-blame can lead to a variety of negative outcomes of an internalizing nature, such as depression, low self-esteem, and withdrawal, thereby suggesting a self-reinforcing cycle of negative socioemotional functioning (see also Dill, Vernberg, & Fonagy, 2004).

Taken together, the findings reported earlier suggest that if children interpret social experiences negatively, inappropriately, and inaccurately, they may prove to be their own worst enemies. Such negative biases are likely to contribute to their already problematic social relationships. In the case of rejected-aggressive children, demonstrated deficits in social-cognitive processing suggest that these children may have difficulty understanding the consequences of their behaviors for others and that their social failures can be attributed to internal, stable causes. In short, they may not claim responsibility for their production of agonistic social behaviors ("They made me do it!") or for their negative social reputations. Indeed, given their social-cognitive inadequacies, rejected-aggressive children may not realize that their interactive styles are perceived negatively by peers. After all, as noted earlier, they do regard aggression as an effective and appropriate means to meet their interactive goals.

Alternatively, the rejected socially withdrawn child may be able to think through interpersonal dilemmas in an adequate, competent manner. Nevertheless, when confronted by the "real-life" social world, withdrawn children may be less able to meet their social goals than are their nonwithdrawn peers. The experience of peer noncompliance noted earlier is likely to have an unfortunate outcome for the sensitive, wary, withdrawn child. It is this type of sensitive rejected child who would attribute social failures to internal, stable characteristics, and who would respond to peer rebuff by expressing (a) loneliness, (b) self-blame, (c) dissatisfaction with his or her social relationships, and (d) negative self-appraisals of social skills.

Self-System Correlates of Peer Acceptance and Rejection

An important repercussion that has been ascribed to the experiences with peers is their effect on the self-concept. In the foundational ideas of Sullivan and of the symbolic interactionists, peer relationships were described as a critical source of the self. Specifically, boys and girls were said to use their peer relationships as important sources of information about themselves. Most *positive* experiences were believed to provide a strong sense of validation that reinforced the perception that one is well-functioning and grounded. Accordingly, research on peer relationships has often addressed theoretically derived hypotheses about the effects of peer experiences on aspects of the self.

Researchers have consistently reported that it is mainly *rejected-withdrawn* children (also variously described as submissive, sensitive, wary) who believe they have poor social skills and relationships (Hymel, Bowker, & Woody, 1993). *Rejected-aggressive* children do not report thinking poorly about their social compe-

tencies or their relationships with peers (Zakriski & Coie, 1996). These findings are in keeping with the results of studies concerning withdrawn and aggressive children conducted in Western cultures; it is only the former group that reports having difficulty with their social skills and peer relationships (Rubin, Chen, & Hymel, 1993).

Given rejected-withdrawn children's negative perceptions of their social competencies and relationships, and given their negative experiences in the peer group, it is not surprising that these children report more loneliness and social detachment than popular children or children who are rejected but aggressive (e.g., Gazelle & Ladd, 2003). These relations have been reported throughout childhood and early adolescence (e.g., Crick & Ladd, 1993; Parkhurst & Asher, 1992).

A further distinction between rejected children is the chronicity of their peer problems. Whereas rejection is temporary for some children, it is an enduring experience for others. Ladd and Troop-Gordon (2003) showed that chronic rejection was related to subsequent views of the self and that these negative self-perceptions partially mediated the relation between peer difficulties and internalizing problems and loneliness.

In summary, although rejected children tend to report that they are less competent, less efficacious, and less satisfied with reference to their social skills and peer relationships, this conclusion appears true only for rejected children who are withdrawn, timid, or submissive. The study of the association between the self and peer relations is part of a large and enduring research tradition, which treats that self as the result of peer processes. More recent research suggests that children who are high and low in self-esteem manage and use their peer relations for different purposes. Research on the association between peer relationships and the self may benefit from the adoption of new perspectives such as the ideas from dynamic systems models of the self.

Children's Friendships: Correlates and Individual Differences

In an earlier section, we described developmental issues pertaining to friendship, such as its understanding by children, its prevalence, features, and functions. In this section, we examine the correlates of friendship and individual differences in those aspects of friendship described earlier.

Children who lack friends may miss out on the advantages thought to be garnered by such relationships.

Furthermore, not only is the presence of friendship viewed as important, but the *quality* of the relationship is also considered significant. Qualitative dimensions of friendship include intimacy, companionship, and emotional and social support. Notably, friendship quality has been positively associated with indices of psychosocial adjustment and functioning, such as self-esteem (Berndt, 1996).

In an attempt to illustrate the distinction between peer acceptance and friendship, several researchers have examined the relation between sociometric status, friendship prevalence, and relationship quality. For example, Parker and Asher (1993) showed that while not all highly accepted children had best friends and not all children low in peer acceptance were without best friendships, highly accepted and average-accepted children were twice as likely as low-accepted children to have a mutual best friend. Additionally, low-accepted children reported qualitatively poorer friendships than the other two groups. From a dyadic perspective, Brendgen, Little, and Krappmann (2000) found that the degree of parallelism in friendship quality, or perceptual concordance, varied as a function of sociometric status. Whereas the perceptions of friendship quality of average-accepted and highly accepted children and their respective best friends were highly correlated, there was little relation between rejected children's own perceptions and their best friends' perceptions of the relationship quality, particularly concerning the extent to which they viewed the relationship as close and being fun.

Although an examination of the relation between sociometric status (group "level") and friendship (dyadic relationship "level") is important, there is also a need to describe how children's *individual* characteristics are related to the prevalence of friendship and the quality of their dyadic relationships with peers. Given that many rejected children appear to be aggressive and/or withdrawn, it is surprising to note that few investigators have examined the friendships of these children. Not all aggressive and withdrawn children and certainly not all rejected children experience later adjustment difficulties. Thus, the best friendships of these children may function protectively and buffer them from later problems. Alternately, some best friendships may actually serve to exacerbate existing problems. An example of the protective role that friendship may play for children who have difficulties in the peer group may be drawn from research by Hodges, Boivin, et al. (1999). These researchers found that peer victimization predicted increases in internalizing and externalizing difficulties during the school year for those children who lacked a mutual best friendship. The relation between peer victimization, internalizing, and externalizing problems was nonsignificant for children who possessed a mutual best friendship, thereby suggesting that friendship may function protectively for children who are victimized by their peers.

We now compare the friendships of those children who appear at greatest risk for peer rejection (i.e., those who have been identified as aggressive or socially withdrawn) with their age-mates who have do not evidence such behavioral or psychological difficulties.

Friendship Prevalence and Quality

Investigators have shown that the majority of aggressive children have a mutual best friendship and are as likely as well-adjusted children to have mutual friends (e.g., Vitaro, Brendgen, & Tremblay, 2000). Aggression, however, does seem to be negatively related to friendship stability (e.g., Hektner, August, & Realmuto, 2000), a finding that is not too surprising considering the adverse nature of aggression. Moreover, aggressive children have friends who are more aggressive and their relationships are more confrontational and antisocial in quality (e.g., Dishion, Eddy, Haas, Li, & Spracklen, 1997). High levels of relational aggression (e.g., threatening friendship withdrawal) *within* the friendship, and high levels of exclusivity/jealously, and intimacy characterize the friendships of relationally aggressive children. In contrast, overtly aggressive children direct their overt aggression *outside* their friendship dyads, and report low levels of intimacy (Grotpeter & Crick, 1996).

The prevalence of best friendships among *young* socially withdrawn children is not significantly different from that among nonwithdrawn children (Ladd & Burgess, 1999), and approximately 60% of withdrawn 8-, 9-, and 10-year-olds have reciprocated friendships (Rubin, Wojslawowicz, Burgess, Booth-LaForce, & Rose-Krasnor, in press; Schneider, 1999). These data suggest that social withdrawal and shyness are individual characteristics that do not influence the formation, prevalence, and maintenance of friendship in childhood.

Relationship qualities have been studied in relation to different subtypes of aggression, such as relational and overt aggression (Grotpeter & Crick, 1996), and proactive and reactive aggression (Poulin & Boivin, 1999). Results from the aforementioned studies suggest that aggressive behaviors may negatively affect the quality of friendships. Recently, it has been shown that the friendships of withdrawn children are viewed as relatively lacking in fun, intimacy, helpfulness and guidance, and validation and caring (Rubin, Wojslawowicz, et al., in press). These findings suggest a "misery loves company" scenario for withdrawn children and their best friends. One may conjure up images of victimized friends coping poorly in the world of peers, images reflected in recent newspaper and television accounts of peer victimization and its untimely consequences.

There is some evidence to suggest that socially withdrawn children are more likely than their age-mates to be *chronically friendless*. In a summer camp study conducted by Parker and Seal (1996), chronically friendless children were rated by their peers to be more shy and timid, to spend more time playing alone, and to be more sensitive than children who possessed a mutual best friendship during the summer camp program. Additionally, counselors rated these friendless children as less mature, less socially skilled, and as displaying more withdrawn and anxious behaviors than children with friends. The aforementioned study is the only investigation to date of chronically friendless children, and the summer camp setting may have influenced the results in a significant fashion. If some socially withdrawn children are *shy* (e.g., Rubin, Burgess, Kennedy, & Stewart, 2003), then establishing friendships amongst unfamiliar others may prove somewhat overwhelming for many of these children. However, in a familiar setting, such as school, withdrawn children may have less difficulty forming and keeping friendships over the course of the school year. Conversely, as noted earlier, social withdrawal increases in salience with age to peers. Thus, it is possible that the negative reputation accorded socially withdrawn children may hinder friendship formation and maintenance processes. In any event, an investigation of the *consistent absence* of friendship among withdrawn and aggressive children relative to their nonwithdrawn, nonaggressive age-mates may prove illuminating.

DISTAL PREDICTORS OF CHILDREN'S SOCIAL SKILLS AND PEER RELATIONSHIPS

The quality of children's extrafamilial social lives is likely a product of factors internal and external to the child. Drawing from Hinde (1987), for example, it seems reasonable to suggest that such *individual* characteristics as biological or dispositional factors (e.g., temperament; self-regulatory mechanisms) may influence children's peer interactions and relationships. It is equally plausible that the *interactions* and *relationships* children experience with their parents are important.

In the following section, we present a brief review of some of the distal factors that may influence children's social interactions and peer relationships. We begin with a short discussion of the role of *individual* or dispositional temperament and biological factors. Following this, we examine the association between the parent-child and child-peer *relationship* systems. We focus primarily on research conducted in the framework of attachment theory. Following our discussion of attachment theory, we examine the relevant literature on parenting beliefs and behaviors.

Temperament, Social Behaviors, and Peer Relationships

Recently, temperament has been construed as constitutionally based individual differences in emotional, motoric, and attentional reactivity and the regulation thereof (Rothbart, Ellis, & Posner, 2004). Researchers who study temperament report that individuals differ not only in the ease with which positive and negative emotions may be aroused (*emotionality*) but also in the ease with which emotions, once aroused, can be *regulated* (Rothbart et al., 2004). In some respects, a better term for emotionality is *reactivity* in that most research on the phenomenon is focused on the extent to which children react to situations or events with anger, irritability, or fear. And again, most contemporary researchers have been interested in the ways in which reactive responses can be *self*-regulated. Thus, researchers have centered on the *effortful self-control* of emotional, behavioral, and attentional processes (Sanson, Hemphill, & Smart, 2004).

The constructs of difficult temperament, activity level, inhibition, and sociability merit special attention in the study of peer interactions and relationships. *Difficult temperament* refers to the frequent and intense expression of negative affect (Thomas & Chess, 1977). Fussiness and irritability would be characteristic of a "difficult" infant or toddler. In reactivity/regulation terminology, the *difficult* child is one whose negative emotions are easily aroused and difficult to soothe or regulate. The *highly active* baby/toddler is one who is easily excited and motorically facile. Again, these children are easily aroused—that is, highly reactive. *Inhibited* infants/toddlers are timid, vigilant, and fearful when faced with novel social stimuli; like the other groups of children, their emotions are easily aroused and difficult to regulate. Finally, children who are outgoing and open in response to social novelty are described as *sociable* (Kagan, 1999).

Each of these temperamental characteristics is relatively stable (e.g., Rothbart, Derryberry, & Hershey, 2000), and each is related to particular constellations of social behaviors that we described earlier as characteristic of either popular or rejected children. The conceptual model that "drives" much of the longitudinal research connecting temperament to peer interactions and relationships is rather straightforward. Temperament processes, such as emotional reactivity or effortful control, are posited to underpin the presentation of given social behaviors; these behaviors, in turn, are thought to predict children's relationships with their peers (e.g., Eisenberg, 2002).

In keeping with this perspective, infants and toddlers who have been identified as having difficult and/or active temperament, or as emotionally reactive are more likely to behave in aggressive, impulsive ways in early childhood (e.g., Hay, Castle, & Davies, 2000; Rubin, Burgess, Dwyer, & Hastings, 2003). Contemporaneous and predictive connections between negative emotionality and/or difficult temperament and children's aggressive and oppositional behavior have been discovered by researchers the world over (e.g., Keenan, Shaw, & Delliquadri, 1998; Russell, Hart, Robinson, & Olson, 2003; Vitaro, Brendgen, & Tremblay, 2002). And, as we noted earlier, undercontrolled, impulsive, and aggressive behavior is associated contemporaneously and predictively with peer relationships characterized by rejection. Indeed, negative emotionality itself has been associated with peer rejection (e.g., Eisenberg, Fabes, Guthrie, & Reiser, 2000).

Similarly, behavioral inhibition, an individual trait identified in infancy and toddlerhood predicts the display of shyness and socially withdrawn behavior in early and middle childhood (Kagan, 1999; Rubin, Burgess, & Hastings, 2002). Contemporaneous connections between behavioral inhibition and children's shy or socially reticent behavior have been found during early and middle childhood and adolescence (e.g., Pfeifer, Goldsmith, Davidson, & Rickman, 2002). Shy, socially

reticent children display less socially competent and prosocial behaviors, employ fewer positive coping strategies, and are more likely to develop anxiety problems than their nonreticent age-mates (e.g., Coplan et al., 1994; Eisenberg, Shepard, Fabes, Murphy, & Guthrie, 1998). Moreover, reticence and social withdrawal has been found to predict peer rejection and victimization from as early as the preschool years (e.g., Gazelle & Ladd, 2003; Hart et al., 2000).

It has been suggested that dispositional characteristics related to *emotion regulation* may lay the basis for the emergence of children's social behaviors and relationships. For example, Rubin, Coplan, Fox, and Calkins (1995) have argued that the social consequences of emotion dysregulation vary in accord with the child's behavioral tendency to approach and interact with peers during free play. They found that sociable children whose approach behaviors lacked regulatory control were disruptive and aggressive; those who were sociable but able to regulate their emotions were socially competent. Unsociable children who were good emotion regulators appeared to suffer no ill effects from their lack of social behavior; when playing alone, they were productive engagers in constructive and exploratory activity. They were neither anxious amongst peers nor rated by parents as having socioemotional difficulties. Unsociable children who were poor emotion regulators were more behaviorally anxious and wary, more reticent than constructive when playing alone, and were viewed by parents as having more internalizing problems than their age-mates. Thus, emotionally dysregulated preschoolers may behave in ways that will elicit peer rejection and inhibit the development of qualitatively adaptive friendships. Further, this is the case for emotionally dysregulated sociable as well as unsociable children.

The results of Rubin et al.'s (1995) study are clearly in keeping with findings from Eisenberg and colleagues' extensive research program on young children's emotional arousal and regulation. Eisenberg and colleagues have consistently found that emotion dysregulation is a concomitant and predictor of behavioral solitude (e.g., Fabes, Hanish, Martin, & Eisenberg, 2002; Spinrad et al., 2004) and externalizing forms of behavior (e.g., Eisenberg, Cumberland, et al., 2001) in the peer group. Relatedly, researchers have found that the abilities to regulate negative emotions and to inhibit the expression of undesirable affect and behavior (regulatory control) are associated with, and predictive of, social competence and peer acceptance (e.g., Eisenberg, Pidada, &

Liew, 2001; Eisenberg, Spinrad, Fabes, Reiser, et al., 2004; Gunnar, Sebanc, Tout, Donzella, & Van Dulmen, 2003; Kochanska, Murray, & Coy, 1997), while an inability to regulate affect is associated with socially incompetent behavior (e.g., Calkins & Dedmon, 2000; Calkins, Gill, Johnson, & Smith, 1999). Importantly, these findings appear to be consistent across cultures (e.g., Eisenberg, Pidada, & Liew, 2001; Zhou, Eisenberg, Wang, & Reiser, 2004).

Temperament and Friendship

Most research associating temperament-related constructs and peer relationships have focused on peer popularity or rejection. There has been little work in which temperament has been associated with aspects of friendship. Stocker and Dunn (1990) found that sociable children were rated as having more positive relationships with friends; highly emotional children had less successful relationships with friends. Dunn and Cutting (1999), in a study of young children, found that negative emotionality was associated with the observed frequency of failed social bids and with less amity directed to the best friend; as a counterpoint, children showed less amity to friends who were inhibited or shy. More recently, in a study of young adolescents, Pike and Atzaba-Poria (2003) reported that sociability was related to positive aspects of perceived friendship quality, whereas negative emotionality was associated with friendship conflict.

Summary

In summary, researchers suggest that individual, dispositionally based characteristics may set the stage for the development of particular types of parent-child relationships and for the development of social behavioral profiles that ultimately predict the quality of children's peer relationships.

Parent-Child Attachment Relationships, Social Behaviors, and Peer Relationships

According to Hartup (1985), parents serve at least three functions in the child's development of social competence and qualitatively positive peer relationships. First, parent-child *interaction* is a context in which many competencies necessary for social interaction develop. Second, the parent-child *relationship* constitutes a safety net permitting the child the freedom to examine features of the social universe, thereby enhancing the development of social skills. Third, it is in the parent-child relationship that the child begins to develop expectations and assumptions about interactions and relationships with other people.

The Parent-Child Attachment Relationship

A basic premise of attachment theory is that the early mother-infant relationship lays the groundwork for children's understanding of, and participation in, subsequent extrafamilial relationships. And, since the quality of attachment relationships with the mother may vary, subsequent social success and relationships with peers is expected to vary as well.

The putative, proximal causes of the development of a secure attachment relationship are the expressions of parental responsivity, warmth, and sensitivity (e.g., Belsky & Cassidy, 1995). The sensitive and responsive parent recognizes the infant's or toddler's emotional signals, considers the child's perspective, and responds promptly and appropriately to the child's needs. In turn, it is posited that the child develops a belief system that incorporates the parent as someone who can be relied on for protection, nurturance, comfort, and security; a sense of trust in relationships results from the secure infant/toddler-parent bond. Furthermore, the child forms a belief that the self is competent and worthy of positive response from others. The process by which a secure attachment relationship is thought to result in the development of social competence and positive relationships with peers may be described briefly as follows. The "internal working model" of the securely attached young child allows him or her to feel secure, confident, and self-assured when introduced to novel settings; this sense of felt security fosters the child's active exploration of the social environment (Sroufe, 1983). In turn, exploration of the social milieu leads to peer interaction and play. And as we noted earlier, peer interaction and play allow children to experience the interpersonal exchange of ideas, perspectives, roles, and actions. From such social interchanges, children develop skills that lead to the development of positive peer relationships.

Alternatively, the development of an insecure attachment relationship is posited to result in the child's developing an internal working model that interpersonal relationships are rejecting or neglectful (Bowlby, 1973). Attachment theorists have suggested also that the expectations and assumptions that infants hold about others, and the means by which they cope with these cognitions, are internalized and carried forward into subsequent relationships. Thus, it has been proposed that, in their subsequent peer relationships, insecure "avoidant" infants are guided by previously reinforced expectations of parental rejection; hence, they are believed to perceive peers as potentially hostile and tend to strike out proactively and aggressively (Troy & Sroufe, 1987). Insecure "ambivalent" infants, alternatively, are thought to be guided by a fear of rejection; consequently, in their extrafamilial peer relationships they are posited to attempt to avoid rejection through passive, adult-dependent behavior and withdrawal from the prospects of peer interaction (Renken, Egeland, Marvinney, Mangelsdorf, & Sroufe, 1989).

The Parent-Child Attachment Relationship and Children's Social Behaviors: Empirical Support

Securely attached infants are more likely than their insecure counterparts to demonstrate socially competent behaviors amongst peers during the toddler (e.g., Pastor, 1981), preschool (e.g., Booth, Rose-Krasnor, & Rubin, 1991), and elementary school periods (e.g., Elicker, Englund, & Sroufe, 1992). Insecure babies, especially those classified as avoidant, later exhibit more hostility, anger, and aggressive behavior in preschool settings than their secure counterparts (e.g., Burgess, Marshall, Rubin, & Fox, 2003; Shaw, Owens, Vondra, Keenan, & Winslow, 1996). Insecure-ambivalent infants are more easily frustrated, and socially inhibited at 2 years than their secure age-mates (e.g., Fox & Calkins, 1993). At 4 years of age, children classified at 1 year as ambivalent have been described as fearful and lacking in assertiveness (Kochanska, 1998). Spangler and Schieche (1998) have reported that of the 16 "C" babies they identified in their research, 15 were rated by their mothers as behaviorally inhibited. As noted earlier, it has been suggested that inhibition in infancy and toddlerhood is a precursor of social withdrawal in early and middle childhood. Finally, evidence that disorganized/disoriented attachment status in infancy predicts the subsequent display of aggression amongst preschool and elementary school peers derives from several sources (e.g., Lyons-Ruth, Easterbrooks, & Cibelli, 1997).

It is also the case that secure and insecure attachments, as assessed in early and middle childhood, as well as in early adolescence are associated contemporaneously with and predictive of adaptive and maladaptive social behaviors respectively. For example, children who experience a secure relationship with their mothers (and fathers) have been found to be more sociable and compe-

tent than their insecure counterparts, whilst insecure children exhibit more aggression and withdrawal (Allen, Moore, Kuperminc, & Bell, 1998; Rose-Krasnor, Rubin, Booth, & Coplan, 1996; Schmidt, DeMulder, & Denham, 2002; Simons, Paternite, & Shore, 2001; Stevenson-Hinde & Marshall, 1999). Extensive reviews of related literature may be found in Thompson (Chapter 2, this *Handbook,* this volume).

The Parent-Child Attachment Relationship and Children's Peer Relationships: Empirical Support

If the quality of the attachment relationship is associated with, and predictive of, patterns of social interaction, it seems logical to propose a relation between attachment status and the child's standing in the peer group. In a recent meta-analysis of the extant literature on links between attachment and peer acceptance, Schneider, Atkinson, and Tardiff (2001) found a small-to-moderate effect size between these domains.

Attachment and Friendship

According to Booth, Rubin, Rose-Krasnor, and Burgess (2004), although associations between attachment security and social competence and peer acceptance are theoretically meaningful, there is an even more compelling rationale for the link between attachment security and *friendship.* From attachment theory, one would expect that the trust and intimacy characterizing secure child-parent relationships should produce an internalized model of relationship expectations that affects the quality of relationships with friends. In support of this theoretically driven expectation, Schneider et al. (2001), in a meta-analysis, found a larger effect size linking attachment security with friendship than with peer relationships more generally.

For example, Youngblade and Belsky (1992) reported that securely attached infants were less likely than insecure infants to have negative and asynchronous friendships at 5 years of age. Freitag, Belsky, Grossmann, Grossmann, and Scheurer-Englisch (1996) found that children who had positive early relationships with their parents were more likely to have a close friend at age 10. Also, secure parent-child attachment in late childhood and early adolescence is associated positively (and contemporaneously) with positive qualities of children's close peer relationships (Lieberman, Doyle, & Markiewicz, 1999; Rubin, Dwyer, et al., 2004). And Clark and Ladd (2000) have reported that parent-child connectedness, an essential element of the attachment bond, is associated with higher levels of harmony and lower levels of conflict in the friendships of young children.

Whether specific attachment classifications predict types of friendships characteristics is, as yet, unknown. Recently, Hodges, Finnegan, and Perry (1999) have suggested that an important feature in close relationships is the balance between autonomy and connectedness. They suggested that this *relationship orientation* or *relationship stance* may be conceptualized and coded as avoidant or preoccupied: An *avoidant* child may be characterized by showing very little emotion on reunion with or on separation from the relationship partner, may avoid the partner when in a state of distress, and renounce the importance of the relationship. A *preoccupied* child may show extreme distress when the relationship partner is needed but absent, and may be acutely sensitive to the possibility of rejection by, and separation from, the partner. Hodges et al. (1999) found that relationship orientation with a best friend could be moderately predicted from the child's relationship orientation with his or her parents, a finding that is explained by attachment theory and Bowlby's (1969/1982) notion of generalized internal working models. Hodges and colleagues (1999) do not consider their measure of relationships stance to be equivalent to an attachment classification. However, their research represents an important step in the direction of matching characteristics of parent-child and friend relationships.

Summary

There is growing evidence that the quality of parent-child attachment relationships is associated with and predictive of qualitatively good friendships. This being the case, we might expect future research to focus on relations between relationships systems and examine whether (and when) children's friendships can augment (or exacerbate) the relations between parent-child attachment and adaptation or maladaptation.

Parenting and Children's Social Behaviors and Peer Relationships

Parental Beliefs

Parents' ideas, beliefs, and perceptions about the development and maintenance of children's social behaviors and relationships predict, and presumably partially explain the development of socially adaptive and maladaptive interactive behaviors and peer relationships in childhood. This is true because parents' child-rearing practices represent a behavioral expression of their ideas

about how children become socially competent, how family contexts should be structured to shape children's behaviors, and how and when children should be taught to initiate and maintain relationships with others (Bugental & Happaney, 2002; Rubin & Burgess, 2002). These ideas about child rearing and about what is acceptable and unacceptable child behavior in the social world are culturally determined. Extended discussions of such cultural determination may be found in Rubin and Chung (in press).

Parents' Beliefs about Adaptive Child Behaviors and Relationships

Parents of socially competent children believe that, in early childhood, they should play an active role in the socialization of social skills via teaching and providing peer interaction opportunities (Rubin, Mills, & Rose-Krasnor, 1989). They believe also that when their children display maladaptive behaviors, it is due to transitory and situationally caused circumstances. Parents whose preschoolers display socially incompetent behaviors, alternatively, are less likely to endorse strong beliefs in the development of social skills (Rubin et al., 1989). Furthermore, they are more likely to attribute the development of social competence to internal factors ("Children are born that way"), to believe that incompetent behavior is difficult to alter, and to believe that interpersonal skills are best taught through direct instructional means (Rubin et al., 1989).

One conclusion that may derive from these findings is that parental involvement in the promotion of social competence is mediated by strong beliefs in the importance of social skills. When a socially competent child demonstrates poor social performance, parents who place a relatively high value on social competence are likely to become the most involved and responsive. Over time, such involvement may be positively reinforced by the child's acquisition of social skills. At the same time, parents are likely to value the social skills displayed by their children, and these children will be perceived as interpersonally competent and capable of autonomous learning. Hence, parental beliefs and child characteristics will influence each other in a reciprocal manner (Rubin, Rose-Krasnor, Bigras, Mills, & Booth, 1996).

The Child as Parental Belief Evocateur

In keeping with the perspective that the parent-child relationship reflects the contributions of both partners, it is important to understand that parental beliefs may be evoked by child characteristics and behavior (Bornstein,

2002). For example, the "problematic" child who demonstrates maladaptive social behaviors and who does not get along with her or his peers is likely to evoke different parental emotions and cognitions than the "normal" child (Bugental, 1992). When this latter group of children behaves in maladaptive or socially inappropriate manners, they may activate parental feelings of concern, puzzlement, and, in the case of aggression, anger. These parental emotions are regulated by the parent's attempts to understand, rationalize, or justify the child's behavior and by the parent's knowledge of the child's social skills history and the known quality of the child's social relationships at home, at school, and in the neighborhood. Thus, in the case of nonproblematic children, the evocative stimulus produces adaptive, solution-focused parental ideation that results in the parent's choice of a reasoned, sensitive, and responsive approach to dealing with the problem behavior (Bugental, 1992). In turn, the child views the parent as supportive and learns to better understand how to behave and feel in similar situations as they occur in the future. As such, a reciprocal connection is developed between the ways and means of adult and child social information processing.

But how does the socially incompetent child's presentation of socially maladaptive behavior affect the parent? In the case of aggressive children, any hostile behavior, whether directed at peers, siblings, or parents may evoke (a) strong parental feelings of anger and frustration (Deater-Deckard & Dodge, 1997; Eisenberg, Gershoff, et al., 2001) and (b) biased attributions that "blame" the child's noxious behavior on traits, intentions, and motives internal to the child (e.g., Strassberg, 1995). These parental cognitions and emotions, predict the use of power assertive and restrictive disciplinary techniques (Colwell, Mize, & Pettit, 2002; Coplan, Hastings, Lagace-Seguin, & Moulton, 2002). This type of low warmth-high control parental response, mediated by affect and beliefs/cognitions about the intentionality of the child behavior, the historical precedence of child aggression, and the best means to control child aggression, is likely to evoke negative affect and cognitions in the child. The result of this interplay between parent and child beliefs, affects, and behavior may be the reinforcement and extension of family cycles of hostility (Carson & Parke, 1996; Dishion, Duncan, Eddy, Fagot, & Fetrow, 1994; Granic & Lamey, 2002).

Parental reactions to social wariness and fearfulness are less well understood. Researchers have found that when children produce a high frequency of socially wary, withdrawn behaviors their parents (a) recognize this as a problem; (b) express feelings of concern, sympathy, guilt, embarrassment, and, with increasing child age, a growing sense of frustration; and (c) are more inclined than parents of nonwary children to attribute their children's social reticence to dispositional traits (Hastings & Rubin, 1999). Perhaps in an attempt to regulate their own expressed guilt and embarrassment emanating from their children's ineffectual behaviors, mothers of socially withdrawn preschoolers indicate that they would react to their children's displays of social withdrawal by providing them with protection and direct instruction (Mills & Rubin, 1998). To release the child from social discomfort, the parents of socially wary children have indicated that they would solve the child's social dilemmas by asking other children for information desired by the child, obtaining objects desired by the child, or requesting that peers allow the child to join them in play (Rubin & Burgess, 2002).

In summary, it is suggested that parental beliefs influence parental behavior; in turn, parental behavior influences the development, maintenance, and inhibition of children's social behaviors, which, as we noted earlier, influence the quality of their peer relationships. Consistent with this view, parents of aggressive and withdrawn children have been found to differ from those of typical children in the ways in which they think about socializing social skills and in the ways that they report reacting to their children's maladaptive behaviors.

Parenting Behaviors, Children's Social Skills, and Peer Relationships

Parents may influence the development of social behaviors, interaction patterns, and ultimately, the quality of their children's peer relationships by (a) providing opportunities for their children to have contact with peers; (b) monitoring of their children's peer encounters (when necessary); (c) coaching their children to deal competently with interpersonal peer-related tasks; and (d) disciplining unacceptable, maladaptive peer directed behaviors (e.g., Parke & O'Neill, 1999).

Parental Coaching and Managing

Research suggests that parents vary widely in the extent of their efforts to provide opportunities for peer interaction for their children and to coach their children in specific social skills. Moreover, the available evidence suggests that parents' efforts in these areas have implications for their young children's success with peers (see Kerns, Cole, & Andrews, 1998; Mize & Pettit, 1997; Pettit, Brown, Mize, & Lindsey, 1998). Ladd and Golter (1988), for example, found that parents who actively arranged peer contacts and who indirectly supervised these contacts had preschoolers who were better liked by their peers. In addition, children whose parents relied on indirect rather than direct monitoring of their children's peer contacts were less hostile toward peers. These findings have been supported in subsequent studies (e.g., Pettit et al., 1998). In a follow-up, short-term longitudinal study, Ladd and Hart (1992) found that mothers' over- and underinvolvement in arranging and monitoring peer contacts could be detrimental to children's social success, at least among boys. Boys whose mothers were moderately involved in initiating their child's peer contacts displayed significant gains in peer status over time compared to boys with over- and underinvolved mothers. Girls made significant gains in peer status only when their own efforts to initiate contact with other children were large in comparison to those of their mothers (i.e., when their mothers were underinvolved).

Finnie and Russell (1988) found that during play with an unfamiliar age-mate, mothers of unpopular children were more likely to avoid supervising their children and to supervise their children less skillfully than mothers of more popular children. Mothers of more popular children were more active and effective in supervising their children's peer related behaviors than mothers of less well-accepted children. In a follow-up study, Russell and Finnie (1990) examined mothers' instructions to their child immediately prior to the child's opportunity to play with an unfamiliar child. Mothers of popular children were more likely than mothers of low-status (rejected and neglected) children to make group-oriented statements during both the anticipatory instruction period as well as during the play session itself. Mothers of low-status children were more disruptive of their children's play.

In summary, research indicates that when mothers are involved in effective ways in coaching their children through difficulties with peers, facilitating their children's play with peers, and providing their children with opportunities to play with peers, their children are more popular among their age-mates. However, all of the research in this area is correlational and virtually none of the extant research is focused on fathers. It is entirely possible that the observed differences between the mothers of socially popular and unpopular or competent and incompetent children are a consequence, rather than the cause, of their children's success with peers. Thus, it would be timely to examine whether very young children identified as being relatively unpopular with peers could "shake" their early reputations if their parents (mothers and fathers) were "trained" in parental monitoring and coaching skills.

Parenting Behaviors

Parents (usually mothers) of unpopular and/or peer rejected children have been reported to use inept, intrusive, harsh, and authoritarian disciplinary and socialization practices more frequently than those of their more popular counterparts (e.g., Carson & Parke, 1996; McDowell & Parke, 2000; Pettit, Clawson, Dodge, & Bates, 1996). These data seem to hold true for parents of preschoolers through elementary school children. Alternately, parents of popular children use more feelings-oriented reasoning and induction, responsivity, warm control (authoritative), and positivity during communication than their unpopular counterparts (e.g., Mize & Pettit, 1997).

In regard to the actual process that links parenting to the child's peer relationships, it is possible to consider that parenting styles may promote particular child behaviors that mark a child for acceptance or rejection. To this end, researchers have demonstrated that mothers of socially competent children are more child-centered, more feelings-oriented, warmer, and more likely to use positive verbalizations, reasoning, and explanations than mothers of less competent children (e.g., Mize & Pettit, 1997; Rose-Krasnor et al., 1996).

With regard to socially incompetent behaviors, researchers have shown consistently that aggressive children have parents who model and inadvertently reinforce aggressive and impulsive behavior, and who are cold and rejecting, physically punitive, and inconsistent in their disciplinary behaviors. In addition to parental rejection and the use of high power-assertive and inconsistent disciplinary strategies, parental permissiveness, indulgence, and lack of supervision have often been found to correlate with children's aggressive behavior (see Rubin & Burgess, 2002, and Dodge et al., Chapter 12, this *Handbook,* this volume, for recent reviews). It may not be difficult to understand these associations given that parental tolerance and neglect of the child's aggressive behavior may actually have the implication of legitimization and encouragement of aggression. Importantly, these findings appear to have cross-cultural universality (e.g., Cheah & Rubin, 2004; Chen & Rubin, 1994; Schneider, Attili, Vermigli, & Younger, 1997).

Relative to the literature on the parenting behaviors associated with undercontrolled, aggressive children little is known about social wariness and withdrawal. Research concerning the parenting behaviors and styles associated with social withdrawal focuses clearly on two potential socialization contributors—overcontrol and overprotection. Parents who use high power-assertive strategies and who place many constraints on their children tend to rear shy, reserved, and dependent children. Thus, the issuance of parental commands combined with constraints on exploration and independence may hinder the development of competence in the social milieu. Restrictive control may also deprive the child of opportunities to interact with peers. It should not be surprising that children who are socially withdrawn are on the receiving end of parental overcontrol and overprotection (e.g., Rubin, Burgess, & Hastings, 2002; Rubin, Cheah, & Fox, 2001). These findings concerning parental overcontrol and restriction stem from very few studies, most of which center on children of preschool age. Furthermore, the contexts in which parents of socially withdrawn children display overcontrol and overprotection have not been well specified. Thus, unlike the literature on the parents of aggressive children, the socialization correlates and causes of social withdrawal are not well-known. This dearth of data represents an open research agenda for future investigation.

Parenting Behaviors and Children's Social Competence: A Model

In summary, there is some support for the contention that parental behavior is associated, not only with the development of children's social competence, but also with their peer relationships (see Ladd & Pettit, 2002, for a review). The assumption has been that parenting leads to social competence or incompetence, which leads to peer acceptance or rejection. This causal model has been tested in a number of studies.

Dishion (1990) examined the relations among grade-school boys' sociometric status, academic skills, antisocial behavior, and several elements of parental discipline practices and family circumstances. Causal modeling suggested that the relation between inept parenting and peer rejection was mediated by boys' antisocial behavior and academic difficulties: Lower levels of parental skill were associated with higher levels of antisocial behavior and lower levels of academic performance; antisocial behavior and poor academic performance, in turn, were associated with higher levels of peer rejection.

These findings have been replicated and extended in a similar study conducted in the People's Republic of China (Chen & Rubin, 1994). The pathway from parental authoritarian, punitive disciplinary practices to child aggression to peer rejection was replicated, but the authors also found that parental warmth and authoritative control predicted social competence, which predicted peer acceptance. These latter results suggest that the pathways to peer acceptance and rejection may be generalized across cultures.

There is also the possibility that the link between parenting and child outcomes of an adaptive or maladaptive nature can be attenuated by the quality of the child's status in the peer group or the quality of his or her friendships. For example, the longitudinal relation between harsh parenting and negative outcomes of an externalizing nature is augmented when children have poor peer relationships (e.g., Criss, Pettit, Bates, Dodge, & Lapp, 2002; Lansford, Criss, Pettit, Dodge, & Bates, 2003). And Schwartz, Dodge, Pettit, and Bates (2000) found that children who experienced harsh home environments in the preschool years were more likely to be victimized by peers in the third and fourth grades; however, this correlation was stronger for those who had a lower number of friendships.

Researchers have shown that the relation between insecurity of attachment and negative outcome can be moderated by friendship quality. Thus an insecure attachment relationship may predict difficulties of an externalizing or internalizing nature, but only for those children or young adolescents who lack friendship or qualitatively rich friendship (e.g., Rubin, Dwyer, et al., 2004). Thus, in recent models pertaining to the links between parenting and adaptive or maladaptive outcome, it appears as if, by middle to late childhood, children's friendships may buffer or exacerbate the statistical associations.

Summary

The existing research supports the general conclusion that socially successful children have mothers (and, where examined, fathers) who are more feelings-oriented, more positive, more skillful, more likely to use inductive reasoning, and less negative and coercive in their interaction with their children than their socially unsuccessful counterparts. The limits that the correlational nature of this workplace on our interpretations should be recognized, however. Although it is likely that parents' behaviors have an influence on their children's behavior and success with peers, it must be acknowledged that parental behavior may be elicited by their children's characteristics (Belsky, 1997; Putnam, Sanson, & Rothbart, 2002). Relatedly, it should be noted that, with few exceptions, research in this area focuses on the *concurrent* relations between parental practices and children's social adjustment with peers and not these relations over time. Thus, although we take this work as generally supportive of a link between early parental behaviors contributing to children's later social success, this link has not been thoroughly demonstrated.

CHILDHOOD PEER EXPERIENCES AND LATER ADJUSTMENT

Our goal, in this section, is to provide a summary of research in which the primary focus has been to identify aspects of childhood peer relationship experiences that predict subsequent adaptation and maladaptation. The predictors we examine fall at the levels of dyadic (friendship) and group (peer acceptance) *relationships*. Although we fully recognize that social behaviors (e.g., aggression), dispositions (e.g., temperament), and interactions (e.g., interactive conflict evoked by differences of opinion) may predict adaptive and malevolent "outcomes," relevant discussions are presented elsewhere in this volume.

Significantly, the associations between the quality of peer relationships in childhood and subsequent difficulties have generally been examined in one of two ways. First, using *case-control* or *follow-back* designs, researchers have asked whether maladjusted and adjusted adolescents or adults differed as children in their adjustment with peers. Second, with the cohort, *prospective*, or *follow-up* design, researchers have asked whether popular and unpopular children differ in their incidence of later psychological and educational adaptation. We provided a lengthy overview of retrospective studies in the previous iteration of this chapter (Rubin, Bukowski, & Parker, 1998). Here, we focus only on studies in which prospective, follow-forward designs have been employed.

Academic Adjustment

For many children and adolescents, the primary venue for their experiences with peers is the school context. School is where many children meet peers, form friendships, and take part in groups. For friendless, rejected, or victimized children, the school must be a less-than-desirable context and certainly a place that is unlikely to promote learning or well-being. This is likely to be the case, not only for the child who was doing poorly in school to begin with, but also for the intellectually competent child who has trouble becoming part of the peer system. For these individuals, withdrawing via truancy or by dropping out may serve as the escape route to avoid constant rejection or victimization by peers. Alternatively, having a friend with whom one can share the struggles associated with acquiring new forms of academic competence may prove entirely helpful. For these reasons, peer relationships have been studied as a form of social engagement and social motivation that has wide ranging positive and negative effects on academic performance and a child's sense of belonging and adjustment (Juvonen & Wentzel, 1996).

It has been shown that adjustment to school derives from several aspects of children's relationships with peers. Wentzel and Asher (1995) found that popular children were viewed as helpful, good students. Rejected/aggressive students, relative to average and rejected/submissive children, showed little interest in school, were perceived by teachers as dependent, and were seen by peers and teachers as inconsiderate, noncompliant, and prone to causing trouble in school. Many of the problems that lead to rejection, such as the display of disruptive and aggressive behavior, make it difficult for a child to adjust to the climate of most classrooms.

These findings were consistent with longitudinal findings reported by Ollendick, Weist, Borden, and Greene (1992) who showed that children who were actively disliked by their peers were anywhere from two to seven times more likely to fail a subsequent grade than better accepted children. Similarly, Coie, Lochman, Terry, and Hyman (1992), in a 3-year longitudinal study, found that higher levels of social rejection predicted later grade retention and poorer adjustment to the transition to middle school. Likewise, based on a 4-year longitudinal study, DeRosier, Kupersmidt, and Patterson (1994) reported that the experience of peer rejection in any 1 of the first 3 years of their study placed children at significantly greater risk for absenteeism in the 4th year, even after statistically controlling for initial levels of absenteeism.

Given these longitudinal connections between peer rejection and later poor school performance and truancy, it is not surprising to learn that children who have troubled relationships with their peers are more likely to drop out of school than are other children. For example, Ollendick and colleagues (1992) found (in a 5-year longitudinal study) that 17.5% of rejected children had dropped out of school before the end of ninth grade compared to 5.4% of popular or average children.

Factors other than peer rejection appear to be important also. Most notably *friendships* appear to influence school adjustment in many ways. In a longitudinal study with a representative sample of 475 12-year-olds, Cairns et al. (1989) found little reason to conclude that peer rejection by itself carries risk of later dropping out. Instead, the most powerful precursors of later dropping out were aggression and academic difficulties, especially when the latter were simultaneously present. They showed that many school dropouts appeared to have satisfactory social lives and, as a result, gravitate to peers who shared their negative dispositions toward school. These conditions, in turn, lead to lower academic performance and, in some cases, school drop out.

These latter findings are important because they show that peer group norms may influence academic performance. For example, Kindermann (1993) identified the subgroups that constituted the larger peer groups in the children's elementary school classrooms. Each group was assessed according to its overall level of the academic motivational orientation. He found that children typically associated with peers who had a motivational orientation similar to their own. Moreover, using a longitudinal design, he found that children's motivational orientations toward school were in accord with the initial orientation of the peer group in which they were constituents. Recently, Hymel, Comfort, Schonert-Reichl, and McDougall (2002) noted that adolescents who drop out of school are more likely than other students to have associated with peers who do not regard school as useful and important. These authors argued that the two variables from the peer system that appear to be associated with school drop out are (1) peer rejection and (2) close association with peers who place little emphasis on academic achievement and active school participation.

Similar factors seem to be important with younger children also. In a series of studies, Ladd and colleagues (Ladd, 1990, 1991; Ladd, Kochenderfer, & Coleman, 1996, 1997) demonstrated the potential influence of close dyadic relationships on academic performance. Ladd (1990) obtained repeated measures of friendship, sociometric status, and school adjustment during the transition to kindergarten. Although children's personal attributes (mental age and prior school experience) predicted early school performance, measures of social adjustment with peers were much better predictors by comparison. Children with many friends at the time of school entry developed more favorable attitudes toward school in the early months than children with fewer friends. Those who maintained their friendships also liked school better as the year went by. Making new friends in the classroom also predicted gains in school performance. By comparison, measures of school performance at the start of the transition to kindergarten did not generally forecast gains in social adjustment. In addition, children who were rejected by peers were less likely than other children to have positive attitudes toward school and they were less likely to show a positive school performance. These findings show clearly that even during the early childhood years, friendships with and acceptance by peers are strongly linked to children's academic success. Because Ladd used a longitudinal design in which initial assessments of academic orientation and peer relationships were accounted for, his findings suggest a causal link between friendship and academic outcome.

In a subsequent study, Ladd, Kochenderfer, and Coleman (1997) examined the association between children's perceptions of best friendship quality in kindergarten and indices of scholastic adjustment (school-related affect, perceptions, involvement, and performance) in grade school (transition from kindergarten to grade school). Their main finding replicated, at the dyadic level, one of the findings observed by Kindermann (1993) at the group level. Specifically, Ladd et al. (1997) reported that children who viewed their friendships as a source of validation or aid, tend to (a) feel happier at school, (b) see their classmates as supportive, and (c) develop positive attitudes toward school.

In two studies, the effect of early adolescent friendship was demonstrated clearly and in richer ways than seen previously. Berndt, Hawkins, and Jiao (1999) showed that adjustment to junior high school was facilitated by engagement in friendships that were stable and of high quality (e.g., rated as high in closeness and support). Wentzel, McNamara-Barry, and Caldwell (2004) also examined friendship and the adjustment to a junior high school. They showed that friendless children were lower in prosocial behavior and higher in affective distress both concurrently and 2 years later. They noted that friends' characteristics can act as a form of social motivation that can either increase or decrease an early adolescent's adjustment to school.

In summary, it appears reasonable to conclude that children's peer relationships play a central role in promoting or maintaining academic adaptation. This role occurs at several levels of peer group analysis: Peer rejection may serve the purpose of making school an unwelcome venue for children and adolescents, and the lack of friends may fail to provide the necessary support for children and adolescents to fare well in school. Alternatively, a child's peer group may actually serve to develop and reinforce poor school-related goals and behaviors. Thus, the role of the peer culture appears too significant to be dismissed in practical efforts designed to encourage promising school aspirations and performance; indeed, this is an area that requires further empirical and practical substantiation in the future.

Psychological Adjustment

Ample evidence exists that difficulties with peers place a child at risk for developing subsequent problems of a psychological nature. Consistent with the general trends of the peer literature, research on the long-term consequences of peer experiences has focused largely on rejection and friendship.

Externalizing Problems

Results of longitudinal studies have indicated that peer rejection in childhood predicts a wide range of *externalizing* problems in adolescence, including delinquency, conduct disorder, attention difficulties, and substance abuse. These findings are not particularly surprising given the well-established link between aggression and peer rejection, and especially given that aggressive-rejected children are more likely to remain rejected over time.

Kupersmidt and Coie (1990) reported the findings of a longitudinal study in which they followed-forward a group of fifth grade children for 7 years. Children identified as sociometrically rejected were twice as likely to be delinquent (35%) in adolescence than was the case for the sample base rate (17%). In a second study, Ollendick et al. (1992) followed sociometrically rejected, neglected, popular, controversial, and average status 9-year-old children for 5 years; at the follow-up, rejected children were perceived by their peers as less likable and more aggressive than popular and average children. Rejected children were also perceived by their teachers

as having more conduct problems, aggression, motor excess, and attention problems than their popular and average counterparts. Moreover, rejected children reported higher levels of conduct disturbance and substance abuse and committed more delinquent offenses than the popular and average children. Controversial children were similar to rejected children on most measures. For example, children in the two groups committed similar numbers of delinquent offenses.

Similar findings concerning the predictive outcomes of rejected status have been reported by Bierman and Wargo (1995) and Coie, Terry, Lenox, Lochman, and Hyman (1995). In both of these longitudinal studies, peer rejection in combination with the early display of aggressive behavior, predicted externalizing problems. More recent research has shown that *early* peer rejection provides a unique increment in the prediction later antisocial outcomes, even when controlling for previous levels of aggression and externalizing problems (Ladd & Burgess, 2001; Miller-Johnson, Coie, Maumary-Gremaud, Bierman, & Conduct Problems Prevention Research, 2002; Miller-Johnson, Coie, Maumary-Gremaud, Lochman, & Terry, 1999; Wentzel, 2003). For example, Laird, Jordan, Dodge, Pettit, and Bates (2001) followed 400 children from early childhood through to adolescence. They reported that sociometric rejection at ages 6 to 9 years predicted externalizing problems in adolescence, even when controlling for the stability of externalizing problems over this age period.

Given the less than perfect stability of rejected status, it would seem reasonable to ask whether psychological risk status is equivalent for children with chronic versus episodic and transient rejection by peers. To address this question, DeRosier, Kupersmidt, and Patterson (1994) followed 640 7- to 9-year-old children for 4 years. They found that children who were more chronically rejected over the first 3 years of the study were at greatest risk for behavior problems in the 4th year, even after controlling for initial level of adjustment. More recently, Miller-Johnson et al. (2002) showed that peer rejection in first grade added incrementally to the prediction of early starting conduct problems in third and fourth grades, over and above the effects of aggression. Similarly, Dodge and colleagues (2003) reported that peer rejection predicted longitudinal "growth" in aggression over time (controlling for original levels of aggression) from early to middle childhood, and from middle childhood to adolescence. These researchers also found a developmental pathway in which peer rejection led to more negative information processing patterns (i.e., hostile cue interpretation), which led to increased aggression. Certainly part of the association between rejection and externalizing involves the network of peer involvement experiences by rejected children. Brendgen, Vitaro, and Bukowski (1998) showed that rejected children were more likely than other boys and girls to associate with delinquent peers and that these associations accounted for their subsequent delinquency. Consistent with expectations related to the process of deviancy training (Dishion et al., 1996), at-risk children, especially boys, who have aggressive friends appear to influence each other with reinforcements and enticements (Bagwell & Coie, 2004) so as to increase each other's aggression. These processes likely explain why gang membership is a good predictor of developmental trajectories of aggression (Lacourse, Nagin, Tremblay, Vitaro, & Claes, 2003). These mechanisms appear to account for the development of substance abuse problems also (Dishion, Capaldi, & Yoerger, 1999; Dishion & Owen, 2002).

Internalizing Problems

Results from a growing number of studies have indicated that anxious-withdrawal is contemporaneously and predictively associated with internalizing problems during the life span, including low self-esteem, anxiety problems, loneliness, and depressive symptoms (e.g., Coplan, Prakash, O'Neil, & Armer, 2004; Gest, 1997). Rubin and colleagues followed a group of children from kindergarten (age 5 years) to the ninth grade (age 14 years). They reported that withdrawal in kindergarten and second grade predicted the following outcomes in fifth grade: peer rejection, self-reported feelings of depression, loneliness, and negative self-worth and teacher ratings of anxiety (Hymel et al., 1990; Rubin & Mills, 1988). In turn, social withdrawal in the fifth grade predicted self-reports of loneliness, depression, negative self-evaluations of social competence, feelings of not belonging to a peer group that could be counted on for social support, and parental assessments of internalizing problems in the ninth grade (Rubin, Chen, McDougall, Bowker, & McKinnon, 1995). Using a follow-back design with a group of adolescents who had been classified according to clique membership, Prinstein and La Greca (2002) found adolescents' self-reports of peer crowd affiliation to be concurrently associated with self-concept and levels of internalizing distress. Their analyses of internalizing trajectories revealed that "Populars/Jocks" had experienced significant declines in internalizing

distress across adolescences whereas "Brains" showed increases in internalizing distress between childhood and adolescence.

Researchers have also recently begun to explore the *unique* role of peer rejection in the prediction of internalizing problems. For example, in a longitudinal study following 405 children from kindergarten to grade 7, Kraatz-Keily, Bates, Dodge, and Pettit (2000) reported that peer rejection predicted increases in both internalizing and externalizing problems over time. Moreover, Burks, Dodge, and Price (1995) found that chronic rejection in middle childhood predicted the subsequent development of internalizing difficulties (depression, loneliness) 6 years hence. Their results held only for boys who had been rejected for 2 consecutive years; chronicity of rejection did not predict internalizing problems for girls. The authors speculated that girls' rejection by the larger peer group is less severe than the lack of close, intimate relationships with a friend.

Relatedly, Gazelle and Ladd (2003) found that shy-anxious kindergarteners who were also excluded by peers displayed a greater stability in anxious solitude through the fourth grade and had elevated levels of depressive symptoms as compared to shy-anxious peers who did not experience peer exclusion. Indeed, Gazelle and Rudolph (2004) recently found that over the course of fifth and sixth grade, high exclusion by peers led anxious solitary youth to maintenance or exacerbate the extent of social avoidance and depression; increased social approach and less depression resulted from the experience of low exclusion.

In understanding the link between peer rejection and psychosocial adjustment, it may also be important to consider the role of children's *perceptions* of their *own* peer rejection. Children's *perceived* rejection has been associated with increases in depression over time (e.g., Kistner, Balthazor, Risi, & Burton, 1999). Moreover, Sandstrom, Cillessen, and Eisenhower (2003) demonstrated that children's self-appraisal of peer rejection was associated with increased internalizing and externalizing problems even after controlling for actual peer rejection. Thus, children's *beliefs* that they are rejected may play an influential role in the development of psychosocial maladjustment.

The majority of the research regarding *friendship* and subsequent internalizing problems has considered the effects of friendship as either a moderator or as a mediator. Hodges, Boivin, et al. (1999) examined whether friendship would moderate the associations between victimization and depressed affect. Using a longitudinal design they showed that young adolescents with friends *and who were victimized* subsequently showed lower levels of depressed affect than did young adolescents who were friendless and victimized. Specifically, for young adolescents without a friend, being victimized at the beginning of the school year predicted increases in internalizing and externalizing behaviors from the beginning to the end of the school year, while there was no link between being victimized and adjustment for those with friends. Relatedly, Rubin et al. (2004) found that when fifth graders (10- to 11-year-olds) reported difficulties in their relationships with their mothers and fathers, having a strong supportive best friendship buffered them from negative self-perceptions and internalizing problems.

The notion that friendship may buffer rejected children from negative outcomes has been examined in a number of recent studies. However, the findings in these studies have been somewhat counterintuitive. For example, Hoza, Molina, Bukowski, and Sippola (1995) and Kupersmidt, Burchinal, and Patterson (1995) reported that having a best friend actually *augmented* negative outcomes for children who were earlier identified as rejected and aggressive. One explanation for these findings emanates from findings noted earlier that the friendship networks of aggressive-rejected children comprise other aggressive children; the existence of a friendship network supportive of maladjusted behavior may actually exacerbate the prospects of a negative developmental outcome for rejected children (Cairns et al., 1989; Tremblay, Mâsse, Vitaro, & Dobkin, 1995). Finally, Nangle, Erdley, Newman, Mason, and Carpenter (2003) examined whether the association between being well-liked by peers (i.e., being accepted) and feelings of loneliness would be explained by the *mediating* effects of friendship. In the model supported by their data, acceptance was an antecedent to friendship, which, in turn, negatively predicted loneliness and depression.

Summary

Studies of the predictive relations between children's peer relationships and their subsequent academic and psychological adjustment generally support the notion that experiences with peers represent a risk factor for maladjustment. The extant data reveal that the types of friends a child may have, or the groups in which she or he participates, may influence individual adaptation.

Despite these conclusions, however, it is important to note that most of the longitudinal studies are typically limited in a few critical ways. First, the design of most

studies precludes conclusions about causality. An interpretation of causality is warranted only when other potential pathways between the initial peer measures and the subsequent adjustment variables have been accounted for (Kupersmidt, Coie, & Dodge, 1990). For example, the initial level of adjustment must be controlled for if an unequivocal conclusion about causal relations is to be reached. Second, the possibility of multicollinearity must be considered. We have noted that there is neither conceptual nor empirical independence between measures of peer experiences taken from different levels of social complexity. For example, measures of aggression and group acceptance are intercorrelated. One repercussion of such associations is that if researchers want to conclude that a given measure from the peer domain predicts some outcome, it is necessary to control for the other measures with which the predictor may be confounded. Third, although the growth of the literature on peer relationships was inspired by studies that followed individuals over long periods, most current studies are of a short duration.

Considering how a set of measures will function together to affect outcome will also satisfy substantive objectives as well as methodological concerns. Inherent in theoretical positions regarding the peer system is the notion that experience in one domain of the peer system may compensate for, or enhance, experience in another domain. For example, if it is true that friends influence one another, the experience of having a friend will vary according to what the friend is like. Or, as we have shown, the experience of being rejected by peers appears to be different for children who are aggressive and those who are nonaggressive. The implication of these concerns regarding the associations among measures from different domains of the peer system is that using a single factor model to understand the link between peer experiences and outcome is likely to result in both an empirical and conceptual dead end.

CONCLUSIONS

In this chapter, we have reviewed literature concerning (a) developmental norms in children's peer interactions, relationships, and groups; (b) the developmental significance of peer interaction, discussion, and shared differences of opinion; (c) the importance of friendship; (d) the significance of social skills and social competence; (e) the assessment of children's peer experiences; (f) the proximal and distal predictors of peer acceptance; and

(g) the outcomes of qualitative differences in peer relationships histories. The study of peer relationships has never been as active or as diverse as it is now. As we have tried to show, remarkable progress has been made in describing and explaining the features, processes, and effects of children's experiences with their age-mates. A consequence of this progress is that peer research must now answer new questions and deal with new challenges. An additional repercussion of our progress is that the gaps in our understanding of the peer system become clear. We address these concerns in this concluding section. Specifically, we identify three current challenges and opportunities for peer research, and we identify three topics that deserve more attention than they have received in the past.

Three Critical Challenges

First, we propose that the efforts to study peer relationships as a system need to be continued and intensified. The study of peer relationships has been frequently predicated on the concept that peer relationships, however construed, must be viewed as either an antecedent or consequence. Consistent with the view that development is a dynamic, multidirectional process (Sameroff & MacKenzie, 2003), the study of peer relationships needs to be understood as a complex system. Children bring various behaviors, needs, and cognitions into their peer experiences at the dyadic and group level. In turn, these individual characteristics affect the features of these experiences and the provisions that children derive from peer experiences leading to changes, for better or worse, in the child's subsequent short-term and long-term functioning. Although this approach has already been widely used, the adoption of a fully integrated model such as the one we have proposed has been rare.

The study of transactional models of development has been aided by the evolution of statistical procedures (e.g., structural equation modeling, growth curve analyses, hierarchical linear modeling, and survival analyses) that allow examination of bidirectional and reciprocal influences in multivariate longitudinal data sets. Although researchers of peer relationships have used these analytic procedures for at least 20 years, the number of investigations incorporating these techniques remains lower than one might expect.

Second, the features and effects of experiences with peers need to be understood according to the larger systems in which they are embedded and according to how they interface with other systems. Opportunities for peer interaction and relationships vary from one culture to another and different cultures ascribe different degrees of significance to them. The "content" of peer interactions and relationships is likely to vary, for example, as a function of how much power is ascribed to kinship structures and by who makes primary decisions about allowable extrafamilial relationships. Because the defining features or characteristics of what it means to be adapted to one's social context will differ across contexts, the impact on adaptation of particular characteristics of peer relationships is likely to vary also. Finally, in a culture, the effect of the peer system is likely to vary according to differences between children in provisions they obtain in their families. Indeed, a central tenet of the seminal views of Sullivan (1953) was that the developmental significance of friendship will be higher for children whose relationships with parents was less than optimal than for other children.

A third challenge concerns the development of interventions to help children who have troubled experiences with peers and to more generally promote and facilitate more positive peer experiences among children. There now exists an extensive literature addressing how to improve children's social skills (Bierman, 2003). Nevertheless, further development of techniques is needed to help children develop healthy friendships, to decrease the frequency and the effects of victimization, to regulate emotions and inhibit maladaptive behavior, and to enhance the power of the peer system as a positive factor in development. It is important to remember that intervention research provides an important assessment of the causal pathways implicated in the link between poor peer relationships and later adjustment. Specifically, through intervention, researchers can learn whether improvements in adjustment with peers also reduce children's relative risk for subsequent adjustment disturbances.

An important feature of the literature on intervention is developmental sensitivity. The role that children's peer relationships play in development appears to vary with age. For example, we have noted that children's ideas about friendship become increasingly abstract with age. Furthermore, children's friendships are posited to play an increasingly important role with age. Yet, little is known about the potential adaptive effects of friendship or about *when* it is in childhood that friendship can serve as an accelerator, promoter, or inhibitor of adaptation or as a buffer against the ill-effects of parental or peer neglect or rejection. This issue of the functional significance of friendship may prove helpful in the planning of intervention programs for children who have poorly developed social skills and peer relationships.

Three Questions in Search of Answers

In spite of its diversity and breadth, at least three fundamental aspects of peer interactions, relationships, and groups are nearly absent from our review. First, *what accounts for interpersonal attraction?* The question of attraction may be implied in many of the topics we have discussed; nevertheless, its explicit presence as a topic of study in the contemporary literature is, at best, weak. This gap is surprising, and regrettable, given the potential significance of interpersonal attraction as a phenomenon at the front end of the relationship process. If we are going to claim that who one befriends or is attracted to makes a difference, knowing something about the factors underlying attraction is necessary. Thus far, two sets of ideas have been proposed. Whereas one model has emphasized general patterns of attraction (i.e., children are generally drawn to helpful peers), another has emphasized the importance of similarity on a dyadic level. Similarity as an explanation of attraction has elicited some empirical scrutiny (e.g., Hamm, 2000; Rubin et al., 1994), but the model has not been pushed hard or analyzed carefully. This inattention is surprising given the ease with which similarity between peers can be studied, especially by exploiting the advantages of such statistical techniques such as multilevel modeling.

Second, *what aspects of peer interactions, relationships, and groups affect boys and girls differently?* The study of sex differences is covered sporadically throughout this chapter and is seen also in Ruble, Martin, and Berenbaum (Chapter 14, this *Handbook,* this volume). There are many exemplary studies of how peer interactions and relationships differ for boys and for girls. A central gap in the literature is the understanding of whether some aspects of peer interactions and relationships affect boys and girls differently. This question is not about whether there are differences between the features of peer interactions and relationships of boys and girls. Instead, it is concerned with potential differences in the functions and the developmental significance of peer experiences for boys and girls. Knowing if and how the peer system works differently for boys and girls would certainly add to our understanding of peer relationships; it would augment our understanding of sexual differentiation as well.

Third, *what are the provisions of peer relationships?* Friendship, acceptance, and popularity have been studied extensively. We know how to measure these constructs, and we know a good deal about their antecedents and their consequences. Yet, we know little about what it is that children and adolescents "get" from these relationships. To be sure there have been theoretical propositions about why friendship is important and how acceptance and rejection can influence child and adolescent development. But there have been few studies of the specific opportunities and experiences that are afforded by friendship, acceptance, and popularity. And there have been fewer studies of the significance of friendship and/or peer acceptance and rejection for children who vary with regard to sex, ethnicity, and behavioral characteristics. Certainly, the role of culture remains to be fully explored. This question is not simply one of description. Research on friendship, for example, is based on claims about the putative provisions of this relationship. Similar comments can be offered about acceptance and, to a lesser extent, popularity. Further inquiry into what these experiences provide for children would help us better understand the value of the theories we have relied on.

Our review is now complete. We have examined that which we know and we have attempted to raise questions about that which we must come to know in the future. There is no doubt that many interesting and important questions remain unanswered. This should not be surprising given that the modern history of peer research began only 35 years ago with Willard Hartup's 1970 chapter in this *Handbook.* But growth begets growth, and it is encouraging to realize that there is no shortage of topics for us to study.

REFERENCES

Abecassis, M., Hartup, W. W., Haselager, G. J. T., Scholte, R. H. J., & van Lieshout, C. F. M. (2002). Mutual antipathies and their significance in middle childhood and adolescence. *Child Development, 73,* 1543–1556.

Achenbach, T. M., McConaughy, S. H., & Howell, C. T. (1987). Child/adolescent behavioral and emotional problems: Implications of cross-informant correlations for situational specificity. *Psychological Bulletin, 101,* 213–232.

Allen, J. D., Moore, C., Kuperminc, G., & Bell, K. (1998). Attachment and adolescent psychosocial functioning. *Child Development, 69,* 1406–1419.

Altermatt, E. R., & Pomerantz, E. M. (2003). The development of competence-related and motivational beliefs: An investigation of similarity and influence among friends. *Journal of Educational Psychology, 95,* 111–123.

Asher, S. R., Parker, J. G., & Walker, D. L. (1996). Distinguishing friendship from acceptance: Implications for intervention and assessment. In W. M. Bukowski, A. F. Newcomb, & W. W. Hartup (Eds.), *The company they keep: Friendship during childhood and adolescence* (pp. 366–405). New York: Cambridge University Press.

Atlas, R., & Pepler, D. J. (1998). Observations of bullying in the classroom. *Journal of Educational Research, 92*(2), 86–99.

Azmitia, M., Lippman, D. N., & Ittel, A. (1999). On the relation of personal experience to early adolescents' reasoning about best friendship deterioration. *Social Development, 8,* 275–291.

Azmitia, M., & Montgomery, R. (1993). Friendship, transactive dialogues, and the development of scientific reasoning. *Social Development, 2,* 202–221.

Bagwell, C. L., & Coie, J. D. (2004). The best friendships of aggressive boys: Relationship quality, conflict management, and rule-breaking behavior. *Journal of Experimental Child Psychology, 88*(1), 5–24.

Bagwell, C. L., Coie, J. D., Terry, R. A., & Lochman, J. E. (2000). Peer clique participation and social status in preadolescence. *Merrill-Palmer Quarterly, 46,* 280–305.

Bandura, A. (1989). Social cognitive theory. In R. Vasta (Ed.), *Annals of child development: Vol. 6. Six theories of child development-Revised formulations and current issues* (pp. 1–60). Greenwich, CT: JAI Press.

Bandura, A., & Walters, R. H. (1963). *Social learning and personality development.* New York: Holt, Rinehart and Winston.

Baumeister, R. F., & Sommer, K. L. (1997). What do men want? Gender differences and two spheres of belongingness—Comment on Cross and Madson, 1997. *Psychological Bulletin, 122,* 38–44.

Beer, B. (2001). Anthropology of friendship. In N. J. Smelser & P. B. Baltes (Eds.), *International encyclopedia of the social and behavioral sciences* (pp. 5805–5808). Kidlington, England: Elsevier.

Belsky, J. (1997). Variation in susceptibility to environmental influence: An evolutionary argument. *Psychological Inquiry, 8,* 182–186.

Belsky, J., & Cassidy, J. (1995). Attachment: Theory and evidence. In M. Rutter, D. Hay, & S. Baron-Cohen (Eds.), *Developmental principles and clinical issues in psychology and psychiatry.* Oxford, England: Blackwell.

Benenson, J. F., Apostoleris, N. H., & Parnass, J. (1997). Age and sex differences in dyadic and group interaction. *Developmental Psychology, 33,* 538–543.

Benenson, J. F., & Christakos, A. (2003). The greater fragility of female's versus male's closest same-sex friendships. *Child Development, 74,* 1123–1129.

Benenson, J. F., Markovits, H., Roy, R., & Denko, P. (2003). Behavioural rules underlying learning to share: Effects of development and context. *International Journal of Behavioural Development, 27,* 116–121.

Benenson, J. F., Nicholson, C., Waite, A., Roy, R., & Simpson, A. (2001). The influence of group size on children's competitive behavior. *Child Development, 72,* 921–928.

Benenson, J. F., Roy, R., Waite, A., Goldbaum, S., Linders, L., & Simpson, A. (2002). Greater discomfort as a proximate cause of sex differences in competition. *Merrill-Palmer Quarterly, 48,* 225–247.

Berndt, T. J. (1996). Friendship quality affects adolescents' self-esteem and social behavior. In W. M. Bukowski, A. F. Newcomb, & W. W. Hartup (Eds.), *The company they keep: Friendship during childhood and adolescence* (pp. 346–365). New York: Cambridge University Press.

Berndt, T. J. (2002). Friendship quality and social development. *Current Directions in Psychological Science, 11,* 7–10.

Berndt, T. J. (2004). Children's friendships: Shifts over a half-century in perspectives on their development and their effects. *Merrill-Palmer Quarterly, 50,* 206–223.

Berndt, T. J., Hawkins, J. A., & Hoyle, S. G. (1986). Changes in friendship during a school year: Effects on children's and adolescents' impressions of friendship and sharing with friends. *Child Development, 57,* 1284–1297.

Berndt, T. J., Hawkins, J. A., & Jiao, Z. (1999). Influences of friends and friendships on adjustment to junior high school. *Merrill-Palmer Quarterly, 45,* 13–41.

Berndt, T. J., & Heller, K. A. (1986). Gender stereotypes and social inferences: A developmental study. *Journal of Personality and Social Psychology, 50,* 889–898.

Berndt, T. J., & Hoyle, S. G. (1985). Stability and change in childhood and adolescent friendships. *Developmental Psychology, 21,* 1007–1015.

Berndt, T. J., & Perry, T. B. (1986). Children's perceptions of friendships as supportive relationships. *Developmental Psychology, 22,* 640–648.

Bierman, K. L. (2003). *Peer rejection: Developmental processes and intervention.* New York: Guilford Publications.

Bierman, K. L., Smoot, D. L., & Aumiller, K. (1993). Characteristics of aggressive-rejected, aggressive (nonrejected), and rejected (nonaggressive) boys. *Child Development, 64,* 139–151.

Bierman, K. L., & Wargo, J. B. (1995). Predicting the longitudinal course associated with aggressive-rejected, aggressive (nonrejected), and rejected (nonaggressive) status. *Development and Psychopathology, 7,* 669–682.

Bigelow, B. J. (1977). Children's friendship expectations: A cognitive developmental study. *Child Development, 48,* 246–253.

Black, B., & Hazan, N. (1990). Social status and patterns of communication in acquainted and unacquainted preschool children. *Developmental Psychology, 26,* 379–387.

Blos, P. (1967). *The second individuation process of adolescence: Vol. 22. Psychoanalytic study of the child.* New York: International Universities Press.

Boivin, M., Dodge, K. A., & Coie, J. D. (1995). Individual-group behavioral similarity and peer status in experimental play groups of boys: The social misfit revisited. *Journal of Personality and Social Psychology, 69,* 269–279.

Boivin, M., Hymel, S., & Bukowski, W. M. (1995). The roles of social withdrawal, peer rejection, and victimization by peers in predicting loneliness and depressed mood in childhood. *Development and Psychopathology, 7,* 765–785.

Bonney, M. E. (1944). Relationship between social success, family size, socioeconomic background, and intelligence among school children grades three to five. *Sociometry, 7,* 26–39.

Booth, C., Rubin, K. H., Rose-Krasnor, L., & Burgess, K. (2004). Attachment and friendship predictors of psychosocial functioning in middle childhood and the mediating roles of social support and self-worth. In K. Kerns & R. A. Richardson (Eds.), *Attachment in middle childhood* (pp. 161–188). New York: Guilford Press.

Booth, C. L., Rose-Krasnor, L., & Rubin, K. H. (1991). Relating preschoolers' social competence and their mothers' parenting behaviors to early attachment security and high-risk status. *Journal of Social and Personal Relationships, 8,* 363–382.

Bornstein, M. H. (2002). Parenting infants. In M. H. Bornstein (Ed.), *Handbook of parenting: Vol. 1. Children and parenting* (2nd ed., pp. 3–43). Mahwah, NJ: Erlbaum.

Bornstein, M. H., & Cheah, C. S. L. (in press). The place of "culture and parenting" in the ecological contextual perspective on developmental science. In K. H. Rubin & O. Boon Chung (Eds.), *Parental beliefs, parenting, and child development in cross-cultural perspective.* London: Psychology Press.

Boulton, M. J. (1996). A comparison of 8- and 11-year-old girls' and boys' participation in specific types of *rough-and-tumble play* and aggressive fighting: Implications for functional hypotheses. *Aggressive Behavior, 22,* 271–287.

Boulton, M. J., Trueman, M., Chau, C., Whitehand, C., & Amatya, K. (1999). Concurrent and longitudinal links between friendships and peer victimization: Implications for befriending interventions. *Journal of Adolescence, 22,* 461–466.

Bowker, A., Bukowski, W., Zargarpour, S., & Hoza, B. (1998). A structural and functional analysis of a two-dimensional model of social isolation. *Merrill-Palmer Quarterly, 44,* 447–463.

Bowlby, J. (1973). *Attachment and loss: Vol. 2. Separation, anxiety and anger.* New York: Basic Books.

Bowlby, J. (1982). *Attachment and loss: Vol. 1. Attachment.* New York: Basic Books. (Original work published 1969)

Brendgen, M., Bowen, F., Rondeau, N., & Vitaro, F. (1999). Effects of friends' characteristics on children's social cognitions. *Social Development, 8,* 41–51.

Brendgen, M., Little, T. D., & Krappmann, L. (2000). Rejected children and their friends: A shared evaluation of friendship quality? *Merrill-Palmer Quarterly, 46*(1), 45–70.

Brendgen, M., Vitaro, F., & Bukowski, W. M. (1998). Affiliation with delinquent friends: Contributions of parents, self-esteem, delinquent behavior, and rejection by peers. *Journal of Early Adolescence, 18*(3), 244–265.

Brendgen, M., Vitaro, F., & Bukowski, W. M. (2000). Deviant friends and early adolescents' emotional and behavioral adjustment. *Journal of Research on Adolescence, 10*(2), 173–189.

Brendgen, M., Vitaro, F., Doyle, A. B., Markiewicz, D., & Bukowski, W. M. (2002). Same-sex peer relations and romantic relationships during early adolescence: Interactive links to emotional, behavioral, and academic adjustment. *Merrill-Palmer Quarterly, 48,* 77–103.

Bronfenbrenner, U. (1944). A constant frame of reference for sociometric research: Pt. 11. Experiment and inference. *Sociometry, 7,* 40–75.

Bronfenbrenner, U., & Crouter, A. C. (1983). The evolution of environmental models in developmental research. In P. H. Mussen (Series Ed.) & W. Kessen (Vol. Ed.), *Handbook of child psychology: Vol. 1. History, theory, and methods* (4th ed., pp. 357–414). New York: Wiley.

Brown, B. B. (1989). The role of peer groups in adolescents' adjustment to secondary school. In T. J. Berndt & G. W. Ladd (Eds.), *Peer relationships in child development* (pp. 188–216). New York: Wiley.

Brown, B. B., Clasen, D. R., & Neiss, J. D. (1987, April). *Smoke through the looking glass: Adolescents' perceptions of peer group status.* Paper presented at the biennial meeting of the Society for Research in Child Development, Baltimore, MD.

Brown, B. B., & Klute, C. (2003). Friends, cliques, and crowds. In G. R. Adams & M. D. Berzonsky (Eds.), *Blackwell handbook of adolescence* (pp. 330–348). Malden, MA: Blackwell.

Bugental, D., & Happaney, K. (2002). Parental attributions. In M. Bornstein (Ed.), *Handbook of parenting: Vol. 3. Being and becoming a parent* (2nd ed., pp. 509–535). Mahwah, NJ: Erlbaum.

Bugental, D. B. (1992). Affective and cognitive processes within threat-oriented family systems. In I. E. Sigel, A. V. McGillicuddy-DeLisi, & J. J. Goodnow (Eds.), *Parental belief systems: The psychological consequences for children* (pp. 219–248). Hillsdale, NJ: Erlbaum.

Buhler, C. (1931). The social behavior of the child. In C. Murchison (Ed.), *A handbook of child psychology.* New York: Russell & Russell.

Buhler, C. (1935). *From birth to maturity: An outline of the psychological development of the child.* London: Routledge & Kegan Paul.

Burhmester, D. (1998). Need fulfillment, interpersonal competence, and the developmental contexts of early adolescent friendship. In W. M. Bukowski, A. Newcomb, & W. W. Hartup (Eds.), *The company they keep: Friendship in childhood and adolescence* (pp. 158–185). New York: Cambridge University Press.

Buhrmester, D., & Furman, W. (1987). The development of companionship and intimacy. *Child Development, 58,* 1101–1103.

Bukowski, W. M., & Cillessen, A. H. N. (Eds.). (1996). *Sociometry then and now: Recent developments in the study of children's peer groups.* San Francisco: Jossey-Bass.

Bukowski, W. M., & Hoza, B. (1989). Popularity and friendship: Issues in theory, measurement, and outcome. In T. J. Berndt & G. W. Ladd (Eds.), *Peer relations in child development* (pp. 15–45). New York: Wiley.

Bukowski, W. M., Hoza, B., & Newcomb, A. F. (1994). Using rating scale and nomination techniques to measure friendships and popularity. *Journal of Social and Personal Relationships, 11,* 485–488.

Bukowski, W. M., Rubin, K. H., & Parker, J. (2001). Social competence. In N. J. Smelser & P. B. Baltes (Eds.) & N. Eisenberg (Sec. Ed.), *International encyclopedia of social and behavioral sciences* (pp. 14258–14264). Oxford, England: Elsevier Science.

Bukowski, W. M., & Sippola, L. K. (2001). Groups, individuals, and victimization: A view of the peer system. In J. Juvonen & S. Graham (Eds.), *Peer harassment in school: The plight of the vulnerable and victimized* (pp. 355–377). New York: Guilford Press.

Bukowski, W. M., Sippola, L. K., & Hoza, B. (1999). Same and other: Interdependency between participation in same- and other-sex friendships. *Journal of Youth and Adolescence, 28,* 439–459.

Bukowski, W. M., Sippola, L., Hoza, B., & Newcomb, A. F. (2000). Pages from a sociometric notebook: An analysis of nomination and rating scale measures of acceptance, rejection, and social preference. In A. Cillessen & W. Bukowski (Eds.), *Recent advances in the measurement of acceptance and rejection in the peer system* (pp. 11–26). San Francisco: Jossey-Bass.

Burgess, K. B., Marshall, P., Rubin, K. H., & Fox, N. A. (2003). Infant attachment and temperament as predictors of subsequent behavior problems and psychophysiological functioning. *Journal of Child Psychology and Psychiatry and Allied Disciplines, 44,* 1–13.

Burgess, K. B., Wojslawowicz, J. C., Rubin, K. H., Rose-Krasnor, L., & Booth, C. L. (2003, April). *The "extended class play": A longitudinal study of its factor structure, reliability, and validity.* Poster resented at the biennial meeting of the Society for Research in Child Development, Tampa, FL.

Burks, V. S., Dodge, K. A., & Price, J. M. (1995). Models of internalizing outcomes of early rejection. *Development and Psychopathology, 7,* 683–696.

Buskirk, A. A., Rubin, K. H., Burgess, K., Booth-LaForce, C. L., & Rose-Krasnor, L. (2004, March). *Loved, hated . . . but never ignored: Evidence for two types of popularity.* Paper presented as part of Symposium on the Many Faces of Popularity at the biennial meeting of the Society for Research in Adolescence, Baltimore, MD.

Cairns, R. B. (1979). *Social development: The origins and plasticity of interchanges.* San Francisco: Freeman.

Cairns, R. B., Gariepy, J. L., & Kindermann, T. (1989). *Identifying social clusters in natural settings.* Unpublished manuscript, University of North Carolina at Chapel Hill, Social Development Laboratory.

Cairns, R. B., Xie, H., & Leung, M. C. (1996). The popularity of friendship and the neglect of social networks: Toward a new balance. In W. M. Bukowski & A. H. N. Cillessen (Eds.), *Sociometry then and now: Recent developments in the study of children's peer groups* (pp. 25–53). San Francisco: Jossey Bass.

Calkins, S. D., & Dedmon, S. A. (2000). Physiological and behavioral regulation in 2-year-old children with aggressive/destructive behavior problems. *Journal of Abnormal Child Psychology, 28,* 103–118.

Calkins, S. D., Gill, K. L., Johnson, M. C., & Smith, C. L. (1999). Emotional reactivity and emotional regulation strategies as predictors of social behavior with peers during toddlerhood. *Social Development, 8*(3), 310–334.

Camodeca, M., Goossens, F. A., Terwogt, M. M., & Schuengel, C. (2002). Bullying and victimization among school-age children: Stability and links to proactive and reactive aggression. *Social Development, 11,* 332–345.

Carson, J. L., & Parke, R. D. (1996). Reciprocal negative affect in parent-child interactions and children's peer competency. *Child Development, 67,* 2217–2226.

Carver, K., Joyner, K., & Udry, J. R. (2003). National estimates of adolescent romantic relationships. In P. Florsheim (Ed.), *Adolescent romantic relations and sexual behavior: Theory, research, and practical implications* (pp. 23–56). Mahwah, NJ: Erlbaum.

Casiglia, A. C., Lo Coco, A., & Zappulla, C. (1998). Aspects of social reputation and peer relationships in Italian children: A cross-cultural perspective. *Developmental Psychology, 34,* 723–730.

Challman, R. C. (1932). Factors influencing friendships among preschool children. *Child Development, 3,* 146–158.

Chang, L., Lei, L., Li, K., Liu, H., Guo, B., Wang, Y., et al. (2005). Peer acceptance and self perceptions of verbal and behavioral aggression and social withdrawal. *International Journal of Behavioral Development, 29,* 48–57.

Cheah, C. S. L., & Rubin, K. H. (2004). A cross-cultural examination of maternal beliefs regarding maladaptive behaviors in preschoolers. *International Journal of Behavioral Development, 28,* 83–94.

Chen, D. W., Fein, G., & Tam, H. P. (2001). Peer conflicts of preschool children: Issues, resolution, incidence, and age-related patterns. *Early Education and Development, 12,* 523–544.

Chen, X., Cen, G., Li, D., & He, Y. (2005). Social functioning and adjustment in Chinese children: The imprint of historical time. *Child Development, 76,* 182–195.

Chen, X., Chang, L., & He, Y. (2003). The peer group as a context: Mediating and moderating effects on the relations between academic achievement and social functioning in Chinese children. *Child Development, 74,* 710–727.

Chen, X., Hastings, P. D., Rubin, K. H., Chen, H., Cen, G., & Stewart, S. L. (1998). Child-rearing practices and behavioral inhibition in Chinese and Canadian toddlers: A cross-cultural study. *Developmental Psychology, 34,* 677–686.

Chen, X., & Rubin, K. H. (1994). Family conditions, parental acceptance, and social competence and aggression in Chinese children. *Social Development, 3,* 269–290.

Chen, X., Rubin, K. H., & Li, B. (1995). Social and school adjustment of shy and aggressive children in China. *Development and Psychopathology, 7,* 337–349.

Chen, X., Rubin, K. H., & Li, D., & Li, Z. (1999). Adolescent outcomes of social functioning in Chinese children. *International Journal of Behavioral Development, 23,* 199–223.

Chen, X., Rubin, K. H., Liu, M., Chen, H., Wang, L., & Li, D. (2003). Compliance in Chinese and Canadian toddlers. *International Journal of Behavioral Development, 27,* 428–436.

Chen, X., Rubin, K. H., & Sun, Y. (1992). Social reputation and peer relationships in Chinese and Canadian children: A cross-cultural study. *Child Development, 63,* 1336–1343.

Chen, X., Zappulla, C., Lo Coco, A., Schneider, B., Kaspar, V., de Oliveira, A. M., et al. (2004). Self-perceptions of competence in Brazilian, Canadian, Chinese, and Italian children: Relations with social and school adjustment. *International Journal of Behavioural Development, 28,* 129–138.

Cillessen, A., & Bukowski, W. (1998). *Sociometry then and now: Building on 6 decades of measuring children's experiences with the peer group.* San Francisco: Jossey-Bass.

Cillessen, A. H., Bukowski, W. M., & Haselager, G. T. (2000). Stability of sociometric categories. In A. Cillessen & W. Bukowski (Eds.), *Recent advances in the measurement of acceptance and rejection in the peer system* (pp. 75–93). San Francisco: Jossey-Bass.

Cillessen, A. H. N., & Mayeux, L. (2004). From censure to reinforcement: Developmental changes in the association between aggression and social status. *Child Development, 75,* 147–163.

Cillessen, A. H., van IJzendoorn, H. W., van Lieshout, C. F., & Hartup, W. W. (1992). Heterogeneity among peer-rejected boys: Subtypes and stabilities. *Child Development, 63,* 893–905.

Clark, K. E., & Ladd, G. W. (2000). Connectedness and autonomy support in parent-child relationships: Links to children's socioemotional orientation and peer relationships. *Developmental Psychology, 36,* 485–498.

Coie, J. D., & Dodge, K. A. (1988). Multiple sources of data on social behavior and social status. *Child Development, 59,* 815–829.

Coie, J. D., Dodge, K. A., & Coppotelli, H. (1982). Dimensions and types of social status: A cross-age perspective. *Developmental Psychology, 18,* 557–570.

Coie, J. D., & Kupersmidt, J. (1983). A behavioral analysis of emerging social status in boys' groups. *Child Development, 54,* 1400–1416.

Coie, J. D., Lochman, J. E., Terry, R., & Hyman, C. (1992). Predicting early adolescent disorder from childhood aggression and peer rejection. *Journal of Consulting and Clinical Psychology, 60,* 783–792.

Coie, J. D., Terry, R., Lenox, K., Lochman, J., & Hyman, C. (1995). Childhood peer rejection and aggression as predictors of stable patterns of adolescent disorder. *Development and Psychopathology, 7,* 697–714.

Collins, W. A. (2003). More than a myth: The developmental significance of romantic relationships during adolescence. *Journal of Research on Adolescence, 13,* 1–24.

Collins, W. A., Maccoby, E. E., Steinberg, L., Hetherington, E. M., & Bornstein, M. H. (2000). Contemporary research on parenting: The case for nature and nurture. *American Psychologist, 55,* 218–232.

Colwell, M. J., Mize, J., & Pettit, G. S. (2002). Contextual determinants of mothers' interventions in young children's peer interactions. *Developmental Psychology, 38,* 492–502.

Connolly, J., Craig, W., Goldberg, A., & Pepler, D. (2004). Mixed-gender groups, dating, and romantic relationships in early adolescence. *Journal of Research on Adolescence, 14,* 185–207.

Connolly, J., Furman, W., & Konarski, R. (2000). The role of peers in the emergence of heterosexual romantic relationships in adolescence. *Child Development, 71*(5), 1395–1408.

Coplan, R. J., Gavinski-Molina, M. H., Lagace-Seguin, D. G., & Wichmann, C. (2001). When girls versus boys play alone: Non-social play and adjustment in kindergarten. *Developmental Psychology, 37,* 464–474.

Coplan, R. J., Hastings, P. D., Lagace-Seguin, D. G., & Moulton, C. E. (2002). Authoritative and authoritarian mothers' parenting goals, attributions, and emotions across different childrearing contexts. *Parenting: Science and Practice, 2,* 1–26.

Coplan, R. J., Prakash, K., O'Neil, K., & Armer, M. (2004). Do you "want" to play? Distinguishing between conflicted shyness and social disinterest in early childhood. *Developmental Psychology, 40*(2), 244–258.

Coplan, R. J., Rubin, K. H., Fox, N. A., Calkins, S., & Stewart, S. L. (1994). Being alone, playing alone, and acting alone: Distinguishing between reticence and passive- and active-solitude in young children. *Child Development, 65,* 129–138.

Crick, N. R., & Bigbee, M. A. (1998). Relational and overt forms of peer victimization: A multi-informant approach. *Journal of Consulting and Clinical Psychology, 66*(2), 337–347.

Crick, N. R., Casas, J. F., & Mosher, M. (1997). Relational and overt aggression in preschool. *Developmental Psychology, 33*(4), 579–588.

Crick, N., & Dodge, K. A. (1994). A review and reformulation of social information processing in children's social adjustment. *Psychological Bulletin, 115,* 74–101.

Crick, N. R., & Grotpeter, J. K. (1995). Relational aggression, gender, and social-psychological adjustment. *Child Development, 66,* 710–722.

Crick, N. R., & Ladd, G. W. (1993). Children's perceptions of their peer experiences: Attributions, loneliness, social anxiety, and social avoidance. *Development Psychology, 29,* 244–254.

Crick, N. R., & Nelson, D. A. (2002). Relational and physical victimization within friendship: Nobody told me there'd be friends like these. *Journal of Abnormal Child Psychology, 30,* 599–607.

Criss, M. M., Pettit, G. S., Bates, J. E., Dodge, K. A., & Lapp, A. L. (2002). Family adversity, positive peer relationships, and children's externalizing behavior: A longitudinal perspective on risk and resilience. *Child Development, 73,* 1220–1237.

Csikszentmihalyi, M., & Larson, R. (1984). *Being adolescent.* New York: Basic Books.

Damon, W., & Killen, M. (1982). Peer interaction and the process of change in children's moral reasoning. *Merrill-Palmer Quarterly, 28,* 347–378.

Davila, J., Steinberg, S. J., Kachadourian, L., Cobb, R., & Fincham, F. (2004). Romantic involvement and depressive symptoms in early and late adolescence: The role of a preoccupied relational style. *Personal Relationships, 11,* 161–178.

Dawe, H. C. (1934). Analysis of two hundred quarrels of preschool children. *Child Development, 5,* 139–157.

Deater-Deckard, K. (2001). Annotation: Recent research examining the role of peer relations in the development of psychopathology. *Journal of Child Psychology and Psychiatry, 42,* 565–579.

Deater-Deckard, K., & Dodge, K. A. (1997). Externalizing behavior problems and discipline revisited: Nonlinear effects and variation by culture, context, and gender. *Psychological Inquiry, 8,* 161–175.

Degirmencioglu, S. M., Urberg, K. A., Tolson, J. M., & Richard, P. (1998). Adolescent friendship networks: Continuity and change over the school year. *Merrill-Palmer Quarterly, 44,* 313–337.

Denton, K., & Zarbatany, L. (1996). Age differences in support processes in conversations between friends. *Child Development, 67,* 1360–1373.

DeRosier, M., Kupersmidt, J., & Patterson, C. (1994). Children's academic and behavioral adjustment as a function of the chronicity and proximity of peer rejection. *Child Development, 65,* 1799–1813.

Dill, E. J., Vernberg, E. M., & Fonagy, P. (2004). Negative affect in victimized children: The roles of social withdrawal, peer rejection, and attitudes toward bullying. *Journal of Abnormal Child Psychology, 32,* 159–173.

Dishion, T. J. (1990). The family ecology of boys' peer relations in middle childhood. *Child Development, 61,* 874–892.

Dishion, T. J., Capaldi, D. M., & Yoerger, K. (1999). Middle childhood antecedents to progressions in male adolescent substance use: An ecological analysis of risk and protection. *Journal of Adolescent Research, 14*(2), 175–205.

Dishion, T. J., Duncan, T. E., Eddy, J. M., Fagot, B. I., & Fetrow, R. (1994). The world of parents and peers: Coercive exchanges and children's social adaptation. *Social Development, 3,* 255–268.

Dishion, T. J., Eddy, M., Haas, E., Li, F., & Spracklen, K. (1997). Friendships and violent behavior during adolescence. *Social Development, 6*(2), 207–223.

Dishion, T. J., McCord, J., & Poulin, F. (1999). When interventions harm: Peer groups and problem behavior. *American Psychologist, 54*(9), 755–764.

Dishion, T. J., & Owen, L. (2002). A longitudinal analysis of friendships and substance use: Bidirectional influence from adolescence to adulthood. *Developmental Psychology, 38*(4), 480–491.

Dishion, T. J., Spracklen, K. M., Andrews, D., & Patterson, G. (1996). Deviancy training in male adolescents friendships. *Behavior Therapy, 27*(3), 373–390.

Dodge, K. A. (1983). Behavioral antecedents of peer social status. *Child Development, 54,* 1386–1399.

Dodge, K. A. (1986). A social information processing model of social competence in children. In M. Perlmutter (Ed.), *Minnesota Symposia on Child Psychology* (Vol. 18, pp. 77–125). Hillsdale, NJ: Erlbaum.

Dodge, K. A., Lansford, J. E., Burks, V. S., Bates, J. E., Pettit, G. S., Fontaine, R., et al. (2003). Peer rejection and social information-processing factors in the development of aggressive behavior problems in children. *Child Development, 74*(2), 374–393.

Dodge, K. A., McClaskey, C. L., & Feldman, E. (1985). A situational approach to the assessment of social competence in children. *Journal of Consulting and Clinical Psychology, 53,* 344–353.

Dunn, J. (1993). *Young children's close relationships: Beyond attachment.* London: Sage.

Dunn, J. (1999). Making sense of the social world: Mindreading, emotion, and relationships. In P. D. Zelazo, J. W. Astington, & D. R. Olson (Eds.), *Developing theories of intention: Social understanding and self-control* (pp. 229–242). Mahwah, NJ: Erlbaum.

Dunn, J. (2004). *Children's friendships: The beginnings of intimacy.* Oxford, England: Blackwell.

Dunn, J., & Cutting, A. (1999). Understanding others and individual differences in friendship interactions in young children. *Social Development, 8,* 201–219.

Dunn, J., Cutting, A., & Fisher, N. (2002). Old friends, new friends: Predictors of children's perspective on their friends at school. *Child Development, 73,* 621–635.

Duran, R. T., & Gauvain, M. (1993). The role of age versus expertise in peer collaboration during joint planning. *Journal of Experimental Child Psychology, 55,* 227–242.

Eckerman, C. O. (1979). The human infant in social interaction. In R. Cairns (Ed.), *The analysis of social interactions: Methods, issues, and illustrations* (pp. 163–178). Hillsdale, NJ: Erlbaum.

Eckerman, C. O., & Stein, M. R. (1990). How imitation begets imitation and toddler's generation of games. *Developmental Psychology, 26,* 370–378.

Eckert, P. (1989). *Jocks and burnouts: Social categories and identity in the high school.* New York: Teachers College Press.

Edwards, C. P. (1992). Cross-cultural perspective on family-peer relations. In R. D. Parke & G. W. Ladd (Eds.), *Family-peer relationships: Modes of linkage* (pp. 285–316). Hillsdale, NJ: Erlbaum.

Eisenberg, N. (2002). Emotion-related regulation and its relation to quality of social functioning. In W. W. Hartup & R. A. Weinberg (Eds.), *Child psychology in retrospect and prospect: In celebration of the 75th anniversary of the Institute of Child Development* (pp. 133–171). Mahwah, NJ: Erlbaum.

Eisenberg, N., Cumberland, A., Spinrad, T. L., Shepard, S. A., Reiser, M., Murphy, B. C., et al. (2001). The relations of regulation and emotionality to children's externalizing and internalizing problem behavior. *Child Development, 72,* 1112–1134.

Eisenberg, N., Fabes, R. A., Guthrie, I. K., & Reiser, M. (2000). Dispositional emotionality and regulation: Their role in predicting quality of social functioning. *Journal of Personality and Social Psychology, 78,* 136–157.

Eisenberg, N., Gershoff, E. T., Fabes, R. A., Shepard, S. A., Cumberland, A. J., Losoya, S. H., et al. (2001). Mothers' emotional expressivity and children's behavior problems and social competence: Mediation through children's regulation. *Developmental Psychology, 37,* 475–490.

Eisenberg, N., Guthrie, I. K., Murphy, B. C., Shepard, S. A., Cumberland, A., & Carlo, G. (1999). Consistency and the development of prosocial dispositions: A longitudinal study. *Child Development, 70,* 1360–1372.

Eisenberg, N., Pidada, S., & Liew, J. (2001). The relations of regulation and negative emotionality to Indonesian children's social functioning. *Child Development, 72,* 1747–1763.

Eisenberg, N., Shephard, S. A., Fabes, R. A., Murphy, B. C., & Guthrie, I. K. (1998). Shyness and children's emotionality, regulation, and coping: Contemporaneous, longitudinal, and across-context relations. *Child Development, 69,* 767–790.

Eisenberg, N., Spinrad, T. L., Fabes, R. A., Reiser, M., Cumberland, A., Shephard, S. A., et al. (2004). The relations of effortful control and impulsivity to children's resiliency and adjustment. *Child Development, 75,* 25–46.

Elicker, J., Englund, M., & Sroufe, L. A. (1992). Predicting peer competence and peer relationships in childhood from early parent-child relationships. In R. Parke & G. Ladd (Eds.), *Family-peer relationships: Modes of linkage* (pp. 77–106). Hillsdale, NJ: Erlbaum.

Elman, N. M., & Kennedy-Moore, E. (2003). *The unwritten rules of friendship: Simple strategies to help your child make friends.* New York: Little, Brown.

Englund, M. M., Levy, A. K., Hyson, D. M., & Sroufe, A. (2000). Adolescent social competence: Effectiveness in a group setting. *Child Development, 71*(4), 1049–1060.

Espelage, D. L., Bosworth, K., & Simon, T. R. (2000). Examining the social context of bullying behaviors in early adolescence. *Journal of Counseling and Development, 78,* 326–333.

Espelage, D., Holt, M., & Henkel, R. (2003). Examination of peer-group contextual effects on aggression during early adolescence. *Child Development, 74,* 205–220.

Fabes, R. A., Hanish, L. D., Martin, C. L., & Eisenberg, N. (2002). Young children's negative emotionality and social isolation: A latent growth curve analysis. *Merrill-Palmer Quarterly, 48,* 284–307.

Farmer, T., Estell, D., Bishop, J., O'Neal, K., & Cairns, B. (2003). Rejected bullies or popular leaders? The social relations of aggressive subtypes of rural African American early adolescents. *Developmental Psychology, 39*(6), 992–1004.

Finnie, V., & Russell, A. (1988). Preschool children's social status and their mothers' behavior and knowledge in the supervisory role. *Developmental Psychology, 24,* 789–801.

Fox, N. A., & Calkins, S. D. (1993). Pathways to aggression and social withdrawal: Interactions among temperament, attachment, and regulation. In K. H. Rubin & J. Asendorpf (Eds.), *Social withdrawal, inhibition, and shyness in childhood* (pp. 81–100). Hillsdale, NJ: Erlbaum.

Freitag, M. K., Belsky, J., Grossmann, K., Grossmann, J. E., & Scheurer-Englisch, H. (1996). Continuity in child-parent relationships from infancy to middle childhood and relations with friendship competence. *Child Development, 67,* 1437–1454.

French, D. C. (2004). The cultural context of friendship. *ISSBD Newsletter, 28,* 19–20.

Furman, W. (1996). The measurement of friendship perceptions: Conceptual and methodological issues. In W. M. Bukowski, A. F. Newcomb, & W. W. Hartup (Eds.), *The company they keep: Friendships in childhood and adolescence* (pp. 41–65). Cambridge: Cambridge University Press.

Furman, W., & Buhrmester, D. (1992). Age and sex differences in perceptions of networks and personal relationships. *Child Development, 63,* 103–115.

Furman, W., Simon, V. A., Shaffer, L., & Bouchey, H. A. (2002). Adolescents' working models and styles for relationships with parents, friends, and romantic partners. *Child Development, 73,* 241–255.

Garton, A. F. (2001). Peer assistance in children's problem solving. *British Journal of Developmental Psychology, 19,* 307–319.

Gavin, L. A., & Furman, W. (1989). Age differences in adolescents' perceptions of their peer groups. *Developmental Psychology, 25,* 827–834.

Gazelle, H., & Ladd, G. W. (2003). Anxious solitude and peer exclusion: A diathesis-stress model of internalizing trajectories in childhood. *Child Development, 74,* 257–278.

Gazelle, H., & Rudolph, K. D. (2004). Moving toward and moving away from the world: Social approach and avoidance trajectories in anxious youth. *Child Development, 75*(3), 829–849.

Gest, S. D. (1997). Behavioral inhibition: Stability and association with adaptation from childhood to early adulthood. *Journal of Personality and Social Psychology, 72,* 467–475.

Gest, S. D., Farmer, T., Carins, B., & Xie, H. (2003). Identifying children's peer social networks in school classrooms: Links between peer reports and observed interactions. *Social Development, 12*(4), 513–529.

Golbeck, S. L. (1998). Peer collaboration and children's representation of the horizontal surface of liquid. *Journal of Applied Developmental Psychology, 19,* 542–572.

Goncu, A. (1993). Development of intersubjectivity in the dyadic play of preschoolers. *Early Childhood Research Quarterly, 8,* 99–116.

Goncu, A., Patt, M. B., & Kouba, E. (2002). Understanding young children's pretend play in context. In P. K. Smith & C. H. Hart (Eds.), *Blackwell handbook of childhood social development* (pp. 418–437). Malden, MA: Blackwell.

Graham, S., & Juvonen, J. (1998). Self-blame and peer victimization in middle school: An attributional analysis. *Developmental Psychology, 34,* 587–599.

Graham, S., & Juvonen, J. (2001). An attributional approach to peer victimization. In J. Juvonen & S. Graham (Eds.), *Peer harassment in school: The plight of the vulnerable and victimized* (pp. 49–72). New York: Guilford Press.

Granic, I., & Lamey, A. V. (2002). Combining dynamic systems and multivariate analyses to compare the mother-child interactions of externalizing subtypes. *Journal of Abnormal Child Psychology, 30,* 265–283.

Grotpeter, J. K., & Crick, N. R. (1996). Relational aggression, overt aggression, and friendship. *Child Development, 67,* 2328–2338.

Gunnar, M. R., Sebanc, A. M., Tout, K., Donzella, B., & Van Dulmen, M. M. H. (2003). Peer rejection, temperament, and cortisol activity in preschoolers. *Developmental Psychobiology, 43,* 346–358.

Guralnick, M. J., Hammond, M. A., & Connor, R. T. (2003). Subtypes of nonsocial play: Comparisons between young children with and without developmental delays. *American Journal of Mental Retardation, 108,* 347–362.

Hamm, J. V. (2000). Do birds of a feather flock together? The variable bases for African American, Asian American, and European American adolescents' selection of similar friends. *Developmental Psychology, 36*(2), 209–219.

Hanfmann, E. P. (1935). Social structure of a group of kindergarten children. *American Journal of Orthopsychiatry, 5,* 407–410.

Hanish, L. D., & Guerra, N. G. (2004). Aggressive victims, passive victims, and bullies: Developmental continuity or developmental change. *Merrill-Palmer Quarterly, 50,* 17–38.

Hansell, S. (1981). Ego development and peer friendship networks. *Sociology of Education, 54,* 51–63.

Hardy, C. L., Bukowski, W. M., & Sippola, L. K. (2002). Stability and change in peer relationships during the transition to middle-level school. *Journal of Early Adolescence, 22,* 117–142.

Harkness, S., & Super, C. M. (2002). Culture and parenting. In M. H. Bornstein (Ed.), *Handbook of parenting: Vol. 2. Biology and ecology of parenting* (2nd ed., pp. 253–280). Mahwah, NJ: Erlbaum.

Harris, J. (1998). *The nurture assumption: Why children turn out the way they do.* New York: Touchstone.

Harris, J. R. (1995). Where is the child's environment? A group socialization theory of development. *Psychological Review, 102,* 458–489.

Hart, C. H., DeWolf, D., Wozniak, P., & Burts, D. C. (1992). Maternal and paternal disciplinary styles: Relations with preschoolers' playground behavioral orientations and peer status. *Child Development, 63,* 879–892.

Hart, C. H., Yang, C., Nelson, L. J., Robinson, C. C., Olsen, J. A., Nelson, D., et al. (2000). Peer acceptance in early childhood and subtypes of socially withdrawn behavior in China, Russia, and the United States. *International Journal of Behavioral Development, 24,* 73–81.

Hartup, W. W. (1970). Peer interaction and social organization. In P. H. Mussen (Ed.), *Carmichael's manual of child psychology* (Vol. 2, pp. 361–456). New York: Wiley.

Hartup, W. W. (1983). Peer relations. In P. H. Mussen (Ed.), *Handbook of child psychology: Vol. 4. Socialization, personality, and social development* (4th ed., pp. 103–196). New York: Wiley.

Hartup, W. W. (1985). Relationships and their significance in cognitive development. In R. A. Hinde, A. Perret-Clermont, & J. Stevenson-Hinde (Eds.), *Social relationships and cognitive development* (pp. 66–82). Oxford, England: Clarendon Press.

Hartup, W. W., & Abecassis, M. (2002). Friends and enemies. In P. K. Smith & C. H. Hart (Eds.), *Blackwell handbook of childhood social development* (pp. 286–306). Malden, MA: Blackwell.

Hartup, W. W., Laursen, B., Stewart, M. A., & Eastenson, A. (1988). Conflicts and the friendship relations of young children. *Child Development, 59,* 1590–1600.

Hartup, W. W., & Stevens, N. (1997). Friendships and adaptation in the life course. *Psychological Bulletin, 121,* 355–370.

Haselager, G. J. T., Cillissen, H. N., van Lieshout, C. F. M., Riksen-Walraven, J. M. A., & Hartup, W. W. (2002). Heterogeneity among peer-rejected boys across middle childhood: Developmental pathways of social behavior. *Child Development, 73,* 446–456.

Haselager, G. J. T., Hartup, W. W., van Lieshout, C. F. M., & Riksen-Walraven, J. M. A. (1998). Similarities between friends and nonfriends in middle childhood. *Child Development, 69,* 1198–1208.

Hastings, P., & Rubin, K. H. (1999). Predicting mothers' beliefs about preschool-aged children's social behavior: Evidence for maternal attitudes moderating child effects. *Child Development, 70*(3), 722–741.

Hawley, P. H. (2002). Social dominance and prosocial and coercive strategies of resource control in preschoolers. *International Journal of Behavioral Development, 26,* 167–176.

Hawley, P. H. (2003). Strategies of control, aggression and morality in preschoolers: An evolutionary perspective. *Journal of Experimental Child Psychology, 85*(3), 213–235.

Hawley, P. H., Little, T. D., & Pasupathi, M. (2002). Winning friends and influencing peers: Strategies of peer influence in late childhood. *International Journal of Behavioral Development, 26,* 466–474.

Hay, D. F. (1985). Learning to form relationships in infancy: Parallel attainments with parents and peers. *Developmental Review, 5,* 122–161.

Hay, D. F., Castle, J., & Davies, L. (2000). Toddlers' use of force against familiar peers: A precursor of serious aggression? *Child Development, 71,* 457–467.

Hay, D. F., Castle, J., Davies, L., Demetriou, H., & Stimson, C. (1999). Prosocial action in very early childhood. *Journal of Child Psychology and Psychiatry, 40,* 905–916.

Hay, D. F., Nash, A., & Pedersen, J. (1983). Interaction between 6-month-old peers. *Child Development, 54,* 557–562.

Hay, D. F., Payne, A., & Chadwick, A. (2004). Peer relations in childhood. *Journal of Child Psychology and Psychiatry, 45,* 84–108.

Hay, D. F., & Ross, H. (1982). The social nature of early conflict. *Child Development, 53,* 105–113.

Hayes, D. S., Gershman, E., & Bolin, L. J. (1980). Friends and enemies: Cognitive bases for preschool children's unilateral and reciprocal friendships. *Child Development, 51,* 1276–1279.

Hays, R. B. (1988). Friendship. In S. W. Duck (Ed.), *Handbook of personal relationships: Theory, research, and interventions* (pp. 391–408). London: Wiley.

Hektner, J. M., August, G. J., & Realmuto, G. M. (2000). Patterns and temporal changes in peeraffiliation among aggressive and nonaggressive children participating in a summer school program. *Journal of Clinical Child Psychology, 29*(4), 603–614.

Henderson, H., Marshall, P., Fox, N. A., & Rubin, K. H. (2004). Psychophysiological and behavioral evidence for varying forms of nonsocial behavior in preschoolers. *Child Development, 75,* 251–263.

Hinde, R. A. (1979). *Towards understanding relationships.* London: Academic Press.

Hinde, R. A. (1987). *Individuals, relationships and culture.* Cambridge: Cambridge University Press.

Hinde, R. A. (1995). A suggested structure for a science of relationships. *Personal Relationships, 2,* 1–15.

Hinde, R. R., & Stevenson-Hinde, J. (1976). Toward understanding relationships: Dynamic stability. In P. Bateson & R. Hinde (Eds.), *Growing points in ethology* (pp. 451–479). Cambridge: Cambridge University Press.

Hinde, R. R., & Stevenson-Hinde, J. (1987). Interpersonal relationships and child development. *Developmental Review, 7,* 1–21.

Hodges, E. V. E., Boivin, M., Vitaro, F., & Bukowski, W. M. (1999). The power of friendship: Protection against an escalating cycle of peer victimization. *Developmental Psychology, 35,* 94–101.

Hodges, E. V. E., & Card, N. A. (Eds.). (2003). *Enemies and the darker side of peer relations.* San Francisco: Jossey-Bass.

Hodges, E. V. E., Finnegan, R. A., & Perry, D. G. (1999). Skewed autonomy-relatedness in preadolescents' conceptions of their relationships with mother, father, and best friend. *Developmental Psychology, 35*(3), 737–748.

Hodges, E. V. E., Malone, M. J., & Perry, D. G. (1997). Individual risk and social risk as interacting determinants of victimization in the peer group. *Developmental Psychology, 33,* 1032–1039.

Hogan, D., & Tudge, J. (1999). Implications of Vygotsky's theory for peer learning. In A. M. O'Donnell & A. King (Eds.), *Cognitive perspectives on peer learning* (pp. 39–65). Mahwah, NJ: Erlbaum.

Hogue, A., & Steinberg, L. (1995). Homophily of internalized distress in adolescent peer groups. *Developmental Psychology, 31,* 897–906.

Hops, H., Albert, A., & Davis, B. (1997). The development of same- and opposite-sex social relations among adolescents: An analogue study. *Social Development, 6*(2), 165–183.

Horn, S. (2003). Adolescents' reasoning about exclusion from social groups. *Developmental Psychology, 39,* 11–84.

Howes, C. (1983). Patterns of friendship. *Child Development, 54,* 1041–1053.

Howes, C. (1988). Peer interaction of young children. *Monographs of the Society for Research in Child Development, 53*(217).

Howes, C. (1992). *The collaborative construction of pretend.* Albany: State University of New York Press.

Howes, C. (1996). The earliest friendships. In W. M. Bukowski, A. F. Newcomb, & W. W. Hartup (Eds.), *The company they keep: Friendship in childhood and adolescence* (pp. 66–86). Cambridge: Cambridge University Press.

Howes, C., Matheson, C. C., & Wu, F. (1992). Friendships and social pretend play. In C. Howes, O. Unger, & C. C. Matheson (Eds.), *The collaborative construction of pretend.* Albany: State University of New York Press.

Howes, C., & Phillipsen, L. (1998). Continuity in children's relationships with peers. *Social Development, 7,* 340–349.

Hoza, B., Molina, B., Bukowski, W. M., & Sippola, L. K. (1995). Aggression, withdrawal and measures of popularity and friendship as predictors of internalizing and externalizing problems during early adolescence. *Development and Psychopathology, 7,* 787–802.

Humphreys, A. P., & Smith, P. K. (1987). Rough-and-tumble, friendship, and dominance in school children: Evidence for continuity and change with age. *Child Development, 58,* 201–212.

Hymel, S. (1986). Interpretations of peer behavior: Affective bias in childhood and adolescence. *Child Development, 57,* 431–445.

Hymel, S., Bowker, A., & Woody, E. (1993). Aggressive versus withdrawn unpopular children: Variations in peer and self-perceptions in multiple domains. *Child Development, 64,* 879–896.

Hymel, S., Comfort, C., Schonert-Reichl, K., & McDougall, P. (2002). Academic failure and school dropout: The influence of peers. In K. Wentzel & J. Juvonen (Eds.), *Social motivation: Understanding children's school adjustment* (pp. 313–335). Cambridge: Cambridge University Press.

Hymel, S., & Rubin, K. H. (1985). Children with peer relationship and social skills problems: Conceptual, methodological, and developmental issues. In G. J. Whitehurst (Ed.), *Annals of Child Development* (Vol. 2, pp. 251–297). Greenwich, CT: JAI Press.

Hymel, S., Rubin, K. H., Rowden, L., & LeMare, L. (1990). Children's peer relationships: Longitudinal predictions of internalizing and externalizing problems from middle to late childhood. *Child Development, 61,* 2004–2021.

James, W. (1890). *The principles of psychology.* New York: Henry Holt.

Joyner, K., & Udry, J. R. (2000). You don't bring me anything but down: Adolescent romance and depression. *Journal of Health and Social Behavior, 41,* 369–391.

Juvonen, J., & Graham, S. (Eds.). (2001). *Peer harassment in school: The plight of the vulnerable and victimized.* New York: Guilford Press.

Juvonen, J., & Wentzel, K. (1996). *Social motivation: Understanding children's school adjustment.* New York: Cambridge University Press.

Kagan, J. (1999). The concept of behavioral inhibition. In L. A. Schmidt & J. Schulkin (Eds.), *Extreme fear, shyness, and social phobia: Origins, biological mechanisms, and clinical outcomes* (pp. 3–13). London: Oxford University Press.

Kandel, D. B. (1978). Homophily, selection, and socialization in adolescent friendships. *American Journal of Sociology, 84,* 427–436.

Keenan, K., Shaw, D., & Delliquadri, E. (1998). Evidence for the continuity of early problem behaviors: Application of a developmental model. *Journal of Abnormal Child Psychology, 26,* 441–452.

Keller, M. (2004a). A cross cultural perspective on friendship research. *Newsletter of the International Society for the Study of Behavioral Development, 28,* 10–14.

Keller, M. (2004b). Self in relationship. In D. K. Lapsley & D. Narvaez (Eds.), *Morality, self, and identity: Essays in honor of Augusto Blasi* (pp. 269–300). Mahwah, NJ: Erlbaum.

Kerns, K. A., Cole, A. K., & Andrews, P. B. (1998). Attachment security, parent peer management practices, and peer relationships in preschoolers. *Merrill-Palmer Quarterly, 44,* 504–522.

Kerns, K. A., Contreras, J. M., & Neal-Barnett, A. M. (Eds.). (2000). *Family and peers: Linking two social worlds.* London: Praeger.

Khatri, P., & Kupersmidt, J. B. (2003). Aggression, peer victimization, and social relationships among Indian youth. *International Journal of Behavioral Development, 27,* 87–95.

Kiesner, J., Poulin, F., & Nicotra, E. (2003). Peer relations across contexts: Individual network homophily and network inclusion in and after school. *Child Development, 74,* 1328–1343.

Killen, M., Crystal, D. S., & Watanabe, H. (2002). Japanese and American children's evaluations of peer exclusion, tolerance of differences, and prescriptions for conformity. *Child Development, 73,* 1788–1802.

Killen, M., Lee-Kim, J., McGlothlin, H., & Stangor, C. (2002). How children and adolescents evaluate gender and racial exclusion. *Monographs of the Society for Research in Child Development, 67*(4).

Killen, M., & Stangor, C. (2001). Children's reasoning about social inclusion and exclusion in peer group contexts. *Child Development, 72,* 174–186.

Killen, M., Stangor, C., Horn, S., & Sechrist, G. B. (2004). Social reasoning about racial exclusion in intimate and nonintimate relationships. *Youth and Society, 35,* 293–322.

Kindermann, T. A. (1993). Natural peer groups as contexts for individual development: The case of children's motivation in school. *Developmental Psychology, 29,* 970–977.

Kindermann, T. A. (1995). Distinguishing "buddies" from "bystanders": The study of children's development within natural peer contexts. In T. A. Kindermann & J. Valsiner (Eds.), *Development of person-context relations* (pp. 205–226). Hillsdale, NJ: Erlbaum.

Kindermann, T. A., McCollam, T. L., & Gibson, E., Jr. (1995). Peer networks and students' classroom engagement during childhood and adolescence. In K. Wentzel & J. Juvonen (Eds.), *Social motivation: Understanding children's school adjustment* (pp. 279–312). New York: Cambridge University Press.

Kistner, J., Balthazor, M., Risi, S., & Burton, C. (1999). Predicting dysphoria from actual and perceived acceptance in childhood. *Journal of Clinical Child Psychology, 28,* 94–104.

Kochanska, G. (1998). Mother-child relationship, child fearfulness, and emerging attachment: A short-term longitudinal study. *Developmental Psychology, 34,* 480–490.

Kochanska, G., Murray, K., & Coy, K. (1997). Inhibitory control as a contributor to conscience in childhood: From toddler to early school age. *Child Development, 68*(2), 263–277.

Kochenderfer, B. J., & Ladd, G. W. (1997). Victimized children's responses to peers' aggression: Behaviors associated with reduced versus continued victimization. *Development and Psychopathology, 9,* 59–73.

Kochenderfer-Ladd, B. (2003). Identification of aggressive and asocial victims and the stability of their peer victimization. *Merrill-Palmer Quarterly, 49*(4), 401–425.

Kochenderfer-Ladd B., & Wardrop, J. L. (2001). Chronicity and instability of children's peer victimization experiences as predictors of loneliness and social satisfaction trajectories. *Child Development, 72,* 134–151.

Kovacs, D. M., Parker, J. G., & Hoffman, L. W. (1996). Behavioral, affective, and social correlates of involvement in cross-sex friendship in elementary school. *Child Development, 67,* 2269–2286.

Kraatz-Keily, M., Bates, J. E., Dodge, K. A., & Pettit, G. S. (2000). A cross-domain analysis: Externalizing and internalizing behaviors during 8 years of childhood. *Journal of Abnormal Child Psychology, 28,* 161–179.

Krappmann, L. (1996). Amicitia, drujba, shin-yu, philia, freundschaft, friendship: On the cultural diversity of a human relationship. In W. M. Bukowski, A. F. Newcomb, & W. W. Hartup (Eds.), *The company they keep: Friendship in childhood and adolescence* (pp. 19–40). Cambridge: Cambridge University Press.

Krasnor, L., & Rubin, K. H. (1983). Preschool social problem solving: Attempts and outcomes in naturalistic interaction. *Child Development, 54,* 1545–1558.

Kupersmidt, J. B., Burchinal, M., & Patterson, C. J. (1995). Developmental patterns of childhood peer relations as predictors of externalizing behavior problems. *Development and Psychopathology, 7,* 649–668.

Kupersmidt, J. B., & Coie, J. D. (1990). Preadolescent peer status, aggression, and school adjustment as predictors of externalizing problems in adolescence. *Child Development, 61,* 1350–1362.

Kupersmidt, J. B., Coie, J. D., & Dodge, K. A. (1990). The role of poor peer relationships in the development of disorder. In S. R. Asher & J. D. Coie (Eds.), *Peer rejection in childhood* (pp. 274–305). Cambridge: Cambridge University Press.

Kupersmidt, J. B., & Dodge, K. A. (Eds.). (2004). *Children's peer relations: From development to intervention.* Washington, DC: American Psychological Association.

Kuttler, A. F., La Greca, A. M., & Prinstein, M. J. (1999). Friendship qualities and social-emotional functioning of adolescents with close, cross-sex friendships. *Journal of Research on Adolescence, 9,* 339–366.

Kuttler, A. F., Parker, J. G., & La Greca, A. M. (2002). Developmental and gender differences in preadolescents' judgments of the veracity of gossip. *Merrill-Palmer Quarterly, 48,* 105–132.

Lacourse, E., Nagin, D., Tremblay, R. E., Vitaro, F., & Claes, M. (2003). Developmental trajectories of boys' delinquent group membership and facilitation of violent behaviors during adolescence. *Development and Psychopathology, 15*(1), 183–197.

Ladd, G. W. (1990). Having friends, keeping friends, making friends, and being liked by peers in the classroom: Predictors of children's early school adjustment? *Child Development, 61,* 312–331.

Ladd, G. W. (1991). Family-peer relations during childhood: Pathways to competence and pathology? *Journal of Social and Personal Relationships, 8,* 307–314.

Ladd, G. W., & Burgess, K. B. (1999). Charting the relationship trajectories of aggressive, withdrawn, and aggressive/withdrawn children during early grade school. *Child Development, 70,* 910–929.

Ladd, G. W., & Burgess, K. B. (2001). Do relational risks and protective factors moderate the linkages between childhood aggression and early psychological and school adjustment? *Child Development, 72,* 1579–1601.

Ladd, G. W., & Golter, B. S. (1988). Parents' initiation and monitoring of children's peer contacts: Predictive of children's peer relations in nonschool and school settings? *Developmental Psychology, 24,* 109–117.

Ladd, G. W., & Hart, C. H. (1992). Creating informal play opportunities: Are parents' and preschoolers' initiations related to children's competence with peers? *Developmental Psychology, 28*(6), 1179–1187.

Ladd, G. W., & Kochenderfer, B. (1996). Linkages between friendship and adjustment during early school transitions. In W. M. Bukowski, A. F. Newcomb, & W. W. Hartup (Eds.), *The company they keep: Friendship in childhood and adolescence* (pp. 322–345). Cambridge: Cambridge University Press.

Ladd, G. W., & Kochenderfer, B. J., & Coleman, C. C. (1996). Friendship quality as a predictor of young children's early school adjustment. *Child Development, 67,* 1103–1118.

Ladd, G. W., & Kochenderfer, B. J., & Coleman, C. C. (1997). Classroom peer acceptance, friendship, and victimization: Distinct relational systems that contribute uniquely to children's school adjustment? *Child Development, 68,* 1181–1197.

Ladd, G. W., & Pettit, G. S. (2002). Parenting and the development of children's peer relationships. In M. H. Bornstein (Ed.), *Handbook of parenting: Vol. 5. Practical issues in parenting* (2nd ed., pp. 269–309). Mahwah, NJ: Erlbaum.

Ladd, G. W., & Troop-Gordon, W. (2003). The role of chronic peer difficulties in the development of children's psychological adjustment problems. *Child Development, 74*(5), 1344–1367.

LaFontana, K. M., & Cillessen, A. H. N. (1998). The nature of children's stereotypes of popularity. *Social Development, 7,* 301–320.

LaFontana, K. M., & Cillessen, A. H. N. (2002). Children's perceptions of popular and unpopular peers: A multimethod assessment. *Developmental Psychology, 38,* 635–647.

Laird, R. D., Jordan, K. Y., Dodge, K. A., Pettit, G. S., & Bates, J. E. (2001). Peer rejection in childhood, involvement with antisocial peers in early adolescence, and the development of externalizing behavior problems. *Development and Psychopathology, 13,* 337–354.

Lansford, J. E., Criss, M. M., Pettit, G. S., Dodge, K. A., & Bates, J. (2003). Friendship quality, peer group affiliation, and peer antisocial behavior as moderators of the link between negative parenting and adolescent externalizing behavior. *Journal of Research on Adolescence, 13,* 161–184.

Lansford, J. E., & Parker, J. G. (1999). Children's interactions in triads: Behavioral profiles and effects of gender and patterns of friendships among members. *Developmental Psychology, 35,* 80–93.

Larkin, R. W. (1979). *Suburban youth in cultural crisis.* New York: Oxford University Press.

Larson, R. W., Brown, B. B., & Mortimer, J. T. (Eds.). (2002). *Adolescents' preparation for the future: Perils and promise—A report of the study group on adolescence in the twenty-first century.* London: Blackwell.

Laursen, B. (1993). Conflict management among close peers. In B. Laursen (Ed.), *Close friendships in adolescence* (pp. 39–54). San Francisco: Jossey-Bass.

Laursen, B., Finkelstein, B. D., & Betts, N. T. (2001). A developmental meta-analysis of peer conflict resolution. *Developmental Review, 21,* 423–449.

Laursen, B., & Hartup, W. W. (1989). The dynamics of preschool children's conflicts. *Merrill-Palmer Quarterly, 35,* 281–297.

Laursen, B., Hartup, W. W., & Koplas, A. L. (1996). Towards understanding peer conflict. *Merrill-Palmer Quarterly, 42,* 76–102.

Laursen, B., & Koplas, A. L. (1995). What's important about important conflicts? Adolescents' perceptions of daily disagreements. *Merrill-Palmer Quarterly, 41,* 536–553.

Laursen, B., Wilder, D., Noack, P., & Williams, V. (2000). Adolescent perceptions of reciprocity, authority, and closeness in relationships with mothers, fathers, and friends. *International Journal of Behavioral Development, 24,* 464–471.

Laursen, B., & Williams, V. A. (1997). Perceptions of interdependence and closeness in family and peer relationships among adolescents with and without romantic partners. In S. Shulman & W. A. Collins (Eds.), *New Directions for Child Development: Vol. 78. Romantic relationships in adolescence—Developmental perspectives* (pp. 3–20). San Francisco: Jossey-Bass.

Leaper, C. (1994). Exploring the consequences of gender segregation on social relationships. In C. Leaper (Ed.), *Childhood gender segregation: Causes and consequences* (pp. 67–86). San Francisco: Jossey-Bass.

Lease, A. M., Kennedy, C. A., & Axelrod, J. L. (2002). Children's social constructions of popularity. *Social Development, 11,* 87–109.

Lease, A. M., Musgrove, K. T., & Axelrod, J. L. (2002). Dimensions of social status in preadolescent peer groups: Likability, perceived popularity, and social dominance. *Social Development, 11,* 508–533.

Legault, F., & Strayer, F. F. (1991). The emergence of sex-segregation in preschool peer groups. In F. F. Strayer (Ed.), *Behaviour, 119,* 285–301.

Lemerise, E. A., & Arsenio, W. F. (2000). An integrated model of emotion processes and cognition in social information processing. *Child Development, 71,* 107–118.

Levin, E., & Rubin, K. H. (1983). Getting others to do what you wanted them to do: The development of children's requestive strategies. In K. Nelson (Ed.), *Child language* (Vol. 4, pp. 157–186). Hillsdale, NJ: Erlbaum.

Lewin, K., Lippitt, R., & White, R. K. (1939). Patterns of aggressive behavior in experimentally created "social climates." *Journal of Social Psychology, 10,* 271–299.

Lewin, M. L., Davis, B., & Hops, H. (1999). Childhood social predictors of adolescent antisocial behavior: Gender differences in predictive accuracy and efficacy. *Journal of Abnormal Child Psychology, 27*(4), 277–292.

Lieberman, M., Doyle, A. B., & Markiewicz, D. (1999). Developmental patterns in security of attachment to mother and father in late childhood and early adolescence: Associations with peer relations. *Child Development, 70,* 202–213.

Little, T. D., Brendgen, M., Wanner, B., & Krappmann, L. (1999). Children's reciprocal perceptions of friendship quality in the sociocultural contexts of East and West Berlin. *International Journal of Behavioral Development, 23,* 63–89.

Little, T. D., Jones, S. M., Henrich, C. C., & Hawley, P. H. (2003). Disentangling the "whys" from the "whats" of aggressive behavior. *International Journal of Behavioral Development, 27,* 122–133.

Liu, M., & Chen, X. (2003). Friendship networks and social, school, and psychological adjustment in Chinese junior high school students. *Psychology in the Schools, 40,* 5–17.

Lorenz, K. (1966). *On aggression.* London: Methuen.

Lyons-Ruth, K., Easterbrooks, M. A., & Cibelli, C. D. (1997). Infant attachment strategies, infant mental lag, and maternal depressive symptoms: Predictors of internalizing and externalizing problems at age seven. *Developmental Psychology, 33,* 681–692.

MacDonald, R. A. R., Miell, D., & Morgan, L. (2000). Social processes and creative collaboration in children. *European Journal of the Psychology of Education, 15,* 405–416.

Masten, A. S., Morrison, P., & Pellegrini, D. S. (1985). A revised class play method of peer assessment. *Developmental Psychology, 3,* 523–533.

Matsumoto, D. (1997). *Culture and modern life.* Pacific Grove, CA: Brooks/Cole.

Maudry, M., & Nekula, M. (1939). Social relations between children of the same age during the first 2 years of life. *Journal of Genetic Psychology, 54,* 193–215.

McCall, G. J. (1988). The organizational life cycle of relationships. In S. W. Duck (Ed.), *Handbook of personal relationships* (pp. 467–484). New York: Wiley.

McDowell, D. J., & Parke, R. D. (2000). Differential knowledge of display rules for positive and negative emotions: Influences from parents, influences on peers. *Social Development, 9,* 415–432.

McNeilly-Choque, M. K., Hart, C. H., Robinson, C. C., Nelson, L. J., & Olsen, S. F. (1996). Overt and relational aggression on the playground: Correspondence among different informants. *Journal of Research in Childhood Education, 11,* 47–67.

Mead, G. H. (1934). *Mind, self, and society.* Chicago: University of Chicago Press.

Miller-Johnson, S., Coie, J. D., Maumary-Gremaud, A., Bierman, K., & Conduct Problems Prevention Research Group. (2002). Peer rejection and aggression and early starter models of conduct disorder. *Journal of Abnormal Child Psychology, 30,* 217–230.

Miller-Johnson, S., Coie, J., Maumary-Gremaud, A., Lochman, J., & Terry, R. (1999). Relationship between childhood peer rejection and aggression and adolescent delinquency severity and type among African-American youth. *Journal of Emotional and Behavioral Disorders, 7,* 137–146.

Mills, R. S. L., & Rubin, K. H. (1998). Are behavioral control and psychological control both differentially associated with childhood aggression and social withdrawal? *Canadian Journal of Behavioral Sciences, 30,* 132–136.

Mize, J., & Pettit, G. S. (1997). Mothers' social coaching, mother-child relationship style and children's peer competence: Is the medium the message? *Child Development, 68,* 312–332.

Moffitt, T. E. (1993). Adolescence-limited and life-course-persistent antisocial behavior: A developmental taxonomy. *Psychological Review, 100,* 674–701.

Moller, L., Hymel, S., & Rubin, K. H. (1992). Sex typing in play and popularity in middle childhood. *Sex Roles, 26,* 331–353.

Moreno, J. L. (1934). *Who shall survive? A new approach to the problem of human interrelations.* Washington, DC: Nervous and Mental Disease.

Mueller, E. (1972). The maintenance of verbal exchanges between young children. *Child Development, 43,* 930–938.

Mueller, E., & Brenner, J. (1977). The origins of social skills and interaction among playgroup toddlers. *Child Development, 48,* 854–861.

Murphy, B. C., & Eisenberg, N. (2001). An integrative examination of peer conflict: Children's reported goals, emotions, and behaviors. *Social Development, 11,* 534–557.

Murphy, L. B. (1937). *Social behavior and child psychology: An exploratory study of some roots of sympathy.* New York: Columbia University Press.

Nangle, D. W., & Erdley, C. A. (Eds.). (2001). *The role of friendship in psychological adjustment.* San Francisco: Jossey-Bass.

Nangle, D. W., Erdley, C. A., Newman, J. E., Mason, C. A., & Carpenter, E. (2003). Popularity, friendship quantity, and friendship quality: Interactive influences on children's loneliness and depression. *Journal of Clinical Child and Adolescent Psychology, 32*(4), 546–555.

National Institute of Child Health and Human Development Early Child Care Research Network. (2001). Child care and children's peer interaction at 24 and 36 months: The National Institute of Child Health and Human Development Study of Early Child Care. *Child Development, 72,* 1478–1500.

Nelson, L. J., Rubin, K. H., & Fox, N. A. (2005). Social and nonsocial behaviors and peer acceptance: A longitudinal model of the development of self-perceptions in children ages 4 to 7 years. *Early Education and Development, 20,* 185–200.

Newcomb, A., & Bagwell, C. (1995). Children's friendship relations: A meta-analytic review. *Psychological Bulletin, 117,* 306–347.

Newcomb, A. F., & Bukowski, W. M. (1983). Social impact and social preference as determinants of children's peer group status. *Developmental Psychology, 19,* 856–867.

Newcomb, A. F., & Bukowski, W. M. (1984). A longitudinal study of the utility of social preference and social impact sociometric classification schemes. *Child Development, 55,* 1434–1447.

Newcomb, A. F., Bukowski, W. M., & Pattee, L. (1993). Children's peer relations: A meta-analyic review of popular, rejected, neglected, controversial, and average sociometric status. *Psychological Bulletin, 113,* 99–128.

Nolen-Hoeksema, S., Girgus, J. S., & Seligman, M. E. (1992). Predictors and consequences of childhood depressive symptoms: A 5-year longitudinal study. *Journal of Abnormal Psychology, 101*(3), 405–422.

Northway, M. L. (1944). Outsiders: A study of the personality patterns of children least acceptable to their age mates. *Sociometry, 7,* 10–25.

Northway, M. L. (1946). Sociometry and some challenging problems of social relations. *Sociometry, 9,* 187–198.

O'Brien, S. F., & Bierman, K. L. (1987). Conceptions and perceived influence of peer groups: Interviews with preadolescents and adolescents. *Child Development, 59,* 1360–1365.

Ollendick, T. H., Weist, M. D., Borden, M. G., & Greene, R. W. (1992). Sociometric status and academic, behavioral, and psychological adjustment: A 5-year longitudinal study. *Journal of Consulting and Clinical Psychology, 60,* 80–87.

Olweus, D. (1978). *Aggression in the schools: Bullies and whipping boys.* Oxford, England: Hemisphere.

Olweus, D. (1984). Stability in aggressive and withdrawn, inhibited behavior patterns. In R. M. Kaplan, V. J. Konecni, & R. W. Novaco (Eds.), *Aggression in children and youth* (pp. 104–136). Den Haag, The Netherlands: Martinus Nijhoff.

Olweus, D. (1993). Victimization by peers: Antecedents and long-term outcomes. In K. H. Rubin & J. B. Asendorpf (Eds.), *Social withdrawal, inhibition and shyness in childhood* (pp. 315–341). Hillsdale, NJ: Erlbaum.

Orobio de Castro, B., Veerman, J. W., Koops, W., Bosch, J. D., & Monshouwer, H. J. (2002). Hostile attribution of intent and aggressive behavior: A meta-analysis. *Child Development, 73*(3), 916–934.

Pakaslahti, L., Karjalainen, A., & Keltikangas-Jarvinen, L. (2002). Relationships between adolescent prosocial problem-solving strategies, prosocial behaviour, and social acceptance. *International Journal of Behavioral Development, 26*(2), 137–144.

Parke, R. D., & O'Neil, R. (1999). Social relationships across contexts: Family-peer linkages. In W. A. Collins & B. Laursen (Eds.), *Minnesota Symposia on Child Psychology* (Vol. 30, pp. 211–239). Hillsdale, NJ: Erlbaum.

Parker, J. G., & Asher, S. R. (1993). Friendship and friendship quality in middle childhood: Links with peer group acceptance and feelings of loneliness and social dissatisfaction. *Developmental Psychology, 29,* 611–621.

Parker, J. G., Saxon, J., Asher, S. R., & Kovacs, D. (1999). Dimensions of children's friendship adjustment: Implications for studying loneliness. In K. J. Rotenberg & S. Hymel (Eds.), *Loneliness in childhood and adolescence.* New York: Cambridge University Press.

Parker, J. G., & Seal, J. (1996). Forming, losing, renewing, and replacing friendships: Applying temporal parameters to the assessment of children's friendship experiences. *Child Development, 67,* 2248–2268.

Parkhurst, J. T., & Asher, S. R. (1992). Peer rejection in middle school: Subgroup differences in behavior, loneliness, and interpersonal concerns. *Developmental Psychology, 28,* 231–241.

Parkhurst, J. T., & Hopmeyer, A. (1998). Sociometric popularity and peer-perceived popularity: Two distinct dimensions of peer status. *Journal of Early Adolescence, 18,* 125–144.

Parten, M. B. (1932). Social participation among preschool children. *Journal of Abnormal and Social Psychology, 27,* 243–269.

Pastor, D. L. (1981). The quality of mother-infant attachment and its relationship to toddlers' initial sociability with peers. *Developmental Psychology, 17,* 326–335.

Pekarik, E. G., Prinz, R. J., Liebert, D. E., Weintraub, S., & Neale, J. M. (1976). The pupil evaluation inventory: A sociometric technique for assessing children's social behavior. *Journal of Abnormal Child Psychology, 4,* 83–97.

Pellegrini, A. D. (2002). Rough-and-tumble play from childhood through adolescence: Development and possible functions. In P. K. Smith & C. H. Hart (Eds.), *Blackwell handbook of childhood social development* (pp. 438–453). London: Blackwell.

Perry, D. G., Perry, L., & Kennedy, E. (1992). Conflict and the development of antisocial behavior. In C. Shantz & W. W. Hartup (Eds.), *Conflict in child and adolescent development* (pp. 301–329). New York: Cambridge University Press.

Pettit, G. S., Brown, E. G., Mize, J., & Lindsey, E. W. (1998). Mothers' and fathers' socializing behaviors in three contexts: Links with children's peer competence. *Merrill-Palmer Quarterly, 44,* 173–193.

Pettit, G. S., Clawson, M. A., Dodge, K. A., & Bates, J. (1996). Stability and change in peer-rejected status: The role of child behavior, parenting, and family ecology. *Merrill-Palmer Quarterly, 42,* 267–294.

Pfeifer, M., Goldsmith, H. H., Davidson, R. J., & Rickman, M. (2002). Continuity and change in inhibited and uninhibited children. *Child Development, 73,* 1474–1485.

Piaget, J. (1932). *The moral judgment of the child.* Glencoe, IL: Free Press.

Piaget, J. (1959). *The language and thought of the child.* New York: Harcourt, Brace, and World.

Pike, A., & Atzaba-Poria, N. (2003). Do sibling and friend relationships share the same temperamental origins? A twin study. *Journal of Child Psychology and Psychiatry and Allied Disciplines, 44,* 598–611.

Pinker, S. (2002). *The blank slate: The modern denial of human nature.* New York: Penguin Putnam.

Pinto, G., Bombi, A. S., & Cordioli, A. (1997). Similarity of friends in three countries: A study of children's drawings. *International Journal of Behavioral Development, 20,* 453–469.

Pope, A. W., Bierman, K., & Mumma, G. H. (1991). Aggression, hyperactivity, and inattention-immaturity: Behavior dimensions associated with peer rejection in elementary school boys. *Developmental Psychology, 27*(4), 663–671.

Poulin, F., & Boivin, M. (1999). Proactive and reactive aggression and boys' friendship quality in mainstream classrooms. *Journal of Emotional and Behavioral Disorders, 7*(3), 168–177.

Poulin, F., & Boivin, M. (2000). The role of proactive and reactive aggression in the formation and development of boys' friendships. *Developmental Psychology, 36,* 233–240.

Prinstein, M., & La Greca, A. M. (2002). Peer crowd affiliation and internalizing distress in childhood and adolescence: A longitudinal follow-back study. *Journal of Research on Adolescence, 12*(3), 325–351.

Prinstein, M. J., & Cillessen, A. (2003). Forms and functions of adolescent peer aggression associated with high levels of peer status. *Merrill-Palmer Quarterly, 49*(3), 310–342.

Putallaz, M. (1983). Predicting children's sociometric status from their behavior. *Child Development, 54,* 1417–1426.

Putallaz, M., & Gottman, J. (1981). An interactional model of children's entry into peer groups. *Child Development, 52*(3), 986–994.

Putnam, S. P., Sanson, A. V., & Rothbart, M. K. (2002). Child temperament and parenting. In M. H. Bornstein (Ed.), *Handbook of parenting: Vol. 1. Children and parenting* (2nd ed., pp. 163–179). Mahwah, NJ: Erlbaum.

Rabiner, D., & Gordon, L. (1992). The coordination of conflicting social goals: Differences between rejected and nonrejected boys. *Child Development, 63,* 1344–1350.

Renken, B., Egeland, B., Marvinney, D., Mangelsdorf, S., & Sroufe, L. A., (1989). Early childhood antecedents of aggression and passive-withdrawal in early elementary school. *Journal of Personality, 57,* 257–281.

Reznick, J. S., Kagan, J., Snidman, N., Gersten, M., Baak, K., & Rosenberg, A. (1986). Inhibited and uninhibited children: A follow-up study. *Child Development, 57,* 660–680.

Richards, W. D. (1995). *NEGOPY 4.30: Manual and user's guide.* Burnaby, British Columbia, Canada: School of Communication, Simon Fraser University.

Robinson, C. C., Anderson, G. T., Porter, C. L., Hart, C. H., & Wouden-Miller, M. (2003). Sequential transition patterns of preschoolers' social interactions during child-initiated play: Is parallel-aware play a bidirectional bridge to other play states? *Early Childhood Research Quarterly, 18,* 3–21.

Rodkin, P. C., Farmer, T. W., Pearl, R., & Van Acker, R. (2000). Heterogeneity of popular boys: Antisocial and prosocial configurations. *Developmental Psychology, 36,* 14–24.

Rodkin, P. C., & Hodges, E. V. E. (2003). Bullies and victims in the peer ecology: Four questions for psychological and school professionals. *School Psychology Review, 32,* 384–401.

Rogoff, B. (1997). Evaluating development in the process of participation: Theory, methods and practice building on each other. In E. Amsel & K. A. Renninger (Eds.), *Change and development: Issues in change, method, and application* (pp. 265–285). Mahwah, NJ: Erlbaum.

Rose, A. (2002). Co-rumination in the friendships of girls and boys. *Child Development, 73,* 1830–1843.

Rose-Krasnor, L. (1997). The nature of social competence: A theoretical review. *Social Development, 6,* 111–135.

Rose-Krasnor, L., Rubin, K. H., Booth, C. L., & Coplan, R. J. (1996). Maternal directiveness and child attachment security as predictors of social competence in preschoolers. *International Journal of Behavioral Development, 19,* 309–325.

Ross, H. S. (1982). The establishment of social games amongst toddlers. *Developmental Psychology, 18,* 509–518.

Ross, H. S., Conant, C., Cheyne, J. A., & Alevizos, E. (1992). Relationships and alliances in the social interactions of kibbutz toddlers. *Social Development, 1,* 1–17.

Ross, H. S., & Lollis, S. P. (1989). A social relations analysis of toddler-peer relationships. *Child Development, 60,* 1082–1091.

Rotenberg, K., & Slitz, D. (1988). Children's restrictive disclosure to friends. *Merrill-Palmer Quarterly, 34,* 203–215.

Rothbart, M. K., Derryberry, D., & Hershey, K. (2000). Stability of temperament in childhood: Laboratory infant assessment to parent report at 7 years. In V. J. Molfese & D. L. Molfese (Eds.), *Temperament and personality development across the life span* (pp. 85–119). Mahwah, NJ: Erlbaum.

Rothbart, M. K., Ellis, L., & Posner, M. I. (2004). Temperament and self-regulation. In R. F. Baumeister & K. D. Vohs (Eds.), *Handbook of self-regulation: Research, theory, and applications* (pp. 357–370). New York: Guilford Press.

Rowe, D. C. (1995). *The limits of family influence: Genes, experience, and behavior.* New York: Guilford Press.

Roy, R., & Benenson, J. F. (2002). Sex and contextual effects on children's use of interference competition. *Developmental Psychology, 38,* 306–312.

Rubin, K. H. (1983). Recent perspectives on sociometric status in childhood: Some introductory remarks. *Child Development, 54,* 1383–1385.

Rubin, K. H. (2001). *The Play Observation Scale (POS).* University of Maryland: Author.

Rubin, K. H. (2003). *The friendship factor: Helping our children navigate their social world—And why it matters for their success and happiness.* New York: Viking Penguin.

Rubin, K. H., Bukowski, W., & Parker, J. G. (1998). Peer interactions, relationships, and groups. In W. Damon (Editor-in-Chief) & N. Eisenberg (Vol. Ed.), *Handbook of child psychology: Vol. 3. Social, emotional, and personality development* (5th ed., pp. 619–700). New York: Wiley.

Rubin, K. H., & Burgess, K. (2002). Parents of aggressive and withdrawn children. In M. Bornstein (Ed.), *Handbook of Parenting* (2nd ed., Vol. 1, 383–418). Hillsdale, NJ: Erlbaum.

Rubin, K. H., Burgess, K. B., Dwyer, K. D., & Hastings, P. (2003). Predicting preschoolers' externalizing behaviors from toddler temperament, conflict, and maternal negativity. *Developmental Psychology, 39,* 164–176.

Rubin, K. H., Burgess, K. B., & Hastings, P. D. (2002). Stability and social-behavioral consequences of toddlers' inhibited temperament and parenting. *Child Development, 73,* 483–495.

Rubin, K. H., Burgess, K. B., Kennedy, A. E., & Stewart, S. (2003). Social withdrawal in childhood. In E. Mash & R. Barkley (Eds.), *Child psychopathology* (2nd ed., pp. 372–406). New York: Guilford Press.

Rubin, K. H., Cheah, C. S. L., & Fox, N. A. (2001). Emotion regulation, parenting, and the display of social reticence in preschoolers. *Early Education and Development, 12,* 97–115.

Rubin, K. H., Chen, X., & Hymel, S. (1993). Socioemotional characteristics of withdrawn and aggressive children. *Merrill-Palmer Quarterly, 39,* 518–534.

Rubin, K. H., Chen, X., McDougall, P., Bowker, A., & McKinnon, J. (1995). The Waterloo longitudinal project: Predicting internalizing and externalizing problems in adolescence. *Development and Psychopathology, 7,* 751–764.

Rubin, K. H., & Chung, O. B. (Eds.). (in press). *Parental beliefs, parenting, and child development in cross-cultural perspective.* London: Psychology Press.

Rubin, K. H., Coplan, R. J., Fox, N. A., & Calkins, S. (1995). Emotionality, emotion regulation, and preschoolers' social adaptation. *Development and Psychopathology, 7,* 49–62.

Rubin, K. H., Daniels-Beirness, T., & Bream, L. (1984). Social isolation and social problem solving: A longitudinal study. *Journal of Consulting and Clinical Psychology, 52,* 17–25.

Rubin, K. H., Dwyer, K. M., Booth, C. L., Kim, A. H., Burgess, K. B., & Rose-Krasnor, L. (2004). Attachment, friendship, and psychosocial functioning in early adolescence. *Journal of Early Adolescence, 24,* 326–356.

Rubin, K. H., Fein, G., & Vandenberg, B. (1983). Play. In P. H. Mussen (Series Ed.) & E. M. Hetherington (Vol. Ed.), *Handbook of child psychology: Vol. 4. Socialization, personality and social development* (4th ed., pp. 693–774). New York: Wiley.

Rubin, K. H., Hastings, P., Chen, X., Stewart, S., & McNichol, K. (1998). Intrapersonal and maternal correlates of aggression, conflict, and externalizing problems in toddlers. *Child Development, 69,* 1614–1629.

Rubin, K. H., Hemphill, S., Chen, X., Hastings, P., Sanson, A., Lo Coco, A., et al. (in press). Parenting beliefs and behaviors: Initial findings from the International Consortium for the Study of Social and Emotional Development (ICSSED). In K. H. Rubin & O. B. Chung (Eds.), *Parental beliefs, parenting, and child development in cross-cultural perspective.* London: Psychology Press.

Rubin, K. H., & Krasnor, L. R. (1986). Social-cognitive and social behavioral perspectives on problem solving. In M. Perlmutter (Ed.), *Minnesota Symposia on Child Psychology: Vol. 18. Cognitive perspectives on children's social and behavioral development* (pp. 1–68). Hillsdale, NJ: Erlbaum.

Rubin, K. H., Lynch, D., Coplan, R., Rose-Krasnor, L., & Booth, C. L. (1994). "Birds of a feather . . .": Behavioral concordances and preferential personal attraction in children. *Child Development, 65,* 1778–1785.

Rubin, K. H., & Mills, R. S. L. (1988). The many faces of social isolation in childhood. *Journal of Consulting and Clinical Psychology, 6,* 916–924.

Rubin, K. H., Mills, R. S. L., & Rose-Krasnor, L. (1989). Maternal beliefs and children's social competence. In B. Schneider, G. Attili, J. Nadel, & R. Weissberg (Eds.), *Social competence in devel-*

opmental perspective (pp. 313–331). Dordrecht, The Netherlands: Kluwer Press.

Rubin, K. H., & Rose-Krasnor, L. (1992). Interpersonal problem solving. In V. B. Van Hasselt & M. Hersen (Eds.), *Handbook of social development* (pp. 283–323). New York: Plenum Press.

Rubin, K. H., Rose-Krasnor, L., Bigras, M., Mills, R. S. L., & Booth, C. (1996). La prediction du comportement parental: Les influences du contexte, des facteurs psychosociaux et des croyances de parents [The prediction of parental behavior: Contextual, psychosocial and cognitive influences]. In G. M. Tarabulsy & R. Tessier (Eds.), *La Développement Emotionnel et Social De l'Enfant* (pp. 11–32). Sainte Foy, Québec, Canada: Presses de l'Universiteé du Québec.

Rubin, K. H., Watson, K., & Jambor, T. (1978). Free play behaviors in pre-school and kindergarten children. *Child Development, 49,* 534–536.

Rubin, K. H., Wojslawowicz, J. C., Burgess, K. B., Booth-LaForce, C., & Rose-Krasnor, L. (in press). The best friendships of shy/withdrawn children: Prevalence, stability, and relationship quality. *Journal of Abnormal Child Psychology.*

Russell, A., & Finnie, V. (1990). Preschool social status and maternal instructions to assist group entry. *Developmental Psychology, 26,* 603–611.

Russell, A., Hart, C. H., Robinson, C. C., & Olsen, S. F. (2003). Children's sociable and aggressive behavior with peers: A comparison of the U.S. and Australia, and contributions of temperament and parenting styles. *International Journal of Behavioral Development, 27,* 74–86.

Ryan, A. M. (2001). The peer group as a context for the development of young adolescent motivation and achievement. *Child Development, 72,* 1135–1150.

Sage, N. A., & Kindermann, T. A. (1999). Peer networks, behavior contingencies, and children's engagement in the classroom. *Merrill-Palmer Quarterly, 45,* 143–171.

Salisch, M. von (2000). The emotional side of sharing, emotional support, and conflict negotiation between siblings and between friends. In R. Mills & S. Duck (Eds.), *Developmental psychology of personal relationships* (pp. 49-–70). Chichester, England: Wiley.

Salmivalli, C., Huttunen, A., & Lagerspetz, K. (1997). Peer networks and bullying in schools. *Scandinavian Journal of Psychology, 38,* 305–312.

Salmivalli, C., & Voeten, M. (2004). Connections between attitudes, group norms, and behaviour in bullying situations. *International Journal of Behavioral Development, 28,* 246–258.

Sameroff, A. J., & MacKenzie, M. J. (2003). Research strategies for capturing transactional models of development: The limits of the possible. *Development and Psychopathology, 15,* 613–640.

Sandstrom, M. J., Cillessen, A. H. N., & Eisenhower, A. (2003). Children's appraisal of peer rejection experiences: Impact on social and emotional adjustment. *Social Development, 12,* 530–550.

Sandstrom, M. J., & Coie, J. D. (1999). A developmental perspective on peer rejection: Mechanisms of stability and change. *Child Development, 70,* 955–966.

Sandstrom, M., & Cramer, P. (2003). Girls' use of defense mechanisms following peer rejection. *Journal of Personality, 71,* 605–627.

Sanson, A., Hemphill, S. A., & Smart, D. (2004). Connections between temperament and social development: A review. *Social Development, 13,* 142–170.

Sawyer, R. K. (1997). *Pretend play as improvisation: Conversation in the preschool classroom.* Mahwah, NJ: Erlbaum.

Schafer, M., Werner, N. E., & Crick, N. R. (2002). A comparison of two approaches to the study of negative peer treatment: General victimization and bully/victim problems among German schoolchildren. *British Journal of Developmental Psychology, 20,* 281–306.

Schmidt, M. E., Demulder, E. K., & Denham, S. (2002). Kindergarten social-emotional competence: Developmental predictors and psychosocial implications. *Early Child Development and Care, 172,* 451–462.

Schneider, B. H. (1999). A multimethod exploration of the friendships of children considered socially withdrawn by their school peers. *Journal of Abnormal Child Psychology, 27,* 115–123.

Schneider, B. H., Atkinson, L., & Tardif, C. (2001). Child-parent attachment and children's peer relations: A quantitative review. *Developmental Psychology, 37*(1), 86–100.

Schneider, B. H., Attili, G., Vermigli, P., & Younger, A. (1997). A comparison of middle class English-Canadian and Italian mothers' beliefs about children's peer-directed aggression and social withdrawal. *International Journal of Behavioral Development, 21,* 133–154.

Schwartz, D. (2000). Subtypes of victims and aggressors in children's peer groups. *Journal of Abnormal Child Psychology, 28*(2), 181–192.

Schwartz, D., Dodge, K. A., Pettit, G. S., & Bates, J. E. (2000). Friendship as a moderating factor in the pathway between early harsh home environment and later victimization in the peer group. *Developmental Psychology, 36*(5), 646–662.

Schwartz, D., Farver, J. M., Chang, L., & Lee-Shin, Y. (2002). Victimization in South Korean children's peer groups. *Journal of Abnormal Child Psychology, 30,* 113–125.

Sebanc, A. M. (2003). The friendship features of preschool children: Links with prosocial behavior and aggression. *Social Development, 12,* 249–268.

Seiffge-Krenke, I. (2003). Testing theories of romantic development from adolescence to young adulthood: Evidence of a developmental sequence. *International Journal of Behavioral Development, 27,* 519–531.

Shatz, M., & Gelman, R. (1973). The development of communication skills: Modifications in the speech of young children as a function of the listener. *Monographs of the Society for Research in Child Development, 38*(38).

Shaw, D., Owens, E. B., Vondra, J. I., Keenan, K., & Winslow, E. B. (1996). Early risk factors and pathways in the development of early disruptive behavior problems. *Development and Psychopathology, 8,* 679–699.

Sherif, M., Harvey, O. J., White, B. J., Hood, W. R., & Sherif, C. (1961). *Inter-group conflict and cooperation: The robbers cave experiment.* Norman: University of Oklahoma Press.

Shrum, W., & Cheek, N. H. (1987). Social structure during the school years: Onset of the degrouping process. *American Sociological Review, 52,* 218–223.

Shulman, S., & Laursen, B. (2002). Adolescent perceptions of conflict in interdependent and disengaged friendships. *Journal of Research on Adolescence, 12,* 353–372.

Silbereisen, R. K. (2000). German unification and adolescents' developmental timetables: Continuities and discontinuities. In L. A. Crockett & R. K. Silbereisen (Eds.), *Negotiating adolescence in times of social change* (pp. 104–122). Cambridge, MA: Cambridge University Press.

Simons, K. J., Paternite, C. E., & Shore, C. (2001). Patterns of parent/adolescent attachment and aggression in young adolescents. *Journal of Early Adolescence, 21,* 182–203.

Simpkins, S. D., & Parke, R. D. (2002). Do friends and nonfriends behave differently? A social relations analysis of children's behavior. *Merrill-Palmer Quarterly, 48,* 263–283.

Slaughter, V., Dennis, M. J., & Pritchard, M. (2002). Theory of mind and peer acceptance in preschool children. *British Journal of Developmental Psychology, 20*(4), 545–564.

Slee, P. T., & Rigby, K. (Eds.). (1998). *Children's peer relations.* New York: Routledge.

Smollar, J., & Youniss, J. (1982). Social development through friendship. In K. H. Rubin & H. S. Ross (Eds.), *Peer relationships and social skills in childhood* (pp. 277–298). New York: Springer-Verlag.

Snyder, J., Brooker, M., Patrick, M. R., Snyder, A., Schrepferman, L., & Stoolmiller, M. (2003). Observed peer victimization during early elementary school: Continuity, growth, and relation to risk for child antisocial and depressive behavior. *Child Development, 74,* 1881–1898.

Spangler, G., & Schieche, M. (1998). Emotional and adrenocortical responses of infants to the strange situation: The differential function of emotional expression. *International Journal of Behavioral Development, 22,* 681–706.

Spinrad, T. L., Eisenberg, N., Harris, E., Fabes, R. A., Kupanoff, K., Ringwald, S., et al. (2004). The relation of children's everyday nonsocial peer play behavior to their emotionality, regulation, and social functioning. *Developmental Psychology, 40,* 67–80.

Sroufe, L. A. (1983). Infant-caregiver attachment and patterns of adaptation in preschool: The roots of maladaptation. In M. Perlmutter (Ed.), *Minnesota Symposia on Child Psychology* (Vol. 16, pp. 41–83). Hillsdale, NJ: Erlbaum.

Sroufe, L. A., & Rutter, M. (1984). The domain of developmental psychopathology. *Child Development, 55,* 17–29.

Stevenson-Hinde, J., & Marshall, P. J. (1999). Behavioral inhibition, heart period, and respiratory sinus arrhythmia: An attachment perspective. *Child Development, 70,* 805–816.

Stewart, S. L., & Rubin, K. H. (1995). The social problem solving skills of anxious-withdrawn children. *Development and Psychopathology, 7,* 323–336.

Stocker, C., & Dunn, J. (1990). Sibling relationships in childhood: Links with friendships and peer relationships. *British Journal of Developmental Psychology, 8,* 227–244.

Stormshak, E. A., Bierman, K. L., Bruschi, C., Dodge, K. A., Coie, J. D., & the Conduct Preventions Research Group. (1999, January/February). The relation between behavior problems and peer preference in different classroom contexts. *Child Development, 70*(1), 169–182.

Strassberg, Z. (1995). Social information processing in compliance situations by mothers of behavior-problem boys. *Child Development, 66*(2), 376–389.

Strayer, F. F., & Strayer, J. (1976). An ethological analysis of social agonism and dominance relations among preschool children. *Child Development, 47,* 980–989.

Strough, J., Swenson, L. M., & Cheng, S. (2001). Friendship, gender and preadolescents' representation of peer collaboration. *Merrill-Palmer Quarterly, 47,* 475–499.

Sullivan, H. S. (1953). *The interpersonal theory of psychiatry.* New York: Norton.

Suttles, G. D. (1970). Friendship as a social institution. In G. McCall, M. McCall, N. Denzin, G. Suttles, & S. Kurth (Eds.), *Social relationships* (pp. 95–135). Chicago: Aldine.

Thomas, A., & Chess, S. (1977). *Temperament and development.* New York: Brunner/Mazel.

Tinbergen, N. (1951). *The study of instinct.* London: Oxford University Press.

Tomada, G., & Schneider, B. H. (1997). Relational aggression, gender, and peer acceptance: Invariance across culture, stability over time, and concordance among informants. *Developmental Psychology, 33,* 601–609.

Tremblay, R. E., Mâsse, L. C., Vitaro, F., & Dobkin, P. L. (1995). The impact of friends' deviant behavior on early onset of delinquency: Longitudinal data from 6 to 13 years of age. *Development and Psychopathology, 7,* 649–668.

Troy, M., & Sroufe, L. A. (1987). Victimization among preschoolers: Role of attachment relationship history. *Journal of the American Academy of Child and Adolescent Psychiatry, 26,* 166–172.

Tudge, J. (1992). Processes and consequences of peer collaborations: A Vygotskian analysis. *Child Development, 63,* 1364–1379.

Urberg, K. A., Degirmencioglu, S. M., & Pilgrim, C. (1997). Close friend and group influence on adolescent cigarette smoking and alcohol use. *Developmental Psychology, 33,* 834–844.

Vandell, D. L., & Mueller, E. (1980). Peer play and friendships during the first 2 years. In H. Foot, A. Chapman, & J. Smith (Eds.), *Friendship and social relations in children* (pp. 181–208). New York: Wiley.

van den Oord, E. J. C., Rispens, J., Goudena, P. P., & Vermande, M. (2000). Some developmental implications of structural aspects of preschoolers' relations with classmates. *Journal of Applied Developmental Psychology, 21,* 619–639.

Vaughn, B. E. (1999). Power is knowledge (and vice versa): A commentary on "On winning some and losing some: A social relations approach to social dominance in toddlers." *Merrill-Palmer Quarterly, 45,* 215–225.

Vaughn, B. E. (2001). Dyadic analyses of friendship in a sample of preschool children attending Head Start: Correspondence between measures. *Child Development, 72,* 862–878.

Vaughn, B. E., Vollenweider, M., Bost, K. K., Azria-Evans, M. R., & Snider, J. B. (2003). Negative interactions and social competence for preschool children in two samples: Reconsidering the interpretation of aggressive behavior for young children. *Merrill-Palmer Quarterly, 49,* 245–278.

Vermande, M., van den Oord, E. J. C. G., Rispens, J., & Goudena, P. P. (2000). Structural characteristics of aggressor-victim relationships in school classes of 4- to 5-year-olds. *Aggressive Behavior, 26,* 11–31.

Vernberg, E. M., Jacobs, A. K., & Hershberger, S. L. (1999). Peer victimization and attitudes about violence during early adolescence. *Journal of Clinical Child Psychology, 28*(3), 386–395.

Vitaro, F., Brendgen, M., & Tremblay, R. E. (2000). Influence of deviant friends on delinquency: Searching for moderator variables. *Journal of Abnormal Child Psychology, 28*(4), 313–325.

Vitaro, F., Brendgen, M., & Tremblay, R. E. (2002). Reactively and proactively aggressive children: Antecedent and subsequent characteristics. *Journal of Child Psychology and Psychiatry and Allied Disciplines, 43,* 495–506.

Vygotsky, L. S. (1978). *Mind in society: The development of higher psychological processes.* Cambridge, MA: Harvard University Press.

Walden, T., Lemerise, E., & Smith, M. C. (1999). Friendship and popularity in preschool classrooms. *Early Education and Development, 10,* 351–371.

Watson, A. C., Nixon, C. L., Wilson, A., & Capage, L. (1999). Social interaction skills and theory of mind in young children. *Developmental Psychology, 35,* 386–391.

Way, N., & Chen, L. (2000). The characteristics, quality, and correlates of friendship among African American, Latino, and Asian American adolescents. *Journal of Adolescent Research, 15,* 274–301.

Wentzel, K. R. (2003). Sociometric status and adjustment in middle school: A longitudinal study. *Journal of Early Adolescence, 23,* 5–28.

Wentzel, K. R., & Asher, S. R. (1995). The academic lives of neglected, rejected, popular, and controversial children. *Child Development, 66,* 754–763.

Wentzel, K. R., McNamara-Barry, C., & Caldwell, K. A. (2004). Friendships in middle school: Influences on motivation and school adjustment. *Journal of Educational Psychology, 96*(2), 195–203.

White, K. J., & Kistner, J. (1992). The influence of teacher feedback on young children's peer preferences and perceptions. *Developmental Psychology, 28,* 933–940.

Wichmann, C., Coplan, R. J., & Daniels, T. (2004). The social cognitions of socially withdrawn children. *Social Development, 13,* 377–392.

Wiseman, R. (2002). *Queen bees and wannabes: Helping your daughter survive cliques, gossip, boyfriends, and other realities of adolescence.* New York: Crown.

Wojslawowicz, J. C., Rubin, K. H., Burgess, K. B., Booth-LaForce, C., & Rose-Krasnor, L. R. (in press). Behavioral characteristics associated with stable and fluid best friendship patterns in middle childhood. *Merrill-Palmer Quarterly.*

Wright, J. C., Giammarino, M., & Parad, H. (1986). Social status in small groups: Individual group similarity and the social "misfit." *Journal of Personality and Social Psychology, 50,* 523–536.

Xie, H., Cairns, B. D., & Cairns, R. B. (2001). Predicting teen motherhood and teen fatherhood: Individual characteristics and peer affiliations. *Social Development, 10,* 488–511.

Xie, H., Cairns, R. B., & Cairns, B. D. (1999). Social networks and configurations in inner-city schools: Aggression, popularity, and implications for students with EBD. *Journal of Emotional and Behavioral Disorders, 7,* 147–155.

Youngblade, L., & Belsky, J. (1992). Parent-child antecedents of 5-year-olds' close friendships: A longitudinal analysis. *Developmental Psychology, 28,* 107–121.

Youngblade, L., Park, K., & Belsky, J. (1993). Measurement of young children's close friendship: A comparison of two independent assessment systems and their associations with attachment security. *International Journal of Behavioral Development, 16,* 563–587.

Zarbatany, L., Hartmann, D., & Rankin, D. (1990). The psychological functions of preadolescent peer activities. *Child Development, 61,* 1067–1080.

Zarbatany, L., McDougall, P., & Hymel, S. (2000). Gender-differentiated experience in the peer culture: Links to intimacy in preadolescence. *Social Development, 9,* 62–79.

Zarbatany, L., Van Brunschot, M., Meadows, K., & Pepper, S. (1996). Effects of friendship and gender on peer group entry. *Child Development, 67,* 2287–2300.

Zakriski, A., & Coie, J. (1996). A comparison of aggressive-rejected and nonaggressive rejected children's interpretations of self-directed and other-directed rejection. *Child Development, 67,* 1048–1070.

Zeller, M., Vannatta, K., Schafer, J., & Noll, R. (2003). Behavioral reputation: A cross-age perspective. *Developmental Psychology, 39,* 129–139.

Zhou, Q., Eisenberg, N., Wang, Y., & Reiser, M. (2004). Chinese children's effortful control and dispositional anger/frustration: Relations to parenting styles and children's social functioning. *Developmental Psychology, 40,* 352–366.

CHAPTER 11

Prosocial Development

NANCY EISENBERG, RICHARD A. FABES, and TRACY L. SPINRAD

Prosocial behavior—voluntary behavior intended to benefit another—is of obvious importance to the quality of interactions between individuals and among groups. However, scientists did not devote much attention to prosocial development prior to 1970, perhaps because the consequences of aggression, criminality, and immorality had greater salience for society.

Prosocial behaviors may be performed for a host of reasons including egoistic, other-oriented, or practical concerns (Boxer, Tisak, & Goldstein, 2004; Eisenberg, 1986). Of particular importance is the subgroup of

Writing of this chapter was supported by a grant from the National Institute of Mental Health to Nancy Eisenberg and Tracy Spinrad and by grants from the National Science Foundation and the National Institute of Child Health and Human Development to Richard A. Fabes. Appreciation also is expressed to Carolyn Zahn-Waxler for comments on earlier drafts of this manuscript.

prosocial behaviors labeled *altruism.* A common definition of altruism is "intrinsically motivated voluntary behavior intended to benefit another"—acts motivated by concern for others or by internalized values, goals, and self-rewards rather than by the expectation of concrete or social rewards or the avoidance of punishment (Eisenberg & Mussen, 1989). However, because it usually is impossible to differentiate between altruistically motivated actions and actions motivated by less noble concerns, it is necessary to focus on the broader domain of prosocial behaviors.

Emotion plays a particularly important role in the development of prosocial values, motives, and behaviors. Especially relevant are empathy-related emotions. Definitions of *empathy* vary; we define it as an affective response that stems from the apprehension or comprehension of another's emotional state or condition, and which is identical or very similar to what the other person is feeling or would be expected to feel.

It is necessary to differentiate empathy from related vicarious emotional responses, particularly sympathy and personal distress. *Sympathy* is an affective response that frequently stems from empathy, but can derive directly from perspective taking or other cognitive processing, including retrieval of information from memory. It consists of feeling sorrow or concern for the distressed or needy other (rather than feeling the same emotion as the other person is experiencing or is expected to experience). *Personal distress* also frequently stems from exposure to another's state or condition; however, it is a self-focused, aversive emotional reaction to the vicarious experiencing of another's emotion (e.g., discomfort, anxiety; see Batson, 1991; Eisenberg, Shea, Carlo, & Knight, 1991). As discussed later, empathy and sympathy have been strongly implicated in prosocial development and action. Thus, these vicarious emotional reactions are discussed to some degree throughout the chapter.

In the initial sections of this chapter, we briefly discuss philosophical perspectives on prosocial development, as well as several grand psychological theories that have influenced the field. Then the empirical literature related to prosocial responding in children is reviewed. Because there have been few recent studies on the role of situational factors such as cost and benefits, situational skills, or mood inductions on prosocial behavior, these topics are not reviewed (see Eisenberg & Fabes, 1998, for a review). In the final

sections of the chapter, a model for integrating the factors believed to relate to prosocial responding is presented briefly, and gaps in the field and future directions are discussed.

In this chapter, we review many of the major topics in the literature on prosocial development. Due to space constraints, we have sometimes built on previously published reviews. We generally have emphasized topics of central importance to prosocial development and issues that have emerged in the past decade or two. Further, we have confined our coverage to a somewhat narrow definition of prosocial responding. For example, the literature on cooperation, the personality trait of agreeableness, or the allocation of rewards generally is not emphasized, although some investigators of prosocial behavior included cooperation as well as other types of prosocial behavior in their index of prosociality (in these cases, we sometimes have included the study with other citations, but often refer to it in listings under "also see . . ."). Again due to space limitations, we often cite the more recent studies when there are numerous reports pertaining to a given issue. Interested readers can refer to the earlier version of this chapter in the fifth edition of this *Handbook* (1998) to obtain additional citations, especially references prior to 1990.

PHILOSOPHICAL ROOTS OF PROSOCIAL BEHAVIOR

Philosophical concepts of prosocial behavior and sympathy often have their roots in religious doctrine. The commandment "Thou shalt love thy neighbor as thyself" is a basic tenet in Judaism and Christianity. Similarly, the parable of the Good Samaritan, who pitied and helped an injured man (Luke 10:29–37), often is cited as an example for Christians. In Buddhism, the *via positiva* outlines the virtues necessary to reach *Nirvana* (ultimate happiness), including *dana* (giving), *metta* (kindness), *mudita* (sympathetic joy), *and karuna* (compassion).

Given the influence of religion in philosophy, it is not surprising that philosophers have discussed the origins of prosocial and moral behaviors for centuries. Of particular relevance, philosophers have debated whether any human action is truly unselfish and, relatedly, the doctrine of ethical egoism (i.e., whether it is unreasonable to behave in a manner contrary to one's own self-interest). According to Thomas Hobbes (1651/1962), a vocal advocate of egoism and self-love, selfishness might produce helping, but the motivation for such prosocial action would primarily be to relieve the helper's own distress. He also believed that the only motivation for cooperative action lay in the fear of some outside agent.

Later philosophers began to refute the doctrine of ethical egoism. Rousseau (1773/1962) believed that human nature was basically good and that humans have an innate sensitivity toward others. In his view, if individuals were able to develop this natural state of nobility and sensitivity, a strong sense of moral obligation to others and concern for the common good would develop. He believed society corrupts this innate moral nature.

Kant (1785/1956) also refuted the doctrine of ethical egoism and argued that if an action is one's duty, that is reason enough to do it, independent of one's own interests. According to Kant, prosocial and moral behavior and values involve one's will and self-control, and stem from universal, impartial principles that are totally detached from emotion.

Nagel (1970) differentiated between pure rational altruism and behavior motivated by sympathy, love, or other emotions. In his view, the involvement of affect in the helping process tainted its purity. In contrast, David Hume (1748/1975) argued that moral emotions such as sympathy, benevolence, and concern for humanity are fundamental incentives of human action and that prosocial behaviors often are based on these incentives. Susceptibility to sympathy and empathy was viewed as an innate human propensity. Similarly, sympathy and related affective responses were core elements of A. Smith's (1759/1982) moral and social system. Smith believed that sympathy was an innate endowment, instigated by the perception of others' conditions and the desire to see them happy for purely altruistic reasons. For Smith, sympathy was not solely a primitive awareness of others' suffering; it was a complex capacity influenced by awareness of aspects of the situation or the person involved.

Lawrence Blum (1980) has been particularly vocal in refuting some of Kant's ideas about the role of emotion in morality. He pointed out that rational processes do not always produce moral action and that the sense of duty (viewed by Kant as rational) is no more immune to the distorting and weakening effects of personal feelings than is sympathy for another. Blum further suggested that because emotions such as sympathy and empathy promote perspective taking and understanding of others, they sometimes produce rationality and may, in addition, induce more and higher quality prosocial behavior than does rationality. Similarly, Slote (2001, 2004) argued that caring is a true virtue that is involved in moral judgment and that empathy is essential to the development of morally based caring about others. Relatedly, current writings on "altruistic (or compassionate) love" (which correlates with sympathy; L.G. Underwood, 2001) and *agape* (altruistic love universalized to all humanity; Post, 2001) in theology and philosophy are relevant to the notions of selfless love and to extending caring to people outside one's ingroup.

In summary, philosophers have viewed people as primarily egoistic, primarily noble and generous, or somewhere in between. Philosophical debate about the nature and existence of altruism is alive and well in contemporary psychology, particularly in social (e.g., Batson & Powell, 2003) and evolutionary (Konner, 2002) psychology. However, it is often difficult to discriminate people's motives and conceptions of their prosocial behavior. Thus, philosophical concerns are not highly salient in developmental work and are reflected primarily in work on moral judgment influenced by cognitive developmental theory.

PSYCHOLOGICAL THEORIES

As might be expected, the grand theories that have had considerable influence on developmental psychology have affected thinking about prosocial development, particularly in the past. Thus, pertinent ideas in psychoanalytic theory, behaviorism and social learning theory, and cognitive developmental theory are discussed briefly. In addition, recent work on prosocial behavior has been influenced by minitheories such as Hoffman's theoretical contributions to understanding empathy (1982, 2000) and socialization (1970, 1983) and Grusec's (e.g., Grusec & Goodnow, 1994) and Staub's (1979, 1992, 2003) thinking about socialization. Some of these conceptual frameworks are referred to briefly later in this chapter.

Psychoanalytic Theory

In Freud's psychoanalytic theory, children are born with innate, irrational sexual and aggressive impulses directed toward self-gratification (the id). They develop a conscience (superego) at about age 4 to 6 years as a means of resolving the conflict between their own hostile and sexual impulses and their fears of parental hostility or the loss of parental love. The superego is the outcome of the process of identification, by which children internalize their same-sex parents' values and introject these values. Once children develop a superego, they may behave prosocially to avoid the guilt inflicted by the conscience for not doing so or based on the internalization of values consistent with prosocial behavior (e.g., Freud, 1933/1968). In many versions of psychoanalytic theory, guilt, self-destructive tendencies, and sexual strivings underlie altruism (Fenichel, 1945; Glover, 1968). Prosocial actions often are defense mechanisms used by the ego (the rational part of personality) to deal with the irrational demands of the superego.

However, Freud and other psychoanalysts sometimes have acknowledged more positive roots of altruism. Freud (1930) asserted, "Individual development seems to us a product of the interplay of two trends, the striving for happiness, generally called 'egoistic,' and the impulse toward merging with others in the community, which we call 'altruistic'" (1930, p. 134). Other theorists such as Ekstein (1978) have built on Freud's emphasis on the importance of the early mother-child relationship for the development of empathy, identification, and internalization.

Perhaps the greatest contribution of psychoanalytic work to theory on prosocial responding is the construct of identification. Social learning theorists in the 1960s and 1970s adapted this construct to refer to children's internalization of parents' norms, values, and standards as a consequence of a positive parent-child relationship (e.g., Hoffman, 1970). This theoretical perspective had a significant impact on the early work on the socialization of altruism.

Behaviorism and Social Learning Theory

Early behaviorists posited that children learn primarily through mechanisms such as conditioning. This perspective is reflected in some of the relatively early work on the role of reinforcement and punishment in promoting prosocial behavior (e.g., Hartmann et al., 1976) and in work concerning the development of empathy through conditioning (Aronfreed, 1970).

Social learning theorists allowed internal cognitive processes to play a greater role. For example, contingencies need not actually occur; people can vicariously learn the likely consequences of a behavior through observation and verbal behavior. Imitation is viewed as a critical process in the socialization of moral behavior and standards (Bandura, 1986).

In current cognitive social learning theory, the interplay of cognition and environmental influences in moral development is complex. According to Bandura (1986; also see Hoffman, 2000), moral rules or standards of behavior are fashioned from information from a variety of sources such as intuition, others' evaluative social reactions, and models. Based on experience, people learn what factors are morally relevant and how much value to attach to each one. Socializers provide information about behavioral alternatives, expectations, and possible contingencies for different courses of action; model moral behaviors; reinforce and punish children for various actions; and influence the development of self-evaluative reactions (e.g., guilt). Moreover, thought, behavior, and environmental events all interact and influence one another, and the individual's attentional and regulatory processes play a role in the learning of moral behavior. Moral and prosocial functioning are thought to be governed by self-reactive responses (e.g., self processes such as self-sanctions, personal agency) and other self-regulatory processes rather than by dispassionate abstract reasoning (Bandura, 2002). Additionally, the regulation of affect has an important influence on prosocial behavior. Support for this argument has been found: Perceived self-efficacy in the regulation of positive affect was related to perceptions of empathic efficacy, which in turn were related to prosocial behavior (Bandura, Caprara, Barbaranelli, Gerbino, & Pastorelli, 2003). Thus, perceived self-efficacy to manage basic affective states plays a pivotal role in the causal processes determining the likelihood of empathic responding and prosocial behavior.

Cognitive Developmental Theory

The cognitive developmental perspective on morality, as represented by the work of Piaget (e.g., 1932/1965) and Kohlberg (e.g., 1969, 1984), concerns primarily the development of moral reasoning and other social cognitive processes rather than moral behavior. Kohlberg described moral development as an invariant, universal, and hierarchical sequence of stages progressing as a function of sociocognitive development (e.g., perspective taking). Kohlberg emphasized the contributions of cognition, particularly perspective taking, to morality and minimized (but did not fully neglect) the contributions of emotion and socialization (Kohlberg, 1969). Moreover, because of Piaget's and Kohlberg's assumption that young children have limited perspective-taking abilities, investigators influenced by cognitive developmental work assumed for years that other-oriented prosocial behavior was not likely to emerge until the early school years.

The cognitive developmental perspective is discussed by Turiel (Chapter 13, this *Handbook,* this volume). Its primary relevance for this chapter is that Kohlberg's theory influenced Eisenberg's (e.g., Eisenberg, 1986) work on prosocial moral reasoning. However, although Eisenberg views sociocognitive development as playing an important role in the development of prosocial moral reasoning, she does not view all stages of prosocial reasoning (especially the higher ones) as universal or as involving the hierarchical integration of lower stages. Rather, environmental and emotional factors are believed to play a considerable role in the development and use of prosocial moral reasoning. Thus, Eisenberg's conception of moral reasoning differs considerably from the traditional cognitive developmental perspective.

Current Conceptual Emphases: Positive Psychology and Positive Youth Development

Positive psychology and positive youth psychology are not fully developed theories, but perspectives that recently have influenced the study of prosocial behavior. Although prosocial behavior was a popular topic of study in the 1970s and early 1980s, interest declined in the late 1980s and the 1990s. Since the late 1990s, there has been a resurgence of interest in the positive aspects of human development, spurred by the positive psychology movement. This movement is an effort to counteract the focus on negative aspects of psychological functioning (e.g., problems with psychological adjustment) and highlight human strengths. As summarized by Seligman and Csikszentmihalyi (2000), the field of positive psychology concerns subjective experiences (e.g., well-being, optimism), positive personal traits (e.g., the capacity for love, interpersonal skills, forgiveness, wisdom), and "civic virtues and the institutions that move individuals toward better citizenship: responsibility, nurturance, altruism, civility, moderation, tolerance, and work ethnic" (p. 1). Similarly, the positive youth development perspective is a strength-based conception of adolescence that highlights plasticity in development and the "poten-

tial for systematic change in behavior . . . as a consequence of mutually influential relationships between the developing person and his or her biology, psychological characteristics, family, community, culture, physicial and designed ecology, and historical niche" (Lerner et al., 2005, p. 13; also see Lerner, Dowling, & Anderson, 2003).

Although prosocial behavior has not been a primary topic of interest for those researchers most associated with the positive psychology movement, some psychologists (Aspinwall & Staudinger, 2003a; Eisenberg & Ota Wang, 2003) have argued that interpersonal and relational strengths such as sympathy, compassion, cooperation, tolerance, and altruism are important topics of investigation for those investigators concerned with positive psychological development. In fact, prosocial and empathic development are discussed in some books on positive psychology (e.g., Aspinwall & Staudinger, 2003b; Lopez & Snyder, 2003), and the positive psychology movement has stimulated renewed interest in prosocial behavior and sympathy by including the topic in various books and conferences. Similarly, caring is viewed as one of five components of positive youth development (along with competence, confidence, connection, and character); thus, some relevant research contains measures of sympathy or related constructs (e.g., Lerner et al., 2005).

Now that the conceptual roots of work on prosocial responding have been reviewed briefly, we turn to the review of the empirical literature. We first examine theory and empirical work on developmental trends in prosocial responding, followed by discussion of the potential origins of prosocial behavior (biological, cultural, and socialization). Next we consider the sociocognitive, empathy-related, dispositional, and situational correlates of prosocial behavior. In the final sections, age and sex differences in prosocial behavior are considered.

BIOLOGICAL DETERMINANTS OF PROSOCIAL BEHAVIOR

In examining the major theoretical and empirical approaches to understanding the determinants of prosocial behaviors, most efforts have been directed at identifying the situational, social, and individual factors that affect the degree to which prosocial behavior is learned and enhanced (see M.S. Clark, 1991; Eisenberg, 1986, for reviews and examples). Relatively little of the empirical work on prosocial behavior has focused on the genetic and neurohormonal substrates of such behavior. The lack of empirical work is somewhat surprising given the attention that genetic, evolutionary, and neurohormonal factors have received in the literature on antisocial, aggressive, and criminal behavior (see Ellis & Hoffman, 1990). As noted by Eisenberg, Fabes, and Miller (1990), some of the biological factors that affect antisocial behavior are also likely to account for variations in prosocial behavior and therefore warrant consideration in any major review of prosocial behavior and development.

Evolutionary Explanations

Prosocial actions such as helping and sharing have frequently been observed among nonhuman animals (e.g., E. O. Wilson, 1975, 1978). Various social insects (such as certain honeybees, ants, and wasps) frequently sacrifice their own lives while defending their hives or nests from intruders. Similarly, some birds give off a warning call that informs other birds of a predator's presence. The call, however, occasionally helps predators locate the call giver, thereby resulting in its capture and death.

Sharing and cooperation also have been observed among nonhuman animals (Trivers, 1971; Wilson, 1975), as have consoling behaviors and empathy among chimpanzees (Preston & de Waal, 2002). Van Lawick-Goodall (1968) reported that chimpanzees often hand over portions of their catch to other chimpanzees who beg for food. Similarly, certain wild African dogs that live in packs share the prey they catch with members of the pack who stay behind to guard the pups. Common to all these examples is that in some way one animal has improved the chances of one or more animals reaching some sort of goal (protection, feeding, care of young, etc.).

Explanations have been proposed for the prosocial actions of animals. Wilson (1975, 1978) and others (e.g., Barash, 1977) have advanced the notion of *kin selection,* which is a broadened view of natural selection. They argue that through self-sacrificing or cooperative actions, the prosocial animal increases the probability that its relatives, who share its genes, will survive and reproduce. Thus, even if the prosocial animal dies, its genes will be passed on to the next generation by its surviving relatives. The genes selected for by evolution contribute to their own perpetuation, regardless of the individual carrying the animal's genes.

The percentage of shared or common genes is hypothesized to be an important determinant of altruism dis-

played among species members—more altruism would be expected to be directed toward more closely related kin than toward distant kin or those who are unrelated (Hastings, Zahn-Waxler, & McShane, 2005). Thus, for kin selection to be effective (in an evolutionary sense), altruists must be able to distinguish between individuals who are their kin and those who are not. Rushton and associates (Rushton, Russell, & Well, 1984) proposed that that there is an innate ability to recognize someone who is genetically similar. Evidence from the study of a wide variety of species supports the conclusion that certain animals may be genetically programmed to identify their own kin (Alberts, 1976; Leon, 1983). Evidence for a similar genetic predisposition in humans is much less clear-cut (Fabes & Filsinger, 1988). There is, however, evidence that humans are more willing to assist others who are genetically related to themselves (Bar-Tal, Bar-Zohar, Greenberg, & Hermon, 1977) and that the degree of biological relatedness is positively associated with willingness to help (Cunningham, 1985/1986). In addition, the more valuable the helpful act is, the more likely it is to come from kin (Borgida, Conner, & Manteufel, 1992; Essock-Vitale & McGuire, 1985). People also are likely to seek out and assist others who are similar to themselves (Eisenberg, 1983; Rushton et al., 1984). Because individuals who share proximity and who are physically similar are likely to share more genes than dissimilar others, the predisposition to help others who are similar may enhance the survival of persons likely to share genes with the altruist.

In many species (including humans), prosocial behavior also is extended toward nonrelatives. Hall and DeVore (1965) described the tendency for baboons to form alliances and fight as a unit in aggressive encounters. Female bluebirds occasionally provide foster parenting to young birds deserted by their mothers (Hayes, Felton, & Cohen, 1985).

Trivers (1971, 1983) uses the term *reciprocal altruism* to explain instances of prosocial behavior that are directed to recipients so distantly related to the organism performing the altruistic act that kin selection can be ruled out. Trivers argues that under certain conditions natural selection favors these altruistic behaviors because in the long run they benefit the organism performing them. Cleaning symbiosis is a case in point. Both host and cleaner benefit from the relationship (e.g., the host is cleaned of parasites and the cleaner is fed and sometimes protected). There also apparently has been selection for the host to avoid eating one's cleaner (Trivers, 1971). These behaviors cannot be explained by kin selection because they are performed by members of one species for the benefit of members of another species.

Another evolutionary explanation of prosocial behavior is that of *group selection* (Wynne-Edwards, 1962). According to this view, altruism among group members may benefit the survival of the group. Thus, groups with altruistic members are less likely to become extinct than groups comprised of nonaltruistic members. This perspective, however, has not received strong support (Boorman & Leavitt, 1980). Group selection works very slowly and it would take an exceedingly long time for an entire group to become extinct. In the short run, selfish members would have a competitive edge over altruistic members (Krebs & Miller, 1985). Altruistic members would die out long before the group does. Therefore, the forces underlying group selection do not appear compatible with the evolution of a group with altruistic members.

In summary, evolutionary perspectives on prosocial behavior suggest that these behaviors result from evolutionary forces (Sober & Wilson, 1998). Prosocial behaviors may have been selected because they (a) increase individuals' survival to reproductive age, (b) increase the reproductive capacity of the individual, and (c) increase either or both of these tendencies in other members of the species that likely carry the same genes. Inherent in this argument is that evolutionary forces favoring altruistic behaviors often come into conflict with those forces that favor behaviors maximizing the survival of the individual. Out of this complex interplay of competing forces comes the potential to act prosocially and to account for individual differences in prosocial responding (Hofer, 1981).

Heritability of Prosocial Tendencies

Twin studies have been used to examine the genetic contribution to individual differences in prosocial responding. In these studies, if the correlation between scores on prosocial responding is higher for identical twins than for fraternal twins, the difference is attributed to genetic effects to the degree that common environmental sources are assumed to be roughly equal for the two types of twins.

In twin studies involving adults' self-reports of prosocial tendencies, researchers have found that genetic factors accounted for between 40% and 70% of the variance in twins' altruism, empathy, and nurturance (Hastings et al., in press). Most of the remaining variance was accounted for by idiosyncratic differences in the environments of the twins rather than by their shared environment (Rushton, Fulker, Neale, Nias, & Eysenck, 1986; also see Davis, Luce, & Kraus, 1994), although in one study of adults, the variance in prosocial behavior was linked primarily to shared and nonshared environment (Krueger, Hicks, & McGue, 2001). It is likely that the common shared variance decreases with age (Scarr & McCartney, 1983; Scourfield, John, Martin, & McGuffin, 2004).

W. Johnson and Krueger (2004) examined the heritability of middle-aged adults' personality traits that likely relate to prosocial qualities. Using twin data, they found that about 50% of the variance in extraversion and neuroticism was explained by genetic influences; however, this was not the case for agreeableness, openness, and conscientiousness. Agreeableness is believed to contribute to, or overlap with, prosocial tendencies (Graziano & Eisenberg, 1997). Thus, although genetics appear to contribute to children's prosocial tendencies, genetically informed studies also provide evidence for the role of the environment in the origins of prosocial behavior.

Relatively few twin studies involve children, and the strength of the heredity estimates has varied somewhat across studies. In one study of 5- to 16-year-olds, the estimate for the genetic contribution was about 52% for parental reports, but considerably higher for teachers' reports of prosocial behavior (Scourfield et al., 2004). In another study, Zahn-Waxler and colleagues (Plomin et al., 1993; Zahn-Waxler, Robinson, & Emde, 1992; Zahn-Waxler, Schiro, Robinson, Emde, & Schmitz, 2001) examined twins' behavioral reactions to simulations of distress in others. Estimates of heritability indicated a significant genetic component for empathic concern, prosocial acts, and maternal reports of prosocial acts at 14 months of age, albeit the variance accounted for was much less than 50% for all but maternal reports (indicating that environmental factors also contributed to prosocial development). At 20 months, empathic concern (sympathy) and prosocial acts continued to evidence significant genetic contributions. Active indifference also showed significant genetic influence at 14 months; however, there was no evidence of heritability for self-distress at either 14 or 20 months (Zahn-Waxler et al., 1992). Plomin et al. (1993) found no evidence of genetic influence on change in a composite index of children's empathy from 14 to 20 months of age, although genetic factors partially accounted for stability over time in empathy.

In follow-ups in which additional twins were added to the sample, empathic concern continued to show evidence of genetic influence at 24 and 36 months, whereas prosocial acts and indifference did so only at 36 months. Mothers' reports of children's prosocial behavior showed a genetic influence only at 14 months; it was predicted by shared environmental variance at older ages (Zahn-Waxler et al., 2001). Moreover, there is evidence that heritable differences may account for toddlers' empathy-related responding toward an unfamiliar adult, whereas shared environmental influences account for concern toward the mother (Robinson, Zahn-Waxler, & Emde, 2001). The differences in the findings reported at earlier and older ages may have been due to the smaller sample in the assessments conducted in the 2nd year of life. Regardless, the magnitude of any genetic influences on these observed measures of concern generally were modest. Moreover, Robinson and colleagues found there was no significant genetic variance in children's positive reactions to others' distress at 14 months; it was moderately strong at 20 months and disappeared again at 24 months (Robinson, Emde, & Corley, 2001). Thus, there appears to be considerable variability in heritability estimates across age and measures of prosocial responding.

The role of genetic and environmental influences in children's prosocial tendencies also has been tested in other types of genetically informed studies. In a study of stepfamilies, Deater-Deckard, Dunn, et al. (2001) found that most of the variance in adults' reports of children's (mostly preschool and school age) prosocial behavior was due to environmental (not genetic) factors, especially aspects of the environment that were not shared by the children, although there was significant variance for shared environmental effects. Moreover, in a study involving only identical pre-school-age twins, Deater-Deckard, Pike, et al. (2001) obtained additional evidence of the role of nonshared environment (e.g., maternal supportive and punitive behaviors) in predicting children's prosocial behavior.

Other evidence relevant for examining the role of genetics in prosocial behavior is found in studies of children with certain genetic abnormalities. Williams syndrome, caused by a microdeletion of part of the long arm of chromosome 7, is associated with a specific personality profile that includes highly sociable, empathic, sympathetic, and prosocial interpersonal behavior (Mervis & Klein-Tasman, 2000), perhaps even more so than for normal children or those with some other disorders such as Prader-Willi or fragile X syndrome (Jones et al., 2000; see Semel & Rosner, 2003). Thus, the highly specific and sensitive social profile of individuals with Williams syndrome suggests that hemizygous deletion of one or more genes is involved in biasing (but not determining) development toward these components of prosocial behavior.

Neurophysiological Underpinnings of Prosocial Responding

Behavioral genetics research provides information regarding the presence and size of genetic contributions to prosocial behavior, but does not identify the conditions or processes of organism-environment interaction through which genotypes are transformed into phenotypes. Research and theory on the neurological processes may provide a mechanism for mediation between genetics and overt behavior (see Hastings et al., 2005, for a recent review). Panksepp (1986) suggested that brain opioids influence the degree to which social contact is reinforcing and that fluctuations in brain opioids and the underlying emotive systems affect altruistic behavior. Panksepp also hypothesized that during social interactions (which are affected by brain opioids), animals may become better attuned to the emotions of their conspecifics and thereby become better able to alleviate their distress when it occurs.

Panksepp asserted that all mammalian helping behavior arises from the "nurturant dictates of brain systems that mediate social bonding and maternal care" (1986, p. 44). This view is consistent with that of MacLean (1985), who argued that the basis for altruism lies in maternal behavior, affiliation, and play, which are mediated in part by the limbic system of the brain. MacLean further suggested that the prefrontal neocortex, which developed relatively recently in evolution and is most distinctive in humans, provides the basis for concern for others and a sense of responsibility and conscience.

There have been direct attempts to identify the neural roots of prosocial behavior and emotions. It has been argued that the perceptual bases of empathy may be "mirror neurons"—neurons that fire not only when a monkey executes an action but also when it observes another monkey or human performing the same action (Gallese, 2001). In addition, Decety and Chaminade

(2003) used positron emission tomography neuroimaging (i.e., PET scanning) to demonstrate that the neural structures known to be involved in emotional responding (e.g., amygdala and the adjacent orbitofrontal cortex and the insula) were activated when people listened to sad stories designed to elicit sympathy; listening to neutral stories did not cause similar neural activation. Increased neural activity was also found in the cortical regions involved in shared motor representations (e.g., dorsal premotor cortex, right inferior parietal lobule)—areas of the brain thought to be important when taking the perspective of others (Ruby & Decety, 2001).

Other researchers have highlighted the importance of frontal cortical activity in sympathetic responses. Harmon-Jones, Vaughn-Scott, Mohr, Sigelman, and Harmon-Jones (2004) found that anger provocation increased left frontal cortical activity and decreased right activity; however, high levels of sympathetic responses were found to eliminate these effects. Moreover, Eslinger and colleagues (1998; Eslinger, Eastin, Grattan, & Van Hoesen, 1996) studied individuals with front lesions and found that when the lesion was in the dorsolateral front system, deficits in cognitive aspects of empathy resulted. In contrast, when lesions were in the orbitofrontal system, deficits in the more emotional aspects of empathy resulted. Such findings suggest that complex neural responses likely are involved in prosocial actions and reactions, a conclusion that is consistent with Panksepp's (1986) assertion that it may be unrealistic to assume that functional unitary brain circuits will be discovered for global constructs such as altruism, sympathy, and prosocial behavior.

In summary, it is likely that biological factors play some role in individual differences in empathy and prosocial behavior. However, much of the relevant research on biological mechanisms comes from work with nonhumans, and existing behavioral genetics work is limited in quantity and scope. Moreover, it is unclear whether some of the aforementioned biological correlates of empathy or prosocial behavior play a causal role in individual differences among people in prosocial tendencies (e.g., they may simply be correlates or consequences of empathy). Pertinent theory is speculative and underdeveloped. Finally, there is evidence that the environment plays a critical role in prosocial development, even in the behavioral genetics research. The key to understanding human prosocial behavior lies in determining how biological factors, prior environmental influences on the child, and the current context jointly affect prosocial behavior and development (with the in-

fluence of biology being probabilistic rather than deterministic; Wachs, 1994).

DEVELOPMENTAL TRENDS IN THE EMERGENCE OF PROSOCIAL TENDENCIES

According to both theory and empirical findings, prosocial behavior and empathy emerge early in life. In this section, we first briefly review Hoffman's theory of the development of prosocial behavior, and we then examine age changes in prosocial behavior and empathy-related responding.

Theory

Hoffman (1982, 2000) proposed a four-level theoretical model that delineates the role of infants' and children's affect and cognitive sense of self-awareness and self-other differentiation in the emergence of prosocial behavior. Specifically, he outlined the developmental shift over time from self-concern in response to others' distress to empathic concern (i.e., sympathy) for others that results in other-oriented prosocial behavior.

In Hoffman's first stage, newborns and infants display rudimentary empathic responses that are manifested as "global empathy." Hoffman argues that the young infant has not acquired a sense of self-other differentiation (at least in regard to emotional states) and experiences empathic distress through one or more of the simpler modes of empathy (e.g., based on reactive crying, conditioning, mimicry). Because young infants cannot differentiate their own distress from that of another, they often experience self-distress in response to another's distress, as evidenced in their reactive crying in response to the sound of another's cry (viewed as a simple form, or precursor, of global empathy). Beginning around the end of the 1st year of life, infants experience *egocentric empathic distress* and are thought to seek comfort for themselves when exposed to others' distress. At this level, infants have begun developing a sense of self as separate from others; however, this sense is quite immature (i.e., they cannot fully differentiate between their own distress and that of another). Thus, the infant is likely to respond to empathic and actual distress situations in the same way.

Early in the 2nd year of life, toddlers begin to make helpful advances toward a victim of distress (i.e., patting, touching). Around the same age, they may intervene by hugging, giving physical assistance, or getting someone else to help (Zahn-Waxler & Radke-Yarrow, 1982). Hoffman labels this level *quasi-egocentric empathic distress*. According to Hoffman (2000), toddlers in this developmental period can differentiate between self and other, although they still do not distinguish well between their own and another's internal states. Nonetheless, toddlers can experience empathic concern for another, rather than solely seek comfort for themselves. They also can and sometimes do try to comfort another person, but such prosocial behavior is likely to involve giving the other person what the toddlers themselves find comforting. Empathy at this level differs from the previous stage because toddlers are not purely egocentric and are more likely to respond with appropriate empathic affect.

Stern (1985) has argued that young children develop a subjective self capable of recognizing the subjectivity of the other earlier than stated by Hoffman (2000). Although this issue has not been resolved, the affect attunement ("a recasting or restatement of a subjective state," p. 161) or emotional resonance between parent and child discussed by Stern—albeit believed to be largely out of the child's conscious awareness—may foster the early development of affective empathy, especially if parents are empathic in their interactions.

Sometime during the 2nd year of life, children enter the period of *veridical empathic distress*. According to Hoffman (1982, 2000), this stage marks the period in which children are increasingly aware of other people's feelings and are capable of understanding that other people's perspectives and feelings may differ from their own. Thus, prosocial actions reflect an awareness of the other person's needs (versus the egocentric empathy of the previous stage), and children can be more accurate in their empathic responses and help others in less egocentric ways. Moreover, with the development of language, children are able to empathize and sympathize with a wider range of emotions than they previously could. However, according to Hoffman, children's empathic responses are restricted to another's immediate, or situation-specific, distress.

As children develop more sophisticated perspective-taking skills and the ability to think abstractly, the ability to experience empathic responses even when the other person is not physically present (e.g., if they hear or read about someone in distress) emerges (Hoffman, 1982). Moreover, by mid to late childhood, children can empathize with another person's general condition or plight. Further, the adolescent is capable of comprehending and responding to the plight of an entire group

or class of people, such as the impoverished or the politically oppressed. Thus, Hoffman (1982) proposed that with increasing cognitive maturation, children are better able to respond with concern to others' distress.

Empirical Studies of the Development of Prosocial Behavior

In this section, we review empirical studies that provide insight into the development of prosocial tendencies. To organize these, we review them according to the ages of the participants in the study.

Infancy and Childhood

Compared with research in older children, adolescents, and adults, research examining prosocial behavior in young children is relatively limited. Nonetheless, there is some empirical support for Hoffman's theory. There is evidence that newborn infants exhibit some form of global empathy as displayed by their reactive crying in response to the cries of another infant (Martin & Clark, 1982; Sagi & Hoffman, 1976). Of particular interest, infants exhibit more distress in response to another infant's crying than to their own (Dondi, Simion, & Caltran, 1999), suggesting that they are biologically predisposed to experience a rudimentary form of empathy. However, some researchers have questioned the interpretation of these findings (Eisenberg & Lennon, 1983); for example, infants may simply find a novel cry to be more aversive than their own cry.

Around 6 months of age, infants will sometimes respond to the cry of another infant by crying, but they frequently ignore it or merely orient toward the peer (Hay, Nash, & Pederson, 1981). By 38 to 61 weeks of age, infants sometimes react to others' distress by orienting and distress cries, but they occasionally display positive affect, such as smiling or laughing (Zahn-Waxler & Radke-Yarrow, 1982).

Thus, it appears that infants are responsive to others' emotional signals. In a study in which mothers expressed sadness or joy in view of their 9-month-old infants, the infants displayed more negative emotional expressions and tended to avert their gaze away from their mothers in the sadness condition and expressed more joy when they viewed their mothers' expressions of joy (Termine & Izard, 1988). Moreover, studies of social referencing show that infants not only are responsive to others' emotional signals, but also make use of them to guide their own behavior in an ambiguous situation (see Saarni, Mumme, & Campos, 1998; Saarni et al., Chapter 5, this *Handbook,* this volume). During the 2nd year of life, toddlers display the ability to discuss their own and others' emotions and show significant improvements in this skill between 18 and 36 months of age (Bretherton, Fritz, Zahn-Waxler, & Ridgeway, 1986). These findings demonstrate that very young children are affected by the emotions they observe in others.

Around 12 to 18 months of age, infants clearly react to others' negative emotions (often with orienting and distress reactions) and sometimes react to others' distress with concerned attention and prosocial behavior, including positive contact and verbal reassurance (Zahn-Waxler, Robinson, et al., 1992). These patterns have been found in interactions with mothers (Zahn-Waxler, Robinson, et al., 1992), siblings (Dunn, 1988), peers (Denham, 1986; Howes & Farver, 1987), and strangers (Johnson, 1982).

In one of the earliest studies of children's sympathy and prosocial behavior, Lois Murphy (1937) found that preschool children reacted to another's distress in a variety of ways. Children's responses ranged from sympathy and prosocial initiations to egocentric and unsympathetic reactions, such as laughing, aggression, or ignoring. These findings have been replicated in other samples with young children (Radke-Yarrow & Zahn-Waxler, 1984; Zahn-Waxler & Radke-Yarrow, 1982; Zahn-Waxler, Radke-Yarrow, Wagner, & Chapman, 1992). Moreover, researchers have found that responsiveness to peers' distress in naturalistic settings is relatively infrequent among toddlers and preschoolers (Caplan & Hay, 1989; Howes & Farver, 1987; Phinney, Feshbach, & Farver, 1986). In a naturalistic study examining toddlers' responses to peers' distress in day care, Lamb and Zakhireh (1997) found that toddlers responded to a peer's distress with prosocial behavior in only 11 out of 345 incidents. Factors that appear to relate to children's prosocial responding include whether a peer's distress persists for a long period or if the particular peer is one who infrequently becomes distressed (Caplan & Hay, 1989).

As proposed by Hoffman (1982, 2000), prosocial behaviors have been associated with indices of cognitive development. Toddlers who display evidence of self-recognition (indicating a self-other distinction) tend to be relatively empathic and are likely to display prosocial behaviors (Bischof-Koehler, 1991; Johnson, 1982; Zahn-Waxler, Radke-Yarrow, et al., 1992; Zahn-Waxler, Schiro, et al., 2001). Further, children's perspective taking (as indexed by their hypothesis testing [e.g.,

attempts to label or understand why the other is distressed] or social referencing) in the 2nd year of life and at age 4 to 5 years has been positively related to their prosocial behaviors (Kiang, Moreno, & Robinson, 2004; Zahn-Waxler, Cole, Welsh, & Fox, 1995; Zahn-Waxler, Robinson, et al., 1992). Similarly, preschool children's emotion knowledge has been positively related to prosocial behavior toward adults who express negative emotion (Denham & Couchoud, 1991) and toward younger siblings (Garner, Jones, & Palmer, 1994).

Other types of prosocial behavior besides sympathetic or comforting responses to others' distress have been examined in young children. The tendency to give objects to other people is common in early childhood, and young children have been observed sharing objects with parents, other adults, siblings, and peers (Hay, 1994). Object sharing seems to emerge around 8 months of age and is increasingly evident during the next year (Hay & Rheingold, 1983). In general, prosocial behavior has been found to increase in the early years of life (Zahn-Waxler & Radke-Yarrow, 1982; Zahn-Waxler, Schiro, et al., 1992, 2001). For example, Zahn-Waxler, Schiro, et al. (1992, 2001) and Robinson et al. (2001) studied toddlers' empathy-related responding to an experimenter and the mother feigning injuries at 14, 20, 24, and 36 months of age. They found an increase with age in empathic concern, hypotheses testing, and prosocial behavior. Van der Mark, van IJzendoorn, and Bakermans-Kranenburg (2002) also found an increase in empathy/prosocial responding (combined) from 16 to 22 months when toddlers' mothers were distressed. Further, Lamb and Zakhireh (1997) found that age was positively related to toddlers' prosocial behavior toward peers.

Moreover, nonempathic responses (e.g., self-oriented distress reactions) seem to decrease in the second and 3rd year of life (Zahn-Waxler, Radke-Yarrow, et al., 1992; Zahn-Waxler et al., 2001). Toddlers' indifference toward another's distress has been found to decline from 14 to 20 months of age and then increase between 24 and 36 months (Zahn-Waxler et al., 2001). Nonetheless, with increasing age, preschoolers are more likely to respond to others' distress with empathy and prosocial behaviors (Hastings, Zahn-Waxler, Robinson, Usher, & Bridges, 2000; Lennon & Eisenberg, 1987; Phinney et al., 1986).

Although many empirical studies have demonstrated the hypothesized increase in prosocial behavior over time, Hay (1994; Hay, Caplan, Castle, & Stimson, 1991) proposed a developmental model which predicted that prosocial action would emerge in the 2nd year of life and *decline* after that. She argued that after the age of 2, prosocial action becomes more regulated such that it is shown to some but not to all potential recipients (e.g., prosocial actions become increasingly differentiated based on gender and personality). In one study with girls and boys in three age cohorts (18 to 24 months, 24 to 30 months, and 30 to 36 months), Hay found the hypothesized decline in sharing with peers between 18 and 24 months of age; however, the trend was not reliable thereafter. In addition, the tendency to share was more stable with older toddlers (24- to 36-month-olds) than with younger toddlers (18- to 24-month-olds; Hay, Castle, Davies, Demetriou, & Stimson, 1999). The fact that Hay and colleagues studied sharing with only familiar peers—and in fact "best friends"—may have contributed to the pattern observed; most studies have not involved this type of sharing context. Additionally, the meaning of prosocial behavior may differ across childhood. At young ages, children may exchange toys as part of simple play or to communicate with their friend about the objects they are using (e.g., to show the peer something about a toy or to interest the peer in it).

To bring coherence to the many studies of age-related change in prosocial behavior, Eisenberg and Fabes (1998) conducted a meta-analysis of relevant studies. Overall, there were significant increases in prosocial behavior within both the infant (less than 3 years of age) and the preschool (3 to 6 years) age groups (effect sizes = .24 and .33). In addition, there were increases in prosocial behavior when comparing the preschool group with either the childhood or adolescent age groups. However, there was no difference between the infancy and preschool periods, perhaps due to the relatively small number of studies that compared these age groups ($n = 11$). In addition, school-age children were higher in prosocial behavior than preschoolers (effect size = .30).

In the meta-analysis, prosocial behavior generally increased across the preschool and school years (also see Benenson, Markovits, Roy, & Denko, 2003). However, some of the findings were based on relatively small samples, particularly for comparisons of the youngest children in these samples. We also recognize that the findings of our meta-analysis were based largely on cross-sectional data and on aggregations of data from studies that varied greatly in their quality and methodologies.

Despite possible age-related changes in children's prosocial behavior, there appears to be considerable interindividual stability in children's levels of prosocial responding. Côté, Tremblay, Nagin, Zoccolillo, and Vitaro (2002) examined the continuity of trajectories for helpfulness across early elementary school (measured annually from age 6 to age 12 years). Generally, children who entered kindergarten with specific levels of helpfulness finished primary school at similar levels. The observed degree of stability in these trajectories was impressive considering that ratings of helpfulness were provided by independent raters (i.e., different teachers at different years).

Adolescence

Age Trends. Prosocial tendencies appear to increase from childhood into adolescence. According to Eisenberg and Fabes's (1998) meta-analysis, adolescents tend to be higher in prosocial behavior than children aged 7 to 12 years, albeit on sharing/donating, but not instrumental helping or comforting. Both young adolescents (13 to 15 years) and older adolescents (16 to 18 years) were higher than elementary school students in their prosocial tendencies (Fabes, Carlo, Kupanoff, & Laible, 1999). Thus, adolescents exhibit more prosocial behavior than do younger children; however, this pattern was noted only for particular types of studies. Although there was not an overall increase in prosocial responding across adolescence (from age 12 to 17 or 18), prosocial behavior increased in adolescence for the few studies of sharing/donating (but not helping), and in experimental/structured studies (but not naturalistic/correlational studies; see Eisenberg & Fabes, 1998; also see Jacobs, Vernon, & Eccles, 2004). Moreover, helping of victims of aggression may actually decline across adolescence (Lindeman, Harakka, & Keltikangas-Jarvinen, 1997; also see Pakaslahti, Karjalainen, & Keltikangas-Jarvinen, 2002).

In the meta-analysis, prosocial behavior directed toward adults did not change with age in adolescence. This finding may primarily reflect findings in the family setting. Investigators have found nonlinear age-related changes or no consistent change in adolescents' and parents' reports of adolescents' parent-directed prosocial behaviors (e.g., Eberly & Montemayor, 1998, 1999; also see Keith, Nelson, Schlabach, & Thompson, 1990), as well as a decline in helpfulness toward parents between fifth and ninth grades (Eberly, Montemayor, & Flannery, 1993).

Based on Hoffman's theory, one would expect an age-related increase in empathy-related responding during adolescence, especially in situations in which empathy or sympathy is directed toward abstract groups (e.g., deprived groups). In studies conducted before about

1986, findings regarding age trends in empathy-related responding in adolescence were inconsistent, although there was some evidence of an increase from childhood into adolescence (e.g., Saklofske & Eysenck, 1983; see Lennon & Eisenberg, 1987). Since 1987, there has been additional longitudinal evidence of an increase in empathy-related responding from 9th to 10th grade, especially for sympathetic concern, and of a decline in personal distress (Davis & Franzoi, 1991). In a cross-sectional study, Strayer and Roberts (1997b) also found that both reported empathic sadness and facial concerned reactions to evocative videotapes (perhaps indicative of sympathy) increased with age from childhood into adolescence (although there was no age difference in affective matching of the emotion in the film). However, some investigators who have conducted cross-sectional studies have obtained mixed evidence of sympathy increasing between 6th and 12th grade (Olweus & Endresen, 1998) or have found little change in sympathy or personal distress from 8th to 11th grades (Karniol, Gabay, Ochion, & Harari, 1998). Finally, a longitudinal study (Eisenberg, Cumberland, Guthrie, Murphy, & Shepard, 2005) did not find change in sympathy from age 15 to 16 into the 20s, although personal distress declined with age. Thus, there may be a modest increase in sympathy with age, especially in early to mid-adolescence, although it is not clear that sympathy increases in mid- and late-adolescence.

The Potential Effects of Adolescents' Participation in Prosocial Service.   A type of prosocial behavior that appears to be much more common in adolescence than at younger ages is volunteering. Approximately half of all adolescents engage in some type of community service or volunteer activity (National Center for Education Statistics, 1997). Volunteerism is an interesting type of prosocial behavior because it generally is sustained over some period of time (rather than performed only once) and is expected to have some enduring effect on youths' prosocial, civic, and personal development.

Although motives for volunteering vary and are sometimes self-related rather than altruistic (Clary & Snyder, 1999), investigators have found that high school students who volunteer appear to benefit from the experience. Of these studies, few have used random assignment (for an exception, see Allen, Philliber, Herrling, & Kuperminc, 1997), although most have included a comparison control group or a pre/post design (see Moore &

Allen, 1996; Yates & Youniss, 1996a). In general, researchers have found volunteering is associated with increases in adolescents' self-esteem and self-acceptance, moral development, and belief in one's personal responsibility to help (Conrad & Hedin, 1982; see Switzer, Simmons, Dew, Regalski, & Wang, 1995, for similar results for a required helping program), as well as concern for social issues and future intended service (Metz, McLellan, & Youniss, 2003).

In a panel design of youth volunteers and nonvolunteers in which the initial levels of variables correlated with volunteering were controlled, volunteering was related to gains in subsequent intrinsic work values and the anticipated importance of community involvement (Johnson, Beebe, Mortimer, & Snyder, 1998). There is also evidence that service participation (voluntary or not) is related to decreases in course failure, truancy, suspension from school, school dropout, disciplinary problems, and pregnancies, as well as with improved reading skills (see Allen, Kuperminc, Philliber, & Herre, 1994; Allen et al., 1997; Calabrese & Schumer, 1986; Moore & Allen, 1996; Switzer et al., 1995; also see Eccles & Barber, 1999). Finally, in a prospective longitudinal study, volunteer work negatively predicted subsequent arrests, even when controlling for the effects of antisocial propensities, prosocial attitudes and behavior, and commitment to conventional lines of action (Uggen & Janikula, 1999). Quality of the program (e.g., allowing adolescents autonomy and choice, being challenging and enjoyable), length of the program (programs 12 weeks or more tend to be more successful than shorter programs), and age of adolescents (in some programs, older youth benefited more) all appear to affect potential benefits of volunteering (Moore & Allen, 1996). Thus, participation in service activities—a common adolescent activity—is related to both prosocial and other developmental outcomes.

Moderators of Age Trends across Childhood and Adolescence

Viewed more generally, the extant literature appears to support the conclusion that as children get older, they exhibit more sympathy and prosocial behavior. This trend does not hold, however, for children of all ages or for all measures of prosocial behavior (see Radke-Yarrow, Zahn-Waxler, & Chapman, 1983; Zarbatany, Hartmann, & Gelfand, 1985). In fact, in the previously mentioned Eisenberg and Fabes (1998) meta-analysis, age differences in prosocial behavior sometimes varied as a function of study characteristics. These differences did not vary as a function of type of prosocial behavior for studies conducted with young children; moreover, across the remaining age group comparisons (involving older children), the magnitude of age differences was relatively constant in size when the type of prosocial behavior was sharing, comforting, or an aggregated index. In contrast, the magnitude of the age-related effect size for instrumental helping varied more across the older age group comparisons. The magnitude of this effect size was relatively high when the type of prosocial behavior was instrumental help for the childhood versus preschool and within-childhood comparisons and relatively low for the adolescent versus childhood and the within-adolescence comparisons.

The magnitude of the effect sizes differed significantly by the method of data collection (e.g., observation, self-report, other-report) only for childhood/ preschool, childhood/childhood, and adolescent/childhood comparison groups. For both the childhood/ preschool and childhood/childhood age comparison groups, effect sizes for age differences were significantly higher when prosocial tendencies were measured with observations or self-reports than when assessed with reports obtained from other people. For the adolescent versus childhood comparisons, effect sizes were significantly higher when measured with observational or other report methods rather than with self-report methods.

For all age-comparison groups, effect sizes were greater in experimental/structured designs than in naturalistic/correlational designs (although the difference was not significant for infant/infant and preschool/ preschool comparisons). Finally, the magnitude of the effect size differed significantly by the target of the prosocial behavior, but this was true only for childhood/preschool, childhood/childhood, and adolescent/ adolescent comparison groups. In the first two age comparison groups, effect sizes were larger when the target was an adult and lowest when the target was unknown/ unspecified (with child targets in between). In contrast, for the adolescent/adolescent comparison, the effect size was greater when the target was a child compared with an adult.

There also were differences in the procedures used to measure prosocial behavior in different age groups. Instrumental help was relatively unlikely to be used as a measure of prosocial behavior with children under 7

years of age. Moreover, naturalistic/correlational designs were relatively likely to be used with very young children, whereas experimental/structured designs were more often used with older children. Additionally, adults were likely to be used as targets of children's prosocial behavior in studies with the youngest and oldest age groups, whereas children were likely to be the potential recipients of prosocial behavior for children not at the age extremes. Thus, age-related differences in prosocial behavior may have varied as a function of differences in study characteristics that differed across age groups.

To explore this possibility, we examined age differences in prosocial behavior while controlling for study characteristics (through hierarchical regression analyses). Age differences in prosocial behavior were found to be smaller as the mean age of the sample increased, as the sample size increased, and in studies published more recently. Moreover, although type of prosocial behavior was related to effect sizes for age prior to controlling for study characteristics, effect sizes were not affected by type of prosocial measure (instrumental help, sharing/ donating, aggregated, comforting) after partialling out other study characteristics. However, after controlling for study characteristics (and not before), a larger increase in prosocial behavior with age was found when prosocial behavior was measured with self- or other-reports rather than with observations.

In brief, the findings of our meta-analysis suggested that age differences in prosocial behavior differed in magnitude as a function of the specific age comparison, the measure of prosocial behavior, and the type of analysis. However, combining across all studies and study characteristics, we still found a significant, positive effect size for age differences in prosocial behavior. Thus, our data support the conclusion that as children get older, prosocial behaviors generally are more likely to occur, although there may be variation within age groups and for various measures and methods.

Processes Potentially Related to Changes with Age in Prosocial Responding

For some theorists, the primary source of the increase in prosocial and altruistic behavior across age is sociocognitive development, including understanding and decoding others' emotions, evaluative processes (evaluating behaviors and situations in terms of moral standards), and planning processes (Krebs & Van Hesteren, 1994).

Aspects of socioemotional responding (e.g., moral emotions, regulatory capacities) also partially account for age-related changes in prosocial behavior (Hart, Burock, London, & Atkins, 2003).

Sociocognitive Processes

As noted by Krebs and Van Hesteren (1994) and Hoffman (1982), attention to the needs of others transforms egoistic affect to other-oriented affect, rendering it increasingly altruistic. Throughout infancy and childhood, children develop an increasingly refined understanding of others' emotional states and cognitive processes, and are better able to decode other people's emotional cues (see Eisenberg, Murphy, & Shepard, 1997, for a review). As is discussed later, such perspective taking and related sociocognitive skills are associated with prosocial responding. Moreover, with age, children are more likely to have the social experience necessary to perceive another's need in social contexts in which overt cues of distress are ambiguous or subtle (see Pearl, 1985), and to distinguish real versus apparent emotional states (Gosselin, Warren, & Diotte, 2002). In addition, younger children appear to weigh costs to the self more than do older children when deciding whether to assist others (see Eisenberg, 1986) and are less attuned to the benefits of prosocial behavior (Lourenco, 1993; Perry, Perry, & Weiss, 1986). These age-related differences in the analysis of costs and benefits likely contribute to age-related differences in prosocial behavior.

Moreover, numerous researchers have suggested that the quality of children's motivation for assisting others changes with age (e.g., Eisenberg, 1986; Erdley & Asher, 1999; Krebs & Van Hesteren, 1994). Bar-Tal, Raviv, and Leiser (1980) proposed that children's helping behavior develops through six stages that differ in quality of motivation. The first three stages involve helping behaviors that are compliant and in which the child anticipates the gain of material rewards (or the avoidance of punishment). The next two stages involve compliance with social demands and concern with social approval and generalized reciprocity. The final stage represents true altruism in which helping is an end in itself.

Bar-Tal and colleagues found some support for their hypothesized developmental changes in children's motives for helping. For example, older children tend to assist more often than do younger children in contexts in which the effects of compliance and rewards or costs are minimized (Bar-Tal, Raviv, et al., 1980; see Bar-Tal, 1982; Eisenberg, 1986). Although Bar-Tal and col-

leagues sought to delineate a developmental sequence in prosocial motivation, the data concerning this issue are inconclusive (i.e., it is unclear whether all their proposed stages actually emerge in the specified order; see Eisenberg, 1986). Nonetheless, children's reported motives for their prosocial behavior change in ways that generally are consistent with Bar-Tal's stages. Although even preschoolers sometimes give simple other-oriented and pragmatic reasons for their peer-directed prosocial actions (Eisenberg, Lundy, Shell, & Roth, 1985; Eisenberg, Pasternack, Cameron, & Tryon, 1984), researchers generally have found a decrease with age in self-oriented, hedonistic reasons for helping and an increase in other-oriented, internalized, and altruistic motives and reasons for prosocial behavior (e.g., Bar-Tal, Raviv, et al., 1980; see Bar-Tal, 1982; Eisenberg, 1986; cf. Hertz-Lazarowitz, 1983).[1] Thus, in general, the evidence of developmental change in children's motives for assisting others is relatively compelling (see Eisenberg, 1986).

Like Bar-Tal (1982), Krebs and Van Hesteren (1994) proposed age-related forms of altruism, ranging from egocentric and exchange stages (e.g., egocentric accommodation and instrumental cooperation, Stages 1 and 2, respectively), to concern with others' evaluation and behaving in a socially acceptable manner (Stage 3), to altruism motivated by the desire to fulfill an internalized sense of social responsibility (e.g., conscientious altruism, Stage 4). The higher level adult stages are motivated by the desire to uphold self-chosen, internalized utilitarian values (e.g., maximizing benefits to all; autonomous altruism, Stage 5), the goal of fostering maximally balanced and integrated social relationships (e.g., upholding the rights of all people, including the self; integrated altruism, Stage 6), and the goal of universal love stemming from a cosmic feeling of oneness with the universe and a selfless ethic of responsible love, service, and sacrifice that is extended to others without regard for merit (universal self-sacrificial love, Stage 7). Of course, children or adolescents would not be expected to obtain the higher level stages. Although Krebs and his colleagues have not explicitly tested the validity of their stages, their position is supported in the data collected

---

[1] Here and throughout the chapter, the abbreviation "cf.," meaning "compare with," signifies "contrast with." It indicates that contrary findings were obtained in a study. "Also see" generally indicates that the results in the listed studies are also relevant to discussion of the issue at hand.

by other investigators concerned with the development of moral reasoning, prosocial behavior, and empathy.

Age-related changes in children's evaluative processes and prosocial-relevant goals are reflected in children's prosocial moral reasoning (i.e., reasoning about moral dilemmas in which one person's needs or wants conflict with those of others in a context where authorities, laws, rules, punishment, and formal obligations play a minimal role). In research on prosocial moral reasoning, individuals typically are presented with hypothetical moral conflicts (e.g., about helping an injured child rather than going to a social event), and their reasoning about the conflicts is elicited.

Based on both cross-sectional and longitudinal research, Eisenberg and her colleagues have identified an age-related sequence of children's prosocial reasoning. Preschool and early elementary school students tend to use primarily hedonistic reasoning or needs-oriented (primitive empathic) prosocial reasoning. Hedonistic reasoning decreases sharply in elementary school and increases slightly in adolescence. Needs-oriented reasoning increases until mid-childhood and then levels off in use. In elementary school, children's reasoning begins to reflect concern with others' approval and enhancing interpersonal relationships, as well as the desire to behave in stereotypically "good" ways. However, such reasoning (particularly approval-oriented reasoning) appears to decline somewhat in high school.

Beginning in late elementary school or thereafter, children begin to express reasoning reflecting abstract principles, internalized affective reactions (e.g., guilt or positive affect about the consequences of one's behavior for others or living up to internalized principles and values), and self-reflective sympathy and perspective taking. Thus, although children and adolescents sometimes verbalize immature modes of reasoning, children's moral reasoning becomes more abstract, somewhat less self-oriented, and increasingly based on values, moral principles, and moral emotions with age (Carlo, Eisenberg, & Knight, 1992; Carlo, Koller, Eisenberg, De-Silva, & Frohlich, 1996; Eisenberg, Carlo, Murphy, & Van Court, 1995; Eisenberg-Berg, 1979; also see Hart et al., 2003; Helwig & Turiel, 2003). As discussed later, these age-related changes are linked to prosocial behavior; thus, the processes reflected in children's moral reasoning likely play some role in the age-related increase in quantity and quality of prosocial behavior. However, these processes may include age-related changes in goals and values, as well as in the sociocog-

nitive skills required for high-level moral reasoning (see Eisenberg, 1986).

Sociocognitive processes may underlie the development of children's prosocial behaviors, but engaging in these processes does not ensure the enacting of prosocial actions. Eisenberg and Fabes (1992) suggested that individuals who are well regulated are relatively likely to engage in costly, other-oriented prosocial behavior. Because regulatory capacities likely increase with age (Eisenberg, Smith, Sadovsky, & Spinrad, 2004), we would expect older children, relative to younger ones, to be more likely to respond sympathetically and with prosocial behavior in emotionally evocative situations. Support for the hypothesized relations between children's prosocial tendencies and their behavioral and emotional regulation is discussed later.

Age Changes in Empathy-Related Responding

Developmental change in both children's emotion regulation and in their sociocognitive skills (e.g., Hoffman, 1982, 2000) would be expected to contribute to age-related changes in prosocial behavior, in part by influencing children's tendencies to respond empathically or sympathetically. Lennon and Eisenberg (1987), in a review of the literature, found that age differences in empathy varied with the specific index of empathy used. In general, self-report of empathy/sympathy was positively associated with age in preschool and elementary school years. Facial/gestural indices appeared to be either inversely related or unrelated to age in the early school years, perhaps due to increases with age in children's ability to mask their emotions. As discussed, more recent studies show some evidence (albeit mixed) for increased empathy-related responding in adolescence.

Eisenberg and Fabes (1998) conducted a separate meta-analysis of age differences in empathy (rather than prosocial behavior) in studies published since 1983 and found an overall unweighted effect size of .24 (favoring older children). Moreover, they found that effect sizes in empathy varied significantly by method; they were significant and larger for observational and self-report indices than for nonverbal (facial/physiological) or other-report measures (for which the effect sizes were not significant).

Vitaglione and Barnett (2003) found evidence that empathic anger on behalf of a victimized person motivates desires to help. As children develop the ability to empathize with others, empathic anger may increasingly motivate prosocial behavior.

Changes in Experience-Based Competence

Developmental changes in children's experience-based competencies also affect their ability to engage in prosocial behavior. Peterson (1983) found that when children were specially trained on relevant tasks, age-related increases in helping evaporated. The data in our meta-analysis (see Eisenberg & Fabes, 1998) also suggested that experience-based developmental competencies may contribute to age-related differences in prosocial behavior. For example, age differences in prosocial behavior were relatively pronounced when the index of prosocial behavior was instrumental helping. Older children may provide more direct, instrumental assistance because they possess greater physical and social competence than do younger children.

Summary

Developmental changes in prosocial behavior are complex and are influenced by methodological factors. Moreover, the precise developmental mechanisms involved in producing these changes are not yet fully explicated and likely involve cognitive, social, motivational/emotional, and physical processes and capabilities. The next wave of research should include studies devoted to identifying when and how age-related changes in the sociocognitive, emotional, and regulatory capabilities jointly affect prosocial responding.

CULTURAL DETERMINANTS OF PROSOCIAL BEHAVIOR

Research on the cultural bases of prosocial responding provides insights into the role of the social environment—in contrast to strictly biological factors—in prosocial development. People in different cultures may differ somewhat genetically from one another, but these differences are unlikely to fully account for any large cultural differences found in human social behavior.

Research in non-Western cultures suggests that societies vary greatly in the degree to which prosocial and cooperative behavior are normative, and such differences appear to affect prosocial development. In field studies of individual cultures, some writers have described societies in which prosocial and communal values and behaviors are (or were in the past) highly valued and common, such as the Aitutaki (a Polynesian island people; Graves & Graves, 1983), the Javanese (e.g., Mul-

der, 1996; Williams, 1991), and the Papago tribe in Arizona (Rohner, 1975; see Eisenberg & Mussen, 1989). In contrast, other social and behavioral scientists have described cultures in which prosocial behaviors were rare and cruelty or hostility was the norm, such as the Ik of Uganda (Turnbull, 1972) or the Alorese (on an island east of Java; Rohner, 1975). Moreover, societal experiments such as the communally oriented kibbutzim in Israel (see Nadler, Romek, & Shapira-Friedman, 1979) support the view that subcultural variations can have a substantial impact on prosocial values and behavior.

The perceived practical value of prosocial behavior varies across cultures; such differences may affect even early socialization. It has been reported that in some cultures such as in West Africa, prosocial behavior is encouraged as early as infancy (e.g., infants are offered objects and then encouraged to return the gifts) to foster sharing and exchange norms believed to bind the social group together (Nsamenang, 1992).

In many cases, reports of cultural differences in prosocial responding are based on single-culture studies and qualitative data (or mere observation/inference). Empirical studies of prosocial behaviors and values sometimes include only one culture, sometimes more. Although the results of the empirical research generally are consistent with qualitative cultural studies in highlighting the importance of culture in prosocial development, little is known about cross-cultural differences in actual (rather than reported) prosocial actions directed toward those who are not part of the child's family or community. Nor is it clear what factors mediate or moderate the cultural factors that have been found.

Laboratory or Adult- and Self-Report Studies

Much of the work on cross-cultural and subcultural variation in prosocial behavior is embedded in the research on cooperation, competition, and reward-allocation behavior. In many studies, the measure of cooperation involved overt self-gain; this work is not reviewed. However, researchers consistently have found that children from traditional rural and semi-agricultural communities and from relatively traditional subcultures (e.g., Mexican American children) are more cooperative than children from urban or Westernized cultures (see Eisenberg & Mussen, 1989).

In other studies, children were asked to make a series of choices concerning the distribution of objects (i.e., chips) to the self and a peer when giving the peer more chips did not change the child's own yield. Brazilian children (Carlo, Roesch, Knight, & Koller, 2001) and Mexican American children generally give more to the peer than do Euro-American children (Kagan & Knight, 1981; Knight, Nelson, Kagan, & Gumbiner, 1982), and the difference for Mexican Americans increases in magnitude from age 5 to 6 years to age 8 to 9 years (Knight & Kagan, 1977b). Sometimes, however, there have been no significant differences between Mexican or Mexican American children and Euro-American children in the selection of options in which the peer could receive more chips than the child (e.g., Kagan & Knight, 1981; Knight, Nelson, Kagan, & Gumbiner, 1982). The tendency to choose more for the peer than for the self is stronger in second- than in third-generation Mexican American children (Knight & Kagan, 1977a), suggesting that acculturation is associated with a decline in prosocial tendencies. Consistent with the latter finding, de Guzman and Carlo (2004) found that acculturation was negatively related to Hispanic adolescents' self-reported prosocial behavior.

In another variation on allocation tasks, some of the choices allow children to give more to the peer at a cost to the self. Mexican American or Mexican children still tend to give more prize chips overall to a peer than do Euro-American children (e.g., Knight, Kagan, & Buriel, 1981). Mexican American children with a stronger ethnic identity have been found to display more concern with others' outcomes on this type of task (Knight, Cota, & Bernal, 1993). On a similar task, Cook Island Polynesian children were more generous than were New Zealand city and rural children of European origin (Graves & Graves, 1983).

In other studies, cross-national or cross-cultural differences in sharing or helping have been examined. Few consistent differences have been found among Western, industrialized countries such as Germany, Russia, Australia, and the United States (e.g., Kienbaum & Trommsdorff, 1999; Russell, Hart, Robinson, & Olsen, 2003), although young Italian adolescents report more prosocial behavior than Hungarian youth, who report more than Czech youth (Caprara, Barbaranelli, Pastorelli, Cermak, & Rosza, 2001). In studies within North and South America, Mexican rural children and Euro-American city children were equally likely to help a peer in a non-competitive context (Kagan & Madsen, 1972) and Mexican American and Euro-American children did not differ in anonymous sharing of candy with an unspecified classmate (Hansen & Bryant, 1980). In contrast,

U.S. first graders shared candy more than did Colombian children of the same age, although some (but not all) of this sharing was passive (i.e., they allowed a peer to take the candies; Pilgrim & Rueda-Riedle, 2002).

More consistent cross-group differences might be found when comparing Eastern and Western cultures. Although Trommsdorff (1995) did not find a difference in German and Japanese 5-year-olds' prosocial behavior with a distressed peer, Stewart and McBride-Chang (2000) found that Asian second graders (from a range of ethnic groups) were more likely than Western Caucasian children in Hong Kong to donate gifts for participating in the study to other children in the classroom who could not participate. Similarly, Rao and Stewart (1999) found that Asian (Chinese Hong Kong and Indian) kindergartners shared more food with a peer than had been found in a sample in the United States, and Asian children were more likely to do so spontaneously and to allow the peer to take some food. Thus, in initial small studies, it appears that Asian children are more likely to engage in prosocial behavior than are Western Caucasian children. This finding may be due to the greater focus on maintaining good relationships with group members (and on the interrelatedness of self and other) in at least some Asian cultures, compared with Western cultures (Markus & Kitayama, 1991).

Naturalistic Observational Research

Systematic observation of prosocial behavior in different cultures is rare. In the classic study by Whiting and Whiting (1975), prosocial behavior was operationalized as a composite index of offering helping (including food, toys, and helpful information), offering support, and making helpful suggestions. Cultures in which children scored relatively high on prosocial behavior (Kenya, Mexico, Philippines) tended to differ from the other three cultures (Okinawa, India, and the United States) on several dimensions. In prosocial cultures, people tended to live together in extended families, the female role was important (with women making major contributions to the economic status of the family), work was less specialized, and the government was less centralized. Further, children's prosocial behavior was associated with early assignment of chores and taking on responsibility for welfare of family members and the family's economic well-being (also see Whiting & Edwards, 1988). Similar to Whiting's data on chores and family structure, Graves and Graves (1983) found that

Aituaki (Polynesian) children, particularly girls, from urban settings performed fewer chores and were less prosocial than were children raised in traditional extended families.

Consistent with some of the aforementioned laboratory research on Asian and Western children's prosocial behavior, Stevenson (1991) found that the observed incidence of sharing, comforting, and helping in Taiwanese, Japanese, and U.S. kindergarten classes was lowest in the United States (albeit relatively high in all groups). Stevenson and others have argued that Chinese and Japanese societies generally put great emphasis on socializing children to be responsible and prosocial toward others in their group (e.g., the family, the classroom, and the society; also see Hieshima & Schneider, 1994). Privileges and social acknowledgment in the classroom are dependent on group rather than on individual accomplishments. Researchers have also suggested that Japanese mothers traditionally use empathic sensitivity in their parenting to promote their children's empathy with them and with others' needs (Lebra, 1994; Trommsdorff & Kornadt, 2003). However, parental valuing of prosocial behavior appears to have declined from the 1950s and 1960s to the 1980s in the People's Republic of China (Lee & Zhan, 1991), so it is unclear whether the findings would be replicated today in Asian countries that are undergoing rapid cultural transitions.

Moral Reasoning, Values, and Beliefs about Social Responsibility

Cultural norms regarding the importance of harmony among people and social responsibility differ across cultures and subcultures. Miller and her colleagues found that Hindu Indians held a broader and more stringent duty-based view of social responsibility than did people in the United States. Hindu Indians, school-age and adult, tended to focus more than North Americans on responsiveness to others' needs when discussing moral conflicts and viewed interpersonal responsibilities as at least as important as justice-related obligations (Miller & Bersoff, 1992). In contrast, people in the United States tended to view interpersonal responsiveness and caring as less obligatory and more of a personal choice, particularly if the other's need was moderate or minor, or if friends or strangers (rather than parents and children) were potential recipients (Miller, Bersoff, & Harwood, 1990). Adults in the United States, for example, were more likely than Indian adults to report that their liking of a needy sibling or colleague affected their

moral responsibility to help that person (Miller & Bersoff, 1998). Both groups, however, reported feeling less obligation to help people on the other side of the world than those in their own town. Miller and Bersoff (1992; Baron & Miller, 2000) argued that a personal morality of interpersonal responsiveness and caring (such as that in the United States) is linked to a strong cultural emphasis on individual rights and autonomy.

The research on prosocial and caring-related moral reasoning is a body of work relevant to an understanding of cross-cultural variation in cognitions about prosocial behavior. Among industrial Western cultures, relatively few cross-cultural differences in prosocial or caring-related reasoning have been noted, although minor differences have been found (see Eisenberg, Boehnke, Schuhler, & Silbereisen, 1985; Eisenberg, Hertz-Lazarowitz, & Fuchs, 1990; Skoe et al., 1999). Moreover, the reasons that German, Polish, Italian, and American adolescents attribute to themselves for helping or not helping were somewhat similar, although some differences have been found (Boehnke, Silbereisen, Eisenberg, Reykowski, & Palmonari, 1989). In general, however, the similarities in the care- or prosocial-related moral reasoning or prosocial self-attributions of individuals from Western cultures are much greater than the differences.

The prosocial-related moral reasoning of children and adults from non-Western or less industrial cultures may differ considerably from that of people from Western cultures, especially with age; however, the pattern is not very consistent. Carlo et al. (1996) found that Brazilian urban adolescents used less internalized (i.e., higher level) prosocial moral reasoning than did adolescents from the United States, although their reasoning was similar otherwise. Kumru, Carlo, Mestre, and Samper (2003) found that Turkish adolescents scored higher than Spanish adolescents on mid-level modes of prosocial moral reasoning (i.e., needs-oriented and stereotypic), whereas Spanish adolescents scored higher on both lower (hedonistic and approval oriented) and higher (internalized) types of moral reasoning. When justifying hypothetical moral decisions involving others' needs, Ma (1989) found that English adolescents were more oriented to their own survival and less to belongingness and to affective and altruistic motives than were Chinese adolescents from Hong Kong and mainland China. However, Stewart and McBride-Chang (2000) found no differences in Western Caucasian and Asian (mostly Chinese) second graders' moral reasoning; and Japanese children's prosocial moral reasoning resembled that of children from urbanized Western cultures (although there are some differences; Munekata & Ninomiya, 1985). In the one study of a nonindustrial, traditional sample, Tietjen (1986) found that although younger Maisen children from Papua New Guinea differed little in their prosocial moral reasoning from children in Western cultures, Maisen adults' moral reasoning was less sophisticated than that of Western adults. Maisen adults' reasoning, however, was probably appropriate for a small traditional society in which others' physical and psychological needs, costs for prosocial behavior, and pragmatic concerns are paramount to everyday life.

Making cross-cultural comparisons can be difficult because cultures differ considerably in their valuing of different types of prosocial action. Hindu Indians viewed prosocial behavior performed because of reciprocity considerations as more moral than did American adults (Miller & Bersoff, 1994). Further, Middle Eastern third graders in Israel seemed to value requested acts of consideration more, and spontaneous acts less, than did Israeli Jewish children of Western heritage (Jacobsen, 1983). Thus, Westerners may value prosocial acts that appear to be based on endogenous motivation more than do people from traditional cultures whereas people from traditional cultures value prosocial actions that reflect responsiveness to others' stated needs and reciprocal obligations.

SOCIALIZATION WITHIN AND OUTSIDE THE FAMILY

Family structure, socialization within the family, and socialization by peers and in the schools may augment or counteract cultural influences. However, the existing research has limitations, including an overreliance on parents' reports of the child's prosocial proclivities and of their own socialization practices or style, the use of very brief observations to measure behavior (which may not be generalizable), and a dearth of data from fathers and from minority and non-Western populations. It is likely that the relations of aspects of parental control and punitiveness to developmental outcomes (including prosocial and moral development) vary somewhat across cultures (Trommsdorff & Kornadt, 2003). Further, most of the work is correlational; thus, causal relations cannot be ascertained. The prevailing view of socialization is that the parent-child relationship is complex, bidirec-

tional, and transactional in influence (Bugental & Grusec, Chapter 7, this *Handbook,* this volume), and this relation is embedded in the macro environment (e.g., family, neighborhood, culture). However, this complexity generally is not reflected in the existing empirical research on the socialization of prosocial behavior.

Demographic Features of Families and Family Members

Intuitively, one might expect children's prosocial behavior to be related to the socioeconomic status (SES) of their families. Poorer children might be expected to horde scarce resources or, due to increased demand for participation in caregiving chores, to be relatively helpful and likely to comfort others in distress (see Whiting & Whiting, 1975).

Findings are inconsistent about the relation of indices of socioeconomic status such as family income or parental education to most types of prosocial behavior (Laible, Carlo, & Raffaelli, 2000; see Eisenberg & Fabes, 1998). However, many of the relevant studies include relatively few study participants. In a large study in England, factors such as social support for parents, favorable housing, and fewer transitions in maternal partner relationships, in addition to higher maternal education, higher family income, and lower levels of financial problems, were associated with higher levels of mother-reported prosocial behavior for school-age children (but less so for 4-year-old younger siblings; Dunn et al., 1998). Furthermore, findings are consistent for adolescents' volunteering behavior. In a large study of volunteerism among at-risk adolescents, family poverty was negatively associated with males' involvement in volunteering and community activity (Lichter, Shanahan, & Gardner, 2002); a similar relation was obtained for both sexes in another large study involving a more representative sample (Hart, Atkins, & Ford, 1998) and in other studies on volunteering in the United States (Huebner & Mancini, 2003; Lichter et al., 2002; National Center for Education Statistics, 1997; Uggen & Janikula, 1999; Youniss, McLellan, Su, & Yates, 1999) and Hong Kong (Chou, 1998). Nonetheless, most of these relations are modest in magnitude.

Findings on the relation of family structure and family size to prosocial behavior are mixed. Rehberg and Richman (1989) found that preschool boys from father-absent homes comforted (but did not help) a peer more than did girls and boys from two-parent homes. Other researchers have not found effects of father absence on measures of prosocial responding (Call, Mortimer, & Shanahan, 1995; Dunn et al., 1998), and some researchers have found that adolescents in two-parent families volunteer more than those in one-parent homes (Huebner & Mancini, 2003; Keith et al., 1990; Lichter et al., 2002; Youniss et al., 1999). Investigators have found that family size and prosocial behavior or sympathy are unrelated (e.g., Chou, 1998; Gelfand, Hartmann, Cromer, Smith, & Page, 1975); that children in a large family volunteer more (Zaff, Moore, Papillo, & Williams, 2003); and that children with siblings are less likely to help in an emergency situation (Staub, 1971b) or to comfort a peer (Rehberg & Richman, 1989). Staub speculated that children from small families are more self-assured and, consequently, are more likely to take initiative and intervene spontaneously to help someone else. In contrast, children in larger families, perhaps due to the need to engage in chores, are particularly likely to learn everyday helping and sharing behaviors. Consistent with this reasoning, Weissbrod (1976) found that large family size was related to slower helping in an emergency but higher levels of generosity.

Findings concerning ordinal position are few and limited in scope. Firstborn children, particularly girls, have been found to be more willing than their peers to give commodities to peers (Sharma, 1988) and to intervene in an emergency (Staub, 1971b). Moreover, older siblings, compared with younger siblings, more often behave prosocially in sibling interactions (Bryant & Crockenberg, 1980; Dunn & Munn, 1986; Furman & Buhrmester, 1985; Stoneman, Brody, & MacKinnon, 1986; Whiting & Whiting, 1975), perhaps due in part to their older age (rather than ordinal position per se) and their greater engagement in chores and caregiving that provide opportunities for prosocial behavior (de Guzman, Edwards, & Carlo, 2005). Other investigators have found no relation between birth order and measures of prosocial responding (e.g., Gelfand et al., 1975; Rheingold, Hay, & West, 1976) or sympathy (Wise & Cramer, 1988), or have obtained mixed findings (Eisenberg, Fabes, Karbon, Murphy, Carlo, et al., 1996). In general, older children seem to be somewhat more prosocial, especially in their actual (rather than reported) prosocial behavior and in interactions with younger children.

Parental Socialization Style and Practices

Many investigators have examined the relations of parenting style and a range of specific socialization prac-

tices to children's prosocial behavior and empathy/sympathy.

Parental Warmth and Quality of the Parent-Child Relationship

Intuitively, it would seem that warm, supportive socializers would rear prosocial children. However, support for this assumption is mixed. In some studies, a positive relation between an index of maternal warmth/support or sensitivity (often versus negativity) and children's and adolescents' prosocial or empathic/sympathetic responding has been obtained, at least for some measures (Asbury, Dunn, Pike, & Plomin, 2003; Bryant & Crockenberg, 1980; Deater-Deckard, Dunn, et al., 2001; Dunn, Cutting, & Fisher, 2002; Eberly et al., 1993; Eberly & Montemayor, 1998; Janssens & Dekovic, 1997; Janssens & Gerris, 1992; Kiang et al., 2004; Krevans & Gibbs, 1996; Laible & Carlo, 2004; Lerner et al., 2005; Robinson, Zahn-Waxler, & Emde, 1994; Strayer & Roberts, 2004b; Zahn-Waxler, Radke-Yarrow, & King, 1979; also see Shek & Ma, 2001). In contrast, other investigators have failed to obtain evidence of a relation between parental warmth (or rejection) and children's prosocial behavior or empathy/sympathy (Eberly & Montemayor, 1999; Iannotti et al., 1992; Kienbaum, Volland, & Ulich, 2001; Koestner, Franz, & Weinberger, 1990; Stewart & McBride-Chang, 2000; Turner & Harris, 1984) or have found very different relations of parental support with children's prosocial behavior and sympathy (Carlo, Roesch, & Melby, 1998). Sometimes the relation of parental warmth to children's prosocial responding has been weak and only significant through mediation; for example, Zhou et al. (2002) found that the relation of parental warmth to elementary school students' facial and self-reported empathy was indirect through its positive relation with parental expressions of positive emotion in contexts involving others' emotions (especially others' positive emotions).

Support for the role of parental nurturance or warmth can be gleaned from several other bodies of data. Parents' report of children's helpfulness is higher for adolescents who share more time and activities with their parents (Eberly & Montemayor, 1998) and when fathers in two-parent families are more involved in child care (Bernadett-Shapiro, Ehrensaft, & Shapiro, 1996). A study in which parenting was assessed with observations (Kochanska, Forman, & Coy, 1999) found that maternal responsivity (contingent, appropriate responding) to their infants at 9 (but not 14) months predicted higher levels of toddlers' empathy/prosocial responsiveness at 22 months (cf. van der Mark et al., 2002). Moreover, Spinrad (1999) found that observed maternal sensitivity to their infants at 10 months was positively related to toddlers' concerned attention at 18 months of age to adults' feigned distress. Further, Clark and Ladd (2000) found that parental connectedness (including mutual parent-child positive engagement, warmth, intimacy, and happy emotional tone, as well as reciprocity) was positively related to kindergartners' teacher-reported prosocial tendencies.

There also is limited evidence that children with secure attachments to their mothers at a young age are more sympathetic at 3.5 years of age (Waters, Hay, & Richters, 1986) and display more prosocial behavior and concern for others at approximately age 5 years (Iannotti et al., 1992; Kestenbaum, Farber, & Sroufe, 1989). In a study with 22-month-old children, the relation between attachment and empathy/sympathy was positive but weak and somewhat inconsistent (Van der Mark et al., 2002). Moreover, adolescents' reports of attachment to their parents have been associated with Turkish early adolescents' empathy/sympathy/perspective taking (Kumru & Edwards, 2003), middle or late adolescents' sympathy/perspective taking and prosocial behavior (Laible, Carlo, & Roesch, 2004; Markiewicz, Doyle, & Brendgen, 2001), and parents' reports of adolescents' helpfulness (Eberly & Montemayor, 1998), albeit not in all studies (de Guzman & Carlo, 2004; Eberly & Montemayor, 1999), and not across 2 years' time (Laible, Carlo, & Raffaelli, 2000). Because securely attached offspring tend to have sensitive and warm parents, the finding of a relation between the security of children's attachments and their prosocial tendencies is indirect support for an association between parental warmth and children's prosocial development.

Why might children with warm parents and secure attachments be more prosocial? Waters et al. (1986) suggested that children with secure attachments differentially attend to their parent, are positively oriented to the parent, are familiar with and reproduce parents' actions, and are responsive to parental control and wish to avoid parental censure. These tendencies would be expected to enhance the effectiveness of parents' attempts to encourage prosocial behavior. Staub (1992) also argued that the quality of early attachments is important to the development of a sense of connection to others and positive valuing of other people—two characteristics with conceptual links to intrinsically based caring for other people (also see Oliner & Oliner, 1988). Nonetheless, in families in which the child or parent has

significant psychological problems, the link between attachment and prosocial behavior or empathy/sympathy may vary in a complex manner (e.g., Radke-Yarrow, Zahn-Waxler, Richardson, Susman, & Martinez, 1994).

It is likely that the degree of association between children's prosocial responding and parental warmth is moderated by other socialization practices. Dekovic and Janssens (1992) found that democratic parenting, involving parental warmth and support, combined with inductions, demandingness, and the provision of suggestions, information, and positive comments, was associated with Dutch children's prosocial behavior as reported by teachers and peers (also see Janssens & Dekovic, 1997). Similarly, Robinson et al. (1994) found that mothers who were relatively negative *and* controlling had children who tended to decrease rather than increase in empathy from 14 to 20 months of age (for those moderate or high in empathy at 14 months). Moreover, as discussed in the section on modeling, socializers who are nurturant *and* model prosocial behavior seem to promote costly prosocial behavior in children (e.g., Yarrow & Scott, 1972; Yarrow, Scott, & Waxler, 1973). Nurturance may serve as a background or contextual variable that enhances the child's receptivity to parental influence, including parental inductions, preachings, and moral standards (Hoffman, 1970).

Inductions

A disciplinary practice of particular importance in the study of prosocial behavior is *parental induction* (i.e., verbal discipline in which the socializer gives explanations or reasons for requiring the child to change his or her behavior; Hoffman, 1970). Hoffman (2000) argued that inductions are likely to promote moral development because they induce an optimal level of arousal for learning (i.e., elicit the child's attention, but are unlikely to disrupt learning). Further, inductions are not likely to be viewed as arbitrary by the child and thereby induce resistance; rather, they focus children's attention on the consequences of their behavior for others, thereby capitalizing on children's capacity to empathize and experience guilt. Hoffman further suggested that over time, inductive messages are experienced as internalized because the child plays an active role in processing the information (which is encoded and integrated with information contained in other inductions) and the focus is on the child's action and its consequences rather than on the parent as the disciplinary agent. Thus, over time, children are likely to remember the causal link between their actions and consequences for others rather than the external pressure or the specific disciplinary context.

Investigators usually have tried to assess the degree to which parents use inductions as a general mode of discipline, not simply to promote prosocial behavior (as for experimental studies on preaching). Inductions vary in their content: They can appeal to justice, including fairness of the consequences of the child's behavior for another; appeal to legitimate authorities; or provide matter-of-fact, nonmoralistic information. In addition, inductions may be focused on the consequences of the child's behavior for either the parent or for the other person involved in the situation (often called peer-oriented inductions). Hoffman (1970) argued that peer-oriented inductions are likely to be most effective because they are most apt to induce sympathy.

There is support for an association between parental use of inductions and children's prosocial tendencies, although significant findings often have been obtained for one sex, age, or socioeconomic status group, or for one measure of prosocial behavior (or empathy/sympathy), and not another. Nonetheless, positive associations have been found in studies in which the type of reasoning was not specified (Bar-Tal, Nadler, & Blechman, 1980; Dlugokinski & Firestone, 1974; Feshbach, 1978; Janssens & Gerris, 1992; Oliner & Oliner, 1988; cf. Trommsdorff, 1991), as well as in those in which parental inductions focused on peers' or others' feelings or states (Hoffman, 1975; Karylowski, 1982; Krevans & Gibbs, 1996; Stanhope, Bell, & Parker-Cohen, 1987). Victim-oriented discipline seems to enhance the level of children's interpersonal understanding (e.g., perspective taking), which is associated with higher guilt, including concern about harm to another (de Veer & Janssens, 1994). Further, inductions that emphasize how others (including the parent) react to children's behavior have been found to predict higher levels of prosocial behavior (Krevans & Gibbs, 1996). Stewart and McBride-Chang (2000) found that parental emphasis on the effects of the child's misbehavior in the family and what others think of the child was positively related to the anonymous donations of Asian children in Hong Kong.

The tone in which inductions are delivered often may contribute to their effectiveness, particularly with young children. Zahn-Waxler, Radke-Yarrow, and King (1979) noted that maternal use of affectively charged explanations, particularly those that included moralizing, was positively associated with toddlers' prosocial behavior in the second and 3rd years of life. Explanations delivered without affect were not effective, per-haps because the toddlers were unlikely to attend or to think that their mother was serious. Similarly, Miller, Eisenberg, Fabes, Shell, and Gular (1989) found that inductions regarding peers were positively related to children's sad reactions to viewing others in distress and, when delivered by mothers with affective intensity, to low levels of facial distress (an index of personal distress rather than sympathy). However, parental inductions delivered in situations involving relatively high degrees of anger, particularly inductions that are guilt-inducing, seem to be associated with low levels of preschoolers' parent-directed prosocial behavior (Denham, Renwick-DeBardi, & Hewes, 1994).

The configuration of parenting practices appears to influence the effectiveness of inductions. They are likely to be more effective at promoting prosocial behavior or empathy when verbalized by parents who typically do not use power-assertive (punitive) techniques (Hoffman, 1963; also see Dlugokinski & Firestone, 1974) or are part of a pattern of democratic or authoritative parenting (Dekovic & Janssens, 1992; Janssens & Gerris, 1992).

Some of the inconsistency in the findings on inductions may stem from a failure by researchers to assess critical dimensions of parental messages. Grusec and Goodnow (1994) argued that internalization of parental messages likely depends on children's accurate perception of the message (including its content, the rules implied in the message, and the parent's intentions and investment in the message) and children's acceptance of it. They suggested that the clarity, redundancy, and consistency of the message, as well as its fit to the child's developmental level, influence children's accurate perception of the message. Children are more likely to accept the message if they perceive it as appropriate, find it motivating (e.g., if it arouses empathy or insecurity), and believe that the value inherent in the message is self-generated. Grusec and Goodnow also hypothesized that parental responsivity or past willingness to comply with the child's wishes promotes the child's willingness to comply with the parent's wishes. Thus, it may be productive to examine the clarity of parents' messages and variables related to children's acceptance of the message as moderators of the relation between parental inductions and children's prosocial behavior.

Power-Assertive, Punitive Techniques of Discipline

Researchers generally have found that socializers' use of power-assertive techniques of discipline such as physical punishment or deprivation of privileges is either unrelated (e.g., Janssens & Gerris, 1992; Kochanska et al., 1999; Zahn-Waxler, Radke-Yarrow, & King, 1979) or negatively related to children's prosocial behavior (Asbury, Dunn, Pike, & Plomin, 2003; Bar-Tal, Nadler, et al., 1980; Deater-Deckard, Dunn, et al., 2001; Dlugokinski & Firestone, 1974; Krevans & Gibbs, 1996), empathy (Janssens & Gerris, 1992; Krevans & Gibbs, 1996), or sympathy (Spinrad et al., 1999). Likewise, a punitive, authoritarian parenting style has been unrelated (Iannotti, Cummings, Pierrehumbert, Milano, & Zahn-Waxler, 1992; Russell et al., 2003, for mothers; also see Diener & Kim, 2004) or negatively related (Dekovic & Janssens, 1992; Hastings et al., 2000; Russell et al., 2003, for fathers) to children's prosocial behavior and sympathy, and its negative relation with sympathy may increase with age (Hastings et al., 2000). Moreover, physical abuse of children has been linked to low levels of children's empathy and prosocial behavior (Howes & Eldredge, 1985; Main & George, 1985; Miller & Eisenberg, 1988; see Koenig, Cicchetti, & Rogosch, 2004, for mixed findings).

Nonetheless, there is a difference between the occasional, measured use of power-assertive techniques in the context of a positive parent-child relationship and the use of punishment as the preferred, predominant mode of discipline. Rescuers of Jews in Nazi Europe reported that the punishment they had received from their parents was not a routine response and was linked to specific behaviors rather than used gratuitously (Oliner & Oliner, 1988). Further, Miller et al. (1989) found that maternal report of using physical techniques (including physical punishment) was positively associated with preschoolers' empathic sadness when viewing others in distress, but only for children whose mothers also used relatively high levels of inductive discipline (cf. Hoffman, 1963).

Punishment can induce immediate compliance with socializers' expectations for prosocial behavior if the socializer monitors the child's behavior (Morris, Marshall, & Miller, 1973), particularly if the contingency between lack of prosocial behavior and punishment is specified (Hartmann et al., 1976). However, these effects often extinguish when punishment is removed (Hartmann et al., 1976), and children tend to attribute prosocial behavior induced by power-assertive techniques to external motives such as fear of detection or punishment (Dix & Grusec, 1983; Smith, Gelfand, Hartmann, & Partlow, 1979). Nonetheless, social disapproval, unlike material punishment (e.g., fines for not helping), has been positively associated with children's

attributing their own donating to internal motives (Smith et al., 1979). Thus, it is possible that social disapproval (verbal punishment) can be used to enhance internally motivated prosocial behavior; indeed, maternal expressions of disappointment have been linked to greater prosocial behavior (Stewart & McBride-Chang, 2000). Although most middle-class mothers in Western cultures such as the United States rarely use punishment (especially physical punishment) to induce helping or in response to children's failure to help (Grusec, 1991; Zahn-Waxler et al., 1979), this may be less true in Asian societies (see Stewart & McBride-Chang, 2000).

Appropriate versus Inappropriate Parental Control

Perhaps the critical issue when thinking about parental punishment and control is whether the degree of power asserted by the parent is perceived as excessive and arbitrary versus reasonable in the given context or culture. Parental demands and expectations for socially responsible and moral behavior (often expressed in an authoritative parenting style) have been associated with socially responsible and prosocial behavior (e.g., Dekovic & Janssens, 1992; Janssens & Dekovic, 1997; Janssens & Gerris, 1992; Lidner-Gunnoe, Hetherington, & Reiss; 1999), adolescents' endorsement of caring values (Pratt, Hunsberger, Pancer, & Alisat, 2003), and caring moral reasoning (Pratt, Skoe, & Arnold, 2004). In contrast, strict, rejecting control has been linked to low levels of sympathy (Laible & Carlo, 2004). Somewhat related, in Western cultures, parental emphasis on adolescents' autonomy also has been linked with prosocial development (Bar-Tal, Nadler, et al., 1980; Pratt et al., 2004); this relation may hold less in early childhood (Clark & Ladd, 2000). In Asian cultures that emphasize parental training and filial piety (Stewart et al., 1998), training of this sort was associated with anonymous prosocial behavior, whereas restrictive control was marginally, negatively related (Stewart & McBride-Chang, 2000). Other researchers have found a positive association between appropriate parental control (rather than leniency) and children's empathy (Bryant, 1987) or girls' (but not boys') sympathy years later in adulthood (Koestner, Franz, & Weinberger, 1990). Analogously, parental monitoring of adolescents' activities was positively related to adolescents' volunteerism in large survey research (Huebner & Mancini, 2003; Zaff et al., 2003). For middle-class families, parental demands for prosocial behavior appear to be part of a child-rearing pattern in which mature behavior is expected (Greenberger & Goldberg, 1989). In contrast, parental valuing of mere compliance, which often may lead to arbitrary overcontrol, has been linked to low levels of children's prosocial behavior with mothers and peers (Eisenberg, Wolchik, Goldberg, & Engel, 1992).

Parental Emphasis on Prosocial Values

Because parents who hold prosocial values would be expected to teach and model prosocial behavior, it is reasonable to expect a relation between parental prosocial values and children's prosocial behavior. Parents' reports of holding prosocial values have been associated with peer nominations of fifth graders' prosocial behavior (including prosocial behavior, guilt, and rule-following; Hoffman, 1975) and older adolescents' caring moral reasoning (Pratt et al., 2004; also see Eisenberg, Wolchik, et al., 1992). Although some investigators have found no evidence of a relation between parental emphasis on prosocial responding (reported or observed) and children's prosocial behavior or empathy (Turner & Harris, 1984), others have obtained mixed (Bryant & Crockenberg, 1980) or positive relations (Trommsdorff, 1991) (also see section on modeling and preachings).

Perhaps the most compelling evidence for the importance of parental prosocial values comes from studies of adults who have displayed unusual acts of altruism. Rescuers in Nazi Europe often recalled learning values of caring from their parents or the other most influential person in their lives (Oliner & Oliner, 1988; also see Hart & Fegley, 1995; London, 1970). Rescuers reported that their parents felt that ethical values were to be extended to all human beings. Interestingly, rescuers did not differ from nonrescuers in reported exposure to nonprosocial values such as honesty or equity. However, real-life moral exemplars often solidify their values or even develop new moral values in adulthood when interacting with other adults who discuss value-related issues and jointly engage in moral activities with the individual (Colby & Damon, 1992). Thus, it is likely that the socialization of other-oriented values, even if it begins in one's family of origin, is a continuing dynamic process.

Modeling

Because of the importance of modeling in social learning theory (e.g., Bandura, 1986), numerous researchers have examined whether children's prosocial behavior varies as a function of exposure to prosocial versus selfish models. Much of the relevant research has been conducted in laboratory studies using strangers or brief acquaintances as models and donating as the index of

prosocial behavior. Thus, the generalizability of much of the laboratory research to real-life settings involving familiar models and to other types of prosocial actions can be questioned. The experimental laboratory literature is supplemented by a smaller body of work, often correlational in design, in which real-life situations and familiar models have been used; and similar results have been obtained in these studies.

In the prototypic laboratory study of modeling prosocial behavior, children earn prizes, tokens, or money by winning a game, view or do not view a model, and then are provided an opportunity to donate to needy children or to children who did not get to play the game. Because this topic was reviewed in considerable detail in Eisenberg and Fabes (1998) and there have been few new studies since 1998, this work is briefly summarized here. In general, children who view a generous model or helpful model are more generous or helpful than those exposed to a control condition (often a model who had no opportunity to donate; e.g., Rice & Grusec, 1975; Rushton & Littlefield, 1979; Rushton & Teachman, 1978) or a selfish model (e.g., Bryan & Walbek, 1970; Rushton, 1975). Further, multiple models may be more effective than inconsistent models for inducing precise imitation of donating (Wilson, Piazza, & Nagle, 1990).

In most laboratory studies of modeling, prosocial behavior is modeled only once; thus, it is impressive that some investigators have obtained evidence of generalization to new behaviors or settings (Midlarsky & Bryan, 1967; Rushton, 1975), although others have not (Rushton & Littlefield, 1979; Rushton & Teachman, 1978). Further, investigators have found effects of modeling days to months later (Israel & Raskin, 1979; Rice & Grusec, 1975; Rushton, 1975; Rushton & Littlefield, 1979; Wilson et al., 1990).

Adults who control valued resources (Grusec, 1971) appear to be relatively powerful models, as are models perceived as competent (Eisenberg-Berg & Geisheker, 1979). Moreover, nurturant prosocial models whom children have just met seem to promote prosocial behavior when the prosocial behavior is not costly and is something they probably want to do (e.g., help when they hear someone in distress; Weissbrod, 1976; also see Staub, 1971a). In contrast, when prosocial behavior involves self-denial (e.g., donations), short-term exposure to a warm model seems to have little effect or may even reduce donating behavior (Grusec, 1971; Midlarsky & Bryan, 1967; Weissbrod, 1976). Thus, short-term noncontingent warmth seems to disinhibit children to do as they please, including assisting distressed others as well as keeping valued commodities for themselves. However, in the classroom context in which warmth probably is not entirely noncontingent, preschool children model the prosocial behaviors and nurturance of adults with whom they have had a relatively extended nurturant relationship (Yarrow & Scott, 1972; Yarrow et al., 1973).

In addition to the laboratory studies, investigators have examined whether children appear to model real-life socializers such as parents. In the first 2 years of life, children do not seem to consistently model maternal sharing or helping of a distressed person (Hay & Murray, 1982; Zahn-Waxler et al., 1979). However, mothers' modeling of helping behaviors (such as participation in household chores) seems to enhance the likelihood of 1- and 2-year-olds helping with similar tasks (Rheingold, 1982). Moreover, the data on real-life altruists suggest an effect of parental modeling. Youth volunteerism has been found to be related to the degree to which their parents volunteer; moreover, the types of voluntary activities chosen by youths tend to be similar to those of their parents (e.g., in providing a social service or working for a cause; Keith et al., 1990; McLellan & Youniss, 2003; National Center for Education Statistics, 1997; also see Hart & Fegley, 1995; Janoski & Wilson, 1995; Stukas, Switzer, Dew, Goycoolea, & Simmons, 1999).

Consistent with the notion that parental modeling fosters children's prosocial tendencies, sympathetic parents, who likely model sympathy, tend to have same-sex elementary school children who are helpful (Fabes, Eisenberg, & Miller, 1990) or prone to sympathy rather than to egoistic personal distress (Eisenberg, Fabes, Carlo, Troyer, et al., 1992; Eisenberg, Fabes, Schaller, Carlo, & Miller, 1991; Eisenberg & McNally, 1993; Fabes et al., 1990). In contrast, links between parental empathy (rather than sympathy) and children's empathy have been mixed, with some researchers obtaining positive relations (Barnett, Howard, King, & Dino, 1980; Strayer & Roberts, 2004b; Trommsdorff, 1991) and others obtaining no relations or inconsistent correlations (e.g., Bernadett-Shapiro, Ehrensaft, & Shapiro, 1996; Strayer & Roberts, 1989). Some parents prone to empathy may become overly aroused and personally distressed, which would be expected to lead to lower levels of helping in many contexts. Multiple mechanisms, including the heritability of emotionality related to sympathy or other characteristics, could explain the significant findings that have been obtained.

In regard to high-cost real-life helping behavior, Rosenhan (1970) found that Caucasian civil rights activists in the late 1950s and 1960s who were highly involved and committed to the cause despite considerable danger and cost reported that their parents were both nurturant and actively involved in working for altruistic and humanitarian causes. In contrast, individuals who were less involved and committed reported that their parents preached prosocial values but often did not practice altruism. Further, rescuers of Jews in Nazi Europe described their parents as having acted in accordance with strong moral convictions (London, 1970; Oliner & Oliner, 1988).

The data from studies of adult altruists are not only correlational in design but involve retrospective data. Even if people's recall of parental practices were unbiased and accurate, it is possible that their altruism stemmed from family factors other than modeling, such as optimal discipline or exposure to prosocial cultural or community values. Nonetheless, research findings on parents of prosocial offspring converge with the experimental laboratory findings that implicate modeling in the development of prosocial tendencies.

Preachings

The verbalizations of adults relevant to prosocial behavior have been examined in nondisciplinary contexts (laboratory situations in which the adult is not responding to the child's misbehavior), as well as in disciplinary situations (e.g., inductions). In studies of the effects of preachings or exhortations, the preacher states what should be done (sometimes in regard to his or her own earnings that can be donated), but does not directly and explicitly direct the child to assist. Often the preacher also gives reasons that one should or should not assist. Preachers may verbalize to themselves, as if thinking through the issue (Eisenberg-Berg & Geisheker, 1979), or direct their preaching to the child (e.g., Bryan & Walbek, 1970; Rushton, 1975). Preachings often are normative in content, with the preacher stating what should be done and stating either prosocial or selfish norms (e.g., "It's a nice thing [not such a nice thing] to give to the crippled children"; Bryan & Walbek, 1970). In a neutral control group, the preacher typically would make normatively neutral statements such as "This game is fun."

Most researchers have found no effects, or inconsistent effects, of normative preachings by nonparental adults on children's donating behavior (e.g., Bryan & Walbek, 1970; cf. Zarbatany, Hartmann, & Gelfand,

1985). However, normative preachings seem to foster generosity if the preacher promoting donating is an adult who is likely to have direct power over the children (Eisenberg-Berg & Geisheker, 1979). In addition, empathy-inducing preachings that emphasize the emotional consequences of assisting for the recipients of aid have been found to elicit more donating in private than do neutral control preachings (Dlugokinski & Firestone, 1974; Eisenberg-Berg & Geisheker, 1979; Perry, Bussey, & Freiberg, 1981; Smith, 1983) or punitive, threatening preachings (Perry et al., 1981). Empathy-inducing preachings also have been found to enhance the effort and success of children in elementary school when helping a peer (Ladd, Lange, & Stremmel, 1983) and have been related to prosocial behavior in another setting or at a later date (Grusec, Saas-Kortsaak, & Simutis, 1978; Smith, 1983).

Not all researchers have found effects of empathy-inducing preachings. The wording in some studies may have led the children to believe that the adult or the beneficiary would be angry at them for not helping, which might evoke reactance rather than empathy (McGrath & Power, 1990), or compliance rather than internalization. Preachings seem to work best if children feel that they have a choice of whether to assist and if the preachings highlight the positive outcomes of helping for another (Grusec, Saas-Kortsaak, & Simutis, 1978; McGrath, Wilson, & Frassetto; 1995). Further, the results of one study suggest that empathic preachings are effective primarily for children who have been exposed to inductive discipline at home (rather than a relatively high degree of power assertion; Dlugokinski & Firestone, 1974).

Prompts and Directives

Children who are instructed or prompted to help or share tend to do so (Gelfand et al., 1975; Hay & Murray, 1982; Israel & Raskin, 1979), and the effects of directive instructions have been found to persist over 11 days (Israel & Brown, 1979) or 4 weeks (Israel & Raskin, 1979). Direct requests for prosocial behavior may be particularly important for younger children because of their limited abilities to understand others' emotions and situational cues (Denham, Mason, & Couchoud, 1995). However, there is evidence that constraining directives are less effective with older children than with younger ones (White & Burnam, 1975), particularly over time (Israel & Raskin, 1979; cf. Israel & Brown, 1979). Highly constraining instructions may induce reactance; moreover, after the early years, children are unlikely to attribute forced behavior to internal reasons

and, consequently, may not enact prosocial behavior in an unsupervised setting (see McGrath & Power, 1990).

Reinforcement for Prosocial Behavior

Consistent with learning theory, concrete (Fischer, 1963) and social (Eisenberg, Fabes, Carlo, et al., 1993; Gelfand et al., 1975; Grusec & Redler, 1980; Rushton & Teachman, 1978; cf. Mills & Grusec, 1989) reinforcements have been found to increase children's prosocial behavior, at least in the immediate context. Further, parental reports of reinforcement for children's sympathetic and prosocial behavior have been associated with girls' (but not boys') concerned or sad reactions to others in distress (Eisenberg, Fabes, Carlo, et al., 1992).

Although concrete rewards may induce prosocial behavior in the given context, the long-term effect of concrete rewards may be negative. Consistent with Lepper's (1983) notion that the provision of concrete rewards undermines intrinsic motivation (and also may induce children to attribute their prosocial actions to external motivation), Szynal-Brown and Morgan (1983) found that third-grade children who were promised tangible rewards if the younger children they tutored did well were less likely to engage in teaching activities during a subsequent free-choice period than were tutors who were not promised rewards for teaching. Those children promised rewards that were not contingent on the pupil's learning were between the aforementioned two groups in regard to teaching, but did not differ significantly from either. Further, Fabes, Fultz, Eisenberg, Plumlee, and Christopher (1989) found that the use of material rewards for school children's helping behavior undermined their subsequent, anonymous prosocial behavior during a free-choice situation, particularly for children whose mothers valued the use of rewards. Moreover, mothers who felt relatively positive about using rewards reported that their children were less prosocial than did mothers who were less enthusiastic about the use of rewards. Rewards may be salient for these children and, consequently, they may be particularly likely to attribute their initial prosocial behavior to the external reward (rather than to an internal motive).

The effects of social reinforcement may vary as a function of type of praise and the age of the child. For young children, reinforcement for prosocial behavior does not seem to increase prosocial tendencies in another setting or over time and may even undermine it (Eisenberg, Wolchik, et al., 1992; Grusec, 1991). Moreover, praise that attributes the children's positive behavior to their dispositional kindness or internal motives (e.g., because they enjoy helping others) appears to be more effective than praise that simply labels the act as positive (Grusec & Redler, 1980; Mills & Grusec, 1989; dispositional attribution is a special type of praise and is discussed in the following subsection). Grusec and Redler (1980) found that social reinforcement for prosocial actions (without an internal attribution) increased elementary school children's prosocial behavior in the immediate context; however, it was associated with the generalization of prosocial behavior to a different, anonymous situation only for 10-year-old children (not for 5- or 8-year-olds). Grusec and Redler (1980) hypothesized that older children may interpret reinforcement for a specific action as having implications for a variety of situations, whereas younger children do not view praise for a given act as having broader relevance.

Provision of Attributions or Dispositional Praise

Elementary school children are likely to behave in a prosocial manner on a subsequent occasion if they initially are induced to behave prosocially and are provided with internal attributions (i.e., dispositional praise) for their actions (e.g., "I guess you're the kind of person who likes to help others whenever you can. Yes, you are a very nice and helpful person"; Grusec & Redler, 1980). Children provided with such praise are more helpful or generous even weeks later than are children who are provided with no attribution (Grusec, Kuczynski, Rushton, & Simutis, 1978; Grusec & Redler, 1980; Holte, Jamruszka, Gustafson, Beaman, & Camp, 1984; cf. Eisenberg, Cialdini, McCreath, & Shell, 1987) or with one attributing prosocial behavior to the fact that the adult experimenter expected such behavior (Grusec, Kuczynski, et al., 1978).

The provision of internal attributions is believed to foster a prosocial self-image that then results in enhanced prosocial behavior (Grusec & Redler, 1980). However, support for this supposition is mixed (e.g., Holte et al., 1984; Mills & Grusec, 1989). If changes in children's self-concepts mediate the effects of dispositional attributions, the provision of internal attributions would not be expected to be effective until children have some understanding of personality traits and their stability. Consistent with this logic, Grusec and Redler (1980) found that the provision of internal attributions was effective in enhancing prosocial behavior both immediately and long term (e.g., a week or more later) for middle and later elementary school children, but not for kindergartners. Further, Eisenberg, Cialdini, McCreath, and Shell (1989) found that children in elementary

school who were induced to engage in prosocial behavior and provided with internal attributions were more helpful if they demonstrated the ability to label traits accurately. Thus, it is possible that an understanding of traits is essential if internal attributions are to foster children's prosocial behavior.

Learning by Doing (and the Foot-in-the-Door Effect)

Children's participation in prosocial activities seems to foster prosocial behavior at a later time, although boys sometimes may exhibit some reactance in the short-term (Staub, 1992). This pattern of findings has been obtained using both experimental procedures (Staub, 1979; although effects may be stronger for older children; Eisenberg, Cialdini, et al., 1987) and in research linking prosocial proclivities to participation in household chores (perhaps particularly those that benefit others; Graves & Graves, 1983; Rehberg & Richman, 1989; Whiting & Whiting, 1975; cf. Gelfand et al., 1975). In some cultures, guided participation (Rogoff, 2003) may be a major way in which children are socialized into a variety of activities, including prosocial ones (Whiting & Whiting, 1975).

In a study of 9- and 14-year-old children, Grusec, Goodnow, and Cohen (1996) found that routine (but not requested) participation in household chores was related to youths' prosocial behavior in the family, but primarily for older youth and girls. Routine participation in chores was not related to helping strangers. Thus, if chores benefit a delimited group of individuals, any prosocial tendencies fostered may not extend to those beyond that group.

Participation in organized youth activities and nonvoluntary service required by school programs also has been linked to prosocial behavior, especially subsequent volunteerism or intentions to volunteer (Metz & Youniss, 2003; Stukas, Switzer, et al., 1999; Youniss & Metz, 2004). In addition, adolescents' and young adults' participation in voluntary community service sometimes has been linked to greater feelings of commitment to helping others (Yates & Youniss, 1996b; see discussion of these programs in the section on adolescence). Of particular interest, Youniss and Metz (2004) found that required school-based service was related to increased volunteerism and intentions to volunteer for students who were less inclined to participate; it had little effect for those students who quickly completed their requirement and went on to participate in voluntary activities. In contrast, Stukas, Snyder, and Clary (1999) found that mandatory volunteerism undermined college students' future intentions to volunteer only for individuals who otherwise would not have been volunteering (i.e., they felt that their service was solely due to external force) or for those who had the preexisting belief that they would not freely choose to engage in any volunteer activities. For most students who are not generally opposed to volunteer service activities and do not focus on external pressures to engage in such activities, mandatory service participation seems likely to increase prosocial responding.

The findings on the effects of practice and compulsory service activities are similar to those obtained by social psychologists studying compliance (i.e., the "foot-in-the-door" effect) in adulthood. Although the processes underlying the findings for adults are not entirely clear (Burger, 1999; Cialdini & Goldstein, 2004), a common explanation is that engaging in the initial prosocial behavior changes the actor's self-perceptions about his or her own prosocial disposition or the actor's attitude about helpfulness. A self-concept explanation is consistent with Eisenberg, Cialdini, et al.'s (1989) finding that the effects of an initial helping experience were primarily for children with a rudimentary understanding of trait labels (because an understanding of traits is necessary for a stable self-concept) and with Eisenberg, Cialdini, et al.'s (1987) finding that practice had an effect only for children old enough to understand consistency in personality. However, there is little direct evidence that a more sophisticated understanding of the stability of personality is necessary for the foot-in-the-door effect to be effective.

It also is possible that engaging in prosocial activities enhances subsequent prosocial behavior because the experience provides empathic rewards, helping skills, and social approval. Further, investigators have argued that service activities can promote identity formation, a sense of personal competence and civic responsibility, and the adoption of prosocial norms, as well as opportunities to learn about systems of meaning (e.g., about society, social injustice; McLellan & Youniss, 2003; Yates & Youniss, 1996a, 1996b, 1998).

Emotion Socialization

Parental practices that help children to cope with their negative emotion in a constructive fashion tend to be associated with children's sympathy (rather than personal distress) and prosocial behavior. This may be partly because children who cannot adequately cope with their emotions tend to become overaroused and ex-

perience a self-focused, aversive response (i.e., personal distress) when confronted with another's distress, whereas children who can regulate their emotions tend to experience sympathy (Eisenberg, Fabes, Murphy, et al., 1994, 1996).

For example, Buck (1984) hypothesized that punitive reactions by parents when children exhibit negative emotion result in children's increased arousal when they experience negative emotion, as well as in attempts to hide such feelings. Eisenberg, Fabes, Schaller, Carlo, and Miller (1991) found that mothers who emphasized to their sons the need to control their own negative emotions (e.g., sadness and anxiety) had sons who exhibited facial and physiological (skin conductance and heart rate) markers of distress when they viewed a sympathy-inducing film, but reported low distress in reaction to the film. Thus, these boys seemed prone to experience distress when confronted with others' distress, but appeared not to want others to know what they were feeling. In contrast, same-sex parents' restrictiveness in regard to emotional displays that could be *hurtful to others* (e.g., gasping at a disfigured person) has been positively related to elementary school children's reports of dispositional and situational sympathy (Eisenberg, Fabes, Schaller, Carlo, & Miller, 1991). Parents who discourage their children from expressing emotions hurtful to others may educate their children about the effects of emotional displays on others. However, maternal restrictiveness in regard to the display of hurtful emotions was associated with distress in kindergarten girls, perhaps because mothers who were restrictive in this regard with kindergarten girls were less supportive in general. Thus, for younger children, such maternal restrictiveness may reflect age-inappropriate restrictiveness or low levels of support (Eisenberg, Fabes, et al., 1992).

Parents can also demonstrate methods of coping with emotions or encourage the use of certain means of coping. Eisenberg, Fabes, Schaller, Carlo, and Miller (1991) found that boys whose parents encouraged them to deal instrumentally with situations causing their own sadness or anxiety were relatively likely to experience sympathy rather than personal distress in empathy-inducing contexts. Further, parents' encouragement of direct problem solving as a way to cope with emotion has been associated with the amount that girls (but not boys) comfort a crying infant (Eisenberg, Fabes, Carlo, et al., 1993).

Mothers' discussions of their own and their children's emotions also seem to relate to children's vicarious emotional responding. When mothers verbally linked the events in an empathy-inducing film with children's own experiences, children exhibited heightened vicarious emotional responding of various sorts (sadness, distress, and sympathy). Further, mothers' references to their own sympathy and sadness and their statements about perspective taking or the film protagonist's feelings or situation were associated with boys' reports of sympathy and sadness (Eisenberg, Fabes, Carlo, et al., 1992). In addition, mothers' reports of trying to find out why their child is feeling badly, helping their children talk about negative emotions, and listening to their children when they are anxious or upset have been associated with girls' comforting of an infant (Eisenberg, Fabes, Carlo, et al., 1993). Similarly, Belden, Kuebli, Pauley, and Kindleberger (2003) found that mothers' questions about their children's emotional reactions, states of mind, or interpretations about the motivation for a good deed performed by their child in the past were positively correlated with children's self-reported empathy. Moreover, Denham and Grout (1992) found that preschoolers' prosocial behavior at school was positively related to mothers' tendencies to explain their own sadness, and Kojima (2000) found that young children's prosocial behaviors with their siblings were positively related to the degree to which their mothers made reference to the sibling's actions and emotional states.

The positive association between parental discussion of emotion and prosocial tendencies has not been found in all studies (Eisenberg, Losoya, et al., 2001; Garner, Jones, Gaddy, & Rennie, 1997; Eisenberg, Fabes, Schaller, Carlo, & Miller, 1991). Trommsdorff (1995) found that German and Japanese mothers who focused on their child's emotions in stressful situations by verbalizing or matching their emotions had 5-year-old daughters who were prone to experience distress rather than sympathy when exposed to another's sadness. Trommsdorff suggested that girls who experience too strong a degree of empathy from their caretaker may experience more distress in empathy-inducing contexts because of less developed self-other differentiation. Another possibility is that some mothers may overarouse their children by focusing too much on distress, with the consequence that the children do not learn to regulate their distress.

It is likely that the manner in which mothers talk about emotional events partially accounts for the degree and valence of the relation between maternal emotion-related verbalizations and children's empathy-

related and prosocial responding. Fabes, Eisenberg, Karbon, Bernzweig, et al. (1994) found that mothers' displays of positive rather than negative emotion while telling their kindergarten-age children empathy-inducing stories were associated with children's sympathy, low personal distress, and relatively high helpfulness on a behavioral task. Mothers displayed more of this positive expressiveness with kindergartners if they viewed their child as reactive to others' distresses. Thus, it appeared as if mothers were reacting to characteristics of their children (i.e., age and emotional vulnerability) and were attempting to buffer younger and vulnerable children from emotional overarousal (also see Zhou et al., 2002). In contrast, for second-grade children, helpfulness, as well as sympathy and low personal distress (assessed with physiological and facial measures), were positively associated with a maternal style that combined warmth with directing the child's attention to the stories. For older children, buffering of negative emotion may not be necessary, whereas it may be important to direct the child's attention to others in a way that does not induce reactance.

In brief, findings are consistent with the view that parental practices that help children regulate their negative emotion to avoid becoming overaroused may foster sympathy and prosocial behavior rather than personal distress. However, there may be a fine line between the parental practices that help children regulate and understand their own emotion and the practices that overly focus children's attention on negative emotion. Moreover, the effects of parental emotion-related practices likely are moderated by individual differences in children's emotional reactivity, regulation, and other aspects of temperament and personality.

Expression of Emotion and Conflict in the Home

Frequency and valence of emotion expressed in the home appear to be linked to children's prosocial behavior, albeit in a complex manner. Parental expression of positive emotion in the family tends to be positively correlated with children's prosocial tendencies (Denham & Grout, 1992; Eisenberg, Fabes, Schaller, Miller, et al., 1991; Garner, Jones, & Miner, 1994), a finding that is consistent with the modest associations between prosocial behavior and parental support, warmth, and sympathy. However, researchers sometimes have found no relations between familial or maternal positive emotion and children's sympathy (Eisenberg, Fabes, Carlo, Troyer, et al., 1992) or prosocial behavior (Denham &

Grout, 1993). These weak relations may be due to the relation between parental positive expressivity and prosocial behavior or sympathy being quadratic or moderated by children's dispositional regulation. Valiente et al. (2004) found that moderate (compared with low or high) levels of parental positive expressivity were most highly, positively related to children's sympathy.

Culture also may moderate the relation between parental expression of positive emotion and children's sympathy. Unlike in the United States, Eisenberg, Liew, and Pidada (2001) did not find a relation between these two constructs in Indonesia. This finding may not be surprising given that anthropological and sociological reports indicate that the expression of high levels of emotion—positive or negative—is discouraged in that culture.

At first glance, findings about negative emotion in the home appear inconsistent and puzzling. Conflict in the family has been positively associated with prosocial behavior toward family members. Even very young children exposed to parental conflict sometimes try to comfort or help their parents, and this tendency increases with age in the early years (Cummings, Zahn-Waxler, & Radke-Yarrow, 1984). Further, siblings (but not peers) exposed to conflict between their mother and another adult seem to try to buffer the stress for one another (Cummings & Smith, 1993). Young children are more likely to respond with prosocial behavior toward a parent, as well as with anger, distress, and support-seeking, if familial conflict is frequent (Cummings, Zahn-Waxler, & Radke-Yarrow, 1981) or is physical in nature (Cummings, Pellegrini, & Notarius, 1989).

Other investigators have examined the relation of prosocial tendencies to reported prevalence of hostile, negative emotion in the home environment or maternal simulations of anger situations. Some investigators have not found significant relations between mothers' reports of dominant negative affect or their own anger directed toward the child and children's observed prosocial behaviors (Garner & Estep, 2001; Garner, Jones, & Miner, 1994; also see Hastings et al., 2000). In contrast, Denham and her colleagues found that preschoolers' real-life prosocial reactions to their peers' emotional displays were negatively related to mothers' reports of the frequency of their own anger at home (Denham & Grout, 1992) and intense maternal simulations of anger (when enacting events in a photograph; Denham et al., 1994), and were positively related to mothers' reports of the ra-

tional expressions of anger (Denham & Grout, 1992). Similarly, high levels of familial or maternal dominant negative emotion (e.g., anger) have been linked to low levels of sympathetic concern and high levels of personal distress, both in the United States (Crockenberg, 1985; Eisenberg, Fabes, Carlo, et al., 1992) and in Indonesia (Eisenberg, Liew, & Pidada, 2001).

To summarize, Cummings and his colleagues found that exposure to conflict involving one or both parents, including ongoing conflict in the home, was related to increased prosocial reactions toward children's mothers and siblings (but not peers; Cummings & Smith, 1993); whereas in other studies, reports and displays of maternal anger and externalizing emotion tend to be associated with low levels of peer-directed prosocial behavior and sympathy, as well as high levels of personal distress. Perhaps exposure to adult conflict undermines children's emotional security and induces distress, resulting in children coping in ways that are likely to minimize the stress in their social environment (see Davies & Cummings, 1994). Because children frequently cannot readily escape from conflict in the home, they may attempt to alleviate their distress by intervening and comforting family members. However, children exposed to high intensity or ongoing parental anger may become overaroused by others' negative emotions and experience self-focused personal distress in reaction to others' negative emotion (see Eisenberg et al., 1994). If this were true, they would be expected to try to escape from dealing with others' distress if possible. Exposure to high levels of anger and conflict may induce attempts by children to minimize self-related negative emotional (and physical) consequences of conflict but likely does not foster the capacity for sympathy or other-oriented (rather than self-oriented) prosocial behavior.

Another reason for the inconsistency in the general pattern of findings for parental expression of dominant (assertive) negative emotion may be that the relation between parental expression of dominant negative emotion in the family and children's sympathy appears to be quadratic, with moderate levels of expressivity being most highly associated with children's sympathy (Valiente et al., 2004). Valiente and colleagues also found a quadratic relation such that children's personal distress was higher for mean and high levels of parental negative expressivity than for low parental negative expressivity. In addition, the relation of parental negative expressivity to children's sympathy appears to be moderated by children's regulation. Valiente and colleagues found a significant negative relation between situational sympathy and parents' negative expressivity, but only for children high in regulation. Furthermore, for children who were moderate or low in regulation, dispositional personal distress was relatively high regardless of the level of parental expression of negative emotion, whereas for well-regulated children, personal distress was low when parents expressed little negative emotion but increased with the level of parental expression of negative emotion.

Negative emotions need not always be harsh and dominant; often emotions such as sadness, fear, and loss are expressed in the home. The findings about the relation between the children's exposure to parents' softer negative emotions and their prosocial tendencies are inconsistent. In studies of children from typical families, maternal report of such submissive negative emotion has been negatively related to children's caregiving toward a younger sibling (Garner, Jones, & Miner, 1994), positively related to girls' (but not boys') sympathy in the United States (Eisenberg, Fabes, Carlo, Troyer, et al., 1992), and negatively related to Indonesian children's sympathy (Eisenberg, Liew, & Pidada, 2001). Further, preschoolers' prosocial reactions to peers' emotions have been related to mothers' low rather than high intensity enacted sadness (Denham et al., 1994). In contrast, children's peer-oriented prosocial actions have not been significantly related to frequency of mothers' reported expressions of sadness or tension at home in front of their child (Denham & Grout, 1992) or mothers' reports of experiencing internalizing negative emotions (Denham & Grout, 1993).

Findings about maternal depression are also mixed. Maternal depression has been linked to lower levels of children's prosocial behavior in general (Dunn et al., 1998), to lower mother- and, to a lesser degree, teacher-reported prosocial behavior but higher child-reported prosocial behavior (Hay & Pawlby, 2003), and to higher empathy or prosocial behavior for some children in some circumstances (Radke-Yarrow et al., 1994; Zahn-Waxler, Cummings, McKnew, & Radke-Yarrow, 1984). Perhaps what is important is whether such emotion is dealt with constructively in the home and if children learn ways to manage emotions such as sadness so that they are likely to experience sympathy rather than personal distress when exposed to others' negative emotion. Denham and Grout (1992) found that mothers' reported expressions of tension or fear and sadness at home were positively related to children's peer-oriented prosocial behavior if mothers expressed their tension in a positive manner or explained their sadness.

Summary of Research on Adults' Socialization-Relevant Practices, Beliefs, and Styles

A constellation of parental practices, beliefs, and characteristics, as well as the emotional atmosphere of the home, seems to be related to children's prosocial development. The findings generally are consistent with Staub's (1992, 2003) assertion that the development of prosocial behavior is enhanced by a sense of connection to others (e.g., through attachment and a benign social environment), exposure to parental warmth (which fosters a positive identity and sense of self as well as attachment), adult guidance, and participation in prosocial activities. Moreover, parents' coaching and other behaviors that teach children to understand and regulate their emotions also are likely related to sympathetic capacities.

Although it is likely that the social environment of children, especially their parents, has a causal effect on prosocial behavior and empathy-related responding, heredity may partially account for such relations, especially when predicting aspects of prosociality based on the experience of empathic emotion (see Caspi & Shiner, Chapter 6, this *Handbook,* this volume). It is possible that prosocial, sympathetic parents have prosocial children because of shared genetic predispositions toward regulation and emotionality. Moreover, biologically based dispositions (e.g., as partly reflected in temperament) undoubtedly play a major role in empathic and prosocial functioning. However, Plomin et al. (1993) found that nonshared (unique) environmental experience accounted for some consistency and for the substantial degree of change in twins' empathy over the early years of life. Similarly, as discussed, there is evidence of shared and especially unshared environmental variance in the prediction of empathy-related responding and prosocial behavior (e.g., Deater-Deckard, Dunn, et al., 2001; Zahn-Waxler et al., 2001). For example, differences in parenting (i.e., warmth versus harsh parenting) partly explain differences in the prosocial behavior of monozygotic twins, especially for parents who treat their twins quite differently (Asbury et al., 2003; also see Deater-Deckard, Pike, et al., 2001). Further, genetic explanations cannot account for findings in experimental studies in which parents were not involved (e.g., many of the studies on modeling, preaching, attributions for helping, directives, and learning by doing). In brief, although biological factors, including genetics, play a major role in prosocial development, environmental factors also play an important role and undoubtedly interact with biological factors.

Most researchers who have studied socialization correlates of prosocial responding have taken into account only the effects of parental behaviors and characteristics on children; the role of the children's behavior and characteristics in the socialization process has been virtually ignored. Yet, as was demonstrated by Valiente et al. (2004), it is highly likely that children's personality and temperament interact with parental characteristics and beliefs in determining the quality of the parent-child relationship and parental socialization efforts. Consistent with the possibility of child effects, adults use more reasoning about the consequences of actions and less bargaining with material rewards to induce prosocial behavior for children who are responsive and attentive than for children who are not (Keller & Bell, 1979). The role of the child and dyadic processes (e.g., mutual parent-child responsivity) in the socialization of prosocial behaviors is a key topic for further attention.

Other Familial and Extrafamilial Influences

People and institutions other than parents in children's environments are potential socializers of children's prosocial actions. Research on the role of nonparental influences is still in the rudimentary stages, and researchers studying environmental influences seldom have simultaneously examined multiple familial models (including multiple family members) or multiple types of potential socializers (e.g., peers and the school context). (For a discussion of the effects of television, see Huston & Wright, 1998).

Siblings

Because siblings are familiar and relatively uninhibited with one another, they would be expected to play a considerable role in the development of children's social understanding and interpersonal skills, including prosocial behavior (Dunn & Munn, 1986). Even 1- to 2-year-old children exhibit prosocial behavior toward their siblings (Dunn & Kendrick, 1982). Preschool-age children enact relatively high rates of comforting behavior to distressed younger siblings (Howe & Ross, 1990; Stewart & Marvin, 1984), but show relatively low rates of responsiveness to unfamiliar younger children (Berman & Goodman, 1984).

Because older siblings often act as caregivers to younger siblings, the sibling relationship provides children with opportunities to learn about others' needs and caring effectively for others. In addition, children with supportive sibling relationships may be less preoccupied with their own feelings of distress, so that they are better able to attend to and understand the feelings and need states of others—promoting prosocial behavior and action (Sawyer et al., 2002). The link between the presence of siblings and prosocial behavior is not always consistent, and it has been argued that the quality of the sibling relationship may be more predictive of children's positive behavior than the mere presence of siblings in the home (Cutting & Dunn, 1999).

As suggested, the child's ordinal position in the sibling dyad probably affects opportunities and expectations for prosocial behavior. Older children are more likely to enact prosocial behaviors directed toward younger siblings and younger siblings accept reciprocal roles by displaying high rates of compliance and modeling (Dunn & Munn, 1986; Stoneman et al., 1986). Moreover, there is evidence that older sisters are particularly likely to engage in prosocial interactions with their siblings (Sawyer et al., 2002; Stoneman et al., 1986; Whiting & Whiting, 1975; cf. Brody, Stoneman, & MacKinnon, 1986). Due to gender roles, older girls may be expected to help, comfort, and teach younger siblings. Tucker and colleagues (Tucker, Updegraff, McHale, & Crouter, 1999) found that older siblings' personal qualities and sibling relationship experiences were related to the empathy of younger sisters, but not younger brothers. By early adulthood, people are less defensive about accepting aid from a sister, particularly from an older sister, than from a brother (especially a younger brother; Searcy & Eisenberg, 1992).

Siblings' prosocial behavior may be related in degree, although the data are sparse and inconsistent. In a study of Japanese children, siblings' prosocial behaviors toward one another were positively related (Kojima, 2000). In contrast, Dunn and Munn (1986) found little correlation between older and younger siblings' prosocial behavior (also see Bryant & Crockenberg, 1980), although younger siblings' cooperation and prosocial behavior were positively related to older siblings' giving and cooperation 6 months later. Furthermore, in that study, siblings who expressed negative affect in a high percentage of their interactions were relatively unlikely to behave prosocially with one another (cf. Stillwell & Dunn, 1985, using a small sample).

Characteristics of siblings may affect the degree of prosocial behavior between them. For example, sibling relationships in families of children with autism were characterized by less intimacy, prosocial behavior, and nurturance than those that occurred between typically developing siblings or a typical child and a sibling with Down syndrome (Kaminsky & Dewey, 2001). Children with autism rarely seek out others for comfort, affection, or help, decreasing the likelihood that siblings respond in a helpful and affectionate way (Knott, Lewis, & Williams, 1995). Thus, when one sibling has difficulty initiating, maintaining, or promoting positive interactions, prosocial and nurturing sibling interactions are likely to be negatively affected.

Because sibling relationships are embedded in the family, it is not surprising that mothers' behaviors are linked to prosocial behavior between siblings. When mothers discussed their newborn's feelings and needs with an older sibling, the older child was more nurturant toward the infant. Further, friendly interest in the infant persisted and predicted prosocial behavior toward the younger sibling 3 years later (Dunn & Kendrick, 1982). Kojima (2000) found that Japanese mothers' references to the actions or emotional states of a sibling were positively correlated with the other child's prosocial interactions with that sibling. In another study, nurturant maternal responsiveness to young daughters' needs was positively related to younger siblings' comforting and sharing with their older sibling. In contrast, mothers' unavailability was associated with older daughters' prosocial behavior toward their younger sibling (Bryant & Crockenberg, 1980). The latter finding is similar to Brody et al.'s (1986) finding that maternal valuing of a separate life from children was associated with older siblings' helping and managing their younger sibling. Perhaps older siblings, especially daughters, are expected to take a nurturant helping role when the mother is unavailable relatively often.

Because sibling caregiving provides children with opportunities to learn about others' perspectives and emotions, children with sibling caregiving experience may develop relatively mature perspective-taking skills and therefore respond relatively appropriately and effectively in caregiving situations (see section on perspective taking). Stewart and Marvin (1984) found a positive relation between perspective taking and sibling caregiving; however, Howe and Ross (1990) did not find this re-

lation (although perspective taking was related to friendly behavior between siblings). In addition, Garner, Jones, and Palmer (1994) found that emotional role-taking skills, but not cognitive perspective taking, predicted sibling caregiving behavior. Perspective taking about emotions may be a more relevant skill for sibling caregiving than is cognitive perspective taking, although the latter has been emphasized in most studies of perspective taking and sibling interactions. A relation between perspective taking and siblings' prosocial behavior may be partly because high perspective-taking siblings are especially likely to be asked by parents to take care of younger siblings (Stewart & Marvin, 1984).

In summary, sibling interactions may be an important context for learning caregiving behaviors (particularly for older siblings) and the development of perspective taking. However, little is known about the ways in which the larger familial context moderates the development of prosocial responding in the sibling relationship.

Peer Influences on Prosocial Development

Developmental theorists frequently have tied the acquisition of morality to processes inherent in social interactions with peers (Piaget, 1932/1965). These theorists have argued that because peer interactions involve the association with equals and, frequently, cooperation, reciprocity, and mutuality, peer interaction may provide an optimal atmosphere for the acquisition of concepts and behaviors reflecting justice, kindness, and concern for another's welfare (Youniss, 1980). Consistent with this view, Tesson, Lewko, and Bigelow (1987) found that prosocial themes pertaining to issues such as reciprocity, sincerity and trust, helping and solving problems, and sensitivity to others' feelings were prominent in 6- to 13-year-old children's reports of the social rules they used in peer relationships. Additionally, having at least one reciprocated friendship has been related to higher levels of prosocial behavior (Wentzel, Barry, & Caldwell, 2004).

Researchers also have found that the quality of children's prosocial behavior directed toward peers and adults differs somewhat, particularly at younger ages. When asked to give examples of kindness directed toward peers, 6- to 14-year-olds tended to cite giving and sharing, playing, physical assistance, understanding, and teaching. In contrast, they cited primarily being good or polite, doing chores, and obeying in regard to kindness toward adults (Youniss, 1980). Further, preschoolers provide more authority- and punishment-related reasons for complying with adults' than peers' requests, and more other-oriented or relational (friendship, liking) motives for complying with peers' requests (Eisenberg, Lundy, et al., 1985). With age, children appear to be slightly more likely to define kindness toward adults in a manner similar to peer-directed kindness; that is, as involving acts demonstrating concern rather than compliance (Youniss, 1980). Thus, peer interactions may provide a context that is conducive to the development of prosocial behavior motivated by other-oriented concerns rather than compliance, particularly for prosocial actions directed toward individuals outside the family.

Other research also is consistent with the notion that peer interactions are important for the development of empathy, sympathy, and an other-orientation. According to maternal reports, infants and toddlers cry more in response to cries of peers than of adults (Zahn-Waxler, Iannotti, & Chapman, 1982). Children observed adults cry relatively infrequently, and when they did, they generally did not cry. When children cried in response to adults' distress, it usually was in reaction to angry interactions such as fights between parents. Moreover, prosocial behavior (when it occurred) was enacted more often in response to a child's than to an adult's distress.

Peers also may affect prosocial development because of their roles as models. Adolescents who volunteer are relatively likely to have friends who feel it is important to engage in activities such as sports, clubs, or school events (Huebner & Mancini, 2003), to do well in school, and to be involved in community and volunteer work (Zaff et al., 2003). In contrast, adolescents are relatively unlikely to report the intention to volunteer if they belong to a crowd that places a high value on having fun (Youniss, Mclellan, & Mazer, 2001; also see Pugh & Hart, 1999). Although such data are only correlational and do not demonstrate causality, prosocial peer models sometimes have been found to be effective in eliciting prosocial behavior in the laboratory (e.g., Owens & Ascione, 1991). Familiarity and liking of peer models may be important factors in influencing children's prosocial behavior: Children may have greater identification with fellow peers and may experience more freedom to try out new behaviors with peers than they do with adults. However, findings in this regard are sparse and are not readily interpretable (see Owens & Ascione, 1991). In one study, children with a history of receiving social reinforcement from peers were more likely to model the donating behavior of a peer from whom they had re-

ceived frequent rewards than the behavior of a nonrewarding peer. In contrast, children with a history of infrequent peer reinforcement imitated the prosocial behavior of a nonrewarding rather than a rewarding peer (Hartup & Coates, 1967). Thus, characteristics of the child and the peer model influence whether children imitate peers' prosocial actions.

Peers sometimes respond in a reinforcing manner to peers' prosocial actions (Eisenberg, Cameron, Tryon, & Dodez, 1981), and such reinforcement may affect children's prosocial behavior. Eisenberg et al. (1981) found that preschool girls (but not boys) who engaged in relatively high levels of spontaneous prosocial behavior were those who received marginally more positive reinforcement for their prosocial actions from peers. However, preschoolers (especially boys) who were high in compliant (requested) prosocial actions received low levels of positive reinforcement for their compliant prosocial actions. Sociable children were relatively likely to receive positive peer reactions when they enacted compliant prosocial actions, and children who responded positively to other children's spontaneous prosocial behaviors were likely to receive positive peer reactions for their own spontaneous and compliant prosocial behavior. Thus, children who were more sociable and positive may have elicited the most peer reinforcement when they engaged in prosocial behavior. A cyclical process may occur in which socially competent children elicit more positive peer reactions for prosocial behavior, which in turn increases their prosocial behavior (with the reverse process occurring for children low in social skills).

Related to this cyclical process, Fabes, Martin, and Hanish (2002) analyzed the degree to which low- and high-prosocial children (i.e., those at least 1 standard deviation below or above the mean in teacher-reported prosociality) interacted with each other. Rarely were low and high prosocial children observed interacting with each other (about 5% of the time). Fabes et al. referred to this as a type of "prosocial segregation." Of importance, the more exposure that preschool children had to prosocial peers at the beginning of the school year, the greater the degree of positive peer interactions later in the school year. In a longitudinal extension of these analyses, Fabes, Moss, Reesing, Martin, and Hanish (2005) found that exposure to prosocial peers was related to heightened prosocial behavior 1 year later. In addition, Wentzel et al. (2004) found that students with initially low levels of prosocial behavior relative to those of their friends improved when exposed to their more prosocial peers, and students with initially higher levels of prosocial behavior decreased their levels of prosocial behavior when exposed to their less prosocial peers. Such findings demonstrate the potential potency of peers as influences on the subsequent likelihood of prosocial and positive development.

Peer interactions seem to provide unique opportunities for prosocial behavior, and peer responses in such contexts may influence the type and degree of potential prosocial responses. The role of peer interaction in older children's and adolescents' prosocial behavior has seldom been examined and little is known about the degree to which the effects of peers are moderated by other variables (e.g., the nature of interactions with other socializers and characteristics of the child, the peer group, or the context) or the exact processes that underlie such influences.

School Programs

Children likely receive considerable moral education and training in school, but little is known about the effects of school experiences on children's prosocial behavior.

One avenue for examining the potential impact of the school context on children's prosocial behavior is to assess the natural occurrence of prosocial behavior in the classroom. Hertz-Lazarowitz (1983; Hertz-Lazarowitz, Fuchs, Sharabany, & Eisenberg, 1989) found that naturally occurring prosocial behaviors in school classrooms (Grades 1 to 12) were relatively rare (only 1.5% to 6.5% of total behaviors). Similarly, researchers usually have noted low frequencies of prosocial behavior in preschool classes, although estimates vary considerably with the operationalization of prosocial behavior (e.g., Caplan & Hay, 1989; Denham & Burger, 1991; Eisenberg et al., 1981; Fabes et al., 2002; Strayer, Wareing, & Rushton, 1979). Further, in studies of preschoolers, teachers rarely reinforced (Eisenberg et al., 1981) or encouraged (Caplan & Hay, 1989) children's prosocial behavior.

Findings such as these suggest that the typical classroom environment may not be conducive to eliciting frequent prosocial interactions among children. Salient and unambiguous expectations regarding prosocial behavior may be necessary to elicit more spontaneous prosocial actions in the classroom. Moreover, structuring classes to provide children with opportunities to help others may promote prosocial behavior. Bizman, Yinon,

Mivtzari, and Shavit (1978) found that Israeli kindergartners enrolled in classes that contained younger peers were more altruistic than those enrolled in classes that were homogeneous in age. Further, elementary school Israeli students in active classrooms in which cooperation and individualized learning were emphasized helped peers more than students in traditional classrooms (Hertz-Lazarowitz et al., 1989).

Some investigators have tried to assess the effects of preschool and day care on children's prosocial development by comparing children who attend preschool with those who do not (e.g., are reared at home). Clarke-Stewart (1981) suggested that attendance at group day care has a temporarily accelerating effect on social development and found that prosocial behavior was higher for children with nonparental care. However, evidence in support of this contention is equivocal. Schenk and Grusec (1987) found that home-care children were more likely than day-care children to behave prosocially in situations involving an adult stranger, whereas the two groups were similar on helping unknown children. Other researchers have produced results indicating that out-of-home care per se does not have any reliable or consistent effects on children's emerging prosocial development (Austin et al., 1991).

Although differences between home versus group care children may be limited, quality of the caregiving situation likely moderates the degree and type of influence preschools have on children's prosocial behavior and attitudes (Love et al., 2003). Quality of the day care or preschool environment has been associated with children's self-regulation (Howes & Olenick, 1986), empathy and social competence (Vandell, Henderson, & Wilson, 1988), considerateness (Phillips, McCartney, & Scarr, 1987), and positive peer-related behaviors (including prosocial behaviors; Broberg, Hwang, Lamb, & Ketterlinus, 1989). Moreover, warm, supportive interactions with teachers have been associated with preschool children's modeling of teachers' prosocial actions (Yarrow et al., 1973), sympathetic-prosocial reactions to distress (Kienbaum, Volland, & Ulich, 2001), and positive interactions among students in the elementary school classroom (Serow & Solomon, 1979). In addition, Howes, Matheson, and Hamilton (1994) found that children classified as securely attached to their current and first preschool teachers were rated as more considerate and empathic with unfamiliar peers than were children classified as having an insecure relationship (especially ambivalent) with their teachers. Contemporaneous teacher-child relationships better differentiated peer-related outcomes for children than did contemporaneous maternal attachment relations or day-care history. Thus, degree and type of influence exerted by school experiences, as well as durability of effects on prosocial responding, probably varies as a function of quality of care received and the child's relationship with the teacher (as well as quality of care received from parents at home).

Based on the previously described literature concerning the socialization of prosocial attitudes and behavior, some investigators have attempted to design school-based programs aimed at fostering prosocial responding. Solomon and colleagues (Solomon, Battistich, Watson, Schaps, & Lewis, 2000; Solomon, Watson, Delucchi, Schaps, & Battistich, 1988) developed a program (The Child Development Project, henceforth referred to as the CDP) in which teachers were trained to maintain positive personal relationships with their students by using a child-centered approach to classroom management that emphasized inductive discipline and student participation in rule-setting. Other aspects of the program were designed to promote social understanding, highlight prosocial values, and provide helping activities; however, these program components were viewed as playing a more limited, supportive role in the program (Battistich, Watson, Solomon, Schaps, & Solomon, 1991).

Across 5 consecutive years of implementation (kindergarten through fourth grade), students in the program classrooms, compared with control classes, generally scored higher on ratings of prosocial behavior. These patterns held when both teachers' general competence and students' participation in cooperative activities were controlled, suggesting that program effects on children's prosocial behavior were not due simply to differences in teacher-initiated cooperative interactions or to more efficiently organized and managed classrooms (Solomon et al., 1988).

Children enrolled in the program (but not children in the control group) evidenced the highest ratings for prosocial behavior and harmony in kindergarten. Thus, it appears that the impact of this program was greatest when first introduced. The degree to which program effects generalized beyond the immediate classroom environment was unclear (Battistich et al., 1991). However, the teachers in the program had only 1 year of experience in implementing the program and the effects may have been more sustained given additional time for teachers to develop their techniques and fully integrate the program into the ongoing routine of the classroom.

In another longitudinal test of the effects of the CDP, the program was used with a cohort of students who began in kindergarten and continued through eighth grade (Solomon, Battistich, & Watson, 1993). Of particular interest, measures of prosocial reasoning and conflict resolution were obtained each year. Comparison students reasoned higher than CDP children at kindergarten, but CDP students reasoned at higher levels from first grade on, although the within-year difference was significant only in second grade. In general, CDP students also evidenced higher conflict resolution scores than comparison students (indicating consideration of others' needs and a reliance on compromise and sharing). Program effects appeared to be greater when combined across years (effects were not consistently significant within years). However, the CDP initially was implemented in schools with mostly advantaged Caucasian children. More recently, the CDP was implemented in six school districts over a 3-year period, with two additional schools in each district serving as comparison groups (Battistich, Schaps, Watson, Solomon, & Lewis, 2000; Solomon et al., 2000). For those schools that made significant progress in implementing the program, students showed positive gains in personal, social, and ethical values, attitudes, and motives, and a reduction of substance abuse and other problem behaviors (also see Battistich, Solomon, Kim, Watson, & Schaps, 1995).

Other school-based programs have been designed to promote empathy. Although some seem to have been minimally effective (e.g., Kalliopuska & Tiitinen, 1991), Feshbach and Feshbach (1982) found that empathy training significantly increased incidents of prosocial behavior in schoolchildren. Moreover, the use of cooperative educational techniques in classroom activities has been found to promote acceptance of others (Johnson & Johnson, 1975), as well as cooperation and prosocial behavior (Hertz-Lazarowitz & Sharan, 1984; Hertz-Lazarowitz, Sharan, & Steinberg, 1980).

Some researchers have developed school-based programs that include a formal curriculum component. Ascione (1992) studied the effects of a humane education program when used with first, second, fourth, and fifth graders for nearly 40 hours over the school year. There was relatively little evidence of an immediate effect for younger children, although there was an effect on humane attitudes a year later (Ascione & Weber, 1993).

Humane attitudes were enhanced for the fourth graders in the immediate posttest and for fourth and fifth graders a year later. Human-directed empathy increased for fourth and fifth graders on both the initial and 1-year posttests.

In summary, although prosocial behavior often may not be directly promoted in the classroom, quality early schooling and supportive relationships between children and their teachers have been associated with the development of prosocial tendencies. Moreover, school-based programs designed to enhance prosocial values, behaviors, and attitudes in children can be effective in fostering children's prosocial attitudes and behaviors. However, most programs have involved relatively weak and short interventions that may not be adequate for some groups of children. Variation in instruction among teachers within a treatment group often is problematic, as is the application of these programs to large and diverse samples. These issues are critical if one hopes to argue that such programs are cost-effective and impactful, especially in contexts where resources and time are limited.

COGNITIVE AND SOCIOCOGNITIVE CORRELATES OF PROSOCIAL DEVELOPMENT

Numerous theorists have hypothesized that cognitive and sociocognitive skills, particularly perspective taking and moral reasoning, foster prosocial responding (Batson, 1991; Eisenberg, 1986; Hoffman, 1982). Moreover, although not discussed, it is likely that certain types of prosocial experiences provide experiences that enhance children's sociocognitive skills (see Eisenberg, 1986, for a review of children's understanding of, and attributions about, their own and others' kindness).

Intelligence, Cognitive Capacities, and Academic Achievement

Because cognitive abilities may underlie the ability to discern others' needs or distress, as well as the capacity to devise ways to respond to others' needs, it would be logical to expect a modest relation between measures of intelligence and prosocial responding, particularly prosocial behavior involving sophisticated cognitive skills. Some investigators have obtained modest to moderate positive correlations between measures of intelli-

gence (e.g., IQ, vocabulary or reading skills, language development, developmental level) and self-reported (Carlo, Hausmann, Christiansen, & Randall, 2003; Cassidy, Werner, Rourke, Lubernis, & Balaraman, 2003; Hart et al., 1998; Ma & Leung, 1991; also see Goodman, 1994) or other measures of prosocial behavior (Krebs & Sturrup, 1982; Slaughter, Dennis, & Pritchard, 2002; van der Mark et al., 2002; Zahn-Waxler et al., 1982; also see Lourenco, 1993; Zaff et al., 2003). Grade point average also has been linked to prosocial goals and behavior (Caprara, Barbaranelli, Pastorelli, Bandura, & Zimbardo, 2000; Huebner & Mancini, 2003; Johnson et al., 1998; Uggen & Janikula, 1999; Wentzel, 2003; Zeldin & Topitzes, 2002; also see Lichter et al., 2002), as have teachers' ratings of school performance combined with grades (e.g., Welsh, Parke, Widaman, & O'Neil, 2001). In addition, there is some support for a positive relation between scores on achievement tests and children's empathy (Feshbach, 1978) or sympathy (Wise & Cramer, 1988), and between academic self-efficacy and prosocial behavior (Bandura et al., 2001, 2003). Not surprisingly, given the array of measures used, some researchers have found no significant relations between tests of intelligence (or scholastic ability) and children's prosocial behavior (e.g., Jennings, Fitch, & Suwalsky, 1987; Turner & Harris, 1984) or have obtained mixed or inconsistent relations with prosocial behavior (e.g., Strayer & Roberts, 1989) or sympathy (Wise & Cramer, 1988). Intelligence and academic skills likely are associated with certain types of prosocial responding or prosocial behavior in some contexts.

Perspective Taking and Understanding of Emotion

As noted, it is commonly assumed that perspective-taking skills increase the likelihood of individuals identifying, understanding, and sympathizing with others' distress or need (e.g., Batson et al., 2003; Eisenberg, Shea, et al., 1991; Feshbach, 1978; Hoffman, 1982). Hoffman (1982) proposed that improvement in young children's perspective taking is critical to children's abilities to differentiate between their own and others' distress and to accurately understand others' emotional reactions. These skills are believed to foster empathy and sympathy and, consequently, more and higher quality prosocial behavior.

Information about others' internal states can be obtained by imagining oneself in another's position or through processes such as accessing stored knowledge, mental associations, and social scripts or deduction (Karniol, 1995). Children also may have "theories" about others' internal states that they use to infer how others feel (see Eisenberg, Murphy, & Shepard, 1997). For convenience, and because it generally is difficult to identify the processes underlying performance on perspective-taking tasks, the term *perspective taking* is used to refer to the ability to engage in any of these processes when they result in knowledge about others' internal states.

Researchers have found an association between perspective taking (broadly defined, and including an understanding of theory of mind) and prosocial behavior (including comforting skills) or empathy/sympathy, although findings sometimes have been obtained for only some of the examined associations (e.g., Bengtsson, 2003; Bengtsson & Johnson, 1992; Bosacki, 2003; Carlo et al., 2003; Cassidy et al., 2003; Charbonneau & Nicol, 2002; Denham, Blair, et al., 2003; Denham & Couchoud, 1991; Denham et al., 1994; Dekovic & Gerris, 1994; Eisenberg, Carlo, et al., 1995; Eisenberg, Zhou, & Koller, 2001; Estrada, 1995; Garner & Estep, 2001; Garner, Jones, & Miner, 1994; Ginsburg et al., 2003; Kumru & Edwards, 2003; Litvack-Miller, McDougall, & Romney, 1997; Roberts & Strayer, 1996; Slaugher et al., 2002; Strayer & Roberts, 2004b; also see Eisenberg & Fabes, 1998; Matsuba & Walker, 2005). Although no such association has been found in a minority of studies (e.g., Astington & Jenkins, 1995; Hughes, White, Sharpen, & Dunn, 2000; Lalonde & Chandler, 1995; Peterson, 1983; Zahn-Waxler et al., 1982), to our knowledge, perspective taking seldom has been significantly negatively related to children's prosocial behavior (e.g., Barrett & Yarrow, 1977; LeMare & Krebs, 1983, for low assertive boys only). Moreover, the match between children's facial reactions and reported reactions to empathy-inducing stimuli (believed to reflect emotional insight) has been positively related to their empathy (Roberts & Strayer, 1996), whereas young adolescents' self-understanding has been associated with high levels of prosocial behavior (Bosacki, 2003).

Positive findings were obtained in many studies although most researchers used single measures of perspective-taking abilities or prosocial behavior rather than more reliable indexes created by aggregation across measures. The association does not seem to be due merely to increases in both perspective taking and prosocial behavior with age; often the age range of the study participants was narrow or findings were maintained when age was controlled (e.g., Garner, Jones, & Palmer, 1994; see Underwood & Moore, 1982). As might be expected, the relation seems to be stronger when there is a match between the type of perspective-taking skills assessed and the type or level of understanding likely to promote prosocial behavior in the given context (Carlo, Knight, Eisenberg, & Rotenberg, 1991). In some circumstances, perspective-taking skills may be unimportant because prosocial actions are enacted in a relatively automatic fashion due to either their low cost or the compelling, crisis-like nature of the situation. In other contexts, prosocial behavior likely is motivated by any number of factors other than knowledge of another's internal states.

Some people may take others' perspectives but lack the motivation, skills, or social assertiveness required to take action. Thus, the relations of measures of perspective taking or emotion understanding with prosocial responding are likely moderated by other variables. Perspective taking has been linked to prosocial behavior for children who are socially assertive (Barrett & Yarrow, 1977; Denham & Couchoud, 1991), but not for children who are less assertive. Similarly, the relation of perspective taking to prosocial behavior sometimes has been mediated or moderated by children's empathic/sympathetic responding (Barnett & Thompson, 1985; Roberts & Strayer, 1996). In one study, children who donated money to help a child who had been burned were those who not only evidenced relatively sophisticated perspective-taking skills, but also were sympathetic and understood units and value of money (Knight, Johnson, Carlo, & Eisenberg, 1994). In another study, perspective taking was not directly related to reported prosocial behavior; it was indirectly related through its prediction of both sympathy and moral reasoning (Eisenberg, Zhou, & Koller, 2001).

In summary, children with higher perspective-taking skills generally are somewhat more prosocial, particularly if their perspective-taking abilities are relevant to the prosocial task and if they have the social skills (e.g., assertiveness) and emotional motivation (e.g., sympathy) to act on the knowledge obtained by perspective taking. Perspective-taking skills may be involved in discerning others' needs, providing sensitive help, and evoking the affective motivation for prosocial action (i.e., sympathy, empathy, or guilt). Moreover, it is likely that children with well-developed perspective-taking abilities have more opportunities to be prosocial; for example, older siblings with better perspective-taking skills are more frequently asked by their mothers to provide caregiving to younger siblings (Stewart & Marvin, 1984).

Person Attributions and Expressed Motives

Although children sometimes may report socially desirable motives or may have little access to their motives (see Eisenberg, 1986, for a discussion of these issues), there appears to be some relation between children's expressed motives and the quantity (e.g., Bar-Tal, Raviv, et al., 1980) or quality (i.e., maturity; see Bar-Tal, 1982) of their prosocial behavior (see Eisenberg, 1986, for a review). As discussed by Eisenberg (1986), it is unclear whether children's motives influence their prosocial responding or if children formulate motives post hoc to the execution of behavior based on self-observation. In support of the former explanation, Smith et al. (1979) found that individual differences in expressed internality of motives were associated with donating, whereas environmental contingencies (e.g., rewards and punishments) that might influence post hoc evaluations were not. In any case, it is likely that people have greater access to their cognitive processes (including motives) when a task is not so overlearned that it can be performed in a mindless manner. Therefore, it is probable that expressed motives are more accurate for prosocial acts that are not performed automatically; that is, when the potential benefactor must consider whether to assist. At this time, data to test this idea are not available (see, however, Eisenberg & Shell, 1986).

Moral Reasoning

In general, investigators have hypothesized that there should be some link between children's moral reasoning and their behavior. Krebs and Van Hesteren (1994) asserted: "[A]dvanced stages give rise to higher quantities of altruism than less advanced stages because they give rise to greater social sensitivity, stronger feelings of responsibility, and so on. . . . We propose that advanced stage-structures give rise for forms of altruism that are (1) purer (i.e., more exclusively devoted to enhancing the welfare of others, as opposed to the self) and (2) deeper (i.e., that benefit others in less superficial and less transient ways) than less advanced structures" (p. 136).

Prosocial actions can be motivated by a range of considerations, including altruistic, pragmatic, and even self-oriented concerns; this attenuates the degree to which one might expect associations between general level of moral reasoning and observed prosocial actions. However, prosocial behavior motivated by a particular type of factor (e.g., sympathy) is likely to be correlated with the types or levels of reasoning reflecting that factor, although not necessarily with an individual's overall level of reasoning.

In published studies involving child participants, prosocial behavior has been inconsistently related to aspects of Piaget's scheme of moral judgment (e.g., intentionality, distributive justice), but generally (albeit not consistently) positively related to Kohlbergian prohibition- and justice-oriented moral reasoning (or modified versions thereof; see Eisenberg, 1986; Eisenberg & Fabes, 1998; Underwood & Moore, 1982). However, there appears to be a stronger correspondence between moral reasoning and prosocial behavior if the moral reasoning dilemma concerns reasoning about prosocial behavior rather than another type of behavior. Levin and Bekerman-Greenberg (1980) found that the strength of the positive relation between reasoning about sharing and actual prosocial behavior was somewhat greater if the dilemma and sharing task were similar in content. Moreover, when researchers have assessed children's moral reasoning about dilemmas involving helping or sharing behavior, generally moral reasoning has been associated in the predicted manner with at least some measures of prosocial behavior (e.g., Carlo & Randall, 2002; Eisenberg, Carlo, et al., 1995; Eisenberg, Miller, et al., 1991; Eisenberg, Zhou, & Koller, 2001; Janssens & Dekovic, 1997; Kumru et al., 2003; Larrieu & Mussen, 1986; Stewart & McBride-Chang, 2000; also see Eisenberg, 1986, and Eisenberg & Fabes, 1998, for reviews). In addition, children who reason at developmentally mature levels are less likely than children who reason at lower levels to say they would discriminate between people close to them and others when deciding whether to help (Eisenberg, 1983; also see Ma, 1992).

Types of reasoning that reflect an other- versus self-orientation or are developmentally mature for the age group are most likely to predict prosocial responding. Hedonistic reasoning and needs-oriented reasoning (i.e., rudimentary other-oriented reasoning) tend to be negatively and positively related, respectively, to prosocial behavior (e.g., Carlo et al., 1996; Carlo et al., 2003; Eisenberg, Boehnke, et al., 1985; Eisenberg, Carlo, et al., 1995; Eisenberg, Miller, et al., 1991; Eisenberg & Shell, 1986). In addition, sometimes a mode of reasoning that is relatively sophisticated for the age group

(Carlo & Randall, 2002; Miller, Eisenberg, Fabes, & Shell, 1996; Schenk & Grusec, 1987) has been significantly associated with prosocial behavior. It is possible that the relation of moral reasoning and prosocial behavior increases with age across adolescence (Pratt et al., 2004) because moral reasoning becomes more mature and internalized with age (Eisenberg, 1986).

The nature of the enacted prosocial behavior also seems to be a critical variable. Higher level self-reported internalized prosocial moral reasoning tends to be positively correlated with adolescents' reports of altruistic prosocial actions and helping in emotional and anonymous situations, whereas lower level reasoning (i.e., approval-oriented or hedonistic) tends to be related positively to reported public helping and negatively to altruism or helping in emotional or dire circumstances (Carlo, Hausmann, et al., 2003). In observational studies, prosocial moral reasoning most often has been significantly positively related to preschoolers' spontaneous sharing behaviors rather than helping behaviors (which, in these studies, generally entailed little cost) or prosocial behaviors performed in compliance with a peer's request (Eisenberg et al., 1984; Eisenberg-Berg & Hand, 1979). Preschoolers' spontaneous prosocial behaviors predict a prosocial, sympathetic orientation across childhood and into early adulthood (Eisenberg, Guthrie, et al., 1999, 2002).

In laboratory studies involving elementary or high school students, prosocial moral reasoning more frequently has been associated with prosocial actions that incur a cost (e.g., donating or volunteering time after school) than with those low in cost (e.g., helping pick up dropped paper clips; Eisenberg, Boehnke, et al., 1985; Eisenberg & Shell, 1986; Eisenberg, Shell, et al., 1987; also see Miller et al., 1996). Eisenberg and Shell (1986) hypothesized that low-cost behaviors are performed rather automatically, without much cognitive reflection, moral or otherwise. In contrast, moral reasoning is likely to be associated with children's prosocial behavior in situations involving a cost because consideration of the cost may evoke cognitive conflict and morally relevant decision making.

It also is likely that other variables moderate the relation between moral judgment and prosocial behavior, particularly for lower level modes of reasoning (at higher levels, moral principles may be sufficient motivation to help). Sympathetic responding is a probable moderator. Consistent with this view, Miller et al. (1996) found that preschoolers who reported sympathy

for hospitalized children *and* who were relatively high in use of needs-oriented reasoning were especially likely to help hospitalized children at a cost to themselves. Affective motivation such as sympathy (and perhaps guilt) often may be necessary to spur the individual to action. Thus, it is important to identify moderators and mediators of the relation between moral reasoning and prosocial responding.

EMPATHY-RELATED EMOTIONAL RESPONDING

As noted, psychologists (e.g., Eisenberg, 1986; Feshbach, 1978; Hoffman, 1982; Staub, 1979) and philosophers (Blum, 1980; Hume, 1748/1975; Slote, 2004) have proposed that prosocial behavior, particularly altruism, often is motivated by empathy or sympathy. Links between empathy or sympathy and prosocial behavior have been presumed to exist both within specific contexts (e.g., Batson, 1991; Eisenberg & Fabes, 1990) and at the dispositional level (i.e., people with a dispositional tendency toward empathy/sympathy are expected to be altruistic in general; Eisenberg & Miller, 1987).

Although many psychologists have assumed that empathy plays a role in prosocial behavior, in a meta-analytic review, Underwood and Moore (1982) found that empathy was *not* significantly related to prosocial behavior. Many of the studies they reviewed were conducted with children, and most involved a particular type of measure—the picture/story measure of empathy. With this type of measure, children are presented with a series of short vignettes, usually illustrated (rather than videotaped), about children in emotionally evocative contexts (e.g., when a child loses his or her dog). After each vignette, the child is asked, "How do you feel?" or a similar question. If children say they felt an emotion similar to that which the story protagonist would be expected to feel, they typically are viewed as empathizing.

The validity of this sort of measure has been questioned, in part because these measures were not very evocative (see Eisenberg & Lennon, 1983; Lennon, Eisenberg, & Carroll, 1983). In fact, the degree of association between measures of empathy-related responding and prosocial behavior appears to vary as a function of the measure of empathy. In a meta-analytic review of the literature, Eisenberg and Miller (1987) found no significant relation between prosocial behavior and picture/story measures (or children's self-reported reactions to enactments or videotapes of others in distress or need). In contrast, there were significant positive associations with prosocial behavior for some non-self-report measures of empathy-related responding and self-report measures for older adolescents and adults. At the time of the Eisenberg and Miller review, there were few published studies including facial or physiological measures or the use of questionnaires with children in preschool or early elementary school.

In recent years, it has become clear that it is essential to differentiate among empathy-related emotional reactions. Batson (1991) hypothesized that sympathy (as defined at the beginning of this chapter, although labeled "empathy" by Batson) is intimately linked with other-oriented motivation and, consequently, with other-oriented, altruistic helping behavior. In contrast, personal distress is viewed as involving the egoistic motivation of alleviating one's own distress; therefore, it is expected to motivate prosocial behavior only when the easiest way to reduce one's own distress is to reduce the other's distress (e.g., when one cannot easily escape contact with the empathy-inducing person).

Consistent with his theorizing, Batson and his colleagues, in laboratory studies with adults, have found that sympathy is more likely to be positively associated with helping than is personal distress when it is easy for people to escape contact with the person needing assistance (see Batson, 1991). In a series of studies, Eisenberg, Fabes, and their colleagues obtained similar findings with children. In their studies, children's prosocial behavior was as anonymous as possible and children did not have to interact in any way with the needy other(s) if they did not want to do so. Eisenberg et al. (1994) argued that people tend to experience personal distress when they are physiologically over-aroused, whereas they experience sympathy when they experience moderate vicarious arousal. Thus, the researchers hypothesized that high levels of autonomic arousal would be associated with personal distress, whereas the reverse would be true for sympathy (except when low arousal is likely an index of no empathy-related responding, especially to a mild stimulus). In addition, heart rate deceleration tends to occur when individuals are oriented to information in the environment outside the self; this is another reason one might expect an association between experiencing sympathy and heart rate deceleration. Across studies in which children were shown empathy-inducing videotapes, children who exhibited facial or physiological (i.e., heart rate deceleration or lower skin conductance)

markers of sympathy tended to be relatively prosocial when given an opportunity to assist someone in the film or people similar to those in the film (e.g., hospitalized children). In contrast, children who exhibited evidence of personal distress (higher heart rate or skin conductance) tended to be less prosocial (Eisenberg, Fabes, et al., 1993; Eisenberg, Fabes, et al., 1990; Eisenberg, Fabes, Karbon, Murphy, Carlo, et al., 1996; Eisenberg, Fabes, Miller, et al., 1989; Fabes, Eisenberg, Karbon, Bernzweig, et al., 1994; Fabes, Eisenberg, Karbon, Troyer, & Switzer, 1994; Miller et al., 1996). Self-report measures in these studies tended to be less consistently related to children's prosocial behaviors (see Eisenberg & Fabes, 1990). Fabes, Eisenberg, and Eisenbud (1993) also found that skin conductance (a marker of personal distress) predicted girls' (but not boys') low *dispositional* (rather than situational) helpfulness (i.e., parental ratings of helpfulness rather than prosocial behavior in the same context). Moreover, facial reactions of sympathy have been linked to prosocial behavior in another context (Eisenberg, Fabes, et al., 1990; Eisenberg, McCreath, & Ahn, 1988).

As one would expect, not all markers of sympathy or personal distress in Eisenberg, Fabes, and their colleagues' research predicted prosocial behavior (or sometimes for both sexes; e.g., Eisenberg, Fabes, Karbon, Murphy, Carlo, et al., 1996; Miller, et al., 1996). In addition, heart rate markers of reactions to empathy-inducing films predicted prosocial behavior within, but not across, contexts (e.g., Eisenberg, Fabes, et al., 1990). Nonetheless, the overall pattern of findings is consistent. Further, other investigators have obtained similar findings. Zahn-Waxler and her colleagues found that sympathetic concern and prosocial actions seemed to co-occur in the behavior of children aged 14 and 26 months (Zahn-Waxler, Robinson, & Emde, 1992; Zahn-Waxler et al., 2001) and 4 to 5 years (Zahn-Waxler et al., 1995), although self-distress in reaction to another's emotion (Zahn-Waxler, Robinson, & Emde, 1992) and arousal (Zahn-Waxler et al., 1995) were unrelated to prosocial behavior in toddlers (also see Trommsdorff, 1995). Zahn-Waxler et al. (1995) also found (a) children's heart rate deceleration during exposure to sadness (at the peak interval) was associated with 3 of 4 measures of prosocial responding, and (b) behavioral/ facial measures of concerned attention were positively related to prosocial behavior directed toward the target of concern. Similarly, Volling (2001) found that preschoolers who turned their backs or moved away from a distressed younger sibling were also more likely to display personal distress reactions. Trommsdorff and Friedlmeier (1999) reported that German children's facial sympathy was positively correlated with intensity of observed helping, unless they were distracted by another task.

Preschoolers' personal distress reactions also have been positively related to the children's tendency to engage in compliant, requested prosocial behaviors in other contexts (Eisenberg, Fabes, et al., 1990; Eisenberg et al., 1988). Compliant prosocial behavior, in contrast to spontaneously emitted prosocial behavior, has been correlated with low assertiveness, low levels of positive peer reinforcement, low levels of positive response to peers' prosocial actions, and low levels of social interaction. Children high in compliant prosocial responding, especially boys, seem to be nonassertive and perhaps are viewed as easy targets by their peers (Eisenberg et al., 1981; Eisenberg et al., 1988; Larrieu, 1984). Unlike frequency of spontaneous sharing, young children's compliant prosocial behaviors generally do not predict their sympathy at older ages, although there are a few correlations of compliant sharing with self-reported measures evident in adolescence and early adulthood (Eisenberg, Guthrie, et al., 1999, 2002). It is possible that young children who exhibit high levels of compliant behavior with peers are relatively low in social competence and emotion regulation, and engage in requested prosocial behaviors as a means of curtailing unpleasant social interactions.

Studies since Eisenberg and Miller's (1987) review support the view that questionnaire measures tapping empathy (Albiero & Lo Coco, 2001; Eisenberg, Miller, et al., 1991; Eisenberg, Shell, et al., 1987; Hoffner & Haefner, 1997; cf. Stewart & McBride-Chang, 2000), sympathy (Eisenberg, Carlo, et al., 1995; Eisenberg, Miller, et al., 1991; Estrada, 1995; Knight et al., 1994; Litvack-Miller et al., 1997), sympathy and empathy combined (e.g., Krevans & Gibbs, 1996), or empathic self-efficacy (i.e., perceived ability to experience empathy/sympathy; Bandura et al., 2003) are positively related to some measures of children's prosocial behavior in Asian (e.g., in Japan; Asakawa, Iwawaki, Mondori, & Minami, 1987), mid-Eastern (Kumru & Edwards, 2003), or European samples (Bandura et al., 2003), as well as in North American samples. Relations between dispositional empathy or sympathy and prosocial behavior seem to be most consistent for self-reported or relatively costly prosocial behavior (Eisenberg, Miller, et al., 1991; Eisenberg, Shell, et al., 1987). Findings for

self-reported empathy are not highly consistent (e.g., Larrieu & Mussen, 1986; Strayer & Roberts, 1989; also see Roberts & Strayer, 1996). However, empathy questionnaires often contain items that may reflect personal distress or sympathy in addition to empathy. Children's self-reported personal distress on questionnaires tends not to be related to children's prosocial behavior (e.g., Eisenberg, Carlo, et al., 1995; Eisenberg, Miller, et al., 1991; Litvack-Miller et al., 1997), although a weak negative relation was obtained with adolescents (Estrada, 1995). It may be that questionnaire measures of personal distress, which have been adapted from work with adults, are not optimal for children.

In brief, recent research findings are consistent with the conclusion that sympathy and sometimes empathy (depending on its operationalization) are positively related to prosocial behavior, whereas personal distress, particularly as assessed with nonverbal measures, is negatively related (or unrelated for self-reports) to prosocial behavior. As might be expected, there is more evidence of associations within contexts than across contexts, although children with a sympathetic disposition appear to be somewhat more prosocial in general than are other children. In addition, there is evidence that the relation of sympathy to prosocial behavior is moderated by dispositional perspective taking (Knight et al., 1994) and moral reasoning (Miller et al., 1996). Thus, it is important to identify dispositional and situational factors that influence when and whether empathy-related situational reactions and dispositional characteristics are related to prosocial behavior.

DISPOSITIONAL AND PERSONALITY CORRELATES OF PROSOCIAL BEHAVIOR

Some, but not all, aspects of personality likely have a substantial genetic basis. Thus, some of the research on personality correlates (particularly those viewed as part of temperament, such as negative emotionality) is relevant to an understanding of the constitutional bases of prosocial behavior and empathy. Moreover, information on the personality correlates of prosocial behavior could provide clues to the environmental origins of prosocial behavior when there is evidence of a link between a given aspect of personality and socialization.

Consistency of Prosocial Behavior

The assertion that there are personality correlates of prosocial behavior implies a more basic assumption: that there is some consistency in children's prosocial responding. Consistency of the existence of an altruistic (or moral) personality has been an issue of debate for many years and continues to be discussed in the social psychological literature (see Batson, 1991; Eisenberg, Guthrie, et al., 2002). The empirical findings are reviewed in some detail in other sources (Eisenberg & Fabes, 1998; Graziano & Eisenberg, 1997) and, consequently, are merely summarized briefly here.

Although findings differ considerably across measures of prosocial responding and age, there is evidence of modest consistency across situations and time. Evidence of consistency is weakest in studies of infants and preschoolers (e.g., Dunn & Munn, 1986; Eisenberg et al., 1984; Strayer & Roberts, 1989), but sometimes modest or even compelling evidence of consistency has been obtained (e.g., Denham et al., 1994; Gill & Calkins, 2003; Kienbaum et al., 2001; Robinson et al., 2001; van der Mark et al., 2002). Although nonsignificant correlations have been obtained in some studies (e.g., Koenig et al., 2004), positive relations among measures of prosocial or empathy-related responding, across situations, raters, or time, often have been obtained in studies of elementary school children (e.g., Dekovic & Janssens, 1992; Hastings et al., 2000; Rushton & Teachman, 1978; Strayer & Roberts, 1997b; Tremblay, Vitaro, Gagnon, Piche, & Royer, 1992, Vitaro, Gagnon, & Tremblay, 1990, 1991; Warden, Cheyne, Christie, Fitzpatrick, & Reid, 2003; Welsh et al., 2001) and particularly adolescents (Davis & Franzoi, 1991; Eberly & Montemayor, 1999; Eisenberg, Carlo, et al., 1995; Goodman, 2001; Savin-Williams, Small, & Zeldin, 1981; Wentzel, 2003). Given the diversity of motives likely to be associated with prosocial- and empathy-related responses, it is impressive that investigators frequently have found significant relations across situations or time, even if many are modest in size.

Sociability and Shyness

Sociability, which likely has a temperamental basis (see Kagan & Fox or Rothbart & Bates, Chapter 3, this *Handbook,* this volume), appears to influence if and when children assist others. In preschool and beyond, children who are prone to participate in activities at school (Jennings et al., 1987), who tend to approach novel people and things (Stanhope et al., 1987), and who are sociable and low in shyness, social anxiety, or social withdrawal are somewhat more likely to help than are other children (Diener & Kim, 2004; Eisenberg, Fabes,

Karbon, Murphy, Carlo, et al., 1996; Hart et al., 2003; Howes & Farver, 1987; Inglés, Hidalgo, Mendéz, & Inderbitzen, 2003; Russell et al., 2003; Silva, 1992; cf. Farver & Branstetter, 1994). Moreover, behavioral inhibition at age 2 years has been associated with lower empathy and prosocial behavior, especially with strangers (Young, Fox, & Zahn-Waxler, 1999). In one study, however (Volling et al., 2004), preschoolers who were high in social fear were relatively likely to provide caregiving to a young sibling during a separation from mother, perhaps because they were especially likely to experience their sibling's distress and were not inhibited in interactions with the sibling.

There is some reason to believe that early adolescents high in evaluative concerns are more prosocial and less aggressive toward others (if one controls for depression; Rudolph & Conley, 2005). Perhaps children and youth prone to social anxiety are particularly likely to engage in prosocial behavior with those they know; they also may be more easily socialized to comply with adults' expectations for prosocial behavior. In one of the few other studies of adolescents, social anxiety was positively correlated with dispositional personal distress but not sympathy (Davis & Franzoi, 1991).

Sociability is particularly likely to be associated with the performance of prosocial behaviors that are spontaneously emitted (rather than in response to a request for assistance; Eisenberg et al., 1981; Eisenberg et al., 1984; Eisenberg-Berg & Hand, 1979) or directed toward an unfamiliar person in an unfamiliar setting (rather than a familiar person at home; Stanhope et al., 1987; Young et al., 1999). Further, extroversion (which includes an element of sociability) was related to elementary school children's helping in an emergency when another peer was present (but not when the child was alone) and to helping that involved approaching the other person; introverts tended to help in ways that did not involve approaching the injured individual (Suda & Fouts, 1980). Thus, sociable children seem to be more prosocial than their less social peers when assisting another involves social initiation or results in social interaction.

Social Competence and Socially Appropriate Behavior

Because prosocial behavior is socially appropriate in many contexts, it is not surprising that children's prosocial behavior often is correlated with indexes of socially appropriate behavior. Although not all researchers have obtained significant results (e.g., Sawyer et al., 2002), prosocial children tend to be viewed by adults as socially skilled and constructive copers (Cassidy et al., 2003; Eisenberg, Fabes, Karbon, Murphy, Wosinski, et al., 1996; Eisenberg, Fabes, Murphy, et al., 1996; Eisenberg, Guthrie, et al., 1997; Inglés et al., 2003; Peterson, Ridley-Johnson, & Carter, 1984) and are high in social problem-solving skills (Marsh, Serafica, & Barenboim, 1981; also see Warden & Mackinnon, 2003), positive social interaction with peers (Farver & Branstetter, 1994; Howes & Farver, 1987; also see Warden & Mackinnon, 2003), developmentally advanced play (Howes & Matheson, 1992), and cooperation (e.g., Dunn & Munn, 1986; Jennings et al., 1987). In addition, sympathy and empathy have been correlated (sometimes over years) with enacted or adult-reported socially competent behavior (Eisenberg & Fabes, 1995; Eisenberg, Fabes, Murphy, Karbon, et al., 1996; Murphy, Shepard, Eisenberg, Fabes, & Guthrie, 1999; see Eisenberg & Miller, 1987) or with self-reports of number of friends (Coleman & Byrd, 2003).

Consistent with the link between socially appropriate behavior and prosocial behavior, preschoolers' prosocial and sympathetic responding have been linked to having a close friend or more friends (Clark & Ladd, 2000; Coleman & Byrd, 2003; Farver & Branstetter, 1994; McGuire & Weisz, 1982; Sebanc, 2003; cf. Huebner & Mancini, 2003), supportive peer relationships (de Guzman & Carlos, 2004; Laible et al., 2000; Lerner et al., 2005; Sebanc, 2003), the receipt of prosocial actions from peers (Persson, 2005), less conflict with friends (Dunn, Cutting, & Fisher, 2002), low levels of peer victimization (Johnson et al., 2002; cf. Coleman & Byrd, 2003), and being popular (rather than rejected) with peers (Caprara et al., 2000; Clark & Ladd, 2000; Coleman & Byrd, 2003; Dekovic & Gerris, 1994; Dekovic & Janssens, 1992; Denham, Blair, et al., 2003; Eisenberg, Fabes, Murphy, et al., 1996; Hampson, 1984; Keane & Calkins, 2004; Pakaslahti & Keltikangas-Jarvinen, 2001; Ramsey, 1988; Slaugher et al., 2002; Tremblay et al., 1992; Warden et al., 2003; Welsh et al., 2001; Wentzel, 2003; Wilson, 2003; also see Haselager, Cillessen, Van Lieshout, Riksen-Walraven, & Hartup, 2002; LaFontana & Cillessen, 2002; Pakaslahti et al., 2002; cf. McGuire & Weisz, 1982). Stability of rejection by peers in early elementary school is predicted by low levels of children's prosocial behavior (Vitaro et al., 1990); children's skill at comforting predicts whether children are rejected, neglected, or accepted by peers (Burleson et al., 1986); and nonsupportive goals or strategies in hypothetical help-giving situations are

linked to having few and lower quality friends (Rose & Asher, 2004). Clark and Ladd (2000) obtained concurrent relations consistent with the hypothesis that children's prosocial tendencies mediate the relation between a positive, warm parent-child relationship and children's peer acceptance and number of mutual friends. In addition, mature prosocial moral reasoning has been positively correlated with sociometric status, as well as with teachers' reports of social competence and low levels of acting-out behavior (Bear & Rys, 1994). Thus, children who are prosocial tend to have positive relationships and interactions with peers.

Degree of social competence or popularity also may affect the types of prosocial behavior children prefer to perform. Hampson (1984) found that popular prosocial adolescents tended to engage in peer-related prosocial behavior, whereas less popular helpers preferred non-peer-related tasks. Peer acceptance may affect children's comfort level when helping peers; alternatively, people who prefer to help in ways that do not involve social contact with peers may be less popular due to their avoidant behavior.

Aggression and Externalizing Problems

Prosocial children are relatively likely to evaluate aggression negatively (Nelson & Crick, 1999) and are low in aggression and externalizing problems (e.g., Caprara, Barbaranelli, & Pastorelli, 2001; Caprara et al., 2000; Crick, Casas, & Mosher, 1997; Denham, Blair, et al., 2003; Diener & Kim, 2004; Goodman, 1994; Hughes et al., 2000; Inglés et al., 2003; Keane & Calkins, 2004; Ma & Leung, 1991; Muris, Meesters, & van den Berg, 2003; Nagin & Tremblay, 2001; Uggen & Janikula, 1999; Warden et al., 2003; Welsh et al., 2001; Wilson, 2003; also see Haselager et al., 2002; Silva, 1992; Slaughter et al., 2002; Youniss, McLellan, Su, & Yates, 1999). Relations are found across time: Hay and Pawlby (2003) found that externalizing problems at age 4 predicted low levels of prosocial behavior at age 11. Furthermore, sympathy (Eisenberg, Fabes, Murphy, et al., 1996; Laible, Carlos, & Raffaelli, 2000; Murphy et al., 1999; Zahn-Waxler et al., 1995) and empathy (Albiero & Lo Coco, 2001; Braaten & Rosen, 2000; Cohen & Strayer, 1996; Endresen & Olweus, 2001; Strayer & Roberts, 2004a; Warden & Mackinnon, 2003; see Miller & Eisenberg, 1988, for a review) have been linked to low levels of externalizing problem behaviors (including aggression or ADHD). Children's and adolescents' self-reported delinquency and externalizing problem behaviors also have been negatively related to their self-reported empathic efficacy (Bandura et al., 2001, 2003).

The relation of prosocial responding to aggression likely varies depending on the actor's motive for engaging in prosocial behavior. Although prosocial actions that involve a positive affective response to an individual and those not motivated by personal gain tend to be negatively related to adolescents' reports of aggression (and their belief that aggression is acceptable), reports of prosocial actions performed for personal gain have been positively related to reported aggressive actions and the acceptance of aggression (Boxer et al., 2004).

The relation between aggressiveness and prosocial behavior may be more complex in the early years than at older ages. Gil and Calkins (2003) found that aggressive toddlers displayed *more* evidence of empathy or concern than less aggressive toddlers. Moreover, Yarrow et al. (1976) found a positive correlation between prosocial and aggressive behavior for preschool boys (but not girls) below the mean in exhibited aggression, whereas there was a negative relation between prosocial behavior and aggression for boys above the mean in aggression. For those young children who are relatively nonaggressive overall, aggression often may be indicative of assertiveness rather than hostility or the intent to harm another (Eisenberg & Mussen, 1989). Moreover, the lack of regulation reflected in aggression may allow young children to approach and exhibit concern toward an unfamiliar adult (the measure of concern used by Gil and Calkins, 2003).

Thus, a negative relation between aggression and prosocial tendencies may develop with age. Although Hastings and colleagues (2000) did not find a relation between concern for others and the behavior problems of 4- to 5-year-olds, children with clinical behavior problems decreased in their concern and were reported by both mothers and themselves to be relatively low in concern by age 6 to 7 years. Moreover, greater concern at 4 to 5 years predicted a decline in the severity of externalizing problems over the 2 years. Thus, the inverse relation between sympathy and externalizing problems seems to begin consolidation during the preschool to early school years.

Assertiveness and Dominance

Assertiveness and dominance also have been associated with frequency and type of children's prosocial behaviors. Assertive children (e.g., those who issue commands or defend their possessions) are relatively high in sym-

pathy versus personal distress reactions (Eisenberg, Fabes, et al., 1990) and prosocial behavior (Barrett & Yarrow, 1977; Denham & Couchoud, 1991; Inglés et al., 2003; Larrieu & Mussen, 1986), particularly spontaneously emitted (unrequested) instances of helping and sharing (Eisenberg et al., 1984; cf. Eisenberg et al., 1981). A certain level of assertiveness may be necessary for many children to spontaneously approach others needing assistance. In contrast, nonassertive, nondominant children tend to be prosocial in response to a request (Eisenberg et al., 1981; Eisenberg et al., 1984; Larrieu, 1984), apparently because they frequently are asked for help or sharing (probably due to their compliance; Eisenberg et al., 1981; Eisenberg, McCreath, & Ahn, 1988). Children who are not simply assertive but seek to dominate others may be low in prosocial behavior (Krebs & Sturrup, 1984).

Self-Esteem and Related Constructs

It appears that there is a positive relation between children's self-esteem and their prosocial tendencies, but more so for older than for younger children. In studies of preschoolers and elementary school children, investigators typically have found no evidence of a relation between self-reports of self-esteem or self-concept and measures of prosocial behavior (Cauley & Tyler, 1989; Rehberg & Richman, 1989). In studies of children in fourth grade to high school, investigators generally have found that prosocial children have a positive self-concept (Laible & Carlo, 2004; Larrieu & Mussen, 1986; Rigby & Slee, 1993; also see Jacobs et al., 2004; cf. Huebner & Mancini, 2003; Karafantis & Levy, 2004), are high in self-efficacy (Bandura et al., 2001, 2003; Lichter et al., 2002; Sugiyama, Matsui, Satoh, Yoshimi, & Takeuchi, 1992), and tend to have prosocial self-schemas (that affect donating when children are self-aware; Froming, Nasby, & McManus, 1998). Johnson et al. (1998) found that girls, but not boys, with higher academic and positive self-esteem in ninth grade were more likely to volunteer in grades 10 to 12. Perhaps young children's self-reports do not adequately tap relevant dimensions of their self-concepts. However, it is also possible that young children's self-concept often is not based on enduring characteristics that are relevant to prosocial responding (see Harter, Chapter 9, this *Handbook*, this volume).

It also is probable that the relation between self-concept or self-esteem and prosocial behavior varies as a function of the psychological significance or quality of the prosocial act. Children who are anxious or emotionally unstable may enact prosocial behaviors to ingratiate, avoid disapproval, or prevent overreactivity to social distress. In fact, there is some evidence that boys who are particularly high in prosocial behavior performed or promised in a public context are anxious, inhibited, and emotionally unstable (Bond & Phillips, 1971; O'Connor, Dollinger, Kennedy, & Pelletier-Smetko, 1979). Similarly, Jacobs et al. (2004) found that although socially confident adolescents were relatively high in self-reported prosocial activities, so were anxious adolescents. Youth who had a low social self-concept but were not worried about their standing with peers were lower in prosocial activities than the socially confident or anxious adolescents.

The association between older children's self-conceptions and prosocial behavior probably is bidirectional in causality. Children who feel good about themselves may be able to focus on others' needs because their own needs are being met; further, they may feel that they have the competencies needed to assist others. In addition, it has been argued that involvement in activities that help others may foster the development of self-efficacy (Yates & Youniss, 1996b). It is reasonable to assume that the performance of socially competent behavior, including prosocial behavior, and children's self-concept are complexly related during development.

Values and Goals

An important component of the self is one's values. Colby and Damon (1992) noted two morally relevant characteristics that were dramatically evident in adult moral exemplars: (1) exemplars' certainty or exceptional clarity about what they believed was right and about their own personal responsibility to act in ways consistent with those beliefs; and (2) the unity of self and moral goals, that is, the central role of exemplars' moral goals in their conceptions of their own identity and the integration of moral and personal goals.

Consistent with Colby and Damon's findings, Hart and Fegley (1995) found that adolescents who demonstrated exceptional commitments to care for others were particularly likely to describe themselves in terms of moral personality traits and goals and to articulate theories of self in which personal beliefs and philosophies were important. Moreover, Pratt et al. (2003) found that adolescents who were more actively involved in community helping activities reported closer agreement with

parents about the importance of moral values for the self 2 years later than did their less involved peers.

More generally, there is evidence that prosocial behavior is positively associated with measures of moral functioning, including other-oriented values and beliefs (Dlugokinski & Firestone, 1974; Janoski, Musick, & Wison, 1998; Larrieu & Mussen, 1986); social responsibility, responsibility goals, or low levels of irresponsibility (Savin-Williams et al., 1981; Wentzel, 2003); integrative goals (i.e., concern with the maintenance and promotion of other individuals or social groups; Estrada, 1995); guilt or need for reparation (Caprara et al., 2001; Chapman, Zahn-Waxler, Cooperman, & Iannotti, 1987); and low levels of moral disengagement (Bandura et al., 2001). Further, adolescents sometimes cite moral values and responsibility for others as reasons for enacting prosocial behaviors (e.g., Carlo, Eisenberg, & Knight, 1992; Eisenberg, Carlo, et al., 1995). Thus, it appears that older children and adolescents who have internalized moral (including altruistic) values and who view morality as central to their self-concept are particularly likely to be altruistic. In addition, prosocial tendencies appear to be linked to relational rather than instrumental goals (Nelson & Crick, 1999) and to collaborative goals in the school environment (Cheung, Ma, & Shek, 1998).

In addition, empathic or sympathetic youth not only exhibit values and a social conscience (Lerner et al., 2005), but also may be more likely than less responsive youth to extend their prosocial behaviors to members outside their own group. Empathic youth are more likely than their less empathic peers to say that they are comfortable being near children who are different from them and who might be viewed negatively (e.g., a child who is depressed, immature, aggressive, overweight, or doing poorly academically; Bryant, 1982; cf. Strayer & Roberts, 1997a). Similarly, sympathetic youth value diversity (Lerner et al., 2005), and school children feel less interpersonal distance from those with whom they empathize/sympathize (Strayer & Roberts, 1997a; see, however, Batson, Chang, Orr, & Rowland, 2002). Inclusive reactions such as these would be expected to enhance prosocial behavior directed toward out-group members (Oliner & Oliner, 1988).

Religiosity

Religiosity (as measured by attending religious services) has been positively related to participation in volunteer activities during adolescence (Huebner & Mancini, 2003; Lichter et al., 2002) and predicts subsequent volunteering behavior in early adulthood (Zaff et al., 2003). Similarly, going to a Catholic or church-based school (but not being Catholic; Youniss, McLellan, Su, & Yates, 1999) predicted adolescents' community service (Youniss, McLellan, & Yates, 1999). Because involvement in church and other community-based youth groups is related to doing volunteer service (McLellan & Youniss, 2003), it is likely that religious institutions provide opportunities for organized prosocial activities. In addition, Youniss, McLellan, and Yates (1999) argued that involvement in church-sponsored services makes it more likely that youth will internalize or adopt the religious rationales provided for engaging in service. More generally, a religious identity, if it involves moral overtones, has been linked with a prosocial personality (Furrow, King, & White, 2004). At this time, it is unclear whether prosocial behavior is differentially linked to identification with, or acceptance of, various religions.

Regulation

In studies involving adult-reported or behavioral measures of self-regulation (generally defined in terms of processes involved in modulating emotional states and behaviors; Eisenberg, Spinrad, & Sadovsky, 2005), prosocial children tend to be relatively well regulated, as well as low in impulsivity (e.g., Eisenberg, Fabes, Karbon, Murphy, Wosinski, et al., 1996; Eisenberg, Fabes, Karlo, Murphy, Wosinski, et al., 1996; Eisenberg, Guthrie, et al., 1997; Moore, Barresi, & Thompson, 1998; Rothbart, Ahadi, & Hershey, 1994; Silva, 1992; Thompson, Barresi, Moore, 1997; Wilson, 2003; also see Deater-Deckard, Dunn, et al., 2001). The association between regulation and prosociality is not surprising because engaging in prosocial actions often requires regulated behavior and emotion (e.g., controlling one's own negative emotion) or involves actions that help regulate others' emotions (Bergin, Talley, & Hamer, 2003). In fact, degree of regulation is a stronger positive predictor of prosocial behavior for children prone to negative emotions such as anger (Diener & Kim, 2004; also see Eisenberg, Guthrie, et al., 1997).

Similarly, sympathy has been associated with high levels of children's regulation (Eisenberg & Fabes, 1995; Eisenberg, Fabes, Murphy, Karbon, et al., 1994; Eisenberg, Fabes, Murphy, et al., 1996; Eisenberg, Liew, & Pidada, 2001; Murphy et al., 1999), whereas personal distress sometimes has been associated with low regulation (Eisenberg, Fabes, Murphy, Karbon, et al., 1994, Ungerer et al., 1990; Valiente et al., 2004; cf. Eisenberg & Fabes, 1995). The few findings for empathy are mixed, some positive (Sneed, 2002), some not (Saklofske & Eysenck, 1983). In addition, resilient children, who may be viewed as optimally regulated, tend to be prosocial and empathic (Atkins, Hart, & Donnelly, 2005; Eisenberg, Guthrie, et al., 1997; Strayer & Roberts, 1989; also see Hart et al., 1998). In contrast, boys with ADHD were found to be lower on empathy than boys without a diagnosis of ADHD. Because children diagnosed with ADHD have low attentional control, these children may be at a disadvantage for the development of empathy and prosocial behavior (Braaten & Rosen, 2000).

It appears that well-regulated children can modulate their vicarious arousal and, consequently, focus their attention on others' emotions and needs rather than on their own aversive vicarious emotion (Trommsdorff & Friedlmeier, 1999). Consistent with this idea, Bengtsson (2003) found that Swedish elementary school students who were high in self-reported empathy and teacher-reported prosocial behavior tended to experience moderate (rather than high) levels of threat and to modulate the emotional significance of empathy-eliciting stimuli through cognitive restructuring (which can be viewed as a mode of emotion regulation). Moreover, well-regulated children would be expected to be relatively likely to sustain their attentional focus on others and to suppress any tendencies to try to avoid contact with distressed or needy individuals.

Findings for measures of physiological emotional regulation are somewhat inconsistent and may vary as a function of age of the child or evocativeness of the empathy-inducing situation. In the relevant studies, physiological emotion-related regulation often is assessed with higher heart rate variance, high vagal tone, or vagal suppression. These intercorrelated measures, especially the latter two, are viewed as reflecting emotion-related physiological regulation based on the control of parasympathetic functioning by the vagal nerve (Porges, Doussard-Roosevelt, & Maiti, 1994; see Rothbart & Bates, Chapter 3, this *Handbook,* this volume). Such measures have been positively related with elementary school students' observed comforting (Eisenberg, Fabes, Karbon, Murphy, Carlo, & Wosinski, 1996) and dispositional sympathy (Fabes et al., 1993), although findings for girls have been positive for maternal report of girls' sympathy

(Fabes et al., 1993), but negative for girls' self-reported sympathy (and positive for boys' sympathy; Eisenberg, Fabes, Murphy, Karbon, Smith, et al., 1996).

Moreover, contrary to expectations, toddlers' vagal suppression in response to a crying infant was *negatively* related to observed concern in response to an adult feigning distress to an injury (Gill & Calkins, 2003). Similarly, Zahn-Waxler et al. (1995) found that preschool children's concerned reactions during the same type of feigned injury task were negatively related to their vagal tone. The same children's vagal tone was weakly negatively related to teacher- (but not parent- or child-reported) prosocial behavior 2 years later (Hastings et al., 2000). Gill and Calkins suggested that a positive relation between concern and physiological regulation might develop with age. Alternatively, it may be difficult to differentiate between personal distress and sympathy with some of the measures (e.g., reactions to feigned distress) typically used with younger children. It is not clear whether the complex pattern of findings is due to age-related factors, to differences in the measures of prosocial behavior used with younger and older children, or to other moderating factors.

Emotionality

Children who are emotionally positive—a characteristic that may be viewed as partly an outcome of emotional regulation—also tend to be prosocial (Denham, 1986; Denham & Burger, 1991; Eisenberg et al., 1981; Garner & Estep, 2001; also see Bandura et al., 2003; cf. Braaten & Rosen, 2000; Denham, Blair, et al., 2003; Farver & Branstetter, 1994) and empathic/sympathetic (Eisenberg, Fabes, Murphy, Karbon, et al., 1996; Robinson et al., 1994; also see Eisenberg et al., 1994; cf. Volling, Herrera, & Poris, 2004). In contrast, the data pertaining to the relation between negative emotionality and prosocial responding are more complex. Prosocial behavior generally (albeit sometimes for one sex or the other) has been negatively related to negative emotionality, including anger, fear, anxiety, or sadness (Bandura et al., 2001; Denham, 1986; Denham & Burger, 1991; Diener & Kim, 2004; Eisenberg, Fabes, Karbon, Murphy, Wosinski, et al., 1996; Hoffner & Haefner, 1997; Ma & Leung, 1991, Tremblay et al., 1992; Volling et al., 2004; Wentzel & McNamara, 1999; also see Caprara, Barbaranelli, Pastorelli, et al., 2001; Strayer & Roberts, 2004a, 2004b; cf. Denham & Burger, 1991; Farver &

Branstetter, 1994; Hart et al., 2003), albeit not for some measures of depression or internalizing problems (Bandura et al., 2003; Goodman, 1994; Hay & Pawlby, 2003; Muris et al., 2003). In addition, intensity of emotional responding in general may be negatively related to prosocial tendencies (Garner & Estep, 2001). However, relations of negative emotionality (intensity and/or frequency) to empathy/sympathy have been negative (Eisenberg, Fabes, Murphy, Karbon, et al., 1996; Eisenberg, Fabes, Shepard, et al., 1998; Murphy et al., 1999; Roberts & Strayer, 1996, for anger; Strayer & Roberts, 2004a; van der Mark et al., 2002), nonsignificant (Braaten & Rosen, 2000; Denham, Blair, et al., 2003), and positive (Saklofske & Eysenck, 1983), although positive findings have been obtained primarily when negative emotionality was measured during the early years and related to empathy (or mixed empathy and sympathy) rather than sympathy (Howes & Farver, 1987; Robinson et al., 1994; Rothbart et al., 1994). There also is some evidence that children who are extremely worried about the well-being of family members are relatively prosocial (Hay & Pawlby, 2003).

Thus, in general, prosocial behavior and sympathy or empathy have been linked to dispositional positive emotionality. Further, low negative emotionality has been consistently associated with children's prosocial behavior, but not young children's empathy/sympathy. The inconsistencies in findings may be partly due to both type and intensity of the negative emotion experienced and type of measure. Relations between negative emotionality and empathy/sympathy or prosocial behavior seem to be negative especially for externalizing types of emotions (e.g., anger) rather than depression, anxiety, or dysphoric emotions (e.g., Laible et al., 2000; Strayer & Roberts, 2004a). Children's anger and frustration seem to be salient to adults and, like aggression, covary inversely with prosocial behaviors and empathy-related emotions.

In addition, intensity of negative emotion may be related to whether people experience sympathy or personal distress, which, in turn, predicts prosocial behavior. Eisenberg et al. (1994) proposed that situational emotional overarousal due to empathy is associated with personal distress, whereas moderate empathic responding is associated with sympathy (also see Hoffman, 1982). If people can maintain their vicarious emotional reactions at a tolerable range, they are likely to vicariously experience the emotion of needy or distressed others, but are relatively unlikely to become overwhelmed by the emotion and, consequently, self-focused. In contrast, people who are overaroused by vicarious negative emotion are expected to experience that emotion as aversive and as a distressed, self-focused reaction (personal distress). Consistent with this view, general negative emotional arousal has been found to result in a self-focus (Wood, Saltzberg, & Goldsamt, 1990), and empathically induced distress reactions are associated with higher skin conductance reactivity than is sympathy (Eisenberg, Fabes, Schaller, Carlo, & Miller, 1991; Eisenberg, Fabes, Schaller, Miller, et al., 1991).

Based on this line of reasoning, Eisenberg and colleagues argued that individual differences in the dispositional tendency to experience sympathy versus personal distress vary as a function of dispositional differences in both typical level of emotional intensity and individuals' abilities to regulate their emotional reactions. People high in effortful regulation (e.g., who have control over their ability to focus and shift attention) are hypothesized to be relatively high in sympathy regardless of their emotional intensity. Well-regulated people would be expected to modulate their negative vicarious emotion and to maintain an optimal level of emotional arousal that has emotional force and enhances attention, but is not so aversive and physiologically arousing that it engenders a self-focus. In contrast, people low in the ability to regulate their emotion, especially if they are emotionally intense, are hypothesized to be low in dispositional sympathy. Further, measures of tendencies to display anger and frustration probably partly reflect low regulation and high emotional reactivity and, consequently, would be expected to relate to personal distress and low prosocial behavior.

Modest support has been obtained for these ideas. As noted, regulation has been linked to high sympathy and low personal distress. Further, low and moderate levels of negative emotional intensity, but not high levels, have been associated with situational concern (Eisenberg & Fabes, 1995) and children who experience more negative emotion than that of the stimulus person eliciting empathy (i.e., become overaroused) are relatively low in empathy/sympathy (Strayer, 1993). In addition, there is limited evidence that unregulated children are low in sympathy regardless of their level of emotional intensity whereas, for moderately and highly regulated children, level of sympathy increases with level of emotional in-

tensity (Eisenberg, Fabes, Murphy, Karbon, et al., 1996; also see Eisenberg et al., 1998).

Thus, there is initial support for the notion that emotional intensity (including intensity of both positive and negative emotions) interacts with regulation in predicting children's sympathy, although the pattern of relations is complex and depends on the type of regulation. For children in mid-elementary school, behavioral regulation was positively related to dispositional sympathy for boys who were average or high, but not low, in the tendency to experience emotions intensely. In contrast, attentional regulation predicted high dispositional sympathy (for both sexes) only for children low in general emotional intensity. For children low in emotional intensity, attentional control may be important in helping children focus on and process others' emotions and needs (Eisenberg et al., 1998).

Positive relations between some measures of negative emotionality and empathy/sympathy in the literature also may be due to empathic or sympathetic people being relatively likely to express or report their emotions (see Roberts & Strayer, 1996), in empathy-inducing contexts (Roberts & Strayer, 1996; also see Eisenberg, Losoya, et al., 2001). In future work on empathy-related reactions, it will be useful to differentiate among types of negative emotion (e.g., externalizing and internalizing emotions), between expressed (i.e., observable) and experienced emotion, and between individuals' general emotional intensity and the intensity of solely negative emotions.

THE ROLE OF RELATIONSHIP HISTORY IN PROSOCIAL BEHAVIOR

The degree to which children are prosocial frequently depends on the identity and characteristics of the potential recipient. Children prefer to help people who are relatively important in their lives, such as family members (e.g., Killen & Turiel, 1998; Rheingold et al., 1976; van der Mark et al., 2002; Young et al., 1999). In adolescence, help is as likely or more likely to be directed toward known peers as toward known, nonfamilial adults (e.g., Zeldin, Savin-Williams, & Small, 1984). Moreover, children often share or help friends or liked peers more than less liked peers (Buhrmester, Goldfarb, & Cantrell, 1992) or acquaintances (Buhrmester et al.,

1992; Farver & Branstetter, 1994; Pilgram & Rueda-Riedle, 2002; Rao & Stewart, 1999). In fact, children as young as age 4 or 5 years or in elementary school report more sympathy toward the plight of a friend or liked peer than toward an acquaintance (Costin & Jones, 1992). Prosocial behavior among friends appears to be motivated by not only liking and concern (Costin & Jones, 1992), but also loyalty, consideration of reciprocity obligations, and the fact that friends more often ask for sharing or help (Birch & Billman, 1986).

Sometimes children are equally prosocial to friends and other peers or even help or share less with friends (Berndt, Hawkins, & Hoyle, 1986). In studies in which children have had to choose between friends and strangers, children apparently sometimes assisted people they did not know well to eliminate inequities between a stranger and a friend because they believed that their friend would understand, they wanted to gain the unknown person's approval or friendship, or they were competing with the friend (Berndt, 1982; Staub & Noerenberg, 1981).

SEX DIFFERENCES IN CHILDREN'S PROSOCIAL BEHAVIOR

Based on stereotypic gender roles, females generally are expected and believed to be more responsive, empathic, and prosocial than males, whereas males are expected to be relatively independent and achievement oriented (e.g., Spence, Helmreich, & Stapp, 1974). Further, cross-cultural work has verified that gender differences in prosocial responding are not limited to only a few cultures and may develop with age. Whiting and Edwards (1973) found that helpfulness and support giving generally were greater for girls than boys across six different cultures, although these differences were significant for older but not younger children. More recent work confirms the cross-cultural tendency of girls to be more prosocial than boys (e.g., Carlo, Reoesch, Knight, & Koller, 2001; Russell et al., 2003).

Despite the prevailing view that females are more prosocial than males, findings vary depending on the age of the actor and the type of prosocial behavior. Eagly and Crowley (1986) conducted a meta-analysis of sex differences in older adolescents' and adults' helping behavior and found that *men* helped more than women, particularly in situations involving instrumental and chivalrous assistance. Sex differences in helping were inconsistent across studies and were successfully predicted by various attributes of the studies. Carlo et al. (2003) also found sex differences varied with type of reported prosocial behavior: Adolescent girls were more likely to report altruistic and emotional prosocial behaviors than were boys; boys were more likely to report prosocial tendencies in public situations; and no sex differences were found in situations involving anonymous or compliant prosocial behavior or helping in dire circumstances. Becker and Eagly (2004) examined extreme forms of prosocial behavior—heroism—and found that men were overrepresented in some forms of heroism (e.g., Carnegie Hero Fund medalists who engaged in life-risking rescue actions), but in other heroic actions (organ donors, peace corps volunteers, holocaust rescuers), the percentage of women was at least equal to and, in several cases, higher than that found for men. Such findings suggest that the qualities associated with different types of prosocial behavior (e.g., the role of risk taking in extremely dangerous heroic acts) more likely explain differences in males' and females' tendencies to engage in prosocial actions than a general sex difference model of prosociality per se.

Eisenberg and Fabes (1998) reported a meta-analysis of sex differences in children's prosocial behavior involving 259 studies yielding a total of 450 effect sizes (M age = 7.93 years). Only one effect size was used per sample (i.e., when different variables were used for a single sample, one was selected randomly). For both the full and partial sample of effect sizes, the mean unweighted effect size was modest (.18) and favored girls. Although effect sizes were significant for all types of prosocial behavior and for various design, method, or recipient characteristics, they varied in strength by the type of prosocial behavior studied. Sex differences were significantly greater when prosocial responding was measured with self-reports or reports from others than with observational methods. The effect size also was significantly greater for aggregated indices or indices reflecting kindness/consideration than for indices reflecting instrumental help, comforting, or sharing, and in correlational/naturalistic studies than in structured/experimental studies. However, the latter two differences disappeared when study characteristics were controlled in regression analyses, probably because self-report measures have been used disproportionately in assessment of kindness/consideration and aggregated indices, and in observational/correlational studies. In addition, sex differences in prosocial behavior were significantly greater when the target was an adult or was unspecified than when the target was another child.

When controlling for other study or participant variables, the sex difference in prosocial behavior was greater for larger samples and when the age span of study participants was relatively small. Instrumental help also was significantly less predictive of sex differences in prosocial behavior than were other types of prosocial indices.

These findings support Eagly and Crowley's (1986) conclusion that sex differences in adults' prosocial behavior vary as a function of the qualities of the studies. In contrast to Eagly and Crowley's findings for adults and older adolescents (combined), Eisenberg and Fabes (1998) found that girls tended to be more prosocial than boys. The finding that the sex difference was weakest for instrumental helping is particularly interesting because many of the studies in the adult literature in which men helped more were assessments of instrumental helping (Eagly & Crowley, 1986).

With increasing age, sex differences in prosocial behavior tended to get larger (see Eisenberg & Fabes, 1998; Fabes, Carlo, Kupanoff, & Laible, 1999). However, the effect for age in the meta-analysis was eliminated once other study qualities were controlled, probably because type of study was associated with age, with older children involved in more naturalistic/correlational studies.

Since the Eisenberg and Fabes' meta-analysis, investigators have continued to find sex differences in reports of children's prosocial behaviors (e.g., Bosacki, 2003; Caprara, Barbaranelli, & Pastorelli, 2001). Peers, especially girls, are more likely to nominate girls as being prosocial and to nominate boys as being bullies (Warden et al., 2003; Warden & Mackinnon, 2003). Fewer differences have been found in some observational studies (Fabes, Martin, & Hanish, 2002; contrast with Zahn-Waxler et al., 2001). To some degree, sex differences in self- and other-reported prosocial behavior may reflect people's conceptions of what boys and girls are *supposed* to be like rather than how they actually behave. Parents emphasize prosocial behaviors and politeness more with their daughters than with their sons (Power & Parke, 1986). Moreover, peers, parents, and teachers tend to perceive girls as more prosocial than either behavioral or self-reported data indicate (Bond & Phillips,

1971; Shigetomi, Hartmann, & Gelfand, 1981). Furthermore, parents have been found to attribute girls' actions to inborn factors significantly more often than boys' actions, whereas boys' prosocial actions are more likely to be viewed as due to environmental factors (Gretarsson & Gelfand, 1988). These findings are consistent with the view that girls' reputations for prosocial behavior are greater than the actual sex difference. In addition, children may self-socialize their prosocial tendencies by means of having their thoughts, emotions, and behavioral scripts conform to parents', teachers', and peers' expectations (Maccoby, 1998). Nonetheless, there is a small sex difference favoring girls even in observational studies (Eisenberg & Fabes, 1998), so there likely is some truth to the stereotype.

Sex differences in the literature may also be due, in part, to biases in measures of prosocial behavior. Zarbatany, Hartmann, Gelfand, and Vinciguerra (1985) argued that measures used to evaluate children's prosocial tendencies include a disproportionate number of sex-biased items favoring girls (items pertaining to feminine activities). They found that masculine items (e.g., helping get a cat out of a tree) elicited endorsements for boys, and feminine-related and neutral items elicited endorsements for girls. Masculine items likely included acts of instrumental helping, the category for which there was the smallest sex difference favoring girls (when study characteristics were controlled) in the meta-analysis.

Findings about sex differences in empathy and sympathy, like those for prosocial behavior, vary with the method used to assess empathy-related responding. As mentioned, Eisenberg and Lennon (1983; also see Lennon & Eisenberg, 1987), in a meta-analytic review, found large differences favoring girls for self-report measures of empathy/sympathy, especially questionnaire indices. No gender differences were found when the measure of empathy was either physiological or unobtrusive observations of nonverbal behavior. In work in which sympathy and personal distress have been differentiated, investigators have obtained similar findings, although they occasionally have found weak (but significant) sex differences in facial reactions (generally favoring females; see Eisenberg, Fabes, Schaller, & Miller, 1989) and in observational assessments of young children using developmentally appropriate stimuli such as puppets to elicit distress (Kienbaum et al., 2001) or feigned distress (Zahn-Waxler et al., 2001). Eisenberg and Lennon (1983) suggested that the general pattern of results was due to differences among measures in the degree to which both the intent of the measure was obvious and people could control their responses. Sex differences were greatest when demand characteristics were high (it was clear what was being assessed) and individuals had conscious control over their responses (i.e., self-report indices were used); gender differences were virtually nonexistent when demand characteristics were subtle and study participants were unlikely to exercise much conscious control over their responding (i.e., physiological indices). Thus, when gender-related stereotypes are activated and people can easily control their responses, they may try to project a socially desirable image to others or to themselves.

Eisenberg and Fabes (1998; Fabes & Eisenberg, 1996) also conducted a follow-up meta-analysis of empathy/sympathy data published since Eisenberg and Lennon's (1983) first review and found an overall unweighted effect size (favoring girls) of .34. Relatively large effect sizes were found in self-report studies (significantly larger than in the studies involving other methods) and in studies in which the targets of the empathic response were unspecified or unknown individuals. Moreover, sex differences were larger for older children. When sex differences were examined by method, significant sex differences favoring girls were obtained for self-report indices (weighted effect size of .60) and observational measures (in which a combination of behavioral and facial reactions usually were used, .29). The gender difference in observed reactions, especially for young children, suggests that there is a real, albeit modest, difference in children's empathy. No sex differences were obtained for nonverbal facial and physiological measures. Further, the sex difference in self-reported empathy/sympathy increased with mean age of the sample (beta = .24). Sex differences in reported empathy may increase as children become more aware of, and perhaps are more likely to internalize, sex-role stereotypes and expectations into their self-image (Karniol et al., 1998).

Although there are no sex differences in prosocial moral reasoning in young children, in later elementary school and beyond, girls use more of some relatively sophisticated types of prosocial moral reasoning, whereas boys sometimes verbalize more of less mature types of reasoning (Eisenberg, Carlo, et al., 1995; Eisenberg, Miller, et al., 1991; also see Jaffee & Hyde, 2000). Moreover, in adolescence, femininity is positively re-

lated to internalized prosocial moral reasoning (but also related to hedonistic reasoning for males; Carlo et al., 1996). It is unclear the degree to which these sex differences, which generally are relatively weak, are due to real differences in moral reasoning or to differences in the ways that adolescent males and females view themselves and desire to be viewed by others.

In summary, although girls appear to be more prosocial than boys, the issue of sex differences in prosocial responding and their origins is far from resolved. It is difficult to determine the degree to which the sex difference reflects a difference in moral or other-orientation versus other factors (e.g., self-presentation). It also is unclear whether the sex difference changes with age. Although age was related to the prosocial effect size in the univariate analysis in our meta-analysis, there was no effect of age when study characteristics were controlled. There is a need to better assess the developmental trajectory of the sex differences and to investigate the origins of sex differences in prosocial behavior.

AN INTEGRATIVE MODEL OF PROSOCIAL ACTION

Based on the available evidence, prosocial action appears to be the outcome of multiple individual (including biological) and situational factors. A simplified model of the major variables believed to contribute to the performance of prosocial behavior (and steps in the process itself) is depicted in Figure 11.1 (see Eisenberg, 1986, for extended discussion of this model). This heuristic model can be used to integrate many of the topics discussed in this chapter.

In our model, biological factors are viewed as having an effect on both the child's individual characteristics (e.g., sociocognitive development, empathy, sociability) and parental interactions with the child (i.e., socialization experiences). The child's individual characteristics and socialization experiences affect one another and, together with objective characteristics of the situation (see Eisenberg & Fabes, 1998, for a review of situational influences), influence how the child interprets events involving another's need or distress in a specific context. For example, individual differences in perspective taking and in decoding skills, which likely are influenced by socialization experiences as well as heritability (e.g., genetic effects on intelligence), may affect whether a child notices another's distress, as might the clarity of the dis-

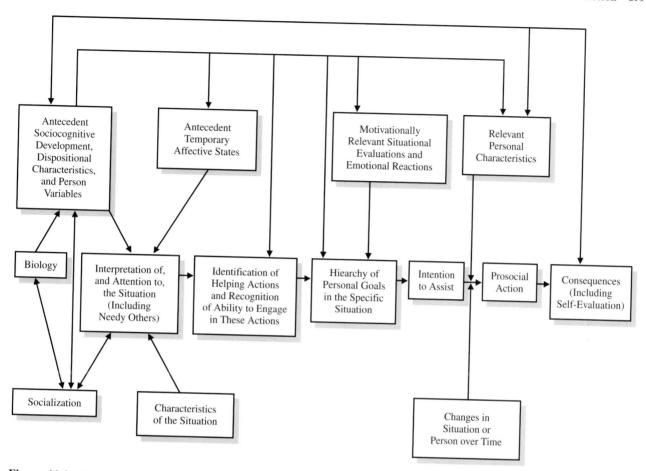

Figure 11.1 Heuristic model of prosocial behavior. Adapted from *Altruistic Emotion, Cognition, and Behavior,* by N. Eisenberg, 1986, Hillsdale, NJ: Erlbaum.

tressed other's nonverbal and verbal cues of emotion (a situational factor). Moreover, socialization influences and person variables likely interact; as discussed, Valiente et al. (2004) found that parental expressivity related differently to children's sympathy and personal distress depending on the children's regulation. It also is likely that antecedent characteristics interact when predicting children's prosocial tendencies; examples were discussed in our review (e.g., between regulation and emotional intensity, or between perspective taking and sympathy; Diener & Kim, 2004; Eisenberg, Fabes, Karbon, Murphy, Wosinski, et al., 1996; Knight et al., 1994).

How the child interprets the situation logically leads to and affects the child's identification of prosocial actions and the child's recognition of his or her ability to engage in these actions. A temporary state such as the child's mood may determine his or her attention to, or interpretation of, a situation (see Eisenberg & Fabes, 1998). Level of arousal seems to alter the ways in which

people interpret others' verbal statements and facial expressions (Clark, Milberg, & Erber, 1983).

In addition, a child who feels capable of assisting must then decide whether he or she intends to assist. The child's emotional reactions (e.g., sympathy or personal distress), relationship with the other person (which affects the child's emotional reactions and perceived costs and benefits of assisting), and attributions about the cause of the other's need or distress (e.g., whether the needy person is responsible for his or her situation) are examples of motivationally relevant situational evaluations and emotional reactions that can play a role in this decision. The decision of whether to engage in prosocial action also is affected by antecedent person variables such as individual differences in concern about social approval, values, personal goals, and self-identity in regard to the trait of altruism (see Figure 11.1).

In the given context, the various relevant moral and nonmoral factors—be they perceived costs and benefits, values, sympathetic emotion, or other factors—influence the individual's relative hierarchy of goals in the particular situation. Often goals, needs, or values conflict in a situation and must be prioritized. This ordering of personal goals undoubtedly varies across individuals and across situations for a given person (see Figure 11.1). In a situation in which important people are present, social approval needs may be salient (particularly for people who value such approval). In another situation in which there are material costs for assisting, valuing of the object to be shared or donated will be particularly relevant for some people (but not others who do not value the commodity). Moreover, if the situation evokes an emotional reaction such as sympathy or personal distress, then other- or self-related goals linked to those emotional reactions will be salient and perhaps activated.

The values, goals, and needs that underlie personal goals and their relative importance (in general and in specific contexts) change with age (e.g., Bar-Tal, Raviv, et al., 1980). An individual's values, goals, and needs, as expressed in his or her prosocial moral reasoning, provide some insight into the child's typical hierarchy of goals, needs, and values (i.e., one's general hierarchy rather than one's hierarchy in a specific context), although, as noted, different factors will be particularly salient in different situations (see Eisenberg, 1986). Because other-oriented values based in part on perspective taking, sympathetic reactions, or the capacity for abstract principles increase with age (Eisenberg, 1986), one would expect prosocial moral goals to rank higher in the hierarchies of older children than in those of young children.

Thus, the hierarchy of an individual's goals or priorities in the particular situation is viewed as determining whether the child wants to assist, as well as the intention to assist. However, even if the child intends to perform a prosocial behavior, he or she may not be able to do so due to the lack of relevant personal competencies (physical, psychological, or material) needed to intervene or provide appropriate helping skills. In addition, the situation may change, as might the potential benefactor's situation, prior to the actual helping opportunity. For example, the potential benefactor may receive help from someone else before the child can assist.

Finally, there are consequences of engaging in prosocial behavior or choosing not to do so. Children who help may develop new helping competencies or sociocognitive skills that can be applied in future situations. Assist-ing another also may affect socializers' efforts to promote the child's prosocial behavior and the degree to which an individual develops a prosocial self-concept (e.g., Eisenberg, Cialdini, et al., 1987). These consequences are reflected in the future in terms of the child's ongoing dispositional or person variables (see Figure 11.1), as well as in the range of the child's prosocial-relevant personal competencies. Thus, there is a cycle by which children's prosocial behavior (or the lack thereof) has consequences for future prosocial responding.

CHALLENGES AND FUTURE DIRECTIONS

As is evident in this review, there is considerable research on antecedents and correlates of children's prosocial responding. This work has provided a rudimentary understanding of the factors that may foster prosocial action, although in many cases, it is premature to confidently assume causation. Many of the deficiencies in the research on prosocial development noted in 1998 still exist. Although there is more research on some topics (e.g., volunteering, personality/person correlates), the field would benefit from new emphases in methods, conceptual frameworks, and empirical foci.

Methodological Issues

In this chapter, we have discussed a few of the mediators and moderators of the bivariate relations associated with the development of prosocial behavior. There is initial evidence that regulation mediates the relation between parental expression of negative emotion and children's sympathy (Eisenberg, Liew, & Pidada, 2001) and that sympathy and prosocial moral reasoning mediate the relation of perspective taking to prosocial behavior (Eisenberg, Zhou, & Koller, 2001). A greater focus on mediation would enhance our understanding of the processes related to prosocial development and behavior. Little is known about factors that mediate the relations of parental inductions or assignment of responsibilities to children and their prosocial behavior or empathy-related responding. Consistent with Hoffman's (2000) thinking, inductions may affect perspective taking and empathy, which then foster prosocial action. Additionally, certain types of interactions with peers or teachers may promote children's understanding of others' emotions and mental states in a manner that in turn fosters sympathy. Sympathy may act as a mediator of the relation of many environmental influences or genetic predispositions (e.g., regulation) to children's prosocial behavior. Examination of such mediational processes requires that investigators refine their conceptual explanations and go beyond looking at global associations to focus on process-oriented explanations.

In contrast, a focus on moderation forces investigators to think about the ways in which predictors of prosocial responding interact in their potential influence. The strength of many predictors of prosocial responding (e.g., perspective taking or parental use of inductions) likely varies based on factors such as sex, age, general parenting style, cultural experiences, personality predispositions, or children's susceptibility to experience empathy or sympathy. We live in a multivariate world, and prosocial behavior in specific situations, is determined by numerous additive and interacting factors. For example, as mentioned, Knight et al. (1994) found that children who donated to needy children were not only high in perspective taking, but also high in sympathy and understood the commodity to be donated (money; also see Eisenberg, Zhou, & Koller, 2001, who found that sympathy and perspective taking jointly predicted prosocial moral reasoning). As noted, parental expression of emotion and children's regulation also interact when predicting children's empathy-related responding (Valiente et al., 2004). Based on the work of Kochanska (1995), who found that children's temperament moderated the relations between maternal gentle discipline and measures of conscience, it is likely that temperament affects the relations of parental practices to children's prosocial tendencies. In addition, it is important to go beyond moderational models to examine the ways in which configurations of numerous variables (e.g., child-rearing practices) predict prosocial outcomes.

Most of the research on prosocial development continues to be correlational. To better examine issues of causality, longitudinal designs and structural equation modeling can be used to test causal hypotheses (although structural modeling can only assess if a causal sequence is consistent with the data and does not prove causality). Longitudinal data are especially important for testing mediated relations; concurrent data provide a weak test of causal, mediated relations. Further, experimental research designs could be used more frequently to test causal assumptions. Although experimental designs usually (but need not) require relatively artificial laboratory situations, researchers have tended to shy away from experiments in the past decade or two. Yet experiments, especially those performed in more natural settings (e.g., at school), can be valuable in testing ideas about causality. Interventions and prevention programs provide a rigorous test of causal relations.

A multimethod approach in the design of studies also is necessary because different methods address somewhat different questions, including questions about causality. Moreover, all methods of measurement have limitations, but these differ for different measures. Thus, the convergence of findings across methods increases one's confidence in the veracity of the findings. In addition, as illustrated by the results of the Eisenberg and Fabes (1998) meta-analyses, certain types of methods tend to be used with certain ages of children, and such confounds may undermine our ability to understand the development of prosocial behavior.

Conceptual and Content-Related Directions

The study of prosocial behavior would benefit from greater integration with conceptual work on related issues. Prosocial behavior can be considered in a manner similar to most interpersonal behaviors—in terms of its social appropriateness and social and personal outcomes both in specific situations and in the long term. In many, but not all, settings, prosocial behavior is a socially appropriate behavior; indeed, prosocial behaviors frequently are used in measures of social competence. Thus, conceptual work on social competence and the development of interpersonal competence in attachment and peer relationships is relevant to the understanding of prosocial development. Moreover, research on moral emotions such as guilt, moral cognitions, and the development of an egoistic or antisocial orientation could be used to a greater degree than in the past to inform our understanding of prosocial behavior, particularly altruism.

As an example, we have seen that individual differences in children's emotionality and their ability to regulate emotional arousal appear to be related to whether children experience sympathy or egoistic, personal distress in helping contexts. Moreover, enactment of prosocial behaviors often involves not only emotional regulation, but also behavioral regulation, particularly if prosocial action requires self-denial. Thus, developmental change and individual differences in children's abilities to inhibit their behavior, delay gratification, and activate behavior when desirable are of considerable importance to understanding prosocial development. Environmental factors associated with optimal regulation and moderate levels of emotional reactivity likely foster prosocial responding, including sympathy. Thus, the growing bodies of literature on the socialization of emotion and coping, as well as cultural influences on emotion and its regulation, are highly relevant to a comprehensive perspective on prosocial development. A better understanding of these issues may be especially useful in delineating the emergence of sympathy and prosocial tendencies in the first years of life when children's regulatory skills are changing rapidly.

Work on prosocial behavior too often has been isolated from work on related topics, and greater integration across content domains would have broad benefits. This situation has improved somewhat in the past decade, especially in the literature on peer relationships and social competence. We have tried to make further inroads in that direction in this chapter, although our attempts were limited by the need to cover much material in a restricted space. Moreover, prosocial behaviors can be characterized as *attractors* ("absorbing" states that pull the behavior of the system from other potential states) that affect the organization of individual and group behaviors (Martin, Fabes, Hanish, & Hollensetin, in press). As such, integration of concepts from dynamic systems may lead to new insights in research and theorizing about prosocial behavior and development.

Advances in some fields of the behavioral sciences are just beginning to provide methods and data that can inform our understanding of prosocial development. Developments in brain-scanning procedures are providing new venues for studying emotion, attention, and decision making and, hence, processes related to sympathy and prosocial behavior. This technology may provide new insights on the role of emotion and attentional processes in prosocial decision making, although it is unlikely to provide in-depth information relevant to the role of antecedent biological and environmental influences on prosocial development.

Finally, not only has the field of prosocial behavior been relatively intellectually isolated from relevant literature on other topics, but investigators studying other issues (e.g., psychopathology, information processing, peer relationships, academic success) also have not attended sufficiently to findings in the domain of prosocial development. The broader field of developmental science would benefit if the boundaries among content areas, as well as across disciplines, were more permeable.

REFERENCES

Alberts, J. R. (1976). Olfactory contributions to behavioral development in rodents. In R. L. Doty (Ed.), *Mammalian olfaction, reproductive processes, and behavior* (pp. 67–95). New York: Academic Press.

Albiereo, P., & Lo Coco, A. (2001). Designing a method to assess empathy in Italian children. In A. C. Bohart & D. J. Stipek (Eds.), *Constructive and destructive behavior: Implications for family, school, and society* (pp. 205–223). Washington, DC: American Psychological Association.

Allen, J. P., Kuperminc, G., Philliber, S., & Herre, K. (1994). Programmatic prevention of adolescent problem behaviors: The role of autonomy, relatedness, and volunteer service in the teen outreach program. *American Journal of Community Psychology, 22,* 617–638.

Allen, J. P., Philliber, S., Herrling, S., & Kuperminc, G. P. (1997). Preventing teen pregnancy and academic failure: Experimental evaluation of a developmentally based approach. *Child Development, 64,* 729–742.

Aronfreed, J. (1970). The socialization of altruistic and sympathetic behavior: Some theoretical and experimental analyses. In J. Macaulay & L. Berkowitz (Eds.), *Altruism and helping behavior* (pp. 103–126). New York: Academic Press.

Asakawa, K., Iwawaki, S., Mondori, Y., & Minami, H. (1987, July). *Altruism in school and empathy: A developmental study of Japanese pupils.* Paper presented at the International Society for the Study of Behavioral Development, Tokyo, Japan.

Asbury, K., Dunn, J. F., Pike, A., & Plomin, R. (2003). Nonshared environmental influences on individual differences in early behavioral development: A monozygotic twin differences study. *Child Development, 74,* 933–943.

Ascione, F. R. (1992). Enhancing children's attitudes about the humane treatment of animals: Generalization to human-directed empathy. *Antrozoos, 5,* 176–191.

Ascione, F. R., & Weber, C. V. (1993, March). *Children's attitudes about the humane treatment of animals and empathy: One-year follow up of a school-based intervention.* Paper presented at the biennial meeting of the Society for Research in Child Development, New Orleans, LA.

Aspinwall, L. G., & Staudinger, U. M. (2003a). Introduction. In L. G. Aspinwall & U. M. Staudinger (Eds.), *A psychology of human strengths: Fundamental questions and future directions for a positive psychology.* Washington, DC: American Psychological Association.

Aspinwall, L. G., & Staudinger, U. M. (2003b). *A psychology of human strengths: Fundamental questions and future directions for a positive psychology.* Washington, DC: American Psychological Association.

Astington, J. W., & Jenkins, J. M. (1995). Theory of mind development and social understanding. *Cognition and Emotion, 9,* 151–165.

Atkins, R., Hart, D., & Donnelly, T. M. (2005). The association of childhood personality type with volunteering during adolescence. *Merrill-Palmer Quarterly, 51,* 145–162.

Austin, A. M. B., Braeger, T., Schvaneveldt, J. D., Lindauer, S. L. K., Summers, M., Robinson, C., et al. (1991). A comparison of helping, sharing, comforting, honesty, and civic awareness for children in home care, day care, and preschool. *Child and Youth Care Forum, 20,* 183–194.

Bandura, A. (1986). *Social foundations of thought and action: A social cognitive theory.* Englewood Cliffs, NJ: Prentice-Hall.

Bandura, A. (2002). Selective moral disengagement in the exercise of moral agency. *Journal of Moral Education, 31,* 101–119.

Bandura, A., Caprara, G. V., Barbaranelli, C., Gerbino, M., & Pastorelli, C. (2003). Role of affective self-regulatory efficacy in diverse sphere of psychosocial functioning. *Child Development, 74,* 769–782.

Bandura, A., Caprara, G. V., Barbaranelli, C., Pastorelli, C., & Regalia, C. (2001). Sociocognitive self-regulatory mechanisms governing transgressive behavior. *Journal of Personality and Social Psychology, 80,* 125–135.

Barash, D. P. (1977). *Sociobiology and behavior.* New York: Elsevier/North-Holland.

Barnett, M. A., & Thompson, S. (1985). The role of perspective taking and empathy in children's Machiavellianism, prosocial behavior and motive for helping. *Journal of Genetic Psychology, 146,* 295–305.

Baron, J., & Miller, J. G. (2000). Limiting the scope of moral obligations to help: A cross-cultural investigation. *Journal of Cross-Cultural Psychology, 31,* 703–725.

Barrett, D. E., & Yarrow, M. R. (1977). Prosocial behavior, social inferential ability, and assertiveness in young children. *Child Development, 48,* 475–481.

Bar-Tal, D. (1982). Sequential development of helping behavior: A cognitive-learning approach. *Developmental Review, 2,* 101–124.

Bar-Tal, D., Bar-Zohar, Y., Greenberg, M. S., & Hermon, M. (1977). Reciprocity behavior in the relationship between donor and recipient and between harmdoer and victim. *Sociometry, 40,* 293–298.

Bar-Tal, D., Nadler, A., & Blechman, N. (1980). The relationship between Israeli children's helping behavior and their perception on parents' socialization practices. *Journal of Social Psychology, 111,* 159–167.

Bar-Tal, D., Raviv, A., & Leiser, T. (1980). The development of altruistic behavior: Empirical evidence. *Developmental Psychology, 16,* 516–524.

Batson, C. D. (1991). *The altruism question: Toward a social-psychological answer.* Hillsdale, NJ: Erlbaum.

Batson, C. D., Chang, J., Orr, R., & Rowland, J. (2002). Empathy, attitudes and action: Can feeling for a member of a stigmatized group motivate one to help the group. *Personality and Social Psychology Bulletin, 28,* 1656–1666.

Batson, C. D., Lishner, D. A., Carpenter, A., Dulin, L., Harjusola-Webb, S., Stocks, E. L., et al. (2003). "... As you would have them do unto you": Does imagining yourself in the other's place simulate moral action? *Personality and Social Psychology Bulletin, 29,* 1190–1201.

Batson, C. D., & Powell, A. A. (2003). Altruism and prosocial behavior. In T. Millon & M. J. Lerner (Eds.), *Handbook of psychology: Vol. 5. Personality and social psychology* (pp. 463–484). New York: Wiley.

Battistich, V., Schaps, E., Watson, M., Solomon, D., & Lewis, C. (2000). Effects of the child development project on students' drug use and other problem behaviors. *Journal of Primary Prevention, 21,* 75–99.

Battistich, V., Watson, M., Solomon, D., Schaps, E., & Solomon, J. (1991). The child development project: A comprehensive program for the development of prosocial character. In W. M. Kurtines & J. L. Gewirtz (Eds.), *Handbook of moral behavior and development: Vol. 3. Application* (pp. 1–34). New York: Erlbaum.

Bear, G. G., & Rys, G. S. (1994). Moral reasoning, classroom behavior, and sociometric status among elementary school children. *Developmental Psychology, 30,* 633–638.

Becker, S. W., & Eagly, A. H. (2004). The heroism of women and men. *American Psychologist, 59,* 163–178.

Belden, A., Kuebli, J., Pauley, D., & Kindleberger, L. (2003, April). *Predicting children's empathy from family talk about past good deeds.* Paper presented at the biennial meeting of the Society for Research in Child Development, Tampa, FL.

Benenson, J. F., Markovits, H., Roy, R., & Denko, P. (2003). Behavioural rules underlying learning to share: Effects of development and context. *International Journal of Behavioral Development, 27,* 116–121.

Bengtsson, H. (2003). Children's cognitive appraisal of others' distressful and positive experiences. *International Journal of Behavioral Development, 27,* 457–466.

Bengtsson, H., & Johnson, L. (1992). Perspective taking, empathy, and prosocial behavior in late childhood. *Child Study Journal, 22,* 11–22.

Bergin, C., Talley, S., & Hamer, L. (2003). Prosocial behaviors of young adolescents: A focus group study. *Journal of Adolescence, 26,* 13–32.

Berman, P. W., & Goodman, V. (1984). Age and sex differences in children's responses to babies: Effects of adults' caretaking requests and instructions. *Child Development, 55,* 1071–1077.

Bernadett-Shapiro, S., Ehrensaft, D., & Shapiro, J. L. (1996). Father participation in childcare and the development of empathy in sons: An empirical study. *Family Therapy, 23,* 77–93.

Berndt, T. J. (1982). The features and effects of friendship in early adolescence. *Child Development, 53,* 1447–1460.

Berndt, T. J., Hawkins, J. A., & Hoyle, S. G. (1986). Changes in friendship during a school year: Effects on children's and adolescents' impressions of friendship and sharing with friends. *Child Development, 57,* 1284–1297.

Birch, L. L., & Billman, J. (1986). Preschool children's food sharing with friends and acquaintances. *Child Development, 57,* 387–395.

Bischof-Kohler, D. (1991). The development of empathy in infants. In M. E. Lamb & H. Keller (Eds.), *Infant development: Perspectives from German-speaking countries* (pp. 245–273). Hillsdale, NJ: Erlbaum.

Bizman, A., Yinon, Y., Mivtzari, E., & Shavit, R. (1978). Effects of the age structure of the kindergarten on altruistic behavior. *Journal of School Psychology, 16,* 154–160.

Blum, L. A. (1980). *Friendship, altruism and morality.* London: Routledge & Kegan Paul.

Boehnke, K., Silbereisen, R. K., Eisenberg, N., Reykowski, J., & Palmonari, A. (1989). The development of prosocial motivation: A cross-national study. *Journal of Cross Cultural Psychology, 20,* 219–243.

Bond, N. D., & Phillips, B. N. (1971). Personality traits associated with altruistic behavior of children. *Journal of School Psychology, 9,* 24–34.

Boorman, S. A., & Leavitt, P. R. (1980). *The genetics of altruism.* New York: Academic Press.

Borgida, E., Conner, C., & Manteufel, L. (1992). Understanding kidney donation: A behavioral decision-making perspective. In S.

Spacapan & S. Oskamp (Eds.), *Helping and being helped* (pp. 183–212). Newbury Park, CA: Sage.

Bosacki, S. L. (2003). Psychological pragmatics in preadolescents: Sociomoral understanding, self-worth, and school behavior. *Journal of Youth and Adolescence, 32,* 141–155.

Boxer, P., Tisak, M. S., & Goldstein, S. E. (2004). Is it bad to be good? An exploration of aggressive and prosocial behavior subtypes in adolescence. *Journal of Youth and Adolescence, 33,* 91–100.

Braaten, E. B., & Rosen, L. A. (2000). Self-regulation of affect in Attention Deficit-Hyperactivity Disorder (ADHD) and non-ADHD boys: Differences in empathic responding. *Journal of Consulting and Clinical Psychology, 68*(2), 313–321.

Bretherton, I., Fritz, J., Zahn-Waxler, C., & Ridgeway, D. (1986). Learning to talk about emotions: A functionalist perspective. *Child Development, 57,* 529–548.

Broberg, A., Hwang, C., Lamb, M., & Ketterlinus, R. D. (1989). Child care effects on socioemotional and intellectual competence in Swedish preschoolers. In J. S. Lande, S. Scarr, & N. Gunzenhauser (Eds.), *Caring for children: Challenge to America* (pp. 49–76). Hillsdale, NJ: Erlbaum.

Brody, G. H., Stoneman, Z., & MacKinnon, C. E. (1986). Contributions of maternal child-rearing practices and play contexts to sibling interactions. *Journal of Applied Developmental Psychology, 7,* 225–236.

Bryan, J. H., & Walbek, N. H. (1970). The impact of words and deeds concerning altruism upon children. *Child Development, 41,* 747–757.

Bryant, B. K. (1982). An index of empathy for children and adolescents. *Child Development, 53,* 413–425.

Bryant, B. K. (1987). Mental health, temperament, family, and friends: Perspectives on children's empathy and social perspective taking. In N. Eisenberg & J. Strayer (Eds.), *Empathy and its development* (pp. 245–270). Cambridge, England: Cambridge University Press.

Bryant, B. K., & Crockenberg, S. B. (1980). Correlates and dimensions of prosocial behavior: A study of female siblings with their mothers. *Child Development, 51,* 529–544.

Buhrmester, D., Goldfarb, J., & Cantrell, D. (1992). Self-presentation when sharing with friends and nonfriends. *Journal of Early Adolescence, 12,* 61–79.

Burger, J. M. (1999). The foot-in-the-door compliance procedure: A multiple-process analysis and review. *Personality and Social Psychology Review, 3,* 303–325.

Burleson, B., Applegate, J. L., Burke, J. A., Clark, R. A., Delia, J. G., & Kline, S. L. (1986). Communicative correlates of peer acceptance in childhood. *Communication Education, 35,* 349–361.

Calabrese, R. L., & Schumer, H. (1986). The effects of service activities on adolescent alienation. *Adolescence, 21,* 675–687.

Call, K. T., Mortimer, J. T., & Shanahan, M. J. (1995). Helpfulness and the development of competence in adolescence. *Child Development, 66,* 129–138.

Caplan, M. Z., & Hay, D. F. (1989). Preschoolers' responses to peers' distress and beliefs about bystander intervention. *Journal of Child Psychology and Psychiatry, 30,* 231–242.

Caprara, G. V., Barbaranelli, C., & Pastorelli, C. (2001). Prosocial behavior and aggression in childhood and pre-adolescence. In A. C. Bohart & D. J. Stipek (Eds.), *Constructive and destructive behavior: Implications for family, school, and society* (pp. 187–203). Washington, DC: American Psychological Association.

Caprara, G. V., Barbaranelli, C., Pastorelli, C., Bandura, A., & Zimbardo, P. G. (2000). Prosocial foundations of children's academic achievement. *Psychological Science, 11,* 302–306.

Caprara, G. V., Barbaranelli, C., Pastorelli, C., Cermak, I., & Rosza, S. (2001). Facing guilt: Role of negative affectivity, need for reparation, and fear of punishment in leading to prosocial behaviour and aggression. *European Journal of Personality, 15,* 219–237.

Carlo, G., Eisenberg, N., & Knight, G. P. (1992). An objective measure of adolescents' prosocial moral reasoning. *Journal of Research on Adolescence, 2,* 331–349.

Carlo, G., Hausmann, A., Christiansen, S., & Randall, B. A. (2003). Sociocognitive and behavioral correlates of a measure of prosocial tendencies for adolescents. *Journal of Early Adolescence, 23,* 107–134.

Carlo, G., Knight, G. P., Eisenberg, N., & Rotenberg, K. (1991). Cognitive processes and prosocial behavior among children: The role of affective attributions and reconciliations. *Developmental Psychology, 27,* 456–461.

Carlo, G., Koller, S. H., Eisenberg, N., DaSilva, M. S., & Frohlich, C. B. (1996). A cross-national study on the relations among prosocial moral reasoning, gender role orientations, and prosocial behaviors. *Developmental Psychology, 32,* 231–240.

Carlo, G., & Randall, B. A. (2002). The development of a measure of prosocial behaviors for late adolescents. *Journal of Youth and Adolescence, 31,* 31–44.

Carlo, G., Roesch, S. C., Knight, G. P., & Koller, S. H. (2001). Between- or within-culture variation? Culture groups as a moderator of the relations between individual differences and resource allocation preferences. *Applied Developmental Psychology, 22,* 559–579.

Carlo, G., Roesch, S. C., & Melby, J. (1998). The multiplicative relations of parenting and temperament to prosocial and antisocial behaviors in adolescence. *Journal of Early Adolescence, 18,* 266–290.

Cassidy, K. W., Werner, R. S., Rourke, M., Zubernis, L. S., & Balarman, G. (2003). The relationship between psychological understanding and positive social behaviors. *Social Development, 12,* 198–221.

Cauley, K., & Tyler, B. (1989). The relationship of self-concept to prosocial behavior in children. *Early Childhood Research Quarterly, 4,* 51–60.

Chapman, M., Zahn-Waxler, C., Cooperman, G., & Iannotti, R. (1987). Empathy and responsibility in the motivation of children's helping. *Developmental Psychology, 23,* 140–145.

Charbonneau, D., & Nicol, A. A. M. (2002). Emotional intelligence and prosocial behaviors in adolescents. *Psychological Reports, 90,* 361–370.

Cheung, P. C., Ma, H. K., & Shek, D. T. L. (1998). Conceptions of success: Their correlates with prosocial orientation and behaviour in Chinese adolescents. *Journal of Adolescence, 21,* 31–42.

Chou, K. L. (1998). Effects of age, gender, and participation in volunteer activities on the altruistic behavior of Chinese adolescents. *Journal of Genetic Psychology, 159,* 195–201.

Cialdini, R. B., & Goldstein, N. (2004). Social influence: Compliance and conformity. *Annual Review of Psychology, 55,* 591–621.

Clark, K. E., & Ladd, G. W. (2000). Connectedness and autonomy support in parent-child relationships: Links to children's socioemotional orientation and peer relationships. *Developmental Psychology, 36,* 485–498.

Clark, M. S. (1991). *Review of personality and social psychology: Prosocial behavior* (Vol. 12). Newbury Park, CA: Sage.

Clark, M. S., Milberg, S., & Erber, R. (1984). Effects of arousal on judgments of others' emotions. *Journal of Personality and Social Psychology, 46,* 551–560.

Clarke-Stewart, K. A. (1981). Observation and experiment: Complementary strategies for studying day care and social development. In S. Kilmer (Ed.), *Advances in Early Education and Day Care* (Vol. 2, pp. 227–250). Greenwich, CN: JAI Press.

Clary, E. G., & Snyder, M. (1999). The motivations to volunteer: Theoretical and practical considerations. *Current Directions in Psychological Science, 8,* 156–159.

Cohen, D., & Strayer, J. (1996). Empathy in conduct-disordered and comparison youth. *Developmental Psychology, 32,* 988–998.

Colby, A., & Damon, W. (1992). *Some do care: Contemporary lives of moral commitment.* Toronto, Ontario, Canada: Free Press.

Coleman, P. K., & Byrd, C. P. (2003). Interpersonal correlates of peer victimization among young adolescents. *Journal of Youth and Adolescence, 32,* 301–314.

Conrad, D., & Hedin, D. (1982). The impact of experiential education on adolescent development. In D. Conrad & D. Hedin (Eds.), *Youth participation and experiential education.* New York: Haworth Press.

Costin, S. E., & Jones, D. C. (1992). Friendship as a facilitator of emotional responsiveness and prosocial interventions among young children. *Developmental Psychology, 28,* 941–947.

Côté, S., Tremblay, R. E., Nagin, D., Zoccolillo, M., & Vitaro, F. (2002). The development of impulsivity, fearfulness, and helpfulness during childhood: Patterns of consistency and change in the trajectories of boys and girls. *Journal of Child Psychology and Psychiatry, 43,* 609–618.

Crick, N. R., Casas, J. F., & Mosher, M. (1997). Relational an overt aggression in preschool. *Developmental Psychology, 33,* 579–588.

Crockenberg, S. (1985). Toddlers' reactions to maternal anger. *Merrill-Palmer Quarterly, 31,* 361–373.

Cummings, J. S., Pellegrini, D. S., & Notarius, C. I. (1989). Children's responses to angry adult behavior as a function of marital distress and history of interparent hostility. *Child Development, 60,* 1035–1043.

Cummings, E. M., & Smith, D. (1993). The impact of anger between adults on siblings' emotions and social behavior. *Journal of Child Psychology and Psychiatry, 34,* 1425–1433.

Cummings, E. M., Zahn-Waxler, C., & Radke-Yarrow, M. (1981). Young children's responses to expressions of anger and affection by others in the family. *Child Development, 52,* 1274–1282.

Cummings, E. M., Zahn-Waxler, C., & Radke-Yarrow, M. (1984). Developmental changes in children's reactions to anger in the home. *Journal of Child Psychology and Psychiatry, 25,* 63–74.

Cunningham, M. R. (1985/1986). Levites and brother's keepers: A sociobiological perspective on prosocial behavior. *Humboldt Journal of Social Relations, 13,* 35–67.

Cutting, A. L., & Dunn, J. (1999). Theory of mind, emotion understanding, language, and family background: Individual differences and interrelations. *Child Development, 70,* 853–865.

Davies, P. T., & Cummings, E. M. (1994). Marital conflict and child adjustment: An emotional security hypothesis. *Psychological Bulletin, 116,* 387–411.

Davis, M. H., & Franzoi, S. (1991). Stability and change in adolescent self-consciousness and empathy. *Journal of Research in Personality, 25,* 70–87.

Davis, M. H., Luce, C., & Kraus, S. J. (1994). The heritability of characteristics associated with dispositional empathy. *Journal of Personality, 62,* 369–391.

Deater-Deckard, K., Dunn, J., O'Connor, T. G., Davies, L., Golding, J., & the ALSPAC Study Team. (2001). Using the stepfamily genetic design to examine gene-environmental processes in child and family functioning. *Marriage and Family Review, 33,* 131–156.

Deater-Deckard, K., Pike, A., Petrill, S. A., Cutting, A. L., Hughes, C., & O'Connor, T. G. (2001). Nonshared environmental processes in social-emotional development: An observational study of identical twin differences in the preschool period. *Developmental Science, 4,* F1–F6.

Decety, J., & Chaminade, T. (2003). Neural correlates of feeling sympathy. *Neuropsychologia, 41,* 127–138.

de Guzman, M. R. T., & Carlo, G. (2004). Family, peer, and acculturative correlates of prosocial development among Latino youth in Nebraska. *Great Plains Research, 14,* 185–202.

de Guzman, M. R. T., Edwards, C. P., & Carlo, G. (2005). Prosocial behaviors in context: A study of the Gukuyu children of Ngecha, Kenya. *Applied Developmental Psychology, 26,* 542–558.

Dekovic, M., & Gerris, J. R. M. (1994). Developmental analysis of social cognitive and behavioral differences between popular and rejected children. *Journal of Applied Developmental Psychology, 15,* 367–386.

Dekovic, M., & Janssens, J. M. A. M. (1992). Parents' child-rearing style and children's sociometric status. *Developmental Psychology, 28,* 925–932.

Denham, S. A. (1986). Social cognition, prosocial behavior, and emotion in preschoolers: Contextual validation. *Child Development, 57,* 194–201.

Denham, S. A., Blair, K. A., DeMulder, E., Levitas, J., Sawyer, K., Auerbach-Major, S., et al. (2003). Preschool emotional competence: Pathway to social competence. *Child Development, 74,* 238–256.

Denham, S. A., & Burger, C. (1991). Observational validation of ratings of preschoolers' social competence and behavior problems. *Child Study Journal, 21,* 185–291.

Denham, S. A., & Couchoud, E. A. (1991). Social-emotional predictors of preschoolers' responses to adult negative emotion. *Journal of Child Psychology and Psychiatry, 32,* 595–608.

Denham, S. A., & Grout, L. (1992). Mothers' emotional expressiveness and coping: Relations with preschoolers' social-emotional competence. *Genetic, Social, and General Psychology Monographs, 118,* 75–101.

Denham, S. A., & Grout, L. (1993). Socialization of emotion: Pathway to preschoolers' emotional and social competence. *Journal of Nonverbal Behavior, 17,* 205–227.

Denham, S. A., Mason, T., & Couchoud, E. A. (1995). Scaffolding young children's prosocial responsiveness: Preschoolers' responses to adult sadness, anger, and pain. *International Journal of Behavioral Development, 18,* 489–504.

Denham, S. A., Renwick-DeBardi, S., & Hewes, S. (1994). Emotional communication between mothers and preschoolers: Relations with emotional competence. *Merrill-Palmer Quarterly, 40,* 488–508.

de Veer, A. J. E., & Janssens, J. M. A. M. (1994). Victim-oriented discipline, interpersonal understanding, and guilt. *Journal of Moral Education, 23,* 165–182.

Diener, M. L., & Kim, D. Y. (2004). Maternal and child predictors of preschool children's social competence. *Applied Developmental Psychology, 25,* 3–24.

Dix, T., & Grusec, J. E. (1983). Parental influence techniques: An attributional analysis. *Child Development, 54,* 645–652.

Dlugokinski, E. L., & Firestone, I. J. (1974). Other centeredness and susceptibility to charitable appeals: Effects of perceived discipline. *Developmental Psychology, 10,* 21–28.

Dondi, M., Simion, F., & Caltran, G. (1999). Can newborns discriminate between their own cry and the cry of another newborn infant? *Developmental Psychology, 35,* 418–426.

Dunn, J. (1988). *The beginnings of social understanding.* Cambridge, MA: Harvard University Press.

Dunn, J., Cutting, A., & Fisher, N. (2002). Old friends, new friends: Predictors of children's perspective on their friends at school. *Child Development, 73,* 621–635.

Dunn, J., Deater-Deckard, K., Pickering, K., O'Connor, T. G., Golding, J., & the ALSPAC Study Team. (1998). Children's adjustment and prosocial behaviour in step-, single-parent, and non-stepfamily settings: Findings from a community study. *Journal of Child Psychology and Psychiatry, 39,* 1083–1095.

Dunn, J., & Kendrick, D. (1982). *Siblings: Love, envy, and understanding.* Cambridge, MA: Harvard University Press.

Dunn, J., & Munn, P. (1986). Siblings and the development of prosocial behavior. *International Journal of Behavioral Development, 9,* 265–284.

Eagly, A. H., & Crowley, M. (1986). Gender and helping behavior: A meta-analytic review of the social psychological literature. *Psychological Bulletin, 100,* 283–308.

Eberly, M. B., & Montemayor, R. (1998). Doing good deeds: An examination of adolescent prosocial behavior in the context of parent-adolescent relationships. *Journal of Adolescent Research, 13,* 403–432.

Eberly, M. B., & Montemayor, R. (1999). Adolescent affection and helpfulness toward parents: A 2-year follow-up. *Journal of Early Adolescence, 19,* 226–248.

Eberly, M. B., Montemayor, R., & Flannery, D. J. (1993). Variation in adolescent helpfulness toward parents in a family context. *Journal of Early Adolescence, 13,* 228–244.

Eccles, J. S., & Barber, B. L. (1999). Student council, volunteering, basketball, or marching band: What kind of extracurricular involvement matters? *Journal of Adolescent Research, 14,* 10–43.

Eisenberg, N. (1983). Children's differentiations among potential recipients of aid. *Child Development, 54,* 594–602.

Eisenberg, N. (1986). *Altruistic emotion, cognition, and behavior.* Hillsdale, NJ: Erlbaum.

Eisenberg, N., Boehnke, K., Schuhler, P., & Silbereisen, R. K. (1985). The development of prosocial behavior and cognitions in German children. *Journal of Cross-Cultural Psychology, 16,* 69–82.

Eisenberg, N., Cameron, E., Tryon, K., & Dodez, R. (1981). Socialization of prosocial behavior in the preschool classroom. *Developmental Psychology, 17,* 773–782.

Eisenberg, N., Carlo, G., Murphy, B., & Van Court, P. (1995). Prosocial development in late adolescence: A longitudinal study. *Child Development, 66,* 1179–1197.

Eisenberg, N., Cialdini, R., McCreath, H., & Shell, R. (1987). Consistency-based compliance: When and why do children become vulnerable? *Journal of Personality and Social Psychology, 52,* 1174–1181.

Eisenberg, N., Cialdini, R. B., McCreath, H., & Shell, R. (1989). Consistency-based compliance in children: When and why do consistency procedures have immediate effects? *Journal of Behavioral Development, 12,* 351–367.

Eisenberg, N., Cumberland, A., Guthrie, I. K., Murphy, B. C., & Shepard, S. A. (2005). Age changes in prosocial responding and moral reasoning in adolescence and early adulthood. *Journal of Research in Adolescence, 15,* 235–260.

Eisenberg, N., & Fabes, R. A. (1990). Empathy: Conceptualization, assessment, and relation to prosocial behavior. *Motivation and Emotion, 14,* 131–149.

Eisenberg, N., & Fabes, R. A. (1992). Emotion, regulation, and the development of social competence. In M. S. Clark (Ed.), *Review of personality and social psychology: Vol. 14. Emotion and social behavior* (pp. 119–150). Newbury Park, CA: Sage.

Eisenberg, N., & Fabes, R. A. (1995). The relation of young children's vicarious emotional responding to social competence, regulation, and emotionality. *Cognition and Emotion, 9,* 203–228.

Eisenberg, N., & Fabes, R. (1998). Prosocial development. In W. Damon (Editor-in-Chief) & N. Eisenberg (Vol. Ed.), *Handbook of child psychology: Vol. 3. Social, emotional, and personality development* (5th ed., pp. 701–778). New York: Wiley.

Eisenberg, N., Fabes, R. A., Carlo, G., Speer, A. L., Switzer, G., Karbon, M., et al. (1993). The relations of empathy-related emotions and maternal practices to children's comforting behavior. *Journal of Experimental Child Psychology, 55,* 131–150.

Eisenberg, N., Fabes, R. A., Carlo, G., Troyer, D., Speer, A. L., Karbon, M., et al. (1992). The relations of maternal practices and characteristics to children's vicarious emotional responsiveness. *Child Development, 63,* 583–602.

Eisenberg, N., Fabes, R. A., Karbon, M., Murphy, B. C., Carlo, G., & Wosinski, M. (1996). Relations of school children's comforting behavior to empathy-related reactions and shyness. *Social Development, 5,* 330–351.

Eisenberg, N., Fabes, R. A., Karbon, M., Murphy, B. C., Wosinski, M., Polazzi, L., et al. (1996). The relations of children's dispositional prosocial behavior to emotionality, regulation, and social functioning. *Child Development, 67,* 974–992.

Eisenberg, N., Fabes, R. A., & Miller, P. A. (1990). The evolutionary and neurological roots of prosocial behavior. In L. Ellis & H. Hoffman (Eds.), *Crime in biological, social, and moral contexts* (pp. 247–260). New York: Praeger.

Eisenberg, N., Fabes, R. A., Miller, P. A., Fultz, J., Mathy, R. M., Shell, R., et al. (1989). The relations of sympathy and personal distress to prosocial behavior: A multimethod study. *Journal of Personality and Social Psychology, 57,* 55–66.

Eisenberg, N., Fabes, R. A., Miller, P. A., Shell, C., Shea, R., & May-Plumlee, T. (1990). Preschoolers' vicarious emotional responding and their situational and dispositional prosocial behavior. *Merrill-Palmer Quarterly, 36,* 507–529.

Eisenberg, N., Fabes, R. A., Murphy, B., Karbon, M., Maszk, P., Smith, M., et al. (1994). The relations of emotionality and regulation to dispositional and situational empathy-related responding. *Journal of Personality and Social Psychology, 66,* 776–797.

Eisenberg, N., Fabes, R. A., Murphy, B. C., Karbon, M., Smith, M., & Maszk, P. (1996). The relations of children's dispositional empathy-related responding to their emotionality, regulation, and social functioning. *Developmental Psychology, 32,* 195–209.

Eisenberg, N., Fabes, R. A., Schaller, M., Carlo, G., & Miller, P. A. (1991). The relations of parental characteristics and practices to children's vicarious emotional responding. *Child Development, 62,* 1393–1408.

Eisenberg, N., Fabes, R. A., Schaller, M., & Miller, P. A. (1989). Intercorrelations and developmental changes in indices of empathy. In N. Eisenberg (Ed.), *New directions in child development* (Vol. 44, pp. 86–126). San Francisco: Jossey-Bass.

Eisenberg, N., Fabes, R. A., Schaller, M., Miller, P. A., Carlo, G., Poulin, R., et al. (1991). Personality and socialization correlates of vicarious emotional responding. *Journal of Personality and Social Psychology, 61,* 459–470.

Eisenberg, N., Fabes, R. A., Shepard, S. A., Murphy, B. C., Jones, J., & Guthrie, I. K. (1998). Contemporaneous and longitudinal prediction of children's sympathy from dispositional regulation and emotionality. *Developmental Psychology, 34,* 910–924.

Eisenberg, N., Guthrie, I., Cumberland, A., Murphy, B. C., Shepard, S. A., Zhou, Q., et al. (2002). Prosocial development in early adulthood: A longitudinal study. *Journal of Personality and Social Psychology, 82,* 993–1006.

Eisenberg, N., Guthrie, I. K., Fabes, R. A., Reiser, M., Murphy, B. C., Holgren, R., et al. (1997). The relations of regulation and emotionality to resiliency and competent social functioning in elementary school children. *Child Development, 68,* 295–311.

Eisenberg, N., Guthrie, I. K., Murphy, B. C., Shepard, S. A., Cumberland, A., & Carlo, G. (1999). Consistency and development of prosocial dispositions: A longitudinal study. *Child Development, 70,* 1360–1372.

Eisenberg, N., Hertz-Lazarowitz, R., & Fuchs, I. (1990). Prosocial moral judgment in Israeli kibbutz and city children: A longitudinal study. *Merrill-Palmer Quarterly, 36,* 273–285.

Eisenberg, N., & Lennon, R. (1983). Gender differences in empathy and related capacities. *Psychological Bulletin, 94,* 100–131.

Eisenberg, N., Liew, J., & Pidada, S. (2001). The relations of parental emotional expressivity with the quality of Indonesian children's social functioning. *Emotion, 1,* 107–115.

Eisenberg, N., Losoya, S., Fabes, R. A., Guthrie, I. K., Reiser, M., Murphy, B. C., et al. (2001). Parental socialization of children's dysregulated expression of emotion and externalizing problems. *Journal of Family Psychology, 15,* 183–205.

Eisenberg, N., Lundy, N., Shell, R., & Roth, K. (1985). Children's justifications for their adult and peer-direct compliant (prosocial and nonprosocial) behaviors. *Developmental Psychology, 21,* 325–331.

Eisenberg, N., McCreath, H., & Ahn, R. (1988). Vicarious emotional responsiveness and prosocial behavior: Their interrelations in young children. *Personality and Social Psychology Bulletin, 14,* 298–311.

Eisenberg, N., & McNally, S. (1993). Socialization and mothers' and adolescents' empathy-related characteristics. *Journal of Research on Adolescence, 3,* 171–191.

Eisenberg, N., & Miller, P. (1987). The relation of empathy to prosocial and related behaviors. *Psychological Bulletin, 101,* 91–119.

Eisenberg, N., Miller, P. A., Shell, R., McNalley, S., & Shea, C. (1991). Prosocial development in adolescence: A longitudinal study. *Developmental Psychology, 27,* 849–857.

Eisenberg, N., Murphy, B., & Shepard, S. (1997). The development of empathic accuracy. In W. Ickes (Ed.), *Empathic accuracy* (pp. 73–116). New York: Guilford Press.

Eisenberg, N., & Mussen, P. (1989). *The roots of prosocial behavior in children.* Cambridge, England: Cambridge University Press.

Eisenberg, N., & Ota Wang, V. (2003). Toward a positive psychology: Social developmental and cultural contributions. In L. G. Aspinwall & U. M. Staudinger (Eds.), *A psychology of human strengths: Fundamental questions and future directions for a positive psychology* (pp. 117–129). Washington, DC: APA Books.

Eisenberg, N., Pasternack, J. F., Cameron, E., & Tryon, K. (1984). The relation of quality and mode of prosocial behavior to moral cognitions and social style. *Child Development, 155,* 1479–1485.

Eisenberg, N., Shea, C. L., Carlo, G., & Knight, G. (1991). Empathy-related responding and cognition: A "chicken and the egg" dilemma. In W. Kurtines & J. Gewirtz (Eds.), *Handbook of moral behavior and development: Vol. 2. Research* (pp. 63–88). Hillsdale, NJ: Erlbaum.

Eisenberg, N., & Shell, R. (1986). The relation of prosocial moral judgment and behavior in children: The mediating role of cost. *Personality and Social Psychology Bulletin, 12,* 426–433.

Eisenberg, N., Shell, R., Pasternack, J., Lennon, R., Beller, R., & Mathy, R. M. (1987). Prosocial development in middle childhood: A longitudinal study. *Developmental Psychology, 24,* 712–718.

Eisenberg, N., Smith, C. L., Sadovsky, A., & Spinrad, T. L. (2004). Effortful control: Relations with emotion regulation, adjustment, and socialization in childhood. In R. F. Baumeister & K. D. Vohs (Eds.), *Handbook of self-regulation: Research, theory, and applications* (pp. 259–282). New York: Guilford Press.

Eisenberg, N., Spinrad, T. L., & Sadovsky, A. (2005). Empathy-related responding in children. In M. Killen & J. G. Smetana (Eds.), *Handbook of moral development* (pp. 517–549). Hillsdale, NJ: Erlbaum.

Eisenberg, N., Wolchik, S., Goldberg, L., & Engel, I. (1992). Parental values, reinforcement, and young children's prosocial behavior: A longitudinal study. *Journal of Genetic Psychology, 153,* 19–36.

Eisenberg, N., Zhou, Q., & Koller, S. (2001). Brazilian adolescents' prosocial moral judgment and behavior: Relations to sympathy, perspective taking, gender-role orientation, and demographic characteristics. *Child Development, 72,* 518–534.

Eisenberg-Berg, N. (1979). The development of children's prosocial moral judgment. *Developmental Psychology, 15,* 128–137.

Eisenberg-Berg, N., & Geisheker, E. (1979). Content of preachings and power of the model/preacher: The effect on children's generosity. *Developmental Psychology, 15,* 168–175.

Eisenberg-Berg, N., & Hand, M. (1979). The relationship of preschooler's reasoning about prosocial moral conflicts to prosocial behavior. *Child Development, 50,* 356–363.

Ekstein, R. (1978). Psychoanalysis, sympathy, and altruism. In L. G. Wispe (Ed.), *Altruism, sympathy, and helping: Psychological and sociological principles* (pp. 165–176). New York: Academic Press.

Ellis, L., & Hoffman, H. (1990). Views of contemporary criminologists on causes and theories of crime. In L. Ellis & H. Hoffman (Eds.), *Crime in biological, social, and moral contexts* (pp. 50–58). New York: Praeger.

Endresen, I. M., & Olweus, D. (2001). Self-reported empathy in Norwegian adolescents: Sex differences, age trends, and relationship to bullying. In A. C. Bohart & D. J. Stipek (Eds.), *Constructive and destructive behavior: Implications for family, school, and society* (pp. 147–165). Washington, DC: American Psychological Association.

Erdley, C. A., & Asher, S. R. (1999). A social goals perspective on children's social competence. *Journal of Emotional and Behavioral Disorders, 7,* 156–167.

Eslinger, P. J. (1998). Neurological and neuropsychological bases of empathy. *European Neurology, 39,* 193–199.

Eslinger, P. J., Easton, A., Grattan, L. M., & Van Hoesen, G. W. (1996). Distinctive forms of partial retrograde amnesia after asymmetric temporal lobe lesions: Possible role of the occipitotemporal gyri in memory. *Cerebral Cortex, 6,* 530–539.

Essock-Vitale, S., & McGuire, M. (1985). Women's lives viewed from an evolutionary perspective: Pt. 2. Patterns of helping. *Ethology and Sociobiology, 6,* 155–173.

Estrada, P. (1995). Adolescents' self-reports of prosocial responses to friends and acquaintances: The role of sympathy-related cognitive, affective, and motivational processes. *Journal of Research on Adolescence, 5,* 173–200.

Fabes, R. A., Carlo, G., Kupanoff, K., & Laible, D. (1999). Early adolescence and prosocial/moral behavior: Pt. 1. The role of individual processes. *Journal of Early Adolescence, 19,* 5–16.

Fabes, R. A., & Eisenberg, N. (1996). *An examination of age and sex differences in prosocial behavior and empathy.* Unpublished manuscript, Arizona State University at Tempe.

Fabes, R. A., Eisenberg, N., & Eisenbud, L. (1993). Behavioral and physiological correlates of children's reactions to others' distress. *Developmental Psychology, 29,* 655–663.

Fabes, R. A., Eisenberg, N., Karbon, M., Bernzweig, J., Speer, A. L., & Carlo, G. (1994). Socialization of children's vicarious emotional responding and prosocial behavior: Relations with mothers' perceptions of children's emotional reactivity. *Developmental Psychology, 30,* 44–55.

Fabes, R. A., Eisenberg, N., Karbon, M., Troyer, D., & Switzer, G. (1994). The relations of children's emotion regulation to their vicarious emotional responses and comforting behavior. *Child Development, 65,* 1678–1693.

Fabes, R. A., Eisenberg, N., & Miller, P. (1990). Maternal correlates of children's vicarious emotional responsiveness. *Developmental Psychology, 26,* 639–648.

Fabes, R. A., & Filsinger, E. E. (1988). Odor communication and parent-child interaction. In E. Filsinger (Ed.), *Biosocial perspectives on the family* (pp. 93–118). Newbury Park, CA: Sage.

Fabes, R. A., Fultz, J., Eisenberg, N., May-Plumlee, T., & Christopher, F. S. (1989). The effects of reward on children's prosocial motivation: A socialization study. *Developmental Psychology, 25,* 509–515.

Fabes, R. A., Martin, C. L., & Hanish, L. D. (2002, October). *The role of sex segregation in young children's prosocial behavior and disposition.* Paper presented at the Groningen Conference on Prosocial Dispositions and Solidarity, Groningen, The Netherlands.

Fabes, R. A., Moss, A., Reesing, A., Martin, C. L., & Hanish, L. D. (2005, October). *The effects of peer prosocial exposure on the quality of young children's social interactions.* Data presented at the annual conference of the National Council on Family Relations, Phoenix, AZ.

Farver, J. A. M., & Branstetter, W. H. (1994). Preschoolers' prosocial responses to their peers' distress. *Developmental Psychology, 30,* 334–341.

Fenichel, O. (1945). *The psychoanalytic theory of neurosis.* New York: Norton.

Feshbach, N. D. (1978). Studies of empathic behavior in children. In B. A. Maher (Ed.), *Progress in experimental personality research* (Vol. 8, pp. 1–47). New York: Academic Press.

Feshbach, N. D., & Feshbach, S. (1982). Empathy training and the regulation of aggression: Potentialities and limitations. *Academic Psychology Bulletin, 4,* 399–413.

Fischer, W. F. (1963). Sharing in preschool children as function of amount and type of reinforcement. *Genetic Psychology Monographs, 68,* 215–245.

Freud, S. (1930). *Civilization and its discontents* (J. Riviere, Trans.). London: Hogarth Press.

Freud, S. (1968). *New introductory lectures on psychoanalysis.* London: Hogarth. (Original work published 1933)

Froming, W. J., Nasby, W., & McManus, J. (1998). Prosocial self-schemas, self-awareness, and children's prosocial behavior. *Journal of Personality and Social Psychology, 75,* 766–777.

Furman, W., & Buhrmester, D. (1985). Children's perceptions of the personal relationships in their social networks. *Developmental Psychology, 21,* 1016–1024.

Gallese, V. (2001). The "Shared Manifold" Hypothesis: From mirror neurons to empathy. *Journal of Consciousness Studies, 8,* 33–50.

Garner, P. W., & Estep, K. M. (2001). Emotional competence, emotion socialization, and young children's peer-related social competence. *Early Education and Development, 12,* 29–48.

Garner, P. W., Jones, D. C., Gaddy, G., & Rennie, K. M. (1997). Low-income mothers' conversations about emotions and their children's emotional competence. *Social Development, 6,* 37–52.

Garner, P. W., Jones, D. C., & Miner, J. L. (1994). Social competence among low-income preschoolers: Emotion socialization practices and social cognitive correlates. *Child Development, 65,* 622–637.

Garner, P. W., Jones, D. C., & Palmer, D. J. (1994). Social cognitive correlates of preschool children's sibling caregiving behavior. *Developmental Psychology, 30,* 905–911.

Gelfand, D. M., Hartmann, D. P., Cromer, C. C., Smith, C. L., & Page, B. C. (1975). The effects of instructional prompts and praise on children's donation rates. *Child Development, 46,* 980–983.

Gill, K. L., & Calkins, S. D. (2003). Do aggressive/destructive toddlers lack concern for others? Behavioral and physiological indicators of empathic responding in 2-year-old children. *Development and Psychopathology, 15,* 55–71.

Ginsburg, H. J., Ogletree, S. M., Silakowski, T. D., Bartels, R. D., Burk, S. L., & Turner, G. M. (2003). Young children's theories of mind about empathic and selfish motives. *Social Behavior and Personality, 31,* 237–244.

Glover, E. (1968). *The birth of the ego.* London: Allen & Unwin.

Goodman, R. (1994). A modified version of the Rutter Parent Questionnaire including extra items on children's strengths: A research note. *Journal of Child Psychology and Psychiatry, 35,* 1483–1494.

Goodman, R. (2001). Psychometric properties of the Strengths and Difficulties Questionnaire. *Journal of the American Academy of Child and Adolescent Psychiatry, 40,* 1337–1345.

Gosselin, P., Warren, M., & Diotte, M. (2002). Motivation to hide emotion and children's understanding of the distinction between real and apparent emotions. *Journal of Genetic Psychology, 163.*

Graves, N. B., & Graves, T. D. (1983). The cultural context of prosocial development: An ecological model. In D. L. Bridgeman (Ed.), *The nature of prosocial development* (pp. 243–264). New York: Academic Press.

Graziano, W. G., & Eisenberg, N. H. (1997). Agreeableness: A dimension of personality. In R. Hogan, J. Johnson, & S. Briggs (Eds.), *Handbook of personality psychology* (pp. 795–824). San Diego, CA: Academic Press.

Greenberger, E., & Goldberg, W. A. (1989). Work, parenting, and the socialization of children. *Developmental Psychology, 25,* 22–35.

Gretarsson, S. J., & Gelfand, D. M. (1988). Mothers' attributions regarding their children's social behavior and personality characteristics. *Developmental Psychology, 24,* 264–269.

Grusec, J. E. (1971). Power and the internalization of self denial. *Child Development, 42,* 93–105.

Grusec, J. E. (1991). Socializing concern for others in home. *Developmental Psychology, 27,* 338–342.

Grusec, J. E., & Goodnow, J. J. (1994). Impact of parental discipline methods on the child's internalization of values: A reconceptualization of current points of view. *Developmental Psychology, 30,* 4–19.

Grusec, J. E., Goodnow, J. J., & Cohen, L. (1996). Household work and the development of concern for others. *Developmental Psychology, 32,* 999–1007.

Grusec, J. E., Kuczynski, L., Rushton, J. P., & Simutis, Z. M. (1978). Modeling, direction instruction, and attributions: Effects on altruism. *Developmental Psychology, 14,* 51–57.

Grusec, J. E., & Redler, E. (1980). Attribution, reinforcement, and altruism: A developmental analysis. *Developmental Psychology, 16,* 525–534.

Grusec, J. E., Saas-Kortsaak, P., & Simutis, Z. M. (1978). The role of example and moral exhortation in the training of altruism. *Child Development, 49,* 920–923.

Hall, K. R. L., & DeVore, I. (1965). Baboon social behavior. In I. DeVore (Ed.), *Primate behavior: Field studies of monkeys and apes* (pp. 53–110). New York: Holt, Rhinehart, & Winston.

Hampson, R. B. (1984). Adolescent prosocial behavior: Peer group and situational factors associated with helping. *Journal of Personality and Social Psychology, 46,* 153–162.

Hansen, B. K., & Bryant, B. K. (1980). Peer influence on sharing behavior of Mexican-American and Anglo-American boys. *Journal of Social Psychology, 110,* 135–136.

Harmon-Jones, E., Vaughn-Scott, K., Mohr, S., Sigelman, J., & Harmon-Jones, C. (2004). The effect of manipulated sympathy and anger on left and right frontal cortical activity. *Emotion, 4,* 95–101.

Hart, D., Atkins, R., & Ford, D. (1998). Urban America as a context for the development of moral identity in adolescence. *Journal of Social Issues, 54,* 513–530.

Hart, D., Burock, D., London, B., & Atkins, R. (2003). Prosocial tendencies, antisocial behavior, and moral development. In A. Slater & G. Bremner (Eds.), *An introduction to developmental psychology* (pp. 334–356). Malden, MA: Blackwell.

Hart, D., & Fegley, S. (1995). Altruism and caring in adolescence: Relations to self-understanding and social judgment. *Child Development, 66,* 1346–1359.

Hartmann, D. P., Gelfand, D. M., Smith, C. L., Paul, S. C., Cromer, C. C., Page, B. C., et al. (1976). Factors affecting the acquisition and elimination of children's donation behavior. *Journal of Experimental Child Psychology, 21,* 328–338.

Hartup, W. W., & Coates, B. (1967). Imitation of a peer as a function of reinforcement from the peer group and rewardingness of the model. *Child Development, 38,* 1003–1016.

Haselager, G. J. T., Cillessen, A. H. N., Van Lieshout, C. F. M., Riksen-Walraven, J. M. A., & Hartup, W. W. (2002). Heterogeneity among peer-rejected boys across middle childhood: Developmental pathways of social behavior. *Developmental Psychology, 38,* 446–456.

Hastings, P. D., Zahn-Waxler, C., & McShane, K. (2005). We are, by nature, moral creatures: Biological bases of concern for others. In M. Killen & J. Smetana (Eds.), *Handbook of moral development* (pp. 483–516). Hillsdale, NJ: Erlbaum.

Hastings, P. D., Zahn-Waxler, C., Robinson, J., Usher, B., & Bridges, D. (2000). The development of concern for others in children with behavior problems. *Developmental Psychology, 36,* 531–546.

Hay, D. F. (1994). Prosocial development. *Journal of Child Psychology and Psychiatry, 35,* 29–71.

Hay, D. F., Caplan, M. Z., Castle, M. Z., & Stimson, C. A. (1991). Does sharing become "rational" in the second year of life? *Developmental Psychology, 27,* 987–993.

Hay, D. F., Castle, J., Davies, L., Demetriou, H., & Stimson, C. A. (1999). Prosocial action in very early childhood. *Journal of Child Psychology and Psychiatry and Allied Disciplines, 40,* 905–916.

Hay, D. F., & Murray, P. (1982). Giving and requesting: Social facilitation of infants' offers to adults. *Infant Behavior and Development, 5,* 301–310.

Hay, D. F., Nash, A., & Pedersen, J. (1981). Responses of 6-month-olds to the distress of their peers. *Child Development, 52,* 1071–1075.

Hay, D. F., & Pawlby, S. (2003). Prosocial development in relation to children's and mothers' psychological problems. *Child Development, 74,* 1314–1327.

Hay, D. F., & Rheingold, H. L. (1983). The early appearance of some valued behaviors. In D. L. Bridgeman (Ed.), *The nature of prosocial development: Interdisciplinary theories and strategies* (pp. 73–94). New York: Academic Press.

Hayes, D. J., Felton, R. R., & Cohen, R. R. (1985). A natural occurrence of foster parenting by a female mountain bluebird. *Auk, 102,* 191–193.

Helwig, C. C., & Turiel, E. (2003). Children's social and moral reasoning. In P. K. Smith & C. H. Hart (Eds.), *Blackwell handbook of childhood social development* (pp. 476–490). Malden, MA: Blackwell.

Hertz-Lazarowitz, R. (1983). Prosocial behavior in the classroom. *Academic Psychology Bulletin, 5,* 319–338.

Hertz-Lazarowitz, R., Fuchs, I., Sharabany, R., & Eisenberg, N. (1989). Students' interactive and non-interactive behaviors in the classroom: A comparison between two types of classrooms in the city and the kibbutz in Israel. *Contemporary Educational Psychology, 14,* 22–32.

Hertz-Lazarowitz, R., & Sharan, S. (1984). Enhancing prosocial behavior through cooperative learning in the classroom. In E. Staub, D. Bar-Tal, J. Karylowski, & J. Reykowski (Eds.), *Development and maintenance of prosocial behavior: International perspectives on positive morality* (pp. 423–443). New York: Plenum Press.

Hertz-Lazarowitz, R., Sharan, S., & Steinberg, R. (1980). Classroom learning style and cooperative behavior of elementary school children. *Journal of Educational Psychology, 72,* 97–104.

Hieshima, J. A., & Schneider, B. (1994). Intergenerational effects on the cultural and cognitive socialization of third- and fourth-generation Japanese Americans. *Journal of Applied Developmental Psychology, 15,* 319–327.

Hobbes, T. (1962). *Leviathan* (M. Oakeshotte, Ed.). New York: Dutton. (Original work published 1651)

Hofer, M. A. (1981). *The roots of human behavior.* San Francisco: Freeman.

Hoffman, M. L. (1963). Parent discipline and the child's consideration for others. *Child Development, 34,* 573–588.

Hoffman, M. L. (1970). Moral development. In P. H. Mussen (Ed.), *Carmichael's manual of child development* (Vol. 2, pp. 261–359). New York: Wiley.

Hoffman, M. L. (1975). Altruistic behavior and the parent-child relationship. *Journal of Personality and Social Psychology, 31,* 937–943.

Hoffman, M. L. (1981). Is altruism part of human nature? *Journal of Personality and Social Psychology, 40,* 121–137.

Hoffman, M. L. (1982). Development of prosocial motivation: Empathy and guilt. In N. Eisenberg (Ed.), *The development of prosocial behavior* (pp. 281–313). New York: Academic Press.

Hoffman, M. L. (1983). Affective and cognitive processes in moral internalization. In E. T. Higgins, D. N. Ruble, & W. W. Hartup (Eds.), *Social cognition and social development: A sociocultural perspective* (pp. 236–274). Cambridge, MA: Cambridge University Press.

Hoffman, M. L. (2000). *Empathy and moral development: Implications for caring and justice.* New York: Cambridge University Press.

Hoffner, C., & Haefner, M. J. (1997). Children's comforting of frightened coviewers: Real and hypothetical television-viewing situations. *Communication Research, 24,* 136–152.

Holte, C. S., Jamruszka, V., Gustafson, J., Beaman, A. L., & Camp, G. C. (1984). Influence of children's positive self-perceptions on donating behavior in naturalistic settings. *Journal of School Psychology, 22,* 145–153.

Howe, N., & Ross, H. S. (1990). Socialization, perspective-taking, and the sibling relationship. *Developmental Psychology, 26,* 160–165.

Howes, C., & Eldredge, R. (1985). Responses of abused, neglected, and non-maltreated children to the behaviors of their peers. *Journal of Applied Developmental Psychology, 6,* 261–270.

Howes, C., & Farver, J. (1987). Toddlers' responses to the distress of their peers. *Journal of Applied Developmental Psychology, 8,* 441–452.

Howes, C., & Matheson, C. C. (1992). Sequences in the development of competent play with peers: Social and social pretend play. *Developmental Psychology, 28,* 961–974.

Howes, C., Matheson, C. C., & Hamilton, C. E. (1994). Maternal, teacher, and child care history correlates of children's relationships with peers. *Child Development, 65,* 264–273.

Howes, C., & Olenick, M. (1986). Family and child care influences on toddlers' compliance. *Child Development, 57,* 202–216.

Huebner, A. J., & Mancini, J. A. (2003). Shaping structured out-of-school time use among youth: The effects of self, family, and friend systems. *Journal of Youth and Adolescence, 32,* 453–463.

Hughes, C., White, A., Sharpen, J., & Dunn, J. (2000). Antisocial, angry, and unsympathetic: "Hard-to-manage" preschoolers' peer problems and possible cognitive influences. *Journal of Child Psychology and Psychiatry and Allied Disciplines, 41,* 169–179.

Hume, D. (1975). *Enquiry into the human understanding* (P. Nidditch, Ed.). Oxford, England: Clarendon Press. (Original work published 1748)

Huston, A. C., & Wright, J. C. (1998). Mass media and children's development. In W. Damon, I. S. Sigel, & K. A. Renninger (Eds.), *Handbook of child psychology* (Vol. 4, 5th ed., pp. 999–1058). New York: Wiley.

Iannotti, R. J., Cummings, E. M., Pierrehumbert, B., Milano, M. J., & Zahn-Waxler, C. (1992). Parental influences on prosocial behavior and empathy in early childhood. In J. M. A. M. Janssens & J. R. M. Gerris (Eds.), *Child rearing: Influence on prosocial and moral development* (pp. 77–100). Amsterdam: Swets & Zeitlinger.

Inglés, C. J., Hidalgo, M. D., Méndéz, F. X., & Inderbitzen, H. M. (2003). The Teenage Inventory of Social Skills: Reliability and validity of the Spanish translation. *Journal of Adolescence, 26,* 505–510.

Israel, A. C., & Brown, M. S. (1979). Effects of directiveness of instructions and surveillance on the production and persistence of children's donations. *Journal of Experimental Child Psychology, 27,* 250–261.

Israel, A. C., & Raskin, P. A. (1979). Directiveness of instructions and modeling: Effects on production and persistence on children's donations. *Journal of Genetic Psychology, 135,* 269–277.

Jacobs, J. E., Vernon, M. K., & Eccles, J. S. (2004). Relations between social self-perceptions, time use, and prosocial or problem behavior during adolescence. *Journal of Adolescent Research, 19,* 45–62.

Jacobsen, C. (1983). What it means to be considerate: Differences in normative expectations and their implications. *Israel Social Science Research, 1,* 24–33.

Jaffee, S., & Hyde, J. S. (2000). Gender differences in moral orientation: A meta-analysis. *Psychological Bulletin, 126,* 703–726.

Janoski, T., Musick, M., & Wilson, J. (1998). Being volunteered? The impact of social participation and pro-social attitudes on volunteering. *Sociological Forum, 13,* 495–519.

Janoski, T., & Wilson, J. (1995). Pathways to volunteerism: Family socialization and status transmission models. *Social Forces, 74,* 271–292.

Janssens, J. M. A. M., & Dekovic, M. (1997). Child rearing, prosocial moral reasoning, and prosocial behaviour. *International Journal of Behavioral Development, 20,* 509–527.

Janssens, J. M. A. M., & Gerris, J. R. M. (1992). Child rearing, empathy and prosocial development. In J. M. A. M. Janssens & J. R. M. Gerris (Eds.), *Child rearing: Influence on prosocial and moral development* (pp. 57–75). Amsterdam: Swets & Zeitlinger.

Jennings, K. D., Fitch, D., & Suwalsky, J. T. (1987). Social cognition and social interaction in 3-year-olds: Is social cognition truly social? *Child Study Journal, 17,* 1–14.

Johnson, D. B. (1982). Altruistic behavior and the development of the self in infants. *Merrill-Palmer Quarterly, 28,* 379–388.

Johnson, D. W., & Johnson, R. T. (1975). *Learning together and alone: Cooperation, competition, and individualization.* Englewood Cliffs, NJ: Prentice-Hall.

Johnson, H. R., Thompson, M. J. J., Wilkinson, S., Walsh, L., Balding, J., & Wright, V. (2002). Vulnerability to bullying: Teacher-reported conduct and emotional problems, hyperactivity, peer relationship difficulties, and prosocial behaviour in primary school children. *Educational Psychology, 22,* 553–556.

Johnson, M. K., Beebe, T., Mortimer, J. T., & Snyder, M. (1998). Volunteerism in adolescence: A process perspective. *Journal of Research on Adolescence, 8,* 309–332.

Johnson, W., & Krueger, R. F. (2004). Genetic and environmental structure of adjectives describing the domains of the big five model of personality: A nationwide U.S. twin study. *Journal of Research in Personality, 38,* 448–472.

Jones, W., Bellugi, U., Lai, Z., Chiles, M., Reilly, J., Lincoln, A., et al. (2000). Hypersociability in Williams syndrome. In U. Bellugi & M. St. George (Eds.), Linking cognitive neuroscience and molecular genetics: New perspectives from Williams syndrome. *Journal of Cognitive Neuroscience, 12*(Suppl. 1), 30–46.

Kagan, S., & Knight, G. P. (1981). Social motives among Anglo-American and Mexican-American children: Experimental and projective measures. *Journal of Research in Personality, 15,* 93–106.

Kagan, S., & Madsen, M. C. (1972). Experimental analyses of cooperation and competition of Anglo-American and Mexican children. *Developmental Psychology, 6,* 49–59.

Kalliopuska, M., & Tiitinen, U. (1991). Influence of two developmental programs on the empathy and prosociability of preschool children. *Perceptual and Motor skills, 72,* 323–328.

Kiang, L., Moreno, A. J., & Robinson, J. L. (2004). Maternal perceptions about parenting predict child temperament, maternal sensitivity, and children's empathy. *Developmental Psychology, 40,* 1081–1092.

Kaminsky, L., & Dewey, D. (2001). Sibling relationships of children with autism. *Journal of Autism and Developmental Disorders, 31,* 339–410.

Kant, E. (1956). *Groundwork of the metaphysics of moral law.* London: Hutchinson. (Original work published 1785)

Karafantis, D. M., & Levy, S. R. (2004). The role of children's lay theories about the malleability of human attributes in beliefs about and volunteering for disadvantaged groups. *Child Development, 75,* 236–250.

Karniol, R. (1995). Developmental and individual differences in predicting others' thoughts and feelings: Applying the transformation rule model. In N. Eisenberg (Ed.), *Review of personality and social psychology: Vol. 15. Social development* (pp. 27–48). Thousand Oaks, CA: Sage.

Karniol, R., Gabay, R., Ochion, Y., & Harari, Y. (1998). Is gender or gender-role orientation a better predictor of empathy in adolescence? *Sex Roles, 39,* 45–59.

Karylowski, J. (1982). Doing good to feel good versus doing good to make others feel good: Some child-rearing antecedents. *School Psychology International, 3,* 149–156.

Keane, S. P., & Calkins, S. D. (2004). Predicting kindergarten peer social status from toddler and preschool problem behavior. *Journal of Abnormal Child Psychology, 32,* 409–423.

Keith, J. G., Nelson, C. S., Schlabach, J. H., & Thompson, C. J. (1990). The relationship between parental employment and three measures of early adolescent responsibility: Family-related, personal, and social. *Journal of Early Adolescence, 10,* 399–415.

Keller, B. B., & Bell, R. Q. (1979). Child effects on adult's method of eliciting altruistic behavior. *Child Development, 50,* 1004–1009.

Kestenbaum, R., Farber, E. A., & Sroufe, L. A. (1989). Individual differences in empathy among preschoolers: Relation to attachment history. *New Directions in Child Development, 44,* 51–64.

Kienbaum, J., & Trommsdorff, G. (1999). Social development of young children in different cultural systems. *International Journal of Early Years Education, 7,* 241–248.

Kienbaum, J., Volland, C., & Ulich, D. (2001). Sympathy in the context of mother-child and teacher-child relationships. *International Journal of Behavioral Development, 25,* 302–309.

Killen, M., & Turiel, E. (1998). Adolescents' and young adults' evaluations of helping and sacrificing for others. *Journal of Research on Adolescence, 8,* 355–375.

Knight, G. P., Cota, M. K., & Bernal, M. E. (1993). The socialization of cooperative, competitive, and individualistic preferences among Mexican American children: The mediating role of ethnic identity. *Hispanic Journal of Behavioral Sciences, 15,* 291–309.

Knight, G. P., Johnson, L. G., Carlo, G., & Eisenberg, N. (1994). A multiplicative model of the dispositional antecedents of a prosocial behavior: Predicting more of the people more of the time. *Journal of Personality and Social Psychology, 66,* 178–183.

Knight, G. P., & Kagan, S. (1977a). Acculturation of prosocial and competitive behaviors among second- and third-generation Mexican-American children. *Journal of Cross-Cultural Psychology, 8,* 273–284.

Knight, G. P., & Kagan, S. (1977b). Development of prosocial and competitive behaviors in Anglo-American and Mexican-American children. *Child Development, 48,* 1385–1394.

Knight, G. P., Kagan, S., & Buriel, R. (1981). Confounding effects of individualism in children's cooperation-competition social motive measures. *Motivation and Emotion, 5,* 167–178.

Knight, G. P., Nelson, W., Kagan, S., & Gumbiner, J. (1982). Cooperative-competitive social orientation and school achievement among Anglo-American and Mexican-American children. *Contemporary Educational Psychology, 7,* 97–106.

Knott, F., Lewis, C., & Williams, T. (1995). Sibling interaction of children with learning disabilities: A comparison of autism and Down's syndrome. *Journal of Child Psychology and Psychiatry, 6,* 965–976.

Kochanska, G. (1985). Children's temperament, mothers' discipline, and security of attachment: Multiple pathways to emerging internalization. *Child Development, 66,* 597–615.

Kochanska, G., Forman, D. R., & Coy, K. C. (1999). Implications of the mother-child relationship in infancy for socialization in the second year of life. *Infant Behavior & Development, 22,* 249–265.

Koenig, A. L., Cicchetti, D., & Rogosch, F. A. (2004). Moral development: The association between maltreatment and young children's prosocial behaviors and moral transgressions. *Social Development, 13,* 87–106.

Koestner, R., Franz, C., & Weinberger, J. (1990). The family origins of empathic concern: A 26-year longitudinal study. *Journal of Personality and Social Psychology, 58,* 709–717.

Kohlberg, L. (1969). Stage and sequence: The cognitive-developmental approach to socialization. In D. A. Goslin (Ed.), *Handbook of socialization theory and research* (pp. 325–480). New York: Rand McNally.

Kohlberg, L. (1984). *Essays on moral development: Vol. 2. The psychology of moral development.* San Francisco: Harper & Row.

Kojima, Y. (2000). Maternal regulation of sibling interactions in the preschool years: Observational study in Japanese families. *Child Development, 71,* 1640–1647.

Konner, M. (2002). Some obstacles to altruism. In S. G. Post & L. G. Underwood (Eds.), *Altruism and altruistic love: Science, philosophy, and religion in dialogue* (pp. 192–211). Oxford, England: Oxford University Press.

Krebs, D., & Miller, D. (1985). Altruism and aggression. In G. Lindzey & E. Aronson (Eds.), *Handbook of social psychology* (pp. 1–71). New York: Random House.

Krebs, D. L., & Sturrup, B. (1982). Role-taking ability and altruistic behavior in elementary school children. *Journal of Moral Education, 11,* 94–100.

Krebs, D. L., & Van Hesteren, F. (1994). The development of altruism: Toward an integrative model. *Developmental Review, 14,* 103–158.

Krevans, J., & Gibbs, J. C. (1996). Parents' use of inductive discipline: Relations to children's empathy and prosocial behavior. *Child Development, 67,* 3263–3277.

Krueger, R. F., Hicks, B. M., & McGue, M. (2001). Altruism and antisocial behavior: Independent tendencies, unique personality correlates, distinct etiologies. *Psychological Science, 12,* 397–402.

Kumru, A., Carlo, G., Mestre, V., & Samper, P. (2003, April). *Prosocial moral reasoning and prosocial behavior among Turkish and Spanish adolescents.* Paper presented at the biennial meeting of the Society for Research in Child Development, Tampa, FL.

Kumru, A., & Edwards, C. P. (2003, April). *Gender and adolescent prosocial behavior within the Turkish family.* Poster presented at the biennial meeting of the Society for Research in Child Development, Tampa, FL.

Laible, D. J., & Carlo, G. (2004). The differential relations of maternal and paternal support and control to adolescent social competence, self-worth, and sympathy. *Journal of Adolescent Research, 19,* 759–782.

Laible, D. J., Carlo, G., & Raffaelli, M. (2000). The differential relations of parent and peer attachment to adolescent adjustment. *Journal of Youth and Adolescence, 29,* 45–59.

Laible, D. J., Carlo, G., & Roesch, S. (2004). Pathways to self-esteem: The role of parent and peer attachment, empathy, and social behaviors. *Journal of Adolescence, 27,* 703–716.

Ladd, G. W., Lange, G., & Stremmel, A. (1983). Personal and situational influences on children's helping behavior: Factors that mediate helping. *Child Development, 54,* 488–501.

LaFontana, K. M., & Cillessen, A. H. N. (2002). Children's perceptions of popular and unpopular peers: A multimethod assessment. *Developmental Psychology, 38,* 635–647.

Lalonde, C. E., & Chandler, M. J. (1995). False belief understanding goes to school: On the social-emotional consequences of coming early or late to a first theory of mind. *Cognition and Emotion, 9,* 167–185.

Lamb, S., & Zakhireh, B. (1997). Toddlers' attention to the distress of peers in a day care setting. *Early Education and Development, 8,* 105–118.

Larrieu, J., & Mussen, P. (1986). Some personality and motivational correlates of children's prosocial behavior. *Journal of Genetic Psychology, 147,* 529–542.

Larrieu, J. A. (1984, March). *Prosocial values, assertiveness, and sex: Predictors of children's naturalistic helping.* Paper presented at the biennial meeting of the Southwestern Society for the Research in Human Development, Denver, CO.

Lebra, T. S. (1994). Mother and child in Japanese socialization: A Japan-United States comparisons. In P. M. Greenfield & R. R. Cocking (Eds.), *Cross-cultural roots of minority child development* (pp. 259–274). Hillsdale, NJ: Erlbaum.

Lee, L. C., & Zhan, G. Q. (1991). Political socialization and parental values in the People's Republic of China. *International Journal of Behavioral Development, 14,* 337–373.

LeMare, L., & Krebs, D. (1983). Perspective-taking and styles of (pro) social behavior in elementary school children. *Academic Psychology Bulletin, 5,* 289–298.

Lennon, R., & Eisenberg, N. (1987). Gender and age differences in empathy and sympathy. In N. Eisenberg & J. Strayer (Eds.), *Empathy and its development* (pp. 195–217). New York: Cambridge University Press.

Lennon, R., Eisenberg, N., & Carroll, J. (1983). The assessment of empathy in early childhood. *Journal of Applied Developmental Psychology, 4,* 295–302.

Leon, M. (1983). Chemical communication in mother-young interaction. In J. Vandenbergh (Ed.), *Pheromones and reproduction in mammals* (pp. 39–75). New York: Academic Press.

Lepper, M. R. (1983). Social-control processes and the internalization of social values: An attributional perspective. In E. T. Higgins, D. N. Ruble, & W. W. Hartup (Eds.), *Social cognition and social development: A sociocultural perspective* (pp. 294–330). Cambridge, England: Cambridge University Press.

Lerner, R. M., Almerigi, J. B., Theokas, C., & Lerner, J. V. (2005). Positive youth development: A view of the issues. *Journal of Early Adolescence, 25,* 10–16.

Lerner, R. M., Dowling, E. M., & Anderson, P. M. (2003). Positive youth development: Thriving as a basis of personhood and civil society. *Applied Developmental Science, 7,* 172–180.

Lerner, R. M., Lerner, J. V., Almerigi, J. B., Theokas, C., Phelps, E., Gestsdottir, S., et al. (2005). Positive youth development, participation in community youth development programs, and community contributions of fifth-grade adolescents: Findings from the first wave of the 4-H study of positive youth development. *Journal of Early Adolescence, 25,* 17–71.

Levin, I., & Bekerman-Greenberg, R. (1980). Moral judgment and moral reasoning in sharing: A developmental analysis. *Genetic Psychological Monographs, 101,* 215–230.

Lichter, D. T., Shanahan, M. J., & Gardner, E. L. (2002). Helping others? The effects of childhood poverty and family instability on prosocial behavior. *Youth & Society, 34,* 89–119.

Lindeman, M., Harakka, T., & Keltikangas-Jarvinen, L. (1997). Age and gender differences in adolescents' reactions to conflict situations: Aggression, prosociality, and withdrawal. *Journal of Youth and Adolescence, 26,* 339–351.

Lindner-Gunnoe, M., Hetherington, E. M., & Reiss, D. (1999). Parental religiosity, parenting style, and adolescent social responsibility. *Journal of Early Adolescence, 19,* 199–225.

Litvack-Miller, W., McDougall, D., & Romney, D. M. (1997). The structure of empathy during middle childhood and its relationship to prosocial behavior. *Genetic, Social, and General Psychology Monographs, 123,* 303–324.

London, P. (1970). The rescuers: Motivational hypotheses about Christians who saved Jews from the Nazis. In J. Macaulay & L. Berkowitz (Eds.), *Altruism and helping behavior* (pp. 241–250). New York: Academic Press.

Lopez, S. J., & Snyder, C. R. (2003). *Positive psychological assessment: A handbook of models and measures.* Washington, DC: American Psychological Association.

Lourenco, O. M. (1993). Toward a Piagetian explanation of the development of prosocial behaviour in children: The force of negational thinking. *British Journal of Developmental Psychology, 11,* 91–106.

Love, J. M., Harrison, L., Sagi-Schwartz, A., van IJzendoorn, J. H., Ross, C., Ungerer, J. A., et al. (2003). Child care quality matters: How conclusions can vary with context. *Child Development, 74,* 1003–1021.

Ma, H. K. (1989). Moral orientation and moral judgment in adolescents in Hong Kong, mainland China, and England. *Journal of Cross Cultural Psychology, 20,* 152–177.

Ma, H. K. (1992). The relation of altruistic orientation to human relationships and moral judgment in Chinese people. *International Journal of Psychology, 27,* 377–400.

Ma, H. K., & Leung, M. C. (1991). Altruistic orientation in children: Construction and validation of the child altruism inventory. *International Journal of Psychology, 26,* 745–759.

Maccoby, E. E. (1998). *The two sexes: Growing up apart, coming together.* Cambridge, MA: Belknap Press.

MacLean, P. D. (1985). Brain evolution relating to family, play and the separation call. *Archives of General Psychiatry, 42,* 405–417.

Main, M., & George, C. (1985). Responses of abused and disadvantaged toddlers to distress in agemates: A study in the day care setting. *Developmental Psychology, 21,* 407–412.

Markiewicz, D., Doyle, A. B., & Brendgen, M. (2001). The quality of adolescents' friendships: Associations with mothers' interpersonal relationships, attachments to parents and friends, and prosocial behaviors. *Journal of Adolescence, 24,* 429–445.

Markus, H. R., & Kitayama, S. (1991). Culture and the self: Implications for cognition, emotion, and motivation. *Psychological Review, 48,* 224–253.

Marsh, D. T., Serafica, F. C., & Barenboim, C. (1981). Interrelationships among perspective taking, interpersonal problem solving and interpersonal functioning. *Journal of Genetic Psychology, 138,* 37–48.

Martin, C. L., Fabes, R. A., Hanish, L. D., & Hollenstein, T. (in press). Social dynamics in the preschool. *Developmental Review.*

Martin, G. B., & Clark, R. D. (1982). Distress crying in neonates: Species and peer specificity. *Developmental Psychology, 18,* 3–9.

Matsuba, M. K., & Walker, L. J. (2005). Young adult moral exemplars: The making of self through stories. *Journal of Research on Adolescence, 15,* 275–287.

McGrath, M. P., & Power, T. G. (1990). The effects of reasoning and choice on children's prosocial behaviour. *International Journal of Behavioural Development, 13,* 345–353.

McGrath, M. P., Wilson, S. R., & Frassetto, S. J. (1995). Why some forms of inductive reasoning are better than others: Effects of cognitive focus, choice, and affect on children's prosocial behavior. *Merrill-Palmer Quarterly, 41,* 347–360.

McGuire, K. D., & Weisz, J. R. (1982). Social cognition and behavior correlates of preadolescent chumship. *Child Development, 53,* 1478–1484.

McLellan, J. A., & Youniss, J. (2003). Two systems of youth service: Determinants of voluntary and required youth community service. *Journal of Youth and Adolescence, 32,* 47–58.

Mervis, C. B., & Klein-Tasman, B. P. (2000). Williams syndrome: Cognition, personality, and adaptive behavior. *Mental Retardation and Developmental Disabilities Research Review, 6,* 148–158.

Metz, E., McLellan, J., & Youniss, J. (2003). Types of voluntary service and adolescents' civic development. *Journal of Adolescent Research, 18,* 188–203.

Metz, E., & Youniss, J. (2003). A demonstration that school-based required service does not deter, but heightens, volunteerism. *Political Science and Politics, 36,* 281–286.

Midlarsky, E., & Bryan, J. H. (1967). Training charity in children. *Journal of Personality and Social Psychology, 5,* 408–415.

Miller, J. G., & Bersoff, D. M. (1992). Culture and moral judgment: How are conflicts between justice and interpersonal responsibilities resolved? *Journal of Personality and Social Psychology, 62,* 541–554.

Miller, J. G., & Bersoff, D. M. (1994). Cultural influences on the moral status of reciprocity and the discounting of endogenous motivation. *Personality and Social Psychology Bulletin, 20,* 592–602.

Miller, J. G., & Bersoff, D. M. (1998). The role of liking in perceptions of the moral responsibility to help: A cultural perspective. *Journal of Experimental Social Psychology, 34,* 443–469.

Miller, J. G., Bersoff, D. M., & Harwood, R. L. (1990). Perceptions of social responsibilities in India and in the United States: Moral imperatives or personal decisions? *Journal of Personality and Social Psychology, 58,* 33–47.

Miller, P., & Eisenberg, N. (1988). The relation of empathy to aggression and externalizing/antisocial behavior. *Psychological Bulletin, 103,* 324–344.

Miller, P. A., Eisenberg, N., Fabes, R. A., & Shell, R. (1996). Relations of moral reasoning and vicarious emotion to young children's prosocial behavior toward peers and adults. *Developmental Psychology, 32,* 210–219.

Miller, P. A., Eisenberg, N., Fabes, R. A., Shell, R., & Gular, S. (1989). Socialization of empathic and sympathetic responding. In N. Eisenberg (Ed.), *The development of empathy and related vicarious responses: New Directions in child development* (pp. 65–83). San Francisco: Jossey-Bass.

Mills, R. S. L., & Grusec, J. (1989). Cognitive, affective, and behavioral consequences of praising altruism. *Merrill-Palmer Quarterly, 35,* 299–326.

Moore, C., Barresi, J., & Thompson, C. (1998). The cognitive basis of future-oriented prosocial behavior. *Social Development, 7,* 198–218.

Morris, W. N., Marshall, H. M., & Miller, R. S. (1973). The effect of vicarious punishment on prosocial behavior in children. *Journal of Experimental Child Psychology, 15,* 222–236.

Moore, C. W., & Allen, J. P. (1996). The effects of volunteering on the young volunteer. *Journal of Primary Prevention, 17,* 231–258.

Mulder, N. (1996). *Inside Indonesian society: Cultural change in Indonesia.* Amsterdam, The Netherlands: Pepin Press.

Munekata, H., & Ninomiya, K. (1985). Development of prosocial moral judgments. *Japanese Journal of Educational Psychology, 33,* 157–164.

Muris, P., Meesters, C., & van den Berg, F. (2003). The Strengths and Difficulties Questionnaire (SDQ): Further evidence for its reliability and validity in a community sample of Dutch children and adolescents. *European Child and Adolescent Psychiatry, 12,* 1–8.

Murphy, B. C., Shepard, S. A., Eisenberg, N., Fabes, R. A., & Guthrie, I. K. (1999). Contemporaneous and longitudinal relations of dispositional sympathy to emotionality, regulation, and social functioning. *Journal of Early Adolescence, 19,* 66–97.

Murphy, L. B. (1937). *Social behavior and child personality: An exploratory study of some roots of sympathy.* New York: Columbia University Press.

Nadler, A., Romek, E., & Shapira-Friedman, A. (1979). Giving in the kibbutz: Pro-social behavior of city and Kibbutz children as affected by social responsibility and social pressure. *Journal of Cross-Cultural Psychology, 10,* 57–72.

Nagel, T. (1970). *The possibility of altruism.* Oxford, England: Clarendon Press.

Nagin, D. S., & Tremblay, R. E. (2001). Parental and early childhood predictors of persistent physical aggression in boys from kindergarten to high school. *Archives of General Psychiatry, 58,* 389–394.

National Center for Education. (1997). *1996 National Household Education Survey: Student participation in community service activity.* Washington, DC: U.S. Department of Education. (NCES 97-331)

Nelson, D. A., & Crick, N. R. (1999). Rose-colored glasses: Examining the social information-processing of prosocial young adolescents. *Journal of Early Adolescence, 19,* 17–38.

Nsamenang, A. B. (1992). *Human development in cultural context: A third-world perspective.* Newbury Park, CA: Sage.

O'Connor, M., Dollinger, S., Kennedy, S., & Pelletier-Smetko, P. (1979). Prosocial behavior and psychopathology in emotionally disturbed boys. *American Journal of Orthopsychiatry, 49,* 301–310.

Oliner, S. P., & Oliner, P. M. (1988). *The altruistic personality: Rescuers of Jews in Nazi Europe.* New York: Free Press.

Olweus, D., & Endresen, I. M. (1998). The importance of sex-of-stimulus object: Age trends and sex differences in empathic responsiveness. *Social Development, 7,* 370–388.

Owens, C. R., & Ascione, F. R. (1991). Effects of the model's age, perceived similarity, and familiarity on children's donating. *Journal of Genetic Psychology, 152,* 341–357.

Pakaslahti, L., Karjalainen, A., & Keltikangas-Jarvinen, L. (2002). Relationships between adolescent prosocial problem-solving strategies, prosocial behaviour, and social acceptance. *International Journal of Behavioural Development, 26,* 137–144.

Pakaslahti, L., & Keltikangas-Jarvinen, L. (2001). Peer-attributed prosocial behavior among aggressive/preferred, aggressive/non-preferred, non-aggressive/preferred, and non-aggressive/non-preferred adolescents. *Personality and Individual Differences, 30,* 903–916.

Panksepp, J. (1986). The psychobiology of prosocial behaviors: Separation distress, play, and altruism. In C. Zahn-Waxler, E. M. Cummings, & R. Iannotti (Eds.), *Altruism and aggression: Biological and social origins* (pp. 19–57). Cambridge, England: Cambridge University Press.

Pearl, R. (1985). Children's understanding of others' need for help: Effects of problem explicitness and type. *Child Development, 56,* 735–745.

Perry, D. G., Bussey, K., & Freiberg, K. (1981). Impact of adults' appeals for sharing on the development of altruistic dispositions in children. *Journal of Experimental Child Psychology, 32,* 127–138.

Perry, L. C., Perry, D. G., & Weiss, R. J. (1986). Age differences in children's beliefs about whether altruism makes the actor feel good. *Social Cognition, 4,* 263–269.

Persson, G. E. B. (2005). Young children's prosocial and aggressive behaviors and their experiences of being targeted for similar behaviors by peers. *Social Development, 14,* 206–228.

Peterson, L. (1983). Influence of age, task competence, and responsibility focus on children's altruism. *Developmental Psychology, 19,* 141–148.

Peterson, L., Ridley-Johnson, R., & Carter, C. (1984). The supersuit: An example of structured naturalistic observation of children's altruism. *Journal of General Psychology, 110,* 235–241.

Phillips, D., McCartney, K., & Scarr, S. (1987). Child-care quality and children's social development. *Developmental Psychology, 23,* 537–543.

Phinney, J., Feshbach, N., & Farver, J. (1986). Preschool children's responses to peer crying. *Early Childhood Research Quarterly, 1,* 207–219.

Piaget, J. (1965). *The moral judgment of the child.* New York: Free Press. (Original work published 1932)

Pilgrim, C., & Rueda-Riedle, A. (2002). The importance of social context in cross-cultural comparisons: First graders in Columbia and the United States. *Journal of Genetic Psychology, 163,* 283–295.

Plomin, R., Emde, R. N., Braungart, J. M., Campos, J., Corley, R., Fulker, D. W., et al. (1993). Genetic change and continuity from 14 to 20 months: The MacArthur Longitudinal Twin Study. *Child Development, 64,* 1354–1376.

Porges, S. W., Doussard-Roosevelt, J. A., & Maiti, A. K. (1994). Vagal tone and the physiological regulation of emotion. *Monographs of the Society for Research in Child Development, 59(2/3,* Serial No. 240), 167–186, 250–283.

Post, S. G. (2001). The tradition of agape. In S. G. Post & L. G. Underwood (Eds.), *Altruism and altruistic love: Science, philosophy, and religion in dialogue* (pp. 51–64). Oxford, England: Oxford University Press.

Power, T. G., & Parke, R. D. (1986). Patterns of early socialization: Mother- and father-infant interaction in the home. *International Journal of Behavioral Development, 6,* 331–341.

Pratt, M. W., Hunsberger, B., Pancer, S. M., & Alisat, S. (2003). A longitudinal analysis of personal values socialization: Correlates of a moral self-ideal in late adolescence. *Social Development, 12,* 563–585.

Pratt, M. W., Skoe, E. E., & Arnold, M. L. (2004). Care reasoning development and family socialization patterns in later adolescence: A longitudinal analysis. *International Journal of Behavioral Development, 28,* 139–147.

Preston, S. D., & de Waal, F. B. M. (2002). Empathy: Its ultimate and proximate bases. *Behavioral and Brain Sciences, 25,* 1–72.

Pugh, M. J., & Hart, D. (1999). Identity development and peer group participation. *New Directions in Child and Adolescent Development, 84,* 55–70.

Radke-Yarrow, M., & Zahn-Waxler, C. (1984). Roots, motives, and patterns in children's prosocial behavior. In E. Staub, D. Bar-Tal, J. Karylowski, & J. Reykowski (Eds.), *Development and maintenance of prosocial behavior: International perspectives on positive behavior* (pp. 81–99). New York: Plenum Press.

Radke-Yarrow, M. R., Zahn-Waxler, C., & Chapman, M. (1983). Children's prosocial dispositions and behavior. In P. H. Mussen (Ed.), *Carmichael's manual of child psychology* (Vol. 4, pp. 469–546). New York: Wiley.

Radke-Yarrow, M., Zahn-Waxler, C., Richardson, D. T., Susman, A., & Martinez, P. (1994). Caring behavior in children of clinically depressed and well mothers. *Child Development, 65,* 1405–1414.

Ramsey, P. G. (1988). Social skills and peer status: A comparison of two socioeconomic groups. *Merrill-Palmer Quarterly, 34,* 185–202.

Rao, N., & Stewart, S. M. (1999). Cultural influences on sharer and recipient behavior: Sharing in Chinese and Indian preschool children. *Journal of Cross-Cultural Psychology, 30,* 219–241.

Rehberg, H. R., & Richman, C. L. (1989). Prosocial behaviour in preschool children: A look at the interaction of race, gender, and family composition. *International Journal of Behavioral Development, 12,* 385–401.

Rheingold, H. L. (1982). Little children's participation in the work of adults, a nascent prosocial behavior. *Child Development, 53,* 114–125.

Rheingold, H. L., Hay, D. F., & West, M. J. (1976). Sharing in the second year of life. *Child Development, 47,* 1148–1158.

Rice, M. E., & Grusec, J. E. (1975). Saying and doing: Effects on observer performance. *Journal of Personality and Social Psychology, 32,* 584–593.

Rigby, K., & Slee, P. T. (1993). Dimensions of interpersonal relation among Australian children and implications for psychological well-being. *Journal of Social Psychology, 133,* 33–42.

Roberts, W., & Strayer, J. (1996). Empathy, emotional expressiveness, and prosocial behavior. *Child Development, 67,* 449–470.

Robinson, J. L., Emde, R. N., & Corley, R. P. (2001). Dispositional cheerfulness: Early genetic and environmental influences. In R. N. Emde & J. K. Hewitt (Eds.), *Infancy to early childhood: Genetic and environmental influences on developmental change* (pp. 163–177). Oxford, England: Oxford University Press.

Robinson, J. L., Zahn-Waxler, C., & Emde, R. N. (1994). Patterns of development in early empathic behavior: Environmental and child constitutional influences. *Social Development, 3,* 125–145.

Robinson, J. L., Zahn-Waxler, C., & Emde, R. N. (2001). Relationship context as a moderator of sources of individual difference in empathic development. In R. N. Emde & J. K. Hewitt (Eds.), *Infancy to early childhood: Genetic and environmental influences on developmental change* (pp. 257–268). Oxford, England: Oxford University Press.

Rogoff, B. (2003). *The cultural nature of human development.* London: Oxford University Press.

Rohner, R. P. (1975). *They love me, they love me not.* New Haven, CT: HRAF Press.

Rose, A. J., & Asher, S. R. (2004). Children's strategies and goals in response to help-giving and help-seeking tasks within a friendship. *Child Development, 75,* 749–780.

Rosenhan, D. L. (1970). The natural socialization of altruistic autonomy. In J. Macaulay & L. Berkowitz (Eds.), *Altruism and helping behavior* (pp. 251–268). New York: Academic Press.

Rothbart, M. K., Ahadi, S. A., & Hershey, K. L. (1994). Temperament and social behavior in childhood. *Merrill-Palmer Quarterly, 40,* 21–39.

Rousseau, J. J. (1962). *Emile.* New York: Columbia University Press. (Original work published 1773)

Ruby, P., & Decety, J. (2001). Effect of subjective perspective taking during simulation of action: A PET investigation of agency. *Nature and Neuroscience, 4,* 546–550.

Rudolph, K. D., & Conley, C. S. (2005). The socioemotional costs and benefits of social-evaluative concerns: Do girls care too much? *Journal of Personality, 73,* 115–137.

Rushton, J. P. (1975). Generosity in children: Immediate and long-term effects of modeling, preaching, and moral judgment. *Journal of Personality and Social Psychology, 31,* 459–466.

Rushton, J. P., Fulker, D. W., Neale, M. C., Nias, D. K. B., & Eysenck, H. J. (1986). Altruism and aggression: The heritability of individual differences. *Journal of Personality and Social Psychology, 50,* 1192–1198.

Rushton, J. P., & Littlefield, C. (1979). The effects of age, amount of modeling, and a success experience on 7- to 11-year-old children's generosity. *Journal of Moral Education, 9,* 55–56.

Rushton, J. P., Russell, R. J. H., & Wells, P. A. (1984). Genetic similarity theory: Beyond kin selection altruism. *Behavior Genetics, 14,* 179–193.

Rushton, J. P., & Teachman, G. (1978). The effects of positive reinforcement, attributions, and punishment on model induced altruism in children. *Personality and Social Psychology Bulletin, 4,* 322–325.

Russell, A., Hart, C. H., Robinson, C. C., & Olsen, S. F. (2003). Children's sociable and aggressive behaviour with peers: A comparison of the United States and Australia, and contributions of temperament and parenting style. *International Journal of Behavioral Development, 27,* 74–86.

Saarni, C., Mumme, D. L., & Campos, J. J. (1998). Emotional development: Action, communication, and understanding. In W. Damon (Editor-in-Chief) & N. Eisenberg (Vol. Ed.), *Handbook of child psychology: Vol. 3. Social, emotional and personality development* (5th ed., pp. 237–309). New York: Wiley.

Sagi, A., & Hoffman, M. L. (1976). Empathic distress in the newborn. *Developmental Psychology, 12,* 175–176.

Saklofske, D. H., & Eysenck, S. B. G. (1983). Impulsiveness and venturesomeness in Canadian children. *Psychological Reports, 52,* 147–152.

Savin-Williams, R. C., Small, S. A., & Zeldin, R. S. (1981). Dominance and altruism among adolescent males: A comparison of ethological and psychological methods. *Ethology and Sociobiology, 2,* 167–176.

Sawyer, K. S., Denham, S., DeMulder, E., Blair, K., Auerbach-Major, S., & Levitas, J. (2002). The contribution of older siblings' reactions to emotions to preschoolers' emotional and social competence. *Marriage and Family Review, 34,* 183–212.

Scarr, S., & McCartney, K. (1983). How people make their own environments: A theory of genotype → environment effects. *Child Development, 54,* 424–435.

Schenk, V. M., & Grusec, J. E. (1987). A comparison of prosocial behavior of children with and without day care experience. *Merrill-Palmer Quarterly, 33,* 231–240.

Scourfield, J., John, B., Martin, N., & McGuffin, P. (2004). The development of prosocial behaviour in children and adolescents: A twin study. *Journal of Child Psychology and Psychiatry, 45,* 927–935.

Searcy, E., & Eisenberg, N. (1992). Defensiveness in response to aid from a sibling. *Journal of Personality and Social Psychology, 62,* 422–433.

Sebanc, A. M. (2003). The friendship features of preschool children: Links with prosocial behavior and aggression. *Social Development, 12,* 249–268.

Seligman, M. E. P., & Csikszentmihalyi, M. (2000). Positive psychology: An introduction. *American Psychologist, 55,* 5–14.

Semel, E., & Rosner, S. R. (2003). *Understanding Williams syndrome: Behavioral patterns and interventions.* Mahwah, NJ: Erlbaum.

Serow, R. C., & Solomon, D. (1979). Classroom climates and students' intergroup behavior. *Journal of Educational Psychology, 71,* 669–676.

Sharma, V. (1988). Effect of birthorder, age and sex on helping behaviour of children. *Indian Journal of Psychometry and Education, 19,* 91–96.

Shek, D. T. L., & Ma, H. K. (2001). Parent-adolescent conflict and adolescent antisocial and prosocial behavior: A longitudinal study in a Chinese context. *Adolescence, 36,* 545–555.

Shigetomi, C. C., Hartmann, D. P., & Gelfand, D. M. (1981). Sex differences in children's altruistic behavior and reputations for helpfulness. *Developmental Psychology, 17,* 434–437.

Silva, F. (1992). Assessing the child and adolescent personality: A decade of research. *Personality and Individual Differences, 13,* 1163–1181.

Skoe, E. E. A., Hansen, K. L., Morch, W.-T., Bakke, I., Hoffmann, T., Larsen, B., et al. (1999). Care-based moral reasoning in Norwegian and Canadian early adolescents: A cross-national comparison. *Journal of Early Adolescence, 19,* 280–291.

Slaughter, V., Dennis, M. J., & Pritchard, M. (2002). Theory of mind and peer acceptance in preschool children. *British Journal of Developmental Psychology, 20,* 545–564.

Slote, M. (2001). *Morals from motives.* Oxford, England: Oxford University Press.

Slote, M. (2004). Autonomy and empathy. *Social Philosophy and Policy Foundation, 21,* 293–309.

Smith, A. (1982). *A theory of moral sentiments.* Indianapolis, IN: Liberty Classics. (Original work published 1759)

Smith, C. L. (1983). Exhortations, rehearsal, and children's prosocial behavior. *Academic Psychology Bulletin, 5,* 261–271.

Smith, C. L., Gelfand, D. M., Hartmann, D. P., & Partlow, M. E. Y. (1979). Children's causal attributions regarding help giving. *Child Development, 50*, 203–210.

Sneed, C. (2002). Correlates and implications for agreeableness in children. *Journal of Psychology, 136*, 59–67.

Sober, E., & Wilson, D. (1998). *Unto others: The evolution and psychology of unselfish behavior.* Cambridge, MA: Harvard University Press.

Solomon, D., Battistich, V., & Watson, M. (1993, March). *A longitudinal investigation of the effects of a school intervention program on children's social development.* Paper presented at the biennial meeting of the Society for Research in Child Development, New Orleans, LA.

Solomon, D., Battistich, V., Watson, M., Schaps, E., & Lewis, C. (2000). A six-district study of educational changes: Direct and mediated effects of the Child Development Project. *Social Psychology of Education, 4*, 3–51.

Solomon, D., Watson, M. S., Delucchi, K. L., Schaps, E., & Battistich, V. (1988). Enhancing children's prosocial behavior in the classroom. *American Educational Research Journal, 25*, 527–554.

Spence, J. T., Helmreich, R. L., & Stapp, J. (1974). The Personal Attributes Questionnaire: A measure of sex-role stereotypes and masculinity-femininity. *JSAS: Catalog of Selected Documents in Psychology, 4*(43, Ms. No. 617).

Spinrad, T. L. (1999, April). *Toddlers' vicarious emotional responses and prosocial behaviors: The role of infant temperament and maternal behavior.* Paper presented at the Society for Research in Child Development, Albuquerque, NM.

Spinrad, T. L., Losoya, S., Eisenberg, N., Fabes, R. A., Shepard, S. A., Cumberland, A., et al. (1999). The relation of parental affect and encouragement to children's moral emotions and behaviour. *Journal of Moral Education, 28*, 323–337.

Stanhope, L., Bell, R. Q., & Parker-Cohen, N. Y. (1987). Temperament and helping behavior in preschool children. *Developmental Psychology, 23*, 347–353.

Staub, E. (1971a). A child in distress: The influence of nurturance and modeling on children's attempts to help. *Developmental Psychology, 5*, 124–132.

Staub, E. (1971b). The use of role playing and induction in children's learning of helping and sharing behavior. *Child Development, 42*, 805–817.

Staub, E. (1979). *Positive social behavior and morality: Vol. 2. Socialization and development.* New York: Academic Press.

Staub, E. (1992). The origins of caring, helping, and nonaggression: Parental socialization, the family system, schools, and cultural influence. In P. M. Oliner, L. Baron, L. A. Blum, D. L. Krebs, & M. Z. Smolenska (Eds.), *Embracing the other: Philosophical, psychological, and historical perspectives on altruism* (pp. 390–412). New York: New York University Press.

Staub, E. (2003). *The psychology of good and evil: Why children, adults, and groups help and harm others.* New York: Cambridge University Press.

Staub, E., & Noerenberg, H. (1981). Property rights, deservingness, reciprocity, friendship: The transactional character of children's sharing behavior. *Journal of Personality and Social Psychology, 40*, 271–289.

Stern, D. N. (1985). *The interpersonal world of the infant: A view from psychoanalysis and developmental psychology.* New York: Basic Books.

Stevenson, H. W. (1991). The development of prosocial behavior in large-scale collective societies: China and Japan. In R. A. Hinde & J. Groebel, (Eds.), *Cooperation and prosocial behaviour* (pp. 89–105). Cambridge, England: Cambridge University Press.

Stewart, R. B., & Marvin, R. S. (1984). Sibling relations: The role of conceptual perspective-taking in the ontogeny of sibling caregiving. *Child Development, 55*, 1322–1332.

Stewart, S. M., & McBride-Chang, C. (2000). Influences on children's sharing in a multicultural setting. *Journal of Cross-Cultural Psychology, 31*, 333–348.

Stewart, S. M., Rao, N., Bond, M. H., Fielding, R., McBride-Chang, C.,& Kennard, B. D. (1998). Chinese dimensions of parenting: Broadening Western predictors and outcomes. *International Journal of Psychology, 33*, 345–358.

Stillwell, R., & Dunn, J. (1985). Continuities in sibling relationships: Patterns of aggression and friendliness. *Journal of Child Psychology and Psychiatry, 26*, 627–637.

Stoneman, Z., Brody, G. H., & MacKinnon, C. E. (1986). Same-sex and cross-sex siblings: Activity choices, roles, behavior, and gender stereotypes. *Sex Roles, 15*, 495–511.

Strayer, F. F., Wareing, S., & Rushton, J. P. (1979). Social constraints on naturally occurring preschool altruism. *Ethology and Sociobiology, 1*, 3–11.

Strayer, J. (1993). Children's concordant emotions and cognitions in response to observed emotions. *Child Development, 64*, 188–201.

Strayer, J., & Roberts, W. (1989). Children's empathy and role taking: Child and parental factors, and relations to prosocial behavior. *Journal of Applied Developmental Psychology, 10*, 227–239.

Strayer, J., & Roberts, W. (1997a). Children's personal distance and their empathy: Indices of interpersonal closeness. *International Journal of Behavioral Development, 20*, 385–403.

Strayer, J., & Roberts, W. (1997b). Facial and verbal measures of children's emotions and empathy. *International Journal of Behavioral Development, 20*, 627–649.

Strayer, J., & Roberts, W. (2004a). Empathy and observed anger and aggression in 5-year-olds. *Social Development, 13*, 1–13.

Strayer, J., & Roberts, W. (2004b). Children's anger, emotional expressiveness, and empathy: Relations with parents' empathy, emotional expressiveness, and parenting practices. *Social Development, 13*, 229–254.

Stukas, A. A., Snyder, M., & Clary, E. G. (1999). The effects of "mandatory volunteerism" on intentions to volunteer. *Psychological Science, 10*, 59–64.

Stukas, A. A., Jr., Switzer, G. E., Dew, M. A., Goycoolea, J. M., & Simmons, R. G. (1999). Parental helping models, gender, and service-learning. *Journal of Prevention and Intervention in the Community, 18*, 5–18.

Suda, W., & Fouts, G. (1980). Effects of peer presence on helping in introverted and extroverted children. *Child Development, 51*, 1272–1275.

Sugiyama, K., Matsui, H., Satoh, C., Yoshimi, Y., & Takeuchi, M. (1992). Effects of self-efficacy and outcome expectation on observational learning of altruistic behavior. *Japanese Journal of Psychology, 63*, 295–302.

Switzer, G. E., Simmons, R. G., Dew, M. A., Regalski, J. M., & Wang, C. (1995). The effect of a school-based helper program on adolescent self-image, attitudes, and behavior. *Journal of Early Adolescence, 15*, 429–455.

Szynal-Brown, C., & Morgan, R. R. (1983). The effects of reward on tutor's behaviors in a cross-age tutoring context. *Journal of Experimental Child Psychology, 36,* 196–208.

Termine, N. T., & Izard, C. E. (1988). Infants' responses to their mothers' expressions of joy and sadness. *Developmental Psychology, 24,* 223–229.

Tesson, G., Lewko, J. H., & Bigelow, B. J. (1987). The social rules that children use in their interpersonal relations. *Contributions of Human Development, 18,* 36–57.

Thompson, C., Barresi, J., & Moore, C. (1997). The development of future-oriented prudence and altruism in preschoolers. *Cognitive Development, 12,* 199–212.

Tietjen, A. (1986). Prosocial reasoning among children and adults in a Papua, New Guinea society. *Developmental Psychology, 22,* 861–868.

Tremblay, R. E., Vitaro, F., Gagnon, C., Piche, C., & Royer, N. (1992). A prosocial scale for the preschool behaviour questionnaire: Concurrent and predictive correlates. *International Journal of Behavioral Development, 15,* 227–245.

Trivers, R. L. (1971). The evolution of reciprocal altruism. *Quarterly Review of Biology, 46,* 35–57.

Trivers, R. L. (1983). The evolution of cooperation. In D. L. Bridgeman (Ed.), *The nature of prosocial development* (pp. 95–112). New York: Academic Press.

Trommsdorff, G. (1991). Child-rearing and children's empathy. *Perceptual Motor Skills, 72,* 387–390.

Trommsdorff, G. (1995). Person-context relations as developmental conditions for empathy and prosocial action: A cross-cultural analysis. In T. A. Kindermann & J. Valsiner (Eds.), *Development of person-context relations* (pp. 189–208). Hillsdale, NJ: Erlbaum.

Trommsdorff, G., & Friedlmeier, W. (1999). Motivational conflict and prosocial behaviour of kindergarten children. *International Journal of Behavioral Development, 23,* 413–429.

Trommsdorff, G., & Kornadt, H.-J. (2003). Parent-child relations in cross-cultural perspective. In L. Kuczynski (Ed.), *Handbook of dynamics in parent-child relations* (pp. 271–306). Thousand Oaks, CA: Sage.

Tucker, C. J., Updegraff, K. A., McHale, S. M., & Crouter, A. C. (1999). Older siblings as socializers of younger siblings' empathy. *Journal of Early Adolescence, 19,* 176–198.

Turnbull, C. M. (1972). *The mountain people.* New York: Simon & Schuster.

Turner, P. H., & Harris, M. B. (1984). Parental attitudes and preschool children's social competence. *Journal of Genetic Psychology, 144,* 105–113.

Uggen, C., & Janikula, J. (1999). Volunteerism and arrest in the transition to adulthood. *Social Forces, 78,* 331–362.

Underwood, B., & Moore, B. (1982). Perspective-taking and altruism. *Psychological Bulletin, 91,* 143–173.

Underwood, L. G. (2001). The human experience of compassionate love: Conceptual mapping and data from selected studies. In S. G. Post & L. G. Underwood (Eds.), *Altruism and altruistic love: Science, philosophy, and religion in dialogue* (pp. 72–88). Oxford, England: Oxford University Press.

Ungerer, J. A., Dolby, R., Waters, B., Barnett, B., Kelk, N., & Lewin, V. (1990). The early development of empathy: Self-regulation and individual differences in the first year. *Motivation and Emotion, 14,* 93–106.

Valiente, C., Eisenberg, N., Fabes, R. A., Shepard, S. A., Cumberland, A., & Losoya, S. H. (2004). Prediction of children's empathy-related responding from their effortful control and parents' expressivity. *Developmental Psychology, 40,* 911–926.

Vandell, D. L., Henderson, V. K., & Wilson, K. S. (1988). A longitudinal study of children with day-care experiences of varying quality. *Child Development, 59,* 1286–1292.

van der Mark, I. L., van IJzendoorn, M. H., & Bakermans-Kranenburg, M. J. (2002). Development of empathy in girls during the second year of life: Associations with parenting, attachment, and temperament. *Social Development, 11,* 451–468.

Van Lawick-Goodall, J. (1968). A preliminary report on expressive movements and communication in the Gombe Stream chimpanzees. In P. Jay (Ed.), *Primates* (pp. 313–374). New York: Holt, Rhinehart, & Winston.

Vitaglione, G. D., & Barnett, M. A. (2003). Assessing a new dimension of empathy: Empathic anger as a predictor of helping and punishing desires. *Motivation and Emotion, 27,* 301–324.

Vitaro, F., Gagnon, C., & Tremblay, R. E. (1990). Predicting stable peer rejection from kindergarten to grade 1. *Journal of Clinical Child Psychology, 19,* 257–264.

Vitaro, F., Gagnon, C., & Tremblay, R. E. (1991). Teachers' and mothers' assessment of children's behaviors from kindergarten to grade 2: Stability and change within and across informants. *Journal of Psychopathology and Behavioral Assessment, 13,* 325–343.

Volling, B. L. (2001). Early attachment relationships as predictors of preschool children's emotion regulation with a distressed sibling. *Early Education and Development, 12,* 185–207.

Wachs, T. D. (1994). Genetics, nurture and social development: An alternative viewpoint. *Social Development, 3,* 66–70.

Warden, D., Cheyne, B., Christie, D., Fitzpatrick, H., & Reid, K. (2003). Assessing children's perceptions of prosocial and anti-social behavior. *Educational Psychology, 23,* 547–567.

Warden, D., & Mackinnon, S. (2003). Prosocial bullies, bullies, and victims: An investigation of their sociometric status, empathy, and social problem-solving strategies. *British Journal of Developmental Psychology, 21,* 367–385.

Waters, E., Hay, D., & Richters, J. (1986). Infant-parent attachment and the origins of prosocial and antisocial behavior. In D. Olweus, J. Block, & M. Radke-Yarrow (Eds.), *Development of antisocial and prosocial behavior: Research, theories, and issues* (pp. 97–125). Orlando, FL: Academic Press.

Weissbrod, C. S. (1976). Noncontingent warmth induction, cognitive style, and children's imitative donation and rescue effort behaviors. *Journal of Personality and Social Psychology, 34,* 274–281.

Welsh, M., Parke, R. D., Widaman, K., & O'Neil, R. (2001). Linkages between children's social and academic competence: A longitudinal analysis. *Journal of School Psychology, 39,* 463–481.

Wentzel, K. R. (2003). Sociometric status and adjustment in middle school: A longitudinal study. *Journal of Early Adolescence, 23,* 5–28.

Wentzel, K. R., Barry, C. M., & Caldwell, K. A. (2004). Friendship in middle school: Influences on motivation and school adjustment. *Journal of Educational Psychology, 96,* 195–203.

Wentzel, K. R., & McNamara, C. C. (1999). Interpersonal relationships, emotional distress, and prosocial behavior in middle school. *Journal of Early Adolescence, 19,* 114–125.

White, G. M., & Burnam, M. A. (1975). Socially cued altruism: Effects of modeling, instructions, and age on public and private donations. *Child Development, 46,* 559–563.

Whiting, B. B., & Edwards, C. P. (1973). A cross-cultural analysis of sex differences in the behavior of children aged 3 through 11. *Journal of Social Psychology, 91,* 171–188.

Whiting, B. B., & Edwards, C. P. (1988). *Children of different worlds.* Cambridge, MA: Harvard University Press.

Whiting, B. B., & Whiting, J. W. M. (1975). *Children of 6 cultures: A psychocultural analysis.* Cambridge, MA: Harvard University Press.

Williams, W. (1991). *Javanese lives: Men and women in modern Indonesian society.* New Brunswick, NJ: Rutgers University Press.

Wilson, B. J. (2003). The role of attentional processes in children's prosocial behavior with peers: Attention shifting and emotion. *Developmental and Psychopathology, 15,* 313–329.

Wilson, C. C., Piazza, C. C., & Nagle, R. J. (1990). Investigation of the effect of consistent and inconsistent behavioral example upon children's donation behaviors. *Journal of Genetic Psychology, 151,* 361–376.

Wilson, E. O. (1975). *Sociobiology: The new synthesis.* Cambridge, MA: Harvard University Press.

Wilson, E. O. (1978). *On human nature.* Cambridge, MA: Harvard University Press.

Wise, P. S., & Cramer, S. H. (1988). Correlates of empathy and cognitive style in early adolescence. *Psychological Reports, 63,* 179–192.

Wood, J. V., Saltzberg, J. A., & Goldsamt, L. A. (1990). Does affect induce self-focused attention? *Journal of Personality and Social Psychology, 58,* 899–908.

Wynne-Edwards, V. C. (1962). *Animal dispersion in relation to social behaviour.* New York: Hafner.

Yarrow, M. R., & Scott, P. M. (1972). Imitation of nurturant and non-nurturant models. *Journal of Personality and Social Psychology, 23,* 259–270.

Yarrow, M. R., Scott, P. M., & Waxler, C. Z. (1973). Learning concern for others. *Developmental Psychology, 8,* 240–260.

Yarrow, M. R., Waxler, C. Z., Barrett, D., Darby, J., King, R., Pickett, M., et al. (1976). Dimensions and correlates of prosocial behavior in young children. *Child Development, 47,* 118–125.

Yates, M., & Youniss, J. (1996a). Community service and political-moral identity in adolescents. *Journal of Research on Adolescence, 6,* 271–284.

Yates, M., & Youniss, J. (1996b). A development perspective on community service in adolescence. *Social Development, 5,* 85–111.

Yates, M., & Youniss, J. (1998). Community service and political identity development in adolescence. *Journal of Social Issues, 43,* 495–512.

Young, S. K., Fox, N. A., & Zahn-Waxler, C. (1999). The relations between temperament and empathy in 2-year-olds. *Developmental Psychology, 35,* 1189–1197.

Youniss, J. (1980). *Parents and peers in social development: A Sullivan-Piaget perspective.* Chicago: University of Chicago Press.

Youniss, J., McLellan, J. A., & Mazer, B. (2001). Voluntary service, peer group orientation, and civic engagement. *Journal of Adolescent Research, 16,* 456–468.

Youniss, J., McLellan, J. A., Su, Y., & Yates, M. (1999). The role of community service in identity development: Normative, unconventional, and deviant orientations. *Journal of Adolescent Research, 14,* 248–261.

Youniss, J., McLellan, J. A., & Yates, M. (1999). Religion, community service, and identity in American youth. *Journal of Adolescence, 22,* 243–253.

Youniss, J., & Metz, E. (2004). *Longitudinal gains in civic development through school-based required service.* Manuscript submitted for publication.

Zaff, J. F., Moore, K. A., Papillo, A. R., & Williams, S. (2003). Implications of extracurricular activity participation during adolescence on positive outcomes. *Journal of Adolescent Research, 18,* 599–630.

Zahn-Waxler, C., Cole, P. M., Welsh, J. D., & Fox, N. A. (1995). Psychophysiological correlates of empathy and prosocial behaviors in preschool children with problem behaviors. *Development and Psychopathology, 7,* 27–48.

Zahn-Waxler, C., Cummings, E. M., McKnew, D., & Radke-Yarrow, M. (1984). Altruism, aggression, and social interactions in young children with a manic-depressive parent. *Child Development, 55,* 112–122.

Zahn-Waxler, C., Iannotti, R., & Chapman, M. (1982). Peers and prosocial development. In K. H. Rubin & H. S. Ross (Eds.), *Peer relationships and social skills in childhood* (pp. 133–162). New York: Springer-Verlag.

Zahn-Waxler, C., & Radke-Yarrow, M. (1982). The development of altruism: Alternative research strategies. In N. Eisenberg (Ed.), *The development of prosocial behavior* (pp. 109–137). New York: Academic Press.

Zahn-Waxler, C., Radke-Yarrow, M., & King, R. A. (1979). Child rearing and children's prosocial initiations toward victims of distress. *Child Development, 50,* 319–330.

Zahn-Waxler, C., Radke-Yarrow, M., & King, R. (1983). Early altruism and guilt. *Academic Psychology Bulletin, 5,* 247–259.

Zahn-Waxler, C., Radke-Yarrow, M., Wagner, E., & Chapman, M. (1992). Development of concern for others. *Developmental Psychology, 28,* 126–136.

Zahn-Waxler, C., Robinson, J., & Emde, R. N. (1992). The development of empathy in twins. *Developmental Psychology, 28,* 1038–1047.

Zahn-Waxler, C., Schiro, K., Robinson, J. L., Emde, R. N., & Schmitz, S. (2001). Empathy and prosocial patterns in young MZ and DZ twins: Development and genetic and environmental influences. In R. N. Emde & J. K. Hewitt (Eds.), *Infancy to early childhood* (pp. 141–162). New York: Oxford University Press.

Zarbatany, L., Hartmann, D. P., & Gelfand, D. M. (1985). Why does children's generosity increase with age: Susceptibility to experimenter influence or altruism? *Child Development, 56,* 746–756.

Zarbatany, L., Hartmann, D. P., Gelfand, D. M., & Vinciguerra, P. (1985). Gender differences in altruistic reputation. *Developmental Psychology, 21,* 97–101.

Zeldin, R. A., Savin-Williams, R. C., & Small, S. A. (1984). Dimensions of prosocial behavior in adolescent males. *Journal of Social Psychology, 123,* 159–168.

Zeldin, S., & Topitzes, D. (2002). Neighborhood experiences, community connection, and positive beliefs about adolescents among urban adults and youth. *Journal of Community Psychology, 30,* 647–669.

Zhou, Q., Eisenberg, N., Losoya, S. H., Fabes, R. A., Reiser, M., Guthrie, I. K., et al. (2002). The relations of parental warmth and positive expressiveness to children's empathy-related responding and social functioning: A longitudinal study. *Child Development, 73,* 893–915.

CHAPTER 12

Aggression and Antisocial Behavior in Youth

KENNETH A. DODGE, JOHN D. COIE, and DONALD LYNAM

Over the past 40 years, crime rates have risen steadily in nearly all countries that keep reasonably accurate records (Rutter, Giller, & Hagell, 1998). More dramatic has been the increase in violent crime by young juveniles in the United States. Even though adult robbery and

homicide arrest rates and assault victimization reports reveal little secular change since 1965, juvenile violent crime rates have risen markedly: Since 1965, the homicide rate by juveniles aged 18 or under has increased by close to 400% (Blumstein, 2000).

The authors wish to thank Lynda Harrison for her careful scrutiny of the text, Amber Runion for assembling over 1,000 references, Terrie Moffitt for her insightful review, and

Nancy Eisenberg for her valuable editing. The first author is grateful for the support of Senior Research Scientist Award 5 K05 DA-015226.

Secular swings in juvenile violence have been especially dramatic. Between 1988 and 1997, the number of juvenile arrests increased by 35% and arrests of juveniles under age 13 for violent crimes increased by 45% (Snyder, 2003). Since then, however, juvenile arrests and violent crime receded back to the level of the 1980s (Blumstein & Wallman, 2000). The decrease in adolescent violence, however, is attributable primarily to decreases in crime among older juveniles. While the aggravated assault arrest rate among older juveniles in 2001 dropped 38% from its peak in 1994, the rate for juveniles under age 13 dropped only 3% (Snyder, 2003). Thus, the violent crime rate among younger children remains dramatically higher than it was 40 years ago. Similarly, the prevalence of psychiatrically diagnosed conduct disorder is several times greater than it was 70, or even 40, years ago, in both the United States (Robins, 1999), and the United Kingdom, even controlling for reporter effects (Collishaw, Maughan, Goodman, & Pickles, 2004).

The annual aggregate burden of crime in the United States now exceeds $1 trillion (D. Anderson, 1999). In the eyes of the U.S. public, crime and violence perennially rank among the most important problems facing this country (Berke, 1994). Both the magnitude of the current problem and the urgency of a solution are represented in the U.S. Surgeon General's national objectives for 2010 to reduce the prevalence of physical fighting among adolescents to less than 32% and to reduce the prevalence of weapon-carrying on high school property to less than 4.9% (U.S. Department of Health and Human Services, 2000).

The rapid swings in U.S. crime rates have been paralleled by growth in research on the development of aggressive and other antisocial behavior. Research in the past 2 decades has increasingly focused on the development of chronically antisocial individuals, in contrast to research on species-wide patterns in aggressive behavior. This shift in emphasis has grown from recognition that a small group of chronically violent youth are responsible for over half of all crimes (Howell, Krisberg, & Jones, 1995), that criminal careers can be charted across the life span beginning in childhood (Blumstein & Cohen, 1987), that career criminals cost society up to $2 million *each* (M. Cohen, 1998), and that citizens may be willing to pay a great deal in extra taxes for interventions that could confidently reduce crime (Cohen, Rust, Steen, & Tidd, 2004).

Four questions guide the organization of this chapter:

1. What is the human species-wide developmental course of aggression and antisocial behavior?

2. What stability and change occur in the life course of individual differences in antisocial behavior?

3. Why do some individuals become more antisocial than others?

4. What promising avenues exist in the prevention and treatment of aggressive behavior in children?

DEFINING THE DOMAIN OF AGGRESSION AND ANTISOCIAL BEHAVIOR

Previous editions of the *Handbook* have restricted the discussion of antisocial behavior to aggression, perhaps because that form of antisocial behavior has been studied most often. Over the past 10 years, research has increasingly emphasized individual differences in aggressive behavior, and this shift has led to the recognition that aggressive behaviors often occur in a context of other antisocial behaviors, such as noncompliance with adults, lying, stealing, destruction of property in the childhood years, and more serious antisocial behaviors such as illegal drug selling, sexual assault, burglary, and other violent crimes. Even the psychiatric diagnosis of conduct disorder has evolved over the past half-century to address the co-occurrence of physical aggression with other forms of aggressive behavior (e.g., verbal aggression) and other antisocial behaviors (e.g., illicit substance use; Robins, 1999). This comorbidity of aggression with other antisocial behaviors suggests that an understanding of the etiology and developmental course of aggression might be enhanced by including it in the broader class of antisocial behaviors (Menard & Elliott, 1994). Substance use and abuse, as well as participation in drug sales activities, have particular significance in any discussion of contemporary antisocial behavior because the increased rate of violence in the United States, especially for teenage males, parallels the rise in certain kinds of illegal substance use in our society. Nonetheless, an explicit treatment of developmental issues relating to substance use and trafficking is not included in this chapter because of space limitations.

Although definitions of aggression and antisocial behavior usually have considerable overlap, there are important differences between them. The definition of aggression embraced by Parke and Slaby (1983), "behavior that is aimed at harming or injuring another person or persons" (p. 50), is similar to the broader definition that Loeber (1985) offered for antisocial behaviors, namely those "that inflict physical or mental harm or property loss or damage on others, and which may or may not constitute the breaking of criminal laws" (p. 6). This latter definition includes aggression but is not restricted to it. Sometimes aggression is defined broadly enough to include property loss or damage, as in the case of instrumental aggression; however, the feature of instrumental aggression that makes it aggressive, in our view, is the use or threat of force to obtain possession. An important difference in the two definitions is the inclusion of intent in the Parke and Slaby (1983) definition, a distinction that we endorse.

Part of the ambiguity in definition arises from the fact that governmental and professional institutions have their own contextually based definitions for antisocial behavioral problems. Loeber's (1985) definition of antisocial behavior makes reference to violations of criminal code. For children and adolescents, legal violations constitute delinquency, although some delinquent acts such as truancy and running away from home do not conform to usual definitions of antisocial behavior. Conversely, fighting and threats of harm occur frequently among school-aged children, and yet these behaviors are rarely considered as a possible cause for arrest even though the same acts by adults would be construed as assault. In education, the terms *Serious Emotional Disturbance* (SED) and *Behavior Disorders* (BD) have been applied to children whose classroom behavior is too disruptive to allow for the education of other children. These children are typically removed to special education classrooms with other similar children. *Conduct disorder* is a psychiatric term that refers to a disorder that is diagnosed by the frequency of problem behaviors exhibited by a child or adolescent across a given period (three or more across a 6-month period). The term is applied to individuals rather than to acts and is considered to reflect a diagnostic syndrome. *Oppositional defiant disorder,* which includes disobedience or disrespect for adults often accompanied by irritability, is a psychiatric syndrome that is distinct from conduct disorder and is most often applied to elementary-school children but is thought to predict conduct disorder. *Antisocial personality disorder* is a chronic psychiatric condition that requires a life-persistent pattern of antisocial behavior (Hinshaw & Anderson, 1996).

In earlier *Handbook* chapters on aggression, including our own, the merits and flaws in various approaches to defining aggression have been discussed at length. As noted earlier, the study of aggression prior to the 1980s focused more on the behavioral analysis of aggression than on individual differences in aggressive behavior and the need for precision in defining aggression was quite obvious. For those who study individual differences, the need for precision in defining aggressive acts is not as important as precision in identifying aggressive persons. Because the identification of aggressive persons often depends on consensus in social judgments by third parties, the need to be clear about what constitutes aggression might not seem important. Nonetheless, the need to be clear about the nature of this judgment invariably brings us back to the definitional issue. The topographical approach to defining aggression, taken from ethology, focuses on the form of the act itself and has been successful with lower-order species but is less reliable with humans because of the greater range of diversity in human aggressive behavior (Hartup & deWit, 1974). Antecedent approaches focus on the conditions eliciting aggression and emphasize the importance of determining the intent involved. This approach has its origins in the concept of the goal response introduced by Dollard, Doob, Miller, Mowrer, and Sears (1939). Defining aggression by the outcome (Buss, 1961) avoids the pitfalls of inferring intention but suffers from other problems. First, injury can result unintentionally from the behavior of others. Second, this definition excludes behaviors that have obvious aggressive intent but fail, somehow, to lead to injury. Third, such an approach emphasizes the instrumental aspect of aggression while ignoring the emotional component. Finally, Walters and Parke (1964) have suggested that aggression is determined by the social judgment of observers operating in a specific cultural context that must be understood as influencing the definition of aggression. Such an approach clearly fits legal approaches to defining guilt (Dodge, 1991) and may be necessary to any culturally sensitive research strategy for studying aggression, but it also suggests the challenge of defining aggression in the abstract. Viewed in the context of various cultures or social contexts, the same act might be classified as aggressive or not depending on how it contrasts with base rates for similar behavior in each of these contexts. Also, identification might depend on the perspectives of those whose resources are being controlled (Hawley, Little, & Pasupathi, 2002). One way to understand this point in the context of contemporary American culture is to note that some acts might be considered as acts of aggression when exhibited by a girl but not when exhibited by a boy.

These problems in defining aggression have led Tremblay, Hartup, and Archer (2005) to suggest that a weakness in the study of aggression is the ambiguity in its definition. We conclude that there is less ambiguity to the definition of aggression than in observers' ability to determine when it has actually occurred. This ambiguity plays itself out in everyday life, leading, perhaps, to much of the conflict and violence that surrounds us. We suggest that most people would readily agree with the very simple definition offered by Parke and Slaby (1983): Aggression is behavior aimed at harming or injuring another person or persons. The problem, as Tremblay and most other reviewers have pointed out, is that it is not always easy to decide whether harm was intended. This ambiguity, in our view, is not a definitional issue but a measurement issue. To confound the conceptual definition with the criterion for measurement is to fall prey to the limits of operationism—a philosophical approach to science that guided much of early experimental psychology. Human aggression may best be viewed as a heterogeneous category of human behavior, defined simply as acts intended to harm others, which requires a multifactor framework (Brain, 1994) to address the measurement problem. In other words, no single statement can adequately bound the acts that we would want to describe as aggressive behaviors. Instead, a judgment is made that relies on cues to intent, outcome potential, biological arousal, and social context. As with many other behavioral constructs, aggression is a "fuzzy set," and unreliability in assessment is part of the price that one pays for investigating an important aspect of human behavior.

DIMENSIONS OF AGGRESSION AND OTHER ANTISOCIAL BEHAVIOR

Because antisocial or disruptive behavior is a heterogeneous set, numerous attempts have been made to establish dimensions of antisocial behavior by factor-analytic or multidimensional scaling techniques. Frick et al. (1993) conducted a meta-analysis of factor-analytic studies of oppositional defiant disorder and conduct disorder behaviors in over 23,000 youth and extracted two dimensions of antisocial behavior. One dimension runs from overt to covert behaviors, a distinction that Loeber and Schmaling (1985) found to be quite robust, and the second dimension ranges in level of destructiveness. The resulting quadrants constitute categories of aggression (overt, high destructive), oppositional behavior (overt, low destructive), property violations (covert, high destructive), and status violations (covert, low destructive).

The category of aggressive behaviors can be further subcategorized into dimensions that reflect both the forms and functions of aggression. Little, Brauner, Jones, Nock, and Hawley (2003a) have demonstrated the validity of a dimensional system from self-reports by 1,723 German adolescents from grades 5 to 10. The form of aggression varies as direct, involving verbal or physical attack, or relational, involving damage to the target's friendships or inclusion in the peer group (Crick & Grotpeter, 1995). The function of aggression is either instrumental, occurring in the anticipation of self-serving outcomes, or reactive, occurring as an angry defensive response to goal blocking or provocation (Little, Jones, Henrich, & Hawley, 2003b). This latter distinction follows from Hartup's (1974) distinction between instrumental and hostile aggression and Dodge, Lochman, Harnish, Bates, and Pettit's (1997) empirical distinction between reactive and proactive aggressive behavior in chronically assaultive youth. Dodge and Coie (1987) demonstrated that reactive and proactive aggressive boys differ in social information-processing patterns. Little et al. (2003b) found that the reactive group showed consistent maladaptive behavior patterns not found in the instrumental group. Finally, adaptive functions of aggressive behavior, such as providing an opportunity for social-cognitive growth in very young children attracting peers' interest (Rodkin, Farmer, Pearl, & Van Acker, 2000), and maintenance of high-influence status in adolescent peer groups (Prinstein & Cillessen, 2003) suggest that the complexity of this behavior pattern may be tied to its robustness to evolutionary threats across the ages (Hawley, 2003).

The perspective of this chapter is that human aggressive behavior, because of its many adaptive features, has evolved to be part of a broader social communication system (Tedeschi & Felson, 1994). Aggression must be interpreted as a social event. It has meaningful subtypes and multiple topographies, antecedents, and functions. To understand processes in specific aggressive events may require subclassification and behavioral analysis. To understand the broader adaptive (and maladaptive) functions of aggression may require integration with other antisocial patterns.

HISTORICAL PERSPECTIVES ON THEORY AND EMPIRICAL INQUIRY

Through the 1980s, scholarly inquiry in aggressive behavior was dominated by broad debates among theorists. These debates addressed the very nature of the human species. The frustration-aggression hypothesis of Dollard et al. (1939) posited a drive theory that aggressive behavior is an inevitable, species-wide response to perceived goal-blocking. They suggested that frustration necessarily results in aggression and that all aggressive behavior is instigated by frustration. This hypothesis led to the first major empirical studies of aggression, and the findings disputed that premise. Berkowitz (1962) noted that frustration does not always lead to aggression but maintained the hypothesis that frustration creates a drivelike readiness to aggress, namely the arousal of anger.

The ethological approach of Lorenz (1966) similarly suggested the inevitability of aggressive behavior but emphasized the instinctual system that relies on internal energy that is generated even in the absence of external stimuli and must be released periodically. Even though empirical studies fail to support this hypothesis, Lorenz contributed the general perspective that the adaptive species-preserving functions of intraspecific aggression are to balance the distribution of the species across a limited ecology, to allow for the natural selection of the fittest of the species through combat, and to promote the selection of the most able family defenders against extraspecific threat. Thus, aggressive behavior has evolved as a necessary, species-preserving, component of human adaptation.

Bandura (1973) hypothesized that aggressive behavior develops through social learning processes, including imitation of aggressive models, direct operant reinforcement for aggressive acts, and vicarious reinforcement through observational learning. Most empirical research on human aggression during the 1970s and 1980s was inspired by this perspective. Bandura acknowledged the biological constraints on human learning but argued that these constraints are much less restrictive than in other species. Biological and genetic theories, other than those relating to instinct, have been posed primarily to account for age and individual differences in aggression and have proliferated in the past decade.

Two other developments have reshaped the nature of theory and empirical enquiry over the past 2 decades. First, the emerging field of developmental psychopathology (D. Shaw, 2003) has come to dominate the study of aggressive development. Microbehavioral analyses of aggressive events have been supplemented by epidemiological studies of individual differences in the life course of aggressive behavior. Models of reciprocal influence, transactional development, and biological-psychosocial interaction have been formulated (Dodge & Pettit, 2003). What has emerged is a theory of the devel-

opment of early starting aggressive behavior that has received growing consensus (Conduct Problems Prevention Research Group, 1992; Moffitt, 1990; Patterson, Reid, & Dishion, 1992). Much less studied and more poorly understood are later-onset patterns of aggressive behavior in adolescence and factors in desistance. The early starter theory incorporates an understanding of how biological factors, sociocultural contexts, and early life experiences with parents, peers, and schooling contribute to the development of enduring patterns of aggressive behavior. Rather than understand these factors as orthogonal influences, the emergent theory highlights the power of the interaction effect between genes and the environment (Caspi et al., 2002) and describes the social-cognitive processes by which children actively relate their experiences to future behavior. Second, methods have been developed to test these theories by identifying trajectories of growth and change over time (Nagin, 1999) and to parse influences that are nested across levels of the individual child who lives in a family nested with neighborhoods and schools (Bryk & Raudenbush, 1992).

CULTURAL DIFFERENCES AND AGGRESSION

How various cultures define aggression is beyond the scope of this chapter, but the impact of culture on the development of aggression and whether developmental models of aggression hold across cultures are important questions addressed here. Emerging literature suggests that many of the developmental processes first studied in the United States operate similarly across cultures, including China (Chang, Schwartz, Dodge, & McBride-Chang, 2003; Chen, Wang, Chen, & Liu, 2002) and Indonesia (Eisenberg, Pidada, & Liew, 2001), but future work may clarify the circumstances in which patterns diverge.

AGGRESSIVE AND ANTISOCIAL DEVELOPMENT IN THE HUMAN SPECIES

Charting species-wide patterns of growth and change in aggressive behavior across the life span is complicated by the qualitatively different measures of aggression across contexts. Even though infancy and toddlerhood represent the periods of highest frequency in aggression, the most dangerously aggressive periods are clearly late adolescence and early adulthood. Different measures of aggressive behavior provide discrepant pictures of aggressive development. Some of these discrepancies imply that the construct of antisocial behavior itself changes across development. Grabbing objects, tattling on others, and homicide are all valid measures, but developmental norms and base rates alter their validity at different ages. Tremblay et al. (2005) and Farrington (1993) suggest that different measures at different ages (e.g., fighting at age 8, vandalism at age 12, and homicide at age 18) may be indicators of the same underlying antisocial construct. Cairns (1979) described the concept of continuity across development as including intraindividual continuity (absolute stability), interindividual continuity (relative stability in rank), organizational continuity (the fact that the organism is fundamentally the same from birth to death), factor structure continuity (whether covariance matrices in variables are identical across ages), process continuity (whether rates of change or factors in change vary across age), and societal or generational continuity (whether the construct is conceptualized similarly across time by societies). Aggressive behavior is such a complex developmental construct partly because even though its intraindividual, factor-structure, and process continuities are weak, its interindividual continuity is strong.

The Emergence of Anger and Physical Aggression in Infancy

The fundamental human emotion of anger is crucial to survival because of its self-regulatory and social communication functions (Lemerise & Dodge, 2000). It prepares the body physiologically and psychologically to initiate self-protective and instrumental activity (Frijda, 1986) and may be an important reason for the adaptation and survival of the species (Lorenz, 1966). When not controlled properly, anger is a source of much human misery.

If anger is functional and innate, when does it emerge, and what are its earliest elicitors? Stenberg and Campos (1990) used a forearm restraint procedure to elicit responses in 1-, 4-, and 7-month-old infants. They grasped the infant's forearms, pulled them together, and held them approximately 6 inches in front of the infant's torso for up to 3 minutes. Even though 1-month-olds did display undifferentiated negative facial expressions, not one of the 16 1-month-olds displayed a discrete anger template that differentiated the anger expression from all other negative expressions. In contrast, 5 of the 16 infants at 4 months and 6 of the 16 infants at 7 months displayed the discrete anger template. Thus, even though the capacity for negative emotional expression is present by 1 month of age, only over the course of the first 4 months of life does a distinct anger response become coordinated.

At what age does anger expression come to have a social communication function? Stenberg and Campos (1990) found that, following restraint, 1-month-olds turned their heads randomly, but 4-month-olds turned their heads toward the frustrator or the frustrator's hands. Immediately following the onset of the first display of anger, 7-month-olds, but not 4-month-olds, turned their heads not toward the frustrator but toward their mothers. Stenberg and Campos (1990) concluded, "By at least 4 months anger facial displays may function as discrete social signals. These signals are at first directed proximally to the immediate source of frustration, but by 7 months they become expressed directly to social objects such as the mother" (pp. 270–271). The failure to observe a discrete anger expression in 1-month-olds does not rule out its existence at this age, because other stimuli might have elicited the anger response or other observational codes might be necessary to detect a different form of anger at an early age. Likewise, if intent-to-harm is a necessary component of aggression as it is defined here, labeling these behaviors as aggressive requires the scientist to make a high level of inference.

Aggression and Conflict in the Second Year of Life

Trivers (1974) suggested that conflict, anger, and aggression increase in frequency and intensity across the 2nd year of life in all mammalian species that undergo a prolonged period of symbiosis between mother and infant. Following a period of total dependence by the infant, the mother is motivated to help the infant achieve independence for survival, but the infant is ambivalent and may be motivated to sustain the mother's attention. The infant's growing size and weight or the birth of a younger sibling may accelerate the mother's interest in pushing the infant/toddler toward independence and the toddler's interest in keeping the mother's attention (Dunn, 1988). Mother-infant conflict is thus inevitable in the 2nd year of life as the individuation process intensifies (Mahler, 1968).

Although individual differences in intensity and ease of recovery from attack can be measured from responses to blood drawn as early as 2 days of life (Keenan, Gunthorpe, & Young, 2002), the stability of individual differences over the first several months of life is modest (Gunnar, Brodersen, & Krueger, 1996). Stable individual differences in anger expression emerge later during the 1st year and into the 2nd year of life (Stifter, Spinrad, & Braungart-Rieker, 1999). The earliest documented observations of peer-directed aggression have been found at the end of the 1st year of life. This period coincides with emerging interest in one's own possessions, in control over one's own activities, and in peer communication. Six-month-olds appear not to be bothered by peers who grab their objects or invade their space (Hay, Nash, & Pedersen, 1983). By 12 months of age, however, infants respond to peer provocations with protest and aggressive retaliation (Caplan, Vespo, Pedersen, & Hay, 1991). Up to half of all peer exchanges among children 12 to 18 months old involve conflict (Holmberg, 1977). Hay and Ross (1982) found that 87% of 21-month-old children participated in at least one conflict during four 15-minute laboratory peer group observation sessions.

Aggression during the Preschool Years

Although physical aggression decreases, verbal aggression increases normatively between 2 and 4 years of age (Cairns, 1979), coinciding with growth in expressive vocabulary. A twin study revealed that the negative correlation between physical aggression and expressive vocabulary in toddlers cannot be dismissed as due to a common genetic origin; rather, the most likely causal path goes from the development of expressive vocabulary to decreases in physical aggression (Dionne, Boivin, Tremblay, Laplante, & Perusse, 2003). But language onset also provides children with a new means of aggressing (e.g., through insults, threats, and name-calling), and the general parental perspective is that problem behavior by toddlers increases during this era. Jenkins, Bax, and Hart (1980) found that parental concerns about behavior problems and management peak at age 3. Other epidemiological studies have revealed high rates (up to 13%) of tantrum, peer fighting, and frustration tolerance problems in 3-year-olds, with declines thereafter (Crowther, Bond, & Rolf, 1981).

Whereas the most frequent elicitors of aggression in infancy are physical discomfort and the need for attention, elicitors become "habit training" in the 3rd year and peer conflicts and conflicts over material possessions (Fabes & Eisenberg, 1992) in the 4th and 5th

years. Caregivers' demands for compliance increase during these years, and the probability of noncompliant responses increases. Klimes-Dougan and Kopp (1999) found that, in response to a clean-up task, rates of noncompliance were 68% among 18-month-olds but as high as 97% among 30-month-olds. Abramovitch, Corter, and Lando (1979) found that siblings become a predominant source of agonistic behavior for preschoolers, with 45% of all interactions between younger and older siblings involving conflict.

Although relatively few sex differences have been found in infancy and toddlerhood in the rate and form of aggressive behaviors, by the time that children interact in naturally occurring preschool groups, the differences become striking (Underwood, 2003), especially in physical aggression.

Aggression during the Elementary School Years

It is not surprising that the start of elementary school is often experienced with a sense of relief by parents, both because behavior management is now shared with a teacher and because the overall level of aggressive behaviors decline. Analyses of mothers' Child Behavior Checklist Reports of the 1,195 children studied by the National Institute of Child Health and Human Development Early Child Care Research Network (2004) indicate "The most frequent form of early aggression, hits others, occurred in about 70% of the sample at ages 2 and 3, but declined to 20% by ages 4 and 5 (kindergarten), and to 12% by third grade" (p. 42). Keenan and Shaw (2003) have suggested that growth in self-control over emotion, known as the development of emotion regulation, is responsible for the decline in aggression during these years. Lingering problems with aggression during this period have been called adaptive disability (AD) and deficient self-regulation by Barkley et al. (2002).

Numerous factors may account for the joint growth in emotion regulation and decline in aggression across the period from 4 to 8 years of age, all of which are subsumed in the development of executive functions. Rapid neural development in the anterior cingulate gyrus during these years has been hypothesized by Posner and Rothbart (1998) to be responsible for the development of effortful control and, indirectly, decreases in aggressive behavior. Mischel (1974) suggested that the emerging ability to delay gratification is a crucial factor in declines in aggression during this era. Through interpersonal exchanges, children acquire cognitive strategies for delaying gratification (e.g., distraction, mentally representing delayed rewards) and effortful control (Eisenberg et al., 2004) that may help them avoid impulsive grabbing of others' possessions and hitting. The ability to delay gratification, in turn, may be aided by the corresponding development of broader representational abilities (Gelman & Baillargeon, 1983), perspective taking (Selman, 1980), empathy (Zahn-Waxler, Radke-Yarrow, & King, 1979), emotion processing (Schultz, Izard, & Bear, 2004), and memory strategies (Brown, Bransford, Ferrara, & Campione, 1983). Replicating the work of Eisenberg et al. (1999), Gilliom, Shaw, Beck, Schonberg, and Lukon (2002) found that the ability to deploy attention-shifting strategies such as seeking information about situational constraints and ignoring frustrating stimuli is associated with anger control at age 42 months and is predictive of teacher-reported externalizing problems at age 6. Eisenberg and Fabes (1999) have articulated a broader theory of emergent emotional self-regulation during this period, with children progressing from externally controlled regulation to internally mediated cognitive controls that lead to reduced aggressive behavior. Quite a different explanation for declines in aggression during this period is that peers begin to provide feedback to aggressors that extinguishes aggression.

With the gradual decline in the rate of aggression comes a shift in its form and function. An increasing proportion of aggressive behaviors becomes directed toward specific dyadic relationships (Coie et al., 1999), and its form becomes increasingly hostile, in contrast with the relatively nonsocial, instrumental nature of aggression in the preschool period. Aggressive behaviors also become more person-directed and relational (Crick & Bigbee, 1998). Finally, covert forms of antisocial behavior such as lying, cheating, and stealing emerge with greater frequency (Loeber, Farrington, Stouthamer-Loeber, & van Kammen, 1998).

Major elicitors of aggression come to include perceived threats and insults to one's ego (Schwartz, Mc-Fadden-Ketchum, Dodge, Pettit, & Bates, 1998). Although the emerging recognition that provocations may be accidental contributes to declines in aggression, the emergent recognition that another may be acting with intentional and hostile motives instigates increased retaliatory, angry responding (Gifford-Smith & Rabiner, 2004). During the early elementary school years, children learn that some actions are unintended but others are under the volitional control of the actor; the result is that the attribution that a peer has acted with hostile intent has an inflammatory effect (Hubbard, Dodge, Cillessen, Coie, & Schwartz, 2001).

An important distinction made during this age period is between reactive and proactive aggression. Animal behaviorists have long distinguished between hostile-affective (reactive) aggression, characterized by intensive patterned autonomic arousal, anger, and defensive postures that lead to frenzied attacks in response to perceived threat, and instrumental (proactive) aggression, characterized by little autonomic activation but highly patterned appetitive behavior oriented toward a reward (Lorenz, 1966). These behaviors have been distinguished reliably in direct observations of children aged 5 to 9 (Coie et al., 1999), teacher ratings, and ratings of violent behaviors in clinical records (Dodge et al., 1997). Vitaro, Brendgen, and Tremblay (2002) found distinct correlates of these two types of aggression in inattentiveness and anxiety (reactives higher) and in overt delinquency (proactives higher). Smithmyer, Hubbard, and Simons (2000) found that proactive aggression is a function of outcome expectancies, whereas reactive aggression grows out of maltreatment and emotion dysregulation (Shields & Cicchetti, 1998).

Although most children aggress less frequently during the elementary school years, a select few become highly troublesome to peers, parents, and teachers (Loeber et al., 1998). It is during the elementary school years that many children, boys especially, are referred to mental health clinics for conduct problems. Lahey and Loeber (1994) have outlined a developmental path for aggressive conduct problems, beginning with oppositional defiant disorder (ODD), which is characterized by temper tantrums and defiant, irritable, blameful, argumentative, and annoying behavior. These behaviors are not uncommon at 4 to 5 years of age (Achenbach & Edelbrock, 1983) but become less common and clinically problematic by age 8 (Loeber, Lahey, & Thomas, 1991). Clinically referred elementary school children typically do not present with these problems as new symptoms; rather, these children have been unable to outgrow problems that have carried over from earlier times (Loeber, Tremblay, Gagnon, & Charlebois, 1989). Some ODD children begin to diversify their deviant repertoire in the elementary school years (usually about age 8 to 11) to include setting fires, lying, fighting, weapon use, and vandalism (Loeber et al., 1998). This pattern is called conduct disorder (CD), and its prevalence in the United States is about 9% of males and 2% of females (American Psychological Association, 1994). Canadian surveys of 3,300 children indicate a prevalence of 7% of males and 3% of females (Offord, Boyle, & Racine, 1989).

Between age 11 and 13, a subset of children who could be diagnosed as CD begin to diversify their deviant behaviors even further to include violent criminal behavior such as mugging, breaking and entering, and forced sex. The group of children whose early aggressive behavior does not dissipate over time has been called early starters (Moffitt, 1993). Broidy et al. (2003) used Nagin and Tremblay's (1999) semiparametric methods to identify trajectories of aggressive development with six independent longitudinal samples from across the world. In all samples, a group of early starting aggressive boys was found to persist in physically aggressive behavior across the ages 7 to 13.

Aggression during the Adolescent Years

Loeber et al. (1998) concluded that most longitudinal studies show decrements in ratings of aggressive behavior as children enter adolescence. However, adolescence is a time when serious acts of violence increase, as age-crime curves regularly demonstrate (e.g., U.S. Department of Justice, 2003), when a second group of youth joins the early starting group in antisocial behavior, and when aggressive behavior broadens to new contexts, including romantic relationships.

Growth of Serious Violence

Data from the National Youth Survey (NYS) of 1,725 youths first surveyed in 1976 (D. Elliott & Huizinga, 1983) indicate that violent offending almost always begins in the adolescent years. Self-reports of serious violent offenses (SVOs, defined as aggravated assault, robbery, or rape, necessarily involving some injury or a weapon) rise sharply from age 12 to 20. The onset hazard rate (first-time offending) for SVOs is almost zero (< 0.5%) through age 11 but doubles between ages 13 and 14 and rises sharply to 5.1% at age 16. The onset rate then halves between ages 16 and 18 and declines to less than 1% after age 20. Thus, over half of the persons who become involved in serious violent offending, prior to age 27, commit their first violent offense between the ages of 14 and 17, and almost all offenders commit their first offense before age 21. Not only is the rise in first-time offending dramatic, but the overall prevalence rates for offending in adolescence are also startlingly high. At the peak age of 17, 19% of males and 12% of females reported committing at least one SVO.

Official arrest records reported by the Federal Bureau of Investigation (FBI; U.S. Department of Justice, 2003) indicate 3 to 4 times lower prevalence rates of SVOs and a similar but lagged (delayed) curvilinear developmental function. At age 17, about 15% of all boys in the United States are arrested (Blumstein, 2000). Of those adolescents who commit offenses, only 15% to 33% are in fact arrested (Farrington, 1989). Of those arrested, about 64% are referred to juvenile or adult court, and of those referred to court, only about 2% to 10% are incarcerated. Thus, very few offenders are ever incarcerated. Because those arrested probably are a very biased group of all offenders, due to gender, socioeconomic, and racial discrimination, arrest records and self-reports provide different pictures of violence (Huizinga & Dunford, 1985). Based solely on arrest records, Weiner (1989) concluded that most first-time SVOs occur between ages 18 and 24. However, as noted by D. Elliott (1994), "If we assume the accuracy of both (self-report and official record) measures, it appears that most first arrests for a violent offense in a serious violent career take place several years after the initiation into this type of behavior and extend into ages where the hazard rate for initiation is close to 0" (p. 10).

Ethnic differences in aggression in the social context of the United States are almost negligible in the elementary school years (Achenbach, 1991) but are more pronounced in adolescence. Arrest record data indicate that even though African American youth make up 15% of the juvenile population, they account for 52% of those arrested for juvenile violent crimes (Dryfoos, 1990). The lifetime chances that an urban African American male will be arrested for an FBI "index" offense (murder, forcible rape, aggravated assault, robbery, burglary, larceny, and auto theft) is 50%, in contrast with 14% for urban White males (Blumstein & Cohen, 1987). The problem is so great that more African American male adolescents are incarcerated or on probation for a crime than are gainfully employed (Edelman, 1992). Self-reports indicate a much narrower race difference in actual behavior, however. The Black-to-White ratio in prevalence of SVOs is about 5 to 4, a statistically significant but substantially small effect (D. Elliott, 1994). When socioeconomic class confounds are controlled, this ratio is reduced to about 7 to 6. D. Elliott (1994) has reported that the higher prevalence rate of self-reported SVOs among African Americans can be almost entirely accounted for by the particularly high risk of onset between the ages of 13 and 16 for African American male adolescents. This age period obviously is a risky one for this group in terms of self-reported SVOs, but an even more tragic time in terms of arrest rates and rates of victimization.

These data suggest common developmental patterns in serious violence that begin with minor aggressive acts and delinquent behaviors in middle childhood and progress to frequent and serious offending by age 17. The initiation of substance use and sexual activity adds incrementally to the risk for increased aggressive behavior during this period (Jessor, Donovan, & Costa, 1991). D. Elliott (1994) concluded that minor forms of delinquent behavior and alcohol use typically precede more serious forms of violence. Thus, the developmental path for a small portion of the population involves progressively serious and violent behaviors, although most offenders usually desist from crime in early adulthood.

Adolescent Culture

In American peer culture, physical aggression and delinquent deviance become more socially acceptable during adolescence (Coie, Terry, Zakriski, & Lochman, 1995). Moffitt (1993) hypothesized that early starting children contribute to the growth of a deviant peer culture by acting as role models and by offering opportunities for deviant behavior. Indeed, some deviant youth begin to hold positive status among peers (Miller-Johnson & Costanzo, 2004). The positive correlation between physical aggression and being disliked by peers dissolves during middle school (Cillessen & Mayeux, 2004), and the base rates of self-reported antisocial behavior rise. In turn, as the contextual normativeness of antisocial behavior increases, the effects of this context are to increase the display of aggressive behavior by individual youth (Espelage, Holt, & Henkel, 2003). The new group of aggressors has been called adolescence-limited by Moffitt (1993), who asserted that this group engages in delinquent behavior only during adolescence.

Violence in Romantic Relationships

Studying a representative birth cohort in New Zealand, Magdol, Moffitt, Caspi, and Silva (1998) found that 32% of late-adolescent males and females reported perpetrating physical aggression in an intimate relationship during the past year. This domain is one of the few in which violence by females equals that by males, although male violence is more likely to result in partner injury (Archer, 2000). Although many individuals who are violent toward intimate partners are also violent in other situations, quite a few display violence only in this context (Holtzworth-Munroe & Stuart, 1994). Indeed, existing theory and research concerning intimate partner violence generally is based on the premise that intimate partner violence is distinct from other forms of violence (Moffitt, Krueger, Caspi, & Fagan, 2000).

Aggression during Adulthood

Most self-report studies indicate that between ages 18 and 25 the overall rate of aggressive behavior declines, and virtually no new cases of antisocial behavior begin in adulthood (Robins, 1966). Sampson and Laub (2003) examined trajectories of adult development in the Glueck sample of delinquents and found that further declines in crime are found after age 35 in all groups of early offenders. In the Cambridge study, Farrington (1993) found that self-reported prevalence of all criminal behaviors, including violence, decreased markedly in early adulthood, for example, self-reports of burglary decreased from 11% at age 18 to 5% at age 21 and 2% at both ages 25 and 32. In the NYS, D. Elliott, Huizinga, and Menard (1989) found that self-reported offending peaked at age 17 and declined linearly in subsequent years. Official arrest record data indicate a similar decline in violent offending in adulthood, although the decline as measured by arrests begins later and is less sharp than that by self-reports (Blumstein, 2000).

An important caveat to these findings is that almost all of these studies fail to include child abuse and spousal battery as instances of violence. Thus, it might be misleading to conclude that adulthood brings about less violence. Straus and Gelles (1990) reported that 16% of American couples report physically assaulting each other, and 11% report physically abusing their children, in the past 12 months; however, systematic epidemiological research that would adequately describe the life course and origins of child and spouse abuse does not yet exist. Huesmann, Eron, Lefkowitz, and Walder (1984) have reported some continuity between peer-directed aggression at age 8 and spousal and child abuse at age 30, suggesting that this behavior may have similar antecedents to other forms of violence.

There is a significant exception to the general pattern of decline in serious violence in early adulthood, for both early-starting and late-starting youth (Coie, 2004). Among African American males, there is no decline in violence from age 22 to 30. Nearly twice as many African Americans continue their violent careers as do Whites; thus, the violent careers of African Americans last longer than they do for Whites (D. Elliott, 1994), in sharp contrast with the finding of few race differences in the propensity for initial violence. It seems that the underclass, especially poor African American males, are unable to escape the system of incarceration, labeling, unemployment, and negative identity once the course of violence begins. As D. Elliott (1994), concluded:

> Once involved in a lifestyle that includes serious forms of violence, theft, and substance use, persons from disadvantaged families and neighborhoods find it very difficult to escape. They have fewer opportunities for conventional adult roles, and they are more deeply embedded in and dependent upon the gangs and the illicit economy that flourish in their neighborhoods. . . . Poverty is related less to the onset of violence than to the continuity of violence, once initiated. (p. 19)

It is important to note that there is no race disparity in continuing violence among persons who are employed at ages 18 to 20 or married or living with a partner. The evidence suggests that those persons who are able to establish stable work and family life and careers, regardless of ethnicity, tend to give up their involvement in criminal violence (Rutter, 1989). As D. Elliott (1994) pointed out, these findings have enormous implications for the focus of intervention, which might be directed toward job training and economic opportunity.

Continuity of Individual Differences in Adulthood

The early starter model of antisocial individuals posits that early starters are more likely to continue breaking the law in their adult years than are the late starters. The distinction between early and late starters, however, cannot be sharply drawn because curves for the onset of offending do not show clear demarcation and some so-called late starters do continue offending in the adult years. Continuity of offending into adult years has been shown by Farrington (1995). Nearly 75% of those convicted of juvenile offenses (at age 10 to 16) were reconvicted between age 17 and 24, and half of the juvenile offenders were reconvicted between age 25 and 32. Thus, although the peak of offending in this study was age 17, a substantial number of juvenile offenders continue in criminal careers well into adulthood.

The continuity of antisocial activity in adulthood takes on other forms besides criminal offending. This heterotypic continuity includes spouse abuse, drunk driving, moving traffic violations, and severe punishment of children (Huesmann, Eron, et al., 1984), what

Pulkkinen (1990) described as a relapsed lifestyle, and less stable marriages that more frequently end in divorce (Caspi, Elder, & Bem, 1987). Longitudinal studies also reflect substantial discontinuity. Not all early-starting antisocial youth become adult offenders or follow the pathway of poor occupational or marital adjustment.

The idea that a stable marriage and regular employment provide support for desistance from crime is consistent with social control theories of crime. Sampson and Laub's (2003) analyses of the Glueck and Glueck (1968) longitudinal study indicated that strong ties to adult institutions, such as work and family, protect one from subsequent criminal behavior among those with a previous history of delinquency. Job stability had a consistently inverse influence on crime and deviance in young adulthood (age 17 to 25) and in later adulthood (age 25 to 32), whereas income did not have effects when other factors were controlled. Following up that part of the sample that had been married at some time, Sampson and Laub found that marital cohesiveness had a significant effect on crime and deviance, independent of other factors. Sampson and Laub (1990) concluded that "job stability is central in explaining adult desistance from crime; however, this effect is reduced among those who were never married, for whom attachment to wife assumes greater relative importance" (p. 621).

GENDER AND AGGRESSION

Long-standing interest in the issue of gender differences in antisocial behavior has typically taken two forms. One is interest in the size of the difference between men and women as a function of developmental phase and the type of antisocial behavior examined. The other focus is on differences in the processes and outcomes of antisocial behavior for males and females. The evidence is stronger in the first case than in the second.

Physical Aggression

Gender differences begin to emerge as early as 3 years of age, particularly for more serious and stable aggression. Crick, Casas, and Mosher (1997) found that teachers rated preschool boys aged 3 to 5 as more aggressive than girls. Kingston and Prior (1995) used annual maternal assessments taken between ages 3 and 8 in the 1,721 participants in the Australian Temperament Project to find that 41 out of the 53 members of a stable aggressive group were boys.

These differences in physical aggression remain stable through childhood and adolescence. Broidy et al. (2003) examined developmental trajectories of physical aggression in six large, well-known, longitudinal samples from three different countries: the Pittsburgh Youth Study and Child Development Project from the United States, the Dunedin and Christchurch studies from New Zealand, and the Montreal and Quebec samples from Canada. These authors found that "girls exhibit lower mean levels of physical aggression than do boys across all four sites with comparable data for boys and girls. Even among girls who exhibit chronic physical aggression across assessment periods, their mean levels of physical aggression are notably lower than those of chronic physically aggressive boys in the same sample" (p. 232). Stanger, Achenbach, and Verhulst (1997) found that boys were more aggressive than girls at every age from 4 to 18, using the aggression subscale of the Child Behavior Checklist (CBC) in a sample of over 2,000 Dutch children.

Antisocial Behavior

Similar sex differences have been observed for antisocial behavior more broadly defined. Stanger et al. (1997) reported that scores on the delinquency subscale of the CBC were higher for boys than girls at every age from 4 to 18. Gender differences on the externalizing subscale, a combination of aggression and delinquency, have been found across 12 different cultures (Crijnen, Achenbach, & Verhulst, 1997). In their intensive examination of gender differences in antisocial behavior using data from the Dunedin Study, Moffitt, Caspi, Rutter, and Silva (2001) reported that males score higher on antisocial behavior from age 5 to age 21 on parent, teacher, informant, and self-reports. The difference between boys and girls, averaged across method, ranged from .15 standard deviations at age 15 to almost a half standard deviation at age 21. Finally, Fergusson and Horwood (2002) examined the offending trajectories from ages 8 until 20 for boys and girls enrolled in the Christchurch study and found that the female offending rate was about half the male offending rate at all ages.

Conduct Disorder

Not surprisingly, similar gender differences are found when CD is examined. In the Virginia Twin Study of Adolescent Development, Simonoff et al. (1997) found a rate for CD of 5.9% for boys compared to 2.8% for girls. This sex ratio is consistent with the ratios obtained from other epidemiological studies. For example, Costello et al. (1996) reported a sex ratio of 4.8:1 in the Great Smoky Mountains study. The sex ratio in the New York State study was 2.3:1 (P. Cohen et al., 1993) and in the Ontario study it was 2.4:1 (Offord et al., 1989).

The gender differences are especially pronounced for more severe conduct problems that begin early. Moffit and Caspi (2001), using data from the Dunedin Study, identified two groups of antisocial individuals using data from age 5 through age 18: life-course persistent (LCP) offenders and adolescent limited (AL) offenders. Twenty-six percent of males were placed into the AL group compared to 18% of females. In contrast, 10% of males were placed in the LCP group compared to only 1% of females. Thus, the male-to-female ratio for the LCP path was 10:1, whereas the sex ratio for the AL path was 1.5:1.

Female Aggression

One type of antisocial behavior for which there is either very little difference between boys and girls (Underwood, 2003) or for which girls actually score higher than boys (Crick & Zahn-Waxler, 2003) has been studied under several terms, each of which is meant to refer to a type of aggression that is more subtle than physical aggression and which may be used preferentially by girls. Indirect aggression has been defined as "a noxious behavior in which the target person is attacked not physically or directly through verbal intimidation but in a circuitous way, through social manipulation" (Kaukiainen et al., 1999). Galen and Underwood (1997) defined social aggression as aggression "directed toward damaging and another's self-esteem, social status, or both" (p. 589). Relational aggression has been defined as "harming others through purposeful manipulation and damage of their peer relationships" (Crick & Grotpeter, 1995, p. 711). Although there may be subtle differences between these conceptions (see Underwood, 2003), they are highly overlapping constructs and we treat them as assessing a single type of aggression that we label, following Underwood, *social aggression*.

Social aggression can be reliably identified using multiple methods in children as young as 3 years old (Crick et al., 1997). An explosion in interest on the topic has resulted in dozens of studies that examine the construct from early childhood until late adolescence. In terms of gender differences, there is agreement that this construct references a form of aggression that is more normative in girls than is physical aggression. There is disagreement, however, as to whether girls are more socially aggressive than boys.

Results are mixed in preschool studies. McNeilly-Choque, Hart, Robinson, Nelson, and Olsen (1996) found that 4- and 5-year-old girls, relative to boys, displayed more relationally aggressive behaviors on the playground and were rated as more relationally aggressive by classmates and teachers. Crick et al. (1997) found that girls were more relationally aggressive than boys according to teacher ratings but not according to peer nominations. A study by Hart, Nelson, Robinson, Olsen, and McNeilly-Choque (1998) of Russian nursery school children failed to find gender differences for relational aggression as did a study of Head Start and community preschool participants (Kupersmidt, Bryant, & Willoughby, 2000).

The issue of gender differences is no clearer in middle childhood. Archer, Pearson, and Westeman (1998), using observational data from a sample of 7- to 11-year-olds in Great Britain, found that girls engaged in more verbal aggression than did boys. However, a cross-cultural study using peer ratings found that boys were rated as more verbally aggressive than girls (Osterman et al., 1994). Tiet, Wasserman, Loeber, McReynolds, and Miller (2001) used parent reports of relational aggression for boys and girls aged 4 to 18 and found no gender differences. However, Crick (1996) used teacher reports to find that girls were more relationally aggressive than boys. Studies using peer nominations are also discordant. Crick and colleagues often report that girls receive more nominations for relational aggression than do boys (e.g., Crick & Grotpeter, 1995). Other studies, using the same methodology, have either failed to find gender differences in relational aggression (e.g., Rys & Bear, 1997) or have found that boys received more nominations for relational aggression than girls (e.g., David & Kistner, 2000).

In adolescence, the picture is the same. Several studies report that girls are more socially aggressive than boys, whereas others find no differences or that boy are more socially aggressive than girls. For example, for verbal aggression, Salmivalli, Kaukiainen, and Lagerspetz (2000) found that 15- and 16-year-old boys were rated by peers as higher in verbal aggression than girls, but Kashani and Shepperd (1990) failed to find gender differences in verbal aggression. For indirect aggression, one study found that girls were more aggressive than boys (Salmivalli et al., 2000) and two other studies failed to find such dif-

ferences (Pakaslahti & Keltigangas-Jarvinen, 2000). Results are also mixed for studies of social aggression (Paquette & Underwood, 1999).

Gender Differences in Process

It is clear that for most forms of antisocial behavior boys are more antisocial than girls. What is not clear, however, is whether the processes that lead to antisocial behavior are the same or different for girls and boys. Moffitt et al. (2001) examined correlations separately for males and females between antisocial behavior and five classes of important risk factors: maternal factors, family factors, cognitive and neurological factors, child behavior factors, and peer factors. Of the 35 correlations examined, 14 differed significantly for males and females. These differences, however, were differences in magnitude rather than direction: All correlations were in the same direction and, in almost every case, the correlation was significant for both males and females.

DETERMINANTS OF INDIVIDUAL DIFFERENCES IN ANTISOCIAL BEHAVIOR

Causes of individual differences in antisocial behavior range from genetic to socialization, and contemporary models integrate these factors through interactions, transactions, moderation, and mediation.

Genetics

It is homiletic to say that antisocial behavior is the result of both nature and nurture. To move beyond homily, we must disentangle these effects and examine their interplay. This is the realm of behavior genetics, which relies on genetically sensitive designs (e.g., twin and adoption studies) to accomplish these goals. Genetically sensitive designs utilize the differing degrees of genetic similarity in relatives (e.g., monozygotic and dizygotic twins, parents and children, stepsiblings) to determine how much of the variance in a trait is due to variation in genetic similarity and environmental similarity.

Contemporary behavior-genetics researchers provide estimates of four types of influences. The first two, additive and nonadditive genetic effects, constitute heritability. The third component, shared environment, indexes the degree to which environmental factors are responsible for the resemblance of family members. The fourth component, nonshared environment, indexes the degree to which environmental factors contribute to differences between family members.

Before examining the estimates themselves, two cautions are important to note. First, it is understood that genetic effects may be mediated environmentally through gene-environment transactions in which genes influence surrounding environments, which, in turn, influence phenotypic expression (cf., Scarr & McCartney, 1983). In behavior genetics studies, the effects of such transactions are included in the heritability estimates and not counted as environmental effects. Second, all estimates are context specific. The influence of genes on behavior varies across social contexts, and a change in the social context may change the relative importance of genes and environment (cf., Dunne et al., 1997).

Even with these cautions, the conclusions from this research regarding the relative influences of genes and environment on antisocial behavior are impossible to escape. Over 100 quantitative genetic studies on antisocial behavior have been published from more than 60 different samples, with over one-third of these published in the past 10 years. As Moffitt (2005) has written, there is a "new look" about the current generation of behavior genetics studies. The samples have grown larger, more representative, and more global. Reports have appeared from large, representative samples in Australia, the Netherlands, Scandanavia, the United Kingdom, and the United States. Statistical techniques have grown more sophisticated. Multiple sources (i.e., self-reports, reports from others, and observational reports) have been utilized to measure antisocial behavior. Finally, research has spanned the entire range of development from early childhood to late adulthood. Two examples of the new behavior genetics approach appear below.

Arseneault et al. (2003) reported on the results of a behavior-genetic analysis among 5-year-old children from the Environmental Risk Longitudinal Twin Study (E-risk), which drew an initial 1,210 families from a national registry of twins born in England and Wales with an over-representation of high-risk families defined as young age of the mother at first birth. Antisocial behavior was assessed using mother, teacher, examiner, and self-reports. In univariate analyses, considering one antisocial behavior variable at a time, heritability estimates ranged from .42 for self-reports to .76 for teacher reports, nonshared environmental estimates ranged from .24 for teacher reports to .58 for child reports, and shared environmental estimates were zero. Multivariate analyses, which included a common latent ASB factor

that combined across raters and contexts as well as four specific factors corresponding to each informant, revealed that 82% of the variance in the common latent factor was influenced by genetic influences with the remaining 18% influenced by nonshared environment. Similarly, moderate proportions of the variance unique to each reporter were accounted for by genetic influences. Thus, measures that combine across social contexts yield estimates that minimize environmental estimates and maximize genetic estimates.

O'Connor, McGuire, Reiss, Hetherington, and Plomin (1998) reported results from the Nonshared Environment and Adolescent Development (NEAD) project. The goals of this project were to identify sources of nonshared environment, estimate its impact on adolescent development, and integrate genetic and environmental models of adolescent development. The sample consisted of 720 same-sex adolescent siblings between 10 and 18 years of age, including monozygotic and dizygotic twins, full siblings, half siblings, and unrelated siblings. Antisocial behavior was assessed using multiple instruments collected from multiple sources. Results from model-fitting analyses yielded estimates of .56 for the genetic component, .25 for shared environment, and .19 for nonshared environment.

Rhee and Waldman (2002) recently meta-analyzed the genetic influences on antisocial behavior from 42 independent twin samples and 10 adoption samples. These studies varied in their operationalizations of antisocial behavior, sources of information, and ages of the participants. The best-fitting model for the data included additive genetic influences (.32), nonadditive genetic influences (.09), shared environmental influences (.16), and nonshared environmental influences (.43). Following this overall analysis, the authors examined potential moderators of the estimates. They found no differences as a function of gender. Differences, however, were identified as functions of operationalization and age. For diagnosis (e.g., CD or antisocial personality disorder), aggression, and antisocial behavior (an omnibus operationalization) a model that included additive genetic, shared, and nonshared environmental influences best fit the data. Heritability estimates were .44, .44, and .47 for diagnosis, aggression, and antisocial behavior, respectively. Estimates for shared and nonshared environment were .11 and .45, .06 and .50, and .22 and .31 for diagnosis, aggression, and antisocial behavior, respectively. For antisocial behavior assessed via criminality, however, the best-fitting model included an additive genetic component (.33), a nonadditive genetic component (.42), and a nonshared environment component (.25). Age also significantly moderated the magnitude of genetic and environmental influences with the magnitude of familial influences decreasing with age and the magnitude of nonfamilial influences increasing. For children, additive genetic effects accounted for 46% of the variance, shared environment accounted for 20%, and nonshared accounted for the remaining 34%. The corresponding figures for adolescents were .43, .16, and .41; for adults, these figures were .41, .09, and .50. In general, these results suggest that there are moderate genetic (.41) and nonshared environmental effects (.43), and small shared environmental effects (.16) on antisocial behavior.

A recent review by Moffitt (2005) came to similar conclusions as Rhee and Waldman. One moderator not examined by Rhee and Waldman (2002), but discussed in detail by Moffitt, is the type of offender in question. Moffitt argues that LCP antisocial behavior may be more heritable than AL antisocial behavior. First, she points to the results from studies of large representative samples of very young twins that yield higher heritability coefficients than those reported by Rhee and Waldman (2002), ranging from 50% for externalizing behaviors among 2- to 3-year-old boys to 76% for teacher reports of antisocial behavior among 5-year-olds. Second, Moffitt points to several studies that have shown higher heritability for the Aggression (around 60%) than the Delinquency (around 30 to 40%) subscales of the CBCL (Achenbach, 1991). She argues that because the Aggression scale measures antisocial personality and physical violence and its scores are relatively stable across development, it is a better measure of LCP antisocial behavior than the delinquency scale, which measures rule-breaking and shows a rise in its mean scores across adolescence. Third, Moffitt points to two studies that have contrasted preadolescent onset antisocial behavior against antisocial behavior that begins during adolescence, showing that preadolescent onset is substantially more heritable. Finally, she points to two studies demonstrating that the heritability of antisocial behavior that persists from adolescence into adulthood is more heritable than antisocial behavior confined to adolescence.

Gene-by-Environment Interactions

Studies of antisocial behavior were among the first to document interactions between genetic and environmen-

tal risk factors. Mednick and Christiansen (1977) provided the first evidence that genetic and environmental risk factors interact to produce offending. Among the 6,000 families in the Danish Adoption Study, 14% of adoptees were convicted when neither their biological nor adoptive parents had been convicted of a crime; 15% were convicted if only their adoptive parent had been convicted; 20% were convicted if only their biological parent had been; finally, 25% were convicted if both their adoptive and biological parents had been convicted.

The dynamic interaction effect was found to be even stronger in several later studies. Cloninger, Sigvardsson, Bohman, and van Knoring (1982), in a sample of 2000 Swedish adoptees, found that 3% were convicted if both biological and rearing environments were normal; 7% offended if only rearing were abnormal; 12% offended in the face of offending in the biological parent; however, 40% offended if both the biological parent offended and the rearing environment was abnormal. Cadoret, Cain, and Crowe (1983), in a sample of 500 adoptees, found that the most antisocial adoptees were those that had birth mothers with antisocial personality disorder or alcoholism *and* came from adoptive homes marked by adverse circumstances. These findings were replicated in a separate sample by Cadoret, Yates, Troughton, Woodworth, and Stewart (1995) who showed that adversity in adoptive homes (e.g., marital or problems, substance use, psychopathology) interacted with antisocial personality disorder in the biological parents to predict childhood and adolescent antisocial behavior. Similar findings have been reported in twin studies as well. Jaffe et al. (in press), in the E-risk twin study, showed that environmental risk interacted with genetic risk to predict CD; physical maltreatment was associated with a 24% increase in the probability of CD among twins at high genetic risk (i.e., having a co-twin with conduct disorder), but only a 2% increase among twins at low risk. Thus, there is a *stronger* environmental impact among subgroups at higher genetic risk.

Caspi et al. (2002) provided evidence for the interaction between a specific gene and environmental risk in predicting antisocial behavior. These authors examined the interaction between childhood maltreatment and a functional polymorphism in the MAO-A gene in 442 males from the Dunedin Multidisciplinary Health and Development Study. The MAO-A gene was chosen because it encodes the MAO-A enzyme, which is responsible for metabolizing neurotransmitters, such as norepinephrine, dopamine, and serotonin, several of which have been linked with antisocial behavior. Caspi et al. reported a significant interaction between childhood maltreatment and MAO-A genotype, such that 85% of the males with the low-activity allele and a history of childhood maltreatment developed some form of antisocial outcome. Importantly, this finding was recently replicated in the 514 male twins from the Virginia Twin Study for Adolescent Behavioral Development (Foley et al., 2004). These authors found an interaction between the MAO-A genotype and childhood adversity (i.e., parental neglect, interparental violence, and inconsistent discipline) in predicting CD. As in the Caspi et al. study, individuals with low MAO-A activity and an adverse childhood environment were the most likely to develop CD. Again, there is a *stronger* environmental impact among subpopulations at higher genetic risk.

Thus, antisocial behavior is quite heritable, especially for LCP antisocial behavior and individuals growing up in risky environments. Genes, and therefore biological factors, play an important role in the causation of antisocial behavior. However, there are several caveats to this conclusion. First, these results do not imply that antisocial behavior is the result of a single gene; as noted by Carey and Goldman (1997) "it defies credulity to imagine that millions of years of primate and the hominid evolution produced a sequence of DNA whose raison d'etre is to forge checks or cheat on income taxes" (p. 249). They do not imply anything about the cause of antisocial behavior in a given individual; heritability is a population statistic. They do not imply immutability; phenylketonuria is a simple single-gene recessive disorder whose ill effects (i.e., mental retardation) can be eliminated by an environmental intervention (i.e., avoiding phenylalanine in the diet). Next, there are caveats about the estimates themselves. As noted earlier, the estimates of genetic effects include gene-environment transactions in which genes influence surrounding environments, which, in turn, influence phenotypic expression. The ratings of aggressive and antisocial behavior typically used (i.e., ratings by teachers, parents, peers, or the self) represent generalized perceptions about someone's aggressive behavior. They necessarily ignore the context-specificity of antisocial behavior. The latent modeling techniques used to composite data from multiple sources (e.g., multiple raters) typically lead to a loss of rater-specific information. Although some information that is lost may be error, at least some substantial portion may reflect the different

contexts in which different raters have observed the individual, which represent real environmental effects. This conclusion is consistent with Arseneault et al.'s (2003) finding that source-specific factors (separate parent, teacher, child, and examiner ratings) were less heritable than the combined factor. Thus, these studies are most relevant to understanding antisocial personalities rather than antisocial behaviors.

There are also conclusions to be drawn about environmental influence. The contribution of shared or common environment to antisocial behavior, although small, is larger than for other psychiatric disorders (Kendler, Prescott, Myers, & Neale, 2003). Consistent with research in other areas, the contribution of nonshared environment is moderate. Taken together, these findings indicate an important role for the environment. However, they do suggest that it is the "person-specific" experiences of individuals in families that are the more important environmental causes.

Dispositional Factors

Personality (i.e., characteristic ways of thinking, feeling, and acting) and its earliest manifestations in temperament have been studied in relation to antisocial behavior for a number of years. The evidence for the influence of both personality and temperament is mounting. Large, prospective studies have shown that early temperament is predictive of antisocial behavior in the preschool period (Keenan, Shaw, Delliquadri, Giovanelli, & Walsh, 1998), childhood (Raine, Reynolds, Venables, Mednick, & Farrington, 1998), and even into adolescence (Caspi et al., 1994). Personality is robustly related to antisocial behavior in childhood (e.g., Krueger, Caspi, Moffitt, White, & Stouthamer-Loeber, 1996) and adulthood (Ball, Tennen, Poling, Kranzler, & Rounsaville, 1997). Thus, the question is no longer is there a relation, but which dimensions of temperament and personality are most strongly related to antisocial behavior?

Temperament

Buss and Plomin (1984, p. 84) define temperament as "inherited personality traits present in early childhood"; thus, we restrict our review to those studies that have measured temperament in early life. Original work on temperament by Thomas, Chess, and Birch (1968) identified nine separable dimensions: (1) activity level, (2) threshold, (3) mood, (4) rhythmicity, (5) approach/withdrawal, (6) intensity, (7) adaptability, (8) distractibility, and (9) attention span/persistence. The authors identified three constellations of these dimensions that they believed were clinically significant: (1) difficult temperament, (2) easy temperament, and (3) slow-to-warm-up temperament. The first of these, difficult temperament, has been frequently examined in the context of antisocial behavior and conduct problems; it refers to children who are irregular in their behavior, tend to withdraw from novel situations, are slow to adapt to environmental change, react intensely, and experience predominantly irritable and negative mood. Several studies have found that early measured difficult temperament is predictive of later antisocial behavior. Bates found that mothers' ratings of infant temperament as early as age 6 months significantly predict mothers' ratings of child conduct problems at age 3 years (Bates, Maslin, & Frankel, 1985) and, to a lesser degree, mothers' CBCL Externalizing Scores at age 7 to 8 years (Bates, Bayles, Bennett, Ridge, & Brown, 1991). Similar results have been obtained from the Australian Temperament Project, a prospective, longitudinal study of temperament and development in a large and representative sample of a whole state population. Kingston and Prior (1995) found that early "difficult" temperament significantly discriminated children whose aggression started early and maintained over time from other aggressive and nonaggressive children.

As noted above, the construct of difficult temperament is a concretion of multiple elements of temperament and is therefore of limited use in understanding which specific elements of temperament are important predictors of outcomes. Studies that have utilized more specific measurements of temperament indicate that the strongest predictors of later antisocial behavior are, borrowing terminology from Rothbart, Ahadi, and Evans (2000), dimensions dealing with fearlessness, irritability/anger/frustration, and effortful control. Many cross-sectional studies and short-term longitudinal studies have found these dimensions to be moderately related to aggression and conduct problems in early, middle, and late childhood (e.g., Lengua, West, & Sandler, 1998). For example, in a study of 214 children aged 4.5 to 8 years, Eisenberg, Cumberland, et al. (2001) found that measures of fear, anger, and control distinguished children with externalizing problems from other children defined when using parent and teacher reports. In one of the strongest demonstrations, Valiente et al. (2003) found that effortful control rated by parents and teachers was related to externalizing problems at age 11 even after controlling for effortful control and externalizing problems 4 years earlier. These results typically hold for mother-reported temperament and observationally assessed temperament (Eisenberg, Cumberland, et al., 2001).

Even more impressive, however, are the results from longer-term longitudinal studies from several countries. Shaw, Gilliom, Ingoldsby, and Nagin (2003) identified developmental trajectories of conduct problems from ages 2 to 8 in a sample of 284 low-income boys from an American city. They found that observed fearlessness at age 2 distinguished the chronically high trajectory group from all other trajectory groups. Raine et al. (1998) found that measures of fearlessness and stimulation seeking at age 3 predicted aggression at age 11 in a sample of 1130 male and female children from the island of Mauritius. Tremblay, Pihl, Vitaro, and Dobkin (1994), using data from the Montreal Longitudinal Study on over 1,000 boys, showed that teacher-rated impulsivity in kindergarten predicted self-reported delinquency at age 13. Finally, the relation between early temperament and later antisocial behavior has also been documented in several papers from the Dunedin Multidisciplinary Study of Health and Development. Caspi, Henry, Moffitt, and Silva (1995) used temperament ratings derived from examiners' behavioral ratings at ages 3 and 5 to find that early lack of control was consistently related to antisocial behavior at 9 and 11 and CD at 13 and 15. Henry, Caspi, Moffitt, and Silva (1996) found this same dimension to predict violent convictions at age 18. Moffitt and Caspi (2001) found that lack of control distinguished LCP offenders from AL offenders.

These findings cohere with theoretical and empirical work on conscience development. Kochanska (1997) posited the existence of two regulatory processes necessary for the adequate development of conscience: (1) affective discomfort and (2) behavioral control. She found that temperamental variations are important to these processes, with fear being important for the first process and inhibitory/effortful control important for the second.

There is also evidence for the interaction between temperament and the socialization context, particularly features of parenting. Coon, Carey, Corley, and Fulker (1992) found that among "difficult-temperament" young children, only those with conjoint maladaptive parenting were at risk for later conduct-disordered behavior. Kochanska (1997) has also reported an interaction between temperament and parenting style in producing compliance (see also Brennan, Hall, Bor, Najman, & Williams, 2003).

Personality

Scientific inquiry in personality development has grown rapidly, as documented by Caspi and Shiner (Chapter 6, this *Handbook,* this volume). J. Miller and Lynam (2001) meta-analyzed 59 studies that examined the relation between antisocial behavior, broadly defined, and one or more structural models of personality. Structural models are derived from basic research in personality and utilize multiple dimensions to organize the vast array of personality traits according to their interrelations. They share the fundamental assumption that a finite number of traits are the basic building blocks of personality, providing comprehensive coverage of human personality. Importantly, there is a great deal of overlap between various structural models (e.g., Five Factor Model; Tellegen's three-factor model, Eysenck's Psychoticism, Extraversion, Neuroticism [PEN] model), making it easier to compare results from different studies. Approximately one-third of the studies examined by J. Miller and Lynam were conducted in samples consisting of children and adolescents. Across the 18 dimensions in the 4 different structural models examined, 8 dimensions showed correlations greater than .25 with antisocial behavior: (1) Five Factor Model (FFM) Agreeableness (negative) and Conscientiousness (negative); (2) Eysenck's Psychoticism (positive); (3) Tellegen's Negative Emotionality (positive) and Constraint (negative); and (4) Cloninger's Novelty Seeking (positive), Self-Directedness (negative), and Cooperativeness (negative). All of these scales can be understood as assessing either Agreeableness or Conscientiousness/Constraint. The strength of these relations did not vary across age, type of sample (institutionalized versus not), or assessment source (e.g., self versus other, official versus self). Other dimensions, theorized to be important to antisocial behavior, such as Neuroticism and Extraversion bore no significant overall relations to antisocial behavior.

These effects are not due to predictor-criterion overlap. The personality inventories contain very little reference to explicitly antisocial behavior; in cases where this is not true, results hold even when overlapping elements are removed (e.g., Krueger et al., 1996). These relations hold prospectively: in a particularly stringent test, Krueger (1999), in the Dunedin Study, found that low levels of constraint and agreeableness at age 18 predicted symptoms of antisocial personality disorder at age 21 above and beyond the effect of antisocial personality disorder at age 18.

Although studied infrequently, there is evidence for personality by context interactions. Lynam et al. (in press) found that impulsivity and neighborhood-socioeconomic status interacted to produce violent and nonviolent offending among 430 boys from the Middle Sample of the Pittsburgh Youth Study, such that impulsivity was more strongly related to self-reported offending in poorer neighborhoods.

Psychopathy

The construct of psychopathy has been studied intensively at the adult level. Interpersonally, the psychopath is grandiose, egocentric, manipulative, forceful, and cold-hearted; affectively, he or she displays shallow emotions, is unable to maintain close-relationships, and lacks empathy, anxiety, and remorse. Behaviorally, the psychopath commits more types of crime, more crimes of any type, and more violent crimes, in or out of prison, than nonpsychopathic counterparts (see Hare, 2003). Lynam and colleagues (i.e., Lynam, 2002; Lynam et al., in press; Miller, Lynam, Widiger, & Leukefeld, 2001) have argued that psychopathy can be understood as a specific constellation of personality traits; in particular, they argue that psychopathy consists of extremely low Agreeableness, low Conscientiousness, a mixture of high and low Neuroticism (i.e., high in angry hostility and impulsiveness and low in anxiety, self-consciousness, and vulnerability), and a mixture of high and low Extraversion (i.e., high in assertiveness and excitement seeking and low in warmth). As a constellation of traits, it warrants mention in the present discussion of dispositional factors, particularly given that several investigators have imported the concept of psychopathy to juveniles (Frick, O'Brien, Wooton, & McBurnett, 1994; Lynam, 1997).

Over 20 studies have examined the relation between juvenile psychopathy and offending. Almost without exception, these studies have found similar relations between psychopathy and antisocial behavior in juveniles as those found in adults. Juvenile psychopathy is moderately strongly related to age at onset (e.g., Corrado, Vincent, Hart, & Cohen, 2004), number and variety of offenses (e.g., Kosson, Cyterski, Steuerwald, Neumann, & Walker-Matthews, 2002), stability of offending across time (e.g., Lynam, 1997), and quantity and quality of aggression (e.g., Frick et al., 1994; Murrie, Cornell, Kaplan, McConville, & Levy-Elkon, 2004). For example, using his Childhood Psychopathy Scale, in a sample of 430 12- to 13-year-old boys from a high-risk study, Lynam (1997) reported that juvenile psychopathy was moderately correlated (rs range from .19 to .39) with past and current delinquency and related to serious delinquency that is stable across time. Kosson et al. (2002) examined correlations between offending history and scores on the Personality Checklist Youth Version (PCL-YV) in a sample of 115 adolescent males on probation. They report that psychopathy scores correlated with the number of nonviolent charges ($r = .35$), number of violent charges ($r = .27$), total number of charges ($r = .42$), and the number of different charges ($r = .45$). These results held across different measurement instruments, reporting sources, samples, and ages.

Moreover, several of these studies have examined the *predictive* relations between juvenile psychopathy and antisocial behavior, including the relation between juvenile psychopathy and institutional infractions (e.g., Edens, Poythress, & Lilienfeld, 1999; Murrie et al., 2004; Stafford & Cornell, 2003). Spain, Douglas, Poythress, and Epstein (2004) administered three psychopathy instruments to 85 male adolescent offenders aged 11 to 18 in a residential treatment facility and found significant relations between the total number of infractions (physical, verbal, and administrative) and each of the psychopathy indices, with rs of .27, .38, and .43 for the PCL-YV, Antisocial Process Screening Device (APSD) and Child Psychopathy Scale (CPS), respectively. Additional studies have examined the predictive relations between juvenile psychopathy measures and recidivism (e.g., Gretton, Hare, & Catchpole, 2004). Corrado et al. (2004) followed 182 male adolescent offenders for, on average, 14.5 months. They found that high scorers on the PCL-YV reoffended earlier than low scorers; this was true for both nonviolent (6.87 months versus 12.33 months) and violent offenses (13.55 months versus 18.17 months). Again, these results mirror those found among adults.

Two studies examined the relation between juvenile psychopathy and treatment outcomes (O'Neil, Lidz, & Heilbrun, 2003; Spain et al., 2004). Using the PCL-YV in a sample of 64 adjudicated youth in a substance treatment program, O'Neil et al. (2003) found that high scorers on the PCL-YV attended the program for fewer days, participated more poorly when they did attend, and showed less clinical improvement across the course of treatment.

Finally, and importantly, several studies have attempted to demonstrate the incremental validity provided by the construct of juvenile psychopathy in predicting antisocial behavior (Lynam, 1997; Murrie et al., 2004; Stafford & Cornell, 2003). Lynam (1997) demonstrated that scores on the CPS were related to concurrent serious delinquency above and beyond social class, IQ, impulsivity, and delinquency. In the strongest demonstrations, studies showed that psychopathy predicted future antisocial behavior above and beyond current antisocial behavior. Murrie et al. (2004), in a sample of 113 incarcerated adolescents, reported that scores on the PCL-YV predicted institutional violence above and beyond previous violence.

Neuropsychological Factors

The idea of a link between the physical health of an individual's brain and his or her level of antisocial behavior has been in the literature for centuries. Benjamin Rush (1812; cited in F. Elliott, 1978, p. 147) referred to the "total perversion of the moral faculties" in people who displayed "innate preternatural moral depravity." Rush further suggested that "there is probably an original defective organization in those parts of the body that are occupied by the moral faculties of the mind." Since Rush's day, there have been numerous advances in our understanding of the human brain and in our ability to measure its functioning. There is strong evidence that antisocial children, adolescents, and adults are impaired, relative to nonantisocial controls, in verbal ability and executive functioning (see Lynam & Henry, 2001, for a review). There is also some indication that antisocial individuals may be impaired in spatial functions, particularly at young ages.

Verbal Ability

One of the most robust correlates of severe conduct problems is impaired verbal ability. Verbal deficits have been found in aggressive toddlers, conduct-disordered children, serious adolescent delinquents, and adult criminals. There have been at least six comprehensive reviews since the first by Prentice and Kelly in 1963; each review includes additional confirming studies (see Lynam & Henry, 2001). The finding of impaired verbal ability in antisocial persons continues to be replicated (e.g., Dery, Toupin, Pauze, Mercier, & Fortin, 1999; Dionne et al., 2003; Fergusson, Lynskey, & Horwood, 1996; Lahey et al., 1995; Lynam, Moffitt, &

Stouthamer-Loeber, 1993; Moffitt, Lynam, & Silva, 1994). Deficient verbal functioning has been found in studies using Verbal IQ tests as well as in those using standard neuropsychological tests.

The Dunedin Multidisciplinary Health and Development Study, a longitudinal study of a birth cohort of over 1,000 subjects who have been studied extensively from birth to age 27 through comprehensive, biannual assessments, has provided some of the strongest evidence. In addition to several biennial IQ assessments, the sample was administered a comprehensive neuropsychological assessment battery when participants were 13 years old. When Moffitt (1990) examined the developmental trajectories of boys with both conduct problems (CP) and hyperactive-impulsive-attention problems (HIA) and boys with only conduct problems or only HIA from age 3 to 15, the comorbid cases were found to have histories of extreme antisocial behavior that remained stable across this period. Their neuropsychological problems were as long-standing as their antisocial behavior. At ages 3 and 5, these boys had scored more than a standard deviation below the age-norm for boys on the Bayley and McCarthy tests of motor coordination; at each age (5, 7, 9, 11, and 13), these boys scored a more than .75 of a standard deviation below the age-norm for boys on verbal IQ (VIQ). Moffitt et al. (1994) demonstrated the ability of deficits in neuropsychological functioning at 13 to predict antisocial behavior in later adolescence. Whether antisocial behavior was measured with self-reports, police reports, or court reports, the poorer a boy's neuropsychological functioning at age 13, the more likely he was to have committed crimes at age 18. The strongest relations were obtained on the verbal and verbal memory factors of the test battery. Not only did scores on verbal and verbal memory factors relate to the early onset of offending, they also related to the persistence of offending across time. In an even more recent report, these same measures of verbal functioning distinguished LCP offenders from AL offenders, defined on the basis of antisocial behavior from ages 5 to 18 (Moffitt & Caspi, 2001).

The relation between poor verbal ability and the persistence of antisocial behavior has also been found among clinic-referred children. Lahey et al. (1995) examined factors related to the persistence of CD across 4 years in a relatively large, prospective study of clinic-referred boys. As expected, low VIQ was related to CD at Time 1. More important, low VIQ was related to the persistence of CD over time, particularly when VIQ was considered in conjunction with a parental history of antisocial personality disorder (APD); only boys with above average VIQ and without a parental history of APD improved across time. Similarly, Farrington and Hawkins (1991) found that low VIQ at age 8 to 10 predicted persistence in crime after the 21st birthday (phi = .23), even after controlling for other predictors. It is important to note that the differences between antisocial and nonantisocial youth remain even after controlling for potential confounds, such as ethnicity (e.g., Lynam et al., 1993), socioeconomic status (e.g., Dery et al., 1999; Lynam et al., 1993, Moffitt, Gabrielli, Mednick, & Schulsinger, 1981), academic attainment (e.g., Denno, 1989; Lynam et al., 1993), test motivation (e.g., Lynam et al., 1993), and the differential detection of low-IQ delinquents (Moffitt & Silva, 1988a).

Executive Functions

Antisocial behavior has been associated with deficiencies in the brain's self-control or executive functions, which include operations such as sustaining attention and concentration, abstract reasoning and concept formation, formulating goals, anticipating and planning, programming and initiating purposive sequences of behavior, and inhibiting unsuccessful, inappropriate, or impulsive behaviors. Evidence of the relation between executive deficits and antisocial behavior has been found among incarcerated subjects, among nonconduct-disordered subjects in laboratory situations, and among general-population samples.

Several studies that have applied batteries of formal tests of executive functions to delinquent subjects have shown that test scores discriminate between antisocial and nonantisocial children and adolescents (see Moffitt, 1990; Lynam & Henry, 2001, for reviews). Multivariate analyses of frontal lobe batteries, for example, the Wisconsin Card Sorting Task, Verbal Fluency, Trails B, Mazes, and the Rey Osterreith Complex Figure Test, with a general population sample in New Zealand (Moffitt & Henry, 1989) have demonstrated that a linear combination of these scores significantly discriminated self-reported early delinquents from nondelinquents. This effect was most robust among the delinquents with co-occurring HIA; differences between this comorbid group and nondisordered controls ranged from two-thirds to over one standard deviation and remained even after controlling for IQ.

Other studies, although not focusing specifically upon executive functions, have reported findings from individual measures typically included in frontal lobe batteries. Berman and Siegal (1976) found that delinquents scored poorly on the Category Test and Trails B. Wolff, Waber, Bauermeister, Cohen, and Ferber (1982) reported delinquency-related impairments on tests of selective attention and on the Stroop Color-Word Test. A number of studies have shown delinquents to score poorly on various tests requiring sequencing of motor behavior (e.g., Brickman, McManus, Grapentine, & Alessi, 1984; Lueger & Gill, 1990).

Recently, several investigators have employed more sophisticated measures, such as the Self-Ordered Pointing (SOP; Petrides & Milner, 1982) task and the Conditional Association Task (CAT; Petrides, 1985), to investigate the relation between aggression and frontal lobe functions, particularly working memory. Positron emission topography studies have found that the SOP is specifically associated with the mid-dorsolateral frontal region, whereas the CAT is specifically associated with the posterior dorsolateral frontal region (Petrides, Alivisatos, Evans, & Meyer, 1993). Lau, Pihl, and Peterson (1995) found that poor performance on these two measures was associated with aggression in a laboratory setting. Giancola and Zeichner (1994) reported that performance on the CAT was associated with intensity of shocks administered to a fictitious opponent in a laboratory setting.

As was the case for verbal deficits, the evidence suggests that poor executive functioning may be especially characteristic of the most antisocial group: boys with symptoms of conduct problems and HIA. In the New Zealand study, adolescent boys who exhibited symptoms of both CD and HIA scored more poorly on neuropsychological tests of executive functions than their peers who had either CD or HIA alone (Moffitt & Henry, 1989; Moffitt & Silva, 1988b). In a companion study of executive functions and conduct problems in the Pittsburgh Youth Study (White et al., 1994), data were gathered on "self-control and impulsivity" using multiple tests and measures for 430 12-year-old boys. The impulsivity measures were strongly related to delinquency at two ages even after controlling for IQ and socioeconomic status; additionally, these measures were related to the 3-year longevity of antisocial behavior, even after controlling for initial levels of delinquency. In a separate study, Aronowitz et al. (1994) reported that adolescents with both CD and HIA performed more poorly on measures of executive function than did CD-only adolescents.

Longitudinal studies have demonstrated that executive function deficits are associated with the stability and continuity of conduct problems. Seguin, Pihl, Harden, Tremblay, and Boulerice (1995) found that boys who exhibited a stable pattern of aggression between the ages of 6 and 12 performed significantly more poorly on measures of executive functions than did unstable aggressive or nonaggressive boys. Seguin, Nagin, Assaad, and Tremblay (in press) have shown that deficits in working memory, an aspect of executive functioning, are most pronounced in adolescents who are consistently high in physical aggression and motoric hyperactivity.

Taken together, these studies suggest that neuropsychological dysfunctions that manifest themselves as poor scores on tests of self-control are linked with early onset and persistence of antisocial behavior. Additionally, the findings in regard to the group comorbid for HIA and CP are of considerable interest in light of evidence that the co-occurrence of CP and HIA may represent a distinct subtype of CD that is particularly severe and persistent and places the child at risk for serious antisocial behavior in adolescence and adulthood.

Spatial Deficits

A few studies suggest that spatial deficits may also characterize severely antisocial children and adolescents, particularly at younger ages (Raine, Yaralian, Reynolds, & Venables, 2002). Dietz, Lavigne, Arend, and Rosenbaum (1997) found that both performance and VIQ were related to externalizing problems in a sample of 2- to 5-year-old children. In perhaps the most compelling report, Raine et al. (2002) examined the relation between verbal and spatial abilities at 3 years of age and antisocial behavior at ages 8 and 17. These authors found that early spatial, not verbal, deficits predicted later antisocial behavior, even after controlling for potential covariates including test behavior and social adversity.

Neuroimaging

Researchers have employed methods that assess both the structural (e.g., computerized tomography, magnetic resonance imaging) and functional (e.g., positron emission tomography, single photon emission computed tomography) characteristics of the brains of antisocial individuals (for reviews, see Bassarath, 2001; Lynam & Henry, 2001). Almost all of these studies have been conducted with adults, using violent, aggressive, criminal, sexual, and/or psychopathic individuals. Results have varied, but where significant findings do emerge, they generally involve dysfunction in the temporal and frontal regions among offenders, a pattern supportive of results found in studies using performance tests. For example, Raine, Lencz, Bihrle, LaCasse, and Colletti (2000) employed structural magnetic resonance imaging in 21 community volunteers with APD and 2 control groups, one consisting of 27 men with substance dependence but without APD and one of 34 men with neither substance dependence nor APD. They found that the APD group had lower prefrontal volumes than both control groups. The few studies that have been conducted in children and adolescents are consistent with the findings among adults. For example, Lyoo, Lee, Jung, Noam, and Renshaw (2002) administered magnetic resonance imaging (MRI) assessments to over 400 children and adolescents with psychiatric disorders and found that the group with attention deficit disorder and CD had more severe levels of white matter signal hyperintensities in the frontal lobes than did controls.

This literature, however, is far from complete, even at the adult level. Reliance on small sample sizes, failure to use noncriminal control groups, and use of a wide variety of types of offenders precludes the drawing of any firm conclusions. The very tentative suggestion is that the results of neuroimaging studies are consistent with results from performance tests of neuropsychological function. However, the two literatures are not integrated, and much future research is needed to explore these issues more fully.

Although it is difficult to demonstrate causality unequivocally in most areas of human behavior, studies of the relation between neuropsychological health and antisocial behavior suggest that neuropsychological deficits can be one cause of serious antisocial behavior. The evidence reviewed suggests that poorer neuropsychological health is associated with more severe antisocial behavior, with moderate effect sizes that survive frequent, conservative controls for other variables. Additionally, several observational studies suggest that poor neuropsychological health is present before the onset of serious antisocial behavior (e.g., Denno, 1989), although there is one published exception. Aguilar, Sroufe, Egeland, and Carlson (2000) found differences between childhood-onset and adolescent-onset offenders in late childhood but not early childhood; methodological problems including the small, nonrepresentative sample and psychometrically weak instruments may account for this

anomaly. Natural experiments in which individuals have sustained severe head injury also suggest that changes in neuropsychological status are associated with changes in antisocial status, with the case of Phineas Gage being the best known. Finally, several studies have tested and ruled out viable third variable explanations of the relation (e.g., Lynam et al., 1993).

Biological Factors

To the degree that temperament, personality, and neuropsychological health are based in biology, the evidence reviewed above demonstrates that biological variables are consistently related to antisocial behavior. In the sections that follow, we examine the relations between more direct indicators of biological function and antisocial behavior. Specifically, we review evidence that links antisocial behavior to pre- and perinatal complications, early exposure to nicotine, neurotransmitter activity, sex hormones, and autonomic reactivity. As we show, each of these factors has been linked to antisocial behavior. Perhaps most interesting, across many studies, the effects of many of these biological variables are strongest under adverse environmental circumstances.

Prenatal and Perinatal Complications

Moffitt's (1993) theory of LCP antisocial behavior posits that prenatal and perinatal complications contribute to the neuropsychological problems that underlie this type of offending. These complications have been examined as predictors of antisocial behavior in multiple studies. At least 6 studies have found associations between minor physical anomalies (MPAs), presumed to be markers for fetal maldevelopment, and antisocial behavior in children (see Raine, 2002, for a review). Arseneault, Tremblay, Boulerice, Seguin, and Saucier (2000) found that MPAs assessed in a sample of 170 males at age 14 predicted violent delinquency at age 17. In several studies, MPAs have been found to interact with social factors to predict antisocial behavior. For example, Brennan, Mednick, and Raine (1997) found that men with both MPAs and high family adversity had the highest rates of adult offending in a sample of male offspring of psychiatrically ill parents. Pine, Coplan, et al. (1997) found that the presence of MPAs interacted with environmental disadvantage to predict CD at age 17.

There have also been a number of studies from large, longitudinal studies in multiple countries examining the relation between birth complications and antisocial behavior. Almost all have found that the relations between birth complications and antisocial behavior are stronger when other psychosocial risk factors are present. In one of the most impressive demonstrations, Raine, Brennan, and Mednick (1994) found that birth complications and maternal rejection at age 1 interacted to predict violent offending at age 18 in a sample of over 4,200 men from Copenhagen. In the follow-up at age 34, the interaction between biological and social risk predicted early onset, serious violent behavior. These findings from Denmark have been replicated in 4 other countries. Piquero and Tibbett (1999), in the Philadelphia Collaborative Perinatal Project, found that the combination of prenatal/perinatal complications and family disadvantage was linked with adult violent offending. Similar results have been obtained in large samples from Sweden (Hodgins, Kratzer, & McNeil, 2001), Finland (Kemppainen, Jokelainen, Jaervelin, Isohanni, & Raesaenen, 2001), and Canada (Arseneault, Tremblay, Boulerice, & Saucier, 2002).

In Utero Exposure to Nicotine

Several large, longitudinal studies in various countries have shown that maternal smoking during pregnancy places the offspring at increased risk for later antisocial behavior. For example, in the Christchurch Health and Development Study, a large, longitudinal study based in Christchurch, New Zealand, Fergusson, Woodward, and Horwood (1998) found that smoking during pregnancy almost doubled the risk for conduct problems in boys, even after controlling for antenatal and postnatal risk factors (see also, Wakschlag et al., 1997; Weissman, Warner, Wickramaratne, & Kandel, 1999). Relations between smoking during pregnancy and later adult offending have also been observed. Brennan, Grekin, and Mednick (1999) found a twofold increase in adult violent offending in the offspring of mothers who smoked in a birth cohort of over 4,000 men. Several studies have found that these relations hold even after controlling many potentially confounding variables, including socioeconomic status, maternal education, mother's age at first birth, family size, parenting behaviors, parental psychopathology, birth weight, and perinatal complications. One study found that the relation between heavy maternal smoking and CP at age 7 persisted even in the face of multiple, well-measured controls; using data from the E-risk study, Maughan, Taylor, Caspi, and Moffitt (2004) found that after controlling for genetic influences, parental antisocial behavior and depression, and family disadvantage the effect of heavy maternal smoking on CP at age 7, but not age 5, remained significant. The models estimated by Maughan et al. are consistent with heavy maternal smoking playing a mediating role between the more distal risk factors and the outcome.

As with other biological variables, there is evidence that smoking during pregnancy interacts with social risks to increase the likelihood of antisocial behavior. Rasanen et al. (1999), using data from a large Finnish birth cohort, found an almost 12-fold increase in recidivistic violent offending through age 26 in offspring whose mothers smoked and who were born into single-parent families.

Autonomic Nervous System Activity

There is extensive evidence for the relation between low resting heart rate and antisocial behavior. In fact, Raine (2002) calls low resting heart rate "the best-replicated biological correlate of antisocial behavior in child and adolescent samples" (p. 418). The relation is present in cross-sectional studies (e.g., Rogeness, Cepeda, Macedo, Fischer, & Harris, 1990) and prospective studies (e.g., Farrington, 1997). Raine, Venables, and Mednick (1997) examined the relation between low resting heart rate at age 3 and antisocial behavior at age 11 in a sample of 1,795 male and female children from Mauritius. These authors found that early low resting heart rate predicted later aggressive behavior. Moreover, these results were the same across gender and ethnicity and held despite controls for various biological, psychological, and psychiatric mediators and confounds. Similar findings have been obtained in other large, prospective studies from England (Farrington, 1997), New Zealand (Moffitt & Caspi, 2001), and Canada (Kindlon et al., 1995). These findings hold after controlling for other variables including physique, exercise, socioeconomic status, motor activity, substance use, and psychosical adversity. Farrington (1997), in the Cambridge Study in Delinquent Development, found that low resting heart rate and poor concentration were the only two risk factors, out of 48 examined, that were independently predictive of violence. Low resting heart rate does not appear to interact with social adversity to increase offending. To the contrary, a single study reports that low resting heart rate is related to antisocial behavior only in children with nonadverse circumstances (Raine, Brennan, & Farrington, 1997).

Sex Hormones

Theoretically, testosterone is a likely candidate as an important biological factor in antisocial behavior. The distribution of testosterone across the population and across development parallels what is known about the distribution of antisocial behavior. Testosterone and antisocial behavior are more concentrated in men than women, and its level increases dramatically across adolescence. In nonhuman animals, the relation between testosterone and aggression has been unequivocally demonstrated through correlational and experimental studies (Turner, 1994). Despite the theoretical appeal, the evidence suggests that testosterone has, at best, a relatively weak correlation with antisocial behavior in humans.

Archer (1991) conducted three meta-analyses, including only 5 to 6 studies each, and found a weak, positive correlation between testosterone and aggression. A more recent, larger, meta-analysis by Book, Starzyk, and Quinsey (2001) confirms Archer's initial results. These authors analyzed 45 independent studies that yielded 54 independent effect sizes. Their correlations ranged from −.28 to .71 with a weighted mean correlation of .14. In contrast to several qualitative reviews, these authors reported that the relation between testosterone and aggression was actually somewhat larger in younger, compared to older samples; this effect of age, however, held for males but not females. Book et al. reported weighted mean correlations of .21, .18, and .10 for participants aged 13 to 20, 21 to 35, and over 35, respectively. Interestingly, there was no difference in the effect size for testosterone across genders.

Not only is the relation between testosterone and aggression relatively weak, the direction of effect is not entirely clear. On one hand, a study by Finkelstein et al. (1997) in hypogonadal adolescents showed that changes in testosterone may instigate changes in aggression. These authors administered depo-testosterone to 35 adolescents in 3-month blocks alternating with placebo at 3 dose levels approximating early, middle, and late pubertal amounts. Results demonstrated significant hormonal effects on physically aggressive behaviors and impulses. On the other hand, there is evidence that dominance may increase testosterone. Archer (1988) reviewed animal studies relating to this question and concluded that dominance or success in conflict often

increases testosterone levels. Observational and experimental research in humans supports this conclusion as well. Schaal, Tremblay, Soussignan, and Susman (1996) examined the relations among testosterone, aggression, and social status in 13-year-old boys whose aggressive behavior and peer status had been assessed continuously for the previous 7 years. They found that testosterone was more closely linked to social dominance than to aggression. Those boys rated by newly acquainted peers as both tough and social leaders had the highest testosterone levels, even though they were not rated by everyday peers and teachers as being high on physical aggression. Boys rated as tough, but not leaders, had testosterone levels no greater than the nontough boys, even though the tough nonleaders were rated highest in physical aggression by peers and teachers. Boys who had been highly aggressive from ages 6 through 12 had lower testosterone levels at age 13 than boys who were consistently low on fighting in elementary school. Salvador, Simon, Suay, and Llorens (1987) studied male judo competitors and found that testosterone levels were positively related to success in competition. Gladue, Boechler, and McCaul (1989) found that winners in a reaction-time competition had elevated testosterone levels after the competition, but losers maintained their original levels. Similar results were obtained even when the contest simply involved coin-tossing (McCaul, Gladue, & Joppa, 1992).

One study has examined the interaction between testosterone and environmental context. Rowe, Maughan, Worthman, Costello, and Angold (2004) examined the relations among testosterone, peer deviance, antisocial behavior, and social dominance in a large sample of boys from the Great Smoky Mountains Study. These authors found that levels of testosterone were related to nonaggressive conduct problems, primarily among boys with deviant peers. Among boys with nondeviant peers, levels of testosterone were related to social dominance but not CP.

Neurotransmitters

The most widely studied of the neurotransmitters in relation to aggression and antisocial behavior is serotonin. There is an extensive research literature, including both human and animal studies, indicating that the central serotonergic system is involved in the regulation of impulsive aggressive behavior (Herbert & Martinez, 2001). Decreased serotonergic functioning has been found among adults with past histories of aggressive acts including violent offenses and suicide (see Asberg, 1994). Specifically, lower concentrations of cerebrospinal fluid (CSF) 5-HIAA, the major metabolite of serotonin, have been found among individuals with past histories of suicide attempts, in violent offenders, in individuals with personality disorders characterized by aggression, and in violent alcoholics (e.g., Tuinier, Verhoeven, & van Praag, 1995; Virkkunen, Eggert, Rawlings, & Linnoila, 1996). Other researchers have indexed platelet levels of monoamine oxidase (MAO), which is responsible for metabolizing both serotonin and dopamine. Although MAO activity is an indirect measure, results from studies using it are consistent with studies that have examined serotonin more directly. Low MAO activity in platelets has been shown to be associated with impulsivity, violent crime, and persistent criminality (e.g., Alm et al., 1994; Belfrage, Lidberg, & Oreland, 1992). In another noninvasive approach, Coccaro (1989) has shown that a blunted prolactin response to fenfluramine challenge, taken as an index of diminished serotonergic response, is associated with impulsive aggression. Some experimental research is also consistent with the idea that levels of serotonin are related to levels of aggression. Cleare and Bond (1995) depleted levels of tryptophan, a serotonin precursor, in a sample of normal male participants. These authors found that among those participants with preexisting aggressive traits, tryptophan depletion increased both subjective feelings and objective ratings of aggression.

In studies of children, however, results are more mixed. Kruesi, Swedo, Leonard, and Rubinow (1990) found, in a sample of children with disruptive behavior disorders, that lower levels of CSF 5-HIAA were related to higher ratings of aggressive behavior. Moreover, Kruesi et al. (1992) found that lower 5-HIAA levels were predictive of aggressive behaviors at a follow-up 2 years later. Other studies have found opposite results. Castellanos et al. (1994) found that CSF 5-HIAA was positively correlated with aggression in 29 boys with attention-deficit hyperactivity disorder (ADHD). Halperin et al. (1994) and Pine et al. (1997) both found that increased prolactin response to fenfluramine challenge, indicating increased serotonergic activity, was related to increased aggression.

One study examined the interaction between neurotransmitters and environments. Moffitt, Caspi, and Fawcett (1997) found that serotonergic activity interacted with a history of family conflict to predict violence at age 21 in the males of the Dunedin study. The nature of the interaction was such that men with high levels of whole blood serotonin, and therefore low levels of serotonin in the brain, and history of psychosocial adversity were the most violent by both official and self-report.

Ecological Factors and Social Stressors

As compelling as constitutional and biological factors are in leading to aggressive behavior, ecological factors play just as strong a role, and an even stronger role for certain indicators of aggression. The 600% increase in juvenile murder arrests between 1965 and 1994 (Blumstein, 2000) and wide variations across countries cannot be accounted for by enduring characteristics such as genes and traits. Ecological contexts surely play a major role in predicting individual differences in aggressive behavior as well.

Culture, Laws, and Policies

Cultural norms and public policies have enormous influence over community-wide rates of aggressive behaviors such as gun violence. Firearm homicide rates, including rates for children, are 12 to 16 times higher in the United States than in the average of 25 other industrialized countries, including Canada, simply because of differences in laws that allow gun ownership (U.S. Department of Health and Human Services, 1997). In the United States, children in the 5 states with the highest levels of gun ownership are 3 times more likely to die from firearm homicide as are children from the 5 states with the lowest levels of gun ownership (M. Miller, Azrael, & Hemenway, 2002). Gun ownership is a product of laws and cultural norms, but surely these factors cannot be dismissed as by-products of genetic or biological variations across states in this country (Wintemute, 2000). Nisbett and Cohen (1996) compiled population-level and laboratory evidence to argue that a "culture of honor" is responsible for consistently higher rates of violence in the American South than in other geographic regions.

Community Factors

The crowded inner city has long been highlighted as a setting for high rates of violence (Hammond & Yung, 1991). In a classic work, C. Shaw and McKay (1942) argued that the three community structural variables of poverty, ethnic heterogeneity, and high residential mobility are associated with high violent crime rates that persist across time, even after the entire population in a community changes. Sampson, Raudenbush, and Earls (1997) used multilevel analyses of adolescents to find large variations in violent behaviors that are associated with structural characteristics across neighborhoods in Chicago. Census tract data document that neighborhood-level scores for the proportions of families characterized by poverty, unemployment, low education, single-parent households, high residential mobility, and low income represent significant risk factors for individual-level conduct problems (Beyers, Bates, Pettit, & Dodge, 2003).

A problem in interpretation of neighborhood and community effects concerns the likelihood of self-migration into neighborhoods by families of varying background characteristics. As Jencks and Mayer (1990) noted, "the most fundamental problem confronting anyone who wants to estimate neighborhoods' effects on children is distinguishing between neighborhood effects and family effects" (p. 119), known as the omitted variable bias or social selection. The problem of self-selection has been partially solved by quasi-experiments in housing afforded by government-assisted housing programs that assign families somewhat randomly into different neighborhoods. Votruba and Kling (2004) analyzed data from the Gautreux Program in Chicago and found that mortality of African American male youth (mainly by violence) varied as a function of neighborhood characteristics related to human capital and work, such as unemployment rates and levels of education among the adults in the neighborhood.

Neighborhood effects go well beyond structural characteristics to social factors such as disorganization and control. These latter factors have been called collective efficacy by Sampson et al. (1997) and are indexed by levels of trust among neighbors, supportive social networks, and the degree to which neighbors "look out for one another." These factors partially mediate the effects of structural factors but also operate independently (Ingoldsby & Shaw, 2002).

Within-Family Ecological Factors

Neighborhood factors influence a child's development at least partly through their effects on the family unit (McLoyd, 1990; Wilson, 1987), and the family social context exerts its own independent effect on antisocial development. The most important of these factors is low

socioeconomic status. Controlling for other community variables, poverty in the family is associated with higher rates of peer-directed aggressive behavior by children (Bradley & Corwyn, 2002), adolescents (Spencer, Dobbs, & Phillips, 1988), and adults (Sampson & Laub, 1994). The potential problem of selection bias into poverty limits confidence in the causal role that family poverty plays in child conduct problems. A recent study by Costello, Compton, Keeler, and Angold (2003) capitalized on the natural experiment afforded by a government policy enabling Native American families in western North Carolina to reap the financial benefits of a new casino in their community. Of the previously poor families, those that were suddenly thrust out of poverty (21.3% of all poor families) had children whose behavioral problem symptoms declined by 40%, whereas never-poor children in the same community displayed no change in symptoms across the same period. This finding might suggest a causal role of family wealth in alleviating these symptoms, although even this natural experiment has a caveat: not all families who received financial benefits were brought out of poverty. Almost 79% of poor families remained below the poverty level even after the casino brought them financial gains (either they squandered the resources or the resources were insufficient to have an enduring impact); their children's symptoms increased by 21% across the same time period. The full effect (combining ex-poor and always-poor families) of the introduction of the casino on child behavior problem symptoms was actually negligible.

McLoyd (1990) has examined the family mechanisms through which poverty might exert its impact. She found that poverty increases single African American parents' psychological distress and impairs their social support systems, which, in turn, diminishes their effectiveness and increases their coerciveness toward their children. These effects, in turn, may lead to child aggression. Consistent with this formulation, Guerra, Huesmann, Tolan, Van Acker, and Eron (1995) found that, among urban Chicagoans, poverty is correlated with stressful life events and a lack of parental involvement in religious support systems and that these two factors, in turn, account for the effect of poverty on peer-nominated aggression. Sampson and Laub (1994) reanalyzed the Glueck and Glueck (1950) longitudinal data set involving 1,000 Depression-era White families and found that the structural variable of family poverty influenced family processes of harsh discipline, low supervision, and poor parent-child attachment, which, in turn, influenced juvenile delinquency. Family process accounted for two-thirds of the effect of poverty on delinquency. Likewise, Dodge, Pettit, and Bates (1994) found that harsh physical discipline by parents accounted for about half of the effect of low socioeconomic status on children's aggressive behavior.

A second major family context factor is marital conflict. Cummings and Davies (2002) accumulated laboratory and naturalistic evidence to determine that ambient conflict increases child aggression. Cummings, Goeke-Morey, and Papp (in press) used daily home diary reports to find that everyday marital conflicts increase children's aggressive behavior. Fergusson and Horwood (1998) found robust correlations between observing domestic violence and later antisocial behavior. The stress of child conduct problems can increase marital conflict, and so the issue of temporal ordering is crucial in understanding the role of this context factor in child behavior. Recent advances in multilevel modeling of developmental trajectories afford the opportunity to evaluate within-individual changes in a child's behavior as a function of an environmental event, reducing the likelihood that the environmental effects can be explained away as being due to correlation with static traits or to reverse causal processes. Malone et al. (2004) followed 356 boys and girls across 10 years, as some of their families experienced divorce, and found that for boys (especially younger boys) the experience of parental divorce increased their externalizing problems in the year of the divorce. Furthermore, these problems continued for several years following divorce. Finally, Jaffee, Moffitt, Caspi, Taylor, and Arseneault (2002) employed a twin research design to find that adult domestic violence accounted for 5% of the variance in child antisocial behavior, even when genetic factors are controlled.

Other early environmental conditions also increase children's aggression, including being born to a teenage (Morash & Rucker, 1989) or single (Blum, Boyle, & Offord, 1988) parent, being raised in a large family (Rutter, Tizard, & Whitmore, 1970), and being parented by convicted felons (Farrington, 1992). These factors are intercorrelated and likely share a common pathway through effects on parenting quality, although they may have more direct effects or may be linked to child aggression through common genes. Furthermore, these risk factors are apparently not merely redundant in their impact on the developing child; rather, their effects are cumulative (Rutter & Garmezy, 1983).

Alternatively, analyses by Bolger, Patterson, Thompson, and Kupersmidt (1995) indicate that the effects of economic hardship are more dramatic among children in the racial majority than among those who are already stressed by the circumstances of racial minority status. Being Black brings numerous social hardships in American society (Ogbu, 1990) and, with these hardships, relative risk for aggressive behavior. The effects of economic hardship, above and beyond the hardships already imposed by racial stratification, are muted for African American children (Bolger et al., 1995).

Non-Family Child Care

The experience of early out-of-home group child care has been posited as a cause of child aggressive behavior (Belsky, 2001). However, families self-select into group child care for a variety of reasons, including attitudes about day care, availability, and ability to pay for other kinds of care (including a parent staying at home). The National Institute of Child Health and Human Development (NICHD) Early Child Care Research Network (2004) study of child care in the United States offers the most comprehensive opportunity to study these effects. Analyses of the 1,081 children in this sample, controlled for many potentially confounding variables, yielded a positive effect size of about one-fourth standard deviation of day care experience on aggressive behavior at age 4.5 years and kindergarten as rated by mothers, caregivers, and teachers. Borge, Rutter, Cote, and Tremblay (2004) analyzed data from the 15,579 families of the Canadian National Longitudinal Survey of Children and Youth to find that once selection factors were taken into account, children reared in homes by their mothers were actually *more* physically aggressive than children reared in group day care. Further analyses of the NICHD study sample by Love et al. (2003) and Votruba-Drzal, Coley, and Chase-Lansdale (2004) indicate that the effect of group day care depends on the quality of that care. Furthermore, the effect of group care must be interpreted in light of the alternative type of care that is available to a child—the quality of available home-rearing may differ across families such that group day care might offer a better *or* worse experience for a child than available alternatives.

A Case of Pervasive Environmental Influence: The Effects of Media Violence

Perhaps no greater cultural influence on children's aggressive development can be found than the effects of viewing violence on television. Meta-analyses (Wood, Wong, & Chachere, 1991) indicate that television violence-viewing accounts for about 10% of the variance in child aggression, which approximately equals the magnitude of effect of cigarette smoking on lung cancer.

Laboratory experiments demonstrate that viewing televised aggressive models results in aggressive behavior toward "Bobo" dolls (Bandura, Ross, & Ross, 1963) and peers (Björkqvist, 1985). Field studies repeatedly demonstrate significant correlations between television-violence viewing and aggressiveness, even when self-selection factors, such as parental supervision and socioeconomic status, are controlled. Eron, Huesmann, Lefkowitz, and Walder (1972) found that boys' television-violence preferences at age 8 predicted aggressiveness at age 18. Follow-ups to age 30 showed that age 8 television violence predicted self-reported aggression and seriousness of criminal arrests, even when social class, intelligence, parenting, age 8 aggression, and age 30 TV violence viewing all were controlled statistically (Huesmann, 1986). Huesmann and Eron (1986) replicated these findings in urban Israel, Poland, and the United States but not in Australia and an Israeli kibbutz. More recently, Huesmann, Moise-Titus, Podolski, and Eron (2003) followed 450 6- to 10-year-old Chicagoan boys and girls for 15 years and found that childhood exposure to television violence predicted a composite adult aggression score that included self-ratings, ratings by others, and crime records, even when early parenting, parent aggression, and socioeconomic status were controlled.

A major moderator of this effect is age of the viewer: the effects hold more strongly for children than for adults (Huesmann & Miller, 1994), perhaps because the effects act more strongly on the individual's development of a repertoire than on the accessing of responses already in one's repertoire. Also, the effects of viewing television violence are greater if the child believes that the violence is real, perhaps because perceived reality increases salience and the encoding of scripts, and if the child identifies with the violent TV character—believes that the character is like the self (Huesmann, Lagerspetz, & Eron, 1984). The family context in which TV violence is viewed is another qualifier, in that children who watch violence without parental supervision and in home contexts in which harsh discipline is utilized are subject to greater influence by TV violence (Singer & Singer, 1981).

Perhaps even more threatening than passive viewing of television violence is the active experience of playing violent video games. C. Anderson (2004) has reviewed the growing laboratory and longitudinal evidence to conclude that chronic experience playing video games that require and reward the shooting of victims on a computer screen increases children's future aggressive behavior, through many of the same psychological mechanisms that hold for viewing television violence.

Processes in Early Family Socialization

There is ample evidence of differences in discipline and parenting practices between families of aggressive children and nonproblem children. Much of the early research on this point was cross-sectional, however, and there has long been recognition of the difficulty in separating cause and effect in these relations (Bell & Harper, 1977). K. Anderson, Lytton, and Romney (1986) demonstrated that parents of normal children will resort to more punitive discipline practices when confronted with conduct-disordered boys than when they manage their own sons. Despite these problems of interpretation, longitudinal, behavior-genetic, and intervention studies show convincingly the causal role of early family socialization.

Mother-Infant Attachment Relationships

The results of longitudinal studies on infant attachment and conduct problems in childhood are mixed. Bates et al. (1991) failed to establish insecure attachment as a predictor of externalizing problems in a predominantly middle-class, two-parent sample followed from infancy into elementary school. The same held for a similar study by Fagot and Kavanagh (1990) and a longitudinal investigation by Lewis, Feiring, McGuffog, and Jaskir (1984). Alternatively, Renken, Egeland, Marvinney, Mangelsdorf, and Sroufe (1989) have repeatedly found insecure attachments to predict childhood behavior problems in a sample from low-income and predominantly single-parent households. Lyons-Ruth found that disorganized attachment status predicted hostile behavior to peers at age 5 (Lyons-Ruth, Alpern, & Repacholi, 1993) and teacher-rated externalizing problems at age 7 (Lyons-Ruth, Easterbrooks, & Davidson, 1995). Finally, D. Shaw et al. (1995) found that insecure attachment, particularly disorganized attachment, predicted CBCL aggression scores at age 5. This latter sample was predominantly lower income, having been recruited from a federally funded nutritional support program for mothers, infants, and children. Greenberg, Spelz, and Deklyen (1993) have argued that secure attachment is a protective factor for infants of low-income, highly stressed mothers but is less crucial to antisocial development in middle-class families. Dishion and Bullock (2002) proposed a general "nurturance hypothesis," whereby parents' positive attention, emotional investment, and behavioral management combine in ways that protect otherwise high-risk children from becoming aggressive.

Support for the interaction between parent-infant warmth and a biological factor comes from Raine, Brennan, and Mednick (1997), who found that Danish males with a history of birth complications and early rejection by the mother (unwanted pregnancy, attempt to abort fetus, and public institutional care of the infant) were at high risk for violent crime by age 19. Of children who had both risk factors, 47% became violent, compared to 20% of those who had just one factor. Thus, the strength of the mother-child bond protected children from later violence, but only for high biological-risk children.

Parental Warmth and Proactive Teaching

Closely related to the attachment construct is the concept of maternal warmth. Bates and Bayles (1988) found maternal affection to be negatively related to externalizing problems in both boys and girls at ages 5 and 6, and Booth, Rose-Krasnor, McKinnon, and Rubin (1994) found maternal warmth at age 4 negatively related to externalizing problems at age 8. As with many other parenting factors, the problem of selection bias and alternate causal paths calls into question whether parental lack of warmth causes child conduct problems or the reverse. Caspi et al. (2004) used a monozygotic twin study that controls for genetic differences to find that maternal expressed emotion (i.e., verbal statements of negative affect about a child) predicted children's antisocial behavior problems. Deater-Deckard (2000) used identical and fraternal twin pairs to reach the same conclusion.

One social-learning explanation for the role of parental warmth is that for a parent to be effective in socializing a child to parental behavior standards, the parent must be seen by the child as a potential source of reward, which occurs through the exchange of warmth. Eisenberg (Eisenberg, Cumberland, et al., 2001; Eisen-

berg, Pidada, & Liew, 2001) found support for a second possible mechanism, that parental negative emotion expression directly interferes with the child's normal development of self-regulation and regulation of emotion, which, in turn, mediate the child's development of externalizing problems (Eisenberg et al., 2003). Cole, Teti, and Zahn-Waxler (2003) found that maternal negative expressed emotion directly observed in laboratory tasks operates through dyadic exchanges with their preschool boys, leading to conduct problems. Zhou et al. (2002) found support for yet another pathway, that parental warmth leads to the child's development of empathy, which is known to protect a child from aggressive behavior.

Pettit, Bates, and Dodge (1997) have introduced the concept of proactive teaching by parents to indicate their positive attempts to teach their child appropriate behavior to prevent later discipline or conduct problems. They found that this construct is orthogonal to warmth and independently predicts child conduct problems.

Family Coercion and Inconsistent Discipline

In their classic longitudinal study of delinquency, Glueck and Glueck (1950) reported that parents of boys who became delinquent were less consistent in their discipline practices than parents of matched control boys who did not become delinquent. In an experimental follow-up of this hypothesis, Parke and Deur (1972) demonstrated that children are less inhibited from behaving aggressively when an adult is inconsistent in administering punishment. The same point has been made about inconsistency between adults when one adult enforces a standard, but the other does not (Sawin & Parke, 1979).

Patterson (Reid, Patterson, & Snyder, 2000) has offered a theory of coercive social learning that goes well beyond inconsistency in parenting as a core feature of antisocial development. According to this functionalist perspective, children who begin to display antisocial behaviors, such as aggression and disruptiveness, in the early school years have been inadvertently trained in the effectiveness of these behaviors by parents. Snyder, Reid, and Patterson (2003) describe coercion training as a four-step process that begins with the aversive intrusion of a family member into the child's activities (e.g., a mother may scold her child for not going to bed). In the second step, the child counterattacks (e.g., by whining, yelling, and complaining that he or she is being picked as the only one being made to go to bed). The third step is the crucial one, for it involves the negative reinforcement that increases the likelihood of future aversive responding by the child: The adult stops her scolding and her demands for compliance. The fourth step is reinforcement of the mother's giving in to the child. When the mother ceases her demands, the child stops the counterattack. According to this theory, it is the conditional probabilities in this sequence that distinguish the early parenting patterns of antisocial children from those of normal children. Observational data from clinical samples (Patterson et al., 1992) indicate that a child's aversive responses to the mother's intrusions in the second step occur two to three times more often in distressed families than in normal families. The success of these child counterattacks is reflected in observations documenting that mothers of aggressive boys more frequently reinforce negatively their sons' aversive responses than do mothers of nonaggressive boys (Snyder & Patterson, 1995). Conversely, mothers of nonaggressive boys more often reinforce the prosocial responses (e.g., talking or positive nonverbal communication) of their sons than do the mothers of aggressive boys. The net result is that children in normal families can be successful with their parents in two ways (aversive and nonaversive behavior), whereas the aggressive boys succeed only with aversive behavior. Furthermore, the coercion training process is a reciprocal family dynamic.

Physical Punishment and Punitiveness

The role of physical punishment in promoting or reducing children's aggressive and antisocial behavior has long been a matter of dispute among professionals and laypersons (Straus, 2005). The practice of spanking children is almost ubiquitous in American culture: 94% of parents of 3- and 4-year-olds use spanking as a discipline technique (Straus & Stewart, 1999). Gershoff's (2002) meta-analysis has revealed a consistent correlation between corporal punishment and child aggressive behavior, although the interpretation of that correlation is still in doubt (Benjet & Kazdin, 2003). Longitudinal investigations have consistently supported the relation between early punishment and later antisocial behavior. Data from the 411 London males of the Cambridge Longitudinal Study (Farrington & Hawkins, 1991) point to harsh discipline practices at age 8 as an important predictor of the early onset of delinquency. McCord's (1991) analyses of the Combridge-Somerville Youth

Study indicated that fathers' use of physical punishment predicted their sons' adult criminal records, even when paternal criminality was controlled.

Although robust, this correlation is moderated by other factors such as the quality of the parent-child relationship and the degree of parent-child warmth (Campbell, 1990). The adverse effects of physical punishment seem to hold only when punishment is administered in the absence of warmth and caring guidance. Deater-Deckard and Dodge (1997) reported that harsh physical discipline was positively correlated with later externalizing problems only among the subset of children who scored below the median in parent-child warmth. Thus, a warm parent-child relationship might buffer a child from deleterious effects of physical punishment.

The cultural context of parenting also moderates the impact of physical punishment. Deater-Deckard, Dodge, Bates, and Pettit (1996) found that physical punishment was positively correlated with later child aggressive behavior among European American families, in which this discipline style occurred relatively rarely. Among African American families, corporal punishment was more common (and normative) and was not correlated with child aggressive outcomes. This finding has been replicated by Lansford et al. (2004), who extended it to other measures of parenting (e.g., including direct observations, responses to hypothetical vignettes, rating scales, and clinical judgments) and later periods in a child's life. The authors hypothesized that it is not physical punishment per se that is responsible for child outcomes. Rather, it is the message that the child receives during the discipline event. Among European American families in which harsh discipline is nonnormative, for a child who receives harsh discipline, the message may be that the parent is rejecting the child. Among African American families, for whom corporal punishment is normative and "good" parenting, the message may be that the parent cares about the child's development. These different messages yield different outcomes, even though the parenting behavior superficially appears the same.

Disentangling the effects of parenting from the behavior of the child that might lead to corporal punishment is yet another problem. P. Cohen and Brook (1995) used cross-lagged analyses of longitudinal data to conclude that physical punishment more strongly predicts growth in conduct problems than the reverse. Stronger evidence regarding the causal role of harsh parenting comes from intervention experiments. Hinshaw et al. (2000) randomly assigned families of children with ADHD to behavioral or medical treatments. The behavioral treatment taught parents to engage in less negative/ineffective discipline strategies. They found that this treatment led to fewer disruptive behavior problems and measures of negative discipline at the end of treatment mediated the effect of assignment to treatment on those outcomes.

Abusive Parenting

The distinction between the use of physical punishment and physically abusive parenting is not simply one of degree. With abuse comes out-of-control, emotionally volatile, and nonnormative actions by a caregiver, which appear to have devastating effects on at least some children. Numerous studies have identified the experience of physical abuse as one of the most important parenting factors in antisocial development. Luntz and Widom (1994) found long-term effects of child abuse on antisocial behavior in a 20-year follow-up of children who had been reported as abused or neglected prior to age 11. Compared with control children matched for age, race, sex, and family socioeconomic status, the abused sample had twice the probability of being diagnosed as having an adult antisocial personality disorder. One of the problems with studies using children who have been identified as abused by child protective services (CPS) is that the experience of abuse is confounded with the actions taken by CPS, including being removed from the home, publicly labeled as abused, and aggregated with deviant children in foster and group-home settings. Dodge, Bates, and Pettit (1990) assessed physical maltreatment in a community sample of preschool children through extended clinical interviews and then followed this sample across childhood. They found short-term effects of maltreatment on aggressive behavior in kindergarten and long-term effects through late adolescence that included school suspensions and physical violence (Lansford et al., 2002).

Given the possibilities that children with particular characteristics might elicit abuse and that common genetic characteristics between parents and child might account for the correlation between abusive parenting and child aggression, Jaffee, Caspi, Moffitt, and Taylor (2004b) studied 1,116 twin pairs in Great Britain and found that physical maltreatment plays a strong causal role in the development of children's antisocial behavior.

At ages 5 and 7, mothers' and teachers' scores on the Child Behavior Checklist were .8 standard deviations higher for abused than nonabused children, controlling for genetic and other factors. Furthermore, Jaffee et al. (2004) found evidence for genetically mediated child effects on corporal punishment, but not on physical maltreatment, suggesting that effects of maltreatment cannot be attributed to genes or child effects.

As research on the effects of child abuse has expanded, it has become important to distinguish among several forms of maltreatment (Cicchetti, 1989). Physical abuse has clear effects on subsequent child aggressive behavior, whereas sexual abuse and neglect have different negative consequences. Fagot, Hagan, Youngblade, and Potter (1989) found important early childhood effects in the observed social behavior of preschool children (ages 3 to 5) who had been sexually abused or were victims of physical abuse and neglect. The physically abused children were more aggressive, less communicative, and more passive than either sexually abused or control children, whereas the sexually abused children were simply more quiet and unresponsive to peers. The physically abused children were more apt to respond to conflicts with aggressive behavior than other children. Sternberg et al. (1993) contrasted 8- to 12-year-old children who had been physically abused by parents in the previous 6 months with others who had witnessed spousal violence but not been abused themselves, or had witnessed violence and been abused. Data on abuse and violence for this Israeli sample came from social workers and the outcome data involved self-reports or mothers' ratings of internalizing or externalizing problems. All 3 vulnerable groups showed more self-reported depression than a demographically matched control group, but only the 2 groups that had been physically abused reported more externalizing problems. Mothers, however, reported more externalizing problems in the two groups who had witnessed domestic violence.

The effects of physical abuse, neglect, and sexual abuse also were contrasted in a summer camp study of 235 children 5- to 11-years-old that included a nonmaltreated matched control group (Manley, Cicchetti, & Barnett, 1994). The subgroups differed on counselor ratings of social competence and behavior problems, but did not differ on peer ratings of disruptiveness or aggressiveness. The sexually abused group was rated by counselors as more socially competent and having fewer behavior problems than the physically abused or the neglected groups, and even somewhat more competent than the nonmaltreated group. The physically abused group had more behavior problems than the nonmaltreated group, with the other two maltreated groups falling between these extreme groups.

Childhood Peer Factors

The peer social context exerts yet another influence on the child's behavioral development. Kellam and Rebok (1992) have found that kindergarten classrooms naturally vary in the incidence of peer-nominated aggression (e.g., in one school, classrooms ranged from 33% to 85% in the proportion of children rated as aggressive), even when assignment to classrooms is random. Clearly, unidentified factors in the ecology of the classroom context account for these differences in aggressive behavior problems. In turn, the ratio of peers who are aggressive influences a child's growing tendency to become aggressive and to value aggression (Stormshak et al., 1999), and these influences last across several years of elementary school (Kellam, Ling, Merisca, Brown, & Ialongo, 1998).

When young aggressive children enter school, they are likely not only to fail academically but also socially, and these two kinds of failure can interact to accelerate the growth of aggressive behavior. There is substantial evidence that aggressive children are likely to be rejected by their peers (Kupersmidt & Dodge, 2004). Although most of the studies have been correlational, making it difficult to determine whether aggression leads to rejection or rejection to aggression, several laboratory play-group studies demonstrate that early aggression leads to later rejection among new, unfamiliar peers.

Coie and Kupersmidt (1983) assembled groups of previously unacquainted fourth grade boys of known sociometric status, one of whom was rejected, and observed them at play for 6 weekly sessions. By the 3rd week, most of the rejected boys were rejected by their new group mates. Verbal and physical aggression were most characteristic of the rejected boys, and in ratings after the last session, there was consensus among group members that the rejected boys most often started fights. In a second study, Dodge (1983) formed groups of 8 previously unacquainted second grade boys who were not selected for social status and observed them for eight sessions. Boys who were observed to make hostile comments and hit other boys most often in initial ses-

sions were likely to be rejected by their new peers in sociometric nominations by the fourth session of play. In a third study, Dodge, Coie, Pettit, and Price (1990) observed groups of 5 or 6 unfamiliar boys at two grade levels (first and third) for five consecutive play sessions. Negative peer status determined at the end of the sessions was associated with both angry reactive aggression and instrumental aggression. Bullying led to disliking only in the third grade groups, suggesting that bullying becomes socially unacceptable by this age.

Three qualifying points need to be made about the relation between childhood aggression and rejection by peers. First, not all aggressive acts are viewed with disapproval by peers. Aggression in response to direct provocation actually is evaluated positively by peers. Children who are seen as standing up for themselves are generally well-liked (Lancelotta & Vaughn, 1989). Second, not all aggressive children are socially rejected by peers. In fact, only about half of the children named by classmates as being highly aggressive are rejected by them. Leadership and other social skills may enable some aggressive children to avoid being rejected (Kupersmidt & Dodge, 2004). Bierman (1986) found differences in the social behavior of rejected versus nonrejected aggressive boys that account for the different evaluations by peers. For example, Bierman, Smoot, and Aumiller (1993) found that boys rated by peers as both aggressive and rejected were more argumentative, more disruptive, and less socially attentive than boys who were aggressive but not rejected.

Finally, the normativeness and cultural context of aggressive behavior moderate the relation between rejection and aggression. Lancelotta and Vaughn (1989) found the correlation between aggression and peer rejection to be much stronger among girls ($r = .73$) than among boys ($r = .37$). The fact that aggression is generally more normative for boys than girls suggests that deviation from norms is likely to result in rejection. Social contextual norms play a significant role in the factors leading to peer rejection. Wright, Giammarino, and Parad (1986) demonstrated the importance of social context in a study of groups of cabin mates in a summer program for behaviorally disturbed boys. Counselor-reported aggression was negatively correlated with peer status in the groups characterized by low levels of aggression, but aggression was uncorrelated with status in the high-aggression groups. Cillessen and Mayeux (2004) followed 905 children from ages 10 to 14, a period when aggressive behavior grows in normativeness.

They found that aggression was increasingly less disliked as children got older, consistent with the hypothesis that when children behave in accordance with group norms they are not disliked.

Findings consistent with a general person-group similarity model positing that deviancy is rejected only if different from group norms have been found in playgroups by Boivin, Dodge, and Coie (1995) and in classrooms by Stormshak et al. (1999). This model also partially explains the developmental differences in the correlation between aggression and popularity: as aggression becomes more normative in early adolescence, its association with social rejection dissipates. The effectiveness and status of bullies also varies with the cultural context in which bullying occurs. Kim, Koh, and Leventhal (2004) found high (40%) prevalence rates for bullying in a sample of 1,756 Korean middle school students and a positive correlation between bullying and high socioeconomic status. In that context, bullying is common among the successful upper class.

Consequences of Peer Rejection

The reason for giving special attention to the peer status consequences of aggressive behavior is that peer rejection appears to contribute to subsequent problems of adaptation, including increased antisocial behavior (Haselager et al., 2002). Ladd (1990) found that rejection by peers in the fall of the kindergarten year predicted declining academic adjustment across the school year. Dodge et al. (2003) found that rejection increases aggressive behavior, especially among children who are aggressive initially. They found that peer rejection in early school years (grades K, 1, and 2) predicted increased aggressive behavior in third grade, even when previous aggression was controlled statistically. Similar findings have been reported by Patterson and Bank (1989), Kupersmidt and Coie (1990), Bierman and Wargo (1995), and Coie (2004).

Adolescent Family Processes

Just as early parenting practices contribute to peer relations problems that exacerbate antisocial behavior during the elementary school years, so, too, parents of adolescents are influenced by their aggressive children but also reciprocally contribute to growth in antisocial behavior during adolescence. Two aspects of parenting appear to be critical to controlling child antisocial activity in early adolescence: discipline practices and parental monitoring. Larzelere and Patterson (1990) used structural equation modeling to find that the linkage between family socioeconomic status, as measured when the boys were in fourth grade, and delinquency, measured in seventh grade from police records and self-report, is mediated by parent management practices measured in sixth grade. Parental management included discipline practices such as consistency, control of parental anger during discipline, and negativity in interactions reflecting aversive comments over trivial incidents, and parental monitoring of the child's activities and associations.

Monitoring is a critical aspect of parenting during adolescence (Dishion & McMahon, 1998). Parental monitoring is particularly important in preventing adolescent involvement with deviant peers. Snyder, Dishion, and Patterson (1986) reported strong path relations between low levels of parental monitoring and increases in deviant peer associations in tenth grade. In their study of 169 adolescent boys living in small, midwestern towns, Simons, Wu, Conger, and Lorenz (1994) found that problems in parental discipline practices (including poor monitoring, harsh discipline, lack of consistency, and ill-defined standards) in seventh grade predicted increased deviant peer associations and police arrests and sanctions in ninth grade.

Not surprisingly, parental monitoring is more important in some circumstances and with some children than others. Pettit, Bates, Dodge, and Meece (1999) found that the positive effects of parental monitoring on keeping antisocial behavior in check were stronger for families living in dangerous neighborhoods than in safe neighborhoods and for children with previous histories of aggressive behavior than nonaggressive children. Thus, youth who are at lower risk do not need, or benefit from, close monitoring as much as high-risk youth. This difference helps explain why parents of low-risk youth (and legislators who fund programs) are sometimes unable to grasp the importance of parent-training and supervised after-school programs for high-risk youth.

Although it is easy to warn parents about the importance of monitoring their adolescents, several studies have demonstrated that it is difficult to monitor certain youth, especially high-risk antisocial youth who begin to engage in covert activities and learn to hide their deviance from their parents (Crouter & Head, 2002). Furthermore, parent-child conflict is extremely stressful for all parties involved, and monitoring can heighten conflict when the parent confronts the youth with evidence of misbehavior. Not surprisingly, early conduct problems lead to *lower* levels of parental monitoring in adolescence (Stattin & Kerr, 2000). Stattin and Kerr (2000) suggested that monitoring is more a consequence than a cause of child antisocial behavior, but other studies have shown that it increases adolescent delinquency beyond the levels that led to poor monitoring (Laird, Pettit, Bates, & Dodge, 2003). Overall, levels of parental monitoring decrease across adolescence, as parents recognize adolescents' desires for greater autonomy and growing maturity to act responsibly on their own (Laird et al., 2003).

Dishion, Nelson, and Bullock (2004) have provided important observational evidence regarding the pattern of parental disengagement with aggressive boys. They videorecorded families of aggressive and nonaggressive boys during interaction tasks in the laboratory and detected patterns of disengagement by parents of aggressive boys. These patterns predicted growth in associations with deviant peers and delinquent outcomes. Ironically and unfortunately, it is the very families for which monitoring and engagement should be increased that it decreases most rapidly, signaling the growing gap between parent and aggressive youth as antisocial behavior becomes more serious.

The constructs of parental monitoring and engagement turn out to include several distinct parenting patterns, each of which has been related to growth in antisocial behavior. Crouter and Head (2002) distinguished between parental monitoring, which involves surveillance of child activities and whereabouts, and knowledge of one's child, which involves seeking information from teachers and the child. Low levels of both constructs have been correlated with past and future child antisocial behavior. These constructs, and discipline practices, are distinguished from a third construct, psychological control, which involves parents' coercive attempts to use guilt and manipulation to control a youth's whereabouts and activities (Barber, 1996). Pettit, Laird, Bates, Dodge, and Criss (2001) found that psychological control strategies grow out of a parent's relationship with a difficult child but, in turn, exacerbate antisocial development and estrangement between the parent and child. Finally, Shumow and Lomax (2002), in a way that is consistent with Baumrind's (1987) construct of authoritative parenting, have suggested that all of these parenting practices are mediated and organized by a parent's sense of efficacy in parenting, and it is the communication of this sense of efficacy that leads to positive outcomes for the child.

Following from Hirschi's (1969) social control theory of antisocial behavior in which a close bond between parent and adolescent is thought to function as a control on antisocial activity, Hawkins and Lishner (1987) reviewed studies that supported the hypothesis that positive parent-child bonding in adolescence is negatively related to adolescent problem behavior. Dishion, French, and Patterson (1995) have challenged the bonding hypothesis on the grounds that these studies fail to control for previous problem-behavior levels and confound bonding with measures of parental monitoring. They cited a multiagent and multimethod measurement study that indicates that there is considerable overlap among these measures of parenting practices. Thus, they argued that parent-child bonding is an outcome of previous conflicts and does not cause future problems; in contrast, parental failure to monitor a child directly increases associations with deviant peers and antisocial behavior.

An important validation of the causal role of parenting practices on adolescent antisocial activity comes from interventions designed to change these practices and reduce antisocial activity. Patterson, Chamberlain, and Reid (1982) evaluated the effects of parent training that used the coercion model as a basis for altering parent behavior and found significant reductions in observed deviant behavior compared with those youth randomly assigned to community practitioners. In a stronger test of the model, Dishion, Patterson and Kavanagh (1991) randomly assigned parents of preadolescents at risk for substance abuse to training in contingency management techniques and found significant reductions in teacher ratings of antisocial behavior compared with youth whose families were assigned to placebo control conditions. Of greatest significance for the validation of the causal role of parenting to antisocial behavior was the fact that improvements in behavior correlated significantly, controlling for baseline behavior, with improvements in observed discipline practices.

Adolescent Peer Processes

Whereas in earlier years when the major influence that peers had on antisocial development was to include or exclude a child from social acceptance, during adolescence the chief peer effect comes from the influence of particular kinds of peer groups. Bagwell, Coie, Terry, and Lochman (2000) have developed a method to identify peer cliques based on a consensus of group members and have found that in preadolescence children organize themselves into different peer cliques that have distinctive features. Aggressive behavior is the primary factor associated with being a central member of deviant peer cliques. Deviant peer cliques offer both a home to attract like-minded antisocial youth (called homophily) and an opportunity to expand the range and severity of antisocial behaviors. The question of social selection versus social influence again looms as a methodological challenge, but current evidence supports both effects. The deviant peer group both assembles antisocial youth and contributes to their antisocial growth. Furthermore, evidence has begun to accumulate that systematic efforts to intervene with antisocial adolescents, which often involve aggregating deviant youth for group interventions, may have iatrogenic effects. This section is organized around the topics of deviant peer group effects, gangs, mechanisms of peer influence in adolescence, and iatrogenic effects of interventions.

Deviant Peer Influences

As noted above, parenting practices in early adolescence can contribute to the disengagement between parent and youth that contributes to gravitation toward deviant friends and peer groups. Undoubtedly, normal developmental processes of autonomy-seeking during this era also contribute to the tendency to seek highly sensational stimuli and to gravitate toward deviant peers. Highly visible antisocial peers come to be viewed positively by a large segment of the adolescent population. Rodkin et al. (2000) identified a subgroup of popular adolescents who are aggressive, cool, and athletic. Cillessen and Mayeux (2004) have documented a general developmental trend for children to move from censuring aggressive peers during elementary school to giving those peers high social status in early adolescence. They also note that this trend is moderated by gender, ethnicity, and the ethnic mix of the peer group, so that the features of popular adolescents depend heavily on the idiosyncratic culture of the peer setting.

In turn, deviant peers come to influence other adolescents in a deviant direction, especially when those peers are central to one's peer clique or have stable friendships with a child. Berndt, Hawkins, and Jiao (1999) found that children who had a stable friendship with a deviant peer were at increased risk for growing in their own deviant behavior as they made the transition from elementary to junior high school. D. Elliott, Huizinga, and Ageton (1985) suggested that the modeling and reinforcement required to produce stronger and more diverse antisocial behavior does not usually come from the family but resides in the deviant peer context. Their longitu-

dinal data on delinquency and substance use from the NYS point to the incremental predictive role of involvement with deviant peers. In support of this conclusion, Patterson, Reid, et al. (1992) found that involvement with deviant peers in grade six predicted subsequent delinquency even controlling for prior antisocial behavior. The deviant peer association construct in this study was formed from parent, peer, and self descriptions of children who "hang around" with peers who get into trouble. Simons et al. (1994) also found that association with deviant peers predicted subsequent arrests.

Keenan, Loeber, Zhang, Stouthamer-Loeber, and van Kammen (1995) examined the effects of deviant peer associations on the onset of disruptive behaviors in two cohorts of the Pittsburgh Youth Study. The onset of delinquency was assessed at 6-month intervals for five successive waves in data collection beginning in fourth grade for one cohort, or in seventh grade for the other. Authority conflict was twice as likely to occur among those disruptive boys who had truant or disobedient best friends as among those who did not, and the odds ratios for the correlation with covert and overt antisocial behavior were 4.3 and 3.4, respectively. The odds ratios for association with deviant peers on predicting disruptive behavior in the following year were 2.2 and 1.9 for covert and overt antisocial behaviors, respectively. Two important features of this study were the fact that onset was the dependent variable, thus controlling for previous disruptive behavior, and that peer influence was tested in a specific type of antisocial activity as a way of examining the extent to which peers truly were models of deviant behavior.

In a contrasting study, Tremblay, Mâsse, Vitaro, and Dobkin (1995) failed to find peer influence on delinquency in a longitudinal study of preadolescents. Mutual best friends were identified for 758 of the 1,034 French-Canadian boys aged 10 to 12. Self-reported overt and covert delinquency assessed 1 year later were predicted by the participants' earlier peer-rated aggressiveness, but the peer-rated aggressiveness of the best friends did not add to the prediction of either covert or overt delinquency. The delinquency of peers in this study was estimated by aggressive reputation and peer influence was restricted to a single best friend rather than a group of friends; however, it is possible that peer influence may be greater at older ages than those studied here. In a follow-up analysis of the same sample, Vitaro et al. (1999) divided the boys according to teacher ratings of their disruptiveness at ages 11 to 12. When the impact of having aggressive-disruptive friends was analyzed by the boys' prior history of conduct problems, Vitaro et al. (1999) found that it was the moderately disruptive boys whose delinquent activity at age 13 showed the negative consequences of deviant friends' influence, in contrast to highly disruptive or socially conforming boys. Thus, it may be the marginally deviant youth who are most susceptible to the influence of deviant peers and are damaged most by placement in highly deviant peer settings (Caprara & Zimbardo, 1996).

One limitation in these studies is that direct measures of group affiliation were not used. A problem with relying on adult or peer estimates of deviant peer influence is that these indices are highly correlated ($r = .89$) with ratings of the target individual's own aggressive behavior (Bagwell et al., 2000), making it difficult to partial out the influence of the target's aggression from estimates of deviant peer influence. Cairns and his associates utilized a more complex approach that was less susceptible to stereotyping on the basis of reputation. They used peer informants to identify the peer clique structure for a school-based peer cohort and then used behavioral characteristics of clique members as an index of clique deviance. Using this approach, they demonstrated that aggressive youth not only tend to associate with other aggressive youth (Cairns, Cairns, Neckerman, Gest, & Gariepy, 1988) but that deviant peer associations influence dropping out of school (Cairns, Cairns, & Neckerman, 1989).

The relation between association with other deviant youth and delinquent activity is well-established in the literature on gangs. Thornberry, Krohn, Lizotte, and Chard-Wierschem (1993) found that gang members accelerated their illegal activity during the time they were associated with their gang and decelerated this activity when they left the gang and were not enmeshed in the gang environment.

Taken together, these findings suggest two important conclusions about deviant peer associations and antisocial behavior. Friendship activities between antisocial youth serve to promote greater deviant behavior, even though, or perhaps because, the interaction quality of the relationship is abrasive. Second, when youth are in a period of antisocial activity, they tend to associate with other antisocial youth, a phenomenon that Kandel (1978) referred to as homophily (like seeking like), but when they are no longer engaged in antisocial activity, they no longer associate with deviant peers.

Although the term homophily suggests a mutual attraction between antisocial adolescents, the quality of

interactions among aggressive youth suggests both positive friendship features like those of nondeviant friends and aversive qualities that are lacking in the relationship of nondeviant friends. In comparing delinquent and nondelinquent 12- to 19-year-olds, Giordano, Cernkovich, and Pugh (1986) found more self-reported conflict between delinquent friends but also more willingness to confide and equivalent amounts of interaction. Gillmore, Hawkins, Day, and Catalano (1992) interviewed preadolescent youth about their friends and nonfriends and found that those who described themselves as frequently getting into trouble were more attached to their conventional friends than to their friends who also get into trouble. These sentiments about friendship mirror Dishion, Patterson, and Griesler's (1994) conclusion that many antisocial friendships are relationships of convenience and not necessarily the preferred choices of these youth. Many of the chronically antisocial youth in the Oregon Youth Study Sample (Dishion et al., 1994) were rejected at age 10 and age 14, and their friendships were of relatively short duration. Thus, part of the dynamics of peer associations for highly antisocial youth may be that they have limited conventional friendship opportunities. Hawkins and Weis (1985) have argued that delinquency often results from a lack of social bonding to the conventional elements of society. The absence of these bonds leads to a lessened influence of conventional rules for behavior, and this contributes to greater antisocial activity.

The reciprocal influence of deviant peer associations and delinquent activity is illustrated in longitudinal findings from the Rochester Youth Developmental Study. Thornberry, Krohn, Lizotte, and Chard-Wierschem (1993) found that associating with deviant peers leads to increased delinquency, partly through the formation and reinforcement of beliefs that it is not wrong to commit delinquent acts. Across time, adolescents who commit delinquent acts are more likely to associate with peers who are also delinquent. Their analyses suggested that bidirectional relationships are necessary to account for longitudinal changes in delinquency, supporting the idea that a dynamic social developmental process is involved.

Delinquent Gangs

The phenomenon of delinquent gangs, particularly in the United States, is an important contemporary manifestation of deviant peer groups (Klein, in press). As Thornberry, Krohn, Lizotte, Smith, and Tobin (2003) have noted, gangs have changed across the past 50 years, as have explanations for their existence, one of the most salient changes being the increased involvement with illegal drug sales. Spergel, Ross, Curry, and Chance (1989, as cited in Goldstein, 1994) have found gangs in all 50 states, with most police and other informants indicating that gang participation and activity were on the increase. Males outnumbered females in gang membership by 20 to 1 and gang crime rates by gender mirrored this ratio. The age range of gang members appear to have extended in both directions across time. Goldstein concluded that the reasons youths join gangs are: "peer friendship, pride, identity development, self esteem enhancement, excitement, the acquisition of resources, and in response to family and community tradition. These goals are often not available to young people through legitimate means in the disorganized and low-income environments from which most gang youth derive" (p. 261).

Even though adolescents join gangs for identity and friendship, one effect of gang involvement, like involvement with deviant peers in general, is increased antisocial activity. Spergel et al. (1989) found that individuals in a gang are 3 times more likely to engage in violent offenses than are those persons not affiliated with a gang. Again, issues of selection bias threaten one's confidence in the conclusion of a causal role for gang membership. However, Thornberry et al. (1993, 2003) used longitudinal analyses to show that becoming involved in a gang increases an adolescent's likelihood of violently offending and that leaving a gang leads to decreases in the likelihood of violently offending. Even more convincingly, Gordon et al. (2004) used fixed-effects models that control for selection to conclude that both selection and socialization effects of gang membership occur among the 858 participants in the 10-year longitudinal Pittsburgh Youth Study.

Mechanisms of Deviant Peer Influence

Since Buehler, Patterson, and Furniss (1966) found that adolescent inmates in a correctional facility tended to reinforce delinquent behaviors and punish behaviors conforming to mainstream social norms, Dishion has examined the interactions of antisocial youth and their friends to understand processes of deviant peer influence. As part of the 13- to 14-year-old assessment of the Oregon Youth Study, friends of the study participants (named by both the boys and their parents) were invited to participate in a peer interaction task (Dishion, Andrews, & Crosby, 1995). Friends of the more antisocial

boys tended to come from the same neighborhood and to provide less satisfying friendships, suggesting that these were friendships of convenience. The behaviors of friends were highly correlated, with antisocial dyads having more negative qualities and more noxious behavior. When highly antisocial dyads (i.e., both had prior police contact and high antisocial ratings) were compared to low antisocial dyads, the high antisocial dyads contingently reciprocated more negative behavior.

In another report of the same set of friendship interaction data, Dishion et al. (1994) found that antisocial dyads engaged in more delinquent talk would tend to reinforce delinquent behavior, than low antisocial dyads. In this latter paper, longitudinal data on antisocial activity and deviant peer associations at ages 10 and 14 suggested a synchrony between the two variables.

Dishion (in press) has proposed a general ecological model of the mechanisms of deviant peer influence that locates the adolescent in a deviant peer group, which, in turn, is located in the larger community. This model posits mechanisms at all levels, beginning with intrapersonal effects of association with deviant peers on cognitive processes by the self and the observing world. Labeling oneself (and of one by others) that comes from mere proximity to a group that is characterized by aggressive behavior may yield self-fulfilling prophecies. Bernberg (2002) found that official processing in juvenile courts systems has adverse effects on subsequent criminal offending once controlling for prior offending, which he attributed to the labeling that comes from the official record. Once the stereotype of a "deviant type" has been established, cognitive processes of stereotype threat (Steele, Spencer, & Aronson, 2002) may operate to disrupt a deviant adolescent's behavior during critical situations, thereby exacerbating deviant behavior. Kaplan and Liu (1994) suggested that self-derogation and helplessness occur when an adolescent is labeled by the mainstream world as a member of a deviant group and that participating in further deviant behavior (in their empirical analyses, drug use and dropping out) restores self-esteem and control.

At the interpersonal level, modeling and positive reinforcement of deviant verbal statements during conversations (called deviancy training) occur in deviant peer groups, leading to increased deviant statements by a youth and serving to mediate the link between early antisocial behavior and young adult problem behavior and adjustment problems (Patterson, Dishion, and Yoerger, 2000). A dynamical systems process has been observed by Granic and Dishion (2002), in which, once ignited, nonlinear acceleration of deviant talk occurs during peer conversations and sometimes leads to a frenzy of deviant statements. Dishion (in press) suggests that, "what is rewarded is not the behavior but the overall set of values, attitudes, and behaviors that accompany a delinquent lifestyle." A contagion effect results, in which deviant behavior proliferates.

Evidence for more specific social learning from deviant peers comes from analyses by Bayer, Pintoff, and Pozen (2004), who analyzed data from 15,000 juveniles serving sentences in 169 Florida correctional facilities. They used facility fixed effects to find that access to peers in prison who have histories of specific crimes (e.g., burglary, felony drug, or weapon-related) leads to facilitation of later crimes of that very same type. These effects are strongest for adolescents who have had initial experience with that type of crime (suggesting a facilitation effect rather than initial exposure effect) and who are exposed to older adolescents than younger adolescents. These findings suggest that deviancy training extends beyond verbal talk to serious crimes, through processes of social learning.

Iatrogenic Effects of Deviant Peer Aggregation

Growing evidence indicates that peer effects on adolescent antisocial behavior occur not only in naturally formed peer groups but also in groups that are formed by government and interventionists. The frightening possibility that well-intentioned interventions can have harmful iatrogenic effects was proposed by Dishion, McCord, and Poulin (1999), with support from the domains of mental health, education, and juvenile justice. In all of these domains, deviant adolescents are routinely aggregated with each other for intervention purposes (e.g., through tracking and special education placement in education, group therapies and group residential homes in mental health, and incarceration and group placements such as boot camps in corrections). These effects provide strong evidence of deviant peer influences because self-selection biases are eliminated through institutional placements.

In mental health, Dishion and Andrews (1995) randomly assigned 119 high-risk boys and girls to one of four treatment conditions: (1) parent focus only, (2) peer focus only, (3) combined parent and peer focus, and (4) control. Analyses revealed adverse effects for peer-focused interventions at both the 1-year and 3-year follow-up. Specifically, subjects in the peer-focus condition showed increases in tobacco use and teacher reports of

delinquent behavior. Feldman, Caplinger, and Wodarski (1983) assigned youth randomly to one of three treatment groups: one composed exclusively of referred deviant youth, one involving nonreferred youth only, and one involving a mix of referred-deviant and nonreferred youth. Deviant children assigned to all-deviant groups had more adverse outcomes than those assigned to mixed groups. Lavallee, Bierman, Nix, and Conduct Problems Prevention Research Group (2005) found that, although random assignment to social skill training groups led to improvements in aggressive behavior overall, the magnitude of this improvement was moderated by characteristics of the peers with whom a child was aggregated. Children assigned to groups with higher levels of peer aggressive behavior improved less.

In education, both tracking children based on academic achievement (Kerckhoff, 1988) and assignment to classrooms with deviant peers for special education (Peetsma, Vergeer, Roeleveld, & Karsten, 2001) are associated with growth in antisocial behavior, including school crimes. Arum and Beattie (1999) found that high school suspensions, which typically involve temporary placement with other suspended students, are associated with a 200% increase in the likelihood of adult incarceration, even after controlling for related risk factors such as family characteristics, socioeconomic status, prior delinquency, and years of education.

In corrections, randomized experiments with juvenile delinquents have demonstrated that assignment to prison visitation and exposure to more deviant inmates (e.g., the "Scared Straight" Program) leads to harmful effects that include later crimes (Petrosino, Turpin-Petrosino, & Finckenauer, 2000). In the most comprehensive meta-analysis to date, Lipsey (in press) examined 396 intervention studies, contrasting group-aggregation versus individually based programs for juvenile delinquency. Studies of prevention programs that intervene with youth in groups show a general pattern of main effects on subsequent offense rates that average about one-third smaller than those of comparable programs that intervene with juveniles individually. Analysis of interactions showed that this effect is concentrated in programs that work with younger juveniles (e.g., age 15 and under) and those that work with lower risk juveniles.

COGNITIVE-EMOTIONAL PROCESSES AS MEDIATORS

A large body of evidence from laboratory, longitudinal, and intervention-experiment studies has accumulated to support the hypotheses that (a) cognitive-emotional processes contribute to antisocial behavioral responding in specific situations, (b) individual differences in cognitive-emotional processes account for a significant proportion of chronic individual differences in aggressive behavior, and (c) cognitive-emotional processes at least partially mediate the effects of socialization on aggressive behavior outcomes. These processes include a variety of constructs from online processing of current social stimuli to latent knowledge structures in memory. This review begins with a discussion of social-situational factors that proximally influence cognitive-emotional processes and then moves to a review of social information processing, followed by a discussion of latent mental structures that guide processing.

Social-Situational Factors That Alter Cognitive-Emotional Processes

Several kinds of situations instigate aggressive behavioral responses through their impact on various aspects of social information processing. These situations are reviewed next.

Factors That Enhance the Attribution of Threat

One of the most consistent findings from laboratory studies is that provocation leads to retaliatory aggression, even in young children (Ferguson & Rule, 1988). Frustration and goal-blocking have long been known to induce anger under both experimental and natural conditions (Berkowitz, 1962). Studies over the past 3 decades have indicated that the *perception* of provocation is far more important than the provocation itself in instigating aggression (Dodge, Murphy, & Buchsbaum, 1984). If a child who is pushed from behind in line at school or who receives an excessively severe punishment from a teacher interprets such an environmental threat as malevolently intended and foreseeable, that child is likely to retaliate aggressively (Dodge et al., 2003). Even kindergarten children can refrain from aggressing when they make a nonmalevolent interpretation of a negative event (Shantz & Voydanoff, 1973). Environmental factors that facilitate a hostile attribution include information about the provocateur as acting consistently negatively over time, distinctively negatively toward the perceiver, and others consensually interpreting the provocateur's actions similarly (Kelley, 1973). Inferences of hostile intent are more likely when the provocateur continues to harm the perceiver despite feedback or threats of punishment, exerts special effort to cause the harm, or seems happy when causing the harm (Rule & Ferguson, 1986). Children also learn when to attribute hostile intent and make moral judgments of a provocateur through socialization (Rule & Ferguson, 1986). Berkowitz (1993) suggested that environmental conditions leading to pervasive negative affect (such as high temperatures, unpleasant living conditions, and foul odors) will also increase the likelihood of anger responses to current threats, even when the unpleasant environmental condition is unrelated to the current threat. He argues that the conscious ascription of blame to the provocateur is not as essential as the experience of displeasure during the time that the stimulus is presented.

It is only a short inferential leap to suggest that attributions of hostile intent and experiences of anger in response to current provocative stimuli become more likely when a child is growing up under circumstances of pervasive violence, harm, and deprivation, such as when others regularly assault the child, when assaults regularly occur toward the child's family, peers, and ethnic group, and when peer groups and family also interpret provocateurs as being hostile. Longitudinal evidence is consistent with this hypothesis. Dodge, Price, Bachorowski, & Newman (1990) found that a history of physical maltreatment in the first 5 years of life leads to hostile attributional biases during elementary school. Dodge et al. (2003) found that chronic peer social rejection during early elementary school years leads to hostile attributional biases during later elementary school. Aber, Gershoff, Ware, and Kotler (2004) found that witnessing family violence around the time of the September 11th disaster predicted children's tendencies to display hostile attributional biases a year later. Cassidy, Kirsh, Scolton, and Parke (1996) found that an early history of insecure attachment to one's mother and the experience of parental rejection were both antecedents of the tendency to display hostile attributional biases during elementary school. Finally, MacBrayer, Milich, and Hundley (2003) found that modeling of hostile attributional biases by mothers is correlated with a child's own tendency to attribute hostility to others.

Factors That Increase the Accessibility of Aggressive Responses

A second mechanism leading to aggressive responding is the accessing of aggressive responses from memory during interpersonal exchanges. Bandura's classic studies (1973, 1983) indicate that "children can acquire entire repertoires of novel aggressive behavior from observing aggressive models and can retain such response patterns over extended periods" (Bandura, 1983, p. 6). Imitation is an evolved characteristic that is present even among neonates (Meltzoff & Moore, 1977). Aggressive models can be observed in a child's family members, community subculture, or mass media. Social learning theory (Bandura, 1983) articulates four processes by which modeling can activate aggressive behavior: (1) directive functions, through which an aggressive response enters a child's repertoire because of the positive consequences for aggressing that are vicariously taught; (2) disinhibitory functions, in which modeled aggression reduces fear of negative consequences; (3) emotional arousal, in which the aggressive model facilitates aggression by arousing observers; and (4) stimulus-enhancing effects, in which the objects used in aggression receive heightened attention and provide instruction for the aggressive use of these objects.

Aggressive models teach more than just specific behaviors. They teach general strategies for acting; when observers synthesize modeled behaviors into patterns that follow regularized sequences, those patterns form *scripts* that are laid down in memory (Huesmann, 1998). Information about the category of aggression, its elicitors, and its consequences constitutes aggressive *schemas* (Shank & Abelson, 1977), which guide attention and interpretation to future stimuli and can therefore enrich scripts for action. Through observation and experience, children develop an understanding of aggression that includes expectations for what produces aggression, how aggression is performed, elements of an aggression category (including emotions and actions), and the likely consequences of this behavior (Rule & Ferguson, 1986). Once having acquired an aggression script, when a child encounters difficult situations, that script governs expectations and prescribes behavioral strategies. Strongly developed scripts, acquired through observational learning, can lead to aggressive responding.

Huesmann (1988) suggested that aggression scripts are developed through active attention to aggressive models. Aggressive behaviors can be acquired through repeated exposure to multiple stimulating aggressive acts in diverse contexts displayed by models who are both heroes and identification figures for the observer, followed by opportunities to practice aggressing with impunity so that complex scripts for aggressing become part of a child's memorial repertoire for extraction in future situations. Living with a violent family or in a neighborhood in which the heroes are violent, interacting with antisocial peers who present repeated chances to act aggressively, and watching TV violence all represent opportunities to learn aggressive scripts.

Priming of Aggressive Constructs

The extraction of aggressive scripts and specific aggressive responses from memory can occur either through active problem solving (Rubin & Krasnor, 1986) or nonconscious priming. Graham and Hudley (1994) demonstrated that "priming" the perception that others' negative actions are intentional can lead to hostile attributional biases, which, in turn, have been related to aggressive behavioral responses.

Berkowitz (1993) suggested that certain stimuli induce an associative network of internal responses that he calls "the anger/aggression syndrome," which include physiological reactions, motor tendencies, feelings, thoughts, and memories. Wyer and Srull (1989) have suggested that these responses are activated through an association in memory between a stimulus and one aspect of the response, which then spreads the activation to the entire syndrome through secondary associations. Priming effects are short-lived but powerful and automatic (Bargh, Chaiken, Raymond, & Hymes, 1995). Wann and Branscombe (1990), for example, found that experimentally giving students the names of aggressive persons in sports increased the likelihood that the student would subsequently attribute hostile intent to an ambiguous target person.

Many factors influence the probability that a particular stimulus will prime aggressive responses. Aggressive script responses that are laid down in memory with great frequency, drama, and recency are likely to be at the top of the "storage bin" and primed (Wyer & Srull, 1989); scripts that have multiple complex associations in memory are likely to be easily and chronically accessible (Bargh & Thein, 1985) because many stimuli can instigate associations to the script. Thus, growing up in an environment in which violence is normative will increase the accessibility of aggressive constructs in future situations. Certain persons who are nonreflective about their own behavior or are in impaired pathological states (Bargh, 1989) are "ripe" for priming effects. Stressful environments may render children vulnerable to aggressive priming. Finally, situational cues that are self-relevant (Strauman & Higgins, 1987), not overly engrossing, but are aggression-related (such as easy access to weapons; Goldstein, 1994) or semantically related to one's ideographic aggressive schema (Carver, Ganellan, Froming, & Chambers, 1983), are likely to have priming effects.

Factors That Dysregulate Emotion Control

Lemerise and Arsenio (2000) suggested that a variety of emotion-related processes mediate aggressive behavior. Although they integrate these processes with a more general social information-processing framework, they argue that the dysregulation of emotion plays a special role that differs from other cognitive processes. They cite studies that relate child aggression to the child's ability to regulate emotion, to understand others' emotion, and to express emotion accurately. The work of Eisenberg et al. (2003, 2004) buttresses the role of emotion-regulatory processes in mediating the development of antisocial behavior. Other studies indicate that these processes develop through experience and account for the relation between life experiences and later behavior; for example, Cummings and Davies (2002) have argued that emotion dysregulation is the process that mediates the relation between witnessing marital conflict and child aggression.

Factors That Enhance the Attractiveness of Aggression

Accessing aggressive behavior from memory is only partly a function of its salience and priming potential; it is also a function of the salience and accessibility of alternatives to aggression, enhanced by modeling. Furthermore, social learning theory stipulates that environments induce aggression by promoting the belief that aggression is normative, morally appropriate, and will lead to desired positive consequences (through reinforcement). According to Bandura (1983), "(In) societies that provide extensive training in aggression, attach prestige to it, and make its use functional, people spend a great deal of time threatening, fighting, maiming, and killing each other" (p. 11).

Bandura (1983) hypothesized that reinforcement can take the form of tangible rewards, social and status rewards, reduction of aversive treatment, and expressions of injury by the victim. Patterson, Littman, and Bricker (1967) found that children who were victimized by peers and who occasionally succeeded in stopping those attacks through counteraggression became more likely to fight in the future; in contrast, those children who avoided peers and thus avoided victimization did not become aggressive over time. Just as powerful as direct reinforcement is the observation of other persons being

reinforced for aggressing. In this case, the person learns through vicarious means that aggression leads to desired consequences. Neuroimaging studies have revealed that the "positive consequences" of aggressing could also be entirely intrapersonal—through activation of the dorsal striatum region of the brain (de Quervain et al., 2004). In other words, no external reward is necessary to reinforce reactive aggressive behaviors, which instead may be reinforced merely by brain activation that is experienced as the intrinsic pleasure experienced in revenge.

Social Information Processing

Social information-processing models of aggressive behavior were initially developed to describe at a proximal level how cognitive and emotional processes lead a child to engage in aggressive behavior in a social event (e.g., Dodge, 1986; McFall, 1982). The conceptual grounding for these models is work in cognitive science on how individuals store and retrieve information (Tulving & Thomson, 1973), distribute processing in parallel and hierarchical fashion (Rumelhart & McClelland, 1986), and ultimately solve problems (Newell & Simon, 1972).

According to current formulations (Dodge & Pettit, 2003; Gifford-Smith & Rabiner, 2004), an individual comes to a social situation with a set of neural pathways that have been honed over time through genetic and experiential factors and a history of social experiences that are represented in memory. The individual is presented with a new set of social cues (e.g., peers gently tease a boy on the playground about his ugly shoes) and responds behaviorally as a function of how he or she processes those cues, which, in turn, is a function of the interaction among biological, memorial, and current-cue factors. Because processing occurs in real time, it can have both conscious and unconscious (and controlled and automatic) components (Rabiner, Lenhart, & Lochman, 1990). As Piaget (1965; Cowan, 1979) noted, processing is a fully emotional, as well as cognitive, phenomenon.

The first step of processing is encoding of the cues. Because the cue array is so overwhelming, the individual employs heuristics to encode only relevant portions. Both deficits (e.g., failure to encode mitigating cues) and biases (e.g., selective attention to hostile features of others' behavior) in encoding could lead an individual to respond aggressively; different biases (e.g., selective failure to encode actual hostile cues) could lead to nonaggressive responding. As cues are encoded, they are interpreted, so the next step is mental representation of the meaning of the cues, particularly with regard to threat and others' intentions. Both biases (e.g., a hostile attributional bias, as dubbed by Nasby, Hayden, & De-Paulo, 1979) and errors (e.g., misinterpreting a benign teasing stimulus as malicious) in mental representation could enhance the likelihood of aggressive responding. The next step in processing is accessing of one or more possible behavioral responses from memory. Through exposure, experience, and evolution, one's interpretation of a stimulus becomes associated with emotional and behavioral responses (e.g., threat-retaliate, disrespect-anger; see desired object, grab it); in some cases, the individual actively generates responses, as in problem solving. Often, single behavioral responses are not accessed; rather, a program of behaviors and expected responses to those behaviors is accessed, as in a script (Huesmann, 1988). Obviously, patterns of response access will be closely linked to the probability of aggressive responding. Accessing a response does not destine one to that response, so the next step of processing is response decision. The individual might evaluate a potential response by its moral acceptability and its instrumental, interpersonal, and intrapersonal outcomes, weight the values of those outcomes, and decide on a course of action. The response that is most positively evaluated (e.g., a boy evaluates that hitting a peer will save face, which is more important than being punished by authority, so he decides to aggress) will likely be enacted. An individual might consider responses simultaneously or sequentially, with varying thresholds of acceptability for enactment. In this context, impulsivity is defined as the lowest possible acceptability (i.e., a child responds with the first response that comes to mind, with no further evaluation). Thus, patterns of impulsivity or positive evaluation for aggressing are likely to eventuate in aggressive behavior. Also, rehearsal of behaviors in one's mind enhances the likelihood of selection, without regard to its likely consequences (Huesmann, 1988). Finally, the selected response gets transformed into behavior, which requires motor and verbal skills. Skill deficiencies in enacting aggressive responses could inhibit those behaviors, whereas skill deficiencies in enacting competent, nonaggressive alternatives could enhance aggressive responding through default.

Because the model describes social behavior as it unfolds in real time, the steps of processing are hypothesized to recycle iteratively (e.g., the child's behavioral response gets a reaction from another person, which becomes the next cue for further encoding) and most likely occurs simultaneously with feedback loops in parallel processing (e.g., in the microsecond of evaluating a potential response, the child encodes a change in a peer's facial expression). As a description of social events, the model has heuristic strength (see Crick & Dodge, 1994, for a review). In addition, the model proposes that individuals develop characteristic styles of processing cues at each step, in domains of situations, and that these processing styles will correlate with individual differences in aggressive behavior. This hypothesis has generated over 200 empirical studies, with generally supportive findings (see reviews by Gifford-Smith & Rabiner, 2004; Dodge & Pettit, 2003).

Selective Attention and Encoding

Using videotaped stimuli to assess the first step of processing, Dodge et al. (2003) found that aggressive children are less able than nonaggressive children to recall relevant social cues. Aggressive children have also been found to attend selectively to aggressive social cues in a stimulus array more than nonaggressive peers do and have difficulty diverting attention from aggressive cues (Gouze, 1987). When encoded cues are used to make interpretations of others' actions, aggressive children use fewer external cues than others do (Dodge & Newman, 1981) and instead rely more on their own stereotypes or simply use the most recently presented cue (Dodge & Tomlin, 1987).

Pollock has creatively used selective attention paradigms with emotional faces as stimuli to understand the influence of physical abuse on selective attention to threat cues as a mechanism in the development of aggressive behavior. Pollak and Tolley-Schell (2003) found that physically abused children demonstrate selective attention to angry faces and reduced attention to happy faces. Further, abused children display relative difficulty in disengaging from angry faces.

Attribution of Intent

Over three dozen studies have shown that, given ambiguous provocation circumstances, aggressive children are more likely than nonaggressive children to make a hostile interpretation of another's intentions. In a typical study, participants are asked to imagine being the object of an ambiguous provocation (e.g., a peer spills water on you) and to make an interpretation of the peer's likely intent (Dodge, 1980). Positive correlations between hostile attributional biases and aggressive behavior have been found in many school-based samples, including 8- to 12-year-old children (Guerra & Slaby, 1989), White children (Dell Fitzgerald & Asher, 1987), African American middle school boys (Graham & Hudley, 1994), Latino children (Graham, Hudley, & Williams, 1992), and British 8- to 10-year-old children (Aydin & Markova, 1979). Hostile attributional biases have also been found in aggressive clinical samples, including children with diagnosed disruptive behavior disorders (MacBrayer et al., 2003), adolescent offenders (Dodge, Price, et al., 1990), incarcerated violent offenders (Slaby & Guerra, 1988), and aggressive boys in residential treatment (Nasby et al., 1979). The findings extend beyond hypothetical situations: Steinberg and Dodge (1983) found similar evidence using a laboratory-based actual social interaction, in which children made attributions about a peer partner.

Although reciprocal effects are likely, prospective analyses by Dodge, Pettit, Bates, and Valente (1995) indicate that hostile attributional biases predict growth in aggressive behavior over time. Finally, experimental intervention with aggressive African American boys in which the focus was to reduce hostile attributional tendencies led to decreased aggressive behavior, relative to a control group (Hudley & Graham, 1993).

Several studies have found that aggressive children also erroneously interpret hostile intent when the stimuli clearly depict benign intentions (Dodge, Murphy, & Buchsbaum, 1984; Dodge, Pettit, McClaskey, & Brown, 1986). Statistical controls indicate that this intention-cue detection deficiency cannot be accounted for by general information-processing deficits or impulsivity (Waldman, 1988) or verbal intelligence (Dodge, Price, et al., 1990).

Accessing Goals

A growing body of research has correlated children's goals with individual differences in aggressive behavior (Erdley & Asher, 1999). Aggressive behavior has been linked to present-oriented (versus future-oriented) goals (Caprara & Zimbardo, 1996), goals in friendships (Rose & Asher, 1998), less-social goals (Murphy & Eisenberg, 2002), and performance-competitive (rather than relational) goals (Asher & Renshaw, 1981). Crick and Dodge (1994) introduced the process of goals accessing as the next step of processing, once the individual has mentally represented the stimulus set. Thus, goals are dynamically formulated online as a joint function of preexisting long-term plans that may reside in memory

and the immediate circumstances of a particular social stimulus. A child may enter a situation with preexisting hopes of establishing a friendship with a peer partner in a game, but the stimulus of losing a game under questionable circumstances may lead the child to formulate a goal of revenge that overwhelms other goals. All situations require the balancing of multiple goals, but little is known about how children redirect their goals during social interactions. Research on executive function deficits in aggressive children suggests that this process may be difficult for aggressive children. Indeed, Taylor and Gabriel (1989) found that aggressive children have difficulty coordinating multiple goals.

Response Access

The next step of processing is behavioral response access. Both the automatic association between social cue representation and aggressive responses and the conscious generation of aggressive solutions to social dilemmas have been implicated in the genesis of aggressive behavior. Shure and Spivack (1980) have found that among preschool children, the number of responses that a child generates to hypothetical social problems is inversely related to that child's rate of aggressive behavior. Among children in elementary school, the quality, not quantity, of responses is linked to aggressive problems. Aggressive children generate high proportions of atypical responses (Ladd & Oden, 1979), bribery and affect manipulation responses (Rubin, Moller, & Emptage, 1987), direct physical aggression responses (Dodge et al., 2003; Waas, 1988), and adult intervention responses (Asher & Renshaw, 1981). They access fewer competent responses, including nonaggressive assertion (Deluty, 1981) and planning responses (Asarnow & Callan, 1985).

Response Decision

There are crucial differences between accessing a response and selecting it for enactment. Across development, children learn to lengthen the time between response accessing and behavior or to withhold impulses altogether, pending a mental evaluation of the likely effects. Barkley et al. (2002) have argued that the inability to inhibit accessed responses is the single major component of ADHD that is responsible for the aggressive behavior problems of these children. Self-reports by aggressive children (Perry, Perry, & Rasmussen, 1986) support the hypothesis that aggressive children have difficulty inhibiting aggressive responses. Slaby and

Guerra (1988) found that aggressive adolescent offenders generate fewer possible outcomes for their own behaviors than others do, suggesting a failure to consider consequences by this group.

Wilson and Herrnstein (1985) proposed that criminal behavior (and aggression more broadly) involves a rational decision in which the participant considers the expectation of benefits and their probabilities (e.g., peer approval or instrumental gain) versus the expectation of costs and their probabilities (e.g., legal punishment or parental disapproval). Crick and Dodge (1994) proposed that children may consider instrumental, interpersonal, intrapersonal, and moral outcomes in their evaluations. They may evaluate a possible behavior by these various outcomes, assign weights (estimates of value) to these categories, and perform mental arithmetic to decide on a behavioral response. Thus, environments that afford a positive cost/benefit ratio will show high rates of aggression. Clarke and Cornish (1983) conducted a rational decision analysis of youthful burglary and found that important deciding factors included whether a house was occupied, whether it had a burglar alarm or dog, and whether it reflected affluence. Not surprisingly, Becker (1974) concludes that offenders typically estimate the risk of being caught as very low (whether valid or not); thus, a rational analysis can still lead to risky (and ill-informed) behavior by some individuals.

As young children develop the ability to represent mentally the anticipated consequences of their behavior (usually, between ages 5 and 10; Werner, 1961), they become more skilled at deciding when to aggress. The rate of their aggression might not necessarily decrease, but their behavior will become more reasoned.

One of the mental actions that can occur during decision making has been called moral disengagement by Bandura (2002). Through socialization, most children learn self-restraints on aggressive behavior that involve anticipatory self-censuring and evaluations that aggression will be punished. Bandura (2002) argued that otherwise moral children perform aggressive acts through processes that disengage the usual self-reactions from such conduct. Several processes can contribute to moral disengagement. Cognitive restructuring can involve justifying aggressive action on the grounds that it will lead to a higher moral end (e.g., self-respect). This restructuring involves the minimization of one's own moral violations by comparing them to more reprehensible acts. This minimizing is particularly easy when a child is growing up amidst truly flagrant inhumanities (e.g.,

child abuse, homicide, rape, or discrimination). Euphemistic labeling (e.g., "trains," "get-back," "just teaching him a lesson"; McCall, 1994) further minimizes the perceived seriousness of the act.

A second set of dissociative processes involves distorting the relation between actions and their effects. When aggressing in a group, individuals can diffuse their own responsibility for their actions or deflect responsibility elsewhere (e.g., to authority, as in Milgram's, 1974, obedience experiments, or to society more broadly in war). A third set of disengagement processes operates on the perceptions of the victims. Dehumanization through labels (e.g., "cracker," "nigger") can lead to self-exoneration for inhumane acts. Modern urban life tends to foster such dehumanization processes as a result of high social mobility, anonymity, and the castelike categorization of persons into in-group and out-group members. Finally, aggressive actions are justified by attributing blame for the action to the victim. Because most aggressive acts occur in a sequence of escalating interpersonal exchanges, aggressors often find it easy to select from the chain of events an act by the victim that "merits" aggressive retaliation. Studies by Bandura, Barbaranelli, Caprara, and Pastorelli (1996) demonstrate that measures of moral disengagement by children based on these concepts are linked to their rates of aggressive behavior and emotional irascibility.

Moral disengagement can occur quickly in a social exchange, but more frequently it evolves gradually through cultural influence and reinforcement for partial disengagement. Children learn across time whether disengagement is allowed, and they learn to disengage more quickly and with less apparent justification in environments that provide little opposition. During this process, the individual misrepresents, minimizes, and disregards the injurious effects of aggression while selectively focusing on the self-enhancing outcomes; diffuses responsibility for the outcomes of aggression; generates palliative comparisons for one's own act of aggression; places euphemistic labels on one's own aggression; and vilifies and dehumanizes the victim of aggression. Bandura et al. (1996) have demonstrated in a longitudinal study of children outside of Rome, Italy, that these processes predict interpersonal aggressive behavior. Even otherwise moral human beings have been found to engage in these processes selectively during the course of morally defended aggressive acts (Bandura, 2002).

When they are experimentally forced to make evaluations and consider consequences, aggressive children, relative to nonaggressive peers, evaluate aggressive responses as more legitimate (Erdley & Asher, 1998), less morally "bad" (Deluty, 1983), more "friendly" (Crick & Ladd, 1990), and globally more acceptable (Crick & Werner, 1998). They expect more positive instrumental outcomes (Egan, Monson, & Perry, 1998), more positive intrapersonal outcomes (Fontaine, Burks, & Dodge, 2002), fewer negative interpersonal outcomes (Quiggle, Panak, Garber, & Dodge, 1992), and fewer sanctional outcomes (Perry et al., 1986) for aggressing. In contrast, aggressive children report lower levels of perceived self-regulatory efficacy for prosocial behaviors and resisting peer pressure (Caprara, Regalia, & Bandura, 2002). Ethnographic analyses of urban communities also support the notion that "codes of violence" support aggressive behavior as the only means of gaining status and avoiding victimization (E. Anderson, 1990).

Enactment

The final step of processing is to transform a selected response into motor and verbal behavior. Socially rejected and aggressive children have been shown to be less competent when asked to enact and role-play nonaggressive socially appropriate behaviors in laboratory settings (Burleson, 1982). One of the difficulties with these studies is that children's enactments may be confounded by other mental processes, such as their expectations about the likely outcomes of behavior, even in laboratory role-play settings.

Mediation of Life Experiences through Acquired Processing Patterns

Each of the processing-aggressive behavior correlations previously described is rather modest in magnitude. These correlations are enhanced by considering the situational context, the type of aggressive behavior, and the profile of processing patterns. Dodge et al. (1986) found that the correlation between processing and aggressive behavior is stronger in situations than across situations (i.e., processing about teasing events relates more strongly to aggressive behavior in response to teasing than to aggressive behavior in peer group entry situations). Also, early-step processing variables (i.e., encoding and hostile attributions) relate more strongly to reactive anger, whereas later-stage processing variables (i.e., response evaluations) relate more strongly to proactive aggression (Crick & Dodge, 1996). Finally, when profiles are assembled or multiple regression techniques are used, the predictability of aggressive behavior from aggregated processing measures is great (Dodge et al., 1986). Findings from 9 samples (1 from Dodge & Price, 1994; 3 from Dodge et al., 1986; 2 from Dodge et al., 2003; 1 from Slaby & Guerra, 1988; and 2 from Weiss, Dodge, Bates, & Pettit, 1992) indicate that processing variables from different steps provide unique increments in predicting aggression, such that multiple correlations range up to .94.

Several studies have found that the effects of adverse life experiences on growth in aggressive behavior are mediated by the child's development of patterns of processing social information. Dodge, Bates, et al. (1990) found that the experience of physical maltreatment is associated with an acquired tendency to become hypervigilant to hostile cues, to attribute hostile intent to others, to access aggressive responses readily, and to evaluate aggressive responses as instrumentally successful. In turn, these social information-processing patterns were found to lead to later aggressive behavior and to account for the effect of maltreatment on aggression in middle school (Dodge et al., 1995).

Eisenberg et al. (2003) found that parents' negative expressed emotion influences the child's social adjustment through its mediating effects on the development of self-regulatory processes, including attention focusing, attention shifting, and inhibitory control. In yet another study, Snyder, Stoolmiller, Wilson, and Yamamoto (2003b) found that parents' responses to child misbehavior lead to growth in the child's antisocial behavior through the mediating process of children's anger regulation.

Latent Knowledge Structures

A growing body of evidence suggests that children's life experiences lead to represented memories that predict future behavioral tendencies through an influence on the way that future social information is processed. This work has been conducted under several different rubrics.

Schemas and Scripts

Social-cognitive theories in psychology (Bargh et al., 1995) suggest that processing of social cues is guided by latent knowledge structures, variously called schemas and scripts, that are stored in memory (Abelson, 1981). These structures are hypothesized to be the evolving representational products of experience, which guide processing of new cues. Baldwin (1992) has described several ways that social knowledge structures exert an impact on social information processing, including selective attention to cues, premature judgments about stimuli, biased interpretations of ambiguous information, and biased expectancies for the outcomes of events.

Huesmann (1988, 1998) has articulated the hypothesis that early development leads children to represent in memory scripts for aggression that include acceptable antecedents, details of context and action, and likely consequences. Graham and Hudley (1994) employed priming techniques from cognitive-social psychology to ascertain that aggressive children have highly accessible aggressive constructs represented in memory. Stromquist and Strauman (1992) asked children to describe freely their social relationships and found that the tendency to use aggressive constructs (both in commission and omission, e.g., "he hits others" and "he stays away from fights") is correlated with aggressive behavior. Burks, Laird, Dodge, Pettit, and Bates (1999) used the Stromquist-Strauman method to find that hostile representations of peer relationships predict later aggressive behavior toward peers. MacKinnon-Lewis, Rabiner, and Starnes (1999) found that cognitive representations of familiar and unfamiliar peers are associated with social maladjustment. Specifically, boys who held negative feelings about known peers at the beginning of the school year were less likely to be accepted by peers 6 months later.

Self-Concept

Self-concept is a knowledge structure that has been hypothesized to relate to aggression (Harter, 1982). However, despite the speculation of psychodynamic theorists (Keith, 1984) that aggressive children must have miserable self-concepts, empirical assessments have not borne out this hypothesis (Crick & Dodge, 1996; Zakriski & Coie, 1996). Even aggressive children who are also socially rejected by peers do not seem to recognize that they are rejected by peers. Zakriski and Coie (1996) reported that aggressive-rejected boys did not see themselves as having been rejected by an experimental confederate playmate even when this was observed to have happened. Hymel, Bowker, and Woody (1993) found that unpopular aggressive children received self-concept scores in academic, athletic, appearance, and social competence domains that were as high as those of average peers, even though objective assessments of their competence in these domains indicated otherwise. Aggressive children appear to blame others rather than themselves for their negative outcomes (Cairns, 1991). The possibility that other-blaming may represent self-defensive mechanisms in aggressive children (Keith, 1984) indicates the inherent difficulty in measuring this latent knowledge structure.

Normative Beliefs

Huesmann (1998) has proposed that children's beliefs about consensual social norms influence children's aggressive behavior. Children learn these norms through perception, identification with reference groups, and personal evaluation. Guerra et al. (1995) assessed children's normative beliefs about the consequences of aggressing and found that (a) the male culture more strongly endorses the use of aggression than does the female culture, (b) the normative endorsement of aggression increases across age during the school years, and (c) these beliefs correlate with aggressive behavior. Zelli, Dodge, Lochman, Laird, and the Conduct Problems Prevention Research Group (1999) found that third graders who hold normative beliefs that aggression is acceptable are relatively likely to engage in deviant social information processing in fourth and fifth grade, which, in turn, is related to aggressive behavior and mediates the effect of beliefs on aggression. The converse relation did not hold as strongly.

Working Models

Bowlby (1980) proposed that early life experiences, especially with regard to an infant's attachment with a caregiver, lead to the formulation of working models of how social relationships operate. These models reside in memory and guide future social behavior. Cassidy, Ziv, Rodenberg, and Woodhouse (2003) found that measures of working models correlate with indices of children's social adjustment. Cassidy et al. (1996) found that children classified as insecurely attached or who reported experiencing parental rejection were more likely to make hostile attributions in response to hypothetical, ambiguous provocations than were other children.

Moral Development and Perspective Taking

Arsenio and Lemerise (2004) have proposed that moral development acts as a distal latent knowledge structure to guide more proximal online processing of social information. The structuralist perspective on cognitive development evolving from Piaget's (1965) theory and research has contributed two major ideas to the quest for understanding the development of antisocial behavior

(Nucci, 2001). First, social and cognitive egocentrism, or the failure to recognize the perspective of social others, has been related to the development of antisocial behavior. Chandler (1973) found that aggressive children's social perspective-taking level, scored in terms of Piagetian developmental levels, was lower than their peers. He then developed an intervention showing young adolescent delinquents videotapes of their own behavior, followed by discussion in which participants were encouraged to take each other's roles, to improve their perspective-taking levels. Those adolescents who participated in the intervention displayed fewer delinquent acts 18 months later than did a control group. Others (e.g., Iannotti, 1978) have been unable to obtain shifts in aggression through role-taking training. There have been some attempts to make children less aggressive by training them to take the affective perspective of others (e.g., Feshbach & Feshbach, 1982), but the results of these efforts have been mixed, at best.

The second major contribution of the structuralist perspective has been to relate moral development to antisocial behavior. The basic hypothesis has been that developmental lags in stages of moral development will lead to antisocial behavior. Blasi (1980) reviewed studies testing the relation between moral judgment and moral action and concluded that a majority of these studies supported Kohlberg's (1986) thesis that higher moral reasoning would lead to personal honesty and altruism. The fact that moral reasoning per se does not always relate to apparently altruistic behavior or resistance to temptation has led to an elaboration of the theory in terms of personal identity: Moral reasoning is related to moral behavior in individuals for whom moral values are central to their self-understanding (Blasi & Oresick, 1986). Recent studies have found correlations between moral reasoning in domains of social encounters (Horn, 2003) and racial exclusion (Killen, Lee-Kim, McGlothlin, & Stangor, 2002) and social adjustment.

TREATMENT AND PREVENTION OF ANTISOCIAL BEHAVIOR

The past decade has witnessed an explosion of randomized trials testing interventions to prevent aggressive behavioral development and to treat conduct disorder. Hinshaw (2002) has noted that intervention experiments offer the opportunity not only to apply the developmental knowledge reviewed in this chapter to improve children's

lives but also to test developmental hypotheses more rigorously. A comprehensive review is beyond the scope of this chapter. Instead, the intervention experiments that will be highlighted are those that include a theoretical basis in a developmental model, random assignment, evaluation of all children assigned to intervention (whether they received it or not), independent replication, long-term follow-up, and blind assessment of outcome. These studies have in common the hypotheses that conduct problem behavior develops (or is maintained) by one or more of the developmental factors reviewed here and that intervention to alter those developmental factors will indirectly lead to the prevention or reduction of aggressive behavior. The interventions range from universal (population-based) to selected (groups identified based on risk factors) to indicated (groups identified based on aggressive behavior) approaches.

Stimulant Medication

The success of psychostimulant medication in treating attention deficits (Frick, 2001), coupled with the known association between early biologically based attention deficits (ADHD) and CD has led to the hypothesis that psychostimulant medication could indirectly reduce conduct problems. The Multimodal Treatment Study of Children with Attention Deficit Hyperactivity Disorder (MTA) is the largest randomized trial test of this hypothesis, albeit with a subgroup of conduct-problem children who have comorbid ADHD. Although psychostimulant treatment (relative to no treatment) was found to be effective in altering attention deficits in this group of 7- to 10-year-olds, by itself it had no substantial impact on oppositional and aggressive behavior (MTA Cooperative Group, 1999). Other trials (reviewed by Frick, 2001) indicate some success of psychostimulants in reducing disruptive behavior; however, Frick points out that "the medication's primary effect may be to enhance the child's responsiveness to other interventions" (p. 600) and that "there is little evidence to date that stimulants reduce conduct problems in children without a comorbid diagnosis of ADHD" (p. 600).

Parent-Based Approaches

A variety of family interventions designed to improve parents' discipline strategies, the quality of parent-child relationships, and parents' monitoring and supervision of children have proven efficacious in reducing aggressive behavior. The basis for most of these interventions is coercion theory by Patterson et al. (1992) and Forehand and McMahon's (1981) behavioral approach. The primary goal of Parent Management Training (PMT) is to alter the pattern of exchanges between parent and child during discipline events so that coercive behavior by each party is extinguished in favor of contingent, consistent, and clear rules that lead to compliance. Parenting behaviors are taught through role-play, practice, completion of homework, and discussion, sometimes with the child present.

Rigorous evaluations have proven this approach to be efficacious. "PMT is probably the most well-investigated therapy technique for children and adolescents . . . and has led to marked improvements in child behavior" (Kazdin, 2003a, pp. 261–262). A meta-analysis by Serketich and Dumas (1996) yielded a large mean effect size of .86 standard deviations for programs with young children (up to age 10). A meta-analysis of programs for delinquent and conduct-disordered children aged 10 to 17 by Woolfendon, Williams, and Peat (2002) yielded a mean effect size of .56. The meta-analysis of 40 studies by Farrington and Welsh (2003) yielded a mean effect size of .32 in preventing delinquency outcomes.

Kazdin (2003b) notes that one of the major problems with PMT approaches is getting families to participate and to complete the intervention. Issues of cultural relevance loom large, and practices to engage parents by focusing on family relationships (as in functional family therapy; Alexander & Parsons, 1982), and by attending to their stressors (Kazdin & Whitley, 2003) have proven important.

Several mediational analyses of PMT have supported the developmental hypothesis that parenting practices themselves play a role in aggressive behavioral growth. Hinshaw et al. (2000) found that child disruptive behavior gains in school as a function of randomly assigned treatment could be accounted for by improvements in parenting practices. Dishion and Kavanagh (2000) reported that changes in parenting accounted for the positive effects of the parent intervention of the Adolescent Transitions Program (ATP) on child antisocial behavior.

For families facing extremely high levels of antisocial behavior in adolescents who are on the verge of incarceration, multisystemic therapy (MST) has proven efficacious (Henggeler et al., 1997, 1998). It is an intensive home-based approach based on an ecological model of possible individual, family, peer, school, and community risk factors in antisocial behavior. A meta-analysis of 11 outcome studies revealed a mean effect size of .55 in reducing antisocial outcomes (Curtis, Ronan, & Bourduin, 2004).

For antisocial youth who are already in the child welfare system, multidimensional treatment foster care (MTFC) has been developed. The MTFC model was originally funded by the Oregon Youth Authority in 1983 to provide a community-based alternative to incarceration for boys with serious and chronic delinquency (Chamberlain, 2003). Two randomized trials have supported the efficacy of MTFC. In the first trial, MTFC boys had significantly lower rates of official and self-reported delinquency in a 12-month follow-up and lower rates of violent offending in a 24-month follow-up than did group-care youth (Chamberlain & Reid, 1998; Eddy, Whaley, & Chamberlain, 2004). A second trial with adolescent girls found that MTFC girls spent fewer days in locked settings, had fewer parent-reported delinquent behaviors, and showed a trend toward fewer arrests at the 12-month follow-up (Leve & Chamberlain, 2005). Eddy and Chamberlain (2000) examined mediational factors in the boys' sample, with several factors mediating the relationship between group condition and boys' criminal referral and self-reported delinquency rates. Mediating variables included close and consistent supervision, effective discipline, adult mentoring, and separation from delinquent peers, all consistent with the developmental model described in this chapter.

Webster-Stratton (1998) has led the move to bring these principles to preventive intervention with high-risk families of preschool-aged children (such as Head Start), with marked short-term success as evaluated by randomized trials. The Triple P-Positive Parenting Program by Sanders, Markie-Dadds, Tully, and Bor (2000) has been adapted for use in universal settings (media), on a selected basis for concerned parents, or in primary care settings, also with success. A different parent-based approach was taken by Olds et al. (1998), who made weekly home visits by a nurse-practitioner to high-risk mothers beginning in pregnancy for 3 years. The visitor provided information about child-rearing, helped problem solve parenting and family issues, and helped bring mothers to financial self-sufficiency. A randomized trial revealed no positive effects on children's conduct problems during elementary school (Kitzman et al., 1997), but, by age 15, 45% of the control group children had been arrested in contrast with just 20% of the intervention group children (Olds et al., 1998). Other home-visiting programs have yielded less favorable long-term effects (Stone, Bendell, & Field, 1988).

School-Based Approaches

The largest school-based approach to reducing aggressive behavior is that implemented by Olweus (1993), which involved the distribution of booklets and videos to teachers and parents in all schools in Norway, focusing on targeted parenting and discipline practices to reduce bullying behaviors. Cross-time evaluations suggest positive effects, but this program has not been evaluated by a randomized trial.

The most well-known classroom-based approach is the Good Behavior Game (GBG), which is a behavior management program designed to reduce disruptive behavior and promote prosocial behavior by group-level contingencies. When implemented in first grade classrooms in randomized trials, it has proven efficacious in reducing disruptive behavior at both proximal (Ialongo et al., 1999) and distal (Ialongo, Poduska, Werthamer, & Kellam, 2001) time points. Van Lier, Muthén, van der Sar, and Crijnen (2004) found that these positive effects could be sustained across 24 months and were strongest for the most disruptive children.

Universally-administered classroom curricula have been developed to teach social-cognitive and social-emotional skills for the purpose of preventing aggressive behavior. Greenberg and Kusche (1993) have found success with their PATHS Program (Providing Alternative Thinking Strategies) in increasing prosocial behavior, and the Conduct Problems Prevention Research Group (1999b) has demonstrated classroom-level success in reducing aggressive behavior with its adaptation of this approach.

Social Cognitive Skills Training

A key component of developmental models of aggressive behavior is the child's social-cognitive skill deficits, including attributional biases, problem solving, and decision making. Based on this model, numerous interventions have been developed to prevent aggressive behavior through enhancement of these skills and reduction of deficits and biases. Graham and Hudley (1993) developed an intervention designed to reduce hostile attributional biases in African American children, with demonstrated short-term success in a randomized trial.

Lochman has developed the Coping Power Program, which is designed to enhance an array of social-cognitive skills in aggressive fourth- and fifth-grade boys. Lochman and Wells (2004) have found positive effects of this program in reducing aggressive behavior as rated by school teachers, which persisted into the following school year, with an effect size of .42. Ross and Ross (1998) used a randomized trial to demonstrate positive effects in preventing reoffending for their program aimed at helping youth to stop and think about social problems, consider alternative strategies, and consider consequences of their actions.

Kazdin (2003a) has developed a variant of this approach that he calls Problem-Solving Skills Training (PSST). When implemented with aggressive children in randomized trials, he has found success in reducing aggressive behavior in both home and school settings that lasts over 12 months, in at least five replicated studies.

Combining Approaches

The developmental model described in this chapter posits risk factors and processes from multiple domains that provide unique, incremental power in predicting aggressive behavior outcomes. Given that single-domain approaches have proven modestly efficacious, several intervention scientists have hypothesized that comprehensive approaches that cross multiple domains would have even more powerful effects. In the MTA Study (Hinshaw et al., 2000), a combined program that included both stimulant medication and parent management training yielded more positive effects on child disruptive behavior than either approach alone. Lochman and Wells (2004) contrasted their child-focused Coping Power program with an enhanced program that added 16 parent-group sessions based on behavioral principles. The comprehensive program yielded more positive effects on child self-reports of covert delinquency than either the child-focused program or a control. Likewise, Kazdin (2003a) found that an intervention that combined parent management training with child problem-solving skills training tended to be more effective than either intervention alone.

Tremblay et al. (1995) implemented an important intervention that combined parent management training based on Patterson's principles with social and problem-solving skills training with groups of 7-year-old boys over a 2-year period. In contrast with a randomly assigned control group, by age 12 the intervention group committed less burglary and were in fewer fights. By age 17, analyses of developmental trajectories revealed that fewer intervention-group boys (16.6%) than control boys (29.5%) followed a trajectory of high levels of physical aggression.

Comprehensive Approaches to Prevention

Several interventions have gone beyond the simple combination of two approaches toward comprehensive approaches that last multiple years. These approaches tend to have greater and longer-lasting impact than other programs.

Reaching Educators, Children, and Parents Program

The RECAP Program (Reaching Educators, Children, and Parents; Weiss, Harris, Catron, & Han, 2003) provided semistructured training with individual children, small peer groups, classroom groups, classroom teachers, and parents. Child components focused on social skills, reattribution training, communication skills, self-control, affect recognition, and relaxation. Parent and teacher components focused on using praise and punishment appropriately, improving adult-child communication, and strengthening the adult-child relationship. This program was administered to children with comorbid externalizing and internalizing problems in a randomized trial that revealed positive effects on teacher, self, and peer ratings of externalizing problem behaviors at 1-year follow-up.

Metropolitan Area Child Study

The Metropolitan Area Child Study (MACS; Metropolitan Area Study Research Group, 2002) nested interventions in a research design that contrasted no treatment, a classroom program, a classroom-plus-small-group peer-skills training program, and a classroom-plus-small-group plus family-intervention program delivered in grades two and three and/or grades five and six. The peer-group component focused on altering normative beliefs about aggression and improving peer social skills, and the family intervention focused on parenting skills and parent-child communication. Outcome analyses revealed that only the fully combined intervention, when delivered in a community-rich context in the early grades, had a positive effect on reducing peer- and teacher-rated aggression, relative to a randomly assigned control group. The peer-group component appeared to have an iatrogenic effect on increasing aggression when administered to older youth in an inner-city context, a finding that is consistent with the deviant peer-contagion hypothesis that bringing deviant peers together only enhances problem outcomes.

Social Development Model

Hawkins, von Cleve, and Catalano (1991) combined parent training in behavior management, teacher training, and child interpersonal cognitive problem-solving skills training with first-grade children in the Social Development Model program. O'Donnell et al. (1995) reported that, by sixth grade, intervention boys from low-income families reported less delinquency than low-income control boys. By age 18, Hawkins, Catalano, Kosterman, Abbott, and Hill (1999) found that the full intervention group (receiving intervention for 6 years from grade one to grade six) reported less violence than a no-treatment control group and an intervention group that received intervention only in grades five and six.

Fast Track

The Conduct Problems Prevention Research Group (CPPRG) designed a 10-year-long intervention that combined family, peer, academic, classroom, and child social-cognitive skill-training components of the developmental model into a cohesive and comprehensive intervention called Fast Track. It was delivered to 445 first-grade children at high risk for adolescent violence and contrasted with a similar number of randomly assigned control-group children. After the 1st year of intervention, compared with the control group, the intervention group displayed higher levels of targeted skills in parenting, social cognition, and reading, and less aggressive behavior (CPPRG, 1999a). These effects on aggressive behavior persisted through third grade (CPPRG, 2002a) and appeared to hold equally well across gender, ethnic, and severity-level groups. Effects have persisted through fifth grade, with about a 25% reduction in cases that could be classified as clinically deviant (CPPRG, 2004). Mediation analyses revealed that intervention effects on outcomes could be partially accounted for gains in targeted areas of intervention, consistent with the premises of the developmental model (CPPRG, 2002b).

Early Comprehensive Approaches

Finally, given the importance of early lack of stimulation of cognitive and social skills in developmental models of aggressive behavior, several comprehensive programs that provide enriched preschool environments coupled with home-visiting for parent support have been evaluated for effects on aggressive behavior.

Perry Preschool Project

The Perry Preschool Project is the most well-known of these efforts. Three-year-old African American children living in poverty were randomly assigned to intervention or control groups. The intervention group was provided daily preschool and weekly home visits for 2 years. The intervention group was rated as less aggressive by teachers at ages 6 to 9, rated as less delinquent by self-report at age 15, had fewer arrests at age 19, and had only half as many arrests by age 27 (Schweinhart, Barnes, & Weikart, 1993).

Child-Parent Center

The Child-Parent Center approach is similar to the Perry Preschool approach in providing preschool along with family support. Long-term evaluations reveal that by age 18 program participants, compared with randomly assigned controls, had fewer nonviolent (17% versus 26%) and violent (9% versus 15%) arrests. A program in Syracuse, New York, revealed similar positive effects (Lally, Mangione, & Honig, 1988), but the well-administered Infant Health and Development Program (IHDP) found no positive long-term effects on conduct problems (McCarton et al., 1997).

CONCLUSIONS AND FUTURE DIRECTIONS

Recent advances reported in this chapter indicate a wide range of risk factors for aggressive and antisocial behavior and numerous processes in its development across the lifespan. These factors cover domains as broad as genes, acquired neuropsychological deficits, personality characteristics, ecological and cultural contexts, family demographics, parenting strategies, peer relations, situational characteristics, and cognitive-emotional skills and biases. The processes range from neurological to social, at intrapersonal, interpersonal, and institutional levels. A simple summing of the bivariate effect sizes of these risk factors in predicting aggressive behavior would reveal a striking paradox. On the one hand, the separate effect sizes would sum to well beyond 100% of the variance in aggression; on the other hand, the sum would not come close to accounting for all of the variance in aggressive behaviors. How can genes account for a full half of the variance while life experiences and situational parameters

account for well over half of the variance, too? Four general conclusions may resolve this paradox, but it is important to recognize that our review of determinant factors includes studies that vary in the degree to which they might evidence causality rather than statistical correlation.

A number of developmental theorists have argued for research designs that strengthen the implication of causality for individual risk factors, but this is not always a straightforward issue because, as Rutter et al. (1998) have noted, "causal processes are neither simple nor unidirectional. They involve indirect chain effects rather than one basic cause, and they can also reflect a two-way interplay between underlying biological features and behavior" (p. 378). The kinds of ABAB designs that were used in behavioral analysis designs to demonstrate causality of situational factors, such as reward contingency, are not applicable to the study of individual differences. Intervention designs have been proposed as one way to approximate this kind of rigor, but interventions that attempt individual change across multiple contexts and across time, as contrasted with lab analogue studies, typically address multiple aspects of the individual or parent functioning. Nonetheless, most of the factors reviewed rely on longitudinal studies that attempt to control for other related risk factors to demonstrate some independence of influence. Some, such as the impact of peer factors, have tracked changes in individual aggressive or antisocial behavior across time in relation to the hypothesized risk factors. Some factors, such as TV viewing, are inextricably confounded with other factors, such as the propensity to choose to watch violent programs or the correlate changes in acceptability of violence in the surrounding culture, and this makes it difficult to determine causality even though the potential for causality seems so inherently compelling.

Conclusion 1: Predictors Differ across Aggressive Acts, Personalities, and Patterns

First, it is necessary to distinguish among predictors of aggressive acts, aggressive personalities, and aggressive patterns. Aggressive acts are largely situationally and contextually determined. Handgun homicides are well modeled by variations in laws, policies, and access to handguns across the world. The probability of an antisocial act of looting is much greater during an electrical blackout than during a well-policed spring afternoon. The occurrence of an act of reactive aggression almost always follows some kind of provocation stimulus and almost never occurs in the absence of such a stimulus. In a hypothetical experiment in which all individuals are exposed equally to all possible situational stimuli, most of the variance in single acts of aggression would occur within (not between) individuals. Individual acts of aggression are poorly predicted by heredity.

Second, stable patterns of aggression are well predicted by individual difference factors like heredity and dispositions. These stable patterns emerge when acts of aggression are aggregated across time and situations. When we look at these personalities, derived by averaging across time and situations, we see the importance of between individual factors. Just as some situations are more likely to lead to aggression, so some people are more likely to act aggressively.

Yet a third kind of aggressive behavior occurs as a contingent pattern. Developmental studies suggest that life experiences have the effect of altering a person's behavior in particular contexts for as long as the contextual parameters remain the same. As an example, the experience of physical abuse teaches a child that the social world is threatening and that aggressive behavior toward peers protects oneself from harm. This pattern of preemptive reactive aggressive behavior will endure as long as the balance of a child's life experiences continues to be threatening. As a second example, contingent reinforcement of aggressive behavior as described in Patterson's coercion theory (Patterson, Reid, & Dishion, 1992) will lead to a pattern of high rates of aggressive behavior, *as long as the contingencies remain in place*. Further complicating the picture is empirical evidence suggesting that these children may inadvertently act in such a way as to maintain the occurrence of threats from others or contingent reinforcement for their aggressive behavior.

Conclusion 2: Risk Factors Operate in Biopsychosocial Symbiotic Development

The second resolution of the paradox in risk factors for aggression comes from an understanding of how risk factors co-occur, interact, and transact. First, the co-occurrence, or correlation, among risk factors suggests that they might share a common origin and might not account for unique portions of the variance in aggressive behavior. Empirical evidence indicates that, for example, the effects of low socioeconomic status, large family size, single-parent status, teenage-parent status, and lack of

parental social support on antisocial behavior are highly redundant and can be accounted for by their correlation with inadequate parenting. Redundancy across all risk factors is not nearly complete, as indicated by the cumulative risk factor modeling pioneered by Rutter (1989).

Second, a large portion of the variance in aggressive behavior is accounted for by interaction effects among risk factors. Merely cumulating nonredundant risk factors will not exhaustively account for the variation in aggressive behavior; rather, one of the most important findings of the past decade is that risk factors often exert their influence contingently—only in the context of another risk factor. Caspi et al.'s (2002) findings that child maltreatment leads to child CD only in the presence of the MAO-A genotype is a prime example. Another example is Dodge et al.'s (2003) finding that peer social rejection enhances risk for growth in aggressive behavior only among a subgroup of children evaluated by their mothers as showing difficult temperament. A third example is Lynam et al.'s (2000) demonstration that impulsivity is a risk factor for delinquency primarily in neighborhoods characterized by poor informal controls.

Third, risk factors transact—they reciprocally influence each other across time. Harsh discipline of a child may lead that child to fail to develop social skills of relating effectively with other persons. In turn, a child who lacks social skills may get into conflicts with peers and adults, leading adults to apply more harsh discipline. Further, these transactions may lead to a transformation in the risk factors. The parent who applies harsh discipline in the above example may find that, over time, repeated conflicts with a child are very stressful and disruptive to family life. As this child moves into adolescence, empirical evidence suggests that this parent may withdraw from interaction, monitoring, and supervision of this child, perhaps to minimize overt conflicts. The child may also play a role in becoming adept at making it difficult for a parent to monitor his or her behavior. The parents' lack of monitoring, coupled with the child's own social rejection by mainstream peers, may lead the child to gravitate toward deviant peers, thus transforming the child's peer status from social rejection to member of a deviant peer group.

The co-occurrences, interaction effects, and transactional mediation effects among risk factors described here are more the rule than the exception in antisocial development. They explain why a simple summing of bivariate effects would yield well beyond 100% of variance "explained" and yet would not exhaustively describe how chronic antisocial behavior develops.

Conclusion 3: A General Consensus Model of the Development of Aggressive Behavior Patterns Is within Reach

Instead of a haphazard array of risk factors that may cumulate, interact, and transact in unknown ways, a rapidly growing body of theory is developing in the field such that a consensus model of the development of aggressive behavior patterns may well cohere in the next decade. The components of this model are described in this chapter, and they include genetic factors, sociocultural contexts, early life experiences (both biological exposures and psychosocial experiences in family and peer domains), middle childhood experiences (in family, peer, and school domains), adolescent experiences (in family, peer, school, and community domains) and transient situational stimuli. The mediating processes of these influences are likely to be intrapersonal, at both neuropsychological and cognitive-emotional levels.

Conclusion 4: The Most Important Discoveries in the Next Decade Will Come from Studies of Gene-Environment Interactions, Modeling of Developmental Trajectories, and Prevention Experiments

Finally, this chapter points to the areas where the most exciting discoveries are likely to occur in the next decade. Three areas seem especially ripe. First, as recent technological advances make it easier and less expensive to identify specific genotypes, studies are likely to test the correlation between various genotypes and indices of aggressive behavior and risk factors associated with aggression. The studies by Caspi et al. (2002), reported in this chapter, provide models for this work. These studies are likely to yield important findings if they are completed with samples for which the measurement of the environment is equally precise. It is anticipated that such studies will reveal interaction effects between genotypes and environmental factors. Replicating such findings and integrating them into coherent theories will challenge this field.

Second, recent methodological advances in the modeling of developmental trajectories and changes in latent classes across time will be applied to longitudinal data sets to reveal patterns in antisocial development, factors that predict trajectories, and life experiences that deflect individuals away from antisocial lives.

Finally, prevention science is maturing at a rapid rate. Randomized clinical trials are proliferating, providing opportunities to test developmental theories. These trials include both large-scale implementations of broad models of multiple risk factors and single-component trials designed to identify specific clinical techniques for achieving behavior change. Evidence is strong that changing parenting behavior and improving social-cognitive skills can alter trajectories of antisocial behavior, supporting the causal role of these factors. Future trials will refine developmental models through the rigor of experiments and will bring the fruits of developmental psychopathology to bear on the crucial problem of violence in children's lives. We anticipate that the next decade's edition of this chapter will benefit greatly from these advances.

REFERENCES

Abelson, R. P. (1981). The psychological status of the script concept. *American Psychologist, 36,* 715–729.

Aber, J. L., Gershoff, E. T., Ware, A., & Kotler, J. A. (2004). Estimating the effects of September 11th and other forms of violence on the mental health and social development of New York City's youth: A matter of context. *Applied Developmental Science, 8,* 111–129.

Abramovitch, R., Corter, C., & Lando, B. (1979). Sibling interaction in the home. *Child Development, 4,* 997–1003.

Achenbach, T. M. (1991). *Manual for the Child Behavior Checklist and 1991 Profile.* Burlington: University of Vermont, Department of Psychiatry.

Achenbach, T. M., & Edelbrock, C. S. (1983). *Manual for the Child Behavior Checklist and Revised Child Behavior Profile.* Burlington: University of Vermont, Department of Psychiatry.

Aguilar, B., Sroufe, L. A., Egeland, B., & Carlson, E. (2000). Distinguishing the early-onset/persistent and adolescence-onset antisocial behavior types: From birth to 16 years. *Development and Psychopathology, 12,* 109–132.

Alexander, J. F., & Parsons, B. V. (1982). *Functional family therapy.* Monterey, CA: Brooks/Cole.

Alm, P. O., Alm, M., Humble, K., Leppert, J., Sörensen, S., Lidberg, L., et al. (1994). Criminality and platelet monoamine oxidase activity in former juvenile delinquents as adults. *Acta Psychiatrica Scandinavica, 89*(1), 41–45.

American Psychiatric Association. (1994). *Diagnostic and statistical manual of mental disorders* (4th ed.). Washington, DC: Author.

Anderson, C. A. (2004). An update on the effects of violent video games. *Journal of Adolescence, 27,* 113–122.

Anderson, D. A. (1999). The aggregate burden of crime. *Journal of Law and Economics, 42,* 611–642.

Anderson, E. (1990). *Streetwise: Race, class, and change in an urban community.* Chicago: University of Chicago Press.

Anderson, K. E., Lytton, H., & Romney, D. M. (1986). Mother's interactions with normal and conduct-disordered boys: Who affects whom? *Developmental Psychology, 22,* 604–609.

Archer, J. (1988). Ethopharmacological approaches to aggressive behavior. *Nordisk Psykiatrisk tidsskrift, 42*(2), 471–477.

Archer, J. (1991). The influence of testosterone on human aggression. *British Journal of Psychology, 82,* 1–28.

Archer, J. (2000). Sex differences in aggression between heterosexual partners: A meta-analytic review. *Psychological Bulletin, 126,* 651–680.

Archer, J., Pearson, N. A., & Westeman, K. E. (1998). Aggressive behavior of children aged 6 to 11: Gender differences and their magnitude. *British Journal of Social Psychology, 27,* 371–384.

Aronowitz, B., Liebowitz, M. R., Hollander, E., Fazzini, E., Durlach-Misteli, C., Frenkel, M., et al. (1994). Neuropsychiatric and neuropsychological findings in conduct disorder and attention-deficit hyperactivity disorder. *Journal of Neuropsychiatry and Clinical Neurosciences, 6*(3), 245–249.

Arseneault, L., Moffitt, T. E., Capsi, A., Taylor, A., Rijsdijk, F. V., Jaffee, S. R., et al. (2003). Strong genetic effects on cross-situational antisocial behavior among 5-year-old children according to mothers, teachers, examiner-observers, and twins' self reports. *Journal of Child Psychology and Psychiatry, 44,* 832–848.

Arseneault, L., Tremblay, R. E., Boulerice, B., & Saucier, J. F. (2002). Obstetrical complications and violent behaviors: Testing two developmental pathways. *Child Development, 73*(2), 496–508.

Arseneault, L., Tremblay, R. E., Boulerice, J. R., Seguin, J. R., & Saucier, J. F. (2000). Minor physical anomalies and family adversity as risk factors for violent delinquency in adolescence. *American Journal of Psychiatry, 157,* 917–923.

Arsenio, W. F., & Lemerise, E. A. (2004). Aggression and moral development: Integrating social information processing and moral domain models. *Child Development, 75,* 985–1002.

Arum, R., & Beattie, I. (1999). High school experience and the risk of adult incarceration. *Criminology, 37,* 515–537.

Asarnow, J. R., & Callan, J. W. (1985). Boys with peer adjustment problems: Social cognitive processes. *Journal of Consulting and Clinical Psychology, 53,* 80–87.

Asberg, M. (1994). Monoamine neurotransmitters in human aggressiveness and violence: A selected review. *Criminal Behaviour and Mental Health, 4*(4), 303–327.

Asher, S. R., & Renshaw, P. D. (1981). Children without friends: Social knowledge and social skill training. In S. R. Asher & J. M. Gottman (Eds.), *The development of children's friendships* (pp. 273–296). Cambridge, England: Cambridge University Press.

Aydin, O., & Markova, I. (1979). Attribution of popular and unpopular children. *British Journal of Social and Clinical Psychology, 18,* 291–298.

Bagwell, C. L., Coie, J. D., Terry, R. A., & Lochman, J. E. (2000). Peer clique participation in middle childhood: Associations with sociometric status and gender. *Merrill-Palmer Quarterly, 46,* 280–305.

Baldwin, M. W. (1992). Relational schemas and the processing of social information. *Psychological Bulletin, 112,* 461–484.

Ball, S. A., Tennen, H., Poling, J. C., Kranzler, H. R., & Rounsaville, B. J. (1997). Personality, temperament, and character dimensions and the *DSM-IV* personality disorders in substance abusers. *Journal of Abnormal Psychology, 106,* 545–553.

Bandura, A. (1973). *Aggression: A social learning analysis.* Englewood Cliffs, NJ: Prentice-Hall.

Bandura, A. (1983). Psychological mechanisms of aggression. In R. G. Geen & E. Donnerstein (Eds.), *Aggression: Theoretical and empirical reviews* (pp. 1–24). New York: Academic Press.

Bandura, A. (2002). Selective moral disengagement in the exercise of moral agency. *Journal of Moral Education, 31,* 101–119.

Bandura, A., Barbaranelli, C., Caprara, G. V., & Pastorelli, C. (1996). Mechanisms of moral disengagement in the exercise of moral agency. *Journal of Personality and Social Psychology, 71,* 364–374.

Bandura, A., Ross, D., & Ross, S. A. (1963). Imitation of film-mediated aggressive models. *Journal of Abnormal and Social Psychology, 66,* 3–11.

Barber, B. K. (1996). Parental psychological control: Revisiting a neglected construct. *Child Development, 67,* 3296–3319.

Bargh, J. A. (1989). Conditional automaticity: Varieties of automatic influence in social perception and cognition. In J. S. Uleman & J. A. Bargh (Eds.), *Unintended thought* (pp. 3–51). New York: Guilford Press.

Bargh, J. A., Chaiken, S., Raymond, P., & Hymes, C. (1995). The automatic evaluation effect: Unconditional automatic attitude activation with a pronunciation task. *Journal of Experimental Social Psychology, 31,* 221–232.

Bargh, J. A., & Thein, R. D. (1985). Individual construct accessibility, person memory, and the recall-judgment link: The case of information overload. *Journal of Personality and Social Psychology, 49,* 1129–1146.

Barkley, R. A., Shelton, T. L., Crosswait, C., Moorehouse, M., Fletcher, K., Barrett, S., et al. (2002). Preschool children with disruptive behavior: Three-year outcome as a function of adaptive disability. *Development and Psychopathology, 14,* 45–67.

Bassarath, L. (2001). Neuroimaging studies of antisocial behavior. *Canadian Journal of Psychiatry, 46,* 728–732.

Bates, J. E., & Bayles, K. (1988). Attachment and the development of behavior problems. In J. Belsky & T. Nezworski (Eds.), *Clinical implications of attachment* (pp. 253–299). Hillsdale, NJ: Erlbaum.

Bates, J. E., Bayles, K., Bennett, D. S., Ridge, B., & Brown, M. M. (1991). Origins of externalizing behavior problems at 8 years of age. In D. J. Pepler & K. H. Rubin (Eds.), *The development and treatment of childhood aggression* (pp. 3–120). Hillsdale, NJ: Erlbaum.

Bates, J. E., Maslin, C. A., & Frankel, K. A. (1985). Attachment security, mother-child interaction, and temperament as predictors of behavior problem ratings at age 3 years. *Growing points of attachment theory and research: Monographs of the Society for Research in Child Development, 50*(1/2, Serial No. 209).

Baumrind, D. (1987). A developmental perspective on adolescent risk taking in contemporary America. In C. E. Irwin Jr. (Ed.), *Adolescent social behavior and health: Vol. 37. New directions for child development* (pp. 3–125). San Francisco: Josey-Bass.

Bayer, P., Pintoff, R., & Pozen, D. (2004). *Building criminal capital behind bars: Social learning in juvenile corrections.* Unpublished manuscript, Yale University.

Becker, G. (1974). Crime and punishment: An economic approach. In G. Becker & W. Landes (Eds.), *Essays in the economics of crime and punishment* (pp. 1–54). New York: Macmillan.

Belfrage, H., Lidberg, L., & Oreland, L. (1992). Platelet monoamine oxidase activity in mentally disordered violent offenders. *Acta Psychiatrica Scandinavica, 85*(3), 218–221.

Bell, R. Q., & Harper, L. V. (1977). *Child effects on adults.* Hillsdale, NJ: Erlbaum.

Belsky, J. (2001). Emanuel Miller Lecture: Developmental risks (still) associated with early child care. *Journal of Child Psychology and Psychiatry, 42,* 845–859.

Benjet, C., & Kazdin, A. E. (2003). Spanking children: The controversies, findings, and new directions. *Clinical Psychology Review, 23,* 197–224.

Berke, R. L. (1994, January 23). Crime joins economic issues as leading worry, poll says. *New York Times.*1.

Berkowitz, L. (1962). *Aggression: A social psychological analysis.* New York: McGraw-Hill.

Berkowitz, L. (1993). Towards a general theory of anger and emotional aggression: Implications of the cognitive-neoassociationistic perspective for the analysis of anger and other emotions. In R. S. Wyer Jr. & T. K. Srull (Eds.), *Advances in social cognition: Vol. 6. Perspectives on anger and emotion* (pp. 1–45). Hillsdale, NJ: Erlbaum.

Berman, A., & Siegal, A. W. (1976). Adaptive and learning skills in juvenile delinquents: A neuropsychological analysis. *Journal of Learning Disabilities, 9,* 51–58.

Bernberg, J. G. (2002). *State reaction life-course outcomes and structural disadvantage: A panel study of the impact of formal criminal labeling on the transition to adulthood.* Albany, NY: State University of New York.

Berndt, T. J., Hawkins, J. A., & Jiao, Z. (1999). Influences of friends and friendships on adjustment to junior high school. *Merrill-Palmer Quarterly, 45,* 13–33.

Beyers, J. M., Bates, J. E., Pettit, G. S., & Dodge, K. A. (2003). Neighborhood structure, parenting processes, and the development of youths' externalizing behaviors: A multilevel analysis. *American Journal of Community Psychology, 31,* 35–53.

Bierman, K. L. (1986). The relation between social aggression and peer rejection in middle childhood. In R. J. Prinz (Ed.), *Advances in behavioral assessment of children and families* (Vol. 2, pp. 151–178). Greenwich, CT: JAI Press.

Bierman, K. L., Smoot, D. L., & Aumiller, K. (1993). Characteristics of aggressive-rejected, aggressive (nonrejected), and rejected (nonaggressive) boys. *Child Development, 64,* 139–151.

Bierman, K. L., & Wargo, J. B. (1995). Predicting the longitudinal course associated with aggressive-rejected, aggressive (non-rejected), and rejected (non-aggressive) status. *Developmental Psychopathology, 7,* 669–682.

Björkqvist, K. (1985). *Violent films, anxiety, and aggression.* Helsinski, Finland: Finnish Society of Sciences and Letters.

Blasi, A. (1980). Bridging moral cognition and moral action: A critical review of the literature. *Psychological Bulletin, 88,* 593–637.

Blasi, A., & Oresick, R. J. (1986). Emotions and cognitions in self-consistency. In D. J. Bearison & H. Zimiles (Eds.), *Thought and emotion* (pp. 147–165). Hillsdale, NJ: Erlbaum.

Blum, H. M., Boyle, M. H., & Offord, D. R. (1988). Single-parent families: Child psychiatric disorder and school performance. *Journal of the American Academy of Child and Adolescent Psychiatry, 27,* 214–219.

Blumstein, A. (2000). Disaggregating the violence trends. In A. Blumstein & J. Wallman (Eds.), *The crime drop in America* (pp. 13–44). New York: Cambridge University Press.

Blumstein, A., & Cohen, J. (1987). Characterizing criminal careers. *Science, 237,* 985–991.

Blumstein, A., & Wallman, J. (Eds.). (2000). *The crime drop in America.* New York: Cambridge University Press.

Boivin, M., Dodge, K. A., & Coie, J. D. (1995). Individual-group behavioral similarity and peer status in experimental play groups of boys: The social misfit revisited. *Journal of Personality and Social Psychology, 69,* 269–279.

Bolger, K. E., Patterson, C. J., Thompson, W. W., & Kupersmidt, J. B. (1995). Psychosocial adjustment among children experiencing persistent and intermittent family economic hardship. *Child Development, 66,* 1107–1129.

Book, A. S., Starzyk, K. B., & Quinsey, V. L. (2001). The relationship between testosterone and aggression: A meta-analysis. *Aggression and Violent Behavior, 6*(6), 579–599.

Booth, C. A., & Rose-Krasnor, L., McKinnon, J., & Rubin, K. H. (1994). Predicting social adjustment in middle childhood: The role of preschool attachment security and maternal style—From family to peer group: Relations between relationship systems [Special issue]. *Social Development, 3,* 189–204.

Borge, A. I. H., Rutter, M., Cote, S., & Tremblay, R. E. (2004). Early childcare and physical aggression: Differentiating social selection and social causation. *Journal of Child Psychology and Psychiatry, 45,* 367–376.

Bowlby, J. (1980). *Attachment and loss: Vol. 3. Loss.* New York: Basic Books.

Bradley, R. H., & Corwyn, R. F. (2002). Socioeconomic status and child development. *Annual Review of Psychology, 53*(1), 371–399.

Brain, P. F. (1994). Hormonal aspects of aggression and violence. In A. J. Reis Jr. & J. A. Roth (Eds.), *Understanding and control of biobehavioral influences on violence* (Vol. 2, pp. 177–244). Washington, DC: National Academy Press.

Brennan, P., Grekin, E. R., & Mednick, S. A. (1999). Maternal smoking during pregnancy and adult male criminal outcomes. *Archives of General Psychiatry, 56,* 215–219.

Brennan, P. A., Hall, J., Bor, W., Najman, J. M., & Williams, G. (2003). Integrating biological and social processes in relationship to early-onset persistent aggression in boys and girls. *Developmental Psychology, 39,* 309–323.

Brennan, P., Mednick, S. A., & Raine, A. (1997). Biosocial interactions and violence: A focus on perinatal factors. In A. Raine, P. Brennan, D. P. Farrington, & S. A. Mednick (Eds.), *Biosocial bases of violence* (pp. 163–174). New York: Plenum Press.

Brickman, A. S., McManus, M., Grapentine, W. L., & Alessi, N. (1984). Neuropsychological assessment of seriously delinquent adolescents. *Journal of the American Academy of Child Psychiatry, 23,* 453–457.

Broidy, L. M., Nagin, D. S., Tremblay, R. E., Brame, B., Dodge, K. A., Fergusson, D., et al. (2003). Developmental trajectories of childhood disruptive behaviors and adolescent delinquency: A six-site, cross-national study. *Developmental Psychology, 39*(2), 222–245.

Brown, A. L., Bransford, J. D., Ferrara, R. A., & Campione, J. C. (1983). Learning, remembering, and understanding. In P. Mussen (Series Ed.) & J. H. Flavell & E. M. Markman (Vol. Eds.), *Handbook of child psychology: Vol. 3. Cognitive development* (4th ed., pp. 77–166). New York: Wiley.

Bryk, A. S., & Raudenbush, S. W. (1992). *Advanced quantitative techniques in the social sciences: Vol. 1. Hierarchical linear models—Applications and data analysis methods.* Newbury Park, CA: Sage.

Buehler, R. E., Patterson, G. R., & Furniss, J. M. (1966). The reinforcement of behavior in institutional settings. *Behavior Research and Therapy, 4,* 157–167.

Burks, V., Laird, R., Dodge, K., Pettit, G., & Bates, J. (1999). Knowledge structures, social information processing, and children's aggressive behavior. *Social Development, 8,* 220–236.

Burleson, B. R. (1982). The development of communication skills in childhood and adolescence. *Child Development, 53,* 1578–1588.

Buss, A. H. (1961). *The psychology of aggression.* New York: Wiley.

Buss, A. H., & Plomin, R. (1984). *Temperament: Early developing personality traits.* Hillsdale, NJ: Erlbaum.

Cadoret, R. J., Cain, C. A., & Crowe, R. R. (1983). Evidence for gene-environment interaction in the development of adolescent antisocial behavior. *Behavior Genetics, 13*(3), 301–310.

Cadoret, R. J., Yates, W. R., Troughton, E., Woodworth, G., & Stewart, M. A. (1995). Genetic-environmental interaction in the genesis of aggressivity and conduct disorders. *Archives of General Psychiatry, 52,* 916–924.

Cairns, R. B. (1979). *Social development: The origins and plasticity of interchanges.* San Francisco: Freeman.

Cairns, R. B. (1991). Multiple metaphors for a singular idea. *Developmental Psychology, 27,* 23–26.

Cairns, R. B., Cairns, B. D., & Neckerman, H. J. (1989). Early school drop-out: Configurations and determinants. *Child Development, 60,* 1437–1452.

Cairns, R. B., Cairns, B. D., Neckerman, H. J., Gest, S. D., & Gariepy, J. L. (1988). Social networks and aggressive behavior: Peer support or peer rejection? *Developmental Psychology, 24,* 815–823.

Campbell, S. B. (1990). *Behavior problems in preschool children: Clinical and developmental issues.* New York: Guilford Press.

Caplan, M., Vespo, J. E., Pedersen, J., & Hay, D. F. (1991). Conflict over resources in small groups of 1- and 2-year-olds. *Child Development, 62,* 1513–1524.

Caprara, G. V., Regalia, C., & Bandura, A. (2002). Longitudinal impact of perceived self-regulatory efficacy on violent conduct. *European Psychologist, 7*(1), 63–69.

Caprara, G. V., & Zimbardo, P. G. (1996). Aggregation and amplification of marginal deviations in the social construction of personality and maladjustment. *European Journal of Personality, 10,* 79–110.

Carey, G., & Goldman, D. (1997). The genetics of antisocial behavior. In J. Breiling & D. M. Stoff (Eds.), *Handbook of antisocial behavior* (pp. 243–254). New York: Wiley.

Carver, C. S., Ganellan, R. J., Froming, W. J., & Chambers, W. (1983). Modeling: An analysis in terms of category accessibility. *Journal of Experimental Social Psychology, 19,* 403–421.

Caspi, A., Elder, G. H., & Bem, D. J. (1987). Moving against the world: Life-course patterns of explosive children. *Development Psychology, 23,* 308–313.

Caspi, A., Henry, B., Moffitt, T. E., & Silva, P. A. (1995). Temperamental origins of child and adolescent behavior problems: From age 3 to age 15. *Child Development, 66,* 55–68.

Caspi, A., McClay, J., Moffitt, T. E., Mill, J., Martin, J., Craig, I. W., et al. (2002). Role of genotype in the cycle of violence in maltreated children. *Science, 297,* 851–854.

Caspi, A., Moffitt, T. E., Silva, P. A., Stouthamer-Loeber, M., Krueger, F. F., & Schmutte, P. S. (1994). Are some people crime-prone? Replications of the personality-crime relationship across countries, genders, races, and methods. *Criminology, 32,* 163–195.

Caspi, A., Moffitt, T. E., Morgan, J., Rutter, M., Taylor, A., Arseneault, L., et al. (2004). Maternal expressed emotion predicts children's antisocial behavior: Using MZ-twin differences to identify environmental effects on behavioral development. *Developmental Psychology, 40,* 149–161.

Cassidy, J., Kirsh, S., Scolton, K., & Parke, R. (1996). Attachment and representations of peer relationships. *Developmental Psychology, 32,* 892–904.

Cassidy, J., Ziv, Y., Rodenberg, M., & Woodhouse, S. (2003, April). *Adolescent perceptions of parents: Associations with adolescent attachment (AAI) and interaction with parents.* Paper presented at the biennial meeting of the Society for Research in Child Development, Tampa, FL.

Castellanos, F. X., Elia, J., Kruesi, M. J., Gulotta, C. S., Mefford, I. N., Potter, W. Z., et al. (1994). Cerebrospinal fluid monoamine metabolites in boys with attention deficit hyperactivity disorder. *Psychiatry Research, 52*(3), 305–316.

Chamberlain, P. (2003). *Treating chronic juvenile offenders: Advances made through the Oregon Multidimensional Treatment Foster Care Model.* Washington, DC: American Psychological Association.

Chamberlain, P., & Reid, J. B. (1998). Comparison of two community alternatives to incarceration for chronic juvenile offenders. *Journal of Consulting and Clinical Psychology, 66,* 624–633.

Chandler, M. J. (1973). Egocentrism and antisocial behavior: The assessment and training of social perspective-taking skills. *Developmental Psychology, 9,* 326–332.

Chang, L., Schwartz, D., Dodge, K. A., & McBride-Chang, C. A. (2003). Harsh parenting in relation to child emotion regulation and aggression. *Journal of Family Psychology, 17*(4), 598–606.

Chen, X., Wang, L., Chen, H., & Liu, M. (2002). Noncompliance and child-rearing attitudes as predictors of aggressive behavior: A longitudinal study in Chinese children. *International Journal of Behavioral Development, 26,* 225–233.

Cicchetti, D. (1989). How research on child maltreatment has informed the study of child maltreatment: Perspectives from developmental psychopathology. In D. Cicchetti & V. Carlson (Eds.), *Child maltreatment: Theory and research on the causes and consequences of child abuse and neglect* (pp. 377–431). New York: Cambridge University Press.

Cillessen, A. H. N., & Mayeux, L. (2004). From censure to reinforcement: Developmental changes in the association between aggression and social status. *Child Development, 75,* 147–163.

Clarke, R. V., & Cornish, D. B. (1983). *Crime control in Britain: A review of policy research.* Albany: State University of New York Press.

Cleare, A. J., & Bond, A. J. (1995). The effect of tryptophan depletion and enhancement on subjective and behavioral aggression in normal male subjects. *Psychopharmacology, 118*(1), 72–81.

Cloninger, C. R., Sigvardsson, S., Bohman, M., & van Knoring, A. L. (1982). Predisposition to petty criminality in Swedish adoptees: Pt. 2. Cross-fostering analyses of gene-environmental interactions. *Archives of General Psychiatry, 39,* 1242–1247.

Coccaro, E. F. (1989). Central serotonin and impulsive aggression. *British Journal of Psychiatry, 155*(Suppl. 8), 52–62.

Cohen, M. A. (1998). The monetary value of saving a high-risk youth. *Journal of Quantitative Criminology, 14,* 5–33.

Cohen, M. A., Rust, R., Steen, S., & Tidd, S. (2004, February). Willingness-to-pay for Crime Control Programs. *Criminology, 42*(1), 86–106.

Cohen, P., & Brook, J. S. (1995). The reciprocal influence of punishment and child behavior disorder. In J. McCord (Ed.), *Coercion and punishment in long-term perspective* (pp. 154–164). Cambridge, England: Cambridge University Press.

Cohen, P., Cohen, J., Kasen, S., Velez, C. N., Hartmark, C., Johnson, J., et al. (1993). An epidemiological study of disorders in late childhood and adolescence: Pt. 1. Age and gender-specific prevalence. *Journal of Child Psychiatry and Psychology, 34,* 851–867.

Coie, J. D. (2004). The impact of negative social experiences on the development of antisocial behavior. In J. B. Kupersmidt & K. A. Dodge (Eds.), *Children's peer relations: From development to intervention* (pp. 243–267). Washington, DC: American Psychological Association.

Coie, J. D., Cillessen, A., Dodge, K. A., Hubbard, J., Schwartz, D., Lemerise, E., et al. (1999). It takes two to fight: A test of relational factors and a method for assessing aggressive dyads. *Developmental Psychology, 35,* 1179–1185.

Coie, J. D., & Kupersmidt, J. B. (1983). A behavioral analysis of emerging social status in boys' groups. *Child Development, 54,* 1400–1416.

Coie, J. D., Terry, R., Zakriski, A., & Lochman, J. E. (1995). Early adolescent social influences on delinquent behavior. In J. McCord (Ed.), *Coercion and punishment in long-term perspectives* (pp. 229–244). New York: Cambridge University Press.

Cole, P. M., Teti, L. O., & Zahn-Waxler, C. (2003). Mutual emotion regulation and the stability of conduct problems between preschool and early school age. *Development and Psychopathology, 15,* 1–18.

Collishaw, S., Maughan, B., Goodman, R., & Pickles, A. (2004). Time trends in adolescent mental health. *Journal of Child Psychology and Psychiatry, 45,* 1350–1362.

Conduct Problems Prevention Research Group. (1992). A developmental and clinical model for the prevention of conduct disorder: The Fast Track program. *Development and Psychopathology, 4,* 509–527.

Conduct Problems Prevention Research Group. (1999a). Initial impact of the Fast Track prevention trial for conduct problems: Pt. 1. The high-risk sample. *Journal of Consulting and Clinical Psychology, 67,* 631–647.

Conduct Problems Prevention Research Group. (1999b). Initial impact of the Fast Track prevention trial for conduct problems: Pt. 2. Classroom effects. *Journal of Consulting and Clinical Psychology, 67,* 648–657.

Conduct Problems Prevention Research Group. (2002a). Evaluation of the first 3 years of the Fast Track prevention trial with children at high risk for adolescent conduct problems. *Journal of Abnormal Child Psychology, 30,* 19–35.

Conduct Problems Prevention Research Group. (2002b). Using the Fast Track randomized prevention trial to test the early-starter model of the development of serious conduct problems. *Development and Psychopathology, 14,* 927–945.

Conduct Problems Prevention Research Group. (2004). The effects of the Fast Track program on serious problem outcomes at the end of elementary school. *Journal of Clinical Child and Adolescent Psychology, 33,* 650–661.

Coon, H., Carey, G., Corley, R., & Fulker, D. W. (1992). Identifying children in the Colorado Adoption Project at risk for conduct disorder. *Journal of the American Academy of Child and Adolescent Psychiatry, 31,* 503–511.

Corrado, R. R., Vincent, G. M., Hart, S. D., & Cohen, I. M. (2004). Predictive validity of the Psychopathy Checklist: Youth version for general and violent recidivism. *Behavioral Sciences and the Law, 22*(1), 5–22.

Costello, E. J., Angold, A., Burns, B., Stangl, D., Tweed, D., & Erklani, A. (1996). The Great Smoky Mountain study of youth: Pt. 1. Prevalence and correlates of *DSM-III-R* disorders. *Archives of General Psychiatry, 53,* 1137–1143.

Costello, E. J., Compton, S. N., Keeler, G., & Angold, A. (2003). Relationships between poverty and psychopathology: A natural experiment. *Journal of the American Medical Association, 290,* 2023–2029.

Cowan, P. (1979). *Piaget with feelings: Cognitive, social, and emotional dimensions.* New York: Holt, Rinehart and Winston.

Crick, N., & Werner, N. (1998). Response decision processes in relational and overt aggression. *Child Development, 69,* 1630–1639.

Crick, N., & Zahn-Waxler, C. (2003). The development of psychopathology in females and males: Current progress and future challenges. *Development and Psychopathology, 15,* 719–742.

Crick, N. R. (1996). The role of overt aggression, relational aggression, and prosocial behavior in the prediction of children's future social adjustment. *Child Development, 67,* 2317–2327.

Crick, N. R., & Bigbee, M. A. (1998). Relational and overt forms of peer victimization: A multi-informant approach. *Journal of Consulting and Clinical Psychology, 66,* 610–617.

Crick, N. R., Casas, J. F., & Mosher, M. (1997). Relational and overt aggression in preschool. *Developmental Psychology, 33,* 589–600.

Crick, N. R., & Dodge, K. A. (1994). A review and reformulation of social information-processing mechanisms in children's social adjustment. *Psychological Bulletin, 115,* 74–101.

Crick, N. R., & Dodge, K. A. (1996). Social-information-processing mechanisms in reactive and proactive aggression. *Child Development, 67,* 993–1002.

Crick, N. R., & Grotpeter, J. K. (1995). Relational aggression, gender, and social-psychological adjustment. *Child Development, 66,* 710–722.

Crick, N. R., & Ladd, G. W. (1990). Children's perceptions of the outcomes of aggressive strategies: Do the ends justify being mean? *Developmental Psychology, 26,* 612–620.

Crijnen, A. A., Achenbach, T. M., & Verhulst, F. C. (1997). Comparisons of problems reported by parents of children in 12 countries: Total problems, externalizing, and internalizing. *Journal of the American Academy of Child and Adolescent Psychiatry, 36,* 1269–1277.

Crouter, A. C., & Head, M. R. (2002). Parental monitoring and knowledge of children. In M. Bornstein (Ed.), *Handbook on parenting: Vol. 3. Being and becoming a parent* (2nd ed., pp. 461–484). Mahwah, NJ: Erlbaum.

Crowther, J. K., Bond, L. A., & Rolf, J. E. (1981). The incidence, prevalence, and severity of behavior disorders among preschool-aged children in day care. *Journal of Abnormal Child Psychology, 9,* 23–42.

Cummings, E. M., & Davies, P. T. (2002). Effects of marital conflict on children: Recent advances and emerging themes in process-oriented research. *Journal of Child Psychology and Psychiatry and Allied Disciplines, 43,* 31–63.

Cummings, E. M., Goeke-Morey, M. C., & Papp, L. M. (in press). Everyday marital conflict and child aggression. *Journal of Abnormal Child Psychology.*

Curtis, N. M., Ronan, K. R., & Bourduin, C. M. (2004). Multisystemic treatment: A meta-analysis of outcome studies. *Journal of Family Psychology, 18,* 411–419.

David, C. F., & Kistner, J. A. (2000). Do positive self-perceptions have a "dark side"? Examination of the link between perceptual bias and aggression. *Journal of Abnormal Child Psychology, 28,* 327–337.

Deater-Deckard, K. (2000). Parenting and child behavioral adjustment in early childhood: A quantitative genetic approach to studying family processes. *Child Development, 71,* 468–484.

Deater-Deckard, K., & Dodge, K. A. (1997). Externalizing behavior problems and discipline revisited: Nonlinear effects and variation by culture, context, and gender. *Psychological Inquiry, 8,* 161–175.

Deater-Deckard, K., Dodge, K. A., Bates, J. E., & Pettit, G. S. (1996). Physical discipline among African-American and European-American mothers: Links to children's externalizing behaviors. *Developmental Psychology, 32,* 1065–1072.

Dell Fitzgerald, P., & Asher, S. R. (1987, August/September). *Aggressive-rejected children's attributional biases about liked and disliked peers.* Paper presented at the 95th annual convention of the American Psychological Association, New York, NY.

Deluty, R. H. (1981). Alternative-thinking ability of aggressive, assertive, and submissive children. *Cognitive Therapy and Research, 5,* 309–312.

Deluty, R. H. (1983). Children's evaluations of aggressive, assertive, and submissive responses. *Journal of Clinical Child Psychology, 12,* 124–129.

Denno, D. J. (1989). *Biology, crime and violence: New evidence.* Cambridge: Cambridge University Press.

de Quervain, D. J.-F., Fischbacher, U., Treyer, V., Schellhammer, M., Schnyder, U., Buck, A., et al. (2004). The neural basis of altruistic punishment. *Science, 305,* 1254–1258.

Dery, M., Toupin, J., Pauze, R., Mercier, H., & Fortin, L. (1999). Neuropsychological characteristics of adolescents with conduct disorders: Association with attention-deficit-hyperactivity and aggression. *Journal of Abnormal Child Psychology, 27*(3), 225–236.

Dietz, K. R., Lavigne, J. V., Arend, R., & Rosenbaum, D. (1997). Relation between intelligence and psychopathology among preschoolers. *Journal of Clinical Child Psychology, 26,* 99–107.

Dionne, G., Boivin, M., Tremblay, R., Laplante, D., & Perusse, D. (2003). Physical aggression and expressive vocabulary in 19-month-old twins. *Developmental Psychology, 39,* 261–273.

Dishion, T. J. (in press). Deviant peer contagion within interventions and programs: An ecological framework for understanding influence mechanisms. In K. A. Dodge & T. J. Dishion (Eds.), *Deviant peer contagion in therapeutic interventions: From documentation to policy.* New York: Guilford Press.

Dishion, T. J., & Andrews, D. W. (1995). Preventing escalation in problem behaviors with high-risk adolescents: Immediate and 1-year outcomes. *Journal of Consulting and Clinical Psychology, 63,* 538–548.

Dishion, T. J., Andrews, D. W., & Crosby, L. (1995). Antisocial boys and their friends in early adolescence: Relationship characteristics, quality, and interactional process. *Child Development, 66,* 139–151.

Dishion, T. J., & Bullock, B. M. (2002). Parenting and adolescent problem behavior: An ecological analysis of the nurturance hypothesis. In J. G. Borkowski & S. L. Ramey (Eds.), *Parenting and the child's world: Influences on academic, intellectual, and social-emotional development* [Monograph]. (pp. 231–249). Mahwah, NJ: Erlbaum.

Dishion, T. J., French, D. C., & Patterson, G. R. (1995). The development and ecology of antisocial behavior. In D. Cicchetti & D. J. Cohen (Eds.), *Developmental psychopathology* (pp. 421–471). New York: Wiley.

Dishion, T. J., & Kavanagh, K. (2000). A multilevel approach to family-centered prevention in schools: Process and outcome. *Addictive Behaviors, 25,* 899–911.

Dishion, T. J., McCord, J., & Poulin, F. (1999). When interventions harm: Peer groups and problem behavior. *American Psychologist, 54*(9), 1–10.

Dishion, T. J., & McMahon, R. J. (1998). Parental monitoring and the prevention of child and adolescent problem behavior: A conceptual and empirical formulation. *Clinical Child and Family Psychology Review, 1,* 61–75.

Dishion, T. J., Nelson, S. N., & Bullock, B. M. (2004). Premature adolescent autonomy: Parent disengagement and deviant peer process in the amplification of problem behavior. *Journal of Adolescence, 27*(5), 515–530.

Dishion, T. J., Patterson, G. R., & Griesler, P. C. (1994). Peer adaptations in the development of antisocial behavior: A confluence model. In L. R. Huesmann (Ed.), *Aggressive behavior: Current perspectives* (pp. 61–95). New York: Plenum Press.

Dishion, T. J., Patterson, G. R., & Kavanagh, K. (1991). An experimental test of the coercion model: Linking theory, measurement, and intervention. In J. McCord & R. Tremblay (Eds.), *Preventing antisocial behavior: Interventions from birth through adolescence* (pp. 253–282). New York: Guilford Press.

Dodge, K. A. (1980). Social cognition and children's aggressive behavior. *Child Development, 51,* 162–170.

Dodge, K. A. (1983). Behavioral antecedents of peer social status. *Child Development, 54,* 1386–1399.

Dodge, K. A. (1986). A social information processing model of social competence in children. In M. Perlmutter (Ed.), *Minnesota Symposia on Child Psychology* (Vol. 18, pp. 77–125). Hillsdale, NJ: Erlbaum.

Dodge, K. A. (1991). The structure and function of reactive and proactive aggression. In D. J. Pepler & K. H. Rubin (Eds.), *The development and treatment of childhood aggression* (pp. 201–218). Hillsdale, NJ: Erlbaum.

Dodge, K. A., Bates, J. E., & Pettit, G. S. (1990). Mechanisms in the cycle of violence. *Science, 250,* 1678–1683.

Dodge, K. A., & Coie, J. D. (1987). Social information processing factors in reactive and proactive aggression in children's peer groups. *Journal of Personality and Social Psychology, 53,* 1146–1158.

Dodge, K. A., Coie, J. D., Pettit, G. S., & Price, J. M. (1990). Peer status and aggression in boys' groups: Developmental and contextual analyses. *Child Development, 61,* 1289–1309.

Dodge, K. A., Lansford, J. E., Burks, V. S., Bates, J. E., Pettit, G. S., Fontaine, R., et al. (2003). Peer rejection and social information-processing factors in the development of aggressive behavior problems in children. *Child Development, 74,* 374–393.

Dodge, K. A., Lockman, J. E., Harnish, J. D., Bates, J. E., & Pettit, G. S. (1997). Reactive and proactive aggression in school children and psychiatrically impaired chronically assaultive youth. *Journal of Abnormal Psychology, 106,* 37–51.

Dodge, K. A., Murphy, R. R., & Buchsbaum, K. (1984). The assessment of intention-cue detection skills in children: Implications for developmental psychopathology [Special issue]. *Child Development, 55,* 163–173.

Dodge, K. A., & Newman, J. P. (1981). Biased decision making processes in aggressive boys. *Journal of Abnormal Psychology, 90,* 375–379.

Dodge, K. A., & Pettit, G. S. (2003). A biophychosocial model of the development of chronic conduct problems in adolescence. *Developmental Psychology, 39*(2), 349–371.

Dodge, K. A., Pettit, G. S., & Bates, J. E. (1994). Socialization mediators of the relation between socioeconomic status and child conduct problems. *Child Development, 65,* 649–665.

Dodge, K. A., Pettit, G. S., Bates, J. E., & Valente, E. (1995). Social information-processing patterns partially mediate the effect of early physical abuse on later conduct problems. *Journal of Abnormal Psychology, 104,* 632–643.

Dodge, K. A., Pettit, G. S., McClaskey, C. L., & Brown, M. (1986). Social competence in children. *Monographs of the Society for Research in Child Development, 51*(2, Serial No. 213).

Dodge, K. A., & Price, J. M. (1994). On the relations between social information processing and socially competent behavior in early school-aged children. *Child Development, 65,* 1385–1398.

Dodge, K. A., Price, J. M., Bachorowski, J. A., & Newman, J. P. (1990). Hostile attributional biases in severely aggressive adolescents. *Journal of Abnormal Psychology, 99,* 385–392.

Dodge, K. A., & Tomlin, A. (1987). Cue utilization as a mechanism of attributional bias in aggressive children. *Social Cognition, 5,* 280–300.

Dollard, J., Doob, L. W., Miller, N. E., Mowrer, O. H., & Sears, R. R. (1939). *Frustration and aggression.* New Haven, CT: Yale University Press.

Dryfoos, J. G. (1990). *Adolescents at risk: Prevalence and prevention.* New York: Oxford University Press.

Dunn, J. (1988). *The beginnings of social understanding.* Cambridge, MA: Harvard University Press.

Dunne, M., Martin, N., Statham, D., Slutske, W., Dinwiddie, S., Bucholz, K., et al. (1997). Genetic and environmental contributions to variance in age at first sexual intercourse. *Psychological Science, 8,* 211–216.

Eddy, J. M., & Chamberlain, P. (2000). Family management and deviant peer association as mediators of the impact of treatment condition on youth antisocial behavior. *Journal of Consulting and Clinical Psychology, 68,* 857–863.

Eddy, J. M., Whaley, R. B., & Chamberlain, P. (2004). The prevention of violent behavior by chronic and serious male juvenile offenders: A 2-year follow-up of a randomized clinical trial. *Journal of Emotional and Behavioral Disorders, 12,* 2–8.

Edelman, M. W. (1992). *The measure of our success.* Boston: Beacon Press.

Edens, J. F., Poythress, N. G., & Lilienfeld, S. O. (1999). Identifying inmates at risk for disciplinary infractions: A comparison of two measures of psychopathy. *Behavioral Sciences and the Law, 17,* 435–443.

Egan, S., Monson, T., & Perry, D. (1998). Social-cognitive influences on change in aggression over time. *Developmental Psychology, 34,* 996–1006.

Eisenberg, N., Cumberland, A., Spinrad, T. L., Fabes, R. A., Shepard, S. A., Reiser, M., et al. (2001). The relations of regulation and emotionality to children's externalizing and internalizing problem behavior. *Development and Psychopathology, 72,* 1112–1134.

Eisenberg, N., & Fabes, R. A. (1999). Emotion, emotion-related regulation, and quality of socioemotional function. In L. Balter & C. S. Tamis-LeMonda (Eds.), *Child psychology: A handbook of contemporary issues.* Philadelphia: Psychology Press/Taylor & Francis.

Eisenberg, N., Fabes, R. A., Murphy, B. C., Shepard, S., Guthrie, I. K., Mazsk, P., et al. (1999). Prediction of elementary school children's socially appropriate and problem behavior from anger reactions at age 4 to 6. *Journal of Applied Developmental Psychology, 20,* 119–142.

Eisenberg, N., Pidada, S., & Liew, J. (2001). The relations of regulation and negative emotionality to Indonesian children's social functioning. *Child Development, 72,* 1747–1763.

Eisenberg, N., Spinrad, T. L., Fabes, R. A., Reiser, M., Cumberland, A., Shepard, S. A., et al. (2004). The relations of effortful control and impulsivity to children's resiliency and adjustment. *Child Development, 75,* 1–22.

Eisenberg, N., Valiente, C., Morris, A. S., Fabes, R. A., Cumberland, A., Reiser, M., et al. (2003). Longitudinal relations among parental emotional expressivity, children's regulation, and quality of socioemotional functioning. *Developmental Psychology, 39,* 3–19.

Elliott, D. S. (1994). Serious violent offenders: Onset, developmental course, and termination—The American Society of Criminology 1993 Presidential Address. *Criminology, 32,* 1–21.

Elliott, D. S., & Huizinga, D. (1983). Social class and delinquent behavior. *Criminology, 21,* 149–177.

Elliott, D. S., Huizinga, D., & Ageton, S. S. (1985). *Explaining delinquency and drug use.* Newbury Park, CA: Sage.

Elliott, D. S., Huizinga, D., & Menard, S. (1989). *Multiple problem youth: Delinquency, substance use, and mental health problems.* New York: Springer-Verlag.

Elliott, F. A. (1978). Neurological aspects of antisocial behavior. In W. H. Reid (Ed.), *The psychopath* (pp. 146–189). New York: Brunner/Mazel.

Erdley, C., & Asher, S. (1998). Linkages between children's beliefs about the legitimacy of aggression and their behavior. *Social Development, 7,* 321–339.

Erdley, C., & Asher, S. (1999). A social goals perspective on children's social competence. *Journal of Emotional and Behavioral Disorders, 7,* 156–167.

Eron, L. D., Huesmann, L. R., Lefkowitz, M. M., & Walder, L. O. (1972). Does television violence cause aggression? *American Psychologist, 27,* 253–263.

Espelage, D. L., Holt, M. K., & Henkel, R. R. (2003). Examination of peer-group contextual effects on aggression during early adolescence. *Child Development, 74,* 205–220.

Fabes, R. A., & Eisenberg, N. (1992). Young children's emotional arousal and anger/aggressive behaviors. In A. Fraezek & H. Zumkley (Eds.), *Socialization and aggression* (pp. 85–102). Berlin, Germany: Springer-Verlag.

Fagot, B. I., Hagan, R., Youngblade, L. M., & Potter, L. (1989). A comparison of the play behaviors of sexually abused, physically abused, and nonabused preschool children. *Topics in Early Childhood Special Education, 9,* 88–100.

Fagot, B. I., & Kavanagh, K. (1990). The prediction of antisocial behavior from avoidant attachment classifications. *Child Development, 61,* 864–873.

Farrington, D. P. (1989). Self-reported and official offending from adolescence to adulthood. In M. W. Klein (Ed.), *Cross-national research in self-reported crime and delinquency* (pp. 399–423). Dordrecht, The Netherlands: Kluwer Press.

Farrington, D. P. (1992). Juvenile delinquency. In J. C. Coleman (Ed.), *The school years* (2nd ed., pp. 123–163). London: Routledge & Kegan Paul.

Farrington, D. P. (1993). The challenge of teenage antisocial behavior. In M. Rutter (Ed.), *Psychosocial disturbances in young people.* Cambridge: Cambridge University Press.

Farrington, D. P. (1995). The development of offending and antisocial behavior from childhood: Key findings from the Cambridge study in delinquent development. *Journal of Child Psychology and Psychiatry, 36,* 1–36.

Farrington, D. P. (1997). The relationship between low resting heart rate and violence. In A. Raine, P. A. Brennan, D. P. Farrington, & S. A. Mednick (Eds.), *Biosocial bases of violence* (pp. 89–106). New York: Plenum Press.

Farrington, D. P., & Hawkins, J. D. (1991). Predicting participation, early onset and later persistence in officially recorded offending. *Criminal Behavior and Mental Health, 1,* 1–33.

Farrington, D. P., & Welsh, B. C. (2003). Family-based prevention of offending: A meta-analysis. *Australian and New Zealand Journal of Criminology, 36*(2), 127–151.

Feldman, R. A., Caplinger, T. E., & Wodarski, J. S. (1983). *The St. Louis conundrum: The effective treatment of antisocial youths.* Englewood Cliffs, NJ: Prentice-Hall.

Ferguson, T. J., & Rule, B. G. (1988). Children's evaluations of retaliatory aggression. *Child Development, 59,* 961–968.

Fergusson, D., Lynskey, M. T., & Horwood, L. J. (1996). Factors associated with continuity and changes in disruptive behavior patterns between childhood and adolescence. *Journal of Abnormal Child Psychology, 24,* 533–553.

Fergusson, D. M., & Horwood, L. J. (1998). Exposure to interparental violence in childhood and psychosocial adjustment in young adulthood. *Child Abuse and Neglect, 22,* 339–357.

Fergusson, D. M., & Horwood, L. J. (2002). Male and female offending trajectories. *Development and Psychopathology, 14,* 159–177.

Fergusson, D. M., Woodward, L. J., & Horwood, J. (1998). Maternal smoking during pregnancy and psychiatric adjustment in late adolescence. *Archives of General Psychiatry, 55,* 721–727.

Feshbach, N. D., & Feshbach, S. (1982). Empathy training and the regulation of aggression: Potentialities and limitations. *Academic Psychology Bulletin, 4,* 399–413.

Finkelstein, J. W., Susman, E. J., Chinchilli, V. M., Kunselman, S. J., d'Arcangelo, M. R., Schwab, J., et al. (1997). Estrogen or testosterone increases self-reported aggressive behaviors in hypogonadal adolescents. *Journal of Clinical Endocrinology and Metabolism, 82,* 2433–2438.

Foley, D. L., Eaves, L. J., Wormley, B., Silberg, J., Maes, H., Kuhn, J., et al. (2004). Childhood adversity, monoamine oxidase A genotype, and risk for conduct disorder. *Archives of General Psychiatry, 61,* 738–744.

Fontaine, R. G., Burks, V. S., & Dodge, K. A. (2002). Response decision processes and externalizing behavior problems in adolescents. *Development and Psychopathology, 14,* 107–122.

Forehand, R., & McMahon, R. (1981). *The noncompliant child.* New York: Guilford Press.

Frick, P. J. (2001). Effective interventions for children and adolescents with conduct disorder. *Canadian Journal of Psychiatry, 46,* 597–608.

Frick, P. J., Lahey, B. B., Loeber, R., Tannenbaum, L., Van Horn, Y., & Christ, M. A. G. (1993). Oppositional defiant disorder and conduct disorder: Pt. 1. Meta-analytic review of factor analyses. *Clinical Psychology Review, 13,* 319–340.

Frick, P. J., O'Brien, B. S., Wooton, J. M., & McBurnett, K. (1994). Psychopathy and conduct problems in children. *Journal of Abnormal Psychology, 103*(4), 700–707.

Frijda, N. (1986). *The emotions.* New York: Cambridge University Press.

Galen, B. R., & Underwood, M. K. (1997). A developmental investigation of social aggression among children. *Developmental Psychology, 33,* 589–600.

Gelman, R., & Baillargeon, R. (1983). A review of some Piagetian concepts. In P. Mussen (Series Ed.) & J. H. Flavell & E. M. Markman (Eds.), *Handbook of child psychology: Vol. 3. Cognitive development* (4th ed., pp. 167–230). New York: Wiley.

Gershoff, E. T. (2002). Parental corporal punishment and associated child behaviors and experiences: A meta-analytic and theoretical review. *Psychological Bulletin, 128,* 539–579.

Giancola, P., & Zeichner, A. (1994). Neuropsychological performance on tests of frontal-lobe functioning and aggressive behavior in men. *Journal of Abnormal Psychology, 103,* 832–835.

Gifford-Smith, M. E., & Rabiner, D. L. (2004). Social information processing and children's social adjustment. In J. Kupersmidt & K. A. Dodge (Eds.), *Children's peer relations: From development to intervention* (pp. 69–84). Washington, DC: American Psychological Association.

Gilliom, M., Shaw, D. S., Beck, J. E., Schonberg, M. A., & Lukon, J. L. (2002). Anger regulation in disadvantaged preschool boys: Strategies, antecedents, and the development of self-control. *Developmental Psychology, 38,* 222–235.

Gillmore, M. R., Hawkins, J. D., Day, L. E., & Catalano, R. F. (1992). Friendship and deviance: New evidence on an old controversy. *Journal of Early Adolescence, 12,* 80–95.

Giordano, P. G., Cernkovich, S. A., & Pugh, M. D. (1986). Friendships and delinquency. *American Journal of Sociology, 91,* 1170–1202.

Gladue, B. A., Boechler, M., & McCaul, K. D. (1989). Hormonal response to competition in human males. *Aggressive Behavior, 15,* 409–422.

Glueck, S., & Glueck, E. (1950). *Unraveling juvenile delinquency.* Cambridge, MA: Harvard University Press.

Glueck, S., & Glueck, E. (1968). *Delinquents and nondelinquents in perspective.* Cambridge, MA: Harvard University Press.

Goldstein, A. P. (1994). Delinquent gangs. In L. R. Huesmann (Ed.), *Aggressive behavior: Current perspectives—Plenum series in social/clinical psychology* (pp. 255–273). New York: Plenum Press.

Gordon, R. A., Lahey, B. B., Kawai, E., Loeber, R., Stouthamer-Loeber, M., & Farrington, D. P. (2004). Antisocial behavior and gang membership: Selection and socialization. *Criminology, 42,* 55–87.

Gouze, K. R. (1987). Attention and social problem solving as correlates of aggression in preschool males. *Journal of Abnormal Child Psychology, 15,* 181–197.

Graham, S., & Hudley, C. (1993). An attributional intervention to reduce peer-directed aggression among African-American boys. *Child Development, 64,* 124–138.

Graham, S., & Hudley, C. (1994). Attributions of aggressive and nonaggressive African-American male early adolescents: A study of construct accessibility. *Developmental Psychology, 30,* 365–373.

Graham, S., Hudley, C., & Williams, E. (1992). Attributional and emotional determinants of aggression among African-American and Latino young adolescents. *Developmental Psychology, 28,* 731–740.

Granic, I., & T. J. Dishion. (2002, May). *Measuring deviant talk between adolescents as an attractor: Predictions to antisocial outcomes* (Invited talk). First Annual Workshop, Linking Dynamic Systems and Reinforcement Mechanisms: Complementarities, Disparities and Data, Port Townsend, WA.

Greenberg, M. T., & Kusche, C. A. (1993). *Promoting social and emotional development in deaf children: The PATHS Project.* Seattle, WA: University of Washington Press.

Greenberg, M. T., Spelz, M. L., & Deklyen, M. (1993). The role of attachment in the early development of disruptive behavior problems. *Development and Psychopathology, 5,* 191–213.

Gretton, H. M., Hare, R. D., & Catchpole, R. (2004). Psychopathy and offending from adolescence to adulthood: A 10-year follow up. *Journal of Consulting and Clinical Psychology, 72,* 636–645.

Guerra, N. G., Huesmann, L. R., Tolan, P. H., Van Acker, R., & Eron, L. D. (1995). Stressful events and individual beliefs as correlates of economic disadvantage and aggression among urban children. *Journal of Consulting and Clinical Psychology, 63,* 518–528.

Guerra, N. G., & Slaby, R. G. (1989). Evaluative factors in social problem solving by aggressive boys. *Journal of Abnormal Child Psychology, 17,* 277–289.

Gunnar, M. R., Brodersen, L., & Krueger, K. (1996). Dampening of adrenocortical responses during infancy: Normative changes and individual differences. *Child Development, 67,* 877–889.

Halperin, J. M., Sharma, V., Siever, L. J., Schwartz, S. T., Matier, K., Wornell, G., et al. (1994). Serotonergic function in aggression and non-aggressive boys with attention deficit hyperactivity disorder. *American Journal of Psychiatry, 151,* 243–248.

Hammond, W. R., & Yung, B. R. (1991). Preventing violence in at-risk African-American youth. *Journal of Health Care for the Poor and Underserved, 2,* 1–16.

Hare, R. D. (2003). *The Hare PCL-R* (2nd ed.). Toronto, Ontario: Multi-Health Systems.

Hart, C. H., Nelson, D. A., Robinson, C. C., Olsen, S. F., & McNeilly-Choque, M. K. (1998). Overt and relational aggression in Russian nursery-school-age children: Parenting style and marital linkages. *Developmental Psychology, 34,* 687–697.

Harter, S. (1982). The perceived competence scale for children. *Child Development, 53,* 89–97.

Hartup, W. W. (1974). Aggression in childhood: Developmental perspectives. *American Psychologist, 29,* 336–341.

Hartup, W. W., & deWit, J. (1974). The development of aggression: Problems and perspectives. In J. deWit & W. W. Hartup (Eds.), *Determinants and origins of aggressive behavior* (pp. 595–615). The Hague, The Netherlands: Mouton.

Haselager, G. J. T., Cillessen, A. H. N., Hartup, W. W., van Lieshout, C. F. M., & Riksen-Walraven, J. M. A. (2002). Heterogeneity among peer rejected boys across middle childhood: Developmental pathways of social behavior. *Developmental Psychology, 38,* 446–456.

Hawkins, J. D., Catalano, R. F., Kosterman, R., Abbott, R., & Hill, K. G. (1999). Preventing adolescent health-risk behaviors by strengthening protection during childhood. *Archives of Paediatrics and Adolescent Medicine, 153,* 226–234.

Hawkins, J. D., & Lishner, D. M. (1987). Schooling and delinquency. In E. H. Johnson (Ed.), *Handbook on crime and delinquency prevention* (pp. 179–221). New York: Greenwood Press.

Hawkins, J. D., von Cleve, E., & Catalano, R. F. (1991). Reducing early childhood aggression: Results of a primary prevention programme. *Journal of the American Academy of Child and Adolescent Psychiatry, 30,* 208–217.

Hawkins, J. D., & Weis, J. G. (1985). The social development model: An integrated approach to delinquency prevention. *Journal of Primary Prevention, 6,* 73–95.

Hawley, P. H. (2003). Strategies of control, aggression, and morality in preschoolers: An evolutionary perspective. *Journal of Experimental Child Psychology, 85,* 213–235.

Hawley, P. H., Little, T. D., & Pasupathi, M. (2002). Winning friends and influencing peers: Strategies of peer influence in late childhood. *International Journal of Behavioral Development, 26,* 466–474.

Hay, D. F., Nash, A., & Pedersen, J. (1983). Interactions between 6-month-olds. *Child Development, 54,* 557–562.

Hay, D. F., & Ross, H. S. (1982). The social nature of early conflict. *Child Development, 53,* 105–113.

Henggeler, S. W., Melton, G. B., Brondino, M. J., Scherer, D. G., & Hanley, J. H. (1997). Multisystemic therapy with violent and chronic juvenile offenders and their families: The role of treatment fidelity in successful dissemination. *Journal of Consulting and Clinical Psychology, 65,* 821–833.

Henggeler, S. W., Schoenwald, S. K., Bourduin, C. M., Rowland, M. D., & Cunningham, P. B. (1998). *Multisystemic treatment of antisocial behavior in children and adolescents.* New York: Guilford Press.

Henry, B., Caspi, A., Moffitt, T. E., & Silva, P. W. (1996). Temperamental and familial predictors of violent and nonviolent criminal convictions: From age 3 to 18. *Developmental Psychology, 32,* 614–623.

Herbert, J., & Martinez, M. (2001). Neural mechanisms underlying aggressive behavior. In J. Hill & B. Maughan (Eds.), *Conduct disorders in childhood and adolescence.* Cambridge: Cambridge University Press.

Hinshaw, S. P. (2002). Intervention research, theoretical mechanisms, and causal processes related to externalizing behavior patterns. *Development and Psychopathology, 14,* 789–818.

Hinshaw, S. P., & Anderson, C. A. (1996). Conduct and oppositional defiant disorder. In E. J. Mash & R. A. Barkley (Eds.), *Child Psychology* (pp. 113–149). New York: Guilford Press.

Hinshaw, S. P., Owens, E. B., Wells, K. C., Kraemer, H. C., Abikoff, H. B., Arnold, L. E., et al. (2000). Family processes and treatment outcome in the MTA: Negative/ineffective parenting practices in relation to multimodal treatment. *Journal of Abnormal Child Psychology, 28,* 555–568.

Hirschi, T. (1969). *Causes of delinquency.* Berkeley: University of California Press.

Hodgins, S., Kratzer, L., & McNeil, T. F. (2001). Obstetric complications, parenting, and risk of criminal behavior. *Archives of General Psychiatry, 58,* 746–752.

Holmberg, M. S. (1977). *The development of social interchange patterns from 12 months to 42 months: Cross-sectional and short-term longitudinal analyses.* Doctoral dissertation. Chapel Hill, NC: University of North Carolina.

Holtzworth-Munroe, A., & Stuart, G. L. (1994). Typologies of male batterers: Three subtypes and the differences among them. *Psychological Bulletin, 116,* 476–497.

Horn, S. S. (2003). Adolescents' reasoning about exclusion from social groups. *Developmental Psychology, 39,* 71–84.

Howell, J. C., Krisberg, B., & Jones, M. (1995). Trends in juvenile crime and youth violence. In J. C. Howell, B. Krisberg, J. D. Hawkins, & J. J. Wilson (Eds.), *Serious, violent, and chronic juvenile offenders* (pp. 1–35). Sage: Thousand Oaks, CA.

Hubbard, J. A., Dodge, K. A., Cillessen, A. H. N., Coie, J. D., & Schwartz D. (2001). The dyadic nature of social information-processing in boys' reactive and proactive aggression. *Journal of Personality and Social Psychology, 80*(2), 268–280.

Hudley, C. A., & Graham, S. (1993). An attributional intervention to reduce peer-directed aggression among African-American boys. *Child Development, 64,* 124–138.

Huesmann, L. R. (1986). Psychological processes promoting the relation between exposure to media violence and aggressive behavior by the viewer. *Journal of Social Issues, 42,* 125–139.

Huesmann, L. R. (1988). An information-processing model for the development of aggression. *Aggressive Behavior, 14,* 13–24.

Huesmann, L. R. (1998). The role of social information processing and cognitive schema in the acquisition and maintenance of habitual aggressive behavior. In R. Green & E. Donnerstein (Eds.), *Human aggression: Theories, research, and implications for social policy* (pp. 73–109). New York: Academic Press.

Huesmann, L. R., & Eron, L. D. (1986). *Television and the aggressive child: A cross-national perspective.* Hillsdale, NJ: Erlbaum.

Huesmann, L. R., Eron, L. D., Lefkowitz, M. M., & Walder, L. O. (1984). Stability of aggression over time and generations. *Developmental Psychology, 20,* 1120–1134.

Huesmann, L. R., Lagerspetz, & Eron, L. D. (1984). Intervening variables in the TV violence aggression relation: Evidence from two countries. *Developmental Psychology, 20,* 746–775.

Huesmann, L. R., & Miller, L. S. (1994). Long-term effects of repeated exposure to media violence in childhood. In L. R. Huesmann (Ed.), *Aggressive behavior: Current perspectives* (pp. 153–186). New York: Plenum Press.

Huesmann, L. R., Moise-Titus, J., Podolski, C., & Eron, L. D. (2003). Longitudinal relations between children's exposure to TV violence and their aggressive and violent behavior in young adulthood: 1977–1992. *Developmental Psychology, 39,* 201–221.

Huizinga, D., & Dunford, F. W. (1985, November). *The delinquent behavior of arrested individuals.* Paper presented at the 1985 annual meeting of the Academy of Criminal Justice Sciences, Las Vegas, NV.

Hymel, S., Bowker, A., & Woody, & E. (1993). Aggressive versus withdrawn unpopular children: Variations in peer and self-perceptions in multiple domains. *Child Development, 64,* 879–896.

Ialongo, N., Poduska, J., Werthamer, L., & Kellam, S. (2001). The distal impact of two first-grade preventive interventions on conduct problems and disorder in early adolescence. *Journal of Emotional and Behavioral Disorders, 9,* 146–160.

Ialongo, N. S., Werthamer, L., Kellam, S. G., Brown, C. H., Wang, S., & Lin, Y. (1999). Proximal impact of two first-grade preventive interventions on the early risk behaviors for later substance abuse, depression, and antisocial behavior. *American Journal of Community Psychology, 27,* 599–641.

Iannotti, R. J. (1978). Effects of role-taking experiences on role-taking, empathy, altruism, and aggression. *Developmental Psychology, 14,* 119–124.

Ingoldsby, E. M., & Shaw, D. S. (2002). Neighborhood contextual factors and early-starting antisocial pathways. *Clinical Child and Family Psychology Review, 5,* 21–55.

Jaffee, S. R., Capsi, A., Moffitt, T. E., Dodge, K. A., Rutter, M., & Taylor, A. (in press). Nature × nurture: Genetic vulnerabilities interact with physical maltreatment to promote conduct problems. *Development and Psychopathology.*

Jaffee, S. R., Caspi, A., Moffitt, T. E., Polo-Tomas, M., Price, T. S., & Taylor, A. (2004a). The limits of child effects: Evidence for genetically mediated child effects on corporal punishment, but not on physical maltreatment. *Developmental Psychology, 40,* 1047–1058.

Jaffee, S. R., Caspi, A., Moffitt, T. E., & Taylor, A. (2004b). Physical maltreatment victim to antisocial child: Evidence of an environmentally mediated process. *Journal of Abnormal Psychology, 113*(1), 44–55.

Jaffee, S. R., Moffitt, T. E., Caspi, A., Taylor, A., & Arseneault, L. (2002). Influence of adult domestic violence on children's internalizing and externalizing problems: An environmentally informative twin study. *Journal of the American Academy of Child and Adolescent Psychiatry, 41,* 1095–1103.

Jencks, C., & Mayer, S. E. (1990). The social consequences of growing up in a poor neighborhood. In L. E. Lynn & M. McGeary (Eds.), *Inner-city poverty in the United States* (pp. 117–135). Washington, DC: National Academy Press.

Jenkins, S., Bax, M., & Hart, H. (1980). Behaviour problems in preschool children. *Journal of Child Psychology and Psychiatry, 21,* 5–18.

Jessor, R., Donovan, J. E., & Costa, F. M. (1991). *Beyond adolescence: Problem behavior and young adult development.* New York: Academic Press.

Jimack, P. (1911). *Introduction to Rousseau's Emile.* London: Dent.

Kandel, D. B. (1978). Homophily, selection, and socialization in adolescent friendships. *American Journal of Sociology, 84,* 427–436.

Kaplan, H. B., & Liu, X. (1994). A longitudinal analysis of mediating variables in the drug use-dropping out relationship. *Criminology, 32,* 415–439.

Kashani, J. H., & Shepperd, J. A. (1990). Aggression in adolescents: The role of social support and personality. *Canadian Journal of Psychiatry, 35,* 311–315.

Kaukiainen, A., Bjorkqvist, K., Lagerspetz, K., Osterman, K., Salmivalli, C., Rothberg, S., et al. (1999). The relationship between social intelligence, empathy, and three types of aggression. *Aggressive Behavior, 25,* 81–89.

Kazdin, A. E. (2003a). Problem-solving skills training and parent management training for conduct disorder. In A. E. Kazdin & J. R. Weisz (Eds.), *Evidence-based psychotherapies for children and adolescents* (pp. 241–262). New York: Guilford Press.

Kazdin, A. E. (2003b). Psychotherapy for children and adolescents. *Annual Review in Psychology, 54,* 253–276.

Kazdin, A. E., & Whitley, M. K. (2003). Treatment of parental stress to enhance therapeutic change among children referred for aggressive and antisocial behavior. *Journal of Consulting and Clinical Psychology, 71,* 504–515.

Keenan, K., Gunthorpe, D., & Young, D. (2002). Patterns of cortical reactivity in African-American neonates from low-income environments. *Developmental Psychobiology, 41,* 1–13.

Keenan, K., Loeber, R., Zhang, Q., Stouthamer-Loeber, M., & van Kammen, W. B. (1995). The influence of deviant peers on the development of boys' disruptive and delinquent behavior: A temporal analysis. *Development and Psychopathology, 7,* 715–726.

Keenan, K., & Shaw, D. S. (2003). Starting at the beginning: Exploring the etiology of antisocial behavior in the first years of life. In B. B. Lahey, T. E. Moffitt, & A. Caspi (Eds.), *Causes of conduct disorder and juvenile delinquency* (pp. 153–181). New York: Guilford Press.

Keenan, K., Shaw, D. S., Delliquadri, E., Giovanelli, J., & Walsh, B. (1998). Evidence for the continuity of early problem behaviors: Application of a developmental model. *Journal of Abnormal Child Psychology, 26,* 441–452.

Keith, C. R. (Ed.). (1984). *The aggressive adolescent: Clinical perspectives.* New York: Free Press.

Kellam, S., Ling, X., Merisca, R., Brown, C. H., & Ialongo, N. (1998). The effect of the level of aggression in the first grade classroom on the course and malleability of aggressive behavior into middle school. *Development and Psychopathology, 10,* 165–185.

Kellam, S. G., & Rebok, G. W. (1992). Building developmental and ethiological theory through epidemiologically based preventive intervention trials. In J. McCord & R. E. Tremblay (Eds.), *Preventing antisocial behavior: Interventions from birth through adolescence* (pp. 162–195). New York: Guilford Press.

Kelley, H. H. (1973). The processes of causal attribution. *American Psychologist, 28,* 107–128.

Kemppainen, L., Jokelainen, J., Jaervelin, M. R., Isohanni, M., & Raesaenen, P. (2001). The one-child family and violent criminality: A 31-year follow-up study of the Northern Finland 1966 birth cohort. *American Journal of Psychiatry, 158,* 960–962.

Kendler, K. S., Prescott, C. A., Myers, J., & Neale, M. C. (2003). The structure of genetic and environmental risk factors for common psychiatric and substance use disorders in men and women. *Archives of General Psychiatry, 60*(9), 929–937.

Kerckhoff, A. C. (1988). Effects of ability and grouping in British secondary schools. *American Sociological Review, 51,* 842–858.

Killen, M., Lee-Kim, J., McGlothlin, H., & Stangor, C. (2002). How children and adolescents evaluate gender and racial exclusion. *Monographs of the Society for Research in Child Development, 67*(4, Serial No. 271).

Kim, Y. S., Koh, Y. J., & Leventhal, B. L. (2004). Prevalence of bullying in Korean middle school students. *Archives of Pediatric and Adolescent Medicine, 158,* 737–741.

Kindlon, D. J., Tremblay, R. E., Mezzacappa, E., Earls, F., Laurent, D., & Schaal, B. (1995). Longitudinal patterns of heart rate and fighting behavior in 9- through 12-year-old boys. *Journal of the American Academy of Child and Adolescent Psychiatry, 34*(3), 371–377.

Kingston, L., & Prior, M. (1995). The development of patterns of stable, transient, and school-age onset aggressive behavior in young children. *Journal of the American Academy of Child and Adolescent Psychiatry, 34,* 348–452.

Kitzman, H., Olds, D. L., Henderson, C. R., Hanks, C., Cole, R., Tatelbaum, R., et al. (1997). Effect of prenatal and infancy home visitation by nurses on pregnancy outcomes, childhood injuries, and repeated childbearing: A randomized controlled trial. *Journal of the American Medical Association, 278,* 644–652.

Klein, M. (in press). Peer effects in naturally occurring groups: The case for street gangs. In K. A. Dodge & T. J. Dishion (Eds.), *Deviant peer contagion in therapeutic interventions: From documentation to policy.* New York: Guilford Press.

Klimes-Dugan, B., & Kopp, C. B. (1999). Children's conflict tactics with mothers: A longitudinal investigation of the toddler and preschool years. *Merrill-Palmer Quarterly, 45,* 226–241.

Kochanska, G. (1997). Multiple pathways to conscience for children with different temperaments: From toddlerhood to age 5. *Developmental Psychology, 33,* 228–240.

Kohlberg, L. (1986). *The Philosophy of Moral Development.* San Francisco: Harper & Row.

Kosson, D. S., Cyterski, T. D., Steuerwald, B. L., Neumann, C. S., & Walker-Matthews, S. (2002). The reliability and validity of the Psychopathy Checklist: Youth Version (PCL:YV) in nonincarcerated adolescent males. *Psychological Assessment, 14*(1), 97–109.

Krueger, R. F. (1999). Personality traits in late adolescence predict mental disorders in early adulthood: A prospective-epidemiological study. *Journal of Personality, 67,* 39–65.

Krueger, R. F., Caspi, A., Moffitt, T. E., White, J., & Stouthamer-Loeber, M. (1996). Delay of gratification, psychopathology, and personality: Is low self-control specific to externalizing problems? *Journal of Personality, 64,* 107–129.

Kruesi, M. J., Hibbs, E. D., Zahn, T. P., Keysor, C. S., Hamburger, S. D., Bartko, J. J., et al. (1992). A 2-year prospective follow-up study of children and adolescents with disruptive behavior disorders: Prediction by cerebrospinal fluid 5-hydroxyindoleacetic acid, homovanillic acid, and autonomic measures? *Archives of General Psychiatry, 49*(6), 429–435.

Kruesi, M. J., Swedo, S., Leonard, H., & Rubinow, D. R. (1990). CSF somatostatin in childhood psychiatric disorders: A preliminary investigation. *Psychiatry Research, 33*(3), 277–284.

Kupersmidt, J. B., Bryant, D., & Willoughby, M. (2000). Prevalence of aggressive behaviors in Head Start and community child care programs. *Behavior Disorders, 26,* 42–52.

Kupersmidt, J. B., & Coie, J. D. (1990). Preadolescent peer status, aggression, and school adjustment as predictors of externalizing problems in adolescence. *Child Development, 61,* 1350–1362.

Kupersmidt, J., & Dodge, K. A. (Eds.). (2004). *Children's peer relations: From development to intervention to policy—A festschrift to honor John D. Coie.* Washington, DC: American Psychological Association.

Ladd, G. W. (1990). Having friends, keeping friends, making friends, and being liked by peers in the classroom: Predictors of children's early school adjustment. *Child Development, 61,* 312–331.

Ladd, G. W., & Oden, S. (1979). The relationship between peer acceptance and children's ideas about helpfulness. *Child Development, 50,* 402–408.

Lahey, B., & Loeber, R. (1994). Framework for a developmental model of oppositional defiant disorder and conduct disorder. In D. Routh (Ed.), *Disruptive behavior disorders in childhood* (pp. 139–180). New York: Plenum Press.

Lahey, B. B., Loeber, R., Hart, E. L., Frick, P. J., Applegate, B., Zhang, Q., et al. (1995). Four-year longitudinal study of conduct disorder in boys: Patterns and predictors of persistence. *Journal of Abnormal Psychology, 104,* 83–93.

Laird, R. D., Pettit, G. S., Bates, J. E., & Dodge, K. A. (2003). Parents' monitoring-relevant knowledge and adolescents' delinquent behavior: Evidence of correlated developmental changes and reciprocal influences. *Child Development, 74,* 752–768.

Lally, J. R., Mangione, P. L., & Honig, A. S. (1988). Syracuse University Family Development Research Program: Long-range impact of an early intervention with low-income children and their families. In D. R. Powell (Ed.), *Parent education as early childhood intervention: Emerging directions in theory, research and practice* (pp. 79–104). Norwood, NJ: Ablex.

Lancelotta, G. X., & Vaughn, S. (1989). Relation between types of aggression and sociometric status: Peer and teacher perceptions. *Journal of Educational Psychology, 81,* 86–90.

Lansford, J. E., Deater-Deckard, K., Dodge, K. A., Bates, J. E., & Pettit, G. S. (2004). Ethnic differences in the link between physical discipline and later adolescent externalizing behaviors. *Journal of Child Psychology and Psychiatry, 45,* 801–812.

Lansford, J. E., Dodge, K. A., Pettit, G. S., Bates, J. E., Crozier, J., & Kaplow, J. (2002). A 12-year prospective study of the long-term effects of early child physical maltreatment on psychological, behavioral, and academic problems in adolescence. *Archives of Pediatrics and Adolescent Medicine, 156,* 824–830.

Larzelere, R. E., & Patterson, G. R. (1990). Parental management: Mediators of the effect of socioeconomic status on early delinquency. *Criminology, 28,* 301–323.

Lau, M. A., Pihl, R. O., & Peterson, J. B. (1995). Provocation, acute alcohol intoxication, cognitive performance and aggression. *Journal of Abnormal Psychology, 104,* 150–155.

Lavallee, K. L., Bierman, K. L., Nix, R. L., & Conduct Problems Prevention Research Group. (2005). The impact of first grade "friendship group" experiences on child social outcomes in the Fast Track Program. *Journal of Abnormal Child Psychology, 33,* 307–324.

Lemerise, E. A., & Arsenio, W. (2000). An integrated model of emotion processes and cognition in social information processing. *Child Development, 71,* 107–118.

Lemerise, E. A., & Dodge, K. A. (2000). The development of anger and hostile interactions. In M. Lewis & J. M. Haviland-Jones

(Ed.), *Handbook of emotions* (2nd ed., pp. 594–606). New York: Guilford Press.

Lengua, L. L., West, S. G., & Sandler, I. N. (1998). Temperament as a predictor of symptomatology in children: Addressing contamination of measures. *Child Development, 69,* 164–181.

Leve, L. D., & Chamberlain, P. (2005). Intervention outcomes for girls referred from Juvenile Justice: Effects on delinquency. *Journal of Abnormal Child Psychology, 33,* 339–347.

Lewis, M., Feiring, C., McGuffog, C., & Jaskir, J. (1984). Predicting psychopathology in 6-year-olds from early social relations. *Child Development, 55,* 123–136.

Lipsey, M. W. (in press). The effects of community-based group treatment for delinquency: A meta-analytic search for cross-study generalizations. In K. A. Dodge & T. J. Dishion (Eds.), *Deviant peer contagion in therapeutic interventions: From documentation to policy.* New York: Guilford Press.

Little, T. D., Brauner, J., Jones, S. M., Nock, M. K., & Hawley, P. H. (2003). Rethinking aggression: A typological examination of the functions of aggression. *Merrill-Palmer Quarterly, 49,* 343–369.

Little, T. D., Jones, S. M., Henrich, C. C., & Hawley, P. H. (2003). Disentangling the "whys" from the "whats" of aggressive behavior. *International Journal of Behavioral Development, 27,* 122–133.

Lochman, J. E., & Wells, K. C. (2004). The coping power program for preadolescent aggressive boys and their parents: Outcome effects at the 1-year follow-up. *Journal of Consulting and Clinical Psychology, 72,* 571–578.

Loeber, R. (1985). Patterns and development of antisocial child behavior. *Annals of Child Development, 2,* 77–116.

Loeber, R., Farrington, D. P., Stouthamer-Loeber, M., & van Kammen, W. B. (1998). *Antisocial behavior and mental health problems: Explanatory factors in childhood and adolescence.* Mahwah, NJ: Erlbaum.

Loeber, R., Lahey, B. B., & Thomas, C. (1991). Diagnostic conundrum of oppositional defiant disorder and conduct disorder. *Journal of Abnormal Psychology, 100,* 379–390.

Loeber, R., & Schmaling, K. B. (1985). Empirical evidence for overt and covert patterns of antisocial conduct problems: A meta-analysis. *Journal of Abnormal Child Psychology, 13,* 337–352.

Loeber, R., Tremblay, R. E., Gagnon, C., & Charlebois, P. (1989). Continuity and desistance in disruptive boys' early fighting in school. *Development and Psychopathology, 1,* 39–50.

Lorenz, K. (1966). *On aggression.* New York: Harcourt.

Love, J. M., Harrison, L., Sagi-Schwartz, A., van IJzendoorn, M. H., Ross, C., Ungerer, J. A., et al. (2003). Child care quality matters: How conclusions may vary with context. *Child Development, 74,* 1021–1033.

Lueger, R., & Gill, K. (1990). Frontal-lobe cognitive dysfunction in conduct disorder adolescents. *Journal of Clinical Psychology, 46,* 696–706.

Luntz, B. K., & Widom, C. S. (1994). Antisocial personality disorders in abused and neglected children grown up. *American Journal of Psychiatry, 151,* 670–674.

Lynam, D. R. (1997). Pursuing the psychopath: Capturing the fledgling psychopath in a nomological net. *Journal of Abnormal Psychology, 106*(3), 425–438.

Lynam, D. R. (2002). Fledgling psychopathy: A view from personality theory. *Law and Human Behavior, 26,* 255–259.

Lynam, D. R., Caspi, A., Moffitt, T. E., Wikström, P. O., Loeber, R., & Novak, S. P. (2000). The interaction between impulsivity and neighborhood context on offending: The effects of impulsivity are stronger in poorer neighborhoods. *Journal of Abnormal Psychology, 109,* 563–574.

Lynam, D. R., & Henry, B. (2001). The role of neuropsychological deficits in conduct disorders. In J. Hill & B. Maughan (Eds.), *Conduct disorders in childhood and adolescence* (pp. 235–263). New York: Cambridge University Press.

Lynam, D. R., Moffitt, T. E., & Stouthamer-Loeber, M. A. (1993). Explaining the relation between IQ and delinquency: Class, race, test motivation, school achievement, or self-control? *Journal of Abnormal Psychology, 102,* 187–196.

Lyons-Ruth, K., Alpern, L., & Repacholi, B. (1993). Disorganized infant attachment classification and maternal psychosocial problems as predictors of hostile-aggressive behavior in the preschool classroom. *Child Development, 64,* 572–585.

Lyons-Ruth, K., Easterbrooks, M. A., & Davidson, C. (1995, April). *Disorganized attachment strategies and mental lag in infancy: Prediction of externalizing problems at seven.* Paper presented at biennial meeting of the Society for Research in Child Development, Indianapolis, IN.

Lyoo, I. K., Lee, H. K., Jung, J. H., Noam, G. G., & Renshaw, P. F. (2002). White matter hyperintensities on magnetic resonance imaging of the brain in children with psychiatric disorders. *Comprehensive Psychiatry, 43,* 361–368.

MacBrayer, E. K., Milich, R., & Hundley, M. (2003). Attributional biases in aggressive children and their mothers. *Journal of Abnormal Psychology, 112,* 698–708.

MacKinnon-Lewis, C., Rabiner, D., & Starnes, R. (1999). Predicting boys' social acceptance and aggression: The role of mother-child interactions and boys' beliefs about peers. *Developmental Psychology, 35,* 632–639.

Magdol, L., Moffitt, T., Caspi, A., & Silva, P. (1998). Hitting without a license: Testing explanations for differences in partner abuse between young adult daters and cohabitators. *Journal of Marriage and the Family, 60,* 41–55.

Mahler, M. (1968). *On human symbiosis and the vicissitudes of individualization.* New York: International Universities Press.

Malone, P. S., Lansford, J. E., Castellino, D. R., Berlin, L. J., Dodge, K. A., Bates, J. E., et al. (2004). Divorce and child behavior problems: Applying latent change score models to life event data. *Structural Equation Modeling, 11*(3), 401–423.

Manley, J. T., Cicchetti, D., & Barnett, D. (1994). The impact of subtype, frequency, chronicity, and severity of child maltreatment on social competence and behavior problems. *Development and Psychopathology, 6,* 121–143.

Maughan, B., Taylor, A., Caspi, A., & Moffitt, T. E. (2004). Prenatal smoking and early childhood conduct problems. *Archives of General Psychiatry, 61,* 836–843.

McCall, N. (1994). *Makes me wanna holler: A young black man in America.* New York: Vintage Books.

McCarton, C. M., Brooks-Gunn, J., Wallace, I. F., Bauer, C. R., Bennett, F. C., Bernbaum, J. C., et al. (1997). Results at age 8 years of early intervention for low-birth-weight premature infants: The infant health and development program. *Journal of the American Medical Association, 277,* 126–132.

McCaul, K. D., Gladue, B. A., & Joppa, M. (1992). Winning, losing, mood, and testosterone. *Hormones and Behavior, 26*(2), 486–504.

McCord, J. (1991). Questioning the value of punishment. *Social Problems, 38,* 167–179.

McFall, R. M. (1982). A review and reformulation of the concept of social skills. *Behavioral Assessment, 4,* 1–33.

McLoyd, V. (1990). The impact of economic hardship on black families and children: Psychological distress, parenting, and socioemotional development. *Child Development, 61,* 311–346.

McNeilly-Choque, M. K., Hart, C. H., Robinson, C. C., Nelson, L. J., & Olsen, S. F. (1996). Overt and relational aggression on the playground: Correspondence among different informants. *Journal of Research in Childhood Education, 11,* 47–67.

Mednick, S. A., & Christiansen, K. O. (1977). *Biosocial bases of criminal behavior.* Oxford, England: Gardner Press.

Meltzoff, A. N., & Moore, M. K. (1977). Imitation of facial and manual gestures by human neonates. *Science, 198,* 75–78.

Menard, S., & Elliott, D. S. (1994). Delinquent bonding, moral beliefs, and illegal behavior: A three-wave panel model. *Justice Quarterly, 11,* 173–188.

Metropolitan Area Child Study Research Group. (2002). A cognitive-ecological approach to preventing aggression in urban settings: Initial outcomes for high-risk children. *Journal of Consulting and Clinical Psychology, 70,* 179–194.

Milgram, S. (1974). *Obedience to authority: An experimental view.* New York: Harper & Row.

Miller, J. D., & Lynam, D. R. (2001). Structural models of personality and their relation to antisocial behavior: A meta-analytic review. *Criminology, 39,* 765–792.

Miller, J. D., Lynam, D. R., Widiger, T. A., & Leukefeld, C. (2001). Personality disorders as extreme variants of common personality dimensions: Can the five-factor model adequately represent psychopathy? *Journal of Personality, 69*(2), 253–276.

Miller, M., Azrael, D., & Hemenway, D. (2002). Firearm availability and unintentional firearm deaths, suicide, and homicide among 5- to 14-year-olds. *Journal of Trauma—Injury, Infection, and Critical Care, 52,* 267–275.

Miller-Johnson, S., & Costanzo, P. (2004). If you can't beat 'em . . . Induce them to join you: Peer-based interventions during adolescence. In J. Kupersmidt & K. A. Dodge (Eds.), *Children's peer relations: From development to intervention* (pp. 209–222). Washington, DC: American Psychological Association.

Mischel, W. (1974). Processes in delay of gratification. In L. Berkowitz (Ed.), *Advances in experimental social psychology* (Vol. 7, pp. 249–292). New York: Academic Press.

Moffitt, T. E. (1990). Juvenile delinquency and attention deficit disorders: Boys' developmental trajectories from age 3 to age 15. *Child Development, 61,* 893–910.

Moffitt, T. E. (1993). Adolescence-limited and life-course-persistent antisocial behavior: A development taxonomy. *Psychological Review, 100,* 674–701.

Moffitt, T. E. (2005). *The new look of behavioral-genetics in developmental psychopathology: Gene-environment interplay in antisocial behaviors.* Unpublished manuscript, Institue of Psychiatry, London.

Moffitt, T. E., & Caspi, A. (2001). Childhood predictors differentiate life-course persistent and adolescence-limited antisocial pathways among males and females. *Development and Psychopathology, 13,* 135–151.

Moffitt, T. E., Caspi, A., & Fawcett, P. (1997). Whole blood serotonin and family background relate to male violence. In A. Raine, P. A. Brennan, D. P. Farrington, & S. A. Mednick (Eds.), *Biosocial bases of violence* (pp. 321–340). New York: Plenum Press.

Moffitt, T. E., Caspi, A., Rutter, M., & Silva, P. A. (2001). *Sex differences in antisocial behavior: Conduct disorder, delinquency, and violence in the Dunedin Longitudinal Study.* Cambridge, England: Cambridge University Press.

Moffitt, T. E., Gabrielli, W. F., Mednick, S. A., & Schulsinger, F. (1981). Socioeconomic status IQ and delinquency. *Journal of Abnormal Psychology, 90,* 152–156.

Moffitt, T. E., & Henry, B. (1989). Neuropsychological assessment of executive functions in self-reported delinquents. *Development and Psychopathology, 1,* 105–118.

Moffitt, T. E., Krueger, R. F., Caspi, A., & Fagan, J. (2000). Partner abuse and general crime: How are they the same? How are they different? *Criminology, 38,* 199–232.

Moffitt, T. E., Lynam, D. R., & Silva, P. A. (1994). Neuropsychological tests predicting persistent male delinquency. *Criminology, 32,* 277–300.

Moffitt, T. E., & Silva, P. A. (1988a). IQ and delinquency: A direct test of the differential detection hypothesis. *Journal of Abnormal Psychology, 97,* 330–333.

Moffitt, T. E., & Silva, P. A. (1988b). Self-reported delinquency, neuropsychological deficit, and history of attention deficit disorder. *Journal of Abnormal Child Psychology, 16,* 553–569.

Morash, M., & Rucker, L. (1989). An exploratory study of the connection of mother's age at child-bearing to her children's delinquency in four data sets. *Crime and Delinquency, 35,* 45–93.

Multimodal Treatment for Attention-Deficit/Hyperactivity Disorder Cooperative Group (MTA). (1999). Fourteen-month randomized clinical trial of treatment strategies for attention-deficit hyperactivity disorder. *Archives of General Psychiatry, 56,* 1073–1086.

Murphy, B. C., & Eisenberg, N. (2002). An integrative examination of peer conflict: Children's reported goals, emotions and behaviors. *Social Development, 11,* 534–557.

Murrie, D. C., Cornell, D. G., Kaplan, S., McConville, D., & Levy-Elkon, A. (2004). Psychopathy scores and violence among juvenile offenders: A multi-measure study. *Behavioral Sciences and the Law, 22*(1), 49–67.

Nagin, D. S. (1999). Analyzing developmental trajectories: A semi-parametric, group-based approach. *Psychological Methods, 4,* 139–177.

Nagin, D. S., & Tremblay, R. (1999). Trajectories of boys' physical aggression, opposition, and hyperactivity on the path to physically violent and nonviolent juvenile delinquency. *Child Development, 70,* 1181–1196.

Nasby, W., Hayden, B., & DePaulo, B. M. (1979). Attributional bias among aggressive boys to interpret unambiguous social stimuli as displays of hostility. *Journal of Abnormal Psychology, 89,* 459–468.

National Institute of Child Health and Human Development Early Child Care Research Network. (2004). Trajectories of physical aggression from toddlerhood to middle childhood. *Monographs of the Society for Research in Child Development, 69*(4, Serial No. 278).

Newell, A., & Simon, H. A. (1972). *Human problem solving.* Englewood Cliffs, NJ: Prentice-Hall.

Nisbett, R. E., & Cohen, D. (1996). *Culture of honor.* Boulder, CO: Westview Press.

Novak, S. P. (2000). The interaction between impulsivity and neighborhood context on offending: The effects of impulsivity are stronger in poorer neighborhoods. *Journal of Abnormal Psychology, 109,* 563–574.

Nucci, L. (2001). *Education in the moral domain.* New York: Cambridge University Press.

O'Connor, T. G., McGuire, S., Reiss, D., Hetherington, E., & Plomin, R. (1998). Co-occurrence of depressive symptoms and antisocial behavior in adolescence: A common genetic liability. *Journal of Abnormal Psychology, 107*(1), 27–37.

O'Donnell, J., Hawkins, J. D., Catalano, R. F., Abbott, R. D., & Day, L. E. (1995). Preventing school failure, drug use and delinquency among low income children: Long-term intervention in elementary schools. *American Journal of Orthopsychiatry, 65,* 87–100.

Offord, D. R., Boyle, M. H., & Racine, Y. A. (1989). Ontario Child Health Study: Correlates of conduct disorder. *Journal of the American Academy of Child and Adolescent Psychiatry, 28,* 856–860.

Ogbu, J. U. (1990). Overcoming racial barriers to equal access. In I. Goodlad & P. Keating (Eds.), *Access to knowledge: An agenda for our nation's schools* (pp. 59–89). New York: College Entrance Examination Board.

Olds, D. L., Henderson, C. R., Cole, R., Eckenrode, J., Kizman, H., Luckey, D., et al. (1998). Long-term effects of nurse home visitation on children's criminal and antisocial behavior: 15-year follow-up of a randomized trial. *Journal of the American Medical Association, 280,* 1238–1244.

Olweus, D. (1993). *Bullying at school: What we know and what we can do.* Cambridge, MA: Blackwell.

O'Neil, M. L., Lidz, V., & Heilbrun, K. (2003). Adolescents with psychopatic characteristics in a substance abusing cohort: Treatment process and outcomes. *Law and Human Behavior, 27,* 299–313.

Osterman, K., Bjorkqvist, K., Lagerspetz, K. M. J., Kaukiainen, A., Huesmann, L. R., & Fraczek, A. (1994). Peer and self-estimated aggression and victimization in 8-year-old children from five ethnic groups. *Aggressive Behavior, 20,* 411–428.

Pakaslahti, L., & Keltigangas-Jarvinen, L. (2000). Comparison of peer, teacher, and self-assessments on adolescent direct and indirect aggression. *Educational Psychology, 20,* 177–190.

Paquette, J. A., & Underwood, M. K. (1999). Young adolescents' experiences of peer victimization: Gender differences in accounts of social and physical aggression. *Merrill-Palmer Quarterly, 45,* 233–258.

Parke, R. D., & Deur, J. L. (1972). Schedule of punishment and inhibition of aggression in children. *Developmental Psychology, 7,* 266–269.

Parke, R. D., & Slaby, R. G. (1983). The development of aggression. In P. Mussen (Series Ed.) & E. M. Hetherington (Ed.), *Handbook of child psychology: Vol. 4. Socialization, personality, and social development* (4th ed., pp. 547–641). New York: Wiley.

Patterson, G. R., & Bank, C. L. (1989). Some amplifying mechanisms for pathologic processes in families. In M. Gunnar & E. Thelen (Eds.), *Minnesota Symposia on child psychology: Systems and development* (pp. 167–210). Hillsdale, NJ: Erlbaum.

Patterson, G. R., Chamberlain, P., & Reid, J. R. (1982). A comparative evaluation of parent training procedures. *Behavior Therapy, 3,* 638–650.

Patterson, G. R., Dishion, T. J., & Yoerger, K. (2000). Adolescent growth in new forms of problem behavior: Macro- and micro-peer dynamics. *Prevention Science, 1,* 3–13.

Patterson, G. R., Littman, R. A., & Bricker, W. (1967). Assertive behavior in children: A step toward a theory of aggression. *Monographs of the Society for Research in Child Development, 32*(5, Serial No. 113).

Patterson, G. R., Reid, J. B., & Dishion, T. J. (1992). *A social learning approach: Vol. 4. Antisocial boys.* Eugene, OR: Castalia Press.

Peetsma, T., Vergeer, M., Roeleveld, J., & Karsten, S. (2001). Inclusion in education: Comparing pupils' development in special and regular education. *Educational Review, 53,* 125–135.

Perry, D. G., Perry, L. C., & Rasmussen, P. (1986). Cognitive social learning mediators of aggression. *Child Development, 57,* 700–711.

Petrides, M. (1985). Deficits on conditional associative-learning tasks after frontal- and temporal-lobe lesions in man. *Neuropsychologia, 23,* 601–614.

Petrides, M., Alivisatos, B., Evans, A., & Meyer, E. (1993). Dissociation of human mid-dorsolateral frontal cortex in memory processing. *Proceedings of the National Academy of Sciences, USA, 90,* 873–877.

Petrides, M., & Milner, B. (1982). Deficits on subject-ordered tasks after frontal- and temporal-lobe lesions in man. *Neuropsychologia, 20,* 249–262.

Petrosino, A., Turpin-Petrosino, C., & Finckenauer, J. O. (2000). Well-meaning programs can have harmful effects!: Lessons from experiments in Scared Straight and other like programs. *Crime and Delinquency, 46,* 354–379.

Pettit, G. S., Bates, J. E., & Dodge, K. A. (1997). Supportive parenting, ecological context, and children's adjustment. *Child Development, 68,* 908–923.

Pettit, G. S., Bates, J. E., Dodge, K. A., & Meece, D. W. (1999). The impact of after-school peer contact on early adolescent externalizing problems is moderated by parental monitoring, neighborhood safety, and prior adjustment. *Child Development, 70,* 768–778.

Pettit, G. S., Laird, R. D., Bates, J. E., Dodge, K. A., & Criss, M. M. (2001). Antecedents and behavior-problem outcomes of parental monitoring and psychological control in early adolescence. *Child Development, 72*(2), 583–598.

Piaget, J. (1965). *The moral judgment of the child.* London: Routledge & Kegan Paul.

Pine, D. S., Coplan, J. D., Wasserman, G. A., Miller, L. S., Fried, J. E., Davies, M., et al. (1997). Neuroendocrine response to fenfluramine challenge in boys. *Archives of General Psychiatry, 54,* 839–846.

Pine, D. S., Shaffer, D., Schonfeld, I. S., & Davies, M. (1997). Minor physical anomalies: Modifiers of environmental risks for psychiatric impairment? *Journal of the American Academy of Child and Adolescent Psychiatry, 36,* 395–403.

Piquero, A., & Tibbett, S. (1999). The impact of per/perinatal disturbances and disadvantaged familial environment in predicting criminal offending. *Studies on Crime and Crime Prevention, 8,* 52–70.

Pollak, S. D., & Tolley-Schell, S. A. (2003). Selective attention to facial emotion in physically abused children. *Journal of Abnormal Psychology, 112,* 323–338.

Posner, M., & Rothbart, M. K. (1998). Attention, self-regulation, and consciousness. *Transactions of the Philosophical Society of London, B,* 1915–1927.

Prentice, N. M., & Kelly, F. J. (1963). Intelligence and delinquency: A reconsideration. *Journal of Social Psychology, 60,* 327–337.

Prinstein, M. J., & Cillessen, A. H. N. (2003). Forms and functions of adolescent peer aggression associated with high levels of peer status. *Merrill-Palmer Quarterly, 49,* 310–342.

Pulkkinen, L. (1990). Adult life-styles and their precursors in the social behavior of children and adolescents. *European Journal of Personality, 4,* 237–251.

Quiggle, N., Panak, W. F., Garber, J., & Dodge, K. A. (1992). Social information processing in aggressive and depressed children. *Child Development, 63,* 1305–1320.

Rabiner, D. L., Lenhart, L., & Lochman, J. E. (1990). Automatic versus reflective social problem solving in relation to children's sociometric status. *Developmental Psychology, 26,* 1010–1016.

Raine, A. (2002). Biosocial studies of antisocial and violent behavior in children and adults: A review. *Journal of Abnormal Child Psychology, 30*(4), 311–326.

Raine, A., Brennan, P., & Farrington, D. P. (1997). Biosocial bases of violence: Conceptual and theoretical issues. In A. Raine, P. A. Brennan, D. P. Farrington, & S. A. Mednick (Eds.), *Biosocial bases of violence* (pp. 1–20). New York: Plenum Press.

Raine, A., Brennan, P., & Mednick, S. A. (1994). Birth complications combined with early maternal rejection at age 1 year predispose to violent crime at age 18 years. *Archives of General Psychiatry, 53,* 984–988.

Raine, A., Brennan, P., & Mednick, S. A. (1997). Interaction between birth complications and early maternal rejection in predisposing to adult violence: Specificity to serious, early onset violence. *American Journal of Psychiatry, 154,* 1265–1271.

Raine, A., Lencz, T., Bihrle, S., LaCasse, L., & Colletti, P. (2000). Reduced prefrontal gray matter volume and reduced autonomic activity in antisocial personality disorder. *Archives of General Psychiatry, 57,* 119–127.

Raine, A., Reynolds, C., Venables, P. H., Mednick, S. A., & Farrington, D. P. (1998). Fearlessness, stimulation-seeking, and large body size at age 3 years as early predispositions to childhood aggression at age 11 years. *Archives of General Psychiatry, 55,* 745–751.

Raine, A., Venables, P. H., & Mednick, S. A. (1997). Low resting heart rate at age 3 years predisposes to aggression at age 11 years: Findings from the Mauritius Joint Child Health Project. *Journal of the American Academy of Child and Adolescent Psychiatry, 36,* 1457–1464.

Raine, A., Yaralian, P. S., Reynolds, C., & Venables, P. H. (2002). Spatial but not verbal cognitive deficits at age 3 years in lifecourse persistent antisocials: A prospective, longitudinal study. *Development and Psychopathology, 14*(1), 25–44.

Rasanen, P., Hakko, H., Isohanni, M., Hodgins, S., Jarvelin, M. R., & Tiihonen, J. (1999). Maternal smoking during pregnancy and risk of criminal behavior among adult male offspring in the northern Finland 1996 birth cohort. *American Journal of Psychiatry, 156,* 857–862.

Reid, J. B., Patterson, G. R., & Snyder, J. (Eds.). (2000). *Antisocial behavior in children and adolescents: A developmental analysis and model for intervention.* Washington, DC: American Psychological Association.

Renken, B., Egeland, B., Marvinney, D., Mangelsdorf, S., & Sroufe, L. A. (1989). Early childhood antecedents of aggression and passive-withdrawal in early elementary school. *Journal of Personality, 57,* 257–281.

Rhee, S. H., & Waldman, I. D. (2002). Genetic and environmental influences on antisocial behavior: A meta-analysis of twin and adoption studies. *Psychological Bulletin, 128,* 490–529.

Robins, L. N. (1966). *Deviant children grown up.* Baltimore: Williams & Wilkins.

Robins, L. N. (1999). A 70-year history of conduct disorder: Variations in definition, prevalence, and correlates. In P. Cohen, C. Slomkowski, & L. N. Robins (Eds.), *Historical and geographical influences of psychopathology* (pp. 37–56). Mahwah, NJ: Erlbaum.

Rodkin, P. C., Farmer, T. W., Pearl, R., & Van Acker, R. (2000). Heterogeneity of popular boys: Antisocial and prosocial configurations. *Developmental Psychology, 36,* 14–24.

Rogeness, G. A., Cepeda, C., Macedo, C. A., Fischer, C., & Harris, W. R. (1990). Differences in heart rate and blood pressure in children with conduct disorder, major depression, and separation anxiety. *Psychiatry Research, 33,* 199–206.

Rose, A., & Asher, S. (1998). Children's goals and strategies in response to conflicts within a friendship. *Developmental Psychology, 35,* 69–79.

Ross, R. R., & Ross, B. D. (1998). Delinquency prevention through cognitive training. *New Education, 10,* 70–75.

Rothbart, M. K., Ahadi, S. A., & Evans, D. E. (2000). Temperament and personality: Origins and outcomes. *Journal of Personality and Social Psychology, 78,* 122–135.

Rowe, R., Maughan, B., Worthman, C. M., Costello, E. J., & Angold, A. (2004). Testosterone, antisocial behavior, and social dominance in boys: Pubertal development and biosocial interaction. *Biological Psychiatry, 55*(5), 546–552.

Rubin, K. H., & Krasnor, L. R. (1986). Social cognitive and social behavioral perspectives on problem solving. In M. Perlmutter (Ed.), *Minnesota Symposia on Child Psychology* (Vol. 18, pp. 1–68). Hillsdale, NJ: Erlbaum.

Rubin, K. H., Moller, L., & Emptage, A. (1987). The preschool behavior questionnaire: A useful index of behavior problems in elementary school-age children. *Canadian Journal of Behavioral Science, 19,* 86–100.

Rule, B. G., & Ferguson, T. J. (1986). The effects of media violence on attitudes, emotions, and cognitions. *Journal of Social Issues, 42,* 29-50.

Rumelhart, D. E., & McClelland, J. L. (1986). *Parallel distributed processing—Exploration in the microstructure of cognition: Vol. 1. Foundations.* Cambridge, MA: MIT Press/Bradford Books.

Rutter, M. (1989). Pathways from childhood to adult life. *Journal of Child Psychology and Psychiatry, 30,* 25–31.

Rutter, M., & Garmezy, N. (1983). Developmental psychopathology. In P. H. Mussen (Series Ed.) & E. M. Hetherington (Vol. Ed.), *Handbook of child psychology: Vol. 4. Socialization, personality and social development* (4th ed., pp. 775–911). New York: Wiley.

Rutter, M., Giller, H., & Hagell, A. (1998). *Antisocial behavior by young people.* Cambridge: Cambridge University Press.

Rutter, M., Tizard, J., & Whitmore, K. (Eds.). (1970). *Education, health, and behavior.* London: Longmans.

Rys, G. S., & Bear, G. G. (1997). Relational aggression and peer relations: Gender and developmental issues. *Merrill-Palmer Quarterly, 43,* 87–106.

Salmivalli, C., Kaukiainen, A., & Lagerspetz, K. (2000). Aggression and socio-metric status among peers: Do gender and type of aggression matter? *Scandinavian Journal of Psychology, 41,* 17–24.

Salvador, A., Simon, V., Suay, F., & Llorens, L. (1987). Testosterone and cortisol responses to competitive fighting in human males: A pilot study. *Aggressive Behavior, 13,* 9–13.

Sampson, R. J., & Laub, J. H. (1990). Crime and deviance over the life course: The salience of adult social bonds. *American Sociological Review, 55,* 609–627.

Sampson, R. J., & Laub, J. H. (1994). Urban poverty and the family context of delinquency: A new look at structure and process in a classic study. *Child Development, 65,* 523–540.

Sampson, R., & Laub, J. (2003). Life-course desisters? Trajectories of crime among delinquent boys followed to age 70. *Criminology, 41*(3), 555–592.

Sampson, R. J., Raudenbush, S. W., & Earls, F. (1997). Neighborhoods and violent crime: A multi-level study of collective efficacy. *Science, 277,* 918–924.

Sanders, M. R., Markie-Dadds, C., Tully, L. A., & Bor, W. (2000). The Triple P-positive Parenting Intervention for parents of children with early onset conduct problems. *Journal of Consulting and Clinical Psychology, 68,* 624–640.

Sawin, D. B., & Parke, R. D. (1979). The effects of interagent inconsistent discipline on children's aggressive behavior. *Journal of Experimental Child Psychology, 28,* 525–538.

Scarr, S., & McCartney, K. (1983). How people make their own environments: A theory of genotype greater than environment effects. *Child Development, 54,* 424–435.

Schaal, B., Tremblay, R., Soussignan, R., & Susman, E. (1996). Male testosterone linked to high social dominance but low physical aggression in early adolescence. *Journal of the American Academy of Child and Adolescent Psychiatry, 34,* 1322–1330.

Schultz, D., Izard, C. E., & Bear, G. (2004). Children's emotion processing: Relations to emotionality and aggression. *Development and Psychopathology, 16,* 371–387.

Schwartz, D., Dodge, K. A., Coie, J. D., Hubbard, J., Cillessen, A., Lemerise, E., et al. (1998). Social cognitive and behavioral correlates of aggression and victimization in boys' play groups. *Journal of Abnormal Child Psychology, 26,* 431–440.

Schwartz, D., McFadyen-Ketchum, S. A., Dodge, K. A., Pettit, G. S., & Bates, J. E. (1998). Peer group victimization as a predictor of children's behavior problems at home and in school. *Development and Psychopathology, 10,* 87–99.

Schweinhart, L. J., Barnes, H. V., & Weikart, D. P. (1993). *Significant benefits: The High/Scope Perry Preschool Study thorough age 27.* Ypsilanti, MI: High/Scope Press.

Seguin, J. R., Nagin, D., Assaad, J. M., & Tremblay, R. E. (in press). Cognitive-neuropsychological function in chronic physical aggression and hyperactivity. *Journal of Abnormal Psychology.*

Seguin, J. R., Pihl, R. O., Harden, P. W., Tremblay, R. E., & Boulerice, B. (1995). Cognitive and neuropsychological characteristics of physically aggressive boys. *Journal of Abnormal Psychology, 104,* 614–624.

Selman, R. (1980). *The growth of interpersonal understanding.* New York: Academic Press.

Serketich, W. J., & Dumas, J. E. (1996). The effectiveness of behavioral parent training to modify antisocial behavior in children: A meta-analysis. *Behavior Therapy, 27,* 171–186.

Shank, R. C., & Abelson, R. (1977). *Scripts, plans, goals, and understanding.* Hillsdale, NJ: Erlbaum.

Shantz, D. W., & Voydanoff, D. A. (1973). Situational effects on retaliatory aggression at three age levels. *Child Development, 44,* 149–153.

Shaw, C., & McKay, H. (1942). *Juvenile delinquency and urban areas.* Chicago: University of Chicago Press.

Shaw, D. S. (2003). Innovative approaches and methods to the study of children's conduct problems. *Social Development, 12,* 322–326.

Shaw, D. S., Gilliom, M., Ingoldsby, E. M., & Nagin, D. S. (2003). Trajectories leading to school-age conduct problems. *Developmental Psychology, 39,* 189–200.

Shaw, D. S., Keenan, K., Owens, E. B., Winslow, E. B., Hood, N., & Garcia, M. (1995, April). *Developmental precursors of externalizing behavior among two samples of low-income families: Ages 1 to 5.* Paper presented at biennial meeting of the Society for Research in Child Development, Indianapolis, IN.

Shields, A., & Cicchetti, D. (1998). Reactive aggression among maltreated children: The contributions of attention and emotion dysregulation. *Journal of Clinical Child Psychology, 27,* 381–395.

Shumow, L., & Lomax, R. (2002). Parental efficacy: Predictor of parenting behavior and adolescent outcomes. *Parenting: Science and Practice, 2,* 127–150.

Shure, M. B., & Spivack, G. (1980). Interpersonal problem-solving as a mediator of behavioral adjustment in preschool and kindergarten children. *Journal of Applied Developmental Psychology, 1,* 29–44.

Simonoff, E., Pickles, A., Meyer, J., Silberg, J. L., Maes, H. H., Loeber, R., et al. (1997). The Virginia Twin Study of Adolescent Behavioral Development: Influences of age, gender, and impairment on rates of disorders. *Archives of General Psychiatry, 54,* 801–808.

Simons, R. L., Wu, C. I., Conger, R. D., & Lorenz, F. O. (1994). Two routes to delinquency: Differences between early and late starters in the impact of parenting and deviant peers. *Criminology, 32,* 247–276.

Singer, J. L., & Singer, D. G. (1981). *Television, imagination, and aggression: A study of preschoolers' play.* Hillsdale, NJ: Erlbaum.

Slaby, R. G., & Guerra, N. G. (1988). Cognitive mediators of aggression in adolescent offenders: Pt. 1. Assessment. *Developmental Psychology, 24,* 580–588.

Smithmyer, C. M., Hubbard, J. A., & Simons, R. F. (2000). Proactive and reactive aggression in delinquent adolescents: Relations to aggression outcome expectancies. *Journal of Clinical Child Psychology, 29,* 86–93.

Snyder, H. N. (2003). *Juvenile arrests 2001.* Washington, DC: U.S. Department of Justice, Office of Justice Programs, Office of Juvenile Justice and Delinquency Prevention.

Snyder, J., Dishion, T. J., & Patterson, G. R. (1986). Determinants and consequences of associating with deviant peers during preadolescence and adolescence. *Journal of Early Adolescence, 6,* 29–43.

Snyder, J., Reid, J., & Patterson, G. (2003). A social learning model of child and adolescent antisocial behavior. In B. B. Lahey, T. E. Moffitt, & A. Caspi (Eds.), *Causes of conduct disorder and juvenile delinquency* (pp. 27–48). New York: Guilford Press.

Snyder, J., Stoolmiller, M., Wilson, M., & Yamamoto, M. (2003). Child anger regulation, parental responses to children's anger displays, and early child antisocial behavior. *Social Development, 12,* 335–360.

Snyder, J. J., & Patterson, G. R. (1995). Individual differences in social aggression: A test of a reinforcement model of socialization in the natural environment. *Behavior Therapy, 26,* 371–391.

Spain, S. E., Douglas, K. S., Poythress, N. G., & Epstein, M. (2004). The relationship between psychopathic features, violence and treatment outcome: The comparison of three youth measures of psychopathic features. *Behavioral Sciences and the Law, 22*(1), 85–102.

Spencer, M. B., Dobbs, B., & Phillips, D. (1988). African-American adolescents: Adaptational processes and socioeconomic diversity in behavioral outcomes. *Journal of Adolescence, 11,* 117–137.

Spergel, I. A., Ross, R. E., Curry, G. D., & Chance, R. (1989). *Youth gangs: Problem and response.* Washington, DC: Office of Juvenile Justice and Delinquency Prevention.

Stafford, E., & Cornell, D. G. (2003). Psychopathy scores predict adolescent inpatient aggression. *Assessment, 10,* 102–112.

Stanger, C., Achenbach, T. M., & Verhulst, F. C. (1997). Accelerated longitudinal comparisons of aggressive versus delinquent syndromes. *Development and Psychopathology, 9,* 43–58.

Stattin, H., & Kerr, M. (2000). Parental monitoring: A reinterpretation. *Child Development, 71,* 1072–1085.

Steele, C. M., Spencer, S. J., & Aronson, J. (2002). Contending with group image: The psychology of stereotype and social identity threat. In M. P. Zanna (Ed.), *Advances in experimental social psychology* (Vol. 34, pp. 379–440). San Diego, CA: Academic Press.

Steinberg, M. D., & Dodge, K. A. (1983). Attributional bias in aggressive adolescent boys and girls. *Journal of Social and Clinical Psychology, 1,* 312–321.

Stenberg, C., & Campos, J. (1990). The development of anger expressions in infancy. In N. Stein, T. Trabasso, & B. Leventhal (Eds.), *Concepts in emotion* (pp. 75–99). Hillsdale, NJ: Erlbaum.

Sternberg, K. J., Lamb, M. E., Greenbaum, C., Cicchetti, D., Dawus, S., Cortes, R. M., et al. (1993). Effects of domestic violence on children's behavior problems and depression. *Developmental Psychology, 29,* 44–52.

Stifter, C. A., Spinrad, T. L., & Baungart-Rieker, J. M. (1999). Toward a developmental model of child compliance: The role of emotion regulation in infancy. *Child Development, 70,* 21–32.

Stone, W. L., Bendell, R. D., & Field, T. M. (1988). The impact of socioeconomic status on teenage mothers and children who received early intervention. *Journal of Applied Developmental Psychology, 9,* 391–408.

Stormshak, E. A., Bierman, K. L., Bruschi, C., Dodge, K. A., Coie, J. D., & the Conduct Problems Prevention Research Group. (1999). The relation between behavior problems and peer preference in different classroom contexts. *Child Development, 70,* 169–182.

Strauman, T. J., & Higgins, E. T. (1987). Automatic activation of self-discrepancies and emotional syndromes: When cognitive structures influence affect. *Journal of Personality and Social Psychology, 53,* 1004–1014.

Straus, M. A. (2005). *The primordial violence: Corporal punishment by parents, cognitive development, and crime.* Walnut Creek, CA: Alta Mira Press.

Straus, M. A., & Gelles, R. J. (1990). How violent are American families. In M. A. Straus & R. J. Gelles (Eds.), *Physical violence in American families* (pp. 95–112). New Brunswick, NJ: Transaction.

Straus, M. A., & Stewart, J. H. (1999). Corporal punishment by American parents: National data on prevalence, chronicity, severity, and duration, in relation to child and family characteristics. *Clinical Child and Family Psychology Review, 2,* 55–70.

Stromquist, V. J., & Strauman, T. J. (1992). Children's social constructs: Pt. 2. Nature, assessment, and association with adaptive and maladaptive behavior. *Social Cognition, 9,* 330–358.

Taylor, A. R., & Gabriel, S. W. (1989, April). *Cooperative versus competitive game-playing strategies of peer accepted and peer rejected children in a goal conflict situation.* Paper presented at the biennial meeting of the Society for Research in Child Development, Kansas City, MO.

Tedeschi, J. T., & Felson, R. B. (1994). *Violence, aggression, and coercive actions.* Washington, DC: American Psychological Association.

Thomas, A., Chess, S., & Birch, H. (1968). *Temperament and behavior disorders in children.* New York: New York University Press.

Thornberry, T. P., Krohn, M. D., Lizotte, A. J., & Chard-Wierschem, D. (1993). The role of juvenile gangs in facilitating delinquent behavior. *Journal of Research in Crime and Delinquency, 30,* 55–87.

Thornberry, T. P., Krohn, M. D., Lizotte, A. J., Smith, C. A., & Tobin, K. (2003). *Gangs and delinquency in developmental perspective.* Cambridge: Cambridge University Press.

Tiet, Q. Q., Wasserman, G. A., Loeber, R., McReynolds, L. S., & Miller, L. S. (2001). Developmental and sex differences in types of conduct problems. *Journal of Child and Family Studies, 10,* 181–197.

Tremblay, R. E., Hartup, W. W., & Archer, J. (Eds.). (2005). *Developmental origins of aggression.* New York: Guilford Press.

Tremblay, R. E., Mâsse, L. C., Vitaro, F., & Dobkin, P. L. (1995). The impact of friend's deviant behavior on early onset of delinquency: Longitudinal data from 6 to 13 years of age. *Development and Psychopathology, 7,* 649–667.

Tremblay, R. E., Pihl, R. O., Vitaro, R., & Dobkin, P. L. (1994). Predicting early onset of male antisocial behavior from preschool behavior. *Archives of General Psychiatry, 51,* 732–739.

Trivers, R. L. (1974). Parental-offspring conflict. *American Zoologist, 46,* 35–57.

Tuinier, S., Verhoeven, W. M. A., & van Praag, H. M. (1995). Cerebrospinal fluid 5-hydroxyindolacetic acid and aggression: A critical reappraisal of the clinical data. *International Clinical Psychopharmacology, 10*(3), 147–156.

Tulving, E., & Thomson, D. M. (1973). Encoding specificity and retrieval processes in episodic memory. *Psychological Review, 80,* 352-373.

Turner, A. K. (1994). Genetic and hormonal influences on male violence. In J. Archer (Ed.), *Male violence* (pp. 233–252). New York: Routledge.

Underwood, M. K. (2003). *Social aggression among girls.* New York: Guilford Press.

U.S. Department of Health and Human Services. (1997). *Morbidity and Mortality Weekly Report, 46*(5). Atlanta, GA: Centers for Disease Control and Prevention.

U.S. Department of Health and Human Services. (2000). *Healthy people 2010: Understanding and improving health and objectives for improving health* (2nd ed., Vols. 1–2). Washington, DC: U.S. Department of Health and Human Services.

U.S. Department of Justice, Federal Bureau of Investigation. (2003). *Crime in the United States: Uniform Crime Reports, 2002.* Washington, DC: U.S. Government Printing Office.

Valiente, C., Eisenberg, N., Smith, C. L., Reiser, M., Fabes, R. A., Losoya, S., et al. (2003). The relations of effortful control and reactive control to children's externalizing problems: A longitudinal assessment. *Journal of Personality, 71,* 1171–1196.

Van Lier, P. A. C., Muthén, B. O., van der Sar, R. M., & Crijnen, A. A. M. (2004). Preventing disruptive behavior in elementary schoolchildren: Impact of a universal classroom-based intervention. *Journal of Consulting and Clinical Psychology, 72,* 467–478.

Virkkunen, M., Eggert, M., Rawlings, R., & Linnoila, M. (1996). A prospective follow-up study of alcoholic violent offenders and fire setters. *Archives of General Psychiatry, 53,* 523–529.

Vitaro, F., Brendgen, M., Pagani, L., Trembley, R. E., & McDuff, P. (1999). Disruptive behavior, peer association, and conduct disorder: Testing the developmental links through early intervention. *Development and Psychopathology, 11,* 287-304.

Vitaro, F., Brendgen, M., & Tremblay, R. E. (2002). Reactively and proactively aggressive children: Antecedent and subsequent characteristics. *Journal of Child Psychology and Psychiatry, 43,* 495–505.

Votruba, M. E., & Kling, J. R. (2004). *Effects of neighborhood characteristics on the mortality of Black male youth: Evidence from Gautreaux* (Working Paper No. 491). Industrial Relations Section, Princeton University.

Votruba-Drzal, E., Coley, R. L., & Chase-Lansdale, P. L. (2004). Child care and low-income children's development: Direct and moderated effects. *Child Development, 75,* 296–312.

Waas, G. A. (1988). Social attributional biases of peer-rejected and aggressive children. *Child Development, 59,* 969-992.

Wakschlag, L. S., Lahey, B. B., Loeber, R., Green, S. M., Gordon, R. A., & Leventhal, B. L. (1997). Maternal smoking during pregnancy and the risk of conduct disorder in boys. *Archives of General Psychiatry, 54,* 670–676.

Waldman, I. D. (1988). *Relationships between noon-social information processing, social perception, and social status in 7- to 12-year-old boys.* Unpublished doctoral dissertation, University of Waterloo, Ontario, Canada.

Walters, R. H., & Parke, R. D. (1964). Social motivation, dependency, and susceptibility to social influence. In L. Berkowitz (Ed.), *Advances in experimental social psychology* (Vol. 1, pp. 231–276). New York: Academic Press.

Wann, D. L., & Branscombe, N. R. (1990). Person perception when aggressive or nonaggressive sport are primed. *Aggressive Behavior, 16,* 27-32.

Webster-Stratton, C. (1998). Preventing conduct problems in Head Start children: Strengthening parenting competencies. *Journal of Consulting and Clinical Psychology, 66,* 715–730.

Weiner, N. A. (1989). Violent criminal careers and "violent career criminals": An overview of the research literature. In N. A. Weiner & M. E. Wolfgang (Eds.), *Violent crime, violent criminals* (pp. 35–138). Newbury Park, CA: Sage.

Weiss, B., Dodge, K. A., Bates, S. E., & Pettit, G. S. (1992). Some consequences of early harsh discipline: Child aggression and a maladaptive social information processing style. *Child Development, 63,* 1321–1335.

Weiss, B., Harris, V., Catron, T., & Han, S. H. (2003). Efficacy of the RECAP intervention program for children with concurrent internalizing and externalizing problems. *Journal of Consulting and Clinical Psychology, 71,* 364–374.

Weissman, M. M., Warner, V., Wickramaratne, P. J., & Kandel, D. B. (1999). Maternal smoking during pregnancy and psychopathology in offspring followed to adulthood. *Journal of the American Academy of Child and Adolescent Psychiatry, 38,* 892–899.

Werner, H. (1961). *Comparative psychology of mental development.* New York: Science Editions. (Original work published 1948)

White, J., Moffitt, T. E., Caspi, A., Bartusch, D. J., Needles, D., & Stouthamer-Loeber, M. (1994). Measuring impulsivity and examining its relation to delinquency. *Journal of Abnormal Psychology, 103,* 192–205.

Wilson, J. Q., & Herrnstein, R. (1985). *Crime and Human Nature.* New York: Simon and Schuster.

Wilson, W. J. (1987). *The truly disadvantaged.* Chicago: University of Chicago Press.

Wintemute, G. (2000). Guns and gun violence. In A. Blumstein & J. Wallman (Eds.), *The crime drop in America* (pp. 45–96). New York: Cambridge University Press.

Wolff, P. H., Waber, D., Bauermeister, M., Cohen, C., & Ferber, R. (1982). The neuropsychological status of adolescent delinquent boys. *Journal of Child Psychology and Psychiatry, 23,* 267–279.

Wood, W., Wong, F. Y., & Chachere, G. (1991). Effects of media violence on viewers' aggression in unconstrained social interaction. *Psychological Bulletin, 109,* 371–383.

Woolfenden, S. R., Williams, K., & Peat, J. (2002). Family and parenting interventions in children and adolescents with conduct disorder and delinquency aged 10 to 17 (Cochrane Review). *The Cochrane Library, 4.* Oxford, England: Update Software.

Wright, J. C., Giammarino, M., & Parad, H. W. (1986). Social status in small groups: Individual-group similarity and the social "misfit." *Journal of Personality and Social Psychology, 50,* 523–536.

Wyer, R. S., Jr., & Srull, T. K. (1989). *Memory and cognition in its social context.* Hillsdale, NJ: Erlbaum.

Zahn-Waxler, C., Radke-Yarrow, M., & King, R. A. (1979). Child-rearing and children's prosocial initiations toward victims of distress. *Child Development, 50,* 319–330.

Zakriski, A. L., & Coie, J. D. (1996). A comparison of aggressive-rejected and nonaggressive-rejected boys' interpretations of self-directed and other-directed rejection. *Child Development, 67,* 1048–1070.

Zelli, A., Dodge, K., Lochman, J., Laird, R., & the Conduct Problems Prevention Research Group. (1999). The distinction between beliefs legitimizing aggression and deviant processing of social cues: Testing measurement validity and the hypothesis that biased processing mediates the effects of beliefs on aggression. *Journal of Personality and Social Psychology, 77,* 150–166.

Zhou, Q., Eisenberg, N., Losoya, S., Fabes, R. A., Reiser, M., Guthrie, I. K., et al. (2002). The relations of parental warmth and positive expressiveness to children's empathy-related responding and social functioning: A longitudinal study. *Child Development, 73,* 893–915.

CHAPTER 13

The Development of Morality

ELLIOT TURIEL

Philosophers have been concerned with the topic of morality for a long time. Socrates is referred to as the "patron saint of moral philosophy" (Frankena, 1963, p. 1). The moral philosophies of Plato and Aristotle included concerns with how individuals acquire or develop morality and how to create the best educational conditions for its acquisition. Moral development has been of central concern in the major psychological theoretical perspectives since the beginning of the twentieth century. Psychoanalytic, behavioristic, Gestalt, and structural-developmental theorists made the study of morality central. The major figures in these approaches, including Sigmund Freud, B. F. Skinner, and Jean Piaget, provided accounts of moral development. Many of the problems raised by them and by moral philosophers over the ages remain part of contemporary discussion.

Psychological research in recent years has produced new findings and changes in assumptions about children's social propensities, social experiences, and ways of framing features of moral development. Nevertheless, many of the issues around definitions of morality, influences of emotions and thought, and the roles of society or cultures are still debated. In these regards, little has changed in theory and research on moral development since the publication of the previous volumes of the *Handbook of Child Psychology* in 1998. This chapter, therefore, covers much of the same ground as the previous version, with an updating of the literature since that time. Because most of the theorizing and research discussed in the previous version of this chapter remains relevant, changes in this version primarily reflect the inclusion of new research conducted during the past few years.

SETTING THE STAGE

Sigmund Freud wrote extensively about morality, incorporating it into his general formulations of individual development in society. Central to his view were the concepts of conscience (tied to the idea of a duality) and concomitant tension between an individual and society. The root of this tension is the incompatibility of psychological and biological needs of individuals and strivings for long-term survival of individuals and the species. The collectivity largely has the function of ensuring survival and protecting people from each other's aggressive tendencies. Through the influences of the collectivity, particularly as reproduced in a family, the individual's needs for instinctual gratification become transformed and displaced in the developmental process to make room for internalized standards (via parents as representatives of society) and internalized emotional mechanisms for regulating behaviors. This transformation, which is grounded in emotions of fear and anxiety and facilitated by positive emotions of love and attachment, largely stems from emotional conflicts producing psychological transformations through the acquisition of a mental agency, a superego, and incorporating moral ideals and guilt as the means for the regulation of conduct.

In the Freudian view, the acquisition of morality results in a duality in the individual, including the forces of the superego and needs for instinctual gratification. The moral side of the duality entails duties to uphold societal norms. Although fulfilling duties entails deep conflicts (most often of an unconscious nature), the duties are felt as inexorable and impersonal. An appropriately internalized morality is invariable and applied inflexibly. In this regard, Freud proposed that women do not adequately internalize a superego. In what has become an infamous statement about gender differences in morality, Freud (1925/1959) said:

> I cannot escape the notion (though I hesitate to give it expression) that for women the level of what is ethically normal is different from what it is in men. Their superego is never so inexorable, so impersonal, so independent of its emotional origins as we require it to be in men. (p. 196)

The important question of gender differences is discussed later with regard to contemporary analyses and debates. Gender is important in analyses of morality because females are in subordinate positions in the social hierarchies of most societies and thereby are not treated equally with males. Inequalities that stem from such social hierarchies or cultural practices and affect women and others (e.g., minorities and people of lower social castes or classes) are discussed in this chapter. In particular, research is considered that has examined the perspectives and moral reactions (through social opposition, resistance, and subversion) of those in subordinate positions.

B. F. Skinner (1971, Chapter 6) presented his position on morality in the latter part of his career and in a largely nontechnical book for a popular audience. In keeping with his behavioristic formulations, Skinner proposed that morality reflects behaviors that have been reinforced (positively or negatively) by value judgments associated with cultural norms. Actions are not intrinsically good or bad but are acquired and performed as a consequence of contingencies of reinforcement. Certain contingencies, consistent with the mores of the group, are social in that they pertain to relationships with others and are governed by verbal reinforcers such as good, bad, right, and wrong. Moreover, social control over behavior is particularly powerful when it is exercised by institutional forces (e.g., religious, governmental, economic, or educational). This is because the reinforcers of "good" and "bad" also take the form of legal, illegal, pious, or sinful acts with their associated rewards and punishments. Learned behaviors stemming from the customary practices of a group are invariant because reinforcement contingencies are maintained. For Skinner, however, learned behaviors do not constitute duties or obligations nor reflect a person's character; rather, they are due to the arrangement of effective social contingencies.

Knowledge and judgments about social relationships were considered central to morality by Jean Piaget, who wrote about the topic mainly in the early part of his career (Piaget, 1932; see also Piaget, 1951/1195a, 1960/1995b). In keeping with his general views of development as stemming from reciprocal interactions of individuals and multiple features of social experiences (entailing constructions of understandings of experiences), Piaget analyzed morality from the perspective of how experiences result in the formation of judgments about social relationships, rules, laws, authority, and social institutions. Piaget's formulations on moral development included the idea that social transmission does not solely result in the reproduction of that which is transmitted but also entails reconstructions. He also proposed that moral development is influenced by a variety of experiences, including emotional reactions (e.g., sympathy, empathy, and respect), relationships with adults, and relationships with other children. In Piaget's view, moral judgments are fundamentally about relationships, with development progressing (a) toward feelings of mutual respect among persons (with a developmentally prior set of feelings entailing a sense of unilateral respect from child to adult or authority), (b) toward concerns with attaining and maintaining social relationships of cooperation (with rules and laws serving ends of cooperation rather than seen as fixed and categorical), (c) toward the formation of concepts of justice, and (d) toward an ability to consider the perspectives of others as possibly different from one's own (thus accounting for subjectivity and intentionality rather than viewing all perspectives as reflecting objective reality). As based on mutual respect, cooperation, and concepts of rules, laws, and duties as serving ends of fairness and justice, the developmentally advanced form of morality, in Piaget's view, is both inexorable and flexible. Moral concepts and goals have an obligatory quality to individuals but are applied flexibly in accord with requirements of situations, appraisal of intentions, and varying perspectives. The less developmentally advanced heteronomous morality of the young child entails conceptions of fixed rules, duties, and obedience to authority. In this regard, too, Piaget proposed gender differences of a less straightforward kind than those proposed by Freud. In some respects, Piaget (1932) viewed the morality of school-age girls as less advanced than boys (specifically, "the legal sense is far less developed in little girls than in boys"; p. 69), whereas in other respects he viewed girls as more advanced than boys (specifically, girls more readily subordinate rules to cooperation and mutual agreement and are "more tolerant and more easily reconciled to innovations"; p. 75).

Another aspect of Piaget's formulation especially relevant to contemporary analyses of culture and morality is the concept of autonomy. Piaget proposed that as morality develops, there is a shift from a heteronomous to an autonomous orientation. Autonomy in this context does not mean that individuals' conceptions of morality are based on the independence of individuals. Indeed,

the ideas of mutual respect and cooperation, key to Piaget's formulation, imply interdependence rather than independence. By autonomy, Piaget (1960/1995b) meant "that the subject participates in the elaboration of norms instead of receiving them ready-made as happens in the case of the norms of unilateral respect that lie behind heteronomous morality" (p. 315). Therefore, Piaget used autonomy in reference to a process in which norms furthering interdependence are elaborated with the participation of the child.

The concept of autonomy, along with the propositions that obligatory moral judgments are applied with flexibility of thought in social contexts, makes for a fundamental contrast between Piagetian and Freudian or behaviorist approaches. In both the Freudian and behaviorist conceptions, the individual's morality is under some kind of psychological compulsion: In the Freudian view, an internalized conscience or superego compels behavior, and in the behavioristic conception, actions are compelled by habits of behavior. Contemporary analyses discussed in this chapter can also be contrasted on these dimensions as well. Contemporary researchers have examined moral judgments and how they are applied in situational and cultural contexts. There are also various psychological and/or biologically based explanations of moral functioning that are based on how psychological mechanisms compel actions. These include genetic traits and genetically based intuitions and emotions. Some explanations are based on propositions of acquired, learned, or internalized features, such as character traits and conscience. Some are based on internalized values, norms, or rules, such as from parents, society, and culture. Some of these explanations imply moral absolutism, such as genes are fixed and conscience or traits of character are regarded as unvarying. Other explanations imply a degree of moral relativism, such as different parents, societies, or cultural ways result in different groups being compelled in different ways.

As already noted, many issues and questions addressed by Freud, Skinner, and Piaget persist in contemporary analyses of moral development. Their theoretical approaches influenced subsequent researchers working from the 1950s to the 1970s, which in turn have influenced contemporary researchers. The following section presents a brief historical overview connecting the ideas of Skinner and Freud to subsequent research of behavioristically oriented thinkers, who also attempted to account for psychoanalytic concepts. The overview includes a consideration of connections between the ideas of Piaget and subsequent cognitively oriented thinkers.

HISTORICAL OVERVIEW: THE FIRST AND SECOND PARTS OF THE TWENTIETH CENTURY

Freud's and Piaget's formulations of morality were produced in the context of a fair amount of interest in the topic among social scientists writing in the early part of the twentieth century (Baldwin, 1896; McDougall, 1908). Another influential direction was established by the French sociologist Emile Durkheim (1925/1961, 1912/1965), whose ideas contrasted with those of Piaget (see Piaget, 1932, chap. 4, for his critique of Durkheim's position). Durkheim conceptualized morality as largely based on sentiments of attachment to the group and respect for its symbols, rules, and authority. According to Durkheim, children's immersion in the group and participation in social life produce a natural attachment to the group and a willing adherence to its moral norms.

Many of the issues put forth in the first part of the twentieth century by Freud, Piaget, and others had a major influence on later research on moral development. It took some time, however, for those influences to have their impact. Whereas there was little research from about the early 1930s until the late 1950s, a great deal of research on moral development has been conducted since the late 1950s to the time of this writing. During the late 1950s and early 1960s, there was steadily increasing interest in the child-rearing antecedents of conscience, guilt, and internalized moral values and behaviors (e.g., Hoffman, 1963; Sears, Maccoby, & Levin, 1957). Although the influence of psychoanalytic theory waned over the years, many of Freud's ideas were incorporated into the work on child rearing, alongside the increasingly influential behavioristic theories of that time. Emphasis was placed on identification as a mechanism for the acquisition of moral values and on guilt and anxiety as the basic motives for the child's inhibition of needs or impulses and adherence to moral values. At about the same time, several researchers turned their attention to direct applications of behavioristic learning principles for explanations of the acquisition of moral behaviors and the role of anxiety and guilt in moral actions (e.g., Aronfreed, 1961; Bandura & Walters, 1963).

The dominant conceptions of morality were, therefore, either based on psychoanalytic explanations of conscience and guilt, as transformed by learning theories, or straightforward behavioristic explanations of moral learning. In either type of formulation, moral development was assumed to be a function of societal control over the individual's interests, needs, or impulses. Since then a major shift, brought about in no small measure by the work of Kohlberg, has occurred in psychologists' approach to morality. Kohlberg critiqued the dominant behavioristic and psychoanalytic conceptions of morality (Kohlberg, 1963, 1964), argued for the need to ground empirical study of moral development on sound philosophical definitions of the domain (Kohlberg, 1970, 1971), and presented his own formulations of the process of moral development (Kohlberg, 1963, 1969), entailing modifications and elaborations of Piaget's (1932) earlier formulations.

Kohlberg provided a comprehensive review of research pertaining to what was then the common wisdom that parental practices of discipline determined the strength and accuracy of the acquisition of conscience and moral behaviors. Kohlberg's review documented that there were no consistent relations between those parental conditions of child rearing postulated to lead to learning and the various measures of conscience or internalized values used at the time (see Kohlberg, 1963, for details). Kohlberg also argued that the measures of moral development generally used in that body of research were inadequate because they entailed projective tests of guilt or anxiety, reactions to story stimuli of little moral importance, ambiguous self-reports by parents of their past child-rearing techniques, and contrived experimental situations of little meaning to children.

The message Kohlberg wanted to convey regarding his methodological critique was not only methodological. The inadequacies in methods were, in Kohlberg's view, tied to theories that were not grounded in any substantive epistemology of the domain. Whereas morality was treated as a substantive epistemological category by many philosophers—from Plato and Aristotle to Hume, Mill, and Kant and contemporary philosophers (e.g., John Rawls)—psychologists attempted to explain its acquisition without considering the definition or meaning of that which is acquired. Kohlberg argued that we could not consider mechanisms of moral acquisition without concern with definitions, meanings, and the substance of morality. This idea was also based on psychological considerations. Kohlberg presumed that social scientists and philosophers were not the only ones who engage in systematic thinking about psychological, social, or moral matters: Laypersons do, too. He rejected the implied duality between the psychologist and the layperson evident in most psychological explanations.

Kohlberg (1968) coined the phrase "the child as a moral philosopher." However, the metaphor was not meant to convey the idea that children engage in reflective intellectual deliberations or formulate conceptual systems of the type seen in the writings of professional moral philosophers. Rather, it was meant to convey the idea that children form ways of thinking through their social experiences, which include substantive understandings of moral concepts like justice, rights, equality, and welfare. Implicit but important assumptions in this formulation are that morality is not solely, or even mainly, imposed on children and that morality is not solely based on avoiding negative emotions like anxiety and guilt. As part of their orientation to social relationships, and especially through taking the perspectives of others, children generate judgments, built on emotions like sympathy, empathy, respect, love, and attachment to which they have a commitment and which are not in conflict with their "natural" or biological dispositions (recall Piaget's definition of moral autonomy).

Kohlberg studied moral development by focusing on how children and adolescents make judgments about conflicts, in hypothetical situations, around issues of life, interpersonal obligations, trust, law, authority, and retribution. He proposed a sequence of six stages, depicting a progression of judgments. Stages 1 and 2, grouped into a "preconventional" level, were primarily based on obedience, punishment avoidance, and instrumental need and exchange. Stages 3 and 4, grouped into a "conventional" level, were based on role obligations, stereotypical conceptions of good persons, and respect for the rules and authority legitimated in the social system. Stages 5 and 6, grouped into a "postconventional" level, were based on contractual agreements, established procedural arrangements for adjudicating conflicts, mutual respect, and differentiated concepts of justice and rights. This sequence was also a reformulation of Piaget's progression from heteronomy to autonomy (Kohlberg, 1963). Kohlberg maintained that respect for rules and authority, which Piaget had attributed to young children at the heteronomous level, does not come about at least until adolescence (Kohlberg's conventional level), and that young children's moral judgments are characterized, instead, by a failure to distinguish

moral value from power, sanctions, and instrumental needs. In turn, Kohlberg proposed that mutual respect and concepts of justice and rights as part of an autonomous system of thought, whose emergence Piaget had placed in late childhood or early adolescence, do not come about until, at the earliest, late adolescence and usually not until adulthood (Kohlberg's postconventional level).

Kohlberg also proposed that the stages represent universal forms of moral judgment among individuals participating in social interactions and perspective taking. He proposed that the stages defined structural features of moral thought, which represented commonalities among cultures in the context of possible differences in the content of morality. By undertaking a series of studies in several cultures, some Western and some non-Western (Kohlberg, 1969), Kohlberg gave greater emphasis than existed before to empirical data to test propositions regarding cultural differences or commonalities in moral judgments. Kohlberg's research, as well as many studies conducted by others, suggested both that there may be similarities across cultures in development through the first three or four stages and that there is much ambiguity of thought corresponding to the higher stages (see Snarey, 1985). As discussed in subsequent sections, the question of cultural differences and commonalities has provoked much controversy. Nevertheless, Kohlberg's work in this regard has been influential in framing discussions of morality and culture around empirical findings.

Kohlberg's influence on subsequent research and theories is, in important respects, separate from the influence of his particular formulation of stages of moral development or even from the general theoretical viewpoint he espoused. Many advance alternative theoretical paradigms, including paradigms based on the idea of the internalization of conscience and values or the idea of culture-based morality. Among those who advance developmental positions influenced by Piaget's theory, many propose formulations divergent from that of Kohlberg. Yet, Kohlberg has influenced discourse about the psychology of moral development in several ways. One is that there is greater recognition of the need to ground psychological explanations in philosophical considerations about morality. Another influence is that in many current formulations morality is not framed by impositions on children due to conflicts between their needs or interests and the requirements of society or the group. Many now think that children are, in an active and positive sense, integrated into their social relationships with adults and peers and that morality is not solely or even primarily an external or unwanted imposition on them. Kohlberg had stressed children's constructions of moral judgments from social interactions. Following Piaget's formulations, Kohlberg proposed that emotions of sympathy for others, spontaneous interests in helping others, and respect were centrally involved in children's moral development, especially as part of the process of taking the perspective of others (Kohlberg, 1969, 1971, 1976).

All the changes in perspectives on moral development cannot be attributed solely to Kohlberg's influence. The issues noted are ones he addressed directly and for which he provided persuasive arguments. Nor do contemporary analyses of moral development exclude elements of the positions taken by behavioristic and psychoanalytic theorists. There are researchers concerned with the internalization of values, the ideas of conscience and self-control, and with emotions like anxiety, shame, and guilt. Nevertheless, the scope of inquiry has been broadened to include and emphasize positive emotions; the intricacies of moral, social, and personal judgments as part of individuals' relations with the social world; and social interactions contributing to development, including with parents, peers, schooling, and culture. Debates now center on the roles of emotions and judgments, on the individual and the collectivity, on the contributions of constructions of moral understandings and culturally based meanings, and on how to distinguish between universally applicable and locally based moralities.

ISSUES, EMPHASES, AND THEORIES

Discussions of moral development seem to involve strongly held and conflicting positions. It is frequently asserted that positions held by others exclude a particular feature of central importance—usually the feature emphasized by those characterizing the other's approach. Portraying others as excluding a feature deemed of central importance extends well beyond debates over moral development. Probably the most common example is seen in the debates over the roles of biology and environment. Those debates seem to be everlasting and there is a recycling of the issues even though periodically there appears something of a consensus that such de-

bates are futile because both biology and environment contribute to psychological functioning and development. One reason for this state of affairs is that the question is usually mischaracterized as whether biology or environment is taken into account rather than *how* each feature is explained. An equally important reason for the continual reemergence of the debates is that these matters are not settled, yet researchers pursuing different and even opposite explanations tend to declare matters settled.

For example, consider assertions about supposedly new disciplines: One labeled cultural psychology (Shweder, 1990a; Shweder & Sullivan, 1993) and the other evolutionary psychology (Cosmides & Tooby, 1989; Tooby, 1987; Wright, 1994). Proponents of cultural psychology maintain that thoughts, meanings, emotions, and behaviors vary by culture. Consequently, they propose that there are no general psychological processes to be discovered: "[T]he mind . . . is content driven, domain specific, and constructively stimulus bound" (Shweder, 1990a, p. 87), with an emphasis on that which is local, contingent, and context-dependent. Cultural psychology is said to be a newly emerging discipline entailing "the study of the way cultural traditions and social practices regulate, express, and transform the human psyche, resulting less in psychic unity for humankind than in ethnic divergences in mind, self, and emotion" (Shweder, 1990a, p. 73).

By contrast, proponents of evolutionary psychology maintain that mind and behavior have a firm evolutionary basis, which makes for a "unity within the species" connecting the peoples of the world. According to evolutionary psychologists, social relationships, and especially relationships between the sexes, including and going well beyond reproductive functions, are highly influenced by evolutionary processes. Evolutionary processes extend to morality: "Altruism, compassion, empathy, love, conscience, the sense of justice—all these things, the things that hold society together, the things that allow our species to think so highly of itself, can now confidently be said to have a firm genetic basis" (Wright, 1994, p. 12). Confidence in a firm genetic basis brings with it confidence in uniformities among people of different cultures: "Evolutionary psychologists are pursuing what is known in the trade as 'the psychic unity of humankind'" (Wright, 1994, p. 26).

Along with the striking confidence expressed by cultural and evolutionary psychologists in discoveries against and for the psychic unity of humankind, they make other parallel claims. They claim that the discipline has discovered knowledge contrary to the established perspective in psychology that will be resisted by those with vested interests in the old paradigm. Cultural psychologists argue that psychology and other social sciences have been dominated by those seeking psychic unity and proposing general psychological mechanisms. Evolutionary psychologists argue that psychology and other social sciences have been dominated by those seeking environmental and cultural explanations.

If the content were omitted, it would appear that cultural and evolutionary psychologists are in agreement about the past and future of psychology. Each asserts that there is a previously dominant paradigm about which its proponents are defensive and resistant to change but which is being displaced by a new paradigm. Yet, they hold contradictory views about which paradigm was previously dominant and which one is taking over. Not only are levels of the state of knowledge and documentation and verification for discoveries exaggerated so that matters are prematurely claimed to be settled, but also opposing positions are characterized as accounting for mainly one type of feature. This is an old story. Behaviorists made similar claims early in the twentieth century. Most notably, Watson (1924) proclaimed that behaviorism was the wave of the future that would replace the prescientific thinking of the mass of people and of psychologists through its experimental approach and the recognition of the ways environment shapes behavior (Turiel, 2004a).

Among theorists of moral development, there seems to be a greater recognition of the viability of competing points of view. However, it is not uncommon to find characterizations of others' explanations of moral development as excluding a feature judged to be of central importance. It is implied that the omission, in itself, invalidates the theoretical point of view. The most frequent examples of this revolve around whether theorists account for emotions or judgments, for social influences or the individual's logical operations, for parental influences or peer influences, and for cultural or individual constructions. There is a tendency to mischaracterize positions as failing to account for this or that instead of recognizing that differences in theoretical perspectives have more to do with how different features (e.g., emotions and judgments) are explained and emphasized. Even when a theorist excludes a particular component

regarded important by others, it is usually mistaken to say that there is a failure to account for the component. Often, the relevance of a component is explicitly excluded. An example is Skinner's (1971) arguments for the exclusion of moral judgments, along with cognition in general, as epiphenomena.

It is important, therefore, to consider how a theoretical perspective frames the relevant issues. In current theoretical perspectives and research programs, it is particularly important to consider how issues like emotion, culture, gender, judgment, social influences, and individual constructions are explained. Indeed, emphases placed on these issues serve to distinguish points of view on moral development. Whereas most explanations of moral development attempt to account for each of these issues, there are differences in the importance and roles given to them that result in varying explanations of morality and its development.

This chapter is organized around theoretical approaches to moral development, with the central issues emphasized. There is a tradition in which morality is defined as the possession of habits or virtues or traits of character, which are usually linked tightly with emotions. In recent years, psychologists have not emphasized habits or traits. Many have moved away from explanations of morality as the formation of internal traits or dispositions of personality. Nonetheless, there are sizable groups, including those concerned with moral education and certain sociologists and social commentators, who rely on the concept of character as linked more to emotions than to reasoning. Some of this literature—that on character and moral education (often referred to as character education)—will not be considered here, as it is the topic of the chapter by Narvaez and Lapsley, Chapter 7, this *Handbook,* Volume 4. Narvaez and Lapsley also consider propositions using the notions of character and moral identity as bridging moral judgments to moral actions (for a critique and alternative view, see Turiel, 2003a). However, I do discuss some views outside of psychology that are presented by social critics and sociologists who link emotions to the formation of character traits and/or habitual moral practices. Their positions have connections to psychological concepts and can be evaluated by psychological evidence. After discussing their positions, I consider, in greater detail, the concepts and research of developmental psychologists who emphasize emotions, influences of parental practices, and conscience. This is followed by discussion of approaches that, though including emotions and judgments, emphasize the role of gender and gender-related experiences in moral development. Then, I consider approaches in which culture is regarded as central and in which fairly sharp distinctions are drawn among moral orientations in different cultures. Next, I discuss approaches emphasizing moral judgments and reciprocal interactions in development. Finally, a perspective is presented based on reciprocal interactions; the domains of personal, social, and moral judgments; and their interplay with cultural practices. I approach each of the positions, and associated research, from the perspectives of their conceptualizations of the moral realm, the theoretical constructs on development, and the ways development is influenced by biological and environmental features.

In the course of this chapter, I do not solely review the different positions on moral development. While presenting the different positions, I comment on and evaluate the positions. Those evaluations are connected to my own views and positions. In the latter parts of the chapter, I discuss my positions, which are shared by a number of colleagues and collaborators.

BUILDING CHARACTER AND STRENGTHENING COMMUNITIES

Some philosophers who trace their roots to Aristotle have proposed explanations of morality as entailing virtues and character. Aristotelian and neo-Aristotelian accounts (e.g., MacIntyre, 1981) have included conceptions of morality as the good life, reflected in habitual practices and in living up to the virtues through action. Although Aristotle linked virtues to tradition, he also believed that traditions should not necessarily remain fixed or immune from criticism. According to Nussbaum (1989), Aristotle's position was "If we reason well we can make progress in lawmaking, just as we do in other arts and sciences" (p. 36). However, the sociologists and social critics who stress the concept of character have not carried over the philosophical substance of the Aristotelian and neo-Aristotelian propositions, at least as interpreted by Nussbaum. Instead, they have used the concepts of character as a means of commenting on the state of American society. It has been proposed that American children's acquisition of moral habits requires a renewed valuing of cultural traditions and commitment to a sense of community, along with a de-emphasis of individualism. Positions emphasizing

community have affinities to Durkheim's (1925/1961) proposition that morality involves a collective sense of solidarity, experienced by individuals as feelings of attachments to and respect for the moral authority embedded in society.

The common themes in these positions are that habits and character traits are at the core of morality and that American society is in moral crisis, decay, or serious decline. Myriad causes have been offered as bringing about the decline. These include the culture of the 1960s (Bloom, 1987); changes in the family (Bloom, 1987; Etzioni, 1993; Wilson, 1993); a failure to attend to traditions (Bennett, 1993; Etzioni, 1993; K. Ryan, 1989; Wynne, 1986, 1989); a failure to provide moral education (Bennett & Delattre, 1978); an onset of radical individualism (Bellah, Madsen, Sullivan, Swidler, & Tipton, 1985; Etzioni, 1993); the influences of feminism (Bloom, 1987); and the teachings of elites (intellectuals, scholars) who, in contradiction with the common sense or natural propensities of ordinary people, create theories hostile to virtues and character (Bennett, 1992; Bloom, 1987; Wilson, 1993).

Character Traits and Moral Sensibilities

Some who lament the moral decline of American society propose that the remedy lies in promoting character in children through firm controls by adults in the family and schools. They find fault in programs of moral education (especially those based on Kohlberg's theories) whose pedagogical aims are to stimulate the development of moral judgments, reflection, or the consideration of alternative moral decisions (see Bennett & Delattre, 1978). Judgment is deemed largely tangential to morality, and its emphasis is said to divert children from learning to behave in habitual ways consistent with traditions and virtues.

It is argued that, instead, there should be an emphasis on the inculcation of traits in children, with a focus on influencing how they act and not on their states of mind (Wynne, 1986). The traits, which are based on traditions of the culture, are transmitted not only through rewards and punishments but also, especially, through the example provided by the consistent actions of adults practicing the values and in the telling and retelling of stories about people behaving in accord with those values. The fundamental traits of character include honesty, compassion, courage, responsibility, self-discipline, and loyalty.

The premise that traits of character are ingrained in cultural traditions and held in respect by the majority of Americans may appear contradictory with the proposition put forth by the same writers that American society has lost its moral compass and is experiencing moral decay (the latter premise suggests that Americans do not possess the necessary traits). This potential contradiction is explained as due to a discrepancy between the beliefs and values of the majority of Americans, who constitute the mainstream, and an apparently highly influential minority of "elites" who "have waged an all-out assault on common sense and the common values of the American people" (Bennett, 1992, p. 13). In ways unspecified, the presumed elites' rejection of the idea of character, their antipathy to the culture, and their embrace of an ideology contrary to the beliefs of most Americans are said to have placed the country in moral crisis.

These propositions are at root paradoxical because if people acquire character and habits through the example of others and if the majority of mainstream Americans maintain the morally proper traits and beliefs, then it would be expected that there are many examples from which children would learn. Presumably, children are exposed to exemplary virtues in most families, schools, and elsewhere. A similar paradox is seen in the propositions of Wilson (1993), another social scientist who shares some of the emphasis on character, while attempting to account for evidence from psychology, anthropology, economics, and biology in formulating a theory of morality and its acquisition based on emotions and innate sociability. Wilson sees a loss of confidence in the use of the language of morality due to a prevailing moral skepticism perpetuated by "intellectuals" who question the scientific bases for morality and who further an ideology of individual autonomy and choice. At the same time, Wilson's explanation of morality is founded on the proposition that a natural moral sense emerged in the process of evolution and that most people's moral behaviors are determined largely by emotions and habits: "Much of the time our inclination toward fair play or our sympathy for the plight of others are immediate and instinctive, a reflex of our emotions more than an act of our intellect. . . . The feelings on which people act are often superior to the arguments that they employ" (Wilson, 1993, pp. 7–8).

In Wilson's formulation, although reasoning, reflection, and deliberation may emerge later in life than the reflexive and habitual, they are less adaptive, from the moral point of view, than the earlier emerging moral sensibilities. Such a reversal of often-held conceptions of development (where reasoning and reflection are advances built on earlier reflexive processes) is based on the idea that morality stems from natural emotions, whose emergence is best facilitated by early experiences in appropriate types of families (i.e., defined by Wilson as intact, heterosexual families where parents provide love, nurturance, and act authoritatively). Evolution, Wilson argues, has selected for attachment or affiliative behavior. In addition to natural selection for reproductive success, with a disposition toward self-interest, there is a biologically based disposition for bonding and attachment that takes the form of sociability. Innate sociability is the overriding component in producing four central "sentiments" that make up the moral life: *sympathy* (allowing people to be affected by the feelings and experiences of others), *fairness* (based on equity, reciprocity, and impartiality), *self-control* (a necessary sensibility because conflicts arise between self-interest and the moral sense), and *duty* or conscience (which dictates actions in the absence of sanctions).

In keeping with a de-emphasis of individuals' reasoning and reflection, Wilson believes that morality is, in most instances, local and parochial. In simple agricultural communities, and in Western cultures prior to the Enlightenment, the moral sense applies to those who are similar and familiar to oneself (kin and the local community). The idea that moral considerations should be universalized is a Western concept stemming from the Enlightenment and the advent of individualism.

The idea that morality is constituted by moral sentiments guiding behavior in instinctive and reflexive ways is akin to the idea that morality comprises habitual behaviors reflecting traits or dispositions. Wilson goes beyond solely describing traits by attempting to explain the sources of moral sensibility in biologically based dispositions toward sociability and attachments. This type of link between emotions and habitual behaviors also has affinities with those who regard emotions as linked to habits based on commitments to community.

Habits and the Communitarian Spirit

As noted, those who believe that individuals need to form tighter and better attachments to communities that transcend individual goals echo the theme of a moral decline in American society. Not surprisingly, the emphasis on community is evident in works of sociologists—

among the most visible are Etzioni's (1993) *The Spirit of Community* (also Etzioni, 1996) and Bellah et al.'s (1985) *Habits of the Heart.* With regard to the moral status of American society, Etzioni (1993) has asserted that because of a waning of traditional values, without an affirmation of new values, "we live in a state of everlasting moral confusion and social anarchy" (p. 12). Bellah et al. (1985) assert that American "individualism may have grown cancerous" (p. vii), and that "we seem to be hovering on the very brink of disaster . . . from the internal incoherence of society" (p. 284). They ask: "How can we reverse the slide toward the abyss?" (p. 284).

The call for a greater sense of community is necessary to reverse a supposed breakdown in society connected to a supposed overemphasis on personal goals and individual rights that is part of the cultural ethos. The cultural ethos of rights and individualism is seen as, in large measure, a contemporary phenomenon at odds with the traditions of social commitment and responsibility. To a good extent, a return to past practices is required. Much of the reason there is a need for a return to past practices and recommitment to moral values, restoration of law and order, and rebuilding of the foundation of society is that Americans have become overly concerned with rights (there has been an "explosion" of rights, and "incessant issuance of new rights") and a concomitant "elevation of the unbridled pursuit of self-interest and greed to the level of social virtue" (Etzioni, 1993, p. 24). However, the call is not for an elimination of all personal rights, but for a renewed balance of rights and responsibilities. To accomplish such a balance, Etzioni recommends a moratorium on virtually all new rights for a decade, a reaffirmation of responsibilities, and a restoration of communities. Essential to the renewal are changes in family structure—ranging from maintaining two-parent families (such as by legislating a lengthy waiting period for remarriage after divorce) to reinstating the ritual of the family meal.

Bellah et al.'s (1985) analyses of late-twentieth-century American culture adopt the idea of "national character"—the American character is firmly, and legitimately from the moral point of view, individualistic. In the past, American individualism was characterized by personal autonomy, self-reliance, and individual initiative, with beliefs in the dignity of the individual, a valuing of equality, and questioning of fixed social ranks and subjugation of persons.

In its traditional form, however, individualism was balanced with commitment to the moral order and attachments to family, church, and community. American society is "hovering on the brink of disaster" and sliding "toward the abyss" because individualism is no longer balanced (Bellah et al., 1985, p. 284). There is now a radical individualism, characterized by isolation, separation, independence from the past (from a "community of memory"), with personal choice and individual fulfillment placed over attachment to family, social institutions (e.g., the church), and community. Moral goals have been transformed into ones of economic effectiveness, self-fulfillment, and personal satisfaction. The proposed solution—the way to avoid the abyss—is to achieve a balance by attenuating individualism and by restoring traditions, a sense of community, and concerns for the common good.

Moral Appraisal and Moral Recommendations

The writings on character and the need for restoration of a sense of community have applied components because much of the focus is on changing society and people. However, the validity of the proposed social recommendations rest on assertions about the moral state of society in the present and past (i.e., moral crisis, decay now and a better moral state of affairs then); about the nature of individuals' morality in the past and present (i.e., firm character traits and commitment to virtues and community then but not now); and about the causes of moral problems in the present (i.e., selfishness, individualism, failures of commitment and community, and changes in family life). Those assertions are subject to social scientific analysis and imply assumptions about the process of successful moral development. It is assumed that in the past morality was acquired through training in character or commitment to family and community and that society was then more successful morally. On that basis, it is assumed that adequate moral development should proceed (and be facilitated) as it did in the past. These assumptions about the psychology of moral development, however, are not grounded on detailed psychological and developmental analyses or empirical evidence. Instead, the line of reasoning rests on certain key untested assumptions.

One is the repeatedly stated assumption of the moral downslide. The causes attributed to the moral decline of the society are quite varied, and many of those causes reflect disagreements about the events with others who would regard them as having promoted moral goals. As examples, many would regard as furthering moral ends events in the 1960s (especially the anti-Vietnam War and civil rights movements), feminism, and the assertion of rights for groups faced with discrimination. Furthermore, the only evidence provided for the sweeping claims of moral decline is some data, open to varying interpretations, on increases (since the 1950s) of rates of suicide, homicide, and out-of-wedlock births (Wynne, 1986).

The vast societal changes over the past two centuries, however, make it very difficult to document whether there has been decay, improvement, or simply patterns of positive and negative changes associated with different realms of social life. To cite some salient examples of morally relevant (and often viewed as positive) societal shifts, there have been changes in (a) race relations and treatment of minority groups; (b) the roles, burdens, and privileges of women; (c) the treatment of children and the conditions of work for children; (d) the workforce and labor relations more generally; (e) the care of the elderly; (f) the levels of political representation of many groups (including women); (g) the numbers of people receiving higher levels of education; and (h) the power and authority relationships among those of higher and lower social classes.

No analyses have been provided of the ways all these changes might constitute some betterment of the lives of people or of how past practices may have produced harm. Even with regard to violence and homicide—for which there are statistics documenting its prevalence in contemporary society—there are good indications that they are traditional in American society and were prevalent in the past (Butterfield, 1995). Moreover, to the extent that there is documentation regarding levels of honesty, it reveals that even in the early part of the twentieth century children exhibited a fair amount of dishonesty in school activities and in experimental tasks (Hartshorne & May, 1928, 1929, 1930). And strikingly similar concerns with moral decay existed in Western countries. During the 1920s, much concern was expressed in the United States regarding the moral state of youth, cultural disintegration, and social chaos (see Fass, 1977). Similarly, in *fin-de-siècle* France (the late 1800s), there were widespread concerns with moral degeneration, national decline, the declining morality of youth (e.g., an explosion of juvenile crime rates), and calls for renewal of the society (see Norris, 1996). In each instance, similar claims were made about moral crisis and decay in society and about the "good old days" (see Turiel, 2002, for discussion of these issues).

These examples demonstrate the complexity of social and moral change through history and suggest that we are seeing stereotypic impressions and speculations of the morality of the present, along with nostalgic views of the past (Turiel, 2002). Without solid evidence of negative changes in the morality of the society, it cannot be concluded that the ways morality was transmitted in the past are the most efficacious (similar considerations apply to claims that recent activities, such as of the 1960s or feminism, have caused moral decay). It may be that the proposed explanations of the process of moral development would hold for the past (and present) even in the absence of any considerations of moral decline. However, the assertions about how morality was transmitted or acquired in the past are themselves undocumented.

At best, the propositions regarding moral development as the acquisition of character traits or as commitment to community must be seen as standing alongside several other competing explanations. However, the basic concepts used still require research so as to know more about the parameters of the habitual, the criteria for an adequate commitment to community, and how these are acquired. Several of the psychological, social, and cultural issues raised by those lamenting the moral state of society arise in research on moral development. For instance, the propositions regarding the family as a central influence on moral development through parental example and training represents only one perspective on the family. Others have attempted to account for the effects of the structure (e.g., extent of a hierarchical structure) of the family, its particular practices in terms of their fairness and justice, and the content of communications and proclaimed ideology. Furthermore, many researchers have given a fair amount of emphasis to the influences of other social experiences (e.g., with peers, in school, or in relation to culture), to the ways children account for heterogeneity of social experiences, and to their ways of constructing judgments about those different dimensions of social experience.

EMPHASIZING EMOTIONS

Emotions have been considered the basis for morality by some philosophers, and have been central in certain psychologists' formulations. As already noted, the Freudian and behavioristic conceptions relied heavily on emotions as the basis for the acquisition of morality— though in different ways from each other. However, both saw the acquisition of morally obligatory actions as a process by which aversive emotions are central to moral learning and maintenance. Therefore, most emphasis was given to emotions of fear, anxiety, shame, and guilt in their explanations of moral acquisition. Aversive emotions were seen as forces that served to transform the individual's natural inclinations into needs and desires in a psychological make-up that included a "conscience" or behaviors consistent with societal norms or values. However, a major shift in thinking about emotions in the late 1970s and through the 1980s entailed a focus on attachment, bonding, love, sympathy, and empathy.

The emphasis on these emotions included continued concerns with the influences of the family (in keeping with Freudian and behavioristic accounts), the role of aversive emotions, and a renewed interest in the evolutionary sources of emotions. Research demonstrating that very young children display positive emotions and affiliate and bond with others was particularly influential in the shift (Dunn, 1987, 1988; Dunn, Brown, & Maguire, 1995; Hoffman, 1991a, 1991b; Kochanska, 1993, 1994). Another set of relevant findings show that young children are sensitive to the interests and well-being of others, producing actions of a prosocial or altruistic nature. That body of research is not reviewed in this chapter as it is the topic of the chapter by Eisenberg, Fabes, and Spinrad in Chapter 11, this *Handbook,* this volume, but the general pattern of findings is that young children engage in acts of sharing and helping or altruism. As put by Zahn-Waxler, Radke-Yarrow, Wagner, and Chapman (1992): "The evidence for early moral internalization, however, highlights the need to reformulate theories emphasizing the egocentricism and narcissism of young children" (p. 133). Studies conducted in the home show that even children under 2 years of age share possessions (e.g., toys) with others, help mothers with household tasks, cooperate in games, and respond to the emotional distress of others (Radke-Yarrow, Zahn-Waxler, & Chapman, 1983). Toddlers and young children, in addition, show comfort and engage in caregiving of others. It also appears that reactions of empathy emerge by age 3 (Lennon & Eisenberg, 1987; Zahn-Waxler et al., 1992). Moreover, distinctions drawn among reactions of empathy have a bearing on the relations of emotions to prosocial or altruistic behaviors (Carlo, 2006; Eisenberg & Fabes, 1990, 1991; Eisenberg, Spinard, & Sadorsky, 2006).

Empathy, defined as an emotional response stemming from another's emotional state, can result in sympathy or "personal distress." Sympathy goes beyond solely experiencing an emotional reaction to another

similar to the other's feelings in that it entails an other-oriented response and concern for that person's well-being. Empathy can also result, by contrast, in personal distress, which entails a self-focused aversive reaction (e.g., anxiety, discomfort) to the distress of another; the motivation is to alleviate one's own aversive state (see Eisenberg & Fabes, 1990, 1991; Eisenberg, Fabes, & Spinrad in Chapter 11, this *Handbook,* this volume, for further discussion). There is also evidence that children's feelings of empathy are related to their prosocial actions (Eisenberg & Miller, 1987; Eisenberg & Strayer, 1987). In particular, measures of facial and psychological indexes of affect have shown that sympathy, and not personal distress, is positively related to prosocial actions motivated by concerns for the welfare of others (Eisenberg & Fabes, 1991).

The research findings on sympathy and prosocial actions are inconsistent with the idea that children, before they have internalized parental values, or societal standards, or have been taught to behave in socially sanctioned ways, will act solely in selfish and self-directed ways when they are not coerced or fearful of detection. It does not necessarily follow that sympathy and spontaneous prosocial behaviors at a very young age reflect innate dispositions or that morality is primarily based on emotions (to be discussed). Moreover, questions still exist regarding the validity of age-related findings in empathic responses, the need to draw further distinctions between closely aligned emotions, and the development of more adequate methods of measurement (Eisenberg & Fabes, 1991). The findings on sympathy and prosocial actions are not inconsistent with emotive positions on morality. In several formulations, it has been proposed that morality is directed more by emotions than reasoning (Dunn, 1987, 1988; Haidt, 2001; Hoffman, 1984, 1991b; Kagan, 1984; Kochanska, 1993, 1994).

A Primacy for Empathy

Empathy has been considered primary in moral development by some who do not rely heavily on associations of unpleasant and pleasant affect with morality. Hoffman (1991a, 1991b, 2000) has put forth a formulation combining emotion due to evolution with internalization, in that "the society's moral norms and values [are made] part of the individual's personal motive system" (1991a, p. 106). In addition to emotion and internalization, this approach includes motives, cognition, moral principles of care and justice, and perspective taking.

Despite the attempt to incorporate all these features, it can be said that primacy is given to emotion because the linchpin is empathy.

Hoffman distinguishes his approach from those giving primacy to moral judgments in that he defines moral actions in motivational terms. A moral act is "a disposition to do something on behalf of another person, or to behave in accord with a moral norm or standard bearing on human welfare or justice" (Hoffman, 1991b, p. 276). The distinction between defining a moral act in terms of moral judgment or motives is not unambiguous (Blasi, 1993; Turiel, 2003a). It could be said that the moral judgments one makes—say that one should come to the aid of another in distress because it is wrong to allow suffering—motivates one to act. The key to the distinction is in the term *disposition* in the definition of a moral act—disposition referring to an emotional reaction that propels action. The main source of moral motives is the feeling of empathy, which is defined as an affective response that does not necessarily match another's affective state. By putting the matter in affective-motivational terms, Hoffman poses the question, "Why act morally?" and answers in terms of feelings that need to be acted on.

Although empathy is regarded as a biological predisposition and a product of natural selection, it is characterized as developing through four stagelike manifestations that are partly determined by changing cognitive capabilities. The first of these stages is characterized simply by the "global" distress felt by infants (during the 1st year) entailing a confusion of the infant's own feelings with those of another. At the second stage of "egocentric" empathy (age of 1 year), the onset of object permanence allows for an awareness that other people are physically distinct from the self and a concern ("sympathetic distress") with another person who is in distress. However, children do not distinguish between their own or other's internal states.

Hoffman further asserts that role taking emerges at about 2 or 3 years of age (this, however, is a controversial issue), allowing for a differentiation of the child's own feelings from those of others. At the third stage, therefore, children are responsive to cues about the other person's feelings and empathize with a range of emotions other than distress (e.g., disappointment, feelings of betrayal). Whereas the third stage is labeled "empathy for another's feelings," the fourth stage, emerging in late childhood is labeled "empathy for another's life conditions." The relevant social cognitions

for the fourth stage are children's awareness of self and others with separate identities. These conceptions allow for awareness that others feel pleasure and pain in their general life experiences. At this stage, empathy is felt in particular situations, as well as for more general life circumstances of others or of groups of people (e.g., the poor or the oppressed).

Whether this sequence of stages is an accurate representation of how children develop is undetermined because the stages were not, for the most part, based on empirical evidence. There is some evidence that infants respond to the actual crying of other infants to a greater extent than to sounds resembling the crying of human infants (Sagi & Hoffman, 1976). However, it is not entirely clear that this type of response is a form of very early empathy. The other stages have not been tested empirically and, instead, rely on illustrations with the types of anecdotal examples previously mentioned. Research by Zahn-Waxler and her colleagues (Hastings, Zahn-Waxler, & McShane, 2006; Zahn-Waxler, Robinson, & Emde, 1992; Zahn-Waxler et al., 1992) does provide some evidence that young children show empathic reactions to the distress of others and attempt to understand the nature of the distress (see Eisenberg, Fabes, & Spinard, Chapter 11, this *Handbook,* this volume, for discussion of further distinctions in the general construct of empathy).

In later writings, Hoffman (2000) attempted to identify situations in which empathic reactions and moral actions occur. He labeled these moral encounters and proposed that five "encompass most of the prosocial domain" (Hoffman, 2000, p. 3). These include situations in which a person is an innocent bystander (witnessing someone in pain or distress), a transgressor (harming or about to harm someone), or a "virtual transgressor" (an imagined harmful act). The two others are situations in which there are "multiple moral claimants" (where a person has to make choices about who to help) and in which there is a clash between caring and justice (between considering others and abstract issues of rights, duty, and reciprocity). These categories are meant to capture the situations that evoke guilt and empathic responses. Empathy is also supposedly associated with a variety of moral reactions, including sympathy, aggression or anger at another who injures people, guilt, and feelings of injustice (empathy due to perceived unfairness of a situation). Indeed, in Hoffman's perspective, moral principles of care and injustice are validated by emotions.

Hoffman invoked a distinction between "cool" and "hot" cognitions with regard to moral principles. Moral principles, in that view, can be so-called cool cognitions because they are detached from emotions. The association of empathy with principles renders them "hot"— morally meaningful and linked to action. At least as common, if not more common, a perspective, especially among philosophers (but also see Baldwin, 1896; Kohlberg, 1971; Piaget, 1932), is that to the extent that moral principles are understood by people in ways that are part of their belief systems and mental functioning, it is not necessary that they receive their force from other elements (like empathy) so as to render them meaningful. Instead, there is a synthesis between judgments and emotions, making it difficult to disentangle the two.

Evolution and Internalization

The formulations of morality emphasizing emotions illustrate that, in many instances, asking whether theories are based on nature or nurture, or biology or environment, is not useful. These positions show a firm orientation to evolutionary-based biological processes and to influences of the family, historical contexts, and culture. Much of the research on the internalization side has focused on the family, examining the types of parental child-rearing practices producing more and stronger incorporations of moral standards by children. A large body of research (for reviews, see Eisenberg, Fabes, & Spinard, Chapter 11, this *Handbook,* this volume; Hoffman, 1970; Maccoby & Martin, 1983) has examined, mainly through self-reports, parental child-rearing practices, along with various measures of moral functioning. Three types of parental practices were identified. One is referred to as power assertion, mainly involving physical punishment, deprivation of goods or privileges, and threats of force. The second, love withdrawal, involves disapproval and other expressions of the removal of affection or emotional supports. The third type, referred to as induction, entails the communication of reasons or explanations for the prescribed behavior, including appeals for concerns with the welfare of others.

Parental reports of their use of these discipline techniques have been correlated with measures of children's guilt (e.g., children's tendencies to confession to misdeeds; projective measures of story completions), an external or internal orientation to moral stories (i.e., if they judge by fear of external sanctions or by an evaluation of the act's wrongness), and whether children resist the temptation to engage in a prohibited act (e.g., often measured in experimental situations). A consistent finding from these studies is that parental practices of induction are the most successful method of discipline (Hoffman, 1970; Hoffman & Saltzstein, 1967; Maccoby & Martin, 1983). Measures reflecting moral development are correlated more with induction than love withdrawal or power assertion. For example, a moral orientation based on fear of sanctions is correlated with parental practices of physical punishment, whereas expressions of guilt and an internal orientation are correlated with parental practices that emphasize explaining reasons for avoiding or engaging in moral actions.

Conscience and Internalization

By including natural or biological features, these perspectives go beyond earlier socialization perspectives by which it was assumed that morality could be adequately defined through consensual norms (Berkowitz, 1964; Maccoby, 1968; Skinner, 1971). However, some contemporary researchers have addressed hypotheses regarding moral internalization—defining morality through consensual norms—with the assumption that morality entails the acquisition of a conscience serving to internally regulate conduct consistent with societal values, norms, or rules (Kochanska, 1993, 1994; Thompson, Mayer, & McGinley, 2006). The concept of conscience, central to Freud's theory, was also central to behavioristic conceptions in which internalization was theorized to be acquired through the anxiety associated with punishments for transgressions (Aronfreed, 1968). Whether it be from a psychoanalytic or behavioristic perspective, the concept of conscience has been used to refer to a mechanism internalized by children for exerting control on needs that would otherwise be acted on: "Conscience is the term that has been used traditionally to refer to the cognitive and affective processes which constitute an internalized moral governor over an individual's conduct" (Aronfreed, 1968, p. 2).

In a contemporary formulation that has affinities with earlier positions on conscience and that includes elements of other socioemotional perspectives, Kochanska (1993, 1994) has examined conscience as regulation due to internalization marking successful socialization as "the gradual developmental shift from external to internal regulation that results in the child's ability to conform to societal standards of conduct and to restrain antisocial or destructive impulses, even in the absence of surveillance" (1993, pp. 325–326). Moreover, the formation of conscience is functional from the societal perspective: "Without reliance on internalized consciences, societies would have to instill ever-present surveillance in all aspects of social life" (Kochanska, 1994, p. 20). This position includes a shift in balance away from natural moral propensities of concerns with the welfare of others back to more of an emphasis on the need to control antisocial and destructive tendencies. Ultimately, it is society that has to control the behavior of individuals, either by instilling control internally in children or through continual and all-encompassing ("in all aspects of social life") external control.

In keeping with the traditional conception of conscience, it was proposed that it is encompassed by "affective discomfort" or the various aversive emotional reactions to acts of transgression and "behavioral control." Reactions of sympathy and empathy contribute to the process of development, but they do so through the anxiety and distress they can arouse in a child. One focus is on anxiety, fear arousal, and discomfort in the process of internalizing moral prohibitions. A significant aspect of this process is that parental socialization contributes greatly through arousal of children's anxiety.

Kochanska and her colleagues have continued this line of research in a series of studies aimed at examining what they refer to as bidirectional models of mother-child relationships. In these cases, the bidirectional conceptualizations of relationships remain within the context of a conception of conscience or morality as the internalization of values, norms, and behaviors established by parents. Some of these studies, for example, were designed to examine the role of children's temperament in the formation of conscience (Kochanska, 1997; Kochanska, Gross, Linn, & Nichols, 2002; Kochanska, Murray, & Coy, 1997). Anxiety, fearfulness, and arousal (e.g., as found for shy children) underlie the affective component of conscience, and impulsivity and inhibition are related to behavioral control. Specifically, impulsive children are more likely to transgress and find it more difficult to internalize conscience than non-impulsive children. Thus, parents' methods of socialization may work differently for children with different temperaments. The practice of induction (which involves explanations and reasoning) may be less effective with impulsive than nonimpulsive children.

In other aspects of the research program, the type of mother-child relationships was correlated with measures of conscience. In particular, measures were obtained of the extent to which mother-child relationships were mutually responsive (Kochanska & Murray, 2000) and entailed secure attachments (Kochanska, Aksan, Knaack, & Rhines, 2004). Greater mutuality in the form of cooperation and shared positive affect was associated with the measures of conscience. Similarly, it has been found that more secure attachments at 14 months of age were correlated with measures of conscience. In this approach, the quality of the mother-child relationship is proposed to influence internalization of and compliance with parental standards. As put by Kochanska et al. (2004), "security may make the child eager to embrace parental demands. A secure child is cooperative and receptive to parental demands, emulates the parent and follows parental suggestions" (p. 1234).

Beyond Family and beyond Incorporation of Societal Standards

Findings on temperament are not consistent. A longitudinal study by Dunn et al. (1995) showed, in contrast with the other studies, that shy children (i.e., inhibited, nonimpulsive, and anxious) scored lower on the same measures of moral orientation than children who were not shy. Dunn et al. also found that along with some positive correlations between nonpower-assertive parental practices and moral orientation, other factors were associated with moral orientation, including the quality of the child's relationships with older siblings (children who had friendlier, more positive relationships with siblings showed higher moral orientation scores) and the child's earlier level of understanding of emotions (children who had shown better emotional understandings at earlier ages scored higher on moral orientation at first grade). Moreover, Dunn et al. found differences among the stories used in the assessments. At kindergarten and first grade, children gave more empathic responses to a physical harm story than to a story dealing with cheating in a game. Correspondingly, more children gave guilt responses (i.e., reparative endings in the story completions) to the physical harm story than to the cheating story.

Findings in the Dunn et al. (1995) study, as well as from a study by Dunn, Cutting, and Demetriou (2000), suggest that influences on moral development extend beyond the practices of parents in disciplining children and that a child's reactions to transgressions are not uniform. Other research indicates that young children's development may proceed in several directions with regard to relationships with parents and in their orientations to morality. Along with an increased awareness of standards, at the age of 2 or 3 years, young children display increased teasing of their mothers, more physical aggression and destruction of objects, and greater interest in what is socially prohibited (Dunn, 1987). Along with greater sympathy and empathy for others, with increasing age children may begin to understand how to manipulate situations and upset others. This increasing complexity of young children's social relationships is also evident by their abilities, by 18 to 36 months, to engage in arguments and counterarguments in disputes with mothers (Dunn & Munn, 1987). By 36 months, children also provide justifications for their positions in disputes with mothers and siblings (see also Kuczynski, Kochanska, Radke-Yarrow, & Girnius-Brown, 1987). Disputes occurred over issues such as rights and needs of persons, conventions (manners, etiquette), and destruction or aggression. Children's emotional reactions also varied by the different kinds of disputes; distress and anger were associated with disputes affecting children's rights and interests. These differentiations and extensions of the influences of social relationships are consistent with a reconceptualization of moral internalization presented by Grusec and Goodnow (1994), Grusec, Goodnow, and Kuczynski (2000), Kuczynski and Hildebrandt (1997), Grusec (2006), and Kuczynski and Navara (2006).

Grusec and Goodnow (1994) maintained that the traditional view of internalization as the process by which children take over the values of society has significant limitations and is not consistent with existing data. A better understanding of the process requires accounting for additional factors, including the nature of the act (the misdeed or transgression), characteristics of parents, the child's perspective on the position of parents, and the child's perceptions of the misdeed. Furthermore, they argue that it is necessary to consider the child's ability to "move beyond the parent's specific position to one of his or her own, a consideration that points to successful socialization as more than an unquestioning adoption of another's position" (Grusec & Goodnow, 1994, p. 4). As summarized by Grusec et al. (2000):

> A significant shift is required to understand the process of socialization. This shift will be facilitated by an explicit interest in the agency of parents and children, that is, in the meanings they construct of each other's behavior, in their capacity for strategic action, and in their ability to behave "as if" the other is also an agent. (p. 205)

In essence, they call for a reorientation in research that would take seriously the idea of reciprocal interactions in explanations of social development. There is evidence (some of which is reviewed by Grusec and Goodnow) that the effectiveness of particular parental practices are not uniform and that parents do not consistently use one type of discipline. Mothers use different reasons for different kinds of transgressions. Smetana (1989b) found that mothers of toddlers used explanations of needs and rights for acts entailing harm to others, whereas they used explanations pertaining to social order and conformity for violations of social conventions. It also appears that mothers vary their methods in accord with the types of standard violated. Working with families of children from 6 to 10 years of age, Chilamkurti and Milner (1993) found that mothers report using reasons or explanations mainly for moral transgressions and forceful verbal commands for conventional transgressions. Furthermore, parents use a combination of power assertion and reasoning in reaction to acts like lying and stealing, whereas reasoning is used in reaction to a child's failure to show concern for others (Grusec & Goodnow, 1994).

Other findings in accord with these propositions stem from studies of children's evaluations of parental discipline, as well as of correspondences between the judgments of children and adults (studies on parent-adolescent relationships are discussed later in the chapter). Catron and Masters (1993) showed that 10- to 12-year-old children and mothers endorsed corporal punishment (spanking) for prudential (i.e., acts harmful to the self, such as opening a bottle of poison) and moral transgressions to a greater extent than for transgressions of social conventions. These findings indicate both that mothers make discriminations in the ways discipline should be used and that by at least 10 years of age children make similar judgments about that type of discipline. Research by Saltzstein, Weiner, and Munk (1995) on judgments about moral intentionality and consequences shows that children evaluate the fairness of mothers' (in hypothetical situations) approval or disapproval of actions in accord with their own judgments regarding those actions. For example, children regard a mother who disapproves of a well-intentioned act resulting in a negative outcome more unfair than a mother who approves it. Moreover, children whose own judgments were based on the actor's intentions made greater distinctions in evaluations of mothers' approval or disapproval than children whose judgments were based on the consequences of the act. All these findings indicate that children apply their judgments to parental acts in ways that involve both acceptance and critical scrutiny.

It has also been found that children's own judgments about intentions and consequences are not concordant with the judgments they attribute to adults (Saltzstein et al., 1987). For acts with positive intentions and negative outcomes, children (incorrectly) believe adults' judgments of wrongness would be harsher than their own; whereas children judge by intentions, they believe that adults' judgments are mainly based on disobedience or rule violations.

These findings indicate that it is necessary to account for the child's perspective and, thereby, view the process of discipline as interactive. In particular, Grusec and colleagues maintained that because children's judgments differ for different types of misdeeds (e.g., moral as opposed to conventional transgressions; Turiel, 1983a), they would evaluate and judge the appropriateness of the reasons given by parents, or others, when disciplining the child. It has been found that children are more responsive to adults' directives when the adults use reasons that correspond to the ways children classify moral actions. For example, when teachers simply point to rule violations in discussing acts like stealing or hitting, children are less responsive than when teachers underscore the welfare of others or fairness (Killen, 1991; Nucci, 1984). It has also been found that children are more likely to share with others when given reasons based on empathy and concern for others than when to adhere to norms (Eisenberg-Berg & Geisheker, 1979).

Several other features of communications from parents to children bear on the effectiveness of discipline. These include verifiability of its truth value, the level of generality of reprimands, whether they are tangential or directly relevant to the misdeed, and whether statements are direct or indirect. Distinctions need to be made in discipline activities to understand how they are interpreted and how they might lead to changes in children's behaviors. Along those lines, it is proposed that characteristics of the parents and children would also make a difference in the ways discipline is interpreted and felt.

Unlike the traditional views of conscience or internalization, the model presented by Grusec and Goodnow includes the idea that internalization is not necessarily the sole desired goal of parents or the only positive outcome from the societal or individual perspectives. Parents may strive for flexibility and initiative on the part of the child rather than simply the adoption of parental standards. They may also be motivated by the goal that children acquire negotiation and thinking skills. Grusec and Goodnow raised the issue of noncompliance for positive goals and thereby raised the specter of social oppo-

sition and resistance. From the perspective of moral development as internalization of parental or societal norms, the good is defined as some form of compliance to the social environment. Social accommodation on the part of the child is thus regarded as the desirable end-state. In a later section, I consider research on opposition and resistance to social norms, societal arrangements, and cultural practices that stem from a moral standpoint.

GENDER, EMOTIONS, AND MORAL JUDGMENTS

The major issues considered thus far—emotion, socialization, and interaction—also have received scrutiny in theory and research on gender differences in moral development. The question of gender differences has been posed regarding many aspects of development (Maccoby & Jacklin, 1974), but it has been of particular controversy in the moral realm because in the early part of the century it was asserted (most notably by Freud) that the morality of females is less developed than that of males, and then, in the latter part of the century, that the morality of females is qualitatively different from that of males (Gilligan, 1977, 1982; Gilligan & Wiggins, 1987). Gilligan and her colleagues maintained that two moral injunctions define two sequences of moral development—the injunction not to treat others unfairly (justice) and the injunction to not turn away from someone in need (care). Gilligan (1982) argued that a morality of care, mainly linked to females, had been overlooked in favor of analyses of justice because mainly males had formulated explanations of moral development. These assertions, however, have generated controversy among students of moral development, as well as in other social scientific disciplines (Abu-Lughod, 1991; Okin, 1989; Stack, 1990), within feminist scholarship (Faludi, 1991) and in journalistic accounts (Pollitt, 1992).

In a way, Gilligan accepts Freud's (1925/1959) contention that women "show less sense of justice than men." She does not accept Freud's contention that women show less moral sense than men because women show more of a sense of the alternative form of care. A morality of justice fails to account for women's moral orientation because it focuses on rules and rights. According to Gilligan (1982), justice links development to the logic of equality and reciprocity, which contrasts with "the logic underlying an ethic of care [which] is a psychological logic of relationships" (p. 73). The morality of care is one of fulfillment of responsibility and avoidance of exploitation and hurt and is linked to concepts of self as attached to social networks, whereas the morality of justice is linked to concepts of self as autonomous and detached from social networks.

It would appear then that the formulation of a morality of care has affinities with those who emphasize emotions. Care entails avoidance of harm and concerns for the welfare of others (sympathy and empathy) and is applied mainly to those in close relationships. Although empathy and sympathy are relevant, this formulation differs in several respects from other perspectives emphasizing emotions. First, the central emotions for morality are defined differently from empathy, sympathy, shame, and guilt and are associated with a different set of experiences and mechanisms for the development of morality. Second, more emphasis is given to judgments in both moralities. And third, there is a sequence of development for the morality of care progressing toward increasing inclusiveness of moral judgments.

Very young children's relationships constitute the groundwork for the types of morality formed by individuals. Two dimensions of relationships are proposed as mechanisms for development at early ages, establishing long-term moral orientations. First, the experience of attachment, which produces awareness that one can affect others and be affected by them, results in discoveries of the ways people care for and hurt one another. Relying on neo-psychoanalytic accounts of identity formation (Chodorow, 1978), there is a basic difference in the social experiences of boys and girls that results, by an early age (3 or 4 years), in differences in their personality and identity. For girls, identity formation occurs in the context of a relationship with another female, the mother, which maintains continuity and in which mothers and daughters see themselves as alike. Most important, in forming her identity as a female, the young girl maintains an attachment with her mother, and thereby development progresses toward creating and sustaining relationships. Thus, the emotions associated with attachment and care are "co-feelings."

For young boys, identity formation occurs in the context of a sense of difference (in both mother and son), and in the process of forming a masculine identity there is separation from the mother and individuation. The consequence is an orientation to differentiations from others and independence on the part of boys. The second related dimension is the inequality that stems from the child's awareness of being smaller, less powerful, and less competent than older children and adults (Gilligan & Wiggins, 1987). For girls, the experience of inequality is not as overwhelming as for boys because girls identify with the object of their attachment (mother). Because boys identify with their fathers without a strong attachment with him, they relate more to the father's authority and power. Inequality and authority are therefore salient for boys, resulting in strivings for equality (part of fairness) and regulation as moral ends.

Gilligan regards the care and justice orientations as systems of moral judgments. In fact, she considers the conception of justice and fairness as one of the two major types of morality and, at least implicitly, accepts the validity of the stages of moral judgment formulated by Kohlberg (1969). The morality of care, too, proceeds through a sequence of transformations culminating in a level of thinking based on universal principles encompassing self and others, with an understanding that self and other are interdependent, violence is destructive, and care benefits others and self. That level of moral judgment is preceded by two less advanced levels, and associated transitions, reflecting a conflict between self and other that constitutes the central moral problem for women. At the first level, there is a focus on caring for the self as a means of survival. At the second level, concepts of responsibility focus on care for dependent persons.

The sequence of women's conceptions of the morality of care was derived from interview studies. The main study entailed interviews of 29 pregnant women (ages 15 to 33 years) about their decision to have or not to have an abortion. Follow-up interviews were conducted with 21 of the women a year after they had made their choices. A necessary feature of this study, according to Gilligan (1982), is that the interviews were about situations faced in the women's own lives. This is because women's moral judgments are tied more closely to contexts than men's. Interviews about hypothetical situations, in her view, are likely to provide misleading information since women attempt to reframe hypothetical situations into real, contextualized ones. Gilligan also asserted that interviews about hypothetical situations are more likely to elicit justice concerns than would interviews about real-life situations. Nevertheless, hypothetical situations (along with judgments about situations generated by participants) have been used to study levels of development of judgments about care (Skoe & Gooden, 1993; Skoe et al., 1999). Those studies indicate that levels of care reasoning are associated with age and that there are some variations by nation in the levels attained by females and males (i.e., Canadian and U. S. females score higher than males, but no gender differences were obtained among Norwegians). Skoe, Eisenberg, and Cumberland (2002) found that self-reports of sympathy by adults are associated with care reasoning.

Gilligan (1982) has argued that the study of the judgments of females serves to correct biases in influential theories of moral development put forth by males who largely overlooked females or who, when they addressed the issue, superficially relegated females' morality of care to a "lesser" form. Freud, for example, included women in his observations and case studies but misinterpreted their care orientation simply as a concern with approval. Gilligan also contends that others, such as Piaget (1932) and Kohlberg (1963), constructed their theories through research with samples of males and then studied females from the inappropriate perspective of male-based theories.

In considering Piaget's ideas, Gilligan imposes certainty where ambiguity exists. Piaget did maintain that girls are less interested than boys with "legal elaboration" and that "the legal sense is far less developed in little girls than in boys" (Piaget, 1932, pp. 69, 75, and quoted in Gilligan, 1977, and Gilligan & Wiggins, 1987). As noted earlier, however, in Piaget's view, the developmentally advanced level of autonomous morality was organized by concerns with mutuality, reciprocity, and cooperation. Piaget saw a strict legal sense for fixed rules that left little room for innovation and tolerance as part of the less advanced form of heteronomous morality. Thus, it is not at all clear that Piaget regarded girls to be less advanced than boys because he thought that girls were oriented to tolerance, innovation with rules, and cooperation. Aside from his studies of children's practices with game rules, Piaget's research was not conducted only with males. Piaget supported his interpretations with many interview excerpts (he did not report statistical analyses) that included both boys and girls.

In contrast, Kohlberg's (1963) original formulation of stages of the development of moral judgments was based on interviews with males only. The first studies assessing Kohlberg's stages that included females showed college-age and adult women scoring at Stage 3 (entailing judgments of morality focused on interpersonal considerations) more than men, and men scoring at higher stages (mainly Stage 4, which entails judgments of morality focused on maintenance of rules, authority,

and social order) more than women (Kohlberg & Kramer, 1969). Briefly speculating on these results, Kohlberg and Kramer (1969) suggested that Stage 3 moral thinking might be functional for the roles of housewives and mothers. The generalizability of this finding, with regard to the stages formulated by Kohlberg, was accepted by Gilligan, but she was critical of the idea that Stage 3 was functional for the roles of housewives or mothers and proposed that instead women's reasoning proceeds through the sequence of the morality of care.

However, the conclusion that women score lower on Kohlberg's stages (as drawn by Kohlberg and Kramer and reaffirmed by Gilligan) has not been supported empirically. Walker (1984, 1991) presented extensive reviews of 80 studies, which included assessments of males and females on Kohlberg's stages. Those analyses reveal little in the way of sex differences on this dimension. In most studies (86% of the samples), no differences were obtained. In some samples (9%), males scored higher than females, but in other samples (6%), it was the reverse. Walker also found that when researchers controlled for educational and occupational levels, no sex differences were observed.

Furthermore, it is not generally accepted that Kohlberg's concept of morality at the most advanced stages actually fails to account for judgments about interdependence and concerns with welfare (Gilligan construed Kohlberg's formulation as focusing on rights, rules, and separation). It has been argued that embedded in Kohlberg's formulations of justice and fairness are considerations of respect for others and ways of maintaining social relationships that are nonexploitive, nonharmful, and that promote the welfare of persons (see Boyd, 1983; Habermas, 1990b; Kohlberg, Levine, & Hewer, 1983; Nunner-Winkler, 1984; Walker, 1991).

Care and Justice as Moral Orientations

Gilligan's propositions have received a good deal of attention, with some providing positive evaluations (Haste, 1993; Shweder & Haidt, 1993), and others pointing to inadequacies in sampling, procedures, research designs, and data analyses (see Colby & Damon, 1983; Greeno & Maccoby, 1986; Luria, 1986; Mednick, 1989). Gilligan's formulation was not based on extensive research but initially on a combination of (a) the argument that a conception of morality as justice did not adequately characterize the moral judgments of females because they were usually assessed in stages lower than males (a conclusion that, as already discussed, does not hold), and (b) subjectively analyzed excerpts from a limited number of boys and girls responding to moral dilemmas in Kohlberg's interview (Gilligan, 1982, Chapter 2).

The construct of a morality of care was also based on the studies of women discussing abortion and of interviews of college students. Those studies were limited in that the samples were small and restricted to either pregnant women discussing one particular contested issue (abortion) or students in elite universities. Perhaps most important, the analyses of interview responses were neither based on systematic coding schemes nor analyzed statistically in any extensive ways (Colby & Damon, 1983; Greeno & Maccoby, 1986; Luria, 1986). Furthermore, the propositions regarding the origins of moral concepts in early relationships entailing inequalities, detachments, and attachments have not been subjected to empirical study.

In subsequent research, a more circumscribed approach was taken, with a focus on defining the proposed orientations of care and justice and on coding (Lyons, 1983) the extent to which males and females use one or the other or combine the two. Studies assessing the distribution of care and justice orientations included male and female adolescents and adults responding to questions about moral conflicts in their lives (Gilligan & Attanucci, 1988). Varying results were obtained. Lyons (1983), for example, found that the majority of females (75%) judged by a care orientation, whereas the majority of males (79%) judged by a rights orientation. Other studies, with more refined analyses, indicated that only a minority of people exclusively use either care or justice orientation and that most use both in one fashion or another (Gilligan & Attanucci, 1988). Those studies also suggested that the justice orientation was used more frequently than care but with a tendency for females to use care more than males and males to use justice more than females. Research with preschoolers revealed no gender differences in care or justice orientations (Cassidy, Chu, & Dahlsgaard, 1997).

These types of studies (see Gilligan, Ward, Taylor, & Bardige, 1988, for reports of additional research) have provided some evidence that care and justice tend to be associated with gender. However, the patterns are not clear-cut because studies also show shifts by context (Johnston, 1988). Perhaps because of the combinations of care and justice found in the reasoning of males and

females, Gilligan and her colleagues appear, in later writings, to be inconsistent or ambiguous about sex differences, asserting that care and justice are concerns that can be part of the thinking of males or females. The conclusion drawn from a meta-analysis of research on care and justice orientations was that neither is used predominantly by women or men, though there is a tendency for females to use more care related reasoning than males (Jaffee & Hyde, 2000).

Moral Judgments, Orientations, and Social Contexts

The ambiguities in the interpretations of gender differences may very well stem from contextual variations in individuals' judgments. Issues of context are considered in propositions regarding justice and care, but in a limited way. In the first place, a broad contextual distinction was drawn through the proposition that the life circumstances of girls and women usually differ from those of boys and men. Especially for females, judgments in the context of a hypothetical situation may differ from judgments in the context of real-life situations (Gilligan, 1982). The inclination to be distant from hypothetical situations may be related to another proposed feature of the psychology of those with a care orientation—that they are more attuned to contextual features than those with a justice orientation. Those with a justice orientation are more likely to abstract from a situation (i.e., decontextualize it) in ways that generate judgments of likeness with other situations.

Because those formulations essentially propose group differences in the ways people approach morality, a more fundamental issue regarding social contexts is unaddressed: People may apply their moral judgments in sufficiently flexible ways to take features of situations into account in coming to decisions. In that case, moral judgments would not be of one type for females or males. Females and males may hold both concepts of justice and concepts regarding the network of social relationships. Individuals may be oriented both to independence and interdependence. How individuals apply these different judgments might depend on the situation. Because of the different roles and status in social networks and hierarchies of women and men, it may also be that they would apply justice and care considerations differently. In some situations, men may even apply considerations regarding social networks and interdependence more than women (e.g., situations in which men wish to maintain the existing network of unequal relationships and role obligations), whereas in some situations women may apply justice considerations more than men (e.g., situations in which women are more sensitive to the injustices of the existing inequalities, networks of role obligations, and interdependence; see Abu-Lughod, 1993; Turiel & Wainryb, 1998; Wainryb & Turiel, 1994). Gilligan treats different moral and personal orientations as general characteristics of individuals.

These multifaceted concerns are not unrelated to the types of childhood experiences proposed to be sources of the different orientations. It was proposed that attachments and detachments are the central social experiences for girls, while inequalities and power are central for boys (Gilligan & Wiggins, 1987). This is surely a one-sided characterization. In certain respects, issues of equalities, inequalities, and power relationships are at least as salient for girls as for boys. Perhaps starting in the family (Okin, 1989), and then in school (Ornstein, 1994) and the wider society, girls confront unequal treatment in more poignant ways than boys. Women, too, experience inequalities and unjust treatment in ways that permeate their family and work experiences (Hochschild, 1989; Nussbaum, 1999, 2000; Okin, 1989; Turiel, 2002). Conversely, issues of attachment and detachment may be salient in the experiences of boys. The prominence of groups, cliques, team sports, and gangs are evidence of the pull for cooperation, attachments, and solidarity pervasive in their experiences. This is not to say that researchers should simply reverse the ways the proposed moral orientations have been linked to gender, but that concerns with justice, fairness, individuation, care, solidarity, and interdependence are all important coexisting aspects of children's social experiences and developing judgments.

A number of studies on how care and justice orientations are used in different hypothetical and real-life situations show that situational contexts affect whether a justice or care orientation is used. A study by Rothbart, Hanley, and Albert (1986) found that more reasoning about rights was used in one of Kohlberg's hypothetical dilemmas (a husband is faced with deciding whether to steal a drug to save his dying wife) than in the real-life situations, but real-life situations produced more reasoning about rights than a Kohlberg hypothetical situation pertaining to physical intimacy.

Therefore, the substance of the situations (e.g., physical intimacy or saving a life), and not only whether they are hypothetical or real-life, has a bearing on people's

judgments. Other studies (Walker, 1991; Walker, de Vries, & Trevethan, 1987) have shown that only a minority makes consistent judgments across the hypothetical and real-life situations, and that about 50% of them showed consistency among the real-life situations. Whereas no sex differences were obtained in children's or adolescents' use of the care orientations on the real-life situations, adult women showed more use of care than men (60% versus 37%). In addition, the real-life conflicts were divided as to whether they involved a specific person or group with whom the subject had or did not have a relationship (labeled personal and impersonal, respectively). Both female and male adults used the care orientation more on personal than impersonal conflicts. Whereas this shows that type of conflict can predict moral orientation better than gender (Walker, 1991), overall the adult women showed more care responses than men. This means that women generated more personal conflicts than men. Therefore, type of orientation is related to the content of the situation (reflecting contextual variations), but women are more likely than men to use the care orientation if they are more likely to perceive moral conflicts as personal rather than impersonal. These findings are generally consistent with findings from other studies (Jaffee & Hyde, 2000; Pratt, Diessner, Hunsberger, Pancer, & Savoy, 1991; Smetana, Killen, & Turiel, 1991).

The findings of these studies indicate that concerns with fairness and with the maintenance of interpersonal relationships do not represent individual differences in moral orientations. Furthermore, numerous studies on the development of moral judgments, considered in subsequent sections, have included females and males in the initial investigations (theory building). Little in the way of sex difference has been obtained in all that research. Some studies are worth noting at this juncture because of their focus on judgments about positive actions toward others. Using stories that pose conflicts between close friendship considerations, personal interests, and the interests of nonclose friendships, Keller and Edelstein (1990, 1993) longitudinally studied the interpersonal concepts of children and adolescents (7 to 15 years). Along with understandings of friendship relationships, there are age-related shifts, but no gender differences, in moral commitments based on obligations, intimacy, and mutuality in relationships. Kahn (1992) put forth a similar proposition on the basis of his findings on children's judgments about positive moral actions (i.e., whether to give money for food to hungry persons). Females were no more likely than males to judge that people should give to, or care for, hungry persons. Moreover, the reasons for these evaluations were mainly consideration of the welfare of others and issues of justice. Whereas younger children emphasized welfare, older girls and boys embedded welfare into concepts of justice.

Politics, Economics, Social Structure, and Women's Perspectives

The proposition that care and justice tend to be organized differently in males and females as a consequence of differences in childhood relationships carries a host of problems, including scientific verification, stereotyping of moral orientations, and the role of politics, economics, and social structure in possible inequalities and power relationships between men and women. Issues pertaining to scientific verification are raised by the assertion that male psychologists have imposed male-oriented formulations of moral development that overlook a major strand of development associated with females. This, however, is a criticism that turns on itself as a vicious cycle. It could be said, for example, that Gilligan's perspective is a consequence of various biases. It could be said that her ideas are colored by her status as a female of a rather advantaged position writing from the perspective of her memberships in a male-dominated field and in a highly elitist, well-endowed, and powerful male-dominated educational institution. The myriad ways that such contexts can determine one point of view or another should be evident if too much credence is given to the ways an individual's characteristics and place color scientific or scholarly analyses. The alternative is to evaluate the arguments and the evidence on their own merits.

A related point made by Gilligan, closer to issues of evidence, is that some researchers (e.g., Kohlberg, 1969) used data from males only to build theory. An analogous criticism applies to the data used by Gilligan to build her theory because her initial findings came from samples of largely White middle-class and upper-middle-class women, most of whom were undergraduates at Harvard and Radcliffe (Pollitt, 1992; Stack, 1990). Gilligan's (1977) focus has been on women's status in society, which is that they are usually in subordinate and vulnerable positions relative to men (see also Nussbaum, 1999, 2000; Okin, 1989, 1996; Turiel, 1996, 2002; Wainryb & Turiel, 1994). However, working-class and racial minority groups are also in vulnerable positions relative to

middle- and upper-class groups. The hierarchical relationships between White middle-class women or men in relation to working-class or minority racial groups pose interesting questions that have not been much investigated. One such question bears on the racial and economic injustices experienced by children in those groups, and its effects on their sensitivity to the issues.

This question was addressed in a study by Stack (1990) of the moral thinking of African American adolescents and adults who were return migrants from the north to rural, southern home places in the United States. She interviewed the participants in the study about dilemmas relevant to their lives and found no differences between responses of the adolescent girls and boys or between adult females and males, all of whom gave more justice than care responses. Stack proposed that African American boys and girls are aware, from an early age, of social and economic injustices. Men and women experience a good deal of injustice in the workplace and other settings and are committed to combating it. Simultaneously, males and females are embedded in extended families, concerning themselves with their own aspirations and the needs of their kin. Stack's findings and theoretical analyses suggest that broader life experiences than identifications, attachments, and separations are central to the development of moral concepts.

Another potential methodological problem in Gilligan's (1982) research is that much of the data used to formulate the levels of care reasoning were derived from interviews about abortion, which is an issue with some unique features that may not generalize to other moral issues. Other research has shown people are divided as to whether abortion should be classified as a moral issue, and those divisions are associated with assumptions people make about the fetus as a person and as constituting a life (Smetana, 1982; Turiel, Hildebrandt, & Wainryb, 1991). Whereas those who assume that the fetus is a life with attributes of personhood judge abortion as morally wrong, those who do not hold to that assumption judge abortion as mainly a decision of personal choice. Moreover, many individuals' assumptions about the status of the fetus as a life include ambiguities and uncertainties resulting in conflicting and contradictory judgments about abortion not evident in the same individuals' judgments about welfare, harm, and life in other contexts (Turiel et al., 1991).

Finally, in contrast with the way the issue has sometimes been couched, women have been involved in the construction of theoretical approaches at variance with the proposition that there are sex differences in moral orientations. Many women, including those writing from a feminist perspective, have taken issue with the proposition that women's morality is mainly one of care and interdependence (e.g., Abu-Lughod, 1991; Colby & Damon, 1983; Mednick, 1989; Nussbaum, 1999; Okin, 1989; Pollitt, 1992; Stack, 1990). These critiques have highlighted the stereotypical nature of gender-linked distinctions, the significance of justice and fairness in women's judgments and life circumstances, how men's concepts of nurturance and interdependence serve to maintain those circumstances, and how economics and social structural arrangements bear on the moral judgments of females and males. Writing from her perspective as a journalist and feminist, Pollitt (1992) has critiqued characterizations of women as nurturing, caring individuals whose concerns are with relationships but not justice, rationality, or logic. Not that Pollitt would exclude nurturing and caring from the purview of women by any means. Rather, it is that women neither have a monopoly on caring nor are they solely caring nurturers of others. Women are caring, cooperative, competitive, assertive of independence, and committed to rights and justice.

The characterization of women as caring and nurturing, according to Pollitt, stereotypes them in traditional and restrictive ways. It is restrictive because it limits real concern with justice, rights, and independence—just as it is restrictive to attribute characteristics of males solely to justice, rights, and autonomy. This stereotyping serves several ends for females and males. The positive end is that it provides women with an equal moral status to men and challenges the division of men as rational and women as irrational. Women are said to develop a type of rationality by which their morality is different and equal to that of men. Despite the greater concern with equality in moral orientations, Pollitt argues that the formulation constitutes a stereotype serving also to reinforce a status quo in which women retain positions subordinate to men. Men encourage the idea that women are concerned with care because men are, in addition to children, the main beneficiaries of women's nurturance.

Pollitt also argues that propositions regarding the sources of women's judgments in early identifications (Chodorow, 1978) overlook the important contributions of their roles in the economic and social structure. Along with its positive aspects, caring is a consequence of economic dependence and subordination in the family. The role of caretaker and nurturer is, in part, imposed by a power structure in which men are in positions

of influence and economic independence (at least middle-class men). Pollitt's argument, it should be stressed, is not that caring and interdependence are negative and independence is positive. Rather, it is that women, too, can appropriately function independently, claiming rights. In particular, the workplace in capitalist society entails autonomy, concerns with personal advancement and rights, along with caring and justice. Women appear less autonomous in the workplace as a consequence of discrimination serving ends of men in positions of power and influence.

The justice of distribution of resources, privileges, and burdens in the family, especially as it affects women, has been analyzed in depth by Okin (1989, 1996). She argues that moral philosophers and social scientists have either ignored the justice of gender relationships or accepted the legitimacy of unequal distributions and unjust treatment by relegating women to traditional roles. In that context, she also maintains that (a) justice and rights are spheres relevant to women's thinking, (b) there is no evidence that women are more inclined to contextualism than universalism, and (c) the idea that women are oriented to care and not universally applicable concepts of rights and justice reinforces traditional stereotypes. In Okin's (1989) view, the distinction between care and justice has been overdrawn:

> The best theorizing about justice, I argue, has integral to it the notions of care and empathy, of thinking of the interests and well-being of others who may be very different from ourselves. It is, therefore, misleading to draw a dichotomy as though they were two contrasting ethics. The best theorizing about justice is not some abstract "view from nowhere," but results from the carefully attentive consideration of *everyone's* point of view [emphasis in original]. (p. 15)

An implication of Okin's contention is that justice needs to be inclusive. Those emphasizing emotions argue, as noted, that an inclusive or universal conception of morality is a Western one, largely promulgated by intellectuals. In other cultures, and perhaps for ordinary people in Western cultures, morality is applied in a local and parochial fashion. A similar position has been taken by those who propose that integrated cultural patterns are central in the development of morality.

EMPHASIZING CULTURE

The idea of cultures forming integrated cohesive patterns diverging from each other goes back at least to the formulations of cultural anthropologists of the early part of the twentieth century. One of the most influential proponents of the idea that cultures form integrated patterns was Ruth Benedict (1934), who proclaimed that "the diversity of cultures can be endlessly documented" (p. 45). Cultural anthropologists of the time also wrote about morality, often taking positions of cultural relativism, in reaction to predominant late-nineteenth-century anthropological assumptions that cultures could be classified in a hierarchy of lower to higher. Usually, Western cultures were placed at the apex of the hierarchy. Cultural anthropologists argued that the classifications of cultures in a hierarchy of progress or development were due to bias in favor of Western cultural values and to intolerance and lack of respect for the equally valid values of other cultures. Along with relativism, therefore, it was asserted that cultures should be treated as different and equal, and each accepted as functioning on its own moral standards with moral ends endemic to its system. Some critics of cultural relativism (e.g., Hatch, 1983) have pointed out that the position actually includes nonrelativistic moral prescriptions. In particular, relativists espouse the values of tolerance (that the validity of other cultures' values and perspectives should be accepted), freedom (that a culture should not be obstructed from following its moral standards), and equality (that a culture's moral standards should be regarded as of equal validity as those of any other).

Benedict (1934) sharply characterized the proposed variations among cultures through an example that many would consider to epitomize moral concerns, transcending time and place, and pertaining to justice, rights, empathy, sympathy, and care:

> We might suppose that in the matter of taking life all peoples would agree in condemnation. On the contrary, in a matter of homicide, it may be held that one is blameless if diplomatic relations have been severed between neighboring countries, or that one kills by custom his first two children, or that a husband has right of life and death over his wife, or that it is the duty of the child to kill his parents before they are old. It may be that those are killed who steal a fowl, or who cut their upper teeth first, or who are born on a Wednesday. (p. 46)

In this way, Benedict encompassed several cultural practices commonly used to illustrate variations in moral codes: parricide, infanticide, and family relationships of deep inequalities. Observations of variations in social practices, thus, were used to argue for the incomparability of the moralities of different cultures, and in that sense empirical observations were used for propositions about the nature of morality (i.e., to define it as local and entailing an acquisition of the standards of the culture). The core of these propositions is that variations in social practices stem from differences in the ways cultures are integrated (Benedict, 1934, p. 46): "A culture, like an individual, is a more or less consistent pattern of thought and action."

In contemporary views of human development, the role of culture has once again been emphasized (Bruner, 1990; Shweder, 1990a; Shweder & Sullivan, 1993) and has become increasingly part of research on moral development. As already seen, those emphasizing emotions include cultural influences as a part of moral acquisition, along with the idea that morality is highly influenced by biologically based propensities. Others assert that culture must be given center stage (Markus & Kitayama, 1991; Miller & Bersoff, 1995; Shweder, 1990a; Shweder, Mahapatra, & Miller, 1987; Shweder, Much, Mahapatra, & Park, 1997; Triandis, 1990). In giving culture center stage, sharp distinctions are drawn between Western and non-Western cultures in morality and concepts of self. Westerners are said to place an emphasis on abstractions, justice, and the autonomy of individuals, whereas non-Westerners are said to place emphasis on concrete contexts, duties, and interdependence. Yet, when discussing Western cultures in the context of critiques of some explanations of moral development, such as Kohlberg's, culturalists end up portraying people in Western cultures as holding both types of orientations (Shweder, 1982; Simpson, 1973).

Shweder (1982), for instance, asserted that Kohlberg's highest stages (Stages 5 and 6), which include the ideas of "society as a social contract" and the "individual as possessing natural and inalienable rights prior to or outside society" (p. 424), are culture specific. However, he also stated that these ideas are the domain of a small segment of Western culture: "If they are advocated at all, and they rarely are, it is among Western educated middle-class adults" (p. 425). The majority of people (nonintellectuals in Western culture and those in non-Western cultures), therefore, hold views that do not revolve around individual autonomy and separateness from society: "Moral exegesis seems to stabilize around the not unreasonable ideas that social roles carry with them an obligation to behave in a certain way, that society is not of our own making, and that self and society are somehow intimately linked (Stages 3 and 4)" (p. 425).

Most often, Shweder's (1986) position is that a variety of systems of rationality exist that are framed by culture. Western cultures have an individualistic orientation (in contrast with the collectivistic orientations of non-Western cultures) focusing on rights and autonomy. Therefore, while asserting that individualism is the central ethos of Western cultures, it is argued that concepts of freedom, contract, and rights are ways of thinking espoused mainly by intellectual elites and not others in the West. Furthermore, whereas these writers often emphasize the role of the elites in Western culture and draw differences in the thinking of elites and laypersons, they seldom do so with non-Western cultures. Because there is mention of elites or leaders in non-Western cultures, it is on the premise that there is consistency in their thinking with that of ordinary people (Shweder, 1986).

Social Communication and Cultural Coherence

Like Benedict, contemporary researchers point to many areas of *moral* diversity that are said to be well documented by anthropologists and historians:

> On the basis of the historical and ethnographic record we know that different people in different times and places have found it quite natural to be spontaneously appalled, outraged, indignant, proud, disgusted, guilty and ashamed by all sorts of things: masturbation, homosexuality, sexual abstinence, polygamy, abortion, circumcision, corporal punishment, capital punishment, Islam, Christianity, Judaism, capitalism, democracy, flag burning, miniskirts, long hair, no hair, alcohol consumption, meat eating, medical inoculations, atheism, idol worship, divorce, widow remarriage, arranged marriage, romantic love marriage, parents and children sleeping in the same bed, parents and children not sleeping in the same bed, women being allowed to work, women not being allowed to work. (Shweder, 1994, p. 26)

The sweep of this statement is breathtaking. Being appalled, outraged, indignant, proud, disgusted, guilty and ashamed are all seen as moral reactions. Most positive and negative reactions are regarded to have a moral component. Moreover, as evident in the long list given of "all sorts of things," many different behaviors can be and have been part of the moral domain. Little is exempt, given that sexuality, hairstyle, clothing style,

love, marriage, sleeping patterns, and work are all included. Despite appearances, it would not be correct to say that these researchers endorse moral relativism (although questions can be raised about this) nor that they regard the reactions to social practices (e.g., women being allowed to work or women not being allowed to work) as arbitrary or fortuitous. This is because particular social practices are proposed to be part of sets of "moral qualities" entailing rights, autonomy, duty, interdependence, and sanctity. In turn, moral qualities are connected to more general patterns that make up cultural communities. Cultures do not simply provide a series of isolated standards, values or codes. Some worlds of moral meaning emphasize rights and justice, others emphasize duties and obligations, each part of general orientations to individualistic (read Western cultures) and collectivistic (read non-Western cultures) conceptions of self, others, and society.

The proposed contrast between individualistic and collectivistic cultural orientations is related to moral conceptions, practices, and appraisals. However, these orientations encompass much more; they are the bases for cultural constructions of how persons are defined, how they interact with each other, how society is defined, and how the goals of persons and the group are established and met (e.g., Geertz, 1984; Markus & Kitayama, 1991; Shweder & Bourne, 1982; Triandis, 1990). As put by Markus and Kitayama (1991): "In many Western cultures there is a faith in the coherent separateness of distinct persons. . . . Achieving the cultural goal of independence requires construing oneself as an individual whose behavior is organized and made meaningful primarily by reference to one's own internal repertoire of thought, feelings, and action" (p. 225). And in the contrasting construal of interdependence "many non-Western cultures insist . . . on the fundamental connectedness of human beings to each other. A normative imperative of these cultures is to maintain this interdependence among individuals" (p. 227).

In these formulations, the United States is often identified as the quintessential individualistic society (also by Bellah et al., 1985), but individualism is also prevalent in other countries such as Australia, Canada, England, and New Zealand (Triandis, 1990). Prototypical collectivistic cultures are found in Japan, India, China, and the Middle East, as well as in Africa, Latin America, and southern Europe (Markus & Kitayama, 1991). The person conceived as an autonomous agent, with personal goals, is central in the individualistic frame, whereas the group as an interconnected and interdependent network of relationships is central in the collectivistic frame. A core feature of individualistic cultures is that the highest value is accorded to the person as *detached* from others and as independent of the social order. People are, therefore, oriented to self-sufficiency, self-reliance, independence, and resistance to social pressure for conformity or obedience to authority. Collectivistic cultures, by contrast, are oriented to tradition, duty, obedience to authority, interdependence, and social harmony (for a general review of evidence, see Oyserman, Coon, & Kemmelmeier, 2002; for conceptual analyses, see Mascolo & Li, 2004).

A significant component of cultural meanings is the kind of moral orientation communicated to children and reproduced by them as they grow into adulthood. Shweder et al. (1987) proposed a distinction between "rights-based" and "duty-based" moralities in their comparisons between the United States and India. In Western cultures, moral authority resides in individuals who voluntarily enter into contracts and promises, with the idea of rights as fundamental (hence a "rights-based" morality). In a contrasting duty-based morality, the social order is the organizing feature of moral rationality. Customary social practices are viewed as part of the natural moral order, so that social practices are seen neither as within individual discretion nor as a function of social consensus (thus the concept of conventionality as agreement in a group is largely absent). The social order dictates specified duties based on roles and status in the social structure, "while the individual per se and his various interior states, preferences, appetites, intentions, or motives are of little interest or concern" (Shweder et al., 1987, pp. 20–21). Moreover, Shweder et al. asserted that in a duty-based culture, individuals are not free to deviate from rules and that there is little conception of a natural right (such as free speech) that might lead to advocating deviation from the socially defined good.

Social Practices and Cultural Coherence

Propositions regarding cultural divergence in "moral rationality" were examined in a study conducted with samples of secular middle- and upper-middle-class children and adults from the United States (Hyde Park in Chicago), and samples of "untouchables" and Brahmans living in the old temple town of Bhubaneswar, Orissa, in India (for research in Brazil, see Haidt, Koller, & Dias,

1993; and in Israel, see Nissan, 1987). In large measure, the research aimed at ascertaining whether a distinction could be drawn across the two cultures between morality, as based on concepts of justice, rights, and welfare, and conventionality, as based on context-specific uniformities serving goals of social coordination—a distinction that had been addressed by others and is considered further in subsequent sections of this chapter (e.g., Nucci, 1981; Smetana, 1981, 1984; Tisak, 1986; Turiel, 1979, 1983a).

Shweder et al. (1987) hypothesized that a distinction between morality and convention is particular to cultures which structure social relationships through the concept of autonomous individuals free to choose by consensus. Accordingly, they included topics of consensual choice in Western cultures such as issues about food, dress, and terms of address. Whereas some items were straightforward (e.g., a son addressing his father by his first name) others included religious and metaphysical considerations for Indians because of their connections to ideas about an afterlife (e.g., a widow wearing jewelry and bright-colored clothing 6 months after the death of her husband, a widow eating fish 2 or 3 times a week). Also many of the items entailed acts on the part of women that might contradict the power and desires of men (e.g., a woman wanting to eat with her husband and elder brother, a son claiming an inheritance over his sister). Shweder et al. (1987) included items reflecting concepts they consider candidates for moral universals (e.g., a father breaking a promise to his son, cutting in line, refusing to treat an injured person) that dealt with justice, harm, reciprocity, theft, arbitrary assault, and discrimination. Still other issues dealt with family practices that might vary by culture, including those bearing on personal liberty, privacy, and equality (considered central themes for Americans), and sanctity, chastity, and respect for status (considered central themes for Indians).

The assessments were adapted, in modified form, from previous research on morality and convention (Turiel, 1983a). Shweder et al. (1987) found that Americans and Indians rank the seriousness of transgressions in very different ways, such that there are high correlations among Americans and among Indians but little correlation between Americans and Indians. There was agreement in judgments about some moral issues between Indians and Americans and a good deal of disagreement on issues pertaining to conventions, liberty, equality, sanctity, chastity, and status. The findings of variations in judgments, aside from the few issues deal-ing with harm, promises, assault, and so on, led Shweder et al. (1987) to conclude that "many things viewed as wrong on one side of the Atlantic are not viewed as wrong on the other side" (p. 51).

On the side of India, according to the findings, more things are regarded as wrong than on the side of the United States. In particular, Indians regarded many breaches pertaining to food, dress, terms of address, and sex roles as wrong, as unalterable, and in some cases as universal. Shweder et al. (1987) maintained that conven-tional thinking "is almost a nonexistent form of thought in our Indian data" (p. 52). Although convention was ex-istent in the American data, it was much less prevalent than found in many other studies conducted in the United States. It was also found that with increasing age Americans judged the issues in more relativistic ways (i.e., judging that the practices are acceptable for other people or in other countries) and were more likely to take situational features into account. By contrast, with increasing age, Indians judged the prohibitions as appli-cable universally and across varying contexts. On the basis of these findings, Damon (1988) has suggested "that moral maturity in some parts of the world implies an ever-expanding tendency to universalize one's moral beliefs, whereas in other parts of the world moral matu-rity means applying one's beliefs flexibly to an array of changing situations" (p. 109). Because it is Indians, in contrast to Americans, who universalize moral judg-ments, Damon's suggestion is in direct opposition to presumptions that moral universality is a post-Enlight-enment Western idea.

In addition to differences in judgments between the two cultural groups, on issues related to food, dress, terms of address, and sex roles, Shweder et al. (1987) found that a number of issues were judged as wrong by both Indians and Americans (these are the candidates for moral universals). Agreement occurred on issues pertaining to harm (e.g., hospital workers ignoring an accident victim, destroying another child's picture, kicking a harmless animal), injustice (e.g., cutting in line, discriminating against invalids), breaking prom-ises, and incest. However, not all issues bearing on dis-crimination or harm were judged as wrong by Indians and Americans. Three issues, in particular, were judged as right by Indians and wrong by Americans. One of these depicted a father who canes his son for a misdeed. Two others pertained to gender relationships. One de-picted a husband who beats his wife "black and blue"

after she disobeys him by going to a movie alone without his permission, and a son who claims most of his de-ceased father's property, not allowing his sister to ob-tain much inheritance. As put by Shweder et al. (1987):

> Oriya Brahmans do not view beating an errant wife as an instance of arbitrary assault, and they do not believe it is unfair to choose the son over the daughter in matters of life and inheritance. . . . [T]hey] believe, that beating a wife who goes to the movies without permission is roughly equivalent to corporal punishment for a private in the army who leaves the military base without permission. For Oriyas there are rationally appealing analogical map-pings between the family unit and military units (differen-tiated roles and status obligations in the service of the whole, hierarchical control, drafting and induction, etc.). One thing the family is not, for Oriyas, is a voluntary asso-ciation among equal individuals. (p. 71)

The overarching principle applied in the analyses of responses to these items is cultural meaning in a moral system. Not considered is that different and varying agendas may be at work in addition to "moral duties." For example, Indians may judge caning a son as right be-cause of their psychological assumptions regarding the effectiveness of physical punishment on learning (see Wainryb, 1991). Also, exerting power and asserting per-sonal entitlements may account for the acceptability, among Indians, of husbands beating their wives and sons claiming an inheritance over their sisters. The analogy between the family and military units ignores some pos-sibly important differences. Is it permissible for a pri-vate in the army to be "beaten black and blue"? What about an officer who leaves the base without permis-sion? Is he not accountable for his actions, as opposed to a husband in the family situation? In that sense, there may be more accountability and reciprocity between people in different ranks in the military than husband and wife in the family. When a husband beats his wife, is it "in the service of the whole" or in the service of the husband's personal interests?

Nevertheless, the examples and analogy point to some hierarchical social relationships, entailing dominance and subordination. Additional items used by Shweder et al. (1987) illustrate hierarchy in the family. Indians judged that it is wrong for a woman to eat with her hus-band's elder brother, that it is wrong for a husband to massage the legs of his wife, and that it is wrong for a husband to cook dinner for his wife. Intimacy should not exist among certain family members, such as between a woman and her husband's elder brother. A husband must not give his wife a massage or cook for her because "The wife is the servant of the husband. The servant should do her work" (Shweder et al., 1997, p. 137).

Another area where hierarchical relationships exist in a traditional culture like India is among people of different castes. Shweder et al. (1987) also propose that the morality of Indians includes the idea of "purity," communicating to children that they should avoid sources of impurity and uncleanliness, and one such source of pollution is contact with people of a lower caste: "Just as the pure must be protected from the impure, the higher status and the lower status must be kept at a distance . . . the culture is providing the child with a practical moral commentary in which one of the many messages is ultimately that menstrual blood, feces, and lower status go together" (pp. 74–75). Again, these practices are attributed to cultural meanings around duties, without consideration of the possibility that they reflect the creation of distance in social relationships that benefit those in positions of power (in a culture that is supposed to be collectivistic and to stress interdependence).

Emotional Forms, Intuitions, and Rapid Processing

The emphasis on the dictates of roles, status, and hierarchy appears to leave little room for the types of moral concerns with justice, harm, and even rights (e.g., that it is wrong to discriminate against invalids) apparent in some of the findings of the Shweder et al. (1987) research. Recognizing that such judgments are made in that non-Western, "sociocentric" culture (as in their own findings and as in interpretations by Turiel, Killen, & Helwig, 1987), Shweder and his colleagues (1990b; Shweder et al., 1997) attenuated somewhat the proposition regarding the separation of a rights-based morality and a duty-based morality and elaborated on it. One elaboration is the proposition that three "ethics" are found the world over: the ethics of autonomy, community, and divinity. Although the inclusion of three ethics broadens the scope of the analyses beyond the dichotomy of rights and duties, it is still presumed that the social order determines the interplay of different types of "goods" in a worldview. Thus, in India, community and divinity are dominant, whereas in the United States autonomy prevails (Shweder et al., 1997). In Indian society, the ethics of autonomy, based on justice, harm, and rights, is subordinated to and in the service of the ethics

of community, which refers to status, hierarchy, and social order, and the ethics of divinity based on concepts of sin, sanctity, duty, and natural order. In the United States, by contrast, there is a "specialization" in the ethics of autonomy, with community, and divinity in even smaller part, providing a background. Reminiscent of Etzioni's (1993) position, Shweder et al. (1997) are of the opinion that the "expertise" in the ethics of autonomy in the United States has led to a wide extension of the concept of rights (e.g., to children or animals), to the desire to be protected from "every imaginable harm" (e.g., from secondary cigarette smoke or psychologically offensive work environments), and to an enlargement of the idea of harm (to include "all-embracing notions as 'harassment,' 'abuse,' 'exploitation,'" p. 142). Shweder et al. (1997) view these extensions as distortions, just as other distortions may occur through the extensions of concepts of community and divinity in Indian culture.

In India, the ethics of autonomy is linked to the idea of a soul, which obligates respect (souls include human and nonhuman animals). More dominant, however, is the ethic of community, in which a person's identity is associated with status and relationships to others to a much greater extent than individuality. Relationships are part of hierarchical orderings in which people in subordinate and dominant positions are obligated to protect and look after each other's interests (e.g., wives should be obedient to husbands and husbands should be responsive to the needs and desires of wives). Shweder et al. (1997) regard this as analogous to feudal ethics, where the feudal lord does for others as much as they do for him (an asymmetrical reciprocity because one person is in a position of dominance and control).

Along with the three types of morality, another set of modifications and extensions of the theory is that cultural content is communicated to individuals who are prepared by evolution with deep emotions to receive and rapidly process the content, making decisions intuitively (Shweder, 1994; Shweder & Haidt, 1993). Moreover, emotions are regarded as "the gatekeeper of the moral world," revealing features of social reality.

The proposition that emotions are linked to intuitions has been extended by Haidt (2001) in ways that render rationality and reasoning largely irrelevant in moral evaluations and decisions (which contrasts with Shweder's, 1986, proposition that people in different cultures maintain different types of rationality). In Haidt's view, immediate, reflexive reactions, such as revulsion, disgust, and sympathy, trigger moral reactions.

Judging acts as wrong involves immediate "gut" reactions of intuitive kinds that do not involve reasoning. For Haidt, the defining feature of "intuitions" is quantitative: They occur rapidly, without effort, automatically, and without intentionality. Haidt proposes that intuitions are due to evolutionary adaptations shaped by culture. Culture provides a context for the expression (referred to as externalization) of built-in moral intuitions. The outcome in children and among adults is a morality that is unique to their culture or group and often includes asymmetrical reciprocity with acceptance of dominance and subordination.

In Haidt's view, humans are reasoning beings only in secondary ways. Reasoning contrasts with intuitions in that it is slow, requires effort, and makes use of evidence. Moral reasoning is used mainly after the fact to justify to self and others why an act is intuitively grasped as wrong "when faced with a social demand for a verbal justification one becomes a lawyer building a case rather than a judge searching for the truth" (Haidt, 2001, p. 814). Moral reasoning is also used to persuade and to rationalize but does not involve choices, rationality, deliberation, or use of evidence. According to Haidt, most people are not concerned with reflection on moral matters. It is philosophers and those with a "high need" for cognition who engage in private or personal reflection.

To the extent that evidence is provided for the proposition that moral evaluations are intuitive, it is from research in nonmoral realms. Haidt cites a number of studies from social psychology that appear to support the idea that people are biased, emotive, intuitive, and unconcerned with evidence. Moreover, Haidt proclaims that research on moral reasoning only reveals what people do in the way of justification to convince others or to rationalize, in a post hoc way, positions they hold for other reasons. However, he does not provide evidence as to how the moral reasoning investigated in so many studies fails to account for moral evaluations or how it is that such reasoning is mainly used for purposes of persuasion and rationalization. A good part of Haidt's argument is based on a few examples. One that he seems to regard as prototypical is that of incest—an example that could be viewed as shared within cultures, yet applicable across cultures, and an evolutionary adaptation. Incest is an act, even when it is specified that it is consensual and there is no risk of pregnancy occurring, to which people react immediately with a gut reaction that it is wrong and are unable to explain why. The specific ex-

ample provided is of a brother and sister who go on vacation and, with all precautions, decide to make love. The act is intuitively grasped as wrong because most people say something like "I don't know, I can't explain it. I just know it's wrong."

A key question is the generality of this type of example (or examples like people judging it wrong to eat dogs, etc.) and whether it applies to people's moral lives more generally and meaningfully. The research discussed in subsequent sections provides a good deal of evidence that children, adolescents, and adults explain many of their moral evaluations in ways that are very different from the way they approach an issue like incest. A number of features in social situations are taken into account, including what has been referred to as informational assumptions or assumptions about reality (see the discussion that follows; for a critique of the emotivist-intuitionist position, see Turiel, 2006).

Justice and Interpersonal Responsibilities

The position taken by Shweder and his colleagues (Shweder, 1986, 2002; Shweder et al., 1987; Shweder et al., 1997) gives more emphasis to systems of rationality in moral judgments than is evident in the proposition that morality is based on intuitions given expression by cultural practices. Moral systems of rationality, as already noted, vary by cultural orientations to self, other, roles, and duties. Social hierarchy is seen to be central in the morality of Hindu Indians, as exemplified by Shweder's view that their morality includes treating the family unit like a military unit and acceptance of the legitimacy of a husband beating his wife "black and blue" when she is disobedient. Another aspect of hierarchy, in this moral orientation, is the necessity of members of the higher caste to avoid contact with members of lower castes (to avoid pollution). Although social hierarchy is portrayed as entailing asymmetrical reciprocity, it also makes for a good deal of distance and separation between males and females and among social classes. Shweder et al.'s (1987) depiction of the family unit as akin to a military unit implies formality and dependence of women (like privates) on men (like commissioned officers). The distance between members of different castes due to the need to avoid pollution makes for very little interdependence or care and concern for the welfare of those of lower castes. These conclusions are at odds with the portrayal of non-Western cultures as oriented to interdependence and social harmony.

Another series of studies comparing Americans and Indians on their judgments about helping others, interpersonal obligations, and justice was based on the proposed cultural distinction between independence and interdependence (Bersoff & Miller, 1993; Miller & Bersoff, 1992, 1995; Miller, Bersoff, & Hardwood, 1990; Miller & Luthar, 1989). In contrast to Gilligan (1982), Miller and her colleagues proposed that variations in judgments about interpersonal obligations and justice reflect cultural, and not gender, differences. Miller and Bersoff (1995) maintained that Gilligan takes a narrow approach to culture by failing to consider differences in cultural meanings that affect individuals' concepts of self and morality. They believe Gilligan's ideas lead to implausible predictions—that concepts of self and morality would be more similar among individuals of the same gender from different cultures (e.g., a secular American woman versus a traditional Hindu Indian woman) than individuals of different genders from similar cultures (e.g., a traditional Hindu Indian man versus a traditional Hindu Indian woman). Miller and Bersoff (1995) further argue that in Gilligan's propositions regarding the influences of early childhood experience there is a failure to consider how they are related to cultural meanings.

Miller and Bersoff (1995) proposed that American women, too, are influenced by the individualistic views of self in their culture and that Indian men are influenced by the relational or interdependent views of the self in their culture. As a consequence, Americans have a "minimalist" view of interpersonal moral obligations that contrasts with the maximalist views of Indians. The thinking of Indians is contextual because self is conceptualized as part of the social order so that duty is not in contradiction with individual desires.

In a study (Miller & Luthar, 1989) comparing Indians and Americans, adults were presented with a set of scenarios depicting transgressions of role-related interpersonal obligations (e.g., a son refusing to care for his elderly parents, a man leaving his wife and children for another woman), and justice (e.g., a college student cheating on a final exam because family responsibilities do not allow time for study, a man leaving the city without paying back a personal loan). It was found that both groups evaluated the justice issues as wrong, but Indians were more likely than Americans to evaluate the interpersonal transgressions as wrong. Correspondingly, each group classified the justice transgressions mainly in moral terms. There was a greater tendency for Indi-

ans to classify the interpersonal transgressions as moral rather than as matters of personal choice and the reverse for Americans.

In addition, a study by Miller et al. (1990) showed that a large majority of Indians judged as wrong actors who, for selfish reasons, failed to help persons in extreme, moderate, or minor need. This was true for relationships between parent and child, best friends, and strangers. The same judgment was made by the large majority of Americans regarding situations of extreme need and situations of moderate need involving parents and children. With regard to the situations of minor need with parents, and moderate need in relationships of friends and strangers, Americans (especially among the oldest groups) were less likely to see helping as an obligation.

Miller and Bersoff (1995) also proposed that selflessness is consistent with a duty-oriented culture and that providing psychological support is consistent with a cultural orientation to voluntary, personal decisions in interpersonal relationships. More generally, for Americans, because of their orientation to individualism, interpersonal relationships are not strictly moral obligations but are seen as either matters of personal choice or as involving a combination of the moral and personal. For Indians, interpersonal relationships are seen as moral obligations that can be given priority over matters of justice or rights.

However, the proposed commitment of Indians to interpersonal obligations is discrepant with the findings of Shweder et al. (1987) showing detachment between castes and among family members. Other aspects of the research conducted by Miller and her colleagues are discrepant with findings obtained by Shweder et al. (1987). In the first place, they (Bersoff & Miller, 1993; Miller & Bersoff, 1992) found that Indians do think in terms of social conventions. Both Indians and Americans judged a violation of a dress code (not related to religious obligations) in social conventional and not moral terms, and these judgments differed from judgments about theft (which was judged in moral terms). Other research (Madden, 1992) conducted in the temple town of Bhubaneswar also showed that there was conventional thinking about nonreligious issues, which was distinct from moral thinking.

Additionally, Miller contends that Indians take contextual features into account to a greater extent than Americans. Evidence for this proposition comes from studies of person descriptions and social explanations indicating that Americans tend to explain behaviors with trait attributions, whereas Indians tend to do so with references to context (Miller, 1984, 1986). Evidence also comes from studies indicating that Indians are less likely than Americans to hold individuals accountable for violations of moral codes, attributing the causes of behavior to contextual features (Bersoff & Miller, 1993; Miller & Luthar, 1989). These propositions about the contextual dependence of duty appear to be in opposition to the Shweder et al. (1987) findings that with age Americans become more relativistic and flexible in their moral judgments and that Indians become more universalistic, applying moral injunctions across contexts. Miller's propositions regarding moral accountability also appear to be different from the view of Shweder et al. (1997) that karma institutionalizes human tendencies to attribute consequences to personal responsibility. "It is a great irony of Western understanding that karma is often misinterpreted as a description of how Indians excuse themselves from responsibility by describing themselves as passive objects of the force of their past actions (p. 152)." According to Shweder et al., some Indians do use an interpretation of karma to account for failures of responsibility, but other Indians are critical of such thinking.

EMPHASIZING JUDGMENT AND RECIPROCAL SOCIAL INTERACTIONS

In several approaches considered thus far, it is, for the most part, proposed that children acquire morality from the family and/or the culture, and that this occurs very early in life. It is presumed that the necessary components of morality emerge very early in life—infants and very young children show positive social behaviors, react with positive emotions to others, and form attachments with them. This presumption, in turn, is linked to the propositions that much of it is naturally derived (through evolution), that much of it is acquired from parents because most of the child's early social experiences are in the family, and that much of it is reflexive and habitual.

The findings that young children show positive moral emotions and actions toward others indicate that the foundations of morality are established in early childhood and do not solely entail the control and inhibition of children's tendencies toward gratifying needs or drives or acting on impulses. However, that the foundations of positive morality are established in early child-

hood does not necessarily establish that significant aspects of development do not occur beyond early childhood; that judgments, deliberations, and reflections are unimportant; or that many experiences, in addition to parental practices, do not contribute. As noted earlier, the theories and research of Piaget and Kohlberg have had much to do with the shift away from conceptualizing morality as entailing self-control over impulses through their demonstrations that children think about the social world, attempt to understand social relationships, form judgments of right and wrong, and thereby engage in reciprocal interactions with others. However, Piaget and Kohlberg thought that extrinsic features, such as basing right and wrong on obedience and sanctions, structure young children's moral judgments. As is discussed, it appears that Piaget and Kohlberg failed to uncover not only the positive nature of young children's moral feelings but also that young children form relatively complex judgments that are not based on extrinsic features.

Moral reasoning is multifaceted and can entail ambiguities and uncertainties, certainties and unreflective apprehension, as well as deliberation and reflection. Whether moral evaluations and judgments are processed very quickly or slowly, with certainty or given pause, with an apparent lack of self-awareness or with reflection and deliberation, depends on the individual's development, the situation or problem confronted, and the points of view of other people. First, how well a concept is understood has a bearing on the rapidity of a moral evaluation. A well-understood concept that is perceived as readily applicable to a particular situation may well be used in rapid fashion and give a false appearance to the outside observer that it is "intuitive" or a habitual practice. The same concept for that individual at an earlier time may have been applied with more uncertainty and less of a sense of being evidently true. That does not mean that a concept, once formed and accepted, will be produced rapidly and without self-awareness in all situations. Ambiguities in a situation, as well as awareness that others take a different point of view, can produce deliberation, awareness of ambiguities, and argumentation.

It will be recalled that Haidt (2001) used the quantitative dimension of rapidity and lack of effort as criteria for designating responses as intuitive and habitual. He referred to social psychological research in nonmoral realms to support the propositions that people's thinking is intuitive, unreflective, and that they do not concern themselves with evidence. However, there is a large body of evidence from developmental and cognitive psychology in realms like number, mathematical reasoning, classification, understandings of space and physics more generally, causality, intentionality, and theories of mind showing that people make judgments that are not necessarily immediate, rapid, and categorical and that can be intentional, deliberative, and reflective. People do reason and are not intuitive in many realms of knowledge. The research also shows that such reasoning can become immediate and rapid. Conceptualizations of, for example, number and arithmetic may be acquired laboriously over time but, once acquired, are applied in rapid fashion (for further discussion, see Turiel, 2006).

Research on young children's psychological understandings also demonstrates that the quantitative dimension of rapidity of response is inadequate as a means for ascertaining whether reasoning is at work. Many studies of children's understandings of others' minds (see Flavell & Miller, 1998) show that cognitive processes of a slow and rapid nature are at work between 3 and 5 years of age. As the research clearly shows, 5-year-old children have an understanding of others' mental states, including beliefs, desires, and intentions. For instance, 5-year-olds readily understand that another person may hold a "false" belief about, for example, the contents of a crayon box that actually contains candy. For adults, this is rapidly understood and readily applied—and it appears to be so also for 5-year-olds. Yet, processes of development and thought are involved in these understandings given that 3-year-olds generally do not answer correctly on tasks assessing false beliefs (or other assessments of understandings of mental states). The rapidity of the cognitive processing of 5- or 6-year-old children can mask the uncertainties and ambiguities in younger children's judgments, as well as the processes of reasoning in the older children. Furthermore, the development of psychological understandings does not stop there. Even adults can face difficulties and ambiguities in understanding the psychological states and behaviors of persons (Ross & Nisbett, 1991).

Research on the moral decisions of people identified by Colby and Damon (1992) as moral exemplars indicated that judgments could include convictions, certainty, *and* openness to new ways of thinking. The search for "truth" and openness to change in thinking do not reflect automatic, reflexive, or intuitively evident truths immediately apparent to an individual. However, the certainty in the thinking of these individuals also leads them to make decisions that much of the time does not require belabored weighing of alternatives. It might

be said that the "moral exemplars" studied by Colby and Damon are among those with more philosophical orientations or a "high need" for cognition. In a later section, however, research is discussed on how reflection and social critique are part of most people's social lives (Turiel, 2003b; Turiel & Perkins, 2004).

Studies of moral development, including several of the ones already considered, suggest alternatives to the propositions that emotions are primary in morality, that moral acquisition is mainly due to effects of parental practices on children, or that morality largely reflects the acquisition of societal standards. Dunn et al. (1995) found differences in the two types of situations they assessed (physical harm and cheating) and documented that relationships with siblings influence development. By 2 or 3 years of age, children display a fair amount of teasing of mothers, physical aggression, destruction of objects, and an increasing ability to engage in arguments and disputes with mothers (Dunn, 1987; Dunn & Munn, 1987). This increasing variety in young children's social relationships is consistent with the findings reviewed by Grusec and Goodnow (1994) showing that parental practices are related to type of misdeed (e.g., moral or conventional), children judge the appropriateness of reasons given by parents when communicating with them, and parents may encourage ways of behaving that differ from those they engage in themselves.

An interactional perspective on parent-child relationships casts a different light on the types of child-rearing practices studied in research on moral development (Turiel, 1983a, 1983b). In addition to how particular practices shape children's behaviors (the focus of much of the research), it is necessary to consider how these very practices constitute forms of social communication. Among the types of child-rearing practices, the most effective (the so-called induction method) entails explanation of reasons for the required behaviors (Hoffman, 1970; Maccoby & Martin, 1983). That explicit communications of this sort are more effective than practices like physical punishment and love-withdrawal suggests that parents and children engage in reciprocal interactions. Another body of findings on parental practices has shown that "authoritative" forms of parenting are more effective than either "authoritarian" or "permissive" forms (Baumrind, 1973, 1989; Maccoby & Martin, 1983; see also Collins & Steinberg, Chapter 16, this *Handbook,* this volume; Parke & Buriel, Chapter 8, this *Handbook,* this volume). One of the features distinguishing authoritative parenting from the others is an emphasis on discussion, communication, and explanation. It is also likely that the types of parental practices that do not emphasize communications entail implicit communications. As implicit communications, the messages are less clear and more open to children's own interpretations. Perhaps this accounts for the findings that the use of physical punishment is connected with greater aggressiveness on the part of children (Hoffman, 1970; Maccoby & Martin, 1983). Physical punishment may convey the implicit message that inflicting physical harm and using a form of aggression is acceptable.

It is also likely that family influences on children's moral development go beyond the effects of parental discipline practices. The structure of family interactions is another important influence, especially as it relates to fairness in arrangements among males and females (Hochschild, 1989; Okin, 1989, 1996). In most families, there exist gender-related inequalities in the distribution of power, the ways goods and privileges are allocated, and the work opportunities encouraged or discouraged. Such structural arrangements and practices may well have an effect on children's development, but this is an area largely neglected in research on family influences.

An interactional perspective, therefore, needs to account for many aspects of family life and social life in addition to family experiences (Turiel, 2004b). One of these that has received some attention from researchers is interaction among peers. Some have followed Piaget's (1932) lead in proposing that peer interactions are important to children's moral development (Damon, 1981, 1988; Youniss, 1980). Piaget maintained that relationships of young children with adults were ones of constraint, whereas relationships with peers are more likely to be ones of cooperation. According to Piaget, because peers are perceived more or less as equals, children are more likely to take their perspectives and see themselves as responsible partners in social interchanges.

Without necessarily presuming that interactions with peers are more conducive than interactions with adults to the development of moral judgments, several researchers have examined the influences of children's relationships with each other. Damon (1981, 1984, 1988) and Youniss (1980) propose that the effects of peer interactions are a consequence of "the coordinating of one's perspective and actions with those of another, rather than through the transmission of information and ideas" (Damon, 1981, p. 165). Furthermore, Damon maintains that important aspects of morality are first learned through play with friends, including norms that may be discrepant with societal standards espoused by adults.

Even norms consistent with those of adults are "discovered" by children through their interactions with friends.

Damon (1988) identified as primary to childhood relationships reciprocity of a symmetrical kind, which is more likely to occur among children than between adults and children because children perceive each other as equals in status and power. Moreover, the mutuality and intimacy that develop among children entail close collaboration and communication and are more likely to foster decisions based on consensual agreements. Children, thereby, come to understand that social rules can be based on cooperation among equals in creating and applying them and not solely on the authority of others. Children, through interactions involving give-and-take, collaborations, the sharing of ideas, openness to new insights, and compromise "co-construct" knowledge and ways of thinking. Co-construction involves children together discovering solutions to problems and encouraging creative thinking.

In the context of research on the development of concepts of distributive justice, experimental work has shown that children change more as a consequence of discussions with peers than with adults (Damon, 1981). Other studies on the influences of peer discussion among college students were conducted in the context of Kohlberg's stages of moral judgments. In these studies, students were paired for discussions about moral dilemmas so as to create disparities in their previously assessed levels of moral judgment. It was found that discussions between those whose levels were only slightly different served to stimulate change (Berkowitz, Gibbs, & Broughton, 1980) and that the most effective types of discussions entailed efforts at transforming each other's meanings into comprehensible forms (Berkowitz & Gibbs, 1983).

Another source of development related to peer interactions occurs through social conflicts (Berkowitz & Gibbs, 1985; Killen & Nucci, 1995), which are common among children, and can stimulate them to take different points of view to restore balance to social situations, to produce ideas as to how to coordinate the needs of others and self, and to consider the rights of others—especially claims of ownership or possession of objects (see Killen & Nucci, 1995, for more extensive discussion). Research by Killen and her colleagues (Killen, 1989; Killen & Naigles, 1995; Killen & Nucci, 1995; Killen & Sueyoshi, 1995; Rende & Killen, 1992) has also demonstrated that in the absence of adult intervention, young children are quite capable of addressing social conflicts and producing resolutions that take the needs and interests of others into account. In another study (Eisenberg, Lundy, Shell, & Roth, 1985), it was found that preschool children justified meeting the requests of peers with references to the needs of others and to their relationships with others (requests of adults, by contrast, were justified with references to authority and punishment).

The Construction of Moral Judgments through Social Interactions

Conflicts, disputes, argumentation, and discussion are all part of social interactions. For many who emphasize the role of judgments in morality, such social interactions are involved in the individual's constructions of moral judgments that are not solely local or derived primarily from parental teachings or from an integrated, consistent cultural pattern. In these positions, generalizable, nonlocal moral judgments are not innately based but constructions through social interactions. A significant aspect of approaches emphasizing judgments is to have an epistemological grounding with regard to the nature of the realm of morality. For a number of researchers, such grounding is provided by philosophical traditions that, as put by Nussbaum (1999), presume that "human beings are above all reasoning beings." Nussbaum has summarized such traditions going back to Immanuel Kant and John Stuart Mill and including contemporary philosophers like Rawls (1971, 1993), Dworkin (1977), Gewirth (1978), and Habermas (1990a, 1990b, 1993) as follows:

> At the heart of this tradition is a twofold intuition about human beings: namely, that all, just by being human, are of equal dignity and worth, no matter where they are situated in society, and that the primary source of this worth is a power of moral choice within them, a power that consists in the ability to plan a life in accordance with one's own evaluations of ends . . . the moral equality of persons gives them a fair claim to certain types of treatment at the hands of society and politics. What this treatment is will be a subject of debate within the tradition, but the shared starting point is that this treatment must do two closely related things. It must respect and promote the liberty of choice, and it must respect and promote the equal worth of persons as choosers. (p. 54)

Nussbaum adds that a basic moral premise in these approaches is that each person be treated as an end and not as a means to other goals. She maintains that emotions are intertwined with moral reasoning. In this view,

morality is not primarily driven by emotions. Emotions involve evaluative appraisals so that "the entire distinction between reason and emotions begins to be called into question, and one can no longer assume that a thinker who focuses on reason is excluding emotion" (Nussbaum, 1999, p. 72). From the psychological perspective, emotional experiences inform the development of thought and, reciprocally, thinking informs the development and maintenance of emotions.

In line with Nussbaum's propositions, the approaches to moral judgments linked to Piaget (1932) and Kohlberg (1963) have considered emotional appraisals important to both the formation of morality and its applications. However, aversive emotions are not the basis of moral judgments. Rather, emotions of sympathy, empathy, and especially respect are central. In Piaget's view, combinations of in-born or very early emerging emotions of fear, affection, and sympathy, as well as vindictiveness and compassion, help form the basis for the development of morality. He regarded instinctive tendencies as "a necessary but not a sufficient condition for the formation of morality" (Piaget, 1932, p. 344), and maintained that "the child's behavior toward persons shows signs from the first of those sympathetic tendencies and affective reactions in which one can easily see the raw material of all subsequent moral behavior. But an intelligent act can only be called logical and a good-hearted impulse moral from the moment that certain norms impress a given structure and rules of equilibrium upon this material" (p. 405). It is especially the combination of fear, affection, and sympathy in relation to adults that are intertwined with social interactions and processes of reasoning that make for the emergence of heteronomy—which includes "unilateral respect" for those in authority. The transformation of unilateral respect into feelings of mutual respect is essential for the emergence of autonomous moral judgments about welfare and justice.

From philosophical perspectives, as well as psychological ones, propositions regarding universalizable moral reasoning are consistent with the idea that morality stems from social experiences and social constructions. One of the most extensive philosophical formulations of the social sources of moral reasoning can be seen in the "neo-Kantian" propositions of Habermas (1993), based on his theory of communicative action and discourse ethics, that morality entails concepts of justice, rights, and welfare (of others and the general welfare). Habermas bridges important distinctions: one between justification and application of moral norms, the other between individual autonomy and social solidarity. Whereas moral principles are justified or grounded in criteria of universalizability and impartiality, situational features are taken into account in their application to concrete instances. Consequently, the way moral principles are understood is a necessary component, as is an understanding of the features of the context. As put by Habermas (1993):

> The principle of universalization that regulates discourses of justification does not exhaust the normative sense of the impartiality of a just judgment. A further principle must be adduced to guarantee the correctness of singular judgments. An impartial judge must assess which of the competing norms of action—whose validity has been established in advance—is most appropriate to a given concrete case once all the relevant features of the given constellation of circumstances have been accorded due weight in the situational description. Thus, principles of appropriateness and the exhaustion of all relevant contextual features come into play here. (p. 129)

Habermas maintained that both autonomy and social solidarity are essential features for those participating in a network of reciprocal expectations. Discourse, communication, and argumentation are the means by which individuals function in a moral world. This places individuals in a collectivity, attempting to maintain social solidarity by submitting their moral principles for verification by others in moral dialogue, reflective discussion, and argumentation. In the process, individuals take positions based on moral concepts but through consensus attempt to achieve resolutions that account for the general welfare and maintenance of solidarity.

Habermas also incorporated developmental research into his philosophical formulations, relying on his revised form of the progression of moral judgments formulated by Kohlberg (the general outline of the stage progression was provided earlier). Like Kohlberg (1976), Habermas regarded stages of perspective taking (Selman, 1980) as part of the process of the formation of moral judgments. However, Habermas's theory of discourse ethics is not dependent on Kohlberg's particular formulation. It would be consistent with psychological formulations that postulate that individuals make moral judgments of a generalizable kind.

Kohlberg's formulations are not further reviewed here, as they have been discussed extensively in previous editions of this *Handbook* (see Hoffman, 1970, and, especially, Rest, 1983). Several researchers, however, have pursued hypotheses based on the stages proposed by Kohlberg. This includes research conducted by Kohlberg and his colleagues tracing developmental changes longitudinally (Colby, Kohlberg, Gibbs, & Lieberman, 1983) and reformulating the specific descriptions of the stages (Colby & Kohlberg, 1987a; Kohlberg, 1984; Kohlberg, Levine, & Hewer, 1983). Other researchers have used Kohlberg's formulations to examine relationships between perspective taking and moral development (e.g., Keller & Edelstein, 1991; Selman, 1980; Walker, 1980), hypotheses regarding the invariance of the stages (Walker, 1982; Walker, de Vries, & Bichard, 1984), and processes by which changes occur (Berkowitz & Gibbs, 1983; Walker & Taylor, 1991).

Some studies have examined family variables and moral judgment, including correspondence between parents' and children's levels (e.g., Hart, 1988b; Walker & Taylor, 1991). Other studies (Hart, 1988a; Hart & Chmiel, 1992) have related personality measures and defense mechanisms to stages of moral judgment. There have also been theoretical formulations aimed at combining aspects of Kohlberg's stage sequence with other variables, such as affect, coping, and stress, to explain unusual moral commitments on the part of individuals (Haste, 1990). Still other research has attempted to extend the analyses to the adult life span, including among the elderly (Pratt, Golding, & Hunter, 1983; Pratt, Golding, Hunter, & Norris, 1988).

Studies were conducted on the influences of attending college on the development of moral judgments (e.g., Rest & Narvaez, 1991). These studies deviate from Kohlberg's procedures in that assessments were made using a paper and pencil questionnaire requesting individuals to rate and rank a series of solutions to moral dilemmas corresponding to the six stages—in contrast with Kohlberg's semistructured clinical interview aimed at ascertaining individuals' ways of thinking (see Rest, 1979, for details on the standardized assessment; see Damon, 1977, Piaget, 1929; Turiel, 1983a, for discussions of the aims and value of the clinical interview method). The research conducted by Rest is also linked to what he refers to as a "Four Component Model" of moral development, including judgment, "sensitivity," motivation, and ego strength (it is detailed in a previous edition of this *Handbook*; Rest, 1983; see also Rest, Narvaez, & Thoma, 1999).

Moral Judgments in Early Childhood and Beyond

Kohlberg's stage formulation, in which young children's moral judgments are based on obedience and sanctions, was derived from responses to complex situations in which competing and conflicting issues are depicted. As an example, the often-cited situation of a man who must decide whether to steal an overpriced drug that might save his wife's life includes considerations of the value of life, property rights, violating the law, interpersonal obligations, and personal responsibilities to each of these. In that sense, Kohlberg was attempting to study judgments in contexts. He constructed hypothetical situations in which the use of readily conceived values (e.g., it is wrong to steal; it is wrong to allow someone to die) would be complicated by situational circumstances (e.g., if you do not steal, you sacrifice a life; if you try to save a life, you violate another's property rights). These situations, however, presented multifaceted problems requiring children to weigh and coordinate competing moral considerations and nonmoral considerations (Turiel, 1978a, 1978b, 1983a, in press-a). The complexity of the judgments required by those situations led to the appearance that young children's moral judgments are contingent on sanctions, are not based on understandings of morality as generalizable, and it is not until after progressing to the fourth stage (usually not until at least adolescence) that morality is distinguished from nonmoral issues (Turiel & Davidson, 1986). Research into several aspects of moral judgments indicates that starting at a young age children make moral judgments that are not based on extrinsic features like obedience and sanctions. These include judgments about distributive justice, social justice in institutional settings, and prosocial actions.

Concepts of Distributive Justice and Fairness of Social Practices

In accord with long-standing presumptions among philosophers (e.g., Aristotle, 1947; Mill, 1863/1963; Rawls, 1971), Damon (1988, p. 31) has placed issues of distributive justice at the forefront of moral concerns. His research on children's concepts of sharing and distribution revealed a developmental progression of moral judgments (Damon, 1975, 1977, 1980, 1988), with indications that very young children are somewhat attuned to sharing. In their 2nd year, children take turns in playing with objects and show awareness that food or candy can be divided. Information regarding how children 4 to 5 years of age and older conceptualize sharing comes from research on children's judgments about hypothetical and real-life situations entailing the distribution of

goods (Damon, 1977, 1980). For example, in one situation, children in a class that made paintings to sell at a school fair must decide how to distribute the proceeds. Children were asked to respond to examples of ways of distributing the money (e.g., on the basis of merit, need, equality, and sex of the children) and to give their ideas on how the money should be distributed. The children were presented with examples of ways of distribution so as to elicit reactions to three categories considered basic in the literature on moral philosophy: equality, merit, and benevolence.

It was found that children's thinking about distributive justice progresses through four levels encompassing equality, merit, and benevolence (though not at the first level). At the first level, concepts of distribution initially are tied to the child's own desires and perspectives. After these initial judgments, children begin to bring in external criteria (such as size or ability). Although these external features ultimately are used to justify a person's desires and goals, this way of thinking leads to other-oriented concepts based on equality, merit, and benevolence. Elementary school-aged children, at the next level, base their judgments on equality; everyone should be given the same amount and receive the same treatment, regardless of merit or need. Next comes a shift to considerations of merit and reciprocity; distribution is based on the need to acknowledge good deeds, hard work, or personal attributes like intelligence. The next shift includes judgments that take benevolence into account, with greater awareness of competing claims and an understanding of the need for compromises to resolve claims in a fair manner. Therefore, by the ages of 10 or 11 years, children take into account merit (hard work, talent), advantages and disadvantages, and other factors (e.g., investment, inheritance).

This developmental sequence was supported by longitudinal findings (see Damon, 1977, 1980). Furthermore, similar patterns of judgment were obtained in studies of behavioral situations in experimental contexts (Gerson & Damon, 1978). Judgments on the "real-life" situations (elicited individually and in group discussions) were highly correlated with judgments on the hypothetical situations, and the same age trends were evidenced. It was also found, however, that personal concerns were coordinated with judgments about distribution to a greater extent in the real-life than the hypothetical situations. For example, children who showed an understanding of merit as a basis for fairness were most likely to apply that understanding when they were themselves in a meritorious position than when they were not. In ways consistent with these findings, Blasi (1993) proposed that an integration of concepts of self and identity contributes to how individuals act on their moral judgments.

An age-related sequence generally corresponding to the levels of concepts of distributive justice has been observed by Thorkildsen (1989a, 1989b, 1991) in children's judgments about the fairness of classroom practices pertaining to "educational goods" (e.g., ways of fostering learning, contests, and testing situations). In one study (Thorkildsen, 1989a), children and adolescents judged the fairness of several different teaching practices as to how faster workers would proceed, relative to slower workers, in a class assignment (e.g., after finishing, faster workers tutor slower ones; faster workers move on to other learning experiences). It was found that younger children focus on equality and older ones on equity. In the focus on equality, there are also shifts with age in the goods considered relevant. The youngest children judged as fair attainment of an equality of rewards, whereas somewhat older children consider as fair those practices that result in equality in schoolwork completed. This is followed by an emphasis on learning as the relevant good where practices that foster equality in learning are judged as fair. Finally, equity in learning is judged as the basis for fairness; it is fair that those capable of learning more than others do so.

Thorkildsen, in other research (1989b), has linked judgments of fair practices to individuals' situational definitions. What is considered a fair classroom practice in the context of a learning activity differed from what is considered fair in a testing situation (e.g., helping slower workers to learn was judged as more fair than helping them on a test). These findings indicate that children coordinate their understandings of the goals of events (e.g., to learn or to demonstrate what one knows), participants' perspectives on those events, and what would constitute a breach of just expectations. Thorkildsen (1989b, 1991) interprets these results as showing that concepts of justice vary in accord with "spheres" of activities (e.g., justice is one thing in economics, another in the family).

Prosocial Moral Judgments

Children's judgments about sharing or distribution pertain to actions beneficial to others and possibly entail sacrifice of self-interests. These are not the only types of positive social actions experienced by children. The term *prosocial* moral reasoning has been used (Eisenberg-Berg, 1979) with reference to judgments about positive social actions (e.g., helping, giving) serving to benefit others in contexts in which a person's actions are not based on rules, laws, or the dictates of authorities. Children were presented with hypothetical situations posing conflicts between the needs and desires of different actors and questioned about whether it would be right to help, give, or share with others at the expense of their own goals (Eisenberg-Berg, 1979). One situation depicted people faced with deciding whether to help feed those of another town who had lost their food in a flood; doing so would present a hardship to them. Other situations included donating blood, helping another who is being mugged or bullied, and helping physically disabled children.

A sequence of five age-related levels in judgments about prosocial actions were identified—a sequence proposed to reflect developmental advances in "capabilities for complex perspective taking and for understanding abstract concepts" (Eisenberg, Miller, Shell, McNalley, & Shea, 1991, p. 849). It was also proposed that the levels do not constitute hierarchical, integrated structures, and that the sequence is not entirely invariant nor necessarily universal (i.e., Eisenberg indicates that some aspects of the levels likely are invariant due to developmental changes in perspective-taking skills and abstract reasoning and that the early levels are more likely to be universal than later ones; Eisenberg, 1986). This implies that an individual's reasoning can be spread over the different types and that the sequence may vary by situations and life circumstances. At the first level, judgments are based on a "hedonistic," self-focused orientation (personal gain is linked to reciprocity with others, based in identification and relationship with another, or liking for the other), whereas at the next level there is an orientation to the needs of others. This is followed by judgments based on stereotypes of good or bad persons, along with concerns with the approval or disapproval of others. The fourth level is characterized by a self-reflective and empathetic orientation, including sympathetic concern and caring for others, and taking the perspective of others. At the fifth level, there is an internalization of affect linked to self-respect and an internalization of laws, norms, duties, and responsibilities, as well as abstract types of reasoning about society, rights, justice, and equality.

A series of longitudinal assessments were conducted following children from preschool to ages 19 to 20 years (Eisenberg, Carlo, Murphy, & Van Court, 1995; Eisenberg, Lennon, & Roth, 1983; Eisenberg et al., 1987, 1991; Eisenberg-Berg & Roth, 1980; Valiente et al., 2003). The longitudinal findings yielded a heterogeneous pattern of changes in prosocial judgments. In broad terms, there was advance on the levels with increasing age and decreased use of the lowest levels. However, along with increased use of the higher levels with age, there were renewed uses of aspects of lower levels. Hedonistic reasoning decreased in mid-adolescence, but in late adolescence, along with increases in self-reflection and empathy, there was some increase in hedonistic reasoning (i.e., in situations where costs of helping were high). The patterns obtained in the longitudinal studies indicate, again, an interaction of different ways of thinking with situational contexts, as do studies in Brazil (Carlo, Koller, Eisenberg, DaSilva, & Frolich, 1996) and on relations of prosocial reasoning to emotions (Miller, Eisenberg, Fabes, & Shell, 1996; for further discussion of this extensive body of research, see Eisenberg, Fabes, & Spinard, Chapter 11, this *Handbook,* this volume).

DOMAIN SPECIFICITY: EMPHASIZING DISTINCTIONS IN JUDGMENTS

Concepts of welfare and justice emerge as central in the development of morality across the diversity of theoretical approaches. Several theorists pursued hypotheses regarding other issues, but their research findings have pointed to welfare and justice as ubiquitous components of moral judgments. Gilligan's (1982) initial emphasis on the division of gender more or less along a care or justice orientation has been largely transformed into the proposition that the two orientations coexist in most individuals, including a substantive concern with justice on the part of females. The proposition that cultures divide more or less on the basis of an orientation to the individual as an autonomous agent with rights or an orientation to the duties of the social order has also been transformed. The research by Miller and her colleagues consistently demonstrated that Indians maintain concepts of justice and welfare (in this regard, little difference was obtained between cultures).

Philosophers, dating back to the formulations of Aristotle, have considered concepts of justice and welfare

central to morality. Aristotle, like many philosophers after him (e.g., Dworkin, 1977; Gewirth, 1978, 1982; Habermas, 1990b; Rawls, 1971), considered justice as "other-regarding," impartial, and as characterized by universality (see Helwig, Turiel, & Nucci, 1996, for further discussion). As already indicated, Piaget's research was consistent with moral epistemologies of this type. However, Piaget proposed that understandings of welfare, justice, and rights did not emerge until after a period in which right and wrong are judged by the word of authorities and the necessity of adhering to their rules. Such "unilateral respect," according to Piaget, reflected young children's heteronomous thinking in which undifferentiated concepts of authority are based on adults' size, power, and knowledge. In this way of thinking, justice is subordinated to obeying rules and authority: "if distributive justice is brought into conflict with adult authority, the youngest subjects will believe authority right and justice wrong" (Piaget, 1932, p. 304). However, several studies conducted in the United States (Braine, Pomerantz, Lorber, & Krantz, 1991; Damon, 1977; Laupa, 1991, 1994; Laupa & Turiel, 1986, 1993; Tisak, 1986) and Korea (Kim, 1998; Kim & Turiel, 1996) have yielded a different portrayal of young children's understandings of authority relations and moral judgments (see Helwig, in press; Turiel & Smetana, 1998, for a discussion of problems in Piaget's propositions regarding young children's moral thinking).

These studies have shown that young children, in evaluating commands by either adults or peers in positions of authority, account for the type of act commanded and the boundaries of the authority's jurisdiction in a social context. Damon (1977) found that young children do not accept the legitimacy of a parent's directive to engage in acts judged to violate moral injunctions such as directives to steal or cause another harm. Other studies (Kim, 1998; Kim & Turiel, 1996; Laupa, 1991, 1994; Laupa & Turiel, 1986, 1993) examined how children account for the type of act commanded and the attributes of persons giving commands (i.e., adult or peer, social position in a school, and attributes like possessing knowledge about rules or an event). With acts entailing theft or physical harm to persons, young children (4 to 6 years) give priority to the act itself rather than the status of the person as in a position of authority. For example, whether they hold positions of authority, commands from peers or adults that children stop fighting were judged as legitimate. Moreover, commands from peers (with or without positions of authority in a school) that children stop fighting were judged as more legitimate than a conflicting command from an adult authority (e.g., a teacher) that children be allowed to continue fighting. By contrast, children do give priority to adult authority over children or other adults who are not in positions of authority for acts like turn-taking and interpretations of game rules.

Children's judgments are not based on respect or reverence for adult authority but on an act's harmful consequences to persons (for a more general discussion of concepts of authority, see Laupa, Turiel, & Cowan, 1995). Children's judgments about harmful consequences emerge early in life along with emotions of sympathy, empathy, and respect (Baldwin, 1896; Piaget, 1932; Turiel, in press-a); at young ages children go well beyond social impulses and the habitual or reflexive, attempting to understand emotions, other persons, the self, and interrelationships (Arsenio, 1988; Arsenio & Lemerise, 2004; Nucci, 1981; Nunner-Winkler & Sodian, 1988; Turiel, 1983a, in press-b). A great deal of research has demonstrated that young children make moral judgments about harm, welfare, justice, and rights, which are different from their judgments about other social domains.

Domains of Social Judgment

Distinguishing morality from other domains presupposes that individuals think about social relationships, emotions, social practices, and social order. It presupposes that thinking about morality has features distinctive from thinking about other aspects of the social world (hence the idea of domain specificity). It also presupposes that individuals' judgments about the social world include domains of importance, which need to be distinguished from morality. Individuals form judgments in the "personal" domain that pertain to actions considered outside the jurisdiction of moral concern or social regulation and legitimately in the jurisdiction of personal choice (Nucci, 1996, 2001; Nucci & Lee, 1993). Individuals also form judgments about social systems, social organization, and the conventions that further the coordination of social interactions in social systems. As summarized in Turiel et al. (1987):

> Conventions are part of constitutive systems and are shared behaviors (uniformities, rules) whose meanings are defined by the constituted system in which they are embedded. Adherence to conventional acts is contingent on

the force obtained from socially constructed and institutionally embedded meanings. Conventions are thus context-dependent and their content may vary by socially constructed meanings. (pp. 169–170)

Morality, too, applies to social systems, but the contrast with convention is that it is not constitutive or defined by existing social arrangements. In this perspective on morality, prescriptions are characterized as obligatory, generalizable, and impersonal to the extent that they stem from concepts of welfare, justice, and rights (Turiel et al., 1987). This type of definition of morality is, in part, derived from criteria given in philosophical analyses where concepts of welfare, justice, and rights are not seen as solely determined by consensus, agreement, or received wisdom. In his *Nichomachean Ethics,* Aristotle drew a distinction of this type, although he couched it as two forms of justice:

> There are two forms of justice, the natural and the conventional. It is natural when it has the same validity everywhere and is unaffected by any view we may take of the justice of it. It is conventional when there is no original reason why it should take one form rather than another and the rule it imposes is reached by agreement after which it holds good. Some philosophers are of the opinion that justice is conventional in all its branches, arguing that a law of nature admits no variation and operates in exactly the same way everywhere—thus fire burns here and in Persia—while rules of justice keep changing before our eyes. It is not obvious what rules of justice are natural and what are legal and conventional, in cases where variation is possible. Yet it remains true that there is such a thing as natural, as well as conventional, justice. (as cited in Winch, 1972, p. 50)

Although Aristotle considered other aspects of morality, including happiness and the good life, which differed from the approaches of philosophers like Dworkin (1977), Gewirth (1978), Habermas (1990a, 1990b), and Rawls (1971), there is overlap among all of them in the propositions that justice is universal (it has the same validity everywhere), it is not legitimated by agreement (as opposed to convention), and it is impartial (not based on personal preference or individual inclinations).

These features of morality are not solely the products of philosophical conceptions but apply also to laypersons' ways of thinking. As noted earlier, children and adolescents in India make judgments about welfare and justice that differ from their judgments about social convention (Bersoff & Miller, 1993; Madden, 1992;

Miller & Bersoff, 1992). Similar findings have been obtained in several other non-Western cultures, including Korea (Song, Smetana, & Kim, 1987), Hong Kong (Yau & Smetana, 2003), Indonesia (Carey & Ford, 1983), Nigeria (Hollos, Leis, & Turiel, 1986), Zambia (Zimba, 1987), Brazil (Nucci, Camino, & Milnitsky-Sapiro, 1996), and Colombia (Ardila-Rey & Killen, 2001). A greater number of studies have evidenced that domain distinctions are made by children and adolescents in Western cultures. Well over 100 studies have examined and supported the validity of the domain distinctions (for comprehensive reviews, see Helwig, Tisak, & Turiel, 1990; Killen, McGlothlin, & Lee-Kim, 2002; Nucci, 2001; Smetana, 1995b, 2006; Tisak, 1995; Turiel, 2002).

One direction of early research on domains was to examine how children make judgments about moral, conventional, and personal issues (e.g., Davidson, Turiel, & Black, 1983; Nucci, 1981; Smetana, 1981; Tisak, 1986; Tisak & Tisak, 1990; Tisak & Turiel, 1984, 1988; Turiel, 1978b, 1983a; Weston & Turiel, 1980). Children were typically presented with a series of social acts or transgressions classified in accord with the distinctions among the domains. Thus, moral actions pertained to physical harm (e.g., hitting others or pushing them down), psychological harm (e.g., teasing, name-calling, or hurting feelings), and fairness or justice (e.g., failing to share, stealing, or destroying others' property). These acts were depicted as intentional and as resulting in negative consequences to others (a few studies also included prosocial actions—Kahn, 1992; Smetana, Bridgeman, & Turiel, 1983). Recent research has also examined in more detail issues of psychological harm (Helwig, Hildebrandt, & Turiel, 1995; Helwig, Zelazo, & Wilson, 2001) and fairness with regard to social exclusion (Killen, Lee-Kim, McGlothlin, & Stangor, 2002; McGlothlin, Killen, & Edmonds, 2005). By contrast, conventional issues pertained to uniformities or regulations serving functions of social coordination (e.g., pertaining to modes of dress, forms of address, table manners, or forms of greeting). Actions that do not entail inflicting harm or violating fairness or rights and that are not regulated formally or informally are consistent with the definition of the personal domain (these issues, in Western culture, include choices of friends, the content of personal correspondence, and recreational activities).

Two dimensions, in particular, have been examined. One pertains to the criteria by which thinking in do-

mains is identified (referred to as *criterion judgments*); the second pertains to the ways individuals reason about courses of action (referred to as *justifications*). Assessments of criterion judgments have included questions as to whether the actions would be right or wrong in the absence of a rule or law, if the act would be all right if permitted by a person in authority (e.g., a teacher in a school context), whether an act would be all right if there were general agreement as to its acceptability, and whether the act would be all right if it were accepted in another group or culture. These studies consistently show that children and adolescents judge that moral issues are obligatory; that they are not contingent on authority dictates, rules or consensus (e.g., that the acts would be wrong even if no rule or law exists about it); or on accepted practices in a group or culture (e.g., the act is wrong even if it were an acceptable practice in another culture). Judgments about moral issues, based on these criteria, are structured by concepts of welfare, justice, and rights. Justifications for these judgments entail preventing harm and promoting welfare, fairness, and rights (Turiel, 1983a, 2002).

However, all social actions and regulations are not judged in these ways. Conventional issues are conceptualized as linked to existing social arrangements and contingent on rules, authority, and existing social or cultural practices. Justifications for judgments about conventional issues are based on understandings of social organization, including the role of authority, custom, and social coordination. Even when conventional transgressions are deemed very important, children still judge them by conventional criteria and justifications (Tisak & Turiel, 1988). Furthermore, nonmoral actions that are not part of the conventionally regulated system are judged to be part of the realm of personal jurisdiction, which defines the bounds of individual authority and establishes distinctions between the self and group (Nucci, 1996, 2001).

The research has focused more on the distinctions among moral, conventional, and personal judgments, as well as ways the domains are manifested in varying aspects of social interactions, and much less on changes in the domains. However, the findings on domain distinctions have far-reaching developmental implications. Because the domains are differentiated at fairly early ages and continue to be so into adulthood, development is not adequately characterized as entailing differentiations between domains. In addition, the domains provide the context for the study of developmental transformations. At least two types of analyses need to be drawn to better understand developmental changes. One would entail analyses of changes in judgments within domains and the other analyses of how the different domains are coordinated.

Research has been done on levels of thinking within the conventional domain (Turiel, 1983a) and the personal domain (Nucci, 2001). Thus far, analyses of changes in thinking within the moral domain are limited. Levels of thinking about distributive justice identified by Damon (1977, 1980) have already been discussed. Other research indicates that young children's moral judgments are grounded in concepts of physical harm and welfare and that older children form greater understandings of psychological harm, fairness, justice, and equal treatment (Davidson et al., 1983; Kahn, 1992; Turiel & Smetana, 1998). In early adolescence, there is also a greater concern with equity as part of fair treatment (Damon, 1977) and efforts to coordinate the fairness of equality and equity. (See Nucci, 2001, chap. 4, for a more extensive discussion of ways of characterizing developmental transformations in the moral domain.)

The research on domains shows that individuals' social judgments are multifaceted, including understandings of right and wrong based on concerns with welfare, justice, and rights that are not simply based on acceptance of societal values, along with understandings of the conventional system of social regulation and coordination judged as relative and context-specific. Starting in early childhood, differentiations are made among moral, conventional, and personal concepts whose origins appear to be based in early social experiences (for more detailed discussions of methods, types of studies, and numbers of studies documenting domain distinctions in criterion judgments and justifications, see Helwig et al., 1990; Smetana, 1995b; Tisak, 1995; Turiel, 1983a).

Several studies were conducted with young children. In one type of study, criterion judgments were assessed among children ranging from about 2 years to about 5 years (Crane & Tisak, 1995a; Nucci & Turiel, 1978; Siegal & Storey, 1985; Smetana, 1981, 1985; Smetana & Braeges, 1990; Smetana, Schlagman, & Adams, 1993; Smetana et al., 1999; Tisak, 1993; Yau & Smetana, 2003). These studies show that a distinction between moral and conventional transgressions becomes more consistent and focused by about the ages of 4 or 5 years. Whereas 2-year-olds do not distinguish the domains,

during their 3rd year children judge moral transgressions to be generally wrong to a greater extent than conventional transgressions. By the end of the 3rd year, children also judge moral transgressions independently of rules or authority (Smetana, 1995b; Smetana & Braeges, 1990). Although 6- or 7-year-old children generally make the distinction on several dimensions, it has been found that they apply it readily to familiar but not unfamiliar issues (Davidson et al., 1983). By the ages of 9 or 10 years, children apply the distinction to both familiar and unfamiliar issues.

Social Judgments and Social Experiences

Just as children's judgments are multifaceted, their social experiences are varied. Some of those variations have already been considered—experiences with parents, siblings, and peers. Children also experience the substance of people's (adults' or children's) reactions to the events around them, including emotional responses to social interactions. An important part of all this is communications among persons, and as already considered, how explicit communications (induction or explanations) may be more effective than implicit communications between parent and child. Among young children's experiences are interactions that differ in the context of dealing with moral, conventional, or personal issues. A series of observational studies in schools, playgrounds, and homes (ages ranging from 2 and 3 years to late childhood) has shown that communications between adults and children, as well as other types of social interactions, are not uniform (Nucci & Nucci, 1982a, 1982b; Nucci & Turiel, 1978; Nucci, Turiel, & Encarnacion-Gawrych, 1983; Nucci & Weber, 1995; Smetana, 1984, 1989b; Tisak, Nucci, Baskind, & Lampling, 1991).

To summarize the findings, children's experiences around moral transgressions (e.g., when one child hits another, a failure to share, or taking another's objects) usually entail communications about the effects of acts on others, the welfare or expectations of others, and attention to the perspectives and needs of others. At an early age, children respond to moral transgressions and focus on the consequences of actions, the pain and injuries experienced, and emotions felt. The observational studies generally show that young children do not respond to conventional transgressions to the extent they respond to moral transgressions. However, adults' responses to conventional transgressions focus on issues of disorder, rule maintenance, authority, and more generally on social organization.

Much more than exposure to directives about rules, standards, or norms is involved in children's social experiences. At the least, social interactions and social communications differ in accord with domains. Furthermore, the distinction between morality and social conventions applies to situations actually experienced (Smetana et al., 1999; Turiel, 2002). The most extensive study showing that this is the case was conducted in the context of social interactions in elementary and junior high schools, where observations were made in classrooms, periods of recess, during lunch, and during transitions from one activity to another (reported in Turiel, 2002, chap. 6). The detailed recording of observations included events or incidents entailing moral or conventional issues and events that involved combinations of the two domains.

The majority of observed events involved transgressions (e.g., around physical harm, issues of fairness, and psychological harm), but some also involved efforts at preventing moral or conventional transgressions. As in prior observational studies, social interactions and communications were, in important respects, different for the moral and conventional events. In reaction to moral events, participants responded with statements about the injurious effects on others, the unfairness of actions, and at times with physical or verbal retaliation. By contrast, reactions to the conventional events focused on rules, sanctions, and commands to refrain from the acts. In this research, unlike most of the prior studies, participants' judgments about the events were assessed shortly after the events had occurred. For the most part, participants negatively evaluated the moral and conventional transgressions and accepted as valid the rules prohibiting the actions. Nevertheless, judgments about the actual moral events differed from judgments about the actual conventional events in ways consistent with previous findings in studies conducted in nonbehavioral contexts. Acts in the moral domain, in contrast with acts in the conventional domain, were judged independently of rules, institutional context, or authority dictates. As examples, generally it was judged that moral acts should be regulated, and that moral acts would be wrong even if a rule did not exist in the school or in a school in another city. It was judged that conventional acts were acceptable if rules did not exist. It was also found that transgressions in the moral domain, in contrast with conventional transgressions, would be wrong even if the teacher dictates that they are acceptable. In turn, justifications for judgments about moral events were mainly based on welfare and justice, whereas for conventional events, justifications were mainly based on considerations of social organization, rules, authority, and tradition. Moreover, these participants made similar judgments and justifications when responding to situations put to them in hypothetical terms.

Social Judgments and Family Interactions

Differences among the domains of social judgment also have a bearing on social interactions in families. In addition to moral and conventional issues, the domain of personal jurisdiction is a salient aspect of social interactions across different age periods. As shown in a study (Nucci & Weber, 1995) of social interactions in the home between children (3 to 4 years of age) and mothers, children are given a fair amount of freedom and discretion with regard to aspects of behavior revolving around personal issues. Mothers allow their children choices in activities, show a willingness to negotiate, and accept challenges from them. Other studies have shown that mothers in the United States (Nucci & Smetana, 1996) and Japan (Yamada, 2004) believe that there are areas of personal jurisdiction to be granted to young children (e.g., clothes, recreational activities, or choices of playmates). American and Japanese mothers also believe that control should be exercised over children's activities that have moral implications, that involve social conventions, and that might be unsafe (see also Killen & Smetana, 1999, on judgments of teachers in the United States). The mothers reported that conflicts occurred with their children over issues of safety and prudence. In the observational studies, as well as the studies of mothers' beliefs, it was found that most allow choice on certain activities, but interact differently with their children over moral, social-conventional, and prudential issues, often placing restrictions on them. Therefore, the discretion mothers allow in the personal domain does not simply reflect a general permissive orientation.

The observational study by Nucci and Weber (1995), along with the research by Dunn and her colleagues (e.g., Dunn & Munn, 1987), show that relationships between parents and children, early on, include conflict and harmony, as well as domain differences in the extent to which parents are directive. This pattern of heterogeneity of social relationships is not, by any means, restricted to early childhood. It is generally accepted that conflicts occur between parents and adolescents (Collins & Laursen, 1992; Smetana, 1995a). Adolescence is a period in which parents have multiple goals for their children and in which personal decisions become more salient. The ways parents and adolescents think about moral, social-conventional, and personal issues in family interactions have been part of an extensive program of research by Smetana and her colleagues (see Smetana, 1995b, 1997, 2002, for reviews). This body of work has included European American and African American working-class and middle-class families and working-class families in Hong Kong. The studies included divorced and two-parent families.

These studies consistently showed that morality is judged to be legitimately regulated and enforced by parents (Smetana, 1988, 1995a, 2000, 2002; Smetana & Daddis, 2002). There is acceptance of parental authority over moral issues by adolescents of varying ages and by their parents in nondivorced and divorced families (Smetana, 1988, 1993, 2000; Smetana & Asquith, 1994; Smetana, Yau, Restrepo, & Braeges, 1991), and with regard to both hypothetical and actual conflicts (Smetana, 1989a; Smetana, Braeges, & Yau, 1991). Smetana (1995a) reports that moral issues are not a frequent source of conflict between parents and adolescents. Adolescents also accept parental regulation over conventions, so that there is a good deal of agreement on those issues as well (Smetana, 1988, 2000; Smetana & Asquith, 1994; Tisak, 1986). Nevertheless, there is greater acceptance on the part of adolescents of parental authority over moral than conventional issues. It is issues in the personal domain, as well as those entailing a combination of personal and conventional considerations, which produce disagreements and conflicts (Smetana, 1988, 1993; Smetana & Asquith, 1994). As with younger children, adolescents identify issues they consider part of personal jurisdiction (some of the issues examined in these studies include spending decisions, appearances, and friendship preferences). European American parents tend to believe that they should have authority to control these activities (judging the activities as part of social convention), whereas adolescents believe that the activities are not legitimately regulated and are part of the realm of personal choice. Moreover, from early to late adolescence, there is an increase in judgments (by both parents and adolescents) that parents do not have authority over personal issues (Smetana, 1988; Smetana & Asquith, 1994). Another type of disagreement occurs when parents judge a set of activities to be part of the personal realm but believe that their child is not old enough to make those choices. Parents accept that the acts can be freely chosen by older people and by their child at an older age. Conflicts occur when adolescents maintain that they should be free to engage in the activities (especially actions involving risks, such as smoking, drinking, and sex). An even sharper sort of disagreement occurs over issues combining conventional and personal considerations (e.g., disputes over order in an adolescent's room because it can be seen as both personal and shared space in the home; see Smetana, 1995a). Typically, clashes between adolescents and parents actually entail different interpretations of the issues. Parents focus on components pertaining to conventional regulations, whereas adolescents focus on personal components.

These patterns of findings hold for African American families, with some differences. As one example, parents in African American families were more likely than European American families to insist on some degree of involvement in the decisions of adolescents as they grew older (Smetana, 2000; Smetana & Gaines, 1999). There also appears to be more concern among the middle-class African American parents with pragmatic and prudential issues (and less with conventional issues). More generally, African American parents are more restrictive of adolescents' freedoms of choices over personal issues and issues that involve conventional and personal matters. Nevertheless, African American adolescents do assert their personal choices and oppose parents. According to Smetana (2006, p. 140), the greater restrictions imposed by African American parents are linked "to their concerns for their children's well-being in an environment where racism and prejudice remain pervasive and where too-early autonomy may carry substantial risks for their children's safety."

The research by Smetana and her colleagues provides evidence that synchrony does not always exist in the ways parents and their children interpret and evaluate social events. Although parents and children alike identify the different domains of judgment, they differ regarding the legitimacy of parental authority over some of the issues. They also differ in their interpretations of events with mixtures of personal and conventional considerations. Adolescents agree with parents in the ways they judge moral events and attribute legitimacy to parental authority. However, children and adolescents do not accept the legitimacy of parental authority with regard to parental directives to engage in acts considered morally wrong (Laupa et al., 1995).

Emotional Attributions and Social Judgments

Observational studies also show that conflicts among siblings usually occur over morally relevant issues, such as possessions, rights, physical harm, and unkindness (Dunn & Munn, 1987). These interactions include feedback from siblings, which reveal negative reactions and feelings, as well as communications, especially from parents, about reasons as to why acts are wrong (Smetana, 1995a). The observational studies suggest that the emotions surrounding moral transgressions may differ from those around conventional transgressions and that social events entail emotional reactions (Arsenio & Lover, 1995). Studies by Arsenio and his colleagues (Arsenio, 1988; Arsenio & Fleiss, 1996; Arsenio & Ford, 1985) have demonstrated that children associate different types of emotional outcomes with different types of social events.

In one study (Arsenio, 1988), children from 5 to 12 years of age, who were presented with descriptions of several different types of acts, gave their assessments of the emotions that would be experienced by different participants (actors, recipients, and observers). For events entailing positive moral actions, such as helping and sharing, children generally attributed positive emotions, like happiness, to the actors. For conventional transgressions, children attributed neutral or somewhat negative emotions (sadness, anger) to the participants. In the case of moral transgressions entailing one person victimizing another (e.g., a child stealing a toy from another), children attributed very negative emotions to the recipients and observers, and attributed somewhat positive emotions to the perpetrators of the acts. The research also showed children could use information about emotional responses to infer the types of experiences that would lead to the emotional reactions. Children, who were presented with descriptions of the emotional reactions of actors and alternative events that may have elicited the emotions, associated different emotions to the different actions; older children were able to do this more accurately than younger ones.

Children's reasons for characters in the events experiencing the emotions attributed to them, too, varied by domain of event and role of participants (Arsenio & Fleiss, 1996). The negative emotions expected of victims of moral transgressions were thought to occur be-cause of the harm, loss, or injury resulting from the acts. For victimizers, however, it was thought that the material gains obtained by them would result in some feelings of happiness. With regard to conventional transgressions, it was thought that negative emotions would be felt by those in authority who tend not to want rules violated (also see Arsenio, Berlin, & O'Desky, 1989).

Thus, children differentiate among the emotions attributed to people in different roles in an event. In particular, they attribute different emotions to victims and those who do the victimizing. The youngest children assumed that those engaging in a transgression would feel positive emotions and the victims would feel negative emotions. The finding that positive emotions are attributed to victimizers is consistent with Nunner-Winkler and Sodian's (1988) finding that the younger children focused on the material outcomes for victimizers. Arsenio's research (e.g., Arsenio & Kramer, 1992) extends those findings by showing that attributions to victims and victimizers are very different, and that young children do not minimize the negative emotions that might be experienced by victims. Also, older children tended to attribute mixed emotions to victimizers, expecting that in addition to positive emotions for a desired outcome, there may be negative feelings due to the effects of their acts on others. Because even among the younger children, the moral transgressions were evaluated as wrong, it would appear that their attributions of positive emotional outcomes to victimizers do not determine their moral judgments about the acts. Instead, with regard to moral evaluations, the victims' reactions seem to be what is taken into account. It also appears that older children give priority to the victim in their moral judgments and understand that a victim's reactions can feed back on the victimizer and produce a mixture of positive and negative reactions (for more extensive discussion, including similar findings of a study conducted in Korea, see Arsenio & Lover, 1995).

Children's understandings of people's emotional reactions to moral and social transgressions bring to bear different realms of understanding. When young children state that a person who engages in a moral transgression feels happy and that the victim feels sad, it is likely that they are making psychological attributions. When older children state that a victimizer may experience a mixture of positive and negative emotions, they may also be making psychological attributions, with awareness that people can simultaneously experience more than one emotion. These interpretations are supported by a study with children (ages 5 to 8 years) from Portugal and Germany (Keller, Lourenco, Malti, & Saalbach, 2003). Assessments were made of children's judgments of right and wrong about acts of stealing and breaking a promise, attributions of emotions to the victimizers, and whether the victimizers should feel a certain way (e.g., happy). Many of the younger children, especially the ones from Portugal, thought that the victimizer would feel happy. Nevertheless, they judged the acts to be wrong and tended to say that it was wrong for the victimizer to feel happy. Older children made the same moral evaluations, but attributed negative emotions to the victimizer. These findings demonstrate that children make psychological attributions that may be less or more coordinated with their moral judgments.

Ambiguities, Uncertainties, and Deliberations

Despite the complexities in understandings of the psychological features of emotions, children do assume that victims of moral transgressions react negatively and they evaluate those transgressions as wrong using the previously mentioned criteria and justifications. The moral reasoning reflected in criterion judgments and justifications includes relatively complex components. Nevertheless, because young children (3- and 4-year-olds) make moral judgments about many situations, such as harming another person for reasons of self-interest or stealing another's property (situations referred to as "prototypical," see Turiel et al., 1987), in an unambiguous way and with certainty, it is said by some (e.g., Haidt, 2001) that their moral responses are easily derived and reflexive, and, in turn, that the judgments are intuitive or naturally given. As pointed out by Piaget (1932) many years ago, however, those presumptions ignore that 3- and 4-year-olds have experienced a fair amount of social interaction as infants and toddlers, and that they have already undergone some development. Piaget was responding to propositions put forth by Antipoff (H. Antipoff, Observations sur la compassion et le sens de la justice chez l'enfant, Archives de Psychologie, XXI, 1928), that a sense of justice involved "an innate and instinctive moral manifestation, which in order to develop really requires neither preliminary experience nor socialization amongst other children. . . . We have an inclusive affective perception, an elementary moral 'structure' which the child seems to possess very easily and which enables him to grasp simultaneously evil and its cause, innocence and guilt. We may say that

what we have here is an *affective perception of justice*" (quoted in Piaget, 1932, p. 228). Piaget noted that because Antipoff observed children who were between the ages of 3 and 9 years her research did not demonstrate innateness. By the age of 3, children would have experienced social interactions, including influences from adults. In addition, moral judgments give the appearance that they are readily derived and reflexive if we consider only their application once they have been constructed, and then only for judgments about relatively straightforward situations in the case of most children.

For some children, the application of their moral judgments to particular kinds of situations can be problematic. Astor (1994) investigated the reasoning of children with histories of violent actions, pursuing the propositions that they had formed moral judgments regarding harm and welfare but, nevertheless, would judge actions in response to various kinds of provocations differently from children who do not engage in violence. Children with or without histories of violent activities evaluated unprovoked acts of violence (e.g., a boy who is mad because he fell down hits his brother) as wrong, and justified their evaluations with moral reasons. Differences between the two groups emerged with regard to acts of violence after provocation (e.g., a boy hits his brother after being teased and called names by him). The group of children without a history of violence evaluated those acts as wrong on the grounds that physically harming another is worse than the provoking acts. By contrast, the group with a history of violence accepted the legitimacy of hitting in those situations on the grounds that it is fair retribution for an unjust action. For those children, therefore, the application of their moral judgments in situations perceived as entailing provocations differed from those who do not often engage in acts of violence (see Butterfield, 1995, for a historical and contemporary analysis of the role of provocation in individuals who have engaged in extremely violent acts).

Another difference from judgments about straightforward situations is seen in judgments about situations that include components from more than one domain (Helwig & Turiel, 2003; Smetana & Turiel, 2003; Turiel, 1989; Turiel & Davidson, 1986). In such situations, the application of moral and social judgments is not entirely straightforward, entailing ambiguities, uncertainties, contradictions, and a good deal of disagreement. Many situations, studied naturalistically (Kelman & Hamilton, 1989) and experimentally (Haney, Banks,

& Zimbardo, 1973; Milgram, 1974), pose conflicts between issues of harm and issues of authority, status, and social organization. Milgram's experiments on obedience to authority, which posed individuals with choices between avoiding harm and adhering to conventional authority-relations, have shown that moral and social decisions can entail uncertainties, emotional and cognitive conflicts, and belabored decision making (Turiel & Smetana, 1984).

Judgments about situations with salient features from more than one domain have been examined in several studies. A study by Killen (1990) presented children with both prototypical situations (e.g., one child hitting another) and "mixed-domain" situations (e.g., choosing between preventing harm or continuing a task to maintain a group activity). Whereas judgments about prototypical events were similar among children, there were differences as to whether children gave priority to the moral or nonmoral features in the mixed-domain situations. Moreover, decisions in the mixed situations involved consideration of the different components, with expressions of conflict (see also Smetana, 1985; Tisak & Tisak, 1990; Turiel, 1983a). It has also been found that older children are better able to coordinate varying components than younger children (Crane & Tisak, 1995b).

The coordination of different domains applies to evaluations and decisions about social inclusion and exclusion (Horn, 2003; Killen, Piscane, Lee-Kim, & Ardila-Rey, 2001; Killen & Stagnor, 2001; Killen, Lee-Kim, et al., 2002; Theimer, Killen, & Stagnor, 2001). Some studies, conducted with preschoolers, children, and adolescents, examined judgments about social exclusion and gender stereotypes (e.g., in doll play or truck play) and racial stereotypes (e.g., in a basketball team or in a math club). The studies examined judgments about straightforward exclusion; these were situations in which a child is excluded because of gender or race. The studies also examined contextualized situations that depicted additional social or group considerations: information was provided about children's past experiences with the activity (child fitting the stereotype has more experience) or their qualifications (equally qualified or the child fitting the stereotype is better qualified). These assessments were made with regard to exclusion in friendships, peer groups, and school contexts.

A central finding is that gender and racial exclusion were judged as wrong in straightforward situations. The judgments were based on moral reasons of fairness and equality. There was a greater tendency to accept exclusion in the contextualized situations. Moreover, these judg-

ments included reasons based on conventional expectations and the need to maintain the goals of a social group (e.g., perform well in a basketball game or math competition). The force of morality in children's thinking about stereotypes and exclusion was also evidenced by effective persuasion of moral reasons influencing changes toward greater inclusion. By contrast, conventional reasons were not effective in changing judgments to an acceptance of exclusion (Killen, Lee-Kim, et al., 2001).

Killen et al. (2002) found that at varying ages exclusion of girls or Black children is judged as wrong on moral grounds and that there are contextual variations in these judgments. For instance, exclusion in friendships was more acceptable than in the other situations. An intriguing finding is that older adolescents were more likely to accept exclusion in friendships and peer groups than younger adolescents.

Information, Assumptions about Reality, and Moral Decisions

The research discussed thus far indicates that there is a good deal of uniformity within and between cultures in the ways certain issues are morally evaluated. However, as is generally known and amply documented by many polls and surveys, sharp differences among people exist in positions taken on issues like abortion, homosexuality, and pornography (Smetana, 1982; Turiel et al., 1991). Research into the judgments of adolescents and adults also shows that individuals display inconsistencies and ambiguities. People differ in their judgments about these issues (and not about issues like killing or rape), in large measure, as a consequence of differences in assumptions about reality or aspects of nature. With regard to abortion, for example, differences were associated with assumptions about the origins of life, with those who assumed the fetus to be a life evaluating abortion as wrong. Those assumptions, however, contained ambiguities in thinking, such that evaluations about abortion were inconsistent across situations and patterns of judgment differed from those usually found with regard to prototypical moral issues (e.g., abortion is wrong but should not be legally restricted because it is a personal decision).

Assumptions of an informational kind about persons, psychological states, biology, and nature represent an additional component to be added to the mix in analyses of social decision making. Wainryb (1991, 1993) has shown that individuals may hold similar concepts about welfare, fairness, and rights but come to different decisions in situations where they apply different informational assumptions. An example is that assumptions about the effectiveness of parental punishment bears on evaluations of physical harm in the context of a parent disciplining a child, whereas, in other contexts, parents inflicting harm on children is commonly judged as unacceptable.

Possible variations in informational assumptions, especially those entailing assumptions about the natural and an afterlife, bear on cultural variations in moral decisions. It has been noted, not infrequently, that differences in such assumptions give the appearance of radical differences in moral concepts, when moral judgments or principles themselves may actually not vary (Asch, 1952; Duncker, 1939; Hatch, 1983). Asch (1952) pointed out that beliefs about an afterlife bear on cultural practices (such as the social practices listed by Benedict, 1934, as evidence of variability in cultural patterns). An example is the cultural practice of putting one's elderly parents to death because "there prevails the belief that people continue into the next world the same existence as in the present and that they maintain the same condition of health and vigor at the time of death" (Asch, 1952, p. 377). According to Asch, a concern with the welfare of one's parents underlies the practice. A similar view was proposed by Hatch (1983): "Judgments of value are always made against a background of existential beliefs and assumptions, consequently what appears to be a radical difference in values between societies may actually reflect different judgments of reality" (p. 67).

Most analyses of culture and morality, however, have not seriously considered the role of judgments of reality. Through consideration of such judgments the findings of Shweder et al. (1987) were reinterpreted by Turiel et al. (1987). In their comparative research of judgments about morality and convention in India and the United States, Shweder et al. presented individuals with some issues pertaining to matters like dress and eating (practices such as a son avoids eating chicken or getting a haircut the day after his father's death or a widow does not eat fish). These issues were supposedly conventional by U.S. standards, given their content, but treated as moral by Indians. Indians treat these as moral issues because of their assumptions about reality—especially about an after-life. As detailed elsewhere (Turiel et al., 1987), classifying acts solely on the basis of whether they involve matters like dress or food entails an overly literal interpretation of how to classify issues in domains (moral or otherwise) that fails to account for the intentions and goals of actors, the surrounding context of the actions, and informational assumptions. This literal interpretation would be akin to classifying any act that causes physical damage or pain to another person as a moral transgression. By that standard, a surgeon's thrust of the knife would be classified a moral transgression, as would the spanking of a child by a parent. Wainryb (1991) has shown that acts of hitting with the intent to harm are judged as morally wrong, whereas spanking is not judged as wrong because it is assumed that the actor's intent is to correct and guide a child's behavior and that he or she believes that spanking is effective.

For several "conventional" issues studied by Shweder et al. (1987), a different picture of their domain status emerges by considering the assumptions of reality surrounding the events. Those assumptions concern beliefs about an afterlife and actions on earth that can adversely affect unobservable entities such as souls and deceased ancestors. Using ethnographic material (presented by Shweder et al., 1987, and Shweder & Miller, 1985), further analyses of the issues were made by Turiel et al. (1987) to account for assumptions about reality. Consider some examples. The practice that a son not eat chicken the day after his father's death is connected to the belief that doing so would result in a failure of the father's soul to receive salvation (Shweder & Miller, 1985, p. 48). It is believed that if a widow were to eat fish regularly, it would cause her great suffering and offend her husband's spirit. If a menstruating woman were to enter the kitchen it would result in great misfortune for the family because the deceased ancestors would leave the household for several generations.

Because in these examples events on earth affect unobserved unearthly occurrences and beings, they illustrate how assumptions about an afterlife contextualize some issues to include potential harm. The cultural differences may thus reflect existential beliefs and not moral principles. The Turiel et al. (1987) reanalysis showed that many issues of this kind pertaining to dress, food, and the like resulted in different judgments between Indians and Americans. By contrast, issues that directly depicted consequences of harm or unfairness to people on earth were judged in the same ways by individuals in both cultures. These reanalyses are consistent with the findings of conventional judgments by Indians.

In the Shweder et al. (1987) American sample, "conventional" issues were more often judged by moral criteria than had been typically found in other studies. In part, this is because many of the issues pertained to practices that restrict the activities of one group and not another (usually restrictions on females and not males).

Americans were simply presented with a description of an act like "a widow eats fish two or three times a week" and asked to evaluate it. Other research with Americans (Vail & Turiel, 1995) has demonstrated that if children are given a little context regarding such practices, and if they are not couched in terms that can be perceived as discriminatory practices, the issues are judged differently. When American children were presented with the issues as cultural practices that apply to everyone (not just one group) they generally judged them by conventional criteria rather than moral criteria.

Informational assumptions also provide people with contexts for their acceptance and tolerance of beliefs that differ from their own. People take into account the informational assumptions held by others when evaluating their actions. For the most part, different moral beliefs are judged as wrong, in nonrelativistic ways, and are not treated with tolerance (Wainryb, 1993; Wainryb & Ford, 1998; Wainryb, Shaw, Langley, Cottam, & Lewis, 2004; Wainryb, Shaw, Laupa, & Smith, 2001). In contrast, beliefs about conventions, tastes of a personal nature, and psychological attributes are judged as acceptable and with tolerance. However, additional findings from these studies show that attitudes toward the beliefs of others are influenced by the informational assumptions held by others. For instance, beliefs with moral implications (e.g., it is alright for parents to hit children) were presented (i.e., for other individuals or in other cultures) as due to the view that such acts are all right or due to particular informational assumptions (e.g., that children who misbehave are possessed by evil sprits that can only be removed by beating the child). The pattern of findings is that such beliefs are judged more tolerantly when they are based on divergent informational assumptions, especially when there is agreement about the informational assumptions in a group or culture (Shaw & Wainryb, 1999; Wainryb et al., 2001). Therefore, informational assumptions and their implications for an actor's intentions contribute to the ways context of events are construed.

The Personal and the Social

Most of the research comparing moral and conventional judgments with judgments in the personal domain has been conducted in Western cultures. From the viewpoint of the proposition that cultures can be divided according to orientations to collectivism and individualism, it would be expected that concepts of personal agency and

jurisdiction are mainly part of Western individualism and not of non-Western collectivism. However, the findings from several studies (Ardila-Rey & Killen, 2001; Miller, Bersoff, & Harwood, 1990; Nucci et al., 1996; Yau & Smetana, 1996, 2003) in non-Western cultures showing that they distinguish areas of personal jurisdiction from moral and conventional regulations are consistent with fundamental propositions in the social theories and philosophical views of James (1890), Dewey (A. Ryan, 1995), and Habermas (1990b, 1993). Each of these writers argued that personal agency and individual freedom cannot be offset from collectivism or social solidarity. They held that the self and the social, individual growth and social engagement, and personhood and social solidarity are not opposing orientations restricted to particular societies.

The development of personal boundaries and their connections to moral development have been elaborated by several researchers (Helwig, 1995a; Nucci, 1996, 2001; Nucci & Lee, 1993; Nucci & Turiel, 2000; Turiel & Wainryb, 1994; Wainryb & Turiel, 1994). Beyond the identification of issues that individuals judge as part of personal jurisdiction, Nucci (2001) maintains that children attempt to establish boundaries between self and other, and that establishing such boundaries facilitates mutual respect and cooperation. Moreover, the process of coming to understand personal boundaries is social and includes interpersonal negotiations primarily around personal and not moral issues (Nucci & Weber, 1995). At a young age, children challenge parental authority to a greater extent in the personal than the moral realm. Interviews with Americans (Nucci & Smetana, 1996), Brazilians (Nucci et al., 1996), and Japanese (Yamada, 2004) further demonstrated that mothers believe children should be allowed discretion over certain activities to encourage a sense of autonomy and personal agency. (For a discussion of the psychological functions of the establishment of personal boundaries, see Nucci, 1996. For a discussion of the negative psychological consequences of over control of personal jurisdiction in U.S. and Japanese adolescents, see Hasebe, Nucci, & Nucci, 2004).

Along with conceptions of philosophers (e.g., Dworkin, 1977), Nucci sees necessary links between the development of a personal sphere and concepts of rights. Concepts of the agency of self and others constitute the locus of the application of freedoms and rights. Indeed, if concepts of personal agency did not develop because persons were defined mainly through connections with the group and embeddedness in the collectivity (as in, e.g., Markus & Kitayama, 1991; Shweder & Bourne, 1982), it would follow that moral concepts of rights and freedoms would not apply.

Although many philosophers have regarded rights as universally significant, little research was conducted on the development of concepts of rights until recently (Clémence, Doise, de Rosa, & Gonzales, 1995; Doise, Clémence, & Spini, 1996; Helwig, 1995a, 1995b, 1997, 1998; Ruck, Abromovitch, & Keating, 1998). Helwig's research examined the judgments of American and Canadian children, adolescents, and adults about freedoms of speech and religion and about a series of situations entailing conflicts between the freedoms and other moral considerations. In response to general questions (e.g., Should people be allowed to express their views or engage in their religious practices? Would it be right or wrong for the government to institute laws restricting the freedoms?), most endorsed the freedoms and judged them as moral rights independent of existing laws that are generalizable to other cultural contexts. They based these judgments on psychological needs (e.g., self-expression, identity, and autonomy), social utility, and democratic principles. Along with the general judgments, however, individuals accepted restrictions on the freedoms when in conflict with other moral considerations (i.e., physical harm, psychological harm, or equality of opportunity). At younger ages, however, there was more likelihood of acceptance of restrictions than at older ages.

In other studies, Helwig (1997, 1998) found that in late adolescence and early adulthood there are also distinctions drawn among contexts in which people in authority can legitimately restrict freedoms (e.g., parents can legitimately restrict children's practice of religion but school or governmental authorities cannot). It has also been found that children of about 6 years of age reason about civil liberties on the basis of needs for personal choices and individual expression, whereas by about 8 years of age they start to consider the societal and democratic aspects of rights (Helwig & Turiel, 2002; Neff & Helwig, 2002; see Helwig, 1998, 2006; Helwig & Kim, 1999, for discussion of changes in children's conceptions of government and democracy). The pattern of the application of rights by contexts is also found in Costa Rica, France, Italy, and Switzerland (Clémence et al., 1995; Doise et al., 1996).

The findings on rights, based on in-depth interviews, are consistent with findings of large-scale surveys of the attitudes of American adults toward civil liberties (McClosky & Brill, 1983; Stouffer, 1955). The surveys tapped the attitudes of large samples (in some cases over 3,000 adults) toward several freedoms (speech, press, assembly, religion privacy, dissent, and divergent lifestyles). When questions of freedoms and rights were put generally or in the abstract (e.g., a belief in freedom of speech for everyone) they were endorsed by large majorities of respondents. However, the surveys also tapped attitudes toward the freedoms in conflict with other moral considerations, such as when they may result in harm to others or may be detrimental to the general welfare. Also assessed were conflicts of freedoms with traditions, community standards, and the maintenance of social order. The results were striking for the ways majorities fail to uphold freedoms and rights in most of those situations. Most Americans do not endorse the very freedoms and rights highlighted in public discourse, evident in public documents (e.g., the United States Constitution and the Bill of Rights), and central to depictions of American culture as individualistic and perhaps overly oriented to rights (as maintained by Bellah et al., 1985; Etzioni, 1993).

The coexistence of concerns with the freedoms and rights of individuals and the welfare of the community supports the contentions of Dewey and Habermas that personal agency and social solidarity go together. Additional research, on the concepts of freedoms and rights of Druze Arabs living in northern Israel (Turiel & Wainryb, 1998), supports Habermas's (1993) view that the coexistence of personal agency and collectivism is not applicable "for Americans alone," and that it extends beyond those who are "heirs to the political thought of a Thomas Paine and a Thomas Jefferson" (p. 114).

The Druze community is tightly knit, living in large measure separately from the rest of the nation of Israel. They constitute a traditional hierarchical society, with strong sanctions for violations of societal norms—especially as applied to women because it is a patriarchal society (Turiel & Wainryb, 1994). Three types of freedoms were studied with adolescents and adults: speech, religion, and reproduction (i.e., freedom to bear the number of children desired). The Druze clearly judge, when put in general terms, that individuals should have noncontingent rights to each freedom.

Individuals were also presented with conflicts depicting freedoms producing physical or psychological harm or having negative effects on community interests. Conflict situations also depicted ways that in the family the exercise of the freedoms by a son, daughter, or wife was in contradiction with the desires and directives of father or husband. The findings from the conflict situations showed that the Druze also think that freedoms should be, in certain situations, subordinated to other concerns, such as when they could cause harm to others. Similarly, in some situations (but not all) it is thought that considerations of community interest should take precedence over the right to exercise the freedoms.

For the most part, however, freedoms and rights of sons, daughters, and wives were not subordinated to the authority of the father or husband. Particularly for religion and reproduction, most upheld the rights and negatively evaluated the father's or husband's efforts to restrict the freedoms. The Druze were more willing to allow restrictions on the freedoms of females (wives and daughters) than males (sons) and, thereby, granted greater authority to men over their wives and daughters.

Concepts of rights, democracy, and political organization appear to extend beyond the heirs of Paine and Jefferson to people in China (Helwig, Arnold, Tan, & Boyd, 2003a). The judgments of adolescents from rural and urban settings regarding democratic and authority-based decision making in peer groups, families, and schools again showed contextual variations. Adolescents understood and supported democratic decision making, with endorsements of children's autonomy and their right to participate in certain decisions. For instance, there was greater support for children's participation in family decisions than in those about a school's curriculum. Similarly, Chinese adolescents expressed preferences for democratic systems of majority rule over nondemocratic systems of meritocracy (Helwig, Arnold, Tan, & Boyd, 2003b). As in studies with Canadians, there was an increase with age in understandings of political participation, the will of the majority, and the protection of minorities.

CULTURE AND CONTEXT REVISITED

The research with the Druze and in China, along with the other research in non-Western cultures, indicates that concepts of rights, welfare, and justice are found across cultures. In the context of these similarities among cultures, however, there are also differences. In addition to differences in assumptions about reality,

there are differences in the degree of hierarchically based distinctions in relationships between males and females and those of different social castes and classes. Many analyses of culture have focused on differences between cultures on these dimensions, interpreting them in accord with the proposition that cultures form integrated patterns represented either by an individualistic or collectivistic orientation. The hierarchical distinctions in gender or castes are said to be connected with the role designations of persons, through which persons are submerged in the group.

It is not at all clear, however, that the presumption of coherent, integrated cultural patterns and associated consistencies in individuals' judgments and actions are in line with other formulations central to the propositions of those emphasizing culture. In particular, the idea of coherence and consistency conflicts with the call for pluralism, and with the core ideas of cultural psychology that the mind is context-dependent, domain-specific, and local. With regard to pluralism, those emphasizing culture often have voiced that there be acceptance of a variety of moral perspectives. Shweder and Haidt (1993) asserted that Gilligan "won the argument for pluralism" (p. 362) by augmenting the traditional views on justice with the care orientation. They also argue that Gilligan's proposition does not go far enough in the quest for pluralism because it does not account for further variations among cultures.

These kinds of arguments are contradictory because descriptions of cultural orientations actually frame most of the elements in Gilligan's formulation of justice as part of Western (or individualistic) morality and most of the elements of the care orientation as part of non-Western (or collectivistic) morality (see Miller & Bersoff, 1995). By describing cultures with integrated patterns of thought, a rather limited form of pluralism or heterogeneity is seen to be in differences between cultures while a unitary or homogeneous orientation (with a lack of pluralism) is imposed within cultures and for individuals. The evidence actually points in the other direction—that there is coexistence, not only within cultures but also for individuals, of care, interdependence, justice, and autonomy. As detailed earlier, the research assessing those dimensions through Gilligan's formulations has shown that care (or collectivistic) and justice (or individualistic) judgments vary by context for females and males. The evidence suggests that the types of contextual distinctions drawn by Gilligan between females' and males' life circumstances are too broad and require further distinctions within each context.

Those emphasizing culture also have maintained that general, "abstract," universal moral principles are inadequate because they fail to account for variations among cultures. However, by locating contextual variations at the cultural level little consideration is given to variations that may be associated with contextual differences within cultures. For a given culture, therefore, constructs like individualism and collectivism end up functioning as general, abstract orientations that apply across contexts and fail to account for domain specificity. Distinctions in judgments by domain mean that individuals have heterogeneous orientations in social thought.

The coexistence of domains stems from a process of development that is not restricted to circumscribed experiences characterized by the family or parental child-rearing practices, more narrowly, or by culture, more broadly. As shown by much of the research considered thus far, social experiences influencing development are varied (with parents, siblings, peers, or social institutions). Through reciprocal interactions, children are engaged in communications, negotiations, compromises, disputes, and conflicts. The research has also shown that the diversity of children's social interactions includes concerns with the desires, goals, and interests of persons (self and others), as well as with the welfare of others and the group.

Culture as Context or Context as Context?

Children's social interactions involve a dynamic interplay of personal goals and social goals, as well as interplay among different social goals. Reciprocity of social interactions means that individuals both participate in cultural practices and can stand apart from culture and take a critical approach to social practices. Typically, there are elements both of harmony and tension or conflict. Moreover, through the development of different domains of judgment, individuals deal with social situations from more than one perspective, taking into account varying features of situations and contexts.

The diversity in judgments of individuals includes domain specificity in people's thinking and contextual variations in the ways judgments are applied. As seen from the research on concepts of freedoms and rights, people in so-called individualistic cultures have multiple social orientations, including concerns with social duties, the collective community, and interdependence, as well as independence, rights, freedoms, and equality. People in so-called traditional, collectivistic cultures endorse traditions, status, and role distinctions, but they also endorse individual freedoms and rights even when in contradiction with status and hierarchy.

Another issue of importance to moral and social functioning that involves contextual variations in judgments and actions is that of honesty. Honesty is often regarded as one of those moral matters that once acquired by the individual will be and should be applied consistently. In some analyses, honesty is a virtue or trait of character that children must be taught to always follow (Bennett, 1993; K. Ryan, 1989; Wynne, 1986). In other perspectives, honesty is linked to the need to maintain trust in social relationships.

Most research has looked at whether children act honestly or in self-serving ways. Dishonest acts are taken to reflect deficiencies in character or the failure to internalize norms of truthfulness (Grinder, 1964; Hartshorne & May, 1928, 1929, 1930). Dishonest behavior can be self-serving and motivated for personal gain; however, issues of honesty are more complicated and are often weighed against other considerations so that there is much variability in the ways people act. For instance, honesty can be in conflict with desires to prevent harm to another. Some researchers who have recognized this type of conflict looked at so-called white lies—lies aimed at sparing the feelings of others (Lewis, 1993). There is only a little research on judgments about conflicts between honesty and preventing more serious harm. An example of how deception has been used to prevent harm is that during World War II many lied and engaged in elaborate deceptions to save people from Nazi concentration camps. No doubt, they gave greater priority to preventing harm and deaths than to honesty.

Recent research that has begun to address these issues shows that people systematically evaluate the consequences of telling the truth or engaging in deception in relation to furthering the welfare of persons, achieving justice, and promoting individual autonomy when it is perceived to be unfairly restricted. One study of this kind looked at, in hypothetical situations, how physicians evaluate deception of insurance companies when it is the only way to obtain approval for treatments or diagnostic procedures for medical conditions of different degrees of severity (Freeman, Rathore, Weinfurt, Schulman, & Sulmasy, 1999). In the two most severe conditions (life-threatening ones), the majority thought that the doctor was justified in engaging in deception. In other conditions, the percentages accepting deception were considerably lower, with the fewest (only 3%) judging that deception was legitimate for purposes of cosmetic surgery. Moreover, there is evidence that physicians actually do engage in deception of insurance companies (Wynia, Cummins, VanGeest, & Wilson, 2000).

Other research has shown a corresponding pattern of contextual differences in judgments of college undergraduates and adults about deception between husbands and wives (Turiel & Perkins, 2004). Participants were presented with several situations entailing deception. One depicted a spouse who tightly controls the family finances, and the other maintains a secret bank account. Other situations involved secretly seeing a friend disliked by the spouse, shopping for clothes, and attending meetings of a support group for a drinking problem (the meetings are kept secret because a spouse does not want the other to attend). These acts were depicted as situations where only a husband works outside the home, with a wife engaging in deception; and the reverse, where only a wife works, with a husband engaging in deception.

Most participants judged deception to be legitimate in some situations. The large majority judged deception by wife or husband acceptable to attend meetings of a support group for a drinking problem. Most also judged it acceptable for the wife to maintain a secret bank account, but fewer judged it acceptable for a husband to engage in such deception even though it is the wife who works and controls the finances. It seems that the more general structure of power in society is taken into account in making these decisions. Males are accorded greater power and control over females, and family relationships are frequently based on the type of injustice that grants greater privileges and entitlements to men over women (Hochschild, 1989; Nussbaum, 1999, 2000; Okin, 1989). Similar patterns were found for situations that involved friendships and shopping (but the differences between judgments about the activities of husbands and wives were not statistically significant).

Another study (Perkins, 2003; see also Turiel & Perkins, 2004) assessed judgments of adolescents who deceive parents or friends. The situations involved parents or peers telling an adolescent to act in ways that might be considered morally wrong (i.e., not to befriend another of a different race; to physically confront another who is teasing him or her); giving directives about

issues of personal choice (not to date someone the parents or peers do not like; not to join a club because they think it is a waste of time); and directives about personal issues with prudential or pragmatic considerations (completing homework; not riding a motorcycle).

Most of the adolescents judged it acceptable to deceive parents about the demands considered morally wrong, viewing it necessary to prevent injustice or harm. The majority also thought that deception was justified when parents interfered with personal choices but that deception was not justified with regard to the prudential matters on the grounds that it is legitimate for parents to concern themselves with the welfare of their children (most thought the restrictions were not legitimate in the case of the moral and personal matters). Fewer judged deception of peers acceptable than deception of parents for the morally relevant and personal issues. Although the adolescents thought that the restrictions directed by peers were not legitimate, they were less likely to accept deception of peers than of parents because friends are in relationships of equality and mutuality and can confront each other about these matters without resorting to deception.

For these adolescents, honesty in social relationships is not a straightforward matter but they do not devalue honesty. Most said, in response to a general question, that lying is wrong, and the large majority thought that it is not justifiable to lie to parents or peers to cover up damage to property. As with the physicians, there are situations in which they believe honesty needs to be subordinated to other considerations. A consistent finding across these studies is that deception and lying are judged wrong, but honesty is nevertheless evaluated in relation to competing moral claims. Social psychological experiments of morally relevant behaviors demonstrate the same phenomenon of variations by contexts. Although these experiments are well-known for their findings of group influences (Latanée & Darley, 1970), conformity (Asch, 1956), obedience (Milgram, 1974), and adherence to roles in social hierarchy (Haney et al., 1973), they actually show that individuals respond in several ways, often with conflict, and that different domains of judgment are used in interpreting the parameters of situations (Turiel, 2002; Turiel & Wainryb, 1994). In each of these types of experiment, behaviors varied by context. In some experimental conditions, people generally obeyed an authority's directives to act in ways that caused physical pain to others (by administering electric shocks), but in other experimental conditions people generally defied the authority's directives to engage in similar acts (Milgram, 1974). Other experiments showed that individuals are influenced by group decisions as to whether to help someone in distress, helping in some situations but not in others (Latanée & Darley, 1970). Similarly, individuals "conform" to the judgments of a group in some situations but contradict the group in others (Asch, 1956).

The behaviors tapped in the experiments are not readily classified as independent and interdependent because of the interweaving of both types of judgment. Consider the research on whether bystanders intervene to help others in distress. An individual is more likely to intervene to help others when alone than when in the presence of others who do not intervene (Latanée & Darley, 1970). Thus, people seem to act in independent ways and take personal initiative when alone, but do so in the service of interdependence because the act furthers the welfare of others. Conversely, when in the presence of others, people are influenced socially in failing to intervene. This social influence, however, simultaneously works against interdependence in the sense that it is at the expense of the welfare of others. A similar analysis applies to experiments on obedience to an authority's commands to inflict pain on another person (Milgram, 1974). To the extent that participants in the experiments adhered to their assigned roles and accepted the authority's status and commands, they acted in ways consistent with a collectivistic orientation. In doing so, however, they acted against an interdependent concern with the welfare of the victim. To the extent that people defied the experimenter, and in that sense acted independently, they were acting in the service of the nonindividualistic goal of promoting the welfare of the victim. The overarching observation is that individuals do not simply obey or disobey nor act as conformists or nonconformists. Rather, they make judgments about the actions of others, social organizational features, and right and wrong (see Ross & Nisbett, 1991, for an analysis of social construal and psychological attributions in these situations).

Asch (1952, 1956) has provided an incisive analysis of the process of social construal. In the experiments on conformity, some participants were asked to judge the length of lines in group settings, where the other participants were confederates of the experimenters who at predetermined times gave incorrect judgments. In

Asch's view, those who gave incorrect perceptual judgments consistent with those of the group were not simply "going along" with others so as to fit into the group but were instead attempting to make sense of a perplexing situation. One component of reality about which people were making judgments was the straightforward physical event regarding the relative lengths of lines. A second component was the actions of other people. Especially once the rest of the group began to give opposing judgments about the length of lines, participants had to make judgments about others' reactions to the physical event. Because the judgments about the lengths of lines were unambiguous and they could see no apparent reason for the others' judgments, they were led to question their own perceptions, perceive a conflict, and give credence to the group judgment. Asch proposed that individuals made a judgment about the total context experienced so that variations in situational features make for differences in the actual "objects of judgment."

Research by Ross, Bierbrauer, and Hoffman (1976) supported Asch's interpretation, through the finding that when participants could attribute the actions of the others in the group to motivation by extrinsic goals (e.g., attaining a material payoff) there was much less conformity than when no motives were specified. If individuals were acting so as to fit into the group, they should have conformed to an equal extent regardless of the perceived motivations of others.

Although it has been recognized that behaviors vary by situations (especially Mischel, 1973) and that research shows conformity, obedience to authority, and group influences among Americans (Kelman & Hamilton, 1989; Milgram, 1974; Ross & Nisbett, 1991), the import of these findings has not often been carried over to characterizations of culture. It seems that those who characterize Western cultures as individualistic attend mainly to one side of the picture.

It is informative that in the fairly recent history of social scientific thought, the opposite side of the picture, reflecting the idea that the individual is submerged into the group, has been portrayed as the dominant cultural orientation in the United States. For example, Fromm (1941) maintained that modern capitalistic societies, including the United States, foster conformity and a loss of personal identity. In Fromm's view, the self is subordinated to others in personal relationships and to the social and economic system. He lamented that the individual is but a "cog in the vast economic machine."

Others writing in the 1950s were popularly received for similar characterizations of the culture (Mills, 1956; Reisman, Glazer, & Denney, 1950; Whyte, 1956) as oriented to conformity and to group dependence, with individual initiative being overwhelmed by economic forces. They proclaimed that bureaucratic and hierarchical social institutions stifle freedoms, personal control, and individual creativity.

Therefore, the culture of the United States (and other Western societies) has been characterized in nearly opposite ways by different social scientists. In a sense, these characterizations capture the opposing attitudes and behaviors evident in research on concepts of freedoms and in the social psychological experiments. However, each of these characterizations provides a one-sided typing (stereotyping?) that fails to account for the heterogeneity of social judgments and behaviors. In line with Asch's analyses, the process of making social judgments, psychological attributions, and construal about social events implies that neither individuals nor cultures are appropriately characterized by a category reflecting consistent, integrated patterns. From this broader conception of individuals in Western culture, it is not plausible to portray their morality as framed only through the ideas of individuals with rights and the freedom to voluntarily enter into contracts.

Tradition, Social Hierarchy, Heterogeneity, and Social Opposition

Many of the findings considered thus far that document heterogeneous moral and social judgments come from research in the United States, but findings were reviewed from non-Western cultures showing that concepts of freedom and rights vary by context. Anthropological research yields direct evidence of contextual variations in the judgments of people in non-Western cultures, including variations in concepts of persons. Spiro's (1993) extensive review of anthropological research shows that concepts of self, as well as other social concepts, vary across individuals in the same society and across societies: "There is much more differentiation, individuation, and autonomy in the putative non-Western self, and much more dependence and interdependence in the putative Western self, than these binary opposite types allow" (p. 117).

Spiro maintained that cultural ideologies and public symbols do not necessarily translate into individuals' conceptions or experiences of self and others. One ex-

ample comes from his research of Buddhism in Burma. A central doctrine of Theravada Buddhism is that there is no soul, ego, or transcendental self, but Spiro found that the Burmese he studied do not maintain these ideas. Instead, "They strongly believe in the very ego or soul that this doctrine denies . . . because they themselves experience a subjective sense of self, the culturally normative concept does not correspond to their personal experience" (Spiro, 1993, p. 119). Ethnographic evidence also shows that self-interested goals and concerns with personal entitlements are part of the thinking of the Balinese, Indians, Pakistanis, Nepalese, and Japanese. In their work, northern Japanese villagers are motivated not so much by group goals as by individual goals of power, self-esteem, and pride (see Spiro, 1993, pp. 134–136). Moreover, village women act in accord with the interests of others, their roles in the family, and "self-serving personal desires." Others have also documented that self-interest, personal goals, and autonomy are significant in the lives of Indians from various backgrounds (Mines, 1988; Misra & Giri, 1995; Neff, 2001), among the Toraja of Indonesia (Hollan, 1992), in China (Helwig et al., 2003a, 2003b; Lau, 1992; Li & Yue, 2004), Bangladesh (Chen, 1995), and Japan (Crystal, 2000; Crystal, Watanabe, & Chen, 2000; Crystal, Watanabe, Weinfurt, & Wu, 1998).

In accord with these findings, several anthropologists (e.g., Abu-Lughod, 1991, 1993; Appadurai, 1988; Clifford, 1988; Strauss, 1992; Wikan, 1991, 1996, 2002) have criticized conceptions of cultures as either homogenous, coherent, and timeless or as embodying integrated, stable sets of meanings and practices readily reproduced in individuals through socialization. Abu-Lughod (1991) argued for the need to include, in analyses of culture, conflicts, disputes, arguments, contradictions, ambiguity, and changes in cultural understandings:

> By focusing on particular individuals and their changing relationships, one would necessarily subvert the most problematic connotations of culture: homogeneity, coherence, and timelessness. Individuals are confronted with choices, struggle with others, make conflicting statements, argue about points of view on the same events, undergo ups and downs in various relationships and changes in their circumstances, and fail to predict what will happen to them or those around them. (p. 154)

Several anthropologists and philosophers (Nussbaum, 1999, 2000; Okin, 1989; Strauss, 1992; Wikan, 1991, 1996) have stressed the need to explore the varying meanings individuals give to the dominant values and practices of the society, so as to ascertain if the actor's point of view looks different from the perspective of dominant institutions and ideologies.

Exploring the individual's understandings of dominant cultural values and practices was one of the aims of another study conducted with the Druze (Wainryb & Turiel, 1994). A second aim was to explore the hypothesis that there is more than one side to cultural practices. The varying perspectives individuals may take render cultural practices more nebulous and multifaceted; thus, a particular type of cultural practice is likely to contain differing messages. Cultural practices around social hierarchies are a case in point. One side of social hierarchy, which has been the focus of cultural analyses, is specified duties and roles, and the submergence of self into a network of interdependence. The other side, however, is that there is a strong sense of independence and personal entitlements embedded in hierarchical arrangements. Examples of where such entitlements hold are for those in higher castes and social classes relative to those in lower castes and classes (Turiel, 1994, 2002, 2003b; Turiel & Wainryb, 2000), and in relationships between males and females. Whereas practices revolving around social hierarchical arrangements convey duties and role prescriptions, they also convey that those in dominant positions have personal autonomy and entitlements—especially due to them by those in subordinate positions.

The research with the Druze examined personal, social, and moral judgments, focusing on decision making in the family regarding various activities of relevance in the community (e.g., choices of occupational and educational activities, household tasks, friendships, or leisure activities). Family decisions were examined because the society is hierarchically organized, with a strong patriarchal tradition. Many restrictions are placed on the activities of females, including their education, work, dress, social affiliations, and leisure time. Men are in control of finances and can easily divorce their wives, while wives cannot easily divorce their husbands. Individuals were presented with conflicts between persons in dominant (i.e., husbands and fathers) and subordinate (i.e., wives, daughters, and sons) positions in the family structure. In one set of situations, a person in a dominant position objects to the choices of a person in a subordinate position (e.g., a husband objects to his wife's decision to take a job); in another set, the person in the subordinate position objects to the choices of the person who is in a dominant position (e.g., a wife objects to her husband's decision to change jobs).

The results showed that Druze males and females think men should have decision-making power and discretion. While most participants judged that wives or daughters should not engage in activities to which a father or husband objects, this was not reciprocal. Most judged that a man is free to choose his activities even if his wife, daughter, or son objects. It was also thought that sons should be able to make their own decisions over objections from their fathers. The inequality in decision making is based on different reasons for the decisions and on different ways of conceptualizing the relationships. Again, there is an interweaving of people's judgments in situations that constitute, for them, different contexts associated with the direction of the dialogue and negotiation. In the context of objections from a man to the activities of his wife or daughter, relationships were viewed in interdependent and hierarchical terms. In the context of objections from a wife or daughter to the activities of her husband or father (as well as a father who objects to a son's activities), the relationships were conceptualized as ones of independence for a person choosing the activities (i.e., men). Males and females attributed interdependence to females and to males in some contexts and both attributed independence to males. However, Druze females were aware of the pragmatics of social relationships in the family and sometimes attributed decision-making authority to males because males have the power to inflict serious negative consequences to those in subordinate positions (e.g., abandonment and divorce). Moreover, females evaluated many of these practices giving men power over the activities of females as unfair.

Analogous findings were obtained in research conducted in India (Neff, 2001) and Colombia (Mensing, 2002). As with the Druze, Indian males were more likely than females to be accorded freedom of choice and independence. In Colombia, too, there is a mixture of judgments about interpersonal obligations and interdependence, on the one hand, and the autonomy of persons, on the other.

The findings of these studies demonstrate the multiple aspects of social hierarchy; in traditional cultures there is a complex picture of judgments about role obligations, prescribed activities, personal independence and entitlements, pragmatic concerns, and fairness. For the activities used in these studies, the Druze judged it more acceptable to impose restrictions on a wife or daughter than was the case when judging the legitimacy of restricting freedoms of speech, religion, or reproduction (as in the Turiel & Wainryb, 1998, study discussed earlier). The multiplicity of individuals' perspectives brings with it both acceptance and opposition to cultural practices. Whereas persons in dominant and subordinate positions share orientations to duties, status, prescribed roles, and personal autonomy, those in subordinate positions are aware of the pragmatics of power relationships and view themselves as having legitimate claims to independence and unmet rights. There is a tendency to restrict analyses of cultures to the public and institutionalized features of cultural practices and to the perspectives of those in a dominant position (i.e., caste, class, and gender). However, the perspectives of those in subordinate positions are significant reflections of culture and provide windows into conflicts, struggles, below-the-surface activities, and the interplay of opposing orientations such as independence and interdependence, or conflict and harmony. Along with participation in cultural practices, there can be distancing from them. Along with acceptance of one's role in the culture, there can be opposition to cultural practices (Turiel, 1998, 2002, 2003b; Turiel & Wainryb, 2000; Wainryb, 1995, 2006; Wainryb & Turiel, 1995).

Conflicts, struggles, and below-the-surface activities have been documented when social practices are examined from the perspective of those in subordinate positions. One example is Abu-Lughod's (1993) studies of Bedouin women in Egypt. Abu-Lughod reported that there are differences and disagreements among group members, conflicts between people, efforts to alter existing practices, and struggles between wives and husbands, and parents and children. Women develop strategies, often hidden from men, to assert their interests. These strategies, which include deception, allow women to avoid unwanted arranged marriages, assert their will against restrictions imposed by men, attain some education, and engage in prohibited leisure activities. A woman who finds some of her husband's demands unacceptable typically attempts to control and even dominate him through connections to her parents and, at a later age, to her grown sons (see also Mernissi's, 1994, reflections on her upbringing in Morocco of the 1940s).

Wikan's (1996) studies in poor neighborhoods of Cairo, Egypt, also revealed conflicts, struggles, and efforts at subverting cultural practices. In the poor areas

of Cairo, women come into conflict with men who try to control their activities. Women attempt to circumvent the effects of inequalities in their relationships with men and express unhappiness with practices like polygamy. Wikan's (1996) general conclusion is that "these lives I depict can be read as exercises in resistance against the state, against the family, against one's marriage, against the forces of tradition or change, against neighborhoods and society—even against oneself. But it is resistance that seems to follow a hidden agenda and to manage and endure in ways that respect the humanity of others" (pp. 6–7; for additional examples of studies in India and Bangladesh, see Chen, 1995; Chowdry, 1994; Menchen, 1989).

Examining the perspective of people in subordinate positions, as well as the way people in dominant positions construe their relationships with persons in subordinate positions, yields an alternative view of social hierarchies from those who have emphasized community as a moral good. Social hierarchy does not solely entail an asymmetrical reciprocity whereby those in dominant positions oversee the welfare of those in subordinate positions. Hierarchy often involves oppression and exploitation (Baumrind, 1997) and the use of status differences to further the self-interest, entitlements, and autonomy of those in positions of power and dominance (Wainryb & Turiel, 1994). When we look beyond public characterizations of social practices and when our analyses are not restricted to the perspectives of those in dominant positions, there is evidence for a conception of cultures as embodying variations in behaviors, diversity in orientations, and conflicting points of view resulting in disagreements, disputes, struggles among people, and acts of social opposition and resistance (Abu-Lughod, 1991; Turiel, 2002; Wikan, 1996, 2002).

Conflicts over inequalities among persons of differing status are not restricted to traditional, hierarchically organized cultures. Gender relationships in Western cultures usually are not strictly hierarchical nor are the activities of females restricted in the same ways as in some traditional cultures. Despite the emphasis on equality in the culture, there is considerable evidence documenting inequalities and struggles between men and women in several spheres of life (see especially Hochschild, 1989; Okin, 1989, 1996; Turiel, 1996). Unequal treatment of women is reflected in their under-representation in the political system, in positions of power and influence in business and the professions, and in fewer opportunities for paid work. In addition, in many fields, women are paid substantially less than men for similar work, even when their qualifications are the same (Okin, 1989). Inequalities are also part of gender relationships in the family, with the interests of men given priority over those of women (Blood & Wolfe, 1960; Blumstein & Schwartz, 1983). Studies of dual-career families document a pervasive pattern in which women are expected to do more of the undesired household tasks, and men have entitlements such as greater time for leisure activities (see Hochschild, 1989, for a review). These conditions provide another example of the interweaving of duties, roles, and assertion of rights and personal entitlements. Often conflicts occur over men's orientation to maintaining role distinctions and role responsibilities in the family and women's concerns that there be greater equality and fairness (Hochschild, 1989; Okin, 1989).

The existence of conflicts, opposition and below-the-surface activities in cultures that include the vantage points of those in subordinate positions as different from those in dominant positions casts a different light on the intersection of gender and cultures. Although there are commonalities and shared experiences between men and women in a culture, the issues are more complicated because women from different cultures also share certain perspectives based on their roles in a hierarchy, the status held, their burdens, and the unfairness experienced. Similarly, men from different cultures share perspectives based on their roles in the hierarchy, their privileges and burdens, and a sense of personal entitlements based on the extent to which they are in dominant positions relative to women.

However, aspects other than gender further complicate perspectives based on social hierarchy. Males and females share dominant or subordinate positions with regard to their status as members of social classes in the hierarchy. It is likely that the perspectives of men or women of lower classes in non-Western and Western cultures have some similarities (as would the perspectives of those of higher classes). Correspondingly, differences exist between people of different social classes in a culture (an interesting comparison, again, is between an upper-middle-class woman and a working-class man with regard to roles in the hierarchy). These considerations have received very little attention in research on social and moral development (for an exception, see the analyses of Nucci et al., 1996, of people from different social classes in Brazil). It would be of

particular interest to consider how in some non-Western societies the economic dependence of women on men, and differential economic status in the caste hierarchy, bear on concepts of interpersonal obligations.

One example of research documenting conflict in a Western society pertaining to social class comes from Willis's (1977) ethnographic analyses of British working-class youth in school settings. Willis documented the conflicts of working-class youth with dominant cultural values and ideology to the extent they are represented by teachers, administrators, and even middle-class students. The working-class adolescents opposed and defied authority, criticized teachers, rejected many of their values, and often failed to adhere to their rules. Moreover, working-class adolescents were critical of other students perceived to be part of mainstream culture. Here, too, there is a mixture of individuation and connection. The working-class youth continually displayed behaviors that were independent and rebellious relative to school authorities, other students, and cultural symbols. Their independence, however, was linked to cohesiveness among working-class adolescents or what Willis referred to as the counterculture group. A corresponding example of tensions between social class groups comes from Wikan's (1996) findings that in Cairo, Egypt, people of poverty engage in resistance against society.

All these examples demonstrate that along with the cohesiveness usually ascribed to cultures, it is necessary to account for conflicts, struggles, ambiguities, and multiple perspectives. Multiple perspectives stem from both the varieties of social experiences and the differentiated domains of social thinking developed by individuals. Distinctions need to be made between culture as publicly conveyed ideologies or as social practices and the ways individuals interpret and make judgments about social experiences. Social and cultural practices can be nebulous, with many sides and connotations. They embody multiple messages and are carried out in multiple ways. It has been documented that experiences influencing social development go well beyond any one type (family, peers, culture) and must be viewed form the perspective of reciprocal interactions. The idea of development stemming from reciprocal interactions suggests that there are discrepancies between cultural ideologies, public documents, official pronouncements, or other manifestations of cultural orientations. More generally, the multiplicity of orientations in cultures, including conflicts and ambiguities, means that morality cannot be simply characterized through particular ideologies like that of individuals with rights and freedom to enter into contracts or that of persons as interconnected in a social order of involuntary duties and roles.

CONCLUSIONS

Heterogeneity and variability in social judgments and actions do not stem solely from the presence of different groups or cultures in a society. The types of variations documented pertain to given cultures and individual members of those cultures. However, those variations are not haphazard, nor do the features of situations simply determine how people will act. Rather, heterogeneity and variation suggest that the thinking of individuals is flexible and takes into account different and varied aspects of the social world. The variety of social experiences is relevant to an understanding of moral development because children attend to much more than one type or context of social experience. Moreover, these and other aspects of a vast social world affect development through reciprocal interactions that include a coordination of emotions, thoughts, and actions.

Very important social and psychological questions are embedded in the existence of social hierarchies within cultures. Do people accept their designated roles in a society even when they are in subordinate positions? Do people embrace cultural practices that grant greater power, control, and privileges to one group over another (such as males over females)? Do people in subordinate positions evaluate social hierarchies positively because of a respect for society or culture even though they hold an unequal status and are in subservient positions? Or do people in such positions perceive the inequalities as wrong and unjust and do they, in one way or another, critique societal arrangements and cultural practices through opposition, resistance, and subversion?

These questions go to the core of how cultures are to be characterized and to how individuals develop morally and socially. Research showing that people oppose cultural practices and act to resist and change societal arrangements and cultural practices they judge unfair leads to the view that morality does not involve compliance, and that its development is neither an accommodation to societal values or norms nor their internalization (Turiel, in press-b).

There is evidence that the origins of opposition and resistance are in childhood (Turiel, 2003b, 2006). Children's social development involves a combination of what can be referred to as cooperative and oppositional orientations. Evidence of the origins of opposition and resistance in early childhood comes from studies showing that young children do not accept rules or authority dictates that are in contradiction with their judgments of what is morally right or wrong (Laupa, 1991; Laupa & Turiel, 1986; Weston & Turiel, 1980). Moreover, there is a coexistence of positive, prosocial actions toward and conflicts with parents, siblings, and peers (Dunn, 1987, 1988; Dunn & Munn, 1985, 1987; Dunn, Brown, & Maguire, 1995; Dunn & Slomkowski, 1992). This combination reflects the multiple judgments that children develop. Children's moral judgments also produce acts of defiance or opposition when they perceive unfairness and harm. The research on deception discussed earlier and the research on family conflicts (Smetana, 1997, 2002) demonstrates that opposition and resistance are part of the lives of adolescents, as well.

As children interact with a varied social world, their development entails the formation of different but systematic types or domains of social reasoning. Whereas morality is an important domain, it needs to be understood alongside and in intersection with other aspects of understandings of the social world. Because the social world is varied, and because there are different domains of social judgment, moral prescriptions are not always applied in the same way. Social situations often require a balancing and coordination of different social and personal considerations related to features of the context. Consequently, although moral prescriptions dictate obligations based on right or wrong and how a person ought to act, they do not dictate rigid rules or maxims. There is more than one way to reach a particular set of goals. Habermas (1993) articulated this feature of morality, particularly in his analyses of how a traditional Kantian view failed to account for context. He argued that rational principles can take different forms in their application in contexts and are subject to change and elaboration through social discourse. However, those who critique abstract moral principles all too often postulate analogously abstract, decontextualized, and general cultural orientations. A critique of moral rationality like that of MacIntyre (1981) originally included the concern that rational principles do not address local and contextual circumstances but resulted (see MacIntyre, 1988) in the propositions that morality best rests on religious tradition and authority and that agreements regarding moral principles should be inculcated through education designed by religious authorities. By relying on a system of religious tradition and authority for moral prescriptions, there is little room for contextual variations.

Especially in the United States, the current political and intellectual climate seems to be one that de-emphasizes thought, reasoning, rationality, and reflective analyses and not infrequently places them under attack. Emotions, with assumptions about their underlying evolutionary biological bases, are frequently regarded as the central determinants of morality along with the authority of the group, religion, or culture. As important as emotions—especially sympathy, empathy, and respect—are for moral functioning, emotions occur in and among persons who can think about them with regard to other people and in relation to complicated social agendas, goals, and arrangements. The relationships among emotions, moral judgments, reflections, and deliberations require a great deal of attention in research and theoretical formulations. Investigators are less likely to address these relationships if reflective analyses are attacked as, at best, irrelevant to the layperson and, at worst, corrupting of individuals and society (Wilson, 1993). Still, scholars critiquing the proposition of rational, deliberative, and reflective moral functioning, themselves engage in those very activities, attempting to persuade others though rational discourse. These human activities are not solely the province of scholars, however. Laypersons (children included), too, deliberate and reason systematically about emotions and morality and engage in discussion and argumentation.

REFERENCES

Abu-Lughod, L. (1991). Writing against culture. In R. E. Fox (Ed.), *Recapturing anthropology: Working in the present* (pp. 137–162). Santa Fe, NM: School of American Research Press.

Abu-Lughod, L. (1993). *Writing women's worlds: Bedouin stories.* Berkeley: University of California Press.

Appadurai, A. (1988). Putting hierarchy in its place. *Cultural Anthropology, 3,* 36–49.

Ardila-Rey, A., & Killen, M. (2001). Middle-class Colombian children's evaluations of personal, moral, and social conventional interactions in the classroom. *International Journal of Behavioral Development, 25,* 246–255.

Aristotle. (1947). Nichomachean ethics. In R. McKeon (Ed.), *Introduction to Aristotle* (pp. 402–404). New York: Random House.

Aronfreed, J. (1961). The nature, variety, and social patterning of moral responses to transgressions. *Journal of Abnormal and Social Psychology, 63,* 223–240.

Aronfreed, J. (1968). *Conduct and conscience: The socialization of internalized control over behavior.* New York: Academic Press.

Arsenio, W. (1988). Children's conceptions of the situational affective consequences of sociomoral events. *Child Development, 59,* 1611–1622.

Arsenio, W., Berlin, N., & O'Desky, I. (1989, April). *Children's and adults' understanding of sociomoral events.* Paper presented at the biennial meeting of the Society for Research in Child Development, Kansas City, MO.

Arsenio, W., & Fleiss, K. (1996). Typical and behaviourally disruptive children's understanding of the emotional consequences of socio-moral events. *British Journal of Developmental Psychology, 14,* 173–186.

Arsenio, W., & Ford, M. (1985). The role of affective information in social-cognitive development: Children's differentiation of moral and conventional events. *Merril-Palmer Quarterly, 31,* 1–18.

Arsenio, W., & Kramer, R. (1992). Victimizers and their victims: Children's conceptions of the mixed emotional consequences of moral transgressions. *Child Development, 63,* 915–927.

Arsenio, W., & Lemerise, E. A. (2004). Aggression and moral development: Integrating social information processing and moral domain models. *Child Development, 75,* 987–1002.

Arsenio, W., & Lover, A. (1995). Children's conceptions of sociomoral affect: Happy victimizers, mixed emotions, and other expectancies. In M. Killen & D. Hart (Eds.), *Morality in everyday life: Developmental perspectives* (pp. 87–128). Cambridge, England: Cambridge University Press.

Asch, S. E. (1952). *Social psychology.* Englewood Cliffs, NJ: Prentice-Hall.

Asch, S. E. (1956). Studies of independence and conformity: A minority of one against a unanimous majority. *Psychological Monographs, 70*(Whole No. 416).

Astor, R. A. (1994). Children's moral reasoning about family and peer violence: The role of provocation and retribution. *Child Development, 65,* 1054–1067.

Baldwin, J. M. (1896). *Social and ethical interpretations in mental development.* New York: Macmillan.

Bandura, A., & Walters, R. (1963). *Social learning and personality development.* New York: Holt, Rinehart and Winston.

Baumrind, D. (1973). The development of instrumental competence through socialization. In A. D. Pick (Ed.), *Minnesota Symposia on Child Psychology* (Vol. 7, pp. 3–46). Minneapolis: University of Minnesota Press.

Baumrind, D. (1989). Rearing competent children. In W. Damon (Ed.), *Child development today and tomorrow* (pp. 349–378). San Francisco: Jossey-Bass.

Baumrind, D. (1997, April). *A correct moral standpoint is not impartial or universalizable.* Paper presented at the biennial meeting of the Society for Research in Child Development, Washington, DC.

Bellah, R. N., Madsen, R., Sullivan, W. M., Swidler, A., & Tipton, S. M. (1985). *Habits of the heart: Individualism and commitment in American life.* New York: Harper & Row.

Benedict, R. (1934). *Patterns of culture.* Boston: Houghton Mifflin.

Bennett, W. J. (1992). *The de-valuing of America: The fight for our culture and our children.* New York: Simon & Schuster.

Bennett, W. J. (1993). *The book of virtues.* New York: Simon & Schuster.

Bennett, W. J., & Delattre, E. J. (1978). Moral education in the schools. *Public Interest, 50,* 81–99.

Berkowitz, L. (1964). *Development of motives and values in a child.* New York: Basic Books.

Berkowitz, M. W., & Gibbs, J. C. (1983). Measuring the developmental features of moral discussion. *Merrill-Palmer Quarterly, 29,* 399–410.

Berkowitz, M. W., & Gibbs, J. C. (1985). The process of moral conflict resolution and moral development. In M. Berkowitz (Ed.), *Peer conflict and psychological growth: New directions for child development* (pp. 71–84). San Francisco: Jossey-Bass.

Berkowitz, M. W., Gibbs, J. C., & Broughton, J. M. (1980). The relation of moral judgment stage disparity to developmental effects of peer dialogues. *Merrill-Palmer Quarterly, 26,* 341–357.

Bersoff, D. M., & Miller, J. G. (1993). Culture, context, and the development of moral accountability judgments. *Developmental Psychology, 29,* 664–676.

Blasi, A. (1993). The development of identity: Some implications for moral functioning. In G. G. Noam & T. E. Wren (Eds.), *The moral self: Building a better paradigm* (pp. 99–121). Cambridge, MA: MIT Press.

Blood, R. O., & Wolfe, D. M. (1960). *Husbands and wives: The dynamics of married living.* Glencoe, IL: Free Press.

Bloom, A. (1987). *The closing of the American mind: How higher education has failed democracy and impoverished the soul of today's students.* New York: Simon & Schuster.

Blumstein, P., & Schwartz, P. (1983). *American couples.* New York: Morrow.

Boyd, D. (1983). Careful justice or just caring: A response to Gilligan. *Proceedings of the Philosophy of Education Society, 38,* 63–69.

Braine, L. G., Pomerantz, E., Lorber, D., & Krantz, D. H. (1991). Conflicts with authority: Children's feelings, actions, and justifications. *Developmental Psychology, 27,* 829–840.

Bruner, J. (1990). *Acts of meaning.* Cambridge, MA: Harvard University Press.

Butterfield, F. (1995). *All God's children: The Boskett family and the American tradition of violence.* New York: Knopf.

Carey, N., & Ford, M. (1983, August). *Domains of social and self-regulation: An Indonesian study.* Paper presented at the meeting of the American Psychological Association, Los Angeles, CA.

Carlo, G. (2006). Care-based and altruistically based morality. In M. Killen & J. G. Smetana (Eds.), *Handbook of moral development* (pp. 551–580). Mahwah, NJ: Erlbaum.

Carlo, G., Koller, S. H., Eisenberg, N., DaSilva, M. S., & Frohlich, C. B. (1996). A cross-national study on the relations among prosocial moral reasoning, gender, role orientations, and prosocial behaviors. *Developmental Psychology, 32,* 231–240.

Cassidy, K. W., Chu, J. Y., & Dahlsgaard, K. K. (1997). Preschoolers' ability to adopt justice and care orientations to moral dilemmas. *Early Education and Development, 8,* 419–434.

Catron, T. F., & Masters, J. C. (1993). Mothers' and children's conceptualizations of corporal punishment. *Child Development, 64,* 1815–1828.

Chen, M. (1995). A matter of survival: Women's right to employment in India and Bangladesh. In M. C. Nussbaum & J. Glover (Eds.), *Women, culture, and development: A study of human capabilities* (pp. 61–75). New York: Oxford University Press.

Chilamkurti, C., & Milner, J. S. (1993). Perceptions and evaluations of child transgressions and disciplinary techniques in high- and low-risk mothers and their children. *Child Development, 64,* 1801–1814.

Chodorow, N. (1978). *The reproduction of mothering.* Berkeley: University of California Press.

Chowdry, P. (1994). *The veiled women: Shifting gender equations in rural Haryana 1880–1990.* Delhi: Oxford University Press.

Clémence, A., Doise, W., de Rosa, A. S., & Gonzalez, L. (1995). Le représentation sociale de droites de l'homme: Une recherche internationale sur l'étendue et les limites de l'universalité. *Journal Internationale de Psychologie, 30,* 181–212.

Clifford, J. (1988). *The predicament of culture: Twentieth-century ethnography, literature, and art.* Cambridge, MA: Harvard University Press.

Colby, A., & Damon, W. (1983). Listening to a different voice: A review of Gilligan's "In a different voice." *Merrill-Palmer Quarterly, 29,* 473–481.

Colby, A., & Damon, W. (1992). *Some do care: Contemporary lives of moral commitment.* New York: Free Press.

Colby, A., & Kohlberg, L. (1987a). *The measurement of moral judgment: Vol. 1. Theoretical foundations and research validation.* New York: Cambridge University Press.

Colby, A., & Kohlberg, L. (with Hewer, A., Candee, D., Gibbs, J. C., & Power, F. C.). (1987b). *The measurement of moral judgment: Vol. 2. Standard issue scoring manual.* New York: Cambridge University Press.

Colby, A., Kohlberg, L., Gibbs, J., & Lieberman, M. (1983). A longitudinal study of moral judgment. *Monographs of the Society for Research in Child Development, 48*(Serial No. 200).

Collins, W. A., & Laursen, B. (1992). Conflict and relationships during adolescence. In C. U. Shantz & W. W. Hartup (Eds.), *Conflict in child and adolescent development* (pp. 216–241). Cambridge, England: Cambridge University Press.

Cosmides, L., & Tooby, J. (1989). Evolutionary psychology and the generation of culture: Pt. 2. Case study—A computational theory of social exchange. *Ethology and Sociobiology, 10,* 51–97.

Crane, D. A., & Tisak, M. (1995a). Does day-care experience affect young children's judgments of home and school rules? *Early Education and Child Development, 6,* 25–37.

Crane, D. A., & Tisak, M. (1995b). Mixed-domain events: The influence of moral and conventional components on the development of social reasoning. *Early Education and Development, 6,* 169–180.

Crystal, D. S. (2000). Concepts of deviance and disturbance in children and adolescents: A comparison between the United States and Japan. *International Journal of Psychology, 35,* 207–218.

Crystal, D. S., Watanabe, H., & Chen, R. S. (2000). Reactions to morphological deviance: A comparison of Japanese and American children and adolescents. *Social Development, 9,* 40–61.

Crystal, D. S., Watanabe, H., Weinfurt, K., & Wu, C. (1998). Concepts of human differences: A comparison of American, Japanese, and Chinese children and adolescents. *Developmental Psychology, 34,* 714–722.

Damon, W. (1975). Early conceptions of positive justice as related to the development of logical operations. *Child Development, 46,* 301–312.

Damon, W. (1977). *The social world of the child.* San Francisco: Jossey-Bass.

Damon, W. (1980). Patterns of change in children's social reasoning: A 2-year longitudinal study. *Child Development, 51,* 1010–1017.

Damon, W. (1981). Exploring children's social cognition on two fronts. In J. M. Flavell & L. Ross (Eds.), *Social cognitive development: Frontiers and possible futures* (pp. 154–175). Cambridge, England: Cambridge University Press.

Damon, W. (1984). Peer education: The untapped potential. *Journal of Applied Developmental Psychology, 5,* 331–343.

Damon, W. (1988). *The moral child: Nurturing children's natural moral growth.* New York: Free Press.

Davidson, P., Turiel, E., & Black, A. (1983). The effect of stimulus familiarity on the use of criteria and justifications in children's social reasoning. *British Journal of Developmental Psychology, 1,* 49–65.

Doise, W., Clémence, A., & Spini, D. (1996). Human rights and social psychology. *British Psychological Society Social Psychology Section Newsletter, 35,* 3–21.

Duncker, K. (1939). Ethical relativity? (An inquiry into the psychology of ethics). *Mind, 48,* 39–53.

Dunn, J. (1987). The beginnings of moral understanding: Development in the second year. In J. Kagan & S. Lamb (Eds.), *The emergence of morality in young children* (pp. 91–112). Chicago: University of Chicago Press.

Dunn, J. (1988). *The beginnings of social understanding.* Cambridge, MA: Harvard University Press.

Dunn, J., Brown, J. R., & Maguire, M. (1995). The development of children's moral sensibility: Individual differences and emotion understanding. *Developmental Psychology, 31,* 649–659.

Dunn, J., Cutting, A. L., & Demetriou, H. (2000). Moral sensibility, understanding others, and children's friendship interactions in the preschool period. *British Journal of Developmental Psychology, 18,* 159–177.

Dunn, J., & Munn, P. (1987). Development of justification in disputes with mother and sibling. *Developmental Psychology, 23,* 791–798.

Dunn, J., & Slomkowski, C. (1992). Conflict and the development of social understanding. In C. U. Shantz & W. W. Hartup (Eds.), *Conflict in child and adolescent development* (pp. 70–92). Cambridge, England: Cambridge University Press.

Durkheim, E. (1961). *Moral education.* Glencoe, IL: Free Press. (Original work published 1925)

Durkheim, E. (1965). *The elementary forms of the religious life.* New York: Free Press. (Original work published 1912)

Dworkin, R. M. (1977). *Taking rights seriously.* Cambridge, MA: Harvard University Press.

Eisenberg, N. (1986). *Altruistic emotion, cognition, and behavior.* Hillsdale, NJ: Erlbaum.

Eisenberg, N., Carlo, G., Murphy, B., & Van Court, N. (1995). Prosocial development in late adolescence: A longitudinal study. *Child Development, 66,* 1179–1197.

Eisenberg, N., & Fabes, R. A. (1990). Empathy: Conceptualization, measurement, and relation to prosocial behavior. *Motivation and Emotion, 14,* 131–149.

Eisenberg, N., & Fabes, R. A. (1991). Prosocial behavior: A multimethod developmental perspective. In M. S. Clark (Ed.), *Review of personality and social psychology* (Vol. 2, pp. 34–61). Newbury Park, CA: Sage.

Eisenberg, N., Guthrie, I. K., Cumberland, A., Murphy, B. C., Shepard, S. A., Zhou, Q., et al. (2002). Prosocial development in early adulthood: A longitudinal study. *Journal of Personality and Social Psychology, 82,* 993–1006.

Eisenberg, N., Lennon, R., & Roth, K. (1983). Prosocial development: A longitudinal study. *Developmental Psychology, 19,* 846–855.

Eisenberg, N., Lundy, T., Shell, R., & Roth, K. (1985). Children's justifications for their adult and peer-directed compliant (prosocial and nonprosocial) behaviors. *Developmental Psychology, 21,* 325–331.

Eisenberg, N., & Miller, P. A. (1987). The relation of empathy to prosocial and related behaviors. *Psychological Bulletin, 101,* 91–119.

Eisenberg, N., Miller, P. A., Shell, R., McNalley, S., & Shea, C. (1991). Prosocial development in adolescence: A longitudinal study. *Developmental Psychology, 27,* 849–857.

Eisenberg, N., Shell, R., Pasternack, J., Lennon, R., Beller, R., & Mathy, R. M. (1987). Prosocial development in middle childhood: A longitudinal study. *Developmental Psychology, 23,* 712–718.

Eisenberg, N., Spinard, T., & Sadovsky, A. (2006). Empathy-related responding in children. In M. Killen & J. G. Smetana (Eds.), *Handbook of moral development* (pp. 517–550). Mahwah, NJ: Erlbaum.

Eisenberg, N., & Strayer, J. (Eds.). (1987). *Empathy and its development.* New York: Cambridge University Press.

Eisenberg-Berg, N. (1979). Development of children's prosocial moral judgment. *Developmental Psychology, 15,* 128–137.

Eisenberg-Berg, N., & Geisheker, E. (1979). Content of preachings and power of the model/preacher: The effect on children's generosity. *Developmental Psychology, 15,* 168–175.

Eisenberg-Berg, N., & Roth, K. (1980). Development of young children's prosocial moral judgment: A longitudinal follow-up. *Developmental Psychology, 16,* 375–376.

Etzioni, A. (1993). *The spirit of community: The reinvention of American society.* New York: Touchstone.

Etzioni, A. (1996). *The new golden rule: Community and morality in a democratic society.* New York: Basic Books.

Faludi, S. (1991). *Backlash: The undeclared war against American women.* New York: Doubleday.

Fass, P. (1977). *The damned and the beautiful: American youth in the 1920s.* New York: Oxford University Press.

Flavell, J. H., & Miller, P. H. (1998). Social cognition. In W. Damon (Editor-in-Chief) & D. Kuhn & R. Siegler (Vol. Eds.), *Handbook of child psychology: Vol. 2. Cognition, perception, and language* (5th edl, pp. 851–898). New York: Wiley.

Frankena, W. K. (1963). *Ethics.* Englewood Cliffs, NJ: Prentice-Hall.

Freeman, V. G., Rathore, S. S., Weinfurt, K. P., Schulman, K. A., & Sulmasy, D. P. (1999). Lying for patients: Physician deception of third-party payers. *Archives of Internal Medicine, 159,* 2263–2270.

Freud, S. (1959). Some psychological consequences of the anatomical distinction between the sexes. In S. Freud (Ed.), *Collected papers* (pp. 186–197). New York: Basic Books.

Fromm, E. (1941). *Escape from freedom.* New York: Holt, Rinehart and Winston.

Geertz, C. (1984). "From the native's point of view": On the nature of anthropological understanding. In R. A. Shweder & R. A. Levine (Eds.), *Culture theory: Essays on mind, self, and emotion* (pp. 123–136). Cambridge, England: Cambridge University Press.

Gerson, R., & Damon, W. (1978). Moral understanding and children's conduct. In W. Damon (Ed.), *Moral development: New directions in child development* (pp. 41–60). San Francisco: Jossey-Bass.

Gewirth, A. (1978). *Reason and morality.* Chicago: University of Chicago Press.

Gilligan, C. (1977). In a different voice: Women's conceptions of self and of morality. *Harvard Educational Review, 47,* 481–517.

Gilligan, C. (1982). *In a different voice: Psychological theory and women's development.* Cambridge, MA: Harvard University Press.

Gilligan, C., & Attanucci, J. (1988). Two moral orientations: Gender differences and similarities. *Merrill-Palmer Quarterly, 34,* 223–237.

Gilligan, C., Ward, J. V., Taylor, J. M., & Bardige, B. (Eds.). (1988). *Mapping the moral domain: A contribution of women's thinking to psychological theory and education.* Cambridge, MA: Harvard University Press.

Gilligan, C., & Wiggins, G. (1987). The origins of morality in early childhood relationships. In J. Kagan & S. Lamb (Eds.), *The emergence of morality in young children* (pp. 277–305). Chicago: University of Chicago Press.

Greeno, C. G., & Maccoby, E. E. (1986). How different is the "different voice?" *Signs, 11,* 313–314.

Grinder, R. E. (1964). Relations between behavioral and cognitive dimensions of conscience in middle childhood. *Child Development, 35,* 881–891.

Grusec, J. E. (2006). The development of moral behavior and conscience from a socialization perspective. In M. Killen & J. G. Smetana (Eds.), *Handbook of moral development* (pp. 243–266). Mahwah, NJ: Erlbaum.

Grusec, J. E., & Goodnow, J. J. (1994). Impact of parental discipline methods on the child's internalization of values: A reconceptualization of current points of view. *Developmental Psychology, 30,* 4–19.

Grusec, J. E., Goodnow, J. J., & Kuczynski, L. (2000). New directions in analyses of parenting contributions to children's acquisition of values. *Child Development, 71,* 205–211.

Habermas, J. (1990a). Justice and solidarity: On the discussion concerning stage 6. In T. E. Wren (Ed.), *The moral domain: Essays in the ongoing discussion between philosophy and the social sciences* (pp. 224–254). Cambridge, MA: MIT Press.

Habermas, J. (1990b). *Moral consciousness and communicative action.* Cambridge, MA: MIT Press.

Habermas, J. (1993). *Justification and application.* Cambridge, MA: MIT Press.

Haidt, J. (2001). The emotional dog and its rational tail: A social intuitionist approach to moral judgment. *Psychological Review, 108,* 814–834.

Haidt, J., Koller, S. H., & Dias, M. G. (1993). Affect, culture, and morality, or is it wrong to eat your dog? *Journal of Personality and Social Psychology, 65,* 613–628.

Haney, C., Banks, C., & Zimbardo, P. (1973). Interpersonal dynamics in a simulated prison. *International Journal of Criminology and Penology, 1,* 69–97.

Hart, D. (1988a). A longitudinal study of adolescents' socialization and identification as predictors of adult moral judgment development. *Merrill-Palmer Quarterly, 34,* 245–260.

Hart, D. (1988b). Self-concept in the social context of the adolescent. In D. Lapsely & F. C. Power (Eds.), *Self, ego, and identity: Integrative approaches* (pp. 71–90). New York: Springer-Verlag.

Hart, D., & Chmiel, S. (1992). Influence of defense mechanisms on moral judgment development: A longitudinal study. *Developmental Psychology, 28,* 722–730.

Hartshorne, H., & May, M. A. (1928). *Studies in the nature of character: Vol. 1. Studies in deceit.* New York: Macmillan.

Hartshorne, H., & May, M. A. (1929). *Studies in the nature of character: Vol. 2. Studies in self-control.* New York: Macmillan.

Hartshorne, H., & May, M. A. (1930). *Studies in the nature of character: Vol. 3. Studies in the organization of character.* New York: Macmillan.

Hasebe, Y., Nucci, L., & Nucci, M. S. (2004). Parental control of the personal domain and adolescent symptoms of psychopathology: A cross-national study in the United States and Japan. *Child Development, 75,* 815–828.

Haste, H. (1990). Moral responsibility and moral commitment: The integration of affect and cognition. In T. E. Wren (Ed.), *The moral domain: Essays in the ongoing discussion between philosophy and the social sciences* (pp. 315–359). Cambridge, MA: MIT Press.

Haste, H. (1993). Morality, self, and sociohistorical context: The role of lay social theory. In G. G. Noam & T. E. Wren (Eds.), *The moral self: Building a better paradigm* (pp. 175–208). Cambridge, MA: MIT Press.

Hastings, P. D., Zahn-Waxler, C., & McShane, K. (2006). We are, by nature, moral creatures: Biological bases of concern for others. In M. Killen & J. G. Smetana (Eds.), *Handbook of moral development* (pp 483–516). Mahwah, NJ: Erlbaum.

Hatch, E. (1983). *Culture and morality: The relativity of values in anthropology.* New York: Columbia University Press.

Helwig, C. C. (1995a). Adolescents' and young adults' conceptions of civil liberties: Freedom of speech and religion. *Child Development, 66,* 152–166.

Helwig, C. C. (1995b). Social context in social cognition. In M. Killen & D. Hart (Eds.), *Morality in everyday life: Developmental perspectives* (pp. 166–200). Cambridge, England: Cambridge University Press.

Helwig, C. C. (1997). The role of agent and social context in judgments of freedom of speech and religion. *Child Development, 68,* 484–495.

Helwig, C. C. (1998). Children's conceptions of fair government and freedom of speech. *Child Development, 69,* 518–531.

Helwig, C. C. (2006). Rights, civil liberties, and democracy across cultures. In M. Killen & J. G. Smetana (Eds.), *Handbook of moral development (pp. 185–210).* Mahwah, NJ: Erlbaum.

Helwig, C. C. (in press). The moral judgment of the child reevaluated: Heteronomy, early morality, and reasoning about social justice and inequalities. In C. Wainryb, J. Smetana, & E. Turiel (Eds.), *Social development, social inequalities, and social justice.* Mahwah, NJ: Erlbaum.

Helwig, C. C., Arnold, M. L., Tan, D., & Boyd, D. (2003a). Chinese adolescents' reasoning about democratic and authority-based decision making in peer, family, and school contexts. *Child Development, 74,* 783–800.

Helwig, C. C., Arnold, M. L., Tan, D., & Boyd, D. (2003b, June). *Mainland Chinese adolescents' judgments and reasoning about democratic government.* Poster presented at the annual meeting of the Jean Piaget Society, Chicago, IL.

Helwig, C. C., Hildebrandt, C., & Turiel, E. (1995). Children's judgments about psychological harm in social context. *Child Development, 66,* 1680–1693.

Helwig, C. C., & Kim, S. (1999). Children's evaluations of decision making procedures: In peer, family, and school contexts. *Child Development, 70,* 502–512.

Helwig, C. C., Tisak, M., & Turiel, E. (1990). Children's social reasoning in context. *Child Development, 61,* 2068–2078.

Helwig, C. C., & Turiel, E. (2002). Civil liberties, autonomy, and democracy: Children's perspectives. *International Journal of Law and Psychiatry, 25,* 253–270.

Helwig, C. C., & Turiel, E. (2003). Children's moral and social reasoning. In P. K. Smith & C. H. Hart (Eds.), *Blackwell handbook of childhood social development* (pp. 475–490). Oxford, England: Blackwell.

Helwig, C. C., Turiel, E., & Nucci, L. P. (1996). The virtues and vices of moral development theorists. *Developmental Review, 16,* 69–107.

Helwig, C. C., Zelazo, P. D., & Wilson, M. (2001). Children's judgments of psychological harm in normal and noncanonical situations. *Child Development, 72,* 66–81.

Hochschild, A. (1989). *The second shift.* New York: Avon.

Hoffman, M. L. (1963). Childrearing practices and moral development: Generalizations from empirical research. *Child Development, 34,* 295–318.

Hoffman, M. L. (1970). Moral development. In P. H. Mussen (Ed.), *Carmichael's manual of child psychology* (Vol. 2, pp. 261–359). New York: Wiley.

Hoffman, M. L. (1984). Empathy, its limitations, and its role in a comprehensive moral theory. In W. M. Kurtines & J. L. Gewirtz (Eds.), *Morality, moral behavior, and moral development: Basic issues in theory and research* (pp. 283–302). New York: Wiley.

Hoffman, M. L. (1991a). Commentary on: Toward an integration of Kohlberg's and Hoffman's moral development theories. *Human Development, 34,* 105–110.

Hoffman, M. L. (1991b). Empathy, social cognition, and moral action. In W. M. Kurtines & J. L. Gewirtz (Eds.), *Handbook of moral behavior and development: Vol. 1. Theory* (pp. 275–301). Hillsdale, NJ: Erlbaum.

Hoffman, M. L. (2000). *Empathy and moral development: Implications for caring and justice.* Cambridge, England: Cambridge University Press.

Hoffman, M. L., & Saltzstein, H. D. (1967). Parent discipline and the child's moral development. *Journal of Personality and Social Psychology, 5,* 45–57.

Hollan, D. (1992). Cross-cultural differences in the self. *Journal of Anthropological Research, 48,* 283–300.

Hollos, M., Leis, P. E., & Turiel, E. (1986). Social reasoning in Ijo children and adolescents in Nigerian communities. *Journal of Cross-Cultural Psychology, 17,* 352–374.

Horn, S. S. (2003). Adolescents reasoning about exclusion from social groups. *Developmental Psychology, 39,* 71–84.

Hume, D. (1966). *An enquiry concerning the principles of morals.* Oxford, England: Clarendon Press. (Original work published 1751)

Jaffee, S., & Hyde, J. H. (2000). Gender differences in moral orientation: A meta-analysis. *Psychological Bulletin, 12,* 703–726.

James, W. (1890). *The principles of psychology.* New York: Holt.

Johnston, D. K. (1988). Adolescents' solutions to dilemmas in fables: Two moral orientations: Two problem solving strategies. In C. Gilligan, J. V. Ward, J. M. Taylor, & B. Bardige (Eds.), *Mapping the moral domain: A contribution of women's thinking to psychological theory and education* (pp. 49–71). Cambridge, MA: Harvard University Press.

Kagan, J. (1984). *The nature of the child.* New York: Basic Books.

Kahn, P. H. (1992). Children's obligatory and discretionary moral judgments. *Child Development, 63,* 416–430.

Keller, M., & Edelstein, W. (1990). The emergence of morality in interpersonal relationships. In T. E. Wren (Ed.), *The moral domain: Essays in the ongoing discussion between philosophy and the social sciences* (pp. 255–282). Cambridge, MA: MIT Press.

Keller, M., & Edelstein, W. (1991). The development of socio-moral meaning making: Domains, categories, and perspective-taking. In W. M. Kurtines & J. L. Gewirtz (Eds.), *Handbook of moral behavior and development: Vol. 1. Theory* (pp. 89–114). Hillsdale, NJ: Erlbaum.

Keller, M., & Edelstein, W. (1993). The development of the moral self from childhood to adolescence. In G. G. Noam & T. E. Wren (Eds.), *The moral self: Building a better paradigm* (pp. 310–336). Cambridge, MA: MIT Press.

Keller, M., Lourenco, O., Malti, T., & Saalbach, H. (2003). The multifaceted phenomenon of "'happy victimizer": A cross-cultural comparison. *British Journal of Developmental Psychology, 21,* 1–18.

Kelman, H. C., & Hamilton, V. L. (1989). *Crimes of obedience: Toward a social psychology of authority and responsibility.* New Haven, CT: Yale University Press.

Killen, M. (1989). Context, conflict, and coordination in social development. In L. T. Winegar (Ed.), *Social interaction and the development of children's understanding* (pp. 119–146). Norwood, NJ: Ablex.

Killen, M. (1990). Children's evaluations of morality in the context of peer, teacher-child and familial relations. *Journal of Genetic Psychology, 151,* 395–410.

Killen, M. (1991). Social and moral development in early childhood. In W. M. Kurtines & J. L. Gewirtz (Eds.), *Handbook of moral behavior and development: Vol. 2. Research* (pp. 115–138). Hillsdale, NJ: Erlbaum.

Killen, M., Lee-Kim, J., McGlothlin, H., & Stagnor, C. (2002). How children and adolescents value gender and racial exclusion. *Monographs of the Society for Research in Child Development, 67*(4, Serial No. 271).

Killen, M., McGlothlin, H., & Lee-Kim, J. (2002). Hetrogeneity in social cognition and culture. In H. Keller, Y. Poortinga, & A. Schoelmerich (Eds.), *Between biology and culture: Perspectives on ontogenetic development* (pp. 159–190). Cambridge, England: Cambridge University Press.

Killen, M., & Naigles, L. (1995). Preschool children pay attention to their addresses: The effects of gender composition on peer disputes. *Discourse Processes, 19,* 329–346.

Killen, M., & Nucci, L. P. (1995). Morality, autonomy, and social conflict. In M. Killen & D. Hart (Eds.), *Morality in everyday life: Developmental perspectives* (pp. 52–86). Cambridge, England: Cambridge University Press.

Killen, M., Pisacane, K., Lee-Kim, J., & Ardila-Rey, A. (2001). Fairness or stereotypes? Young children's priorities when evaluating group exclusion and inclusion.*Developmental Psychology, 37,* 587–596.

Killen, M., & Smetana, J. G. (1999). Social interactions in preschool classrooms and the development of young children's conceptions of the personal. *Child Development, 70,* 486–501.

Killen, M., & Stangor, C. (2001). Children's reasoning about social inclusion and exclusion in gender and race peer group contexts. *Child Development, 72,* 174–186.

Killen, M., & Sueyoshi, L. (1995). Conflict resolution in Japanese social interactions. *Early Education and Development, 6,* 313–330.

Kim, J. M. (1998). Korean children's concepts of adult and peer authority and moral reasoning. *Developmental Psychology, 34,* 947–955.

Kim, J. M., & Turiel, E. (1996). Korean and American children's concepts of adult and peer authority. *Social Development, 5,* 310–329.

Kochanska, G. (1993). Toward a synthesis of parental socialization and child temperament in early development of conscience. *Child Development, 64,* 325–347.

Kochanska, G. (1994). Beyond cognition: Expanding the search for the early roots of internalization, and conscience. *Developmental Psychology, 30,* 20–22.

Kochanska, G. (1997). Multiple pathways to conscience for children with different temperaments: From toddlerhood to age 5. *Developmental Psychology, 33,* 228–240.

Kochanska, G., Aksan, N., Knaack, A., & Rhines, H. M. (2004). Maternal parenting and children's conscience: Early security as a moderator. *Child Development, 75,* 1229–1242.

Kochanska, G., Gross, J. N., Lin, M., & Nichols, K. E. (2002). Guilt in young children: Development, determinants, and relations with a broader system of standards. *Child Development, 73,* 461–482.

Kochanska, G., & Murray, K. T. (2000). Mother-child mutually responsive orientation and conscience development: From toddler to early school age. *Child Development, 71,* 417–431.

Kochanska, G., Murray, K. T., & Coy, K. C. (1997). Inhibitory control as a contributor to conscience in childhood: From toddler to early school age. *Child Development, 68,* 263–277.

Kohlberg, L. (1963). Moral development and identification. In H. W. Stevenson (Ed.), *Child psychology: 62nd yearbook of the National Society for the Study of Education* (pp. 277–332). Chicago: University of Chicago Press.

Kohlberg, L. (1964). Development of moral character and moral ideology. In M. L. Hoffman & L. W. Hoffman (Eds.), *Review of child development research* (Vol. 1, pp. 283–432). New York: Sage.

Kohlberg, L. (1968). The child as a moral philosopher. *Psychology Today, 2,* 25–30.

Kohlberg, L. (1969). Stage and sequence: The cognitive-developmental approach to socialization. In D. Goslin (Ed.), *Handbook of socialization theory and research* (pp. 347–480). Chicago: Rand McNally.

Kohlberg, L. (1970). Education for justice: A modern statement of the Platonic view. In N. F. Sizer & T. R. Sizer (Eds.), *Moral education: Five lectures* (pp. 56–83). Cambridge, MA: Harvard University Press.

Kohlberg, L. (1971). From is to ought: How to commit the naturalistic fallacy and get away with it in the study of moral development. In T. Mischel (Ed.), *Psychology and genetic epistemology* (pp. 151–235). New York: Academic Press.

Kohlberg, L. (1976). Moral stages and moralization: The cognitive developmental approach. In T. Lickona (Ed.), *Moral development and behavior: Theory, research, and social issues* (pp. 31–53). New York: Holt, Rinehart and Winston.

Kohlberg, L. (1984). *Essays on moral development: The psychology of moral development.* San Francisco: Harper & Row.

Kohlberg, L., & Kramer, R. (1969). Continuities and discontinuities in childhood and adult moral development. *Human Development, 12,* 93–120.

Kohlberg, L., Levine, C., & Hewer, A. (1983). Moral stages: A current formulation and a response to critics. *Contributions to Human Development, 10,* 104–166.

Kuczynski, L., & Hildebrandt, N. (1997). Models of conformity and resistance in socialization theory. In J. E. Grusec & L. Kucynski (Eds.), *Parenting and the internalization of values: A handbook of contemporary theory* (pp. 227–256). New York: Wiley.

Kuczynski, L., Kochanska, G., Radke-Yarrow, M., & Girnius-Brown, O. (1987). A developmental interpretation of young children's noncompliance. *Developmental Psychology, 23,* 799–806.

Kuczynski, L., & Navara, G. S. (2006). Sources of innovation and change in socialization, internalization, and acculturation. In M.

Killen & J. G. Smetana (Eds.), *Handbook of moral development* (pp. 299–330). Mahwah, NJ: Erlbaum.

Latanée, B., & Darley, J. M. (1970). *The unresponsive bystander: Why doesn't he help?* New York: Appleton-Crofts.

Lau, S. (1992). Collectivism's individualism: Value preference, personal control, and the desire for freedom among Chinese in mainland China, Hong Kong, and Singapore. *Personality and Individual Differences, 13,* 361–366.

Laupa, M. (1991). Children's reasoning about three authority attributes: Adult status, knowledge, and social position. *Developmental Psychology, 27,* 321–329.

Laupa, M. (1994). "Who's in charge?" Preschool children's concepts of authority. *Early Childhood Research Quarterly, 9,* 1–17.

Laupa, M., & Turiel, E. (1986). Children's conceptions of adult and peer authority. *Child Development, 57,* 405–412.

Laupa, M., & Turiel, E. (1993). Children's concepts of authority and social contexts. *Journal of Educational Psychology, 85,* 191–197.

Laupa, M., Turiel, E., & Cowan, P. A. (1995). Obedience to authority in children and adults. In M. Killen & D. Hart (Eds.), *Morality in everyday life: Developmental perspectives* (pp. 131–165). Cambridge, England: Cambridge University Press.

Lennon, R., & Eisenberg, N. (1987). Gender and age differences in empathy and sympathy. In N. Eisenberg & J. Strayer (Eds.), *Empathy and its development* (pp. 195–217). New York: Cambridge University Press.

Lewis, M. (1993). The development of deception. In M. Lewis & C. Saarni (Eds.), *Lying and deception in everyday life* (pp. 90–105). New York: Guilford Press.

Li, J., & Yue, X. (2004). Self in learning in Chinese children. In M. F. Mascolo & J. Li (Eds.), *New directions in child and adolescent development: Vol. 104. Culture and developing selves—Beyond dichotomization* (pp. 27–44). San Francisco: Jossey-Bass.

Luria, Z. (1986). A methodological critique. *Signs, 11,* 318.

Lyons, N. P. (1983). Two perspectives: On self, relationships, and morality. *Harvard Educational Review, 53,* 125–145.

Maccoby, E. E. (1968). The development of moral values and behavior in childhood. In J. A. Clausen (Ed.), *Socialization and society* (pp. 227–269). Boston: Little, Brown.

Maccoby, E. E., & Jacklin, C. N. (1974). *The psychology of sex differences.* Stanford, CA: Stanford University Press.

Maccoby, E. E., & Martin, J. A. (1983). Socialization in the context of the family: Parent-child interaction. In P. Mussen (Series Ed.) & E. M. Hetherington (Vol. Ed.), *Handbook of child psychology: Vol. 4. Socialization, personality, and social development* (4th ed., pp. 1–102). New York: Wiley.

MacIntyre, A. (1981). *After virtue: A study in moral theory.* Notre Dame, IN: University of Notre Dame Press.

MacIntyre, A. (1988). *Whose justice? Which rationality?* Notre Dame, IN: University of Notre Dame Press.

Madden, T. (1992). *Cultural factors and assumptions in social reasoning in India.* Unpublished doctoral dissertation, University of California, Berkeley.

Markus, H. R., & Kitayama, S. (1991). Culture and the self: Implications for cognition, emotion, and motivation. *Psychological Review, 98,* 224–253.

Mascolo, M. F., & Li, J. (Eds.). (2004). *New Directions in child and adolescent development: Beyond dichotomization—Culture and developing selves.* San Francisco: Jossey-Bass.

McClosky, M., & Brill, A. (1983). *Dimensions of tolerance: What Americans believe about civil liberties.* New York: Russell Sage.

McDougall, W. (1908). *An introduction to social psychology.* London: Methuen.

McGlothlin, H., Killen, M., & Edmonds, C. (2005). European-American children's intergroup attitudes about peer relationships. *British Journal of Developmental Psychology, 23,* 227–249.

Mednick, M. T. (1989). On the politics of psychological constructs: Stop the bandwagon, I want to get off. *American Psychologist, 44,* 1118–1123.

Mencher, J. P. (1989). Women agricultural labourers and landowners in Kerala and Tamil Nadu: Some questions about gender and autonomy in the household. In M. Krishnaraj & K. Chanana (Eds.), *Gender and the household domain: Social and cultural dimensions* (pp. 117–141). London: Sage.

Mensing, J. F. (2002). *Collectivism, individualism, and interpersonal responsibilities in families: Differences and similarities in social reasoning between individuals in poor, urban families in Colombia and the United States.* Unpublished doctoral dissertation, University of California, Berkeley.

Mernissi, F. (1994). *Dreams of trespass: Tales of a harem girlhood.* Reading, MA: Addison-Wesley.

Milgram, S. (1974). *Obedience to authority.* New York: Harper & Row.

Mill, J. S. (1963). *On liberty.* London: Oxford University Press. (Original work published 1863)

Miller, J. G. (1984). Culture and the development of everyday social explanation. *Journal of Personality and Social Psychology, 46,* 961–978.

Miller, J. G. (1986). Early cross-cultural commonalities in social explanation. *Developmental Psychology, 22,* 514–520.

Miller, J. G., & Bersoff, D. M. (1992). Culture and moral judgment: How are conflicts between justice and interpersonal responsibilities resolved? *Journal of Personality and Social Psychology, 62,* 541–554.

Miller, J. G., & Bersoff, D. M. (1995). Development in the context of everyday family relationships: Culture, interpersonal morality, and adaption. In M. Killen & D. Hart (Eds.), *Morality in everyday life: Developmental perspectives* (pp. 259–282). Cambridge, England: Cambridge University Press.

Miller, J. G., Bersoff, D. M., & Harwood, R. L. (1990). Perceptions of social responsibilities in India and in the United States: Moral imperatives or personal decisions? *Journal of Personality and Social Psychology, 58,* 33–47.

Miller, J. G., & Luthar, S. (1989). Issues of interpersonal responsibility and accountability: A comparison of Indians' and Americans' moral judgments. *Social Cognition, 7,* 237–261.

Miller, P. A., Eisenberg, N., Fabes, R. A., & Shell, R. (1996). Relations of moral reasoning and vicarious emotion to young children's prosocial behavior toward peers and adults. *Developmental Psychology, 32,* 210–219.

Mills, C. W. (1956). *White collar: The American middle-class.* New York: Oxford University Press.

Mines, M. (1988). Conceptualizing the person: Hierarchial society and individual autonomy in India. *American Anthropologist, 90,* 568–579.

Mischel, W. (1973). Toward a cognitive social learning reconceptualization of personality. *Psychological Review, 80,* 252–283.

Misra, G., & Giri, R. (1995). Is Indian self predominantly interdependent? *Journal of Indian Psychology, 13,* 16–29.

Neff, K. D. (2001). Judgments of personal autonomy and interpersonal responsibility in the context of Indian spousal relationships: An examination of young people's reasoning in Mysore, India. *British Journal of Developmental Psychology, 19,* 233–257.

Neff, K. D., & Helwig, C. C. (2002). A constructivist approach to understanding the development of reasoning about rights and authority within cultural contexts. *Cognitive Development, 17,* 1429–1450.

Nissan, M. (1987). Moral norms and social conventions: A cross-cultural comparison. *Developmental Psychology, 23,* 719–725.

Norris, K. (1996, February). *Lying in the age of innocence: The deceitful child in Fin-de-Siecle France.* Paper presented at the Society for French Historical Studies annual meeting, Boston, MA.

Nucci, L. P. (1981). The development of personal concepts: A domain distinct from moral or social concepts. *Child Development, 52,* 114–121.

Nucci, L. P. (1984). Evaluating teachers as social agents: Students' ratings of domain appropriate and domain inappropriate teacher responses to transgressions. *American Educational Research Journal, 21,* 367–378.

Nucci, L. P. (1996). Morality and the personal sphere of action. In E. Reed, E. Turiel, & T. Brown (Eds.), *Values and knowledge* (pp. 41–60). Hillsdale, NJ: Erlbaum.

Nucci, L. P. (2001). *Education in the moral domain.* Cambridge, England: Cambridge University Press.

Nucci, L. P., Camino, C., & Milnitsky-Sapiro, C. (1996). Social class effects on Northeastern Brazilian children's conceptions of areas of personal choice and social regulation. *Child Development, 67,* 1223–1242.

Nucci, L. P., & Lee, J. (1993). Morality and personal autonomy. In G. G. Noam & T. Wren (Eds.), *The moral self: Building a better paradigm* (pp. 123–148). Cambridge, MA: MIT Press.

Nucci, L. P., & Nucci, M. S. (1982a). Children's responses to moral and social conventional transgressions in free-play settings. *Child Development, 53,* 1337–1342.

Nucci, L. P., & Nucci, M. S. (1982b). Children's social interactions in the context of moral and conventional transgressions. *Child Development, 53,* 403–412.

Nucci, L. P., & Smetana, J. G. (1996). Mother's concepts of young children's areas of personal freedom. *Child Development, 67,* 1870–1886.

Nucci, L. P., & Turiel, E. (1978). Social interactions and the development of social concepts in preschool children. *Child Development, 49,* 400–407.

Nucci, L. P., & Turiel, E. (2000). The moral and the personal: Sources of social conflicts. In L. P. Nucci, G. Saxe, & E. Turiel (Eds.), *Culture, thought, and development* (pp. 115–137). Mahwah, NJ: Erlbaum.

Nucci, L. P., Turiel, E., & Encarnacion-Gawrych, G. (1983). Children's social interactions and social concepts: Analyses of morality and convention in the Virgin Islands. *Journal of Cross-Cultural Psychology, 14,* 469–487.

Nucci, L. P., & Weber, E. (1995). Social interactions in the home and the development of young children's conceptions of the personal. *Child Development, 66,* 1438–1452.

Nunner-Winkler, G. (1984). Two moralities? A critical discussion of an ethic of care and responsibility versus an ethic of rights and justice. In W. M. Kurtines & J. L. Gewirtz (Eds.), *Morality, moral behavior, and moral development: Basic issues in theory and research* (pp. 348–364). New York: Wiley.

Nunner-Winkler, G., & Sodian, B. (1988). Children's understanding of moral emotions. *Child Development, 59,* 1323–1328.

Nussbaum, M. (1989, December 7). Recoiling from reason [Review of the book *Whose justice? Which rationality?*]. *New York Review of Books, 36,* 41.

Nussbaum, M. C. (1999). *Sex and social justice.* New York: Oxford University Press.

Nussbaum, M. C. (2000). *Women and human development: The capabilities approach.* Cambridge, England: Cambridge University Press.

Okin, S. M. (1989). *Justice, gender, and the family.* New York: Basic Books.

Okin, S. M. (1996). The gendered family and the development of a sense of justice. In E. S. Reed, E. Turiel, & T. Brown (Eds.), *Values and knowledge* (pp. 61–74). Hillsdale, NJ: Erlbaum.

Ornstein, P. (1994). *Schoolgirls: Young women, self esteem, and the confidence gap.* New York: Doubleday.

Oyserman, D., Coon, H. M., & Kemmelmeier, M. (2002). Rethinking individualism and collectivism: Evaluation of theoretical assumptions and meta-analyses. *Psychological Bulletin, 128,* 3–72.

Perkins, S. A. (2003). *Adolescent reasoning about lying in close relationships.* Unpublished doctoral dissertation, University of California, Berkeley.

Piaget, J. (1929). *The child's conception of the world.* London: Routledge & Kegan Paul.

Piaget, J. (1932). *The moral judgment of the child.* London: Routledge & Kegan Paul.

Piaget, J. (1995a). Egocentric thought and sociocentric thought. In J. Piaget (Ed.), *Sociological studies* (pp. 270–286). London: Routledge. (Original work published 1951)

Piaget, J. (1995b). *Sociological studies.* London: Routledge. (Original work published 1960)

Pollitt, K. L. (1992). Are women really superior to men? *Nation,* 799–807.

Pratt, M. W., Diessner, R., Hunsberger, B., Pancer, S. M., & Savoy, K. (1991). Four pathways in the analysis of adult development and aging: Comparing analyses of reasoning about personal-life dilemmas. *Psychology and Aging, 6,* 666–675.

Pratt, M. W., Golding, G., & Hunter, W. (1983). Aging as ripening: Character and consistency of moral judgment in young, mature, and older adults. *Human Development, 26,* 277–288.

Pratt, M. W., Golding, G., Hunter, W., & Norris, J. (1988). From inquiry to judgment: Age and sex differences in patterns of adult moral thinking and information-seeking. *International Journal of Aging and Human Development, 27,* 109–124.

Radke-Yarrow, M., Zahn-Waxler, C., & Chapman, M. (1983). Children's prosocial dispositions and behavior. In P. Mussen (Series Ed.) & E. M. Hetherington (Vol. Ed.), *Handbook of child psychology: Vol. 4. Socialization, personality, and social development* (4th ed., pp. 469–545). New York: Wiley.

Rawls, J. (1971). *A theory of justice.* Cambridge, MA: Harvard University Press.

Rawls, J. (1993). *Political liberalism.* New York: Columbia University Press.

Reisman, D. (with N. Glazer & R. Denney). (1950). *The lonely crowd: A study of the changing American character.* New York: Doubleday.

Rende, R., & Killen, M. (1992). Social interactional antecedents of object conflict. *Early Childhood Research Quarterly, 1,* 551–563.

Rest, J. (1979). *Development in judging moral issues.* Minneapolis: University of Minnesota Press.

Rest, J. (1983). Morality. In P. Mussen (Series Ed.) & J. H. Flavell & E. Markman (Vol. Eds.), *Handbook of child psychology: Vol. 3. Cognitive development* (4th ed., pp. 920–990). New York: Wiley.

Rest, J., & Narvaez, D. (1991). The college experience and moral development. In W. M. Kurtines & J. L. Gewirtz (Eds.), *Handbook*

of moral behavior and development: Vol. 2. Research (pp. 229–245). Hillsdale, NJ: Erlbaum.

Rest, J. D., Narvaez, M., & Thoma, S. (1999). *Postconventional moral thinking: A neo-Kohlbergian approach.* Mahwah, NJ: Erlbaum.

Ross, L., Bierbrauer, G., & Hoffman, S. (1976). The role of attributional processes in conformity and dissent: Revisiting the Asch situation. *American Psychologist, 31,* 148–157.

Ross, L., & Nisbett, R. M. (1991). *The person and the situation: Perspectives on social psychology.* Philadelphia: Temple University Press.

Rothbart, M. K., Hanley, D., & Albert, M. (1986). Gender differences in moral reasoning. *Sex Roles, 15,* 645–653.

Ruck, M. D., Abramovitch, R., & Keating, D. P. (1998). Children's and adolescents' understandings of rights: Balancing nurturance and self-determination. *Child Development, 69,* 404–417.

Ryan, A. (1995). *John Dewey and the high tide of American liberalism.* New York: Norton.

Ryan, K. (1989). In defense of character education. In L. P. Nucci (Ed.), *Moral development and character education: A dialogue* (pp. 3–18). Berkeley, CA: McCutchan.

Sagi, A., & Hoffman, M. L. (1976). Empathic distress in the newborn. *Developmental Psychology, 32,* 720–729.

Saltzstein, H. D., Weiner, S., & Munk, J. (1995). *Children's judgments of the fairness of mothers who approve/disapprove good and bad intended acts.* Unpublished manuscript, City University of New York.

Saltzstein, M. D., Weiner, A. S., Munk, J. S., Supraner, A., Blank, R., & Schwarz, R. P. (1987). Comparison between children's own moral judgments and those they attribute to adults. *Merrill-Palmer Quarterly, 33,* 33–51.

Sears, R. R., Maccoby, E. E., & Levin, M. (1957). *Patterns of child reasoning.* Evanston, IL: Row-Peterson.

Selman, R. L. (1980). *The growth of interpersonal understanding: Developmental and clinical analyses.* New York: Academic Press.

Shaw, L., & Wainryb, C. (1999). The outsider's perspective: Young adults' judgments of social practices of other cultures. *British Journal of Developmental Psychology, 17,* 451–471.

Shweder, R. A. (1982). Liberalism as destiny. *Contemporary Psychology, 27,* 421–424.

Shweder, R. A. (1986). Divergent rationalities. In D. W. Fiske & R. A. Shweder (Eds.), *Metatheory in social science: Pluralism and subjectivities* (pp. 163–196). Chicago: University of Chicago Press.

Shweder, R. A. (1990a). Cultural psychology—What is it. In J. W. Stigler, R. A. Shweder, & G. Herdt (Eds.), *Cultural psychology: Essays on comparative human development* (pp. 1–43). Cambridge, England: Cambridge University Press.

Shweder, R. A. (1990b). In defense of moral realism: Reply to Gabennesch. *Child Development, 61,* 2060–2067.

Shweder, R. A. (1994). Are moral intuitions self-evident truths? *Criminal Justice Ethics, 13,* 24–31.

Shweder, R. A. (2002). "What about female genital mutilation?" And why understanding culture matters in the first place. In R. A. Shweder, M. Minow, & H. R. Markus (Eds.), *Engaging cultural differences: The multicultutral challenge in liberal democracies* (pp. 216–251). New York: Russell Sage Foundation.

Shweder, R. A., & Bourne, E. J. (1982). Does the concept of person vary cross-culturally. In A. J. Marsella & G. M. White (Eds.), *Cultural conceptions of mental health and therapy* (pp. 97–137). Boston: Reidel.

Shweder, R. A., & Haidt, J. (1993). The future of moral psychology: Truth, intuition, and the pluralist way. *Psychological Science, 4,* 360–356.

Shweder, R. A., Mahapatra, M., & Miller, J. G. (1987). Culture and moral development. In J. Kagan & S. Lamb (Eds.), *The emergence of morality in young children* (pp. 1–83). Chicago: University of Chicago Press.

Shweder, R. A., & Miller, J. G. (1985). The social construction of the person: How is it possible. In K. J. Gergen & K. Davis (Eds.), *The social construction of the person* (pp. 41–69). New York: Springer-Verlag.

Shweder, R. A., Much, N. C., Mahapatra, M., & Park, L. (1997). The "big three" of morality (autonomy, community, and divinity) and the "big three" explanations of suffering. In A. Brandt & P. Rozin (Eds.), *Morality and health* (pp. 119–169). Stanford, CA: Stanford University Press.

Shweder, R. A., & Sullivan, M. A. (1993). Cultural psychology: Who needs it? *Annual Review of Psychology, 44,* 497–523.

Siegal, M., & Storey, R. M. (1985). Day care and children's conceptions of moral and social rules. *Child Development, 56,* 1001–1008.

Simpson, E. L. (1973). Moral development research: A case study of scientific cultural bias. *Human Development, 17,* 81–106.

Skinner, B. F. (1971). *Beyond freedom and dignity.* New York: Knopf.

Skoe, E. E., Eisenberg, N., & Cumberland, A. (2002). The role of reported emotion in real-life and hypothetical moral dilemmas. *Personality and Social Psychology Bulletin, 28,* 962–973.

Skoe, E. E., & Gooden, A. (1993). Ethic of care, justice, identity and gender: An extension and replication. *Merrill-Palmer Quarterly, 40,* 109–117.

Skoe, E. E., Hansen, K. L., Morch, W., Bakke, I., Hoffman, T., Larsen, B., et al. (1999). Care-based moral reasoning in Norwegian and Canadian adolescents: A cross-national comparison. *Journal of Early Adolescence, 19,* 280–291.

Smetana, J. G. (1981). Preschool conceptions of moral and social rules. *Child Development, 52,* 1333–1336.

Smetana, J. G. (1982). *Concepts of self and morality: Women's reasoning about abortion.* New York: Praeger.

Smetana, J. G. (1984). Toddlers' social interactions regarding moral and conventional transgressions. *Child Development, 55,* 1767–1776.

Smetana, J. G. (1985). Preschool children's conceptions of transgressions: Effects of varying moral and conventional domain-related attributes. *Developmental Psychology, 21,* 18–29.

Smetana, J. G. (1988). Adolescents' and parents' conceptions of parental authority. *Child Development, 59,* 321–335.

Smetana, J. G. (1989a). Adolescents' and parents' reasoning about actual family conflict. *Child Development, 60,* 1052–1067.

Smetana, J. G. (1989b). Toddlers' social interactions in the context of moral and conventional transgressions in the home. *Developmental Psychology, 25,* 499–508.

Smetana, J. G. (1993). Conceptions of parental authority in divorced and married mothers and their adolescents. *Journal of Research in Adolescence, 3,* 19–40.

Smetana, J. G. (1995a). Context, conflict, and constraint in adolescent-parent authority relationships. In M. Killen & D. Hart (Eds.), *Morality in everyday life: Developmental perspectives* (pp. 225–255). Cambridge, England: Cambridge University Press.

Smetana, J. G. (1995b). Morality in context: Abstractions, ambiguities, and applications. In R. Vasta (Ed.), *Annals of child development* (Vol. 10, pp. 83–130). London: Jessica Kingsley.

Smetana, J. G. (1997). Parenting and the development of social knowledge reconceptualized: A social domain analysis. In J. E. Grusec & L. Kuczynski (Eds.), *Parenting and the internalization of values* (pp. 162–192). New York: Wiley.

Smetana, J. G. (2000). Middle class African American adolescents' and parents' conceptions of parental authority and parenting practices: A longitudinal investigation. *Child Development, 71,* 1672–1686.

Smetana, J. G. (2002). Culture, autonomy, and personal jurisdiction in adolescent-parent relationships. In H. W. Reese & R. Kail (Eds.), *Advances in child development and behavior* (Vol. 29, pp. 51–87). New York: Academic Press.

Smetana, J. G. (2006). Social domain theory: Consistencies and variations in children's moral and social judgments. In M. Killen & J. G. Smetana (Eds.), *Handbook of moral development* (pp. 119–153). Mahwah, NJ: Erlbaum.

Smetana, J. G., & Asquith, P. (1994). Adolescents' and parents' conceptions of parental authority and adolescent autonomy. *Child Development, 65,* 1147–1162.

Smetana, J. G., & Braeges, J. L. (1990). The development of toddler's moral and conventional judgments. *Merrill-Palmer Quarterly, 36,* 329–346.

Smetana, J. G., Braeges, J. L., & Yau, J. (1991). Doing what you say and saying what you do: Reasoning about adolescent-parent conflict in interviews and interactions. *Journal of Adolescent Research, 6,* 276–295.

Smetana, J. G., Bridgeman, D. L., & Turiel, E. (1983). Differentiation of domains and prosocial behaviors. In D. L. Bridgeman (Ed.), *The nature of prosocial development: Interdisciplinary theories and strategies* (pp. 163–183). New York: Academic Press.

Smetana, J. G., & Daddis, C. (2002). Domain-specific antecedents of psychological control and parental monitoring: The role of parenting beliefs and practices. *Child Development, 73,* 563–580.

Smetana, J. G., & Gaines, C. (1999). Adolescent-parent conflict in middle-class African-American families. *Child Development, 70,* 1447–1463.

Smetana, J. G., Killen, M., & Turiel, E. (1991). Children's reasoning about interpersonal and moral conflicts. *Child Development, 62,* 629–644.

Smetana, J. G., Schlagman, N., & Adams, P. W. (1993). Preschool children's judgments about hypothetical and actual transgressions. *Child Development, 64,* 202–214.

Smetana, J. G., Toth, S., Cicchetti, D., Bruce, J., Kane, P., & Daddis, C. (1999). Maltreated and nonmaltreated preschoolers' conceptions of hypothetical and actual moral transgressions. *Developmental Psychology, 35,* 269–281.

Smetana, J. G., & Turiel, E. (2003). Morality during adolescence. In G. R. Adams & M. Berzonsky (Eds.), *Blackwell handbook of adolescence* (pp. 247–268). Oxford, England: Blackwell.

Smetana, J. G., Yau, J., Restrepo, A., & Braeges, J. (1991). Adolescent-parent conflict in married and divorced families. *Developmental Psychology, 27,* 1000–1010.

Snarey, J. (1985). Cross-cultural universality of social-moral development: A critical review of Kohlbergian research. *Psychological Bulletin, 97,* 202–232.

Song, M. J., Smetana, J. G., & Kim, S. Y. (1987). Korean children's conceptions of moral and conventional transgressions. *Developmental Psychology, 23,* 577–582.

Spiro, M. (1993). Is the Western conception of the self "peculiar" within the context of the world cultures? *Ethos, 21,* 107–153.

Stack, C. (1990). Different voices, different visions: Race, gender, and moral reasoning. In R. Ginsberg & A. Tsing (Eds.), *The negotiation of gender in American society* (pp. 19–27). Boston: Beacon Press.

Stouffer, S. (1955). *Communism, conformity and civil liberties.* New York: Doubleday.

Strauss, C. (1992). Models and motives. In R. G. D'Andrade & C. Strauss (Eds.), *Human motives and cultural models* (pp. 1–20). Cambridge, England: Cambridge University Press.

Theimer, C. E., Killen, M., & Stangor, C. (2001). Young children's evaluations of exclusion in gender-stereotypic peer contexts. *Developmental Psychology, 37,* 18–27.

Thompson, R. A., Meyer, S., & McGinley, M. (2006). Understanding values in relationships: The development of conscience. In M. Killen & J. G. Smetana (Eds.), *Handbook of moral development* (pp. 267–298). Mahwah, NJ: Erlbaum.

Thorkildsen, T. A. (1989a). Justice in the classroom: The student's view. *Child Development, 60,* 323–334.

Thorkildsen, T. A. (1989b). Pluralism in children's reasoning about social justice. *Child Development, 60,* 965–972.

Thorkildsen, T. A. (1991). Defining social goods and distributing them fairly: The development of conceptions of fair testing practices. *Child Development, 62,* 852–862.

Tisak, M. S. (1986). Children's conceptions of parental authority. *Child Development, 57,* 166–176.

Tisak, M. S. (1993). Preschool children's judgments of moral and personal events involving physical harm and property damage. *Merrill-Palmer Quarterly, 39,* 375–390.

Tisak, M. S. (1995). Domains of social reasoning and beyond. In R. Vista (Ed.), *Annals of child development* (Vol. 11, pp. 95–130). London: Jessica Kingsley.

Tisak, M. S., Nucci, L., Baskind, D., & Lampling, M. (1991, August). *Preschool children's social interactions: An observational study.* Paper presented at the annual meeting of the American Psychological Association, San Francisco, CA.

Tisak, M. S., & Tisak, J. (1990). Children's conceptions of parental authority, friendship, and sibling relations. *Merrill-Palmer Quarterly, 36,* 347–367.

Tisak, M. S., & Turiel, E. (1984). Children's conceptions of moral and prudential rules. *Child Development, 55,* 1030–1039.

Tisak, M. S., & Turiel, E. (1988). Variation in seriousness of transgressions and children's moral and conventional concepts. *Developmental Psychology, 24,* 352–357.

Tooby, J. (1987). The emergence of evolutionary psychology. In D. Pines (Ed.), *Emerging synthesis in science* (pp. 67–76). Santa Fe, NM: Santa Fe Institute.

Triandis, H. C. (1990). Cross-cultural studies of individualism and collectivism. In J. J. Berman (Ed.), *Nebraska Symposium on Motivation: Vol. 37. Cross-cultural perspectives* (pp. 41–133). Lincoln: University of Nebraska Press.

Turiel, E. (1978a). The development of concepts of social structure: Social convention. In J. Glick & K. A. Clarke-Stewart (Eds.), *The development of social understanding* (pp. 25–107). New York: Gardner Press.

Turiel, E. (1978b). Social regulation and domains of social concepts. In W. Damon (Ed.), *Social cognition: New directions for child development* (pp. 45–74). San Francisco: Jossey-Bass.

Turiel, E. (1979). Distinct conceptual and developmental domains: Social convention and morality. In H. E. Howe & G. B. Keasey (Eds.), *Nebraska Symposium on Motivation: Vol. 25. Social cognitive development* (pp. 77–116). Lincoln: University of Nebraska Press.

Turiel, E. (1983a). *The development of social knowledge: Morality and convention.* Cambridge, England: Cambridge University Press.

Turiel, E. (1983b). Interaction and development in social cognition. In E. T. Higgins, D. N. Ruble, & W. W. Hartup (Eds.), *Social cognition and social development: A sociocultural perspective* (pp. 333–355). Cambridge, England: Cambridge University Press.

Turiel, E. (1989). Domain-specific social judgments and domain ambiguities. *Merril-Palmer Quarterly, 35,* 89–114.

Turiel, E. (1994). Morality, authoritarianism, and personal agency. In R. J. Sternberg & P. Ruzgis (Eds.), *Personality and intelligence* (pp. 271–299). Cambridge, England: Cambridge University Press.

Turiel, E. (1996). Equality and hierarchy: Conflict in values. In E. S. Reed, E. Turiel, & T. Brown (Eds.), *Values and knowledge* (pp. 71–102). Hillsdale, NJ: Erlbaum.

Turiel, E. (1998). Notes from the underground: Culture, conflict, and subversion. In J. Langer & M. Killen (Eds.), *Piaget, evolution, and development* (pp. 271–296). Mahwah, NJ: Erlbaum.

Turiel, E. (2002). *The culture of morality: Social development, context, and conflict.* Cambridge, England: Cambridge University Press.

Turiel, E. (2003a). Morals, motives, and actions. In L. Smith, C. Rogers, & P. Tomlinson (Eds.), *Development and motivation: Joint perspectives* (Monograph Series II, Serial No. 2, pp. 29–40). Leicester, England: British Journal of Educational Psychology.

Turiel, E. (2003b). Resistance and subversion in everyday life. *Journal of Moral Education, 32,* 115–130.

Turiel, E. (2004a). Historical lessons: The value of pluralism in psychological research. *Merrill-Palmer Quarterly, 50,* 535–545.

Turiel, E. (2004b). The many faces of parenting. In J. G. Smetana (Ed.), *Changing boundaries of parental authority during adolescence: New directions in child and adolescent development* (pp. 79–88). San Francisco: Jossey-Bass.

Turiel, E. (2006). Thought, emotions, and social interactional processes in moral development. In M. Killen & J. G. Smetana (Eds.), *Handbook of moral development (pp. 7–36).* Mahwah, NJ: Erlbaum.

Turiel, E. (in press-a). The multiplicity of social norms: The case for psychological constructivism and social epistemologies. In L. Smith & J. Voneche (Eds.), *Norms and development.* Cambridge, UK: Cambridge University Press.

Turiel, E. (in press-b). The trouble with the ways morality is used and how they impede social equality and social justice. In C. Wainryb, J. Smetana, & E. Turiel (Eds.), *Social development, social inequalities, and social justice.* Mahwah, NJ: Erlbaum.

Turiel, E., & Davidson, P. (1986). Heterogeneity, inconsistency, and asynchrony in the development of cognitive structures. In I. Levin (Ed.), *Stage and structure: Reopening the debate* (pp. 106–143). Norwood, NJ: Ablex.

Turiel, E., Hildebrandt, C., & Wainryb, C. (1991). Judging social issues: Difficulties, inconsistencies and consistencies. *Monographs of the Society for Research in Child Development, 56*(Serial No. 224).

Turiel, E., Killen, M., & Helwig, C. C. (1987). Morality: Its structure, functions and vagaries. In J. Kagan & S. Lamb (Eds.), *The emergence of moral concepts in young children* (pp. 155–244). Chicago: University of Chicago Press.

Turiel, E., & Perkins, S. A. (2004). Flexibilities of mind: Conflict and culture. *Human Development, 47,* 158–178.

Turiel, E., & Smetana, J. G. (1984). Social knowledge and social action: The coordination of domains. In W. M. Kurtines & J. L. Gewirtz (Eds.), *Morality, moral behavior, and moral development: Basic issues in theory and research* (pp. 261–282). New York: Wiley.

Turiel, E., & Smetana, J. G. (1998). Limiting the limits on domains: Comments on Fowler and heteronomy. *Merrill-Palmer Quarterly, 44,* 293–312.

Turiel, E., & Wainryb, C. (1994). Social reasoning and the varieties of social experience in cultural contexts. In H. W. Reese (Ed.), *Advances in child development and behavior* (Vol. 25, pp. 289–326). New York: Academic Press.

Turiel, E., & Wainryb, C. (1998). Concepts of freedoms and rights in a traditional hierarchically organized society. *British Journal of Developmental Psychology, 16,* 375–395.

Turiel, E., & Wainryb, C. (2000). Social life in cultures: Judgments, conflicts, and subversion. *Child Development, 71,* 250–256.

Vail, S., & Turiel, E. (1995). *Children's judgments about others' social practices.* Unpublished manuscript, University of California, Berkeley.

Valiente, C., Eisenberg, N., Smith, C. L., Reiser, M., Fabes, R. A., Losoya, S., et al. (2003). The relations of effortful control and reactive control to children's externalizing problems: A longitudinal assessment. *Journal of Personality, 71,* 1171–1196.

Wainryb, C. (1991). Understanding differences in moral judgments: The role of informational assumptions. *Child Development, 62,* 840–851.

Wainryb, C. (1993). The application of moral judgments to other cultures: Relativism and universality. *Child Development, 64,* 924–933.

Wainryb, C. (1995). Reasoning about social conflicts in different cultures: Druze and Jewish children in Israel. *Child Development, 66,* 390–401.

Wainryb, C. (2006). Moral development in culture: Diversity, tolerance, and justice. In M. Killen & J. G. Smetana (Eds.), *Handbook of moral development* (pp. 211–240). Mahwah, NJ: Erlbaum.

Wainryb, C., & Ford, S. (1998). Young children's evaluations of acts based on beliefs different from their own. *Merrill-Palmer Quarterly, 44,* 484–503.

Wainryb, C., Shaw, L. A., Langley, M., Cottam, K., & Lewis, R. (2004). Children's thinking about diversity of belief in the early school years: Judgments of relativism, tolerance, and disagreeing persons. *Child Development, 75,* 687–703.

Wainryb, C., Shaw, L. A., Laupa, M., & Smith, K. (2001). Childrens', adolescents', and young adults' thinking about different types of disagreements. *Developmental Psychology, 37,* 373–386.

Wainryb, C., & Turiel, E. (1994). Dominance, subordination, and concepts of personal entitlements in cultural contexts. *Child Development, 65,* 1701–1722.

Wainryb, C., & Turiel, E. (1995). Diversity in social development: Between or within cultures. In M. Killen & D. Hart (Eds.), *Morality in everyday life: Developmental perspectives* (pp. 283–313). Cambridge, England: Cambridge University Press.

Walker, L. J. (1980). Cognitive and perspective-taking prerequisites for moral development. *Child Development, 51,* 131–139.

Walker, L. J. (1982). The sequentiality of Kohlberg's stages of moral development. *Child Development, 53,* 1330–1336.

Walker, L. J. (1984). Sex differences in the development of moral reasoning: A critical review. *Child Development, 55,* 677–691.

Walker, L. J. (1991). Sex differences in moral reasoning. In W. M. Kurtines & J. L. Gewirtz (Eds.), *Handbook of moral behavior and development: Vol. 2. Research* (pp. 333–364). Hillsdale, NJ: Erlbaum.

Walker, L. J., de Vries, B., & Bichard, S. L. (1984). The hierarchical nature of stages of moral development. *Developmental Psychology, 20,* 960–966.

Walker, L. J., de Vries, B., & Trevethan, S. D. (1987). Moral stages and moral orientations in real-life and hypothetical dilemmas. *Child Development, 58,* 842–858.

Walker, L. J., & Taylor, J. H. (1991). Stage transitions in moral reasoning: A longitudinal study of developmental processes. *Developmental Psychology, 27,* 330–337.

Watson, J. B. (1924). *Behaviorism.* New York: The People's Institute.

Weston, D. R., & Turiel, E. (1980). Act-rule relations: Children's concepts of social rules. *Developmental Psychology, 16,* 417–424.

Whyte, W. H. (1956). *The organization man.* New York: Simon & Schuster.

Wikan, U. (1991). Toward an experience-near anthropology. *Cultural Anthropology, 6,* 285–305.

Wikan, U. (1996). *Tomorrow, God willing: Self-made destinies in Cairo.* Chicago: University of Chicago Press.

Wikan, U. (2002). *Generous betrayal: Politics of culture in the new Europe.* Chicago: University of Chicago Press.

Willis, P. (1977). *Learning to labor: How working class kids get working class jobs.* New York: Columbia University Press.

Wilson, J. Q. (1993). *The moral sense.* New York: Free Press.

Winch, P. (1972). *Ethics and action.* London: Routledge & Kegan Paul.

Wright, R. (1994). *The moral animal: The new science of evolutionary psychology.* New York: Pantheon Books.

Wynia, M. K., Cummins, D. S., VanGeest, J. B., & Wilson, I. B. (2000). Physician manipulation of reimbursement rules for patients: Between a rock and a hard place. *Journal of the American Medical Association, 283,* 1858–1865.

Wynne, E. A. (1986). The great tradition in education: Transmitting moral values. *Educational Leadership, 43,* 4–9.

Wynne, E. A. (1989). Transmitting traditional values in contemporary schools. In L. P. Nucci (Ed.), *Moral development and character education: A dialogue* (pp. 19–36). Berkeley, CA: McCutchan.

Yamada, H. (2004). Japanese mothers' views of young children's areas of personal discretion. *Child Development, 75,* 164–179.

Yau, J., & Smetana, J. G. (1996). Adolescent-parent conflict among Chinese adolescents in Hong Kong. *Child Development, 67,* 1262–1275.

Yau, J., & Smetana, J. G . (2003). Conceptions of moral, social-conventional, and personal events among Chinese preschoolers in Hong Kong. *Child Development, 74,* 647–658.

Youniss, J. (1980). *Parents and peers in social development: A Sullivan-Piaget perspective.* Chicago: University of Chicago Press.

Zahn-Waxler, C., Radke-Yarrow, M., Wagner, E., & Chapman, M. (1992). Development of concern for others. *Developmental Psychology, 28,* 126–136.

Zahn-Waxler, C., Robinson, J. L., & Emde, R. N. (1992). The development of empathy in twins. *Developmental Psychology, 28,* 1038–1047.

Zimba, R. F. (1987). *A study of forms of social knowledge in Zambia.* Unpublished doctoral dissertation, Purdue University, West Lafayette, IN.

CHAPTER 14

Gender Development

DIANE N. RUBLE, CAROL LYNN MARTIN, and SHERI A. BERENBAUM

Being born a girl or a boy has implications that carry considerably beyond chromosomal, hormonal, and genital differences. Virtually all of human functioning has a gendered cast—appearance, mannerisms, communication, temperament, activities at home and outside, aspirations, and values. In this chapter, we consider the developmental processes involved in sustaining this gender system. How does a girl come to think of herself as a girl? When and why do children prefer same-sex playmates and activities? Do the sexes really differ cognitively? Do children's beliefs about the sexes influence their own behavior?

The issues surrounding gender span many controversial and intriguing topics. Given the broad scope of topics, the many studies that have been conducted, and space restrictions, however, we limit our coverage to updating the last *Handbook* chapters on gender development (Huston, 1983; Ruble & Martin, 1998). To maintain continuity, we build on the framework that Huston (1983) carefully developed, and that we (Ruble

& Martin, 1998) modified and expanded. The multidimensional framework provides a good way to organize the area, and it helps to direct new research efforts.

In our 1998 chapter, we began by presenting general issues and trends in research on gender development. We refer interested readers to the previous chapter for: (a) a brief historical review of the broad perspectives (developmental and social psychological, evolutionary and, anthropological and sociological) that have shaped current theorizing about gender development; and (b) a brief description of central conceptual and methodological issues in the areas of sex differences, gender stereotyping, masculinity/femininity, gender schemas, and gender categories.

Our current review is organized in three major sections. First, we present a detailed *description* of what aspects of gender are changing across age, including sex differences, using a modified version of the matrix of gender-related constructs and content presented in previous editions (Huston, 1983; Ruble & Martin, 1998).

This chapter is dedicated to our mothers, Edith Berenbaum, and, in loving memory, to Marjorie W. Nelesen and Carolyn I. Martin. We are grateful to Faith Greulich and Matt DiDonato for assistance in gathering materials and organizing references. We are also grateful to Meredith Bachman, David Perry, and Martin Trautner for a number of very helpful suggestions, and to Elaine Blakemore for sharing her reviews of the literature on sex differences in physical skills, cognitive abilities, personality, and social behavior. Preparation of this chapter was facilitated by a Research Award (MH37215) from the National Institute of Mental Health to D. Ruble, and by Research Awards from National Institute of Child Heath and Human Development to Carol Martin (HD45816) and to Sheri Berenbaum (HD19644).

Second, we consider the *causes* of developmental and sex difference trends from three major theoretical orientations—biological, socialization, and cognitive—emphasizing aspects that have generated the most controversy. Finally, we suggest conclusions and future research directions. A source of continuing debate concerns terminology, especially sex versus gender. For many scholars, the debate involves assumptions of causality, with "gender" used for socially based characteristics and "sex" used for biologically based characteristics. Because causality is more complex than such a system implies, we instead adopt Deaux's (1993) terminology: *sex* refers to the demographic categories of female and male, and *gender* refers to judgments or inferences about the sexes, such as stereotypes, roles, and masculinity and femininity. Even this system is difficult to apply unequivocally, so we are not rigid about its application. In general, we use the term *gender* except when comparisons explicitly involve girls and boys or men and women as a category—for example, *sex differences* and *sex segregation*.

THE DEVELOPMENT OF GENDER-RELATED CONSTRUCTS AND CONTENT

In this section, we update earlier reviews of the developmental course of the components of gender, using our modification (Ruble & Martin, 1998) of Huston's (1983) multidimensional matrix (see Table 14.1).

TABLE 14.1   A Matrix of Gender-Typing: Constructs by Content (All Entries Are Examples)

Content Area	A. Concepts or Beliefs	B. Identity or Self-Perception	C. Preferences	D. Behavioral Enactment
1. *Biological/categorical sex.*	1A. Gender awareness, labeling, and constancy.	1B. Personal sense of self as male or female.	1C. Wish to be male or female.	1D. Displaying bodily attributes of one's gender (e.g., clothing, body type, or hair); transvestism, transsexualism.
2. *Activities and interests:* Toys, play activities, occupations, household roles, or tasks.	2A. Knowledge of gender stereotypes or beliefs about toys, activities, and so on.	2B. Self-perception of interests and activities as related to gender.	2C. Preference for toys, games, or activities.	2D. Engaging in gender-typed play, activities, occupations, or achievement tasks.
3. *Personal-social attributes:* Personality traits, social behaviors, and abilities.	3A. Knowledge of gender stereotypes or beliefs about personality or role-appropriate social behavior.	3B. Perception of own traits and abilities (e.g., on self-rating questionnaires).	3C. Preference or wish to have gender-linked attributes.	3D. Displaying gender-typed traits (e.g., aggression, dependence) and abilities (e.g., math).
4. *Social relationships:* Sex of peers, friends, lovers; or play qualities.	4A. Concepts about norms for gender-based relationships.	4B. Self-perception of own patterns of friendships, relationships, or sexual orientation.	4C. Preference for social interactions or judgments about social relationships based on sex or gender.	4D. Engaging in social activity with others on the basis of sex or gender (e.g., same-sex peer play).
5. *Styles and symbols:* Gestures, speech patterns (e.g., tempo), appearance, or body image.	5A. Awareness of gender-related symbols or styles.	5B. Self-perception of non-verbal stylistic characteristics or body image.	5C. Preference for gender-typed stylistic or symbolic objects or personal characteristics.	5D. Manifesting gender-typed verbal and nonverbal behavior.
6. *Values regarding gender.*	6A. Knowledge of greater value attached to one sex or gender role than the other.	6B. Self-perceptions associated with group identification.	6C. In-group/out-group biases, prejudice, or attitudes toward egalitarian roles.	6D. In-group/out-group discrimination.

The four Constructs (columns) are: Concepts or Beliefs, Identity or Self-Perception, Preferences, and Behavioral Enactment. The six Contents (rows) are: Biological/Categorical Sex, Activities and Interests, Personal-Social Attributes, Social Relationships, Styles and Symbols, and Values. Definitions and examples are provided in the cells of the table. Our review is divided by matrix cells (ordered by row headings), beginning with a review of the literature on biological/categorical sex. The sections are designated with the numbers and letters corresponding to the cells in the matrix.

The matrix is organized around the content areas to allow for consistencies and variations in each content domain to be recognized. The matrix remains useful, especially in pinpointing areas needing additional research, and in providing clear distinctions among aspects of gender-typing. The multidimensional nature of gender-typing is evident in examining patterns across cells. The drawback of using the matrix is that it presents a rather piecemeal and atheoretical picture of gender development. Furthermore, there are some difficulties in distinguishing some of the constructs and content domains (e.g., preferences and behavior) and in ensuring that common developmental trends across cells are identified. The major theories of gender development that help to integrate the material will be presented and evaluated following the matrix review. These theories posit consistencies across certain cells of the matrix. For instance, several theories hold that concepts or beliefs about a content area, such as stereotypes about activities and interests, influence preferences and adoption of these attributes. Some theories suggest that gender identity influences preferences and adoption of attributes more broadly. This revision also reflects areas that have received recent attention: early gender labeling and identity, children with "disorders of sex development" (previously termed "intersex conditions"), and body image. Because this is a revision of our prior chapter and because of major space limitations, we have deleted most references from the prior edition, and instead cite Ruble and Martin (1998), suggesting that the reader look there for original citations.

Biological/Categorical Sex (1)

The literature on biological/categorical sex spans a wide array of well-researched topics, including gender identity, gender constancy, and intersex conditions. Many of these issues are controversial and the topics have wide-ranging theoretical importance. A key issue concerns how and when do children learn about their placement in a gender group. This issue has been theoretically important, especially in untangling biological and environmental contributors to gender identity.

Concepts or Beliefs (1A)

Making Gender Distinctions. How early can children discriminate the sexes? Recent research using habituation and preferential looking paradigms suggests that infants as young as 3 to 4 months of age are capable of distinguishing between males and females in a categorical manner (e.g., Quinn, Yahr, Kuhn, Slater, & Pascalis, 2002). Subsequently, as described in a recent review (Martin, Ruble, & Szkrybalo, 2002), 9- to 11-month-olds can discriminate faces by sex, habituate to faces of both sexes, and make intermodal associations (e.g., among female faces and voices). It has not always been clear whether infants have established gender categories prior to testing or whether ad hoc categories are formed during the testing. Recent research suggests that infant performance is influenced by experiences prior to the experiment; for instance, the sex of the primary caretaker influences infants' preferences for male or female faces (Quinn et al., 2002). Thus, these studies suggest that before children can walk or talk, they have in place perceptual categories that distinguish "male" from "female."

When can children label the sexes? Early research suggested that most children cannot reliably sort pictures of males and females until after 30 months of age (S. K. Thompson, 1975). With other measures, however, many children appear to understand and use gender labels much earlier (e.g., Fagot & Leinbach, 1989; Weinraub et al., 1984). For example, in two recent studies, most 24- and 28-month-old children chose the correct picture in response to experimenter-provided gender labels (A. Campbell, Shirley, & Caygill, 2002; G. D. Levy, 1999).

These findings imply that many children understand gender labels by their second birthday. Research with other methods suggests that gender labeling may occur even earlier. For example, in a preferential looking paradigm, 50% of 18-month-old girls showed knowledge of gender labels ("lady" or "man") but boys did not, and 50% of 18- and 24-month-old boys and girls showed above chance understanding of the label boy (Poulin-Dubois, Serbin, & Derbyshire, 1998). Other evidence suggests that gender words occur early in vocabulary development (Stennes, Burch, Sen, & Bauer, 2005); parents report that the words "boy," "girl," and "man" are understood by many toddlers by 22 months (Fenson et al., 1994). In a longitudinal study (Zosuls, Greulich, Haddad, Ruble, & Tamis-LeMonda, 2006), parent diaries indicated that, by 22 months of age, 56% of boys and 86% of girls had at least one gender label in their productive vocabulary (e.g., boy/girl; man/lady). Taken together, these findings suggest a need to revise prior conclusions that children do not understand gender labels until 2½ years.

What cues are used to discriminate or label the sexes? Perceptual discriminations made before 6 months of age may be based on facial features alone, without hair styles/length or clothing cues (Quinn et al., 2002). In verbal labeling, young children rely heavily on hair cues, believing that figures with blonde, curly, long hair are females (Intons-Peterson, 1988a), but some preschoolers can recognize genital differences when realistic pictures are used (S. L. Bem, 1989). Recent data suggest that 3-year-olds can identify a neutral figure as a man or a woman using clothes and voice, with hair a better cue for identifying the figure as a woman than a man and face and body type better for identifying the figure as a man (Zucker, Yoannidis, & Abramovitch, 2001). In a developmental study that eliminated hairstyle and clothing cues so that facial structure was the only relevant cue children as young as 7 years could accurately identify the sex of adult faces; but accurate identification of child faces was not found until 9 years (Wild et al., 2000). Other research also suggests that children are able to distinguish gender in adults before they do so in children (e.g., Poulin-Dubois et al., 1998; Weinraub et al., 1984). In short, perceptually discriminating males from females (in habituation and visual preference studies) is based on minimal cues and occurs in infancy, but verbal identification of male or female shows a more complex developmental course.

Gender Constancy. One of the most controversial and compelling ideas in the literature is "gender constancy." As proposed by Kohlberg (1966), children's developing sense of the permanence of categorical sex ("I am a girl and will always be a girl") is a critical organizer and motivator for learning gender concepts and behaviors. Slaby and Frey (1975) demonstrated that children move through a series of stages: first learning to identify their own and others' sex (basic gender identity or labeling), next learning that gender remains stable over time (gender stability), and finally learning that gender is a fixed and immutable characteristic that is not altered by superficial transformations in appearance or activities (gender consistency). These stages were confirmed in other research, including cross-cultural studies (e.g., De Lisi & Gallagher, 1991). The first stage is acquired by age 3, and typically much younger, as discussed earlier. The second stage (stability) is acquired between 3 and 5 years in the United States (L. Taylor, Ruble, Cyphers, Greulich, & Shrout, 2006), but may be later in other countries (Ruble, Trautner, Shrout, & Cyphers, 2006). There is considerable controversy, however, about when children acquire consistency understanding, and thus full constancy. In this section, we focus on this age issue. In later sections, we review the evidence concerning the consequences of acquiring gender constancy.

From a cognitive developmental perspective, children would not be expected to show a complete understanding of constancy until they mastered conservation, usually during the concrete operational period (5 to 7 years of age; Maccoby, 1990). Moreover, recent research suggests that constancy is closely associated with probably the most relevant element of operational thinking: understanding the distinction between appearance and reality (Trautner, Gervai, & Nemeth, 2003). Studies designed to pinpoint the development of constancy show a wide age range with some finding complete understanding in children as young as 3 to 4 years (e.g., S. L. Bem, 1989), but others failing to find it in most 7-year-olds (e.g., De Lisi & Gallagher, 1991).

A number of methodological and theoretical issues may underlie the discrepancies, including sample variations, the use of verbal questions about hypothetical transformations versus actual transformations, whether children's justifications are included in the criteria for understanding constancy, and the degree of realism of the measure and context (Ruble & Martin, 1998). Much of the discrepancy appears to be due to the consistency questions. Many children who first gave nonconstant responses to a consistency question (e.g., responding that Jack would be a girl if he wore lipstick) later gave the correct answer when asked if the child was *really* a girl or a boy, suggesting that they were originally responding to what sex they thought the child was *pretending* to be (Martin & Halverson, 1983). Thus, in many studies, constancy may be *under*estimated. However, several studies show a dip in scores on consistency questions appearing sometime after age 3 to 4 years followed by a recovery between 5 to 9 years (e.g., De Lisi & Gallagher, 1991; Yee & Brown, 1994), suggesting perhaps that high levels of constancy in very young children may be *over*estimates of their understanding.

These problems with consistency items raise important questions about interpreting scores on constancy measures. Are high constancy scores in 3-year-olds pseudo-constancy (Emmerich, Goldman, Kirsh, & Sharabany, 1977), or are 3- and 4-year-olds capable of true constancy (e.g., S. L. Bem, 1989)? Recent research examining consistency scores with and without justifications suggests that high constancy scores by 3- to 5-year-olds are eliminated when justifications are included (L. Taylor et al., 2006). This is because young children generally do not provide a constancy-relevant justification for their responses (e.g., "It doesn't matter if he's wearing a dress, he'll always be a boy"), but rather focus on irrelevant details (e.g., "He still has a boy's face"). Thus, young children may focus more on gender categories than on role conflicts, and thus their response is simple: "Jack is a boy; of course he would still be a boy." As children grow older, conflicting gender role information may become more salient and may interfere with the application of the categorical distinction, contributing to errors on consistency questions. In support, some studies indicate that the dip in consistency scores occurs at approximately the same time that there is an increase in children's use of social norms to explain their answers (e.g., "If Jack wore lipstick, Jack would be a girl; boys can't wear lipstick"; Szkrybalo & Ruble, 1999). Finally, the recovery of constancy after age 5 years may represent an integration of understanding categorical distinctions with understanding gender role norms.

In summary, the age at which children attain complete constancy understanding has yet to be completely resolved. This issue remains important because of its implications for predicted associations between constancy and outcomes such as learning gender stereotypes or developing gender-typed preferences (see Cognitive Developmental Theory section). Care must be taken because the "errors" of older children may not reflect a lack of understanding and because high level responding among 3- to 4-year-olds may not reflect a true understanding of constancy.

Beliefs about the Origins of Gender Group Differences.   Do children believe that the sexes differ be-cause of biological factors, or do they believe differences are more likely due to societal factors, such as how children are raised? This issue is important, in part, because it may provide insight about when and why children show changes in flexibility in their gender-related perceptions and behaviors at different ages.

Several studies indicate that adults believe sex differences are based more on socialization than biological factors (e.g., Martin & Parker, 1995; Neff & Terry-Schmitt, 2002). In children and adolescents, attributions of differences to biological factors seem to decrease with age (J. Smith & Russell, 1984). When preschoolers were asked about the outcome of a child being raised by members of only one sex, they attributed characteristics to the target children based on their sex rather than on the basis of the rearing environment (M. G. Taylor, 1996).

Identity or Self-Perception (1B)

Gender identity is a person's sense of self as a male or female (Zucker & Bradley, 1995). At its most basic, this understanding is anatomical, but also includes feelings about a person's biological sex and behavioral self-presentation as male or female. Research on gender identity has generally followed two separate paths: (1) the typical development of *self*-awareness as male or female or (2) variations in gender identity. These two paths have also differed in their emphases, with the former focusing on cognitive aspects of gender identity and the latter on affective aspects.

Typical Developmental Course.   Normative developmental research has focused on the age at which children attain basic gender identity because a child's awareness of being a boy or a girl is considered by cognitive theorists to motivate gender-typed behavior (Constantinople, 1979; Martin et al., 2002). Most children can accurately label their sex and place a picture of themselves with other same-sex children by 27 to 30 months, but recent research suggests that attaining basic gender identity occurs earlier for many children (e.g., A. Campbell et al., 2002; Zosuls et al., 2006).

Variations in Core Gender Identity.   Recent work in typical children shows variability in several affective aspects of gender identity that relate to sex, age, and subsequent adjustment; this is discussed elsewhere (e.g., 1C, 2B) because it is not concerned with core identity as male or female. We focus here on research concerned with the etiology of core gender identity and its disorders, which has been studied in two clinical populations. The first is children born with ambiguous genitalia because of disorders of sex development (intersex conditions) or boys who lack a penis due to a surgical accident or congenital defect. It was long believed that children adopt an identity consistent with their rearing, regardless of biological sex, as long as gender assignment is done early in life (before 18 to 30 months), is unambiguous, and genital appearance is made concordant with rearing sex (e.g., Money & Ehrhardt, 1972). This resulted in female rearing for such children because it is easier to construct female genitalia than male genitalia. Questions about this position (e.g., Imperato-McGinley, Peterson, Gautier, & Sturla, 1979) became prominent in the past decade (Colapinto, 2000; M. Diamond & Sigmundson, 1997; Reiner & Gearhart, 2004). Systematic evidence shows that gender identity is not determined simply by either biology or rearing, and that gender identity may change even in adulthood (see Biological Approaches).

The second population involves individuals with gender identity problems whose biological sex is not in doubt (for details, see Zucker & Bradley, 1995). Since 1980, the *Diagnostic and Statistical Manual* (*DSM*) of the American Psychiatric Association has included Gender Identity Disorder of Childhood (GIDC) for children who show both identity problems (e.g., wishing to be the other sex) and cross-gender behavior (e.g., wearing clothes and playing with toys typical of the other sex; Zucker, 2004). Children with GIDC show extreme sex-atypical behavior and are not androgynous. The revised *DSM* includes separate criteria for children versus adolescents and adults reflecting developmental differences in clinical presentation.

There are no epidemiological data on the prevalence of GIDC. Estimates suggest 2% to 5% of the population have GIDC or subclinical variants (Zucker & Bradley, 1995). Boys are referred for treatment more than girls, 3 to 6 times more in childhood, but only 1.2 to 1.3 times more in adolescence (Zucker, 2004). This may reflect referral bias due to cultural factors; for example, beliefs that girls may outgrow cross-gender behavior, and less tolerance of cross-gender behavior in boys than in girls. Girls display more extreme cross-gender behavior than boys before a clinical assessment is obtained (Zucker & Bradley, 1995).

Gender-atypical behavior in GIDC children usually begins during the preschool years but may begin earlier

(Zucker & Bradley, 1995). Early signs include wearing other-sex clothing, preoccupation with other-sex toys, and gender confusion or mislabeling. Children with GIDC develop gender concepts later than do typical children (Zucker et al., 1999). Extreme gender-atypicality may lead to peer ostracism in childhood and adolescence (Zucker & Bradley, 1995). Long-term outcome of children with extreme cross-gender identity is better studied in boys than in girls, with most showing bisexual and homosexual orientation without gender dysphoria, but a minority remaining identified with the other sex (Zucker, 2004). Individuals diagnosed with GID in adolescence are more likely than those diagnosed in childhood to persist with GID into adulthood (Zucker, 2004), suggesting reduced plasticity of gender identity with age, and perhaps some misdiagnoses.

Several broad factors have been hypothesized to cause GIDC, including hormones, temperament, family dysfunction, and encouragement of cross-sex behaviors (Zucker & Bradley, 1995). Research on gender identity raises questions about assumptions of the last 30 years. If stereotypes are less prevalent, why are children referred to clinics if they behave in a way considered normal for the other sex? If goals for boys and girls are the same, why is it considered a problem for boys to play with dolls? Perhaps it is because children with GIDC are rigid in their sex-atypicality, and likely to be teased and victimized by peers (Zucker & Bradley, 1995), to have behavioral and emotional problems (Egan & Perry, 2001; Zucker & Bradley, 1995), and to become homosexual adults (a problem for some parents).

Is GIDC truly a psychiatric disorder? It is unclear if emotional distress in GIDC is intrinsic or a consequence of social responses (Bartlett, Vasey, & Bukowski, 2000). A distinction has been made between discomfort with one's biological sex and discomfort with the gender role prescribed for one's sex, with GIDC to be reserved only for the former (Bartlett et al., 2000), but there is disagreement about whether most children with GIDC truly wish to be the other sex (Bartlett et al., 2000; Bartlett, Vasey, & Bukowski, 2003; Zucker, 2002).

Preferences (1C)

How satisfied are children with their sex? Very few children in Western cultures say they want to be the other sex, although more girls wish to be boys than vice versa (Antill, Cotton, Russell, & Goodnow, 1996; Goldman & Goldman, 1982), with this difference increasing into adolescence but decreasing from the 1950s to the

1980s (Ruble & Martin, 1998). Parents of 4- to 11-year-old clinic-referred children report 1% to 16% of boys and 4% to 8% of girls wish to be the other sex, compared to 0% to 2% of boys and 2% to 5% of girls from a nonclinic sample (Zucker & Bradley, 1995). Among typical fourth to eighth graders, gender-contentedness was higher in boys than in girls and negatively correlated with age (Egan & Perry, 2001).

Behavioral Enactment (1D)

Despite wide varieties of socialization pressures, cultural differences, and even biological influences, most children develop a clear sense of self as male or female and master the roles generally associated with their assigned sex. There are separate criteria in the *DSM* for GID of childhood and of adolescence/adulthood, but both sets of criteria require for diagnosis a specific *pattern* of feelings and behavior. Some adults with GID have sex-reassignment surgery. Among adult males with GID, there is heterogeneity in other aspects of gender-related behavior; for example, there is an equal distribution of those sexually attracted to biological males or females (Blanchard, 1989).

Activities and Interests (2)

Are there parallels in the development of children's concepts and beliefs about gender-related activities and interests and their self-perceptions, preferences, and behaviors? This question is important for understanding the mechanisms driving children's behavior. Do self-reported preferences and behavioral measures of children's activities and interests yield similar trends? Processes governing conscious choices may be quite different from those governing behavior. For instance, self-reports may involve demand characteristics more than behavioral measures.

Concepts or Beliefs (2A)

Earlier *Handbook* reviews have concluded that stereotypes about clothing, activities, toys, and games are known as early as age 2½ (Huston, 1983; Ruble & Martin, 1998). Recent work suggests that children are aware of some stereotypes even before 2½ years (Martin et al., 2002; C. F. Miller, Trautner, & Ruble, 2006; Powlishta et al., 2001). On nonverbal looking-time tasks, infants have some knowledge of activities and objects associated with each gender. For example, one study using a preferential looking-time paradigm showed that 18- and 24-month-old girls (but not boys) were able to match gender-typed toys (e.g., doll/car) with the face of a boy or a girl (Serbin, Poulin-Dubois, Colburne, Sen, & Eichstedt, 2001). Other studies have examined infants' responses to mismatches, which purportedly lead to longer looking times because they involve surprise or novelty. For example, 24-month-old boys and girls paid significantly more attention to gender-inconsistent pictures than consistent pictures, but only when they involved female-typical behavior (e.g., man putting on make-up; Serbin, Poulin-Dubois, & Eichstedt, 2002).

Looking-time studies are promising for understanding children's earliest understanding of gender, suggesting that children as young as 18 months begin to link activities to gender, but further research is needed before clear conclusions can be drawn. Nevertheless, studies using other paradigms provide some converging evidence for early developing stereotypes (A. Campbell et al., 2002; Poulin-Dubois, Serbin, Eichstedt, Sen, & Beissel, 2002). Taken together, these recent studies suggest that some children understand concrete gender stereotypes by 2 years of age, but that the level of such understanding found depends on the measure, the stereotype, and the child's sex.

Stereotype knowledge of child and adult activities and occupations increases rapidly between ages 3 and 5 (reaching a ceiling by kindergarten or first grade) depending on the particular item (e.g., Blakemore, 2003). A meta-analysis of developmental studies of stereotype knowledge (Signorella, Bigler, & Liben, 1993) suggested that gender stereotypes are well developed at the end of preschool, showing further change only when a broad range of topics is examined.

Most stereotype measures assess knowledge at a relatively simple level, identifying which gender category is associated with particular objects, so it is not surprising to find high levels of stereotyping in very young children. Studies assessing stereotype knowledge in different ways, however, suggest continued development throughout childhood. For example, free descriptions of what boys, girls, grown-up women, and grown-up men are like show increasing use of stereotypes with age from preschool through fifth grade (C. F. Miller, Lurye, Zosuls, & Ruble, 2006). Further, horizontal stereotypic associations (attribute to attribute) develop later than vertical associations (male/female label to attribute; Ruble & Martin, 1998). For example, children 8 years or older can use attribute information about a target to make horizontal associations about other stereotypic attributes (e.g., judge that a girl who likes a male-typical game will also choose a male-typical after-school activity; Lobel, Gewirtz, Pras, Shoeshine-Rokach, & Ginton, 1999), but 6-year-olds are limited in these horizontal associations (Martin, Wood, & Little, 1990).

What kinds of stereotypes do children learn first? Although this question has not been systematically addressed, there are some interesting clues. Very young children (around 26 months) appear to be most aware of gender differences associated with adult possessions (e.g., shirt and tie), roles, physical appearance, and abstract characteristics associated with gender (e.g., softness), and 5 to 6 months later show evidence of awareness of stereotypes about children's toys (Ruble & Martin, 1998). In free descriptions, preschool children are most likely to refer to dolls and appearance (e.g., dresses or jewelry) for girls and toys and behaviors (e.g., hits or action heroes) for boys (C. F. Miller, Lurye, et al., 2006). During the elementary school years, the range of and extent to which occupations, sports, and school tasks or subjects are differentially associated with males and females continues to increase (Ruble & Martin, 1998; C. F. Miller, Lurye, et al., 2006).

Do stereotypes become more flexible with age? Clear developmental trends are difficult to describe because *flexibility* means many things: for instance, the willingness to apply an attribute to both sexes rather than just to one or the other, or the recognition of the relativity of stereotypes (e.g., that norms could be different in another culture). The term has been applied either to changes in knowledge (e.g., about variability or relativity) or to personal acceptance of stereotypes, with the latter being closer in meaning to attitudes or values that the sexes "should" be different. Ideally, these latter trends would be reviewed in the Values section below. However, it is difficult to distinguish between knowledge and attitudes on the basis of currently available measures; thus, all are reviewed here. And because it is difficult to define flexibility precisely, we use the term "flexible" to apply to any nonrigid application of stereotypic items, whether because of knowledge or because of personal attitudes.

Based largely on a comparison of studies that allow children to classify items as equally appropriate for both sexes (i.e., "both" responding), prior *Handbook* chapters concluded that after about 7 years of age, children's knowledge of stereotypes continues to increase but that their acceptance of stereotypes as inflexible or being morally right begins to decline (Huston, 1983; Ruble & Martin, 1998). For example, interview studies suggest that with age, children increasingly recognize the cultural

relativity of gender norms, though this understanding appears to reach a ceiling at some point during middle elementary school (e.g., Blakemore, 2003; L. Taylor et al., 2006). In addition, a meta-analysis of stereotype attitudes and knowledge studies showed that "both" responding for questions worded "who can" or "who should" engage in an activity increase with age among elementary school children (Signorella et al., 1993). Studies using conceptually similar measures that do not rely on "both" responses show similar trends (C. F. Miller, Trautner, et al., 2006). Interestingly, the meta-analysis revealed curvilinear age trends, with flexibility of association or attitudes lowest when children begin school.

Recent longitudinal studies support these conclusions. For example, flexibility of occupational stereotyping increased between second and sixth grades (Helwig, 1998). Also, children given a measure of stereotyping annually from ages 5 to 10 showed a peak in rigidity at either 5 or 6 years of age and then a dramatic increase in flexibility 2 years later (Trautner et al., 2005). Notably, analyses of individual differences in stereotyping showed that neither the level nor timing of peak rigidity affected this developmental trajectory, suggesting that all children follow the same basic developmental path of stereotype rigidity and flexibility across development, despite variations in when it begins and what level it reaches.

Taken together, these data suggest that children entering elementary school have extensive knowledge about which activities are linked to being male or female. Until approximately 7 to 8 years of age, when horizontal associations emerge, stereotypes are held quite rigidly, perhaps because younger children do not seem to recognize that there can be individual variation in masculinity and femininity within the male and female categories.

Beyond flexibility and rigidity, certain developmental trends often vary for girls and boys. As revealed in meta-analysis (Signorella et al., 1993), preschool girls scored higher than boys on stereotype knowledge (see also O'Brien et al., 2000), but no clear sex differences were found in flexibility. Similarly, in free descriptions of males and females, preschool to fifth grade girls used more stereotypic terms than did boys (C. F. Miller, Lurye, et al., 2006). But, by middle childhood, girls have more flexible stereotypes (e.g., L. Miller & Budd, 1999; Whitley, 1997), including cultures outside the United States (Zammuner, 1987). Finally, children view the male role as more rigidly proscribed than the female role (e.g., Henshaw, Kelly,

& Gratton, 1992). In short, some, but not all, studies suggest that girls are both more knowledgeable and, after the preschool years, more flexible in their personal acceptance of gender stereotypes, whereas boys hold stereotypic views more rigidly and are held to them more by others.

Stereotyped knowledge, rigidity/flexibility, and inferences have also been found to vary across ethnicity/cultures by some researchers. Given the relatively limited number of studies, it is premature to draw definitive conclusions. When differences are found, however, relative to children of European origin, Hispanic/Latino children (e.g., B. A. Bailey & Nihlen, 1990) and Asian children (Lobel, Gruber, Govrin, & Mashraki-Pedhatzur, 2001) have shown greater stereotyping, whereas African American children have shown less (e.g., Albert & Porter, 1988; but see Liben & Bigler, 2002, for an exception). Even countries that share a European background vary with respect to degree of stereotyping. For example, Italian children were more likely to stereotype toys and activities than were Dutch children (Zammuner, 1987). It would be interesting to examine the extent to which developmental trends and types of earliest stereotypes (e.g., appearance) generalize beyond Western cultures.

Predictions and evidence concerning changes in flexibility during adolescence have been mixed. Gender-related beliefs and behaviors may become intensified (e.g., J. P. Hill & Lynch, 1983), as an adolescent's newly emerging identity as a sexual being may lead to heightened concerns about gender role expectations and increased polarization of attitudes. In contrast, continuing cognitive maturation should facilitate a more flexible and relativistic view of gender norms (Eccles, 1987). Most indexes of stereotype flexibility show an increase through early adolescence (Liben & Bigler, 2002). Studies of changes between early and later adolescence show mixed results depending on the nature of the stereotype, the measure, and the sex of the participants (Ruble & Martin, 1998; Whitley, 1997).

Identity or Self-Perception (2B)

To what extent is there a connection between children's activities and interests and their self-perceptions and identities? For example, do children perceive their interests and activities as related to their gender (e.g., they like trucks because they are boys)? Examining developmental changes in such connections is important for theories of gender development, discussed later, which suggest that developmental changes in gender identity influence gender differentiation. As Liben and Bigler (2002) suggest, it is important to examine the direction of effects: Does identity influence activities and interests or do activities and interests influence identity? Unfortunately, research has not focused on such questions, but rather on what kinds of activities children prefer (see 2C) or how children perceive themselves in term of traits (see 3B).

Some recent research is indirectly relevant to such issues. Perry and colleagues' research on gender identity in children (e.g., Egan & Perry, 2001) addresses two components closely connected to activities and interests. *Gender typicality* is thought to reflect children's idiosyncratic weighting and integration of diverse information about their gender-related interests and activities (Perry, 2004), so that different children feel gender typical for different reasons (e.g., athletic prowess versus competence in math and science). *Felt pressure* refers to pressure felt from parents, peers, and the self to conform to gender stereotypes. In terms of developmental trends, Perry (2004) suggested that felt pressure may develop in preschool but that perceived typicality may not emerge until later when children engage in social comparison. Such hypotheses remain to be tested. Available data suggest few age effects among elementary school children over age 7 (e.g., Egan & Perry, 2001). Further research into the developmental course of these identity-related beliefs is important, in part because children who feel gender typical and who experience little pressure for gender conformity are less distressed than other children (Carver, Yunger, & Perry, 2003).

Other relevant research involves the relation between self-concept and academic interests and abilities (e.g., Byrne & Gavin, 1996; Marsh, Byrne, & Yeung, 1999). Stereotypic patterns are found: Boys' academic self-concept is correlated more strongly with math than with verbal self-perceptions, and the reverse is true for girls (Skaalvick & Rankin, 1990). Even first grade children show some effects of gendered self-beliefs: math is relevant for boys' self-concepts but not for girls' (Entwisle, Alexander, Pallas, & Cadigan, 1987). Such relations are important because children may avoid courses or future occupations that are believed to be unimportant or irrelevant for their academic self-concept. For example, over time, girls gave lower ratings to liking of math and the importance of math competence for self-concept, and such values were related to enrollment in advanced math and physics in high school (Eccles, 1989). Students' views of future selves also appear to involve stereotypic activities and interests, with boys more likely to see their futures emphasizing science, numbers, reasoning, and girls more likely to see futures emphasizing people, culture, and self-expression; this future divide was more extensive for college than high school students (Lips, 2004).

Preferences (2C)

Unfortunately, it is difficult to discern clear developmental trends for activity and interest preferences because conclusions depend on variables used. For example, some studies focus on sex differences in interest in female- or male-typical activities (e.g., does the gender gap in interest in math increase at adolescence) and infer greater flexibility of preferences during developmental periods when those differences are smaller. Such an approach cannot inform us, however, about changes in relative interests (e.g., in math versus language arts) for males versus females. For example, in some cases, small sex differences may be driven by girls' relatively greater or lesser interests in male-typical versus female-typical activities. In such cases, the girls may have become more flexible but not the boys. Other studies examine developmental trends within sex for different types of activities (e.g., female typical, male typical, and neutral). Increasing flexibility would be shown for girls, for example, by decreasing interest in female-typical activities and increasing interest in male-typical and neutral activities. Relative interest in activities may be determined by a number of factors other than gender typicality. For example, girls' liking of tea sets and household chores may decline with age but imply nothing about developmental trends in interest in other female-typical activities. They may have switched to jump ropes or pajama parties. Such interpretational difficulties also apply to behavioral engagement in gender-typical activities (see 2D). Thus, for both preferences and behaviors, the conclusions drawn about developmental changes depend on which comparison is made, even in the same study (e.g., see McHale, Shanahan, Updegraff, Crouter, & Booth, 2004). Space limitations preclude detailed review of studies examining age and sex differences in gender-typed preferences to resolve conflicting conclusions across studies, but we call attention to some of these difficulties when discrepant developmental patterns are found.

Infancy.   Recent research has examined gender-typed preferences in infancy, using nonverbal methods.

In a longitudinal study of children tested at 3, 9, and 18 months, A. Campbell, Shirley, Heywood, and Crook (2000) examined whether children would look longer at gender-typical than atypical activities and toys. There was some evidence that boys but not girls showed gender-typed preferences at 9 and 18 months. One problem interpreting the data is that both boys and girls showed a strong preference for male-typical activities, which involved much more gross motor activity (e.g., wrestling versus whispering). A cross-sectional study using a similar paradigm (Serbin et al., 2001) showed that 12-month-old boys and girls preferred looking at dolls over trucks, with no sex difference. At 18 and 23 months, however, clear preferences were observed, with boys looking more at trucks and girls looking more at dolls. Despite the small number of studies and inconsistent results, the preferential-looking paradigm appears promising, and the data provide preliminary evidence that gender-typed preferences may begin before 2 years of age.

Preschool.   Recent research (e.g., Servin, Bohlin, & Berlin, 1999) supports earlier conclusions that trends for toy and activity preferences are similar to those for stereotypes: an increase in gender-typed preferences during the preschool years, with well-established preferences by 5 years, and more gender-typed preferences for boys than for girls (Huston, 1983; Ruble & Martin, 1998). There are qualifications to these conclusions. First, preferences vary tremendously by activity. Because some measures ask about chores (e.g., Sex Role Learning Inventory [SERLI]; Edelbrock, & Sugawara, 1978), children's preferences are not strongly gender-typed, even though their stereotype knowledge is (Serbin, Powlishta, & Gulko, 1993; Turner, Gervai, & Hinde, 1993). For other play activities (e.g., trucks, dolls), gender-consistent preferences are very strong, over 80% at age 4 and reaching 100% by age 7 (Emmerich & Shepard, 1982). Second, the size of the sex difference varies by activity. Because SERLI items for boys are mostly play things, whereas for girls they are household chores, it is not surprising that girls consistently show less clear same-gender preferences (Serbin et al., 1993; Welch-Ross & Schmidt, 1996). When other items are used, boys do not always show greater gender-typing (e.g., Serbin et al., 1993). Nevertheless, even using other measures, many studies still suggest that girls are less likely to prefer same-gender activities than are boys (e.g., Perry, White, & Perry, 1984; Turner et al., 1993).

Middle Childhood. Because some aspects of stereotyping become less rigid but also more elaborated as children move into middle school, activity/interest preferences might also be expected to change at this time. Early studies showed that boys' and girls' preferences follow different developmental paths after age 5, with boys showing increasingly stereotyped preferences and girls remaining stable or declining (Huston, 1983). More recent research has shown mixed support for this conclusion. In some cases, a sex by age interaction was found (e.g., Helwig, 1998); but other studies showed that gender-typed preference scores for both sexes were stable between kindergarten/first grade and fifth/sixth grade (e.g., Egan & Perry, 2001; Serbin et al., 1993) or declined (Welch-Ross & Schmidt, 1996).

The mixed results may be due to variations across studies in the kind of preferences assessed (Ruble & Martin, 1998). Also, patterns may vary depending on whether assessment involves children's preferences for same-gender activities or rejection of other-gender activities. For example, in a longitudinal study, Aubry, Ruble, and Silverman (1999) found that preferences for gender-atypical items declined steeply between preschool and third grade, whereas preferences for gender-typical items were relatively stable across age. In addition, Bussey and Perry (1982) found that third and fourth grade boys rejected gender-atypical behavior more than girls, but there was no sex difference in preferences regarding gender-typical behavior. In short, it appears that when gender-typed preferences increase with age, it is likely to reflect avoidance of other-sex activities and interests; and when a sex difference is observed, it is likely to show that boys are more rigidly gender-typed during the middle grades.

Adolescence. As for stereotypes (see 2A), researchers have asked whether children's gender-related preferences become intensified or more egalitarian as children enter adolescence. Preferences generally become more flexible between middle childhood and early adolescence (e.g., Katz & Ksansnak, 1994), but flexibility regarding certain kinds of interests, may decline during this period. For example, in a meta-analysis of computer-related attitudes and self-efficacy beliefs, Whitley (1997) found a small but significant overall sex difference ($d = .23$) showing that males were more positive than girls about computers at all ages, but this difference peaked at high school. Recent longitudinal research from 1st to 12th grades showed that sex differ-

ences in subjective task values (e.g., interest, importance, or usefulness) for gender-typed school activities (e.g., math, language arts, sports) did not all increase at adolescence, thus failing to support theories of gender intensification (Fredricks & Eccles, 2002). Other research has found clear sex differences in adolescents' interests in academic subjects. In a study of high school students in the United States, Taiwan, and Japan, boys in all cultures were more likely to report preferences for mathematics, science, and physical education, and girls were more likely to report preferences for language arts, music, and art (E. M. Evans, Schweingruber, & Stevenson, 2002).

Some studies suggest that an increase in flexibility during adolescence occurs only or primarily for girls (e.g., Ruble & Martin, 1998). One recent longitudinal study, however, showed this increasing flexibility from sixth to seventh grade only for girls' endorsement of feminine occupations; otherwise, preferences for activities and occupations were reasonably stable across this 2-year period (Liben & Bigler, 2002). A similar pattern of results was reported in a longitudinal study among middle school-age Australian children (Antill et al., 1996). As Liben and Bigler (2002) speculate, the reduction in some gender-typed preferences by adolescent girls may indicate both increasing tolerance for females to engage in male-typical roles and recognition that male-typical activities and roles have higher status.

In short, the dominant finding is that girls are less rigid in their stereotypic toy and activity preferences than are boys. With few exceptions, this difference appears at all ages. Although some evidence suggests an increase in flexibility in middle childhood and adolescence, particularly for girls, findings are mixed. Gender differences in growth trajectories appear to be domain specific, and are likely to be influenced by changing stereotypes (e.g., math) and opportunities (e.g., sports; Fredricks & Eccles, 2002).

Behavioral Enactment (2D)

Children's engagement in gender-stereotypical activities has been examined in a wide range of settings, including free-play in home, school, and laboratory observations, as well as household chores, television preferences, and school courses selected. Some studies suggest that boys and girls show at least some differential play by as early 2 years of age (e.g., A. Campbell et al., 2002). Whether gender-typed toy play emerges prior to 2 years of age is less clear. In one study, the toy play of infants aged 10, 14, and 18 months was observed during structured free play with parents (Roopnarine, 1986). Girls played more with dolls and offered toys to parents more than did boys. The results of this study have been interpreted to show gender-typed play by 10 months, but the samples for each age group were too small to detect interactions and tests within age were not conducted. Moreover, it was not clear if play was child or parent initiated. Other studies of unconstrained free play by children younger than 2 years have reported mixed results (Ruble & Martin, 1998). For example, in a longitudinal study, girls played more with female-typical toys (e.g., kitchen set, princess outfit) than with male-typical toys (e.g., tool set, baseball outfit) or neutral toys at 18 months and at 30 months, but boys did not show sex-differentiated play until 36 months (Katz & Kofkin, 1997). In another study, 12- to 14-month-old boys played longer than girls with male-typical toys, but the sexes did not differ significantly in play with female-typical toys (though the means were in the expected direction; Servin et al., 1999). By 36 months, both boys and girls played longer with gender-typical than atypical toys. Thus, the former study suggests that gender-typing may emerge at a younger age in girls, and the latter study suggests that gender-typing may emerge earlier in boys. This apparent discrepancy in showing earlier gender-typed play in girls versus boys may reflect a difference in the operationalization of gender-typed behavior: that is, showing more play with same-sex compared to other-sex play versus showing sex differences in play with specific toys. Indeed, a recent study using both operationalizations supports this conclusion. Zosuls et al. (2006) found that, at 17 and 21 months, girls engaged in more gender-typed play (doll versus truck) than boys did. Nevertheless, boys played more with the truck than girls did. Thus, although some gender-differentiated play may be found among infants and toddlers, this trend increases dramatically with age such that clear and strong findings that both boys and girls play more with gender-typical toys are seen at 36 months.

During preschool, the two sexes engage in such different activities, they are almost like two separate cultures: girls play more frequently with dolls, tea and kitchen sets, dress-up, and engage in fantasy play involving household roles, glamour, and romance, whereas boys play with transportation and construction toys, and engage in fantasy play involving action heroes, aggression, and themes of danger (Dunn & Hughes, 2001; Maccoby, 1998). For example, an analysis of the stories told by preschool children revealed that boys and girls became increasingly polarized across a school year (Nicolopoulou, 1997): Most girls' stories involved themes of family relationships with virtually no aggression or violence; the reverse was true for boys. The research also suggests that gender-typical activity involvement increases dramatically during the preschool years. For example, in one large study, parents from the United Kingdom, the United States, and the Netherlands reported on their preschool children's activities and interests (Golombok & Rust, 1993). There was a steady increase in sex-differential involvement between 18 and 60 months, with parents reporting much less overlap in the interests of boys and girls at 5 than at 2 years. In another large study of parent reports' of children's use of time among a diverse sample, sex differences in some activities such as video games increased dramatically between 2 to 7 years of age, and at 3 to 4 years of age, girls spent more time than boys on personal care, social interaction, and chores (Huston, Wright, Marquis, & Green, 1999).

Do boys show stronger evidence of gender-typed toy play, as some researchers have suggested (e.g., A. Campbell et al., 2000)? The studies described earlier suggest that, if anything, infant girls are more likely to play with gender-typical versus atypical toys than are boys. By preschool age, this pattern changes. Studies of young children show mixed results (Ruble & Martin, 1998). The evidence is clearest for children's willingness to play with other-gender toys. Young boys appear to avoid highly stereotyped other-gender behavior more than do girls (e.g., Bussey & Bandura, 1992).

Sex differences in interests and activities persist into middle childhood and adolescence. Several studies reveal clear gender-typing across a variety of domains: sports, household jobs, toys owned, and interests/hobbies (Antill, Russell, Goodnow, & Cotton, 1993; McHale, Kim, Whiteman, & Crouter, 2004; McHale, Shanahan, et al., 2004). Boys and girls differ in the themes that draw their interest: girls like to read adventures, ghost/horror, animal, school-related, relationship/romance stories, and poetry more than boys do. Boys like to read science fiction/fantasy, sports, and war/spy stories, comic books, and joke books more than girls do (Coles & Hall, 2002; C. Hall & Coles, 1999). Girls tend to develop stories with affectionate themes; boys use aggressive themes. Boys and girls also differ in the themes in drawings, with boys depicting mechanical and moving objects and girls depicting human figures, flowers, and butterflies (Iijima, Arisaka, Minamoto, & Arai, 2001).

A few studies have found changes in gender-typed behavior in adolescence that support the gender intensification hypothesis, especially for girls. With age, girls spend more time in interpersonal activities, personal care, and household chores and less time in sports; for boys, participation in sports either remains stable or increases (Ruble & Martin, 1998). Of particular current interest is how such interests may be affected by increased opportunities for girls' sports participation afforded by Title IX, the Educational Amendments Act (e.g., McHale, Kim, et al., 2004), especially given links between athletic activity and adjustment (Pedersen & Seidman, 2004). A recent longitudinal diary study examining middle elementary and adolescent girls' relative involvement in female- versus male-typical activities (most of the latter involving sports) found that behaviors were least stereotypical at age 13 but that involvement in male-typical activities declined in middle adolescence (8th to 10th grades; McHale, Shanahan, et al., 2004).

Finally, a few studies have looked specifically at gender-atypical behavior early in development, in part because such behaviors are related to later homosexuality (J. M. Bailey & Zucker, 1995; D. J. Bem, 1996; Green, 1987) and are associated with difficulties in psychological adjustment (Egan & Perry, 2001; Yunger, Carver, & Perry, 2004). Some aspects of gender-atypical behavior are uncommon in early and middle childhood, such as playing more with other-sex children than same-sex children (e.g., Maccoby, 1998; Martin & Fabes, 2001). But, other forms of gender-atypical behavior are not uncommon, particularly among girls: for example, studies of toy play typically find that girls will play with both boy-typical and girl-typical toys, with both boys and girls becoming more interested in boy-typical activities (especially sports) and less interested in girl-typical activities across middle childhood (Sandberg & Meyer-Bahlburg, 1994).

Personal-Social Attributes (3)

Section 3 addresses questions similar to Section 2, but with respect to personal-social attributes (e.g., traits, abilities, and behaviors) rather than activities and interests. For instance, do the traits that children ascribe to themselves show parallel trends to gender-typed beliefs about the traits that girls and boys should have or do they occur independently of belief systems? The main behaviors being examined are those typically considered in the very large literature on sex differences (e.g., aggression, nurturance, ability at math or English), except that we focus on developmental changes in such differences.

Concepts or Beliefs (3A)

Many studies of the development of stereotypes about personal-social attributes have used a measure based on the Sex Stereotype Questionnaire, in which children are told stories about masculine and feminine traits and are asked to select whether the stories fit better with a male or female figure (Best et al., 1977). The original studies of U.S. participants showed that the knowledge of kindergartners was little better than chance, with a large increase in knowledge between kindergarten and third grade, and continuing steady increase in knowledge throughout elementary school, such that the knowledge level of high school students approached that of college students on whom the measure was standardized (J. E. Williams & Best, 1990). Recent research confirms that gender stereotype knowledge of personal-social attributes emerges at approximately 5 years of age and increases steadily throughout childhood (e.g., Powlishta, Sen, Serbin, Poulin-Dubois, & Eichstedt, 2001; Serbin et al., 1993; Signorella et al., 1993). This pattern occurs across cultures even if the level and actual content of the stereotypes differ (Gibbons, 2000; J. E. Williams & Best, 1990; Zammuner, 1987). Interestingly, both adults and children apply trait stereotypes more strongly to child than to adult targets (Powlishta, 2000). In addition, the extent of trait stereotyping and the nature of developmental trends vary across methods. For example, children made stronger distinctions between boys and girls on social (aggression and prosocial behavior) and academic (math and spelling competence) stereotypes when direct comparisons between males and females were made than when they were not (Heyman & Legare, 2004). Children younger than 5 years of age often show little evidence of trait stereotyping. Instead, preschool children tend to attribute positive characteristics to their own sex and negative characteristics to the other (Ruble & Martin, 1998). This bias may peak at age 5 (Urberg, 1982), though it continues at least into middle elementary school (Heyman & Legare, 2004).

Are any particular trait stereotypes learned earlier than 5 years of age? Such data may provide clues about how young children structure their initial learning about gender categories. Multiple studies have reported that 2- to 4-year-old children distinguish between boys and girls on particular traits (e.g., cruel), emotions (e.g., fearful), or trait-related behaviors (e.g., hits; can't fix things; Ruble & Martin, 1998). Some recent evidence suggests that preschoolers may even have quite sophisticated knowledge about aggression, an attribute likely to be highly salient in preschool classrooms, with preschool children associating physical aggression with males and relational aggression with females (Giles & Heyman, 2005). Thus, preschoolers may be most aware of differentials along a power dimension, as they apply high power adjectives to boys (e.g., strong, fast, hit) and adjectives related to fear and helplessness to girls (e.g., can't fix bike, need help, cry a lot, fearful). Children also use a general evaluative dimension in which males are labeled negatively (e.g., aggressive, cruel) and females are labeled positively (e.g., affectionate, nice). Even in free descriptions, when they are not explicitly cued with particular choices, preschool and kindergarten girls (but not boys) frequently use negative, power-linked terms to describe boys (e.g., plays rough; mean); whereas kindergarten (but not preschool) boys and girls frequently use positive evaluative terms (e.g., nice/sweet/kind) to describe girls (C. F. Miller, Lurye, et al., 2006). As Serbin et al. (1993) suggested, young children may apply a general stereotype that girls are sugar and spice . . . and boys are snakes and snails. Interestingly, early stereotypes appear to highlight distinctions identified as two of the three most important dimensions of meaning (i.e., power and valence; Osgood, Suci, & Tannenbaum, 1957).

As with concrete activities and objects, flexibility in beliefs about gender-typed traits increases following a period of rigidity after they are learned (Trautner et al., 2005). Developmental trends for traits appear similar to those for activities and interests with a peak in rigidity as children enter school and a subsequent increase with age in flexibility (Signorella et al., 1993). Relatively few studies have extended beyond elementary school, but, for the most part, the pattern seems similar to that described earlier for activities: Flexibility increases through early adolescence (Ruble & Martin, 1998) and is often higher for girls (Antill et al., 1996). Research directly comparing younger and older adolescents suggests that trait flexibility may stabilize or decline during high school (e.g., Neff & Terry-Schmitt, 2002).

Moreover, one study showed this curvilinear pattern using a combination of cross-sectional and longitudinal analyses (Alfieri, Ruble, & Higgins, 1996), with flexibility increasing through the 1st year of junior high school and then declining.

Thus, consistent with the earlier conclusions concerning concrete stereotypes, stereotypes about traits show fluctuating flexibility throughout the adolescent years in response to two opposing influences—increasing cognitive flexibility and increasing pressures to conform to gender stereotypes in preparation for sexual roles and adult status (Eccles, 1987; Katz & Ksansnak, 1994). In addition, variations across studies in the assessment of flexibility affect conclusions about these developmental changes.

Identity or Self-Perception (3B)

In the 1970s and 1980s, researchers explored sex differences in gender role orientation using "masculine" and "feminine" characteristics, but later research showed these characteristics to be better conceptualized as instrumental and expressive traits. How early do children view themselves in terms of these personality traits and do these patterns change over time? Only tentative conclusions can be drawn because of methodological differences across studies. In studies with 3- to 4-year-olds, both sexes endorse socially desirable characteristics, and their perceptions of themselves are beginning to differentiate along gender-typed lines but not yet enough to show a significant difference. For 5-year-olds, the findings are mixed. By age 8 to 9 years, however, most but not all studies show that boys and girls rate themselves in terms of gender-typed patterns of traits (Ruble & Martin, 1998) and this continues into adolescence (Klingenspor, 2002; Washburn-Ormachea, Hillman, & Sawilowsky, 2004). Cross-sectional studies suggest that self-perceptions of instrumental and expressive traits become more sex-differentiated with age up through early adolescence, even though considerable overlap remains between the sexes (Ruble & Martin, 1998).

The stability of children's endorsements of gender-typed personality traits is of interest because some theorists expect that certain life events will influence their adoption. Testing the gender intensification hypothesis (J. P. Hill & Lynch, 1983), many longitudinal studies have focused on the preadolescent to adolescent time span. Only limited support for gender intensification has been found, mainly for increased sex differences in masculinity/instrumentality. Other studies show a general pattern of stability over time, or that both masculinity/instrumentality and femininity/expressiveness increase with age (Ruble & Martin, 1998). In a recent longitudinal study designed to examine how instrumentality and expressivity in adolescence were influenced by children's earlier activities and experiences with same-sex and other-sex peers and family members, the findings showed support for gender socialization occurring through children's activities and social partners for instrumental traits but not for expressive traits (McHale, Kim, et al., 2004).

The study of gendered personality traits has changed direction in recent years. Rather than emphasizing sex differences per se, many of the recent studies examine a wide array of correlates of instrumental and expressive characteristics. For example, 6- to 11-year-old children with instrumental traits reported higher levels of motivation when competing with other children (Conti, Collins, & Picariello, 2001). In adolescents, there are positive associations between expressivity and positive outcomes such as perspective taking, sympathy, and having an ethic of caring (Carlo, Eisenberg, Koller, DaSilva, & Frohlich, 1996; Eisenberg, Zhou, & Koller, 2001; Karniol, Grosz, & Schorr, 2003). Others have examined links between instrumental and expressive characteristics and social judgments (Lobel, Bar-David, Gruber, Lau, & Bar-Tal, 2000; Lobel et al., 1999). Understanding the association between depression and other internalizing disorders and gender role orientation has become a dominant theme in the past 10 years with expressivity being positively linked (Broderick & Korteland, 2002) and instrumentality negatively linked (Marcotte, Alain, & Gosselin, 1999). Importantly, in adolescents, instrumentality partially mediated the relationship between sex and internalizing symptoms, and expressivity fully mediated the relation between sex and externalizing symptoms (M. L. Hoffman, Powlishta, & White, 2004). Thus, gendered personality characteristics appear to account for what are commonly thought to be differences between the sexes in adjustment outcomes.

Personality researchers have investigated how the sexes compare on the major dimensions of personality, specifically, the Big Five. Over the ages of 12 to 18, girls scored higher than boys on Neuroticism, Extraversion, Openness, and Agreeableness (McCrae et al., 2002) and did not differ in Conscientiousness. Girls increased in Neuroticism and both sexes increased in Openness as they grew older. The increase in Neuroticism may reflect hormonal changes and/or transitions in schooling and is consistent with increases in depression for girls during adolescence (McCrae et al., 2002).

Finally, in terms of gender-linked dimensions of self-concept, when sex differences are found, they are small and follow gender-typed patterns (e.g., Eccles et al., 1989; Wilgenbusch & Merrell, 1999). Boys' self-concepts tend to be higher in math, sports, and physical appearance and girls' self-concepts tend to be higher in music, and verbal/reading ability, and sometimes social competence (Hay, Ashman, & Van Kraayenoord, 1998; Klomsten, Skaalvik, & Espnes, 2004; Marsh, Craven, & Debus, 1998; Watt, 2004). Sex differences develop early and remain relatively consistent over time with a few exceptions (Cole et al., 2001; Jacobs, Lanza, Osgood, Eccles, & Wigfield, 2002; Wigfield et al., 1997).

Do young girls and boys share the same perceptions of their beliefs about school performance? In a cross-cultural study of over 3,000 children in second to sixth grade, children's achievement in specific domains closely matched their competence-related beliefs, suggesting that they have realistic self-assessments. However, in contexts where girls achieved better than boys, their self-assessments were equal to boys, not higher. Girls did not credit themselves with being talented even when they performed better than boys (Stetsenko, Little, Gordeeva, Grasshof, & Oettingen, 2000).

Preferences (3C)

Do children prefer certain kinds of gender-linked personality traits for themselves? In our consideration of the findings in the previous section (B3), we discussed a closely related issue: how children perceive their current or actual selves in terms of such traits—that is, their identity. Few researchers have examined trait preferences, even though preferred characteristics may influence children's future behavior. In one relevant study, Swedish children aged 11 to 18 years rated characteristics of their ideal self (Intons-Peterson, 1988b). Both sexes endorsed several instrumental qualities (e.g., never gives up) and several expressive qualities (e.g., kind). Only 19 of 59 characteristics showed sex differences, but these were not the top-rated characteristics (except "gentle," which was rated more highly by females). With age, the importance of expressive characteristics increased and instrumental traits decreased. It is curious that there has been so little research on this issue, given recent work on the dimensions of gender identity (Egan & Perry, 2001). Future research should examine the potential significance of variations in children's perceptions of what "kind" of boy or girl they would like to be.

Behavioral Enactment (3D)

As in past *Handbooks* (Huston, 1983; Ruble & Martin, 1998), we do not review individual studies in the voluminous literature on sex differences in traits and abilities. Instead, we focus on meta-analyses, which provide quantitative summaries, including effect sizes (here *d,* the difference in means between the sexes expressed in standard deviation units), and analyses showing whether effects change across characteristics of the population (e.g., age) or study (e.g., subjectivity of measurement, year of publication). Guidelines for effect size (Cohen, 1988) suggest that *d* of .2 is small (85% overlap in distributions), .5 is moderate (67% overlap) and probably noticeable, and .8 is large (53% overlap) and very noticeable (by convention, *d* is calculated as the male mean minus the female mean, so positive values reflect males higher than females and negative values females higher than males). Much has been written about benefits and limitations of meta-analysis, but we note two points: First, small mean differences can be associated with large differences at the tails of the distributions; second, meta-analyses assume that the distribution of scores in the two sexes is the same, with one shifted away from the other. We focus on developmental trends in sex differences and whether differences are larger in some domains than others. Our review relies heavily on Blakemore's recent summary of sex differences in physical skills, cognition, personality, and social behavior, which includes empirical studies and meta-analyses, covering studies through 2004 (Blakemore, Berenbaum, & Liben, 2006).

Physical and Motor Skills. Meta-analyses of activity level (e.g., D. W. Campbell & Eaton, 1999) show an increasing sex difference with age: infants *d* = .20, preschool *d* = .44, elementary school *d* = .64, with the differences largest in familiar, nonthreatening settings and when peers are present. Sex differences in physical and motor skills generally relate to girls' earlier neurological development and better fine motor skills and boys' greater muscle strength. Boys are slightly stronger

than girls in early childhood, becoming more so through childhood and after puberty—for example, the sex difference in grip strength is .25 to .50 in early childhood, .50 to 1.0 in middle childhood, and 1.0 to 2.0 in adolescence (Sartorio, Lafrotuna, Pogliaghi, & Trecate, 2002; J. R. Thomas & French, 1985). There are few sex differences in milestones of reaching, sitting, crawling, and walking, but differences in motor skills begin to appear in the 2nd year. Abilities that depend on neurological development, such as eye-hand coordination and toilet training, develop earlier in girls than in boys (Blakemore et al., 2006). Data from a large sample of children aged 5 to 18 show that girls develop sooner than boys on fine motor skills and upper body tasks, whereas boys do better on tasks requiring rapid movement (Largo et al., 2001a, 2001b). Meta-analysis (J. R. Thomas & French, 1985) and recent studies (Blakemore et al., 2006) show males to be better than females on many motor tasks, with the largest differences in throwing velocity and distance, whereas females excel on fine eye-motor and flexibility tasks. Sex differences in many (but not all) physical and motor abilities increase with age, and much of boys' increasing superiority appears to reflect their greater practice of these skills, in part from involvement in sports (Blakemore et al., 2006), although biological factors likely also play a role (Kimura, 1999).

Cognitive Skills. There are no sex differences in overall intellectual ability, but the sexes differ in the *pattern* of cognitive abilities (for reviews see Halpern, 2000; Kimura, 1999). The biggest cognitive sex difference is in spatial ability. There are several ways to parse the domain (Halpern, 2000; Linn & Petersen, 1985), but males outperform females in most aspects of spatial ability, with the size of the difference varying across abilities. More is known about differences in adults than in children because many tests are too difficult for children and tests that are used with children measure multiple abilities. The largest sex difference is in mental rotation, especially rotation of objects in three dimensions: *d* = .56 to 1.0 in adolescents and adults, and about .40 in children (Blakemore et al., 2006; Halpern, 2000). There are also differences in spatial perception, which requires recognition of the vertical or horizontal (*d* = .4), targeting (i.e., hitting a target with a ball; *d* = 1.0; Kimura, 1999), and abilities related to navigating in the real world (Blakemore et al., 2006; Halpern, 2000). There is a huge sex disparity in National Geography Bee winners (despite equal participation from boys and girls); the sex ratio increases at each level of competition, so that in most years, all 10 finalists are boys (Liben, 1995). There do not appear to be sex differences in visualization (e.g., hidden figures), but this may be due to visualization tests measuring multiple abilities. There is one spatial domain in which females outperform males: memory for spatial location ($d = -1.0$; Blakemore et al., 2006; Kimura, 1999).

The sexes differ in mathematic abilities, with the differences again varying by type of ability and age. Meta-analyses show a greater male advantage in selected samples (Hyde, Fennema, & Lamon, 1990) and on certain standardized tests (e.g., SAT, $d = .4$; Hyde & Frost, 1993). There is no sex difference in mathematical concepts; females outperform males in computation, especially before puberty ($d = -.14$); and males outperform females on problem-solving tasks, especially at older ages ($d = .29$ by high school; Hyde et al., 1990). Girls receive higher grades in mathematics than boys, as they do in all classes. Girls now take almost the same number of math classes as boys do, but boys still perform better on standardized tests after course-taking has been considered. There are a variety of factors that may contribute to the sex difference in math, including biological factors, spatial ability, strategies used to solve math problems, attitudes toward math, and stereotype threat (Blakemore et al., 2006).

Females outperform males on verbal tasks, again with the difference varying across ability and age. Girls have a small advantage in language learning in early childhood, but boys catch up by age 6 (e.g., Bornstein, Hahn, & Haynes, 2004; Huttenlocher, Haight, Bryk, Seltzer, & Lyons, 1991). Boys are more likely than girls to have disorders of spoken and written language (Halpern, 2000; Hyde & McKinley, 1997). Meta-analyses (Hyde & Linn, 1988) show that males are better than females in analogies ($d = .22$), but females have a small advantage over males in other verbal skills: $d = -.11$ for overall verbal skills, $d = -.20$ for general verbal ability tests, $d = -.02$ for vocabulary, $d = -.03$ for reading comprehension, $d = -.09$ for essay writing, and $d = -.33$ for speech production. A summary of several large studies of adolescents showed larger sex differences than reported in meta-analyses in reading comprehension (0 to $-.3$) and writing ($-.5$ to $-.6$; Hedges & Nowell, 1995); the latter is consistent with national data on writing proficiency (Halpern, 2000). Females also do better than males on verbal

abilities not included in meta-analyses, such as phonological processing, $d = -.5$ to -1.0 (Majeres, 1997, 1999), verbal fluency, $d = -.5$ to -1.0 (Halpern, 2000), and verbal learning and memory, $d = -.5$ (Halpern, 2000; Hedges & Nowell, 1995; Kimura, 1999; Kramer, Delis, & Daniel, 1988). Females' superior learning and recall of lists of common objects is largely due to their use of efficient clustering strategies ($d = -.5$). Females also outperform males on perceptual speed, with small to moderate differences ($d = -.2$ to $-.6$).

There are also sex differences in variability in cognitive abilities, particularly in spatial and mathematical abilities (Hedges & Nowell, 1995). For example, more than twice as many males as females have high spatial ability, and the same sex ratio is found on SAT Math scores above the 95th percentile.

Some have argued that cognitive sex differences have declined across time (e.g., Feingold, 1988; but compare to Hedges & Nowell, 1995), but methodological issues make it difficult to know if these changes are real. Such trends might reflect factors correlated with publication year, such as sampling (e.g., college enrollment shifted from overwhelming male to predominant female, changing sex differences in selectivity), publishing trends (e.g., greater likelihood that nonsignificant findings are published now than previously), and use of tests that never showed large sex differences (Halpern, 2000).

Subjective Well-Being and Self-Evaluation. A variety of indicators show that females experience lower levels of well-being than males. Females are more likely than males to be clinically depressed and to exhibit more depressive symptoms, beginning in adolescence, with likely contributors being hormonal changes at puberty (e.g., Angold, Costello, & Worthman, 1998), and girls' greater risk factors before puberty combined with greater challenges in adolescence (Nolen-Hoeksema & Girgus, 1994). Meta-analyses of global self-esteem reveal small but consistent effects (.2 to .3) favoring males (Kling, Hyde, Showers, & Buswell, 1999; Major, Barr, Zubek, & Babey, 1999; Wilgenbusch & Merrell, 1999), with differences appearing around age 10 and perhaps increasing in late adolescence.

The prevalence of some mental disorders varies by sex. For example, in childhood and adolescence, there is male preponderance of speech and language disorders, Autism, Attention-Deficit/Hyperactivity Disorder (ADHD), Oppositional and Conduct Disorder, and female preponderance of Separation Anxiety Disorder; in adulthood, males predominate in substance abuse, females in Dysthymic Disorder, Generalized Anxiety Disorder, and certain phobias (for specific data, see Hartung & Widiger, 1998). Reported sex ratios may be biased by sampling issues and problems with *DSM* criteria (Hartung & Widiger, 1998).

Personality Traits and Social Behavior. The question of whether males and females display the attributes that are stereotypically associated with them, such as aggression and dependency, has been the subject of meta-analyses. Studies of aggression have yielded some of the most consistent findings for any domain, at least for children. Boys engage in more aggressive behaviors than girls ($d = .5$; Knight, Fabes, & Higgins, 1996; Maccoby & Jacklin, 1974). Differences emerge early in life and are found cross-culturally, suggesting that biological factors may be involved (Maccoby & Jacklin, 1974). There is controversy over whether the sex difference in aggression decreases or increases with age (Knight et al., 1996; Ruble & Martin, 1998). The discrepancy reflects a larger difference with observational measures, more often used with children than with adolescents and adults (Knight et al., 1996). Sex differences in aggression vary by context; for example, differences are larger when aggression is spontaneous rather than provoked or required in experimental situations (Bettencourt & Kernahan, 1997; Bettencourt & Miller, 1996). There are large sex differences in real-world aggression: Men commit more violent crimes than women, and the more serious the crime, the more the sex difference is apparent (Rutter, Giller, & Hagell, 1998). Males take more risks than females do throughout childhood and into early adulthood ($d = .2$), contributing to their higher rates of injury (Byrnes, Miller, & Schafer, 1999). Girls engage in social or relational aggression (i.e., behaviors intended to damage another's friendships and social status) more than they engage in physical aggression, but it is not clear whether they engage in it more than boys do (e.g., Underwood, Scott, Galperin, Bjornstad, & Sexton, 2004).

Despite stereotypes that females are more helpful and oriented to the needs of others, there are not strong and consistent sex differences in children's prosocial behavior. Sex differences tend to be small, and the likelihood of finding them varies by study characteristics (Eisenberg & Fabes, 1998; Eisenberg, Martin, & Fabes, 1996). Meta-analysis of helping behavior shows girls to help others more than boys (Eisenberg & Fabes, 1998), but the reverse is true for adults, partly

because studies with adults often involve helping that is heroic and instrumental—more consistent with the male role. Girls interact more with babies than do boys, with the magnitude of the difference depending on the context (Blakemore et al., 2006). Much attention has focused on sex differences in level and orientation of moral reasoning (Gilligan, 1982). Meta-analyses suggest no sex differences in level of morality (Walker, 1984, 1986). In four data sets, males had a slightly higher stage of morality at some ages, and females did at other ages, but all effects were very small (Dawson, 2002). There are small differences in the type of moral arguments used: Females are more likely than males to use a morality of caring ($d = -.28$) and less likely to use a morality of justice ($d = .19$), with the largest effects seen during adolescence and young adulthood (Jaffee & Hyde, 2000).

Stereotypes suggest that females are more passive and dependent, and more easily influenced than males, but this is not empirically verified. Differences are particularly small for observational and experimental studies of children interacting with parents and peers, but girls are rated by others as dependent, possibly because of stereotypes (Maccoby & Jacklin, 1974). Meta-analyses show women to be more easily influenced than men ($d > -.3$), with effects of context (Ruble & Martin, 1998). Females are more likely to be helped than males ($d = -.5$), although this may reflect perceptions about females' dependence and not that they need help (Ruble & Martin, 1998). Nevertheless, females may be more likely to seek help of certain kinds and more willing to accept help (see Eisenberg et al., 1996, for review).

Are females more socially oriented and sensitive as stereotypes suggest? Meta-analyses in some areas suggest that they are. Girls and boys do not differ in ability to understand what others are thinking or feeling, but women appear to be better than men at decoding others' emotions and have a greater tendency to take the perspective of another (Eisenberg et al., 1996). In addition, females at all ages are more accurate at decoding emotions from visual and auditory stimuli, $d = -.25$ (e.g., J. A. Hall, Carter, & Horgan, 2000). Girls are better than boys at decoding the facial emotions of others; effects are small ($d = -.13$ to $-.18$), except in infancy ($d = -.70$ to $-.92$; McClure, 2000). Females also appear to be more socially expressive and responsive, with moderate to large effects, for example, for social gazing, expression of emotion, and general facial expressiveness (Ruble & Martin, 1998).

Emotionality. Females are believed to be more emotional, which generally means more anxious, fearful, more easily upset, and more empathic and emotionally expressive, whereas males are believed to express more anger and to be more likely to hide or deny emotional reactions. As described earlier, there are sex differences in anxiety and depression.

Adult men and women differ in emotional expressiveness and in expression accuracy. Females show more expression than males in faces ($d = -.45$) and gestures ($d = -.27$; J. A. Hall et al., 2000). They are also more accurate in conveying emotions, spontaneously and posed ($d = -.25$), in facial cues but not in voice (J. A. Hall et al., 2000). The sexes differ in patterns of emotional responding, with women generally reporting more sadness, fear, shame, and guilt, and men reporting more anger. Cross-cultural data suggest the universality of these differences (Fischer, Rodriguez Mosquera, van Vianen, & Manstead, 2004). With respect to the development of emotion, Eisenberg et al. (1996) provide the following account on the basis of their review. During infancy and toddler years, few consistent sex differences in the expression of emotion are found, although males may exhibit more irritability and anger, and girls more fearfulness. During the early elementary school years, boys start to hide negative emotions, such as sadness, and girls express less anger and emotions such as disappointment that might hurt others' feelings. By adolescence, girls report more sadness, shame, and guilt, and say they experience emotions more intensely, whereas boys are more likely to deny experiencing these emotions.

Empathy is slightly more likely to be displayed by females than males, with differences dependent on methodology and context (Eisenberg et al., 1996). For example, self-report measures show large differences favoring females, but physiological or unobtrusive observations do not (Eisenberg & Fabes, 1998). Meta-analysis supports the idea that individuals' self-perceptions are biased by their stereotypes (Ickes, Gesn, & Graham, 2000).

Summary. The sex differences reported by Maccoby and Jacklin (1974) in their comprehensive review have been well documented, and work since has expanded the categorization of sex differences. Differences are found for aspects of spatial, mathematical, and verbal skills, with effects largest for spatial abilities and on standardized tests, but questions remain about the age at which these differences first appear. Males are more physically aggressive than females and

more likely to take risks. Females are better at expressing and decoding emotions than are males. There are also strong and consistent sex differences in activity level and physical and motor skills. Overall, sex-difference patterns vary considerably by content area, developmental level, and context. In general, personal-social behaviors show negligible to moderate differences but no large differences, whereas interests and abilities show differences across the full range of effect sizes (for details of effect sizes, see Blakemore et al., 2006; Halpern, 2000).

Social Relationships (4)

Children's gendered social relationships include peer relationships and friendships and sexual relationships. To what extent do children's concepts, self-perceptions, preferences, and enactment show parallels in this domain? When do children develop knowledge about the desirability of relationships with same-sex playmates, and what is the developmental course of children's preferences and behaviors regarding same- and other-sex relationships?

Concepts or Beliefs (4A)

Children have different conceptions of relationships with girls and boys and these views change developmentally. Young children understand that certain relationships are more acceptable than others (i.e., same-sex play and friendships are more acceptable than other-sex play and friendships). For instance, children showed strong stereotypes about others' relationships (i.e., they believe boys prefer to play with other boys more than with girls) that increased from 4 to 6 years, and these beliefs correlated with same-sex play partner preferences (Martin, Fabes, Evans, & Wyman, 1999).

Knowledge about sex differences in relationships increases with age. Young children show little evidence of knowing how boys' and girls' play differs (e.g., that girls play inside more than boys; Martin et al., 1999). Preschoolers recognized that boys prefer to play in groups but not that they have more shared friendships than girls. By grade 2, children believe that boys have more shared friendships, and by grade 6, they recognize that friends have access to more information about each other than nonfriends (Markovits, Benenson, & Dolenszky, 2001). Older children (9 to 11 years) believe that, for competitive but not for cooperative games (i.e., those games that boys may be more likely to play), playing in larger groups is more enjoyable than playing in dyads (Benenson, Gordon, & Roy, 2000).

Children's conceptions of friendship differ by sex (Ladd, 2005). By middle to late childhood, girls regard friendships as higher in positive qualities (i.e., intimacy and closeness) than do boys, but the sexes have similar levels of conflict in these relationships. In conflict situations, girls place greater priority on relationship goals (such as wanting to maintain a friendship) and boys are more likely to try to seek control over friends (Rose & Asher, 1999). In early and middle adolescence, girls' friendships focus on issues of intimacy, love, and communion, whereas boys' friendships tend to focus on agency, power, and excitement (Rose, 2002). Because of the greater intimacy of girls' relationships, they are more fragile and prone to disruption through divulging of confidential information during conflict (Benenson & Christakos, 2003).

Insights about gendered relationships can be gleaned from research on how children evaluate exclusion. About 30% to 50% of preschool children used gender stereotypes to condone exclusion during play, especially in situations involving activities rather than roles. Although children have stereotypes about play with peers that are used in certain situations, principles of equity and fairness may override their use (Theimer, Killen, & Stangor, 2001).

Identity or Self-Perception (4B)

Although many scholars argue that it is best to study gender as it is constructed within a social context, little attention has been paid to how children perceive themselves in terms of their social relationships. To what degree do children incorporate stereotypic beliefs into their self-concepts about their relationships, and how do their gender identities relate to relationship choices? There is little developmental research on such questions. Some evidence has been obtained from gender-atypical children. For instance, tomboys report liking boys as playmates more than other girls do (J. M. Bailey, Bechtold, & Berenbaum, 2002), and children with GIDC report preferences for other-sex playmates (Zucker & Bradley, 1995). However, identity is not consistently linked to relationship preferences: Girls with early androgen exposure but with female gender identity show some tendency to prefer boys as playmates (Berenbaum & Snyder, 1995).

The association between identity and relationships has also been studied in the context of sexuality. Sexual identity is often but not always related to sexual behav-

ior. Sexual identity is a person's identity in relation to preferred sexual partners and it may not correspond with sexual behavior. For instance, a person may engage in sex with same-sex others without identifying as gay or lesbian. Sexual identity is presumed to be later developing and more dependent on social, historical, and cultural factors than is sexual orientation (Savin-Williams & Diamond, 2000). Women are less likely to report congruence between sexual behavior and identities (Dempsey, Hillier, & Harrison, 2001; L. M. Diamond, 2000) and are more likely to change their sexual identity (L. M. Diamond, 1998; Savin-Williams & Diamond, 2001), suggesting that sexual identity is more fluid for women than men (Baumeister, 2000; L. M. Diamond, 2003b).

Preferences (4C)

Children's self-reported preferences for same-sex peers have been widely documented (behavioral choices are described in 4D). Preschool, kindergarten, and middle school children consistently like same-sex (known or unknown) peers and prefer them as friends more than other-sex peers, and this tendency increases with age until adolescence when other-sex interests become apparent and strong same-sex preferences decreases (Lobel et al., 2000; Powlishta, Serbin, Doyle, & White, 1994; Serbin et al., 1993; Sippola, Bukowski, & Noll, 1997). Young children maintain same-sex preferences even when unknown children have nontraditional interests (see Ruble & Martin, 1998, for review), although the extent of gender-nonnormative behavior may moderate these preferences, especially for boys (Zucker, Wilson-Smith, Kurita, & Stern, 1995; also see Bussey & Bandura, 1992). In adolescence, boys with cross-sex interests are not liked but girls' interests do not appear to matter as much to ratings of liking (Lobel et al., 1999).

Behavioral Enactment (4D)

Young girls and boys differ in how they act in their social relationships but both sexes show strong same-sex preferences in the types of relationships they choose. As children grow older, the sex-differentiated nature of their relationships changes to reflect interest in sexual relationships.

Play Qualities of Girls and Boys. Boys and girls differ in their play qualities. Interactions among boys are marked by rough-and-tumble play, attempts to attain dominance, and constrictive interaction styles, whereas interactions among girls are more often cooperative and enabling of others (Ruble & Martin, 1998). Even by preschool, a number of differences can be identified in the play styles of boys and girls. Boys often play further away from adults than do girls (Benenson, Morash, & Petrakos, 1998; A. Campbell, Shirley, & Candy, 2004), so their play is less supervised and may be more peer- than adult-oriented (Fabes, Martin, Hanish, 2003; Martin & Fabes, 2001). The differences between girls' and boys' play tends to be exaggerated in groups versus dyads (Fabes et al., 2003). Boys show higher activity level, more exercise play, and more rough-and-tumble play (Di Pietro, 1981; Eaton & Enns, 1986; Fabes et al., 2003; Martin & Fabes, 2001; Pellegrini, 1987; Pellegrini & Smith, 1998). Rough-and-tumble play may exacerbate sex segregation because boys initiate this type of play and girls withdraw from it (Pellegrini & Smith, 1998).

Play qualities and games continue to show sex differences as children age. In middle childhood, boys are more likely than girls to be involved in ball games and fantasy play and are more physically aggressive. Girls are more likely to be involved in conversations, sedentary play, skipping, verbal games, and positive affect during play (Blatchford, Baines, & Pellegrini, 2003). Girls tend to self-disclose and provide greater emotional support, spend more time talking to, and report feeling more intimate with their friends than do boys (Buhrmester, 1996; Lansford & Parker, 1999). Girls engage in co-rumination, extensively discussing problems, and focusing on negative feelings (Rose, 2002).

Both sexes tend to interact in small groups of two or three members, but from about the age of 5, boys are more likely than girls to associate in larger groups (Fabes, Martin, & Hanish, 2003; Maccoby, 2002). Boys are involved in larger organized group games and occupy more space on playgrounds than do girls. This difference appears even in young children who are not yet playing team sports. It appears that dyadic play is not a function of the kinds of activities or materials involved in play. For example, in one study boys and girls showed different patterns of interaction when given the same materials to use however they wanted: Boys organized themselves into larger groups and engaged in coordinated activities, whereas girls formed dyads with more prolonged interactions. These patterns were more pronounced at age 6 than at age 4 (Benenson, Apostoleris, & Parnass, 1997). Group size influences how children play: Larger groups promote competition and conflict, especially in boys, whereas dyadic interaction promotes consideration of others' interests, less competition, and more emotional support (Benenson et al., 2002; Benenson, Nicholson, Waite, Roy, & Simpson, 2001; Roy & Benenson, 2002). Boylike behavior may result not from the direct influence of individual boys' personalities or temperaments but from boys' tendencies to respond in particular ways in boy groups (Maccoby, 2002). In contrast, girls' behavior appears to be more similar across different play contexts (Benenson et al., 2002; Trautner, 1995). How children play in groups also depends on the play partner. Boys engage in more active play with other boys than with girls. The reverse pattern is found for girls: They are more active with boys. Both sexes adjust their behavior somewhat to fit their play partners' styles, but other-sex group encounters are relatively rare, so likely have little overall impact on children (Fabes, Martin, & Hanish, 2003).

Development of Sex Segregation. One of the most pervasive sex differences involves whom children choose as play partners (Maccoby, 1998). Children and adolescents consistently report spending more time with same-sex peers and siblings (McHale, Kim, et al., 2004). Whereas many sex differences are quite small, sex accounts for a very large proportion of the variance (70% to 85%) in children's play partners (Maccoby, 1998; Martin & Fabes, 2001). Sex segregation appears to be universal, occurring in many higher species of nonhuman primates (Wallen, 1996) and in Western and non-Western societies, although the extent depends on the number of children available, their ages (e.g., Whiting & Edwards, 1988), and the setting (highest when children have more playmate choices and in less structured settings; Maccoby, 1998). Sex segregation is evident early in the school term (Martin, Fabes, Hanish, & Hollenstein, in press) and is influenced by activity involvement: Boys were more likely to segregate when involved in a competitive game than during a less competitive game (Boyatzis, Mallis, & Leon, 1999). Whether there are individual differences in the stability of sex segregation has received attention because of its importance in identifying causes of segregation. Although stability has been reported to be low or modest (e.g., M. L. Hoffman & Powlishta, 2001; Maccoby & Jacklin, 1987), it is high when larger samples and extensive observations are used (Martin & Fabes, 2001).

Sex segregation emerges at an early age: for girls, by 27 months; for boys, by 36 months (La Freniere, Strayer, & Gauthier, 1984). Other studies confirm this pattern of emergence (Ruble & Martin, 1998). Sex segregation is evident in social networks and in friendship choices. By preschool, children spend little time with other-sex peers:

Only about 10% of children's interactions occur solely with a child of the other sex and about 25% involve mixed-sex groups (Fabes, Martin, & Hanish, 2003). In very young children, other-sex friends are common, but other-sex friendships decline from 1 to 6 years of age (Howes, 1988). In middle childhood, sex segregation becomes even more pronounced (Maccoby, 1998). By middle childhood, only about 15% of children have other-sex friends (Kovacs, Parker, & Hoffman, 1996). Throughout childhood, boys and girls prefer same-sex friends and have more positive interactions with them as compared to other-sex friends (Vaughn, 2001). Nonetheless, some young children develop friendships with other-sex children and these often go underground during school hours. Prior to adolescence, both girls and boys expect greater enjoyment in interaction with same-sex peers, but these expectations vary depending on setting (Strough & Covatto, 2002).

During adolescence, peer networks change. In early adolescence, children congregate in small cliques of same-sex peers and have same-sex friends (Bukowski, Sippola, & Hoza, 1999) but, by middle adolescence, although same-sex preferences are still obvious, heterosexual dating couples also become apparent and various types of other-sex relationships emerge (Sippola, 1999). In middle adolescence, about 40% to 50% of young people have romantic relationships; by later adolescence, most have experienced a romantic relationship (e.g., Connolly, Craig, Goldberg, & Pepler, 1999). Even with the increase in other-sex relationships, girls (but not boys) report feeling more comfortable with same-sex peers (Lundy, Field, & McBride, 1998). Longitudinal data across grades 9 to 11 show that children's same-sex networks remained about the same while their other-sex networks increased in size (Richards, Crowe, Larson, & Swarr, 1998) and other-sex networks facilitated romantic relationships by helping adolescents to meet potential partners (Connolly, Furman, & Konarski, 2000).

Sibling interactions influence adolescent friendships, especially for girls. For example, girls who had a brother were more likely to report using control strategies with friends than girls who had a sister (Updegraff, McHale, & Crouter, 2000). Sibling interactions appear to provide children with opportunities seldom available in school for learning about other-sex interactions (McHale, Crouter, & Tucker, 1999).

Few children report preferences for other-sex relationships. Girls with early androgen exposure, tomboys, and children with GIDC are somewhat more likely than typical girls to prefer other-sex playmates (J. M. Bailey et al., 2002; Berenbaum & Snyder, 1995; Zucker & Bradley, 1995). Sexual minority youth (e.g., homosexual) report predominantly same-sex peer networks, but friendships differ by sex, with males reporting more other-sex friends than same-sex friends and females reporting more same-sex friends than other-sex friends (L. M. Diamond & Dube, 2002).

Causes of Sex Segregation. Why do children show sex-segregated interactions? Many potential explanations have been proposed to account for sex segregation, involving both distal and proximal mechanisms. For instance, evolutionary theorists propose that selection factors increase the likelihood that the sexes will be drawn together in same-sex dyads or groups, which are hypothesized to prepare children for adult roles (Geary, 1999; Geary & Bjorklund, 2000).

A proximal explanation involves behavioral similarity, i.e., individuals are drawn to others who behave similarly to themselves. Many dimensions of behavioral similarity have been proposed including physiological and temperament differences between the sexes (e.g., Fabes, 1994; Serbin, Moller, Gulko, Powlishta, & Colburne, 1994). For example, children who are active and like rough-and-tumble play may be more inclined to play with boys than with girls (Fabes, Shepard, Guthrie, & Martin, 1997; M. L. Hoffman & Powlishta, 2001; Martin, Fabes, et al., 2006; Pellegrini & Smith, 1998). Computer simulations of preschool children's play show that real play patterns can be mimicked by using simple rules based on compatibility along a few behavioral and affective dimensions (Griffin, Hanish, Martin, & Fabes, 2003; Schmidt, Griffin, Hanish, Martin, & Fabes, 2004).

Children may also sex segregate because of their gender theories or cognitions (i.e., they believe they will be similar to same-sex others; Martin, 1994; Martin & Dinella, 2002; Martin et al., 2002). Evidence supports this idea: children's beliefs that they are similar to their own sex and different from the other sex have been found to predict children's observed sex segregation (Martin et al., 2006). Behavioral similarity and gender-based theories are not mutually exclusive and may both act to influence sex segregation (Barbu, Le-Maner-Idrissi, & Jouanjean, 2000; Martin et al., 2006). A recent proposal about sex segregation based on dynamic systems theory integrates these earlier explanations (Martin et al., in press): Children's interactions are considered to be a dynamic system in which children's partner choices are influenced by many small and large forces working in concert—including behavioral, cognitive, and social forces—and each of these contribute to the formation and maintenance of peer relationships and groups.

A number of fascinating questions remain about sex segregation. What characterizes children who consistently play with other-sex peers and what enables them to cross boundaries (Sroufe, Bennett, Englund, Urban, & Shulman, 1993; Thorne, 1993)? What are the circumstances that promote and inhibit socialization by same- and other-sex peers? By what processes do peers influence one another, and which children are most vulnerable to peer influence (see Socialization Approaches section)?

Development of Sexual Behavior and Orientation. In 4B, we discussed how sexual identity can be discrepant from sexual behavior. In this section, we focus on sexual attraction and behavior, and briefly on theories that consider how all domains of sexuality develop. Interestingly, with few exceptions (e.g., Hyde & Jaffee, 2000), most of the research and theorizing on the development of sexual orientation concerns the development of orientation in sexual minorities, even though a complete picture of sexual development requires understanding the experience, meaning, and development of same-sex and other-sex sexuality in all individuals (L. M. Diamond, 2003a).

On average, sexual attraction begins at age 10, but varies by sex, culture, and sexual orientation (Herdt & McClintock, 2000). Much recent research has focused on same-sex sexual orientation and posits stages marked by awareness of same-sex attractions in late childhood/early adolescence, and then a period of testing and exploration, and finally the adoption of a sexual minority label, disclosing sexual identity to others, and involvement in same-sex romantic relationships. This developmental course is more typical for males than for females. Sexual minority men experience earlier same-sex sexual attractions and behavior than do sexual minority women (L. M. Diamond, 1998; Savin-Williams & Diamond, 2001). For males, there is more congruence between the sex of the person of sexual and romantic attractions (i.e., they are attracted to and fall in love with people of the same sex); for females, the link between desire and love may be looser (L. M. Diamond, 2000, 2004). Thus, different models are needed to describe the development of sexual orientation in men versus women (Savin-Williams & Diamond, 2000).

Interesting precursors to sexual orientation have been identified. Some evidence of early gender atypicality is apparent in individuals who grow up to identify themselves as homosexual or bisexual. Boys (more so than girls) with gender identity issues are more likely to have homosexual or bisexual orientations than are other children (Zucker & Bradley, 1995). A meta-analytic review suggests that homosexual individuals are more likely than heterosexual individuals to report retrospectively cross-gender interests in childhood (effect size for men = 1.3; women = 1.0; J. M. Bailey & Zucker, 1995).

The origins of sexual orientation have been hotly debated. The core of the debate concerns whether sexual orientation is innate. Although some authors have suggested that social factors relate to homosexuality or bisexuality, many others have examined genetic, hormonal, and brain structural evidence to suggest a biological component (e.g., LeVay, 1993). Biological contributors to sexual orientation also may work indirectly through an influence on temperament, which in turn may influence feelings of gender atypicality. Feeling gender atypical may lead to viewing the self as more similar to the other sex and may promote feelings of eroticism toward the relatively unfamiliar same-sex others (D. J. Bem, 1996, 2000). Alternatively, identity may drive behavioral changes. Children questioning their heterosexuality may begin to engage in gender-atypical behavior and develop self-perceptions in line with their newly developing identity as a sexual minority (Carver, Egan, & Perry, 2004).

Styles and Symbols (5)

Gendered styles and symbols range from body image and hairstyles to speech patterns and communication. Do children know the gendered meanings of voices, interaction and communication styles, gestures, hairstyles, and clothing? To what extent are their self-perceptions, preferences, and behavioral patterns in these domains gender-typed? Most research in styles and symbols concerns communication patterns and, more recently, body image. Although communication involves both substantive and stylistic variations, to be consistent with the last *Handbook* chapter, we continue to cover this material in the styles and symbols section.

Concepts or Beliefs (5A)

Young children know gender-related symbolic associations. For example, preschoolers have clear stereotypes about colors and associate physical cues such as colors and clothing with gender-typed interests in others (e.g., Picariello, Greenberg, & Pillemer, 1990). As discussed in the last *Handbook* chapter, in studies of metaphorical associations, children attribute to boys things that are angular, rough, and dangerous (e.g., a bear), and to girls things that are soft, light, and graceful (e.g., a butterfly). Children select toys using metaphorical cues rather than known stereotypes when these are in conflict (e.g., a pink truck may be appealing to girls).

Hairstyles and clothing (and adornment in general) are important external stylistic markers strongly associated with gender and are learned at a very young age. In a study of stereotypic norms and their violations (see 6C; Blakemore, 2003), 100% of first grade children knew the norms for girls' and boys' clothing and hairstyles, and by third grade for play styles. Appearance cues appear to be more important for girls than boys. When asked to tell what they know about the sexes (a measure of the accessibility of stereotypes), girls provided more appearance stereotypes than boys, and both sexes provided more appearance stereotypes when describing girls than when describing boys (C. F. Miller, Lurye, et al., 2006).

Children demonstrate stereotypic knowledge about speech patterns and roles associated with the sexes. When children ages 4 to 7 were asked to enact their father's speech, they used a deeper-pitched voice and loud voice; when enacting their mother's speech, they tended to use higher-pitched voice, exaggerated intonation, and female-stereotyped vocabulary (Andersen, 1996). Young children also illustrate stereotypic knowledge of gendered language, recognizing the links between sex and gendered linguistic markers, such as "adorable" as a female-type word, and intensifiers (e.g., so, very) as markers of female speech (Gleason & Ely, 2002).

Children begin to develop body image stereotypes about others concerning weight around age 5 (Hendy, Gustitus, & Leitzel-Schwalm, 2001). It appears that children also develop a preference for muscular male bodies at a young age (Spitzer, Henderson, & Zivian, 1999). These stereotypes relate to children's own body perceptions as they grow older (see 5B).

Identity or Self-Perception (5B)

To understand how children view themselves as gendered in their style, we review evidence concerning clothing preferences, types of mannerisms, and body image. Although the evidence on these topics has been sparse, recent interest in body image has provided a clearer picture of the extent to which identity and self-perception are evidenced through stylistic and symbolic markers.

Clothing Styles and Mannerisms. Dress and mannerism provide ways to actively construct gender yet have not been well studied. Many interesting questions need to be addressed (see Ruble & Martin, 1998). Are children who select their own clothing aware of the effects of their choices? What are the links between gender identity and adoption of gender-typical styles and mannerisms?

Body Image. Extensive research has demonstrated that images of one's body play a significant role in predicting depression, eating disorders, and low self-esteem, especially in adolescent girls (e.g., J. K. Thompson, Heinberg, Altabe, & Tantleff-Dunn, 1999). At age 5, both sexes are similar in body image (i.e., girls do not yet show more body dissatisfaction; Hendy et al., 2001). Between 6 and 8 years of age, sex differences appear, with girls showing more body dissatisfaction than boys, and more desire to be thin (e.g., A. J. Hill & Pallin, 1998; Ricciardelli & McCabe, 2001; Schur, Sanders, & Steiner, 2000; Tiggemann & Wilson-Barrett, 1998), which are consistent over time and related to disordered eating behavior and eating attitudes (Davison, Markey, & Birch, 2002; Ricciardelli & McCabe, 2001). Preadolescents show similar patterns of sex differences in body image and dissatisfaction (K. Thomas, Ricciardelli, & Williams, 2000). Body image concerns for boys center on being more muscular (McCabe & Ricciardelli, 2003; Smolak, Levine, & Thompson, 2001) and for girls on weight.

The sex difference in body image continues in adolescence (Byely, Archibald, Graber, & Brooks-Gunn, 2000). A large percentage of adolescent girls report significant body dissatisfaction (J. K. Thompson et al., 1999), which is linked with emotional distress, appearance rumination, and unnecessary cosmetic surgery (Ohring, Graber, & Brooks-Gunn, 2002; J. K. Thompson et al., 1999), as well as depression and disordered eating (e.g., Grant et al., 1999; Stice & Bearman, 2001; Stice & Whitenton, 2002). A number of studies link body image to media and societal pressures for attractiveness and thinness for females (Smolak et al., 2001; Stice & Whitenton, 2002; J. K. Thompson & Stice, 2001; Werthein, Koerner, & Paxton, 2001). Peer pressure affects body dissatisfaction (Carlson Jones, 2001; Vincent & McCabe, 2000). A recent study demonstrated that changes in boys' body dissatisfaction over adolescence related to internalization of the male muscular ideal; girls' body dissatisfaction related to their body mass, social comparisons, and appearance conversations with friends (Carlson Jones, 2004). Body dissatisfaction is associated in girls with earlier pubertal maturation (Ohring et al., 2002) and, in both sexes, with maternal pressure to lose weight (Ricciardelli & McCabe, 2001).

Preferences (5C)

Anecdotal data suggest that young children express strong preferences to dress in a way that indicates their sex, regardless of parents' preferences, with girls preferring frilly dresses and bows and boys, baseball caps and sneakers. But, few studies have addressed verbal preferences (see 4D for research on adoption of styles of dress).

In one study of 5- to 10-year-olds, children preferred same-sex peers dressed in stereotypic or neutral clothing over children dressed in counter-stereotypic clothing (Albers, 1998). They also associated play activities with clothing styles, indicating that they may form broader stereotypes about the characteristics of gender normative versus nonnormative children.

Color preferences have been examined in a number of studies mostly in adults. Although the pattern is not replicated in every study, it appears that young adults often show stereotypic color preferences: Females prefer pinks but not darker reds, and males prefer shades of blues (Ellis & Ficek, 2001). Some people, especially females, have genes that provide additional color discrimination, and this may contribute to sex differences in color preferences (Jameson, Highnote, & Wasserman, 2001). There is speculation that color preferences are linked to sex differences in the visual centers of brain and that these differences contribute to children's sex-typed toy choices (Alexander, 2003).

Although very little work has been done to assess whether girls and boys show different artistic preferences or produce different images, one study found that by the age of 4, children preferred gender-stereotypic art and both sexes showed equally extreme patterns of gender-typed preferences. Furthermore, both girls and boys produced gender-stereotypic art (as rated by judges; also see Boyatzis & Albertini, 2000). It is particularly interesting to find these preferences at such a young age. Also, the degree to which the art was gender-typed is surprising: even when it was non-representational, judges determined that it was "masculine" or "feminine" based on color use and shapes that were drawn (Boyatzis & Eades, 1999).

Behavioral Enactment (5D)

Both verbal and non-verbal forms of expression may communicate information about gender, either intention-ally or unintentionally. The extent to which males and females differ in their use of language and non-verbal communication styles has been of interest to researchers because these differences may reflect differences in power and status; however, a number of studies suggest that they may also vary depending on context.

Communication Styles. Research on adults has demonstrated that women and men differ in styles of speaking and nonverbal communication, and has examined how these differences reflect roles and context (Ruble & Martin, 1998). The same issues are apparent in the developmental literature. Although it is difficult to disentangle stylistic from context effects, some evidence suggests that both of these views may hold merit, and that they should be viewed as complementary (Leaper & Smith, 2004). And it is important to keep in mind that although sex differences are found, the similarities in girls' and boys' styles are more apparent.

Consistent stylistic effects have been identified in recent studies. Although researchers often find more similarities than differences, girls use strategies to demonstrate their attentiveness, responsiveness, and support, whereas boys use strategies to demand attention and establish dominance. Girls tend to use affiliative and help-seeking speech acts; boys tend to use controlling and domineering exchanges (Leaper, Tenenbaum, & Shaffer, 1999; Leman, Ahmed, & Ozarow, 2005; B. R. Thompson, 1999). Meta-analysis shows sex differences in children's language use (Leaper & Smith, 2004). Girls differed from boys by being more talkative ($d = -.11$), using more affiliative speech (language used to establish or maintain contacts with others; $d = -.26$) and less self-assertive speech (language used to influence others; $d = .11$). For many of these sex differences, there is an increase between preschool and elementary school. However, girls were more talkative only in early childhood (1 to 2½ years, $d = -.32$).

Evidence also has accumulated concerning situational differences in children's communicative behavior. In meta-analyses (Leaper & Smith, 2004), sex of partner influenced the magnitude of sex differences in language use. For instance, sex differences in assertive speech were evident in same-sex interactions ($d = .18$) but not in mixed-sex interactions ($d = .04$). Sex differences in affiliative speech were larger in unstructured situations ($d = -.65$) than in structured situations ($d = -.20$). A number of other studies also have demonstrated context effects (e.g., Holmes-Lonergan, 2003; Leaper et al., 1999; Leman et al., 2005). Culture also influences communicative styles. For example, African-American adolescent girls were less likely to show gender-typed forms of communication than were White girls (Leaper et al., 1999).

Nonverbal Communication.   Early studies reveal girls and boys to use different mannerisms and gestures, with girls more likely to use limp wrists, arm flutters, and flexed elbows when walking, boys to put hands-on-hips more than girls, and gender nonnormative boys to exhibit feminine mannerisms (Ruble & Martin, 1998). In college students, observed gender-related physical characteristics and mannerisms (e.g., deep voice and broad shoulders) have been found to relate to personality traits, interests, roles, and gender identity in men but not women, suggesting some coherence in the various domains of gender for men (Aube, Norcliffe, & Koestner, 1995).

Children use gestures to communicate even before they use language, and boys and girls do so differently. Parents' ratings of their children's gestures and symbolic play actions (e.g., feeding a doll with a spoon) revealed sex differences from $9\frac{1}{2}$ to 36 months of age (but not before; Fenson et al., 1994; Stennes et al., 2005).

Clothing and Appearance.   Clothing, jewelry, cosmetics, and hairstyles provide a wealth of information about a person's sex, socioeconomic background, status, lifestyle, nationality, and age. Parents use clothing to mark the sex of their children for strangers, and these cues are accurately interpreted much of the time (Ruble & Martin, 1998). In adults, much has been written about how women actively construct their identity through the "gendering" of their clothing. Little interest has been shown in children's construction of gender or the extent to which they are aware of using clothing as markers of gender, possibly because there is an assumption that parents choose children's clothing.

In the few studies that have examined this issue, the findings are clear: Children prefer to dress in sex-appropriate clothing, and girls particularly prefer feminine clothing. Ruble and her colleagues (Greulich, Ruble, Khuri, & Cyphers, 2001; Ruble, 2004) describe how girls between the ages of 3 to 6 years often become quite insistent on wearing clothes that are highly female stereotypic, such as pink frilly dresses, a phenomenon she has labeled PFD. This may be one of the strongest gender effects found in childhood. Further research is needed to assess whether these gendered enactments in the early years relate to other forms of gendered behav-

ior and whether they are indicative of stable individual differences in gender roles.

As children make their own clothing choices, they may signal their gender-related interests or roles by selecting particular styles and rejecting others. For instance, a girl with interest in "masculine" activities and sports may wear boyish pants, T-shirts, and athletic shoes rather than dresses and pink clothing. Clothing choices of tomboys are more masculine than those of nontomboys (Dinella & Martin, 2003). Wearing clothing typically associated with the other sex—"cross-dressing"—is common in children identified as having GIDC and this may partly signal their atypical preferences.

It is unclear whether clothing choices are practical or serve as signals for others. Interesting questions about whether children's clothing choices (e.g., dresses) preclude certain activity choices (e.g., rough-and-tumble play) remain. Girls who dress in feminine styles may be reluctant to engage in active or dirty activities because of their clothing, and/or they may rigidly adhere to gender norms (Ruble & Martin, 1998). Moreover, a cycle may develop in which girls' clothing choices modify their behavior, decreasing their competence for certain activities over time, leading to even less interest in those activities. Any factor that modifies children's interests may have a large impact on later abilities and behavior.

Values Regarding Gender (6)

What are children and adolescents' evaluative beliefs and preferences about gender? At what age do they become aware that males and females may be differentially valued, and how does that affect their self-perceptions, personal preferences, and behaviors such as discrimination? This section examines these questions using a range of different types of evaluations.

Concepts or Beliefs (6A)

In many cultures, more positive evaluations are applied to men and masculine activities than to women and feminine activities (e.g., Berscheid, 1993). When do children become aware of the cultural values placed on the sexes? The social psychological literature has distinguished between personal evaluations (i.e., private regard) about a social group (in this case, male versus female) and perceptions of others' evaluations (i.e., public regard; Sellers, Smith, Shelton, Rowley, & Chavous, 1998). Almost no research has directly examined children's public regard for gender (e.g., beliefs that men are highly regarded by others; see Ruble et al.,

2004, for a review). Kohlberg (1966) hypothesized that at a very young age, children are attentive to sex differences in power, and research on stereotype knowledge described earlier is consistent with this hypothesis. One study examining the development of knowledge about cultural values suggests that children older than 10 years perceive that females are devalued. For example, when asked to describe what would happen if they woke up one day to find they had changed sex, 11-, 14-, and 18-year-olds in Sweden and the United States offered different evaluations of the male and female role, acknowledging gender-based discrimination, greater restrictions for females, and the lower value of the female role (Intons-Peterson, 1988a). A recent study found that children may be aware of gender discrimination as young as 5 to 7 years, but more so at 8 to 10 years (Brown & Bigler, in press). Discrimination was perceived, however, only when children were explicitly told that it was a possible reason why a teacher might respond more favorably to a boy than to a girl (or vice-versa). Girls but not boys were more likely to perceive such discrimination against girls than against boys.

Identity or Self-Perception (6B)

As children begin to recognize that males and females are differentially valued, their own self-perceptions may be affected when their identity as a group member is salient. According to social identity theory (Tajfel, 1978), the social categories into which individuals are divided have evaluative implications and thus consequences for self-esteem. For example, girls who attribute their failure on a computer project to the idea that girls are incompetent in this domain may experience sadness and shame (Lutz & Ruble, 1995). These ideas have received little direct empirical attention with children. Although considerable evidence suggests that girls evaluate themselves more negatively than boys in many situations (Ruble, Greulich, Pomerantz, & Gochberg, 1993), the specific link to gender values is not clear. The results of one study suggest that as 5- to 8-year-old children learn about positive and negative traits associated with the sexes, they gradually begin to view themselves in terms of such traits (Aubry et al., 1999). Presumably, the level of private or public regard for their own sex may show associations with self-esteem. One program of research has reported results consistent with this hypothesis. For one aspect of private regard (i.e., feeling content with one's gender, such as liking to be a girl), Perry and his colleagues have shown a positive relation

with self-esteem and other indices of adjustment among third to eighth grade children (Carver et al., 2003; Egan & Perry, 2001). Another kind of private regard (i.e., believing that one's sex is superior, such as believing that girls are friendlier than boys) was not associated with self-esteem in these studies. This hypothesis has not been tested for public regard, however, and represents an important direction for future research. Future research should also examine self-perceptions in situations in which categorical group identification is more or less salient. Finally, as Eckes and Trautner (2000) suggest, future research needs to examine the influence on gender-related self-evaluations of cultural forces, such as variations in cultural views of femininity and masculinity or the importance of adhering to gender norms. For example, the relations reported earlier between private regard and adjustment may differ by race and ethnicity (Corby, Hodges, & Perry, in press).

Preferences (6C)

How do children personally evaluate gender categories and related activities and interests? Do they view males and masculine activities as somehow better or more valued? Do they view cross-gender behavior or traits as wrong? One problem with examining personal values about gender (i.e., private regard) is that they are rarely measured directly by, for example, asking children whether they think it is better to be a man or woman or to do masculine or feminine jobs. Instead, such values must be inferred from related measures. In this section, evidence regarding three types of gender-related values is examined: (1) in-group biases, (2) prejudice against females, and (3) attitudes about egalitarian gender roles.

In-Group/Out-Group Biases. According to cognitive theories, children's growing awareness of their membership in one sex category is likely to create a number of identity validation processes, one of which is to view one's own sex, the "in-group," more favorably than the other (Kohlberg, 1966; Martin & Halverson, 1981; Tajfel, 1978). In a direct examination of this prediction, 3- to 11-year-olds in South Wales were asked how they "feel" about girls and boys (Yee & Brown, 1994). By age 5, both girls and boys were markedly more positive about their own sex than about the other sex, and even 3-year-old girls (but not boys) showed significant in-group favoritism. Children also tend to show in-group evaluative biases in assigning more positive than negative traits to their own sex in the early and middle school years (Ruble & Martin, 1998), particularly when asked to make a direct comparison between males and females (Heyman & Legare, 2004). This positivity bias declines with age, at least after age 4 to 5 years (e.g., Heyman & Legare, 2004; Powlishta et al., 1994) and the decline is often stronger for girls (Egan & Perry, 2001; Yee & Brown, 1994). Finally, in-group biases may be inferred from findings that children show greater liking for peers of their own sex (e.g., Heyman, 2001), and typically play with same-sex others after the age of 3 (Maccoby, 1998; see Section 4C). Overall, there is considerable evidence of in-group evaluative biases, especially among preschool children.

Prejudice against Women.   One reason for the high level of interest in gender development is a search for the origins of women's disadvantaged status in most cultures. Is there any evidence that, aside from in-group biases, children value males more than females, and if so, how early does this begin? Interestingly, despite general cultural biases attributing greater prestige and power to males (and some evidence that children are aware of such status differences by middle childhood—see 6A), most of the available evidence suggests that children are more likely to derogate males than females. For example, Yee and Brown (1994) found that although both boys and girls felt more positively about their own sex, boys were described in more negative terms overall. Similarly, Heyman (2001) found that children's interpretations of ambiguous behavior were more negative for male than female targets. It would be interesting in future research to examine judgments about adult males and females.

Why do children not show this expected devaluation of females relative to males? Young children may be particularly attentive to attributes implying moral goodness, such as helpfulness and conformity with adult norms (Paley, 1988; Ruble & Dweck, 1995). As children begin to stereotypically associate such attributes more with females than with males (see 3A; "girls are sugar and spice and everything nice"), they may initially value females more. Indeed, this positive evaluation of females continues to some extent into adulthood (Eagly, Mladinic, & Otto, 1991). However, for adults, cultural standards emphasize masculine attributes of prestige, power, and competence (Powlishta, 2000). As Glick and Fiske (1996) argue, prejudice toward women may be characterized as ambivalent: Women are often portrayed as nice but incompetent. As these adult standards

are acquired, evaluations of females would be expected to decline relative to evaluations of males and to be characterized as ambivalent in this way. Indeed, a recent developmental analysis suggests that gender prejudice moves from a simple form of childhood hostility toward the other sex to a complex and ambivalent set of adult attitudes that combine, particularly for men, both hostile and benevolent forms of prejudice (Glick & Hilt, 2000).

Some evidence reviewed in our prior *Handbook* chapter indirectly supports this account (Ruble & Martin, 1998). A recent study of perceived competencies of men and women in gender-typed occupations found that children as young as 5- to 7-years-old view males as more competent overall (G. D. Levy, Sadovsky, & Troseth, 2000). In an interesting experimental study, 11- to 12-year-olds but not 6- to 8-year-olds evaluated novel occupations portrayed with male workers as higher in prestige than identical jobs portrayed with female workers (Liben, Bigler, & Krogh, 2001). Both studies found that even younger children evaluated existing occupations traditionally performed by males as higher in status.

Egalitarian Attitudes.   Do children think it is desirable for individuals to be free to engage in whatever behaviors they prefer, or do they feel it is wrong to engage in activities not stereotypically associated with one's gender? There are several types of relevant data. Especially close to the notion of values are studies that ask what males, females, or both "should" be like or do. As described in Section 2A, meta-analysis suggests a curvilinear developmental trend, such that values about gender may increase in rigidity until 5 to 7 years of age but subsequently become more flexible, at least through early adolescence (Signorella et al., 1993).

Another approach is to examine developmental trends in children's personal evaluations (good or bad) of individuals who engage in cross-gender behavior. It seems reasonable to expect that such evaluations would show curvilinear developmental trends similar to those just described for stereotypic attitudes. Some research is consistent with this prediction. For example, negative reactions to atypical behavior (e.g., desire not to be friends with a boy who wears nail polish) increased between 3 to 5 years of age but decreased between 5 to 7 years (L. Taylor et al., 2006), and gender-atypical behavior was evaluated more negatively by kindergartners and eighth graders than by children in middle elementary school (Stoddart & Turiel, 1985). Other studies have found very different developmental patterns, however, suggesting that some negative reactions may be relatively stable (G. D. Levy, Taylor, & Gelman, 1995) or increase between preschool and middle elementary school (Carter & McCloskey, 1984). In a promising attempt to explore possible reasons for these discrepancies across studies, Blakemore (2003) examined developmental changes in 3- to 11-year-old's reactions to several different types of gender norm violations. Unfortunately, no clear pattern emerged. Negative evaluations of norm violations increased with age for many items but were unrelated or curvilinearly related to age for other items, with no clear linkages between age trends and characteristics of the items. One clear finding was that when an age difference was found, older children evaluated norm violations by boys more negatively than did younger children.

Thus, the exact nature of developmental trends in children's reactions to atypical behavior varies with the sex of target, the type of target behavior, and the type of reaction assessed. Unfortunately, it remains unclear exactly what processes underlie such differences. Further, although sex of target differences are not always found, when they are, boys are judged more negatively for violating norms than are girls (Antill et al., 1996; Zucker et al., 1995), especially when they involve appearance (Blakemore, 2003). Finally, past research has suggested sex differences in egalitarian attitudes among children. Boys are often more negative about gender norm violations than are girls (e.g., Blakemore, 2003), and girls are more likely to consider it wrong to exclude another child from an activity simply because it violates gender norms (e.g., allowing a boy to participate in a ballet class; Killen & Stangor, 2001).

Another approach addresses attitudes about role equality, with such research suggesting that attitudes become more flexible or egalitarian with age in contrast to developmental changes in reactions to gender norm violations, as described earlier (e.g., Huston & Alvarez, 1990; L. Taylor et al., 2006). Sex differences in such trends have been found, however. Studies examining attitudes toward equal roles, using, for example, the Attitudes toward Women Scale (e.g., "Girls should have the same freedoms as boys"; Galambos, Petersen, Richards, & Gitelson, 1985), suggest that boys value gender equality less than girls and become increasingly negative between sixth and eighth grades, whereas girls become increasingly positive (e.g., Galambos, Almeida, & Petersen, 1990). More recent research has shown a similar sex difference in valuing equality regarding involve-

ment in careers and shared household demands, with older adolescent boys (relative to girls and younger adolescent boys) having more traditional role-differentiated attitudes, such as believing that working is detrimental to the family for women but not for men (Jackson & Tein, 1998).

Behavioral Enactment, Adoption (6D)

Values are expressed in behavior through overt indices of preferential or discriminatory treatment. A common paradigm for examining discriminatory behavior is a reward allocation task in which individuals are asked to distribute resources to different groups or individuals based on performance and personal attributes. Although some research has shown in-group favoritism based on ethnicity, only one study to our knowledge has examined such behaviors as a function of sex (Yee & Brown, 1994). In this study, girls tended to give rewards on the basis of in-group favoritism, whereas boys tended to reward on the basis of equity. Although these trends did not vary significantly across age (3 to 11 years), it is noteworthy that at age 3, both boys and girls gave nicer prizes to girls regardless of actual performance, and the clearest indication of in-group favoritism for both sexes occurred at age 5. Values are also expressed in the way children respond to cross-gender behavior. Children, especially boys, who deviate from gender norms suffer more from peer ridicule (Zucker, 1990) and peer rejection (Cohen-Kettenis, Owen, Kaijser, Bradley, & Zucker, 2003). Thorne (1993) found that boys who violated norms for masculinity were teased, shunned, or referred to as "girls."

Summary of Developmental Trends

The extensive data base on gender development produces the following portrait. By 1 year of age, many infants respond to gender cues. Most children learn to label themselves and others as male and female by 2½ years of age (and many before age 2), show some limited understanding of gender stereotypes, play more often with same- rather than other-gender toys (especially dolls and cars), and show the first signs of more positive contacts toward same- rather than other-sex peers. In addition, early indication of GIDC may be seen at this age. Three-year-old children master gender stability, show better than chance responding to measures of gender stereotyping of children's toys and activities, colors, and certain traitlike characteristics, and state gender-typed play preferences.

During the remaining preschool years (age 4 to 5), most indices of gender knowledge and behavior increase dramatically. Many children show complete gender constancy understanding, are able to link traits to gender (especially power-related and evaluative traits), show ingroup positivity biases, and expect same-sex peers to play together. In addition, sex differences in a few personal-social characteristics, such as aggression and decoding facial expressions, are seen at this time. This also appears to be an age of heightened gender rigidity.

A number of important changes in gender development occur during the elementary school years. Children develop more complex stereotypic associations and add more information to their stereotypes. During middle elementary school, children become aware of male-favored status differences and, at the same age, girls are more likely than boys to prefer to be the other sex. Elementary school children also show increasingly flexible stereotypic beliefs through, at least, early adolescence, and girls often become more flexible in their activity preferences and behaviors. A few indices do not show increasing flexibility, however, such as children's segregation into same-sex groupings, which remains high during elementary school, and negative evaluations of peers who engage in cross-gender behavior. Sex differences in certain spatial skills and emotional perception and expression are seen in middle childhood and increase with age.

Finally, further changes are found during adolescence. Some evidence supports the existence of gender intensification after early adolescence. A few studies suggest that stereotyping becomes somewhat less flexible. Trends for preferences are less clear and appear to diverge for males and females, with boys less likely to become flexible. However, in middle adolescence, both sexes show gender-typed activities and interests in many contexts (i.e., at home or school) and sexual identity may emerge. In addition, sex differences in mathematical problem solving, physical skills, and depression emerge or increase during adolescence. Taken together, the various trends show a number of parallel developments among cognitions, preferences, and behavior.

The development of the multidimensional matrix by Huston (1983) marked an important turning point in the study of gender. By disentangling the various content domains, she gave researchers a clearer picture of the many aspects of gender that exist. Furthermore, developmental researchers were sensitized to the implicit assumption underlying much of the thinking in the area—that gender-typing in one domain will predict gender-typing in another. Rather than assuming unity in measures, developmentalists have been faced with the issue of how to assess each aspect of gender and have begun using multimethod assessments to discover whether relations exist among the various aspects. In future research, it will be interesting to incorporate a recently proposed third dimension of the matrix: levels of analysis (Eckes & Trautner, 2000).

What is the state of the field regarding the unity of gender-typing constructs? The multidimensionality of gender-typing (e.g., Antill et al., 1993; Hort, Leinbach, & Fagot, 1991; Serbin et al., 1993) has been inferred from failures to find relations among gender-related variables, but is most often used to refer to failures to find connections between gender-typed preferences or behavior and emerging cognitions about gender. Nevertheless, it appears that basic knowledge about one's own sex and the sex of others does develop at about the same time as gender-typed behavior and may influence that behavior (see Cognitive Approaches section).

It may be informative to examine issues of unity among subsets of variables. For instance, much of gender differentiation may be thought of as a set of *self* variables, and it may be productive to examine to what extent coherence appears among such variables as categorical gender, the development of gender identity, preferences for same-sex playmates, interests in gender-typed activities, and later preferences for other-sex sexual partners. Many of these components in the matrix did show parallel developmental trends, but it is unclear whether they cohere within individuals, so associations and causal relations need to be assessed in longitudinal or, in some cases, experimental studies (e.g., varying the salience of gender labels). It would also be productive to examine whether individual differences show stability over time. Are 3-year-old girls who dress in pink frilly dresses, play primarily with girls, and play with dolls likely to become 9-year-olds who avoid sports, show feminine interpersonal characteristics, and select female-typical occupations? To date, there has been relatively little research about such issues (Maccoby, 2002; McHale, Crouter, & Whiteman, 2003), though retrospective studies suggest that some early gender-typed interests may continue into middle childhood and adolescence (e.g., Giuliano, Popp, & Knight, 2000).

One interesting benefit of the matrix framework (Table 14.1) is that gaps in the literature can easily be identified. Although relatively clear conclusions can now be drawn about the development of gender-related stereotypes, verbal preferences, and behaviors (especially regarding concrete activities and interests and relationships), much less is known about corresponding trends in children's gender-related self-perceptions and identity (Column B) or about the development of children's gender-related values and attitudes (Row 6).

In summary, the matrix has been particularly useful in studying questions about the relations among the various constructs and content domains. We agree with Huston (1983) that gender researchers should take the multidimensionality of gender-typing seriously, but we also recommend avoiding the assumption that no unity exists at all. The likelihood of finding expected correlations may be influenced by a number of factors (Aubry et al., 1999; C. F. Miller, Trautner, et al., 2006). Thus, researchers should base examinations of cross-construct associations on careful theoretical and methodological analyses of which, and under what conditions, relations are expected.

THEORETICAL ANALYSIS OF GENDER DEVELOPMENT

In this section, we analyze possible processes underlying the developmental and sex differences trends we have just described, focusing on three broad approaches: (1) biological, (2) socialization, and (3) cognitive. These three perspectives have historically represented the dominant theories applied to gender development, but it has become increasingly difficult to make clear distinctions among them, because intersections across perspectives drive much of current theorizing and research. Particularly problematic is the distinction between socialization and cognitive perspectives because current theories incorporate elements of both. To facilitate comparisons with prior reviews, we have maintained these labels, but call attention to their limits at various places. In each section, we use mechanisms derived from each of the theoretical perspectives to describe gender development and consider the evidence relevant to the most pressing issues in each theoretical orientation.

Biological Approaches

Biological perspectives have gained in visibility and acceptability. Converging data from multiple methods (facilitated by methodological advances) provide compelling support for biological contributors to gender de-

velopment. The nature-nurture debate has given way to questions about the mechanisms by which biology and the social environment work together to produce behavior. Political and social implications of sex differences are not dependent on their causes. Biological factors do not imply determinism, because behaviors with a strong biological influence may be relatively easy to modify, as exemplified by the diet used to prevent retardation in children with phenylketonuria. Environmental factors do not imply free will and easy malleability, because social forces may be difficult to counteract, as exemplified by racism.

Biological approaches to gender development emphasize the parallels between physical and psychological sexual differentiation. The brain is part of the body and the brain underlies behavior, so it should not be surprising that the same factors that govern sexual differentiation of the body—genes and hormones—also govern sexual differentiation of the brain and thus behavior. Further, it is logical for there to be a biological basis for the sex differences in reproductive and related behaviors essential for the survival of our species. Thus, biological approaches generally focus on *distal* evolutionary explanations of gender development and *proximal* mechanisms mediated by genes and hormones.

Evolutionary Psychology

Evolutionary psychologists view behavior as the result of adaptive pressures, so that our brains—and, therefore, our behaviors—developed to solve problems faced by our ancestors, and good solutions enabled them to survive and reproduce. The sexes have faced different adaptive pressures related to differences in reproduction: Women have a greater physical investment than men in childbearing (gestation and postnatal support), leading them to be careful in choosing a mate, and leading men to compete for mates; men cannot be certain of the paternity of offspring that they rear. These pressures are hypothesized to result in behavioral sex differences seen in contemporary society, including females' greater interest in babies and males' greater aggression and preferences for multiple sex partners (Buss, 2000; Geary, 1998).

There are many appeals to an evolutionary approach: It places behavior on an equal footing with physical characteristics, correctly conceptualizes behavior (as other characteristics) as adaptation to problems faced by our ancestors, and provides a single explanation for a range of sex differences. Nevertheless, evolutionary theories are currently incomplete because they do not make unique predictions (results often can be explained by other theories, such as social learning), are difficult to falsify (there are no methods available to decide whether a behavior "evolved" because it was adaptive or a by-product of another trait), and concern factors that make all boys and men similar to each other and different from all girls and women (but not all men and women behave in ways predicted by evolutionary theory).

Comparative Approaches

Another perspective on evolution relies on cross-species comparisons to understand the origins of behavior in developmental and cultural context. Its value for understanding sex-related behavior can be seen in two recent papers. The first described a sex difference in wild chimpanzees in learning to use tools to fish for termites. Compared to males, female chimps learned at a younger age and were more likely to use techniques resembling those of their mothers (Lonsdorf, Eberly, & Pusey, 2004). The second paper described a study of toy preferences in vervet monkeys, showing sex differences paralleling those seen in children (Alexander & Hines, 2002).

A comparative approach seems promising for examining the development of sex-related behavior, given evidence that primates, and perhaps other animals, learn from others in their social groups and that they form and use cognitive categories and concepts that can be generalized and adapted to new circumstances (E. K. Miller, Nieder, Freedman, & Wallis, 2003). It is important to know, for example, whether juvenile monkeys sex segregate (Maccoby, 1998), what gender concepts they have, and how they use knowledge of sex membership (their own and other's) in their behavior. Comparative studies can also provide information about proximal mechanisms that can be studied in human beings, such as characteristics underlying toy preferences.

Parallels between Physical and Psychological Sexual Differentiation

Evolutionary and comparative approaches put human gender development into context. Proximal explanations focus on biological mechanisms accounting for differences between males and females, specifically processes of physical sexual differentiation.

Genetic sex is determined at conception. The difference between the sexes is determined by a gene on one of 23 pairs of chromosomes. Females have two X chromosomes, males one X and one Y, with the latter con-

taining *SRY* (the sex-determining region). The two sexes start out with the same sets of structures that differentiate into male or female gonads, internal reproductive organs, and genitals (Grumbach, Hughes, & Conte, 2002). The path to male development is initiated by *SRY,* which causes the indifferent gonad to develop into testes at about weeks 6 to 7 of gestation. After this, sexual differentiation largely depends on hormones secreted by the gonads, particularly androgens; estrogens have little role during prenatal development. Although both sexes produce and respond to androgens and estrogens, there are large sex differences in the concentrations of these hormones. The external genitalia start out the same in the two sexes; high levels of androgen beginning at prenatal weeks 7 to 8 cause male external genitalia to develop. Although this normally occurs only in males, females can develop masculinized genitalia if they are exposed to high levels of androgen early in development. Female-typical development is largely a default process, occurring when *SRY* is absent and androgen is low, but completely normal female development requires other genes. Hormones exert effects through cell receptors, so complete masculinization requires both high levels of androgen and functioning androgen receptors.

Hormonal Influences on Behavior and Brain in Nonhuman Animals

Hormones are also responsible for sexual differentiation of the brain and behavior. In nonhuman species, exposure to androgens early in development because of experimental manipulations or natural variations (e.g., females who gestate in the uterus between two males) causes masculinization of sex-typed sexual, social, and cognitive behaviors. Similarly, experimental manipulations and natural variations in levels of androgens and estrogens later in life (e.g., estrus cycle variations, menopause) alter behavior.

Several principles from animal studies have implications for human behavioral development (for reviews, see Becker, Breedlove, Crews, & McCarthy, 2002; Ryan & Vandenbergh, 2002; Wallen, 2005). First, hormones affect behavior in two ways: (1) by producing permanent changes to brain structures and the behaviors they subserve, usually early in life ("organizational" effects) and (2) by producing temporary alterations to the brain and behavior (through ongoing changes to neural circuitry) as the hormones circulate in the body, primarily throughout adolescence and adulthood ("activational" effects; although the distinction between organizational and activational hormone effects is not absolute). Second, there are multiple sensitive periods for permanent effects of hormones, and these periods may differ for the brain and the genitals. The human sex difference in testosterone is largest during prenatal weeks 8 to 24, postnatal months 1 to 5, and puberty through adulthood (Smail, Reyes, Winter, & Faiman, 1981). The key sensitive period for human brain and behavioral sexual differentiation has been considered to occur right after the genitals differentiate, but other times may be important. For example, some behaviors in monkeys are masculinized by androgen exposure early (but not late) in gestation, whereas other behaviors are masculinized by exposure late (but not early) in gestation (Goy, Bercovitch, & McBrair, 1988). Third, the specific form of the hormone affecting behavior differs across species and across behavior within species. For example, androgen masculinizes behavior through conversion (aromatization) to estradiol in rodents but appears to affect behavior directly in primates (Wallen & Baum, 2002). Fourth, effects of hormones may be quite specific so that different behaviors are affected by different hormones acting at different times in development. For example, in rodents, androgen given early in development produces permanent changes in spatial learning, whereas ovarian estrogen given at puberty and beyond affects memory.

Human Behavioral Effects of Prenatal Hormones

It is not possible to investigate the effects of hormones in people by manipulating their levels, but much has been learned from children and adults whose hormone levels were atypical for their sex during early development as a result of genetic disease or maternal ingestion of drugs during pregnancy to prevent miscarriage. Evidence from these natural experiments has been supplemented by data from normal individuals with typical variations in hormones.

Congenital Adrenal Hyperplasia. The most extensively studied natural experiment, congenital adrenal hyperplasia (CAH) is a genetic disease in which the fetus is exposed to high levels of androgens beginning early in gestation because of an enzyme defect affecting cortisol production. Females with CAH have external genitalia masculinized to varying degrees, but they have ovaries and a uterus and are fertile. Most girls are diagnosed at birth and treated with cortisol to reduce androgen excess (or they will experience rapid growth and

early puberty) and surgically to feminize their genitalia. If sexual differentiation of human behavior is affected by androgens present during critical periods of development, females with CAH should be behaviorally more masculine and less feminine than a comparison group of females without CAH. And they are in many, but not all, ways, as described below. Males with CAH have few prenatal effects and are treated postnatally with cortisol to maintain growth and prevent early puberty and other consequences of the disease. They are reared as boys, develop male gender identity, and generally display male-typical behavior (for reviews, see Berenbaum, 2001, 2004; Meyer-Bahlburg, 2001).

In early studies, girls with CAH were reported to be tomboys, and this was interpreted to reflect behavioral effects of androgen (Money & Ehrhardt, 1972). Interpretation was complicated by methodology (e.g., nonblind interviews, small samples, inadequate comparisons), factors associated with the disease and treatment (e.g., other hormones), and the possibility that behavior resulted from parent treatment in response to the appearance of the girls' genitals (Quadagno, Briscoe, & Quadagno, 1977).

Subsequent studies addressing these problems found girls with CAH to be masculinized and defeminized in aspects of their feelings, preferences, and behavior. In childhood and adolescence, girls with CAH reported being more interested in male-typical occupations than in female-typical occupations (Berenbaum, 1999; Servin, Nordenström, Larsson, & Bohlin, 2003), and they reported liking and engaging more with boys' toys and activities and less with girls' toys and activities than did typical girls (e.g., Berenbaum, 1999; Berenbaum & Snyder, 1995; Servin et al., 2003). Girls with CAH were more likely than control girls to report preferences for boy playmates (Berenbaum & Snyder, 1995; Hines & Kaufman, 1994; Servin et al., 2003).

Differences have also been observed in behavior. Girls with CAH aged 3 to 12 played with boys' toys more than comparison girls (Berenbaum & Snyder, 1995; Nordenström, Servin, Bohlin, Larsson, & Wedell, 2002; Servin et al., 2003). When choosing a toy to keep, about 50% of girls with CAH chose a transportation toy, whereas no control girl did (Berenbaum & Snyder, 1995; Servin et al., 2003). They drew pictures with masculine characteristics (e.g., moving objects, dark colors, a bird's-eye perspective), as opposed to those with feminine characteristics (e.g., human figures, flowers, light colors; Iijima et al., 2001). There have been no studies directly observing peer choices in girls with CAH.

Evidence is accruing that masculinized preferences and play in girls with CAH result directly from prenatal androgen. Play with boys' toys has been related to the degree of prenatal androgen excess inferred from genetic defect and other indicators of disease severity (Berenbaum, Duck, & Bryk, 2000; Nordenström et al., 2002). Effects of parent socialization have not been demonstrated. For example, the amount of time that girls with CAH played with boys' toys was not increased when parents were present (Nordenström et al., 2002); parents wished that their daughters with CAH were *less* masculine than they were (and wished that their daughters without CAH were more masculine than they were; Servin et al., 2003); and parents of girls with CAH were observed to encourage them to play with *girls'* toys (Pasterski et al., 2005). The lack of evidence for parent effects on masculinized behavior in girls with CAH is consistent with data from androgenized female monkeys showing mothers' behaviors to be unrelated to offsprings' masculine behavior (Goy et al., 1988). Although these results strongly suggest that the boy-typical activities and interests of girls with CAH are due to prenatal androgen excess, it is possible that differential parent treatment is subtle and best detected in within-family designs (McHale et al., 1999).

Females with CAH appear to be masculinized and defeminized in other domains. Compared to typical females, adolescent and adult females with CAH reported that they would be more likely to use aggression in a conflict situation (Berenbaum & Resnick, 1997) and that they were less maternal and nurturant (Helleday, Edman, Ritzen, & Siwers, 1993). Parents reported that girls with CAH were less interested in babies than were their unaffected sisters (Leveroni & Berenbaum, 1998). These findings are less firmly established than those on activities and interests, and no studies have examined behavioral enactment of these characteristics or studied their associations with degree of prenatal androgen or parental treatment.

Beginning in childhood and continuing into adulthood, females with CAH have been found to score higher on spatial tasks (Berenbaum, 2001; Hines, Fane, et al., 2003). This difference has not been observed in all studies, perhaps due to low statistical power associated with relatively small samples and a moderate-size effect. Similar considerations apply in interpreting lack of differences between CAH and typical females on measures of other abilities, such as perceptual speed and verbal fluency (Berenbaum, 2001).

Gender identity is typical in the majority of girls and women with CAH, although degree of identification may be reduced compared to typical females (Berenbaum & Bailey, 2003; Hines, Brook, & Conway, 2004). Gender change in females with CAH is uncommon but still more common than in the general population (Meyer-Bahlburg et al., 1996; Zucker et al., 1996). Degree of prenatal androgen excess and genital appearance do not appear to contribute to variations in gender identity. Finally, women with CAH are more likely than typical women to have bisexual or homosexual orientation, although most are exclusively heterosexual (Hines et al., 2004; Zucker et al., 1996).

Complete Androgen Insensitivity Syndrome. In this rare condition, XY males produce male-typical levels of androgen, but lack cell receptors allowing them to respond to the hormones. Consequently, they have female-typical genitalia and are reared as girls. They provide an opportunity to study the behavioral effects of genes on the Y chromosome and the nature of the hormone responsible for human behavioral sexual differentiation. If androgen affects behavior through conversion to estrogen (as happens in rodents), individuals with complete androgen insensitivity syndrome (CAIS) should be masculinized as a result of normal male levels of androgen converted in the brain to normal male levels of estrogen (estrogen receptors are normal). But, if the important hormone is androgen itself (or its other forms), individuals with CAIS should have female-typical gender development because they cannot respond to the high levels present. Gender development might also be masculinized by effects of genes on the Y chromosome, as suggested by animal studies (de Vries et al., 2002).

There is little evidence about gender development in CAIS, especially in childhood because it is rare and generally not diagnosed until menarche fails to occur. Limited data show individuals with CAIS to be female-typical with respect to gender identity, sexual orientation, and masculinity and femininity of interests (e.g., Hines, Ahmed, & Hughes, 2003). Female-typical gender development in CAIS could result from low androgens or rearing as girls, and argue against a role for aromatized estrogen or specific genes on the Y chromosome, but definitive answers await additional study.

Other evidence against a role for aromatized estrogens comes from females whose mothers were treated with diethylstilbestrol (DES), which used to be prescribed for pregnancy complications and which masculinizes aspects of brain and behavior in female rodents. Studies have generally found DES-exposed women to be similar to their unexposed sisters on measures of gender role and cognition; differences in brain organization and sexual orientation are not consistently found (reviewed in Cohen-Bendahan, van de Beek, & Berenbaum, 2005).

Boys without a Penis. Much attention has been directed to rare clinical conditions in which boys are lacking a penis but all other aspects of sexual differentiation are male-typical. Until recently, these children were usually reared as females, because it was believed that gender identity is determined by rearing and that normal psychological development depends on having normal-looking genitalia (although some surgical correction is now possible, the penis will never look or function normally; Money & Ehrhardt, 1972). There are two primary situations in which a boy might lack a penis: (1) ablatio penis—the penis is lost through an accident, such as a mishandled circumcision, and (2) cloacal exstrophy—a rare congenital defect affecting the bladder and external genitalia, causing a malformed or absent penis but otherwise normal male-typical physical development.

Because these conditions are rare, psychological outcome data come from case reports and small studies. Much attention has been focused on an individual born a boy but reared as a girl after a mishandled circumcision. Although early reports suggested that this child adapted well to the female assignment (Money & Ehrhardt, 1972), later reports revealed considerable unhappiness with the assignment, resulting in self-reassignment to the male sex (Colapinto, 2000; M. Diamond & Sigmundson, 1997). This was interpreted to show the primacy of biology in determining gender identity, but close inspection of the evidence suggests a complex picture. The child was reared as a boy early in life (the accident happened at age 7 months, reassignment was made in the 2nd year, and the initial feminizing genital surgery was not completed until 21 months), so there was a long and perhaps sensitive period when he was reared as a boy. Further, another individual with a similar history but with earlier female reassignment had a female identity (Bradley, Oliver, Chernick, & Zucker, 1998). Although

differing in gender identity, both cases had similar masculinized interests (e.g., occupation) and sexual orientation (i.e., arousal to women).

Boys with cloacal exstrophy reared as girls are also heterogeneous with respect to gender identity, but it is unclear what accounts for the variability. In a recent study of 14 children, 6 or 8 (depending on the criteria) were stated to identify as male, which was taken as evidence for biological determination of gender identity (Reiner & Gearhart, 2004). But, interpretation is difficult because of unsystematic and subjective assessments, likely effects of interviewer expectations, and some conflating of gender identity with male-typical activity interests. Further, gender change may arise not just from biology, but in response to complex social conditions, for example, a mismatch between behavior and parent expectations or peer stigmatization for atypical interests. Although much attention has been directed to that study, it is probably not representative of gender identity outcome in boys with cloacal extsrophy reared as girls: A recent review shows that the majority identify as girls (Meyer-Bahlburg, 2005).

Evidence from males with ablatio penis and cloacal exstrophy shows the importance of biological influences on activities and interests, consistent with the importance of androgen seen in CAH and CAIS. Gender identity, however, is not simply related to prenatal androgen (or to the Y chromosome), given the variability in outcome both within and across studies of ablatio penis, cloacal exstrophy, and other disorders of sexual differentiation such as micropenis and partial androgen insensitivity syndrome (e.g., Meyer-Bahlburg, 2005; Wisniewski et al., 2001; Zucker, 1999).

Normal Variations in Prenatal Hormones. Considerable progress has been made in examining the generalizability of results obtained in clinical populations. This involves studies of childhood or adult gender-related behavior in relation to hormones obtained in early development from umbilical cord blood, amniotic fluid, or mother's blood during pregnancy (although none directly measure fetal hormone levels) or to markers of prenatal hormones (for review of methods and findings, see Cohen-Bendahan et al., 2005).

A project examining umbilical cord blood in relation to behavior in infancy and childhood generally found few associations that would have been predicted from studies in nonhuman animals and human clinical samples (e.g., Jacklin, Wilcox, & Maccoby, 1988). Two problems make it difficult to interpret findings: (1) timing of hormone sampling is not optimal (the likely sensitive time for hormonal influences on brain development is prenatal rather than neonatal), and (2) the umbilical cord contains blood from both mother and fetus.

Two projects studied hormones in amniotic fluid in relation to later behavior. Most analyses revealed nonsignificant associations (Finegan, Niccols, & Sitarenois, 1992; Grimshaw, Sitarenios, & Finegan, 1995; Knickmeyer, Baron-Cohen, Raggatt, & Taylor, 2004; Knickmeyer et al., 2005; Lutchmaya, Baron-Cohen, & Raggatt, 2002a, 2002b) although testosterone was associated with some traits that show sex differences: Testosterone in girls was positively correlated with speed of mental rotation at age 7 (Grimshaw et al., 1995), and testosterone in boys was negatively correlated with eye contact in infancy (Lutchmaya, Baron-Cohen, & Raggatt, 2002a) and positively correlated with restricted interests at age 4 (Knickmeyer et al., 2004). It is unclear whether negative findings indicate lack of association between behavior and testosterone within the normal range or study limitations (e.g., behavioral measures that do not show sex differences, small samples, single measure of testosterone, limited variability in testosterone).

Two studies examining hormones in mother's blood during pregnancy found markers of high testosterone to be associated with masculinized gender role behavior in daughters. A broad measure of gender role behavior in adult females was found to be associated with their own hormones in adulthood, hormones in mother's blood during pregnancy, and their interaction (e.g., Udry, 2000). High levels of masculinizing hormones were suggested to be associated with masculinized behavior, but detailed results were not reported and the specific hormone associated with behavior varied across reports. Consistent with suggestions that prenatal weeks 8 to 24 are the key sensitive period, behavior was related to hormones during the second trimester only. In children aged 3½ years, mother-reported involvement in boy-typical activities was highest in girls whose mothers had high levels of testosterone in blood samples collected between weeks 5 and 36 of gestation (Hines, Golombok, Rust, Johnston, & Golding, 2002). In boys, activities were not related to maternal testosterone.

Increasingly, studies in typical samples have examined associations between behavior and morphological measures considered "markers" of prenatal hormone exposure. For example, fingerprint patterns, relative finger lengths, and otoacoustic emissions (sounds produced by the ear) have been related to a host of gender-related traits, most prominently sexual orientation, spatial ability, and activity interests. Potentially valuable as nonintrusive, easily collected, retrospective measures of prenatal hormone exposure that can be used at all ages, these markers are not yet suitable for widespread use given insufficient validation (Cohen-Bendahan et al., 2005).

Hormone Influences in Adolescence

Do the changes in sex hormones and physical appearance at adolescence contribute to gender development? Research on pubertal change has focused on possible relations with two general categories of behavior. First, emotion-related characteristics (e.g., negative affect, anxiety, self-esteem, and aggression) are studied because some sex differences in distress and psychopathology emerge at puberty and because hormones are thought to account for adolescents' moodiness. Second, cognitive abilities are studied also because of an emergence or increase in sex differences at puberty (although some sex differences emerge earlier, see 3D) and because variations in abilities have been associated with variations in circulating hormones in adults.

Emotion, Aggression, and Problem Behavior. Hormonal increases at pubertal onset generally do not appear to increase negative affect or moodiness in the normal range (Buchanan, Eccles, & Becker, 1992; Susman et al., 1998). But they appear to increase girls' risk for serious depression at puberty, especially in those with genetic vulnerability (Angold, Costello, Erkanli, & Worthman, 1999).

Related studies have examined associations between hormones and affect across the entire pubertal transition. Not surprisingly, such relations are neither simple nor large (and thus not always found; reviewed by Brooks-Gunn, Petersen, & Compas, 1995; Buchanan et al., 1992). For example, in one study of negative affect in girls aged 10 to 14, hormones accounted for 4% of the variance, social factors 8% to 18%, and the interaction of negative life events and pubertal factors 9% to 15% (Brooks-Gunn & Warren, 1989). Absolute hormone levels might be less important than the *changes* in levels (Buchanan et al., 1992).

Hormone effects are clearer in studies linking hormones to aggression and behavior problems, particularly in boys (Buchanan et al., 1992; Susman et al., 1987). In an experimental study of hormone treatment of children with delayed puberty, testosterone in boys and estrogen in girls increased self-reported aggression (Finkelstein et al., 1997). Circulating testosterone is weakly related to aggression, $r = .14$ from a meta-analysis, similar in males and females, but with larger effects in adolescents than in adults (perhaps due to maximal variability in both measures at this age; Book, Starzyk, & Quinsey, 2001). Even when associations between hormones and behavior are observed, it is difficult to determine causality. For example, testosterone levels increase in adult sports players who win, and in their fans (e.g., Bernhardt, Dabbs, Fielden, & Lutter, 1998; Booth, Shelley, Mazur, Tharp, & Kittok, 1989), with mood a possible mediator of winning's effect on testosterone (e.g., McCaul, Gladue, & Joppa, 1992). Testosterone may not affect aggression per se but may affect social dominance (i.e., attempt to achieve social power such as leadership; e.g., Mazur & Booth, 1998; Rowe, Maughan, Worthman, Costello, & Angold, 2004). Behavioral effects of testosterone also depend on social context: In a longitudinal study of psychopathology, testosterone was related to nonaggressive symptoms of Conduct Disorder in boys with deviant peers and to leadership in boys with nondeviant peers (Rowe et al., 2004).

Other studies have examined affective changes in relation to hormonal changes across the life span beyond puberty; for example, those associated with the menstrual cycle or menopause. In general, these studies find little association between hormones and mood (see Klebanov & Ruble, 1994, for review of menstrual cycle effects), although hormones may trigger depression in vulnerable individuals (Steiner, Dunn, & Born, 2003).

Timing of pubertal onset has behavioral significance (Steinberg & Morris, 2001; Weichold, Silbereisen, & Schmitt-Rodermund, 2003). Early-maturing girls have more emotional distress and problem behavior (e.g., delinquency, substance use, early sexuality) than on-time peers (e.g., Ge, Conger, & Elder, 1996) and these problems persist into adulthood (Weichold et al., 2003). Among boys, late maturers have low self-esteem compared to on-time peers, whereas early maturers are more popular and have better self-image (Ruble & Martin, 1998) but are more likely to engage in delinquent, antisocial, and sexual behaviors and substance use (J. M. Williams & Dunlop, 1999). The relative contributions to behavior of specific aspects of pubertal change, and of social and psychological factors initiated by those changes are being investigated. Social factors that mediate and moderate these effects, especially in girls, include association with older and other-sex peers, childhood problems, parenting practices, and neighborhoods (Caspi, Lynam, Moffitt, & Silva, 1993; Ge, Brody, Conger, Simons, & Murry, 2002; Weichold et al., 2003).

Cognition.   Circulating hormones relate to patterns of cognitive abilities. Most evidence comes from observational studies in adults, although some confirmation comes from studies in which hormones are administered exogenously (Berenbaum, Moffat, Wisniewski, & Resnick, 2003; Hampson, 2002; Liben et al., 2002). Verbal fluency and memory are enhanced by circulating estrogens beginning at least in adolescence. Spatial ability is enhanced by moderate levels of androgen in adults, that is, levels that are high for normal females and low for normal males. Two recent studies of hormones at puberty produced conflicting results, with one finding effects of testosterone on spatial ability in boys and girls (Davison & Susman, 2001) and another finding no effects of testosterone in boys or of estrogen in girls (Liben et al., 2002).

Interpretive Issues in Studying Hormone Effects in Adolescence.   Some of the inconsistencies and puzzles about effects of hormones in adolescence reflect the complexity of the effects and the challenges of assessing pubertal hormones. Self- and parent-reports of pubertal development are not good proxies for hormonal status (Dorn, Susman, Nottelmann, Inoff-Germain, & Chrousos, 1990). Even direct hormone assays are limited unless they are repeated to capture intraindividual variability and the pulsatile nature of hormone secretion and are sensitive enough to detect small variations across individuals, especially during early puberty when estrogen levels are below sensitivity limits of conventional assays (J. L. Cameron, 2004).

The multiple determinants of adolescent development have become increasingly obvious, and it is important to study how biological factors exert effects indirectly and interact with social factors to produce gender-related changes during adolescence (e.g., Ruble & Martin, 1998; Susman, 1997). School transitions, to junior high and then to high school, for example, affect children's self-perceptions and mood, especially for girls. Gender identification or socialization processes prior to adolescence may differentially affect girls' and boys' reactions to adolescent transitions.

Brain Structure and Function

Ultimately, all aspects of gender development are mediated through the brain. The brain changes in response to environmental events, but there has been less study of the ways in which brain sex differences are shaped by behavioral differences than the reverse. Research concerning structural and functional similarities and differences in male and female brains has increased dramatically with the availability of imaging techniques, including structural magnetic resonance imaging (MRI) to observe fine-grained details of brain structure and functional magnetic resonance imaging (fMRI) to measure brain activation in response to specific tasks, such as looking at emotional pictures or solving a problem. A review of this literature is beyond the scope of this chapter, but we provide a sample of the work and sources for additional information.

Overall Brain Structure.   Research comparing the brain sizes and structures of men and women has a checkered history. Overall, the brain size of men tends to be 10% to 15% larger than for women, with much of the difference due to differences in body size (Halpern, 2000). Contemporary research has focused less on overall brain size than on sex differences in specific parameters of brain structure and specific brain regions, and whether differences within sex relate to behavior or abilities. There may be sex differences in concentration of gray and white matter (containing cell bodies and fiber tracts, respectively). Some, but not all, studies suggest that females have more cortical gray matter (e.g., Good et al., 2001; Rabinowicz, Dean, Petetot, & de Courten-Myers, 1999; Witelson, Glezer, & Kigar, 1995), whereas males have more white matter (e.g., De Bellis et al., 2001; Giedd et al., 1999). This might have implications for processes involving coordination among multiple brain areas.

Organization of the Cerebral Hemispheres.
Early research on sex differences focused on the two cerebral hemispheres. In most people, the left hemisphere is specialized for language tasks and the right for perceptual and spatial processing, with some variation among individuals in the extent to which the brain is lateralized. Meta-analysis shows that women are somewhat less lateralized than men, but the difference is small (Voyer, 1996). These functional differences have parallels in structure: Men show more morphological asymmetry than women in parts of the brain, including cerebral hemispheric volume, patterning of gyri and sulci, language-related areas, and distribution of gray matter (Good et al., 2001; Kovalev, Kruggel, & von Cramon, 2003; Yücel et al., 2001). Sex differences in lateralization have been hypothesized to account for differences in cognition and behavior (L. J. Harris, 1978; J. Levy, 1974), but there is little direct evidence. Prenatal testosterone has been suggested to influence lateralization, but effects are likely to be small and difficult to observe, so it is not surprising that results are inconsistent (Bryden, McManus, & Bulman-Fleming, 1994; Mathews et al., 2004). There may also be sex differences in the organization of the brain within the hemispheres (Kimura, 1999).

Regional Brain Structures.   Sex differences in the size of specific brain regions are suggested to underlie cognitive and behavioral sex differences, for example, differences in orbital frontal cortex or amygdala underlying differences in emotion and differences in temporal lobe relating to language (for summaries and illustrative results, see Goldstein et al., 2001; Nopoulos, Flaum, O'Leary, & Andreasen, 2000; Raz et al., 2004). Results are inconsistent across studies, in part because of methodological variability, sample heterogeneity, and high statistical errors due to small samples and many regions examined. Furthermore, large brain size does not always mean optimal function. Developmental changes in the brain, including sex differences, are only beginning to be understood (Giedd, 2004; Giedd et al., 1999; Gogtay et al., 2004).

The preoptic area of the anterior hypothalamus is of interest because it has a high density of hormone receptors and is sexually dimorphic in nonhuman animals (Wallen & Baum, 2002). One of four nuclei of the human anterior hypothalamus (INAH-3) has consistently been found to be smaller in women than in men and may also be smaller in homosexual than in heterosexual men (e.g., LeVay, 1993).

There is also much interest in the corpus callosum (CC), a bundle of fibers connecting the left and right cerebral hemispheres and allowing transfer of information between the hemispheres. A report on autopsied brains showed certain portions of the CC, especially the splenium, to be more bulbous and larger in women than in men (de Lacoste-Utamsing & Holloway, 1982). Subsequent studies and meta-analyses, most using MRI in normal individuals, are inconsistent, with some suggesting that women do have a larger CC after adjustment for brain size (Driesen & Raz, 1995), and others concluding that they do not (Bishop & Wahlsten, 1997). Sex differences in CC are potentially important because women's reduced lateralization might be associated with more communication between the hemispheres.

There is need to study the behavioral significance of sex differences in brain size and to consider that correlates of size may differ by sex. In one study (Davatzikos & Resnick, 1998), CC (particularly splenium) size was positively correlated with cognitive performance in women but not in men.

Regional Brain Function.   Paralleling MRI studies on sex differences in the *size* of specific brain regions are fMRI studies examining sex differences in the *activation* of specific regions in response to psychologically relevant stimuli or tasks. We illustrate work focusing on brain regions that might underlie sex differences in cognition or emotion. In a study of language processing (Shaywitz et al., 1995), women and men activated different brain regions as they decided if nonsense words rhymed, with women using both the left and right inferior frontal gyrus for the task and men using only the left. There was little overlap between the sexes in patterns of brain activation, but the activation difference did not translate into a performance difference, perhaps because the task was easy. In a study of navigation, men and women activated different regions as they went through a three-dimensional virtual-reality maze, which men performed more quickly than women. Men were more likely to use the left hippocampus and women the right parietal and prefrontal regions—a difference suggested to reflect processing differences—that is, men's use of geometric cues versus women's use of landmarks (Grön, Wunderlich, Spitzer, Tomczak, & Riepe, 2000).

The amygdala has been a focus because of its role in processing emotion (Hamann & Canli, 2004). Meta-analysis (Wager, Phan, Liberzon, & Taylor, 2003) revealed no sex difference in overall activation to emotional stimuli, but men show greater lateralized activation, consistent with their generally increased hemispheric asymmetry. Recent studies showed sex differences in specific aspects of emotional processing

(Hamann & Canli, 2004), including sexual arousal (Hamann, Herman, Nolan, & Wallen, 2004).

Hormones and the Brain.   Empirical studies are beginning to test hypotheses about the role of hormones in brain sex differences and about the ways that the brain mediates behavioral effects of prenatal and circulating hormones. Initial imaging studies of brain structure in females with CAH have not shown them to differ from controls (Merke et al., 2003). Future work might focus on task-specific brain *activation* related to activity interests and spatial ability, examining brain regions likely to subserve those behaviors (e.g., parietal lobe and hippocampus for spatial ability). With respect to circulating hormones, there is some evidence that estrogen affects gender-related cognition through effects on brain activity (Maki & Resnick, 2001). Future work might focus on how pubertal hormones affect the brain differently in the sexes, resulting in the rise in depression in girls and aggression in boys.

Integration and Conclusions

The biologically-oriented work of the past few years has enhanced knowledge about hormonal influences on gender development and potential neural mechanisms that mediate both hormone effects and environmental input. Just as sex hormones affect the body, they also influence behavior. Hormones present during early development (organizational effects) play a substantial role in aspects of gender development, particularly self-perception, preferences, and behavioral enactment (columns B, C, and D of the matrix) of some content areas. Prenatal androgens influence activities and interests (row 2 in the matrix), some personal-social attributes (row 3), such as interest in babies and spatial abilities, and aspects of gender-based social relationships, such as play and sexual partners (row 4), with smaller effect on psychological aspects of categorical sex (row 1). Most evidence comes from individuals with clinical conditions, primarily girls with CAH. The limitations of these natural experiments are being overcome, and there is increasing confirmation from typical samples for behavioral effects of hormones.

Many important questions remain unanswered about hormone effects on gender development. Do prenatal hormones affect gender-related styles and values (rows 5 and 6) or concepts and beliefs (column A) of any content area? How do prenatal and pubertal hormones affect the *development* of gender-typing? Why do hormones have different effects on different characteristics, with prenatal androgen having a big effect on some (e.g., activities and interests), a modest effect on others (e.g., sexual orientation), and a small effect on still others (e.g., gender identity)? Biological and social moderators of hormone effects likely vary across aspects of gender-typing and account for variations within and between the sexes. What are the psychological mechanisms that mediate the effects? For example, what is it about boys' toys that makes them attractive to children who have been exposed to high levels of androgen during prenatal development? Infant males and females differ in some sensory and perceptual characteristics (McGuinness & Pribram, 1979) and perhaps androgen effects on these characteristics mediate effects on toy play (Alexander, 2003). Hormones also affect peripheral structures, such as muscles, and these might affect behavior.

Sex hormone increases during adolescence do not have many direct behavioral effects within the normal range, but they may increase girls' depression and boys' aggressiveness and behavior problems. The complexity of hormone-behavior links is highlighted by evidence showing that behavioral changes at puberty may be mediated by social and psychological changes, such as peer associations. Sex hormones circulating in the body throughout adolescence and adulthood influence gender-related behavior, but generally different aspects than are influenced by prenatal hormones, with particular effects of estrogen on memory, and androgen on social dominance.

Brain structure and function also differ in some ways between the sexes, including regions involved in gender-related behavior. But it is necessary to make the explicit link between the brain and behavior and to show how the links are forged—for example, how structural differences are produced by prenatal exposure to sex hormones, and how patterns of brain activation are affected by sex-differential experience and circulating sex hormones at puberty. An area that has been neglected concerns neural processing of gender concepts and beliefs. Is gender processed in the brain in the same way as other categories? What are the neural correlates of stereotyping? How does the brain change with interventions to reduce stereotyping, and what does that tell us about the formation and maintenance of stereotypes?

There is increasingly sophisticated understanding of biological effects and recognition that they are not im-

mutable. Genes are activated or suppressed by environmental factors. Hormones and brain functioning are almost certainly influenced by the different environments in which girls and boys are raised, by their different toy and activity choices, and by joint effects of genes and the social environment.

Socialization Approaches

Gender permeates every aspect of a child's social environment. In Bronfenbrenner's (1977) terms, the meaning of gender is communicated through the cultural values and practices of the macrosystem (e.g., power and economic differentials between men and women), which in turn influence the microsystems a child experiences at home, school, and neighborhood (Leaper, 2002). But how do we conceptualize the direct and interactive effects of these various influences? Which features from the environment are noticed and incorporated into gender development, *and* by what processes? In this section, we tackle such questions as we summarize the past 10 to 15 years of socialization research.

Socialization Processes

In the 1970 *Handbook,* Mischel presented the social learning perspective on the development of gender-typing. This perspective calls attention to direct reinforcement for conformity to gender norms, as when adults compliment a girl when she wears a dress but not when she wears pants. In addition, social learning theories (as well as other theories: e.g., S. L. Bem, 1981; Kohlberg, 1966; Martin & Halverson, 1981) emphasize the importance of observational learning. Children may engage in more same- rather than other-sex behavior because they are differentially exposed to same-sex models (Crouter, Manke, & McHale, 1995), and children's tendencies to segregate by sex means that they are exposed more often to same-sex peers than other-sex peers (Maccoby, 1998; Martin & Fabes, 2001).

In the past 30 years, social learning perspectives have undergone a number of modifications and elaborations (Bandura, 1986). Social cognitive theory was recently applied to gender development by Bussey and Bandura (1999), highlighting a central role for cognitive processes. For example, when children attend to same-sex models, they are assumed to focus on and extract information about how behaviors are enacted, the sequencing of events, and the consequences associated with enacting behavior. We describe social cognitive theory in this section on socialization processes, rather than in the following section on cognitive processes, because it focuses on traditional learning principles of reinforcement and observation in the initial stages of gender development (Liben & Bigler, 2002).

Bussey and Bandura's (1999) description of these principles improved on early accounts in several ways. Generalized imitation of same-sex models had not been found in earlier research (Huston, 1983; Maccoby & Jacklin, 1974), and Bussey and Bandura showed the importance of the conditions under which children imitate behavior. For example, children may not imitate a single same-sex model, but they are likely to learn from multiple models engaged in the same activity.

Moreover, in social cognitive theory, observational learning is not confined to imitation of same-sex models. Instead, children learn abstract rules and styles of modeled behaviors. By attending to models of both sexes, children construct notions of "appropriate" appearance, occupations, and behavior for each sex, and use these stereotypes to develop complex concepts about gender-appropriate behavior. Thus, a boy may develop a unique style of rough-and-tumble play based on observations of multiple boys engaging in different games and girls not participating. Further, children's performance of these learned behaviors depends on incentives and sanctions associated with the outcomes of engaging in these behaviors. Through such experiences, children develop outcome expectancies and self-efficacy beliefs that become linked to gender-related behaviors, which serve to motivate and regulate gender role conduct. Although such regulatory processes are originally environmentally determined, Bussey and Bandura (1999) describe a period in early development when they become internalized, as children administer self-praise or self-sanctions in relation to a set of personal standards for gender conduct.

Finally, these environmental events are not viewed as the only source of gender learning in social cognitive theory. Instead, a triadic reciprocal model of causation is proposed, in which personal (i.e., cognitive, affective, and biological factors), behavioral, and environmental factors interact to determine gender-related conduct (see Bandura, 1986; Bussey & Bandura, 1999, for details).

In the following sections, we review the evidence regarding the impact on gender development of social ex-

periences/socialization processes in the family, among peers, at school, and via the media. These studies speak to the general social learning principles of reinforcement and observational learning, though few have examined the shift from external to internal regulation. The only study directly examining this issue suggested that children learn to guide their own gender-linked conduct with self-evaluative reactions between 3 to 4 years of age (Bussey & Bandura, 1992), but the lack of longitudinal data and other limitations (Martin et al., 2002) preclude definitive conclusions.

Gender Socialization in the Family

The family provides many types of socialization experiences, including models of gender roles and differences in the ways sons and daughters are raised. The following sections outline effects of family socialization experiences on several aspects of children's gender development.

Encouragement of Gender-Typed Activities and Interests. Caregivers influence gender development by providing boys and girls with distinct social contexts (e.g., toys and room furnishings; Pomerleau, Bolduc, Malcuit, & Cossette, 1990; Rheingold & Cook, 1975). Gender-typed environments may subtly channel children's preferences and engagement in activities.

Meta-analysis of parents' differential treatment of boys and girls (Lytton & Romney, 1991) showed the clearest effect for encouragement of gender-typed activities (versus areas such as personality traits). For example, parents offer gender-stereotypic toys to children during free play, and they are more responsive when children are engaged in same-gender play than when they are engaged in other-gender play. The effect was moderate ($d = .43$), somewhat stronger for fathers than for mothers, and decreased with the child's age. Recent research on this pattern (e.g., Caldera & Sciaraffa, 1998) extended it to cultures other than middle-class Caucasian (e.g., Raffaelli & Ontai, 2004) and revealed other means of parental encouragement of gender-typed play (Leaper, 2002). For example, communication patterns between mothers and their preschool children depended on whether children were engaged in gender-typical or gender-atypical play (Leaper, Leve, Strasser, & Schwartz, 1995). Nevertheless, other research suggests that parents often treat young children in nonstereotypic ways, such as buying gender neutral toys for children when they are not requested by the child (e.g., Fisher-Thompson, 1993). Thus, contemporary efforts to foster sex-differentiated play may often be subtle or limited, and many parents may make conscious efforts to encourage egalitarian behaviors.

What is the effect of encouraging gender-typed play? In our last review (Ruble & Martin, 1998), we concluded that parents of very young children appear to promote precocious learning of gender distinctions when they encourage gender-typed play. Encouragement of particular activities may also influence children's learning of cognitive and social skills (Caldera et al., 1999). Boys' toys, such as blocks, model building, and manipulative toys, encourage the development of visual/spatial skills, problem solving, independent learning, self-confidence, and creativity, whereas dolls and domestic items provide girls with practice in learning rules, imitating behaviors, using adults as sources of help, and solving familiar problems (Martin & Dinella, 2002). Parents may also provide daughters and sons differential experiences that foster different social cognitive skills (Leaper, 2002). For example, parents' greater focus on explanations of scientific content in museums for boys than for girls may foster boys' greater interest in and knowledge about science (Crowley, Callanan, Tenenbaum, & Allen, 2001). In addition, parents' assignment of household chores along gender stereotyped lines (Antill et al., 1996) may have implications beyond learning particular skills. For example, children's involvement in family care work has been associated positively with prosocial concerns (Grusec, Goodnow, & Cohen, 1996).

In our last review (Ruble & Martin, 1998), we indicated that little is known about the role of parental encouragement of gender-typed play on subsequent play preferences and behaviors. That is still the case; it is still not clear how important parent socialization is to the emergence of individual differences in young children's preferences and displays of relatively female- or male-typical behavior. Some research has found significant but weak correlations between parent behaviors and children's preferences and behaviors, such as a relation between encouragement of physical behaviors by parents and children's physical play with peers (Lindsey & Mize, 2001). As Eisenberg, Wolchik, Hernandez, and Pasternack (1985) suggested, an important "tool" for gender socialization is channeling or shaping, as when socializing agents structure the environment in a way that limits choices, such as providing only dolls for girls

and trucks for boys. Given this kind of control, parents may not need to differentially encourage certain kinds of play during actual interactions, because the situation dictates the desired behavior.

Encouragement of Gender-Typed Personal-Social Attributes.   Huston (1983) concluded that parental socialization practices influence the development of gender-typed personality characteristics in children. Meta-analysis (Lytton & Romney, 1991), however, failed to find significant effects for amount of interaction, encouragement of achievement, warmth and responsiveness, encouragement of dependency, restrictiveness/low encouragement of independence, disciplinary strictness, or clarity of communication/use of reasoning. But some limitations in the analysis suggest that it is premature to conclude that the only way parents treat boys and girls differently is by encouraging gender-typed behavior, especially because conclusions depend on how studies are combined to compute effect sizes. For most domains, studies showed effects in both directions, but reasons for heterogeneity were not explored. Moreover, a focus on broad socialization domains, such as warmth or restrictiveness, may mask significant specific effects, such as the extent of supportive versus directive speech (McHale et al., 2003). Broad groupings may also obscure effects when socialization practices in different domains have similar effects. For instance, sex differences in self-evaluative processes may be linked to seemingly quite distinct socialization practices (Leaper, 2002) such as differential control versus autonomy-granting in the home (e.g., Pomerantz & Ruble, 1998) and greater encouragement of empathy and feelings of responsibility in girls than in boys (e.g., Zahn-Waxler, Cole, & Barrett, 1991). Because such socialization processes cut across the different domains, it would be difficult to identify them in meta-analysis.

Recent research suggests promising approaches to examining when and how boys and girls are treated differently in the family. One important new direction focuses on context and the recognition that parental socialization is embedded in a larger family system (McHale et al., 2003). For example, families' sensitivity to gender-related differential treatment may be exacerbated when there are both boys and girls in the house. Consistent with this idea, parents respond more differentially to boys and girls in mixed-sex than same-sex sibling dyads (McHale et al., 2003). A particularly interesting finding is that siblings from mixed-sex dyads with a traditional father exhibited the most sex-typed leisure activities and parent-child activities (McHale et al., 1999).

A second new direction focuses on the subtleties of gender socialization practices, suggesting that they may be implicit rather than explicit (Gelman, Taylor, & Nguyen, 2004). For example, microanalysis of everyday social interactions among the Kaluli showed how mothers use language and games to teach children adult gender roles and characteristics, even though direct reference to gender only occurs when norms are violated (Schieffelin, 1990). Recent research has identified a number of subtleties in gender-related language and communication. Pomerantz and Ruble (1998) found that although overall communication of control in the home did not differ for girls and boys, control communications were more often accompanied by autonomy granting messages for boys than for girls. In an analysis of mothers' speech patterns during reading of stories, mothers explicitly espoused egalitarian views but implicitly made gender concepts salient, for example, through labeling of gender and contrasting male and female gender categories (Gelman et al., 2004).

Although sex-differential socialization practices may be subtle, complex, and context-dependent, parents do show different treatment of sons and daughters in some very important ways that are broader than the assignments of chores or encouragement of activities or traits (Leaper, 2002). For example, mothers' tendencies to be more talkative with daughters than sons may contribute to sex-differentiated language learning (Leaper, Anderson, & Sanders, 1998). Parents also vary the nature and frequency of their discussion of emotions with young sons and daughters (e.g., Fivush, Brotman, Buckner, & Goodman, 2000). Such gender-differentiated patterns of parent-child interaction in the domain of emotions may contribute to boys learning to control their emotions and girls learning to express them (Eisenberg, Cumberland, & Spinrad, 1998).

Parents also hold stereotypic beliefs that boys and girls have different attributes and skills, even when they are not different. For example, mothers of 11-month-olds underestimated girls' motor skills and overestimated boys' skills, but tests showed no sex differences in motor performance (Mondschein, Adolph, & Tamis-LeMonda, 2002). In a different domain, parents expected sons to find science easier and more interesting than daughters, despite a lack of difference in performance (Tenenbaum & Leaper, 2003). Such beliefs and expectations appear to influence adults' perceptions and behaviors toward their children, and even the children's own perceptions and behaviors. In an impressive program of research, Eccles and her colleagues (e.g., Fredricks & Eccles, 2002) found that parents who hold stronger stereotypes regarding the capabilities of boys and girls in English, math, and sports had differential expectations regarding their own children's abilities in these subjects, which were in turn related to the children's performance and self-perceptions of competence, even when actual ability levels were controlled. Such relations appear to be mediated, in part, by parents' tendencies to provide different experiences for sons and daughters, such as enrolling sons more often in sports programs.

Finally, early studies suggested that differential treatment may also occur through reciprocal role enactment processes in which fathers encourage femininity in daughters and mothers encourage masculinity in sons (Huston, 1983; Ruble & Martin, 1998). Parents may also feel a greater commonality and responsibility for socializing same-sex children, and thereby exert closer control over them. Because most children spend more time with female than male caregivers, such responses may represent a significant type of differential treatment, though it has been relatively understudied.

Role Models in the Home. In what ways do parents act as role models, thereby influencing their children's attitudes and behaviors? Maternal employment has been associated with less stereotyped concepts and beliefs in both boys and girls and less gender-typed preferences and behaviors in girls (Ruble & Martin, 1998). Relations between maternal employment and egalitarian beliefs and behaviors may reflect access to nontraditional role models, but other variables associated with maternal employment are probably also involved, such as nontraditional attitudes in the home or exposure to different kinds of information outside the home (L. O. Hoffman, 1989; McHale et al., 2003).

Despite the many processes that might lead maternal employment to be associated with nontraditional beliefs, findings are inconsistent. Many other factors likely moderate the relation between maternal employment and children's gender traditionality, such as mothers' reasons for working (Katz & Boswell, 1986) and father's involvement (Grych & Clark, 1999). Furthermore, maternal employment may reflect socioeconomic status, which is itself related to nontraditional gender concepts.

When demographic variables were controlled in one study, there were few effects of maternal employment on gender concepts and preferences (Serbin et al., 1993). Failures to find effects of maternal employment in recent research may also be due to the prevalence of maternal employment, which both reduces variability and exposes children to women in the workplace, regardless of whether their own mother works outside the home.

A few studies have examined effects of other nontraditional family roles on gender development. An egalitarian division of labor in the home (or father involvement) relates to many aspects of children's gender development, such as less traditional occupational and peer preferences (Serbin et al., 1993), and less traditional gender role attitudes and behaviors (McHale et al., 2003), although such effects are not consistently found (e.g., Weisner, Garnier, & Loucky, 1994).

Parental Attitudes and Values.   To what extent are children's gender concepts related to general measures of gender orientation in the home, such as parents' perceptions of their own attributes, attitudes about equality, or nonegalitarian lifestyles? Early research suggested that caregivers who view themselves in traditional terms or who hold traditional attitudes foster the learning of gender distinctions in their children, such as earlier learning of gender labels and stereotype knowledge (Ruble & Martin, 1998). Some recent research has failed to confirm this (O'Brien et al., 2000), perhaps because the children were beyond toddler age.

Parental attitudes have also been associated with children's gender-typing, including the distribution of gender-typed chores to sons and daughters (e.g., Blair, 1992) and children's own gender attitudes (e.g., McHale et al., 1999). Such relations are not always consistent across different measures of gender-typing, even in the same study, and are often moderated by other factors such as birth order (McHale et al., 1999). For example, meta-analysis of the relation between parents' gender schemas and child outcomes (Tenenbaum & Leaper, 2002) showed that effects were large for parent-daughter pairs and for parents of older children and adolescents.

Research would benefit from an approach recognizing cultural and historical variations in gendered attitudes (Leaper, 2002; McHale et al., 2003). For example, adult African Americans (especially women) are likely to reject traditional gender divisions (Kane, 2000), many Latin cultures are marked by strong gender role divisions (Raffaelli & Ontai, 2004), and data from the National Opinion Research Center's General Social Surveys for 1974 to 1994 suggest a shift toward egalitarian gender role attitudes in the United States (R. J. Harris & Firestone, 1998).

Alternative Family Structures: Single Parenting and Gay and Lesbian Parenting.   Nontraditional families are interesting because role modeling and differential reinforcement are likely to differ from those in two-parent heterosexual families. For example, single parents may have less gendered roles than those in two-parent families. Because mothers usually have custody, children receive less exposure to male role models at home. To the extent that fathers take responsibility for masculinizing sons (Huston, 1983; McHale et al., 2003), father absence should be associated with less traditional gender-typing in boys. Early studies (Huston, 1983) including meta-analysis (Stevenson & Black, 1988) showed very small effects of paternal absence on gender development, so perhaps it is not surprising that recent research is mixed (e.g., Stevens, Golombok, Beveridge & Avon Logitudinal Study of Parents and Children Study Team, 2002). Effects may be subtle (Leaper et al., 1995), occur only for cognitive variables, such as stereotypic knowledge (Serbin et al., 1993), or vary across behavior and child age and sex (e.g., older father-absent boys are more stereotypical in overt behavior, particularly aggression; effects are generally lacking in girls, except perhaps on femininity in adolescence).

These effects are important theoretically. For example, nontraditional gender role attitudes of African American children may relate to the prevalence of children reared by a working, single mother (Leaper, 2002). Further, findings that boys but not girls are affected by paternal absence support theories emphasizing identification and modeling. Minimal effects for girls, however, are inconsistent with hypotheses about reciprocal role socialization processes (e.g., E. Williams, Radin, & Allegro, 1992). Perhaps these processes are important in adolescence and account for earlier findings (Huston, 1983) that father absence is associated with difficult heterosexual relationships in adolescent girls.

Not surprisingly, other types of nontraditional family structures are also associated with less traditional gender-typing in children. For example, girls raised by lesbian couples show less female-typical clothing, activity, and occupational preferences relative to girls raised by heterosexual couples (Stacey & Biblarz, 2001), although effects are small and children from these families are within conventional gender norms (Patterson, 2000). Research efforts should be directed to specific processes in the home (e.g., division of labor; parental attitudes) rather than the family structure itself (McHale et al., 2003).

Sibling Effects. Do children learn gender-related attributes and interests from their siblings? Early research showed that children with few or no siblings are more likely to have gender egalitarian beliefs, suggesting that siblings promote gender-typing (Ruble & Martin, 1998). Recent research suggests stronger socialization effects of siblings than of parents (McHale et al., 2003), but sibling effects are inconsistent, depending on age, birth order, and whether they are the same sex (Crouter et al., 1995; McHale et al., 2003). Although sibling relationships have generally been conceptualized in terms of modeling, they may also be characterized by needs to individuate, especially in adolescence (McHale, Updegraff, Helms-Erikson, & Crouter, 2001).

Gender Socialization at School

Schools provide a wide array of gender-related messages to children. Their structures provide gender messages because men tend to be in positions of power and women are teachers of younger children. Teachers treat boys and girls differently and hold differential expectations of their abilities. Classrooms provide children with opportunities to learn about the consequences of behavior through observing peers.

Differential Treatment. Teachers interact differently with girls and boys at every level of schooling. Teachers of infants and toddlers may shape behavior by reinforcing stereotypic expectations about girls' and boys' behavior even when no sex differences are evident. Preschool teachers encourage gender-appropriate play and discourage gender-inappropriate play. Throughout the school years, teachers not only interact and attend more to boys than to girls but also interrupt them less (see Ruble & Martin, 1998). Effects vary across grade, with teachers in lower grades showing more sex-differentiated responses than do high school teachers, except that high school boys continue to receive more criticism from teachers than do girls. In high school, teacher responsiveness depends on the sex of the teacher and the course subject (Hopf & Hatzichristou, 1999).

For instance, female mathematics teachers and language teachers of both sexes interacted more with male than female students (Duffy, Warren, & Walsh, 2002).

An interesting issue is whether teacher responsiveness reflects bias or students' willingness to volunteer answers. Elementary school teachers called on boys more than girls, but girls and boys were equally likely to be called on when they volunteered (Altermatt, Jovanovic, & Perry, 1998), whereas high school teachers' greater interactions with male students were not driven by boys' verbal comments to teachers (Duffy et al., 2002).

Teachers hold differentiated views of girls and boys. They believe that elementary school boys are better than girls in science and math (e.g., Tiedemann, 2000). They also view girls' and boys' classroom behavior differently; for instance, lying and cheating are seen to be more undesirable in girls than boys, and hyperactivity and quarrelsomeness are more serious for boys than girls (Borg, 1998). However, in naturalistic settings, teachers form relatively accurate perceptions of students based on children's characteristics (e.g., achievement and motivation) and only occasionally rely on stereotypes about sex (Madon et al., 1998). Much attention has been paid to whether teachers develop self-fulfilling prophecies of students' abilities and whether these beliefs account for student success. Overall, these effects are small, but may endure (A. E. Smith, Jussim, & Eccles, 1999). Effects may be more pronounced for some children than others; for instance, girls in mathematics classes may be more negatively influenced by low teacher expectations than girls in female-stereotypic classes (McKown & Weinstein, 2002).

Finally, school practices may foster perceptions of sex differences. Boys and girls may be kept in segregated groups for even minor activities such as standing in line. Differing contexts and activities may influence behavior. The highly structured activities of girls may elicit higher rates of feminine-typed social behaviors, such as asking for help, whereas the low-structured activities of boys may elicit higher rates of masculine-typed behaviors, such as leadership attempts toward peers; alternatively, children may engage in structures that allow them to display their preferred behaviors (Ruble & Martin, 1998).

Role Models in School. Schools provide children with gender-related information through roles played by men and women. Men are disproportionately represented in positions of power and administration, whereas women are often teachers, particularly in the early grades. Only in older grades are children likely to have male teachers, and these are often in male-typical classes such as mathematics and science.

There are two main issues relevant to the impact of role models on gender development. First, does exposure to male teachers affect gender concepts? The dearth of male teachers in elementary school and its implications for gender-typing has generated considerable debate, but little research has directly examined this question (Hopf & Hatzichristou, 1999). Some data suggest that male teachers foster nontraditional gender beliefs and preferences and nontraditional views of teachers perhaps because they are in female-typical roles (Ruble & Martin, 1998).

Second, is same-sex education better than coed-education? The evidence is mixed. Some evidence suggest that same-sex education has a positive effect on females' achievement (e.g., Lee & Bryk, 1986; Mael, 1998), whereas other recent studies do not show that these classes are better for girls' or boys' achievement or in changing gender conceptions (Harker, 2000; Signorella, Frieze, & Hershey, 1996; Warrington & Younger, 2003).

Peers

Classic studies in the 1970s and 1980s explored peers' roles in socializing gender development through reinforcement and role modeling. Although these processes continue to be emphasized as mechanisms involved in peer socialization, another approach has become prominent—children are broadly socialized through exposure to same-sex peers. This "separate cultures" perspective presumes that children spend a significant amount of time with their own sex and thus selectively learn the behaviors and interaction styles associated with their own sex and not much about other-sex interactions and play styles (Leaper, 1994; Maccoby, 1998; Thorne, 1986).

Differential Treatment.   Most studies of peer reinforcement of gender-appropriate behavior were conducted by Fagot and colleagues during the 1970s and 1980s (e.g., Fagot, 1977), and there are few recent studies. These classic studies showed that, by age 3, children respond differentially to gender-typed behavior in others (Huston, 1983; Ruble & Martin, 1998). Peers responded to boys' assertive behavior more than to girls'

(Fagot & Hagan, 1985) and were more negative to boys who engaged in female-typical behaviors, especially those who did not engage in male-typical behaviors (Fagot, 1984). Recent research on differential treatment, rather than examining reinforcement, focuses on rejection or dislike. Both sexes dislike others who are aggressive, but girls are more negative about externalizing behavior in peers, and boys are more negative about anxious and depressed behaviors, suggesting that both sexes are more tolerant of gender-typed behavior (Waas & Graczyk, 1999). Children of both sexes exhibiting extreme gender-nonnormative behaviors are teased and disliked by peers, with boys receiving more teasing for their behavior than girls (Zucker & Bradley, 1995).

Peer Models.   Although peers are presumed to socialize gender development by serving as role models, this has not been well studied. Early studies demonstrated that children learn standards for gender-appropriate behavior through observation, as discussed earlier. It is less clear whether peer modeling of gender-inconsistent behavior can promote change. Simply observing peer models engage in gender-inconsistent behavior did not change young children's behavior unless the model's behavior was reinforced (Katz & Walsh, 1991). Under certain circumstances, other-sex role models can dissuade children from "own-sex appropriate" preferences, but children also consider the perceived appropriateness of the activities encouraged (Harrison & O'Neill, 2000).

Children and adolescents may also try to live up to images of what behavior is "cool" or leads to popularity and high status. Preadolescent boys achieve status via athletic ability, toughness, and social skills, whereas girls' status relates to physical appearance, social skills, and parents' socioeconomic status. Characteristics valued by high school students vary by sex and ethnicity: For Caucasian adolescents, both sexes value peers who are high achievers; for African American and Latino adolescents, girls value peers who are high achievers but boys devalue achievers (Graham, Taylor, & Hudley, 1998).

Socialization in Sex-Segregated Play.   Increasing recognition has been given to peers' role in gender development because of the opportunities they provide to learn interactional styles and behaviors (see Ladd, 2005; Leaper, 1994; Maccoby, 1998 for reviews). In particular, emphasis has been given to the role of sex-segregated groups and how this produces "separate cultures" (Maccoby, 1998; Thorne, 1986) because children's time with same-sex peers exposes them more to same-sex than other-sex behaviors and interaction styles, narrowing their behavioral repertoire. "The essence of these cultures is a set of socially shared cognitions, including common knowledge and mutually congruent expectations, and common interests in specific themes and scripts that distinguish the two sexes" (Maccoby, 2002, p. 57). Although this perspective has gained broad support, it has also been questioned for its ability to adequately capture the complexity of children's social interactions, particularly influences of social contexts, and variations in play partners (see Thorne, 1993; Underwood, 2003; Zarbatany, McDougall, & Hymel, 2000).

What is the evidence for the power of peers on children's gender development? Although not all the evidence is consistent on these points, sex segregation in certain settings with older children may lessen gender-stereotypes; for example, there is some evidence that all-female schools and math classes promote nontraditional attitudes (e.g., Lee & Bryk, 1986), allow greater exposure to successful role models, and reduce differential teacher responsiveness and peer pressures compared to mixed-sex groupings (Ruble & Martin, 1998). Sex segregation in play situations with younger children shows a different pattern. With same-sex peers, children practice gender-typed play with toys and learn behavioral patterns that facilitate interaction with their own sex and limit interaction with the other sex (Leaper, 1994; Maccoby, 1998). A recent study (Martin & Fabes, 2001) suggests a *social dosage effect* in children's socialization by peers, in which preschool children with higher levels of same-sex play early in the school year increased in gender-typed behaviors later in the school year more than children who had lower levels of same-sex play, and these effects were beyond those that initially drew children into sex-segregated groups. Boys increased in rough-and-tumble play, aggression, gender-typed activities, and playing away from teachers; girls decreased activity and aggression and increased gender-typed play and play near adults. In young children, sex-segregated interactions appear to have the potential to move the behavior of girls and boys in gender-typed directions even with relatively limited exposure.

Sex-segregated play also influences school readiness (Fabes, Martin, Hanish, Anders, & Madden-Derdich, 2003; Martin & Dinella, 2002) and can facilitate or ex-

acerbate existing behavioral tendencies. For example, highly arousable children who play with same-sex peers show changes in behavior problems—increased for boys and decreased for girls. Playing with other highly arousable boys does not appear to help boys regulate their behavior, but girls' calm play may help arousable girls learn control (Fabes et al., 1997). Although it is difficult to disentangle the consequences of peer socialization from the selection factors that draw that children together, analyses suggest a transactional pattern at work (Hanish, Martin, Fabes, Leonard, & Herzog, 2005; Martin, Fabes, Hanish, Leonard, & Danella, 2006).

Many interesting questions about peer socialization remain unanswered. A particularly important question concerns the nature of the processes that enable peers to influence children's gender development. Addressing this issue requires identification of the varied nature of peer relationships and the effects of such variations (Gest, Graham-Bermann, & Hartup, 2001). Future research also should identify the situations and processes that lead to different outcomes (e.g., more versus less stereotyping) associated with sex-segregated environments.

Observational Learning from the Media

Children spend much of their free time watching television, so it is not surprising that media effects are a central issue in gender development. Exposure to popular media has greatly expanded—there are hundreds of cable channels, many more music channels, and increased access through DVDs, TiVo, and videos. Other powerful forms of media, such as computers and the Internet, also provide children with extensive exposure to messages about gender (Roberts, Foehr, Rideout, & Brodie, 1999; Subrahmanyam, Kraut, Greenfield, & Gross, 2001; Vandewater, Shim, & Caplovitz, 2004). Correlations have been demonstrated between exposure to media and many types of behavior (e.g., drug use, sexual behavior, and aggression), leading researchers to argue for powerful and pervasive media influences on child development (Ward, 2003).

Both sexes spend much of their time watching television, and boys do so more than girls throughout childhood (Huston et al., 1999) but not in adolescence (Huston & Wright, 1998). Boys also spend more time than girls playing video games, watching sports, cartoons, action-adventure, and fantasy programming, and using computers, whereas girls spend more time watching relationship and comedy programming, with the differences increasing across childhood (Huston et al., 1999; Lemish, Liebes, & Seidmann, 2001; Subrahmanyam et al., 2001; Wright et al., 2001) and in adolescence (Roberts & Foehr, 2004). Children are aware of sex differences in entertainment preferences: Three- to 9-year-olds recognize that action adventure programming should be appealing to boys more than girls (Oliver & Green, 2001).

Despite social changes of the late 1900s, the sexes continue to be portrayed in stereotypic ways, with some improvements (see Huston & Wright, 1998). Messages transmitted through the media are still highly stereotypic, teaching about and reinforcing traditional gender roles (Signorielli, 2001).

There are two broad concerns about media portrayals of the sexes. First, under-representation of females suggests devaluation. Early studies showed strong bias, with more males than females presented in virtually every domain (except daytime soap operas), and females occupying about one quarter to one third of televised roles (Signorielli, 1993). Underrepresentation of females has continued (Signorielli & Bacue, 1999).

Second, the sexes are portrayed in stereotypic ways regarding occupations, personality characteristics, social relationships, appearance, dress styles, and the value and desirability of roles. Some small changes have been made, such as portraying women in somewhat more prestigious careers (Signorielli & Bacue, 1999), but there continues to be stereotyping of occupational and appearance portrayals. For example, women tend to be young, thin, provocatively dressed, and beautiful, whereas men tend to be older and muscular (Signorielli & Bacue, 1999). Men are less likely than women to be portrayed cooking, cleaning, washing dishes, and shopping (Kaufman, 1999). The personality characteristics demonstrated by the sexes also continue to be stereotypic (Signorielli, 1993) and women are presented as sex objects more than men (Coltrane & Messineo, 2000; Lin, 1998). Gender-typing of roles also has been common in commercials (Furnham, 1999).

Children's programs present a more gender-typed picture of the world than do adult programs. Males outnumber females in all types of programming, including educational ones, as much as four or five to one in cartoons (Signorielli, 2001). Characters' roles continue to be stereotyped, although less than in the past. Female cartoon characters in the 1990s were more likely to be assertive, intelligent, and independent than characters

10 to 20 years earlier, but were still shown in traditional roles (i.e., emotional, romantic, and domestic). Male characters in the 1990s were presented as being more intelligent, more technical, and more aggressive but also less boastful than earlier characters (T. L. Thompson & Zerbinos, 1995).

Children's literature contains stereotypic messages about gender roles, although less so now than in the past. Girls, however, are still depicted as dependent and needing help more often than boys. Even "nonsexist" books show females in relatively limited roles (Diekman & Murnen, 2004). Girls are now more likely to be portrayed in masculine roles but boys are seldom shown possessing feminine traits (L. Evans & Davies, 2000). Females continue to be underrepresented in illustrations even when they are evenly portrayed as main characters in picture books (Gooden & Gooden, 2001). Classic children's literature also shows children in stereotyped characters (see Ruble & Martin, 1998).

Media for adolescents depict the sexes in stereotypic ways. In music-oriented broadcasting (and accompanying advertisements), women are underrepresented, and 10 times more likely to be dressed in revealing clothing than are men (Sommers-Flanagan, Sommers-Flanagan, & Davis, 1993). Video games are violent and stereotypic, with women often portrayed as sex objects (Dietz, 1998). Teen magazines for girls are highly stereotyped, with much attention paid to physical appearance, body weight, and relationships with others; magazines for boys provide entertainment and information about hobbies and activities (Malkin, Wornian, & Chrisler, 1999).

The Influence of Gender-Stereotypic Portrayals of the Sexes. What role does television play in children's gender socialization? It is very difficult to study the causal influence of something so pervasive in our culture. Researchers have used correlational and longitudinal studies, and natural experiments to determine whether media influences gender-related behavior and attitudes.

Some correlational studies report that children who are heavy, consistent television viewers generally hold more stereotypic beliefs about the sexes than light viewers (e.g., Huston et al., 1992). Children as young as age 5 are aware of gender stereotypes on television and are able to predict whether males or females would be in particular roles on television (Durkin & Nugent, 1998). For adolescents, frequent exposure to sexually oriented media (i.e., soap operas, music videos) is associated with more stereotypical and casual attitudes about sex (Ward, 2003). The major problem with such studies is determining the direction of influence. Television may be influencing beliefs or heavier viewers find television more appealing because it presents images that are consistent with their beliefs.

Meta-analyses of experimental and nonexperimental studies show an association between frequent television viewing and more stereotypic beliefs about gender roles (e.g., Morgan & Shanahan, 1997). Effect sizes are small ($r = .10$) but meaningful because they are consistent and because so many people are exposed to television that it is difficult to find unexposed individuals, thereby making large effects unlikely. However, it is difficult to draw firm conclusions from the correlational studies because of the inability to determine the cause of the association.

Therefore, important data come from longitudinal studies examining relations between television viewing at one time and gender-related attitudes and behavior later in time. For example, an extensive examination of viewing habits of preschoolers and a follow-up of attitudes, behavior, and achievement in adolescence (Anderson, Huston, Schmitt, Linebarger, & Wright, 2001) suggests that messages counter to gender-typed norms have longer-term effects than gender-typed messages: Positive relations between early exposure to educational television and school achievement were more pronounced for boys than girls; negative relations between watching violence and school achievement were stronger in girls.

The most convincing evidence for television's impact comes from a natural experiment in Canada: the introduction of television into towns that had been unable to receive it. In one town, children held less traditional gender attitudes than comparison children before television was introduced; but 2 years after television was introduced, they showed sharp increases in traditional attitudes (Kimball, 1986).

Summary. The range of media options has expanded rapidly over the last decade. Despite changes in the representation and portrayal of the sexes, the media continue to provide a window onto a highly stereotyped world. The ways in which media messages affect children's lives have yet to be fully determined. The background "wash" of gender stereotyping messages certainly provides an overabundance of inaccurate information about the sexes. But it is not enough to know

about children's media use. We need to investigate how children understand the messages and how they use them.

Integration and Conclusions

Gender socialization processes at home, at school, in interaction with peers, and through the media all contribute to gender differentiation in most areas identified in Table 14.1—concepts, preferences, behaviors, and values. Many studies fail to find expected associations, however, or find them only under some conditions. For example, studies using social learning principles to *change* stereotypic beliefs and behaviors have met with little success (Ruble & Martin, 1998). Careful theoretical analysis suggests that interventions attentive to developmental factors and using combinations of strategies may prove more successful (Bigler, 1999).

It is clear that the social world is gender-typed, but it is less clear how this influences gender development. The findings highlight the complexity of gender socialization processes and the need for fine-grained analysis to understand when and how social agents influence gender development. It is relatively rare to focus on a specific process underlying differential socialization, such as via the development of personal gender standards or different attributions for performance. Instead, most studies test a relatively simple hypothesis—that boys and girls are treated differently or exposed to models of differential behavior. Although many findings are intuitively compelling, the nature of the mediating process and its causal direction are often unclear. For example, an interesting and consistent finding is that advanced gender knowledge in young children is associated with encouragement of gender-differentiated play and traditional role modeling in the home, but it is unclear which aspects of the home environment are most important—is it differential responding, traditional attitudes, or the father's lack of involvement in activities at home? Are multiple socialization processes involved or does a single process underlie these various relations?

Cognitive Approaches

Cognitive approaches to the study of gender development have received considerable attention and there is a rapidly growing body of work on how cognitions affect gender development. Although cognitive approaches share many similarities (see Martin et al., 2002, for a review), different theories focus on different sorts of cognitions and different mechanisms linking cognitions to beliefs and behavior. We examine three cognitive theories of gender development: (1) cognitive developmental, (2) gender schemas, and (3) identification with males or females as a group. Although other theories also refer to cognitive mechanisms (e.g., Bussey & Bandura, 1999), the three theories discussed here share key fundamental assumptions, explicitly described in the integration section that follows.

Cognitive Developmental Theory and the Role of Gender Constancy

Kohlberg (1966) first posited the importance of developmental changes in children's gender understanding for organizing other aspects of gendered behavior and thinking. He proposed that gender development involves an active construction of the meaning of gender categories, initiated internally by the child rather than externally by socializing agents. This idea that children socialize themselves into gender roles was pioneering, but the mechanisms driving their socialization efforts were not articulated (Huston, 1983; Martin & Little, 1990). According to Kohlberg (1966), children's understanding that sex categorization does not change was an essential motivator for children to acquire gender roles, stating that "a child's gender identity can provide a stable organizer of the child's psychosexual attitudes only when he is categorically certain of its unchangeability" (p. 95). Once children acquire this sense of gender identity, they are presumed to be actively involved in gender self-socialization as they become increasingly motivated to behave like members of their own sex. Given Kohlberg's emphasis on understanding unchangeability, many researchers not surprisingly concluded that gender consistency—children's understanding of the permanence of sex categorization across situational changes—was the critical component for motivating children to learn and to adhere to gender roles (see Section 1A for a review of the stages of gender constancy), implying that children should show few gender-typed preferences and behaviors until they have attained this level of understanding.

Review of the Evidence. Over the years, cognitive developmental theory (CDT) has been reformulated in a number of ways (Ruble & Martin, 1998). For example, understanding of gender constancy is no longer expected to be antecedent to all gender knowledge and gender differentiation. Instead, constancy understanding is viewed as a point of increased susceptibility to gender-relevant information as well as a period of consolidation for conclusions about gender-appropriate activities (Ruble, 1994). Thus, children's engagement in gender-typed behavior prior to age 5—an observation even Kohlberg (1966) referred to—does not by itself contradict the basic tenets of contemporary CDT. Cognitive developmental theorists recognize that biological and socialization processes may lead very young children to show gender-typed preferences and behaviors prior to understanding constancy but constancy understanding is expected to exert an effect once it emerges.

Specifically, CDT predicts higher levels of gender constancy to be associated with increased responsiveness to gender-related information and more rigid application of gender norms. Indeed, as reviewed recently (Martin et al., 2002), many studies show positive relationships between level of gender constancy and aspects of gender development: selective attention to same-sex models; same-sex imitation; same-sex activity, clothing, and peer preferences; gender stereotype knowledge; and heightened responsiveness to gender cues. As Huston (1983) noted, however, there have been many mixed or null findings; and that has been true in more recent research as well (e.g., G. D. Levy, 1998; Zucker et al., 1999). Comparisons across studies are difficult because of varying operationalizations of constancy (see 1A). For example, prior research suggests that scoring only the simple responses to constancy questions (without justifications) may overestimate children's level of understanding, thereby making it difficult to interpret failures to find predicted relations between constancy and behavior in preschool children.

Interestingly, increased responsiveness to gendered information is found more often to relate to lower levels of gender constancy such as gender stability or basic identity. Only rarely has the highest level of constancy, gender consistency, been associated with other indices of gender development (Ruble & Martin, 1998). This is important because it implies that Kohlberg was right about the motivational significance of knowledge and identification with gender categories (Maccoby, 1990), but this process may begin earlier than Kohlberg thought—prior to a full understanding of gender consistency.

Supporting this idea, two recent studies have taken a developmental approach to relations between stability understanding and gender-related outcomes. In a cross-sectional study described earlier (L. Taylor et al., 2006), stability scores increased with age and reached ceiling at 5 years in parallel with age-related increases in gender-typed beliefs and preferences. Moreover, stability understanding mediated the relation between age and some of these outcome variables. Increases in consistency understanding were not predictive of increases in gender-typing. In a longitudinal study, stability understanding was related to levels of and increases in stereotypic knowledge and rigidity—for example, beliefs that "only" boys could play with trucks (Ruble et al., 2006).

Evaluating Gender Constancy.   There is currently little empirical support for the idea that gender consistency is a crucial component of gender development. Instead, lower levels of gender constancy are key—namely, identity and stability. It would be valuable to pay attention to the psychological processes that underlie relations between different components of constancy and gender-related outcomes. For example, does understanding gender identity elicit the kind of group identification described by social identity and schema theorists (see later sections) or reflect the motivational attachment to one's group suggested by Kohlberg (1966)? If so, the emphasis on consistency, due largely to its association with conservation, may have been misleading.

Does gender consistency have any important consequences for gender development? Firm conclusions are difficult to draw because of methodological limitations, but it is possible to examine competing hypotheses about the role of full constancy understanding (i.e., including consistency) in gender development. The first hypothesis is that children show strongest adherence to gender-related behaviors prior to attainment of gender consistency because they are afraid that cross-sex behaviors may transform them to the other sex. Once consistency is attained, they are free to defy gender norms (Huston, 1983). Thus, the attainment of consistency should be associated with decreased rigidity. The second hypothesis is that children show a linear increase in adherence to gender norms in relation to gender consistency (Warin, 2000) and do not become more flexible until a few years after the attainment of full constancy when stereotypes become more flexible (Ruble, 1994).

Additional findings in the study described earlier (L. Taylor et al., 2006) support the first hypothesis. Among children aged 3 to 7 years, increasing age was associated both with higher levels of consistency understanding and with higher levels of flexibility of gender-related beliefs. Moreover, consistency understanding mediated the relation between age and some indices of flexibility. Nevertheless, as described earlier, support for the second hypothesis has been found when stability understanding, rather than consistency, represents constancy. Future research using longitudinal designs is needed to clarify these relations.

In short, there are problems with the construct of gender constancy and its presumed relation to gender-related beliefs, preferences, and behaviors. Such relations are more complex than initially hypothesized. The evidence indicates that complete understanding of constancy does not serve the initial organizing function that Kohlberg (1966) proposed but may serve other important functions, such as promoting an increase in flexibility. Lower levels of constancy—identity and sometimes stability—do show some of the predicted associations. Whether such relations are best understood as reflecting the motivational processes Kohlberg described or alternative formulations remains for future research to decide.

Gender Schema Theory

Several versions of gender schema theory (GST) were proposed in the early 1980s, with one version emphasizing developmental changes (Liben & Signorella, 1980; Martin & Halverson, 1981) and another emphasizing individual differences (S. L. Bem, 1981; Marcus, Crane, Bernstein, & Siladi, 1982). Although they differ in focus, variations of GST all assume that children are actively involved in gender development.

Gender schemas are interrelated networks of mental associations representing information about the sexes. Schemas are not passive copies of the environment, but instead they are active constructions, prone to errors and distortions. Two types of schemas were initially formulated: (1) the superordinate schema containing list-like information about the sexes; and (2) the own-sex schema, a narrow schema containing detailed action plans for self-relevant information (Martin & Halverson, 1981). Gender schemas also have been conceived in other ways (Ruble & Stangor, 1986), including "lenses" that color perception and thinking (S. L. Bem, 1993) and scripts (G. D. Levy & Boston, 1994). Schemas are viewed as dynamic knowledge representations changing in response to situations and age and as having content that varies with culture and with individual social experiences and preferences.

Gender schema theory has been reviewed and updated recently (Martin et al., 2002). The major elaborations involve increased clarity about self- and other-schemas (Hannover, 2000), emphasis on the interplay between gender schemas and social environments (Martin & Dinella, 2002), descriptions of the dynamic nature of gender schemas (Martin, 2000; Martin & Dinella, 2001), and descriptions of processes that influence stereotyping (Barbera, 2003) and contribute to schema maintenance (Hughes & Seta, 2003).

Schematic consistency refers to children's tendencies to bring their attention, actions, and memories in line with their gender schemas. Once they identify themselves as boys or girls, children seek details and scripts for same-sex activities, show in-group biases, and become more sensitive to sex differences. Children are motivated to behave according to gender norms as a means of defining themselves and attaining cognitive consistency. The links between gender cognitions and behavior are presumed to occur through selective attention to and memory for own-sex relevant information and through motivation to be similar to same-sex others. Gender schemas are organizers of gender development but not the sole causes of gendered behavior (Martin et al., 2002).

Developing Gender Schemas. The development of gender schemas involves learning actual gender-related regularities in the environment and constructing other gender-related patterns, some of which may not exist in reality. Infants are assumed to attend to statistical regularities and to form categories and concepts based on them. Evidence regarding infant and child perception and categorization confirms these ideas. Infants notice even weak covariations or statistical regularities in some domains (e.g., Saffran, Aslin, & Newport, 1996). For gender categorization, sex differences in physical appearance (e.g., height, body shape) and styles (e.g., clothing, hairstyles) likely make learning even easier and increase the salience of gender categories for processing information. Furthermore, parents, media, peers, and the culture highlight the functional utility of gender categories and transmit information about sex-related differences (e.g., "boys don't wear pink"). Research confirms that children are more likely to use categories to make judgments of others when the categories are both physically salient and functional (e.g., teachers line children up by groups; Bigler, Brown, & Markell, 2001; Bigler, Jones, & Lobliner, 1997).

Furthermore, children add to their schemas by using processes that are less veridical, for instance, by forming illusory correlations (Susskind, 2003), exaggerating between-group differences and within-group similarities (see section on identification with social categories), and drawing inferences from limited information. Schemas also are responsive to a child's own preferences: Preferences for a particular activity may modify a child's stereotypes (Liben & Bigler, 2002; Martin, Eisenbud, & Rose, 1995).

Individual Differences in Gender Schemas. The content and application of gender schemas varies across situations and children. Some children will stereotype a broader range of information in their environments than others, and each child develops his or her own personal view of gender. This idea is similar to those proposed by other theorists (e.g., Egan & Perry, 2001; Perry, 2004; Spence, 1999) that each child develops an idiosyncratic set of cognitions about gender (e.g., gender relevance beliefs, Perry, 2004) that are particularly relevant for determining his or her view of gender typicality. Individuals differ in how fully developed, elaborated, and accessible their gender schemas are (Hannover, 2000; Liben & Bigler, 2002; Signorella et al., 1993), and these factors relate to how schemas influence behavior and thinking (S. L. Bem, 1981), although this line of reasoning has not been fully explored. However, both earlier (see Ruble & Martin, 1998) and recent research (Lobel et al., 1999, 2000) shows the importance of some types of individual differences in the use of gender to process information.

Gender Schemas and Inferences. A major contribution of GST has been in showing how gender schemas guide children's gender-based inferences and judgments. Early studies showed how children of different ages rely on gender schemas to make social judgments (see Ruble & Martin, 1998) and recent research has expanded on this work using more varied judgments and age groups. Some researchers have examined gender-related social judgments in very young children (Bauer, Liebl, & Stennes, 1998). Other researchers have examined social judgments in adolescents to determine how judgments depend on the adolescent's and the target's characteristics (Lobel et al., 1999, 2000). Giles and Heyman (2005) found that children use gender schemas to make judgments about sex differences in forms of aggression. Preschool children believed that girls were more likely to engage in relational aggression and boys in physical aggression. Interestingly, children showed memory distortions when information was inconsistent with their stereotypic beliefs. By age 8 or 9, children show evidence of using gender schemas to make judgments about which sex will play particular musical instruments, and their own preferences are similar to their stereotypes (Harrison & O'Neill, 2000, 2003).

Several studies have explored how children use social categories (e.g., sex) to make judgments in novel and ambiguous situations. In novel situations, children use gender to make generalizations about unfamiliar characteristics (Gelman, Collman, & Maccoby, 1986). For example, when 3½-year-olds were told the preferences of a girl and a boy for nongender-typed objects (e.g., pizza), they projected these preferences to sex-unspecified others based only on their proper names (Bauer & Coyne, 1997). Children also use gender schemas to evaluate and explain behavior. For instance, when told about a boy or girl who spilled some milk, children evaluated the behavior of boys more negatively and were more likely to draw general conclusions based on the behavior of boys than when girls spilled the milk, which can be interpreted as a "boys are bad" stereotype (Giles & Heyman, 2004; Heyman, 2001; Heyman & Gelman, 2000).

Memory and Illusory Correlations.   Early evidence supported the predictions from GST that children selectively attend to and remember schematically consistent information and supported the idea that they distort information that does not fit their schemas into schema-consistent information (Ruble & Martin, 1998). Recent work confirms and extends these findings. When 6-, 8-, and 10-year-old children appraised the risk of injury for boys and girls in various activities, boys were rated as having a lower chance of injury than girls in the same activity. Children appear to develop the belief that girls are more fragile than boys, even though evidence shows boys experience more injuries than do girls (Morrongiello, Midgett, & Stanton, 2000). Consistent with an own-sex schema bias in memory, young children (3 to 6 years) and adults remember own-sex objects better than other-sex objects (Cherney & Ryalls, 1999). Age may moderate these effects. Younger, but not older, children recalled more information from stories containing gender-consistent activities than other stories (Conkright, Flannagan, & Dykes, 2000). Furthermore, GST posits that children should show illusory correlations: They should remember that schema-consistent information occurred more frequently than schema-

inconsistent or neutral information, even when each is presented an equal number of times. Illusory correlations have been demonstrated in second grade children, although their extent depends on how frequently information is presented (Susskind, 2003).

Gender Schemas and Behavior.   Central to GST is the idea that gender group membership organizes gender development. This idea is shared among several theoretical views, so it is discussed in the Integration of Perspectives section. Gender schema theory also assumes that superordinate schemas (i.e., stereotypes) organize and guide behavior, and this idea is similar to Kohlberg's notion that children self-socialize using the guidance of their stereotypes. Extensive summaries of the evidence regarding the cognitive underpinnings of gender development have been recently published (Martin et al., 2002), so only a brief discussion of both of these issues is presented in the Integration of Perspectives section.

The Role of Identification with a Social Category

Social categorization approaches emphasize gender identification occurring at a group level. Categorization represents the cognitive mechanism that segments, classifies, and orders the environment, and the resulting social groupings provide a system of orientation for self-reference (Tajfel & Turner, 1979). Social identities are socially meaningful categories that individuals consider descriptive of themselves or their group (Thoits & Virshup, 1997). In a recent review, Ashmore, Deaux, and McLaughlin-Volpe (2004) suggested that "collective identity" describes this sense of being a member of a group, and thus we have shifted our terminology from *social identity,* as used in our last *Handbook* chapter, to *collective identity.*

Considerable effort has been devoted to showing how identification with a particular social category (involving a comparison with other social categories) promotes a sense of belonging and connectedness but also may lead to stereotyping of out-group members and prejudice and intergroup conflict (Hewstone, Rubin, & Willis, 2002; Tajfel & Turner, 1979). Despite the importance of social category beliefs, we know little about how they develop over the elementary school years (Ruble et al., 2004). We examine three elements of collective identity particularly relevant to a developmental analysis of gender: (1) the *consequences* of a sense of "we," (2) the *mul-*

tidimensional nature of collective identity, and (3) the *contextual* influences on collective identity.

Consequences.   Collective identities serve several different purposes and have significant personal and interpersonal consequences (Brewer & Brown, 1998; Hewstone et al., 2002). Social identity theory (Tajfel & Turner, 1979) proposes that identification with a group and comparison across groups jointly serve individuals' striving for positive self-concept. Collective identity also affects individuals' desires to look and act in identity-consistent ways. The motivational consequences of social group membership take many forms. For example, group membership shapes personal values and interests, in turn influencing effort and performance. Individuals whose gender identity is central to their self-definitions may value tasks associated with their sex and devalue those associated with the other sex (e.g., Wigfield & Eccles, 2000). Experimental work demonstrates that simply labeling an ambiguous activity as associated with one sex affects performance (Martin & Dinella, 2002; C. F. Miller, Trautner, et al., 2006).

Social identity theory also explains behavior of high- and low-status members, and thus asymmetries in gender-typing of boys and girls. The high-status group would be expected to strive to maintain its advantage, consistent with findings that boys emphasize stereotypic differences more than do girls and are more rigidly gender-typed, as reported earlier. This is supported by an experimental study: When novel groups of unequal status were created, in-group biases developed only in members of high-status groups (Bigler et al., 2001).

Finally, the mere act of categorizing individuals into social groups changes the nature of interpersonal perceptions and behaviors (Tajfel, 1978), for example, increasing perception of between-group differences and within-group similarity and increasing in-group favoritism. Such changes occur even if the social categories are arbitrary, for example, wearing different colored shirts (Bigler et al., 1997). Does this mean that as early as 3 years of age, children exhibit gender prejudice? Recent analyses suggest that in-group favoritism does not necessarily imply out-group derogation or prejudice because much past research has confounded in-group positivity and out-group negativity (J. A. Cameron, Alvarez, Ruble, & Fuligni, 2001). Social categorization and in-group positivity are probably universal aspects of human social groups, but out-group

hostility requires social-structural and motivational conditions not inherent to collective identity formation (Brewer, 2001). For example, prejudice against women is more likely when they violate gender stereotypes or participate in male-dominated domains (Eagly & Mladinic, 1994). To illustrate, "girls' efforts to 'beat the boys' in areas where boys may be tacitly expected to do better, such as playground athletics, are likely to provoke resentment and active attempts at exclusion on the part of boys" (Lutz & Ruble, 1995, p. 144).

Gender is probably one of the earliest and most salient social categories available, so children's self-identification as members of the group of males or females is likely to affect substantially their self-concepts, preferences, and behaviors. An important issue concerns the emergence of this sense of "we boys" or "we girls" (Maccoby, 1998). Although gender labeling and identity begin before age 2 (see 1A), it seems unlikely that this initial understanding involves a sense of belonging to a group, or perceived similarity to other group members. By 2 to 3 years of age, however, children can sort pictures, including their own, according to gender category, suggesting the beginning of a sense of group identification. By 5 years, children spontaneously categorize people by gender (Bennett, Sani, Hopkins, Agostinie, & Mallucchi, 2000).

Subsequent to categorization, children should evaluate their own group positively and out-groups negatively. Research on gender-related group bias is consistent with this prediction, as reviewed earlier (6C). Whether preschoolers' in-group favoritism (e.g., liking and feeling more similar to same-sex others) directly reflects the emergence of collective identity is controversial, however, and this issue represents an important direction for future research.

Another area for research concerns the evaluations of individual boys and girls in relation to gender categories. Research with adults suggests that not all in-group members are evaluated positively: Individuals who deviate from in-group social category norms are evaluated more negatively than those who support the norms (Marques, Abrams, Paez, & Martinez-Taboada, 1998). Although it is clear that children show in-group biases from an early age, it is not clear when they adopt a discerning approach to interpersonal evaluation. At what point in development, for example, do children's evaluations depend on an individual's fit to group norms rather than just in-group/out-group membership? Research on developmental changes in children's inferences from categorical information (being male or female) versus typicality information (masculine or feminine interests) suggests that the latter does not affect judgments about individuals until age 8 or later (see Gender Schema section).

Multidimensional Nature. Contemporary analyses emphasize that the significance of group identity depends on more than simple self-labeling (e.g., Ashmore et al., 2004). Thus, gender identity should be conceptualized as multidimensional, including, for example, the centrality/importance of gender to self-concept, personal evaluation of one's gender, and feelings about oneself in relation to gender (i.e., typicality, contentedness, or felt pressure for gender conformity; Egan & Perry, 2001; Ruble et al., 2004). There is little work on the emergence of these components of identity, but gender appears to be central to young children relative to other social identities (Ruble et al., 2004; L. Taylor et al., 2006). Moreover, different components have different consequences for self-esteem and interpersonal relationships. For example, social-identity theorists emphasize the process of deriving self-esteem from identification with a valued group, but children also evaluate themselves on the basis of noticing how well their self-perceived gender-typing matches gender norms (e.g., Bussey & Bandura, 1999; Egan & Perry, 2001). Recent research suggests that certain combinations of different components of identity may create problems. Specifically, children who feel gender atypical but also feel pressure for gender conformity are particularly likely to have low self-esteem. Thus, focusing on the emergence and consequences of different components of gender identity represents a promising direction for future research.

Context.   There are several ways in which context influences collective identity related to gender. First, gender salience varies with context, for example, being the only child of a particular sex in a group (e.g., McGuire, McGuire, Child, & Fujioka, 1978). Second, when social categories are emphasized, such as when gender is used for classroom organization, children process information in terms of that category (Bigler, 1995). Experimental research on collective identity formation and consequences in middle elementary school children has been critical in understanding such processes (e.g., Bigler et al., 1997), suggesting three crucial environmental/group factors: (1) functional use

(e.g., having boys and girls line up separately to go out for recess), (2) perceptual salience (e.g., distinctive clothing and hair styles), and (3) the presence of group-to-attribute links (e.g., specific mention that boys' do X, or observation that this is the case).

Third, stereotypes are representations of social groups formed in a specific intergroup context rather than stored concepts waiting to be activated. This suggests that the exact nature of gender stereotypes depends on the specific comparison. Consistent with this view, children's descriptions of their gender in-group changed significantly with changes in frame of reference (whether they were first asked about an other-sex adult or an other-sex child; Sani & Bennett, 2001); for example, boys described boys as brave, big, and strong when the contrast was girls, but as talkative when the contrast was men (Sani, Bennett, Mullally, & MacPherson, 2003).

Finally, Maccoby (1998, 2002) has described a context-dependent collective gender identity process occurring in preschool, with gender-linked qualities constructed and maintained at the level of the group of "we girls" and "we boys" rather than at the level of the individual. For example, preschool children in the same classrooms show increasing divergence across the school year in the stories they tell and the fantasy play they enact, even though such gender differentiation may not be the same as general cultural stereotypes about boys and girls (Paley, 1984; Richner & Nicolopoulou, 2001). These observations raise a number of interesting questions. What is the connection between collective identity as a girl or boy versus gender-based group identity in school? Is there a gradual incorporation of culture-based gender identity norms into these group level norms, perhaps as children are shaped by peers perceived as gender "enforcers" or gender "police" (Martin & Fabes, 2001)? Do children who never attend preschool show less gender-typed behavior in later years? It is important to explore such questions and examine long-term consequences of group-based gender identity for individual level gender-typing.

Summary and Conclusions across the Three Cognitive Approaches

These three cognitive approaches have a number of commonalities, but differ in emphases. First, they hypothesize that gender cognitions act to organize and interpret information and they provide the standards that guide behavior, but they emphasize different cognitions. Kohlberg (1966) emphasized the importance of the stability and constancy of gender concepts, but newer formulations of CDT are similar to GST and category identification perspectives in emphasizing the significance for gender development of basic categorization as a girl or boy. Each theory also has unique perspectives. Social category perspectives focus on how individuals relate to social groups, CDT on the stability and consistency of gender understanding, and GST on the range of gender-related knowledge structures that influence gender development.

Second, central to these theories is the view that children actively seek out and construct rules about gender at an early age. Children are intrinsically motivated to build on their gender schemas and to develop gendered standards for their own behavior as they strive to understand the significance of their gender category. The active construction of gender is one of the most intriguing yet understudied aspects of cognitive theories. Cognitive theorists are interested in the processes of "gender construction" that allow for the gathering and organizing of both accurate and inaccurate information about the sexes. How do children derive faulty conclusions, distorted perceptions, inaccurate recall, and idiosyncratic norms about gender? Why are children quick to use a single sex-related pairing to develop a broad rule; for example, after seeing Mom drink coffee and Dad tea, deciding that "females drink coffee." How does this relate to other types of cognitive overgeneralization?

Third, these cognitive approaches focus on development—the relative waxing and waning of gender knowledge and its use and implications for behavior. Children move from awareness of categorical distinctions when they learn about gender (construction/information gathering) to rigid application of those distinctions during "consolidation" (Ruble, 1994) or "schema confirmation" (Welch-Ross & Schmidt, 1996) to later flexibility in applying gender knowledge (integration and schema deployment; Trautner et al., 2005). Are these phaselike shifts in the rigidity of gender knowledge parallel to other elements of gender development (e.g., Ruble, 1994)? How do changes in broad cognitive skills play a role in gender development (Bigler, 1995)?

Concerns have been raised about the overemphasis on cognitive factors in gender development. For instance, gender identity has been argued to not be central to gender development, even for same-sex modeling (Bussey & Bandura, 1999). The two main arguments against the

importance of cognitive factors reflect some misunderstandings. First, there is a widespread but erroneous assumption that cognitions must not affect gender development if they occur later than gendered behavior (e.g., Bandura & Bussey, 2004; A. Campbell et al., 2002). But cognitive theorists do not argue that this cannot occur and, instead, focus on the organizational and motivational function of gender concepts (see Martin, Ruble, & Szkrybalo, 2004). Moreover, as discussed earlier, recent evidence from infants and toddlers suggests early development of gender cognitions (e.g., Martin, et al., 2002). It is important to examine whether and how such early gender concepts influence the emergence of early gender-typed behaviors.

Second, it is often suggested that evidence fails to show associations between gender cognitions and behavior. This evidence has been extensively reviewed (Martin et al., 2002, 2004), so we only summarize it here. Most evidence focuses on two types of gender cognitions: (1) gender identity/labeling of the sexes and (2) gender stereotypes.

Concerning the evidence linking gender identity (group membership) and behavior, few studies have examined these types of relationships. Unfortunately, most studies have used gender labeling as a proxy for gender identity understanding, but it may not be equivalent. In these studies, using young children, gender labeling is related to preferences for same-sex peers and some behaviors but shows mixed relations with toy play (Fagot, 1985; Fagot, Leinbach, & Hagan, 1986; O'Brien & Huston, 1985; Weinraub et al., 1984). In older children, relations are found between gender labeling/membership, preferences, and stereotype knowledge (Martin & Little, 1990). Limited longitudinal data provide the clearest evidence. Children who engage in early gender labeling show increased gender-typed play in the toddler years relative to those who are later labelers (Fagot & Leinbach, 1989; Zosuls et al., 2006). Thus, the data support a link between gender labeling/identity and gender-related preferences and behavior, suggesting that this form of basic gender knowledge provides an organizational structure for further gender development.

Concerning links between gender stereotypes and behavior, both correlational and experimental studies provide relevant information about the role of cognitions. A number of studies have compared, at a global level, stereotype knowledge and behavior or preferences, but these do not provide a direct assessment of whether particular stereotypes influence behavioral choices. Only a few studies have examined direct links between children's gender stereotypes and behavior, and interpretations of findings from these studies are limited by a variety of methodological issues. Nonetheless, the studies that have used similar items for knowledge and preferences tend to find that the two are related (Aubry et al., 1999; C. F. Miller, Trautner, et al., 2006; Serbin et al., 1993). In older children and adolescents, there are links between stereotypes and interests, although the direction of causation is unclear (Liben & Bigler, 2002).

Experimental studies provide strong and consistent support for the organizational influence of gender stereotypes: Gender stereotypes influence children's behavior, motivation and interests, and memory for information (for review see Martin & Dinella, 2002; Martin et al., 2002). In these studies, children are shown novel toys given gender-typed labels ("boys like the things in this box better than girls do"), and then their behavior, and/or memory is assessed (e.g., Bradbard, Martin, Endsley, & Halverson, 1986). Consistency in findings is striking across studies—from different laboratories, using obvious and subtle labels (e.g., Davies, 1989), with children of many ages, and using ploys to reduce demand characteristics: When toys are stereotyped, either with overt or covert gender cues, children respond according to whether the toy is perceived to be appropriate or inappropriate for their own sex (Martin et al., 2002).

In sum, these three cognitive perspectives focus on the role of gender-related cognitions in organizing and motivating gender development, influencing what children attend to and remember, how they make social judgments, and how they behave. A large body of evidence supports these ideas, including studies of gender identity, stability, and the importance of gender categories in directing and organizing processing, affect, and behavior.

An Integration of Perspectives

The three broad approaches to the understanding of gender-typing—biological, socialization, and cognitive—generally focus on specific topics and concerns unique to each approach. Biological researchers have directed attention to the pathway from sex hormones to brain structure and function to gender-related preferences and behaviors and have not considered effects of gendered environments on brain structure or hormone levels, or of biological influences on gender-related concepts or beliefs. Social developmentalists have focused on two issues that differentiate cognitive and social-learning approaches. The first issue concerns the temporal sequencing of gender awareness and gender-typing: Do children learn the consequences of behavior and then use patterns of rewards to derive gender identity, or does the formation of gender identity and understanding of gender category drive gender-typing? The second issue is less well defined but underlies the philosophical foundation of the theories. It concerns the factors that determine self-concept: Is it reinforcement history or desire to adhere to a gendered cognitive structure? Because of this intense focus on a few issues, other interesting aspects of each theory have been relatively neglected, and the developmental focus has been primarily on the preschool years.

To understand gender-typing, we need to listen to messages from separate perspectives and to devise ways to integrate the three approaches in meaningful ways. Huston's (1983) plea for biological and social psychologically oriented researchers to combine their efforts is beginning to be realized in conversation, if not yet in data. Research findings are accumulating about the wide range of influences on particular gendered behaviors, suggesting several promising avenues for future research using multiple approaches.

Lessons can be learned from nonhuman primates. Behavioral sex differences in monkeys result from hormonally influenced predispositions to engage in certain behaviors, but the ultimate expression is shaped by the social environment in which the animal develops (Wallen, 1996). For example, sex differences in rough-and-tumble play occur in all rearing environments, with the *size* of the difference affected by the environment, whereas differences in aggressive and submissive behaviors are found only in certain rearing situations. Behaviors that show consistent sex differences across social context are most affected by prenatal androgens. Existing evidence in human children is consistent with this: Prenatal androgens have the largest effect on activities and interests, which also show large sex differences across cultures. It is important to study context in hormonally informative samples; for example, are differences in aggression between girls with and without CAH apparent primarily when aggression is spontaneous and not when it is provoked?

Children come into this world with certain predispositions that are manifested and exaggerated or suppressed by the environment in which they are reared, and those with sex-atypical predispositions provide a unique opportunity to examine this developmental process with respect to gender-related behavior. Hypotheses derived from cognitive/schema and socialization theories can be tested in girls with CAH or typical girls with high levels of prenatal testosterone. Doing so makes clear that biology is a process, unfolding across development, manifested through and moderated by the social environment, thereby challenging researchers to develop hypotheses about the *ways* in which biological factors affect behavior.

Consider some outstanding questions about gender development that can be informed by such studies. What is the role of gender identity and awareness in gender-typing—how do girls with CAH develop female gender identity but interest in boys' toys? How does socialization occur—do girls with CAH model others on the basis of their female-typical gender identity or their male-typical interests? What is the basis of sex-segregation—do girls with CAH play with girls who share their identity, boys who share their interests, or children who share their play style or strategy for influencing others (which have not yet been studied in CAH)? Does the effectiveness of the environment vary with biology—do girls with CAH benefit from practice in spatial ability more than typical girls do?

The key questions about gender development—for example, how do gender identity and gendered behaviors develop and how does gender socialization operate—require creative thinking across disciplinary boundaries and perspectives. Answers require a willingness to suspend narrow conceptualizations of gender and old biases. Using multidisciplinary teams, multiple perspectives, and broader conceptualizations of underlying mechanisms and processes should enable significant strides in understanding the complexities of gender differentiation.

CONCLUSIONS AND FUTURE DIRECTIONS

One of the difficulties in compiling research on gender is that it cuts across areas and is relevant to virtually every topic, ranging from brain sex differences to children's identification with gender in all of its complexities. Controversies frequently arise that do not occur with regularity in many other areas, such as the questioning of the research enterprise itself, confusion about

terms for major constructs, and the political implications of the findings. Despite, or perhaps because of the controversies, the study of gender attracts scientists from many disciplines, each bringing to the enterprise different interests and strategies. The pluralism of views provides many insights into the diverse issues covered in gender studies.

Several broad themes are apparent from the literature that we reviewed for this chapter. First, interest in all sorts of biological factors has marked the literature of the past 10 years. In accord with this interest are suggestions that biological factors may play a more prominent role in behavior, thinking, and gender identity than has been previously considered. Thus, this section of the chapter received a major revision in the present edition. Second, social and cognitive theories have moved more closely together but continue to disagree about some issues, and these theoretical debates drive a surprising amount of gender-typing research. In the present revision, we expanded discussion of identification with social groups as important theoretical processes to consider in future research. Third, developmental researchers have taken Huston's (1983) admonitions to heart: They have included multiple components of gender-typing in studies, are less prone to infer broadly about gender-typing from one measure, and recognize the distinctions among various content domains and constructs. Fourth, new methods have played an important role in the research that has been undertaken in the past 10 years. For instance, sophisticated testing procedures have allowed researchers to begin to understand what infants and young children know about gender.

Many new and intriguing ideas are emerging in the field that may spark interest and lead researchers to think about gender in novel and interesting ways. There is renewed interest in process and change in gender development. Social learning theorists have concentrated efforts on cognitive mechanisms underlying observational learning (Bussey & Bandura, 1999). Cognitive theorists have considered how shifts from early gender concepts to more consolidated ones influence information processing and memory (Martin et al., 2002; Ruble, 1994). There is increasing interest in the changing nature of gendered personal identities and stereotypes in context (e.g., Sani & Bennett, 2001). Gender researchers should explore in even more depth the issues of context and variability, given their importance in development. Biological perspectives also encourage the study of change because predispositions are manifested and moderated by the organism's transactions with the environment.

The idea that gender is constructed in a social context has many interesting possibilities for future research. The idea of the social construction of gender has generally meant that we must investigate how we see others in gendered ways, using gender cues. But it also suggests that we need to examine how individuals construct their own multifaceted gender cues and how they believe these cues work in social interactions. For instance, do individuals strive for balance in their gender cues to present a particular image? Does a woman who is assertive and dominant choose to dress in a feminine way to offset perceptions of masculinity? Appearance, clothing, adornment, mannerisms all become more important to study, given that they are visible cues that are often used to read and construct gender.

Questions about mental health and self-esteem also require more research efforts. In the 1970s, mental health was thought to be associated with androgyny. Recent research has provided alternative views and suggested that different elements of gender identity relate differentially to personal and interpersonal adjustment (e.g., Egan & Perry, 2001). For example, adjustment variables were found to be positively associated with self-perceptions of gender typicality and contentedness, but negatively associated with felt pressure for gender conformity in fourth to eighth graders (Carver et al., 2003; Egan & Perry, 2001). These associations remained after controlling for children's perceptions of self-efficacy for gender-typed activities, implying that gender identity has implications for adjustment beyond gender-linked competencies. Such research represents promising new directions, taking seriously the idea of the multidimensionality of gender. Which particular domains of gender influence positive self-regard? Why are preadolescent girls more likely to show declines in self-esteem than boys? Which factors related to gender may be risk versus buffering factors?

Gender in relationships is an idea that promotes many new and interesting views. Peers' contributions to socialization have been at the forefront of recent research because sex segregation probably provides the impetus for many sex differences seen in adults (Maccoby, 1998, 2002). The role of parents in socialization continues to be of interest, but perhaps with some different emphases on subtle forms of socialization. Research suggests that children with rigid cross-gender roles may be more likely than others to show later maladjustment. Does this mean that parents should not encourage cross-gender interests for fear of inducing psychological problems in their children? We also know surprisingly little about the effects of androgynous interests.

A final comment about current directions in the field: Despite the number of exciting new directions and increased interest in certain age periods, such as infancy, it was surprising to note the relative dearth of research on adolescents and adolescent transitions. This is puzzling, given the significance of changes during adolescence for gender development (e.g., acceptance of one's male or female body and reproductive functions, forming a sexual orientation, establishing new forms of relationships with same-sex and other-sex peers, and decisions regarding future gender roles). Although many researchers have been intrigued by notions of gender intensification during this developmental phase, empirical research, including measures suitable for research with adolescents, has been relatively rare. A few recent studies examining gender subgroups and crowd types (e.g., druggies, brains) suggests that future theorizing about gender development would benefit from greater attention to adolescence (Eccles & Barber, 1999; Eckes, Trautner, & Behrendt, 2005).

In conclusion, the study of gender is a monumental undertaking, shared by individuals from many fields. Constantinople (1979) used the metaphor about four blind men studying an elephant to describe how gender researchers have focused on individual parts of the elephant, with each one assuming that the animal was best described by the part they were studying. No one recognized the whole animal. Gender researchers must continue to be careful about building global concepts based on partial information. However, we now have some sense of the size of the animal, its capacities, and its general framework. The picture is far from complete but the process of identification has certainly continued to be intriguing.

REFERENCES

Albers, S. M. (1998). The effect of gender-typed clothing on children's social judgments. *Child Study Journal, 28,* 137–159.

Albert, A. A., & Porter, J. R. (1988). Children's gender-role stereotypes: A sociological investigation of psychological models. *Sociological Forum, 3*(2), 184–210.

Alexander, G. M. (2003). An evolutionary perspective of sex-typed toy preferences: Pink, blue, and the brain. *Archives of Sexual Behavior, 32,* 7–14.

Alexander, G. M., & Hines, M. (2002). Sex differences in response to children's toys in nonhuman primates (*Cercopithecus aethiops sabaeus*). *Evolution and Human Behavior, 23,* 467–479.

Alfieri, T. J., Ruble, D. N., & Higgins, E. T. (1996). Gender stereotypes during adolescence: Developmental changes and the transition to Junior High School. *Developmental Psychology, 32,* 1129–1137.

Altermatt, E. R., Jovanovic, J., & Perry, M. (1998). Bias or responsivity? Sex and achievement-level effects on teachers' classroom questioning practices. *Journal of Educational Psychology, 90*(3), 516–527.

Anderson, D. R., Huston, A. C., Schmitt, K. L., Linebarger, D. L., & Wright, J. C. (2001). Early childhood television viewing and adolescent behavior: The recontact study. *Monographs of the Society for Research in Child Development, 66,* 1–147.

Andersen, E. S. (1996). A cross-cultural study of children's register knowledge. In D. I. Slobin, J. Gerhardt, A. Kyratzis, & J. Guo (Eds.), *Social interaction, social context, and language: Essays in honor of Susan Ervin-Tripp* (pp. 125–142). Hillsdale, NJ: Erlbaum.

Angold, A., Costello, E. J., Erkanli, A., & Worthman, C. M. (1999). Pubertal changes in hormone levels and depression in girls. *Psychological Medicine, 29,* 1043–1053.

Angold, A., Costello, E. J., & Worthman, C. M. (1998). Puberty and depression: The roles of age, pubertal status and pubertal timing. *Psychological Medicine, 28,* 51–61.

Antill, J. K., Cotton, S., Russell, G., & Goodnow, J. J. (1996). Measures of children's sex-typing in middle childhood, II. *Australian Journal of Psychology, 48*(1), 35–44.

Antill, J. K., Russell, G., Goodnow, J. J., & Cotton, S. (1993). Measures of children's sex typing in middle childhood. *Australian Journal of Psychology, 45*(1), 25–33.

Ashmore, R. D., Deaux, K., & McLaughlin-Volpe, T. (2004). An organizing framework for collective identity: Articulation and significance of multidimensionality. *Psychological Bulletin, 130,* 80–114.

Aube, J., Norcliffe, H., & Koestner, R. (1995). Physical characteristics and the multifactorial approach to the study of gender characteristics. *Social Behavior and Personality, 23*(1), 69–82.

Aubry, S., Ruble, D. N., & Silverman, L. B. (1999). The role of gender knowledge in children's gender-typed preferences. In L. Balter & C. S. Tamis-LeMonda (Eds.), *Child psychology: A handbook of contemporary issues* (pp. 363–390). New York: Psychology Press.

Bailey, B. A., & Nihlen, A. S. (1990). Effect of experience with nontraditional workers on psychological and social dimensions of occupational sex-role stereotyping by elementary school children. *Psychological Reports, 66,* 1273–1282.

Bailey, J. M., Bechtold, K. T., & Berenbaum, S. A. (2002). Who are tomboys and why should we study them? *Archives of Sexual Behavior, 31,* 333–341.

Bailey, J. M., & Zucker, K. J. (1995). Childhood sex-typed behavior and sexual orientation: A conceptual and quantitative review. *Developmental Psychology, 31,* 43–55.

Bandura, A. (1986). *Social foundations of thought and action: A social cognitive theory.* Englewood Cliffs, NJ: Prentice-Hall.

Bandura, A., & Bussey, K. (2004). On broadening the cognitive, motivational, and sociocultural scope of theorizing about gender development and functioning: Comment on Martin, Ruble, and Szkrybalo (2002). *Psychological Bulletin, 130*(5), 691–701.

Barbera, E. (2003). Gender schemas: Configuration and activation processes. *Canadian Journal of Behavioural Science, 35*(3), 176–184.

Barbu, S., Le-Maner-Idrissi, G., & Jouanjean, A. (2000). The emergence of gender segregation: Towards an integrative perspective. *Current Psychology Letters: Behavior, Brain, and Cognition, 3,* 7–18.

Bartlett, N. H., Vasey, P. L., & Bukowski, W. M. (2000). Is gender identity disorder in children a mental disorder? *Sex Roles, 43,* 753–785.

Bartlett, N. H., Vasey, P. L., & Bukowski, W. M. (2003). Cross-sex wishes and gender identity disorder in children: A reply to Zucker, 2002. *Sex Roles, 49,* 191–192.

Bauer, P. J., & Coyne, M. J. (1997). When the name says it all: Preschoolers' recognition and use of the gendered nature of common proper names. *Social Development, 6,* 271–291.

Bauer, P. J., Liebl, M., & Stennes, L. (1998). Pretty is to dress as brave is to suitcoat: Gender-based property-to-property inferences by $4^{1}/_{2}$-year-old children. *Merrill-Palmer Quarterly, 44,* 355–377.

Baumeister, R. F. (2000). Gender differences in erotic plasticity: The female sex drive as social flexible and responsive. *Psychological Bulletin, 126,* 247–374.

Becker, J. B., Breedlove, S. M., Crews, D., & McCarthy, M. M. (Eds.). (2002). *Behavioral endocrinology* (2nd ed.). Cambridge, MA: MIT Press.

Bem, D. J. (1996). Exotic becomes erotic: A developmental theory of sexual orientation. *Psychological Review, 103*(2), 320–335.

Bem, D. J. (2000). Exotic becomes erotic: Interpreting the biological correlates of sexual orientation. *Archives of Sexual Behavior, 29,* 531–548.

Bem, S. L. (1981). Gender schema theory: A cognitive account of sex typing. *Psychological Review, 88,* 354–364.

Bem, S. L. (1989). Genital knowledge and gender constancy in preschool children. *Child Development, 60,* 649–662.

Bem, S. L. (1993). *The lenses of gender: Transforming the debate on sexual inequality.* New Haven, CT: Yale University Press.

Benenson, J. F., Apostoleris, N., & Parnass, J. (1997). Age and sex differences in dyadic and group interaction. *Developmental Psychology, 33,* 538–543.

Benenson, J. F., & Christakos, A. (2003). The greater fragility of females' versus males' closest same-sex friendships. *Child Development, 74,* 1123–1129.

Benenson, J. F., Gordon, A. J., & Roy, R. (2000). Children's evaluative appraisals of competition in tetrads versus dyads. *Small Group Research, 31,* 635–652.

Benenson, J. F., Meaiese, R., Dolenszky, E., Dolensky, N., Sinclair, N., & Simpson, A. (2002). Group size regulates self-assertive versus self-deprecating responses to interpersonal competition. *Child Development, 73,* 1818–1829.

Benenson, J. F., Morash, D., & Petrakos, H. (1998). Gender differences in emotional closeness between preschool children and their mothers. *Sex Roles, 38,* 975–985.

Benenson, J. F., Nicholson, C., Waite, A., Roy, R., & Simpson, A. (2001). The influence of group size on children's competitive behavior. *Child Development, 72,* 921–928.

Bennett, M., Sani, F., Hopkins, N., Agostini, L., & Mallucchi, L. (2000). Children's gender categorization: An investigation of automatic processing. *British Journal of Developmental Psychology, 18,* 97–102.

Berenbaum, S. A. (1999). Effects of early androgens on sex-typed activities and interests in adolescents with congenital adrenal hyperplasia. *Hormones and Behavior, 35,* 102–110.

Berenbaum, S. A. (2001). Cognitive function in congenital adrenal hyperplasia. *Endocrinology and Metabolism Clinics of North America, 30,* 173–192.

Berenbaum, S. A. (2004). Androgen and behavior: Implications for the treatment of children with disorders of sexual differentiation. In O. H. Pescovitz & E. A. Eugster (Eds.), *Pediatric endocrinology: Mechanisms, manifestations, and management* (pp. 275–284). Philadelphia: Lippincott, Williams, & Wilkins.

Berenbaum, S. A., & Bailey, J. M. (2003). Effects on gender identity of prenatal androgens and genital appearance: Evidence from girls with congenital adrenal hyperplasia. *Journal of Clinical Endocrinology and Metabolism, 88,* 1102–1106.

Berenbaum, S. A., Duck, S. C., & Bryk, K. (2000). Behavioral effects of prenatal versus postnatal androgen excess in children with 21-hydroxylase-deficient congenital adrenal hyperplasia. *Journal of Clinical Endocrinology and Metabolism, 85*(2), 727–733.

Berenbaum, S. A., Moffat, S., Wisniewski, A. B., & Resnick, S. M. (2003). Neuroendocrinology: Cognitive effects of sex hormones. In M. de Haan & M. H. Johnson (Eds.), *The cognitive neuroscience of development* (pp. 207–235). New York: Psychology Press.

Berenbaum, S. A., & Resnick, S. M. (1997). Early androgen effects on aggression in children and adults with congenital adrenal hyperplasia. *Psychoneuroendocrinology, 22,* 505–515.

Berenbaum, S. A., & Snyder, E. (1995). Early hormonal influences on childhood sex-typed activity and playmate preferences: Implications for the development of sexual orientation. *Developmental Psychology, 31,* 31–42.

Bernhardt, P. C., Dabbs, J. M., Fielden, J. A., & Lutter, C. D. (1998). Testosterone changes during vicarious experiences of winning and losing among fans at sporting events. *Physiology and Behavior, 65,* 59–62.

Best, D. L., Williams, J. E., Cloud, J. M., Davis, S. W., Robertson, L. S., Edwards, J. R., et al. (1977). The development of sex-trait stereotypes. *Child Development, 48,* 1375–1384.

Bettencourt, B. A., & Kernahan, C. (1997). A meta-analysis of aggression in the presence of violent cues: Effects of gender differences and aversive provocation. *Aggressive Behavior, 23,* 447–456.

Bettencourt, B. A., & Miller, N. (1996). Gender differences in aggression as a function of provocation: A meta-analysis. *Psychological Bulletin, 119,* 422–447.

Bigler, R. S. (1995). The role of classification skill in moderating environmental effects on children's gender stereotyping: A study of the functional use of gender in the classroom. *Child Development, 66,* 1072–1087.

Bigler, R. S. (1999). Psychological interventions designed to counter sexism in children: Empirical limitations and theoretical foundations. In W. G. Swann, J. H. Langlois, & L. A. Gilbert (Eds.), *Sexism and stereotypes in modern society.* Washington, DC: American Psychological Association.

Bigler, R. S., Brown, C. S., & Markell, M. (2001). When groups are not created equal: Effects of group status on the formation of intergroup attitudes in children. *Child Development, 72*(4), 1151–1162.

Bigler, R. S., Jones, L. C., & Lobliner, D. B. (1997). Social categorization and the formation of intergroup attitudes in children. *Child Development, 68,* 530–543.

Bishop, K. M., & Wahlsten, D. (1997). Sex differences in the human corpus callosum: Myth or reality? *Neuroscience and Biobehavioral Reviews, 21,* 581–601.

Blair, S. L. (1992). The sex-typing of children's household labor: Parental influences on daughters' and sons' housework. *Youth and Society, 24*(2), 178–203.

Blakemore, J. E. O. (2003). Children's beliefs about violating gender norms: Boys shouldn't look like girls and girls shouldn't act like boys. *Sex Roles, 48*(9/10), 411–419.

Blakemore, J. E. O., Berenbaum, S. A., & Liben, L. S. (2006). *Gender development.* Book in preparation, Mahwah, NJ: Erlbaum.

Blanchard, R. (1989). The classification and labeling of nonhomosexual gender dysphorias. *Archives of Sexual Behavior, 18,* 315–334.

Blatchford, P., Baines, E., & Pellegrini, A. (2003). The social context of school playground games: Sex and ethnic differences and changes over time after entry to junior high. *British Journal of Developmental Psychology, 21,* 481–505.

Book, A. S., Starzyk, K. B., & Quinsey, V. L. (2001). The relationship between testosterone and aggression: A meta-analysis. *Aggression and Violent Behavior, 6,* 579–599.

Booth, A., Shelley, G., Mazur, A., Tharp, G., & Kittok, R. (1989). Testosterone, and winning and losing in human competition. *Hormones and Behavior, 23,* 556–571.

Borg, M. G. (1998). Secondary school teachers' perception of pupils' undesirable behaviours. *British Journal of Educational Psychology, 68,* 67–79.

Bornstein, M. H., Hahn, C. S., & Haynes, O. M. (2004). Specific and general language performance across early childhood: Stability and gender considerations. *First Language, 24,* 267–304.

Boyatzis, C., & Eades, J. (1999). Gender differences in preschoolers' and kindergartners' artistic production and preference. *Sex Roles, 41,* 627–638.

Boyatzis, C., Mallis, M., & Leon, I. (1999). Effects of game type on children's gender-based peer preferences: A naturalistic observational study. *Sex Roles, 40*(1/2), 93–105.

Boyatzis, C. J., & Albertini, G. (2000). A naturalistic observation of children drawing: peer collaboration processes and influences in children's art. In C. Boyatzis & M. Watson (Eds.), *New directions for child and adolescent development* (Vol. No. 90, pp. 31–48). San Francisco: Jossey-Bass.

Bradbard, M. R., Martin, C. L., Endsley, R. C., & Halverson, C. F. (1986). Influence of sex stereotypes on children's exploration and memory: A competence versus performance distinction. *Developmental Psychology, 22*(4), 481–486.

Bradley, S. J., Oliver, G. D., Chernick, A. B., & Zucker, K. J. (1998). Experiment of nurture: Ablatio penis at 2 months, sex reassignment at 7 months, and a psychosexual follow-up in young adulthood. *Pediatrics, 102,* 1–5.

Brewer, M. B. (2001). Ingroup identification and intergroup conflict: When does ingroup love become outgroup hate. In R. D. Ashmore, L. Jussim, & D. Wilder (Eds.), *Social identity, intergroup conflict, and conflict reduction* (pp. 2–41). New York: Oxford University Press.

Brewer, M. B., & Brown, R. J. (1998). Intergroup relations. In D. T. Gilbert, S. T. Fiske, & G. Lindzey (Eds.), *The handbook of social psychology* (Vol. 2, 4th ed., pp. 554–594). New York: McGraw-Hill.

Broderick, P. C., & Korteland, C. (2002). Coping style and depression in early adolescence: Relationships to gender, gender role, and implicit beliefs. *Sex Roles, 46*(7/8), 201–213.

Bronfenbrenner, U. (1977). Toward an experimental ecology of human development. *American Psychologist, 32,* 513–531.

Brooks-Gunn, J., Petersen, A. C., & Compas, B. E. (1995). Physiological processes and the development of childhood and adolescent depression. In I. M. Goodyear (Ed.), *The depressed child and adolescent: Developmental and clinical perspectives* (pp. 91–109). New York: Cambridge University Press.

Brooks-Gunn, J., & Warren, M. P. (1989). Biological and social contributions to negative affect in young adolescent girls. *Child Development, 60,* 40–55.

Brown, C. S., & Bigler, R. S. (in press). Children's perceptions of gender discrimination. *Developmental Psychology.*

Bryden, M. P., McManus, I. C., & Bulman-Fleming, M. B. (1994). Evaluating the empirical support for the Geschwind-Behan-Galaburda model of cerebral lateralization. *Brain and Cognition, 26,* 103–167.

Buchanan, C. M., Eccles, J. S., & Becker, J. B. (1992). Are adolescents the victims of raging hormones: Evidence for activational effects of hormones on moods and behavior at adolescence. *Psychological Bulletin, 111,* 62–107.

Buhrmester, D. (1996). Need fulfillment, interpersonal competence and the developmental contexts of early adolescent friendship. In W. M. Bukowski, A. F. Newcomb, & W. W. Hartup (Eds.), *The company they keep: Friendship in childhood and adolescence* (pp. 158–185). New York: Cambridge University Press.

Bukowski, W. M., Sippola, L. K., & Hoza, B. (1999). Same and other: Interdependency between participation in same- and other-sex friendships. *Journal of Youth and Adolescence, 28*(4), 439–459.

Buss, D. M. (2000). Desires in human mating. *Annals of the New York Academy of Sciences, 907,* 39–49.

Bussey, K., & Bandura, A. (1992). Self-regulatory mechanisms governing gender development. *Child Development, 63,* 1236–1250.

Bussey, K., & Bandura, A. (1999). Social cognitive theory of gender development and differentiation. *Psychological Review, 106,* 676–713.

Bussey, K., & Perry, D. G. (1982). Same-sex imitation: The avoidance of cross-sex models or the acceptance of same-sex models? *Sex Roles, 8,* 773–785.

Byely, L., Archibald, A. B., Graber, J., & Brooks-Gunn, J. (2000). A prospective study of familial and social influences on girls' body image and dieting. *International Journal of Eating Disorders, 28,* 155–164.

Byrne, B. M., & Gavin, D. A. W. (1996). The Shavelson model revisited: Testing for structure of academic self-concept across pre-, early, and late adolescence. *Journal of Educational Psychology, 88,* 215–228.

Byrnes, J. P., Miller, D. C., & Schafer, W. D. (1999). Gender differences in risk taking: A meta-analysis. *Psychological Bulletin, 1999,* 367–383.

Caldera, Y. M., McDonald-Culp, A., O'Brien, M., Truglio, R., Alvarez, M., & Huston, A. C. (1999). Children's play preferences, construction play with blocks, and visual-spatial skills: Are they related? *International Journal of Behavioral Development, 23,* 855–872.

Caldera, Y. M., & Sciaraffa, M. A. (1998). Parent-toddler play with feminine toys: Are all dolls the same? *Sex Roles, 39,* 657–668.

Cameron, J. A., Alvarez, J. M., Ruble, D. N., & Fuligni, A. J. (2001). Children's lay theories about ingroups and outgroups: Reconceptualizing research on "prejudice." *Personality and Social Psychology Review, 5,* 118–128.

Cameron, J. L. (2004). Interrelationships between hormones, behavior, and affect during adolescence: Understanding hormonal, physical, and brain changes occurring in association with pubertal activation of the reproductive axis—Introduction to Part III. *Annals of the New York Academy of Sciences, 1021,* 110–123.

Campbell, A., Shirley, L., & Candy, J. (2004). A longitudinal study of gender-related cognition and behaviour. *Developmental Science, 7,* 1–9.

Campbell, A., Shirley, L., & Caygill, L. (2002). Sex-typed preferences in three domains: Do 2-year-olds need cognitive variables? *British Journal of Psychology, 50,* 590–593.

Campbell, A., Shirley, L., Heywood, C., & Crook, C. (2000). Infants' visual preference for sex-congruent babies, children, toys and activities: A longitudinal study. *British Journal of Developmental Psychology, 18,* 479–498.

Campbell, D. W., & Eaton, W. O. (1999). Sex differences in the activity level of infants. *Infant and Child Development, 8,* 1–17.

Carlo, G., Eisenberg, N., Koller, S., DaSilva, M. S., & Frohlich, C. B. (1996). A cross-national study on the relations among prosocial moral reasoning, gender role orientations, and prosocial behaviors. *Developmental Psychology, 32,* 231–240.

Carlson-Jones, D. (2001). Social comparison and body image: Attractiveness comparisons to models and peers among adolescent girls and boys. *Sex Roles, 45,* 645–664.

Carlson-Jones, D. (2004). Body image among adolescent girls and boys: A longitudinal study. *Developmental Psychology, 40,* 823–835.

Carter, D. B., & McCloskey, L. A. (1984). Peers and the maintenance of sex-typed behavior: The development of children's conceptions of cross-gender behavior in their peers. *Social Cognition, 2,* 294–314.

Carver, P. R., Egan, S. K., & Perry, D. G. (2004). Children who question their heterosexuality. *Developmental Psychology, 40,* 43–53.

Carver, P. R., Yunger, J. L., & Perry, D. G. (2003). Gender identity and adjustment in middle childhood. *Sex Roles, 49,* 95–109.

Caspi, A., Lynam, D., Moffitt, T. E., & Silva, P. A. (1993). Unraveling girls' delinquency: Biological, dispositional, and contextual contributions to adolescent misbehavior. *Developmental Psychology, 29,* 19–30.

Cherney, I. D., & Ryalls, B. O. (1999). Gender-linked differences in the incidental memory of children and adults. *Journal of Experimental Child Psychology, 72*(4), 305–328.

Cohen, J. (1988). *Statistical power analysis for the behavioral sciences* (2nd ed.). New York: Academic Press.

Cohen-Bendahan, C. C., van de Beek, C., & Berenbaum, S. A. (2005). Prenatal sex hormone effects on child and adult sex-typed behavior: Methods and findings. *Neuroscience and Biobehavioral Reviews, 29,* 353–384.

Cohen-Kettenis, P. T., Owen, A., Kaijser, V. G., Bradley, S. J., & Zucker, K. J. (2003). Demographic characteristics, social competence, and behavior problems in children with gender identity disorder: A cross-national, cross-clinic comparative analysis. *Journal of Abnormal Child Psychology, 31,* 41–53.

Colapinto, J. (2000). *As nature made him: The boy who was raised as a girl.* New York: HarperCollins.

Cole, D. A., Maxwell, S. E., Martin, J. M., Peeke, L. G., Seroczynski, A. D., Tram, J. M., et al. (2001). The development of multiple domains of child and adolescent self-concept: A cohort sequential longitudinal design. *Child Development, 72*(6), 1723–1746.

Coles, M., & Hall, C. (2002). Gendered readings: Learning from children's reading choices. *Journal of Research on Reading, 25*(1), 96–108.

Coltrane, S., & Messineo, M. (2000). The perpetuation of subtle prejudice: Race and gender imagery in 1990s television advertising. *Sex Roles, 42*(5/6), 363–389.

Conkright, L., Flannagan, D., & Dykes, J. (2000). Effects of pronoun type and gender role consistency on children's recall and interpretation of stories. *Sex Roles, 43*(7/8), 481–497.

Connolly, J., Craig, W., Goldberg, A., & Pepler, D. (1999). Conceptions of cross-sex friendships and romantic relationships in early adolescence. *Journal of Youth and Adolescence, 28,* 481–494.

Connolly, J., Furman, W., & Konarski, R. (2000). The role of peers in the emergence of heterosexual romantic relationships in adolescence. *Child Development, 71*(5), 1395–1408.

Constantinople, A. (1979). Sex-role acquisition. In search of the elephant. *Sex Roles, 5,* 121–132.

Conti, R., Collins, M. A., & Picariello, M. L. (2001). The impact of competition on intrinsic motivation and creativity: Considering gender, gender segregation, and gender role orientation. *Personality and Individual Differences, 31,* 1273–1289.

Corby, B. C., Hodges, E. V. E., & Perry, D. G. (in press). Gender identity and adjustment in Black, Hispanic, and White preadolescents. *Developmental Psychology.*

Crouter, A. C., Manke, B. A., & McHale, S. M. (1995). The family context of gender intensification in early adolescence. *Child Development, 66,* 317–329.

Crowley, K., Callanan, M. A., Tenenbaum, H. R., & Allen, E. (2001). Parents explain more often to boys than to girls during shared scientific thinking. *Psychological Science, 12,* 258–261.

Davatzikos, C., & Resnick, S. M. (1998). Sex differences in anatomic measures of interhemispheric connectivity: Correlations with cognition in women but not men. *Cerebral Cortex, 8*(7), 635–640.

Davies, D. R. (1989). The effects of gender-typed labels on children's performance. *Current Psychology: Research and Reviews, 8*(4), 267–272.

Davison, K. K., Markey, C. N., & Birch, L. L. (2002). A longitudinal examination of patterns in girls' weight concerns and body dissatisfaction from age 5 to 9 years. *International Journal of Eating Disorders, 33,* 320–332.

Davison, K. K., & Susman, E. J. (2001). Are hormone levels and cognitive ability related during early adolescence? *International Journal of Behavioral Development, 25,* 416–428.

Dawson, T. L. (2002). New tools, new insights: Kohlberg's moral judgment stages revisited. *International Journal of Behavioral Development, 26,* 154–166.

Deaux, K. (1993). Commentary: Sorry, wrong number—A reply to Gentile's call (Special Section: Sex or gender?). *Psychological Science, 4*(2), 125–126.

De Bellis, M. D., Keshavan, M. S., Beers, S. R., Hall, J., Frustaci, K., Masalehdan, A., et al. (2001). Sex differences in brain maturation during childhood and adolescence. *Cerebral Cortex, 11,* 552–557.

de Lacoste-Utamsing, C., & Holloway, R. L. (1982). Sexual dimorphism in the corpus callosum. *Science, 216,* 1431–1432.

De Lisi, R., & Gallagher, A. M. (1991). Understanding of gender stability and constancy in Argentinean children. *Merrill-Palmer Quarterly, 37,* 483–502.

Dempsey, D., Hillier, L., & Harrison, L. (2001). Gendered explorations among same-sex attracted young people in Australia. *Journal of Adolescence, 24,* 67–81.

De Vries, G. J., Rissman, E. F., Simerly, R. B., Yang, L. Y., Scordalakes, E. M., Auger, C. J., et al. (2002). A model system for study of sex chromosome effects on sexually dimorphic neural and behavioral traits. *Journal of Neuroscience, 22,* 9005–9014.

Diamond, L. M. (1998). Development of sexual orientation among adolescent and young adult women. *Developmental Psychology, 34,* 241–250.

Diamond, L. M. (2000). Sexual identity attractions, and behavior among young sexual-minority women over a 2-year period. *Developmental Psychology, 36,* 241–250.

Diamond, L. M. (2003a). New paradigms for research on sexual-minority and heterosexual youth. *Journal of Clinical Child and Adolescent Psychology, 32,* 490–498.

Diamond, L. M. (2003b). What does sexual orientation orient? A biobehavioral model distinguishing romantic love and sexual desire. *Psychological Review, 110*(1), 173–192.

Diamond, L. M., & Dube, E. M. (2002). Friendship and attachment among heterosexual and sexual-minority youths: Does the gender of your friend matter? *Journal of Youth and Adolescence, 31*(2), 155–166.

Diamond, M., & Sigmundson, H. K. (1997). Sex reassignment at birth: Long-term review and clinical implications. *Archives of Pediatric and Adolescent Medicine, 151,* 298–304.

Diekman, A. B., & Murnen, S. K. (2004). Learning to be little women and little men: The inequitable gender equality of nonsexist children's literature. *Sex Roles, 50*(5/6), 373–385.

Dietz, T. L. (1998). An examination of violence and gender role portrayals in video games: Implications for gender socialization and aggressive behavior. *Sex Roles, 38*(5/6), 425–442.

Dinella, L., & Martin, C. L. (2003, April). *Gender stereotypes, gender identity, and preferences of self-identified tomboys and traditional girls.* Paper presented at the meetings of the Society for Research in Child Development, Tampa, FL.

Di Pietro, J. A. (1981). Rough and tumble play: A function of gender. *Developmental Psychology, 17,* 50–58.

Dorn, L. D., Susman, E. J., Nottelmann, E. D., Inoff-Germain, G., & Chrousos, G. P. (1990). Perceptions of puberty: Adolescent, parent, and health care personnel. *Developmental Psychology, 26,* 322–329.

Driesen, N. R., & Raz, N. (1995). The influence of sex, age, and handedness on corpus callosum morphology: A meta-analysis. *Psychobiology, 23,* 240–247.

Duffy, J., Warren, K., & Walsh, M. (2002). Classroom interactions: Gender of teacher, gender of student, and classroom subject. *Sex Roles, 45*(9/10), 579–593.

Dunn, J., & Hughes, C. (2001). "I got some swords and you're dead!": Violent fantasy, antisocial behavior, friendship, and moral sensibility in young children. *Child Development, 72,* 491–505.

Durkin, K., & Nugent, B. (1998). Kindergarten children's gender-role expectations for television actors. *Sex Roles, 38*(5/6), 387–402.

Eagly, A. H., & Mladinic, A. (1994). Are people prejudiced against women? Some answers from research on attitudes, gender stereotypes, and judgments of competence. In W. Stroebe & M. Hewstone (Eds.), *European review of social psychology* (Vol. 5, pp. 1–35). New York: Wiley.

Eagly, A. H., & Mladinic, A., & Otto, S. (1991). Are women evaluated more favorably than men? An analysis of attitudes, beliefs, and emotions. *Psychology of Women Quarterly, 15,* 203–216.

Eaton, W. O., & Enns, L. R. (1986). Sex differences in human motor activity level. *Psychological Bulletin, 100,* 19–28.

Eccles, J. S. (1987). Adolescence: Gateway to gender-role transcendence. In D. B. Carter (Ed.), *Current conceptions of sex roles and sex typing: Theory and research* (pp. 225–241). New York: Praeger.

Eccles, J. S. (1989). Bringing young women to math and science. In M. Crawford & M. Gentry (Eds.), *Gender and thought* (pp. 36–58). New York: Springer-Verlag.

Eccles, J. S., & Barber, B. L. (1999). Student council, volunteering, basketball, or marching band: What kinds of extracurricular involvement matters? *Journal of Adolescent Research, 14*(1), 10–43.

Eccles, J. S., Wigfield, A., Flanagan, C. A., Miller, C., Reuman, D. A., & Yee, D. (1989). Self-concepts, domain values, and self-esteem: Relations and changes at early adolescence. *Journal of Personality, 57,* 283–310.

Eckes, T., & Trautner, H. M. (Eds.). (2000). *The developmental social psychology of gender.* Mahwah, NJ: Erlbaum.

Eckes, T., Trautner, H. M., & Behrendt, R. (2005). Gender subgroups and intergroup perception: Adolescents' views of own-gender and other-gender groups. *Journal of Social Psychology, 145,* 85–111.

Edelbrock, C., & Sugawara, A. I. (1978). Acquisition of sex-typed preferences in preschool children. *Developmental Psychology, 14,* 614–623.

Egan, S. K., & Perry, D. G. (2001). Gender identity: A multidimensional analysis with implications for psychosocial adjustment. *Developmental Psychology, 37,* 451–463.

Eisenberg, N., Cumberland, A., & Spinrad, T. L. (1998). Parental socialization of emotion. *Psychology Inquiry, 9,* 241–273.

Eisenberg, N., & Fabes, R. A. (1998). Prosocial development. In W. Damon (Ed.), *Handbook of child psychology* (5th ed., Vol. 3, pp. 701–778). New York: Wiley.

Eisenberg, N., Martin, C. L., & Fabes, R. A. (1996). Gender development and gender effects. In D. Berliner & R. Calfee (Eds.), *Handbook of educational psychology* (pp. 358–396). New York: Prentice-Hall International.

Eisenberg, N., Wolchik, S. A., Hernandez, R., & Pasternack, J. (1985). Parental socialization of young children's play: A short-term longitudinal study. *Child Development, 56,* 1506–1513.

Eisenberg, N., Zhou, Q., & Koller, S. (2001). Brazilian adolescents' prosocial moral judgment and behavior: Relations to sympathy, perspective taking, gender-role orientation, and demographic characteristics. *Child Development, 72*(2), 518–534.

Ellis, L., & Ficek, C. (2001). Color preferences according to gender and sexual orientation. *Personality and Individual Differences, 31,* 1375–1379.

Emmerich, W., Goldman, K. S., Kirsh, B., & Sharabany, R. (1977). Evidence for a transitional phase in the development of gender constancy. *Child Development, 48,* 930–936.

Emmerich, W., & Shepard, K. (1982). Development of sex-differentiated preferences during late childhood and adolescence. *Developmental Psychology, 18,* 406–417.

Entwisle, D. R., Alexander, K. L., Pallas, A. M., & Cadigan, D. (1987). The emergence of academic self-image of first graders: Its response to social structure. *Child Development, 58,* 1190–1206.

Evans, E. M., Schweingruber, H., & Stevenson, H. W. (2002). Gender differences in interest and knowledge acquisition: The United States, Japan, and Taiwan. *Sex Roles, 47,* 153–167.

Evans, L., & Davies, K. (2000). No sissy boys here: A content analysis of the representation of masculinity in elementary school reading textbooks. *Sex Roles, 42,* 255–270.

Fabes, R. A. (1994). Physiological, emotional, and behavioral correlates of gender segregation. In C. Leaper (Ed.), *New directions for child development: Vol. 65. Childhood gender segregation—Causes and consequences* (pp. 19–34). San Francisco: Jossey-Bass.

Fabes, R. A., Martin, C. L., & Hanish, L. D. (2003). Young children's play qualities in same-, other-, and mixed-sex peer groups. *Child Development, 74,* 921–932.

Fabes, R. A., Martin, C. L., Hanish, L. D., Anders, M. C., & Madden-Derdich, D. A. (2003). Early school competence: The roles of sex-segregated play and effortful control. *Developmental Psychology, 39,* 848–858.

Fabes, R. A., Shepard, A. S., Guthrie, I. K., & Martin, C. L. (1997). Roles of temperamental arousal and gender segregated play in young children's social adjustment. *Developmental Psychology, 33*(4), 693–702.

Fagot, B. I. (1977). Consequences of moderate cross-gender behavior in preschool children. *Child Development, 48,* 902–907.

Fagot, B. I. (1984). The child's expectations of differences in adult male and female interactions. *Sex Roles, 11*(7/8), 593–600.

Fagot, B. I. (1985). Changes in thinking about early sex role development. *Developmental Review, 5*(1), 83–98.

Fagot, B. I., & Hagan, R. (1985). Aggression in toddlers' responses to the assertive acts of boys and girls. *Sex Roles, 12*(3/4), 341–351.

Fagot, B. I., & Leinbach, M. (1989). The young child's gender schema: Environmental input, internal organization. *Child Development, 60,* 663–672.

Fagot, B. I., Leinbach, M. D., & Hagan, R. (1986). Gender labeling and the adoption of sex-typed behaviors. *Developmental Psychology, 22,* 440–443.

Feingold, A. (1988). Cognitive gender differences are disappearing. *American Psychologist, 43,* 95–103.

Fenson, L., Dale, P. S., Resznick, J. S., Bates, E., Thale, D. J., & Pethick, S. J. (1994). Variability in early communicative development. *Monographs of the Society for Research in Child Development, 59*(5), v–173.

Finegan, J. K., Niccols, G. A., & Sitarenois, G. (1992). Relations between testosterone levels and cognitive abilities at 4 years. *Developmental Psychology, 28,* 1075–1089.

Finkelstein, J. W., Susman, E. J., Chinchilli, V. M., Kunselman, S. J., D'Arcangelo, M. R., Schwab, J., et al. (1997). Estrogen or testosterone increases self-reported aggressive behaviors in hypogonadal adolescents. *Journal of Clinical Endocrinology and Metabolism, 82,* 2433–2438.

Fischer, A. H., Rodriguez Mosquera, P. M., van Vianen, A. E., & Manstead, A. S. (2004). Gender and culture differences in emotion. *Emotion, 4,* 87–94.

Fisher-Thompson, D. (1993). Adult toy purchase for children: Factors affecting sex-typed toy selection. *Journal of Applied Developmental Psychology, 14,* 385–406.

Fivush, R., Brotman, M. A., Buckner, J. P., & Goodman, S. H. (2000). Gender differences in parent-child emotion narratives. *Sex Roles, 42,* 233–253.

Fredricks, J. A., & Eccles, J. S. (2002). Children's competence and value beliefs from childhood through adolescence: Growth trajectories in two male-sex-typed domains. *Developmental Psychology, 38,* 519–533.

Furnham, A. (1999). Sex-role stereotyping in television commercials: A review and comparison of fourteen studies done on five continents over 25 years. *Sex Roles, 41*(5/6), 413–437.

Galambos, N. L., Almeida, D. M., & Petersen, A. C. (1990). Masculinity, femininity, and sex role attitudes in early adolescence: Exploring gender intensification. *Child Development, 61*(6), 1905–1914.

Galambos, N. L., Petersen, A. C., Richards, M., & Gitelson, I. B. (1985). The attitudes toward women scale for adolescents (AWSA): A study of reliability and validity. *Sex Roles, 13*(5/6), 343–356.

Ge, X., Brody, G. H., Conger, R. D., Simons, R. L., & Murry, V. M. (2002). Contextual amplification of pubertal transition effects on deviant peer affiliation and externalizing behavior among African American children. *Developmental Psychology, 38,* 42–54.

Ge, X., Conger, R. D., & Elder, G. H. (1996). Coming of age too early: Pubertal influences on girls' vulnerability to psychological distress. *Child Development, 67,* 386–400.

Geary, D. C. (1998). *Male, female: The evolution of human sex differences.* Washington, DC: American Psychological Association.

Geary, D. C. (1999). Evolution and developmental sex differences. *Current Directions in Psychological Science, 8,* 115–120.

Geary, D. C., & Bjorklund, D. F. (2000). Evolutionary developmental psychology. *Child Development, 71,* 57–65.

Gelman, S. A., Collman, P., & Maccoby, E. E. (1986). Inferring properties from categories versus inferring categories from properties: The case of gender. *Child Development, 57,* 396–404.

Gelman, S. A., Taylor, M. G., & Nguyen, S. P. (2004). Mother-child conversations about gender. *Monographs of the Society for Research in Child Development, 69*(1), vii–127.

Gest, S. D., Graham-Bermann, S. A., & Hartup, W. W. (2001). Peer experience: Common and unique features of number of friendships, social network centrality, and sociometric status. *Social Development, 10*(1), 23–40.

Gibbons, J. L. (2000). Gender development in cross-cultural perspective. In T. Eckes & H. S. Trautner (Eds.), *The developmental social psychology of gender* (pp. 389–415). Mahwah, NJ: Erlbaum.

Giedd, J. N. (2004). Structural magnetic resonance imaging of the adolescent brain. *Annals of the New York Academy of Sciences, 1021,* 77–85.

Giedd, J. N., Blumenthal, J., Jeffries, N. O., Castellanos, F. X., Liu, H., Zijdenbos, A., et al. (1999). Brain development during childhood and adolescence: A longitudinal MRI study. *Nature Neuroscience, 2,* 861–863.

Giles, J. W., & Heyman, G. D. (2004). When to cry over spilled milk: Young children's use of category information to guide inferences about ambiguous behavior. *Journal of Cognition and Development, 5,* 359–386.

Giles, J. W., & Heyman, G. D. (2005). Young children's beliefs about the relationship between gender and aggressive behavior. *Child Development, 76,* 107–121.

Gilligan, C. (1982). *In a different voice: Psychological theory and women's development.* Cambridge, MA: Harvard University Press.

Giuliano, T. A., Popp, K. E., & Knight, J. L. (2000). Footballs versus Barbies: Childhood play activities as predictors of sport participation by women. *Sex Roles, 42,* 159–181.

Gleason, J. B., & Ely, R. (2002). Gender differences in language development. In A. McGillicuddy-De Lisi & R. De Lisi (Eds.), *Biology, society, and behavior: Vol. 21. The development of sex differences in cognition* (pp. 127–154). Westport, CN: Ablex.

Glick, P., & Fiske, S. T. (1996). The ambivalent sexism inventory: Differentiating hostile and benevolent sexism. *Journal of Personality and Social Psychology, 70,* 491–512.

Glick, P., & Hilt, L. (2000). Combative children to ambivalent adults: The development of gender prejudice. In T. Eckes & H. M. Trautner (Eds.), *The developmental social psychology of gender* (pp. 243–272). Mahwah, NJ: Erlbaum.

Gogtay, N., Giedd, J. N., Lusk, L., Hayashi, K. M., Greenstein, D., Vaituzis, A. C., et al. (2004). Dynamic mapping of human cortical development during childhood through early adulthood. *Proceedings of the National Academy of Sciences, 101,* 8174–8179.

Goldman, R., & Goldman, J. (1982). *Children's sexual thinking.* London: Routledge & Kegan Paul.

Goldstein, J. M., Seidman, L. J., Horton, N. J., Makris, N., Kennedy, D. N., Caviness, V. S., et al. (2001). Normal sexual dimorphism of the adult human brain assessed by in vivo magnetic resonance imaging. *Cerebral Cortex, 11,* 490–497.

Golombok, S., & Rust, J. (1993). The pre-school activities inventory: A standardized assessment of gender role in children. *Psychological Assessment, 5,* 131–136.

Good, C. D., Johnsrude, I., Ashburner, J., Henson, R. N. A., Friston, K. J., & Frackowiak, R. S. J. (2001). Cerebral asymmetry and the effects of sex and handedness on brain structure: A voxel-based morphometric analysis of 465 normal adult human brains. *NeuroImage, 14,* 685–700.

Gooden, A. M., & Gooden, M. A. (2001). Gender representation in notable children's picture books: 1995–1999. *Sex Roles, 45*(1/2), 89–101.

Goy, R. W., Bercovitch, F. B., & McBrair, M. C. (1988). Behavioral masculinization is independent of genital masculinization in prenatally androgenized female rhesus macaques. *Hormones and Behavior, 22,* 552–571.

Graham, S., Taylor, A. Z., & Hudley, C. (1998). Exploring achievement values among ethnic minority early adolescents. *Journal of Educational Psychology, 90,* 606–620.

Grant, K., Lyons, A., Landis, D., Cho, M., Scudiero, M., Reynolds, L., et al. (1999). Gender, body image, and depressive symptoms among low-income African American adolescents. *Journal of Social Issues, 55,* 299–315.

Green, R. (1987). *The "sissy boy syndrome" and the development of homosexuality.* New Haven, CT: Yale University Press.

Greulich, F. K., Ruble, D. N., Khuri, J., & Cyphers, L. (2001, April). *What parents say about children's gender-typed behavior.* Poster presentation at the Society for Research in Child Development Conference, Minneapolis, MN.

Griffin, W. A., Hanish, L. D., Martin, C. L., & Fabes, R. A. (2003). Modeling playgroups in children: Determining validity and veridicality. In D. L. Sallach, C. M. Macal, & M. J. North (Eds.), *Agent 2003: Challenges in social simulation.* Chicago: University of Chicago and Argonne National Laboratory.

Grimshaw, G. M., Sitarenios, G., & Finegan, J. K. (1995). Mental rotation at 7 years: Relations with prenatal testosterone levels and spatial play experience. *Brain and Cognition, 29,* 85–100.

Grön, G., Wunderlich, A. P., Spitzer, M., Tomczak, R., & Riepe, M. W. (2000). Brain activation during human navigation: Gender-different neural networks as substrate of performance. *Nature Neuroscience, 3,* 404–408.

Grumbach, M. M., Hughes, I. A., & Conte, F. A. (2002). Disorders of sex differentiation. In P. R. Larsen, H. M. Kronenberg, S. Melmed, & K. S. Polonsky (Eds.), *Williams textbook of endocrinology* (10th ed., pp. 842–1002, 2003). Philadelphia: Saunders.

Grusec, J. E., Goodnow, J. J., & Cohen, L. (1996). Household work and the development of concern for others. *Developmental Psychology, 32,* 999–1007.

Grych, J. H., & Clark, R. (1999). Maternal employment and development of the father-infant relationship in the first year. *Developmental Psychology, 35,* 893–903.

Hall, C., & Coles, M. (1999). *Children's reading choices.* London: Routledge.

Hall, J. A., Carter, J. D., & Horgan, T. G. (2000). Gender differences in nonverbal communication of emotion. In A. H. Fischer (Ed.), *Gender and emotion* (pp. 97–117). Cambridge, England: Cambridge University Press.

Halpern, D. F. (2000). *Sex differences in cognitive abilities* (3rd ed.). Mahwah, NJ: Erlbaum.

Hamann, S., & Canli, T. (2004). Individual differences in emotional processing. *Current Opinion in Neurobiology, 14,* 233–238.

Hamann, S., Herman, R. A., Nolan, C. L., & Wallen, K. (2004). Men and women differ in amygdala response to visual sexual stimuli. *Nature Neuroscience, 7,* 411–416.

Hampson, E. (2002). Sex differences in human brain and cognition: The influence of sex steroids in early and adult life. In J. B.

Becker, S. M. Breedlove, D. Crews, & M. M. McCarthy (Eds.), *Behavioral endocrinology* (2nd ed., pp. 579–628). Cambridge, MA: MIT Press.

Hanish, L. D., Martin, C. L., Fabes, R. A., Leonard, S., & Herzog, M. (2005). Peer contagion effects on young children's externalizing symptomatology. *Journal of Abnormal Child Psychology, 33*(3), 267–281.

Hannover, B. (2000). Development of the self in gendered contexts. In T. Eckes & H. M. Trautner (Eds.), *The developmental social psychology of gender* (pp. 177–206). Mahwah, NJ: Erlbaum.

Harker, R. (2000). Achievement, gender and the single-sex/co-ed debate. *British Journal of Sociology of Education,* 203–218.

Harris, L. J. (1978). Sex differences in spatial ability: Possible environmental, genetic, and neurological factors. In M. Kinsbourne (Ed.), *Asymmetrical functions of the brain* (pp. 405–522). London: Cambridge University Press.

Harris, R. J., & Firestone, J. M. (1998). Changes in predictors of gender role ideologies among women: A multivariate analysis. *Sex Roles, 38*(3/4), 239–252.

Harrison, A. C., & O'Neill, S. A. (2000). Children's gender-typed preferences for musical instruments: An intervention study. *Psychology of Music, 28,* 81–97.

Harrison, A. C., & O'Neill, S. A. (2003). Preferences and children's use of gender-stereotyped knowledge about musical instruments: Making judgments about other children's preferences. *Sex Roles, 49*(7/8), 389–400.

Hartung, C. M., & Widiger, T. A. (1998). Gender differences in the diagnosis of mental disorders: Conclusions and controversies of the *DSM-IV. Psychological Bulletin, 123,* 260–278.

Hay, I., Ashman, A. F., & Van Kraayenoord, C. E. (1998). The influence of gender, academic achievement, and non-school factors upon pre-adolescent self-concept. *Educational Psychology, 18*(4), 461–471.

Hedges, L. V., & Nowell, A. (1995). Sex differences in mental test scores, variability, and numbers of high-scoring individuals. *Science, 269,* 41–45.

Helleday, J., Edman, G., Ritzen, E. M., & Siwers, B. (1993). Personality characteristics and platelet MAO activity in women with Congenital Adrenal Hyperplasia (CAH). *Psychoneuronendocrinology, 18,* 343–354.

Helwig, A. A. (1998). Gender-role stereotyping: Testing theory with a longitudinal sample. *Sex Roles, 38,* 403–423.

Hendy, H. M., Gustitus, C., & Leitzel-Schwalm, J. (2001). Social cognitive predictors of body image in preschool children. *Sex Roles, 44*(9/10), 557–569.

Henshaw, A., Kelly, J., & Gratton, C. (1992). Skipping's for girls: Children's perceptions of gender roles and gender preferences. *Educational Research, 34*(3), 229–235.

Herdt, G., & McClintock, M. (2000). The magical age of 10. *Archives of Sexual Behavior, 29,* 587–606.

Hewstone, M., Rubin, M., & Willis, H. (2002). Intergroup bias. *Annual Review of Psychology, 53*(1), 575–604.

Heyman, G. D. (2001). Children's interpretation of ambiguous behavior: Evidence for a "boys are bad" bias. *Social Development, 10,* 230–247.

Heyman, G. D., & Gelman, S. A. (2000). Preschool children's use of trait labels to make inductive inferences. *Journal of Experimental Child Psychology, 77,* 1–19.

Heyman, G. D., & Legare, C. H. (2004). Children's beliefs about gender differences in the academic and social domains. *Sex Roles, 50*(3/4), 227–239.

Hill, A. J., & Pallin, V. (1998). Dieting awareness and low self-worth: Related issues in 8-year-old girls. *International Journal of Eating Disorders, 24,* 405–413.

Hill, J. P., & Lynch, M. E. (1983). The intensification of gender-related role expectations during early adolescence. In J. Brooks-Gunn & A. C. Petersen (Eds.), *Girls at puberty: Biological and psychosocial perspectives* (pp. 201–228). New York: Plenum Press.

Hines, M., Ahmed, F., & Hughes, I. A. (2003). Psychological outcomes and gender-related development in complete androgen insensitivity syndrome. *Archives of Sexual Behavior, 32,* 93–101.

Hines, M., Brook, C., & Conway, G. S. (2004). Androgen and psychosexual development: Core gender identity, sexual orientation, and recalled gender role behavior in women and men with Congenital Adrenal Hyperplasia (CAH). *Journal of Sex Research, 41,* 75–81.

Hines, M., Fane, B. A., Pasterski, V. L., Mathews, G. A., Conway, G. S., & Brook, C. (2003). Spatial abilities following prenatal androgen abnormality: Targeting and mental rotations performance in individuals with congenital adrenal hyperplasia. *Psychoneuroendocrinology, 28,* 1010–1026.

Hines, M., Golombok, S., Rust, J., Johnston, K. J., Golding, J., & Avon Longitudinal Study of Parents and Children Study Team. (2002). Testosterone during pregnancy and gender role behavior of preschool children: A longitudinal, population study. *Child Development, 73,* 1678–1687.

Hines, M., & Kaufman, F. (1994). Androgen and the development of human sex-typical behavior: Rough-and-tumble play and sex of preferred playmates in children with Congenital Adrenal Hyperplasia (CAH). *Child Development, 65,* 1042–1053.

Hoffman, L. O. (1989). Effects of maternal employment in the two-parent family. Children and their development—Knowledge base, research agenda, and social policy application [Special issue]. *American Psychologist, 44*(2), 283–292.

Hoffman, M. L., & Powlishta, K. K. (2001). Gender segregation in childhood: A test of the interaction style theory. *Journal of Genetic Psychology, 162*(3), 298–313.

Hoffman, M. L., Powlishta, K. K., & White, K. J. (2004). An examination of gender differences in adolescent adjustment: The effect of competence on gender role differences in symptoms of psychopathology. *Sex Roles, 50*(11/12), 795–810.

Holmes-Lonergan, H. A. (2003). Preschool children's collaborative problem-solving interactions: The role of gender, pair type, and task. *Sex Roles, 48*(11, 12), 505–517.

Hopf, D., & Hatzichristou, C. (1999). Teacher gender-related influences in Greek schools. *British Journal of Educational Psychology, 69,* 1–18.

Hort, B. E., Leinbach, M. D., & Fagot, B. I. (1991). Is there coherence among components of gender acquisition? *Sex Roles, 24,* 195–208.

Howes, C. (1988). Relations between child care and schooling. *Developmental Psychology, 24,* 53–57.

Hughes, F. M., & Seta, C. E. (2003). Gender stereotypes: Children's perceptions of future compensatory behavior following violations of gender roles. *Sex Roles, 49*(11, 12), 685–691.

Huston, A. C. (1983). Sex-typing. In E. M. Hetherington (Ed.), *Handbook of child psychology: Vol. 4. Socialization, personality, and social development* (pp. 387–467). New York: Wiley.

Huston, A. C., & Alvarez, M. M. (1990). The socialization context of gender role development in early adolescence. In R. Montemayor, G. R. Adams, & T. P. Gullotta (Eds.), *From childhood to adolescence: A transitional period?* (pp. 156–179). Newbury Park: Sage.

Huston, A. C., Dunnerstein, E., Fairchild, H., Feshbach, N. D., Katz, P. A., Murray, J. P., et al. (1992). *Big world, small screen: The role of television in American society*. Lincoln: University of Nebraska Press.

Huston, A. C., & Wright, J. C. (1998). Mass media and children's development. In I. E. Sigel & K. A. Renninger (Eds.), *Handbook of child psychology: Vol. 4. Child psychology in practice* (5th ed., pp. 999–1058). New York: Wiley.

Huston, A. C., Wright, J. C., Marquis, J., & Green, S. B. (1999). How young children spend their time: Television and other activities. *Developmental Psychology, 35,* 921–925.

Huttenlocher, J., Haight, W., Bryk, A., Seltzer, M., & Lyons, T. (1991). Early vocabulary growth: Relation to language input and gender. *Developmental Psychology, 27,* 236–248.

Hyde, J. S., Fennema, E., & Lamon, S. J. (1990). Gender differences in mathematics performance: A meta-analysis. *Psychological Bulletin, 107,* 139–155.

Hyde, J. S., & Frost, L. A. (1993). Meta-analysis in the psychology of women. In F. L. Denmark & M. A. Paludi (Eds.), *Psychology of women: A handbook of issues and theories* (pp. 67–103). Westport, CT: Greenwood Press.

Hyde, J. S., & Jaffee, S. R. (2000). Becoming a heterosexual adult: The experiences of young women. *Journal of Social Issues, 56,* 283–296.

Hyde, J. S., & Linn, M. C. (1988). Gender differences in verbal ability: A meta-analysis. *Psychological Bulletin, 104,* 53–69.

Hyde, J. S., & McKinley, N. M. (1997). Gender differences in cognition: Results from meta-analyses. In P. J. Caplan, M. Crawford, J. S. Hyde, & J. T. E. Richardson (Eds.), *Gender differences in human cognition* (pp. 30–51). New York: Oxford University Press.

Ickes, E., Gesn, P. R., & Graham, T. (2000). Gender differences in empathic accuracy: Differential ability or differential motivation? *Personal Relationships, 7,* 95–109.

Iijima, M., Arisaka, O., Minamoto, F., & Arai, Y. (2001). Sex differences in children's free drawings: A study on girls with congenital adrenal hyperplasia. *Hormones and Behavior, 40,* 99–104.

Imperato-McGinley, J., Peterson, R. E., Gautier, T., & Sturla, E. (1979). Androgens and the evolution of male gender identity among male pseudohermaphrodites with 5-alpha-reductase deficiency. *New England Journal of Medicine, 300,* 1233–1237.

Intons-Peterson, M. J. (1988a). *Children's concepts of gender.* Norwood, NJ: Ablex.

Intons-Peterson, M. J. (1988b). *Gender concepts of Swedish and American youth.* Hillsdale, NJ: Erlbaum.

Jacklin, C. N., Wilcox, K. T., & Maccoby, E. E. (1988). Neonatal sex-steroid hormones and cognitive abilities at 6 years. *Developmental Psychobiology, 21,* 567–574.

Jackson, D. W., & Tein, J. (1998). Adolescents' conceptualization of adult roles: Relationships with age, gender, work, goal, and maternal employment. *Sex Roles, 38*(11/12), 987–1008.

Jacobs, J. E., Lanza, S., Osgood, D. W., Eccles, J. S., & Wigfield, A. (2002). Changes in children's self-competence and values: Gender and domain differences across grades 1 through 12. *Child Development, 73,* 509–527.

Jaffee, S., & Hyde, J. S. (2000). Gender differences in moral orientation: A meta-analysis. *Psychological Bulletin, 126,* 703–726.

Jameson, K. A., Highnote, S. M., & Wasserman, L. M. (2001). Richer color experience in observers with multiple photopigment opsin genes. *Psychonomic Bulletin and Review, 8,* 244–261.

Kane, E. W. (2000). Racial and ethnic variations in gender-related attitudes. *Annual Review of Sociology, 26,* 419–439.

Karniol, R., Grosz, E., & Schorr, I. (2003). Caring, gender role orientation, and volunteering. *Sex Roles, 49*(1/2), 11–19.

Katz, P. A., & Boswell, S. (1986). Flexibility and traditionality in children's gender roles. *Genetic, Social, & General Psychology Monographs, 112*(1), 103–147.

Katz, P. A., & Kofkin, J. A. (1997). Race, gender, and young children. In S. S. Luthar, J. A. Burack, D. Cicchetti, & J. Weisz (Eds.), *Developmental psychopathology: Perspectives on adjustment, risk, and disorder* (pp. 51–74). New York: Cambridge University Press.

Katz, P. A., & Ksansnak, K. R. (1994). Developmental aspects of gender role flexibility and traditionality in middle childhood and adolescence. *Developmental Psychology, 30*(2), 272–282.

Katz, P. A., & Walsh, V. (1991). Modification of children's gender-stereotyped behavior. *Child Development, 62,* 338–351.

Kaufman, G. (1999). The portrayal of men's family roles in television commercials. *Sex Roles, 41*(5/6), 439–458.

Killen, M., & Stangor, C. (2001). Children's social reasoning about inclusion and exclusion in gender and race peer group contexts. *Child Development, 72*(1), 174–186.

Kimball, M. M. (1986). Television and sex-role attitudes. In T. M. Williams (Ed.), *The impact of television: A natural experiment in three communities* (pp. 265–301). Orlando, FL: Academic Press.

Kimura, D. (1999). *Sex and cognition.* Cambridge, MA: MIT Press.

Klebanov, P. K., & Ruble, D. N. (1994). Toward an understanding of women's experience of menstrual cycle symptoms. In V. J. Adesso, D. M. Reddy, & R. Fleming (Eds.), *Psychological perspectives on women's health* (pp. 183–221). Washington, DC: Taylor & Francis.

Kling, K. C., Hyde, J. S., Showers, C. J., & Buswell, B. N. (1999). Gender differences in self-esteem: A meta-analysis. *Psychological Bulletin, 125,* 470–500.

Klingenspor, B. (2002). Gender-related self discrepancies and bulimic eating behavior. *Sex Roles, 47*(1/2), 51–64.

Klomsten, A. T., Skaalvik, E. M., & Espnes, G. A. (2004). Physical self-concept and sports: Do gender differences still exist? *Sex Roles, 50*(1/2), 119–127.

Knickmeyer, R., Baron-Cohen, S., Raggatt, P., & Taylor, K. (2004). Foetal testosterone, social relationships, and restricted interests in children. *Journal of Child Psychology and Psychiatry, 46*(2), 198–210.

Knickmeyer, R. C., Wheelwright, S., Taylor, K., Raggatt, P., Hackett, G., & Baron-Cohen, S. (2005). Gender-typed play and amniotic testosterone. *Developmental Psychology, 41,* 517–528.

Knight, G. P., Fabes, R. A., & Higgins, D. A. (1996). Concerns about drawing causal inferences from meta-analyses: An example in the study of gender differences in aggression. *Psychological Bulletin, 119,* 410–421.

Kohlberg, L. A. (1966). A cognitive-developmental analysis of children's sex role concepts and attitudes. In E. E. Maccoby (Ed.), *The development of sex differences* (pp. 82–173). Stanford, CA: Stanford University Press.

Kovacs, D. M., Parker, J. G., & Hoffman, L. W. (1996). Behavioral, affective, and social correlates of involvement in cross-sex friendship in elementary school. *Child Development, 67,* 2269–2286.

Kovalev, V. A., Kruggel, F., & von Cramon, D. Y. (2003). Gender and age effects in structural brain asymmetry as measured by MRI texture analysis. *NeuroImage, 19,* 895–905.

Kramer, J. H., Delis, D. C., & Daniel, M. (1988). Sex differences in verbal learning. *Journal of Clinical Psychology, 44,* 907–915.

Ladd, G. W. (2005). *Peer relationships and social competence of children and adolescents.* New Haven, CT: Yale University Press.

La Freniere, P., Strayer, F. F., & Gauthier, R. (1984). The emergence of same-sex affiliative preferences among preschool peers: A developmental/ethological perspective. *Child Development, 55*(5), 1958–1965.

Lansford, J. E., & Parker, J. G. (1999). Children' interactions in triads: Behavioral profiles and effects of gender and patterns of friendships among members. *Developmental Psychology, 35*, 80–93.

Largo, R. H., Caflisch, J. A., Hug, F., Muggli, K., Molnar, A. A., Molinari, L., et al. (2001a). Neuromotor development from 5 to 18 years: Pt. 1. Timed performance. *Developmental Medicine and Child Neurology, 43*, 436–443.

Largo, R. H., Caflisch, J. A., Hug, F., Muggli, K., Molnar, A. A., Molinari, L., et al. (2001b). Neuromotor development from 5 to 18 years: Pt. 2. Associated movements. *Developmental Medicine and Child Neurology, 43*, 444–453.

Leaper, C. (1994). Exploring the consequences of gender segregation on social relationships. In C. Leaper (Ed.), *Childhood gender segregation: Causes and consequences* (pp. 67–86). San Francisco: Jossey-Bass.

Leaper, C. (2002). Parenting girls and boys. In M. H. Bornstein (Ed.), *Handbook of parenting: Children and parenting* (pp. 189–225). Mahwah, NJ: Erlbaum.

Leaper, C., Anderson, K. J., & Sanders, P. (1998). Moderators of gender effects on parents' talk to their children: A meta-analysis. *Developmental Psychology, 34*(1), 3–27.

Leaper, C., Leve, L., Strasser, T., & Schwartz, R. (1995). Mother-child communication sequences: Play activity, child gender, and marital status effects. *Merrill-Palmer Quarterly, 41*, 307–327.

Leaper, C., & Smith, T. E. (2004). A meta-analytic review of gender variations in children's language use: Talkativeness, affiliative speech, and assertive speech. *Developmental Psychology, 40*, 993–1027.

Leaper, C., Tenenbaum, H. R., & Shaffer, T. G. (1999). Communication patterns of African American girls and boys from low-income, urban backgrounds. *Child Development, 70*, 1489–1503.

Lee, V. E., & Bryk, A. S. (1986). Effects of single-sex secondary schools on student achievement and attitudes. *Journal of Educational Psychology, 78*(5), 381–395.

Leman, P. J., Ahmed, S., & Ozarow, L. (2005). Gender, gender relations, and the social dynamics of children's conversations. *Developmental Psychology, 41*, 64–74.

Lemish, D., Liebes, T., & Seidmann, V. (2001). Gendered media meanings and uses. In S. Livingstone & M. Bovill (Eds.), *Children and their changing media environment* (pp. 263–282). Mahwah, NJ: Erlbaum.

LeVay, S. (1993). *The sexual brain.* Cambridge, MA: MIT Press.

Leveroni, C. L., & Berenbaum, S. A. (1998). Early androgen effects on interest in infants: Evidence from children with congenital adrenal hyperplasia. *Developmental Neuropsychology, 14*, 321–340.

Levy, G. D. (1998). Effects of gender constancy and figure's height and sex on young children's gender-typed attributions. *Journal of General Psychology, 125*, 65–88.

Levy, G. D. (1999). Gender-typed and non-gender-typed category awareness in toddlers. *Sex Roles, 41*, 851–873.

Levy, G. D., & Boston, M. B. (1994). Preschoolers' recall of own-sex and other-sex gender scripts. *Journal of Genetic Psychology, 155*(3), 369–371.

Levy, G. D., Sadovsky, A. L., & Troseth, G. L. (2000). Aspects of young children's perceptions of gender-typed occupations. *Sex Roles, 42*(11/12), 993–1006.

Levy, G. D., Taylor, M. G., & Gelman, S. A. (1995). Traditional and evaluative aspects of flexibility in gender roles, social conventions, moral rules, and physical laws. *Child Development, 66*, 515–531.

Levy, J. (1974). Psychobiological implications of bilateral asymmetry. In S. J. Dimond & J. G. Beaumont (Eds.), *Hemisphere function in the human brain* (pp. 121–183). New York: Wiley.

Liben, L. S. (1995). Psychology meets geography: Exploring the gender gap on the national geography bee. *Psychological Science Agenda, 8*, 8–9.

Liben, L. S., & Bigler, R. S. (2002). The developmental course of gender differentiation. *Monographs of the Society for Research in Child Development, 67*(2), 1–147.

Liben, L. S., Bigler, R. S., & Krogh, H. R. (2001). Pink and blue collar jobs: Children's judgments of job status and job aspirations in relation to sex of worker. *Journal of Experimental Child Psychology, 79*, 346–363.

Liben, L. S., & Signorella, M. L. (1980). Gender-related schemata and constructive memory in children. *Child Development, 51*, 11–18.

Liben, L. S., Susman, E. J., Finkelstein, J. W., Chinchilli, V. M., Kunselman, S. J., Schwab, J., et al. (2002). The effects of sex steroids on spatial performance: A review and an experimental clinical investigation. *Developmental Psychology, 38*, 236–253.

Lin, C. A. (1998). Uses of sex appeals in prime-time television commercials. *Sex Roles, 38*(5/6), 461–475.

Lindsey, E. W., & Mize, J. (2001). Contextual differences in parent-child play: Implications for children's gender role development. *Sex Roles, 44*(3/4), 155–176.

Linn, M., & Petersen, A. (1985). Emergence and characterization of sex differences in spatial ability: A meta-analysis. *Child Development, 56*, 1479–1498.

Lips, H. M. (2004). The gender gap in possible selves: Divergence of academic self-views among high school and university students. *Sex Roles, 50*(5/6), 357–371.

Lobel, T. E., Bar-David, E., Gruber, R., Lau, S., & Bar-Tal, Y. (2000). Gender schema and social judgments: A developmental study of children from Hong Kong. *Sex Roles, 43*, 19–42.

Lobel, T. E., Gewirtz, J., Pras, R., Schoeshine-Rokach, M., & Ginton, R. (1999). Preadolescents' social judgments: The relationship between self-endorsements of traits and gender-related judgments of female peers. *Sex Roles, 40*(5/6), 483–498.

Lobel, T. E., Gruber, R., Govrin, N., & Mashraki-Pedhatzur, S. (2001). Children's gender-related inferences and judgments: A cross-cultural study. *Developmental Psychology, 37*, 839–846.

Lonsdorf, E. V., Eberly, L. E., & Pusey, A. E. (2004). Sex differences in learning in chimpanzees. *Nature, 428*, 715–716.

Lundy, B., Field, T., & McBride, C. K. (1998). Same-sex and opposite-sex best friend interactions among high school juniors and seniors. *Adolescence, 33*(130), 279–289.

Lutchmaya, S., Baron-Cohen, S., & Raggatt, P. (2002a). Foetal testosterone and eye contact in 12-month-old human infants. *Infant Behavior and Development, 25*, 327–335.

Lutchmaya, S., Baron-Cohen, S., & Raggatt, P. (2002b). Foetal testosterone and vocabulary size in 18- and 24-month-old infants. *Infant Behavior and Development, 24*, 418–424.

Lutz, S. E., & Ruble, D. N. (1995). Children and gender prejudice: Context, motivation, and the development of gender conceptions. In R. Vasta (Ed.), *Annals of child development* (Vol. 10, pp. 131–166). London: Jessica Kingsley.

Lytton, H., & Romney, D. M. (1991). Parents' differential socialization of boys and girls: A meta-analysis. *Psychological Bulletin, 109*, 267–296.

Maccoby, E. E. (1990). The role of gender identity and gender constancy in sex-differentiated development. In D. Schroder (Ed.), *The legacy of Lawrence Kohlberg: New directions for child development* (pp. 5–20). San Francisco: Jossey-Bass.

Maccoby, E. E. (1998). *The two sexes: Growing apart and coming together*. Cambridge, MA: Harvard University Press.

Maccoby, E. E. (2002). Gender and group process: A developmental perspective. *Current Directions in Psychological Sciences, 11,* 54–58.

Maccoby, E. E., & Jacklin, C. N. (1974). *The psychology of sex differences*. Stanford, CA: Stanford University Press.

Maccoby, E. E., & Jacklin, C. N. (1987). Gender segregation in childhood. In W. R. Hayne (Ed.), *Advances in child development and behavior* (Vol. 20, pp. 239–287). Orlando, FL: Academic Press.

Madon, S., Jussim, L., Keiper, S., Eccles, J. S., Smith, A., & Palumbo, P. (1998). The accuracy and power of sex, social class, and ethnic stereotypes: A naturalistic study in person perception. *Personality and Social Psychology Bulletin, 24*(12), 1304–1318.

Mael, F. A. (1998). Single-sex and coeducational schooling: Relationships to socioemotional and academic development. *Review of Educational Research, 68*(2), 101–129.

Majeres, R. L. (1997). Sex differences in phonetic processing: Speed of identification of alphabetical sequences. *Perceptual and Motor Skills, 85,* 1243–1251.

Majeres, R. L. (1999). Sex differences in phonological processes: Speeded matching and word reading. *Memory and Cognition, 27,* 246–253.

Major, B., Barr, L., Zubek, J., & Babey, S. H. (1999). Gender and self-esteem: A meta-analysis. In W. B. Swann & J. H. Langlois (Eds.), *Sexism and stereotypes in modern society: The gender science of Janet Taylor Spence* (pp. 223–253). Washington, DC: American Psychological Association.

Maki, P. M., & Resnick, S. M. (2001). Effects of estrogen on patterns of brain activity at rest and during cognitive activity: A review of neuroimaging studies. *NeuroImage, 14,* 789–801.

Malkin, A. R., Wornian, K., & Chrisler, J. C. (1999). Women and weight: Gendered messages on magazine covers. *Sex Roles, 40*(7/8), 647–655.

Marcotte, D., Alain, M., & Gosselin, M. (1999). Gender differences in adolescent depression: Gender-typed characteristics or problem-solving deficits? *Sex Roles, 41,* 31–48.

Marcus, H., Crane, M., Bernstein, S., & Siladi, M. (1982). Self-schemas and gender. *Journal of Personality and Social Psychology, 42,* 38–50.

Markovits, H., Benenson, J., & Dolenszky, E. (2001). Evidence that children and adolescents have internal models of peer interactions that are gender differentiated. *Child Development, 72,* 879–886.

Marques, J., Abrams, D., Paez, D., & Martinez-Taboada, C. (1998). The role of categorization and in-group norms in judgments of groups and their members. *Journal of Personality and Social Psychology, 75*(4), 976–988.

Marsh, H. W., Byrne, B. M., & Yeung, A. S. (1999). Causal ordering of academic self-concept and achievement: Reanalysis of a pioneering study and revised recommendations. *Educational Psychologist, 34,* 154–157.

Marsh, H. W., Craven, R., & Debus, R. (1998). Structure, stability, and development of young children's self-concepts: A multicohort-multioccasion study. *Child Development, 69,* 1030–1053.

Martin, C. L. (1994). Cognitive influences on the development and maintenance of gender segregation. In L. Campbell (Ed.), *New directions for child development: Vol. 65. Childhood gender segregation—Causes and consequences* (pp. 35–51). San Francisco: Jossey-Bass.

Martin, C. L. (2000). Cognitive theories of gender development. In T. Eckes & H. M. Trautner (Eds.), *The developmental social psychology of gender* (pp. 91–121). Mahwah, NJ: Erlbaum.

Martin, C. L., & Dinella, L. M. (2001). Gender development: Gender schema theory. In *Encyclopedia of women and gender* (Vol. 1, pp. 507–521). New York: Academic Press.

Martin, C. L., & Dinella, L. M. (2002). Children's gender cognitions, the social environment, and sex differences in cognitive domains. In A. McGillicuddy-De Lisi & R. De Lisi (Eds.), *Biology, society, and behavior: The development of sex differences in cognition* (pp. 207–239). Westport, CT: Ablex.

Martin, C. L., Eisenbud, L., & Rose, H. (1995). Children's gender-based reasoning about toys. *Child Development, 66,* 1453–1471.

Martin, C. L., & Fabes, R. A. (2001). The stability and consequences of young children's same-sex peer interactions. *Developmental Psychology, 37,* 431–446.

Martin, C. L., Fabes, R. A., Evans, S. M., & Wyman, H. (1999). Social cognition on the playground: Children's beliefs about playing with girls versus boys and their relations to sex segregated play. *Journal of Social and Personal Relationships, 16,* 751–771.

Martin, C. L., Fabes, R. A., Hanish, L. D., & Hollenstein, T. (in press). Social dynamics in the preschool. *Developmental Review.*

Martin, C. L., Fabes, R. A., Hanish, L. D., Leonard, S., Dinella, L. (2006). *The roles of behavioral compatibility and gender cognitions in sex-segregated play.* Unpublished manuscript.

Martin, C. L., & Halverson, C. (1981). A schematic processing model of sex typing and stereotyping in children. *Child Development, 52,* 1119–1134.

Martin, C. L., & Halverson, C. F. (1983). Gender constancy: A methodological and theoretical analysis. *Sex Roles, 9,* 775–790.

Martin, C. L., & Little, J. K. (1990). The relation of gender understanding to children's sex-typed preferences and gender stereotypes. *Child Development, 61,* 1427–1439.

Martin, C. L., & Parker, S. (1995). Folk theories about sex and race differences. *Personality and Social Psychology Bulletin, 21,* 45–57.

Martin, C. L., Ruble, D. N., & Szkrybalo, J. (2002). Cognitive theories of early gender development. *Psychological Bulletin, 128,* 903–933.

Martin, C. L., Ruble, D. N., & Szkrybalo, J. (2004). Recognizing the centrality of gender identity and stereotype knowledge in gender development and moving toward theoretical integration: Reply to Bandura and Bussey. *Psychological Bulletin, 130*(5), 702–710.

Martin, C. L., Wood, C. H., & Little, J. K. (1990). The development of gender stereotype components. *Child Development, 61,* 1891–1904.

Mathews, G. A., Fane, B. A., Pasterski, V. L., Conway, G. S., Brook, C., & Hines, M. (2004). Androgen influences on neural asymmetry: Handedness and language lateralization in individuals with congenital adrenal hyperplasia. *Psychoneuroendocrinology, 29,* 810–822.

Mazur, A., & Booth, A. (1998). Testosterone and dominance in men. *Behavioral and Brain Sciences, 21,* 353–397.

McCabe, M. P., & Ricciardelli, L. A. (2003). Body image and strategies to lose weight and increase muscle among boys and girls. *Health Psychology, 22*(1), 39–46.

McCaul, K. D., Gladue, B. A., & Joppa, M. (1992). Winning, losing, mood, and testosterone. *Hormones and Behavior, 26,* 486–504.

McClure, E. B. (2000). A meta-analytic review of sex differences in facial expression processing and their development in infants, children, and adolescents. *Psychological Bulletin, 126,* 424–453.

McCrae, R. R., Costa, P. T., Terracciano, A., Parker, W. D., Mills, C. J., De Fruyt, F., et al. (2002). Personality trait development from age 12 to age 18: Longitudinal, cross-sectional, and cross-cultural analyses. *Journal of Personality and Social Psychology, 83*(6), 1456–1468.

McGuinness, D., & Pribram, K. H. (1979). The origins of sensory bias in the development of gender differences in perception and cognition. In M. Bortner (Ed.), *Cognitive growth and development* (pp. 3–56). New York: Brunner/Mazel.

McGuire, W. J., McGuire, C. V., Child, P., & Fujioka, T. (1978). Salience of ethnicity in the spontaneous self-concept as a function of one's ethnic distinctiveness in the social environment. *Journal of Personality and Social Psychology, 36,* 511–520.

McHale, S. M., Crouter, A. C., & Tucker, C. J. (1999). Family context and gender role socialization in middle childhood: Comparing girls to boys and sisters to brothers. *Child Development, 70,* 990–1004.

McHale, S. M., Crouter, A. C., & Whiteman, S. D. (2003). The family contexts of gender development in childhood and adolescence. *Social Development, 12*(1), 125–148.

McHale, S. M., Kim, J., Whiteman, S., & Crouter, A. C. (2004). Links between sex-typed time use in middle-childhood and gender development in early adolescence. *Developmental Psychology, 40,* 868–881.

McHale, S. M., Shanahan, L., Updegraff, K. A., Crouter, A. C., & Booth, A. (2004). Developmental and individual differences in girls' sex-typed activities in middle childhood and adolescence. *Child Development, 75*(5), 1575–1593.

McHale, S. M., Updegraff, K. A., Helms-Erikson, H., & Crouter, A. C. (2001). Sibling influence on gender development in middle childhood and early adolescence: A longitudinal study. *Developmental Psychology, 37,* 115–125.

McKown, C., & Weinstein, R. S. (2002). Modeling the role of child ethnicity and gender in children's differential response to teacher expectations. *Journal of Applied Social Psychology, 32,* 159–184.

Merke, D. P., Fields, J. D., Keil, M. F., Vaituzis, A. C., Chrousos, G. P., & Giedd, J. N. (2003). Children with classic congenital adrenal hyperplasia have decreased amygdala volume: Potential prenatal and postnatal hormonal effects. *Journal of Clinical Endocrinology and Metabolism, 88,* 1760–1765.

Meyer-Bahlburg, H. F. L. (2001). Gender and sexuality in congenital adrenal hyperplasia. *Endocrinology and Metabolism Clinics of North America, 30*(1), 155–171.

Meyer-Bahlburg, H. F. L. (2005). Gender identity outcome in female-raised 46, XY persons with penile agenesis, cloacal exstrophy of the bladder, or penile ablation. *Archives of Sexual Behavior, 34,* 423–438.

Meyer-Bahlburg, H. F. L., Gruen, R. S., New, M. I., Bell, J. J., Morishima, A., Shimshi, M., et al. (1996). Gender change from female to male in classical congenital adrenal hyperplasia. *Hormones and Behavior, 30,* 319–332.

Miller, C. F., Lurye, L., Zosuls, K., & Ruble, D. N. (2006). *Developmental changes in the accessibility of gender stereotypes.* Manuscript in preparation.

Miller, C. F., Trautner, H. M., & Ruble, D. N. (2006). The role of gender stereotypes in children's preferences and behavior. In C. Tamis-LeMonda & L. Balter (Eds.), *Child psychology: A handbook of contemporary issues* (2nd ed.). Philadelphia: Psychology Press.

Miller, E. K., Nieder, A., Freedman, D. J., & Wallis, J. D. (2003). Neural correlates of categories and concepts. *Current Opinion in Neurobiology, 13,* 198–203.

Miller, L., & Budd, J. (1999). The development of occupational sex-role stereotypes, occupational preferences, and academic subject preferences in children at ages 8, 12, and 16. *Educational Psychology, 19,* 17–35.

Mondschein, E. R., Adolph, K. E., & Tamis-LeMonda, C. S. (2000). Gender bias in mothers' expectations about infant crawling. *Journal of Experimental Child Psychology, 77*(4), 304–316.

Money, J., & Ehrhardt, A. A. (1972). *Man and woman, boy and girl.* Baltimore: Johns Hopkins University Press.

Morgan, M., & Shanahan, J. (1997). Two decades of cultivation research: An appraisal and meta-analysis. In B. R. Burleson (Ed.), *Communication yearbook* (Vol. 20, pp. 1–46). Thousand Oaks, CA: Sage.

Morrongiello, B. A., Midgett, C., & Stanton, K. (2000). Gender biases in children's appraisals of injury risk and other children's risk-taking behaviors. *Journal of Experimental Child Psychology, 77,* 317–336.

Neff, K. D., & Terry-Schmitt, L. N. (2002). Youths' attributions for power-related gender differences: Nature, nurture, or God? *Cognitive Development, 17*(2), 1185–1202.

Nicolopoulou, A. (1997). Worldmaking and identity formation in children's narrative play-acting. In B. Cox & C. Lightfoot (Eds.), *Sociogenic perspectives in internalization* (pp. 157–187). Hillsdale, NJ: Erlbaum.

Nolen-Hoeksema, S., & Girgus, J. S. (1994). The emergence of gender differences in depression during adolescence. *Psychological Bulletin, 115,* 424–443.

Nopoulos, P., Flaum, M., O'Leary, D. S., & Andreasen, N. C. (2000). Sexual dimorphism in the human brain: Evaluation of tissue volume, tissue composition, and surface anatomy using magnetic resonance imaging. *Psychiatry Research, 98*(1), 1–13.

Nordenström, A., Servin, A., Bohlin, G., Larsson, A., & Wedell, A. (2002). Sex-typed toy play behavior correlates with the degree of prenatal androgen exposure assessed by CYP21 genotype in girls with congenital adrenal hyperplasia. *Journal of Clinical Endocrinology and Metabolism, 87,* 5119–5124.

O'Brien, M. H., & Huston, A. C. (1985). Development of sex-typed play behavior in toddlers. *Developmental Psychology, 21,* 866–871.

O'Brien, M. H., Peyton, V., Mistry, R., Hruda, L., Jacobs, A., Caldera, Y., et al. (2000). Gender-role cognition in 3-year-old boys and girls. *Sex Roles, 42,* 1007–1025.

Ohring, R., Graber, J. A., & Brooks-Gunn, J. (2002). Girls' recurrent and concurrent body dissatisfaction: Correlates and consequences over 8 years. *International Journal of Eating Disorders, 31,* 404–415.

Oliver, M. B., & Green, S. (2001). Development of gender differences in children's responses to animated entertainment. *Sex Roles, 45*(1/2), 67–88.

Osgood, C. E., Suci, G. J., & Tannenbaum, P. H. (1957). *The measurement of meaning.* Urbana: University of Illinois Press.

Paley, V. G. (1984). *Boys and girls: Superheroes in the doll corner.* Chicago: University of Chicago Press.

Paley, V. G. (1988). *Bad guys don't have birthdays: Fantasy play at four.* Chicago: University of Chicago Press.

Pasterski, V. L., Geffner, M. E., Brain, C., Hindmarsh, P., Brook, C., & Hines, M. (2005). Prenatal hormones and postnatal socialization by parents as determinants of male-typical toy play in girls with congenital adrenal hyperplasia. *Child Development, 76,* 264–278.

Patterson, C. J. (2000). Family relationships of lesbian and gay men. *Journal of Marriage and the Family, 62,* 1052–1069.

Pedersen, S., & Seidman, E. (2004). Team sports achievement and self-esteem development among urban adolescent girls. *Psychology of Women Quarterly, 28,* 412–422.

Pellegrini, A. D. (1987). Rough-and-tumble play: Developmental and educational significance. *Educational Psychologist, 22,* 23–43.

Pellegrini, A. D., & Smith, P. K. (1998). Physical active play: The nature and function of a neglected aspect of play. *Child Development, 69*(3), 577–598.

Perry, D. G. (2004, April). *Gender identity and gender relevance beliefs: Two components of a causal cognitive system underlying gender differentiation?* Paper presented at the Gender Development Conference, San Francisco, CA.

Perry, D. G., White, A. J., & Perry, L. C. (1984). Does early sex typing result from children's attempts to match their behavior to sex role stereotypes? *Child Development, 55,* 2114–2121.

Picariello, M. L., Greenberg, D. N., & Pillemer, D. B. (1990). Children's sex-related stereotyping of colors. *Child Development, 61,* 1453–1460.

Pomerantz, E., & Ruble, D. N. (1998). A multidimensional perspective of control: Implications for the development of sex differences in self-evaluation and depression. In J. Heckhausen & C. Dweck (Eds.), *Motivation and self-regulation across the life span* (pp. 159–184). New York: Cambridge University Press.

Pomerleau, A., Bolduc, D., Malcuit, G., & Cossette, L. (1990). Pink or blue: Environmental gender stereotypes in the first 2 years of life. *Sex Roles, 22,* 359–367.

Poulin-Dubois, D., Serbin, L. A., & Derbyshire, A. (1998). Toddlers' intermodal and verbal knowledge about gender. *Merrill-Palmer Quarterly, 44,* 338–354.

Poulin-Dubois, D., Serbin, L. A., Eichstedt, J. A., Sen, M. G., & Beissel, C. F. (2002). Men don't put on make-up: Toddlers' knowledge of the gender stereotyping of household activities. *Social Development, 11*(2), 166–181.

Powlishta, K. K. (2000). The effect of target age on the activation of gender stereotypes. *Sex Roles, 42*(3/4), 271–282.

Powlishta, K. K., Sen, M. G., Serbin, L. A., Poulin-Dubois, D., & Eichstedt, J. A. (2001). From infancy through middle childhood: The role of cognitive and social factors in becoming gendered. In R. K. Unger (Ed.), *Handbook of the psychology of women and gender* (pp. 116–132). New York: Wiley.

Powlishta, K. K., Serbin, L. A., Doyle, A., & White, D. C. (1994). Gender, ethnic, and body type biases: The generality of prejudice in children. *Developmental Psychology, 30*(4), 526–536.

Quadagno, D. M., Briscoe, R., & Quadagno, J. S. (1977). Effects of perinatal gonadal hormones on selected nonsexual behavior patterns: A critical assessment of the non-human and human literature. *Psychological Bulletin, 84,* 62–80.

Quinn, P. C., Yahr, J., Kuhn, A., Slater, A. M., & Pascalis, O. (2002). Representation of the gender of human faces by infants: A preference for female. *Perception, 31,* 1109–1121.

Rabinowicz, T., Dean, D. E., Petetot, J. M., & de Courten-Myers, G. M. (1999). Gender differences in the human cerebral cortex: More neurons in males, more processes in females. *Journal of Child Neurology, 14*(2), 98–107.

Raffaelli, M., & Ontai, L. L. (2004). Gender socialization in Latino/a families: Results from two retrospective studies. *Sex Roles, 50,* 287–299.

Raz, N., Gunning-Dixon, F., Head, D., Rodrique, K. M., Williamson, A., & Acker, J. D. (2004). Aging, sexual dimorphism, and hemispheric asymmetry of the cerebral cortex: Replicability of regional differences in volume. *Neurobiology of Aging, 25,* 377–396.

Reiner, W. G., & Gearhart, J. P. (2004). Discordant sexual identity in some genetic males with cloacal exstrophy assigned to female sex at birth. *New England Journal of Medicine, 350,* 333–341.

Rheingold, H. L., & Cook, K. V. (1975). The contents of boys' and girls' rooms as an index of parents' behavior. *Child Development, 46,* 445–463.

Ricciardelli, L. A., & McCabe, M. P. (2001). Children's body image concerns and eating disturbance: A review of the literature. *Clinical Psychology Review, 21,* 325–344.

Richards, M. H., Crowe, P. A., Larson, R., & Swarr, A. (1998). Developmental patterns and gender differences in the experience of peer companionship during adolescence. *Child Development, 69,* 154–163.

Richner, E. S., & Nicolopoulou, A. (2001). The narrative construction of differing conceptions of the person in the development of young children's social understanding. *Early Education and Development, 12*(3), 393–432.

Roberts, D., & Foehr, U. (2004). *Kids and media in American.* Cambridge, England: Cambridge University Press.

Roberts, D., Foehr, U., Rideout, V., & Brodie, M. (1999). *Kids and media and the new millennium.* Menlo Park, CA: Henry J. Kaiser Family Foundation.

Roopnarine, J. L. (1986). Mothers' and fathers' behaviors toward the toy play of their infant sons and daughters. *Sex Roles, 14,* 59–68.

Rose, A. J. (2002). Co-rumination in the friendships of girls and boys. *Child Development, 73,* 1830–1843.

Rose, A. J., & Asher, S. R. (1999). Children's goals and strategies in response to conflicts within a friendship. *Developmental Psychology, 35,* 69–79.

Rowe, R., Maughan, B., Worthman, C. M., Costello, E. J., & Angold, A. (2004). Testosterone, antisocial behavior, and social dominance in boys: Pubertal development and biosocial interaction. *Biological Psychiatry, 55,* 546–552.

Roy, R., & Benenson, J. F. (2002). Sex and contextual effects on children's use of interference competition. *Developmental Psychology, 38,* 306–312.

Ruble, D. N. (1994). A phase model of transitions: Cognitive and motivational consequences. *Advances in Experimental Social Psychology, 26,* 163–214.

Ruble, D. N. (2004, April). *Gender identity development.* Paper presented at the Gender Development Conference, San Francisco, CA.

Ruble, D. N., Alvarez, J. M., Bachman, M., Cameron, J. A., Fuligni, A. J., Garcia Coll, C., et al. (2004). The development of a sense of "we": The emergence and implications of children's collective identity. In M. Bennett & F. Sani (Eds.), *The development of the social self* (pp. 29–76). East Sussex, England: Psychology Press.

Ruble, D. N., & Dweck, C. (1995). Self-conceptions, person conceptions, and their development. In N. Eisenberg (Ed.), *Review of personality and social psychology: Vol. 15. Social development* (pp. 109–135). Thousand Oaks, CA: Sage.

Ruble, D. N., Greulich, F., Pomerantz, E. M., & Gochberg, G. (1993). The role of gender-related processes in the development of sex differences in self-evaluation and depression. *Journal of Affective Disorders, 29,* 97–128.

Ruble, D. N., & Martin, C. (1998). Gender development. In N. Eisenberg (Ed.), *Handbook of child psychology: Vol. 3. Personality and social development* (5th ed., pp. 933–1016). New York: Wiley.

Ruble, D. N., & Stangor, C. (1986). Stalking the elusive schema: Insights from development and social-psychological analyses of gender schemas. *Social Cognition, 4,* 227–261.

Ruble, D. N., Trautner, H. M., Shrout, P., & Cyphers, L. (2006). *Longitudinal analysis of the consequences of children's understanding of gender stability.* Manuscript in preparation.

Rutter, M., Giller, H., & Hagell, A. (1998). *Antisocial behavior by young people.* Cambridge: Cambridge University Press.

Ryan, B. C., & Vandenbergh, J. G. (2002). Intrauterine position effects. *Neuroscience and Biobehavioral Reviews, 26,* 665–678.

Saffran, J. R., Aslin, R. N., & Newport, E. L. (1996). Statistical learning by 8-month-old infants. *Science, 274,* 1926–1928.

Sandberg, D. E., & Meyer-Bahlburg, H. F. L. (1994). Variability in middle childhood play behavior: Effects of gender, age, and family background. *Archives of Sexual Behavior, 23,* 645–663.

Sani, F., & Bennett, M. (2001). Contextual variability in young children's gender in group stereotypes. *Social Development, 10,* 221–229.

Sani, F., Bennett, M., Mullally, S., & MacPherson, J. (2003). On the assumption of fixity in children's stereotypes: A reappraisal. *British Journal of Developmental Psychology, 99,* 113–124.

Sartorio, A., Lafrotuna, C. L., Pogliaghi, S., & Trecate, L. (2002). The impact of gender, body dimension, and body composition on hand-grip strength in healthy children. *Journal of Endocrinological Investigation, 25,* 431–435.

Savin-Williams, R. C., & Diamond, L. (2000). Sexual identity trajectories among sexual-minority youths: Gender comparisons. *Archives of Sexual Behavior, 29,* 607–627.

Schieffelin, B. B. (1990). *The give and take of everyday life: Language socialization of Kaluli children.* New York: Cambridge University Press.

Schmidt, S. K., Griffin, W. A., Hanish, L. D., Martin, C. L., & Fabes, R. A. (2004). PlayMate: New data, new rules, and model validity. *Proceedings of the Agent 2004 Conference on Social Dynamics: Interaction, Reflexivity and Emergence,* C. M. Macal, D. Sallach, & M. J. North (Eds.). Chicago: Argonne National Laboratory and the University of Chicago.

Schur, E. A., Sanders, M., & Steiner, H. (2000). Body dissatisfaction and dieting in young children. *International Journal of Eating Disorders, 27,* 74–82.

Sellers, R. M., Smith, M., Shelton, J. N., Rowley, S. A. J., & Chavous, T. M. (1998). Multidimensional model of racial identity: A reconceptualization of African American racial identity. *Personality and Social Psychology Review, 2,* 18–39.

Serbin, L. A., Moller, L. C., Gulko, J., Powlishta, K. K., & Colburne, K. A. (1994). The emergence of gender segregation in toddler playgroups. In W. Damon (Series Ed.) & C. Leaper (Vol. Ed.), *New directions for child development: Vol. 65. Childhood gender segregation—Causes and consequences* (pp. 7–18). San Francisco: Jossey-Bass.

Serbin, L. A., Poulin-Dubois, D., Colburne, K. A., Sen, M. G., & Eichstedt, J. A. (2001). Gender stereotyping in infancy: Visual preferences for and knowledge of gender-stereotyped toys in the second year. *International Journal of Behavioral Development, 25*(1), 7–15.

Serbin, L. A., Poulin-Dubois, D., & Eichstedt, J. A. (2002). Infants' response to gender-inconsistent events. *Journal of Infancy, 3*(4), 531–542.

Serbin, L. A., Powlishta, K. K., & Gulko, J. (1993). The development of sex-typing in middle childhood. *Monographs of the Society for Research in Child Development, 58*(Serial No. 232, Whole issue).

Servin, A., Bohlin, G., & Berlin, L. (1999). Sex differences in 1-, 3-, and 5-year-olds' toy-choice in a structured play-session. *Scandinavian Journal of Psychology, 40,* 43–48.

Servin, A., Nordenström, A., Larsson, A., & Bohlin, G. (2003). Prenatal androgens and gender-typed behavior: A study of girls with mild and severe forms of congenital adrenal hyperplasia. *Developmental Psychology, 39,* 440–450.

Shaywitz, B. A., Shaywitz, S. E., Pugh, K. R., Constable, R. T., Skudlarski, P., Fulbright, R. K., et al. (1995). Sex differences in the functional organization of the brain for language. *Nature, 373,* 607–609.

Signorella, M. L., Bigler, R. S., & Liben, L. S. (1993). Developmental differences in children's gender schemata about others: A meta-analytic review. *Developmental Review, 13,* 147–183.

Signorella, M. L., Frieze, I. H., & Hershey, S. W. (1996). Single-sex versus mixed-sex classes and gender schemata in children and adolescents. *Psychology of Women Quarterly, 20,* 599–607.

Signorielli, N. (1993). Television, the portrayal of women, and children's attitudes. In G. L. Berry & J. K. Samen (Eds.), *Children and television: Images in a changing sociocultural world.* Newbury Park, CA: Sage.

Signorielli, N. (2001). Television's gender role images and contribution to stereotyping: Past, present, future. In D. Singer & J. Singer (Eds.), *Handbook of children and the media* (pp. 341–358). Thousand Oaks, CA: Sage.

Signorielli, N., & Bacue, A. (1999). Recognition and respect: A content analysis of prime-time television characters across 3 decades. *Sex Roles, 40*(7/8), 527–544.

Sippola, L. K. (1999). Getting to know the "other": The characteristics and developmental significance of other-sex relationships in adolescence. *Journal of Youth and Adolescence, 28*(4), 407–418.

Sippola, L. K., Bukowski, W. M., & Noll, R. B. (1997). Dimensions of liking and disliking underlying the same-sex preference in childhood and early adolescence. *Merrill-Palmer Quarterly, 43,* 591–609.

Skaalvik, E. M., & Rankin, R. J. (1990). Math, verbal, and general academic self-concept: The internal/external frame of reference model and gender differences in self-concept structure. *Journal of Educational Psychology, 82,* 546–554.

Slaby, R. G., & Frey, K. S. (1975). Development of gender constancy and selective attention to same-sex models. *Child Development, 52,* 849–856.

Smail, P. J., Reyes, F. I., Winter, J. S. D., & Faiman, C. (1981). The fetal hormone environment and its effect on the morphogenesis of the genital system. In S. J. Kogan & E. S. E. Hafez (Eds.), *Pediatric andrology* (pp. 9–19). Den Haag, The Netherlands: Martinus Nijhoff.

Smith, A. E., Jussim, L., & Eccles, J. S. (1999). Do self-fulfilling prophecies accumulate, dissipate, or remain stable over time? *Journal of Personality and Social Psychology, 77*(3), 548–565.

Smith, J., & Russell, G. (1984). Why do males and females differ? Children's beliefs about sex differences. *Sex Roles, 11,* 1111–1120.

Smolak, L., Levine, M. P., & Thompson, J. K. (2001). The use of the sociocultural attitudes towards appearance questionnaire with middle school boys and girls. *International Journal of Eating Disorders, 29,* 216–223.

Sommers-Flanagan, R., Sommers-Flanagan, J., & Davis, B. (1993). What's happening on music television? A gender role content analysis. *Sex Roles, 28,* 745–753.

Spence, J. T. (1999). Thirty years of gender research: A personal chronicle. In W. B. Swann, J. H. Langlois, & L. A. Gilbert (Eds.), *Sexism and stereotypes in modern society: The gender science of Janet Taylor Spence* (pp. 255–289). Washington, DC: American Psychological Association.

Spitzer, B. L., Henderson, K. A., & Zivian, M. T. (1999). Gender differences in population versus media body sizes: A comparison over 4 decades. *Sex Roles, 40,* 545–565.

Sroufe, L. A., Bennett, C., Englund, M., Urban, J., & Shulman, S. (1993). The significance of gender boundaries in preadolescence: Contemporary correlates and antecedents of boundary violation and maintenance. *Child Development, 64,* 455–466.

Stacey, J., & Biblarz, T. J. (2001). (How) does the sexual orientation of parents matter? *American Sociological Review, 66,* 159–183.

Steinberg, L., & Morris, A. S. (2001). Adolescent development. *Annual Review of Psychology, 52,* 83–110.

Steiner, M., Dunn, E., & Born, L. (2003). Hormones and mood: From menarche to menopause and beyond. *Journal of Affective Disorders, 74,* 67–83.

Stennes, L. M., Burch, M. M., Sen, M. G., & Bauer, P. J. (2005). A longitudinal study of gendered vocabulary and communicative action in young children. *Developmental Psychology, 41,* 75–88.

Stetsenko, A., Little, T. D., Gordeeva, T., Grasshof, M., & Oettingen, G. (2000). Gender effects in children's beliefs about school performance: A cross-cultural study. *Child Development, 71*(2), 517–527.

Stevens, M., Golombok, S., Beveridge, M., & Avon Longitudinal Study of Parents and Children Study Team. (2002). Does father absence influence children's gender development? Findings from a general population study of preschool children. *Parenting: Science and Practice, 2*(1), 47–60.

Stevenson, M. R., & Black, K. N. (1988). Paternal absence and sex-role development: A meta-analysis. *Child Development, 59,* 793–814.

Stice, E., & Bearman, S. K. (2001). Body image and eating disturbances prospectively predict growth in depressive symptoms in adolescents girls: A growth curve analysis. *Developmental Psychology, 37,* 597–607.

Stice, E., & Whitenton, K. (2002). Risk factors for body dissatisfaction in adolescent girls: A longitudinal investigation. *Developmental Psychology, 38,* 669–678.

Stoddart, T., & Turiel, E. (1985). Children's concepts of cross-gender activities. *Child Development, 56,* 1241–1252.

Strough, J., & Covatto, A. M. (2002). Context and age differences in same- and other-gender peer preferences. *Social Development, 11*(3), 346–361.

Subrahmanyam, K., Kraut, R., Greenfield, P., & Gross, E. (2001). New forms of electronic media: The impact of interactive games and the internet on cognition, socialization, and behavior. In D. Singer & J. Singer (Eds.), *Handbook of children and the media* (pp. 73–99). Thousand Oaks, CA: Sage.

Susman, E. J. (1997). Modeling developmental complexity in adolescence: Hormones and behavior in context. *Journal of Research on Adolescence, 7,* 283–306.

Susman, E. J., Finkelstein, J. W., Chinchilli, V. M., Schwab, J., Liben, L. S., D'Arcangelo, M. R., et al. (1998). The effect of sex hormone replacement therapy on behavior problems and moods in adolescents with delayed puberty. *Journal of Pediatrics, 133,* 521–525.

Susman, E. J., Inoff-Germain, G., Nottelmann, E. D., Loriaux, D. L., Cutler, G. B., & Chrousos, G. P. (1987). Hormones, emotional dispositions, and aggressive attributes in young adolescents. *Child Development, 58,* 1114–1134.

Susskind, J. E. (2003). Children's perception of gender-based illusory correlations: Enhancing preexisting relationships between gender and behavior. *Sex Roles, 48*(11/12), 483–494.

Szkrybalo, J., & Ruble, D. N. (1999). "God made me a girl": Gender constancy judgments and explanations revisited. *Developmental Psychology, 35,* 392–402.

Tajfel, H. (1978). Social categorization, social identity and social comparison. In H. Tajfel (Ed.), *Differentiation between social groups: Studies in the social psychology of intergroup relations* (pp. 61–76). London: Academic Press.

Tajfel, H., & Turner, J. (1979). An integrative theory of intergroup conflict. In W. Austin & S. Wochel (Eds.), *The social psychology of intergroup relations* (pp. 33–47). Monterey, CA: Brooks/Cole.

Taylor, L., Ruble, D. N., Cyphers, L., Greulich, F. K., & Shrout, P. E. (2006). *The role of gender constancy in early gender development.* Manuscript submitted for publication.

Taylor, M. G. (1996). The development of children's beliefs about social and biological aspects of gender differences. *Child Development, 67,* 1555–1571.

Tenenbaum, H. R., & Leaper, C. (2002). Are parents' gender schemas related to their children's gender-related cognitions? A meta-analysis. *Developmental Psychology, 38,* 615–630.

Tenenbaum, H. R., & Leaper, C. (2003). Parent-child conversations about science: Socialization of gender inequities. *Developmental Psychology, 39,* 34–47.

Theimer, C. E., Killen, M., & Stangor, C. (2001). Young children's evaluations of exclusion in gender-stereotypic peer contexts. *Developmental Psychology, 37,* 18–27.

Thoits, P. A., & Virshup, L. K. (1997). Me's and we's: Forms and functions of social identities. In R. D. Ashmore & L. J. Jussim (Eds.), *Self and identity: Vol. 1. Fundamental issues—Rutgers series on self and social identity* (pp. 106–133). New York: Oxford University Press.

Thomas, J. R., & French, K. E. (1985). Gender differences across age in motor performance: A meta-analysis. *Psychological Bulletin, 98,* 260–282.

Thomas, K., Ricciardelli, L. A., & Williams, R. J. (2000). Gender traits and self-concept as indicators of problem eating and body dissatisfaction among children. *Sex Roles, 43*(7/8), 441–458.

Thompson, B. R. (1999). Gender differences in preschoolers' help-eliciting communication. *Journal of Genetic Psychology, 160,* 357–369.

Thompson, J. K., Heinberg, L. J., Altabe, M., & Tantleff-Dunn, S. (1999). *Exacting beauty: Theory, assessment, and treatment of body image disturbances.* Washington, DC: American Psychological Association.

Thompson, J. K., & Stice, E. (2001). Thin-ideal internalization: Mounting evidence for a new risk factor for body-image disturbance and eating pathology. *Current Directions in Psychological Science, 10,* 181–183.

Thompson, S. K. (1975). Gender labels and early sex-role development. *Child Development, 46,* 339–347.

Thompson, T. L., & Zerbinos, E. (1995). Gender roles in animated cartoons: Has the picture changed in 20 years? *Sex Roles, 32*(9/10), 651–673.

Thorne, B. (1986). Girls and boys together, but mostly apart. In W. W. Hartup & Z. Rubin (Eds.), *Relationship and development* (pp. 167–184). Hillsdale, NJ: Erlbaum.

Thorne, B. (1993). *Gender play: Girls and boys in school.* New Brunswick, NJ: Rutgers University Press.

Tiedemann, J. (2000). Parents' gender stereotypes and teachers' beliefs as predictors of children's concept of their mathematical ability in elementary school. *Journal of Educational Psychology, 92,* 144–151.

Tiggemann, M., & Wilson-Barrett, E. (1998). Children's figure ratings: Relationship to self-esteem and negative stereotyping. *International Journal of Eating Disorders, 23,* 83–88.

Trautner, H. M. (1995). Boys' and girls' play behavior in same-sex and opposite-sex pairs. *Journal of Genetic Psychology, 156,* 5–21.

Trautner, H. M., Gervai, J., & Nemeth, R. (2003). Appearance-reality distinction and development of gender constancy understanding in children. *International Journal of Behavioral Development, 27*(3), 275–283.

Trautner, H. M., Ruble, D. N., Cyphers, L., Kirsten, B., Behrendt, R., & Hartmann, P. (2005). Rigidity and flexibility of gender stereotypes in children: Developmental or differential? *Infant and Child Development, 14,* 365–380.

Turner, P. J., Gervai, J., & Hinde, R. A. (1993). Gender-typing in young children: Preferences, behavior and cultural differences. *British Journal of Developmental Psychology, 11,* 323–342.

Udry, J. R. (2000). Biological limits of gender construction. *American Sociological Review, 65,* 443–457.

Underwood, M. K. (2003). *Social aggression among girls.* New York: Guilford Press.

Underwood, M. K., Scott, B. L., Galperin, M. B., Bjornstad, G. J., & Sexton, A. M. (2004). An observational study of social exclusion under varied conditions: Gender and developmental differences. *Child Development, 75,* 1538–1555.

Updegraff, K. A., McHale, S. M., & Crouter, A. C. (2000). Adolescents' sex-typed friendship experiences: Does having a sister versus a brother matter? *Child Development, 71,* 1597–1610.

Urberg, K. A. (1982). The development of the concepts of masculinity and femininity in young children. *Sex Roles, 8,* 659–668.

Vandewater, E. A., Shim, M., & Caplovitz, A. G. (2004). Linking obesity and activity level with children's television and video game use. *Journal of Adolescence, 27,* 71–85.

Vaughn, L. M. (2001). Teaching and learning in the primary care setting. In R. Baker (Ed.), *Handbook of pediatric primary care* (2nd ed.). Philadelphia: Lippincott, Willliams & Wilkins.

Vincent, M. A., & McCabe, M. P. (2000). Gender differences among adolescents in family and peer influences on body dissatisfaction, weight loss, and binge eating disorders. *Journal of Youth and Adolescence, 29*(2), 205–221.

Voyer, D. (1996). On the magnitude of laterality effects and sex differences in functional lateralities. *Laterality, 1,* 51–83.

Waas, G. A., & Graczyk, P. A. (1999). Child behaviors leading to peer rejection: A view from the peer group. *Child Study Journal, 29*(4), 291–307.

Wager, T. D., Phan, K. L., Liberzon, I., & Taylor, S. F. (2003). Valence, gender, and lateralization of functional brain anatomy in emotion: A meta-analysis of findings from neuroimaging. *NeuroImage, 19,* 513–531.

Walker, L. J. (1984). Sex differences in the development of moral reasoning: A critical review. *Child Development, 55,* 677–691.

Walker, L. J. (1986). Sex differences in the development of moral reasoning: A rejoinder to Baumrind. *Child Development, 57,* 522–526.

Wallen, K. (1996). Nature needs nurture: The interaction of hormonal and social influences on the development of behavioral sex differences in rhesus monkeys. *Hormones and Behavior, 30,* 364–378.

Wallen, K. (2005). Hormonal influences on sexually differentiated behavior in nonhuman primates. *Frontiers in Neuroendocrinology, 26,* 7–26.

Wallen, K., & Baum, M. J. (2002). Masculinization and defeminization in altricial and precocial mammals: Comparative aspects of steroid hormone action. In D. W. Pfaff, A. P. Arnold, A. M. Etgen, S. E. Fahrbach, & R. T. Rubin (Eds.), *Hormones, brain and behavior* (Vol. 4, pp. 385–423). New York: Academic Press.

Ward, L. M. (2003). Understanding the role of entertainment media in the sexual socialization of American youth: A review of empirical research. *Developmental Review, 23,* 347–388.

Warin, J. (2000). The attainment of self-consistency through gender in young children. *Sex Roles, 42,* 209–231.

Warrington, M., & Younger, M. (2003). "We decided to give it a twirl": Single-sex teaching in English comprehensive schools. *Gender and Education, 15,* 339–350.

Washburn-Ormachea, J. M., Hillman, S. B., & Sawilowsky, S. S. (2004). Gender and gender-role orientation differences on adolescents' coping with peer stressors. *Journal of Youth and Adolescence, 33,* 31–40.

Watt, H. M. G. (2004). Development of adolescents' self-perception, values, and task perceptions according to gender and domain in 7th- through 11th-grade Australian students. *Child Development, 75,* 1556–1572.

Weichold, K., Silbereisen, R. K., & Schmitt-Rodermund, E. (2003). Short-and long-term consequences of early versus late physical maturation in adolescents. In C. Hayward (Ed.), *Puberty and psychopathology* (pp. 241–276). Cambridge, MA: Cambridge University Press.

Weinraub, M., Clemens, L. P., Sockloff, A., Etheridge, R., Gracely, E., & Myers, B. (1984). The development of sex role stereotypes in the third year: Relationships to gender labeling, gender identity, sex-typed toy preferences, and family characteristics. *Child Development, 55,* 1493–1503.

Weisner, T. S., Garnier, H., & Loucky, J. (1994). Domestic tasks, gender egalitarian values and children's gender typing in current and nonconventional families. *Sex Roles, 30*(1/2), 23–54.

Welch-Ross, M. K., & Schmidt, E. R. (1996). Gender-schema development and children's constructive story memory: Evidence for a developmental model. *Child Development, 67,* 820–835.

Wertheim, E. H., Koerner, J., & Paxton, S. J. (2001). Longitudinal predictors of restrictive eating and bulimic tendencies in three different age groups of adolescent girls. *Journal of Youth and Adolescence, 30,* 69–81.

Whiting, B. B., & Edwards, C. P. (1988). *Children of different worlds.* Cambridge, MA: Harvard University Press.

Whitley, B. E. (1997). Gender differences in computer-related attitudes: A meta-analysis. *Computers in Human Behavior, 13*(1), 1–22.

Wigfield, A., & Eccles, J. S. (2000). Expectancy-value theory of achievement motivation. *Contemporary Educational Psychology, 25,* 68–81.

Wigfield, A., Eccles, J. S., Yoon, K. S., Harold, R. D., Abreton, A. J., Freedman-Doan, C., et al. (1997). Changes in children's competence beliefs and subjective task values across the elementary school years: A 3-year study. *Journal of Educational Psychology, 89,* 451–469.

Wild, H. A., Barrett, S. E., Spence, M. J., O'Toole, A. J., Cheng, Y. D., & Brooke, J. (2000). Recognition and sex categorization of adult's and children's faces: Examining performance in the absence of sex-stereotyped cues. *Journal of Experimental Child Psychology, 77,* 269–291.

Wilgenbusch, T., & Merrell, K. W. (1999). Gender differences in self-concept among children and adolescents: A meta-analysis of multidimensional studies. *School Psychology Quarterly, 14,* 101–120.

Williams, E., Radin, N., & Allegro, T. (1992). Sex role attitudes of adolescents reared primarily by their fathers: An 11-year follow-up. *Merrill-Palmer Quarterly, 38*(4), 457–476.

Williams, J. E., & Best, D. L. (1990). *Measuring sex stereotypes: A multination study.* Newbury Park, CA: Sage.

Williams, J. M., & Dunlop, L. C. (1999). Pubertal timing and self-reported delinquency among male adolescents. *Journal of Adolescence, 22,* 157–171.

Wisniewski, A. B., Migeon, C., Gearhart, J. P., Rock, J. A., Berkovitz, G. D., Plotnick, L. P., et al. (2001). Congenital micropenis: Long-term medical, surgical, and psychosexual follow-up of individuals raised male or female. *Hormone Research, 56,* 3–11.

Witelson, S. F., Glezer, I. I., & Kigar, D. L. (1995). Women have greater density of neurons in posterior temporal cortex. *Journal of Neuroscience, 15,* 3418–3428.

Wright, J. C., Huston, A. C., Vandewater, E. A., Bickham, D. S., Scantlin, R. M., Kotler, J. A., et al. (2001). American children's use of electronic media in 1997: A national study. *Journal of Applied Developmental Psychology, 22,* 31–47.

Yee, M., & Brown, R. (1994). The development of gender differentiation in young children. *British Journal of Social Psychology, 33,* 183–196.

Yücel, M., Stuart, G. W., Maruff, P., Velakoulis, D., Crowe, S. F., Savage, G., et al. (2001). Hemispheric and gender-related differences in the gross morphology of the anterior cingulate/paracingulate cortex in normal volunteers: An MRI morphometric study. *Cerebral Cortex, 11*(1), 17–25.

Yunger, J. L., Carver, P. R., & Perry, D. G. (2004). Does gender identity influence children's psychological well-being? *Developmental Psychology, 40,* 582–582.

Zahn-Waxler, C., Cole, P. M., & Barrett, K. C. (1991). Guilt and empathy: Sex differences and implications for the development of depression. In J. Garber & K. A. Dodge (Eds.), *The development of emotion regulation and dysregulation* (pp. 243–272). Cambridge: Cambridge University Press.

Zammuner, V. L. (1987). Children's sex-role stereotypes: A cross-cultural analysis. In P. Shaver & C. Hendrick (Eds.), *Review of personality and social psychology: Sex and gender* (pp. 272–293). Newbury Park, CA: Sage.

Zarbatany, L., McDougall, P., & Hymel, S. (2000). Gender-differentiated experience in the peer culture: Links to intimacy in preadolescence. *Social Development, 9,* 62–79.

Zosuls, K. M., Greulich, F., Haddad, M. E., Ruble, D. N., & Tamis-LeMonda, C. (2006). *Understanding gender labels and sex-typed play behavior before two years of age: A longitudinal analysis.* Manuscript submitted for publication.

Zucker, K. J. (1990). Psychosocial and erotic development in cross-gender identified children. *Canadian Journal of Psychiatry, 35,* 487–495.

Zucker, K. J. (1999). Intersexuality and gender identity differentiation. *Annual Review of Sex Research, 10,* 1–69.

Zucker, K. J. (2002). A factual correction to Bartlett, Vasey, and Bukowski's (2000) "Is gender identity disorder in children a mental disorder?" *Sex Roles, 46,* 263–264.

Zucker, K. J. (2004). Gender identity development and issues. *Child and Adolescent Psychiatric Clinics of North America, 13*(3), 551–568.

Zucker, K. J., & Bradley, S. J. (1995). *Gender identity disorder and psychosexual problems in children and adolescents.* New York: Guilford Press.

Zucker, K. J., Bradley, S. J., Kuksis, M., Pecore, K., Birkenfeld-Adams, A., Doering, R. W., et al. (1999). Gender constancy judgments in children with gender identity disorder: Evidence for a developmental lag. *Archives of Sexual Behavior, 28*(6), 475–502.

Zucker, K. J., Bradley, S. J., Oliver, G., Blake, J., Fleming, S., & Hood, J. (1996). Psychosexual development of women with congenital adrenal hyperplasia. *Hormones and Behavior, 30,* 300–318.

Zucker, K. J., Wilson-Smith, D. N. W., Kurita, J. A., & Stern, A. (1995). Children's appraisals of sex-typed behavior in their peers. *Sex Roles, 33*(11/12), 703–725.

Zucker, K. J., Yoannidis, T., & Abramovitch, R. (2001). The relation between gender labeling and gender constancy in preschool children. *Scandinavian Journal of Sexology, 4,* 107–113.

CHAPTER 15

Development of Achievement Motivation

ALLAN WIGFIELD, JACQUELYNNE S. ECCLES, ULRICH SCHIEFELE, ROBERT W. ROESER, and PAMELA DAVIS-KEAN

Work on the development of children's achievement motivation has continued to flourish since the fifth edition of this *Handbook* was published in 1998. In this chapter, we update Eccles, Wigfield, and Schiefele's (1998) chapter on motivation from the previous edition of the *Handbook*. Motivational psychologists study what moves people to act and why people think and do what they do (Pintrich, 2003; Weiner, 1992). Motivation energizes and directs actions, and so it has great relevance to many important developmental outcomes. Achievement motivation refers more specifically to motivation relevant to performance on tasks in which standards of excellence are operative. Because much of the work on motivation in developmental and educational psychology has focused on achievement motivation, we emphasize it in this chapter.

We would like to thank Ellen Skinner and Nancy Eisenberg for helpful comments on an earlier version of this chapter. The work contributed to this chapter was completed when Dr. Roeser was a visiting scholar at the Steinhardt School of Education, New York University.

How can we conceptualize broadly the nature of motivation, its influences on behavior, and its development? Motivation is most directly observable in the level of energy in individuals' behaviors. Researchers studying motivation posit various sources of this energy. Historically, drives, needs, and reinforcements were proposed as the primary sources (see Eccles et al., 1998; Pintrich & Schunk, 2002; Weiner, 1992), and needs continue to be prominent in one major current motivational theory. However, much current theory and research on motivation focuses on individuals' beliefs, values, and goals as primary influences on motivation (Eccles & Wigfield, 2002). This implies that the processes influencing motivation are cognitive, conscious, affective, and often under control of the individual. We focus on the belief, value, and goal constructs prominent in current theoretical models in this chapter.

With respect to influences on behavior, children's motivation relates to their choices about which tasks and activities to do, the persistence with which they pursue those activities, the intensity of their engagement in them, and their performance on them. Depending on their motivation, some individuals approach particular activities with great persistence and enthusiasm, whereas others seek to avoid these activities. Thus, motivation influences the ways in which individuals' do or do not participate in different activities. Once engaged in an activity, motivation can influence how diligently and in what ways the activity is pursued. Fundamentally, motivational theorists and researchers work to understand the motivational predictors of choice, persistence, and effort (Eccles et al., 1998).

With respect to development, there are important changes in children's motivation as they grow up. The prevailing pattern of change with respect to achievement motivation for many children is a decline over the school years. We discuss the reasons for this decline in this chapter. There are also important individual and group differences in the development of motivation. Many researchers have focused on gender differences in motivation, and there is increasing interest in cultural differences in motivation. We highlight work on both kinds of differences, with a particular emphasis on culture and motivation because much work on this topic has been done over the past decade. Although current theoretical perspectives often emphasize psychological beliefs, values, and goals as crucial to motivation, children's motivational development also is strongly influenced by different socialization agents, such as parents, teachers, and peers, and by the contexts in which they develop. We discuss these influences in this chapter. Indeed, a hallmark of much recent work on motivation is a concern for how different contexts influence motivation (Urdan, 1999).

To present the work on motivation, we organize our chapter in a similar fashion to the one published in the previous edition of this *Handbook,* with some deletions and some additions. To incorporate the new work into the chapter, we deleted or shortened the sections of the chapter focusing on the history of the field. Readers can consult that chapter (Eccles et al., 1998) or Weiner (1992) for this history. To explain the nature of motivation, we begin with a discussion of current theories. Some theories discussed in our previous chapter receive less attention this time and some more attention based on our assessment of their current influence on the field. We then discuss how children's motivation develops. We nest our discussion of group differences in motivation in this section because these differences are developmen-

tal in nature—they emerge during children's development. Next, we turn to how children's motivation is socialized in the home, school, and by peers. We conclude with a brief overall assessment of the state of theory and research in the achievement motivation field.

CURRENT THEORETICAL PERSPECTIVES ON MOTIVATION

Current achievement motivation theories continue to emphasize children's beliefs, values, and goals as prominent influences on motivation. This means that many theorists adopt a social cognitive perspective on the nature of motivation (Eccles et al., 1998; Pintrich, 2003). Central constructs of interest to motivation theorists include (a) self-efficacy, perceptions of control, and other competence-related beliefs; (b) the goals (both specific and general) children have for learning and other activities; (c) children's interest and intrinsic motivation for learning; and (d) children's valuing of achievement. Although the study of beliefs, goals, and values remains strong, self-determination theorists continue to emphasize the role of basic psychological needs and how they influence motivation.

As Eccles et al. (1998) did we organize our discussion of motivation theories and research around three broad motivation-related questions children can ask themselves: "Can I do this task?" "Do I want to do this task and why?" and "What do I have to do to succeed on this task?" The first two questions primarily are motivational, whereas the third merges cognitive and motivational variables crucial to the regulation of achievement behavior. Some theories include constructs that deal with all of these questions, but even so we find these questions to be a useful way to organize the theories and constructs.

Theories Concerned Primarily with the Question: "Can I Do This Task?"

Competence-related beliefs—including individuals' beliefs about their competence, self-efficacy, and expectancies for success; attributions and beliefs about intelligence; and sense of control over outcomes—relate directly to the question: "Can I do this task?" and remain prominent in theory and research on achievement motivation (e.g., Elliot & Dweck, 2005). In general, when children answer this question affirmatively, they try harder, persist longer, perform better and are motivated to select more challenging tasks.

Self-Efficacy Theory

Bandura's (1977, 1997) construct of self-efficacy is a major part of his broader social cognitive model of learning and development. Bandura defines self-efficacy as individuals' confidence in their ability to organize and execute a given course of action to solve a problem or accomplish a task. He emphasizes human agency and self-efficacy perceptions as major influences on individuals' achievement strivings, including performance, choice, and persistence. Bandura (1997) characterizes self-efficacy as a multidimensional construct that can vary in strength (i.e., positive or negative), generality (i.e., relating to many situations or only a few), and level of difficulty (i.e., feeling efficacious for all tasks or only easy tasks).

An important distinction in Bandura's (1997) model is different kinds of expectancies for success. He distinguished between two kinds of expectancy beliefs: (1) outcome expectations—beliefs that certain behaviors, like practice, will lead to certain outcomes, like improved performance; and (2) efficacy expectations—beliefs about whether one can perform the behaviors necessary to produce the outcome (e.g., I can practice sufficiently hard to win the next tennis match). Individuals can believe that a certain behavior will produce a certain outcome (i.e., outcome expectation) but may not believe they can do that behavior (i.e., efficacy expectation). Bandura therefore proposed that individuals' efficacy expectations rather than outcome expectancies are the major determinant of goal setting, activity choice, willingness to expend effort, and persistence (see Bandura, 1997).

Bandura proposed that individuals' perceived self-efficacy is determined primarily by four things: Previous performance (i.e., succeeding leads to a stronger sense of personal efficacy); vicarious learning (i.e., watching models succeed or fail on tasks); verbal encouragement by others; and one's physiological reactions (i.e., overarousal and anxiety/worry leading to a lower sense of personal efficacy). His stress on these four determinants reflects the link of this theory with both behaviorist and social learning traditions. In addition, Bandura acknowledged the influence of causal attributions on people's self-efficacy. However, Bandura argued that causal attributions only influence behavior

through their impact on efficacy beliefs. Bandura (1995) extended the self-efficacy model by discussing how collective efficacy along with individual efficacy also can be a strong influence on achievement strivings.

The self-efficacy construct has been applied to behavior in many domains, including school, health, sports, therapy, occupational choice, and even snake phobia (see Bandura, 1997, for a comprehensive review). The evidence is supportive of his theoretical predictions with respect to efficacy's influences on performance and choice. For example, high self-efficacy predict subsequent performance, course enrollment, and occupational choice (see Bandura, 1997; Pajares, 1996; Schunk & Pajares, 2002); we discuss some of the particular findings in a later section.

Bandura (1997) systematically discussed why he believes self-efficacy theory provides a fuller and richer depiction of the causal relations of self-beliefs to behavior than do other theories focused on self-referent beliefs, including theories of self-concept, locus of control, effectance motivation, control beliefs, perceived competence beliefs, and possible selves, among others. He argued that self-efficacy is defined more precisely and is more task and situation specific than many of these other beliefs and therefore should relate more strongly to behavior. However, some of the distinctions among these constructs may be less clear than Bandura proposed. For instance, researchers measuring both self-concept and self-efficacy in the same study often have found it difficult to distinguish the two constructs empirically (Skaalvik & Bong, 2003; Skaalvik & Rankin, 1996). Bong and Clark (1999) and Skaalvik and Bong (2003) provide a good discussion of conceptual and methodological similarities and differences between self-efficacy and self-concept.

Like many social cognitive-based theories, self-efficacy theory can be criticized for its overly rational and information-processing approach. How accurate are individuals at judging their efficacy, how do these calibrations vary over age, and how much are our decisions influenced by a rational judgment of our competence to do an activity? Further, the focus on one major variable as the major predictor of performance and choice perhaps is too limiting.

Self-Concept and Self-Worth Theories

Harter (1998; Chapter 9, this *Handbook,* this volume) presents comprehensive reviews of the work on self-concept, and so we only include a brief discussion of it here. Work on self-concept is relevant to this section of the chapter in two main respects. First, many of the most widely used measures of self-concept, such as those developed by Harter (1982) and Marsh (1989), assess perceived competence as the major dimension of self-concept. Thus, self-concept as measured by these instruments is beliefs about one's competence in different areas.

Second, a variety of researchers have examined the relationship between self-concept and achievement, one of the outcomes of great interest to motivation researchers. For many years, researchers debated about the causal direction between self-concept and achievement, with some proposing that growth in self-concept produces growth in achievement, and others proposing just the opposite (see Marsh, 1990b). Many of the studies that purportedly tested these relations used designs that were not adequate to test fully either position (see Marsh & Yeung, 1997, for discussion of these design problems). Recently, a number of researchers utilizing longitudinal designs found that relations between self-concept and achievement are reciprocal. These reciprocal relations have been observed in studies of children of different ages, including children as young as age 7 (Guay, Marsh, & Boivin, 2003). These findings (finally) move the field away from the seemingly intractable question of "which causes which" to the more reasonable conclusion that each variable has causal influence on the other. Such findings provide support for the important role of social cognitive and behavioral variables in the study of motivation.

Self-worth, or our overall evaluation of our worth as a person, continues to be an important variable relevant to motivation as well. Covington and his colleagues (e.g., Covington, 1992; Covington & Dray, 2002) provide the most complete motivational analysis of self-worth, arguing that individuals have a strong desire to protect their self-worth in achievement settings. Schools often focus on the demonstration of relative competence, and Covington argued that to maintain self-worth in school children must protect their competence. Children who do less well than their peers are most at risk for losing self-worth, and so they can develop strategies, such as not trying or procrastinating, as a way to try to protect their sense of competence. These strategies may provide some short-term benefits with respect to self-worth protection but, over the long term, actually work against children. Covington and his colleagues have written about ways in which school environments can be changed to lessen the emphasis on relative competence

of children, thereby allowing more children to maintain a sense of self-worth in school.

Researchers also continue to study other self-processes that guide, direct, and motivate behaviors in ways other than self-worth maintenance (e.g., Garcia & Pintrich, 1994; Markus & Wurf, 1987). For example, Markus and her colleagues discuss how "possible future selves" motivate behavior. Possible selves, the vision individuals have of themselves in the future, include both hoped-for (I will pass geometry) and feared (I will not pass geometry) components. Because possible selves are not identical to one's current self-concept, they motivate the individual by providing goals that the individual tries to attain and outcomes that the individual tries to avoid to achieve his or her image. Whether the possible self is attained depends on many things, one of which is the individual's current perceived competence.

Attribution Theory and Theories about Beliefs about Intelligence and Ability

Attribution theory concerns individuals' explanations (or attributions) for their successes and failures and how these attributions influence subsequent motivation (Graham, 1991; Weiner, 1985, 2004, 2005). Weiner and his colleagues identified the most frequently used attributions (i.e., ability, effort, task difficulty, and luck), and classified these and other attributions into the different causal dimensions of stability (i.e., stable or unstable), locus of control (i.e., internal or external), and controllability (i.e., under one's volition or not). For instance, ability is classified as internal, stable, and uncontrollable. Each of these dimensions has important psychological consequences that influence subsequent motivation and behavior. The stability dimension relates most directly to expectancies for success and failure, locus of control to affective reactions to success and failure, and controllability to help giving. For instance, attributing failure to lack of ability leads to lowered expectancies for success and negative affect like shame (Weiner, 1985; see Eccles et al., 1998, for more detailed review).

Attribution theory was quite dominant in the motivation field for many years, but its influence has waned to an extent recently. Despite this, there still is great interest in the motivation field in perceptions of ability and also of effort. Indeed, some theorists (most notably, Carol Dweck) working in the attribution tradition have become interested in individuals' beliefs about the nature of ability and the implications of these beliefs for their motivation and effort. Dweck and her colleagues (e.g., Dweck, 2002; Dweck & Leggett, 1988) posited that children can hold one of two views of intelligence or ability. Children holding an *entity* view of intelligence believe that intelligence is a stable trait. Children holding an *incremental* view of intelligence believe that intelligence is changeable, so that it can be increased through effort. Note that this differs from the traditional attribution theory view, which is that ability is a stable characteristic. In Dweck's work there is more than one way to view one's ability.

Dweck and her colleagues (Dweck, 2002; Dweck & Leggett, 1988) have discussed how children's conceptions of ability and intelligence can have important motivational consequences. Dweck (2002) argued that children holding an entity theory of intelligence are motivated to look smart and protect their sense of ability. Children believing intelligence can change focus on learning and improvement. When children do poorly, believing that their ability has a limited capacity means that failure is more debilitating. Some children holding this view will believe they have little chance of ever doing well because their ability cannot be improved. Children holding this belief can become "learned helpless" in achievement settings; we discuss learned helplessness later. In contrast, believing effort can improve performance in important ways can mean that children will continue to try even if they are not doing well on a given task (see Dweck & Leggett, 1988; Nicholls, 1984, 1990, for further discussion).

Dweck and Leggett (1988) tied children's beliefs about intelligence to their achievement goals, as we see in a later section. Children holding an incremental view of intelligence tend to have mastery or learning goals, whereas children holding an entity view have performance goals. Further, Dweck and Leggett broadened their analysis to other domains, contrasting the relative benefits of incremental versus entity views about social relationships and moral development. In each case, they argued that the incremental view has many benefits to children (see also Dweck, 2002).

Control Theories

Building on the seminal early work of Rotter (1966) and Crandall, Katkovsky, and Crandall (1965) on internal and external locus of control, theorists have elaborated broader conceptual models of control. Connell (1985), for example, added *unknown control* as a third control belief category and argued that younger children are particularly likely to use this category. He developed and validated to a scale to assess external control (i.e.,

"powerful others"), internal control (i.e., effort and ability), and unknown control for cognitive, physical, social, and general activities. Connell and Wellborn (1991) then integrated control beliefs into the self-determination framework that proposes the fundamental psychological needs for competence, autonomy, and relatedness (see Deci & Ryan, 1985; R. M. Ryan, 1992; R. M. Ryan & Deci, 2000a, further discussion later). They linked control beliefs to competence needs: Children who believe they control their achievement outcomes should feel more competent. They hypothesized that the extent to which these needs are fulfilled is influenced by the following characteristics of their family, peer, and school contexts: (a) the amount of structure, (b) the degree of autonomy provided, and (c) the level of involvement in the children's activities.

Ellen Skinner and her colleagues (e.g., Skinner, 1995; Skinner, Chapman, & Baltes, 1988) proposed a more elaborate model of control beliefs. This model includes three critical control-related beliefs: (1) strategy beliefs, (2) control beliefs, and (3) capacity beliefs. Strategy beliefs concern the expectation that particular causes can produce certain outcomes; these causes include Weiner's (2005) various causal attributions and Connell's (1985) unknown control. Control beliefs are the expectations individuals have that they can produce desired events and prevent undesired ones. Capacity beliefs are the expectations that one has access to the means needed to produce various outcomes. Skinner (1995) proposed that control beliefs are a major determinant of actions, leading to outcomes that are interpreted by the individual and subsequently influence their control beliefs, starting the cycle again.

Skinner distinguished her position from self-efficacy theories by noting that self-efficacy theorists discuss connections between agents and means primarily as expectancies that the individual can produce some outcome; thus outcomes are contingent on one's responses. In contrast, she argued that her capacity beliefs relate to potential as well as actual means. Further, an individual can have strong capacity beliefs for different means without believing that any of the means are necessarily effective (see also R. M. Ryan, 1992).

Finally, Skinner, Connell, and their colleagues have broadened their discussion of perceived control and its influences by developing a model of the relations among context, the self, action, and outcomes (e.g., Connell, Spencer, & Aber, 1994; Skinner & Wellborn, 1994). They proposed that when contexts are set up in a way that allows the needs of competence, relatedness, and autonomy to be supported, individuals will be engaged more fully in activities, which leads to positive developmental outcomes. Contexts that are not supportive of these needs lead to disengagement. Further, the ways in which these needs are fulfilled determine engagement in different activities. When the needs are fulfilled, children will be fully engaged. When one or more of the needs is not fulfilled, children will become disaffected. Connell et al. (1994) and Skinner and Belmont (1993) conducted studies in classroom settings that supported these linkages. We discuss the implications of these findings in the section on how school contexts influence children's motivation.

Modern Expectancy-Value Theory

Modern expectancy-value theories (e.g., Eccles-Parsons et al., 1983; Feather, 1982; Heckhausen, 1977; Pekrun, 1993; Wigfield & Eccles, 2000, 2002b) are based in Atkinson's (1957, 1964) original expectancy-value model in that they link achievement performance, persistence, and choice most directly to individuals' expectancy-related and task-value beliefs. However, they differ from Atkinson's theory in several ways: First, both the expectancy and value components are more elaborate and are linked to a broader array of psychological and social/cultural determinants. Second, they are grounded more in real-world achievement tasks than the laboratory tasks often used to test Atkinson's theory. We focus here on the ability and expectancy portion of Eccles and her colleagues' model; see Eccles et al. (1998) for review of some other modern expectancy-value models.

The Eccles et al. Expectancy-Value Model. Eccles-Parsons and her colleagues elaborated and tested one expectancy-value model of achievement-related choices (see Eccles, 1987, 1993; Eccles & Wigfield, 1995; Eccles-Parsons et al., 1983; Wigfield & Eccles, 2000, 2002b). This model focuses on the social psychological influences on choice and persistence. Choices are seen to be influenced by both negative and positive task characteristics and all choices are assumed to have costs associated with them precisely because one choice often eliminates other options. Much of their work focuses on individual differences and gender differences in decisions regarding which courses to take, what careers to seek, and what activities to pursue.

The theoretical model is depicted in Figure 15.1. Expectancies and values are assumed to directly influence performance, persistence, and task choice. Expectan-

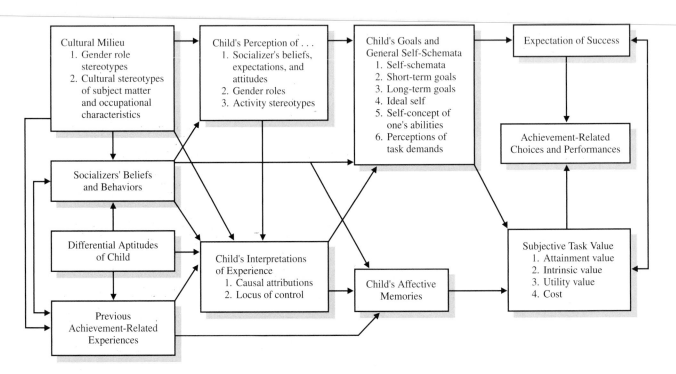

Figure 15.1 Eccles and colleagues' motivational model of achievement performance and choice.

cies and values are assumed to be influenced by task-specific beliefs such as perceptions of competence, perceptions of the difficulty of different tasks, and individuals' goals and self-schema. These social cognitive variables are influenced by individuals' perceptions of other peoples' attitudes and expectations for them and by their own interpretations of their previous achievement outcomes. Individuals' task-perceptions and interpretations of their past outcomes are assumed to be influenced by the socializer's behavior and beliefs and by the cultural milieu and unique historical events.

Eccles-Parsons et al. (1983) defined expectancies for success as children's beliefs about how well they will do on upcoming tasks, either in the immediate or longer-term future. These expectancy beliefs are measured in a manner analogous to measures of Bandura's (1997) personal efficacy expectations: Thus, in contrast to Bandura's claim that expectancy-value theories focus on outcome expectations, the focus in this model is on personal or efficacy expectations.

Eccles-Parsons et al. (1983) defined beliefs about ability as children's evaluations of their competence in different areas; this definition is similar to those of researchers like Covington (1992), Harter (e.g., Harter, 1982, 1990), and Marsh and his colleagues (e.g., Marsh, 1990a). In measuring ability beliefs, Eccles and her colleagues measure individuals' beliefs about how good they are at a certain activity, how good they are relative to other individuals, and how good they are relative to their performance on other activities. This approach is somewhat different from the way in which self-efficacy often is measured. Many self-efficacy measures do not include the comparative items but instead focus solely on individuals' judgments of their own capabilities (Bandura, 1997; Pajares, 1996).

In this model, ability beliefs and expectancies for success are distinguished theoretically in that ability beliefs are seen as beliefs about competence in a given domain, in contrast to one's expectancies for success on a specific upcoming task. However, their empirical work has shown that children and adolescents do not distinguish between these two different levels of beliefs (e.g., Eccles & Wigfield, 1995; Eccles, Wigfield, Harold, & Blumenfeld, 1993). Even though these constructs can be theoretically distinguished from each other, in real-world achievement situations they are highly related and thus empirically indistinguishable. Eccles and her colleagues have found that children's expectancy-related beliefs have direct effects on their subsequent perfor-

mance and indirect effects on their intentions to continue doing activities and actual choices of doing so (e.g., Meece, Wigfield, & Eccles, 1990).

In sum, a variety of theories continue to focus on competence-related beliefs as having a major impact on motivation. As we have seen, there are differences in how the competence and control constructs are defined and measured in these theoretical models. These distinctions among the various constructs are important theoretically, but, empirically and practically, the constructs are highly related. A further proliferation of these constructs does not seem necessary, and perhaps by examining more closely relations among them we can determine which of them is the most viable.

Theories Concerned with the Question: "Do I Want to Do This Task and Why?"

Theories dealing with efficacy, expectancy, and control beliefs provide powerful explanations of individuals' performance on different kinds of achievement tasks. However, these theories do not systematically address another important motivational question: "Do I *want* to do the task?" Even if people are certain they can do a task, they may not want to engage in it, and so they may not be strongly motivated to approach it. Further, individuals often have different purposes or goals for doing different activities, which also can impact their motivation for doing the task. The theories presented next focus on these kinds of issues.

Modern Expectancy-Value Theories: The Importance of Task Value

We discussed in the previous section the expectancy and competence belief portions of expectancy-value models. Here we focus on the task value part of the model. Eccles and her colleagues have done much of this work. However, it is important to acknowledge Feather's (1982, 1988, 1992) contributions (see Eccles et al., 1998, for more detailed discussion of his work). Feather looked at broader values and task-specific values in several studies of students' choices of college majors and activities. Finding values to be strongly predictive of these choices, he also found that students' expectancies for success and values were positively rather than inversely related.

Eccles, Wigfield, and Colleagues' Work on Subjective Task Values.   Eccles-Parsons and her colleagues (1983) defined four motivational components of task value: (1) attainment value, (2) intrinsic value, (3) utility value, and (4) cost. They defined attainment value as the personal importance of doing well on the task, and also linked this aspect of task value to the relevance of engaging in a task for confirming or disconfirming salient aspects of one's self-schema, such as perceived gender role, ethnic identity, or other salient aspect of self.

Intrinsic value is the enjoyment the individual gets from performing the activity, or the subjective interest the individual has in the subject. This component of value is similar in certain respects to the construct of intrinsic motivation as defined by Harter (1981), and by Deci and his colleagues (e.g., Deci & Ryan, 1985; R. M. Ryan & Deci, 2000a), and to the constructs of interest and flow as defined by Csikszentmihalyi (1988), Renninger (1990), and Schiefele (1991). However, like the debates about the different competence-related belief constructs, there have been discussions in the literature about the differences among these related constructs as well.

Utility value is determined by how well a task relates to current and future goals, such as career goals. A task can have positive value to a person because it facilitates important future goals, even if he or she is not interested in the task for its own sake. For instance, students often take classes that they do not particularly enjoy but that they need to take to pursue other interests, to please their parents, or to be with their friends. In one sense, this component captures the more extrinsic reasons for engaging in a task. But it also relates directly to individuals' internalized short- and long-term goals.

Finally, Eccles and her colleagues identified "cost" as a critical component of value (Eccles, 1987; Eccles-Parsons et al., 1983). Cost is conceptualized as the negative aspects of engaging in the task, such as performance anxiety and fear of failure or of success and the amount of effort needed to succeed. It also is defined by the lost opportunities that result from making one choice rather than another. When a child chooses to do her homework this may mean she will not have time to instant message her friends, truly a major cost for some children. This aspect of task values has been less studied than the others, even though it likely plays an important role in individuals' choices. Indeed, Battle and Wigfield (2003) found that the perceived psychological costs of attending graduate school were a negative predictor of college students' intentions to enroll in graduate school.

Eccles and her colleagues and others (e.g., Bong, 2001) have assessed the links of expectancies and values to performance and choice (see Wigfield & Eccles, 2002b, for review). They have shown that ability self-concepts and expectancies for success directly predict performance in mathematics, English, computer activities, and sport activities, even when previous performance is controlled. Children's task values predict course plans and enrollment decisions more strongly than do expectancy-related beliefs. Eccles (1994) found that both expectancies and values predict career choices. These results illustrate the importance of looking not only at competence and expectancy beliefs but also at achievement values in understanding individuals' performance and choice.

Valuing Particular Learning Activities Now and in the Future. Brophy (1999) edited a special issue of the journal *Educational Psychologist* devoted to the value aspects of learning. In his article in this issue, he noted that we still know relatively little about how children's values and interests for particular learning activities develop and how different learning opportunities influence children's valuing of them. He made the intriguing proposal that we should think of a motivational zone of proximal development (ZPD) along with a cognitive ZPD as we consider ways to enhance children's learning and motivation. When learning activities are in a child's motivational ZPD they can come to appreciate the importance of the activity and will be more likely to engage in it. If a learning activity is too far above a student's motivational ZPD the student will be less likely to engage in the activity, or appreciate its importance. Brophy also proposed that the cognitive and motivational ZPD's may interact to influence students' learning and engagement, and he discussed ways in which children's valuing of learning can be fostered. We return to these ideas in a later section.

Husman, Lens, and their colleagues have discussed another important values-related construct, future time perspective (FTP; Husman & Lens, 1999; Kaufman & Husman, 2004; Lens, 1986), building on earlier work on the role of the future in motivation by theorists such as Raynor (1982). They noted that much of the work in the motivation field focuses on motivation for immediate tasks and activities. This motivation obviously is important for students' engagement in learning, but students also know that a major purpose of education is to prepare them for the future. Therefore, if students believe that current educational activities are useful to them in the long run, they are more likely to be motivated to achieve. Husman, Lens, and their colleagues have done a series of studies on FTP, showing that when students see the value of educational activities to their future success they are more positively motivated, self-regulated, and achieve higher grade point averages (GPAs). They refer to the *instrumentality* of these activities to the future as the key predictive variable. With respect to Eccles and colleagues' definitions of aspects of task value, it appears that FTP focuses on the utility and (possibly) the attainment aspects rather than the interest aspect. However, Husman (1998) has shown some relations of future instrumentality to intrinsic motivation.

In sum, expectancy-value models continue to be prominent. We noted in our previous chapter that research has focused to a much greater extent on expectancy-related rather than value aspects of this model. That picture has changed some over the past several years. Yet, more work is needed on the nature of children's achievement values and how they develop. We also need more work on how the links of expectancies and values to performance and choice change across ages (see Eccles, 1993; Wigfield, 1994) and on the links between expectancies and values (see Jacobs, Lanza, Osgood, Eccles, & Wigfield, 2002). Both Eccles (1984) and Bandura (1997) propose a positive association between expectancy related beliefs and task values, and research supports this (e.g., Wigfield et al., 1997). The role of FTP in expectancy-value models also deserves continued study.

Like self-efficacy theory, modern expectancy-value theory can be criticized for emphasizing overly rational cognitive processes leading to motivation and behavior. Such criticisms are likely to be particularly apropos when these models are considered from a developmental perspective (see Wigfield, 1994). However, the impressive body of research showing the relations of expectancy and values to different kinds of performance and choice supports the continuing viability of these models. Furthermore, as conceptualized by Eccles and her colleagues, values are linked to more stable self-schema and identity constructs and choice is not necessarily the result of conscious, rational, decision-making processes (see Eccles, 1987; Eccles & Harold, 1992). By including affective memories, culturally based stereotypes, and identity-related constructs and processes as part of the theoretical system, Eccles and her colleagues

have allowed for less rational and conscious processes in motivated behavioral choices.

Intrinsic Motivation Theories

There is a fundamental distinction in the motivation literature between *intrinsic* motivation and *extrinsic* motivation. When individuals are intrinsically motivated, they do activities for their own sake and out of interest in the activity. When extrinsically motivated, individuals do activities for instrumental or other reasons, such as receiving a reward (see Sansone & Harackiewicz, 2000b). There is continuing debate about the pros and cons of intrinsic and extrinsic motivation, and a growing consensus that these two constructs should not be treated as polar opposites. Rather, they often both operate in different situations, and may even form a continuum.

Much of the work on intrinsic motivation stemmed from White's (1959) seminal article on effectance motivation: He argued persuasively that both people and at least some animals are motivated by curiosity and interest in developing their competence rather than just by rewards or the satisfaction of basic bodily needs. This influential article had a strong influence on the views of Edward Deci and Richard Ryan, whose self-determination theory of intrinsic motivation is the main focus in this section.

Self-Determination Theory. Deci, Ryan, and their colleagues' self-determination theory (SDT) is an organismic theory of development that has a particular focus on the role of motivation in development and learning (e.g., Deci & Ryan, 1985, 2002b; Deci, Vallerand, Pelletier, & Ryan, 1991; R. M. Ryan & Deci, 2000a). Broadly, self-determined behavior is behavior that originates from the self and that results from the individual utilizing his or her volition. Deci, Ryan, and their colleagues suggest that when individuals' behavior is self-determined they are psychologically healthier and tend to be intrinsically motivated. Indeed, they make a specific link between intrinsic motivation and self-determination, arguing that intrinsic motivation is only possible when individuals freely choose their own actions—they are self-determined.

Deci, Ryan, and their colleagues propose that there are three basic or fundamental human psychological needs: (1) the need for competence, (2) the need for autonomy, and (3) the need for relatedness (Deci & Ryan, 2002b; R. M. Ryan & Deci, 2002). For healthy development to occur, these needs must be met. Further, these needs are a basis for motivation. For instance, the need for competence is the major reason why people seek out optimal stimulation and challenging activities. The need for autonomy refers most directly to volition and self-determination; Deci and Ryan argue that this sense of volition is necessary for optimum motivation. R. M. Ryan (1992) discussed the importance of distinguishing between competence and autonomy. He argued that models that focus primarily on competence, like self-efficacy theory, do not make this distinction clear enough. Individuals can act competently and demonstrate their competence but still be doing so under the control of others. R. M. Ryan compared such actions to those of a robot, rather than a self-determined individual, and argued that intrinsic motivation only occurs when individuals are both autonomous and competent. The proposal that autonomy is a basic human need has led to much interesting research on topics such as choice and how providing children and adults with choice influences their intrinsic motivation.

Relatedness refers to the need to be connected with others. This need was added to the theory after the other two, and reflects Deci and Ryan's beliefs that individuals must have strong connections to others for optimum development to occur. In their view, the need for autonomy does not imply total independence; connections with others also are important to optimum development.

Deci, Ryan, and colleagues go beyond the extrinsic-intrinsic motivation dichotomy in their discussion of *internalization*, which is the process of transferring the regulation of behavior from outside to inside the individual (see Deci, Koestner, & Ryan, 1999; Grolnick, Gurland, Jacob, & Decourcey, 2002). They developed a taxonomy to describe different types of motivation involved in the process of going from external to more internalized regulation of motivation. This taxonomy forms a continuum. At one extreme is *amotivation*, which as the name implies means an absence of motivation to act. Next are several types of extrinsic motivation that range from least to most autonomous. In order, these are:

- *External:* Regulation coming from outside the individual
- *Introjected:* Internal regulation based on feelings that he or she should or has to do the behavior
- *Identified:* Internal regulation of behavior that is based on the utility of that behavior (e.g., studying hard to get grades to get into college)
- *Integrated:* Regulation based on what the individual thinks is valuable and important to the self

Each of these levels also is associated with different kinds of motivation. For instance, extrinsic rewards are most salient for external regulation, and at each subsequent level motivation become more internalized.

Deci, Ryan, and their colleagues have developed scales to measure these different levels of regulation. They have tested their continuum idea by looking at how related the different kinds of motivation are. For instance, R. M. Ryan and Connell (1989) assessed children's external, introjected, identified, and intrinsic reasons for doing schoolwork, and found that these correlations formed a simplex pattern (see also Vallerand et al., 1993). The levels of regulation closer to one another in the continuum were more highly related than those further apart, which they took as evidence for their placement on the continuum. Further, they found that the more extrinsically motivated the students were, the less invested they were in their schoolwork.

One major focus of Deci, Ryan, and their colleagues' research and theorizing has been how extrinsic rewards can undermine intrinsically motivated behavior. They call this portion of their theory cognitive evaluation theory. They and others (e.g., Lepper & Green, 1978) described different conditions under which rewards can be undermining; the most notable is when rewards are controlling, which reduces the individual's perceptions of autonomy over their own learning. When rewards provide individuals with information about how they are doing rather than focus on controlling them, the undermining effects do not occur. In 1994, Cameron and Pierce published a meta-analysis of this research in which they questioned the strength of these undermining effects, arguing that they occurred only in very limited circumstances if at all. This article led to a series of commentaries and reactions and further meta-analyses of the findings regarding the undermining effects of rewards on intrinsically motivated behavior, with many claims and counter-claims about the adequacy of the meta-analytic techniques used and ways of parsing the findings (see Deci et al., 1999; Lepper & Henderlong, 2000; R. M. Ryan & Deci, 2000b; Sansone & Harackiewicz, 2000b, for a summary of this debate). We believe that Deci, Ryan, and their colleagues have replied effectively to Cameron and Pierce's various arguments against the undermining effects of extrinsic motivation. Yet, this debate was useful because it served to clarify the conditions under which extrinsic motivators do undermine intrinsically motivated behaviors and so moved the field ahead in important ways.

SDT has been a dominant theoretical model and one that has generated a great deal of research. It is a broad model that encompasses a variety of constructs and that integrates many important issues with respect to the development of motivation. The theory, however, has been the subject of some criticism. A number of questions have been raised about Deci and Ryan's contention that there are three basic psychological needs (see Pintrich, 2003). Other questions have been raised about the universality of these needs and whether they operate similarly in different cultures. For instance, in cultures defined as less individualistic and more collectivist does the need for autonomy take on the same importance? This question currently is the focus of a great deal of research (Reeve, Deci, & Ryan, 2004). There also has been debate in SDT on the role of choice in helping children fulfill their need for autonomy (Reeve, Nix, & Hamm, 2003). Finally, although the continuum from extrinsic to intrinsic motivation is intriguing, there is some concern that intrinsic motivation as defined in this way only describes a very limited set of activities that people do during their daily lives. This perhaps constrains intrinsic motivation too much.

Flow Theory. Csikszentmihalyi (1988) discusses intrinsically motivated behavior in terms of the immediate subjective experience that occurs when people are engaged in the activity. Interviews with climbers, dancers, chess players, basketball players, and composers revealed that these activities yield a specific form of experience—labeled flow—characterized by: (a) holistic feelings of being immersed in, and of being carried by, an activity; (b) merging of action and awareness; (c) focus of attention on a limited stimulus field; (d) lack of self-consciousness; and (e) feeling in control of one's actions and the environment. Flow is only possible when people feel that the opportunities for action in a given situation match their ability to master the challenges. The challenge of an activity may be something concrete or physical, like the peak of a mountain to be scaled, or it can be something abstract and symbolic, like a set of musical notes to be performed, a story to be written, or a puzzle to be solved. Further research has shown that both the challenges and skills must be relatively high before a flow experience becomes possible (Massimini & Carli, 1988).

At first sight, the theories of Deci and Ryan and Csikszentmihalyi seem to be very different. Deci and Ryan (1985, 2002b) explain intrinsic motivation by assuming innate, basic needs, whereas Csikszentmihalyi stresses subjective experience. We suggest that this difference reflects two sides of the same coin. As K. Schneider (1996) has argued, a person has to distinguish between immediate reasons (e.g., enjoyment) and ultimate reasons of behavior (e.g., survival). Intrinsically motivated behavior can be conducive to ultimate goals even though the actor is only motivated by immediate incentives. A typical case is exploratory or play behavior. Both types of behavior help to increase an individual's competence, but they are usually performed because they are exciting, pleasurable, or enjoyable. This distinction between immediate and ultimate causes of behavior makes it possible to reconcile the positions of Deci and Ryan and Csikszentmihalyi. Deci and Ryan (1985) focus on ultimate reasons of behavior, whereas Csikszentmihalyi (1988) focuses mainly on immediate reasons. Csikszentmihalyi and Massimini (1985) have suggested that the experience of flow is a reward that ensures that individuals will seek to increase their competence. According to Csikszentmihalyi, the repeated experience of flow is only possible when individuals seek out increasingly challenging tasks and expand their competencies to meet these challenges. Thus, the experience of flow should reinforce behaviors underlying development.

Individual Difference Theories of Intrinsic Motivation. Until recently, intrinsic motivation researchers like Deci and Ryan and Csikszentmihalyi have dealt with conditions, components, and consequences of intrinsic motivation without making a distinction between intrinsic motivation as a state versus intrinsic motivation as a traitlike characteristic. However, interest in traitlike individual differences in intrinsic motivation has increased recently, particularly among educational psychologists (see Gottfried, 1985, 1990; Gottfried, Fleming, & Gottfried, 2001; Harter, 1981; Nicholls, 1984, 1989; Schiefele, 1996a, 1996b; Schiefele & Schreyer, 1994). These researchers define this enduring intrinsic motivational orientation by three components: (1) preference for hard or challenging tasks, (2) learning that is driven by curiosity or interest, and (3) striving for competence and mastery. The second component is most central to the idea of intrinsic motivation. Both preference for hard tasks and striving for competence can be linked to either extrinsic or more general need achievement motivation. Nonetheless, empirical findings suggest that the three components are highly correlated. In addition, evidence suggests that high levels of traitlike intrinsic motivation facilitate positive emotional experience and well-being (Matsumoto & Sanders, 1988; R. M. Ryan & Deci, 2000a), self-esteem (R. M. Ryan, Connell, & Deci, 1985), high academic achievement (Cordova & Lepper, 1996; Schiefele & Schreyer, 1994), creativity (e.g., Hennessey, 2000), self-regulation, and persistence (Cordova & Lepper, 1996; Pelletier, Fortier, Vallerand, & Brière, 2001; Pintrich & Schrauben, 1992; Schiefele & Schreyer, 1994). As a consequence, many have suggested that the development of an intrinsic motivational orientation should be fostered in the home and the classroom (e.g., Brophy, 1999; Dewey, 1913; Lepper & Chabay, 1985).

Interest Theories

Closely related to the notion of intrinsic motivation is work on the concept of "interest" (P. A. Alexander, Kulikowich, & Jetton, 1994; Hidi, 2001; Krapp, 2002; Renninger, 2000; Renninger, Hidi, & Krapp, 1992; Schiefele, 1991, 2001; Tobias, 1994). Hidi and Harackiewicz (2000) propose that interest is more specific than intrinsic motivation, which is a broader motivational characteristic (see also Deci, 1992, 1998). Researchers studying interest differentiate between individual and situational interest. Individual interest is a relatively stable evaluative orientation toward certain domains; situational interest is an emotional state aroused by specific features of an activity or a task. Two aspects or components of individual interest are distinguishable (Schiefele, 1996a, 2001): (1) feeling-related valences and (2) value-related valences. Feeling-related valences refer to the feelings that are associated with an object or an activity itself—feelings like involvement, stimulation, or flow. Value-related valences refer to the attribution of personal significance or importance to an object. In addition, both feeling-related and value-related valences are directly related to the object rather than to the relation of this object to other objects or events. For example, if students associate mathematics with high personal significance because mathematics can help them get prestigious jobs, we would not speak of interest. Although feeling-related and value-related valences are highly correlated (Schiefele, 1996a), it is useful to differentiate between them because some individual interests are likely based primarily on feelings, whereas others' interests are more likely to be based on personal significance (see Eccles, 1984; Wigfield & Eccles, 1992). Further research is necessary to validate this assumption.

Much of the research on individual interest has focused on its relation to the quality of learning (see P. A. Alexander et al., 1994; Hidi, 2001; Renninger, Ewen, & Lasher, 2002; Schiefele, 1996a, 1996b, 1999). In general, there are significant but moderate relations between interest and text learning. Importantly, interest is more strongly related to indicators of deep-level learning (e.g., recall of main ideas, coherence of recall, responding to deeper comprehension questions, and representation of meaning) than to surface-level learning (e.g., responding to simple questions or verbatim representation of text; Schiefele, 1996b, 1999; Schiefele & Krapp, 1996). Findings by Ainley, Hidi, and Berndorff (2002) and Hidi (2001) suggest that attentional processes, affect, and persistence mediate the effects of interest on text learning.

There is also ample evidence that subject matter interest is positively related to school achievement (cf. Schiefele, Krapp, & Winteler, 1992). Recent studies suggest that interest particularly predicts achievement when there is a context that allows for choice. Specifically, Köller, Baumert, and Schnabel (2001) found that interest in mathematics predicts achievement only at higher grade levels when students have a choice between more or less advanced courses. The "effect" of interest on achievement was partly mediated by choice of course level. However, there was also a direct path from interest to achievement even when controlling for prior achievement.

Most of the research on situational interest has focused on the characteristics of academic tasks that create interest (e.g., Hidi, 2001; Schraw & Lehman, 2001). Among others, the following text features were found to arouse situational interest: personal relevance, novelty, vividness, and comprehensibility (Chen, Darst, & Pangrazi, 2001; Schraw, Bruning, & Svoboda, 1995; Wade, Buxton, & Kelly, 1999). Empirical evidence has provided strong support for the relation between situational interest and text comprehension and recall (see reviews by Hidi, 2001; Schiefele, 1996a, 1999; Wade, 1992).

Goal Theories

Work on achievement goals and goal orientations has flourished since the publication of our previous chapter. This work can be organized into three relatively distinct areas (see Pintrich, 2000a). One group of researchers has focused on the properties of goals for specific learning activities. These researchers (e.g., Bandura, 1986; Schunk, 1991) focus on goals' proximity, specificity, and level of challenge and have shown that specific, proximal, and somewhat challenging goals promote both self-efficacy and improved performance. A second group of researchers defined and investigated broader goal orientations students have toward their learning, focusing primarily on three broad orientations: (1) a mastery or learning orientation, (2) an ego or performance orientation, and (3) a work-avoidant orientation. These orientations refer to broader approaches children take to their learning, rather than goals for specific activities, although goal orientations can also influence the approach one takes to a specific task. A third group focuses on the content of children's goals, proposing that there are many different kinds of goals individuals can have in achievement settings, including both academic and social goals (e.g., Ford, 1992; Wentzel, 1991b). We focus in this section on the work of the latter two groups.

Goal Orientation Theory. Researchers (e.g., Ames, 1992; Blumenfeld, 1992; Butler, 1993; Dweck & Leggett, 1988; Maehr & Midgley, 1996; Nicholls, 1984) initially distinguished two broad goal orientations that students can have toward their learning. First, the *learning, task-involved,* or *mastery* goal orientation means that the child is focused on improving their skills, mastering material, and learning new things. Questions such as "How can I do this task?" and "What will I learn?" reflect task-involved goals. Second, the *performance* or *ego* orientation means that the child focuses on maximizing favorable evaluations of their competence and minimizing negative evaluations of competence. In addition, Nicholls and his colleagues (e.g., Nicholls, Cobb, Yackel, Wood, & Wheatley, 1990) and Meece (1991, 1994) have described a *work-avoidant* goal orientation, which means that the child does not wish to engage in academic activities.

The different terms used to label these goal orientations occurred because different researchers were working on them simultaneously, with each having a somewhat distinctive view of each orientation (see Pintrich, 2000a; Thorkildsen & Nicholls, 1998, for discussion of the intellectual roots of different researchers' definitions of these goal orientations). For instance, Dweck and Leggett (1988) proposed that children's goal orientations stem from their theories of intelligence that were described earlier. Children believing intelligence is malleable tend to hold a learning (mastery) goal orientation, and children adopting the entity view take on performance goals. By contrast, Ames (1992) focused primarily on classroom antecedents of these goal orientations, rather than characteristics of children, which implies that goal orientations are more a product of context rather than the person and so may vary more widely across different achievement situations. We acknowledge that the different terminology used by these theorists reflects some important distinctions in the conceptualization of these goal orientations, but also believe that the similarities are stronger than the distinctions between them (see Midgley, Kaplan, & Middleton, 2001; Pintrich, 2000a, for a similar conclusion). We will use the terms *mastery* and *performance* goal orientations in this chapter.

One of the newer directions in goal orientation theory is further differentiation of these two broad goal orientations into approach and avoidance components (Elliot, 1999, 2005). This occurred first for the performance goal orientation, beginning with work by Elliot and Harackiewicz (1996) and Skaalvik (1997), among others. These further distinctions emerged for two main reasons. Empirically, findings concerning the outcomes of having a performance goal orientation were somewhat contradictory, leading researchers to wonder why this occurred. Theoretically, Elliot and Harackiewicz noted that traditional achievement motivation theories, such as Atkinson's (1957) expectancy-value model, included both approach and avoidance motives. By contrast, most modern theories focus primarily on the approach aspect, thus overlooking the importance of avoidance motivation.

Therefore, Elliot and Harackiewicz (1996) proposed approach and avoidance aspects of performance goals, as did Skaalvik (1997). Performance-approach goals refer to the students' desire to demonstrate competence and outperform others. Performance-avoidance goals involve the desire to avoid looking incompetent. Researchers began to disentangle the effects of these two kinds of performance orientations. As we see later, there is evidence that performance-approach goals can have a positive impact on different outcomes, such as grades, whereas the impact of performance-avoidance goals is nearly always negative.

Elliot (1999; Elliott & McGregor, 2001) and Pintrich (2000c) proposed that the mastery goal orientation also may be divided into approach and avoid components. Elliot and McGregor stated that the assumption was made that mastery goals always referred to approach situations, rather than avoidance situations, which they believe does not provide a full characterization of situations to which mastery goals apply. They argued that mastery-avoidance goals include such things as working to avoid misunderstanding or the use of standards to not be wrong when doing an achievement activity. As Elliot and McGregor and Pintrich both note, perfectionists may be characterized as holding mastery-avoidance goals. Elliot and McGregor (2001) developed items to assess mastery-avoidance goals and found (in a study of college students) that these items factored separately from items measuring the other three kinds of goal orientations. The antecedents (as perceived by the participants) of mastery-avoidance goals were not as positive as antecedents of mastery-approach goals. These results are intriguing, but much more work is needed to establish the meaningfulness of this new category.

There is a growing body of research documenting the consequences of adopting one or the other of these goal orientations. Researchers have used a variety of methodologies in this work—including classroom observations (Ames & Archer, 1988), interviews (Dowson & McInerney, 2003), and questionnaire-based studies—often using Midgley and her colleagues' Patterns of Adaptive Learning Scale (PALS; Midgley et al., 1998). Experimental manipulations of students' goal orientations also have been done, by introducing achievement tasks in a way that fosters either mastery or performance goals (e.g., Graham & Golan, 1991). The results concerning mastery orientation are quite consistent and positive (see E. M. Anderman, Austin, & Johnson, 2002; Pintrich, 2000a, 2000c; Urdan, 1997, for review). When children are mastery oriented, they are more highly engaged in learning, use deeper cognitive strategies, and are intrinsically motivated to learn. Elliot and McGregor (2001) found that mastery-avoidance goals are associated with a mixture of outcomes, including subsequent test anxiety, mastery-approach goals, and performance-approach goals. Based on this and other work, researchers have proposed that schools should work to foster mastery goal orientations rather than performance goal orientations, and school reform efforts to do just that have been undertaken (e.g., Maehr & Midgley, 1996). We discuss some of this work in a later section of this chapter.

As noted earlier, the research on performance goals is somewhat less consistent, in part because of the methodological confounding of performance-avoidance and performance-approach goals. When these two aspects of performance goals are unconfounded, researchers find that performance-avoidance goals have negative consequences for students' motivation and learning (e.g., Elliot & Harackiewicz, 1996; Middleton & Midgley, 1997; Skaalvik, 1997). Performance-approach goals relate positively to academic self-concept, task value, and performance (at least in college students) but not to intrinsic motivation to learn (see Harackiewicz, Barron, Pintrich, Elliot, & Thrash, 2002, for review).

The distinction between performance-approach and performance-avoidance goals, and evidence showing that performance-approach goals relate to positive motivational and achievement outcomes, led Harckiewicz, Barron, and Elliot (1998) and Pintrich (2000a, 2000c) to call for a revision of goal theory that acknowledges the positive effects of performance-approach goals, and also the need to look at how different goals relate to different outcomes. Traditional (or *normative* to use the term adopted by Harackiewicz et al.) goal theory argues for the benefits of mastery goals and the costs of performance goals. Pintrich (2000b) studied eighth grade students' goal orientations, and identified four groups of children crossing high and low mastery and performance goal orientations. He found that students with a combination of high mastery and high performance-approach goal orientations were similar with respect to a variety of motivational outcomes to a group of students who were high in mastery but low in performance goal orientations. This finding does not support the normative theory view that only mastery goal orientations lead to positive developmental outcomes and was one impetus for the call for a revised goal orientation theory.

Midgley et al. (2001) disputed these claims, arguing that the costs of performance-avoidance goals are clearly documented and that the benefits of performance-approach goals are not as clearly established in the literature. They also noted that performance-approach goals may benefit some students (e.g., boys, older students) rather than others (e.g., girls, younger students), and that we do not yet have enough information about how performance-approach goals operate in other groups of children. They also pointed out that benefits of performance goals identified by researchers may be in part due to the focus of our educational system on standards, assessments, and performance rather than effort and improvement, which they argue is a better approach to schooling.

In response, Harackiewicz et al. (2002) argued that the evidence for the positive effects of performance-approach goals is clearer than Midgley et al. (2001) stated that it was, and they continued to propose the multiple goal perspective (that both mastery and performance goals can benefit different educational outcomes) is the more viable approach to goal orientation theory. They noted a number of areas of research that now are needed to assess each of these perspectives. In a final response, Kaplan and Middleton (2002) took a broader perspective and focused on what the purposes of schooling should be. In their view, the purposes of schooling should be knowledge growth and the fostering of a love of learning, rather than performance per se, and thus for them a mastery orientation continues to be more desirable, even if performance-approach goals relate to some positive educational outcomes in our current educational system (see also Roeser, 2004a, for further elaboration of these ideas). So this debate appears to be at different levels. At one level is the concern for how the specific goal orientations relate to different kinds of outcomes in our current educational system. The second level concerns what that system should focus on rather than an acceptance of the current system and its strong performance emphasis.

This healthy debate among goal orientation theorists should move the field ahead, as more research is done to look at the benefits and costs of different kinds of goal orientations, and as we consider further the nature and purposes of schooling and their influence on the development of students' goals and motivation. We believe the move beyond the perhaps too simplistic two-goal orientation theory is welcome, but acknowledge that more work is needed both on performance-approach and (especially) mastery-avoidance goals to evaluate their effects, and in the case of mastery-avoidance goals, to document their existence. Work on achievement goal orientations also needs to look more carefully at how different achievement domains (e.g., math, science, English) might impact achievement goal orientations and their effects (see Meece, 1991, 1994). Finally, Brophy (2005) noted recently that goal orientation theorists need to investigate further the frequency of occurrence of performance goals in school situations, arguing that students may not spontaneously generate such goals very frequently.

The Goal Content Approach: Academic and Social Goals. Building on Ford's (1992) work defining a taxonomy of human goals, Wentzel has examined the multiple goals of children in achievement settings (see Wentzel, 1991b, 1993, 2002b, for review of this work). Her view on goals differs from the goal orientation theorists in that she focuses on the *content* of children's goals to guide and direct behavior, rather than the criteria a person uses to define success or failure (i.e., mastery versus performance). In this sense, these goals are like the goals and self-schema that relate to attainment value hierarchies in the Eccles-Parsons et al. (1983) expectancy value. However, she does view these goals as contributing to children's competence in particular situations. Wentzel primarily has focused on academic and social goals and their relations to a variety of outcomes.

Wentzel has demonstrated that both social and academic goals relate to adolescents' school performance and behavior (Wentzel, 2002b). For instance, she found that the goals related to school achievement include seeing oneself as successful, dependable, wanting to learn new things, and wanting to get things done. Higher achieving students have higher levels of both social responsibility and achievement goals than lower achieving students. Similarly, Wentzel (1994) documented the association among middle school children's prosocial goals of helping others, academic prosocial goals like sharing learning with classmates, peer social responsibility goals like following through on promises made to peers, and academic social responsibility goals like doing what the teacher says to do. Prosocial goals (particularly academic prosocial goals) related positively to peer acceptance. She also found positive relations between prosocial goals and children's grades and even IQ scores (Wentzel, 1989, 1996).

Although it appears valuable to have multiple goals, Wentzel (2002b) discussed the difficulty some children may have coordinating these multiple goals. Can students manage a variety of social and academic goals? This question also applies to the multiple goal perspective in goal orientation theory. Having multiple goals may be especially challenging for younger children, whose resources to manage such goals may be limited.

Building in part on Wentzel's work, researchers increasingly are interested in how social relations and the social context influences students' goals and other aspects of motivation (e.g., L. H. Anderman, 1999; Patrick, 1997; A. M. Ryan, 2001). L. H. Anderman (1999) proposed a number of mechanisms by which students' social experiences in school relate to their motivation. These include the extent to which students feel a part of the school or at least some activities in the school, how much they endorse social responsibility goals, and the kinds of relationships they have with peers. We return to some of these points later.

Summary

Work on interest, intrinsic motivation, values, and goals continues to thrive, and the knowledge base in these areas is beginning to rival that on competence-related beliefs, although it still lags behind to a degree. We need additional work on the relations among these various constructs and a closer look at the developmental trajectories that they take.

Theories Concerned with the Question: "What Do I Have to Do to Succeed on This Task?"

We discussed in the previous version of our chapter that researchers were becoming increasingly interested in linkages between motivation, self-regulation, and cognitive processes. This work has grown over the past several years. In this section, we discuss work on the following topics: (a) motivation and the regulation of behavior; (b) motivation and volition; (c) relations of motivation to cognitive processes and conceptual change; and (d) academic help seeking.

Social Cognitive Theories of Self-Regulation and Motivation

Reviewing the extensive literature on the self-regulation of behavior is beyond the scope of the chapter (see Boekarts, Pintrich, & Zeidner, 2000, for a comprehensive review of models of self-regulation from a variety of different fields in psychology). These models take a variety of different conceptual and methodological approaches. There are two approaches to self-regulation that relate most directly to our focus on the development of motivation in this chapter. First is self-determination theory; we mention it only briefly here because it was discussed earlier. This theory proposes that individuals are intrinsically motivated when they are self-determined or are the source of their own behavior (Deci & Ryan, 2002b; R. M. Ryan & Deci, 2002). R. M. Ryan and Deci discuss the internalization process, which essentially involves the individual taking greater control over her own behavior, leading to greater intrinsic motivation. Grolnick et al. (2002) review the development of self-determination and how it is influenced by experiences at home and in school; we discuss some

of this work in the Socialization of Motivation section of this chapter.

A second approach to self-regulation particularly relevant to this chapter is the social cognitive perspective, and there are several models in this tradition. We focus on the recent work of Pintrich, Schunk, Zimmerman, and their colleagues because they directly link motivation to self-regulation; see Schunk and Zimmerman (1994) and Eccles et al. (1998) for review of earlier work on self-regulation.

Zimmerman (1989) described self-regulated students as being metacognitively, motivationally, and behaviorally active in their own learning processes and in achieving their own goals and active in their use of cognitive strategies for learning; thus motivation plays an important part in self-regulation. Recent social cognitive models of self-regulation (e.g., Pintrich, 2000c; Schunk & Ertmer, 2000; Zimmerman, 2000) divide the regulation of behavior into three phases: (1) forethought, (2) performance and volitional control, and (3) self-reflection. We focus on how motivation relates to each of these phases. *Forethought* involves planning one's behavior, and Zimmerman stated that there are two major aspects of forethought: (1) analyzing the task or activity that needs to be done and (2) motivating oneself to undertake the activity. Zimmerman focused on goal setting, self-efficacy, and interest and value as the key aspects of motivation during this phase. When students are efficacious about their ability to regulate their behavior, set goals and commit to them, and value what they are doing, they will be more likely to begin an activity. Zimmerman also noted that having a mastery goal orientation might facilitate task engagement and self-regulation of achievement behaviors.

Performance refers to self-regulation as the individual actually is doing the activity. What is crucial for the regulation of performance is focusing attention on the activity and monitoring how one is doing, through processes of self-observation. Schunk and Ertmer (2000) also noted that maintaining self-efficacy and monitoring progress toward the achievement of goals are important motivational aspects of the performance process. During *self-reflection and reaction,* individuals interpret the outcomes of their activities by making attributions for their success and failure and by evaluating whether they achieved their goals. Affective reactions are likely here as well. When individuals achieve the expected outcome they experience satisfaction; when they don't, various negative affective reactions can occur (see Pintrich, 2000c).

Wigfield and Eccles (2002b) discussed the particular roles achievement values may take in different aspects of the regulation of behavior. They argued that the social cognitive models of self-regulation focus primarily on self-efficacy and goals as the motivational factors influencing self-regulation, although some attention has been paid to values. Schunk and Ertmer (2000) discussed how the value of an activity is an important part of the forethought or preengagement phase of self-regulation; when activities are valued, students will devote more time both to planning for them and doing them. Rheinberg, Vollmeyer, and Rollett (2000) specified different questions individuals pose to themselves concerning potential links of their actions to desired outcomes. One of the questions is a "values" question: Are the consequences of the action important enough to me? If the answer is yes, the individual more likely will undertake the action; if no, engagement is less likely. Wigfield and Eccles discussed two additional roles values may play in the regulation of behavior. Values may help individuals determine which of different (and potentially conflicting) goals to pursue. During the self-reflection phase, after an activity is completed, students' valuing of the activity likely influences their likelihood to continue to engage in the activity.

Wolters (2003) discussed the importance of regulating one's motivation along with regulating one's behavior and cognition (see also Pintrich, 2000c). He posited that motivational regulation is one part of the broader self-regulatory process. The regulatory aspect in this instance refers to individuals' cognitive awareness of and control over their own motivation, but Wolters noted that motivation regulation and motivation itself likely are strongly related. He argued further that the regulation of motivation might be most needed when individuals encounter obstacles as they are attempting to do various achievement activities, even activities that they initially were quite motivated to do. Wolters discussed a variety of motivation regulation strategies. These include creating consequences for one's own behavior (when I finish my homework, I can play the videogame I want to play), attempting to modify activities one is doing to make them more interesting, and engaging in goal-oriented self talk (reminding oneself of the purposes for which the activity was undertaken in the first place), among others, including managing one's efficacy perceptions and controlling the kinds of attributions for success and failure that are made. One interesting regulatory strategy is self-handicapping, which involves things like waiting until the last minute to study for a test, and setting up other obstacles to performance. Although this regulatory strategy may provide students with good excuses for not doing well, its potential costs likely outweigh its benefits. Another potentially less positive strategy is called defensive pessimism in which individuals believe that they are unprepared and will do poorly on an exam or assignment, which spurs them to work harder. Defensive pessimists often perform well, but the desirability of this strategy is questionable.

In sum, social cognitive models of self-regulation consider many of the aspects of motivation that we are reviewing in this chapter, including self-efficacy, goals, achievement values, and interest. Researchers are beginning to focus on the regulation of motivation and how it fits into the broader models of self-regulation of achievement behaviors. Self-regulation of behavior and motivation processes require relatively sophisticated cognitive processes, which can be problematic for young children (see Pintrich & Zusho, 2002; Wigfield & Eccles, 2002b; Zimmerman, 2000, for a discussion of the development of self-regulatory processes). We return to this issue later.

Theories of Motivation and Volition

The term *volition* refers to both the strength of will needed to complete a task and diligence of pursuit (Corno, 1993, 2004; Kuhl, 2000). Zimmerman (2000) and other theorists proposing social cognitive models of self-regulation include volition as part of the regulation of achievement behavior, but Corno argued that volition is a broader concept than self-regulation because volition includes personality characteristics, aptitudes, and other cognitive processes (see also Corno & Kanfer, 1993). Researchers studying volition also argue for a clear distinction between motivation and volition; motivation brings the individual to an activity, but volitional processes carry him or her through the activity (see Corno, 2004).

Kuhl (1987) proposed several specific volitional strategies to explain persistence in the face of distractions and other opportunities; including cognitive, emotional, motivational, and environmental control strategies (see Eccles et al., 1998, for review of these strategies). Corno (1993) provided several examples of the volitional challenges students face, including coordinating multiple demands and desires like doing homework, watching TV, or calling a friend; dealing with the many distractions in any particular context like a classroom; and clarifying often vaguely specified goals and assignments.

There currently is some debate between volitional theorists and social cognitive self-regulation theorists (see Corno, 2004; Wolters, 2003; Zimmerman & Schunk, 2002). The social cognitive theorists argue that the "hard" distinction between motivation as the intention to act and volition as the control of action is drawn to strongly by volitional theorists. Wolters (2003) notes that the regulation of motivation can occur both in the phase leading up to action and the action phase itself, and so sees regulatory process as integrated across both. Corno (2004) continued to argue for the motivation-volition distinction but stated that volition can involve reassessing motivational goals as well.

Theories Linking Motivation and Cognition

Motivation researchers increasingly are interested in how motivation and cognition influence one another (see Eccles et al., 1998, for work done on this topic in the 1980s and early 1990s). In a seminal article, Pintrich, Marx, and Boyle (1993) discussed links of motivation and cognition, with specific reference to conceptual change. They argued that traditional "cold" cognitive psychological models of conceptual change, which focus on conceptual change resulting from dissatisfaction with one's current conceptions, and the intelligibility, plausibility, and fruitfulness of the new conception, do not consider the motivational and contextual factors that influence conceptual development. They identified a variety of contextual and motivational factors that can influence this process (see also Pintrich & Schrauben, 1992); we briefly note some of the motivation factors here.

Pintrich et al. (1993) focused on goal orientation, interest and value, and self-efficacy as motivational factors influencing conceptual change. They reviewed work showing that mastery goal orientations relate to deeper cognitive processing and more sophisticated cognitive strategy use. As discussed earlier, students' valuing of achievement relates to their choices of activities, and when they are interested in an activity deeper cognitive processing occurs. Similarly, students with higher self-efficacy use more elaborate and better cognitive strategies (see Schunk, 1991). Each of these motivational beliefs and values can be influenced by the classroom context (a point we return to later). Based on this, Pintrich et al. concluded that conceptual change is a "hot" rather than a cold process.

This work clearly indicates motivation's role in conceptual change and engagement in cognitive processing. However, Pintrich (2003) discussed that there still is lit-tle information on motivation's relations to basic cognitive activity such as the activation, acquisition, and development of knowledge, and he called for research in this area. He also argued that motivational beliefs might be represented cognitively in similar ways to other kinds of content knowledge (see Winne & Marx, 1989, for a similar view that motivational thoughts and beliefs are governed by the basic principles of cognitive psychology). Cognitive psychologists have developed detailed depictions of knowledge representation, and some of these likely could be applied to motivational beliefs. We have focused so far on motivation's relations to cognition; Pintrich also argued that cognition likely influences motivation and that researchers need to address these complex and likely cyclical relations.

Academic Help Seeking

Some researchers have argued that another important aspect of self-regulation and volition is knowing when help is needed (Newman, 2002; A. M. Ryan, Pintrich, & Midgley, 2001). Children learn to do many tasks on their own; indeed, schools and parents often encourage children to become independent and self-reliant. However, there are times when children need help. Both Nelson-Le Gall and her colleagues (e.g., Nelson-Le Gall & Glor-Shieb, 1985; Nelson-Le Gall & Jones, 1990) and Newman and his colleagues (e.g., Newman, 1994, 2002; Newman & Goldin, 1990; Newman & Schwager, 1995) have articulated models of children's help seeking that stress the difference between appropriate and inappropriate help seeking. Appropriate help seeking (labeled *instrumental* help seeking by Nelson-Le Gall and *adaptive* help seeking by Newman) involves deciding that one doesn't understand how to complete a problem after having tried to solve it on one's own, figuring out what and whom to ask, developing a good question to get the needed help, and processing the information received appropriately to complete the problem-solving task.

Adaptive help seeking can foster motivation by keeping children engaged in an activity when they experience difficulties. However, many children, and often the children that need the most help, are unwilling to ask for it in many classrooms, likely because they are concerned that asking for help will make them appear to others that they lack competence (A. M. Ryan, Gheen, & Midgley, 1998; A. M. Ryan et al., 2001). There are developmental differences here as well; younger children are more likely to ask for help than are older children. Newman (2002) described conditions under which children are more or less likely to ask for help; these conditions include both characteristics of children and of the learning environments they experience. When children are self-regulated and perceive they are competent they are more likely to ask for help when it is needed. Teachers can facilitate help seeking by showing concern for children; focusing on mastery goals, improvement, and effort; and facilitating peer collaboration in the classroom.

Summary

Work on links between motivation, self-regulation, and cognition has burgeoned over the last several years. This integrative work is crucial for a better understanding of the learning process and children's achievement, and likely will continue to grow. Developmental issues remain front and center in this work, as the complex regulation of achievement and other kinds of behaviors poses many challenges for young children in particular. We need more information about the development of these processes and models that take account of them.

THE DEVELOPMENT OF MOTIVATION: WITHIN-PERSON CHANGE AND GROUP DIFFERENCES

Developmental and educational psychologists have focused on two major developmental questions:

1. How do the different beliefs, values, and goals defined in the different theories develop during childhood and adolescence?

2. What explains the emergence of individual differences in motivation?

Different sources of influence have been considered: Within-person changes resulting from growth and maturation in cognitive processing, emotional development, or other individual characteristics; socially mediated developmental changes resulting from systematic age-related changes in the social contexts children experience at home, in school and among peers as they grow up; and socially mediated influences that differ across individuals and contexts. These different sources often interact with one another, but the nature of this interaction is rarely studied. Consequently, we have organized our discussion of the development of motivation, and of individual differences in motivation, around these broad categories of influence. First, we present work on within-person changes, beginning with work on children's early self-evaluations, and then describe the

work on within-person changes in the constructs discussed thus far. We also include a consideration of the development of certain motivational problems. Also discussed in this section is the development of sex and ethnic differences in children's motivation. We include this work in this section because they emerge during children's development. The next major section considers how various socialization agents influence children's motivation.

Within-Person Change in Motivation

Some researchers have looked at very young children's reactions to success and failure, reactions which likely provide the foundation for the development of the different motivational beliefs, values, and goals discussed in this chapter. Heckhausen (1987) found that children between 2.5 and 3.5 years start to show self-evaluative, nonverbal expressions following a successful or unsuccessful action. The earliest indicators of achievement motivation were facial expressions of joy after success and sadness after failure. The experience of success (around 30 months) preceded the experience of failure (around 36 months). Several months later, children showed postural expressions of pride and shame following success and failure. When competing with others, 3- and 4-year-old children initially showed joy after winning and sadness after losing. It was only when they looked at their competitor that they expressed pride and shame.

Stipek, Recchia, and McClintic (1992) identified three stages of development in young children's self-evaluations: The children younger than 22 months were neither concerned with others' evaluation of their performance nor self-reflective in their evaluations. However, they did show positive emotional reactions to accomplishing a task and negative emotions when they did not. Thus, unlike Heckhausen, Stipek, et al. found that reactions to success and failure occurred at the same time in development. Two-year-olds reacted more to others' evaluations by seeking approval when they did well and turning away when they did poorly. After age 3, the children were able to evaluate their own performance, without needing to see how adults reacted to that performance, and engaged in more autonomous self-evaluation. Children age 3 and older also reacted more strongly to winning and losing than did younger children.

Dweck and her colleagues (e.g., Burhans & Dweck, 1995; Heyman, Dweck, & Cain, 1992; Smiley & Dweck, 1994; see Dweck, 2002, for review) also have done interesting work on young children's reactions to failure; we review this work more completely later when we discuss the development of learned helplessness. Generally, their findings show that some preschool children already react quite negatively to failure, reactions that may lead to later learned helplessness in response to failure.

Taken together, these studies show that reactions to success and failure begin early in the preschool years, likely laying the groundwork for the development of motivation in the middle childhood years and beyond. The results concerning children's reactions to failure are particularly important because they suggest that children are more sensitive to failure in the preschool years than was once believed (see Dweck, 2002).

The Development of Competence-Related Beliefs

Much of the work on the development of children's achievement-related beliefs has looked at the development of children's ability and expectancy-related beliefs (e.g., see Dweck & Elliott, 1983; Stipek & Mac Iver, 1989, for reviews of the early work on this topic). We discuss three kinds of changes in these beliefs: (1) change in their factorial structure, (2) change in mean levels, and (3) change in children's understanding of them.

The Factor Structure of Children's Competence-Related Beliefs. Eccles et al. (1998) reviewed factor analytic research showing that children as young as age 5 or 6 appear to have distinctive competence perceptions among different academic and nonacademic domains of competence. Since that review researchers have looked at even younger children and found that these children also have differentiated competence-related beliefs (Mantzicoupolus, French, & Maller, 2004; Marsh, Ellis, & Craven, 2002). This does not mean that there is no change or refinement in children's beliefs from kindergarten through high school. The pattern of correlations of self-concept factors differs in meaningful ways for younger and older children (Marsh & Ayotte, 2003). Younger children use fewer of the scale points when responding to the items on the questionnaires, and their responses correlate less well with both their teachers' and their parents' estimates of their competencies (Eccles, Wigfield, et al., 1993; Wigfield et al., 1997).

Eccles and Wigfield (1995) and Eccles, Wigfield, et al. (1993) also have used factor analytic strategies to assess whether children's competence beliefs and expectancies for success are distinct constructs. Analyses of both children's and adolescents' responses indicate the ratings of their current competence, expectancies for success, and perceived performance load on the same fact or, suggesting that these components comprise a single concept for children age 6 to 18.

Change in the Mean Level of Children's Competence-Related Beliefs. Another well-established finding in the literature is that children's competence beliefs for different tasks decline across the elementary school years and through the high school years (see Dweck & Elliott, 1983; Eccles et al., 1998; Stipek & Mac Iver, 1989, for review). Many young children are quite optimistic about their competencies in different areas, and this optimism changes to greater realism and (sometimes) pessimism for many children. To illustrate, in Nicholls (1979) most first graders ranked themselves near the top of the class in reading ability, and there was no correlation between their ability ratings and their performance level. By contrast the 12-year-olds' ratings were more dispersed and correlated highly with school grades (.70 or higher). Recently, researchers in the United States have examined change over the entire elementary and secondary school years in children's competence beliefs for math, language arts, and sports (Jacobs et al., 2002; Fredericks & Eccles, 2002), and Watt (2004) looked at change across middle and senior high school years in Australia. Jacobs et al. examined change in children's competence for math, language arts, and sports across grades 1 through 12. Children's perceptions in each area were strongly positive early on. However, the overall pattern of change was a decline in each domain. There were some differences across domain with respect to when the strongest changes occurred, particularly in language arts and math. In language arts, the strongest declines occurred during elementary school and then little change was observed after that. In sports, the change accelerated during the high school years. The decline in math competence beliefs was steady over time. Fredericks and Eccles and Watt also found declines over time in competence beliefs and values, although the specific trends were somewhat different across these studies.

One caveat about this general "optimism early and realism later" pattern should be noted. As just discussed, researchers observing children's reactions to failure find that some preschool children already reacted negatively to failure (see Dweck, 2002; Stipek et al., 1992). Dweck notes that during the preschool years, children likely do not have a clearly defined notion of what ability is. So these earlier negative reactions to failure may not mean that children doubt their ability, as their views of ability still are taking shape. But the connection between these reactions and level of ability beliefs likely begins to develop early in the school years, and children reacting negatively to failure early on may be more likely to be pessimistic about their abilities later.

In summary, children's competence beliefs and expectancies for success become more negative as they get older. The negative changes in children's competence-related beliefs have been explained in two ways: (1) Because children become much better at understanding, interpreting, and integrating the evaluative feedback they receive, and engage in more social comparison with their peers, children become more accurate or realistic in their self-assessments, leading some to become relatively more negative (see Dweck & Elliott, 1983; Nicholls, 1984; Ruble, 1983; Stipek & Mac Iver, 1989); (2) Because school environment changes in ways that makes evaluation more salient and competition between students more likely, some children's self-assessments will decline as they get older (e.g., see Eccles & Midgley, 1989; Wigfield, Byrnes, & Eccles, in press; Wigfield, Eccles, & Pintrich, 1996). We return to this issue of how school environments influence children's motivation later.

There are two important limitations to this work on mean-level change in the development of competence beliefs. First, most of it is normative, in the sense that researchers report overall mean differences in their studies. We thus know less about patterns of changes in different groups of children and adolescents, although there is some information about this (e.g., Harter, Whitesell, & Kowalski, 1992; Wigfield, Eccles, Mac Iver, Reuman, & Midgley, 1991). Wigfield et al. (1991) found that this pattern of change varied somewhat for children high or low in math ability. Second, the measures used in this work either are at the school level or (more frequently) at the domain-specific level. It is possible that children's beliefs about their competence for more particular activities may show different patterns of change, and we know little about this. We also know little about how children arrive at judgments of their competence in something as broad as reading or science; do they simply average their performance in a variety of different relevant tasks or use a more elaborate strategy (see Assor & Connell, 1992; Winne & Jamieson-Noel, 2002, for discussion of issues regarding measurement of individuals' beliefs and how individuals calibrate their beliefs)?

Finally, one other set of findings relevant to the issue of mean-level change should be mentioned. Longitudinal studies looking at relations of children's competence beliefs over time show that these beliefs become increasingly stable as children get older (e.g., Eccles et al., 1989; Wigfield et al., 1997). Even by the middle of the elementary school years, children's competence beliefs correlate quite highly across a 1-year period, with the correlations reaching as high as .74. Thus, by early adolescence there is much stability in these beliefs, even though the overall pattern of change is the decline just discussed. The implication of these findings is that individuals tend to maintain their relative position in their group, even as the group's mean declines.

Changes in Children's Understanding of Competence-Related Beliefs. The research on both the structure of and mean level differences in children's beliefs does not tell us about children's understanding of these constructs, because the questionnaire methodology used in these studies requires children to respond to researcher-defined constructs rather than generate their own definitions of a given construct. But it is important to understand how children conceptualize the different constructs to interpret comparisons of different-aged children's beliefs meaningfully.

Dweck (2002) described important developmental changes in children's understandings of ability. During the preschool years and into kindergarten, children do not have a clear sense of ability as a characteristic that determines outcomes, but as discussed earlier they do react to success and failure experiences. Part of this reaction is to think they are good when they do well and bad when they do poorly; indeed, Dweck argues that conceptions of goodness and badness are primary at this time. During the early school years concepts of ability begin to emerge, and children see ability as distinct from other qualities and also differentiate their ability across domains. They often think of ability as changeable, and use normative rather than comparative standards to judge ability, but some children begin to see ability as a stable characteristic. As children move through these ages, social comparison takes on increasing importance. Children's beliefs about ability also become more accurate, in the sense of correlating more strongly with performance measures. Between ages 10 and 12, children differentiate more clearly ability, effort, and performance, but they also see how they interrelate. These children more often use comparative standards in judging ability. More children come to view ability as capacity (or take an *entity* view of intelligence, to use Dweck's term), which means they are less likely to believe that with increased effort their ability will improve.

Researchers have investigated children's understanding of ability, effort, task difficulty, and intelligence (see Eccles et al., 1998, for review). Nicholls and his colleagues found a developmental progression between ages 5 and 12 with respect to children's beliefs about ability, effort, and performance (Nicholls, 1978; Nicholls & Miller, 1984). They found four relatively distinct levels of reasoning: At level one (ages 5 to 6), effort, ability, and performance are not clearly by cause and effect. At level two (ages 7 to 9), effort is seen as the primary cause of performance outcomes. At level three (ages 9 to 12), children begin to differentiate ability and effort as causes of outcomes, but they do not always apply this distinction. Finally, at level four, adolescents clearly differentiate ability and effort, and they understand the notion of ability as capacity. They also believe that ability can limit the effects of additional effort on performance and that ability and effort are often related to each other in a compensatory manner and, consequently, success requiring a great deal of effort likely reflects limited ability.

As we discuss in more detail later in the section presenting work on Learned Helplessness, these different views of ability and intelligence have important implications for children's reactions to success and failure, particularly their reactions to failure. As Dweck and her colleagues have discussed, children with an entity view of ability are more likely to give up following failure, because they are less likely to believe that additional effort will improve their performance, because their ability is fixed. By contrast, children with an incremental view are more likely to continue to strive after failure because they think their ability can change.

Pomerantz and Saxon (2001; see also Pomerantz & Ruble, 1997) added another distinction to this discussion. They distinguished between (in their terms) "conceptions of ability as stable to external forces," and "conceptions of ability as stable to internal forces." Stability of ability with respect to external forces "is the view that ability is unlikely to be influenced by forces external to the individual possessing the ability (e.g., situational changes)" (Pomerantz & Saxon, 2001, p. 153). Pomerantz and Saxon argued that as children get older they increasingly hold this view about ability and a number of other characteristics, with the implication that

children see individuals' behaviors as relatively consistent across types of activities and over time. Pomerantz and Saxon see conceptions of ability as stable to internal forces as analogous to Dweck's (2002) entity theory of ability. One reason they see these as similar is that Dweck and her colleagues operationalize the entity view of ability as the belief that ability is not under one's own control (e.g., Cain & Dweck, 1995). For instance, one item from Cain and Dweck's measure of views of intelligence is "You're a certain amount smart, and you can't really do much to change it" (p. 153). The individual cannot do much to change his or her ability. Pomerantz and Saxon proposed that the latter, but not the former, conception about the nature of ability could have negative consequences for motivation and achievement.

They studied these two conceptions of ability in a sample of fourth through sixth grade children. Concepts of ability as stable to external forces were measured by the researchers describing to participants another child as either smart or not very smart at schoolwork, and then having children rate the other child's ability at four time points and in four situations. Similar procedures were used to measure social ability. Differences between children's ratings of the other's ability and the initial description were used to determine how much children believed that the other children's ability was stable with respect to external forces. Ability as stable with respect to internal forces was measured using Cain and Dweck's (1995) scale. Results showed that the two kinds of conceptions were inversely (but weakly) related. Children's beliefs that ability was stable with respect to external forces increased over time, and their conceptions of ability as stable with respect to internal forces decreased over time. Believing that ability is stable with respect to external forces correlated positively with the importance children attached to being competent, a preference for challenge, positive perceptions of competence, and academic performance. The opposite pattern of relations occurred for perceptions that ability is stable with respect to internal forces. It should be noted that both sets of correlations were relatively weak.

Pomerantz and Saxon (2001) concluded that seeing ability as stable, at least with respect to external forces, actually is a positive belief for children to have because of the pattern of its relations with other motivational beliefs and performance. By contrast, believing that ability is stable with respect to internal forces has negative implications for motivation and performance. Thus, it is not stability per se but the type of stability that is crucial. Further, they noted that viewing ability as stable with respect to external forces was a more stable belief over time than was viewing ability as stable with respect to internal forces. These intriguing findings provide a more subtle representation of the impact of having "stable" beliefs on motivational and performance outcomes. However, because many of the observed relations were rather weak (albeit significant), this potentially important distinction requires further research. Further, both Dweck's work and Nicholls' work suggests that children increasingly view ability as stable as they get older, whereas Pomerantz and Saxon found just the opposite with respect to beliefs about stability of ability with respect to internal causes. This apparent contradiction needs to be resolved.

In sum, work on children's understanding of ability converges with the factor analytic work in the sense of showing that young children differentiate ability into different areas. However, this work shows that younger and older children have different ideas about the nature of ability and its relations to effort, other achievement beliefs, and performance, which means we must take some care in how we interpret the factor analytic findings. Using the same scales to measure perceived ability at different ages may be problematic given the apparent differences in how younger and older children understand ability.

Development of Efficacy Beliefs

There has not been extensive research on the development of efficacy beliefs per se, although the work on ability beliefs and expectancies is directly relevant. Instead, research on children's self-efficacy has focused primarily on interventions to enhance the self-efficacy and school performance of low-achieving children (e.g., see Schunk, 1994; Schunk & Pajares, 2002). Extant work on the development of efficacy shows that children's efficacy beliefs increase across age. Shell, Colvin, and Bruning (1995) found that fourth graders had lower self-efficacy beliefs for reading and writing than did 7th and 10th graders, and the 7th graders efficacy beliefs were lower than 10th graders beliefs (see Zimmerman & Martinez-Pons, 1990, for similar findings). The inconsistency of these findings with those on children's competence beliefs just discussed likely reflects the self-efficacy measure used by Shell et al. Their instrument measured children's estimates of their efficacy on specific reading and writing skills rather than more general beliefs about competence reading and writing; the more specific beliefs should be higher among older children. Also, as noted earlier efficacy beliefs usually are

not measured comparatively, whereas many measures of competence beliefs include comparisons of a child's ability with that of others. The latter kind of measure may be more likely to show declines over age.

Bandura (1997) and Schunk and Pajares (2002) discussed factors influencing the development of self-efficacy. They proposed that children who have mastery experiences in which they exert some control over their environments develop the earliest sense of personal agency. Through these experiences, infants learn that they can influence and control their environments. Parents and other adults can facilitate the growth of this sense of agency by the kinds of experiences they provide children. If parents do not provide infants with these experiences, they are not likely to develop a strong a sense of personal agency. Second, because self-efficacy requires the understanding that the *self* produced an action and an outcome, Bandura argued that a more mature sense of self-efficacy should not emerge until children have at least a rudimentary self-concept and can recognize that they are distinct individuals, which happens sometime during the 2nd year of life (see Harter, 1998). Through the preschool period, children are exposed to extensive performance information that should be crucial to their emerging sense of self-efficacy. However, just how useful such information is likely depends on the child's ability to integrate it across time, contexts, and domains; Schunk and Pajares discuss the challenges children face in doing so. More work is needed to understand how children become able to integrate diverse sources of information about their performances (e.g., information about their own performance, and social comparison information) to develop a stable of self-efficacy. Schunk and Pajares also discuss the crucial role peers can play in the development, or demise, of self-efficacy.

Finally, Schunk and Pajares (2002) and Bandura (1997) stressed the importance of school environments for developing and supporting a high sense of efficacy or possibly undermining it if support is not provided. We return later to a discussion of how this can occur.

Development of Control Beliefs

Work on perceived control done in the 1980s and 1990s showed that there are developmental patterns in these beliefs. Weisz (1984) found that younger children actually believe they have greater control over chance events than do older children. Similarly, Connell (1985) found a decrease in the endorsement of all three of his locus of control constructs (internal control, powerful others control, and unknown control) from third through ninth grade. Like Weisz's findings, the unknown belief results suggest that older children have a clearer understanding of what controls achievement outcomes. However, the older children also rated the other two sources of control as less important, making interpretation of these findings difficult.

Skinner examined age differences in both the structure and the mean levels of means-ends beliefs (see Skinner, 1995), and found the factor structure becomes increasingly complex as children get older. She also found the largest mean-level differences on some of the means-ends beliefs. At all ages between 7 and 12, children believe effort is the most effective means. In contrast, older children are much less likely to believe that luck is an effective means than younger children. As in Connell (1985), belief in the relevance of unknown control and powerful others also decreased across age levels.

In a landmark 3-year longitudinal study, Skinner, Gembeck-Zimmer, and Connell (1998) assessed the development of perceived control in children and early adolescents and how it predicted student engagement in school. Their cohort-sequential design encompassed third through seventh grade children. Skinner et al. measured overall control beliefs, beliefs about the strategies needed to do well in school (including the strategies of effort, ability, powerful others, luck, and unknown), and beliefs about the capacity to access one's effort, ability, powerful others, and luck. They also measured children's engagement in school and their perceptions of the structure and involvement provided by teachers, examining predictive relations among these variables.

Skinner et al. (1998) found that perceived control showed a curvilinear pattern of change, being stable at first, increasing slightly through fourth grade, and then declining after fifth grade. Student engagement declined during middle school, as did students' perceptions that teachers provided structure and were involved with them. Changes in perceived control related to changes in engagement, and change in the teacher-context variables predicted change in perceived control. Specifically, children initially either high or low in perceived control decreased in their control perceptions if they perceived that teachers were providing less structure and were less involved with them. A number of interesting age differences in the predictors of engagement and control emerged. Younger children's beliefs about their capacity to exert effort were a stronger predictor, whereas for older children it was their beliefs about their ability.

Grades predicted perceived control more strongly for older than younger children. Skinner et al. also suggested that the context provided by teachers may provide a stronger role in the development of perceived control for younger than for older children. Skinner et al. also examined how the constructs they measured varied across different subgroups in their sample, and thus went beyond the normative approach often taken in this area.

This fascinating study provides a rich depiction of the development of perceived control, and how it relates to students' engagement in the classroom. While rich in many respects, the measures of both academic performance and perceived control were done at the general level (see Eccles, 1998, for discussion of this and other issues with respect to this study). Based on work we reviewed earlier, these beliefs (and performances) likely vary across different areas. The measure of teacher context also focused on just a few features of the classroom context. Nevertheless, the study provides a model for how to study the development of motivational processes.

In overall summary of competence-related beliefs, there are numerous changes in children's competence and control beliefs. These changes include structural change, mean level change, and change in children's understanding of the constructs. We need more complex longitudinal studies such as those of Jacobs et al. (2002) and Skinner et al. (1998) to examine these changes over time, for different groups, and in relation to other contextual and psychological factors.

Development of Subjective Task Values

Eccles, Wigfield, and their colleagues examined age-related changes in both the structure and mean levels of children's valuing of different activities. In Eccles, Wigfield, et al. (1993) and Eccles and Wigfield (1995), children's competence-expectancy beliefs and subjective values *within* the domains of math, reading, and sports formed distinct factors at all grade levels from 1st through 12th. Thus, even during the very early elementary grades children appear to have distinct beliefs about what they are *good* at and what they *value*. The distinction between various subcomponents of subjective task value appear to differentiate more gradually (Eccles, Wigfield, et al., 1993; Eccles & Wigfield, 1995). Children in early elementary school differentiate task value into two components: (1) interest and (2) utility/importance. In contrast, children in grades 5 through 12 differentiate task value into the three major subcomponents (attainment value/personal importance, interest, and utility value) outlined by Eccles-Parsons et al. (1983). These results suggest that the interest component differentiates out first, followed later by the distinction between utility and attainment value.

As with competence-related beliefs, studies generally show age-related decline in children's valuing of certain academic tasks (e.g., see Eccles et al., 1998; Wigfield & Eccles, 2002b, for review). Jacobs et al. (2002), in the study described earlier in the section on the development of competence beliefs, found that children's valuing of the domains of math, language arts, and sports declined. As was the case for competence beliefs, children's valuing of language arts declined most during elementary school and then leveled off. By contrast, children's valuing of math declined the most during high school (see also Fredericks & Eccles, 2002).

Researchers have not addressed changes in children's understandings of the components of task value identified by Eccles-Parsons et al. (1983), although there likely are age-related differences in these understandings. An 8-year-old is likely to have a different sense of what it means for a task to be "useful" than an 11-year-old does. Further, it also is likely that there are differences across age in which of the components of achievement values are most dominant. Wigfield and Eccles (1992) suggested that interest may be especially salient during the early elementary school grades with young children's activity choices being most directly related to their interests. Young children likely try many different activities for a short time before developing a more stable opinion regarding which activities they enjoy the most. As children get older, the perceived utility and personal importance of different tasks likely become more salient, particularly as they develop more stable self-schema and long-range goals and plans. These developmental predictions need to be tested.

A related developmental question is how children's developing competence beliefs relate to their developing subjective task values. According to both the Eccles-Parsons et al. (1983) model and Bandura's (1997) self-efficacy theory, ability self-concepts should influence the development of task values. In support of this prediction, Mac Iver, Stipek, and Daniels (1991) found that changes in junior high school students' competence beliefs over a semester predicted change in children's interest much more strongly than vice versa. Does the same causal ordering occur in younger children? Bandura (1997) argued that interests emerge out of a child's sense of self-efficacy and that children should be more

interested in challenging than in easy tasks. Taking a developmental perspective, Wigfield (1994) proposed that initially young children's competence and task-value beliefs are likely to be relatively independent of each other. This independence would mean that children might pursue some activities in which they are interested regardless of how good or bad they think they are at the activity. Over time, particularly in the achievement domains, children may begin to attach more value to activities on which they do well for several reasons: First, through processes associated with classical conditioning, the positive affect a child experiences when he or she does well should become attached to the activities yielding success (see Eccles, 1984). Second, lowering the value a child attaches to activities that he or she is having difficulty with is likely to be an effective way to maintain a positive global source of efficacy and self-esteem (Eccles, 1984; Harter, 1990). Thus, at some point, the two kinds of beliefs should become more positively related to one another.

In partial support of this view, Wigfield et al. (1997) found that relations between children's competence beliefs and subjective values in different domains indeed are stronger among older than younger elementary school-aged children. Jacobs et al. (2002) found that changes in competence beliefs predicted changes in children's valuing of the activities, accounting for as much as 40% of the variance in change in children's valuing of the activities. This suggests that the causal direction in this relation goes from competence beliefs to values, but more longitudinal work is needed to assess this possibility.

Development of Interest and Intrinsic Motivation

Eccles et al. (1998) summarized work on the early development of children's interests, which shows that children have general or universal interests at first, which become more specific relatively quickly (see also Todt, 1990). Todt argued that this early differentiation eventually leads to individual differences in interests in the social versus the natural sciences. The next phase of interest development—between 3 and 8 years of age—is characterized by the formation of gender-specific interests. According to Kohlberg (1966), the acquisition of gender identity leads to gender-specific behaviors, attitudes, and interests. Children strive to behave consistently with their gender identity and, thus, evaluate activities or objects as consistent with their gender identity more positively than other activities or objects.

As a consequence, boys and girls develop gender role stereotyped interests (see Eccles, 1987; Ruble & Martin, 1998).

At the next stage (ages 9 to 13), the emerging self-concept is assumed to be linked more directly to social group affiliation and cognitive ability, leading to occupational interests consistent with a child's social class and ability self-concepts (see Cook et al., 1996). The final stage (occurring after age 13 or 14) is characterized by an orientation to the internal, unique self leading to more differentiated and individualized vocational interests, based on abstract concepts of self (e.g., of personality). Thus, the development of vocational interests is a process of continuous elimination of interests that do not fit the self-concepts of a child's gender, social group affiliation, ability, and then personal identity (Todt, 1990). This process is assumed to depend mainly on the general cognitive development of the child or adolescent.

Changing needs or motives across the life span can influence the development of interests. A good example is the increasing interest in biology and psychology during puberty. The need to know oneself and to cope with rapid bodily and psychological changes seems to foster interest in biological and psychological domains of knowledge at this age (Todt, 1990).

Consistent with studies of American children (e.g., Eccles, Wigfield, et al., 1993; Gottfried et al., 2001; Harter, 1981; Wigfield et al., 1991), several European researchers have found that that interest and intrinsic motivation in different subject areas decline across the school years. This is especially true for the natural sciences and mathematics (e.g., Hedelin & Sjoberg, 1989), particularly during the early adolescent years. Pekrun (1993) found that intrinsic motivation stabilized after eighth grade, and Gottfried et al. (2001) reported surprisingly high stability coefficients for intrinsic motivation measured across a 1-year period for children ages 13 and above.

Baumert (1995) argued that the decline in school-related interests during adolescence reflects a more general developmental process in which the adolescents discover new fields of experience that lead to new interests and reduce the dominant influence of school. In contrast, other researchers have suggested that changes in a number of instructional variables like clarity of presentation, monitoring of what happens in the classroom, supportive behavior, cognitively stimulating experi-

ences, self-concept of the teacher (educator versus scientist), and achievement pressure may contribute to declining interest in school mathematics and science (e.g., Eccles & Midgley, 1989).

Development of Children's Goal Orientations

There still is not a large body of work on the development of children's goals and goal orientations (see E. M. Anderman et al., 2002, for review of extant work). Instead, most of the work has focused on relations of goals to ability beliefs and on how different instructional contexts influence achievement goals. For instance, Dweck and her colleagues looked at relations of children's beliefs about ability and their goal orientations and found that performance-goal oriented children only show mastery behavior when their perceived ability is high. By contrast, mastery-oriented children engage in mastery-oriented behavior irrespective of their perceived ability (Burhans & Dweck, 1995; Smiley & Dweck, 1994). Butler and her colleagues have done an elegant series of studies in which they have shown how different learning conditions (competitive or noncompetitive; performance or mastery focused) influence children's subsequent motivation and found quite interesting differences in motivation depending on these conditions (see Eccles et al., 1998, for review).

Maehr, Midgley, and their colleagues conducted a number of studies looking at how classroom instructional practices relate to children's goal orientations and how these relations may change over time. L. H. Anderman and E. M. Anderman (1999) reported that adolescents endorse performance goals more than mastery goals. A major reason for this likely is that schools increasingly emphasize performance goals as children get older. One clear example of this is how evaluations of different kinds proliferate and have stronger consequences for adolescents' futures. Midgley (2002) and colleagues' work has shown two major things with respect to this point: (1) Elementary school teachers focus on mastery-oriented goals to a greater extent than do middle school teachers, and (2) middle school students perceive school as more performance oriented than do elementary school students. Thus, any observed changes in children's goal orientations seem very bound up in changes in the school goal culture. We return to this issue later.

Goal orientations often are studied at a relatively general level, but some researchers have looked at goal orientations toward particular school activities. Meece and Miller (2001) studied the development during elementary school of students' goal orientations in reading and writing, looking at performance goals, mastery goals, and work-avoidant goals. They found that children's goal orientation were reasonably stable over a 1-year period; the lagged correlations were .44 for task-mastery goals, .58 for performance goals, and .45 for work-avoidant goals. With respect to change over time, following prediction children's mastery goals decreased over time. Contrary to prediction, performance goals did as well. The pattern of change in work-avoidant goals was less consistent.

There is much less work on the development of the content of children's goals. Thus, we know very little about how the contents of children's goals vary across age and context.

Development of Self-Regulation and Volition

Eccles et al. (1998) reviewed work establishing two general developmental points concerning self-regulation. First, children's ability to self-regulate increases dramatically across the toddler period (Bullock & Lutkenhaus, 1988) due to increases in ability to focus on both the outcomes of their behaviors and the behaviors themselves (see Mischel & Mischel, 1983), increases in understanding of the self as a causal agent (Bandura, 1997; Jennings, 1991; Skinner, 1995), and increases in both the ability and desire to evaluate the success or failure of their achievement efforts (Heckhausen, 1987; Stipek et al., 1992). Second, parents play a critical role in the extent to which children regulate their own behavior. For instance, both the ways parents define and organize tasks for the children, and the control strategies they use, have a big impact on very young children's ability to regulate their behavior (e.g., use of indirect commands, verbal controls, and reasoning facilitates the early development of self-regulation, see Kopp, 1991).

From the self-determination theory perspective, development involves the process of internalization, where children take increasing control over their own behavior and thus become more self-determined (see Deci & Ryan, 2002b). Grolnick and her colleagues (2002) discussed the important role of autonomy support in the development of self-determination and intrinsic motivation. They reviewed research showing that when parents and teachers support children's autonomy, children have more positive competence beliefs, greater intrinsic mo-

tivation, and higher self-esteem. Along with autonomy support Grolnick et al. stressed the roles of affective support, involvement in children's lives, and the provision of adequate structure in children's environments as fostering the development of self-determination.

Turning to self-regulated learning, Zimmerman (2000) proposed a four-step developmental sequence of self-regulation. Children first learn effective strategies by observing successful models and focusing on process goals. Second, children imitate the strategies, following what the model did relatively closely. Third, they learn to use the strategies apart from the model; Zimmerman called this self-controlled learning. Although children do the strategies on their own, they still are dependent on the model. Finally, in the self-regulated phase children begin both to use the strategies in different situations and to tailor them to their own purposes. They also focus more on outcome goals. Research is beginning to show that individuals' ability to learn different behaviors relates to the kind of regulatory training they experience. Kitsantas, Zimmerman, and Cleary (2000) found that novice students learned best when learning from models rather than simply receiving performance feedback on their own performance. Zimmerman and Kitsantas (1999) found that as students moved through the levels of regulatory skill they learned more efficiently when focused on outcome goals rather than process goals because the former matched more clearly their level of self-regulation.

Pintrich and Zusho (2002) also discussed the development of self-regulation, discussing both phases of self-regulation, like those we discussed earlier, and different areas that need to be regulated (i.e., cognition, motivation, behavior, and context). Like Eccles et al. (1998) they noted that children become more efficient at regulating their cognition and behavior, and possibly their motivation, as they get older. However, they also discussed that older children may know how to regulate these areas but often do not, reflecting the pervasive competence/performance distinction that occurs in many areas of psychology. Pintrich and Zusho reviewed specific aspects of cognition and motivation that relate to the ability to self-regulate learning and behavior. With respect to motivation, a child's level of efficacy, degree of interest in the activity, and goals for the activity all relate to their self-regulation. When children are efficacious, interested in the activity they are doing, and hold learning goals, they are more likely to regulate their behavior to accomplish a certain activity (see also Wolters, 2003). Further, there are potentially interesting developmental issues with respect to how each of these motivational constructs may relate to the regulation of achievement behavior. For instance, younger children's competence and efficacy beliefs relate less closely to their actual behavior and (particularly with respect to competence beliefs) often are overly optimistic, which may mean that younger children do not see the need to carefully regulate their actions to produce an outcome. As competence beliefs and performance become more closely calibrated, this likely changes. With respect to goal orientations, if mastery goals become less prevalent and performance goals more prevalent then self-regulation may decline (but see Pintrich, 2000b, on multiple pathways to different outcomes).

With respect to the use of different self-regulatory strategies, Zimmerman and Martinez-Pons (1990) found a complex pattern of differences across age in use of these strategies by older children and adolescents. Researchers have not yet systematically tested how strategies, goals, and self-efficacy interact to influence the regulation of learning in different-aged children. Additionally, it would be useful to compare Zimmerman's model with Deci and Ryan's discussion of the development of internalized regulation.

There is some developmental work on volitional strategies. For example, Kuhl and Kraska (1989), in German and Mexican elementary school-aged children, found increases in children's ability to use all of the strategies except for emotion control. But more developmental work is needed here as well.

The Development and Remediation of Motivational Problems

Many children begin to experience motivational problems during the school years. We focus on three motivational problems that have received the most attention in the literature: (1) test anxiety, (2) learned helplessness, and (3) apathy. The first two of these problems are tied to beliefs about not being able to do different activities, whereas the third emerges when children devalue achievement related activities.

Anxiety

Anxiety and test anxiety are estimated to interfere with the learning and performance, particularly in evaluative situations, of as many as 10 million children and adolescents in the United States (Hill & Wigfield, 1984; Tobias, 1985; Wigfield & Eccles, 1989). This problem likely will get worse as evaluation and accountability become more emphasized in schools (Deci & Ryan, 2002a; Zeidner, 1998). Anxiety often is conceptualized as having two components—worry and emotionality—with worry referring to cognitive ruminations and emotionality referring to physiological reactions (see Morris, Davis, & Hutchings, 1981). Researchers have focused on the cognitive/worry aspect of anxiety because worry is more strongly and negatively related to performance than emotionality (e.g., Morris et al., 1981; Sarason, 1980).

Researchers (e.g., Dusek, 1980; Hill & Wigfield, 1984; Wigfield & Eccles, 1989; Zeidner, 1998) postulate that high anxiety emerges when parents have overly high expectations and put too much pressure on their children, but few studies have tested this proposition. Anxiety continues to develop across the school years as children face more frequent evaluation, social comparison, and (for some) experiences of failure; to the extent that schools emphasize these characteristics, anxiety becomes a problem for more children (Hill & Wigfield, 1984). With a few important exceptions (e.g., Silverman, La Greca, & Wasserstein, 1995; Vasey & Daleiden, 1994; Zeidner, 1998), work on anxiety has diminished. One reason for this is the argument that anxiety is simply the flip side of negative judgments about one's ability and efficacy. For instance, Nicholls (1976) concluded that many items on one of the major scales used to measure anxiety, the Test Anxiety Scale for Children, refer to negative ability beliefs. When he separated the ability and anxiety items, the ability items related more strongly to indicators of achievement than the anxiety items (cf. Bandura, 1997; Meece et al., 1990). Second, is increasing interest in other kinds of emotions and their relations to motivation and achievement (see Pekrun, 2000).

Anxiety Intervention Programs

Many programs have been developed to reduce anxiety (Denny, 1980; Wigfield & Eccles, 1989; Zeidner, 1998). Earlier intervention programs, emphasizing the emotionality aspect of anxiety, focused on relaxation and desensitization techniques. Although these programs did reduce anxiety, they did not always lead to improved performance, and the studies had serious methodological flaws. Anxiety intervention programs linked to the worry aspect of anxiety focus on changing the negative, self-deprecating thoughts of anxious individuals and replacing them with more positive, task-focused thoughts (e.g., see Denny, 1980; Meichenbaum & Butler, 1980). These programs have been more successful both in lowering anxiety and improving performance.

Learned Helplessness

"Learned helplessness . . . exists when an individual perceives the termination of failure to be independent of his responses" (Dweck & Goetz, 1978, p. 157). Eccles et al. (1998) reviewed the early work (primarily by Dweck and her colleagues) on how helpless and mastery-oriented children differ in their responses to failure (see also Dweck & Elliott, 1983; Dweck & Leggett, 1988). When confronted by difficulty (or failure), mastery-oriented children persist, stay focused on the task, and sometimes even use more sophisticated strategies. In contrast, helpless children's performance deteriorates, they ruminate about their difficulties, and often begin to attribute their failures to lack of ability. Further, helpless children adopt the entity view that their intelligence is fixed, whereas mastery-oriented children adopt the incremental view of intelligence.

As noted earlier, the "optimism to realism" pattern of change in children's ability-related belief led some researchers to conclude that helplessness is less likely to occur in younger children. Dweck and her colleagues' more recent work (e.g., Burhans & Dweck, 1995) shows that in fact some young (5- and 6-year-old) children respond quite negatively to failure feedback, showing the helpless pattern and judging themselves to be bad people (cf. Stipek et al., 1992). Indeed, they proposed that young children's helplessness is based more on their judgments that their worth as persons is contingent on their performance than on having a mature entity view of intelligence. This work suggests an important developmental modification to Dweck and Legget's (1988) model of learned helpless versus mastery-oriented motivational styles that is based in beliefs about intelligence and goals.

What else influences the emergence of individual differences in learned helplessness in children? Dweck and Goetz (1978) stressed that whether children receive feedback, their failures are due to lack of ability or lack of skills and effort from parents and teachers. In support, Hokoda and Fincham (1995) found that mothers of helpless third grade children (in comparison to mothers of mastery-oriented children) gave fewer positive affective comments to their children, were more likely to respond to their children's lack of confidence in their ability by telling them to quit, were less responsive to their children's bids for help, and did not focus them on mastery goals. Dweck and Lennon (2001) found that students' perceptions that their parents had entity views of intelligence (measured by the kinds of feedback they would provide their children about different achievement outcomes) predicted their own views of intelligence. For instance, students perceiving their parents had an entity view were more likely themselves to have an entity view.

Alleviating Learned Helplessness

Various training techniques (including operant conditioning and providing specific attributional feedback) have been used successfully to change children's failure attributions from lack of ability to lack of effort, improving their task persistence and performance (e.g., Andrews & Debus, 1978; Dweck, 1975; Forsterling, 1985). Two problems with these approaches have been noted. First, what if the child is already trying very hard? Then, the attribution retraining may be counterproductive. Second, telling children to "try harder" without providing specific strategies designed to improve performance is likely to backfire if the children increase their efforts and still do not succeed. Therefore, some researchers advocate using strategy retraining in combination with attribution retraining to provide lower achieving and/or learned helpless children with specific ways to remedy their achievement problems. Borkowski and his colleagues, for example, have shown that a combined program of strategy instruction and attribution retraining is more effective than strategy instruction alone in increasing reading motivation and performance in underachieving students (e.g., Borkowski, Weyhing, & Carr, 1988; Paris & Byrnes, 1989).

Student Apathy

Apathy has more to do with students' sense of the value of participating in different activities rather than their beliefs about whether they are capable of accomplishing the activity. Children who are apathetic about learning or participating in other activities do not find much worthwhile to do in school or in other situations; they may even be so alienated from these activities that they actively resist attempts to get them involved. Brophy (2004) contended that apathy is the most serious motivational problem that teachers most contend with in their students—more serious than learned helplessness or anxiety. The apathy construct has some overlap with the construct of amotivation in SDT (Vallerand et al., 1993).

There has not been a lot of research on the development of apathy, but different researchers have discussed possible reasons for it. These range from broad social and cultural explanations to more psychologically oriented ones. Ogbu's (1992) discussion of why some minority children do well in school and others do not is an example of a broad cultural approach to this issue. Children who believe their ethnic or racial group is excluded from meaningful participation in the economic structure of this country may find little reason to engage in the school activities said to be needed to obtain good occupations. Ogbu has argued that such children often become oppositional to participation in school activities, resisting attempts of teachers to engage them in learning activities. We return to this issue later. A more psychological perspective on apathy can be drawn from Markus and Nurius's (1986) work on possible selves. Markus and Nurius argued that possible selves provide an important motivational force for engagement in different activities such as school or sport activities. If children do not see much of a future for themselves in these or other domains, they may not see much reason to be involved in school or other activities designed to prepare them for the future, and so they may be very apathetic about becoming involved in such activities.

We noted that apathy stems from the devaluing of different kinds of activities rather than from children's perceptions of their competence to accomplish them, but the interplay of competence beliefs and values may play a crucial role in the development of apathy. Recall our earlier discussion of how children maintain their self-worth by valuing those activities at which they are competent and devaluing activities where they are doing less well. Children doing poorly in school may begin to devalue school achievement, as a way to protect their self-esteem (see Covington, 1992). This devaluing could lead to apathy, again as a self-protective mechanism. Engaging in learning has risks, particularly for students not doing well, and one way to protect against those risks is to be apathetic about learning.

Finally, there likely are different developmental trajectories for the development of apathy. We noted two major possibilities to this point: (1) children who perceive few opportunities for themselves or for their group and so come to devalue school, or (2) children who begin to do poorly in school and so begin to devalue it as a way to protect their self-esteem. We use school activities to illustrate these points, but it should be noted that these patterns could occur for other kinds of activities as well. Another trajectory occurs for students doing well in school during the early school years and who come from backgrounds and cultural groups who generally have succeeded in our society, but who decide (for a variety of reasons) to no longer engage in school. These children may become alienated from school and therefore apathetic about participating in school activities (National Research Council [NRC], 2004). To date, there is little developmental work on any of these trajectories, but it should be undertaken.

Summary

In summary, work on anxiety, learned helplessness, and apathy shows that some children suffer from motivational problems that may debilitate their performance in achievement situations and may lead them to disengage from school and other achievement activities. Although most of the work in developmental and educational psychology has focused on these problems, there likely are other important motivational problems as well. In particular, some children may set maladaptive achievement goals, and others may have difficulties regulating their achievement behaviors. More comprehensive work on these kinds of motivational problems and how they affect children's achievement is needed.

The Development of Gender Differences in Motivation

Despite recent efforts to increase the participation of women in advanced educational training and high-status professional fields, women are still underrepresented in many fields, particularly those associated with technology, physics and applied mathematics, and at the highest levels of almost all fields (see Wigfield, Battle, Keller, & Eccles, 2002). Efforts to understand these persistent sex differences in achievement patterns have produced a proliferation of theories and research (see McGillicuddy-DeLisi & DeLisi, 2002, for review). Eccles and her colleagues originally proposed their expectancy-value model of achievement choices (see Figure 15.1) as an effort to organize this disparate research into a comprehensive theoretical framework (see Eccles-Parsons et al., 1983; Wigfield & Eccles, 2002b). This model predicts that people will be most likely to enroll in courses and choose careers that they think they will do well in and that have high task value for them. Expectations for success depend on the confidence the individual has in his or her intellectual abilities and on the individual's estimations of the difficulty of the course or activity. These beliefs have been shaped by the individual's experiences with the subject matter, by the individual's subjective interpretation of those experiences (e.g., Does the person think that her/his successes are a consequence of high ability or lots of hard work?), and by cultural stereotypes regarding both the difficulty of the course and the distribution of relevant talents across various subgroups. The value of a particular course is also influenced by several factors, including the following: Does the person like doing the subject material? How well does the course fit with the individual's self-concepts, goals, and values? Is the course seen as instrumental in meeting one of the individual's long- or short-range goals? Have the individual's parents or counselors insisted that the course be taken or, conversely, have other people tried to discourage the individual from taking the course? Does taking the course interfere with other goals and values activities? Existing evidence, reviewed next, supports the conclusion that gender-role socialization and internalization are likely to lead to gender differences in each of these broad motivational categories, which in turn could contribute to the underrepresentation of women in many high achievement-oriented occupations and activities (see Eccles, 1994).

Gender Differences in Competence-Related Beliefs, Causal Attributions, and Control Beliefs

Gender differences (often favoring males) in competence beliefs are often reported, particularly in gender-role stereotyped domains and on novel tasks, and these differences are apparent as early as kindergarten or first grade, if not before. For example, gifted and high-achieving females are more likely to underestimate both their ability level and their class standing (Frome & Eccles, 1995). In other studies, the gender difference depends on the gender-role stereotyping of the activity. For example, boys hold higher competence beliefs than girls for math and sports, even after all relevant skill-level differences are controlled; in contrast, girls have higher competence beliefs than boys for reading and English, music and arts, and social studies. Recent work (Jacobs et al., 2002) shows that the gender differences in competence beliefs in math narrow during adolescence, but those in English remain. Further, the extent to which children endorse the cultural stereotypes regarding which sex is likely to be most talented in each domain predicts the extent to which girls and boys distort their ability, self-concepts, and expectations in the gender stereotypic direction (Eccles & Harold, 1991). However, these sex differences are generally relatively small when they are found (Marsh, 1989).

Gender differences are also sometimes found for locus of control, with girls having higher internal locus of responsibility scores for both positive and negative achievement events and the older girls had higher internality for negative events than did the younger girls (Crandall et al., 1965). These two developmental patterns resulted in the older girls accepting more blame for negative events than the older boys (cf. Dweck & Goetz, 1978). Connell (1985) found that boys attributed their outcomes more than girls to either powerful others or unknown causes in both the cognitive and social domains.

This greater propensity for girls to take personal responsibility for their failures, coupled with their more frequent attribution of failure to lack of ability (a stable, uncontrollable cause) has been interpreted as evidence of greater learned helplessness in females (see Dweck & Licht, 1980). However, evidence for gender differences on behavioral indicators of learned helplessness is quite mixed. In most studies of underachievers, boys outnumber girls 2 to 1 (see McCall, Evahn, & Kratzer, 1992). Similarly, boys are more likely than girls to be referred by their teachers for motivational problems and are more likely to drop out of school before completing high school. More consistent evidence exists that females, compared to males, select easier laboratory tasks, avoid challenging and competitive situations, lower their expectations more following failure, shift more quickly to a different college major when their grades begin to drop, and perform more poorly than they are capable of on difficult, timed tests (see Dweck & Licht, 1980; S. J. Spencer, Steele, & Quinn, 1999).

Gender differences also emerge regularly in studies of anxiety (e.g., Hill & Sarason, 1966; Meece et al., 1990). However, Hill and Sarason suggested that boys may be more defensive than girls about admitting anxiety on questionnaires. In support of this suggestion, Lord, Eccles, and McCarthy (1994) found that test anxiety was a more significant predictor of poor adjustment to junior high school for boys even though the girls reported higher mean levels of anxiety.

Closely related to the anxiety findings, S. J. Spencer et al. (1999) documented another motivational mechanism likely to undermine females' performance on difficult timed tests: stereotype vulnerability. They hypothesize that members of social groups (like females) stereotyped as being less competent in a particular subject area (like math) will become anxious when asked to do difficult problems because they are afraid the stereotype might be true of them. This vulnerability is also likely to make them respond more negatively to failure feedback, leading to lowering their expectations and their confidence in their ability to succeed. They gave college students a difficult math test under different conditions: (a) after being told that males typically do better on this test, (b) after being told that males and females typically do about the same, or (c) after gender differences were not mentioned. The women scored lower than the males only in the first condition.

In sum, when gender differences emerge on competence-related measures of motivation, they are both consistent with gender-role stereotypes and are likely mediators of gender differences in various types of achievement-related behaviors and choices.

Gender Differences in Achievement Values

Eccles, Wigfield and their colleagues have found gender-role stereotypic differences in both children's and adolescents' valuing of sports, social activities, and English that begin quite early during children's development (e.g., Eccles et al., 1989; Eccles, Wigfield, et al., 1993; Wigfield et al., 1991). In Eccles, Wigfield, et al. (1993), girls also valued instrumental music more than boys. Earlier work showed gender differences in math value favoring boys emerging during adolescence (Eccles, 1984), but more recent studies show that boys and girls value math equally during adolescence (Jacobs et al., 2002). Although boys and girls now appear to value math equally, girls are less interested in science (with the exception of biology) and engineering than are boys, and they enroll much less frequently in these majors in college (see Wigfield et al., 2002, for review). Eccles et al. (1998) reviewed the work on the psychological

processes that underlie some of these sex differences in children's achievement values.

Disidentification.   Earlier, we discussed the relationship between values and competence-related beliefs. Drawing on the writings of William James (1892/1963), we suggested that children will lower the value they attach to particular activities or subject areas if they lack confidence in these areas to maintain their self-esteem (see also Harter, 1990). S. J. Spencer et al. (1999) suggested a similar phenomenon related to stereotype vulnerability. They hypothesized that women will disidentify with those subject areas in which females are stereotyped as less competent than males. By disidentifying with these areas, the women will not only lower the value they attach to these subject areas, they will also be less likely to experience pride and positive affect when they are doing well in these subjects. Consequently, these subjects should become irrelevant to their self-esteem. These hypotheses need further testing.

The Development of Group Differences in Motivation: The Roles of Culture, Ethnicity, and Immigration

As is the case in many areas of psychology (see Graham, 1992), less is known about the motivation of children from racial and ethnic groups other than European Americans. However, work in this area is growing quickly, with much of it focusing on the academic problems and prospects of African American (see Hare, 1985; Meece & Kurtz-Costes, 2001; Slaughter-Defoe, Nakagawa, Takanishi, & Johnson, 1990), Mexican American (e.g., Padilla & Gonzalez, 2001; Portes & Rumbaut, 2001), and Asian American youth (Fuligni & Tseng, 1999; S. J. Lee, 1994), both those born in this country and those who have immigrated here. Motivation theorists increasingly are interested in the applicability of their theoretical models to diverse groups of children. For instance, in a recent volume edited by McInerney and Van Etten (2004), theorists representing many of the theoretical perspectives reviewed in this chapter discussed the role of culture in their theoretical views, and whether their theories are applicable in different cultures.

This is an important time for renewed interest in how culture, ethnicity, and immigration relate to children's academic motivation, achievement, and future educational plans and attainments, as emerging and ongoing demographic trends in the United States and in developed countries all over the world show that large-scale immigration is taking place. For instance, in the United States today, the school-aged population stands at about 54 million individuals and is as large and diverse as it has ever been in U.S. history (U.S. Department of Education, 2003a). As of 2002, approximately 40% of the entire school-aged population was a member of an ethnic group other than European American, a large jump from the early 1970s that is due mainly to large-scale immigration from Mexico and certain East Asian countries (U.S. Department of Education, 2002). Thus, a significant proportion of the school-aged population today, approximately 20%, are "New Americans" who are growing up in immigrant families (Portes & Rumbaut, 2001; Suarez-Orozco & Suarez-Orozco, 2001).

This chapter is about motivation and not achievement, but it is important to understand achievement differences across groups to understand motivational differences. There are many individual differences in given groups, but overall Asian American children (both recent immigrants and those born here) perform better than many European American children. These two groups continue to outperform African American children and Latino and Mexican American children. Mexican American children have a very high school drop out rate relative to these other groups (U.S. Department of Education, 2003b).

There are interesting generational and gender differences in these effects. For instance, despite traditional socialization practices in many cultures that can exert strong pressures on females toward traditional gender roles associated with the home and not achievement in the outside world (e.g., Olson, 1997), there is evidence that second-generation immigrant females, like U.S. born females in general, tend to outperform their male counterparts in school and aspire to go further educationally and occupationally as well (Portes & Rumbaut, 2001). Understanding motivational dynamics behind these achievement differences is an important task, so we now turn to a discussion of the development of differences in motivation across different racial and ethnic groups.

Researchers interested in issues of culture, motivation, and achievement have examined the ways in which: (a) culture informs the development of self, motives, and behavioral scripts associated with achievement

(e.g., Markus & Kitayama, 1991; Ogbu, 1981); (b) culture shapes group members' construal of the meaning of success and failure before and after achievement experiences (e.g., Grant & Dweck, 2001; Heine et al., 2001); (c) culture influences how universal and individual psychological needs are expressed (e.g., Chirkov, Ryan, Kim, & Kaplan, 2003); and (d) culture influences engagement in the classroom (e.g., Greeno, Collins, & Resnick, 1996; Hickey & McCaslin, 2001; Roeser & Nasir, in press). We focus on the first three in this section, and the fourth in the School Level Characteristics and Student Motivation section.

Contemporary cultural psychology focuses on variation in the self linked to culture-specific socialization practices. A major distinction in this work is between socialization practices anchored in more individualistic (priority placed on goals and preferences of the self) and those anchored in more collectivist (priority placed on needs and norms of the group) cultural traditions (Triandis & Suh, 2002). Markus and Kitayama (1991) developed the notion of "cultural frame" as a way of describing how cultural socialization practices come to literally inform the self. Cultural frames are meaning systems comprised of language, tacit social understandings, and scripts for enacting these social understandings in daily life. Individual's self-construals (i.e., the individual's understandings about what it means to be a person in the world) are a critical component of these cultural frames. Markus and Kitayama (1991) outlined two different cultural frames, each associated with a specific self-construal: (1) independence and (2) interdependence. In the independent construal of self, individuals come to see themselves as autonomous, self-contained, unique from others, and assertive in pursuing personal goals and desires. In contrast, in the interdependent self-construal, individuals assign primary significance to others in defining the self, feel a fundamental sense of connectedness to others, and attend, first and foremost, to social roles, in-group norms, and obligations and responsibilities to others (see Oyserman, Coon, & Kemmelmeier, 2002, for a comprehensive review of different strands of research on these two construals). Self-construals are assumed to be the seedbed of goals and motives, including one's achievement-related goals and motives.

Although just beginning, research relating culture to motivation in this area tends to examine how (culturally informed) self-construals influence (a) the kinds of motivations that are prevalent for members of different cultural groups (the issue of approach and avoidance motivation), (b) the kinds of values and goals that are taken up into the self by members of different cultural groups (the issue of diversity in goal content), and (c) the kinds of meanings that individuals from different cultural groups make both before and after engaging with an achievement task (issues of meaning and appraisal). For example, Elliot, Chirkov, Kim, and Sheldon (2001) hypothesized that individualistic self-construals should promote approach motivation in which goals associated with self-assertion are focal; in contrast, interdependent self-construals should promote avoidance motivation in which goals associated with the reduction of group discord are focal. They found some support for these hypotheses in a cross-cultural study of college students. Among non-Asian college students, small correlations exist between self-as-independent and approach goals and between self-as-interdependent and avoidance goals. Both Asian American college students and students from more collectivist societies (Korea and Russia) report higher levels of avoidance motivation than European American college students.

These findings are consistent with studies suggesting that both the level and impact of avoidance motivation on achievement may be greater among individuals from cultural groups that emphasize interdependence and group membership. For instance, Eaton and Dembo (1997) found that the fear of failure (an avoidance motive) best predicted ninth grade Asian and Asian American students' performance on an intellectual task; in contrast, the non-Asian students' performance was best predicted by their beliefs about the incremental nature of intelligence, the importance of effort, and their self-efficacy. The authors interpreted these findings in relation to cultural dimensions of Asian cultures such as collectivism in which avoidance motives serve the function of maintaining group harmony.

Looking more directly at the association of culture to individual's view of such basic universal needs as autonomy, Chirkov et al. (2003) tested the proposition that individuals can "take up" cultural practices associated with collectivism and individualism in either a self-determined (autonomous) or an other-controlled (heteronomous) way in a study of undergraduates in Turkey, Russia, the United States, and South Korea. Defining autonomy by individuals' self-reported level of internalization of various collectivist or individualistic cultural

practices, they found considerable variation in the extent to which individuals in any culture took up and internalized supposedly focal cultural practices. Despite this variation, Americans saw their culture as relatively individualistic, South Koreans saw their culture as relatively collectivistic, and Russians saw their culture as a mixture of both. Further, the greater the degree of internalization of any type of cultural practice (whether collectivist or individualist), the greater the association of that belief with well-being. The extension of this work to examine how such cultural orientations, and their level of internalization, affect young people's goals and values in relation to education is just beginning.

Researchers also have looked at racial and ethnic group differences in the achievement beliefs, values, and goals we have been discussing and we turn to that work next.

Racial and Ethnic Group Differences in Children's Competence, Control, and Attribution Beliefs

Graham (1994) reviewed the literature on differences between African American and European American students on such motivational constructs as need for achievement, locus of control, achievement attributions, and ability beliefs and expectancies. She concluded that, in general, the differences are not very large. Further, she argued that many existing studies have not adequately distinguished between race and socioeconomic status, making it very difficult to interpret any differences that emerge. Cooper and Dorr (1995) did a meta-analysis of many of the same studies reviewed by Graham. There were important points of agreement across the two reviews, but Cooper and Dorr concluded that there is evidence suggesting race differences in need for achievement favoring Whites, especially in lower socioeconomic status (SES) and younger samples.

Research on competence beliefs and expectancies has revealed more optimism among African American children than among European American children, even when the European American children are achieving higher marks (e.g., H. W. Stevenson, Chen, & Uttal, 1990). But more important, in H. W. Stevenson et al. (1990), the European American children's ratings of their ability related significantly to their performance but the African American children's did not. Graham (1994) suggested the following explanations: (a) African American and European American children may use different social comparison groups to help judge their own abilities; and (b) African American children may say they are doing well to protect their general self-esteem, and may also devalue or *dis*identify academic activities at which they do poorly to protect their self-esteem. However, neither of these explanations has been adequately tested. If African American children's competence-related beliefs indeed do not predict their school performance, questions must be raised about how relevant the theories considered in this chapter are for understanding these children's motivation.

Racial and Ethnic Group Differences in Achievement Values and Goals

There are few ethnic comparative studies specifically focused on the kinds of achievement values measured by Eccles, Wigfield, and their colleagues, or of the kinds of goals measured by Nicholls, Dweck, Ames, and Wentzel. Researchers studying minority children's achievement values have focused instead on the broader valuing of school by minority children and their parents. In general, these researchers find that minority children and parents highly value school (particularly during the elementary school years) and have high educational aspirations for their children (e.g., Galper, Wigfield, & Seefeldt, 1997; H. W. Stevenson et al., 1990). However, the many difficulties associated with poverty may make these educational aspirations difficult to attain (see Duncan, Brooks-Gunn, & Klebanov, 1994; Huston, McLoyd, & Coll, 1994; McLoyd, 1990).

In two studies that did examine between-group differences in the achievement values among Latino, African American, and White youth, Graham, Taylor, and Hudley (1998) and Graham and Taylor (2002) used a peer nomination technique to assess group differences in achievement values. Participants indicated which children in their class they admired, respected, and wanted to be like, and Graham and her colleagues argued that this is one way to gauge what children value. Results showed that White, Latino, and African American girls chose high-achieving girls as those whom they admired, respected, and wanted to be like. For boys, this was only true for White boys; the other two groups of boys admired low achievers more. In a third study, they looked at this issue developmentally, and found that in second and fourth grades all children were more likely to nominate higher achievers. In seventh grade, the sex-differentiated pattern for the different groups emerged. This intriguing work needs to be followed up to look more closely at why the nomination patterns shift be-

tween fourth and seventh grades; and what it is about entering adolescent and puberty that seems to cause many African and Mexican American youth to endorse values and role-models that exclude school achievement (e.g., Tatum, 1997).

In a study of high school students in Australia, McInerney, Hinkley, Dowson, and Van Etten (1998) tested whether significant cultural differences between Anglo, immigrant, and Aboriginal Australians would eventuate in different achievement goal profiles. They found that Aboriginals were lower on mastery and performance goals compared to the Anglo and immigrant Australians. Nonetheless, mastery goals were positively associated with achievement for all groups. That mastery goals may be interpreted differently by members of different cultural groups—mastery as a means of self-improvement and role fulfillment (interdependent self) or mastery as a means of self-improvement and personal success (independent self)—may explain why this goal seems to operate effectively across a wide diversity of cultural settings (Urdan, 1997).

Race, Ethnicity, and Motivation at the Interface between Expectancies and Values

Researchers interested in ethnic and racial differences in achievement have proposed models linking social roles, competence-related beliefs, and values. For example, Steele (1992, 1997) proposed stereotype vulnerability and disidentification to help explain the underachievement of African American students (see also Aronson, 2002; Aronson & Steele, 2005): Confronted throughout their school career with mixed messages about their competence and their potential and with the widespread negative cultural stereotypes about their academic potential and motivation, African American students should find it difficult to concentrate fully on their school work due to the anxiety induced by their stereotype vulnerability (for support see Steele & Aronson, 1995). In turn, to protect their self-esteem, they should disidentify with academic achievement leading to both a lowering of the value they attach to academic achievement and a detachment of their self-esteem from both positive and the negative academic experiences. In support, several researchers have found that academic self-concept of ability is less predictive of general self-esteem for some African American children (Winston, Eccles, Senior, & Vida, 1997). A key mediator of this process is African Americans beliefs about the nature of their intelligence (Dweck & Leggett, 1988). In a recent experimental intervention with college students, Aronson, Fried, and Good (2001) found that by encouraging African American college students to adopt a mind-set in which they viewed their own intelligence as malleable, there were able to increase their enjoyment and engagement in academics as well as their grades compared to controls. This exciting research suggests interventions at the level of the meaning of intelligence and the purpose of learning may bear fruit for ameliorating the effect of stereotype threat on the achievement of African Americans.

Fordham and Ogbu (1986) have made a similar argument linking African American students' perception of limited future job opportunities to lowered academic motivation: Because society and schools give African American youth the dual message that academic achievement is unlikely to lead to positive adult outcomes for them and that they are not valued by the system, some African American youth may create an oppositional culture that rejects the value of academic achievement. Ogbu (1992) discussed how this dynamic will be stronger for involuntary minorities who continue to be discriminated against by mainstream American culture (e.g., African Americans) than for voluntary minority immigrant groups (e.g., recent immigrants from Southeast Asia). Although voluntary minorities have initial barriers to overcome due to language and cultural differences, these barriers can be overcome somewhat more easily than the racism faced by involuntary minorities, giving voluntary minorities greater access to mainstream culture and its benefits. This analysis is intriguing, but it may oversimplify the nature of different kinds of immigrants and does not attend enough to individual differences in these groups.

Contrary to this view, several investigators found no evidence of greater disidentification with school among African American students (e.g., M. B. Spencer, Noll, Stoltzfus, & Harpalani, 2001; Steinberg, Dornbusch, & Brown, 1992; Taylor, Casten, Flickinger, Roberts, & Fulmore, 1994). But several studies show that disidentification, particularly as a result of inequitable treatment and failure experiences at school, undermines achievement and academic motivation (e.g., see Finn, 1989; Taylor et al., 1994). Some students, particularly members of involuntary minority groups, may have these experiences as they pass through the secondary school system. Longitudinal studies of the process of

disidentification and how to ameliorate it when it occurs are needed.

In summary, as researchers continue to highlight the importance of understanding racial, ethnic, and immigrant variations in educational achievement given the demographic trends in our society (Kao & Thompson, 2003; Portes & Rumbaut, 2001), a deeper understanding of the role of academic motivational processes in explaining such variation in achievement behavior among different cultural, ethnic, and racial groups will continue to be critical topics of study in the developmental literature, as will further work that will help us to understand better the factors influencing the development of motivation in diverse groups of children (Graham, 1994; Pintrich, 2003).

THE SOCIALIZATION OF MOTIVATION: PARENTAL INFLUENCES

In the previous edition of this chapter, Eccles et al. (1998) reviewed the early literature on how parents influence child motivation through socialization process. In the past decade, the socialization research has become more focused and has begun to examine the various processes and pathways where socialization strategies might be exerting their influence (see Collins, Maccoby, Steinberg, Hetherington, & Bornstein, 2000). The research has also become more general as the research has moved from the laboratory settings in which researchers link specific parenting practices to specific motivational constructs but generalizability is limited to large-scale nationally representative studies of child development and parenting (e.g., Panel Study of Income Dynamics-Child Development Supplement, National Longitudinal Study of Youth, and Early Childhood Longitudinal Study) that use global indicators of parenting practices and beliefs and examine how they link to motivational and performance outcomes. This transition to more complicated examination of socialization processes has been motivated by both advances in theory as well as advances in statistical and analytic techniques that have allowed for more complicated analyses of parent influence to be examined and for moderators and mediators of this influence to be taken into account. In both small- and large-scale studies, there have been attempts to link parenting practices both to their an-

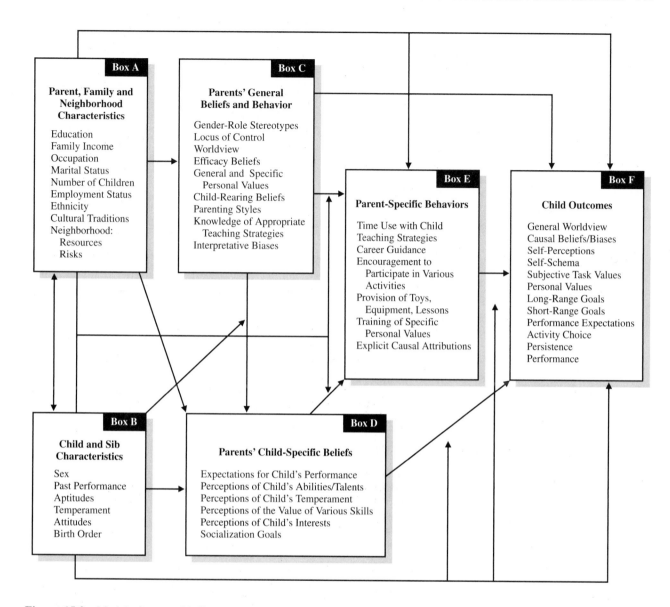

Figure 15.2   Model of parental influences on children's motivation and achievement.

tecedents and to their socialization consequences. Figure 15.2 provides a general overview of the types of associations tested. Although this specific model was proposed and elaborated by Eccles and her colleagues (Barber & Eccles, 1992; Eccles, 1989, 1993; Eccles & Harold, 1993), similar social cognitive mediational models of parental behavior and influence have been proposed by several other researchers (e.g., K. L. Alexander & Entwisle, 1988; Bronfenbrenner & Morris, 1998; Clark, 1983; J. J. Goodnow & Collins, 1990; Grolnick & Slowiaczek, 1994; H. W. Stevenson et al., 1990).

Although there is extensive work on some components of this model, very few studies include the several components underlying parenting behaviors outlined in Box E. Much of this literature focuses on the association of the exogenous characteristics (Boxes A and B) with parents' beliefs (Box C) or child outcomes (Box F)—for example, linking family socioeconomic status and/or ethnicity with parents' child-specific beliefs (Box D), specific parenting practices (Box E), and children's academic outcomes (Box F; Entwisle & Alexander, 1990; B. Schneider & Coleman, 1993; Steinberg et al., 1992; H. W.

Stevenson et al., 1990). Recently, however, research is beginning to appear that directly examines the mediating and moderating hypotheses implied in Figure 15.2 on achievement outcomes (Corwyn & Bradley, 2003; Davis-Kean, 2005; Davis-Kean & Magnuson, 2004). In general, this research has focused on the role that parent beliefs and behaviors may play in the socialization of achievement motivation in the individual child. This research indicates that parent's beliefs and behaviors are critical in setting a climate for children's motivation development by providing various activities or resources in the home environment that may provide stimulation to pursue various activities across time. For example, recent work on activity involvement suggests that parents play a role in promoting certain types of involvement in academic and sports domain in the early elementary years and that this emphasis translates into greater interest and motivation to continue with these activities over time and to choose course work and extracurricular activities consistent with these activities in adolescence (Simpkins, Fredricks, Davis-Kean, & Eccles, in press). Only in the past few years, this specific research has started to develop, and the research remains quite general; for example, linking family SES and general family socialization styles to general school achievement, achievement motivation, and other general motivational constructs such as mastery orientation, learned helplessness, and school engagement.

Family Demographic Characteristics

Researchers in sociology, economics, and psychology have documented the importance of factors such as family structure, family size, parents' financial resources, parents' education, parents' occupation, community characteristics, and dramatic changes in the family's economic resources in shaping children's academic motivation and achievement (e.g., K. L. Alexander & Entwisle, 1988; Corwyn & Bradley, 2003; Marjoribanks, 2002; Teachman, Paasch, & Carver, 1997; Thompson, Alexander, & Entwisle, 1988; Yeung, Linver, & Brooks-Gunn, 2002). Several mechanisms could account for these associations. First, family demographics could affect children's motivation indirectly through their association with both parent beliefs and practices and the opportunity structures in the child's environment. For example, parents with more

education are more likely to (a) believe that involvement in their children's education and intellectual development is important, (b) be actively involved with the children's education, and (c) have intellectually stimulating materials in their home (e.g., Davis-Kean & Magnuson, 2004; DeBaryshe, Patterson, & Capaldi, 1993; B. Schneider & Coleman, 1993).

Second, some demographic characteristics could influence motivation indirectly through the competing demands they place on parents' time and energy. For example, the negative association of single-parent status, time spent at work, and large family size on children's school achievement might reflect the fact that these factors reduce the time and energy parents have for engaging their children in activities that foster high motivation (e.g., Marjoribanks, 2002; B. Schneider & Coleman, 1993). Similarly, the psychological stress associated with some demographic factors could influence parents' ability to engage in the kinds of behaviors associated with high motivation. Ample evidence documents how much harder the job of parenting becomes when the family lives in a high-risk neighborhood or is financially stressed (e.g., Conger et al., 2002; Elder, Eccles, Ardelt, & Lord, 1995; Furstenberg, Cook, Eccles, Elder, & Sameroff, 1999; McLoyd, 1990; Mistry, Vandewater, Huston, & McLoyd, 2002). Such parents not only have limited resources to implement whatever strategies they think might be effective but also have to cope with more external stressors than middle-class families living in stable, resource-rich neighborhoods. Not surprisingly, their children also evidence less positive motivation toward conventional school success.

Third, demographic characteristics can also affect parents' perceptions of, and expectations for, their children. Both parent educational level and family income are related positively to parents' expectations regarding both their children's immediate school success and long-term educational prospects (e.g., K. L. Alexander & Entwisle, 1988; Davis-Kean, Malanchuk, Peck, & Eccles, 2003; Teachman et al., 1997). Similarly, divorced parents have lower expectations for their children's academic achievement (Barber & Eccles, 1992). Ogbu has highlighted this mechanism as one way poverty and anticipated discrimination can undermine academic motivation in some minority populations: If parents believe that there are limited opportunities for their children to obtain conventional forms of success, they are likely to shift their socialization efforts toward other goals and interests (Fordham & Ogbu, 1986; Ogbu, 1985).

Fourth, demographic characteristics can influence parents' beliefs and behaviors, and children's outcomes, in even less direct ways like those associated with role modeling. Family demographic characteristics are often associated with things like parents' jobs and leisure-time activities and with the kinds of role models children see outside the home. These behaviors and models can influence children's achievement goals, values, and self-perceptions through observational learning (Furstenberg et al., 1999; Kohn, 1997). Very little work has addressed this hypothesis directly. Instead, the mechanisms are typically inferred from correlational findings.

Fifth, demographic characteristics such as culture and ethnicity can influence parents' behaviors and children's motivation through mechanisms linked directly to values, goals, and general belief systems (e.g., Garcia Coll & Pachter, 2002; Gutman & Midgley, 2000; Luster, Rhoades, & Haas, 1989). For example, Ogbu (1985) has argued that parents value those characteristics that they assume will help their children succeed in their world. Other scholars describe cultural differences in valued activities, motivational orientation, and behavioral styles (e.g., H. W. Stevenson et al., 1990; Super & Harkness, 2002). Such differences can affect the socialization of motivated behavior through variations in: (a) valued activities (e.g., athletic versus musical competence), (b) valued goals (e.g., communal goals versus individualistic goals, mastery versus performance goals, doing versus being goals), and (c) approved means of achieving one's goals (e.g., competitive versus cooperative means). Further, there are cultural differences in the extent to which perceived family obligations influence children's motivation and achievement. Urdan and Giancarlo (2001) found that children from collectivist cultures had a stronger sense of obligation to their families that extended to the importance of doing well in school. Roeser, Lowe, Sattler, Gehlbach, and Strobel (2003) examined two kinds of family obligation goals that might motivate eighth grade Latino's academic achievement—those associated with making their parents proud through academic accomplishment (approach goals); and those associated with avoiding dishonoring the family through academic failure (avoidance goals). Compared to European American early adolescents, the Latino adolescents were more likely to endorse the pur-

suit of both types of goals (Roeser & Rodriquez, 2004), and family goals predicted Latino students' language achievement in school even after controlling for a host of sociodemographic, cognitive aptitude, and other motivational variables.

Researchers studying cultural differences in school achievement found cultural differences in parents' expectations and achievement-related beliefs and linked them to cultural differences in achievement. For example the work by H. W. Stevenson and his colleagues has demonstrated that European American parents, compared to Japanese parents, overestimate their children's academic abilities, are less aware of their children's academic difficulties, and are more satisfied with school performance that falls below their expectations (e.g., Crystal & Stevenson, 1991). Similarly, H. W. Stevenson et al. (1990) found differences in parents' achievement beliefs across African American, Hispanic, and European American parents in the United States.

In summary, there are many ways for family demographic characteristics to directly or indirectly affect motivation. However, even though family demographic characteristics have been linked repeatedly to children's school achievement; their effects are almost always indirect and mediated by their association with parents' beliefs, practices, and psychological resources. In addition, parents' beliefs and psychological and social resources can override the effects of even the most stressful demographic characteristics on children's school achievement and motivation (e.g., Clark, 1983; McLoyd, 1990). Finally, there are often complex interactions among various demographic characteristics in predicting either parenting beliefs and practices or child outcomes.

General Child-Rearing Climate

Historically, researchers studying parental influence have focused on the impact of the general patterns and philosophy of child rearing on children's overall orientation toward achievement. Researchers have related a set of general behaviors and beliefs to the development of self-esteem, achievement motivation, locus of control, sense of personal efficacy, and so on. The variables investigated have included the general emotional warmth and supportiveness in the home (e.g., Connell, Halpren-Felsher, Clifford, Crichlow, & Usinger, 1995; Gutman, Sameroff, & Eccles, 2002; Wagner & Phillips, 1992); valuing of achievement (e.g., Clark, 1983; DeBaryshe, 1995); general parental child-rearing beliefs, theories, values, and goals, as well as sex-typed goals and cultural beliefs, goals, and values (e.g., Goodnow & Collins, 1990; Miller & Davis, 1992); general child-rearing style, as well as authority structure, discipline tactics, and general interaction patterns (e.g., DeBaryshe et al., 1993; Lord et al., 1994; Steinberg et al., 1992; Yee & Flanagan, 1985); parental locus of control and personal efficacy (Bandura, 1997; Gutman et al., 2002); and communicative style and teaching style (McGillicuddy-DeLisi & Sigel, 1991). Similarly, researchers have documented the benefits of active involvement with, and monitoring of, children's and adolescents' school work (e.g., Clark, 1993; Connell et al., 1994; Eccles, 1993; B. Schneider & Coleman, 1993; Steinberg et al., 1992; H. W. Stevenson et al., 1990).

Several investigators have stressed an integrated view of how these various parenting characteristics work together to produce optimal motivational outcomes. For example, Grolnick and Ryan (1989) stressed the interplay of three components of general parenting in promoting self-determination in children and adolescents: (1) involvement and interest in the child's activities, (2) support for autonomous behaviors, and (3) adequate structure (e.g., Connell & Wellborn, 1991; Skinner, 1990). Grolnick and colleagues (2002) suggest that these parenting behaviors are important in helping children form a sense of autonomy and interest in activities that leads to greater achievement performance and a reduction in learning problems. Similarly, Csikszentmihalyi, Rathunde, and Whalen (1993) suggest the positive motivational development is optimized when there is appropriate synergy in the family's provision of support, harmony, involvement, and freedom. Finally, Eccles (1993) stressed the importance of emotional support, role models, and the right balance between structure, control, challenge, and developmentally appropriate levels of support for autonomy. This balance depends on cultural systems, on the specific context in which the family is living, the age of the child, and other individual characteristics.

Although the magnitude of effects varies by race/ethnicity, sex, social-economic class, and nationality, there is consensus that these general parental practices do impact on a variety of indicators of children's motivation and motivated behavior (e.g., Eccles, 1993; D. L. Stevenson & Baker, 1987). The results are consistent with three general principles: (1) appropriate levels of structure (as evident in Vygotsky's notion of appropriate scaffolding and Hunt and Paraskevopoulos's, 1980, no-

tion of good match), (2) consistent and supportive parenting, and (3) observational learning. Families who know enough about their child to provide the right amount of challenge with the right amount of support seem more likely to produce highly competent and motivated children. These parents are also likely to be able to adjust their behavior to meet the changing developmental needs and competencies of their children. Families that provide a positive emotional environment are more likely to produce children who want to internalize the parents' values and goals and therefore want to imitate the behaviors being modeled by their parents. Consequently, children growing up in these homes are likely to develop a positive achievement orientation if their parents provide such a model and value those specific tasks, goals, and means of achieving one's goals valued by their parents.

General Beliefs

Researchers have shown that parents' general beliefs such as valuing of achievement and school competence, general parental child-rearing beliefs and theories, values and goals, sex-typed ideologies and goals, and culturally based beliefs, goals, and values are linked to parenting behaviors in the school achievement arena in the predicted direction (e.g., Eccles, 1993; Eccles, Freedman-Doan, Fromme, Jacobs, & Yoon, 2000; Goodnow & Collins, 1990; Jacobs & Eccles, 2000; Miller, 1988; Sigel et al., 1992). We are beginning to know more about how these general beliefs relate to specific behaviors and motivational beliefs across various achievement-related activity domains. Figure 15.2 depicts a general overview of how one might think about these interrelationships. Several important questions are suggested by this depiction: First, what is the relation of parents' general beliefs and practices to domain and child-specific parental beliefs, values, and practices? For example, do parents' gender-role stereotypes affect their perceptions of their own child's abilities in various activity domains? Relevant research is reviewed later.

Similarly, do parents' beliefs regarding the nature of ability affect their motivational parenting? Dweck has hypothesized that different ways of viewing the nature of ability and incompetence account for individual differences in academic achievement orientation (Dweck, 2002). As discussed earlier, children who think that incompetence is a temporary and modifiable state should respond to failure with increased mastery efforts more than children who think that current incompetence is a sign of insufficient aptitude that cannot be modified. Parents also likely differ in their beliefs regarding the origins of individual differences in competence, the meaning of failure, and the most adaptive responses to failure. These beliefs should influence both their response to their children's failures and their efforts to help their children acquire new competencies and interests. Hokoda and Fincham (1995) provide support for these ideas.

Second, do cultural beliefs about things like the nature of ability affect the attributions parents' provide to their children for the child's successes and failures? Hess and his colleagues (e.g., Hess, Chih-Mei, & McDevitt, 1987; Holloway, 1988) and Stevenson and his colleagues (Lee, Ichikama, & Stevenson, 1987; H. W. Stevenson et al., 1990) have found that Japanese and Chinese parents make different causal attributions than European American parents for their children's school performances, with Japanese and Chinese parents emphasizing effort and hard work and European American parents emphasizing natural talent. Similarly, cultural differences in beliefs regarding the nature of ability and competence should relate to the kinds of statements parents make to their children about the origins of individual differences in performance—statements such as "You have to be born with math talent" versus "Anyone can be good at math if they just work hard enough" (Holloway, 1988; H. W. Stevenson et al., 1990). An interesting cross-cultural difference in the relation between the age of the child and parents' beliefs regarding ability is also emerging. Knight (1981) found that European Australian parents become more nativist in their view of their children's cognitive abilities as their children get older. In contrast, Japanese mothers become less nativist as their children get older.

Child-Specific Beliefs, Values, and Perceptions: Parents as Interpreters of Competence-Relevant Information

Parents hold many specific beliefs about their children's abilities, which affect motivationally linked outcomes, such as the well-established positive link between parents' educational expectations and academic motivation and performance (e.g., K. L. Alexander, Entwisle, & Bedinger, 1994; Brooks-Gunn, Guo, & Furstenberg, 1993; Davis-Kean, Eccles, & Schnabel, 2002; Grolnick & Slowiaczek, 1994; V. E. Lee & Croninger, 1994; B. Schneider & Coleman, 1993). Along with others, Eccles (1993) suggested the follow-

ing specific parental beliefs as particularly likely influences on children's motivation:

- Causal attributions for their children's performance in each domain
- Perceptions of the difficulty of various tasks for their children
- Expectations for their children's probable success and confidence in their children's abilities
- Beliefs regarding the value of various tasks and activities coupled with the extent to which parents believe they should encourage their children to master various tasks
- Differential achievement standards across various activity domains
- Beliefs about the external barriers to success coupled with beliefs regarding both effective strategies to overcome these barriers and their own sense of efficacy to implement these strategies for each child

Such beliefs and messages, particularly those associated with parents' perceptions of their children's competencies and likely success, influence children's self-beliefs and task beliefs (e.g., Fredricks & Eccles, 2002; Frome & Eccles, 1998; Miller, Manhal, & Mee, 1991; Pallas, Entwisle, Alexander, & Stluka, 1994; H. W. Stevenson et al., 1990). For example, parents' perceptions of their adolescents' abilities are significant predictors of adolescents' estimates of their own ability and interest in math, English, and sports even after the significant positive relation of the child's actual performance to both the parents' and adolescents' perceptions of the adolescents' domain-specific abilities is controlled (Eccles, 1993; Fredricks & Eccles, 2002; Jacobs, 1992; Jacobs & Eccles, 1992). Furthermore, Eccles and her colleagues found support for the hypothesized causal direction of this relationship using longitudinal panel analyses (Eccles, 1993; Eccles et al., 2000; Fredricks & Eccles, 2002; Yoon, Wigfield, & Eccles, 1993). In addition, in this same longitudinal study (The Michigan Study of Adolescent Life Transitions—MSALT), there was a negative relation between mothers' perceptions of their adolescents' English ability and the adolescents' perceptions of their own math ability. Individuals use a variety of information in deciding how good they are in various domains including their relative performances across various domains (i.e., they may decide they are very good at math because they find it easier to do better in math than in other school subjects; see Eccles, 1987; Marsh, 1990a). These results suggest that a similar phenomenon may characterize the impact of parents' perceptions of their children's abilities on the development of the children's self-perceptions. The adolescents in this study had lower estimates of their math ability than one would have predicted based on their teachers' and their mothers' rating of their math ability if their mothers also thought that they were better in English than in math (Eccles et al., 1993).

Influences on Parents' Perceptions of Their Children's Competencies. How do parents' form their impressions of their children's abilities? Parents appear to rely quite heavily on objective feedback, such as school grades (K. L. Alexander, Entwisle, & Bedinger, 1994; Arbreton & Eccles, 1994). The causal attributions parents make for their children's performances should also influence parents' perceptions. Support for this hypothesis is provided by Arbreton, Eccles, & Harold's (1994) longitudinal study. They found that parents' attributions of success to talent lead to increments in the parents' perceptions of their children's abilities in math, English, and sports and decrements in parents' estimates of how hard their children will have to work to be successful in math, English, and sports even after appropriate controls for prior performance and prior ability ratings are included.

Researchers have also assessed sex of child effects on parents' attributional patterns to help explain the gender role stereotypic distortions in parents' impression of their children's academic and nonacademic abilities that exist from a very early age on, even after one controls for actual performance differences (e.g., Eccles, 1993, 1994; Jacobs, 1992; Jacobs & Eccles, 1992). For example, in Jacobs (1992), mothers gave gender-role stereotypic causal attributions for their adolescent children's successes and failures in mathematics, English and sports: Sons' successes in math and sports were more likely to be attributed to natural talent than daughters'; daughters' success in English was more likely to be attributed to natural talent than sons'. Furthermore, as predicted, the sex differences in these mothers' ratings of their adolescents' abilities in each domain were substantially reduced once these sex differences in the mothers' causal attributions was controlled, supporting the hypothesis that parents' gender-role stereotyped causal attributions mediate parents' gender-role stereotyped perceptions of their children's math competence.

Using path-analytic techniques, Jacobs and Eccles (1992) tested whether parents' gender-role stereotypes generalized to their perceptions of their own children's ability. They found that parents who endorsed a gender-role stereotype regarding which sex is most interested in, and has the most natural talent for, math, English, and sports also distorted their ratings of their own children's abilities in each of these domains in the gender-role stereotypic direction.

Child-Specific Beliefs, Values, and Perceptions: Parents as Interpreters of Task Value

Parents may convey differential task values through explicit rewards and encouragement for participating in some activities rather than others. Similarly, parents may influence children's interests and aspirations, particularly with regard to future educational and vocational options, through explicit and implicit messages they provide as they counsel children or work with them on different academic activities (e.g., Eccles & Harold, 1993; Jacobs & Eccles, 2000; Tenenbaum & Leaper, 2003). For instance, Tenenbaum and Leaper found that fathers used higher order conceptual language when discussing physics activities with sons than with daughters, which gave boys and girls different messages about their ability in science. Whether this encouragement directly affects either the value the children attach to math or their participation in math activities has not been established.

Provisions of Specific Experiences at Home

There is ample evidence that parents influence their children's motivation through the specific types of learning experiences they provide for their children. For example, researchers have shown that reading to preschool children and providing reading materials in the home predicts the children's later reading achievement and motivation (e.g., Davis-Kean & Eccles, 2003; Linver, Brooks-Gunn, & Kohen, 2002; Wigfield & Asher, 1984). Such experience likely influences the child's skill levels and interest in doing these activities, both of which have a positive impact on the child's transition into elementary school and subsequent educational success (Entwisle & Alexander, 1993). Similarly, by providing the specific toys, home environment, and cultural and recreational activities for their children, parents structure their children's experiences (Jacobs, Davis-Kean, Bleeker, Eccles, & Malanchuk, 2004). However, the extent to which these experiences actually influence children's motivation should depend on the affective and motivational climate that is created by parents when the children are engaged with any particular experience. Finally, the differential provision of such experiences to girls and boys and to children from various ethnic groups might explain group differences in subsequent motivation to engage various types of achievement activities (see Jacobs et al., 2004, for discussion relating to gender).

Another avenue through which parents indirectly influence the provisions in the home is the way they manage the family. Parents manage the resources and time of their children and thus choose or help in choosing activities for their child that may increase interest and competence in these areas (Davis-Kean & Eccles, 1999; Simpkins et al., in press). Many parents try to organize and arrange their children's social environments to promote opportunities, to expose their children to particular experiences and value systems, and to restrict dangers and exposure to undesirable influences. Consider, for example, the amount of attention some parents give to the choice of child care during early childhood, to picking a place to live, and to selecting appropriate after-school and summer activities for their children to ensure desirable schools and appropriate playmates for their children and to help their children acquire particular skills and interests. In the arena of school achievement, parents' engagement in managing their children's experiences in relation to intellectual skills (e.g., reading, acquisition of general information, and mastering school assignments) is directly and powerfully related to children's subsequent academic success even in stressful contexts such as poverty (Furstenberg et al., 1999). Given the consistency of the evidence in this one domain, understanding the specific ways parents organize and manage their children's experiences across a wide range of activities is a promising approach to understanding how parents shape individual differences in specific skills, self-perceptions, interests, and activity preferences. For example, children are most likely to acquire those skills that their parents make sure they have the opportunity to learn and practice.

Summary

The studies reviewed suggest a multivariate model of the relation between antecedent child-rearing variables and the development of achievement orientation: The development of achievement motivation likely depends on the presence of several variables interacting with each other and mediating and moderating children's motivation. Specifically, proper timing of demands creates a situation in which the child can develop his or her sense of competence in dealing with his environment. An optimally warm and supportive environment creates a situation in which the child will choose his parents as role models. The presence of high yet realistic expectations creates a demand situation in which the child will perform in accord with the expectancies of the parents. Finally, the ability level of the child must be such that attainment of the expected level of performance is within his or her capacity. All these factors, as well as the availability of appropriate role models, are essential for the child to develop a positive, achievement orientation. The exact way this orientation will be manifest is likely dependent on the values the child has learned, which are directly influenced by the culture in which the family lives and the social roles that the child is being socialized to assume.

THE SOCIALIZATION OF MOTIVATION: INFLUENCES OF SCHOOL/INSTRUCTIONAL CONTEXTS AND SCHOOL TRANSITIONS

In this section, we review work on two broad topics: (1) how teachers, classroom contexts, and school contexts influence motivation; and (2) how school transitions influence children's motivation. Given space limitations, we provide only an overview of the types of work being done in these areas. There is a continuing trend for motivational researchers to study contextual influences on motivation and the work on motivation in context has burgeoned since the last edition of this *Handbook* was published (see Hickey & McCaslin, 2001; Urdan, 1999, for further discussion of this topic).

Much of the recent work is directly related to notions inherent in person-environment fit perspectives. The researchers, either implicitly or explicitly, assume that motivation will be optimized in learning settings that meet individual's basic and developmental needs. The exact nature of the basic or universal needs has been articulated in various ways. As discussed earlier, Deci, Ryan, Connell, and their colleagues focus attention on three basic needs: (1) competence, (2) relatedness, and (3) autonomy (e.g., R. M. Ryan & Deci, 2002). Eccles suggested that the need to matter (e.g., to make a real and meaningful difference in one's social world) is an additional universal value likely to influence achievement-related motivation particularly as individuals' mature into and through adolescence (Eccles, 2004). Eccles, Midgley, and their colleagues (e.g., Eccles, Midgley, et al., 1993) articulated a set of changing developmental needs that are often not met in school settings as children move from elementary school into secondary school. We believe that many of the constructs discussed in the next sections relate directly to these basic and developmental needs and thus influence individuals' motivation through their impact on the individuals' believing and feeling that their cognitive, emotional, and social needs are being met.

Teacher Beliefs and General Instructional Practices in the Classroom

There are several beliefs teachers have about their students and instructional practices they undertake that influence children's motivation. We discuss each in turn.

Teachers' General Expectations and Sense of Their Own Efficacy

Both teachers' general expectations for their students' performance and teachers' confidence in their own teaching efficacy (e.g., confidence in their ability to influence their students through their teaching) predict students' school achievement likely through their impact are on students' sense of competence. When teachers hold high generalized expectations for student achievement and students perceive these expectations, students achieve more, experience a greater sense of esteem and competence as learners, and resist involvement in problem behaviors during both childhood and adolescence (Eccles, Midgley, et al., 1993; V. E. Lee & Smith, 2001; NRC, 2004; Weinstein, 1989). Similarly, teachers who feel they are able to reach even the most difficult students, who believe in their ability to affect students' lives, and who believe that teachers are an important factor in determining developmental outcomes communicate such positive expectations and beliefs to their students (V. E. Lee & Smith, 2001; Midgley, Feldlaufer, & Eccles, 1989; Roeser, Marachi, & Gehlbach, 2002; Tschannen-Moran, Woolfolk-Hoy, & Hoy, 1998). Such expectations, when communicated to students, become internalized in positive self-appraisals that enhance both feelings of competence and worth, which enhance engagement in the learning tasks offered in school (V. E. Lee & Smith, 2001; NRC, 2002; Roeser, Eccles, & Sameroff, 1998).

Differential Teacher Expectations

Equally important are the differential expectations teachers hold for various individuals in the same classroom and the differential treatment practices that sometimes accompany these expectations. These person-specific expectations may be one of the most direct social influences on students' feelings of competence in classrooms. The research indicates that teacher-expectancy effects are mediated by the ways in which teachers interact with the students for whom they have high versus low expectations (Brophy, 1985; Eccles-Parsons et al., 1983; Rosenthal, 1974; Weinstein, 1989). Whether the effects are positive or negative depends on the exact nature of these interactions. For example, a teacher can respond to low expectation by providing the kinds of help and structure that increase the student's sense of competence and ability to master the material being presented. Alternatively, the teacher can respond in ways that communicate low expectations and little hope that the student will be able to master the material. In the latter case, the students' own sense of competence should decrease and the student should disengage from the classroom's learning agenda as much as is possible. Teachers' expectations for individual students are directly related to how well the student has done in the past (Jussim, Eccles, & Madon, 1996). What is critical is how these perceptions translate into the teachers' actual behavioral interactions with each of the students in the class.

A great deal of this work has focused on differential treatment related to gender, racial/ethnic group, and/or social class. There are small but fairly consistent negative effects of low teacher expectations on girls (for math and science), on minority children (for all subject areas), and on children from lower social class family backgrounds (again, for all subject areas; see Baron, Tom, & Cooper, 1985; Eccles & Wigfield, 1985; Ferguson, 1998; Jussim et al., 1996).

Teacher-Student Relationships

Many researchers have stressed the importance of human relationships for human development; the clearest exemplars of this view in the motivation field are self-determination theorists, who posit relatedness as a basic human need (Baumeister & Leary, 1995; R. M. Ryan & Deci, 2002). Consistent with these suggestions, there is strong evidence for the importance of positive teacher-student relationships and a sense of belonging for children's development in school (L. H. Anderman, 1999; Furrer & Skinner, 2003; Lynch & Cicchetti, 1997;

Wentzel, 2002a). Teachers who are trusting, caring, and respectful of students provide the kind of social-emotional support adolescents need to approach, engage, and persist on academic learning tasks and to develop positive achievement-related self-perceptions and values, high self-esteem, and a sense of belonging and emotional comfort at school (Eccles et al., 1998; C. Goodnow, 1993; Midgley et al., 1989; Roeser & Eccles, 2000; Roeser, Midgley, & Urdan, 1996). In addition, teachers represent one stable source of adult models and mentors for children in a highly complex society. Teachers can provide guidance and assistance when social-emotional or academic problems arise, and they may be particularly important in promoting developmental competence when conditions in the family and neighborhood do not (Eccles et al., 1998; Lord et al., 1994; Simmons & Blyth, 1987).

Classroom Management

Work related to classroom management focuses on two general issues: (1) orderliness/predictability and (2) control/autonomy. We focus on the latter because issues of autonomy are so important to student motivation in this culture. Many researchers believe that classroom practices that support student autonomy are critical for fostering intrinsic motivation to learn and for supporting socioemotional development during childhood and adolescence (Deci & Ryan, 1985; Grolnick et al., 2002). Support for this hypothesis has been found in both laboratory and field-based studies (Deci & Ryan, 1985; Grolnick & Ryan, 1987). However, it is also critical that the teacher supports student autonomy in a context of adequate structure and orderliness (Skinner & Belmont, 1993). This issue is complicated by the fact that the right balance between adult-guided structure and opportunities for student autonomy changes as the students mature: Older students desire more opportunities for autonomy and less adult-controlled structure. To the extent that the students do not experience these changes in the balance between structure and opportunities for autonomy as they pass through kindergarten to 12th grade, their school motivation should decline as they get older.

The Nature of Academic Work

Many researchers believe that the meaningfulness of the academic work influences sustained attention, high investment of cognitive and affective resources in learning, and strong identification with educational goals and aims (NRC, 2004). In general, research supports this hypothesis: For example, students' reports of high levels of boredom in school, low interest, and perceived irrelevance of the curriculum are associated with poor attention, diminished achievement, disengagement, and finally, alienation from school (e.g., Jackson & Davis, 2000; NRC, 2004; Roeser, Eccles, & Strobel, 1998; Roeser, Strobel, & Quihuis, 2002). Unfortunately, evidence from several different perspectives suggests that the curriculum to which most students are exposed is often not particularly meaningful from either a cultural or a developmental perspective. Several researchers suggest that the disconnect of traditional curricula from the experiences of several cultural groups can explain the alienation of some group members from the educational process, sometimes leading to school drop out (Dehyle & LeCompte, 1999; Fordham & Ogbu, 1986; Sheets & Hollins, 1999; Valencia, 1991). There is also a disconnect between increases in students' cognitive sophistication, life experiences, and identity needs and the nature of the curriculum as students move from the elementary into the secondary school years (Jackson & Davis, 2000; V. E. Lee & Smith, 2001; NRC, 2004). As one indication of this, middle school students report higher rates of boredom than elementary school students when doing schoolwork, especially passive work (e.g., listening to lectures), especially in social studies, math, and science (Larson & Richards, 1991). This could lead to some of the apathy problems discussed earlier.

Integrated Approaches to Within-Classroom Experiences

We have seen an increase over the past 20 years in studies that look at multiple aspects of the classroom simultaneously. During the past 8 years, this approach, in contrast to looking at single classroom or teacher characteristics one at a time, has predominated in keeping with our increasingly integrated view of motivation. In this section, we provide examples of this more integrated approach.

Rosenholtz and Simpson (1984) hypothesized that individualized versus whole group instruction, ability grouping practices, and the relatively public versus private nature of feedback work together to create a classroom environment that fundamentally shapes children's school motivation. Specifically, they argued that these practices make ability differences salient and thereby undermine motivation, particularly of low-achieving students, by increasing the salience of extrinsic motivators and ego-focused learning goals. Such motivational orientations are hypothesized to lead to greater incidence of social comparison behaviors and to increased perception of one's abilities as fixed entities rather than malleable ones. Mac Iver (1987) provided support for some of these predictions. More recently, the work of Midgley, Maehr, and their colleagues has shown that school reform efforts designed to reduce these types of classroom practices, particularly those associated with socially comparative feedback and reward systems, and teachers' use of competitive motivational strategies have positive consequences for adolescents' academic motivation, persistence on difficult learning tasks, and socioemotional development (Maehr & Midgley, 1996; Midgley, 2002).

Drawing on similar insights from different theoretical traditions, Guthrie, Wigfield, and their colleagues developed an instructional program in reading (Concept Oriented Reading Instruction—CORI) focused on enhancing students' reading motivation along with their reading comprehension. The program integrates instruction in reading and science and is based in part on principles derived from self-determination theory, self-efficacy theory, and expectancy-value theory (Wigfield & Tonks, 2004). Teachers work to enhance students' motivation by providing content goals for their learning and by having students engage in hands-on activities in science that tie to the content goals. Students have a variety of interesting texts in their classrooms that tie directly to the hands-on activities and content goals. They are given autonomy with respect to which books to read, which questions to address, and the nature of the projects that they do. Students also collaborate extensively with each other (Guthrie, Wigfield, & Perencevich, 2004). Guthrie, Wigfield, Barbosa, et al. (2004) found that CORI students surpassed students experiencing a cognitively based strategy instruction reading program in both reading motivation and reading comprehension. The more general implication of these results is that when teachers utilize teaching practices known to enhance student motivation, their motivation does indeed grow.

Gender Differences in Classroom Experiences

Research on gender differences in achievement is another example of an attempt to identify a broad set of classroom characteristics that influence students' motivation; due to space limitations we discuss the example of gender differences in interest in math, physical science, and engineering (see Wigfield, Byrnes, & Eccles, in press, for a more detailed review). Courses in these subject areas are often taught in a manner that females find either boring, irrelevant to their interests, or threatening (Eccles, 1989; Hoffmann & Haeussler, 1995). Females respond more positively to math and science instruction when it is taught in a cooperative or individualized manner rather than a competitive manner, when it is taught from an applied/person centered perspective rather than a theoretical/abstract perspective, when it is taught using a hands-on approach rather than a book-learning approach, when the teacher avoids sexism in its many subtle forms, and when the examples used to teach general concepts reflect both stereotypically female and male interests (e.g., using the heart as an illustration of the principles associated with pumps). The reason often given for these effects is the fit of the teaching style and format with females' values, goals, motivational orientation, and learning styles (see Eccles, 1989; Krapp, Hidi, & Renninger, 1992). Interestingly, more males are also motivated by these same approaches suggesting that these characteristics fit well with a broad range of human needs.

Experiences of Racial/Ethnic Discrimination in Classrooms

Researchers interested in the relatively poor academic performance of children from some ethnic/racial groups have suggested another classroom level experience as critical for academic motivation and achievement: experiences of racial/ethnic discrimination (Fordham & Ogbu, 1986; Garcia Coll et al., 1996; Roeser et al., 1998; Ruggiero & Taylor, 1995; Taylor et al., 1994; Wong, Eccles, & Sameroff, 2003). Whereas elementary school-aged children may lack the requisite social understandings and cognitive skills to judge discrimination experiences (though not always—see Quintana & Vera, 1999), and may also have too little life exposure to such incidents to make them impactful; beginning in early adolescence, young people are more likely to say they have experienced discrimination, and these experiences are negatively associated with young people's mental health and, sometimes, their motivation in school (Quintana & Vera, 1999; Roeser et al., 1998; Szalacha et al., 2003).

Two types of discrimination have been discussed: (1) anticipation of future discrimination in the labor market, which might be seen as undermining the long-term benefits of education (Fordham & Ogbu, 1986); and (2) the impact of daily experiences of discrimination on one's mental health and academic motivation (Wong et al., 2003). Wong et al. found that anticipated future discrimination leads to increases in African American youth's motivation to do well in school, which in turn leads to increases in academic performance. In this sample, anticipated future discrimination appeared to motivate the youth to do their very best so that they would be maximally equipped to deal with future discrimination (Eccles, 2004). In contrast, daily experiences of racial discrimination from their peers and teachers led to declines in school engagement and confidence in one's academic competence and grades, along with increases in depression and anger. In a study of Asian, Mexican, Central and South American immigrant high school students growing up in major metropolitan areas of the United States, Portes and Rumbaut (2001) found that a majority of youth in their sample reported feeling discriminated at school and in other settings. The major sources of this perceived discrimination were White classmates, teachers, and neighbors. Such experiences were associated with greater feelings of depression among the youth. In a sample of Mexican American high school students in California, perceived discrimination in school was found to have a strong, negative multivariate relation to school belonging (Roeser, 2004b).

Wong et al. (2003) also found that a strong, positive African American social identity helped to buffer these negative effects. These results suggest a possible buffering effect of ethnic identity on the potential debilitating effects of perceived discrimination, perhaps because a strong connection to one's ethnic group provides a context of shared meaning around issues of discrimination that assist group members in defusing its potential negative impact on the self and therefore, on motivation to succeed (Szalacha et al., 2003).

It is also critical in this discussion to consider the quality of the educational institutions that serve many of these youth. Thirty-seven percent of African American youth and 32% of Hispanic youth, compared to 5% of European American and 22% of Asian youth, are enrolled in the 47 largest city school districts in this country; in addition, African American and Latino youth attend some of the poorest school districts in this country. Twenty-eight percent of the youth enrolled in city schools live in poverty and 55% are eligible for free or reduced cost lunch, suggesting that class may be as important (or more important) as race in the differences that emerge. Teachers in these schools report feeling less safe than teachers in other school districts, dropout rates are the highest, and achievement levels at all grades are the lowest (Council of the Great City Schools,

1992). Finally, schools that serve these populations are less likely than schools serving more advantaged populations to offer either high quality remedial services or advanced courses and courses that facilitate the acquisition of higher order thinking skills and active learning strategies. Even children who are extremely motivated may find it difficult to perform well under these educational circumstances. These facts highlight the importance of focusing on the conjoint influences that poverty, discrimination, and debilitating work conditions for (often under qualified) teachers can have on the educational motivation, achievement, and attainments of African and Latin American youth.

School Level Characteristics and Student Motivation

Researchers suggest that variations at the school level in the climate and general expectations regarding student potential affect the development of both teachers and students in very fundamental ways (e.g., Bandura, 1997; Bryk, Lee, & Holland, 1993; Darling-Hammond, 1997; V. E. Lee & Smith, 2001; Mac Iver, Reuman, & Main, 1995; NRC, 2004). For example, Bryk et al. (1993) pointed out how the culture in Catholic schools is fundamentally different from the culture in most public schools in ways that positively affect academic motivation and achievement. This culture (school climate) values academics, has high expectations that all children can learn, and affirms the belief that the business of school is learning. Similarly, V. E. Lee and Smith (2001) showed that between-school differences in teachers' sense of their own personal efficacy as well as their confidence in the general ability of the teachers at their school to teach all students accounted, in part, for between-school differences in adolescents' high school performance and motivation. Finally, Maehr, Midgley, and their colleagues have argued that a school-level emphasis on different achievement goals creates a school psychological environment that affects students' academic beliefs, affect, and behavior (e.g., Maehr & Midgley, 1996; Midgley, 2002). For example, because schools' use of public honor rolls and assemblies for the highest achieving students, class rankings on report cards, and differential curricular offerings for students of various ability levels make relative ability, competition, and social comparison salient; these practices can create a school-level ability rather than mastery/task focus. In contrast, schools can promote a school-level focus on discovery, effort and improvement, and academic mastery by focusing school-wide recognition efforts on academic effort and improvement as well as on a wide range of competencies that include as many students as possible and by implementing practices that emphasize learning and task mastery such as block scheduling, interdisciplinary curricular teams, and cooperative learning (see also Finn, 1989; Fiqueira-McDonough, 1986; Roeser et al., 1998).

Academic Tracks/Curricular Differentiation

Curricular tracking (e.g., college track course sequences versus general or vocational education sequences) is another important school-level contextual feature that is quite common in secondary schools (Oakes, Gamoran, & Page, 1992). Differentiated curricular tracking influences adolescents' school experiences in two important ways: First, tracking determines the quality and kinds of opportunities to learn each student receives (Oakes et al., 1992); second, it determines exposure to different peers and thus, to a certain degree, the nature of social relationships that youth form in school (Fuligni, Eccles, & Barber, 1995).

Despite years of research on the impact of tracking practices, few strong and definitive answers have emerged. The results vary depending on the outcome assessed, the group studied, the length of the study, the control groups used for comparison, and the specific nature of the context in which these practices are manifest. The situation is complicated by the fact that conflicting hypotheses about the likely direction and the magnitude of the effect emerge depending on the theoretical lens one uses to evaluate the practice. The best justification for these practices derives from a person-environment fit perspective. Students are more motivated to learn if the material can be adapted to their current competence level. There is some evidence consistent with this perspective for children placed in high ability classrooms, high within-class ability groups, and college tracks (Fuligni et al., 1995; Kulik & Kulik, 1987; Pallas et al., 1994). The results for adolescents placed in low ability and noncollege tracks do not confirm this hypothesis. By and large, when long-term effects are found for this group of students, they are negative primarily because these adolescents are typically provided with inferior educational experience and support (Dreeban & Barr, 1988; Oakes et al., 1992; Pallas et al., 1994). Low track placement is related to poor attitudes toward school, feelings of incompetence, and problem behaviors both in

school (e.g., nonattendance, crime, misconduct) and in the broader community (e.g., drug use, arrests) as well as to educational attainments (Oakes et al., 1992).

Yet another way to think about the impact of ability grouping on development is by its impact on peer groups: Between-classroom ability grouping and curricular differentiation promotes continuity of contact among adolescents with similar levels of achievement and engagement with school. For those doing poorly in school, such practices can structure and promote friendships among students who are similarly alienated from school and are more likely to engage in risky or delinquent behaviors (Dryfoos, 1990). The "collecting" of adolescents with poor achievement or adjustment histories also places additional burdens on teachers who teach these classes (Oakes et al., 1992).

Another important and controversial aspect of curriculum tracking involves how students get placed in different classes and how difficult it is for students to move between class levels as their academic needs and competencies change once initial placements have been made. These issues are important both early in a child's school career (e.g., Pallas et al., 1994) and later in adolescence when course placement is linked directly to the kinds of educational options that are available to the student after high school. Minority youth, particularly African American and Hispanic boys, are more likely to be assigned to low ability classes and noncollege bound curricular tracks than other groups; furthermore, many of these youth were sufficiently competent to be placed in higher ability level classes (Dornbusch, 1994; Oakes et al., 1992).

Extracurricular Activities

Schools differ in the extent to which they provide a variety of extracurricular activities for their students. Research on extracurricular activities has documented a positive link between adolescents' extracurricular activities and high school GPA, strong school engagement, and high educational aspirations (see Eccles & Barber, 1999; Holland & Andre, 1987). This work has also documented the protective value of extracurricular activity participation in reducing dropout rates as well as involvement in delinquent and other risky behaviors (e.g., Mahoney & Cairns, 1997; McNeal, 1995). Participation in sports, in particular, has been linked to lower likelihood of school dropout and higher rates of college attendance (Deeter, 1990; Eccles & Barber, 1999; McNeal, 1995), especially among low achieving and blue-collar male athletes (Holland & Andre, 1987). These effects likely reflect the impact of extracurricular activities on students' sense of belonging in the school, as well as on the increased likelihood of participation leading to good relationships with particular teachers.

School Transitions and Motivational Development

We reviewed earlier normative developmental work showing that many aspects of children's motivation decline as they go through school. These declines are most marked as children make major school transitions (e.g., from elementary school into middle or junior high school and then again into high school). In this section, we briefly review the research focused on explaining these developmental declines.

Transition into and through Elementary School

Entrance into kindergarten and then the transition from kindergarten to first grade introduces several systematic changes in children's social worlds (see Pianta, Rimm-Kaufman, & Cox, 1999). First, classes are age stratified, making within-age ability social comparison much easier. Second, formal evaluations of competence by "experts" begin. Third, formal ability grouping begins usually with reading group assignment. Fourth, peers have the opportunity to play a much more constant and salient role in children' lives. Each of these changes should impact children's motivational development (Pianta et al., 1999). Unfortunately, very little longitudinal research has focused on this transition. We do know that many of the gains made in high quality preschool programs for children living in poverty can be lost as the children move into elementary school, although there are notable exceptions (Ramey & Ramey, 1999). In addition, we know that early school transitions are changing and will continue to change during this decade, with a stronger focus on academic aspects of schooling beginning earlier and earlier (Pianta & Cox, 1999). These transitions are happening earlier as more and more students begin school at earlier ages. In addition, the population of children is getting increasingly diverse and many public schools (particularly in urban and rural settings) now serve large groups of children living in poverty. The impact of these kinds of changes, and changes stemming from the No Child Left Behind Act, on students' motivation needs to be studied.

Instead, most of the research on the early elementary school years has focused on individual differences in the link between children's early school experiences and their subsequent development. This research suggests significant long-term consequences of children's experiences in the early school years, particularly experiences associated with ability grouping and within-class differential teacher treatment. For example, teachers use a variety of information to assign first graders to reading groups including temperamental characteristics like interest and persistence, race, gender, and social class (e.g., K. L. Alexander, Dauber, & Entwisle, 1993; Brophy & Good, 1974). K. L. Alexander et al. (1993) demonstrated that differences in first grade reading group placement and teacher-student interactions predict subsequent motivation and achievement even after controlling for initial differences in reading competence. Furthermore, these effects are mediated by both differential instruction and the amplifying impact of ability group placement on parents' and teachers' views of the children's abilities, talents, and motivation (Pallas et al., 1994).

These findings are important because they point to early school years as critical for subsequent school achievement. They are also important because they bring attention to the potential role of elementary schools in reproducing the economic stratification that exists in our society. Elementary schools are located in the communities they serve; thus, there can be great variations in the populations different schools serve, as well as in the curriculum offered, and the resources available, at different schools. Interestingly, in analyses of data from their Baltimore School Study, Entwisle and Alexander (1999) found that low SES and high SES children progressed equally during the school year when school was in session. Differences in performance emerged over the summer when school is not in session, with the low SES children losing more ground in what they are able to do over the summer than the high SES children.

We reviewed earlier the research showing that many children's motivation declines during the elementary school years. Researchers doing this work suggest that these changes reflect a combination of cognitive changes in the children and contextual changes in the classrooms (although more longitudinal studies are needed to assess these explanations fully). More specifically, children's ability to use social comparison information increases over the elementary school years making it easier for them to compare their relative ability with that other children (Ruble, 1983). This change should lead some children to lower their confidence in their own ability to master the school material (Eccles, 1984). Similarly, it is possible that teachers increase their use of social comparative information and their emphasis on ability as entity based rather than incremental. The increasing emphases as children go through school on evaluation and performance outcomes also likely play a strong role (Maehr & Midgley, 1996). More work is needed to test these hypotheses.

Transitions from Elementary School into Secondary School

As was true in 1998, most of the research on secondary school transition effects has focused on the transition to middle or junior high school. But more work is coming out on the transition into high school. Because the principles underlying the declines in students' motivation are quite similar across these two transitions, we focus on these principles rather than the specific grade levels at which the transitions are made.

As noted earlier, there are substantial declines in academic motivation and achievement across the upper elementary and secondary school years, including changes in grades, interest in school, perceptions of competence in different areas, and increases in performance goals at the expense of mastery goals (see Eccles et al., 1998; B. Schneider & Coleman, 1993, for reviews). These changes are particularly large for students who are doing poorly (either emotionally or academically) in school (Lord et al., 1984). These changes are also likely to be especially problematic for children from low SES communities and families, children who find the school curriculum particularly meaningless and children who find the school climate particularly unsupportive and uncomfortable.

In explaining such changes, Eccles et al. (1998) discussed how the multiple changes that occur during this time period (puberty, school transitions, changing relations with parents, increasing cognitive maturity, increasing concern with identity, increasing sexuality and heterosociality, and increasing focus on peer relationships) likely have an impact on students' motivation and achievement. They also discussed how differences in school environments between elementary and secondary schools could contribute to these changes (see also Eccles & Roeser, 2003; NRC, 2004; Wigfield & Eccles, 2002b; Wigfield & Tonks, 2002). Traditional secondary schools differ structurally in important ways from ele-

mentary schools. Most secondary schools are substantially larger than elementary schools. As a result, students' friendship networks often are disrupted as they attend classes with students from several different schools. In addition, students are likely to feel more anonymous and alienated because of the large size of many secondary schools. Finally, the opportunity to participate in and play leadership roles in school activities often decline over these school transitions due to the limited number of slots in such niches and the increasing size of the student body. These kinds of changes should affect the students' sense of belonging as well as their sense of social competence.

The nature of instruction also changes: Secondary school instruction is organized and taught departmentally—making it likely that secondary school teachers teach several different groups of students each day and are unlikely to teach any particular students for more than 1 year. This departmental structure can create a number of difficulties for students. First, the curriculum often is not integrated across different subjects. Second, students typically have several teachers each day with little opportunity to interact with any one teacher on any dimension except the academic content of what is being taught and disciplinary issues. As a result, the likelihood of students and teachers forming close, supportive bonds is much less in secondary than in elementary schools. This result can be problematic for a number of reasons. First, it could reduce the likelihood that a teacher will be able to identify whether a particular student is having problems and make an appropriate referral recommendation. Second, it could reduce the likelihood that a teacher will have time to provide adequate instructional supports for students who need extra academic help. Both of these changes are likely to undermine low-performing students' sense of competence and sense of belonging.

Finally, grading systems are more likely to be based on social comparative performance, ability-level tracking via curricular tracking is common, and teachers are more likely to hold entity, rather than incremental, views of ability differences (Eccles & Midgley, 1989; Wigfield, Eccles, & Pintrich, 1996). These characteristics, in turn, are likely to lead to an increase in performance rather than mastery goal focus in the classroom and the school building. As noted earlier, these changes are likely to undermine low performing students' sense of competence. Because the nature of these changes is so dramatic at the shift from elementary school to middle or junior high school, it is not surprising that there is a major decline in motivation for many students as they make this transition.

Recent work on the transition to high school suggests that similar changes occur at this transition (V. E. Lee & Smith, 2001; Mac Iver et al., 1995; NRC, 2004; Wehlage, Rutter, Smith, Lesko, & Fernandez, 1989). For example, high schools are typically even larger and more bureaucratic than middle and junior high schools. V. E. Lee and Smith (2001) provide numerous examples that the sense of community among teachers and students is undermined by the size and bureaucratic structure of most high schools. There is little opportunity for students and teachers to get to know each other and, likely as a consequence, there is distrust between them and little attachment to a common set of goals and values. There is also little opportunity for the students to form mentorlike relationships with the teachers and there is little effort to make instruction meaningful to the students. Such environments are likely to undermine the motivation and involvement of many students, especially those not doing particularly well academically or who are alienated from the values of the adults in the high school.

Furthermore, research based on both teacher and student reports shows that schools become more socially comparative and competitive in orientation as students progress from elementary to middle to high school (Roeser et al., 2002). The coincidence of declining social support and increased social comparison and competition at both the middle and high school levels likely contribute to some adolescents' decisions, those who are already on the margins of the school community, to withdraw from school prior to graduation. For example, Fine (1991) documented how these kinds of secondary school practices cumulate to drive out students who are not doing very well academically. In a large study of students in the Chicago public schools, Roderick and Camburn (1999) showed how failure rates increase dramatically after students made the transition to high school (this was particularly true for minority students), and how early failures in high school strongly predict later poor performance. Other studies of ethnic minority youth document the negative impact of alienating and noninclusive high school practices on school engagement and achievement of students of color (e.g., Darling-Hammond, 1997; Deyhle & LeCompte, 1999; Ferguson, 1998; Jackson & Davis, 2000; Taylor et al., 1994; Valencia, 1991). More work is needed on this transition point.

School Experiences as Related to Ethnic and Cultural Identity Formation

As noted earlier, typical secondary school practices may be particularly problematic for adolescents from cultural minority groups. Adolescence is the prime developmental period for identity development. A great deal of work in the past 10 to 15 years has focused on the potential disconnect between what goes on in typical American secondary schools and the goals, values, and experiences of cultural minority groups in the United States (see Meece & Kurtes-Costes, 2001; Okagaki, 2001).

Much of this work has focused on how individuals from different ethnic and cultural groups navigate the sometimes disparate social worlds of home and school by "managing" the relation of their in-school identity with broader aspects of their social identities (e.g., Roeser et al., 2003). Perhaps the most well-known view of how members of different ethnic minorities manage, or rather fail to manage, aspects of their ethnic/racial and student identities is that of John Ogbu and Signthia Fordham, some of whose work was reviewed earlier. These authors highlighted the identity conflicts that members of particular ethnic minority groups may experience between ethnic loyalty and school identification. Another view of how members of traditionally disenfranchised groups address these kinds of potential identity conflicts comes from scholars such as Oetting and Beauvais (1991) and Lafromboise, Coleman, and Gerton (1993). These authors have pointed to the strategies that members of nonmajority groups use to develop bicultural identities—those that integrate a sense of ethnic pride and engagement with activities of the majority culture in a complementary rather than conflictual way (Phinney & Devich-Navarro, 1997). This work underscores how some members of stigmatized ethnic minority groups integrate their sense of ethnic pride and their pursuit of success in school, with the presumption that success in school is defined as a "majority" activity. In this instance, neither ethnic loyalty nor commitment to education "gives way" to the other. Evidence for the existence of such subgroups among Mexican American youth, for example, has been found at the middle school (Roeser et al., 2003) and high school level (Matute-Bianchi, 1986).

The emerging literature on social identities and academic identity among ethnic minorities (see Wigfield & Wagner, 2005) raises several possibilities concerning what Roeser and his colleagues (2003) have called "school identity configurations." Young people from

TABLE 15.1 Recommendations for Restructuring Middle Grades Schools

Recommendations from the Carnegie Council on Adolescent Development

1. Turn large schools into smaller learning communities.
2. All students should receive a common core of high-level knowledge.
3. All students should be given the opportunity to succeed.
4. Teachers and school administrators should have decision-making authority.
5. Middle grades teachers should receive special preparation for working with early adolescents.
6. Early adolescents' fitness and health should be a strong focus of middle school education.
7. Families should be involved in middle schools.
8. School-community connections need to be established.

Recommendations from the National Middle School Association

1. Middle school educators should be knowledgeable about young adolescents.
2. The middle school curriculum should be responsive to the needs of young adolescents.
3. There should be a range of organizational arrangements in middle schools.
4. Instructional strategies should be varied.
5. There should be full exploratory programs in different schools.
6. Comprehensive advising and counseling should be provided for all students.
7. All students should make continual progress.
8. Evaluation procedures should be compatible with the nature of young adolescents.
9. Teachers should have time for cooperative planning.
10. Each middle school should have a positive school climate.

various nonmajority ethnic groups may integrate their sense of ethnic pride and school commitment in the ways described by those who study biculturalism. Others may manage different facets of identities inside and outside of school by code switching in the ways that scholars such as Fordham (1988) have proposed, whereas some individuals who have difficulty managing different dimensions of identity may show oppositional patterns of disengagement as described by Fordham and Ogbu (1986). However, such conflicts are not confined to ethnic minority youth but rather are a broader phenomena characteristic of many adolescents (Arroyo & Zigler, 1995; Roeser et al., 2003).

Middle School Reform Efforts and Student Motivation

Based in part on the research just reviewed, proposals by middle schools experts, and the *Turning Points* report written by the Carnegie Council on Adolescent Development, middle school reform has become very popular (see Carnegie Foundation, 1989; Jackson & Davis, 2000;

Midgley & Edelin, 1998). There is growing consensus about what kinds of changes should be made in middle grades schools (Lipsitz, Mizell, Jackson, & Austin, 1997). One structural change adopted in many school districts has been to move the transition to middle school from after to before sixth grade. However, this change on its own accomplishes little and often simply moves the transitional problems 1 year earlier in the students' development. What is more important is changing school organization and instructional practices in systematic ways (Mac Iver & Epstein, 1993). Both the Carnegie Council on Adolescent Development and the National Middle Schools Association have made recommendations for how middle schools should be changed; a summary of their recommendations is presented in Table 15.1. As can be seen in the table, there is much overlap between these recommendations. The broadest goal of these recommendations is to provide developmentally appropriate education for early adolescents.

There are a number of important ways in which these recommendations have been implemented in different middle schools. One is replacing departmentalized curriculum structures with teams of teachers working with the same group of students. This practice allows groups of teachers to spend more time with the same group of adolescents, thus getting to know them better. It also allows for greater integration across the curriculum. Teachers who serve as advisors and counselors have become more prevalent, so that adolescents can develop closer relationships with their teachers. To create smaller learning communities in often-large middle schools, "schools within schools" have been created, in part through the teaming approach just discussed. This is particularly likely to occur for the youngest group in a middle school, whether they are fifth graders, sixth graders, or seventh graders. Cooperative learning practices are used more frequently, in part to reduce the use of ability grouping or tracking.

Lipsitz and her colleagues (1997) discussed middle school reform efforts across the country. They focused in particular on three sets of middle schools in Illinois, Michigan, and Indiana in which reform efforts in line with the recommendations included in Table 15.1 have been undertaken in meaningful ways. Felner et al. (1997) reported systematic evaluations of the schools in the Illinois network. They conducted longitudinal studies in schools implementing fully the recommendations from the Carnegie Council, comparing them with schools implementing the recommendations to a degree and not at all. The comparison schools are matched carefully on demographic and other characteristics. Felner et al. obtained measures of students' achievement, school attitudes, and behavior problems. Preliminary analyses indicate that schools in which the implementation has been fullest have higher achieving students. Students in these schools report higher self-esteem and fewer worries about bad things happening to them in schools; the teachers report fewer behavior problems. These results provide encouraging support for the efficacy of the reform efforts. One crucial point made by Felner et al. is that comprehensive reform is needed. Schools in which one or two of the recommendations have been implemented, or schools in which the implementation of several recommendations has proceeded slowly, have not been as successful. Unfortunately, as noted earlier, many schools are just beginning to implement change, or are doing so selectively.

There is not yet a great deal of information about how reform efforts have affected students' motivation. Felner and his colleagues measured self-esteem but not the different aspects of motivation we have discussed in this chapter. Mac Iver and his colleagues began a middle school reform effort (Mac Iver & Plank, 1997; Mac Iver, Young, & Washburn, 2002) focused on schools serving early adolescents who live in high poverty areas. The program involves the implementation of many of the recommendations discussed in this section: detracking the schools, using cooperative learning extensively, team teaching, offering a challenging core curriculum (including algebra) to all students, and providing advising services. Preliminary results for both achievement and motivation outcomes are encouraging.

As mentioned earlier, Maehr and Midgley (1996) used goal theory to work with teachers and administrators to change the culture organization and climate of a middle school and an elementary school in a city in Michigan. The school-university team worked extensively to restructure the school toward a focus on mastery goal; they spent 3 years in each school. At the middle school, they focused on creating teams of teachers, "schools within the school," lessening the use of ability grouping practices, and changing the student recognition patterns so that not just the "honor roll" students were recognized. They also worked to loosen the rigid bell schedule so that longer class periods were sometimes possible. Changing the school culture in the middle school was very difficult due to some teachers' (especially the math teachers) resistance to change, par-

ticularly with respect to doing away with grouping, difficulties in adjusting the rigid middle school bell schedule to accommodate teaming and flexible class scheduling, and parents' objections that their high-achieving students did not receive enough recognition. However, despite these difficulties, the changes had positive effects on students' motivation (E. M. Anderman, Maehr, & Midgley, 1999).

In contrast, much less work has been done on high school reform effort and the results of this work are less consistent (NRC, 2004). Reform efforts have followed similar principles aimed at creating schools that better meet the competence, belonging, autonomy, and mattering needs of the adolescent students. As is true for the middle school reform efforts, when these principles are well implemented, improvements in students' motivation, school engagement, and academic performance are obtained (NRC, 2004). But successfully implementing these kinds of changes has proven to be very difficult at the high school level.

THE SOCIALIZATION OF MOTIVATION: ROLES OF PEERS

How might peers affect motivation and achievement? We focus on four possible links: (1) the role of social comparison in self-evaluation, (2) the relation between social competence and school motivation/achievement, (3) peers as co-learners, and (4) the reinforcing and socializing mechanism in peer groups.

Social Comparison and Self-Evaluation

Given the importance of ability self-concepts in all motivational theories, understanding the role that peers play in self-evaluation is critical to our understanding of motivation. Researchers interested in social comparison have addressed this issue, focusing specifically on age-related increases in children's use of social comparison information in forming perceptions of their own abilities. In general, older children and adolescents use social comparison more often and more accurately in forming their own self-evaluations than younger children (e.g., Ruble, 1994). Ruble (1994) also suggested that the use of social comparison may increase during transitional phases in a child's life like the school transitions discussed earlier. Together these transitional processes and the age-related increases in the use of social comparison make adolescents exceptionally vulnerable to the motivational consequences of such comparisons (Eccles, Midgley, et al., 1993; Fuligni et al., 1995). Cultural background (either in terms of gender or ethnic group) also likely influences the extent and the type of social comparison. Finally, as noted earlier, social comparison processes are very sensitive to social context, particularly those linked to the types of classroom experiences linked to performance versus mastery orientation.

Social Competence and Motivation

Many studies document the positive association of good social skills with both better performance and higher motivation in school (e.g., Asher & Coie, 1990; Juvonen & Wentzel, 1996; Wentzel, 1998). Further, social competence and social support can help ease school transitions (Birch & Ladd, 1996; Lord et al., 1994; Rubin, Bukowski, & Parker, 1998; Rubin, Coplan, Chen, Buskirk, & Wojslawowicz, 2005). The exact mechanisms underlying these associations are just beginning to be understood. Some suggest that the association represents the influence of some underlying form of inherited intelligence or temperament/motivational orientation that facilitates the acquisition of both social and academic competence (e.g., Martin, Drew, Gaddis, & Moseley, 1988; Wentzel, 1991b). Others focus on the link between social support and mental health: Children should be able to focus more of their attention on learning if they feel socially supported and well-liked by both their peers and the adults in their learning context and if they feel that they belong (Furrer & Skinner, 2003; C. Goodnow, 1993; Lynch & Cicchetti, 1997; Roeser et al., 1996; Sage & Kindermann, 1999). Well-liked children may also place more value on learning in such a context.

Peers as Co-Learners

The extensive work on the advantages of cooperative learning provides another link between peers and motivation. This work suggests that doing learning activities in a social context is usually more fun and, thus, more intrinsically interesting (Slavin, 1995; Stevens & Slavin, 1995). Peers also help each other understand and learn the material through group discussion, sharing of resources, modeling academic skills, and interpreting and clarifying the tasks for each other (Schunk, 1987). Each of these characteristics should influence achievement through its impact on children's expectations for success, their valuing of the activity, and their focus on learning rather than performance goals.

Peer Group Influences

Much of the classic work on peer influences on school achievement focused on the negative effects of peer groups on children's commitment to doing well in school (see Brown, 1990, 2004, for review). More recently, researchers have investigated the specific mechanisms by which peer groups can have either a positive or negative affect on motivation across various activity settings. These researchers document that children cluster together in peer groups sharing similar motivational orientations and activity preferences and that such clustering reinforces and strengthens their existing motivational orientation and activity preferences over time (e.g., Guay, Boivin, & Hodges, 1999; Kindermann, Mc-Collam, & Gibson, 1996; A. M. Ryan, 2001). Altermatt and Pomerantz (2003) found in a study of early adolescents that best friends' report-card grades were similar, as were their beliefs about their competence in different subject areas. In addition, friends had significant (but modest) influences on each others' grades and motivational beliefs across the 2 school years studied. Whether such effects are positive or negative depends on the nature of the peer groups' motivational orientation. High-achieving children who seek out other high achievers as friends develop even more positive academic motivation over time. In contrast, low achievers who join a low-achieving peer group should become even less motivated to do school work and more motivated to engage in other activities more consistent with their peer group's values (see Brown, 2004; Kindermann, 1993; Kindermann et al., 1996).

The role of peer group influence varies across ages, with peers in an especially important role in relation to motivation and achievement during adolescence for two reasons: First, adolescents are more aware of, and concerned about, peer-group acceptance and spend much more unsupervised time with peers groups than younger children (Brown, 2004). Consequently, adolescents should be especially vulnerable to peer group influences on their goals, interests, and values. In addition, however, the potential negative impact of peers may be especially problematic for some adolescents' academic achievement motivation. For example, early adolescents rate social activities as very important and more enjoyable than most other activities, particularly academic activities (Eccles et al., 1989; Wigfield et al., 1991). Consequently, to the extent that one's peer group devalues academic achievement relative to other goals and activities, the adolescents should shift their focus away from academic pursuits to maintain peer acceptance. Finally, given other changes associated with adolescent development, it is quite likely that a substantial number of adolescents will be recruited into such a peer group. Some of these adolescents will be recruited into gangs—a particularly problematic peer group in terms of antisocial behavior and low school achievement (Battin-Pearson, Thornberry, Hawkins, & Krohn, 1998; NRC, 2004).

Another growing concern about the impact of peers on children's school motivation focuses on bullying and peer violence at school. Fighting increases during the middle school years, and more students are bullied in middle school than in either elementary or high school (Juvonen, Le, Kaganoff, Augustine, & Constant, 2004). Being bullied is associated with many negative developmental outcomes, including loneliness, depression, and social anxiety, as well as lower school performance (Juvonen & Graham, 2001; Juvonen, Nishina, & Graham, 2001). Increasing percentages of both middle and high school students report concerns about their safety in school, which distracts them from their school learning and can lead to motivational disengagement from school (Brand, Felner, Shim, Seitsinger, & Dumas, 2003). Creating safer school environments where bullying and other forms of violence are less likely is an important priority to maximize all students' school engagement and motivation.

CONCLUSIONS

Research on the development of children's motivation remains vibrant. Many of the same theories that were reviewed in the previous chapter in this *Handbook* continue to be influential, although the influence of some theories has waned, and others grown. Research in these different theoretical traditions is giving us a more complete understanding of the development of motivation across the childhood and adolescent years.

We believe the research since the last edition of this *Handbook* was published has made especially important advances in the following areas. First, we have learned much about contextual influences on motivation and how children's motivation varies across different contexts, such as in different kinds of families, and different school contexts. We have long known that motivation is not solely a characteristic of the individual, but the new emphasis on "motivation in context" has brought that point out much more clearly (Hickey & McCaslin, 2001; Urdan, 1999). Further, as we understand better contextual influences in schools and other settings that influence motivation, we are making progress in developing ways to foster the development of children's motivation in these settings (e.g., Guthrie, Wigfield, & Perencevich, 2004; Maehr & Midgley, 1996). Through this intervention work the often-noted declines in children's motivation can be reversed or avoided.

Second, we have learned much about the development of motivation in diverse groups of children in this country and others. Although much remains to be done in this area, motivation researchers increasingly include diverse samples in their work, revising their theories to incorporate culture more clearly in their models, and testing their theories in diverse groups (see the McInerney & Van Etten, 2004 volume for good examples of this work). Following Graham's (1994) call, much of this work is looking at variation *within* different cultural groups, rather than comparisons across groups. This is an important trend because we need to know much more about variation in motivation within different groups rather than how one group's mean level of motivation compares to the mean level of another group.

Third, progress has been made in understanding the relations between motivation, cognition, and self-regulation, which provides us with a more complete picture of children's functioning in different kinds of achievement settings (e.g., Boekaerts et al., 2000; Pintrich, 2003; Wolters, 2003; Zimmerman, 2000). Yet, as Pintrich notes, much work remains to be done on this topic, as there is (potentially) great complexity in these relations. Along with the relations of motivation, cognition, and self-regulation, there has been increasing interest in research on relations between motivation and affect (e.g., Pekrun, 2000; Pintrich, 2003), and we think this work will grow over the next few years. Understanding relations among the different motivational beliefs, values, and goals; cognitive processes; and the regulation of behavior and affect is a major priority for the next several years.

Another important advance over the past 8 years is the growing concern for how motivation constructs are defined, and there are attempts to specify the similarities and differences in related constructs (e.g., self-efficacy and expectations for success). A particular example of this is Murphy and Alexander's (2000) article in their special issue of *Contemporary Educational* Psychology devoted to motivational terminology, but others have contributed to these efforts as well (e.g., Bandura, 1997; Pintrich, 2003; Schunk & Pajares, 2002; Wigfield & Eccles, 2000). As motivation terminology becomes increasingly clearly defined, theoretical clarity, and the similarities and differences across different theories, also should be better understood. Indeed, we believe it may be time for greater integration across some of the major theories of motivation rather than a continued proliferation of theories focused primarily on one or two constructs.

Finally, in a chapter for the *Handbook of Child Psychology* we think it important to note that there needs to be more truly developmental work on the nature and development of motivation. Many researchers have focused on individual differences and group differences in motivation, but not always on motivational development. One important developmental issue that needs more attention is how children at different ages understand their own motivational beliefs, values, and goals. The only such belief that has been investigated systematically in this way is children's conceptions of the nature of ability. This work has shown clearly that children have rather different conceptions of ability at different ages, which has many implications for our understanding of how motivation operates at different ages, as well as for how we measure children's sense of ability. Such work has not been done with the other major belief, value, and goal constructs discussed in this chapter, and this work should be undertaken.

There have been important methodological advances that allow us to study the development of motivation in increasingly sophisticated ways. Studies we reviewed earlier by Jacobs et al. (2002), Skinner et al. (1998), and Watt (2004) are good examples, and there are other examples in the literature. These researchers (and others) are using newly developed statistical methods to analyze short- and long-term change in the belief, value, and goal constructs that impact motivation. These researchers also are examining what explains different patterns of change in children's beliefs, values, and goals. Continuing such work will lead to an even better understanding of the *development* of motivation. Coupling such work with investigations into the *processes* involved in motivation's relations to outcomes also will advance the field.

REFERENCES

Ainley, M., Hidi, S., & Berndorff, D. (2002). Interest, learning, and the psychological process that mediate their relationship. *Journal of Educational Psychology, 94,* 545–561.

Alexander, K. L., Dauber, S. L., & Entwisle, D. R. (1993). First-grade classroom behavior: Its short- and long-term consequences for school performance. *Child Development, 64,* 801–803.

Alexander, K. L., & Entwisle, D. (1988). Achievement in the first 2 years of school: Patterns and processes. *Monographs of the Society for Research in Child Development, 53*(2, Serial No. 218).

Alexander, K. L., Entwisle, D. R., & Bedinger, S. D. (1994). When expectations work: Race and socioeconomic differences in school performance. *Social Psychology Quarterly, 57,* 283–299.

Alexander, P. A., Kulikowich, J. M., & Jetton, T. L. (1994). The role of subject-matter knowledge and interest in the processing of linear and nonlinear texts. *Review of Educational Research, 64,* 201–252.

Altermatt, E. R., & Pomerantz, E. M. (2003). The development of competence-related and motivational beliefs: An investigation of similarity and influence among friends. *Journal of Educational Psychology, 95,* 111–123.

Ames, C. (1992). Classrooms: Goals, structures, and student motivation. *Journal of Educational Psychology, 84,* 261–271.

Ames, C., & Archer, J. (1988). Achievement goals in the classroom: Students' learning strategies and motivation processes. *Journal of Educational Psychology, 80,* 260–267.

Anderman, E. M., Austin, C. C., & Johnson, D. M. (2002). The development of goal orientation. In A. Wigfield & J. S. Eccles (Eds.), *Development of achievement motivation* (pp. 197–220). San Diego, CA: Academic Press.

Anderman, E. M., Maehr, M. L., & Midgley, C. (1999). Declining motivation after the transition to middle school: Schools can make a difference. *Journal of Research and Development in Education, 32,* 131–147.

Anderman, L. H. (1999). Expanding the discussion of social perceptions and academic outcomes: Mechanisms and contextual influences. In T. Urdan (Ed.), *Advances in motivation and achievement* (Vol. 11, pp. 303–336). Greenwich, CT: JAI Press.

Anderman, L. H., & Anderman, E. M. (1999). Social predictors of changes in students' achievement goal orientations. *Contemporary Educational Psychology, 25,* 21–37.

Andrews, G. R., & Debus, R. L. (1978). Persistence and the causal perception of failure: Modifying cognitive attributions. *Journal of Educational Psychology, 70,* 154–166.

Arbreton, A. J. A., & Eccles, J. S. (1994, April). *Mother's perceptions of their children during the transition from kindergarten to formal schooling: The effect of teacher evaluations on parents' expectations for their early elementary school children.* Paper presented at the annual meeting of the American Educational Research Association Conference, New Orleans, LA.

Arbreton, A. J., Eccles, J. S., & Harold, R. (1994, April). *Parents' perceptions of their children's competence: The role of parents attributions.* Paper presented at the biennial meeting of the Society for Research on Adolescence, San Diego, CA.

Aronson, J. (2002). Stereotype threat: Contending and coping with unnerving expectations. In J. Aronson (Ed.), *Improving academic achievement: Impact of psychological factors on education* (pp. 279–301). San Diego, CA: Academic Press.

Aronson, J., Fried, C. B., & Good, C. (2001). Reducing the effects of stereotype threat on African American college students by shaping theories of intelligence. *Journal of Experimental Social Psychology, 58,* 3–11.

Aronson, J., & Steele, C. M. (2005). Stereotypes and the fragility of academic competence, motivation, and self-concept. In A. J. Elliot & C. S. Dweck (Eds.), *Handbook of competence and motivation* (pp. 436–456). New York: Guilford Press.

Arroyo, C., & S-Zigler, E. (1995). Racial identity, academic achievement, and the psychological well being of economically disadvantaged adolescents. *Journal of Personality and Social Psychology, 69,* 903–914.

Asher, S. R., & Coie, J. D. (Eds.). (1990). *Peer rejection in childhood.* Cambridge, England: Cambridge University Press.

Assor, A., & Connell, J. P. (1992). The validity of students' self-reports as measures of performance affecting self-appraisals. In D. H. Schunk & J. L. Meece (Eds.), *Student perceptions in the classroom* (pp. 25–47). Hillsdale, NJ: Erlbaum.

Atkinson, J. W. (1957). Motivational determinants of risk taking behavior. *Psychological Review, 64,* 359–372.

Atkinson, J. W. (1964). *An introduction to motivation.* Princeton, NJ: Van Nostrand.

Bandura, A. (1977). Self-efficacy: Toward a unifying theory of behavioral change. *Psychological Review, 84,* 191–215.

Bandura, A. (1986). *Social foundations of thought and action: A social cognitive theory.* Englewood Cliffs, NJ: Prentice-Hall.

Bandura, A. (1995). Exercise of personal and collective efficacy in changing societies. In A. Bandura (Ed.), *Self-efficacy in changing societies* (pp. 1–45). Cambridge, England: Cambridge University Press.

Bandura, A. (1997). *Self-efficacy: The exercise of control.* New York: Freeman.

Barber, B., & Eccles, J. S. (1992). A developmental view of the impact of divorce and single parenting on children and adolescents. *Psychological Bulletin, 111,* 108–126.

Baron, R. M., Tom, D. Y. H., & Cooper, H. M. (1985). Social class, race, and teacher expectations. In J. B. Dusek (Ed.), *Teacher expectancies* (pp. 251–269). Hillsdale, NJ: Erlbaum.

Battin-Pearson, S. R., Thornberry, T. P., Hawkins, J. D., & Krohn, M. D. (1998). *Gang membership, delinquent peers, and delinquent behavior* (Report No. 1-11). Washington, DC: U.S. Department of Justice.

Battle, A., & Wigfield, A. (2003). College women's value orientations toward family, career, and graduate school. *Journal of Vocational Behavior, 62,* 56–75.

Baumeister, R. F., & Leary, M. R. (1995). The need to belong: Desire for interpersonal attachments as a fundamental human motivation. *Psychological Bulletin, 117,* 497–529.

Baumert, J. (1995, April). *Gender, science interest, teaching strategies and socially shared beliefs about gender roles in seventh graders: A multi-level analysis.* Paper presented at the annual meeting of the American Educational Research Association, San Francisco, CA.

Birch, S. H., & Ladd, G. W. (1996). Interpersonal relationships in the school environment and children's early school adjustment: The role of teachers and peers. In J. Juvonen & K. R. Wentzel (Eds.), *Social motivation: Understanding children's school adjustment* (pp. 199–225). New York: Cambridge University Press.

Blumenfeld, P. C. (1992). Classroom learning and motivation: Clarifying and expanding goal theory. *Journal of Educational Psychology, 84,* 272–281.

Boekaerts, M., Pintrich, P. R., & Zeidner, M. (2000). *Handbook of self-regulation.* San Diego, CA: Academic Press.

Bong, M. (2001). Role of self-efficacy and task value in predicting college students' course enrollments and intentions. *Contemporary Educational Psychology, 26,* 553–570.

Bong, M., & Clark, R. E. (1999). Comparison between self-concept and self-efficacy in academic motivation research. *Educational Psychologist, 34,* 139–154.

Borkowski, J. G., Weyhing, R. S., & Carr, M. (1988). Effects of attributional retraining on strategy-based reading comprehension in learning-disabled student. *Journal of Educational Psychology, 80,* 46–53.

Brand, S., Felner, R., Shim, M., Seitsinger, A., & Dumas, T. (2003). Middle school improvement and reform: Development and validation of a school-level assessment of climate, cultural pluralism, and school safety. *Journal of Educational Psychology, 95,* 570–588.

Bronfenbrenner, U., & Morris, P. A. (1998). The ecology of environmental processes. In W. Damon (Series Ed.) & R. M. Lerner (Vol. Ed.), *Handbook of child psychology* (5th ed., Vol. 1, pp. 993–1028). New York: Wiley.

Brooks-Gunn, J., Guo, G., & Furstenberg, F. F., Jr. (1993). Who drops out of and who continues beyond high school? A 20-year follow up of Black urban youth. *Journal of Research on Adolescence, 3,* 271–294.

Brophy, J. E. (1985). Teacher-student interaction. In J. B. Dusek (Ed.), *Teacher expectations* (pp. 303–328). Hillsdale, NJ: Erlbaum.

Brophy, J. E. (1999). Toward a model of the value aspects of motivation in education: Developing appreciation for particular learning domains and activities. *Educational Psychologist, 34,* 75–85.

Brophy, J. E. (2004). *Motivating students to learn* (2nd ed.). Mahwah, NJ: Erlbaum.

Brophy, J. E., & Good, T. L. (1974). *Teacher-student relationships: Causes and consequences.* New York: Holt, Rinehart and Winston.

Brown, B. B. (1990). Peer groups and peer culture. In S. S. Feldman & G. R. Elliott (Eds.), *At the threshold: The developing adolescent* (pp. 171–196). Cambridge, MA: Harvard University Press.

Brown, B. B. (2004). Adolescents' relationships with peers. In R. M. Lerner & L. D. Steinberg (Eds.), *Handbook of adolescent psychology* (2nd ed., pp. 363–394). Hoboken, NJ: Wiley.

Bryk, A. S., Lee, V. E., & Holland, P. B. (1993). *Catholic schools and the common good.* Cambridge, MA: Harvard University Press.

Bullock, M., & Lutkenhaus, P. (1988). The development of volitional behaviors in the toddler years. *Child Development, 59,* 664–674.

Burhans, K. K., & Dweck, C. S. (1995). Helplessness in early childhood: The role of contingent worth. *Child Development, 66,* 1719–1738.

Butler, R. (1993). Effects of task- and ego-achievement goals on information seeking during task engagement. *Journal of Personality and Social Psychology, 65,* 18–31.

Cain, K., & Dweck, C. S. (1995). The development of children's achievement motivation patterns and conceptions of intelligence. *Merrill-Palmer Quarterly, 41,* 25–52.

Cameron, J., & Pierce, W. D. (1994). Reinforcement, reward, and intrinsic motivation: A meta-analysis. *Review of Educational Research, 64,* 363–424.

Carnegie Council on Adolescent Development. (1989). *Turning points: Preparing American youth for the twenty-first century.* Washington, DC: Author.

Chen, A., Darst, P. W., & Pangrazi, R. P. (2001). An examination of situational interest and its sources. *British Journal of Educational Psychology, 71,* 383–400.

Chirkov, V., Ryan, R. M., Kim, Y., & Kaplan, U. (2003). Differentiating autonomy from individualism and independence: A self-determination theory perspective on internalization of cultural orientations and well-being. *Journal of Personality and Social Psychology, 84,* 97–110.

Clark, R. (1983). *Family life and school achievement: Why poor Black children succeed or fail.* Chicago: University of Chicago Press.

Clark, R. (1993). Homework parenting practices that positively affect student achievement. In N. F. Chavkin (Ed.), *Families and schools in a pluralistic society* (pp. 53–71). Albany: State University of New York Press.

Collins, W. A., Maccoby, E. E., Steinberg, L., Hetherington, E. M., & Bornstein, M. H. (2000). Contemporary research on parenting: The case for nature and nurture. *American Psychologist, 55,* 218–232.

Conger, R. D., Wallace, L. E., Sun, Y., Brody, G., McLoyd, V., Simons, R. L., et al. (2002). Economic pressure in African-American families: A replication and extension of the family stress model. *Developmental Psychology, 38,* 179–193.

Connell, J. P. (1985). A new multidimensional measure of children's perception of control. *Child Development, 56,* 1018–1041.

Connell, J. P., Halpern-Felsher, B. L., Clifford, E., Crichlow, W., & Usinger, P. (1995). Hanging in there: Behavioral, psychological, and contextual factors affecting whether African-American adolescents stay in high school. *Journal of Adolescent Research, 10,* 41–63.

Connell, J. P., Spencer, M. B., & Aber, J. L. (1994). Educational risk and resilience in African American youth: Context, self, and action outcomes in school. *Child Development, 65,* 493–506.

Connell, J. P., & Wellborn, J. G. (1991). Competence, autonomy, and relatedness: A motivational analysis of self-system processes. In R. Gunnar & L. A. Sroufe (Eds.), *Minnesota Symposia on Child Psychology* (Vol. 23, pp. 43–77). Hillsdale, NJ: Erlbaum.

Cook, T. D., Church, M. B., Ajanaku, S., Shadish, W. R., Kim, J. R., & Cohen, R. (1996). The development of occupational aspirations and expectations among inner-city boys. *Child Development, 67,* 3368–3385.

Cooper, H., & Dorr, N. (1995). Race comparisons on need for achievement: A meta-analytic alternative to Graham's narrative review. *Review of Educational Research, 65,* 483–508.

Cordova, D. I., & Lepper, M. R. (1996). Intrinsic motivation and the process of learning: Beneficial effects of contextualization, personalization, and choice. *Journal of Educational Psychology, 88,* 715–730.

Corno, L. (1993). The best-laid plans: Modern conceptions of volition and educational research. *Educational Researcher, 22,* 14–22.

Corno, L. (2004). Work habits and study styles: Volition in education. *Teachers College Press, 106,* 1669–1694.

Corno, L., & Kanfer, R. (1993). The role of volition in learning and performance. In L. Darling-Hammond (Ed.), *Review of research in education* (Vol. 29, pp. 301–342). Washington, DC: American Educational Research Association.

Corwyn, R. F., & Bradley, R. F. (2003). *Family process mediators of the relation between SES and child outcomes.* Unpublished manuscript, University of Arkansas at Little Rock.

Council of the Great City Schools. (1992). *National urban education goals: Baseline indicators, 1990–1991.* Washington, DC: Author.

Covington, M. V. (1992). *Making the grade: A self-worth perspective on motivation and school reform.* New York: Cambridge University Press.

Covington, M. V., & Dray, E. (2002). The developmental course of achievement motivation: A need-based approach. In A. Wigfield & J. S. Eccles (Eds.), *Development of achievement motivation* (pp. 33–56). San Diego, CA: Academic Press.

Crandall, V. C., Katkovsky, W., & Crandall, V. J. (1965). Children's beliefs in their own control of reinforcements in intellectual-academic achievement situations. *Child Development, 36,* 91–109.

Crystal, D. S., & Stevenson, H. W. (1991). Mothers' perceptions of children's problems with mathematics: A cross-national comparison. *Journal of Educational Psychology, 83,* 372–376.

Csikszentmihalyi, M. (1988). The flow experience and its significance for human psychology. In M. Csikszentmihalyi & I. S. Csikszentmihalyi (Eds.), *Optimal experience* (pp. 15–35). Cambridge, MA: Cambridge University Press.

Csikszentmihalyi, M., & Massimini, F. (1985). On the psychological selection of bio-cultural information. *New Ideas in Psychology, 3,* 15–38.

Csikszentmihalyi, M., Rathunde, K., & Whalen, S. (1993). *Talented teenagers: The roots of success and failure.* New York: Cambridge University Press.

Darling-Hammond, L. (1997). *The right to learn: A blueprint for creating schools that work.* San Francisco: Jossey-Bass.

Davis-Kean, P. E. (2005). The influence of parent education and family income on child achievement: The indirect role of parental expectations and the home environment. *Journal of Family Psychology, 19,* 294–304.

Davis-Kean, P. E., & Eccles, J. S. (1999). *It takes a village to raise a child: A social executive functioning and community management perspective.* University of Michigan, Ann Arbor, MI.

Davis-Kean, P. E., & Eccles, J. S. (2003). Influences and barriers to better parent-school collaborations. *Laboratory for Student Success Review, 2*(1), 4–5.

Davis-Kean, P. E., Eccles, J. S., & Schnabel, K. U. (2002, August). *How the home environment socializes a child: The influence of SES on child outcomes.* Paper presented at the International Society for the Study of Behavioral Development, Ottawa, Canada.

Davis-Kean, P. E., & Magnuson, K. A. (2004). *The importance of parents' education on child outcomes.* Unpublished manuscript.

Davis-Kean, P. E., Malanchuk, O., Peck, S. C., & Eccles, J. S. (2003, March). *Parental influence on academic outcomes: Do race and SES matter?* Paper presented at the biennial meeting of the Society for Research on Child Development, Tampa, FL.

DeBaryshe, B. D. (1995). Maternal belief systems: Linchpin in the home reading process. *Journal of Applied Developmental Psychology, 15,* 1–20.

DeBaryshe, B. D., Patterson, G. R., & Capaldi, D. M. (1993). A performance model for academic achievement in early adolescence. *Developmental Psychology, 29,* 795–804.

Deci, E. L. (1992). The relation of interest to the motivation of behavior: A self-determination theory perspective. In K. A. Renninger, S. Hidi, & A. Krapp (Eds.), *The role of interest in learning and development* (pp. 43–70). Hillsdale, NJ: Erlbaum.

Deci, E. L. (1998). The relation to interest to motivation and human needs: The self-determination theory viewpoint. In L. Hoffman, A. Krapp, K. A. Renninger, & J. Baumert (Eds.), *Interest and learning* (pp. 146–162). Kiel, Germany: IPN Press.

Deci, E. L., Koestner, R., & Ryan, R. M. (1999). A meta-analytic review of experiments examining the effects of extrinsic motivation on intrinsic rewards. *Psychological Bulletin, 125,* 627–668.

Deci, E. L., & Ryan, R. M. (1985). *Intrinsic motivation and self-determination in human behavior.* New York: Plenum Press.

Deci, E. L., & Ryan, R. M. (2002a). The paradox of achievement: The harder you push, the worse it gets. In J. Aronson (Ed.), *Improving academic achievement: Impact of psychological factors on education* (pp. 61–87). San Diego, CA: Academic Press.

Deci, E. L., & Ryan, R. M. (2002b). Self-determination research: Reflections and future directions. In E. L. Deci & R. M. Ryan (Eds.), *Handbook of self-determination theory research* (pp. 431–441). Rochester, NY: University of Rochester Press.

Deci, E. L., Vallerand, R. J., Pelletier, L. C., & Ryan, R. M. (1991). Motivation and education: The self-determination perspective. *Educational Psychologist, 26,* 325–346.

Deeter, T. E. (1990). Remodeling expectancy and value in physical activity. *Journal of Sport and Exercise Psychology, 12,* 83–91.

Denny, D. R. (1980). Self-control approaches to the treatment of test anxiety. In I. G. Sarason (Ed.), *Test anxiety: Theory, research, and applications* (pp. 209–243). Hillsdale, NJ: Erlbaum.

Dewey, J. (1913). *Interest and effort in education.* Boston: Riverside Press.

Deyhle, D., & LeCompte, M. (1999). Cultural differences in child development: Navaho adolescents in middle schools. In R. H. Sheets & E. R. Hollins (Eds.), *Racial and ethnic identity in school practices: Aspects of human development* (pp. 123–140). Mahwah, NJ: Erlbaum.

Dornbusch, S. M. (1994, February). *Off the track.* Presidential address at the biennial meeting of the Society for Research on Adolescence, San Diego, CA.

Dowson, M., & McInerney, D. M. (2003). What do students say about their motivational goals? Towards a more complex and dynamic perspective on student motivation. *Contemporary Educational Psychology, 28,* 91–113.

Dreeban, R., & Barr, R. (1988). Classroom composition and the design of instruction. *Sociology of Education, 61,* 129–142.

Dryfoos, J. G. (1990). *Adolescents at risk: Prevalence and prevention.* Oxford, England: Oxford University Press.

Duncan, G. J., Brooks-Gunn, J., & Klevbanov, P. K. (1994). Economic deprivation and early childhood development. *Child Development, 65,* 296–318.

Dusek, J. B. (1980). The development of test anxiety in children. In I. G. Sarason (Ed.), *Test anxiety: Theory, research, and applications* (pp. 87–110). Hillsdale, NJ: Erlbaum.

Dweck, C. S. (1975). The role of expectations and attributions in the alleviation of learned helplessness. *Journal of Personality and Social Psychology, 31,* 674–685.

Dweck, C. S. (2002). The development of ability conceptions. In A. Wigfield & J. S. Eccles (Eds.), *Development of achievement motivation* (pp. 57–88). San Diego, CA: Academic Press.

Dweck, C. S., & Elliott, E. S. (1983). Achievement motivation. In P. H. Mussen (Ed.), *Handbook of child psychology* (3rd ed., Vol. 4, pp. 643–691). New York: Wiley.

Dweck, C. S., & Goetz, T. E. (1978). Attributions and learned helplessness. In J. H. Harvey, W. Ickes, & R. F. Kidd (Eds.), *New directions in attribution research* (Vol. 2, pp. 155–179). Hillsdale, NJ: Erlbaum.

Dweck, C. S., & Leggett, E. (1988). A social-cognitive approach to motivation and personality. *Psychological Review, 95,* 256–273.

Dweck, C. S., & Lennon, C. (2001, April). *Person versus process focused parenting: Impact on achievement motivation.* Paper presented at the biennial meeting of the Society for Research in Child Development, Minneapolis, MN.

Dweck, C. S., & Licht, B. G. (1980). Learned helplessness and intellectual achievement. In J. Garber & M. E. P. Seligman (Eds.),

Human helplessness: Theory and applications. New York: Academic Press.

Eaton, M. J., & Dembo, M. H. (1997). Differences in the motivational beliefs of Asian American and non-Asian students. *Journal of Educational Psychology, 89,* 433–440.

Eccles, J. S. (1984). Sex differences in achievement patterns. In T. Sonderegger (Ed.), *Nebraska Symposium on Motivation* (Vol. 32, pp. 97–132). Lincoln: University of Nebraska Press.

Eccles, J. S. (1987). Gender roles and women's achievement-related decisions. *Psychology of Women Quarterly, 11,* 135–172.

Eccles, J. S. (1989). Bringing young women to math and science. In M. Crawford & M. Gentry (Eds.), *Gender and thought: Psychological perspectives* (pp. 36–57). New York: Springer-Verlag.

Eccles, J. S. (1993). School and family effects on the ontogeny of children's interests, self-perceptions, and activity choice. In J. Jacobs (Ed.), *Nebraska Symposium on Motivation: Vol. 40. Developmental perspectives on motivation* (pp. 145–208). Lincoln: University of Nebraska Press.

Eccles, J. S. (1994). Understanding women's educational and occupational choices: Applying the Eccles et al. model of achievement-related choices. *Psychology of Women Quarterly, 18,* 585–609.

Eccles, J. S. (1998). Commentary: Individual differences and the development of perceived control. *Monographs of the Society for Research in Child Development, 6*(2/3, Serial No. 254), 221–231.

Eccles, J. S. (2004). Schools, academic motivation, and stage-environment fit. In R. M. Lerner & L. Steinberg (Eds.), *Handbook of adolescent psychology* (2nd ed., pp. 125–153). Hoboken, NJ: Wiley.

Eccles, J. S., & Barber, B. L. (1999). Student council, volunteering, basketball, or marching band: What kind of extracurricular involvement matters? *Journal of Adolescent Research, 14,* 10–43.

Eccles, J. S., Freedman-Doan, C., Fromme, P., Jacobs, J., & Yoon, K. S. (2000). Gender-role socialization in the family: A longitudinal approach. In T. Eckes & H. M. Trautner (Eds.), *The developmental social psychology of gender* (pp. 333–360). Mahwah, NJ: Erlbaum.

Eccles, J. S., & Harold, R. D. (1991). Gender differences in sport involvement: Applying the Eccles' expectancy-value model. *Journal of Applied Sport Psychology, 3,* 7–35.

Eccles, J. S., & Harold, R. D. (1992). Gender differences in educational and occupational patterns among the gifted. In N. Colangelo, S. G. Assouline, & D. L. Amronson (Eds.), *Proceedings from the 1991 Henry B. and Jocelyn Wallace National Research Symposium on Talent Development* (pp. 3–29). Unionville, NY: Trillium Press.

Eccles, J. S., & Harold, R. D. (1993). Parent-school involvement during the early adolescent years. *Teachers' College Record, 94,* 568–587.

Eccles, J. S., Jacobs, J., Harold, R., Yoon, K. S., Arbreton, A., & Freedman-Doan, C (1993). Parents and gender role socialization during the middle childhood and adolescent years. In S. Oskamp & M. Costanzo (Eds.), *Gender issues in contemporary society* (pp. 59–83). Newbury Park: Sage.

Eccles, J. S., & Midgley, C. (1989). Stage/environment fit: Developmentally appropriate classrooms for early adolescents. In R. Ames & C. Ames (Eds.), *Research on motivation in education* (Vol. 3, pp. 139–181). New York: Academic Press.

Eccles, J. S., Midgley, C., Wigfield, A., Reuman, D., Mac Iver, D., & Feldlaufer, H. (1993). Negative effects of traditional middle-schools on students' motivation. *Elementary School Journal, 93,* 553–574.

Eccles, J. S., & Roeser, R. W. (2003). Schools as developmental contexts. In G. Adams & M. D. Berzonsky (Eds.), *Blackwell*

Handbook of Adolescence (pp. 129–148). Malden, MA: Blackwell Publishing.

Eccles, J. S., & Wigfield, A. (1985). Teacher expectations and student motivation. In J. B. Dusek (Ed.), *Teacher expectations* (pp. 185–217). Hillsdale, NJ: Erlbaum.

Eccles, J. S., & Wigfield, A. (1995). In the mind of the achiever: The structure of adolescents' academic achievement related-beliefs and self-perceptions. *Personality and Social Psychology Bulletin, 21,* 215–225.

Eccles, J. S., & Wigfield, A. (2002). Motivational beliefs, values, and goals. *Annual Review of Psychology, 53,* 109–132.

Eccles, J. S., Wigfield, A., Flanagan, C., Miller, C., Reuman, D., & Yee, D. (1989). Self-concepts, domain values, and self-esteem: Relations and changes at early adolescence. *Journal of Personality, 57,* 283–310.

Eccles, J. S., Wigfield, A., Harold, R., & Blumenfeld, P. B. (1993). Age and gender differences in children's self- and task perceptions during elementary school. *Child Development, 64,* 830–847.

Eccles, J. S., Wigfield, A., & Schiefele, U. (1998). Motivation to succeed. In W. Damon (Series Ed.) & N. Eisenberg (Vol. Ed.), *Handbook of child psychology* (5th ed., Vol. 3, pp. 1017–1095). New York: Wiley.

Eccles-Parsons, J., Adler, T. F., Futterman, R., Goff, S. B., Kaczala, C. M., Meece, J. L., et al. (1983). Expectancies, values, and academic behaviors. In J. T. Spence (Ed.), *Achievement and achievement motivation* (pp. 75–146). San Francisco: Freeman.

Elder, G. H., Eccles, J. S., Ardelt, M., & Lord, S. (1995). Inner-city parents under economic pressure: Perspectives on the strategies of parenting. *Journal of Marriage and the Family, 6,* 81–86.

Elliot, A. J. (1999). Approach and avoidance motivation and achievement goals. *Educational Psychologist, 34,* 169–189.

Elliot, A. J. (2005). A conceptual history of the achievement goal construct. In A. J. Elliot & C. S. Dweck (Eds.), *Handbook of competence and motivation* (pp. 52–72). New York: Guilford Press.

Elliot, A. J., Chirkov, V. I., Kim, Y., & Sheldon, K. M. (2001). A cross-cultural analysis of avoidance (relative to approach) personal goals. *Psychological Science, 6,* 505–510.

Elliot, A. J., & Dweck, C. S. (Eds.). (2005). *Handbook of competence and motivation.* New York: Guilford Press.

Elliot, A. J., & Harackiewicz, J. M. (1996). Approach and avoidance goals and intrinsic motivation: A mediational analysis. *Journal of Personality and Social Psychology, 70,* 461–475.

Elliot, A. J., & McGregor, H. (2001). A 2 × 2 achievement goal framework. *Journal of Personality and Social Psychology, 80,* 501–509.

Entwisle, D. R., & Alexander, K. L. (1990). Beginning school math competence: Minority and majority comparisons. *Child Development, 61,* 454–471.

Entwisle, D. R., & Alexander, K. L. (1993). Entry into school: The beginning school transition and educational stratification in the United States. *Annual Review of Sociology, 19,* 401–423.

Entwisle, D. R., & Alexander, K. L. (1999). Early schooling and social stratification. In R. C. Pianta & M. J. Cox (Eds.), *The transition to kindergarten* (pp. 13–38). Baltimore: Paul H. Brookes.

Feather, N. T. (1982). Expectancy: Value approaches—Present status and future directions. In N. T. Feather (Ed.), *Expectations and actions: Expectancy-value models in psychology* (pp. 395–420). Hillsdale, NJ: Erlbaum.

Feather, N. T. (1988). Values, valences, and course enrollment: Testing the role of personal values within an expectancy—Value framework. *Journal of Educational Psychology, 80,* 381–391.

Feather, N. T. (1992). Values, valences, expectations, and actions. *Journal of Social Issues, 48,* 109–124.

Felner, R. D., Jackson, A. W., Kasak, D., Mulhall, P., Brand, S., & Flowers, N. (1997). The impact of school reform for the middle years: Longitudinal study of a network engaged in turning points-based comprehensive school transformation. *Phi Delta Kappan, 78,* 528–532, 541–550.

Ferguson, R. F. (1998). Teachers' perceptions and expectations and the Black-White test score gap. In C. Jencks & M. Phillips (Eds.), *The Black-White test score gap* (pp. 273–317). Washington, DC: Brookings Institute Press.

Fine, M. (1991). *Framing dropouts: Notes on the politics of an urban public high school.* Albany: State University of New York Press.

Finn, J. D. (1989). Withdrawing from school. *Review of Educational Research, 59,* 117–142.

Figueira-McDonough, J. (1986). School context, gender, and delinquency. *Journal of Youth and Adolescence, 15,* 79–98.

Ford, M. E. (1992). *Human motivation: Goals, emotions, and personal agency beliefs.* Newbury Park, CA: Sage.

Fordham, S. (1988). Racelessness as a factor in Black students' school success: Pragmatic strategy or pyrrhic victory. *Harvard Educational Review, 58,* 54–84.

Fordham, S., & Ogbu, J. U. (1986). Black students' school success: Coping with "the burden of 'acting White.'" *Urban Review, 18,* 176–206.

Forsterling, F. (1985). Attributional retraining: A review. *Psychological Bulletin, 98,* 495–512.

Fredericks, J., & Eccles, J. S. (2002). Children's competence and value beliefs from childhood through adolescence: Growth trajectories in two male sex-typed domains. *Developmental Psychology, 38,* 519–533.

Frome, P., & Eccles J. (1995, April). *Underestimation of academic ability in the middle school years.* Poster presented at the bienniel meeting of the Society for Research on Child Development, Indianapolis, IN.

Frome, P. M., & Eccles, J. S. (1998). Parents' influence on children's achievement-related perceptions. *Journal of Personality and Social Psychology, 74*(2), 435–452.

Fuligni, A. J., Eccles, J. S., & Barber, B. L. (1995). The long-term effects of seventh-grade ability grouping in mathematics. *Journal of Early Adolescence, 15,* 58–89.

Fuligni, A. J., & Tseng, V. (1999). Family obligation and the academic motivation of adolescents from immigrant and American-born families. In T. Urdan (Ed.), *Advances in motivation and achievement: Vol. 11. The role of context* (pp. 159–183). Stamford, CT: JAI Press.

Furrer, C., & Skinner, E. (2003). Sense of relatedness as a factor in children's academic engagement and performance. *Journal of Educational Psychology, 95,* 148–162.

Furstenberg, F., Cook, T., Eccles, J., Elder, G., & Sameroff, A. (1999). *Managing to make it: Urban families in adolescent success.* Chicago: University of Chicago Press.

Galper, A., Wigfield, A., & Seefeldt, C. (1997). Head Start parents' beliefs about their children's abilities, task values, and performance on different activities. *Child Development, 68,* 897–907.

Garcia, T., & Pintrich, P. R. (1994). Regulating motivation and cognition in the classroom: The role of self-schemas and self-regulatory strategies. In D. H. Schunk & B. J. Zimmerman (Eds.), *Self-regulation of learning and performance: Issues and educational applications* (pp. 127–154). Hillsdale, NJ: Erlbaum.

Garcia Coll, C. T., Crnic, K., Hamerty, G., Wasik, B. H., Jenkins, R., Vazquez Garcia, H., et al. (1996). An integrative model for the study of developmental competencies in minority children. *Child Development, 20,* 1891–1914.

Garcia Coll, C., & Pachter, L. M. (2002). Ethnic and minority parenting. In M. Bornstein (Ed.), *Handbook of parenting* (2nd ed., Vol. 4, pp. 1–20). Mahwah, NJ: Erlbaum.

Goodnow, C. (1993). Classroom belonging among early adolescent students: Relationships to motivation and achievement. *Journal of Early Adolescence, 13*(1), 21–43.

Goodnow, J. J., & Collins, W. A. (1990). *Development according to parents: The nature, sources, and consequences of parents' ideas.* London: Erlbaum.

Gottfried, A. E. (1985). Academic intrinsic motivation in elementary and junior high school students. *Journal of Educational Psychology, 77*(6), 631–645.

Gottfried, A. E. (1990). Academic intrinsic motivation in young elementary school children. *Journal of Educational Psychology, 82,* 525–538.

Gottfried, A. E., Fleming, J. S., & Gottfried, A. W. (2001). Continuity of academic intrinsic motivation from childhood through late adolescence: A longitudinal study. *Journal of Educational Psychology, 93,* 3–13.

Graham, S. (1991). A review of attribution theory in achievement contexts. *Educational Psychology Review, 3,* 5–38.

Graham, S. (1992). Most of the subjects were European American and middle class: Trends in published research on African Americans in selected APA journals 1970–1989. *American Psychologist, 47,* 629–639.

Graham, S. (1994). Motivation in African Americans. *Review of Educational Research, 64,* 55–117.

Graham, S., & Golan, S. (1991). Motivational influences on cognition: Task involvement, ego involvement, and depth of information processing. *Journal of Educational Psychology, 83,* 187–194.

Graham, S., & Taylor, A. Z. (2002). Ethnicity, gender, and the development of achievement values. In A. Wigfield & J. S. Eccles (Eds.), *Development of achievement motivation* (pp. 123–146). San Diego, CA: Academic Press.

Graham, S., Taylor, A. Z., & Hudley, C. (1998). Exploring achievement values among ethnic minority early adolescents. *Journal of Educational Psychology, 90,* 606–620.

Grant, H., & Dweck, C. S. (2001). Cross-cultural responses to failure: Considering outcome attributions with different goals. In F. Salili, C. Y. Chui, & Y. Y. Hong (Eds.), *Student motivation: The culture and context of learning* (pp. 203–219). New York: Plenum Press.

Greeno, J. G., Collins, A. M., & Resnick, L. B. (1996). Cognition and learning. In D. C. Berliner & R. C. Calfee (Eds.), *Handbook of educational psychology* (pp. 15–46). London: Prentice-Hall International.

Grolnick, W. S., Gurland, S. T., Jacob, K. F., & Decourcey, W. (2002). The development of self-determination in middle childhood and adolescence. In A. Wigfield & J. S. Eccles (Eds.), *Development of achievement motivation* (pp. 147–171). San Diego, CA: Academic Press.

Grolnick, W. S., & Ryan, R. M. (1987). Autonomy in children's learning: An experimental and individual difference investigation. *Journal of Personality and Social Psychology, 52,* 890–898.

Grolnick, W. S., & Ryan, R. M. (1989). Parent styles associated with children's self-regulation and competence in schools. *Journal of Educational Psychology, 8,* 143–154.

Grolnick, W. S., & Slowiaczek, M. L. (1994). Parents' involvement in children's schooling: A multidimensional conceptualization and motivational model. *Child Development, 65,* 237–252.

Guay, F., Boivin, M., & Hodges, E. V. E. (1999). Predicting change in academic achievement: A model of peer experiences and self-system processes. *Journal of Educational Psychology, 91,* 105–115.

Guay, F., Marsh, H. W., & Boivin, M. (2003). Academic self-concept and academic achievement: Developmental perspectives on their causal ordering. *Journal of Educational Psychology, 95,* 124–136.

Guthrie, J. T., Wigfield, A., Barbosa, P., Perencevich, K. C., Taboada, A., Davis, M. H., et al. (2004). Increasing reading comprehension and engagement through concept oriented reading instruction. *Journal of Educational Psychology, 96,* 403–423.

Guthrie, J. T., Wigfield, A., & Perencevich, K. (Eds.). (2004). *Motivating reading comprehension: Concept oriented reading instruction.* Mahwah, NJ: Erlbaum.

Gutman, L., & Midgley, C. (2000). The role of protective factors in supporting the academic achievement of poor African American students during the middle school transition. *Journal of Youth and Adolescence, 29,* 223–248.

Gutman, L. M., Sameroff, A. J., & Eccles, J. S. (2002). The academic achievement of African American students during early adolescence: An examination of multiple risk, promotive, and protective factors. *American Journal of Community Psychology, 30,* 367–399.

Harackiewicz, J. M., Barron, K. E., & Elliot, A. J. (1998). Rethinking achievement goals: When are they adaptive for college students and why? *Educational Psychologist, 33,* 1–21.

Harackiewicz, J. M., Barron, K. E., Pintrich, P. R., Elliot, A. J., & Thrash, T. M. (2002). Revision of achievement goal theory: Necessary and illuminating. *Journal of Educational Psychology, 94,* 638–645.

Hare, B. R. (1985). Stability and change in self-perceptions and achievement among African American adolescents: A longitudinal study. *Journal of African American Psychology, 11,* 29–42.

Harter, S. (1981). A new self-report scale of intrinsic versus extrinsic orientation in the classroom: Motivational and informational components. *Developmental Psychology, 17,* 300–312.

Harter, S. (1982). The Perceived Competence Scale for Children. *Child Development, 53,* 87–97.

Harter, S. (1990). Causes, correlates and the functional role of global self-worth: A life-span perspective. In J. Kolligian & R. Sternberg (Eds.), *Perceptions of competence and incompetence across the life-span* (pp. 67–98). New Haven, CT: Yale University Press.

Harter, S. (1998). The development of self-representations. In W. Damon (Series Ed.) & N. Eisenberg (Vol. Ed.), *Handbook of child psychology* (5th ed., Vol. 3, pp. 553–617). New York: Wiley.

Harter, S., Whitesell, N. R., & Kowalski, P. (1992). Individual differences in the effects of educational transitions on young adolescents' perceptions of competence and motivational orientation. *American Educational Research Journal, 29,* 809–835.

Heckhausen, H. (1977). Achievement motivation and its constructs: A cognitive model. *Motivation and Emotion, 1,* 283–329.

Heckhausen, H. (1987). Emotional components of action: Their ontogeny as reflected in achievement behavior. In D. Gîrlitz & J. F. Wohlwill (Eds.), *Curiosity, imagination, and play* (pp. 326–348). Hillsdale, NJ: Erlbaum.

Hedelin, L., & Sjîberg, L. (1989). The development of interests in the Swedish comprehensive school. *European Journal of Psychology of Education, 4,* 17–35.

Heine, S. J., Lehman, D. R., Ide, E., Leung, C., Kitayama, S., Takata, T., et al. (2001). Divergent consequences of success and failure in Japan and North America: An investigation of self-improving motivations and malleable selves. *Journal of Personality and Social Psychology, 81,* 599–615.

Hennessey, B. A. (2000). Rewards and creativity. In C. Sansone & J. M. Harackiewicz (Eds.), *Intrinsic and extrinsic motivation: The search for optimal motivation and performance* (pp. 55–78). San Diego: Academic Press.

Hess, R. D., Chih-Mei, C., & McDevitt, T. M. (1987). Cultural variations in family beliefs about children's performance in mathematics: Comparisons among People's Republic of China, Chinese-American, and Caucasian-American families. *Journal of Educational Psychology, 70,* 179–188.

Heyman, G. D., Dweck, C. S., & Cain, K. M. (1992). Young children's vulnerability to self-blame and helplessness: Relationships to beliefs about goodness. *Child Development, 63,* 401–415.

Hickey, D. T., & McCaslin, M. (2001). A comparative, sociocultural analysis of context and motivation. In S. Volet & S. Jarvela (Eds.), *Motivation in learning contexts: Theoretical advances and methodological implications* (pp. 33–55). Elmsford, NY: Pergamon Press.

Hidi, S. (2001). Interest, reading, and learning: Theoretical and practical considerations. *Educational Psychology Review, 13,* 191–209.

Hidi, S., & Harackiewicz, J. (2000). Motivating the academically unmotivated: A critical issue for the twenty-first century. *Review of Educational Research, 70,* 151–180.

Hill, K. T., & Sarason, S. B. (1966). The relation of test anxiety and defensiveness to test and school performance over the elementary school years: A further longitudinal study. *Monographs for the Society for Research in Child Development, 31*(2, Serial No. 104).

Hill, K. T., & Wigfield, A. (1984). Test anxiety: A major educational problem and what to do about it. *Elementary School Journal, 85,* 105–126.

Hoffmann, L., & Haeussler, P. (1995, April). *Modification of interests by instruction.* Paper presented at the annual meeting of the American Educational Research Association in San Francisco, CA.

Hokoda, A., & Fincham, F. D. (1995). Origins of children's helpless and mastery achievement patterns in the family. *Journal of Educational Psychology, 87,* 375–385.

Holland, A., & Andre, T. (1987). Participation in extracurricular activities in secondary school: What is known, what needs to be known? *Review of Educational Research, 57,* 437–466.

Holloway, S. D. (1988). Concepts of ability and effort in Japan and the United States. *Review of Educational Research, 58,* 327–345.

Hunt, J. M., & Paraskevopoulos, J. (1980). Children's psychological development as a function of the inaccuracy of their mothers' knowledge of their abilities. *Journal of Genetic Psychology, 136,* 285–298.

Husman, J. (1998). *The effects of perceptions of the future on intrinsic motivation.* Unpublished doctoral dissertation, University of Texas at Austin.

Husman, J., & Lens, W. (1999). The role of the future in the study of motivation. *Educational Psychologist, 34,* 113–125.

Huston, A. C., McLoyd, V., & Coll, C. G. (1994). Children and poverty: Issues in contemporary research. *Child Development, 65,* 275–282.

Jackson, A. W., & Davis, G. A. (2000). *Turning points 2000: Educating adolescents in the twenty-first century.* New York: Teachers College Press.

Jacobs, J. E. (1992). The influence of gender stereotypes on parent and child math attitudes. *Journal of Educational Psychology, 83,* 518–527.

Jacobs, J. E., Davis-Kean, P. E., Bleeker, M., Eccles, J. S., & Malanchuk, O. (2004). "I can do it but I don't want to": The impact of parents, interests, and activities on gender differences in math. In A. Gallagher & J. Kaufman (Eds.), *Gender differences in mathematics* (pp. 246–263). New York: Cambridge University Press.

Jacobs, J. E., & Eccles, J. S. (1992). The influence of parent stereotypes on parent and child ability beliefs in three domains. *Journal of Personality and Social Psychology, 63,* 932–944.

Jacobs, J. E., & Eccles, J. S. (2000). Parents, task values, and real-life achievement-related choices. In C. Sansone & J. M. Harackiewicz (Eds.), *Intrinsic and extrinsic motivation: The search for optimal motivation and performance* (pp. 405–439). San Diego, CA: Academic Press.

Jacobs, J., Lanza, S., Osgood, D. W., Eccles, J. S., & Wigfield, A. (2002). Ontogeny of children's self-beliefs: Gender and domain differences across grades 1 through 12. *Child Development, 73,* 509–527.

James, W. (1963). *Psychology.* New York: Fawcett. (Original work published 1892)

Jennings, K. D. (1991). Early development of mastery motivation and its relation to the self-concept. In M. Bullock (Ed.), *The development of intentional action: Vol. 22. Contributions to human development—Cognitive, motivational, and interactive processes* (pp. 1–13). Basel, Switzerland: Karger.

Jussim, L., Eccles, J., & Madon, S. (1996). Social perception, social stereotypes, and teacher expectations: Accuracy and the quest for the powerful self-fulfilling prophecy. In L. Berkowitz (Ed.), *Advances in experimental social psychology* (pp. 281–388). New York: Academic Press.

Juvonen, J., & Graham, S. (Eds.). (2001). *Peer harassment in school: The plight of the vulnerable and victimized.* New York: Guilford Press.

Juvonen, J., Le, V. N., Kaganoff, T., Augustine, C., & Constant, L. (2004). *Focus on the wonder years: Challenges facing the American middle school.* Santa Monica, CA: Rand Corporation.

Juvonen, J., Nishnia, A., & Graham, S. (2001). Self-views and peer perceptions of victim status among early adolescents. In J. Juvonen & S. Graham (Eds.), *Peer harassment in school: The plight of the vulnerable and victimized* (pp. 105–124). New York: Guilford Press.

Juvonen, J., & Wentzel, K. R. (Eds.). (1996). *Social motivation: Understanding children's school adjustment.* New York: Cambridge University Press.

Kao, G., & Thompson, J. S. (2003). Racial and ethnic stratification in educational achievement and attainment. *Annual Review of Sociology, 29,* 417–442.

Kaplan, A., & Middleton, M. (2002). Should childhood be a journey or a race? Response to Harackiewicz et al. *Journal of Educational Psychology, 94,* 646–648.

Kauffman, D. F., & Husman, J. (2004). Effects of time perspective on student motivation: Introduction to a special issue. *Educational Psychology Review, 16,* 1–7.

Kindermann, T. A. (1993). Natural peer groups as contexts for individual development: The case of children's motivation in school. *Developmental Psychology, 29,* 970–977.

Kindermann, T. A., McCollam, T. L., & Gibson, E., Jr. (1996). In peer networks and students' classroom engagement during childhood and adolescence. In K. Wentzel & J. Juvonen (Eds.), *Social motivation: Understanding children's school adjustment* (pp. 279–312). Cambridge, England: Cambridge University Press.

Kitsantas, A., Zimmerman, B. J., & Cleary, T. (2000). The role of observation and emulation in the development of athletic self-regulation. *Journal of Educational Psychology, 92,* 811–817.

Knight, R. (1981). Parents' beliefs about cognitive development: The role of experience. In A. R. Nesdale, C. Pratt, R. Grieve, J. Field, D. Illingworth, & J. Hogben (Eds.), *Advances in child development: Theory and research* (pp. 226–229). Perth: University of Western Australia Press.

Kohlberg, L. (1966). A cognitive-development analysis of children's sex-role concepts and attitudes. In E. E. Maccoby (Ed.), *The Development of sex differences* (pp. 81–72). Stanford, CA: Stanford University Press.

Kohn, M. L. (1997). *Class and conformity: A study in values, with a reassessment.* Chicago: University of Chicago Press.

Köller, O., Baumert, J., & Schnabel, K. (2001). Does interest matter? The relationship between academic interest and achievement in mathematics. *Journal of Research in Mathematics Education, 32,* 448–470.

Kopp, C. B. (1991). Young children's progression to self-regulation. In M. Bullock (Ed.), *The development of intentional action: Vol. 22. Contributions to human development—Cognitive, motivational, and interactive processes.* Basel, Switzerland: Karger.

Krapp, A. (2002). Structural and dynamic aspects of interest development: Theoretical considerations from an ontogenetic perspective. *Learning and Instruction, 12,* 383–409.

Krapp, A., Hidi, S., & Renninger, K. A. (1992). Interest, learning and development. In K. A. Renninger, S. Hidi, & A. Krapp (Eds.), *The role of interest in learning and development* (pp. 3–25). Hillsdale, NJ: Erlbaum.

Kuhl, J. (1987). Action control: The maintenance of motivational states. In F. Halisch & J. Kuhl (Eds.), *Motivation, intention, and volition* (pp. 279–307). Berlin, Germany: Springer-Verlag.

Kuhl, J. (2000). A functional design approach to motivation and self-regulation: The dynamics of personality systems and interactions. In M. Boekaerts, P. R. Pintrich, & M. Zeidner (Eds.), *Handbook of self-regulation* (pp. 111–169). San Diego, CA: Academic Press.

Kuhl, J., & Kraska, K. (1989). Self-regulation and metamotivation: Computational mechanisms, development, and assessment. In R. Kanfer, P. L. Ackerman, & R. Cudeck (Eds.), *Abilities, motivation, and methodology* (pp. 343–374). Hillsdale, NJ: Erlbaum.

Kulik, J. A., & Kulik, C. L. (1987). Effects of ability grouping on student achievement. *Equity and Excellence, 23,* 22–30.

Lafromboise, T., Coleman, H. L. K., & Gerton, J. (1993). Psychological impact of biculturalism: Evidence and theory. *Psychological Bulletin, 114,* 395–412.

Larson, R. W., & Richards, M. H. (1991). Boredom in the middle school years: Blaming schools versus blaming students. *American Journal of Education, 99,* 418–443.

Lee, S., Ichikawa, V., & Stevenson, H. S. (1987). Beliefs and achievement in mathematics and reading: A cross-national study of Chinese, Japanese, and American children and their mothers. In M. Maehr (Ed.), *Advances in motivation and achievement* (Vol. 7, pp. 149–179). Greenwich, CT: JAI Press.

Lee, S. J. (1994). Beyond the model-minority stereotype: Voices of high- and low-achieving Asian American students. *Anthropology and Education Quarterly, 25,* 413–429.

Lee, V. E., & Croninger, R. G. (1994). The relative importance of home and school in development of literacy skills for middle-grade students. *American Journal of Education, 102*(3), 286–329.

Lee, V. E., & Smith, J. (2001). *Restructuring high schools for equity and excellence: What works.* New York: Teachers College Press.

Lens, W. (1986). Future time perspective: A cognitive-motivational construct. In D. R. Brown & J. Veroff (Eds.), *Frontiers of motivational psychology* (pp. 173–190). New York: Springer-Verlag.

Lepper, M. R., & Chabay, R. W. (1985). Intrinsic motivation and instruction: Conflicting views on the role of motivational processes in computer-based education. *Educational Psychologist, 20,* 217–230.

Lepper, M. R., & Green, D. (1978). *The hidden cost of rewards: New perspectives on the psychology of human motivation.* Hillsdale, NJ: Erlbaum.

Lepper, M. R., & Henderlong, J. (2000). Turning "play" into "work": 25 years of research on intrinsic versus extrinsic motivation. In C. Sansone & J. M. Harackiewicz (Eds.), *Intrinsic and extrinsic motivation: The search for optimal motivation and performance* (pp. 257–307). San Diego, CA: Academic Press.

Linver, M. R., Brooks-Gunn, J., & Kohen, D. E. (2002). Family processes as pathways from income to young children's development. *Developmental Psychology, 38,* 719–734.

Lipsitz, J., Mizell, M. H., Jackson, A. W., & Austin, L. M. (1997). Speaking with one voice: A manifesto for middle-grades reform. *Phi Delta Kappan, 78,* 533–540.

Lord, S., Eccles, J. S., & McCarthy, K. (1994). Risk and protective factors in the transition to junior high school. *Journal of Early Adolescence, 14,* 162–199.

Luster, T., Rhoades, K., & Hass, B. (1989). The relation between parental values and parenting behavior: A test of the Kohn hypothesis. *Journal of Marriage and the Family, 51,* 139–147.

Lynch, M., & Cicchetti, D. (1997). Children's relationships with adults and peers: An examination of elementary and junior high school students. *Journal of School Psychology, 35*(1), 81–99.

Mac Iver, D. (1987). Classroom factors and student characteristics predicting students' use of achievement standards during ability self-assessment. *Child Development, 58,* 1258–1271.

Mac Iver, D. J., & Epstein, J. L. (1993). Middle grades research: Not yet mature, but no longer a child. *Elementary School Journal, 93,* 519–533.

Mac Iver, D. J., & Plank, J. B. (1997). Improving urban schools: Developing the talents of students placed at risk. In J. L. Irvin (Ed.), *What current research says to the middle level practitioner* (pp. 243–256). Columbus, OH: National Middle School Association.

Mac Iver, D. J., Reuman, D. A., & Main, S. R. (1995). Social structuring of school: Studying what is, illuminating what could be. *Annual Review of Psychology, 46,* 375–400.

Mac Iver, D. J., Stipek, D. J., & Daniels, D. H. (1991). Explaining within-semester changes in student effort in junior high school and senior high school courses. *Journal of Educational Psychology, 83,* 201–211.

Mac Iver, D. J., Young, E. M., & Washburn, B. (2002). Instructional practices and motivation during middle school (with special attention to science). In A. Wigfield & J. S. Eccles (Eds.), *The development of achievement motivation* (pp. 333–351). San Diego, CA: Academic Press.

Maehr, M. L., & Midgley, C. (1996). *Transforming school cultures.* Boulder, CO: Westview Press.

Mahoney, J. L., & Cairns, R. B. (1997). Do extracurricular activities protect against early school dropout? *Developmental Psychology, 33,* 241–253.

Mantzicopoulos, P., French, B. F., & Maller, S. J. (2004). Factor structure of the Pictorial Scale of Perceived Competence and Social Acceptance with two pre-elementary samples. *Child Development, 75,* 1214–1228.

Marjoribanks, K. (2002). *Family and school capital: Towards a context theory of students' school outcomes.* Dordrecht, The Netherlands: Kluwer Academic.

Markus, H. R., & Kitayama, S. (1991). Culture and the self: Implications for cognition, emotion, and motivation. *Psychological Review, 98,* 224–253.

Markus, H. R., & Nurius, P. (1986). Possible selves. *American Psychologist, 41,* 954–969.

Markus, H. R., & Wurf, E. (1987). The dynamic self-concept: A social psychological perspective. *Annual Review of Psychology, 38,* 299–337.

Marsh, H. W. (1989). Age and sex effects in multiple dimensions of self-concept: Preadolescence to early adulthood. *Journal of Educational Psychology, 81,* 417–430.

Marsh, H. W. (1990a). A multidimensional, hierarchical self-concept: Theoretical and empirical justification. *Educational Psychology Review, 2,* 77–171.

Marsh, H. W. (1990b). The causal ordering of academic self-concept and academic achievement: A multiwave, longitudinal analysis. *Journal of Educational Psychology, 82,* 646–656.

Marsh, H. W., & Ayotte, V. (2003). Do multiple dimensions of self-concept become more differentiated with age: The differential distinctiveness hypothesis. *Journal of Educational Psychology, 95,* 687–706.

Marsh, H. W., Ellis, L. A., & Craven, R. G. (2002). How do preschool children feel about themselves? Unraveling measurement and multidimensional self-concept structure. *Developmental Psychology, 38,* 376–393.

Marsh, H. W., & Yeung, A. S. (1997). Causal effects of academic self-concept on academic achievement: Structural equation models of longitudinal data. *Journal of Educational Psychology, 89,* 41–54.

Martin, R., Drew, K., Gaddis, L., & Moseley, M. (1988). Prediction of elementary school achievement from preschool temperament: Three studies. *School Psychology Review, 17,* 125–137.

Massimini, F., & Carli, M. (1988). The systematic assessment of flow in daily experience. In M. Csikszentmihalyi & I. S. Csikszentmihalyi (Eds.), *Optimal experience: Psychological studies of flow in consciousness* (pp. 266–287). New York: Cambridge University Press.

Matsumoto, D., & Sanders, M. (1988). Emotional experiences during engagement in intrinsically and extrinsically motivated tasks. *Motivation and Emotion, 12,* 353–369.

Matute-Bianchi, M. E. (1986). Ethnic identities and patterns of school success and failure among Mexican-descent and Japanese-American students in a California high school: An ethnographic analysis. *American Journal of Education, 95,* 233–255.

McCall, R. B., Evahn, C., & Kratzer, L. (1992). *High school underachievers: What do they achieve as adults?* Newbury Park, CA: Sage.

McGillicuddy-DeLisi, A., & DeLisi, R. (2002). Emergent themes in the development of sex differences in cognition. In A. McGillicuddy-DeLisi & R. DeLisi (Eds.), *Biology, society, and behavior: The development of sex differences in cognition* (pp. 243–258). Westport, CT: Ablex.

McGillicuddy-DeLisi, A. V., & Sigel, I. E. (1991). Family environments and children's representational thinking. In S. Sivern (Ed.), *Advances in reading/language research* (Vol. 5, pp. 63–90). Greenwich, CT: JAI Press.

McInerney, D. M., Hinkley, J., Dowson, M., & Van Etten, S. (1998). Aboriginal, Anglo, and immigrant Australian students' motivational beliefs about personal academic success: Are there cultural differences? *Journal of Educational Psychology, 90,* 621–629.

McInerney, D. M., & Van Etten, S. (2004). Big theories revisited: The challenge. In D. M. McInerney & S. Van Etten (Eds.), *Big theories revisited: Vol. 4. Research on sociocultural influences on motivation and learning* (pp. 1–13). Greenwich, CT: Information Age Press.

McLoyd, V. C. (1990). The impact of economic hardship on African American families and children: Psychological distress, parenting, and socioemotional development. *Child Development, 61,* 311–346.

McNeal, R. B. (1995). Extracurricular activities and high school dropouts. *Sociology of Education, 68,* 62–81.

Meece, J. L. (1991). The classroom context and students' motivational goals. In M. Maehr & P. Pintrich (Eds.), *Advances in motivation and achievement* (Vol. 7, pp. 261–286). Greenwich, CT: JAI Press.

Meece, J. L. (1994). The role of motivation in self-regulated learning. In D. H. Schunk & B. J. Zimmerman (Eds.), *Self-regulation of learning and performance* (pp. 25–44). Hillsdale, NJ: Erlbaum.

Meece, J. L., & Kurtz-Costes, B. (2001). Introduction: The schooling of ethnic minority children and youth. *Educational Psychologist, 36,* 1–7.

Meece, J. L., & Miller, S. D. (2001). A longitudinal analysis of elementary school students' achievement goals in literacy activities. *Contemporary Educational Psychology, 26,* 454–480.

Meece, J. L., Wigfield, A., & Eccles, J. S. (1990). Predictors of math anxiety and its consequences for young adolescents' course enrollment intentions and performances in mathematics. *Journal of Educational Psychology, 82,* 60–70.

Meichenbaum, D., & Butler, L. (1980). Toward a conceptual model of the treatment of test anxiety: Implications for research and treatment. In I. G. Sarason (Ed.), *Test anxiety: Theory, research, and applications.* Hillsdale, NJ: Erlbaum.

Middleton, M. J., & Midgley, C. (1997). Avoiding the demonstration of lack of ability: An unexplored aspect of goal theory. *Journal of Educational Psychology, 89,* 710–718.

Midgley, C. (2002). *Goals, goal structures, and adaptive learning.* Mahwah, NJ: Erlbaum.

Midgley, C., & Edelin, K. C. (1998). Middle school reform and early adolescent well-being: The good news and the bad. *Educational Psychologist, 33,* 195–206.

Midgley, C., Feldlaufer, H., & Eccles, J. S. (1989). Student/teacher relations and attitudes toward mathematics before and after the transition to junior high school. *Child Development, 60,* 981–992.

Midgley, C., Kaplan, A., & Middleton, M. (2001). Performance-approach goals: Good for what, for whom, and under what circumstances? *Journal of Educational Psychology, 93,* 77–87.

Midgley, C., Kaplan, A., Middleton, M., Maehr, M. L., Urdan, T., Anderman, L. H., et al. (1998). The development and validation of scales assessing students' achievement goal orientations. *Contemporary Educational Psychology, 23,* 113–131.

Miller, S. A. (1988). Parents' beliefs about children's cognitive development. *Child Development, 59,* 259–285.

Miller, S. A., & Davis, T. L. (1992). Beliefs about children: A comparative study of mothers, teachers, peers, and self. *Child Development, 63,* 1251–1265.

Miller, S. A., Manhal, M., & Mee, L. L. (1991). Parental beliefs, parental accuracy, and children's cognitive performance: A search for causal relations. *Developmental Psychology, 27,* 267–276.

Mischel, W., & Mischel, C. (1983). Development of children's knowledge of self-control strategies. *Child Development, 54,* 603–619.

Mistry, R. S., Vandewater, E. A., Houston, A. C., & McLoyd, V. C. (2002). Economic well-being and children's social adjustment: The role of family process in an ethnically diverse low-income sample. *Child Development, 73,* 935–951.

Morris, L. W., Davis, M. A., & Hutchings, C. J. (1981). Cognitive and emotional components of anxiety: Literature review and a revised worry-emotionality scale. *Journal of Educational Psychology, 73,* 541–555.

Murphy, P. K., & Alexander, P. A. (2000). A motivated exploration of motivation terminology. *Contemporary Educational Psychology, 25,* 3–53.

National Research Council. (2004). *Engaging schools: Fostering high school students' motivation to learn.* Washington, DC: National Academies Press.

Nelson-Le Gall, S., & Glor-Sheib, S. (1985). Help seeking in elementary classrooms: An observational study. *Contemporary Educational Psychology, 10,* 58–71.

Nelson-Le Gall, S., & Jones, E. (1990). Cognitive-motivational influences on task-related help-seeking behavior of Black children. *Child Development, 61,* 581–589.

Newman, R. S. (1994). Adaptive help-seeking: A strategy of self-regulated learning. In D. H. Schunk & B. J. Zimmerman (Eds.), *Self-regulation of learning and performance: Issues and educational applications* (pp. 283–301). Hillsdale, NJ: Erlbaum.

Newman, R. S. (2002). What do I need to do to succeed . . . when I don't understand what I am doing!? Developmental influences on students' adaptive help-seeking. In A. Wigfield & J. S. Eccles (Eds.), *Development of achievement motivation* (pp. 285–306). San Diego, CA: Academic Press.

Newman, R. S., & Goldin, L. (1990). Children's reluctance to seek help with schoolwork. *Journal of Educational Psychology, 82,* 92–100.

Newman, R. S., & Schwager, M. T. (1995). Students' help seeking during problem solving: Effects of grade, goals, and prior achievement. *American Educational Research Journal, 94,* 3–17.

Nicholls, J. G. (1976). When a test measures more than its name: The case of the Test Anxiety Scale for Children. *Journal of Consulting and Clinical Psychology, 20,* 321–326.

Nicholls, J. G. (1978). The development of the concepts of effort and ability, perceptions of academic attainment, and the understanding that difficult tasks require more ability. *Child Development, 49,* 800–814.

Nicholls, J. G. (1979). Development of perception of own attainment and causal attributions for success and failure in reading. *Journal of Educational Psychology, 71,* 94–99.

Nicholls, J. G. (1984). Achievement motivation: Conceptions of ability, subjective experience, task choice, and performance. *Psychological Review, 91,* 328–346.

Nicholls, J. G. (1989). *The competitive ethos and democratic education.* Cambridge, MA: Harvard University Press.

Nicholls, J. G. (1990). What is ability and why are we mindful of it? A developmental perspective. In R. J. Sternberg & J. Kolligian (Eds.), *Competence considered* (pp. 11–40). New Haven, CT: Yale University Press.

Nicholls, J. G., Cobb, P., Yackel, E., Wood, T., & Wheatley, G. (1990). Students' theories of mathematics and their mathematical knowledge: Multiple dimensions of assessment. In G. Kulm (Ed.), *Assessing higher order thinking in mathematics* (pp. 137–154). Washington, DC: American Association for the Advancement of Science.

Nicholls, J. G., & Miller, A. T. (1984). The differentiation of the concepts of difficulty and ability. *Child Development, 54,* 951–959.

Oakes, J., Gamoran, A., & Page, R. N. (1992). Curriculum differentiation: Opportunities, outcomes, and meanings. In P. Jackson (Ed.), *Handbook of research on curriculum* (pp. 570–608). New York: Macmillan.

Oetting, E., & Beauvais, F. (1991). Orthogonal cultural identification theory: The cultural identification of minority adolescents. *International Journal of Addictions, 25,* 655–685.

Ogbu, J. (1981). Origins of human competence: A cultural-ecological perspective. *Child Development, 52,* 413–429.

Ogbu, J. (1985). Cultural ecology of competence among inner-city Blacks. In H. McAdoo & J. McAdoo (Eds.), *Black children social, educational, and parental environments.* Newbury Park, CA: Sage.

Ogbu, J. (1992). Understanding cultural diversity and learning. *Educational Researcher, 21,* 5–14.

Okagaki, L. (2001). Triarchic model of minority children's school achievement. *Educational Psychologist, 36,* 9–20.

Olson, L. (1997). *Made in America: Immigrant students in our public schools.* New York: New Press.

Oyserman, D., Coon, H. M., & Kemmelmeier, M. (2002). Rethinking individualism and collectivism: Evaluation of theoretical assumptions and meta-analyses. *Psychological Bulletin, 128,* 3–72.

Padilla, A. M., & Gonzalez, R. (2001). Academic performance of immigrant and U.S. born Mexican heritage students: Effects of schooling in Mexico and Bilingual/English language instruction. *American Educational Research Journal, 38,* 727–742.

Pajares, F. (1996). Self-efficacy beliefs in academic settings. *Review of Educational Research, 66,* 543–578.

Pallas, A. M., Entwisle, D. R., Alexander, K. L., & Stluka, M. F. (1994). Ability-group effects: Instructional, social, or institutional? *Sociology of Education, 67,* 27–46.

Paris, S. G., & Byrnes, J. P. (1989). The constructivist approach to self-regulation and learning in the classroom. In B. J. Zimmerman & D. H. Schunk (Eds.), *Self-regulated learning and academic achievement: Theory, research, and practice* (pp 169–200). New York: Springer-Verlag.

Patrick, H. (1997). Social self-regulation: Exploring the relations between children's social relationships, academic self-regulation, and school performance. *Educational Psychologist, 32,* 209–220.

Pekrun, R. (1993). Facets of adolescents' academic motivation: A longitudinal expectancy-value approach. In M. Maehr & P. Pintrich (Eds.), *Advances in motivation and achievement* (Vol. 8, pp. 139–189). Greenwich, CT: JAI Press.

Pekrun, R. (2000). A social-cognitive, control-value theory of achievement emotions. In J. Heckhausen (Ed.), *Motivational psychology of human development* (pp. 143–163). Oxford, England: Elsevier.

Pelletier, L. G., Fortier, M. S., Vallerand, R. J., & Brière, N. M. (2001). Associations among perceived autonomy support, forms of self-regulation, and persistence: A prospective study. *Motivation and Emotion, 25,* 279–306.

Phinney, J. S., & Devich-Navarro, M. (1997). Variations in bicultural identification among African-American and Mexican-American adolescents. *Journal of Research on Adolescence, 7,* 3–32.

Pianta, R. C., & Cox, M. J. (1999). The changing nature of the transition to school: Trends for the next decade. In R. C. Pianta & M. J. Cox (Eds.), *The transition to kindergarten* (pp. 363–379). Baltimore: Paul H. Brookes.

Pianta, R. C., Rimm-Kaufman, S. E., & Cox, M. J. (1999). Introduction: An ecological approach to kindergarten transition. In R. C. Pianta & M. J. Cox (Eds.), *The transition to kindergarten* (pp. 3–12). Baltimore: Paul H. Brookes.

Pintrich, P. R. (2000a). An achievement goal theory perspective on issues in motivation terminology, theory, and research. *Contemporary Educational Psychology, 25,* 92–104.

Pintrich, P. R. (2000b). Multiple pathways, multiple goals: The role of goal orientation in learning and achievement. *Journal of Educational Psychology, 92,* 54–555.

Pintrich, P. R. (2000c). The role of goal orientation in self-regulated learning. In M. Boekaerts, P. R. Pintrich, & M. Zeidner (Eds.), *Handbook of self-regulation* (pp. 451–502). San Diego, CA: Academic Press.

Pintrich, P. R. (2003). A motivational science perspective on the role of student motivation in learning and teaching contexts. *Journal of Educational Psychology, 95,* 667–686.

Pintrich, P. R., Marx, R. W., & Boyle, R. A. (1993). Beyond cold conceptual change: The role of motivational beliefs and classroom contextual factors in the process of conceptual change. *Review of Educational Research, 63,* 167–199.

Pintrich, P. R., & Schrauben, B. (1992). Students' motivational beliefs and their cognitive engagement in classroom academic tasks. In D. Schunk & J. Meece (Eds.), *Student perceptions in the classroom* (pp. 149–183). Hillsdale, NJ: Erlbaum.

Pintrich, P. R., & Schunk, D. H. (2002). *Motivation in education: Theory, research, and application* (2nd ed.). Englewood Cliffs, NJ: Merrill-Prentice-Hall.

Pintrich, P. R., & Zusho, A. (2002). The development of academic self-regulation: The role of cognitive and motivational factors. In A. Wigfield & J. S. Eccles (Eds.), *Development of achievement motivation* (pp. 250–284). San Diego, CA: Academic Press.

Pomerantz, E. M., & Ruble, D. N. (1997). Distinguishing multiple dimensions of conceptions of ability: Implications for self-evaluation. *Child Development, 68,* 1165–1180.

Pomerantz, E. M., & Saxon, J. L. (2001). Conceptions of ability as stable and self-evaluative processes: A longitudinal examination. *Child Development, 72,* 152–173.

Portes, A., & Rumbaut, R. G. (2001). *Legacies: The story of the immigrant second generation.* Berkeley: University of California Press.

Quintana, S. M., & Vera, E. M. (1999). Mexican-American children's ethnic identity, understanding of ethnic prejudice, and parental ethnic socialization. *Hispanic Journal of Behavioral Sciences, 21,* 387–404.

Ramey, C. T., & Ramey, S. l. (1999). Beginning school for children at risk. In R. C. Pianta & M. J. Cox (Eds.), *The transition to kindergarten* (pp. 217–251). Baltimore: Paul H. Brookes.

Raynor, J. O. (1982). Future orientation, self-evaluation, and achievement motivation: Use of an expectancy X value theory of personality functioning and change. In N. T. Feather (Ed.), *Expectations and actions: Expectancy-value models in psychology* (pp. 97–124). Hillsdale, NJ: Erlbaum.

Reeve, J., Deci, E. L., & Ryan, R. M. (2004). Self-determination theory: A dialectical framework for understanding sociocultural influences on student motivation. In D. M. McInerney & S. Van Etten (Eds.), *Big theories revisited: Vol. 4. Sociocultural influences on motivation and learning* (pp. 31–60). Greenwich, CT: Information Age Press.

Reeve, J., Nix, G., & Hamm, D. (2003). Testing models of the experience of self-determination in intrinsic motivation and the conundrum of choice. *Journal of Educational Psychology, 95,* 375–392.

Renninger, K. A. (1990). Children's play interests, representation, and activity. In R. Fivush & J. Hudson (Eds.), *Knowing and remembering in young children*(pp. 127–165). Cambridge, England: Cambridge University Press.

Renninger, K. A. (2000). Individual interest and its implications for understanding intrinsic motivation. In C. Sansone & J. M. Harackiewicz (Eds.), *Intrinsic and extrinsic motivation* (pp. 373–404). San Diego, CA: Academic Press.

Renninger, K. A., Ewen, L., & Lasher, A. K. (2002). Individual interest as context in expository text and mathematical word problems. *Learning and Instruction, 12,* 467–491.

Renninger, K. A., Hidi, S., & Krapp, A. (Eds.). (1992). *The role of interest in learning and development.* Hillsdale, NJ: Erlbaum.

Rheinberg, F., Vollmeyer, R., & Rollett, W. (2000). Motivation and action in self-regulated learning. In M. Boekaerts, P. R. Pintrich, & M. Zeidner (Eds.), *Handbook of self-regulation* (pp. 503–529). San Diego, CA: Academic Press.

Roderick, M., & Camburn, E. (1999). Risk and recovery from course failure in the early years of high school. *American Educational Research Journal, 36,* 303–344.

Roeser, R. W. (2004a). Competing schools of thought in achievement goal theory. In M. L. Maehr & P. R. Pintrich (Eds.), *Advances in motivation and achievement: Vol. 13. Motivating students, improving schools* (pp. 265–299). New York: Elsevier.

Roeser, R. W. (2004b, July). *The diversity of selfways in school during adolescence project.* Paper presented at the annual meeting of William T. Grant Faculty Scholars Program, Vail, CO.

Roeser, R. W., & Eccles, J. S. (2000). Schooling and mental health. In A. J. Sameroff, M. Lewis, & S. M. Miller (Eds.), *Handbook of developmental psychopathology* (2nd ed., 135–156). New York: Plenum Press.

Roeser, R. W., Eccles, J. S., & Sameroff, A. J. (1998). Academic and emotional functioning in early adolescence: Longitudinal relations, patterns, and prediction by experience in middle school. *Development and Psychopathology, 10,* 321–352.

Roeser, R. W., Eccles, J. S., & Strobel, K. (1998). Linking the study of schooling and mental health: Selected issues and empirical illustrations at the level of the individual. *Educational Psychologist, 33,* 153–176.

Roeser, R. W., Lowe, A., Sattler, R., Gehlbach, H., & Strobel, K. R. (2003, April). *On identity and motivation to learn among Latino adolescents: Patterns, dynamics, and relation to educational outcomes.* Paper presented at the annual meeting of the American Educational Research Association, Chicago, IL.

Roeser, R. W., Marachi, R., & Gehlbach, H. (2002). A goal theory perspective on teachers' professional identities and the contexts of teaching. In C. M. Midgley (Ed.), *Goals, goal structures, and patterns of adaptive learning* (pp. 205–241). Hillsdale, NJ: Erlbaum.

Roeser, R. W., Midgley, C., & Urdan, T. C. (1996). Perceptions of the school psychological environment and early adolescents' psychological and behavioral functioning in school: The mediating role of goals and belonging. *Journal of Educational Psychology, 88,* 408–422.

Roeser, R. W., & Nasir, N. (in press). Identity and self processes in school learning, achievement and well-being. In P. Alexander & P. H. Winne (Eds.), *Handbook of educational psychology* (2nd ed.). Mahwah, NJ: Erlbaum.

Roeser, R. W., & Rodriquez, R. (2004, April). *On academic motivation, achievement, and the diversity of selfways in school during early adolescence.* Paper presented at the annual meeting of American Educational Research Association, San Diego, CA.

Roeser, R. W., Strobel, K. R., & Quihuis, G. (2002). Studying early academic motivation, social-emotional functioning, and engagement in learning: Variable- and person-centered approaches. *Anxiety, Stress, and Coping, 15,* 345–368.

Rosenholtz, S. J., & Simpson, C. (1984). The formation of ability conceptions: Developmental trend or social construction? *Review of Educational Research, 54,* 31–63.

Rosenthal, R. (1974). *On the social psychology of the self-fulfilling prophecy: Further evidence for Pygmalion effects and their mediating mechanisms.* New York: MSS Modular Publications.

Rotter, J. B. (1966). Generalized expectancies for internal versus external control of reinforcement. *Psychological Monographs, 80,* 1–28.

Rubin, K. H., Bukowski, W., & Parker, J. G. (1998). Peer interactions, relationships, and groups. In W. Damon (Series Ed.) & N. Eisenberg (Vol. Ed.), *Handbook of child psychology* (5th ed., Vol. 3, pp. 619–700). New York: Wiley.

Rubin, K. H., Coplan, R., Chen, X., Buskirk, A. A., & Wojslawowicz, J. C. (2005). Peer relationships in childhood. In M. Bornstein & M. Lamb (Eds.), *Developmental science: An advanced textbook* (5th ed., p. 469–512). Mahwah, NJ: Erlbaum.

Ruble, D. (1983). The development of social comparison processes and their role in achievement-related self-socialization. In E. T. Higgins, D. N. Ruble, & W. W. Hartup (Eds.), *Social cognition and social development: A sociocultural perspective* (pp. 134–157). New York: Cambridge University Press.

Ruble, D. N. (1994). A phase model of transitions: Cognitive and motivational consequences. In M. Zanna (Ed.), *Advances in experimental social psychology* (Vol. 26, pp. 163–214). New York: Academic Press.

Ruble, D. N., & Martin, C. L. (1998). Gender development. In W. Damon (Series Ed.) & N. Eisenberg (Vol. Ed.), *Handbook of child psychology* (5th ed., Vol. 3, pp. 933–1016). New York: Wiley.

Ruggerio, K. M., & Taylor, D. M. (1995). Coping with discrimination: How disadvantaged group members perceive the discrimination that confronts them. *Journal of Personality and Social Psychology, 68*, 826–838.

Ryan, A. M. (2001). The peer group as a context for the development of young adolescents' motivation and achievement. *Child Development, 72*, 1135–1150.

Ryan, A. M., Gheen, M. H., & Midgley, C. (1998). Why do some students avoid asking for help? An examination of the interplay among students' academic self-efficacy, teachers' social-emotional role, and the classroom goal structure. *Journal of Educational Psychology, 90*, 528–535.

Ryan, A. M., Pintrich, P. R., & Midgley, C. (2001). Avoiding seeking help in the classroom: Who and why? *Educational Psychology Review, 13*, 93–114.

Ryan, R. M. (1992). Agency and organization: Intrinsic motivation, autonomy, and the self in psychological development. In J. Jacobs (Ed.), *Nebraska Symposium on Motivation* (Vol., 40, pp. 1–56). Lincoln: University of Nebraska Press.

Ryan, R. M., & Connell, J. P. (1989). Perceived locus of causality and internalization: Examining reasons for acting in two domains. *Journal of Personality and Social Psychology, 57*, 749–761.

Ryan, R. M., Connell, J. P., & Deci, E. L. (1985). A motivational analysis of self-determination and self-regulation in education. In C. Ames & R. Ames (Eds.), *Research on motivation in education: Vol. 2. The classroom milieu* (pp. 13–51). London: Academic Press.

Ryan, R. M., & Deci, E. L. (2000a). Self-determination theory and the facilitation of intrinsic motivation, social development, and well-being. *American Psychologist, 55*, 68–78.

Ryan, R. M., & Deci, E. L. (2000b). When rewards compete with nature: The undermining of intrinsic motivation and self-regulation. In C. Sansone & J. M. Harackiewicz (Eds.), *Intrinsic and extrinsic motivation: The search for optimal motivation and performance* (pp. 13–54). San Diego, CA: Academic Press.

Ryan, R. M., & Deci, E. L. (2002). An overview of self-determination theory: An organismic-dialectical perspective. In E. L. Deci & R. M. Ryan (Eds.), *Handbook of self-determination theory research* (pp. 3–33). Rochester, NY: University of Rochester Press.

Sage, N. A., & Kindermann, T. A. (1999). Peer networks, behavior contingencies, and children's engagement in the classroom. *Merrill-Palmer Quarterly, 45*, 143–171.

Sansone, C., & Harackiewicz, J. M. (Eds.). (2000a). *Intrinsic and extrinsic motivation: The search for optimal motivation and performance.* San Diego, CA: Academic Press.

Sansone, C., & Harackiewicz, J. M. (2000b). Looking beyond rewards: The problem and promise of intrinsic motivation. In C. Sansone & J. M. Harackiewicz (Eds.), *Intrinsic and extrinsic motivation: The search for optimal motivation and performance* (pp. 1–9). San Diego, CA: Academic Press.

Sarason, I. G. (1980). Introduction to the study of test anxiety. In I. G. Sarason (Ed.), *Test anxiety: Theory, research, and application* (pp. 3–14). Hillsdale, NJ: Erlbaum.

Schiefele, U. (1991). Interest, learning, and motivation. *Educational Psychologist, 26*, 299–323.

Schiefele, U. (1996a). *Motivation und lernen mit texten* [Motivation and text learning]. Goettingen, Germany: Hogrefe & Huber.

Schiefele, U. (1996b). Topic interest, text representation, and quality of experience. *Contemporary Educational Psychology, 21*, 3–18.

Schiefele, U. (1999). Interest and learning from text. *Scientific Studies of Reading, 3*, 257–279.

Schiefele, U. (2001). The role of interest in motivation and learning. In J. M. Collis & S. Messick (Eds.), *Intelligence and personality: Bridging the gap in theory and measurement* (pp. 163–194). Mahwah, NJ: Erlbaum.

Schiefele, U., & Krapp, A. (1996). Topic interest and free recall of expository text. *Learning and Individual Differences, 8*, 141–160.

Schiefele, U., Krapp, A., & Winteler, A. (1992). Interest as a predictor of academic achievement: A meta-analysis of research. In K. A. Renninger, S. Hidi, & A. Krapp (Eds.), *The role of interest in learning and development* (pp. 183–212). Hillsdale, NJ: Erlbaum.

Schiefele, U., & Schreyer, I. (1994). Intrinsische lernmotivation und lernen [Intrinsic motivation and learning]. *Zeitschrift für Pädagogische Psychologie, 8*, 1–13.

Schneider, B., & Coleman, J. S. (1993). *Parents, their children, and schools.* Boulder, CO: Westview Press.

Schneider, K. (1996). Intrinsically motivated activity as an example of creativity and related behavioral systems. In H. Heckhausen & J. Kuhl (Eds.), *Motivation, volition, and action.* Goettingen, Germany: Hogrefe & Huber.

Schraw, G., Bruning, R., & Svoboda, C. (1995). Sources of situational interest. *Journal of Reading Behavior, 27*, 1–17.

Schraw, G., & Lehman, S. (2001). Situational interest: A review of the literature and directions for future research. *Educational Psychology Review, 13*, 23–52.

Schunk, D. H. (1987). Peer models and children's behavioral change. *Review of Educational Research, 57*, 149–174.

Schunk, D. H. (1991). Goal setting and self-evaluation: A social cognitive perspective on self-regulation. In M. L. Maehr & P. R. Pintrich (Eds.), *Advances in motivation and achievement* (Vol. 7, pp. 85–113). Greenwich, CT: JAI Press.

Schunk, D. H. (1994). Self-regulation of self-efficacy and attributions in academic settings. In D. H. Schunk & B. J. Zimmerman (Eds.), *Self-regulation of learning and performance* (pp. 75–99). Hillsdale, NJ: Erlbaum.

Schunk, D. H., & Ertmer, P. A. (2000). Self-regulation and academic learning: Self-efficacy enhancing interventions. In M. Boekaerts, P. R. Pintrich, & M. Zeidner (Eds.), *Handbook of self-regulation* (pp. 631–649). San Diego, CA: Academic Press.

Schunk, D. H., & Pajares, F. (2002). The development of academic self-efficacy. In A. Wigfield & J. S. Eccles (Eds.), *Development of achievement motivation* (pp. 15–32). San Diego, CA: Academic Press.

Schunk, D. H., & Zimmerman, B. J. (Eds.). (1994). *Self-regulation of learning and performance.* Hillsdale, NJ: Erlbaum.

Sheets, R. H., & Hollins, E. R. (Eds.). (1999). *Racial and ethnic identity in school practices: Aspects of human development.* Mahwah, NJ: Erlbaum.

Shell, D. F., Colvin, C., & Bruning, R. H. (1995). Self-efficacy, attribution, and outcome expectancy mechanisms in reading and writing achievement: Grade-level and achievement-level differences. *Journal of Educational Psychology, 87,* 386–398.

Silverman, W. K., La Greca, A. M., & Wasserstein, S. (1995). What do children worry about? Worries and their relations to anxiety. *Child Development, 66,* 671–686.

Simmons, R. G., & Blyth, D. A. (1987). *Moving into adolescence: The impact of pubertal change and school context.* Hawthorn, NY: Aldine de Gruyter.

Simpkins, S. D., Fredricks, J. A., Davis-Kean, P. E., & Eccles, J. S. (in press). Healthy mind, healthy habits: The influence of activity involvement in middle childhood. In A. C. Huston & M. N. Ripke (Eds.), *Middle childhood: Contexts of development.* New York: Cambridge University Press.

Skaalvik, E. (1997). Self-enhancing and self-defeating ego orientation: Relations with task and task avoidance orientation, achievement, self-perceptions, and anxiety. *Journal of Educational Psychology, 89,* 71–81.

Skaalvik, E. M., & Bong, M. (2003). Self-concept and self-efficacy revisited: A few notable differences and important similarities. In H. W. Marsh, R. Craven, & D. M. McInerney (Eds.), *International advances in self research* (pp. 67–90). Greenwich, CT: Information Age Publishing.

Skaalvik, E. M., & Rankin, R. J. (1996, April). *Self-concept and self-efficacy: Conceptual analysis.* Paper presented at the annual meeting of the American Educational Research Association in New York.

Skinner, E. A. (1990). Age differences in the dimensions of perceived control during middle childhood: Implications for developmental conceptualizations and research. *Child Development, 61,* 1882–1890.

Skinner, E. A. (1995). *Perceived control, motivation, and coping.* Thousand Oaks, CA: Sage.

Skinner, E. A., & Belmont, M. J. (1993). Motivation in the classroom: Reciprocal effects of teacher behavior and student engagement across the school year. *Journal of Educational Psychology, 85,* 571–581.

Skinner, E. A., Chapman, M., & Baltes, P. B. (1988). Control, means-ends, and agency beliefs: A new conceptualization and its measurement during childhood. *Journal of Personality and Social Psychology, 54,* 117–133.

Skinner, E. A., Gembeck-Zimmer, M. J., & Connell, J. P. (1998). Individual differences and the development of perceived control. *Monographs of the Society for Research in Child Development, 6*(2/3, Serial No. 254), 1–220.

Skinner, E. A., & Wellborn, J. G. (1994). Coping during childhood and adolescence: A motivational perspective. In D. Featherman, R. Lerner, & M. Perlmutter (Eds.), *Life-span development and behavior* (pp. 91–133). Hillsdale, NJ: Erlbaum.

Slaughter-Defoe, D. T., Nakagawa, K., Takanishi, R., & Johnson, D. J. (1990). Toward cultural/ecological perspectives on schooling and achievement in African- and Asian-American children. *Child Development, 61,* 363–383.

Slavin, R. E. (1995). *Cooperative learning* (2nd ed.). Boston: Allyn & Bacon.

Smiley, P. A., & Dweck, C. S. (1994). Individual differences in achievement goals among young children. *Child Development, 65,* 1723–1743.

Spencer, M. B., Noll, E., Stoltzfus, J., & Harplani, V. (2001). Identify and school adjustment: Revising the "Acting White" assumption. *Educational Psychologist, 36,* 31–44.

Spencer, S. J., Steele, M., & Quinn, D. M. (1999). Stereotype threat and women's math performance. *Journal of Experimental Social Psychology, 35,* 4–28.

Steele, C. (1997). A threat in the air: How stereotypes shape intellectual identity and performance. *American Psychologist, 52,* 613–629.

Steele, C. M. (1992, April). Race and the schooling of Black Americans. *Atlantic Monthly, 269*(4), 68–78.

Steele, C. M., & Aronson, J. (1995). Stereotype threat and the intellectual test performance of African-Americans. *Journal of Personality and Social Psychology, 69,* 797–811.

Steinberg, L., Dornbusch, S., & Brown, B. (1992). Ethnic differences in adolescents achievements: An ecological perspective. *American Psychologist, 47,* 723–729.

Stevens, R. J., & Slavin, R. E. (1995). The cooperative elementary school: Effects on students' achievement, attitudes, and social relations. *American Educational Research Journal, 32,* 321–351.

Stevenson, D. L., & Baker, D. P. (1987). The family-school relation and the child's school performance. *Child Development, 58,* 1348–1357.

Stevenson, H. W., Chen, C., & Uttal, D. H. (1990). Beliefs and achievement: A study of Black, White, and Hispanic children. *Child Development, 61,* 508–523.

Stipek, D. J., & Mac Iver, D. (1989). Developmental change in children's assessment of intellectual competence. *Child Development, 60,* 521–538.

Stipek, D. J., Recchia, S., & McClintic, S. M. (1992). Self-evaluation in young children. *Monographs of the Society for Research in Child Development, 57*(2, Serial No. 226).

Suarez-Orozco, C., & Suarez-Orozco, M. (2001). *Children of Immigration.* Cambridge, MA: Harvard University Press.

Super, C. M., & Harkness, S. (2002). Culture structures the environment for development. *Human Development, 45,* 270–274.

Szalacha, L. A., Erkut, S., Garcia-Coll, C., Alarcon, O., Fields, J. P., & Ceder, I. (2003). Discrimination and Puerto Rican children's and adolescents' mental health. *Cultural Diversity and Ethnic Minority Psychology, 9,* 141–155.

Tatum, B. D. (1997). *"Why are all the Black kids sitting together in the cafeteria?" and other conversations about race.* New York: Basic Books.

Taylor, R. D., Casten, R., Flickinger, S., Roberts, D., & Fulmore, C. D. (1994). Explaining the school performance of African-American adolescents. *Journal of Research on Adolescence, 4,* 21–44.

Teachman, J., Paasch, K., & Carver, K. (1997). Social capital and the generation of human capital. *Social Forces, 75,* 1–17.

Tenenbaum, H. R., & Leaper, C. (2003). Parent-child conversations about science: The socialization of gender inequities? *Developmental Psychology, 39,* 34–47.

Thompson, M. S., Alexander, K. L., & Entwisle, D. R. (1988). Household composition, parental expectations, and school achievement. *Social Forces, 67,* 424–451.

Thorkildsen, T., & Nicholls, J. G. (1998). Fifth graders' achievement orientations and beliefs: Individual and classroom differences. *Journal of Educational Psychology, 90,* 179–201.

Tobias, S. (1985). Test anxiety: Interference, deficient skills, and cognitive capacity. *Educational Psychologist, 20,* 135–142.

Tobias, S. (1994). Interest, prior knowledge, and learning. *Review of Educational Research, 64,* 37–54.

Todt, E. (1990). Development of interest. In H. Hetzer (Ed.), *Applied developmental psychology of children and youth.* Wiesbaden, Germany: Quelle & Meyer.

Triandis, H. C., & Suh, E. M. (2002). Cultural influences on personality. *Annual Review of Psychology, 53,* 133–160.

Tschannen-Moran, M., Woolfolk Hoy, A., & Hoy, W. K. (1998). Teacher efficacy: Its meaning and measure. *Review of Educational Research, 68,* 202–248.

Urdan, T. C. (1997). Achievement goal theory: Past results, future directions. In P. R. Pintrich & M. L. Maehr (Eds.), *Advances in motivation and achievement* (Vol. 10, pp. 99–142). Greenwich, CT: JAI Press.

Urdan, T. C. (Ed.). (1999). *The role of context: Advances in motivation and achievement* (Vol. 11). Greenwich, CT: JAI Press.

Urdan, T., & Giancarlo, C. (2001). A comparison of motivational and critical thinking orientations across ethnic groups. In D. M. McInerney & S. V. Etten (Eds.), *Research on sociocultural influences on motivation and learning* (Vol. 1, pp. 37–60). Greenwich, CT: Information Age Publishing.

U.S. Department of Education, National Center for Education Statistics. (2002). *The condition of education, 2002.* Washington, DC: Author. (NCES 2002-025, sect. 1).

U.S. Department of Education, National Center for Education Statistics. (2003a). *Projections of education statistics to 2013.* Washington, DC: U.S. Government Printing Office. (NCES 2004-013)

U.S. Department of Education, National Center for Education Statistics. (2003b). *Digest of education statistics, 2002.* Washington, DC: Author. (NCES 2003-060, chap 2)

Valencia, R. R. (Ed.). (1991). *Chicano school failure and success: Research and policy agendas for the 1990s.* London: Falmer Press.

Vallerand, R. J., Pelletier, L. G., Blais, M. R., Brière, N. M., Senécal, C. B., & Vallières, E. F. (1993). On the assessment of intrinsic, extrinsic, and amotivation in education: Evidence on the concurrent and construct validity of the Academic Motivation Scale. *Educational and Psychological Measurement, 53,* 159–172.

Vasey, M. W., & Daliedon, E. L. (1994). Worry in children. In G. Davey & F. Tallis (Eds.), *Worrying: Perspectives on theory, assessment, and treatment* (pp. 185–207). Chichester, West Sussex, England: Wiley.

Wade, S. E. (1992). How interest affects learning from text. In K. A. Renninger, S. Hidi, & A. Krapp (Eds.), *The role of interest in learning and development* (pp. 255–277). Hillsdale, NJ: Erlbaum.

Wade, S. E., Buxton, W. M., & Kelly, M. (1999). Using think-alouds to examine reader-text interest. *Reading Research Quarterly, 34,* 194–216.

Wagner, B. M., & Phillips, D. A. (1992). Beyond beliefs: Parent and child behaviors and children's perceived academic competence. *Child Development, 63,* 1380–1391.

Watt, H. (2004). Development of adolescents' self-perceptions, values, and task perceptions. *Child Development, 75,* 1556–1574.

Wehlage, G., Rutter, R., Smith, G., Lesko, N., & Fernandez, R. (1989). *Reducing the risk: Schools as communities of support.* Philadelphia: Falmer Press.

Weiner, B. (1985). An attributional theory of achievement motivation and emotion. *Psychological Review, 92,* 548–573.

Weiner, B. (1992). *Human motivation: Metaphors, theories, and research.* Newbury Park, CA: Sage.

Weiner, B. (2004). Attribution theory revisited: Cultural plurality and theoretical unity. In D. M. McInerney & S. Van Etten (Eds.), *Big theories revisited: Vol. 4. Sociocultural influences on motivation and learning* (pp. 13–30). Greenwich, CT: Information Age Press.

Weiner, B. (2005). Motivation from an attribution perspective and the social psychology of perceived competence. In A. J. Elliot & C. S. Dweck (Eds.), *Handbook of competence and motivation* (pp. 73–84). New York: Guilford Press.

Weinstein, R. S. (1989). Perception of classroom processes and student motivation: Children's views of self-fulfilling prophecies. In R. E. Ames & C. Ames (Eds.), *Research on motivation in education* (Vol. 3, pp. 187–221). New York: Academic Press.

Weisz, J. P. (1984). Contingency judgments and achievement behavior: Deciding what is controllable and when to try. In J. G. Nicholls (Ed.), *The development of achievement motivation* (pp. 107–136). Greenwich, CT: JAI Press.

Wentzel, K. R. (1989). Adolescent classroom grades, standards for performance, and academic achievement: An interactionist perspective. *Journal of Educational Psychology, 81,* 131–142.

Wentzel, K. R. (1991b). Social competence at school: Relation between social responsibility and academic achievement. *Review of Educational Research, 61,* 1–24.

Wentzel, K. R. (1993). Does being good make the grade? Social behavior and academic competence in middle school. *Journal of Educational Psychology, 85,* 357–364.

Wentzel, K. R. (1994). Relations of social goal pursuit to social acceptance, and perceived social support. *Journal of Educational Psychology, 86,* 173–182.

Wentzel, K. R. (1996). Social goals and social relationships as motivators of school adjustment. In J. Juvonen & K. R. Wentzel (Eds.), *Social motivation: Understanding school adjustment* (pp. 226–247). New York: Cambridge University Press.

Wentzel, K. R. (1998). Social relationships and motivation in middle school: The role of parents, teachers, and peers. *Journal of Educational Psychology, 90,* 202–209.

Wentzel, K. (2002a). Are effective teachers like good parents? Teaching styles and student adjustment in early adolescence. *Child Development, 73,* 287–301.

Wentzel, K. R. (2002b). The contribution of social goal setting to children's school adjustment. In A. Wigfield & J. S. Eccles (Eds.), *Development of achievement motivation* (pp. 222–246). San Diego, CA: Academic Press.

White, R. H. (1959). Motivation reconsidered: The concept of competence. *Psychological Review, 66,* 297–333.

Wigfield, A. (1994). Expectancy: Value theory of achievement motivation—A developmental perspective. *Educational Psychology Review, 6,* 49–78.

Wigfield, A., & Asher, S. R. (1984). Social and motivational influences on reading. In P. D. Pearson, R. Barr, M. L. Kamil, & P. Mosenthal (Eds.), *Handbook of reading research* (pp. 423–452). New York: Longman.

Wigfield, A., Battle, A., Keller, L., & Eccles, J. S. (2002). Sex differences in motivation, self-concept, career aspirations, and career choice: Implications for cognitive development. In A. McGillicuddy-DelLisi & R. DeLisi (Eds.), *Biology, society, and behavior: The development of sex differences in cognition* (pp. 93–124). Greenwich, CT: Ablex.

Wigfield, A., Byrnes, J. B., & Eccles, J. S. (in press). Adolescent development. In P. A. Alexander & P. Winne (Eds.), *Handbook of educational psychology* (2nd ed.). Mahwah, NJ: Erlbaum.

Wigfield, A., & Eccles, J. S. (1989). Test anxiety in elementary and secondary school students. *Educational Psychologist, 24,* 159–183.

Wigfield, A., & Eccles, J. (1992). The development of achievement task values: A theoretical analysis. *Developmental Review, 12,* 265–310.

Wigfield, A., & Eccles, J. S. (2000). Expectancy: Value theory of motivation. *Contemporary Educational Psychology, 25,* 68–81.

Wigfield, A., & Eccles, J. S. (2002a). Children's motivation during the middle school years. In J. Aronson (Ed.), *Improving academic achievement: Contributions of social psychology* (pp. 159–184). San Diego, CA: Academic Press.

Wigfield, A., & Eccles, J. S. (2002b). The development of competence beliefs and values from childhood through adolescence. In A. Wigfield & J. S. Eccles (Eds.), *Development of achievement motivation* (pp. 92–120). San Diego, CA: Academic Press.

Wigfield, A., Eccles, J. S., Mac Iver, D., Reuman, D., & Midgley, C. (1991). Transitions at early adolescence: Changes in children's domain-specific self-perceptions and general self-esteem across the transition to junior high school. *Developmental Psychology, 27,* 552–565.

Wigfield, A., Eccles, J. S., & Pintrich, P. R. (1996). Development between the ages of 11 and 25. In D. C. Berliner & R. C. Calfee (Eds.), *Handbook of educational psychology* (pp. 148–185). New York: Macmillan.

Wigfield, A., Eccles, J. S., Yoon, K. S., Harold, R. D., Arbreton, A., Freedman-Doan, C., et al. (1997). Changes in children's competence beliefs and subjective task values across the elementary school years: A 3-year study. *Journal of Educational Psychology, 89,* 451–469.

Wigfield, A., & Tonks, S. (2002). Adolescents' expectancies for success and achievement task values. In F. Pajares & T. Urdan (Eds.), *Academic motivation of adolescents* (pp. 53–82). Greenwich, CT: Information Age Publishing.

Wigfield, A., & Tonks, S. (2004). The development of motivation for reading. In J. T. Guthrie, A. Wigfield, & K. C. Perencevich (Eds.), *Motivating reading comprehension: Concept oriented reading instruction* (pp. 249–272). Mahwah, NJ: Erlbaum.

Wigfield, A., & Wagner, A. L. (2005). Competence, motivation, and identity development during adolescence. In A. J. Elliot & C. S. Dweck (Eds.), *Handbook of competence and motivation* (pp. 222–239). New York: Guilford Press.

Winne, P. H., & Jamieson-Noel, D. L. (2002). Exploring students' calibration of self-reports about study tactics and achievement. *Contemporary Educational Psychology, 27,* 551–572.

Winne, P. H., & Marx, R. W. (1989). A cognitive-process analysis of motivation within classroom tasks. In C. Ames & R. E. Ames (Eds.), *Research on motivation in education* (Vol. 3, pp. 223–257). San Diego, CA: Academic Press.

Winston, C., Eccles, J. S., Senior, A. M., & Vida, M. (1997). The utility of an expectancy/value model of achievement for understanding academic performance and self-esteem in African-American and European-American adolescents. *Zeitschrift Fur Padagogische Psychologie, 11,* 177–186.

Wolters, C. A. (2003). Regulation of motivation: Evaluating an underemphasized aspect of self-regulated learning. *Educational Psychologist, 38,* 189–206.

Wong, C. A., Eccles, J. S., & Sameroff, A. J. (2003). The influence of ethnic discrimination and ethnic identification on African-Americans adolescents' school and socioemotional adjustment. *Journal of Personality, 71,* 1197–1232.

Yee, D. K., & Flanagan, C. (1985). Family environments and self-consciousness in early adolescence. *Journal of Early Adolescence, 5,* 59–68.

Yeung, W. J., Linver, M. R., & Brooks-Gunn, J. (2002). How money matters for young children's development: Parental investment and family processes. *Child Development, 73,* 1861–1879.

Yoon, K. S., Wigfield, A., & Eccles, J. S. (1993, April). *Causal relations between mothers' and children's beliefs about math ability: A structural equation model.* Paper presented at the annual meeting of the American Educational Research Association, Atlanta.

Zeidner, M. (1998). *Test anxiety: The state of the art.* New York: Plenum Press.

Zimmerman, B. J. (1989). A social cognitive view of self-regulated learning. *Journal of Educational Psychology, 81,* 329–339.

Zimmerman, B. J. (2000). Attaining self-regulation: A social cognitive perspective. In M. Boekaerts, P. R. Pintrich, & M. Zeidner (Eds.), *Handbook of self-regulation* (pp. 13–39). San Diego, CA: Academic Press.

Zimmerman, B. J., & Kitasantas, A. (1999). Acquiring writing revision skill: Shifting from process to outcome self-regulatory goals. *Journal of Educational Psychology, 91,* 241–250.

Zimmerman, B. J., & Martinez-Pons, M. (1990). Student differences in self-regulated learning: Relating grade, sex, and giftedness to self-efficacy and strategy use. *Journal of Educational Psychology, 82,* 51–59.

Zimmerman, B. J., & Schunk, D. H. (2002). Reflections on theories of self-regulated learning and academic achievement. In B. J. Zimmerman & D. H. Schunk (Eds.), *Self-regulated learning and academic achievement: Theoretical perspectives* (2nd ed., pp. 289–308). Mahwah, NJ: Erlbaum.

CHAPTER 16

Adolescent Development in Interpersonal Context

W. ANDREW COLLINS and LAURENCE STEINBERG

The study of adolescence began with Hall's (1904) two-volume work, *Adolescence: Its Psychology and Its Relations to Physiology, Anthropology, Sociology, Sex, Crime, Religion, and Education.* Hall's vision blended attention to individual and contextual factors, as well as basic and applied concerns, and this breadth of perspective continues to characterize research on adolescence today. The most prominent line of study, however, has focused on individual attributes as the hallmarks of psychosocial development and on parents as the most significant source of influence. The contemporary vitality of that tradition is evident in the publication of no fewer than

three recent handbook chapters (Collins & Laursen, 2004b; Granic, Dishion, & Hollenstein, 2003; Grotevant, 1998) and other widely cited reviews (e.g., Steinberg, 2001; Steinberg & Silk, 2002) on family influences and parent-child relationships as contexts of adolescent development.

As the twentieth century came to an end, the individualistic orientation and dominance of family influences gradually broadened to include *relational* processes in development (Collins & Laursen, 2004a). Rather than focusing exclusively on outcomes such as achievement, competence, self-esteem, psychopathology and other problems of individual functioning, researchers began to attend to adolescents' abilities for high-quality affiliations, to seek support effectively from others, and to cooperate and collaborate on formal and informal tasks (Collins, Gleason, & Sesma, 1997; Epstein, 1989; Savin-Williams & Berndt, 1990). Researchers also recognized

The authors thank the editor of this volume, as well as Willard W. Hartup and Brett Laursen, for helpful comments on earlier versions of this chapter. In addition, we are grateful to Amy Luckner and Jessica Siebenbruner for their assistance in preparation of the manuscript.

that extrafamilial interpersonal relationships contributed significantly to both individual and relational competence in childhood and adolescence (for reviews, see B. Brown, 2004; Collins, Maccoby, Steinberg, Hetherington, & Bornstein, 2000; Darling, Hamilton, & Shaver, 2003; Hartup, 1996). Socialization and acculturation increasingly were viewed as occurring in networks of relationships in both proximal (e.g., neighborhood or ethnic communities) and distal (e.g., societal or cultural) contexts (Brewer & Caporael, 1990; Cooper, 1994; Masten et al., 1995).

This more relational orientation has transformed traditional approaches to research on adolescence in two ways. First, it has led to findings that yield a vastly different picture of the social world of adolescents than the prevailing view in the middle decades of the past century (e.g., Allen & Land, 1999; Collins & Laursen, 2004b; Grotevant, 1998). Researchers now recognize that adolescents of different ages differ in their capacities as relationship partners and that social contacts during adolescence differ from those of childhood. Although family relationships remain salient, the proportion of time that adolescents spend with persons outside of the family increases, and these extrafamilial relationships serve many of the same functions that previously were considered the exclusive province of family relationships during childhood (Collins & Laursen, 2004b). Today, research on adolescents' social relationships has been refocused to include interest in interpersonal *transformations* in which the properties and conditions of relationships within and outside of the family change without subverting the bond between parent and child (Collins, 1995).

Second, an increased emphasis on relationships has altered perspectives on the nature and course of psychosocial achievements that long have been regarded as touchstones of adolescent development. One is the development of a sense of *independence,* including both behavioral and emotional autonomy from parents. The other is the development of *interdependence* by forming connections with others in which mutual influence and support can occur. Of these complementary tasks, the former has received the lion's share of empirical and theoretical attention (Collins, 2003; Zimmer-Gembeck & Collins, 2003), probably because of the emphasis in Western culture on attaining abilities for functioning outside of the family of origin. At the same time, experiences in adolescence long have been considered primary

to the process of establishing emotionally intimate relationships with peers and sexual relationships with romantic partners. Increasingly, research is encompassing the facilitating role of both familial and extrafamilial relationships in achieving age-appropriate independence, as well as the formation and maintenance of effective relations with others (for reviews, see Collins, Gleason, et al., 1997; Collins & Laursen, 2004b).

The topic of this chapter is the nature and significance of familial and extrafamilial relationships during adolescence and their role in the development of the competencies associated with independence and interdependence. The chapter begins with a brief overview of research and theory pertaining to three key processes of individual development: (1) biological maturation, (2) cognitive development, and (3) changes in social definitions and expectations. Three sections then examine links between individual development and salient interpersonal contexts. The first of these is an overview of three dominant conceptual perspectives in current research on adolescent interpersonal experiences: (1) ecological models; (2) models of interpersonal interaction and influence; and (3) biosocial models, including evolutionary and behavioral genetics approaches. The second subsection addresses family relationships and extrafamilial relationships as salient interpersonal contexts of adolescent development. Our discussion of extrafamilial contexts emphasizes interpersonal features of peer groups and of close relationships with friends and of romantic interests. The third section on links between relationships and individual development addresses the impact of settings such as schools, workplaces, volunteer activities, leisure pursuits, and neighborhoods on developmentally significant interpersonal experiences. The subsequent section then outlines the role of interpersonal contexts in the development of independence and interdependence. The importance given to these two complementary processes in psychosocial development varies across cultures, and even among subcultural and social-status groups in cultures, and these realities of adolescent development recur throughout the chapter.

The chapter concludes with reflections on current knowledge of the extensive interrelations among the interpersonal and other contexts of contemporary adolescence. A key theme of this part of the chapter is the futility of searching for singular answers to questions about *which* experiences are developmentally optimal and the potential benefits of attending to more nuanced questions of *how* and *under what conditions* developmentally positive outcomes are likely.

DEFINING FEATURES OF ADOLESCENCE AND PSYCHOSOCIAL DEVELOPMENT

Two decades ago Hill (1983) proposed three principles that remain fundamental to contemporary views of the period. First, biological, cognitive, and social definitional changes are defining features of adolescent social and personality development. Second, social and personality development in adolescence involves transformations in existing psychological capacities rather than new issues that arise for the first time at adolescence. Third, the impact of biological, cognitive, and social-definitional changes on personality and social development is moderated by the proximal and distal contexts in which these changes occur.

The transitions that form the tacit boundaries of the period—one from childhood into adolescence and one from adolescence into adulthood—have received unequal attention, with far more attention having been devoted to the study of the entrance into adolescence than to the transition out of it. Since the mid-1970s the early (ages 10 to 13) and middle (ages 14 to 17) portions of adolescence have dominated psychologists' interests, while the psychosocial transition between adolescence and adulthood—though of considerable interest to sociologists and anthropologists concerned with educational attainment, labor force participation, and family formation—has been largely ignored. Although several writers (Arnett, 2000; Keniston, 1970) have noted that the transition between adolescence and adulthood has been lengthened in contemporary society, this observation has not yet generated a great deal of empirical research on the psychological implications of this social change.

A full discussion of the specific nature of biological, cognitive, and social definitional changes in adolescence is beyond the scope of this chapter. Comprehensive reviews may be found in Susman and Rogol (2004), with regard to puberty; Keating (2004), with regard to cognitive development; and Modell and Goodman (1990) and Schlegel and Barry (1991), with regard to changes in social status and social definition. In the following subsections, we briefly emphasize some key im-

plications of these changes for psychosocial development and interpersonal relationships.

Biological Change

Researchers have focused considerable attention on the co-occurrence of changes in psychological functioning and interpersonal relationships and hormonal and somatic changes of puberty. Indeed, the study of puberty and its impact on social and emotional development is one of the oldest and most enduring topics in the field, beginning with the classic studies of early- and late-maturing youth conducted by Jones and associates (M. Jones, 1957, 1965; M. Jones & Bayley, 1950; M. Jones & Mussen, 1958; Mussen & M. Jones, 1957, 1958) and continuing today (e.g., Ge, Brody, Conger, Simons, & Murry, 2002; Ge, Conger, & Elder, 2001; Ge et al., 2003).

Puberty is best understood as a lengthy process that is set in motion long before any external manifestations of biological change are evident (Susman & Rogol, 2004). Recent studies, enabled by advances in measuring and monitoring endocrine and neuroendocrine activity, have illuminated the exceedingly complex hormonal changes associated with the chief physical manifestations of puberty. These include rapid acceleration in height and weight, which is typically referred to as the "adolescent growth spurt," and emergence of secondary sex characteristics (changes in the genitals and breasts; the growth of pubic, facial, and body hair; and the further development of the external sex organs). The endocrinological changes that stimulate these somatic transformations occur across multiple hypothalamic-pituitary-end organ axes—most notably, the hypothalamic-pituitary-gonadal (HPG) and the hypothalamic-pituitary-adrenal (HPA) axes. There is considerable variability in the timing and pace of pubertal maturation, owing to both genetic and environmental factors, with some early-maturing girls showing signs of puberty as early as 7 and some late-maturing boys not displaying any signs of puberty as late as 14. Generally, girls mature approximately 2 years earlier than boys (Eveleth & Tanner, 1990).

There is no simple answer to the question: "How does puberty affect the psychological development and social relationships of the adolescent?" The answer depends on the gender of the adolescent, the particular aspect of puberty in question, the adolescent's pubertal stages, the timing and pace of pubertal change, and the broader context in which puberty takes place. Studying the relation between pubertal and psychological development is further complicated by the fact that the timing of puberty is itself influenced by social factors. The exact mechanisms remain unknown, but several studies indicate that girls reared in hostile or distant family environments mature somewhat earlier than their peers. This finding implies that the often reported link between pubertal maturation and parent-adolescent conflict may be reciprocal rather than unidirectional (Ellis & Garber, 2000; Ellis, McFadyen-Ketchum, Dodge, Pettit, & Bates, 1999; Graber, Brooks-Gunn, & Warren, 1995; Moffitt, Caspi, Belsky, & Silva, 1992; Steinberg, 1988).

Despite this complexity, a few broad generalizations can be drawn about puberty and adolescent psychological development. First, the direct effects of hormonal changes at puberty are surprisingly small in magnitude, especially given popular stereotypes of adolescent moodiness or unpredictability as the products of "raging hormones" (Buchanan, Eccles, & Becker, 1992; Flannery, Torquati, & Lindemeier, 1994; Susman & Rogol, 2004). There is some evidence that negative affect may be higher during periods of relatively more rapid hormonal change than during periods in which hormonal levels are changing more gradually. In addition, some evidence suggests that adolescents' affect may be more closely linked to levels of adrenal hormones than to levels of gonadal hormones. Generally, however, studies of direct hormone-behavior relations in adolescence have yielded inconsistent and largely unimpressive findings (Buchanan et al., 1992). Second, links between psychological functioning and puberty are stronger when somatic indicators of puberty are measured rather than endocrinological ones (Susman & Rogol, 2004). This pattern suggests that puberty may affect psychological functioning chiefly through its impact on appearance, which likely transforms both self-conceptions and social interactions. Third, studies examining the impact of pubertal timing (i.e., the adolescent's level of pubertal maturation relative to his or her peers or to norms established for a specific chronological age) yield stronger findings than studies examining the impact of pubertal status per se (i.e., which stage of puberty the adolescent is in; Susman & Rogol, 2004).

A fourth and final psychosocial implication of biological maturation comes from well-documented associations between early pubertal maturation and higher rates of negative affect (including clinical depression)

among girls (Aro & Taipale, 1987; Ge et al., 2003; Graber, Brooks-Gunn, & Warren, in press; Hayward et al., 1997; Stice, Presnell, & Bearman, 2001) and higher rates of problem behavior (including antisocial behavior and substance use) among both girls (Dick, Rose, Pulkkinen, & Kaprio, 2001; Flannery, Rowe, & Gulley, 1993; Ge, Conger, & Elder, 1996; Graber, Brooks-Gunn, & Galen, 1999; Magnusson, Stättin, & Allen, 1986; Stice et al., 2001; Wiesner & Ittel, 2002; Wichstrom, 2001) and boys (Andersson & Magnusson, 1990; Dick et al., 2001; Silbereisen, Kracke, & Crockett, 1990; Wichstrom, 2001; Williams & Dunlop, 1999). Prevailing theories point to two potential mechanisms for this connection: (1) the negative impact of puberty on body image among girls (Petersen, 1988; Wichstrom, 2001) and (2) the increased likelihood of early maturers having older friends, which may lead early maturers to experiment with various risky behaviors when they are younger and relatively immature (Magnusson et al., 1986). Notably, the link between early maturation and negative affect among girls is particularly strong in Western countries where cultural beliefs about attractiveness emphasize thinness. This observation is consistent with other research showing that correlates of early and late maturation vary across cultures, societies, neighborhoods, and even schools (Caspi, Lynam, Moffitt, & Silva, 1993; Dick, Rose, Viken, & Kaprio, 2000; Dyer & Tiggemann, 1996; Richards, Boxer, Petersen, & Albrecht, 1990; Silbereisen, Petersen, Albrecht, & Kracke, 1989).

Studies of pubertal maturation and changes in social relationships fall into two broad categories. One group of studies has tracked changes in parent-adolescent relationships, especially parent-adolescent conflict, as a function of pubertal maturation. Overall, the effects of pubertal timing on parent-adolescent conflict are larger and more robust than those of pubertal status (for reviews, see Collins & Laursen, 2004b; Laursen & Collins, 1994). Meta-analyses (e.g., Laursen, Coy, & Collins, 1998) have revealed a small positive linear association between pubertal status and negative affect in parent-adolescent interchanges but not between pubertal status and the *rate* of parent-adolescent conflict. In other words, as adolescents mature, they do not fight with their parents more often, but when they do, the fighting tends to be more intense (Laursen et al., 1998). Generally, early-maturing sons and daughters experience more frequent and more intense parent-child conflict than adolescents who mature on-time or late. Several explanations have been offered, most suggesting that parents do not agree with adolescents that physical precocity is a sufficient basis for granting greater autonomy. The effects of pubertal maturation on parent-adolescent harmony are less well-studied. A few investigations of this have suggested that pubertal maturation may be associated with diminished closeness, manifested mainly in increased privacy-seeking on the part of the adolescent and diminished physical affection between teenagers and parents, but the effects are small and inconsistent across studies (Collins & Laursen, 2004b; Montemayor, 1983, 1986).

The other broad class of studies of the impact of puberty on relationships examines the role of puberty in adolescents' sexual behavior. This literature shows that a complete understanding of the role of puberty in adolescent sexual behavior necessitates examining biological and social influences in interaction with each other rather than focusing on either set of influences alone (Billy & Udry, 1985; E. Smith, Udry, & Morris, 1985; Udry, Talbert, & Morris, 1986). Adolescents become sexually active in part because of increases in sex hormones at puberty and in part because sexual activity becomes accepted in their peer group. Consistent with this, adolescents who mature earlier than their peers are also likely to have sexual intercourse earlier, as a consequence of both biological and social factors (Lam, Shi, Ho, Stewart, & Fan, 2002; B. Miller, Norton, Fan, & Christopherson, 1998).

Although motivation to have sex appears to be hormonally driven in both sexes, influences on actual sexual activity are both hormonal and social and differ somewhat between males and females (Savin-Williams & Diamond, 2004). Among both males and females, initial *interest* in sex, as well as arousal in response to sexual stimuli, is influenced primarily by the pubertal surge in sex hormones (E. Smith et al., 1985; Udry, 1990; Udry et al., 1986). Links between hormonal change and sexual *activity,* however, are stronger among males than females. Some evidence indicates that boys whose friends are sexually active are themselves more likely to be involved in sex, apparently because boys tend to have friends who are at a similar level of pubertal development and who therefore are likely to have similar androgen levels and rates of sexual activity.

Because male adolescents are traditionally more likely to initiate sex than female adolescents, girls' sexual activity is influenced both by their sex drive and their receptivity to males' sexual advances. Perhaps because of this, numerous studies show that social factors are far more important in influencing girls' involvement in sexual intercourse than boys' (Crockett, Bingham, Chopak, & Vicary, 1996; Savin-Williams & Diamond, 2004; Udry & Billy, 1987). Among girls with high levels of androgens, for example, those who have sexually permissive attitudes and sexually active friends are more likely to engage in intercourse than those with more conservative attitudes and inactive or less active friends. Conversely, among girls whose social environment is less encouraging of sex, even those girls with high levels of androgens are unlikely to be sexually active. One explanation for this sex difference is that boys develop in an environment that is more uniformly tolerant and encouraging of sexual behavior than girls do, thus permitting the direct effects of hormonal changes on sexual activity to be more easily realized among males.

There is strong evidence that the impact of pubertal maturation on adolescent psychosocial development is more likely to be interpersonally mediated than to result from the direction action of hormonal change on mood or emotional functioning. This conclusion is supported by evidence of three kinds: (1) findings that the effects of puberty are stronger when observable manifestations of changes in physical appearance, rather than hormonal indices, are used to measure maturation; (2) results showing that pubertal timing, which necessarily involves some sort of social comparison, is a better predictor of psychosocial functioning than pubertal status; and (3) indications that the impact of puberty on psychological functioning is moderated by the social context in which adolescents mature.

Cognitive Change

During early adolescence, individuals show marked improvements in reasoning (especially deductive reasoning), information processing (in both efficiency and capacity), and expertise. Abstract, multidimensional, planful, and hypothetical thinking also increases from late childhood into middle adolescence. According to a recent review (Keating, 2004), it is probably more sensible to view improvements in thinking as involving an interrelated "suite" of changes than to search for a single driving force that accounts for the multiple advances in thinking that occur during adolescence.

After a period of relative inactivity during the late 1980s and early 1990s, the study of intellectual development during adolescence has been revitalized in two ways. First, research in developmental neuroscience has redirected attention to the study of structural and functional aspects of brain development (e.g., Casey, Giedd, & Thomas, 2000; Giedd et al., 1999; Sowell, Trauner, Gamst, & Jernigan, 2002; Spear, 2000). These studies have pointed to significant growth and change in multiple regions of the prefrontal cortex throughout the course of adolescence, especially with respect to processes of myelination and synaptic pruning (both of which increase the efficiency of information processing; Huttenlocher, 1994; Paus et al., 1999; Sowell et al., 2002). These changes are believed to undergird improvements in executive functioning (i.e., long-term planning, metacognition, self-evaluation, self-regulation, and the coordination of affect and cognition; Keating, 2004). Improved connectivity between regions of the prefrontal cortex and several areas of the limbic system also occur during adolescence, and this restructuring likely affects evaluations and responses to both risk and reward (Martin et al., 2002; Spear, 2000). Substantial changes also apparently occur in brain systems that regulate the ways in which individuals process and respond to social stimuli, such as facial displays of affective states (E. Nelson, Leibenluft, McClure, & Pine, 2005). Whether and to what extent these changes in brain structure and function are linked to processes of pubertal maturation is not known. Some aspects of brain development are coincident with, and likely linked to, neuroendocrinological changes occurring at the time of puberty, but others appear to take place along a different, and later, timetable. Disentangling the first set from the second is an important challenge for the field (see Dahl, 2001).

A second relatively new direction examines cognitive development as it plays out in social contexts and, in particular, as cognitive functioning affects the development of judgment, decision making, and risk taking (Cauffman & Steinberg, 2000; Fried & Reppucci, 2001; Maggs, Almeida, & Galambos, 1995; D. Miller & Byrnes, 1997; Scott, Reppucci, & Woolard, 1995; Steinberg & Cauffman, 1996). New perspectives emphasize that adolescent thinking in the real world is a function of social and emotional, as well as cognitive, processes; thus, a full account of the ways in which the intellectual changes of adolescence affect social and emotional development must address the ways in which affect and cognition interact (Keating, 2004). Studies of adoles-cents' reasoning and problem solving using laboratory-based measures of intellectual functioning may provide better information about adolescents' potential competence than about their actual performance in everyday settings, where judgment and decision making are likely affected by emotional states and social influences (Steinberg, 2003). Thus, although studies of responses to hypothetical dilemmas involving the perception and appraisal of risk show few reliable age differences after middle adolescence (e.g., Beyth-Marom, Austin, Fischoff, Palmgren, & Jacobs-Quadrel, 1993), studies of actual risk taking (e.g., risky driving and unprotected sexual activity) indicate that adolescents are significantly more likely than adults to make risky decisions. One reasonable hypothesis is that adults and adolescents age 16 and older share the same logical competencies but that age differences in social and emotional factors, such as susceptibility to peer influence or impulse control, contribute to age differences in actual decision making (Steinberg & Scott, 2003).

Similarly, although it is reasonable to assume that the intellectual advances of adolescence transform, and are transformed by, individuals' relationships with parents, peers, and other individuals, direct examinations of this proposition are surprisingly infrequent. Research on links between the cognitive changes of adolescence and social or emotional development during the period more typically has examined age-related differences in social cognition rather than the relation between cognitive advances and changes in social relationships.

An extensive literature, however, has shown that the ways in which individuals think about others becomes more abstract, more differentiated, and more multidimensional during adolescence (for a review, see Eisenberg & Morris, 2004). Recent studies have attempted to clarify the conditions under which relatively more advanced displays of social cognition are likely. These efforts have included attention to gender and cultural differences in certain aspects of social cognition, such as prosocial reasoning (e.g., Boehnke, Silbereisen, Eisenberg, Reykowski, & Palmonari, 1989; Jaffee & Hyde, 2000) and impression formation (e.g., Crystal, Watanabe, Weinfurt, & Wu, 1998), as well as efforts to examine links between social cognition and social behavior. The findings imply that patterns of social cognitive development vary both as a function of the content under consideration and the emotional and social context in which the reasoning occurs. As an example, reasoning about moral dilemmas becomes more principled over the course of adolescence, but thinking about real-life problems often is less advanced than that seen when adolescents are asked to reason about hypothetical situations. When individuals perceive that they will be hurt severely by morally advanced actions (e.g., defending someone in the face of being punished oneself), they are less likely to reason at a higher moral level (Sobesky, 1983).

The correlation between adolescents' moral reasoning and their moral behavior is especially likely to break down when individuals define issues as personal choices rather than ethical dilemmas (e.g., when using drugs is seen as a personal matter rather than a moral issue; Kuther & Higgins-D'Alessandro, 2000). Similarly, when faced with a logical argument, adolescents are more likely to accept faulty reasoning or shaky evidence when they agree with the substance of the argument than when they do not (Klaczynski, 1997; Klaczynski & Gordon, 1996). In other words, social reasoning is influenced not only by adolescents' basic intellectual abilities but also by their desires, motives, and interests.

Although advances in hypothetical thinking and social perspective taking are presumed to stimulate the development of more egalitarian relationships with parents and more intimate relationships with peers, most work in this area has focused on links between cognitive development and parent-adolescent conflict, to the neglect of research on the ways in which more mature reasoning may permit the adolescent to establish a closer, more sympathetic relationship with his or her parents. For example, studies of family interaction and moral reasoning generally indicate that adolescents who display relatively more advanced reasoning and social perspective taking are more likely to have parents who are warm and supportive and who engage the adolescent in discussions in which the young person is encouraged to express independent opinions (Boyes & Allen, 1993; Grotevant & Cooper, 1985; Hauser, Powers, & Noam, 1991; M. Pratt, Arnold, A. Pratt, & Diessner, 1999; Walker & Taylor, 1991), whereas adolescents with parents who are challenging but critical, hostile, and intolerant of the adolescent's assertiveness demonstrate less sophisticated reasoning. Furthermore, whereas high-conflict, challenging interactions between parents and adolescents are associated with adolescents who are likely to engage in less mature reasoning (Walker & Hennig, 1999; Walker, Hennig, & Krettenauer, 2000), comparably challenging and conflictual interactions between adolescents and their peers is associated with

more mature reasoning (Walker et al., 2000). These associations have been reported in multiple studies. Though consistent with reciprocal influences between social interactions and cognitive change, the cross-sectional nature of most research on the topic makes it impossible to answer questions of causality. Research that examines developmental changes in cognitive abilities assessed over time and under varying social and emotional conditions is needed to elucidate this complex interplay among contexts and intrapersonal and interpersonal processes.

Changes in Social Definition

Changes in social definition refer to changes in the legal or social standing of the adolescent that ordinarily carry with them changes in rights, privileges, or responsibilities. In nonindustrialized societies, such changes are typically marked by ceremonial rites of passage and transformations in the adolescent's appearance or form of address designed to signify to members of the community that the young person either has transitioned out of childhood or has entered into adulthood. Often, adolescents undergo two different rites of passage—one marking the beginning of adolescence, and one marking its conclusion (Schlegel & Barry, 1991). In industrialized societies, where ceremonial rites of passage are not universal and are idiosyncratic to particular religious or cultural groups, the social recognition of the adolescent is rarely a public event. Nevertheless, changes in social definition do occur in contemporary society through the legal regulation of the transition to adulthood—in the form of laws concerning the age at which individuals are eligible for employment in the formal labor force, driving, voting, autonomous medical or financial decision making, and the purchase of regulated substances such as alcohol and tobacco (Scott & Woolard, 2004).

Compared to biological or cognitive maturation, the social and emotional implications of the changes in social definition during adolescence have received much less attention. Adolescents' psychosocial development may be influenced in important ways by changes in social definition. As examples, receipt of a driver's license may diminish parental monitoring, facilitate the maintenance of romantic relationships, and change the dynamics of peer interactions; entrance into the formal labor force may provide additional financial autonomy not ordinarily associated with the receipt of an allowance and thereby transform power relationships in the family; and the ability to obtain contraception without parental consent may alter patterns of sexual activity. A reasonable hypothesis is that attaining various adult privileges may affect adolescents' perceptions of their own independence and competence. Some research has examined how adolescents' self-conceptions are affected by paid employment (e.g., Mortimer, 2003), but associations between other changes in social definition and adolescent psychological functioning have not been studied.

Biological and cognitive changes, as well as altered expectations regarding adolescent behavior, thus both stimulate and reflect the central role of interpersonal processes in adolescent development. The remaining sections of the chapter examine these processes and their significance for individual development in the adolescent years.

CONCEPTUAL PERSPECTIVES ON ADOLESCENT DEVELOPMENT IN INTERPERSONAL CONTEXTS

Theories of adolescent development provide overlapping accounts of differences and changes in interpersonal contexts, but contrasting explanations of their significance for individual psychosocial development. *Ecological perspectives* view individuals and relationships as features of larger contexts in which the elements are multilayered and interconnected. *Interpersonal perspectives* focus on patterns of interaction and affect in social interactions and the principles by which close relationships exert pressures toward continuity and coherence. *Biosocial perspectives* emphasize intrapersonal biological and motivational pressures toward engaging in relationships and adapting them to changing contexts. This section elaborates these three views.

Ecological Perspectives

The ecological perspective on adolescence construes context as a series of nested environments, each level of which is embedded in a larger level (Bronfenbrenner, 1979). Although most studies of the role of context in shaping adolescent behavior and development are studies of single contexts examined in isolation from one another, the ecological perspective provides a conceptual framework for investigating more complex interactions between persons and environments. Three premises are especially important in this regard.

The first premise is that proximal settings are connected to each other, in that events that occur in one setting often have ramifications for individual behavior and development in another. Socialization in the family context influences how adolescents behave in the peer group (e.g., B. Brown, Mounts, Lamborn, & Steinberg, 1993; Fuligni & Eccles, 1993), peer influence processes affect how adolescents behave in the classroom (e.g., Mounts & Steinberg, 1995; Steinberg, Dornbusch, & B. Brown, 1992), experiences in the workplace affect family relationships and behavior in school (e.g., Mortimer, 2003; Steinberg, Fegley, & Dornbusch, 1993), and so on.

Second, these proximal settings are contained in broader institutional and community contexts that shape the structure of settings and influence what takes place in them (Duncan & Raudenbush, 2001; Jencks & Mayer, 1990). This realization has stimulated considerable research in recent years on neighborhood influences on adolescent development (Leventhal & Brooks-Gunn, 2004). Qualities of neighborhoods are now known to influence the functioning of adolescents' families and friendship networks (Furstenberg, T. Cook, Eccles, Elder, & Sameroff, 1999). Parents interact with their children differently in poor neighborhoods than they do in more affluent ones; as a consequence, adolescent development may vary across neighborhood contexts (McLoyd, 1990). Similarly, schools exist in communities, and characteristics of communities—urban versus rural or tightly knit versus impersonal—influence the ways in which schools are organized and operate (Eccles, 2004).

A third premise is that proximal settings and the broader environments that contain them (macrosystems) are located in particular historical, social, economic, political, geographical, and cultural contexts. These contexts in turn are linked to the nature, structure, function, organization, and influence of all levels of the environment (Larson & Wilson, 2004). In addition, important social and economic events—wars, economic depressions, or natural disasters—shape proximal and distal settings in important ways that have ramifications for individuals' behavior and development (Elder, 1998).

The preeminence of contextual perspectives on adolescent development during the past several decades stands in stark contrast to the emphasis placed on studies of intraindividual development during the 1950s, 1960s, and 1970s. During that period, grand theories of adolescent development, such as Freud's theory of detachment (1958), Erikson's theory of identity development (1968), or Piaget's theory of formal operations

(Inhelder & Piaget, 1958), defined the empirical agenda. Even a cursory examination of articles in today's scientific journals reveals just how much the influence of these intraindividual perspectives has waned and has been supplanted by less theoretically driven studies of the contexts in which adolescents develop.

Two important ramifications of the ascendance of contextual perspectives deserve comment. First, research on social and personality development in adolescence has shifted away from the description of processes of normative social and emotional development toward an emphasis on diversity in adolescent experiences attributable to variations in the family, peer group, school, workplace, and neighborhood. As a result, recent research on adolescence has tended to emphasize individual differences in behavior, psychosocial functioning, and mental health far more than universal (or, at least, putatively universal) aspects of social or emotional maturation. Second, as Steinberg and Morris (2001) noted, "No comprehensive theories of normative adolescent development have emerged to fill the voids created by the declining influence of Freud, Erikson, and Piaget. Instead, the study of adolescence has come to be organized around a collection of 'mini-theories'— frameworks designed to explain only small pieces of the larger puzzle. As a consequence, although the field of adolescence research is certainly much bigger now than before, it is less coherent and, in a sense, less developmental than it had been in the past" (pp. 101–102).

One attempt to bridge developmental and contextual approaches has involved the study of "stage-environment fit." This approach identifies whether a given context or set of contexts provides opportunities for processes of normative development to unfold along an appropriate timetable. Studies of stage-environment fit, which examine the match between a context and the developmental needs associated with a particular period, should not be confused with studies of "person-environment fit," which examine the match between individual characteristics such as temperament and the contexts in which the individuals live (e.g., Stice & Gonzales, 1998). The former emphasize development, whereas the latter focus on individual differences. An example of stage-environment fit research is the study of the mismatch between the typical social climate of middle or junior high schools and the capabilities and psychosocial needs of young adolescents (e.g., Eccles et al., 1993). Underlying this work is the hypothesis that the normative press toward behavioral independence clashes with the overly rigid and inflexible nature of most educational environments for early adolescents, hindering healthy development. Similar themes appear in research on family relationships that distinguishes between patterns of interaction that seem consonant with the young person's interests in being granted greater emotional and behavioral autonomy versus those that stifle the adolescent's independence striving (e.g., Allen, Hauser, Bell, & O'Connor, 1994; Fuligni & Eccles, 1993). The ecological perspective thus integrates consideration of individual changes and the contexts (including relational ones) that facilitate or interfere with those changes.

Interpersonal Perspectives

Interpersonal perspectives emphasize how adolescents' experiences in social relationships change and how these changes, in turn, contribute to individual development. At least three formulations exemplify interpersonal perspectives on development during adolescence. The three differ primarily in the degree to which changes in dyadic relationships are attributed to individual maturation or to constraints and demands from larger contexts (e.g., schools). All three, however, assign a significant developmental role to the interactions that occur within dyads and social groups.

Interdependence Models

In interdependence models, joint patterns of actions, cognitions, and emotions between two individuals are the primary locus of contextual influences on individuals (Hinde, 1997; Kelley et al., 1983; Laursen & Bukowski, 1997). A *close relationship* is one in which two persons are highly interdependent; they interact with each other frequently, across a variety of settings and tasks, and exert considerable influence on each others' thoughts and actions (Berscheid, Snyder, & Omoto, 1989; Kelley et al., 1983; Repinski, 1992). Defining closeness by the degree of interdependence between two persons avoids potential confounds between the degree to which adolescents are interdependent with their relationship partners and the emotional qualities of those relationships, which can be either positive or negative (Berscheid et al., 1989).

During adolescence interdependencies in family relationships continue, though often in different forms than in earlier life, and interdependencies with friends and romantic partners become more apparent (Collins & Laursen, 2004a). In parent-child relationships, expectancies must be adjusted on both sides to preserve sufficient interdependence to assure parents a continuing role in facilitating development (Collins, 1995; Darling & Steinberg, 1993). In peer relationships, skills must be developed for maintaining interdependence on the basis of shared interests, commitments, and intimacy, even when contact is relatively infrequent (Parker & Gottman, 1989). In both types of relationships, discrepancies in the expectancies of the relationship partners may stimulate conflicts, but these conflicts often stimulate adjustments of expectancies that gradually restore harmony (Collins, 1995).

The process by which discrepant perceptions mediate changes in interactions has yet to be examined directly, although Collins (1995) offered one possible model. Seeking to explain how both stability and change are inextricably involved in the natural history of relationships, including those involving adolescents, the model begins with the assumption that interactions between parents and children are mediated by cognitive and emotional processes associated with *expectancies* about the behavior of the other person. In periods of rapid developmental change, such as the transition to adolescence, parents' expectancies often are violated, generating emotional turmoil and conflict and stimulating parents and children to realign their expectancies appropriately. In younger and older age groups, change may occur more gradually, so that discrepancies are both less frequent and less salient than in periods of rapid multiple changes. Baumrind (1991) and Holmbeck (1996) also have proposed models implying links between individual development and adaptations in parent-adolescent relationships. Interdependence models thus provide for both continuity and change during development, two requirements for the development of independence and interdependence.

Attachment Perspectives

In contrast to the behavioral emphasis of interdependence views, attachment formulations emphasize the strong emotional ties between parents and adolescents. As a mutually regulated system, parents and children collaborate in maintaining the qualities of parent-child relationships. Relationship qualities are based in emotions associated with feelings of security and insecurity (Bowlby, 1982). Although the qualities and functions of these relationships are presumed to be inherently stable over time (Allen & Land, 1999), specific forms and modes of interaction between parent and child differ from one age period to another, reflecting the developing capabilities and needs of the child and parent and

the varying challenges associated with age-graded tasks and settings.

Attachment in adolescence is distinctive, both behaviorally and cognitively, from attachment in earlier relationships. Compared to children, adolescents manifest emotional ties to their parents subtly and often privately, often through such behaviors as friendly teasing and small acts of concern, as well as shared activities and self-disclosure. Cognitive advances in adolescence make possible more complex and integrated views regarding experiences that involve caregiving, caretaking, and confidence in the availability of significant others. Consequently, adolescents are increasingly attuned to both the similarities and the differences between relationships with parents, other significant adults, friends, and eventually romantic partners and offspring (Allen & Land, 1999; Furman & Wehner, 1994).

Despite these differing attachment behaviors, the functions of secure relationships for adolescents are similar to the functions for infants. Whereas security in infancy facilitates exploration of the immediate environment, security in adolescence provides a sense of confidence in family support for explorations outside of the family, thus facilitating relationships with peers and other adults (Collins & Sroufe, 1999). Longitudinal findings have shown that measures of the quality of caregiver-child relationships in infancy and early childhood forecast measures of quality in relationships with romantic partners in adolescence and even in adulthood (Collins, Hennighausen, Schmit, & Sroufe, 1997; Collins & Van Dulmen, 2006b).

Attachment formulations may appear to emphasize the development of interdependence to the potential detriment of appropriate independence. A key implication of attachment views, however, is that a history of sensitive, responsive interactions and strong emotional bonds facilitates adaptation during the transitions of adolescence—transitions that permit functioning outside the immediate sphere of close relationships, while simultaneously transforming existing bonds into more age-appropriate ones (Collins, 1995; Collins & Sroufe, 1999).

Social-Psychological Perspectives

The distinctive developmental issues of adolescence reflect the multiple adaptations required during the transition from childhood to adulthood (Combrinck-Graham, 1985; Lewin, 1931; Simmons & Blyth, 1987). Adolescent transitions are due partly to the physical changes of puberty and the emergence of behavior commonly expected of physically adult, reproductively mature individuals, but also to age-graded changes in expectations, tasks, and settings (Bandura, 1964). In the social-psychological perspective, this confluence of maturational changes and age-graded shifts in tasks and settings can affect the psychosocial adaptation of individuals more extensively than either can alone (Simmons & Blyth, 1987). A well documented instance is the deleterious impact on seventh grade girls' self-esteem when pubertal maturation, the onset of dating, and a shift from elementary to junior high school coincide (Simmons & Blyth, 1987; Simmons, Burgeson, & Reef, 1988).

The impact of adolescent transitions on interpersonal relationships has three major sources. One is the increase in ambient anxiety and tension from adapting to the multiple changes of early adolescence. Another is that some difficulties in adjusting to the world beyond the family are imported into family relationships, perhaps because families provide relatively safe settings for expressing the bewilderment, anger, and frustration that cannot be expressed freely with nonfamily members (Hartup, 1979; Youniss, 1980). A third is the pressure to diminish dependency on the family to adapt successfully to extrafamilial contexts (Brooks-Gunn, Petersen, & Eichorn, 1985; R. Lerner, 1985). These latter pressures frequently affect psychosocial variables that may play a role in diverse relationships (e.g., self-esteem, perceived independence, value placed on independence, perceived acceptance, methods of control, and implicit timetables for "acting older"; Collins, 1995; Simmons & Blyth, 1987). Parental role confusion and satisfaction also have an impact on the transitions of this period (Silverberg & Steinberg, 1990; Wynne, 1984), a convergence of life-course issues in the two generations that has been frequently cited as a likely source of difficulties in parent-adolescent relationships (e.g., Hill, 1987; Rossi, 1987; Silverberg & Steinberg, 1990). Family development perspectives regard the life-cycle changes experienced by offspring as having ramifications for family systems, which in turn affect the individual development of both parents and children (Combrinck-Graham, 1985; Wynne, 1984).

The social-psychological viewpoint, like other interpersonal perspectives, implies an increase and then a decrease in relationship difficulties from early to late adolescence (Collins & Laursen, 2004b). The course of development may be more episodic than other theories imply, however. For example, social age-grading implies that adolescents will encounter periodic recurrence of shifts in age-related social expectancies; similarly, changes could recur in connection with changes in family status (e.g., Combrinck-Graham, 1985; Wynne, 1984). An alternate, but conceptually consistent, prediction is that early adolescence might be the primary period of change, with gradual restabilization as appropriate accommodations are made to further age- or status-related transitions. Relationship changes may vary, moreover, as a function of timing of puberty. Hill (1988) has suggested that very early pubertal timing for girls may result in long-lasting perturbations in relationships, but the reasons for a different pattern of resolution for this group than for other timing-of-puberty groups are not readily apparent. One possibility, suggested several decades ago by Peskin (1967), is that very early puberty (which characterizes early-maturing girls) occurs well before mature "ego skills" have developed, leaving the adolescent vulnerable to developmental difficulties.

Summary Comment

Interpersonal perspectives elaborate ecological views of the role of social systems in adolescent development by describing the dynamics of adaptation in the proximal arena of close relationships. A particular strength of interpersonal formulations is the implied balance between continuity and change. This balance fosters the simultaneous growth of abilities for autonomous functioning and the capacities required for forming healthy, well-functioning relationships outside of the family and maintaining positive connections in the family.

Biosocial Perspectives

Biosocial perspectives on development in interpersonal contexts come largely from evolutionary psychology and research on behavior genetics, especially more recent work based on molecular genetics and multivariate models of genetic-environment influence. Although the evolutionary view deals primarily with tendencies and processes characteristic of human adolescents in general and that of behavior genetics with individual differences among adolescents, together they provide a picture of the ways in which intraindividual biological processes are relevant to understanding variations in interpersonal experiences during the adolescent years.

Evolutionary Perspectives

In view of the importance of the development of reproductive capability as a defining feature of adolescence, it is not surprising that theorists have drawn on evolutionary perspectives (more specifically, the perspectives of sociobiology and behavioral ecology) in attempting to account for transformations in social relations during the period. The basic argument is that the attainment of reproductive capability should be accompanied by changes in social relationships that increase reproductive fitness (Weisfeld, 1999). This general notion has been used to explain a wide range of social phenomena in adolescence, including the establishment of dominance hierarchies among adolescent males (Savin-Williams, 1979), distancing in the parent-adolescent relationship during puberty (Steinberg, 1989), the emergence of romantic relationships in adolescence (Gray & Steinberg, 1999; Laursen & Jensen-Campbell, 1999), processes of mate selection (Steinberg & Belsky, 1996), the differential patterns of social relationships evinced by early versus late maturers (Belsky, Steinberg, & Draper, 1991; Ellis et al., 1999), and the development of both internalizing (Cyranowski, Frank, Young, & Shear, 2000) and externalizing (Steinberg & Belsky, 1996) problems. In each case, theorists have suggested ways in which the social phenomenon in question might be viewed as a strategic behavior that originally evolved to facilitate the dispersal of an individual's genes in subsequent generations.

Evolutionary perspectives on adolescent social development are grounded in the observation that many social behaviors seen among human adolescents share a great deal in common with those seen among adolescents in other mammalian species and, in particular, with adolescents among other primates—for example, transformations in parent-child relationships at puberty. As is the case among humans, among most nonhuman primates living in the wild, pubertal maturation is generally accompanied by increased distance in the parent-child relationship, either by increased physical distance or heightened aggression; in many primate species, juveniles leave the natal group at puberty, either voluntarily or forcibly (Caine, 1986; Steinberg, 1989). The human and animal studies combined suggest that reproductive maturation may be inhibited by physical closeness to parents and accelerated by distance from them (see also Belsky et al., 1991). Sociobiological explanations of this phenomenon are plausible in that postpubertal distance in the parent-child relationship would minimize inbreeding and thereby increase reproductive fitness (Steinberg, 1989). The fact that parallel changes in parent-child relations occur during puberty across different primate species adds an important new twist to the standard psychoanalytic interpretation of increased parent-adolescent bickering at puberty because monkeys and apes probably do not harbor unresolved Oedipal tension. Although the cross-species similarities do not argue against psychological accounts of transformations in family relations (e.g., such transformations are the result of independence seeking on the part of the adolescent). The fact that parent-adolescent distance occurs routinely at puberty across primate species suggests that it probably has played some role in primate evolution. Similar arguments have been made about the adaptive significance of other "problematic" aspects of adolescent social behavior such as risk taking (Steinberg & Belsky, 1996).

Behavioral Genetics

Growing interest in understanding the joint influence of biology and environment has led to an increase in behavioral genetics research in recent years focused specifically on adolescent social development. Most of this work has employed an additive statistical model, where the variance of a psychological or interpersonal characteristic is partitioned among three components: genetic influences, shared environmental influences (i.e., facets of the environment that family members, such as siblings, share in common), and nonshared environmental influences (i.e., facets of the environment that family members do not share in common; Plomin & Daniels, 1987). Both genetic and nonshared environmental influences, such as parental differential treatment, peer relations, and school experiences, are particularly strong in adolescence. In contrast, shared environmental factors, such as socioeconomic status, neighborhood quality, and parental psychopathology, are less influential (e.g., McGue, Sharma, & Benson, 1996; Pike, McGuire, Hetherington, Reiss, & Plomin, 1996).

Genetic factors contribute to individual variations in social behavior during adolescence, including aggression, antisocial behavior, and delinquency. These individual differences in aggression appear to have a more substantial genetic basis than other behaviors, although both shared and nonshared influences on aggression and other externalizing behaviors have been identified (Deater-Deckard & Plomin, 1999; Eley, Lichenstein, & Stevenson, 1999; Spotts, Neiderhiser, Hetherington, & Reiss, 2001). Genetic factors also have been linked to adolescent internalizing problems, such as risk for suicide and depressed mood (Blumenthal & Kupfer, 1988; Jacobson & Rowe, 1999).

Nonproblem behaviors such as self-perceptions of scholastic competence, athletic competence, physical appearance, social competence, and general self-worth also are highly heritable, with little evidence for shared environmental influences and only modest evidence for nonshared environmental influences (McGuire et al., 1999). Intelligence in adolescence (as indexed by IQ) is strongly influenced by heredity as well; and these genetic influences compound over time, becoming stronger determinants of IQ-test performance than family environmental influences (Loehlin, Willerman, & Horn, 1988). Parental education moderates the heritability of IQ, however. Genetic influences are stronger in families with highly educated parents, consistent with the general notion that heritability estimates are generally higher in more favorable environments (Rowe, Jacobson, & van den Oord, 1999).

One of the most important findings to emerge in recent years is that assessments of the adolescent's family environment via adolescent or parent reports—measures previously presumed to assess the environment—also may reflect features of the parents' genetic make-up, which in turn affect individuals' perceptions and descriptions of their family situations (Plomin, Reiss, Hetherington, & Howe, 1994). Genetic factors contribute significantly to actual and reported levels of conflict, support, and involvement in the family (Neiderhiser, Reiss, Hetherington, & Plomin, 1999), in part, because adolescents who display hostile and antisocial behaviors are more likely to elicit negative behaviors from their parents than adolescents less prone to these problems (Ge et al., 2002). Genetic influences on family relations become even more pronounced as adolescents mature, perhaps because older adolescents have more influence in family relationships (Elkins, McGue, & Iacono, 1997).

An important note is that most psychological traits and behaviors are influenced by *both* nature and nurture and that, among environmental influences, the nonshared component generally contributes more heavily to individual characteristics than shared environment does (Plomin & Daniels, 1987). On average, shared family environment explains only 5% to 10% of the variance in psychological behaviors and attitudes (Collins et al., 2000). Research findings also indicate that variation in the family climate, as opposed to the adolescent behavior or personality trait in question, across sibling and parent-adolescent relationships is explained more by shared influences than nonshared ones (Bussell et al., 1999).

Summary Comment

Ecological, interpersonal, and biosocial perspectives are neither mutually exclusive nor incompatible. Rather, they address different levels of analysis and together promise a richer understanding of the significance of adolescents' interpersonal contexts than any single perspective alone. Developmental systems models (e.g., Magnusson & Stättin, 1998; Sameroff, 1983) incorporate these multiple perspectives. Such models are daunting, both conceptually and methodologically, and few examples exist of thoroughgoing application to research on adolescents. Nevertheless, awareness of the contrasting and the overlapping implications of multiple perspectives provides a useful touchstone for appraising findings from research on adolescent development in interpersonal contexts.

SIGNIFICANT INTERPERSONAL RELATIONSHIPS DURING ADOLESCENCE

The psychosocial challenges of adolescence arise in rapidly diversifying personal and social contexts. This section addresses both relationships established in earlier life periods (e.g., with family members, long-time peers) and those that emerge during adolescence (e.g., with secondary school classmates, romantic interests, extrafamilial adult mentors). In each case, we consider distinctive features of particular types of relationships, the developmental course of these relationships during adolescence, the contributions of the maturation and changes in social expectations that define adolescence, and the significance of relationship changes for adolescent development. We give particular attention to the importance of differing relationships for accomplishing the psychosocial tasks of independence and interdependence.

Familial Relationships and Influences

The role of the family in social development is arguably the most studied topic in the field of adolescence (Steinberg, 2001). Because the literature on parent-adolescent relations has been reviewed so frequently, so extensively, and so recently (Collins & Laursen, 2004b; Grotevant, 1998; Steinberg & Silk, 2002), our brief discussion is oriented toward articulating the major themes and conclusions on the topic.

Research on adolescent development in the family context has focused almost exclusively on adolescents' relationships with their parents or stepparents. Far less is known about relations with brothers or sisters, and almost nothing is known about relationships with family members other than siblings or parents. Given the changing demography of adolescence and the relative increase in the proportion of adolescents from ethnic minority groups in which extended family members are especially important, research on the variations and impact of relationships with grandparents, aunts, uncles, and cousins would be a valuable addition to the literature. Extant research on African American adolescents indicates that, for example, social support from extended family members is an important resource for inner-city adolescents growing up in single-parent homes (Mason, Cauce, Gonzales, & Hiraga, 1994; Salem, Zimmerman, & Notaro, 1998; Taylor, 1996; Taylor, Casten, & Flickinger, 1993; Taylor & Roberts, 1995). Support from kin, in particular, appears to increase single parents' effectiveness in child rearing, and this, in turn, tends to limit adolescents' misbehavior.

Scholars interested in parent-adolescent relationships generally have asked two related questions. First, how do family relationships change over the course of adolescence (i.e., What is the impact of adolescence on the family)? Second, how does adolescent adjustment vary as a function of variations in the parent-adolescent relationship (i.e., What is the impact of the family on the adolescent)?

Transformations in Family Relationships

Researchers have tracked changes in parent-child relations across three different dimensions: (1) autonomy (the extent to which the adolescent is under the control of the parents); (2) conflict (the extent to which the parent-adolescent relationship is contentious or hostile); and (3) harmony (the extent to which the parent-adolescent relationship is warm, involved, and emotionally close; Collins & Laursen, 2004b; Collins & Repinski, 1994). Generally, the most important transformations in family relationships occur during the early portion of the period. Many theorists have argued that the biological, cognitive, and social changes of early adolescence disturb an equilibrium that had been established during middle childhood and that it is not until middle or even late adolescence that a new equilibrium is in place (Collins, 1995).

Autonomy-related changes are probably the most salient of the relational transformations in the family context during adolescence. Adolescents' early attempts at establishing behavioral autonomy in the family frequently precipitate conflict between parents and teenagers, especially during early adolescence (Collins, 1995). As a result, young adolescents may interrupt their parents more often during family discussions but have little impact—a state of affairs that may lead to escalating conflict (Steinberg, 1981). By middle adolescence, however, teenagers behave much more like adults, and thus may no longer need to assert their opinions through interruptions or immature behavior (Grotevant, 1998). Greater freedom to spend time outside of direct parental supervision also may diminish the frequency of autonomy-related struggles. During adolescence, a shift occurs from patterns of influence and interaction that are asymmetrical and unequal to ones in which parents and their adolescent children are on a more equal footing (Collins, 1995).

Despite firmly held popular notions and pervasive media portrayals of conflict as the hallmark of family relations during this period, research has established that frequent, high-intensity, angry fighting is not normative during adolescence (Collins & Laursen, 2004b; Steinberg, 1990). Although fighting is not a central feature of normative family relationships in adolescence, however, nattering or bickering is. Smetana (1995) and colleagues (Smetana & Asquith, 1994; Smetana, Crean, & Daddis, 2002; Smetana & Daddis, 2002; Yau & Smetana, 1996) have argued that much parent-adolescent conflict results from changes in the adolescent's reasoning about the legitimacy of parental authority. Parents and adolescents often squabble over matters that are defined by parents as moral or prudential issues but by adolescents as questions of personal choice and, accordingly, as less appropriate for parental regulation. With increasingly more sophisticated reasoning abilities, adolescents gradually better appreciate distinctions among the personal, the prudential, and the moral, and they begin to challenge parental authority when they believe it is not legitimate. Adolescents appear less likely to challenge parental authority when they identify a source of disagreement as a moral or prudential (rather than personal) issue (Smetana & Daddis, 2002).

Many of the frustrations associated with parent-adolescent conflict may be related less to the content of the conflict and more to the manner in which conflict is typically resolved. Conflicts between teenagers and parents tend to be resolved not through compromise but through submission (i.e., giving in) or disengagement (i.e., walking away; Laursen & Collins, 1994). Compared with conflicts between adolescents and their friends, conflicts between adolescents and their parents are more apt to involve neutral or angry affect and less likely to involve positive affect (R. Adams & Laursen, 2001).

Until recently, it was widely assumed that parent-child conflict followed the course of an inverted U-shaped curve across the adolescent period (e.g., Montemayor, 1983). A recent meta-analysis of studies of parent-adolescent conflict failed to support the commonly held view that parent-child conflict rises and then falls across adolescence, however (Laursen et al., 1998). Rather, a linear decline occurs in the frequency of parent-adolescent conflict in early and middle adolescence, and during this same period expressions of negative affect during conflict increases. Thus, the curvilinear pattern in conflict reported by some investigators may be the result of conflating conflict frequency (which may decline) and conflict intensity (which may rise). Also unclear is the extent to which changes in rate or intensity of conflict are associated with pubertal change as opposed to age (Laursen et al., 1998; Paikoff & Brooks-Gunn, 1991).

Although there is less consensus on the extent of changes in positive affect than on autonomy or conflict, the existing evidence suggests that subjective feelings of closeness and objective measures of interdependence decrease across the adolescent years (Collins & Repinski, 2001; Laursen & Williams, 1997), as does the amount of time parents and adolescents spend together (Larson, Richards, Moneta, Holmbeck, & Duckett, 1996). Relative to preadolescents, adolescents report less companionship and intimacy with parents (Buhrmester & Furman, 1987) and report lower feelings of acceptance by parents and less satisfaction with family life (Hill, 1988). Although perceptions of relationships remain generally warm and supportive, both adolescents and parents report less frequent expressions of positive emotions and more frequent expressions of negative emotions when compared with parents and preadolescent children. After a decrease in early adolescence, older teens report more positive affect during family interactions (Larson et al., 1996). It is important to note that children who had warm relationships with their parents during preadolescence are likely to remain

close and connected with their parents during adolescence, even though the frequency and quantity of positive interactions may be somewhat diminished (Collins & Laursen, 2004b).

The Influence of Parenting on Adjustment

Drawing a distinction between *parenting style* and *parenting practices* helps to clarify the relation between parenting and adolescent adjustment (Darling & Steinberg, 1993). Parenting style refers to the overall emotional climate of the parent-child relationship, as indicated by variations in autonomy, harmony, and conflict. Parenting practices, in contrast, are specific, goal-directed attempts by the parent to socialize the adolescent in a particular fashion (e.g., toward high academic achievement or away from experimentation with alcohol). Practices are more or less independent from parenting style, in that similar practices can be carried out against very different stylistic backdrops. More important, the same parenting practice may have different outcomes in the context of one style than another (Darling & Steinberg, 1993; Steinberg, Lamborn, Dornbusch, & Darling, 1992).

Many researchers employ a typological approach to the study of parenting style in which families are categorized into one of several groups based on multiple dimensions of the parent-child relationship. The most influential and well-known approach (Maccoby & Martin, 1983; also see Baumrind, 1991) groups parents into four categories based on levels of responsiveness and demandingness. *Authoritative* parents are warm, firm, and accepting of the adolescent's individuality (Barber, 1994; Gray & Steinberg, 1999). Parents who are very demanding but not responsive are labeled *authoritarian*. Authoritarian parents place a high value on obedience and conformity and tend to favor more punitive, absolute, and forceful disciplinary measures. They tend not to encourage independent behavior and, instead, place a good deal of importance on restricting the child's autonomy. A parent who is very responsive but not at all demanding is labeled *indulgent* (or permissive). Indulgent parents place relatively few demands on the child's behavior, giving the child a high degree of freedom to act as she or he wishes. Parents who are neither demanding nor responsive are labeled *indifferent*. Indifferent parents minimize the time and energy that they must devote to interacting with their child. In extreme cases, indifferent parents may be neglectful.

A vast literature has linked higher levels of psychosocial competence to rearing by authoritative parents than to rearing by authoritarian, indulgent, or indifferent parents. Adolescents from authoritative homes are relatively more responsible, more self-assured, more adaptive, more creative, more curious, more socially skilled, and more successful in school. In contrast, adolescents from authoritarian homes are more dependent, more passive, less socially adept, less self-assured, and less intellectually curious; those from indulgent households are often less mature, more irresponsible, more conforming to their peers, and less able to assume positions of leadership; and those reared in indifferent homes are disproportionately impulsive and more likely to be involved in delinquent behavior and in precocious experiments with sex, drugs, and alcohol (Fuligni & Eccles, 1993; Kurdek & Fine, 1994; Lamborn, Mounts, Steinberg, & Dornbusch, 1991; Petit, Laird, Dodge, Bates, & Criss, 2001; Pulkkinen, 1982; Steinberg, 2001; Steinberg, Lamborn, Darling, Mounts, & Dornbusch, 1994). Although occasional exceptions to these general patterns have been noted, the evidence linking authoritative parenting and healthy adolescent development is remarkably strong, and it comes from studies of a wide range of ethnicities, social classes, and family structures, not only in the United States (e.g., Clark, Novak, & Dupree, 2002; Dornbusch, Ritter, Liederman, Roberts, & Fraleigh, 1987; Forehand, Miller, Dutra, & Chance, 1997; Hetherington, Henderson, & Reiss, 1999; S. Kim & Ge, 2000; Matza, Kupersmidt, & Glenn, 2001; Steinberg, Mounts, Lamborn, & Dornbusch, 1991) but in parts of the world as diverse as Iceland (Adalbjarnardottir & Hafsteinsson, 2001), India (Carson, Chowdhury, Perry, & Pati, 1999), China (Pilgrim, Luo, Urberg, & Fang, 1999), and Palestine (Punamaki, Qouta, & Sarraj, 1997).

Research also consistently indicates that adolescents who have experienced indifferent, neglectful, or abusive parenting disproportionately experience problems in mental health and development, such as depression and a variety of behavior problems, including, in cases of physical abuse, aggression toward others (Crittenden, Claussen, & Sugarman, 1994; Pittman & Chase-Lansdale, 2001; Sheeber, Hops, Alpert, Davis, & Andrews, 1997; Strauss & Yodanis, 1996). Severe psychological abuse (excessive criticism, rejection, or emotional harshness) appears to be linked to the most deleterious outcomes (Dubé et al., 2003; Haj-Yahia, Musleh, & Haj-Yahia, 2002; McGee, Wolfe, & Wilson, 1997; Rohner, Bourque, & Elordi, 1996; Simons, Johnson, & Conger, 1994).

It is important to acknowledge possible bidirectional influence in these associations (W. Cook, 2001; C. Lewis, 1981; Stice & Barrera, 1995). Adolescents who are aggressive, dependent, or less psychosocially mature in other ways may provoke parental behavior that is excessively harsh, passive, or distant (Rueter & R. Conger, 1998). In contrast, adolescents who are responsible, self-directed, curious, and self-assured may elicit from their parents warmth, flexible guidance, and verbal give-and-take. In all likelihood, links between adolescent competence and authoritative parenting may be the result of a reciprocal cycle in which the child's psychosocial maturity leads to authoritative parenting, which in turn leads to the further development of maturity (J. Lerner, Castellino, & Perkins, 1994; Repetti, 1996; Steinberg, Elmen, & Mounts, 1989). One 9-year longitudinal study found that, for example, adolescents' and parents' negative feelings toward each other were reciprocally related over time. The more negative adolescents felt, the more this led to negative feelings on the part of their parents, and vice versa (K. Kim, R. Conger, Lorenz, & Elder, 2001).

Much research on parenting style addresses the independent, additive, and interactive effects of variations in autonomy, harmony, and conflict on adolescent adjustment. Although largely cross-sectional and, consequently, limited in its ability to inform questions of causality, studies of parent-adolescent relationships and adolescent adjustment have yielded remarkably consistent findings. Across a variety of outcomes, adolescents fare best in households characterized by a climate of warmth, in which they are encouraged both to be "connected" to their parents and to express their own individuality (Allen, Hauser, O'Connor, Bell, & Eickholt, 1996; Cooper, Grotevant, & Condon, 1983; Grotevant & Cooper, 1985; Hauser et al., 1991; Hauser & Safyer, 1994; Hodges, Finnegan, & Perry, 1999; McElhaney & Allen, 2001). Adolescents who report feeling relatively closer to their parents score higher than other adolescents on measures of psychosocial development, including self-reliance (Steinberg & Silverberg, 1986); behavioral competence, including school performance (Hill, 1987; Maccoby & Martin, 1983); and psychological well-being, including self-esteem (Harter, 1983). Adolescents who report feeling close to their parents also score lower than comparison groups on measures of psychological or social problems (e.g., drug use, depression, deviant behavior, and impulse control; Allen, Hauser, Eickholt, Bell, & O'Connor, 1994; Garber, Robinson, & Valentiner, 1997; Ge, Best, Conger, & Simons, 1996; Jessor & Jessor, 1977). The benefits of a balance between autonomy and connectedness also are evident in research on family decision making. Adolescents fare better when their families engage in joint decision making in which the adolescent plays an important role but parents remain involved in the eventual resolution, rather than unilateral decision making by the parent or adolescent (Lamborn, Dornbusch, & Steinberg, 1996).

Problems in psychosocial adjustment commonly occur when parents are either highly constraining or insufficiently involved. Adolescents whose parents are intrusive or overprotective, for example, may have difficulty individuating from them, which may lead to depression, anxiety, and diminished social competence (Holmbeck et al., 2000; McElhaney & Allen, 2001). Alternatively, those adolescents who are granted autonomy but who feel distant or detached from their parents score poorly on measures of psychological adjustment (Allen et al., 1996; Chen & Dornbusch, 1998; Fuhrman & Holmbeck, 1995; Lamborn & Steinberg, 1993; R. Ryan & Lynch, 1989). In short, the characteristics of parent-adolescent relationships moderate the impact of parental practices on adolescent behavior and adjustment.

Research findings on parent-adolescent conflict further illustrate this point. Parent-child conflict that occurs in the context of hostile and contentious interactions is associated with negative adolescent adjustment and behaviors. Apparently, the emotional climate of the relationship, rather than the conflict per se, may distinguish adaptive from maladaptive parent-adolescent quarreling (Smetana, 1995). Mild conflict between parents and adolescents actually may be functional in development, in that disagreements may be a mechanism through which adolescents signal changing self-conceptions and expectations for independence (Collins, 1995; Holmbeck & Hill, 1991; Steinberg, 1990). Conflict with parents also may facilitate the development of conflict-resolution skills, assertiveness, and role-taking skills (Cooper et al., 1983; Smetana, Yau, & Hanson, 1991). The positive effects of conflict, however, appear to occur only in parent-adolescent relationships that are also characterized by a high degree of cohesion or harmony (R. Adams & Laursen, 2001).

An important vehicle through which parents remain connected to adolescents without constraining them un-

duly is monitoring (Crouter & Head, 2002). Parental monitoring and supervision are correlated highly with positive adjustment and academic achievement among adolescents (Lamborn et al., 1991; Linver & Silverberg, 1997; Patterson & Stouthamer-Loeber, 1984). Stättin and Kerr recently have argued that the beneficial outcomes often attributed by researchers to effective parental monitoring may actually have little to do with monitoring and may merely be the end result of a parent-adolescent relationship in which the adolescent willingly discloses information to the parent (Kerr & Stättin, 2000; Stättin & Kerr, 2000). Indeed, a close examination of many widely used measures of parental monitoring reveals that researchers often conflate parental *monitoring* with parental *knowledge,* which can be gained through many means other than direct surveillance (e.g., voluntary disclosure by the adolescent). Although one recent analysis suggests that parental monitoring is a deterrent to adolescent problem behavior above and beyond that attributable to knowledge derived from other sources (Fletcher, Steinberg, & Williams-Wheeler, 2004), Stättin and Kerr's work points up the importance of distinguishing between what parents do and what they know. It is especially important that researchers interested in parental monitoring take care to ensure that the measurement of this construct is precise and that, perhaps, parental knowledge of their adolescent's behavior (and how the knowledge is obtained) be measured separately.

Findings on the significance of parenting during adolescence underscore the value of examining multiple parenting dimensions simultaneously to obtain a more accurate reading of the overall emotional climate of the parent-adolescent relationship. Parental attempts at control may be experienced differently in the context of a harmonious relationship than in the context of an adversarial one. Though once regarded largely as matter of parenting practices, the contributions of parents to adolescent development are now recognized as a complex interplay of parental actions, parent-adolescent relationships, and the larger contexts impinging on both.

Ethnic Variations

In the United States, the topic of ethnic differences in parent-adolescent relationships has received a great deal of attention in recent years, as researchers have attempted to keep pace with the changing demography of U.S. society. The studies generally have found that authoritative parenting is less prevalent among African

American, Asian American, or Hispanic American families than among White families, no doubt reflecting the fact that parenting practices are often linked to cultural values and beliefs (Dornbusch et al., 1987; Smetana & Chuang, 2001; Steinberg, Dornbusch, et al., 1992; Yau & Smetana, 1996). Nevertheless, even though authoritative parenting is less common in ethnic minority families, its links to adolescent adjustment appear to be positive in all ethnic groups (Amato & Fowler, 2002; Knight, Virdin, & Roosa, 1994; Mason, Cauce, Gonzales, & Hiraga, 1996; Steinberg, Dornbusch, et al., 1992; Walker-Barnes & Mason, 2001).

Research also has indicated that authoritarian parenting is more prevalent among ethnic minority than among White families, even after taking ethnic differences in socioeconomic status into account (Chao, 1994; Dornbusch et al., 1987; Steinberg, Lamborn, et al., 1992). In contrast to research on authoritative parenting, which suggests similar effects across ethnic groups, research on authoritarian parenting indicates that the adverse effects of this style of parenting may be greater among White youngsters than among ethnic minority youth (Chao, 1994; Dornbusch et al., 1987; Lamborn et al., 1996; Morrison Gutman, Sameroff, & Eccles, 2002; Ruiz, Roosa, & Gonzales, 2002; Schweingruber & Kalil, 2000; Steinberg et al., 1994).

At least two explanations have been offered for this finding. First, because ethnic minority families are more likely to live in dangerous communities, authoritarian parenting, with its emphasis on control, may be less harmful than in more positive settings and may even carry some benefits. Second, the distinction between authoritative versus authoritarian parenting may not always make sense when applied to parents from other cultures (Chao, 1994, 2001; Gonzales, Cauce, & Mason, 1996). For example, non-White parents frequently combine a very high degree of strictness (similar to White authoritarian parents) with warmth (similar to White authoritative parents; Formoso, Ruiz, & Gonzales, 1997; Rohner & Pettengill, 1985; Smetana & Gaines, 1999; Yau & Smetana, 1996). If researchers accustomed to studying White families focus too much on parents' strictness when observing family relationships, they may mislabel other ethnic groups' approaches to child rearing—which appear very controlling, but which are neither aloof nor hostile—as authoritarian when they are not (Gonzales et al., 1996).

Ethnic groups in the United States also differ in the expression of intimacy between adolescents and parents.

Some of these differences may have more to do with recency of immigration into the United States than with ethnicity per se. One study of late adolescents found that, for example, Vietnamese American and Chinese American individuals felt less comfortable talking to their parents about such intimate matters as sex or dating than did Filipino Americans or Mexican Americans, who in turn felt less comfortable than European Americans. The researchers speculated that these differences reflected ethnic differences in norms of formality in family relationships, especially in relationships between adolescents and their fathers (Cooper, Baker, Polichar, & Welsh, 1994). Other studies indicate that ethnic minority American adolescents, more than White adolescents, are likely to believe that it is important to respect, assist, and support their family (Fuligni, Tseng, & Lam, 1999), although ethnic differences in adolescents' *beliefs* and *expectations* appear to be more sizable than ethnic differences in how adolescents and their parents actually interact. Indeed, except for families who are recent immigrants to the United States, relations between American adolescents and their parents appear surprisingly similar across ethnic groups (Fuligni, 1998).

Relationships with Siblings

Less is known about adolescents' relations with their brothers and sisters than with their parents. During adolescence relationships with siblings, and especially with younger siblings, generally become more egalitarian but also more distant and less emotionally intense (Buhrmester & Furman, 1990; Cole & Kerns, 2001). Despite these changes, the quality of sibling relationships between childhood and adolescence remains remarkably stable, and siblings who are relatively closer during middle childhood also are relatively closer as young adolescents (Dunn, Slomkowski, & Beardsall, 1994).

Early adolescents commonly describe their relationships with siblings and with parents similarly in terms of power differentials and the degree to which the relationship provides assistance and satisfaction (Furman & Buhrmester, 1985; Raffaelli & Larson, 1987). By contrast, sibling relationships are perceived as more similar to friendships than to parent-adolescent relationships with respect to the provision of companionship and the importance of the relationship (Furman & Buhrmester, 1985; Raffaelli & Larson, 1987). As children mature from childhood to early adolescence, conflict increasingly typifies sibling relationships (Brody, Stoneman, &

McCoy, 1994), with adolescents reporting more negativity in their sibling relationships compared to their relationships with friends (Buhrmester & Furman, 1990). Negative interactions between siblings are especially common in families under economic stress (K. Conger, R. D. Conger, & Elder, 1994). Like conflicts in parent-adolescent relationships, high levels of sibling conflict in early adolescence gradually diminish as adolescents move into middle and late adolescence. As siblings mature, relations become more egalitarian and supportive, and, as with the parent-adolescent relationship, siblings become less influential as adolescents expand their relations outside the family (Hetherington et al., 1999).

Several researchers have uncovered important connections among parent-child, sibling, and peer relationships in adolescence. Extensive findings imply that the quality of parent-adolescent relationships may influence the quality of relations among adolescent siblings, which in turn influences adolescents' relationships with peers (e.g., Brody et al., 1994; MacKinnon-Lewis, Starnes, Volling, & Johnson, 1997; Paley, Conger, & Harold, 2000; Reese-Weber, 2000), though the causal status of these interrelations has yet to be conclusively documented. Harmony and cohesiveness in parent-adolescent relationships are associated with less sibling conflict and more positive sibling relationships, whereas adolescents who experience maternal rejection and negativity are more likely to display aggression with siblings (e.g., Hetherington et al., 1999). Moreover, children and adolescents learn much about social relationships from sibling interactions, and they may bring this knowledge and experience to friendships outside the family (Brody et al., 1994; McCoy, Brody, & Stoneman, 1994; Updegraff, McHale, & Crouter, 2000). In poorly functioning families, aggression between unsupervised siblings may provide a training ground for learning, practicing, and perfecting antisocial and aggressive behavior (Bank, Reid, & Greenley, 1994; Slomkowski, Rende, K. Conger, Simons, & R. Conger, 2001).

The quality of sibling relationships has been linked not only to adolescents' peer relations but also to their adjustment in general (Seginer, 1998; Stocker, Burwell, & Briggs, 2002). Positive sibling relationships contribute to adolescents' academic competence, sociability, autonomy, and self-worth (e.g., Hetherington et al., 1999; Rowe, Rodgers, Meseck-Bushey, & St. John, 1989). A close sibling relationship can partially ameliorate the negative effects of not having friends in school

(East & Rook, 1992), and siblings can serve as sources of advice and guidance (Tucker, Barber, & Eccles, 1997; Tucker, McHale, & Crouter, 2001). At the same time, siblings are often similar in problem behaviors (K. Conger, R. Conger, & Elder, 1997; Slomkowski et al., 2001), such as early sexual activity, early pregnancy (e.g., East & Jacobson, 2001; East & Kiernan, 2001), drug use, and antisocial behavior (e.g., Ardelt & Day, 2002; Bullock & Dishion, 2002; Rowe et al., 1989). These similarities raise the question of whether older siblings' problem behaviors are a risk factor for younger siblings.

As one might expect, unequal treatment from mothers or fathers often is associated with conflict among siblings (Brody, Stoneman, & Burke, 1987) and also with problematic individual outcomes such as depression and antisocial behavior (Reiss et al., 1995). Studies show that differences in siblings' real and perceived family experiences are related to different patterns of development (Anderson, Hetherington, Reiss, & Howe, 1994; Barrett Singer & Weinstein, 2000; K. Conger & R. Conger, 1994; Mekos, Hetherington, & Reiss, 1996). In general, better adjusted adolescents are more likely than their siblings to report that their relationship with their mother was close, their relations with brothers or sisters were friendly, they were involved in family decision making, and they were given a high level of responsibility around the house (Daniels, Dunn, Furstenberg, & Plomin, 1985). Studies show that youngsters, especially as they get older, generally appreciate the reasons why parents treat siblings differently and document that sibling relationships are strained only when this differential treatment is perceived as unfair (Feinberg, Neiderhiser, Simmens, Reiss, & Hetherington, 2000; Kowal & Kramer, 1997).

Extrafamilial Relationships and Influences

Relationships with peers differ from those with family members in the distribution of power between participants and the permanence of the affiliation (Laursen & Bukowski, 1997). Peer relationships, moreover, are voluntary and transitory; participants freely initiate and dissolve interconnections. Neither party in peer relationships can impose the terms of social interaction on the other (Piaget, 1932/1965); whether an affiliation persists hinges on mutually satisfactory terms and outcomes (Laursen & Hartup, 2002). These distinctive features of relationships among peers provide potentially important opportunities that differ from the socialization experiences that families provide and that are key to mastering skills for both independence and interdependence.

This section examines networks of relationships beyond the family. We emphasize the nature and significance of friendships and of romantic relationships during adolescence and also address the extent and implications of interrelations among personal relationships.

Social Networks and Social Status

Adolescents typically affiliate with one or more peer groups, which are commonly distinguished as *cliques* (relatively small networks of friends or persons sharing common interests or activities) or *crowds* (loose aggregations based on members' common reputations for certain attitudes, interests, or behaviors). Once formed, these groups tend to remain relatively closed to newcomers, although boundaries may become more permeable in the senior high school years. According to recent estimates, almost half of high school students are associated with one crowd, about one-third are associated with two or more crowds, and about one-sixth do not fit into any crowd (Strouse, 1999).

Cliques exist in childhood and adulthood, as well as adolescence. Adolescent cliques, however, differ from both childhood and adult cliques in the bases for membership, as well as the degree of "cliquishness." Although common interests and shared activities are important determinants of clique membership at all ages, cliques during adolescence also are important in establishing individuals' status in the social hierarchy of the high school (Eder, 1985).

In contrast, reputation-based crowds do not emerge until the early or middle adolescent years and typically become much less prominent by late adolescence. The emergence, ascendance, and decline of crowds may be linked to the normative course of adolescent psychosocial development. For example, crowds may serve as an identity "way station" or placeholder during the period between individuation from parents and establishment of a coherent personal identity (Newman & Newman, 2001). Adolescents who feel relatively more confident in their identity may consider crowd affiliations less important than those who are more uncertain. By high school, many adolescents report that being part of a crowd stifles identity and self-expression (Larkin, 1979; Varenne, 1982)—a perception that may account partly for the instability in crowd identification during

middle and late adolescence. Research with a national sample showed that two-thirds of individuals changed crowds between grades 10 and 12 (Kinney, 1993; Strouse, 1999).

Little is known about the long-term implications of identifying with particular crowds, with the exception of youth who belong to delinquent crowds (e.g., B. Brown et al., 1993; Cairns & Cairns, 1994; Dishion, 2000; Patterson, DeBaryshe, & Ramsey, 1989). Some writers argue that the tendency of group members to exaggerate the positive features of their own group while disparaging the features of others groups may be beneficial to identity development, whereas others deplore the same process as perpetuating socially dysfunctional in-group versus out-group patterns (e.g., Stone & Brown, 1998). Crowd membership has been linked to academic success and failure, which may constrain later developmentally important opportunities (B. Brown et al., 1993). A possible, but little examined, moderating factor in these outcomes is whether the crowds are specific to school contexts rather than out-of-school settings (Kiesner, Poulin, & Nicotra, 2003). Though suggestive, findings on sequelae of crowd membership during adolescence require more extensive and differentiated studies than are now available.

Friendships

The visibility of crowd memberships notwithstanding, friendships are arguably the most prominent and significant feature of social relationships during adolescence. Adolescents commonly report that friends are their most important extrafamilial resources and influences, and relationships with friends consistently are implicated in variations in adolescent competence and well-being (for reviews, see B. Brown, 2004; Hartup & Abecassis, 2002). Moreover, self-perceived competence in friendships is a significant component of overall competence during adolescence (Masten et al., 1995). Experiences with friends appear both to influence and moderate social adaptation and academic competence (Cairns & Cairns, 1994) and provide a prototype for later close relationships (Furman & Wehner, 1994; Sullivan, 1953).

The Identity of Friends

The broad outlines of friendship formation, processes, and links to individual development have been described extensively. Adolescents choose as friends other adolescents who are similar to them on some dimensions and dissimilar on others. For example, European Americans and Asian Americans have friends who are similar in substance use and academic orientation but dissimilar in the importance given to ethnicity in self-definition, whereas African American adolescents show the reverse pattern (Hamm, 2000). It may be that affiliating with others who are somewhat dissimilar is more comfortable for asserting and developing one's own identity. Such affiliative preferences may be somewhat fluid as adolescents engage and resolve identity issues. This fluidity, as well as school transitions and more diverse involvement in school and extracurricular activities (e.g., choices of courses, sports, or other activities), almost certainly contributes to the considerable instability in friendships during adolescence (Hardy, Bukowski, & Sippola, 2002; Way, Cowal, Gingold, Pahl, & Bissessar, 2001). Changing friendship patterns can be beneficial if an adolescents' new associates are more prosocial or espouse more positive goals than former associates did (e.g., Berndt, Hawkins, & Jiao, 1999; Mulvey & Aber, 1988).

Though less often studied than same-sex friendships, cross-sex friendships are a common experience in adolescence, with slightly fewer than half (47%) of adolescents reporting a cross-sex friendship (Kuttler, La Greca, & Prinstein, 1999). Acknowledging mixed-gender friendships in social groups is more common in adolescence than in middle childhood, when gender segregation is the norm in mixed-gender groups (Maccoby, 1990). Affiliations with other-sex, as well as same-sex, friends are correlated with self-perceived competence (Darling, Dowdy, Van Horn, & Caldwell, 1999).

Concepts of Friendship

The changing features of friendships during adolescence parallel increasingly complex and sophisticated beliefs about and expectations of friendships (Furman & Wehner, 1994; Selman, 1980; Youniss & Smollar, 1985). Adolescents increasingly regard companionship and sharing as a necessary, but no longer sufficient, condition for closeness in friendships; commitment and intimacy are expected as well, especially among females (Youniss & Smollar, 1985). For example, adolescents, more than children, view friends' behaviors and emotions as historical, biological, and social factors affecting the individual (Livesley & Bromley, 1973; Selman, 1980). This shift to more complex understanding of behavior between friends may account partly for adolescents' perceptions that their current friendship-making

abilities are inferior to their abilities in this domain in middle childhood (Barry & Wigfield, 2002).

Research on cognitive development and peer relationships has provided little compelling evidence regarding whether developmental changes in reasoning during early adolescence lead to changes in social competence or vice-versa or, even more likely, whether there is a reciprocal relationship between the two (for a review, see Eisenberg & Morris, 2004). For example, friendships become more intimate during adolescence in ways that imply improved perspective taking, abstract thinking, and meta-cognition (Savin-Williams & Berndt, 1990), but no study has yet made these connections explicit. Similarly, links between adolescents' understanding of the structure and organization of cliques and crowds undoubtedly depends on cognitive advances (B. Brown, 2004), although this relation has not been examined directly; neither do cross-sectional studies of individual differences in cognitive maturity typically inform questions about age differences, developmental change, or cause and effect.

Linking cognitive development to close relationships with peers is further complicated by the fact that adolescents' reasoning skills, like those of adults, often may be overridden in ambiguous or multifaceted situations or those to which stereotypes can be readily applied, so that both attentiveness to shared values and concerns can be undermined (Horn, 2003; Rest, 1983). Similarly, in studies of logical reasoning, easily accessible heuristics often trump logic (e.g., Klaczynski, 1997; Klaczynski & Gordon, 1996). Moreover, although adolescent changes are extensive and profound, conceptions of friendships now appear to remain malleable into the 20s. Conceptual refinements in late adolescence and the transition to early adulthood may reflect adjustments to the distinctive experiences of that period, which may require modifications to previously held expectations of friends (Baxter, Dun, & Sahlstein, 2001). Brain development that supports advances in executive regulatory functions and social information processing may account partly for the continued development of relationship-relevant cognitive skills as early adulthood nears (E. Nelson et al., 2005; Siegel, 1999).

Friendship Quality

Developmental changes in understanding of friendships is only one contrast between adolescents' friendships and children's friendships (Rubin, Bukowski, & Parker, 1998). Mutuality, self-disclosure, and intimacy (defined as reciprocal feelings of self-disclosure and shared activities) increase markedly (Furman & Buhrmester, 1992; Sharabany, Gershoni, & Hofmann, 1981) during adolescence. Intimacy in particular is related to satisfaction with friendships during early and middle adolescence (Hartup, 1996).

Paradoxically, conflicts also are more likely between friends than between acquaintances in both childhood and adolescence. Among adolescents, topics of conflict reflect current concerns, with older adolescents reporting more conflicts regarding disrespect in private interactions with peers, and young adolescents voicing more concern about instances of disrespect and undependability that occur in public (Shulman & Laursen, 2002). Still, compared to middle childhood conflicts with friends, conflicts decline during adolescence, and those that occur are increasingly likely to be resolved effectively and are less likely to disrupt relationships (Laursen & Collins, 1994; Laursen, Finkelstein, & Betts, 2001). Having primarily opposite-gender friends may signal social incompetence and rejection by same-gender peers for some adolescents, but may be a marker of a high level of social competence and acceptance in the peer group for others (Bukowski, Sippola, & Hoza, 1999). The quality of friendships of mixed-gender friendships appears to differentiate among these relationships more for boys than the converse. Boys describe their friendships with girls as more rewarding than their friendships with other boys, but girls do not report more satisfying friendships with boys than with other girls (J. Thomas & Daubman, 2001), perhaps because friendships with girls tend to be generally more intimate and supportive than friendships with boys (Kuttler et al., 1999).

Developmental Significance

Interest in adolescents' friendships has thrived largely because consistent findings attest that friendships are developmentally significant features of adolescent experience (for reviews, see Hartup, 1996; Hartup & Abecassis, 2002). The line of reasoning that emerges from these findings is as follows: Friendships are primary settings for the acquisition of skills, ranging from social competencies to motor performance (e.g., athletics, dancing) to cognitive abilities (Hartup, 1996). Poor quality adolescent friendships (e.g., those low in supportiveness and intimacy) are associated with multiple outcomes, including incidence of loneliness, depression, and decreases in achievement in school and work settings (Hartup, 1996). Difficult, conflictful relations

with peers, especially if chronic in an individual's history, have been linked persistently to negative personal and social characteristics of the individuals involved (e.g., Abecassis, Hartup, Haselager, Scholte, & van Lieshout, 2002).

During adolescence, perceptions of parents as primary sources of support decline and perceived support from friends increases, such that friendships are perceived as providing roughly the same (Helsen, Vollebergh, & Meeus, 2000; Scholte, van Lieshout, & van Aken, 2001) or greater (Furman & Buhrmester, 1992) support as parental relationships. High-quality friendships become increasingly important as sources of support for adolescents' experiencing emotional problems. Recent findings have documented that adolescents receiving little support from parents and greater support from friends report more emotional problems (Helsen et al., 2000). These results are consonant with other findings showing stronger contributions of parental than peer relationships to increased risk for depression among youth at risk for affective problems (Aseltine, Gore, & Colten, 1994). Of the relatively few studies that address both parent and peer influences, however, few have considered possibilities other than simple additive ones. One exception to this shows that parental involvement with adolescents moderates the peer influences on drinking behavior (Wood, Read, Mitchell, & Brand, 2004). In an area long dominated by simplistic views of parent-peer cross-pressures on adolescent behavior, more nuanced views are both eminently plausible and badly needed.

Gender-Related Patterns

Gender differences are integral to friendship expectations of both children and adolescents (Markovits, Benenson, & Dolenszky, 2001). Indeed, girls typically report greater companionship, intimacy, prosocial support and esteem support in their close friendships than boys do (Kuttler et al., 1999). Closeness to friends, however, may create a vulnerability that could account for some negative features of girls' relationships. For example, females' current friendships tend to be of shorter duration than males' friendships, and more females than males report both actions that have harmed existing friendships and histories of dissolved friendships (Benenson & Christakos, 2003). The greater emotional intensity of girls', as compared to boys', friendships and the resulting potential vulnerability when friendship ends have been hypothesized as risk factors for depression and as one explanation for the emergence of gender differences in internalized distress during adolescence (Cyranowski et al., 2000).

Summary Comment

Despite its salience in research, the topic of friendships as a feature of interpersonal contexts during adolescence is still in an early stage. Much important descriptive work has been done, to be sure, but studies of explanatory processes are still lacking. Among the questions requiring more urgent attention are those involving group differences (e.g., gender and racial-ethnic variations in friendship) and individual differences (e.g., the friendships of high-functioning, well adjusted adolescents versus the relationships of adolescents who appear to be less well adjusted) in the nature and significance of close friendships.

Romantic Relationships

Romantic interests are both normative and salient during the adolescent years. In the United States, 25% of 12-year-olds report having had a romantic relationship in the past 18 months; by age 18, more than 70% do (Carver, Joyner, & Udry, 2003). Zani (1991) reported similar rates of involvement for studies of European youth. Despite the obvious centrality of these relationships, however, research on adolescent romantic relationships was both meager and superficial until the last decade of the twentieth century. This section distills key points from this currently burgeoning area of study.

Contexts of Romantic Development

Romantic feelings and the initiation of dating commonly have been attributed to hormonal changes. Most current findings imply that, however, the growing nature and significance of romantic relationships during adolescence and early adulthood stem as much from a culture that emphasizes and hallows romance and sexuality as from physical maturation. Social and cultural expectations, especially age-graded behavioral norms, independently influence the initiation of dating (Dornbusch et al., 1981; Feldman, Turner, & Araujo, 1999; Meschke & Silbereisen, 1997).

Relationships with peers are a primary context for the transmission and realization of these expectations (B. Brown, 2004; Giordano, 2003). Adolescents regard being in a romantic relationship as central to "belonging" and status in the peer group (Connolly, Craig, Goldberg, & Pepler, 1999; Levesque, 1993). The link

may be a transactional one: Peer networks support early romantic coupling, and romantic relationships facilitate connections with other peers (Connolly, Furman, & Konarski, 2000; Milardo, 1982; for reviews, see B. Brown, 2004; Furman, 1999; Giordano, 2003). Other studies have documented the impact of the extensiveness of peer networks for involvement in dating (Connolly & Johnson, 1996; Taradash, Connolly, Pepler, Craig, & Costa, 2001).

Mixed-gender peer groups appear to be especially significant settings for the development of romantic relationships. Several scholars have recently documented the role of these groups (Connolly, Craig, Goldberg, & Pepler, 2004; Connolly et al., 2000; Feiring, 1999; for reviews, see B. Brown, 2004; Collins & Van Dulmen, 2006b; Giordano, 2003). According to Connolly et al. (2004), among fifth and eighth graders, participation in mixed-gender peer groups normatively preceded involvement in dyadic romantic relationships. This progression partly reflects the tendency to incorporate dating activities with mixed-gender affiliations. For these young adolescents, group-based romantic activities were more stable than other dating contexts. At the same time, being with mixed-gender groups promotes proximity and common ground that enhance two adolescents' attraction to each other (Connolly & Goldberg, 1999).

Developmental Course

By middle adolescence, most individuals have been involved in at least one romantic relationship; and, by the early years of early adulthood, most are currently participating in an ongoing romantic relationship (Carver et al., 2003). Middle and late adolescents (approximately, ages 14 to 18) balance time spent with romantic partners with continued participation in same-sex cliques, gradually decreasing time in mixed-sex groups; by early adulthood, time with romantic partners increases further at the expense of involvement with friends and crowds (Reis, Lin, Bennett, & Nezlek, 1993).

Most current findings portray normative experiences of adolescent romance as part of a continuous progression toward the romantic relationships of adulthood. After age 17, adolescents are no more or less likely to be involved in a romantic relationship than at earlier ages (Collins & Van Dulmen, 2006a). Older adolescents, however, tend to emphasize personal compatibility rather than focusing solely on superficial features of appearance and social status (Levesque, 1993); and couple interactions often are marked by greater interdependence and more communal orientations than was the case in early adolescent relationships (Laursen & Jensen-Campbell, 1999). In general, differences between mid-adolescents and 25-year-olds reflect increasing differentiation and complexity of thoughts about romantic relationships but continuity in relationship motives, concerns, and expectations. In a longitudinal analysis of relationship narratives (Waldinger et al., 2002), the structure and complexity of narratives increased between middle adolescence and age 25, whereas narrative themes were surprisingly similar across the 8- to 10-year gap between waves of the study. A desire for closeness was a dominant theme in the relationships of participants at both ages. Themes of distance also were present at both ages, although in adolescence this theme was characterized by actually being on one's own, whereas at age 25 the emphasis was on making autonomous decisions. Because U.S. respondents are highly likely to reflect the wish for independence throughout adulthood, these findings imply greater continuity than discontinuity between early adults and both foregoing and succeeding periods, although explicit comparisons have not yet been reported.

Developmental Significance

Accumulating findings imply that variations in qualities of dating and romantic relationships are associated with psychosocial development during adolescence (Furman & Shaffer, 2003). Variations in the *timing* of involvement in both romantic relationships and sexual activity also have been linked to adolescent behavior and development. Findings typically have identified early dating and sexual activity as risk factors for current and later problem behaviors and social and emotional difficulties (e.g., Davies & Windle, 2000; Zimmer-Gembeck, Siebenbruner, & Collins, 2001). At the same time, having a romantic relationship and having a relationship of high quality are associated positively with romantic self-concept and, in turn, with feelings of self-worth (Connolly & Konarski, 1994; Kuttler et al., 1999); longitudinal evidence indicates that, by late adolescence, self-perceived competence in romantic relationships emerges as a reliable component of general competence (Masten et al., 1995). Several writers have suggested that romantic relationships may be implicated in key processes of identity formation during adolescence, though no research currently supports this hypothesis (e.g., Furman & Shaffer, 2003; Sullivan, 1953). The findings linking adolescent romantic relationships and psychosocial development generally do not substantiate

causal connections between the two, though correlational findings document associations that should be explained. For example, longitudinal research with a German sample (Seiffge-Krenke & Lang, 2002) showed that quality of romantic relationships in middle adolescence was significantly and positively related to commitment in other relationships in early adulthood.

The developmental significance of romantic relationships depends more heavily on the behavioral, cognitive, and emotional processes that occur in the relationship than on the age of initiation and the degree of dating activity that a young person experiences (Collins, 2003). Interactions with romantic partners are associated with distinctive patterns of experience for adolescents. Adolescents in romantic relationships, for example, report experiencing more conflict than other adolescents (Laursen, 1995). Moreover, conflict resolution between late-adolescent romantic partners more often involves compromise than does conflict resolution in early adolescent romantic pairs (Feldman & Gowen, 1998). Mood swings, a stereotype of adolescent emotional life, are more extreme for those involved in romantic relationships (Larson, Clore, & Wood, 1999). Participants in the National Longitudinal Study of Adolescent Health who had begun romantic relationships in the past year manifested more symptoms of depression than adolescents not in romantic relationships (Joyner & Udry, 2000). This elevation may be due to breakups, rather than to involvement in a romantic relationship per se. Indeed, the most common trigger of the first episode of a major depressive disorder is a romantic breakup (Monroe, Rohde, Seeley, & Lewinsohn, 1999).

Little information is available on how time devoted to romantic relationships is spent or how teenage romantic partners behave toward one another. Without such information, it is difficult to identify possible functions of the relationships, whether positive or negative, for long-term growth (Collins, 2003).

Individual Differences

Variations in relationship expectancies reflect prior relationship experiences. Adolescents who have poor relationships with parents and peers appear to be at risk for later physical and relational aggression with romantic partners (J. R. Linder & Collins, 2005; J. L. Linder, Crick, & Collins, 2002). Moreover, the cognitive and behavioral syndrome known as *rejection sensitivity* arises from experiences of rejection in parent-child relationships and also in relations with peers and, possibly, romantic partners. Rejection sensitivity in turn predicts expectancies of rejection that correlate strongly with both actual rejection and lesser satisfaction in subsequent relationships (Downey, Bonica, & Rincon, 1999). Similarly, individual differences in the history of attachment security in relationships with caregivers in early life and in accounts of those relationships in early adulthood are correlated with characteristics of romantic relationships in early adulthood (Collins & Van Dulmen, 2006b). Other individual differences play a role as well. Initial findings (e.g., Connolly & Konarski, 1994) imply that adolescent relationships parallel adult relationships in the relevance of individual partners' self-esteem, self-confidence, and physical attractiveness to the timing, frequency, duration, and quality of relationships (Long, 1989; Mathes, Adams, & Davies, 1985; Samet & Kelly, 1987).

Summary Comment

B. Brown (2004) has observed that neither affiliations nor close relationships with peers, whether friends or romantic partners, can be regarded as uniformly positive or negative influences in adolescent development. This conclusion echoes Hartup's (1996) influential appraisal that the nature and extent of impact is not a main effect of whether an adolescent has mutual relationships with other adolescents, but is moderated significantly by the identity of the other and the quality of the relationships. This relatively recent realization promises both a more complex and more informative recognition of the relevance of peers and romantic partners to adolescent development.

Interrelations of Relationships

Adolescents' relationships with family members and with peers become increasingly interrelated over time. Despite the stereotype of incompatible or contradictory influences of parents and friends, parent-child relationships set the stage for both the selection of friends and the management of these relationships (Parke & Buriel, 1998). Links between qualities of friendships and romantic relationships, as well as between family and romantic relationships, are equally impressive (Collins, Hennighausen, et al., 1997). At the same time, relationships with parents, friends, and romantic partners serve overlapping, but distinctive, functions. Typical exchanges in each of these types of dyads differ accordingly. Displaying safe-haven and secure-base behaviors with best friends is associated positively with displaying

these behaviors with dating partners. Perhaps, the growing importance of romantic relationships makes the common relationship properties across types of relationships more apparent than before. Equally likely, the parallels between early adults' relationships reflect their common similarity to prior relationships with parents and peers (Owens, Crowell, Treboux, O'Connor, & Pan, 1995; Waters, Merrick, Treboux, & Albersheim, 2000).

Similarity, however, is not the only indicator of relations among these relationships. For example, adolescents with insecure or otherwise unsatisfying relationships with parents initiate dating and sexual activity earlier than adolescents with more positive family relationships. The quality of these apparently compensatory early involvements, however, is typically poorer than that of extrafamilial relationships for youth with more beneficent family histories (Collins & Van Dulmen, 2006b). In comparison to childhood relationships, the diminished distance and greater intimacy in adolescents' peer relationships may both satisfy affiliative needs and also contribute to socialization for relations among equals. Intimacy with parents provides nurturance and support but may be less important than friendships for socialization to roles and expectations in late adolescence and early adulthood (Collins & Laursen, 2004a; Laursen & Bukowski, 1997). As noted earlier, research also points to important interrelations among adolescents' relationships with siblings and with friends. The nature and processes of these developmentally significant interrelations of relationships promise to become an increasingly prominent focus of future research.

SOCIAL INSTITUTIONS AS CONTEXTS FOR ADOLESCENT PSYCHOSOCIAL DEVELOPMENT

Relationships with family members, friends, and romantic partners exist in a broader context of social institutions that also contribute to psychosocial development. These contributions are largely mediated through close relationships. These relationships also may moderate the impact of contexts on adolescents. Parent-adolescent and peer relationships in dangerous neighborhoods, for instance, appear to differ from those in safe ones, and the organization of schools with respect to age-grading and school transitions may strongly affect the structure, nature, and importance of peer relationships. This section outlines the role of neighborhoods, schools, and social settings that potentially transform the interpersonal worlds of adolescents.

Neighborhoods

Research on the ways in which neighborhoods influence adolescent development has expanded greatly since 1990 (Leventhal & Brooks-Gunn, 2004). The main challenge in research on neighborhood influences is demonstrating that neighborhood conditions affect adolescents' development above and beyond the influence of proximal contexts such as families and peer groups. These efforts typically require comparing adolescents whose family situations are similar, but who live in very different types of neighborhoods. In addition, a few researchers have tracked the psychological development and behavior of adolescents before and after their families moved from a poor neighborhood into a more advantaged one (e.g., Ludwig, Duncan, & Hirschfield, 2001).

Most research has focused on the effects of neighborhood poverty, although other characteristics of neighborhoods (e.g., the ethnic composition, crime rate, or availability of social service programs) potentially impinge on adolescents' relationships and development (Brooks-Gunn, Duncan, Klebanov, & Sealand, 1993; Coulton & Pandey, 1992; Duncan, 1994; Ensminger, Lamkin, & Jacobson, 1996; Sampson, 1997). Evidence from both cross-sectional and longitudinal studies documents the negative effects of poor neighborhoods on behavior and mental health, above and beyond effects attributable to family poverty or attending an underfunded school. Adolescents from impoverished urban communities are more likely than adolescents from equally poor households in better neighborhoods to bear children as teenagers, to become involved in criminal activity, and to achieve less in high school (Leventhal & Brooks-Gunn, 2004). Findings generally support the inference that it is the absence of affluent neighbors, rather than the presence of poor neighbors, which elevates risks for adolescents from impoverished communities (Duncan, 1994; Ensminger et al., 1996; Leventhal & Brooks-Gunn, 2004). Although virtually all neighborhood research has focused on urban adolescents, growing up in poor *rural* communities also appears harmful to adolescents' development and well-being (McLoyd, 1990), but whether the effects of urban and rural poverty reflect the same processes is not known.

Three different mechanisms have been suggested by which neighborhood conditions affect the behavior and development of adolescents (Leventhal & Brooks-Gunn, 2004). First, neighborhood conditions shape the norms that guide individuals' values and behaviors. Poverty in neighborhoods breeds social isolation and social disorganization, undermining a neighborhood's sense of "collective efficacy" (the extent to which neighbors trust each other, share common values, and can count on each other to monitor the activities of youth in the community; Sampson, Raudenbush, & Earls, 1997). As a consequence, deviant peer groups more readily form and influence the behavior of adolescents in these communities. Rates of teen pregnancy, school failure, and antisocial behavior are all higher in neighborhoods in which collective efficacy is low (J. Ainsworth, 2002; N. Bowen, G. Bowen, & Ware, 2002; G. Bowen & Chapman, 1996; Brooks-Gunn et al., 1993; Herrenkohl et al., 2000; Paschall & Hubbard, 1998; Sampson, 1997; Sampson & Laub, 1994; Simons, Johnson, Beaman, R. Conger, & Whitbeck, 1996; Tolan, Gorman-Smith, & Henry, 2003). Some writers (e.g., Crane, 1991; Simons et al., 1996) further suggest that social problems are contagious under conditions of low collective efficacy. For example, adolescents who associate with delinquent peers are more likely to be drawn into criminal and delinquent activity (Simons et al., 1996). Similarly, adolescents who live in neighborhoods with high rates of teenage childbearing encounter relatively greater tolerance of this behavior, which in turn can affect their own attitudes toward premarital childbearing (Baumer & South, 2001; South & Baumer, 2000).

Second, stressors associated with neighborhood poverty undermine the quality of parenting in families, potentially affecting adolescent development adversely. Across all ethnic groups, poverty has been linked to harsh, inconsistent, and punitive parenting (Bradley, Corwyn, Burchinal, McAdoo, & García Coll, 2001; R. Conger et al., 1992; McLoyd, 1990; Patterson, Reid, & Dishion, 1992; Ramirez-Valles, Zimmerman, & Juarez, 2002; Simons et al., 1996). Ineffective parental supervision and low levels of adult social support, in turn, are associated with antisocial activity (G. Bowen & Chapman, 1996; Hoffman, 2003; Lynam et al., 2000; McCabe, Barnett, & Robbins, 1996). Furthermore, adolescents in poor neighborhoods frequently are exposed to chronic community violence, which increases the risk of behavioral and emotional problems (Biafora, Warheit, Vega, & Gil, 1994; DuRant, Cadenhead, Pendergrast, Slavens, & Linder, 1994; Osofsky, 1997; Stevenson, 1998; Vermeiren, Ruchkin, Leckman, Deboutte, & Schwab-Stone, 2002).

Third, adolescents in poor neighborhoods have access to fewer resources than do those who grow up in more advantaged communities. As a result, adolescents in poor communities have fewer opportunities to engage in activities that facilitate positive development and lower likelihood of receiving assistance when they are having difficulties (Leventhal & Brooks-Gunn, 2004); adolescents in communities with relatively greater resources, such as higher quality schools, are at lower risk for antisocial behavior (Kowaleski-Jones, 2000). Moreover, in neighborhoods with higher levels of resources and greater feelings of cohesion, adults' beliefs about teenagers tend to be more favorable, probably because the casual interactions between adults and adolescents in these settings are more positive than the interactions in less advantaged environments (Zeldin & Topitzes, 2002).

Although experts agree that neighborhoods exert an impact on adolescent behavior and development, the estimated strength of neighborhood influences is fairly modest once the likely contributions of other, more proximal influences are taken into account. Furthermore, most of the impact of neighborhoods on adolescent development appears to be indirect, transmitted through social relationships in families, peer groups, or schools (D. Jones, Forehand, Brody, & Armistead, 2002; Schwartz, Hopmeyer-Gorman, Toblin, & Abou-ezzeddine, 2003; Teitler & Weiss, 2000). Studying relevant mediating processes and those through which neighborhood conditions moderate the impact of relationships on adolescent development is likely to be more fruitful than searching for direct neighborhood effects. It is worth noting that the cumulative impact of multiple contexts appears to matter more than any single context alone in explaining why some adolescents are more successful than others (T. Cook, Herman, Phillips, & Settersten, 2002). Simply put, the greater number of positive features an adolescent's environment contains, the better off he or she will be; conversely, the more sources of contextual risk adolescents are exposed to, the greater their chances of developing problems (Gutman, Sameroff, & Eccles, 2002; Herrenkohl et al., 2000; D. Jones et al., 2002).

Schools

Adolescents in industrialized societies typically change schools at least once during their teenage years, and researchers have devoted considerable attention to the nature and impact of school transitions. Research suggests that school transitions can disrupt the academic performance, behavior, and self-image of adolescents, but this disruption generally appears temporary. Over time, most youngsters adapt successfully to changing schools, especially when other contexts—family and peer relationships, for example—remain stable and supportive and when the new school environment is well suited for adolescents (Anderman & Midgley, 1996; DuBois, Eitel, & Felner, 1994; Gillock & Reyes, 1996; Koizumi, 1995; Lord, Eccles, & McCarthy, 1994; Teachman, Paasch, & Carver, 1996; Wigfield & Eccles, 1994).

Not all students experience the same degree of stress when changing schools (Fenzel, 2001; Roeser, Eccles, & Freedman-Doan, 1999). Students who have more academic and psychosocial problems before making a school transition cope less successfully with it (Anderman, 1998; Berndt & Mekos, 1995; E. Carlson et al., 1999; Murdock, Anderman, & Hodge, 2000; Roeser et al., 1999; Safer, 1986). More vulnerable adolescents, those with fewer sources of social support, and those moving into more impersonal schools may be relatively more susceptible to the adverse consequences of changing schools. Poor inner-city youngsters appear to be especially likely to show transition-related negative decrements in self-esteem, achievement, classroom preparation, perceptions of the school environment, reports of social support, and participation in extracurricular activities (Eccles, 2004; Seidman, Aber, Allen, & French, 1996; Seidman, Allen, Aber, Mitchell, & Feinman, 1994). Interpersonal relationships play a role, as well. Adolescents who have close friends before and during the transition tend to adapt more successfully to the new school, although the benefits of staying with one's friends may accrue only to students who had been doing well previously; students who had been doing poorly adjust better if they enroll in a different school, away from their friends (Schiller, 1999).

One of the most commonly reported findings on adolescent school transitions is that students' academic motivation and school grades drop as they move into middle or junior high school (Eccles, 2004; Gentry, Gable, & Rizza, 2002; Gutman & Midgley, 2000; Murdock et al., 2000). Students' self-esteem also declines during this transition but increases somewhat during the early high school years. These findings suggest that the initial decline reflects students' temporary difficulties in adapting to the shift from an elementary to a secondary school environment (Wigfield, Eccles, Mac Iver, Reuman, & Midgley, 1991). Several features of secondary schools may be involved. Because scores on standardized achievement tests do not decline during this same time, the decline in school grades may reflect changes in grading practices and student motivation rather than in students' knowledge or ability. Some difficulties may stem primarily from the failure of middle and junior high schools to meet the particular developmental needs of young adolescents. Eccles (2004; Eccles, Lord, & Midgley, 1991; Eccles et al., 1993; Roeser et al., 1999) has argued that junior high schools are larger and less personal than elementary schools and that, moreover, middle and junior high school teachers hold different beliefs about students than do elementary school teachers—even when they teach students of the same chronological age (Midgley, Berman, & Hicks, 1995). Teachers in junior high schools are less likely to trust their students and more likely to emphasize discipline, which creates a mismatch between what students at this age desire (more independence) and what their teachers provide (more control). Further, junior high teachers tend more than others to believe that students' abilities are fixed and not easily modified through instruction—a belief that interferes with their students' achievement (Eccles, 2004).

Eccles' findings are consonant with findings that adolescents attending more personal, less departmentalized schools do better than those in more rigid and more anonymous schools (Lee & J. Smith, 1993). Generally, changing schools also is easier on students who move into small rather than large institutions (Russell, Elder, & Conger, 1997). Moreover, studies of the immediate classroom environment indicate that the same factors that influence positive adolescent adjustment at home are important at school. Students achieve and are engaged more in school when they attend schools that are both responsive and demanding. In addition, academic functioning and psychological adjustment each affect the other, so that a school climate in which teachers are supportive and relationships between students and teachers are positive, but also demanding, enhances both adolescents' psychological well-being and their achievement (Blum & Rinehart, 2000; Eccles, 2004; Gutierrez, 2000; Phillips, 1997; Roeser & Eccles, 1998; Roeser, Eccles, & Sameroff, 1998). Both students and teachers are more satisfied in classes that combine a moderate degree of structure with high student involvement and high teacher support, a finding that has emerged in studies of both White and non-White students (Langer, 2001; Wentzel, 2002). Students in classes that are too task oriented, especially when they also emphasize teacher control, tend to feel anxious, uninter-

ested, and unhappy (Moos, 1978). Students in schools in which teachers are supportive but firm and maintain high, well-defined standards for behavior and academic work have stronger bonds to their school and more positive achievement motives; these beliefs and emotions, in turn, lead to fewer problems, better attendance, lower rates of delinquency, more supportive friendships, and higher scores on tests of achievement (Eccles, 2004; Roeser et al., 1998; A. Ryan & Patrick, 2001; Way & Pahl, 2001).

The Workplace

Most American adolescents—a far larger proportion than elsewhere in the world—hold paid jobs during the school year. For example, about three-quarters of American high school juniors hold jobs during the school year, whereas only one-quarter of Japanese and Taiwanese juniors do (Larson & Verma, 1999). Paid employment during the school year is even rarer in most European countries and virtually nonexistent in many, such as France, Hungary, Russia, and Switzerland; in European countries where adolescents are employed during the school year, they tend to work very few hours each week and are employed in more informal jobs, like babysitting (Flammer & Schaffner, 2003). Although European adolescents are less likely than their American counterparts to hold paying part-time jobs during the school year, they are more likely to work in school-sponsored or government-sponsored apprenticeships (Hamilton & Hamilton, 2004; Kantor, 1994; Mortimer, 2003).

Most employed students spend considerable amounts of time in the workplace. Not surprisingly, the impact of paid employment on the psychosocial development of adolescents has been the focus of numerous studies (see Staff, Mortimer, & Uggen, 2004, for a detailed review). This research has addressed three broad questions: (1) whether working helps adolescents develop a sense of responsibility; (2) whether working interferes with other activities, such as school or extracurricular participation; and (3) whether working promotes the development of negative behaviors, such as drug and alcohol use. Most research has been cross-sectional, but several longitudinal studies of the impact of employment on adolescent development have distinguished between characteristics of adolescents that predict entry into the labor force versus characteristics that appear to develop as a consequence of employment. Generally, the effects of employment largely depend on the number of hours worked each week rather than the type of job held. Several studies suggest deleterious consequences of employment when time at work exceeds 20 hours per week. In smaller doses, however, working seems to have neither a positive or negative effect on adolescents' psychological development (for a recent review, see Staff et al., 2004).

With respect to the questions that have driven research on adolescent work, research findings provide no support for the popular belief that holding a job fosters the development of responsibility or other positive aspects of psychosocial development (Mortimer & Johnson, 1998; Steinberg et al., 1993; Wright, Cullen, & Williams, 1997). Indeed, adolescents who have jobs are more likely than nonworkers to express cynical attitudes toward work and to endorse unethical business practices (Steinberg, Greenberger, Garduque, Ruggiero, & Vaux, 1982). Although working may help adolescents become more responsible when their work makes a genuine contribution to their family's welfare, as it often did during the Great Depression (Elder, 1974), most contemporary adolescents work mainly to earn their own spending money.

Regarding the impact of working on adolescents' involvement in other activities, most notably schooling, findings show unequivocally that adolescents who work long hours are absent from school more often, are less likely to participate in extracurricular activities, report enjoying school less, spend less time on their homework, and earn lower grades. Although the impact on students' actual grades and achievement test scores is small (Barton, 1989), students who work a great deal report paying less attention in class, exerting less effort on their studies, and skipping class more frequently (Steinberg & Dornbusch, 1991). These results occur both because youngsters who are less interested in school choose to work longer hours and because working long hours leads to disengagement from school—meaning that intensive employment during the school year most threatens the school performance of those students who can least afford to have their academic performance decline (Mihalic & Elliott, 1997; Schoenhals, Tienda, & Schneider, 1998; Steinberg & Cauffman, 1995; Warren, 2002).

Regarding the impact of working on negative behavior and adjustment, evidence suggests links between working long hours and increases in aggression, school misconduct, precocious sexual activity, and minor delinquency (Gottfredson, 1985; Rich & S. Kim, 2002; Wright et al., 1997). Smoking, drinking, and drug use are also higher among teenage workers than nonworkers, especially among students who work long hours (e.g., Bachman & Schulenberg, 1993; Mihalic & Elliott, 1997; Mortimer & Johnson, 1998; Steinberg et al., 1993; Wu, Schlenger, & Galvin, 2003).

Leisure Settings

Adolescents in industrialized societies have a considerable amount of time to devote to activities of their choosing. Although systematic research on the ways in which leisure influences adolescent development has begun only recently (J. Brown & Cantor, 2000; Larson & Verma, 1999; Roberts, Henriksen, & Foehr, 2004; Staff et al., 2004; Verma & Larson, 2003), it is apparent that, for U.S. adolescents, leisure typically occupies more waking hours (between 40% and 50%) than do school and work combined (between 35% and 40%; Larson, 2000). Teenagers spend more time in leisure activities than they do in school-related activities, more time alone than with members of their family, and considerably more time "wired" to music, the Internet, or television than "tuned into" the classroom (Csikszentmihalyi & Larson, 1984; Roberts et al., 2004; Shanahan & Flaherty, 2001; Staff et al., 2004).

Use of free time varies widely among individuals. In one study of American youth that tracked time use over the high school years (Shanahan & Flaherty, 2001), several distinct groups of students emerged. One especially busy group (about one-third of the sample in all grades) spent considerable time in a wide range of activities, including extracurricular activities, paid work, schoolwork, time with friends, and household chores. A second group, which made up about one-fourth of the sample, was similarly busy but did not hold a paying job. A third group, whose numbers increased from about 12% in the ninth grade to 20% in the 12th grade, devoted substantial time to a paying job but spent little time on other activities. A fourth group (roughly 20%) did not spend time in work or extracurricular activities but spent a substantial amount of time socializing with friends. Although adolescents' time use patterns changed somewhat with age, individuals who were busy at the beginning of high school typically were likely to be busy throughout high school. Overall, the results suggest that adolescents' free time is not best thought of as a "zero-sum" phenomenon, where involvement in one activity necessarily displaces involvement in another. Rather, there are very busy, well-rounded adolescents, who have substantial time commitments across many different activities, and not-so-busy adolescents, who do not. Generally, the relatively busier adolescents also were better adjusted and more achievement-oriented than their classmates, but whether their better adjustment caused or resulted from their busy schedules could not be determined.

Adolescents choose their leisure activities, whereas their time at school and work mainly is dictated by others (e.g., teachers or supervisors); not surprisingly, studies show that adolescents report being in a better mood during leisure activities than during school or work (Csikszentmihalyi & Larson, 1984). Leisure activities that are both structured and voluntary (e.g., sports, hobbies, artistic activities, or clubs) seem to carry special benefits for adolescents' psychological well-being (Larson, 2000). When in school, adolescents report moderate levels of concentration but very low levels of motivation or interest in what they are doing. With friends and when participating in unstructured leisure activities (e.g., watching TV), teenagers report moderate levels of motivation and interest but low levels of concentration. It is only when adolescents are playing sports or involved in the arts, a hobby, or some sort of extracurricular organization that they report high levels of *both* concentration and interest. Participation in structured leisure activities, such as hobbies or sports, has been shown to be the most positive way for adolescents to spend free time, in terms of their psychological development (McHale, Crouter, & Tucker, 2001).

Researchers have spent considerable time studying links between extracurricular participation and psychological development, but firm conclusions are difficult because few studies separate cause and effect. For example, although researchers generally find that extracurricular participants have higher self-esteem than nonparticipants, it is not clear whether students with high self-esteem are simply more likely to volunteer for extracurricular activities, whether participation makes students feel better about themselves, or whether some other factor (e.g., having positive family relationships) is associated both with extracurricular participation and with better mental health (Gore, Farrell, & Gordon, 2001; Spreitzer, 1994). Findings from the few studies that tracked students over time imply that participation in an extracurricular activity—especially in athletics or fine arts—improves students' performance in school and reduces the likelihood of dropping out; deters delinquency, drug use, and other types of risk taking; and enhances students' psychological well-being and social

status (Broh, 2002; Eder & Kinney, 1995; Mahoney & Cairns, 1997; J. McNeal, 1995; Savage & Holcomb, 1999). Extracurricular activities are especially beneficial among adolescents whose network of friends also participates in the same activity—an indicator, perhaps, of membership in a peer group that is involved in prosocial activities that revolve around the school (Mahoney, 2000). Finally, extracurricular activities may foster psychosocial development because of the opportunities for relationships with adults such as coaches or mentors. Although this possibility has received scant attention from researchers, recent studies show that the development of close relationships with nonfamilial adults is a normative and beneficial part of adolescence in many communities (Beam, Chen, & Greenberger, 2002; Greenberger, Chen, & Beam, 1998; Rhodes, Grossman, & Resche, 2000).

The impact of the media on teenagers' behavior and development has been the subject of extensive debate but little conclusive scientific research. One formidable problem in interpreting studies of media use and adolescent development is the difficulty of disentangling cause and effect, because adolescents *choose* which mass media they are exposed to (Roberts et al., 2004). Thus, although studies have documented that adolescents who watch a lot of television and movies are significantly more troubled (e.g., bored, unhappy, and in trouble at home or school) than adolescents who watch less often, it is not known whether large doses of mass media cause problems; more plausibly, adolescents with more problems watch more TV, perhaps as a way of distracting themselves from their troubles (Roberts & Foehr, 2003). Similarly, although students who watch relatively more TV and videos and listen to relatively more music earn lower grades in school than their peers, it is impossible to say whether high media use leads to poor school performance, results from poor school performance, or is correlated with poor school performance because of some other factor (e.g., adolescents with poor family relationships both watch a lot of TV and do badly in school).

These inferential problems notwithstanding, a few generalizations about media usage and adolescent development have enough supportive evidence, however indirect, to generate some consensus among experts in the area. Most of the relevant research has focused on television, and the bulk of the research has focused on the three topics: sex, violence, and drugs. Exposure of adolescents to programs with sex, violence, and drug use is considerable (Roberts et al., 2004).

Studies that unequivocally demonstrate that exposure to messages about sex, violence, and drugs causes changes in adolescents' behavior, however, are rare. The strongest evidence is in the area of violence; numerous studies have shown that repeated exposure to violent imagery on television leads to aggressive behavior in children and youth, especially among those who have prior histories of aggression (e.g., Johnson, Cohen, Smailes, Kasen, & Brook, 2002). Exposure to violence has been linked conclusively—though not exclusively—to aggressive behavior toward others, heightened tolerance of violence, and greater desensitization to the effects of violence on others (Cantor, 2000; Roberts et al., 2004). Data linking exposure to messages about sex and drugs to actual sexual activity or drug use are less compelling than those linking violence and aggressive behavior (Strasburger & Donnerstein, 1999).

Summary Comment

In general, research on institutional and leisure-time influences on adolescents and the relationships of which they are part documents forces that often determine the nature and extent of interpersonal influences in adolescent development. In some cases (e.g., the contributions of neighborhoods), contexts constrain or amplify dyadic and group effects. In others (e.g., leisure, media use), largely extrarelational experiences directly contribute to the behavior patterns and expectations that help to shape adolescents' orientations to current and future roles. Capturing these complex interrelations among levels of influence is a continuing challenge in research on adolescent development in interpersonal contexts.

INTERPERSONAL CONTEXTS AND THE PSYCHOSOCIAL TASKS OF ADOLESCENCE

Adolescence has long been viewed as a period of tension between two developmental tasks: (1) increasing connections to others beyond the family and conformity to societal expectations, while simultaneously (2) attaining individual competence and autonomy from the influence of others. Implicitly, researchers have weighted questions of how adolescents separate themselves from others more heavily than questions of how they form connections and close relationships. Balance has been restored partially by recent research on intimate and romantic relationships in adolescence (e.g., Collins, 2003; Furman, Brown, & Feiring, 1999), but studies of autonomy and identity still far exceed studies of close relationships.

The focus of this section is independence and interdependence in relation to psychosocial development. An overarching issue is the contributions of interpersonal contexts to both of these psychosocial tasks during adolescence.

Developing a Sense of Independence

The imbalance between the study of autonomy and the study of connectedness in adolescence has resulted from several factors. First, the study of human development has long been dominated by Western views of mental health and maturity, which emphasize the development of personal agency and self-definition over the growth of interpersonal competence and social interconnectedness (Baumeister & Tice, 1986). Second, the study of adolescence in particular has been characterized by the strong, enduring influence of psychoanalytic and neoanalytic theory, both of which have stressed the significance of adolescence as a period for the full maturation of ego skills, including those involving self-regulation (Blos, 1967, 1979) and the development of a sense of personal identity (Erikson, 1968). Finally, scholars of adolescence historically have attended particularly to the processes through which adolescents separate or distance themselves from authority figures, especially parents (Collins, Gleason, et al., 1997; Steinberg, 1990). As a result, adolescence continues to be cast as a critical period for the development of autonomy, and researchers remain intensely interested in questions of how and along what timetable individuals establish independence.

Independence is a multifaceted construct that refers, somewhat loosely, to a lengthy list of phenomena that vary in their interrelatedness. The definition of adolescent autonomy suggested by Douvan and Adelson in 1966 remains a helpful starting point for discussing what it means to become "independent." These writers identified three broad types of autonomy: *emotional autonomy,* which refers to the subjective feelings of independence, especially in relation to parents; *behavioral autonomy,* which refers to the capacity for independent decision making and self-governance; and *value autonomy,* which refers to the development of an independent world view that is grounded in a set of overarching principles and beliefs.

This subsection emphasizes research on emotional and behavioral autonomy. Research on the development of value autonomy in adolescence, generally discussed with reference to moral development, has been extensively reviewed elsewhere (Eisenberg & Morris, 2004; Rest, 1983). However, the development of independent religious and political beliefs in adolescence has received only scant attention from developmental psychologists in recent years and more concerted study is needed.

We begin with three introductory observations about the study of independence in adolescence. First, although the development of independence is usually cast as an individual accomplishment (i.e., the adolescent becomes "an autonomous person"), the development of autonomy almost always implies independence *from or in relation to* some person (e.g., a parent), group, or institution. Consequently, the development of autonomy necessarily involves both a change in individual capacity (e.g., in the ability of the adolescent to make independent decisions) and a change in the individual's relationships with other individuals or institutions that deliberately or unintentionally influence or control the adolescent's feelings, behavior, or beliefs (e.g., in the extent to which the adolescent is permitted or encouraged by parents to make independent decisions or by the law to engage in autonomous decision making; Collins, Gleason, et al., 1997). Because of this, studying the development of independence in adolescence necessarily requires attention to the social context in which it takes place.

Second, independence is both a process and an outcome. In the realm of emotional autonomy, one can think of individuation not only as the process through which adolescents reformulate views of themselves, their parents, and the parent-child relationship but also as the end state of emotional maturity that emerges from this reformulation (Josselson, 1980). In the realm of behavioral autonomy, one can think of the renegotiation of family rules and regulations as the process through which adolescents establish more freedom from parental control and also as the family's acceptance of a new, more egalitarian division of authority between adolescent and parent that results from this renegotiation (Collins, 1995). And in the realm of value autonomy, one can study the process through which adolescents come to question the values and beliefs handed down by parents or other authorities and the adolescents' adoption of a system of moral, religious, or political beliefs based on their own views (Eisenberg & Morris, 2004). Relative to research on independence as an outcome, research on independence as a process is relatively sparse; consequently, we know far more about the characteristics of adolescents who are individuated, capable of independent decision making, or principled in their beliefs, than we do about the interpersonal and intraindividual transformations that facilitated these outcomes.

Third, it is important to note that independence, as defined here, is valued differently in different cultural contexts (Feldman & Quatman, 1988). Among cultural and socioeconomic groups that value individual autonomy more than demonstrations of collective responsibility (e.g., middle-class European Americans), the capacity to function without depending on parents, to make personal decisions that contradict the desire of the group, and to voice one's own opinions, even if they challenge those of one's elders, is seen as a highly desirable trait, and adolescents who do not demonstrate sufficient emotional or behavioral autonomy are viewed as psychosocially immature. Among groups in which attending to the good of the larger collective is more important than the exercise of personal choice (e.g., middle-class Japanese, working-class Mexican Americans), however, establishing emotional independence from parents, making decisions without the input of one's elders, and endorsing values or beliefs that go against those of one's family often are seen in a negative light (e.g., Rothbaum, Pott, Azuma, Miyake, & Weisz, 2000).

One interesting but relatively unstudied question is whether the correlates and consequences of independence in adolescence vary across groups that differ in their views of its value. For example, whereas individuation tends to be associated with higher self-esteem among American youth, it is associated with lower self-esteem among Asian adolescents (Chun & MacDermid, 1997). A related question concerns the ways in which adolescents, especially those whose families are recent immigrants, are affected by growing up in a social context in which they are encouraged by some individuals (e.g., teachers or peers) to behave independently but expected by others (e.g., parents or extended family) to sacrifice personal autonomy for the sake of the larger group. Generally, families who have emigrated from a culture that is relatively slower to grant adolescents autonomy to a culture where autonomy is granted sooner follow timetables for adolescent independence that fall somewhere between the two extremes. This tendency has been documented in studies both of Chinese immigrants in America and Australia (Rosenthal & Feldman, 1990) and of East German immigrants in the former West Germany (Silbereisen & Schmitt-Rodermund, 1995).

Recognizing that the development of independence is simultaneously an individual and interpersonal phenomenon poses methodological difficulties. Often, researchers assess the capacity for self-regulation or some other sort of independent functioning, ignoring the fact that manifestations of autonomy (whether emotional, behavioral, or cognitive) typically take place in interpersonal contexts. An illustration comes from research on developmental changes in resistance to peer influence in which adolescents typically respond to a series of hypothetical dilemmas requiring them to choose between a course of action that is self-determined and one that is demanded by their friends. In this paradigm, individuals who less often endorse the course of action recommended by the peer group are characterized as relatively more autonomous. Findings from research in which autonomy is operationalized in this way imply that the development of autonomy follows a J-shaped function, with resistance to peer influence declining between the ages of 10 and 14 or so and then increasing into late adolescence (Berndt, 1979; Steinberg & Silverberg, 1986).

It is tempting to conclude from this research that middle adolescence is a time of heightened susceptibility to peer influence (and, thus, diminished behavioral independence). This may be the case, but interpreting the findings of studies like these is difficult without information about developmental changes in the real or perceived degree of coercive pressure exerted by adolescent peer groups. Individuals' capacity to maintain autonomy in the face of peer pressure actually may remain constant during adolescence, whereas the amount of pressure from peers to comply with the group's norms and preferences may increase. If so, changes in the strength of peer group pressure, and not in individuals' capacity to resist it, may account for apparent declines in behavioral independence around age 14. Adolescents' likelihood of capitulating to peer-group influence may be a joint product of their capacity for autonomous behavior and the peer group's tolerance of individual members' independent decision making. Few studies, however, have been designed to distinguish between these contrasting processes (but see B. Brown, Clasen, & Eicher, 1986).

Similar conceptual and methodological challenges inhere in the study of emotional and value autonomy. Adolescents' subjective sense of independence, especially in the context of the parent-adolescent relationship, inevitably is influenced by the extent to which their parents encourage, accept, or hamper emotional autonomy. Some parents become distressed by their teenager's striving for emotional independence, whereas others relish this same development (Silverberg & Steinberg, 1990). Yet, measures of emotional autonomy that simply assess the adolescent's subjective feelings of independence from parents do not ordinarily distinguish between individuals who have achieved this state with their parents' blessings or assistance and those who have had to struggle to establish their independence. It is not known whether this distinction makes a difference (e.g., whether the mental health correlates of emotional autonomy vary as a function of the degree to which the adolescent's independence was facilitated, tolerated, or fought by his or her parents). Similarly, some adolescents who have developed an independent world view may have achieved this degree of ideological autonomy through parental encouragement of independent thinking, whereas others may have had to struggle to assert their independent opinions. Research on adolescent autonomy would benefit from more systematic efforts to understand the processes through which emotional, behavioral, and value autonomy develop and from investigations that examine the relation between aspects of adolescent adjustment and variations in the process as well as outcome of the adolescent's move toward independence.

Emotional and behavioral autonomy undoubtedly are interrelated, although little is known about whether and how changes in adolescents' subjective feelings of independence affect, or are affected by, changes in capacities for independent behavior. For example, are adolescents who see themselves as emotionally autonomous from parents more likely than other adolescents to demonstrate independent decision making in the peer group? Similarly, do experiences in independent decision making outside the family promote the development of emotional autonomy in relation to parents? The notion that growth in one aspect of independence necessarily translates into growth in another is hardly self-evident. Indeed, one interesting possibility is that emotional autonomy from parents, especially when gained at a relatively early age, results in becoming more, not less, susceptible to the influence of peers and, accordingly, less behaviorally independent in that context.

Emotional Autonomy

The development of emotional autonomy involves increases in adolescents' subjective sense of his or her independence, especially in relation to parents or parental figures. At least in the early stages of adolescence, feeling emotionally autonomous is achieved in part by separating oneself from and arguing with one's parents; through this process, the relationship is transformed and the adolescent develops both a new behavioral repertoire and a new image of his or her parents (Collins, 1995; Steinberg, 1990). In this sense, the development of emotional autonomy is not primarily an intrapsychic transformation in which the adolescent comes to see him- or herself as more grown up, but an interpersonal transformation, in which patterns of interaction between the adolescent and parents shift through a process of mutual (if not always willing) renegotiation. At the end of this transformative process are three interrelated outcomes: a changed adolescent, who now views him- or herself in a different light; a changed parent, who now views his or her child (and perhaps him- or herself) in a different light; and a changed parent-child relationship, which is likely to be somewhat more egalitarian (Collins, 1995).

The starting point for most discussions of emotional autonomy and its development is the psychodynamic perspective on adolescence. In this perspective, the development of emotional independence during adolescence is conceptualized as independence *from* parents, parent-adolescent conflict is seen as a normative manifestation of the detachment process, and parent-adolescent harmony, at least in the extreme, is viewed as developmentally stunting and symptomatic of intrapsychic immaturity (A. Freud, 1958). Orthodox analytic views of the detachment process gave way in the last quarter of the twentieth century to more tempered, neoanalytic theories that cast the development of emotional independence in terms of the adolescent's *individuation* or *sense of identity* rather than limiting the phenomenon to his or her detachment from parents. The development of emotional autonomy begins with individuation from parents (Blos, 1967, 1979) and ends with the achievement of a sense of identity (Erikson, 1968).

Theory and research recently has shifted toward the idea that emotional autonomy results from a progressive negotiation between adolescent and parents over issues related to the granting and exercise of adolescent autonomy (Collins, 1995; Collins, Gleason, et al., 1997). Thus, the process of individuation is less about the adolescent's attempt to separate from his or her parents than about a transformation in the implicit and explicit assumptions and beliefs that shape interactions among family members. This is not to say that all elements of this negotiation process are conscious or deliberate, the involved parties are always agreeable participants, or the everyday experience of renegotiating the terms of the parent-adolescent relationship is necessarily pleasant.

This new view of emotional autonomy, however, emphasizes the different ways in which adolescents and parents construe their relationship, the different expectations that they bring to the kitchen table, the different frames they use to interpret their experiences with one another, and the ways in which these cognitions shape patterns of interaction among family members (Collins, 1995; Larson & Richards, 1994; Smollar & Youniss, 1985). Accordingly, assessments of emotional autonomy have relied both on self-report measures of individuation (e.g., Lamborn & Steinberg, 1993; R. Ryan & Lynch, 1989; Steinberg & Silverberg, 1986) in which adolescents are asked questions about their perceptions of themselves (e.g., "I go to my parents for help before trying to solve a problem myself"), their parents (e.g., "My parents hardly ever make mistakes"), and the parent-adolescent relationship (e.g., "There are some things about me that my parents do not know"), and also on observational techniques, in which interactions between parents and adolescents are recorded and subsequently coded for displays of assertiveness and individuality on the part of the adolescent and for evidence of the facilitation or hindrance of the adolescent's assertion of autonomy by his or her parents (e.g., Hauser et al., 1991). Currently, the most widely used coding system for this purpose is that developed by Hauser, Allen, and their associates (Allen, Hauser, Bell, et al., 1994; Allen, Hauser, Eickholt, et al., 1994; Allen, Hauser, O'Connor, & Bell, 2002; Allen et al., 1996; Hauser et al., 1991; Hauser & Safyer, 1994).

Empirical research on the development of emotional autonomy implies a reciprocal process of intraindividual and interpersonal change in which the adolescents' growing sense of emotional independence affects, is affected by, and manifests itself in their relations with others. Several conclusions have emerged from work in this area. First, over the course of adolescence, individuals' subjective sense of independence increases significantly, as indicated by feelings of separateness from their parents and changes in their perceptions of them, with older adolescents less likely than preadolescents to idealize their parents or believe in their omnipotence (Steinberg & Silverberg, 1986). Notably, although this process begins early in adolescence, typically with the deidealization of parents and challenges to parental authority, it unfolds over the entire adolescent period, and fully mature images of one's parents do not begin to appear until very late in adolescence, around the time that the adolescent is likely to be in the midst of the identity crisis described by Erikson (Smollar & Youniss, 1985).

Second, numerous studies show that the development of emotional autonomy is a far more gradual and far less dramatic phenomenon than originally suggested in "storm and stress" perspectives on adolescence (Collins & Laursen, 2004b; Steinberg, 1990). Detachment from parental ties is neither the norm, nor is it associated with positive adjustment or psychological well-being (Allen et al., 1996; Chen & Dornbusch, 1998; Frank, Avery, & Laman, 1988; Fuhrman & Holmbeck, 1995; Lamborn & Steinberg, 1993; Mahoney, Schweder, & Stättin, 2002; R. Ryan & Lynch, 1989). No studies suggest that active rebellion or unrelenting oppositionalism is necessary to later healthy psychosocial development, and many studies indicate that the overt repudiation of parents by the adolescent likely forecasts problems, not success, in the development of emotional independence (Fuhrman & Holmbeck, 1995; Steinberg, 1990). Furthermore, although the development of emotional autonomy is not characterized by individual psychological upheaval or excessive familial turbulence, it may be associated with mild distress among parents, especially mothers. This issue has not been studied, however, in samples other than White, working- and middle-class families (Silverberg & Steinberg, 1987, 1990; Steinberg, 2001; Steinberg & Silverberg, 1987).

Third, whereas the process of individuation appears to be especially significant during early adolescence, identity development is salient in late adolescence and early adulthood. Indeed, research on identity development indicates few age differences in early, or even middle, adolescence; rather, the end of the adolescent decade appears to be the critical time for the development of a coherent sense of identity (Archer, 1982; Nurmi, 2004; Waterman, 1982). Thus, the process of discovering *that* one has a separate identity (the process of individuation) precedes the process of discovering *what* that identity is (the process of identity development). Middle adolescence is important as the time during which the psychosocial concerns of adolescence shift from individuation from parents to the establishment of a sense of identity. Peers, in close relationships as well as in groups, undoubtedly play a crucial role in this transition (B. Brown, 2004). No research, however, has examined possible connections between the processes of individuation in early adolescence and identity development in late adolescence.

Fourth, the most visible autonomy-related transformations in family relations, such as the widely reported increase in bickering and squabbling over matters of parental authority, occur relatively early in the period (Steinberg, 1981). The timing of these changed family patterns suggests that interpersonal changes that reflect the development of emotional autonomy precede some of the intrapsychic changes associated with gains in self-governance, which may not take place until the middle portion of the period, or in the development of a sense of identity, which takes place relatively late in adolescence. Although more longitudinal studies of the links between intrapsychic and interpersonal aspects of emotional autonomy are needed, one plausible hypothesis is that changes in the parent-adolescent relationship lead to, rather than follow from, changes in the adolescent's subjective sense of self-reliance (Holmbeck & Hill, 1991; Steinberg, 1990). In other words, the interpersonal may drive the intrapsychic, rather than the reverse.

Finally, there are sizable individual differences in the extent to which significant others in the adolescent's life permit or encourage the development of emotional independence, and these differences are meaningfully related to measures of adolescent psychosocial adjustment, especially in the realms of self-reliance, self-perceptions, and mental health. Many studies, involving both observational and self-report measures, indicate that the development of emotional independence is facilitated by parents who are warm but not intrusive. This recurring finding is consistent with the view that adolescents are more self-confident and less prone to depression and other forms of internalization when they feel close to parents and simultaneously feel free to individuate from them (Allen, Hauser, Eickholt, et al., 1994; Grotevant & Cooper, 1986; Hodges et al., 1999). In contrast, positive mental health and the development of emotional autonomy are linked negatively to parenting that is either excessively controlling (which may be experienced by the adolescent as passive aggression) or overtly hostile (Allen, Hauser, Eickholt, et al., 1994; Holmbeck et al., 2000; McElhaney & Allen, 2001; Pavlidis & McCauley, 1995). Extreme psychological control, including various forms of love withdrawal and guilt induction, has been shown to be especially incompatible with the development of emotional autonomy (Barber, 1996; Pomerantz, 2001). The same factors that are associated with the development of healthy individuation—parental warmth, involvement, and the tolerance of expressions of individuality—also appear to contribute to the development of a healthy sense of identity, lending further support to the notion that these phenomena are interrelated (Grotevant & Cooper, 1986; Perosa, Perosa, & Tam, 1996).

Behavioral Autonomy

Behavioral autonomy encompasses multiple capacities involved with self-reliance, but the construct of behavioral independence has appeared in two very different forms in research on adolescence (see Hill & Holmbeck, 1986). In one, behavioral autonomy refers to the capacity for competent self-governance in the absence of external guidance or monitoring, as when, for example, an adolescent is able to function on his or her own without parents in a new or challenging situation or behave ethically when outside the purview of adult supervision. In the other, behavioral autonomy also refers to the capacity to function independently in the face of *excessive* external influence, when, for example, the adolescent must be able to resist peer pressure to behave in a way that goes against his or her better judgment or personal preferences. Both of these situations require self-reliance, but whether these very different aspects of behavioral independence (i.e., the ability to function responsibly without guidance or in the presence of strong external influence) develop concomitantly has not received adequate research attention, nor has the broader issue of whether the expression of behavioral autonomy is stable across contexts. It is quite easy to imagine, for example, a young person who functions competently while alone but who behaves irresponsibly when in the presence of peers or one who is slavishly dependent on parents when around the house but who stands up for herself when with friends.

Research on the development of behavioral autonomy has for the most part been conducted in the broader framework of socialization research, guided mainly by social learning theory. Investigators have studied features of family contexts that covary with responsible independence, manifested in self-reliance, personal accountability, and appropriate responses to social influence. Two specific lines of work have dominated: studies of the development of responsibility (e.g., Cauffman & Steinberg, 2000; Greenberger & Sorenson, 1974; Lamborn et al., 1991; Steinberg et al., 1994) and studies of resistance to peer pressure, especially in antisocial situations (Berndt, 1979; B. Brown et al., 1986; Erick-

son, Crosnoe, & Dornbusch, 2000; Krosnick & Judd, 1982; Steinberg & Silverberg, 1986). According to these socialization models, parents facilitate the development of behavioral autonomy in four chief ways: (1) by serving as models of competent decision-makers; (2) by encouraging independent decision making in the family context; (3) by rewarding independent decision making outside the family context; and (4) by instilling in the adolescent a more general sense of self-efficacy through the use of parenting that is both responsive and demanding (Darling & Steinberg, 1993). Unfortunately, the sizable intercorrelations among these features of parenting make it impossible to specify which of these processes is most important.

As with research on emotional autonomy, behavioral autonomy sometimes has been examined as a quality of the adolescent's psychological capability or functioning (e.g., studies of age or gender differences in self-reliance) and sometimes as a quality of the adolescent's relationships with parents (e.g., studies of independence seeking or independence granting) or peers (e.g., studies of resistance to peer influence). When conceptualized as an individual phenomenon, assessment generally has taken four forms:

1. Adolescent self-report of global tendencies, using personality inventories that pose direct questions about self-reliance or personal responsibility (e.g., Greenberger & Sorenson, 1974)

2. Adolescent self-report of his or her performance of specific tasks indicative of independent functioning (e.g., the completion of school assignments, money management, punctuality at work; e.g., Mortimer, 2003)

3. Adolescent responses to hypothetical dilemmas that ask the individual to report how he or she would behave in various situations (e.g., when tempted to do something antisocial) and under varying social conditions (e.g., with peers versus alone; e.g., Ford, Wentzel, Wood, Stevens, & Siesfeld, 1990)

4. Assessments of the adolescent's independence made by parents or teachers (a method more popular in the past than currently; e.g., Bronfenbrenner, 1961)

Studies of behavioral autonomy as a quality of the parent-child relationship generally rely on questionnaires requiring parents and, independently, adolescents to report on how familial decisions are made (e.g., unilaterally by parents, jointly, or unilaterally by the adolescent; e.g., Dornbusch et al., 1987).

The fact that expressions of behavioral autonomy likely vary as a function of who else is present at the time makes it difficult to draw generalizations about the developmental course of behavioral independence as an overall capacity. Most studies that ask adolescents to gauge their own level of self-reliance (e.g., Steinberg & Silverberg, 1986) find a linear increase in this trait over the course of adolescence, but it is not clear whether adolescents' own appraisal of their capacity for responsible autonomy is consistent with their actual performance across varied situations. For example, whereas the period between age 11 and 14 is characterized by gains in subjective reports of responsibility, the same period is characterized by a decline in resistance to peer influence. Indeed, even in research on susceptibility to social influence, studies indicate different developmental timetables with respect to resistance to parental influence (which tends to increase linearly over the course of adolescence) and resistance to peer influence (which follows an U-shaped pattern, declining between ages 11 and 14 but increasing thereafter; Berndt, 1979). Although few studies have charted developmental changes in parental autonomy-granting, early adolescence is likely to be an important time for changes, with most parents relinquishing unilateral control over an increasingly wider array of everyday issues involving the adolescent and most families undergoing the sorts of transformations in family relations described in the previous section on emotional autonomy. Because they appear to progress along similar developmental timetables, adolescents' reports of their own sense of self-reliance may more closely reflect their assessment of their growing emotional and behavioral independence in relation to their parents rather than changes in their relations with peers.

The period between early and middle adolescence, from around age 13 until 15, appears to be an important transitional time in the development of behavioral autonomy, because adolescents become increasingly motivated to seek independence from parents during this period, while not yet having the psychosocial maturity for mature self-regulation when alone or in the company of their friends. Recent advances in developmental neuroscience have led several writers to link findings from studies of brain maturation to findings from studies of self-governance (e.g., Steinberg et al., in press). Changes in the limbic system that impel the adolescent toward sensation seeking and risk taking, both of which require greater independence from parental control, pre-

cede the maturation of the prefrontal cortex, which undergirds various aspects of executive function, affecting self-regulation, impulse control, planning, and foresight. This disjunction creates a gap that some writers have likened to "starting the engines with an unskilled driver" (C. Nelson et al., 2002, p. 515). This gap between the degree of autonomy adolescents seek and are granted, on the one hand, and their actual capacity for self-governance, on the other, may leave individuals prone to poor judgment, so that they place themselves in difficult or challenging situations before having developed the capacity for mature self-regulation (Steinberg & Scott, 2003).

Several investigators have examined ethnic and cross-cultural differences in adolescents' and parents' expectations for behavioral autonomy. Feldman and her colleagues, for example, have examined this issue by asking parents and adolescents from both Asian and Anglo cultural groups to fill out a "teen timetable"—a questionnaire that asks at what age one would expect an adolescent to be permitted to engage in various behaviors that signal autonomy (e.g., "spend money however you want," "go out on dates," "go to rock concerts with friends"; Feldman & Wood, 1994). In general, Anglo adolescents and their parents living in America, Australia, or Hong Kong have earlier expectations for adolescent autonomy than do Asian adolescents and parents from these same countries (Feldman & Quatman, 1988; Rosenthal & Feldman, 1990). Because of this, adolescents from Asian families may be less likely to seek autonomy from their parents than are their Anglo counterparts. In general, adolescents' mental health is most positive when their desires for autonomy match their expectations for what their parents are willing to grant (Juang, J. Lerner, McKinney, & von Eye, 1999). Not surprisingly, adolescents believe that individuals should be granted autonomy earlier than parents do (Ruck, Peterson-Badali, & Day, 2002).

Studies of expectations for behavioral autonomy have failed to find consistent sex or birth-order differences in age expectations for behavioral independence, contrary to the popular belief that boys expect more autonomy than girls or that later-born adolescents are granted earlier freedom because their older siblings have paved the way. Sex and birth-order differences in the extent to which parents *grant* autonomy do exist, though the pattern varies depending on the particular constellation of sons and daughters in the household and the parents' attitudes toward sex roles. Although parents are generally thought to be more controlling of daughters than sons, this is relatively more likely in households where parents have traditional views of gender roles (Bumpus, Crouter, & McHale, 2001). Gender differences in the extent to which adolescents are granted independence appear to be especially pronounced in African American households. Relative to other ethnic groups, African American boys are given relatively more freedom but girls are given less (Bulcroft, Carmody, & Bulcroft, 1996). Contrary to expectation, parents grant more autonomy to first-borns than to second-borns, especially when the first-born is a girl and the second-born is a boy (Bumpus et al., 2001). Adolescents' expectations for autonomy may be highly influenced by the ways in which peers are treated by parents. Consistent with this, adolescents who "feel" older seek more independence than their same-aged peers who "feel" younger (Galambos, Kolaric, Sears, & Maggs, 1999).

Summary Comment

The purportedly individual process of developing independence is embedded in the interpersonal contexts of family and peer relationships. Though rarely conceptualized as a systemic phenomenon, the emergence of evidence on the likely interacting processes of brain development, transformations in parent-child relationships, and the ascendance of extrafamilial networks implies that a developmental systems perspective is the minimum adequate conceptual framework for studying the development of autonomy.

Developing a Sense of Interdependence

Interdependence is the norm in societies throughout the world. The emphasis on independence in industrialized cultures is relative not absolute (Goodnow, 2002; Goodnow, Miller, & Kessel, 1995). Adolescents in most cultures strive to be connected with others, whether as members of pairs, families, or larger groups. The significance of interdependence for developing adolescents is apparent in several ways. Adolescents in diverse industrialized societies generally now enjoy more discretionary time than in other historical periods; in many cultures (e.g., East Asian countries or Hispanic communities in the United States), a large proportion of the time not devoted to schooling is spent with family members (Cooper, 1994; Larson & Verma, 1999; Rothbaum et al., 2000). Although European American middle-class ado-

lescents in the United States spend less time with family members during adolescence than before, the amount of time actually spent talking with family members declines negligibly over these years (Larson et al., 1996) and appears to exceed the time that non-Western youth typically spend talking with their families (Stevenson et al., 1990; B. Whiting & Edwards, 1988). In addition, time with peers increases gradually during adolescence (Larson & Richards, 1991), and most adolescents claim to have several good friends and one or more best friends (Hartup & Abecassis, 2002). The centrality of interdependence is also apparent in the importance adolescents assign to interpersonal competence during the adolescent years. Longitudinal findings indicate that, by late adolescence, self-perceived competence in close relationships (e.g., with romantic partners) emerges as a reliable component of self-perceptions of general competence (Masten et al., 1995).

Developmental task analyses imply that achieving interdependence in adolescence is part of a process begun at birth (Buhrmester & Furman, 1987). *Attachment* to caregivers forms a substrate on which other attachments can be built, and the processes of forming and transforming attachments continues into adulthood as a component of interdependence. Same-gender peer relationships during childhood provide initial experiences of *intimacy*, but intimate relationships with opposite-sex peers typically first develop during adolescence (Savin-Williams & Berndt, 1990; Sullivan, 1953). Some rudiments of *sexuality* are present in infancy and childhood, but sexual activity itself generally begins during adolescence, bringing with it issues of relationships, social and personal responsibility, health, and safety (Brooks-Gunn & Paikoff, 1997; Simon & Gagnon, 1969; Udry, 1990). Interdependence is thus both a multifaceted construct comprised of several closely related but not redundant competencies, and an ongoing process in which each person affects, and is affected by, the other. Attachment, or the capacity to form interpersonal bonds, is a—perhaps the—foundational skill involved in developing interdependence.

The focus of this section is the three psychosocial goals comprising the task of interdependence: (1) attachment, (2) intimacy, and (3) sexuality. With respect to each we ask, first, what is the nature of the psychosocial task? Second, what is its developmental course? Third, how are the tasks related to the maturational and social issues that frame adolescent experiences? Fourth, what experiences, especially in interpersonal relationships, facilitate or hamper the achievement of interdependence during adolescence?

Attachment

The construct of attachment in infant-caregiver relationships refers to a relatively unique or distinct connection, which supports infants' efforts to feel safe from threatening conditions and to be regulated emotionally. These internal emotional experiences are manifested in the organization of the infant's behavior to maintain proximity with the caregiver, especially in novel or threatening circumstances. Infants may feel secure with multiple partners, though these may vary in the degree to which the infant feels secure in them (Cassidy, 1999; Weinfield, Sroufe, Egeland, & E. Carlson, 1999). According to M. Ainsworth (1989), infant behaviors with attachment partners are prototypes of attachments at every age, including those that occur outside of the biological family. These relationships illustrate four defining criteria for differentiating attachment relationships from other close relationships: proximity seeking, secure-base behavior (free exploration in the presence of the other person); safe-haven behavior (turning first to the other person when facing a perceived threat); and distress over involuntary separations (see Waters & Cummings, 2000, for a discussion of the significance of secure-base behavior after childhood).

Two largely compatible explanations have been offered for links between attachments with caregivers and those in later extrafamilial relationships. One is a carry-forward model, in which functions and representations of caregiver-child attachment relationships (*internal working models*) organize expectations and behaviors in later relationships (e.g., Waters & Cummings, 2000). Research findings document correspondences between early insecure attachment and poor peer relationships in adolescence (e.g., Weinfield, Ogawa, & Sroufe, 1997) and between security, as assessed in the Adult Attachment Interview, and peers' reports of resiliency, undercontrol, hostility, and anxiety (Kobak & Sceery, 1988). A second explanation is that relationships with caregivers prior to adolescence expose individuals to components of effective relating, such as empathy, reciprocity, and self-confidence, which shape interactions in other, later relationships (e.g., Collins & Sroufe, 1999; Sroufe & Fleeson, 1988). In turn, childhood and adolescent friendships serve as templates for subsequent close relationships outside of

the family (Furman & Wehner, 1994; Sullivan, 1953; Youniss, 1980). For example, recent findings substantiate links between representations of romantic relationships and representations of other close relationships, especially relationships with friends; and these interrelated expectancies parallel interrelations in features like support and control (Furman, Simon, Shaffer, & Bouchey, 2002; Furman & Wehner, 1994). Studies of the same individuals from birth to age 19 suggest that these two pathways may be part of a single process. In longitudinal studies, representations of attachment throughout childhood and also social behavior during the same period both have been predicted by early attachment relationships, and interactions between behavior and representations across time in turn have been found to predict social competence at age 19 (Carlson, Sroufe, & Egeland, 2004).

Maintaining interdependence in adolescence and early adulthood, however, involves relative redistributions of relationship functions. Adolescents' perceptions of parents as primary sources of support generally decline, whereas perceived support from friends increases, such that friendships are seen as providing roughly the same (Helsen et al., 2000; Scholte et al., 2001) or greater (Furman & Buhrmester, 1992) support as parental relationships. This process especially implicates friends and romantic interests, the individuals with whom early adults most like to spend time (proximity seeking) and with whom they most want to be when feeling down (safe-haven function; M. Ainsworth, 1989; Cassidy, 2001; Waters & Cummings, 2000). This shift in attachments requires a cognitive and emotional maturity that rarely is achieved before late adolescence (M. Ainsworth, 1989). In the process, attachment is transformed from caregiving of one partner by the other to that of mutual caregiving between the two partners (Allen & Land, 1999; Cassidy, 2001; Waters & Cummings, 2000). Although parents are just as likely as friends to be the primary source from which late adolescents and early adults seek advice and on which they depend (Fraley & Davis, 1997), Hazan and Zeifman (1994) have suggested that the apparent overlap among relationships at this time implies that components of attachment relationships (namely, maintaining proximity, using the other as a safe haven, and using the other as a secure base) also become characteristic of relationships with extrafamilial partners.

The significance of attachment for individuals and their relationships both before and during adolescence is apparent in longitudinal findings. For example, secure early attachment in caregiving relationships predicts the features of relationships with extrafamilial partners during adolescence (Sroufe & Fleeson, 1988). Similarly, early attachment security predicts competence with peers both during middle childhood (the elementary school years) and during adolescence. The combination of early experiences of caregiving and competence in peer relationships in preschool and middle childhood predicts adolescent competence more strongly than any of these assessments alone (Sroufe, Egeland, & Carlson, 1999). Likewise, early caregiving experiences significantly predict hostility in interactions with romantic partners in early adulthood over and above the contributions of proximal relationships with peers and parents (Collins & Van Dulmen, 2006b).

Attachments assessed during adolescence and early adulthood also predict quality of relationships. Representations of attachment in earlier life, as assessed by the Adult Attachment Interview (AAI; Main, Kaplan, & Cassidy, 1985; see also Kobak, Cole, Ferenz-Gillies, Fleming, & Gamble, 1993) have been linked significantly to characteristics of relationships with parents in adolescence and early adulthood (Becker-Stoll & Fremmer-Bombik, 1997). Researchers also have documented remarkable correspondence between AAI classifications and an individual's actual manifestations of security in relationships with their caregiver in infancy, as assessed by the Strange Situation (Waters et al., 2000). Exceptions to this general continuity also are consistent with the hypothesis that current functioning reflects a combination of relationship history and current experiences (Carlson et al., 2004; Sroufe, Egeland, Carlson, & Collins, in press; for a critical perspective, see M. Lewis, Feiring, & Rosenthal, 2000). For example, Weinfield, Sroufe, and Egeland (2000) reported that disruptive life events often undermine continuity from early attachment assessments to early adult attachment assessments in a risk sample, whereas Waters et al. (2000) found significant continuities in a largely stable middle-class sample. Finally, individuals' security in caregiver relationships during infancy significantly predicted representations of romantic relationships, as assessed by the Current Relationships Interview (CRI; Crowell & Owens, 1996), at age 21. Other things being equal, a foundation of interdependence in early life appears to be a significant forerunner of continued interdependence in one's closest relationships in adolescence and adulthood.

Whether adolescent attachments contribute uniquely to future adaptation and well-being is still largely unknown. Suggestive recent findings, however, come from a 2-year longitudinal study implying considerable stability of attachment beginning in 9th and 10th grades (Allen, McElhaney, Kuperminc, & Jodl, 2004). More extensive evidence is accumulating slowly, partly because few valid, reliable measures of adolescents' current attachments exist. Conceptually sound, well-validated measures of attachment, such as the AAI (Main et al., 1985), are of questionable validity for some samples of adolescents. Moreover, some instruments carry the label "attachment," but do not systematically assess M. Ainsworth's (1989) criteria for distinguishing attachment relationships from other close relationships. Nor have these instruments been validated longitudinally against attachment measures that do address these criteria, such as the Strange Situation or the AAI (Crowell, Fraley, & Shaver, 1999). The most widely used such instrument, Armsden and Greenberg's Inventory of Parent and Peer Attachment (IPPA, 1984), reliably measures certain features of relationships that overlap with the features of secure attachments, such as degree of mutual trust, quality of communication between partners, and degree of anger and alienation. Although IPPA scores cannot substitute for valid measures of attachment, the scores have yielded interesting age-related patterns that are relevant to interdependence during adolescence and even into early adulthood. For example, in a recent study linking IPPA scores with measures of romantic relationships, relationship quality with mothers and decreasing quality of relationships with father during adolescence were associated with greater expectations of rejection in relationships with friends and romantic partners (Ho, 2004). Other researchers have documented significant positive correlations between poor quality relationships with parents and peers, as assessed by the IPPA, and aggression and victimization toward partners in romantic relationships in early adulthood (J. L. Linder et al., 2002).

Summary Comment

Achieving the psychosocial tasks of interdependence thus implies building on earlier relationship patterns to form and maintain further stable interdependencies during and beyond adolescence. Attachment perspectives have yielded compelling evidence that interpersonal contexts are significant not only in achieving adolescents' interdependence goals but also in providing a foundation for competent independent functioning as well (Allen & Land, 1999; R. Thompson, 1999).

Intimacy

Intimacy has been defined in several ways. In the widely accepted definition proposed by Reis and Shaver (see also Reis & Patrick, 1996):

> Intimacy is an interpersonal process within which two interaction partners experience and express feelings, communicate verbally and nonverbally, satisfy social motives, augment or reduce social fears, talk and learn about themselves and their unique characteristics, and become "close" (psychologically and often physically). (1988, p. 387)

As a psychosocial task of adolescence, intimacy refers to experiencing this mutual openness and responsiveness in at least some relationships with age-mates. Interdependence is a necessary, but not sufficient, condition for intimacy. If interdependence declines, intimacy may be less likely or less satisfying (Prager, 2000; Reis & Patrick, 1996; Reis & Shaver, 1988).

The development of capabilities for intimacy during adolescence undoubtedly builds on the hallmark physical, cognitive, and social changes of the period. Concepts of friendship first incorporate notions of intimacy in early adolescence (Furman & Bierman, 1984). In contrast to the relatively large number of studies linking these changes to the growth of independence, few studies have examined their links to changing patterns of intimacy with peers. Nevertheless, many scholars speculate that adolescents become increasingly capable of intimate relationships as more sophisticated understanding of social relations emerges and as adolescents' ability to infer the thoughts of feelings of others sharpens (e.g., Selman, 1980).

The interpersonal roots of emerging intimacy during adolescence have been studied more extensively. Generally, findings confirm links between the quality of adolescents' relationships (i.e., the degree of openness and support experienced with close associates) and the nature of family relationships in earlier periods, as well as changes in the abilities of relationship partners during adolescence (Collins & Van Dulmen, 2006a). For example, in one longitudinal study parent involvement during childhood predicted closeness to parents during adolescence, with stronger links between childhood father involvement in childhood and closeness to father at age 16 for girls than for boys (Flouri & Buchanan, 2002). Fur-

thermore, the degree of flexible control, cohesion, and respect for privacy experienced in families has been linked positively to intimacy in late-adolescent romantic relationships, with especially strong associations emerging for women (Feldman, Gowen, & Fisher, 1998). In contrast, degree of negative emotionality in parent-adolescent dyads predicted degree of negative emotionality and poor quality interactions with romantic partners in late adolescence (K. Kim et al., 2001). This association appears to be mediated by negative affect and ineffective monitoring and discipline in parent-adolescent relationships (R. Conger, Cui, Bryant, & Elder, 2000).

In relationships with peers, larger amounts of time with peers and correspondingly less time with adults during adolescence may contribute to the development of intimacy by increasing comfort with peers and encouraging self-disclosure, as well as openness to others' self-revelations. Shared interest in mastering the distinctive contexts and social systems of adolescence also stimulates a desire to communicate with peers, and biological changes associated with puberty also may occasion more frequent discussion with peers, who may offer a more comfortable arena than parent-child relationships for discussing issues of physical changes, sex, and dating. Opportunities for intimacy may be one reason why friendships occupy increasing amounts of time during adolescence. The superficial sharing of activities that sufficed between childhood friends is supplanted, during adolescence, by the potential for mutual responsiveness, concern, loyalty, trustworthiness, and respect for confidence between adolescent friends (Furman & Bierman, 1984; Newcomb & Bagwell, 1995). According to Sullivan (1953), the theoretical fountainhead of research in the area, friendship in preadolescence and adolescence meets a basic psychological need to overcome loneliness, an idea that is similar to Baumeister and Leary's (1995) recent proposal that humans have an evolved need to belong. In Sullivan's view, same-sex peers develop the psychological capacity to achieve intimacy by overcoming loneliness through close friendships with same-sex peers (*chumships*).

Increases during adolescence in mutuality, self-disclosure, and intimacy with friends (defined as reciprocal feelings of self-disclosure and engagement in activities) have been documented in several studies (Furman & Buhrmester, 1992; Sharabany et al., 1981). Sharabany et al. (1981) reported, from age 10 to age 16, adolescents increasingly reported frankness, spontaneity, knowing, and sensitivity toward friends. Trust and loyalty, as well as taking and imposing, were characteristics of communication with friends throughout this age range.

Gender differences in both extent and significance of intimacy are both common and widely discussed. During adolescence, girls' friendships consistently involve more knowing and sensitivity, more giving and sharing, and more taking and imposing than boys' friendships do (e.g., Sharabany et al., 1981; Youniss & Smollar, 1985). McNelles and Connolly (1999) found that with increasing age both girls and boys in grades 9, 10, and 11 in a Canadian sample increasingly engaged in discussion and self-disclosure with close friends and were equally successful in sustaining shared affect between them. In this study, the two genders differed primarily in the manner in which intimacy was established, with boys more often manifesting intimacy in the context of shared activities than girls did and girls more likely than boys to attain intimacy through discussion and self-disclosure. One interesting by-product of this gender difference is the relatively greater tendency for adolescent girls to engage in "co-rumination," which may leave them more susceptible than boys to the development of depressive symptomatology (Rose, 2002).

Intimacy in opposite-sex friendships, although not uncommon among late adolescents (Kuttler et al., 1999), emerges relatively late. Sharabany et al. (1981) found that not until the 9th and 11th grades were opposite-sex friendships rated very high in intimacy. Little is known about the intimacy of these friendships relative to those of same-gender pairs (but see Sippola, 1999, for relevant evidence), the typical role of intimacy in networks of same-gender and opposite-gender friends, or the developmental significance of placing high relative importance on opposite-gender over same-gender friendships.

Adolescent friendships appear to provide critical interpersonal experiences for both genders that both shape later close relationships and support individual psychosocial growth (Furman & Wehner, 1994; Sullivan, 1953). Qualities of friendships in middle and late adolescence appear to be linked to concurrent qualities of romantic relationships (Collins & Van Dulmen, in press; Furman et al., 2002). Representations of friendships and romantic relationships are interrelated as well. Displaying safe-haven and secure-base behaviors with best friends is correlated positively with these behaviors in dating relationships (Treboux, Crowell, Owens, & Pan, 1994). Perhaps the growing importance of romantic

relationships calls attention to the commonalities across types of relationships. It is equally likely that the parallels between early adults' relationships reflect their common similarity to prior relationships with parents and peers (Collins & Van Dulmen, 2006a; R. Conger et al., 2000; Owens et al., 1995; Waters et al., 2000). The nature and processes of these developmentally significant relations among relationships is a promising area for further study.

Intimacy also may enhance other aspects of psychosocial development. In particular, intimacy with peers has been implicated in identity development. In an influential early essay, Elkind (1967) depicted the opportunity to share perceptions and feelings with other adolescents as one of the main ways in which adolescents overcome egocentric beliefs that others are preoccupied with their behavior (the imaginary audience) or that their experiences are unique (the personal fable). Erikson (1968) regarded intimacy in early adulthood as emerging from identity achievement, which enables individuals to engage in sharing with others without feeling excessively vulnerable personally. Little evidence bears on either Elkind's or Erikson's predictions. Some studies have shown that young adults who are relatively advanced in identity achievement, as assessed in Marcia's (1980) classification scheme, also are more likely than those in less advanced classifications to have formed intimate relationships (Dyk & G. Adams, 1990; Fitch & G. Adams, 1983; Orlofsky, Marcia, & Lesser, 1973; Tesch & Whitbourne, 1982). Although these correlational findings do not address the causal implications of Erikson's developmental formulation, multiple findings imply that high-quality friendships—those that are intimate and in which the adolescent feels supported and cared for—are associated with a range of positive outcomes, including school engagement and positive self-esteem and mental health, and poor-quality relationships consistently are associated with the converse (e.g., Berndt & Keefe, 1992; Dubow, Tisak, Causey, Hryshko, & Reid, 1991; for reviews, see B. Brown, 2004; Hartup, 1996).

Summary Comment

Intimacy as an aspect of interdependence, though rooted in key family experiences and same-sex friendships prior to adolescence, is largely an emergent of adolescent development. Research findings, however, have revealed more about the observable characteristics of adolescent friendships than about the meaning of deeper, less discernible qualities like intimacy. As interest in close relationships grows in diverse fields, not just in developmental psychology, renewed focus on the nature and course of intimacy as a human capacity undoubtedly will require more concerted attention.

Sexuality

The psychosocial task of sexuality refers to adjusting to a sexually maturing body, managing sexual desires, forming sexual attitudes and values and learning about others' expectations, experimenting with sexual behaviors, and integrating these dimensions into one's sense of self (Crockett, Raffaelli, & Moilanen, 2003). As with other aspects of physical and psychological change during adolescence, psychosocial sexuality reflects complex exposure to social roles, behaviors, mores, and values, as well as biological changes. The focus of this section is social, attitudinal, and emotional aspects of sexuality rather than sexual behavior per se (e.g., patterns of sexual behavior, rates of sexual intercourse, or contraceptive use; for a recent comprehensive review of these topics, see Savin-Williams & Diamond, 2004).

Key elements of sexual response are present well before gonadal puberty. For example, sexual attraction is evident in diverse societies by the age of 10, the age at which adrenal puberty (adrenarche) occurs (Herdt & McClintock, 2000). The main developmental issues of psychosocial sexuality during the adolescent period, thus, are not biological ones but social ones. Pubertal changes and their endocrinological antecedents mainly affect the frequency and intensity of sexual arousal in both sexes. These latter sequelae are highly correlated with sexual activity of various kinds among both females and males, although their significance is moderated by social relationships and social context, especially among females (B. Miller et al., 1998).

Sexual fantasizing typically appears earliest and remains the most common adolescent sexual experience (Halpern, Udry, Campbell, & Suchindran, 1993; Katachadourian, 1990). Erotic fantasies appear to be followed by the initiation of masturbation, "making out," and sexual intercourse of various kinds (B. Miller et al., 1998; E. Smith & Udry, 1985). This sequence appears to be typical of European American youth, whereas the order in which these sexual experiences occur is less predictable for African American youth (E. Smith & Udry, 1985). Ethnic and racial differences are espe-

cially marked in the prevalence of intercourse and in the speed with which adolescents progress to intercourse from other sexual activity (Blum et al., 2000; Katchadourian, 1990).

Other generalizations about the normative development of psychosocial sexuality are difficult, because expectations, attitudes, and values vary considerably across cultural, societal, and ethnic-racial contexts (Brewster, 1994; Eyre, Auerswald, Hoffman, & Millstein, 1998; Eyre, Read, & Millstein, 1997; Paige & Paige, 1985; T. Smith, 1994; J. Whiting, Burbank, & Ratner, 1986), and even across neighborhoods (Billy, Brewster, & Grady, 1994; Ku, Sonenstein, & Pleck, 1993; for reviews, see Brooks-Gunn & Paikoff, 1997; Crockett et al., 2003; Savin-Williams & Diamond, 2004). For example, societal indicators of sexual behavior, contraceptive practices, sexually transmitted diseases, and early pregnancy among the United States and other Western nations parallel variations between those countries in prevalent attitudes about the desirability and appropriateness of sexual experimentation during adolescence and the proper goals of sexuality education (Fine, 1988), the impact of family relationships on sexual behavior (e.g., Weinstein & Thornton, 1989; for a review, see B. Miller, Benson, & Galbraith, 2001), and processes and peer norms of sexual behavior (e.g., Billy & Udry, 1985; for a review, see Crockett et al., 2003).

In the United States, social and cultural expectations account partly for changes in attitudes and values regarding sexuality since the middle of the twentieth century: (a) An increased proportion of both males and females now express approval of premarital intercourse when it occurs in the context of an affectionate relationship; and (b) a larger proportion of females now engage in sexual activity during the middle adolescent years than had done so in past decades (Moore & Rosenthal, 1993). Though often attributed to a "sexual revolution," the changes have occurred so gradually that the term *sexual evolution* may be more appropriate.

Social and interpersonal processes undoubtedly also contribute to persistent differences between the genders and between adolescents with heterosexual versus homosexual preferences in component tasks of achieving maturity in psychosocial sexuality. Evidence on these comparisons is not adequately balanced in that studies of girls' subjective experiences of sexuality are more numerous than studies of boys' experiences and many more studies focus on heterosexual adolescents than on homosexual or bisexual youth. Nevertheless, contrasting challenges are apparent. For example, girls, who are judged more harshly than boys for engaging in some types of sexual activities, are more likely than boys to express ambivalence about their sexuality and to fear harsh judgments if they are viewed as sexually active (Graber et al., 1999; Hillier, Harrison, & Warr, 1997; Moore & Rosenthal, 1993). Similarly, in contrast to females with heterosexual orientations, females with preferences for same-gender partners appear to experience more fluidity in their sexual-identity labels during adolescence (Diamond, 2000; for other research on bisexual attractions, see Weinberg, Williams, & Pryor, 1994).

Understanding the development of psychosocial sexuality is complicated further by the sizable individual differences in attitudes and values pertaining to relationships and sexual expression. Evidence of such differences comes from research showing that a sample of Australian adolescents could be differentiated according to five "styles" of psychosocial sexuality: (1) sexually naive, (2) sexually unassured, (3) sexually competent, (4) sexually adventurous, and (5) sexually driven (Buzwell & Rosenthal, 1996). These clusters varied correspondingly in tendencies toward sexual risk taking, a finding which implies that appropriate differentiation might be needed for interventions such as sex-education programs and campaigns to reduce the risk of teenage pregnancy or to promote safe sexual practices. Gender and sexual-orientation variations also are apparent. Females generally appear to emphasize emotional aspects of relationships as contexts for sexual behavior, whereas males more often emphasize physical satisfaction and release (Moore & Rosenthal, 1993), though within-gender views are highly variable (S. Thompson, 1995). Similarly, current evidence implies that the risk of social and emotional isolation in sexual relationships may be relatively greater for gay, lesbian, and bisexual adolescents of both genders than for adolescents with heterosexual orientations. Sanctions against explicit displays of same-sex romance in adolescence may make the maintenance of a more "normalized" emotional relationship difficult because sexual-minority youth often find it difficult to engage in many of the social and interpersonal activities that their heterosexual peers are permitted to enjoy (Diamond & Savin-Williams, 2003).

Further sources of individual variation in the development of psychosocial sexuality include significant others, especially relationships and processes involving family members, best friends, and romantic partners.

Longitudinal and cross-sectional evidence alike implicates positive parent-adolescent relationships in delayed initiation of intercourse, less frequent intercourse, and fewer sexual partners (e.g., Feldman & Brown, 1993; K. Miller, Sabo, Farrell, Barnes, & Melnick, 1998; for reviews, see Brooks-Gunn & Paikoff, 1997; B. Miller et al., 2001; Savin-Williams & Diamond, 2004). Peers, especially best friends, also contribute to individual differences in sexual expectations, attitudes, and behaviors, albeit more so among girls than boys (e.g., East, Felice, & Morgan, 1993; Whitbeck, Conger, & Kao, 1993). For European American males, though apparently not for African American males, a similar association may reflect selection of friends with similar activities and values (e.g., Bauman & Ennett, 1996; Billy, Rodgers, & Udry, 1984; Rowe et al., 1989).

Sexuality most often has been regarded as a source of developmental difficulties and risks during adolescence. This assumption stems partly from a concern about the impact of precocious sexual experience on normative developmental timetables and abilities and prevailing moral values regarding sexuality outside of marriage, especially for the very young, and partly from concerns about sexual exploitation, pregnancy, and health risks from early sexual activity (Brooks-Gunn & Paikoff, 1997; Savin-Williams & Diamond, 2004). Most studies have emphasized these and other dysfunctional outcomes; research findings consistently have shown that adolescents who become sexually active at a young age (typically, initiating intercourse before age 16) generally exhibit relatively greater risk for problematic outcomes, compared to adolescents who defer sexual activity. Indeed, early onset of sexual activity, rather than sexual activity per se, appears to account for the association between sexual activity and problematic psychosocial development. The link almost certainly is mediated by relative psychosocial immaturity and by a general orientation to unconventionality among early active teenagers (Jessor, Costa, Jessor, & Donovan, 1983). As a group, these adolescents tend to be less achievement oriented, more alienated from their parents, and more likely to exhibit other problem behaviors such as drug or alcohol abuse (e.g., Davies & Windle, 2000; Neeman, Hubbard, & Masten, 1995; B. Thomas & Hsiu, 1993; Zimmer-Gembeck et al., 2001).

Several theoretical formulations, bolstered by supportive findings from empirical research, view these associations as part of a cluster of behaviors defined as problems because they represent "transition proneness," or a pattern of earlier-than-usual transitions to behaviors that are typically expected of adults but not of adolescents (e.g., Bingham & Crockett, 1996; Capaldi, Crosby, & Stoolmiller, 1996; Costa, Jessor, Donovan, & Fortenberry, 1995; Jessor, Donovan, & Costa, 1991; Tubman, Windle, & Windle, 1996). This inference is bolstered by findings that later initiation of intercourse and less frequent intercourse for those who do begin early are inversely related to both religiosity (Rostosky, Wilcox, Comer Wright, & Randall, in press; Whitbeck, Yoder, Hoyt, & Conger, 1999) and high levels of educational aspirations and achievement (Jessor et al., 1983; Ohannessian & Crockett, 1993; Whitbeck et al., 1999). In a 4-year longitudinal study, self-restraint at age 10 to 11 predicted having had fewer sexual partners at the later time (Feldman & Brown, 1993). By contrast, sexual activity is associated with risk proneness (Rawlings, Boldero, & Wiseman, 1995). Contrary to common expectations, however, correlations between delayed intercourse and self-esteem generally have been negligible (e.g., Crockett et al., 1996; Whitbeck et al., 1999), although more depressed girls are at risk for higher levels for sexual activity (Whitbeck et al., 1999).

One concern about early sexual behavior is that a premature focus on sexual expression may interfere with successful integration of physical sexuality with attitudinal, emotional, and identity components. For example, Maccoby (1998) has observed that sexually adventurous female adolescents, unlike their male counterparts, may experience social condemnation, peer derision, and stereotyping that interfere with more positive developmental opportunities. Savin-Williams (1996) has suggested that negative social sanctions, stigmatization, and personal identity struggles may account partly for current findings showing a high rate of attempted suicide, emotional distress, school problems, and alcohol and drug abuse among self-identified gay, lesbian, and bisexual youth. Although some researchers question the validity of these findings (Savin-Williams, personal communication, October 22, 2004), many adolescents, regardless of sexual orientation, report negative experiences stemming from perceived pressure to engage in sexual activity, which they did not desire or for which they felt unready. These individuals disproportionately reported guilt and self-doubt following sexual experimentation, which colored feelings about subsequent sexual experiences (Moore & Rosenthal, 1993; Savin-Williams, 1996; Zani, 1991).

Unfortunately, relatively little research has been devoted to examining the hypothesized psychological advantages of integrating physical and psychosocial aspects of sexuality during adolescence, especially for sexual-minority youth. Contemporary views regard mature sexuality in the psychosocial sense as developmentally healthy rather than problematic (e.g., Brooks-Gunn & Paikoff, 1997; Carpenter, 2001; Savin-Williams & Diamond, 2004; Tolman, 1994; Tolman, Spencer, Rosen-Reynoso, & Porche, 2004). Accordingly, many observers have advocated that public school sex-education efforts include more detailed and comprehensive programs that directly address issues of attitudes, values, and responsible sexual decision making (including decisions to abstain from sexual activity), in contrast to the largely ineffective current models based exclusively on abstinence (Landry, Kaeser, & Richards, 1999). Some experts are cautiously optimistic that a combination of school-based sex education and community-based health clinics could reduce the rate of teenage pregnancy by providing the information about contraception, sex, and pregnancy that sexually active adolescents need (e.g., Frost & Forrest, 1995; Tiezzi, Lipshutz, Wrobleski, Vaughan, & McCarthy, 1997). Even more broadly based programs may be needed, as in one highly effective combination of service learning with classroom discussions about life options (Allen, Philliber, Herrling, & Kuperminc, 1997). Efforts like these integrate sexuality into a framework of healthy interdependence (i.e., focused on the relational aspects of sexuality) and independence (i.e., focused on responsible and self-governed sexual behavior).

Summary Comment

Interdependence implies a cluster of interrelated psychosocial competencies. Thus far, researchers have focused primarily on the separate tasks of attachment, intimacy, and sexuality but have given little attention to the interrelations among them. Isolated findings suggest that, for example, questions about the role of attachment in the development of intimacy (e.g., Cassidy, 2001; Collins & Sroufe, 1999) and the degree to which sexuality is integrated with intimacy and commitment in early adulthood (e.g., Bogaert & Sadava, 2002; Collins, Hennighausen, & Sroufe, 1998) deserve further attention. These and other questions regarding the extent of such linkages and the processes by which they occur promise to illuminate the nature of adolescent development in relational contexts.

CONCLUDING THEMES

Research on adolescence, which was moribund halfway through the twentieth century, now is a vital and productive area of developmental psychology. Professional organizations are flourishing, and scholarly journals and multiple major volumes of reviews (e.g., G. Adams & Berzonsky, 2003; R. Lerner & Steinberg, 2004) attest to the quantity and quality of archival research and the desire of scholars and scholars-in-training for authoritative sources in the field. In a sense, the study of adolescence has attained its majority.

As in other vital subfields of psychology, research on adolescence reflects significant theoretical and empirical themes in psychology generally and developmental psychology in particular. One such theme, the importance of contextual as well as traditionally intraindividual forces in human functioning, has become a hallmark of research on adolescence during the past 2 decades (e.g., Grotevant, 1998; Larson & Wilson, 2004; R. Lerner & Steinberg, 2004). Initially focused largely on institutional, economic, and cultural conditions, contemporary interest in context is now realizing the vision of developmental systems theorists (e.g., Bronfenbrenner, 1979; Magnusson & Stättin, 1998; Sameroff, 1983). The emphasis has shifted from external, often distal forces as moderating influences on intrapersonal processes to processes by which intraindividual processes are engaged in dynamic interplay with both proximal (e.g., interpersonal) and distal (e.g., economic systems) environments.

This chapter underscores how this more inclusive view is expanding understanding of the nature and significance of psychological functioning during adolescence. Extensive findings substantiate long-standing speculations that perceptions and expectancies emanating from society and culture, via interactions with salient members of social networks, mediate the psychological and behavioral impact of pubertal changes. Expanded knowledge of brain development and function is clarifying many previously veiled processes that contribute to this interactive nexus of influences. Likewise, the extent and nature of interrelated social processes in diverse interpersonal contexts, from those typifying relationships with parents and siblings to those more typical of expanding networks of peers, is moving the field beyond simplistic notions of the distinctiveness and separateness of family and extrafamilial influences that characterized the writings of adolescent researchers for three quarters of a century (Collins & Laursen, 2004a).

Full-fledged realizations of developmental systems formulations in research designs and statistical analyses remain a goal for the future, but an appreciation of the extensive interconnections among individual and contextual factors has contributed greatly to the creative thrust in contemporary research with adolescents.

Although the overall level of activity and the gains accrued from studying phenomena of adolescence are impressive, some topics have received less attention and less rigorous investigation than others. Consequently, some fundamental facets of growth and change in adolescence are understood only marginally better today than at the time of the publication of the previous edition of this *Handbook*. Whereas the study of social influences has advanced remarkably, cognitive development and intellectual performance in adolescence have been addressed in relatively few recent studies. Similarly, emotional development and self-regulation, both key elements in the transition from childhood to adulthood, have attracted only tangential attention from adolescence researchers. These topics represent a growing interest in the development of positive competence as a complement to the long-standing emphasis on deficits in competence as factors in maladaptation during and beyond adolescence. Several of the key psychosocial tasks that for decades have served as theoretical and conceptual hallmarks of adolescence, such as the development of the capacity for mature intimacy in close relationships, are the focus of only a minority of the research findings reported each year. Autonomy and identity arguably are exceptions to this generalization, but even when these widely studied aspects of adolescent functioning are brought into research, the purpose is to assess an adolescent's current status rather than to examine the nature and course of development toward mature functioning during adolescence and beyond.

This unevenness in research emphases challenges researchers to complement the vigorous attention to contexts of adolescent development with renewed attention to developmental issues. From questions of how adolescents function differently in relationships with different partners, in varying ethnic or cultural milieu, or in relatively disadvantaged versus relatively more advantaged environments, research should move to questions of how variations in self-regulatory competence or in capacities for seeking gratification for one's partner as well as oneself in sexual relationships emerge from characteristic interpersonal experiences in families, peer networks, school, and community experiences. Such questions push the boundaries of widely used research designs and statistical methods, but rapidly emerging innovations in the field imply that many current limitations may be overcome in the near future (R. Lerner & Steinberg, 2004).

In addition to greater emphasis on developmental processes, more attention to psychological processes generally would enhance research on adolescence. At present, studies focus heavily on individual and relational correlates of antecedent and contemporaneous aspects of development (e.g., behavior problems in relation to parental styles or peer-group values) or as contributors to later competence (e.g., parent-adolescent interactions as predictors of later interactions with dating partners). Relatively few studies examine the mediating processes that account for these links (for exemplary exceptions, see B. Brown et al., 1993; E. Carlson et al., 2004; R. Conger et al., 2000; K. Kim et al., 2001). Greater attention to biopsychosocial processes derived from current theories would move research beyond the descriptive level toward more comprehensive understanding of adolescent functioning.

The goal of research on adolescence is the same in the 1st decade of the twenty-first century as it was 100 years ago: to illuminate the nature and significance of the multiple transitions embedded in achieving maturity. For the most part researchers have set their sights on documenting *which* persons and circumstances influence adolescents most and *to what extent* these influences account for variability in the maturity of adolescents. The advances of recent decades have come primarily from the realization that the candidate variables of interest extend to the diverse interpersonal, institutional, societal, and cultural contexts in which adolescents encounter opportunities, demands, resources, and obstacles relevant to psychological maturation. In the next decade, a more comprehensive understanding of the nature and course of achieving maturity promises to come from extending the question of *which* influences to questions of *how* and *through what processes* adolescents develop the capacities for healthy independence and healthy interdependence in a complex world.

REFERENCES

Abecassis, M., Hartup, W. W., Haselager, G. J. T., Scholte, R. H. J., & van Lieshout, C. F. M. (2002). Mutual antipathies and their significance in middle childhood and adolescence. *Child Development, 75*(5), 1543–1556.

Adalbjarnardottir, S., & Hafsteinsson, L. G. (2001). Adolescents' perceived parenting styles and their substance use: Concurrent and longitudinal analyses. *Journal of Research on Adolescence, 11*(4), 401–423.

Adams, G. R., & Berzonsky, M. D. (Eds.). (2003). *Blackwell handbook of adolescence.* Malden, MA: Blackwell.

Adams, R., & Laursen, B. (2001). The organization and dynamics of adolescent conflict with parents and friends. *Journal of Marriage and the Family, 63,* 97–110.

Ainsworth, J. W. (2002). Why does it take a village? The mediation of neighborhood effects on educational achievement. *Social Forces, 81*(1), 117–152.

Ainsworth, M. S. (1989). Attachments beyond infancy. *American Psychologist, 44*(4), 709–716.

Allen, J., Hauser, S., Bell, K., & O'Connor, T. (1994). Longitudinal assessment of autonomy and relatedness in adolescent-family interactions as predictors of adolescent ego development and self-esteem. *Child Development, 65,* 179–194.

Allen, J., Hauser, S., Eickholt, C., Bell, K., & O'Connor, T. (1994). Autonomy and relatedness in family interactions as predictors of expressions of negative adolescent affect. *Journal of Research on Adolescence, 4,* 535–552.

Allen, J., Hauser, S., O'Connor, T., Bell, K., & Eickholt, C. (1996). The connection of observed hostile family conflict to adolescents' developing autonomy and relatedness with parents. *Development and Psychopathology, 8,* 425–442.

Allen, J. P., Hauser, S. T., O'Connor, T. G., & Bell, K. L. (2002). Prediction of peer-rated adult hostility from autonomy struggles in adolescent-family interactions. *Development and Psychopathology, 14,* 123–137.

Allen, J. P., & Land, D. (1999). Attachment in adolescence. In J. Cassidy & P. R. Shaver (Eds.), *Handbook of attachment: Theory, research, and clinical applications* (pp. 319–335). New York: Guilford Press.

Allen, J. P., McElhaney, K. B., Kuperminc, G. P., & Jodl, K. M. (in press). Stability and change in attachment security across adolescence. *Child Development, 75,* 1792–1805.

Allen, J. P., Philliber, S., Herrling, S., & Kuperminc, G. P. (1997). Preventing teen pregnancy and academic failure: Experimental evaluation of a developmentally based approach. *Child Development, 68*(4), 729–742.

Amato, P. R., & Fowler, F. (2002). Parenting practices, child adjustment, and family diversity. *Journal of Marriage and the Family, 64*(3), 703–716.

Anderman, E. (1998). The middle school experience: Effects on math and science achievement of adolescents with LD. *Journal of Learning Disabilities, 31,* 128–138.

Anderman, E., & Midgley, C. (1996, March). *Changes in achievement goal orientations after the transition to middle school.* Paper presented at the biennial meeting of the Society for Research on Adolescence, Boston, MA.

Anderson, E., Hetherington, E. M., Reiss, D., & Howe, G. (1994). Parents' nonshared treatment of siblings and the development of social competence during adolescence. *Journal of Family Psychology, 8,* 303–320.

Andersson, T., & Magnusson, D. (1990). Biological maturation in adolescence and the development of drinking habits and alcohol abuse among young males: A prospective longitudinal study. *Journal of Youth and Adolescence, 19,* 33–42.

Archer, S. (1982). The lower age boundaries of identity development. *Child Development, 53,* 1551–1556.

Ardelt, M., & Day, L. (2002). Parents, siblings, and peers: Close social relationships and adolescent deviance. *Journal of Early Adolescence, 22*(3), 310–349.

Armsden, G., & Greenberg, M. T. (1984). *The inventory of parent and peer attachment: Individual differences and their relationship to psychological well-being in adolescence.* Unpublished manuscript, University of Washington.

Arnett, J. (2000). Emerging adulthood: A theory of development from the late teens through the twenties. *American Psychologist, 55,* 469–480.

Aro, H., & Taipale, V. (1987). The impact of timing of puberty on psychosomatic symptoms among 14- to 16-year-old Finnish girls. *Child Development, 58,* 261–268.

Aseltine, R. H., Gore, S., & Colten, M. E. (1994). Depression and the social developmental context of adolescence. *Journal of Personality and Social Psychology, 67*(2), 252–263.

Bachman, J., & Schulenberg, J. (1993). How part-time work intensity relates to drug use, problem behavior, time use, and satisfaction among high school seniors: Are these consequences or merely correlates? *Developmental Psychology, 29,* 220–235.

Bandura, A. (1964). The stormy decade: Fact or fiction? *Psychology in the Schools, 1,* 224–231.

Bank, L., Reid, J., & Greenley, K. (1994, February). *Middle childhood predictors of adolescent and early adult aggression.* Paper presented at the biennial meeting of the Society for Research on Adolescence, San Diego, CA.

Barber, B. (1994). Cultural, family, and personal contexts of parent-adolescent conflict. *Journal of Marriage and the Family, 56,* 375–386.

Barber, B. (1996). Parental psychological control: Revisiting a neglected construct. *Child Development, 67,* 3296–3319.

Barrett Singer, A. T., & Weinstein, R. S. (2000). Differential parental treatment predicts achievement and self-perceptions in two cultural contexts. *Journal of Family Psychology, 14*(3), 491–509.

Barry, C. M., & Wigfield, A. (2002). Self-perceptions of friendship-making ability and perceptions of friends' deviant behavior: Childhood to adolescence. *Journal of Early Adolescence, 22*(2), 143–172.

Barton, P. (1989). *Earning and learning.* Princeton, NJ: National Assessment of Educational Progress, Educational Testing Service.

Bauman, K. E., & Ennett, S. T. (1996). On the importance of peer influence for adolescent drug use: Commonly neglected considerations. *Addiction, 91*(2), 185–198.

Baumeister, R., & Tice, D. (1986). How adolescence became the struggle for self: A historical transformation of psychological development. In J. Suls & A. Greenwald (Eds.), *Psychological perspectives on the self* (Vol. 3, pp. 183–201). Hillsdale, NJ: Erlbaum.

Baumeister, R. F., & Leary, M. R. (1995). The need to belong: Desire for interpersonal attachments as a fundamental human motivation. *Psychological Bulletin, 117*(3), 497–529.

Baumer, E. P., & South, S. J. (2001). Community effects on youth sexual activity. *Journal of Marriage and the Family, 63*(2), 540–554.

Baumrind, D. (1991). Effective parenting during the early adolescent transition. In P. A. Cowan & E. M. Hetherington (Eds.), *Advances in family research* (Vol. 2, pp. 111–163). Hillsdale, NJ: Erlbaum.

Baxter, L. A., Dun, T., & Sahlstein, E. (2001). Rules for relating communicated among social network members. *Journal of Social and Personal Relationships, 18*(2), 173–199.

Beam, M. R., Chen, C., & Greenberger, E. (2002). The nature of adolescents' relationship with their "very important" nonparental adults. *American Journal of Community Psychology, 30,* 305–325.

Becker-Stoll, F., & Fremmer-Bombik, E. (1997, April). *Adolescent-mother interaction and attachment: A longitudinal study.* Paper presented at the biennial meeting of the Society for Research in Child Development, Washington, DC.

Belsky, J., Steinberg, L., & Draper, P. (1991). Childhood experience, interpersonal development, and reproductive strategy: An evolutionary theory of socialization. *Child Development, 62,* 647–670.

Benenson, J. F., & Christakos, A. (2003). The greater fragility of females' versus males' closest same-sex friendships. *Child Development, 74*(4), 1123–1129.

Berndt, T. (1979). Developmental changes in conformity to peers and parents. *Developmental Psychology, 15,* 608–616.

Berndt, T., & Mekos, D. (1995). Adolescents' perceptions of the stressful and desirable aspects of the transition to junior high. *Journal of Research on Adolescence, 5,* 123–142.

Berndt, T. J., Hawkins, J. A., & Jiao, Z. (1999). Influences of friends and friendships on adjustment to junior high school. *Merrill-Palmer Quarterly, 45*(1), 13–41.

Berndt, T. J., & Keefe, K. (1992). Friends' influence on adolescents' perceptions of themselves in school. In D. H. Schunk & J. L. Meece (Eds.), *Students' perceptions in the classroom* (pp. 51–73). Hillsdale, NJ: Erlbaum.

Berscheid, E., Snyder, M., & Omoto, A. M. (1989). Issues in studying close relationships. In C. Hendrick (Ed.), *Close relationships* (pp. 63–91). Newbury Park, CA: Sage.

Beyth-Marom, R., Austin, L., Fischoff, B., Palmgren, C., & Jacobs-Quadrel, M. (1993). Perceived consequences of risky behaviors: Adults and adolescents. *Developmental Psychology, 29,* 549–563.

Biafora, F., Jr., Warheit, G., Vega, W., & Gil, A. (1994). Stressful life events and changes in substance use among a multiracial/ethnic sample of adolescent boys. *American Journal of Community Psychology, 22,* 296–311.

Billy, J. O. G., Brewster, K. L., & Grady, W. R. (1994). Contextual effects of the sexual behavior of adolescent women. *Journal of Marriage and the Family, 56*(2), 387–404.

Billy, J. O. G., Rodgers, J. L., & Udry, J. R. (1984). Adolescent sexual behavior and friendship choice. *Social Forces, 62,* 653–678.

Billy, J. O. G., & Udry, J. R. (1985). The influence of male and female best friends on adolescents' sexual behavior. *Adolescence, 20,* 21–32.

Bingham, C. R., & Crockett, L. J. (1996). Longitudinal adjustment patterns of boys and girls experiencing early, middle, and late sexual intercourse. *Developmental Psychology, 32,* 647–658.

Blos, P. (1967). The second individuation process of adolescence. In R. S. Eissler, A. Freud, H. Hartmann, & M. Kris (Eds.), *Psychoanalytic study of the child* (Vol. 22, pp. 162–186). New York: International Universities Press.

Blos, P. (1979). *The adolescent passage.* New York: International Universities Press.

Blum, R., & Rinehart, P. (2000). *Reducing the risk: Connections that make a difference in the lives of youth.* Minneapolis: Division of General Pediatrics and Adolescent Health, University of Minnesota.

Blum, R. W., Beuhring, T., Shew, M. L., Bearinger, L. H., Sieving, R. E., & Resnick, M. D. (2000). The effects of race/ethnicity, income, and family structure on adolescent risk behaviors. *American Journal of Public Health, 90*(12), 1879–1884.

Blumenthal, S. J., & Kupfer, D. J. (1988). Overview of early detection and treatment strategies for suicidal behavior in young people. *Journal of Youth and Adolescence, 17*(1), 1–23.

Boehnke, K., Silbereisen, R. K., Eisenberg, N., Reykowski, J., & Palmonari, A. (1989). Developmental pattern of prosocial motivation: A cross national study. *Journal of Cross Cultural Psychology, 20*(3), 219–243.

Bogaert, A. F., & Sadava, S. (2002). Adult attachment and sexual behavior. *Personal Relationships, 9*(2), 191–204.

Bowen, G. L., & Chapman, M. V. (1996). Poverty, neighborhood danger, social support, and the individual adaptation among "at risk" youth in urban areas. *Journal of Family Issues, 17,* 641–666.

Bowen, N. K., Bowen, G. L., & Ware, W. B. (2002). Neighborhood social disorganization, families, and the educational behavior of adolescents. *Journal of Adolescent Research, 17,* 468–490.

Bowlby, J. (1982). *Attachment and loss* (2nd ed.). New York: Basic Books. (Original work published 1962)

Boyes, M., & Allen, S. (1993). Styles of parent-child interaction and moral reasoning in adolescence. *Merrill-Palmer Quarterly, 39,* 551–570.

Bradley, R. H., Corwyn, R. F., Burchinal, J., McAdoo, H., & García Coll, C. (2001). The home environments of children in the United States: Pt. 2. Relationships with behavioral development through age thirteen. *Child Development, 72*(6), 1868–1886.

Brewer, M. B., & Caporael, L. R. (1990). Selfish genes versus selfish people: Sociobiology as origin myth. *Motivation and Emotion, 14*(4), 237–243.

Brewster, K. L. (1994). Race differences in sexual activity among adolescent women: The role of neighborhood characteristics. *American Sociological Review, 59*(3), 408–424.

Brody, G., Stoneman, Z., & Burke, M. (1987). Child temperaments, maternal differential treatment, and sibling relationships. *Developmental Psychology, 23,* 354–362.

Brody, G., Stoneman, Z., & McCoy, J. (1994). Forecasting sibling relationships in early adolescence from child temperaments and family processes in middle childhood. *Child Development, 65,* 771–784.

Broh, B. A. (2002). Linking extracurricular programming to academic achievement: Who benefits and why? *Sociology of Education, 75*(1), 69–95.

Bronfenbrenner, U. (1961). Some family antecedents of responsibility and leadership in adolescents. In L. Petrullo & B. Bass (Eds.), *Leadership and interpersonal behavior* (pp. 239–272). New York: Holt, Rinehart and Winston.

Bronfenbrenner, U. (1979). *The ecology of human development.* Cambridge, MA: Harvard University Press.

Brooks-Gunn, J., Duncan, G., Klebanov, P., & Sealand, N. (1993). Do neighborhoods influence child and adolescent development? *American Journal of Sociology, 99,* 353–395.

Brooks-Gunn, J., & Paikoff, R. (1997). Sexuality and developmental transitions during adolescence. In J. Schulenberg & J. L. Maggs (Eds.), *Health risks and developmental transitions during adolescence* (pp. 190–219). New York: Cambridge University Press.

Brooks-Gunn, J., Petersen, A. C., & Eichorn, D. (1985). The study of maturational timing effects in adolescence. *Journal of Youth and Adolescence, 14*(3), 149–161.

Brown, B. (2004). Adolescents' relationships with peers. In R. Lerner & L. Steinberg (Eds.), *Handbook of adolescent psychology* (2nd ed., pp. 363–394). Hoboken, NJ: Wiley.

Brown, B., Clasen, D., & Eicher, S. (1986). Perceptions of peer pressure, peer conformity dispositions, and self-reported behavior among adolescents. *Developmental Psychology, 22,* 521–530.

Brown, B., Mounts, N., Lamborn, S., & Steinberg, L. (1993). Parenting practices and peer group affiliation in adolescence. *Child Development, 64,* 467–482.

Brown, J. D., & Cantor, J. (2000). An agenda for research on youth and the media. In J. D. Brown & J. Cantor (Eds.), The mass media and adolescents' health. *Journal of Adolescent Health, 27*(Suppl. 1), 2–7.

Buchanan, C., Eccles, J., & Becker, J. (1992). Are adolescents the victims of raging hormones? Evidence for activational effects of hormones on moods and behavior at adolescence. *Psychological Bulletin, 111,* 62–107.

Buhrmester, D., & Furman, W. (1987). The development of companionship and intimacy. *Child Development, 58,* 1101–1113.

Buhrmester, D., & Furman, W. (1990). Perceptions of sibling relationships during middle childhood and adolescence. *Child Development, 61,* 1387–1396.

Bukowski, W. M., Sippola, L. K., & Hoza, B. (1999). Same and other: Interdependency between participation in same- and other-sex friendships. *Journal of Youth and Adolescence, 28*(4), 439–459.

Bulcroft, R., Carmody, D., & Bulcroft, K. (1996). Patterns of parental independence giving to adolescents: Variations by race, age, and gender of child. *Journal of Marriage and the Family, 58,* 866–883.

Bullock, B. M., & Dishion, T. J. (2002). Sibling collusion and problem behavior in early adolescence: Toward a process model for family mutuality. *Journal of Abnormal Child Psychology, 30*(2), 143–153.

Bumpus, M. F., Crouter, A. C., & McHale, S. M. (2001). Parental autonomy granting during adolescence: Exploring gender differences in context. *Developmental Psychology, 37*(2), 163–173.

Bussell, D., Neiderhiser, J., Pike, A., Plomin, R., Simmens, S., Howe, G. W., et al. (1999). Adolescents' relationships to siblings and mothers: A multivariate genetic analysis. *Developmental Psychology, 35,* 1248–1259.

Buzwell, S., & Rosenthal, D. (1996). Constructing a sexual self: Adolescents' sexual self-perceptions and sexual risk-taking. *Journal of Research on Adolescence, 6*(4), 489–513.

Caine, N. (1986). Behavior during puberty and adolescence. In G. Mitchell & J. Erwin (Eds.), *Comparative primate biology: Vol. 2A. Behavior, conservation, and ecology* (pp. 327–361). New York: Alan R. Liss.

Cairns, R. B., & Cairns, B. D. (1994). *Lifelines and risks: Pathways of youth in our time.* New York: Cambridge University Press.

Cantor, J. (2000). Media violence. *Journal of Adolescent Health, 27,* 30–34.

Capaldi, D. M., Crosby, L., & Stoolmiller, M. (1996). Predicting the timing of first sexual intercourse for at-risk adolescent males. *Child Development, 67*(2), 344–359.

Carlson, E. A., Sroufe, L. A., Collins, W. A., Jimerson, S., Weinfield, N., Hennighausen, K., et al. (1999). Early environmental support and elementary school adjustment as predictors of school adjustment in middle adolescence. *Journal of Adolescent Research, 14,* 72–94.

Carlson, E. A., Sroufe, L. A., & Egeland, B. (2004). The construction of experience: A longitudinal study of representation and behavior. *Child Development, 75*(1), 66–83.

Carpenter, L. M. (2001). The ambiguity of "having sex": The subjective experience of virginity loss in the United States. *Journal of Sex Research, 38,* 127–139.

Carson, D., Chowdhury, A., Perry, C., & Pati, C. (1999). Family characteristics and adolescent competence in India: Investigation of youth in southern Orissa. *Journal of Youth and Adolescence, 28,* 211–233.

Carver, K., Joyner, K., & Udry, J. R. (2003). National estimates of adolescent romantic relationships. In P. Florsheim (Ed.), *Adolescent romantic relations and sexual behavior: Theory, research, and practical implications* (pp. 23–56). Mahwah, NJ: Erlbaum.

Casey, B. J., Giedd, J. N., & Thomas, K. M. (2000). Structural and functional brain development and its relation to cognitive development. *Biological Psychology, 54,* 241–257.

Caspi, A., Lynam, D., Moffitt, T., & Silva, P. (1993). Unraveling girls' delinquency: Biological, dispositional, and contextual contributions to adolescent misbehavior. *Developmental Psychology, 29,* 19–30.

Cassidy, J. (1999). The nature of the child's ties. In J. Cassidy & P. R. Shaver (Eds.), *Handbook of attachment: Theory, research, and clinical applications* (pp. 3–20). New York: Guilford Press.

Cassidy, J. (2001). Truth, lies, and intimacy: An attachment perspective. *Attachment and Human Development, 3*(2), 121–155.

Cauffman, E., & Steinberg, L. (2000). (Im)maturity of judgment in adolescence: Why adolescents may be less culpable than adults. *Behavioral Sciences and the Law, 18,* 1–21.

Chao, R. (1994). Beyond parental control and authoritarian parenting style: Understanding Chinese parenting through the cultural notion of training. *Child Development, 65,* 1111–1119.

Chao, R. (2001). Extending research on the consequences of parenting style for Chinese Americans and European Americans. *Child Development, 72*(6), 1832–1843.

Chen, Z.-Y., & Dornbusch, S. M. (1998). Relating aspects of adolescent emotional autonomy to academic achievement and deviant behavior. *Journal of Adolescent Research, 13*(3), 293–319.

Chun, Y.-J., & MacDermid, S. M. (1997). Perceptions of family differentiation, individuation, and self-esteem among Korean adolescents. *Journal of Marriage and the Family, 59*(2), 451–462.

Clark, R., Novak, J. D., & Dupree, D. (2002). Relationship of perceived parenting practices to anger regulation and coping strategies in African American adolescents. *Journal of Adolescence, 25*(4), 373–384.

Cole, A., & Kerns, K. A. (2001). Perceptions of sibling qualities and activities of early adolescents. *Journal of Early Adolescence, 21*(2), 204–226.

Collins, W. A. (1995). Relationships and development: Family adaptation to individual change. In S. Shulman (Ed.), *Close relationships and socioemotional development* (pp. 128–154). New York: Ablex.

Collins, W. A. (2003). More than a myth: The developmental significance of romantic relationships during adolescence. *Journal of Research on Adolescence, 13*(1), 1–24.

Collins, W. A., Gleason, T., & Sesma, A., Jr. (1997). Internalization, autonomy, and relationships: Development during adolescence. In J. E. Grusec & L. Kuczynski (Eds.), *Parenting and children's internalization of values* (pp. 78–102). New York: Wiley.

Collins, W. A., Hennighausen, K. H., Schmit, D. T., & Sroufe, L. A. (1997). Developmental precursors of romantic relationships: A longitudinal analysis. In S. Shulman & W. A. Collins (Eds.), *Romantic relationships in adolescence: Developmental perspectives* (pp. 69–84). San Francisco: Jossey-Bass.

Collins, W. A., Hennighausen, K. H., & Sroufe, L. A. (1998, June). Developmental precursors of intimacy in romantic relationships: A longitudinal analysis. In W. A. Collins (Chair), *Intimacy in childhood and adolescence: Developmental perspectives on relationships.* Symposium conducted at the International Conference on Personal Relationships, Saratoga Springs, NY.

Collins, W. A., & Laursen, B. (2004a). Changing relationships, changing youth: Interpersonal contexts of adolescent development. *Journal of Early Adolescence, 24,* 55–62.

Collins, W. A., & Laursen, B. (2004b). Parent-adolescent relationships and influences. In R. Lerner & L. Steinberg (Eds.), *Handbook of adolescent psychology* (2nd ed., pp. 331–361). New York: Wiley.

Collins, W. A., Maccoby, E., Steinberg, L., Hetherington, E. M., & Bornstein, M. (2000). Contemporary research on parenting: The case for nature and nurture. *American Psychologist, 55,* 218–232.

Collins, W. A., & Repinski, D. J. (1994). Relationships during adolescence: Continuity and change in interpersonal perspective. In R. Montemayor, G. R. Adams, & T. P. Gullotta (Eds.), *Personal relationships during adolescence* (pp. 7–36). Thousand Oaks, CA: Sage.

Collins, W. A., & Repinski, D. J. (2001). Parents and adolescents as transformers of relationships: Dyadic adaptations to developmental change. In J. R. M. Gerris (Ed.), *Dynamics of parenting: International perspectives on nature and sources of parenting* (pp. 429–443). Leuven, The Netherlands: Garant Publishers.

Collins, W. A., & Sroufe, L. A. (1999). Capacity for intimate relationships: A developmental construction. In W. Furman, C. Feiring, & B. B. Brown (Eds.), *Contemporary perspectives on adolescent romantic relationships* (pp. 123–147). New York: Cambridge University Press.

Collins, W. A., & Van Dulmen, M. (2006a). Friendships and romantic relationships in emerging adulthood: Continuities and discontinuities. In J. J. Arnett & J. Tanner (Eds.), *Emerging adults in America: Coming of age in the 21st century* (pp. 219–234). Washington, DC: American Psychological Association.

Collins, W. A., & Van Dulmen, M. (2006b). "The course of true love(s). . .": Origins and pathways in the development of romantic relationships. In A. Booth & A. Crouter (Eds.), *Romance and sex in adolescence and emerging adulthood: Risks and opportunities* (pp. 63–86). Mahwah, NJ: Erlbaum.

Combrinck-Graham, L. (1985). A developmental model for family systems. *Family Process, 24*(2), 139–150.

Conger, K., & Conger, R. D. (1994). Differential parenting and change in sibling differences in delinquency. *Journal of Family Psychology, 8,* 287–302.

Conger, K., Conger, R. D., & Elder, G., Jr. (1994). Sibling relationships during hard times. In R. Conger & G. Elder Jr. (Eds.), *Families in troubled times: Adapting to change in rural America* (pp. 235–252). New York: Aldine.

Conger, K., Conger, R. D., & Elder, G., Jr. (1997). Parents, siblings, psychological control, and adolescent adjustment. *Journal of Adolescent Research, 12,* 113–138.

Conger, R. D., Conger, K., Elder, G., Jr., Lorenz, F., Simons, R., & Whitbeck, L. (1992). A family process model of economic hardship and adjustment of early adolescent boys. *Child Development, 63,* 526–541.

Conger, R. D., Cui, M., Bryant, C. M., & Elder, G. H., Jr. (2000). Competence in early adult romantic relationships: A developmental perspective on family influences. *Journal of Personality and Social Psychology, 79,* 224–237.

Connolly, J. A., Craig, W., Goldberg, A., & Pepler, D. (1999). Conceptions of cross-sex friendships and romantic relationships in early adolescence. *Journal of Youth and Adolescence, 28,* 481–494.

Connolly, J., Craig, W., Goldberg, A., & Pepler, D. (2004). Mixed-gender groups, dating, and romantic relationships in early adolescence. *Journal of Research on Adolescence, 14,* 185–207.

Connolly, J., Furman, W., & Konarski, R. (2000). The role of peers in the emergence of heterosexual romantic relationships in adolescence. *Child Development, 71*(5), 1395–1408.

Connolly, J. A., & Goldberg, A. (1999). Romantic relationships in adolescence: The role of friends and peers in their emergence and development. In W. Furman, B. B. Brown, & C. Feiring (Eds.), *The development of romantic relationships in adolescence* (pp. 266–290). New York: Cambridge University Press.

Connolly, J. A., & Johnson, A. (1996). Adolescents' romantic relationships and the structure and quality of their close interpersonal ties. *Personal Relationships, 3,* 185–195.

Connolly, J. A., & Konarski, R. (1994). Peer self-concept in adolescence: Analysis of factor structure and of associations with peer experience. *Journal of Research on Adolescence, 4*(3), 385–403.

Cook, T. D., Herman, M. R., Phillips, M., & Settersten, R. A., Jr. (2002). Some ways in which neighborhoods, nuclear families, friendship groups, and schools jointly affect changes in early adolescent development. *Child Development, 73*(4), 1283–1309.

Cook, W. L. (2001). Interpersonal influence in family systems: A social relations model analysis. *Child Development, 72*(4), 1179–1197.

Cooper, C., Baker, H., Polichar, D., & Welsh, M. (1994). Values and communication of Chinese, European, Filipino, Mexican, and Vietnamese American adolescents with their families and friends. In S. Shulman & W. A. Collins (Eds.), *The role of fathers in adolescent development: New directions for child development* (pp. 73–89). San Francisco: Jossey-Bass.

Cooper, C. R. (1994). Cultural perspectives on continuity and change in adolescents' relationships. In R. Montemayor, G. R. Adams, & T. P. Gullotta (Eds.), *Personal relationships during adolescence* (pp. 78–100). Thousand Oaks, CA: Sage.

Cooper, C. R., Grotevant, H. D., & Condon, S. (1983). Individuality and connectedness in the family as a context for adolescent identity formation and role taking skill. In H. D. Grotevant & C. R. Cooper (Eds.), *Adolescent development in the family* (pp. 43–60). San Francisco: Jossey-Bass.

Costa, F. M., Jessor, R., Donovan, J. E., & Fortenberry, J. D. (1995). Early initiation of sexual intercourse: The influence of psychosocial unconventionality. *Journal of Research on Adolescence, 5*(1), 93–121.

Coulton, C., & Pandey, S. (1992). Geographic concentration of poverty and risk to children in urban environments. *American Behavioral Scientist, 35,* 238–257.

Crane, J. (1991). The epidemic theory of ghettos and neighborhood effects on dropping out and teenage childbearing. *American Journal of Sociology, 96,* 1226–1259.

Crittenden, P., Claussen, A., & Sugarman, D. (1994). Physical and psychological maltreatment in middle childhood and adolescence. *Development and Psychopathology, 6,* 145–164.

Crockett, L., Bingham, C., Chopak, J., & Vicary, J. (1996). Timing of first sexual intercourse: The role of social control, social learning and problem behavior. *Journal of Youth and Adolescence, 25,* 89–111.

Crockett, L. J., Raffaelli, M., & Moilanen, K. L. (2003). Adolescent sexuality: Behavior and meaning. In G. R. Adams & M. D. Berzonsky (Eds.), *Blackwell handbook of adolescence* (pp. 371–392). Malden, MA: Blackwell.

Crouter, A. C., & Head, M. R. (2002). Parental monitoring and knowledge of children. In M. Bornstein (Ed.), *Handbook on parenting* (2nd ed., pp. 461–484). Mahwah, NJ: Erlbaum.

Crowell, J., & Owens, G. (1996). *Current relationship interview and scoring system* (Version 2). Unpublished manuscript, State University of New York at Stony Brook.

Crowell, J. A., Fraley, R. C., & Shaver, P. R. (1999). Measurement of individual differences in adolescent and adult attachment. In J. Cassidy & P. R. Shaver (Eds.), *Handbook of attachment: Theory, research, and clinical applications* (pp. 434–465). New York: Guilford Press.

Crystal, D., Watanabe, H., Weinfurt, K., & Wu, C. (1998). Concepts of human differences: A comparison of American, Japanese, and Chinese children and adolescents. *Developmental Psychology, 34,* 714–722.

Csikszentmihalyi, M., & Larson, R. W. (1984). *Being adolescent.* New York: Basic Books.

Cyranowski, J., Frank, E., Young, E., & Shear, K. (2000). Adolescent onset of the gender difference in lifetime rates of major depression. *Archives of General Psychiatry, 57,* 21–27.

Dahl, R. E. (2001). Affect regulation, brain development, and behavioral/emotional health in adolescence. *CNS Spectrums, 6*(1), 1–12.

Daniels, D., Dunn, J., Furstenberg, F., Jr., & Plomin, R. (1985). Environmental differences within the family and adjustment differences within pairs of adolescent siblings. *Child Development, 56,* 764–774.

Darling, N., Dowdy, B. B., Van Horn, M. L., & Cadwell, L. L. (1999). Mixed-sex settings and the perception of competence. *Journal of Youth and Adolescence, 28*(4), 461–480.

Darling, N., Hamilton, S. F., & Shaver, K. H. (2003). Relationships outside the family: Unrelated adults. In G. R. Adams & M. D. Berzonsky (Eds.), *Blackwell handbook of adolescence* (pp. 349–370). Malden, MA: Blackwell.

Darling, N., & Steinberg, L. (1993). Parenting style as context: An integrative model. *Psychological Bulletin, 113,* 487–496.

Davies, P. T., & Windle, M. (2000). Middle adolescents' dating pathways and psychosocial adjustment. *Merrill-Palmer Quarterly, 46*(1), 90–118.

Deater-Deckard, K., & Plomin, R. (1999). An adoption study of etiology of teacher and parent reports of externalizing behavior problems in middle childhood. *Child Development, 70,* 144–154.

Diamond, L. M. (2000). Passionate friendships among adolescent sexual-minority women. *Journal of Research on Adolescence, 10,* 191–209.

Diamond, L. M., & Savin-Williams, R. C. (2003). Explaining diversity in the development of same-sex sexuality among young women. In L. D. Garnets & D. C. Kimmel (Eds.), *Psychological perspectives on lesbian, gay, and bisexual experiences* (2nd ed., pp. 130–148). New York: Columbia University Press.

Dick, D., Rose, R., Pulkkinen, L., & Kaprio, J. (2001). Measuring puberty and understanding its impact: A longitudinal study of adolescent twins. *Journal of Youth and Adolescence, 30*(4), 385–400.

Dick, D. M., Rose, R. J., Viken, R. J., & Kaprio, J. (2000). Pubertal timing and substance use: Associations between and within families across late adolescence. *Developmental Psychology, 36*(2), 180–189.

Dishion, T. J. (2000). Cross-setting consistency in early adolescent psychopathology: Deviant friendships and problem behavior sequelae. *Journal of Personality, 68,* 1109–1126.

Dornbusch, S., Carlsmith, J., Gross, R., Martin, J., Jennings, D., Rosenberg, A., et al. (1981). Sexual development, age, and dating: A comparison of biological and social influences upon one set of behaviors. *Child Development, 52,* 179–185.

Dornbusch, S., Ritter, P., Liederman, P., Roberts, D., & Fraleigh, M. (1987). The relation of parenting style to adolescent school performance. *Child Development, 58,* 1244–1257.

Douvan, E., & Adelson, J. (1966). *The adolescent experience.* New York: Wiley.

Downey, G., Bonica, C., & Rincon, C. (1999). Rejection sensitivity and adolescent romantic relationships. In W. Furman & B. B. Brown (Eds.), *The development of romantic relationships in adolescence* (pp. 148–174). New York: Cambridge University Press.

Dubé, S. R., Felitti, V. J., Dong, M., Chapman, D. P., Giles, W. H., & Anda, R. F. (2003). Childhood abuse, neglect, and household dysfunction and the risk of illicit drug use: The adverse childhood experiences study. *Pediatrics, 111*(3), 564–572.

DuBois, D., Eitel, S., & Felner, R. (1994). Effects of family environment and parent-child relationships on school adjustment during the transition to early adolescence. *Journal of Marriage and the Family, 56,* 405–414.

Dubow, E. F., Tisak, J., Causey, D., Hryshko, A., & Reid, G. (1991). A 2-year longitudinal study of stressful life events, social support, and social problem-solving skills: Contributions to children's behavioral and academic adjustment. *Child Development, 62,* 583–599.

Duncan, G. (1994). Families and neighbors as sources of disadvantage in the schooling decisions of White and Black adolescents. *American Journal of Education, 103,* 20–53.

Duncan, G., & Raudenbush, S. (2001). Neighborhoods and adolescent development: How can we determine the links. In A. Booth & A. C. Crouter (Eds.), *Does it take a village? Community effects on children, adolescents, and families* (pp. 105–130). Mahwah, NJ: Erlbaum.

Dunn, J., Slomkowski, C., & Beardsall, L. (1994). Sibling relationships from the preschool period through middle childhood and early adolescence. *Developmental Psychology, 30,* 315–324.

DuRant, R., Cadenhead, C., Pendergrast, R., Slavens, G., & Linder, C. (1994). Factors associated with the use of violence among urban Black adolescents. *American Journal of Public Health, 84,* 612–617.

Dyer, G., & Tiggemann, M. (1996). The effects of school environment on body concerns in adolescent women. *Sex Roles, 34,* 127–138.

Dyk, P. H., & Adams, G. R. (1990). Identity and intimacy: An initial investigation of three theoretical models using cross-lag panel correlations. *Journal of Youth and Adolescence, 19*(2), 91–110.

East, P., & Rook, K. (1992). Compensatory patterns of support among children's peer relationships: A test using school friends, nonschool friends, and siblings. *Developmental Psychology, 28,* 163–172.

East, P. L., Felice, M. E., & Morgan, M. C. (1993). Sisters' and girlfriends' sexual and childbearing behavior: Effects on early adolescent girls' sexual outcomes. *Journal of Marriage and the Family, 55*(4), 953–963.

East, P. L., & Jacobson, L. J. (2001). The younger siblings of teenage mothers: A follow-up of their pregnancy risk. *Developmental Psychology, 37*(2), 254–264.

East, P. L., & Kiernan, E. A. (2001). Risks among youths who have multiple sisters who were adolescent parents. *Family Planning Perspectives, 33*(2), 75–80.

Eccles, J. (2004). Schools, academic motivation, and stage-environment fit. In R. Lerner & L. Steinberg (Eds.), *Handbook of adolescent psychology* (2nd ed., pp. 125–153). Hoboken, NJ: Wiley.

Eccles, J., Lord, S., & Midgley, C. (1991). What are we doing to early adolescents? The impact of educational contexts on early adolescents. *American Journal of Education, 99,* 521–542.

Eccles, J., Midgley, C., Wigfield, A., Buchanan, C., Reuman, D., Flanagan, C., et al. (1993). Development during adolescence: The impact of stage-environment fit on young adolescents' experiences in schools and families. *American Psychologist, 48,* 90–101.

Eder, D. (1985). The cycle of popularity: Interpersonal relations among female adolescence. *Sociology of Education, 58,* 154–165.

Eder, D., & Kinney, D. (1995). The effect of middle school extracurricular activities on adolescents' popularity and peer status. *Youth and Society, 26,* 298–324.

Eisenberg, N., & Morris, A. (2004). Moral cognitions and prosocial responding in adolescence. In R. Lerner & L. Steinberg (Eds.), *Handbook of adolescent psychology* (2nd ed., pp. 155–188). Hoboken, NJ: Wiley.

Elder, G. H., Jr. (1974). *Children of the Great Depression.* Chicago: University of Chicago Press.

Elder, G. H., Jr. (1998). The life course and human development. In W. Damon (Editor-in-Chief) & R. Lerner (Vol. Ed.), *Handbook of child psychology: Vol. 1. Theoretical models of human development* (5th ed., pp. 939–991). New York: Wiley.

Eley, T., Lichenstein, P., & Stevenson, J. (1999). Sex differences in the etiology of aggressive and nonaggressive antisocial behavior: Results from two twin studies. *Child Development, 70,* 155–168.

Elkind, D. (1967). Egocentrism in adolescence. *Child Development, 38,* 1025–1034.

Elkins, I., McGue, M., & Iacono, W. (1997). Genetic and environmental influences on parent-son relationships: Evidence for increasing genetic influence during adolescence. *Developmental Psychology, 33,* 351–363.

Ellis, B., & Garber, J. (2000). Psychosocial antecedents of variation in girls' pubertal timing: Maternal depression, stepfather presence, and marital and family stress. *Child Development, 71,* 485–501.

Ellis, B., McFadyen-Ketchum, S., Dodge, K., Pettit, G., & Bates, J. (1999). Quality of early family relationships and individual differences in the timing of pubertal maturation in girls: A longitudinal test of an evolutionary model. *Journal of Personality and Social Psychology, 77,* 387–401.

Ensminger, M., Lamkin, R., & Jacobson, N. (1996). School leaving: A longitudinal perspective including neighborhood effects. *Child Development, 67,* 2400–2416.

Epstein, J. L. (1989). The selection of friends: Changes across the grades and in different school environments. In T. J. Berndt & G. W. Ladd (Eds.), *Peer relationships in child development* (pp. 158–187). New York: Wiley.

Erickson, K., Crosnoe, R., & Dornbusch, S. M. (2000). A social process model of adolescent deviance: Combining social control and differential association perspectives. *Journal of Youth and Adolescence, 29*(4), 395–425.

Erikson, E. (1968). *Identity: Youth and crisis.* New York: Norton.

Eveleth, P., & Tanner, J. (1990). *Worldwide variation in human growth* (2nd ed.). New York: Cambridge University Press.

Eyre, S. L., Auerswald, C., Hoffman, V., & Millstein, S. G. (1998). Fidelity management: African-American adolescents' attempts to control the sexual behavior of their partners. *Journal of Health Psychology, 3*(3), 393–406.

Eyre, S. L., Read, N. W., & Millstein, S. G. (1997). Adolescent sexual strategies. *Journal of Adolescent Health, 4,* 286–293.

Feinberg, M. E., Neiderhiser, J. M., Simmens, S., Reiss, D., & Hetherington, E. M. (2000). Sibling comparison of differential parental treatment in adolescence: Gender, self-esteem, and emotionality as mediators of the parenting-adjustment association. *Child Development, 71*(6), 1611–1628.

Feiring, C. (1999). Gender identity and the development of romantic relationships in adolescence. In W. Furman, B. B. Brown, & C. Feiring (Eds.), *The development of romantic relationships in adolescence* (pp. 175–210). New York: Cambridge University Press.

Feldman, S., & Quatman, T. (1988). Factors influencing age expectations for adolescent autonomy: A study of early adolescents and parents. *Journal of Early Adolescence, 8,* 325–343.

Feldman, S., & Wood, D. (1994). Parents' expectations for preadolescent sons' behavioral autonomy: A longitudinal study of correlates and outcomes. *Journal of Research on Adolescence, 4,* 45–70.

Feldman, S. S., & Brown, N. L. (1993). Family influences on adolescent male sexuality: The mediational role of self-restraint. *Social Development, 2*(1), 15–35.

Feldman, S. S., & Gowen, L. K. (1998). Conflict negotiation tactics in romantic relationships in high school students. *Journal of Youth and Adolescence, 27*(6), 691–717.

Feldman, S. S., Gowen, L. K., & Fisher, L. (1998). Family relationships and gender as predictors of romantic intimacy in young adults: A longitudinal study. *Journal of Research on Adolescence, 8*(2), 263–286.

Feldman, S. S., Turner, R., & Araujo, K. (1999). Interpersonal context as an influence on sexual timetables of youths: Gender and ethnic effects. *Journal of Research on Adolescence, 9,* 25–52.

Fenzel, L. (2001). Prospective study of changes in global self-worth and strain during the transition to middle school. *Journal of Early Adolescence, 20*(1), 93–116.

Fine, M. (1988). Sexuality, schooling, and adolescent females: The missing discourse of desire. *Harvard Educational Review, 58*(1), 29–53.

Fitch, S., & Adams, G. (1983). Ego identity and intimacy statuses: Replication and extension. *Developmental Psychology, 19,* 839–845.

Flammer, A., & Schaffner, B. (2003). Adolescent leisure across European nations. *New Directions for Child and Adolescent Development, 99,* 65–78.

Flannery, D., Rowe, D., & Gulley, B. (1993). Impact of pubertal status, timing, and age on adolescent sexual experience and delinquency. *Journal of Adolescent Research, 8,* 21–40.

Flannery, D., Torquati, J., & Lindemeier, L. (1994). The method and meaning of emotional expression and experience during adolescence. *Journal of Adolescent Research, 9,* 8–27.

Fletcher, A. C., Steinberg, L., & Williams-Wheeler, M. (2004). Parental influences on adolescent problem behavior: A response to Stattin and Kerr. *Child Development, 75,* 781–796.

Flouri, E., & Buchanan, A. (2002). What predicts good relationships with parents in adolescence and partners in adult life: Findings from the 1958 British birth cohort. *Journal of Family Psychology, 16,* 186–198.

Ford, M., Wentzel, K., Wood, D., Stevens, E., & Siesfeld, G. A. (1990). Processes associated with integrative social competence: Emotional and contextual influences on adolescent social responsibility. *Journal of Adolescent Research, 4,* 405–425.

Forehand, R., Miller, K., Dutra, R., & Chance, M. (1997). Role of parenting in adolescent deviant behavior: Replication across and within two ethnic groups. *Journal of Consulting and Clinical Psychology, 65,* 1036–1041.

Formoso, D., Ruiz, S., & Gonzales, N. (1997, March). *Parent-adolescent conflict: Resolution strategies reported with African-American, Mexican-American, and Anglo-American families.* Paper presented at the biennial meeting of the Society for Research in Child Development, Washington, DC.

Fraley, R. C., & Davis, K. E. (1997). Attachment formation and transfer in young adults' close friendships and romantic relationships. *Personal Relationships, 4*(2), 131–144.

Frank, S., Avery, C., & Laman, M. (1988). Young adults' perceptions of their relationships with their parents: Individual differences in connectedness, competence, and emotional autonomy. *Developmental Psychology, 24,* 729–737.

Freud, A. (1958). Adolescence. In R. Eissler, A. Freud, H. Hartman, & M. Kris (Eds.), *Psychoanalytic study of the child* (Vol. 13, pp. 255–278). New York: International Universities Press.

Fried, C. S., & Reppucci, N. (2001). Criminal decision-making: The development of adolescent judgment, criminal responsibility, and culpability. *Law and Human Behavior, 25*(1), 45–61.

Frost, J., & Forrest, J. (1995). Understanding the impact of effective teenage pregnancy prevention programs. *Family Planning Perspectives, 27,* 188–195.

Fuhrman, T., & Holmbeck, G. (1995). A contextual-moderator analysis of emotional autonomy and adjustment in adolescence. *Child Development, 66,* 793–811.

Fuligni, A. (1998). Authority, autonomy, and parent-adolescent conflict and cohesion: A study of adolescents from Mexican, Chinese, Filipino, and European backgrounds. *Developmental Psychology, 34,* 782–792.

Fuligni, A., & Eccles, J. (1993). Perceived parent-child relationships and early adolescents' orientation toward peers. *Developmental Psychology, 29,* 622–632.

Fuligni, A., Tseng, V., & Lam, M. (1999). Attitudes toward family obligations among American adolescents from Asian, Latin American, and European backgrounds. *Child Development, 70,* 1030–1044.

Furman, W. (1999). Friends and lovers: The role of peer relationships in adolescent romantic relationships. In W. A. Collins & B. Laursen (Eds.), *Minnesota Symposia on Child Psychology: Vol. 30. Relationships as developmental contexts* (pp. 133–154). Hillsdale, NJ: Erlbaum.

Furman, W., & Bierman, K. L. (1984). Children's conceptions of friendship: A multimethod study of developmental changes. *Developmental Psychology, 20*(5), 925–931.

Furman, W., Brown, B., & Feiring, C. (Eds.). (1999). *Contemporary perspectives on adolescent romantic relationships.* New York: Cambridge University Press.

Furman, W., & Buhrmester, D. (1985). Children's perceptions of the personal relationships in their social networks. *Developmental Psychology, 21,* 1016–1024.

Furman, W., & Buhrmester, D. (1992). Age and sex differences in perceptions of networks of personal relationships. *Child Development, 63,* 103–115.

Furman, W., & Shaffer, L. (2003). The role of romantic relationships in adolescent development. In P. Florsheim (Ed.), *Adolescent romantic relations and sexual behavior: Theory, research, and practical implications* (pp. 3–22). Mahwah, NJ: Erlbaum.

Furman, W., Simon, V. A., Shaffer, L., & Bouchey, H. A. (2002). Adolescents' working models and styles for relationships with parents, friends, and romantic partners. *Child Development, 73*(1), 241–255.

Furman, W., & Wehner, E. A. (1994). Romantic views: Toward a theory of adolescent romantic relationships. In R. Montemayor, G. R. Adams, & T. Gullotta (Eds.), *Personal relationships during adolescence* (pp. 168–195). Thousand Oaks, CA: Sage.

Furstenberg, F., Jr., Cook, T., Eccles, J., Elder, G. H., Jr., & Sameroff, A. (1999). *Managing to make it: Urban families and adolescent success.* Chicago: University of Chicago Press.

Galambos, N., Kolaric, G., Sears, H., & Maggs, J. (1999). Adolescents' subjective age: An indicator of perceived maturity. *Journal of Research on Adolescence, 9,* 309–337.

Garber, J., Robinson, N., & Valentiner, D. (1997). The relation between parenting and adolescent depression: Self-worth as a mediator. *Journal of Adolescent Research, 12,* 12–33.

Ge, X., Best, K., Conger, R. D., & Simons, R. (1996). Parenting behaviors and the occurrence and co-occurrence of adolescent depressive symptoms and conduct problems. *Developmental Psychology, 32,* 717–731.

Ge, X., Brody, G. H., Conger, R. D., Simons, R. L., & Murry, V. (2002). Contextual amplification of pubertal transition effects on deviant peer affiliation and externalizing behavior among African American children. *Developmental Psychology, 38*(1), 42–54.

Ge, X., Conger, R. D., & Elder, G. H., Jr. (1996). Coming of age too early: Pubertal influences on girls' vulnerability to psychological distress. *Child Development, 67,* 3386–3400.

Ge, X., Conger, R. D., & Elder, G. H., Jr. (2001). Pubertal transition, stressful life events, and the emergence of gender differences in adolescent depressive symptoms. *Developmental Psychology, 37*(3), 404–417.

Ge, X., Kim, I. J., Brody, G. H., Conger, R. D., Simons, R. L., Gibbons, F. X., et al. (2003). It's about timing and change: Pubertal transition effects on symptoms of major depression among African American youths. *Developmental Psychology, 39*(3), 430–439.

Gentry, M., Gable, R. K., & Rizza, M. G. (2002). Students' perceptions of classroom activities: Are there grade-level and gender differences? *Journal of Educational Psychology, 94*(3), 539–544.

Giedd, J. N., Blumenthal, J., Jeffries, N. O., Castellanos, F. X., Liu, H., Zijdenbos, A., et al. (1999). Brain development during childhood and adolescence: A longitudinal MRI study. *Nature Neuroscience, 2,* 861–863.

Gillock, K. L., & Reyes, O. (1996). High school transition-related changes in urban minority students' academic performance and perceptions of self and school environment. *Journal of Community Psychology, 24*(3), 245–261.

Giordano, P. C. (2003). Relationships in adolescence. *Annual Review of Sociology, 29,* 257–281.

Gonzales, N., Cauce, A., & Mason, C. (1996). Interobserver agreement in the assessment of parental behavior and parent-adolescent conflict: African American mothers, daughters, and independent observers. *Child Development, 67,* 1483–1498.

Goodnow, J. J. (2002). Adding culture to studies of development: Toward changes in procedure and theory. *Human Development, 45*(4), 237–245.

Goodnow, J. J., Miller, P. J., & Kessel, F. (Eds.). (1995). *Cultural practices as contexts for development.* San Francisco: Jossey-Bass.

Gore, S., Farrell, F., & Gordon, J. (2001). Sports involvement as protection against depressed mood. *Journal of Research on Adolescence, 11*(1), 119–130.

Gottfredson, D. (1985). Youth employment, crime, and schooling: A longitudinal study of a national sample. *Developmental Psychology, 21,* 419–432.

Graber, J. A., Brooks-Gunn, J., & Galen, B. R. (1999). Betwixt and between: Sexuality in the context of adolescent transitions. In R. Jessor (Ed.), *New perspectives on adolescent risk behavior* (pp. 270–316). New York: Cambridge University Press.

Graber, J. A., Brooks-Gunn, J., & Warren, M. P. (1995). The antecedents of menarcheal age: Heredity, family environment, and stressful life events. *Child Development, 66,* 346–359.

Graber, J. A., Brooks-Gunn, J., & Warren, M. P. (in press). Pubertal effects on adjustment in girls: Moving from demonstrating effects to identifying pathways. *Journal of Youth and Adolescence.*

Granic, I., Dishion, T. J., & Hollenstein, T. (2003). The family ecology of adolescence: A dynamic systems perspective on normative development. In G. R. Adams & M. D. Berzonsky (Eds.), *Blackwell handbook of adolescence* (pp. 60–91). Malden, MA: Blackwell.

Gray, M., & Steinberg, L. (1999). Adolescent romance and the parent-child relationship: A contextual perspective. In W. Furman, B. Brown, & C. Feiring (Eds.), *Contemporary perspectives on adolescent romantic relationships* (pp. 235–265). New York: Cambridge University Press.

Greenberger, E., Chen, C., & Beam, M. R. (1998). The role of "very important" nonparental adults in adolescent development. *Journal of Youth and Adolescence, 27*(3), 321–343.

Greenberger, E., & Sorenson, A. (1974). Toward a concept of psychosocial maturity. *Journal of Youth and Adolescence, 3,* 329–358.

Grotevant, H. D. (1998). Adolescent development in family contexts. In W. Damon (Editor-in-Chief) & N. Eisenberg (Vol. Ed.), *Handbook of child psychology: Vol. 3. Social, emotional, and personality development* (5th ed., pp. 1097–1149). New York: Wiley.

Grotevant, H. D., & Cooper, C. R. (1985). Patterns of interaction in family relationships and development of identity formation in adolescence. *Child Development, 56,* 415–428.

Grotevant, H. D., & Cooper, C. R. (1986). Individuation in family relationships: A perspective on individual differences in the development of identity and role-taking skill in adolescence. *Human Development, 29,* 82–100.

Gutierrez, R. (2000). Advancing African American urban youth in mathematics: Unpacking the success of one math department. *American Journal of Education, 109*(1), 63–111.

Gutman, L. M., & Midgley, C. (2000). The role of protective factors in supporting the academic achievement of poor African American students during the middle school transition. *Journal of Youth and Adolescence, 29*(2), 223–248.

Gutman, L. M., Sameroff, A. J., & Eccles, J. S. (2002). The academic achievement of African American students during early adolescence: An examination of multiple risk, promotive, and protective factors. *American Journal of Community Psychology, 30,* 367–399.

Haj-Yahia, M. M., Musleh, K., & Haj-Yahia, Y. (2002). The incidence of adolescent maltreatment in Arab society and some of its psychological effects. *Journal of Family Issues, 23*(8), 1032–1064.

Hall, G. S. (1904). *Adolescence: Its psychology and its relations to physiology, anthropology, sociology, sex, crime, religion, and education* (Vols. 1–2). Englewood Cliffs, NJ: Prentice-Hall.

Halpern, C. T., Udry, J. R., Campbell, B., & Suchindran, C. (1993). Relationships between aggression and pubertal increases in testosterone: A panel analysis of adolescent males. *Social Biology, 40*(1/2), 8–24.

Hamilton, S., & Hamilton, M. (2004). Contexts for mentoring: Adolescent-adult relationships in workplaces and communities. In R. Lerner & L. Steinberg (Eds.), *Handbook of adolescent psychology* (2nd ed., pp. 395–428). Hoboken, NJ: Wiley.

Hamm, J. V. (2000). Do birds of a feather flock together? The variable bases for African American, Asian American, and European American adolescents' selection of similar friends. *Developmental Psychology, 36*(2), 209–219.

Hardy, C. L., Bukowski, W. M., & Sippola, L. K. (2002). Stability and change in peer relationships during the transition to middle-level school. *Journal of Early Adolescence, 22,* 117–142.

Harter, S. (1983). Developmental perspectives on the self-system. In P. H. Mussen (Series Ed.) & E. M. Hetherington (Vol. Ed.), *Handbook of child psychology: Vol. 4. Socialization, personality, and social development* (4th ed., pp. 275–385). New York: Wiley.

Hartup, W. W. (1979). The social worlds of childhood. *American Psychologist, 34*(10), 944–950.

Hartup, W. W. (1996). The company they keep: Friendships and their developmental significance. *Child Development, 67*(1), 1–13.

Hartup, W. W., & Abecassis, M. (2002). Friends and enemies. In P. K. Smith & C. H. Hart (Eds.), *Blackwell handbook of childhood and social development* (pp. 286–306). Malden, MA: Blackwell.

Hauser, S., Powers, S., & Noam, G. (1991). *Adolescents and their families.* New York: Free Press.

Hauser, S., & Safyer, A. (1994). Ego development and adolescent emotions. *Journal of Research on Adolescence, 4,* 487–502.

Hayward, C., Killen, J., Wilson, D., Hammer, L., Litt, I., Kraemer, H., et al. (1997). Psychiatric risk associated with early puberty in adolescent girls. *Journal of the American Academy of Child and Adolescent Psychiatry, 36,* 255–261.

Hazan, C., & Zeifman, D. (1994). Sex and the psychological tether. In K. Bartholomew & D. Perlman (Eds.), *Attachment processes in adulthood* (pp. 151–178). London: Jessica Kingsley.

Helsen, M., Vollebergh, W., & Meeus, W. (2000). Social support from parents and friends and emotional problems in adolescence. *Journal of Youth and Adolescence, 29*(3), 319–335.

Herdt, G., & McClintock, M. (2000). The magical age of 10. *Archives of Sexual Behavior, 29*(6), 587–606.

Herrenkohl, T. I., Maguin, E., Hill, K. G., Hawkins, J., Abbott, R. D., & Catalano, R. F. (2000). Developmental risk factors for youth violence. *Journal of Adolescent Health, 26*(3), 176–186.

Hetherington, E. M., Henderson, S., & Reiss, D. (1999). Adolescent siblings in stepfamilies: Family functioning and adolescent adjustment. *Monographs of the Society for Research in Child Development, 64*(Serial No. 259).

Hill, J. P. (1983). Early adolescence: A framework. *Journal of Early Adolescence, 3,* 1–21.

Hill, J. P. (1987). Research on adolescents and their families: Past and prospect. In C. E. Irwin (Ed.), *Adolescent social behavior and health: Vol. 37. New directions for child development* (pp. 13–31). San Francisco: Jossey-Bass.

Hill, J. P. (1988). Adapting to menarche: Family control and conflict. In M. Gunnar & W. A. Collins (Eds.), *Development during the transition to adolescence* (pp. 43–77). Hillsdale, NJ: Erlbaum.

Hill, J. P., & Holmbeck, G. (1986). Attachment and autonomy during adolescence. In G. Whitehurst (Ed.), *Annals of child development* (Vol. 3, pp. 145–189). Greenwich, CT: JAI Press.

Hillier, L., Harrison, L., & Warr, D. (1997). "When you carry a condom all the boys will think you want it": Negotiating competing discourses about safe sex. *Journal of Adolescence, 21,* 15–29.

Hinde, R. A. (1997). *Relationships: A dialectical perspective.* East Sussex, England: Psychology Press.

Ho, M. J. (2004, April). Adolescent attachment to parents: Predicting later rejection sensitivity. In D. Welsh (Chair), *The development of adolescent romantic relationships: The role of attachment.* Symposium conducted at the conference of the Society for Research on Adolescence, Baltimore, MD.

Hodges, E., Finnegan, R., & Perry, D. (1999). Skewed autonomy-relatedness in preadolescents' conceptions of their relationships with mother, father, and best friend. *Developmental Psychology, 35,* 737–748.

Hoffman, J. P. (2003). A contextual analysis of differential association, social control, and strain theories of delinquency. *Social Forces, 81*(3), 753–785.

Holmbeck, G. N. (1996). A model of family relational transformations during the transition to adolescence: Parent-adolescent conflict and adaptation. In J. A. Graber, J. Brooks-Gunn, & A. C. Petersen (Eds.), *Transitions in adolescence: Interpersonal domains and context* (pp. 167–199). Mahwah, NJ: Erlbaum.

Holmbeck, G. N., & Hill, J. P. (1991). Conflictive engagement, positive affect, and menarche in families with seventh-grade girls. *Child Development, 62,* 1030–1048.

Holmbeck, G. N., Shapera, W., Westhoven, V., Johnson, S., Millstein, R., & Hommeyer, J. (2000, March). *A longitudinal study of observed and perceived parenting behaviors and autonomy development in families of young adolescents with spina bifida.* Paper presented at the biennial meeting of the Society for Research on Adolescence, Chicago, IL.

Horn, S. S. (2003). Adolescents' reasoning about exclusion from social groups. *Developmental Psychology, 39,* 71–84.

Huttenlocher, P. (1994). Synaptogenesis, synapse elimination, and neural plasticity in human cerebral cortex. In C. Nelson (Ed.), *Threats to optimal development: Integrating biological, psychological, and social risk factors* (Vol. 27, pp. 35–54). Hillsdale, NJ: Erlbaum.

Inhelder, B., & Piaget, J. (1958). *The growth of logical thinking from childhood to adolescence.* New York: Basic Books.

Jacobson, K., & Rowe, D. (1999). Genetic and environmental influences on the relationships between family connectedness, school connectedness, and adolescent depressed mood: Sex differences. *Developmental Psychology, 35,* 926–939.

Jaffee, S., & Hyde, J. S. (2000). Gender differences in moral orientation: A meta-analysis. *Psychological Bulletin, 126,* 703–726.

Jencks, C., & Mayer, S. (1990). The social consequences of growing up in a poor neighborhood. In L. E. Lynn Jr. & G. H. McGeary (Eds.), *Inner-city poverty in the United States* (pp. 111–186). Washington, DC: National Academy Press.

Jessor, R., Costa, F., Jessor, L., & Donovan, J. E. (1983). Time of first intercourse: A prospective study. *Journal of Personality and Social Psychology, 44,* 608–620.

Jessor, R., Donovan, J. E., & Costa, F. M. (1991). *Beyond adolescence: Problem behavior and young adult development.* New York: Cambridge University Press.

Jessor, R., & Jessor, S. (1977). *Problem behavior and psychosocial development: A longitudinal study of youth.* New York: Academic Press.

Johnson, J. G., Cohen, P., Smailes, E. M., Kasen, S., & Brook, J. S. (2002). Television viewing and aggressive behavior during adolescence and adulthood. *Science, 295*(5564), 2468–2471.

Jones, D. J., Forehand, R., Brody, G., & Armistead, L. (2002). Psychosocial adjustment of African American children in single-mother families: A test of three risk models. *Journal of Marriage and the Family, 64*(1), 105–115.

Jones, M. C. (1957). The later careers of boys who were early- or late-maturing. *Child Development, 28,* 113–128.

Jones, M. C. (1965). Psychological correlates of somatic development. *Child Development, 36,* 899–911.

Jones, M. C., & Bayley, N. (1950). Physical maturing among boys as related to behavior. *Journal of Educational Psychology, 41,* 129–148.

Jones, M. C., & Mussen, P. (1958). Self-conceptions, motivations, and inter-personal attitudes of early- and late-maturing girls. *Child Development, 29,* 491–501.

Josselson, R. (1980). Ego development in adolescence. In J. Adelson (Ed.), *Handbook of adolescent psychology* (pp. 188–210). New York: Wiley.

Joyner, K., & Udry, J. R. (2000). "You don't bring me anything but down": Adolescent romance and depression. *Journal of Health and Social Behavior, 41,* 369–391.

Juang, L., Lerner, J., McKinney, J., & von Eye, A. (1999). The goodness of fit in autonomy timetable expectations between Asian-Americans late adolescents and their parents. *International Journal of Behavioral Development, 23,* 1023–1048.

Kantor, H. (1994). Managing the transition from school to work: The false promise of youth apprenticeship. *Teachers College Record, 95,* 442–461.

Katchadourian, H. (1990). Sexuality. In S. S. Feldman & G. R. Elliott (Eds.), *At the threshold: The developing adolescent* (pp. 330–351). Cambridge, MA: Harvard University Press.

Keating, D. (2004). Cognitive and brain development. In R. Lerner & L. Steinberg (Eds.), *Handbook of adolescent psychology* (2nd ed., pp. 45–84). Hoboken, NJ: Wiley.

Kelley, H. H., Berscheid, E., Christensen, A., Harvey, J. H., Huston, T. L., Levinger, G., et al. (1983). *Close relationships.* New York: Freeman.

Keniston, K. (1970). Youth: A "new" stage of life. *American Scholar, 39,* 631–641.

Kerr, M., & Stättin, H. (2000). What parents know, how they know it, and several forms of adolescent adjustment: Further support for a reinterpretation of monitoring. *Developmental Psychology, 36,* 366–380.

Kiesner, J., Poulin, F., & Nicotra, E. (2003). Peer relations across contexts: Individual-network homophily and network inclusion in and after school. *Child Development, 74*(5), 1328–1343.

Kim, K., Conger, R. D., Lorenz, F. O., & Elder, G. H., Jr. (2001). Parent-adolescent reciprocity in negative affect and its relation to early adult social development. *Developmental Psychology, 37*(6), 775–790.

Kim, S., & Ge, X. (2000). Parenting practices and adolescent depressive symptoms in Chinese American families. *Journal of Family Psychology, 14*(3), 420–435.

Kinney, D. A. (1993). From nerds to normals: The recovery of identity among adolescents from middle school to high school. *Sociology of Education, 66,* 21–40.

Klaczynski, P. A. (1997). Bias in adolescents' everyday reasoning and its relationships with intellectual ability, personal theories, and self-serving motivation. *Developmental Psychology, 33,* 273–283.

Klaczynski, P. A., & Gordon, D. (1996). Everyday statistical reasoning during adolescence and young adulthood: Motivational, general ability, and developmental influences. *Child Development, 67,* 2873–2891.

Knight, G., Virdin, L., & Roosa, M. (1994). Socialization and family correlates of mental health outcomes among Hispanic and Anglo American children: Consideration of cross-ethnic scalar equivalence. *Child Development, 65,* 212–224.

Kobak, R. R., Cole, H. E., Ferenz-Gillies, R., Fleming, W. S., & Gamble, W. (1993). Attachment and emotion regulation during mother-teen problem solving: A control theory analysis. *Child Development, 64*(1), 231–245.

Kobak, R. R., & Sceery, A. (1988). Attachment in late adolescence: Working models, affect regulation, and representations of self and others. *Child Development, 59*(1), 135–146.

Koizumi, R. (1995). Feelings of optimism and pessimism in Japanese students' transition to junior high school. *Journal of Early Adolescence, 15,* 412–428.

Kowal, A., & Kramer, L. (1997). Children's understanding of parental differential treatment. *Child Development, 68,* 113–126.

Kowaleski-Jones, L. (2000). Staying out of trouble: Community resources and problem behavior among high-risk adolescents. *Journal of Marriage and the Family, 62*(2), 449–464.

Krosnick, J., & Judd, C. (1982). Transitions in social influence at adolescence: Who induces cigarette smoking? *Developmental Psychology, 18,* 359–368.

Ku, L., Sonenstein, F. L., & Pleck, J. H. (1993). Neighborhood, family, and work: Influences on the premarital behaviors of adolescent males. *Social Forces, 72*(2), 479–503.

Kurdek, L., & Fine, M. (1994). Family acceptance and family control as predictors of adjustment in young adolescents: Linear, curvilinear, or interactive effects. *Child Development, 65,* 1137–1146.

Kuther, T. L., & Higgins-D'Alessandro, A. (2000). Bridging the gap between moral reasoning and adolescent engagement in risky behavior. *Journal of Adolescence, 23*(4), 409–422.

Kuttler, A., La Greca, A. M., & Prinstein, M. J. (1999). Friendship qualities and social-emotional functioning of adolescents with close, cross-sex friendships. *Journal of Research on Adolescence, 9*(3), 339–366.

Lam, T., Shi, H., Ho, L., Stewart, S. M., & Fan, S. (2002). Timing of pubertal maturation and heterosexual behavior among Hong Kong Chinese adolescents. *Archives of Sexual Behavior, 31*(4), 359–366.

Lamborn, S., Dornbusch, S., & Steinberg, L. (1996). Ethnicity and community context as moderators of the relation between family decision-making and adolescent adjustment. *Child Development, 66,* 283–301.

Lamborn, S., Mounts, N., Steinberg, L., & Dornbusch, S. (1991). Patterns of competence and adjustment among adolescents from authoritative, authoritarian, indulgent, and neglectful families. *Child Development, 62,* 1049–1065.

Lamborn, S., & Steinberg, L. (1993). Emotional autonomy redux: Revisiting Ryan and Lynch. *Child Development, 64,* 483–499.

Landry, D., Kaeser, L., & Richards, C. (1999). Abstinence promotion and the provision of information about contraception in public school district sexuality education policies. *Family Planning Perspectives, 31,* 280–286.

Langer, J. A. (2001). Beating the odds: Teaching middle and high school students to read and write well. *American Educational Research Journal, 38*(4), 837–880.

Larkin, R. W. (1979). *Suburban youth in cultural crisis.* New York: Oxford University Press.

Larson, R. W. (2000). Toward a psychology of positive youth development. *American Psychologist, 55,* 170–183.

Larson, R. W., Clore, G. L., & Wood, G. A. (1999). The emotions of romantic relationships. In W. Furman, B. B. Brown, & C. Feiring (Eds.), *Contemporary perspectives on romantic relationships* (pp. 19–49). New York: Cambridge University Press.

Larson, R. W., & Richards, M. (1991). Daily companionship in late childhood and early adolescence: Changing developmental contexts. *Child Development, 62,* 284–300.

Larson, R. W., & Richards, M. (1994). *Divergent realities: The emotional lives of mothers, fathers, and adolescents.* New York: Basic Books.

Larson, R. W., Richards, M. H., Moneta, G., Holmbeck, G., & Duckett, E. (1996). Changes in adolescents' daily interactions with their families from 10 to 18: Disengagement and transformation. *Developmental Psychology, 32,* 744–754.

Larson, R. W., & Verma, S. (1999). How children and adolescents spend time across the world: Work, play, and developmental opportunities. *Psychological Bulletin, 125,* 701–736.

Larson, R. W., & Wilson, S. (2004). Adolescence across place and time: Globalization and the changing pathways to adulthood. In R. Lerner & L. Steinberg (Eds.), *Handbook of adolescent psychology* (2nd ed., pp. 299–330). Hoboken, NJ: Wiley.

Laursen, B. (1995). Conflict and social interaction in adolescent relationships. *Journal of Research on Adolescence, 5*(1), 55–70.

Laursen, B., & Bukowski, W. M. (1997). A developmental guide to the organization of close relationships. *International Journal of Behavioral Development, 21*(4), 747–770.

Laursen, B., & Collins, W. (1994). Interpersonal conflict during adolescence. *Psychological Bulletin, 115,* 197–209.

Laursen, B., Coy, K., & Collins, W. A. (1998). Reconsidering changes in parent-child conflict across adolescence: A meta-analysis. *Child Development, 69,* 817–832.

Laursen, B., Finkelstein, B. D., & Betts, N. (2001). A developmental meta-analysis of peer conflict resolution. *Developmental Review, 21*(4), 423–449.

Laursen, B., & Hartup, W. W. (2002). The origins of reciprocity and social exchange in friendships. In W. G. Graziano & B. Laursen (Eds.), *New directions for child and adolescent development: Vol. 95. Social exchange in development* (pp. 27–40). San Francisco: Jossey-Bass.

Laursen, B., & Jensen-Campbell, L. A. (1999). The nature and functions of social exchange in adolescent romantic relationships. In W. Furman, B. B. Brown, & C. Feiring (Eds.), *The development of romantic relationships in adolescence* (pp. 50–74). New York: Cambridge University Press.

Laursen, B., & Williams, V. (1997). Perceptions of interdependence and closeness in family and peer relationships among adolescents with and without romantic partners. In S. Shulman & W. A. Collins (Eds.), *Romantic relationships in adolescence* (pp. 3–20). San Francisco: Jossey-Bass.

Lee, V., & Smith, J. (1993). Effects of school restructuring on the achievement and engagement of middle-grade students. *Sociology of Education, 66,* 164–187.

Lerner, J., Castellino, D., & Perkins, D. (1994, February). *The influence of adolescent behavioral and psychosocial characteristics on maternal behaviors and satisfaction.* Paper presented at the biennial meeting of the Society for Research on Adolescence, San Diego, CA.

Lerner, R. (1985). Adolescent maturational change and psychosocial development: A dynamic interactional perspective. *Journal of Youth and Adolescence, 14,* 355–372.

Lerner, R., & Steinberg, L. (2004). The scientific study of adolescence: Past, present, and future. In R. Lerner & L. Steinberg (Eds.), *Handbook of adolescent psychology* (2nd ed., pp. 1–12). Hoboken, NJ: Wiley.

Leventhal, T., & Brooks-Gunn, J. (2004). Diversity in developmental trajectories across adolescence: Neighborhood influences. In R. Lerner & L. Steinberg (Eds.), *Handbook of adolescent psychology* (2nd ed., pp. 451–486). Hoboken, NJ: Wiley.

Levesque, R. J. R. (1993). The romantic experience of adolescents in satisfying love relationships. *Journal of Youth and Adolescence, 22,* 219–251.

Lewin, K. (1931). Environmental forces in child behavior and development. In C. Murchison (Ed.), *Handbook of child psychology* (2nd ed., pp. 590–625). Worcester, MA: Clark University Press.

Lewis, C. (1981). The effects of parental firm control. *Psychological Bulletin, 90,* 547–563.

Lewis, M., Feiring, C., & Rosenthal, S. (2000). Attachment over time. *Child Development, 71*(3), 707–720.

Linder, J. L., Crick, N. R., & Collins, W. A. (2002). Relational aggression and victimization in young adult romantic relationships: Associations with perceptions of parent, peer, and romantic relationships quality. *Social Development, 11,* 69–86.

Linder, J. R., & Collins, W. A. (2005). Parent and peer predictors of physical aggression and conflict management in romantic relationships in early adulthood. *Journal of Family Psychology 19,* 252–262.

Linver, M., & Silverberg, S. B. (1997). Maternal predictors of adolescent achievement: Differential prediction of as function of adolescent gender. *Journal of Early Adolescence, 17,* 294–318.

Livesley, W. J., & Bromley, D. B. (1973). *Person perception in childhood and adolescence.* New York: Wiley.

Loehlin, J. C., Willerman, L., & Horn, J. M. (1988). Human behavior genetics. *Annual Review of Psychology, 39,* 101–133.

Long, B. H. (1989). Heterosexual involvement of unmarried undergraduate females in relation to self-evaluations. *Journal of Youth and Adolescence, 18,* 489–500.

Lord, S., Eccles, J., & McCarthy, K. (1994). Surviving the junior high transition: Family processes and self-perceptions as protective and risk factors. *Journal of Early Adolescence, 14,* 162–199.

Ludwig, J., Duncan, G., & Hirschfield, P. (2001). Urban poverty and juvenile crime: Evidence from a randomized housing-mobility experiment. *Quarterly Journal of Economics, 116,* 665–679.

Lynam, D. R., Caspi, A., Moffitt, T. E., Wikstroem, P.-O., Loeber, R., & Novak, S. (2000). The interaction between impulsivity and neighborhood context on offending: The effects of impulsivity are stronger in poorer neighborhoods. *Journal of Abnormal Psychology, 109*(4), 563–574.

Maccoby, E. E. (1990). Gender and relationships. *American Psychologist, 45,* 513–520.

Maccoby, E. E. (1998). *The two sexes: Growing up apart, coming together.* Cambridge, MA: Harvard University Press.

Maccoby, E. E., & Martin, J. (1983). Socialization in the context of the family: Parent-child interaction. In E. M. Hetherington (Ed.), *Handbook of child psychology: Vol. 4. Socialization, personality, and social development* (4th ed., pp. 1–101). New York: Wiley.

MacKinnon-Lewis, C., Starnes, R., Volling, B., & Johnson, S. (1997). Perceptions of parenting as predictors of boys' sibling and peer relations. *Developmental Psychology, 33,* 1024–1031.

Maggs, J., Almeida, D., & Galambos, N. (1995). Risky business: The paradoxical meaning of problem behavior for young adolescents. *Journal of Early Adolescence, 15,* 344–362.

Magnusson, D., & Stättin, H. (1998). Person-context interaction theories. In W. Damon (Editor-in-Chief) & R. Lerner (Vol. Ed.), *Handbook of child psychology: Vol. 1. Theoretical models of human development* (5th ed., pp. 685–760). New York: Wiley.

Magnusson, D., Stättin, H., & Allen, V. (1986). Differential maturation among girls and its relation to social adjustment in a longitudinal perspective. In P. Baltes, D. Featherman, & R. Lerner (Eds.), *Life span development and behavior* (Vol. 7, pp. 134–172). Hillsdale, NJ: Erlbaum.

Mahoney, J. L. (2000). School extracurricular activity participation as a moderator in the development of antisocial patterns. *Child Development, 71*(2), 502–516.

Mahoney, J. L., & Cairns, R. (1997). Do extracurricular activities protect against early school dropout? *Developmental Psychology, 33,* 241–253.

Mahoney, J. L., Schweder, A. E., & Stättin, H. (2002). Structured after-school activities as a moderator of depressed mood for adolescents with detached relations to their parents. *Journal of Community Psychology, 30*(1), 69–86.

Main, M., Kaplan, N., & Cassidy, J. (1985). Security in infancy, childhood, and adulthood: A move to the level of representation. *Monographs of the Society for Research in Child Development, 50*(1/2, Serial No. 209), 66–104.

Marcia, J. (1980). Ego identity development. In J. Adelson (Ed.), *Handbook of adolescent psychology* (pp. 159–187). New York: Wiley.

Markovits, H., Benenson, J., & Dolenszky, E. (2001). Evidence that children and adolescents have internal models of peer interactions that are gender differentiated. *Child Development, 72*(3), 879–886.

Martin, C. A., Kelly, T. H., Rayens, M., Brogli, B. R., Brenzel, A., Smith, W., et al. (2002). Sensation seeking, puberty and nicotine, alcohol and marijuana use in adolescence. *Journal of American Academy of Child and Adolescent Psychiatry, 41*(12), 1495–1502.

Mason, C., Cauce, A. M., Gonzales, N., & Hiraga, Y. (1994). Adolescent problem behavior: The effect of peers and the moderating role of father absence and the mother-child relationship. *American Journal of Community Psychology, 22,* 723–743.

Mason, C., Cauce, A. M., Gonzales, N., & Hiraga, Y. (1996). Neither too sweet nor too sour: Problem peers, maternal control, and problem behavior in African American adolescents. *Child Development, 67,* 2115–2130.

Masten, A. S., Coatsworth, J. D., Neeman, J., Gest, S. D., Tellegen, A., & Garmezy, N. (1995). The structure and coherence of competence from childhood through adolescence. *Child Development, 66*(6), 1635–1659.

Mathes, E. W., Adams, H. E., & Davies, R. M. (1985). Jealousy: Loss of relationship rewards, loss of self-esteem, depression, anxiety, and anger. *Journal of Personality and Social Psychology, 48*(6), 1552–1561.

Matza, L. S., Kupersmidt, J. B., & Glenn, D. (2001). Adolescents' perceptions and standards of their parents as a function of sociometric status. *Journal of Research on Adolescence, 11*(3), 245–272.

McCabe, K., Barnett, D., & Robbins, E. (1996, March). *Optimistic future orientation and adjustment among inner city African-American youth.* Paper presented at the biennial meeting of the Society for Research on Adolescence, Boston, MA.

McCoy, J., Brody, G., & Stoneman, Z. (1994). A longitudinal analysis of sibling relationships as mediators of the link between family processes and youths' best friendships. *Family Relations: Journal of Applied Family and Child Studies, 43*(4), 400–408.

McElhaney, K. B., & Allen, J. P. (2001). Autonomy and adolescent social functioning: The moderating effect of risk. *Child Development, 72,* 220–231.

McGee, R., Wolfe, D., & Wilson, S. (1997). Multiple maltreatment experiences and adolescent behavior problems: Adolescents' perspectives. *Development and Psychopathology, 9,* 131–149.

McGue, M., Sharma, A., & Benson, P. (1996). The effects of common rearing on adolescent adjustment: Evidence from a U.S. adoption cohort. *Developmental Psychology, 32,* 604–613.

McGuire, S., Manke, B., Saudino, K., Reiss, D., Hetherington, E. M., & Plomin, R. (1999). Perceived competence and self-worth during adolescence: A longitudinal behavioral genetic study. *Child Development, 70,* 1283–1296.

McHale, S. M., Crouter, A. C., & Tucker, C. J. (2001). Free-time activities in middle childhood: Links with adjustment in early adolescence. *Child Development, 72,* 1764–1778.

McLoyd, V. (1990). The impact of economic hardship on Black families and children: Psychological distress, parenting, and socioemotional development. *Child Development, 61,* 311–346.

McNeal, J. (1995). Extracurricular activities and high school dropouts. *Sociology of Education, 68,* 62–81.

McNelles, L. R., & Connolly, J. A. (1999). Intimacy between adolescent friends: Age and gender differences in intimate affect and intimate behaviors. *Journal of Research on Adolescence, 9*(2), 143–159.

Mekos, D., Hetherington, E. M., & Reiss, D. (1996). Sibling differences in problem behavior and parental treatment in nondivorced and remarried families. *Child Development, 67,* 2148–2165.

Meschke, L. L., & Silbereisen, R. K. (1997). The influence of puberty, family processes, and leisure activities on the timing of first experience. *Journal of Adolescence, 20*(4), 403–418.

Midgley, C., Berman, E., & Hicks, L. (1995). Differences between elementary and middle school teachers and students: A goal theory approach. *Journal of Early Adolescence, 15,* 90–113.

Mihalic, S., & Elliot, D. (1997). Short- and long-term consequences of adolescent work. *Youth and Society, 28,* 464–498.

Milardo, R. M. (1982). Friendship networks in developing relationships: Converging and diverging social environments. *Social Psychology Quarterly, 45,* 162–172.

Miller, B., Benson, B., & Galbraith, K. A. (2001). Family relationships and adolescent pregnancy risk: A research synthesis. *Developmental Review, 21,* 1–38.

Miller, B., Norton, M., Fan, X., & Christopherson, C. (1998). Pubertal development, parental communication, and sexual values in relation to adolescent sexual behaviors. *Journal of Early Adolescence, 18,* 27–52.

Miller, D., & Byrnes, J. (1997). The role of contextual and personal factors in children's risk taking. *Developmental Psychology, 33,* 814–823.

Miller, K. E., Sabo, D. F., Farrell, M. P., Barnes, G. M., & Melnick, M. J. (1998). Athletic participation and sexual behavior in adolescents: The different worlds of boys and girls. *Journal of Health and Social Behavior, 39*(2), 108–123.

Modell, J., & Goodman, M. (1990). Historical perspectives. In S. Feldman & G. Elliott (Eds.), *At the threshold: The developing adolescent* (pp. 93–122). Cambridge, MA: Harvard University Press.

Moffitt, T., Caspi, A., Belsky, J., & Silva, P. (1992). Childhood experience and the onset of menarche: A test of a sociobiological model. *Child Development, 63,* 47–58.

Monroe, S. M., Rohde, P., Seeley, J. R., & Lewinsohn, P. M. (1999). Life events and depression in adolescence: Relationship loss as a prospective risk factor for first onset of major depressive disorder. *Journal of Abnormal Psychology, 108*(4), 606–614.

Montemayor, R. (1983). Parents and adolescents in conflict: All families some of the time and some families most of the time. *Journal of Early Adolescence, 3,* 83–103.

Montemayor, R. (1986). Family variation in parent-adolescent storm and stress. *Journal of Adolescent Research, 1,* 15–31.

Moore, S., & Rosenthal, D. (1993). *Sexuality in adolescence.* New York: Routledge.

Moos, R. (1978). A typology of junior high and high school classrooms. *American Educational Research Journal, 15,* 53–66.

Morrison Gutman, L., Sameroff, A. J., & Eccles, J. S. (2002). The academic achievement of African American students during early adolescence: An examination of multiple risk, promotive, and protective factors. *American Journal of Community Psychology, 30*(3), 367–399.

Mortimer, J. (2003). *Working and growing up in America.* Cambridge, MA: Harvard University Press.

Mortimer, J., & Johnson, M. (1998). New perspectives on adolescent work and the transition to adulthood. In R. Jessor & M. Chase (Eds.), *New perspectives on adolescent risk behavior* (pp. 425–496). New York: Cambridge University Press.

Mounts, N., & Steinberg, L. (1995). An ecological analysis of peer influence on adolescent grade point average and drug use. *Developmental Psychology, 31,* 915–922.

Mulvey, E. P., & Aber, M. S. (1988). Growing out of delinquency: Development and desistance. In R. Jerkins & W. Brown (Eds.), *The abandonment of delinquent behavior: Promoting the turn-around* (pp. 99–116). New York: Praeger.

Murdock, T. B., Anderman, L. H., & Hodge, S. A. (2000). Middle-grade predictors of students' motivation and behavior in high school. *Journal of Adolescent Research, 15*(3), 327–351.

Mussen, P., & Jones, M. C. (1957). Self-conceptions, motivations, and interpersonal attitudes of late- and early-maturing boys. *Child Development, 28,* 243–256.

Mussen, P., & Jones, M. C. (1958). The behavior-inferred motivations of late- and early-maturing boys. *Child Development, 29,* 61–67.

Neeman, J., Hubbard, J., & Masten, A. S. (1995). The changing importance of romantic relationship involvement to competence from childhood to late adolescence. *Development and Psychopathology, 7,* 727–750.

Neiderhiser, J., Reiss, D., Hetherington, E. M., & Plomin, R. (1999). Relationships between parenting and adolescent adjustment over time: Genetic and environmental contributions. *Developmental Psychology, 35,* 680–692.

Nelson, C., Bloom, F., Cameron, J., Amaral, D., Dahl, R., & Pine, D. (2002). An integrative, multidisciplinary approach to the study of brain-behavior relations in the context of typical and atypical development. *Development and Psychopathology, 14,* 499–520.

Nelson, E., Leibenluft, E., McClure, E., & Pine, D. (2005). The social re-orientation of adolescence: A neuroscience perspective on the process and its relation to psychopathology. *Psychological Medicine, 35,* 163–174.

Newcomb, A. F., & Bagwell, C. L. (1995). Children's friendship relations: A meta-analytic review. *Psychological Bulletin, 117*(2), 306–347.

Newman, B. M., & Newman, P. R. (2001). Group identity and alienation: Giving the we its due. *Journal of Youth and Adolescence, 30*(5), 515–538.

Nurmi, J.-E. (2004). Socialization and self-development: Channeling, selection, adjustment, and reflection. In R. Lerner & L. Steinberg (Eds.), *Handbook of adolescent psychology* (2nd ed., pp. 85–124). Hoboken, NJ: Wiley.

Ohannessian, C. M., & Crockett, L. J. (1993). A longitudinal investigation of the relationship between educational investment and adolescent sexual activity. *Journal of Adolescent Research, 8*(2), 167–182.

Orlofsky, J., Marcia, J., & Lesser, I. (1973). Ego identity status and the intimacy versus isolation crisis of young adulthood. *Journal of Personality and Social Psychology, 27,* 73–88.

Osofsky, J. (Ed.). (1997). *Children in a violent society.* New York: Guilford Press.

Owens, G., Crowell, J., Treboux, D., O'Connor, E., & Pan, H. (1995). The prototype hypothesis and the origins of attachment working models: Adult relationships with parents and romantic partners. *Monographs of the Society for Research in Child Development, 60*(2/3, Serial No. 244), 216–233.

Paige, K. E., & Paige, J. M. (1985). *Politics and reproductive rituals.* Berkeley: University of California Press.

Paikoff, R., & Brooks-Gunn, J. (1991). Do parent-child relationships change during puberty? *Psychological Bulletin, 110,* 47–66.

Paley, B., Conger, R. D., & Harold, G. T. (2000). Parents' affect, adolescent cognitive representations, and adolescent social development. *Journal of Marriage and the Family, 62*(3), 761–776.

Parke, R. D., & Buriel, R. (1998). Socialization in the family: Ethnic and ecological perspectives. In W. Damon (Editor-in-Chief) & N. Eisenberg (Vol. Ed.), *Handbook of child psychology: Vol. 3. Social, emotional, and personality development* (5th ed., pp. 463–552). New York: Wiley.

Parker, J. G., & Gottman, J. M. (1989). Social and emotional development in a relational context: Friendship interaction from early childhood to adolescence. In T. J. Berndt & G. W. Ladd (Eds.), *Peer relationships in child development* (pp. 95–131). New York: Wiley.

Paschall, M., & Hubbard, M. (1998). Effects of neighborhood and family stressors on African American male adolescents' self-worth and propensity for violent behavior. *Journal of Consulting and Clinical Psychology, 66*(5), 825–831.

Patterson, G., & Stouthamer-Loeber, M. (1984). The correlation of family management practices and delinquency. *Child Development, 55,* 1299–1307.

Patterson, G. R., DeBaryshe, B. D., & Ramsey, E. (1989). A developmental perspective on antisocial behavior. *American Psychologist, 44,* 329–335.

Patterson, G. R., Reid, J., & Dishion, T. (1992). *Antisocial boys.* Eugene, OR: Castalia.

Paus, T., Zijdenbos, A., Worsley, K., Collins, D. L., Blumenthal, J., Giedd, J. N., et al. (1999). Structural maturation of neural pathways in children and adolescents: In vivo study. *Science, 283,* 1908–1911.

Pavlidis, K., & McCauley, E. (1995, March). *Autonomy and relatedness in family interactions with depressed adolescents.* Paper presented at the biennial meeting of the Society for Research in Child Development, Indianapolis, IN.

Perosa, L., Perosa, S., & Tam, H. (1996). The contribution of family structure and differentiation to identity development in females. *Journal of Youth and Adolescence, 25,* 817–837.

Peskin, H. (1967). Pubertal onset and ego functioning: A psychoanalytic approach. *Journal of Abnormal Psychology, 72,* 1–15.

Petersen, A. C. (1988). Adolescent development. *Annual Review of Psychology, 39,* 583–607.

Pettit, G. S., Laird, R. D., Dodge, K. A., Bates, J. E., & Criss, M. M. (2001). Antecedents and behavior-problem outcomes of parental monitoring and psychological control in early adolescence. *Child Development, 72*(2), 583–598.

Phillips, M. (1997). What makes schools effective? A comparison of the relationships of communitarian climate and academic climate to mathematics achievement and attendance during middle school. *American Educational Research Journal, 34,* 633–662.

Piaget, J. (1965). *The moral judgment of the child.* New York: Harcourt Brace Jovanovich. (Original work published 1932)

Pike, A., McGuire, S., Hetherington, E. M., Reiss, D., & Plomin, R. (1996). Family environment and adolescent depressive symptoms and antisocial behavior: A multivariate genetic analysis. *Developmental Psychology, 32,* 590–604.

Pilgrim, C., Luo, Q., Urberg, K. A., & Fang, X. (1999). Influence of peers, parents, and individual characteristics on adolescent drug use in two cultures. *Merrill-Palmer Quarterly, 45,* 85–107.

Pittman, L. D., & Chase-Lansdale, P. (2001). African American adolescent girls in impoverished communities: Parenting style and adolescent outcomes. *Journal of Research on Adolescence, 11*(2), 199–224.

Plomin, R., & Daniels, D. (1987). Why are children in the same family so different from one another? *Behavioral and Brain Sciences, 10,* 1–60.

Plomin, R., Reiss, D., Hetherington, E. M., & Howe, G. (1994). Nature and nurture: Genetic contributions to measures of the family environment. *Developmental Psychology, 30,* 32–43.

Pomerantz, E. (2001). Parent child socialization: Implications for the development of depressive symptoms. *Journal of Family Psychology, 15*(3), 510–525.

Prager, K. J. (2000). Intimacy in personal relationships. In C. Hendrick & S. S. Hendrick (Eds.), *Close relationships: A sourcebook* (pp. 229–242). Thousand Oaks, CA: Sage.

Pratt, M. W., Arnold, M. L., Pratt, A. D., & Diessner, R. (1999). Predicting adolescent moral reasoning from family climate: A longitudinal study. *Journal of Early Adolescence, 19,* 148–175.

Pulkkinen, L. (1982). Self-control and continuity from childhood to adolescence. In P. Baltes & O. Brim (Eds.), *Life-span development and behavior* (Vol. 4, pp. 63–105). New York: Academic Press.

Punamaki, R., Qouta, S., & Sarraj, E. E. (1997). Models of traumatic experiences and children's psychological adjustment: The roles of perceived parenting and the children's own resources and activity. *Child Development, 68,* 718–728.

Raffaelli, M., & Larson, R. W. (1987). *Sibling interactions in late childhood and early adolescence.* Paper presented at the biennial meeting of the Society for Research in Child Development, Baltimore, MD.

Ramirez-Valles, J., Zimmerman, M. A., & Juarez, L. (2002). Gender differences of neighborhood and social control processes: A study of the timing of first intercourse among low-achieving, urban, African American youth. *Youth and Society, 33*(3), 418–441.

Rawlings, D., Boldero, J., & Wiseman, F. (1995). The interaction of age with impulsiveness and venturesomeness in the prediction of adolescent sexual behavior. *Personality and Individual Differences, 19*(1), 117–120.

Reese-Weber, M. (2000). Middle and late adolescents' conflict resolution skills and siblings: Associations with interparental and parent-adolescent conflict resolution. *Journal of Youth and Adolescence, 29*(6), 697–711.

Reis, H. T., Lin, Y., Bennett, M. E., & Nezlek, J. B. (1993). Change and consistency in social participation during early adulthood. *Developmental Psychopathology, 29,* 633–645.

Reis, H. T., & Patrick, B. C. (1996). Attachment and intimacy: Component processes. In E. T. Higgins & A. Kruglanski (Eds.), *Social psychology: Handbook of basic principles* (pp. 367–389). New York: Guilford Press.

Reis, H. T., & Shaver, P. (1988). Intimacy as an interpersonal process. In S. Duck (Ed.), *Handbook of personal relationships: Theory, research, and interventions* (pp. 367–389). Chichester, England: Wiley.

Reiss D., Hetherington, E. M., Plomin, R., Howe, G., Simmens, S., Henderson S., et al. (1995). Genetic questions for environmental studies. *Archives of General Psychiatry, 52,* 925–936.

Repetti, R. (1996). The effects of perceived daily social and academic failure experiences on school-age children's subsequent interactions with parents. *Child Development, 67,* 1467–1482.

Repinski, D. J. (1992). *Closeness in parent-adolescent relationships: Contrasting interdependence, emotional tone, and a subjective rating.* Unpublished doctoral dissertation, University of Minnesota.

Rest, J. (1983). Morality. In P. H. Mussen (Series Ed.) & J. Flavell & E. Markman (Vol. Eds.), *Handbook of child psychology: Vol. 3. Cognitive development* (4th ed., pp. 556–629). New York: Wiley.

Rhodes, J. E., Grossman, J. B., & Resche, N. L. (2000). Agents of change: Pathways through which mentoring relationships influence adolescents' academic adjustment. *Child Development, 71,* 1662–1671.

Rich, L. M., & Kim, S.-B. (2002). Employment and the sexual and reproductive behavior of female adolescents. *Perspectives on Sexual and Reproductive Health, 34*(3), 127–134.

Richards, M. H., Boxer, A., Petersen, A., & Albrecht, R. (1990). Relation of weight to body image in pubertal girls and boys from two communities. *Developmental Psychology, 26,* 313–321.

Roberts, D., & Foehr, U. (2003). *Kids and media in America: Patterns of use at the millennium.* New York: Cambridge University Press.

Roberts, D., Henriksen, L., & Foehr, U. (2004). Adolescents and media. In R. Lerner & L. Steinberg (Eds.), *Handbook of adolescent psychology* (2nd ed., pp. 487–521). Hoboken, NJ: Wiley.

Roeser, R., & Eccles, J. (1998). Adolescents' perceptions of middle school: Relation to longitudinal changes in academic and psychological adjustment. *Journal of Research on Adolescence, 8,* 123–158.

Roeser, R., Eccles, J., & Freedman-Doan, C. (1999). Academic functioning and mental health in adolescence: Patterns, progressions, and routes from childhood. *Journal of Adolescent Research, 14,* 135–174.

Roeser, R., Eccles, J., & Sameroff, A. (1998). Academic and emotional functioning in early adolescence: Longitudinal relations, patterns, and prediction by experience in middle school. *Development and Psychopathology, 10,* 321–352.

Rohner, R., Bourque, S., & Elordi, C. (1996). Children's perceptions of corporal punishment, caretaker acceptance, and psychological adjustment in a poor, biracial Southern community. *Journal of Marriage and the Family, 58,* 842–852.

Rohner, R., & Pettengill, S. (1985). Perceived parental acceptance-rejection and parental control among Korean adolescents. *Child Development, 56,* 524–528.

Rose, A. (2002). Co-rumination in friendships of girls and boys. *Child Development, 73,* 1830–1843.

Rosenthal, D., & Feldman, S. (1990). The acculturation of Chinese immigrants: The effects on family functioning of length of residence in two cultural contexts. *Journal of Genetic Psychology, 151,* 493–514.

Rossi, A. S. (1987). Parenthood in transition: From lineage to child to self-orientation. In J. Lancaster, J. Altmann, A. Rossi, & L. Sherrod (Eds.), *Parenting across the life span: Biosocial dimensions* (pp. 31–81). New York: Aldine de Gruyter.

Rostosky, S. S., Wilcox, B. L., Comer Wright, M. L., & Randall, B. A. (in press). Religiosity as a predictor of adolescent sexual behavior: A review of the evidence. *Journal of Adolescent Research.*

Rothbaum, F., Pott, M., Azuma, H., Miyake, K., & Weisz, J. (2000). The development of close relationships in Japan and the United States: Paths of symbiotic harmony and generative tension. *Child Development, 71,* 1121–1142.

Rowe, D., Jacobson, K., & van den Oord, E. (1999). Genetic and environmental influences on vocabulary IQ: Parental education level as moderator. *Child Development, 70,* 1151–1162.

Rowe, D. C., Rodgers, J. L., Meseck-Bushey, S., & St. John, C. (1989). Sexual behavior and nonsexual deviance: A sibling study of their relationship. *Developmental Psychopathology, 25*(1), 61–69.

Rubin, K. H., Bukowski, W., & Parker, J. G. (1998). Peer interactions, relationships, and groups. In W. Damon (Editor-in-Chief) & N. Eisenberg (Vol. Ed.), *Handbook of child psychology: Vol. 3. Social, emotional, and personality development* (5th ed., pp. 619–700). New York: Wiley.

Ruck, M., Peterson-Badali, M., & Day, D. M. (2002). Adolescents' and mothers' understanding of children's rights in the home. *Journal of Research on Adolescence, 12*(3), 373–398.

Rueter, M., & Conger, R. D. (1998). Reciprocal influences between parenting and adolescent problem-solving behavior. *Developmental Psychology, 34,* 1470–1482.

Ruiz, S. Y., Roosa, M. W., & Gonzales, N. A. (2002). Predictors of self-esteem for Mexican-American and European American youths: A reexamination of the influence of parenting. *Journal of Family Psychology, 16*(1), 70–80.

Russell, S., Elder, G. H., Jr., & Conger, R. D. (1997, April). *School transitions and academic achievement.* Paper presented at the biennial meeting of the Society for Research in Child Development, Washington, DC.

Ryan, A. M., & Patrick, H. (2001). The classroom social environment and changes in adolescents' motivation and engagement during middle school. *American Educational Research Journal, 38*(2), 437–460.

Ryan, R., & Lynch, J. (1989). Emotional autonomy versus detachment: Revisiting the vicissitudes of adolescence and young adulthood. *Child Development, 60,* 340–356.

Safer, D. (1986). The stress of secondary school for vulnerable students. *Journal of Youth and Adolescence, 15,* 405–417.

Salem, D., Zimmerman, M., & Notaro, P. (1998). Effects of family structure, family process, and father involvement on psychosocial outcomes among African American adolescents. *Family Relations, 47,* 331–341.

Sameroff, A. J. (1983). Developmental systems: Contexts and evolution. In P. H. Mussen (Series Ed.) & W. Kessen (Vol. Ed.), *Handbook of child psychology: Vol. 1. History, theory, and methods* (4th ed., pp. 237–294). New York: Wiley.

Samet, N., & Kelly, E. W. (1987). The relationship of steady dating to self-esteem and sex role identity among adolescents. *Adolescence, 22*(85), 231–245.

Sampson, R. (1997). Collective regulation of adolescent misbehavior: Validation results from eighty Chicago neighborhoods. *Journal of Adolescent Research, 12,* 227–244.

Sampson, R., & Laub, J. (1994). Urban poverty and the family context of delinquency: A new look at structure and process in a classic study. *Child Development, 65,* 523–540.

Sampson, R., Raudenbush, S., & Earls, F. (1997). Neighborhoods and violent crime: A multilevel study of collective efficacy for children. *Science, 277,* 918–924.

Savage, M., & Holcomb, D. (1999). Adolescent female athletes' sexual risk-taking behaviors. *Journal of Youth and Adolescence, 28,* 595–602.

Savin-Williams, R. C. (1979). Dominance hierarchies in groups of adolescents. *Child Development, 50,* 923–935.

Savin-Williams, R. C. (1996). Dating and romantic relationships among gay, lesbian, and bisexual youths. In R. C. Savin-Williams & K. M. Cohen (Eds.), *The lives of lesbians, gays, and bisexuals: Children to adults* (pp. 166–180). Fort Worth, TX: Harcourt Brace Jovanovich.

Savin-Williams, R. C., & Berndt, T. J. (1990). Friendship and peer relations. In S. S. Feldman & G. R. Elliott (Eds.), *At the threshold: The developing adolescent* (pp. 277–307). Cambridge, MA: Harvard University Press.

Savin-Williams, R. C., & Diamond, L. (2004). Sex. In R. Lerner & L. Steinberg (Eds.), *Handbook of adolescent psychology* (2nd ed., pp. 189–231). Hoboken, NJ: Wiley.

Schiller, K. (1999). Effects of feeder patterns on students' transition to high school. *Sociology of Education, 72,* 216–233.

Schlegel, A., & Barry, H. (1991). *Adolescence: An anthropological inquiry.* New York: Free Press.

Schoenhals, M., Tienda, M., & Schneider, B. (1998). The educational and personal consequences of adolescent employment. *Social Forces, 77,* 723–762.

Scholte, R. H. J., van Lieshout, C. F. M., & van Aken, M. A. G. (2001). Perceived relationship support in adolescence: Dimensions, configurations, and adolescent adjustment. *Journal of Research on Adolescence, 11*(1), 71–94.

Schwartz, D., Hopmeyer-Gorman, A., Toblin, R. L., & Abou-ezzeddine, T. (2003). Describing the dark side of preadolescents' peer experiences: Four questions (and data) on preadolescents' enemies. In E. V. E. Hodges & N. A. Card (Eds.), *New directions for child and adolescent development: Vol. 102. Enemies and the darker side of peer relations* (pp. 55–72). San Francisco: Jossey-Bass.

Schweingruber, H. A., & Kalil, A. (2000). Decision making and depressive symptoms in Black and White multigenerational teen-parent families. *Journal of Family Psychology, 14*(4), 556–569.

Scott, E., Reppucci, N., & Woolard, J. (1995). Evaluating adolescent decision making in legal contexts. *Law and Human Behavior, 19,* 221–244.

Scott, E., & Woolard, J. (2004). The legal regulation of adolescence. In R. Lerner & L. Steinberg (Eds.), *Handbook of adolescent psychology* (2nd ed., pp. 523–550). Hoboken, NJ: Wiley.

Seginer, R. (1998). Adolescents' perceptions of relationships with older siblings in the context of other close relationships. *Journal of Research on Adolescence, 8,* 287–308.

Seidman, E., Aber, J. L., Allen, L., & French, S. (1996). The impact of the transition to high school on the self-system and perceived social context of poor urban youth. *American Journal of Community Psychology, 24,* 489–515.

Seidman, E., Allen, L., Aber, J. L., Mitchell, C., & Feinman, J. (1994). The impact of school transitions in early adolescence on the self-system and perceived social context of poor urban youth. *Child Development, 65,* 507–522.

Seiffge-Krenke, I., & Lang, J. (2002, April). Forming and maintaining romantic relations from early adolescence to young adulthood: Evidence of a developmental sequence. In S. Shulman & I. Seiffge-Krenke (Co-chairs), *Antecedents of the quality and stability of adolescent romantic relationships.* Symposium conducted at the biennial meeting of the Society for Research on Adolescence, New Orleans, LA.

Selman, R. (1980). *The growth of interpersonal understanding.* New York: Academic Press.

Shanahan, M. J., & Flaherty, B. P. (2001). Dynamic patterns of time use in adolescence. *Child Development, 72*(2), 385–401.

Sharabany, R., Gershoni, R., & Hofmann, J. (1981). Girlfriend, boyfriend: Age and sex differences in intimate friendship. *Developmental Psychology, 17,* 800–808.

Sheeber, L., Hops, H., Alpert, A., Davis, B., & Andrews, J. (1997). Family support and conflict: Prospective relations to adolescent depression. *Journal of Abnormal Child Psychology, 25,* 333–344.

Shulman, S., & Laursen, B. (2002). Adolescent perceptions of conflict in interdependent and disengaged friendships. *Journal of Research on Adolescence, 12*(3), 353–372.

Siegel, D. J. (1999). *The developing mind: Toward a neurobiology of interpersonal experience.* New York: Guilford Press.

Silbereisen, R. K., Kracke, B., & Crockett, L. J. (1990, March). *Timing of maturation and adolescent substance use.* Paper presented at the biennial meeting of the Society for Research on Adolescence, Atlanta, GA.

Silbereisen, R. K., Petersen, A. C., Albrecht, H., & Kracke, B. (1989). Maturational timing and the development of problem behavior: Longitudinal studies in adolescence. *Journal of Early Adolescence, 9,* 247–268.

Silbereisen, R. K., & Schmitt-Rodermund, E. (1995). German immigrants in Germany: Adaptation of adolescents' timetables for autonomy. In M. Hofer, P. Noack, & J. Youniss (Eds.), *Psychological responses to social change: Human development in changing environments* (pp. 105–125). Berlin, Germany: W. de Gruyter.

Silverberg, S., & Steinberg, L. (1990). Psychological well-being of parents at midlife: The impact of early adolescent children. *Developmental Psychology, 26,* 658–666.

Silverberg, S. B., & Steinberg, L. (1987). Adolescent autonomy, parent-adolescent conflict, and parental well-being. *Journal of Youth and Adolescence, 16*(3), 293–312.

Simmons, R. G., & Blyth, D. A. (1987). *Moving into adolescence.* Hawthorne, NY: Aldine de Gruyter.

Simmons, R. G., Burgeson, R., & Reef, M. J. (1988). Cumulative change at entry to adolescence. In M. R. Gunnar & W. A. Collins (Eds.), *Development during the transition to adolescence* (pp. 123–150). Hillsdale, NJ: Erlbaum.

Simon, W., & Gagnon, J. (1969). On psychosexual development. In D. Goslin (Ed.), *Handbook of socialization theory and research* (pp. 733–752). Chicago: Rand McNally.

Simons, R., Johnson, C., & Conger, R. D. (1994). Harsh corporal punishment versus quality of parental involvement as an explanation of adolescent maladjustment. *Journal of Marriage and the Family, 56,* 591–607.

Simons, R. L., Johnson, C., Beaman, J., Conger, R. D., & Whitbeck, L. (1996). Parents and peer group as mediators of the effect of community structure on adolescent problem behavior. *American Journal of Community Psychology, 24,* 145–171.

Sippola, L. K. (1999). Getting to know the "other": The characteristics and developmental significance of other-sex relationships in adolescence. *Journal of Youth and Adolescence, 28,* 407–418.

Slomkowski, C., Rende, R., Conger, K. J., Simons, R. L., & Conger, R. D. (2001). Sisters, brothers, and delinquency: Social influence during early and middle adolescence. *Child Development, 72,* 271–283.

Smetana, J. (1995). Parenting styles and conceptions of parental authority during adolescence. *Child Development, 66,* 299–316.

Smetana, J., & Asquith, P. (1994). Adolescents' and parents' conceptions of parental authority and personal autonomy. *Child Development, 65,* 1147–1162.

Smetana, J., & Chuang, S. (2001). Middle-class African American parents' conceptions of parenting in the transition to adolescence. *Journal of Research on Adolescence, 11,* 177–198.

Smetana, J., Crean, H. F., & Daddis, C. (2002). Family processes and problem behaviors in middle-class African American adolescents. *Journal of Research on Adolescence, 12*(2), 275–304.

Smetana, J., & Daddis, C. (2002). Domain-specific antecedents of parental psychological control and monitoring: The role of parenting beliefs and practices. *Child Development, 73*(2), 563–580.

Smetana, J., & Gaines, C. (1999). Adolescent-parent conflict in middle-class African-American families. *Child Development, 70*(6), 1447–1463.

Smetana, J., Yau, J., & Hanson, S. (1991). Conflict resolution in families with adolescents. *Journal of Research on Adolescence, 1,* 189–206.

Smith, E., & Udry, J. R. (1985). Coital and noncoital sexual behaviors of White and Black adolescents. *American Journal of Public Health, 75,* 1200–1203.

Smith, E., Udry, J. R., & Morris, N. (1985). Pubertal development and friends: A biosocial explanation of adolescent sexual behavior. *Journal of Health and Social Behavior, 26,* 183–192.

Smith, T. W. (1994). Attitudes towards sexual permissiveness: Trends, correlates, and behavioral connections. In A. S. Rossi (Ed.), *Sexuality across the life course* (pp. 63–97). Chicago: University of Chicago Press.

Smollar, J., & Youniss, J. (1985, April). *Transformation in adolescents' perceptions of parents.* Paper presented at the biennial meeting of the Society for Research in Child Development, Baltimore, MD.

Sobesky, W. (1983). The effects of situational factors on moral judgments. *Child Development, 54,* 575–584.

South, S. J., & Baumer, E. P. (2000). Deciphering community and race effects on adolescent premarital childbearing. *Social Forces, 78*(4), 1379–1407.

Sowell, E. R., Trauner, D. A., Gamst, A., & Jernigan, T. L. (2002). Development of cortical and subcortical brain structures in childhood and adolescence: A structural MRI study. *Developmental Medicine and Child Neurology, 44,* 4–16.

Spear, P. (2000). The adolescent brain and age-related behavioral manifestations. *Neuroscience and Biobehavioral Reviews, 24,* 417–463.

Spotts, E. L., Neiderhiser, J. M., Hetherington, E. M., & Reiss, D. (2001). The relation between observational measures of social problem solving and family antisocial behavior: Genetic and environmental influences. *Journal of Research on Adolescence, 11*(4), 351–374.

Spreitzer, E. (1994). Does participation in interscholastic athletics affect adult development. *Youth and Society, 25,* 368–387.

Sroufe, L. A., Egeland, B., & Carlson, E. A. (1999). One social world: The integrated development of parent-child and peer relationships. In W. A. Collins & B. Laursen (Eds.), *Minnesota Symposium on Child Psychology: Vol. 30. Relationships as developmental context* (pp. 241–262). Hillsdale, NJ: Erlbaum.

Sroufe, L. A., Egeland, B., Carlson, E., & Collins, W. A. (in press). The place of early attachment in developmental context. In K. E. Grossmann, K. Grossmann, & E. Waters (Eds.), *The power of longitudinal attachment research: From infancy and childhood to adulthood.* New York: Guilford Publications.

Sroufe, L. A., & Fleeson, J. (1988). The coherence of family relationships. In R. A. Hinde & J. Stevenson-Hinde (Eds.), *Relationships within families: Mutual influences* (pp. 27–47). Oxford, England: Oxford University Press.

Staff, J., Mortimer, J., & Uggen, C. (2004). Work and leisure in adolescence. In R. Lerner & L. Steinberg (Eds.), *Handbook of adolescent psychology* (2nd ed., pp. 429–450). Hoboken, NJ: Wiley.

Stättin, H., & Kerr, M. (2000). Parental monitoring: A reinterpretation. *Child Development, 71*(4), 1072–1085.

Steinberg, L. (1981). Transformations in family relations at puberty. *Developmental Psychology, 17,* 833–840.

Steinberg, L. (1988). Reciprocal relation between parent-child distance and pubertal maturation. *Developmental Psychology, 24,* 122–128.

Steinberg, L. (1989). Pubertal maturation and parent-adolescent distance: An evolutionary perspective. In G. R. Adams, R. Montemayor, & T. Gullotta (Eds.), *Advances in adolescent development* (Vol. 1, pp. 71–97). Beverly Hills, CA: Sage.

Steinberg, L. (1990). Autonomy, conflict, and harmony in the family relationship. In S. S. Feldman & G. R. Elliott (Eds.), *At the threshold: The developing adolescent* (pp. 255–276). Cambridge, MA: Harvard University Press.

Steinberg, L. (2001). We know some things: Adolescent-parent relationships in retrospect and prospect. *Journal of Research on Adolescence, 11,* 1–19.

Steinberg, L. (2003). Is decision-making the right framework for the study of adolescent risk-taking. In D. Romer (Ed.), *Reducing adolescent risk: Toward an integrated approach* (pp. 18–24). Thousand Oaks, CA: Sage.

Steinberg, L., & Belsky, J. (1996). A sociobiological perspective on psychopathology in adolescence. In D. Cicchetti & S. Toth (Eds.), *Rochester Symposium on Developmental Psychopathology* (Vol. 7, pp. 93–124). Rochester, NY: University of Rochester Press.

Steinberg, L., & Cauffman, E. (1995). The impact of employment on adolescent development. In R. Vasta (Ed.), *Annals of child development* (Vol. 11, pp. 131–166). London: Jessica Kingsley.

Steinberg, L., & Cauffman, E. (1996). Maturity of judgment in adolescence: Psychosocial factors in adolescent decision-making. *Law and Human Behavior, 20,* 249–272.

Steinberg, L., Dahl, R., Keating, D., Kupfer, D., Masten, A., & Pine, D. (in press). Psychopathology in adolescence: Integrating affective neuroscience with the study of context. In D. Cicchetti (Ed.), *Developmental Psychopathology.* Hoboken, NJ: Wiley.

Steinberg, L., & Dornbusch, S. (1991). Negative correlates of part-time work in adolescence: Replication and elaboration. *Developmental Psychology, 17,* 304–313.

Steinberg, L., Dornbusch, S., & Brown, B. (1992). Ethnic differences in adolescent achievement: An ecological perspective. *American Psychologist, 47,* 723–729.

Steinberg, L., Elmen, J., & Mounts, N. (1989). Authoritative parenting, psychosocial maturity, and academic success among adolescence. *Child Development, 60,* 1424–1436.

Steinberg, L., Fegley, S., & Dornbusch, S. (1993). Negative impact of part-time work on adolescent adjustment: Evidence from a longitudinal study. *Developmental Psychology, 29,* 171–180.

Steinberg, L., Greenberger, E., Garduque, L., Ruggiero, M., & Vaux, A. (1982). Effects of working on adolescent development. *Developmental Psychology, 18,* 385–395.

Steinberg, L., Lamborn, S., Darling, N., Mounts, N., & Dornbusch, S. (1994). Over-time changes in adjustment and competence among adolescents from authoritative, authoritarian, indulgent, and neglectful families. *Child Development, 65,* 754–770.

Steinberg, L., Lamborn, S., Dornbusch, S., & Darling, N. (1992). Impact of parenting practices on adolescent achievement: Authoritative parenting, school involvement, and encouragement to succeed. *Child Development, 63,* 1266–1281.

Steinberg, L., & Morris, A. (2001). Adolescent development. *Annual Review of Psychology, 52,* 83–110.

Steinberg, L., Mounts, N., Lamborn, S., & Dornbusch, S. (1991). Authoritative parenting and adolescent adjustment across various ecological niches. *Journal of Research on Adolescence, 1,* 19–36.

Steinberg, L., & Scott, E. S. (2003). Less guilty by reason of adolescence: Developmental immaturity, diminished responsibility, and the juvenile death penalty. *American Psychologist, 58*(12), 1009–1018.

Steinberg, L., & Silk, J. (2002). Parenting adolescents. In M. Bornstein (Ed.), *Handbook of parenting: Vol. 1. Children and parenting* (2nd ed., pp. 103–133). Mahwah, NJ: Erlbaum.

Steinberg, L., & Silverberg, S. (1986). The vicissitudes of autonomy in early adolescence. *Child Development, 57,* 841–851.

Steinberg, L., & Silverberg, S. (1987). Influences on marital satisfaction during the middle stages of the family life cycle. *Journal of Marriage and the Family, 49,* 751–760.

Stevenson, H., Jr. (1998). Raising safe villages: Cultural-ecological factors that influence the emotional adjustment of adolescents. *Journal of Black Psychology, 24*(1), 44–59.

Stevenson, H. W., Lee, S., Chen, C., Stigler, J. W., Hsu, C.-C., Kitamura, S., et al. (1990). Contexts of achievement: A study of American, Chinese, and Japanese children. *Monographs of the Society for Research in Child Development, 55*(1/2, Serial No. 221).

Stice, E., & Barrera, M., Jr. (1995). A longitudinal examination of the reciprocal relations between perceived parenting and adolescents' substance use and externalizing behaviors. *Developmental Psychology, 31,* 322–334.

Stice, E., & Gonzales, N. (1998). Adolescent temperament moderates the relation of parenting to antisocial behavior and substance use. *Journal of Adolescent Research, 13*(1), 5–31.

Stice, E., Presnell, K., & Bearman, S. (2001). Relation of early menarche to depression, eating disorders, substance abuse, and comorbid psychopathology among adolescent girls. *Developmental Psychology, 37*(5), 608–619.

Stocker, C. M., Burwell, R. A., & Briggs, M. L. (2002). Sibling conflict in middle childhood predicts children's adjustment in early adolescence. *Journal of Family Psychology, 16*(1), 50–57.

Stone, M. R., & Brown, B. B. (1998). In the eye of the beholder: Adolescents' perceptions of peer crowd stereotypes. In R. E. Muuss & H. D. Porton (Eds.), *Adolescent behavior and society: A book of readings* (5th ed., pp. 158–169). New York: McGraw-Hill.

Strasburger, V., & Donnerstein, E. (1999). Children, adolescents, and the media: Issues and solutions. *Pediatrics, 103,* 129–139.

Strauss, M., & Yodanis, C. (1996). Corporal punishment in adolescence and physical assaults on spouses in later life: What accounts for the link? *Journal of Marriage and the Family, 58,* 825–841.

Strouse, D. L. (1999). Adolescent crowd orientations: A social and temporal analysis. In J. A. McLellan & M. J. V. Pugh (Eds.), *The role of peer groups in adolescent social identity: Exploring the importance of stability and change* (pp. 37–54). San Francisco: Jossey-Bass.

Sullivan, H. S. (1953). *The interpersonal theory of psychiatry.* New York: Norton.

Susman, E., & Rogol, A. (2004). Puberty and psychological development. In R. Lerner & L. Steinberg (Eds.), *Handbook of adolescent psychology* (2nd ed., pp. 15–44). Hoboken, NJ: Wiley.

Taradash, A., Connolly, J. A., Pepler, D., Craig, W., & Costa, M. (2001). The interpersonal context of romantic autonomy in adolescence. *Journal of Adolescence, 24*(3), 365–377.

Taylor, R. (1996). Adolescents' perceptions of kinship support and family management practices: Association with adolescent adjustment in African American families. *Developmental Psychology, 32*, 687–695.

Taylor, R., Casten, R., & Flickinger, S. (1993). The influence of kinship social support on the parenting experiences and psychosocial adjustment of African-American adolescents. *Developmental Psychology, 29*, 382–388.

Taylor, R., & Roberts, D. (1995). Kinship support and maternal and adolescent well-being in economically disadvantaged African-American families. *Child Development, 66*, 1585–1597.

Teachman, J., Paasch, K., & Carver, K. (1996). Social capital and dropping out of school early. *Journal of Marriage and the Family, 58*, 773–783.

Teitler, J. O., & Weiss, C. C. (2000). Effects of neighborhood and school environments on transitions to first sexual intercourse. *Sociology of Education, 73*(2), 112–132.

Tesch, S. A., & Whitbourne, S. K. (1982). Intimacy and identity status in young adults. *Journal of Personality and Social Psychology, 43*(5), 1041–1051.

Thomas, B. S., & Hsiu, L. T. (1993). The role of selected risk factors in predicting adolescent drug use and its adverse consequences. *International Journal of the Addictions, 28*(14), 1549.

Thomas, J. J., & Daubman, K. A. (2001). The relationship between friendship quality and self-esteem in adolescent girls and boys. *Sex Roles, 45*(1/2), 53–65.

Thompson, R. (1999). Early attachment and later development. In J. Cassidy & P. R. Shaver (Eds.), *Handbook of attachment: Theory, research, and clinical applications* (pp. 265–286). New York: Guilford Press.

Thompson, S. (1995). *Going all the way: Teenage girls' tales of sex, romance and pregnancy.* New York: Hill & Wang.

Tiezzi, L., Lipshutz, J., Wrobleski, N., Vaughan, R., & McCarthy, J. (1997). Pregnancy prevention among urban adolescents younger than 15: Results of the "In Your Face" program. *Family Planning Perspectives, 29*, 173–176, 197.

Tolan, P., Gorman-Smith, D., & Henry, D. B. (2003). The developmental ecology of urban males' youth violence. *Developmental Psychology, 39*(2), 274–291.

Tolman, D. L. (1994). Doing desire: Adolescent girls' struggles for/with sexuality. *Gender and Society, 8*(3), 324–342.

Tolman, D. L., Spencer, R., Rosen-Reynoso, M., & Porche, M. V. (2004). Sowing the seeds of violence in heterosexual relationships: Early adolescents narrate compulsory heterosexuality. *Journal of Social Issues, 59*(1), 159–178.

Treboux, D., Crowell, J. A., Owens, G., & Pan, H. S. (1994, February). *Attachment behaviors and working models: Relations to best friendship and romantic relationships.* Paper presented at the Society for Research on Adolescence, San Diego, CA.

Tubman, J. G., Windle, M., & Windle, R. C. (1996). Cumulative sexual intercourse patterns among middle adolescents: Problem behavior precursors and concurrent health risk behaviors. *Journal of Adolescent Health, 18*(3), 182–191.

Tucker, C., Barber, B., & Eccles, J. S. (1997). Advice about life plans and personal problems in late adolescent sibling relationships. *Journal of Youth and Adolescence, 26*, 63–76.

Tucker, C., McHale, S. M., & Crouter, A. C. (2001). Conditions of sibling support in adolescence. *Journal of Family Psychology, 15*(2), 254–271.

Udry, J. R. (1990). Hormonal and social determinants of adolescent sexual initiation. In J. Bancroft & J. Reinisch (Eds.), *Adolescence and puberty* (pp. 70–87). New York: Oxford University Press.

Udry, J. R., & Billy, J. O. G. (1987). Initiation of coitus in early adolescence. *American Sociological Review, 52*, 841–855.

Udry, J. R., Talbert, L., & Morris, N. (1986). Biosocial foundations for adolescent female sexuality. *Demography, 23*, 217–230.

Updegraff, K., McHale, S. M., & Crouter, A. C. (2000). Adolescents' sex-typed friendship experiences: Does having a sister versus or brother matter? *Child Development, 71*(6), 1597–1610.

Varenne, H. (1982). Jocks and freaks: The symbolic structure of the expression of social interaction among American senior high school students. In G. Spindler (Ed.), *Doing the ethnography of schooling* (pp. 213–235). New York: Holt, Rinehart and Winston.

Verma, S., & Larson, R. W. (Eds.). (2003). *Examining adolescent leisure time across cultures.* San Francisco: Jossey-Bass.

Vermeiren, R., Ruchkin, V., Leckman, P. E., Deboutte, D., & Schwab-Stone, M. (2002). Exposure to violence and suicide risk in adolescents: A community study. *Journal of Abnormal Child Psychology, 30*(5), 529–537.

Waldinger, R. J., Diguer, L., Guastella, F., Lefebvre, R., Allen, J., Luborsky, L., et al. (2002). The same old song?—Stability and change in relationship schemas from adolescence to young adulthood. *Journal of Youth and Adolescence, 31*(1), 17–29.

Walker, L. J., & Hennig, K. H. (1999). Parenting style and the development of moral reasoning. *Journal of Moral Education, 28*, 359–374.

Walker, L. J., Hennig, K. H., & Krettenauer, T. (2000). Parent and peer contexts for children's moral reasoning development. *Child Development, 71*, 1033–1048.

Walker, L. J., & Taylor, J. (1991). Family interaction and the development of moral reasoning. *Child Development, 62*, 264–283.

Walker-Barnes, C. J., & Mason, C. A. (2001). Ethnic difference in the effect of parenting on gang involvement and gang delinquency: A longitudinal, hierarchical linear modeling perspective. *Child Development, 72*(6), 1814–1831.

Warren, J. (2002). Reconsidering the relationship between student employment and academic outcomes: A new theory and better data. *Youth and Society, 33*(3), 366–393.

Waterman, A. (1982). Identity development from adolescence to adulthood: An extension of theory and a review of research. *Developmental Psychology, 18*, 341–358.

Waters, E., & Cummings, E. M. (2000). A secure base from which to explore close relationships. *Child Development, 71*(1), 164–172.

Waters, E., Merrick, S., Treboux, D., Crowell, J., & Albersheim, L. (2000). Attachment security in infancy and early adulthood: A 20-year longitudinal study. *Child Development, 71*(3), 684–689.

Way, N., Cowal, K., Gingold, R., Pahl, K., & Bissessar, N. (2001). Friendship patterns among African American, Asian American, and Latino adolescents from low-income families. *Journal of Social and Personal Relationships, 18*, 29–53.

Way, N., & Pahl, K. (2001). Individual and contextual predictors of perceived friendship quality among ethnic minority, low-income adolescents. *Journal of Research on Adolescence, 11*(4), 325–349.

Weinberg, M. S., Williams, C. J., & Pryor, D. W. (1994). *Dual attraction: Understanding bisexuality.* New York: Oxford University Press.

Weinfield, N., Ogawa, J., & Sroufe, L. A. (1997). Early attachment as a pathway to adolescent peer competence. *Journal of Research on Adolescence, 7,* 241–265.

Weinfield, N. S., Sroufe, L. A., & Egeland, B. (2000). Attachment from infancy to young adulthood in a high-risk sample: Continuity, discontinuity and their correlates. *Child Development, 71*(3), 695–702.

Weinfield, N. S., Sroufe, L. A., Egeland, B., & Carlson, E. A. (1999). The nature of individual differences in infant-caregiver attachment. In J. Cassidy & P. Shaver (Eds.), *Handbook of attachment: Theory, research, and clinical application* (pp. 68–88). New York: Guilford Press.

Weinstein, M., & Thornton, A. (1989). Mother-child relations and adolescent sexual attitudes and behaviors. *Demography, 26*(4), 563–577.

Weisfeld, G. (1999). *Evolutionary principles of human adolescence.* New York: Basic Books.

Wentzel, K. (2002). Are effective teachers like good parents? Teaching styles and student adjustment in early adolescence. *Child Development, 73*(1), 287–301.

Whitbeck, L. B., Conger, R. D., & Kao, M. (1993). The influence of parental support, depressed affect, and peers on the sexual behaviors of adolescent girls. *Journal of Family Issues, 14*(2), 261–278.

Whitbeck, L. B., Yoder, K. A., Hoyt, D. R., & Conger, R. D. (1999). Early adolescent sexual activity: A developmental study. *Journal of Marriage and the Family, 61*(4), 934–946.

Whiting, B. B., & Edwards, C. P. (1988). *Children of different worlds.* Cambridge, MA: Harvard University Press.

Whiting, J. W., Burbank, V. K., & Ratner, M. S. (1986). The duration of maidhood across cultures. In J. B. Lancaster & B. A. Hamburg (Eds.), *School-age pregnancy and parenthood: Biosocial dimensions* (pp. 273–302). Hawthorne, NY: Aldine de Gruyter.

Wichstrom, L. (2001). The impact of pubertal timing on adolescents' alcohol use. *Journal of Research on Adolescence, 11*(2), 131–150.

Wiesner, M., & Ittel, A. (2002). Relations of pubertal timing and depressive symptoms to substance use in early adolescence. *Journal of Early Adolescence, 22*(1), 5–23.

Wigfield, A., & Eccles, J. S. (1994). Children's competence beliefs, achievement values, and general self-esteem: Change across elementary and middle school. *Journal of Early Adolescence, 14,* 107–138.

Wigfield, A., Eccles, J. S., Mac Iver, D., Reuman, D., & Midgley, C. (1991). Transitions during early adolescence: Changes in children's domain-specific self-perceptions and general self-esteem across the transition to junior high school. *Developmental Psychology, 27,* 552–565.

Williams, J., & Dunlop, L. (1999). Pubertal timing and self-reported delinquency among male adolescents. *Journal of Adolescence, 22,* 157–171.

Wood, M. D., Read, J. P., Mitchell, R. E., & Brand, N. H. (2004). Do parents still matter? Parent and peer influences on alcohol involvement among recent high school graduates. *Psychology of Addictive Behaviors, 18*(1), 19–30.

Wright, J., Cullen, F., & Williams, N. (1997). Working while in school and delinquent involvement: Implications for social policy. *Crime and Delinquency, 43,* 203–221.

Wu, L., Schlenger, W., & Galvin, D. (2003). The relationship between employment and substance abuse among students aged 12 to 17. *Journal of Adolescent Health, 32*(1), 5–15.

Wynne, L. C. (1984). Communication patterns and family relations of children at risk for schizophrenia. In N. F. Watt & E. J. Anthony (Eds.), *Children at risk for schizophrenia: A longitudinal perspective* (pp. 551–556). New York: Cambridge University Press.

Yau, J., & Smetana, J. (1996). Adolescent-parent conflict among Chinese adolescents in Hong Kong. *Child Development, 67,* 1262–1275.

Youniss, J. (1980). *Parents and peers in the social environment: A Sullivan Piaget perspective.* Chicago: University of Chicago Press.

Youniss, J., & Smollar, J. (1985). *Adolescent relations with mothers, fathers, and friends.* Chicago: University of Chicago Press.

Zani, B. (1991). Male and female patterns in the discovery of sexuality during adolescence. *Journal of Adolescence, 14,* 163–178.

Zeldin, S., & Topitzes, D. (2002). Neighborhood experiences, community connection, and positive beliefs about adolescents among urban adults and youth. *Journal of Community Psychology, 30*(6), 647–669.

Zimmer-Gembeck, M., & Collins, W. A. (2003). Autonomy development during adolescence. In G. Adams & M. Berzonsky (Eds.), *Blackwell handbook of adolescence* (pp. 175–204). Oxford, England: Blackwell.

Zimmer-Gembeck, M. J., Siebenbruner, J., & Collins, W. A. (2001). Diverse aspects of dating: Associations with psychosocial functioning from early to middle adolescence. *Journal of Adolescence, 24,* 1–24.

Author Index

Subject Index

For Reference

Not to be taken from this room